AMERICA IN LITERATURE

Volume

I

AMERICA IN LITERATURE

General Editor: Theodore L. Gross

VOLUME I
PART I. THE FIRST TWO CENTURIES
David Levin
The University of Virginia

PART II. THE ROMANTIC ERA
Theodore L. Gross
The City College of New York

VOLUME II
PART III. THE AGE OF REALISM
Alan Trachtenberg
Yale University

PART IV. THE TWENTIETH CENTURY
Benjamin DeMott
Amherst College

AMERICA IN LITERATURE

VOLUME I

David Levin
THE UNIVERSITY OF VIRGINIA

Theodore L. Gross
THE CITY COLLEGE OF NEW YORK

JOHN WILEY & SONS
NEW YORK   SANTA BARBARA   LONDON   SYDNEY   TORONTO

CREDITS

William Bradford: from OF PLYMOUTH PLANTATION by William Bradford. Copyright 1952, by Samuel Eliot Morison. Reprinted by permission of Alfred A. Knopf, Inc.

John Winthrop: From A Model of Christian Charity by John Winthrop. Reprinted by permission of the Massachusetts Historical Society.

(Acknowledgments are continued on page 1911.)

LIBRARY OF CONGRESS CATALOGING IN PUBLICATION DATA:
Main entry under title:

America in literature.

    Bibliography: v. 1, p.
    Includes indexes.
    1. American literature. 2. United States—
Literary collections. 3. United States—Civilization.
I. Gross, Theodore L.
PS509.U52A38   810'.9   76-49486
ISBN 0-471-32808-1

Printed in the United States of America

10 9 8 7 6 5 4 3 2 1

Preface

America is a civilization whose literature cannot be fully understood apart from the culture that has helped to shape it. When the achievement of a novelist or poet is viewed in the context of his time, the work assumes a meaning it can never possess alone; it becomes a dominant feature in the social and literary record of the nation rather than an isolated artifact. *America in Literature* is an attempt to reflect organically the most urgent ideas of our nation as they have risen from the roots of the American soil and issued through the American mind and imagination.

In form, *America in Literature* is as interdisciplinary as the culture itself. Although the dominant expression is literary and is represented by the essential authors who must be included in any record of artistic achievement, other disciplines illuminate a common heritage. As Bryant, Cooper, Whitman, and Twain draw verbal landscapes of the American scene, their contemporaries, Cole, Mount, Heade, and Bingham, create paintings of the same land, nourished by similar concepts of nature, and man, and God, and society. As Emerson, Thoreau, and Hawthorne write literary masterpieces concerned with the reformation of the human heart, others seek to translate these ideas into social action: Horace Mann in education; Margaret Fuller in woman's rights; Dorothea Dix in prison reform; and Frederick Douglass through the abolition of slavery. F. Scott Fitzgerald shows the reader how the American rich are different from the American poor, but Edward Dahlberg and Robert Coles speak intimately and powerfully of "bottom dogs" in a democracy, even though their voices may be less conventionally artistic; they, too, must be included in a record of American civilization. Artemus Ward satirizes Lincoln's thought in words less reverential than those of Whitman and Lincoln himself. The autobiographies of Elizabeth Ashbridge, Benjamin Franklin, Charlotte Forten, and Randolph Bourne; the spirituals of blacks and Indians; the architecture of Horatio Greenough, Louis Sullivan, and Frank Lloyd Wright; the historical documents of John Adams, Thomas Jefferson, James Madison, and Abraham Lincoln; the photographs of Matthew Brady and Walker Evans—these various forms of expression help to create the mosaic of a complex culture and involve us in the real texture of actual American lives.

The interdisciplinary approach of *America in Literature* depends upon a view of national culture that is organic. If Puritanism is the primary force of early American civilization, how may we represent it most vividly and comprehensively? Should we restrict ourselves to a few poems and sermons, or should we include diaries, histories, paintings, and architectural reproductions of homes and landscapes in order to recreate the full sense of life as it was lived in the seventeenth and eighteenth centuries? Can we truly understand slavery by reading only Thoreau, Whitman, and Twain, or might we not have a deeper sense of its complexity and cutting edge by also hearing John C. Calhoun and Daniel Webster, looking at contemporary cartoons and photographs, listening to songs and battle hymns, and reading the journalism of William Lloyd Garrison and Wendell Phillips, the slave narratives, and the sociological treatises and tracts of the time? In the modern period, technocracy can be interpreted not only by artists like Norman Mailer and James Baldwin, but also by those who affect all of us in our daily lives: practitioners of film and television, creators of photographs and posters, the participants in interviews, and voices in tape recordings.

Clearly American civilization is more complex than the traditional and almost exclusively literary presentation it has been accorded. As authors who have participated in the general critical attempt to view literature in the fullest cultural context, we have sought to redress the balance, to present a record of American civilization as well as of American literature, "to come to a hard bottom and rocks in place," as Thoreau admonished us to do, "which we can call *reality*"—an *American reality.*

In order to broaden the range of our selections, we have been compelled to make certain arbitrary decisions regarding space. We are deeply aware that no account of American civilization would be complete without the inclusion of major creations of considerable length, and we urge the reader to possess the following books as a minimal list of masterpieces: *The Pioneers, The Scarlet Letter, Walden, Moby Dick, Huckleberry Finn, The Portrait of a Lady, The Rise of Silas Lapham, An American Tragedy, The Sun Also Rises, The Sound and the Fury, The Great Gatsby,* and *Invisible Man.* It did not seem a wise use of space to reprint these or other comparable works, since they are readily available in paperback editions, but they obviously should have a primary place in any discussion of the materials presented in American civilization.

Inevitably, certain ideas have dominated our record: democratization and its effect on the poor, the wealthy, and minorities; the conflict between nature and technocracy; the myth of the West that has shaped the imagination of writers, painters, and humorists; the artistic response to evil and sin that is so central to our most deeply creative authors. But if one theme has seemed of special urgency at the end of

America's fourth century, it has been the tension between personal expression and mutual dependency, announced in Whitman's famous inscription, "One's-self I sing, a simple separate person,/Yet utter the word Democratic, the word En-Masse," and repeated for the twentieth century in John Dewey's reminder that a democracy is a "conjoint communicated experience." Many have profited from this land; too many have been excluded from its riches and its power. And, together with the record of artistic achievement in America, we have sought to reflect this tension that preoccupies us—to borrow a word from William Carlos Williams—in the "dailiness" of our lives.

Within the limits of two volumes, we have attempted to view American civilization contextually, and the reader will discover that much of the writing is arranged in clusters of experience. Thus the pamphlets and tracts of black authors like Jupiter Hammond, Absalom Jones, and William Hamilton are grouped together as early commentaries on slavery; Emerson's "Divinity School Address" is seen in the context of transcendentalist expression, and Thoreau's "Civil Disobedience" is placed with other works concerning reform; the observations of Frederick Jackson Turner, Henry Adams, William James, Thorstein Veblen, and George Santayana are grouped together in "Expressions of Social Thought"; the essays of John Dewey, Randolph Bourne, and Van Wyck Brooks are juxtaposed in a section entitled "The Case for Cultural Revolution"; the writings of Jane Addams, W. E. B. DuBois, Edward Dahlberg, James Agee, Richard Wright, Ralph Ellison, James Baldwin, Robert Coles, and N. Scott Momaday point toward the possibility of a "new society" in which we care more about all of the Americans who constitute, in Gwendolyn Brooks' image, "our mutual estate." Great authors naturally transcend movements, and their writings are presented as the expression of their unique sensibilities; but we have also introduced the social and historical record without which their works of art lose meaning.

While we share the principles of *American in Literature,* as four discrete editors we have individual approaches to these principles, reflected in our own quite personal idioms. It would be a contradiction of purpose to suppress or deny our individual voices, and we have not done so; we have allowed ourselves the freedom of personal expression, even of idiosyncrasy. Although we present the fundamental documents of American civilization—certainly those major literary works of prose, poetry, and drama—and are as informative as space will allow, we always interpret these materials, hoping to provoke the reader into his own interpretation. There is one vision in *America in Literature,* but four distinct angles of that vision. We invite the reader to provide his own angle of vision, to make our book complete.

The shifting patterns of democracy and the contradictory elements of a mobile society do not yield readily to any formal structure and, through this formidable record, we have followed the natural direction of those who have articulated the meaning of America. The result, we hope, is a reflection of our nation that will persuade the reader who touches this book that he touches not merely a book, but a culture— the whole way of life of a people.

Theodore L. Gross

Acknowledgments

During the many years in which this manuscript was developing, a number of people have given the editors invaluable help, ranging from scholarly advice and research concerning texts and biography to collation and proofreading. We are grateful to these people and regret that space does not allow us to mention all of their names. Certain individuals, however, have been so helpful that they must be mentioned.

In terms of the sort of book that would seem appropriate to the contemporary student, we received significant advice from Elizabeth Wooten Cowan, Texas A & M University; Carl H. Klaus, The University of Iowa; James A. Parrish, University of South Florida, Tampa; Louis D. Rubin, Jr., University of North Carolina at Chapel Hill; Michael F. Shugrue, The College of Staten Island, CUNY; Eugene Soules, Sonoma State College; and Neal Woodruff, Coe College.

David Levin wishes to thank Sacvan Bercovitch, Columbia University; Louise Gentry, formerly of the University of Virginia; Alfred Habegger (now at the University of Kansas), who helped him while a graduate student at Stanford; William L. Hedges, Goucher College; Alan B. Howard, University of Virginia; James Jubak, who did a great deal of research for him at the University of Virginia; Louise Lynch, who did excellent research for him while an undergraduate at the University of Virginia; Michael McGiffert, College of William and Mary; Raymond Nelson, University of Virginia; Helen Saltman, whose dissertation at the University of California (Los Angeles) provided him with a John Adams manuscript; Daniel B. Shea, Washington University, who introduced him to the narrative of Elizabeth Ashbridge and directed him to the best text of Jonathan Edwards' spiritual autobiography; Frank Shuffelton, University of Rochester; Kenneth Silverman, New York University, who gave him copies of some unpublished letters by Cotton Mather; Roberta Simon, who helped him in research at the University of Virginia; Louise Stokes, who assisted him in research in Cambridge, Massachusetts; and Walter Wenska, College of William and Mary. Patricia M. Levin read every word of the text with him in proof.

Theodore L. Gross is particularly grateful to Arthur Waldhorn and Arthur Zeiger of the City College of New York for editing large sections of the manuscript and for discussing the broader implications of these volumes. His administrative assistant, Theresa Romanelli, was extremely helpful in keeping the records of both volumes in order and in typing. Selma Gross helped design the structure of Part II and reviewed the headnotes scrupulously.

As general editor, I wish to express my personal appreciation to the staff at John Wiley who worked on *America in Literature:* Vivian Kahane for her final editing; Debra Schwartz for her production supervision; and Andrea Stingelin for her extensive work on permissions. My deepest gratitude is to Thomas O. Gay, without whom *America in Literature* would not have been realized. From conception to reality, and at every stage of development, Mr. Gay monitored the progress of this anthology. He exhibited a rare sensitivity to a complex task, and I am grateful for his devotion to the project and for his continuous support.

Although the individual sections are the responsibility of their respective editors, I should note that certain selections were handled by another editor within the project; in this sense as well as in the continual discussions we have had with one another, *America in Literature* expresses the common view of the four editors. David Levin wrote the headnote to William Ellery Channing; Theodore Gross wrote the headnotes to the Southern Agrarians, James Weldon Johnson, Claude McKay, Jean Toomer, Countee Cullen, Langston Hughes, Adrienne Rich, Michael Harper, Don Lee, Melvin Tolson and Gwendolyn Brooks; Alan Trachtenberg wrote the head note to Walt Whitman.

Theodore L. Gross

Contents

PART I: THE FIRST TWO CENTURIES, 1630-1820

EDWARD TAYLOR (1645-1729)   283

II. Early Virginians
390

III. Testaments of Eighteenth-Century Experience
433

IV. The Revolution and the Republic
553

V. Beginnings of American Romanticism
731

PART II: THE ROMANTIC ERA, 1819-1868
801

I. The American Scene
820

III. Varieties of Thought:
Religious, Social, and Political Reform
1543

PART I

THE FIRST TWO CENTURIES

1630-1820

INTRODUCTION

The student of American literature during the first two centuries of English colonization ought to begin by settling some awkward problems of definition and proportion. Problems for the editors and for teachers, they must also be clear to students. By American literature we mean literature written in English by people who came to settle in the territory that eventually became the United States of America. We exclude English Canadian literature; the *Relations* written in French by Jesuit missionaries, even those written among the Iroquois on what became United States soil; and the writings of early Spanish missionaries. Other exclusions are less simple. Some scholars regard Captain John Smith as one of the first American writers, because he acted vigorously in helping to establish the first successful English colony and because his narratives helped, as in his story of Pocahontas, to establish some of the earliest episodes in a new American mythology. We include him here (perhaps arbitrarily) as an English commentator on the New World who lived here for a time but did not really settle.

Even less precisely familiar today than the definition of *American* is our conception of seventeenth- and eighteenth-century literature. Since contemporary literary life is dominated by fiction, poetry, drama, and criticism, one might reasonably expect the study of American literature to begin with the earliest achievements in those genres, and many survey courses on American literature before the Civil War do spend only a very brief time on the literature written before 1820, so that their emphasis may fall on the major works of imaginative literature in the 1830's, 1840's, and 1850's. We believe, however, that in choosing to study American literature we commit ourselves to a particular kind of literary history. We might properly have chosen to study a few of the best American writers and their works as a part of English literature, or as part of the literature of Western Civilization, or in many other useful ways, from the development of the short story to a comparison of the great ethical values in world literature. By choosing to study a *nation's* literature, we commit ourselves chronologically as well as geographically. We don't study seventeenth-century American writers chiefly because they influenced Nathaniel Hawthorne and Ralph Waldo Emerson—although that influence is considerable—but because they were the important writers of their time, because they wrote the most powerful expressions of the human values, aspirations, and experience of Americans in their time. Although they did not use the term "creative imagination," they applied the faculties we understand in that term to create a voluminous literature concerning fundamental issues of religious and political destiny. They wrote so much that we could spend an entire academic year reading the published works of the seventeenth century alone. With few exceptions (most of them in the poetry) our subject is a literature of utility—sermons, histories, descriptions of the land, autobiographical narratives and meditations, and political tracts and essays. These are the forms in which the best writers of the day addressed their contemporaries.

By 1800 the situation has changed, and by 1860 it has been completely transformed. Clergymen and politicians continue to publish sermons, essays, and books in those years, and histories and autobiographies continue to flourish, but the best writers are then working in other forms and the volume of fiction, poetry, and literary essays has grown prodigiously, crowding out of our pages most sermons, theological controversies, histories, and political exposition. In this one volume, then, a reader can see a major shift in the *definition* of our central literature simply by reading our table of contents. At the time of the Civil War, history was still considered a fit subject for the man of letters, and one can still see the value of sermons and religious lectures in the debates of Ralph Waldo Emerson and Andrews Norton in the 1830's, but by then American literary talent was no longer concerned primarily with religion or statesmanship. More than a century later, though we have recently seen a revival of critical interest in history and autobiography, nobody urges us to study the sermons of Billy Graham or even the late Reinhold Niebuhr as examples of exposition. One reason for the difference is that the best literary talent has worked elsewhere, and another is that the definition of literature has more or less quietly changed so that usually none but so-called imaginative works are formally studied. In our own day, moreover, the task of literary history has been profoundly complicated by the immense volume of literature published in the United States—more than 13,000 separate titles in 1973 alone, more than 10 times the American output of the entire seventeenth century.

Similarly large discrepancies in volume between the nineteenth century and the seventeenth oblige us to make large concessions in our chronological apportionment of space, even in this first volume. Although allotted more space here than in almost any comparable anthology, American literature of the first 200 years occupies fewer of our pages than the literature of the subsequent 30 to 40 years. And the pedagogical consequence is more than simply quantitative. Scholarly custom still tends to regard the first period of American literary history as two centuries long, with asymmetrical subdivisions that allot roughly 140 years (1620–1760) to the colonizing age; 20 years (1760–1780) to the American Revolution and its causes; and 40 years (1781–1820) to the "early national" period or the literature of the early republic. Forewarned of such arbitrary anomalies, both the readers and we ourselves should beware the danger of assuming that the intellectual and cultural changes over two centuries are as slight as those of a single generation. Students should also bear in mind one other fact that can be easily forgotten, even though it is obvious. Many of the longer works—novels and romances by Cooper, Hawthorne, and Melville, for example—are available in relatively inexpensive editions, and they could not be adequately represented in an anthology; shorter works that are not separately available will naturally occupy a disproportionate amount of space in an anthology. By excluding Hawthorne's, Melville's, and Cooper's novels, we do not say that they are less important than Bradford's history *Of Plymouth Plantation,* which is out of print, or less important than the shorter works that are collected here.

A student recently asked whether, if William Faulkner and Ernest Hemingway had been writing fiction in the seventeenth century, we would still assign sermons and histories as works of literature. Amusing as it is to consider that anachronistic fantasy, the supposition begs the question. At least one reason why the modern novel and short story did not then exist is that the community's affirmative and negative values made such literature impossible. Nathaniel Hawthorne gave a fundamentally sound version of the negative values when he remarked in 1850 that his Puritan ancestors would have been horrified to learn that their descendant had become a mere storyteller. But the affirmative values are even more important to our understanding of early American literature. It was the sermon, the diary or meditation, the personal narrative, the history, the political essay or tract, that best articulated the human experience and aspirations of seventeenth-century New England men and women.

By arranging our Introduction according to such genres we invite comparisons of substance and technique within unfamiliar literary forms, and we underline the importance of recognizing their differing functions. But of course we do not thereby deny the relevance of early American literature to the other major themes in these volumes or to the lives of modern Americans. One major purpose in studying any literature is in some way to apprehend the experience of others and compare it with our own. The study of any remote literature gives us the valuable opportunity to observe both how distant people differ from ourselves and how they resemble us. When we perceive how seventeenth-century Puritans, for example, dealt with complexity in their emotional lives, their political life, and their literature, we replace a stereotype that each of us has known since childhood with historical men and women from whose life and literature we still have the ability to learn.

Our own secular age, moreover, has some special reasons for understanding the seventeenth-century Puritans and the Revolutionary leaders. Of course we find among both those early groups the American origins of continuing habits and values, from the so-called work ethic to the belief in a commonwealth, a community "knit together as in a body," with a special destiny to perform exemplary missions in the world. But our peculiar opportunity to understand the early Puritans has more to do with self-criticism, doubt, and uncertainty than with a conviction of high manifest destiny. We, like them, live with the real possibility of an apocalypse that could occur in our own lifetime. Without the aid of psychiatry or psychoanalysis they, like us, lived within a psychological theory that told them they could not really know their own motives. "Suspect thyself much," Thomas Shepard told his congregation, and despite the self-assurance implicit in the effort to make Boston "a city on a hill," a beacon lighting the true way for all the world, the Puritans' experience during the first century of settlement gave them much reason to doubt their ability to recognize how to do God's will as a collective people any better than sinning individuals could do His will in their private lives. Especially in the second and third generations, the American Puritans found themselves committed to doing God's will in history but perplexed about how to discover that will, and at last profoundly uncertain of the direction in which history, which they believed to be always under divine control, was actually moving. Like many young American reformers of the 1960's and 1970's, the Puritans were convinced that they must build a new society by replacing the corrupt forms of the Establishment and returning to an idealized, primitive model. In both church government and civil government they strove to revive the principles set forth in the Bible and exemplified in the primitive Christian churches. But as they prospered they found that churches lost their unity, many young people failed to join their parents as church members, and (as Thomas Hooker had foreseen on his departure from England) "Adversity had slain her Thousands; Prosperity would slay her Ten Thousands." Before the end of the seventeenth century (although the decline of religious faith has been exaggerated), ministers and historians were exhorting the people to return not only to the principles of the first Christian century, but also to the example of the first Puritan settlers of New England.

We must begin by looking at that example, since American literature as we have defined it here begins among the Puritan colonists who first emigrated to New England in the third and fourth decades of the seventeenth century. In 1630, 10 years after the founding of Plymouth Plantation by a group of Congregational Separatists (who had "separated" from the Church of England), Governor William Bradford began writing his history, *Of Plymouth Plantation,* just as a much larger and more richly financed migration was settling Massachusetts Bay. Both of these Puritan colonies, unlike their predecessor in Jamestown, Virginia, were led by people committed to a strong sense of religious community and an equally strong conviction (especially in Massachusetts Bay) that they must justify their enterprise in England. Their formal writing therefore becomes a part of our literary record even before their landing. The Plymouth colonists drew up the Mayflower Compact (which is reprinted here as part of Bradford's history), and John Winthrop delivered his sermon "A Model of Christian Charity" on board the *Arbella* during the founders' voyage to Massachusetts Bay. Especially in Massachusetts Bay, where a printing press was established at Cambridge within the first decade of settlement (1639), cultural and spiritual life depended on the word—both the exegesis of God's Word in the Bible and the extended debate over how to proceed in church and state. Throughout the seventeenth century, people gathered twice every Sunday for a church service dominated by sermons that often lasted more than an hour and sometimes more than two hours. On Thursdays, moreover, all the neighboring ministers gathered in Boston and some other communities to hear the weekly lecture, assigned on a rotating basis to different preachers for the discussion of some difficult or timely question of theology or law.

1. HISTORIES

We begin with history, because the concept of the covenanted community and its mission or vocation lies at the heart of the enterprise, and the combined experience of triumph and painful loss, of exhilarating assurance and perplexed struggle to understand and justify, establishes a social context for much of the more personal literature. As we speak of Puritans in the broad general terms that brevity forces us to use, the histories written by Puritans remind us that these writers differed from each other, that their political life in church and state was filled with controversy even though they generally agreed in their theories of history, and that the histories written in this country during the first half-century of settlement were written by the victors in the several controversies. (Thomas Morton is a singular exception, but of course he was no Puritan and he published his book in exile from New England.)

Puritan historians wrote in the conviction that history developed according to a divine plan and that Providence controlled events. God's will, they believed, had been partly revealed to men in the Bible and in the physical world, whose laws men could use to their own benefit. As history unfolded, then, God also revealed His secret will in the actual course of events—and sometimes by extraordinary intervention, as when He saved the ship carrying fugitive Pilgrims during a terrible storm in the North Sea (see Bradford's history, below p. 34). Christians, they believed, are bound by the Covenant of Grace, a solemn compact to act in the world for the glory of God after He has freely given each of them the faith that is the necessary condition of their salvation from the Hell to which their own sins, as descendants of the fallen Adam and Eve, would otherwise have condemned them.

These people saw history as a grand drama enacted for the glory of God, and they felt obliged to think of themselves both in the practical, political world of seventeenth-century England and America and in the context of Biblical history. Adam and Eve had lived under a Covenant of Works, which had obliged them to obey God's law, but which their descendants were unable to fulfill after the Fall. God had then offered a Covenant of Grace to Abraham (Genesis, 17) with a free promise to save him and his descendants, and after the Crucifixion that covenant had been extended to all faithful believers in Jesus Christ, the Son of God whose vicarious sacrifice "paid their debt" for them. (See Edward Taylor's "Meditation 112," Second Series, below, pp. 289-290.) The true church had been corrupted by papal authorities after a few centuries, and its glorious Reformation, begun by Martin Luther in the sixteenth century, was continuing more than 100 years later as reformers tried to purify the various established churches and, especially in America, to build new church discipline according to the austere simplicity of the Biblical model. This practical world was filled with "antitypes" who enacted roles analogous to those of the original "types" in the Bible— as William Bradford resembled Moses, for example (in Cotton Mather's history, not in Bradford's!), and as the emigrants in Bradford's history and others resembled the people of Israel leaving Egypt. In heavily allegorical narratives such as the first book of Bradford's history and Edward Johnson's *Wonder Working Providence of Sion's Saviour in New England,* Puritan historians stressed Biblical typology. In the more mundane sections of Bradford's second book, John Winthrop's *General History of New England,* and Cotton Mather's *Magnalia Christi Americana,* while typology continued to function in important ways, the search for an understanding of worldly causes often predominated as the historian tried to apprehend the ways in which particular phenomena could be related to the grand design. If he could not see the pattern, he could at least leave a faithful record for others to interpret in the better light of the future.

For all their dogmatic tendencies, then, and despite their belief that history moved toward a spectacular event in which Jesus would return to reign on earth for 1000 years, Puritan historians believed in an essentially progressive view of their calling. Just as they were able to correct the errors of their predecessors, so they believed that their successors would have still more light. Their own grand challenge, meanwhile, was to set down for the glory of God and the edification of posterity a moving narrative in which readers could see both the universal types—the lives of the saints in conflict with the agents of darkness—and the unique characters of a particular time in New England, related of course to their Biblical types but nonetheless peculiar to their own time and place. Myles Standish, John Robinson, Thomas Morton, Roger Williams, Anne Hutchinson, William Bradford, John Winthrop (in Mather's history), and Sir William Phips—all these figures are unique personalities as they appear in the histories reprinted here. The challenge for the reader, to whom all saints and sinners may at first look like simple abstractions, is to look closely enough (perhaps even reread) to perceive the distinctions.

The most important change in American historiography during the century that separates Cotton Mather from Washington Irving was the replacement of a kingly Providence by natural laws and individual human choice. Here we represent the secular histories of eighteenth-century Virginia and Massachusetts, respectively, through two of the best writers, Robert Beverley and Thomas Hutchinson. Beverley's history of seventeenth-century Virginia was published only three years after Cotton Mather's *Magnalia Christi Americana,* but it seems to issue from a different world. Providence and the Devil have virtually disappeared. Self-interest prevails as the motive of too many officials, but the historian's worldly intelligence and curiosity concentrate more on delineating human behavior than on judging it morally or seeking its meaning in the Providential design. As the principles of the Enlightenment spread through the American colonies, historians tended to avoid large theoretical statements or at least to screen the reader from any explicit view of their historical assumptions. The most noticeable quality in Beverley and Hutchinson, both Anglicans who were virtually untouched by the movement toward Deism, is their detachment from any personal identification with the ancestors whose actions they narrate.

Of course there are other kinds of history written in eighteenth-century America. We might have chosen Jonathan Edwards's unfinished *History of the Work of Redemption,* Cadwallader Colden's *History of the Five Indian Nations* (1727), David Ramsay's *History of the Revolution in South Carolina* (1785), Jeremy Belknap's *History of New Hampshire* (1784), or Mercy Otis Warren's *History of the Rise, Progress, and Termination of the American Revolution* (1805). In the grand patriotic rhetoric of Mrs. Warren's three-volume work, one quickly sees parallels to the tone of Cotton Mather and other Puritans. But the prevailing quality of eighteenth-century American historiography is represented in Beverley and Hutchinson: dispassionate, perhaps ironic, rationally interested in the working out of human destiny according to laws which, though not easily read by human observers, are not subject to the arbitrary will of God. The changes in thought that underlie these differences are set forth more specifically in our introductions to Benjamin Franklin, Jonathan Edwards, Charles Chauncy, Thomas Jefferson, Thomas Paine, and John Adams.

By the time Washington Irving sat down to write his mock-heroic history of New York (1809), a rich body of historical literature ranging over two centuries could be studied. Irving's anticlimactic title, promising to trace the history from the beginning of the world to the end of the Dutch dynasty, mocks the pretentiousness of many earlier histories that began with the Reformation and quickly descended to tiny Massachusetts colonies, and he also mocked the grandiloquence of some Revolutionary histories and (later) Cotton Mather's *Magnalia*. But the works of William Bradford (still at that time unpublished), Edward Johnson, Cotton Mather, Thomas Hutchinson, Robert Beverley, William Byrd, II, Cadwallader Colden, Mercy Otis Warren, David Ramsay, and John Marshall constituted an admirable tradition on which Irving and other romantic historians of the nineteenth century were able to build in their own efforts to place American history in the context of the European past.

2. DIARIES AND AUTOBIOGRAPHIES

Autobiographical literature, which flourishes with new intensity in our own time, has always been one of the most vigorous American forms. Among colonists whose experience was new or even unique, the natural impulse to keep a record produced a vast quantity of private narrative and reflection, and of course readers in Europe and America eagerly read those narratives that were published. Narratives of exploration, adventure, and captivity had a strong motivation and attractiveness for readers and writers of all religions, but again the circumstances of Puritan—and, later, of Quaker—settlement combined with particular religious doctrines to give personal narratives a special significance.

The comforting ideal of a covenanted community modified but could not erase a crucial fact of Puritanism and other versions of Reformed Protestantism: salvation was an individual experience. The most important spiritual event in an individual life was that of regeneration, conversion from sin to a gracious repentance and then to a genuine desire to live in the world for the glory of God. Puritans were essentially Calvinists. They believed that all men and women were naturally sinful as a consequence of Adam's original sin and that nobody could possibly earn God's forgiveness or grace. Grace was freely given, generously given to a few people by a merciful God who had every justification for condemning everyone. The naturally sinful person might rail against the will of the sovereign God in protest against such a state of affairs. A gracious person would gladly surrender his own will to that of a God so generous as not only to forgive an unworthy sinner but to fill him with joy.

To understand that joy, which is too often omitted from retrospective accounts of Puritan religion, one must recognize that the essential fact of Puritan belief was a conviction of God's majesty, His sovereignty, His glory. The earth existed for God's glory, not for man's use or delight. The true purpose of life was to glorify God. Human happiness both in this world and the next depended, as Perry Miller has said, on recognizing that one's own happiness was *not* the chief goal of life.

In consequence of that awesome doctrine, the converted Christian (or saint, as the elected person was called) often felt an overwhelming sense of human unworthiness when measured against such perfect majesty. The sovereign God was a Creator and Lawgiver who did not have to appeal to His fallible creature's sense of justice. A thing was not first of all reasonable and just, one English Puritan wrote, and then afterward willed by God. It was first of all willed by God, and thereupon *became* reasonable and just. In this way of thinking Christians strove not to think of the Lord as thrusting sinners down into Hell, but (in an image Jonathan Edwards used in the next century) of men and women heavy with sin, standing on a rotten covering over Hell from which God's merciful hand alone held them up and kept them from falling *of their own weight* into the damnation they deserved. (See below, p. 341.)

Let us return to joy. Both as a positive good to be sought and as a release from dreadful anxiety, the experience of grace became for many men and women the highest spiritual and psychological good. John Winthrop, a disciplined leader capable of making tough decisions to banish Roger Williams, Anne Hutchinson, and John Wheelwright, could nevertheless write in his journal of being "ravished . . . with unspeakable joy" during a meditation on the love between Christ and himself; "methought my soul had as familiar and sensible society with Him as any wife could have with the kindest husband; I desired no other happiness but to be embraced of Him. . . . I forgot to look after my supper, and some things that my heart lingered after before; then came such a calm of comfort over my heart, as revived my spirits, set my mind and conscience at sweet liberty and peace." The poet Anne Bradstreet told her children she was disappointed to find after her conversion that the joy of Christians was not so "constant" as she had supposed it would be, but she declared that she had "tasted of the hidden manna that the world knows not," and that in grateful awareness of such realities and such promises she would hold out against the temptations of doubt, corruption, despair, and even atheism that continued to afflict her. And more than a century after the founding of Massachusetts, Jonathan Edwards wrote perhaps the most meticulous account of the psychological experience of grace. Despite an increase in worldliness throughout the society, *some* writers upheld this emphasis on the splendor of God's glory, and the joy of sharing it, in every period from 1630 to 1860. One can find it in these pages, for example, in Emerson's *Nature* and his Divinity School Address, and in Thoreau's *Walden*.

But as Anne Bradstreet told her children, the Christian's spiritual life was not easy after conversion. Theoretically, at least, and in many lives all too actually, the converted Puritan lived at the center of an endless dialectic between assurance and doubt. The saints' assurance of salvation depended on their renouncing all claims that placed any value or confidence in themselves. They had to become convinced that they did not deserve to be redeemed and that they could not earn salvation. If convinced of their inadequacy but unable to attain a conviction of faith, they might fall into the sin of despair—a beginning of the hell on earth into which Satan tries to seduce the Soul in Edward Taylor's *God's Determinations Touching His Elect,* and into which the title character of Nathaniel Hawthorne's "Young Goodman Brown" falls. In the real life of the seventeenth century both Increase and Cotton Mather felt the threat of this terror long after they had become eminent preachers, and John Cotton was already a respected tutor at Emmanuel College, Cambridge, when he heard a sermon about "the misery of those who had only a negative righteousness, or a civil, sober, honest blamelessness before men." He suffered "disconsolate apprehensions" for the next three years before a more settled assurance "filled him with sacred joy."

Of course strong social forces in the community encouraged the children of saints to quiet their most troublesome doubts and find the freedom to act. The Covenant of Grace was usually interpreted as a divine promise to redeem the descendants of those whom Providence had chosen (or elected) for salvation, and there was even good practical evidence that an extraordinary number of ministers' sons in New England went to Harvard College and became ministers themselves. The Mather family not only produced many ministers, but not until the fourth generation did one adult descendant die without apparently having been given clear signs of election. Yet the command to "suspect thyself much" was always to be remembered, and even relatively worldly temperaments such as that of Samuel Sewall could become entangled in intricate personal doubts from which the achievement of active faith and benevolent action could seem an immense psychological relief, a virtual liberation. (See below, pp. 209–210.)

In the churches, moreover, the desire to purify worship and to follow Biblical example soon led a number of congregations to require that each prospective new member make a public confession of faith and of his religious experience—to edify other members with evidence of the various ways in which the Holy Spirit descended on the elect, and to allow prudent Elders of the church to help the applicant decide whether the apparent calling had genuinely come from above—self-deception being a great temptation. That emphasis on public or at least official scrutiny reinforced the strong pressure for self-examination and the natural desire to share personal experience with others. In various ways the requirement of public confession became controversial throughout the two centuries between the Antinomian crisis (1637) and Emerson's Divinity School Address (1838), and differences in the historical circumstances did not materially weaken the concentration on individual experience and belief, or on the value of articulating them verbally. Puritans and Friends (or Quakers) had especially strong reasons for writing spiritual autobiographies, diaries or journals to aid in self-examination, and meditative poems. Even Edward Taylor's *God's Determinations* concentrates on the Soul's effort to find the courage to claim membership in the church. And Jonathan Edwards's spiritual autobiography (which has usually been reprinted in our century under the title "Personal Narrative") sets forth a careful record of the differences between false and genuine experience of saving grace.

But of course religious experience was not the only personal experience of the colonists, and even among Puritan and Quaker writers, as Daniel B. Shea has shown, the outer world, the world in which all such Protestants had resolved to act for the glory of God, could dominate the narrative. The narratives of Indian captivity, usually designed to praise God for remarkable deliverance, appealed also to the reader's curiosity and racial prejudice concerning Indian life, and to the taste for adventure and horror. Elizabeth Ashbridge's fine narrative and some of Anne Bradstreet's best poems (as well as her brief spiritual autobiography) say as much about the life struggle of a seventeenth- or eighteenth-century woman as about private religious experience. Among writers whom we cannot call Puritan, moreover—those in whose work the self-examination is unarticulated and perfunctory (as in William Byrd's diary) or chiefly ethical and practical (as in *The Autobiography of Benjamin Franklin*)—social observation and experience take over the narrative. In New England, at least, one can find a potential link between the pious Puritans and Franklin in the methodical passages of Cotton Mather's so-called Diary. Thomas Jefferson, on the other hand, represents the self almost exclusively through public action.

3. SERMONS AND RELIGIOUS EXPOSITION

Throughout the first two centuries of New England settlement the literary leaders were with few exceptions clergymen, and the tradition of oratory behind William Ellery Channing, Ralph Waldo Emerson, Daniel Webster, and Theodore Parker was created largely by preachers of sermons. The function of that central act in Congregational churches was first to teach the truth to the people and then to make it a "convicting" truth by applying the lesson to the auditors' hearts. The style was therefore relatively unembellished. God's altar, said the translators who edited the *Bay Psalm Book,* needs not our polishings. Propositions and doctrine were generally set forth in plain declarations under numbered headings. Arguments, often called reasons, were then developed for the respective propositions, and *Uses* or the *Application* would then be directed to the auditors' own situation. The central target of most preaching in the seventeenth century was the heart or will of the individual persons—not only for the conversion of unregenerate sinners but also for renewing the commitment of the saints themselves. It was in these "Uses" that the sermons reached their rhetorical and emotional heights. Just as emotion without understanding was spiritually useless and even dangerous, so a rational understanding of doctrine had no spiritual value until the mind and heart accepted its significance by receiving it as a genuinely personal experience. It was in Uses, then, that emotional and figurative language most often appeared, and in the kind of anxious perplexity that we have already described one can see why the eager acceptance of a call to action would be followed with relief—especially if it provided in action a way of transcending logical difficulties. One of the best examples in the literature is the passage (below, p. 123) in which Thomas Shepard, having used all his reasoning power to argue that very few people shall be saved and that one cannot save oneself, urges his congregation to *strive* to be among those to be saved. For, as Thomas Hooker declared, though preaching did not save sinners, it might be the means through which the Lord prepares the heart to receive His free gift of grace.

There were essentially three other kinds of sermon in the period before the nineteenth century: the doctrinal sermon, especially at the weekly lecture assigned (as in Boston) alternately to the ministers of the community and usually attended by their colleagues as well; the Election Sermon, preached annually on Election Day and usually devoted to some national or social issue; and the revival sermon, which though usually logical (when delivered from New England pulpits) concentrated almost exclusively on stirring the congregation to repentance. The revivals began in the latter part of the seventeenth century in western Massachusetts and recurred periodically thereafter, most intensely in 1734 and from 1740 to 1742, when the Great Awakening of religious enthusiasm stirred the American colonies north and south, and England and some European communities as well.

4. POETRY

The early settlers wrote a great quantity and a considerable variety of verse. Perhaps the most successful of all the poems was Michael Wigglesworth's *The Day of Doom* (1662), which is too long in its 224 stanzas to be reprinted here. That is a didactic representation of the Day of Judgment, making doctrine memorable in internal rhyme and pounding fourteeners (14 beats to the line):

219
The Saints behold with courage bold,
and thankful wonderment,
To see all those that were their foes
thus sent to punishment:
Then do they sing unto their King
a Song of endless Praise:
They praise his Name, and do proclaim
that just are all his ways.

But much of the poetry was not in any social sense didactic, and a respectable quantity of seventeenth-century verse dealt with the ordinary experience of this world—sexual love, personal loss, natural observation. Both Anne Bradstreet and Edward Taylor wrote dramatic dialogues as well as meditations and other lyric poems. Taylor also wrote one poem on a spider catching a fly, and another on a wasp chilled with cold. Roger Williams incorporated brief poems on the significance of American Indian life into his *Key into The Language of America*. Cotton Mather wrote hymns for his private fasts, and some elegies, epitaphs, and acrostics; he translated some psalms into blank verse and wrote some heroic couplets on the barbarousness of cruel schoolmasters. John Wilson and others wrote anagrams, usually to honor the dead. Nicholas Noyes and others wrote prefatory poems and elegies. And of course the scholarly editors of *The Bay Psalm Book* strove to translate the Hebrew into rhythmic English verse without altering the sacred sense.

In the eighteenth century the quantity and variety continued to flourish, but religious verse became less dominant even in New England, and Virginia, Pennsylvania, and New York contributed heavily to the flood of published verse as printers throughout the colonies produced almanacs and journals. Here we have not reproduced any of the ephemeral verse of the early eighteenth century, for we have allowed Benjamin Franklin's witty verse proverbs to represent the typical wit, and in the later years we have let the poems of Royall Tyler (including his skillful prologue to *The Contrast*), Philip Freneau, and Joel Barlow represent the great quantity of comical and patriotic poetry that was published in the last quarter of the century. The strength of mock-heroic verse, especially in Barlow's *The Hasty Pudding,* is best appreciated through a contrast to the grandiose epics that he and some of his fellow Connecticut Wits wrote, but those epics—*The Columbiad* and Timothy Dwight's *The Conquest of Canaan,* for example—are too long to be included here.

5. POLITICAL AND PHILOSOPHICAL EXPOSITION

To some degree American literature was forced by circumstances to be concerned with political theory from the very beginning. In Virginia as well as New England the establishment of colonial government raised questions almost immediately about the relationship of legislative to executive authority and of the colonists to authorities in England. Discussion of the subject was especially urgent in New England, because so many people came at one time to found Massachusetts Bay, where several towns were founded at once, and because the colonists brought their charter with them. They therefore had no obligation to report, as the first Virginia and Plymouth colonists had done, to company officials in England.

Determined to establish a "Bible Commonwealth" where the city on a hill would set an example for the Christian world, the leaders of Massachusetts Bay faced new and sometimes unforeseen problems of government. They first met the great difficulty that has always confronted revolutionaries and reformers: they found that the complexities of established power were quite different from the relatively simple opposition they had maintained as oppressed reformers resisting the Establishment in England. They had always lived within an established church, for example, and had demanded the liberty to worship in a simpler way within it. Now they were almost immediately forced to consider what kind of authority they would establish over the several congregations scattered about the Bay. How much authority would the civil government have in religious matters? Everybody seemed to agree that the governor would have to be a layman and that in that sense the church and the state would be separated, but the leaders had to decide whether any but church members would be allowed to vote, and to what degree individual congregations, which were now no longer subject to the authority of bishops or even presbyters, could be limited in their collective action. Similar questions existed in the churches themselves. Who could be baptized? Who was entitled to the sacraments and to membership in the church, and what standards were to be applied in judging eligibility? When could a minister leave his congregation to become associated with another? Both the religious and the civil polity, in short, had to be created virtually anew. It is that necessity and that experience that, as much as any particular ideas, make the seventeenth-century colonists precursors of the American Revolution.

But of course the ideas themselves are important. On few of them did all the colonists or all their leaders agree. Some of the ideas that prevailed were fashioned in hot controversy, and some that lost (most notoriously Roger Williams's defense of religious toleration) eventually triumphed in the Bill of Rights a century and a half later. The founders of Massachusetts Bay were not democrats—indeed, they feared democracy as much as their descendant John Adams and other Revolutionary leaders would come to fear it, because they were certain that it would end in despotism. If the people be governors, one leader asked, who shall be governed? But all the Puritan leaders did believe that all human government must be limited, because even among Christians any man would in time surely use all the power that was given to him. They established an annual election for the governorship, and although John Winthrop and his associates used cunning and the threat of force to control the election of 1637 it is nonetheless a moving experience, during the unfinished term of a president who was obliged to resign, to read Winthrop's speech to the General Court (1645) on natural and civil liberty. Winthrop insisted there that although the legislature had just acquitted him of exceeding his authority the people had every right to remove an official who had betrayed his oath to serve them faithfully. They must, he said, endure until the next annual election official errors that were committed in good faith, for elected officials were not professionally trained to govern.

Insistence on the rights of Englishmen began in both Massachusetts and Virginia in the latter half of the seventeenth century. The first real troubles between London and Massachusetts Bay came soon after the Restoration in 1660 when the royal government of Charles II began to assert some control—especially over religious discrimination and maritime commerce—in a colony that had been virtually independent for a generation. The mutual suspicion of colony and home government was intensified by the bloody history of religious persecution and conflict that had culminated in civil war and in the execution of Charles I, under the regime of Oliver Cromwell, whom the Massachusetts leaders had of course supported.

In the controversy during the 1660's, the defense of colonial prerogative reversed old positions. Now it was the Puritans who found themselves under attack for the religious intolerance of their colonial government. To the dismay of many friends in Massachusetts, Oliver Cromwell himself had instituted a limited religious toleration and now, while in England Puritan ministers were for a time being silenced once again by royal authority, the government of Massachusetts was ordered to desist from persecuting Quakers and to allow Anglicans to worship freely. In one of the saddest episodes in New England history, a group of Quakers who had been whipped and banished, had persisted in returning to bear witness to their faith and to the harshness of the authorities. Four Quakers had then been hanged in Boston. Reluctantly, the Massachusetts authorities desisted from physical punishment of Quakers, but as Hutchinson's history and Samuel Sewall's diary indicate (below, pp. 517, 213) Quaker witnesses continued to shock respectable churchgoers with bizarre appearances, and eventually, as the pamphlet of Isaac Backus indicates, it was the Baptists who carried on the eighteenth-century battle for complete religious liberty in New England.

The intricate conflict between Massachusetts and the royal government intensified in complex ways during the reign of Charles II, and eventually the precious charter that John Winthrop had brought with him was revoked in 1684. The provincial rule of Sir Edmund Andros in the 1680's was so offensive to many people in Boston that it provoked an actual rebellion in 1689, as soon as news was received that James II had been deposed in England. The significance of Massachusetts appeals to Englishmen's rights in that controversy is clearly stated in Cotton Mather's biography of Sir William Phips. (See below, pp. 262–265.)

Similar conflicts, without the same religious base, troubled the relationship between Virginia and the royal authorities during the same period, and as the other colonies developed in the early decades of the eighteenth century local and imperial interests clashed more often. The selections here from Thomas Paine—who was a mature man before he emigrated from England to Pennsylvania during the year before the Revolution—Benjamin Franklin, Thomas Jefferson, and James Madison must represent a large body of political exposition that came from outside New England. The Virginia literary tradition developed more slowly than that of Massachusetts, for her settlement had been less densely concentrated at first, her economy less commercial, and (above all) her sense of purpose less intensely ideological. But in the controversies with royal governors during the seventeenth century, in the writings of men like Beverley and Byrd, and in the tradition of legal and literary education in London as well as at the College of William and Mary, Virginia had developed a strong tradition of sophisticated political expression. Thomas Jefferson, like Benjamin Franklin, is a figure of too large a genius to be confined within a political context, but his skill as a writer found its most important expression in political affairs.

Although French and other continental ideas had considerable influence, the great English minds of John Locke (1632–1704) and Isaac Newton (1642–1727) can stand as representative of the major differences between the thought of the founding generations in Virginia and Massachusetts and that of the Revolutionary leaders. Although Locke actually devised an abortive plan for aristocratic titles to be established in the Carolinas, and although Newton spent much of his later life working on chronologies of Biblical prophecy, their writings gave authority to the replacement of a sovereign God and a sovereign monarch by natural law and the natural rights of men. Many Americans came to believe that the goal of life was not the glory of God but the pursuit of happiness. Despite the brilliant dissent of Jonathan Edwards (see below, p. 313), prevailing opinion in the latter half of the eighteenth century read Newton's lesson in a way that can be summed up in the title of Philip Freneau's poem "On the Uniformity and Perfection of Nature" (below, p. 699).

When John Winthrop distinguished between natural and civil liberty in 1645, he insisted that natural liberty was the liberty to live as we like, as impulsively as beasts, as wickedly as the worst of sinners, and he declared that civil liberty, under covenanted Christian authority, was a liberty "to that only which is good, just, and honest." Thomas Paine and Thomas Jefferson appealed to the natural rights of men, the so-called economy of Nature, the authority of the human Understanding, the moral sense, common sense. Students of early American literature have a chance to examine the differences and the affinities between those worlds.

Two large minority groups, the one declining in population and the other increasing, remained outside this political world, although they were profoundly affected by its actions and their status offered a profound challenge to its most humane assumptions. Thomas Jefferson estimated that nearly one-half the population of Virginia in 1782 consisted of African slaves, and the United States census of 1790 counted 750,000 Afro-Americans in a total national population of 4 million. Not only in occasional pamphlets like Samuel Sewall's *The Selling of Joseph* (1700) and John Woolman's *Journal,* but in writings and speeches by free black citizens and by a few slaves, the ideal of equal rights was memorably advanced before black and white audiences. The famous, stirring letter of Benjamin Banneker to Thomas Jefferson and the powerful addresses of Absalom Jones and William Hamilton form an indispensable commentary on the political ideals of the new republic—a commentary intensified by the beautiful music of the spirituals that appear later on in this volume, and by the slave narratives and autobiographies that are represented here by the chapter from *Narrative of the Life of . . . an American Slave* by Frederick Douglass.

The American Indians in the eighteenth century did not write poems or speeches in English, but their oral literature deserves to be represented briefly here to remind us of the complex culture that was displaced by European encroachment and simplified in American literature of the nineteenth century. Indians were of course the subject of much American writing in English, much of it prejudiced, self-serving, and misinformed. Indian speeches, moreover, were sometimes apparently delivered in English, and in any case the translations through which we now know them are the versions that their Anglo-American contemporaries read and that Anglo-American novelists and dramatists exploited to create some of the conventional Indian figures of historical romance and romantic history.

6. DIALOGUE, FICTION, FABLE, AND DRAMA

Perhaps the earliest version of American fiction was the dialogue between old and young Congregationalists in which William Bradford worked out some controverted principles, and some obviously dramatic elements enliven sermons like the one that we have reprinted from Thomas Shepard's *The Sincere Convert*. Shepard sets up a vigorous contrast in brief questions by a hypothetical objector to his doctrines, and pithy, rhythmic answers of his own. (See below, pp. 121–123.) Cotton Mather, too, wrote some political fables, and Benjamin Franklin, having opened his journalistic career under the pseudonym of Mrs. Silence Dogood in Boston, established his position in Philadelphia with Socratic dialogues and the universally successful *Poor Richard Improved* (or *The Way to Wealth*), which he cast in the form of a narrative by Poor Richard. But the hostility to drama and fiction had not softened much by the time that Royall Tyler, happening to be in New York on politico-military business in 1787, saw a performance of *The School for Scandal* and suddenly composed *The Contrast*. Tyler had apparently participated in some clandestine performances of tragedies with other Harvard students during the early years of the Revolution, and H. H. Brackenridge and others had written heroic dramas during the Revolution. Even in the 1740's writers as different as Benjamin Franklin, who reprinted Samuel Richardson's *Pamela,* and Jonathan Edwards had seen moral value in the sentimental novel. Yet drama did not really flourish until much later, and fiction had only begun to attract a number of American writers by the end of the eighteenth century. It is in the mock-epic narrative of *Modern Chivalry*, the psychological novels of Charles Brockden Brown, and the sketches and tales of Washington Irving that American fiction begins to achieve deep social penetration and technical originality. Only with Irving's *The Sketch Book* (1820) did an American writer of fiction achieve great financial success, and not until James Fenimore Cooper's *The Spy* (1821) did that kind of triumph come to an American novelist.

American literature of the first two centuries sounded major themes that would echo through some of the best achievements of the next 150 years: the nature of the commonwealth; the threat, the grandeur, and beauty of the landscape; the limits of individual liberty and governmental authority; the riddle of American guilt and American destiny; and the quest for union with the divine and for self-expression. In the literature of those years the literary imagination expands to conceive of ways to build the new church and the new society, and at other times it turns inward to seek ways of expressing the inexpressible—an experience of joy or guilt that makes the individual will wish alternately to become united with, lost in, or annihilated by the divine spirit of the Creator. And alongside that self, described by Jonathan Edwards and Cotton Mather, the personal literature of the eighteenth century ranges the ingenious, tolerant, guilt-free selves of Benjamin Franklin, John Adams, and Thomas Jefferson, the observant mind of William Bartram, the conscientiously un-self-conscious Elizabeth Ashbridge, and the self-taught presence of Benjamin Banneker showing the Secretary of State that a black man is after all capable of intellectual achievement.

A NOTE ON THE EARLY TEXTS

In all of Part I except the selections from Edward Taylor and Benjamin Franklin, we have normalized spelling and capitalization according to modern usage. Because punctuation and italics often serve important rhetorical functions in seventeenth- and eighteenth-century works, we have reproduced those peculiarities of the original texts, except for a few meaningless practices (commas before the beginning or end of parentheses). When Cotton Mather (p. 254) says that Sir William Phips's temperament cut "rather like a *hatchet*, than like a *razor*," and that no difficulties could "put by the *edge* of his resolutions," both the author and the printer intend to call attention to the wordplay, although not with the very heavy emphasis that italics would now convey.

I
The Literature of New England Puritanism

A.
THE SEVENTEENTH CENTURY

Our Introduction has described the major ideas and genres of American Puritan writers. Here we arrange the literature chronologically according to the authors' birth dates, and we set off the first century after the settlement of Boston (and the composition of William Bradford's first book about Plymouth Plantation) in 1630 from the extraordinary revival of religion known as the Great Awakening in the fourth and fifth decades of the eighteenth century. Within what now seems the narrow range of Puritan thought, seventeenth-century New England writers established a firm tradition of historical, autobiographical, and devotional literature that sounded themes to which American writers would return for another 200 years. The newness of the country, the puzzle of American destiny, the nature of the just political system, the limits of liberty, the value of the examined self, the significance of American Indian culture, the study of contemporaneous history, the relationship between individual experience in this world and the soul's eternal fate or the grand design of Providence—all these subjects are represented in a way that affects American writers long after the specific religious doctrines of seventeenth-century New England Puritanism have lost most of their power in American society. As we have argued in the Introduction, however, the continuing significance of American Puritanism cannot be properly understood unless one tries to understand it in its own terms.

WILLIAM BRADFORD

(1590-1657)

William Bradford was elected to replace the first governor of Plymouth Plantation, who died in 1621, a few months after the founding of the colony, and in the annual elections during the rest of Bradford's life he was reelected 30 times. As a signer of the Mayflower Compact and governor for virtually all of the colony's first three decades, he had unique qualifications for writing the history of the people who came to be known as Pilgrims. He gave them that name in his history, he had been with them since the beginning of their long journey, and he had the best supply of original documents for the narrative.

Bradford was born at Austerfield, Yorkshire. When his mother remarried after his father's death, he was reared by his grandfather and uncles, who prepared him to become a farmer. His life changed sharply, however, when he was converted by a nonconformist preacher at the age of fifteen or sixteen. He became a member of the Separatist congregation at Scrooby in 1606, and three years later he was one of those young men whose exciting departure from Hull for the

All the published versions of this unfinished work take some liberties with the punctuation. The sections reprinted here have been edited for this anthology from a photographic facsimile of the original manuscript (1896) and then checked for errors against the only modern edition that was based directly on the original manuscript, Samuel Eliot Morison's *Of Plymouth Plantation*, 1952. Morison's superb notes are reprinted here with permission of the publisher, Alfred A. Knopf. Morison's edition is the most readable, but it normalizes punctuation and paragraphing according to modern usage and thus changes the rhythm of the prose. Here we have normalized spelling and capitalization according to modern practice, but we have retained Bradford's punctuation (except for obviously accidental inconsistencies or inconsistent peculiarities such as commas before the beginning or end of parentheses). We believe that the periods that occur in the manuscript above the ordinary line are not meant to be full stops and that Bradford's sentences are often much longer than any previous editor has understood them to be. The periods that we have printed above the line [·] represent our judgment that the sentence continues without a complete stop. Except for its neglect of this question and for a few other errors noted by Morison, the best edition that reproduces Bradford's orthography is *History of Plymouth Plantation 1620-1647*, 2 vols., ed. Worthington C. Ford, 1912.

Studies include G. F. Willison, *Saints and Strangers*, 1945; Bradford Smith, *Bradford of Plymouth*, 1951; George D. Langdon, Jr., *Pilgrim Colony: A History of New Plymouth, 1620-1691*, 1966; Alan B. Howard, "Art and History in Bradford's *Of Plymouth Plantation*, *William and Mary Quarterly*, 3d ser., 28 (1971): 237-266; David Levin, "William Bradford: The Value of Puritan Historiography," in *Major Writers of Early American Literature*, ed. Everett H. Emerson, 1972, pp. 11-31.

Netherlands is so movingly described in the second chapter of his history. From then on he served under the spiritual leaders John Robinson and William Brewster, whom he describes (respectively) as the representative pastor and elder in the history. He moved from Amsterdam to Leyden with the congregation later in 1609, he learned the trade of weaving (farming being impractical for men who owned no land in that new country), he married in 1613, and he managed somehow to educate himself in humane letters, so that by the time he began to write the history he knew Dutch and French as well as the Latin and Greek to which he had been introduced in grammar school, and he had laid a foundation for the study of Hebrew that filled his leisure hours (and blank pages in the bound volume of his history) during the last years of his life.

Bradford began writing the history *Of Plymouth Plantation* in 1630, the tenth year of settlement, when a much larger group of English Puritans had founded the Massachusetts Bay Colony in Boston, Cambridge, and other towns. In that first year of composition, he wrote the whole of Book I, bringing the narrative down to 1621. Then he apparently abandoned the history until he began writing again in 1646, and internal evidence shows that he wrote the last sections in 1650. The manuscript was used by later historians of New England in the seventeenth and eighteenth centuries, but disappeared during the American Revolution and was not found again until it turned up in an English library in the middle of the nineteenth century. More than two centuries after Bradford's death, it was published for the first time.

Bradford exemplifies the great strength that Puritanism gave, along with the prejudices we so easily recognize, to the historian. He set the story of his little community in the large history of Christianity, and especially of the Reformation, which he believed the Separatists were perfecting by restoring "the primitive order, liberty, and beauty" of the very first Christian churches. That is why it is so important for the selection in this anthology to begin at the beginning of Bradford's work rather than to follow the usual practice of opening in the ninth chapter, with the Pilgrims (and the reader) at sea. Long before the Mayflower sails for America, Bradford has established the historical context and pattern for much of his narrative. His Puritan beliefs naturally lead him to stress the community's dependence on Providence, and of course he regarded history as a means of celebrating the glory of God. But we must take care to notice how splendidly his historical imagination manages to construct the narrative so that the Pilgrims (as in Chapter 2) have nothing else to rely on except their faith in Providence. Repeatedly the Lord delivers them less spectacularly than by miraculously intervening to quell a storm at sea. His more characteristic way of delivering them is to let His intelligent people puzzle out the earthly, humane reasons for relying on their faith in Providence. Because he is a Puritan justifying God's ways, along with his own community's ways, to mankind, Bradford feels obliged to show in some detail how "necessity forced a way" for the oppressed saints, and to reveal the dialectical pattern in which they move from perplexity to hope, from disease to remedy, and from prosperity to unforeseen complexities. With a Puritan's passion for justification, he fills his narrative with documents, and especially with letters, that not only help to characterize the principal actors and forces but also show us the incontrovertible evidence on which the characters' decisions and his own historical judgments have been based. Sometimes those documents seem tedious; often they give character and event a deeper complexity.

This first American historiographical masterpiece thus derives as much of its strength from the author's historical intelligence and from his Puritan preconceptions as from his celebrated magnanimity and his justly celebrated style. Students reading him for the first time will not want to overlook those qualities, either. With the Puritan's interest in typology, Bradford provides in his history a mythic representation of the grand, painful emigration, the journey over a perilous sea to a safe haven, that still has a deep meaning for all immigrants and their descendants. He makes of his Pilgrims a heroic but simple community, striving against persecutors, against natural terrors, against the strangeness of a European exile, an American wilderness, and a succession of ruinous confidence men to do their duty in the world for the glory of God. And with a mixture of pride and dismay he shows their colony prospering "from small beginnings" even as its growing size and complexity threaten and virtually destroy the original ideal of the covenant, a spiritual community knit together as in a body.

The first book, comprising about one-fifth of the whole, was written as a coherent narrative. When he resumed the narrative about 16 years later, Bradford divided the chapters annually. The selections from Book II are taken from a year in the middle 1620's and a year in the early 1640's, but both were written no earlier than 1646.

Of Plymouth Plantation

And first of the occasion, and inducements thereunto; the which that I may truly unfold, I must begin at the very root, and rise of the same. The which I shall endeavor to manifest in a plain style; with singular regard unto the simple truth in all things, at least as near as my slender judgment can attain the same.

CHAPTER I

It is well known unto the godly, and judicious, how ever since the first breaking out of the light of the gospel, in our honorable nation of England (which was the first of nations, whom the Lord adorned therewith, after that gross darkness of popery which had covered, and overspread the Christian world) what wars, and oppositions ever since, Satan hath raised, maintained, and continued against the Saints,[1] from time, to time, in one sort or other. Sometimes by bloody death and cruel torments, other whiles imprisonments, banishments, and other hard usages. As being loath his kingdom should go down, the truth prevail; and the churches of God revert to their ancient purity; and recover, their primitive [primative] order, liberty, and beauty. But when he could not prevail by these means, against the main truths of the gospel, but that they began to take rooting in many places; being watered with the blood of the martyrs, and blessed from Heaven with a gracious increase he then began to take him to his ancient stratagems, used of old against the first Christians [·] that when by the bloody, and barbarous persecutions of the heathen emperors, he could not stop, and subvert the course of the gospel; but that it speedily overspread, with a wonderful celerity, the then best known parts of the world [·] he then began to sow errors, heresies, and wonderful dissensions amongst the professors[2] themselves (working upon their pride, and ambition, with other corrupt passions, incident to all mortal men; yea to the saints themselves in some measure) by which woeful effects followed; as not only bitter contentions, and heartburnings, schisms, with other horrible confusions [·] but Satan took occasion and advantage thereby to foist in a number of vile ceremonies, with many unprofitable canons, and decrees which have since been as snares, to many poor, and peaceable souls, even to this day. So as in the ancient times, the persecutions by the heathen, and their emperors was not greater than of the Christians one against other [—] the Arians, and other their complices, against the orthodox and true Christians. As witnesseth Socrates in his second book[.][3] His words are these:

> The violence truly (saith he) was no less than that of old, practiced towards the Christians when they were compelled, and drawn to sacrifice to idols; for many endured sundry kinds of torment, often rack-

[1] Bradford uses the word *Saint* in the Biblical sense, as one of God's chosen people, or a church member, not one of those canonized by the Roman Catholic Church.

[2] *Professor*, as used by Bradford and by Puritans generally, had no educational connotation; it merely meant one who professed Christianity.

[3] Socrates Scholasticus, Greek historian of the 5th century A.D. His Ecclesiastical History translated by Meredith Hanmer was printed in London in 1577. Bradford's quotation is from lib. ii chap. 22.

ings, and dismembering of their joints; confiscating of their goods; some bereaved of their native soil; others departed this life under the hands of the tormentor, and some died in banishment, and never saw their country again etc.

The like method Satan hath seemed to hold in these later times, since the truth began to spring, and spread after the great defection made by Antichrist that man of sin[.][4]

For to let pass the infinite examples in sundry nations, and several places of the world, and instance in our own [·] when as that old serpent could not prevail by those fiery flames and other his cruel tragedies which he (by his instruments) put in ure,[5] everywhere in the days of Queen Mary, and before [·] he then began another kind of war, and went more closely to work, not only to oppugn, but even to ruinate and destroy the kingdom of Christ, by more secret and subtle means[,] by kindling the flames of contention, and sowing the seeds of discord, and bitter enmity amongst the professors (and seeming reformed) themselves. For when he could not prevail (by the former means) against the principal doctrines of faith; he bent his force against the holy discipline, and outward regiment of the kingdom of Christ, by which those holy doctrines should be conserved, and true piety maintained amongst the saints, and people of God.

Mr. Fox[6] recordeth, how that besides those worthy martyrs and confessors which were burned in Queen Mary's days and otherwise tormented[,] "Many (both students, and others) fled out of the land, to the number of 800 [·] and became several congregations [·] at Wesel, Frankfort, Basel, Emden, Markpurge, Strasburg, and Geneva, etc." Amongst whom (but especially those at Frankfort[)] began that bitter war of contention, and persecution about the ceremonies, and service book, and other popish and antichristian stuff the plague of England to this day (which are like the high places in Israel; which the prophets cried out against, and were their ruin), which the better part sought (according to the purity of the gospel) to root out, and utterly to abandon [·] and the other part (under veiled pretences for their own ends, and advancements) sought as stiffly, to continue, maintain, and defend [·] as appeareth by the discourse thereof published in print, anno 1575 (a book that deserves better to be known, and considered).[7]

[4] 2 Thessalonians ii.3.

[5] I.e., into practice.

[6] Acts and Mon[uments]: pag. 1587 edition 2 (Bradford). His reference is to John Fox *Acts and Monuments* (familiarly known as the *Book of Martyrs*) p. 1587 of 2nd edition.

[7] William Whittingham *Brieff Discours of the Troubles begonne at Franckford*, printed at Zurich or Geneva in 1575. The row was between the Marian exiles who wished to abolish "service books" altogether (which Bradford and the entire left wing of English Protestantism believed should have been done), and those who adopted the typically English compromise of a Book of Common Prayer. The Marian exiles, or some of them, wished to reorganize the church on congregational principles which they believed alone to be sanctioned by the New Testament.

The one side labored to have the right worship of God, and discipline of Christ, established in the church, according to the simplicity of the gospel; without the mixture of men's inventions. And to have, and to be ruled by the laws of God's Word; dispensed in those offices, and by those officers of Pastors, Teachers, and Elders, etc, according to the Scriptures. The other party (though under many colors, and pretenses) endeavored to have the episcopal dignity (after the popish manner) with their large power, and jurisdiction, still retained; with all those courts, canons, and ceremonies, together with all such livings, revenues, and subordinate officers, with other such means, as formerly upheld their antichristian greatness and enabled them with lordly, and tyrannous power, to persecute the poor servants of God. This contention was so great, as neither the honor of God, the common persecution; nor the mediation of Mr. Calvin, and other worthies of the Lord, in those places could prevail with those thus episcopally minded; but they proceeded by all means to disturb the peace of this poor persecuted church. Even so far as to charge (very unjustly, and ungodlily; yet prelate-like) some of their chief opposers, with rebellion, and high treason against the Emperor, and other such crimes.

And this contention died not with Queen Mary; nor was left beyond the seas, but at her death these people returning into England under gracious Queen Elizabeth [·] many of them being preferred to bishoprics and other promotions, according to their aims and desires [·] that inveterate hatred against the holy discipline of Christ in His church[8] hath continued to this day. Insomuch that for fear it should prevail, all plots, and devices have been used to keep it out, incensing the Queen and State against it as dangerous for the commonwealth; and that it was most needful that the fundamental points of religion should be preached in those ignorant, and superstitious times; and to win the weak and ignorant they might retain divers harmless ceremonies, and though it were to be wished that divers things were reformed, yet this was not a season for it. And many the like to stop the mouths of the more godly [·] to bring them on to yield to one ceremony after another, and one corruption after another; by these wiles beguiling some, and corrupting others till at length they began to persecute all the zealous professors in the land (though they knew little what this discipline meant) both by word, and deed if they would not submit to their ceremonies, and become slaves to them, and their popish trash, which have no ground in the Word of God, but are relics of that man of sin. And the more the light of the gospel grew, the more they urged their subscriptions to these corruptions. So as (notwithstanding all their former pretenses, and fair colors) they whose eyes God had not justly blinded, might easily see whereto these things tended.

[8] Bradford means the Congregational discipline. His account of church history during Elizabeth's reign is of course a partisan one, unfair to the acts and the motives of everyone not in the left wing of Protestantism.

And to cast contempt the more upon the sincere servants of God; they opprobriously, and most injuriously, gave unto, and imposed upon them, that name of puritans; which is said the Novatians (out of pride) did assume and take unto themselves.[9] And lamentable it is to see the effects which have followed; Religion hath been disgraced, the godly grieved, afflicted, persecuted, and many exiled, sundry have lost their lives in prisons, and otherways. On the other hand, sin hath been countenanced; ignorance, profaneness, and atheism increased, and the papists encouraged to hope again for a day.[°]

---

[9] Eusebius lib. vi chap. 42 (Bradford [in margin]). The Novatians were an obscure sect of the 3rd century. The term *Puritan*, like *Quaker*, was originally one of reproach, not accepted until nearly the close of the 17th century by the people to whom it was applied. The Puritans called themselves "God's people."

[°] Sixteen years after he had written these lines, Bradford added the following commentary on the blank page facing this one. With the Puritans now in firm control of the English government, and the bishops deposed, Bradford exults in celebration of what he takes to be the Lord's power. Notice, however, that his commentary opens with an emphatic recognition of his own ignorance of coming historical events at the time he wrote the chapter.—D.L.

A Late Observation, as it Were, by the Way, Worthy to be Noted

Full little did I think, that the downfall of the bishops, with their courts, canons and ceremonies, etc. had been so near, when I first began these scribbled writings (which was about the year 1630, and so pieced up at times of leisure afterward) or that I should have lived, to have seen, or heard of the same; but it is the Lord's doing, and ought to be marvelous in our eyes! [Psalm cxviii. 23.] Every plant which mine heavenly Father hath not planted (saith our Saviour) shall be rooted up. Matthew xv.13. I have snared thee, and thou art taken, O Babel (Bishops) and thou wast not aware; thou art found, and also caught, because thou hast striven against the Lord. Jeremiah L.24. But will they needs strive? Against the truth, against the servants of God, what and against the Lord Himself? Do they provoke the Lord to anger? Are they

stronger than He? 1 Corinthians x.22. No, no, they have met with their match. Behold, I come unto thee, O proud man, saith the Lord God of hosts; for thy day is come, even the time that I will visit thee. Jeremiah L.31. May not the People of God now say (and these poor people among the rest), "The Lord hath brought forth our righteousness; come let us declare in Zion the work of the Lord our God." Jeremiah li.10. Let all flesh be still before the Lord; for He is raised up out of His holy place. Zechariah ii.13.

In this case, these poor people may say (among the thousands of Israel) "When the Lord brought again the captivity of Zion, we were like them that dream." Psalm cxxvi.1. "The Lord hath done great things for us, whereof we rejoice." Verse 3. "They that sow in tears, shall reap in joy. They went weeping, and carried precious seed, but they shall return with joy, and bring their sheaves." Verses 5, 6.

Do you not now see the fruits of your labors, O all ye servants of the Lord? That have suffered for His truth, and have been faithful witnesses of the same, and ye little handful amongst the rest, the least amongst the thousands of Israel? [Micah v.2] You have not only had a seed time, but many of you have seen the joyful harvest, should you not then rejoice? Yea, and again rejoice, and say, Hallelujah, Salvation, and glory, and honor, and power, be to the Lord our God; for true, and righteous are His judgments." Revelation xix.1, 2.

But thou wilt ask What is the matter, What is done? Why, art thou a stranger in Israel, that thou shouldst not know what is done? Are not those Jebusites overcome that have vexed the people of Israel so long, even

(Footnote continued next page.)

This made that holy man Mr. Perkins[10] cry out in his exhortation to repentance, upon Zephaniah II:

> Religion (saith he) hath been amongst us this thirty-five years; but the more it is published, the more it is contemned, and reproached of many, etc. Thus not profaneness, nor wickedness; but religion itself is a byword, a mockingstock, and a matter of reproach; so that in England at this day, the man, or woman that begins to profess religion, and serve God, must resolve with himself to sustain mocks, and injuries even as though he lived amongst the enemies of religion.

And this common experience hath confirmed, and made too apparent.

But that I may come more near my intendment; when as by the travail, and diligence of some godly and zealous preachers, and God's blessing on their labors; as in other places of the land, so in the North parts, many became enlightened by the Word of God, and had their ignorance and sins discovered unto them, and began by His grace to reform their lives, and make conscience of their ways. The work of God was no sooner manifest in them; but presently they were both scoffed, and scorned by the profane multitude; and the ministers urged with the yoke of subscription, or else must be silenced; and the poor people were so vexed with apparitors, and pursuivants[11] and the commissary courts, as truly their affliction was not small; which, notwithstanding they bore sundry years with much patience, till they were occasioned (by the continuance, and increase of these troubles, and other means which the Lord raised up in those days) to see further into things by the light of the Word of God. How not only these base and beggarly ceremonies were unlawful; but also that the lordly, and tyrannous

holding Jerusalem till David's days, and been as thorns in their sides, so many ages; and now began to scorn that any David should meddle with them [2 Samuel v.6-9]; they began to fortify their tower, as that of the old Babylonians; but those proud Anakims were thrown down, and their glory laid in the dust. [Joshua xi.21-2] The tyrannous Bishops are ejected, their courts dissolved, their canons forceless, their service cashiered, their ceremonies useless, and despised; their plots for popery prevented, and all their superstitions discarded, and returned to Rome from whence they came, and the monuments of idolatry rooted out of the land. And the proud and profane supporters, and cruel defenders of these (as bloody papists and wicked atheists, and their malignant consorts) marvelously overthrown. And are not these great things? Who can deny it?

But who hath done it? Who, even He that

sitteth on the white horse, who is called Faithful, and true, and judgeth, and fighteth righteously. Revelation xix.11. Whose garments are dipped in blood, and His name was called the Word of God. (verse 13) For He shall rule them with a rod of iron; for it is He that treadeth the winepress of the fierceness and wrath of God Almighty. And He hath upon His garment, and upon His thigh a name written, The King of Kings, and Lord of Lords. Verses 15, 16.

Anno Domini 1646.   Hallelujah

[10] William ("Painful") Perkins, a graduate of Emmanuel College, Cambridge, whose works were much esteemed by all branches of Puritans. The quotation is from his *Exposition of Christ's Sermon Upon the Mount* (1618) p. 421.

[11] Officers of the Church of England whose duty was to enforce conformity.

power of the prelates, ought not to be submitted unto; which thus (contrary to the freedom of the gospel) would load and burden men's consciences; and by their compulsive power make a profane mixture of persons, and things in the worship of God. And that their offices and callings; courts, and canons, etc. were unlawful, and antichristian; being such as have no warrant in the Word of God; but the same that were used in popery, and still retained. Of which a famous author thus writeth in his Dutch commentaries: [12]

At the coming of King James into England; The new king (saith he) found there established the reformed religion, according to the reformed religion of King Edward VI, retaining, or keeping still the spiritual state of the bishops, etc. after the old manner, much varying, and differing from the reformed churches, in Scotland, France, and the Netherlands, Emden, Geneva, etc. whose reformation is cut, or shapen much nearer the first Christian churches, as it was used in the Apostles' times.

So many therefore (of these professors) as saw the evil of these things (in these parts) and whose hearts the Lord had touched with heavenly zeal for His truth; they shook off this yoke of antichristian bondage [·] and as the Lord's free people, joined themselves (by a covenant of the Lord) into a church estate, in the fellowship of the gospel to walk in all His ways, made known, or to be made known unto them (according to their best endeavors) whatsoever it should cost them, the Lord assisting them. [13] And that it cost them something this ensuing history will declare.

These people became two distinct bodies, or churches; and in regard of distance of place did congregate severally; for they were of sundry towns and villages, some in Nottinghamshire, some of Lincolnshire and some of Yorkshire, where they border nearest together. In one of these churches (besides others of note) was Mr. John Smith, [14] a man of able gifts, and a good preacher; who afterwards was chosen their pastor. But these afterwards falling into some errors in the Low Countries, there (for the most part) buried themselves, and their names.

[12] Emanuel van Meteren *General History of the Netherlands* (London 1608) xxv.119. Bradford's reference, to which he adds this remark: "The reformed churches shapen much near[er] the primitive pattern than England, for the[y] cashier the Bishops with all their courts, canons, and ceremonies, at the first; and left them amongst the popish tr[ash] to which they per[tained]." Bradford passes over the fact that James I at the Hampton Court Conference in 1604 gave full opportunity of self-expression to the Puritans, who so exasperated him with their demands that he declared he would make them conform to the Church of England, "or . . . harry them out of the land, or else do worse."

[13] A paraphrase of the words of the covenant that people made when they formed a Separatist (later called Congregational) church.

[14] An alumnus of Christ's College, Cambridge, who seceded from the Church of England in 1605 and preached to the Separatist church at Gainsborough. This congregation emigrated in 1608 to Amsterdam, where Smith embraced a number of strange opinions and his church broke up.

But in this other church (which must be the subject of our discourse) besides other worthy men, was Mr. Richard Clyfton a grave and reverend preacher; who by his pains and diligence had done much good, and under God had been a means of the conversion of many. And also that famous and worthy man Mr. John Robinson, who afterwards was their pastor for many years, till the Lord took him away by death [·] also Mr. William Brewster a reverent man, who afterwards was chosen an elder of the church and lived with them till old age.[15]

But after these things; they could not long continue in any peaceable condition; but were hunted, and persecuted on every side, so as their former afflictions were but as flea-bitings in comparison of these which now came upon them. For some were taken, and clapped up in prison, others had their houses beset and watched night and day, and hardly escaped their hands; and the most were fain to flee and leave their houses and habitations, and the means of their livelihood. Yet these and many other sharper things which afterward befell them, were no other than they looked for, and therefore were the better prepared to bear them by the assistance of God's grace and Spirit; yet seeing themselves thus molested, and that there was no hope of their continuance there [·] by a joint consent they resolved to go into the Low Countries where they heard was freedom of religion for all men; as also how sundry from London, and other parts of the land had been exiled, and persecuted for the same cause, and were gone thither; and lived at Amsterdam, and in other places of the land. So after they had continued together about a year, and kept their meetings every Sabbath, in one place, or other, exercising the worship of God amongst themselves, notwithstanding all the diligence and malice of their adversaries; they seeing they could no longer continue in that condition, they resolved to get over into Holland as they could. Which was in the year 1607 and 1608 of which more at large in the next chap[ter.]

CHAPTER II
OF THEIR DEPARTURE INTO HOLLAND AND THEIR TROUBLES THEREABOUT, WITH SOME OF THE MANY DIFFICULTIES THEY FOUND AND MET WITHAL. ANNO 1608

Being thus constrained to leave their native soil and country, their lands and livings, and all their friends, and familiar acquaintance, it was much; and thought marvelous by many. But to go into a country they knew not (but by

[15] Richard Clyfton and John Robinson also were Cambridge alumni in holy orders who separated. Clyfton and William Brewster organized the Separatist congregation at Scrooby, Nottinghamshire, which Bradford joined as a young man. The sentence on Brewster is written in a different ink from the rest of the chapter, having been inserted after the Elder's death in 1643.

hearsay) where they must learn a new language, and get their livings they knew not how, it being a dear place and subject to the miseries of war, it was by many thought an adventure almost desperate, a case intolerable, and a misery worse than death. Especially seeing they were not acquainted with trades, nor traffic (by which that country doth subsist) but had only been used to a plain country life, and the innocent trade of husbandry. But these things did not dismay them (though they did sometimes trouble them) for their desires were set on the ways of God, and to enjoy His ordinances, but they rested on His providence, and knew Whom they had believed. Yet this was not all, for though they could not stay, yet were they not suffered to go, but the ports, and havens were shut against them; so as they were fain to seek secret means of conveyance, and to bribe and fee the mariners, and give extraordinary rates for their passages.[1] And yet were they often times betrayed (many of them) and both they, and their goods intercepted and surprised, and thereby put to great trouble, and charge, of which I will give an instance, or two, and omit the rest.

There was a large company of them purposed to get passage at Boston in Lincolnshire, and for that end, had hired a ship wholly to themselves; and made agreement with the master to be ready at a certain day, and take them, and their goods in, at a convenient place, where they accordingly would all attend in readiness. So after long waiting, and large expenses (though he kept not day with them) yet he came at length, and took them in, in the night. But when he had them, and their goods aboard; he betrayed them, having beforehand complotted with the searchers, and other officers so to do. Who took them, and put them into open boats, and there rifled and ransacked them, searching them to their shirts for money, yea even the women further than became modesty, and then carried them back into the town, and made them a spectacle, and wonder to the multitude; which came flocking on all sides to behold them. Being thus first, by these catchpoll officers, rifled, and stripped of their money, books, and much other goods; they were presented to the magistrates and messengers sent to inform the Lords of the Council of them; and so they were committed to ward. Indeed the magistrates used them courteously, and showed them what favor they could; but could not deliver them, till order came from the Council table. But the issue was that after a month's imprisonment, the greatest part were dismissed, and sent to the places from whence they came, but seven of the principal were still kept in prison, and bound over to the assizes.

The next spring[2] after, there was another attempt made by some of these and others; to get over at another place. And it so fell out, that they light of[3] a Dutchman at Hull, having a ship of his own belonging to Zealand; they

---

[1] In England, as in other European nations at the time, a license was required to go abroad, and such licenses were commonly refused to Roman Catholics and dissenters. This first at- tempt of the Scrooby congregation to flee was in the fall of 1607.

[2] Of 1608.

[3] Happened upon.

made agreement with him, and acquainted him with their condition, hoping to find more faithfulness in him, than in the former of their own nation; he bade them not fear, for he would do well enough. He was (by appointment) to take them in between Grimsby, and Hull, where was a large common a good way distant from any town. Now against the prefixed time, the women, and children, with the goods, were sent to the place in a small bark, which they had hired for that end; and the men were to meet them by land. But it so fell out, that they were there a day before the ship came, and the sea being rough, and the women very sick prevailed with the seamen to put into a creek hard by, where they lay on ground at low water. The next morning the ship came, but they were fast, and could not stir until about noon; in the meantime the shipmaster (perceiving how the matter was) sent his boat, to be getting the men aboard whom he saw ready, walking about the shore. But after the first boatful was got aboard, and she was ready to go for more, the master espied a great company (both horse, and foot) with bills, and guns, and other weapons (for the country was raised to take them) the Dutchman seeing that, swore (his country's oath), *sacremente;* and having the wind fair weighed his anchor, hoised sails and away. But the poor men which were got aboard, were in great distress for their wives, and children, which they saw thus to be taken, and were left destitute of their helps; and themselves also, not having a cloth to shift them with, more than they had on their backs (and some scarce a penny about them), all they had being aboard the bark. It drew tears from their eyes, and anything they had, they would have given to have been ashore again; but all in vain, there was no remedy; they must thus sadly part. And afterward endured a fearful storm at sea, being fourteen days or more before they arrived at their port; in seven whereof they neither saw sun, moon nor stars, and were driven near the coast of Norway; the mariners themselves often despairing of life; and once with shrieks and cries, gave over all, as if the ship had been foundered in the sea and they sinking without recovery. But when man's hope, and help wholly failed, the Lord's power, and mercy appeared in their recovery; for the ship rose again, and gave the mariners courage again to manage her. And if modesty would suffer me, I might declare with what fervent prayers they cried unto the Lord in this great distress (especially some of them), even without any great distraction when the water ran into their mouths, and ears; and the mariners cried out We sink, we sink; they cried (if not with miraculous, yet with a great height, or degree, of divine faith) Yet Lord Thou canst save; Yet Lord Thou canst save; with such other expressions as I will forbear. Upon which the ship did not only recover, but shortly after the violence of the storm began to abate; and the Lord filled their afflicted minds with such comforts as everyone cannot understand. And in the end brought them to their desired haven, where the people came flocking [,] admiring their deliverance, the storm having been so long and sore in which much hurt had been done, as the master's friends related unto him in their congratulations.

But to return to the others where we left; the rest of the men that were in greatest danger, made shift to escape away before the troop could surprise them; those only staying that best might, to be assistant unto the women. But pitiful it was to see the heavy case of these poor women in this distress; what weeping, and crying on every side, some for their husbands, that were carried away in the ship as is before related [·] others not knowing what should become of them, and their little ones; others again melted in tears, seeing their poor little ones hanging about them, crying for fear, and quaking with cold. Being thus apprehended, they were hurried from one place to another, and from one justice to another; till in the end they knew not what to do with them [·] for to imprison so many women and innocent children, for no other cause (many of them) but that they must go with their husbands; seemed to be unreasonable, and all would cry out of them, and to send them home again was as difficult, for they alleged (as the truth was) they had no homes to go to, for they had either sold, or otherwise disposed of their houses, and livings. To be short, after they had been thus turmoiled a good while; and conveyed from one constable to another, they were glad to be rid of them in the end upon any terms; for all were wearied, and tired with them. Though in the meantime they (poor souls) endured misery enough; and thus in the end necessity forced a way for them.

But that I be not tedious in these things, I will omit the rest, though I might relate many other notable passages and troubles which they endured, and underwent in these their wanderings, and travels both at land, and sea; but I haste to other things. Yet I may not omit the fruit that came hereby, for by these so public troubles; in so many eminent places, their cause became famous, and occasioned many to look into the same; and their godly carriage, and Christian behavior was such, as left a deep impression in the minds of many. And though some few shrunk, at these first conflicts and sharp beginnings (as it was no marvel) yet many more came on, with fresh courage, and greatly animated others. And in the end notwithstanding all these storms of opposition, they all gat over at length, some at one time, and some at another; and some in one place, and some in another [·] and met together again according to their desires, with no small rejoicing.[4]

From CHAPTER III
OF THEIR SETTLING IN HOLLAND, AND THEIR MANNER OF LIVING, AND ENTERTAINMENT THERE

Being now come into the Low Countries, they saw many goodly and fortified cities, strongly walled, and guarded with troops of armed men. Also they

---

[4] About 125 members of the Scrooby congregation "gat over" to Amsterdam, including the two ministers Clyfton and Robinson, William Brewster and Bradford himself.

heard a strange, and uncouth language, and beheld the different manners, and customs of the people, with their strange fashions, and attires; all so far differing from that of their plain country villages (wherein they were bred, and had so long lived) as it seemed they were come into a new world. But these were not the things they much looked on, or long took up their thoughts; for they had other work in hand, and another kind of war to wage, and maintain [·] For though they saw fair, and beautiful cities, flowing with abundance of all sorts of wealth, and riches [·] yet it was not long before they saw the grim, and grisly face of poverty coming upon them like an armed man;[1] with whom they must buckle; and encounter; and from whom they could not fly, but they were armed with faith, and patience against him, and all his encounters; and though they were sometimes foiled, yet by God's assistance they prevailed, and got the victory.

Now when Mr. Robinson, Mr. Brewster, and other principal members were come over (for they were of the last and stayed to help the weakest over before them) such things were thought on as were necessary for their settling, and best ordering of the church affairs. And when they had lived at Amsterdam about a year, Mr. Robinson (their pastor) and some others of best discerning, seeing how Mr. John Smith and his company, was already fallen into contention with the church that was there before them [·] and no means they could use, would do any good to cure the same, and also that the flames of contention were like to break out in that ancient church itself (as afterwards lamentably came to pass) which things they prudently foreseeing, thought it was best to remove; before they were any way engaged with the same [·] though they well knew it would be much to the prejudice of their outward estates; both at present, and in likelihood in the future, as indeed it proved to be.

THEIR REMOVAL TO LEYDEN

For these, and some other reasons they removed to Leyden,[2] a fair, and beautiful city, and of a sweet situation, but made more famous by the university wherewith it is adorned, in which (of late) had been so many learned men.[3] But wanting that traffic by sea which Amsterdam enjoys, it was not so beneficial for their outward means of living, and estates. But being now here pitch[ed] they fell to such trades, and employments as they best could; valuing peace, and their spiritual comfort above any other riches whatso-

---

[1] Proverbs xxiv.34.

[2] A formal application was made to the Burgomasters of Leyden by the Pilgrims, to settle in that city, and was granted 12 Feb. 1609. Text in 1912 ed. Bradford I 39–40.

[3] The University of Leyden, founded in 1575, had in the space of a single generation become one of the first in Christendom, with scholars such as Scaliger, Heinsius, Arminius, Vorstius, Golius, and Cluvier on its several faculties.

ever. And at length they came to raise a competent, and comfortable living, but with hard, and continual labor.[4]

. . .

CHAPTER IV
SHOWING THE REASONS, AND CAUSES OF
THEIR REMOVAL

After they had lived in this city about some eleven or twelve years (which is the more observable being the whole time of that famous truce between that state and the Spaniards)[1] and sundry of them were taken away by death; and many others began to be well stricken in years (the grave mistress of Experience having taught them many things) those prudent governors, with sundry of the sagest members began both deeply to apprehend their present dangers, and wisely to foresee the future; and think of timely remedy. In the agitation of their thoughts, and much discourse of things hereabout; at length they began to incline to this conclusion, of removal to some other place [·] not out of any newfangledness, or other such like giddy humor, by which men are oftentimes transported to their great hurt, and danger [·] but for sundry weighty, and solid reasons; some of the chief of which, I will here briefly touch. And first they saw, and found by experience, the hardness of the place, and country to be such; as few in comparison would come to them; and fewer that would bide it out, and continue with them [·] for many that came to them, and many more that desired to be with them; could not endure the great labor, and hard fare, with other inconveniences, which they underwent, and were contented with. But though they loved their persons, approved their cause, and honored their sufferings; yet they left them, as it were weeping, as Orpah did her mother-in-law Naomi;[2] or as those Romans did Cato in Utica, who desired to be excused, and borne with, though they could not all be Catos. For many, though they desired to enjoy the ordinances of God in their purity, and the liberty of the Gospel with them [·] yet (alas) they admitted of bondage, with danger of conscience; rather than to

[4] D. Plooij *The Pilgrim Fathers from a Dutch Point of View* (1932) is the principal authority on the Pilgrim Fathers in Leyden; but Henry Martyn Dexter *England and Holland of the Pilgrims* had already made extensive researches into their life there. He found that of 131 English in the city at that time, 86 of which belonged to the Pilgrim company, 57 occupations were represented, most of them having something to do with cloth making. Bradford himself is described in the local records as a fustian maker. Brewster and Winslow ran a printing press where Puritan tracts that could not get a license in England were published.

[1] The twelve years' truce was signed on 30 March 1609, and therefore was due to end in 1621. Although war was then renewed, the Netherlands had powerful allies such as France, Sweden, and several German States already engaged with Spain in the Thirty Years' War, at the end of which, in the Treaty of Westphalia (1648), Spain recognized the independence of the United Netherlands.

[2] Ruth i.14.

endure these hardships, yea, some preferred, and chose the prisons in England rather than this liberty in Holland, with these afflictions.[3] But it was thought that if a better, and easier place of living could be had; it would draw many, and take away these discouragements. Yea their pastor would often say, that many of those that both wrote, and preached now against them, if they were in a place, where they might have liberty, and live comfortably, they would then practice as they did.

Secondly they saw, that though the people generally, bore all these difficulties very cheerfully, and with a resolute courage, being in the best, and strength of their years; yet old age began to steal on many of them (and their great, and continual labors, with other crosses, and sorrows, hastened it before the time) so as it was not only probably thought, but apparently seen, that within a few years more, they would be in danger to scatter (by necessities pressing them) or sink under their burdens, or both. And therefore according to the divine proverb, that a wise man seeth the plague when it cometh, and hideth himself, Proverbs xxii.3 [·] so they like skillful and beaten soldiers were fearful, either to be entrapped, or surrounded by their enemies; so as they should neither be able to fight, nor fly [·] and therefore thought it better to dislodge betimes, to some place of better advantage; and less danger, if any such could be found.

Thirdly, as necessity was a taskmaster over them so they were forced to be such, not only to their servants, but (in a sort°) to their dearest children; the which as it did not a little wound the tender hearts of many a loving father, and mother; so it produced likewise sundry sad; and sorrowful effects. For many of their children; that were of best dispositions, and gracious inclinations (having learned[4] to bear the yoke in their youth) and willing to bear part of their parents' burden, were (oftentimes) so oppressed with their heavy labors; that though their minds were free and willing, yet their bodies bowed under the weight of the same, and became decrepit in their early youth, the vigor of nature being consumed in the very bud as it were. But that which was more lamentable, and of all sorrows most heavy to be borne; was that many of their children, by these occasions (and the great licentiousness of youth in that country)[5] and the manifold temptations of the place, were drawn away by evil examples into extravagant, and dangerous courses, getting the reins off their necks, and departing from their parents. Some

[3] It may seem strange that it should seem easier to emigrate to the American wilderness than to a Dutch city; but the Netherlands were overpopulated in relation to the economic system of that day, and the standard of living in the handicrafts, the only occupations open to English immigrants, was low.

° Bradford opens the parenthesis before *but*. [D I.]

[4] Lamentations iii.27.

[5] The Dutch, curiously enough, did not "remember the Sabbath Day to keep it holy" in the strict sense that other Calvinists did. Sunday after church was a day of feasting and merrymaking, especially for children. This was one of the conditions that the English community found most obnoxious.

became soldiers, others took upon them far voyages by sea; and other some worse courses, tending to dissoluteness, and the danger of their souls; to the great grief of their parents, and dishonor of God. So that they saw their posterity would be in danger to degenerate, and be corrupted.[6]

Lastly (and which was not least) a great hope, and inward zeal they had of laying some good foundation (or at least to make some way thereunto) for the propagating, and advancing the gospel of the kingdom of Christ in those remote parts of the world; yea though they should be, but even as stepping-stones, unto others for the performing of so great a work.

These, and some other like reasons, moved them to undertake this resolution of their removal; the which they afterward prosecuted with so great difficulties, as by the sequel will appear.

The place they had thoughts on, was some of those vast, and unpeopled countries of America, which are fruitful, and fit for habitation; being devoid of all civil inhabitants; where there are only savage, and brutish men, which range up, and down, little otherwise than the wild beasts of the same. This proposition being made public, and coming to the scanning of all, it raised many variable opinions amongst men, and caused many fears, and doubts amongst themselves. Some from their reasons, and hopes conceived; labored to stir up and encourage the rest to undertake, and prosecute the same; others again out of their fears, objected against it, and sought to divert from it; alleging many things, and those neither unreasonable, nor unprobable [·] as that it was a great design, and subject to many unconceivable perils, and dangers, as (besides the casualties of the seas, which none can be freed from) the length of the voyage was such, as the weak bodies of women, and other persons worn out with age, and travail (as many of them were) could never be able to endure. And yet if they should, the miseries of the land, which they should be exposed unto, would be too hard to be borne; and likely, some or all of them together, to consume, and utterly to ruinate them. For there they should be liable to famine, and nakedness and the want in a manner of all things. The change of air, diet, and drinking of water,[7] would infect their bodies with sore sicknesses, and grievous diseases. And also those which should escape, or overcome these difficulties, should yet be in continual danger: of the savage people, who are cruel, barbarous, and most treacherous, being most furious in their rage, and merciless where they overcome;

[6] Both Nathaniel Morton in *New Englands Memoriall* p. 3, and Edward Winslow in *Hypocrisie Unmasked* p. 89 stressed the fear of the Pilgrims lest their children lose their language and nationality. And their fear of the Dutch "melting pot" was well taken; for the offspring of those English Puritans who did not emigrate to New England or return to England became completely amalgamated with the local population by 1660.

[7] It was a general opinion of the time, which Bradford on sundry occasions shows that he shared, that water was an unwholesome beverage, as indeed it was when drawn from a contaminated well in a city or farmyard. The common table beverages of poor families in England and Holland were beer and cider.

not being content only to kill, and take away life, but delight to torment men in the most bloody manner that may be; flaying some alive with the shells of fishes, cutting off the members, and joints of others by piecemeal; and broiling on the coals; eat the collops of their flesh in their sight whilst they live, with other cruelties horrible to be related.[8] And surely it could not be thought but the very hearing of these things, could not but move the very bowels of men to grate within them, and make the weak to quake, and tremble. It was further objected, that it would require greater sums of money to furnish such a voyage (and to fit them with necessaries) than their consumed estates would amount to; and yet they must as well look to be seconded with supplies, as presently to be transported. Also many precedents of ill success, and lamentable miseries befallen others, in the like designs, were easy to be found, and not forgotten to be alleged. Besides their own experience, in their former troubles, and hardships, in their removal into Holland; and how hard a thing it was for them to live in that strange place, though it was a neighbor country, and a civil and rich commonwealth.

It was answered, that all great, and honorable actions, are accompanied with great difficulties; and must be both enterprised, and overcome with answerable courages. It was granted the dangers were great, but not desperate; the difficulties were many, but not invincible. For though there were many of them likely, yet they were not certain; it might be sundry of the things feared, might never befall; others by provident care and the use of good means might in a great measure be prevented; and all of them (through the help of God) by fortitude, and patience, might either be borne, or overcome. True it was that such attempts were not to be made, and undertaken without good ground, and reason; not rashly, or lightly as many have done for curiosity, or hope of gain etc. But their condition was not ordinary; their ends were good and honorable; their calling lawful, and urgent; and therefore they might expect the blessing of God in their proceeding. Yea though they should lose their lives in this action, yet might they have comfort in the same, and their endeavors would be honorable. They lived here but as men in exile, and in a poor condition; and as great miseries might possibly befall them in this place; for the twelve years of truce were now out, and there was nothing but beating of drums; and preparing for war, the events whereof are always uncertain. The Spaniard might prove as cruel, as the savages of America; and the famine, and pestilence, as sore here as there; and their liberty less to look out for remedy. After many other particular things answered, and alleged on both sides, it was fully concluded by the major part, to put this design in execution, and to prosecute it by the best means they could.

[8] As the Netherlands was then the principal center for the publication of illustrated narratives of voyages, the Pilgrims had a wide choice of literature from which to acquire a healthy respect for the Indians and an aversion to taking up a new abode within reach of the Spaniards

CHAPTER IX
OF THEIR VOYAGE, AND HOW THEY PASSED
THE SEA; AND OF THEIR SAFE ARRIVAL AT
CAPE COD

September 6. These troubles being blown over, and now all being compact together in one ship, they put to sea again with a prosperous wind, which continued divers days together, which was some encouragement unto them; yet according to the usual manner many were afflicted with seasickness. And I may not omit here a special work of God's providence; there was a proud and very profane young man, one of the seamen, of a lusty able body, which made him the more haughty; he would alway be condemning the poor people in their sickness, and cursing them daily with grievous execrations; and did not let to tell them, that he hoped to help to cast half of them overboard before they came to their journey's end, and to make merry with what they had; and if he were by any gently reproved, he would curse and swear most bitterly. But it pleased God before they came half seas over, to smite this young man with a grievous disease, of which he died in a desperate manner; and so was himself the first that was thrown overboard, thus his curses light on his own head; and it was an astonishment to all his fellows, for they noted it to be the just hand of God upon him.

After they had enjoyed fair winds, and weather for a season, they were encountered many times with cross winds, and met with many fierce storms, with which the ship was shroudly[1] shaken, and her upper works made very leaky; and one of the main beams in the midships was bowed and cracked, which put them in some fear that the ship could not be able to perform the voyage. So some of the chief of the company (perceiving the mariners to fear the sufficiency of the ship, as appeared by their mutterings) they entered into serious consultation with the master, and other officers of the ship, to consider in time of the danger; and rather to return, than to cast themselves into a desperate, and inevitable peril. And truly there was great distraction, and difference of opinion amongst the mariners themselves; fain would they do what could be done for their wages' sake (being now near half the seas over) and on the other hand they were loath to hazard their lives too desperately. But in examining of all opinions, the master and others affirmed they knew the ship to be strong, and firm under water, and for the buckling of the main beam, there was a great iron screw the passengers brought out of Holland, which would raise the beam into his place[;] the which being done, the carpenter, and master affirmed that with a post put under it, set firm in the lower deck, and otherways bound he would make it sufficient. And as for the decks and upper works they would caulk them as well as they could, and though with the working of the ship they would not long keep staunch, yet

[1] An old form of *shrewdly* in its original meaning *wickedly*.

there would otherwise be no great danger, if they did not overpress her with sails; so they committed themselves to the will of God, and resolved to proceed. In sundry of these storms the winds were so fierce, and the seas so high, as they could not bear a knot of sail, but were forced to hull,[2] for divers days together; and in one of them as they thus lay at hull in a mighty storm, a lusty[3] young man (called John Howland) coming upon some occasion above the gratings, was with a seele[4] of the ship thrown into sea; but it pleased God, that he caught hold of the topsail halyards, which hung overboard, and ran out at length, yet he held his hold (though he was sundry fathoms under water) till he was hauled up by the same rope to the brim of the water; and then with a boat hook, and other means got into the ship again and his life saved, and though he was something ill with it, yet he lived many years after, and became a profitable member, both in church and commonwealth. In all this voyage there died but one of the passengers, which was (William Butten, a youth, servant to Samuel Fuller), when they drew near the coast. But to omit other things (that I may be brief) after long beating at sea, they fell with that land which is called Cape Cod;[5] the which being made, and certainly known to be it they were not a little joyful. After some deliberation had amongst themselves; and with the master of the ship; they tacked about; and resolved to stand for the southward (the wind and weather being fair) to find some place, about Hudson's River for their habitation.[6] But after they had sailed that course about half the day, they fell

---

[2] To heave or lay-to under very short sail and drift with the wind.

[3] Lively, merry; no sexual connotation. Howland, a servant of Governor Carver, rose to be one of the leading men of the Colony.

[4] Roll or pitch.

[5] At daybreak 9/19 Nov. 1620, they sighted the Highlands of Cape Cod. Full discussion in W. Sears Nickerson *Land Ho!—1620* chap. iv.

[6] This is the only direct statement in the *History* as to whither the *Mayflower* was bound. I see no reason to doubt its accuracy. It is borne out by Bradford's own journal in *Mourt's Relation* (see Chap. x note 2, below): "We made our course south-southwest, purposing to go to a river ten leagues to the south of the Cape, but at night the wind being contrary, we put round again for the Bay of Cape Cod." Although the mouth of the Hudson is nearer 15 than 10 leagues south of the Cape in latitude, the Pilgrims' knowledge of New England geography was far from exact, and the Hudson was doubt-

less meant. The Virginia Company, which had granted the Peirce Patent which the Pilgrims brought with them, had a right to colonize up to lat. 41° N, which included Manhattan Island. The Dutch did not settle Manhattan (the famous $24 purchase) until 1626, although they claimed the region by virtue of Hudson's voyage in 1609; the English never admitted their claim, and the Pilgrims, who certainly had heard of the Hudson River and Long Island Sound from the several Dutch voyages thither before 1620, doubtless hoped to be first at the natural center for fur trade and fishing, and were glad to rely on their Patent from the Virginia Company both for local self-government and for protection from Dutch encroachment. John Pory, the Secretary of Virginia who visited Plymouth Colony in 1622 (see below, chap. xiii), reported that "their voyage was intended for Virginia." They carried letters, he says, from Sir Edwin Sandys and John Ferrar to Governor Sir George Yeardley recommending "that he should give the best advice
(Footnote continued next page.)

amongst dangerous shoals; and roaring breakers, and they were so far entangled therewith, as they conceived themselves in great danger, and the wind shrinking upon them withal, they resolved to bear up again for the Cape; and thought themselves happy to get out of those dangers, before night overtook them, as by God's good providence they did; and the next day[7] they got into the Cape Harbor[8] where they rid in safety. A word or two by the way of this cape, it was thus first named by Captain Gosnold, and his company;[9] Anno 1602 and after by Captain Smith was called Cape James; but it retains the former name amongst seamen. Also that point which first showed those dangerous shoals unto them, they called Point Care, and Tucker's Terror, but the French and Dutch to this day call it Malabar, by reason of those perilous shoals, and the losses they have suffered there.[10]

Being thus arrived in a good harbor, and brought safe to land, they fell upon their knees and blessed the God of Heaven,[11] who had brought them over the vast, and furious ocean, and delivered them from all the perils, and miseries thereof; again to set their feet on the firm and stable earth, their proper element. And no marvel if they were thus joyful, seeing wise Seneca was so affected with sailing a few miles on the coast of his own Italy; as he affirmed, that he had rather remain twenty years on his way by land, than pass by sea to any place in a short time; so tedious and dreadful was the same unto him.[12]

But here I cannot but stay, and make a pause, and stand half amazed at this poor people's present condition; and so I think will the reader, too, when he well considers the same. Being thus passed the vast ocean, and a sea of troubles before in their preparation (as may be remembered by that which went before) they had now no friends to welcome them, nor inns to entertain, or refresh their weatherbeaten bodies; no houses, or much less

he could for trading in Hudson's River." Champlin Burrage *John Pory's Lost Description of Plymouth* (1918) p. 35. The theory that Master Jones of the *Mayflower* was bribed by the Dutch to set the Pilgrims ashore at a safe distance from Manhattan has a respectable antiquity but no basis in fact. No seaman who has weathered Cape Cod needs any better explanation than a head wind on unbuoyed Pollock Rip to explain why the *Mayflower* turned back.

[7] Nov. 11/21, 1620. Thus the *Mayflower's* passage from Plymouth took 65 days.

[8] Now Provincetown Harbor.

[9] Because they took much of that fish there (Bradford).

[10] The location of these places is discussed by W. Sears Nickerson chap. iii. He believes that the original Point Care and Tucker's Terror (so named by Gosnold) and Mallebarre (named by Champlain) were at Nauset Harbor. The name Mallebarre later became transferred to Monomoy, which is called Cape Malabar in the *Atlantic Neptune* (1774), Anthony Finley's *New General Atlas* (1832), U. S. Coast Survey Chart No. 11 (1860), *Black's General Atlas American Edition* (1879), and E. G. Perry *A Trip Around Cape Cod* (1898) p. 206. Thereafter it drops out, except as a name for John Alden's yachts.

[11] Daniel ii.19.

[12] Epistle 53 (Bradford). The sentence is in Seneca *ad Lucilium Epistulae Morales* liii §5: *Et ego quocumque navigare debuero, vicesimo anno perveniam.*

towns to repair to, to seek for succor; it is recorded in Scripture[13] as a mercy to the Apostle and his shipwrecked company, that the barbarians showed them no small kindness in refreshing them, but these savage barbarians, when they met with them (as after will appear) were readier to fill their sides full of arrows than otherwise. And for the season it was winter, and they that know the winters of that country, know them to be sharp and violent, and subject to cruel and fierce storms, dangerous to travel to known places, much more to search an unknown coast. Besides what could they see, but a hideous and desolate wilderness, full of wild beasts, and wild men—and what multitudes there might be of them they knew not; neither could they (as it were) go up to the top of Pisgah, to view from this wilderness, a more goodly country to feed their hopes; for which way soever they turned their eyes (save upward to the heavens) they could have little solace or content, in respect of any outward objects, for summer being done, all things stand upon them with a weather-beaten face; and the whole country (full of woods and thickets) represented a wild and savage hue; if they looked behind them, there was the mighty ocean which they had passed, and was now as a main bar, and gulf, to separate them from all the civil parts of the world. If it be said they had a ship to succor them, it is true; but what heard they daily from the master and company? But that with speed they should look out a place (with their shallop) where they would be, at some near distance; for the season was such, as he would not stir from thence, till a safe harbor was discovered by them, where they would be, and he might go without danger; and that victuals consumed apace, but he must and would keep sufficient for themselves, and their return. Yea it was muttered by some, that if they got not a place in time, they would turn them, and their goods ashore, and leave them. Let it also be considered what weak hopes of supply, and succor, they left behind them, that might bear up their minds in this sad condition, and trials they were under; and they could not but be very small; it is true, indeed, the affections and love of their brethren at Leyden was cordial and entire towards them, but they had little power to help them, or themselves; and how the case stood between them, and the merchants, at their coming away hath already been declared. What could now sustain them, but the Spirit of God and His grace? May not, and ought not the children of these fathers rightly say, "Our fathers were Englishmen which came over this great ocean, and were ready to perish in this wilderness, but they cried unto the Lord and He heard their voice, and looked on their adversity,"[14] etc. "Let them therefore praise the Lord, because He is good; and His mercies endure forever. Yea, let them which have been redeemed of the Lord, shew how He hath delivered them, from the hand of the oppressor [·] when they wandered in the desert wilderness out of the way, and found no city to dwell in, both hungry, and thirsty, their soul was overwhelmed in them. Let them

---

[13] Acts xxviii (Bradford); verse 2.   [14] Deuteronomy xxvi.5, 7 (Bradford).

confess before the Lord His lovingkindness, and His wonderful works before the sons of men."[15]

CHAPTER X
SHOWING HOW THEY SOUGHT OUT A PLACE OF HABITATION; AND WHAT BEFELL THEM THEREABOUT

Being thus arrived at Cape Cod the 11th of November, and necessity calling them to look out a place for habitation (as well as the master's and mariners' importunity); they having brought a large shallop with them out of England, stowed in quarters in the ship, they now got her out, and set their carpenters to work to trim her up, but being much bruised and shattered in the ship with foul weather, they saw she would be long in mending. Whereupon a few of them tendered themselves, to go by land and discover those nearest places, whilst the shallop was in mending, and the rather because as they went into that harbor there seemed to be an opening some two or three leagues off, which the master judged to be a river.[1] It was conceived there might be some danger in the attempt, yet seeing them resolute they were permitted to go; being sixteen of them well armed under the conduct of Captain Standish,[2] having such instructions given them as was thought meet. They set forth the 15th of November and when they had marched about the space of a mile by the seaside they espied five or six persons, with a dog coming towards them, who were savages, but they fled from them, and ran up into the woods, and the English followed them, partly to see if they could speak with them, and partly to discover if there might not be more of them lying in ambush, but the Indians seeing themselves thus followed, they again forsook the woods, and ran away on the sands as hard as they could, so as they could not come near them, but followed them by the track of their feet sundry miles, and saw that they had come the same way. So night coming on they made their rendezvous and set out their sentinels, and rested in quiet that night, and the next morning followed their track till they had headed a

[15] Psalm cvii.1, 2, 4, 5, 8 (Bradford).

[1] Looking south from Provincetown Harbor where the Pilgrims then were, the high land near Plymouth looks like an island on clear days, suggesting that there is a river or arm of the sea between it and Cape Cod.

[2] Myles Standish, scion of an old Lancashire family, was now about 36 years old. A soldier of fortune in the wars of the Netherlands, he was engaged either by Weston or the Carver-Cushman committee to go with the colonists and handle their military affairs. Though a "stranger" to the Leyden Pilgrims, Standish, like John Alden the hired cooper, became one of their staunchest supporters. Bradford,

Hopkins, and Tilley accompanied Standish. More details on these exploring expeditions will be found in the extracts from Bradford's and Winslow's Journals which were published in London in 1622 as *A Relation or Iournall of the beginning and proceedings of the English Plantation setled at Plimoth in New England, by certain English Aduenturers both Merchants and others.* As the authors' names did not appear, and the preface was signed "G. Mourt," this is generally called *Mourt's Relation* (although who Mourt was, nobody knows). Several times reprinted, it is included in Alexander Young *Chronicles of the Pilgrim Fathers* (1841).

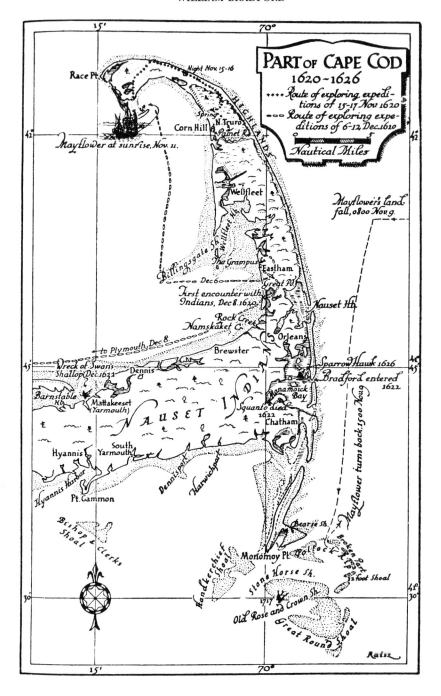

PART OF CAPE COD
1620~1626

•••• Route of exploring expeditions of 15-17 Nov 1620
--- Route of exploring expeditions of 6-12 Dec 1620

Nautical Miles

great creek and so left the sands, and turned another way into the woods, but they still followed them by guess, hoping to find their dwellings, but they soon lost both them, and themselves, falling into such thickets as were ready to tear their clothes, and armor in pieces, but were most distressed for want of drink; but at length they found water and refreshed themselves, being the first New England water they drunk of, and was now in great thirst as pleasant unto them as wine, or beer, had been in foretimes. Afterwards they directed their course to come to the other shore for they knew it was a neck of land they were to cross over, and so at length got to the seaside; and marched to this supposed river, and by the way found a pond[3] of clear fresh water, and shortly after a good quantity of clear ground, where the Indians had formerly set corn; and some of their graves; and proceeding further they saw new stubble where corn had been set the same year, also they found where lately a house had been where some planks and a great kettle was remaining, and heaps of sand newly paddled with their hands, which they digging up, found in them divers fair Indian baskets filled with corn, and some in ears, fair and good of divers colors, which seemed to them a very goodly sight (having never seen any such before), this was near the place of that supposed river they came to seek; unto which they went, and found it to open itself into two arms with a high cliff of sand in the entrance,[4] but more like to be creeks of salt water than any fresh for aught they saw; and that there was good harborage for their shallop, leaving it further to be discovered by their shallop when she was ready. So their time limited them being expired, they returned to the ship, lest they should be in fear of their safety; and took with them, part of the corn, and buried up the rest, and so, like the men from Eshcol carried with them of the fruits of the land, and showed their brethren;[5] of which, and their return they were marvelously glad, and their hearts encouraged.

After this the shallop being got ready they set out again, for the better discovery of this place, and the master of the ship desired to go himself, so there went some thirty men, but found it to be no harbor for ships but only for boats;[6] there was also found two of their houses covered with mats, and

---

[3] The pond that gives its name to Pond Village, Truro.

[4] Pamet River, a salt creek that almost bisects the Cape in Truro. The place where they found the corn is still called Corn Hill. It runs along the Bay side, just north of Little Pamet River.

[5] Numbers xiii.23-6.

[6] This second exploring expedition, which started by boat, 28 Nov., made for the mouth of the Pamet River (later called Cold Harbor), which still is good for boats only. Readers interested in further details may profitably consult Mourt's Relation, the 1865 edition of which, edited by Henry Martyn Dexter, has an excellent map with details of the routes. This second expedition ranged up and down the valleys of the Pamet and Little Pamet Rivers, and returned to Cape Cod Harbor on 30 Nov. by the shallop. The Indians who lived in this region were the Nauset; they built arborlike wigwams of boughs bent over and stuck in the ground at both ends, woven by smaller boughs into a stout frame and covered with woven mats or strips of bark. Descendants of the Nauset still survive in the village of Mashpee on Cape Cod.

sundry of their implements in them, but the people were run away, and could not be seen, also there was found more of their corn, and of their beans of various colors; the corn, and beans they brought away, purposing to give them full satisfaction when they should meet with any of them (as about six months afterward they did, to their good content). And here is to be noted a special providence of God, and a great mercy to this poor people, that here they got seed to plant them corn the next year; or else they might have starved, for they had none, nor any likelihood to get any till the season had been past (as the sequel did manifest) neither is it likely they had, had this, if the first voyage had not been made, for the ground was now all covered with snow, and hard frozen; but the Lord is never wanting unto His in their greatest needs, let His holy name have all the praise.

The month of November being spent in these affairs, and much foul weather falling in; the 6th of December they sent out their shallop again with ten of their principal men,[7] and some seamen, upon further discovery intending to circulate that deep bay of Cape Cod; the weather was very cold, and it froze so hard as the spray of the sea lighting on their coats, they were as if they had been glazed, yet that night betimes they got down into the bottom of the bay, and as they drew near the shore they saw some ten or twelve Indians very busy about something; they landed about a league or two from them,[8] and had much ado to put ashore anywhere[,] it lay so full of flats. Being landed it grew late, and they made themselves a barricado with logs and boughs as well as they could in the time, and set out their sentinel and betook them to rest, and saw the smoke of the fire the savages made that night. When morning was come they divided their company, some to coast along the shore in the boat, and the rest marched through the woods to see the land if any fit place might be for their dwelling; they came also to the place where they saw the Indians the night before, and found they had been cutting up a great fish like a grampus[9] being some two inches thick of fat like a hog, some pieces whereof they had left by the way; and the shallop found

---

[7] The names of the ten (from *Mourt's Relation*) are Standish, Carver and his servant Howland, Bradford, Winslow, John and Edward Tilley, Richard Warren, Stephen Hopkins and his servant Doten; also the pilots, John Clarke and Robert Coppin, and the master gunner and three sailors, whose names are unknown. *Mourt's Relation* states that after the return of the second exploring expedition there was much debate on board the *Mayflower* whether they should settle at Pamet River, at Agawam (the later Ipswich), which looked good on Captain John Smith's map, at Cape Ann, or at Plymouth. On the strength of the recommendations of Coppin,

who had been to Plymouth on a previous voyage and offered to pilot them thither, they decided to investigate that place before deciding.

[8] Somewhere in the present Eastham, at one of the several beaches (Kingsbury, Campground, Silver Spring), north of the Great Pond. The tide along this shore runs out very far. The barricade where they passed the night was (according to H. M. Dexter's researches) a few hundred yards northwest of the Great Pond.

[9] This was probably one of the blackfish (*Globicephala melaena*) that frequently get stranded on Cape Cod.

two more of these fishes dead on the sands, a thing usual after storms in that place by reason of the great flats of sand that lie off.

So they ranged up and down all that day, but found no people, nor any place they liked; when the sun grew low, they hasted out of the woods to meet with their shallop, to whom they made signs to come to them into a creek hard by, [10] the which they did at high water; of which they were very glad, for they had not seen each other, all that day since the morning. So they made them a barricado (as usually they did every night) with logs, stakes, and thick pine boughs the height of a man, leaving it open to leeward, partly to shelter them from the cold, and wind (making their fire in the middle, and lying round about it) and partly to defend them from any sudden assaults of the savages, if they should surround them; so being very weary they betook them to rest. But about midnight they heard a hideous, and great cry, and their sentinel called Arm arm, so they bestirred them and stood to their arms, and shot off a couple of muskets and then the noise ceased. They concluded it was a company of wolves, or such like wild beasts; for one of the seamen told them he had often heard such a noise in Newfoundland. So they rested till about five of the clock in the morning; for the tide and their purpose to go from thence, made them be stirring betimes, so after prayer they prepared for breakfast, and it being day dawning it was thought best to be carrying things down to the boat; but some said it was not best to carry the arms down, others said they would be the readier, for they had lapped them up in their coats from the dew, but some three or four would not carry theirs till they went themselves, yet as it fell out the water being not high enough, they laid them down on the bank side, and came up to breakfast. But presently, all on the sudden they heard a great and strange cry, which they knew to be the same voices, they heard in the night, though they varied their notes, and one of their company being abroad came running in and cried, Men, Indians, Indians; and withal their arrows came flying amongst them, their men ran with all speed to recover their arms, as by the good providence of God they did. In the meantime, of those that were there ready two muskets were discharged at them, and two more stood ready in the entrance of their rendezvous but were commanded not to shoot till they could take full aim at them, and the other two charged again with all speed, for there were only four had arms there, and defended the barricado which was first assaulted; the cry of the Indians was dreadful, especially when they saw their men run out of the rendezvous, towards the shallop to recover their arms, the Indians wheeling about upon them, but some running out with coats of mail on, and cutlasses in their hands, they soon got their arms and let fly amongst them, and quickly stopped their violence. Yet there was

[10] The mouth of Herring River, in the present Eastham. The beach north of the river mouth, where the action about to be described took place, is still called First Encounter Beach.

a lusty man, and no less valiant, stood behind a tree within half a musket shot, and let his arrows fly at them, he was seen [to] shoot three arrows which were all avoided, he stood three shot of a musket till one taking full aim at him, and made the bark or splinters of the tree fly about his ears, after which he gave an extraordinary shriek; and away they went all of them, they[11] left some to keep the shallop, and followed them about a quarter of a mile and shouted once or twice, and shot off two or three pieces, and so returned. This they did, that they might conceive that they were not afraid of them or any way discouraged.

Thus it pleased God to vanquish their enemies, and give them deliverance; and by His special providence so to dispose that not any one of them, were either hurt, or hit, though their arrows came close by them, and on every side [of] them; and sundry of their coats, which hung up in the barricado, were shot through, and through. Afterwards they gave God solemn thanks, and praise, for their deliverance, and gathered up a bundle of their arrows, and sent them into England afterward by the master of the ship, and called that place the First Encounter. From hence they departed, and coasted all along, but discerned no place likely for harbor; and therefore hasted to a place, that their pilot (one Mr. Coppin who had been in the country before) did assure them was a good harbor which he had been in, and they might fetch it before night; of which they were glad, for it began to be foul weather. After some hours' sailing, it began to snow, and rain, and about the middle of the afternoon, the wind increased; and the sea became very rough; and they broke their rudder, and it was as much as two men could do to steer her with a couple of oars. But their pilot bade them be of good cheer for he saw the harbor, but the storm increasing, and night drawing on, they bore what sail they could to get in, while they could see; but herewith they broke their mast in three pieces and their sail fell overboard, in a very grown sea, so as they had like to have been cast away; yet by God's mercy they recovered themselves, and having the flood[12] with them struck

[11] I.e., the English.

[12] I.e., the flood tide. The mean rise and fall of tide there is about 9 ft. Plymouth Bay, even today when well buoyed, is a bad place to enter in thick weather with a sea running and night coming on. For if you do not steer for the Gurnet, the high point that marks the northern entrace to Plymouth Bay, you run afoul of Browns Bank, which breaks all over in heavy weather or at low tide; in 1620 a part of this bank was dry at all tides. Coppin, I believe, mistook the Gurnet for Saquish Head; and Saquish for Goose Point; steering between them so as to enter the harbor, he was unnerved by seeing the breakers in Saquish Cove. Mr. Gershom Bradford, late of

the U. S. Hydrographic Survey, has a different interpretation: that the storm blew from the NE, not the SE, that the shallop clung to the shoreline and worked through the boat channel between Browns Bank and Long Beach, and that the cove full of breakers was Warrens Cove east of Long Beach. In either case, it is clear that the rowers, encouraged by the "lusty seaman" at the steering oar, managed to weather Saquish Head, behind which they found shelter and good anchorage late in the night of Friday 8 Dec. 1620. They spent Saturday and Sunday 9 and 10 Dec. on Clarks Island, and made the famous "landing" on the 11th.

into the harbor. But when it came to, the pilot was deceived in the place, and said the Lord be merciful unto them, for his eyes never saw that place before; and he, and the master's mate would have run her ashore, in a cove full of breakers before the wind but a lusty seaman which steered, bade those which rowed if they were men, about with her, or else they were all cast away; the which they did with speed, so he bid them be of good cheer, and row lustily for there was a fair sound before them, and he doubted not, but they should find one place or other, where they might ride in safety. And though it was very dark, and rained sore; yet in the end they got under the lee of a small island and remained there all that night in safety. But they knew not this to be an island till morning, but were divided in their minds, some would keep the boat for fear they might be amongst the Indians; others were so wet and cold, they could not endure, but got ashore, and with much ado got fire (all things being so wet) and the rest were glad to come to them, for after midnight the wind shifted to the northwest, and it froze hard. But though this had been a day, and night of much trouble, and danger unto them; yet God gave them a morning of comfort and refreshing (as usually He doth to His children) for the next day was a fair sunshining day, and they found themselves to be on an island secure from the Indians; where they might dry their stuff, fix their pieces, and rest themselves, and gave God thanks for His mercies, in their manifold deliverances. And this being the last day of the week, they prepared there to keep the Sabbath; on Monday they sounded the harbor, and found it fit for shipping; and marched into the land, and found divers cornfields, and little running brooks, a place as (they supposed) fit for situation,[13] at least it was the best they could find, and the season, and their present necessity made them glad to accept of it. So they returned to their ship again with this news to the rest of their people, which did much comfort their hearts.

On the 15th of December they weighed anchor to go to the place they had discovered, and came within two leagues of it, but were fain to bear up again, but the 16th day the wind came fair, and they arrived safe in this harbor. And afterwards took better view of the place, and resolved where to

---

[13] Here is the only contemporary authority for the "Landing of the Pilgrims on Plymouth Rock" on Monday, 11/21 Dec. 1620. It is clear that the landing took place from the shallop, not the *Mayflower*, which was then moored in Provincetown Harbor; that no women were involved in it, and no Indians or anyone else were on the receiving end. Nor is it clear that they landed on the large boulder since called Plymouth Rock. That boulder was identified in 1741 by Elder John Faunce, aged 95, as the "place where the forefathers landed," and although he probably only meant to say that they used it as a landing place, for it would have been very convenient for that purpose at half tide, everyone seems to have assumed that they "first" landed there. The exploring party may have landed anywhere between Captain's Hill and the Rock.

pitch their dwelling; and the 25th day began to erect the first house, for common use to receive them, and their goods.[14]

The Second Book

The rest of this history (if God give me life, and opportunity) I shall for brevity's sake, handle by way of annals, noting only the heads of principal things, and passages as they fell in order of time; and may seem to be profitable to know or to make use of. And this may be as the Second Book.[1]

From CHAPTER XI
THE REMAINDER OF ANNO 1620

[THE MAYFLOWER COMPACT]

I shall a little return back, and begin with a combination made by them before they came ashore; being the first foundation of their government in this place [·] occasioned partly by the discontented, and mutinous speeches that some of the strangers amongst them had let fall from them in the ship; that when they came ashore they would use their own liberty; for none had power to command them, the patent they had being for Virginia, and not for New England, which belonged to another government with which the Virginia Company had nothing to do[1] [·] and partly that such an act by them

---

[14] *Mourt's Relation* p. 23 says that after the *Mayflower's* arrival in Plymouth Bay on 16/26 Dec. the men explored the bay again and debated whether to settle at Plymouth, the mouth of Jones River (the present Kingston), or on Clark's Island. They decided on the first because much of the land was already cleared and a fort on the hill—now Burial Hill—could command the surrounding country; and because "a very sweet brook"—the Town Brook—"runs under the hillside."

[1] I have added chapter numbers for the reader's convenience (Bradford started to do so but crossed out "the 11 chapter"); and I have broken up some of the longer chapters with subheadings in square brackets. It must be remembered that Bradford's year begins 25 March and extends through 24 March of the following year; and he often extends his narrative into the following summer before starting another chapter.

[1] This, as we have seen, was correct; the Pilgrims were now in New England, as the "Northern Parts of Virginia" had just been renamed, and the patent that they brought with them was invalid. With mutiny threatened, something had to be done; and the church covenants, or compacts, with which all Puritans were familiar, suggested this Compact. Moreover, John Robinson had suggested (see Appendix IV) that they broaden the base of their local government; and the Virginia Company of London, immediately after sealing the Pilgrims' patent and those of other Particular Plantations on 2 Feb. 1620, voted "that such Captains and Leaders of Particular Plantations that shall go there to inhabit by virtue of their Grants, and plant themselves, their tenants and servants in Virginia, shall have liberty, till a form of Government be here settled for them, associating (Footnote continued next page.)

done (this their condition considered) might be as firm as any patent; and in some respects more sure.

The form was as following [·][2]

IN THE NAME OF GOD AMEN.

We whose names are underwritten, the loyal subjects of our dread Sovereign Lord King James by the Grace of God, of Great Britain, France, and Ireland King, Defender of the Faith, etc.

Having undertaken, for the Glory of God, and advancement of the Christian Faith and Honor of our King and Country, a Voyage to plant the First Colony in the Northern Parts of Virginia [·] do by these presents solemnly and mutually in the presence of God, and one of another; Covenant, and Combine ourselves together into a Civil Body Politic; for our[3] better ordering, and preservation and furtherance of the ends aforesaid; and by virtue hereof to enact, constitute, and frame such just and equal Laws, Ordinances, Acts, Constitutions, and Offices, from time to time, as shall be thought most meet and convenient for the general good of the Colony: unto which we promise all due submission and obedience. In witness whereof we have hereunder subscribed our names at Cape Cod the 11th of November, in the year of the reign of our Sovereign Lord King James of England, France, and Ireland the eighteenth and of Scotland the fifty-fourth. Anno Domini 1620.

After this they chose, or rather confirmed Mr. John Carver (a man godly and well approved amongst them) their Governor for that year. And after they had provided a place for their goods, or common store (which were long in unlading for want of boats, foulness of the winter weather, and sickness of divers), and begun some small cottages[4] for their habitation; as time would admit they met and consulted of laws; and orders, both for their

with them divers of the gravest and discreetest of their Companies, to make Orders, Ordinances and Constitutions for the better ordering and directing of their servants and business, provided they be not repugnant to the Laws of England." (*Records of Virginia Company* I 303.) Thus, the Pilgrims would have had a right to form a government even if they had settled within the boundaries of Virginia and had been encouraged to do so.

[2] The original document has disappeared, so this may be regarded as the most authentic text of the Compact. It was first printed in *Mourt's Relation* (1622) and that text differs from this only by the dropping of an occasional *the*, *and*, and *at*. Nathaniel Morton

printed it in *New Englands Memoriall* (1669), together with the names of the 41 signers. See Appendix XIII below, where signers' names are distinguished by an asterisk.

[3] Bradford scratched out y^e and substituted *our*. This and other corrections suggest that he collated his own text with the original document.

[4] The subject of early housing at Plymouth has been covered exhaustively in Harold R. Shurtleff *The Log Cabin Myth* (1939) chap. v. On the basis of this and other researches a one-room frame house with a thatched roof, representing one of these first cottages, has been constructed by Plimoth Plantation, Inc. on the Plymouth waterfront, near the Rock.

civil, and military government, as the necessity of their condition did require, still adding thereunto as urgent occasion in several times, and as cases did require.

In these hard and difficult beginnings they found some discontents and murmurings arise amongst some, and mutinous speeches and carriages in other; but they were soon quelled, and overcome, by the wisdom, patience, and just and equal carriage of things, by the Governor and better part which clave faithfully together in the main.

[THE STARVING TIME]

But that which was most sad, and lamentable, was, that in two or three months' time half of their company died, especially in January and February, being the depth of winter, and wanting houses and other comforts; being infected with the scurvy and other diseases, which this long voyage and their inaccommodate condition had brought upon them; so as there died some times two or three of a day, in the foresaid time, that of 100 and odd persons, scarce fifty remained.[5] And of these in the time of most distress there was but six or seven sound persons; who to their great commendations, be it spoken, spared no pains, night nor day, but with abundance of toil and hazard of their own health, fetched them wood[,] made them fires, dressed them meat, made their beds, washed their loathsome clothes, clothed and unclothed them. In a word, did all the homely, and necessary offices for them, which dainty and queasy stomachs cannot endure to hear named and all this willingly and cheerfully, without any grudging in the least, showing herein their true love unto their friends and brethren; a rare example and worthy to be remembered. Two of these seven were Mr. William Brewster their reverend Elder, and Myles Standish their Captain and military commander (unto whom myself, and many others were much beholden in our low, and sick condition), and yet the Lord so upheld these persons as in this general calamity they were not at all infected either with sickness, or lameness. And what I have said of these, I may say of many others who died in this general visitation and others yet living [·] that whilst they had health, yea or any strength continuing they were not wanting to any that had need of them; and I doubt not but their recompense is with the Lord.

But I may not here pass by, another remarkable passage not to be forgotten. As this calamity fell among the passengers that were to be left here to plant; and were hasted ashore and made to drink water, that the seamen might have the more beer, and one[6] in his sickness desiring but a small can

---

[5] Of the 102 *Mayflower* passengers who reached Cape Cod, 4 died before she made Plymouth; and by the summer of 1621 the total deaths numbered 50. Only 12 of the original 26 heads of families and 4 of the original 12 unattached men or boys were left; and of the women who reached Plymouth, all but a few died. Doubtless many of the deaths took place on board the *Mayflower* at anchor, since there was not enough shelter ashore for all; and Plymouth Harbor is so shallow that she was moored about 1½ nautical miles from the Rock.

[6] Which was this author himself (Bradford).

of beer, it was answered that if he were their own father he should have none; the disease began to fall amongst them also, so as almost half of their company died before they went away, and many of their officers and lustiest men; as the boatswain, gunner, three quartermasters the cook and others [·] at which the Master was something strucken and sent to the sick ashore and told the Governor he should send for beer for them that had need of it, though he drunk water homeward bound; but now amongst his company there was far another kind of carriage in this misery, than amongst the passengers. For they that before had been boon companions in drinking, and jollity in the time of their health and welfare, began now to desert one another in this calamity, saying they would not hazard their lives for them, they should be infected by coming to help them in their cabins, and so after they came to lie by it; would do little or nothing for them, but if they died let them die. But such of the passengers as were yet aboard showed them what mercy they could, which made some of their hearts relent, as the boatswain and some others who was a proud young man, and would often curse, and scoff at the passengers; but when he grew weak they had compassion on him and helped him, then he confessed he did not deserve it at their hands, he had abused them in word and deed; O (saith he) you, I now see show your love like Christians indeed one to another, but we let one another lie, and die like dogs. Another lay cursing his wife, saying if it had not been for her he had never come this unlucky voyage, and anon cursing his fellows saying he had done this, and that for some of them, he had spent so much, and so much, amongst them, and they were now weary of him, and did not help him having need, another gave his companion all he had, if he died, to help him in his weakness; he went and got a little spice and made him a mess of meat once, or twice; and because he died not so soon as he expected, he went amongst his fellows, and swore the rogue would cozen him, he would see him choked before he made him any more meat; and yet the poor fellow died before morning.

[INDIAN RELATIONS]

All this while the Indians came skulking about them, and would sometimes show themselves aloof off, but when any approached near them, they would run away; and once they stole away their tools where they had been at work and were gone to dinner.[7] But about 16th of March, a certain Indian came boldly amongst them, and spoke to them in broken English which they could

[7] *Mourt's Relation* adds more details. On every fair day the men worked building houses. On 8 Jan. 1621 Master Jones and some of the men caught three seal and a codfish, and Francis Billington, the *Mayflower's* bad boy, sighted from a treetop "a great sea, as he thought," but found it to be a lake; it is still called Billington's Sea. On 9 Jan. the 20-foot-square common house for stores was completed except for the roof, and the house lots were laid out. On the 12th two men went afield to cut thatch, accompanied by a mastiff bitch and a spaniel. The dogs flushed a deer and the men gave chase, got lost and were benighted. Terrified at the howling of (Footnote continued next page.)

well understand, but marveled at it; at length they understood by discourse with him, that he was not of these parts, but belonged to the eastern parts where some English ships came to fish, with whom he was acquainted, and could name sundry of them by their names, amongst whom he had got his language. He became profitable to them in acquainting them with many things concerning the state of the country in the east parts where he lived, which was afterwards profitable unto them; as also of the people here, of their names, number and strength, of their situation and distance from this place, and who was chief amongst them. His name was Samoset;[8] he told them also of another Indian whose name was Squanto, a native of this place, who had been in England and could speak better English than himself. Being after some time of entertainment, and gifts dismissed, a while after he came again, and five more with him, and they brought again all the tools that were stolen away before, and made way for the coming of their great Sachem, called Massasoit. Who about four or five days after came with the chief of his friends, and other attendance with the aforesaid Squanto. With whom after friendly entertainment, and some gifts given him, they made a peace with him (which hath now continued this 24 years)[9] in these terms [·]

1. That neither he nor any of his, should injure or do hurt to any of their people,
2. That if any of his, did hurt to any of theirs; he should send the offender, that they might punish him.

wolves, which they mistook for lions, they passed an unhappy night but got back next day. On the 14th the common house caught fire and the thatched roof was consumed; Bradford was lying sick abed inside but escaped. On the 19th John Goodman, one of the hunters, beat off two wolves that chased the spaniel. On 9 Feb. Master Jones shot five wild geese and found a deer killed by the Indians and being eaten by wolves. On the 16th a man out fowling saw twelve Indians; these were they who stole the tools. After that some of the ordnance from the *Mayflower* was mounted on the hill. On 3 March the wind turned south and "birds sang in the woods most pleasantly."

[8] Samoset was an Algonkian sagamore of Pemaquid Point, Maine, a region much frequented by English fishermen. He probably shipped with Capt. Dermer from Monhegan to Cape Cod shortly before the Pilgrims landed and worked his way overland to Plymouth. He conveyed 12,000 acres of Pemaquid Point to one John Brown in 1625, and lived until about 1653. One of the best historical paintings of the Pilgrims is that of this scene by Charles Hoffbauer in the New England Mutual Life Insurance building, Boylston Street, Boston.

[9] This passage dates Bradford's writing of this chapter not earlier than 1644. Massasoit, chief of the Wampanoag, had his principal seat at Sowams in the present town of Barrington, R. I. On this first visit he was accompanied by his brother and 60 warriors. *Mourt's Relation*, p. 36, describes the meeting, the exchange of presents, and speeches interpreted by Squanto. The Pilgrims "conducted him to an house then in building, where we placed a green rug and three or four cushions. Then instantly came our Governor, with drum and trumpet after him, and some few musketeers. After salutations, our Governor kissing his hand, the King kissed him; and so they sat down. The Governor called for some strong water and drunk to him; and he drunk a great draught, that made him sweat all the while after." The treaty thus concluded was faithfully kept until the reign of Massasoit's son Metacom, better known as King Philip.

3. That if anything were taken away from any of theirs, he should cause it to be restored; and they should do the like to his.
4. If any did unjustly war against him, they would aid him; if any did war against them, he should aid them.
5. He should send to his neighbors confederates, to certify them of this, that they might not wrong them but might be likewise comprised in the conditions of peace.
6. That when their men came to them, they should leave their bows and arrows behind them.

After these things he returned to his place called Sowams,[10] some 40 mile from this place, but Squanto continued with them, and was their interpreter, and was a special instrument, sent of God for their good beyond their expectation, he directed them how to set their corn, where to take fish, and to procure other commodities, and was also their pilot to bring them to unknown places for their profit, and never left them till he died. He was a native of this place, and scarce any left alive besides himself; he was carried away with divers others by one Hunt, a master of a ship,[11] who thought to sell them for slaves in Spain, but he got away for England and was entertained by a merchant in London, and employed to Newfoundland and other parts, and lastly brought hither into these parts, by one Mr. Dermer, a gentleman employed by Sir Ferdinando Gorges and others, for discovery, and other designs in these parts.

·   ·   ·

But to return; the spring now approaching, it pleased God the mortality began to cease amongst them; and the sick and lame recovered apace, which put as [it] were new life into them; though they had borne their sad affliction with much patience and contentedness, as I think any people could do, but it was the Lord which upheld them, and had beforehand prepared them; many having long borne the yoke, yea, from their youth.[12] Many other smaller matters I omit, sundry of them having been already published in a journal made by one of the company,[13] and some other passages of journeys and relations already published to which I refer those, that are willing to know them more particularly. And being now come to the 25th of March I shall begin the year 1621.

[10] For the history of this place see Thomas W. Bicknell *Sowams* (1908).
[11] Squanto or Tisquantum appears to have been the sole survivor of the Patuxet tribe. Kidnapped there by Capt. Thomas Hunt in 1614, he had the curious career that Bradford says; he jumped Capt. Dermer's ship in 1618 and made his way to the site of Plymouth, where he found himself to be the sole survivor of his tribe, wiped out in the pestilence of 1617.
[12] Lamentations iii.26.
[13] *Mourt's Relation*—see Chap. x note 2, above.

[The Thomas Morton Affair: Merrymount (1628)]

. . . In the meantime, it [the trade in wampum] makes the Indians of these parts rich and powerful and also proud thereby, and fills them with pieces, powder and shot, which no laws can restrain, by reason of the baseness of sundry unworthy persons, both English, Dutch and French, which may turn to the ruin of many. Hitherto the Indians of these parts had no pieces nor other arms but their bows and arrows, nor of many years after; neither durst they scarce handle a gun, so much were they afraid of them. And the very sight of one (though out of kilter) was a terror unto them. But those Indians to the east parts, which had commerce with the French, got pieces of them, and they in the end made a common trade of it. And in time our English fishermen, led with the like covetousness, followed their example for their own gain. But upon complaint against them, it pleased the King's Majesty to prohibit the same by a strict proclamation, commanding that no sort of arms or munition should by any of his subjects be traded with them.

About some three or four years before this time there came over one Captain Wollaston (a man of pretty parts) and with him three or four more of some eminency, who brought with them a great many servants, with provisions, and other implements for to begin a plantation [·] and pitched themselves in a place within the Massachusetts, which they called after their Captain's name, Mount Wollaston [·] amongst whom was one Mr. Morton, who it should seem had some small adventure (of his own or other men's) amongst them; but had little respect amongst them, and was slighted by the meanest servants.[1] Having continued there some time, and not finding things to answer their expectations, nor profit to arise as they looked for [·] Captain Wollaston takes a great part of the servants, and transports them to Virginia, where he puts them off at good rates, selling their time to other men; and writes back to one Mr. Rasdall (one of his chief partners, and accounted their merchant) to bring another part of them to Virginia likewise, intending to put them off there as he had done the rest. And he (with the consent of the said Rasdall) appointed one Fitcher to be his Lieutenant, and govern the remains of the Plantation, till he or Rasdall returned to take further order thereabout. But this Morton abovesaid having more craft, than honesty (who

---

[1] Nothing certain is known about Capt. Wollaston's antecedents; for various guesses see 1912 ed. Bradford II 45-6. Of Thomas Morton "of Merrymount" there is an extensive literature, the best being Charles Francis Adams *Three Episodes of Massachusetts History* and introduction to the Prince Society edition of Morton's *New English Canaan*; Charles E. Banks brought out more facts about him in Massachusetts Historical Society *Proceedings* LVIII 147-86. It is clear that he was a well-educated gentleman with a tendency to get into fights and lawsuits, a lawyer of Clifford's (not Furnival's) Inn, who had "left his country for his country's good."

had been a kind of pettifogger; of Furnival's Inn), in the others' absence, watches an opportunity (commons being but hard amongst them) and got some strong drink and other junkets, and made them a feast; and after they were merry, he began to tell them, he would give them good counsel; You see (saith he) that many of your fellows are carried to Virginia; and if you stay till this Rasdall return, you will also be carried away and sold for slaves with the rest. Therefore I would advise you, to thrust out this Lieutenant Fitcher; and I having a part in the Plantation, will receive you as my partners, and consociates; so may you be free from service, and we will converse, trade[,] plant and live together as equals, and support, and protect one another, or to like effect.

This counsel was easily received, so they took opportunity, and thrust Lieutenant Fitcher out o' doors, and would suffer him to come no more amongst them; but forced him to seek bread to eat and other relief from his neighbors, till he could get passages for England. After this they fell to great licentiousness, and led a dissolute life, pouring out themselves into all profaneness; and Morton became Lord of misrule and maintained (as it were) a School of Atheism. And after they had got some goods into their hands, and got much by trading with the Indians; they spent it as vainly, in quaffing, and drinking; both wine, and strong waters in great excess (and as some reported) £ 10 worth in a morning. They also set up a maypole, drinking and dancing about it many days together inviting the Indian women for their consorts, dancing and frisking together (like so many fairies, or furies, rather) and worse practices [·] as if they had anew revived and celebrated the feasts of the Roman goddess Flora; or the beastly practices of the mad Bacchanalians; Morton likewise (to show his poetry) composed sundry rhymes, and verses, some tending to lasciviousness, and others to the detraction and scandal of some persons, which he affixed to this idle, or idol maypole.[2] They changed also the name of their place, and instead of calling it Mount Wollaston they call it Merry-mount, as if this jollity would have lasted ever. But this continued not long, for after Morton was sent for England (as follows to be declared) shortly after came over that worthy gentleman Mr. John Endecott,

[2] Morton gives some of the verses, which he says "puzzled the Separatists most pitifully to expound," in his *New English Canaan* (the book which he wrote to get even with the Pilgrims), pp. 277-81. The best is a drinking song, of which one verse goes:

Give to the Nymph that's free from scorn
No Irish stuff nor Scotch over-worn.
Lasses in beaver coats, come away,
Ye shall be welcome to us night and day.

    Then drink and be merry, merry,
      merry boys,

Let all your delight be in Hymen's
    joys;
Io! to Hymen, now the day is come,
About the merry Maypole take a room.

It perhaps should be explained that the "Irish stuff" and "Scotch" were not whisky but woolens. Neither whisky nor rum had as yet appeared in New England; the only strong liquors known were aqua vitae and brandy.

who brought over a patent under the broad seal for the government of the Massachusetts; who visiting those parts caused that maypole to be cut down, and rebuked them for their profaneness, and admonished them, to look there should be better walking, so they or others now changed the name of their place again, and called it Mount Dagon.[3]

Now to maintain this riotous prodigality, and profuse excess; Morton (thinking himself lawless) and hearing what gain the French, and fishermen, made by trading of pieces, powder, and shot to the Indians [·] he as the head of this consortship, began the practice of the same in these parts; and first he taught them how to use them, to charge, and discharge, and what proportion, of powder, to give the piece, according to the size, or bigness of the same; and what shot to use for fowl, and what for deer. And having thus instructed them, he employed some of them to hunt, and fowl for him so as they became far more active, in that employment, than any of the English; by reason of their swiftness of foot, and nimbleness of body, being also quick-sighted, and by continual exercise well knowing the haunts of all sorts of game [·] So as when they saw the execution that a piece would do, and the benefit that might come by the same; they became mad (as it were) after them, and would not stick to give any price (they could attain to) for them; accounting their bows, and arrows but baubles in comparison of them.

And here I may take occasion to bewail the mischief that this wicked man began in these parts; and which since base covetousness, prevailing in men that should know better, has now at length got the upper hand, and made this thing common (notwithstanding any laws to the contrary) so as the Indians are full of pieces all over, both fowling pieces, muskets, pistols etc. They have also their molds to make shot, of all sorts, as musket bullets, pistol bullets, swan and goose shot, and of smaller sorts; yea some have seen them have their screw-plates to make screw-pins themselves when they want them, with sundry other implements, wherewith they are ordinarily better fitted, and furnished than the English themselves. Yea it is well known that they will have powder, and shot, when the English want it, nor cannot get it; and that in a time of war, or danger; as experience hath manifested, that when lead hath been scarce, and men for their own defense would gladly have given, a groat a pound; which is dear enough; yet hath it been bought up, and sent to other places, and sold to such as trade it with the Indians, at 12*d* the pound. And it is like they give 3*s* or 4*s* the pound, for they will have it at any rate. And these things have been done in the same times, when some of their neighbors and friends, are daily killed by the Indians, or are in danger thereof and live but at the Indians' mercy. Yea some (as they have acquainted them with all other things) have told them how gunpowder is made, and all the materials in it, and that they are to be had in their own

---

[3] After the god of the Philistines—Judges xvi.23. The site of Merrymount or Mount Wollaston is marked on Route 3, in Quincy.

land; and I am confident could they attain to make saltpeter, they would teach them to make powder. O the horribleness of this villainy! How many both Dutch and English have been lately slain by those Indians thus furnished; and no remedy provided; nay, the evil more increased, and the blood of their brethren sold for gain (as is to be feared) and in what danger all these colonies are in is too well known. O that princes and parliaments would take some timely order to prevent this mischief and at length to suppress it; by some exemplary punishment upon some of these gain-thirsty murderers, for they deserve no better title; before their colonies in these parts be overthrown by these barbarous savages, thus armed with their own weapons, by these evil instruments; and traitors to their neighbors; and country!

But I have forgot myself, and have been too long in this digression; but now to return. This Morton having thus taught them the use of pieces, he sold them all he could spare, and he and his consorts determined to send for many out of England, and had by some of the ships sent for above a score: The which being known; and his neighbors meeting the Indians in the woods armed with guns in this sort, it was a terror unto them who lived stragglingly and were of no strength in any place. And other places (though more remote) saw this mischief would quickly spread over all, if not prevented. Besides, they saw they should keep no servants, for Morton would entertain any, how vile soever, and all the scum of the country or any discontents would flock to him from all places, if this nest was not broken, and they should stand in more fear of their lives and goods in short time from this wicked and debauched crew than from the savages themselves.

So sundry of the chief of the straggling plantations meeting together, agreed by mutual consent to solicit those of Plymouth (who were then of more strength than them all) to join with them to prevent the further growth of this mischief; and suppress Morton and his consorts before they grew to further head and strength. Those that joined in this action, and after contributed to the charge of sending him for England, were from Piscataqua, Naumkeag, Winnisimmet, Wessagusset, Nantasket, and other places where any English were seated.[4] Those of Plymouth being thus sought to by their messengers and letters, and weighing both their reasons, and the common danger, were willing to afford them their help; though themselves had least

---

[4] In Bradford's *Letter Book* there is a list of the plantations that contributed, and the amount. Roger Conant and the remnants of the Cape Ann fishing colony, then at Naumkeag (Salem), contributed £1 10s; planters at the Piscataqua, £2 10s; Jeffrey and Burslem at Wessagusset (Weymouth), £2; the widow Thompson on Thompson's Island, Boston Harbor, 15s; William Blackstone at Shawmut (Boston), 12s; Edward Hilton at Cocheco (Dover, N. H.), £1; and Plymouth itself, £2 10s. John Oldham and his friends at Nantasket (Hull) and Maverick at Winnisimmet (Chelsea) apparently gave nothing, but it is clear that Plymouth was acting for the "United Nations" of New England, and that Myles Standish was a U. N. commander.

cause of fear or hurt. So to be short, they first resolved jointly to write to him, and in a friendly, and neighborly way to admonish him to forbear those courses, and sent a messenger with their letters to bring his answer. But he was so high as he scorned all advice, and asked who had to do with him; he had and would trade pieces with the Indians, in despite of all, with many other scurrilous terms full of disdain. They sent to him a second time and bade him be better advised and more temperate in his terms, for the country could not bear the injury he did; it was against their common safety, and against the King's proclamation; he answered in high terms as before; and that the King's proclamation was no law, demanding what penalty was upon it: it was answered, more than he could bear, His Majesty's displeasure, but insolently he persisted, and said the King was dead and his displeasure with him, and many the like things [·] and threatened withal that if any came to molest him, let them look to themselves for he would prepare for them [·] upon which they saw there was no way but to take him by force, and having so far proceeded, now to give over would make him far more haughty and insolent. so they mutually resolved to proceed, and obtained of the Governor of Plymouth to send Captain Standish and some other aid with him, to take Morton by force. The which accordingly was done, but they found him to stand stiffly in his defense, having made fast his doors, armed his consorts, set divers dishes of powder and bullets ready on the table; and if they had not been over-armed with drink, more hurt might have been done. They summoned him to yield, but he kept his house, and they could get nothing but scoffs, and scorns from him. But at length fearing they would do some violence to the house, he and some of his crew came out, but not to yield, but to shoot; but they were so steeled with drink as their pieces were too heavy for them; himself with a carbine (overcharged, and almost half filled, with powder and shot, as was after found), had thought to have shot Captain Standish; but he stepped to him, and put by his piece, and took him; neither was there any hurt done to any of either side; save that one was so drunk, that he ran his own nose upon the point of a sword that one held before him, as he entered the house, but he lost but a little of his hot blood.[5] Morton they brought away to Plymouth where he was kept; till a ship went from the Isle of Shoals for England with which he was sent, to the Council of New England; and letters written to give them information of his course, and carriage; and also one, was sent at their common charge, to inform their Honors more particularly, and to prosecute against him. But he fooled of the messenger, after he was gone from hence and though he went for England yet nothing was done to him not so much as rebuked, for aught was heard; but returned

---

[5] Morton's account naturally differs. According to his *New English Canaan* pp. 285-7, "Captain Shrimpe," as he calls Standish, and his army of eight "came within danger like a flock of wild geese, as if they had been tailed one to another, as colts to be sold at a fair," but "Mine Host" generously yielded to avoid bloodshed.

the next year. Some of the worst of the company were dispersed, and some, of the more modest kept the house till he should be heard from. But I have been too long about so unworthy a person and bad a cause.

.   .   .

[LONGEVITY OF THE PILGRIM FATHERS]

I cannot but here take occasion,* not only to mention, but greatly to admire the marvelous providence of God! That notwithstanding the many changes, and hardships that these people went through, and the many enemies they had, and difficulties they met withal; that so many of them should live to very old age! It was not only this reverend man's condition (for one swallow makes no summer as they say) but many more of them did the like, some dying about, and before this time, and many still living; who attained to sixty years of age, and to sixty-five, divers to seventy and above, and some near eighty as he did. It must needs be more than ordinary, and above natural reason that so it should be. For it is found in experience, that change of air, famine, or unwholesome food, much drinking of water, sorrows, and troubles, etc., all of them are enemies to health, causes of many diseases, consumers of natural vigor, and the bodies of men and shorteners of life. And yet of all these things they had a large part, and suffered deeply in the same; they went from England to Holland, where they found, both worse air, and diet, than that they came from; from thence (enduring a long imprisonment as it were in the ships at sea) into New England; and how it hath been with them here, hath already been shown; and what crosses, troubles, fears, wants, and sorrows they had been liable unto is easy to conjecture. So as in some sort, they may say with the Apostle, 2 Corinthians xi.26, 27, they were in journeyings often, in perils of waters, in perils of robbers, in perils of their own nation, in perils among the heathen, in perils in the wilderness, in perils in the sea, in perils among false brethren; in weariness, and painfulness, in watching often, in hunger, and thirst, in fasting often, in cold and nakedness. What was it then that upheld them? It was God's visitation that preserved their spirits. Job x.12: Thou hast given me life, and grace, and thy visitation hath preserved my spirit. He that upheld the Apostle upheld them, They were persecuted, but not forsaken, cast down, but perished not. 2 Corinthians iv.9. As unknown, and yet known; as dying, and behold we live; as chastened, and yet not killed. 2 Corinthians vi.9. God, it seems, would have all men to behold, and observe such mercies, and works of His providence as

*Having discussed the life and death in 1643
of William Brewster, aged about 80. [D.L.]

these are towards His people; that they in like cases might be encouraged, to depend upon God, in their trials, and also to bless His name when they see His goodness towards others. Man lives not by bread only. Deuteronomy viii.3. It is not by good and dainty fare, by peace, and rest, and heart's ease, in enjoying the contentments and good things of this world only, that preserves health, and prolongs life; God in such examples would have the world see, and behold that He can do it without them; and if the world will shut their eyes, and take no notice thereof, yet He would have His people, to see, and consider it. Daniel could be better liking with pulse, than others were with the king's dainties. Jacob though he went from one nation, to another people, and passed through famine, fears, and many afflictions yet he lived till old age, and died sweetly, and rested in the Lord; as infinite others of God's servants have done; and still shall do (through God's goodness) notwithstanding all the malice of their enemies; when the branch of the wicked shall be cut off before his day. Job xv.32. and the bloody, and deceitful men shall not live half their days; Psalm lv.23. . . .

[THE NEW ENGLAND CONFEDERATION AND THE NARRAGANSETTS, 1643]

By reason of the plottings of the Narragansetts ever since the Pequots' War the Indians were drawn into a general conspiracy against the English in all parts, as was in part discovered the year before; and now made more plain and evident by many discoveries and free confessions of sundry Indians upon several occasions from divers places, concurring in one. With such other concurring circumstances as gave them sufficiently to understand the truth thereof. And to think of means how to prevent the same and secure themselves. Which made them enter into this more near union and confederation following.

These were the articles of agreement in the union and confederation which they now first entered into. And in this their first meeting held at Boston the day and year abovesaid, amongst other things they had this matter of great consequence to consider on:

The Narragansetts, after the subduing of the Pequots, thought to have ruled over all the Indians about them. But the English, especially those of Connecticut, holding correspondency and friendship with Uncas, sachem of the Mohegan Indians which lived near them (as the Massachusetts had done with the Narragansetts) and he had been faithful to them in the Pequot War, they were engaged to support him in his just liberties and were contented that such of the surviving Pequots as had submitted to him should remain with him and quietly under his protection. This did much increase his power and augment his greatness, which the Narragansetts could not endure to see. But Miantonomo,[1] their chief sachem, an ambitious and politic man, sought

---

[1] Miantonomo, a nephew of Canonicus, was apparently jealous of the favor shown by the English to their faithful ally, Uncas.

privately and by treachery, according to the Indian manner, to make him away by hiring some to kill him. Sometime they assayed to poison him; that not taking, then in the night time to knock him on the head in his house or secretly to shoot him, and suchlike attempts. But none of these taking effect, he made open war upon him (though it was against the covenants both between the English and them, as also between themselves and a plain breach of the same). He came suddenly upon him with 900 or 1000 men, never denouncing any war before. The other's power at that present was not above half so many, but it pleased God to give Uncas the victory and he slew many of his men and wounded many more; but the chief of all was, he took Miantonomo prisoner.

And seeing he was a great man, and the Narragansetts a potent people and would seek revenge, he would do nothing in the case without the advice of the English, so he, by the help and direction of those of Connecticut, kept him prisoner till this meeting of the Commissioners. The Commissioners weighed the cause and passages as they were clearly represented and sufficiently evidenced betwixt Uncas and Miantonomo; and the things being duly considered, the Commissioners apparently saw that Uncas could not be safe whilst Miantonomo lived; but either by secret treachery or open force, his life would be still in danger. Wherefore they thought he might justly put such a false and blood-thirsty enemy to death; but in his own jurisdiction, not in the English plantations. And they advised in the manner of his death all mercy and moderation should be showed, contrary to the practice of the Indians, who exercise tortures and cruelty. And Uncas having hitherto showed himself a friend to the English, and in this craving their advice, if the Narragansett Indians or others shall unjustly assault Uncas for this execution, upon notice and request the English promise to assist and protect him as far as they may against such violence.

This was the issue of this business. The reasons and passages hereof are more at large to be seen in the acts and records of this meeting of the Commissioners. And Uncas followed this advice and accordingly executed him in a very fair manner according as they advised, with due respect to his honor and greatness.[2] But what followed on the Narragansetts' part will appear hereafter.

[2] The alleged "fair manner" was being bound and slain by a hatchet wielded by Uncas's brother. "This disgraceful proceeding," as Hodge's *Handbook* terms it, has lain heavily on the New England conscience ever since; and it is strongly suspected that the Confederation wished to make an example of Miantonomo because he had sold land to Roger Williams and Samuel Gorton. A monument was erected to Miantonomo in 1841 at the scene of his murder in Norwich, Conn., and several vessels of the United States Navy have been named after him; a better tribute to his "honor and greatness" than being dispatched with a hatchet.

THE BAY PSALM BOOK

(1640)

The pride of the new press established in Cambridge in 1639 was *The Whole Book of Psalmes Faithfully Translated into English Metre,* the first book published in the American colonies. It was written by Richard Mather (1596–1669), John Eliot (1604–1690), and Thomas Weld (1595–1661). Determined to translate the sacred Hebrew as accurately as possible, yet aware that translation must include some effort to retain poetic form, Richard Mather wrote an intelligent preface explaining the editors' predicament and their principles. The book was revised in the third edition (1651) by the President of Harvard College, Henry Dunster, and Richard Lyon.

The Psalms

23 A PSALM OF DAVID

The Lord to me a shepherd is, want therefore shall not I.
2 He in the folds of tender-grass, doth cause me down to lie:
   To waters calm me gently leads (3) Restore my soul doth he:
   he doth in paths of righteousness: for his name's sake lead me.
4 Yea though in valley of death's shade I walk, none ill I'll fear:
   because thou art with me, thy rod, and staff my comfort are.
5 For me a table thou hast spread, in presence of my foes:
   thou dost anoint my head with oil, my cup it over-flows.
6 Goodness & mercy surely shall all my days follow me:
   and in the Lord's house I shall dwell so long as days shall be.

PSAL: XXIII. A PSALM OF DAVID

The Lord to me a shepherd is: want therefore shall not I.
2 He in the folds of tender grass doth make me down to lie:
He leads me to the waters still. (3) Restore my soul doth he;
In paths of righteousness, he will for his name's sake lead me.

4 In valley of death's shade although I walk I'll fear none ill:
For thou with me thy rod, also thy staff me comfort will.
5 Thou hast 'fore me a table spread, in presence of my foes.
Thou dost anoint with oil my head, my cup it over-flows.

[6] Goodness and mercy my days all shall surely follow me:
And in the Lord's house dwell I shall so long as days shall be.

[From Dunster-Lyon revision, 1651]

JOHN WINTHROP

(1588-1649)

From Cotton Mather at the end of the seventeenth century to Edmund S. Morgan in the twentieth, the best American historians have represented John Winthrop as a strong, temperate man who governed firmly but often acted leniently in his effort to establish "a City upon a Hill," an American beacon that would show Europeans that God's people here strove to do right in the world for the glory of God. He has invariably been compared to William Bradford, for both men were repeatedly elected governor during the critical decades of the earliest colonization; both wrote histories, unpublished during their own lives, of early colonial days; and both lived to address the rising generation in a mixture of celebration and lament concerning an infant colony's thriving health and the apparent decline from the original founders' zealous piety, from their ideal of a closely knit community.

Winthrop, of course, had a much more imposing family than Bradford's. Like many other leaders of the Massachusetts Bay Company, Winthrop attended Cambridge University (Trinity College), and although he did not take a degree there, he did marry an heiress and he became a lawyer and a Justice of the Peace at Groton, where his father was lord of the manor. Ten years before the emigration to New England, Winthrop succeeded to his father's position. He was elected governor of The Massachusetts Bay Company in 1629, the year before he emigrated, and he was one of the chief authors of the decision to bring the company's charter to America rather than leave it (as the settlers of Plymouth Plantation had been forced to leave theirs) in the hands of a group of company officers in England.

The History of New England from 1630 To 1649, from which the selection is taken, was edited by James Savage, New Edition, 2 vols., 1853. A. Forbes edited *The Winthrop Papers,* 5 vols., 1929-1945.

An early biography is R. C. Winthrop, *Life and Letters of John Winthrop, 1864-1867.* A more modern treatment is Edmund S.

Morgan, *The Puritan Dilemma: The Story of John Winthrop,* 1958. See also Richard S. Dunn, *Puritans and Yankees: The Winthrop Dynasty of New England,* 1962; D. B. Rutman, *Winthrop's Boston,* 1965, argues forcibly against unqualified generalizations about the Puritans.

During the remaining 19 years of his life, Winthrop was elected governor or deputy governor more than a dozen times. He was deputy governor during the Antinomian crisis of 1636–1637, and it was his election to the governorship after an extremely tense series of political maneuvers that gave opponents of the Antinomians control of the civil government. In that controversy and a number of others he exerted a

Portrait of Governor John Winthrop, anon. (School of Van Dyke) *(American Antiquarian Society.)*

tough, resourceful political skill which a critical observer might consider ruthless, but both his writing and his documented conduct also reveal an unmistakable spirit of charity, self-restraint, and leniency. Like William Bradford, Winthrop had a passion to explain and justify his controversial actions, and in doing so he made some of the most memorable statements of Puritan political theory. Like Jonathan Edwards (the revivalist who was born more than a century after Winthrop), Winthrop had a capacity for being "ravished" with an inexpressible joy when visited by a suddenly renewed awareness of God's glory.

The two selections reprinted here are central statements of Puritan political and communal faith. Winthrop preached "A Modell of Christian Charity" aboard the *Arbella* during the voyage of the first large group of emigrants from England to Massachusetts Bay. His emphasis on justice and mercy in civil affairs anticipates the allegorical debate between Justice and Mercy in Edward Taylor's poem "God's Determinations Touching His Elect" (see below, pp. 294–297), and his appeal at the end, to honor the Covenant and create a "city upon a hill," is the first of many American claims to a special historical mission, a peculiar opportunity and an extraordinary obligation to set an example for the world.

The passages from Winthrop's *History of New England from 1630 to 1649* recount controversies with Roger Williams, whose extremely sensitive conscience and inquisitive, searching mind provoked a number of theological and civil crises before the civil authorities decided that he must be banished. Notice the marked difference between the circumstantial details of Winthrop's narrative of the brutal beating administered by Nathaniel Eaton (pp. 83–85) and the restrained abstractness of the narrative concerning Williams. In both episodes, however, the central point seems to be not only civil order or justice, but a concern for convincing a fellow man of his error or sin and of the justice in the community's proceeding. The will of Robert Keane, who is charged here with profiteering, has been edited by Bernard Bailyn and published in a Harper Torchbooks Edition. Keane's case leads to a discussion of covetousness and an effort to define its civil consequences and limits, and the definition by Winthrop and Cotton shows how far Puritan authorities were from advocating a free market.

In the passage on the 1645 controversy, Winthrop was himself the central figure. Both the detachment of his narrative tone and the substance of his speech to the General Court (which has often been reprinted since Cotton Mather first published it in his biography of Winthrop) exemplify Winthrop's resolution to establish and justify a government faithful to the covenant and to his version of civil or federal liberty.

From A Model of Christian Charity[1]

Written On Board the Arbella,
On the Atlantic Ocean.

God Almighty in His most holy and wise providence hath so disposed of the condition of mankind, as in all times some must be rich some poor, some high and eminent in power and dignity; others mean and in subjection.[2]

THE REASON HEREOF.

1. REAS: *First*, to hold conformity with the rest of His works, being delighted to show forth the glory of His wisdom in the variety and difference of the creatures and the glory of His power, in ordering all these differences for the preservation and good of the whole, and the glory of His greatness that as it is the glory of princes to have many officers, so this great King will have many stewards counting Himself more honored in dispensing His gifts to man by man, than if He did it by His own immediate hand.

2. REAS: *Secondly*, That He might have the more occasion to manifest the work of His spirit: first, upon the wicked in moderating and restraining them: so that the rich and mighty should not eat up the poor, nor the poor, and despised rise up against their superiors, and shake off their yoke; secondly in the regenerate in exercising His graces in them, as in the great ones, their love, mercy, gentleness, temperance etc., in the poor and inferior sort, their faith, patience, obedience etc:

3. REAS: Thirdly, that every man might have need of other, and from hence they might be all knit more nearly together in the bond of brotherly affection: from hence it appears plainly that no man is made more honorable than another or more wealthy etc., out of any particular and singular respect to himself but for the glory of his Creator and the common good of the creature, man; therefore God still reserves the property of these gifts to Himself as Ezek: 16. 17. He there calls wealth His gold and His silver etc.

---

[1] The following text and notes are reprinted with permission from *Winthrop Papers, Volume II, 1623-1630*, published by the Massachusetts Historical Society, Boston, 1931.

Copy, apparently contemporary or nearly so, in the Library of the New York Historical Society. . . . Like many tracts of the time, the work appears to have been circulated in manuscript. A letter of the Reverend Henry Jacie to John Winthrop, Jr., written January, 1634-35, during a visit of the latter to England, says, "We shall be further indebted to you if you can procure the Map, the Patents Copy, the Model of Charity (also what Oath is taken), Mr. Higginsons Letter, and the Petition to our Ministers for praying for them, made at their going, which is in print." . . . The copy belonging to the New York Historical Society seems to be one of those prepared for circulation. In one or two instances errors of the copyist make the text unintelligible. Several blank spaces left by the copyist, which we have filled in within brackets, probably represent in some cases words which he could not read, in others references left incomplete in the original.

[2] This may be compared with the "difference betwene principalitie and popularie" stated in "Common Greuances," I. 307.

Prov: 3. 9. He claims their service as His due honor the Lord with thy riches etc. All men being thus (by divine Providence) ranked into two sorts, rich and poor; under the first, are comprehended all such as are able to live comfortably by their own means duly improved; and all others are poor according to the former distribution. There are two rules whereby we are to walk one towards another: JUSTICE and MERCY. These are always distinguished in their act and in their object, yet may they both concur in the same subject in each respect; as sometimes there may be an occasion of showing mercy to a rich man, in some sudden danger of distress, and also doing of mere justice to a poor man in regard of some particular contract etc. There is likewise a double law by which we are regulated in our conversation one towards another: in both the former respects, the law of nature and the law of grace, or the moral law or the law of the Gospel, to omit the rule of justice as not properly belonging to this purpose otherwise than it may fall into consideration in some particular cases: by the first of these laws man as he was enabled so withall [is] commanded to love his neighbor as himself upon this ground stands all the precepts of the moral law, which concerns our dealings with men. To apply this to the works of mercy this law requires two things[:] first[,] that every man afford his help to another in every want or distress[;] secondly, that he perform this out of the same affection, which makes him careful of his own good according to that of our Saviour[,] Math: (7.12) Whatsoever ye would that men should do to you. This was practiced by Abraham and Lot in entertaining the angels and the old man of Gibea.[3]

The law of grace or the Gospel hath some difference from the former as in these respects first the law of nature was given to man in the estate of innocency; this of the Gospel in the estate of regeneracy: secondly, the former propounds one man to another, as the same flesh and image of God, this as a brother in Christ also, and in the communion of the same spirit and so teacheth us to put a difference between Christians and others. Do good to all especially to the household of faith;[4] upon this ground the Israelites were to put a difference between the brethren of such as were strangers though not of the Canaanites. Thirdly. The law of nature could give no rules for dealing with enemies for all are to be considered as friends in the estate of innocency, but the Gospel commands love to an enemy. Proof: If thine enemy hunger feed him; love your enemies do good to them that hate you. Math: 5.44.

This law of the Gospel propounds likewise a difference of seasons and occasions: there is a time when a Christian must sell all and give to the poor as they did in the Apostles' times. There is a time also when a Christian (though they give not all yet) must give beyond their ability, as they of

[3] Genesis, xviii–xix, where the marginal comments in the Genevan version may also be read with profit, as they undoubtedly were read by Winthrop; Judges, xix. 16–21.
[4] Galatians, vi. 10.

Macedonia. Cor: 2. 6. Likewise community of perils calls for extraordinary liberality and so doth community in some special service for the Church. Lastly, when there is no other means whereby our Christian brother may be relieved in this distress, we must help him beyond our ability, rather than tempt God, in putting him upon help by miraculous or extraordinary means.

This duty of mercy is exercised in the kinds, giving, lending, and forgiving.

QUEST. What rule shall a man observe in giving in respect of the measure?

ANS. If the time and occasion be ordinary he is to give out of his abundance—let him lay aside, as God hath blessed him. If the time and occasion be extraordinary he must be ruled by them; taking this withall, that then a man cannot likely do too much especially, if he may leave himself and his family under probable means of comfortable subsistence.

OBJECTION. A man must lay up for posterity, the fathers lay up for posterity and children and he is worse than an infidel that provideth not for his own.[5]

ANS: For the first, it is plain, that it being spoken by way of comparison it must be meant of the ordinary and usual course of fathers and cannot extend to times and occasions extraordinary; for the other place the Apostle speaks against such as walked inordinately, and it is without question, that he is worse than an infidel who through his own sloth and voluptuousness shall neglect to provide for his family.

OBJECTION. The wise mans eyes are in his head (saith Solomon)[6] and foreseeth the plague, therefore we must forecast and lay up against evil times when he or his may stand in need of all he can gather.

ANS: This very argument Solomon useth to persuade to liberality. Eccle: (ii.i.) Cast thy bread upon the waters etc.: for thou knowest not what evil may come upon the land. Luke 16: Make you friends of the riches of iniquity; you will ask how this shall be? Very well. For first he that gives to the poor lends to the Lord, and He will repay him even in this life an hundred fold to him or his. The righteous is ever merciful and lendeth and his seed enjoyeth the blessing; and besides we know what advantage it will be to us in the day of account, when many such witnesses shall stand forth for us to witness the improvement of our talent. And I would know of those who plead so much for laying up for time to come, whether they hold that to be Gospel, Math: 16. 19: Lay not up for yourselves treasures upon earth etc., if they acknowledge it what extent will they allow it; if only to those primitive times let them consider the reason whereupon our Saviour grounds it, the first is that they are subject to the moth, the rust, the thief. Secondly, they will steal away the heart, where the treasure is there will the heart be also. The reasons are of like force at all times therefore the exhortation must be general and perpetual which [applies] always in respect of the love and

[5] I Timothy, v. 8.   [6] Ecclesiastes, ii. 14.

affection to riches and in regard of the things themselves when any special service for the church or particular distress of our brother do call for the use of them; otherwise it is not only lawful but necessary to lay up as Joseph did to have ready upon such occasions, as the Lord (whose stewards we are of them) shall call for them from us: Christ gives us an instance of the first, when He sent His disciples for the ass, and bids them answer the owner thus: the Lord hath need of him;[7] so when the Tabernacle was to be built his [servant][8] sends to his people to call for their silver and gold etc.; and yields them no other reason but that it was for his work, when Elisha comes to the widow of Sareptah[9] and finds her preparing to make ready her pittance for herself and family, he bids her first provide for him, he challengeth first God's part which she must first give before she must serve her own family, all these teach us that the Lord looks that when He is pleased to call for His right in anything we have, our own interest we have must stand aside, till His turn be served; for the other we need look no further than to that of John 1: he who hath this world's goods and seeth his brother to need, and shuts up his compassion from him, how dwelleth the love of God in him, which comes punctually to this conclusion: if thy brother be in want and thou canst help him, thou needst not make doubt, what thou shouldst do, if thou lovest God thou must help him.

QUEST: What rule must we observe in lending?

ANS: Thou must observe whether thy brother hath present or probable, or possible means of repaying thee, if there be none of these, thou must give him according to his necessity, rather than lend him as he requires; if he hath present means of repaying thee, thou art to look at him, not as an act of mercy, but by way of commerce, wherein thou art to walk by the rule of justice, but, if his means of repaying thee be only probable or possible then is he an object of thy mercy: thou must lend him, though there be danger of losing it, Deut: 15. 7. If any of thy brethren be poor etc. thou shalt lend him sufficient that men might not shift off this duty by the apparent hazard, he tells them that though the year of jubilee were at hand (when he must remit it, if he were not able to repay it before) yet he must lend him and that cheerfully:[10] it may not grieve thee to give him (saith he) and because some might object, why so I should soon impoverish my self and my family, he adds with all thy work etc. for our Saviour, Math: 5. 42. From him that would borrow of thee turn not away.

QUEST: What rule must we observe in forgiving?

ANS: Whether thou didst lend by way of commerce or in mercy, if he have nothing to pay thee [thou] must forgive him (except in cause where thou hast a surety or a lawful pledge) Deut. 15. 2. Every seventh year the

---

[7] Matthew, xxi. 2–3.

[8] Zerubbabel. Ezra, iii; Haggai, ii, with the Genevan marginal comments.

[9] I Kings, xvii. 8–24; Luke, v. 26.

[10] Deuteronomy, xv. 7–11; Leviticus, xxv. 35–42.

creditor was to quit that which he lent to his brother if he were poor as appears ver: 8[4]: save when there shall be no poor with thee. In all these and like cases Christ was [has?] a general rule, Math: 7. 22. Whatsoever ye would that men should do to you do ye the same to them also.

QUEST: What rule must we observe and walk by in cause of community of peril?

ANS: The same as before, but with more enlargement towards others and less respect towards ourselves, and our own right[;] hence it was that in the primitive Church they sold all, had all things in common, neither did any man say that that which he possessed was his own[11] likewise in their return out of the Captivity, because the work was great for the restoring of the Church and the danger of enemies was common to all Nehemiah exhorts the Jews to liberality and readiness in remitting their debts to their brethren, and disposeth liberally of his own to such as wanted and stands not upon his own due, which he might have demanded of them,[12] thus did some of our forefathers in times of persecution here in England, and so did many of the faithful in other churches whereof we keep an honorable remembrance of them, and it is to be observed that both in Scriptures and latter stories of the churches that such as have been most bountiful to the poor saints especially in these extraordinary times and occasions God hath left them highly commended to posterity, as Zacheus, Cornelius, Dorcas,[13] Bishop Hooper,[14] the Cutler of Brussels and divers others observe again that the Scripture gives no caution to restrain any from being over liberal this way; but all men to the liberal and cheerful practice hereof by the sweetest promises, as to instance one for many, Isaiah 58. 6: Is not this the fast that I have chosen to loose the bonds of wickedness, to take off the heavy burdens to let the oppressed go free and to break every yoke, to deal thy bread to the hungry and to bring the poor that wander into thy house, when thou seest the naked to cover them etc. Then shall thy light break forth as the morning, and thy health shall grow speedily, thy righteousness shall go before thee, and the glory of the Lord shall embrace thee, then thou shalt call and the Lord shall answer thee etc. 2. 10: If thou pour out thy soul to the hungry, then shall thy light spring out in darkness, and the Lord shall guide thee continually, and satisfy thy soul in draught, and make fat thy bones, thou shalt be like a watered garden, and they shall be of thee that shall build the old waste places etc. On the contrary most heavy curses are laid upon such as are straightened toward the Lord and his people Judg: 5. [23] Curse ye Meroshe because the[y] came not

---

[11] Acts, ii. 44-45; iv. 32-35.

[12] Nehemiah, v. Among the pithy Genevan marginal comments on this chapter one may be noted: "By nature the rich is no better than the poore."

[13] Luke, xix. 8-10; Acts, ix. 36-42 and x.

[14] Bishop John Hooper, famous Protestant martyr, burned at the stake at Gloucester, February 9, 1555. "In his Hall there was daily a table spread with good store of victuals, and beset with poore folke of the City of *Worcester* by turns, who were served by four at a Messe, with whole and wholesome meat." Thomas Fuller, *Abel Redevivus* (London, 1651), 173.

to help the Lord etc. Pro: [21. 13] He who shutteth his ears from hearing the cry of the poor, he shall cry and shall not be heard: Math: 25. [41] Go ye cursed into everlasting fire etc. [42] I was hungry and ye fed me not. Cor: 2. 9. 16. [6.] He that soweth sparingly shall reap sparingly.

Having already set forth the practice of mercy according to the rule of God's law, it will be useful to lay open the grounds of it also being the other part of the Commandment and that is the affection from which this exercise of mercy must arise, the Apostle tells us that this love is the fulfilling of the law,[15] not that it is enough to love our brother and so no further but in regard of the excellency of his parts giving any motion to the other as the soul to the body and the power it hath to set all the faculties on work in the outward exercise of this duty[—]as when we bid one make the clock strike he doth not lay hand on the hammer which is the immediate instrument of the sound but sets on work the first mover or main wheel, knowing that will certainly produce the sound which he intends; so the way to draw men to the works of mercy is not by force of argument from the goodness or necessity of the work, for though this course may enforce a rational mind to some present act of mercy as is frequent in experience, yet it cannot work such a habit in a soul as shall make it prompt upon all occasions to produce the same effect but by framing these affections of love in the heart which will as natively bring forth the other, as any cause doth produce the effect.

The definition which the Scripture gives us of love is this: love is the bond of perfection.[16] First, it is a bond, or ligament. Secondly, it makes the work perfect. There is no body but consists of parts and that which knits these parts together gives the body its perfection, because it makes each part so contiguous to other as thereby they do mutually participate with each other, both in strength and infirmity in pleasure and pain, to instance in the most perfect of all bodies, Christ and His church make one body: the several parts of this body considered apart before they were united were as disproportionate and as much disordering as so many contrary qualities or elements but when Christ comes and by His spirit and love knits all these parts to Himself and each to other, it is become the most perfect and best proportioned body in the world. Eph: 4. 16. "Christ by whom all the body being knit together by every joint for the furniture thereof according to the effectual power which is in the measure of every perfection of parts a glorious body without spot or wrinkle the ligaments hereof being Christ or His love for Christ is love. 1 John: 4. 8. So this definition is right. Love is the bond of perfection.

From hence we may frame these conclusions.

1. First all true Christians are of one body in Christ. 1 Cor. 12. 12. 13. 17. [27.] Ye are the body of Christ and members of [your?] part.

[15] Romans, xiii. 10.

[16] Colossians, iii. 14. The Genevan version reads "love, which is the bond of perfectnesse."

2. The ligaments of this body which knit together are love.
3. No body can be perfect which wants its proper ligaments.
4. All the parts of this body being thus united are made so contiguous in a special relation as they must needs partake of each other's strength and infirmity, joy, and sorrow, weal and woe. 1 Cor: 12. 26. If one member suffers all suffer with it, if one be in honor, all rejoice with it.
5. This sensibleness and sympathy of each other's conditions will necessarily infuse into each part a native desire and endeavor, to strengthen defend preserve and comfort the other.[17]

. . .

It rests now to make some application of this discourse by the present design which gave the occasion of writing of it. Herein are 4 things to be propounded: first the persons, secondly, the work, thirdly, the end, fourthly the means.

1. For the persons, we are a Company professing ourselves fellow members of Christ, in which respect only though we were absent from each other many miles, and had our employments as far distant, yet we ought to account our selves knit together by this bond of love, and live in the exercise of it, if we would have comfort of our being in Christ, this was notorious in the practice of the Christians in former times, as is testified of the Waldenses from the mouth of one of the adversaries Aeneas Sylvius, mutuo [solent amare] penè antequam norint, they use to love any of their own religion even before they were acquainted with them.
2. For the work we have in hand, it is by a mutual consent through a special overruling providence, and a more than an ordinary approbation of the churches of Christ to seek out a place of cohabitation and consortship under a due form of government both civil and ecclesiastical. In such cases as this the care of the public must oversway all private respects, by which not only conscience,[18] but mere civil policy doth bind us; for it is a true rule that particular estates cannot subsist in the ruin of the public.
3. The end is to improve our lives to do more service to the Lord[,] the comfort and increase of the body of Christ whereof we are members[,] that ourselves and posterity may be the better preserved from the common corruptions of this evil world to serve the Lord and work out our salvation under the power and purity of His holy ordinances.

---

[17] Omitted here are a number of Biblical examples and a description, from Biblical examples, of "how this love comes to be wrought."

[18] The copyist wrote "consequence," above which a later hand has interlined "conscience."

4. For the means whereby this must be effected, they are two fold, a conformity with the work and end we aim at, these we see are extraordinary, therefore we must not content ourselves with usual ordinary means. Whatsoever we did or ought to have done when we lived in England, the same must we do and more also where we go: That which the most in their churches maintain as a truth in profession only, we must bring into familiar and constant practice, as in this duty of love we must love brotherly without dissimulation,[19] we must love one another with a pure heart fervently,[20] we must bear one another's burdens,[21] we must not look only on our own things, but also on the things of our brethren, neither must we think that the Lord will bear with such failings at our hands as He doth from those among whom we have lived, and that for three Reasons.

1. In regard of the more near bond of marriage, between Him and us, wherein He hath taken us to be His after a most strict and peculiar manner which will make Him the more jealous of our love and obedience. So he tells the people of Israel, you only have I known of all the families of the earth, therefore will I punish you for your transgressions.[22]

2. Because the Lord will be sanctified in them that come near Him. We know that there were many that corrupted the service of the Lord, some setting up altars before His own, others offering both strange fire and strange sacrifices also; yet there came no fire from heaven, or other sudden judgment upon them as did upon Nadab and Abihu[23] who yet we may think did not sin presumptuously.

3. When God gives a special commission He looks to have it strictly observed in every article. when He gave Saul a commission to destroy Amaleck He indented with him upon certain articles and because he failed in one of the least, and that upon a fair pretense, it lost him the kingdom, which should have been his reward, if he had observed his commission:[24] Thus stands the cause between God and us, we are entered into covenant with Him for this work, we have taken out a commission, the Lord hath given us leave to draw our own articles. We have professed to enterprise these actions upon these and these ends, we have hereupon besought Him of favor and blessing: Now if the Lord shall please to hear us, and bring us in peace to the place we desire, then hath He ratified this covenant and sealed our commission, [and] will expect a strict performance of the articles contained in it, but if we shall neglect the observation of these articles which are the

[19] Romans, xii. 9–10.

[20] I Peter, i. 22.

[21] Galatians, vi. 2.

[22] Amos, iii. 2.

[23] Leviticus, x. 1–2.

[24] I Samuel, xv; xxviii. 16–18.

ends we have propounded, and dissembling with our God, shall fall to embrace this present world and prosecute our carnal intentions, seeking great things for ourselves and our posterity, the Lord will surely break out in wrath against us, be revenged of such a perjured people, and make us know the price of the breach of such a covenant.

Now the only way to avoid this shipwreck and to provide for our posterity is to follow the counsel of Micah, to do justly, to love mercy, to walk humbly with our God.[25] For this end, we must be knit together in this work as one man, we must entertain each other in brotherly affection, we must be willing to abridge our selves of our superfluities, for the supply of others' necessities, we must uphold a familiar commerce together in all meekness, gentleness, patience and liberality, we must delight in each other, make others' conditions our own, rejoice together, mourn together, labor, and suffer together, always having before our eyes our commission and community in the work, our community as members of the same body, so shall we keep the unity of the Spirit in the bond of peace,[26] the Lord will be our God and delight to dwell among us, as His own people and will command a blessing upon us in all our ways, so that we shall see much more of His wisdom, power, goodness, and truth than formerly we have been acquainted with, we shall find that the God of Israel is among us, when ten of us shall be able to resist a thousand of our enemies, when He shall make us a praise and glory, that men shall say of succeeding plantations: the Lord make it like that of New England: for we must consider that we shall be as a city upon a hill,[27] the eyes of all people are upon us; so that if we shall deal falsely with our God in this work we have undertaken and so cause Him to withdraw His present help from us, we shall be made a story and a by-word through the world, we shall open the mouths of enemies to speak evil of the ways of God and all professors for God's sake; we shall shame the faces of many of God's worthy servants, and cause their prayers to be turned into curses upon us till we be consumed out of the good land whither we are going: and to shut up this discourse with that exhortation of Moses that faithful servant of the Lord in his last farewell to Israel (Deut. 30). Beloved, there is now set before us life, and good, death and evil in that we are commanded this day to love the Lord our God, and to love one another, to walk in His ways and to keep His Commandments and His Ordinance, and His laws, and the articles of our covenant with Him that we may live and be multiplied, and that the Lord our God may bless us in the land whither we go to possess it: But if our hearts shall turn away so that we will not obey, but shall be seduced and worship [serve *cancelled*] other gods our pleasures, and profits, and serve them; it is propounded unto us this day, we shall surely perish out of the good land whither we pass over this vast sea to possess it;

[25] Micah, vi. 8.
[26] Ephesians, iv. 3.
[27] Matthew, v. 11.

Therefore let us choose life,
that we, and our seed,
may live; by obeying His
voice, and cleaving to Him,
for He is our life, and
our prosperity.

From The History of New England[1]

[REBUKE OF ROGER WILLIAMS]

[December 27, 1633] The Governor and Assistants met at Boston, and took into consideration a treatise, which Mr. Williams (then of Salem) had sent to them, and which he had formerly written to the Governor and Council of Plymouth, wherein, among other things, he disputes their right to the lands they possessed here, and concluded that, claiming by the King's grant, they could have no title, nor otherwise, except they compounded with the natives. For this, taking advice with some of the most judicious ministers (who much condemned Mr. Williams's error and presumption), they gave order, that he should be convented at the next court, to be censured, etc. There were three passages chiefly whereat they were much offended: 1, for that he chargeth King James to have told a solemn public lie, because in his patent he blessed God that he was the first Christian prince that had discovered this land; 2, for that he chargeth him and others with blasphemy for calling Europe Christendom, or the Christian world: 3, for that he did personally apply to our present king, Charles, these three places in the Revelations, viz., [blank.]

Mr. Endicott being absent, the Governor wrote to him to let him know what was done, and withal added divers arguments to confute the said errors, wishing him to deal with Mr. Williams to retract the same, etc. Whereto he returned a very modest and discreet answer. Mr. Williams also wrote to the Governor, and also to him and the rest of the Council, very submissively, professing his intent to have been only to have written for the private satisfaction of the Governor etc., of Plymouth, without any purpose to have stirred any further in it, if the Governor here had not required a copy of him; withal offering his book, or any part of it, to be burnt.

At the next court he appeared *penitently,* and gave satisfaction of his intention and loyalty. So it was left, and nothing done in it.

• • •

---

[1] The text reprinted here is from the *History of New England from 1630 to 1649 . . .,* ed. James Savage, Boston, 1853, volume I.

[January 24, 1633] The Governor and Council met again at Boston, to consider of Mr. Williams's letter, etc., when, with the advice of Mr. Cotton and Mr. Wilson,[2] and weighing his letter, and further considering of the aforesaid offensive passages in his book (which, being written in very obscure and implicative phrases, might well admit of doubtful interpretation), they found the matters not to be so evil as at first they seemed. Whereupon they agreed, that, upon his retractation, etc., or taking an oath of allegiance to the King, etc., it should be passed over.

· · ·

[THE CROSS CUT OUT OF THE FLAG: WILLIAMS AND ENDICOTT, 1634][3]

[November 5, 1634] At the Court of Assistants complaint was made by some of the country (viz., Richard Brown of Watertown, in the name of the rest) that the ensign at Salem was defaced, viz. one part of the red cross taken out. Upon this, an attachment was awarded against Richard Davenport, ensign-bearer, to appear at the next court to answer. Much matter was made of this, as fearing it would be taken as an act of rebellion, or of like high nature, in defacing the King's colors; though the truth were, it was done upon this opinion, that the red cross was given to the King of England by the Pope, as an ensign of victory, and so a superstitious thing, and a relic of antichrist. What proceeding was hereupon, will appear after, at next court, in the first month (for, by reason of the great snows and frosts, we used not to keep courts in the three winter months).

· · ·

[April 30, 1635] The Governor and Assistants sent for Mr. Williams. The occasion was, for that he had taught publicly, that a magistrate ought not to tender an oath to an unregenerate man, for that we thereby have communion with a wicked man in the worship of God, and cause him to take the name of God in vain. He was heard before all the ministers, and very clearly confuted. Mr. Endicott was at first of the same opinion, but he gave place to the truth.

[May 6] A general court was held at Newtown, where John Haynes, Esq., was chosen governor, Richard Bellingham, Esq., deputy governor, and Mr. Hough and Mr. Dummer chosen assistants to the former; and Mr. Ludlow, the late deputy, left out of the magistracy. The reason was, partly, because the people would exercise their absolute power, etc., and partly upon some

[2] John Cotton and John Wilson were the two ministers in Boston at the time.

[3] This incident is the basis for Nathaniel Hawthorne's "Endicott and the Red Cross."

speeches of the deputy, who protested against the election of the Governor as void, for that the deputies of the several towns had agreed upon the election before they came, etc. But this was generally discussed, and the election adjudged good.

Mr. Endicott was also left out, and called into question about the defacing the cross in the ensign; and a committee was chosen, viz., every town chose one (which yet were voted by all the people), and the magistrates chose four, who, taking the charge to consider of the offense, and the censure due to it, and to certify the court, after one or two hours' time, made report to the court, that they found his offense to be great, viz., rash and without discretion, taking upon him more authority than he had, and not seeking advice of the court, etc.; uncharitable, in that he, judging the cross, etc., to be a sin, did content himself to have reformed it at Salem, not taking care that others might be brought out of it also; laying a blemish also upon the rest of the magistrates, as if they would suffer idolatry, etc., and giving occasion to the state of England to think ill of us;—for which they adjudged him worthy admonition, and to be disabled for one year from bearing any public office; declining any heavier sentence, because they were persuaded he did it out of tenderness of conscience, and not of any evil intent.

．　　．　　．

[July 8] At the general court, Mr. Williams of Salem was summoned, and did appear. It was laid to his charge, that, being under question before the magistracy and churches for divers dangerous opinions, viz. 1, that the magistrate ought not to punish the breach of the first table,[4] otherwise than in such cases as did disturb the civil peace; 2, that he ought not to tender an oath to an unregenerate man; 3, that a man ought not to pray with such, though wife, child, etc.; 4, that a man ought not to give thanks after the sacrament nor after meat, etc.; and that the other churches were about to write to the church of Salem to admonish him of these errors; notwithstanding the church had since called him to [the] office of a teacher. Much debate was about these things. The said opinions were adjudged by all, magistrates and ministers (who were desired to be present), to be erroneous, and very dangerous, and the calling of him to office, at that time, was judged a great contempt of authority. So, in fine, time was given to him and the church of Salem to consider of these things till the next general court, and then either to give satisfaction to the court, or else to expect the sentence; it being professedly declared by the ministers (at the request of the court to give

---

[4] That is, the first of the Ten Commandments (Exodus 20.3): "Thou shalt have none other gods before me." Quoted from the Geneva Bible.

their advice), that he who should obstinately maintain such opinions (whereby a church might run into heresy, apostasy, or tyranny, and yet the civil magistrate could not intermeddle) were to be removed, and that the other churches ought to request the magistrates so to do.

. . .

Salem men had preferred a petition, at the last general court, for some land in Marblehead Neck, which they did challenge as belonging to their town; but, because they had chosen Mr. Williams their teacher, while he stood under question of authority, and so offered contempt to the magistrates, etc., their petition was refused till, etc. Upon this the church of Salem write to other churches, to admonish the magistrates of this as a heinous sin, and likewise the deputies; for which, at the next general court, their deputies were not received until they should give satisfaction about the letter.

[August 16] . . . Mr. Williams, pastor of Salem, being sick and not able to speak, wrote to his church a protestation, that he could not communicate with the churches in the Bay; neither would he communicate with them,[5] except they would refuse communion with the rest; but the whole church was grieved herewith.

. . .

[October] At this general court, Mr. Williams, the teacher at Salem, was again convented, and all the ministers in the Bay being desired to be present, he was charged with the said two letters,—that to the churches, complaining of the magistrates for injustice, extreme oppression, etc., and the other to his own church, to persuade them to renounce communion with all the churches in the Bay, as full of antichristian pollution, etc. He justified both these letters, and maintained all his opinions; and, being offered further conference or disputation, and a month's respite, he chose to dispute presently. So Mr. Hooker was appointed to dispute with him, but could not reduce him from any of his errors. So, the next morning, the court sentenced him to depart out of our jurisdiction within six weeks, all the ministers, save one, approving the sentence; and his own church had him under question also for the same cause; and he, at his return home, refused communion with his own church, who openly disclaimed his errors, and wrote an humble submission to the magistrates, acknowledging their fault in joining with Mr. Williams in that letter to the churches against them, etc.

[5] That is, with the members of the Salem congregation, unless they would refuse to associate formally with the other congregations of the colony.

[A CRUEL SCHOOLMASTER]

[October 4?] At the general court at Boston, one Mr. Nathaniel Eaton, brother to the merchant at Quilipiack, was convented and censured. The occasion was this: He was a schoolmaster, and had many scholars, the sons of gentlemen and others of best note in the country, and had entertained one Nathaniel Briscoe, a gentleman born, to be his usher, and to do some other things for him, which might not be unfit for a scholar. He had not been with him above three days but he fell out with him for a very small occasion, and, with reproachful terms, discharged him, and turned him out of his doors; but, it being then about eight of the clock after the Sabbath, he told him he should stay till next morning, and, some words growing between them, he struck him and pulled him into his house. Briscoe defended himself, and closed with him, and, being parted, he came in and went up to his chamber to lodge there. Mr. Eaton sent for the constable, who advised him first to admonish him, etc., and if he could not, by the power of a master, reform him, then he should complain to the magistrate. But he [Eaton] caused his man to fetch him a cudgel, which was a walnut tree plant, big enough to have killed a horse, and a yard in length, and, taking his two men with him, he went up to Briscoe, and caused his men to hold him till he had given him two hundred stripes about the head and shoulders, etc., and so kept him under blows (with some two or three short intermissions) about the space of two hours, about which time Mr. Shepard and some others of the town came in at the outcry, and so he gave over. In this distress Briscoe gat out his knife, and struck at the man that held him, but hurt him not. He also fell to prayer (supposing he should have been murdered), and then Mr. Eaton beat him for taking the name of God in vain. After this Mr. Eaton and Mr. Shepard (who knew not then of these passages) came to the Governor and some other of the magistrates, complaining of Briscoe for his insolent speeches, and for crying out murder and drawing his knife, and desired that he might be enjoined to a public acknowledgment, etc. The magistrates answered, that they must first hear him speak, and then they would do as they should see cause. Mr. Eaton was displeased at this, and went away discontented, etc., and, being after called into the court to make answer to the information, which had been given by some who knew the truth of the case, and also to answer for his neglect and cruelty, and other ill usage towards his scholars, one of the elders (not suspecting such miscarriages by him) came to the Governor, and showed himself much grieved, that he should be publicly produced, alleging, that it would derogate from his authority and reverence among his scholars, etc. But the cause went on notwithstanding, and he was called, and these things laid to his charge in the open court. His answers were full of pride and disdain, telling the magistrates, that they should not need to do anything herein, for he was intended to leave his employment.

And being asked, why he used such cruelty to Briscoe his usher, and to other his scholars (for it was testified by another of his ushers and divers of his scholars, that he would give them between twenty and thirty stripes at a time, and would not leave till they had confessed what he required), his answer was, that he had this rule, that he would not give over correcting till he had subdued the party to his will. Being also questioned about the ill and scant diet of his boarders (for, though their friends gave large allowance, yet their diet was ordinarily nothing but porridge and pudding, and that very homely), he put it off to his wife. So the court dismissed him at present, and commanded him to attend again the next day, when, being called, he was commanded to the lower end of the table (where all offenders do usually stand) and, being openly convict[ed] of all the former offenses, by the oaths of four or five witnesses, he yet continued to justify himself; so, it being near night, he was committed to the marshal till the next day. When the court was set in the morning, many of the elders came into the court (it being then private for matter of consultation) and declared how, the evening before, they had taken pains with him, to convince him of his faults; yet, for divers hours, he had still stood to his justification; but, in the end, he was convinced, and had freely and fully acknowledged his sin, and that with tears; so as they did hope he had truly repented, and therefore desired of the court that he might be pardoned, and continued in his employment, alleging such further reasons as they thought fit. After the elders were departed, the court consulted about it, and sent for him, and there, in the open court, before a great assembly, he made a very solid, wise, eloquent, and serious (seeming) confession, condemning himself in all the particulars, etc. Whereupon, being put aside, the court consulted privately about his sentence, and, though many were taken with his confession, and none but had a charitable opinion of it; yet, because of the scandal of religion, and offense which would be given to such as might intend to send their children hither, they all agreed to censure him, and put him from that employment. So, being called in, the Governor, after a short preface, etc., declared the sentence of the court to this effect, viz: that he should give Briscoe £30, fined 100 marks, and debarred teaching of children within our jurisdiction. A pause being made, and expectation that (according to his former confession) he would have given glory to God, and acknowledged the justice and clemency of the court, the Governor giving him occasion, by asking him if he had aught to say, he turned away with a discontented look, saying, "If sentence be passed, then it is to no end to speak." Yet the court remitted his fine to £20, and willed Briscoe to take but £20.

The church at Cambridge, taking notice of these proceedings, intended to deal with him. The pastor moved the Governor, if they might, without offense to the court, examine other witnesses. His answer was, that the court would leave them to their own liberty; but he saw not to what end they should do it, seeing there had been five already upon oath, and those whom they should examine should speak without oath, and it was an ordinance of God, that by the mouths of two or three witnesses every matter should be established. But he soon discovered himself; for, ere the church could come to deal with him, he fled to Pascataquack, and, being pursued and apprehended by the Governor there, he again acknowledged his great sin in flying, etc., and promised (as he was a Christian man) he would return with the messengers. But, because his things he carried with him were aboard a bark there, bound to Virginia, he desired leave to go fetch them, which they assented unto, and went with him (three of them) aboard with him. So he took his truss and came away with them in the boat; but, being come to the shore, and two of them going out of the boat, he caused the boatsmen to put off the boat, and because the third man would not go out, he turned him into the water, where he had been drowned, if he had not saved himself by swimming. So he returned to the bark, and presently they set sail and went out of the harbor. Being thus gone, his creditors began to complain; and thereupon it was found, that he was run in debt about £1000, and had taken up most of this money upon bills he had charged into England upon his brother's agents, and others whom he had no such relation to. So his estate was seized, and put into commissioners' hands, to be divided among his creditors, allowing somewhat for the present maintenance of his wife and children. And, being thus gone, the church proceeded and cast him out. He had been sometimes initiated among the Jesuits, and, coming into England, his friends drew him from them, but, it was very probable, he now intended to return to them again, being at this time about thirty years of age, and upwards. See after.

.   .   .

[EXCESSIVE PROFITS: ROBERT KEANE]

[November] At a general court holden at Boston, great complaint was made of the oppression used in the country in sale of foreign commodities; and Mr. Robert Keane, who kept a shop in Boston, was notoriously above others observed and complained of; and, being convented, he was charged with many particulars; in some, for taking above six-pence in the shilling profit; in some above eight-pence; and, in some small things, above two for one; and being hereof convict[ed] (as appears by the records), he was fined £200, which came thus to pass: the deputies considered, apart, of his fine, and set it at £200; the magistrates agreed but to £100.[6] So, the court being divided, at length it was agreed, that his fine should be £200, but he should pay but

[6] The deputies were, in effect, the lower house of elected representatives and the   magistrates the upper.

£100, and the other should be respited to the further consideration of the next general court. By this means the magistrates and deputies were brought to an accord, which otherwise had not been likely, and so much trouble might have grown, and the offender escaped censure. For the cry of the country was so great against oppression, and some of the elders and magistrates had declared such detestation of the corrupt practice of this man (which was the more observable, because he was wealthy and sold dearer than most other tradesmen, and for that he was of ill report for the like covetous practice in England, that incensed the deputies very much against him). And sure the course was very evil, especial circumstances considered: 1. he being an ancient professor of the Gospel: 2. a man of eminent parts: 3. wealthy, and having but one child: 4. having come over for conscience's sake, and for the advancement of the Gospel here: 5. having been formerly dealt with and admonished, both by private friends and also by some of the magistrates and elders, and having promised reformation; being a member of a church and commonwealth now in their infancy, and under the curious observation of all churches and civil states in the world. These added much aggravation to his sin in the judgment of all men of understanding. Yet most of the magistrates (though they discerned of the offense clothed with all these circumstances) would have been more moderate in their censure: 1. Because there was no law in force to limit or direct men in point of profit in their trade. 2. Because it is the common practice, in all countries, for men to make use of advantages for raising the prices of their commodities. 3. Because (though he were chiefly aimed at, yet) he was not alone in this fault. 4. Because all men through the country, in sale of cattle, corn, labor, etc., were guilty of the like excess in prices. 5. Because a certain rule could not be found out for an equal rate between buyer and seller, though much labor had been bestowed in it, and divers laws had been made, which, upon experience, were repealed, as being neither safe nor equal. Lastly, and especially, because the law of God appoints no other punishment but double restitution; and, in some cases, as where the offender freely confesseth, and brings his offering, only half added to the principal. After the court had censured him, the church of Boston called him also in question, where (as before he had done in the court) he did, with tears, acknowledge and bewail his covetous and corrupt heart, yet making some excuse for many of the particulars, which were charged upon him, as partly by pretense of ignorance of the true price of some wares, and chiefly by being misled by some false principles, as 1. That, if a man lost in one commodity, he might help himself in the price of another. 2. That is, through want of skill or other occasion, his commodity cost him more than the price of the market in England, he might then sell it for more than the price of the market in New England, etc. These things gave occasion to Mr. Cotton, in his public exercise the next lecture day,[7] to lay open the error of such false principles, and to give some rules of direction in the case.

Some false principles were these:—

1. That a man might sell as dear as he can, and buy as cheap as he can.
2. If a man lose by casualty of sea, etc., in some of his commodities, he may raise the price of the rest.
3. That he may sell as he bought, though he paid too dear, etc., and though the commodity be fallen, etc.
4. That, as a man may take the advantage of his own skill or ability, so he may of another's ignorance or necessity.
5. Where one gives time for payment, he is to take like recompense of one as of another.

The rules for trading were these:—

1. A man may not sell above the current price, i.e., such a price as is usual in the time and place, and as another (who knows the worth of the commodity) would give for it, if he had occasion to use it; as that is called current money, which every man will take, etc.
2. When a man loseth in his commodity for want of skill, etc., he must look at it as his own fault or cross, and therefore must not lay it upon another.
3. Where a man loseth by casualty of sea, or, etc., it is a loss cast upon himself by Providence, and he may not ease himself of it by casting it upon another; for so a man should seem to provide against all providences, etc., that he should never lose; but where there is a scarcity of the commodity, there men may raise their price; for now it is a hand of God upon the commodity, and not the person.
4. A man may not ask any more for his commodity than his selling price, as Ephron to Abraham, the land is worth thus much.

The cause being debated by the church, some were earnest to have him excommunicated; but the most thought an admonition would be sufficient. Mr. Cotton opened the causes, which required excommunication, out of that in 1 Cor. 5. 11. The point now in question was, whether these actions did declare him to be such a covetous person, etc. Upon which he showed, that it is neither the habit of covetousness (which is in every man in some degree), nor simply the act, that declares a man to be such, but when it appears, that

---

[7] John Cotton thus gave a leading minister's view of the ethical issues, speaking at the regular Thursday lecture, at which one of the ministers would address a current religious topic that had practical significance.

a man sins against his conscience, or the very light of nature, and when it appears in a man's whole conversation. But Mr. Keane did not appear to be such, but rather upon an error in his judgment, being led by false principles; and, beside, he is otherwise liberal, as in his hospitality, and in church communion, etc. So, in the end, the church consented to an admonition.[8]

●   ●   ●

[WINTHROP ON NATURAL AND CIVIL LIBERTY—1645[9]]

[May 14] The day appointed being come, the court assembled in the meeting house at Boston. Divers of the elders were present, and a great assembly of people. The deputy governor [John Winthrop himself], coming in with the rest of the magistrates, placed himself beneath within the bar, and so sat uncovered. Some question was in the court about his being in that place (for many both of the court and the assembly were grieved at it). But the deputy telling them, that, being criminally accused, he might not sit as a judge in that cause, and if he were upon the bench, it would be a great disadvantage to him, for he could not take that liberty to plead the cause, which he ought to be allowed at the bar, upon this the court was satisfied.

The petitioners having declared their grievances, etc., the deputy craved leave to make answer, which was to this effect, viz., that he accounted it no disgrace, but rather an honor put upon him, to be singled out from his brethren in the defense of a cause so just (as he hoped to make that appear) and of so public concernment. And although he might have pleaded to the petition, and so have demurred in law, upon three points, 1, In that there is nothing laid to his charge, that is either criminal or unjust; 2, if he had been mistaken either in the law or in the state of the case, yet whether it were such as a judge is to be called in question for as a delinquent, where it doth not appear to be wickedness or wilfulness; for in England many erroneous judgments are reversed, and errors in proceedings rectified, and yet the judges not called in question about them; 3, in that being thus singled out from three other of the magistrates,[10] and to answer by himself for some things, which were the act of a court, he is deprived of the just means of his defense, for many things may be justified as done by four which are not

[8] The individual congregation in Puritan Boston punished the serious transgressions of fellow members—by excommunication, warning, or censure—whether or not the civil or

[9] Winthrop, as deputy-governor, was charged by some deputies with having ex-

ceeded his authority. He insisted upon a public trial before the magistrates. Throughout this account the term "the deputy" means the Deputy-Governor, Winthrop himself.

[10] The magistrates, including the Deputy-Governor, had judicial as well as legislative duties.

warrantable if done by one alone, and the records of a court are a full justification of any act, while such record stands in force. But he was willing to waive this plea, and to make answer to the particular charges, to the end that the truth of the case, and of all proceedings thereupon might appear to all men.

Hereupon the court proceeded to examine the whole cause. The deputy justified all the particulars laid to his charge, as that upon credible information of such a mutinous practice, and open disturbance of the peace, and slighting of authority, the offenders were sent for, the principal by warrant to the constable to bring them, and others by summons, and that some were bound over to the next court of assistants, and others that refused to be bound were committed; and all this according to the equity of laws here established, and the custom and laws of England, and our constant practice here these fifteen years. And for some speeches he was charged with as spoken to the delinquents, when they came before him at his house, when none were present with him but themselves, first, he appealed to the judgment of the court, whether delinquents may be received as competent witnesses against a magistrate in such a case; then, for the words themselves, some he justified, some he explained so as no advantage could be taken of them, as that he should say, that the magistrates could try some criminal causes without a jury, that he knew no law of God or man, which required a judge to make known to the party his accusers (or rather witnesses) before the cause came to hearing. But two of them charged him to have said, that it was against the law of God and man so to do, which had been absurd, for the deputy professed he knew no law against it, only a judge may sometimes, in discretion, conceal their names, etc., lest they should be tampered with, or conveyed out of the way, etc.

Two of the magistrates and many of the deputies were of opinion that the magistrates exercised too much power, and that the people's liberty was thereby in danger; and other of the deputies (being about half) and all the rest of the magistrates were of a different judgment, and that authority was overmuch slighted, which, if not timely remedied, would endanger the commonwealth, and bring us to a mere democracy. By occasion of this difference, there was not so orderly carriage at the hearing, as was meet, each side striving unseasonably to enforce the evidence, and declaring their judgments thereupon, which should have been reserved to a more private debate (as after it was), so as the best part of two days was spent in this public agitation and examination of witnesses, etc. This being ended, a committee was chosen of magistrates and deputies, who stated the case, as it appeared upon the whole pleading and evidence, though it cost much time, and with great difficulty did the committee come to accord upon it.

The case being stated and agreed, the magistrates and deputies considered it apart, first the deputies, having spent a whole day, and not attaining to any issue, sent up to the magistrates to have their thoughts about it, who taking it into consideration (the deputy always withdrawing when that matter came into debate), agreed upon these four points chiefly; 1. That the petition was false and scandalous, 2. That those who were bound over, etc., and others that were parties to the disturbance at Hingham, were all offenders, though in different degrees, 3. That they and the petitioners were to be censured, 4. That the Deputy-Governor ought to be acquit and righted, etc. This being sent down to the deputies, they spent divers days about it, and made two or three returns to the magistrates, and though they found the petition false and scandalous, and so voted it, yet they would not agree to any censure. The magistrates, on the other side, were resolved for censure, and for the deputy's full acquittal. The deputies being thus hard held to it, and growing weary of the court, for it began [May] 14, and brake not up (save one week) till [July] 5, were content they should pay the charges of the court. After, they were drawn to consent to some small fines, but in this they would have drawn in lieutenant Emes to have been fined deeply, he being neither plaintiff nor defendant, but an informer only, and had made good all the points of his information, and no offense found in him, other than that which was after adjudged worthy admonition only; and they would have imposed the charges of the court upon the whole trained band at Hingham,[11] when it was apparent, that divers were innocent, and had no hand in any of these proceedings. The magistrates not consenting to so manifest injustice, they sent to the deputies to desire them to join with them in calling in the help of the elders[12] (for they were now assembled at Cambridge from all parts of the United Colonies, and divers of them were present when the cause was publicly heard, and declared themselves much grieved to see that the Deputy-Governor should be called forth to answer as a delinquent in such a case as this was, and one of them, in the name of the rest, had written to him to that effect, fearing lest he should apprehend over deeply of the injury, etc.) but the deputies would by no means consent thereto, for they knew that many of the elders understood the cause, and were more careful to uphold the honor and power of the magistrates than themselves well liked of, and many of them (at the request of the elder and others of the church of Hingham during this court) had been at Hingham, to see if they could settle peace in the church there, and found the elder and others the petitioners in great fault, etc. After this (upon motion of the deputies) it was agreed to refer the cause to arbitrators, according to an order of court, when the magistrates and deputies cannot agree, etc. The magistrates named six of the elders of the next towns, and left it to them to choose any three or four of

[11] The original issue concerned the election of an officer of the militia (or trained band) in the town of Hingham.

[12] Here the ministers (but usually also the lay officers) of the various congregations. The United Colonies had been organized in 1643 by Massachusetts Bay, New Plymouth, Connecticut (Hartford), and New Haven.

them, and required them to name six others. The deputies finding themselves now at the wall, and not daring to trust the elders with the cause, they sent to desire that six of themselves might come and confer with the magistrates, which being granted, they came, and at last came to this agreement, viz., the chief petitioners and the rest of the offenders were severally fined (all their fines not amounting to 50 pounds), the rest of the petitioners to bear equal share to 50 pounds more towards the charges of the court (two of the principal offenders were the deputies of the town, Joshua Hubbert and Bozone Allen, the first was fined 20 pounds, and the other 5 pounds), Lieutenant Emes to be under admonition, the Deputy-Governor to be legally and publicly acquit of all that was laid to his charge.

According to this agreement, [July] 3, presently after the lecture the magistrates and deputies took their places in the meeting house, and the people being come together, and the Deputy-Governor placing himself within the bar, as at the time of the hearing, etc., the Governor read the sentence of the court, without speaking any more, for the deputies had (by importunity) obtained a promise of silence from the magistrates. Then was the Deputy-Governor desired by the court to go up and take his place again upon the bench, which he did accordingly, and the court being about to arise, he desired leave for a little speech, which was to this effect.

I suppose something may be expected from me, upon this charge that is befallen me, which moves me to speak now to you; yet I intend not to intermeddle in the proceedings of the court, or with any of the persons concerned therein. Only I bless God, that I see an issue of this troublesome business. I also acknowledge the justice of the court, and, for mine own part, I am well satisfied, I was publicly charged, and I am publicly and legally acquitted, which is all I did expect or desire. And though this be sufficient for my justification before men, yet not so before the God, who hath seen so much amiss in my dispensations (and even in this affair) as calls me to be humble. For to be publicly and criminally charged in this court, is matter of humiliation (and I desire to make a right use of it), notwithstanding I be thus acquitted. If her father had spit in her face (saith the Lord concerning Miriam), should she not have been ashamed seven days? Shame had lien upon her, whatever the occasion had been. I am unwilling to stay you from your urgent affairs, yet give me leave (upon this special occasion) to speak a little more to this assembly. It may be of some good use, to inform and rectify the judgments of some of the people, and may prevent such distempers as have arisen amongst us. The great questions that have troubled the country, are about the authority of the magistrates and the liberty of the people. It is yourselves who have called us to this office, and being called by you, we have our authority from God, in way of an ordinance, such as hath the image of God eminently stamped upon it, the contempt and violation whereof hath been vindicated with examples of divine vengeance.[13] I entreat you to consider, that when you choose magistrates, you take them from among yourselves, men subject to like passions as you are. Therefore when you see infirmities in us, you should reflect upon your own, and that would make you bear the more with us, and not be severe censurers of the failings of your magistrates, when you have continual experience of the like infirmities in yourselves and others. We account him a good servant, who breaks not his covenant. The covenant between you and us is the oath you have taken of us, which is to this purpose, that we shall govern you and judge your causes by the rules of God's laws and our own, according to our best skill. When you agree with a workman to build you a ship or house, etc., he undertakes as well for his skill as for his faithfulness, for it is his profession, and you pay him for both. But when you call one to be a magistrate, he doth not profess nor undertake to have sufficient skill for that office, nor can you furnish him with gifts, etc., therefore you must run the hazard of his skill and ability. But if he fail in faithfulness, which by his oath he is bound unto, that he must answer for. If it fall out that the case be clear to common apprehension, and the rule clear also, if he transgress here, the error is not in the skill, but in the evil of the will: it must be required of him. But if the case be doubtful, or the rule doubtful, to men of such understanding and parts as your magistrates are, if your magistrates should err here, yourselves must bear it.

For the other point concerning liberty, I observe a great mistake in the country about that. There is a twofold liberty, natural (I mean as our nature is now corrupt) and civil or federal. The first is common to man with beasts and other creatures. By this, man, as he stands in relation to man simply, hath liberty to do what he lists; it is a liberty to evil as well as to good. This liberty is incompatible and inconsistent with authority, and cannot endure the least restraint of the most just authority. The exercise and maintaining of this liberty makes men grow more evil, and in time to be worse than brute beasts: omnes sumus licentia deteriores.[14] This is that great enemy of truth and peace, that wild beast, which all the ordinances of God are bent against, to restrain and subdue it. The other kind of liberty I call civil or federal, it may also be termed moral, in reference to the covenant between God and man, in the moral law, and the politic covenants and constitutions, amongst men themselves. This liberty is the proper end and object of authority, and cannot subsist without it; and it is a liberty to that only which is good, just, and honest. This liberty you are to stand for, with the hazard (not only of your goods, but) of your lives, if need be. Whatsoever crosseth this, is not authority, but a distemper thereof. This liberty is maintained and exercised in a way of subjection to authority; it is of the same kind of liberty wherewith

[13] Here Winthrop refers to the covenant, or sacred contract, binding a society governed by individually covenanted church members to obey the Lord, whose protection they believed depended on their fidelity to Him.

[14] We are all the worse for license.

Christ hath made us free. The woman's own choice makes such a man her husband; yet being so chosen, he is her lord, and she is to be subject to him, yet in a way of liberty, not of bondage; and a true wife accounts her subjection her honor and freedom, and would not think her condition safe and free, but in her subjection to her husband's authority. Such is the liberty of the church under the authority of Christ, her king and husband; his yoke is so easy and sweet to her as a bride's ornaments; and if through frowardness or wantonness, etc., she shake it off, at any time, she is at no rest in her spirit, until she take it up again; and whether her lord smiles upon her, and embraceth her in his arms, or whether he frowns, or rebukes, or smites her, she apprehends the sweetness of his love in all, and is refreshed, supported, and instructed by every such dispensation of his authority over her. On the other side, ye know who they are that complain of this yoke and say, let us break their bands, etc., we will not have this man to rule over us. Even so, brethren, it will be between you and your magistrates. If you stand for your natural corrupt liberties, and will do what is good in your own eyes, you will not endure the least weight of authority, but will murmur, and oppose, and be always striving to shake off that yoke; but if you will be satisfied to enjoy such civil and lawful liberties, such as Christ allows you, then will you quietly and cheerfully submit unto that authority which is set over you, in all the administrations of it, for your good. Wherein, if we fail at any time, we hope we shall be willing (by God's assistance) to hearken to good advice from any of you, or in any other way of God; so shall your liberties be preserved, in upholding the honor and power of authority amongst you.

The Deputy-Governor having ended his speech, the court arose, and the magistrates and deputies retired to attend their other affairs. Many things were observable in the agitation and proceedings about this case. It may be of use to leave a memorial of some of the most material, that our posterity and others may behold the workings of Satan to ruin the colonies and churches of Christ in New England, and into what distempers a wise and godly people may fall in times of temptation; and when such have entertained some false and plausible principles, what deformed superstructures they will raise thereupon, and with what unreasonable obstinacy they will maintain them.

Some of the deputies had seriously conceived, that the magistrates affected an arbitrary government, and that they had (or sought to have) an unlimited power to do what they pleased without control, and that, for this end, they did strive so much to keep their negative power in the general court.[15] This caused them to interpret all the magistrates' actions and speeches (not complying exactly with their own principles) as tending that

[15] That is, a veto over actions taken by the deputies.

way, by which occasions their fears and jealousies increased daily. For prevention whereof they judged it not unlawful to use even extrema remedia,[16] as if salus populi[17] had been now the transcendent rule to walk by, and that magistracy must be no other, in effect, than a ministerial office, and all authority, both legislative, consultative, and judicial, must be exercised by the people in their body representative. . . .

[16] Extreme remedy.   [17] The health or safety of the people.

THOMAS SHEPARD

(1605–1649)

Thomas Shepard was one of the most effective Puritan preachers in England and New England, and both his autobiography and his sermons are among the documents most important for an understanding of seventeenth-century American literature. "Suspect thyself much," he told his congregation in the sermon that is reprinted here, and in his autobiography (unpublished during his lifetime), he demonstrated in some harrowing passages that he had practiced what he preached. It is the relationship between doubt and faith that lies at the heart of these two literary forms in Puritan New England. Twentieth-century students have a special opportunity to appreciate that early literature because our own exposure to doubt should enable us to see the intensity of both impulses: the yearning for assurance of faith, and the doubt of one's own salvation.

Shepard was born in Towcester, England, into a family that would now be considered remarkably short-lived. He was orphaned in early childhood; both he and his son and namesake, who was also a New England minister, died in their middle forties, and his grandson, a prodigious scholar and minister who was a close friend of Cotton Mather's, died in his twenties.

Brought up by his older brother, Shepard went to Emmanuel College, Cambridge, where many of the Puritan clergy were educated. Only two years after his ordination in 1628, he was silenced by order of

The standard text is *The Works of Thomas Shepard*, 3 vols., 1853. The autobiography and journal have been edited by Michael McGiffert, *God's Plot: The Paradoxes of Puritan Piety, Being the Autobiography of Thomas Shepard*, 1972. A good background work is Samuel Eliot Morison, *Builders of the Bay Colony*, 1930.

Archbishop Laud, and he spent the next four years as tutor and chaplain in a wealthy Puritan family. In 1634 he tried to emigrate to New England, but when his ship, nearly destroyed, was forced back to England in a fierce storm, he had to hide from Archbishop Laud's agents during the rest of the winter. Both his first son and his wife had died before the end of 1636. From 1635 to 1649 Shepard was a powerful force in New England. As Thomas Hooker's successor in Newtown (later Cambridge), he was influential in the founding and early nurture of Harvard College, in the crucial synod that denounced the Antinomian heresies in 1637, and in preparation for the Cambridge Platform of 1648, which established New England Congregational doctrine for the next half-century. Shepard had married Thomas Hooker's daughter in 1637, and after her death he married for the third time in 1647.

Cotton Mather's biography of Jonathan Mitchel cites Mitchel's response to the sermon that is reprinted here, the fifth sermon in the series later published as *The Sincere Convert,* on the small number of those that are to be saved by God's mercy:

"I had little savor on my spirit before God [Mitchel said]: but a terrible and excellent sermon of Mr. Shepard's awakened me. He taught, that there are some who seem to be found and sav'd by Christ, and yet afterwards they perish. These things terrified me (and I wish they had stuck fast in me!), lest I should only seem to belong unto Christ, and lest I should thus go unto Death. . . ."

Notice that the sermon begins with a flat, plain statement of the doctrine and that the preacher keeps the auditor close to the logical outline of his argument by numbering his topics and the objections and answers. The sermon becomes a moving statement of Puritan faith and of the individual soul's predicament as Shepard proceeds systematically through a series of arguments from historical experience, from Scriptural authority, and from common life to try to convict each auditor (as apparently he did actually convict Jonathan Mitchel). The logical progression of the powerful argument moves nearer to the main purpose of the sermon, Application, the appeal to each auditor's sense of his own vulnerability. Not only are there nine easy ways to go to hell, but there are 14 answers to 14 likely objections that a confident sinner might raise in defense of his own security. Everything depends at last on our seeing the purpose that Mitchel felt in hearing the sermon: the highest pitch of Puritan fervor, the true (if harsh) poetry of Puritan religious experience, comes when Shepard seems sure to have driven his auditors to the threshold of despair with his arguments that no effort of their own can save them. Oh *strive,* then, he cries, to be one of those that are saved. *Labor* to be among those who are not lost.

The purpose of such preaching was to cure through a strict application of a traumatic lesson, and a proper understanding of the anxiety that might be induced in the listener will help us to see the power of his willingness to strive, however illogically, for liberation and for psychological as well as spiritual salvation.

Shepard's autobiography needs no elaborate explanation, but the same variation between faith and doubt, security and anxiety, should be noticed in the very structure of the narrative. The autobiography was first published in 1832. It has recently been reprinted in an excellent new edition edited by Michael McGiffert, *God's Plot: The Paradoxes of Puritan Piety* (University of Massachusetts Press, 1972). Omitted here, besides three brief sections within the narrative, are a long preface addressed to Shepard's son and namesake, and some concluding notes on "good things I have received from the Lord."

The text and notes are from the McGiffert edition. McGiffert does not capitalize the pronoun referring to the deity.

From The Autobiography of Thomas Shepard

T. {My Birth and Life} S.

In the year of Christ 1604[1] upon the fifth day of November, called the powder treason day, and that very hour of the day wherein the Parliament should have been blown up by Popish priests, I was then born, which occasioned my father to give me this name Thomas, because he said I would hardly believe that ever any such wickedness should be attempted by men against so religious and good Parliament. My father's name was William Shepard, born in a little poor town in Northamptonshire called Fossecut near Towcester, and being a prentice to one Mr. Bland, a grocer, he married one of his daughters of whom he begat many children—three sons: John, William, and Thomas; and six daughters: An[na], Margaret, Mary, Elizabeth, Hester, Sarah—of all which only John, Thomas,[2] Anna, and Margaret are still living in the town where I was born, viz., Towcester in Northamptonshire, six miles distant from the town of Northampton in old England. I do well remember my father and have some little remembrance of my mother. My father was a wise, prudent man, the peacemaker of the place, and toward his latter end much blessed of God in his estate and in his soul, for there being

---

[1] An error for 1605.

[2] Evidently a slip of the pen, since Shepard did not live in Towcester after completing his studies at Emmanuel College.

no good ministry in the town he was resolved to go and live at Banbury in Oxfordshire under a stirring ministry, having bought a house there for that end. My mother was a woman much afflicted in conscience, sometimes even unto distraction of mind, yet was sweetly recovered again before she died, and I being the youngest she did bear exceeding great love to me and made many prayers for me. But she died when I was about four years old, and my father lived and married a second wife now dwelling in the same town, of whom he begat two children, Samuel and Elizabeth, and died when I was about ten years of age. But while my father and mother lived, when I was about three years old, there was a great plague in the town of Towcester which swept away many in my father's family, both sisters and servants. I being the youngest and best beloved of my mother was sent away the day the plague brake out to live with my aged grandfather and grandmother in Fossecut, a most blind town and corner, and those I lived with also being very well to live yet very ignorant. And there was I put to keep geese and other such country work all that time, much neglected of them, and afterward sent from them unto Adthrop, a little blind town adjoining, to my uncle, where I had more content but did learn to sing and sport as children do in those parts and dance at their Whitsun Ales, until the plague was removed and my dear mother dead who died not of the plague but of some other disease after it. And being come home, my sister An[na] married to one Mr. Farmer, and my sister Margaret loved me much, who afterward married to my father's prentice, viz., Mr. Waples. And my father married again—to another woman who did let me see the difference between my own mother and a stepmother: she did seem not to love me but incensed my father often against me; it may be that it was justly also for my childishness. And having lived thus for a time, my father sent me to school to a Welshman, one Mr. Rice, who kept the Free School in the town of Towcester, but he was exceeding curst and cruel and would deal roughly with me and so discouraged me wholly from desire of learning that I remember I wished oftentimes myself in any condition to keep hogs or beasts rather than to go to school and learn. But my father at last was visited with sickness, having taken some cold upon some pills he took, and so had the hickets[3] with his sickness a week together, in which time I do remember I did pray very strongly and heartily for the life of my father and made some covenant, if God would do it, to serve him the better as knowing I should be left alone if he was gone. Yet the Lord took him away by death, and so I was left fatherless and motherless when I was about ten years old, and was committed to my stepmother to be educated who therefore had my portion which was £100 which my father left me. But she neglecting my education very much, my brother John, who was my only brother alive, desired to have me out of her hands and to have

---

[3] I.e., hiccoughs.

me with him, and he would bring me up for the use of my portion. And so at last it was granted, and so I lived with this my eldest brother who showed much love unto me and unto whom I owe much, for him God made to be both father and mother unto me. And it happened that the cruel schoolmaster died and another[4] came into his room to be a preacher also in the town, who was an eminent preacher in those days and accounted holy but afterward turned a great apostate and enemy to all righteousness and I fear did commit the impardonable sin. Yet it so fell out by God's good providence that this man stirred up in my heart a love and desire of the honor of learning, and therefore I told my friends I would be a scholar. And so the Lord blessed me in my studies and gave me some knowledge of the Latin and Greek tongues, but much ungrounded in both. But I was studious because I was ambitious of learning and being a scholar, and hence when I could not take notes of the sermon I remember I was troubled at it and prayed the Lord earnestly that he would help me to note sermons. And I see cause of wondering at the Lord's providence therein, for as soon as ever I had prayed (after my best fashion) then for it, I presently the next Sabbath was able to take notes who the precedent Sabbath could do nothing at all that way. So I continued till I was about fifteen years of age and then was conceived to be ripe for the University, and it pleased the Lord to put it into my brother's heart to provide and to seek to prepare a place for me there, which was done in this manner: one Mr. Cockerell,[5] Fellow of Emmanuel College in Cambridge, being a Northamptonshire man, came down into the country to Northampton and so sent for me, who upon examination of me gave my brother encouragement to send me up to Cambridge. And so I came up, and though I was very raw and young, yet it pleased God to open the hearts of others to admit me into this College a pensioner,[6] and so Mr. Cockerell became my tutor. But I do here wonder and I hope shall bless the Lord forever in heaven that the Lord did so graciously provide for me, for I have oft thought what a woeful estate I had been left in if the Lord had left me in the profane, ignorant town of Towcester where I was born, that the Lord should pluck me out of that sink and Sodom, who was the least in my father's house, forsaken of father and mother, yet that the Lord should fetch me out from thence by such a sweet hand.

The first two years I spent in Cambridge was in studying and in much neglect of God and private prayer which I had sometime used, and I did not regard the Lord at all unless it were at some fits. The third year, wherein I was Sophister, I began to be foolish and proud and to show myself in the

---

[4] William Cluer, a graduate of Emmanuel, became master of the school on September 23, 1617.

[5] Daniel Cockerell, M.A., 1612, Fellow, 1612-21.

[6] Shepard was admitted pensioner on February 10, 1619/20.

public schools, and there to be a disputer about things which now I see I did not know then at all but only prated about them. And toward the end of this year when I was most vile (after I had been near unto the gates of death by the smallpox the year before), the Lord began to call me home to the fellowship of his grace, which was in this manner:

(1) I do remember that I had many good affections (but blind and unconstant) oft cast into me since my father's sickness by the spirit of God wrastling with me, and hence I would pray in secret. And hence when I was at Cambridge I heard old Doctor Chaderton,[7] the Master of the College, when I came, and the first year I was there to hear him upon a Sacrament day my heart was much affected, but I did break loose from the Lord again. And half a year after I heard Mr. Dickinson common-place in the chapel upon those words—I will not destroy it for ten's sake (Genesis 19)[8]—and then again was much affected, but I shook this off also and fell from God to loose and lewd company, to lust and pride and gaming and bowling and drinking. And yet the Lord left me not, but a godly scholar, walking with me, fell to discourse about the misery of every man out of Christ, viz., that whatever they did was sin, and this did much affect me. And at another time when I did light in godly company I heard them discourse about the wrath of God and the terror of it and how intolerable it was, which they did present by fire: how intolerable the torment of that was for a time—what then would eternity be! And this did much awaken me, and I began to pray again. But then by loose company I came to dispute in the schools and there to join to loose scholars of other colleges and was fearfully left of God and fell to drink with them. And I drank so much one day that I was dead drunk, and that upon a Saturday night, and so was carried from the place I had drink at and did feast at unto a scholar's chamber, one Basset of Christ's College, and knew not where I was until I awakened late on that Sabbath and sick with my beastly carriage. And when I awakened I went from him in shame and confusion, and went out into the fields and there spent that Sabbath lying hid in the cornfields where the Lord, who might justly have cut me off in the midst of my sin, did meet me with much sadness of heart and troubled my soul for this and other my sins which then I had cause and leisure to think of. And now when I was worst he began to be best unto me and made me resolve to set upon a course of daily meditation about the evil of sin and my own ways. Yet although I was troubled for this sin, I did not know my sinful nature all this while.

(2) The Lord therefore sent Doctor Preston[9] to be Master of the College,

[7] Laurence Chaderton, Master of Emmanuel, 1584-1622

[8] Correctly, Genesis 18:32.

[9] John Preston (1587-1628), one of the most influential Puritan preachers and writers of his generation, served as Master of Emmanuel from 1622 to 1628.

and, Mr. Stone[10] and others commending his preaching to be most spiritual and excellent, I began to listen unto what he said, and the first sermon he preached was Romans 12—be renewed in the spirit of your mind—in opening which point, viz., the change of heart in a Christian, the Lord so bored my ears as that I understood what he spake and the secrets of my soul were laid open before me—the hypocrisy of all my good things I thought I had in me—as if one had told him of all that ever I did, of all the turnings and deceits of my heart, insomuch as that I thought he was the most searching preacher in the world. And I began to love him much and to bless God I did see my frame and my hypocrisy and self and secret sins, although I found a hard heart and could not be affected with them.

(3) I did therefore set more constantly (viz., 1624, May 3) upon the work of daily meditation, sometimes every morning but constantly every evening before supper, and my chief meditation was about the evil of sin, the terror of God's wrath, day of death, beauty of Christ, the deceitfulness of the heart, etc., but principally I found this my misery: sin was not my greatest evil, did lie light upon me as yet, yet I was much afraid of death and the flames of God's wrath. And this I remember: I never went out to meditate in the fields but I did find the Lord teaching me somewhat of myself or himself or the vanity of the world I never saw before. And hence I took out a little book I have every day into the fields and writ down what God taught me lest I should forget them, and so the Lord encouraged me and I grew much. But in my observation of myself I did see my atheism, I questioned whether there were a God, and my unbelief, whether Christ was the Messiah, whether the Scriptures were God's word or no. I felt all manner of temptations to all kind of religions, not knowing which I should choose, whether education might not make me believe what I have believed, and whether if I had been educated up among the Papists I should not have been as verily persuaded that Popery is the truth or Turkism is the truth, and at last I heard of Grindleton,[11] and I did question whether that glorious estate of perfection might not be the truth and whether old Mr. Rogers' *Seven Treatises* and the

[10] Samuel Stone (1602-1663) graduated from Emmanuel in the same year as Shepard. Suspended for Nonconformity in 1630, he went three years later to New England where with Thomas Hooker he served the churches at Newtown and Hartford.

[11] The "Grindletonians," judging from the writings of their leader, Roger Brereley (or Brierley), curate at Grindleton in Yorkshire, were spiritual seekers and perfectionists. They were regarded by their critics as antinomians or "familists" who held "that we must not now go by motives but by motions and that when God comes to dwell in a man He so fills the soul that there is no more lusting." Stephen Denison, *The White Wolfe* (London, 1627), p. 39. John Winthrop attributed the antinomianism of Anne Hutchinson to Grindletonian inspiration. Brereley himself was exonerated of antinomianism by the Archbishop of York in 1628.

Practice of Christianity,[12] the book which did first work upon my heart, whether these men were not all legal men and their books so, but the Lord delivered me at last from them. And in the conclusion after many prayers, meditations, duties, the Lord let me see three main wounds in my soul: (1) I could not feel sin as my greatest evil; (2) I could do nothing but I did seek myself in it and was imprisoned there, and though I desired to be a preacher, yet it was honor I did look to like a vile wretch in the use of God's gifts I desired to have; (3) I felt a depth of atheism and unbelief in the main matters of salvation and whether the Scriptures were God's word. These things did much trouble me and in the conclusion did so far trouble me that I could not read the Scriptures or hear them read without secret and hellish blasphemy, calling all into question and all Christ's miracles, and hereupon I fell to doubt whether I had not committed the impardonable sin. And because I did question whether Christ did not cast out devils from Beelzebub, etc., I did think and fear I had, and now the terrors of God began to break in like floods of fire into my soul. For three quarters of a year this temptation did last, and I had some strong temptations to run my head against walls and brain and kill myself. And so I did see, as I thought, God's eternal reprobation of me, a fruit of which was this dereliction to these doubts and darkness, and I did see God like a consuming fire and an everlasting burning, and myself like a poor prisoner leading to that fire, and the thought of eternal reprobation and torment did amaze my spirits, especially at one time upon a Sabbath day at evening, and when I knew not what to do (for I went to no Christian and was ashamed to speak of these things), it came to my mind that I should do as Christ: when he was in an agony he prayed earnestly. And so I fell down to prayer, and being in prayer I saw myself so unholy and God so holy that my spirits began to sink, yet the Lord recovered me and poured out a spirit of prayer upon me for free mercy and pity, and in the conclusion of the prayer I found the Lord helping me to see my unworthiness of any mercy and that I was worthy to be cast out of his sight and to leave myself with him to do with me what he would, and there and never until then I found rest. And so my heart was humbled·and cast down, and I went with a stayed heart unto supper late that night and so rested here, and the terrors of the Lord began to assuage sweetly.[13] Yet when these were gone I felt my

[12] Richard Rogers, preacher at Wethersfield, Essex, was a prominent figure in the rise of Puritanism. Haller calls his *Seven Treatises,* published in 1603, "the first important exposition of the code of behavior which expressed . . . the Puritan . . . conception of the spiritual and moral life" (*The Rise of Puritanism* [New York: Harper and Row, Torchbook Edition, 1957], p. 36). The *Practice of Chris-* *tianity* was an abbreviated edition of the earlier work.

[13] Shortly before his departure from England, Shepard summarized this experience for the benefit of a troubled inquirer:

> . . . you desire me to tell you how myself came to the cure of atheistical thoughts, and whether they did wear

(Footnote continued next page.)

senselessness of sin and bondage to self and unconstancy and losing what the Lord had wrought and my heartlessness to any good and loathing of God's ways. Whereupon walking in the fields the Lord dropped this meditation into me: Be not discouraged therefore because thou art so vile, but make this double use of it: (1) loathe thyself the more; (2) feel a greater need and put a greater price upon Jesus Christ who only can redeem thee from all sin— and this I found of wonderful use to me in all my course whereby I was kept from sinkings of heart and did beat Satan as it were with his own weapons. And I saw Christ teaching me this before any man preached any such thing unto me. And so the Lord did help me to loathe myself in some measure and to say oft: Why shall I seek the glory and good of myself who am the greatest enemy, worse than the Devil can be, against myself, which self ruins me and blinds me, etc.? And thus God kept my heart exercised, and here I began to forsake my loose company wholly and to do what I could to work upon the hearts of other scholars and to humble them and to come into a way of holy walking in our speeches and otherwise. But yet I had no assurance Christ was mine.

out, or whether they were rationally overthrown.

I answer, at first they did wear out, meeting with fruitless and dead-hearted company, which was at the university.

The Lord awakened me again, and bid me beware lest an old sore broke out again. And this I found, that strength of reason would commonly convince my understanding that there was a God, but I felt it utterly insufficient to persuade my will of it unless it was by fits, when, as I thought, God's Spirit moved upon the chaos of those horrible thoughts; and this, I think, will be found a truth.

I did groan under the bondage of those unbelieving thoughts, looking up, and sighing to the Lord, that if he were as his works and word declared him to be, he would be pleased to reveal himself by his own beams, and persuade my heart by his own Spirit of his essence and being, which if he would do, I should account it the greatest mercy that ever he showed me. And after grievous and heavy perplexities, when I was by them almost forced to make an end of myself and sinful life, and to be mine own executioner, the Lord came between the bridge and the water, and set me out of anguish of spirit, . . . to pray unto him for light in the midst of so great darkness. In which time he revealed himself, manifested his love, stilled all those raging thoughts, gave return in great measure of them; so that, though I could not read the Scripture without blasphemous thoughts before, now I saw a glory, a majesty, a mystery, a depth in it, which fully persuaded, and which light (I desire to speak it to the glory of his free grace, seeing you call me to it) is not wholly put out, but remains, while I desire to walk closely with him, unto this day. And thus the Lord opened mine eyes, and cured me of this misery; and if any such base thoughts come (like beggars to my door) to my mind, and put these scruples to me, I used to send them away with this answer: Why shall I question that truth which I have both known and seen?

Certain Select Cases Resolved (London, 1648), p. 142.

(4) The Lord therefore brought Dr. Preston to preach upon that text, I Corinthians 1:30: Christ is made unto us wisdom, righteousness, sanctification, and redemption. And when he had opened how all the good I had, all the redemption I had, it was from Jesus Christ, I did then begin to prize him and he became very sweet unto me, although I had heard many a time Christ freely offered by his ministry if I would come in and receive him as Lord and Saviour and Husband. But I found my heart ever unwilling to accept of Christ upon these terms; I found them impossible for me to keep that condition, and Christ was not so sweet as my lust. But now the Lord made himself sweet to me and to embrace him and to give up myself unto him. But yet after this I had many fears and doubts.

(5) I found therefore the Lord revealing free mercy and that all my help was in that to give me Christ and to enable me to believe in Christ and accept of him, and here I did rest.

(6) The Lord also letting me see my own constant vileness in everything put me to this question: Why did the Lord Jesus keep the law, had no guile in his heart, had no unbrokenness but holiness there? Was it not for them that did want it? And here I saw Christ Jesus righteousness for a poor sinner's ungodliness, but yet questioning whether ever the Lord would apply this and give this unto me.

(7) The Lord made me see that so many as receive him, he gives power to be the sons of God (John 1:12), and I saw the Lord gave me a heart to receive Christ with a naked hand, even naked Christ, and so the Lord gave me peace.

· · ·

So when I had preached awhile at Earle's Colne about half a year the Lord saw me unfit and unworthy to continue me there any longer, and so the Bishop of London, Mountain,[14] being removed to York and Bishop Laud (now Archbishop) coming in his place, a fierce enemy to all righteousness and a man fitted of God to be a scourge to his people, he presently (having been not long in the place) but sent for me up to London and there, never asking me whether I would subscribe (as I remember) but what I had to do to preach in his diocese, chiding also Dr. Wilson for setting up this lecture in his diocese, after many railing speeches against me, forbade me to preach, and not only so, but if I went to preach anywhere else his hand would reach me.[15] And so God put me to silence there which did somewhat humble me,

---

[14] George Mountaigne (or Mountain) (1569–1628), successively Bishop of Lincoln, London, and Durham, 1617–28, was a staunch ally of Laud's High-Church party. His term as Archbishop of York was cut short after less than four months by his death.

[15] The following passage is reprinted with spelling and punctuation modernized from Thomas Prince, *A Chronological History of New England, in the form of Annals . . .*, new ed. (Boston, 1826), pp. 338-39. "I have by me," Prince wrote, "a manuscript of Mr.

(Footnote continued next page.)

for I did think it was for my sins the Lord set him thus against me. Yet when I was thus silenced the Lord stirred me up friends. The house of the Harlakendens were so many fathers and mothers to me, and they and the people would have me live there though I did nothing but stay in the place. But remaining about half a year after this silencing among them, the Lord let me see into the evil of the English ceremonies, cross, surplice, and kneeling, and the Bishop of London, *viz.*, Laud, coming down to visit, he cited me to appear before him at the Court at Reldon[16] where, I appearing, he asked me what I did in the place, and I told him I studied; he asked me what—I told him the fathers; he replied I might thank him for that, yet charged me to depart the place. I asked him whither should I go. To the University, said he. I told him I had no means to subsist there, yet he charged me to depart the place. Now about this time I had great desire to change my estate by marriage, and I had been praying three year before that the Lord would carry me to such a place where I might have a meet yoke fellow. And I had a call at this time to go to Yorkshire to preach there in a gentleman's house, but I did not desire to stir till the Bishop fired me out of this place. For the Bishop having thus charged me to depart, and being two days after to visit at Dunmow in Essex, Mr. Weld, Mr. Daniel Rogers, Mr. Ward, Mr. Marshall, Mr.

Shepard's, written with his own hand, in which are these words."

December 16, 1630. I was inhibited from preaching in the diocese of London by Dr. Laud, bishop of that diocese. As soon as I came in the morning, about eight of the clock, falling into a fit of rage, he asked me what degree I had taken in the University. I answered him, I was a Master of Arts. He asked me, Of what College? I answered, Of Emmanuel. He asked how long I had lived in his diocese. I answered, Three years and upwards. He asked who maintained me all this while, charging me to deal plainly with him, adding withal that he had been more cheated and equivocated with by some of my malignant faction than ever was man by Jesuit, at the speaking of which words he looked as though blood would have gushed out of his face and did shake as if he had been haunted with an ague fit, to my apprehension by reason of his extreme malice and secret venom. I desired him to excuse me. He fell then to threaten me and withal to bitter railing, calling me all to naught, saying, You prating coxcomb! Do you think all the learning is in your brain? He pronounced his sentence thus: I charge you that you neither preach, read, marry, bury, or exercise any ministerial function in any part of my diocese, for if you do, and I hear of it, I will be upon your back and follow you wherever you go, in any part of the kingdom, and so everlastingly disenable you. I besought him not to deal so, in regard of a poor town. Here he stopped me in what I was going on to say. A poor town! You have made a company of seditious, factious Bedlams, and what do you prate to me of a poor town? I prayed him to suffer me to catechise in the Sabbath days in the afternoon, He replied, Spare your breath; I will have no such fellows prate in my diocese. Get you gone, and now make your complaints to whom you will! So away I went, and blessed be God that I may go to him.

[16] Perhaps Peldon, near Colchester, Essex.

Wharton[17] consulted together whether it was best to let such a swine to root up God's plants in Essex and not to give him some check. Whereupon it was agreed upon privately at Braintree that some should speak to him and give him a check. So Mr. Weld and I traveling together had some thoughts of going to New England, but we did think it best to go first unto Ireland and preach there, and to go by Scotland thither. But when we came to the church Mr. Weld stood and heard without (being excommunicated by him); I, being more free, went within. And after sermon Mr. Weld went up to hear the Bishop's speech and being seen to follow the Bishop the first thing he did was to examine Mr. Weld what he did to follow him and to stand upon holy ground. Thereupon he was committed to pursuivant and bound over to answer it at the High Commission. But when Mr. Weld was pleading for himself, and that it was ignorance that made him come in, the Bishop asked him whither he intended to go, whether to New England, and if so whether I would go with him. While he was thus speaking I came into the crowd and heard the words. Others bid me go away, but neglecting to do it, a godly man pulled me away with violence out of the crowd. And as soon as ever I was gone the apparitor calls for Mr. Shepard, and the pursuivant was sent presently after to find me out. But he that pulled me away (Mr. Holbeach[18] by name, a schoolmaster at Felsted in Essex) hastened our horses and away we rid as fast as we could. And so the Lord delivered me out of the hand of that lion a third time. And now I perceived I could not stay in Colne without danger, and hereupon receiving a letter from Mr. Ezekiel Rogers,[19] then living at Rowley in Yorkshire, to encourage me to come to the knight's house, called Sir Richard Darley, dwelling at a town called Buttercrambe, and the knight's two sons, viz., Mr. Henry and Mr. Richard Darley, promising me £20 a year for their part, and the knight promising me my table, and the letters sent to me crying with that voice of the man of Macedonia, Come and help us. Hereupon I resolved to follow the Lord to so remote and strange a place, the rather because I might be far from the hearing of the malicious Bishop Laud who had threatened me if I preached anywhere. So when I was determined to go, the gentlemen sent a man to me to be my guide in my journey, who coming with me, with much grief of heart I forsook Essex and Earle's Colne and they me, going, as it were, now I knew not whither.

---

[17] Daniel Rogers: son of Richard Rogers; lecturer at Wethersfield, Essex. Mr. Ward: probably Nathaniel Ward (1578-1653), then rector of Stondon Massey, Essex; later pastor at Ipswich in Massachusetts; author of *The Simple Cobler of Agawam*. Mr. Marshall: Stephen Marshall, vicar of Finchingfield, Essex. Mr. Wharton: Samuel Wharton, vicar of Felsted, Essex.

[18] Martin Holbeach, headmaster of Felsted School, where a number of prominent Puritans were educated.

[19] Ezekiel Rogers (1590-1661), son of Richard; at that time rector of Rowley St. Peter, Yorkshire; pastor at Rowley in Massachusetts, 1639-60.

The reasons which swayed me to come to New England were many. (1) I saw no call to any other place in old England nor way of subsistence in peace and comfort to me and my family. (2) Divers people in old England of my dear friends desired me to go to New England, there to live together, and some went before and writ to me of providing a place for a company of us, one of which was John Bridge,[20] and I saw divers families of my Christian friends who were resolved thither to go with me. (3) I saw the Lord departing from England when Mr. Hooker and Mr. Cotton were gone, and I saw the hearts of most of the godly set and bent that way, and I did think I should feel many miseries if I stayed behind. (4) My judgment was then convinced not only of the evil of ceremonies but of mixed communion and joining with such in sacraments, though I ever judged it lawful to join with them in preaching. (5) I saw it my duty to desire the fruition of all God's ordinances which I could not enjoy in old England. (6) My dear wife did much long to see me settled there in peace and so put me on to it. (7) Although it was true I should stay and suffer for Christ, yet I saw no rule for it now the Lord had opened a door of escape. Otherwise I did incline much to stay and suffer, especially after our sea storms. (8) Though my ends were mixed and I looked much to my own quiet, yet the Lord let me see the glory of those liberties in New England and made me purpose, if ever I should come over, to live among God's people as one come out from the dead, to his praise, though since I have seen as the Lord's goodness, so my own exceeding weakness to be as good as I thought to have been. And although they did desire me to stay in the north and preach privately, yet (1) I saw that this time could not be long without trouble from King Charles; (2) I saw no reason to spend my time privately when I might possibly exercise my talent publicly in New England; (3) I did hope my going over might make them to follow me; (4) I considered how sad a thing it would be for me to leave my wife and child (if I should die) in that rude place of the north where was nothing but barbarous wickedness generally, and how sweet it would be to leave them among God's people, though poor; (5) My liberty in private was daily threatened, and I thought it wisdom to depart before the pursuivants came out, for so I might depart with more peace and less trouble and danger to me and my friends. And I knew not whether God would have me to hazard my person and comfort of me and all mine for a disorderly manner of preaching privately (as it was reputed) in those parts. So after I had preached my farewell sermon at Newcastle I departed from the north in a ship laden with coals for Ipswich, about the beginning of June, after I had been about a year in the north, the Lord having blessed some few sermons and notes to divers in Newcastle from whom I parted filled with their love. And so the Lord gave us a speedy voyage from thence to Ipswich in old

[20] John Bridge preceded Hooker to New-town and remained there when Hooker's congregation left. He served as deacon, selectman, and deputy to the General Court.

England, whither I came in a disguised manner with my wife and child and maid, and stayed a while at Mr. Russell's house, another while at Mr. Collins his house, and then went down to Essex to the town where I had preached, *viz.*, Earle's Colne, to Mr. Richard Harlakenden's house where I lived privately but with much love from them all, as also from Mr. Joseph Cooke, and also with friends at London and Northamptonshire.[21] And truly I found this time of my life wherein I was so tossed up and down and had no place of settling, but kept secret in regard of the bishops, the most uncomfortable and fruitless time to my own soul especially that ever I had in my life. And therefore I did long to be in New England as soon as might be, and the rather because my wife, having weaned her first son Thomas, had conceived again and was breeding, and I knew no place in England where she could lie in without discovery of myself, danger to myself and all my friends that should receive me, and where we could not but give offense to many if I should have my child not baptized. And therefore, there being divers godly Christians resolved to go toward the latter end of the year if I would go, I did therefore resolve to go that year, the end of that summer I came from the north. And the time appointed for the ship to go out was about a month or fortnight before Michaelmas (as they there call it); the ship was called the *Hope of Ipswich;* the master of it (a very able seaman) was Mr. Gurling who professed much love to me, who had got this ship of 400 ton from the Danes, and as some report, it was by some fraud. But he denied it, and, being a man very loving and full of fair promises of going at the time appointed and an able seaman, hence we resolved to adventure that time, though dangerous in regard of the approaching winter.

Now here the Lord's wonderful terror and mercy to us did appear. For being come to Ipswich with my family at the time appointed, the ship was not ready, and we stayed six or eight weeks longer than the time promised for her going. And so it was very late in the year and very dangerous to go to sea, and indeed if we had gone, doubtless we had all perished upon the seas, it being so extreme cold and tempestuous winter, but yet we could not go back when we had gone so far. And the Lord saw it good to chastise us for rushing onward too soon and hazarding ourselves in that manner, and I had many fears, and much darkness (I remember) overspread my soul, doubting of our way, yet I say we could not now go back. Only I learnt from that time never to go about a sad business in the dark, unless God's call within as well as that without be very strong and clear and comfortable.

So that in the year 1634, about the beginning of the winter, we set sail from Harwich, and, having gone some few leagues onto the sea, the wind stopped us that night, and so we cast anchor in a dangerous place. And on the morning the wind grew fierce and rough against us full, and drave us

[21] John Russell and Joseph Cooke crossed with Shepard in 1635; Edward Collins set-tled in Cambridge in the same year or the next.

toward the sands, but the vessel, being laden too heavy at the head, would not stir for all that which the seamen could do, but drave us full upon the sands near Harwich harbor. And the ship did grate upon the sands and was in great danger, but the Lord directed one man to cut some cable or rope in the ship, and so she was turned about and was beaten quite backward toward Yarmouth, quite out of our way. But while the ship was in this great danger a wonderful, miraculous providence did appear to us, for one of the seamen, that he might save the vessel, fell in when it was in that danger and so was carried out a mile or more from the ship and given for dead and gone. The ship was then in such danger that none could attend to follow him, and when it was out of danger it was a very great hazard to the lives of any that should take the skiff to seek to find him. Yet it pleased the Lord that, being discerned afar off floating upon the waters, three of the seamen adventured out upon the rough waters, and at last, about an hour after he fell into the sea (as we conjectured), they came and found him floating upon the waters, never able to swim but supported by a divine hand all this while. When the men came to him they were glad to find him, but concluded he was dead, and so got him into the skiff, and when he was there tumbled him down as one dead. Yet one of them said to the rest, Let us use what means we can if there be life to preserve it, and thereupon turned his head downward for the water to run out, and having done so the fellow began to gasp and breathe. Then they applied other means they had, and so he began at last to move and then to speak, and by that time he came to the ship he was pretty well and able to walk. And so the Lord showed us his great power, whereupon a godly man in the ship then said: This man's danger and deliverance is a type of ours, for he did fear dangers were near unto us, and that yet the Lord's power should be shown in saving of us. For so indeed it was. For the wind did drive us quite backward out of our way and gave us no place to anchor at until we came unto Yarmouth Roads, an open place at sea yet fit for anchorage, but otherwise a very dangerous place. And so we came thither through many uncomfortable hazards within thirty hours and cast anchor in Yarmouth Roads, which when we had done upon a Saturday morning the Lord sent a most dreadful and terrible storm of wind from the west, so dreadful that to this day the seamen call it Windy Saturday, that it also scattered many ships in divers coasts at that time, and divers ships were cast away. One among the rest, which was the seamen's ship who came with us from Newcastle, was cast away, and he and all his men perished. But when the wind thus arose, the master cast all his anchors, but the storm was so terrible that the anchors broke and the ship drave toward the sands where we could not but be cast away, whereupon the master cries out that we were dead men, and thereupon the whole company go to prayer. But the vessel still drave so near to the sands that the master shot off two pieces of ordnance to the town for help to save the passengers. The town perceived it and thousands came upon the walls of Yarmouth and looked upon us, hearing we were New England men [this word doubtful], and pitied much and gave us for gone because they saw other ships perishing near unto us at that time, but could not send any help unto us though much money was offered by some to hazard themselves for us. So the master not knowing what to do, it pleased the Lord that there was one Mr. Cock, a drunken fellow but no seaman yet one that had been at sea often and would come in a humor unto New England with us; whether it was to see the country or no I cannot tell, but sure I am God intended it for good unto us to make him an instrument to save all our lives. For he persuaded the master to cut down his mainmast. The master was unwilling to it and besotted, not sensible of ours and his own loss. At last this Cock calls for hatchets, tells the master, If you be a man, save the lives of your passengers, cut down your mainmast. Hereupon he encouraged all the company who were forlorn and hopeless of life, and the seamen presently cut down the mast aboard, just at that very time wherein we all gave ourselves for gone to see neither old nor New England nor faces of friends anymore, there being near upon 200 passengers in the ship. And so when the mast was down, the master had one little anchor left and cast it out, but the ship was driven away toward the sands still, and the seamen came to us and bid us look (pointing to the place) where our graves should shortly be, conceiving also that the wind had broke off this anchor also. So the master professed he had done what he could and therefore now desired us to go to prayer. So Mr. Norton[22] in one place and myself in another part of the ship, he with the passengers, and myself with the mariners above decks, went to prayer and committed our souls and bodies unto the Lord that gave them. Immediately after prayer the wind began to abate, and the ship stayed, for the last anchor was not broke (as we conceived) but only rent up with the wind, and so drave and was drawn along plowing the sands with the violence of the wind, which abating after prayer (though still very terrible) the ship was stopped just when it was ready to be swallowed up of the sands, a very little way off from it. And so we rid it out, yet not without fear of our lives though the anchor stopped the ship, because the cable was let out so far that a little rope held the cable, and the cable the little anchor, and the little anchor the great ship in this great storm. But when one of the company perceived that we were so strangely preserved, had these words, That thread we hang by will save us, for so we accounted of the rope fastened to the anchor, in comparison of the fierce storm. And so indeed it did, the Lord showing his dreadful power toward us and yet his unspeakable rich mercy to us who in depths of mercy heard, nay helped, us where we could not cry through the disconsolate fears we had out of these depths of seas and miseries. This deliverance was so great that I then did think if ever the Lord did bring me to shore again I should live like one come and risen

---

[22] John Norton (1606-63), curate at Bishop's Stortford, Hertfordshire; pastor at Ipswich in Massachusetts, 1636-53, and at Boston, 1653-63.

from the dead. This is one of those living mercies the Lord hath shown me, a mercy to myself, to my wife and child then living, and to my second son Thomas who was in this storm but in the womb of his dear mother who might then have perished and been cut off from all hope of means and mercy, and unto my dear friends then with me, viz., brother Champney, Frost, Goffe, [23] and divers others, most dear saints, and also to all with me. And how would the name of the Lord suffered if we had so perished; that the Lord Jesus should have respect to me so vile and one at that time full of many temptations and weaknesses, amazed much and deeply afraid of God's terror, yet supported. I desire this mercy may be remembered of my children and their children's children when I am dead and cannot praise the Lord in the land of the living anymore. And so we continued that night, many sick, many weak and discouraged, many sad hearts. Yet upon the Sabbath morning we departed and went out of the ship—I fear a little soon, for we should have spent that day in praising of him. Yet we were afraid of neglecting a season of providence in going out while we had a calm, and many sick folk were unfit for that work and had need of refreshing at shore.

So upon the Sabbath-day morning boats came to our vessel from the town, and so my dear wife and child went in the first boat. But here the Lord saw that these waters were not sufficient to wash away my filth and sinfulness, and therefore he cast me into the fire as soon as ever I was upon the sea in the boat, for there my first-born child, very precious to my soul and dearly beloved of me, was smitten with sickness; the Lord sent a vomiting upon it whereby it grew faint, and nothing that we could use could stop its vomiting, although we had many helps at Yarmouth, and this was a very bitter affliction to me. And the Lord now showed me my weak faith, want of fear, pride, carnal content, immoderate love of creatures and of my child especially, and begot in me some desires and purposes to fear his name. But yet the Lord would not be entreated for the life of it, and after a fortnight's sickness at last it gave up the ghost when its mother had given it up to the Lord, and was buried at Yarmouth where I durst not be present lest the pursuivants should apprehend me and I should be discovered, which was a great affliction and very bitter to me and my dear wife. And hereby I saw the Lord did come near to me, and I did verily fear the Lord would take away my wife also, if not myself not long after. And these afflictions, together with the Lord's crossing us and being so directly against our voyage, made me secretly willing to stay and suffer in England, and my heart was not so much toward New England. Yet this satisfied me, that seeing there was a door opened of escape, why should I suffer? And I considered how unfit I was to go to such a good land with such an unmortified, hard, dark, formal, hypocritical heart, and therefore no wonder if the Lord did thus cross me. And

[23] Richard Champney crossed with Shepard in the *Defense* in 1635; Edmund Frost and Edward Goffe came the same year in another ship. All three settled in Cambridge where they held high posts in town and church.

the Lord made me fear my affliction came in part for running too far in a way of separation from the mixed assemblies in England, though I bless God I have ever believed that there are true churches in many parishes in England where the Lord sets up able men and ministers of his gospel, and I have abhorred to refuse to hear any able ministers in England.

So that now I having buried my first born and being in great sadness and not knowing where to go nor what to do, the Lord sent Mr. Roger Harlakenden and my brother Samuel Shepard[24] to visit me after they had heard of our escape at sea, who much refreshed us and clave to me in my sorrows. And being casting about where to go and live, Mr. Bridge,[25] then minister in Norwich, sent for me to come and live with him, and being come, one Mistress Corbet who lived five miles off Norwich, an aged, eminent, godly gentlewoman, hearing of my coming and that by being with Mr. Bridge might hazard his liberty by countenancing of me, she did therefore freely offer to me a great house of hers standing empty at a town called Bastwick, and there the Lord stirred up her heart to show all love to me, which did much lighten and sweeten my sorrows. And I saw the Lord Jesus' care herein to me and saw cause of trusting him in times of straits, who set me in such a place where I lived for half a year, all the winter long, among and with my friends (Mr. Harlakenden dwelling with me and bearing all the charge of housekeeping) and far from the notice of my enemies, where we enjoyed sweet fellowship one with another and also with God, in a house which was fit to entertain any prince for fairness and greatness and pleasantness. Here the Lord hid us all the winter long, and when it was fit to travel in the spring we went up to London, Mr. Harlakenden not forsaking me all this while, for he was a father and mother to me. And when we came to London to Mistress Sherborne, not knowing what to do nor where to live privately, the Lord provided a very private place for us where my wife was brought to bed and delivered of my second son Thomas, and none but our friends did know of it. And so by this means my son was not baptized until we came to New England the winter following, being born in London, April 5, 1635. One remarkable deliverance my wife had when we were coming up to London. Mr. Burrows, the minister, kindly entertained us about a fortnight in the way, and when my wife was there, being great with child, she fell down from the top of a pair of stairs to the bottom, yet the Lord kept her and the child also safe from that deadly danger. When we had been also at London for a time and began to be known in the place, my wife was brought to bed. The Lord put it into our hearts to remove to another place in Mr. Eldred's house in London which stood empty, and the very night we were all come away then came the pursuivants and others to search after us, but the Lord delivered us out of their hands. And so, when the Lord had recov-

---

[24] Samuel Shepard went with his brother in the *Defense*, listed as a servant to Roger Harlakenden.

[25] William Bridge, a Cambridge graduate.

ered my wife, we began to prepare for a removal once again to New England.

And the Lord seemed to make our way plain (1) because I had no other call to any place in England, (2) many more of God's people resolved to go with me, as Mr. Roger Harlakenden and Mr. Champney, etc.; (3) the Lord saw our unfitness and the unfitness of our going the year before, and therefore giving us good friends to accompany us and good company in the ship, we set forward, about the tenth of August, 1635, with myself, wife, and my little son Thomas, and other precious friends, having tasted much of God's mercy in England and lamenting the loss of our native country when we took our last view of it. In our voyage upon the sea the Lord was very tender of me and kept me from the violence of seasickness. In our coming we were refreshed with the society of Mr. Wilson,[26] Mr. Jones,[27] by their faith and prayers and preaching. The ship we came in was very rotten and unfit for such a voyage, and therefore the first storm we had, we had a very great leak which did much appal and affect us. Yet the Lord discovered it unto us, when we were thinking of returning back again, and much comforted our hearts. We had many storms, in one of which my dear wife took such a cold and got such weakness as that she fell into a consumption of which she afterward died. And also the Lord preserved her with the child in her arms from imminent and apparent death, for by the shaking of the ship in a violent storm her head was pitched against an iron bolt, and the Lord miraculously preserved the child and recovered my wife. This was a great affliction to me and was a cause of many sad thoughts in the ship how to behave myself when I came to New England. My resolutions I have written down in my little book. And so the Lord after many sad storms and wearisome days and many longings to see the shore, the Lord brought us to the sight of it upon October 2, anno 1635, and upon October the third we arrived with my wife, child, brother Samuel, Mr. Harlakenden, Mr. Cooke, etc., at Boston with rejoicing in our God after a longsome voyage, my dear wife's great desire being now fulfilled, which was to leave me in safety from the hand of my enemies and among God's people, and also the child under God's precious ordinances.

Now when we came upon shore we were kindly saluted and entertained by many friends and were the first three days in the house of Mr. Coddington, being treasurer at that time, and that with much love.[28]

---

[26] John Wilson (1588-1667), teacher of the church at Boston, had crossed with Winthrop in 1630. He was returning in 1635 from his second visit to England.

[27] John Jones (1593-1665), pastor at Concord, 1635-44, and Fairfield, Connecticut, 1644-65.

[28] William Coddington (1601-1678), a leading citizen of Boston from 1630 to 1638 when, having supported Anne Hutchinson, he removed to Aquidneck where he helped found Newport and served as governor both of Aquidneck and later of the united plantations of Rhode Island and Providence. He was a successful merchant; late in life he became a Quaker.

When we had been here two days, upon the Monday, October 5, we came (being sent for by friends at Newtown) to them to my brother Mr. Stone's house. And that congregation being upon their removal to Hartford at Connecticut, myself and those that came with me found many houses empty and many persons willing to sell, and hence our company bought off their houses to dwell in until we should see another place fit to remove unto. But having been here some time, divers of our brethren did desire to sit still and not to remove further, partly because of the fellowship of the churches, partly because they thought their lives were short and removals to new plantations full of troubles, partly because they found sufficient for themselves and their company. Hereupon there was a purpose to enter into church fellowship, which we did the year after about the end of the winter,[29] a fortnight after which my dear wife Margaret died, being first received into church fellowship which, as she much longed for, so the Lord did so sweeten it unto her that she was hereby exceedingly cheered and comforted with the sense of God's love, which continued unto her last gasp.

No sooner were we thus set down and entered into church fellowship but the Lord exercised us and the whole country with the opinions of Familists, begun by Mistress Hutchinson, raised up to a great height by Mr. Vane[30] too suddenly chosen governor, and maintained too obscurely by Mr. Cotton, and propagated too boldly by the members of Boston and some in other churches, by means of which division by these opinions the ancient and received truth came to be darkened, God's name to be blasphemed, the churches' glory diminished, many godly grieved, many wretches hardened, deceiving and being deceived, growing worse and worse. The principal opinion and seed of all the rest was this, *viz.*, that a Christian should not take any evidence of God's special grace and love toward him by the sight of any graces or conditional evangelical promises to faith or sanctification, in way of ratiocination (for this was evidence and so a way of works), but it must be without the sight of any grace, faith, holiness, or special change in himself, by immediate revelation in an absolute promise. And because that the whole scriptures do give such clear, plain, and notable evidences of favor to persons called and sanctified, hence they said that a second evidence might be taken from hence but no first evidence. But from hence it arose that, as all error is fruitful, so this opinion did gender about a hundred monstrous opinions in the country, which the elders perceiving, having used all private brotherly means with Mr. Cotton first and yet no healing hereupon, they publicly preached both against opinions publicly and privately maintained, and I account it no small mercy to myself that the Lord kept me from that contagion and gave me any heart or light to see through those devices of

[29] Winthrop's *Journal* has an account of the ceremonies under date of February 1, 1636.

[30] Sir Henry Vane (1613–62) was defeated by John Winthrop in March, 1637, after one term as governor of the Bay Colony. His departure from Massachusetts in August of the same year deprived the Hutchinsonians of their principal lay supporter.

men's heads, although I found it a most uncomfortable time to live in contention. And the Lord was graciously pleased by giving witness against them
to keep this poor church spotless and clear from them. This division in the
church began to trouble the commonwealth. Mr. Wheelwright, a man of a
bold and stiff conceit of his own worth and light, preached (as the Court
judged) a seditious sermon,[31] stirring up all sorts against those that preached
a covenant of works, meaning all the elders in the country that preach
justification by faith and assurance of it by sight of faith and sanctification,
being enabled thereto by the spirit. The troubles thus increasing and all
means used for crushing and curing these sorts, a synod was thought of and
called from the example, Acts 15, wherein by the help of all the elders
joined together those errors through the grace and power of Christ were
discovered, the defenders of them convinced and ashamed, the truth established, and the consciences of the saints settled, there being a most wonderful presence of Christ's spirit in that assembly, held at Cambridge, anno
1637, about August, and continued a month together in public agitations, for
the issue of this synod was this:

(1). The Pequot Indians were fully discomfited, for as the opinions arose,
wars did arise, and when these began to be crushed by the ministry of
the elders and by opposing Mr. Vane and casting him and others from
being magistrates, the enemies began to be crushed and were perfectly subdued by the end of the synod.

(2). The magistrates took courage and exiled Mr. Wheelwright, Mistress
Hutchinson, and divers Islanders,[32] whom the Lord did strangely discover, giving most of them over to all manner of filthy opinions, until
many that held with them before were ashamed of them, and so the
Lord within one year wrought a great change among us.

· · ·

The year after those wars in the country, God having taken away my first
wife, the Lord gave me a second, the eldest daughter of Mr. Hooker, a
blessed stock. And the Lord hath made her a great blessing to me to carry on
matters in the family with much care and wisdom, and to seek the Lord God
of her father.

The first child I had by her (being a son) died (through the weakness of
the midwife) before it saw the sun, even in the very birth. The second
(whom the Lord I bless hath hitherto spared), viz., my little Samuel, is yet

---

[31] John Wheelwright (1594-1679), later pastor at Hampton, New Hampshire, and Salisbury, Massachusetts, preached the Fast Day
sermon, January 19, 1030/37.

[32] The Islanders were the inhabitants of
Aquidneck, many of whom were Hutchinson
exiles.

living. The third son, viz., my son John, after sixteen weeks departed on the Sabbath-day morning, a day of rest, to the bosom of rest to him who gave it, which was no small affliction and heartbreaking to me that I should provoke the Lord to strike at my innocent children for my sake.

The Lord thus afflicting yet continued peace to the country, that amazing mercy, when all England and Europe are in a flame. The Lord hath set me and my children aside from the flames of the fires in Yorkshire and Northumberland whence if we had not been delivered I had been in great afflictions and temptations, very weak and unfit to be tossed up and down and to bear violent persecution. The Lord therefore hath showed his tenderness to me and mine in carrying me to a land of peace, though a place of trial, where the Lord hath made the savage Indians who conspired the death of all the English by Miantonomo upon a sudden, if Uncas could have been cut off first who stood in their way, and determined an open war upon us by the privy suggestions of some neutral English on the Island, to seek for peace from us upon our own terms without bloodshed, August 26, 1645.

But the Lord hath not been wont to let me live long without some affliction or other, and yet ever mixed with some mercy, and therefore, April the second, 1646, as he gave me another son, John, so he took away my most dear, precious, meek and loving wife in childbed after three weeks lying in, having left behind her two hopeful branches, my dear children Samuel and John. This affliction was very heavy to me, for in it the Lord seemed to withdraw his tender care for me and mine which he graciously manifested by my dear wife; also refused to hear prayer when I did think he would have harkened and let me see his beauty in the land of the living in restoring her to health again; also in taking her away in the prime of her life when she might have lived to have glorified the Lord long; also in threatening me to proceed in rooting out my family, and that he would not stop, having begun here, as in Eli for not being zealous enough against the sins of his son. And I saw that if I had profited by former afflictions of this nature I should not have had this scourge. But I am the Lord's, and he may do with me what he will. He did teach me to prize a little grace gained by a cross as a sufficient recompense for all outward losses. But this loss was very great. She was a woman of incomparable meekness of spirit, toward myself especially, and very loving, of great prudence to take care for and order my family affairs, being neither too lavish nor sordid in anything, so that I knew not what was under her hands. She had an excellency to reprove for sin and discerned the evils of men. She loved God's people dearly and studious to profit by their fellowship, and therefore loved their company. She loved God's word exceedingly and hence was glad she could read my notes which she had to muse on every week. She had a spirit of prayer beyond ordinary of her time and experience. She was fit to die long before she did die, even after the death of her first-born, which was a great affliction to her, but her work not being done then, she lived almost nine years with me and was the comfort of my life to me, and the last sacrament before her lying in seemed to be full of Christ and thereby fitted for heaven. She did oft say she should not outlive this child, and when her fever first began (by taking some cold) she told me so, that we should love exceedingly together because we should not live long together. Her fever took away her sleep; want of sleep wrought much distemper in her head and filled it with fantasies and distractions, but without raging. The night before she died she had about six hours unquiet sleep, but that so cooled and settled her head that when she knew none else so as to speak to them, yet she knew Jesus Christ and could speak to him, and therefore as soon as she awakened out of sleep she brake out into a most heavenly, heartbreaking prayer after Christ, her dear redeemer, for the spirit of life, and so continued praying until the last hour of her death—Lord, though I unworthy; Lord, one word, one word, etc.—and so gave up the ghost. Thus God hath visited and scourged me for my sins and sought to wean me from this world, but I have ever found it a difficult thing to profit even but a little by the sorest and sharpest afflictions.

From The Sincere Convert

THE FIFTH SERMON: [FEW ARE SAVED][1]

"That those that are saved are very few; and that those that are saved, are saved with very much difficulty. Strait is the gate, and narrow is the way that leadeth unto life, and few there be that find it," Mat. 7.14.

Here are two parts.

1. The paucity of them that shall be saved: *few find the way thither.*

2. The difficulty of being saved: *Strait and narrow is the way and gate unto life.*

Hence arise two doctrines.

1. That the number of them that shall be saved is very small, *Luke* 13.24. the Devil hath his drove, and swarms to go to hell, as fast as bees to their hive; Christ hath his *flock*, and that is but *a little stock;* hence God's children are called *jewels, Mat.* 3.17. which commonly are kept secret, in respect of the other lumber in the house; hence they are called *strangers* and *pilgrims*, which are   *Doct. 1.*

Luk. 12.32.

---

[1] The text is from the revised London edition of 1655, which Shepard is said to have supervised.

very few in respect of the inhabitants of the country through which they pass: hence they are called *sons of God,* 1 *John* 3. 2. *Of the blood royal,* which are few in respect of common subjects.

But see the truth of this point in these two things.　　　*Few saved*

First, look to all ages and times of the world. Secondly, to　*in all ages.*
all places and persons in the world, and we shall see few men　　　　*1.*
were saved.

1. Look to all ages, and we shall find but a handful saved. As soon as ever the Lord began to keep house, and there were but two families in it, there was a bloody *Cain* living, and a good　*As the world*
Abel slain. And as the world increased in number, so in　*increased in*
wickedness, *Gen.* 6. 12. it is said, "All flesh had corrupted　*number, so in*
their ways," and amongst so many thousand men, not one　*wickedness.*
righteous but *Noah,* and his family; and yet in the Ark there crept in a cursed *Cham.*

Afterwards as *Abraham's* posterity increased, so we see their sin abounded. When his posterity was in *Egypt,* where one would think, if ever men were good, now it would appear, being so heavily afflicted by *Pharaoh,* being so many miracles miraculously delivered by the hand of *Moses,* yet most of these "God was wroth with," *Heb.* 3. 12. and only two of them, *Caleb* and *Joshua* went into *Canaan,* a type of heaven. Look into *Solomon's* time, what glorious times! what great profession was there then! Yet after his death, *ten tribes* fell to the odious sin of idolatry, following the command of *Jeroboam* their king. Look further into *Isaiah's*　*Isai. 1. 9.*
time, where there were multitudes of sacrifices and prayers, *Isa.* 1. 11. yet then there was but a *remnant,* nay a very *little* remnant that should be saved. And look to the time of Christ's coming in the flesh (for I pick out the best time of all) when one would think　*Joh. 1. 11.*
by such sermons he preached, such miracles he wrought, such a life as he led, all the *Jews* would have entertained him, yet it is said, "He came unto his own, and they received him not." So few, that Christ himself admires at one good *Nathaniel,* "Behold an Israelite in whom there is no guile." In the Apostles' time, many indeed were converted, but few comparatively, and amongst the best Churches many bad: as that at　*Rev. 3. 4.*
Philippi, Phil. 3. 18. Many had a name to live, but were dead,　*Acts 20.*
and few only kept their garments unspotted. And presently af-　*28, 29, 30.*
ter the Apostles' time, *many grievous wolves came and devoured the sheep;* and so in succeeding ages, *Rev.* 12. 9. "All the earth wondered at the whore in scarlet."

And in *Luther's* time,[2] when the light began to arise again, he　*Luther.*
saw so many carnal gospellers, that he breaks out in one sermon,

---

[2] Martin Luther (1483-1546) publicly deplored corrupt practices among Christians　both before and after his excommunication in 1520.

into these speeches, "God grant I may never live to see those bloody days that are coming upon an ungodly world." *Latimer*[3] heard so much profaneness in his time, that he thought verily doomsday was just at hand. And have not our ears heard censuring those in the *Palati-* *Latimer.* *nate,*[4] where (as 'tis reported) many have fallen from the glorious gospel to popery, as fast as leaves fall in *autumn?* Who would have thought there had lurked such hearts under such a show of detesting popery, as was among them before? And at Christ's coming, *shall he find faith on the earth?*

2. Let us look into all places and persons, and see how few shall be saved. The world is now split into four parts, *Europe, Asia, Africa,* and *America;* and the three biggest parts are drowned in a deluge of profaneness and superstition; they do not so much as profess Christ; you may see the sentence of death written on these men's foreheads. *Jer.* 10. *ult.* But *II. Few shall be saved in all places.* let us look upon the best part of the world, and that is *Europe,* how few shall be saved there? First, the *Grecian* *Jer. 10. 25.* Church, howsoever now in these days, their good patri- *Pour out thy* arch of *Constantinople*[5] is about a general Reformation *fury upon the* among them, and hath done much good; yet are they for *heathen that* the present, and have been for the most part of them, *know thee not,* without the saving means of knowledge. They content *and upon the* themselves with their old superstitions, having little or no *families that* preaching at all. And for the other parts, as *Italy, Spain,* *call not upon* *France, Germany,* for the most part they are popish; and *thy name, etc.* see the end of these men, 2 *Thes* 2. 9, 10, 11, 12. And now amongst them that carry the badge of honesty, I will not speak what mine ears have heard, and my heart believes concerning other churches: I will come into our own Church of *England,* which is *Few shall be* the most flourishing church in the world: never had *saved in England.* church such preachers, such means; yet have we not *1 Cor. 1. 29.* some chapels and churches stand as dark lanterns without light, where people are led with blind, or idle, or licentious ministers, and so both fall into the ditch?

Nay, even amongst them that have the means of grace, but few shall be saved. It may be sometimes amongst ninety-nine in a parish, Christ sends a minister to call some one lost sheep among them, *Mat.* 13. Three grounds were bad where the seed was sown, and *Luke 15. 24. 25.* only one ground good. It's a strange speech of *Chrysos-*

[3] Hugh Latimer (1480?-1535) was an English Protestant martyr, executed for heresy.

[4] A section of Germany where some of the worst fighting of the 'Thirty Years' War (1618-1648) between Catholics and Protestants was fought.

[5] This official of the Greek Orthodox Church (1620-1638) was severely punished and at last executed for his public declaration of Protestant beliefs.

tom[6] in his fourth sermon to the people of *Antioch,* where he was much beloved and did much good: "How many do you think," saith he, "shall be saved in this city? It will be an hard speech to you, but I will speak it; though here be so many thousands of you, yet there cannot be found an hundred that shall be saved, and I doubt of them too; for what villany is there among youth? what sloth in old men?" and so he goes on. So say I, never tell me we are baptized, and are Christians, and trust to Christ; let us but separate the goats from the sheep, and exclude none but such as the Scripture doth, and sets a cross upon their doors, with, *Lord have mercy upon them,* and we shall see only few in the city shall be saved.

Chrysostom thought in Antioch, an hundred could not be saved.

1. Cast out all the *profane people* among us, as drunkards, swearers, whores, liars, which the Scripture brands for black sheep, and condemns them in an hundred places.

Those which the Scripture excludes from salvation.
1. The profane.

2. Set by all *civil men,* that are but wolves chained up, tame devils, swine in a fair meadow, that pay all they owe, and do nobody any harm, yet do none any great good, that plead for themselves and say, "Who can say black is mine eye?" These are righteous men, whom Christ never came to call; *for He came not to call the righteous, but sinners to repentance.*

2. The civil men.

3. Cast by all *hypocrites,* that like stage-players, in the sight of others, act the parts of kings, and honest men; when look upon them in their tyring house, they are but base varlets.

3. The hypocrites.

4. *Formal professors,* and *carnal gospellers,* that have a thing like *faith* and like *sorrow,* and like *true repentance,* and like *good desires,* but yet they be but pictures, they deceive others and themselves too, 2 *Tim.* 3. 5.

4. The formal professors.

Set by these four sorts, how few then are to be saved, even among them that are hatched in the bosom of the Church?

First, here then is an use of *encouragement.* Be not discouraged by the name of singularity. What? do you think yourself wiser than others? and shall none be saved but such as are so precise as ministers prate? Are you wiser than others that you think none shall go to heaven but yourself? I tell you if you would be saved, you must be singular men, not out of *faction,* but out of *conscience, Acts* 24. 16.

Use 1. Of encouragement.

Tit. 2. 14.

Secondly, here is matter of *terror* to all those that be of opinion, that few shall be saved; and therefore when they are convinced of the danger of sin by the Word, they fly to this shelter, "If I be damned, it will be woe to many more beside me then"; as though most should not be damned. Oh yes, the most of them

Use 2. Of terror.

---

[6] Chrysostom (345?-407), one of the Puritans' favorites among church fathers, preached in Antioch before he became patriarch of Constantinople.

that live in the Church shall perish; and this made an *hermit* which *Theodoret*[7] mentions, to live 15 years in a cell in a desolate wilderness, with nothing but bread and water, and yet doubted after all his sorrow, whether he should be saved or no. Oh! God's wrath is heavy, which thou shalt one day bear.

Thirdly, this ministreth *exhortation* to all *confident people*, that think they believe and say, they doubt not but to be saved, and hence do not much fear death. Oh! learn hence to suspect and fear your estates, and fear it so much, that thou canst not be quiet until thou hast got *Use 3. Of exhortation to all confident people.* some assurance thou shalt be saved. When Christ told his disciples that one of them should betray him, they all said, "Master, is it I?" but if he had said, eleven of them should betray him, all except one, would they not all conclude, "Surely it is I"? If the Lord had said, only *few* shall be damned, every man might fear, "It may be it is I"; but now he says *most* shall, every man may cry out and say, "Surely it is I." No humble heart, but is driven to and fro with many stinging fears this way; yet there is a generation of presumptuous, brazen-faced, bold people, that confidently think of themselves, as the *Jews* of the *Pharisees* (being so holy and strict) that if God save but two in the world, they shall make one. *Presumptuous men think of themselves as the Jews did of the Pharisees.*

The child of God indeed *is bold as a lion;* but he hath God's spirit and promise, assuring him of his eternal welfare. But I speak of divers that have no sound ground to prove this point (which they pertinaciously defend) that they shall be saved. This confident humor rageth most of all in our old professors at large, who think, that's a jest indeed, that having been of a good belief so long, that they now should be so far behind-hand, as to begin the work, and lay the foundation anew. And not only *Confidence rages most in professors at large.* among these, but amongst divers sorts of people whom the Devil never troubles, because he is sure of them already, and therefore cries peace in their ears, whose *consciences* never trouble them, because *that* hath shut its eyes; and hence they sleep, and sleeping dream, that God is merciful unto them, and will be so; yet never see they are deceived, until they awake with the flames of hell about their ears; and the *world* troubles them not, they have their hearts' desire here, because they are friends to it, and so enemies to God. *The devil never troubles some men, because he is sure of them already.* And *ministers* never trouble them, for they have none such as are fit for that work near them; or if they have, they can sit and sleep in the church, and

---

[7] Bishop of Cyrrhus, 423–449.

choose whether they will believe him. And their friends never trouble them, because they are afraid to displease them. And God himself never troubles them, because that time is to come hereafter. This one truth well pondered and thought on, may damp thine heart and make thy conscience fly in thy face, and say, *Thou art the man;* it may be there are better in hell than thyself that art so

Friends never reprove some men, because of displeasing them.

confident; and therefore tell me what hast thou to say for thyself, that thou shalt be saved? In what thing hast thou gone beyond them that *think they are rich and want nothing, who yet are poor, blind, miserable, and naked?*

Thou wilt say happily, first, I have left my sins I once lived in, and am now no drunkard, no swearer, no liar, etc.   *Obj. 1.*

I answer, thou mayest be washt from thy mire (the pollution of the world) and yet be a swine in God's account, 2 *Pet.* 2.20. thou   *Answ.* mayest live a blameless, innocent, honest, smooth life, and yet be a miserable creature still, *Phil.* 3. 6.

But I pray, and that often.   *Obj. 2.*

This thou mayest do, and yet never be saved, *Isai.* 1. 11. "To what purpose is your multitude of sacrifices?" Nay, thou mayest   *Answ.* pray with much affection, with a good heart, as thou thinkest, yet a thousand miles off from being saved, *Prov.* 1. 28.

But I fast sometimes, as well as pray.   *Obj. 3.*

So did the Scribes and Pharisees, even twice a week, which could not be public, but private fasts. And yet this righteousness   *Answ.* could never save them.

But I hear the word of God, and like the best preachers.   *Obj. 4.*

This thou mayst do too, and yet never be saved. Nay, thou mayst so hear, as to receive much *joy* and comfort in hearing,   *Answ. Ezek. 33. 31, 32.* nay, to believe and catch hold on Christ, and so say and think *He is thine,* and yet not be saved: as the stony ground did, *Matth.* 13. who heard the word with *joy,* and for a *season believed.*

I read the Scriptures often.   *Obj. 5.*

This you may do too, and yet never be saved; as the Pharisees, who were so perfect in reading the Bible, that Christ needed but   *Answ.* only say, "It hath been said of old time," for they knew the text and place well enough without intimation.

But I am grieved and am sorrowful, and repent for my sins past.   *Obj. 6.*

Judas did thus, *Mat.* 27. 3. he repents himself with a legal repentance for fear of hell, and with a natural sorrow for dealing so   *Answ.* unkindly with Christ, in betraying not only blood, but innocent blood. True humiliation is ever accompanied with hearty reformation.

Oh! but I love good men, and their company.   *Obj. 7.*

So did the *five foolish virgins* love the company, and (at the time of *extremity*) the very *oil* and grace of the *wise*, yet they were locked out of the gates of mercy.   *Answ.*

But God hath given me more *knowledge* than others, or than I myself had once.   *Obj. 8.*

This thou mayest have, and be able to teach others, and think so of thyself too, and yet never be saved.   *Answ.*   *Rom. 2. 18.*

But I keep the Lord's day strictly.   *Obj. 9.*

So did the Jews, whom yet Christ condemned, and were never saved.   *Answ.*

I have very many *good desires* and *endeavors* to get heaven.   *Obj. 10.*

These thou and thousands may have, and yet miss of heaven.   *Answ.*

Many still seek to enter in at that narrow gate, and not be able.   *Luke 13. 24.*

True, thou wilt say, many men do many duties, but without any *life* or *zeal:* I am zealous.   *Obj. 11.*

So thou mayest be, and yet never be saved, as *Jehu; Paul* was zealous when he was a Pharisee, and if he was so for a false religion, and a bad cause, why much more mayest thou   *Answ.*   *Phil. 3. 6. 11.* be for a good cause; so zealous as not only to cry out against profaneness in the wicked, but civil honesty of others, and hypocrisy of others, yea, even of the coldness of the best of God's people: thou mayest be the forehorse in the team, and the ringleader of good exercises amongst the best men (as *Joash* a wicked king was the first that complained of the negligence of his best officers in not repairing the Temple) and so stir them up unto it; nay, thou mayest be so forward, as to be persecuted, and not yield an inch, nor shrink in the wetting,   *2 Chron. 24. 4, 5, 6.* but mayest manfully and courageously stand it out in time of persecution, as the *thorny ground* did: so zealous thou mayest be, as to like best of, and to flock most unto the most zealous preachers, that search men's consciences best, as the whole country of *Judea* came flocking to *John's* ministry, and delighted to hear him for a season; nay, thou mayest be [so] zealous as to take sweet delight in doing of all these things, *Isa. 58. 2, 3.* "They delight in approaching near unto God," yet come short of heaven.

But thou wilt say, "True many a man rides post, that breaks his neck at last: many a man is zealous, but his fire is soon   *Obj. 12.* quenched, and his zeal is soon spent; they hold not out; whereas I am constant, and persevere in godly courses."

So did that young man, yet he was a graceless man, *Mat. 19. 20.* "All these things have I done from my youth: what lack I yet?"   *Answ,*

It is true, hypocrites may persevere, but they know them-   *Obj. 13.*
selves *to be naught* all the while, and so deceive others: but I am
persuaded that I am in *God's* favor, and in a safe and happy estate, since I do
all with a good heart for God.

This thou mayest verily think of thyself, and yet be deceived,
and damned, and go to the Devil at last. "There is a way," saith   *Answ.*
Solomon, "that seemeth right to a man, but the end thereof is the way of
death." For he is an hypocrite not only that makes a seeming
outward show of what he hath not, but also that hath a true   *Prov. 14. 12.*
show of what indeed there is not. The first sort of hypocrites
deceive others only; the latter having some inward, yet common work, deceive themselves too, *Jam.* 1. 26. "If any man seem to be religious" (so many
are, and so deceive the world) but it is added, "deceiv-
ing his own soul." Nay, thou mayest go so fairly, and live   *Some hypocrites*
so honestly, that all the best Christians about thee may   *deceive them-*
think well of thee, and never suspect thee, and so may-   *selves, some*
est pass through the world, and die with a deluded com-   *deceive others.*
fort, that thou shalt go to heaven, and be canonized for
a saint in thy funeral sermon, and never know thou art counterfeit, till the
Lord brings thee to thy strict and last examination, and so thou receivest that
dreadful sentence, *Go ye cursed.* So it was with the *five*
foolish virgins that were never discovered by the *wise,*   *Mar. 25.*
nor by themselves, until the gate of grace was shut upon   *The five*
them. If thou hast therefore no better evidences to show   *foolish virgins.*
for thyself, that thine estate is good, than these, I'll not
give a pin's point for all thy flattering false hopes of being saved: but it may
be thou hast never yet come so far as to this pitch; and if not, Lord, what will
become of thee? Suspect thyself much, and when in this shipwreck of souls
thou seest so many thousands sink, cry out, and conclude, It's a wonder of
wonders, and a thousand and a thousand to one, if ever thou comest safe to
shore.

Oh! strive then to be one of them that shall be saved, though
it cost thee thy blood, and the loss of all that thou hast, labor to   *Use 4.*
go beyond all those that go so far, and yet perish at the last. Do   *Strive to*
not say, that seeing so few shall be saved, therefore this discour-   *be saved.*
ageth me from seeking, because all my labor may be in vain. Consider that
Christ here makes another and a better use of it, *Luk.* 3. 24. "Seeing that
many shall seek and not enter, therefore," saith he, "strive to enter in at the
strait gate"; venture at least, and try what the Lord will do for thee.

Wherein doth the child of God (and so how may I) go beyond
these hypocrites that go so far?   *Quest.*

In three things principally.

Answ.

First, no unregenerate man, though he go never so far, let him do never so much, but he lives in some one sin or other, secret or open, little or great. *Judas* went far, but he was covetous. *Herod*[8] went far, but he loved his *Herodias*. Every dog hath his kennel, every swine hath his swill, and every wicked man his lust; for no unregenerate man hath fruition of God to content him, and there is no man's heart but it must have some good to content it, which good is to be found only in the fountain of all good, and that is God; or in the cistern,

Wherein a child of God goeth beyond an hypocrite. 1. No unregenerate man but lives in some known sin.

and that is in the creatures: hence a man having lost full content in God, he seeks for, and feeds upon contentment in the creature which he makes a God to him, and here lies his lust or sin, which he must needs live in. Hence, ask those men that go very far, and take their penny for good silver, and commend themselves for their good desires: I say, ask them, if they have no sin; "Yes," say they, "who can live without sin?" And so they give way to sin, and therefore live in sin; nay, commonly, all the duties, prayers, care, and zeal of the best hypocrites are to hide a lust; as the whore in the *Proverbs*, that wipes her mouth, and goes to the Temple, and pays her vows; or to feed a lust, as *Jehu* his zeal against *Baal*, was to get a kingdom.[9] There remains a root of bitterness in the best hypocrites, which howsoever it be lopped off sometimes by sickness or horror of conscience, and a man hath purposes never to commit again, yet there it secretly lurks; and though it seemeth to be bound and conquered by the *Word*, or by *prayer*, or by outward *crosses*, or while the hand of God is upon

Hypocrites like the whore in the Proverbs, *or like* Jehu, *zealous against* Baal, *but for their own ends.*

a man, yet the inward strength and power of it remains still; and therefore when temptations, like strong *Philistines*, are upon this man again, he breaks all vows, promises, bonds of God, and will save the life of his sin.

Secondly, no unregenerate man or woman ever came to be poor in spirit, and so to be carried out of all duties unto Christ: if it were possible for them to forsake and break loose for ever from all sin, yet here they stick as

2. Unregenerate men are not poor in spirit.

the Scribes and Pharisees, and so like zealous *Paul* before his conversion, they fasted and prayed, and kept the Sabbath, but they rested in their legal righteousness, and in the performance of these and the like duties. Take the

---

[8] King Herod ordered the execution of John the Baptist after the Queen, Herodias, told her daughter (whom Herod had promised anything she wanted) to ask for the head of John. Mark 6:14-28.

[9] See II Kings Chapters 9 and 10. Jehu slew the descendants of King Ahab and obliterated the worship of Baal, but was himself punished for the worship of other idols.

best hypocrite that hath the most strong persuasions of God's love to him, and ask him, why he hopes to be saved. He will answer, "I pray, read, hear, love good men, cry out of the sins of the time." And tell him again, that an hypocrite may climb these stairs and go as far; he will reply, "True indeed, but they do not what they do with a sound heart, but to be seen of men." Mark now, how these men feel a good heart in themselves, and in all things they do, and therefore feel not a want of all good, which is poverty of spirit, and therefore here they fall short. *Isai. 66. 2.* there were divers hypocrites forward for the worship of God in the *God looks* Temple, but God loathes these, because not poor in spirit, to *on the poor* them only it is said the Lord will look. I have seen many *in spirit.* professors very forward for all good duties, but as ignorant of Christ when they are sifted, as blocks. And if a man (as few do) know not Christ, he must rest in his duties, because he knows not Christ, to whom he must go and be carried if ever he be saved. I have heard of a man that being condemned to die, thought to escape the gallows, and to save himself from hanging by a certain gift he said he had of whistling; so men seek to save themselves by their gifts of *knowledge*, gifts of *memory*, gifts of *prayer*, and when they see they must die for their sins, this is the ruin of many a soul, that though he forsake Egypt and his sins, and fleshpots there, and will never be so as he hath been, yet he never cometh into *Canaan*, but loseth himself and his soul in a wilderness of many *duties*, and there perisheth.

Thirdly, if any unregenerate man come unto *Christ*, he never gets into *Christ*, that is, never takes his *eternal* *3. Unregenerate* *rest* and *lodging in Jesus Christ only, Heb. 4. 4. Judas* *men never take* *followed Christ for the bag*, he would have the *bag* and *their rest in* *Christ* too. The young man came unto Christ to be his *Christ only.* disciple, but he would have *Christ* and the *world* too; they will not content themselves with Christ alone, nor with the world alone, but make their markets out of both, like whorish wives, that will please their husbands and others too. Men in distress of conscience, if they have comfort from Christ, they are contented; if they have salvation from hell by Christ, they are contented: but Christ himself contents them not. Thus far an hypocrite goes not. So much for the first doctrine observed out of the text. I come now to the second. *Doct. 2.*

Doct. 2. *That those that are saved, are saved with much* *Salvation* *difficulty: or it is a wonderful hard thing to be saved.* *difficult.*

The gate is strait, and therefore a man must sweat and strive to enter; both the entrance is difficult, and the progress of salvation too. *Jesus Christ* is not got with a wet finger.[10] It is not wishing and desiring to be saved, will bring men to heaven; hell's mouth is full of *good wishes*. It is not shedding a

---

[10] That is, neither by holding up a wet finger to see which way the wind blows, nor by wetting a finger to turn the pages of a book more easily.

tear at a sermon, or blubbering now and then in a corner, and saying over thy prayers, and crying God mercy for thy sins, will save thee. It is not *Lord have mercy upon us*, will do thee good. It is not coming constantly to church; these are easy matters. But it is a tough work, a wonderful hard matter to be saved, 1 *Pet.* 4. 18. Hence the way to heaven is compared to a *race*, where a man must put forth all his strength, and stretch every limb, and all to get forward. Hence a Christian's life is compared to *wrestling, Eph.* 6. 12. All the policy and power of hell buckle together against a Christian, therefore he must look to himself, or else he falls. Hence it is compared to *fighting,* 2 *Tim.* 4. 7. a man must fight against the *Devil,* the *world, himself;* who shoot poisoned bullets in the soul, where a man must kill or be killed. God hath not lined the way to Christ with velvet, nor strewed it with rushes. He will never feed a slothful humor in man, who will be saved *Salvation compared to fighting.* if Christ and heaven would drop into their mouths, and if any would bear their charges thither: If *Christ* might be bought for a few cold wishes, and lazy desires, he would be of small reckoning amongst men, who would say, *lightly come lightly go.* Indeed *Christ's yoke is easy* in itself, and when a man is got into Christ, nothing is so sweet; but for a carnal dull heart, it is hard to draw in it; for,

There are 4 strait gates which everyone must pass through before he can enter into heaven.

Four strait gates to be past through before we can enter into heaven.

1. There is the strait gate of *humiliation:* God saveth none, but first he humbleth them, now it is hard to pass through the gates and flames of hell; for a heart as stiff as a stake, to bow; as hard as a stone, to bleed for the least prick, not to mourn for one sin, but all sins; and not for a fit, but all a man's lifetime; oh it is hard for a man to suffer himself to be loaded with sin, and pressed to *1. The strait gate of humiliation.* death for sin, so as never to love sin more, but to spit in the face of that which he once loved as dearly as his life. It is easy to drop a tear or two, and be sermon-sick; but to have a heart rent *for* sin, and *from* sin, this is true humiliation, and this is hard.

2. The strait gate of *faith, Eph.* 1. 19. It's an easy matter to presume, but hard to believe in Christ. It is easy for a man that was never humbled, to believe and say, " 'Tis *2. Of the strait gate of faith.* but believing": but it is an hard matter for a man humbled, when he sees all his sins in order before him, the *Devil* and *conscience* roaring upon him, and crying out against him, and God frowning upon him, now to call God *Father,* is an hard work. *Judas* had rather be hanged than believe. It is hard to see a Christ as a rock to stand upon, when we are overwhelmed with sorrow of heart for sin. It is hard to prize Christ above ten thousand words of pearl: 'tis hard to desire Christ, and nothing but Christ; hard to follow Christ all the

day long, and never to be quiet till he is got in thine arms, and then with *Simeon* to say, "Lord now lettest thou thy servant depart in peace."

3. The strait gate of *repentance*. It is an easy matter for a man to confess himself to be a sinner, and to cry God forgiveness until next time: but to have a bitter sorrow and to turn from all sin, and to return to God, and all the ways of God; which is true repentance indeed; this is hard.

3. Of the strait gate of repentance.

4. The strait gate of *opposition of devils*, the *world*, and a man's own *self*, who knock a man down when he begins to look towards Christ and heaven.

4. Strait opposition.

Hence learn, that every easy way to heaven is a false way, although ministers should preach it out of their pulpits, and angels should publish it out of heaven.

Use 5. Of instruction.

Now there are nine easy ways to heaven (as men think), all which lead to hell.

1. The common broad way, wherein a whole parish may all go a breadth in it; tell these people they shall be damned; their answer is, then woe to many more besides me.

Nine false ways to salvation discovered.
1. The broad way.

2. The way of *civil education*, whereby many wild natures are by little and little tamed, and like wolves are chained up easily when they are young.

2. The way of civil education.

3. *Balam's*[11] way of *good wishes*, whereby many people will confess their ignorance, forgetfulness, and that they cannot make such shows as others do, but they thank God

3. The way of good wishes.

their hearts are as good, and God for his part accepts (say they) the will for the deed. And, *My son give me thine heart;* the heart is all in all, and so long they hope to do well enough. Poor deluded creatures thus think to break through armies of *sins, devils, temptations,* and to break open the very gates of heaven with a few good wishes; they think to come to their journey's end without legs, because their hearts are good to God.

4. The way of *formality*, whereby men rest in the *performance* of most or of all *external duties* without inward life, *Mark.* 1. 14. Every man must have some *religion*, some

4. The way of formality.

fig-leaves to hide their nakedness. Now this religion must be either true religion, or the false one; if the true, he must either take up the power of it, but that he will not, because it is burdensome; or the *form* of it, and this being easy men embrace it as their God, and will rather lose their lives than their religion thus taken up. This form of religion is the easiest religion in the world; partly, because it easeth men of trouble of conscience, quieting that:

[11] See Numbers, Chapters 22-24.

Thou has sinned, saith conscience, and God is offended, take a book and pray, keep thy conscience better, and bring thy Bible with thee. Now conscience is silent, being charmed down with the form of religion, as the Devil is driven away (as they say) with holy water; partly also because the form of religion credits a man, partly because it is easy in itself; it's of a light carriage, being *The consciences of unregenerate men are often silenced with a form of religion.* but the shadow and picture of the substance of religion; as now, what an easy matter it is to come to church? They hear (at least outwardly) very attentively an hour and more, and then to turn to a proof, and to turn down a leaf, here's the form. But now to spend Saturday night, and all the whole Sabbath day morning, in trimming the lamp, and in getting oil in the heart to meet the Bridegroom the next day, and so meet Him in the Word, and there to tremble at the voice of God, and suck the breast while it is open, and when the word is done, to go aside privately, and there to chew upon the word, there to lament with tears all the vain thoughts in duties, deadness in *hearing,* that is hard, because this is the power of godliness, and this men will not take up: so for private *prayer,* what an easy matter is it for a man to say over a few prayers out of some *devout book,* or to repeat some old prayer got by heart since a child, or to have two or three short-winded wishes for God's mercy in the morning and at night; this form is easy: but now to prepare the heart by serious meditation of God and man's self before he prays, then to come to God with a bleeding hunger-starved heart, not only with a desire, but with a warrant, I must have such or such a mercy, and there to wrestle with God, although it be an hour or two together for a blessing, this is too hard; men think none do thus, and therefore they will not.

Fifthly, the way of *presumption,* whereby men having seen their sins, catch hold easily upon God's mercy, and snatch comforts, before they are reached out unto them. *5. The way of presumption.* There is no word of comfort in the book of God intended for such as *regard iniquity in their hearts,* though they do not act it in their lives. Their only comfort is, that the sentence of damnation is not yet executed upon them.

Sixthly, the way of *sloth,* whereby men lie still, and say God must do all; if the Lord would set up a pulpit at the alehouse door, it may be they would hear oftener. If God will *6. The way of sloth.* always thunder, they will always pray; if strike them now and then with sickness, God shall be paid with good words and promises enow, that they will be better if they live; but as long as peace lasts, they will run to Hell as fast as they can; and if God will not catch them, they care not, they will not return.

Seventhly, the way of *carelesness,* when men feeling many difficulties, pass through some of them, but not all, and what they cannot get *now,* they feed themselves with *7. The way of carelessness.*

a false hope they shall *hereafter:* they are content to be called precisions, and fools, and crazy brains, but they want brokenness of heart, and they will pray (it may be) for it, and pass by that difficulty; but to keep the wound always open, this they will not do, to be always sighing for help, and never to give themselves rest till their hearts are humbled; that they will not; *these have a name to live, yet are dead.*

Eighthly, the way of *moderation* or honest discretion, *Rev.* 3. 16. which indeed is nothing but lukewarmness of the soul, and that is, when a man contrives and cuts out *8. The way of moderation.* such a way to heaven, as he may be hated of none, but please all, and so do anything for a quiet life, and so sleep in a whole skin. The Lord saith, "He that will live godly, must suffer persecution": No, not so, Lord. Surely (think they) if men were discreet and wise, it would prevent a great deal of trouble and opposition in good courses; this man will commend those that are most zealous, if they were but wise; if he meet with a black-mouthed forswearer, he will not reprove him, lest he be displeased with him; if he meet with an honest man, he'll yield to all he saith, that so he may commend him; and when he meets them both together, they shall be both alike welcome (whatever he thinks) to his house and table, because he would fain be at peace with all men.

Ninthly, and lastly, the way of self-love, whereby a man fearing terribly he shall be damned, useth diligently all means whereby he shall be saved. Here is the strongest diffi- *9. The way of self-love.* culty of all, to row against the stream, and to hate a man's self, and then to follow Christ fully.

THOMAS HOOKER

(1586?-1647)

Before he arrived in Hartford as one of the founders of Connecticut, Thomas Hooker had to travel a circuitous and dangerous route. Son of a yeoman farmer in Leicestershire, England, he did his undergraduate

See Cotton Mather, "The Light of the Western Churches, or the Life of Mr. Thomas Hooker," in *Magnalia Christi Americana*, III (1702): 57-68. A new biography by Frank Shuffelton is scheduled for publication in 1977. Charles M. Andrews, *The Beginnings of Connecticut*, 1934, is an excellent background work.

Modern scholarship includes Norman Pettit, *The Heart Prepared: Grace and Conversion in Puritan Spiritual Life*, 1966; Alfred Habegger, "Preparing the Soul for Christ: The Contrasting Sermon Forms of John Cotton and Thomas Hooker," *American Literature*, 41 (1969): 342-354.

The text is from the 1656 edition.

and graduate work at Emmanuel College, Cambridge, where he gained an excellent reputation as a theologian and preacher. He earned extraordinary notice throughout England as a healer of sick souls after he had ministered to a despairing noblewoman whose family had virtually given up hope for her sanity. As a preacher he had great success in what was called "preparation" of the heart, affecting auditors by his sympathy and his example so that they yearned to seek the salvation that could not really be earned but could only be given to them. Hooker's Puritanism kept him from winning formal settlement in a church appropriate to his talents, and the inquisitiveness of Archbishop Laud's men obliged him first to leave the pulpit and become a schoolteacher, then to flee to Amsterdam and Delft, before he followed his congregation to Massachusetts. He barely escaped arrest while preparing for the voyage from England to America in 1633, and even after his arrival in Cambridge (then Newtown) he was not settled. He and many of his congregation moved to Hartford, over the objections of leading Boston ministers and the General Court, in 1636.

In Hartford Hooker became the political as well as the religious patriarch. Even in Massachusetts, where he had already done important service to the government as a critic of Roger Williams and by refuting John Endicott's daring claim that the cross must be cut out of the flag, Hooker retained strong influence. He was called to serve as Moderator at the Synod that resolved the Antinomian controversy in 1637. Again in 1643, he made the first successful effort to establish a confederation of the New England colonies, and at the same time he served with his old rival John Cotton as moderator in a meeting held to resist tendencies away from Congregational polity toward Presbyterianism.

It is as a preacher that Hooker deserves his place in American literature. While insisting that preaching must be reasonable and that auditors must not be seduced with deceptive rhetoric, Hooker believed that the essential target of a sermon was the heart. It wasn't enough, he said, to be up and stirring about in the house in hopes that the sinner would wake up. Instead the minister had an obligation to "pinch the sluggard in his sleep." A true sight of sin, he argued in one of his most frequently reprinted sermons, requires that we see sin not only clearly but "convictingly"; we must know not only the history of sin with our understandings but the nature of sin by recognizing it in our own hearts.

In that doctrine, as in the emphasis on popular consent as the foundation of government, Hooker, though not a democrat, stressed the democratic tendencies in Puritanism and in provincial literary aesthetics. In his preface to the *Survey of the Sum of Church Discipline* he sounded one of the first notes of a theme that has often been echoed in American literary apologetics. This book, he wrote, "comes out of the wilderness" and therefore is written in a "plain style." Hardworking planters have enough to do in trying to keep warm; they must "leave the cuts and lace to those that study to go fine," he says. He will not please "the niceness of men's palates." Those "that covet more sauce than meat must find cooks to their mind."

In the ninth sermon of *The Application of Redemption,* Hooker concentrates on the plain meaning of Biblical words, on plain reasoning about ordinary human psychology, and plain analogies to ordinary planting and engrafting, to explain the doctrine of "preparation" before he applies the lesson to the hearts of his auditors. Follow the proper method, he insists. Move from contrition to humiliation. His technique and his tone here are much more conciliatory than those of Shepard in *The Sincere Convert;* although the doctrine is virtually the same, the emphasis here falls more consistently on hope.

From The Application of Redemption, by the Effectual Work of the Word and Spirit of Christ, for the Bringing Home of Lost Sinners to God

THE NINTH BOOK: [THE HEART MUST BE BROKEN]

ISAIAH, 57.15.

Thus saith he that is the high, and the lofty one that inhabiteth eternity, whose name is holy; I dwell in the high and the holy place, with him also that is of a contrite and humble spirit.

The work of preparation having two parts:

first, The Lord's manner of dispensation: He is pleased to deal with the soul, for the setting up the praise of His rich and glorious grace: and therefore with a holy kind of violence He plucks the sinner from his sins unto Himself, and His Christ. This hath been dispatched already in the former discourse.

The second now follows: and that is the frame and disposition which is wrought in the hearts of such as the Lord hath purposed to save, and to whom He hath dispensed himself in that gracious work of His.

This disposition consists especially in two things:
Contrition, Humiliation.

That so I may follow the phrase of Scripture, and retain the Lord's own words in the text, where the Lord saith, that He dwells with him that is of *an humble and contrite heart.*

To omit all manner of coherence, and other circumstances, we will pass all the other specials in the verse, and point at that particular which will suit our proceeding, and may afford ground to the following discourse, that we may go no further than we see the pillar of fire, the Lord in His truth to go before us. We shall fasten then upon the last words only, as those that fit our intendment.

To make way for ourselves in short, there is one word alone to be opened, that so the point may be better fitted for our Application; we must know what it is *to dwell,* or how *God* is said to *dwell in a contrite and humble heart.*

Answer, To dwell implies three things.

First, that the Lord owns such as those in whom He hath an especial interest, and claims a special propriety, as though He left all the rest of mankind to lie waste as a common, that the world and the Devil, and sin may possess, and use at their pleasure, reserving the honor of His justice, which by a strong hand He will exact as a tribute due to Himself out of all things in heaven and earth, and hell and all; but persons whom He thus fits, He reserves for His own special improvement. As princes and persons of place and quality, do lease out, and let some forests and commons to the inhabitants bordering thereabout, reserving some acknowledgment of fealty and royalty to themselves, but the choice and best palaces or granges of greatest worth, and profit, they reserve for their own peculiar to inhabit in. So here, the Lord leaseth out the world, and the wicked in it to the Devil and his angels, and instruments, reserving royalty and prerogative to Himself, as that He will have His homage and acknowledgment of dependence upon Himself; but His broken-hearted ones are His own for His own improvement, *Deut.* 32.8,9. *When the most High divided to the nations their inheritance and separated the sons of* Adam, *He set the bounds of His people according to the number of the children of Israel, for the Lord's portion is His people Israel, the lot of His inheritance: Ye are the Temple of the living God;* 2 Cor. 6.16. Yea, to them the Lord Himself says, *Ye are my people, and they shall say, Thou art my God,* Zach. 13. last. Therefore He professeth, that though in the course of His Providence He goes on progress over all the world, yet He takes up His dwelling and abode amongst His own people. For,

Secondly, Where a man dwells, as he owns the house, for he takes up his abode there, it is the place of his residence; we say any may know where to seek men, or where to find them, at home, at their own house: That's the difference between inning and dwelling; we inn at a place in our passing by, when we take repast only, and bait,[1] but depart presently, intending not to stay; but where we dwell we settle our abode, we take up our stand there, and stir no further. So the Lord is said then to dwell in the soul, when He vouchsafes the constant expression of His peculiar presence and assistance to the soul. True it is that the Lord fills heaven and earth with His presence, yea, the heaven of heavens is not able to contain Him, *Jer.* 23.24. His infinite Being is everywhere, and one and the same everywhere in regard of Himself; because His being is most simple, and not subject to any shadow of change, being all one with Himself. Yet He is said to take up His abode in a special manner, when He doth put forth the peculiar expression of His Work; as in heaven He dwells, because He puts forth the constant expression of His Glory, and that in the full brightness of it without any alteration and change. Here in this spiritual temple, the souls of His saints, He puts forth the peculiar expression of the constant assistance of His blessed Spirit. *I will pray the Father, and He shall send you another Comforter, who shall abide with you forever,* John 14.16. 1 Joh. 2.23. *Ye have received an anointing which abideth in you.*

Dwelling, if it be attributed to the chiefest inhabitant and owner of the house, it implies also the ruling and ordering of the occasions that come under hand there, the exercising of the government of the house and family where the owner is, and dwells. He that lodgeth at a house as a stranger, comes to an inn as a passenger, he takes what he finds, hath what he can receive of kindness and courtesy; but the owner is the commander of the house where he dwells, and the orderer of all the affairs that appertain thereunto. So doth the Lord with a broken heart. Thus we are said to *live in the Spirit, and to walk in the Spirit,* Gal. 5.25. And it's that which follows by inference upon this ground, *John* 15.4.5. *If I abide in you, and you abide in me, you shall bring forth much fruit;* and therefore it's added also in this place, that the Lord dwells in the contrite and humble heart *to receive the spirit of* the contrite ones, they yield themselves to be acted by Him, and they shall be acted and quickened by Him to eternal life.

3.

So that the full meaning is, The contrite and humble heart is such to whom the Lord vouchsafes acceptance, special presence and abode, and peculiar guidance; He owns him, abides with him, and rules in him for ever.

True, it is said Christ dwells in our hearts by faith, *Eph.* 3.17. and as many as believe in Him, they receive Him, *John* 1.12. That is done as by the next and immediate hand, by which we lay hold on Christ, and give entertainment to Him; but unless the heart be broken and humbled, we cannot receive faith, that we may receive Christ. *And while the soul is thus breaking and humbling, faith also is coming in* a right sense, rightly understood; whereof we shall speak somewhat largely, if the Lord give us leave to come to that place.

---

[1] That is, *eat,* especially during a journey.

The words thus opened, the point is the very letter of the text, which looks full upon every hearer or reader that will look upon the text.

The Heart must be broken and humbled, before the Lord will own it as His, take up His abode with it, and rule in it. Doctrine.

There must be contrition and humiliation before the Lord comes to take possession; the house must be aired and fitted before it comes to be inhabited, swept by brokenness and emptiness of spirit, before the Lord will come to set up His abode in it. This was typified in the passage of the children of Israel towards the promised land; they must come into, and go through a vast and a roaring wilderness, where they must be bruised with many pressures, humbled under many overbearing difficulties, they were to meet withal before they could possess that good land which abounded with all prosperity, flowed with milk and honey. The truth of this type, the prophet Hosea explains and expresseth at large in the Lord's dealing with His people in regard of their spiritual condition, *Hos.* 2.14, 15. *I will lead her into the wilderness,* and break her heart with many bruising miseries, and then I will speak kindly to her heart, and will give her the valley of Acbor for a door of hope; the story you may recall out of *Jos.* 7.28. when Achan had offended in the execrable thing, and the hearts of the Israelites were discomfited and failed, like water spilt upon the ground, because they had caused the Lord to depart away from them, the text says, they having found out the offender by lot, they stoned him, and they said thou hast troubled Israel, we will trouble thee, and they called it the Valley of Achor, and after that God supported their hearts with hope, and encouraged them with success, both in prevailing over their enemies, and in possessing the land. So it shall be spiritually, the valley of consternation, perplexity of spirit, and brokenness of heart, is the very gale and entrance of any sound hope, and assured expectation of good. This I take to be the true meaning and intendment of the place, and part of the description of a good hearer, *Luke* 8.15. "Who with an honest and good heart receives the word, and keeps it, by strong hand, and brings forth fruit with patience"; the fruit is obedience, patience is part of sanctification, and the holy disposition of heart, that must be in the heart, that brings and bears such fruit, that which makes the heart good is faith in vocation, which enables the soul to lay hold upon Christ in the word, and from Him to receive that lively virtue of patience, and readiness to every holy word and work. And *an honest heart is a contrite and humble heart,* so rightly prepared that faith is infused, and the soul thereby carried unto Christ, and quickened with patience to persevere in good duties. As we say of grounds before we cast in seed; there is two things to be attended there, it must be a fit ground, and a fat ground; the ground is fit when the weeds and green sward are plowed up, and the soil there, and made mold: And this is done in contrition and humiliation; then it must be a fat ground, the soil must have heart, we say the

135
THE APPLICATION OF REDEMPTION

ground is plowed well, and lies well, but it's worn out, it's out of heart: Now faith fats the soil, furnisheth the soul with ability to fasten upon Christ, and so to receive the seed of the Word, and the graces of sanctification, and thence it produceth good fruit in obedience: upon this condition God's favor is promised, *Psal.* 34.18. "The Lord is nigh to them that be of a contrite spirit, and saveth them that be of a broken heart." *Isai.* 61.3. "He gives the garment of praise to those that have had the spirit of heaviness"; it will fruit none, fit none, it's prepared for none but such, it's their livery only. Upon this condition it is obtained, *Mat.* 18.3. "Unless ye be converted, and become as little children, ye can in no wise enter into the kingdom of heaven." 2 *Chron.* 33.12. It's said of Manasseh, he humbled himself greatly, and made supplication, and the Lord was intreated of him; such persons and services are highly accepted, *Psal.* 51.17."A broken and contrite heart O God, thou wilt not despise," nay, He will undoubtedly accept of it.

The reasons of the point are taken, partly in regard of the heart, which without these will neither be fitted nor enabled to act upon God in Christ for any good; partly in regard of God, all His ordinances and dispensations will be unprofitable, and unable to do that good which He intends, and we need.

To the first in regard of our hearts; those lets and impediments which put a kind of incapability, yea, and impossibility upon the soul, whereby the coming of faith into the heart, and *Reas[on] 1.* so the entrance and residence of the spirit are hindered, are by this disposition wrought, and removed. These impediments are two:

The first which stops the way and work of faith is, a settled kind of contentedness in [the] corrupt condition, and the blind, yet bold and *1.* presumptuous confidence that a natural man hath, and would maintain of his good condition. Each man sits down willingly, well apaid with his own estate and portion, sees no need of any change, and therefore not willing to hear of it. Each man is so full of self-love that he is loth to pass a sentence against his own soul, to become a judge and self-condemner, and consequently an executioner of all his hopes and comforts at once, and so put his happiness and help out of his own hand. Besides, we are naturally afraid (out of the privy, yet direful guilt of our own consciences) to profess the wretchedness of our own miserable and damnable condition, as to put it upon a peremptory conclusion, and that beyond question, I am undone, I am a damned man, in the gall of bitterness, in the bonds of iniquity, lest they should stir such horrors, which they are neither able to quiet, not yet able to bear. And therefore out of the presumption of their own hearts, they would easily persuade and delude themselves, they have no cause to alter their condition, and therefore they should not endeavor it. Hence the carnal heart is said to bear up himself against all the assaults of the Word, *Deut.* 29.19. *When all the curses of the law were denounced* with never so much evidence, yet the presumptuous sinner *blesseth himself,* promiseth all good to himself, and secretly feeds himself with vain hopes that he shall attain it, therefore he will not stir to seek for a better estate, nor yet receive it if offered, *Job* 22.17. "They say unto the Almighty, depart from us, we desire not the knowledge of his ways": do ministers press them, do others persuade them to a more serious and narrow search, to get more grounded assurance of their estate in grace, they profess they bid them to their loss, they think they need not be better, nor do they desire to be other. It is impossible upon these terms that ever the soul should be carried by faith unto God.

For to be contented and quieted with our condition, as that which best pleaseth, and yet to seek out for another, are things contradictory. And yet this faith doth, for he that is in Christ, is a new creature, behold all things are become new, 2 *Cor.* 5.17. he must have new comforts, new desires, new hopes, therefore the heart must be broken to pieces under the weight of the evil of sin, and the curses due to the old condition, before this will part; for that the word here used with great elegancy and pregnancy implies, viz. by an oppressing weight to be pashed to powder and dust. So the psalmist useth it *Psal.* 90.3. Thou turnest man to powder, to the dust of death: when a man's composition is dissolved, and the body returned again into its first principle; so the word here by way of resemblance, implies that the soul should find his corruption his greatest oppression, so that the composition betwixt sin and his soul should be dissolved and taken down, and the nature of man return to his first principles, and primitive disposition, that he sees an absolute necessity to change, and then he will seek and be willing to receive a change: *The whole need no physician,* and therefore will not seek; *but the sick* that need, will be content to receive; the issue is, if the soul be contented with its sinful condition, and would not have a change, then it cannot be under the power of faith, or receive that which will bring a change; but before the soul be broken under the pressure of sin, it would not have a change, therefore so long it cannot be under the power of faith.

Be it granted that the soul finds sin as a plague, and therefore would be preserved from the evil of it: the second impediment which wholly *2.* keeps out faith is this, when the sinner expects supply and succor from its own sufficiency, either outward excellencies, abilities of nature, or common graces, or the beauty of some performances which issue from any of these. For this is natural to all men ever since innocency, that since the staff was put into his own hand, and then needed not, nay should not deny their own strength, therefore to this day this practice of old *Adam* remaining still in all his posterity, they will scramble for their own comforts and try the utmost of their own strength, to help themselves rather than be beholding to another to help them: hence in cases of conscience and trouble, men are so ready to resolve, so apt and free to promise and profess amendment, what they will do, and others shall see it as well as they resolve it, and so alas it comes to nothing in conclusion, either they fall back unto their base courses, when horror and fear is over, or else wasting away into a wearish formality, and so perish in their hypocrisy. This is an apparent bar to faith, which is the going out of the soul to fetch all life and power from another. Now wholly to be in ourselves, and to stay upon our own ability, and yet to go out of himself to Christ, and receive all from his sufficiency, are things which cannot stand together, *I came not to call the righteous, Mat.* 9.13. *While they sought to establish their own righteousness,* they did not submit to the righteousness of God.

Hence therefore the second work of humiliation is required, whereby God plucks away all his props, and emptieth him wholly of what he hath or seemeth to have. For pride (unto which humiliation is opposite) is but the rankness of praise, and praise is a fruit of a cause by counsel, that hath power to do or not to do this or that, as he sees fit: humiliation is the utter nothingness of the soul, that we have no power, it's not in our choice to dispose of ourselves, nor yet to dispose of that which another gives, nor yet safe to repine at his dispose: in a word, as in a scion before it be engrafted into another flock, it must be cut off from the old, and pared, and then implanted. In contrition we are cut off; in humiliation pared, and so fit to be implanted into Christ by faith.

In regard of God, without this disposition His Word will not, nay cannot take any place in us, or prevail with us for our good: counsels, and commands, and comforts, or whatever dispensations, they fall as water upon a rock, when administered to a hard heart, they enter not, prevail not, profit not at all. As Christ told the Jews, John, 8.37. "My word takes no place in you," and *Zach.* 7.11, 12. "They hardened their hearts as an adamant," etc. *Reas[on] 2.*

A word of terror to dash the hopes, and sink the hearts of all haughty and hard-hearted sinners, God owns not such, will never vouchsafe His gracious presence with them or His blessing upon them for good; be where they will, dwell where they will, the Lord is not with them, nor will dwell in them, by His comforting, quickening, saving presence: hear and fear then all you stout-hearted, stubborn, and rebellious creatures, whose consciences can evidence that the day is yet to dawn, the hour yet to come, that ever you found your sins a pressure to you, they have been your pastime and delight in which you have pleased yourselves, so far from being troubled for your evils that it is your only trouble you may not commit them with content, and without control, you are troubled with admonitions, and counsels, and commands, and threatenings that cross you in your sins. You were never broken-hearted here for your abominations, know assuredly that you will burn for them one day; your proud hearts were never abased, and laid in the dust, the Lord will ruinate both you and them. Never expect a good look from God, set your heart at rest for that, you may draw the eyes of others after you, make many of your deluded followers and favorites to look upon you, but the Lord will not come near, nor once cast a loving look towards you, *Psal.* 138.6. "Though the Lord be high, He hath respect to the lowly, but He knows the proud afar off." Nay, the great God of heaven and *Use, 1.*

earth is up in arms against thee, He is upon the march to work thy destruction, *James*, 4.6. "The Lord resists the proud, but He gives grace to the humble"; all grace is in His gift, and He doles it only to the bruised and abased; but there is no thought nor expectation that thou shalt receive any grace, nay, that grace that thy rebellious and proud heart hath opposed and resisted, will work thy own ruin. Thou art the mark of God's direful indignation and vengeance, He plants all His forces against thee; if all the wisdom in heaven can contrive thy confusion, all the power in heaven work it, all the justice there determine it, it shall be done. God is nigh to them that are of a contrite heart, He saveth such as be of a broken spirit, *Psal.* 34.18, true, and mark it, *of such*, but such thou art not, such thou deridest, scornest, whose hearts fail them under the weight of their abominations, thou lookest at them as mopish, silly, despicable men, well, such you shall see saved forever, when such untamed, presumptuous, proud wretches as thou art shall be turned into hell.

But we do see our sins, and have had many girds and galls of conscience for them.

Obj.[ection]

True, it may be there hath been some blows upon thine heart, conscience it hath smitten thee, the hammer of the

Ans.[wer]

Word, it hath laid some strokes, but it hath not broken thy heart to this day; and that is thus discerned (to go no further now than the very expression of the text).

If thy soul be beaten to powder with this oppression of thy distempers (for so this brokenness of heart was opened before) then as it is with the hardest flints, when they are broken to dust, they are easily yielding, and give way to take the impression of the hand, or whatever is laid upon them: the stone which out of its hardness before, opposed and started aside from the strongest stroke that was laid, now it's turned into dust the least and easiest touch leaves a print and impression upon it; so it is expounded, as appears in this opposition, 2 *Chron.* 30.8. "Be not stiff-necked, but yield yourselves." Observe then, is it so? When the power of the Word comes, the Scriptures are pregnant, arguments undeniable, counsels sweet, reproofs sharp and seasonable, yet thy heart shifts and starts aside, and hits back the authority of the truth, which thou canst not gainsay. The heart may be battered, but it was never broken, it may be overpowered and awed, but it was never humbled to this day. It's that of *Prov.* 3.32. The froward in heart is an abomination to the Lord, but the upright, he that lies level, and bows to the truth, are His delight. A froward man, that is, he that turns off from the authority of the truth: Is this thy temper? thy heart was never broken to dust to this day, but frampful[2] and froward, know thou art an abomination to the Lord. If thou shouldst go to heaven to dwell there, truly God would go out of heaven, He would not dwell with thee.

[2] Greedily self-indulgent, reveling.

Pharaoh is the pattern of all proud hearts, he hardened himself in his wickedness against the word of the Lord. But a broken and humble heart, either lies right, or will come right, it will come to that bent of the rule that is revealed: hard things make that which is most soft to assimilate to them: easy and yielding things assimilate to whatever they close: so water in a round vessel takes that form, in a three square vessel, takes that. So here.

Instruction, to teach us to delight in such, to desire the society of such as are contrite and humble men, to dwell there where God dwells; seem their persons never so mean, their conditions never so *Use, 2.* base, their estates never so low, themselves never so despicable, yet if they be men of broken spirits, God is with them. Go into their societies as men that resolve to go to the Court; for where the King is, the Court is; and where God is, heaven is: the Lord hath two thrones, the one of glory in heaven, where He is all in all to His; another here on earth, an humble heart, where He doth all only of Himself, and for Himself. Therefore as they in *Zachary*, 8. last, "Ten men shall lay hold on the skirt of a Jew, and they shall say, we will go with you, for we have heard God is with you." Much more here, for the Lord is not only with humble hearts, but He dwells in them; we should therefore entertain such servants into our families, such inhabitants into plantations, and such members into congregations, for so you entertain God Himself; resolve as Ruth to Naomi: "Entreat me not to forsake thee, for where thou livest, I will live, thy people shall be my people, thy God my God, where those diest I will die, and there will I be buried, and nothing but death shall part thee and me."[3] Nay, go further, ye blessed spirits (say) death shall not part us, I will be broken-hearted with you, and humble with you, and God shall dwell in us, and we shall dwell with Him in heaven forever. Oh now ye are right, keep here, and be happy here for ever.

Exhortation: to persuade us all, and to prevail with us to take the right way to enjoy God's presence, not only to seek for mercy, *Use, 3.* but seek it in God's order, not only to covet God's presence, but in God's manner; labor to be humble and broken-hearted Christians: then expect we may that the Lord will manifest the presence of His grace and spirit with us, and in us, but not else: every man catcheth at Christ, and mercy, and comfort, but not in a right method, and therefore they lose Him, and their labor also. This is God's order: first be humble and broken, and then He will revive your spirits with His presence, 2 Cor. 6.19. "Come out from among them, and touch no unclean thing; then I will receive you, and be a father to you." In a word, strive to enter in at the strait gate of contrition and humiliation, and then you will hit the right way to Christ and eternal life.

---

[3] Ruth 1:16.

ROGER WILLIAMS

(c. 1603-1683)

Defender of religious liberty, founder of Rhode Island (1644), friend to the American Indian, Roger Williams represents in his publications and in his public actions the conscientious, pious side of Puritanism. His uncompromising search for pure ways of expressing grace in action led him not only to secede from the Anglican Church, in which he had taken holy orders after he had distinguished himself as a scholar in Cambridge, but also to win the unique distinction of banishment from both Plymouth Plantation and Massachusetts Bay. He offended the leaders of Boston in the very first years of colonization by refusing to accept their call to the ministry there. He insisted that they first make a public declaration of repentance for having worshiped with the unregenerate while in England: He "durst not officiate," he said, "to an unseparated people." He supported (some say ordered) Governor Endicott's excision of the cross from the British flag. He insisted that the Indians be paid for every foot of land taken over by the English colonists. He declared that the state had no power to coerce any citizen's conscience in spiritual matters, because spiritual error was a matter to be corrected only by spiritual means, as spiritual allegiance was too sacred to allow contamination from the force of civil authority.

For holding views like these, and especially for preaching them and acting on them, Williams was banished after he had served as Teacher in Salem and then, after an interlude in Plymouth, had returned to Salem. He continued to wage spiritual war with the Boston authorities in pamphlets such as *The Bloody Tenet of Persecution* (1644), and his spiritual quest eventually led him through a brief period of Baptist beliefs to acceptance of perpetual inquiry for new religious truth, when he adopted the religious principles of the Seekers.

Even as we recognize why the civil authorities were provoked to

The modern edition is *The Works of Roger Williams,* ed. Perry Miller, 7 vols., 1963, which is a revision of *The Complete Writings of Roger Williams,* eds. J. H. Trumbull, S. L. Caldwell, J. R. Bartlett, 1866-1874, 1963.

A biography is Ola E. Winslow, *Master Roger Williams,* 1957. Modern criticism includes Perry Miller, *Roger Williams: His Contribution to the American Tradition,* 1953; Edmund S. Morgan, *Roger Williams: The Church and the State,* 1967; Sacvan Bercovitch, "Typology in Puritan New England: The Williams-Cotton Controversy Reassessed," *American Quarterly,* 19 (1967): 166-192; H. Chupack, *Roger Williams,* 1969; J. Garrett, *Roger Williams, Witness Beyond Christendom,* 1971.

banish so intelligent and persistent a gadfly, we should remember that Williams, like the Antinomians who were also banished, expressed an essential quality in Puritanism, a quality that did not disappear from Massachusetts or from American literature when Williams and Ann Hutchinson were separately expelled. Civil authorities often found individual consciences inconvenient and even dangerous, and they and sympathetic religious leaders worked patiently to instruct misguided consciences like Williams's. But despite every safeguard to protect orthodoxy, the aspiring, inquiring mind and the individual conscience were built into the system. Deviant consciences have kept the Puritan heritage alive in our literature ever since the days of Roger Williams.

A Key Into the Language of America sets out to describe some Indian manners and to gain moral instruction from them in the way of meditation and analogy. Williams not only perceives but artfully designs his chapters to exploit a relationship between language and manners, and his simple poems point the way to the didactic use of Indian civility and self-denial in American literature of the eighteenth and nineteenth centuries. Compare Benjamin Franklin's "Remarks Upon the Savages of North America" (below, pp. 498-503). The Bloody Tenet of Persecution is the first in a series of pamphlets in which Williams debated with John Cotton. (Despite his admission of Quakers and Jews to Rhode Island when he later headed the government there, Williams did not avoid public debate with religious dissenters. He challenged George Fox, founder of the Society of Friends, to a debate there and actually did debate with three of Fox's followers.)

From A Key into the Language of America[1]

TO MY DEAR AND WELLBELOVED FRIENDS AND COUNTRYMEN, IN OLD AND NEW ENGLAND.

I present you with a key; I have not heard of the like, yet framed, since it pleased God to bring that mighty continent of America to light: others of my countrymen, have often and excellently, and lately written of the country (and none that I know beyond the goodness and worth of it).

This key, respects the native language of it, and happily may unlock some rarities concerning the natives themselves, not yet discovered.

[1] The text is reprinted from *Collections of the Rhode Island Historical Society*, Providence, 1827, vol. I.

I drew the materials in a rude lump at sea, as a private help to my own memory, that I might not by my present absence lightly lose what I had so dearly bought in some few years' hardship and charges among the barbarians; yet being reminded by some, what pity it were to bury those materials in my grave at land or sea; and withal, remembering how oft I have been importuned by worthy friends of all sorts, to afford them some helps this way.

I resolved (by the assistance of the most High) to cast those materials into this key, pleasant and profitable for all, but specially for my friends residing in those parts:

A little key may open a box, where lies a bunch of keys.

With this I have entered into the secrets of those countries, wherever English dwell about two hundred miles, between the French and Dutch plantations; for want of this, I know what gross mistakes myself and others have run into.

There is a mixture of this language north and south, from the place of my abode, about six hundred miles; yet within the two hundred miles (aforementioned) their dialects do exceedingly differ; yet not so, but (within that compass) a man may by this help, converse with thousands of natives all over the country: and by such converse it may please the Father of Mercies to spread civility (and in His own most holy season) Christianity; for one candle will light ten thousand, and it may please God to bless a little leaven to season the mighty lump of those peoples and territories.

It is expected, that having had so much converse with these natives, I should write some little of them.

Concerning them (a little to gratify expectation) I shall touch upon four heads:

First, by what names they are distinguished.

Secondly, their original and descent.

Thirdly, their religion, manners, customs, etc.

Fourthly, that great point of their conversion.

To the first, their names are of two sorts:

First, those of the English giving: as natives, savages, Indians, wild-men (so the Dutch call them wilden), Abergeny men, pagans, barbarians, heathen.

Secondly, their names, which they give themselves.

I cannot observe, that they ever had (before the coming of the English, French, or Dutch amongst them) any names to difference themselves from strangers, for they knew none; but two sorts of names they had, and have amongst themselves.

First, general, belonging to all natives, as Nínnuock, Ninnimissinûwock, Eniskeetompaûwog, which signifies men, folk, or people.

Secondly, particular names, peculiar to several nations of them amongst themselves, as Nanhigganêuck, Massachusêuck, Cawasumséuck, Cowwe-sêuck, Quintikóock, Quinnipiéuck, Pequttóog, etc.

They have often asked me, why we call them Indians, natives, etc. and understanding the reason, they will call themselves Indians in opposition to English etc.

For the second head proposed, their original and descent.

From Adam and Noah that they spring, it is granted on all hands.

But for their later descent and whence they came into those parts, it seems as hard to find, as to find the wellhead of some fresh stream, which running many miles out of the country to the salt ocean, hath met with many mixing streams by the way. They say themselves, that they have sprung and grown up in that very place, like the very trees of the wilderness.

They say that their great god Cowtantowwit created those parts, as I observed in the chapter of their religion. They have no clothes, books, nor letters, and conceive their fathers never had; and therefore they are easily persuaded that the God that made Englishmen is a greater God, because He hath so richly endowed the English above themselves: but when they hear that about sixteen hundred years ago, England and the inhabitants thereof were like unto themselves, and since have received from God, clothes, books, etc. they are greatly affected with a secret hope concerning themselves.

Wise and judicious men with whom I have discoursed, maintain their original to be northward from Tartaria: and at my now taking ship, at the Dutch plantation, it pleased the Dutch governor (in some discourse with me about the natives) to draw their line from Iceland, because the name Sackmakan (the name for an Indian Prince, about the Dutch) is the name for a prince in Iceland.

Other opinions I could number up: under favor I shall present (not mine opinion, but) my observations to the judgment of the wise.

First, others (and myself) have conceived some of their words to hold affinity with the Hebrew.

Secondly, they constantly anoint their heads as the Jews did.

Thirdly, they give dowries for their wives as the Jews did.

Fourthly (and which I have not so observed amongst other nations as amongst the Jews, and these) they constantly separate their women (during the time of their monthly sickness) in a little house alone by themselves four or five days, and hold it an irreligious thing for either father or husband or any male to come near them.

They have often asked me if it be so with women of other nations, and whether they are so separated: and for their practice they plead nature and tradition. Yet again I have found a greater affinity of their language with the Greek tongue.

2. As the Greeks and other nations, and ourselves call the seven stars (or Charles Wain, the bear), so do they Mosk, or Paukunnawaw the bear.

3. They have many strange relations of one Wétucks, a man that wrought great miracles amongst them, and walking upon the waters, etc. with some kind of broken resemblance to the Son of God.

Lastly, it is famous that the Sowwest (Sowaniu) is the great subject of their discourse. From thence their traditions. There they say (at the southwest) is the court of their great god Cautántowwit: at the southwest are their forefathers' souls: to the southwest they go themselves when they die; from the southwest came their corn, and beans out of their great god Cautántowwit's field: and indeed the further northward and westward from us their corn will not grow, but to the southward better and better. I dare not conjecture in these uncertainties, I believe they are lost, and yet hope (in the Lord's holy season) some of the wildest of them shall be found to share in the blood of the Son of God. To the third head, concerning their religion, customs, manners etc. I shall here say nothing, because in those thirty-two chapters of the whole book, I have briefly touched those of all sorts, from their birth to their burials, and have endeavored (as the nature of the work would give way) to bring some short observations and applications home to Europe from America.

Therefore fourthly, to that great point of their conversion so much to be longed for, and by all New English so much pretended, and I hope in truth.

For myself I have uprightly labored to suit my endeavors to my pretenses: and of later times (out of desire to attain their language) I have run through varieties of intercourses with them day and night, summer and winter, by land and sea, particular passages tending to this, I have related divers, in the chapter of their religion.

Many solemn discourses I have had with all sorts of nations of them, from one end of the country to another (so far as opportunity, and the little language I have could reach).

I know there is no small preparations in the hearts of multitudes of them. I know their many solemn confessions to myself, and one to another of their lost wandering conditions.

I know strong convictions upon the consciences of many of them, and their desires uttered that way.

I know not with how little knowledge and grace of Christ the Lord may save, and therefore neither will despair or report much.

But since it hath pleased some of my worthy countrymen to mention (of late in print) Wequash, the Pequot captain, I shall be bold so far to second their relations, as to relate mine own hopes of him (though I dare not be so confident as others).

Two days before his death, as I past up to Quinnihticut[2] River it pleased my worthy friend Mr. Fenwick whom I visited at his house in Saybrook Fort at the mouth of that river, to tell me that my old friend Wequash lay very

---

[2] Connecticut.

sick: I desired to see him, and himself was pleased to be my guide two mile[s] where Wequash lay.

Amongst other discourse concerning his sickness and death (in which he freely bequeathed his son to Mr. Fenwick) I closed with him concerning his soul: he told me that some two or three year[s] before he had lodged at my house, where I acquainted him with the condition of all mankind, and his own in particular, how God created man and all things: how man fell from God, and of his present enmity against God, and the wrath of God against him until repentance: said he, "Your words were never out of my heart to this present"; and said he, "Me much pray to Jesus Christ." I told him so did many English, French and Dutch, who had never turned to God, nor loved Him: he replied in broken English: "Me so big naughty heart, me heart all one stone!" Savory expressions using to breathe from compunct and broken hearts, and a sense of inward hardness and unbrokenness. I had many discourses with him in his life, but this was the sum of our last parting until our general meeting.

Now because this is the great inquiry of all men: what Indians have been converted? what have the English done in those parts? what hopes of the Indians receiving the knowledge of Christ!

And because to this question some put an edge from the boast of the Jesuits in Canada and Maryland, and especially from the wonderful conversions made by the Spaniards and Portugals in the West Indies, besides what I have here written, as also, besides what I have observed in the chapter of their religion; I shall further present you with a brief additional discourse concerning this great point, being comfortably persuaded that that Father of Spirits, who was graciously pleased to persuade Japhet[3] (the Gentiles) to dwell in the tents of Shem (the Jews) will in His holy season (I hope approaching) persuade these gentiles of America to partake of the mercies of Europe, and then shall be fulfilled what is written by the Prophet Malachi, from the rising of the sun (in Europe) to the going down of the same (in America) my name shall be great among the gentiles.[4] So I desire to hope and pray,

Your unworthy countryman,

Roger Williams.

DIRECTIONS FOR THE USE OF THE LANGUAGE.

1. A dictionary or grammar way I had consideration of, but purposely avoided, as not so accommodate to the benefit of all, as I hope, this form is.

---

[3] The third son of Noah, and believed by some to have been the progenitor of Indo-Europeans. See Genesis 9:18-29.

[4] Malachi 1:11.

2. A dialogue also I had thoughts of, but avoided for brevity's sake, and yet (with no small pains) I have so framed every chapter and the matter of it, as I may call it an implicit dialogue.

3. It is framed chiefly after the Narragansett dialect, because most spoken in the country, and yet (with attending to the variation of peoples and dialects) it will be of great use in all parts of the country.

4. Whatever your occasion be either of travel, discourse, trading etc. turn to the table which will direct you to the proper chapter.

5. Because the life of all language is in the pronunciation, I have been at the pains and charges to cause the accents, tones or sounds to be affixed, (which some understand according to the Greek language, acutes, graves, circumflexes) for example, in the second leaf in the word Ewò He: the sound or tone must not be put on "e," but "wö" where the grave accent is.

In the same leaf, in the word "Ascowequássin," the sound must not be on any of the syllables, but on "quáss," where the acute or sharp sound is.

In the same leaf, in the word "Anspaumpmaûntam," the sound must not be on any other syllable but "maûn" where the circumflex or long sounding accent is.

6. The *English* for every *Indian* word or phrase stands in a straight line directly against the *Indian:* yet sometimes there are two words for the same thing (for their language is exceeding copious, and they have five or six words sometimes for one thing) and then the English stands against them both; for example in the second leaf.

Cowáuncakmish
    and   I pray your favor.
Cuckquénamish,

AN HELP
TO THE NATIVE LANGUAGE
OF THAT PART OF AMERICA CALLED
NEW ENGLAND

CHAPTER I
OF SALUTATION

OBSERVATION

The natives are of two sorts (as the English are) some more rude and clownish, who are not so apt to salute, but upon salutation resalute lovingly. Others, and the general, are sober and grave, and yet cheerful in a mean, and as ready to begin a salutation as to resalute, which yet the English generally begin, out of desire to civilize them.

"What cheer, Nétop," is the general salutation of all English toward them. "Nétop" is friend. "Netompaûog," friends.

They are exceedingly delighted with salutations in their own language.

Neèn, Keèn, Ewò,	I, you, he
Keénkaneen	You and I
Ascowequássin	
Ascowequassunnúmmis,	Good morrow,
Askuttaaquompsín,	How do you?
Asnpaumpmaúntam,	I am very well.
Taubút paump maúntaman,	I am glad you are well.
Cowaúnckamish,	My service to you.

OBSERVATION

This word upon special salutations they use, and upon some offense conceived by the *sachem* or prince against any; I have seen the party reverently do obeisance, by stroking the prince upon both his shoulders, and using this word,

Cowaúnckamish and Cuckquénamish	I pray your favor
Cowaúnkamuck,	He salutes you
Aspaumpmáuntam Sachim,	How doth the prince?
Aspaumpmáuntam commíttamus,	How doth your wife?
Aspaumpmaúntamwock cummuckiaûg?	How doth your children?
Konkeeteâug,	They are well.
Táubot ne paump maunthéttit,	I am glad they are well.
Túnna Cowâum?	Whence came you?
Tuckôteshana,	
Yò nowaum,	I came that way.
Náwwatucknóteshem,	I came from far.
Mattaâsu nóteshem,	I came from hard by.
Wêtu,	An house.
Wetuômuck nóteshem,	I came from the house.
Acâwmuck nóteshem,	I came over the water.
Otàn,	A town.
Otânick nóteshem,	I came from the town.

OBSERVATION

In the Narragansett country (which is the chief people in the land) a man shall come to many towns, some bigger, some lesser, it may be a dozen in twenty miles' travel.

OBSERVATION

"Acawmenóakit," "old England," which is as much as "from the Land on the other side": hardly are they brought to believe that that water is three thousand English mile over or thereabouts.

Tunnock kuttòme,	Whither go you?
Wékick nittóme,	To the house.
Nékick,	To my house.
Kékick,	To your house.
Tuckowêkin,	Where dwell you?
Tuckuttîin,	Where keep you?
Matnowetuómeno,	I have no house.

OBSERVATION

As commonly a single person hath no house, so after the death of a husband or wife, they often break up house, and live here and there a while with friends to allay their excessive sorrows.

Tou wutt in?	Where lives he?
Awânickâchick,	Who are these?
Awaùn ewò?	Who is that?
Túnna úmwock,	
Tunna Wutshaûock,	Whence come they?
Yo nowêkin,	I dwell here.
Yo ntiîn,	I live here.
Eîu or Nnîu?	Is it so?
Nùx,	Yea.
Mat-nippompitámmen,	I have heard nothing.
Wésuonck,	A name.
Tocketussawêitch,	What is your name?
Taantússawese?	Do you ask my name?
Ntússawese,	I am called, etc.
Matnowesuónckane,	I have no name.

OBSERVATION

Obscure and mean persons amongst them have no names: *nullius numeri* etc. as the Lord Jesus foretells His followers that their names should be cast out, Luk. 6.22. as not worthy to be named etc. Again, because they abhor to name the dead (Death being the King of Terrors to all natural men: and though the natives hold the soul to live ever, yet not holding a resurrection they die and mourn without hope). In that respect I say, if any of their sachems or neighbors die who were of their names, they lay down those names as dead.

Nowánnehick nowésuonck—I have forgot my name. Which is common amongst some of them, this being one incivility amongst the more rustical sort, not to call each other by their names, but Keen, You, Ewo, He, etc.

Tahéna,	What is his name?
Tahossowêtam,	What is the name of it?
Tahéttamen,	What call you this?
Teáqua,	What is this?
Yò néepoush,	Stay or stand here
Máttapsh,	Sit down.
Noónshem,	
Non ânum,	I cannot.
Tawhitch Kuppee Yaúmen,	What come you for?
Téaqua Kunnaúnta men,	What do you fetch?
Chenock cuppeeyau mis?	When came you?
Maish-Kitummayi,	Just even now.
Kitummayi nippeéam,	I came just now.
Yò committamus,	Is this your wife?
Yò cuppáppoos,	Is this your child?
Yò cummúckquachucks,	Is this your son?
Yò cuttaunis,	Is this your daughter?
Wunnêtu,	It is a fine child.
Tawhich neepou weéye an,	Why stand you
Pucqúatchick?	without doors?
Tawhítch mat pe titeáyean?	Why come you not in?

OBSERVATION

In this respect they are remarkably free and courteous, to invite all strangers in; and if any come to them upon any occasion, they request them to come in, if they come not in of themselves.

Awássish,	Warm you.
Máttapsh yóteg,	Sit by the fire.
Tocketúnnawem,	What say you?
Keén nétop,	Is it your friend.
Peeyàush nétop,	Come hither friend.
Pétitees,	Come in.
Kunnúnni,	Have you seen me?
Kunnúnnous,	I have seen you.
Taubot mequaun namêan,	I thank you for your kind remembrance.
Taûbotneanawáyean,	I thank you.
Taûbotne aunana mêan,	I thank you for your love.

OBSERVATION

I have acknowledged amongst them an heart sensible of kindnesses and have reaped kindness again from many, seven years after, when I myself had forgotten, etc. Hence the Lord Jesus exhorts His followers to do good for evil; for otherwise sinners will do good for good, kindness for kindness, etc.

Cowàmmaunsh,	I love you.
Cowammaunûck,	He loves you.
Cowámmaus,	You are loving.
Cowáutam,	Understand you.
Nowaûtam,	I understand.
Cowâwtam tawhitche nippeeyaumen,	Do you know why I come?
Cowannántam,	Have you forgotten?
Awanagusàntowosh,	Speak English.
Eenàntowash,	Speak Indian.
Cutehanshish aùmo,	How many were you in company?
Kúnnishishem?	Are you alone.
Nníshishem,	I am alone.
Naneeshuumo,	There be two of us.
Nanshwishâwmen,	We are four.
Npiuckshâwmen,	We are ten.
Neesneechecktashaûmen,	We are twenty, etc.
Nquitpausucko washâwmen,	We are an one hundred.
Comishoonhómmis,	Did you come by boat?
Kuttiakewushaùmis,	Came you by land?
Meshnomishoon hómmin,	I came by boat.
Meshntiauké wushem,	I came by land.
Nippenowàntawem,	I am of another language.
Penowantowawhettûock,	They are of a divers language.
Matnowawtauhettémina,	We understand not each other.
Nummaûchenèm,	I am sick.
Cummaúchenem,	Are you sick?
Tashúckunne cummauchenaûmis,	How long have you been sick?
Nummauchêmin or Ntannetéimmin,	I will be going.
Saùop cummauchêmin,	You shall go tomorrow.
Maúchish or Anakish,	Be going.
Kuttannawshesh,	Depart.
Maùchié or Annittui,	He is gone.

Kautanaûshant,	He being gone.
Mauchéhettit	
or	When they are gone?
Kautanawshàwhettit,	
Kukkowêtous,	I will lodge with you.
Yò Cówish,	Do lodge here.
Hawúnshech,	Farewell.
Chánock wonck cup peeyeàmen,	When will you be here again?
Nétop tattà,	My friend, I cannot tell.

From these courteous salutations, observe in general there is a savor of civility and courtesy even amongst these wild Americans, both amongst themselves and towards strangers.

More particular:

1. The courteous pagan shall condemn
    uncourteous Englishmen,
  Who live like foxes, bears and wolves,
    Or lion in his den.

2. Let none sing blessings to their souls,   5
    For that they courteous are:
  The wild barbarians with no more
    Than nature, go so far;

3. If nature's sons both wild and tame,
    Humane and courteous be: 10
  How ill becomes it sons of God
    To want humanity?

.   .   .

Whosoever cometh in when they are eating, they offer them to eat of that which they have, though but little enough prepared for themselves. If any provision of *fish* or *flesh* come in, they make their neighbors partakers with them.

If any stranger come in, they presently give him to eat of what they have; many a time, and at all times of the night (as I have fallen in travel upon their houses) when nothing hath been ready, have themselves and their wives, risen to prepare me some refreshing.

THE OBSERVATION GENERAL FROM THEIR EATING, ETC.

It is a strange *truth*, that a man shall generally find more free entertainment and refreshing amongst these *barbarians*, than amongst thousands that call themselves Christians.

More particular:

1. Coarse bread and water's most their fare,
   O England's diet fine;
   Thy cup runs o'er with plenteous store
   Of wholesome beer and wine.

2. Sometimes God gives them fish or flesh,   5
   Yet they're content without;
   And what comes in they part to friends
   And strangers round about.

3. God's providence is rich to His,
   Let none distrustful be;   10
   In wilderness, in great distress,
   These ravens have fed me.

CHAPTER III
CONCERNING SLEEP AND LODGING

Nsowwushkâwmen,	I am weary.
Nkàtaquaum,	I am sleepy.
Kukkovetoùs,	Shall I lodge here?
Yo nickowémen?	Shall I sleep here?
Kukkowéti,	Will you sleep here?
Wunnégin, cówish,	Welcome, sleep here.
Nummouaquômen,	I will lodge abroad.
Puckquátchick nickouêmen,	I will sleep without the doors,

Which I have known them contentedly do, by a fire under a tree, when sometimes some *English* have (for want of familiarity and language, with them) been fearful to entertain them. In summertime I have known them lie abroad often themselves, to make room for strangers, *English*, or others.

Mouaquómitea,	Let us lie abroad.
Cowwêtuck,	Let us sleep.
Kukkóuene?	Sleep you?
Cowwêke,	Sleep, sleep.
Cowwêwi,	He is asleep.
Cowwêwock,	They sleep.
Askukkówene?	Sleep you yet?
Takitíppocat,	It is a cold night.
Wekitíppocat,	It is a warm night.
Wauwháutaw ánawat, and Wawhautowâvog,	There is an alarm, or, there is great shouting.

Howling and shouting is their alarm; they having no drums nor trumpets: but whether an enemy approach, or fire break out, this alarm passeth from house to house; yea, commonly, if any *English* or *Dutch* come amongst them, they give notice of strangers by this sign; yet I have known them buy and use a Dutch trumpet, and known a *Native* make a good drum in imitation of the *English*.

Mat annauke, or Mattannoukanash,	A fine sort of mats to sleep on.
Maskituash,	Straw to lie on.
Wuddtúckqunash, ponamáuta,	Let us lay on wood.

This they do plentifully when they lie down to sleep winter and summer, abundance they have and abundance they lay on: their fire is instead of our bedclothes. And so, themselves and any that have occasion to lodge with them, must be content to turn often to the fire if the night be cold, and they who first wake must repair the fire.

Mauataúnamoke,	Mend the fire.
Mauataunamútta,	Let us mend the fire.
Tokêtuck,	Let us wake.
Askuttokémis,	Are you not awake yet?
Tókish, Tókeke,	Wake wake.
Tókinish,	Wake him.
Kitumyái tokéan,	As soon as I wake.
Ntunnaquômen,	I have had a good dream.
Nummattaquômen,	I have had a bad dream.

When they have had a bad dream, which they conceive to be a threatening from God, they fall to prayer at all times of the night, especially early before day: so *David's* zealous heart to the true and living God: *"At midnight will I rise,"* etc. *"I prevented the dawning of the day,"* etc. Psal. 119, etc.

Wunnakukkussaquaùm,	You sleep much.
Peeyauntam,	He prays.
Peeyâuntamwock,	They pray.
Túnna kukkowémis,	Where slept you?
Awaun wéick kukkouémis,	At whose house did you sleep?

I once traveled to an island of the wildest in our parts, where in the night an Indian (as he said) had a vision or dream of the sun (whom they worship for a god) darting a beam into his breast which he conceived to be the messenger of his death: this poor native called his friends and neighbors, and prepared some little refreshing for them, but himself was kept waking and fasting in great humiliations and invocations for ten days and nights: I was alone (having traveled from my bark, the wind being contrary) and little could I speak to them to their understandings especially because of the change of their dialect or manner of speech from our neighbors: yet so much (through the help of God) I did speak, of the *true* and *living only wise God*, of the creation: of man, and his *fall* from God, etc. that at parting many burst forth, "Oh when will you come again, to bring us some more news of this God?"

THEIR SLEEPING: THE OBSERVATION GENERAL

Sweet rest is not confined to soft beds, for, not only God gives His beloved sleep on hard lodgings: but also nature and custom gives sound sleep to these Americans on the earth, on a board or mat. Yet how is *Europe* bound to God for better lodging, etc.

More particular:

1. God gives them sleep on ground, on straw,
        on sedgy mats or board:
    When English softest beds of down,
        sometimes no sleep afford.

2. I have known them leave their house and mat,   5
        to lodge a friend or stranger,
    When Jews and Christians oft have sent
        Christ Jesus to the manger.

3. 'Fore day they invocate their gods,
        Though many false and new: 10
    O how should that God worshipt be,
        who is but one and true?

from CHAPTER VII: OF THEIR PERSONS AND PARTS OF BODY

.   .   .

THE GENERAL OBSERVATION FROM THE PARTS OF THE BODY

Nature knows no difference between Europe and Americans in blood, birth, bodies, etc. God having of one blood made all mankind, Acts 17, and all by nature being children of wrath, Ephes, 2.

More particularly:

Boast not proud English, of thy birth and blood
Thy brother Indian is by birth as good.
Of one blood God made him, and thee, and all.
As wise, as fair, as strong, as personal.
By nature, wrath's his portion, thine, no more   5
Till grace his soul and thine in Christ restore.
Make sure thy second birth, else thou shalt see
Heaven ope to Indians wild, but shut to thee.

From The Bloody Tenet of Persecution, for Cause of Conscience, in a Conference between Truth and Peace[1]

To every courteous reader.

While I plead the cause of *truth* and *innocency* against the bloody *doctrine* of *persecution* for cause of *conscience*, I judge it not unfit to give *alarm* to myself, and all men to prepare to be *persecuted* or hunted for cause of *conscience*.

Whether thou standest charged with ten or but two *talents*, if thou huntest any for cause of *conscience*, how canst thou say thou followest the *Lamb* of *God* who so abhorred that practice?

If *Paul*, if *Jesus Christ* were present here at *London*, and the *question* were proposed what *religion* would they approve of: the *Papists*, *Prelatists*, *Presbyterians*, *Independents*, etc. would each say, "Of mine, of mine."

But put the second question, if one of the several sorts should by *major vote* attain the *sword* of steel: what weapons doth Christ Jesus authorize them to fight with in His cause? Do not all men hate the *persecutor*, and every *conscience* true or false complain of cruelty, tyranny? etc.

Two *mountains* of crying *guilt* lie heavy upon the backs of all that name the name of *Christ* in the eyes of *Jews*, *Turks* and *Pagans*.

First, the blasphemies of their *idolatrous inventions*, *superstitions*, and most *unchristian conversations*.

Secondly, the bloody, irreligious and inhumane *oppressions* and *destructions* under the mask or veil of the name of *Christ*, etc.

O how like is the *jealous Jehovah*, the consuming fire to end these present *slaughters* in a greater slaughter of the holy witnesses? *Rev.* 11.

Six years preaching of so much truth of *Christ* (as that time afforded in K. *Edward's* days) kindles the flames of Q. Mary's bloody *persecutions*.

Who can now but expect that after so many scores of years *preaching* and *professing* of more *truth*, and amongst so many great *contentions* amongst the very best of *Protestants*, a fiery furnace should be heat, and who sees not now the *fires* kindling?[2]

---

[1] Reprinted from the Narragansett Club Publications edition, ed. Samuel Caldwell, III (Providence, 1867). Williams and John Cotton debated liberty of conscience in a number of tracts published between 1643, with the Puritans in control of Parliament, and 1652. *The Bloody Tenet*, published anonymously, was burned by order of Parliament because of some implicitly democratic political ideas.

[2] Edward VI, 1547-1553, and Queen Mary, 1553-1558. In Mary's time many Protestants were burned at the stake.

I confess I have little hopes till those flames are over, that this discourse against the *doctrine* of *persecution* for cause of *conscience* should pass current (I say not amongst the *wolves* and *lions,* but even amongst the *sheep* of *Christ* themselves) yet *liberavi animam meam,*[3] I have not hid within my *breast* my *souls* belief: and although sleeping on the bed either of the pleasures or profits of sin thou thinkest thy conscience bound to smite at him that dares to waken thee? Yet in the midst of all these *civil* and *spiritual wars* I hope we shall agree in these particulars.

First, however the proud (upon the advantage of an higher earth or ground) overlook the poor and cry out *schismatics, heretics, etc.* shall *blasphemers* and *seducers* escape unpunished etc. Yet there is a sorer punishment in the *gospel* for despising of *Christ* than *Moses,* even when the despiser of *Moses* was put to death without mercy, *Heb.* 10. 28, 29. "He that believeth not shall be damned," *Mark* 16. 16.

Secondly, whatever worship, ministry, ministration, the best and purest are practiced without *faith* and true persuasion that they are the true institutions of God, they are sin, sinful worships, ministries, etc. And however in civil things we may be servants unto men, yet in divine and spiritual things the poorest *peasant* must disdain the service of the highest *prince:* "Be ye not the servants of men," I Cor. 14.

Thirdly, without search and trial no man attains this faith and right persuasion, I *Thes.* 5. "Try all things."

In vain have *English-Parliaments* permitted *English Bibles* in the poorest *English* houses, and the simplest man or woman to search the Scriptures, if yet against their soul's persuasion from the Scripture, they should be forced (as if they lived in *Spain* or *Rome* itself without the sight of a *Bible*) to believe as the Church believes.

Fourthly, having tried, we must hold fast, I *Thessal.* 5. upon the loss of a crown, *Revel.* 13. we must not let go for all the flea bitings of the present afflictions, etc. having bought truth dear, we must not sell it cheap, not the least grain of it for the whole world, no not for the saving of souls, though our own most precious; least of all for the bitter sweetening of a little vanishing pleasure.

For a little puff of credit and reputation from the changeable breath of uncertain sons of men.

For the broken bags of riches on eagles' wings: For a dream of these, any or all of these which on our deathbed vanish and leave tormenting stings behind them: oh, how much better is it from the love of truth, from the love of the Father of lights, from whence it comes, from the love of the Son of God, who is the way and the truth, to say as He, *John* 18. 37. "For this end was I born, and for this end came I into the world that I might bear witness to the truth."

[3] I have freed my soul.

ANNE BRADSTREET

(1612-1672)

In some of her poems and in her brief spiritual autobiography, Anne Bradstreet achieves the most moving literary statement of what it meant to be a woman and a Puritan in seventeenth-century New England. She had been brought up in the comfortable English household of her father, Thomas Dudley, steward to an eminent English Puritan family, and when she was only sixteen, she was married to Simon Bradstreet, steward to a similar family. When her husband and her father decided to emigrate to Massachusetts Bay in 1630, she involuntarily became, at 18, one of the founders of the colony—although, as she later confessed in her autobiography, both the idea and the actual experience appalled her. Even in America, as Ann Stanford has pointed out, the best available society would not long be accessible to the young woman if her husband's plans dictated another move. Having settled in the small but lively intellectual community of Ipswich, where she had access to several literary minds (including that of Nathanael Ward, author of "The Simple Cobler of Agawam"), she was distressed by her husband's decision that the family must soon move to Andover. As her husband grew to an eminence that eventually won him the governorship of the colony, Anne Bradstreet bore eight children, ran the large household, and in isolation though not in solitude wrote her prose meditations and her poems.

In 1650 a volume of Bradstreet's poems was published without her supervision and apparently without her consent, under the title *The Tenth Muse Lately Sprung up in America*. Embarrassed by the printer's

The standard text is *The Works of Anne Bradstreet*, ed. J. H. Ellis, 1867. *The Works of Anne Bradstreet* was edited by Jeannine Hensley, 1967 (with modern spelling and punctuation). Ann Stanford, *Anne Bradstreet: The Worldly Puritan*, 1974 is the best recent critical and biographical book on the poet.

John Berryman's fine poem, *Homage to Mistress Bradstreet*, 1956, deserves a sympathetic reading. Recent studies include Austin Warren, *Rage for Order*, 1948: J. J.

Pierry, *Anne Bradstreet*, 1965: Hyatt H. Waggoner, *American Poetry from the Puritans to the Present*, 1968; Alvin H. Rosenfeld, "Anne Bradstreet's 'Contemplations'; Patterns in Form and Meaning," *New England Quarterly*, 43 (1970): 79-96; Elizabeth Wade White, *Anne Bradstreet, The Tenth Muse*, 1971.

The text is taken from the J. H. Ellis edition, but the spelling has been modernized.

errors, she planned a revised edition, but none was published until after her death.

Scholars have traditionally followed Anne Bradstreet's own acknowledgment and pointed out her indebtedness to Joshua Sylvester's translation of the French Calvinist poet Du Bartas, but Ann Stanford and others have recently stressed her emulation of Sir Philip Sidney and Edmund Spenser, and her explicit declaration of independence from Du Bartas' example. She began to learn her craft in Ipswich in the 1630's, dedicating some of her early poems to Sidney, Du Bartas, and Queen Elizabeth. She also wrote in the 1630's and 1640's a series of "quaternions" on "The Four Seasons," the "Four Ages of Man," the "Four Elements," and the "Four Humors," and during the Civil War in England some commentaries in verse on current political and religious issues. Those public poems make up much of *The Tenth Muse*, but her best achievements are in *Contemplations* and in the sometimes awkward but often moving "domestic" poems, not originally printed in *The Tenth Muse*. Her poems addressed to her husband, whether absent on public employment or present before the birth of a child, and the prose letter to her children that constitutes her spiritual autobiography give us powerful statements of a dramatic tension between faith and doubt, between resignation to the social or divine realities and assertion of one's own wishes.

That tension represents the central experience of many Puritans besides Anne Bradstreet. She is not embarrassed to tell her children that she has been tempted by atheism or that she was disappointed to learn after her conversion how infrequently a member of the elect felt the full joy of the Lord's presence. But she has "known the hidden manna that the world knows not," she says, and in memory of such tastes, such sweetness, she will yet stand firm against the Devil. She is not embarrassed to express her sexual love for her husband, the sun through whose heat she bore their children, but she cautions him to persevere in their mutual love (as the true saints were believed to persevere) in a way that always subordinates human to divine love:

> Then while we live, in love let's so persever
> That when we live no more, we may live ever.

It is the self-assertion of the human being's natural will that has attracted many twentieth-century readers, including the poet John Berryman, to Anne Bradstreet's poetry. In some of those poems (on the burning of her house, or before the birth of one of her children, or on the death of her grandchild), the declaration of grief or worldly affection comes through much more strongly than the prescribed resignation to the will of God. Some readers therefore find the "true" meaning of Bradstreet's poetry in the welling up of personal feeling for husband, for child and grandchild, for furniture and keepsakes destroyed in a fire, and for the need to protect a child from "stepdame's injury." Students may come closer to a full apprehension of Bradstreet's representativeness, both as a seventeenth-century woman and as a Puritan, if they remember the toughness of the Puritan creed. A naive young woman might expect before her conversion that regenerate Christians live in constant joy, but such expositors of the creed as Thomas Shepard warned that "Jesus Christ is not got with a wet finger," by turning the pages of a book or putting up that wet finger to see which way the wind blows. The way to Christ, Shepard warns, is not lined with velvet; it is a wonderfully tough work to arrive at the saving way. Jonathan Mitchel could declare bitterly upon the death of his child that the Lord "spits in my face," but the answer to such resentful feelings, however conventional it may seem to us, was as much a part of the typical experience as the resentment itself, and the answer, for Bradstreet as for the others cited here, took account of the rebellious, self-asserting questioning. The center of Bradstreet's poetic sensibility is in the intelligence that remembers it has known the hidden manna that the world knows not, even as worldly affection rises to overwhelm that memory.

Epitaph for her Father, Thomas Dudley (1653)

Within this tomb a patriot lies
That was both pious, just and wise,
To truth a shield, to right a wall,
To sectaries a whip and maul,
A magazine of history,
A prizer of good company,
In manners pleasant and severe
The good him loved, the bad did fear,
And when his time with years was spent
If some rejoiced, more did lament.

An Epitaph on My Dear and Ever-Honored Mother Mrs. Dorothy Dudley, Who Deceased December 27. 1643, and of Her Age, 61

Here lies,
A worthy matron of unspotted life,
A loving mother and obedient wife,
A friendly neighbor, pitiful to poor,
Whom oft she fed, and clothed with her store;   5
To servants wisely awful, but yet kind,
And as they did, so they reward did find;
A true instructor of her family,
The which she ordered with dexterity.
The public meetings ever did frequent,   10
And in her closet constant hours she spent;
Religious in all her words and ways,
Preparing still for death, till end of days:
Of all her children, children, lived to see,
Then dying, left a blessed memory.   15

Contemplations

Some time now past in the autumnal tide,
When Phoebus[1] wanted but one hour to bed,
The trees all richly clad, yet void of pride,
Where gilded o'er by his rich golden head.
Their leaves and fruits seemed painted, but was true   5
Of green, of red, of yellow, mixed hue,
Rapt were my senses at this delectable view.

2
I wist not what to wish, yet sure thought I,
If so much excellence abide below;
How excellent is He that dwells on high?   10
Whose power and beauty by His works we know.
Sure He is goodness, wisdom, glory, light,
That hath this under world so richly dight:
More heaven than earth was here, no winter and no night.

[1] The sun.

3

Then on a stately oak I cast mine eye,   15
Whose ruffling top the clouds seemed to aspire;
How long since thou wast in thine infancy?
Thy strength, and stature, more thy years admire,
Hath hundred winters past since thou wast born?
Or thousand since thou brakest thy shell of horn   20
If so, all these as nought, eternity doth scorn.

4

Then higher on the glistering Sun I gaz'd,
Whose beams was shaded by the leavie tree,
The more I look'd, the more I grew amazed,
And softly said, What glory's like to thee?   25
Soul of this world, this universe's eye,
No wonder, some made thee a deity:
Had I not better known (alas), the same had I.

5

Thou as a bridegroom from thy chamber rushes,[2]
And as a strong man, joys to run a race,   30
The morn doth usher thee, with smiles and blushes,
The Earth reflects her glances in thy face.
Birds, insects, animals with vegative,
Thy heat from death and dullness doth revive:
And in the darksome womb of fruitful nature dive.   35

6

Thy swift annual, and diurnal course,
Thy daily straight, and yearly oblique path,
Thy pleasing fervor, and thy scorching force,
All mortals here the feeling knowledge hath
Thy presence makes it day, thy absence night,   40
Quaternal seasons caused by thy might:
Hail creature, full of sweetness, beauty and delight.

7

Art thou so full of glory, that no eye
Hath strength, thy shining rays once to behold?
And is thy splendid throne erect so high?   45
As to approach it, can no earthly mould.
How full of glory then must thy Creator be?
Who gave this bright light luster unto thee:
Admired, adored for ever, be that Majesty.

[2] See Psalms 19:4-5.

8

Silent alone, where none or saw, or heard,   50
In pathless paths I led my wand'ring feet,
My humble eyes to lofty skies I reared
To sing some song, my mazed Muse thought meet.
My great Creator I would magnify,
That nature had thus decked liberally: 55
But Ah, and Ah, again, my imbecility!

9

I heard the merry grasshopper then sing,
The black-clad cricket bear a second part,
They kept one tune, and played on the same string,
Seeming to glory in their little art.   60
Shall creatures abject, thus their voices raise?
And in their kind resound their Maker's praise:
Whilst I as mute, can warble forth no higher lays[?]

10

When present times look back to ages past,
And men in being fancy those are dead,   65
It makes things gone perpetually to last,
And calls back months and years that long since fled.
It makes a man more aged in conceit
Than was Methuselah, or's grandsire great:[3]
While of their persons and their acts his mind doth treat.   70

11

Sometimes in Eden fair, he seems to be,
Sees glorious Adam there made lord of all,
Fancies the apple, dangle on the tree,
That turned his sovereign to a naked thrall.
Who like a miscreant's driven from that place,   75
To get his bread with pain, and sweat of face,
A penalty imposed on his backsliding race.

12

Here sits our grandame in retired place,
And in her lap, her bloody Cain new-born,
The weeping imp oft looks her in the face,   80
Bewails his unknown hap, and fate forlorn;
His mother sighs, to think of Paradise,
And how she lost her bliss, to be more wise,
Believing him that was, and is, father of lies.

[3] See Genesis 5:18-27.

13

Here Cain and Abel come to sacrifice, [4]   85
Fruits of the earth, and fatlings each do bring,
On Abel's gift the fire descends from skies,
But no such sign on false Cain's offering;
With sullen hateful looks he goes his ways.
Hath thousand thoughts to end his brother's days,   90
Upon whose blood his future good he hopes to raise.

14

There Abel keeps his sheep, no ill he thinks,
His brother comes, then acts his fratricide,
The virgin Earth of blood her first draught drinks
But since that time she often hath been cloyed;   95
The wretch with ghastly face and dreadful mind,
Thinks each he sees will serve him in his kind,
Though none on earth but kindred near then could he
    find.

15

Who fancies not his looks now at the bar,
His face like death, his heart with horror fraught,   100
Nor malefactor ever felt like war,
When deep despair, with wish of life hath fought,
Branded with guilt, and crushed with treble woes,
A vagabond to Land of Nod he goes.
A city builds, that walls might him secure from foes.   105

16

Who thinks not oft upon the father's ages.
Their long descent how nephews' sons they saw,
The starry observations of those sages,
And how their precepts to their sons were law,
How Adam sighed to see his progeny,   110
Clothed all in his black sinful livery,
Who neither guilt, nor yet the punishment could fly.

17

Our life compare we with their length of days
Who to the tenth of theirs doth now arrive?
And though thus short, we shorten many ways,   115
Living so little while we are alive;
In eating, drinking, sleeping, vain delight
So unawares comes on perpetual night,
And puts all pleasures vain unto eternal flight.

[4] See Genesis 4.

18

When I behold the heavens as in their prime,   120
And then the earth (though old) still clad in green,
The stones and trees, insensible of time,
Nor age nor wrinkle on their front are seen;
If winter come and greenness then do fade,
A spring returns, and they more youthful made;   125
But man grows old, lies down, remains where once he's
    laid.

19

By birth more noble than those creatures all,
Yet seems by nature and by custom cursed,
No sooner born, but grief and care makes fall
That state obliterate he had at first: 130
Nor youth, nor strength, nor wisdom spring again
Nor habitations long their names retain,
But in oblivion to the final day remain.

20

Shall I then praise the heavens, the trees, the earth
Because their beauty and their strength last longer?   135
Shall I wish there, or never to had birth,
Because they're bigger, and their bodies stronger?
Nay, they shall darken, perish, fade and die,
And when unmade, so ever shall they lie,
But man was made for endless immortality.   140

21

Under the cooling shadow of a stately elm
Close sat I by a goodly river's side,
Where gliding streams the rocks did overwhelm;
A lonely place, with pleasures dignified.
I once that loved the shady woods so well,   145
Now thought the rivers did the trees excel,
And if the sun would ever shine, there would I dwell.

22

While on the stealing stream I fixt mine eye,
Which to the longed-for ocean held its course,
I marked, nor crooks, nor rubs that there did lie   150
Could hinder ought, but still augment its force.
O happy flood, quoth I, that holds thy race
Till thou arrive at thy beloved place,
Nor is it rocks or shoals that can obstruct thy pace

23

Nor is't enough, that thou alone may'st slide,   155
But hundred brooks in thy clear waves do meet,
So hand in hand along with thee they glide
To Thetis'[5] house, where all embrace and greet:
Thou emblem true of what I count the best,
O could I lead my rivulets to rest,   160
So may we press to that vast mansion, ever blest.

24

Ye fish, which in this liquid region 'bide,
That for each season, have your habitation,
Now salt, now fresh where you think best to glide
To unknown coasts to give a visitation,   165
In lakes and ponds you leave your numerous fry,
So nature taught and yet you know not why?
You wat'ry folk that know not your felicity.

25

Look how the wantons frisk to taste the air,
Then to the colder bottom straight they dive,   170
Eftsoon to Neptune's glassy hall repair
To see what trade they great ones there do drive,
Who forage o'er the spacious sea-green field,
And take the trembling prey before it yield,
Whose armor is their scales, their spreading fins their   175
    shield.

26

While musing thus with contemplation fed,
And thousand fancies buzzing in my brain,
The sweet-tongued philomel perched o'er my head,
And chanted forth a most melodious strain
Which rapt me so with wonder and delight,   180
I judged my hearing better than my sight,
And wished me wings with her a while to take my flight.

27

O merry Bird (said I) that fears no snares,
That neither toils nor hoards up in thy barn,
Feels no sad thoughts nor cruciating cares   185
To gain more good, or shun what might thee harm
Thy clothes ne'er wear, thy meat is everywhere,
Thy bed a bough thy drink the water clear,
Reminds not what is past, nor what's to come dost fear.

[5] That is, to the sea, where Thetis, one of the
Nereids and mother of Achilles, lived.

28

The dawning morn with songs thou dost prevent,   190
Sets hundred notes unto thy feathered crew,
So each one tunes his pretty instrument,
And warbling out the old, begin anew,
And thus they pass their youth in summer season,
Then follow thee into a better region,   195
Where winter's never felt by that sweet airy legion.

29

Man at the best a creature frail and vain,
In knowledge ignorant, in strength but weak,
Subject to sorrows, losses, sickness, pain,
Each storm his state, his mind, his body break,   200
From some of these he never finds cessation,
But day or night, within, without, vexation,
Troubles from foes, from friends, from dearest, near'st
    relation.

30

And yet this sinful creature, frail and vain,
This lump of wretchedness, of sin and sorrow,   205
This weather-beaten vessel wracked with pain,
Joys not in hope of an eternal morrow;
Nor all his losses, crosses and vexation,
In weight, in frequency and long duration
Can make him deeply groan for that divine translation: 210

31

The mariner that on smooth waves doth glide,
Sings merrily, and steers his bark with ease,
As if he had command of wind and tide,
And now become great master of the seas;
But suddenly a storm spoils all the sport,   215
And makes him long for a more quiet port,
Which 'gainst all adverse winds may serve for fort.

32

So he that saileth in this world of pleasure,
Feeding on sweets, that never bit of th' sour,
That's full of friends, of honor and of treasure,   220
Fond fool, he takes this earth ev'n for heav'n's bower.
But sad affliction comes and makes him see
Here's neither honor, wealth, nor safety;
Only above is found all with security.

33

O Time the fatal wrack of mortal things,   225
That draws oblivion's curtains over kings,
Their sumptuous monuments, men know them not,
Their names without a record are forgot,
Their parts, their ports, their pomp's all laid in th' dust
Nor wit nor gold, nor buildings scape times rust;   230
But he whose name is graved in the white stone[6]
Shall last and shine when all of these are gone.

Before the Birth of One
of Her Children

All things within this fading world hath end,
Adversity doth still our joys attend;
No ties so strong, no friends so dear and sweet,
But with death's parting blow is sure to meet.
The sentence past is most irrevocable,   5
A common thing, yet oh inevitable;
How soon, my Dear, death may my steps attend,
How soon't may be thy lot to lose thy friend,
We both are ignorant, yet love bids me
These farewell lines to recommend to thee,   10
That when that knot's untied that made us one,
I may seem thine, who in effect am none.
And if I see not half my days that's due,
What nature would, God grant to yours and you;
The many faults that well you know I have,   15
Let be interred in my oblivious grave;
If any worth or virtue were in me,
Let that live freshly in thy memory
And when thou feel'st no grief, as I no harms,
Yet love thy dead, who long lay in thine arms: 20
And when thy loss shall be repaid with gains
Look to my little babes my dear remains.
And if thou love thyself, or loved'st me
These O protect from step-dame's injury.
And if chance to thine eyes shall bring this verse,   25
With some sad sighs honor my absent hearse;
And kiss this paper for thy love's dear sake,
Who with salt tears this last farewell did take.

[6] See Revelation 2:17.

To My Dear and Loving Husband

If ever two were one, then surely we.
If ever man were loved by wife, then thee;
If ever wife was happy in a man,
Compare with me ye women if you can.
I prize thy love more than whole mines of gold,   5
Or all the riches that the East doth hold.
My love is such that rivers cannot quench,
Nor ought but love from thee, give recompense.
Thy love is such I can no way repay,
The heavens reward thee manifold, I pray.   10
Then while we live, in love let's so persever,
That when we live no more, we may live ever.

A Letter to Her Husband, Absent upon Public Employment

My head, my heart, mine eyes, my life, nay more,
My joy, my magazine of earthly store,
If two be one, as surely thou and I,
How stayest thou there, whilst I at Ipswich lie?
So many steps, head from the heart to sever   5
If but a neck, soon should we be together:
I like the Earth this season, mourn in black,
My Sun is gone so far in's zodiac,[1]
Whom whilst I'joyed, nor storms, nor frosts I felt,
His warmth such frigid colds did cause to melt.   10
My chilled limbs now numbed lie forlorn;
Return, return sweet Sol from Capricorn,
In this dead time, alas, what can I more
Than view those fruits which through thy heat I bore?
Which sweet contentment yield me for a space,   15
True living pictures of their father's face.
O strange effect! now thou art southward gone,
I weary grow, the tedious day so long;
But when thou northward to me shalt return,

---

[1] Her husband, here characterized as the sun, has gone (figuratively) to Capricorn, a sign of the zodiac representing winter, and she asks him to return to the sign of Cancer, the summer of her own warm heart, or breast.

I wish my Sun may never set, but burn   20
Within the Cancer of my glowing breast,
The welcome house of him my dearest guest.
Where ever, ever stay, and go not thence,
Till nature's sad decree shall call thee hence;
Flesh of thy flesh, bone of thy bone,   25
I here, thou there, yet both but one.

In Memory of My Dear Grandchild Elizabeth Bradstreet, Who Deceased August, 1665, Being a Year and Half Old

Farewell dear babe, my heart's too much content,
Farewell sweet babe, the pleasure of mine eye,
Farewell fair flower that for a space was lent,
Then ta'en away unto eternity.
Blest babe why should I once bewail thy fate,   5
Or sigh thy days so soon were terminate;
Sith thou art settled in an everlasting state.

2

By nature trees do rot when they are grown,
And plums and apples thoroughly ripe do fall,
And corn and grass are in their season mown,   10
And time brings down what is both strong and tall.
But plants new set to be eradicate,
And buds new blown, to have so short a date,
Is by His hand alone that guides nature and fate.

On My Dear Grandchild Simon Bradstreet, Who Died on 16 November, 1669, Being but a Month, and One Day Old

No sooner come, but gone, and fall'n asleep,
Acquaintance short, yet parting caused us weep,
Three flowers, two scarcely blown, the last i' th' bud,

Cropt by th' Almighty's hand; yet is He good,
With dreadful awe before Him let's be mute, 5
Such was His will, but why, let's not dispute,
With humble hearts and mouths put in the dust,
Let's say He's merciful as well as just,
He will return, and make up all our losses,
And smile again, after our bitter crosses. 10
Go pretty babe, go rest with sisters twain
Among the blest in endless joys remain.

Verses Upon the Burning of Our House July 10th, 1666

In silent night when rest I took
For sorrow near I did not look
I wakened was with thund'ring noise
And piteous shrieks of dreadful voice.
That fearful sound of "Fire!" and "Fire!" 5
Let no man know is my desire.
I, starting up, the light did spy,
And to my God my heart did cry
To strengthen me in my distress
And not to leave me succorless. 10
Then, coming out, beheld a space
The flame consume my dwelling place.
And when I could no longer look,
I blest His name that gave and took,
That laid my goods now in the dust. 15
Yea, so it was, and so 'twas just.
It was His own, it was not mine,
Far be it that I should repine;
He might of all justly bereft
But yet sufficient for us left. 20
When by the ruins oft I past
My sorrowing eyes aside did cast,
And here and there the places spy
Where oft I sat and long did lie:
Here stood that trunk, and there that chest, 25
There lay that store I counted best.
My pleasant things in ashes lie,
And them behold no more shall I.
Under thy roof no guest shall sit,
Nor at thy table eat a bit. 30

No pleasant tale shall e'er be told,
Nor things recounted done of old.
No candle e'er shall shine in thee,
Nor bridegroom's voice e'er heard shall be.
In silence ever shall thou lie,   35
Adieu, Adieu, all's vanity.
Then straight I 'gin my heart to chide,
And did thy wealth on earth abide?
Didst fix thy hope on mold'ring dust?
The arm of flesh didst make thy trust?   40
Raise up thy thoughts above the sky
That dunghill mists away may fly.
Thou hast an house on high erect,
Framed by that mighty Architect,
With glory richly furnished,   45
Stands permanent though this be fled.
It's purchased and paid for too
By Him who hath enough to do.
A price so vast as is unknown
Yet by His gift is made thine own;   50
There's wealth enough, I need no more,
Farewell, my pelf, farewell my store.
The world no longer let me love,
My hope and treasure lies above.

Meditations Divine and Moral.

I.

There is no object that we see; no action that we do; no good that we enjoy;
no evil that we feel, or fear, but we may make some spiritu[a]l advantage of
all: and he that makes such improvement is wise, as well as pious.

II.

Many can speak well, but few can do well. We are better scholars in the
theory than the practique part, but he is a true Christian that is a proficient
in both.

III.

Youth is the time of getting, middle age of improving, and old age of spending; a negligent youth is usually attended by an ignorant middle age, and
both by an empty old age. He that hath nothing to feed on but vanity and lies
must needs lie down in the bed of sorrow.

IV.

A ship that bears much sail, and little or no ballast, is easily overset; and that man, whose head hath great abilities, and his heart little or no grace, is in danger of foundering.

IX.

Sweet words are like honey, a little may refresh, but too much gluts the stomach.

X.

Divers children have their different natures; some are like flesh which nothing but salt will keep from putrefaction; some again like tender fruits that are best preserved with sugar: those parents are wise that can fit their nurture according to their nature.

XVII.

Few men are so humble as not to be proud of their abilities; and nothing will abase them more than this,—What hast thou, but what thou hast received? Come give an account of thy stewardship.

To My Dear Children[1]

This book by any yet unread,
I leave for you when I am dead,
That, being gone, here you may find
What was your living mother's mind.   5
Make use of what I leave in love
And God shall bless you from above.

My dear children,

I, knowing by experience that the exhortations of parents take most effect when the speakers leave to speak, and those especially sink deepest which are spoke latest—and being ignorant whether on my death bed I shall have opportunity to speak to any of you, much less to all—thought it the best, whilst I was able to compose some short matters (for what else to call them I know not) and bequeath to you, that when I am no more with you, yet I

---

[1] This brief spiritual autobiography was not published in the poet's lifetime.

may be daily in your remembrance (although that is the least in my aim in what I now do), but that you may gain some spiritual advantage by my experience. I have not studied in this you read to show my skill, but to declare the truth—not to set forth myself, but the glory of God. If I had minded the former, it had been perhaps better pleasing to you—but seeing the last is the best, let it be best pleasing to you.

The method I will observe shall be this—I will begin with God's dealing with me from my childhood to this day.

In my young years, about 6 or 7 as I take it, I began to make conscience of my ways, and what I knew was sinful, as lying, disobedience to parents, etc. I avoided it. If at any time I was overtaken with the like evils, it was as a great trouble. I could not be at rest till by prayer I had confessed it unto God. I was also troubled at the neglect of private duties, though too often tardy that way. I also found much comfort in reading the Scriptures, especially those places I thought most concerned my condition, and as I grew to have more understanding, so the more solace I took in them.

In a long fit of sickness which I had on my bed I often communed with my heart, and made my supplication to the most High who set me free from that affliction.

But as I grew up to be about 14 or 15 I found my heart more carnal, and sitting loose from God, vanity and the follies of youth take hold of me.

About 16, the Lord laid His hand sore upon me and smote me with the smallpox. When I was in my affliction, I besought the Lord, and confessed my pride and vanity and He was entreated of me, and again restored me. But I rendered not to Him according to the benefit received.

After a short time I changed my condition and was married, and came into this country, where I found a new world and new manners, at which my heart rose. But after I was convinced it was the way of God, I submitted to it and joined to the church at Boston.

After some time I fell into a lingering sickness like a consumption, together, with a lameness, which correction I saw the Lord sent to humble and try me and do me good: and it was not altogether ineffectual.

It pleased God to keep me a long time without a child, which was a great grief to me, and cost me many prayers and tears before I obtained one, and after him gave me many more, of whom I now take the care, that as I have brought you into the world, and with great pains, weakness, cares, and fears brought you to this, I now travail in birth again of you till Christ be formed in you.

Among all my experiences of God's gracious dealings with me I have constantly observed this, that He hath never suffered me long to sit loose from Him, but by one affliction or other hath made me look home, and search what was amiss—so usually thus it hath been with me that I have no sooner felt my heart out of order, but I have expected correction for it, which most commonly hath been upon my own person, in sickness, weakness, pains, sometimes on my soul, in doubts and fears of God's displeasure, and my sincerity towards Him, sometimes He hath smote a child with a sickness, sometimes chastened by losses in estate—and these times (through His great mercy) have been the times of my greatest getting and advantage, yea I have found them the times when the Lord hath manifested the most love to me. Then have I gone to searching, and have said with David, Lord search me and try me, see what ways of wickedness are in me, and lead me in the way everlasting:[2] and seldom or never but I have found either some sin I lay under which God would have reformed, or some duty neglected which He would have performed. And by His help I have laid vows and bonds upon my soul to perform His righteous commands.

If at any time you are chastened of God, take it as thankfully and joyfully as in greatest mercies, for if ye be His ye shall reap the greatest benefit by it. It hath been no small support to me in times of darkness when the Almighty hath hid His face from me, that yet I have had abundance of sweetness and refreshment after affliction, and more circumspection in my walking after I have been afflicted. I have been with God like an untoward child, that no longer than the rod has been on my back (or at least in sight) but I have been apt to forget Him and myself too. Before I was afflicted I went astray, but now I keep Thy statutes.

I have had great experience of God's hearing my prayers, and returning comfortable answers to me, either in granting the thing I prayed for, or else in satisfying my mind without it; and I have been confident it hath been from Him, because I have found my heart through His goodness enlarged in thankfulness to Him.

I have often been perplexed that I have not found that constant joy in my pilgrimage and refreshing which I supposed most of the servants of God have; although He hath not left me altogether without the witness of His holy spirit, who hath oft given me His word and set to His seal that it shall be well with me. I have sometimes tasted of that hidden manna that the world knows not, and have set up my Ebenezer,[3] and have resolved with myself that against such a promise, such tastes of sweetness, the gates of hell shall never prevail. Yet have I many times sinkings and droopings, and not enjoyed that felicity that sometimes I have done. But when I have been in darkness and seen no light, yet have I desired to stay myself upon the Lord.

And, when I have been in sickness and pain, I have thought if the Lord would but lift up the light of His countenance upon me, although He ground me to powder, it would be but light to me; yea, oft have I thought were I in hell itself, and could there find the love of God toward me, it would be a heaven. And, could I have been in heaven without the love of God, it would

[2] Psalms 139:23-24.
[3] After a victory of Israel over the Philistines, the prophet Samuel set up a stone to commemorate the Lord's help, and he called the monument Ebenezer. "Hitherto," says Samuel in the Geneva version of the Bible, "hath the Lord holpen us." I Samuel 7:10-12. Hitherto, Bradstreet echoes implicitly, the Lord has helped me.

have been a hell to me; for, in truth, it is the absence and presence of God that makes heaven or hell.

Many times hath Satan troubled me concerning the verity of the Scriptures, many times by atheism how I could know whether there was a God; I never saw any miracles to confirm me, and those which I read of how did I know but they were feigned. That there is a God my reason would soon tell me by the wondrous works that I see, the vast frame of the heaven and the earth, the order of all things, night and day, summer and winter, spring and autumn, the daily providing for this great household upon the earth, the preserving and directing of all to its proper end. The consideration of these things would with amazement certainly resolve me that there is an Eternal Being. But how should I know He is such a God as I worship in Trinity, and such a Saviour as I rely upon? Though this hath thousands of times been suggested to me, yet God hath helped me over. I have argued thus with myself. That there is a God I see. If ever this God hath revealed himself, it must be in His Word, and this must be it or none. Have I not found that operation by it that no human invention can work upon the soul? Hath not judgments befallen divers who have scorned and contemned it? Hath it not been preserved through all ages maugre[4] all the heathen tyrants and all of the enemies who have opposed it? Is there any story but that which shows the beginnings of times, and how the world came to be as we see? Do we not know the prophecies in it fulfilled which could not have been so long fore-told by any but God Himself?

When I have got over this block, then have I another put in my way, that admit this be the true God whom we worship, and that be His Word, yet why may not the Popish religion be the right? They have the same God, the same Christ, the same word: they only interpret it one way, we another.

This hath sometimes stuck with me, and more it would, but the vain fooleries that are in their religion, together with their lying miracles and cruel persecutions of the saints, which admit were they as they term them, yet not so to be dealt withal.

The consideration of these things and many the like would soon turn me to my own religion again.

But some new troubles I have had since the world has been filled with blasphemy, and sectaries, and some who have been accounted sincere Christians have been carried away with them, that sometimes I have said, Is there faith upon the earth? and I have not known what to think. But then I have remembered the works of Christ that so it must be, and if it were possible, the very elect should be deceived. Behold, saith our Saviour, I have told you before. That hath stayed my heart, and I can now say, Return, O my Soul, to thy rest, upon this rock Christ Jesus will I build my faith; and, if I perish, I perish. But I know all the Powers of Hell shall never prevail against it. I

---

[4] Despite.

know whom I have trusted, and whom I have believed, and that He is able to keep that I have committed to His charge.

Now to the King, immortal, eternal and invisible, the only wise God, be honor and glory for ever and ever. Amen.

This was written in much sickness and weakness, and is very weakly and imperfectly done; but, if you can pick any benefit out of it, it is the mark which I aimed at.

PHILIP PAIN

(d. 1668)

What do we do about a writer who wrote one memorable poem? Of Philip Pain very little is known except that he was lost at sea at about the age of 16, and that after his death a small volume of his Meditations was published. The eighth of those Meditations is printed here because it is one of the best lyrics written in seventeenth-century America. Notice that the poem requires no special allegiance to Puritan doctrine, or even to Christianity. Its power may be equally strong whether deep thinking conceives of annihilation or of the risk of eternal damnation.

The poem is taken from *Daily Meditations* (reproduced from the original edition of 1668), with Introduction by Leon Howard, 1936.

Meditation 8

Scarce do I pass a day, but that I hear
Some one or other's dead; and to my ear
Me thinks it is no news; but oh, did I
Think deeply on it, what it is to die,
My pulses all would beat, I should not be
Drown'd in this deluge of security.

MARY WHITE ROWLANDSON

(c. 1635-c.1678)

Mrs. Rowlandson belongs to a large group of early American authors who did not consider themselves as writers and whose entire contribution to letters consists of a single life story or a personal narrative. Her *Narrative of Captivity and Restoration* was one of the earliest and most widely reprinted pamphlets in a *genre* that has become known as the Narrative of Indian Captivity and that persisted in a variety of forms through the nineteenth century. Wife of a minister in Lancaster, Massachusetts, Mary Rowlandson was captured in a raid during King Philip's War (in February, 1676) and taken west with her three surviving children, after her captors had mortally wounded one. Ransomed for 20 pounds in May, 1676, and eventually reunited with her children, she wrote the *Narrative* in an effort to communicate her experience, to glorify the Lord her Redeemer, and to disseminate the moral significance of both her sufferings and her Providential rescue. Notice, too, that despite her indignation and the ineradicably diabolical prejudice against Indians, she does struggle to describe and in some way to comprehend Indian manners, beliefs, and attitudes.

The Narrative appears in *"Narratives of the Indian Wars, 1675-1699,"* ed. Charles H. Lincoln, 1913, pp. 107-168 and Richard D. Van Der Beets, *Held Captive by the Indians: Selected Narratives; 1642-1836,* 1973.

For background to the "Narrative" see Á. Keiser, *The Indian In American Literature,* 1933, and R. H. Pearce, "The Significances of the Captivity Narrative," *American Literature,* XIX (1947): 1-20.

From The Sovereignty and Goodness of God[1]

A NARRATIVE OF THE CAPTIVITY AND RESTORATION OF MRS. MARY ROWLANDSON

On the tenth of February 1675,[2] came the Indians with great numbers upon Lancaster: their first coming was about sun-rising; hearing the noise of some guns, we looked out; several houses were burning, and the smoke ascending

[1] Cambridge, 1682. The text and some of the notes here are from *Narratives of the Indian Wars,* ed. C. H. Lincoln, New York, 1913.

[2] Since the New Year began on March 25, we would now write this date as 1676. D.L.

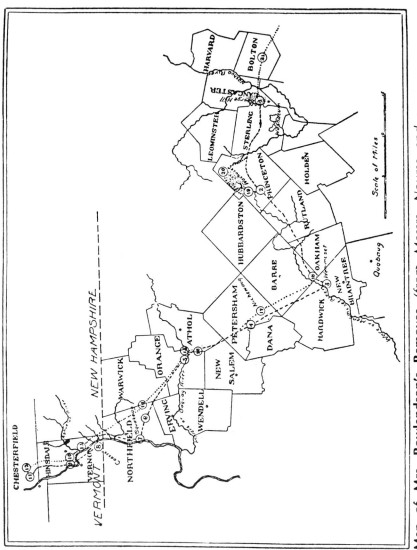

Map of Mrs. Rowlandson's Removes *(from Messrs. Nourse and Thayer's edition of the Narrative.)*

178

to heaven. There were five persons taken in one house, the father, and the mother, and a sucking child, they knocked on the head; the other two they took and carried away alive. There were two others, who being out of their garrison upon some occasion were set upon; one was knocked on the head, the other escaped: another there was who running along was shot and wounded, and fell down; he begged of them his life, promising them money (as they told me) but they would not hearken to him but knocked him in head, and stript him naked, and split open his bowels. Another seeing many of the Indians about his barn, ventured and went out, but was quickly shot down. There were three others belonging to the same garrison who were killed; the Indians getting up upon the roof of the barn, had advantage to shoot down upon them over their fortification. Thus these murderous wretches went on, burning, and destroying before them.

At length they came and beset our own house, and quickly it was the dolefullest day that ever mine eyes saw. The house stood upon the edge of a hill; some of the Indians got behind the hill, others into the barn, and others behind any thing that could shelter them; from all which places they shot against the house, so that the bullets seemed to fly like hail; and quickly they wounded one man among us, then another, and then a third. About two hours (according to my observations, in that amazing time) they had been about the house before they prevailed to fire it (which they did with flax and hemp, which they brought out of the barn, and there being no defense about the house, only two flankers[3] at two opposite corners and one of them not finished) they fired it once and one ventured out and quenched it, but they quickly fired it again, and that took. Now is the dreadful hour come, that I have often heard of (in time of war, as it was the case of others) but now mine eyes see it. Some in our house were fighting for their lives, others wallowing in their blood, the house on fire over our heads, and the bloody heathen ready to knock us on the head, if we stirred out. Now might we hear mothers and children crying out for themselves, and one another, "Lord, what shall we do?" Then I took my children (and one of my sisters, hers) to go forth and leave the house: but as soon as we came to the door and appeared, the Indians shot so thick that the bullets rattled against the house, as if one had taken an handful of stones and threw them, so that we were fain to give back. We had six stout dogs belonging to our garrison, but none of them would stir, though another time, if any Indian had come to the door, they were ready to fly upon him and tear him down. The Lord hereby would make us the more to acknowledge His hand, and to see that our help is always in Him. But out we must go, the fire increasing, and coming along behind us roaring, and the Indians gaping before us with their guns, spears, and hatchets to devour us. No sooner were we out of the house, but my brother-in-law (being before wounded, in defending the house, in or near the

[3] Flankers were projections from which blank walls (curtains) could be enfiladed.

throat) fell down dead, whereat the Indians scornfully shouted, and hallowed, and were presently upon him, stripping off his clothes, the bullets flying thick, one went through my side, and the same (as would seem) through the bowels and hand of my dear child in my arms. One of my elder sister's children, named William, had then his leg broken, which the Indians perceiving, they knocked him on head. Thus were we butchered by those merciless heathen, standing amazed, with the blood running down to our heels. My eldest sister being yet in the house, and seeing those woeful sights, the infidels hauling mothers one way, and children another, and some wallowing in their blood: and her elder son telling her that her son William was dead, and myself was wounded, she said, "And, Lord, let me die with them;" which was no sooner said, but she was struck with a bullet, and fell down dead over the threshold. I hope she is reaping the fruit of her good labors, being faithful to the service of God in her place. In her younger years she lay under much trouble upon spiritual accounts, till it pleased God to make that precious Scripture take hold of her heart, 2 Cor. 12. 9. "And He said unto me, my Grace is sufficient for thee." More than twenty years after I have heard her tell how sweet and comfortable that place was to her. But to return: the Indians laid hold of us, pulling me one way, and the children another, and said, "Come, go along with us;" I told them they would kill me: they answered, If I were willing to go along with them, they would not hurt me.

Oh the doleful sight that now was to behold at this house! "Come, behold the works of the Lord, what desolations He has made in the Earth."[4] Of thirty-seven persons who were in this one house, none escaped either present death, or a bitter captivity, save only one,[5] who might say as he, Job 1.15, "And I only am escaped alone to tell the news." There were twelve killed, some shot, some stabbed with their spears, some knocked down with their hatchets. When we are in prosperity, oh the little that we think of such dreadful sights, and to see our dear friends, and relations lie bleeding out their heart-blood upon the ground. There was one who was chopped into the head with a hatchet, and stripped naked, and yet was crawling up and down. It is a solemn sight to see so many Christians lying in their blood, some here, and some there, like a company of sheep torn by wolves, all of them stripped naked by a company of hell-hounds, roaring, singing, ranting, and insulting, as if they would have torn our very hearts out; yet the Lord by His almighty power preserved a number of us from death, for there were twenty-four of us taken alive and carried captive.

I had often before this said, that if the Indians should come, I should choose rather to be killed by them than taken alive but when it came to the trial my mind changed; their glittering weapons so daunted my spirit, that I

---

[4] Psalm 8.

[5] The person escaping was Ephraim Roper. The size of the garrison as given by contemporary writers varies from 37 to 55, of whom three Kettle children escaped in some way unknown to Mrs. Rowlandson.

chose rather to go along with those (as I may say) ravenous beasts, than that moment to end my days; and that I may the better declare what happened to me during that grievous captivity, I shall particularly speak of the several removes we had up and down the wilderness.

THE FIRST REMOVE

Now away we must go with those barbarous creatures, with our bodies wounded and bleeding, and our hearts no less than our bodies. About a mile we went that night, up upon a hill within sight of the town, where they intended to lodge. There was hard by a vacant house (deserted by the English before, for fear of the Indians). I asked them whether I might not lodge in the house that night to which they answered, "What will you love English men still?" This was the dolefullest night that ever my eyes saw. Oh, the roaring, and singing and dancing, and yelling of those black creatures in the night, which made the place a lively resemblance of hell. And as miserable was the waste, that was there made of horses, cattle, sheep, swine, calves, lambs, roasting pigs, and fowl (which they had plundered in the town) some roasting, some lying and burning, and some boiling to feed our merciless enemies; who were joyful enough though we were disconsolate. To add to the dolefulness of the former day, and the dismalness of the present night: my thoughts ran upon my losses and sad bereaved condition. All was gone, my husband gone (at least separated from me, he being in the Bay,[6] and to add to my grief, the Indians told me they would kill him as he came homeward) my children gone, my relations and friends gone, our house and home and all our comforts within door, and without, all was gone (except my life) and I knew not but the next moment that might go too. There remained nothing to me but one poor wounded babe, and it seemed at present worse than death that it was in such a pitiful condition, bespeaking compassion, and I had no refreshing for it, nor suitable things to revive it. Little do many think what is the savageness and brutishness of this barbarous enemy, ay, even those that seem to profess more than others among them, when the English have fallen into their hands.

Those seven that were killed at Lancaster the summer before upon a Sabbath day, and the one that was afterward killed upon a weekday, were slain and mangled in a barbarous manner, by one-eyed John,[7] and Marlborough's Praying Indians, which Capt. Mosely brought to Boston, as the Indians told me.

---

[6] That is, in Boston, near the Bay, and in the colony of Massachusetts Bay.

[7] One-eyed John was known also as Monoco and Apequinsah. "Marlborough's Praying Indians" means the settlement of Christianized Indians at Marlborough, Massachusetts. On

August 30, 1675, Captain Samuel Mosely, "being instigated thereunto by some people of those parts, no lovers of the Christian Indians, sent down to Boston with a guard of sol-

(Footnote continued next page.)

THE SECOND REMOVE[8]

But now, the next morning, I must turn my back upon the town, and travel with them into the vast and desolate wilderness, I knew not whither. It is not my tongue, or pen can express the sorrows of my heart, and bitterness of my spirit, that I had at this departure: but God was with me, in a wonderful manner, carrying me along, and bearing up my spirit, that it did not quite fail. One of the Indians carried my poor wounded babe upon a horse, it went moaning all along, "I shall die, I shall die." I went on foot after it, with sorrow that cannot be expressed. At length I took it off the horse, and carried it in my arms till my strength failed, and I fell down with it: then they set me upon a horse with my wounded child in my lap, and there being no furniture upon the horse back, as we were going down a steep hill, we both fell over the horse's head, at which they like inhumane creatures laughed, and rejoiced to see it, though I thought we should there have ended our days, as overcome with so many difficulties. But the Lord renewed my strength still, and carried me along, that I might see more of His power; yea, so much that I could never have thought of, had I not experienced it.

After this it quickly began to snow, and when night came on, they stopped: and now down I must sit in the snow, by a little fire, and a few boughs behind me, with my sick child in my lap; and calling much for water, being now (through the wound) fallen into a violent fever. My own wound also growing so stiff, that I could scarce sit down or rise up; yet so it must be, that I must sit all this cold winter night upon the cold snowy ground, with my sick child in my arms, looking that every hour would be the last of its life; and having no Christian friend near me, either to comfort or help me. Oh, I may see the wonderful power of God, that my spirit did not utterly sink under my affliction: still the Lord upheld me with His gracious and merciful spirit, and we were both alive to see the light of the next morning.

THE THIRD REMOVE.[9]

The morning being come, they prepared to go on their way. One of the Indians got up upon a horse, and they set me up behind him, with my poor

diers, pinioned and fastened with lines from neck to neck, fifteen of those Indians that lived with others of them upon their own lands, and in their own fort at Okonhomesitt near Marlborough, where they were orderly settled and were under the English conduct." In Daniel Gookin's *Historical Account of the Doings and Sufferings of the Christian Indians of New England,* from which the above is quoted, the question of the guilt of the Marlborough Indians is discussed at length by that constant friend of the converts. *Transactions of the American Antiquarian Society,* II, 454-461.

[8] The second remove was to Princeton, Massachusetts, near Mount Wachusett.

[9] The third remove, February 12-27, ended at an Indian village, Menameset (Wenimesset), on the Ware River, in what is now New Braintree. Quabaug was Brookfield.

sick babe in my lap. A very wearisome and tedious day I had of it; what with my own wound, and my child's being so exceeding sick, and in a lamentable condition with her wound. It may be easily judged what a poor feeble condition we were in, there being not the least crumb of refreshing that came within either of our mouths, from Wednesday night to Saturday night, except only a little cold water. This day in the afternoon, about an hour by sun, we came to the place where they intended, *viz.* an Indian town, called Wenimesset, norward of Quabaug. When we were come, oh, the number of pagans (now merciless enemies) that there came about me, that I may say as David, Psal. 27. 13, "I had fainted, unless I had believed," etc.[10] The next day was the Sabbath:[11] I then remembered how careless I had been of God's holy time, how many Sabbaths I had lost and misspent, and how evilly I had walked in God's sight; which lay so close unto my spirit, that it was easy for me to see how righteous it was with God to cut off the thread of my life, and cast me out of His presence forever. Yet the Lord still showed mercy to me, and upheld me; and as He wounded me with one hand, so He healed me with the other. This day there came to me one Robert Pepper (a man belonging to Roxbury) who was taken in Captain Beers his fight,[12] and had been now a considerable time with the Indians; and up with them almost as far as Albany, to see King Philip, as he told me, and was now very lately come into these parts.[13] Hearing, I say, that I was in this Indian town, he obtained leave to come and see me. He told me, he himself was wounded in the leg at Captain Beers his fight; and was not able some time to go, but as they carried him, and as he took oaken leaves and laid to his wound, and through the blessing of God he was able to travel again. Then I took oaken leaves and laid to my side, and with the blessing of God it cured me also; yet before the cure was wrought, I may say, as it is in Psal. 38. 5, 6. "My wounds stink and are corrupt, I am troubled, I am bowed down greatly, I go mourning all the day long." I sat much alone with a poor wounded child in my lap, which moaned night and day, having nothing to revive the body, or cheer the spirits of her, but instead of that, sometimes one Indian would come and tell me one hour, that your master will knock your child in the head, and then a second, and then a third, your master will quickly knock your child in the head.

This was the comfort I had from them, miserable comforters are ye all, as he said.[14] Thus nine days I sat upon my knees, with my babe in my lap, till my flesh was raw again; my child being even ready to depart this sorrowful

---

[10] "Unless I had believed to see the goodness of the Lord in the land of the living."

[11] Sunday, February 13.

[12] Captain Beers, attempting to relieve the garrison of Northfield, was slain with most of his men, September 4, 1675.

[13] Philip's headquarters during the winter had been somewhat east of Albany in New York.

[14] I.e., as Job said. Job 16:2.

world, they bade me carry it out to another wigwam (I suppose because they would not be troubled with such spectacles) whither I went with a very heavy heart, and down I sat with the picture of death in my lap. About two hours in the night, my sweet babe like a lamb departed this life, on Feb. 18, 1675. It being about six years, and five months old. It was nine days from the first wounding, in this miserable condition, without any refreshing of one nature or other, except a little cold water. I cannot, but take notice, how at another time I could not bear to be in the room where any dead person was, but now the case is changed; I must and could lie down by my dead babe, side by side all the night after. I have thought since of the wonderful goodness of God to me, in preserving me in the use of my reason and senses, in that distressed time, that I did not use wicked and violent means to end my own miserable life. In the morning, when they understood that my child was dead they sent for me home to my master's wigwam: (by my master in this writing, must be understood Quanopin,[15] who was a sagamore, and married King Philip's wife's sister; not that he first took me, but I was sold to him by another Narragansett Indian, who took me when first I came out of the garrison). I went to take up my dead child in my arms to carry it with me, but they bid me let it alone: there was no resisting, but go I must and leave it. When I had been at my master's wigwam, I took the first opportunity I could get, to go look after my dead child: when I came I asked them what they had done with it? Then they told me it was upon the hill: then they went and showed me where it was, where I saw the ground was newly dug, and there they told me they had buried it: there I left that child in the wilderness, and must commit it, and myself also in this wilderness condition, to Him who is above all. God having taken away this dear child, I went to see my daughter Mary, who was at this same Indian town, at a wigwam not very far off, though we had little liberty or opportunity to see one another. She was about ten years old, and taken from the door at first by a Praying Indian and afterward sold for a gun. When I came in sight, she would fall aweeping; at which they were provoked, and would not let me come near her, but bade me be gone; which was a heart-cutting word to me. I had one child dead, another in the wilderness, I knew not where, the third they would not let me come near to: "Me" (as he said) "have ye bereaved of my children, Joseph is not, and Simeon is not, and ye will take Benjamin also, all these things are against me."[16] I could not sit still in this condition, but kept walking from one place to another. And as I was going along, my heart was even overwhelmed with the thoughts of my condition, and that I should have children, and a nation which I knew not ruled over them. Whereupon I earnestly entreated the Lord, that He would consider my low estate, and

---

[15] Quinnapin was the husband of Weetamoo, the widow of Alexander, already referred to as the Queen of Pocasset. Mrs. Rowlandson became a servant to this wife. He had as well two other squaws.

[16] The lament of Jacob in Genesis 42:36.

show me a token for good, and if it were His blessed will, some sign and hope of some relief. And indeed quickly the Lord answered, in some measure, my poor prayers: for as I was going up and down mourning and lamenting my condition, my son came to me, and asked me how I did; I had not seen him before, since the destruction of the town, and I knew not where he was, till I was informed by himself, that he was amongst a smaller parcel of Indians, whose place was about six miles off; with tears in his eyes, he asked me whether his sister Sarah was dead; and told me he had seen his sister Mary; and prayed me, that I would not be troubled in reference to himself. The occasion of his coming to see me at this time, was this: there was, as I said, about six miles from us, a small plantation of Indians, where it seems he had been during his captivity: and at this time, there were some forces of the Indians gathered out of our company, and some also from them (among whom was my son's master) to go to assault and burn Medfield: in this time of the absence of his master, his dame brought him to see me. I took this to be some gracious answer to my earnest and unfeigned desire. The next day, *viz.* to this, the Indians returned from Medfield,[17] all the company, for those that belonged to the other small company, came through the town that now we were at. But before they came to us, oh! the outrageous roaring and hooping that there was: they began their din about a mile before they came to us. By their noise and hooping they signified how many they had destroyed (which was at that time twenty-three). Those that were with us at home, were gathered together as soon as they heard the hooping, and every time that the other went over their number, these at home gave a shout, that the very earth rung again: and thus they continued till those that had been upon the expedition were come up to the sagamore's wigwam; and then, oh, the hideous insulting and triumphing that there was over some Englishmen's scalps that they had taken (as their manner is) and brought with them. I cannot but take notice of the wonderful mercy of God to me in those afflictions, in sending me a Bible. One of the Indians that came from Medfield fight, had brought some plunder, came to me, and asked me, if I would have a Bible, he had got one in his basket. I was glad of it, and asked him, whether he thought the Indians would let me read? He answered yes: so I took the Bible, and in that melancholy time, it came into my mind to read first the 28. Chap. of Deut.,[18] which I did, and when I had read it, my dark heart wrought on this manner, that there was no mercy for me, that the blessings were gone, and the curses come in their room, and that I had lost my opportunity. But the Lord helped me still to go on reading till I came to Chap. 30 the seven first verses, where I found, there was mercy promised

[17] The Medfield fight . . . occurred on February 21; fifty houses were burned.

[18] Ch. 28 of Deuteronomy is occupied with a recital of blessings for obedience to God and curses for disobedience.

again, if we would return to Him by repentance; and though we were scattered from one end of the earth to the other, yet the Lord would gather us together, and turn all those curses upon our enemies. I do not desire to live to forget this Scripture, and what comfort it was to me.

Now the Indians began to talk of removing from this place, some one way, and some another. There were now besides myself nine English captives in this place (all of them children, except one woman). I got an opportunity to go and take my leave of them; they being to go one way, and I another, I asked them whether they were earnest with God for deliverance, they told me, they did as they were able, and it was some comfort to me, that the Lord stirred up children to look to Him. The woman *viz.* Goodwife Joslin told me, she should never see me again, and that she could find in her heart to run away; I wished her not to run away by any means, for we were near thirty miles from any English town, and she very big with child, and had but one week to reckon; and another child in her arms, two years old, and bad rivers there were to go over, and we were feeble, with our poor and coarse entertainment. I had my Bible with me, I pulled it out, and asked her whether she would read; we opened the Bible and lighted on Psal. 27, in which Psalm we especially took notice of that, *ver. ult.*, "Wait on the Lord, Be of good courage, and He shall strengthen thine heart, wait I say on the Lord."[19]

THE FOURTH REMOVE[20]

And now I must part with that little company I had. Here I parted from my daughter Mary (whom I never saw again till I saw her in Dorchester, returned from captivity) and from four little cousins and neighbors, some of which I never saw afterward: the Lord only knows the end of them. Amongst them also was that poor woman before mentioned, who came to a sad end, as some of the company told me in my travel: she having much grief upon her spirit, about her miserable condition, being so near her time, she would be often asking the Indians to let her go home; they not being willing to that, and yet vexed with her importunity, gathered a great company together about her, and stripped her naked, and set her in the midst of them; and when they had sung and danced about her (in their hellish manner) as long as they pleased, they knocked her on head, and the child in her arms with her: when they had done that, they made a fire and put them both into it, and told the other children that were with them, that if they attempted to go home, they would serve them in like manner: the children said, she did not shed one tear, but prayed all the while. But to return to my own journey; we traveled about half a day or little more, and came to a desolate place in

---

[19] Psalms 27:14.
[20] The fourth remove occupied February 28 to March 3. The camp was between Ware River and Miller's River, at the Indian village of Nichewaug in modern Petersham.

the wilderness, where there were no wigwams or inhabitants before; we came about the middle of the afternoon to this place, cold and wet, and snowy, and hungry, and weary, and no refreshing, for man, but the cold ground to sit on, and our poor Indian cheer.

Heartaching thoughts here I had about my poor children, who were scattered up and down among the wild beasts of the forest: my head was light and dizzy (either through hunger or hard lodging, or trouble or altogether) my knees feeble, my body raw by sitting double night and day, that I cannot express to man the affliction that lay upon my spirit, but the Lord helped me at that time to express it to Himself. I opened my Bible to read, and the Lord brought that precious Scripture to me, Jer. 31. 16. "Thus saith the Lord, refrain thy voice from weeping, and thine eyes from tears, for thy work shall be rewarded, and they shall come again from the land of the enemy." This was a sweet cordial to me, when I was ready to faint, many and many a time have I sat down, and wept sweetly over this Scripture. At this place we continued about four days.

• • •

Our family being now gathered together (those of us that were living) the South Church in Boston hired an house for us: then we removed from Mr. Shepard's, those cordial friends, and went to Boston, where we continued about three quarters of a year: still the Lord went along with us, and provided graciously for us. I thought it somewhat strange to set up housekeeping with bare walls; but as Solomon says, "Money answers all things,"[21] and that we had through the benevolence of Christian friends, some in this town, and some in that, and others: and some from England, that in a little time we might look, and see the house furnished with love. The Lord hath been exceeding good to us in our low estate, in that when we had neither house nor home, nor other necessaries; the Lord so moved the hearts of these and those towards us, that we wanted neither food, nor raiment for ourselves or ours, Prov. 18. 24. "There is a friend which sticketh closer than a brother." And how many such friends have we found, and now living amongst? And truly such a friend have we found him to be unto us, in whose house we lived, *viz.* Mr. James Whitcomb, a friend unto us near hand, and afar off.

I can remember the time, when I used to sleep quietly without workings in my thoughts, whole nights together, but now it is other ways with me. When all are fast about me, and no eye open, but His who ever waketh, my thoughts are upon things past, upon the awful dispensation of the Lord towards us; upon His wonderful power and might, in carrying of us through so many difficulties, in returning us in safety, and suffering none to hurt us. I remember in the night season, how the other day I was in the midst of thousands of enemies, and nothing but death before me: it is then hard work to persuade myself, that ever I should be satisfied with bread again. But now

[21] Ecclesiastes 10:19.

we are fed with the finest of the wheat, and, as I may say, with honey out of the rock:[22] instead of the husk, we have the fatted calf: the thoughts of these things in the particulars of them, and of the love and goodness of God towards us, make it true of me, what David said of himself, Psal. 6. 5. "I watered my couch with my tears."[23] Oh! the wonderful power of God that mine eyes have seen, affording matter enough for my thought to run in, that when others are sleeping mine eyes are weeping.

I have seen the extreme vanity of this world: one hour I have been in health, and wealth, wanting nothing: but the next hour in sickness and wounds, and death, having nothing but sorrow and affliction.

Before I knew what affliction meant, I was ready sometimes to wish for it. When I lived in prosperity, having the comforts of the world about me, my relations by me, my heart cheerful, and taking little care for anything; and yet seeing many, whom I preferred before myself, under many trials and afflictions, in sickness, weakness, poverty, losses, crosses, and cares of the world I should be sometimes jealous lest I should have my portion in this life, and that Scripture would come to my mind, Heb. 12. 6. "For whom the Lord loveth He chasteneth, and scourgeth every son whom He receiveth." But now I see the Lord had His time to scourge and chasten me. The portion of some is to have their afflictions by drops, now one drop and then another; but the dregs of the cup, the wine of astonishment, like a sweeping rain that leaveth no food, did the Lord prepare to be my portion. Affliction I wanted, and affliction I had, full measure (I thought) pressed down and running over; yet I see, when God calls a person to anything, and through never so many difficulties, yet He is fully able to carry them through and make them see, and say they have been gainers thereby. And I hope I can say in some measure, as David did, "It is good for me that I have been afflicted."[24] The Lord hath showed me the vanity of these outward things. That they are the vanity of vanities, and vexation of spirit; that they are but a shadow, a blast, a bubble, and things of no continuance. That we must rely on God Himself, and our whole dependence must be upon Him. If trouble from smaller matters begin to arise in me, I have something at hand to check myself with, and say, why am I troubled? It was but the other day that if I had had the world, I would have given it for my freedom, or to have been a servant to a Christian. I have learned to look beyond present and smaller troubles, and to be quieted under them, as Moses said, Exod. 14. 13. "Stand still and see the salvation of the Lord."

[22] Psalms 81:16.

[23] More exactly, Psalms 6:6.

[24] Psalms 119:71.

SAMUEL DANFORTH

(1626–1674)

The first American historian to praise Samuel Danforth's Election-Day sermon on New England's *Errand into the Wilderness* was Cotton Mather, whose brief biography of Danforth remains the best. In our own day Perry Miller made the sermon famous by choosing Danforth's title for a very successful book of his own essays on American Puritanism. Miller emphasized the ambiguity in the word *errand* and in the Puritans' attitude toward the wilderness. The founders had come to New England on essential business of the Lord's, on an errand of the first importance to Europe and all Christendom: to establish churches and governments that would serve as models for the Western world. But within 20 years they found themselves betrayed by the very successes of their friends in England, who reluctantly but nonetheless decisively accepted the necessity of religious toleration. New England's errand in the wilderness, Miller perceived, thus became trivialized in the usual modern sense of the errand. And as successive preachers called on the young generations to be faithful to the original errand of their ancestors the historical context implied a decline into provincialism from which the local people could never recover, for the grand errand of the founders was no longer accessible to them.

The power of the appeal was strong, however, as any American reader of Danforth's sermon will recognize even after three centuries. Although the Puritans' attitude toward the wilderness was a hostile one—they wished, in Cotton Mather's words, to convert a "desert" into a "garden"—they still took pride, as Thomas Hooker had done, in the tough self-denial that survival in the wilderness had required of them, and of course Danforth's biblical text shows that they had Scriptural precedent for that kind of pride. Danforth's *Errand,* moreover, is a good example of two overlapping subcategories of Puritan sermon. It is one of the "election sermons," preached annually on Election Day and usually published. Election sermons tended to focus on questions of public behavior, or "national" accountability for private misconduct, and the purpose or mission of the covenanted community, and

The modern edition is *The Wall and the Garden: Selected Massachusetts Election Sermons, 1670–1775,* ed. A. W. Plumstead, 1968. For a biography of Danforth, see Cotton Mather, *Magnalia Christi Americana,* 1702. Modern scholarship includes Perry Miller, *Errand in the Wilderness,* 1956, and Sacvan Bercovitch, "Horologicals to Chronometricals: The Rhetoric of the Jeremiad," *Literary Monographs,* 3 (1970): 3–124; and Plumstead's introduction to *The Wall and the Garden.*

they continued to have public importance down to the time of the Revolution, long after the prevailing theology had renounced or quietly abandoned Calvinist doctrines. It is this occasion for which Arthur Dimmesdale, in Hawthorne's *The Scarlet Letter,* prepares his very best work, and (as A. W. Plumstead has shown) the theme of Dimmesdale's sermon resembles Danforth's *Errand.*

The second category is that of the "jeremiad," sermons that lamented the decline from the high principles and practices of the founders, recounted the sins of the present generation, and called on it to re-own the covenant that bound it to the high vocation of the founders.

Danforth's second sermon here is a brief statement read at the grave of his three young children, all of whom died in 1659 of a mysterious respiratory ailment ("bladders in the windpipe"), which Cotton Mather says was identified and found to be subject to surgical treatment only after the Danforth children's deaths. The grieving father's statement was not printed in his lifetime, but Mather did print it from the manuscript in his life of Danforth in *Magnalia Christi Americana.* Like some of Anne Bradstreet's poems, this sermon shows us how a literate Puritan tried to give adequate public expression to both his human grief and his resigned faith, as the judgments of an inscrutable power were bewilderingly pronounced through catastrophic events.

Danforth was known in his undergraduate days at Harvard as a singularly conscientious student who declined to recite the "blasphemies" of Greek and Roman writers "without washing my mouth upon it!" After teaching briefly at Harvard, he joined the legendary John Eliot as Pastor at Roxbury, where he preached for the last 24 years of his life. He was known as a vigilant monitor of his congregation's personal conduct and as a man who did not flinch from blunt admonitions. As an avocation he also did some independent work in astronomy, especially in studying the comet that "alarmed the whole world in 1664."

From A Brief Recognition of New England's Errand Into The Wilderness.[1]

"What went ye out into the wilderness to see? A reed shaken with the wind?

"But what went ye out for to see? A man clothed in soft raiment? Behold, they that wear soft clothing are in kings' houses.

"But what went ye out for to see? A prophet? Yea, I say unto you, and more than a prophet" (Matt. 11. 7-9).

These words are our Saviour's proem to His illustrious encomium of John the Baptist. John began his ministry not in Jerusalem nor in any famous city

[1] Cambridge, Mass., 1671.

of Judea, but in the wilderness, i.e., in a woody, retired, and solitary place, thereby withdrawing himself from the envy and preposterous zeal of such as were addicted to their old traditions and also taking the people aside from the noise and tumult of their secular occasions and businesses, which might have obstructed their ready and cheerful attendance unto his doctrine. The ministry of John at first was entertained by all sorts with singular affection: There "went out to him Jerusalem, and all Judea, and all the region round about Jordan" (Matt. 3. 5); but after awhile the people's fervor abated, and John being kept under restraint divers months, his authority and esteem began to decay and languish (John 5. 35). Wherefore our Saviour, taking occasion from John's messengers coming to Him, after their departure gives an excellent e[u]logy and commendation of John to the intent that he might ratify and confirm his doctrine and administration and revive his authority and estimation in the hearts and consciences of the people.

This e[u]logy our Saviour begins with an elegant dialogism which the rhetorician calleth communication, gravely deliberating with His hearers and seriously enquiring to what purpose they went out into the wilderness and what expectation drew them thither. Wherein we have: 1. The general question and main subject of His inquisition; 2. the particular enquiries; 3. the determination of the question.

The general question is, "What went ye out into the wilderness to see?" He saith not, "Whom went ye out to hear," but "What went ye out to see?"

.   .   .

The meaning then of this first enquiry is, "Went ye out into the wilderness to see a light, vain, and inconstant man, one that could confess and deny and deny and confess the same truth?" This interrogation is to be understood negatively and ironically, q.d., "Surely ye went not into the desert to behold such a ludicrous and ridiculous sight, a man like unto a reed shaken with the wind." Under the negation of the contrary levity our Saviour sets forth one of John's excellencies, viz., his eminent constancy in asserting the truth. The winds of various temptations both on the right hand and on the left blew upon him, yet he wavered not in his testimony concerning Christ; "he confessed, and denied not; but confessed" the truth [John 1. 20].

.   .   .

Doctrine. *Such as have sometime left their pleasant cities and habitations to enjoy the pure worship of God in a wilderness are apt in time to abate and cool in their affection thereunto; but then the Lord calls upon them seriously and thoroughly to examine themselves, what it was that drew them into the wilderness, and to consider that it was not the expectation of ludicrous levity nor of courtly pomp and delicacy, but of the free and clear dispensation of the Gospel and kingdom of God.*

This doctrine consists of two distinct branches; let me open them severally.

Branch I. Such as have sometime left their pleasant cities and habitations to enjoy the pure worship of God in a wilderness are apt in time to abate and cool in their affection thereunto. To what purpose did the children of Israel leave their cities and houses in Egypt and go forth into the wilderness? Was it not to "hold a feast to the Lord," and to "sacrifice to the God of their fathers"? That was the only reason which they gave of their motion to Pharaoh (Exod. 5. 1, 3); but how soon did they forget their errand into the wilderness and corrupt themselves in their own inventions? Within a few months after their coming out of Egypt, "they make a calf in Horeb, and worship the molten image, and change their glory into the similitude of an ox that eateth grass" (Psal. 106. 19, 20; Exod. 32. 7, 8). Yea, for the space of forty years in the wilderness, while they pretended to sacrifice to the Lord, they indeed worshipped the stars and the host of heaven and together with the Lord's tabernacle carried about with them the tabernacle of Moloch (Amos 5. 25, 26; Acts 7. 42, 43). And how did they spend their time in the wilderness but in tempting God and in murmuring against their godly and faithful teachers and rulers, Moses and Aaron (Psal. 95. 8)? To what purpose did the children of the captivity upon Cyrus his proclamation, leave their houses which they had built and their vineyards and oliveyards which they had planted in the province of Babylon and return to Judea and Jerusalem, which were now become a wilderness? Was it not that they might build the house of God at Jerusalem and set up the temple-worship? But how shamefully did they neglect that great and honorable work for the space of above forty years? They pretended that God's time was not come to build his house because of the rubs and obstructions which they met with, whereas all their difficulties and discouragements hindered not their building of stately houses for themselves (Hag. 1. 2-4). To what purpose did Jerusalem and all Judea and all the region round about Jordan leave their several cities and habitations and flock into the wilderness of Judea? Was it not to see that burning and shining light which God had raised up? To hear his heavenly doctrine and partake of that new sacrament which he administered? O how they were affected with his rare and excellent gifts! with his clear, lively, and powerful ministry! The kingdom of heaven pressed in upon them with a holy violence and the violent, the zealous, and affectionate hearers of the gospel took it by force (Matt. 11. 12; Luke 16. 16). They leapt over all discouragements and impediments, whether outward, as legal rites and ceremonies, or inward, the sense of their own sin and unworthiness, and pressed into the kingdom of God as men rush into a theater to see a pleasant sight or as soldiers run into a besieged city to take the spoil thereof; but their hot fit is soon over, their affection lasted but for an hour, i.e., a short season (John 5. 35).

.   .   .

Branch II. When men abate and cool in their affection to the pure worship of God which they went into the wilderness to enjoy, the Lord calls upon them seriously and thoroughly to examine themselves, what it was that drew them into the wilderness, and to consider that it was not the expectation of ludicrous levity nor of courtly pomp and delicacy, but of the free and clear dispensation of the Gospel and kingdom of God. Our Saviour knowing that the people had lost their first love and singular affection to the revelation of His grace by the ministry of His herald John, He is very intense in examining them, what expectation drew them into the wilderness. He doth not once nor twice but thrice propound that question, "What went ye out into the wilderness to see?" Yea in particular He enquires whether it were to see a man that was like to "a reed shaken with the wind," or whether it were to see "a man clothed like a courtier," or whether it were to see a "prophet," and then determines the question, concluding that it was to see a great and excellent prophet and that had not they seen rare and admirable things in him they would never have gone out into the wilderness unto him.

The reason is because the serious consideration of the inestimable grace and mercy of God in the free and clear dispensation of the Gospel and kingdom of God is a special means to convince men of their folly and perverseness in undervaluing the same, and a sanctified remedy to recover their affections thereunto. The Lord foreseeing the defection of Israel after Moses his death, commands him to write that prophetical song recorded in Deuteronomy 32 as a testimony against them, wherein the chief remedy which he prescribes for the prevention and healing of their apostasy is their calling to remembrance God's great and signal love in manifesting Himself to them in the wilderness, in conducting them safely and mercifully, and giving them possession of their promised inheritance (ver. 7-14). And when Israel was apostatized and fallen, the Lord, to convince them of their ingratitude and folly, brings to their remembrance His deliverance of them out of Egypt, His leading them through the wilderness for the space of forty years, and not only giving them possession of their enemies' land but also raising up even of their own sons, prophets, faithful and eminent ministers, and of their young men Nazarites, who being separated from worldly delights and encumbrances were patterns of purity and holiness—all which were great and obliging mercies. Yea the Lord appeals to their own consciences whether these his favors were not real and signal (Amos 2. 10, 11). The prophet Jeremiah, that he might reduce the people from their backsliding, cries in the ears of Jerusalem with earnestness and boldness, declaring unto them that the Lord remembered how well they stood affected towards him when he first chose them to be his people and espoused them to himself; how they followed him in the wilderness and kept close to him in their long and wearisome passage through the uncultured desert; how they were then consecrated to God and set apart for his worship and service, as the first fruits are wont to be sequestered and devoted to God; and thereupon expostulates with them for their forsaking the Lord, and following after their idols (Jer. 2. 2, 3, 5, 6). Surely our Saviour's dialogism with His hearers in my text is not a mere rhetorical elegancy to adorn His testimony concerning John, but a clear and strong conviction of their folly in slighting and despising that which they sometime so highly pretended unto, and a wholesome admonition and direction how to recover their primitive affection to his doctrine and administration.

Use I. Of solemn and serious inquiry to us all in this general assembly is whether we have not in a great measure fogotten our errand into the wilderness. You have solemnly professed before God, angels, and men that the cause of your leaving your country, kindred, and fathers' houses and transporting yourselves with your wives, little ones, and substance over the vast ocean into this waste and howling wilderness, was your liberty to walk in the faith of the Gospel with all good conscience according to the order of the Gospel, and your enjoyment of the pure worship of God according to His institution without human mixtures and impositions. Now let us sadly consider whether our ancient and primitive affections to the Lord Jesus, His glorious Gospel, His pure and spiritual worship, and the order of His house, remain, abide, and continue firm, constant, entire, and inviolate. Our Saviour's reiteration of this question, "What went ye out into the wilderness to see?" is no idle repetition but a sad conviction of our dullness and backwardness to this great duty and a clear demonstration of the weight and necessity thereof. It may be a grief to us to be put upon such an inquisition, as it is said of Peter, "Peter was grieved because He said unto him the third time, Lovest thou me?" (John 21. 17); but the Lord knoweth that a strict and rigid examination of our hearts in this point is no more than necessary. Wherefore let us call to remembrance the former days and consider whether "it was not then better with us than it is now" [Hos. 2. 7].

In our first and best times the kingdom of heaven brake in upon us with a holy violence and every man pressed into it. What mighty efficacy and power had the clear and faithful dispensation of the Gospel upon your hearts? How affectionately and zealously did you entertain the kingdom of God? How careful were you, even all sorts, young and old, high and low, to take hold of the opportunities of your spiritual good and edification, ordering your secular affairs (which were wreathed and twisted together with great variety) so as not to interfere with your general calling, but that you might attend upon the Lord without distraction? How diligent and faithful in preparing your hearts for the reception of the Word, "laying apart all filthiness and superfluity of naughtiness," that you might "receive with meekness the ingraffed[2] word, which is able to save your souls" [Jas. 1. 21], "and purging out all malice, guile, hypocrisies, envies, and all evil speakings, and as newborn babes, desiring the sincere milk of the Word, that ye might grow

---

[2] Engrafted.

thereby" [I Pet. 2. 1, 2]? How attentive in hearing the everlasting Gospel, "watching daily at the gates of wisdom, and waiting at the posts of her doors, that ye might find eternal life, and obtain favor of the Lord" [Prov. 8. 34, 35]? Gleaning day by day in the field of God's ordinances, even among the sheaves, and gathering up handfuls, which the Lord let fall of purpose for you, and at night going home and beating out what you had gleaned, by meditation, repetition, conference, and therewith feeding yourselves and your families. How painful were you in recollecting, repeating, and discoursing of what you heard, whetting the Word of God upon the hearts of your children, servants, and neighbors? How fervent in prayer to almighty God for His divine blessing upon the seed sown, that it might take root and fructify? O what a reverent esteem had you in those days of Christ's faithful ambassadors that declared unto you the word of reconciliation! "How beautiful" were "the feet of them that preached the Gospel of peace, and brought the glad tidings of salvation!" [Rom. 10. 15]. You "esteemed them highly in love for their work's sake" [I Thess. 5. 13]. Their persons, names, and comforts were precious in your eyes; you counted yourselves blessed in the enjoyment of a pious, learned, and orthodox ministry; and though you ate the bread of adversity and drank the water of affliction, yet you rejoiced in this, that your eyes saw your teachers, they were not removed into corners, and your ears heard a word behind you saying, "This is the way, walk ye in it," when you turned to the right hand and when your turned to the left (Isa. 30. 20, 21). What earnest and ardent desires had you in those days after communion with Christ in the holy sacraments? With desire you desired to partake of the seals of the covenant. You thought your evidences for heaven not sure nor authentic unless the broad seals of the kingdom were annexed. What solicitude was there in those days to "seek the Lord after the right order" [I Chron. 15. 13]? What searching of the holy Scriptures, what collations among your leaders, both in their private meetings and public councils and synods, to find out the order which Christ hath constituted and established in His house? What fervent zeal was there then against sectaries and heretics and all manner of heterodoxies? "You could not bear them that were evil" [Rev. 2. 2] but tried them that pretended to new light and revelations, and found them liars.[3] What pious care was there of sister churches, that those that wanted[4] breasts might be supplied and that those that wanted peace, their dissensions might be healed? What readiness was there in those days to call for the help of neighbor elders and brethren in case of any difference or division that could not be healed at home? What reverence was there then of the sentence of a council as being decisive and issuing the controversy, according to that ancient proverbial saying, "They shall surely

---

[3] The allusion here is to the so-called Antinomians, and Anne Hutchinson, Roger Williams, and others.

[4] That is, lacked, or needed, nourishment.

ask counsel of Abel: and so they ended the matter" (II Sam. 20. 18)? What holy endeavors were there in those days to propagate religion to your children and posterity, training them up in the nurture and admonition of the Lord, keeping them under the awe of government, restraining their enormities and extravagancies, charging them to know the God of their fathers and serve Him with a perfect heart and willing mind, and publicly asserting and maintaining their interest in the Lord and in His holy covenant and zealously opposing those that denied the same?

And then had the churches "rest" throughout the several colonies and were "edified; and walking in the fear of the Lord, and in the comfort of the Holy Ghost, were multiplied" [Acts 9. 31]. O how your faith grew exceedingly! You proceeded from faith to faith, from a less to a greater degree and measure, growing up in Him who is our head and receiving abundance of grace and of the gift of righteousness, that you might reign in life by Jesus Christ. O how your love and charity towards each other abounded! O what comfort of love! What bowels[5] and mercies! What affectionate care was there one of another! What a holy sympathy in crosses and comforts, weeping with those that wept and rejoicing with those that rejoiced!

But who is there left among you that saw these churches in their first glory and how do you see them now? Are they not in your eyes in comparison thereof as nothing? "How is the gold become dim! how is the most fine gold changed!" [Lam. 4. 1]. Is not the temper, complexion, and countenance of the churches strangely altered? Doth not a careless, remiss, flat, dry, cold, dead frame of spirit grow in upon us secretly, strongly, prodigiously? They that have ordinances are as though they had none; and they that hear the Word as though they heard it not; and they that pray as though they prayed not; and they that receive sacraments as though they received them not; and they that are exercised in the holy things using them by the by as matters of custom and ceremony, so as not to hinder their eager prosecution of other things which their hearts are set upon. Yea and in some particular congregations amongst us is there not instead of a sweet smell, a stink; and instead of a girdle, a rent; and instead of a stomacher, a girding with sackcloth; and burning instead of beauty?[6] Yea "the vineyard is all overgrown with thorns, and nettles cover the face thereof, and the stone wall thereof is broken down" (Prov. 24. 31). Yea and that which is the most sad and certain sign of calamity approaching: "Iniquity aboundeth, and the love of many waxeth cold" (Matt. 24. 12). Pride, contention, worldliness, covetousness, luxury, drunkenness, and uncleanness break in like a flood upon us and good men

---

[5] Compare Samuel Sewall ("My bowels yearn for Mrs. Denison") and Edward Taylor ("God's tender bowels run out streams of grace"). The bowels are thought of here as the source of human affections.

[6] The controversies referred to here—especially the stink and the rent—probably include the founding of the Third Church (the Old South) in Boston, in 1669, by discontented members of the First.

grow cold in their love to God and to one another. If a man be cold in his bed let them lay on the more clothes that he may get heat; but we are like to David in his old age: "They covered him with clothes, but he gat no heat" (I Kings 1. 1). The Lord heaps mercies, favors, blessings upon us and loads us daily with His benefits, but all His love and bounty cannot heat and warm our hearts and affections. Well the furnace is able to heat and melt the coldest iron; but how oft hath the Lord cast us into the hot furnace of affliction and tribulation and we have been scorched and burnt, yet not melted but hardened thereby (Isa. 63. 17)? How long hath God kept us in the furnace day after day, month after month, year after year? But all our afflictions, crosses, trials have not been able to keep our hearts in a warm temper.

Now let me freely deliberate with you what may be the causes and grounds of such decays and languishings in our affections to, and estimation of, that which we came into the wilderness to enjoy. Is it because "there is no bread, neither is there any water; and our soul loatheth this light bread" (Num. 21. 5)? "Our soul is dried away: and there is nothing at all, besides this manna, before our eyes" (Num. 11. 6). What, is manna no bread? Is this angelical food light bread which cannot satisfy but starves the soul? Doth our soul loathe the bread of heaven? The Lord be merciful to us; the full soul loatheth the honeycomb (Prov. 27. 7).

·   ·   ·

But though unbelief be the principal yet it is not the sole cause of our decays and languishings; inordinate worldly cares, predominant lusts, and malignant passions and distempers stifle and choke the Word and quench our affections to the kingdom of God (Luke 8. 14). The manna was gathered early in the morning; when the sun waxed hot, it melted (Exod. 16. 21). It was a fearful judgment on Dathan and Abiram that the earth opened its mouth and swallowed them up.[7] How many professors of religion are swallowed up alive by earthly affections? Such as escape the lime pit of Pharisaical hypocrisy fall into the coal pit of Sadducean atheism and epicurism. Pharisaism and Sadduceism do almost divide the professing world between them. Some split upon the rock of affected ostentation of singular piety and

If any question how seasonable such a discourse may be upon such a day as this, let him consider Haggai 2. 10–14:

In the four and twentieth day of the ninth month, in the second year of Darius, came the word of the Lord by Haggai the prophet, saying, "Thus saith the Lord of hosts; Ask now the priests concerning the law,

[7] Numbers 17:31–32.

saying, 'If one bear holy flesh in the skirt of his garment, and with his skirt do touch bread, or pottage, or wine, or oil, or any meat, shall it be holy?' " And the priests answered and said, "No." Then said Haggai, "If one that is unclean by a dead body touch any of these, shall it be unclean?" And the priests answered and said, "It shall be unclean." Then answered Haggai, and said, "So is this people, and so is this nation before me," saith the Lord; "and so is every work of their hands; and that which they offer there is unclean."

It was an high and great day wherein the prophet spake these words and an holy and honorable work which the people were employed in. For this day they laid the foundation of the Lord's temple (ver. 18). Nevertheless, the Lord saw it necessary this very day to represent and declare unto them the pollution and uncleanness both of their persons and of their holy services, that they might be deeply humbled before God and carry on their present work more holily and purely. What was their uncleanness? Their eager pursuit of their private interests took off their hearts and affections from the affairs of the house of God. It seems they pleased themselves with this, that the altar stood upon its bases and sacrifices were daily offered thereon and the building of the Temple was only deferred until a fit opportunity were afforded, free from disturbance and opposition; and having now gained such a season they are ready to build the Temple. But the Lord convinceth them out of the Law that their former negligence was not expiated by their daily sacrifices, but the guilt thereof rendered both the nation and this holy and honorable work which they were about vile and unclean in the sight of God. And having thus shown them their spiritual uncleanness, He encourageth them to go on with the work in hand, the building of the Temple, promising them from this day to bless them (ver. 19).

Use II. Of exhortation, to excite and stir us all up to attend and prosecute our errand into the wilderness. To what purpose came we into this place and what expectation drew us hither? Surely not the expectation of ludicrous levity. We came not hither to see "a reed shaken with the wind." Then let not us be reeds—light, empty, vain, hollow-hearted professors, shaken with every wind of temptation—but solid, serious, and sober Christians, constant and steadfast in the profession and practice of the truth, "trees of righteousness, the planting of the Lord, that He may be glorified" [Isa. 61. 3], holding fast the profession of our faith without wavering.

"Alas there is such variety and diversity of opinions and judgments that we know not what to believe."[8]

Were there not as various and different opinions touching the person of Christ even in the days of his flesh? Some said that He was John the Baptist,

[8] Now Danforth, like Shepard in *The Sincere Convert*, sets up a dialogue between the preacher and a dissenting auditor.

some Elias, others Jeremias, or one of the old prophets. Some said He was a gluttonous man and a wine-bibber, a friend of publicans and sinners; others said He was a Samaritan and had a devil; yet the disciples knew what to believe. "Whom say ye that I am? Thou art Christ, the Son of the living God" (Matt. 16. 15, 16). The various heterodox opinions of the people serve as a foil or tinctured leaf to set off the luster and beauty of the orthodox and apostolical faith. This is truly commendable, when in such variety and diversity of apprehensions you are not biased by any sinister respects, but discern, embrace, and profess the truth as it is in Christ Jesus.

But to what purpose came we into the wilderness and what expectation drew us hither? Not the expectation of courtly pomp and delicacy. We came not hither to see men clothed like courtiers. The affectation of courtly pomp and gallantry is very unsuitable in a wilderness. Gorgeous attire is comely in princes' courts if it exceed not the limits of Christian sobriety; but excess in kings' houses escapes not divine vengeance. "I will punish the princes, and the kings' children, and all such as are clothed with strange apparel" (Zeph. 1. 8). The pride and haughtiness of the ladies of Zion in their superfluous ornaments and stately gestures brought wrath upon themselves, upon their husbands, and upon their children, yea and upon the whole land (Isa. 3. 16-26). How much more intolerable and abominable is excess of this kind in a wilderness, where we are so far removed from the riches and honors of princes' courts?

To what purpose then came we into the wilderness and what expectation drew us hither? Was it not the expectation of the pure and faithful dispensation of the Gospel and kingdom of God? The times were such that we could not enjoy it in our own land, and therefore having obtained liberty and a gracious patent from our sovereign, we left our country, kindred, and fathers' houses, and came into these wild woods and deserts where the Lord hath planted us and made us "dwell in a place of our own, that we might move no more, and that the children of wickedness might not afflict us any more" (II Sam. 7. 10). What is it that distinguisheth New England from other colonies and plantations in America? Not our transportation over the Atlantic Ocean, but the ministry of God's faithful prophets and the fruition of his holy ordinances. Did not the Lord bring "the Philistines from Caphtor, and the Assyrians from Kir" as well as "Israel from the land of Egypt" (Amos 9. 7)? But "by a prophet the Lord brought Israel out of Egypt, and by a prophet was he preserved" (Hos. 12. 13). What, is the price and esteem of God's prophets and their faithful dispensations now fallen in our hearts?

The hardships, difficulties, and sufferings which you have exposed yourselves unto that you might dwell in the house of the Lord and leave your little ones under the shadow of the wings of the God of Israel, have not been few nor small. And shall we now withdraw ourselves and our little ones from under those healing wings and lose that full reward which the Lord hath in His heart and hand to bestow upon us? Did we not with Mary choose this for our part, "to sit at Christ's feet, and hear His word" [Luke 10. 39]? And do we now repent of our choice and prefer the honors, pleasures, and profits of the world before it? "You did run well; who doth hinder you that you should not obey the truth?" (Gal. 5. 7).

.   .   .

[A Funeral Sermon at the Grave of his Children][1]

In *December* 1659 the (until then unknown) malady of *bladders in the wind-pipe*, invaded and removed many children; by opening of one of them the malady and remedy (too late for very many) were discovered. Among those many that thereby expired, were the three children of the Reverend Mr. S. D., the eldest of whom (being upward of five years and half; so gracious and intelligent were her expressions and behavior both living and dying, and so evident her faith in Christ) was a luculent commentary on that marvellous prophecy, that the child should die an hundred years old. How the sorrowful father entertained this solemn providence may be partly gathered from what he expressed unto such as came to attend his branches unto their graves; of which may be said, as was said of *Job*, "In all this he sinned not."[2] He saw meet to pen down the minutes of what he spake, and they are faithfully taken out of his own manuscript.

My Friends,
    If any that see my grief should say unto me as the *Danites* unto *Micah*, "What aileth thee?" I thank God, I cannot answer as he did, "They have taken away my Gods."[3] My heart was indeed somewhat set upon my *children*, especially the eldest; but they were none of my Gods, none of my portion; my portion is whole and untoucht unto this day. To understand myself, and to communicate unto my hearers, the spiritual meaning and compass of the law and rule, and nature of gospel obedience hath been my design and work, upon which I have employed much reading and study, and what faith, hope, love, patience, etc. the glorious wisdom, power and mercy of God do oblige us to render. I have endeavored to set forth before you, what if God will now try whether they were mere notions and speculations that I spake, or whether I believe as I spake, and whether there be any divine spark in my heart? I remember him that said to *Abraham*, "Hereby I know that thou fearest Me, in that thou hast not withheld from Me thy son,

---

[1] With an introductory paragraph by Cotton Mather, the following text is taken from *Magnalia Christi Americana* (London, 1702).

[2] Job 2:10. Job at first did not complain sinfully, though under great affliction.

[3] Judges 18:23-24.

thine only son."[4] It is the pleasure of God, that (besides all that may be gained by reading, and studying, and preaching) I should learn and teach obedience by the things that I suffer. The holy fire is not to be fetcht for you, out of such a flint, as I am, without smiting. Not long before these strokes light upon us, it pleased God marvellously to quicken our hearts (both mine and my wife's) and to stir up in us most earnest desires after Himself: and now He hath taken our children, will He accept us unto freer and fuller communion with Himself, blessed be His holy name. I trust the Lord hath done, what He hath done in wisdom, and faithfulness, and dear love, and that in taking these pleasant things from me, He exerciseth and expresseth as tender affection unto me, as I now express towards them in mourning for the loss of them. I desire with *Ephraim*, "to bemoan myself," etc. Jer. 31. 18, 19. O that I might hear the Lord answering me, as He did *Ver.* 20.[5] It is meet to be said to God, "We have borne chastisement, we will not offend; what we see not, teach Thou us; and if we have done iniquity, we will do so no more,"[6] we know, and God much more knows enough in us, and by us to justify His repeated strokes, tho' we cannot tax ourselves with any known way of disobedience. My desire is, that none may be overmuch dismayed at what hath befallen us; and let no man by any means be offended. Who may say to the Lord, "What dost Thou?" I can say from my heart, tho' what is come upon us is very dreadful and amazing, yet I consent unto the will of God that it is good. Doth not the goldsmith cast his metal into the furnace? And you husbandmen, do you not cause the flail to pass over your grain, not that you hate your wheat, but that you desire pure bread? Had our children replied when we corrected them, we could not have borne it: but, poor hearts, they did us reverence; how much rather should we be subject to the Father of spirits and live. You know, that nine years since, I was in a desolate condition without father, without mother, without wife, without children: but what a father, and mother, and wife have been bestowed upon me, and are still continued tho' my children are removed. And above all, although I cannot deny, but that it pierceth my very heart to call to remembrance the voice of my dear children, calling "Father, father!" a voice, now not heard: yet I bless God, it doth far more abundantly refresh and rejoice me, to hear the Lord continually calling unto me, "My son, my son! My son, despise not the chastening of the Lord, nor faint thou when thou art corrected of Him."[7] And blessed be God, that doth not despise the affliction of the afflicted, nor hides His face from him. 'Twas the consideration that God had sanctified and

---

[4] Genesis 22:12. Abraham prepared to obey a divine command that he offer up his son as a sacrifice, whereupon the command was rescinded.

[5] ". . . I will surely have compassion upon him, saith the Lord."

[6] Job 34:31–32.

[7] Proverbs 3:11.

glorified Himself, by striking an holy awe and dread of His majesty into the hearts of His people, that made *Aaron* hold his peace:[8] and if the Lord will glorify Himself by my family, by these awful strokes upon me, quickning parents unto their duty, and awakening their children to seek after the Lord, I shall desire to be content, tho' my name be cut off: and I beseech you be earnest with the Lord for us, that He would keep us from sinning against Him: and that He would teach us to sanctify His name, and tho' our dear branches have forsaken us, yet that He that hath promised to be with His children in six troubles and in seven, would not forsake us. My heart truly would be consumed, and would even die within me, but that the good will of Him that dwelt in the burning bush, and His good word of promise are my *trust* and *stay.*

[8] Leviticus 10:3.

SAMUEL SEWALL

(1652–1730)

Ever since its first publication by the Massachusetts Historical Society nearly 100 years ago, *The Diary of Samuel Sewall* has served historians and literary scholars as an extremely valuable document. Because Sewall wrote the kind of diary that briefly mentioned daily events and personal actions more than it strove to analyze or express his deepest feelings, historians have found his record useful. He kept the diary for 56 years (1674–1729), during most of which he lived near the center of spiritual and political power in Boston, so that his record often concerns important historical figures and events. It often gives us a clear picture of New England social and intellectual life, and some quick, sharply lined characterizations of famous men, including both Increase and Cotton Mather.

Sewall was born in Bishop Stoke, Hampshire, England. His father

The best modern text, with excellent annotation, is *The Diary of Samuel Sewall, 1674-1729,* 2 vols., ed. M. Halsey Thomas, 1973. The diary was first published in the fifth series of *Collections of the Massachusetts Historical Society,* 1878, and that edition is still so valuable that Thomas bases many of his notes on it. Sidney Kaplan has edited *The Selling of Joseph,* 1969.
A biography of Sewall is Ola E. Winslow, *Samuel Sewall of Boston,* 1964.

and grandfather had already emigrated to New England but had returned to their native country during the ascendancy of Oliver Cromwell. Sewall's father returned to Newbury, Massachusetts in 1659, and two years later, when Samuel was only nine, sent for his family to settle permanently with him in Newbury. Samuel received the best education that New England could provide: some years as the private pupil of a minister named Thomas Parker, and then four years at Harvard College, where Sewall received his A.B. in 1671. He took his second degree (A.M.) in 1674, having taught undergraduates in the College as a Fellow for two years, and then he went on to his career as merchant and judge. The very first entry in his famous diary describes his teaching method in a physics class for "junior sophisters"—reading through the textbook twice over a period of three months.

In a ceremony performed by the governor of Massachusetts Bay, Sewall married Hannah Hull, daughter of the mint-master of the colony, in 1676, and from then on he lived in his father-in-law's house in Boston the life of an influential, wealthy citizen. At various times he served in the legislature, as magistrate and judge, as an Overseer of Harvard College, and as a member of the Governor's Council. His most memorable civil assignment was as a Judge on the Special Court of Oyer and Terminer, appointed to hear and determine cases during the notorious witchcraft trials of 1692. His most famous single literary statement, a bill of public confession put up and read aloud in the church to which he belonged in 1697, asks forgiveness for his part in those trials. (His great courage in that action has been exaggerated by modern commentators, for he wrote the petition to be read on a day set aside by the legislature for *general* fasting throughout Massachusetts in contrition for the injustices of 1692. Sewall's own family had very recently suffered deaths and other reverses, which he attributed to Providential retribution for his sins.) Sewall remained a judge for the rest of his life.

Sewall's *The Selling of Joseph* (1700), one of the earliest antislavery tracts published in New England, was an expression of conscience concerning an issue that had troubled him for some time. He says that he had long been "much dissatisfied" with the slave trade and had felt "a strong inclination to write something about it; but it wore off." Reviving the subject later when he read a commentary on biblical views concerning servants, Sewall noticed an apparently Providential coincidence: just as he was thinking about reviving the plan to write a tract, "in came Brother Belknap to shew me a Petition he intended to present to the General Court for the freeing of a Negro and his wife, who were unjustly held in bondage."

Both *The Selling of Joseph* and the diary passages concerning his doubts about Providential judgments and his worthiness to join the church show us a Sewall who was intelligently and deeply concerned about grave issues, and who integrated that concern with the events in his private life. In that context, which has been too often omitted from anthologies of American literature, his amusing, observant, and yet somehow obtuse account of his courtship of Madame Winthrop (1720) will not give a one-sided view of the man.

From The Diary of Samuel Sewall[1]

[JOINING THE CHURCH]

Oct. 22. Musing at noon and troubled at my untowardness in worship, God, He holp me to pray, Come, Lord Jesus, come quickly to put me into a better frame, taking possession of me. Troubled that I could love Christ no more, it came into my mind that Christ had exhibited Himself to be seen in the Sacrament, the Lord's Supper, and I conceived that my want of love was, that I could see Christ no more clearly. *Vid.* Mr. Thacher Dec. 10. 2^d Answer to the objection under 2^d Reason. *Vid.* Mr. Shepard, Dec. 15. Use 3. *Vid.* Mr. Thacher, Decr 17. Direction 9. which I am sure was spoken to me.[2] The Lord set it home efficaciously by His Spirit, that I may have the perfect love which casts out fear.

Oct. 23. Went from Boston about five T.P. [*tempore post-meridiano*] to Milton, there accidentally meeting with Moses Collier, Mr. Senderlen and I went on to Hingham, to John Jacobs. *Oct. 24,* Tuesday, went from thence to Plymouth, about noon, refreshed there. *Note,* James Percival met us there, and so we went cheerfully together from thence about 2. T.P.; got to Sandwich about a quarter of an hour by sun: lodged at Percivals with Mr. Senderlen. *Oct. 25,* Wednesday, breakfasted at Stephen Skiphs. He, Percival and I rode out about 12 miles, within sight of Martha's Vineyard, to look [at] horses: at last happily came on 11, whereof five [are?] my father's, viz, three chestnut colored mares, and 2 colts: put them in Mr. Bourn's sheep-pen all night. *Note.* Supper at Mr. Smith's, good supper. *Oct. 26, Thursday,* took up the young four-year-old mare, slit the two near ears of the colts, their color was a chestnut sorrel, whitish manes and tails. The bigger had all his hoofs white: the lesser all black. Both stone-colts. The hair of the tails cut square

---

[1] The text is the edition of M. Halsey Thomas, New York, 1973.

[2] In these three allusions to sermons by Thomas Shepard and Peter Thacher, Sewall illustrates how closely the numbered sections of sermons were sometimes annotated and studied by those who heard them.

with a knife. After this Mr. Smith rode with me and showed me the place which some had thought to cut, for to make a passage from the South Sea to the North: said 'twas about a mile and a half between the utmost flowing of the two seas in Herring River and Scusset, the land very low and level, Herring River exceeding pleasant by reason that it runs pretty broad, shallow, of an equal depth, and upon white sand. Showed me also the 3 hills on the which 4 towns kept warders, before which was such an isthmus of about 3 miles and barren plain, that scarce anything might pass unseen. Monument Harbor said to be very good. *Note.* Had a very good supper at Mr. Dexter's. Being in trouble how to bring along my mare, in came one Downing and Benjamin his son, who, being asked, to my gladness promised assistance. *Oct. 27*, got very well to Plymouth, tailing my mare, and Ben strapping her on, though we were fain to come over the cliffs the upper way because of the flowing tide. There saw acorns upon bushes about a foot high, which they call running oak; it is content with that stature. From Plymouth Ben and his father mounted a trifle before me, I waved my hat and handkerchief to them, but they left me to toil with my tired jade: was fain at last to untail and so drive them before me, at last ride and lead the mare with great difficulty. When came to Jones's bridge (supposing the house had been just by) put the bridle on the horse's neck, drove him on the bridge, holding the halter in my hand. When I came on the other side, could not catch my horse, but tired myself leading my tired mare sometimes on the left hand into the marsh, sometimes on the right hand: at last left him, went to the bridge to ensure myself of the path, so led her to Tracy's about ½ mile. He not at home, could scarce get them to entertain me, though 'twas night. At length his son John put up my mare, then took up his own horse, and so helped me to look for mine, but could not find him: after his father and he went on foot, and met him almost at the house, saddle cover lost, which John found in the morn. *Oct. 28*, Saturday, Goodman Tracy directed and set me in the way, so I went all alone to the end, almost, of rocky plain, then, by God's good providence, Mr. Senderlen overtook me, so we came along cheerfully together, called at my Aunt's [*in Braintree*], refreshed, left my tired jade there, set out to Boston-ward about half an hour by sun, and got well home before shutting in, praised be God. *Note.* Seeing the wonderful works of God in the journey, I was thereby more persuaded of His justice, and inability to do any wrong: put in mind likewise of Mr. Thacher's sermon, Oct. 22.

> The humble springs of stately Sandwich Beach
> To all inferiors may observance teach,
> They (without complement) do all concur,
> Praying the sea, accept our duty, sir,
> He mild severe, I've (now) no need: and when—
> As you are come: go back and come again.

A hall from the Seth story house in Essex, Massachusetts, c. 1684.
(Courtesy, The Henry Francis du Pont Winterthur Museum.)

The Paul Revere house, built on the site of Rev. Increase Mather's house in North Square, Boston, in the late 1670's and restored in the twentieth century. (*Lynn McLaren/Rapho-Photo Researchers.*)

Novem. 6. Very cold blustering weather. *Note,* I and John went on board of Mr. Downe, to see father's horse and my mare shipped. 7, clear weather. *Wednesday,* cloudy. In the night great deal of rain fell. *Thurs.* Thanksgiving day, cloudy, sultry, wind, S. E. *Friday, Nov. 10* clears up, westerly, wind roars. Mr. Downe sets sail.

Nov. 11. Brave, mild, clear weather, and fresh gale of wind.

Novem. 27, 1676, about 5 M. Boston's greatest fire brake forth at Mr. Moors, through the default of a tailor boy, who rising alone and early to work, fell asleep and let his light fire the house, which gave fire to the next, so that about fifty landlords were despoiled of their housing. N. B. the house of the man of God, Mr. Mather, and Gods house were burnt with fire.[3] Yet God mingled mercy, and sent a considerable rain, which gave check in great measure to the (otherwise) masterless flames: lasted all the time of the fire, though fair before and after. Mr. Mather saved his books and other goods.

• • •

March 13. Capt. Lake, the remainder of his corpse, was honorably buried: Captains and Commissioners carried: no Magistrate save Major Clark there because of the Court. I was not present because it was Tuesday.[4]

March 14. Visited Mr. Willard, and so forgot to go to the meeting at Mr. Smith's.

• • •

Mar. 15, even. Was holp affectionately to argue in prayer the promise of being heard because asking in Christ's name.

March 16. Dr. Alcock dies about midnight. *Note,* Mrs. Williams told us presently after duties how dangerously ill he was, and to get John to go for his grandmother. I was glad of that information, and resolved to go and pray earnestly for him; but going into the kitchen, fell into discourse with Tim about metals, and so took up the time. The Lord forgive me and help me not to be so slack for time to come, and so easy to disregard and let die so good a resolution. Dr. Alcock was 39 years old.[5]

---

[3] Increase Mather's house and the Second Church, in which he preached, were burned in this fire.

[4] Captain Thomas Lake was, with several others, surprised and killed by the Indians, on 14 August 1676, near a fort on Arowsick Island, Maine, during the continuance of the war at the eastward. He had escaped to another island, and his fate was not known, nor his mangled body recovered, till many months afterward. His monument may be seen on Copp's Hill. M.H.S.EDS., in the 1878 edition.

[5] Dr. Samuel Alcock (Harvard 1659) was the son of Dr. George Alcock of Roxbury; his tuition at college was paid in considerable part by his father's patients, who are credited on the college books with barley malte, wheatt, a small weather [sheep], 3 small lambes, a turkey, 3 checkenes, etc. *Sibley,* and *C.S.M,* xxxi, 204. M H Thomas's note.

March 19, 1676/7 Dr. Alcock was buried, at whose funeral I was. After it, went to Mr. Thacher's. He not within, so walkt with Capt. Scottow on the Change till about 5, then went again, yet he not come. At last came Elder Rainsford, after, Mr. Thacher, who took us up into his chamber; went to prayer, then told me I had liberty to tell what God had done for my soul. After I had spoken, prayed again. Before I came away told him my temptations to him alone, and bade him acquaint me if he knew anything by me that might hinder justly my coming into church. He said he thought I ought to be encouraged, and that my stirring up to it was of God.

March 19, 1676/7 Accidentally going to look about the woman of Cana,[6] Mr. Chauncy's sermons on her, I at first dash turned to that sermon of the 7th and 14 March.

March 21, 1676/7. Father and self rode to Dorchester to the fast, which is the first time that ever I was in that *[new]* meetinghouse. So was absent from the private meetings.

March 21. Mane. God helped me affectionately to pray for a communication of His Spirit in attending on Him at Dorchester, and the night before I read the 9th and 10th of Nehemiah, out of which Mr. Mather happened to take his text, which he handled to good purpose, and more taking it was with me because I had perused those chapters for my fitting to attend on that exercise. Mr. Flint prayed admirably in the morn, and pressed much our inability to keep covenant with God, and therefore begged God's Spirit. Mr. Thacher began the afternoon: then Mr. Flint preached and so concluded.

Note. I have been of a long time loth to enter into strict bonds with God, the sinfulness and hypocrisy of which God hath showed me by reading of a sermon that Mr. *[Cornelius]* Burgess preached before the House of Commons, Nov. 17, 1640, and by the forementioned sermons and prayers. *Omnia in bonum mihi vertas, O Deus.*[7] I found the sermon accidentally in Mr. Norton's study.

Remember, since I had thoughts of joining to the church, I have been exceedingly tormented in my mind, sometimes lest the Third Church [*the South*] should not be in God's way in breaking off from the old. (I resolved to speak with Mr. Torrey about that, but he passed home when I was called to business at the warehouse. Another time I got Mr. Japheth Hobart to promise me a meeting at our house after lecture,—but she that is now his wife, being in town, prevented him.) Sometimes with my own unfitness and want of grace: yet through importunity of friends, and hope that God might communicate Himself to me in the ordinance, and because of my child (then hoped for) its being baptised, I offered myself, and was not refused. Besides what I had written, when I was speaking [*about admission to the church*] I

---

[6] For whom Jesus performed the first of His miracles, according to John 2:1-11.

[7] Turn all to good for me, O God. John Norton, a minister, had tutored Increase Mather and others.

resolved to confess what a great sinner I had been, but going on in the method of the paper, it came not to my mind. And now that scruple of the church vanished, and I began to be more afraid of myself. And on Saturday Goodman Walker[8] came in, who used to be very familiar with me. But he said nothing of my coming into the Church, nor wished God to show me grace therein, at which I was almost overwhelmed, as thinking that he deemed me unfit for it. And I could hardly sit down to the Lord's Table.[9] But I feared that if I went away I might be less fit next time, and thought that it would be strange for me who was just then joined to the church, to withdraw, wherefore I stayed. But I never experienced more unbelief. I feared at least that I did not believe there was such an one as Jesus Christ, and yet was afraid that because I came to the ordinance without belief, that for the abuse of Christ I should be stricken dead; yet I had some earnest desires that Christ would, before the ordinance were done, though it were when He was just going away, give me some glimpse of Himself; but I perceived none. Yet I seemed then to desire the coming of the next Sacrament day, that I might do better, and was stirred up hereby dreadfully to seek God who many times before had touched my heart by Mr. Thacher's praying and preaching more than now. The Lord pardon my former grieving of His Spirit, and circumcise my heart to love Him with all my heart and soul.

March 22. 23. Plenty of rain after a great deal of dry and pleasant weather. In the afternoon of the 23[d.] Seth and I gather what herbs we could get, as yarrow, garglio, etc.

March 26, 1677. Mr. Philips arrives from Scotland, brings the news of the messengers' arrival about the beginning of December. They send letters of the latter end of January. Brought likewise the lamentable news of Mr. Samuel Danforth's death, of the small pox.

March 30, 1677. I, together with Gilbert Cole, was admitted into Mr. Thacher's church, making a solemn covenant to take the Lord Jehovah for our God, and to walk in brotherly love and watchfulness to edification. Goodman Cole first spake, then I, then the relations[10] of the women were read: as we spake so were we admitted; then altogether covenanted. Prayed before and after.

Mar. 31. Old Mr. Oakes[11] came hither, so I wrote a letter to his son, after this tenor:

---

[8] Goodman was a title, like Mr., for good men, usually church members, qualified to serve on a jury. Robert Walker was a member of the Third Church, which Sewall had just joined.

[9] It was a grave sin to come to the Lord's Table—to take communion—if one had not received grace and professed a true faith in Jesus.

[10] Here Sewall struggles to find signs that his conversion was genuine. Each new member prepared and delivered to the congregation an account or relation of his or her religious experience.

[11] Father of Urian Oakes, who was President of Harvard College.

SIR, I have been, and am, under great exercise of mind with regard to my spiritual estate. Wherefore I do earnestly desire that you would bear me on your heart tomorrow in prayer, that God would give me a true godly sorrow for sin, as such: love to Himself and Christ, that I may admire His goodness, grace, kindness in that way of saving man, which I greatly want. I think I shall sit down tomorrow to the Lord's table, and I fear I shall be an unworthy partaker. Those words, "If your own hearts condemn you, God is greater, and knoweth all things,"[12] have often affrighted me.

SAMUEL SEWALL

April 1, 1677. About two of the clock at night I waked and perceived my wife ill: asked her to call Mother. She said I should go to prayer, then she would tell me. Then I rose, lighted a candle at Father's fire, that had been raked up from Saturday night, kindled a fire in the chamber, and after 5 when our folks up, went and gave Mother warning. She came and bade me call the midwife, Goodwife Weeden, which I did. But my wife's pains went away in a great measure after she was up; toward night came on again, and about a quarter of an hour after ten at night, April 2, Father and I sitting in the great hall, heard the child cry, whereas we were afraid 'twould have been 12 before she would have been brought to bed. Went home with the midwife about 2 o'clock, carrying her stool, whose parts were included in a bag. Met with the watch at Mr. Rock's brew house, who bade us stand, enquired what we were. I told the woman's occupation, so they bade God bless our labors, and let us pass. The first woman the child sucked was Bridget Davenport.

April 3. Cousin Flint came to us. She said we ought to lay scarlet on the child's head for that it had received some harm. Nurse Hurd watches. *April 4.* Clear cold weather. Goodwife Ellis watches. *April 7,* Saturday, first labored to cause the child suck his mother, which he scarce did at all. In the afternoon my wife set up, and he sucked the right breast bravely, that had the best nipple.

April 8, 1677. Sabbath day, rainy and stormy in the morning, but in the afternoon fair and sunshine, though a blustering wind; so Eliz. Weeden, the midwife, brought the infant to the Third Church when sermon was about half done in the afternoon, Mr. Thacher preaching. After sermon and prayer, Mr. Thacher prayed for Capt. Scottow's cousin and it, then I named him John, and Mr. Thacher baptized him into the name of the Father, Son. and H. Ghost. The Lord give the father and son may be convinced of and washed from sin in the blood of Christ.

April 9, morn. Hot and gloomy with scattered clouds: about 11 clock there fell a considerable storm of hail, after that it thundered a pretty while.

[12] See 1 John 3:20.

[Note] The child sucked his mother's left breast well as she laid in the bed, notwithstanding the shortness of the nipple.

April 4th was at the 15th Meeting, kept at our house in the little hall, because of my wife's weakness. Mr. Scottow spoke to Is. 27. 9. *prin.*.

April 11 Stormy, blustering fore part, left raining a little before night. Went to the 16th Meeting at B. East's, where Br. Edward Allen and John Hayward spake to John 6. 57, which was very suitable for me, and I hope God did me some good at that meeting as to my love to Christ. We heard after of the slaughter of some persons at York by the Indians, among whom was Isaac Smith, who went thither about boards. This is Isaac Smith of Winnesimmet.

April 9, 1677. Seth Shove began to go to school to Mr. Smith.

April 18. My father-in-law and I went on foot to Dorchester, so were not at the Meeting. 'Twas a cold blustering day, as the last of March, and almost all this month has been very cold. Mr. Adams at supper told of his wife being brought to bed of a son about three weeks before, whom he named Eliphelet.

April 25. even. Mr. Gershom and Nehemiah Hobart gave me a visit.

April 27, Friday. Hannah Henchman and Susannah Everenden with two eastern women taken into church. Warm fair weather these two days. *April 28.* Considerable claps of thunder.

April 28, 1677. Mr. Moody was here, he told me that Mr. Parker[13] died last Tuesday, and was buried on Thursday. Mr. Hubbard preached his funeral sermon. The Lord give me grace to follow my dear master as he followed Christ, that I may at last get to heaven whither he has already gone.

April 30. Went to Mr. Urian Oakes, carried him 50 shillings, discoursed largely with him concerning my temptations: he exhorted me to study the Doctrine of Christ well, to read Dr. Goodwin. Spake to him of the Doctor's death: he told me that he died of a cough and cold which he caught standing in the cold after being hot in going from the ferry. Told me 'twas not safe to conceive a resemblance of Christ in one's mind any more than to picture Him. Read to me occasionally part of his sermon yesterday, wherein he amply proved the confirmation and gathering together in a head the elect angels in Christ Heb. 12. 22, 33: *cum multis aliis.*[14]

Note. [May Training, no date] I went out this morning without private prayer and riding on the Common, thinking to escape the soldiers (because of my fearful horse); notwithstanding there was a Company at a great distance which my horse was so transported at that I could no way govern him, but was fain to let him go full speed, and hold my hat under my arm. The

---

[13] Sewall's former teacher.   [14] With many others.

wind was norwest, so that I suppose I took great cold in my ear thereby, and also by wearing a great thick coat of my father's part of the day, because it rained, and then leaving it off. However it was, I felt my throat ill, the danger of which I thought had been now over with the winter, and so neglected it too much, relapsed, and grew very sick of it from Friday to Monday following, which was the worst day: after that it mended. Mr. Mather visited me and prayed on that day.

May 5, Saturday: Mr. Giliam arrived from the straits. *May 9,* Mr. Tanner arrived from London, wherein came Mr. Thacher who brought news of the death of Mr. George Alcock, he died of the pox: also *May 11* Mr. Thacher and his Sister Davenport were here.

May 15. Mr. Anderson's vessel arrived; as for himself, he died yesterday about 4 of the clock. *T. pomer.* [*i.e., tempore post-meridiano.*]

May 16, went to the 17th Meeting at B. Hills, where B. Tapin and Cousin Savage spake to Heb. 10. 24.

May 30 went to the 18th Meeting at Mr. Wings, where Mr. Thacher spake to the 4 last verses of 92 Psal.

June 4. Went to Plymouth. *June 6.* Returned.

June 13. Went to the 19th Meeting at B. Williams, where G. Needham and my father spake to Ps. 119. 11.

June 17. Sabbath day about 7 m, John Sewall had a convulsion fit. He was asleep in the cradle, and suddenly started, trembled, his fingers contracted, his eyes starting and being distorted. I went to Mr. Brackenbury, and thence to Charlestown, and set him to the child.

June the nineteenth he had another about noon.

June 21, 1677. Just at the end of the sermon (it made Mr. Allen break off the more abruptly) one Torrey, of Roxbury, gave a sudden and amazing cry which disturbed the whole assembly. It seems he had the falling sickness. Tis to be feared the Quaker disturbance and this are ominous.

July 8, 1677. New Meeting House [*the third, or South*] *Mane:* In sermon time there came in a female Quaker, in a canvas frock, her hair disheveled and loose like a periwig, her face as black as ink, led by two other Quakers, and two other followed. It occasioned the greatest and most amazing uproar that I ever saw. Isaiah I. 12, 14.[15]

July 11th 1677 Cousin Daniel Quinsey came home to our house, sailing by night from the lands in Mr. Hammond's boat, otherwise he had not been suffered to come on shore for that some of the ship (Genner's) died of the pox and one is still sick.

---

[15] Nathaniel Hawthorne dramatizes a similar episode in "The Gentle Boy."

[RETRIBUTION AND REPENTANCE FOR
JUDGING THE WITCHES]

Decr 21. A very great snow is on the gound.[16] I go in the morn to Mr. Willard, to entreat him to choose his own time to come and pray with little Sarah: he comes a little before night, and prays very fully and well. Mr. Mather, the President, had prayed[17] with her in the time of the Court's sitting. *Decr 22.* being Catechising day, I give Mr. Willard a note to pray for my daughter publicly, which he did. *Note,* this morn Madam Elisa. Bellingham came to our house and upbraided me with setting my hand to pass Mr. Wharton's account to the Court, where he obtained a judgment for Eustace's farm. I was wheedled and hectored into that business, and have all along been uneasy in the remembrance of it: and now there is one come who will not spare to lay load. The Lord take away my filthy garments, and give me change of raiment. This day I remove poor little Sarah into my bedchamber, where about break of day *Decr 23.* she gives up the ghost in Nurse Cowell's arms. Born, Nov. 21. 1694. Neither I nor my wife were by: Nurse not expecting so sudden a change, and having promised to call us. I thought of Christ's words, "Could you not watch with me one hour!" and would fain have sat up with her: but fear of my wife's illness, who is very valetudinarious, made me to lodge with her in the new hall, where was called by Jane's cry to take notice of my dead daughter. Nurse did long and pathetically ask our pardon that she had not called us, and said she was surprised. Thus this very fair day is rendered foul to us by reason of the general sorrow and tears in the family. Master Cheever was here the evening before, I desired him to pray for my daughter. The chapter read in course on December 23. m. was Deut. 22. which made me sadly reflect that I had not been so thoroughly tender of my daughter; nor so effectually careful of her defense and preservation as I should have been. The good Lord pity and pardon and help for the future as to those God has still left me.

Decr 24. Sam. recites to me in Latin, Mat. 12. from the 6th to the end of the 12th verse. The 7th verse did awfully bring to mind the Salem tragedy.[18]

6th day, Decr 25, 1696. We bury our little daughter. In the chamber, Joseph in course reads Ecclesiastes 3^d—a time to be born and a time to die—Elisabeth, Rev. 22., Hannah, the 38th Psalm. I spoke to each, as God helped, to our mutual comfort I hope. I ordered Sam. to read the 102.

---

[16] "The winter of 1696 was as cold as had been known from the first arrival of the English; slays and loaded sleds passing great part of the time upon the ice from Boston as far as Nantasket. Greater losses in trade had never been known than what were net with in this year; nor was there, at any time after the first year, so great a scarcity of food; nor was grain ever at a higher price." *Hutchinson, Hist.,* (1936), ii, 76n. (M. H. Thomas's note.)

[17] Increase Mather, President of Harvard College.

[18] "If ye had known what this meaneth, I will have mercy and not sacrifice, ye would not have condemned the guiltless."

Psalm. Elisha Cooke, Edw. Hutchinson, John Baily, and Josia Willard bear my little daughter to the tomb.

Note. Twas wholly dry, and I went at noon to see in what order things were set; and there I was entertained with a view of, and converse with, the coffins of my dear Father Hull, Mother Hull, Cousin Quinsey, and my six children: for the little posthumous was now took up and set in upon that that stands on John's: so are three, one upon another twice, on the bench at the end. My mother lies on a lower bench, at the end, with head to her husband's head: and I ordered little Sarah to be set on her grandmother's feet. 'Twas an awful yet pleasing treat; having said, "The Lord knows who shall be brought hither next," I came away.

Mr. Willard prayed with us the night before; I gave him a ring worth about 20ˢ. Sent the President one, who is sick of the gout. He prayed with my little daughter. Mr. Oakes, the physician. Major Townsend, Speaker, of whose wife I was a [pall] bearer, and was joined with me in going to Albany and has been civil and treated me several times. Left a ring at Madam Cooper's for the Governor. Gave not one pair of gloves save to the bearers.[19] Many went to the Church this day, I met them coming home, as went to the tomb. *7ᵗʰ day Decʳ 26.* Roger Judd tells me of a ship arriv'd at Rhode Island from England, and after, that Mr. Ive has written that most judged the King of France was dead, or dying. Ship comes from New Castle, several weeks after the Falkland.

Janʸ 1, 6ᵗʰ day 1696/7. One with a trumpet sounds a Levit at our window just about break of day, bids me good morrow and wishes health and happiness to attend me. I was awake before, and my wife, so we heard him: but went not to the window, nor spake a word. The Lord fit me for His coming in whatsoever way it be. Mr. Willard had the Meeting at his house to day, but we had no invitation to be there as is usual.

On the 22ᵗʰ of May I buried my abortive son; so neither of us were then admitted of God to be there, and now the owners of the family admit us not: it may be I must never more hear a sermon there. The Lord pardon all my sins of omission and commission and by His almighty power make me meet to be partaker of the inheritance with the saints in light. *Second-day Janʸ 11, 1696/7* God helped me to pray more than ordinarily, that He would make up our loss in the burial of our little daughter and other children, and that would give us a child to serve Him, pleading with Him as the Institutor of marriage, and the Author of every good work. Janʸ 15, Gridley's wife dies in child-bed.

Copy of the bill I put up on the Fast day;[20] giving it to Mr. Willard as he

[19] It was customary to give gloves to friends who attended a funeral.   [20] January 14, 1697.

passed by, and standing up at the reading of it, and bowing when finished; in the afternoon.

Samuel Sewall, sensible of the reiterated strokes of God upon himself and family; and being sensible, that as to the guilt contracted, upon the opening of the late Commission of Oyer and Terminer at Salem (to which the order for this Day relates) he is, upon many accounts, more concerned than any that he knows of, desires to take the blame and shame of it, asking pardon of men, and especially desiring prayers that God, who has an unlimited authority, would pardon that sin and all other his sins; personal and relative: and according to His infinite benignity, and sovereignty, not visit the sin of him, or of any other, upon himself or any of his, nor upon the land: but that He would powerfully defend him against all temptations to sin, for the future; and vouchsafe him the efficacious, saving conduct of His Word and Spirit.

*Jan*y 26. 1696/7 I lodged at Charlestown, at Mrs. Shepard's, who tells me Mr. Harvard[21] built that house, I lay in the chamber next the street. As I lay awake past midnight, in my meditation, I was affected to consider how long ago God had made provision for my comfortable lodging that night; seeing that was Mr. Harvard's house: and that led me to think of heaven the house not made with hands, which God for many thousands of years has been storing with the richest furniture (saints that are from time to time placed there), and that I had some hopes of being entertained in that magnificent convenient palace, every way fitted and furnished. These thoughts are very refreshing to me.

[COURTSHIP IN OLD AGE: MADAM WINTHROP]*

[*October*] 11th [*1720*] I write a few lines to Madam Winthrop to this purpose: "Madam, these wait on you with Mr. Mayhew's sermon, and account of the state of the Indians on Martha's Vineyard. I thank you for your unmerited favors of yesterday; and hope to have the happiness of waiting on you tomorrow before eight a-clock after noon. I pray God to keep you, and give you a joyful entrance upon the two hundred and twenty-ninth year of Christopher Columbus his discovery; and take leave, who am, Madam, your humble servant.

S.S.

---

[21] John Harvard, who died only a year after he had settled in Charlestown, bequeathed half of his estate and all of his books to the little college that afterward was given his name.

* Widowed after 49 years of marriage, Sewall began to court a widow named Winthrop two years after his wife's death. The extraordinary detail has made this passage one of the most widely reprinted of all colonial documents. The negotiations failed, perhaps for want of a coach and wig. [D.L.]

A silver bowl by Jeremiah Dummer (1645-1718). *(Yale University Art Gallery, Mabel Brady Garvan Collection.)*

Sent this by Deacon Green, who delivered it to Sarah Chickering, her Mistress not being at home.

8ʳ 12. Give Mr. Whittemore and Willard their oath to Dr. Mather's inventory. Visit Mr. Cooper. Go to the Meeting at the Widow Emons's: Mr. Manly prayed, I read half Mr. Henry's 12th Chapter of the Lord's Supper. Sung 1, 2, 3, 4, 5, 10, and 12th Verses of the 30th Psalm. Brother Franklin concluded with prayer. At Madam Winthrop's steps I took leave of Capt Hill, etc.

Mrs. Anne Cotton came to door (twas before 8.) said Madam Winthrop was within, directed me into the little room, where she was full of work behind a stand; Mrs. Cotton came in and stood. Madam Winthrop pointed to her to set me a chair. Madam Winthrop's countenance was much changed from what 'twas on Monday, looked dark and lowering. At last, the work (black stuff or silk) was taken away, I got my chair in place, had some converse, but very cold and indifferent to what 'twas before. Asked her to acquit me of rudeness if I drew off her glove. Enquiring the reason, I told her twas great odds between handling a dead goat, and a living lady. Got it off. I told her I had one petition to ask of her, that was, that she would take off the negative she laid on me the third of October; she readily answered she could not, and enlarg'd upon it; she told me of it so soon as she could; could not leave her house, children, neighbors, business. I told her she might

Silver tea kettle and stand by Joseph Richardson of Philadelphia (1711–1784). *(Yale University Art Gallery, Mabel Brady Garvan Collection.)*

Silver sugar box by Richard Coney of Boston, c. 1685. (*Courtesy, Museum of Fine Arts, Boston, gift of Mrs. J. R. Churchill.*)

do some good to help and support me. Mentioning Mrs. Gookin, Nath, the widow Weld was spoken of; said I had visited Mrs. Denison. I told her Yes! Afterward I said, if after a first and second vagary she would accept of me returning, her victorious kindness and good will would be very obliging. She thanked me for my book (Mr. Mayhew's sermon), but said not a word of the letter. When she insisted on the negative, I prayed there might be no more thunder and lightning, I should not sleep all night. I gave her Dr. Preston, The Church's Marriage and the Church's Carriage, which cost me 6 shillings at the sale.[22] The door standing open, Mr. Airs came in, hung up his hat, and sat down. After awhile, Madam Winthrop moving, he went out. Jonathan Eyre looked in, I said "How do ye," or "Your servant Mr. Eyre:" but heard no word from him. Sarah filled a glass of wine, she drank to me, I to her; she sent Juno home with me with a good lantern, I gave her 6 pence and bid her thank her mistress. In some of our discourse, I told her I had rather go to the stone-house adjoining to her, than to come to her against her mind. Told her the reason why I came every other night was lest I should drink too deep draughts of pleasure. She had talked of Canary, her kisses were to me better than the best Canary. Explained the expression concerning Columbus.

8^r 13. I tell my son and daughter Sewall, that the weather was not so fair as I apprehended. Mr. Sewall preached very well in Mr. Wadsworth's turn. Mr. Williams of Weston and Mr. Odlin dine with us. Text was the excellency of the knowledge of Christ.

Friday, 8^r 14. Made a dinner for my son and daughter Cooper. At table in the best room were sister Stoddard, daughter Cooper, His Excellency, Mrs. Hannah Cooper, Brother Stoddard, S. S., Mr. Joseph Sewall, Mr. Cooper, Mr. Sewall of Brooklin, Mrs. Rand, Mrs. Gerrish, daughter of Brooklin. Mr. Gerrish, Clark and Rand sat at a side-table.

8^r 15. Sent my son Cooper, Pareus, 3 books.

8^r 15. I dine on fish and oil at Mr. Stoddard's. Capt. Hill wished me joy of my proceedings i. e. with M[*adam*] Winthrop; Sister Cooper applauded it, spake of visiting her: I said her complaisance of her visit would be obliging to me.

8^r 16. *L. Day,* I upbraided myself that could be so solicitous about earthly things; and so cold and indifferent as to the love of Christ, who is altogether lovely. Mr. Prince administered. Dined at my son's with Mr. Cutler, and Mr. Shurtleff. Mr. Cutler preaches in the afternoon from Ezek. 16. 30, "How weak is thy heart." Son reads the order for the thanksgiving.

---

[22] *The Golden Scepter held forth to the humble. VVith the Chvrches Dignitie by her Marriage. And The Chvrches Dvtie in her Carriage.* In three Treatises . . . By the late learned and reverend Divine, John Preston (London, 1638). This was a volume of 461 pages which Sewall probably bought at the Auction Sale of Choice Books newly imported from Great Britain, sold at the Sign of the Magpy, 4 July 1720. (M. H. Thomas's note.)

8ʳ 17. *Monday,* give Mr. Danˡ Willard, and Mr. Pelatiah Whittemore their oaths to their accounts; and Mr. John Briggs to his, as they are attornies to Dr. Cotton Mather, administrator to the estate of Nathan Howell deceased. In the evening I visited Madam Winthrop, who treated me courteously, but not in clean linen as sometimes. She said she did not know whether I would come again, or no. I asked her how she could so impute inconstancy to me. (I had not visited her since Wednesday night being unable to get over the indisposition received by the treatment received that night, and *I must* in it seemed to sound like a made piece of formality.) Gave her this day's Gazette. Heard David Jeffries say the Lord's Prayer, and some other portions of the Scriptures. He came to the door, and asked me to go into chamber, where his grandmother was tending little Katee, to whom she had given physic; but I chose to sit below. Dr. Noyes and his wife came in, and sat a considerable time; had been visiting son and daughter Cooper. Juno came home with me.

8ʳ 18. Visited Madam Mico, who came to me in a splendid dress. I said, It may be you have heard of my visiting Madam Winthrop, her sister. She answered, her sister had told her of it. I asked her good will in the affair. She answered, if her sister were for it, she should not hinder it. I gave her Mr. Homes's sermon. She gave me a glass of Canary, entertained me with good discourse, and respectful remembrance of my first wife. I took leave.

8ʳ 19. Midweek, visited Madam Winthrop; Sarah told me she was at Mr. Walley's, would not come home till late. I gave her Hannah's 3 oranges with her duty, not knowing whether I should find her or no. Was ready to go home: but said if I knew she was there, I would go thither. Sarah seemed to speak with pretty good courage, she would be there. I·went and found her there, with Mr. Walley and his wife in the little room below. At 7 a-clock I mentioned going home; at 8. I put on my coat, and quickly waited on her home. She found occasion to speak loud to the servant, as if she had a mind to be known. Was courteous to me; but took occasion to speak pretty earnestly about my keeping a coach: I said 'twould cost £100. per annum: she said 'twould cost but £40. Spake much against John Winthrop, his falseheartedness. Mr. Eyre came in and sat awhile; I offered him Dr. Increase Mather's Sermons, whereof Mr. Appleton's Ordination Sermon was one; said he had them already. I said I would give him another. Exit. Came away somewhat late.

8ʳ 20. Mr. Colman preaches from Luke 15. 10. "Joy among the Angels:" made an excellent discourse.

At Council, Col. Townsend spake to me of my hood: should get a wig. I said 'twas my chief ornament: I wore it for sake of the day. Brother Odlin, and Sam, Mary, and Jane Hirst dine with us. Promised to wait on the Governor about 7. Madam Winthrop not being at Lecture, I went thither first; found her very serene with her daughter Noyes, Mrs. Dering, and the widow

Shipreeve sitting at a little table, she in her armed chair. She drank to me, and I to Mrs. Noyes. After awhile prayed the favor to speak with her. She took one of the candles, and went into the best room, closed the shutters, sat down upon the couch. She told me Madam Usher had been there, and said the coach must be set on wheels, and not by rusting. She spake something of my needing a wig. Asked me what her sister said to me. I told her, she said, If her sister were for it, she would not hinder it. But I told her, she did not say she would be glad to have me for her brother. Said, I shall keep you in the cold, and ask her if she would be within tomorrow night, for we had had but a running feast. She said she could not tell whether she should, or no. I took leave. As were drinking at the Governor's, he said: In England the ladies minded little more than that they might have money, and coaches to ride in. I said, And New England brooks its name. At which Mr. Dudley smiled. Governor said they were not quite so bad here.

8ʳ 21. *Friday,* My son, the minister, came to me p. m. by appointment and we pray one for another in the Old Chamber; more especially respecting my courtship. About 6. a-clock I go to Madam Winthrop's; Sarah told me her Mistress was gone out, but did not tell me whither she went. She presently ordered me a fire; so I went in, having Dr. Sibbes's *Bowels*[23] with me to read. I read the two first sermons, still nobody came in: at last about 9. a-clock Mr. Jonathan Eyre came in; I took the opportunity to say to him as I had done to Mrs. Noyes before, that I hoped my visiting his mother would not be disagreeable to him; he answered me with much respect. When 'twas after 9. a-clock, he of himself said he would go and call her, she was but at one of his brothers': a while after I heard Madam Winthrop's voice, inquiring something about John. After a good while and clapping the garden door twice or thrice, she came in. I mentioned something of the lateness; she bantered me, and said I was later. She received me courteously. I asked when our proceedings should be made public: she said, They were like to be no more public than they were already. Offered me no wine that I remember. I rose up at 11 a-clock to come away, saying I would put on my coat, she offered not to help me. I prayed her that Juno might light me home, she opened the shutter, and said 'twas pretty light abroad; Juno was weary and gone to bed. So I came home by starlight as well as I could. At my first coming in, I gave Sarah five shillings. I wrote Mr. Eyre his name in his book with the date Octobʳ 21. 1720. It cost me 8 shillings. Jehovah jireh![24] Madam told me she had visited M. Mico, Wendell, and Wᵐ Clark of the South

Octobʳ 22. Daughter Cooper visited me before my going out of town, staid till about sunset. I brought her going near as far as the orange tree.

---

[23] Richard Sibbes, *Bowels Opened: Or, A Discovery Of The Neare and Deare Love, Union and Communion betwixt Christ, and the Church* (London, 1641).

[24] That is, God will provide. See Genesis 22:14.

Coming back, near Leg's Corner, little David Jeffries saw me, and looking upon me very lovingly, asked me if I was going to see his grandmother? I said, Not tonight. Gave him a penny, and bid him present my service to his grandmother.

Octob^r 24. I went in the hackney coach through the Common, stopt at Madam Winthrop's (had told her I would take my departure from thence). Sarah came to the door with Katee in her arms: but I did not think to take notice of the child. Called her mistress. I told her, being encouraged by David Jeffries' loving eyes, and sweet words, I was come to enquire whether she could find in her heart to leave that house and neighborhood, and go and dwell with me at the Southend; I think she said softly, Not yet. I told her it did not lie in my hands to keep a coach. If I should, I should be in danger to be brought to keep company with her neighbor Brooker (he was a little before sent to prison for debt). Told her I had an antipathy against those who would pretend to give themselves; but nothing of their estate. I would a proportion of my estate with myself. And I supposed she would do so. As to a periwig, my best and greatest friend, I could not possibly have a greater, began to find me with hair before I was born, and had continued to do so ever since; and I could not find in my heart to go to another. She commended the book I gave her, Dr. Preston, the Church's Marriage; quoted him saying 'twas inconvenient keeping out of a fashion commonly used. I said the time and tide did circumscribe my visit. She gave me a dram of black cherry brandy, and gave me a lump of the sugar that was in it. She wished me a good journey. I prayed God to keep her, and came away. Had a very pleasant journey to Salem.

8^r 25. Sent a letter of it to my son by Wakefield, who delivered it not till Wednesday; so he visited her not till Friday p. m. and then presented my service to her.

8^r 27. Kept the Thanksgiving at Salem. Mr. Fisk preached very well from Ephes. 5. 20. Giving thanks always—dine at Col. Brown's.

[October] 29. 7. Hold court in the morn. Had a pleasant journey home a little before sunset.

[October] 30. 1. Mrs. Phillips and her son sit in their pew.

[October] 31. 2. She proves her husband's will. At night I visited Madam Winthrop about 6. p. m. They told me she was gone to Madam Mico's. I went thither and found she was gone; so returned to her house, read the Epistles to the Galatians, Ephesians in Mr. Eyre's Latin Bible. After the clock struck 8. I began to read the 103rd Psalm. Mr. Wendell came in from his warehouse. Asked me if I were alone? Spake very kindly to me, offered me to call Madam Winthrop. I told him, she would be angry, had been at M. Mico's; he helped me on with my coat and I came home: left the Gazett in the Bible, which told Sarah of, bid her present my service to M. Winthrop, and tell her I had been to wait on her if she had been at home.

Novr 1. I was so taken up that I could not go if I would.

Novr 2. Midweek, went again, and found Mrs. Alden there, who quickly went out. Gave her[25] about ½ pound of sugar almonds, cost 3 shillings per pound. Carried them on Monday. She seemed pleased with them, asked what they cost. Spake of giving her a hundred pounds per annum if I died before her. Asked her what sum she would give me, if she should die first? Said I would give her time to consider of it. She said she heard as if I had given all to my children by deeds of gift. I told her 'twas a mistake, Point Judith was mine etc. That in England, I owned, my father's desire was that it should go to my eldest son; 'twas 20£ per annum; she thought 'twas forty. I think when I seemed to excuse pressing this, she seemed to think 'twas best to speak of it; a long winter was coming on. Gave me a glass or two of Canary.

Novr 4th Friday, Went again about 7. a-clock; found there Mr. John Walley and his wife: sat discoursing pleasantly. I showed them Isaac Moses's [*an Indian*] writing. Madam W. served comfits to us. After awhile a table was spread, and supper was set. I urged Mr. Walley to crave a blessing; but he put it upon me. About 9. they went away. I asked Madam what fashioned necklace I should present her with, she said, None at all. I asked her whereabout we left off last time; mentioned what I had offered to give her; asked her what she would give me; she said she could not change her condition: she had said so from the beginning; could not be so far from her children, the Lecture. Quoted the Apostle Paul affirming that a single life was better than a married. I answered that was for the present distress. Said she had not pleasure in things of that nature as formerly: I said, you are the fitter to make me a wife. If she held in that mind, I must go home and bewail my rashness in making more haste than good speed. However, considering the supper, I desired her to be within next Monday night, if we lived so long. Assented. She charged me with saying, that she must put away Juno, if she came to me: I utterly denied it, it never came in my heart; yet she insisted upon it; saying it came in upon discourse about the Indian woman that obtained her freedom this Court. About 10. I said I would not disturb the good orders of her house, and came away. She not seeming pleased with my coming away. Spake to her about David Jeffries, had not seen him.

Monday, Novr 7th My son prayed in the Old Chamber. Our time had been taken up by son and daughter Cooper's visit; so that I only read the 130th and 143rd. Psalm. 'Twas on the account of my courtship. I went to Mad. Winthrop; found her rocking her little Katee in the cradle. I excused my coming so late (near eight). She set me an armed chair and cushion; and so the cradle was between her armed chair and mine. Gave her the remnant of my almonds; she did not eat of them as before; but laid them away; I said I came to enquire whether she had altered her mind since Friday, or remained of the same mind still. She said, Thereabouts. I told her I loved her, and was so fond as to think that she loved me: she said had a great respect for me. I told her, I had made her an offer, without asking any advice; she had so many to advise with, that 'twas a hindrance. The fire was come to one short brand besides the block, which brand was set up in end; at last it fell to pieces, and no recruit was made: she gave me a glass of wine. I think I repeated again that I would go home and bewail my rashness in making more haste than good speed. I would endeavor to contain myself, and not go on to solicit her to do that which she could not consent to. Took leave of her. As came down the steps she bid me have a care. Treated me courteously. Told her she had entered the 4th year of her widowhood. I had given her the newsletter before: I did not bid her draw off her glove as sometime I had done. Her dress was not so clean as sometime it had been. Jehovah jireh!

The Selling of Joseph[1]

> *Forasmuch as* liberty *is in real*
> *value next unto* life: *None ought*
> *to part with it themselves, or*
> *deprive others of it, but*
> *upon most mature*
> *consideration.*

The numerousness of slaves at this day in the province, and the uneasiness of them under their slavery, hath put many upon thinking whether the foundation of it be firmly and well laid; so as to sustain the vast weight that is built upon it. It is most certain that all men, as they are the sons of *Adam*, are coheirs; and have equal right unto liberty, and all other outward comforts of life. "God hath given the earth [with all its commodities] unto the sons of Adam," *Psal* 115. 16. "And hath made of one blood, all nations of men, for to dwell on all the face of the earth, and hath determined the times before appointed, and the bounds of their habitation: that they should seek the Lord. Forasmuch then as we are the offspring of God" etc.

Act 17. 26, 27, 29. Now although the title given by the last Adam, doth infinitely better men's estates, respecting God and themselves; and grants them a most beneficial and inviolable lease under the broad seal of heaven, who were before only tenants at will: yet through the indulgence of God to our first parents after the Fall, the outward estate of all and every of their children, remains the same, as to one another. So that originally, and natu-

---

[1] Boston, 1700.

rally, there is no such thing as slavery. *Joseph*[2] was rightfully no more a slave to his brethren, than they were to him: and they had no more authority to *sell* him, than they had to *slay* him. And if *they* had nothing to do to sell him; the *Ishmaelites* bargaining with them, and paying down twenty pieces of silver, could not make a title. Neither could *Potiphar*[3] have any better interest in him than the Ishmaelites had. *Gen.* 37. 20, 27, 28. For he that shall in this case plead *alteration of property,* seems to have forfeited a great part of his own claim to humanity. There is no proportion between twenty pieces of silver, and LIBERTY. The commodity itself is the claimer. If *Arabian* gold be imported in any quantities, most are afraid to meddle with it, though they might have it at easy rates; lest if it should have been wrongfully taken from the owners, it should kindle a fire to the consumption of their whole estate. 'Tis pity there should be more caution used in buying a horse, or a little lifeless dust; than there is in purchasing men and women: whenas they are the offspring of God, and their liberty is,

> . . . *Auro pretiosior Omni.*[4]

And seeing God hath said, "He that stealeth a man and selleth him, or if he be found in his hand, he shall surely be put to death." Exod. 21. 16. This law being of everlasting equity, wherein man stealing is ranked amongst the most atrocious of capital crimes: what louder cry can there be made of that celebrated warning,

> *Caveat Emptor!*[5]

And all things considered, it would conduce more to the welfare of the province, to have white servants for a term of years, than to have slaves for life. Few can endure to hear of a Negro's being made free;[6] and indeed they can seldom use their freedom well; yet their continual aspiring after their forbidden liberty, renders them unwilling servants. And there is such a disparity in their conditions, color and hair, that they can never embody with us, and grow up into orderly families, to the peopling of the land: but still remain in our body politic as a kind of extravasate blood. As many Negro men as there are among us, so many empty places there are in our Train Bands, and the places taken up of men that might make husbands for our daughters. And the sons and daughters of *New England* would become more

---

[2] The story of Joseph and his brothers begins in Genesis 37.

[3] The Pharaoh's chief steward, who bought Joseph as a slave from the Ishmaelites, to whom Joseph's brothers had sold him, Genesis 39.

[4] More precious than all gold.

[5] Let the buyer beware.

[6] Here Sewall appeals to, and himself expresses, racially prejudiced beliefs and anxieties about sexual union that have persisted through three centuries. See Winthrop Jordan, *White over Black.*

like *Jacob,* and *Rachel,*[7] if this slavery were thrust quite out of doors. More-over it is too well known what temptations masters are under, to connive at the fornication of their slaves; lest they should be obliged to find them wives, or pay their fines. It seems to be practically pleaded that they might be lawless; 'tis thought much of, that the law should have satisfaction for their thefts, and other immoralities; by which means, "Holiness to the Lord," is more rarely engraven upon this sort of servitude. It is likewise most lament-able to think, how in taking Negroes out of *Africa,* and selling of them here, That which God has joined together men do boldly rend asunder; men from their country, husbands from their wives, parents from their children. How horrible is the uncleanness, mortality, if not murder, that the ships are guilty of that bring great crowds of these miserable men, and women. Methinks, when we are bemoaning the barbarous usage of our friends and kinsfolk in *Africa:* it might not be unseasonable to enquire whether we are not culpable in forcing the *Africans* to become slaves amongst ourselves. And it may be a question whether all the benefit received by *Negro* slaves, will balance the accompt of cash laid out upon them; and for the redemption of our own enslaved friends out of *Africa.* Besides all the persons and estates that have perished there.

Obj. 1. *These blackamoors are of the posterity of* Cham, *and therefore are under the curse of slavery.*[8] Gen. 9. 25, 26, 27.

Answ. Of all offices, one would not beg this; *viz.* uncalled for, to be an executioner of the vindictive wrath of God; the extent and duration of which is to us uncertain. If this ever was a commission; how do we know but that it is long since out of date? Many have found it to their cost, that a prophetical denunciation of judgment against a person or people, would not warrrant them to inflict that evil. If it would, *Hazael* might justify himself in all he did against his master, and the *Israelites,* from 2 *Kings* 8.10, 12.[9]

But it is possible that by cursory reading, this text may have been mis-taken. For *Canaan* is the person cursed three times over, without the men-tioning of *Cham.* Good expositors suppose the curse entailed on him, and that this prophecy was accomplished in the extirpation of the *Canaanites,* and in the servitude of the *Gibeonites.*[10] *Vide Pareum.* Whereas the black-moors are not descended of *Canaan,* but of *Cush.* Psal. 68. 31. "Princes shall come out of Egypt [Mizraim] Ethiopia [Cush] shall soon stretch out her hands unto God." Under which names, all *Africa* may be comprehended;

---

[7] Rachel was Jacob's second wife, mother of Joseph and Benjamin. Genesis 29-35.

[8] The younger son of Noah saw his father naked, and thus provoked this curse when Noah awoke: "Cursed be Canaan: a servant of servants shall he be unto his brethren." Despite Sewall's textual criticism of this idea (below), it has persisted into the twentieth century.

[9] Elisha prophesies that Hazael will do great evil "unto the children of Israel," burning their cities, killing their young men, and slaughtering infants and pregnant women.

[10] See Joshua 9:14-27

and their promised conversion ought to be prayed for. *Jer.* 13.23. "Can the Ethiopian change his skin?" This shows that black men are the posterity of *Cush:* who time out of mind have been distinguished by their color. And for want of the true, *Ovid* assigns a fabulous cause of it.

> *Sanguine tum credunt in corpora summa vocato*
> *Æthiopum populos nigrum traxisse colorem.*
>
> Metamorph. lib. 2.[11]

Obj. 2. *The* Nigers *are brought out of a pagan country, into places where the gospel is preached.*

Answ. Evil must not be done, that good may come of it. The extraordinary and comprehensive benefit accruing to the Church of God, and to *Joseph* personally, did not rectify his brethren's sale of him.

Obj. 3. *The* Africans *have wars one with another: our ships bring lawful captives taken in those wars.*

Answ. For ought is known, their wars are much such as were between *Jacob's* sons and their brother *Joseph.* If they be between town and town; provincial, or national: every war is upon one side unjust. An unlawful war can't make lawful captives. And by receiving, we are in danger to promote, and partake in their barbarous cruelties. I am sure, if some gentlemen should go down to the *Brewsters* to take the air, and fish: and a stronger party from *Hull* should surprise them, and sell them for slaves to a ship outward bound: they would think themselves unjustly dealt with; both by sellers and buyers. And yet 'tis to be feared, we have no other kind of title to our *Nigers.* "Therefore all things whatsoever ye would that men should do to you, do ye even so to them: for this is the Law and the Prophets." Matt. 7.12.

Obj. 4. Abraham *had servants bought with his money, and born in his house.*

Answ. Until the circumstances of *Abraham's* purchase be recorded, no argument can be drawn from it. In the meantime, charity obliges us to conclude, that he knew it was lawful and good.

It is observable that the *Israelites* were strictly forbidden the buying, or selling one another for slaves. *Levit.* 25.39,46. *Jer.* 34.8. . . . 22.[12] And God gaged His blessing in lieu of any loss they might conceipt [conceive] they suffered thereby. *Deut.* 15. 18.[13] And since the partition wall is broken

---

[11] The reference is to Ovid's Metamorphoses, Book 2, which says, "Men believe that at that time the Ethiopians became black, because the heat drew their blood toward the outside of their bodies."

[12] This text not only prohibits buying and selling slaves but also prophesies that the retribution will include burning the cities of Judah.

[13] This text reminds the owner that the six years' service of his bondservant has been worth twice the value of a hired servant, and the owner is promised the Lord's blessing if he will obey the command to liberate every bondservant after six years.

down, inordinate self-love should likewise be demolished. God expects that Christians should be of a more ingenuous and benign frame of spirit. Christians should carry it to all the world, as the *Israelites* were to carry it one towards another. And for men obstinately to persist in holding their neighbors and brethren under the rigor of perpetual bondage, seems to be no proper way of gaining assurance that God has given them spiritual freedom. Our blessed Saviour has altered the measures of the ancient love-song, and set it to a most excellent new tune, which all ought to be ambitious of learning. *Matt.* 5. 43,44. *John* 13.34. These *Ethiopians,* as black as they are; seeing they are the sons and daughters of the first *Adam,* the brethren and sisters of the last Adam, and the offspring of God; they ought to be treated with a respect agreeable.

Servitus perfecta voluntaria, inter Christianum & Christianum, ex parte servi patientis sæpe est licita quia est necessaria: sed ex parte domini agentis, & procurando & exercendo, vix potest esse licita: quia non convenit regulæ illi generali: Quæcunque volueritis ut faciant vobis homines, ita & vos facite eis. Matt. 7.12.

Perfecta servitus pænæ, non potest jure locum habere, nisi ex delicto gravi quod ultimum supplicium aliquo modo meretur: quia Libertas ex naturali æstimatione proxime accedit ad vitam ipsam, & eidem a multis præferri solet.

Ames. Cas. Consc. Lib. 5.
Cap. 23. Thes. 2, 3.[14]

[14] William Ames, *Conscience with the Power and Cases Thereof* (London, 1643) translates the Latin thus (Book 5, p. 160): "Perfect servitude, so it be voluntary, is on the patient's part often lawful between Christian and Christian because indeed it is necessary: but on the master's part who is the agent, in procuring and exercising the authority, it is scarce lawful; in respect, it thwarts that general Canon, 'What you would have men do unto you, even so do unto them.' Matth. 17.12.

"Perfect servitude, by way of punishment, can have no place by right, unless for some heinous offense, which might deserve the severest punishment, to wit, death: because our liberty in the natural account, is the very next thing to life itself, yea by many is preferred before it."

COTTON MATHER

(1663–1728)

Cotton Mather, the prodigious grandson of John Cotton and Richard Mather, was also the eldest son of Increase Mather, an eminent minister in his own right who from the boy's early childhood "designed"

Portrait of Cotton Mather in the last year of his life. He was 65 on February 12, 1728. Mezzotint, 1727, by Peter Pelham *(The Granger Collection).*

him for the ministry, and who then had the pleasure of bringing him into his own church as Pastor before Cotton Mather was 20 years old. For more than 40 years the father and son served respectively as Teacher and Pastor of the Second Church of Boston. Besides preaching often in his own church and in others, Cotton Mather fulfilled the pastoral duties of a very large congregation and acted vigorously in politics and community affairs. He founded a group of young men's organizations, a scientific discussion group, and an organization of black men. He wrote the Declaration of Merchants and Gentlemen that was published as a broadside to support the eviction of the royal governor during the Glorious Revolution of 1689. He wrote the Return of Several Ministers that advised the special court trying the witchcraft cases of 1692. He worked hard with the New England Company to improve Indian churches and to alleviate Indian poverty. He led the movement for inoculation against smallpox. And somehow he managed to write more books and tracts than any other American of the seventeenth or eighteenth century.

Mather's place in American literature depends mainly on his immense folio church-history of New England, *Magnalia Christi Americana*. That sprawling epic begins by echoing Vergil's *Aeneid* ("I write the *Wonders* of the Christian Religion, flying from the Depravations of *Europe*, to the *American Strand*"), but its great strength is in the cumulative number of biographies that comprise three of its first four books. Under the influence of his eminent personal heritage and the proud but anxious needs of a third generation seemingly in flight from the founders' principles, Mather wrote the lives of the saints who had founded and nurtured New England. The historical key to Mather's achievement in those biographies is his ability to demonstrate the uniqueness of individual personalities and historical circumstances even as he virtually overwhelms us with evidence that this is hagiography, that these are the uniformly allegorical lives of Christians on their way to Glory. The two lives reprinted here exemplify that combi-

The standard reference work for the writings of Cotton Mather is Thomas J. Holmes, *Cotton Mather: A Bibliography of His Works,* 3 vols., 1940 (including commentary by several scholars on individual works).

Good editions are *The Diary of Cotton Mather,* 2 vols., ed. Worthington C. Ford, 1912; *Selections from Cotton Mather,* ed. Kenneth Murdock, 1926.

The standard biography is still Barrett Wendell, *Cotton Mather, The Puritan Priest,* 1891 (rpt., 1963).

Recent scholarship includes David Levin, "Introduction," to *Bonifacius, An Essay upon the Good* by Cotton Mather, 1966 (reprinted in Sacvan Bercovitch ed, *The American Puritan Imagination,* 1974); Robert Middlekauff, *The Mathers: Three Generations of Puritan Intellectuals,* 1971; Sacvan Bercovitch, "Cotton Mather," in *Major Writers of Early American Literature,* ed. Everett H. Emerson, 1972; and Sacvan Bercovitch, *The Puritan Origins of the American Self, 1975.*

nation of variety within essential sameness. No reader is likely to confuse the fat, choleric, uneducated treasure-seeker, Sir William Phips—
whose cry of "Thanks be to God, we're made!" rings through American
history and literature for all acquisitive children of destiny—with Winthrop and Bradford, the literate patriarchs of Plymouth and Massachusetts Bay. But the underlying allegorical resemblance is there in Mather's title, in the plain honesty of this man who trusts Providence, and
in his perplexity as he tries to know when or why Providence will grant
him a splendid victory over Catholic enemies at one point and a humiliating defeat at another.

The life of Phips, like many others in Mather's *Magnalia,* had been
published separately, but in the *Magnalia* it appears in a special context. After an introductory book on the founding, Mather writes the
lives of the governors, with a concern for the nature of civil liberty and
the rights of Englishmen as well as for Christian piety. He was the first
historian to see the importance of reprinting John Winthrop's now
celebrated speech on the difference between natural and civil or federal liberty (see above, pp. 91–93), and one of the first to base an
account of the bloodless Revolution of 1689 on principles and issues
that were to clash again in 1775. The third book, the Lives of the Ministers, shows by forcibly if sometimes monotonously repetitive example how dozens of promising or successful lives were transformed by
religious conversion, resistance to Anglican "ceremonies," persecution
under Archbishop Laud, and then emigration into the "wilderness" or
"desert" of America. The remaining four books deal with the history of
Harvard College, the documentary records of New England Congregational doctrines during the seventeenth century, the remarkable inter-
ventions of Providence in New England affairs, and finally "The Wars
of the Lord"—not only wars against Indian and French opponents but
invasions by witches, Quakers, and, in the last years of the century,
confidence-men.

Of Mather's many other works, the most important are probably his
"Reserved Memorials," published in 1912 under the misleading title
The Diary of Cotton Mather and still in print under that title today;
Bonifacius (better known by its running title, *Essays to Do Good*),
1710; *The Christian Philosopher* (essays on Nature and piety), 1712;
Manuductio ad Ministerium, advice to young students and ministers,
1726; and two other manuscripts that were not published during Mather's lifetime, *Curiosa Americana* (letters to the Royal Society in England, which elected him a member in 1713) and *Biblia Americana* (an
immense biblical commentary that has never been edited or published).

Ever since 1692, when he played a debatable role in the Salem
witchcraft trials, Mather has been a controversial figure in American

legend and literary history. Readers of this anthology will find his negative image in Washington Irving's "The Legend of Sleepy Hollow." In that tradition Mather is ridiculed as a credulous, superstitious, meddling, pedantic figure or scorned as a vengeful bigot. For generations, moreover, he has also been defended as a humane, conscientious, liberal man. Passionately pious, proud, vain, he was obsessed with his place in history. He felt obliged to welcome and to disseminate the new scientific revelations of his time, and he was convinced—partly by Biblical and historical study and partly by extraordinary revelations from an angel—that his own lifetime would see the beginning of the Millennium and that Boston could become the New Jerusalem. Although some interpreters believe that he was chained to the past, other critics condemn him for surrendering old virtues to the new opportunism, old piety to the new contentment with mere moralizing and do-gooding. He himself thought that he was conserving, communicating, and extending the best knowledge and pious tradition of the founders for use in the glorious new world. He was not marketing religion, but trying to bring religion into the market. He was trying to do good in the world for the glory of God. With Jonathan Edwards in the next generation, Mather was one of the last of our intellectual leaders to believe with equal strength in the reality of the invisible world of devils and angels, and the new world of scientific inquiry.

Magnalia Christi Americana Book II[1]

CHAPTER IV
NEHEMIAS AMERICANUS.[2] THE LIFE OF
JOHN WINTHROP, ESQ; GOVERNOR OF THE
MASSACHUSET COLONY

Quicunq; Venti erunt, Ars nostra certe non aberit. Cicer.[3]

§1. Let *Greece* boast of her patient *Lycurgus*, the *lawgiver*, by whom *diligence, temperance, fortitude* and *wit* were made the *fashions* of a therefore long-lasting and renowned commonwealth; let *Rome* tell of her devout *Numa*, the *lawgiver*, by whom the most famous commonwealth saw *peace*

[1] The text is the London edition of 1702. The translation and initialed notes are by Kenneth B. Murdock, in *Selections from Cotton Mather*, New York, 1926.

[2] "The American Nehemiah." Nehemiah rebuilt the walls of Jerusalem.

[3] "Whatever winds shall blow, our art surely shall not die." Cicero.

Magnalia Christi Americana:

OR, THE

Ecclesiastical History

OF

NEW-ENGLAND,

FROM

Its First Planting in the Year 1620. unto the Year of our LORD, 1698.

In Seven BOOKS.

I. Antiquities: In Seven Chapters. With an Appendix.

II. Containing the Lives of the Governours, and Names of the Magistrates of *New-England:* In Thirteen Chapters. With an Appendix.

III. The Lives of Sixty Famous Divines, by whose Ministry the Churches of *New-England* have been Planted and Continued.

IV. An Account of the University of *Cambridge* in *New-England*; in Two Parts. The First contains the Laws, the Benefactors, and Vicissitudes of *Harvard College*; with Remarks upon it. The Second Part contains the Lives of some Eminent Persons Educated in it.

V. Acts and Monuments of the Faith and Order in the Churches of *New-England*, passed in their Synods; with Historical Remarks upon those Venerable Assemblies; and a great Variety of Church-Cases occurring, and resolved by the Synods of those Churches: In Four Parts.

VI. A Faithful Record of many Illustrious, Wonderful Providences, both of Mercies and Judgments, on divers Persons in *New-England:* In Eight Chapters.

VII. *The Wars of the Lord.* Being an History of the Manifold Afflictions and Disturbances of the Churches in *New-England*, from their Various Adversaries, and the Wonderful Methods and Mercies of God in their Deliverance: In Six Chapters: To which is subjoined, An Appendix of Remarkable Occurrences which *New-England* had in the Wars with the *Indian* Salvages, from the Year 1688, to the Year 1698.

By the Reverend and Learned *COTTON MATHER*, M. A. And Pastor of the North Church in *Boston, New-England.*

LONDON:

Printed for *Thomas Parkhurst*, at the *Bible* and *Three Crowns* in *Cheapside.* MDCCII.

Title page of Cotton Mather's Church history, 1702. *(Rare Book Division, New York Public Library, Astor, Lenox, and Tilden Foundations.)*

triumphing over extinguished *war,* and cruel *plunders,* and *murders* giving place to the more mollifying exercises of his *religion.* Our *New England* shall tell and boast of her WINTHROP, a *lawgiver,* as patient as *Lycurgus,* but not admitting any of *his* criminal disorders; as devout as *Numa,* but not liable to any of *his* heathenish madnesses; a *governor* in whom the excellencies of *Christianity* made a most improving addition unto the *virtues,* wherein even without *those* he would have made a *parallel* for the great men of *Greece,* or of *Rome,* which the pen of a *Plutarch* has eternized.

§2. A stock of *heroes* by right should afford nothing but what is *heroical;* and nothing but an extreme degeneracy would make any thing less to be expected from a stock of *Winthrops.* Mr. *Adam Winthrop,* the son of a worthy gentleman wearing the same name, was himself a worthy, a discreet, and a learned gentleman, particularly eminent for *skill* in the *law,* nor without remark for *love* to the *Gospel,* under the reign of King *Henry* VIII. And brother to a memorable *favorer* of the *reformed religion* in the days of Queen *Mary,* into whose hands the famous martyr *Philpot* committed his *papers,* which afterwards made no inconsiderable part of our *martyr-books.* This Mr. *Adam Winthrop* had a son of the same name also, and of the same endowments and employments with his father; and this third *Adam Winthrop* was the father of that renowned *John Winthrop,* who was the father of *New England,* and the founder *of a colony,* which upon many accounts, like *him* that founded it, may challenge the *first place* among the *English* glories of *America.*[4] Our JOHN WINTHROP thus born at the mansion house of his ancestors, at *Groton* in *Suffolk,* on *June* 12. 1587.[5] enjoyed afterwards an agreeable education. But though he would rather have devoted himself unto the study of Mr. *John Calvin,* than of Sir *Edward Cook;* nevertheless, the accomplishments of a *lawyer,* were those wherewith Heaven made his chief opportunities to be serviceable.

§3. Being made, at the unusually early age of *eighteen,* a *Justice of Peace,*[6] his virtues began to fall under a more general observation; and he not only so *bound himself to the behavior* of a *Christian,* as to become exemplary for a conformity to the *laws* of *Christianity* in his own conversation, but also discovered a more than ordinary measure of those qualities, which adorn an *officer of humane society.* His *justice* was impartial, and used the *balance* to weigh not the *cash,* but the *case* of those who were before him: *Prosopolatria,* he reckoned as bad as *Idololatria.*[7] His *wisdom* did exquisitely temper things according to the *art of governing,* which is a business of more contrivance than the *seven arts of the schools: oyer* still went before *terminer* in all his administrations:[8] his *courage* made him *dare to do right,*

---

[4] Mr. R. C. Winthrop in his *Life and Letters of John Winthrop* (2d ed.), 1, 12, 13, calls attention to some possible errors in this paragraph. [K.B.M.]

[5] According to later biographers, January 12, 1587–88. [K.B.M.]

[6] R. C. Winthrop, *op. cit.* 1, 223. [K.B.M.]

[7] "Worship of persons" as bad as "worship of idols." [K.B.M.]

[8] "Hearing" before "judging." [K.B.M.]

and fitted him to stand among the *lions*, that have sometimes been the *supporters* of the throne:[9] all which virtues he rendered the more illustrious, by *emblazoning* them with the constant *liberality* and *hospitality* of a *gentleman*. This made him the *terror* of the wicked, and *delight* of the sober, the *envy* of the many, but the *hope* of those who had any *hopeful design* in hand for the common good of the nation, and interests of religion.

§4. Accordingly when the *noble design* of carrying a colony of *Chosen People* into an *American* wilderness, was by *some* eminent persons undertaken, *this* eminent person was, by the consent of all, *chosen* for the *Moses*, who must be the leader of so great an undertaking: and indeed nothing but a *Mosaic spirit* could have carried him through the *temptations*, to which either his *farewell* to his *own land*, or his *travel* in a *strange land*, must needs expose a gentleman of his *education*. Wherefore having sold a fair estate of six or seven hundred a year, he transported himself with the effects of it into *New England* in the year 1630 where he spent it upon the service of a famous plantation founded and formed for the seat of the most *reformed Christianity*: and continued there, conflicting with *temptations*, of all sorts, as many years as the *nodes* of the *Moon* take to dispatch a revolution.[10] Those persons were never concerned in a *new plantation*, who know not that the unavoidable difficulties of such a thing, will call for all the *prudence* and *patience* of a mortal man to encounter therewithal; and they must be very insensible of the influence, which the *just wrath* of Heaven has permitted the *devils* to have upon *this world*, if they do not think that the difficulties of a *new plantation*, devoted unto the *evangelical worship* of our Lord Jesus Christ, must be yet more than ordinary. How *prudently*, how *patiently*, and with how much resignation to our Lord Jesus Christ, our brave *Winthrop* waded through these *difficulties*, let posterity consider with admiration. And know, that as the *picture* of this their *governor*, was, after his *death*, hung up with honor in the *state house* of his country, so the *wisdom, courage,* and holy *zeal* of his *life*, were an example well-worthy to be copied by all that shall succeed in *government*.

§5. Were he now to be considered only as a *Christian*, we might therein propose him as greatly imitable. He was a very *religious* man; and as he strictly kept his *heart*, so he kept his *house*, under the laws of *piety; there* he was every day constant in holy duties, both morning and evening, and on the *Lord's days*, and *Lectures;* though he *wrote* not after the preacher, yet such was his *attention*, and such his *retention* in *hearing*, that he repeated unto his *family* the *sermons* which he had heard in the congregation. But it is chiefly as a *governor* that he is now to be considered. Being the *governor* over the considerablest part of *New England*, he maintained the figure and honor of

[9] "Let judges also remember, that Solomon's throne was supported by lions on both sides: let them be lions, but yet lions under the throne." Bacon, *Essay of Judicature.* [K.B.M.]

[10] The time required for a revolution of the nodes of the moon is 186 years. [K.B.M.]

his place with the spirit of a true *gentleman;* but yet with such obliging *condescension* to the circumstances of the colony, that when a certain troublesome and malicious calumniator, well known in those times, printed his libelous *nicknames* upon the chief persons here, the worst *nickname* he could find for the Governor, was *John Temper-well;* and when the calumnies of that ill man caused the Archbishop to summon one Mr. *Cleaves* before the King, in hopes to get some accusation from him against the country, Mr. *Cleaves* gave such an account of the Governor's laudable carriage in all respects, and the serious devotion wherewith prayers were both publicly and privately made for His Majesty, that the King expressed himself most highly *pleased* therewithal, only *sorry* that so worthy a person should be no better accommodated than with the hardships of *America*. He was, indeed, a *governor,* who had most exactly studied that book, which pretending to teach *politics,* did only contain *three leaves,* and but *one word* in each of those leaves, which word was "MODERATION." Hence, though he were a zealous enemy to all *vice,* yet his *practice* was according to his *judgment* thus expressed; *in the infancy of plantations, justice should be administered with more lenity than in a settled state; because people are more apt then to transgress; partly out of ignorance of new laws and orders, partly out of oppression of business, and other straits.* [LENTO GRADU[11]] *was the old rule; and if the strings of a new instrument be wound up unto their height, they will quickly crack.* But when some leading and learned men took offense at his conduct in this matter, and upon a *conference* gave it in as their opinion, *that a stricter discipline was to be used in the beginning of a plantation, than after its being with more age established and confirmed,* the Governor being readier to see *his own* errors than *other men's,* professed his purpose to endeavor their satisfaction with less of *lenity* in his administrations. At that *conference* there were drawn up several other *articles* to be observed between the Governor and the rest of the Magistrates, which were of this import: *that the Magistrates,* as far as might be, should aforehand ripen their *consultations,* to produce that *unanimity* in their *public votes,* which might make them liker to the *voice of God; that if differences* fell out among them in their public meetings, they should speak only to the *case,* without any reflection, with all due *modesty,* and but by way of *question;* or desire the deferring of the *cause* to further time; and after *sentence* to intimate privately no *dislike; that* they should be more *familiar,* friendly and open unto each other, and more frequent in their *visitations,* and not any way expose each other's *infirmities,* but seek the *honor* of each other, and all the Court; *that* one Magistrate shall not *cross* the proceedings of another, without first advising with him; and *that* they should in all their appearances abroad, be so circumstanced as to prevent all contempt of authority; and *that* they should support and strengthen all *under officers.* All of which *articles* were observed by no man more than by the *Governor* himself.

[11] "By slow degrees."

§6. But whilst he thus did as our *New English Nehemiah*, the part of a *ruler* in managing the public affairs of our *American Jerusalem*, when there were *Tobijahs* and *Sanballats* enough to vex him,° and give him the experiment of *Luther's* observation, *Omnis qui regit, est tanquam signum, in quod omnia Jacula, Satan & Mundus dirigunt;* he made himself still an exacter *parallel* unto that Governor of *Israel*, by doing the part of a *neighbor* among the distressed people of the *new plantation*. To teach them the *frugality* necessary for those times, he abridged himself of a thousand comfortable things, which he had allowed himself elsewhere: his *habit* was not that *soft raiment*, which would have been disagreeable to a *wilderness;* his *table* was not covered with the *superfluities* that would have invited unto *sensualities: water* was commonly his *own drink*, though he gave wine to *others*. But at the time his *liberality* unto the needy was even beyond measure generous; and therein he was continually causing *"The blessing of him that was ready to perish to come upon him, and the heart of the widow and the orphan to sing for joy:*[12] But none more than those of deceased *ministers*, whom he always treated with a very singular compassion; among the instances whereof we still enjoy with us the worthy and now aged son of that Reverend *Higginson*, whose death left his family in a wide world soon after his arrival here, publicly acknowledging the charitable *Winthrop* for his *foster father.*[13] It was oftentimes no small trial unto his *faith*, to think, *How a table for the people should be furnished when they first came into the wilderness!* And for very many of the people, his *own good works* were needful, and accordingly employed for the answering of his *faith*. Indeed, for a while the Governor was the *Joseph*, unto whom the whole body of the people repaired when their *corn* failed them: and he continued relieving of them with his *open-handed bounties*, as long as he had any stock to do it with; and a lively *faith* to *see* the return of the *bread after many days*, and not *starve* in the days that were to pass till that *return* should be *seen*, carried him cheerfully through those expenses. Once it was observable, that on *Feb. 5. 1630.* when he was distributing the last handful of *the meal in the barrel* unto a poor man distressed by the wolf *at the door*, at that instant they spied a ship arrived at the harbor's mouth laden with *provisions* for them all. Yea, the Governor sometimes made his own *private purse* to be the *public;* not by *sucking* into it, but by *squeezing* out of it; for when the *public treasure* had nothing in it, he did himself defray the charges of the *public*. And having learned that lesson of our Lord, *that it is better to give, than to receive*, he did, at the General Court when he was a third time chosen Governor, make a speech unto this purpose, "That he had received gratuties from diverse towns,

---

° When Nehemiah rebuilt the wall of Jerusalem, Sanballat and Tobijah mocked him and threatened to break it down. Nehemiah 4:7-17. [D.L.]

[12] Job 29:11-13.

[13] John, son of Francis Higginson. He wrote an "Attestation" prefixed to the *Magnalia*.

which he accepted with much comfort and content; and he had likewise received civilities from particular persons, which he could not refuse without incivility in himself: nevertheless, he took them with a trembling heart, in regard of God's word, and the conscience of his own infirmities; and therefore he desired them that they would not hereafter take it ill if he refused such presents for the time to come." 'Twas his custom also to send some of his family upon errands, unto the houses of the poor about their *mealtime,* on purpose to *spy* whether they *wanted;* and if it were found that they *wanted,* he would make *that* the opportunity of sending supplies unto them. And there was one passage of his *charity* that was perhaps a little *unusual:* in an hard and long winter, when *wood* was very scarce at *Boston,* a man gave him a private *information,* that a needy person in the neighborhood stole *wood* sometimes from *his* pile: whereupon the Governor in a seeming anger did reply, "Does he so? I'll take a course with him; go, call that man to me, I'll warrant you I'll cure him of stealing!" When the man came, the Governor considering that if he had *stolen,* it was more out of *necessity* than *disposition,* said unto him, *"Friend, it is a severe winter, and I doubt you are but meanly provided for wood; wherefore I would have you supply your self at my woodpile till this cold season be over."* And he then merrily asked his friends, *whether he had not effectually cured this man of stealing his wood?*

§7.   One would have imagined that so *good* a man could have had no *enemies;* if we had not had a daily and woeful experience to convince us, that *goodness* itself will *make* enemies. It is a wonderful speech of *Plato* (in one of his books, *De Republica*) "For the trial of true virtue, 'tis necessary that a good man μηδὲν αδικῶν, δόξαν ἔχει την μεγίστην αδικιας. Tho' he do no unjust thing, should suffer the infamy of the greatest injustice." The Governor had by his unspotted *integrity,* procured himself a great reputation among the *people;* and then the crime of *popularity* was laid unto his charge by such, who were willing to deliver him from the danger of having *all men speak well of him.* Yea, there were persons eminent both for figure and for number, unto whom it was almost *essential* to *dislike* everything that came from *him;* and yet *he* always maintained an amicable correspondence with them; as believing that they acted according to their judgment and conscience, or that their eyes were held by some *temptation* in the worst of all their oppositions. Indeed, his *right works* were so many, that they exposed him unto the *envy* of his neighbors; and of such *power* was that *envy,* that sometimes he could not *stand before it;* but it was by *not standing* that he most effectually *withstood* it all. Great attempts were sometimes made among the *freemen,* to get him left out from his place in the *government* upon little pretenses, lest by the too *frequent choice* of one man, the *government* should cease to be by *choice;* and with a particular aim at *him,* sermons were preached at the Anniversary Court of *Election,* to dissuade the *freemen* from choosing *one man* twice together. This was the reward of his *extraordinary serviceableness!* But when these attempts *did* succeed, as they sometimes *did,* his profound *humility* appeared in that *equality of mind,* wherewith he applied himself cheerfully to serve the country in whatever station their *votes* had allotted for him. And one year when the *votes* came to be numbered, there were found six less for Mr. *Winthrop,* than for another gentleman who then stood in competition: but several other persons regularly tendering their *votes* before the *election* was published, were, upon a very frivolous objection, refused by some of the Magistrates, that were afraid lest the *election* should at last fall upon Mr. *Winthrop:* which though it was well perceived, yet such was the *self-denial,* of this *patriot,* that he would not permit any notice to be taken of the injury. But these *trials* were nothing in comparison of those harsher and harder *treats,* which he sometimes had from the *frowardness* of not a few in the days of their *paroxysms;* and from the *faction* of some against him, not much unlike that of the *Piazzi* in *Florence* against the family of the *Medici:* all of which he at last conquered by conforming to the famous *judge's* motto, *Prudens qui Patiens.* [14] The oracles of God have said, "Envy is rottenness to the bones;" and *Guliclmus Parisiensis* [15] applies it unto rulers, who are as it were the *bones* of the societies which they belong unto: "Envy," says he, "is often found among them, and it is rottenness unto them." Our *Winthrop* encountered this *envy* from others, but conquered it, by being free from it himself.

§8. Were it not for the sake of introducing the exemplary skill of this wise man, *at giving soft answers,* one would not choose to relate those instances of *wrath,* which he had sometimes to encounter with; but he was for his *gentleness,* his *forbearance,* and his *longanimity,* a pattern so worthy to be written *after,* that something must here be written *of* it. He seemed indeed never to speak any other language than that of *Theodosius:* "If any man speak evil of the Governor, if it be thro' lightness, 'tis to be contemned; if it be thro' madness, 'tis to be pitied; if it be thro' injury, 'tis to be remitted." Behold, reader, the *meekness* of *wisdom* notably exemplified! There was a time when he received a very sharp letter from a gentleman, who was a member of the Court, but he delivered back the letter unto the messengers that brought it with such a Christian speech as this: "I am not willing to keep such a matter of provocation by me!" Afterwards, the same gentleman was compelled by the scarcity of provisions to send unto him that he would sell him some of his cattle; whereupon the Governor prayed him to accept what he had sent for as a *token* of his good will; but the gentleman returned him this answer: "Sir, your overcoming of your self hath overcome me;" and afterwards gave demonstration of it. The *French* have a saying, that *Un*

---

[14] "He is prudent who is patient."
[15] William, who became Bishop at Paris, in 1228. [K. B. M.]

honeste homme, est un homme mesle! A *good* man is a *mixed* man; and there hardly ever was a more sensible *mixture* of those two things, *resolution* and *condescension,* than in this good man. There was a time when the Court of *Election,* being for fear of tumult, held at *Cambridge, May* 17. 1637, the sectarian part of the country, who had the year before gotten a *governor* more unto their mind, had a project now to have confounded the *election,* by demanding that the *court* would consider a *petition* then rendered before their proceeding thereunto. Mr. *Winthrop* saw that this was only a trick to throw all into confusion, by putting off the *choice* of the *Governor* and *Assistants* until the *day* should be over; and therefore he did, with a strenuous *resolution,* procure a disappointment unto that mischievous and ruinous contrivance. Nevertheless, Mr. *Winthrop* himself being by the voice of the Freemen in this exigency chosen the *Governor,* and all of the other party left out, that ill-affected party discovered the *dirt* and *mire,* which remained with them, after the *storm* was over; particularly the *sergeants,* whose office 'twas to attend the *Governor,* laid down their *halberds;* but such was the *condescension* of this Governor, as to take no present notice of this anger and contempt, but only order some of his own servants to take the *halberds:* and when the country manifested their deep resentments of the affront thus offered him, *he* prayed them to *overlook* it. But it was not long before a compensation was made for these things by the *doubled respects* which were from all parts paid unto him. Again, there was a time when the suppression of an *Antinomian* and *Familistical* faction, which extremely threatened the ruin of the country, was generally thought much owing unto this renowned man;[16] and therefore when the friends of that faction could not wreak their displeasure on him with any *politic* vexations, they set themselves to do it by *ecclesiastical* ones. Accordingly when a sentence of *banishment* was passed on the ringleaders of those disturbances, who

—*Maira & Terras, Cælumq; profundum,*
Quippe ferant, Rapidi, secum, vertantq; per Auras;[17]

many at the church of *Boston,* who were then that way too much inclined, most earnestly solicited the Elders of that church, whereof the Governor was a *member,* to call him forth as an *offender* for passing of that sentence. The *Elders* were unwilling to do any such thing; but the Governor under-

---

[16] Both the disputed election and the Antinomian controversy, which eventually led to the banishment of Anne Hutchinson, are described here in a way that puts Winthrop in the best possible light. The issues are complex. See *The Antinomian Controversy,* *1636-1638; a Documentary History,* David D. Hall comp., Middletown, Conn., 1968.

[17] "Swift bear with them sea and earth and the lofty sky, and drive them through the air."

standing the *ferment* among the *people,* took that occasion to make a speech in the congregation to this effect.

> *Brethren,* understanding that some of you have desired that I should answer for an *offense* lately taken among you; had I been called upon so to do, I would, *first,* have advised with the Ministers of the country, whether the *church* had power to call in question the *civil court;* and I would, *secondly,* have advised with the rest of the *court,* whether I might discover their counsels unto the *church.* But though I know that the reverend *Elders* of this church, and some others, do very well apprehend that the *church* cannot enquire into the proceedings of the *court;* yet for the satisfaction of the weaker who do not apprehend it, I will declare my mind concerning it. If the *church* have any such power, they have it from the Lord Jesus Christ; but the Lord Jesus Christ hath disclaimed it, not only by *practice,* but also by *precept,* which we have in his Gospel, *Mat. 20. 25, 26.* It is true indeed, that *Magistrates,* as they are *church-members,* are accountable unto the *church* for their failings; but that is when they are out of their calling. When *Uzziah* would go offer incense in the *temple,* the officers of the *church* called him to an account, and withstood him; but when *Asa* put the Prophet in prison, the officers of the *church* did not call *him* to an account for *that.*[18] If the *magistrate* shall in a *private way* wrong any man, the *church* may call him to an account for it; but if he be in pursuance of a course of *justice,* though the thing that he does be *unjust,* yet he is not accountable for it before the *church.* As for myself I did nothing in the causes of any of the *brethren,* but by the advice of the *Elders* of the *church.* Moreover, in the *oath* which I have taken there is this clause, 'In all causes wherein you are to give your vote, you shall do as in your judgment and conscience you shall see to be just, and for the public good.' And I am satisfied, it is most for the glory of God, and the *public good,* that there has been such a *sentence* passed; yea, those *brethren* are so divided from the *rest* of the country in their opinions and practices, that it cannot stand with the *public peace* for them to continue with us; *Abraham* saw that *Hagar* and *Ishmael* must be sent away.[19]

By such a speech he marvellously convinced, satisfied and mollified the *uneasy brethren* of the church; *Sic cunctus Pelagi cecidit Fragor—.*[20] And after a little patient waiting, the *differences* all so wore away, that the

---

[18] For Uzziah, see 2 Chronicles 26:16–21; for Asa, 2 Chronicles 16:7–11.

[19] Genesis 10:1–16; 21:9–14.

[20] "So all the din of the sea subsided."

church, merely as a token of respect unto the Governor, when he had newly met with some *losses* in his estate, sent him a present of several *hundreds* of pounds. Once more there was a time, when some active spirits among the *Deputies* of the colony, by their endeavors not only to make themselves a *court of judicature*, but also to take away the *negative* by which the *Magistrates* might check their *votes*, had like by over-driving to have run the whole government into something too *democratical*. And if there were a town in *Spain* undermined by *coneys*, another town in *Thrace* destroyed by *moles*, a third in *Greece* ranversed by *frogs*, a fourth in *Germany* subverted by *rats;* I must on this occasion add, that there was a country in *America* like to be confounded by a *swine*. A certain *stray sow* being found, was claimed by two several persons with a claim so equally maintained on both sides, that after six or seven years *hunting* the business, from one court unto another, it was brought at last into the *General Court*, where the final determination was, *that it was impossible to proceed unto any judgment in the case.* However in the debate of this matter, the *negative* of the *upper house* upon the *lower* in that Court was brought upon the stage; and agitated with so hot a zeal, that a *little more and all had been in the fire.* In these agitations the Governor was informed that an offense had been taken by some eminent persons, at certain passages in a discourse by him written thereabout; whereupon with his usual *condescendency*, when he next came into the General Court, he made a speech of this import.

I understand, that some have *taken* offense at something that I have lately written; which *offense* I desire to remove now, and begin this year in a reconciled state with you all. As for the *matter* of my writing, I had the concurrence of my *brethren;* it is a point of *judgment* which is not at my own disposing. I have examined it over and over again, by such *light* as God has given me, from the rules of *religion, reason,* and *custom;* and I see no cause to retract any thing of it: wherefore I must enjoy my *liberty* in *that*, as *you* do yourselves. But for the *manner, this,* and all that was blameworthy in it, was wholly *my own;* and whatsoever I might allege for my own justification therein before *men,* I waive it, as now setting myself before another *Judgment Seat.* However, what I wrote was upon *great provocation*, and to vindicate myself and others from great aspersion; yet that was no sufficient warrant for me to allow any *distemper of spirit* in myself; and I doubt I have been too prodigal of my *brethren's reputation;* I might have maintained my cause without casting any blemish upon others, when I made that my conclusion. *And now let religion and sound reason give judgment in the case;* it looked as if I arrogated too much unto *myself,* and too little to *others.* And when I made that profession, *that I would maintain what*

I wrote before all the world, though such words might modestly be spoken, yet I perceive an unbeseeming *pride* of my own heart breathing in them. For these failings I ask pardon both of God and man.

Sic ait, & dicto citius Tumida Æquora placat,
Collectasq; fugat Nubes, Solemq; reducit.[21]

This *acknowledging disposition* in the Governor, made them all *acknowledge*, that he was truly a *man of an excellent spirit*. In fine, the *victories* of an *Alexander*, an *Hannibal*, or a *Caesar* over *other men*, were not so glorious, as the *victories* of this great man over *himself*, which also at last proved *victories* over *other men*.

§9.   But the stormiest of all the *trials*° that ever befell this gentleman, was in the year 1645 when he was in *title* no more than *Deputy-Governor* of the colony. If the famous *Cato*[22] were forty-four times called into judgment, but as often acquitted; let it not be wondered, and if our famous *Winthrop* were one time so. There happening certain seditious and mutinous practices in the town of *Hingham*, the *Deputy-Governor* as legally as prudently interposed his *authority* for the checking of them: whereupon there followed such an *enchantment* upon the minds of the *Deputies* in the General Court, that upon a scandalous petition of the delinquents unto *them*, wherein a pretended invasion made upon the *liberties* of the *people* was complained of, the *Deputy-Governor* was most irregularly called forth unto an ignominious *hearing* before them in a vast assembly; whereto with a *sagacious humility* he *consented*, although he showed them how he might have *refused* it. The result of that *hearing* was that notwithstanding the touchy *jealousy* of the *people* about their *liberties* lay at the bottom of all this prosecution, yet Mr. *Winthrop* was publicly acquitted, and the offenders were severally fined and censured. But Mr. *Winthrop* then resuming the place of *Deputy-Governor* on the bench, saw cause to speak unto the *root of the matter* after this manner.

I shall not now speak any thing about the past *proceedings* of this Court, or the *persons* therein concerned. Only I bless God that I see an issue of this troublesome affair. I am well satisfied that I was publicly *accused*, and that I am now publicly *acquitted*. But though I am justified before *men*, yet it may be the *Lord* hath seen so much amiss in my administrations, as calls me to be *humbled;* and indeed for me to have been thus charged by *men*, is itself a matter of *humiliation*, whereof I

[21] "So he spoke, and thus quickly calmed the swelling sea, put to rout the gathered clouds, and brought back the sun."

° Compare Winthrop's own account of this crisis, above, pp. 91-93. [D. L.]
[22] Roman statesman (95-46 B. C.)

desire to make a right use before the *Lord*. If *Miriam's*[23] father spit in her face, she is to be *ashamed*. But give me leave before you go, to say something that may rectify the *opinions* of many *people*, from whence the *distempers* have risen that have lately prevailed upon the *body* of *this* people. The questions that have troubled the country have been about the *authority of the magistracy*, and the *liberty of the people*. It is *you* who have called *us* unto this office; but being thus *called*, we have our *authority* from *God;* it is the *ordinance* of *God*, and it hath the *image* of God stamped upon it; and the contempt of it has been vindicated by *God*, with terrible examples of his vengeance. I entreat you to consider, that when you choose *Magistrates*, you take them from among yourselves, *men subject unto like passions with yourselves*. If you see *our* infirmities, reflect on *your own*, and you will not be so severe censurers of *ours*. We count him a *good servant* who *breaks not his covenant;* the *Covenant* between *us* and *you*, is the *oath* you have taken of *us*, which is to this purpose: *that we shall govern you, and judge your causes, according to God's laws, and our own, according to our best skill*. As for our *skill*, you must run the hazard of it; and if there be an error, not in the *will*, but only in the *skill*, it becomes *you* to bear it. Nor would I have you to mistake in the point of your own *liberty*. There is a *liberty* of corrupt nature, which is affected both by *men* and *beasts*, to do what they list; and this *liberty* is inconsistent with *authority*, impatient of all restraint; by this *liberty*, *Sumus Omnes Deteriores;*[24] 'Tis the grand enemy of *truth* and *peace*, and all the ordinances of God are bent against it. But there is a civil, a moral, a federal *liberty*, which is the proper end and object of *authority; it* is a *liberty* for that only which is *just* and *good;* for this *liberty* you are to stand with the hazard of your very *lives;* and whatsoever crosses it, is not *authority*, but a *distemper* thereof. This *liberty* is maintained in a way of *subjection* to *authority;* and the *authority* set over you, will in all administrations for your good be quietly submitted unto, by all but such as have a disposition to *shake off the yoke*, and lose their true *liberty*, by their murmuring at the honor and power of *authority*.

The *spell* that was upon the eyes of the people being thus dissolved, their *distorted* and *enraged* notions of things all vanished; and the people would not afterwards entrust the helm of the *weather-beaten* bark in any other hands, but Mr. *Winthrop's*, until he died.

§10.   Indeed such was the *mixture* of *distant qualities* in him, as to make a most admirable *temper;* and his having a certain *greatness of soul*, which rendered him grave, generous, courageous, resolved, well-applied, and every way a *gentleman* in his demeanor, did not hinder him from taking sometimes

[23] See Numbers 12:14.   [24] "We are all the worse."

the old *Romans'* way to avoid confusions, namely, *Cedendo;*[25] or from discouraging some things which are agreeable enough to most that wear the name of *gentlemen.* Hereof I will give no instances, but only *oppose* two passages of his life.

In the year 1632, the Governor, with his Pastor Mr. *Wilson,* and some other gentlemen, to settle a good understanding between the two colonies, travelled as far as *Plymouth,* more than forty miles, through an howling wilderness, no better accommodated in those early days, than the *princes* that in *Solomon's* time saw *servants on horseback,* or than *Genus* and *Species* in the old epigram, *going on foot.* The difficulty of the *walk,* was abundantly compensated by the honorable, *first* reception, and *then* dismission, which they found from the rulers of *Plymouth;* and by the good correspondence thus established between the new colonies, who were like the floating bottles wearing this motto, *Si Collidimur, Frangimur.*[26] But there were at this time in *Plymouth* two ministers, leavened so far with the humors of the *rigid separation,* that they insisted vehemently upon the unlawfulness of calling any *unregenerate* man by the name of *goodman such an one,* until by their indiscreet urging of this whimsey, the place began to be disquieted. The wiser people being troubled at these trifles, they took the opportunity of Governor *Winthrop's* being *there,* to have the thing publicly propounded in the congregation; who in answer thereunto, distinguished between a *theological* and a *moral goodness;* adding, that when *juries* were first used in *England,* it was usual for the *crier,* after the names of persons fit for that service were called over, to bid them all, "Attend, good men, and true;" whence it grew to be a *civil custom* in the *English nation,* for neighbors living by one another, to call one another *goodman such an one:* And it was pity now to make a stir about a *civil custom,* so innocently introduced.° And that speech of Mr. *Winthrop's* put a lasting stop to the little idle, whimsical *conceits,* then beginning to grow obstreperous. Nevertheless there was one *civil custom* used *in* (and in few *but*) the *English nation,* which this gentleman did endeavor to abolish in *this country;* and that was *the usage of drinking to one another.* For although by *drinking to one another,* no more is meant than an act of *courtesy,* when one going to *drink,* does invite another to do so too, for the same ends with himself; nevertheless the Governor (not altogether unlike *to Cleomenes,* of whom 'tis reported by *Plutarch,* ἄκοντι οὐδεὶς ποτήριον προσέφερε, *Nolenti poculum nunquam præbuit,*[27]) considered the *impertinency* and *insignificancy* of this usage, as to any of *those ends* that are usually pretended for it; and that indeed it ordinarily served for *no ends* at all, but only to provoke persons unto *unseasonable,* and perhaps *unreason-*

---

[25] "By yielding."

[26] "If we collide, we break."

° Consider this paragraph in your reading of Nathaniel Hawthorne's story "Young Good man Brown," below.

[27] "Never offered drink to one who was unwilling."

able drinking, and at last produce that abominable *health-drinking*, which the *Fathers* of old so severely rebuked in the *pagans* and which the *Papists* themselves do condemn, when their casuists pronounce it, *Peccatum mortale, provocare ad Æquales Calices, & Nefas Respondere.*[28] Wherefore in his own most hospitable house he left it off, not out of any silly or stingy *fancy*, but merely that by his *example* a greater *temperance*, with *liberty* of *drinking*, might be recommended, and sundry *inconveniences* in drinking avoided; and his *example* accordingly began to be much followed by the sober people in *this country*, as it now also begins to be among persons of the *highest* rank in the *English nation* itself; until an *order of Court* came to be made against that *ceremony* in drinking, and then the *old wont* violently returned, with a *Nitimur in Vetitum.*[29]

§11. *Many were the afflictions of this righteous man!* He lost much of his estate in a ship, and in an *house*, quickly after his coming to *New England*, besides the prodigious expense of it in the difficulties of his first coming hither. Afterwards his assiduous application unto the public *affairs* (wherein *Ipse se non habuit, postquam Respublica eum Gubernatorem habere capit*)[30] made him so much to neglect his own *private interests*, that an *unjust steward* ran him 2500 *l.* in debt before he was aware; for the payment whereof he was forced, many years before his decease, to sell the most of what he had left unto him in the country. Albeit, by the observable blessing of God upon the *posterity* of this *liberal man*, his children all of them came to fair estates, and lived in good fashion and credit. Moreover, he successively buried three *wives;* the first of which was the daughter and heiress of Mr. *Forth*, of *Much Stambridge*[31] in *Essex*, by whom he had *wisdom with an inheritance;* and an excellent son. The second was the daughter of Mr. *William Clopton*, of *London*, who died with her child, within a very little while. The third was the daughter of the truly worshipful Sir *John Tyndal*, who made it her whole care to please, first *God*, and then her *husband;* and by whom he had four sons, which survived and honored their father. And unto all these, the addition of the *distempers*, ever now and then raised in the *country*, procured unto him a very singular share of trouble; yea, so hard was the measure which he found even among pious men, in the temptations of a *wilderness*, that when the *thunder* and *lightning* had smitten a *windmill*, whereof he was owner, some had *such things in their heads*, as publicly to reproach this *charitablest* of men, as if the *voice of the Almighty* had rebuked, I know not what *oppression*, which they *judged* him guilty of: which things I would not have mentioned, but that the instances may fortify the expectations of my *best readers* for such afflictions.

---

[28] "It is a mortal sin to challenge anyone to a drinking match, and to accept such a challenge."

[29] "We strive for what is forbidden."

[30] "He did not possess himself after the state began to possess him as governor."

[31] Or Great Stambridge. [K. B. M.]

§12.   He that had been for his attainments, as they said of the blessed *Macarius*, a Παιδαριογερων, *"An old man, while a young one,"* and that had in his *young days* met with many of those *ill days,* whereof he could say, he had *little pleasure in them;* now found *old age* in its infirmities advancing *earlier* upon him, than it came upon his much longer lived progenitors. While he was yet seven years off of that which we call *the grand climacter-ical,*[32] he felt the approaches of his *dissolution;* and finding he could say,

> *Non Habitus, non ipse Color non Gressus Euntis,*
> *Non Species Eadem, quæ fuit ante, manet,*[33]

he then wrote this account of himself: "Age now comes upon me, and infirmities therewithal, which makes me apprehend that the time of my departure out of this world is not far off. However our times are all in the Lord's hand, so as we need not trouble our thoughts how long or short they may be, but how we may be found faithful when we are called for." But at last when *that year* came, he took a *cold* which turned into a *fever,* whereof he lay *sick* about a month, and in that *sickness,* as it hath been observed, that there was allowed unto the *serpent* the *bruising of the heel;*[34] and accordingly at the *heel* or the *close* of our lives the *old serpent* will be nibbling more than ever in our lives before; and when the Devil sees that we shall shortly be, *where the wicked cease from troubling,* that *Wicked One* will *trouble* us more than ever; so this eminent saint now underwent sharp conflicts with the *Tempter,* whose *wrath* grew *great,* as the *time* to exert it grew *short;* and he was buffeted with the disconsolate thoughts of black and sore *desertions,* wherein he could use that sad representation of his own condition:

> *Nuper Eram Judex; Jam Judicor; Ante Tribunat,*
> *Subsistens paveo, Judicor ipse modo.*[35]

But it was not long before those *clouds* were dispelled, and he enjoyed in his holy soul the *great consolations of God!* While he thus lay *ripening* for heaven, he did out of obedience unto the *ordinance* of our Lord, send for the *Elders of the church* to *pray* with him; yea, they and the whole church *fasted* as well as *prayed* for him; and in that *fast* the venerable *Cotton*[36] preached on *Psal.* 35. 13, 14. "When they were sick, I humbled myself with fasting; I

---

[32] The sixty-third year of life. [K. B. M.]

[33] "There remains not the appearance, not even the color, not the way of life, and not the same aspect, of that which was before."

[34] Genesis 3:15.

[35] "Once I was a judge: now I am judged. I stand trembling before the tribunal, now I myself am judged."

[36] Rev. John Cotton, grandfather of Cotton Mather.

behaved myself as though he had been my friend or brother; I bowed down heavily, as one that mourned for his mother": from whence I find him raising that observation, "The sickness of one that is to us as a friend, a brother, a mother, is a just occasion of deep humbling our souls with fasting and prayer"; and making this application:

> Upon this occasion we are now to attend this duty for a *Governor*, who has been to us as a *friend* in his *counsel* for all things, and *help* for our *bodies* by *physick*, for our *estates* by *law*, and of whom there was no fear of his becoming an *enemy*, like the *friends* of *David*: a *Governor* who has been unto us as a *brother*; not usurping *authority* over the Church; often speaking his *advice*, and often contradicted, even by young men, and some of low degree; yet not replying, but offering satisfaction also when any supposed offenses have arisen; a *Governor* who has been unto us as a *mother*, parent-like distributing his *goods* to brethren and neighbors at his first coming: and *gently* bearing our *infirmities* without taking notice of them.

> *Such* a *Governor* after he had been more than *ten* several times by the people chosen their *Governor*, was *New England* now to lose; who having, like *Jacob*, first left his *counsel* and *blessing* with his children gathered about his bedside; and, like *David*, *served his generation by the will of God*, he *gave up the ghost* and *fell asleep* on *March. 26. 1649*. Having, like the dying Emperor *Valentinian*, this above all his other *victories* for his triumphs, *his overcoming of himself*.

The words of *Josephus* about *Nehemiah*, the Governor of *Israel*, we will now use upon this Governor of *New England*, as his

EPITAPH.

'Ανὴρ ἐγένετο χρηστὸσ τὴν φύσιν, καὶ δίκαιος,
Καὶ περὶ τοὺς ὁμοευνεῖς φιλοτιμότατος:
Μνημεῖον ἰώνιον ἀυτω καταλιπὼν τὰ τῶν
'Ιεροσολύμων Τείχη:[37]

VIR FUIT INDOLE BONUS, AC JUSTUS:
ET POPULARIUM GLORIÆ AMANTISSIMUS:
QUIBUS ETERNUM RELIQUIT MONUMENTUM,
      Novanglorum MOENIA.

[37] "He was a man by nature good and just, and most zealous for honor for his countrymen, leaving for them an eternal memorial— the walls of Jerusalem." The Latin paraphrase that follows, substitutes New England for Jerusalem.

FROM
THE
LIFE
OF HIS EXCELLENCY
SIR *WILLIAM PHIPS,* KNT.
LATE
GOVERNOR
OF
NEW ENGLAND

[THE KNIGHT OF HONESTY: HIS RISE FROM POVERTY TO WEALTH]

§   If such a renowned chemist, as *Quercetanus,*[1] with a whole tribe of *laborers in the fire,* since that learned man, find it no easy thing to make the common part of mankind believe, that they can take a *plant* in its more vigorous consistence, and after a due *maceration, fermentation* and *separation,* extract the *salt* of that *plant,* which, as it were, in a *chaos,* invisibly reserves the *form* of the whole, with its vital principle; and, that keeping the *salt* in a *glass* hermetically sealed, they can, by applying a *soft fire* to the *glass,* make the *vegetable* rise by little and little out of its *ashes,* to surprise the spectators with a notable illustration of that *resurrection,* in the faith whereof the *Jews* returning from the graves of their friends, pluck up the *grass* from the earth, using those words of the Scripture thereupon, "Your bones shall flourish like an herb"; 'Tis likely, that all the observations of such writers, as the incomparable *Borellus,*[2] will find it hard enough to produce our belief, that the *essential salts* of *animals* may be so prepared and preserved, that an ingenious man may have the whole *Ark of Noah* in his own study, and raise the fine *shape* of an *animal* out of its ashes at his pleasure; and, that by the like method from the *essential salts of human dust,* a philosopher may, without any criminal *necromancy,* call up the *shape* of any *dead* ancestor from the dust whereinto his body has been incinerated. The *Resurrection of the Dead,* will be as just, as great an article of our *creed,* although the *relations* of these learned men should pass for *incredible romances:* but yet there is an *anticipation* of that blessed *Resurrection,* carrying in it some resemblance of these *curiosities,* which is performed, when we do in a *book,* as in a *glass,* reserve the history of our departed *friends;* and by bringing our *warm affections* unto such an history, we revive, as it were, out of their *ashes,* the true *shape* of those friends, and bring to a fresh view, what was *memorable* and *imitable* in them. Now, in as much as *mortality* has

---

[1] Joseph Du Chesne, or Quercetanus (1544-1609), was a Paracelsan physician interested in alchemy. His book *The Practice of Chemical and Hermetical Physic,* trans. Thomas Timme, was published in London in 1605.

[2] Giovanni Alphonso Borelli (1608-1679), Italian physiologist.

done its part upon a considerable person, with whom I had the honor to be well acquainted, and a person as *memorable* for the wonderful *changes* which befell him, as *imitable* for his *virtues* and *actions* under those *changes;* I shall endeavor, with the *chemistry* of an impartial *historian,* to *raise* my friend so far out of his *ashes,* as to show him again unto the world; and if the character of *heroic virtue* be for a man to *deserve well of mankind, and be great in the purpose and success of essays to do so,* I may venture to promise my reader such example of *heroic virtue,* in the story whereto I invite him, that he shall say, it would have been little short of a *vice in me,* to have withheld it from him. Nor is it any *partiality* for the memory of my deceased friend, or any other sinister design whatsoever, that has invited me to this undertaking; but I have undertaken this matter from a sincere desire that the ever-glorious Lord JESUS CHRIST may have the glory of His *power* and *goodness,* and of His *Providence,* in what He did for such a person, and in what He disposed and assisted that person to do for Him. Now, *may He assist my writing, even He that prepared the subject, whereof I am to write!*

§2. So *obscure* was the *original* of that memorable person, whose *actions* I am going to relate, that I must, in a way of writing, like that of *Plutarch,*° prepare my reader for the intended relation, by first searching the *archives* of antiquity for a *parallel.* Now, because we will not *parallel* him with *Eumenes,*[3] who, though he were the son of a poor carrier, became a governor of mighty provinces; nor with *Marius,*† whose mean parentage did not hinder his becoming a glorious defender of his country, and seven times the chief magistrate of the chiefest city in the universe; nor with *Iphicrates,*[4] who became a successful and renowned general of a great people, though his father were a *cobler;* nor with *Diocletian,*[5] the son of a poor *scrivener;* nor with *Bonosus,*[6] the son of a poor *schoolmaster,* who yet came to sway the scepter of the *Roman* Empire; nor, lastly, will I compare him to the more late example of the celebrated *Mazarini,*‡ who though no gentleman by his extraction, and one so sorrily educated, that he might have wrote *man,* before he could write at all,[7] yet ascended unto that grandeur, in the memory of many yet living, as to umpire the most important affairs of *Christendom:* we will decline looking any further in that *hemisphere* of the world, and make the *hue and cry throughout* the regions of *America,* the *New World,* which he, that is becoming the subject of our history, by his *nativity,*

° Greek biographer, A. D. 46?-120?, author of *Parallel Lives.* Mather's device here is to set up parallels of his own.

[3] Secretary to Philip of Macedon and Alexander the Great (c. 362-316 B. C.).

† Gaius Marius, Roman general and consul, 155?-86 B. C.

[4] Iphicrates (c. 415-353 B. C.), Athenian general during campaigns against Sparta and Corinth.

[5] Roman emperor, 284-305.

[6] Bonosus, in the third century A. D.

‡Giulio Mazarini, 1602-1661, Italian-born French cardinal who was chief minister to Louis XIV.

[7] That is, was a man before he learned to write.

belonged unto. And in *America*, the first that meets me, is *Francisco Pizarro*,[8] who, though a *spurious offspring*, exposed when a *babe* in a church porch, at a sorry village of *Navarre*, and afterwards employed while he was a *boy* in keeping of cattle, yet, at length, stealing into *America*, he so thrived upon his adventures there, that upon some discoveries, which with an handful of men he had in a desperate expedition made of *Peru*, he obtained the King of *Spain's* commission for the conquest of it, and at last so incredibly enriched himself by the conquest, that he was made the first Vice-Roy of *Peru*, and created Marquess of *Anatilla*.

To the latter and highest part of that story, if anything hindered His Excellency Sir WILLIAM PHIPS, from affording of a *parallel*, it was not the want either of *design*, or of *courage*, or of *conduct* in himself, but it was the fate of a *premature mortality*. For my reader now being satisfied, that a person's being *obscure* in his *original*, is not always a just prejudice to an expectation of *considerable matters* from him; I shall now inform him, that this our PHIPS was born *Feb. 2. A. Dom.* 1650 at a despicable plantation on the River of *Kennebec*, and almost the furthest village of the eastern settlement of *New England*. And as the *father* of that man, which was as great a blessing as *England* had in the age of that man, was a *smith*,[9] so a *gunsmith*, namely, *James Phips*, once of *Bristol*, had the honor of being the *father* to him, whom we shall presently see, made by the God of Heaven as great a blessing to *New England*, as that country could have had, if they themselves had pleased. His fruitful *mother*, yet living, had no less than *twenty-six* children, whereof *twenty-one* were sons; but equivalent to them all was WILLIAM, one of the youngest, whom his *father* dying, left young with his *mother*, and with her he lived, *keeping of sheep in the wilderness*, until he was eighteen years old; at which time he began to feel some further dispositions of mind from that *Providence* of God which *took him from the sheep-folds, from following the ewes great with young, and brought him to feed his people*.[10] Reader, enquire no further who was his *father*? Thou shalt anon see that he was, as the *Italians* express it, *a son to his own labors!*

§3.   His friends earnestly solicited him to settle among them in a plantation of the *east;* but he had an unaccountable *impulse* upon his mind, persuading him, as he would privately hint unto some of them, *that he was born to greater matters*. To come at those *greater matters*, his first contrivance was to bind himself an apprentice unto a *ship-carpenter* for four years, in which time he became a master of the *trade* that once in a vessel of more than *forty thousand tons* repaired the ruins of the earth, *Noah's*, I mean; he then betook himself an hundred and fifty miles further afield, even to *Boston*, the chief town of *New England*, which being a place of the most business and resort in those parts of the world, he expected there more commodiously to

---

[8] 1470?-1541.

[9] Mather refers to Thomas Cromwell, father of Oliver Cromwell.

[10] Psalms 78:71.

pursue the *Spes Majorum & Meliorum*,[11] hopes which had inspired him. At *Boston*, where it was that he now learned first of all, to *read* and *write*, he followed his trade for about a year; and by a laudable deportment, so recommended himself, that he married a young gentlewoman of good repute, who was the widow of one Mr. *John Hull*, a well-bred merchant, but the daughter of one Captain *Roger Spencer*, a person of good fashion, who having suffered much damage in his estate, by some unkind and unjust actions, which he bore with such patience, that for fear of thereby injuring the public, he would not seek satisfaction. *Posterity* might afterward see the reward of his *patience* in what Providence hath now done for one of his own *posterity*. Within a little while after his marriage, he indented with several persons in *Boston*, to build them a ship at *Sheepscot* River, two or three leagues eastward of *Kennebec;* where having launched the ship, he also provided a *lading* of lumber to bring with him, which would have been to the advantage of all concerned. But just as the ship was hardly finished, the barbarous *Indians* on that river, broke forth into an open and cruel war upon the *English;* and the miserable people, surprised by so sudden a storm of blood, had no refuge from the infidels, but the *ship* now finishing in the harbor. Whereupon he left his intended *lading* behind him, and instead thereof, carried with him his old neighbors and their families, free of all charges, to *Boston;* so the *first action* that he did, after he was his own man, was to *save his father's house*, with the rest of the neighborhood, from ruin, but the disappointment which befell him from the loss of his other *lading*, plunged his affairs into greater embarrassments with such as had employed him.

[THE SEARCH FOR SPANISH TREASURE]

§4.   But he was hitherto no more than beginning to make *scaffolds* for further and higher *actions!* He would frequently tell the gentlewoman his wife that he should yet be *captain of a king's ship*, that he should come to have the *command of better men* than he was now accounted himself, and, that he should be owner of a *fair brick house* in the *green lane* of *North Boston*, and, that, it may be, this would not be all that the Providence of God would bring him to. She entertained these passages with a sufficient incredulity; but he had so *serious* and *positive* an expectation of them, that it is not easy to say, what was the *original* thereof. He was of an enterprising *genius*, and naturally disdained *littleness*, but his disposition for *business* was of the *Dutch* mold, where, with a little show of *wit*, there is as much *wisdom* demonstrated, as can be shown by any nation. His talent lay not in the *airs* that serve chiefly for the pleasant and sudden turns of *conversation*; but he

[11] Hopes of greater and better things.

might say, as *Themistocles*,° "Though he could not play upon a fiddle, yet he knew how to make a little city become a great one." He would *prudently* contrive a weighty undertaking, and then patiently pursue it unto the end. He was of an inclination, cutting rather like a *hatchet*, than like a *razor;* he would propose very considerable matters to himself, and then so *cut through* them, that no difficulties could put by the *edge* of his resolutions. Being thus of the *true temper*, for doing of *great things*, he betakes himself to the *sea*, the right *scene* for such things; and upon advice of a *Spanish wreck* about the *Bahamas*, he took a voyage thither; but with little more success, than what just served him a little to furnish him for a voyage to *England;* whither he went in a vessel, not much unlike that which the *Dutchmen* stamped on their *first coin*, with these words about it: *Incertum quo Fata ferant.*[12] Having first informed himself that there was another *Spanish wreck*, wherein was lost a mighty treasure, hitherto undiscovered, he had a strong impression upon his mind that *he* must be the discoverer; and he made such representations of his design at *Whitehall*, that by the year 1683 he became the captain of a *king's ship*, and arrived at *New England* commander of the *Algier Rose*, a frigate of eighteen guns, and ninety-five men.

§5.   To relate all the *dangers* through which he passed, both by sea and land, and all the tiresome trials of his *patience*, as well as of his *courage*, while year after year the most vexing accidents imaginable delayed the success of his design, it would even tire the patience of the reader: for very great was the experiment that Captain *Phips* made of the *Italian* observation, "He that can't suffer both good and evil, will never come to any great preferment." Wherefore I shall supersede all journal of his voyages to and fro, with reciting one instance of his conduct, that showed him to be a person of no contemptible capacity. While he was captain of the *Algier Rose*, his men growing weary of their unsuccessful enterprise, made a mutiny, wherein they approached him on the quarter-deck, with drawn swords in their hands, and required him to join with them in running away with the ship, to drive a trade of piracy on the *South Seas*. Captain *Phips*, though he had not so much of a weapon as an *ox-goad*, or a *jawbone* in his hands, yet like another *Shamgar* or *Samson*,[13] with a most undaunted fortitude, he rushed in upon them, and with the blows of his bare hands, *felled* many of them, and *quelled* all the rest. But this is not the instance which I intended: that which I intend is, that (as it has been related unto me) one day while his frigate lay careening,[14] at a desolate *Spanish* island, by the side of a rock, from whence they had laid a bridge to the shore, the men, whereof he had

---

° Athenian warrior and political leader, 527?-460? B. C., who commanded and won the naval battle at Salamis.

[12] "It is uncertain where the fates will carry me."

[13] Samson was so strong that he killed 1000

Philistine men with the jawbone of an ass. Judges 15:13-16. Shamgar (Judges 3:31) "killed 600 Philistines with an oxgoad, and he too delivered Israel."

[14] I.e., lay on her side, so that the bottom might be cleaned and calked. [K. B. M.]

about an *hundred*, went all, but about eight or ten, to divert themselves, as they pretended, in the *woods* where they all entered into an *agreement*, which they signed in a ring, that about seven a clock that evening they would seize the Captain, and those eight or ten, which they knew to be true unto him, and leave them to perish on this island, and so be gone away unto the *South Sea* to *seek their fortune*. Will the reader now imagine, that Captain *Phips* having advice of this plot but about an hour and half before it was to be put in execution, yet within *two hours* brought all these rogues down upon their knees to beg for their lives? But so it was! For these knaves considering that they should want a *carpenter* with them in their *villanous expedition*, sent a messenger to fetch unto them the *carpenter*, who was then at work upon the vessel, and unto him they showed their *articles*, telling him what he must look for if he did not *subscribe* among them. The *carpenter*, being an honest fellow, did with much importunity prevail for one half hour's time to consider of the matter; and returning to work upon the vessel, with a *spy* by them set upon him, he feigned himself taken with a fit of the *colic*, for the relief whereof he suddenly run unto the Captain in the great cabin for a *dram;* where, when he came, his business was only in brief, to tell the Captain of the horrible distress which he was fallen into; but the Captain bid him as briefly return to the rogues in the *woods*, and sign their *articles*, and leave *him* to provide for the rest. The *carpenter* was no sooner gone, but Captain *Phips* calling together the few friends (it may be seven or eight) that were left him aboard, whereof the gunner was one, demanded of them, whether they would stand by him in the extremity, which he informed them was now come upon him; whereto they replied, *They would stand by him, if he could save them;* and he answered, *By the help of God he did not fear it.* All their provisions had been carried ashore to a tent, made for that purpose there; about which they had placed several great guns to defend it, in case of any *assault* from *Spaniards*, that might happen to come that way. Wherefore Captain *Phips* immediately ordered those guns to be silently drawn and turned; and so pulling up the bridge, he charged his great guns aboard, and brought them to bear on every side of the tent. By this time the *army of rebels* comes out of the woods; but as they drew near to the tent of provisions, they saw such a change of circumstances, that they cried out, "We are betrayed!" And they were soon confirmed in it, when they heard the Captain with a stern fury call to them, "Stand off, ye wretches, at your peril!" He quickly saw them cast into a more than ordinary confusion, when they saw *him* ready to fire his great guns upon them, if they offered one step further than he permitted them: and when he had signified unto them his *resolve* to abandon them unto all the desolation which they had purposed for *him*, he caused the *bridge* to be again laid, and his men begun to take the provisions aboard. When the wretches beheld what was coming upon them, they fell to very humble entreaties; and at last fell down upon their knees, protesting *that they never had any thing against him, except only his unwillingness to go away with the King's ship upon the* South-Sea *design, but upon all other accounts, they would choose rather to live and die with him, than with any man in the world; however, since they saw how much he was dissatisfied at it, they would insist upon it no more, and humbly begged his pardon.* And when he judged that he had kept them on their *knees* long enough, he having first secured their *arms*, received them aboard; but he immediately weighed anchor, and arriving at *Jamaica*, he turned them off. Now with a small company of other men he sailed from thence to *Hispaniola*, where by the policy of his address, he fished out of a very old *Spaniard*, (or *Portuguese*) a little advice about the true spot where lay the *wreck* which he had been hitherto seeking, as unprosperously, as the *chemists* have their *aurific Stone:* [15] that it was upon a *reef of shoals*, a few leagues to the northward of *Port de la Plata*, upon *Hispaniola*, [16] a port so called, it seems, from the landing of some of the *shipwrecked* company, with a boat full of plate, saved out of their sinking frigate: nevertheless, when he had searched very narrowly the spot, whereof the old *Spaniard* had advised him, he had not hitherto exactly lit upon it. Such *thorns* did vex his affairs while he was in the *Rose frigate;* but none of all these things could retund the edge of his expectations to find the *wreck;* with such expectations he returned then into *England*, that he might there better furnish himself to prosecute a *new discovery;* for though he judged he might, by proceeding a little further, have come at the right *spot*, yet he found his present company too ill a crew to be confided in.

§6.   So *proper* was his behavior, that the best noblemen in the kingdom now admitted him into their conversation; but yet he was opposed by powerful enemies, that clogged his affairs with such demurrages, and such *disappointments*, as would have wholly discouraged his designs, if his patience had not been *invincible. He who can wait, hath what he desireth.* This his indefatigable *patience*, with a proportionable *diligence*, at length overcame the difficulties that had been thrown in his way; and prevailing with the Duke of *Albemarle*, and some other persons of quality, to fit him out, he set sail for the *fishing-ground*, which had been so well *baited* half an hundred years before: and as he had already discovered his *capacity for business* in many considerable actions, he now added unto those discoveries, by not only *providing* all, but also by *inventing* many of the instruments necessary to the prosecution of his intended *fishery*. Captain *Phips* arriving with a ship and a *tender* at *Port de la Plata*, made a stout *canoe* of a stately *cotton tree*, so large as to carry eight or ten oars, for the making of which *periagua* (as they call it) he did, with the same industry that he did every thing else, employ his own *hand* and *adze*, and endure no little hardship, lying abroad in the woods

---

[15] That is, "gold-producing" stone, the "philosopher's stone."   [16] Haiti.

many nights together. This *periagua*, with the *tender*, being anchored at a place convenient, the *periagua* kept busking to and again,[17] but could only discover a *reef of rising shoals* thereabouts, called *the Boilers*, which rising to be within two or three feet of the surface of the sea, were yet so steep, that a ship striking on them, would immediately sink down, who could say, *how many fathoms* into the ocean? Here they could get no other pay for their long *peeping* among the *Boilers*, but only such as caused them to think upon returning to their captain with the *bad news* of their total disappointment. Nevertheless, as they were upon the return, one of the men looking over the side of the *periagua*, into the calm water, he spied a *sea feather*,[18] growing, as he judged, out of a rock; whereupon they had one of their *Indians* to dive and fetch this *feather*, that they might however carry home *something* with them, and make, at least, as fair a *triumph* as *Caligula's*.[19] The *diver* bringing up the *feather*, brought therewithal a surprising story: that he perceived a number of *great guns* in the *watery world* where he had found his *feather;* the *report* of which *great guns* exceedingly astonished the whole company; and at once turned their *despondencies* for their ill success into *assurances,* that they had now lit upon the *true spot* of ground which they had been looking for; and they were further confirmed in these *assurances,* when upon further diving, the *Indian* fetcht up a *sow,* as they styled it, or a lump of silver, worth perhaps two or three hundred pounds. Upon this they prudently *buoyed* the place, that they might readily find it again; and they went back unto their captain whom for some while they distressed with nothing but such *bad news,* as they formerly thought they must have carried him: nevertheless, they so slipt in the sow of silver on one side under the table, where they were now sitting with the Captain, and hearing him express his resolutions to wait still patiently upon the Providence of God under these disappointments, that when he should look on one side he might see that *odd thing* before him. At last he *saw* it; seeing it, he cried out with some agony "Why? What is this? Whence comes this?" And then, with changed countenances, they told him *how,* and *where* they got it: "Then," said he, "Thanks be to God! We are made;" and so away they went, all hands to work; wherein they had this one further piece of remarkable prosperity, that whereas if they had first fallen upon that part of the *Spanish wreck*, where the pieces of eight had been stowed in bags among the ballast, they had seen a more laborious, and less enriching time of it: now, most happily, they first fell upon that room in the *wreck* where the *bullion* had been stored up; and they so prospered in this *new fishery*, that in a little while they had, without

[17] Periagua is for piragua, a long narrow canoe, made of the hollowed trunk of a tree. "To busk to and again" meant, in nautical parlance, "to cruise about." [K. B. M.]

[18] A kind or coral or polyp. [K. B. M.]

[19] The Roman Emperor from 37 to 41. Caligula's "triumph" occurred in 40 A. D. when, having raised two new legions for a possible invasion of Germany, he abandoned the enterprise and returned to Rome, with little to show but some seashells gathered on the French coast. His demand for a triumphal celebration was postponed.

the loss of any man's life, brought up *thirty-two tuns* of silver, for it was now come to measuring of silver by *tuns*.[20] Besides which, one *Adderly* of *Providence*, who had formerly been very helpful to Captain *Phips* in the search of this *wreck*, did upon former agreement meet him now with a little vessel here; and *he*, with his few hands, took up about *six tuns* of silver, whereof nevertheless he made so little use, that in a year or two he died at *Bermudas*, and as I have heard, he ran *distracted* some while before he died. Thus did there once again come into the light of the sun, a treasure which had been half an hundred years *groaning under the waters:* and in this time there was grown upon the plate a crust like *limestone*, to the thickness of several inches; which crust being broken open by irons contrived for that purpose, they knockt out whole bushels of rusty pieces of eight which were grown thereinto. Besides that incredible treasure of plate in various forms, thus fetched up, from seven or eight fathoms under water, there were vast riches of *gold*, and *pearls*, and *jewels*, which they also lit upon; and indeed, for a more comprehensive *invoice*, I must but summarily say, *all that a* Spanish *frigate uses to be enricht withal.* Thus did they continue *fishing* till their provisions failing them, 'twas time to be gone; but before they went, Captain *Phips* caused *Adderly* and his folk to swear that they would none of them discover[21] the place of the *wreck*, or come to the place any more till the next year, when he expected again to be there himself. And it was also remarkable, that though the sows came up still so fast, that on the very last day of their being there, they took up *twenty*, yet it was afterwards found, that they had in a manner wholly cleared that room of the ship where those *massy things* were stowed.

But there was one extraordinary distress which Captain *Phips* now found himself plunged into: for his men were come out with him upon seamen's wages, at so much *per* month; and when they saw such vast litters of silver *sows* and *pigs*, as they called them,, come on board them at the Captain's call, they knew not how to bear it, that they should not *share* all among themselves, and be gone to lead *a short life and a merry*, in a climate where the arrest of those that had hired them should not reach them. In this terrible distress he made his vows unto Almighty God, that if the Lord would carry him safe home to *England* with what *He* had now given him, *to suck of the abundance of the seas, and of the treasures hid in the sands*,[22] he would for ever devote himself unto the interests of the Lord *Jesus Christ*, and of His people, especially in the *country* which he did himself originally belong unto. And he then used all the obliging *arts* imaginable to make his men true unto him, especially by assuring them, that besides their *wages*, they should have ample *requitals* made unto them; which if the rest of his employers would

[20] "Tun" as a measure of gold meant 1,00,000 guilders, florins, etc. Whether Mather uses it in this sense here, or simply as equivalent to "ton," is not clear. [K. B. M.]

[21] That is, disclose.

[22] Deuteronomy 33:19.

not agree unto, he would himself distribute his *own share* among them. Relying upon the word of one whom they had ever found worthy of their *love,* and of their *trust,* they declared themselves *content:* but still keeping a most careful eye upon them, he hastened back for *England* with as much *money* as he thought he could then safely *trust* his vessel withal; not counting it safe to supply himself with necessary provisions at any nearer port, and so return unto the *wreck,* by which delays he wisely feared lest all might be lost, more ways than one. Though he also left so much behind him, that many from divers parts made very considerable voyages of *gleanings* after his *harvest:* which came to pass by certain *Bermudians,* compelling of *Adderly's* boy, whom they *spirited* away with them, to tell them the exact place where the *wreck* was to be found. Captain *Phips* now coming up to *London* in the year 1687, with near *three hundred thousand pounds sterling* aboard him, did acquit himself with such an exemplary honesty, that partly by his fulfilling his assurances to the seamen, and partly by his exact and punctual care to have his employers defrauded of nothing that might conscientiously belong unto them, he had less than *sixteen thousand pounds* left unto himself: as an acknowledgment of which *honesty* in him, the Duke of *Albemarle* made unto his wife, whom he never saw, a present of a *golden cup,* near a thousand pound in value. The character of an *honest man* he had so merited in the whole course of his life, and especially in this last act of it, that this, in conjunction with his other serviceable qualities, procured him the favors of the greatest persons in the nation; and *he that had been so diligent in his business, must now stand before kings, and not stand before mean men.*° There were indeed certain *mean men,* if base, little, dirty tricks, will entitle men to meanness, who urged the King to seize his *whole cargo,* instead of the tenths, upon his first arrival; on this pretense, that he had not been rightly informed of the *true state of the case,* when he granted the *patent,* under the protection whereof these *particular men* had made themselves masters of all this mighty treasure; but the King replied, that he had been *rightly informed* by Captain *Phips* of the whole matter, as it now proved; and that it was the slanders of one then present, which had, unto his damage, hindered him from hearkening to the information: wherefore he would give them, he said, no disturbance; they might keep what they had got; but Captain *Phips,* he saw, was a person of that honesty, fidelity and ability, that he should not want his countenance. Accordingly the King, in consideration of the service done by him, in bringing such a treasure into the nation, conferred upon him the honor of *knighthood;* and if we now reckon him *a Knight of the Golden Fleece,* the style or title might pretend unto some circumstances that would justify it. Or call him, if you please, *the Knight of Honesty;* for it was *honesty* with *industry* that raised him; and he became a mighty river, without the

° Proverbs 22:29. Compare Benjamin Franklin, below, pp. 480–481.

running in of muddy water to make him so. Reader, now make a pause, and behold *one raised by God!*

[*PIETAS IN PATRIAM:* HIS PATRIOTISM DURING THE GLORIOUS REVOLUTION
IN NEW ENGLAND]

§7.   I am willing to employ the testimonies of others, as much as may be, to support the credit of my history: and therefore, as I have hitherto related no more than what there are others enough to avouch; thus I shall choose the words of an ingenious person printed at *London* some years ago, to express the sum of what remains, whose words are these:

> It has always been Sir *William Phips's* disposition to seek the *wealth* of his people with as great zeal and unweariedness, as our *publicans* use to seek their *loss* and *ruin.* At first it seems they were in hopes to gain this gentleman to their party, as thinking him *good natured,* and easy to be flattered out of his understanding; and the more, because they had the advantage of some, no very good, treatment that Sir *William* had formerly met with from the people and government of *New England.* But Sir *William* soon showed them, that what they expected would be his *temptation* to lead them into their *little tricks,* he embraced as a glorious opportunity to show his *generosity* and *greatness of mind;* for, in imitation of the greatest worthies that have ever been, he rather chose to join in the defense of his country, with some persons who formerly were none of his friends, than become the head of a *faction,* to its ruin and desolation. It seems this noble disposition of Sir *William,* joined with that capacity and good success wherewith he hath been attended, in raising himself by such an occasion, as it may be, all things considered, has *never happened to any before him,* makes these men apprehensive;—and it must needs heighten their trouble to see, that he neither hath, nor doth spare himself, nor anything that is near and dear unto him, in promoting the good of his native country.

When Sir *William Phips* was *per ardua* & *aspera,*[23] thus raised into an *higher orb,* it might easily be thought that he could not be without charming temptations to take the *way on the left hand.* But as the Grace of God kept him in the midst of none of the strictest company, unto which his affairs daily led him, from abandoning himself to the lewd vices of *gaming, drinking, swearing* and *whoring,* which the men *that made* England *to sin,* debauched so many of the gentry into, and he deserved the salutations of the *Roman* poet:

---

[23] "Through difficulties and hardships."

Cum Tu, inter scabiem tantam, & Contagia Lucri,
Nil parvum sapias, & adhuc Sublimia cures:[24]

Thus he was worthy to pass among the instances of *heroic virtue* for that humility that still adorned him: he was *raised,* and though he prudently accommodated himself to the *quality* whereto he was now *raised,* yet none could perceive him to be *lifted up.* Or, if this were not *heroic,* yet I will relate one thing more of him that must certainly be accounted so. He had in his own country of *New England* met with *provocations* that were enough to have alienated any man living, that had no more than *flesh and blood* in him, from the service of it; and some that were enemies to that country, now lay hard at him to join with them in their endeavors to ravish away their *ancient liberties.* But this *gentleman* had studied another way to *revenge* himself upon his country, and that was to serve it in all *its* interests, with all of *his,* even with his *estate,* his *time,* his *care,* his *friends,* and his very *life!* The old *heathen* virtue of PIETAS IN PATRIAM, or LOVE TO ONES COUNTRY, he turned into *Christian;* and so notably exemplified it, in all the rest of his *life,* that it will be an essential *thread* which is to be now interwoven into all that remains of his *history,* and his *character.* Accordingly though he had the offers of a very gainful place among the *Commissioners of the Navy,* with many other invitations to settle himself in *England,* nothing but a return to *New England* would content him. And whereas the charters of *New England* being taken away,° there was a governor imposed upon the territories with as *arbitrary* and as *treasonable* a *commission,* perhaps, as ever was heard of; a *commission,* by which the Governor, with three or four more, none of whom were chosen by the people, had power to make what *laws* they would, and levy *taxes,* according to their own humors, upon the people; and he himself had power to send the best men in the land more than ten thousand miles out of it, as he pleased: and in the execution of his power, the country was every day suffering intolerable *invasions* upon their *proprieties,* yea, and the lives of the best men in the territory began to be practiced upon: Sir *William Phips* applied himself to consider what was the most significant thing that could be done by him for that poor people in their present circumstances. Indeed, when King *James* offered, as he did, unto Sir *William Phips* an opportunity to ask what he pleased of him, Sir *William* generously prayed for nothing but *this,* that New England *might have its lost privileges restored.* The King then replied, *Any thing but that!* Whereupon

[24] "You, amid so great a leprosy and contagion of avarice, are wise, and seek higher things."

° The charter of Massachusetts Bay had been revoked in 1684, and a royal governor, Sir Edmund Andros, had been appointed and had claimed or asserted many of the powers that Mather specifies here. Andros was deposed by an uprising on April 18, 1689, just after the news of the glorious revolution in England had arrived in Massachusetts.

he set himself to consider what was the next *thing* that he might ask for the service, not of himself, but of his *country.* The result of his consideration was, that by petition to the King, he obtained, with expense of some hundreds of *guineas,* a *patent,* which constituted him *the High Sheriff of that country,*[25] hoping, by his deputies in that office, to supply the country still with conscientious juries, which was the only method that the *New Englanders* had left them to secure any thing that was dear unto them. Furnished with this *patent,* after he had, in company with Sir *John Narborough,* made a second visit unto the wreck (not so advantageous as the former for a reason already mentioned) in his way he returned unto *New England,* in the summer of the year 1688, able, after five years absence, to entertain his lady with some accomplishment of his predictions; and then built himself a *fair brick house* in the very *place* which we foretold, the reader can tell how many *sections* ago. But the *infamous government* then rampant there, found a way wholly to put by the execution of this *patent;* yea, he was like to have had his *person* assassinated in the face of the sun, before his own door, which with some further designs then in his mind, caused him within a few weeks to take another voyage for *England.*

§8.   It would require a long summer's day to relate the miseries which were come, and coming in upon poor *New England,* by reason of the *arbitrary government* then imposed on them; a *government* wherein as old *Wendover* says of the time, when *strangers* were domineering over *subjects* in *England*: *Judicia committebantur Injustis, Leges Exlegibus, Pax Discordantibus, Justitia Injuriosis,*[26] and foxes were made the administrators of justice to the *poultry;* yet some *abridgment* of them is necessary for the better understanding of the matters yet before us. Now to make this *abridgment* impartial, I shall only have recourse unto a little book, printed at *London,* under the title of *The Revolution of* New-England *Justified;*[27] wherein we have a *narrative of the grievances* under the maladministration of that government, written and signed by the chief gentlemen of the *Governor's Council;* together with the *sworn testimonies* of many good men, to prove the several articles of the *declaration,* which the *New Englanders* published against their oppressors. It is in that book demonstrated:

That the Governor neglecting the greater number of his *Council,* did adhere principally to the advice of a *few strangers,* who were persons without any *interest* in the country, but of declared *prejudice* against it, and had plainly laid their *designs* to make an unreasonable *profit* of the poor people:

[25] Provost Marshal-general of New England.

[26] "Judgments were entrusted to the unjust, laws to outlaws, peace to quarrelers, and justice to wrongdoers." Wendover was Roger de Wendover, historian, who died in 1236.

[27] Published in 1691 and attributed to Increase Mather, this pamphlet was reprinted in W. H. Whitmore's *Andros Tracts,* Boston, 1868-1874, where it is listed as perhaps the work of William Stoughton.

and *four* or *five* persons had the absolute rule *over a territory, the most considerable of any belonging to the crown.*

That when *laws* were proposed in the *Council,* tho' the *major* part at any time dissented from them, yet if the Governor were positive, there was no fair *counting* the number of *councilors* consenting, or dissenting, but the laws were immediately *engrossed, published* and *executed.*

That this *Junto* made a *law,* which prohibited the inhabitants of any *town* to meet about their *town affairs* above *once* in a year; for fear, you must note, of their having any opportunity to complain of *grievances.*

That they made another *law,* requiring all masters of *vessels,* even *shallops* and *woodboats,*[28] to give *security,* that no man should be transported in them, except his name had been so many days posted up: whereby the pockets of a few *leeches* had been filled with *fees,* but the whole trade of the country destroyed; and all attempts to obtain a *redress* of these things obstructed; and when this *act* had been strenuously opposed in council at *Boston,* they carried it as far as *New York,* where a crew of them enacted it.

That without any *Assembly,* they levied on the people a *penny* in the pound of all their *estates,* and twenty-pence *per* head, as *poll-money,* with a penny in the pound for *goods* imported, besides a vast *excise* on wine; rum; and other *liquors.*

That when among the inhabitants of *Ipswich,* some of the principal persons modestly gave reasons why they could not choose a *commissioner* to *tax* the town, until the King should first be petitioned for the liberty of an *Assembly,* they were committed unto *jail* for it, as an *high misdemeanor,* and were denied an *Habeas Corpus,* and were dragged many miles out of their own county to answer it at a court in *Boston;* where *jurors* were pickt for the turn, that were not *free-holders,* nay, that were mere *sojourners;* and when the prisoners pleaded the privileges of *Englishmen, that they should not be taxed without their own consent;*[29] they were told, *that those things would not follow them to the ends of the earth:* as it had been before them in *open Council,* no one in the Council contradicting it, "You have no more privleges left you, but this, that you are not bought and sold for slaves": and in fine, they were all *fined* severely, and laid under great *bonds* for their good behavior; besides all which, the *hungry officers* extorted *fees* from them that amounted unto an hundred and threescore pounds; whereas in *England,* upon the like prosecution, the *fees* would not have been ten pounds in all. After which fashion the *townsmen* of many other places were also served.

That these Men giving out that the *charters* being lost, all the title that the people had unto their lands was lost with them; they began to *compel* the people everywhere to take *patents* for their lands: and accordingly *Writs of Intrusion* were issued out against the chief gentlemen in the territory, by the

[28] Small boats used for transporting wood.

[29] This grievance and others of the 1680's were quite similar to those of the American Revolution 90 years later.

terror whereof, many were actually driven to petition for *patents,* that they might quietly enjoy the lands that had been fifty or sixty years in their possession; but for these *patents* there were such exorbitant prices demanded, that fifty pounds could not purchase for its owner an estate not worth *two hundred,* nor could all the money and movables in the territory have defrayed to charges of *patenting* the lands at the hands of these *crocodiles:* besides the considerable *quit-rents* for the King. Yea, the Governor caused the lands of *particular persons* to be measured out, and given to his creatures: and some of his Council petitioned for the *commons* belonging to several towns; and the *agents* of the towns going to get a *voluntary subscription* of the inhabitants to maintain their title at law, they have been dragged forty or fifty miles to answer as criminals at the next assizes; the officers in the meantime extorting three pounds *per* man for fetching them.

That if these *Harpies,* at any time, were a little *out of money,* they found ways to imprison the *best men* in the country; and there appeared not the least *information* of any crime exhibited against them, yet they were put unto intolerable expenses by these greedy oppressors, and the benefit of an *Habeas Corpus* not allowed unto them.

That packt and pickt *juries* were commonly made use of, when under a pretended *form of law,* the trouble of some honest and worthy men was aimed at; and these also were hurried out of their own counties to be tried, when *juries* for the turn were not like to be found there. The *greatest rigor* being used still towards the *soberest sort* of people, whilst in the meantime the most horrid enormities in the world, committed by others, were overlooked.

That the public ministry of the Gospel, and all *schools of learning,* were discountenanced unto the utmost.

And several more such abominable things, too notorious to be denied, even by a *Randolphian*[30] impudence itself, are in that book proved against that *unhappy government.* Nor did that most ancient set of the *Phœnician shepherds,* who screwed the government of *Egypt* into their hands, as old *Manethon*[31] tells us, by their *villanies,* during the reigns of those tyrants, make a *shepherd* more of an *abomination* to the *Egyptians* in all after ages, than these *wolves* under the name of *shepherds* have made the remembrance of their *French government*[32] an *abomination* to all posterity among the *New Englanders:* a *government,* for which, now, reader, as fast as thou wilt, get ready this epitaph:

---

[30] Edward Randolph, an English official in the colonies at the time, was detested by Mather and by many other New Englanders.

[31] Egyptian historian, third century B.C.

[32] The colonists fondly believed that Andros and his followers were secretly in league with the French against England.

Nulla quæsita Scelere Potentia diuturna.[33]

It was under the resentments of these things that Sir *William Phips* returned into *England* in the year 1688. In which *twice-wonderful year* such a *revolution* was wonderfully accomplished upon the whole government of the *English* nation, that *New England,* which had been a *specimen* of what the whole nation was to look for, might justly hope for a share in the general deliverance. Upon this occasion Sir *William* offered his best assistances unto that eminent person,[34] who a little before this revolution betook himself unto *Whitehall,* that he might there lay hold on all opportunities to procure some relief unto the oppressions of that afflicted country. But seeing the *New English* affairs in so able an hand, he thought the best stage of *action* for him would now be *New England* itself; and so with certain instructions from none of the least considerable persons at *Whitehall,* what service to do for his country, in the spring of the year 1689 he hastened back unto it. Before he left *London,* a messenger from the abdicated king tendered him the government of *New England,* if he would accept it: but as that excellent Attorney General, Sir *William Jones,* when it was proposed that the *plantations* might be governed without *assemblies,* told the King *that he could no more grant a commission to levy money on his subjects there, without their consent by an assembly, than they could discharge themselves from their allegiance to the* English *Crown.* So Sir *William Phips* thought it his duty to refuse a *government without an assembly,* as a thing that was treason in the very *essence* of it; and instead of petitioning the succeeding princes, that his *patent* for *High Sheriff* might be rendered effectual, he joined in petitions, that *New England* might have its own old *patent* so restored, as to render ineffectual *that,* and all other grants that might cut short any of its ancient privileges. But when Sir *William* arrived at *New England,* he found a new face of things; for about an hundred Indians in the *eastern parts* of the country, had unaccountably begun a war upon the *English* in *July,* 1688, and though the Governor then in the *western parts* had immediate advice of it, yet he not only delayed and neglected all that was necessary for the *public defense,* but also when he at last returned, he manifested a most furious displeasure against those of the Council, and all others that had forwarded any one thing for the security of the inhabitants; while at the same time he dispatched some of his creatures upon secret errands unto *Canada,* and set at liberty some of the most murderous *Indians* which the *English* had seized upon.

· · ·

[33] "No power achieved by wrongdoing is lasting."   [34] Increase Mather, the writer's father.

[JOINING THE CHURCH]

When Sir *William Phips* was now returned unto his *own house*, he began to bethink himself, like *David*,[35] concerning the *House* of the *God* who had surrounded him with so many favors in *his own;* and accordingly he applied himself unto the *North Church* in *Boston*,[36] that with his open profession of his hearty subjection to the *Gospel* of the Lord Jesus Christ, he might have the *ordinances* and the *privileges* of the *gospel* added unto his other enjoyments. One thing that quickened his resolution to do what might be in this matter expected from him, was a passage which he heard from a minister preaching on the title of the *fifty-first* Psalm: "To make a public and an open profession of repentance, is a thing not misbecoming the greatest man alive. It is an honor to be found among the repenting people of God, though they be in circumstances never so full of suffering." *A famous knight going with other Christians to be crowned with martyrdom, observed that his fellow sufferers were in chains, from which the sacrificers had, because of his quality, excused him; whereupon he demanded, that he might wear chains as well as they.* "For," *said he,"* "I would be a knight of that order too;" *there is among ourselves a repenting people of God, who by their confessions at their admissions to His table, do signalize their being so; and thanks be to God that we have so little of suffering in our circumstances. But if any man count himself grown too big to be a* knight of that order, *the Lord Jesus Christ Himself will one day be ashamed of that man!* Upon this excitation, Sir *William Phips* made his address unto a *Congregational church*, and he had therein one thing to propound unto himself, which few persons of his age, so well satisfied in *infant baptism* as he was, have then to ask for. Indeed, in the primitive times, although the *lawfulness of infant baptism*, or the precept and pattern of *Scripture* for it, was never so much as once made a question, yet we find *baptism* was frequently delayed by persons upon several superstitious and unreasonable accounts, against which we have such church fathers as *Gregory Nazianzen, Gregory Nyssen, Basil, Chrysostom, Ambrose,* and others, employing a variety of argument. But Sir *William Phips* had hitherto delayed his *baptism*, because the years of his childhood were spent where there was no settled minister, and therefore he was now not only willing to attain a good satisfaction of his own internal and practical *Christianity*, before his receiving that *mark* thereof, but he was also willing to receive it among those *Christians* that seemed most sensible of the *bonds* which it laid them under. Offering himself therefore, first unto the *baptism*, and then unto the *Supper* of the Lord, he presented unto the Pastor of the church, with his own *handwriting*, the following *instrument;* which because of the exemplary *devotion* therein expressed, and the remarkable *history*

[35] See II Samuel 7:1-20.
[36] The Second Church of Boston, of which

Cotton and Increase Mather were ministers.

which it gives of several occurrences in his life, I will here faithfully transcribe it, without adding so much as one word unto it.

The first of God's making me sensible of my *sins*, was in the year 1674 by hearing your father preach concerning, *The Day of Trouble near.*[37] It pleased Almighty God to smite me with a deep sense of my miserable condition, who had lived until then in the world, and had *done nothing for God*. I did then begin to think *what I should do to be saved?* And did bewail my *youthful days*, which I had spent *in vain:* I did think that I would begin to mind the *things of God*. Being then some time under your father's ministry, much troubled with my *burden*, but thinking on that Scripture, "Come unto me, you that are weary and heavy laden, and I will give you rest;"[38] I had some thoughts of drawing as near to the communion of the Lord *Jesus* as I could; but the ruins which the *Indian wars* brought on my affairs, and the entanglements which my following the *sea* laid upon me, hindered my pursuing the welfare of my own soul as I ought to have done. At length God was pleased to smile upon my *outward concerns*. The various *providences*, both merciful and afflictive, which attended me in my travels, were sanctified unto me, to make me *acknowledge God in all my ways*. I have divers times been in danger of my *life*, and I have been brought to see that I owe my *life* to Him that has given a *life* so often to me: I thank God, He hath brought me to see myself altogether unhappy, without an interest in the Lord Jesus Christ, and to close heartily with Him, desiring Him to execute *all His offices* on my behalf. I have now, for some time, been under serious *resolutions*, that I would avoid whatever I should know to be displeasing unto God, and that I would *serve him all the days of my life*. I believe *no man will repent the service of such a master*. I find myself *unable* to keep such *resolutions*, but my serious *prayers* are to the Most High, that He would *enable* me. God hath done so much for me, that I am sensible I owe myself to Him; *To Him would I give myself, and all that He has given to me*. I can't express His mercies to me. But as soon as ever God had smiled upon me with a turn of my affairs, I had laid myself under the VOWS of the Lord, *that I would set myself to serve His people, and churches here, unto the utmost of my capacity*. I have had great offers made me in *England;* but the churches of *New England* were those which my heart was most set upon. I knew, *that if God had a people anywhere, it was here:* and I *resolved to rise and fall with them;* neglecting very great advantages for my worldly interest, that I might come and enjoy the ordinances of the Lord Jesus here. It has been my

[37] Increase Mather preached, and later printed, this sermon. [K. B. M.]   [38] Matthew 11:28.

trouble, that since I came home I have made no more haste to get into the *House of God*, where *I desire to be:* especially having heard so much about the *evil* of that omission. I can do little for God, but I desire to wait upon Him in His ordinances, and to live to His honor and glory. My being born in a part of the country, where I had not in my *infancy* enjoyed the *first sacrament* of the *New Testament*, has been something of a *stumbling block* unto me. But though I have had proffers of *baptism* elsewhere made unto me, I resolved rather to defer it, until I might enjoy it in the communion of these churches; and I have had awful impressions from those words of the Lord Jesus in *Matth.* 8. 38. "Whosoever shall be ashamed of Me, and of My words, of him also shall the Son of Man be ashamed." When God had blessed me with something of the world, I had no trouble so great as this, *lest it should not be in mercy;* and I trembled at nothing more than being *put off with a portion here.* That I may make sure of *better things*, I now offer myself unto the communion of this church of the Lord JESUS.

Accordingly on *March 23. 1690*° after he had in the congregation of *North Boston* given himself up, *first unto the Lord, and then unto his people*, he was *baptized*, and so received into the *communion* of the faithful there.

§10. Several times, about, before and after *this time*, did I hear him express himself unto this purpose:

I have no need at all to look after any further advantages for myself in this world; I may sit still at home, if I will, and enjoy my ease for the rest of my life; but I believe that I should offend God in my doing so: for I am now in the prime of my age and strength, and, I thank God, I can undergo hardship: He only knows how long I have to live; but I think 'tis my duty to venture my life in doing of good, before an useless old age comes upon me: wherefore I will now expose myself while I am able, and as far as I am able, for the service of my country: I was born for others, as well as myself.

I say, many a time have I heard him so express himself: and agreeable to this generous *disposition* and *resolution* was all the rest of his life. About this time *New England* was miserably *briared* in the perplexities of an *Indian War;* and the savages in the *eastern* part of the country, issuing out from their inaccessible *swamps*, had for many months made their cruel depredations upon the poor *English* planters, and surprised many of the plantations on the frontiers, into ruin. The *New Englanders* found, that while they continued only on the *defensive* part, their *people* were thinned, and their *trea-*

°The Church Records, as copied by Mr. Robbins in his *History of the Second Church*, say March 8, 1690.

sures wasted, without any hopes of seeing a period put unto the *Indian tragedies;* nor could an army greater than *Xerxes's* have easily come at the seemingly contemptible handful of *Tawnies*[39] which made all this disturbance; or, *Tamerlane,* the greatest conqueror that ever the world saw, have made it a business of no *trouble* to have *conquered* them: they found, that they were like to make no weapons reach their enswamped adversaries, except Mr. *Milton* could have shown them how

> *To have pluckt up the hills with all their load,*
> *Rocks, waters, woods, and by their shaggy tops,*
> *Up-lifting, bore them in their hands, therewith*
> *The rebel host to've over-whelm'd------*[40]

So it was thought that the *English* subjects, in these regions of *America,* might very properly take this occasion to make an attempt upon the *French,* and by reducing them under the *English* government, put an eternal period at once unto all their troubles from the *Frenchified pagans.* This was a motion urged by Sir *William Phips* unto the General Court of the *Massachusetts Colony;* and he then made unto the Court a brave *offer* of his own person and estate, for the service of the public in their present extremity, as far as they should see cause to make use thereof. Whereupon they made a *first essay* against the *French,* by sending a naval force, with about seven hundred men, under the conduct of Sir *William Phips,* against *L'Acady*[41] and *Nova Scotia;* of which action we shall give only this general and summary account; that Sir *William Phips* set sail from *Nantasket, April 28. 1690,* arriving at *Port Royal, May 11,* and had the fort quickly surrendered into his hands by the *French* enemy, who despaired of holding out against him. He then took possession of that province for the *English* crown, and having demolished the fort, and sent away the garrison, administered unto the planters an *oath of allegiance* to King *William* and Queen *Mary,* he left what order he thought convenient for the government of the place, until further order should be taken by the Governor and Council of the *Massachussetts Colony,* unto whom he returned *May 30* with an acceptable account of his expedition, and accepted a place among the *Magistrates* of that colony, to which the *freemen* had chosen him at their *anniversary election* two days before.

. . .

[39] A name for the Indians, because of their "tawny" skins. [K. B. M.]

[41] Acadia.

[40] Paraphrased from *Paradise Lost,* vi. 643-47. [K. B. M.]

[APPOINTMENT AS GOVERNOR]

Sir *Henry Ashurst*, and Mr. *Increase Mather*, well knowing the agreeable disposition to do good, and the king and his country service, which was in Sir *William Phips*, whom they now had with them, all this while prosecuting his design for *Canada*, they did unto the council board nominate *him* for the GOVERNOR of *New England*. And Mr. *Mather* being by the Earl of *Nottingham* introduced unto His Majesty, said:

Sir,
I do, in the behalf of New England, most humbly thank Your Majesty, in that you have been pleased, by a charter, to restore English liberties unto them, to confirm them in their properties, and to grant them some peculiar privileges. I doubt not, but that your subjects there will demean themselves with that dutiful affection and loyalty to Your Majesty, as that you will see cause to enlarge your royal favors towards them. And I do most humbly thank Your Majesty, in that you have been pleased to give leave unto those that are concerned for New England to nominate their governor.

Sir William Phips has been accordingly nominated by us at the council board. He hath done a good service for the Crown, by enlarging your dominions, and reducing of Nova Scotia to your obedience. I know that he will faithfully serve Your Majesty to the utmost of his capacity; and if Your Majesty shall think fit to confirm him in that place, it will be a further obligation on your subjects there.

The effects of all this was, that Sir *William Phips* was now invested with a commission under the King's broad seal to be *Captain General*, and *Governor in Chief* over the Province of the *Massachusetts Bay* in *New England:* Nor do I know a person in the world that could have been proposed more acceptable to the body of the people throughout *New England*, and on that score more likely and able to serve the King's interests among the people there, under the changes in some things unacceptable, now brought upon them. He had been a *Gideon*, [42] who had more than once ventured his life to save his country from their enemies; and they now, with universal satisfaction said, "Thou shalt rule over us." Accordingly, having with Mr. *Mather* kissed the King's hand on *January 3d, 1691*, he hastened away to his government; and arriving at *New England* the fourteenth of *May* following, attended with the *Nonsuch frigate*, both of them were welcomed with the loud acclamations of the long *shaken* and *shattered* country, whereto they were now returned with a settlement so full of happy privileges.

•   •   •

[42] Hebrew conqueror of the Midianites. See Judges 6-8.

[THE SALEM WITCHCRAFT TRIALS]

§16.   About the time of our blessed Lord's coming to reside on earth, we read of so many *possessed with devils,* that it is commonly thought the *number* of such miserable *energumens*[43] was then increased above what has been usual in other ages; and the *reason* of that increase has been made a matter of some enquiry. Now though the *devils* might herein design by *preternatural operations* to blast the *miracles* of our Lord Jesus Christ, which point they gained among the blasphemous *Pharisees;* and the *devils* might herein also design a villainous *imitation* of what was coming to pass in the *incarnation* of our Lord Jesus Christ, wherein *God* came to *dwell in flesh;* yet I am not without suspicion, that there may be something further in the conjecture of the learned *Bartholinus*[44] hereupon, who says, it was *Quod judæi præter modum, Artibus Magicis dediti Dæmonem Advocaverint,* the *Jews,* by the frequent use of *magical tricks,* called in the *devils* among them.

It is very certain, there were hardly any people in the world grown more fond of *sorceries,* than that unhappy people: the *Talmuds* tell us of the little *parchments* with words upon them, which were their common *amulets,* and of the *charms* which they muttered over *wounds,* and of the various *enchantments* which they used against all sorts of disasters whatsoever. It is affirmed in the *Talmuds,* that no less than twenty-four scholars in one school were killed by *witchcraft;* and that no less than *fourscore* persons were hanged for *witchcraft* by one judge in one day. The *gloss* adds upon it, *that the women of* Israel *had generally fallen to the practice of witchcrafts;* and therefore it was required, that there should be still chosen into the council one skillful in the *arts of sorcerers,* and able thereby to discover who might be guilty of those *black arts* among such as were accused before them.

Now the arrival of Sir *William Phips* to the government of *New England,* was at a time when a governor would have had occasion for all the skill in *sorcery,* that was ever necessary to a *Jewish councillor;* a time when scores of poor people had newly fallen under a prodigious *possession of devils,* which it was then generally thought had been by *witchcrafts* introduced. It is to be confessed and bewailed, that many inhabitants of *New England,* and young people especially, had been led away with little *sorceries,* wherein they *did secretly those things that were not right against the Lord their God;* they would often cure hurts with *spells,* and practice detestable conjurations with *sieves,* and *keys,* and *peas,* and *nails,* and *horseshoes,* and other implements, to learn the things for which they had a forbidden and impious curiosity. Wretched books had stolen into the land, wherein fools were instructed how to become able fortunetellers: among which, I wonder that a blacker brand is not set upon that fortunetelling wheel, which that sham scribler, that goes

[43] Persons possessed by devils.

[44] Probably Caspar Bartholin (1585-1629), a Dutch medical scholar, who wrote a book on anatomy and one on astrology.

under the letters of *R. B.* has promised in his *Delights for the Ingenious,* as an *honest and pleasant recreation:*[45] and by these books, the minds of many had been so poisoned, that they studied this *finer witchcraft,* until, 'tis well, if some of them were not betrayed into what is grosser, and more sensible and capital. Although these *diabolical divinations* are more ordinarily committed perhaps all over the *whole world,* than they are in the country of *New England,* yet, that being a country devoted unto the worship and service of the Lord JESUS CHRIST above the *rest of the world,* He signalized His vengeance against these wickednesses, with such extraordinary dispensations as have not been often seen in other places.

The *devils* which had been so played withal, and, it may be, by some few criminals more explicitly engaged and employed, now broke in upon the country, after as astonishing a manner as was ever heard of. Some scores of people, first about *Salem,* the center and first-born of all the towns in the colony, and afterwards in several other places, were arrested with many *preternatural vexations* upon their bodies, and a variety of cruel torments, which were evidently inflicted from the *demons,* of the *invisible world.* The people that were *infected* and *infested* with such *demons,* in a few days' time arrived unto such a *refining alteration* upon their eyes, that they could see their tormentors; they saw a *devil* of a little *stature,* and of a tawny *color,* attended still with *specters* that appeared in more human circumstances.

These *tormentors* tendered unto the afflicted a *book,* requiring them to *sign* it, or to *touch* it at least, in token of their consenting to be lifted in the service of the *Devil;* which they refusing to do, the *specters* under the command of that *black man,* as they called him, would apply themselves to torture them with prodigious molestations.

The afflicted wretches were horribly *distorted* and *convulsed;* they were *pinched* black and blue: *pins* would be run everywhere in their flesh; they would be *scalded* until they had *blisters* raised on them; and a thousand other things before hundreds of witnesses were done unto them, evidently *preternatural:* for if it were *preternatural* to keep a rigid *fast* for *nine,* yea, for *fifteen* days together; or if it were *preternatural* to have one's hands *tied* close together with a *rope* to be plainly seen, and then by *unseen hands* presently pulled up a great way from the earth before a crowd of people; such *preternatural* things were endured by them.

But of all the *preternatural* things which befell these people, there were none more *unaccountable* than those, wherein the prestigious *demons* would ever now and then cover the most *corporeal* things in the world with a *fascinating mist* of *invisibility.* As now; a person was cruelly assaulted by a *specter,* that, she said, run at her with a *spindle,* though nobody else in the

---

[45] Nathaniel Crouch, using the initials R. B.,
published his *Delights for the Ingenious* in
London in 1684. [K. B. M.]

room could see either the *specter* or the *spindle:* At last, in her agonies, giving a snatch at the *specter,* she pulled the *spindle* away; and it was no sooner got into her hand, but the other folks then present beheld that it was indeed a real, proper, iron *spindle;* which when they locked up very safe, it was nevertheless by the *demons* taken away to do farther mischief.°

Again, a person was haunted by a most abusive *specter,* which came to her, she said, with a *sheet* about her, though seen to none but herself. After she had undergone a deal of tease from the annoyance of the *specter,* she gave a violent *snatch* at the *sheet* that was upon it; wherefrom she tore a corner, which in her hand immediately was beheld by all that were present, a palpable corner of a *sheet:* and her father, which was now holding of her, *catched,* that he might *keep* what his daughter had so strangely seized; but the *specter* had like to have wrung his hand off, by endeavoring to wrest it from him: however he still held it; and several times this odd accident was renewed in the family. There wanted not the *oaths* of good credible people to these particulars.

Also, it is well known, that these wicked *specters* did proceed so far as to steal several quantities of money from diverse people, part of which individual money was dropt sometimes out of the air, before sufficient *spectators,* into the hands of the afflicted, while the *specters* were urging them to subscribe their *covenant with death.* Moreover, *poisons* to the standers-by, wholly *invisible,* were sometimes forced upon the afflicted; which when they have with much reluctancy swallowed, they have *swollen* presently, so that the common medicines for *poisons* have been found necessary to relieve them: yea, sometimes the *specters* in the *struggles* have so dropt the *poisons,* that the standers-by have smelt them, and viewed them, and beheld the *pillows* of the miserable stained with them.

Yet more, the miserable have complained bitterly of *burning rags* run into their forcibly distended *mouths;* and though nobody could see any such *clothes,* or indeed *any fires* in the chambers, yet presently the *scalds* were seen plainly by everybody on the mouths of the complainers and not only the *smell,* but the *smoke* of the burning sensibly filled the chambers.

Once more, the miserable exclaimed extremely of *branding irons* heating at the fire on the hearth to mark them; now though the standers-by could see no *irons,* yet they could see distinctly the *print* of them in the ashes, and *smell* them too as they were carried by the *not-seen furies,* unto the poor creatures for whom they were intended; and those poor creatures were thereupon so *stigmatized* with them, that they will bear the *marks* of them to their dying day. Nor are these the *tenth part* of the *prodigies* that fell out among the inhabitants of *New England.*

°Compare the pink ribbon that Goodman Brown clutches, near the climax of Nathaniel Hawthorne's story "Young Goodman Brown," below:

Flashy people may *burlesque* these things, but when hundreds of the most sober people in a country, where they have as much *mother wit* certainly as the rest of mankind, know them to be *true,* nothing but the absurd and froward spirit of *Sadducism*[46] can question them. I have not yet mentioned so much as one thing that will not be justified, if it be required by the *oaths* of more considerate persons than any that can ridicule these odd *phenomena.*

But the worst part of this astonishing *tragedy* is yet behind; wherein Sir *William Phips,* at last being dropt, as it were from the *machine of heaven,* was an instrument of easing the distresses of the land, now *so darkened by the wrath of the Lord of Hosts.* There were very worthy men upon the spot where the *assault from hell* was first made, who apprehended themselves called from the *God of Heaven,* to sift the business unto the bottom of it; and indeed, the continual *impressions,* which the outcries and the havocs of the *afflicted people* that lived nigh unto them caused on their minds, gave no little edge to this apprehension.

The persons were men eminent for *wisdom* and *virtue,* and they went about their enquiry into the matter, as *driven* unto it by a *conscience* of duty to God and the world. They did in the first place take it for granted, that there are *witches,* or wicked children of men, who upon *covenanting* with, and *commissioning* of *evil spirits,* are attended by their ministry to accomplish the things desired of them: to satisfy them in which persuasion, they had not only the *assertions* of the *Holy Scripture;* assertions, which the *witch advocates* cannot evade without shifts, too foolish for any *prudent* or too profane for any *honest* man to use; and they had not only the well-attested *relations* of the gravest authors from *Bodin* to *Bovet,* and from *Binsfeld* to *Bromhal* and *Baxter;*[47] to deny all which, would be as reasonable as to turn the chronicles of all nations into romances of *Don Quixote* and the *Seven Champions,*[48] but they had also an *ocular demonstration* in one, who a little before had been executed for *witchcraft,* when *Joseph Dudley,* Esq; was the Chief Judge. There was one whose *magical images* were found, and who *confessing her deeds* (when a jury of doctors returned her *compos mentis*) actually showed the whole court, by what *ceremonies* used unto them, she directed her *familiar spirits* how and where to cruciate the objects of her malice; and the experiments being made over and over again before the whole court, the *effect* followed exactly in the hurts done to people at a distance from her. The existence of such *witches* was now taken for granted by those good men, wherein so far the generality of reasonable men have

---

[46] The spirit of the Sadducees, who denied the existence of angels and spirits. [K. B. M.]

[47] Mather might easily have extended indefinitely his list of learned writers who had up-

held the reality of witchcraft. [K. B. M.]

[48] *The Famous History of the Seven Champions of Christendom,* by Richard Johnston, a romance first printed in 1596. [K. B. M.]

thought *they ran well*,[49] and they soon received the *confessions* of some *accused* persons to confirm them in it; but then they took one thing more for granted, wherein 'tis now as generally thought they *went out of the way*.[50] The afflicted people vehemently accused several persons in several places, that the *specters* which afflicted them, did exactly resemble *them;* until the importunity of the accusations did provoke the magistrates to examine them. When many of the *accused* came upon their examination, it was found, that the *demons* then a thousand ways abusing of the poor *afflicted* people, had with a marvellous exactness *represented* them; yea, it was found, that many of the *accused,* but casting their eye on the *afflicted,* the *afflicted,* though their faces were never so much another way, would fall down and lie in a sort of a swoon, wherein they would continue, whatever hands were laid upon them, until the hands of the *accused* came to touch them, and *then* they would revive immediately: and it was found, that various kinds of *natural actions,* done by many of the *accused* in or to their own bodies, as *leaning, bending, turning* awry, or *squeezing* their hands, or the like, were presently attended with the like things *preternaturally* done upon the bodies of the *afflicted,* though they were so far asunder, that the *afflicted* could not at all observe the *accused.*

It was also found, that the flesh of the afflicted was often *bitten* at such a rate, that not only the *print of teeth* would be left on their *flesh,* but the very *slaver* of spittle too: and there would appear just such a *set of teeth* as was in the *accused,* even such as might be clearly distinguished from other people's. And usually the *afflicted* went through a terrible deal of seeming difficulties from the tormenting *specters,* and must be long waited on, before they could get a breathing space from their *torments* to give in their testimonies.

Now many good men[51] took up an opinion, that the *Providence* of God would not permit an *innocent person* to come under such a *spectral representation;* and that a concurrence of so many circumstances would prove an *accused* person to be in a *confederacy* with the *demons* thus afflicting of the neighbors; they judged, that except these things might amount unto a *conviction,* it would scarce be possible ever to *convict* a *witch;* and they had some *philosophical schemes* of *witchcraft,* and of the method and manner wherein *magical poisons* operate, which further supported them in their opinion.

Sundry of the *accused* persons were brought unto their *trial,* while this opinion was yet prevailing in the minds of the *judges* and the *juries,* and

[49] That is, they were right.

[50] Here Mather describes spectral evidence, and in the following paragraphs the controversy over its admission as evidence in the court. Here again, compare Hawthorne's "Young Goodman Brown."

[51] Including the Chief-Justice and Deputy-governor of the colony, William Stoughton.

perhaps the most of the people in the country, then mostly suffering; and though against some of them that were tried there came in so much *other evidence* of their diabolical compacts that some of the most *judicious*, and yet *vehement* opposers of the notions then in vogue, publicly declared, *had they themselves been on the bench, they could not have acquitted them;*[52] nevertheless, divers were condemned, against whom the *chief evidence* was founded in the *spectral exhibitions.*

And it happening, that some of the *accused* coming to confess themselves *guilty,* their *shapes* were no more seen by any of the *afflicted,* though the confession had been kept never so secret, but instead thereof the *accused* themselves became in all vexations just like the *afflicted;* this yet more confirmed many in the opinion that had been taken up.

And another thing that quickened them yet more to act upon it, was, that the afflicted were frequently entertained with *apparitions* of *ghosts* at the same time that the *specters* of the supposed *witches* troubled them: which *ghosts* always cast the beholders into far more consternation than any of the *specters;* and when they exhibited themselves, they cried out of being *murdered* by the *witchcrafts,* or other violences of the persons represented in the *specters.* Once or twice these apparitions were seen by others at the very same time that they showed themselves to the *afflicted;* and seldom were they seen at all, but when something unusual and suspicious had attended the death of the party thus appearing.

The *afflicted* people many times had never heard anything before of the persons appearing in *ghost,* or of the persons *accused* by the *apparitions;* and yet the accused upon examination have confessed the murders of those very persons, though these *accused* also knew nothing of the *apparitions* that had come in against them; and the *afflicted* persons likewise, without any private agreement or collusion, when successively brought into a room, have all asserted the same *apparitions* to be there before them: these *murders* did seem to call for an enquiry.

On the other part, there were many persons of great judgment, piety and experience, who from the beginning were very much dissatisfied at these proceedings; they feared lest the *Devil* would get so far into the *faith* of the people, that for the sake of many *truths,* which they might find him telling of them, they would come at length to believe all his *lies,* whereupon what a desolation of *names,* yea, and of *lives* also, would ensue, a man might without much *witchcraft* be able to prognosticate; and they feared, lest in such an extraordinary descent of *wicked spirits* from their *high places* upon us, there might such *principles* be taken up, as, when put into *practice,* would unavoidably cause the *righteous to perish with the wicked,* and procure the

---

[52] A virtual quotation from the postscript to Increase Mather's *Cases of Conscience concerning Evil Spirits Personating Men,* the book that probably put an end to the executions by denouncing spectral evidence.

bloodshed of persons like the *Gibeonites,* whom some learned men suppose to be under a false pretense of *witchcraft,* by *Saul* exterminated.[53]

However uncommon it might be for *guiltless persons* to come under such unaccountable circumstances, as were on so many of the accused, they held *some things there are, which if suffered to be common, would subvert government, and disband and ruin human society, yet God sometimes may suffer such things to evene, that we may know thereby how much we are beholden to Him for that restraint which He lays upon the infernal spirits, who would else reduce a world into a chaos.* They had already known of one at the town of *Groton* hideously agitated by *devils,* who in her fits cried out much against a very godly woman in the town, and when that woman approached unto her, though the eyes of the creature were never so shut, she yet manifested a violent sense of her approach: but when the gracious woman thus impeached, had prayed earnestly with and for this creature, then instead of crying out against her any more, she owned, that she had in all been deluded by the *Devil.* They now saw, that the more the *afflicted* were hearkened unto, the more the number of the *accused* increased; until at last many scores were *cried out* upon, and among them, some, who by the *unblamableness,* yea, and *serviceableness* of their whole conversation, had obtained the just reputation of *good people* among all that were acquainted with them. The character of the *afflicted* likewise added unto the common distaste; for though some of *them* too were *good people,* yet others of them, and such of them as were most flippant at *accusing,* had a far other character.

In fine, the country was in a dreadful *ferment,* and wise men foresaw a long train of dismal and bloody consequences. Hereupon they first advised, that the *afflicted* might be kept asunder in the closest privacy; and one particular person (whom I have cause to know)[54] in pursuance of this advice, offered himself singly to provide accommodations for any *six* of them, that so the success of more than ordinary *prayer* with *fasting,* might, with *patience,* be *experienced,* before any other courses were taken.

And Sir *William Phips* arriving to his government, after this *ensnaring horrible storm* was begun, did consult the neighboring minsiters of the province, who made unto His Excellency and the Council a return (drawn up at their desire by Mr *Mather* the Younger,[55]° as I have been informed) wherein they declared:

---

[53] See I Samuel 28, and II Samuel 1-5. There is no firm record of the reason for which Saul executed the Gibeonites.

[54] Cotton Mather himself.

[55] Cotton Mather. The "as I have been inform'd" is part of his attempt to retain his anonymity, since the life of Phips was first published with no author's name. When it appeared in the *Magnalia,* Mather was known as its author, but he did not alter the phrasing of the original edition.(K. B. M.)

° Mather also omits from his history here the last paragraph of the Return, which recommends "the speedy and vigorous prosecution of such as have rendered themselves obnoxious, according to the direction given in the Laws of God, and the wholesome statutes of the *English* nation for the detection of witchcrafts."

We judge, that in the prosecution of these and all such witchcrafts, *there is need of a very critical and exquisite caution: lest by too much credulity for things received only upon the* Devil's authority, *there be a door opened for a long train of miserable consequences, and Satan get an advantage over us; for* we should not be ignorant of his devices.

As in complaints upon witchcrafts, *there may be matters of* enquiry, *which do not amount unto matters of* presumption; *and there may be matters of* presumption, *which yet may not be reckoned matters of* conviction; *so 'tis necessary that all proceedings thereabout be managed with an* exceeding tenderness *towards those that may be complained of; especially if they have been persons formerly of an* unblemished reputation.

When the first enquiry *is made into the circumstances of such as may lie under any just suspicion of* witchcrafts, *we could wish that there may be admitted as little as is possible of such* noise, company, *and* openness, *as may too hastily expose them that are examined; and that there may nothing be used as a* test *for the trial of the suspected, the lawfulness whereof may be doubted among the people of God: but that the directions given by such judicious writers as* Perkins *and* Bernard, *be consulted in such a case.*

Presumptions, *whereupon persons may be committed, and much more* convictions, *whereupon persons may be condemned as guilty of* witchcrafts, *ought certainly to be more considerable, than barely the* accused *persons being* represented *by a* specter *to the afflicted: inasmuch as it is an undoubted and a notorious thing, that a* demon *may, by God's permission, appear even to ill purposes in the shape of an* innocent, *yea, and a* virtuous *man: nor can we* esteem *alterations made in the* sufferers, *by a* look *or* touch *of the* accused, *to be an infallible evidence of guilt; but frequently liable to be abused by the Devil's* legerdemains.

We know not whether some remarkable affronts *given to the* Devils, *by our disbelieving of those testimonies whose whole force and strength is from* them *alone, may not put a period unto the progress of a direful calamity begun upon us, in the* accusation *of so many persons, whereof, we hope, some are yet* clear from the great transgression *laid unto their charge.*

The ministers of the province also being jealous lest this *counsel* should not be duly followed, requested the President of *Harvard* College[56] to compose and publish (which he did) some *cases of conscience* referring to these difficulties: in which treatise he did, with demonstrations of incomparable *reason* and *reading*, evince it, that *Satan* may appear in the shape of an *innocent* and a *virtuous* person, to afflict those that suffer by the *diabolical molestations:*

---

[56] Increase Mather.

and that the *ordeal* of the *sight*, and the *touch*, is not a conviction of a *covenant* with the Devil, but liable to great exceptions against the *lawfulness*, as well as the *evidence* of it: and that either a free and fair *confession* of the criminals, or the oath of two credible persons proving such things against the person accused, as none but such as have a familiarity with the Devil can know, or do, is necessary to the proof of the crime. Thus,

> *Cum misit Natura Feras, & Monstra per Orbem,*
> *Misit & Alciden qui Fera Monstra domet.*[57]

The *Dutch* and *French* ministers in the Province of *New York*, having likewise about the same time their judgment asked by the *Chief Judge* of that province, who was then a gentleman of *New England*, they gave it in under their hands, that if we believe no *venefic witchcraft*, we must renounce the *Scripture* of God, and the *consent* of almost all the world; but that yet the *apparition* of a person afflicting another, is a very insufficient proof of a *witch;* nor is it inconsistent with the holy and righteous government of God over men, to permit the affliction of the neighbors, by devils in the *shape* of *good men;* and that a *good name*, obtained by a *good life*, should not be lost by mere *spectral accusations*.

Now upon a deliberate review of these things, His Excellency first *reprieved*, and then *pardoned* many of them that had been condemned; and there fell out several strange things that caused the spirit of the country to run as vehemently upon the *acquitting* of all the *accused*, as it by mistake ran at first upon the *condemning* of them. Some that had been zealously of the mind, that the *devils* could not in the *shapes* of good men afflict other men, were terribly confused, by having their own *shapes*, and the *shapes* of their most intimate and valued friends, thus abused. And though more than twice twenty had made such voluntary, and harmonious, and uncontrolable confessions, that if they were all *sham*, there was therein the greatest violation made by the efficacy of the *invisible world*, upon the *rules of understanding human affairs*, that was ever seen since *God made man upon the earth*, yet they did so recede from their *confessions*, that it was very clear, some of them had been hitherto, in a sort of a *preternatural dream*, wherein they had said *of themselves*, they *knew not what themselves*.

In fine, the last courts that sat upon this *thorny business* finding that it was impossible to penetrate into the whole meaning of the things that had happened, and that so many *unsearchable cheats* were interwoven into the *conclusion* of a mysterious business, which perhaps had not crept thereinto at the *beginning* of it, they *cleared* the *accused* as fast as they *tried* them; and within a little while the *afflicted* were most of them delivered out of their *troubles* also: and the land had peace restored unto it, by the *God of peace, treading Satan under foot. Erasmus,* among other historians, does tell us, that

[57] "When Nature sent animals and monsters throughout the world, she sent also Hercules to subjugate them."

at a town in *Germany,* a *demon* appearing on the top of a chimney, threatened that he would set the town on *fire,* and at length scattering some ashes abroad, the whole town was presently and horribly burnt unto the ground.

Sir *William Phips* now beheld such *demons* hideously scattering *fire* about the country, in the exasperations which the minds of men were on these things rising unto; and therefore when he had well canvased a *cause,* which perhaps might have puzzled the wisdom of the wisest men on earth to have managed, without any *error* in their administrations, he thought, if it would be any *error* at all, it would certainly be the *safest* for him to put a stop unto all future prosecutions, as far as it lay in him to do it.

He did so, and for it he had not only the printed acknowledgments of the *New Englanders,* who publicly thanked him, *as one of the tribe of* Zebulun, *raised up from among themselves, and* spirited *as well as* commissioned *to be the* steersman *of a vessel befogged in the* Mare Mortuum[58] *of* witchcraft, *who now so happily* steered *her course, that she escaped shipwreck, and was safely again moored under the Cape of* Good Hope; *and cut asunder the* Circean *knot of enchantment, more difficult to be dissolved than the famous* Gordian *one of old.*

But the QUEEN also did him the honor to write unto him those gracious letters, wherein Her Majesty commended his conduct in these *inexplicable* matters. And I did right in calling these matters *inexplicable.* For if, after the Kingdom of *Sweden* (in the year 1669, and 1670) had some hundreds of their children by night often carried away by *specters* to an *hellish rendezvous,* where the monsters that so *spirited* them, did every way *tempt* them to associate with them; and the judges of the kingdom, after *extraordinary supplications* to heaven, upon a strict enquiry, were so satisfied with the *confessions* of more than twenty of the *accused,* agreeing exactly unto the *depositions* of the *afflicted,* that they put several scores of *witches* to death, whereupon the confusions came unto a period; yet after all, the chiefest persons in the kingdom would question whether there were any *witchcrafts* at all in the whole affair; it must not be wondered at, if the people of *New England* are to this hour full of *doubts,* about the *steps* which were taken, while a *war* from the *invisible world* was terrifying of them; and whether they did not kill some of their *own side* in the *smoke* and *noise* of this dreadful *war.* And it will be yet less wondered at, if we consider, that we have seen the whole *English Nation* alarmed with a *plot,* and both *Houses of Parliament,* upon good grounds, voting their sense of it, and many persons most justly *hanged, drawn and quartered,* for their share in it: when yet there are enough, who to this day will pretend, that they cannot comprehend how much of it is to be accounted *credible.* However, having related these wonderful passages, whereof, if the *veracity* of the relator in any one point be contested, there are whole *clouds of witnesses* to vindicate it, I will take my

[58] "Dead Sea."

leave of the matter with an wholesome caution of *Lactantius,* which, it may be, some other parts of the world besides *New England* may have occasion to think upon: *Efficiunt Dæmones, ut quæ non sint, sic tamen, quasi sint, conspicienda Hominibus exhibeant.*[59]

But the *Devils* being thus vanquished, we shall *next* hear, that some of his most devoted and resembling *children* are so too.

．　．　．

[HIS APPEARANCE AND DISPOSITION]

§18.　Reader, 'tis time for us to view a little more to the *life,* the *picture* of the person, the *actions* of whose *life* we have hitherto been looking upon. Know then, that for his *exterior,* he was one *tall,* beyond the common set of men, and *thick* as well as *tall,* and *strong* as well as *thick:* he was, in all respects, exceedingly *robust,* and able to conquer such difficulties of *diet* and of *travel,* as would have killed most men alive: nor did the *fat,* whereinto he grew very much in his later years, take away the vigor of his motions.

He was well-set, and he was therewithal of a very *comely,* though a very *manly* countenance: a countenance where any true skill in *physiognomy* would have read the characters of a *generous mind.* Wherefore passing to his *interior,* the very first thing which there offered itself unto observation, was a most incomparable *generosity.*

And of this, besides the innumerable instances which he gave in his usual hatred of *dirty* or *little* tricks, there was one instance for which I must freely say, *I never saw three men in this world that equalled him;* this was his wonderfully *forgiving spirit.* In the vast variety of *business,* through which he *raced* in his time, he met with many and mighty *injuries;* but although I have heard all that the most venomous *malice* could ever *hiss* at his memory, I never did hear unto this hour, that he did ever once deliberately *revenge an injury.*

Upon certain *affronts* he has made sudden *returns* that have showed *choler* enough, and he has by *blow,* as well as by *word,* chastised *incivilities:* he was, indeed, sufficiently impatient of being *put upon;* and when *base men,* surprising him at some *disadvantages* (for else few men durst have done it) have sometimes drawn upon him, he has, without the *wicked madness* of a *formal duel,* made them feel that he knew how to *correct fools.* Nevertheless, he ever declined a *deliberate revenge* of ˙a *wrong* done unto him; though few men upon *earth* have, in their *vicissitudes,* been furnished with such fre-

---

[59] "Devils so work that things which are not appear to men as if they were real." Lactantius (c. 240-320), one of Mather's favorite writers, was a scholar who served as tutor to the eldest son of Constantine. One of his religious works is called *The Anger of God* (314).

quent *opportunities* of *revenge*, as *heaven* brought into the hands of this *gentleman*.

Under great provocations, he would commonly say, " 'Tis no matter, let them alone; some time or other they'll see their weakness and rashness, and have occasion for me to do them a kindness: and they shall then see I have quite forgotten all their baseness." Accordingly 'twas remarkable to see it, that few men ever did *him* a mischief, but those men afterwards had occasion for him to do *them* a *kindness;* and he did the *kindness* with as forgetful a *bravery*, as if the *mischief* had never been done at all. The Emperor *Theodosius* himself could not be readier to *forgive*,[60] so worthily did he verify that observation.

> *Quo quisque est Major, magis est Placabilis Ira,*
> *Et Faciles Motus, Mens Generosa capit.*[61]

In those places of *power* whereto the providence of God by several *degrees* raised him, it still fell out so, that before his *rise* thereunto he underwent such things as he counted very hard *abuses*, from those very persons over whom the divine providence afterwards gave him the *ascendant*.

. . .

[60] An allusion to Theodosius I, who won over the Goths, by honors paid to their fallen leader, Athanaric. (K. B. M.)

[61] "The greater one is, the more one is placable in wrath, and a generous mind is easily moved."

A Meditation on Gravity[1]

I am continually entertained with *weighty body*, or *matter* tending to the *center of gravity:* or attracted by matter. I feel it in my own. The *cause* of this *tendency*, 'tis the glorious GOD! *Great GOD, Thou givest this matter such a tendency; Thou keepest it in its operation!* There is no other cause for *gravity*, but the *will* and *work* of the glorious GOD. I am now effectually convinced of that ancient confession, and must effectuously make it, "He is not far from every one of us." When I see a thing moving or settling that way which its *heavy nature* carries it, I may very justly think, and I would often form the thought, "It is the glorious GOD who now carries this matter such a way." When *matter* goes *downward*, my spirit shall therefore mount *upward*,

[1] This meditation is published with the consent of the University of Virginia, from Mather's manuscript Paterna, an autobiographical book that he left for his son. Compare his book of observations on Nature, *The Christian Philosopher*, 1721.

in acknowledgment of the GOD who orders it. I will no longer complain, "Behold, I go forward, but He is not there; and backward, but I cannot perceive Him: on the left hand, where He does work, but I cannot behold Him: He hideth himself on the right hand, that I cannot see Him." No, I am now taught where to meet with Him; even at every turn. *He knows the way that I take;* I cannot stir forward or backward, but I *perceive* Him in the *weight* of every *matter. My way* shall be to improve this as a *weighty argument* for the being of a GOD. I will argue from it, "Behold, there is a God, whom I ought forever to love and serve and glorify." Yea, and if I am tempted unto the doing of any wicked thing, I may reflect, that it cannot be done without some *action,* wherein *the power of matter* operates. But then I may carry on the reflection: "How near, how near am I to the glorious GOD, whose commands I am going to violate! Matter keeps His laws; but, O my soul, wilt thou break His laws? How shall I do this wickedness and therein deny the GOD, who not only is above, but also is exerting His power in the very matter upon which I make my criminal misapplications!"

EDWARD TAYLOR

(1645-1729)

For nearly 60 years after his graduation from Harvard College, Edward Taylor lived in the frontier town of Westfield, Massachusetts, where he survived the Indian wars, tended the souls of his congregation as pastor, treated the people's bodies as physician, defended the traditional side in theological disputes, and wrote but did not publish the largest body of serious verse that any American poet achieved before the

The standard edition is *The Poems of Edward Taylor,* ed. Donald E. Stanford, 1960. See also *The Poetical Works of Edward Taylor,* ed. Thomas H. Johnson, 1939.

Critical estimates are Norman S. Grabo, *Edward Taylor,* 1961 and Donald E. Stanford, *Edward Taylor,* 1965. Recent criticism includes Michael J. Colacurcio, "God's Determinations Touching Half-Way Membership: Occasion and Audience in Edward Taylor," *American Literature,* 39 (1967): 298–314; Alan B. Howard, "The World as Emblem: Language and Vision in the Poetry of Edward Taylor," *American Literature,* 44 (1972): 359–384;

Karl Keller, *The Example of Edward Taylor,* 1975; Albert Gelpi, *The Tenth Muse,* 1975.

The text is from the edition of Donald E. Stanford, New Haven, 1960. Because some of the spelling and capitalization in this frequently "metaphysical" verse might change the meaning if modernized, I have reproduced the peculiarities of Stanford's text, and his substantive notes as well, with permission from The Yale University Press and The Princeton University Press.

nineteenth century. Since the rediscovery and first publication of Taylor's *Meditations* and *God's Determination Touching His Elect* in the 1930's, a great quantity of scholarly and critical commentary has been devoted to his work, and some of his sermons, his long *Metrical History of Christianity,* and his brief spiritual autobiography have been reproduced in one form or another. Taylor's continuing value as a poet depends on his *Preparatory Meditations* and on *God's Determinations.*

Although the Preface and two or three of the concluding poems in *God's Determinations* have often been printed separately, they lose much of their force and meaning outside the larger design. For that reason and because they illuminate Puritan religious culture and the Puritan psyche, an unusually large selection of the poems from *God's Determinations* is reprinted here. In narrative and dramatic form *God's Determinations* traces the spiritual life of the Elect from the Fall of Adam to the secure establishment of a particular saint in the church, the coach in which the covenanted elect "bowl and swim" to glory. From the Creation of the world and the Fall, Taylor moves through dramatic explanation of the logic behind man's plight and regeneration—most effectively in the dialogue between Justice and Mercy—to the successful struggle of a soul to overcome despair and, with the help of direct appeals to Christ and the counsel of a church member, dare to accept the supportive discipline and fellowship of a covenanted church. As the conflict between Justice and Mercy is a meeting of opposite tendencies in the early dialogue, so the struggle between the soul's desire and fear shows us the conscientious Puritan's psychological plight near the end, and the triumph of Mercy over Justice, faith over doubt, desire over fear, is aptly represented by the joyous movement of Christ's coach toward the heavenly City. The success of the poem, at its best, derives from Taylor's skillful representation of the logical conflicts of irreconcilable essences, the telling accuracy of Satan's accusations, the ingenuity of Satan's arguments against true faith. It is in such antitheses that Taylor most admirably fixes the peculiarly narrow line on which the Puritan had to plot his life. "Justice not done no justice is," but "Justice in Justice must adjudge Thee just [that is, justified] If Thou in Mercy's Mercy put thy trust." Presumptuous desire was a sin in Thomas Shepard's time as well as Taylor's, but so was the excessive fear that led to despair, and Taylor's poem had especial relevance to the third-generation people who might be too hesitant to profess their faith and approach the Lord's Table. (Compare the selection from Samuel Sewall's diary, above, pp. 204–212.)

Taylor's *Preparatory Meditations* were written at regular intervals over a number of years, as preparation for the sacrament of communion. The self-examination here is that of a confident believer who is "counted" among the Lord's gold but who must ask self-critically for reassurance. Sometimes he is overwhelmed by his sense of divine goodness to him; sometimes, like Anne Bradstreet, John Winthrop, and Jonathan Edwards, he asks for revival of a powerful experience that has been followed by relative deadness.

The imagery and technique of the Meditations has been the subject of much discussion, ranging from the claim that Taylor was a displaced and anachronistic Metaphysical poet, secretly pouring out his repressed love of sense and ornament in unorthodox verse, to the stronger argument that he was a thoroughly orthodox Calvinist. Some of the most valuable recent work has considered Taylor's use of typology and his indebtedness to the Emblem books.

Preparatory Meditations and Other Lyrics

FIRST SERIES

6. ANOTHER MEDITATION AT THE SAME TIME

Undated.

Am I thy Gold? Or Purse, Lord, for thy Wealth;
    Whether in mine, or mint refinde for thee?
Ime counted so, but count me o're thyselfe,
    Lest gold washt face, and brass in Heart I bee.
    I Feare my Touchstone touches when I try   5
    Mee, and my Counted Gold too overly.

Am I new minted by thy Stamp indeed?
    Mine Eyes are dim; I cannot clearly see.
Be thou my Spectacles that I may read
    Thine Image, and Inscription stampt on mee.   10
    If thy bright Image do upon me stand
    I am a Golden Angell in thy hand.

Lord, make my Soule thy Plate: thine Image bright
    Within the Circle of the same enfoile.
And on its brims in golden Letters write   15
    Thy Superscription in an Holy style.
    Then I shall be thy Money, thou my Hord:
    Let me thy Angell bee, bee thou my Lord.

THE EXPERIENCE

Undated.

Oh! that I alwayes breath'd in such an aire,
    As I suckt in, feeding on sweet Content!
Disht up unto my Soul ev'n in that pray're
    Pour'de out to God over last Sacrament.
        What Beam of Light wrapt up my sight to finde   5
        Me neerer God than ere Came in my minde?

Most strange it was! But yet more strange that shine
    Which filld my Soul then to the brim to spy
My Nature with thy Nature all Divine
    Together joyn'd in Him thats Thou, and I.   10

Flesh of my Flesh, Bone of my Bone. There's run
Thy Godhead, and my Manhood in thy Son.

Oh! that that Flame which thou didst on me Cast
    Might me enflame, and Lighten ery where.
Then Heaven to me would be less at last   15
    So much of heaven I should have while here.
        Oh! Sweet though Short! Ile not forget the same.
        My neerness, Lord, to thee did me Enflame.

I'le Claim my Right: Give place, ye Angells Bright.
    Ye further from the Godhead stande than I.   20
My Nature is your Lord; and doth Unite
    Better than Yours unto the Deity.
        Gods Throne is first and mine is next: to you
        Onely the place of Waiting-men is due.

Oh! that my Heart, thy Golden Harp might bee   25
    Well tun'd by Glorious Grace, that e'ry string
Screw'd to the highest pitch, might unto thee
    All Praises wrapt in sweetest Musick bring.
        I praise thee, Lord, and better praise thee would
        If what I had, my heart might ever hold.   30

38. MEDITATION. 1 JOH. 2.1.
AN ADVOCATE WITH THE FATHER

6.5m [July] *1690.*

Oh! What a thing is Man? Lord, Who am I?
    That thou shouldst give him Law (Oh! golden Line)

To regulate his Thoughts, Words, Life thereby.
    And judge him Wilt thereby too in thy time.
A Court of Justice thou in heaven holdst   5
    To try his Case while he's here housd on mould.

How do thy Angells lay before thine eye
    My Deeds both White, and Black I dayly doe?
How doth thy Court thou Pannellst there them try?
    But flesh complains. What right for this? let's know.   10
    For right, or wrong I can't appeare unto't.
    And shall a sentence Pass on such a suite?

Soft; blemish not this golden Bench, or place.
    Here is no Bribe, nor Colourings to hide
Nor Pettifogger to befog the Case   15
    But Justice hath her Glory here well tri'de.
    Her spotless Law all spotted Cases tends.
    Without Respect or Disrespect them ends.

God's Judge himselfe: and Christ Atturny is,
    The Holy Ghost Regesterer is founde.   20
Angells the sergeants are, all Creatures kiss
    The booke, and doe as Evidences abounde.
    All Cases pass according to pure Law
    And in the sentence is no Fret, nor flaw.

What saist, my soule? Here all thy Deeds are tri'de.   25
    Is Christ thy Advocate to pleade thy Cause?
Art thou his Client? Such shall never slide.
    He never lost his Case: he pleads such Laws
    As Carry do the same, nor doth refuse
    The Vilest sinners Case that doth him Choose.   30

This is his Honour, not Dishonour: nay
    No Habeas-Corpus gainst his Clients came
For all their Fines his Purse doth make down pay.
    He Non-Suites Satan's Suite or Casts the Same.
    He'l plead thy Case, and not accept a Fee.   35
    He'l plead Sub Forma Pauperis for thee.

My Case is bad. Lord, be my Advocate.
    My sin is red: I'me under Gods Arrest.
Thou hast the Hint of Pleading; plead my State.
    Although it's bad thy Plea will make it best.   40
    If thou wilt plead my Case before the King:
    I'le Waggon Loads of Love, and Glory bring.

Detail of the Joseph Tapping stone, King's Chapel, Boston, 1678. *(Reprinted by permission of Allen Ludwig and Wesleyan University Press.)*

SECOND SERIES

112. MEDITATION. 2 COR. 5.14.
IF ONE DIED FOR ALL THEN ARE ALL DEAD

15.12m [Feb.] *1712.*

Oh! Good, Good, Good, my Lord. What more Love yet.
    Thou dy for mee! What, am I dead in thee?
What did Deaths arrow shot at me thee hit?
    Didst slip between that flying shaft and mee?
    Didst make thyselfe Deaths marke shot at for mee?   5
    So that her Shaft shall fly no far than thee?

Di'dst dy for mee indeed, and in thy Death
    Take in thy Dying thus my death the Cause?
And lay I dying in thy Dying breath,
    According to Graces Redemption Laws?   10
    If one did dy for all, it needs must bee
    That all did dy in one, and from death free.

Infinities fierce firy arrow red
    Shot from the splendid Bow of Justice bright
Did smite thee down, for thine. Thou art their head.   15
    They di'de in thee. Their death did on thee light.
    They di'de their Death in thee, thy Death is theirs.
    Hence thine is mine, thy death my trespass clears.

How sweet is this: my Death lies buried
    Within thy Grave, my Lord, deep under ground,   20
It is unskin'd, as Carrion rotten Dead.
    For Grace's hand gave Death its deadly wound.
    Deaths no such terrour on th'Saints blesst Coast.
    Its but a harmless Shade: No walking Ghost.

The Painter lies: the Bellfrey Pillars weare   25
    A false Effigies now of Death, alas!
With empty Eyeholes, Butter teeth, bones bare
    And spraggling arms, having an Hour Glass
    In one grim paw. Th'other a Spade doth hold
    To shew deaths frightfull region under mould.   30

Whereas its Sting is gone: its life is lost.
    Though unto Christless ones it is most Grim
Its but a Shade to Saints whose path it Crosst.
    Or Shell or Washen face, in which she sings
    Their Bodies in her lap a Lollaboy   35
    And sends their Souls to sing their Masters joy.

Lord let me finde Sin, Curse and Death that doe
    Belong to me ly slain too in thy Grave.
And let thy law my clearing hence bestow
    And from these things let me acquittance have.   40
    The Law suffic'de: and I discharg'd, Hence sing
    Thy praise I will over Deaths Death, and Sin.

HUSWIFERY

Undated.

Make me, O Lord, thy Spining Wheele compleate.
    Thy Holy Worde my Distaff make for mee.
Make mine Affections thy Swift Flyers neate
    And make my Soule thy holy Spoole to bee.
    My Conversation make to be thy Reele   5
    And reele the yarn thereon spun of thy Wheele.

Make me thy Loome then, knit therein this Twine:
    And make thy Holy Spirit, Lord, winde quills:
Then weave the Web thyselfe. The yarn is fine.
    Thine Ordinances make my Fulling Mills.   10
    Then dy the same in Heavenly Colours Choice,
    All pinkt with Varnisht Flowers of Paradise.

Then cloath therewith mine Understanding, Will,
    Affections, Judgment, Conscience, Memory
My Words, and Actions, that their shine may fill   15
    My wayes with glory and thee glorify.
    Then mine apparell shall display before yee
    That I am Cloathd in Holy robes for glory.

THE EBB AND FLOW

Undated.

When first thou on me Lord wrought'st thy Sweet Print,
    My heart was made thy tinder box.
    My 'ffections were thy tinder in't.
        Where fell thy Sparkes by drops.
Those holy Sparks of Heavenly Fire that came   5
Did ever catch and often out would flame.

But now my Heart is made thy Censar trim,
    Full of thy golden Altars fire,
    To offer up Sweet Incense in
        Unto thyselfe intire: 10

I finde my tinder scarce thy sparks can feel
That drop out from thy Holy flint and Steel.

Hence doubts out bud for feare thy fire in mee
    'S a mocking Ignis Fatuus
    Or lest thine Altars fire out bee,
        Its hid in ashes thus.'
Yet when the bellows of thy Spirit blow
Away mine ashes, then thy fire doth glow.

15

From God's Determinations Touching His Elect: and the Elect's Combat in their Conversion, and Coming up to God in Christ, Together with the Comfortable Effects thereof.

THE PREFACE

Infinity, when all things it beheld
In Nothing, and of Nothing all did build,

Upon what Base was fixt the Lath, wherein
He turn'd this Globe, and riggalld it so trim?
Who blew the Bellows of his Furnace Vast?   5
Or held the Mould wherein the world was Cast?
Who laid its Corner Stone? Or whose Command?[1]
Where stand the Pillars upon which it stands?
Who Lac'de and Fillitted the earth so fine,
With Rivers like green Ribbons Smaragdine?   10
Who made the Sea's its Selvedge, and it locks
Like a Quilt Ball within a Silver Box?
Who Spread its Canopy? Or Curtains Spun?
Who in this Bowling Alley bowld the Sun?
Who made it always when it rises set   15
To go at once both down, and up to get?
Who th'Curtain rods made for this Tapistry?
Who hung the twinckling Lanthorns in the Sky?
Who? who did this? or who is he? Why, know
Its Onely Might Almighty this did doe.   20
His hand hath made this noble worke which Stands
His Glorious Handywork not made by hands.
Who spake all things from nothing; and with ease
Can speake all things to nothing, if he please.
Whose Little finger at his pleasure Can   25
Out mete ten thousand worlds with halfe a Span:
Whose Might Almighty can by half a looks
Root up the rocks and rock the hills by th'roots.
Can take this mighty World up in his hande,
And shake it like a Squitchen or a Wand.   30
Whose single Frown will make the Heavens shake
Like as an aspen leafe the Winde makes quake.
Oh! what a might is this Whose single frown
Doth shake the world as it would shake it down?
Which All from Nothing fet, from Nothing, All: 35
Hath All on Nothing set, lets Nothing fall.
Gave All to nothing Man indeed, whereby
Through nothing man all might him Glorify.
In Nothing then imbosst the brightest Gem
More pretious than all pretiousness in them.   40
But Nothing man did throw down all by Sin:
And darkened that lightsom Gem in him.
      That now his Brightest Diamond is grown
      Darker by far than any Coalpit Stone.

[1] See Job 38:4–8.

THE EFFECTS OF MANS APOSTASY

While man unmarr'd abode his Spirits all
In Vivid hue were active in their hall,
This Spotless Body, here and there mentain
Their traffick for the Universall gain.
Till Sin Beat up for Volunteers. Whence came   5
A thousand Griefs attending on the same.
Which march in ranck, and file, proceed to make
A Battery, and the fort of Life to take.
Which when the Centinalls did spy, the Heart
Did beate alarum up in every part.   10
The Vitall Spirits apprehend thereby[1]
Exposde to danger great the suburbs ly,
The which they do desert, and speedily
The Fort of Life the Heart, they Fortify.
The Heart beats up still by her Pulse to Call   15
Out of the outworks her train Souldiers all
Which quickly come hence: now the Looks grow pale
Limbs feeble too: the Enemies prevaile.
Do scale the Outworks where there's Scarce a Scoute
That can be Spi'de sent from the Castle out.   20
        Man at a muze, and in a maze doth stand,
While Feare the Generall of all the Band
Makes inroads on him: then he Searches why,
And quickly Findes God stand as Enemy.
Whom he would fain subdue, yet Fears affright   25
In Varnishing their Weapons in his Sight.
Troops after troops, Bands after Bands do high,
Armies of armed terrours drawing nigh:
He lookes within, and sad amazement's there,
Without, and all things fly about his Eares.   30
Above, and sees Heaven falling on his pate,
Below and spies th'Infernall burning lake,
Before and sees God storming in his Face,
Behinde, and spies Vengeance persues his trace.
To stay he dares not, go he knows not where   35
From God he can't, to God he dreads for Feare.
To Dy he Dreads; For Vengeance's due to him;
To Live he must not, Death persues his Sin:

---

[1] *Vital Spirits.* The vital spirits in 17th-century psychology were composed of airy and fiery matter, which resided in the heart and were dispersed by the arteries; they helped carry out the decisions of the sensible soul.

He Knows not what to have, nor what to loose
Nor what to do, nor what to take or Choose: 40
Thus over Stretcht upon the Wrack of Woe,
Bereav'd of Reason, he proceeds now so,
Betakes himself unto his Heels in hast,
Runs like a Madman till his Spirits wast,
Then like a Child that fears the Poker Clapp   45
Him on his face doth on his Mothers lap
Doth hold his breath, lies still for fear least hee
Should by his breathing lowd discover'd bee.
Thus on his face doth see no outward thing
But still his heart for Feare doth pant within.   50
Doth make its Drummer beate so loud it makes
The Very Bulworks of the City Quake:
Yet gets no aide: Wherefore the Spirits they
Are ready all to leave, and run away.
For Nature in this Pannick feare scarce gives   55
Him life enough, to let him feel he lives.
Yet this he easily feels, he liveth in
A Dying Life, and Living Death by Sin,
Yet in this Lifeless life wherein he lies,
Some Figments of Excuses doth devise   60
That he may Something say, when rain'd,[2] although
His Say seems nothing, and for nought will go.
But while he Sculking on his face close lies
Espying nought, the Eye Divine him spies.
Justice and Mercy then fall to debate   65
Concerning this poore fallen mans estate,
Before the Bench of the Almighties Breast
Th' ensuing Dialogues hint their Contest.

From A DIALOGUE BETWEEN JUSTICE AND MERCY

Offended Justice comes in fiery Rage,
    Like to a Rampant Lyon new assaild,
Array'd in Flaming fire now to engage,
    With red hot burning Wrath poore man unbaild.
      In whose Dread Vissage sinfull man may spy   5
      Confounding, Rending, Flaming Majesty.

Out Rebell, out (saith Justice) to the Wrack,
    Which every joynt unjoynts, doth streatch, and strain,
Where Sinews tortur'de are untill they Crack

---

[2] That is, arraigned. [D.L.]

And Flesh is torn asunder grain by grain.   10
What Spit thy Venom in my Face! Come out
To handy gripes seing thou are so stoute.

Mercy takes up the Challenge, Comes as meeke
    As any Lamb, on mans behalfe, she speakes
Like new blown pincks, breaths out perfumed reech   15
    And doth revive the heart before it breaks.
    Justice (saith Mercy) if thou Storm so fast,
    Man is but dust that flies before thy blast.

JUSTICE: My Essence is ingag'de, I cannot bate,
    Justice not done no Justice is; and hence   20
I cannot hold off of the Rebells pate
    The Vengeance he halls down with Violence.
    If Justice wronged be she must revenge:
    Unless a way be found to make all friends.

MERCY: My Essence is engag'de pitty to show.   25
    Mercy not done no Mercy is. And hence
I'le put my shoulders to the burden so
    Halld on his head with hands of Violence.
    As Justice justice evermore must doe:
    So Mercy Mercy evermore must show.   30

JUSTICE: I'le take thy Bond: But know thou this must doe.
    Thou from thy Fathers bosom must depart:
And be incarnate like a slave below
    Must pay mans Debts unto the utmost marke.
    Thou must sustain that burden, that will make   35
    The Angells sink into th' Infernall lake.

Nay on thy shoulders bare must beare the smart
    Which makes the Stoutest Angell buckling cry
Nay makes thy Soule to Cry through griefe of heart,
    ELI, ELI, LAMA SABACHTANI.[1]   40
    If this thou wilt, come then, and do not spare.
    Beare up the Burden on thy Shoulders bare.

MERCY: All this I'le do, and do it o're and o're,
    Before my Clients Case shall ever faile.
I'le pay his Debt, and wipe out all his Score   45
    And till the pay day Come I'le be his baile.
    I Heaven, and Earth do on my shoulders beare,
    Yet down I'le throw them all rather than Spare.

           .   .   .

---

[1] ELI, ELI, LAMA SABACHTANI, Cf. Matt. 27:46.

JUSTICE: Lest that the Soule in Sin securely ly,
    And do neglect Free Grace, I'le steping in   140
Convince him by the Morall Law, whereby
      Ile'st se in what a pickle he is in
      For all he hath, for nothing stand it shall
      If of the Law one hair breadth short it fall.

MERCY: And lest the Soule should quite discourag'de stand   145
    I will step in, and smile him in the face,
Nay I to him will hold out in my hand
      The golden scepter of my Rich-Rich Grace.
      Intreating him with smiling lips most cleare
      At Court of Justice in my robes t'appeare.   150

JUSTICE: If any after Satans Pipes do Caper
    Red burning Coales from hell in Wrath I gripe,
And make them in his face with Vengeance Vaper,
      Untill he dance after the Gospell Pipe.
      Whose Sun is Sin, when Sin in Sorrows shrow'd,   155
      Their Sun of Joy sets in a grievous Cloud.

MERCY: When any such are startled from ill,
    And cry help, help, with tears, I will advance
The Musick of the Gospell Minsterill,
      Whose strokes they strike, and tunes exactly dance.   160
      Who mourn when Justice frowns, when Mercie playes
      Will to her sounding Viall Chant out Praise.

JUSTICE: The Works of Merit-Mongers I will weigh
    Within the Ballance of the sanctuary:
Their Matter, and their Manner I will lay   165
      Unto the Standard-Rule t'see how they Vary.
      Whosoever trust doth to his golden deed
      Doth rob a barren Garden for a Weed.

                •   •   •

JUSTICE: You that Extenuate your sins, come see
    Them in Gods multiplying Glass: for here
Your little sins will just like mountains bee,
      And as they are just so they Will appeare.   190
      Who doth a little sin Extenuate
      Extends the same, and two thereof doth make.

MERCY: A little sin is sin: and is Sin Small?
    Excuse it not, but aggrivate it more.
Lest that your little Sin asunder fall   195
    And two become, each bigger than before.
    Who scants his sin will scarce get grace to save.
    For little Sins, but little pardons have.

JUSTICE: Unto the Humble Humble Soule I say,
    Cheer up, poor Heart, for satisfi'de am I.   200
For Justice nothing to thy Charge can lay,
    Thou hast Acquittance in thy surety.
    The Court of Justice thee acquits: therefore
    Thou to the Court of Mercy are bound o're.

MERCY: My Dove, come hither linger not, nor stay.   205
    Though thou among the pots hast lain, behold
Thy Wings with Silver Colours I'le o're lay:
    And lay thy feathers o're with yellow gold.
    Justice in Justice must adjudge thee just:
    If thou in Mercies Mercy put thy trust.   210

MANS PERPLEXITY WHEN CALLED TO AN ACCOUNT

      Justice, and Mercy ending their Contest,
    In such a sort, now thrust away the Desk.
    And other titles come in Majesty,
    All to attend Almighty royally.
    Which sparkle out, call man to come and tell   5
    How he his Cloath defild and how he fell?

      He on his skirts with Guilt, and Filth out peeps
    With Pallid Pannick Fear upon his Cheeks,
    With Trembling joynts, and Quiverring Lips, doth quake
    As if each Word he was about to make,   10
    Should hackt a sunder be, and Chopt as small
    As Pot herbs for the pot before they Call
    Upon the Understanding to draw neer,
    By tabbering on the Drum within the eare.

His Spirits are so low they'l scarce afford   15
Him Winde enough to wast a single word
Over the Tongue unto one's eare: yet loe,
This tale at last with sobs, and sighs lets goe,
Saying, my Mate procurde me all this hurt,
Who threw me in my best Cloaths in the Dirt.   20

     Thus man hath lost his Freehold by his ill:
Now to his Land Lord tenent is at Will.
And must the Tenement keep in repare
Whate're the ruins, and the Charges are.
Nay, and must mannage war against his Foes.   25
Although ten thousand strong, he must oppose.
Some seeming Friends prove secret foes, which will
Thrust Fire i'th'thatch, nay stob, Cut throate and kill.
Some undermine the Walls: Some knock them down,
And make them tumble on the Tenents Crown.   30
     He's then turned out of Doors, and so must stay,
     Till's house be rais'd against the Reckoning day.

GODS SELECTING LOVE IN THE DECREE

     Man in this Lapst Estate at very best,
A Cripple is and footsore, sore opprest,
Can't track Gods Trace but Pains, and pritches prick
Like poyson'd splinters sticking in the Quick.
Yet jims in th'Downy path with pleasures spread   5
As 'twas below him on the Earth to tread.
Can prance, and trip within the way of Sin,
Yet in Gods path moves not a little wing.

     Almighty this foreseing, and withall
That all this stately worke of his would fall   10
Tumble, and Dash to pieces Did in lay
Before it was too late for it a Stay.
Doth with his hands hold, and uphold the same.
Hence his Eternall Purpose doth proclaim.
Whereby transcendently he makes to shine   15
Transplendent Glory in his Grace Divine.
Almighty makes a mighty sumptuous feast:
Doth make the Sinfull Sons of men his guests.
But yet in speciall Grace he hath to some,
(Because they Cripples are, and Cannot come)   20
He sends a Royall Coach forth for the same,
To fetch them in, and names them name by name.

A Royall Coach whose scarlet Canopy
O're silver Pillars, doth expánded ly:
All bottomed with purest góld refin'de,   25
And inside o're with lovely Love all linde.
Which Coach indeed you may exactly spy
All mankinde splits in a Dicotomy.
  For all ride to the feast that favour finde.
  The rest do slite the Call and stay behinde.   30

  O! Honour! Honour! Honours! Oh! the Gain!
And all such Honours all the saints obtain.
It is the Chariot of the King of Kings:
That all who Glory gain, to glory brings.
Whose Glory makes the rest, (when spi'de) beg in.   35
Some gaze and stare. Some stranging at the thing.
Some peep therein; some rage thereat, but all,
Like market people seing on a stall,
Some rare Commodity Clap hands thereon
And Cheapen't hastily, but soon are gone.   40
For hearing of the price, and wanting pay
Do pish thereat, and Coily pass away.
So hearing of the terms, whist, they'le abide
At home before they'l pay so much to ride.
But they to whom its sent had rather all,   45
Dy in this Coach, than let their journey fall.
They up therefore do get, and in it ride
Unto Eternal bliss, while down the tide
The other scull unto eternall woe;
By letting slip their former journey so.   50
For when they finde the Silver Pillars fair
The Golden bottom pav'de with Love as rare,
To be the Spirits sumptuous building cleare,
When in the Soul his Temple he doth reare
And Purple Canopy to bee (they spy)   55
All Graces Needlework and Huswifry;
Their stomachs rise: these graces will not down.
They think them Slobber Sawces: therefore frown.
They loath the same, wamble keck, heave they do:
Their Spleen thereat out at their mouths they throw,   60
Which while they do, the Coach away doth high
Wheeling the Saints in't to eternall joy.
  These therefore and their journey now do come
  For to be treated on, and Coacht along.

THE SOUL ACCUSED [BY SATAN] IN ITS SERVING GOD.

When thou dost go to serve thy God, behold
What greate Distractions do thy Soule infold?
How thy Religious Worship's much abusde?
And with Confusion greate thy Soul's amus'de?
What thoughts to God on Errand dost thou send   5
That have not Sin therein, or in the End?
In Holy-Waters I delight to fish
For then I mudd them, or attain a Dish,
Of Holy things. I oft have Chiefest part,
And Cutting: nay do Carve the fat, and heart.   10
For in Gods worship still thy heart doth cling
Unto and follows toyish Earthly things.
And what thou offer'st God his Holy Eye
Sees, is an Offering of Hypocrisy.
And if thou saw'st no hell, nor heaven; I see,   15
My Soule for thine, thy Soule and mine agree.
What then's thy Love to God, and Piety?
Is it not selfish? And Comes in by th'by?
For selfe is all thine aim; not God thine end:
And what Delight hath he in such a friend?   20
Lip Love is little else, but such a ly,
As makes the matter but Hypocrisy.

What's thy Repentance? Can'st thou come and show
By those salt Rivers which do Ebb, and Flow
By th'motion of that Ocean Vast within,   25
Of pickled sorrow rising for thy Sin?
For Sin prooves very Costly unto all.
It Cost Saint Peter bitter tears, and Paul.
Thy joy is groundless, Faith is false, thy Hope
Presumption, and Desire is almost broke.   30
Zeale Wildfire is, thy Pray'res are sapless most,
Or like the Whistling of some Dead mans Ghost:
Thy Holy Conference is onely like
An Empty Voice that tooteth through a pipe.
Thy Soule doth peep out at thine Eares, and Eyes   35
To bless those bawbles that are earthly toyes.
But when Gods Words in at those Windows peepe
To kiss thy Soul, thy Soul lies dead asleep.
Examine but thy Conscience, her reply,
Will suite hereto: For Conscience dare not ly.   40

When did thine Eyes run down for sin as sin,
That thus thy heart runs up with joy to sing?
    Thy sins do sculk under a flowrisht paint.
    Hence thou a Sinner art, or I a Saint.

SOUL: Well, Satan, well: with thee I'le parle no more.   45
But do adjure thee hence: begone therefore.
If I as yet was thine, I thus do say
I from thy flag would quickly flag away.
    Begone therefore; to him I'le send a groane
    Against thee drawn, who makes my heart his Throne.   50

DOUBTS FROM THE WANT OF GRACE ANSWERD [BY A SAINT, A MEMBER OF THE CHURCH]

SOUL: Such as are Gracious grow in Grace therefore
Such as have Grace, are Gracious evermore.
Who sin Commit are sinfull: and thereby
They grow Ungodly. So I feare do I.

SAINT: Such as are Gracious, Graces have therefore   5
They evermore desire to have more.
But such as never knew this dainty fare
Do never wish them 'cause they dainties are.

SOUL: Alas! alas! this still doth me benight.
I've no desire, or no Desire aright.   10
And this is Clear: my Hopes do witherd ly,
Before their buds breake out, their blossoms dy.

SAINT: When fruits do thrive, the blossom falls off quite.
No need of blossoms when the seed is ripe.
The Apple plainly prooves the blossoms were.   15
Thy withred Hopes hold out Desires as Cleare.

SOUL: Alas! my Hopes seem but like blasted fruit.
Dead on the Stoole before it leaves its root.
For if it lively were a growth it hath,
And would be grown e're this to Saving Faith.   20

SAINT: ° ° ° ° ° ° ° ° ° ° ° ° ° ° I'le make most plain
° °

Which lively is, layes hold on Christ too, though
Thou deemst it doth like blasted blossoms show.

SOUL: If it was so, then Certainly I should,   25
With Faith Repentance have. But, oh! behold,
This Grace leaves not in mee a single print.
Mine Eyes are Adamant, my Heart is Flint.

SAINT: Repentance is not argued so from Tears.
As from the Change that in the Soul appears.   30
And Faith Ruld by the Word. Hence ever spare
To mete Repentance out by Satans square.

SOUL: I fear Repentance is not Genuine.
Its Feare that makes me from my sins decline.
And if it was, I should delight much more,   35
To bathe in all Gods Ordinances pure.

SAINT: And dost thou not? Poore Soule, thou dost I know.
Why else dost thou Relent, and sorrow so?
But Satan doth molest thee much to fling
Thee from thy Dutie into e'ry Sin.   40

·   ·   ·

SOUL: Had I but any Sparke of Grace, I might
Have much more than I have with much delight.
How can I trust to you? You do not know
Whether I have a Grain of Grace, or no.   90

SAINT: You think you might have more: you shall have so,
But if you'd all at once, you could not grow.
And if you could not grow, you'd grieving fall.
All would not then Content you, had you all.
Should Graces Floodgate thus at once breake down   95
You most would lose, or else it would you drown.
He'l fill you but by drops that so he may
Not drown you in't, nor Cast a Drop away.

SOME OF SATAN'S SOPHISTRY.

The Tempter greatly seeks, though secretly,
     With an Ath'istick Hoodwinke man to blinde,
That so the Footsteps of the Deity
     Might stand no longer stampt upon his minde.
     Which when he can't blot out, by blinding quite,   5
     He strives to turn him from the Purer Light.

With Wiles enough, he on his thoughts intrudes,
    That God's a Heape of Contradictions high,
But when these thoughts man from his thoughts excludes
    Thou knowst not then (saith he) this Mystery.   10
    And when the first String breaks, he strives to bring
    Into sins brambles by the other string.

When God Calls out a Soule, he subtilly
    Saith God is kinde: you need not yet forsake
Your Sins: but if he doth, he doth reply,   15
    Thou'st outstood Grace. Justice will vengeance take.
    He'l tell you you Presume on Grace, to fright
    You to despare, beholding Justice bright.

Though just before mans mountain sins were mites,
    His mites were nothing. Now the scales are turn'd.   20
His mites are mountains now, of mighty height
    And must with Vengeance-Lightening be burn'd.
    Greate Sins are Small, till men repent of Sin:
    Then Small are far too big to be forgi'n.

While man thinks slightly, that he will repent,   25
    There's time enough (saith he), it's easly done.
But when repent he doth, the time is spent,
    Saith he, it is too late to be begun.
    To keep man from't, it's easly done, saith he,
    To dant him in't, he saith, it Cannot bee.   30

So Faith is easy till the Soule resolves
    To Live to Christ, and upon Christ rely.
Then Saving Faith he bold presumption Calls.
    Hast thou (saith he) in Christ propriety?
    The Faithfulls Faith, he stiles Presumption great,   35
    But the Presumptuous, theirs is Faith Compleat.

Nay though the Faith be true he acts so sly,
    As to raise doubts: and then it must not do:
Unless Assurance do it Certify:
    Which if it do, it douts of it also.   40
    Faith is without Assurance shuffled out,
    And if Assurance be, that's still a Doubt.

But should the Soule assured once, once Doubt,
    Then his Assurance no Assurance is:
Assurance doth assure the Soul right out   45
    Leave not a single Doubt to do amiss.
    But Satan still will seeke to Pick an hole
    In thy Assurance to unsure thy Soul.

Should any Soule once an Assurance get,
    Into his hands, soon Satans Pick-Lock key   50
With Sinfull Wards Unlocks his Cabinet
    To Steal the Jewell in it thence away.
    The Soul thus pillag'de, droops unto the grave.
    It's greater grief to lose than not to have.

He doth molest the Soule, it cannot see   55
    Without Assurance Extraordinary
Which should it have, it would soon take to bee
    A Mere Delusion of the Adversary.
    Assurance would not serve, should God Convay
    It in an Usuall or Unusuall way.   60

Thus I might search, Poor Soul, the Magazeen
    Of Gospell Graces over: I might paint
Out Satan sculking each side each unseen
    To Hoodwinck Sinners, and to hopple Saints.
    For he to dim their Grace, and slick up sin   65
    Calls Brass bright Gold, bright Golde but brass or tin.

He tempts to bring the soul too low or high,
    To have it e're in this or that extream:
To see no want or want alone to eye:
    To keep on either side the golden mean.   70
    If it was in't to get it out he'l 'ledge,
    Thou on the wrong side art the Pale or Hedge.

When God awakes a Soule he'l seeke to thrust
    It on Despare for want of Grace or get
And puff't with Pride, or in Securety hush't   75
    Or Couzen it with Graces Counterfet.
    Which if he can't he'l Carp at Grace, and raile
    And say, this is not Grace, it thus doth faile.

And thus he strives with Spite, Spleen, bitter Gall
    That Sinners might Dishonour God Most high: 80
That Saints might never honour God at all.
    That those in Sin, Those not in Grace might dy.
    And that the Righteous, Gracious, Pious, Grave,
    Might have no Comfort of the Grace they have.

Lest you be foild herewith, watch well unto   85
    Your Soul, that thrice Ennobled noble Gem:
For Sins are flaws therein, and double woe
    Belongs thereto if it be found in them.
    Are Flaws in Venice Glasses bad? What in
    Bright Diamonds? What then in man is Sin?   90

OUR INSUFFICIENCY TO PRAISE GOD
SUITABLY, FOR HIS MERCY

Should all the World so wide to atoms fall
    Should th'Aire be shred to motes, should we
    Se all the Earth hackt here so small
        That none Could smaller bee?
Should Heaven, and Earth be Atomizd, we guess   5
The Number of these Motes were numberless.

But should we then a World each Atom deem,
    Where dwell as many pious men
    As all these Motes the world Could teem
        Were it shred into them?   10
Each Atom would the World surmount wee guess
Whose men in number would be numberless.

But had each pious man, as many Tongues
    At singing all together then
    The Praise that to the Lord belongs   15
        As all these Atoms men?
Each man would sing a World of Praise, we guess,
Whose Tongues in number would be numberless.

And had each Tongue, as many Songs of Praise
    To sing to the Almighty ALL   20
    As all these men have Tongues to raise
        To him their Holy Call?
Each Tongue would tune a World of Praise, we guess
Whose songs in number would be numberless.

Nay, had each song as many Tunes most sweet   25
    Or one intwisting in't as many,
    As all these Tongues have songs most meet
        Unparallelld by any?
Each song a world of Musick makes we guess
Whose Tunes in number would be numberless.   30

Now should all these Conspire in us that we
    Could breath such Praise to thee, Most High?
    Should we thy Sounding Organs be
        To ring such Melody?
Our Musick would the World of Worlds out ring   35
Yet be unfit within thine Eares to ting.

Thou didst us mould, and us new mould when wee
    Were worse than mould we tread upon.
    Nay Nettles made by Sin wee bee.
        Yet hadst Compassion.   40
Thou hast pluckt out our Stings; and by degrees
Hast of us, lately Wasps, made Lady-Bees.

Though e're our Tongues thy Praises due can fan
    A Weevle with the World may fly,
    Yea fly away: and with a span   45
        We may out mete the Sky.
Though what we can is but a Lisp, We pray
Accept thereof. We have no better pay.

THE SOUL ADMIRING THE GRACE OF THE CHURCH ENTERS INTO CHURCH FELLOWSHIP

How is this City, Lord, of thine bespangled
    With Graces shine?
With Ordinances alli'de, and inam'led,
    Which are Divine?
Walld in with Discipline her Gates obtaine   5
Just Centinalls with Love Imbellisht plain.

Hence glorious, and terrible she stands;
    That Converts new
Seing her Centinalls of all demand
    The Word to shew;   10
Stand gazing much between two Passions Crusht
Desire, and Feare at once which both wayes thrust.

Thus are they wrackt. Desire doth forward screw
    To get them in,
But Feare doth backward thrust, that lies purdue,   15
    And slicks that Pin.
You cannot give the word, Quoth she, which though
You stumble on't its more than yet you know.

But yet Desires Screw Pin doth not slack:
    It still holds fast.
But Fears Screw Pin turns back or Screw doth Crack   20
    And breaks[1] at last.
Hence on they go, and in they enter: where
Desire Converts to joy: joy Conquours Fear.

[1] orig: slips.

They now enCovenant With God: and His: 25
    They thus indent.
The Charters Seals belonging unto this
    The Sacrament
So God is theirs avoucht, they his in Christ.
In whom all things they have, with Grace are splic'te.   30

Thus in the usuall Coach of Gods Decree
    They bowle and swim
To Glory bright, if no Hypocrisie
    Handed them in.
For such must shake their handmaid off lest they   35
Be shakt out of this Coach, or dy in th'way.

       •   •   •

THE SOULS ADMIRATION HEREUPON

What I such Praises sing! How can it bee?
    Shall I in Heaven sing?
What I, that scarce durst hope to see
    Lord, such a thing?
    Though nothing is too hard for thee: 5
    One Hope hereof seems hard to mee.

What, Can I ever tune those Melodies
    Who have no tune at all?
Not knowing where to stop nor Rise,
    Nor when to Fall.   10
    To sing thy Praise I am unfit.
    I have not learn'd my Gam-Ut yet.

But should these Praises on string'd Instruments
    Be sweetly tun'de? I finde
I nonplust am: for no Consents   15
    I ever minde.
    My Tongue is neither Quill, nor Bow:
    Nor Can my Fingers Quavers show.

But was it otherwise I have no Kit:
    Which though I had, I could   20
Not tune the strings, which soon would slip
    Though others should.
    But should they not, I cannot play:
    But for an F should strike an A.

And should thy Praise upon Winde Instruments   25
    Sound all o're Heaven Shrill?
My Breath will hardly through such Vents
    A Whistle fill,
      Which though it should, its past my spell
      By Stops, and Falls to sound it Well.   30

How should I then, joyn in such Exercise?
    One sight of thee'l intice
Mine Eyes to heft: Whose Extasies
    Will stob my Voice.
      Hereby mine Eyes will bind my Tongue.   35
      Unless thou, Lord, do Cut the thong.

What Use of Uselesse mee, then there, poore snake?
    There Saints, and Angels sing,
Thy Praise in full Cariere, which make
    The Heavens to ring.   40
      Yet if thou wilt thou Can'st me raise
      With Angels bright to sing thy Praise.

THE JOY OF CHURCH FELLOWSHIP RIGHTLY ATTENDED

In Heaven soaring up, I dropt an Eare
    On Earth: and oh! sweet Melody:
And listening, found it was the Saints who were
    Encoacht for Heaven that sang for Joy.
      For in Christs Coach they sweetly sing;   5
      As they to Glory ride therein.

Oh! joyous hearts! Enfir'de with holy Flame!
    Is speech thus tassled with praise?
Will not your inward fire of Joy contain;
    That it in open flames doth blaze?   10
      For in Christ's Coach Saints sweetly sing,
      As they to Glory ride therein.

And if a string do slip, by Chance, they soon
    Do screw it up again: whereby
They set it in a more melodious Tune   15
    And a Diviner Harmony.
      For in Christs Coach they sweetly sing
      As they to Glory ride therein.

In all their Acts, publick, and private, nay
    And secret too, they praise impart.   20
But in their Acts Divine and Worship, they
    With Hymns do offer up their Heart.
    Thus in Christs Coach they sweetly sing
    As they to Glory ride therein.
Some few not in; and some whose Time, and Place   25
    Block up this Coaches way do goe
As Travellers afoot, and so do trace
    The Road that gives them right thereto
    While in this Coach these sweetly sing
    As they to Glory ride therein.   30

B.
THE GREAT AWAKENING

The revival known as the Great Awakening in the 1740's had origins and effects far beyond the limits of New England. Throughout western Europe and the American colonies—whether among new sects of German pietists who remained at home or emigrated to Pennsylvania; among Methodists in the British Isles; or among Baptists, Quakers, and Scotch-Irish Presbyterians in New Jersey, Connecticut, North Carolina, or Virginia—a profound concern for religion forced theological and related social issues upon the attention of both secular and religious leaders. The movement was so powerful that Benjamin Franklin, a skeptical Deist, noted the transformed behavior of youths in Philadelphia soon after the Calvinist Jonathan Edwards described the new spiritual interest of youths in Northampton, which had become known as "the most enthusiastical town in New England." Here we represent the social and literary power of the Awakening through the rigorous theological and psychological writings of Jonathan Edwards; the spiritual autobiographies of Edwards and two unlettered people who suffered for their faith, the Baptist Nathan Cole and the Quaker Elizabeth Ashbridge; and the measured criticism of "enthusiasm" by one of the leading Boston ministers, Charles Chauncy, the most articulate of the religious authorities who deplored the revivalists' excesses.

JONATHAN EDWARDS

(1703-1758)

Jonathan Edwards, more exclusively than any other major figure in American literature, bases his claim to eminence on the power and clarity of his intelligence. His exact observation and lucid (though often unpunctuated) exposition are evident in essays written when he was only 11 years old, and (in his early to middle teens) in his precocious notes on "The Mind"—notes that he wrote while studying John Locke's *Essay Concerning Human Understanding* during his undergraduate days at Yale. But the central experience of Edwards' life, as he tells us in his spiritual autobiography, was an overpowering sense of divine glory that came upon him while he read the Bible, and again while he was walking in his father's pasture in Windsor, Connecticut in January 1723. That experience not only led the young man to dedicate himself and all his possessions to the service of God; he also claimed, years later, that it had given him a completely new sense, a sixth "sense of the heart," which changed the very quality of his perceptions in the natural world. By imperceptible degrees, moreover, he found that he had given up his objections to some difficult theological tenets, such as the absolute sovereignty of God. And now he found

Several volumes of a modern edition of Jonathan Edwards' works have been published by the Yale University Press, and as that project, begun under the general editorship of the late Perry Miller, continues, the volumes supersede inadequate earlier editions. A one-volume collection is *Jonathan Edwards: Representative Selections*, ed. Clarence Faust and Thomas H. Johnson, 1935.

An early biography, still extremely valuable, is Samuel Hopkins, *The Life and Character of the Late Reverend Mr. Jonathan Edwards*, 1765 (reprinted in *Jonathan Edwards, a Profile*, ed. David Levin, 1969). Recent assessments are Ola E. Winslow, *Jonathan Edwards*, 1940; Perry Miller, *Jonathan Edwards*, 1949; A. O. Alridge, *Jonathan Edwards*, 1964; Edward Griffin, *Jonathan Edwards*, 1966; Richard Bushman, "Jonathan Edwards as a Great Man," *Soundings*, 52 (1969): 15-46; Roland A. DeLattre, *Beauty and Sensibility in the Thought of Jonathan Edwards*, 1968; Daniel B. Shea, Jr., *Spiritual Autobiography in Early America*, 1968; William J. Scheick, *The Writings of Jonathan Edwards: Theme, Motif, and Style*, 1975.

that he had not only a belief in their truth but a delightful sense of their fitness, an affectionate conviction of their "excellency." The emotional power of that conviction pervades all of Edwards' major works.

The whole works and selections that are reprinted here are arranged to encourage appreciation of the logical structure in Edwards' thought without ignoring chronology or the central religious experience. In the brief note called "Existence," young Edwards reasons precociously from the new psychology of Locke and the new optics of Sir Isaac Newton that the only true existence is in the complete stable idea in the mind of God. The sermon called "A Divine and Supernatural Light" (1734) was published in the year of the first extraordinary religious revival in Edwards' church at Northampton, Massachusetts, five years after he had succeeded his famous grandfather, Solomon Stoddard, as the minister there. This sermon is a rational argument to show (as the full title plainly says) both the scriptural authority and the philosophical reasonableness of belief that God *immediately* imparts a new, supernatural sense to those whom He has elected as recipients of saving grace. The spiritual autobiography (1739?) represents Edwards' meticulous effort, 16 years after the event, to use his own intense experience as the basis for a careful definition of the differences between the illusion of grace and the real thing. His recurrent emphasis on the language of sensory perception and on what *appears* to be true to him is neither an exercise in self-celebration nor an effort to boast (near the end) of his superior sense of his own wickedness. Instead, it is an extraordinarily fine description of a subjective experience, including the difficulty of articulating verbally a nonverbal, supralogical awareness. The first part of the sermon called "The Justice of God in the Damnation of Sinners" contains a remarkably concise version of Edwards' elaborate defense of the doctrine—including his brilliant application of Newtonian ideas of cause and effect to the problem of imputing Adam's original sin to all of Adam's descendants. The "Application" of that sermon is omitted here, but in the famous sermon that Edwards preached at Enfield in 1741—often reprinted as "Sinners in the Hands of an Angry God"—the affecting message, terrible for many, hopeful for a few, is quietly aimed at the heart of each sinner in the congregation. Images of weight are just as important as the more often noted reminders of eternal fire: there is no reason, Edwards says to each sinner in the audience, why you do not immediately fall of your own weight through the rotten covering between you and Hell—no reason except the merciful hand of God that holds you up.

The point of such preaching was to save sinners, to shock them into a sensible apprehension of their true peril before it was too late. As in traditional Protestantism, every Christian had a strong obligation to understand doctrine, but the essential change was a change in attitude, in inclination, a matter for "the affections." Edwards' greatest works deal with the psychology of religious affection and the nature of true virtue. In both these works, which grew out of his experience and observation during the revival in Northampton in 1734 and the Great Awakening of the 1740's, students of American literature can see a startling foreshadowing—even in this Calvinist's form—of the transcendental vision that was to dominate some of the best American literature in the nineteenth century. Edwards defined true virtue as disinterested benevolence, or "consent to Being in general"—a total harmony with the divine will, and a willing *expression* of benevolence, in addition to the mere "complacence" in having praiseworthy traits.

The emphatic passage from Edwards' long work on *The Freedom of the Will* reveals how passionately Edwards believed that some of the main foundations for belief in free will and moral agency were insupportably flimsy; the passage also reveals the great emotional power that Edwards' writing could acquire through the sheer accumulation of logical weight—especially when he was demolishing the inadequately examined assumptions of his opponents. The meditations in *Images or Shadows of Divine Things* place him in the line that connects the tradition of biblical typology, the tradition of Meditation, and the symbolism of nineteenth-century American writers such as Emerson, Hawthorne, Thoreau, and Melville.

Edwards' career as a minister had a tragic quality. After the triumphs of the revivals in the 1730's and 1740's, he came into irreconcilable conflict with some of his congregation, especially over his increasingly strict requirements for church membership. In 1750, after 23 years as the pastor, he was dismissed by the congregation, and he, the greatest American religious thinker of the century, was even forbidden by his congregation to preach a series of sermons defending his theological position. He retired to the Indian mission at Stockbridge, where he wrote some of his major works, and he left there only a few weeks before his death in 1758. He had barely begun his duties as President of the College that became Princeton, when he became fatally ill after he had been inoculated for smallpox.

Existence[1]

[Edwards' theology depended on his belief in God as the central Being, in whom all goodness is constituted and who also expresses more benevolence than we can con-

[1] The text is from *"The Mind" of Jonathan Edwards: A Reconstructed Text*, by Leon Howard, Berkeley and Los Angeles: University of California Press, 1963.

ceive of in any other being. Before reading Edwards' other writings then, it is useful to consider a brief statement in which he used contemporary theories of perception and motion to support his conviction that all creation depends at every instant on the action of one eternal mind. These paragraphs from "Notes on the Mind" were written when Edwards was at Yale, before he was seventeen.]

If we had only the sense of seeing, we should not be as ready to conclude the visible world to have an existence independent of perception, as we do; because the ideas we have by the sense of feeling, are as much mere ideas, as those we have by the sense of seeing. But we know, that the things that are objects of this sense, all that the mind views by seeing, are merely mental existences; because all these things, with all their modes, do exist in a looking-glass, where all will acknowledge, they exist only mentally.

It is now agreed upon by every knowing philosopher, that colors are not really in the things, no more than pain is in a needle; but strictly nowhere else but in the mind. But yet I think that color may have an existence out of the mind, with equal reason as anything in body has any existence out of the mind, beside the very substance of the body itself, which is nothing but the divine power, or rather the constant exertion of it. For what idea is that, which we call by the name of body? I find color has the chief share in it. 'Tis nothing but color, and figure, which is the termination of this color, together with some powers, such as the power of resisting, and motion, etc. that wholly makes up what we call body. And if that, which we principally mean by the thing itself, cannot be said to be in the thing itself, I think nothing can be. If color exists not out of the mind, then nothing belonging to body, exists out of the mind but resistance, which is solidity, and the termination of this resistance, with its relations, which is figure, and the communication of this resistance, from space to space, which is motion; though the latter are nothing but modes of the former. Therefore, there is nothing out of the mind but resistance. And not that neither, when nothing is actually resisted. Then, there is nothing but the power of resistance. And as resistance is nothing else but the actual exertion of God's power, so the power can be nothing else, but the constant law or method of that actual exertion. And how is there any resistance, except it be in some mind, in idea? What is it that is resisted? It is not color. And what else is it? It is ridiculous to say, that resistance is resisted. That, does not tell us at all what is to be resisted. There must be something resisted before there can be resistance; but to say resistance is resisted, is ridiculously to suppose resistance, before there is any thing to be resisted. Let us suppose two globes only existing, and no mind. There is nothing there, *ex confesso*, but resistance. That is, there is such a law, that the space within the limits of a globular figure shall resist. Therefore, there is nothing there but a power, or an establishment. And if there be any resistance really out of the mind, one power and establishment must resist another establishment and law of resistance, which is exceedingly ridiculous. But yet it cannot be otherwise, if any way out of the mind. But now it is easy to conceive of resistance, as a mode of an idea. It is easy to conceive of such a power, or constant manner of stopping or resisting a color. The idea may be resisted, it may move, and stop and rebound; but how a mere power, which is nothing real, can move and stop, is inconceivable, and it is impossible to say a word about it without contradiction. The world is therefore an ideal one; and the law of creating, and the succession, of these ideas is constant and regular.

[28.] *Coroll.* I. How impossible is it, that the world should exist from Eternity, without a Mind.

From A Divine and Supernatural Light [1]

IMMEDIATELY IMPARTED TO THE SOUL BY THE SPIRIT OF GOD, SHOWN TO BE BOTH A SCRIPTURAL, AND RATIONAL DOCTRINE; IN A SERMON PREACHED AT NORTHAMPTON

[The first two of Edwards' three sections, as he describes them below, are reprinted here.]

MATTHEW xvi. 17. *And Jesus answered and said unto him, blessed art thou Simon Barjona; for flesh and blood hath not revealed it unto thee, but My Father which is in Heaven.*

Christ says these words to *Peter,* upon occasion of his professing his faith in Him as the Son of God. Our Lord was enquiring of his disciples, who men said He was; not that He needed to be informed, but only to introduce and give occasion to what follows. They answer, that some said He was *John* the *Baptist,* and some *Elias,* and others *Jeremias* or one of the prophets. When they had thus given an account who others said He was, CHRIST asks them, who they said He was. *Simon Peter,* whom we find always zealous and forward, was the first to answer; he readily replied to the question, *Thou art* CHRIST *the Son of the living* GOD.

UPON this occasion CHRIST says as He does *to* him and *of* him in the text: in which we may observe,

1. THAT *Peter* is pronounced blessed on this account. *Blessed art thou—* "Thou art an happy man, that thou art not ignorant of this, that I am CHRIST *the son of the living God.* Thou art distinguishingly happy. Others are blinded, and have dark and deluded apprehensions, as you have now given

[1] Boston, 1734.

an account, some thinking that I am *Elias,* and some that I am *Jeremias,* and some one thing, and some another; but none of them thinking right, all of them misled. Happy art thou, that art so distinguished as to know the truth in this matter."

2. THE evidence of this his happiness declared; *viz.* that GOD and He *only* had *revealed it* to him. This is an evidence of his being *blessed.*

First, as it shows how peculiarly favored he was of GOD, above others. *q.d.*[2] "How highly favored art thou, that others that are wise and great men, the scribes, Pharisees, and rulers, and the nation in general, are left in darkness, to follow their own misguided apprehensions, and that thou shouldst be singled out, as it were by name, that My heavenly Father should thus set His love on *thee Simon Bar-jona.* This argues thee *blessed,* that thou should'st thus be the object of GOD's distinguishing love."

Secondly, IT evidences his blessedness also, as it intimates that this knowledge is above any that *flesh and blood* can *reveal.* "This is such knowledge as My *Father which is in heaven* only can give: it is too high and excellent to be communicated by such means as other knowledge is. Thou art *blessed,* that thou knowest that which GOD alone can teach thee."

THE original of this knowlege is here declared; both negatively and positively. *Positively,* as GOD is here declared the author of it. *Negatively,* as 'tis declared that *flesh and blood* had *not revealed it.* GOD is the Author of all knowledge and understanding whatsoever: He is the Author of the knowledge, that is obtained by human learning: He is the Author of all moral prudence, and of the knowledge and skill that men have in their secular business. Thus it is said of all in *Israel* that were *wisehearted,* and skilled in embroidering, that GOD had *filled* them *with the spirit of wisdom.* Exod. 28.[3]

GOD is the Author of such knowledge; but yet not so but that *flesh and blood reveals it.* Mortal men are capable of imparting the knowledge of human arts and sciences, and skill in temporal affairs. GOD is the Author of such knowledge by those means: *flesh and blood* is made use of by GOD as the *mediate* or *second* cause of it; He conveys it by the power and influence of natural means. But this spiritual knowledge, spoken of in the text, is what *God* is the Author of, and none else: He *reveals it* and *flesh and blood reveals it not.* He imparts this knowledge immediately, not making use of any intermediate natural causes, as He does in other knowledge.

What had passed in the preceding discourse naturally occasioned CHRIST to observe this; because the disciples had been telling, how others did not know Him, but were generally mistaken about Him, and divided and confounded in their opinions of Him; but *Peter* had declared his assured faith that He was the *Son of God.* Now it was natural to observe, how it was not *flesh and blood* that had *revealed it to* him, but GOD; for if this knowledge

---

[2] q.d., *quasi dicat,* as if he should say.

were dependent on natural causes or means, how came it to pass that they, a company of poor fishermen, illiterate men, and persons of low education, attained to the knowledge of the truth; while the scribes and Pharisees, men of vastly higher advantages, and greater knowledge and sagacity in other matters, remained in ignorance? This could be owing only to the gracious distinguishing influence and revelation of the SPIRIT of GOD. Hence, what I would make the subject of my present discourse from these words, is this

DOCTRINE, VIZ.

That there is such a thing, as A SPIRITUAL *and* DIVINE LIGHT, *immediately imparted to the soul by* GOD, *of a different nature from any that is obtained by natural means.*

IN what I say on this subject at this time, I would

I. SHOW what this *divine light* is.

II. How it is given *immediately by* GOD, and not *obtained by natural means.*

III. SHOW the truth of the doctrine.

AND then conclude with a brief improvement.

I. I would show *what this* spiritual and divine light *is.* And in order to it would show,

First, IN a few things *what it is not.* And here,

1. THOSE *convictions that natural men may have of their sin and misery* is not *this* spiritual and divine light. Men in a natural condition may have convictions of the guilt that lies upon them, and of the anger of GOD, and their danger of divine vengeance. Such convictions are from *light* or sensibleness of truth: that some sinners have a greater conviction of their guilt and misery than others, is because some have more *light,* or more of an apprehension of truth than others. And this *light* and conviction may be from the Spirit of GOD; *the* SPIRIT *convinces* men *of sin:* but yet nature is much more concerned in it than in the communication of that *spiritual and divine light* that is spoken of in the *doctrine;* 'tis from the Spirit of GOD only as assisting *natural principles,* and not as infusing any new *principles. Common grace* differs from *special,* in that it influences only by assisting of *nature;* and not by imparting *grace,* or bestowing any thing *above* nature. The *light* that is obtained, is wholly *natural,* or of no superior *kind* to what mere *nature* attains to; tho' more of *that kind* be obtained, than would be obtained if men were left wholly to themselves. Or *in other words, common grace* only assists the faculties of the soul to do that more fully, which they do by *nature; as natural* conscience, or reason, will by mere *nature* make a man sensible of guilt, and will accuse and condemn him when he has done amiss. Conscience is a *principle natural* to men; and the work that it doth *naturally,* or of itself, is to give an apprehension of *right* and *wrong;* and to suggest to the mind the

relation that there is between right and wrong, and a retribution. The Spirit of GOD, in those convictions which unregenerate men sometimes have, assists conscience to do this work in a further degree, than it would do if they were left to themselves: He helps it against those things that tend to stupefy it, and obstruct its exercise. But in the *renewing* and *sanctifying* work of the HOLY GHOST, those things are wrought in the soul that are *above* nature; and of which there is nothing of the like kind in the soul *by* nature; and they are caused to exist in the soul habitually, and according to such a stated constitution or law, that lays such a foundation for exercises in a continued course, as is called a *principle* of nature. Not only are remaining *principles* assisted to do their work more freely and fully, but those *principles* are restored that were utterly destroyed by the Fall; and the mind thence-forward habitually exerts those acts that the dominion of sin had made it as wholly destitute of, as a dead body is of vital acts.

The Spirit of GOD acts in a very different manner in the one case, from what He doth in the other. He may indeed act *upon* the mind of a natural man; but He acts *in* the mind of a saint as an *indwelling vital principle.* He acts upon the mind of an unregenerate person as an *extrinsic occasional agent;* for in acting upon them He doth not unite Himself to them; for notwithstanding all His influences that they may be the subjects of, they are still *sensual having not the spirit. Jude* 19. But He unites Himself with the mind of a saint, takes him for His temple, actuates and influences him as a new, *supernatural principle* of life and action. There is this difference; that the Spirit of GOD in acting in the soul of a godly man, exerts and communicates Himself there in His own proper nature. Holiness is the proper nature of the Spirit of GOD. The HOLY SPIRIT operates in the minds of the godly, by uniting Himself to them, and living in them, and exerting His own nature in the exercise of their faculties. The Spirit of GOD may act upon a creature, and yet not, in acting communicate Himself. The Spirit of GOD may act upon inanimate creatures; as the *Spirit moved upon the face of the waters,* in the beginning of the creation: so the Spirit of GOD may act upon the minds of men, many ways, and communicate Himself no more than when he acts upon an inanimate creature. *For instance.* He may excite thoughts in them, may assist their natural reason and understanding, or may assist other natural principles, and this without any union with the soul, but may act, as it were, as upon an external object. But as He acts in His holy influences, and spiritual operations, He acts in a way of peculiar communication of Himself; so that the subject is thence denominated *spiritual.*

2. THIS spiritual and divine light *don't consist in any impression made upon the imagination.* 'Tis no *impression* upon the mind, as tho' one saw any thing with the bodily eyes: 'tis no *imagination* or *idea* of an outward *light* or glory, or any beauty of form or countenance, or a visible luster or brightness of any object. The *imagination* may be strongly impressed with such things;

but this is not *spiritual light*. Indeed when the mind has a lively discovery of spiritual things, and is greatly affected by the power of divine light, it may, and probably very commonly doth, much affect the *imagination:* so that *impressions* of an outward beauty or brightness, may accompany those spiritual discoveries. But *spiritual light* is not that *impression upon the imagination,* but an exceeding different thing from it. Natural men may have lively *impressions* on their *imaginations;* and we can't determine but that the Devil, *who transforms himself into an angel of light,* may cause *imaginations* of an outward beauty, or visible glory, and of sounds and speeches, and other such things; but these are things of a vastly inferior nature to *spiritual light.*

3. THIS spiritual light *is not the suggesting of any new truths, or propositions not contained in the Word of* GOD. This suggesting of new truths or doctrines to the mind, independent of any antecedent revelation of those propositions, either in word or writing, is inspiration; such as the prophets and apostles had, and such as some enthusiasts pretend to. But this *spiritual light* that I am speaking of, is quite a different thing from inspiration: it reveals no new doctrine, it suggests no new proposition to the mind, it teaches no new thing of GOD, or CHRIST, or another world, not taught in the Bible; but only gives a due apprehension of those things that are taught in the word of GOD.

4. 'Tis not every affecting view that men have of the things of religion, *that is this* spiritual and divine light. Men by mere principles of nature are capable of being *affected* with things that have a special relation to religion, as well as other things. A person by mere nature, for instance, may be liable to be *affected* with the story of JESUS CHRIST, and the sufferings He underwent, as well as by any other tragical story: he may be the more *affected* with it from the interest he conceives mankind to have in it: yea, he may be *affected* with it without believing it; as well as a man may be *affected* with what he reads in a romance, or sees acted in a stage play. He may be *affected* with a lively and eloquent description of many pleasant things that attend the state of the blessed in Heaven; as well as his imagination be entertained by a romantic description of the pleasantness of fairy land, or the like. And that common belief of the truth of *the things of religion,* that persons may have from education, or otherwise, may help forward their *affection.* We read in Scripture of many that were greatly *affected* with things of a religious nature, who yet are there presented as wholly graceless, and many of them very ill men. A person therefore may have *affecting views of the things of religion,* and yet be very destitute of *spiritual light. Flesh* and *blood* may be the author of this: one man may give another an *affecting view* of divine things with but common assistance; but GOD alone can give a *spiritual* discovery of them.

BUT I proceed to show,

Secondly, positively, WHAT *this* spiritual and divine light *is.*

AND it may be thus described, *a true sense of the divine excellency of the things revealed in the Word of* GOD, *and a conviction of the truth and reality of them, thence arising.*

THIS *spiritual light* primarily consists in the former of these, *viz.* a real sense and apprehension of the divine excellency of things revealed in the Word of GOD. A spiritual and saving conviction of the truth and reality of these things, arises from such a sight of their divine excellency and glory; so that this conviction of their truth is an effect and natural consequence of this sight of their divine glory. There is therefore in this *spiritual light,*

1. *A true sense of the divine and superlative excellency of the things of religion;* a real sense of the excellency of GOD and JESUS CHRIST, and of the work of redemption, and the ways and works of GOD revealed in the Gospel. There is a *divine* and *superlative* glory in these things; an excellency that is of a vastly higher kind, and more sublime nature, than in other things; a glory greatly distinguishing them from all that is earthly and temporal. He that is spiritually *enlightened* truly apprehends and sees it, or has a sense of it. He don't merely rationally believe that GOD is glorious, but he has a sense of the gloriousness of GOD in his heart. There is not only a rational belief that GOD is holy, and that holiness is a good thing; but there is a sense of the loveliness of GOD's holiness. There is not only a speculatively judging that GOD is gracious, but a sense how amiable GOD is upon that account; or a sense of the beauty of this divine attribute.

THERE is a twofold understanding or knowledge of good that GOD has made the mind of man capable of. The *first,* that which is merely *speculative* and *notional:* as when a person only speculatively judges, that anything is, which by the agreement of mankind, is called good or excellent, *viz.* that which is most to general advantage, and between which and a reward there is a suitableness; and the like. And the *other* is that which consists in the sense of the heart: as when there is a sense of the beauty, amiableness, or sweetness of a thing; so that the heart is sensible of pleasure and delight in the presence of the *idea* of it. In the *former* is exercised merely the speculative faculty, or the understanding strictly so called, or as spoken of in distinction from the will or disposition of the soul. In the *latter* the will, or inclination, or heart, are mainly concerned.

THUS there is a difference between *having an opinion* that GOD is holy and gracious, and *having a sense* of the loveliness and beauty of that holiness and grace. There is a difference between *having a rational judgment* that honey is sweet, and *having a sense* of its sweetness. A man may have the *former,* that knows not how honey tastes; but a man can't have the latter unless he has an *idea* of the taste of honey in his mind. So there is a difference between *believing* that a person is beautiful, and *having a* sense of his beauty. The *former* may be obtained by hearsay, but the *latter* only by seeing the countenance. There is a wide difference between mere *speculative, ra-*

tional judging anything to be excellent, and *having* a sense of its sweetness, and beauty. The *former* rests only in the head, speculation only is concerned in it; but the heart is concerned in the *latter*. When the heart is sensible of the beauty and amiableness of a thing, it necessarily feels pleasure in the apprehension. It is implied in a person's being heartily sensible of the loveliness of a thing, that the *idea* of it is sweet and pleasant to his soul; which is a far different thing from having a rational opinion that it is excellent.

2. THERE *arises from this* sense of divine excellency of things contained in the Word of GOD, a *conviction of the truth and reality of them: and that either* directly, *or* indirectly.

First, *indirectly,* and that two ways.

1. As *the prejudices that are in the heart, against* the truth of divine things, *are hereby removed; so that the mind becomes susceptive of the due force of rational arguments for their truth.* The mind of man is naturally full of *prejudices against the truth of divine things:* it is full of enmity against the doctrines of the Gospel; which is a disadvantage to those *arguments* that prove their *truth,* and causes them to lose their force upon the mind. But when a person has discovered to him the divine excellency of Christian doctrines, this destroys the enmity, removes those *prejudices*, and sanctifies the reason, and causes it to lie open to the *force of arguments for their truth.*

HENCE was the different effect that CHRIST's miracles had to convince the disciples, from what they had to convince the scribes and Pharisees. Not that they had a stronger reason, or had their reason more improved; but their reason was sanctified, and those blinding *prejudices*, that the scribes and Pharisees were under, were removed by the sense they had of the excellency of CHRIST, and His doctrine.

2. IT *not only removes the hindrances of reason, but positively helps reason.* It makes even the speculative notions the more lively. It engages the attention of the mind, with the more fixedness and intenseness to that kind of objects; which causes it to have a clearer view of them, and enables it more clearly to see their mutual relations, and occasions it to take more notice of them. The *ideas* themselves that otherwise are dim, and obscure, are by this means impressed with the greater strength, and have a light cast upon them; so that the mind can better judge of them. As he that beholds the objects on the face of the earth, when the light of the sun is cast upon them, is under greater advantage to discern them in their true forms, and mutual relations, than he that sees them in a dim starlight or twilight.

The mind having a sensibleness of the excellency of divine objects, dwells upon them with delight; and the powers of the soul are more awakened and enlivened to employ themselves in the comtemplation of them, and exert themselves more fully and much more to the purpose. The beauty and sweetness of the objects draws on the faculties, and draws forth their exercises: so that reason itself is under far greater advantages for its proper and free exercises, and to attain its proper end, free of darkness and delusion. But,

SECONDLY, a true sense of the divine excellency of the things of GOD's Word doth more *directly* and *immediately* convince of the truth of them; and that because the excellency of these things is so superlative. There is a beauty in them that is so divine and godlike, that is greatly and evidently distinguishing of them from things merely human, or that men are the inventors and authors of; a glory that is so high and great, that when clearly seen, commands assent to their divinity and reality. When there is an actual and lively discovery of this beauty and excellency, it won't allow of any such thought as that it is an human work, or the fruit of men's invention. This evidence that they, that are spiritually *enlightened*, have of the truth of the things of religion, is a kind of *intuitive* and *immediate* evidence. They believe the doctrines of GOD's Word to be divine, because they see divinity in them, i.e. they see a divine, and transcendent, and most evidently distinguishing glory in them; such a glory as, if clearly seen, don't leave room to doubt of their being of GOD, and not of men.

SUCH a conviction of the truth of religion as this, arising, these ways, from a sense of the divine excellency of them, is that true spiritual conviction, that there is in saving faith. And this original of it, is that by which it is most essentially distinguished from that common assent, which unregenerate men are capable of.

II. I proceed now to the second thing proposed, *viz.* to show *how this light is immediately given by* GOD, *and not obtained by natural means.* And here,

1. *'Tis not intended that the natural faculties are not made use of in it.* The *natural faculties* are the subject of this light: and they are the subject in such a manner, that they are not merely passive, but active in it; the acts and exercises of man's understanding are concerned and made use of in it. GOD in letting in this *light* into the soul, deals with man according to his nature, or as a rational creature; and makes use of his human *faculties*. But yet this *light* is not the less *immediately* from GOD for that; tho' the *faculties are made use of,* 'tis as the subject and not as the cause; and that acting of the *faculties* in it, is not the cause, but is either implied in the thing itself (in the *light* that is imparted) or is the consequence of it. As the use that we make of our eyes in beholding various objects, when the sun arises, is not the cause of the light that discovers those objects to us.

2. *'Tis not intended that outward means have no concern in this affair.* As I have observed already, 'tis not in this affair, as it is in inspiration, where new truths are suggested: for here is by this *light* only given a due apprehension of the same truths that are revealed in the Word of GOD; and therefore it is not given without the Word. The Gospel is made use of in this affair: this *light* is the *light of the glorious gospel of* CHRIST 2. *Cor.* iv. 4. The Gospel is

as a glass, by which this *light* is conveyed to us. 1 *Cor.* xiii. 12. "Now we see through a glass"—but,

3. WHEN it is said that this *light* is given immediately by GOD, and not obtained by natural means, *hereby is intended, that 'tis given by* GOD *without making use of any means that operate by their own power, or a natural force.* GOD makes use of means; but 'tis not as mediate causes to produce this effect. There are not truly any second causes of it; but it is produced by GOD *immediately.* The Word of GOD is no proper cause of this effect: It don't operate by any *natural force* in it. The Word of GOD is only made use of to convey to the mind the subject matter of this saving instruction: and this indeed it doth convey to us by *natural force* or influence. It conveys to our minds these and those doctrines; it is the cause of the notion of them in our heads, but not of the sense of the divine excellency of them in our hearts. Indeed a person can't have *spiritual light* without the Word. But that don't argue, that the Word properly causes that *light.* The mind can't see the excellency of any doctrine, unless that doctrine be first in the mind; but the seeing the excellency of the doctrine may be immediately from the Spirit of GOD; tho' the conveying of the doctrine or proposition itself may be by the Word. So that the notions that are the subject matter of this *light,* are conveyed to the mind by the Word of GOD; but that due sense of the heart, wherein this *light* formally consists, is immediately by the Spirit of GOD. *As for instance,* that notion that there is a CHRIST and that CHRIST is holy and gracious, is conveyed to the mind by the Word of GOD: but the sense of the excellency of CHRIST by reason of that holiness and grace, is nevertheless immediately the work of the HOLY SPIRIT.

•   •   •

Spiritual Autobiography
[Personal Narrative]

[Often reprinted in the twentieth century as "Personal Narrative," this work was first published, after Edwards' death, in Samuel Hopkins' biography (1765). The text here follows that first printing, from which all later versions have deleted some important sentences. Only the spelling and capitalization have been modernized here.]

I had a variety of concerns and exercises about my soul from my childhood; but had two more remarkable seasons of awakening, before I met with that change, by which I was brought to those new dispositions, and that new sense of things, that I have since had. The first time was when I was a boy, some years before I went to college, at a time of remarkable awakening in my father's congregation. I was then very much affected for many months, and concerned about the things of religion, and my soul's salvation; and was abundant in duties. I used to pray five times a day in secret, and to spend much time in religious talk with other boys; and used to meet with them to pray together. I experienced I know not what kind of delight in religion. My mind was much engaged in it, and had much self-righteous pleasure; and it was my delight to abound in religious duties. I, with some of my school-mates joined together, and built a booth in a swamp, in a very secret and retired place, for a place of prayer. And besides, I had particular secret places of my own in the woods, where I used to retire by myself; and used to be from time to time much affected. My affections seemed to be lively and easily moved, and I seemed to be in my element, when engaged in religious duties. And I am ready to think, many are deceived with such affections, and such a kind of delight, as I then had in religion, and mistake it for grace.

But in process of time, my convictions and affections wore off; and I entirely lost all those affections and delights, and left off secret prayer, at least as to any constant performance of it; and returned like a dog to his vomit, and went on in ways of sin.

Indeed, I was at some times very uneasy, especially towards the latter part of the time of my being at college. 'Till it pleased God, in my last year at college, at a time when I was in the midst of many uneasy thoughts about the state of my soul, to seize me with a pleurisy; in which He brought me nigh to the grave, and shook me over the pit of hell.

But yet, it was not long after my recovery, before I fell again into my old ways of sin. But God would not suffer me to go on with any quietness; but I had great and violent inward struggles: 'till after many conflicts with wicked inclinations, and repeated resolutions, and bonds that I laid myself under by a kind of vows to God, I was brought wholly to break off all former wicked ways, and all ways of known outward sin; and to apply myself to seek my salvation, and practice the duties of religion: but without that kind of affection and delight, that I had formerly experienced. My concern now wrought more by inward struggles and conflicts, and self-reflections. I made seeking my salvation the main business of my life. But yet it seems to me, I sought after a miserable manner: which has made me some times since to question, whether ever it issued in that which was saving; being ready to doubt, whether such miserable seeking was ever succeeded. But yet I was brought to seek salvation, in a manner that I never was before. I felt a spirit to part with all things in the world, for an interest in Christ. My concern continued and prevailed, with many exercising thoughts and inward stuggles; but yet it never seemed to be proper to express my concern that I had, by the name of terror.

From my childhood up, my mind had been wont to be full of objections against the doctrine of God's sovereignty, in choosing whom He would to eternal life, and rejecting whom He pleased; leaving them eternally to perish, and be everlastingly tormented in hell. It used to appear like a horrible doctrine to me. But I remember the time very well, when I seemed to be convinced, and fully satisfied, as to this sovereignty of God, and His justice in thus eternally disposing of men, according to His sovereign pleasure. But never could give an account, how, or by what means, I was thus convinced; not in the least imagining, in the time of it, nor a long time after, that there was any extraordinary influence of God's spirit in it; but only that now I saw further, and my reason apprehended the justice and reasonableness of it. However, my mind rested in it; and it put an end to all those cavils and objections, that had 'till then abode with me, all the preceding part of my life. And there has been a wonderful alteration in my mind, with respect to the doctrine of God's sovereignty, from that day to this; so that I scarce ever have found so much as the rising of an objection against God's sovereignty, in the most absolute sense, in showing mercy to whom He will show mercy, and hardening and eternally damning whom He will. God's absolute sovereignty, and justice, with respect to salvation and damnation, is what my mind seems to rest assured of, as much as of any thing that I see with my eyes; at least it is so at times. But I have often times since that first conviction, had quite another kind of sense of God's sovereignty, than I had then. I have often since, not only had a conviction, but a *delightful* conviction. The doctrine of God's sovereignty has very often appeared, an exceeding pleasant, bright and sweet doctrine to me: and absolute sovereignty is what I love to ascribe to God. But my first conviction was not with this.

The first that I remember that ever I found any thing of that sort of inward, sweet delight in God and divine things, that I have lived much in since, was on reading those words, I Tim. i. 17. "Now unto the king eternal, immortal, invisible, the only wise God, be honor and glory for ever and ever, Amen." As I read the words, there came into my soul, and was as it were diffused thro' it, a sense of the glory of the Divine Being; a new sense, quite different from any thing I ever experienced before. Never any words of scripture seemed to me as these words did. I thought with myself, how excellent a being that was; and how happy I should be, if I might enjoy that God, and be wrapt up to God in Heaven, and be as it were swallowed up in Him. I kept saying, and as it were singing over these words of scripture to myself; and went to prayer, to pray to God that I might enjoy Him; and prayed in a manner quite different from what I used to do; with a new sort of affection. But it never came into my thought, that there was any thing spiritual, or of a saving nature in this.

From about that time, I began to have a new kind of apprehensions and ideas of Christ, and the work of redemption, and the glorious way of salvation by Him. I had an inward, sweet sense of these things, that at times came into my heart; and my soul was led away in pleasant views and contemplations of them. And my mind was greatly engaged, to spend my time in reading and meditating on Christ; and the beauty and excellency of His person, and the lovely way of salvation, by free grace in Him. I found no books so delightful to me, as those that treated of these subjects. Those words Cant. ii. I. used to be abundantly with me: "I am the Rose of Sharon, the lily of the valleys." The words seemed to me, sweetly to represent, the loveliness and beauty of Jesus Christ. And the whole Book of Canticles used to be pleasant to me; and I used to be much in reading it, about that time. And found, from time to time, an inward sweetness, that used, as it were, to carry me away in my contemplations; in what I know not how to express otherwise, than by a calm, sweet abstraction of soul from all the concerns of this world; and a kind of vision, or fixed ideas and imaginations, of being alone in the mountains, or some solitary wilderness, far from all mankind, sweetly conversing with Christ, and wrapt and swallowed up in God. The sense I had of divine things, would often of a sudden as it were, kindle up a sweet burning in my heart; an ardor of my soul, that I know not how to express.

Not long after I first began to experience these things, I gave an account to my father, of some things that had passed in my mind. I was pretty much affected by the discourse we had together. And when the discourse was ended, I walked abroad alone, in a solitary place in my father's pasture, for contemplation. And as I was walking there, and looked up on the sky and clouds; there came into my mind, a sweet sense of the glorious majesty and grace of God, that I know not how to express. I seemed to see them both in a sweet conjunction: majesty and meekness joined together: it was a sweet and gentle, and holy majesty; and also a majestic meekness; an awful sweetness; a high, and great, and holy gentleness.

After this my sense of divine things gradually increased, and became more and more lively, and had more of that inward sweetness. The appearance of every thing was altered: there seemed to be, as it were, a calm, sweet cast, or appearance of divine glory, in almost every thing. God's excellency, His wisdom, His purity and love, seemed to appear in every thing; in the sun, moon and stars; in the clouds, and blue sky; in the grass, flowers, trees; in the water, and all nature; which used greatly to fix my mind. I often used to sit and view the moon, for a long time; and so in the day time, spent much time in viewing the clouds and sky, to behold the sweet glory of God in these things: in the mean time, singing forth with a low voice, my contemplations of the Creator and Redeemer. And scarce any thing, among all the works of nature, was so sweet to me as thunder and lightning. Formerly, nothing had been so terrible to me. I used to be a person uncommonly terrified with thunder: and it used to strike me with terror, when I saw a thunder-storm rising. But now, on the contrary, it rejoiced me. I felt God at the first appearance of a thunder-storm. And used to take the opportunity at such times to fix myself to view the clouds, and see the lightnings play, and hear the majestic and awful voice of God's thunder: which often times was exceeding entertaining, leading me to sweet contemplations of my great and glorious God. And while I viewed, used to spend my time, as it always seemed natural to me, to sing or chant forth my meditations; to speak my thoughts in soliloquies, and speak with a singing voice.

I felt then a great satisfaction as to my good estate. But that did not content me. I had vehement longings of soul after God and Christ, and after more holiness; wherewith my heart seemed to be full, and ready to break: which often brought to my mind, the words of the psalmist, Psal. cxix. 28. "My soul breaketh for the longing it hath." I often felt a mourning and lamenting in my heart, that I had not turned to God sooner, that I might have had more time to grow in grace. My mind was greatly fixed on divine things; I was almost perpetually in the contemplation of them. Spent most of my time in thinking of divine things, year after year. And used to spend abundance of my time, in walking alone in the woods, and solitary places, for meditation, soliloquy and prayer, and converse with God. And it was always my manner, at such times, to sing forth my contemplations. And was almost constantly in ejaculatory prayer, wherever I was. Prayer seemed to be natural to me; as the breath, by which the inward burnings of my heart had vent.

The delights which I now felt in things of religion, were of an exceeding different kind, from those forementioned, that I had when I was a boy. They were totally of another kind; and what I then had no more notion or idea of, than one born blind has of pleasant and beautiful colors. They were of a more inward, pure, soul-animating and refreshing nature. Those former delights, never reached the heart; and did not arise from any sight of the divine excellency of the things of God; or any taste of the soul-satisfying, and life-giving good, there is in them.

My sense of divine things seemed gradually to increase, 'till I went to preach at New York; which was about a year and a half after they began. While I was there, I felt them, very sensibly, in a much higher degree, than I had done before. My longings after God and holiness, were much increased. Pure and humble, holy and heavenly Christianity, appeared exceeding amiable to me. I felt in me a burning desire to be in everything a complete Christian; and conformed to the blessed image of Christ: and that I might live in all things, according to the pure, sweet and blessed rules of the Gospel. I had an eager thirsting after progress in these things. My longings after it, put me upon pursuing and pressing after them. It was my continual strife day and night, and constant inquiry, How I should be more holy, and live more holily, and more becoming a child of God, and disciple of Christ. I sought an increase of grace and holiness, and that I might live an holy life, with vastly more earnestness, than ever I sought grace, before I had it. I used to be continually examining myself, and studying and contriving for likely ways and means, how I should live holily, with far greater diligence and earnestness, than ever I pursued any thing in my life: but with too great a dependence on my own strength; which afterwards proved a great damage to me. My experience had not then taught me, as it has done since, my extreme feebleness and impotence, every manner of way; and the innumerable and bottomless depths of secret corruption and deceit, that there was in my heart. However, I went on with my eager pursuit after more holiness; and sweet conformity to Christ.

The Heaven I desired was a heaven of holiness; to be with God, and to spend my eternity in divine love, and holy communion with Christ. My mind was very much taken up with contemplations on heaven, and the enjoyments of those there; and living there in perfect holiness, humility and love. And it used at that time to appear a great part of the happiness of heaven, that there the saints could express their love to Christ. It appeared to me a great clog and hindrance and burden to me, that what I felt within, I could not express to God, and give vent to, as I desired. The inward ardor of my soul, seemed to be hindered and pent up, and could not freely flame out as it would. I used often to think, how in heaven, this sweet principle should freely and fully vent and express itself. Heaven appeared to me exceeding delightful as a world of love. It appeared to me, that all happiness consisted in living in pure, humble, heavenly, divine love.

I remember the thoughts I used then to have of holiness. I remember I then said sometimes to myself, I do certainly know that I love holiness, such as the Gospel prescribes. It appeared to me, there was nothing in it but what was ravishingly lovely. It appeared to me, to be the highest beauty and amiableness, above all other beauties: that it was a *divine* beauty; far purer than any thing here upon earth; and that everything else, was like mire, filth, and defilement, in comparison of it.

Holiness, as I then wrote down some of my comtemplations on it, appeared to me to be of a sweet, pleasant, charming, serene, calm nature. It seemed to me, it brought an inexpressible purity, brightness, peacefulness and ravishment to the soul: and that it made the soul like a field or garden of God, with all manner of pleasant flowers; that is all pleasant, delightful and undisturbed; enjoying a sweet calm, and the gently vivifying beams of the sun. The soul of a true Christian, as I then wrote my meditations, appeared like such a little white flower, as we see in the spring of the year; low and humble on the ground, opening its bosom, to receive the pleasant beams of the sun's glory; rejoicing as it were, in a calm rapture; diffusing around a sweet fragrancy; standing peacefully and lovingly, in the midst of other flowers round about; all in like manner opening their bosoms, to drink in the light of the sun.

There was no part of creature-holiness, that I then, and at other times, had so great a sense of the loveliness of, as humility, brokenness of heart and poverty of spirit: and there was nothing that I had such a spirit to long for.

My heart as it were panted after this, to lie low before God, and in the dust; that I might be nothing, and that God might be all; that I might become as a little child.

While I was there at New York, I sometimes was much affected with reflections on my past life, considering how late it was, before I began to be truly religious; and how wickedly I had lived 'till then: and once so as to weep abundantly, and for a considerable time together.

On January 12, 1722–3 I made a solemn dedication of myself to God, and wrote it down; giving up myself, and all that I had to God; to be for the future in no respect my own; to act as one that had no right to himself, in any respect. And solemnly vowed to take God for my whole portion and felicity; looking on nothing else as any part of my happiness, nor acting as if it were: and His law for the constant rule of my obedience: engaging to fight with all my might, against the world, the flesh and the devil, to the end of my life. But have reason to be infinitely humbled, when I consider, how much I have failed of answering my obligation.

I had then abundance of sweet religious conversation in the family where I lived, with Mr. John Smith, and his pious mother. My heart was knit in affection to those, in whom were appearances of true piety; and I could bear the thoughts of no other companions, but such as were holy, and the disciples of the blessed Jesus.

I had great longings for the advancement of Christ's kingdom in the world. My secret prayer used to be in great part taken up in praying for it. If I heard the least hint of any thing that happened in any part of the world, that appeared to me, in some respect or other, to have a favorable aspect on the interest of Christ's kingdom, my soul eagerly catched at it; and it would much animate and refresh me. I used to be earnest to read public newsletters, mainly for that end; to see if I could not find some news favorable to the interest of religion in the world.

I very frequently used to retire into a solitary place, on the banks of Hudson's river, at some distance from the city, for contemplation on divine things, and secret converse with God; and had many sweet hours there. Sometimes Mr. Smith and I walked there together, to converse of the things of God; and our conversation used much to turn on the advancement of Christ's kingdom in the world, and the glorious things that God would accomplish for His church in the latter days.

I had then, and at other times, the greatest delight in the holy Scriptures, of any book whatsoever. Often-times in reading it, every word seemed to touch my heart. I felt an harmony between something in my heart, and those sweet and powerful words. I seemed often to see so much light, exhibited by every sentence, and such a refreshing ravishing food communicated, that I could not get along in reading. Used often-times to dwell long on one sentence, to see the wonders contained in it; and yet almost every sentence seemed to be full of wonders.

I came away from New York in the month of April, 1723, and had a most bitter parting with Madam Smith and her son. My heart seemed to sink within me, at leaving the family and city, where I had enjoyed so many sweet and pleasant days. I went from New York to Weathersfield by water. As I sailed away, I kept sight of the city as long as I could; and when I was out of sight of it, it would affect me much to look that way, with a kind of melancholy mixed with sweetness. However, that night after this sorrowful parting, I was greatly comforted in God at Westchester, where we went ashore to lodge: and had a pleasant time of it all the voyage to Saybrook. It was sweet to me to think of meeting dear Christians in heaven, where we should never part more. At Saybrook we went ashore to lodge on Saturday, and there kept sabbath; where I had a sweet and refreshing season, walking alone in the fields.

After I came home to Windsor, remained much in a like frame of my mind, as I had been in at New York, but only sometimes felt my heart ready to sink, with the thoughts of my friends at New York. And my refuge and support was in contemplations on the heavenly state; as I find in my diary of May 1, 1723. It was my comfort to think of that state, where there is fulness of joy; where reigns heavenly, sweet, calm and delightful love, without alloy; where there are continually the dearest expressions of this love; where is the enjoyment of the persons loved, without ever parting; where these persons that appear so lovely in this world, will really be inexpressibly more lovely, and full of love to us. And how sweetly will the mutual lovers join together to sing the praises of God and the Lamb! How full will it fill us with joy, to think, that this enjoyment, these sweet exercises will never cease or come to an end; but will last to all eternity!

Continued much in the same frame in the general, that I had been in at New York, till I went to New Haven, to live there as tutor of the college; having some special seasons of uncommon sweetness: particularly once at Boston, in a journey from Boston, walking out alone in the fields. After I went to New Haven, I sunk in religion; my mind being diverted from my eager and violent pursuits after holiness, by some affairs that greatly preplexed and distracted my mind.

In September, 1725, was taken ill at New Haven; and endeavoring to go home to Windsor, was so ill at the North Village, that I could go no further: where I lay sick for about a quarter of a year. And in this sickness, God was pleased to visit me again with the sweet influences of His spirit. My mind was greatly engaged there on divine, pleasant contemplations, and longings of soul. I observed that those who watched with me, would often be looking out for the morning, and seemed to wish for it. Which brought to my mind those words of the psalmist, which my soul with sweetness made its own language. "My soul waitest for the Lord, more than they that watch for the morning, I say, more than they that watch for the morning." And when the light of the morning came and the beams of the sun came in at the windows, it refreshed my soul from one morning to another. It seemed to me to be some image of the sweet light of God's glory.

I remember, about that time, I used greatly to long for the conversion of some that I was concerned with. It seemed to me, I could gladly honor them, and with delight be a servant to them, and lie at their feet, if they were but truly holy.

But some time after this, I was again greatly diverted in my mind, with some temporal concerns, that exceedingly took up my thoughts, greatly to the wounding of my soul: and went on through various exercises, that it would be tedious to relate, that gave me much more experience of my own heart, than ever I had before.

Since I came to this town,[1] I have often had sweet complacency in God, in views of His glorious perfections, and the excellency of Jesus Christ. God has appeared to me, a glorious and lovely being, chiefly on the account of His holiness. The holiness of God has always appeared to me the most lovely of all His attributes. The doctrines of God's absolute sovereignty, and free grace, in showing mercy to whom He would show mercy; and man's absolute dependence on the operations of God's Holy Spirit, have very often appeared to me as sweet and glorious doctrines. These doctrines have been much my delight. God's sovereignty has ever appeared to me, as great part of His glory. It has often been sweet to me to go to God, and adore Him as a sovereign God, and ask sovereign mercy of Him.

I have loved the doctrines of the Gospel: they have been to my soul like green pastures. The Gospel has seemed to me to be the richest treasure; the treasure that I have most desired, and longed that it might dwell richly in me. The way of salvation by Christ, has appeared in a general way, glorious and excellent, and most pleasant and beautiful. It has often seemed to me, that it would in a great measure spoil heaven, to receive it in any other way. That text has often been affecting and delightful to me, Isai. xxxii. 2. "A man shall be an hiding place from the wind, and a covert from the tempest" etc.

It has often appeared sweet to me, to be united to Christ; to have Him for my head, and to be a member of His body: and also to have Christ for my teacher and prophet. I very often think with sweetness and longings and pantings of soul, of being a little child, taking hold of Christ, to be led by Him through the wilderness of this world. That text, Matth. xviii. at the beginning, has often been sweet to me, "Except ye be converted, and become as little children" etc. I love to think of coming to Christ, to receive salvation of Him, poor in spirit, and quite empty of self; humbly exalting Him alone; cut entirely off from my own root, and to grow into, and out of Christ: to have God in Christ to be all in all; and to live by faith on the Son of God, a life of humble, unfeigned confidence in Him. That Scripture has

[1] Northampton.

often been sweet to me, Psal. cxv. I. "Not unto us, O Lord, not unto us, but unto Thy name give glory, for Thy mercy, and for Thy truth's sake." And those words of Christ, *Luk. x.* 21. "In that hour Jesus rejoiced in spirit, and said, I thank thee, O Father, Lord of heaven and earth, that Thou hast hid these things from the wise and prudent, and hast revealed them unto babes: even so Father, for so it seemed good in Thy sight." That sovereignty of God that Christ rejoiced in, seemed to me to be worthy to be rejoiced in; and that rejoicing of Christ, seemed to me to show the excellency of Christ, and the spirit that He was of.

Sometimes only mentioning a single word, causes my heart to burn within me: or only seeing the Name of Christ, or the name of some attribute of God. And God has appeared glorious to me, on account of the Trinity. It has made me have exalting thoughts of God, that He subsists in three persons; Father, Son and Holy Ghost.

The sweetest joys and delights I have experienced, have not been those that have arisen from a hope of my own good estate; but in a direct view of the glorious things of the Gospel. When I enjoy this sweetness, it seems to carry me above the thoughts of my own safe estate. It seems at such times a loss that I cannot bear, to take off my eye from the glorious, pleasant object I behold without me, to turn my eye in upon myself, and my own good estate.

My heart has been much on the advancement of Christ's kingdom in the world. The histories of the past advancement of Christ's kingdom, have been sweet to me. When I have read histories of past ages, the pleasantest thing in all my reading has been, to read of the kingdom of Christ being promoted. And when I have expected in my reading, to come to any such thing, I have lotted[2] upon it all the way as I read. And my mind has been much entertained and delighted, with the Scripture promises and prophecies, of the future glorious advancement of Christ's kingdom on earth.

I have sometimes had a sense of the excellent fulness of Christ, and His meetness and suitableness as a Saviour; whereby He has appeared to me, far above all, the chief of ten thousands. And His blood and atonement has appeared sweet, and His righteousness sweet; which is always accompanied with an ardency of spirit, and inward strugglings and breathings and groanings, that cannot be uttered, to be emptied of myself, and swallowed up in Christ.

Once, as I rid out into the woods for my health, *Anno* 1737; and having lit from my horse in a retired place, as my manner commonly has been, to walk for divine contemplation and prayer; I had a view, that for me was extraordinary, of the glory of the Son of God; as mediator between God and man; and His wonderful, great, full, pure and sweet grace and love, and meek and

---

[2] That is, counted on it.

gentle condescension. This grace, that appeared to me so calm and sweet, appeared great above the heavens. The person of Christ appeared ineffably excellent, with an excellency great enough to swallow up all thought and conception, which continued, as near as I can judge, about an hour; which kept me, the bigger part of the time, in a flood of tears, and weeping aloud. I felt withal, an ardency of soul to be, what I know not otherwise how to express, than to be emptied and annihilated; to lie in the dust, and to be full of Christ alone; to love Him with a holy and pure love; to trust in Him; to live upon Him; to serve and follow Him, and to be totally wrapt up in the fullness of Christ; and to be perfectly sanctified and made pure, with a divine and heavenly purity. I have several other times, had views very much of the same nature, and that have had the same effects.

I have many times had a sense of the glory of the third person in the Trinity, in His office of sanctifier; in His holy operations communicating divine light and life to the soul. God in the communications of His Holy Spirit, has appeared as an infinite fountain of divine glory and sweetness; being full and sufficient to fill and satisfy the soul: pouring forth itself in sweet communications, like the sun in its glory, sweetly and pleasantly diffusing light and life.

I have sometimes had an affecting sense of the excellency of the Word of God, as a word of life; as the light of life; a sweet, excellent, life-giving word: accompanied with a thirsting after that word, that it might dwell richly in my heart.

I have often since I lived in this town, had very affecting views of my own sinfulness and vileness; very frequently so as to hold me in a kind of loud weeping, sometimes for a considerable time together: so that I have often been forced to shut myself up. I have had a vastly greater sense of my own wickedness, and the badness of my heart, since my conversion, than ever I had before. It has often appeared to me, that if God should mark iniquity against me, I should appear the very worst of all mankind; of all that have been since the beginning of the world to this time: and that I should have by far the lowest place in hell. When others that have come to talk with me about their soul concerns, have expressed the sense they have had of their own wickedness, by saying that it seemed to them, that they were as bad as the devil himself; I thought their expressions seemed exceeding faint and feeble, to represent my wickedness. I thought I should wonder, that they should content themselves with such expressions as these, if I had any reason to imagine, that their sin bore any proportion to mine. It seemed to me, I should wonder at myself, if I should express *my* wickedness in such feeble terms as they did.

My wickedness, as I am in myself, has long appeared to me perfectly ineffable, and infinitely swallowing up all thought and imagination; like an infinite deluge, or infinite mountains over my head. I know not how to express better, what my sins appear to me to be, than by heaping infinite upon infinite, and multiplying infinite by infinite. I go about very often, for this many years, with these expressions in my mind, and in my mouth, "Infinite upon infinite. Infinite upon infinite!" When I look into my heart, and take view of my wickedness, it looks like an abyss infinitely deeper than hell. And it appears to me, that were it not for free grace, exalted and raised up to the infinite height of all the fulness and glory of the great Jehovah, and the arm of His power and grace stretched forth, in all the majesty of His power, and in all the glory of His sovereignty; I should appear sunk down in my sins infinitely below hell itself, far beyond sight of every thing, but the piercing eye of God's grace, that can pierce even down to such a depth, and to the bottom of such an abyss.

And yet, I ben't in the least inclined to think, that I have a greater conviction of sin than ordinary. It seems to me, my conviction of sin is exceeding small, and faint. It appears to me enough to amaze me, that I have no more sense of my sin. I know certainly, that I have very little sense of my sinfulness. That my sins appear to me so great, don't seem to me to be, because I have so much more conviction of sin than other Christians, but because I am so much worse, and have so much more wickedness to be convinced of. When I have had these turns of weeping and crying for my sins, I thought I knew in the time of it, that my repentance was nothing to my sin.

I have greatly longed of late, for a broken heart, and to lie low before God. And when I ask for humility of God, I can't bear the thoughts of being no more humble, than other Christians. It seems to me, that tho' their degrees of humility may be suitable for them; yet it would be a vile self-exaltation in me, not to be the lowest in humility of all mankind. Others speak of their longing to be humbled to the dust. Tho' that may be a proper expression for them, I always think for myself, that I ought to be humbled down below hell. 'Tis an expression that it has long been natural for me to use in prayer to God. I ought to lie infinitely low before God.

It is affecting to me to think, how ignorant I was, when I was a young Christian, of the bottomless, infinite depths of wickedness, pride, hypocrisy and deceit left in my heart.

I have vastly a greater sense, of my universal, exceeding dependence on God's grace and strength, and mere good pleasure, of late, than I used formerly to have; and have experienced more of an abhorrence of my own righteousness. The thought of any comfort or joy, arising in me, on any consideration, or reflection on my own amiableness, or any of my performances or experiences, or any goodness of heart or life, is nauseous and detestable to me. And yet I am greatly afflicted with a proud and self-righteous spirit; much more sensibly, than I used to be formerly. I see that serpent rising and putting forth its head, continually, everywhere, all around me.

Tho' it seems to me, that in some respects I was a far better Christian, for two or three years after my first conversion, than I am now; and lived in a more constant delight and pleasure: yet of late years, I have had a more full and constant sense of the absolute sovereignty of God, and a delight in that sovereignty; and have had more of a sense of the glory of Christ, as a mediator, as revealed in the Gospel. On one Saturday night in particular, had a particular discovery of the excellency of the Gospel of Christ, above all other doctrines; so that I could not but say to myself; "This is my chosen light, my chosen doctrine": and of Christ, "This is my chosen prophet." It appeared to me to be sweet beyond all expression to follow Christ, and to be taught and enlightened and instructed by Him; to learn of Him, and live to Him.

Another Saturday night, January, 1738-9, had such a sense, how sweet and blessed a thing it was, to walk in the way of duty, to do that which was right and meet to be done, and agreeable to the holy mind of God; that it caused me to break forth into a kind of loud weeping, which held me some time; so that I was forced to shut myself up, and fasten the doors. I could not but as it were cry out, "How happy are they which do that which is right in the sight of God! They are blessed indeed, they are the happy ones!" I had at the same time, a very affecting sense, how meet and suitable it was that God should govern the world, and order all things according to His own pleasure; and I rejoiced in it, that God reigned, and that His will was done.

From The Justice of God in the Damnation of Sinners.[1]

ROM. III. 19.
—That every mouth may be stopped—

ROM. III. 19.
—That every mouth may be stopped—

Doctrine: "It is just with God eternally to cast off and destroy sinners." For this is the punishment which the law condemns to.—The truth of this doctrine may appear by the joint consideration of two things, *viz.* man's *sinfulness*, and God's *sovereignty*.

I. It appears from the consideration of man's sinfulness. And that whether we consider the infinitely evil nature of all sin, or how much sin men are guilty of.

1. If we consider the infinite evil and heinousness of sin in general, it is not unjust in God to inflict what punishment is deserved; because the very no-

[1] Boston, 1773. A posthumous edition.

tion of deserving any punishment is, that it may be justly inflicted. A deserved punishment and a just punishment are the same thing. To say that one *deserves* such a punishment, and yet to say that he does not *justly* deserve it, is a contradiction; and if he justly deserves it, then it may be justly *inflicted.*

Every crime or fault deserves a greater or less punishment, in proportion as the crime itself is greater or less. If any fault deserves punishment, then so much the greater the fault, so much the greater is the punishment deserved. The faulty nature of any thing is the formal ground and reason of its desert of punishment; and therefore the more any thing hath of this nature, the more punishment it deserves. And therefore the terribleness of the degree of punishment, let it be never so terrible, is no argument against the justice of it, if the proportion does but hold between the heinousness of the crime and the dreadfulness of the punishment; so that if there be any such thing as a fault infinitely heinous, it will follow that it is just to inflict a punishment for it that is infinitely dreadful.

A crime is more or less heinous, according as we are under greater or less *obligations* to the contrary. This is self-evident; because it is herein that the criminalness or faultiness of any thing consists, that it is contrary to what we are obliged or bound to, or what *ought* to be in us. So the faultiness of one being hating another, is in proportion to his obligation to love him. The crime of one being despising and casting contempt on another, is proportionately more or less heinous, as he was under greater or less obligations to honor him. The fault of disobeying another, is greater or less, as anyone is under greater or less obligations to obey him. And therefore, if there be any being that we are under infinite obligations to love, and honor, and obey, the contrary towards him must be infinitely faulty.

Our obligation to love, honor, and obey any being, is in proportion to his loveliness, honorableness, and authority; for that is the very meaning of the words. When we say anyone is very lovely, it is the same as to say, that he is one very much to be loved. Or if we say such a one is more honorable than another, the meaning of the words is, that he is one that we are more obligated to honor. If we say anyone has great authority over us, it is the same as to say, that he has great right to our subjection and obedience.

But God is a being *infinitely* lovely, because He hath infinite excellency and beauty. To have infinite excellency and beauty, is the same thing as to have infinite loveliness. He is a Being of infinite greatness, majesty, and glory; and therefore He is infinitely honorable. He is infinitely exalted above the greatest potentates of the earth, and highest angels in heaven; and therefore He is infinitely more honorable than they. His authority over us is infinite; and the ground of His right to our obedience is infinitely strong; for He is infinitely worthy to be obeyed Himself, and we have an absolute, universal, and infinite dependence upon Him.

So that sin against God, being a violation of infinite obligations, must be a crime infinitely heinous, and so deserving of infinite punishment.—Nothing is more agreeable to the common sense of mankind, than that sins committed against anyone, must be proportionably heinous to the dignity of the being offended and abused; as it is also agreeable to the Word of God, 1 Sam. ii. 25. "If one man sin against another, the Judge shall judge him;" (*i. e.* shall judge him, and inflict a finite punishment, such as finite judges can inflict;) "but if a man sin against the Lord, who shall entreat for him?" This was the aggravation of sin that made Joseph afraid of it, Gen. xxxix. 9. "How shall I commit this great wickedness and sin against God?" This was the aggravation of David's sin, in comparison of which he esteemed all others as nothing, because they were infinitely exceeded by it. Psalm li. 4. "Against Thee, Thee only, have I sinned."—The *eternity* of the punishment of ungodly men renders it infinite; and it renders it no more than infinite; and therefore renders no more than proportionable to the heinousness of what they are guilty of.

If there be *any* evil or faultiness in sin against God, there is certainly *infinite* evil; for if it be any fault at all, it has an infinite aggravation, viz. that it is against an infinite object. If it be ever so small upon other accounts, yet if it be any thing, it has one infinite dimension; and so is an infinite evil. Which may be illustrated by this: if we suppose a thing to have infinite length, but no breadth and thickness (a mere mathematical line), it is nothing: but if it have *any* breadth and thickness, though never so small, and infinite length, the quantity of it is infinite; it exceeds the quantity of any thing, however broad, thick, and long, wherein these dimensions are all finite.

So that the objections made against the *infinite* punishment of sin, from the necessity, or rather previous certainty of the futurition of sin, arising from the unavoidable original corruption of nature, if they argue anything, argue against *any* faultiness at all: for if this necessity or certainty leaves *any* evil at all in sin, that fault must be *infinite* by reason of the infinite object.

But every such objector as would argue from hence, that there is no fault at all in sin, confutes himself, and shows his own insincerity in his objection. For at the same time that he objects, that men's acts are necessary, and that this kind of necessity is inconsistent with faultiness in the act, his own practice shows that he does not believe what he objects to be true: otherwise why does he at all *blame* men? Or why are such persons at all displeased with men, for abusive, injurious and ungrateful acts towards them? Whatever they pretend, by this they show that indeed they do believe that there is no necessity in men's acts that is inconsistent with blame. And if their objection be this, that this previous certainty is by God's own ordering, and that where God orders an antecedent certainty of acts, He transfers all the fault from the actor on Himself; their practice shows, that at the same time they do not believe this, but fully believe the contrary: for when they are abused by men, they are displeased with *men*, and not with *God* only.

The light of nature teaches all mankind, that when an injury is *voluntary*, it is faulty, without any consideration of what there might be previously to determine the futurition of that evil act of the will. And it really teaches this as much to those that object and cavil most as to others; as their universal practice shows. By which it appears, that such objections are insincere and perverse. Men will mention others' corrupt nature when they are injured, as a thing that aggravates their crime, and that wherein their faultiness partly consists. How common is it for persons, when they look on themselves greatly injured by another, to inveigh against him, and aggravate his baseness, by saying, "He is a man of a most perverse spirit: he is naturally of a selfish, niggardly, or proud and haughty temper: he is one of a base and vile disposition." And yet men's natural and corrupt dispositions are mentioned as an excuse for them, with respect to their sins against God, as if they rendered them blameless.

2. That it is just with God eternally to cast off wicked men, may more abundantly appear, if we consider how much sin they are guilty of. From what has been already said, it appears, that if men are guilty of sin but in one particular, that is sufficient ground of their eternal rejection and condemnation. If they are *sinners*, that is enough. Merely this, might be sufficient to keep them from ever lifting up their heads, and cause them to smite on their breasts, with the publican that cried, "God be merciful to me a sinner." But sinful men are full of sin; principles and acts of sin; their guilt is like great mountains, heaped one upon another, till the pile is grown up to heaven. They are totally corrupt, in every part, in all their faculties; in all the principles of their nature, their understandings and wills; and in all their dispositions and affections. Their heads, their hearts, are totally depraved; all the members of their bodies are only instruments of sin; and all their senses, seeing, hearing, tasting, etc. are only inlets and outlets of sin, channels of corruption. There is nothing but sin, no good at all. Rom. vii. 18. "In me (that is, in my flesh) dwelleth no good thing." There is all manner of wickedness. There are the seeds of the greatest and blackest crimes. There are principles of all sorts of wickedness against men; and there is all wickedness against God. There is pride; there is enmity; there is contempt; there is quarrelling; there is atheism; there is blasphemy. There are these things in exceeding strength; the heart is under the power of them, is sold under sin, and is a perfect slave to it. There is hard-heartedness, hardness greater than that of a rock, or an adamant-stone. There is obstinacy and perverseness, incorrigibleness and inflexibleness in sin, that will not be overcome by threatenings or promises, by awakenings or encouragements, by judgments or mercies, nei-

ther by that which is terrifying, nor that which is winning. The very blood of God our Saviour will not win the heart of a wicked man.

And there are actual wickednesses without number or measure. There are breaches of every command, in thought, word, and deed; a life full of sin; days and nights filled up with sin; mercies abused, and frowns despised; mercy and justice, and all the divine perfections, trampled on; and the honor of each person in the Trinity trod in the dirt. Now if one sinful word or thought has so much evil in it, as to deserve eternal destruction, how do they deserve to be eternally cast off and destroyed that are guilty of so much sin!

II. If with man's sinfulness, we consider God's *sovereignty*, it may serve further to clear God's justice in the eternal rejection and condemnation of sinners, from men's cavils and objections. I shall not now pretend to determine precisely what things are and what things are not proper acts and exercises of God's holy sovereignty; but only, that God's sovereignty extends to the following things:

1. That such is God's sovereign power and right, that He is originally under no *obligation* to keep men from sinning; but may in His providence permit and *leave* them to sin. He was not obliged to keep either angels or men from falling. It is *unreasonable* to suppose, that God should be obliged, if He makes a reasonable creature capable of knowing His will, and receiving a law from Him, and being subject to His moral government, at the same time to make it *impossible* for him to sin, or break His law. For if God be obliged to this, it destroys all use of any commands, laws, promises or threatenings, and the very notion of any moral government of God over those reasonable creatures. For to what purpose would it be, for God to give such and such laws, and declare His holy will to a creature, and annex promises and threatenings to move him to his duty, and make him careful to perform it, if the creature at the same time has this to think of, that God is *obliged* to make it *impossible* for him to break His laws? How can God's threatenings move to care or watchfulness, when, at the same time, God is obliged to render it impossible that he should be exposed to the threatenings? Or, to what purpose is it for God to give a law at all? For according to this supposition, it is God, and not the creature that is under the law. It is the lawgiver's care, and not the subject's to see that His law is obeyed; and this care is what the lawgiver is absolutely obliged to! If God be *obliged* never to *permit* a creature to fall, there is an end of all divine laws, or government, or authority of God over the creature; there can be no manner of use of these things.

God *may permit* sin, though the being of sin will *certainly* ensue on that permission; and so, by permission, He may dispose and order the event. If there were any such thing as chance, or mere contingence, and the very notion of it did not carry a gross absurdity (as might easily be shown that it does), it would have been very unfit that God should have left it to mere chance, whether man should fall or no. For chance, if there should be any such thing, is undesigning and blind. And certainly it is more fit that an event of so great importance, and which is attended with such an infinite train of great consequences, should be disposed and ordered by infinite *wisdom*, than that it should be left to blind *chance*.

If it be said, that God need not have interposed to render it impossible for man to sin, and yet not leave it to mere contingence or blind chance neither; but might have left it with man's *free-will*, to determine whether to sin or no: I answer, if God did leave it to man's free-will, without any *sort of disposal, or ordering* (or rather, *adequate cause*) in the case, whence it should be previously *certain* how that free-will should determine, then still that first determination of the will must be merely contingent or by chance. It could not have any antecedent act of the will to determine it; for I speak now of the very first act or motion of the will, respecting the affair that may be looked upon as the prime ground and highest source of the event. To suppose this to be determined by a foregoing act is a contradiction. God's disposing this determination of the will by His *permission*, does not at all infringe the liberty of the creature. It is in no respect any more inconsistent with liberty, than mere chance or contingence. For if the determination of the will from blind, undesigning chance, it is no more from the agent himself, or from the will itself, than if we suppose, in the case, a wise divine disposal by permission.

2. It was fit that it should be at the ordering of the divine wisdom and good pleasure, whether every particular man should stand for himself, or whether the first father of mankind should be appointed as the moral and federal head and representative of the rest. If God has not liberty in this matter to determine either of these two as He pleases, it must be because determining that the first father of men should represent the rest, and not that every one should stand for himself, is *injurious* to mankind. For if it be not injurious, how is it unjust? But it is not injurious to mankind: for there is nothing in the nature of the case itself, that makes it better that each man should stand for himself, than that all should be represented by their common father; as the least reflection or consideration will convince any one. And if there be nothing in the nature of the thing that makes the former better for mankind than the latter, then it will follow, that they are not hurt in God's choosing and appointing the latter, rather than the former; or, which is the same thing, that it is not injurious to mankind.

3. When men are fallen, and become sinful, God by His sovereignty has a right to determine about their redemption as He pleases. He has a right to determine whether He will redeem any, or not. He might, if He had pleased, have left all to perish, or might have redeemed all. Or, He may redeem some, and leave others; and if He doth so, He may take whom He pleases, and leave whom He pleases. To suppose that all have forfeited His favor,

and deserved to perish, and to suppose that He may not leave any one individual of them to perish, implies a contradiction; because it supposes that such an one has a claim to God's favor, and is not justly liable to perish: which is contrary to the supposition.

It is meet that God should order all these things according to His own pleasure. By reason of His greatness and glory, by which He is infinitely above all, He is worthy to be sovereign, and that His pleasure should in all things take place. He is worthy that He should make Himself His end, and that He should make nothing but His own wisdom His rule in pursuing that end, without asking leave or counsel of any, and without giving account of any of His matters. It is fit that He who is absolutely perfect, and infinitely wise, and the fountain of all wisdom, should determine everything (that He effects) by His own will, even things of the greatest importance. It is meet that He should be thus sovereign, because He is the first being, the eternal being, whence all other beings are. He is the creator of all things; and all are absolutely and universally dependent on Him; and therefore it is meet that He should act as the sovereign possessor of heaven and earth.

•   •   •

From Sinners in the Hands of an Angry God[1]

[The sermon that Edwards preached at Enfield on July 8, 1741 is perhaps the most widely known of all his works. Convinced that an extraordinary revival of religion (now called the Great Awakening), then in progress, would bring to repentance before the Lord one of the greatest harvests of souls in Christian history, Edwards quietly but relentlessly preached in a way that would make his very words act as stimuli to force irresistible images on the minds of his auditors, many of whom moaned and wept.

The text was Deuteronomy 32:35, "Their foot shall slide in due time," and Edwards iterated allusions to weight, as he does in the first three paragraphs of the Application. Before coming to the Application, Edwards argued 10 logical "reasons" to support his insistence that "nothing keeps wicked men at any one moment out of hell, but the mere pleasure of God." The point was not merely to terrify people, but to "awaken" them.]

APPLICATION

The USE may be of *awakening* to unconverted persons in this congregation. This that you have heard is the case of every one of you that are out of Christ. That world of misery, that lake of burning brimstone is extended abroad under you. *There* is the dreadful pit of the glowing flames of the

[1] The text is the 1741 edition.

wrath of God; there is hell's wide gaping mouth open; and you have nothing to stand upon, nor anything to take hold of: there is nothing between you and hell but the air; 'tis only the power and mere pleasure of God that holds you up.

You probably are not sensible of this; you find you are kept out of hell, but don't see the hand of God in it, but look at other things, as the good state of your bodily constitution, your care of your own life, and the means you use for you own preservation. But indeed these things are nothing; if God should withdraw His hand, they would avail no more to keep you from falling, than the thin air to hold up a person that is suspended in it.

Your wickedness makes you as it were heavy as lead, and to tend downwards with great weight and pressure towards hell; and if God should let you go, you would immediately sink and swiftly descend and plunge into the bottomless gulf, and your healthy constitution, and your own care and prudence, and best contrivance, and all your righteousness, would have no more influence to uphold you and keep you out of hell, than a spider's web would have to stop a falling rock. Were it not that so is the sovereign pleasure of God, the earth would not bear you one moment; for you are a burden to it; the Creation groans with you; the creature is made subject to the bondage of your corruption, not willingly; the sun don't willingly shine upon you to give you light to serve sin and Satan; the earth don't willingly yield her increase to satisfy your lusts; nor is it willingly a stage for your wickedness to be acted upon; the air don't willingly serve you for breath to maintain the flame of life in your vitals, while you spend your life in the service of God's enemies. God's creatures are good, and were made for men to serve God with, and don't willingly subserve to any other purpose, and groan when they are abused to purposes so directly contrary to their nature and end. And the world would spew you out, were it not for the sovereign hand of Him who hath subjected it in hope. There are the black clouds of God's wrath now hanging directly over your heads, full of the dreadful storm, and big with thunder; and were it not for the restraining hand of God it would immediately burst forth upon you. The sovereign pleasure of God for the present stays His rough wind; otherwise it would come with fury, and your destruction would come like a whirlwind, and you would be like the chaff of the summer threshing floor.

The wrath of God is like great waters that are dammed for the present; they increase more and more, and rise higher and higher, till an outlet is given, and the longer the stream is stopped, the more rapid and mighty is its course, when once it is let loose. 'Tis true, that Judgment against your evil works has not been executed hitherto; the floods of God's vengeance have been withheld; but your guilt in the meantime is constantly increasing, and you are every day treasuring up more wrath; the waters are continually rising and waxing more and more mighty; and there is nothing but the mere pleasure of God that holds the waters back that are unwilling to be stopped, and press hard to go forward; if God should only withdraw His hand from the floodgate, it would immediately fly open, and the fiery floods of the fierceness and wrath of God would rush forth with inconceivable fury, and would come upon you with omnipotent power; and if your strength were ten thousand times greater than it is, yea ten thousand times greater than the strength of the stoutest, sturdiest devil in hell, it would be nothing to withstand or endure it.

The bow of God's wrath is bent, and the arrow made ready on the string, and Justice bends the arrow at your heart, and strains the bow, and it is nothing but the mere pleasure of God, and that of an angry God, without any promise or obligation at all, that keeps the arrow one moment from being made drunk with your blood.

Thus are all you that never passed under a great change of heart, by the mighty power of the SPIRIT of GOD upon your souls; all that were never born again, and made new creatures, and raised from being dead in sin, to a state of new, and before altogether unexperienced light and life (however you may have reformed your life in many things, and may have had religious affections, and may keep up a form of religion in your families and closets, and in the house of God, and may be strict in it), you are thus in the hands of an angry God; 'tis nothing but His mere pleasure that keeps you from being this moment swallowed up in everlasting destruction.

However unconvinced you may now be of the truth of what you hear, by and by you will be fully convinced of it. Those that are gone from being in the like circumstances with you, see that it was so with them; for destruction came suddenly upon most of them, when they expected nothing of it, and while they were saying, *Peace and safety:* Now they see, that those things that they depended on for peace and safety, were nothing but thin air and empty shadows.

The God that holds you over the pit of hell, much as one holds a spider, or some loathsome insect, over the fire, abhors you, and is dreadfully provoked; His wrath towards you burns like fire; He looks upon you as worthy of nothing else, but to be cast into the fire; He is of purer eyes than to bear to have you in His sight; you are ten thousand times so abominable in His eyes as the most hateful venomous serpent is in ours. You have offended Him infinitely more than a stubborn rebel did his prince: and yet 'tis nothing but His hand that holds you from falling into the fire every moment: 'tis to be ascribed to nothing else, that you did not go to hell the last night; that you was suffered to awake again in this world, after you closed your eyes to sleep: and there is no other reason to be given why you have not dropped into hell since you arose in the morning, but that God's hand has held you up; there is no other reason to be given why you han't gone to hell since you have sat here in the house of God, provoking His pure eyes by your sinful wicked manner of attending His solemn worship: Yea, there is nothing else that is to be given as a reason why you don't this very moment drop down into hell.

O Sinner! Consider the fearful danger you are in: 'Tis a great furnace of wrath, a wide and bottomless pit, full of the fire of wrath, that you are held over in the hand of that God, whose wrath is provoked and incensed as much against you as against many of the damned in hell: You hang by a slender thread, with the flames of divine wrath flashing about it, and ready every moment to singe it, and burn it asunder; and you have no interest in any mediator, and nothing to lay hold of to save yourself, nothing to keep off the flames of wrath, nothing of your own, nothing that you have ever done, nothing that you can do, to induce God to spare you one moment.

And consider here more particularly several things concerning that wrath that you are in such danger of.

1. *Whose* wrath it is! It is the wrath of the infinite GOD. If it were only the wrath of man, tho' it were of the most potent prince, it would be comparatively little to be regarded. The wrath of kings is very much dreaded, especially of absolute monarchs, that have the possessions and lives of their subjects wholly in their power, to be disposed of at their mere will. Prov 20. 2, *The fear of a King is as the roaring of a lion; whoso provoketh him to anger, sinneth against his own soul.* The subject that very much enrages an arbitrary prince, is liable to suffer the most extreme torments, that human art can invent or human power can inflict. But the greatest earthly potentates, in their greatest majesty and strength, and when clothed in their greatest terrors, are but feeble, despicable worms of the dust, in comparison of the great and almighty Creator and King of heaven and earth: it is but little that they can do, when most enraged, and when they have exerted the utmost of their fury. All the kings of the earth before GOD are as grasshoppers, they are nothing and less than nothing: both their love and their hatred is to be despised. The wrath of the great King of Kings is as much more terrible than theirs, as His majesty is greater. Luke 12. 4, 5. *And I say unto you my friends, be not afraid of them that kill the body, and after that have no more that they can do: But I will forewarn you whom ye shall fear; fear Him, which after He hath killed, hath power to cast into hell; yea, I say unto you, fear Him.*

2. 'Tis the *fierceness* of His wrath that you are exposed to. We often read of the *fury* of God; as in Isai. 59. 18. *According to their deeds, accordingly will He repay fury to His adversaries.* So Isai. 66. 15. *For behold, the Lord will come with fire, and with chariots like a whirlwind, to render His anger with fury, and His rebukes with flames of fire.* And so in many other places. So we read of God's *fierceness.* Rev. 19. 15. There we read of the *winepress of the fierceness and wrath of Almighty God.* The words are exceeding terrible: if it had only been said, *the wrath of God,* the words would have

implied that which is infinitely dreadful: but 'tis not only said so, but *the fierceness and wrath of God:* the Fury of God! the Fierceness of Jehovah! Oh how dreadful that must be! Who can utter or conceive what such expressions carry in them! But it is not only said so, but *the fierceness and wrath of ALMIGHTY GOD.* As tho' there would be a very great manifestation of His almighty power, in what the fierceness of His wrath should inflict, as tho' Omnipotence should be as it were enraged, and exerted, as men are wont to exert their strength in the fierceness of their wrath. Oh! then, what will be the consequence! What will become of the poor worm that shall suffer it! Whose hands can be strong? And whose heart endure? To what a dreadful, inexpressible, inconceivable depth of misery must the poor creature be sunk, who shall be the subject of this!

Consider this, you that are here present, that yet remain in an unregenerate state. That God will execute the fierceness of His anger, implies that He will inflict wrath without any pity: when God beholds the ineffable extremity of your case, and sees your torment so vastly disproportioned to your strength, and sees how your poor soul is crushed and sinks down, as it were, into an infinite gloom, He will have no compassion upon you, He will not forbear the executions of His wrath, or in the least lighten His hand; there shall be no moderation or mercy, nor will God then at all stay His rough wind; He will have no regard to your welfare, nor be at all careful lest you should suffer too much, in any other sense than only that you shall not suffer beyond what strict justice requires: nothing shall be withheld, because it's so hard for you to bear. Ezek. 8. 18, *Therefore will I also deal in* fury; *mine eye shall not spare, neither will I have pity; and tho' they cry in mine ears with a loud voice, yet I will not hear them.* Now God stands ready to pity you; this is a day of mercy; you may cry now with some encouragement of obtaining mercy: but when once the day of mercy is past, your most lamentable and dolorous cries and shrieks will be in vain; you will be wholly lost and thrown away of God, as to any regard to your welfare; God will have no other use to put you to but only to suffer misery; you shall be continued in being to no other end; for you will be a vessel of wrath fitted to destruction; and there will be no other use of this vessel but only to be filled full of wrath: God will be so far from pitying you when you cry to Him, that 'tis said He will only *laugh and mock,* Prov. 1. 25, 26, etc.

How awful are those words, Isai. 63. 3. which are the words of the great God: *I will tread them in Mine anger, and will trample them in My fury, and their blood shall be sprinkled upon My garments, and I will stain all My raiment.* 'Tis perhaps impossible to conceive of words that carry in them greater manifestations of these three things, *viz.* contempt and hatred, and fierceness of indignation. If you cry to God to pity you, He will be so far from pitying you in your doleful case, or showing you the least regard or favor, that instead of that He'll only tread you under foot: and tho' He will know that you can't bear the weight of Omnipotence treading upon you, yet He won't regard that, but He will crush you under his feet without mercy; He will crush out your blood, and make it fly, and it shall be sprinkled on His garments, so as to stain all His raiment. He will not only hate you, but He will have you in the utmost contempt; no place shall be thought fit for you, but under His feet, to be trodden down as the mire of the streets.

3. The misery you are exposed to is that which God will inflict to that end, that He might *show* what the *wrath* of JEHOVAH is. God hath had it on His heart to show to angels and men, both how excellent His love is, and also how terrible His wrath is. Sometimes earthly kings have a mind to show how terrible *their* wrath is, by the extreme punishments they would execute on those that provoke 'em. *Nebuchadnezzar,* that mighty and haughty monarch of the *Chaldean* Empire, was willing to show *his* wrath, when enraged with *Shadrach, Meschech,* and *Abednego;* and accordingly gave order that the burning fiery furnace should be het seven times hotter than it was before;[2] doubtless it was raised to the utmost degree of fierceness that humane art could raise it; but the great GOD is also willing to show *His wrath,* and magnify His awful majesty and mighty power in the extreme sufferings of His enemies. Rom. 9. 22, *What if God willing to show* HIS *wrath, and to make His power known, endured with much long-suffering the vessels of wrath fitted to destruction?* And seeing this is His design, and what He has determined, to show how terrible the unmixed, unrestrained wrath, the fury and fierceness of JEHOVAH is, He will do it to effect. There will be something accomplished and brought to pass, that will be dreadful with a witness. When the great and angry God hath risen up and executed His awful vengeance on the poor sinner; and the wretch is actually suffering the infinite weight and power of His indignation, then will God call upon the whole universe to behold that awful majesty, and mighty power that is to be seen in it. Isai. 33. 12, 13, 14. *And the people shall be as the burnings of lime, as thorns cut up shall they be burnt in the fire. Hear ye that are far off what I have done; and ye that are near acknowledge My might. The sinners in Zion are afraid, fearfulness hath surprised the hypocrites etc.*

Thus it will be with you that are in an unconverted state, if you continue in it; the infinite might, and majesty and terribleness of the Omnipotent GOD shall be magnified upon you, in the ineffable strength of your torments: you shall be tormented in the presence of the holy angels, and in the presence of the Lamb; and when you shall be in this state of suffering, the glorious inhabitants of heaven shall go forth and look on the awful spectacle, that they may see what the wrath and fierceness of the Almighty is, and

[2] See Daniel 3:19-30.

when they have seen it, they will fall down and adore that great Power and Majesty. Isai. 66. 23, 24, *And it shall come to pass, that from one new moon to another, and from one sabbath to another, shall all flesh come to worship before Me, saith the Lord; and they shall go forth and look upon the carcasses of the men that have transgressed against Me; for their worm shall not die, neither shall their fire be quenched, and they shall be an abhorring unto all flesh.*

4. It is *everlasting* wrath. It would be dreadful to suffer this fierceness and wrath of Almighty God one moment; but you must suffer it to all eternity: there will be no end to this exquisite horrible misery: When you look forward, you shall see a long forever, a boundless duration before you, which will swallow up your thoughts, and amaze your soul; and you will absolutely despair of ever having any deliverance, any end, any mitigation, any rest at all; you will know certainly that you must wear out long ages, millions of millions of ages, in wrestling and conflicting with this almighty merciless vengeance; and then when you have so done, when so many ages have actually been spent by you in this manner, you will know that all is but a point to what remains. So that your punishment will indeed be infinite. Oh who can express what the state of a soul in such circumstances is! All that we can possibly say about it, gives but a very feeble faint representation of it, 'tis inexpressible and inconceivable: for *who knows the power of God's anger?*

How dreadful is the state of those that are daily and hourly in danger of this great wrath, and infinite misery! But this is the dismal case of every soul in this congregation, that has not been born again, however moral and strict, sober and religious they may otherwise be. Oh that you would consider it, whether you be young or old. There is reason to think, that there are many in this congregation now hearing this discourse, that will actually be the subjects of this very misery to all eternity. We know not who they are, or in what seats they sit, or what thoughts they now have: it may be they are now at ease, and hear all these things without much disturbance, and are now flattering themselves that they are not the persons: promising themselves that they shall escape. If we knew that there was one person, and but one, in the whole congregation that was to be the subject of this misery, what an awful thing would it be to think of! If we knew who it was, what an awful sight would it be to see such a person! How might all the rest of the congregation lift up a lamentable and bitter cry over him! But alas! instead of one, how many is it likely will remember this discourse in hell! And it would be a wonder if some that are now present, should not be in hell in a very short time, before this year is out. And it would be no wonder if some person that now sits here in some seat of this meeting-house in health, and quiet and secure, should be there before tomorrow morning.

Treatise of Religious Affections[1]

From PART II, SECTIONS 1 AND 2:
SHOWING WHAT ARE NO CERTAIN SIGNS
THAT RELIGIOUS AFFECTIONS ARE TRULY
GRACIOUS, OR THAT THEY ARE NOT.

If anyone, on the reading of what has been just now said, is ready to acquit himself, and say, "I am not one of those who have no religious affections; I am often greatly moved with the consideration of the great things of religion;" let him not content himself with this, that he has religious affections. For (as was observed before) as we ought not to reject and condemn all affections, as though true religion did not at all consist in affection; so on the other hand, we ought not to approve of all, as though everyone that was religiously affected, had true grace, and was therein the subject of the saving influences of the Spirit of God: and that therefore the right way is to distinguish among religious affections, between one sort and another. Therefore let us now endeavor to do this: and in order to it, I would do two things.

    I. I would mention some things, which are no signs one way or the other, either that affections are such as true religion consists in, or that they are otherwise; that we may be guarded against judging of affections by false signs.

    II. I would observe some things, wherein those affections which are spiritual and gracious, differ from those which are not so, and may be distinguished and known.

First, I would take notice of some things, which are no signs that affections are gracious, or that they are not.

1.'Tis no sign one way or the other, that religious affections are very great, or raised very high.

Some are ready to condemn all high affections: if persons appear to have their religious affections raised to an extraordinary pitch, they are prejudiced against them, and determine that they are delusions, without further inquiry. But if it be as has been proved, that true religion lies very much in religious affections, then it follows, that if there be a great deal of true religion, there will be great religious affections; if true religion in the hearts of men, be raised to a great height, divine and holy affections will be raised to a great height.

---

[1] The text is the edition of the Yale University Press, edited by John E. Smith, New Haven, 1959, pp. 127-135.

Love is an affection; but will any Christian say, men ought not to love God and Jesus Christ in a high degree? And will any say, we ought not to have a very great hatred of sin, and a very deep sorrow for it? Or that we ought not to exercise a high degree of gratitude to God, for the mercies we receive of Him, and the great things He has done for the salvation of fallen men? Or that we should not have very great and strong desires after God and holiness? Is there any who will profess, that his affections in religion are great enough; and will say, "I have no cause to be humbled, that I am no more affected with the things of religion than I am, I have no reason to be ashamed, that I have no greater exercises of love to God, and sorrow for sin, and gratitude for the mercies which I have received"? Who is there that will go and bless God, that he is affected enough with what he has read and heard, of the wonderful love of God to worms and rebels, in giving His only begotten Son to die for them, and of the dying love of Christ; and will pray that he mayn't be affected with them in any higher degree, because high affections are improper, and very unlovely in Christians, being enthusiastical, and ruinous to true religion?

Our text plainly speaks of great and high affections, when it speaks of rejoicing with joy unspeakable and full of glory: here the most superlative expressions are used, which language will afford. And the Scriptures often require us to exercise very high affections: thus in the first and great commandment of the law, there is an accumulation of expressions, as though words were wanting to express the degree, in which we ought to love God; "Thou shalt love the Lord thy God, with all thy heart, with all thy soul, with all thy mind, and with all thy strength." So the saints are called upon to exercise high degrees of joy: "Rejoice," says Christ to His disciples, "and be exceedingly glad" (Matt. 5:12). So it is said, "Let the righteous be glad; let them rejoice before God; yea, let them exceeding rejoice" (Ps. 68:3). So in the same Book of Psalms, the saints are often called upon to "shout for joy"; and in Luke 6:23 "to leap for joy." So they are abundantly called upon to exercise high degrees of gratitude for mercies, to praise God with all their hearts, with hearts lifted up in the ways of the Lord, and their souls magnifying the Lord, singing His praises, talking of His wondrous works, declaring His doings, etc.

And we find the most eminent saints in Scripture, often professing high affections. Thus the Psalmist speaks of his love, as if it were unspeakable; "Oh how love I thy Law!" (Ps. 119:97). So he expresses a great degree of hatred of sin; "Do I not hate them, O Lord, that hate Thee? And am I not grieved with them that rise up against Thee? I hate them with perfect hatred" (Ps. 139:21-22). He also expresses a high degree of sorrow for sin: he speaks of his sins going over his head, as an heavy burden, that was too heavy for him; and of his roaring all the day, and his moisture's being turned into the drought of summer, and his bones being as it were broken with sorrow.

So he often expresses great degrees of spiritual desires, in a multitude of the strongest expressions which can be conceived of; such as his longing, his soul's thirsting as a dry and thirsty land where no water is, his panting, his flesh and heart crying out, his soul's breaking for the longing it hath, etc. He expresses the exercises of great and extreme grief for the sins of others, "Rivers of water run down mine eyes, because they keep not Thy law" (Ps. 119:136). And ver. 53: "Horror hath taken hold upon me, because of the wicked that forsake Thy law." He expresses high exercises of joy, "The king shall joy in thy strength and in thy salvation how greatly shall he rejoice!" (Ps. 21:1) "My lips shall greatly rejoice, when I sing unto Thee" (Ps. 71:23). "Because Thy loving-kindness is better than life, my lips shall praise Thee. Thus will I bless Thee, while I live: I will lift up my hands in Thy name: my soul shall be satisfied as with marrow and fatness, and my mouth shall praise Thee with joyful lips: when I remember Thee upon my bed, and meditate on Thee in the night watches; because Thou hast been my help, therefore in the shadow of Thy wings will I rejoice" (Ps. 63:3-7).

· · ·

'Tis often foretold of the church of God, in her future happy seasons here on earth, that they shall exceedingly rejoice; "They shall walk, O Lord, in the light of Thy countenance: in Thy name shall they rejoice all the day, and in Thy righteousness shall they be exalted" (Ps. 89:15-16). "Rejoice greatly, O daughter of Zion, shout, O daughter of Jerusalem; behold thy King cometh," etc. (Zech. 9:9). The same is represented in innumerable other places. And because high degrees of joy are the proper and genuine fruits of the gospel of Christ, therefore the angel calls this gospel, "good tidings of great joy, that should be to all people."

The saints and angels in heaven, that have religion in its highest perfection, are exceedingly affected with what they behold and contemplate, of God's perfections and works. They are all as a pure heavenly flame of fire, in their love, and in the greatness and strength of their joy and gratitude: their praises are represented, as the voice of many waters, and as the voice of a great thunder. Now the only reason why their affections are so much higher than the holy affections of saints on earth, is, they see the things they are affected by, more according to their truth, and have their affections more conformed to the nature of things. And therefore, if religious affections in men here below, are but of the same nature and kind with theirs, the higher they are, and the nearer they are to theirs in degree, the better; because therein they will be so much the more conformed to truth, as theirs are.

From these things it certainly appears, that religious affections being in a very high degree, is no evidence that they are not such as have the nature of true religion. Therefore they do greatly err, who condemn persons as enthusiasts, merely because their affections are very high.

And on the other hand, 'tis no evidence that religious affections are of a spiritual and gracious nature, because they are great. 'Tis very manifest by the Holy Scripture, our sure and infallible rule to judge of things of this nature, that there are religious affections which are very high, that are not spiritual and saving. The apostle Paul speaks of affections in the Galatians, which had been exceedingly elevated, and which yet he manifestly speaks of, as fearing that they were vain, and had come to nothing, "Where is the blessedness you spake of? for I bear you record, that if it had been possible, you would have plucked out your own eyes, and have given them to me" (Gal. 4:15).

· · ·

2. 'Tis no sign that affections have the nature of true religion, or that they have not, that they have great effects on the body.

All affections whatsoever, have in some respect or degree, an effect on the body. As was observed before, such is our nature, and such are the laws of union of soul and body, that the mind can have no lively or vigorous exercise, without some effect upon the body. So subject is the body to the mind, and so much do its fluids, especially the animal spirits, attend the motions and exercises of the mind, that there can't be so much as an intense thought, without an effect upon them. Yea, 'tis questionable, whether an embodied soul ever so much as thinks one thought, or has any exercise at all, but that there is some corresponding motion or alteration of motion, in some degree, of the fluids, in some part of the body. But universal experience shows, that the exercise of the affections, have in a special manner a tendency, to some sensible effect upon the body. And if this be so, that all affections have some effect on the body, we may then well suppose, the greater those affections be, and the more vigorous their exercise (other circumstances being equal) the greater will be the effect on the body. Hence it is not to be wondered at, that very great and strong exercises of the affections, should have great effects on the body. And therefore, seeing there are very great affections, both common and spiritual; hence it is not to be wondered at, that great effects on the body, should arise from both these kinds of affections. And consequently these effects are not signs, that the affections they arise from, are of one kind or the other.

Great effects on the body certainly are no sure evidences that affections are spiritual; for we see that such effects oftentimes arise from great affections about temporal things, and when religion is no way concerned in them. And if great affections about secular things that are purely natural, may have these effects, I know not by what rule we should determine, that high affections about religious things, which arise in like manner from nature, can't have the like effect.

Nor on the other hand, do I know of any rule any have to determine, that gracious and holy affections, when raised as high as any natural affections, and have equally strong and vigorous exercises, can't have a great effect on the body. No such rule can be drawn from reason: I know of no reason, why a being affected with a view of God's glory should not cause the body to faint, as well as a being affected with a view of Solomon's glory.

.   .   .

That such ideas of God's glory, as are sometimes given in this world, have a tendency to overbear the body, is evident, because the Scripture gives us an account, that this has sometimes actually been the effect of those external manifestations God has made of Himself, to some of the saints, which were made to that end, viz. to give them an idea of God's majesty and glory. Such instances we have in the prophet Daniel, and the apostle John. Daniel giving an account of an external representation of the glory of Christ, says, "And there remained no strength in me, for my comeliness was turned into corruption, and I retained no strength" (Dan. 10:8). And the apostle John giving an account of a like manifestation made to him, says, "And when I saw Him, I fell at His feet as dead" (Rev. 1:17). 'Tis in vain to say here, these were only external manifestations or symbols of the glory of Christ, which these saints beheld: for though it be true, that they were outward representations of Christ's glory, which they beheld with their bodily eyes; yet the end and use of these external symbols or representations, was to give to these prophets an idea of the thing represented, and that was the true divine glory and majesty of Christ, which is His spiritual glory; they were made use of only as significations of this spiritual glory, and thus undoubtedly they received them, and improved them, and were affected by them. According to the end, for which God intended these outward signs, they received by them a great and lively apprehension of the real glory and majesty of God's nature, which they were signs of; and thus were greatly affected, their souls swallowed up, and their bodies overborne. And I think, they are very bold and daring, who will say God cannot, or shall not give the like clear and affecting ideas and apprehensions of the same real glory and majesty of His nature, to none of His saints, without the intervention of any such external shadows of it.

.   .   .

A Careful and Strict Inquiry into the Modern Prevailing Notions of That Freedom of Will, Which Is Supposed to Be Essential to Moral Agency, Virtue and Vice, Reward and Punishment, Praise and Blame.[1]

PART IV

From SECTION 2.

THE FALSENESS AND INCONSISTENCE OF THAT METAPHYSICAL NOTION OF ACTION, AND AGENCY, WHICH SEEMS TO BE GENERALLY ENTERTAINED BY THE DEFENDERS OF THE ARMINIAN DOCTRINE CONCERNING LIBERTY, MORAL AGENCY, ETC.

One thing that is made very much a ground of argument and supposed demonstration by Arminians,[2] in defense of the forementioned principles, concerning moral agency, virtue, vice, etc. is their *metaphysical notion of agency and action*. They say, unless the soul has a self-determining power, it has no power of "action"; if its volitions be not caused by itself, but are excited and determined by some extrinsic cause, they can't be the soul's own "acts"; and that the soul can't be "active," but must be wholly "passive," in those effects which it is the subject of necessarily, and not from its own free determination.

Mr. Chubb lays the foundation of his scheme of liberty, and of his arguments to support it, very much in this position, that man is an agent, and capable of action. Which doubtless is true: but *self-determination* belongs to his notion of "action," and is the very essence of it. Whence he infers that it is impossible for a man to act and be acted upon, in the same thing, at the same time; and that nothing that is an action, can be the effect of the action of another: and he insists, that a "necessary agent," or an agent that is necessarily determined to act, is a "plain contradiction."

---

[1] Boston, 1754. The text here is from the Yale edition, edited by Paul Ramsey, New Haven, 1957.

[2] The term that Edwards and others applied to those who believed in the "prevailing notions" identified in his title.

But those are a precarious sort of demonstrations, which men build on the meaning that they arbitrarily affix to a word; especially when that meaning is abstruse, inconsistent, and entirely diverse from the original sense of the word in common speech.

That the meaning of the word "action," as Mr. Chubb and many others use it, is utterly unintelligible and inconsistent, is manifest, because it belongs to their notion of an action, that 'tis something wherein is no passion or passiveness; that is (according to their sense of passiveness) it is under the power, influence or action of no cause. And this implies, that action has no cause, and is no effect: for to be an effect implies *passiveness*, or the being subject to the power and action of its cause. And yet they hold, that the mind's *action* is the effect of its own determination, yea, the mind's free and voluntary determination; which is the same with free choice. So that action is the effect of something preceding, even a preceding act of choice: and consequently, in this effect the mind is passive, subject to the power and action of the preceding cause, which is the foregoing choice, and therefore can't be active. So that here we have this contradiction, that action is always the effect of foregoing choice; and therefore can't be action; because it is *passive* to the power of that preceding causal choice; and the mind can't be active and passive in the same thing, at the same time. Again, they say, necessity is utterly inconsistent with action, and a necessary action is a contradiction; and so their notion of action implies contingence, and excludes all necessity. And therefore their notion of action implies, that it has no necessary dependence or connection with anything foregoing; for such a dependence or connection excludes contingence, and implies necessity. And yet their notion of action implies necessity, and supposes that it is necessary, and can't be contingent. For they suppose, that whatever is properly called action, must be determined by the will and free choice; and this is as much as to say, that it must be necessary, being dependent upon, and determined by something foregoing; namely, a foregoing act of choice. Again, it belongs to their notion of action, of that which is a proper and mere act, that it is the beginning of motion, or of exertion of power; but yet it is implied in their notion of action, that it is not the beginning of motion or exertion of power, but is consequent and dependent on a preceding exertion of power, viz. the power of will and choice: for they say there is no proper action but what is freely *chosen;* or, which is the same thing, determined by a foregoing act of free choice. But if any of them shall see cause to deny this, and say they hold no such thing as that every action is chosen, or determined by a foregoing choice; but that the very first exertion of will only, undetermined by any preceding act, is properly called action; then I say, such a man's notion of action implies necessity; for what the mind is the subject of without the determination of its own previous choice, it is the subject of necessarily, as to any hand that free choice has in the affair; and without any ability the mind has to prevent it, by any will or election of its own: because by the supposition it precludes all previous acts of the will or choice in the case, which might prevent it. So that it is again, in this other way, implied in their notion of act, that it is both necessary and not necessary. Again, it belongs to their notion of an "act," that it is no effect of a predetermining bias or preponderation, but springs immediately out of indifference; and this implies that it can't be from foregoing choice, which is foregoing preponderation: if it be not habitual, but occasional, yet if it causes the act, it is truly previous, efficacious and determining. And yet, at the same time, 'tis essential to their notion of an act, that it is what the agent is the author of freely and voluntarily, and that is, by previous choice and design.

So that according to their notion of an act, considered with regard to its consequences, these following things are all essential to it; viz. that it should be necessary, and not necessary; that it should be from a cause, and no cause; that it should be the fruit of choice and design, and not the fruit of choice and design; that it should be the beginning of motion or exertion, and yet consequent on previous exertion; that it should be before it is; that it should spring immediately out of indifference and equilibrium, and yet be the effect of preponderation; that it should be self-originated, and also have its original from something else; that it is what the mind causes itself, of its own will, and can produce or prevent, according to its choice or pleasure, and yet what the mind has no power to prevent, it precluding all previous choice in the affair.

So that an act, according to their metaphysical notion of it, is something of which there is no idea; 'tis nothing but a confusion of the mind, excited by words without any distinct meaning, and is an absolute nonentity; and that in two respects: (1) there is nothing in the world that ever was, is, or can be, to answer the things which must belong to its description, according to what they suppose to be essential to it. And (2) there neither is, nor ever was, nor can be, any notion or idea to answer the word, as they use and explain it. For if we should suppose any such notion, it would many ways destroy itself. But 'tis impossible, any idea or notion should subsist in the mind, whose very nature and essence, which constitutes it, destroys it. If some learned philosopher, who had been abroad, in giving an account of the curious observations he had made in his travels, should say, he "had been in Tierra del Fuego, and there had seen an animal, which he calls by a certain name, that begat and brought forth itself, and yet had a sire and a dam distinct from itself; that it had an appetite, and was hungry before it had being; that his master, who led him, and governed him at his pleasure, was always governed by him, and driven by him as he pleased; that when he moved, he always took a step before the first step; that he went with his head first, and yet always went tail foremost; and this, though he had neither head nor tail": it would be no impudence at all, to tell such a traveler, though a learned man, that he himself had no notion or idea of such an animal as he gave an account of, and never had, nor ever would have.

As the forementioned notion of action is very inconsistent, so it is wholly diverse from the original meaning of the word. The more usual signification of it in vulgar speech, seems to be some motion or exertion of power, that is voluntary, or that is the *effect* of the will; and is used in the same sense as "doing": and most commonly 'tis used to signify *outward* actions. So thinking is often distinguished from acting; and desiring and willing, from doing.

Besides this more usual and proper signification of the word "action," there are other ways in which the word is used that are less proper, which yet have place in common speech. Oftentimes 'tis used to signify some motion or alteration in inanimate things, with relation to some object and effect. So the spring of a watch is said to act upon the chain and wheels; the sunbeams, to act upon plants and trees; and the fire, to act upon wood. Sometimes the word is used to signify motions, alterations, and exertions of power, which are seen in corporeal things, *considered absolutely;* especially when these motions seem to arise from some internal cause which is *hidden;* so that they have a greater resemblance of those motions of our bodies, which are the effects of internal volition, or invisible exertions of will. So the fermentation of liquor, the operations of the loadstone, and of electrical bodies, are called the action of these things. And sometimes the word "action" is used to signify the exercise of thought, or of will and inclination: so meditating, loving, hating, inclining, disinclining, choosing and refusing, may be sometimes called acting; though more rarely (unless it be by philosophers and metaphysicians) than in any of the other senses.

But the word is never used in vulgar speech in that sense which Arminian divines use it in, namely, for the self-determinate exercise of the will, or an exertion of the soul that arises without any necessary connection with anything foregoing. If a man does something voluntarily, or as the effect of his choice, then in the most proper sense, and as the word is most originally and commonly used, he is said to act: but whether that choice or volition be self-determined, or no, whether it be connected with foregoing habitual bias, whether it be the certain effect of the strongest motive, or some extrinsic cause, never comes into consideration in the meaning of the word.

And if the word "action" is arbitrarily used by some men otherwise, to suit some scheme of metaphysics or morality, no argument can reasonably be founded on such a use of this term, to prove anything but their own pleasure. For divines and philosophers strenuously to urge such arguments, as though they were sufficient to support and demonstrate a whole scheme of moral philosophy and divinity, is certainly to erect a mighty edifice on the sand, or rather on a shadow. And though it may now perhaps, through custom, have become natural for 'em to use the word in this sense (if that may be called a sense or meaning, which is so inconsistent with itself) yet this don't prove that it is agreeable to the natural notions men have of things, or that there can be anything in the creation that should answer such a meaning. And though they appeal to experience, yet the truth is, that men are so far from experiencing any such thing, that it is impossible for 'em to have any conception of it.

If it should be objected, that "action" and "passion" are doubtless words of a contrary signification; but to suppose that the agent, in its action, is under the power and influence of something extrinsic, is to confound action and passion, and make 'em the same thing—

I answer, that action and passion are doubtless, as they are sometimes used, words of opposite signification; but not as signifying opposite *existences*, but only opposite *relations*. The words "cause" and "effect" are terms of opposite signification; but nevertheless, if I assert that the same thing may at the same time, in different respects and relations, be both cause and effect, this will not prove that I confound the terms. The soul may be both active and passive in the same thing in different respects, active with relation to one thing, and passive with relation to another. The word "passion" when set in opposition to *action* or rather *activeness*, is merely a relative term: it signifies no effect or cause, nor any proper existence; but is the same with *passiveness*, or a being passive, or a being acted upon by something.

* * *

From Images or Shadows of Divine Things[1]

3. Roses grow upon briars, which is to signify that all temporal sweets are mixt with bitter. But what seems more especially to be meant by it is that pure happiness, the crown of glory, is to be come at in no other way than by bearing Christ's cross, by a life of mortification, self-denial, and labor, and bearing all things for Christ. The rose, that is chief of all flowers, is the last thing that comes out. The briary, prickly bush grows before that; the end and crown of all is the beautiful and fragrant rose.

4. The heavens' being filled with glorious, luminous bodies is to signify the glory and happiness of the heavenly inhabitants, and amongst these the sun signifies Christ and the moon the church.

8. Again it is apparent and allowed that there is a great and remarkable analogy in God's works.[2] There is a wonderful resemblance in the effects

---

[1] Meditations unpublished in Edwards' lifetime but published under this title, edited by Perry Miller. New Haven: Yale University Press, 1948.

[2] Here the parallel to R.W. Emerson and H.D. Thoreau is especially noticeable. Compare Emerson's *Nature.*

which God produces, and consentaneity in His manner of working in one thing and another throughout all nature. It is very observable in the visible world; therefore it is allowed that God does purposely make and order one thing to be in agreeableness and harmony with another. And if so, why should not we suppose that He makes the inferior in imitation of the superior, the material of the spiritual, on purpose to have a resemblance and shadow of them? We see that even in the material world, God makes one part of it strangely to agree with another, and why is it not reasonable to suppose He makes the whole as a shadow of the spiritual world? (Vid. Image 59.)

12. We are told that marriage is a great mystery, as representing the relation between Christ and the church. (Eph. 5.32). By mystery can be meant nothing but a type of what is spiritual. And if God designed this for a type of what is spiritual, why not many other things in the constitution and ordinary state of human society and the world of mankind? (Images 5, 9, 56.)

13. Thus I believe the grass and other vegetables growing and flourishing, looking green and pleasant as it were, ripening, blossoming, and bearing fruit from the influences of the heavens, the rain and wind and light and heat of the sun, to be on purpose to represent the dependence of our spiritual welfare upon God's gracious influences and the effusions of His holy spirit. I am sure there are none of the types of the Old Testament are more lively images of spiritual things. And we find spiritual things very often compared to them in Scripture.

14. The sun's so perpetually, for so many ages, sending forth his rays in such vast profusion, without any diminution of his light and heat, is a bright image of the all-sufficiency and everlastingness of God's bounty and goodness.

15. And so likewise are rivers, which are ever flowing, that empty vast quantities of water every day and yet there is never the less to come. The spirit communicated and shed abroad, that is to say, the goodness of God, is in Scripture compared to a river, and the trees that grow and flourish by the river's side through the benefit of the water represent the saints who live upon Christ and flourish through the influences of His spirit. (Jer. 17.8; Ps. 1.3; Num. 24.6.)

21. The purity, beauty, sublimity, and glory of the visible heavens as one views it in a calm and temperate air, when one is made more sensible of the height of them and of the beauty of their color, when there are here and [there] interposed little clouds, livelily denotes the exaltedness and purity of the blessedness of the heavenly inhabitants. How different is the idea from

that which we have in the consideration of the dark and dire caverns and abyss down in the depths of the earth! This teaches us the vast difference between the state of the departed saints and of damned souls; it shows the ineffable glory of the happiness of the one and the unspeakable dolefullness and terrors of the state of the other. (See Image 212.)

NATHAN COLE

(c.1711–c.1765)

Nathan Cole's narrative of his spiritual life has often been quoted in part, to give a sense of the extreme changes that the Great Awakening wrought in the lives of some ordinary folk. Our selection, edited from the manuscript in the Connecticut Historical Society, can stand here as another of those remarkable works in which an untrained writer, under the influence of strong conviction, records a moving representation of early American life. Not Jonathan Edwards himself (with whose narrative of his own conversion Cole's account should be compared), gives us so powerful a representation of the popular excitement in the revival as Nathan Cole the farmer achieves from the moment that he drops his plow and goes running off to ride to the meeting before the Reverend Mr. Whitefield has stopped preaching. But it is also important to notice that excitement is not all, not even in narratives of the Awakening. Cole's report of his tortured struggle, and of his wife's interminable despair, shows that the community often became engaged in the cyclical drama of one psyche's quest for grace.

Commentary on Nathan Cole may be found in Edwin S. Gaustad, *The Great Awakening in New England,* 1957; Daniel B. Shea, Jr., *Spiritual Autobiography in Early America,* 1968.

The text is edited from the manuscript, printed here with the permission of the Connecticut Historical Society. The complete text, edited by Michael J. Crawford, was published for the first time in *William and Mary Quarterly,* 3rd Ser., 33 (1976): 89–126.

From The Spiritual Travels
of Nathan Cole

I was born Feb 15th 1711 and born again Octo 1741—

When I was young I had very early convictions; but after I grew up I was an Arminian[1] until I was near 30 years of age; I intended to be saved by my own works such as prayers and good deeds.

Now it pleased God to send Mr. Whitefield[2] into this land; and my hearing of his preaching at Philadelphia, like one of the old apostles, and many thousands flocking to hear him preach the Gospel, and great numbers were converted to Christ; I felt the Spirit of God drawing me by conviction; I longed to see and hear him, and wished he would come this way. I heard he was come to New York and the Jerseys and great multitudes flocking after him under great concern for their souls which brought on my concern more and more hoping soon to see him but next I heard he was at Long Island; then at Boston and next at Northampton; then on a sudden, in the morning about 8 or 9 of the clock there came a messenger and said Mr. Whitefield preached at Hartford and Weathersfield yesterday and is to preach at Middletown this morning at ten of the clock, I was in my field at work, I dropped my tool that I had in my hand and ran home to my wife, telling her to make ready quickly to go and hear Mr Whitefield preach at Middletown, then run to my pasture for my horse with all my might; fearing that I should be too late; having my horse I with my wife soon mounted the horse and went forward as fast as I thought the horse could bear, and when my horse got much out of breath I would get down and put my wife on the saddle and bid her ride as fast as she could and not stop or slack for me except I bade her and so I would run until I was much out of breath; and then mount my horse again, and so I did several times to favor my horse; we improved every moment to get along as if we were fleeing for our lives; all the while fearing we should be too late to hear the sermon, for we had twelve miles to ride double in little more than an hour and we went round by the upper housen parish and when we came within about half a mile or a mile of the road that comes down from Hartford Weathersfield and Stepney to Middletown; on high land I saw before me a cloud or fog rising; I first thought it came from the great river, but as I came nearer the road, I heard a noise something like a low rumbling thunder and presently found it was the noise of horses' feet

[1] In this context, someone who believes he might earn his own salvation by voluntary obedience to the Law.

[2] George Whitefield, a great Methodist preacher whose tours of the colonies in 1739 and 1741 also impressed Benjamin Franklin and Jonathan Edwards.

coming down the road and this cloud was a cloud of dust made by the horses' feet; it arose some rods into the air over the tops of hills and trees and when I came within about 20 rods of the road, I could see men and horses slipping along in the cloud like shadows and as I drew nearer it seemed like a steady stream of horses and their riders, scarcely a horse more than his length behind another, all of a lather and foam with sweat, their breath rolling out of their nostrils every jump; every horse seemed to go with all his might to carry his rider to hear news from heaven for the saving of souls, it made me tremble to see the sight, how the world was in a struggle; I found a vacancy between two horses to slip in mine and my wife said law our clothes will be all spoiled, see how they look, for they were so covered with dust, that they looked almost all of a color coats, hats, shirts, and horses: We went down in the stream but heard no man speak a word all the way for 3 miles but everyone pressing forward in great haste and when we got to Middletown old meeting house there was a great multitude it was said to be— 3 or 4000 of people assembled together; we dismounted and shook off our dust; and the ministers were then coming to the meeting house; I turned and looked towards the great river and saw the ferry boats running swift backward and forward bringing over loads of people and the oars rowed nimble and quick; everything men horses and boats seemed to be struggling for life; the land and banks over the river looked black with people and horses all along the 12 miles I saw no man at work in his field, but all seemed to be gone—when I saw Mr Whitefield come upon the scaffold he looked almost angelical; a young, slim, slender youth before some thousands of people with a bold undaunted countenance, and my hearing how God was with him everywhere as he came along it solemnized my mind; and put me into a trembling fear before he began to preach; for he looked as if he was clothed with authority from the Great God; and a sweet solemn solemnity sat upon his brow. And my hearing him preach, gave me a heart wound; by God's blessing: my old foundation was broken up, and I saw that my right- eousness would not save me; then I was convinced of the doctrine of elec- tion: and went right to quarreling with God about it; because that all I could do would not save me; and He had decreed from eternity who should be saved and who not: I began to think I was not elected, and that God made some for heaven and me for hell. And I thought God was not just in so doing, I thought I did not stand on even ground with others, if as I thought; I was made to be damned; my heart then rose against God exceedingly, for his making me for hell; now this distress lasted almost two years:—Poor—Me— Miserable me.—It pleased God to bring on my convictions more and more, and I was loaded with the guilt of sin, I saw I was undone for ever; I carried such a weight of sin in my breast or mind, that it seemed to me as if I should sink into the ground every step; and I kept all to myself as much as I could; I went month after month mourning and begging for mercy, I tried every way I could think to help myself, but all ways failed:—Poor me it took away most all my comfort of eating, drinking, sleeping, or working. Hell fire was most always in my mind; and I have hundreds of times put my fingers into my pipe when I have been smoking to feel how fire felt:—And to see how my body could bear to lie in Hell fire forever and ever. Now my countenance was sad so that others took notice of it; sometimes I had some secret hope in the mercy of God; that sometime or other He would have mercy on me; and so I took some hopes, and thought I would do all that I could do, and remove all things out of the way that might possibly be an hindrance; and I thought I must go to my honored father and mother and ask their forgiveness for everything I had done amiss toward them in all my life: if they had anything against me; I went and when I came near the house one of my brothers was there, and asked me what was the matter with me: I told him I did not feel well, and passed by; but he followed and asked again what was the matter I gave him the same answer, but said he something is the matter more than ordinary for I see it in your countenance: I refused to tell at present.—Poor me—I went to my father and mother and told them what I came for: and asked them to forgive me everything they had against me concerning my disobedience or whatever else it might be; they said they had not anything against me, and both fell aweeping like children for joy to see me so concerned for my soul. Now when I went away I made great resolutions that I would forsake everything that was sinful; and do to my uttermost everything that was good; and at once I felt a calm in my mind, and I had no desire to anything that was sin as I thought; but here the Devil thought to catch me on a false hope, for I began to think that I was converted, for I thought I felt a real change in me. But God in His mercy did not leave me here to perish; but in the space of ten days I was made to see that I was yet in the gall of bitterness; my convictions came on again more smart than ever—poor me—Oh then I longed to be in the condition of some good man; there I am in heaven, but take care of yourself and always remember every day that your poor brother is in hell fire.—Misery—miserable me; my brother got out of his chair and went to speak to me, but he could not for weeping and went out of the house; and went away home and told my father and mother what I had said to him, and they were greatly distressed for me, and thought in the morning they would come and see me; but their distress grew so great for me that they could not stay but came in the night. And when they came into the house Mother seemed to bring heaven into the house; but there was no heaven for me: She said Oh Nathan will you despair of the mercy of God, do not for a thousand of worlds, don't despair of the mercy of God, for He can have mercy at the very last gasp; I told her there was no mercy for me; I was going right down to hell, for I cannot feel grieved for myself, I can't relent, I can't weep for myself, I cannot shed one tear for my sins; I am a gone creature: Oh Nathan says she I have been so myself that I could not shed one tear if I might have had all the world for it; and the next moment I could cry as freely for joy as ever I could for anything in the world: Oh said she I know how you feel now, O if God should shine into your soul now it would almost take away your life, it would almost part soul and body; I beg of you not to despair of the mercy of God. I told her I could not bear to hear her talk so; for I cannot pray, my heart is as hard as a stone, do be gone, let me alone: do go home; you cannot do me any good, I am past all help of men or means, either for soul or body, and after some time I persuaded them to go away; and there I lay all night in such a condition until sometime the next day with pining thoughts in my mind that my soul might die with my body; and there came somebody in with a great armful of dry wood and laid it on the fire, and went out and it burnt up very briskly; as I lay on my bed with my face toward the fire looking on, with these thoughts in my mind, Oh that I might creep into that fire and lie there and burn to death and die forever soul and body; Oh that God would suffer it—Oh that God would suffer it.—Poor soul—and while these thoughts were in my mind, God appeared unto me and made me skringe: before whose face the heavens and the earth fled away; and I was shrinked into nothing; I know not whether I was in the body or out, I seemed to hang in open air before God, and He seemed to speak to me in an angry and sovereign way what won't you trust your soul with God; my heart answered O yes, yes, yes; before I could stir my tongue or lips, and then He seemed to speak again, and say, may not God make one vessel to honor and another to dishonor and not let you know it; my heart answered again O yes yes before I could stir my tongue or lips. Now while my soul was viewing God, my fleshly part was working imaginations and saw many things which I will omit to tell at this time. When God appeared to me everything vanished and was gone in the twinkling of an eye, as quick as a flash of lightning; but when God disappeared or in some measure withdrew, everything was in its place again and I was on my bed.

My heart was broken; my burden was fallen off my mind; I was set free, my distress was gone, and I was filled with a pining desire to see Christ's own words in the Bible; and I got up off my bed being alone; and by the help of chairs I got along to the window where my Bible was and I opened it and the first place I saw was the 15th chapter of John—on Christ's own words and they spake to my very heart and every doubt and scruple that rose in my heart about the truth of God's Word was took right off; and I saw the whole train of scriptures all in a connection, and I believe I felt just as the apostles felt the truth of the Word when they writ it, every leaf and line and letter smiled in my face; I got the Bible up under my chin and hugged it; it was sweet and lovely; the word was nigh me in my hand, then I began to pray and to praise God; I could say Oh my God, and then I could think of no expression good enough to speak to Him, He was altogether lovely and then

I would fall down into a muse and look back into my past life to see how I had lived and it seemed as if my very heart strings would break with sorrow and grief, to see how I had lived in abuse to this God I saw; then I began to pray and to praise God again, and I could say Oh my God and then I could not find words good enough to speak to His praise; then I fell into a muse and looked back on my past life; and saw what an abominable unbeliever I had been, O now I could weep for joy and sorrow, now I had true mourning for sin and never before now I saw sin to be right against God; now my heart and soul were filled as full as they could hold with joy and sorrow now I perfectly felt truth: now my heart talked with God; now everything praised God; the trees, the stone, the walls of the house and everything I could set my eyes on, they all praised God; and while I was weeping, sobbing and sighing, as if my heart would break; there came somebody and opened the door and spake to me, but I made no answer nor turned to see who it was: but I remembered I knew the voice but soon forgot who it was: presently my wife came into the room and asked me what I cried for; I gave her little or no answer, she stood a while and went out again; for I was swallowed up in God.

.   .   .

Now Christians had heard of my discovery and rejoiced: one was now sick and sent for me to come and see him the first opportunity. I went and when I was come into his house he said O cousin Cole come and sit down and tell me what God has done for your soul—I hear joyful news of you. I gave him a relation of it; he said I never heard a better scriptural conversion in my life; you have reason to bless God: I wondered what made the man talk so, now I was so ignorant about conversion in its nature, that I dared not believe it was conversion for fear of falling short and resting on a false hope: for I had been almost in the very mouth of hell and had such a sense of it that I wanted to be sure of an interest in Christ: now other Christians called this conversion but I dared not believe it; but soon Mr Leavensworth came here to preach, and in his sermon he took 4 tracks of experience and went through one and another; and then another, and every time he came through he would say, if this be your case you have never found God to this very day. Now I knew I had gone a deal further than this, but he went on the 4th track and he seemed to strike my very heart strings now I thought if he threw these away I was a gone creature for all what I had met with, for I knew it was really my experience: but when he had gone through he said if this be your case you have really found God and you are happy creatures: well I thought you are but a man you may be mistaken I dared not believe yet that I was converted for fear of coming short of heaven: for I had been almost in hell and I was afraid of coming there again; but I came home and borrowed all the books that I could find that treated on the nature of conversion, and with the Bible they all built me up more and more, and I lived a heaven upon earth in my mind, but yet I had not the sealing evidence until about 3 months after; one day as I went out into my field to work when I went out of my door; I fell into a prayer and continued so until I came to the place of my work and then I had a glorious sight.

It seemed as if I really saw the gate of heaven by an eye of faith, and the way for sinners to get to heaven by Jesus Christ; as plain as ever I saw anything with my bodily eyes in my life, I looked round to see if I could see any poor creature; I thought that I could almost point and show them the strait way to heaven by Jesus Christ: I saw what free grace was; I saw how stubborn and willful man was; I saw it was nothing but accepting of Christ's righteousness and the match was made; I saw I was saved by Christ, here I thought I had the sealings of the Holy Ghost; and here I had evidences clear. . . . within about six months I had a turn of extreme darkness; the reason was I had such a sense of the misery of the damned in hell; that I began to reason with God thus; why will not less punishment do, why should they eternally suffer such extreme torment; will not less do; and while I was reasoning thus, God withdrew and hid His face from me, and left me in Egyptian darkness. . . . Now I knew what David meant when he said my flesh trembleth for fear of thee; for when I lay on my bed it shook like a popple leaf; but on the third day at night I was reading in my martyr book about Mr Bradford's faith and Mr. Philpott's explanation on it where he says if a man wants to know if he be converted or not let him not climb up to heaven to know, but let him descend into himself to know; and that moment this cloud went off; and the clear light of God's countenance broke into my soul again, glory be to God, then I lived about three months very clear. . . .

Now I had lived so long without much entanglings in the world that I began to think I should always keep the world off at arm's end as it were. But as I was talking about it with an old Christian, he told me he knew the spot of ground I stood upon; says he you stand upon the top of Mount Pisgah, and you see the promised land and you think you shall presently be there; but you will find you must come down off of this mount, and must travel through a rough wilderness yet and have the sons of Anak to encounter with yet; before you get there; Ay thought I you think so but I don't; but presently I found his words true.

.　　.　　.

. . . Natural men do not understand the things of God's spirit; so that when I tell my conversion to them, many times I tell it in the following form;— Suppose that I had a captain's commission and a band of soldiers under me or with me, and I went with my soldiers (or sins) to fight against a great good general (or God) and I had a bitter enmity against this general, and hated him, trying with all my might to kill him, and he looks me right in the face, and sees me shoot right at him in order to kill him with all my might, and he sees and knows my own soldiers (or sins) fall right upon me and bind me hand and foot before his face and eyes; and then flee and leave me so bound on the ground in his sight, there lying hopeless and helpless; and I know that if I had him in such a condition I would soon kill him; but he seeth me so and comes right up with his sword drawn in his hands; and as I so view him I have no reason to expect mercy from him; for I would have been glad of the like opportunity to have killed him; and he knew it; so coming up he looks me right in the face, I scringe and expect nothing but death in a moment; knowing that I deserve it and have no heart to ask for mercy because undeserved; with angry countenance he puts the sword to my breast; and says will you yield, I say yes, yes, yes, with all my heart, and I am glad I may yield before the sword goes through me; now this great general immediately cuts off all my bands and sets me at liberty; and never hurts me; and all enmity I ever had against him is gone, and pure love fills the place, now I have found the best friend ever man had; now I shall never be afraid of him to hurt me again; now I can lie and sleep securely in his bosom; now I will never trust my own soldier (or sins) any more now I have found such a friend which I once hated and though I highly deserved death yet he slew me not.—So remarkable was my conversion and change from enmity to love—This [analogous explanation] might have been inserted sooner.

. . .

. . . Again June 1763 my wife being grieved by her friends; and the loss of a brother; caused her to fall into a melancholy way; and she was in great darkness so as at last to border hard upon despair, and then lost the use of her reason and understanding; as Nebuchadnezzar[3] did, and so hath continued now this five years and no alteration: and in December following the dropsy and scurvy humors fell down again into my legs; and the doctors used many means; but all seemed to be in vain, so that about the mid of winter the doctor yielded to let it have its course; only to try things that were thought likely to kill or cure; which things did help me some; my friends and neighbors would come to see me, and say they thought I had not long to stay here; and others would say they thought I never should do any more work; now all this was the Lord's doings; and proved a great blessing to me, He brought me into a fiery furnace; the pain in my legs was exceeding great for 2 or 3 months they swelled, burned, ached, and smarted continually and scarce was there any sound skin from my knees to my toes, so I kept house

---

[3] King of Babylon. See Daniel 4:15-31.

3 months and was laid by in all six months from labor, excepting a few chores. Now all this time my wife was by me crying out in her distress Oh dreadful Oh dreadful dreadful, dreadful, dreadful, and I was sitting three months or thereabouts in the furnace of purification and the sound of dreadful from my wife continually in my ears night and day almost: now all this time God gave me a sweet submission to His will, and a sweet measure of patience; I had not the least hard thought of God's dealings with me; He laid on His rod very smart but yet in mercy: He let me know I had need of it; and why and wherefore He did it; and let me know He did not chastise and correct me in anger nor wrath; but in mercy: and in covenant faithfulness; He gave me a sweet gospel frame and temper of mind, heart, and soul; I had not the least hard thought or anything of that nature, as I could discern in me; He gave me them sweet tempers of soul, that the promises of life are made too; for weeks together, if not months; all in me that belonged to the old Adam seemed to be wholly slain; all sinful nature seemed to lie. . . .

ELIZABETH ASHBRIDGE

(1713–1755)

Almost everything that a student can be told about this remarkable woman appears in her autobiography, one of those early American documents that win an untrained but nonetheless gifted writer a place in literary history by the force of her experience, her character, and her powerful need to set them down for the critical instruction of others. As Daniel Shea has demonstrated, this spiritual autobiography not only deserves comparison with the best Puritan and Quaker narratives, but it transcends the usual limits of the genre through its simple, candid portrayal of the second of Mrs. Ashbridge's three husbands (who becomes, for a time, the main character in the work) and through its convincing representation of attitudes toward women in eighteenth-century England and America.

The selection here consists of the second half of the autobiography. The first half describes Mrs. Ashbridge's elopement as a young girl in England and, after her first husband's death, her physical and spiritual travels in Ireland and America, where she married a schoolteacher

An early edition of Elizabeth Ashbridge's work is *Remarkable Experiences in the Life of Elizabeth Ashbridge*, ed. Edmund Hatcher, 1927. See also Daniel B. Shea, Jr., *Spiritual Autobiography in Early America*, 1968.

named Sullivan and continued to be troubled by feelings of guilt and religious hope and fear. She married a Friend named Aaron Ashbridge after the death of the husband who plays so large a part in her narrative.

From
Some Account of the Early Part
of the Life of Elizabeth Ashbridge,
. . . Written by Herself[1]

I now began to think of my relations in Pennsylvania, whom I had not yet seen. My husband gave me liberty to visit them, and I obtained a certificate from the priest, in order that, if I made any stay, I might be received as a member of the church wherever I came. My husband accompanied me to the Blazingstar Ferry, saw me safely over, and then returned. In my way, I fell from my horse, and, for several days, was unable to travel. I abode at the house of an honest Dutchman, who, with his wife, paid me the utmost attention, and would have no recompence for their trouble. I left them with deep sentiments of gratitude for their extraordinary kindness, and they charged me, if ever I came that way again, to lodge with them. I mention this, because I shall have occasion to allude to it hereafter.

When I came to Trenton Ferry, I felt no small mortification on hearing that my relations were all Quakers, and, what was worst of all, that my aunt was a preacher. I was exceedingly prejudiced against this people, and often wondered how they could call themselves Christians. I repented my coming, and was almost inclined to turn back; yet, as I was so far on my journey, I proceeded, though I expected but little comfort from my visit. How little was I aware it would bring me to the knowledge of the truth!

I went from Trenton to Philadelphia by water, and from thence to my uncle's on horseback. My uncle was dead, and my aunt married again; yet, both she and her husband received me in the kindest manner. I had scarcely been three hours in the house, before my opinion of these people began to alter. I perceived a book lying upon the table, and, being fond of reading, took it up; my aunt observed me, and said, "Cousin, that is a Quaker's book." She saw I was not a Quaker, and supposed I would not like it. I made her no answer, but queried with myself, what can these people write about? I have heard that they deny the Scriptures, and have no other bible than

[1] Written before 1755. The text is the Philadelphia edition of 1807.

George Fox's[2] Journal, denying, also, all the holy ordinances. But, before I had read two pages, my heart burned within me, and, for fear I should be seen, I went into the garden. I sat down, and, as the piece was short, read it before I returned, though I was often obliged to stop to give vent to my tears. The fulness of my heart produced the involuntary exclamation of, "My God, must I, if ever I come to the knowledge of Thy truth, be of this man's opinion, who has sought Thee as I have done; and must I join this people, to whom, a few hours ago, I preferred the papists. O, Thou God of my salvation, and of my life, who hath abundantly manifested Thy long suffering and tender mercy, in redeeming me as from the lowest hell, I beseech Thee to direct me in the right way, and keep me from error; so will I perform my covenant, and think nothing too near to part with for Thy name's sake. O, happy people, thus beloved of God!" After having collected myself, I washed my face, that it might not be perceived I had been weeping. In the night I got but little sleep; the enemy of mankind haunted me with his insinuations, by suggesting that I was one of those that wavered, and not steadfast in faith; and advancing several texts of Scripture against me, as that, in the latter days, there should be those who would deceive the very elect; that of such were the people I was among, and that I was in danger of being deluded. Warned in this manner (from the right source as I thought), I resolved to be aware of those deceivers, and, for some weeks, did not touch one of their books. The next day, being the first of the week, I was desirous of going to church, which was distant about four miles; but, being a stranger, and having no one to go with me, I gave up all thoughts of that, and, as most of the family were going to meeting, I went there with them. As we sat in silence, I looked over the meeting, and said to myself, "How like fools these people sit; how much better would it be to stay at home, and read the Bible, or some good book, than come here and go to sleep." As for me I was very drowsy; and, while asleep, had nearly fallen down. This was the last time I ever fell asleep in a meeting. I now began to be lifted up with spiritual pride, and to think myself better than they; but this disposition of mind did not last long. It may seem strange that, after living so long with one of this society at Dublin, I should yet be so much a stranger to them. In answer, let it be considered that, while I was there, I never read any of their books, nor went to one meeting; besides, I had heard such accounts of them, as made me think that, of all societies, they were the worst. But He who knows the sincerity of the heart, looked on my weakness with pity; I was permitted to see my error, and shown that these were the people I ought to join.

A few weeks afterwards, there was an afternoon meeting at my uncle's, at which a minister named William Hammans was present. I was highly prejudiced against him when he stood up, but I was soon humbled; for he preached the Gospel with such power that I was obliged to confess it was

---

[2] George Fox (1624-1691) founded the Society of Friends.

the truth. But, though he was the instrument of assisting me out of many doubts, my mind was not wholly freed from them. The morning before this meeting I had been disputing with my uncle about baptism, which was the subject handled by this minister, who removed all my scruples beyond objection, and yet I seemed loath to believe that the sermon I had heard proceeded from divine revelation. I accused my aunt and uncle of having spoken of me to the Friend; but they cleared themselves, by telling me, that they had not seen him, since my coming, until he came into the meeting. I then viewed him as the messenger of God to me, and, laying aside my prejudices, opened my heart to receive the truth; the beauty of which was shown to me, with the glory of those who continued faithful to it. I had also revealed to me the emptiness of all shadows and types, which, though proper in their day, were now, by the coming of the Son of God, at an end, and everlasting righteousness, which is a work in the heart, was to be established in the room thereof. I was permitted to see that all I had gone through was to prepare me for this day; and that the time was near, when it would be required of me, to go and declare to others what the God of mercy had done for my soul; at which I was surprised, and desired to be excused, lest I should bring dishonor to the truth, and cause His holy name to be evil spoken of.

Of these things I let no one know. I feared discovery, and did not even appear like a Friend.

I now hired to keep school, and, hearing of a place for my husband, I wrote, and desired him to come, though I did not let him know how it was with me.

I loved to go to meetings, but did not love to be seen going on week-days, and therefore went to them, from my school, through the woods. Notwithstanding all my care, the neighbors (who were not Friends), soon began to revile me with the name of Quaker; adding, that they supposed I intended to be a fool, and turn preacher. Thus did I receive the same censure, which, about a year before, I had passed on one of the handmaids of the Lord in Boston. I was so weak, that I could not bear the reproach. In order to change their opinion, I went into greater excess of apparel than I had freedom to do, even before I became acquainted with Friends. In this condition I continued till my husband came, and then began the trial of my faith.

Before he reached me, he heard I was turned Quaker; at which he stamped, and said, "I had rather have heard she was dead, well as I love her; for, if it be so, all my comfort is gone. He then came to me; it was after an absence of four months; I got up and said to him, "My dear, I am glad to see thee."[3] At this, he flew into a great rage, exclaiming, "The devil thee, thee, thee, don't thee me." I endeavored, by every mild means, to pacify him;

---

[3] Friends used the familiar *thee* instead of *you*, and some used it in both the nominative and objective cases. Others, including Elizabeth Ashbridge, continued to use *thou* for the nominative and *thee* for the objective case. Presumably, she had called her husband *you* before her conversion. The shock of her greeting is evident in his response.

and, at length, got him fit to speak to my relations. As soon after this as we were alone, he said to me, "And so I see your Quaker relations have made you one"; I replied, that they had not (which was true), I never told them how it was with me. He said he would not stay amongst them; and, having found a place to his mind, hired, and came directly back to fetch me, walking, in one afternoon, thirty miles to keep me from meeting the next day, which was first day.[4] He took me, after resting this day, to the place where he had hired, and to lodgings he had engaged at the house of a churchwarden. This man was a bitter enemy of Friends, and did all he could to irritate my husband against them.

Though I did not appear like a Friend,[5] they all believed me to be one. When my husband and he used to be making their diversions and reviling, I sat in silence, though now and then an involuntary sigh broke from me; at which he would say, "There, did not I tell you your wife was a Quaker, and she will become a preacher." On such an occasion as this, my husband once came up to me, in a great rage, and shaking his hand over me, said, "You had better be hanged in that day." I was seized with horror, and again plunged into despair, which continued nearly three months. I was afraid that, by denying the Lord, the heavens would be shut against me. I walked much alone in the woods, and there, where no eye saw, or ear heard me, lamented my miserable condition. Often have I wandered, from morning till night, without food. I was brought so low that my life became a burden to me; and the Devil seemed to vaunt that, though the sins of my youth were forgiven me, yet now I had committed an unpardonable sin, and hell would inevitably be my portion, and my torments would be greater than if I had hanged myself at first.

In the night, when, under this painful distress of mind, I could not sleep, if my husband perceived me weeping, he would revile me for it. At length, when he and his friend thought themselves too weak to overset me, he went to the priest at Chester, to inquire what he could do with me. This man knew I was a member of the [Anglican] Church, for I had shown him my certificate. His advice was, to take me out of Pennsylvania, and settle in some place where there were no Quakers. My husband replied, he did not care where we went, if he could but restore me to my natural liveliness of temper. As for me, I had no resolution to oppose their proposals, nor much cared where I went. I seemed to have nothing to hope for. I daily expected to be made a victim of divine wrath, and was possessed with the idea that this would be by thunder.

[4] That is, Sunday. Quakers and many Puritans did not use pagan names but only numbers for months or days. See the Winthrop, Sewall, and Mather entries, above.

[5] That is, did not dress in the usual manner of Quaker women.

When the time of removal came, I was not permitted to bid my relations farewell; and, as my husband was poor, and kept no horse, I was obliged to travel on foot. We came to Wilmington, fifteen miles, and from thence to Philadelphia by water. Here we stopt at a tavern, where I became the spectacle and discourse of the company. My husband told them his wife had become a Quaker, and he designed, if possible, to find out a place where there was none: (thought I) I was once in a condition to deserve that name, but now it is over with me. O that I might, from a true hope, once more have an opportunity to confess the truth; though I was sure of all manner of cruelties, I would not regard them. Such were my concerns, while he was entertaining the company with my story, in which he told them that I had been a good dancer, but now he could get me neither to dance or sing. One of the company then started up, and said, "I'll fetch a fiddle, and we'll have a good dance"; a proposal with which my husband was pleased. When the fiddle was brought, my husband came and said to me, "My dear, shake off that gloom, and let us have a civil dance; you would, now and then, when you were a good churchwoman, and that's better than a stiff Quaker." I had taken up the resolution not to comply with his request, whatever might be the consequence; this I let him know, though I durst say little, for fear of his choleric temper. He pulled me round the room, till the tears fell from my eyes, at the sight of which the musician stopt, and said, "I'll play no more; let your wife alone." There was a person in company that came from Freehold, in East Jersey, who said, "I see your wife's a Quaker, but, if you'll take my advice you need not go so far as you intend; come and live with us; we'll soon cure her of her Quakerism, and we want a schoolmaster and schoolmistress too." He consented, and a happy turn it was for me, as will shortly be seen. The answer of peace was afforded me, for refusing to dance; I rejoiced more than if I had been made mistress of much riches, and, with tears, prayed, "Lord, I dread to ask, and yet without Thy gracious pardon, I am miserable. I therefore fall down before Thy throne, imploring mercy at Thy hand. O Lord, once more, I beseech Thee, try my obedience, and then, in whatsoever Thou commandest, I will obey Thee, and not fear to confess Thee before men." My cries were heard, and it was shown to me, that He delights not in the death of a sinner. My soul was again set at liberty, and I could praise Him.

In our way to Freehold, we visited the kind Dutchman, whom I have mentioned in a former part of this narrative. He made us welcome, and invited us to pass a day or two with him. During our stay, we went to a large meeting of Presbyterians, held not only for worship, but business, in particular, the trial of one of their priests, who had been charged with drunkenness, was to come on. I perceived such great divisions among the people, respecting who should be their shepherd, that I pitied them. Some insisted on having the old offender restored; others wished to have a young man they had on trial for some weeks; others, again, were for sending to New England for a minister. In reply, one who addressed himself to the chief speaker observed, "Sir, when we have been at the expense (which will not be trifling) of fetching this gentleman from New England, perhaps he'll not stay with us." "Don't you know how to make him stay?" said another. "No Sir." "I'll tell you; give him a large salary, and I'll engage he'll stay." I listened attentively to the debate, and most plainly it appeared to me, that these mercenary creatures were all actuated by one and the same motive, which was, not the regard for souls, but the love of money. One of these men, called a reverend divine, whom these people almost adored, had, to my knowledge, left his flock in Long Island, and removed to Philadelphia, where he could get more money. I have myself heard some on the Island say that they had almost impoverished themselves in order to keep him; but, being unable to equal what he was offered at Philadelphia, he left them. Surely these are the shepherds who regard the fleece more than the flock, and in whose mouths are lies, when they say that they are the ambassadors of Christ, whose command it is, "Freely ye have received, freely give."

In our way to Freehold, as we came to Stony Brook, my husband turned towards me, and tauntingly said, "Here's one of Satan's synagogues, don't you long to be in it; I hope to see you cured of your new religion." A little further on, we came to a large run of water, over which there was no bridge, and, being strangers, we knew no way to avoid passing through it. He carried over our clothes, which we had in bundles; and, taking off my shoes, I walked through in my stockings. It was in the 12th month; the weather was very cold, and a fall of snow lay on the ground. It was the concern of my heart, that the Lord would sanctify all my afflictions to me, and give me patience to bear them. After walking nearly a mile, we came to a house, which proved to be a sort of tavern. My husband called for some spirituous liquors, and I got some weakened cider mulled, which rendered me extremely sick; so that, after we were a little past the house, being too faint to proceed, I fell down. "What's the matter now?" said my husband, "what, are you drunk? Where's your religion now?" He knew I was not drunk, and, at that time, I believe he pitied me, although he spoke in this manner. After I was a little recovered, we went on, and came to another tavern, where we lodged. The next day, as we journeyed, a young man, driving an empty cart, overtook us. We asked him to let us ride, and he readily granted the request. I had known the time when I would not have been seen in a cart, but my proud heart was humbled, and I did not now regard the look of it. This cart belonged to a man in Shrewsbury, and was to go through the place of our destination. We soon had the care of the team to ourselves, through a failure of the driver, and arrived with it at Freehold. My husband would have had me stay here, while he went to see the team safe home; I told him, No; since he had led me through the country like a vagabond, I would not stay behind him. We therefore went together, and lodged, that night, at the house of the owner of the cart. The next day, on our return to Freehold, we met a man riding full speed, who, stopping, said to my husband, "Sir, are you a schoolmaster?" He answered, "Yes." "I am come," replied the stranger, "to tell you of two new schoolhouses, two miles apart, each of which wants a master." How this person came to hear of us, who arrived but the night before, I never knew. I was glad he was not called a Quaker, lest it should have been thought a plot by my husband, to whom I turned and said, "My dear, look on me with pity, if thou hast any affection left for me, which I hope thou hast, for I am not conscious of having done any thing to alienate it. Here is an opportunity to settle us both, and I am willing to do all in my power, towards getting an honest livelihood." After a short pause, he consented to go with the young man. In our way, we came to the house of a worthy Friend, who was a preacher, though we did not know it. I was surprised to see the people so kind to us. We had not been long in the house, till we were invited to lodge there for the night, being the last of the week. My husband accepted the invitation, saying, "My wife has had a tedious travel, and I pity her." These kind expressions affected me, for I heard them very seldom. The Friend's kindness could not proceed from my appearing like a Quaker, because I had not yet altered my dress. The woman of the house, after we had concluded to stay, fixed her eyes upon me, and said, "I believe thou hast met with a deal of trouble," to which I made but little answer. My husband observing they were of that sort of people, whom he had so much endeavored to shun, gave us no opportunity for discourse that night; but, the next morning, I let my friend know a little of my situation.

When meeting-time came, I longed to go, but dared not to ask my husband's leave. As the Friends were getting ready themselves, they asked him if he would accompany them, observing, that they knew those who were to be his employers, and, if they were at meeting, would speak to them. He consented. The woman Friend then said, "And wilt thou let thy wife go too"; which request he denied; but she answered his objections so prudently that he could not be angry, and at last consented. I went with joy, and a heavenly meeting it was. My spirit did rejoice in the God of my salvation. May I ever, in humility, preserve the remembrance of His tender mercies to me.

By the end of the week, we got settled in our new situation. We took a room, in a Friend's house, one mile from each school, and eight from the meeting-house. I now deemed it proper to let my husband see I was determined to join with Friends. When first day came, I directed myself to him in this manner: "My dear, art thou willing to let me go to meeting?" He flew into a rage, and replied "No you sha'n't." Speaking firmly, I told him, "That, as a dutiful wife, I was ready to obey all his lawful commands; but, when they imposed upon my conscience, I could not obey him. I had already wronged myself, in having done it too long; and though he was near to me, and, as a wife ought, I loved him, yet God, who was nearer than all the world to me, had made me sensible that this was the way in which I ought to go. I added, that this was no small cross to my own will; but I had given up my heart, and I trusted that He who called for it would enable me, for the remainder of my life, to keep it steadily devoted to His service; and I hoped I should not, on this account, make the worse wife." I spoke, however, to no purpose;—he continued inflexible.

I had now put my hand to the plough, and resolved not to draw back; I therefore went without leave. I expected he would immediately follow and force me back, but he did not. I called at the house of one of the neighbors, and, getting a girl to show me the way, I went on rejoicing, and praising God in my heart.

Thus, for some time, I had to go eight miles on foot to meeting, which I never thought hard. My husband had a horse, but he would not suffer me to ride on it; nor, when my shoes were worn out, would he let me have a new pair; but, though he hoped, on this account, to keep me from meeting, it did not hinder me:—I have tied them round with strings to keep them on.

Finding that all the means he had yet used could not alter my resolutions, he several times struck me with severe blows. I endeavored to bear all with patience, believing that the time would come when he would see I was in the right. Once he came up to me, took out his penknife, and said, "If you offer to go to meeting tomorrow, with this knife I'll cripple you, for you shall not be a Quaker." I made him no answer. In the morning, I set out as usual; he did not attempt to harm me. Having despaired of recovering me himself, he fled, for help, to the priest, whom he told, that I had been a very religious woman, in the way of the Church of England, of which I was a member, and had a good certificate from Long Island; and I was now bewitched, and had turned Quaker, which almost broke his heart; and, therefore, he desired that, as he was one who had the care of souls, he would come and pay me a visit, and use his endeavors to reclaim me, which he hoped, by the blessing of God, would be done. The priest consented, and fixed the time for his coming, which was that day two weeks, as he said he could not come sooner. My husband came home extremely pleased, and told me of it. I replied, with a smile, I trusted I should be enabled to give a reason for the hope within me; yet I believed, at the same time, that the priest would never trouble himself about me, which proved to be the case. Before the day he appointed came, it was required of me, in a more public manner, to confess to the world what I was. I felt myself called to give up to prayer in meeting. I trembled, and would freely have given up my life to be excused. What rendered the required service harder on me was, that I was not yet taken under the care of Friends; and was kept from requesting to be so, for fear I should bring a scandal on the society. I begged to be excused till I had joined, and then I would give up freely. The answer was, "I am a covenant-keeping God, and the word that I spake to thee, when I found thee in distress, even that I would never forsake thee, if thou wouldst be obedient to what I should make known unto thee, I will assuredly make good. If thou refusest, My spirit shall not always strive. Fear not, I will make way for thee through all thy difficulties, which shall be many, for My name's sake; but, be faithful, and I will give thee a crown of life." To this language I answered "Thy will, O God, be done; I am in Thy hand, do with me according to Thy word"; and I then prayed.

This day, as usual, I had gone to meeting on foot. While my husband (as he afterwards told me) was lying on the bed, these words crossed his mind: "Lord, where shall I fly to shun Thee," etc. upon which he arose, and, seeing it rain, got the horse and set off to fetch me, arriving just as the meeting broke up. I got on horseback as quickly as possible, lest he should hear I had been speaking; he did hear of it nevertheless, and, as soon as we were in the woods, began with saying, "Why do you mean thus to make my life unhappy? What, could you not be a Quaker, without turning fool in this manner?" I answered in tears, "My dear, look on me with pity, if thou hast any; canst thou think that I, in the bloom of my days, would bear all that thou knowest of, and much that thou knowest not of, if I did not feel it my duty." These words touched him, and, he said, "Well, I'll e'en give you up; I see it won't avail to strive; if it be of God I cannot overthrow it; and, if of yourself, it will soon fall." I saw the tears stand in his eyes, at which I was overcome with joy, and began already to reap the fruits of my obedience. But my trials were not yet over. The time appointed for the priest to visit me arrived, but no priest appeared. My husband went to fetch him, but he refused, saying he was busy, which so displeased my husband that he never went to hear him again, and, for some time, went to no place of worship.

My faith was now assaulted in another way, so strongly, that all my former trials were but trifling to it. This exercise came upon me unexpectedly, by hearing a woman speak of a book she had read, in which it was asserted that Christ was not the Son of God. A voice within me seemed to answer "No more He is, it's all a fancy, and the contrivance of men." Thus again was I filled with inexpressible trouble, which continued three weeks; and again did I seek desolate places, where I might make my moan. I have lain whole nights without sleep. I thought myself deserted of God, but did not let go my trust in Him. I kept alive a hope that He who had delivered me as it were out of the paw of the bear, and the jaws of the lion, would in His own good time, deliver me from this temptation also. This was, at length, my experience; and I found the truth of His words, that all things shall work together for the good of those who love and fear Him. My present exercises were to prepare me for further services in His cause; and it is necessary for His ministers to experience all conditions, that they may thereby be abler to speak to them.

This happened just after my first appearance as a minister, and Friends had not been to talk with me. They did not well know what to do, till I had appeared again, which was not for some time, when the Monthly Meeting appointed four Friends to pay me a visit. They left me well satisfied with the conference, and I joined the Society. My husband still went to no place of worship. One day he said to me, "I would go to meeting, only I'm afraid I shall hear your clack, which I cannot bear." I used no persuasions. When meeting-time came, he got the horse, took me behind him, and went. For several months, if he saw me offer to rise, he went out; till, one day, I rose before he was aware and then, as he afterwards owned, he was ashamed to do it.

From this time he left off the practice, and never hindered me from going to meeting. Though he did not take up the cross, yet his judgment was convinced; and, sometimes, melting into tears, he would say to me, "My dear, I have seen the beauty there is in the truth, and that thou hast followed the right way, in which I pray God to preserve thee." I told him, that I hoped He who had given me strength would also favor him. "O," said he, "I cannot bear the reproach thou dost, to be called turn-coat, and become a laughing-stock to the world; but I'll no longer hinder thee." This I considered a favor, and a little hope remained that my prayers, on his account, would he heard.

We lived in a small house by ourselves, which, though mean, and though we had little to put in it, our bed being no better than chaff, I was truly content. The only desires I had were for my own preservation, and to be blessed with the reformation of my husband. He was connected with a set of men who he feared would make game of him, which indeed they already did; asking him when he designed to commence preacher, for they saw he intended to turn Quaker, and seemed to love his wife better since she became one than before. They used to come to our house, and provoked him to sit up and drink with them, sometimes till near day, while I have been sorrowing in a stable. Once, as I sat in this condition, I heard him say to his company, "I can't bear any longer to afflict my poor wife in this manner; for, whatever you may think of her, I do believe she's a good woman." He then came to me and said, "Come in, my dear, God has given thee a deal of patience: I'll put an end to this practice." This was the last time they sat up at night.

My husband now thought that if he was in any place where it was not known he had been so bitter against Friends, he could do better. I objected to this, fearing it would not be for his benefit. Frequently, in a broken and affectionate manner, he condemned his ill usage of me. I answered, that I hoped it had been for my good, and therefore desired he would not be afflicted on that account. According to the measure of grace received, I did what I could, both by example and precept, for his good. My advice was for him to stay where he was, as I was afraid he would grow weaker in his good resolutions, if he removed.

All I could say would not avail. Hearing of a place at Bordentown, he went thither, but was not suited. He next removed to Mount Holly,[6] where he settled. We had each of us a good school; we soon got our house pretty well furnished, and might have done very well. Nothing seemed wanting to complete my happiness, except the reformation of my husband, which I had much reason to doubt I should not see soon. It fell out according to my fears. He addicted himself much to drinking, and grew worse than before. Sorrow was again my lot, I prayed for patience to bear my afflictions, and to submit to the dispensations of Providence. I murmured not; nor do I recollect that I ever uttered any harsh expressions except on one occasion. My husband coming home a little intoxicated (a state in which he was very fractious), and, finding me at work by a candle, he put it out, fetching me, at the same time, a box on the ear, and saying, "You don't earn your light." At this unkind usage, which I had not been used to for the last two years, I was somewhat angry, and said, "Thou art a vile man." He struck me again; but my anger had cooled, and I received the blow without so much as a word in return. This also displeased him, and he went on in a distracted like manner, uttering such expressions of despair as, he believed he was predestined to damnation, and he did not care how soon God struck him dead. I said very little, till, at length, in the bitterness of my soul, I broke out into these expressions: "Lord, look down on my afflictions, and deliver me by some means or other." My prayer was granted, but in such a manner that I thought it would have killed me. He went to Burlington, where he got drunk, and enlisted to go as a common soldier to Cuba, in the year 1740. I had drunk many bitter cups, but this seemed the bitterest of them all. A thousand times I blamed myself for making such a request, which I was afraid had displeased God, who had, in displeasure, granted it for my punishment.

I have since had cause to believe that he was benefited by his rash act, as, in the army, he did what he could not at home;—he suffered for the testimony of truth. When they came to prepare for an engagement, he refused to fight; he was whipt, and brought before the General, who asked him, why he enlisted if he would not fight. "I did it," said he, "in a drunken frolic, when the Devil had the better of me; but now my judgment is convinced I ought not to fight, neither will I, whatever I suffer. I have but one life, and you may take that if you please, for I'll never take up arms." He adhered to this resolution. By their cruel usage of him in consequence, he was so much disabled that the General sent him to Chelsea Hospital, near London. Within nine months afterwards, he died at this place, and I hope made a good end.

[6]. The home of John Woolman (1720–1772), a Friend whose Journal is represented below, pp. 506–514.

Having been obliged to say much of his ill usage to me, I have thought it my duty to say what I could in his favor. Although he was so bad, I never thought him the worst of men. If he had suffered religion to have had its perfect work, I should have been happy in the lowest situation of life. I have had cause to bless God, for enabling me, in the station of a wife, to do my duty, and now that I am a widow, I submit to His will. May I still be preserved by the arm of Divine Power; may I never forget the tender mercies of my God, the remembrance of which often boweth my soul in humility before His throne, and I cry, "Lord! what was I, that Thou shouldst have revealed to my soul the knowledge of Thy truth, and have done so much for one who deserved Thy displeasure? Mayst Thou, O God, be glorified, and I abased. It is Thy own works that praise Thee; and, of a truth, to the humble soul, Thou makest every bitter thing sweet."[7]

[7] The widow paid her husband's debts (nearly 80 pounds) by teaching school and sewing, and in 1746, she married Aaron Ashbridge. In 1753 she went to Ireland on a religious mission. There she became ill and died nearly two years later after a long and painful illness.

CHARLES CHAUNCY

(1705–1789)

Charles Chauncy, grandson of the second president of Harvard, is a key figure in the transition from seventeenth-century Puritan Calvinism to the liberal theology that developed into Boston Unitarianism. At his ordination in the First Church of Boston in 1724, Cotton Mather gave the right hand of fellowship, and near the end of his long career Chauncy served as one of the moral leaders of the American Revolution.

Chauncy had begun as an orthodox Calvinist minister, and he remained for decades a firm trinitarian, capable of preaching a stern warning to sinners after a major earthquake in the 1750's. But he was appalled by the excesses of the Great Awakening. His revulsion was given a personal motive when one "enthusiastical" revivalist came to

For Chauncy's life see Edward Griffin, "A Biography of Charles Chauncy," unpublished dissertation, 1966, and the earlier Williston Walker, *Ten New England Leaders,* 1901. See also Alan Heimert, *Religion and the American Mind: From the Great Awakening to the Revolution,* 1966.

The text is from the first edition, Boston, 1742.

the door of Chauncy's house and warned Chauncy that he not only was unqualified to preach but was bound for Hell. Chauncy became the most effective antagonist to Jonathan Edwards in published controversy over the emotional methods and results of the revival. Although Edwards agreed that many excesses, including some frighteningly destructive ones, accompanied the revival, he was more concerned with the "distinguishing marks of a work of the Spirit of God" than with the popular misreading of those signs or the Satanic counterfeit of them. Chauncy came more and more to insist on "reasonable" religion and to condemn the self-indulgence and the destructiveness of "enthusiasm," which in those days meant an excess of emotion.

It is a mistake to assume, as some readers have done, that Chauncy used reason and Edwards relied on emotion. Their disagreement was rather that Edwards' cogent argument led him inexorably to center the religious life in a total change in the affections. Chauncy was strongly influenced not only by rational argument but also by a simple conviction that a certain decorum must hold in truly religious conduct and that God, though omnipotent, chose to treat human beings as rational beings. This kind of emphasis led him long after the Great Awakening eventually to reject the sternly punishing God of the Puritans as a shocking libel, a monstrous invention. He became increasingly concerned with benevolence as a characteristic of the Deity, and in 1784 he published anonymously an essay called *The Benevolence of the Deity,* one of the precursors of American Unitarianism.

During the Great Awakening, Chauncy published controversial works in answer to Jonathan Edwards and the English Methodist George Whitefield. Besides the sermon reprinted here, his major challenge to Edwards is *Seasonable Thoughts on The State of Religion in New England,* 1743.

From Enthusiasm Described and Caution'd Against[1]

I COR. XIV. 37

If any man among you think himself to be a PROPHET, *or* SPIRITUAL, *let him acknowledge that the things that I write unto you are the commandments of the* LORD.

Many things were amiss in the *Church* of *Corinth,* when *Paul* wrote this Epistle to them. There were envyings, strife and divisions among them, on account of their ministers. Some cried up one, others another: one said, I am

---

[1] Boston, 1742.

of Paul, another I am of Appollos. They had formed themselves into parties, and each party so admired the teacher they followed, as to reflect unjust contempt on the other.

Nor was this their only fault. A spirit of pride prevailed exceedingly among them. They were conceited of their gifts, and too generally disposed to make an ostentatious show of them. From this vainglorious temper proceeded the forwardness of those that had the *gift* of *tongues*, to speak in languages which others did not understand, to the disturbance, rather than edification of the church: and from the same principle it arose, that they spake not by turns, but several at once, in the same place of worship, to the introducing such confusion, that they were in danger of being thought mad.

Nor were they without some pretense to justify these disorders. Their great plea was, that in these things they were guided by the Spirit, acted under His immediate influence and direction. This seems plainly insinuated in the words I have read to you. "If any man think himself to be a prophet, or spiritual, let him acknowledge that the things that I write unto you are the commandments of the Lord." As if the apostle had said, you may imagine yourselves to be *spiritual* men, to be under a divine afflatus in what you do; but 'tis all imagination, mere pretense, unless you pay a due regard to the *commandments* I have here *wrote to you;* receiving them not as the *word of man, but of* God. Make trial of your spiritual pretenses by this rule: If you can submit to it, and will order your conduct by it, well; otherwise you only cheat yourselves, while you think yourselves to be *spirtual* men, or *prophets:* you are nothing better than enthusiasts; your being acted by Spirit, immediately guided and influenced by Him, is mere pretense; you have no good reason to believe any such thing.

From the words thus explained, I shall take occasion to discourse to you upon the following particulars.

    I. I shall give you some account of *enthusiasm,* in its *nature* and *influence.*

   II. Point you to a rule by which you may judge of persons, whether they are under the influence of *enthusiasm.*

 III. Say what may be proper to guard you against this unhappy turn of mind.

The whole will then be followed with some suitable Application

I. I am in the first place, to give you some account of *enthusiasm*. And as this a thing much talked of at present, more perhaps than at any other time that has passed over us, it will not be thought unseasonable, if I take some pains to let you into a true understanding of it.

The word, from its etymology, carries in it a good meaning, as signifying *inspiration from* God: in which sense, the prophets under the Old Testament, and the apostles under the New, might properly be called *enthusiasts*. For they were under a divine influence, spake as moved by the HOLY GHOST, and did such things as can be accounted for in no way, but by recurring to an immediate extraordinary power, present with them.

But the word is more commonly used in a bad sense, as intending an *imaginary*, not a *real* inspiration: according to which sense, the *enthusiast* is one, who has a conceit of himself as a person favored with the extraordinary presence of the *deity*. He mistakes the workings of his own passions for divine communications, and fancies himself immediately inspired by the SPIRIT of GOD, when all the while, he is under no other influence than that of an over-heated imagination.

The cause of this *enthusiasm* is a bad temperament of the blood and spirits; 'tis properly a disease, a sort of madness: and there are few; perhaps none at all, but are subject to it, tho' none are so much in danger of it as those, in whom *melancholy* is the prevailing ingredient in their constitution. In these it often reigns; and sometimes to so great a degree, that they are really beside themselves, acting as truly by the blind impetus of a wild fancy, as tho' they had neither reason nor understanding.

And various are the ways in which their *enthusiasm* discovers itself.

Sometimes, it may be seen in their countenance. A certain wildness is discernible in their general look and air; especially when their imaginations are moved and fired.

Sometimes, it strangely loosens their tongues, and gives them such an energy, as well as fluency and volubility in speaking, as they themselves, by their utmost efforts, can't so much as imitate, when they are not under the enthusiastic influence.

Sometimes, it affects their bodies, throws them into convulsions and distortions, into quakings and tremblings. This was formerly common among the people called *Quakers*. I was myself, when a lad, an eyewitness to such violent agitations and foamings, in a boisterous female speaker, as I could not behold but with surprise and wonder.

Sometimes, it will unaccountably mix itself with their conduct, and give it such a tincture of that which is freakish or furious, as none can have an idea of, but those who have seen the behavior of a person in a frenzy.

Sometimes, it appears in their imaginary peculiar intimacy with heaven. They are, in their own opinion, the special favorites of GOD, have more familiar converse with Him than other good men, and receive immediate, extraordinary communications from Him. The thoughts, which suddenly rise up in their minds, they take for suggestions of the SPIRIT; their very fancies are divine illuminations; nor are they strongly inclined to anything, but 'tis an impulse from GOD, a plain revelation of His will.

And what extravagances, in this temper of mind, are they not capable of, and under the specious pretext too of paying obedience to the authority of

GOD? Many have fancied themselves acting by immediate warrant from heaven, while they have been committing the most undoubted wickedness. There is indeed scarce anything so wild, either in *speculation* or *practice*, but they have given into it: they have, in many instances, been blasphemers of GOD, and open disturbers of the peace of the world.

But in nothing does the *enthusiasm* of these persons discover itself more, than in the disregard they express to the dictates of *reason*. They are above the force of argument, beyond conviction from a calm and sober address to their understandings. As for them, they are distinguished persons; GOD himself speaks inwardly and immediately to their souls. "They see the light infused into their understandings, and cannot be mistaken; 'tis clear and visible there, like the light of bright sunshine; shows itself and needs no other proof but its own evidence. They feel the hand of GOD moving them within, and the impulses of His SPIRIT; and cannot be mistaken in what they feel. Thus they support themselves, and are sure reason hath nothing to do with what they see and feel. What they have a sensible experience of, admits no doubt, needs no probation".[2] And in vain will you endeavor to convince such persons of any mistakes they are fallen into. They are certainly in the right, and know themselves to be so. They have the SPIRIT opening their understandings and revealing the truth to them. They believe only as He has taught them: and to suspect they are in the wrong is to do dishonor to the SPIRIT; 'tis to oppose His dictates, to set up their own wisdom in opposition to His, and shut their eyes against that light with which He has shined into their souls. They are not therefore capable of being argued with; you had as good reason with the wind.

And as the natural consequence of their being thus sure of everything, they are not only infinitely stiff and tenacious, but impatient of contradiction, censorious and uncharitable: they encourage a good opinion of none but such as are in their way of thinking and speaking. Those, to be sure, who venture to debate with them about their errors and mistakes, their weaknesses and indiscretions, run the hazard of being stigmatized by them as poor unconverted wretches, without the SPIRIT, under the government of carnal reason, enemies to GOD and religion, and in the broad way to hell.

They are likewise positive and dogmatical, vainly fond of their own imaginations, and invincibly set upon propagating them: and in the doing of this, their powers being awakened, and put as it were, upon the stretch, from the strong impressions they are under, that they are authorized by the immediate command of GOD Himself, they sometimes exert themselves with a sort of *ecstatic* violence: and 'tis this that gives them the advantage, among the less knowing and judicious, of those who are modest, suspicious of themselves, and not too assuming in matters of conscience and salvation. The extraor-

[2] John Locke, *An Essay Concerning Human Understanding*, Book IV, Ch. 19.

dinary fervor of their minds, accompanied with uncommon bodily motions, and an excessive confidence and assurance gains them great reputation among the populace; who speak of them as *men* of GOD in distinction from all others, and too commonly hearken to, and revere their dictates, as tho' they really were, as they pretend, immediately communicated to them from the DIVINE SPIRIT.

This is the nature of *enthusiasm*, and this its operation, in a less or greater degree, in all who are under the influence of it. 'Tis a kind of religious frenzy, and evidently discovers itself to be so, whenever it rises to any great height.

And much to be pitied are the persons who are seized with it. Our compassion commonly works towards those, who, while under distraction, fondly imagine themselves to be kings and emperors: and the like pity is really due to those, who, under the power of *enthusiasm*, fancy themselves to be *prophets; inspired of God*, and *immediately called and commissioned by Him to deliver His messages to the world:* and tho' they should run into disorders, and act in a manner that cannot but be condemned, they should notwithstanding be treated with tenderness and lenity; and the rather, because they don't commonly act so much under the influence of a *bad mind*, as a *deluded imagination*. And who more worthy of Christian pity than those, who, under the notion of serving GOD and the interest of religion, are filled with zeal, and exert themselves to the utmost, while all the time they are hurting and wounding the very cause they take so much pains to advance. 'Tis really a pitiable case: and tho' the honesty of their intentions won't legitimate their bad actions, yet it very much alleviates their guilt: we should think as favorably of them as may be, and be disposed to judge with mercy, as we would hope to obtain mercy.

But I come

II. In the second place, to point you to a *rule* by which you may judge of persons, whether they are *enthusiasts*, mere pretenders to the immediate guidance and influence of the SPIRIT. And this is, in general, *a regard to the Bible, an acknowledgment that the things therein contained are the commandments of GOD*. This is the rule in the text. And 'tis an infallible rule of trial in this matter: we need not fear judging amiss, while we keep closely to it.

'Tis true, it won't certainly follow, that a man, pretending to be a *prophet*, or *spiritual*, really is so, if he owns the *Bible*, and receives the truths therein revealed as the mind of GOD: but the conclusion, on the other hand, is clear and certain; if he pretends to be conducted by the SPIRIT, and disregards the Scripture, pays no due reverence to *the things there delivered as the commandments of GOD*, he is a mere pretender, be his pretenses ever so bold and confident, or made with ever so much seeming seriousness, gravity, or solemnity. . . .

And it deserves particular consideration, whether the suffering, much more the encouraging WOMEN, yea, GIRLS to speak in the assemblies for religious worship, is not a plain breach of that *commandment of the* LORD,[3] wherein it is said, "Let your WOMEN keep silence in the churches; for it is not permitted to them to speak—it is a shame: for WOMEN to speak in the church." After such an express constitution, designedly made to restrain WOMEN from speaking in the church, with what face can such a practice be pleaded for? They may pretend, they are moved by the SPIRIT, and such a thought of themselves may be encouraged by others; but if the apostle *spake by the* SPIRIT, when he delivered *this commandment,* they can't *act by the* SPIRIT, when they break it. 'Tis a plain case, these FEMALE EXHORTERS are condemned by the apostle; and if 'tis the *commandment of the* LORD, that they should not speak, they are *spiritual* only in their own thoughts, while they attempt to do so.

The last thing I shall mention as written by the apostle, is that which obliges to a *just decorum in speaking* in the *house of GOD.* It was an extravagance these *Corinthians* had fallen into, their speaking many of them together, and upon different things, while in the same place of worship. "How is it, brethren," says the apostle? "When ye come together, everyone hath a psalm; hath a doctrine; hath a tongue; hath a revelation; hath an interpretation." It was this that introduced the confusion and noise, upon which the apostle declares, if an unbeliever should come in among them, he would take them to be mad.[4] And the *commandment* he gives them to put a stop to this disorder, is, that they should *speak in course, one by one,* and so as that *things might be done to edifying.*[5]

And whoever the persons are, who will not acknowledge what the apostle has here said is the *commandment of* GOD, and act accordingly, are influenced by another spirit than that which moved in him, be their impressions or pretenses what they will. The disorder of EXHORTING, and PRAYING, and SINGING, and LAUGHING, *in the same house of worship, at one and the same time,* is as great as was that, the apostle blames in the *church of Corinth:* and whatever the persons, guilty of such gross irregularity may imagine, and however they may plead their being under the influence of the SPIRIT, and moved by Him, 'tis evidently a breach upon common order and decency; yea, a direct violation of the *commandment of* GOD, written on purpose to prevent such disorders: and to pretend the direction of the SPIRIT in such a flagrant instance of extravagant conduct, is to reproach the blessed SPIRIT, who is not, as the apostle's phrase is, "the author of confusion, but of peace, as in all the churches of the saints."

[3] I Corinthians 14:34.　　　　　　　[5] 26, 27.
[4] v. 23.

In these, and all other instances, let us compare men's pretenses to the SPIRIT by the SCRIPTURE: and if their conduct is such as can't be reconciled with an *acknowledgment of the things therein revealed, as the commandments of* GOD, their pretenses are vain, they are *prophets* and *spiritual,* only in their own proud imaginations. I proceed now to

III. The third thing, which is to caution you against giving way to *enthusiastic impressions.* And here much might be said,

I might warn you from the *dishonor* it reflects upon the SPIRIT of GOD. And perhaps none have more reproached the blessed SPIRIT, than men pretending to be under His extraordinary guidance and direction. The veriest fancies, the vainest imaginations, the strongest delusions, they have fathered on Him. There is scarce any absurdity in *principle,* or irregularity in *practice,* but He has been made the patron of it.—And what a stone of stumbling has the wildness of *enthusiasm* been to multitudes in the world? What prejudices have been hereby excited in their minds against the very being of the SPIRIT? What temptations have been thrown in their way to dispute His OFFICE as the SANCTIFIER and COMFORTER of GOD's people? And how have they been overcome to disown HIS WORK, when it has been really wrought in the hearts of men?

I might also warn you from the damage it has done in the world. No greater mischiefs have arisen from any quarter. It is indeed the genuine source of infinite evil. POPERY itself hasn't been the mother of more and greater blasphemies and abominations. It has made strong attempts to destroy all property, to make all things common, *wives* as well as *goods.*—It has promoted faction and contention; filled the church oftentimes with confusion, and the state sometimes with general disorder.—It has, by its pretended spiritual interpretations, made void the most undoubted laws of GOD. It has laid aside the *gospel sacraments* as weak and carnal things; yea, this *superior light within* has, in the opinion of thousands, rendered the *Bible* a *useless dead letter.*—It has made men fancy themselves to be *prophets* and *apostles;* yea, some have taken themselves to be CHRIST JESUS; yea, the blessed GOD Himself. It has, in one word, been a pest to the church in all ages, as great an enemy to real and solid religion, as perhaps the grossest *infidelity.*[6]

I might go on and warn you from the danger of it to yourselves. If you should once come under the influence of it, none can tell whither it would carry you. There is nothing so wild and frantic but you may be reconciled to it. And if this should be your case, your recovery to a right mind would be one of the most difficult things in nature. There is no coming at a thorough-paced *enthusiast.* He is proof against every method of dealing with him.

[6] Undoubted instances of these, and many other things of a like nature, are well known to such as are, in any measure, acquainted with the *history* of the *church.* [Chauncy's note.]

Would you apply to him from reason? That he esteems a carnal thing, and flees from it as from the most dangerous temptation. Would you rise higher, and speak to him from *Scripture?* It will be to as little purpose. For if he pays any regard to it, 'tis only as it falls in with his own preconceived notions. He interprets the Scripture by *impulses* and *impressions,* and sees no meaning in it, only as he explains it from his own fancy.—'Tis infinitely difficult [to] convince a man grown giddy and conceited under the false notion, that the good SPIRIT teaches him everything. His apprehended inspiration sets him above all means of conviction. He rather despises than hearkens to the most reasonable advices that can be given him.

But as the most suitable guard against the first tendencies towards *enthusiasm,* let me recommend to you the following words of counsel.

1. Get a true understanding of the *proper work of the* SPIRIT; and don't place it in those things wherein the Gospel does not make it to consist. The work of the SPIRIT is different now from what it was in the first days of Christianity. Men were then favored with the extraordinary presence of the SPIRIT. He came upon them in miraculous gifts and powers; as a spirit of prophecy, of knowledge, of revelation, of tongues, of miracles: but the SPIRIT is not now to be expected in these ways. His grand business lies in preparing men's minds for the grace of GOD, by true *humiliation,* from an apprehension of sin, and the necessity of a *Saviour;* then in working in them *faith* and *repentance,* and such a *change* as shall *turn them from the power of sin and Satan unto* GOD; and in fine, by carrying on the good work He has begun in them; assisting them in duty, strengthening them against temptation, and in a word, preserving them blameless thro' faith unto salvation: and all this He does by the *word* and *prayer,* as the great means in the accomplishment of these purposes of mercy.

Herein, in general, consists the work of the SPIRIT. It does not lie in giving men *private revelations,* but in opening their minds to understand the *public ones* contained in the Scripture. It does not lie in *sudden impulses* and *impressions,* in *immediate calls* and *extraordinary missions.* Men mistake the business of the SPIRIT, if they understand by it such things as these. And 'tis, probably, from such unhappy mistakes, that they are at first betrayed into *enthusiasm.* Having a wrong notion of the *work of* the SPIRIT, 'tis no wonder if they take the uncommon sallies of their own minds for His influences.

. . .

3. Make use of the *Reason* and *Understanding* GOD has given you. This may be thought an ill-advised direction, but 'tis as necessary as either of the former. Next to the *Scripture,* there is no greater enemy to *enthusiasm,* than *reason.* 'Tis indeed impossible a man should be an *enthusiast,* who is in the just exercise of his understanding; and 'tis because men don't pay a due

regard to the sober dictates of a well informed mind, that they are led aside by the delusions of a vain imagination. Be advised then to show yourselves men, to make use of your reasonable powers; and not act as the *horse* or *mule,* as tho' you had no understanding.

'Tis true, you must not go about to set up your own *reason* in *opposition* to *revelation:* nor may you entertain a thought of making *reason* your *rule* instead of *Scripture.*[7] The Bible, as I said before, is the *great rule* of religion, the grand test in matters of salvation: but then you must use your reason in order to understand the *Bible:* nor is there any other possible way, in which, as a reasonable creature, you should come to an understanding of it.

You are, it must be acknowledged, in a corrupt state. The fall has introduced great weakness into your reasonable nature. You can't be too sensible of this; nor of the danger you are in of making a wrong judgment, thro' prejudice, carelessness, and the undue influence of sin and lust. And to prevent this, you can't be too solicitous to get your *nature sanctified:* nor can you depend too strongly upon the divine grace to assist you in your search after truth: and 'tis in the way of due dependence on GOD, and the influences of His SPIRIT, that I advise you to the use of your reason: and in this way, you must make use of it. How else will you know what is a revelation from GOD? What should hinder your entertaining the same thought of a *pretended* revelation, as of a *real* one, but your reason discovering the falsehood of the one, and the truth of the other? And when in the enjoyment of an undoubted revelation from GOD, as in the case of the *Scripture,* how will you understand its meaning, if you throw by your reason? How will you determine, that this, and not that, is its true sense, in this and the other place? Nay, if no reasoning is to be made use of, are not all the senses that can be put on Scripture equally proper? Yea, may not the most contrary senses be received at the same time, since reason only can point out the inconsistency between them? And what will be sufficient to guard you against the most monstrous extravagancies, in *principle* as well as *practice,* if you give up your understandings? What have you left, in this case, to be a check to the wantoness of your imagination? What should hinder your following every idle fancy, 'till you have lost yourselves in the wilds of falsehood and inconsistency?

You may, it is true, misuse your reason: and this is a consideration that should put you upon a due care, that you may use it well; but no argument why you should not use it at all: and indeed, if you should throw by your

[7] In this warning and the rest of the paragraph, Chauncy expresses the essential terms of the battle that soon came to preoccupy Unitarians as they struggled to liberate themselves from Puritan dogma without encour- aging infidelity. One can see later versions of this struggle in Channing's "Unitarian Christianity" (below, pp. 1561 ff.) and Emerson's Divinity School address (below, pp. 1587 ff.).

reason as a useless thing, you would at once put yourselves in the way of all manner of delusion.

But, it may be, you will say, you have committed yourselves to the guidance of the SPIRIT; which is the best preservative. Herein you have done well; nothing can be objected against this method of conduct: only take heed of mistakes, touching the SPIRIT's *guidance*. Let me inquire of you, how is it the SPIRIT preserves from delusion? Is it not by opening the understanding, and enabling the man, in the due use of his reason, to perceive the truth of the things of GOD and religion? Most certainly: and, if you think of being led by the SPIRIT without understanding, or in opposition to it, you deceive yourselves. The SPIRIT of GOD deals with men as *reasonable* creatures: and they ought to deal with themselves in like manner. And while they do thus, making a wise and good use of the understanding GOD has given them, they will take a proper means to prevent their falling into delusions; nor will there be much danger of their being led aside by *enthusiastic* heat and imagination.

4. You must not lay too great stress upon the *workings* of your *passions* and *affections*. These will be excited, in a less or greater degree, in the business of religion: and 'tis proper they should. The passions, when suitably moved, tend mightily to awaken the *reasonable powers,* and put them upon a lively and vigorous exercise. And this is their proper use: and when addressed to, and excited to this purpose, they may be of good service: whereas we shall mistake the right use of the passions, if we place our religion *only* or *chiefly,* in the heat and fervor of them. The *soul* is the *man:* and unless the *reasonable nature* is suitably wrought upon, the *understanding* enlightened, the *judgment* convinced, the *will* persuaded, and the *mind* entirely changed, it will avail but to little purpose; tho' the passions should be set all in a blaze. This therefore you should be most concerned about. And if while you are solicitous that you may be in transports of affection, you neglect your more noble part, your reason and judgment, you will be in great danger of being carried away by your imaginations. This indeed leads directly to *enthusiasm:* and you will in vain, endeavor to preserve yourselves from the influence of it, if you aren't duly careful to keep your passions in their proper place, under the government of a well informed understanding. While the passions are uppermost, and bear the chief sway over a man, he is in an unsafe state: none knows what he may be brought to. You can't therefore be too careful to keep your passions under the regimen of a *sober judgment.* 'Tis indeed a matter of necessity, as you would not be led aside by delusion and fancy.

· · ·

[Use] 2. Let none, from what has been offered, entertain prejudices in their minds against the *operations* of the SPIRIT. There is such a thing as His influence upon the hearts of men. No consistent sense can be put upon a great part of the *Bible,* unless this be acknowledged for a truth: nor is it any objection against its being so, that there has been a great deal of *enthusiasm* in the world, many who have mistaken the motions of their own passions for divine operations. This, it must be acknowledged, should make us cautious; putting us upon a careful examination of whatever offers itself, as a communication from the SPIRIT, that we deceive not ourselves: but it's no argument, why we should conceive a flighty thought, either of the SPIRIT, or His influences, really made upon the minds of men. Much less is it a just ground of exception against the SPIRIT's *operations,* that they may be counterfeited; that men may make an appearance, as if they were acted by the SPIRIT, when, all the while, they have no other view in their pretenses, but to serve themselves. This has often been the case; and points it out as a matter of necessity, that we take heed to ourselves, if we would not be imposed upon by a *fair show,* and *good words:* but at the same time, 'tis no reason why we should think the worse of the blessed SPIRIT, or of those influences that are really *His.*

Let us be upon our guard as to this matter. Many, from what they have seen or heard of the strange conduct of men, pretending to be under *divine impressions,* have had their minds insensibly leavened with prejudices against the things of the SPIRIT. O let it be our care, that we be not thus wrought upon! And the rather, lest it should prove the ruin of our souls. This, perhaps, we may not be afraid of: but the danger is great, if we take up wrong notions of the SPIRIT, or encourage an unbecoming thought of His influences in the business of salvation, lest we should grieve the *good* SPIRIT, and He should leave us to perish in a state of alienation from GOD, and true holiness.

'Tis worthy our particular remark, it is by the powerful operation of the Holy SPIRIT on the hearts of men, that they are changed from the love and practice of sin, to the love and practice of holiness; and have those tempers formed in them, whereby they are made meet for the glory to be hereafter revealed: nor can this be done, in any way, without the *special influence* of the blessed SPIRIT.

And is it likely, *He* should be present with men to such gracious purposes, if they suffer their minds to be impressed with contemptuous thoughts of Him? If they begin to call in question His *office,* as the *great dispenser of divine grace,* or look upon His operations as all delusion and imagination.

·   ·   ·

3. Let not any think *ill* of religion, because of the *ill* representation that is made of it by *enthusiasts.* There may be danger of this; especially, in regard of those who have not upon their minds a serious sense of GOD and the things

of another world. They may be ready to judge of religion from the *copy* given them of it, by those who are too much led by their fancies; and to condemn it, in the gross, as a wild, imaginary, inconsistent thing. But this is to judge too hastily and rashly. Religion ought not to suffer in the opinion of any, because of the imprudencies or extravagancies of those, who call themselves the friends of it. Anything may be abused: nor is there anything, but has actually been abused. And why should any think the worse of religion, because some who make more than ordinary pretenses to it, set it forth in an ugly light by their conduct relative to it?

There is such a thing as real religion, let the conduct of men be what it will; and 'tis, in its nature, a sober, calm, reasonable thing: nor is it an objection of any weight against the sobriety or reasonableness of it, that there have been *enthusiasts,* who have acted as tho' it was a wild, imaginary business. We should not make our estimate of religion as exhibited in the behavior of men of a *fanciful* mind; to be sure, we should not take up an ill opinion of it, because in the example they give of it, it don't appear so amiable as we might expect. This is unfair. We should rather judge of it from the conduct of men of a *sound judgment;* whose lives have been such a uniform, beautiful transcript of that which is just and good, that we can't but think well of religion, as displayed in their example.

.   .   .

II
Early Virginians

Less heavily settled than New England in the seventeenth century, less abundantly supplied with clerical graduates of English universities, and less dependent on religious controversies for the settlement of major public issues, Virginia developed a literary tradition more slowly and less intensively than did Massachusetts and Connecticut. In the early works of John Smith, moreover, and the historical prose of Robert Beverley and William Byrd II, the two best Virginian writers of the early eighteenth century, Virginians expressed a secular emphasis that gives a strikingly different cast to their literary tradition. Some excellent sermons were of course written and preached in seventeenth-century Virginia, and many of the planters were genuinely religious. But the characteristic expression that stands behind the great achievements of Virginia's culture in the late-eighteenth-century prose of Thomas Jefferson and James Madison is secular and relatively detached from the kind of anxious self-examination we have seen in New England writers from Shepard to Edwards.

JOHN SMITH

(1579-1631)

In legend, literature, and fact the first settlers of Jamestown, Virginia stand in sharp contrast to the dedicated Pilgrims whom William Brad-

The standard edition is *Travels and Works of Captain John Smith, President of Virginia and Admiral of New England, 1580-1631,* 2 vols., ed. Edwards Arber, re-edited with an introduction by A. G. Bradley, 1910.

Good background works are Samuel Eliot Morison, *The European Discovery of America: The Northern Voyages,* Moses Coit Tyler, *History of American Literature, 1607-1765,* 1878, 18-38; Philip Barbour, *The Three Worlds of Captain John Smith,* 1964; Frances Mossiter, *Pocahontas: The Life and The Legend, 1976.*

ford describes in *Of Plymouth Plantation,* but the Virginians suffered just as much in their first years as the Pilgrims did, and their survival was just as extraordinary. Smith's representation of himself and his fellow colonists differs strikingly from Bradford's account. Here, of course, there is no congregational community before the emigration, nor any heavy emphasis on religious motivation. Too few practical workers belong to the original group of emigrants, and too many have fantastic hopes of easy wealth. The leader, moreover, is a swashbuckling character whose third-person description of his own exploits sounds more like the bravado of Miles Standish than the cool self-effacement of Bradford. Yet the first English colony did survive at Jamestown, and after we discount some of Smith's inventions and exaggerations, we must allow him great credit for the achievement.

Smith remained in Virginia for only two-and-a-half years, whereupon he returned for five years to England. He wrote his *A True Relation of Virginia* in the first year of colonization and, after exploring the coast of New England in 1614, he published *A Description of New England* (1616). Eight years later he published *The General History of Virginia, New England, and the Summer Isles,* from which our selection is taken.

Trained as a soldier, and tested in continental wars and in capture by pirates, Smith was also an able writer. We include him here because the legend of his rescue by Pocahontas, and his confrontation with the Indians, contribute to American letters a myth different from that of the suffering Pilgrims but equally long-lived and equally characteristic of English settlement in the wilderness.

From The General History of New England

[CAPTAIN SMITH AND POCAHONTAS]

[As Henry Adams demonstrated in his first professional historical publication, John Smith embellished his earlier account of Pocahontas in a way that made himself seem more heroic and the entire episode more exciting. Smith, like Bradford, wrote of himself in the third person and became a prominent figure in the legend of American character and American origins. As Robert Beverley tells us Pocahontas, having been brought to England, died there before Smith could arrange to see her again. She and Squanto, in Bradford's history, are precursors of other Indian and black characters who save the lives of white characters in American literature.]

The next voyage he proceeded so far that with much labor by cutting of trees asunder he made his passage; but when his barge could pass no farther, he left her in a broad bay out of danger of shot, commanding none should go

Ætatis suæ 21. Aº.1616.

Matoaks als Rebecka daughter to the mighty Prince
Powhatan Emperour of Attanoughkomouck als Virginia
converted and baptized in the Chriſtian faith, and
Wife to the worth Mr Tho: Rolff.

An anonymous picture of Pocahontas, 1616. *(National Portrait Gallery, Smithsonian Institutition, Washington, D.C.)*

ashore till his return: himself with two English and two savages went up higher in a canoe, but he was not long absent, but his men went ashore, whose want of government, gave both occasion and opportunity to the savages to surprise one *George Cassen*, whom they slew, and much failed not to have[1] cut of[f] the boat and all the rest.

[1] "Much failed not to have" means "almost."

Smith little dreaming of that accident, being got to the marshes at the river's head, twenty miles in the desert, had his two men slain (as is supposed) sleeping by the canoe, whilst himself by fowling sought them victual, who finding he was beset with 200 savages, two of them he slew, still defending himself, with the aid of a savage his guid[e], whom he bound to his arm with his garters, and used him as a buckler, yet he was shot in his thigh a little, and had many arrows that stuck in his clothes but no great hurt, till at last they took him prisoner.

When this news came to *Jamestown*, much was their sorrow for his loss, few expecting what ensued.

Six or seven weeks those barbarians kept him prisoner, many strange triumphs and conjurations they made of him, yet he so demeaned himself amongst them, as he not only diverted them from surprising the fort, but procured his own liberty, and got himself and his company such estimation amongst them, that those savages admired him more than their own *Quiyouckosucks*.

The manner how they used and delivered him, is as followeth.

The savages having drawn from *George Cassen* whether Captain *Smith* was gone, prosecuting that opportunity they followed him with 300 bowmen, conducted by the King of *Pamaunkee*, who in divisions searching the turnings of the river, found Robinson and Emry by the fireside, those they shot full of arrows and slew. Then finding the Captain, as is said, that used the savage that was his guide as his shield (three of them being slain and divers other so galled) all the rest would not come near him. Thinking thus to have returned to his boat, regarding them, as he marched, more than his way, [Smith] slipped up to the middle in an oozy creek & his savage with him, yet durst they not come to him till being near dead with cold, he threw away his arms. Then according to their composition they drew him forth and led him to the fire, where his men were slain. Diligently they chafed his benumbed limbs.

He demanding for their captain, they showed him *Opechankanough*, King of Pamaunkee, to whom he gave a round ivory double compass dial. Much they marveled at the playing of the fly and needle, which they could see so plainly, and yet not touch it, because of the glass that covered them. But when he demonstrated by that globe-like jewel, the roundness of the earth, and skies, the sphere of the sun, moon, and stars, and how the sun did chase the night round about the world continually; the greatness of the land and sea, the diversity of nations, variety of complexions, and how we were to them antipodes, and many other such like matters, they all stood as amazed with admiration.

Notwithstanding, within an hour after they tied him to a tree, and as many as could stand about him prepared to shoot him, but the King holding up the compass in his hand, they all laid down their bows and arrows, and in a triumphant manner led him to Orapaks, where he was after their manner kindly feasted, and well used.

Their order in conducting him was thus; drawing themselves all in file, the King in the midst had all their pieces and swords borne before him. Captain *Smith* was led after him by three great savages, holding him fast by each arm: and on each side six went in file with their arrows nocked. But arriving at the town (which was but only thirty or forty hunting houses made of mats, which they remove as they please, as we our tents) all the women and children staring to behold him, the soldiers first all in file performed the form of a Bissom[2] so well as could be, and on each flank, officers as sergeants to see them keep their orders. A good time they continued this exercise, and then cast themselves in a ring, dancing in such several postures, and singing and yelling out such hellish notes and screeches; being strangely painted, every one his quiver of arrows, and at his back a club; on his arm a fox or an otter's skin, or some such matter for his vambrace;[3] their heads and shoulders painted red, with oil and *Pocones*[4] mingled together, which scarlet-like color made an exceeding handsome show; his bow in his hand, and the skin of a bird with her wings abroad dried, tied on his head, a piece of copper, a white shell, a long feather, with a small rattle growing at the tail of their snakes tied to it, or some such like toy. All this while *Smith* and the King stood in the midst guarded, as before is said; and after three dances they all departed. *Smith* they conducted to a long house, where thirty or forty tall fellows did guard him; and ere long more bread and venison was brought him than would have served twenty men, I think his stomach at that time was not very good; what he left they put in baskets and tied over his head. About midnight they set the meat again before him, all this time not one of them would eat a bit with him, till the next morning they brought him as much more, and then did they eat all the old, and reserved the new as they had done the other, which made him think they would fat him to eat him. Yet in this desperate estate to defend him from the cold, one *Maocassater* brought him his gown, in requital of some beads and toys Smith had given him at his first arrival in Virginia.

Two days after, a man would have slain him (but that the guard prevented it) for the death of his son, to whom they conducted him to recover the poor man then breathing his last. *Smith* told them that at *Jamestown* he had a water would do it, if they would let him fetch it, but they would not permit that; but made all the preparations they could to assault *Jamestown*, craving his advice, and for recompense he should have life, liberty, land, and women. In part of a table book he wrote his mind to them at the fort, what

[2] A military formation.

[3] Armor to protect the forearm.

[4] Bloodroot.

was intended, how they should follow that direction to affright the messengers, and without fail send him such things as he wrote for, and an inventory with them. The difficulty and danger he told the savages, of the mines, great guns, and other engines, exceedingly affrighted them; yet according to his request they went to Jamestown, in as bitter weather as could be of frost and snow, and within three days returned with an answer.

But when they came to *Jame[s] town,* seeing men sally out as he had told them they would, they fled; yet in the night they came again to the same place where he had told them they should receive an answer, and such things as he had promised them; which they found accordingly, and with which they returned with no small expedition, to the wonder of them all that heard it, that he could either divine, or the paper could speak.

Then they led him to the *Youthtanunds,* the *Mattapanients,* the *Payankatanks,* the *Nantaughtacunds,* and *Onawmanients* upon the rivers of *Rappahannock,* and *Potomac,* over all those rivers, and back again by divers other several nations, to the King's habitation at Pamaunkee, where they entertained him with most strange and fearful conjurations;

As if near led to hell,
Amongst the devils to dwell.

Not long after, early in a morning a great fire was made in a longhouse, and a mat spread on the one side, as on the other; on the one they caused him to sit, and all the guard went out of the house, and presently came skipping in a great grim fellow, all painted over with coal, mingled with oil; and many snakes' and weasels' skins stuffed with moss, and all their tails tied together, so as they met on the crown of his head in a tassel; and round about the tassel was as a coronet of feathers, the skins hanging round about his head, back, and shoulders, and in a manner covered his face; with a hellish voice, and a rattle in his hand. With most strange gestures and passions he began his invocation, and environed the fire with a circle of meal; which done, three more such like devils came rushing in with the like antique tricks, painted half black, half red: but all their eyes were painted white, and some red strokes like Mutchato's [mustachios] along their cheeks. Round about him those fiends danced a pretty while, and then came in three more as ugly as the rest, with red eyes, and white strokes over their black faces. At last they all sat down right against him, three of them on the one hand of the chief priest, and three on the other. Then all with their rattles began a song, which ended, the chief priest laid down five wheat corns; then straining his arms and hands with such violence that he sweat, and his veins swelled, he began a short oration; at the conclusion they all gave a short groan, and they laid down three grains more. After that, began their song again, and then another oration, ever laying down so many corns as before, till they had twice encircled the fire; that done, they took a bunch of little sticks prepared for that purpose, continuing still their devotion, and at the end of every song and oration, they laid down a stick betwixt the divisions of corn. Till night, neither he nor they did either eat or drink; and then they feasted merrily, with the best provisions they could make. Three days they used this ceremony; the meaning whereof, they told him, was to know if he intended them well or no. The circle of meal signified their country, the circles of corn the bounds of the sea, and the sticks his country. They imagined the world to be flat and round, like a trencher, and they in the midst.

After this they brought him a bag of gunpowder, which they carefully preserved till the next spring, to plant as they did their corn; because they would be acquainted with the nature of that seed.

Opitchapam the King's brother, invited him to his house, where, with as many platters of bread, fowl, and wild beasts as did environ him, he bid him welcome; but not any of them would eat a bit with him, but put up all the remainder in baskets.

At his return to Opechancanough's, all the King's women, and their children, flocked about him for their parts; as a due by custom, to be merry with such fragments.

But his waking mind in hideous dreams did oft see wondrous shapes,
Of bodies strange, and huge in growth, and of stupendous makes.

At last they brought him to *Meronocomoco*, where was *Powhatan*, their emperor. Here more than two hundred of those grim courtiers stood wondering at him, as he had been a monster; till *Powhatan* and his train had put themselves in their greatest braveries. Before a fire upon a seat like a bedstead, he sat covered with a great robe, made of raccoon skins, and all the tails hanging by. On either hand did sit a young wench of 16 or 18 years, and along on each side the house, two rows of men, and behind them as many women, with all their heads and shoulders painted red; many of their heads bedecked with the white down of birds; but every one with something, and a great chain of white beads about their necks.

At his entrance before the King, all the people gave a great shout. The Queen of *Appamatuck* was appointed to bring him water to wash his hands, and another brought him a bunch of feathers, instead of a towel, to dry them: having feasted him after their best barbarous manner they could, a long consultation was held; but the conclusion was, two great stones were brought before Powhatan: then as many as could laid hands on him, dragged him to them, and thereon laid his head, and being ready with their clubs, to beat out his brains, *Pocahontas,* the King's dearest daughter, when no entreaty could prevail, got his head in her arms, and laid her own upon his to save him from death: whereat the Emperor was contented he should live to make him hatchets, and her bells, beads, and copper; for they thought him as well of all occupations as themselves. For the King himself will make his own robes, shoes, bows, arrows, pots; plant, hunt, or do any thing so well as the rest.

> They say he bore a pleasant show,
> But sure his heart was sad.
> For who can pleasant be, and rest,
> That lives in fear and dread:
> And having life suspected, doth
> It still suspected lead.

Two days after, *Powhatan,* having disguised himself in the most fearfulest manner he could, caused Captain *Smith* to be brought forth to a great house in the woods, and there upon a mat by the fire to be left alone. Not long after, from behind a mat that divided the house, was made the most dolefulest noise he ever heard; then *Powhatan,* more like a devil than a man, with some two hundred more as black as himself, came unto him and told him now they were friends, and presently he should go to *Jamestown,* to send him two great guns, and a grindstone, for which he would give him the country of *Capahowosick,* and for ever esteem him as his son *Nantaquoud.*

So to *Jamestown* with 12 guides *Powhatan* sent him. That night they quartered in the woods, he still expecting (as he had done all this long time of his imprisonment) every hour to be put to one death or other: for all their feasting. But almighty God (by His divine providence) had mollified the hearts of those stern barbarians with compassion. The next morning betimes they came to the fort; where *Smith,* having used the savages with what kindness he could, he showed *Rawhunt, Powhatan's* trusty servant, two demi-Culverings[5] and a millstone to carry *Powhatan:* they found them somewhat too heavy; but when they did see him discharge them, being loaded with stones, among the boughs of a great tree loaded with icicles, the ice and branches came so tumbling down, that the poor savages ran away half dead with fear. But at last we regained some conference with them, and gave them such toys; and sent to *Powhatan,* his women, and children such presents, as he gave them in general full content.

Now in *Jamestown* they were all in combustion, the strongest preparing once more to run away with the pinnace; which with the hazard of his life,

5 Cannon.

with Sakre falcon[6] and musket shot, *Smith* forced now the third time to stay or sink.

Some, no better then they should be, had plotted with the President, the next day to have put him to death by the Levitical law,[7] for the lives of *Robinson* and *Emry;* pretending the fault was his that had led them to their ends: but he quickly took such order with such lawyers, that he laid them by the heels till he sent some of them prisoners for *England.*

[6] Cannon.
[7] See Leviticus 24:17, which prescribes capital punishment for murder.

ROBERT BEVERLEY
(c. 1673–1722)

Like Governors Bradford, Winthrop, and Hutchinson in New England, Robert Beverley enters American literature as the historian of a colony in whose government he served. Beverley was born in Virginia, educated in England, and appointed and elected to various colonial offices, including the House of Burgesses, after his return. He wrote *The History and Present State of Virginia* during a long interlude in England from 1705 to 1706, allegedly to correct what he considered the outrageous errors in a work on the same subject by John Oldmixon.

The tone of Beverley's work is entirely different from that of his New England predecessors and contemporaries. Beverley represents himself as a literate, ironic gentleman whose indignant objection to the bickering of the founders, for example, must be expressed in the worldly-wise irony of an observer too shrewd to have believed that such gentlemen might be unselfish. And of course Beverley's view of history gives little space to Providence and none to the Devil. Beverley belongs to the generation of Cotton Mather, but the only wonders in this history are of the natural world, and the tone is closer to that of William Byrd than to Mather's. Beverley, though sometimes condescending toward the Indians, also portrays them as virtually noble savages.

The text is taken from *The History and Present State of Virginia,* ed. Louis B. Wright, 1968. Wright's introduction is a valuable critical essay, with some biographical information. The best critical study is in Lewis P. Simpson, *The Dispossessed Garden: Pastoral and History in Southern Literature,* 1975.

The History and Present State of Virginia

From CHAPTER I
SHOWING WHAT HAPPENED IN THE FIRST ATTEMPTS TO SETTLE VIRGINIA, BEFORE THE DISCOVERY OF CHESAPEAKE BAY

¶I. The learned and valiant Sir *Walter Raleigh* having entertained some deeper and more serious considerations upon the state of the earth, than most other men of his time, as may sufficiently appear by his incomparable book, *The History of the World:* and having laid together the many stories then in *Europe* concerning *America;* the native beauty, riches, and value of this part of the world; and the immense profits the *Spaniards* drew from a small settlement or two thereon made; resolved upon an adventure for further discoveries.

According to this purpose, in the year of our Lord, 1583, he got several men of great value and estate to join with him in an expedition of this nature: and for their encouragement obtained Letters Patents from Queen *Elizabeth*, bearing date the 25th of *March*, 1584, for turning their discoveries to their own advantage.

¶2. In *April* following they set out two small vessels under the command of Capt. *Philip Amidas,* and Capt. *Arthur Barlow;* who, after a prosperous voyage, anchored at the inlet by *Roanoke*, at present under the government of North *Carolina*. They made good profit of the *Indian* truck, which they bought for things of much inferior value, and returned. Being over-pleased with their profits, and finding all things there entirely new, and surprising; they gave a very advantageous account of matters; by representing the country so delightful, and desirable; so pleasant, and plentiful; the climate, and air, so temperate, sweet, and wholesome; the woods, and soil, so charming, and fruitful; and all other things so agreeable, that paradise itself seemed to be there, in its first native luster.

They gave particular accounts of the variety of good fruits, and some whereof they had never seen the like before; but above all, that there were grapes in such abundance, as was never known in the world: stately tall large oaks, and other timber; red cedar, cypress, pines, and other evergreens, and sweetwoods; for tallness and largeness exceeding all they had ever heard of: wild fowl, fish, deer, and other game in such plenty, and variety; that no epicure could desire more than this New World did seem naturally to afford.

And, to make it yet more desirable, they reported the native *Indians* (which were then the only inhabitants) so affable, kind, and good-natured; so uncultivated in learning, trades, and fashions; so innocent, and ignorant of all manner of politics, tricks, and cunning; and so desirous of the company of the *English:* that they seemed rather to be like soft wax, ready to take any impression, than any ways likely to oppose the settling of the *English* near them: they represented it as a scene laid open for the good and gracious Q. *Elizabeth,* to propagate the Gospel in, and extend her dominions over: as if purposely reserved for Her Majesty, by a peculiar direction of Providence, that had brought all former adventures in this affair to nothing: and to give a further taste of their discovery, they took with them, in their return for *England,* two men of the native *Indians,* named *Wanchese* and *Manteo.*

¶3. Her Majesty accordingly took the hint, and espoused the project, as far as her present engagements in war with *Spain* would let her; being so well pleased with the account given, that as the greatest mark of honor she could do the discovery, she called the country by the name of *Virginia;* as well, for that it was first discovered in her reign, a virgin queen; as that it did still seem to retain the virgin purity and plenty of the first creation, and the people their primitive innocence: for they seemed not debauched nor corrupted with those pomps and vanities, which had depraved and enslaved the rest of mankind; neither were their hands hardened by labor, nor their minds corrupted by the desire of hoarding up treasure: they were without boundaries to their land; and without property in cattle; and seemed to have escaped, or rather not to have been concerned in the first curse, *of getting their bread by the sweat of their brows:* for, by their pleasure alone, they supplied all their necessities; namely, by fishing, fowling and hunting; skins being their only clothing; and these too, five-sixths of the year thrown by: living without labor, and only gathering the fruits of the earth when ripe, or fit for use: neither fearing present want, nor solicitous for the future, but daily finding sufficient afresh for their subsistence.

¶4. This report was backed, nay much advanced, by the vast riches and treasure mentioned in several merchants' letters from *Mexico* and *Peru,* to their correspondents in *Spain;* which letters were taken with their ships and treasure, by some of ours in Her Majesty's service, in prosecution of the *Spanish* wars: this was encouragement enough for a new adventure, and set people's invention at work, till they had satisfied themselves, and made sufficient essays for the further discovery of the country. Pursuant whereunto Sir *Richard Grenville,* the chief of Sir *Walter Raleigh's* associates, having obtained seven sail of ships, well laden with provision, arms, ammunition, and spare men to make a settlement, set out in person with them early in the spring of the succeeding year, to make further discoveries, taking back the two *Indians* with him; and according to his wish, in the latter end of *May,* arrived at the same place, where the *English* had been the year before: there he made a settlement, sowed beans and peas, which he saw come up and grow to admiration while he stayed, which was about two months; and having made some little discoveries more in the *sound* to the southward, and got some treasure in skins, furs, pearl, and other rarities of the country, for things of inconsiderable value, he returned for *England*, leaving one hundred and eight men upon *Roanoke* Island, under the command of Mr. *Ralph Lane*, to keep possession.

¶5.   As soon as Sir *Richard Grenville* was gone, they, according to order and their own inclination, set themselves earnestly about discovering the country, and ranged about a little too indiscreetly up the rivers, and into the land backward from the rivers, which gave the *Indians* a jealousy of their meaning: for they cut off several stragglers of them, and had laid designs to destroy the rest, but were happily prevented. This put the *English* upon the precaution of keeping more within bounds, and not venturing themselves too defenseless abroad, who till then had depended too much upon the natives' simplicity and innocence.

After the *Indians* had done this mischief, they never observed any real faith towards those *English:* for being naturally suspicious and revengeful themselves, they never thought the *English* could forgive them; and so by this jealousy, caused by the cowardice of their nature, they were continually doing mischief.

The *English*, notwithstanding all this, continued their discoveries, but more carefully than they had done before, and kept the *Indians* in some awe, by threatening them with the return of their companions again with a greater supply of men and goods: and, before the cold of the winter became uneasy, they had extended their discoveries near an hundred miles along the sea coast to the northward; but not reaching the southern cape of *Chesapeake* Bay in *Virginia*, they had as yet found no good harbor.

¶6.   In this condition they maintained their settlement all the winter, and till *August* following; but were much distressed for want of provisions, not having learned to gather food, as the *Indians* did, nor having conveniencies like them of taking fish and fowl: besides, being now fallen out with the *Indians*, they feared to expose themselves to their contempt and cruelty; because they had not received the supply they talked of, and which had been expected in the spring.

All they could do under these distresses, and the despair of the recruits promised them this year, was only to keep a good looking out to seaward, if, perchance, they might find any means of escape, or recruit. And, to their great joy and satisfaction, in *August* aforesaid, they happened to espy, and make themselves be seen to Sir *Francis Drake's* fleet, consisting of twenty-three sail, who being sent by Her Majesty upon the coast of *America*, in search of the *Spanish* treasures, had orders from Her Majesty to take a view of this plantation, and see what assistance or encouragement it wanted: their first petition to him was to grant them a fresh supply of men and provisions, with a small vessel, and boats to attend them; that so if they should be put to distress for want of relief, they might embark for *England*. This was as readily granted by Sir *Francis Drake* as asked by them; and a ship was appointed them, which ship they began immediately to fit up, and supply plentifully with all manner of stores for a long stay; but while they were a doing this, a great storm arose, and drove that very ship (with some others) from her anchor to sea, and so she was lost for that occasion.

Sir *Francis* would have given them another ship, but this accident coming on the back of so many hardships which they had undergone, daunted them, and put them upon imagining that Providence was averse to their designs: and now having given over, for that year, the expectation of their promised supply from *England,* they consulted together, and agreed to desire Sir *Francis Drake* to take them along with him, which he did.

Thus their first intention of settlement fell, after discovering many things of the natural growth of the country, useful for the life of man, and beneficial to trade, they having observed a vast variety of fish, fowl and beasts; fruits, seeds, plants, roots, timber-trees, sweet-woods and gums: they had likewise attained some little knowledge in the language of the *Indians,* their religion, manners, and ways of correspondence one with another; and been made sensible of their cunning and treachery towards themselves.

¶7.   While these things were thus acting in *America,* the adventurers in *England* were providing, tho' too tediously, to send them recruits. And tho' it was late before they could dispatch them (for they met with several disappointments, and had many squabbles among themselves). However, at last they provided four good ships, with all manner of recruits suitable for the colony, and Sir *Walter Raleigh* designed to go in person with them.

Sir *Walter* got his ship ready first, and fearing the ill consequence of a delay, and the discouragement it might be to those that were left to make a settlement, he set sail by himself. And a fortnight after him Sir *Richard Grenville* sailed with the three other ships.

Sir *Walter* fell in with the land at Cape *Hatteras,* a little to the southward of the place, where the 108 men had been settled, and after search not finding them, he returned: however, Sir *Richard,* with his ships, found the place where he had left the men, but entirely deserted, which was at first a great disheartening to him, thinking them all destroyed, because he knew not that Sir *Francis Drake* had been there, and taken them off; but he was a little better satisfied by *Manteo's* report, that they were not cut off by the *Indians,* tho' he could give no good account what was become of them. However, notwithstanding this seeming discouragement, he again left fifty men in the same island of *Roanoke,* built them houses necessary, gave them two years' provision, and returned.

¶8.   The next summer, being *Anno* 1587. Three ships more were sent, under the command of Mr. *John White,* who himself was to settle there as governor with more men, and some women, carrying also plentiful recruits of provisions.

In the latter end of *July* they arrived at *Roanoke* aforesaid, where they again encountered the uncomfortable news of the loss of these men also; who (as they were informed by *Manteo*) were secretly set upon by the *Indians,* some cut off, and the others fled, and not to be heard of, and their place of habitation now all grown up with weeds. However, they repaired the houses on *Roanoke,* and sat down there again.

The 13th of *August* they christened *Manteo,* and styled him Lord of *Dassamonpeak,* an *Indian* nation so called, in reward of the fidelity he had shown to the *English* from the beginning; who being the first *Indian* that was made a Christian in that part of the world, I thought it not amiss to remember him.

On the same occasion also may be mentioned the first child there born of Christian parentage, *viz.* a daughter of Mr. *Ananias Dare.* She was born the 18th of the same *August* upon *Roanoke,* and, after the name of the country, was christened *Virginia.*

This seemed to be a settlement prosperously made, being carried on with much zeal and unanimity among themselves. The form of government consisted of a governor and twelve counselors, incorporated by the name of the governor and assistants of the city of *Raleigh* in *Virginia.*

Many nations of the *Indians* renewed their peace, and made firm leagues with the corporation: the chief men of the *English* also were so far from being disheartened at the former disappointments, that they disputed for the liberty of remaining on the spot; and by mere constraint compelled Mr. *White,* their governor, to return for *England,* to negotiate the business of their recruits and supply, as a man the most capable to manage that affair, leaving at his departure one hundred and fifteen in the corporation.

¶9.   It was above two years before Mr. *White* could obtain any grant of supplies; and then, in the latter end of the year 1589 he set out from *Plymouth* with three ships, and sailed round by the *Western* and *Carribbee* Islands, they having hitherto not found any nearer way: for tho' they were skilled in navigation, and understood the use of the globes, yet did example so much prevail upon them, that they chose to sail a thousand leagues about, rather than attempt a more direct passage.

Towards the middle of *August,* 1590 they arrived upon the coast, at Cape *Hatteras,* and went to search upon *Roanoke* for the people; but found, by letters on the trees, that they were removed to *Croatan,* one of the islands forming the *sound*, and southward of *Roanoke* about twenty leagues, but no sign of distress. Thither they designed to sail to them in their ships; but a storm arising in the meanwhile, lay so hard upon them, that their cables broke; they lost three of their anchors, were forced to sea; and so returned home, without ever going near those poor people again for sixteen years following: and it is supposed, that the *Indians* seeing them forsaken by their country, and unfurnished of their expected supplies, cut them off: for to this day they were never more heard of.

Thus, after all this vast expense and trouble, and the hazard and loss of so many lives, Sir *Walter Raleigh*, the great projector and furtherer of these discoveries and settlements, being under trouble, all thoughts of further prosecuting these designs, lay dead for about twelve years following.

· · ·

CHAPTER II
CONTAINING AN ACCOUNT OF THE FIRST SETTLEMENT OF CHESAPEAKE BAY, IN VIRGINIA, BY THE CORPORATION OF LONDON ADVENTURERS, AND THEIR PROCEEDINGS DURING THEIR GOVERNMENT BY A PRESIDENT AND COUNCIL ELECTIVE

¶13. The merchants of *London, Bristol, Exeter* and *Plymouth*, soon perceived what great gains might be made of a trade this way, if it were well managed, and colonies could be rightly settled; which was sufficiently evinced by the great profits some ships had made, which had not met with ill accidents. Encouraged by this prospect, they joined together in a petition to King *James* the First; showing forth, that it would be too much for any single person to attempt the settling of colonies, and to carry on so considerable a trade: they therefore prayed His Majesty to incorporate them, and enable them to raise a joint stock for that purpose, and to countenance their undertaking.

His Majesty did accordingly grant their petition, and by letters patents bearing date the 10th of *April*, 1606, did in one patent incorporate them into two distinct companies to make two separate colonies, *viz.* "Sir *Tho. Gates*, Sir *George Summers*, Knights; Mr. *Richard Hackluit*, Clerk Prebend of *Westminster*, and *Edward-Maria Wingfield*, Esq; adventurers of the City of *London*, and such others as should be joined unto them of that colony, which should be called, *the First Colony*; with liberty to begin their first plantation and seat, at any place upon the coast of *Virginia*, where they should think fit and conve[ni]ent between the degrees of 34 and 41 of northern latitude: and that they should extend their bounds from the said first seat of their plantation and habitation, fifty *English* miles along the sea coast each way; and include all the lands within an hundred miles directly over-against the same seacoast, and also back into the mainland one hundred miles from the seacoast: and that no other should be permitted or suffered to plant or inhabit behind, or on the back of them towards the mainland, without the express license of the council of that colony thereunto in writing first had and obtained. And for the second colony, to *Tho. Hanham, Rawleigh Gilbert, William Parker,* and *George Popham,* Esqs; of the town of *Plymouth,* and all others who should be joined to them of that colony; with liberty to begin their first plantation and seat at any place upon the coast of *Virginia,* where they should think fit, between the degrees of 38 and 45 of northern latitude, with the like liberties and bounds as the first colony: provided they did not seat within an hundred miles of them."

¶14.   By virtue of this patent, Capt. *John Smith* was sent by the *London* Company in *December,* 1606, on his voyage with three small ships; and a commission was given to him, and to several other gentlemen, to establish a colony, and to govern by a president, to be chosen annually, and council, who should be invested with sufficient authorities and powers. And now all things seemed to promise a plantation in good earnest. Providence seemed likewise very favorable to them: for tho' they designed only for that part of *Virginia* where the hundred and fifteen were left, and where there is no security of harbor: yet, after a tedious voyage of passing the old way again, between the *Carribbee* Islands and the main, he, with two of his vessels, luckily fell in with *Virginia* itself, that part of the continent now so called, anchoring in the mouth of the Bay of *Chesapeake:* and the first place they landed upon, was the southern cape of that bay, which they named Cape *Henry,* and the northern Cape *Charles,* in honor of the King's two eldest sons; and the first great river they searched whose *Indian* name was *Powhatan,* they called *James* River, after the King's own name.

¶15.   Before they would make any settlement here, they made a full search of *James* River; and then by an unanimous consent pitched upon a *peninsula* about fifty miles up the river; which, besides the goodness of the soil, was esteemed as most fit, and capable to be made a place both of trade and security, two-thirds thereof being environed by the main river, which affords good anchorage all along, and the other third by a small narrow river, capable of receiving many vessels of an hundred tons, quite up as high as till it meets within thirty yards of the main river again, and where generally in springtides it overflows into the main river: by which means the land they chose to pitch their town upon, has obtained the name of an island. In this back river ships and small vessels may ride lashed to one another, and moored ashore secure from all wind and weather whatsoever.

The town, as well as the river, had the honor to be called by King *James's* name. The whole island thus enclosed contains about two thousand acres of high land, and several thousands of very good and firm marsh, and is an extraordinary good pasture as any in that country.

By means of the narrow passage, this place was of great security to them from the *Indian* enemy: and if they had then known of the biting of the worm in the salts, they would have valued this place upon that account also, as being free from that mischief.

¶16.   They were no sooner settled in all this happiness and security, but they fell into jars and dissensions among themselves, by a greedy grasping at the *Indian* treasures, envying and overreaching one another in that trade.

After five weeks' stay before this town, the ships returned home again, leaving one hundred and eight men settled in the form of government before spoken of.

After the ships were gone, the same sort of feuds and disorders happened continually among them, to the unspeakable damage of the plantation.

The *Indians* were the same there as in all other places; at first very fair and friendly, tho' afterwards they gave great proofs of their deceitfulness. However, by the help of the *Indian* provisions, the *English* chiefly subsisted till the return of the ships the next year; when two vessels were sent thither full-freighted with men and provisions for supply of the plantation, one of which only arrived directly, and the other being beat off to the *Carribbee* Islands, did not arrive till the former was sailed hence again.

¶17.   In the interval of these ships returning from *England*, the *English* had a very advantageous trade with the *Indians;* and might have made much greater gains of it, and managed it both to the greater satisfaction of the *Indians*, and the greater ease and security of themselves; if they had been under any rule, or subject to any method in trade, and not left at liberty to outvie or outbid one another; by which they not only cut short their own profit, but created jealousies and disturbances among the *Indians*, by letting one have a better bargain than another: for they being unaccustomed to barter, such of them as had been hardest dealt by in their commodities, thought themselves cheated and abused; and so conceived a grudge against the *English* in general, making it a national quarrel: and this seems to be the original cause of most of their subsequent misfortunes by the *Indians*.

What also gave a greater interruption to this trade, was an object that drew all their eyes and thoughts aside, even from taking the necessary care for their preservation, and for the support of their lives; which was this; they found in a neck of land, on the back of *Jamestown Island*, a fresh stream of water springing out of a small bank, which washed down with it a yellow sort of dust isinglass, which being cleansed by the fresh streaming of the water, lay shining in the bottom of that limpid element, and stirred up in

them an unseasonable and inordinate desire after riches: for they, taking all
to be gold that glistered, run into the utmost distraction, neglecting both the
necessary defense of their lives from the *Indians*, and the support of their
bodies by securing of provisions; absolutely relying, like *Midas*, upon the
almighty power of gold, thinking, that where this was in plenty nothing could
be wanting: but they soon grew sensible of their error; and found that if this
gilded dirt had been real gold, it could have been of no advantage to them.
For, by their negligence, they were reduced to an exceeding scarcity of
provisions, and that little they had, was lost by the burning of their town,
while all hands were employed upon this imaginary golden treasure; so that
they were forced to live for some time upon the wild fruits of the earth, and
upon crabs, muscles, and such like, not having day's provision beforehand; as
some of the laziest *Indians*, who have no pleasure in exercise, and won't be
at the pains to fish and hunt: and, indeed, not so well as they neither; for by
this careless neglecting of their defense against the *Indians*, many of 'em
were destroyed by that cruel people; and the rest durst not venture abroad,
but were forced to be content with what fell just into their mouths.

¶18.   In this condition they were, when the first ship of the two before-
mentioned came to their assistance, but their golden dreams overcame all
difficulties: they spoke not, nor thought of any thing but gold, and that was
all the lading that most of them were willing to take care for; accordingly
they put into this ship all the yellow dirt they had gathered, and what skins
and furs they had trucked for; and filling her up with cedar, sent her away.

After she was gone, the other ship arrived, which they stowed likewise
with this supposed gold dust, designing never to be poor again; filling her up
with cedar and clapboard.

Those two ships being thus dispatched, they made several discoveries in
James River, and up *Chesapeake* Bay, by the undertaking and management
of Capt. *John Smith:* and the year 1608 was the first year in which they
gathered *Indian* corn of their own planting.

While these discoveries were making by Capt. *Smith,* matters run again
into confusion in *Jamestown;* and several uneasy people, taking advantage of
his absence, attempted to desert the settlement, and run away with the small
vessel that was left to attend upon it; for Capt. *Smith* was the only man
among them that could manage the discoveries with success, and he was the
only man too that could keep the settlement in order. Thus the *English*
continued to give themselves as much perplexity by their own distraction, as
the *Indians* did by their watchfulness and resentments.

¶19.   *Anno* 1609, *John Laydon* and *Anna Burrows* were married together,
the first Christian marriage in that part of the world: and the year following
the plantation was increased to near five hundred men.

This year *Jamestown* sent out people, and made two other settlements; one at *Nansamond* in *James River*, above thirty miles below *Jamestown*, and the other at *Powhatan*, six miles below the falls of *James River* (which last was bought of *Powhatan* for a certain quantity of copper), each settlement consisting of about a hundred and twenty men. Some small time after another was made at *Kiquotan* by the mouth of *James River*.

From CHAPTER III
*SHOWING WHAT HAPPENED AFTER THE
ALTERATION OF THE GOVERNMENT FROM AN
ELECTIVE PRESIDENT TO A COMMISSIONATED
GOVERNOR, UNTIL THE DISSOLUTION OF THE
COMPANY*

¶20.   In the meanwhile the treasurer, council, and company of *Virginia* adventurers in *London*, not finding that return and profit from the adventures they expected; and rightly judging that this disappointment, as well as the idle quarrels in the colony, proceeded from a mismanage[ment] of the government; petitioned His Majesty, and got a new patent with leave to appoint a governor.

Upon this new grant they sent out nine ships, and plentiful supplies of men and provisions; and made three joint commissioners or governors in equal power, *viz.* Sir *Thomas Gates*, Sir *George Summers*, and Capt. *Newport*. They agreed to go all together in one ship.

This ship, on board of which the three governors had embarked, being separated from the rest, was put to great distress in a severe storm; and after three days and nights constant baling and pumping, was at last cast ashore at *Bermudas*, and there staved, but by good providence the company was preserved.

Notwithstanding this shipwreck, and extremity they were put to, yet could not this common misfortune make them agree. The best of it was, they found plenty of provisions in that island, and no *Indians* to annoy them: but still they quarrelled amongst themselves, and none more than the two knights; who made their parties, built each of them a cedar vessel, one called the *Patience*, the other the *Deliverance*, and used what they gathered of the furniture of the old ship for rigging, and fish oil, and hogs' grease mixed with lime and ashes instead of pitch and tar: for they found great plenty of *Spanish* hogs in this island, which are supposed to have swam ashore from some wrecks, and there afterwards increased.

¶21.   While these things were acting in *Bermudas*, Capt. *Smith* being very much burnt by the accidental firing of some gunpowder, as he was upon a discovery in his boat, was forced for his cure sake, and the benefit of a surgeon, to take his passage for *England* in a ship that was then upon the point of sailing.

Several of the nine ships that came out with the three governors arrived, with many of the passengers; some of which in their humors would not submit to the government there, pretending the new commission destroyed the old one; that governors were appointed instead of a president, and that they themselves were to be of the council; and so would assume an independent power, inspiring the people with disobedience; by which means they became frequently exposed in great parties to the cruelty of the *Indians;* all sorts of discipline was laid aside, and their necessary defense neglected; so that the *Indians* taking advantage of those divisions, formed a stratagem to destroy them root and branch, and indeed they did cut many of 'em off, by massacring whole companies at a time; so that all the out-settlements were deserted, and the people that were not destroyed took refuge in *Jamestown,* except the small settlement at *Kiquotan,* where they had built themselves a little fort, and called it *Algernoon* Fort: and yet, for all this, they continued their disorders, wasting their old provisions, and neglecting to gather others; so that they who remained alive were all near famished, having brought themselves to that pass, that they durst not stir from their own doors to gather the fruits of the earth, or the crabs and mussels from the waterside: much less to hunt or catch wild beasts, fish or fowl, which were found in great abundance there. They continued in these scanty circumstances till they were at last reduced to such extremity, as to eat the very hides of their horses, and the bodies of the *Indians* they had killed; and sometimes also upon a pinch they would not disdain to dig them up again to make a homely meal of after they had been buried. And that time is to this day remembered by the name of the *Starving Time.*

Thus a few months' indiscreet management brought such an infamy upon the country, that to this day it cannot be wiped away: and the sicknesses occasioned by this bad diet, or rather want of diet are unjustly remembered to the disadvantage of the country, as a fault in the climate; which was only the foolishness and indiscretion of those who assumed the power of governing. I call it assumed because the new commission mentioned, by which they pretended to be of the council, was not in all this time arrived, but remained in *Bermudas* with the new governors.

Here I can't but admire the care, labor, courage and understanding that Capt. *John Smith* showed in the time of his administration; who not only founded, but also preserved all these settlements in good order, while he was amongst them. And without him, they had certainly all been destroyed, either by famine, or the enemy long before; tho' the country naturally afforded subsistence enough, even without any other labor than that of gathering and preserving its spontaneous provisions.

For the first three years that Capt. *Smith* was with them, they never had in that whole time above six months' *English* provisions. But as soon as he had left 'em to themselves, all went to ruin; for the *Indians* had no longer any fear for themselves, or friendship for the *English*. And six months after this gentleman's departure, the 500 men that he left were reduced to three-score; and they too must of necessity have starved, if their relief had been withheld a week longer.

¶22.   In the mean time, the three governors put to sea from *Bermudas* in their two small vessels, with their company, to the number of one hundred and fifty, and in fourteen days, *viz.* the 25th of *May*, 1610 they arrived both together in *Virginia;* and went with their vessels up to *Jamestown*, where they found the small remainder of the five hundred men, in that melancholy way I just now hinted.

¶23.   Sir *Thomas Gates*, Sir *George Summers*, and Capt. *Newport*, the governors, were very compassionate of their condition; and called a council, wherein they informed them, that they had but sixteen days' provision aboard; and therefore desired to know their opinion, whether they would venture to sea under such a scarcity: or if they resolved to continue in the settlement, and take their fortunes; they would stay likewise, and share the provisions among them; but desired that their determination might be speedy. They soon came to the conclusion of returning for *England:* but because their provisions were short, they resolved to go by the Banks of *Newfoundland,* in hopes of meeting with some of the fishermen (this being now the season) and dividing themselves among their ships for the greater certainty of provision, and for their better accommodation.

According to this resolution, they all went aboard, and fell down to *Hog Island* the 9th of *June* at night, and the next morning to *Mulberry Island* Point, which is eighteen miles below *Jamestown*, and thirty above the mouth of the river; and there they spied a longboat, which the Lord *Delaware* (who was just arrived with three ships) had sent before him up the river sounding the channel. His Lordship was made sole governor, and was accompanied by several gentlemen of condition. He caused all the men to return again to *Jamestown;* resettled them with satisfaction, and stayed with them till *March* following; and then being very sick, he returned for *England*, leaving about two hundred in the colony.

¶24.   On the 10th of *May*, 1611, Sir *Thomas Dale* being then made governor, arrived with three ships, which brought supplies of men, cattle and hogs. He found them growing again into the like disorders as before, taking no care to plant corn, and wholly relying upon their store, which then had but three months' provisions in it. He therefore set them to work about corn, and tho' it was the middle of *May* before they began to prepare the ground, yet they had an indifferent good crop.

¶25.   In *August* the same year Sir *Thomas Gates* arrived at *Jamestown* with six ships more, and with a plentiful supply of hogs, cattle, fowls, etc. with a good quantity of ammunition, and all other things necessary for a new colony, and besides this a reinforcement of three hundred and fifty chosen men. In the beginning of *September* he settled a new town at *Arrahattuck*, about fifty miles above *Jamestown*, paling in the neck above two miles from the point, from one reach of the river to the other. Here he built forts and sentry-boxes, and in honor of *Henry* Prince of *Wales*, called it *Henrico*. And also run a Palissado on the other side of the river at *Coxendale*, to secure their hogs.

·   ·   ·

[THE MASSACRES OF 1622]

¶.45. *Anno*, 1622, inferior courts were first appointed by the General Assembly, under the name of *County Courts*, for trial of minute causes; the Governor and Council still remaining judges of the supreme court of the colony. In the meantime, by the great increase of people, and the long quiet they had enjoyed among the *Indians*, since the marriage of *Pocahontas*, and the accession of *Oppechancanough* to the imperial crown; all men were lulled into a fatal security, and became everywhere familiar with *Indians*, eating, drinking and sleeping amongst them; by which means they became perfectly acquainted with all our *English* strength, and the use of our arms: knowing at all times, when and where to find our people; whether at home, or in the woods; in bodies, or dispersed; in condition of defense, or indefensible. This exposing of their weakness gave them occasion to think more contemptibly of them, than otherwise, perhaps, they would have done; for which reason they became more peevish, and more hardy to attempt anything against them.

¶.46. Thus upon the loss of one of their leading men (a war captain, as they call him) who was likewise supposed to be justly killed, *Oppechancanough* took affront, and in revenge laid the plot of a general massacre of the *English*, to be executed on the 22d of *March*, 1622, a little before noon, at a time when our men were all at work abroad in their plantations, dispersed and unarmed. This hellish contrivance was to take effect upon all the several settlements at one and the same instant, except on the Eastern Shore, whither this plot did not reach. The *Indians* had been made so familiar with the *English*, as to borrow their boats and canoes to cross the rivers in, when they went to consult with their neighboring *Indians* upon this execrable conspiracy. And, to color their design the better, they brought presents of deer, turkeys, fish and fruits to the *English* the evening before. The very morning of the massacre, they came freely and unarmed among them, eating with them, and behaving themselves with the same freedom and friendship as formerly, till the very minute they were to put their plot in execution. Then they fell to work all at once everywhere, knocking the *English* unawares on the head, some with their hatchets, which they call *tomahauks*, others with the hoes and axes of the *English* themselves, shooting at those who escaped the reach of their hands; sparing neither age nor sex, but destroying man, woman and child, according to their cruel way of leaving none behind to bear resentment. But whatever was not done by surprise that day, was left undone, and many that made early resistance escaped.

By the account taken of the *Christians* murdered that morning, they were found to be three hundred forty-seven, most of them falling by their own instruments, and working tools.

¶.47.   The massacre had been much more general, had not this plot been providentially discovered to the *English* some hours before the execution. It happened thus:

Two *Indians* that used to be employed by the *English* to hunt for them, happened to lie together, the night before the massacre, in an *Englishman's* house, where one of them was employed. The *Indian* that was the guest fell to persuading the other to rise and kill his master, telling him, that he would do the same by his own the next day. Whereupon he discovered the whole plot that was designed to be executed on the morrow. But the other, instead of entering into the plot, and murdering his master, got up (under pretense of going to execute his comrade's advice) went into his master's chamber, and revealed to him the whole story that he had been told. The master hereupon arose, secured his own house, and before day got to *Jamestown*, which, together with such plantations as could receive notice time enough, was saved by this means; the rest, as they happened to be watchful in their defense, also escaped: but such as were surprised, were massacred. Captain *Croshaw* in his vessel at *Patowmeck*, had notice also given him by a young *Indian*, by which means he came off untouched.

¶.48.   The occasion upon which *Oppechancanough* took affront was this. The war captain mentioned before to have been killed, was called *Nemattanow*. He was an active *Indian*, a great warrior, and in much esteem among them; so much, that they believed him to be invulnerable, and immortal, because he had been in very many conflicts, and escaped untouched from them all. He was also a very cunning fellow, and took great pride in preserving and increasing this their superstition concerning him, affecting everything that was odd and prodigious to work upon their admiration. For which purpose he would often dress himself up with feathers after a fantastic manner, and by much use of that ornament, obtained among the *English* the nickname of *Jack of the Feather*.

This *Nemattanow* coming to a private settlement of one *Morgan*, who had several toys which he had a mind to, persuaded him to go to *Pamunky* to

dispose of them. He gave him hopes what mighty bargains he might meet
with there, and kindly offered him his assistance. At last *Morgan* yielded to
his persuasion: but was no more heard of; and it is believed, that *Nemattanow* killed him by the way, and took away his treasure. For within a few
days, this *Nemattanow* returned to the same house with *Morgan's* cap upon
his head; where he found two sturdy boys, who asked for their master. He
very frankly told them, he was dead. But they, knowing the cap again,
suspected the villain had killed their master, and would have had him before
a Justice of Peace: but he refused to go, and very insolently abused them.
Whereupon they shot him down, and as they were carrying him to the
Governor, he died.

As he was dying, he earnestly pressed the boys to promise him two
things; first, that they would not tell how he was killed; and, secondly, that
they would bury him among the *English*. So great was the pride of this vain
heathen, that he had no other thoughts at his death, but the ambition of
being esteemed after he was dead, as he had endeavored to make them
believe of him while he was alive, *viz.* that he was invulnerable and immortal; tho' his increasing faintness convinced himself of the falsity of both. He
imagined that being buried among the *English,* perhaps, might conceal his
death from his own nation, who might think him translated to some happier
country. Thus he pleased himself to the last gasp with the boys' promises to
carry on the delusion. This was reckoned all the provocation given to that
haughty and revengeful man *Oppechancanough,* to act this bloody tragedy,
and to take indefatigable pains to engage in so horrid villany all the kings and
nations bordering upon the *English* settlements, on the western shore of
Chesepeake.

¶.49.   This gave the *English* a fair pretense of endeavoring the total
extirpation of the *Indians,* but more especially of *Oppec[h]ancanough,* and
his nation. Accordingly they set themselves about it, making use of the *Roman* maxim ("Faith is not to be kept with heretics") to obtain their ends.
For, after some months' fruitless pursuit of them, who could too dexterously
hide themselves in the woods, the *English* pretended articles of peace, giving
them all manner of fair words and promises of oblivion. They designed
thereby (as their own letters now on record, and their own actions thereupon, prove) to draw the *Indians* back, and entice them to plant their corn
on their habitations nearest adjoining to the *English;* and then to cut it up
when the summer should be too far spent to leave them hopes of another
crop that year; by which means they proposed to bring them to want necessaries, and starve. And the *English* did so far accomplish their ends, as to
bring the *Indians* to plant their corn at their usual habitations, whereby they
gained an opportunity of repaying them some part of the debt in their own
coin; for they fell suddenly upon them, cut to pieces such of them as could
not make their escape, and afterwards totally destroyed their corn.

¶.50.   Another effect of the massacre of the *English*, was the reducing all their settlements again to six or seven in number, for their better defense. Besides, it was such a disheartening to some good projects, then just advancing, that to this day they have never been put in execution, namely, the glasshouses in *Jamestown*, and the ironwork at *Falling Creek*, which has been already mentioned. The massacre fell so hard upon this last place, that no soul was saved, but a boy and a girl, who, with great difficulty, hid themselves.

The superintendent of this ironwork had also discovered a vein of lead ore, which he kept private, and made use of it to furnish all the neighbors with bullets and shot. But he being cut off with the rest, and the secret not having been communicated, this lead mine could never after be found; till Colonel *Byrd*, some few years ago, prevailed with an *Indian*, under pretense of hunting, to give him a sign, by dropping his *tomahawk* at the place (he not daring publicly to discover it, for fear of being murdered). The sign was accordingly given, and the company at that time found several pieces of good lead ore upon the surface of the ground, and marked the trees thereabouts: notwithstanding which, I know not by what witchcraft it happens, but no mortal to this day could ever find that place again, tho' it be upon part of the Colonel's own possessions. And so it rests, till time and thicker settlements discover it.

¶.51.   Thus the company of adventurers having, by those frequent acts of mismanagement, met with vast losses and misfortunes; many grew sick of it, and parted with their shares; and others came into their places, and promoted the sending in fresh recruits of men and goods. But the chief design of all parties concerned was to fetch away the treasure from thence, aiming more at sudden gain, than to form any regular colony, or establish a settlement in such a manner, as to make it a lasting happiness to the country.

Several gentlemen went over upon their particular stocks, separate from that of the company, with their own servants and goods, each designing to obtain land from the government, as Capt. *Newport* had done; or, at least, to obtain patents according to the regulation for granting lands to adventurers. Others sought their grants of the company in *London*, and obtained authorities and jurisdictions, as well as land, distinct from the authority of the government, which was the foundation of great disorder, and the occasion of their following misfortunes. Among others, one Capt. *Martin*, having made very considerable preparations towards a settlement, obtained a suitable grant of land, and was made of the council there. But he grasping still at more, hankered after dominion, as well as possession, and caused so many differences, that at last he put all things into distraction; insomuch, that the *Indians*, still seeking revenge, took advantage of these dissensions, and fell foul again of the *English*, gratifying their vengeance with new bloodshed.

¶.52.   The fatal consequences of the company's maladministration cried so loud, that King *Charles* the First, coming to the crown of *England*, had a tender concern for the poor people that had been betrayed thither, and lost. Upon which consideration he dissolved the company in the year 1626, reducing the country and government into his own immediate direction, appointing the governor and council himself, and ordering all patents and process to issue in his own name; reserving only to himself an easy quitrent of two shillings for every hundred acres of land, and so *pro rato.*

From Book III
Of the Indians, their Religion, Laws, and Customs, in War and Peace.

CHAPTER I
Of the Persons of the Indians, *and their Dress*

¶.I.   The *Indians* are of the middling and largest stature of the *English:* they are straight and well proportioned, having the cleanest and most exact limbs in the world: they are so perfect in their outward frame, that I never heard of one single *Indian,* that was either dwarfish, crooked, bandy-legged, or otherwise misshapen. But if they have any such practice among them, as the *Romans* had, of exposing such children till they died, as were weak and misshapen at their birth, they are very shy of confessing it, and I could never yet learn that they had.

Their color, when they are grown up, is a chestnut brown and tawny; but much clearer in their infancy. Their skin comes afterwards to harden and grow blacker, by greasing and sunning themselves. They have generally coal black hair, and very black eyes, which are most commonly graced with that sort of squint which many of the *Jews* are observed to have. Their women are generally beautiful, possessing an uncommon delicacy of shape and features, and wanting no charm, but that of a fair complexion.

¶.2.   The men wear their hair cut after several fanciful fashions, sometimes greased, and sometimes painted. The great men, or better sort, preserve a long lock behind for distinction. They pull their beards up by the roots with a mussel-shell; and both men and women do the same by the other parts of their body for cleanliness sake. The women wear the hair of the head very long, either hanging at their backs, or brought before in a single lock, bound up with a fillet of peak, or beads; sometimes also they wear it neatly tied up in a knot behind. It is commonly greased, and shining black, but never painted.

Tab. 2. Is an *Indian* man in his Summer Dress.

The upper part of his hair is cut short, to make a ridge, which stands up like the comb of a cock, the rest is either shorn off, or knotted behind his ear. On his head are stuck three feathers of the wild turkey, pheasant, hawk, or such like. At his ear is hung a fine shell with pearl drops. At his breast is a tablet or fine shell, smooth as polished marble, which sometimes also has etched on it, a star, half-moon, or other figure, according to the maker's fancy. Upon his neck, and wrists, hang strings of beads, peak and roenoke. His apron is made of a deer skin, gashed round the edges, which hang like tassels or fringe; at the upper end of the fringe is an edging of peak, to make it finer. His quiver is of a thin bark; but sometimes they make it of the skin of a fox, or young wolf, with the head hanging to it, which has a wild sort of terror in it; and to make it yet more warlike, they tie it on with the tail of a panther, buffalo, or such like, letting the end hang down between their legs. The pricked lines on his shoulders, breast and legs, represent the figures painted thereon. In his left hand he holds a bow, and in his right an arrow. The mark upon his shoulder blade, is a distinction used by the Indians *in travelling, to show the nation they are of. And perhaps is the same with that which Baron* Lahontan *calls the arms and heraldry of the* Indians. *Thus the several lettered marks, are used by several other nations about* Virginia, *when they make a journey to their friends and allies.*

The landskip [landscape] is a natural representation of an Indian *field.*

Tab. 3. Is two *Indian* Men in their Winter Dress.

Seldom any but the elder people wore the winter cloaks (which they call match-coats), till they got a supply of European goods; and now most have them of one sort or other in the cold winter weather. Fig. I. wears the proper Indian *match-coat, which is made of skins, dressed with the fur on, sewed together, and worn with the fur inwards, having the edges also gashed for beauty sake. On his feet are* moccasins. *By him stand some* Indian *cabins on the banks of the river. Fig. 2. wears the* Duffield *match-coat bought of the* English, *on his head is a coronet of peak, on his legs are stockings made of Duffields: that is, they take a length to reach from the ankle to the knee, so broad as to wrap round the leg; this they sew together, letting the edges stand out an inch beyond the seam. When this is on, they garter below knee, and fasten the lower end in the* moccasin.

The people of condition of both sexes, wear a sort of coronet on their heads, from 4 to 6 inches broad, open at the top, and composed of peak, or beads, or else of both interwoven together, and workt into figures, made by a nice mixture of the colors. Sometimes they wear a wreath of dyed furs; as likewise bracelets on their necks and arms. The common people go bare-headed, only sticking large shining feathers about their heads, as their fancies lead them.

From Robert Beverley, "The History and Present State of Virginia," London, 1705. *(Rare Book Division, New York Public Library, Astor, Lenox, and Tilden Foundations.)*

From Robert Beverley, "The History and Present State of Virginia," London, 1705. *(Rare Book Division, New York Public Library, Astor, Lenox, and Tilden Foundations.)*

¶.3.   Their clothes are a large mantle, carelessly wrapped about their bodies, and sometimes girt close in the middle with a girdle. The upper part of this mantle is drawn close upon the shoulders, and the other hangs below their knees. When that's thrown off, they have only for modesty sake a piece of cloth, or a small skin, tied round their waist, which reaches down to the middle of the thigh. The common sort tie only a string round their middle, and pass a piece of cloth or skin round between their thighs, which they turn at each end over the string.

Their shoes, when they wear any, are made of an entire piece of buckskin; except when they sew a piece to the bottom, to thicken the sole. They are fastened on with running strings, the skin being drawn together like a purse on the top of the foot, and tied round the ankle. The *Indian* name of this kind of shoe is *moccasin.*

But because a draught of these things will inform the reader more at first view, than a description in many words, I shall present him with the following prints; wherein he is to take notice, that the air of the face, as well as the ornaments of the body, are exactly represented, being all drawn by the life.

WILLIAM BYRD, II

(1674-1744)

One of the wealthiest men in colonial America, William Byrd lived and wrote as an eighteenth-century Virginia gentleman, with much of the elegance that nineteenth-century myths attributed to that stereotype, but with more learning, more hard work, and more coarseness than

The standard edition of Byrd's most significant work is *William Byrd's Histories of the Dividing Line*, ed. W. K. Boyd, 1929, from which the following text is taken. Other texts include Mark Van Doren, *A Journey to the Land of Eden*, 1928; *The Secret Diary of William Byrd of Westover, 1709-1712*, ed. Louis B. Wright and Marion Tinling, 1941; *Another Secret Diary of William Byrd of Westover, 1739-1741, With Letters and Literary Exercises, 1696-1726*, ed. M. H. Woodfin, trans. and collated by Marion Tinling, 1942; *The London Diary*, ed. Louis B. Wright and Marion Tinling, 1950.

Biographies and critical estimates include R. C. Beatty, *William Byrd of Westover*, 1932; Louis B. Wright, *The First Gentleman of Virginia*, 1950; Carl Dolmetsch, *William Byrd*, to be published; Pierre Marambavo, *William Byrd of Westover (1674-1744)*, 1971; and Lewis P. Simpson, "William Byrd and the South," *Early American Literature*, 7 (1972): 187-195. See also Professor Simpson's important general study, *The Dispossessed Garden*, 1975; and Donald T. Siebert, "William Byrd's Histories of the Line: The Fashioning of a Hero," *American Literature*, 47 (1976), 535-551.

those myths ever recognized. Like Robert Beverley, Byrd was educated in England, and he spent much time there in later years as a representative of the Virginia colony, which he also served through most of his life as a member of either The House of Burgesses or The Supreme Council. At home, where he accumulated one of the best private libraries in the American colonies, he worked hard in the supervision of his immense plantation, he served on a commission to establish a boundary line between Virginia and North Carolina, he observed a routine of classical reading, he sent letters to the Royal Society and to personal friends in England, he supervised the construction of his mansion at Westover, and he entertained extravagantly.

The diary that Byrd kept reveals none of the introspection that one finds in the private papers of Samuel Sewall, Michael Wigglesworth, or Cotton Mather. Byrd is consistently faithful in his religious observance. His daily record characteristically begins with the litany "I said my prayers and danced my dance and ate boiled milk for breakfast," and concludes with "I had good thoughts, good health, Thank God Almighty." But he expresses no more emotion in recording those religious feelings than in listing his daily reading in classical or Hebrew literature. One can learn much about the manners of Byrd's class and about his daily routine from these diaries and from his secret London diary, which has recently been decoded and published, but the deepest feelings are not articulated.

Byrd's most valuable literary works are *The History of the Dividing Line, The Secret History of the Dividing Line,* and *A Progress to the Mines.* In all these works he comments perceptively on the history and manners of his countrymen, whom he describes with memorable precision and wit. His irreverent comments on William Penn show that he understood the practice of raillery, and his comments on the Virginian founders who "detested work more than famine" show that his wit did not spare his neighbors or his ancestors. The chapter reprinted here established the framework of colonial history within which Byrd sets his particular observations of his own region.

From
History of the Dividing Line
[Between Virginia and North Carolina]
Run in the Year 1728[1]

[INTRODUCTION]

Before I enter upon the journal of the line between Virginia and North Carolina, it will be necessary to clear the way to it, by showing how the other British colonies on the main have, one after the other, been carved out of Virginia, by grants from His Majesty's royal predecessors. All that part of the northern American continent now under the dominion of the King of Great Britain, and stretching quite as far as the Cape of Florida, went *at first under the general name of Virginia.*

The only distinction, in those early days, was, that all the coast to the southward of Chesapeake Bay was called South Virginia, and all to the northward of it, North Virginia.

The first settlement of this fine country was owing to that great ornament of the British nation, Sir Walter Raleigh, who obtained a grant thereof from Queen Elizabeth of ever-glorious memory, by letters patent, dated March the 25th, 1584.

But whether that gentleman ever made a voyage thither himself is uncertain; because those who have favored the public with an account of his life mention nothing of it. However, thus much may be depended on, that Sir Walter invited sundry persons of distinction to share in his charter, and join their purses with his in the laudable project of fitting out a colony to Virginia.

Accordingly, 2 ships were sent away that very year, under the command of his good friends Amidas and Barlow, to take possession of the country in the name of his royal mistress, the Queen of England.

These worthy commanders, for the advantage of the trade winds, shaped their course first to the Caribbee Islands, thence stretching away by the Gulf of Florida, drop anchor not far from Roanoke Inlet. They ventured ashore near that place upon an island now called Colleton Island, where they set up the arms of England, and claimed the adjacent country in right of their sovereign lady, the Queen; and this ceremony being duly performed, they kindly invited the neighboring Indians to traffic with them.

These poor people at first approacht the English with great caution, having heard much of the treachery of the Spaniards, and not knowing but these strangers might be as treacherous as they. But, at length, discovering a kind

---

[1] Our modern text is based on the edition prepared by William K. Boyd, Raleigh: The North Carolina Historical Commission, 1929.

of good nature in their looks, they ventured to draw near, and barter their skins and furs, for the baubles and trinkets of the English.

These first adventurers made a very profitable voyage, raising at least a thousand per cent. upon their cargo. Amongst other Indian commodities, they brought over some of the bewitching vegetable, tobacco. And this being the first that ever came to England, Sir Walter thought he could do no less than make a present of some of the brightest of it to his royal mistress, for her own smoking.

The Queen graciously accepted of it, but finding her stomach sicken after two or three whiffs, it was presently whispered by the Earl of Leicester's faction, that Sir Walter had certainly poisoned her. But Her Majesty soon recovering her disorder, obliged the Countess of Nottingham and all her maids to smoke a whole pipe out amongst them.

As it happened some ages before to be the fashion to saunter to the Holy Land, and go upon other quixot[ic] adventures, so it was now grown the humor to take a trip to America. The Spaniards had lately discovered rich mines in their part of the West Indies, which made their maritime neighbors eager to do so too. This modish frenzy being still more inflamed by the charming account given of Virginia, by the first adventurers, made many fond of removing to such a paradise.

Happy was he, and still happier she, that could get themselves transported, fondly expecting their coarsest utensils, in that happy place, would be of massy silver.

This made it easy for the company to procure as many volunteers as they wanted for their new colony; but, like most other undertakers who have no assistance from the public, they starved the design by too much frugality; for, unwilling to launch out at first into too much expense, they shipt off but few people at a time, and those but scantily provided. The adventurers were, besides, idle and extravagant, and expected they might live without work in so plentiful a country.

These wretches were set ashore not far from Roanoke Inlet, but by some fatal disagreement, or laziness, were either starved or cut to pieces by the Indians.

Several repeated misadventures of this kind did, for some time, allay the itch of sailing to this New World; but the distemper broke out again about the year 1606. Then it happened that the Earl of Southampton and several other persons, eminent for their quality and estates, were invited into the company, who applied themselves once more to people the then almost abandoned colony. For this purpose they embarkt about an hundred men, most of them reprobates of good families, and related to some of the company, who were men of quality and fortune.

The ships that carried them made a shift to find a more direct way to Virginia, and ventured thro the Capes into the Bay of Chesapeake. The same night they came to an anchor at the mouth of Powhatan, the same as James River, where they built a small fort at a place called Point Comfort.

This settlement stood its ground from that time forward in spite of all the blunders and disagreement of the first adventurers, and the many calamities that befell the colony afterwards.

The six gentlemen who were first named of the company by the crown, and who were empowered to choose an annual president from among themselves, were always engaged in factions and quarrels, while the rest detested work more than famine. At this rate the colony must have come to nothing, had it not been for the vigilance and bravery of Capt. Smith, who struck a terror into all the Indians round about. This gentleman took some pains to persuade the men to plant Indian corn, but they look upon all labor as a curse. They chose rather to depend upon the musty provisions that were sent from England: and when they failed they were forct to take more pains to seek for wild fruits in the woods, than they would have taken in tilling the ground. Besides, this exposed them to be knockt on the head by the Indians, and gave them fluxes into the bargain, which thinned the plantation very much. To supply this mortality, they were reinforct the year following with a greater number of people, amongst which were fewer gentlemen and more laborers, who, however, took care not to kill themselves with work.

These found the first adventurers in a very starving condition, but relieved their wants with the fresh supply they brought with them. From Kiquotan they extended themselves as far as Jamestown, where like true Englishmen, they built a church that cost no more than fifty pounds, and a tavern that cost five hundred.[2]

They had now made peace with the Indians, but there was one thing wanting to make that peace lasting. The natives could, by no means, persuade themselves that the English were heartily their friends, so long as they disdained to intermarry with them. And, in earnest, had the English consulted their own security and the good of the colony—had they intended either to civilize or convert these gentiles, they would have brought their stomachs to embrace this prudent alliance.

The Indians are generally tall and well-proportioned, which may make full amends for the darkness of their complexions. Add to this, that they are healthy and strong with constitutions untainted by lewdness, and not enfeebled by luxury. Besides, morals and all considered, I can't think the Indians were much greater heathens than the first adventurers, who, had they been good Christians, would have had the charity to take this only method of converting the natives to Christianity. For, after all that can be said, a sprightly lover is the most prevailing missionary that can be sent amongst these, or any other infidels.

[2] Boyd points out that there is no documentary support for Byrd's statement that Jamestown had a tavern in the first 16 years.

Besides, the poor Indians would have had less reason to complain that the English took away their land, if they had received it by way of portion with their daughters. Had such affinities been contracted in the beginning, how much bloodshed had been prevented, and how populous would the country have been, and, consequently, how considerable? Nor would the shade of the skin have been any reproach at this day; for if a Moor may be washt white in 3 generations, surely an Indian might have been blancht in two.

The French, for their parts, have not been so squeamish in Canada, who upon trial find abundance of attraction in the Indians. Their late Grand Monarch thought it not below even the dignity of a Frenchman to become one flesh with this people, and therefore ordered 100 livres for any of his subjects, man or woman, that would intermarry with a native.

By this piece of policy we find the French interest very much strengthened amongst the savages, and their religion, such as it is, propagated just as far as their love. And I heartily wish this well-concerted scheme don't hereafter give the French an advantage over His Majesty's good subjects on the northern continent of America.

About the same time New England was pared off from Virginia by letters patent, bearing date April the 10th, 1608. Several gentlemen of the town and neighborhood of Plymouth obtained this Grant, with the Lord Chief Justice Popham at their head.

Their bounds were specified to extend from 38 to 45 degrees of northern latitude, with a breadth of one hundred miles from the seashore. The first 14 years, this company encountered many difficulties, and lost many men, tho' far from being discouraged, they sent over numerous recruits of Presbyterians, every year, who for all that, had much ado to stand their ground, with all their fighting and praying.

But about the year 1620, a large swarm of Dissenters fled thither from the severities of their stepmother, the Church. These saints conceiving the same aversion to the copper complexion of the natives, with that of the first adventurers to Virginia, would, on no terms, contract alliances with them, afraid perhaps, like the Jews of old, lest they might be drawn into idolatry by those strange women.

Whatever disgusted them I can't say, but this false delicacy creating in the Indians a jealousy that the English were ill affected towards them, was the cause that many of them were cut off, and the rest exposed to various distresses.

This reinforcement was landed not far from Cape Cod, where, for their greater security they built a fort, and near it a small town, which in honor of the proprietors, was called New Plymouth. But they still had many discouragements to struggle with, tho' by being well supported from home, they by degrees triumpht over them all.

Their brethren, after this, flocked over so fast, that in a few years they extended the settlement one hundred miles along the coast, including Rhode Island and Martha's Vineyard.

Thus the colony throve apace, and was thronged with large detachments of Independents and Presbyterians, who thought themselves persecuted at home.

Tho' these people may be ridiculed for some pharisaical particularities in their worship and behavior, yet they were very useful subjects, as being frugal and industrious, giving no scandal or bad example, at least by any open and public vices. By which excellent qualities they had much the advantage of the southern colony, who thought their being members of the Established Church sufficient to sanctify very loose and profligate morals. For this reason New England improved much faster than Virginia, and in seven or eight years New Plymouth, like Switzerland, seemed too narrow a territory for its inhabitants.

For this reason, several gentlemen of fortune purchased of the company that canton of New England now called Massachusetts colony. And King James confirmed the purchase by his royal charter, dated March the 4th, 1628. In less than 2 years after, above 1000 of the Puritanical sect removed thither with considerable effects, and these were followed by such crowds, that a proclamation was issued in England, forbidding any more of His Majesty's subjects to be shipt off. But this had the usual effect of things forbidden, and served only to make the wilful Independents flock over the faster. And about this time it was that Messrs. Hampden and Pym, and (some say) Oliver Cromwell, to show how little they valued the King's authority, took a trip to New England.

In the year 1630, the famous city of Boston was built, in a commodious situation for trade and navigation, the same being on a peninsula at the bottom of Massachusetts Bay.

This town is now the most considerable of any on the British continent, containing at least 8,000 houses and 40,000 inhabitants.[3] The trade it drives, is very great to Europe, and to every part of the West Indies, having near 1,000 ships and lesser vessels belonging to it.

Altho the extent of the Massachusetts colony reached near one hundred and ten miles in length, and half as much in breadth, yet many of its inhabitants, thinking they wanted elbow-room, quitted their old seats in the year 1636, and formed 2 new colonies: that of Connecticut and New Haven. These King Charles the 2d erected into one government in 1664,[4] and gave them many valuable privileges, and among the rest, that of choosing their own governors. The extent of these united colonies may be about seventy miles long and fifty broad.

Besides these several settlements, there sprang up still another, a little more northerly, called New Hampshire. But that consisting of no more than two counties, and not being in condition to support the charge of a distinct

[3] Probably Boston was less than half as populous as Byrd believed it to be.

[4] Actually, 1662.

government, was glad to be incorporated with that of Massachusetts, but upon condition, however, of being named in all public acts, for fear of being quite lost and forgot in the coalition.

In like manner New Plymouth joined itself to Massachusetts, except only Rhode Island, which, tho' of small extent, got itself erected into a separate government by a charter from King Charles the 2d, soon after the Restoration, and continues so to this day.

These governments all continued in possession of their respective rights and privileges till the Year 1683,[5] when that of Massachusetts was made void in England by a quo warranto.

In consequence of which the King was pleased to name Sir Edmund Andros his first governor of that colony. This gentleman, it seems, ruled them with a rod of iron till the Revolution,[6] when they laid unhallowed hands upon him, and sent him prisoner to England.

This undutiful proceeding met with an easy forgiveness at that happy juncture. King William and his Royal Consort were not only pleased to overlook this indignity offered to their governor, but being made sensible how unfairly their charter had been taken away, most graciously granted them a new one.

By this some new franchises were given them, as an equivalent for those of coining money and electing a governor, which were taken away. However, the other colonies of Connecticut and Rhode Island had the luck to remain in possession of their original charters, which to this day have never been called in question.

The next country dismembered from Virginia was New Scotland [Nova Scotia], claimed by the crown of England in virtue of the first discovery by Sebastian Cabot. By color of this title, King James the First granted it to Sir William Alexander by patent, dated September the 10th, 1621.

But this patentee never sending any colony thither, and the French believing it very convenient for them, obtained a surrender of it from their good friend and ally, King Charles the 2d, by the Treaty of Breda. And, to show their gratitude, they stirred up the Indians soon after to annoy their neighbors of New England. Murders happened continually to His Majesty's subjects by their means, till Sir William Phips took their town of Port Royal, in the year 1690. But as the English are better at taking than keeping strong places, the French retook it soon, and remained masters of it till 1710, when General Nicholson wrested it, once more, out of their hands.

Afterwards the Queen of Great Britain's right to it was recognized and confirmed by the treaty of Utrecht.

Another limb lopt off from Virginia was New York, which the Dutch seized very unfairly, on pretense of having purchased it from Captain Hud-

[5] Actually, 1684. [6] April 18, 1689.

son, the first discoverer. Nor was their way of taking possession of it a whit more justifiable than their pretended title.

Their West India Company tampered with some worthy English skippers (who had contracted with a swarm of English Dissenters to transport them to Hudson River) by no means to land them there, but to carry them some leagues more northerly.[7]

This Dutch finesse took exactly, and gave the company time soon after to seize the Hudson River for themselves. But Sir Samuel Argall, then governor of Virginia, understanding how the King's subjects had been abused by these republicans, marcht thither with a good force, and obliged them to renounce all pretensions to that country.[8] The worst of it was, the knight depended on their parole to ship themselves to Brazil, but took no measures to make this slippery people as good as their word.

No sooner was the good Governor retired, but the honest Dutch began to build forts and strengthen themselves in their ill-gotten possessions; nor did any of the King's liege people take the trouble to drive these intruders thence. The Civil War in England, and the confusions it brought forth, allowed no leisure to such distant considerations. Tho tis strange that the Protector, who neglected no occasion to mortify the Dutch, did not afterwards call them to account for this breach of faith. However, after the Restoration, the King sent a squadron of his ships of war, under the command of Sir Robert Carr, and reduced that province to his obedience.

Some time after, His Majesty was pleased to grant that country to His Royal Highness, the Duke of York, by letters patent, dated March the 12th, 1664. But to show the modesty of the Dutch to the life, tho they had no shadow of right to New York, yet they demanded Surinam, a more valuable country, as an equivalent for it, and our able ministers at that time had the generosity to give it them.

But what wounded Virginia deepest was the cutting off MARYLAND from it, by charter from King Charles the 1st, to Sir George Calvert, afterwards Lord Baltimore, bearing the date the 20th of June, 1632. The truth of it is, it begat much speculation in those days, how it came about that a good Protestant king should bestow so bountiful a grant upon a zealous Roman Catholic. But 'tis probable it was one fatal instance amongst many other of His Majesty's complaisance to the Queen.

However that happened, 'tis certain this province afterwards proved a commodious retreat for persons of that communion. The memory of the gunpowder treason plot was still fresh in everybody's mind, and made Eng-

---

[7] This paragraph repeats a suspicion held against the captain of the *Mayflower* by some Pilgrims, but given no credit in Bradford's history *Of Plymouth Plantation* or in modern scholarship.

[8] The historicity of this expedition of 1613 has been challenged by modern scholars.

land too hot for Papists to live in, without danger of being burnt with the Pope, every 5th of November; for which reason legions of them transplanted themselves to Maryland in order to be safe, as well from the insolence of the populace as the rigor of the government.

Not only the gunpowder treason, but every other plot, both pretended and real, that has been trumpt up in England ever since, has helpt to people his Lordship's propriety.

But what has proved most serviceable to it was the grand rebellion against King Charles the 1st, when everything that bore the least tokens of popery was sure to be demolisht, and every man that profest it was in jeopardy of suffering the same kind of martyrdom the Roman priests do in Sweden.

Soon after the reduction of New York, the Duke was pleasd to grant out of it all that tract of land included between Hudson and Delaware Rivers, to the Lord Berkley and Sir George Carteret, by deed dated June the 24th, 1664. And when these grantees came to make partition of this territory, His Lordship's moiety was called West Jersey, and that to Sir George, East Jersey.

But before the date of this grant, the Swedes began to gain footing in part of that country; tho, after they saw the fate of New York, they were glad to submit to the King of England, on the easy terms of remaining in their possessions, and rendering a moderate quitrent. Their posterity continue there to this day, and think their lot cast in a much fairer land than Dalicarlia. [9]

The proprietors of New Jersey, finding more trouble than profit in their new dominions, made over their right to several other persons, who obtained a fresh grant from His Royal Highness, dated March 14th, 1682.

Several of the grantees, being Quakers and Anabaptists, failed not to encourage many of their own persuasion to remove to this peaceful region. Amongst them were a swarm of Scots Quakers, who were not tolerated to exercise the gifts of the spirit in their own country.

Besides the hopes of being safe from persecution in this retreat, the new proprietors inveigled many over by this tempting account of the country: that it was a place free from those 3 great scourges of mankind, priests, lawyers, and physicians. Nor did they tell a word of a lie, for the people were yet too poor to maintain these learned gentlemen, who, everywhere, love to be paid well for what they do; and, like the Jews, can't breathe in a climate where nothing is to be got.

The Jerseys continued under the government of these proprietors till the year 1702, when they made a formal surrender of the dominion to the Queen, reserving however the property of the soil to themselves. So soon as

[9] A Swedish province.

the bounds of New Jersey came to be distinctly laid off, it appeared that there was still a narrow slip of land, lying betwixt that colony and Maryland. Of this, William Penn, a man of much worldly wisdom, and some eminence among the Quakers, got early notice, and by the credit he had with the Duke of York, obtained a patent for it, dated March the 4th, 1680 [1681].

It was a little surprising to some people how a Quaker should be so much in the good graces of a popish prince; tho, after all, it may be pretty well accounted for. This ingenious person had not been bred a Quaker; but, in his earlier days, had been a man of pleasure about the town. He had a beautiful form and very taking address, which made him successful with the ladies, and particularly with a mistress of the Duke of Monmouth. By this gentlewoman he had a daughter, who had beauty enough to raise her to be a duchess, and continued to be a toast full 30 Years.[10]

But this amour had like to have brought our fine gentleman in danger of a duel, had he not discreetly sheltered himself under this peaceable persuasion. Besides, his father having been a flag-officer in the navy, while the Duke of York was Lord High Admiral, might recommend the son to his favor. This piece of secret history I thought proper to mention, to wipe off the suspicion of his having been popishly inclined.

This gentleman's first grant confined him within pretty narrow bounds, giving him only that portion of land which contains Buckingham, Philadelphia and Chester Counties. But to get these bounds a little extended, he pusht his interest still further with His Royal Highness, and obtained a fresh grant of the three lower counties, called New Castle, Kent and Sussex, which still remained within the New York patent, and had been luckily left out of the grant of New Jersey.

The six counties being thus incorporated, the proprietor dignified the whole with the name of Pennsylvania.

The Quakers flockt over to this country in shoals, being averse to go to heaven the same way with the bishops. Amongst them were not a few of good substance, who went vigorously upon every kind of improvement; and thus much I may truly say in their praise, that by diligence and frugality, for which this harmless sect is remarkable, and by having no vices but such as are private, they have in a few years made Pennsylvania a very fine country.

The truth is, they have observed exact justice with all the natives that border upon them; they have purchased all their lands from the Indians; and tho they paid but a trifle for them, it has procured them the credit of being more righteous than their neighbors. They have likewise had the prudence to treat them kindly upon all occasions, which has saved them from many wars and massacres wherein the other colonies have been indiscreetly involved.

[10] There seems to be no basis for this story or for the denouement in the next paragraph.

The truth of it is, a people whose principles forbid them to draw the carnal sword, were in the right to give no provocation.

Both the French and the Spaniards had, in the name of their respective monarchs, long ago taken possession of that part of the northern continent that now goes by the name of Carolina; but finding it produced neither gold nor silver, as they greedily expected, and meeting such returns from the Indians as their own cruelty and treachery deserved, they totally abandond it. In this deserted condition that country lay for the space of 90 years, till King Charles the 2d, finding it a DERELICT, granted it away to the Earl of Clarendon and others, by his royal charter, dated March the 24th, 1663. The boundary of that grant towards Virginia was a due west line from Luck Island (the same as Colleton Island), lying in 36 degrees n. latitude, quite to the South Sea.

But afterwards Sir William Berkeley, who was one of the grantees and at that time governor of Virginia, finding a territory of 31 miles in breadth between the inhabited part of Virginia and the above-mentioned boundary of Carolina, advised the Lord Clarendon of it. And His Lordship had interest enough with the King to obtain a second patent to include it, dated June the 30th, 1665.

This last grant describes the bounds between Virginia and Carolina in these words: "To run from the north end of Corotuck Inlet, due west to Weyanoke Creek, lying within or about the degree of thirty-six and thirty minutes of northern latitude, and from thence west, in a direct line, as far as the South Sea."[11] Without question, this boundary was well known at the time the charter was granted, but in a long course of years Weyanoke Creek lost its name, so that it became a controversy where it lay. Some ancient persons in Virginia affirmed it was the same with Wicocon, and others again in Carolina were as positive it was Nottoway River.

In the mean time, the people on the frontiers entered for land, and took out patents by guess, either from the King or the Lords Proprietors. But the Crown was like to be the loser by this incertainty, because the terms both of taking up and seating land were easier much in Carolina. The yearly taxes to the public were likewise there less burdensome, which laid Virginia under a plain disadvantage.

This consideration put that government upon entering into measures with North Carolina, to terminate the dispute, and settle a certain boundary between the two colonies. All the difficulty was, to find out which was truly Weyanoke Creek. The difference was too considerable to be given up by either side, there being a territory of 15 miles betwixt the two streams in controversy.

---

[11] Accurate on the boundaries but not accurately quoted.

However, till that matter could be adjusted, it was agreed on both sides, that no lands at all should be granted within the disputed bounds. Virginia observed this agreement punctually, but I am sorry I can't say the same of North Carolina. The great officers of that province were loath to lose the fees accruing from the grants of land, and so private interest got the better of public spirit; and I wish that were the only place in the world where such politics are fashionable.

All the steps that were taken afterwards in that affair, will best appear by the report of the Virginia Commissioners, recited in the Order of Council given at St. James's, March the 1st, 1710, set down in the Appendix.

It must be owned, the report of those gentlemen was severe upon the then commissioners of North Carolina, and particularly upon Mr. [Edward] Moseley. I won't take upon me to say with how much justice they said so many hard things, tho it had been fairer play to have given the parties accused a copy of such representations, that they might have answered what they could for themselves.

But since that was not done, I must beg leave to say thus much in behalf of Mr. Moseley, that he was not much in the wrong to find fault with the quadrant produced by the surveyors of Virginia because that instrument placed the mouth of Nottoway River in the latitude of 37 degrees; whereas, by an accurate observation made since, it appears to line in 36° 30′ ½′, so that there was an error of near 30 minutes, either in the instrument or in those who made use of it.

Besides, it is evident the mouth of Nottoway River agrees much better with the latitude, wherein the Carolina Charter supposed Weyanoke Creek (namely, in or about 36 degrees and 30 minutes), than it does with Wicocon Creek, which is about 15 miles more southerly.

III
Testaments of Eighteenth-Century Experience

All of the following selections are in some sense personal statements of mid-eighteenth-century American character. Benjamin Franklin is a writer of such major importance to American letters that no single category can contain the variety of his work; he might just as well appear, for example, in the chapter on the Revolution and the Republic. But the variety of *personae* and forms in which he expressed himself, from his first days as a young printer and journalist to the last section of his autobiography nearly 60 years later, repeatedly brings a strong individual intelligence into the public arena to reason prudently on small or large questions of public welfare. And in John Woolman, William Bartram, and Hector St. John de Crèvecoeur a less subtle conscientious faith brings a single observer into reflective action on the nature of American society and (for the latter two) the special personal significance of North American Nature. Thomas Hutchinson, who as royal governor of Massachusetts became in the 1770's one of the most unpopular men in America, stands here as the author of the best eighteenth-century history of early Massachusetts, a mind whose cool intelligence declares itself independent of ancestral prejudices, both familial and provincial.

BENJAMIN FRANKLIN

(1706–1790)

Our conception of this great man is so closely tied to his own writing that it is difficult to imagine him as a man sitting down to report on actions that occurred apart from his literary or polemical composition. From the time of his first publication, moreover, there was a certain disguise as well as self-expression in his writing, for as he cheerfully tells us in his autobiography he not only wrote that first piece under the pseudonym of Mrs. Silence Dogood but concealed the author's actual identity from the editor, his own brother. For almost 70 years thereafter Benjamin Franklin's achievements, whether in politics or letters or science, bring us back to recognizing his practice and his extraordinary skill as a writer. He first appeared as Mrs. Silence Dogood, he made his first fortune and his original fame as Richard Saunders, author of *Poor Richard's Almanac,* he often appeared in his own *Pennsylvania Gazette* as a fictitious character in a dialogue, and even toward the end of his life, as a plain republican diplomat in France and as the wise old narrator in his autobiography, he enjoyed playing roles.

Both in his writing and in his private, civic, and political action Franklin links the culture of Puritan Boston to the freethinking republicanism of the American Revolution. Although he tells us that he was converted to Deism by some anti-Deistic books in his father's library, he also acknowledges his father's strong influence on his character,

The standard edition is *The Papers of Benjamin Franklin,* ed. Leonard W. Labaree and others, 1959–   . Seventeen volumes have been published, covering the years through 1770, but including the autobiography. For the remaining years *The Writings of Benjamin Franklin,* 10 vols., ed. A. H. Smyth, 1905–1907 will suffice until the Labaree edition has been completed. Max Farrand has edited *The Autobiography of Benjamin Franklin: A Restoration of a "Fair Copy,"* 1949, and *Benjamin Franklin's Memoirs: A Parallel Text Edition,* 1949. In 1950, Verner W. Crane collected and edited *Benjamin Franklin's Letters to the Press, 1758–1775.*

Biographical studies are Carl Van Doren, *Benjamin Franklin,* 1938, Carl L. Becker,

Benjamin Franklin, A Biographical Sketch, 1946; I. Bernard Cohen, *Benjamin Franklin: His Contributions to the American Tradition,* 1953; Richard Amacher, *Benjamin Franklin,* 1962. Critical studies include Bruce I. Granger, *Benjamin Franklin, An American Man of Letters,* 1964; David Levin, "The Autobiography of Benjamin Franklin: The Puritan Experimenter in Life and Art," *Yale Review,* 53 (1964): 258–275; Robert F. Sayre, *The Examined Self: Benjamin Franklin, Henry Adams, Henry James,* 1964; Alfred O. Aldridge, *Benjamin Franklin and Nature's God,* 1967; Ralph Ketcham, *Benjamin Franklin,* 1965; James A. Sappenfield, *A Sweet Instruction: Franklin's Journalism as a Literary Apprenticeship,* 1973.

An engraving of Benjamin Franklin at 60, from a painting by D. Martin.
(Inventor, Edward Savage, Yale University Art Gallery, Mabel Brady Garvan Collection.)

and he acknowledges Cotton Mather, John Bunyan, John Milton, and Daniel Defoe as well. Franklin's emphasis on industry, frugality, utility, the value of diligence in one's calling, the dangers of self-indulgence, and above all the importance of community service—all these have origins in Puritanism, though of course the meaning of piety has been transformed. And before one condemns the presumptuousness in Franklin's outline for the course in the art of virtue, one should notice both the unmistakably humorous, self-critical paragraph with which his narrative of that experiment begins, and the clear recognition (implicit in his metaphor of weeding a garden and in his purchase of a book with ivory pages) that the task of self-improvement is never done, that new faults will always "peep out" from surprising directions while one is concentrating one's attention on eradicating the old ones. What Franklin does in the autobiography is to make himself representative of his time and his country—the young man learning by experience to build a strong character and, with a combination of luck, prudence, and shrewdness, to make his way in the world to a respectable position from which he can enjoy the pleasure of serving the community, the world of science, and the republic. Insofar as he expects his own experience to serve as a model for others, he preaches the doctrine of enlightened self-interest, which he had defined in 1735 in the dialogue called "A Man of Sense." It is important to recognize the difference between his faith that honesty (for example) is the best policy and the cynical view (which he rejected) that one should be *dis*honest if dishonesty became profitable.

The *Autobiography* was written in Franklin's old age, at four different times beginning when he was 65. The selections in this anthology, though necessarily dominated by that masterpiece, are intended to represent his literary achievement at different times and in different modes. "A Man of Sense" is one of many dialogues published in Franklin's newspaper, *The Pennsylvania Gazette,* before he was 30. *The Way to Wealth,* first published as "Poor Richard Improved," was Franklin's introduction to the twenty-fifth annual edition of *Poor Richard's Almanac.* And the later essays indicate the variety of subject and form in Franklin's later years.

A few brief lines can suffice to review Franklin's extraordinary career, which the reader of his autobiography will do well to remember was presumably well-known to prospective readers in his own time, when Franklin was the first man to be called the father of his country. Apprenticed to his brother James for training as a printer, Franklin ran away when he was only 16 and found work as a printer in Philadelphia. After a misadventure in England, where he was sent on a false promise by the governor of Pennsylvania, Franklin returned to Philadelphia and established himself as a successful printer and journalist, retiring from full-time work at the age of 42. He became a civic and political leader, head of the popular party in many conflicts with the proprietors and later with the royal government. He invented the Franklin stove and bifocal eyeglasses, and he performed successful electrical experiments that won him recognition throughout the Western world. He made extraordinary improvements in local and continental services, from volunteer fire companies, street lighting, and street cleaning to an Albany plan of union for the colonies and a much more efficient postal service. Finally, he was a national representative and leader throughout the Revolution and the early years of the Republic—as agent of the Massachusetts House in London, as a member of the committee to draft the Declaration of Independence, as a diplomatic representative to France during the critical negotiations for the alliance in the 1770's, and as a delegate and an effective speaker during the Constitutional Convention in 1787. When he died in 1790 he was probably (with George Washington) the most beloved man in Europe and North America. The changes in his reputation in the nineteenth and twentieth centuries would form an excellent introduction to changing ethical standards in American civilization.

For the Franklin selections, which can be easily read in the original form, we have not modernized spelling and capitalization, so that students may have available one of the clearest writers of eighteenth-century American prose approximately as contemporaries might have read him.

Slippery Sidewalks[1]

Mr. Franklin,

Walking the Street on one of these late slippery Mornings, I caught two terrible Falls, which made me, by way of Precaution for the future, get my Shoes frosted before I went home:[2] for I am a stiff old Fellow, and my Joints none of the most pliant. At the Door before which I fell last, stood a Gentleman-like Looby, with a couple of Damsels, who all made themselves wonderful merry with my Misfortune: And had not a good Woman, whose Door I had just passed, come and helped me up, I might for ought I know, have given them an Hour's Diversion before I found my Legs again. This good Woman, Heaven bless her, had sprinkled Ashes before her Door: I wish her long Life and better Neighbours. I have reason to think the merry People would not have risen so early, and exposed themselves to the Air, that cold Morning, were it not for the sake of enjoying such Entertainments as I

---

[1] The text is the Yale edition of Franklin's papers, Volume I. Printed in *The Pennsylvania Gazette*, January 11, 1732/3.

[2] That is, fitted with an iron spike at the heel.

afforded them. But they were not alone in the Thing; I saw before I got home, twenty other Gigglers, all employ'd at their Doors in the same Manner. Strange Perverseness of Disposition! to delight in the Mishaps which befal People who have no way disoblig'd us. My Shoes, as I have said, being frosted, I intend the next slippery Time to make a Tour throughout the Town, and take a general List of all the Housekeepers, whom I will divide into three Classes. The humane, kind, compassionate, benevolent Class, I shall easily distinguish by the Ashes at their Doors, as God's People were distinguish'd in Ægypt by the Sprinkling of their Door-posts. The malicious and ill-natured Class I shall know by their Mirth at every Fall or accidental Slip of the Passengers in the Street. The indifferent, thoughtless Class, are the rest. As every Man that walks upon uneven Ice, hazards at each Step his Limbs; methinks some Honours ought to be decreed those of my first Class, proportionate to what the Romans gave him that sav'd the Life of a Fellow-Citizen: They shall, however, be sure of my Respect and Friendship. With regard to those of my two latter Classes, I am resolved, I will not so much as civilly salute one of them, I will not give one of them the Wall,[3] I will not make Room for any of them at a Fire, nor hand them any Thing at a Table, I will not direct a Customer to one of them, if any of my first Class deal in the same Things: In short, I will be as cross-grain'd towards them as 'tis possible for a good-natur'd old Man to be; who is Your Friend and Reader,

N.N.

[3] An old expression for a particular act of courtesy or deference, dating from the time when one who walked nearest to the wall of a building was less likely to encounter sewage flowing in the middle of the street or thrown from an upper window toward the central gutter in the street.

On Literary Style[1]

To the Printer of the *Gazette*.

There are few Men, of Capacity for making any considerable Figure in Life, who have not frequent Occasion to communicate their Thoughts to others in *Writing;* if not sometimes publickly as Authors, yet continually in the Management of their private Affairs, both of Business and Friendship: and since, when ill-express'd, the most proper Sentiments and justest Reasoning lose much of their native Force and Beauty, it seems to me that there is scarce any Accomplishment more necessary to a Man of Sense, than that of *Writing well* in his Mother Tongue: But as most other polite Acquire-

[1] From the Yale edition, Volume I. The essay was published in *The Pennsylvania Gazette,* August 2, 1733.

Franklin wrote this paper for his club, the Junto, an informal group organized for self-education and intellectual exchange during his early days in Philadelphia.

ments, make a greater Appearance in a Man's Character, this however useful, is generally neglected or forgotten.
self-education and intellectual exchange during his early days in Philadelphia.

I believe there is no better Means of learning to write well, than this of attempting to entertain the Publick now and then in one of your Papers. When the Writer conceals himself, he has the Advantage of hearing the Censure both of Friends and Enemies, express'd with more Impartiality. And since, in some degree, it concerns the Credit of the Province, that such Things as are printed be performed tolerably well, mutual Improvement seems to be the Duty of all Lovers of Writing: I shall therefore frankly request those of others in Return.

I have thought in general, that whoever would write so as not to displease good Judges, should have particular Regard to these three Things, viz. That his Performance be *smooth, clear,* and *short:* For the contrary Qualities are apt to offend, either the Ear, the Understanding, or the Patience.

'Tis an Observation of Dr. Swift,[3] that modern Writers injure the Smoothness of our Tongue, by omitting Vowels wherever it is possible, and joining the harshest Consonants together with only an Apostrophe between; thus for *judged,* in it self not the smoothest of Words, they say *judg'd;* for *disturbed, disturb'd,* etc. It may be added to this, says another, that by changing *eth* into *s,* they have shortned one Syllable in a multitude of Words, and have thereby encreased, not only the *Hissing,* too offensive before, but also the great Number of Monosyllables, of which, without great Difficulty, a smooth Sentence cannot be composed. The Smoothness of a Period is also often Hurt by Parentheses, and therefore the best Writers endeavour to avoid them.

To write *clearly,* not only the most expressive, but the plainest Words should be chosen. In this, as well as in every other Particular requisite to Clearness, Dr. Tillotson[4] is an excellent Example. The Fondness of some Writers for such Words as carry with them an Air of Learning, renders them unintelligible to more than half their Countrymen. If a Man would that his Writings have an Effect on the Generality of Readers, he had better imitate that Gentleman, who would use no Word in his Works that was not well understood by his Cook-maid.

A too frequent Use of Phrases ought likewise to be avoided by him that would write clearly. They trouble the Language, not only rendring it extreamly difficult to Foreigners, but make the Meaning obscure to a great number of English Readers. Phrases, like learned Words, are seldom used without Affectation; when, with all true Judges, the simplest Stile is the most beautiful.

But supposing the most proper Words and Expressions chosen, the Per-

[3] Jonathan Swift (1667-1745).
[4] John Tillotson (1630-1694), Archbishop of Canterbury, whose prose was widely admired.

formance may yet be weak and obscure, if it has not *Method*. If a Writer would *persuade*, he should proceed gradually from Things already allow'd, to those from which Assent is yet with-held, and make their Connection manifest. If he would *inform*, he must advance regularly from Things known to things unknown, distinctly without Confusion, and the lower he begins the better. It is a common Fault in Writers, to allow their Readers too much Knowledge: They begin with that which should be the Middle, and skipping backwards and forwards, 'tis impossible for any one but he who is perfect in the Subject before, to understand their Work, and such an one has no Occasion to read it. Perhaps a Habit of using good Method, cannot be better acquired, than by learning a little Geometry or Algebra.

Amplification, or the Art of saying Little in Much, should only be allowed to Speakers. If they preach, a Discourse of considerable Length is expected from them, upon every Subject they undertake, and perhaps they are not stock'd with naked Thoughts sufficient to furnish it out. If they plead in the Courts, it is of Use to speak abundance, tho' they reason little; for the Ignorant in a Jury, can scarcely believe it possible that a Man can talk so much and so long without being in the Right. Let them have the Liberty then, of repeating the same Sentences in other Words; let them put an Adjective to every Substantive, and double every Substantive with a Synonima; for this is more agreeable than hauking, spitting, taking Snuff, or any other Means of concealing Hesitation. Let them multiply Definitions, Comparisons, Similitudes and Examples. Permit them to make a Detail of Causes and Effects, enumerate all the Consequences, and express one Half by Metaphor and Circumlocution: Nay, allow the Preacher to tell us whatever a Thing is negatively, before he begins to tell us what it is affirmatively; and suffer him to divide and subdivide as far as *Two and fiftiethly*. All this is not intolerable while it is not written. But when a Discourse is to be bound down upon Paper, and subjected to the calm leisurely Examination of nice Judgment, every Thing that is needless gives Offence; and therefore all should be retrenched, that does not directly conduce to the End design'd. Had this been always done, many large and tiresome Folio's would have shrunk into Pamphlets, and many a Pamphlet into a single Period. However, tho' a multitude of Words obscure the Sense, and 'tis necessary to abridge a verbose Author in order to understand him; yet a Writer should take especial Care on the other Hand, that his Brevity doth not hurt his Perspicuity.

After all, if the Author does not intend his Piece for general Reading, he must exactly suit his Stile and Manner to the particular Taste of those he proposes for his Readers. Every one observes, the different Ways of Writing and Expression used by the different Sects of Religion; and can readily enough pronounce, that it is improper to use some of these Stiles in common, or to use the common Stile, when we address some of these Sects in particular.

To conclude, I shall venture to lay it down as a Maxim, *That no Piece can properly be called good, and well written, which is void of any Tendency to benefit the Reader, either by improving his Virtue or his Knowledge*. This Principle every Writer would do well to have in View, whenever he undertakes to write. All Performances done for meer Ostentation of Parts, are really contemptible; and withal far more subject to the Severity of Criticism, than those more meanly written, wherein the Author appears to have aimed at the Good of others. For when 'tis visible to every one, that a Man writes to show his Wit only, all his Expressions are sifted, and his Sense examined, in the nicest and most ill-natur'd manner; and every one is glad of an Opportunity to mortify him. But, what a vast Destruction would there be of Books, if they were to be saved or condemned on a Tryal by this Rule!

Besides, Pieces meerly humorous, are of all Sorts the hardest to succeed in. If they are not natural, they are stark naught; and there can be no real Humour in an Affectation of Humour.

Perhaps it may be said, that an ill Man is able to write an ill Thing well; that is, having an ill Design, and considering who are to be his Readers, he may use the properest Stile and Arguments to attain his Point. In this Sense, that is best wrote, which is best adapted to the Purpose of the Writer.

I am apprehensive, dear Readers, lest in this Piece, I should be guilty of every Fault I condemn, and deficient in every Thing I recommend; so much easier it is to offer Rules than to practise them. I am sure, however, of this, that I am Your very sincere Friend and Servant.

A Man of Sense[1]

Mr. Franklin,

Being the other Day near the Meeting-House Corner with some Gentlemen, in the open Street, I heard the following Piece of Conversation; and penn'd it down as soon as I came home. I am confident it varies scarce any thing from what really passed; and as it pleased the By-standers, it may possibly please the Publick, if you give it a Place in your Paper.

It not being proper to name the Persons discoursing, I shall call one of them Socrates, his manner of Arguing being in my Opinion, somewhat like that of Socrates: And, if you please, the other may be Crito. I am Yours, etc.

A.A.

Socrates. Who is that well-dress'd Man that passed by just now?

Crito. He is a Gentleman of this City, esteem'd a *Man of Sense*, but not very honest.

---

[1] The text is the Yale edition, Volume I. This dialogue was printed in *The Pennsylvania Gazette*, February 11, 1734|5.

S. The Appellation of *a Man of Sense* is of late frequently given, and seems to come naturally into the Character of every Man we are about to praise: But I am at some Loss to know whether a Man who *is not honest* can deserve it.

C. Yes, doubtless; There are many vicious Men who are nevertheless Men of very good Sense.

S. You are of Opinion, perhaps, that a Man of Knowledge is *a Man of Sense.*

C. I am really of that Opinion.

S. Is the Knowledge of Push-pin, or of the Game at Ninepins, or of Cards and Dice, or even of Musick and Dancing, sufficient to constitute the Character of a Man of Sense?

C. No certainly; there are many silly People that understand these Things tolerably well.

S. Will the Knowledge of Languages, or of Logic and Rhetoric serve to make a Man of Sense?

C. I think not; for I have known very senseless Fellows to be Masters of two or three Languages; and mighty full of their Logic, or their Rhetoric.

S. Perhaps some Men may understand all the Forms and Terms of Logic, or all the Figures of Rhetoric, and yet be no more able to convince or to perswade, than others who have not learnt those Things?

C. Indeed I believe they may.

S. Will not the Knowledge of the Mathematicks, Astronomy, and Natural Philosophy, those sublime Sciences, give a Right to the Character of *a Man of Sense?*

C. At first Sight I should have thought they might: But upon Recollection I must own I have known some Men, Masters of those Sciences, who, in the Management of their Affairs, and *Conduct of their Lives,* have acted very weakly, I do not mean viciously but foolishly; and therefore I cannot find in my Heart to allow 'em the Character of *Men of Sense.*

S. It seems then, that no Knowledge will serve to give this Character, but the Knowledge of our *true Interest;* that is, of what is best to be done in all the Circumstances of Humane Life, in order to arrive at our main End in View, HAPPINESS.

C. I am of the same Opinion. And now, as to the Point in Hand, I suppose you will no longer doubt whether a vicious Man may deserve the Character of a Man of Sense, since 'tis certain that there are many Men who *know* their true Interest, etc. and are therefore *Men of Sense,* but are nevertheless vicious and dishonest Men, as appears from the whole Tenour of their Conduct in Life.

S. Can Vice consist with any Man's true Interest, or contribute to his Happiness?

C. No certainly; for in Proportion as a Man is vicious he loses the Favour of God and Man, and brings upon himself many Inconveniences, the least of which is capable of marring and demolishing his Happiness.

S. How then does it appear that those vicious Men have the Knowledge we have been speaking of, which constitutes *a Man of Sense*, since they act directly contrary?

C. It appears by their Discoursing perfectly well upon the Subjects of Vice and Virtue, when they occur in Conversation, and by the just Manner in which they express their Thoughts of the pernicious Consequences of the one, and the happy Effects of the other.

S. Is it the Knowledge of all the Terms and Expressions proper to be used in Discoursing well upon the Subject of making a good Shoe, that constitutes a Shoemaker; or is it the Knowing how to go about it and do it?

C. I own it is the latter, and not the former.

S. And if one who could only *talk finely* about Shoemaking, were to be set to work, would he not presently discover his Ignorance in that Art?

C. He would, I confess.

S. Can the Man who is only able to talk justly of Virtue and Vice, and to say that "Drunkenness, Gluttony and Lewdness destroy a Man's Constitution; waste his Time and Substance, and bring him under many Misfortunes (to the Destruction of his Happiness) which the contrary Virtues would enable him to avoid;" but notwithstanding his talking thus, continues in those Vices; can such a Man deserve the Character of a Temperate and Chaste Man? Or does not that Man rather deserve it, who having *a thorough Sense* that what the other has said is true, *knows* also *how* to resist the Temptation to those Vices, and embrace Virtue with a hearty and steady Affection?

C. The latter, I acknowledge. And since Virtue is really the true Interest of all Men; and some of those who talk well of it, do not put it in Practice, I am now inclined to believe they speak only by rote, retailing to us what they have pick'd out of the Books or Conversation of wise and virtuous Men; but what having never enter'd or made any Impression on their Hearts, has therefore no Influence on the Conduct of their Lives.

S. Vicious Men, then, do not appear to have that Knowledge which constitutes *the Man of Sense*.

C. No, I am convinced they do not deserve the Name. However, I am afraid, that instead of *defining* a Man of Sense we have now entirely *annihilated* him: For if the Knowledge of his true Interest in all Parts of the Conduct of Life, and a constant Course of Practice agreeable to it, are essential to his Character, I do not know where we shall find him.

S. There seems no necessity that to be a Man of Sense, he should never make a Slip in the Path of Virtue, or in Point of Morality; provided he is sensible of his Failing and diligently applys himself to rectify what is done amiss, and to prevent the like for the future. The best Arithmetician may err in casting up a long Account; but having found that Error, he *knows how* to mend it, and immediately does so; and is notwithstanding that Error, an Arithmetician; But he who *always* blunders, and cannot correct his Faults in Accounting, is no Arithmetician; nor is the habitually-vicious Man *a Man of Sense.*

C. But methinks 'twill look hard, that all other Arts and Sciences put together, and possess'd by one Man in the greatest Perfection, are not able to dignify him with the Title of *a Man of Sense,* unless he be also a Man of Virtue.

S. We shall agree, perhaps, that one who is *a Man of Sense,* will not spend his Time in learning such Sciences as, if not useless in themselves, will probably be useless to him?

C. I grant it.

S. And of those which may be useful to him, that is, may contribute to his Happiness, he ought, if he is a Man of Sense to know how to make them so.

C. To be sure.

S. And of those which may be useful, he will not (if he is a Man of Sense) acquire all, except that One only which is the most useful of all, to wit, the Science of Virtue.

C. It would, I own, be inconsistent with his Character to do so.

S. It seems to follow then, that the vicious Man, tho' Master of many Sciences, must needs be an ignorant and foolish Man; for being, as he is vicious, of consequence unhappy, either he has acquired only the useless Sciences, or having acquired such as might be useful, he knows not how to make them contribute to his Happiness; and tho' he may have every other Science, he is ignorant that the SCIENCE OF VIRTUE is of more worth, and of more consequence to his Happiness than all the rest put together. And since he is ignorant of what *principally* concerns him, tho' it has been told him a thousand Times from Parents, Press, and Pulpit, the Vicious Man however learned, cannot be *a Man of Sense,* but is a Fool, a Dunce, and a Blockhead.

The Way to Wealth[1]
(Poor Richard Improved)

Courteous Reader,

I have heard that nothing gives an Author so great Pleasure, as to find his Works respectfully quoted by other learned Authors. This Pleasure I have seldom enjoyed; for tho' I have been, if I may say it without Vanity, an

---

[1] Published in *Poor Richard's Almanac* for 1758, the twenty-fifth anniversary of that annual publication, this essay or story was printed separately as *Poor Richard Improved* and then as *The Way to Wealth.* The text is the Yale edition, Volume I.

eminent Author of Almanacks annually now a full Quarter of a Century, my Brother Authors in the same Way, for what Reason I know not, have ever been very sparing in their Applauses; and no other Author has taken the least Notice of me, so that did not my Writings produce me some solid *Pudding,* the great Deficiency of *Praise* would have quite discouraged me.

I concluded at length, that the People were the best Judges of my Merit; for they buy my Works; and besides, in my Rambles, where I am not personally known, I have frequently heard one or other of my Adages repeated, with, *as Poor Richard says,* at the End on't; this gave me some Satisfaction, as it showed not only that my Instructions were regarded, but discovered likewise some Respect for my Authority; and I own, that to encourage the Practice of remembering and repeating those wise Sentences, I have sometimes *quoted myself* with great Gravity.

Judge then how much I must have been gratified by an Incident I am going to relate to you. I stopt my Horse lately where a great Number of People were collected at a Vendue[2] of Merchant Goods. The Hour of Sale not being come, they were conversing on the Badness of the Times, and one of the Company call'd to a plain clean old Man, with white Locks, *Pray, Father Abraham, what think you of the Times? Won't these heavy Taxes quite ruin the Country? How shall we be ever able to pay them? What would you advise us to?*—Father Abraham stood up, and reply'd, If you'd have my Advice, I'll give it you in short, for a *Word to the Wise is enough,* and *many Words won't fill a Bushel,* as *Poor Richard says.* They join'd in desiring him to speak his Mind, and gathering round him, he proceeded as follows:

Friends, says he, and Neighbours, the Taxes are indeed very heavy, and if those laid on by the Government were the only Ones we had to pay, we might more easily discharge them; but we have many others, and much more grievous to some of us. We are taxed twice as much by our *Idleness,* three times as much by our *Pride,* and four times as much by our *Folly,* and from these Taxes the Commissioners cannot ease or deliver us by allowing an Abatement. However let us hearken to good Advice, and something may be done for us; *God helps them that help themselves,* as Poor Richard says, in his Almanack of 1733.

It would be thought a hard Government that should tax its People one tenth Part of their *Time,* to be employed in its Service. But *Idleness* taxes many of us much more, if we reckon all that is spent in absolute *Sloth,* or doing of nothing, with that which is spent in idle Employments or Amusements, that amount to nothing.[3] *Sloth,* by bringing on Diseases, absolutely shortens Life. *Sloth, like Rust, consumes faster than Labour wears, while the*

---

[2] An auction or sale.

[3] In the rest of this paragraph, and periodically thereafter, the playfulness of Franklin's tone here can be best appreciated through an oral reading of the "sermon," with attention to variations in the rhythms of the proverbs juxtaposed together, and to repetitions of *Poor Richard* and *Poor Dick.*

used Key is always bright, as Poor Richard says. But *dost thou love Life, then do not squander Time, for that's the Stuff Life is made of,* as Poor Richard says. How much more than is necessary do we spend in Sleep! forgetting that *The sleeping Fox catches no Poultry,* and that *there will be sleeping enough in the Grave,* as Poor Richard says. If Time be of all Things the most precious, *wasting Time* must be, as Poor Richard says, *the greatest Prodigality,* since, as he elsewhere tells us, *Lost Time is never found again;* and what we call *Time-enough, always proves little enough:* Let us then be up and be doing, and doing to the Purpose; so by Diligence shall we do more with less Perplexity. *Sloth makes all Things difficult, but Industry all easy,* as Poor Richard says; and *He that riseth late, must trot all Day, and shall scarce overtake his Business at Night.* While *Laziness travels so slowly, that Poverty soon overtakes him,* as we read in Poor Richard, who adds, *Drive thy Business, let not that drive thee;* and *Early to Bed, and early to rise, makes a Man healthy, wealthy and wise.*

So what signifies *wishing* and *hoping* for better Times. We may make these Times better if we bestir ourselves. *Industry need not wish,* as Poor Richard says, and *He that lives upon Hope will die fasting.*[4] *There are no Gains, without Pains;* then *Help Hands, for I have no Lands,* or if I have, they are smartly taxed. And, as Poor Richard likewise observes, *He that hath a Trade hath an Estate,* and *He that hath a Calling hath an Office of Profit and Honour;* but then the *Trade* must be worked at, and the *Calling* well followed, or neither the *Estate,* nor the *Office,* will enable us to pay our Taxes. If we are industrious we shall never starve; for, as Poor Richard says, *At the working Man's House Hunger looks in, but dares not enter.* Nor will the Bailiff nor the Constable enter, for *Industry pays Debts, while Despair encreaseth them,* says Poor Richard. What though you have found no Treasure, nor has any rich Relation left you a Legacy, *Diligence is the Mother of Good luck,* as Poor Richard says, and *God gives all Things to Industry.* Then *plough deep, while Sluggards sleep, and you shall have Corn to sell and to keep,* says Poor Dick. Work while it is called To-day, for you know not how much you may be hindered To-morrow, which makes Poor Richard say, *One To-day is worth two To-morrows;* and farther, *Have you somewhat to do To-morrow, do it To-day.* If you were a Servant, would you not be ashamed that a good Master should catch you idle? Are you then your own Master, *be ashamed to catch yourself idle,* as Poor Dick says. When there is so much to be done for yourself, your Family, your Country, and your gracious King, be up by Peep of Day; *Let not the Sun look down and say, Inglorious here he lies.* Handle your Tools without Mittens; remember that *the Cat in Gloves catches no Mice,* as Poor Richard says. 'Tis true there is much to be done,

---

[4] In the original version (1736) the last word was *farting*—either a printer's error or a more startling conclusion.

and perhaps you are weak handed, but stick to it steadily, and you will see great Effects, for *constant Dropping wears away Stones,* and by *Diligence and Patience the Mouse ate in two the Cable;* and *little Strokes fell great Oaks,* as Poor Richard says in his Almanack, the Year I cannot just now remember.

Methinks I hear some of you say, *Must a Man afford himself no Leisure?* I will tell thee, my Friend, what Poor Richard says, *Employ thy Time well if thou meanest to gain Leisure;* and, *since thou art not sure of a Minute, throw not away an Hour.* Leisure, is Time for doing something useful; this Leisure the diligent Man will obtain, but the lazy Man never; so that, as Poor Richard says, a *Life of Leisure and a Life of Laziness are two Things.* Do you imagine that Sloth will afford you more Comfort than Labour? No, for as Poor Richard says, *Trouble springs from Idleness, and grievous Toil from needless Ease. Many without Labour, would live by their* Wits *only, but they break for want of Stock.* Whereas Industry gives Comfort, and Plenty, and Respect: *Fly Pleasures, and they'll follow you. The diligent Spinner has a large Shift;* and *now I have a Sheep and a Cow, every Body bids me Good morrow;* all which is well said by Poor Richard.

But with our Industry, we must likewise be *steady, settled* and *careful,* and oversee our own Affairs *with our own Eyes,* and not trust too much to others; for, as Poor Richard says,

> *I never saw an oft removed Tree,*
> *Nor yet an oft removed Family,*
> *That throve so well as those that settled be.*

And again, Three Removes is as bad as a Fire; and again, *Keep thy Shop, and thy Shop will keep thee;* and again, *If you would have your Business done, go; If not, send.* And again,

> *He that by the Plough would thrive,*
> *Himself must either hold or drive.*

And again, *The Eye of a Master will do more Work than both his Hands;* and again, *Want of Care does us more Damage than Want of Knowledge;* and again, *Not to oversee Workmen, is to leave them your Purse open.* Trusting too much to others Care is the Ruin of many; for, as the Almanack says, *In the Affairs of this World, Men are saved, not by Faith, but by the Want of it;* but a Man's own Care is profitable; for, saith Poor Dick, *Learning is to the Studious,* and *Riches to the Careful,* as well as *Power to the Bold,* and *Heaven to the Virtuous.* And farther, *If you would have a faithful Servant, and one that you like, serve yourself.* And again, he adviseth to Circumspection and Care, even in the smallest Matters, because sometimes *a little Neglect may breed great Mischief;* adding, *For want of a Nail the Shoe was lost;*

for want of a Shoe the Horse was lost; and for want of a Horse the Rider was lost, being overtaken and slain by the Enemy, all for want of Care about a Horse-shoe Nail.

So much for Industry, my Friends, and Attention to one's own Business; but to these we must add *Frugality,* if we would make our *Industry* more certainly successful. A Man may, if he knows not how to save as he gets, *keep his Nose all his Life to the Grindstone,* and die not worth a *Groat* at last. *A fat Kitchen makes a lean Will,* as Poor Richard says; and,

> *Many Estates are spent in the Getting,*
> *Since Women for Tea forsook Spinning and Knitting,*
> *And Men for Punch forsook Hewing and Splitting.*

If you would be wealthy, says he, in another Almanack, *think of Saving as well as of Getting: The Indies have not made Spain rich, because her* Outgoes *are greater than her* Incomes. Away then with your expensive Follies, and you will not have so much Cause to complain of hard Times, heavy Taxes, and chargeable Families; for, as Poor Dick says,

> *Women and Wine, Game and Deceit,*
> *Make the Wealth small, and the Wants great.*

And farther, *What maintains one Vice, would bring up two Children.* You may think perhaps, That a *little* Tea, or a *little* Punch now and then, Diet a *little* more costly, Clothes a *little* finer, and a *little* Entertainment now and then, can be no *great* Matter; but remember what Poor Richard says, *Many* a Little *makes a Mickle;* and farther, *Beware of* little *Expences; a small Leak will sink a great Ship;* and again, *Who Dainties love, shall Beggars prove;* and moreover, *Fools make Feasts, and wise Men eat them.*

Here you are all got together at this Vendue of *Fineries and Knicknacks.* You call them *Goods,* but if you do not take Care, they will prove *Evils* to some of you. You expect they will be sold *cheap,* and perhaps they may for less than they cost; but if you have no Occasion for them, they must be *dear* to you. Remember what Poor Richard says, *Buy what thou hast no Need of, and ere long thou shalt sell thy Necessaries.* And again, *At a great Pennyworth pause a while:* He means, that perhaps the Cheapness is *apparent* only, and not *real;* or the Bargain, by straitning thee in thy Business, may do thee more Harm than Good. For in another Place he says, *Many have been ruined by buying good Pennyworths.* Again, Poor Richard says, *'Tis foolish to lay out Money in a Purchase of Repentance;* and yet this Folly is practised every Day at Vendues, for want of minding the Almanack. *Wise Men,* as Poor Dick says, *learn by others Harms, Fools scarcely by their own;* but, *Felix *quem faciunt aliena Pericula cautum.*[5] Many a one, for the Sake of Finery on the Back, have gone with a hungry Belly, and half starved their Families; *Silks and Sattins, Scarlet and Velvets,* as Poor Richard says, *put out the Kitchen Fire.* These are not the *Necessaries* of Life; they can scarcely be called the *Conveniencies,* and yet only because they look pretty, how many *want* to *have* them. The *artificial* Wants of Mankind thus become more numerous than the *natural;* and, as Poor Dick says, *For one* poor *Person, there are an hundred* indigent. By these, and other Extravagancies, the Genteel are reduced to Poverty, and forced to borrow of those whom they formerly despised, but who through *Industry* and *Frugality* have maintained their Standing; in which Case it appears plainly, that a *Ploughman on his Legs is higher than a Gentleman on his Knees,* as Poor Richard says. Perhaps they have had a small Estate left them, which they knew not the Getting of; they think *'tis Day, and will never be Night;* that a little to be spent out of *so much,* is not worth minding; *(a Child and a Fool,* as Poor Richard says, *imagine Twenty Shillings and Twenty Years can never be spent)* but, *always taking out of the Meal-tub, and never putting in, soon comes to the Bottom;* then, as Poor Dick says, *When the Well's dry, they know the Worth of Water.* But this they might have known before, if they had taken his Advice; *If you would know the Value of Money, go and try to borrow some;* for, *he that goes a borrowing goes a sorrowing;* and indeed so does he that lends to such People, when he goes *to get it in again.* Poor Dick farther advises, and says,

> *Fond* Pride of Dress, *is sure a very Curse;*
> *E'er* Fancy *you consult, consult your Purse.*

And again, *Pride is as loud a Beggar as Want, and a great deal more saucy.* When you have bought one fine Thing you must buy ten more, that your Appearance may be all of a Piece; but Poor Dick says, *'Tis easier to* suppress *the first Desire, than to* satisfy *all that follow it.* And 'tis as truly Folly for the Poor to ape the Rich, as for the Frog to swell, in order to equal the Ox.

> *Great Estates may venture more,*
> *But little Boats should keep near Shore.*

'Tis however a Folly soon punished; for *Pride that dines on Vanity sups on Contempt,* as Poor Richard says. And in another Place, *Pride breakfasted with Plenty, dined with Poverty, and supped with Infamy.* And after all, of

[5] Roughly, a Latin version of the proverb just quoted.

what Use is this *Pride of Appearance*, for which so much is risked, so much is suffered? It cannot promote Health, or ease Pain; it makes no Increase of Merit in the Person, it creates Envy, it hastens Misfortune.

> *What is a Butterfly? At best*
> *He's but a Caterpillar drest.*
> *The gaudy Fop's his Picture just,*

as Poor Richard says.

But what Madness must it be to *run in Debt* for these Superfluities! We are offered, by the Terms of this Vendue, *Six Months Credit;* and that perhaps has induced some of us to attend it, because we cannot spare the ready Money, and hope now to be fine without it. But, ah, think what you do when you run in Debt; *You give to another Power over your Liberty.* If you cannot pay at the Time, you will be ashamed to see your Creditor; you will be in Fear when you speak to him; you will make poor pitiful sneaking Excuses, and by Degrees come to lose your Veracity, and sink into base downright lying; for, as Poor Richard says, *The second Vice is Lying, the first is running in Debt.* And again, to the same Purpose, *Lying rides upon Debt's Back.* Whereas a freeborn Englishman ought not to be ashamed or afraid to see or speak to any Man living. But Poverty often deprives a Man of all Spirit and Virtue: *'Tis hard for an empty Bag to stand upright,* as Poor Richard truly says. What would you think of that Prince, or that Government, who should issue an Edict forbidding you to dress like a Gentleman or a Gentlewoman, on Pain of Imprisonment or Servitude? Would you not say, that you are free, have a Right to dress as you please, and that such an Edict would be a Breach of your Privileges, and such a Government tyrannical? And yet you are about to put yourself under that Tyranny when you run in Debt for such Dress! Your Creditor has Authority at his Pleasure to deprive you of your Liberty, by confining you in Goal for Life, or to sell you for a Servant, if you should not be able to pay him! When you have got your Bargain, you may, perhaps, think little of Payment; but *Creditors,* Poor Richard tells us, *have better Memories than Debtors;* and in another Place says, *Creditors are a superstitious Sect, great Observers of set Days and Times.* The Day comes round before you are aware, and the Demand is made before you are prepared to satisfy it. Or if you bear your Debt in Mind, the Term which at first seemed so long, will, as it lessens, appear extreamly short. *Time* will seem to have added Wings to his Heels as well as Shoulders. *Those have a short Lent,* saith Poor Richard, *who owe Money to be paid at Easter.* Then since, as he says, *The Borrower is a Slave to the Lender, and the Debtor to the Creditor,* disdain the Chain, preserve your Freedom; and maintain your Independency: *Be industrious* and *free;* be *frugal* and *free.* At present, perhaps, you may think yourself in thriving Circumstances, and that you can bear a little Extravagance without Injury; but,

> *For Age and Want, save while you may;*
> *No Morning Sun lasts a whole Day,*

as Poor Richard says. Gain may be temporary and uncertain, but ever while you live, Expence is constant and certain; and *'tis easier to build two Chimnies than to keep one in Fuel,* as Poor Richard says. So *rather go to Bed supperless than rise in Debt.*

> *Get what you can, and what you get hold;*
> *'Tis the Stone that will turn all your Lead into Gold,*

as Poor Richard says. And when you have got the Philosopher's Stone, sure you will no longer complain of bad Times, or the Difficulty of paying Taxes.

This Doctrine, my Friends, is *Reason* and *Wisdom;* but after all, do not depend too much upon your own *Industry,* and *Frugality,* and *Prudence,* though excellent Things, for they may all be blasted without the Blessing of Heaven; and therefore ask that Blessing humbly, and be not uncharitable to those that at present seem to want it, but comfort and help them. Remember Job suffered, and was afterwards prosperous.

And now to conclude, *Experience keeps a dear School, but Fools will learn in no other, and scarce in that;* for it is true, *we may give Advice, but we cannot give Conduct,* as Poor Richard says: However, remember this, *They that won't be counselled, can't be helped,* as Poor Richard says: And farther, That *if you will not hear Reason, she'll surely rap your Knuckles.*

Thus the old Gentleman ended his Harangue. The People heard it, and approved the Doctrine, and immediately practised the contrary, just as if it had been a common Sermon; for the Vendue opened, and they began to buy extravagantly, notwithstanding all his Cautions, and their own Fear of Taxes. I found the good Man had thoroughly studied my Almanacks, and digested all I had dropt on those Topicks during the Course of Five-and-twenty Years. The frequent Mention he made of me must have tired any one else, but my Vanity was wonderfully delighted with it, though I was conscious that not a tenth Part of the Wisdom was my own which he ascribed to me, but rather the *Gleanings* I had made of the Sense of all Ages and Nations. However, I resolved to be the better for the Echo of it; and though I had at first determined to buy Stuff for a new Coat, I went away resolved to wear my old One a little longer. *Reader,* if thou wilt do the same, thy Profit will be as great as mine. I am, as ever, Thine to serve thee,

RICHARD SAUNDERS. JULY 7, 1757.

The Autobiography of Benjamin Franklin[1]

From PART ONE

[EARLY LIFE, TO HIS DEPARTURE FOR ENGLAND]

Twyford, at the Bishop of St. Asaph's 1771.

Dear Son,[2]

I have ever had a Pleasure in obtaining any little Anecdotes of my Ancestors. You may remember the Enquiries I made among the Remains of my Relations when you were with me in England; and the Journey I took for that purpose. Now imagining it may be equally agreeable to you to know the Circumstances of *my* Life, many of which you are yet unacquainted with; and expecting a Weeks uninterrupted Leisure in my present Country Retirement, I sit down to write them for you. To which I have besides some other Inducements. Having emerg'd from the Poverty and Obscurity in which I was born and bred, to a State of Affluence and some Degree of Reputation in the World, and having gone so far thro' Life with a considerable Share of Felicity, the conducing Means I made use of, which, with the Blessing of God, so well succeeded, my Posterity may like to know, as they may find some of them suitable to their own Situations, and therefore fit to be imitated. That Felicity, when I reflected on it, has induc'd me sometimes to say, that were it offer'd to my Choice, I should have no Objection to a Repetition of the same Life from its Beginning, only asking the Advantage Authors have in a second Edition to correct some Faults of the first. So would I if I might, besides corr[ectin]g the Faults, change some sinister Accidents and Events of it for others more favourable, but tho' this were deny'd, I should still accept the Offer. However, since such a Repetition is not to be expected, the next Thing most like living one's Life over again, seems to be a *Recollection* of that Life; and to make that Recollection as durable as possible, the putting it down in Writing. Hereby, too, I shall indulge the Inclination so natural in old Men, to be talking of themselves and their own past Actions, and I shall indulge it, without being troublesome to others who thro' respect to Age might think themselves oblig'd to give me a Hearing, since this may be read or not as any one pleases. And lastly, (I may as well confess it, since my Denial of it will be believ'd by no body) perhaps I shall a good deal gratify my own *Vanity*. Indeed I scarce ever heard or saw the introductory Words, *Without Vanity I may say*, &c. but some vain thing immediately follow'd.

[1] The book, never really completed, was not published in Franklin's lifetime. The best edition is the Yale University Press edition (1964), which is adopted here. The complex history of the publication of Franklin's Memoirs is described in the Yale edition.

[2] William, who was then 41 years old and governor of New Jersey.

Most People dislike Vanity in others whatever Share they have of it themselves, but I give it fair Quarter wherever I meet with it, being persuaded that it is often productive of Good to the Possessor and to others that are within his Sphere of Action: And therefore in many Cases it would not be quite absurd if a Man were to thank God for his Vanity among the other Comforts of Life.

And now I speak of thanking God, I desire with all Humility to acknowledge, that I owe the mention'd Happiness of my past Life to his kind Providence, which led me to the Means I us'd and gave them Success. My Belief of this, induces me to *hope*, tho' I must not *presume*, that the same Goodness will still be exercis'd towards me in continuing that Happiness, or in enabling me to bear a fatal Reverse, which I may experience as others have done, the Complexion of my future Fortune being known to him only: and in whose Power it is to bless to us even our Afflictions.

The Notes one of my Uncles (who had the same kind of Curiosity in collecting Family Anecdotes) once put into my Hands, furnish'd me with several Particulars relating to our Ancestors. From these Notes I learnt that the Family had liv'd in the same Village, Ecton in Northamptonshire, for 300 Years, and how much longer he knew not (perhaps from the Time when the Name *Franklin* that before was the Name of an Order of People, was assum'd by them for a Surname, when others took Surnames all over the Kingdom). (Here a Note) on a Freehold of about 30 Acres, aided by the Smith's Business which had continued in the Family till his Time, the eldest Son being always bred to that Business. A Custom which he and my Father both followed as to their eldest Sons. When I search'd the Register at Ecton, I found an Account of their Births, Marriages and Burials, from the Year 1555 only, there being no Register kept in that Parish at any time preceding. By that Register I perceiv'd that I was the youngest Son of the youngest Son for 5 Generations back.

.   .   .

This obscure Family of ours was early in the Reformation, and continu'd Protestants thro' the Reign of Queen Mary, when they were sometimes in Danger of Trouble on Account of their Zeal against Popery. They had got an English Bible, and to conceal and secure it, it was fastned open with Tapes under and within the Frame of a Joint Stool. When my Great Great Grandfather read in it to his Family, he turn'd up the Joint Stool upon his Knees, turning over the Leaves then under the Tapes. One of the Children stood at the Door to give Notice if he saw the Apparitor coming, who was an Officer of the Spiritual Court. In that Case the Stool was turn'd down again upon its feet, when the Bible remain'd conceal'd under it as before. This Anecdote I had from my Uncle Benjamin. The Family continu'd all of the Church of England till about the End of Charles the 2ds Reign, when some of the

Ministers that had been outed for Nonconformity, holding Conventicles in Northamptonshire, Benjamin and Josiah adher'd to them, and so continu'd all their Lives. The rest of the Family remain'd with the Episcopal Church. Josiah, my Father, married young, and carried his Wife with three Children unto New England, about 1682. The Conventicles having been forbidden by Law, and frequently disturbed, induced some considerable Men of his Acquaintance to remove to that Country, and he was prevail'd with to accompany them thither, where they expected to enjoy their Mode of Religion with Freedom. By the same Wife he had 4 Children more born there, and by a second Wife ten more, in all 17, of which I remember 13 sitting at one time at his Table, who all grew up to be Men and Women, and married. I was the youngest Son and the youngest Child but two, and was born in Boston, N. England.

My Mother the 2d Wife was Abiah Folger, a Daughter of Peter Folger, one of the first Settlers of New England, of whom honourable mention is made by Cotton Mather, in his Church History of that Country, (entitled Magnalia Christi Americana) as a *godly learned Englishman,* if I remember the words rightly. I have heard that he wrote sundry small occasional Pieces, but only one of them was printed which I saw now many Years since. It was written in 1675, in the homespun Verse of that Time and People, and address'd to those then concern'd in the Government there. It was in favour of Liberty of Conscience, and in behalf of the Baptists, Quakers, and other Sectaries, that had been under Persecution; ascribing the Indian Wars and other Distresses, that had befallen the Country to that Persecution, as so many Judgments of God, to punish so heinous an Offence; and exhorting a Repeal of those uncharitable Laws. The whole appear'd to me as written with a good deal of Decent Plainness and manly Freedom. The six last concluding Lines I remember, tho' I have forgotten the two first of the Stanza, but the Purport of them was that his Censures proceeded from *Goodwill,* and therefore he would be known as the Author,

> because to be a Libeller, (says he)
> I hate it with my Heart.
> From Sherburne Town[3] where now I dwell,
> My Name I do put here,
> Without Offence, your real Friend,
> It is Peter Folgier.

My elder Brothers were all put Apprentices to different Trades. I was put to the Grammar School at Eight Years of Age, my Father intending to devote me as the Tithe of his Sons to the Service of the Church. My early Readiness

---

[3] In the Island of Nantucket [Franklin's note]

in learning to read (which must have been very early, as I do not remember when I could not read) and the Opinion of all his Friends that I should certainly make a good Scholar, encourag'd him in this Purpose of his. My Uncle Benjamin too approv'd of it, and propos'd to give me all his Shorthand Volumes of Sermons I suppose as a Stock to set up with, if I would learn his Character. I continu'd however at the Grammar School not quite one Year, tho' in that time I had risen gradually from the Middle of the Class of that Year to be the Head of it, and farther was remov'd into the next Class above it, in order to go with that into the third at the End of the Year. But my Father in the mean time, from a View of the Expence of a College Education which, having so large a Family, he could not well afford, and the mean Living many so educated were afterwards able to obtain, Reasons that he gave to his Friends in my Hearing, altered his first Intention, took me from the Grammar School, and sent me to a School for Writing and Arithmetic kept by a then famous Man, Mr. Geo. Brownell, very successful in his Profession generally, and that by mild encouraging Methods. Under him I acquired fair Writing pretty soon, but I fail'd in the Arithmetic, and made no Progress in it.

At Ten Years old, I was taken home to assist my Father in his Business, which was that of a Tallow Chandler and Sope-Boiler. A Business he was not bred to, but had assumed on his Arrival in New England and on finding his Dying Trade would not maintain his Family, being in little Request. Accordingly I was employed in cutting Wick for the Candles, filling the Dipping Mold, and the Molds for cast Candles, attending the Shop, going of Errands, &c. I dislik'd the Trade and had a strong Inclination for the Sea; but my Father declar'd against it; however, living near the Water, I was much in and about it, learnt early to swim well, and to manage Boats, and when in a Boat or Canoe with other Boys I was commonly allow'd to govern, especially in any case of Difficulty; and upon other Occasions I was generally a Leader among the Boys, and sometimes led them into Scrapes, of which I will mention one Instance, as it shows an early projecting public Spirit, tho' not then justly conducted. There was a Salt Marsh that bounded part of the Mill Pond, on the Edge of which at Highwater, we us'd to stand to fish for Minews. By much Trampling, we had made it a mere Quagmire. My Proposal was to build a Wharf there fit for us to stand upon, and I show'd my Comrades a large Heap of Stones which were intended for a new House near the Marsh, and which would very well suit our Purpose. Accordingly in the Evening when the Workmen were gone, I assembled a Number of my Playfellows, and working with them diligently like so many Emmets, sometimes two or three to a Stone, we brought them all away and built our little Wharff. The next Morning the Workmen were surpriz'd at Missing the

Stones; which were found in our Wharff; Enquiry was made after the Removers; we were discovered and complain'd of; several of us were corrected by our Fathers; and tho' I pleaded the Usefulness of the Work, mine convinc'd me that nothing was useful which was not honest.

I think you may like to know Something of his Person and Character. He had an excellent Constitution of Body, was of middle Stature, but well set and very strong. He was ingenious, could draw prettily, was skill'd a little in Music and had a clear pleasing Voice, so that when he play'd Psalm Tunes on his Violin and sung withal as he sometimes did in an Evening after the Business of the Day was over, it was extreamly agreable to hear. He had a mechanical Genius too, and on occasion was very handy in the Use of other Tradesmen's Tools. But his great Excellence lay in a sound Understanding, and solid Judgment in prudential Matters, both in private and publick Affairs. In the latter indeed he was never employed, the numerous Family he had to educate and the straitness of his Circumstances, keeping him close to his Trade, but I remember well his being frequently visited by leading People, who consulted him for his Opinion in Affairs of the Town or of the Church he belong'd to and show'd a good deal of Respect for his Judgment and Advice. He was also much consulted by private Persons about their Affairs when any Difficulty occur'd, and frequently chosen an Arbitrator between contending Parties. At his Table he lik'd to have as often as he could, some sensible Friend or Neighbour, to converse with, and always took care to start some ingenious or useful Topic for Discourse, which might tend to improve the Minds of his Children. By this means he turn'd our Attention to what was good, just, and prudent in the Conduct of Life;[4] and little or no Notice was ever taken of what related to the Victuals on the Table, whether it was well or ill drest, in or out of season, of good or bad flavour, preferable or inferior to this or that other thing of the kind; so that I was bro't up in such a perfect Inattention to those Matters as to be quite Indifferent what kind of Food was set before me; and so unobservant of it, that to this Day, if I am ask'd I can scarce tell, a few Hours after Dinner, what I din'd upon. This has been a Convenience to me in travelling, where my Companions have been sometimes very unhappy for want of a suitable Gratification of their more delicate because better instructed Tastes and Appetites.

My Mother had likewise an excellent Constitution. She suckled all her 10 Children. I never knew either my Father or Mother to have any Sickness but that of which they dy'd, he at 89 and she at 85 Years of age. They lie buried together at Boston, where I some Years since plac'd a Marble stone over their Grave with this Inscription

---

[4] Compare John Winthrop's phrase, "good, just, and honest," in his definition of Civil or federal liberty, above, p. 92.

Josiah Franklin
And Abiah his Wife
Lie here interred.
They lived lovingly together in Wedlock
Fifty-five Years.
Without an Estate or any gainful Employment,
By constant labour and Industry,
With God's Blessing,
They maintained a large Family
Comfortably;
And brought up thirteen Children,
and seven Grand Children
Reputably.
From this Instance, Reader,
Be encouraged to Diligence in thy Calling,
And distrust not Providence.
He was a pious & prudent Man,
She a discreet and virtuous Woman.
Their youngest Son,
In filial Regard to their Memory,
Places this Stone.
J.F. born 1655—Died 1744. Ætat 89
A.F. born 1667—died 1752—85

By my rambling Digressions I perceive my self to be grown old. I us'd to write more methodically. But one does not dress for private Company as for a publick Ball. 'Tis perhaps only Negligence.

To return. I continu'd thus employ'd in my Father's Business for two Years, that is till I was 12 Years old; and my Brother John, who was bred to that Business having left my Father, married and set up for himself at Rhodeisland, there was all Appearance that I was destin'd to supply his Place and be a Tallow Chandler. But my Dislike to the Trade continuing, my Father was under Apprehensions that if he did not find one for me more agreable, I should break away and get to Sea, as his Son Josiah had done to his great Vexation. He therefore sometimes took me to walk with him, and see Joiners, Bricklayers, Turners, Braziers, &c. at their Work, that he might observe my Inclination, and endeavour to fix it on some Trade or other on Land. It has ever since been a Pleasure to me to see good Workmen handle their Tools; and it has been useful to me, having learnt so much by it, as to be able to do little Jobs my self in my House, when a Workman could not readily be got; and to construct little Machines for my Experiments while the Intention of making the Experiment was fresh and warm in my Mind. My Father at last fix'd upon the Cutler's Trade, and my Uncle Benjamin's

Son Samuel who was bred to that Business in London being about that time establish'd in Boston, I was sent to be with him some time on liking. But his Expectations of a Fee with me displeasing my Father, I was taken home again.

From a Child I was fond of Reading, and all the little Money that came into my Hands was ever laid out in Books. Pleas'd with the Pilgrim's Progress, my first Collection was of John Bunyan's Works, in separate little Volumes. I afterwards sold them to enable me to buy R. Burton's Historical Collections; they were small Chapmen's Books and cheap, 40 or 50 in all. My Father's little Library consisted chiefly of Books in polemic Divinity, most of which I read, and have since often regretted, that at a time when I had such a Thirst for Knowledge, more proper Books had not fallen in my Way, since it was now resolv'd I should not be a Clergyman. Plutarch's Lives there was, in which I read abundantly, and I still think that time spent to great Advantage. There was also a Book of Defoe's, called an Essay on Projects,[5] and another of Dr. Mather's, call'd Essays to do Good which perhaps gave me a Turn of Thinking that had an Influence on some of the principal future Events of my Life.

This Bookish Inclination at length determin'd my Father to make me a Printer, tho' he had already one Son, (James) of that Profession. In 1717 my Brother James return'd from England with a Press and Letters to set up his Business in Boston. I lik'd it much better than that of my Father, but still had a Hankering for the Sea. To prevent the apprehended Effect of such an Inclination, my Father was impatient to have me bound to my Brother. I stood out some time, but at last was persuaded and signed the Indentures, when I was yet but 12 Years old. I was to serve as an Apprentice till I was 21 Years of Age, only I was to be allow'd Journeyman's Wages during the last Year. In a little time I made great Proficiency in the Business, and became a useful Hand to my Brother. I now had Access to better Books. An Acquaintance with the Apprentices of Booksellers, enabled me sometimes to borrow a small one, which I was careful to return soon and clean. Often I sat up in my Room reading the greatest Part of the Night, when the Book was borrow'd in the Evening and to be return'd early in the Morning lest it should be miss'd or wanted. And after some time an ingenious Tradesman Mr. Matthew Adams who had a pretty Collection of Books, and who frequented our Printing House, took Notice of me, invited me to his Library, and very kindly lent me such Books as I chose to read. I now took a Fancy to Poetry, and made some little Pieces. My Brother, thinking it might turn to account encourag'd me, and put me on composing two occasional Ballads. One was

---

[5] Daniel Defoe, *Essay upon Projects* (London, 1697), proposed voluntary associations for life insurance, etc. Cotton Mather's *Bonifacius* (Boston, 1710) bore the running title *Essays to Do Good*. Mather's book stresses ingenuity in the devising of ways to do good in the community (for the glory of God).

called the *Light House Tragedy*, and contain'd an Account of the drowning of Capt. Worthilake with his Two Daughters; the other was a Sailor Song on the Taking of *Teach* or Blackbeard the Pirate. They were wretched Stuff, in the Grubstreet Ballad Stile, and when they were printed he sent me about the Town to sell them. The first sold wonderfully, the Event being recent, having made a great Noise. This flatter'd my Vanity. But my Father discourag'd me, by ridiculing my Performances, and telling me Verse-makers were generally Beggars; so I escap'd being a Poet, most probably a very bad one. But as Prose Writing has been of great Use to me in the Course of my Life, and was a principal Means of my Advancement, I shall tell you how in such a Situation I acquir'd what little Ability I have in that Way.

There was another Bookish Lad in the Town, John Collins by Name, with whom I was intimately acquainted. We sometimes disputed, and very fond we were of Argument, and very desirous of confuting one another. Which disputacious Turn, by the way, is apt to become a very bad Habit, making People often extreamly disagreable in Company, by the Contradiction that is necessary to bring it into Practice, and thence, besides souring and spoiling the Conversation, is productive of Disgusts and perhaps Enmities where you may have occasion for Friendship. I had caught it by reading my Father's Books of Dispute about Religion. Persons of good Sense, I have since observ'd, seldom fall into it, except Lawyers, University Men, and Men of all Sorts that have been bred at Edinborough. A Question was once some how or other started between Collins and me, of the Propriety of educating the Female Sex in Learning, and their Abilities for Study. He was of Opinion that it was improper; and that they were naturally unequal to it. I took the contrary Side, perhaps a little for Dispute sake. He was naturally more eloquent, had a ready Plenty of Words, and sometimes as I thought bore me down more by his Fluency than by the Strength of his Reasons. As we parted without settling the Point, and were not to see one another again for some time, I sat down to put my Arguments in Writing, which I copied fair and sent to him. He answer'd and I reply'd. Three or four Letters of a Side had pass'd, when my Father happen'd to find my Papers, and read them. Without entring into the Discussion, he took occasion to talk to me about the Manner of my Writing, observ'd that tho' I had the Advantage of my Antagonist in correct Spelling and pointing (which I ow'd to the Printing House) I fell far short in elegance of Expression, in Method and in Perspicuity, of which he convinc'd me by several Instances. I saw the Justice of his Remarks, and thence grew more attentive to the *Manner* in Writing, and determin'd to endeavour at Improvement.

About this time I met with an odd Volume of the Spectator.[6] It was the third. I had never before seen any of them. I bought it, read it over and over,

---

[6] A daily paper written almost exclusively by Joseph Addison and Richard Steele in 1711–1712 and broadly accepted as a model of style, especially for essayists.

and was much delighted with it. I thought the Writing excellent, and wish'd if possible to imitate it. With that View, I took some of the Papers, and making short Hints of the Sentiment in each Sentence, laid them by a few Days, and then without looking at the Book, try'd to compleat the Papers again, by expressing each hinted Sentiment at length and as fully as it had been express'd before, in any suitable Words, that should come to hand.

Then I compar'd my Spectator with the Original, discover'd some of my Faults and corrected them. But I found I wanted a Stock of Words or a Readiness in recollecting and using them, which I thought I should have acquir'd before that time, if I had gone on making Verses, since the continual Occasion for Words of the same Import but of different Length, to suit the Measure, or of different Sound for the Rhyme, would have laid me under a constant Necessity of searching for Variety, and also have tended to fix that Variety in my Mind, and make me Master of it. Therefore I took some of the Tales and turn'd them into Verse: And after a time, when I had pretty well forgotten the Prose, turn'd them back again. I also sometimes jumbled my Collections of Hints into Confusion, and after some Weeks, endeavour'd to reduce them into the best Order, before I began to form the full Sentences, and compleat the Paper. This was to teach me Method in the Arrangement of Thoughts. By comparing my work afterwards with the original, I discover'd many faults and amended them; but I sometimes had the Pleasure of Fancying that in certain Particulars of small Import, I had been lucky enough to improve the Method or the Language and this encourag'd me to think I might possibly in time come to be a tolerable English Writer, of which I was extreamly ambitious.

My Time for these Exercises and for Reading, was at Night, after Work or before Work began in the Morning; or on Sundays, when I contrived to be in the Printing House alone, evading as much as I could the common Attendance on publick Worship, which my Father used to exact of me when I was under his Care: And which indeed I still thought a Duty; tho' I could not, as it seemed to me, afford the Time to practise it.

When about 16 Years of Age, I happen'd to meet with a Book, written by one Tryon,[7] recommending a Vegetable Diet. I determined to go into it. My Brother being yet unmarried, did not keep House, but boarded himself and his Apprentices in another Family. My refusing to eat Flesh occasioned an Inconveniency, and I was frequently chid for my singularity. I made my self acquainted with Tryon's Manner of preparing some of his Dishes, such as Boiling Potatoes or Rice, making Hasty Pudding, and a few others, and then propos'd to my Brother, that if he would give me Weekly half the Money he paid for my Board I would board my self. He instantly agreed to it, and I

---

[7] Thomas Tryon, *The Way to Health, long Life and Happiness, or a Discourse of Temperance* (London, 1691).

presently found that I could save half what he paid me. This was an additional Fund for buying Books: But I had another Advantage in it. My Brother and the rest going from the Printing House to their Meals, I remain'd there alone, and dispatching presently my light Repast, (which often was no more than a Bisket or a Slice of Bread, a Handful of Raisins or a Tart from the Pastry Cook's, and a Glass of Water) had the rest of the Time till their Return, for Study, in which I made the greater Progress from that greater Clearness of Head and quicker Apprehension which usually attend Temperance in Eating and Drinking. And now it was that being on some Occasion made asham'd of my Ignorance in Figures, which I had twice failed in learning when at School, I took Cocker's Book of Arithmetick, and went thro' the whole by my self with great Ease. I also read Seller's and Sturmy's Books of Navigation,[8] and became acquainted with the little Geometry they contain, but never proceeded far in that Science. And I read about this Time Locke on Human Understanding, and the Art of Thinking by Messrs. du Port Royal.[9]

While I was intent on improving my Language, I met with an English Grammar (I think it was Greenwood's) at the End of which there were two little Sketches of the Arts of Rhetoric and Logic, the latter finishing with a Specimen of a Dispute in the Socratic Method. And soon after I procur'd Xenophon's Memorable Things of Socrates, wherein there are many Instances of the same Method. I was charm'd with it, adopted it, dropt my abrupt Contradiction, and positive Argumentation, and put on the humble Enquirer and Doubter. And being then, from reading Shaftsbury and Collins,[10] become a real Doubter in many Points of our Religious Doctrine, I found this Method safest for my self and very embarassing to those against whom I used it, therefore I took a Delight in it, practis'd it continually and grew very artful and expert in drawing People even of superior Knowledge into Concessions the Consequences of which they did not foresee, entangling them in Difficulties out of which they could not extricate themselves, and so obtaining Victories that neither my self nor my Cause always deserved.[11]

I continu'd this Method some few Years, but gradually left it, retaining only the Habit of expressing my self in Terms of modest Diffidence, never using when I advance any thing that may possibly be disputed, the Words,

---

[8] John Seller, *An Epitome of the Art of Navigation* (London, 1681), and Samuel Sturmy, *The Mariner's Magazine; or, Sturmy's Mathematical and Practical Arts* (London, 1669).

[9] John Locke, *Essay Concerning Human Understanding* (1690). Antoine Arnauld and Pierre Nicole, of Port Royal, published in 1662 *Logic: or the Art of Thinking*, translated into English in London, 1687.

[10] The Third Earl of Shaftsbury

(1671-1713) was one of the most powerful influences on the moral philosophy of Franklin and other contemporaries. Anthony Collins (1676-1729) was a prominent Deist.

[11] Notice here that Franklin has higher standards than mere success or "victory." He has a separate way of evaluating what he and his cause "deserved." Compare his discussion of "vicious actions," below, p. 491.

Certainly, undoubtedly, or any others that give the Air of Positiveness to an Opinion; but rather say, I conceive, or I apprehend a Thing to be so or so, It appears to me, or I should think it so or so for such and such Reasons, or I imagine it to be so, or it is so if I am not mistaken. This Habit I believe has been of great Advantage to me, when I have had occasion to inculcate my Opinions and persuade Men into Measures that I have been from time to time engag'd in promoting. And as the chief Ends of Conversation are to *inform,* or to be *informed,* to *please* or to *persuade,* I wish wellmeaning sensible Men would not lessen their Power of doing Good by a Positive assuming Manner that seldom fails to disgust, tends to create Opposition, and to defeat every one of those Purposes for which Speech was given us, to wit, giving or receiving Information, or Pleasure: For if you would *inform,* a positive dogmatical Manner in advancing your Sentiments, may provoke Contradiction and prevent a candid Attention. If you wish Information and Improvement from the Knowledge of others and yet at the same time ex-press your self as firmly fix'd in your present Opinions, modest sensible Men, who do not love Disputation, will probably leave you undisturb'd in the Possession of your Error; and by such a Manner you can seldom hope to recommend your self in *pleasing* your Hearers, or to persuade those whose Concurrence you desire. Pope says, judiciously,

> *Men should be taught as if you taught them not,*
> *And things unknown propos'd as things forgot,*

farther recommending it to us,

> *To speak tho' sure, with seeming Diffidence.*

And he might have coupled with this Line that which he has coupled with another, I think less properly,

> *For Want of Modesty is Want of Sense.*

If you ask why, *less properly,* I must repeat the Lines;

> *Immodest Words admit of no Defence;*
> *For Want of Modesty is Want of Sense.*[12]

---

[12] The editors of the Yale edition point out that these lines were written not by Alexander Pope—whose *Essay on Criticism* Franklin has just quoted correctly—but by Wentworth Dillon, Earl of Roscommon, *Essay on Translated Verse* (1684), lines 113-114. There *decency,* not *modesty,* is the correct word.

Now is not *Want of Sense* (where a Man is so unfortunate as to want it) some Apology for his *Want of Modesty?* and would not the Lines stand more justly thus?

> Immodest Words admit *but this* Defence,
> That Want of Modesty is Want of Sense.

This however I should submit to better Judgments.

My Brother had in 1720 or 21, begun to print a Newspaper. It was the second that appear'd in America, and was called *The New England Courant.* The only one before it, was *the Boston News Letter.*[13] I remember his being dissuaded by some of his Friends from the Undertaking, as not likely to succeed, one Newspaper being in their Judgment enough for America. At this time 1771 there are not less than five and twenty. He went on however with the Undertaking, and after having work'd in composing the Types and printing off the Sheets I was employ'd to carry the Papers thro' the Streets to the Customers. He had some ingenious Men among his Friends who amus'd themselves by writing little Pieces for this Paper, which gain'd it Credit, and made it more in Demand; and these Gentlemen often visited us. Hearing their Conversations, and their Accounts of the Approbation their Papers were receiv'd with, I was excited to try my Hand among them. But being still a Boy, and suspecting that my Brother would object to printing any Thing of mine in his Paper if he knew it to be mine, I contriv'd to disguise my Hand, and writing an anonymous Paper I put it in at Night under the Door of the Printing House. It was found in the Morning and communicated to his Writing Friends when they call'd in as usual. They read it, commented on it in my Hearing, and I had the exquisite Pleasure, of finding it met with their Approbation, and that in their different Guesses at the Author none were named but Men of some Character among us for Learning and Ingenuity.

I suppose now that I was rather lucky in my Judges: And that perhaps they were not really so very good ones as I then esteem'd them. Encourag'd however by this, I wrote and convey'd in the same Way to the Press several more Papers, which were equally approv'd, and I kept my Secret till my small Fund of Sense for such Performances was pretty well exhausted, and then I discovered[14] it; when I began to be considered a little more by my Brother's Acquaintance, and in a manner that did not quite please him, as he

---

[13] Again Franklin's memory erred. The *Courant* was the fourth Boston newspaper but, as the Yale editors point out, James Franklin did print the second paper, *The Boston Gazette,* for a while.

[14] Disclosed. These were the Dogood letters, written as if by a Mrs. Silence Dogood, whom Franklin doubtless named for Cotton Mather's *Essays to Do Good* in those days when Mather was a controversial figure.

thought, probably with reason, that it tended to make me too vain. And perhaps this might be one Occasion of the Differences that we frequently had about this Time. Tho' a Brother, he considered himself as my Master, and me as his Apprentice; and accordingly expected the same Services from me as he would from another; while I thought he demean'd me too much in some he requir'd of me, who from a Brother expected more Indulgence. Our Disputes were often brought before our Father, and I fancy I was either generally in the right, or else a better Pleader, because the Judgment was generally in my favour: But my Brother was passionate and had often beaten me, which I took extreamly amiss; and thinking my Apprenticeship very tedious, I was continually wishing for some Opportunity of shortening it, which at length offered in a manner unexpected.[15]

One of the Pieces in our News-Paper, on some political Point which I have now forgotten, gave Offence to the Assembly. He was taken up, censur'd and imprison'd for a Month by the Speaker's Warrant, I suppose because he would not discover his Author. I too was taken up and examin'd before the Council; but tho' I did not give them any Satisfaction, they contented themselves with admonishing me, and dismiss'd me; considering me perhaps as an Apprentice who was bound to keep his Master's Secrets. During my Brother's Confinement, which I resented a good deal, notwithstanding our private Differences, I had the Management of the Paper, and I made bold to give our Rulers some Rubs in it, which my Brother took very kindly, while others began to consider me in an unfavourable Light, as a young Genius that had a Turn for Libelling and Satyr. My Brother's Discharge was accompany'd with an Order of the House, (a very odd one) *that James Franklin should no longer print the Paper called the New England Courant.* There was a Consultation held in our Printing House among his Friends what he should do in this Case. Some propos'd to evade the Order by changing the Name of the Paper; but my Brother seeing Inconveniences in that, it was finally concluded on as a better way, to let it be printed for the future under the Name of *Benjamin Franklin.* And to avoid the Censure of the Assembly that might fall on him, as still printing it by his Apprentice, the Contrivance was, that my old Indenture should be return'd to me with a full Discharge on the Back of it, to be shown on Occasion; but to secure to him the Benefit of my Service I was to sign new Indentures for the Remainder of the Term, which were to be kept private. A very flimsy Scheme it was, but however it was immediately executed, and the Paper went on accordingly under my Name for several Months. At length a fresh Difference arising between my Brother and me, I took upon me to assert my Freedom, presuming that he would not venture to produce the new Indentures. It was not fair

[15] *Note.* I fancy his harsh and tyrannical Treatment of me, might be a means of impressing me with that Aversion to arbitrary Power that has stuck to me thro' my whole Life. [Franklin's note.]

in me to take this Advantage, and this I therefore reckon one of the first Errata of my Life: But the Unfairness of it weigh'd little with me, when under the Impressions of Resentment, for the Blows his Passion too often urg'd him to bestow upon me. Tho' he was otherwise not an ill-natur'd Man: Perhaps I was too saucy and provoking.

When he found I would leave him, he took care to prevent my getting Employment in any other Printing-House of the Town, by going round and speaking to every Master, who accordingly refus'd to give me Work. I then thought of going to New York as the nearest Place where there was a Printer: and I was the rather inclin'd to leave Boston, when I reflected that I had already made myself a little obnoxious to the governing Party; and from the arbitrary Proceedings of the Assembly in my Brother's Case it was likely I might if I stay'd soon bring myself into Scrapes; and farther that my indiscrete Disputations about Religion began to make me pointed at with Horror by good People, as an Infidel or Atheist. I determin'd on the Point: but my Father now siding with my Brother, I was sensible that if I attempted to go openly, Means would be used to prevent me. My Friend Collins therefore undertook to manage a little for me. He agreed with the Captain of a New York Sloop for my Passage, under the Notion of my being a young Acquaintance of his that had got a naughty Girl with Child, whose Friends would compel me to marry her, and therefore I could not appear or come away publickly. So I sold some of my Books to raise a little Money, Was taken on board privately, and as we had a fair Wind in three Days I found my self in New York near 300 Miles from home, a Boy of but 17, without the least Recommendation to or Knowledge of any Person in the Place, and with very little Money in my Pocket.

My Inclinations for the Sea, were by this time worne out, or I might now have gratify'd them. But having a Trade, and supposing my self a pretty good Workman, I offer'd my Service to the Printer of the Place, old Mr. Wm. Bradford, (who had been the first Printer in Pensilvania, but remov'd from thence upon the Quarrel of Geo. Keith). He could give me no Employment, having little to do, and Help enough already: But, says he, my Son at Philadelphia has lately lost his principal Hand, Aquila Rose, by Death. If you go thither I believe he may employ you. Philadelphia was 100 Miles farther. I set out, however, in a Boat for Amboy, leaving my Chest and Things to follow me round by Sea. In crossing the Bay we met with a Squall that tore our rotten Sails to pieces, prevented our getting into the Kill, and drove us upon Long Island. In our Way a drunken Dutchman, who was a Passenger too, fell over board; when he was sinking I reach'd thro' the Water to his shock Pate and drew him up so that we got him in again. His Ducking sober'd him a little, and he went to sleep, taking first out of his Pocket a Book which he desir'd I would dry for him. It prov'd to be my old favourite Author Bunyan's Pilgrim's Progress in Dutch, finely printed on good Paper with copper Cuts, a Dress better than I had ever seen it wear in its own

Language. I have since found that it has been translated into most of the Languages of Europe, and suppose it has been more generally read than any other Book except perhaps the Bible. Honest John was the first that I know of who mix'd Narration and Dialogue, a Method of Writing very engaging to the Reader, who in the most interesting Parts finds himself as it were brought into the Company, and present at the Discourse. Defoe in his Cruso, his Moll Flanders, Religious Courtship, Family Instructor, and other Pieces, has imitated it with Success. And Richardson has done the same in his Pamela, &c.

When we drew near the Island we found it was at a Place where there could be no Landing, there being a great Surff on the stony Beach. So we dropt Anchor and swung round towards the Shore. Some People came down to the Water Edge and hallow'd to us, as we did to them. But the Wind was so high and the Surff so loud, that we could not hear so as to understand each other. There were Canoes on the Shore, and we made Signs and hallow'd that they should fetch us, but they either did not understand us, or thought it impracticable. So they went away, and Night coming on, we had no Remedy but to wait till the Wind should abate, and in the mean time the Boatman and I concluded to sleep if we could, and so crouded into the Scuttle with the Dutchman who was still wet, and the Spray beating over the Head of our Boat, leak'd thro' to us, so that we were soon almost as wet as he. In this Manner we lay all Night with very little Rest. But the Wind abating the next Day, we made a Shift to reach Amboy before Night, having been 30 Hours on the Water without Victuals, or any Drink but a Bottle of filthy Rum: The Water we sail'd on being salt.

In the Evening I found my self very feverish, and went in to Bed. But having read somewhere that cold Water drank plentifully was good for a Fever, I follow'd the Prescription, sweat plentifully most of the Night, my Fever left me, and in the Morning crossing the Ferry, I proceeded on my Journey, on foot, having 50 Miles to Burlington, where I was told I should find Boats that would carry me the rest of the Way to Philadelphia.

It rain'd very hard all the Day, I was thoroughly soak'd and by Noon a good deal tir'd, so I stopt at a poor Inn, where I staid all Night, beginning now to wish I had never left home. I cut so miserable a Figure too, that I found by the Questions ask'd me I was suspected to be some runaway Servant, and in danger of being taken up on that Suspicion. However I proceeded the next Day, and got in the Evening to an Inn within 8 or 10 Miles of Burlington, kept by one Dr. Brown.

He entered into Conversation with me while I took some Refreshment, and finding I had read a little, became very sociable and friendly. Our Acquaintance continu'd as long as he liv'd. He had been, I imagine, an itinerant Doctor, for there was no Town in England, or Country in Europe, of which he could not give a very particular Account. He had some Letters, and was ingenious, but much of an Unbeliever, and wickedly undertook some Years after to travesty the Bible in doggrel Verse as Cotton[16] had done Virgil. By this means he set many of the Facts in a very ridiculous Light, and might have hurt weak minds if his Work had been publish'd: but it never was. At his House I lay that Night, and the next Morning reach'd Burlington. But had the Mortification to find that the regular Boats were gone, a little before my coming, and no other expected to go till Tuesday, this being Saturday. Wherefore I return'd to an old Woman in the Town of whom I had bought Gingerbread to eat on the Water, and ask'd her Advice; she invited me to lodge at her House till a Passage by Water should offer: and being tired with my foot Travelling, I accepted the Invitation. She understanding I was a Printer, would have had me stay at that Town and follow my Business, being ignorant of the Stock necessary to begin with. She was very hospitable, gave me a Dinner of Ox Cheek with great Goodwill, accepting only a Pot of Ale in return. And I tho't my self fix'd till Tuesday should come. However walking in the Evening by the Side of the River a Boat came by, which I found was going towards Philadelphia, with several People in her. They took me in, and as there was no Wind, we row'd all the Way; and about Midnight not having yet seen the City, some of the Company were confident we must have pass'd it, and would row no farther, the others knew not where we were, so we put towards the Shore, got into a Creek, landed near an old Fence with the Rails of which we made a Fire, the Night being cold, in October, and there we remain'd till Daylight. Then one of the Company knew the Place to be Cooper's Creek a little above Philadelphia, which we saw as soon as we got out of the Creek, and arriv'd there about 8 or 9 a Clock, on the Sunday morning, and landed at the Market street Wharff.

I have been the more particular in this Description of my Journey, and shall be so of my first Entry into that City, that you may in your Mind compare such unlikely Beginnings with the Figure I have since made there. I was in my Working Dress, my best Cloaths being to come round by Sea. I was dirty from my Journey; my Pockets were stuff'd out with Shirts and Stockings; I knew no Soul, nor where to look for Lodging. I was fatigu'd with Travelling, Rowing and Want of Rest. I was very hungry, and my whole Stock of Cash consisted of a Dutch Dollar and about a Shilling in Copper. The latter I gave the People of the Boat for my Passage, who at first refus'd it on Account of my Rowing; but I insisted on their taking it, a Man being sometimes more generous when he has but a little Money than when he has plenty, perhaps thro' Fear of being thought to have but little.

Then I walk'd up the Street, gazing about, till near the Market House I met a Boy with Bread. I had made many a Meal on Bread, and inquiring where he got it, I went immediately to the Baker's he directed me to in

[16] Charles Cotton, *Scarronides*. (London, 1664).

second Street; and ask'd for Bisket, intending such as we had in Boston, but they it seems were not made in Philadelphia, then I ask'd for a threepenny Loaf, and was told they had none such: so not considering or knowing the Difference of Money and the greater Cheapness nor the Names of his Bread, I bad him give me three penny worth of any sort. He gave me accordingly three great Puffy Rolls. I was surpriz'd at the Quantity, but took it, and having no room in my Pockets, walk'd off, with a Roll under each Arm, and eating the other. Thus I went up Market Street as far as fourth Street, passing by the Door of Mr. Read, my future Wife's Father, when she standing at the Door saw me, and thought I made as I certainly did a most awkward ridiculous Appearance. Then I turn'd and went down Chestnut Street and part of Walnut Street, eating my Roll all the Way, and coming round found my self again at Market Street Wharff, near the Boat I came in, to which I went for a Draught of the River Water, and being fill'd with one of my Rolls, gave the other two to a Woman and her Child that came down the River in the Boat with us and were waiting to go farther. Thus refresh'd I walk'd again up the Street, which by this time had many clean dress'd People in it who were all walking the same Way; I join'd them, and thereby was led into the great Meeting House of the Quakers near the Market. I sat down among them, and after looking round a while and hearing nothing said, being very drowzy thro' Labour and want of Rest the preceding Night, I fell fast asleep, and continu'd so till the Meeting broke up, when one was kind enough to rouse me. This was therefore the first House I was in or slept in, in Philadelphia.

Walking again down towards the River, and looking in the Faces of People, I met a young Quaker Man whose Countenance I lik'd, and accosting him requested he would tell me where a Stranger could get Lodging. We were then near the Sign of the Three Mariners. Here, says he, is one Place that entertains Strangers, but it is not a reputable House; if thee wilt walk with me, I'll show thee a better. He brought me to the Crooked Billet in Water-Street. Here I got a Dinner. And while I was eating it, several sly Questions were ask'd me, as it seem'd to be suspected from my youth and Appearance, that I might be some Runaway. After Dinner my Sleepiness return'd: and being shown to a Bed, I lay down without undressing, and slept till Six in the Evening; was call'd to Supper; went to Bed again very early and slept soundly till the next Morning. Then I made my self as tidy as I could, and went to Andrew Bradford the Printer's. I found in the Shop the old Man his Father, whom I had seen at New York, and who travelling on horse back had got to Philadelphia before me. He introduc'd me to his Son, who receiv'd me civilly, gave me a Breakfast, but told me he did not at present want a Hand, being lately supply'd with one. But there was another Printer in town lately set up, one Keimer, who perhaps might employ me; if not, I should be welcome to lodge at his House, and he would give me a little Work to do now and then till fuller Business should offer.

The old Gentleman said, he would go with me to the new Printer: And when we found him, Neighbour, says Bradford, I have brought to see you a young Man of your Business, perhaps you may want such a One. He ask'd me a few Questions, put a Composing Stick in my Hand to see how I work'd, and then said he would employ me soon, tho' he had just then nothing for me to do. And taking old Bradford whom he had never seen before, to be one of the Towns People that had a Good Will for him, enter'd into a Conversation on his present Undertaking and Prospects; while Bradford not discovering that he was the other Printer's Father, on Keimer's saying he expected soon to get the greatest Part of the Business into his own Hands, drew him on by artful Questions and starting little Doubts, to explain all his Views, what Interest he rely'd on, and in what manner he intended to proceed. I who stood by and heard all, saw immediately that one of them was a crafty old Sophister, and the other a mere Novice. Bradford left me with Keimer, who was greatly surpriz'd when I told him who the old Man was.

Keimer's Printing House I found, consisted of an old shatter'd Press, and one small worn-out Fount of English, which he was then using himself, composing in it an Elegy on Aquila Rose before-mentioned, an ingenious young Man of excellent Character much respected in the Town, Clerk of the Assembly, and a pretty Poet. Keimer made Verses, too, but very indifferently. He could not be said to write them, for his Manner was to compose them in the Types directly out of his Head; so there being no Copy, but one Pair of Cases, and the Elegy likely to require all the Letter, no one could help him. I endeavour'd to put his Press (which he had not yet us'd, and of which he understood nothing) into Order fit to be work'd with; and promising to come and print off his Elegy as soon as he should have got it ready, I return'd to Bradford's who gave me a little Job to do for the present, and there I lodged and dieted. A few Days after Keimer sent for me to print off the Elegy. And now he had got another Pair of Cases, and a Pamphlet to reprint, on which he set me to work.

These two Printers I found poorly qualified for their Business. Bradford had not been bred to it, and was very illiterate; and Keimer tho' something of a Scholar, was a mere Compositor, knowing nothing of Presswork. He had been one of the French Prophets[17] and could act their enthusiastic Agitations. At this time he did not profess any particular Religion, but something of all on occasion; was very ignorant of the World, and had, as I afterwards found, a good deal of the Knave in his Composition. He did not like my Lodging at Bradford's while I work'd with him. He had a House indeed, but without Furniture, so he could not lodge me: But he got me a Lodging at Mr. Read's before-mentioned, who was the Owner of his House. And my Chest and Clothes being come by this time, I made rather a more respect-

---

[17] Millennarian Protestants who had to leave Catholic France for England in 1706.

able Appearance in the Eyes of Miss Read, than I had done when she first happen'd to see me eating my Roll in the Street.

I began now to have some Acquaintance among the young People of the Town, that were Lovers of Reading with whom I spent my Evenings very pleasantly and gaining Money by my Industry and Frugality, I lived very agreably, forgetting Boston as much as I could, and not desiring that any there should know where I resided, except my Friend Collins who was in my Secret, and kept it when I wrote to him. At length an Incident happened that sent me back again much sooner than I had intended.

I had a Brother-in-law, Robert Holmes, Master of a Sloop, that traded between Boston and Delaware. He being at New Castle 40 Miles below Philadelphia, heard there of me, and wrote me a Letter, mentioning the Concern of my Friends in Boston at my abrupt Departure, assuring me of their Goodwill to me, and that every thing would be accommodated to my Mind if I would return, to which he exhorted me very earnestly. I wrote an Answer to his Letter, thank'd him for his Advice, but stated my Reasons for quitting Boston fully, and in such a Light as to convince him I was not so wrong as he had apprehended.

Sir William Keith Governor of the Province, was then at New Castle, and Capt. Holmes happening to be in Company with him when my Letter came to hand, spoke to him of me, and show'd him the Letter. The Governor read it, and seem'd surpriz'd when he was told my Age. He said I appear'd a young Man of promising Parts, and therefore should be encouraged: The Printers at Philadelphia were wretched ones, and if I would set up there, he made no doubt I should succeed; for his Part, he would procure me the publick Business, and do me every other Service in his Power. This my Brother-in-Law afterwards told me in Boston. But I knew as yet nothing of it; when one Day Keimer and I being at Work together near the Window, we saw the Governor and another Gentleman (which prov'd to be Col. French, of New Castle) finely dress'd, come directly across the Street to our House, and heard them at the Door. Keimer ran down immediately, thinking it a Visit to him. But the Governor enquir'd for me, came up, and with a Condescension and Politeness I had been quite unus'd to, made me many Compliments, desired to be acquainted with me, blam'd me kindly for not having made my self known to him when I first came to the Place, and would have me away with him to the Tavern where he was going with Col. French to taste as he said some excellent Madeira. I was not a little surpriz'd, and Keimer star'd like a Pig poison'd. I went however with the Governor and Col. French, to a Tavern the Corner of Third Street, and over the Madeira he propos'd my Setting up my Business, laid before me the Probabilities of Success, and both he and Col. French assur'd me I should have their Interest and Influence in procuring the Publick Business of both Governments. On my doubting whether my Father would assist me in it, Sir

William said he would give me a Letter to him, in which he would state the Advantages, and he did not doubt of prevailing with him. So it was concluded I should return to Boston in the first Vessel with the Governor's Letter recommending me to my Father. In the mean time the Intention was to be kept secret, and I went on working with Keimer as usual, the Governor sending for me now and then to dine with him, a very great Honour I thought it, and conversing with me in the most affable, familiar, and friendly manner imaginable.

About the End of April 1724, a little Vessel offer'd for Boston. I took Leave of Keimer as going to see my Friends. The Governor gave me an ample Letter, saying many flattering things of me to my Father, and strongly recommending the Project of my setting up at Philadelphia, as a Thing that must make my Fortune. We struck on a Shoal in going down the Bay and sprung a Leak, we had a blustring time at Sea, and were oblig'd to pump almost continually, at which I took my Turn. We arriv'd safe however at Boston in about a Fortnight. I had been absent Seven Months and my Friends had heard nothing of me; for my Br. Holmes was not yet return'd; and had not written about me. My unexpected Appearance surpriz'd the Family; all were however very glad to see me and made me Welcome, except my Brother. I went to see him at his Printing-House: I was better dress'd than ever while in his Service, having a genteel new Suit from Head to foot, a Watch, and my Pockets lin'd with near Five Pounds Sterling in Silver. He receiv'd me not very frankly, look'd me all over, and turn'd to his Work again. The Journey-Men were inquisitive where I had been, what sort of a Country it was, and how I lik'd it? I prais'd it much, and the happy Life I led in it; expressing strongly my Intention of returning to it; and one of them asking what kind of Money we had there, I produc'd a handful of Silver and spread it before them, which was a kind of Raree-Show they had not been us'd to, Paper being the Money of Boston. Then I took an Opportunity of letting them see my Watch: and lastly, (my Brother still grum and sullen) I gave them a Piece of Eight to drink and took my Leave. This Visit of mine offended him extreamly. For when my Mother some time after spoke to him of a Reconciliation, and of her Wishes to see us on good Terms together, and that we might live for the future as Brothers, he said, I had insulted him in such a Manner before his People that he could never forget or forgive it. In this however he was mistaken.

My Father receiv'd the Governor's Letter with some apparent Surprize; but said little of it to me for some Days; when Capt. Homes returning, he show'd it to him, ask'd if he knew Keith, and what kind of a Man he was: Adding his Opinion that he must be of small Discretion, to think of setting a Boy up in Business who wanted yet 3 Years of being at Man's Estate. Homes said what he could in favour of the Project; but my Father was clear in the Impropriety of it; and at last gave a flat Denial to it. Then he wrote a civil Letter to Sir William thanking him for the Patronage he had so kindly offered me, but declining to assist me as yet in Setting up, I being in his Opinion too young to be trusted with the Management of a Business so important, and for which the Preparation must be so expensive.

My Friend and Companion Collins, who was a Clerk at the Post-Office, pleas'd with the Account I gave him of my new Country, determin'd to go thither also: And while I waited for my Fathers Determination, he set out before me by Land to Rhode-island, leaving his Books which were a pretty Collection of Mathematicks and Natural Philosophy, to come with mine and me to New York where he propos'd to wait for me. My Father, tho' he did not approve Sir William's Proposition was yet pleas'd that I had been able to obtain so advantageous a Character from a Person of such Note where I had resided, and that I had been so industrious and careful as to equip my self so handsomely in so short a time: therefore seeing no Prospect of an Accommodation between my Brother and me, he gave his Consent to my Returning again to Philadelphia, advis'd me to behave respectfully to the People there, endeavour to obtain the general Esteem, and avoid lampooning and libelling to which he thought I had too much Inclination; telling me, that by steady Industry and a prudent Parsimony, I might save enough by the time I was One and Twenty to set me up, and that if I came near the Matter he would help me out with the rest. This was all I could obtain, except some small Gifts as Tokens of his and my Mother's Love, when I embark'd again for New-York, now with their Approbation and their Blessing.

The Sloop putting in at Newport, Rhodeisland, I visited my Brother John, who had been married and settled there some Years. He received me very affectionately, for he always lov'd me. A Friend of his, one Vernon, having some Money due to him in Pensilvania, about 35 Pounds Currency, desired I would receive it for him, and keep it till I had his Directions what to remit it in. Accordingly he gave me an Order. This afterwards occasion'd me a good deal of Uneasiness. At Newport we took in a Number of Passengers for New York: Among which were two young Women, Companions, and a grave, sensible Matron-like Quaker-Woman with her Attendants. I had shown an obliging readiness to do her some little Services which impress'd her I suppose with a degree of Good-will towards me. Therefore when she saw a daily growing Familiarity between me and the two Young Women, which they appear'd to encourage, she took me aside and said, Young Man, I am concern'd for thee, as thou has no Friend with thee, and seems not to know much of the World, or of the Snares Youth is expos'd to; depend upon it those are very bad Women, I can see it in all their Actions, and if thee art not upon thy Guard, they will draw thee into some Danger: they are Strangers to thee, and I advise thee in a friendly Concern for thy Welfare, to have no Acquaintance with them. As I seem'd at first not to think so ill of them as she did, she mention'd some Things she had observ'd and heard that had escap'd my Notice; but now convinc'd me she was right. I thank'd her for her kind Advice, and promis'd to follow it. When we arriv'd at New York, they told me where they liv'd, and invited me to come and see them: but I avoided it. And it was well I did: For the next Day, the Captain miss'd a Silver Spoon and some other Things that had been taken out of his Cabbin, and knowing that these were a Couple of Strumpets, he got a Warrant to search their Lodgings, found the stolen Goods, and had the Thieves punish'd. So tho' we had escap'd a sunken Rock which we scrap'd upon in the Passage, I thought this Escape of rather more Importance to me.

At New York I found my Friend Collins, who had arriv'd there some Time before me. We had been intimate from Children, and had read the same Books together. But he had the Advantage of more time for reading, and Studying and a wonderful Genius for Mathematical Learning in which he far outstript me. While I liv'd in Boston most of my Hours of Leisure for Conversation were spent with him, and he continu'd a sober as well as an industrious Lad; was much respected for his Learning by several of the Clergy and other Gentlemen, and seem'd to promise making a good Figure in Life: but during my Absence he had acquir'd a Habit of Sotting with Brandy; and I found by his own Account and what I heard from others, that he had been drunk every day since his Arrival at New York, and behav'd very oddly. He had gam'd too and lost his Money, so that I was oblig'd to discharge his Lodgings, and defray his Expences to and at Philadelphia: Which prov'd extreamly inconvenient to me. The then Governor of N York, Burnet, Son of Bishop Burnet hearing from the Captain that a young Man, one of his Passengers, had a great many Books, desired he would bring me to see him. I waited upon him accordingly, and should have taken Collins with me but that he was not sober. The Governor treated me with great Civility, show'd me his Library, which was a very large one, and we had a good deal of Conversation about Books and Authors. This was the second Governor who had done me the Honour to take Notice of me, which to a poor Boy like me was very pleasing.

We proceeded to Philadelphia. I received on the Way Vernon's Money, without which we could hardly have finish'd our Journey. Collins wish'd to be employ'd in some Counting House; but whether they discover'd his Dramming by his Breath, or by his Behaviour, tho' he had some Recommendations, he met with no Success in any Application, and continu'd Lodging and Boarding at the same House with me and at my Expence. Knowing I had that Money of Vernon's he was continually borrowing of me, still promising Repayment as soon as he should be in Business. At length he had got so much of it, that I was distress'd to think what I should do, in case of being call'd on to remit it. His Drinking continu'd about which we sometimes quarrel'd, for when a little intoxicated he was very fractious. Once in a Boat on the Delaware with some other young Men, he refused to row in his Turn: I will be row'd home, says he. We will not row you, says I. You must or stay all Night on the Water, says he, just as you please. The others said, Let us row; what signifies it? But my Mind being soured with his other Conduct, I continu'd to refuse. So he swore he would make me row, or throw me overboard; and coming along stepping on the Thwarts towards me, when he came up and struck at me I clapt my Hand under his Crutch, and rising pitch'd him head-foremost into the River. I knew he was a good Swimmer, and so was under little Concern about him; but before he could get round to lay hold of the Boat, we had with a few Strokes pull'd her out of his Reach. And ever when he drew near the Boat, we ask'd if he would row, striking a few Strokes to slide her away from him. He was ready to die with Vexation, and obstinately would not promise to row; however seeing him at last beginning to tire, we lifted him in; and brought him home dripping wet in the Evening. We hardly exchang'd a civil Word afterwards; and a West India Captain who had a Commission to procure a Tutor for the Sons of a Gentleman at Barbadoes, happening to meet with him, agreed to carry him thither. He left me then, promising to remit me the first Money he should receive in order to discharge the Debt. But I never heard of him after.

The Breaking into this Money of Vernon's was one of the first great Errata of my Life. And this Affair show'd that my Father was not much out in his Judgment when he suppos'd me too young to manage Business of Importance. But Sir William, on reading his Letter, said he was too prudent. There was great Difference in Persons, and Discretion did not always accompany Years, nor was Youth always without it. And since he will not set you up, says he, I will do it my self. Give me an Inventory of the Things necessary to be had from England, and I will send for them. You shall repay me when you are able; I am resolv'd to have a good Printer here, and I am sure you must succeed. This was spoken with such an Appearance of Cordiality, that I had not the least doubt of his meaning what he said. I had hitherto kept the Proposition of my Setting up a Secret in Philadelphia, and I still kept it. Had it been known that I depended on the Governor, probably some Friend that knew him better would have advis'd me not to rely on him, as I afterwards heard it as his known Character to be liberal of Promises which he never meant to keep. Yet unsolicited as he was by me, how could I think his generous Offers insincere? I believ'd him one of the best Men in the World.

I presented him an Inventory of a Little Printing House, amounting by my Computation to about £100 Sterling. He lik'd it, but ask'd me if my being on the Spot in England to chuse the Types and see that every thing was good of the kind, might not be of some Advantage. Then, says he, when there, you may make Acquaintances and establish Correspondencies in the Bookselling and Stationary Way. I agreed that this might be advantageous. Then says he, get yourself ready to go with Annis; which was the annual Ship, and the only one at that Time usually passing between London and Philadelphia. But it would be some Months before Annis sail'd, so I continu'd working with Keimer, fretting about the Money Collins had got from me, and in daily

Apprehensions of being call'd upon by Vernon, which however did not happen for some Years after.

I believe I have omitted mentioning that in my first Voyage from Boston, being becalm'd off Block Island, our People set about catching Cod and hawl'd up a great many. Hitherto I had stuck to my Resolution of not eating animal Food; and on this Occasion, I consider'd with my Master Tryon, the taking every Fish as a kind of unprovok'd Murder, since none of them had or ever could do us any Injury that might justify the Slaughter. All this seem'd very reasonable. But I had formerly been a great Lover of Fish, and when this came hot out of the Frying Pan, it smelt admirably well. I balanc'd some time between Principle and Inclination: till I recollected, that when the Fish were opened, I saw smaller Fish taken out of their Stomachs: Then thought I, if you eat one another, I don't see why we mayn't eat you. So I din'd upon Cod very heartily and continu'd to eat with other People, returning only now and then occasionally to a vegetable Diet. So convenient a thing it is to be a *reasonable Creature*, since it enables one to find or make a Reason for every thing one has a mind to do.[18]

Keimer and I liv'd on a pretty good familiar Footing and agreed tolerably well: for he suspected nothing of my Setting up. He retain'd a great deal of his old Enthusiasms, and lov'd Argumentation. We therefore had many Disputations. I us'd to work him so with my Socratic Method, and had trapann'd him so often by Questions apparently so distant from any Point we had in hand, and yet by degrees led to the Point, and brought him into Difficulties and Contradictions that at last he grew ridiculously cautious, and would hardly answer me the most common Question, without asking first, *What do you intend to infer from that?* However it gave him so high an Opinion of my Abilities in the Confuting Way, that he seriously propos'd my being his Colleague in a Project he had of setting up a new Sect. He was to preach the Doctrines, and I was to confound all Opponents. When he came to explain with me upon the Doctrines, I found several Conundrums which I objected to unless I might have my Way a little too, and introduce some of mine. Keimer wore his Beard at full Length, because somewhere in the Mosaic Law it is said, *thou shalt not mar the Corners of thy Beard.*[19] He likewise kept the seventh day Sabbath; and these two Points were Essentials with him. I dislik'd both, but agreed to admit them upon Condition of his adopting the Doctrine of using no animal Food. I doubt, says he, my Constitution

---

[18] This paragraph is one of the most extraordinarily skillful passages in early American literature. It not only sets principle and inclination against one another in a way that shows the limits of reason in the Age of Reason. The very organization and rhythm mimic the action: the balance as Franklin deliberates, the decisive *Then* as he rationalizes, and the easy movement as he dines. The witty conclusion echoes the Applications of Puritan sermons and anticipates the punch lines of Thoreau's *Walden*—"as if you could kill time without injuring eternity."

[19] Leviticus 19:27.

will not bear that. I assur'd him it would, and that he would be the better for it. He was usually a great Glutton, and I promis'd my self some Diversion in half-starving him. He agreed to try the Practice if I would keep him Company. I did so and we held it for three Months. We had our Victuals dress'd and brought to us regularly by a Woman in the Neighbourhood, who had from me a List of 40 Dishes to be prepar'd for us at different times, in all which there was neither Fish Flesh nor Fowl, and the whim suited me the better at this time from the Cheapness of it, not costing us above 18d. Sterling each, per Week. I have since kept several Lents most strictly, Leaving the common Diet for that, and that for the common, abruptly, without the least Inconvenience: So that I think there is little in the Advice of making those Changes by easy Gradations. I went on pleasantly, but poor Keimer suffer'd grievously, tir'd of the Project, long'd for the Flesh Pots of Egypt, and order'd a roast Pig. He invited me and two Women Friends to dine with him, but it being brought too soon upon table, he could not resist the Temptation, and ate it all up before we came.

I had made some Courtship during this time to Miss Read. I had a great Respect and Affection for her, and had some Reason to believe she had the same for me: but as I was about to take a long Voyage, and we were both very young, only a little above 18. it was thought most prudent by her Mother to prevent our going too far at present, as a Marriage if it was to take place would be more convenient after my Return, when I should be as I expected set up in my Business. Perhaps too she thought my Expectations not so wellfounded as I imagined them to be.

My chief Acquaintances at this time were, Charles Osborne, Joseph Watson, and James Ralph; All Lovers of Reading. The two first were Clerks to an eminent Scrivener or Conveyancer in the Town, Charles Brogden; the other was Clerk to a Merchant. Watson was a pious sensible young Man, of great Integrity. The others rather more lax in their Principles of Religion, particularly Ralph, who as well as Collins had been unsettled by me, for which they both made me suffer. Osborne was sensible, candid, frank, sincere, and affectionate to his Friends; but in litterary Matters too fond of Criticising. Ralph, was ingenious, genteel in his Manners, and extreamly eloquent; I think I never knew a prettier Talker. Both of them great Admirers of Poetry, and began to try their Hands in little Pieces. Many pleasant Walks we four had together on Sundays into the Woods near Skuylkill, where we read to one another and conferr'd on what we read.

Ralph was inclin'd to pursue the Study of Poetry, not doubting but he might become eminent in it and make his Fortune by it, alledging that the best Poets must when they first began to write, make as many Faults as he did. Osborne dissuaded him, assur'd him he had no Genius for Poetry, and advis'd him to think of nothing beyond the Business he was bred to; that in the mercantile way tho' he had no Stock, he might by his Diligence and Punctuality recommend himself to Employment as a Factor, and in time acquire wherewith to trade on his own Account. I approv'd the amusing one's self with Poetry now and then, so far as to improve one's Language, but no farther. On this it was propos'd that we should each of us at our next Meeting produce a Piece of our own Composing, in order to improve by our mutual Observations, Criticisms and Corrections. As Language and Expression was what we had in View, we excluded all Considerations of Invention, by agreeing that the Task should be a Version of the 18th Psalm, which describes the Descent of a Deity. When the Time of our Meeting drew nigh, Ralph call'd on me first, and let me know his Piece was ready. I told him I had been busy, and having little Inclination had done nothing. He then show'd me his Piece for my Opinion; and I much approv'd it, as it appear'd to me to have great Merit. Now, says he, Osborne never will allow the least Merit in any thing of mine, but makes 1000 Criticisms out of mere Envy. He is not so jealous of you. I wish therefore you would take this Piece, and produce it as yours. I will pretend not to have had time, and so produce nothing: We shall then see what he will say to it. It was agreed, and I immediately transcrib'd it that it might appear in my own hand. We met. Watson's Performance was read: there were some Beauties in it: but many Defects. Osborne's was read: It was much better. Ralph did it Justice, remark'd some Faults, but applauded the Beauties. He himself had nothing to produce. I was backward, seem'd desirous of being excus'd, had not had sufficient Time to correct; &c. but no Excuse could be admitted, produce I must. It was read and repeated; Watson and Osborne gave up the Contest; and join'd in applauding it immoderately. Ralph only made some Criticisms and propos'd some Amendments, but I defended my Text. Osborne was against Ralph, and told him he was no better a Critic than Poet; so he dropt the Argument. As they two went home together, Osborne express'd himself still more strongly in favour of what he thought my Production, having restrain'd himself before as he said, lest I should think it Flattery. But who would have imagin'd, says he, that Franklin had been capable of such a Performance; such Painting, such Force! such Fire! he has even improv'd the Original! In his common Conversation, he seems to have no Choice of Words; he hesitates and blunders; and yet, good God, how he writes! When we next met, Ralph discover'd the Trick, we had plaid him, and Osborne was a little laught at. This Transaction fix'd Ralph in his Resolution of becoming a Poet. I did all I could to dissuade him from it, but He continued scribbling Verses, till Pope cur'd him.[20] He became however a pretty good Prose Writer. More of him hereafter.

But as I may not have occasion again to mention the other two, I shall just remark here, that Watson died in my Arms a few Years after, much la-

---

[20] By writing a severe critique of Ralph's verse after Ralph and Franklin had gone to England.

mented, being the best of our Set. Osborne went to the West Indies, where he became an eminent Lawyer and made Money, but died young. He and I made a serious Agreement, that the one who happen'd first to die, should if possible make a friendly Visit to the other, and acquaint him how he found things in that Separate State. But he never fulfill'd his Promise.

The Governor, seeming to like my Company, had me frequently to his House; and his Setting me up was always mention'd as a fix'd thing. I was to take with me Letters recommendatory to a Number of his Friends, besides the Letter of Credit to furnish me with the necessary Money for purchasing the Press and Types, Paper, &c. For these Letters I was appointed to call at different times, when they were to be ready, but a future time was still named. Thus we went on till the Ship whose Departure too had been several times postponed was on the Point of sailing. Then when I call'd to take my Leave and Receive the Letters, his Secretary, Dr. Patrick Baird, came out to me and said the Governor was extreamly busy, in writing, but would be down at Newcastle before the Ship, and there the Letters would be delivered to me.

Ralph, tho' married and having one Child, had determined to accompany me in this Voyage. It was thought he intended to establish a Correspondence, and obtain Goods to sell on Commission. But I found afterwards, that thro' some Discontent with his Wifes Relations, he purposed to leave her on their Hands, and never return again. Having taken leave of my Friends, and interchang'd some Promises with Miss Read, I left Philadelphia in the Ship, which anchor'd at Newcastle. The Governor was there. But when I went to his Lodging, the Secretary came to me from him with the civillest Message in the World, that he could not then see me being engag'd in Business of the utmost Importance; but should send the Letters to me on board, wish'd me heartily a good Voyage and a speedy Return, &c. I return'd on board, a little puzzled, but still not doubting.

Mr. Andrew Hamilton, a famous Lawyer of Philadelphia, had taken Passage in the same Ship for himself and Son: and with Mr. Denham a Quaker Merchant, and Messrs. Onion and Russel Masters of an Iron Work in Maryland, had engag'd the Great Cabin; so that Ralph and I were forc'd to take up with a Birth in the Steerage: And none on board knowing us, were considered as ordinary Persons. But Mr. Hamilton and his Son (it was James, since Governor) return'd from New Castle to Philadelphia, the Father being recall'd by a great Fee to plead for a seized Ship. And just before we sail'd Col. French coming on board, and showing me great Respect, I was more taken Notice of, and with my Friend Ralph invited by the other Gentlemen to come into the Cabin, there being now Room. Accordingly we remov'd thither.

Understanding that Col. French had brought on board the Governor's Dispatches, I ask'd the Captain for those Letters that were to be under my

Care. He said all were put into the Bag together; and he could not then come at them; but before we landed in England, I should have an Opportunity of picking them out. So I was satisfy'd for the present, and we proceeded on our Voyage. We had a sociable Company in the Cabin, and lived uncommonly well, having the Addition of all Mr. Hamilton's Stores, who had laid in plentifully. In this Passage Mr. Denham contracted a Friendship for me that continued during his Life. The Voyage was otherwise not a pleasant one, as we had a great deal of bad Weather.

When we came into the Channel, the Captain kept his Word with me, and gave me an Opportunity of examining the Bag for the Governor's Letters. I found none upon which my Name was put, as under my Care; I pick'd out 6 or 7 that by the Hand writing I thought might be the promis'd Letters, especially as one of them was directed to Basket the King's Printer, and another to some Stationer. We arriv'd in London the 24th of December, 1724. I waited upon the Stationer who came first in my Way, delivering the Letter as from Gov. Keith. I don't know such a Person, says he: but opening the Letter, O, this is from Riddlesden; I have lately found him to be a compleat Rascal, and I will have nothing to do with him, nor receive any Letters from him. So putting the Letter into my Hand, he turn'd on his Heel and left me to serve some Customer. I was surprized to find these were not the Governor's Letters. And after recollecting and comparing Circumstances, I began to doubt his Sincerity. I found my Friend Denham, and opened the whole Affair to him. He let me into Keith's Character, told me there was not the least Probability that he had written any Letters for me, that no one who knew him had the smallest Dependance on him, and he laught at the Notion of the Governor's giving me a Letter of Credit, having as he said no Credit to give. On my expressing some Concern about what I should do: He advis'd me to endeavour getting some Employment in the Way of my Business. Among the Printers here, says he, you will improve yourself; and when you return to America, you will set up to greater Advantage.

We both of us happen'd to know, as well as the Stationer, that Riddlesden the Attorney, was a very Knave. He had half ruin'd Miss Read's Father by drawing him in to be bound for him. By his Letter it appear'd, there was a secret Scheme on foot to the Prejudice of Hamilton (Suppos'd to be then coming over with us), and that Keith was concern'd in it with Riddlesden. Denham, who was a Friend of Hamilton's, thought he ought to be acquainted with it. So when he arriv'd in England, which was soon after, partly from Resentment and Ill-Will to Keith and Riddlesden, and partly from Good Will to him: I waited on him, and gave him the Letter. He thank'd me cordially, the Information being of Importance to him. And from that time he became my Friend, greatly to my Advantage afterwards on many Occasions.

But what shall we think of a Governor's playing such pitiful Tricks, and imposing so grossly on a poor ignorant Boy! It was a Habit he had acquired. He wish'd to please every body; and having little to give, he gave Expectations. He was otherwise an ingenious sensible Man, a pretty good Writer, and a good Governor for the People, tho' not for his Constituents the Proprietaries, whose Instructions he sometimes disregarded. Several of our best Laws were of his Planning, and pass'd during his Administration.

. . .

From PART TWO

[PROJECTS AND THE ART OF VIRTUE: PHILADELPHIA, 1742]

The Objections, and Reluctances I met with in Soliciting the Subscriptions [for a public library], made me soon feel the Impropriety of presenting one's self as the Proposer of any useful Project that might be suppos'd to raise one's Reputation in the smallest degree above that of one's Neighbours, when one has need of their Assistance to accomplish that Project. I therefore put my self as much as I could out of sight, and stated it as a Scheme of a *Number of Friends*, who had requested me to go about and propose it to such as they thought Lovers of Reading. In this way my Affair went on more smoothly, and I ever after practis'd it on such Occasions; and from my frequent Successes, can heartily recommend it. The present little Sacrifice of your Vanity will afterwards be amply repaid. If it remains a while uncertain to whom the Merit belongs, some one more vain than yourself will be encourag'd to claim it, and then even Envy will be dispos'd to do you Justice, by plucking those assum'd Feathers, and restoring them to their right Owner.

This Library afforded me the means of Improvement by constant Study, for which I set apart an Hour or two each Day; and thus repair'd in some Degree the Loss of the Learned Education my Father once intended for me. Reading was the only Amusement I allow'd my self. I spent no time in Taverns, Games, or Frolicks of any kind. And my Industry in my Business continu'd as indefatigable as it was necessary. I was in debt for my Printing-house, I had a young Family coming on to be educated, and I had to contend with for Business two Printers who were establish'd in the Place before me. My Circumstances however grew daily easier: my original Habits of Frugality continuing. And my Father having among his Instructions to me when a Boy, frequently repeated a Proverb of Solomon, *"Seest thou a Man diligent in his Calling, he shall stand before Kings, he shall not stand before mean Men."*[21] I from thence consider'd Industry as a Means of obtaining Wealth

---

[21] Proverbs 22.29. Compare Mather's "Life of Phips," above, p. 259.

and Distinction, which encourag'd me, tho.' I did not think that I should ever literally stand before Kings, which however has since happened.—for I have stood before five, and even had the honour of sitting down with one, the King of Denmark, to Dinner.

We have an English Proverb that says,

> He that would thrive
> Must ask his Wife;

it was lucky for me that I had one as much dispos'd to Industry and Frugality as my self. She assisted me chearfully in my Business, folding and stitching Pamphlets, tending Shop, purchasing old Linen Rags for the Paper-makers, &c. &c. We kept no idle Servants, our Table was plain and simple, our Furniture of the cheapest. For instance my Breakfast was a long time Bread and Milk, (no Tea) and I ate it out of a twopenny earthen Porringer with a Pewter Spoon. But mark how Luxury will enter Families, and make a Progress, in Spite of Principle. Being call'd one Morning to Breakfast, I found it in a China Bowl with a Spoon of Silver. They had been bought for me without my knowledge by my Wife, and had cost her the enormous Sum of three and twenty Shillings, for which she had no other Excuse or Apology to make, but that she thought *her* Husband deserv'd a Silver Spoon and China Bowl as well as any of his Neighbours. This was the first Appearance of Plate and China in our House, which afterwards in a Course of Years as our Wealth encreas'd augmented gradually to several Hundred Pounds in Value.

I had been religiously educated as a Presbyterian; and tho' some of the Dogmas of that Persuasion, such as the Eternal Decrees of God, Election, Reprobation &c. appear'd to me unintelligible, others doubtful, and I early absented myself from the Public Assemblies of the Sect, Sunday being my Studying-Day, I never was without some religious Principles; I never doubted, for instance, the Existence of the Deity, that he made the World, and govern'd it by his Providence; that the most acceptable Service of God was the doing Good to Man; that our Souls are immortal; and that all Crime will be punished and Virtue rewarded either here or hereafter; these I esteem'd the Essentials of every Religion, and being to be found in all the Religions we had in our Country I respected them all, tho' with different degrees of Respect as I found them more or less mix'd with other Articles which without any Tendency to inspire, promote or confirm Morality, serv'd principally to divide us and make us unfriendly to one another. This Respect to all, with an Opinion that the worst had some good Effects, induc'd me to avoid all Discourse that might tend to lessen the good Opinion another might have of his own Religion; and as our Province increas'd in People and new Places of worship were continually wanted, and generally erected by voluntary Contribution, my Mite for such purpose, whatever might be the Sect, was never refused.[22]

Tho' I seldom attended any Public Worship, I had still an Opinion of its Propriety, and of its Utility when rightly conducted, and I regularly paid my annual Subscription for the Support of the only Presbyterian Minister or Meeting we had in Philadelphia. He us'd to visit me sometimes as a Friend, and admonish me to attend his Administrations, and I was now and then prevail'd on to do so, once for five Sundays successively. Had he been, *in my Opinion,* a good Preacher perhaps I might have continued, notwithstanding the occasion I had for the Sunday's Leisure in my Course of Study: But his Discourses were chiefly either polemic Arguments, or Explications of the peculiar Doctrines of our Sect, and were all to me very dry, uninteresting and unedifying, since not a single moral Principle was inculcated or enforc'd, their Aim seeming to be rather to make us Presbyterians than good Citizens. At length he took for his Text that [eighth] Verse of the 4th Chapter of Philippians, *Finally, Brethren, Whatsoever Things are true, honest, just, pure, lovely, or of good report, if there be any virtue, or any praise, think on these Things;* and I imagin'd in a Sermon on such a Text, we could not miss of having some Morality: But he confin'd himself to five Points only as meant by the Apostle, viz. 1. Keeping holy the Sabbath Day. 2. Being diligent in Reading the Holy Scriptures. 3. Attending duly the Publick Worship. 4. Partaking of the Sacrament. 5. Paying a due Respect to God's Ministers. These might be all good Things, but as they were not the kind of good Things that I expected from that Text, I despaired of ever meeting with them from any other, was disgusted, and attended his Preaching no more. I had some Years before compos'd a little Liturgy or Form of Prayer for my own private Use, viz. in 1728. entitled, *Articles of Belief and Acts of Religion.* I return'd to the Use of this, and went no more to the public Assemblies. My Conduct might be blameable, but I leave it without attempting farther to excuse it, my present purpose being to relate Facts, and not to make Apologies for them.

It was about this time that I conceiv'd the bold and arduous Project of arriving at moral Perfection.[23] I wish'd to live without committing any Fault at any time; I would conquer all that either Natural Inclination, Custom, or Company might lead me into. As I knew, or thought I knew, what was right and wrong, I did not see why I might not *always* do the one and avoid the other. But I soon found I had undertaken a Task of more Difficulty than I

[22] Here the Yale editors point out quite properly that Franklin not only tolerated but financially helped a variety of sects, and that he was among the three most generous contributors to a fund for a synagogue in Philadelphia.

[23] The following paragraphs are probably the most famous, and the most often misunderstood, of Franklin's autobiography. The detached irony and amused self-criticism become evident when this first paragraph, and especially the first sentence, are read slowly, aloud. Compare the codfish episode, above, p. 176.

had imagined. While my *Attention was taken up* in guarding against one Fault, I was often surpriz'd by another. Habit took the Advantage of Inattention. Inclination was sometimes too strong for Reason. I concluded at length, that the mere speculative Conviction that it was our Interest to be compleatly virtuous, was not sufficient to prevent our Slipping, and that the contrary Habits must be broken and good ones acquired and established, before we can have any Dependance on a steady uniform Rectitude of Conduct. For this purpose I therefore contriv'd the following Method.

In the various Enumerations of the moral Virtues[24] I had met with in my Reading, I found the Catalogue more or less numerous, as different Writers included more or fewer Ideas under the same Name. Temperance, for Example, was by some confin'd to Eating and Drinking, while by others it was extended to mean the moderating every other Pleasure, Appetite, Inclination or Passion, bodily or mental, even to our Avarice and Ambition. I propos'd to myself, for the sake of Clearness, to use rather more Names with fewer Ideas annex'd to each, than a few Names with more Ideas; and I included under Thirteen Names of Virtues all that at that time occurr'd to me as necessary or desirable, and annex'd to each a short Precept, which fully express'd the Extent I gave to its Meaning.

These Names of Virtues with their Precepts were

1. TEMPERANCE.

Eat not to Dulness.
Drink not to Elevation.

2. SILENCE.

Speak not but what may benefit others or yourself. Avoid trifling Conversation.

3. ORDER.

Let all your Things have their Places. Let each Part of your Business have its Time.

4. RESOLUTION.

Resolve to perform what you ought. Perform without fail what you resolve.

---

[24] Notice that these are the moral or instrumental virtues, and that piety, for example, is not one of them.

5. FRUGALITY.

Make no Expence but to do good to others or yourself: i.e. Waste nothing.

6. INDUSTRY.

Lose no Time. Be always employ'd in something useful. Cut off all unnecessary Actions.

7. SINCERITY.

Use no hurtful Deceit.
Think innocently and justly; and, if you speak, speak accordingly.

8. JUSTICE.

Wrong none, by doing Injuries or omitting the Benefits that are your Duty.

9. MODERATION.

Avoid Extreams. Forbear resenting Injuries so much as you think they deserve.

10. CLEANLINESS.

Tolerate no Uncleanness in Body, Cloaths or Habitation.

11. TRANQUILITY.

Be not disturbed at Trifles, or at Accidents common or unavoidable.

12. CHASTITY.

Rarely use Venery but for Health or Offspring; Never to Dulness, Weakness, or the Injury of your own or another's Peace or Reputation.

13. HUMILITY.

Imitate Jesus and Socrates.

My Intention being to acquire the *Habitude* of all these Virtues, I judg'd it would be well not to distract my Attention by attempting the whole at once, but to fix it on one of them at a time, and when I should be Master of that, then to proceed to another, and so on till I should have gone thro' the thirteen. And as the previous Acquisition of some might facilitate the Acquisition of certain others, I arrang'd them with that View as they stand above. *Temperance* first, as it tends to procure that Coolness and Clearness of Head, which is so necessary where constant Vigilance was to be kept up, and Guard maintained, against the unremitting Attraction of ancient Habits, and the Force of perpetual Temptations. This being acquir'd and establish'd, *Silence* would be more easy, and my Desire being to gain Knowledge at the same time that I improv'd in Virtue, and considering that in Conversation it was obtain'd rather by the use of the Ears than of the Tongue, and therefore wishing to break a Habit I was getting into of Prattling, Punning and Joking, which only made me acceptable to trifling Company, I gave *Silence* the second Place, This, and the next, *Order,* I expected would allow me more Time for attending to my Project and my Studies; RESOLUTION, once become habitual, would keep me firm in my Endeavours to obtain all the subsequent Virtues; *Frugality* and *Industry,* by freeing me from my remaining Debt, and producing Affluence and Independence, would make more easy the Practice of *Sincerity* and *Justice,* etc. etc. Conceiving then that agreable to the Advice of Pythagoras in his Golden Verses daily Examination would be necessary, I contriv'd the following Method for conducting that Examination.

I made a little Book in which I allotted a Page for each of the Virtues. I rul'd each Page with red Ink, so as to have seven Columns, one for each Day of the Week, marking each Column with a Letter for the Day. I cross'd these Columns with thirteen red Lines, marking the Beginning of each Line with the first Letter of one of the Virtues, on which Line and in its proper Column I might mark by a little black Spot every Fault I found upon Examination to have been committed respecting that Virtue upon that Day.

I determined to give a Week's strict Attention to each of the Virtues successively. Thus in the first Week my great Guard was to avoid every the least Offence against Temperance, leaving the other Virtues to their ordinary Chance, only marking every Evening the Faults of the Day. Thus if in the first Week I could keep my first Line marked T clear of Spots, I suppos'd the Habit of that Virtue so much strengthen'd and its opposite weaken'd, that I might venture extending my Attention to include the next, and for the following Week keep both Lines clear of Spots. Proceeding thus to the last, I could go thro' a Course compleat in Thirteen Weeks, and four Courses in a Year. And like him who having a Garden to weed,[25] does not attempt to eradicate all the bad Herbs at once, which would exceed his Reach and his Strength, but works on one of the Beds at a time, and having accomplish'd

[25] This image suggests that the process may well be endless, or perennial.

the first proceeds to a Second; so I should have, (I hoped) the encouraging Pleasure of seeing on my Pages the Progress I made in Virtue, by clearing successively my Lines of their Spots, till in the End by a Number of Courses, I should be happy in viewing a clean Book after a thirteen Weeks daily Examination.

Form of the Pages

TEMPERANCE							
Eat not to Dulness. *Drink not to Elevation.*							
	S	M	T	W	T	F	S
T	••	•		•		•	
S	•	•	•		•	•	•
O			•			•	
R		•			•		
F			•				
I							
S							
J							
M							
Cl.							
T							
Ch.							
H							

This my little Book had for its Motto these Lines from Addison's *Cato*;

> *Here will I hold: If there is a Pow'r above us,*
> *(And that there is, all Nature cries aloud*
> *Thro' all her Works) he must delight in Virtue,*
> *And that which he delights in must be happy.*

Another from Cicero.

> *O Vitæ Philosophia Dux! O Virtutum indagatrix, expultrixque viti-*
> *orum! Unus dies bene, et ex preceptis tuis actus, peccanti immortalitati*
> *est anteponendus.* [26]

Another from the Proverbs of Solomon speaking of Wisdom or Virtue;

> *Length of Days is in her right hand, and in her Left Hand Riches and*
> *Honours; Her Ways are Ways of Pleasantness, and all her Paths are*
> *Peace.*
>
> III, 16, 17.

And conceiving God to be the Fountain of Wisdom, I thought it right and necessary to solicit his Assistance for obtaining it; to this End I form'd the following little Prayer, which was prefix'd to my Tables of Examination; for daily Use.

> *O Powerful Goodness! bountiful Father! merciful Guide! Increase in*
> *me that Wisdom which discovers my truest Interests; Strengthen my*
> *Resolutions to perform what that Wisdom dictates. Accept my kind*
> *Offices to thy other Children, as the only Return in my Power for thy*
> *continual Favours to me.*

I us'd also sometimes a little Prayer which I took from Thomson's Poems. viz

> *Father of Light and Life, thou Good supreme,*
> *O teach me what is good, teach me thy self!*
> *Save me from Folly, Vanity and Vice,*
> *From every low Pursuit, and fill my Soul*
> *With Knowledge, conscious Peace, and Virtue pure,*
> *Sacred, substantial, neverfading Bliss!* [27]

---

[26] The Yale editors identify and translate this passage thus: *Tusculan Disputations,* v, ii, 5. Several lines of the original are omitted after *vitiorum.* "Oh philosophy, guide of life! Oh searcher out of virtues and expeller of vices! . . . One day lived well and according to thy precepts is to be preferred to an eternity of sin."

[27] From James Thomson, *The Seasons.*

The Precept of *Order* requiring that *every Part of my Business should have its allotted Time,* one Page in my little Book contain'd the following Scheme of Employment for the Twenty-four Hours of a natural Day,

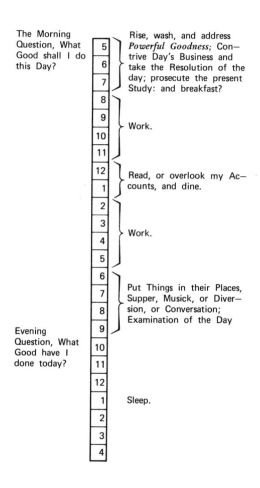

The Morning Question, What Good shall I do this Day?

Hour	
5	Rise, wash, and address *Powerful Goodness*; Con— trive Day's Business and take the Resolution of the day; prosecute the present Study: and breakfast?
6	
7	
8	Work.
9	
10	
11	
12	Read, or overlook my Ac— counts, and dine.
1	
2	Work.
3	
4	
5	
6	Put Things in their Places, Supper, Musick, or Diver— sion, or Conversation; Examination of the Day
7	
8	
9	

Evening Question, What Good have I done today?

Hour	
10	
11	
12	
1	Sleep.
2	
3	
4	

I enter'd upon the Execution of this Plan for Self Examination, and continu'd it with occasional Intermissions for some time. I was surpriz'd to find myself so much fuller of Faults than I had imagined, but I had the Satisfaction of seeing them diminish. To avoid the Trouble of renewing now and then my little Book, which by scraping out the Marks on the Paper of old Faults to make room for new Ones in a new Course, became full of Holes: I transferr'd my Tables and Precepts to the Ivory Leaves[28] of a Memorandum Book, on which the Lines were drawn with red Ink that made a durable Stain, and on those Lines I mark'd my Faults with a black Lead Pencil, which Marks I could easily wipe out with a wet Sponge. After a while I went thro' one Course only in a Year, and afterwards only one in several Years, till at length I omitted them entirely, being employ'd in Voyages and Business abroad with a Multiplicity of Affairs, that interfered, but I always carried my little Book with me.

My Scheme of ORDER, gave me the most Trouble, and I found, that tho' it might be practicable where a Man's Business was such as to leave him the Disposition of his Time, that of a Journey-man Printer for instance, it was not possible to be exactly observ'd by a Master, who must mix with the World, and often receive People of Business at their own Hours. *Order* too, with regard to Places for Things, Papers, &c. I found extreamly difficult to acquire. I had not been early accustomed to *Method,* and having an exceeding good Memory, I was not so sensible of the Inconvenience attending Want of Method. This Article therefore cost me so much painful Attention and my Faults in it vex'd me so much, and I made so little Progress in Amendment, and had such frequent Relapses, that I was almost ready to give up the Attempt, and content my self with a faulty Character in that respect. Like the Man who in buying an Ax of a Smith my neighbour, desired to have the whole of its Surface as bright as the Edge; the Smith consented to grind it bright for him if he would turn the Wheel. He turn'd while the Smith press'd the broad Face of the Ax hard and heavily on the Stone, which made the Turning of it very fatiguing. The Man came every now and then from the Wheel to see how the Work went on; and at length would take his Ax as it was without farther Grinding. No, says the Smith, Turn on, turn on; we shall have it bright by and by; and yet 'tis only speckled. Yes, says the Man; but— *I think I like a speckled Ax best.* And I believe this may have been the Case with many who having for want of some such Means as I employ'd found the Difficulty of obtaining good, and breaking bad Habits, in other Points of Vice and Virtue, have given up the Struggle, and concluded that *a speckled Ax was best.* For something that pretended to be Reason was every now and then suggesting to me, that such extream Nicety as I exacted of my self might be a kind of Foppery in Morals, which if it were known would make me ridiculous; that a perfect Character might be attended with the Inconvenience of being envied and hated; and that a benevolent Man should allow a few Faults in himself, to keep his Friends in Countenance.

[28] Here again, and in the next paragraph, Franklin reminds the reader that the task is endless.

In Truth I found myself incorrigible with respect to *Order;* and now I am grown old, and my Memory bad, I feel very sensibly the want of it. But on the whole, tho' I never arrived at the Perfection I had been so ambitious of obtaining, but fell far short of it, yet I was by the Endeavour a better and a happier Man than I otherwise should have been, if I had not attempted it; As those who aim at perfect Writing by imitating the engraved Copies, tho' they never reach the wish'd for Excellence of those Copies, their Hand is mended by the Endeavour, and is tolerable while it continues fair and legible.

And it may be well my Posterity should be informed, that to this little Artifice, with the Blessing of God, their Ancestor ow'd the constant Felicity of his Life down to his 79th Year in which this is written. What Reverses may attend the Remainder is in the Hand of Providence: But if they arrive the Reflection on past Happiness enjoy'd ought to help his Bearing them with more Resignation. To *Temperance* he ascribes his long-continu'd Health, and what is still left to him of a good Constitution. To *Industry* and *Frugality* the early Easiness of his Circumstances, and Acquisition of his Fortune, with all that Knowledge which enabled him to be an useful Citizen, and obtain'd for him some Degree of Reputation among the Learned. To *Sincerity* and *Justice* the Confidence of his Country, and the honourable Employs it conferr'd upon him. And to the joint Influence of the whole Mass of the Virtues, even in the imperfect State he was able to acquire them, all that Evenness of Temper, and that Chearfulness in Conversation which makes his Company still sought for, and agreable even to his younger Acquaintance. I hope therefore that some of my Descendants may follow the Example and reap the Benefit.

It will be remark'd that, tho' my Scheme was not wholly without Religion there was in it no Mark of any of the distinguishing Tenets of any particular Sect. I had purposely avoided them; for being fully persuaded of the Utility and Excellency of my Method, and that it might be serviceable to People in all Religions, and intending some time or other to publish it, I would not have any thing in it that should prejudice any one of any Sect against it. I purposed writing a little Comment on each Virtue, in which I would have shown the Advantages of possessing it, and the Mischiefs attending its opposite Vice; and I should have called my Book the ART *of Virtue,* because it would have shown the *Means* and *Manner* of obtaining Virtue, which would have distinguish'd it from the mere Exhortation to be good, that does not instruct and indicate the Means; but is like the Apostle's Man of verbal Charity, who only, without showing to the Naked and the Hungry *how* or where they might get Cloaths or Victuals, exhorted them to be fed and clothed. *James* II, 15, 16.[29]

[29] "15. If a brother or sister be naked, and destitute of daily food, 16. And one of you say unto them, Depart in peace, be ye warmed and filled; notwithstanding ye give them not those things which are needful to the body; what doth it profit?"

But it so happened that my Intention of writing and publishing this Comment was never fulfilled. I did indeed, from time to time put down short Hints of the Sentiments, Reasonings, &c. to be made use of in it; some of which I have still by me: But the necessary close Attention to private Business in the earlier part of Life, and public Business since, have occasioned my postponing it. For it being connected in my Mind with a *great and extensive Project* that required the whole Man to execute, and which an unforeseen Succession of Employs prevented my attending to, it has hitherto remain'd unfinish'd.

In this Piece it was my Design to explain and enforce this Doctrine, that vicious Actions are not hurtful because they are forbidden, but forbidden because they are hurtful, the Nature of Man alone consider'd: That it was therefore every one's Interest to be virtuous, who wish'd to be happy even in this World.[30] And I should from this Circumstance, there being always in the World a Number of rich Merchants, Nobility, States and Princes, who have need of honest Instruments for the Management of their Affairs, and such being so rare have endeavoured to convince young Persons, that no Qualities were so likely to make a poor Man's Fortune as those of Probity and Integrity.

My List of Virtues contain'd at first but twelve: But a Quaker Friend having kindly inform'd me that I was generally thought proud; that my Pride show'd itself frequently in Conversation; that I was not content with being in the right when discussing any Point, but was overbearing and rather insolent; of which he convinc'd me by mentioning several Instances; I determined endeavouring to cure myself if I could of this Vice or Folly among the rest, and I added *Humility* to my List, giving an extensive Meaning to the Word. I cannot boast of much Success in acquiring the *Reality* of this Virtue; but I had a good deal with regard to the *Appearance* of it. I made it a Rule to forbear all direct Contradiction to the Sentiments of others, and all positive Assertion of my own. I even forbid myself agreable to the old Laws of our Junto, the Use of every Word or Expression in the Language that imported a fix'd Opinion; such as *certainly, undoubtedly,* &c. and I adopted instead of them, *I conceive, I apprehend,* or *I imagine* a thing to be so or so, or it so appears to me at present. When another asserted something, that I thought an Error, I deny'd my self the Pleasure of contradicting him abruptly, and of showing immediately some Absurdity in his Proposition; and in answering I began by observing that in certain Cases or Circumstances his Opinion would be right, but that in the present case there *appear'd* or *seem'd* to me some Difference, &c. I soon found the Advantage of this Change in my

---

[30] Here one must notice the qualifications ("the nature of man alone considered," and "even in this world") and the objective reality of "vicious actions": some actions are vicious. The essential doctrine here is that of "enlightened self-interest." Compare "A Man of Sense," above, pp. 442–443.

Manners. The Conversations I engag'd in went on more pleasantly. The modest way in which I propos'd my Opinions, procur'd them a readier Reception and less Contradiction; I had less Mortification when I was found to be in the wrong, and I more easily prevail'd with others to give up their Mistakes and join with me when I happen'd to be in the right. And this Mode, which I at first put on, with some violence to natural Inclination, became at length so easy and so habitual to me, that perhaps for these Fifty Years past no one has ever heard a dogmatical Expression escape me. And to this Habit (after my Character of Integrity) I think it principally owing, that I had early so much Weight with my Fellow Citizens, when I proposed new Institutions, or Alterations in the old; and so much Influence in public Councils when I became a Member. For I was but a bad Speaker, never eloquent, subject to much Hesitation in my choice of Words, hardly correct in Language, and yet I generally carried my Points.

In reality there is perhaps no one of our natural Passions so hard to subdue as *Pride*. Disguise it, struggle with it, beat it down, stifle it, mortify it as much as one pleases, it is still alive, and will every now and then peep out and show itself. You will see it perhaps often in this History. For even if I could conceive that I had compleatly overcome it, I should probably by [be] proud of my Humility.

Thus far written at Passy 1784.

Rules
By Which
A Great Empire May Be
Reduced To A Small One;
Presented to A Late Minister,
When He Entered Upon His
Administration[1]

An ancient Sage boasted, that, tho' he could not fiddle, he knew how to make a *great city* of a *little one*. The science that I, a modern simpleton, am about to communicate, is the very reverse.

I address myself to all ministers who have the management of extensive dominions, which from their very greatness are become troublesome to govern, because the multiplicity of their affairs leaves no time for *fiddling*.

---

[1] *The Gentleman's Magazine*, Vol. XLIII,
September, 1773. p. 441.

I. In the first place, gentlemen, you are to consider, that a great empire, like a great cake, is most easily diminished at the edges. Turn your attention, therefore, first to your *remotest* provinces; that, as you get rid of them, the next may follow in order.

II. That the possibility of this separation may always exist, take special care the provinces are never incorporated with the mother country; that they do not enjoy the same common rights, the same privileges in commerce; and that they are governed by *severer* laws, all of *your enacting*, without allowing them any share in the choice of the legislators. By carefully making and preserving such distinctions, you will (to keep to my simile of the cake) act like a wise gingerbread-baker, who, to facilitate a division, cuts his dough half through in those places where, when baked, he would have it *broken to pieces*.

III. Those remote provinces have perhaps been acquired, purchased, or conquered, at the *sole expence* of the settlers, or their ancestors, without the aid of the mother country. If this should happen to increase her *strength*, by their growing numbers, ready to join in her wars; her *commerce*, by their growing demand for her manufactures; or her *naval power*, by greater employment for her ships and seamen, they may probably suppose some merit in this, and that it entitles them to some favour; you are therefore to *forget it all, or resent it*, as if they had done you injury. If they happen to be zealous whigs, friends of liberty, nurtured in revolution principles, *remember all that* to their prejudice, and resolve to punish it; for such principles, after a revolution is thoroughly established, are of *no more use;* they are even *odious* and *abominable*.

IV. However peaceably your colonies have submitted to your government, shewn their affection to your interests, and patiently borne their grievances; you are to *suppose* them always inclined to revolt, and treat them accordingly. Quarter troops among them, who by their insolence may *provoke* the rising of mobs, and by their bullets and bayonets *suppress* them. By this means, like the husband who uses his wife ill *from suspicion*, you may in time convert your *suspicions* into *realities*.

V. Remote provinces must have *Governors* and *Judges*, to represent the Royal Person, and execute everywhere the delegated parts of his office and authority. You ministers know, that much of the strength of government depends on the *opinion* of the people; and much of that opinion on the *choice of rulers* placed immediately over them. If you send them wise and good men for governors, who study the interest of the colonists, and advance their prosperity, they will think their King wise and good, and that he wishes the welfare of his subjects. If you send them learned and upright men for Judges, they will think him a lover of justice. This may attach your provinces more to his government. You are therefore to be careful whom you recommend for those offices. If you can find prodigals, who have ruined their fortunes, broken gamesters or stockjobbers, these may do well as *governors;*

for they will probably be rapacious, and provoke the people by their extortions. Wrangling proctors and pettifogging lawyers, too, are not amiss; for they will be for ever disputing and quarrelling with their little parliaments. If withal they should be ignorant, wrongheaded, and insolent, so much the better. Attornies' clerks and Newgate solicitors will do for *Chief Justices*, especially if they hold their places *during your pleasure;* and all will contribute to impress those ideas of your government, that are proper for a people *you would wish to renounce it.*

VI. To confirm these impressions, and strike them deeper, whenever the injured come to the capital with complaints of mal-administration, oppression, or injustice, punish such suitors with long delay, enormous expence, and a final judgment in favour of the oppressor. This will have an admirable effect every way. The trouble of future complaints will be prevented, and Governors and Judges will be encouraged to farther acts of oppression and injustice; and thence the people may become more disaffected, and at length desperate.

VII. When such Governors have crammed their coffers, and made themselves so odious to the people that they can no longer remain among them, with safety to their persons, *recall and reward* them with pensions. You may make them *baronets* too, if that respectable order should not think fit to resent it. All will contribute to encourage new governors in the same practice, and make the supreme government, *detestable.*

VIII. If, when you are engaged in war, your colonies should vie in liberal aids of men and money against the common enemy, upon your simple requisition, and give far beyond their abilities, reflect that a penny taken from them by your power is more honourable to you, than a pound presented by their benevolence; despise therefore their voluntary grants, and resolve to harass them with novel taxes. They will probably complain to your parliaments, that they are taxed by a body in which they have no representative, and that this is contrary to common right. They will petition for redress. Let the Parliaments flout their claims, reject their petitions, refuse even to suffer the reading of them, and treat the petitioners with the utmost contempt. Nothing can have a better effect in producing the alienation proposed; for though many can forgive injuries, *none ever forgave contempt.*

IX. In laying these taxes, never regard the heavy burthens those remote people already undergo, in defending their own frontiers, supporting their own provincial governments, making new roads, building bridges, churches, and other public edifices, which in old countries have been done to your hands by your ancestors, but which occasion constant calls and demands on the purses of a new people. Forget the *restraints* you lay on their trade for *your own* benefit, and the advantage a *monopoly* of this trade gives your exacting merchants. Think nothing of the wealth those merchants and your manufacturers acquire by the colony commerce; their encreased ability thereby to pay taxes at home; their accumulating, in the price of their commodities, most of those taxes, and so levying them from their consuming customers; all this, and the employment and support of thousands of your poor by the colonists, you are *intirely to forget.* But remember to make your arbitrary tax more grievous to your provinces, by public declarations importing that your power of taxing them has *no limits;* so that when you take from them without their consent one shilling in the pound, you have a clear right to the other nineteen. This will probably weaken every idea of *security in their property,* and convince them, that under such a government they *have nothing they can call their own;* which can scarce fail of producing the *happiest consequences!*

X. Possibly, indeed, some of them might still comfort themselves, and say, "Though we have no property, we have yet *something* left that is valuable; we have constitutional *liberty,* both of person and of conscience. This King, these Lords, and these Commons, who it seems are too remote from us to know us, and feel for us, cannot take from us our *Habeas Corpus* right, or our right of trial *by a jury of our neighbours;* they cannot deprive us of the exercise of our religion, alter our ecclesiastical constitution, and compel us to be Papists, if they please, or Mahometans." To annihilate this comfort, begin by laws to perplex their commerce with infinite regulations, impossible to be remembered and observed; ordain seizures of their property for every failure; take away the trial of such property by Jury, and give it to arbitrary Judges of your own appointing, and of the lowest characters in the country, whose salaries and emoluments are to arise out of the duties or condemnations, and whose appointments are *during pleasure.* Then let there be a formal declaration of both Houses, that opposition to your edicts is *treason,* and that any person suspected of treason in the provinces may, according to some obsolete law, be seized and sent to the metropolis of the empire for trial; and pass an act, that those there charged with certain other offences, shall be sent away in chains from their friends and country to be tried in the same manner for felony. Then erect a new Court of Inquisition among them, accompanied by an armed force, with instructions to transport all such suspected persons; to be ruined by the expence, if they bring over evidences to prove their innocence, or be found guilty and hanged, if they cannot afford it. And, lest the people should think you cannot possibly go any farther, pass another solemn declaratory act, "that King, Lords, Commons had, hath, and of right ought to have, full power and authority to make statutes of sufficient force and validity to bind the unrepresented provinces IN ALL CASES WHATSOEVER." This will include *spiritual* with temporal, and, taken together, must operate wonderfully to your purpose; by convincing them, that they are at present under a power something like that spoken of in the scriptures, which can not only *kill their bodies,* but *damn their souls* to all eternity, by compelling them, if it pleases, *to worship the Devil.*

XI. To make your taxes more odious, and more likely to procure resistance, send from the capital a board of officers to superintend the collection, composed of the most *indiscreet, ill-bred,* and *insolent* you can find. Let these have large salaries out of the extorted revenue, and live in open, grating luxury upon the sweat and blood of the industrious; whom they are to worry continually with groundless and expensive prosecutions before the abovementioned arbitrary revenue Judges; *all at the cost of the party prosecuted,* tho' acquitted, because *the King is to pay no costs.* Let these men, *by your order,* be exempted from all the common taxes and burthens of the province, though they and their property are protected by its laws. If any revenue officers are *suspected* of the least tenderness for the people, discard them. If others are justly complained of, protect and reward them. If any of the under officers behave so as to provoke the people to drub them, promote those to better offices: this will encourage others to procure for themselves such profitable drubbings, by multiplying and enlarging such provocations, and *all will work towards the end you aim at.*

XII. Another way to make your tax odious, is to misapply the produce of it. If it was originally appropriated for the *defence* of the provinces, the better support of government, and the administration of justice, where it may be *necessary,* then apply none of it to that *defence,* but bestow it where it is *not necessary,* in augmented salaries or pensions to every governor, who has distinguished himself by his enmity to the people, and by calumniating them to their sovereign. This will make them pay it more unwillingly, and be more apt to quarrel with those that collect it and those that imposed it, who will quarrel again with them, and all shall contribute to your *main purpose,* of making them *weary of your government.*

XIII. If the people of any province have been accustomed to support their own Governors and Judges to satisfaction, you are to apprehend that such Governors and Judges may be thereby influenced to treat the people kindly, and to do them justice. This is another reason for applying part of that revenue in larger salaries to such Governors and Judges, given, as their commissions are, *during your pleasure* only; forbidding them to take any salaries from their provinces; that thus the people may no longer hope any kindness from their Governors, or (in Crown cases) any justice from their Judges. And, as the money thus misapplied in one province is extorted from all, probably *all will resent the misapplication.*

XIV. If the parliaments of your provinces should dare to claim rights, or complain of your administration, order them to be harrassed with *repeated dissolutions.* If the same men are continually returned by new elections, adjourn their meetings to some country village, where they cannot be accommodated, and there keep them *during pleasure;* for this, you know, is your PREROGATIVE; and an excellent one it is, as you may manage it to promote discontents among the people, diminish their respect, and *increase their disaffection.*

XV. Convert the brave, honest officers of your *navy* into pimping tide-waiters and colony officers of the *customs*. Let those, who in time of war fought gallantly in defence of the commerce of their countrymen, in peace be taught to prey upon it. Let them learn to be corrupted by great and real smugglers; but (to shew their diligence) scour with armed boats every bay, harbour, river, creek, cove, or nook throughout the coast of your colonies; stop and detain every coaster, every wood-boat, every fisherman, tumble their cargoes and even their ballast inside out and upside down; and, if a penn'orth of pins is found un-entered, let the whole be seized and confiscated. Thus shall the trade of your colonists suffer more from their friends in time of peace, than it did from their enemies in war. Then let these boats crews land upon every farm in their way, rob the orchards, steal the pigs and the poultry, and insult the inhabitants. If the injured and exasperated farmers, unable to procure other justice, should attack the aggressors, drub them, and burn their boats; you are to call this *high treason and rebellion*, order fleets and armies into their country, and threaten to carry all the offenders three thousand miles to be hanged, drawn, and quartered. *O! this will work admirably!*

XVI. If you are told of discontents in your colonies, never believe that they are general, or that you have given occasion for them; therefore do not think of applying any remedy, or of changing any offensive measure. Redress no grievance, lest they should be encouraged to demand the redress of some other grievance. Grant no request that is just and reasonable, lest they should make another that is unreasonable. Take all your informations of the state of the colonies from your Governors and officers in enmity with them. Encourage and reward these *leasing-makers;* secrete their lying accusations, lest they should be confuted; but act upon them as the clearest evidence; and believe nothing you hear from the friends of the people: suppose all *their* complaints to be invented and promoted by a few factious demagogues, whom if you could catch and hang, all would be quiet. Catch and hang a few of them accordingly; and the *blood of the Martyrs* shall *work miracles* in favour of your purpose.

XVII. If you see *rival nations* rejoicing at the prospect of your disunion with your provinces, and endeavouring to promote it; if they translate, publish, and applaud all the complaints of your discontented colonists, at the same time privately stimulating you to severer measures, let not that *alarm* or offend you. Why should it, since you all mean *the same thing?*

XVIII. If any colony should at their own charge erect a fortress to secure their port against the fleets of a foreign enemy, get your Governor to betray that fortress into your hands. Never think of paying what it cost the country, for that would look, at least, like some regard for justice; but turn it into a citadel to awe the inhabitants and curb their commerce. If they should have lodged in such fortress the very arms they bought and used to aid you in your conquests, seize them all; it will provoke like *ingratitude* added to *robbery*. One admirable effect of these operations will be, to discourage every other colony from erecting such defences, and so your enemies may more easily invade them; to the great disgrace of your government, and of course *the furtherance of your project.*

XIX. Send armies into their country under pretence of protecting the inhabitants; but, instead of garrisoning the forts on their frontiers with those troops, to prevent incursions, demolish those forts, and order the troops into the heart of the country, that the savages may be encouraged to attack the frontiers, and that the troops may be protected by the inhabitants. This will seem to proceed from your ill will or your ignorance, and contribute farther to produce and strengthen an opinion among them, *that you are no longer fit to govern them.*

XX. Lastly, invest the General of your army in the provinces, with great and unconstitutional powers, and free him from the controul of even your own Civil Governors. Let him have troops enow under his command, with all the fortresses in his possession; and who knows but (like some provincial Generals in the Roman empire, and encouraged by the universal discontent you have produced) he may take it into his head to set up for himself? If he should, and you have carefully practised these few *excellent rules* of mine, take my word for it, all the provinces will immediately join him; and you will that day (if you have not done it sooner) get rid of the trouble of governing them, and all the *plagues* attending their *commerce* and connection from henceforth and for ever.

Q. E. D.

Remarks Concerning the Savages of North America[1]

Savages we call them, because their Manners differ from ours, which we think the Perfection of Civility; they think the same of theirs.

Perhaps, if we could examine the Manners of different Nations with Impartiality, we should find no People so rude, as to be without any Rules of Politeness; nor any so polite, as not to have some Remains of Rudeness.

The Indian Men, when young, are Hunters and Warriors; when old, Counsellors; for all their Government is by Counsel of the Sages; there is no Force, there are no Prisons, no Officers to compel Obedience, or inflict

---

[1] Printed as a pamphlet in Philadelphia, 1784. Compare Roger Williams's Key into the Language of America, above, p. 161.

Punishment. Hence they generally study Oratory, the best Speaker having the most Influence. The Indian Women till the Ground, dress the Food, nurse and bring up the Children, and preserve and hand down to Posterity the Memory of public Transactions. These Employments of Men and Women are accounted natural and honourable. Having few artificial Wants, they have abundance of Leisure for Improvement by Conversation. Our laborious Manner of Life, compared with theirs, they esteem slavish and base; and the Learning, on which we value ourselves, they regard as frivolous and useless. An Instance of this occurred at the Treaty of Lancaster, in Pennsylvania, *anno* 1744, between the Government of Virginia and the Six Nations. After the principal Business was settled, the Commissioners from Virginia acquainted the Indians by a Speech, that there was at Williamsburg a College, with a Fund for Educating Indian youth; and that, if the Six Nations would send down half a dozen of their young Lads to that College, the Government would take care that they should be well provided for, and instructed in all the Learning of the White People. It is one of the Indian Rules of Politeness not to answer a public Proposition the same day that it is made; they think it would be treating it as a light matter, and that they show it Respect by taking time to consider it, as a Matter important. They therefore deferr'd their Answer till the Day following; when their Speaker began, by expressing their deep Sense of the kindness of the Virginia Government, in making them that Offer; 'for we know,' says he, 'that you highly esteem the kind of Learning taught in those Colleges, and that the Maintenance of our young Men, while with you, would be very expensive to you. We are convinc'd, therefore, that you mean to do us Good by your Proposal; and we thank you heartily. But you, who are wise, must know that different Nations have different Conceptions of things; and you will therefore not take it amiss, if our Ideas of this kind of Education happen not to be the same with yours. We have had some Experience of it; Several of our young People were formerly brought up at the Colleges of the Northern Provinces; they were instructed in all your Sciences; but, when they came back to us, they were bad Runners, ignorant of every means of living in the Woods, unable to bear either Cold or Hunger, knew neither how to build a Cabin, take a Deer, or kill an Enemy, spoke our Language imperfectly, were therefore neither fit for Hunters, Warriors, nor Counsellors; they were totally good for nothing. We are however not the less oblig'd by your kind Offer, tho' we decline accepting it and, to show our grateful Sense of it, if the Gentlemen of Virginia will send us a Dozen of their Sons, we will take great Care of their Education, instruct them in all we know, and make *Men* of them.'

Having frequent Occasions to hold public Councils, they have acquired great Order and Decency in conducting them. The old Men sit in the foremost Ranks, the Warriors in the next, and the Women and Children in the hindmost. The Business of the Women is to take exact Notice of what passes, imprint it in their Memories (for they have no Writing), and communicate it to their Children. They are the Records of the Council, and they preserve Traditions of the Stipulations in Treaties 100 Years back; which, when we compare with our Writings, we always find exact. He that would speak, rises. The rest observe a profound Silence. When he has finish'd and sits down, they leave him 5 or 6 Minutes to recollect, that, if he has omitted any thing he intended to say, or has any thing to add, he may rise again and deliver it. To interrupt another, even in common Conversation, is reckon'd highly indecent. How different this is from the conduct of a polite British House of Commons, where scarce a day passes without some Confusion, that makes the Speaker hoarse in calling to *Order;* and how different from the Mode of Conversation in many polite Companies of Europe, where, if you do not deliver your Sentence with great Rapidity, you are cut off in the middle of it by the Impatient Loquacity of those you converse with, and never suffer'd to finish it!

The Politeness of these Savages in Conversation is indeed carried to Excess, since it does not permit them to contradict or deny the Truth of what is asserted in their Presence. By this means they indeed avoid Disputes; but then it becomes difficult to know their Minds, or what Impression you make upon them. The Missionaries who have attempted to convert them to Christianity, all complain of this as one of the great Difficulties of their Mission. The Indians hear with Patience the Truths of the Gospel explain'd to them, and give their usual Tokens of Assent and Approbation; you would think they were convinc'd. No such matter. It is mere Civility.

A Swedish Minister, having assembled the chiefs of the Susquehanah Indians, made a Sermon to them, acquainting them with the principal historical Facts on which our Religion is founded; such as the Fall of our first Parents by eating an Apple, the coming of Christ to repair the Mischief, his Miracles and Suffering, &c. When he had finished, an Indian Orator stood up to thank him. 'What you have told us,' says he, 'is all very good. It is indeed bad to eat Apples. It is better to make them all into Cyder. We are much oblig'd by your kindness in coming so far, to tell us these Things which you have heard from your Mothers. In return, I will tell you some of those we have heard from ours. In the Beginning, our Fathers had only the Flesh of Animals to subsist on; and if their Hunting was unsuccessful, they were starving. Two of our young Hunters, having kill'd a Deer, made a Fire in the Woods to broil some Part of it. When they were about to satisfy their Hunger, they beheld a beautiful young Woman descend from the Clouds, and seat herself on that Hill, which you see yonder among the blue Mountains. They said to each other, it is a Spirit that has smelt our broiling Venison, and wishes to eat of it; let us offer some to her. They presented her with the Tongue; she was pleas'd with the Taste of it, and said, "Your kindness shall be rewarded; come to this Place after thirteen Moons, and you shall find something that will be of great Benefit in nourishing you and your Children to the latest Generations." They did so, and, to their Surprise, found Plants they had never seen before; but which, from that ancient time, have been constantly cultivated among us, to our great Advantage. Where her right Hand had touched the Ground, they found Maize; where her left hand had touch'd it, they found Kidney-Beans; and where her Backside had sat on it, they found Tobacco.' The good Missionary, disgusted with this idle Tale, said, 'What I delivered to you were sacred Truths; but what you tell me is mere Fable, Fiction, and Falsehood.' The Indian, offended, reply'd, 'My brother, it seems your Friends have not done you Justice in your Education; they have not well instructed you in the Rules of common Civility. You saw that we, who understand and practise those Rules, believ'd all your stories; why do you refuse to believe ours?'

When any of them come into our Towns, our People are apt to crowd round them, gaze upon them, and incommode them, where they desire to be private; this they esteem great Rudeness, and the Effect of the Want of Instruction in the Rules of Civility and good Manners. 'We have,' say they, 'as much Curiosity as you, and when you come into our Towns, we wish for Opportunities of looking at you; but for this purpose we hide ourselves behind Bushes, where you are to pass, and never intrude ourselves into your Company.'

Their Manner of entring one another's village has likewise its Rules. It is reckon'd uncivil in travelling Strangers to enter a Village abruptly, without giving Notice of their Approach. Therefore, as soon as they arrive within hearing, they stop and hollow, remaining there till invited to enter. Two old Men usually come out to them, and lead them in. There is in every Village a vacant Dwelling, called *the Strangers' House*. Here they are plac'd, while the old Men go round from Hut to Hut, acquainting the Inhabitants, that Strangers are arriv'd, who are probably hungry and weary; and every one sends them what he can spare of Victuals, and Skins to repose on. When the Strangers are refresh'd, Pipes and Tobacco are brought; and then, but not before, Conversation begins, with Enquiries who they are, whither bound, what News, &c.; and it usually ends with offers of Service, if the Strangers have occasion of Guides, or any Necessaries for continuing their Journey; and nothing is exacted for the Entertainment.

The same Hospitality, esteem'd among them as a principal Virtue, is practis'd by Private Persons; of which Conrad Weiser, our Interpreter, gave me the following Instance. He had been naturaliz'd among the Six Nations, and spoke well the Mohock Language. In going thro' the Indian Country, to carry a Message from our Governor to the Council at Onondaga, he call'd at the Habitation of Canassatego, an old Acquaintance, who embrac'd him, spread Furs for him to sit on, plac'd before him some boil'd Beans and Venison, and mix'd some Rum and Water for his Drink. When he was well refresh'd, and had lit his Pipe, Canassatego began to converse with him; ask'd how he had far'd the many Years since they had seen each other; whence he then came; what occasion'd the Journey, &c. Conrad answered all his Questions; and when the Discourse began to flag, the Indian, to continue it, said, 'Conrad, you have lived long among the white People, and know something of their Customs; I have been sometimes at Albany, and have observed, that once in Seven Days they shut up their Shops, and assemble all in the great House; tell me what it is for? What do they do there?' 'They meet there,' says Conrad, 'to hear and learn *good Things*.' 'I do not doubt,' says the Indian, 'that they tell you so; they have told me the same; but I doubt the Truth of what they say, and I will tell you my Reasons. I went lately to Albany to sell my Skins and buy Blankets, Knives, Powder, Rum, &c. You know I us'd generally to deal with Hans Hanson; but I was a little inclin'd this time to try some other Merchant. However, I call'd first upon Hans, and asked him what he would give for Beaver. He said he could not give any more than four Shillings a Pound; "but," says he, "I cannot talk on Business now; this is the Day when we meet together to learn *Good Things*, and I am going to the Meeting." So I thought to myself, "Since we cannot do any Business to-day, I may as well go to the meeting too," and I went with him. There stood up a Man in Black, and began to talk to the People very angrily. I did not understand what he said; but, perceiving that he look'd much at me and at Hanson, I imagin'd he was angry at seeing me there; so I went out, sat down near the House, struck Fire, and lit my Pipe, waiting till the Meeting should break up. I thought too, that the Man had mention'd something of Beaver, and I suspected it might be the Subject of their Meeting. So, when they came out, I accosted my Merchant. "Well, Hans," says I, "I hope you have agreed to give more than four Shillings a Pound." "No," says he, "I cannot give so much; I cannot give more than three shillings and sixpence." I then spoke to several other Dealers, but they all sung the same song,—Three and sixpence,—Three and sixpence. This made it clear to me, that my Suspicion was right; and, that whatever they pretended of meeting to learn *good Things*, the real purpose was to consult how to cheat Indians in the Price of Beaver. Consider but a little, Conrad, and you must be of my Opinion. If they met so often to learn *good Things*, they would certainly have learnt some before this time. But they are still ignorant. You know our Practice. If a white Man, in travelling thro' our Country, enters one of our Cabins, we all treat him as I treat you; we dry him if he is wet, we warm him if he is cold, we give him Meat and Drink, that he may allay his Thirst and Hunger; and we spread soft Furs for him to rest and sleep on; we demand nothing in return. But, if I go into a white Man's House at Albany, and ask for Victuals and Drink, they say, "Where is your Money?" and if I have none, they say, "Get out, you Indian Dog." You see they have not yet learned those little *Good Things*, that we need no

Meetings to be instructed in, because our Mothers taught them to us when
we were Children; and therefore it is impossible their Meetings should be, as
they say, for any such purpose, or have any such Effect; they are only to
contrive *the Cheating of Indians in the Price of Beaver.*'

Note.—It is remarkable that in all Ages and
Countries Hospitality has been allow'd as the
Virtue of those whom the civiliz'd were
pleas'd to call Barbarians. The Greeks celebrated the Scythians for it. The Saracens possess'd it eminently, and it is to this day the
reigning Virtue of the wild Arabs. St. Paul, too, in the Relation of his Voyage and Shipwreck on the Island of Melita says the Barba-
rous People shewed us no little kindness; for
they kindled a fire, and received us every
one, because of the present Rain, and because of the Cold.

Letter To Ezra Stiles[1]

Philad^a, March 9, 1790.

Reverend and Dear Sir,

I received your kind Letter of Jan'y 28, and am glad you have at length
received the portrait of Gov'r Yale from his Family, and deposited it in the
College Library. He was a great and good Man, and had the Merit of doing
infinite Service to your Country by his Munificence to that Institution. The
Honour you propose doing me by placing mine in the same Room with his,
is much too great for my Deserts; but you always had a Partiality for me, and
to that it must be ascribed. I am however too much obliged to Yale College,
the first learned Society that took Notice of me and adorned me with its
Honours, to refuse a Request that comes from it thro' so esteemed a Friend.
But I do not think any one of the Portraits you mention, as in my Possession,
worthy of the Place and Company you propose to place it in. You have an
excellent Artist lately arrived. If he will undertake to make one for you, I
shall cheerfully pay the Expence; but he must not delay setting about it, or
I may slip thro' his fingers, for I am now in my eighty-fifth year, and very
infirm.

I send with this a very learned Work, as it seems to me, on the antient
Samaritan Coins, lately printed in Spain, and at least curious for the Beauty
of the Impression. Please to accept it for your College Library. I have subscribed for the Encyclopædia now printing here, with the Intention of presenting it to the College. I shall probably depart before the Work is finished,

[1] This letter, in answer to a request from the
president of Yale, is one of the last that
Franklin wrote. The text is from the Smyth edition of Franklin's writings. Remember
that the *Autobiography* had not yet been
published.

but shall leave Directions for its Continuance to the End. With this you will receive some of the first numbers.

You desire to know something of my Religion. It is the first time I have been questioned upon it. But I cannot take your Curiosity amiss, and shall endeavour in a few Words to gratify it. Here is my Creed. I believe in one God, Creator of the Universe. That he governs it by his Providence. That he ought to be worshipped. That the most acceptable Service we render to him is doing good to his other Children. That the soul of Man is immortal, and will be treated with Justice in another Life respecting its Conduct in this. These I take to be the fundamental Principles of all sound Religion, and I regard them as you do in whatever Sect I meet with them.

As to Jesus of Nazareth, my Opinion of whom you particularly desire, I think the System of Morals and his Religion, as he left them to us, the best the World ever saw or is likely to see; but I apprehend it has received various corrupting Changes, and I have, with most of the present Dissenters in England, some Doubts as to his Divinity; tho' it is a question I do not dogmatize upon, having never studied it, and think it needless to busy myself with it now, when I expect soon an Opportunity of knowing the Truth with less Trouble. I see no harm, however, in its being believed, if that Belief has the good Consequence, as probably it has, of making his Doctrines more respected and better observed; especially as I do not perceive, that the Supreme takes it amiss, by distinguishing the Unbelievers in his Government of the World with any peculiar Marks of his Displeasure.

I shall only add, respecting myself, that, having experienced the Goodness of that Being in conducting me prosperously thro' a long life, I have no doubt of its Continuance in the next, though without the smallest Conceit of meriting such Goodness. My Sentiments on this Head you will see in the Copy of an old Letter enclosed,[2] which I wrote in answer to one from a zealous Religionist, whom I had relieved in a paralytic case by electricity, and who, being afraid I should grow proud upon it, sent me his serious though rather impertinent Caution. I send you also the Copy of another Letter, which will shew something of my Disposition relating to Religion. With great and sincere Esteem and Affection, I am, Your obliged old Friend and most obedient humble Servant

B. Franklin.

P.S. Had not your College some Present of Books from the King of France? Please to let me know, if you had an Expectation given you of more, and the Nature of that Expectation? I have a Reason for the Enquiry.

I confide, that you will not expose me to Criticism and censure by publishing any part of this Communication to you. I have ever let others enjoy

[2] Probably the letter written to Joseph Huey, in 1757.

their religious Sentiments, without reflecting on them for those that appeared to me unsupportable and even absurd. All Sects here, and we have a great Variety, have experienced my good will in assisting them with Subscriptions for building their new Places of Worship; and, as I have never opposed any of their Doctrines, I hope to go out of the World in Peace with them all.

JOHN WOOLMAN

(1720-1772)

Both in his life and in his celebrated written work, John Woolman bears exemplary witness to central principles of the Society of Friends: plainness, self-discipline, conscientious behavior to express human brotherhood in daily life. Born near Mount Holly, New Jersey, Woolman grew up on a farm in the discipline of a Quaker Meeting, and then he became a tailor in Mount Holly. As he came to a number of conscientious decisions about social ethics, he tested them against the judgment of local Friends and then began to make a practice of visiting other communities as a witness for the new principles. In this way he served as a kind of itinerant preacher in a religious society that had no paid clergy. In Mount Holly, for example, he had begun to draw wills for neighbors who wanted legal or literary assistance, and he found that his conscience objected to his preparing any will that bequeathed slaves along with other property. Within a few years he was bearing his often unwelcome testimony on that issue to Friends in other parts of the Middle Atlantic colonies, and even to North Carolina. He thus became one of the most effective antislavery influences, and one of the chief defenders of the poor in eighteenth-century America, and he traveled to England (in steerage, because he objected

The most recent edition is The Journal and Major Essays of John Woolman, ed. Phillips P. Moulton, 1971. An earlier edition is The Journal and Essays of John Woolman, ed. Amelia Gummere, 1927, which includes a biography.

Biographies include Janet Whitney, John Woolman, American Quaker, 1942; C. O. Peare, John Woolman, Child of Light,

1954. For critical appraisals, see W. Forrest Altman, "John Woolman's Reading of the Mystics," Bulletin of the Friends' Historical Association, 48 (1959): 103-115; Edwin H. Cady, John Woolman, 1965; Frederick B. Tolles, Quakers and the Atlantic Culture, 1960; Daniel B. Shea, Jr., Spiritual Autobiography in Early America, 1968.

to the luxury and the carved images in the cabins) to seek aid from English Friends in the antislavery movement. But he died of smallpox soon after his arrival.

The first chapter of Woolman's *Journal,* which was not published till after his death, deserves comparison with the spiritual autobiographies of Jonathan Edwards and Anne Bradstreet, and with Henry Thoreau's *Walden* and *The Autobiography of Benjamin Franklin.* It is also one of the most valuable sources for an understanding of the importance of both self-discipline and community discipline to the life of a Friend. As Woolman clearly shows us, the inner light was not to be confused with one's first impulse to speak on any question, and one had a strict obligation to seek and learn from the counsel of other Friends. In *A Plea for the Poor,* which has been reprinted in aid of workingmen's movements since the abolition of slavery, Woolman established an economic attitude that puts him in touch with nineteenth-century American writers such as Melville, and with Irish and English social reformers in the 1830's and the 1890's.

Nor was he politically unsuccessful in his own time. As early as 1758, four years after he had written "Some Considerations on the Keeping of Negroes," Woolman persuaded the Philadelphia Meeting to advise all Quakers to emancipate their slaves, and in the same decision the Meeting voted to exclude all those who bought or sold slaves from participating in the Society's business affairs. Woolman's arguments in such matters were strengthened by his own example. Unlike many Friends who accumulated large estates, he gave up his flourishing retail business in 1756 because it was too prosperous, and a few years later he stopped wearing dyed clothes and resolved again to limit his material things to necessities.

From The Journal of John Woolman[1]

CHAPTER I

1720

I have often felt a motion of love to leave some hints of my experience of the goodness of God: and pursuant thereto, in the 36 year of my age, I begin this work.

I was born in Northampton, in Burlington county, in West Jersey, in the year of our Lord 1720 and before I was seven years old, I began to be

[1] The edition is that of Phillips P. Moulton.

acquainted with the operations of Divine Love. Through the care of my parents, I was taught to read near as soon as I was capable of it, and as I went from school one seventh-day, I remember, while my companions went to play by the way, I went forward out of sight, and sitting down, I read the twenty-second chapter of the Revelations: "He showed me a pure River of Water of Life, clear as Crystal, proceeding out of the Throne of God and of the Lamb," etc. and in the reading of it, my mind was drawn to seek after that Pure Habitation, which I then believed God had prepared for His servants. The place where I sat, and the sweetness that attended my mind, remain fresh in my memory.

This and the like gracious visitations, had that effect upon me, that when boys used ill language, it troubled me, and through the continued mercies of God, I was preserved from it. The pious instructions of my parents were often fresh in my mind when I happened to be among wicked children, and were of use to me.

My parents having a large family of children, used frequently on first-days after meeting, to put us to read in the Holy Scriptures, or some religious books, one after another, the rest sitting by without much conversation, which I have since often thought was a good practice. From what I had read, I believed there had been in past ages, people who walked in uprightness before God in a degree exceeding any that I knew, or heard of, now living: and the apprehension of their being less steadiness and firmness amongst people in this age than in past ages, often troubled me while I was still young.

I had a dream about the ninth year of my age as follows: I saw the moon rise near the west, and run a regular course eastward, so swift that in about a quarter of an hour, she reached our meridian, when there descended from her a small cloud on a direct line to the earth, which lighted on a pleasant green about twenty yards from the door of my father's house (in which I thought I stood) and was immediately turned into a beautiful green tree. The moon appeared to run on with equal swiftness, and soon set in the east, at which time the sun arose at the place where it commonly doth in the summer, and shining with full radiance in a serene air, it appeared as pleasant a morning as ever I saw.

All this time I stood still in the door, in an awful frame of mind, and I observed that as heat increased by the rising sun, it wrought so powerfully on the little green tree, that the leaves gradually withered, and before noon it appeared dry and dead. There then appeared a being, small of size, moving swift from the north southward, called a *"Sun Worm."*

Tho' I was a child, this dream was instructive to me. Another thing remarkable in my childhood was, that once as I went to a neighbor's house, I saw, on the way, a robin sitting on her nest, and as I came near she went off, but having young ones, flew about, and with many cries expressed her concern for them. I stood and threw stones at her, till one striking her, she fell down dead. At first I was pleased with the exploit, but after a few minutes was seized with horror, as having in a sportive way killed an innocent creature while she was careful for her young. I beheld her lying dead, and thought those young ones for which she was so careful must now perish for want of their dam to nourish them; and after some painful considerations on the subject, I climbed up the tree, took all the young birds, and killed them supposing that better than to leave them to pine away and die miserably: and believed in this case, that scripture proverb was fulfilled, "The tender mercies of the wicked are cruel."[2] I then went on my errand, but, for some hours, could think of little else but [the cruelties I had committed, and was much troubled.]

Thus He whose tender mercies are over all His works, hath placed that in the human mind which incites to exercise goodness towards every living creature and this being singly attended to, people become tender-hearted and sympathizing; but being frequently and totally rejected, the mind shuts itself up in a contrary disposition.

About the twelfth year of my age, my father being abroad, my mother reproved me for some misconduct, to which I made an undutiful reply and the next first-day, as I was with my father returning from Meeting, he told me he understood I had behaved amiss to my mother, and advised me to be more careful in future. I knew myself blamable, and in shame and confusion remained silent. Being thus awakened to a sense of my wickedness, I felt remorse in my mind, and getting home, I retired and prayed to the Lord to forgive me; and I do not remember that I ever after that, spoke unhandsomely to either of my parents, however foolish in some other things.

Having attained the age of sixteen, I began to love wanton company: and though I was preserved from profane language or scandalous conduct, still I perceived a plant in me which produced much wild grapes. Yet my Merciful Father forsook me not utterly, but at times through His grace I was brought seriously to consider my ways, and the sight of my backsliding affected me with sorrow: but for want of rightly attending to the reproofs of instruction, vanity was added to vanity, and repentance. Upon the whole my mind was more and more alienated from the Truth, and I hastened towards destruction. While I meditate on the gulf towards which I traveled, and reflect on my youthful disobedience, my heart is affected with sorrow.

Advancing in age, the number of my acquaintance increased, and thereby my way grew more difficult. Though I had heretofore found comfort in reading the Holy Scriptures, and thinking on heavenly things, I was now estranged therefrom. I knew I was going from the flock of Christ, and had no resolution to return, hence serious reflections were uneasy to me, and youthful vanities and diversions my greatest pleasure. Running in this road I found

---

[2] Proverbs 12:10.

many like myself, and we associated in that which is reverse to true friendship: but in this swift race it pleased God to visit me with sickness, so that I doubted of recovering: and then did darkness, horror and amazement, with full force seize me, even when my pain and distress of body was very great. I thought it would have been better for me never to have had a being, than to see the day which I now saw. I was filled with confusion, and in great affliction both of mind and body, I lay and bewailed myself. I had not confidence to lift up my cries to God, whom I had thus offended; but in a deep sense of my great folly I was humbled before Him, and at length that Word which is as a fire and a hammer, broke and dissolved my rebellious heart, and then my cries were put up in contrition, and in the multitude of His mercies I found inward relief, and felt a close engagement, that if He was pleased to restore my health, I might walk humbly before Him.

After my recovery, this exercise remained with me a considerable time, but, by degrees, giving way to youthful vanities, they gained strength, and getting with wanton young people I lost ground. The Lord had been very gracious, and spoke peace to me in the time of my distress, and I now most ungratefully turned again to folly, on which account, at times, I felt sharp reproof, but did not get low enough to cry for help. I was not so hardy as to commit things scandalous, but to exceed in vanity, and promote mirth, was my chief study. Still I retained a love and esteem for pious people, and their company brought an awe upon me. My dear parents several times admonished me in the fear of the Lord, and their admonition entered into my heart, and had a good effect for a season, but not getting deep enough to pray rightly, the tempter when he came found entrance. I remember once having spent a part of a day in wantonness, as I went to bed at night, there lay in a window near my bed a Bible, which I opened, and first cast my eye on the text, "We lie down in our shame, and our confusion covers us."[3] This I knew to be my case, and meeting with so unexpected a reproof, I was somewhat affected with it, and went to bed under remorse of conscience, which I soon cast off again.

Thus time passed on, my heart was replenished with mirth and wantonness, while pleasing scenes of vanity were presented to my imagination, till I attained the age of eighteen years, near which time I felt the judgments of God in my soul like a consuming fire, and looking over my past life, the prospect was moving. I was often sad, and longed to be delivered from those vanities; then again my heart was strongly inclined to them, and there was in me a sore conflict. At times I turned to folly, and then again sorrow and confusion took hold of me. In a while I resolved totally to leave off some of my vanities, but there was a secret reserve in my heart, of the more refined part of them, and I was not low enough to find true peace. Thus for some months, I had great troubles and disquiet, there remaining in me an unsub-

[3] Jeremiah 3:25.

jected will, which rendered my labors fruitless, till at length, through the merciful continuance of heavenly visitations, I was made to bow down in spirit before the Most High. I remember one evening I had spent some time in reading a pious author, and walking out alone, I humbly prayed to the Lord for His help, that I might be delivered from those vanities which so ensnared me. . . . Thus being brought low He helped me, and as I learned to bear the Cross, I felt refreshment to come from His presence: but not keeping in that strength which gave victory I lost ground again, the sense of which greatly afflicted me and I sought deserts and lonely places, and there with tears did confess my sins to God, and humbly craved help of Him, and I may say with reverence He was near to me in my troubles, and in those times of humiliation opened my ear to discipline.

I was now led to look seriously at the means by which I was drawn from the pure Truth, and I learned this. That if I would live in the life which the faithful servants of God lived in, I must not go into company as heretofore in my own will, but all the cravings of sense must be governed by a divine principle. In times of sorrow and abasement these instructions were sealed upon me, and I felt the power of Christ prevail over all selfish desires, so that I was preserved in a good degree of steadiness, and being young and believing at that time that a single life was best for me, I was strengthened to keep from such company as had often been a snare to me.

I kept steady to meetings, spent first-days in the afternoon chiefly in reading the Scriptures and other good books, and was early convinced in my mind that true religion consisted in an inward life, wherein the heart doth love and reverence God the Creator, and learn to exercise true justice and goodness, not only toward all men, but also toward the brute creatures. That as the mind was moved by an inward principle to love God as an invisible, incomprehensible Being, by the same principle it was moved to love Him in all His manifestations in the visible world. That as by His breath the flame of life was kindled in all animal and sensible creatures, to say we love God as unseen, and at the same time exercise cruelty toward the least creature moving by his life, or by life derived from Him, was a contradiction in itself.

I found no narrowness respecting sects and opinions, but believe that sincere upright-hearted people, in every society who truly love God were accepted of Him.

As I lived under the Cross, and simply followed the openings of Truth, my mind from day to day was more enlightened, my former acquaintance were left to judge of me as they would, for I found it safest for me to live in private and keep these things sealed up in my own breast. While I silently ponder on that change which was wrought in me, I find no language equal to it, nor any means to convey to another a clear idea of it. I looked upon the works of God in this visible Creation, and an awfulness covered me. my heart was tender and often contrite, and a universal love to my fellow creatures increased in me. This will be understood by such who have trodden in the same path.

Some glances of real beauty is perceivable in their faces, who dwell in true meekness. Some tincture of true harmony in the sound of that voice to which divine Love gives utterance, and some appearance of right order in their temper and conduct, whose passions are fully regulated, yet all these do not fully show forth that inward life to such who have not felt it; but this white stone and new name is known rightly to such only who have it.

Now tho' I had been thus strengthened to bear the Cross, I still found myself in great danger, having many weaknesses attending me, and strong temptations to wrestle with, in the feeling whereof I frequently withdrew into private places, and often with tears besought the Lord to help me, whose gracious ear was open to my cry.

All this time I lived with my parents, and wrought on the plantation, and having had schooling pretty well for a planter, I used to improve winter evenings, and other leisure times, and being now in the twenty-first year of my age, a man in much business at shopkeeping and baking, asked me if I would hire with him to tend shop and keep books. I acquainted my father with the proposal, and, after some deliberation it was agreed for me to go. I had for a considerable time found my mind less given to husbandry than heretofore, having often in view some other way of living.

At home I had lived retired, and now having a prospect of being much in the way of company, I felt frequent and fervent cries in my heart to God the Father of mercies, that He would preserve me from all taint and corruption. That in this more public employ, I might serve Him my Gracious Redeemer, in that humility and self-denial with which I had been in a small degree exercised in a very private life.

The man who employed me furnished a shop in Mount Holly, about five miles from my father's house and six from his own and there I lived alone, and tended his shop. Shortly after my settlement here, I was visited by several young people, my former acquaintances, who knew not but vanities would be as agreeable to me now as ever, and at these times I cried unto the Lord in secret for wisdom and strength, for I felt myself encompassed with difficulties, and had fresh occasion to bewail the follies of time past, in contracting a familiarity with a libertine people. And as I had now left my father's house outwardly, I found my Heavenly Father to be merciful to me beyond what I can express.

By day I was much among people, and had many trials to go through, but in evenings I was mostly alone, and may with thankfulness acknowledge, that in those times the spirit of supplication was often poured upon me, under which I was frequently exercised, and felt my strength renewed.

In a few months after I came here, my master bought several Scotch menservants, from on board a vessel, and brought them to Mount Holly to sell and having sold several the rest were left with me, one of which was taken sick, and died. The latter part of his sickness, he, being delirious, used to curse and swear most sorrowfully, and after he was buried, I was left to sleep alone the next night in the same chamber where he died. I perceived in me a timorousness: I knew however I had not injured the man, but had assisted in taking care of him according to my capacity, and I was not free to ask anyone, on that occasion, to sleep with me: nature was feeble, but every trial was a fresh incitement to give myself up wholly to the service of God, for I found no helper like Him in times of trouble.

After a while my former acquaintance gave over expecting me as one of their company, and I began to be known to some whose conversation was helpful to me. And now, as I had experienced the love of God, through Jesus Christ, to redeem me from many pollutions, and to be a constant succor to me through a sea of conflicts, with which no person was fully acquainted, and as my heart was often enlarged in this heavenly principle, so I felt a tender compassion for the youth who remained entangled in the same snares which had entangled me. From one month to another, this love and tenderness increased, and my mind was more strongly engaged for the good of my fellow-creatures. I went to meetings in an awful frame of mind, and endeavored to be inwardly acquainted with the language of the True Shepherd, and one day being under a strong exercise of spirit, I stood up, and said some words in a meeting, but not keeping close to the divine opening, I said more than was required of me and being soon sensible of my error, I was afflicted in mind some weeks, without any light or comfort, even to that degree that I could take satisfaction in nothing. I remembered God, and was troubled and in the depth of my distress He had pity upon me, and sent the Comforter. I then felt forgiveness for my offense, and my mind became calm and quiet, being truly thankful to my Gracious Redeemer for His mercies. And after this, feeling the spring of divine love opened, and a concern to speak, I said a few words in meeting in which I found peace, this I believe was about six weeks from the first time, and as I was thus humbled and disciplined under the Cross, my understanding became more strengthened to distinguish the language of the pure Spirit which inwardly moves upon the heart, and taught me to wait in silence sometimes many weeks together, until I felt that rise which prepares the creature to stand like a trumpet, through which the Lord speaks to his flock.

From an inward purifying, and steadfast abiding under it, springs a lively operative desire for the good of others. All faithful people are not called to the public ministry but whoever are called to it, are called to minister of that which they have tasted and handled spiritually. The outward modes of worship are various, but wheresoever men are true ministers of Jesus Christ, it is from the operation of His Spirit upon their hearts, first purifying them, and thus giving them a feeling sense of the conditions of others. This truth was early fixed in my mind, and I was taught to watch the pure opening, and to take heed lest while I was standing to speak, my own will should get uppermost, and cause me to utter words from worldly wisdom, and depart from the channel of the true gospel ministry.

In the management of my outward affairs I may say with thankfulness I found Truth to be my support, and I was respected in my master's family who came to live in Mount Holly within two years after my going there [1742].

About the twenty-third year of my age I had many fresh and heavenly openings, in respect to the care and providence of the Almighty over His creatures in general, and over man as the most noble amongst those which are visible, and being clearly convinced in my judgment that to place my whole trust in God was best for me, I felt renewed engagements that in all things I might act on an inward principle of Virtue, and pursue worldly business no further than as Truth opened my way therein.

About the time called Christmas I observed many people from the country, and dwellers in town, who resorting to public houses, spent their time in drinking and vain sports, tending to corrupt one another, on which account I was much troubled. At one house in particular there was much disorder, and I believed it was a duty laid on me to go and speak to the master of that house. I considered I was young, and that several elderly friends in town had opportunity to see these things, and though I would gladly have been excused, yet I could not feel my mind clear. The exercise was heavy, and as I was reading what the Almighty said to Ezekiel, respecting his duty as a watchman, the matter was set home more clearly, and then with prayer and tears, I besought the Lord for His assistance, who in loving kindness gave me a resigned heart. Then at a suitable opportunity, I went to the public house, and seeing the man amongst a company, I went to him and told him I wanted to speak with him, so we went aside, and there in the fear and dread of the Almighty I expressed to him what rested on my mind, which he took kindly, and afterward showed more regard to me than before. In a few years after he died, middle-aged, and I often thought that had I neglected my duty in that case, it would have given me great trouble and I was humbly thankful to my Gracious Father, who had supported me therein.

My employer having a Negro woman sold her, and directed me to write a bill of sale, the man being waiting who had bought her. The thing was sudden, and though the thoughts of writing an instrument of slavery for one of my fellow creatures felt uneasy, yet I remembered I was hired by the year; that it was my master who directed me to do it, and that it was an elderly man, a member of our Society who bought her, so through weakness I gave way, and wrote it, but at the executing it I was so afflicted in my mind, that I said before my master and the friend, that I believed slavekeeping to be a practice inconsistent with the Christian religion: this in some degree abated my uneasiness, yet as often as I reflected seriously upon it I thought

I should have been clearer, if I had desired to be excused from it, as a thing against my conscience, for such it was. And some time after this a young man of our Society,[4] spake to me to write an instrument of slavery, he having lately taken a Negro into his house. I told him I was not easy to write it, for though many people kept slaves in our Society as in others, I still believed the practice was not right, and desired to be excused from doing the writing. I spoke to him in good will, and he told me, that keeping slaves was not altogether agreeable to his mind, but that the slave being a gift made to his wife, he had accepted of her.

[4] The Society of Friends.

THOMAS HUTCHINSON

(1711-1780)

Anne Hutchinson was banished from seventeenth-century Boston because of the civil danger implicit in her uncompromising religious ideas. Thomas Hutchinson, one of her descendants, was forced to leave his beloved Massachusetts nearly 150 years later because he believed that his duty required him to support the Crown. He was Lieutenant Governor and Chief Justice in 1765, when a mob protesting the Stamp Act looted and wrecked his house, and he was Governor at the time of the Boston Tea Party in 1773. Soon afterward he left for England to consult about ways to deal with the crisis, and he never did return to his native land. He had served in political and judicial posts over a period of 36 years before his departure—as Speaker of the House, as member of the Governor's Council, as Chief Justice. All his property was confiscated during the Revolution.

Hutchinson's admirable *History of Massachusetts Bay* owes much to his political career and something to his political difficulties. With access to government documents and a thorough knowledge of eighteenth-century colonial government, Hutchinson wrote the best eighteenth-century account of early Massachusetts and (when allowance is made for his Loyalist preferences) one of the best accounts of Provin-

The standard edition, from which the following selection is taken, is Thomas Hutchinson, *History of the Colony of Massachusetts Bay*, 3 vols., ed. Lawrence

S. Mayo, 1936. A sympathetic modern biography is Bernard Bailyn, *The Ordeal of Thomas Hutchinson*, 1974.

Portrait of Mrs. Jonathan Winthrop, 1773, by John Singleton Copley (1738–1815). *(The Metropolitan Museum of Art, Morris K. Jessup Fund, 1931.)*

cial Massachusetts in the eighteenth century. He used his enforced leisure during his exile to revise and complete his *History*.

Although sometimes virtually colorless, Hutchinson's *History* is distinguished by the dispassionate observation of a detached, humane intellect, as in the sections reprinted here. No Puritan, Hutchinson writes of seventeenth-century issues as a tolerant son of the Enlightenment. He remains unattached to either his beleaguered ancestor or her antagonists, whose impassioned religious loyalties he represents as distastefully antiquated. In his account of the Quakers, his criticism is more emphatic, anticipating the indignation that Nathaniel Hawthorne expresses in the next century. Compare "Young Goodman Brown," below, pp. 1200ff., and "The Gentle Boy." Elsewhere, Hutchinson's own experience in the royal administration of a hostile colony enabled him to sympathize with the plight of commissioners sent on an impossible mission from Massachusetts Bay to England in 1663. And he was even able to write of his own troubles with extraordinary restraint. His *History* deserves to be compared with those of John Winthrop and Cotton Mather.

From History of Massachusetts Bay[1]

[THE PERSECUTION OF THE QUAKERS]

In the year 1656, began what has been generally, and not improperly, called the persecution of the Quakers.° Two years before, an order had been made, that every inhabitant who had in their custody any of the books of John Reeves and Lodowick Muggleton, "who pretend to be the two last witnesses and prophets of Jesus Christ," which books were said to be full of blasphemies, should bring or send them in to the next magistrate, within one month, on pain of ten pounds for each book remaining in any person's hands after that time. [I do not mention these persons as being Quakers.] No person appeared professing the opinions of the Quakers until July 1656, when Mary Fisher† and Ann Austin arrived from Barbados. A few weeks after arrived in

---

[1] The text is the Harvard edition, edited by Lawrence Mayo. Unless initialed "D.L.," the numbered notes are Mayo's; Hutchinson's notes are indicated with asterisks and daggers. [D.L.]

° This sect made its first appearance in England, in the year 1652. They soon spread themselves into America.

† Mary Fisher travelled as far as Adrianople,

and coming near the grand vizier's camp, she procured a man to inform him that there was an English woman had something to declare from the great God to the great Turk. She was introduced, and delivered her message, &c. *New-England judged, by G. Bishop.* She fared better among the Turks than among christians.

the ship Speedwell of London, Rober Lock master, nine more of these itinerants, whose names "after the flesh," the language they used to the officers sent to make enquiry, were William Brend, Thomas Thurston, Christopher Holder, John Copeland, Richard Smith, Mary Prince, Dorothy Waugh, Sarah Gibbons, and Mary Witherhead.‡ On the 8th of September, they were brought before the court of assistants, and being examined, and each of them questioned how they could make it appear that God sent them, after a pause they answered, that they had the same call which Abraham had to go out of his country; to other questions they gave rude and contemptuous answers, which is the reason assigned for committing them to prison. A great number of their books which they had brought over, with intent to scatter them about the country, were seized and reserved for the fire. Soon after this, as the Governor was going from the public worship on the Lord's day to his own house, several gentlemen accompanying him, Mary Prince called to him from a window of the prison, railing at and reviling him, saying, Woe unto thee, thou art an oppressor; and denouncing the judgments of God upon him. Not content with this she wrote a letter, to the Governor and magistrates, filled with opprobrious stuff. The Governor sent for her twice from the prison to his house, and took much pains to persuade her to desist from such extravagancies. Two of the ministers were present, and with much moderation and tenderness endeavored to convince her of her errors, to which she returned the grossest railings, reproaching them as hirelings, deceivers of the people, Baal's priests, the seed of the serpent, of the brood of Ishmael and the like.

The court passed sentence of banishment against them all, and required the master of the ship in which they came, to become bound with sureties, to the value of five hundred pounds, to carry them all away,° and caused them to be committed to prison until the ship should be ready to sail. At this time there was no special provision by law for the punishment of Quakers; they came within a colony law against heretics in general. At the next sessions of the general court, the 14th of October following, an act passed, laying a penalty of one hundred pounds upon the master of any vessel who should bring a known Quaker into any part of the colony, and requiring him to give security to carry him back again; that the Quaker should be immediately sent to the house of correction and whipped twenty stripes, and afterwards kept to hard labor until transportation. They also laid a penalty, of five pounds, for importing, and the like for dispersing Quakers' books, and severe penalties for defending their heretical opinions. And the next year, an additional law was made, by which all persons were subjected to the penalty of

‡ Mr. Neale says they came from Rhode Island. I take this account from the records of the superior court. See a letter from the president, &c. of Rhode Island in the appendix, shewing the sense they had of the Quakers at that time.

° I cannot find what law they had for this.

forty shillings for every hour's entertainment given to any known Quaker, and any Quaker, after the first conviction, if a man was to lose one ear, and a second time the other; a woman, each time to be severely whipped; and the third time, man or woman, to have their tongues bored through with a red hot iron; and every Quaker, who should become such in the colony, [was] subjected to the like punishments. In May 1658, a penalty of ten shillings was laid on every person present at a Quaker's meeting, and five pounds upon every one speaking at such meeting. Notwithstanding all this severity, the number of Quakers as might well have been expected, increasing rather than diminishing,* in October following, a further law was made for punishing with death all Quakers who should return into the jurisdiction after banishment.† That some provision was necessary against these people, so far as they were disturbers of civil peace and order, every one will allow; but such sanguinary laws against particular doctrines or tenets in religion are not to be defended. The most that can be said for our ancestors is, that they tried gentler means at first, which they found utterly ineffectual, and that they followed the example of the authorities in most other states and in most ages of the world, who, with the like absurdity, have supposed every person could and ought to think as they did, and [with] the like cruelty have punished such as appeared to differ from them. We may add, that it was with reluctance that these unnatural laws were carried into execution, as we shall see by a further account of proceedings. Nicholas Upshall was apprehended in October 1656, fined twenty pounds, and banished for reproaching the magistrates and speaking against the law made against Quakers, and returning in 1659 was imprisoned.‡ At the same court, William Robinson, Marma-

---

* This is the ordinary consequence of pity and compassion for the sufferers. And although it has been observed that persecution tends to frighten men from coming into a country, yet it was a characteristic of this sect, at the beginning of it, to court persecution, and to submit to death, with an infatuation equal to that of some Roman Catholic priests carrying their religion into China or Tartary.

† Great opposition was made to this law, the magistrates were the most zealous, and in general for it; but it was rejected at first by the deputies, afterwards, upon reconsideration, concurred by 12 against 11, with an amendment that the trial should be by a special jury. Capt. Edward Hutchinson[2] and Capt. Thomas Clark,[3] two of the court, desired leave to enter their dissent against this law. *New-England judged.*

[2] Edward Hutchinson (1613?-1675) of Boston was the eldest son of William and Anne Hutchinson; he was a very useful citizen. He lost his life in King Philip's War. The fact that his daughter Anne married "a Dyer, of Newport," may account for his feeling on this subject. He was a great-grandfather of Governor Thomas Hutchinson. See *The Diary and Letters of Thomas Hutchinson* (edited by Peter Orlando Hutchinson), II, 464-465.

[3] Thomas Clark (d. 1678) was a Boston merchant. In 1662 he became Speaker of the House, and in 1673 an Assistant.

‡ Nicholas Upshall was a member of Boston church, a very old man. When he was banished, he went first to Plymouth, where people were forbade entertaining him; but some that were more compassionate, prevailed upon the authority to suffer him to tarry until the spring. *New-England judged.*

duke Stephenson, Mary Dyer and Nicholas Davis were brought to trial. The first gave no particular account of himself. Stephenson had made a public disturbance in the congregation at Boston the 15th of June before. He acknowledged himself to be one of those the world called Quakers, and declared that in the year 1656, at Shipton in Yorkshire, as he was at plough he saw nothing but heard an audible voice saying, "I have ordained thee to be a prophet to the nations," &c.

DYER declared that she came from Rhode Island* to visit the Quakers, that she was of their religion, which she affirmed was the truth, and that the light within her was the rule, &c.

DAVIS came from Barnstable, he came into court with his hat on, confessed he had forsaken the ordinances and resorted to the Quakers. The jury found, "that they were all Quakers." Robinson was whipped 20 stripes for abusing the court, and they were all banished on pain of death.

PATIENCE SCOTT, a girl of about 11 years of age, came I suppose from Providence, her friends lived there, and professing herself to be one of those whom the world in scorn calls Quakers, was committed to prison, and afterwards brought to court. The record stands thus. "The court duly considering the malice of Satan and his instruments by all means and ways to propagate error and disturb the truth, and bring in confusion among us, that Satan is put to his shifts to make use of such a child, not being of the years of discretion, nor understanding the principles of religion, judge meet so far to slight her as a Quaker, as only to admonish and instruct her according to her capacity, and so discharge her, Capt. Hutchinson undertaking to send her home." Strange, such a child should be imprisoned! it would have been horrible if there had been any further severity.†

ROBINSON, Stephenson and Dyer, at the next general court, were brought upon trial, and "for their rebellion, sedition, and presumptuous obtruding

* Her husband or son, William Dyer,[4] was secretary of that colony.

[4] William Dyer, the Secretary of Rhode Island, was the husband of Mary Dyer. He spelt his name "Dyre" as Hutchinson does in this instance. He was a milliner in London before coming to New England. In Massachusetts he became a follower of Wheelwright and accordingly was disarmed, disfranchised, and virtually driven out. He took refuge at Newport, R. I. Mrs. Dyer, who had distinguished herself by walking out of the meeting with Mrs. Hutchinson when the latter was excommunicated, accompanied him. Between 1650 and 1657 she was in England, where she became a Quaker.

There is a life of Mary Dyer by Horatio

Rogers. For a contemporary account of the sufferings of this group see *A Call from Death to Life* (1660). For a modern account, written from the Quaker point of view, see Richard Price Hallowell, *The Quaker Invasion of Massachusetts*, or Rufus M. Jones, *The Quakers in the American Colonies*.

† Bishop says, that they cut off the right ear of Holder, Copeland, and Rous in the prison, and that Catherine Scott, mother of Patience Scott, reproving them for a deed of darkness, they whipped her ten stripes; though they allowed her to be otherwise of blameless conversation and well bred, being a minister's daughter in England. *New-England judged.*

themselves after banishment upon pain of death," were sentenced to die; the two first were executed the 27th of October.° Dyer, upon the petition of William Dyer her son, was reprieved, on condition that she departed the jurisdiction in 48 hours; and if she returned, to suffer the sentence. She was carried to the gallows, and stood with a rope about her neck until the others were executed. She was so infatuated as afterwards to return, and was executed June 1st, 1660.† The court thought it advisable to publish a vindication of their proceedings; they urge the example of England in the provision made against Jesuits, which might have some weight against a charge brought from thence, but in every other part of their vindication, as may well be supposed from the nature of the thing, there is but the bare shadow of reason. Christopher Holder, who had found the way into the jurisdiction again, was, at this court, banished upon pain of death. At the same court, seven or eight persons were fined, some as high as ten pounds, for entertaining Quakers; and Edward Wharton,[5] for piloting them from one place to another, was ordered to be whipped twenty stripes and bound to his good behavior. Divers others were then brought upon trial, "for adhering to the cursed sect of Quakers, not disowning themselves to be such, refusing to give civil respect, leaving their families and relations, and running from place to place vagabonds like," and Daniel Gold was sentenced to be whipped thirty stripes, Robert Harper[6] fifteen, and they, with Alice Courland, Mary Scott and Hope Clifton, banished upon pain of death; William Kingsmill whipped fifteen stripes, Margaret Smith, Mary Trask[7] and Provided Southwick[8] ten stripes each, and Hannah Phelps admonished.

° Mr. Winthrop, the Governor of Connecticut, labored to prevent their execution, and Col. Temple went to the court and told them, "that if according to their declaration, they desired their lives absent, rather than their deaths present, he would carry them away and provide for them at his own charge; and if any of them should return, he would fetch them away again." This motion was well liked by all the magistrates except two or three, and they proposed it to the deputies the next day, but those two or three magistrates, with the deputies, prevailed to have execution done. *New-England judged.*

† Being asked what she had to say, why sentence should not be executed. She answered, that she denied their law, came to bear witness against it, and could not chuse but come and do as formerly. This is the same Mary Dyer, who in the year 1637 was banished for her familistical tenets

[5] Edward Wharton of Salem (*d.* 1678) was a long-suffering Quaker. In 1658 he was whipped for expressing sympathy for Robinson and Stephenson, and again later on for piloting some Quakers from Lynn to Salem. In spite of these and other punishments he continued to reside in Salem until his death. Whittier, in "The King's Missive" rightly calls him "much scourged Wharton."

[6] Robert Harper was of Sandwich, in the Plymouth Colony.

[7] Mary Trask was the wife of Henry Trask of Salem. She was a sister of Provided Southwick, another Quaker.

[8] Provided Southwick of Salem and her brother Daniel were also fined for persistent Quakerism. When the fines were not paid, the General Court ordered them sold "to any of the English nation at Virginia or Barbadoes." Happily the sentence was not carried out.

THE compassion of the people was moved, and many resorted to the prison day and night, and upon a representation of the keeper, a constant watch was kept round the prison to keep people off.°

JOSEPH NICHOLSON and Jane his wife were also tried and found Quakers, as also Wendlock Christopherson,[9] who declared in court, that the Scripture is not the Word of God; and Mary Standley, and all sentenced to banishment, &c. as was soon after Benjamin Bellflower; but John Chamberlain,[10] though he came with his hat on, yet, refusing directly to answer, the jury found him, "much inclining to the cursed opinions of the Quakers," and he escaped with an admonition.†

NICHOLSON and his wife returned, and were apprehended, but upon their petition, had liberty with several others then in prison, to go for England. Christopherson returned also, and was sentenced to die. It is said he desired the court to consider what they had gained by their cruel proceedings.

For the last man (says he) that was put to death here, are five come in his room, and if you have power to take my life from me, God can raise up the same principle of life in ten of His servants, and send them among you in my room, that you may have torment upon torment.‡

He was ordered to be executed the fifth day sevennight after the 14th of March 1660, afterwards reprieved till the 13th of June; but he was set at liberty upon his request to the court, and went out of the jurisdiction.

BELLFLOWER[11] afterwards, in court, renounced his opinions, as also William King (Kingsmill I suppose) the only instances upon record. Chamberlain was afterwards apprehended again, and found a Quaker, and committed to close prison; but no further sentence appears.

° The pillory served for a pulpit to George Fox. He preached to the populace, and made so many converts that they delivered him in a tumultuous manner, and set a clergyman, who had been instrumental in Fox's punishment, upon the same pillory. *Volt. letters.*

[9] Wendlock Christopherson is usually called Wenlock Christison in New England history. Banished from Massachusetts, he went to Plymouth where he was imprisoned for fourteen weeks, "tied neck and heels together," in cold winter weather, and flogged. He returned to Boston and was sentenced to be hanged. The sentence was not carried into execution, however. For his career in Massa-

chusetts and elsewhere see Samuel A. Harrison, *Wenlock Christison and the Early Friends in Talbot County, Maryland.*

[10] John Chamberlain was a currier in Boston.
† [Their forms in law proceedings were loose and irregular.]
‡ *New-England judged.*
[11] Benjamin Bellflower lived in Reading, Mass. He "came into Court with his hat cockt: remaineing on his head. & refusing to pull it of w commanded. & said he could justifie his accon by yᵉ Scripture." Hallowell's *Quaker Invasion*, p. 160, quoting from Massachusetts Archives.

In September 1660, William Ledea[12] was tried and convicted of being a Quaker, and sentenced to banishment, &c. but returning and being apprehended, the general court gave him liberty, notwithstanding, to go to England with Nicholson and others; but he refused to leave the country, and was brought upon trial for returning into the jurisdiction after sentence of banishment, acknowledged himself to be the person, but denied their authority, and told the court, that, "with the spirit they called the Devil, he worshipped God; that their ministers were deluders, and they themselves murderers." He was told that he might have his life and be at liberty if he would. He answered, I am willing to die, I speak the truth. The court took great pains to persuade him to leave the country, but to no purpose. The jury brought him in guilty, and he was sentenced to die, and suffered accordingly March 14th, 1660.

MARY WRIGHT, of Oyster-bay, was tried at the court in September 1660. She said she came to do the will of the Lord, and to warn them to lay by their carnal weapons and laws against the people of God, told the court they thirsted for blood. The court asked her what she would have them do, she said, "repent of your bloodshed and cruelty and shedding the blood of the innocent Wm. Robinson, Marmaduke Stephenson, and Mary Dyer." She said, her tears were her meat many days and nights before she gave up herself to this work of the Lord, but added, that if she had her liberty, she would be gone quickly. Being found a Quaker, she was banished.

EDWARD WHARTON, who had been whipped before, was now indicted for being a Quaker, convicted and sentenced to imprisonment and afterwards to banishment. Judah Brown and Peter Pierson stood mute. They were sentenced to be whipped at the cart's tail in Boston, Roxbury and Dedham.

JOHN SMITH, of Salem, for making disturbance at the ordination of Mr. Higginson, crying out, "What you are going about to set up, our God is pulling down," was committed to prison by order of the court.

PHILIP VERIN[13] was also tried and imprisoned, Josias Southwick,[14] first banished and returning, whipped at the cart's tail, and John Burstowe bound to his good behavior. These are all° who were tried by the court of assistants,

[12] William Ledea is identified by Savage as William Leddra of Boston. His appealing letter to his friends, written the day before he was hanged, is printed in William Sewel, *History of the Quakers* (1844), I, 338–340.

[13] Philip Verin came to New England in 1635 from New Sarum (Salisbury), England. He settled at Salem.

[14] Josias or Josiah was another member of the Southwick family of Salem. He was "constrained to take an opportunity that presented four days after to pass to England by Barbardoes." *An Abstract of the Sufferings of the Quakers* (1733), I, 386.

° George Bishop mentions several who suffered corporal punishment by order of particular magistrates or the county courts, of whom I find no notice any where else. *New England judged.*

[George Bishop (*d.* 1668) was the author of *New England Judged not by Man's but the Spirit of the Lord* (London, 1661), a strong narrative of the sufferings of the Quakers in New England, 1650–1660. D.L.]

or by the general court. Some at Salem, Hampton, Newbury and other places, for disorderly behavior, putting people in terror, coming into the congregations and calling to the minister in the time of public worship, declaring their preaching, &c. to be an abomination to the Lord, and other breaches of the peace, were ordered to be whipped by the authority of the county courts, or particular magistrates. At Boston, one George Wilson, and at Cambridge, Elizabeth Horton,[15] went crying through the streets, that the Lord was coming with fire and sword to plead with them. Thomas New-house went into the meeting-house at Boston with a couple of glass bottles, and broke them before the congregation, and threatened, "Thus will the Lord break you in pieces." Another time, M. Brewster[16] came in with her face smeared and as black as a coal. Deborah Wilson went through the streets of Salem, naked as she came into the world,† for which she was well whipped. For these and such like disturbances, they might be deemed proper subjects either of a mad-house or house of correction, and it is to be lamented that any greater severities were made use of. After all that may be said against these measures, it evidently appears, that they proceeded not from personal hatred and malice against such disordered persons, nor from any private sinister views, as is generally the case with unjust punishments inflicted in times of party rage and discord, whether civil or religious, but merely from a false zeal and an erroneous judgment. In support of their proceedings, they brought several texts of the Old Testament. "Come out of her my people," &c. "If thy brother entice thee to serve other gods, thou shalt surely put him to death," and "for speaking lies in the name of the Lord, his father shall thrust him through when he prophesieth"; and the example of Solomon, who first laid Shimei under restraint, and then for his breach put him to death; as also many passages of the New Testament requiring subjection to magistrates, &c. and thus from a zeal to defend the holy religion they professed, they went into measures directly opposite to its true spirit, and the great design of publishing it to the world.

THAT I may finish what relates to the Quakers, it must be further observed, that their friends in England solicited and at length obtained an order from the King, Sept. 9th, 1661, requiring that a stop should be put to all capital or corporal punishment of those of his subjects called Quakers,

---

[15] Elizabeth Horton is called Hooten by William Sewel, who describes her sufferings in detail in his *History of the Quakers* (1844), I, 412-413.

[16] Margaret Brewster. Her trial, in 1677, is quoted by Richard Price Hallowell in his *Quaker Invasion of Massachusetts*, pp. 193-202.

† One of the sect apologizing for this behavior said, "If the Lord did stir up any of his daughters to be a sign of the nakedness of others, he believed it to be a great cross to a modest woman's spirit, but the Lord must be obeyed." Another quoted the command in Isaiah, cap. 20. R. Williams. One Faubord, of Grindleton, carried his enthusiasm still higher, and was sacrificing his son in imitation of Abraham, but the neighbors hearing the lad cry, broke open the house and happily prevented it.

and that such as were obnoxious should be sent to England. Whatever opinion they might have, of the force of orders from the crown controlling the laws of the colony, they prudently complied with this instruction, and suspended the execution of the laws against Quakers, so far as respected corporal punishment, until further order. Indeed, before the receipt of this letter, but probably when they were in expectation of it, all that were in prison were discharged and sent out of the colony. The laws were afterwards revived so far as respected vagabond Quakers, whose punishment was limited to whipping, and, as a further favor, through three towns only. But there was little or no room for carrying the laws into execution; for after these first excursions they became in general an orderly people, submitting to the laws, except such as relate to the militia and the support of the ministry, and in their scruples as to those, they have, from time to time, been indulged. At present they are esteemed as being of good morals, friendly and benevolent in their disposition, and I hope will never meet with any further persecution on account of their peculiar tenets or customs. May the time never come again, when the government shall think that by killing men for their religion they do God good service.

. . .

WILLIAM BARTRAM

(1739–1823)

Euopean writers began describing the American landscape and its fauna in the very first expeditions. William Bartram was probably the most distinguished writer and observer before the nineteenth century to concentrate his literary skill on reporting his own extensive observations. Bartram was the son of a botanist who had also gained distinction for his American studies, and the son's most important achievement, *Travels through North And South Carolina, Georgia, East and West Florida . . .* (Philadelphia, 1791), continued the father's work. William Bartram's *Travels* was widely read in Europe and England, and Mark Van Doren has pointed out that both Coleridge and Wordsworth used it.

A modern edition is *The Travels of William Bartram,* ed. Mark Van Doren, with introduction by John L. Lowes, 1940. A *Naturalist's Edition,* was edited by Francis Harper, 1958. Biographies include N. B. Fagin, *William Bartram, Interpreter of the American Landscape,* 1933; Ernest Earnest, *John and William Bartram, Botanists and Explorers,* 1940.

Bartram's *Travels* belongs to the kind of autobiographical narrative that public figures like Thomas Jefferson and John Adams wrote. His conception of his literary *persona* is that of a public self represented in conscientious action. He has to write in some detail about his own feelings, but almost always in relation to what his eye observes, and as a representative human rather than a uniquely personal response to the land. Early in the book, when a companion who has promised to accompany him decides to abandon the enterprise, Bartram expresses relief:

> Our views were probably totally opposite; he, a young mechanic on his adventures, seemed to be actuated by no other motives, than either to establish himself in some well-inhabited part of the country, where, by following his occupation, he might be enabled to procure, without much toil and danger, the necessaries and conveniences of life; or by industry and frugality, perhaps establish his fortune. Whilst I, continuously impelled by a restless spirit of curiosity, in pursuit of new productions of nature, my chief happiness consisted in tracing and admiring the infinite power, majesty, and perfection of the great Almighty Creator, and in the contemplation, that through divine aid and permission, I might be instrumental in discovering, and introducing into my native country, some original productions of nature, which might become useful to society. Each of our pursuits was perhaps equally laudable; and, upon this supposition, I was quite willing to part with him upon amicable terms.

Introspection and self-revelation of the early Puritan or mid-twentieth-century psychological varieties do not appear in Bartram's *Travels;* even in subjective passages the reader is placed at a distance. But the alligators are memorable.

The selection here is roughly the first half of Part II, Chapter V.

Travels through North and South Carolina, East and West Florida, . . . [1]

From PART II—CHAPTER V

Being desirous of continuing my travels and observations higher up the river, and having an invitation from a gentleman who was agent for, and resident

[1] Philadelphia, 1791.

at, a large plantation, the property of an English gentleman, about sixty miles higher up, I resolved to pursue my researches to that place; and having engaged in my service a young Indian, nephew to the white captain, he agreed to assist me in working my vessel up as high as a certain bluff, where I was, by agreement, to land him, on the west or Indian shore, whence he designed to go in quest of the camp of the white trader, his relation.

Provisions and all necessaries being procured, and the morning pleasant, we went on board and stood up the river. We passed for several miles on the left, by islands of high swamp land, exceedingly fertile, their banks for a good distance from the water, much higher than the interior part, and sufficiently so to build upon, and be out of the reach of inundations. They consist of a loose black mold, with a mixture of sand, shells, and dissolved vegetables. The opposite Indian coast is a perpendicular bluff, ten or twelve feet high, consisting of a black sandy earth, mixed with a large proportion of shells, chiefly various species of fresh water cochleæ and mytuli. Near the river, on this high shore, grew corypha palma, magnolia grandiflora, live oak, callicarpa, myrica cerifera, hibiscus spinifex, and the beautiful evergreen shrub called wild lime or tallow nut. This last shrub grows six or eight feet high, many erect stems spring from a root; the leaves are lanceolate and entire, two or three inches in length and one in breadth, of a deep green color, and polished; at the foot of each leaf grows a stiff sharp thorn; the flowers are small and in clusters, of a greenish yellow color, and sweet scented; they are succeeded by a large oval fruit, of the shape and size of an ordinary plum, of a fine yellow color when ripe; a soft sweet pulp covers a nut which has a thin shell, enclosing a white kernel somewhat of the consistence and taste of the sweet almond, but more oily and very much like hard tallow, which induced my father, when he first observed it, to call it the tallow-nut.

At the upper end of this bluff is a fine orange grove. Here my Indian companion requested me to set him on shore, being already tired of rowing under a fervid sun, and having for some time intimated a dislike to his situation. I readily complied with his desire, knowing the impossibility of compelling an Indian against his own inclinations, or even prevailing upon him by reasonable arguments, when labor is in the question. Before my vessel reached the shore, he sprang out of her and landed, when uttering a shrill and terrible whoop, he bounded off like a roebuck, and I lost sight of him. I at first apprehended, that as he took his gun with him, he intended to hunt for some game and return to me in the evening. The day being excessively hot and sultry, I concluded to take up my quarters here until next morning.

The Indian not returning this morning, I set sail alone. The coasts on each side had much the same appearance as already described. The palm-trees here seem to be of a different species from the cabbage tree; their straight trunks are sixty, eighty, or ninety feet high, with a beautiful taper, of a bright ash color, until within six or seven feet of the top, where it is a fine green color, crowned with an orb of rich green plumed leaves; I have measured the stem of these plumes fifteen feet in length, besides the plume, which is nearly the same length.

The little lake, which is an expansion of the river, now appeared in view; on the east side are entensive marshes, and on the other high forests and orange groves, and then a bay, lined with vast cypress swamps, both coasts gradually approaching each other, to the opening of the river again, which is in this place about three hundred yards wide. Evening now drawing on, I was anxious to reach some high bank of the river, where I intended to lodge; and agreeably to my wishes, I soon after discovered, on the west shore, a little promontory, at the turning of the river, contracting it here to about one hundred and fifty yards in width. This promontory is a peninsula, containing about three acres of high ground, and is one entire orange grove, with a few live oaks, magnolias, and palms. Upon doubling the point, I arrived at the landing, which is a circular harbor, at the foot of the bluff, the top of which is about twelve feet high; the back of it is a large cypress swamp, that spreads each way, the right wing forming the west coast of the little lake, and the left stretching up the river many miles, and encompassing a vast space of low grassy marshes. From this promontory, looking eastward across the river, I beheld a landscape of low country, unparalleled as I think; on the left is the east coast of the little lake, which I had just passed; and from the orange bluff at the lower end, the high forests begin, and increase in breadth from the shore of the lake, making a circular sweep to the right, and contain many hundred thousand acres of meadow; and this grand sweep of high forests encircles, as I apprehend, at least twenty miles of these green fields, interspersed with hommocks or islets of evergreen trees, where the sovereign magnolia and lordly palm stand conspicuous. The islets are high shelly knolls on the sides of creeks or branches of the river, which wind about and drain off the superabundant waters that cover these meadows during the winter season.

The evening was temperately cool and calm. The crocodiles began to roar and appear in uncommon numbers along the shores and in the river. I fixed my camp in an open plain, near the utmost projection of the promontory, under the shelter of a large live oak, which stood on the highest part of the ground, and but a few yards from my boat. From this open, high situation, I had a free prospect of the river, which was a matter of no trivial consideration to me, having good reason to dread the subtle attacks of the alligators, who were crowding about my harbor. Having collected a good quantity of wood for the purpose of keeping up a light and smoke during the night, I began to think of preparing my supper, when, upon examining my stores, I found but a scanty provision. I thereupon determined, as the most expeditious way of supplying my necessities, to take my bob and try for some trout. About one hundred yards above my harbor began a cove or bay of the river out of which opened a large lagoon. The mouth or entrance from the river to it was narrow, but the waters soon after spread and formed a little lake, extending into the marshes: its entrance and shores within I observed to be verged with floating lawns of the pistia and nymphea and other aquatic plants; these I knew were excellent haunts for trout.

The verges and islets of the lagoon were elegantly embellished with flowering plants and shrubs; the laughing coots with wings half spread were tripping over the little coves, and hiding themselves in the tufts of grass; young broods of the painted summer teal, skimming the still surface of the waters, and following the watchful parent unconscious of danger, were frequently surprised by the voracious trout; and he, in turn, as often by the subtle greedy alligator. Behold him rushing forth from the flags and reeds. His enormous body swells. His plaited tail brandished high, floats upon the lake. The waters like a cataract descend from his opening jaws. Clouds of smoke issue from his dilated nostrils. The earth trembles with his thunder. When immediately from the opposite coast of the lagoon, emerges from the deep his rival champion. They suddenly dart upon each other. The boiling surface of the lake marks their rapid course, and a terrific conflict commences. They now sink to the bottom folded together in horrid wreaths. The water becomes thick and discolored. Again they rise, their jaws clap together, re-echoing through the deep surrounding forests. Again they sink, when the contest ends at the muddy bottom of the lake, and the vanquished makes a hazardous escape, hiding himself in the muddy turbulent waters and sedge on a distant shore. The proud victor exulting returns to the place of action. The shores and forests resound his dreadful roar, together with the triumphing shouts of the plaited tribes around, witnesses of the horrid combat.

My apprehensions were highly alarmed after being a spectator of so dreadful a battle. It was obvious that every delay would but tend to increase my dangers and difficulties, as the sun was near setting, and the alligators gathered around my harbor from all quarters. From these considerations I concluded to be expeditious in my trip to the lagoon, in order to take some fish. Not thinking it prudent to take my fusee with me, lest I might lose it overboard in case of a battle, which I had every reason to dread before my return, I therefore furnished myself with a club for my defense, went on board, and penetrating the first line of those which surrounded my harbor, they gave way; but being pursued by several very large ones, I kept strictly on the watch, and paddled with all my might towards the entrance of the lagoon, hoping to be sheltered there from the multitude of my assailants; but ere I had half-way reached the place, I was attacked on all sides, several endeavoring to overset the canoe. My situation now became precarious to the last degree: two very large ones attacked me closely, at the same instant, rushing up with their heads and part of their bodies above the water, roaring terribly and belching floods of water over me. They struck their jaws together so close to my ears, as almost to stun me, and I expected every moment to be dragged out of the boat and instantly devoured. But I applied my weapons so effectually about me, though at random, that I was so successful as to beat them off a little; when, finding that they designed to renew the battle, I made for the shore, as the only means left me for my preservation; for, by keeping close to it, I should have my enemies on one side of me only, whereas I was before surrounded by them; and there was a probability, if pushed to the last extremity, of saving myself, by jumping out of the canoe on shore, as it is easy to outwalk them on land, although comparatively as swift as lightning in the water. I found this last expedient alone could fully answer my expectations, for as soon as I gained the shore, they drew off and kept aloof. This was a happy relief, as my confidence was, in some degree, recovered by it. On recollecting myself, I discovered that I had almost reached the entrance of the lagoon, and determined to venture in, if possible, to take a few fish, and then return to my harbor, while day-light continued; for I could now, with caution and resolution, make my way with safety along shore; and indeed there was no other way to regain my camp, without leaving my boat and making my retreat through the marshes and reeds, which, if I could even effect, would have been in a manner throwing myself away, for then there would have been no hopes of ever recovering my bark, and returning in safety to any settlements of men. I accordingly proceeded, and made good my entrance into the lagoon, though not without opposition from the alligators, who formed a line across the entrance, but did not pursue me into it, nor was I molested by any there, though there were some very large ones in a cove at the upper end. I soon caught more trout than I had present occasion for, and the air was too hot and sultry to admit of their being kept for many hours, even though salted or barbecued. I now prepared for my return to camp, which I succeeded in with but little trouble, by keeping close to the shore; yet I was opposed upon re-entering the river out of the lagoon, and pursued near to my landing (though not closely attacked), particularly by an old daring one, about twelve feet in length, who kept close after me; and when I stepped on shore and turned about, in order to draw up my canoe, he rushed up near my feet, and lay there for some time, looking me in the face, his head and shoulders out of water. I resolved he should pay for his temerity, and having a heavy load in my fusee, I ran to my camp, and returning with my piece, found him with his foot on the gunwale of the boat, in search of fish. On my coming up he withdrew sullenly and slowly into the water, but soon returned and placed himself in his former position, looking at me, and seeming neither fearful nor any way disturbed. I soon dispatched him by lodging the contents of my gun in his head, and then proceeded to cleanse and prepare my fish for supper; and accordingly took them out of the boat, laid them down on the sand close to the water, and began to scale them; when, raising my head, I saw before me, through the clear water, the head and shoulders of a very large alligator, moving slowly towards me. I instantly stepped back, when with a sweep of his tail, he brushed off several of my fish. It was certainly most providential that I looked up at that instant, as the monster would probably, in less than a minute, have seized and dragged me into the river. This incredible boldness of the animal disturbed me greatly, supposing there could now be no reasonable safety for me during the night, but by keeping continually on the watch: I therefore, as soon as I had prepared the fish, proceeded to secure myself and effects in the best manner I could. In the first place, I hauled my bark upon the shore, almost clear out of the water, to prevent their oversetting or sinking her; after this, every movable was taken out and carried to my camp, which was but a few yards off; then ranging some dry wood in such order as was the most convenient, I cleared the ground round about it, that there might be no impediment in my way, in case of an attack in the night, either from the water or the land; for I discovered by this time, that this small isthmus, from its remote situation and fruitfulness, was resorted to by bears and wolves. Having prepared myself in the best manner I could, I charged my gun, and proceeded to reconnoitre my camp and the adjacent grounds; when I discovered that the peninsula and grove, at the distance of about two hundred yards from my encampment, on the land side, were invested by a cypress swamp, covered with water, which below was joined to the shore of the little lake, and above to the marshes surrounding the lagoon; so that I was confined to an islet exceedingly circumscribed, and I found there was no other retreat for me, in case of an attack, but by either ascending one of the large oaks, or pushing off with my boat.

It was by this time dusk, and the alligators had nearly ceased their roar, when I was again alarmed by a tumultuous noise that seemed to be in my harbor, and therefore engaged my immediate attention. Returning to my camp, I found it undisturbed, and then continued on to the extreme point of the promontory, where I saw a scene, new and surprising, which at first threw my senses into such a tumult, that it was some time before I could comprehend what was the matter; however, I soon accounted for the prodigious assemblage of crocodiles at this place, which exceeded every thing of the kind I had ever heard of.

How shall I express myself so as to convey an adequate idea of it to the reader, and at the same time avoid raising suspicions of my veracity? Should I say, that the river (in this place) from shore to shore, and perhaps near half a mile above and below me, appeared to be one solid bank of fish, of various kinds, pushing through this narrow pass of St. Juan's into the little lake, on their return down the river, and that the alligators were in such incredible numbers, and so close together from shore to shore, that it would have been easy to have walked across on their heads, had the animals been harmless? What expressions can sufficiently declare the shocking scene that for some minutes continued, whilst this mighty army of fish were forcing the pass? During this attempt, thousands, I may say hundreds of thousands, of them were caught and swallowed by the devouring alligators. I have seen an alligator take up out of the water several great fish at a time, and just squeeze them betwixt his jaws, while the tails of the great trout flapped about his eyes and lips, ere he had swallowed them. The horrid noise of their closing jaws, their plunging amidst the broken banks of fish, and rising with their prey some feet upright above the water, the floods of water and blood rushing out of their mouths, and clouds of vapor issuing from their wide nostrils, were truly frightful. This scene continued at intervals during the night, as the fish came to the pass. After this sight, shocking and tremendous as it was, I found myself somewhat easier and more reconciled to my situation; being convinced that their extraordinary assemblage here was owing to the annual feast of fish; and that they were so well employed in their own element, that I had little occasion to fear their paying me a visit.

It being now almost night, I returned to my camp, where I had left my fish broiling, and my kettle of rice stewing; and having with me oil, pepper, and salt, and excellent oranges hanging in abundance over my head (a valuable substitute for vinegar) I sat down and regaled myself cheerfully. Having finished my repast, I rekindled my fire for light, and whilst I was revising the notes of my past day's journey, I was suddenly roused with a noise behind me toward the main land. I sprang up on my feet, and listening, I distinctly heard some creature wading the water of the isthmus. I seized my gun and went cautiously from my camp, directing my steps towards the noise: when I had advanced about thirty yards, I halted behind a coppice of orange trees, and soon perceived two very large bears, which had made their way through the water, and had landed in the grove, about one hundred yards distance from me, and were advancing towards me. I waited until they were within thirty yards of me: they there began to snuff and look towards my camp: I snapped my piece, but it flashed, on which they both turned about and galloped off, plunging through the water and swamp, never halting, as I suppose, until they reached fast land, as I could hear them leaping and plunging a long time. They did not presume to return again, nor was I molested by any other creature, except being occasionally awakened by the whooping of owls, screaming of bitterns, or the wood-rats running amongst the leaves.

The wood-rat is a very curious animal. It is not half the size of the domestic rat; of a dark brown or black color; its tail slender and shorter in proportion, and covered thinly with short hair. It is singular with respect to its ingenuity and great labor in the construction of its habitation, which is a conical pyramid about three or four feet high constructed with dry branches, which it collects with great labor and perseverance, and piles up without any apparent order; yet they are so interwoven with one another, that it would take a bear or wild-cat some time to pull one of these castles to pieces, and allow the animals sufficient time to secure a retreat with their young.

The noise of the crocodiles kept me awake the greater part of the night; but when I arose in the morning, contrary to my expectations, there was perfect peace; very few of them to be seen, and those were asleep on the shore. Yet I was not able to suppress my fears and apprehensions of being attacked by them in future; and indeed yesterday's combat with them, notwithstanding I came off in a manner victorious, or at least made a safe retreat, had left sufficient impression on my mind to damp my courage; and it seemed too much for one of my strength, being alone in a very small boat, to encounter such collected danger. To pursue my voyage up the river, and be obliged every evening to pass such dangerous defiles, appeared to me as perilous as running the gauntlet betwixt two rows of Indians armed with knives and fire-brands. I however resolved to continue my voyage one day longer, if I possibly could with safety, and then return down the river, should I find the like difficulties to oppose. Accordingly I got every thing on board, charged my gun, and set sail, cautiously, along shore. As I passed by Battle lagoon, I began to tremble and keep a good look-out; when suddenly a huge alligator rushed out of the reeds, and with a tremendous roar came up, and darted as swift as an arrow under my boat, emerging upright on my lee quarter, with open jaws, and belching water and smoke that fell upon me like rain in a hurricane. I laid soundly about his head with my club, and beat him off; and after plunging and darting about my boat, he went off on a straight line through the water, seemingly with the rapidity of lightning, and entered the cape of the lagoon. I now employed my time to the very best advantage in paddling close along shore, but could not forbear looking now and then behind me, and presently perceived one of them coming up again. The water of the river hereabouts was shoal and very clear; the monster came up with the usual roar and menaces, and passed close by the side of my boat, when I could distinctly see a young brood of alligators, to the number of one hundred or more, following after her in a long train. They kept close together in a column, without straggling off to the one side or the other; the young appeared to be of an equal size, about fifteen inches in length, almost black, with pale yellow transverse waved clouds or blotches, much like rattlesnakes in color. I now lost sight of my enemy again.

Still keeping close along shore, on turning a point or projection of the river bank, at once I beheld a great number of hillocks or small pyramids, resembling hay-cocks, ranged like an encampment along the banks. They stood fifteen or twenty yards distant from the water, on a high marsh, about four feet perpendicular above the water. I knew them to be the nests of the crocodile, having had a description of them before; and now expected a furious and general attack, as I saw several large crocodiles swimming abreast of these buildings. These nests being so great a curiosity to me, I was determined at all events immediately to land and examine them. Accordingly, I ran my bark on shore at one of their landing-places, which was a sort of nick or little dock, from which ascended a sloping path or road up to the edge of the meadow, where their nests were; most of them were deserted, and the great thick whitish egg-shells lay broken and scattered upon the ground round about them.

The nests or hillocks are of the form of an obtuse cone, four feet high and four or five feet in diameter at their bases; they are constructed with mud, grass and herbage. At first they lay a floor of this kind of tempered mortar on the ground, upon which they desposit a layer of eggs, and upon this a stratum of mortar, seven or eight inches in thickness, and then another layer of eggs; and in this manner one stratum upon another, nearly to the top. I believe they commonly lay from one to two hundred eggs in a nest; these are hatched, I suppose, by the heat of the sun; and perhaps the vegetable substances mixed with the earth, being acted upon by the sun, may cause a small degree of fermentation, and so increase the heat in those hillocks. The ground for several acres about these nests showed evident marks of a continual resort of alligators; the grass was every where beaten down, hardly a blade or straw was left standing; whereas, all about, at a distance, it was five or six feet high, and as thick as it could grow together. The female, as I imagine, carefully watches her own nest of eggs until they are all hatched; or perhaps while she is attending her own brood, she takes under her care and protection as many as she can get at one time, either from her own particular nest or others; but certain it is, that the young are not left to shift for themselves; for I have had frequent opportunities of seeing the female alligator leading about the shores her train of young ones, just as a hen does her brood of chickens; and she is equally assiduous and courageous in defending the young, which are under her care, and providing for their subsistence; and when she is basking upon the warm banks, with her brood around her, you may hear the young ones continually whining and barking like young puppies. I believe but few of a brood live to the years of full growth and magnitude, as the old feed on the young as long as they can make prey of them.

The alligator when full grown is a very large and terrible creature, and of prodigious strength, activity and swiftness in the water. I have seen them twenty feet in length, and some are supposed to be twenty-two or twenty-three feet. Their body is as large as that of a horse; their shape exactly resembles that of a lizard, except their tail, which is flat or cuneiform, being compressed on each side, and gradually diminishing from the abdomen to the extremity, which, with the whole body is covered with horny plates or squammæ, impenetrable when on the body of the live animal, even to a rifle ball, except about their head and just behind their fore-legs or arms, where it is said they are only vulnerable. The head of a full grown one is about three feet, and the mouth opens nearly the same length; their eyes are small in proportion, and seem sunk deep in the head, by means of the prominency of the brows; the nostrils are large; inflated and prominent on the top, so that the head in the water resembles, at a distance, a great chunk of wood floating about. Only the upper jaw moves, which they raise almost perpendicular, so as to form a right angle with the lower one. In the forepart of the upper jaw, on each side, just under the nostrils, are two very large, thick, strong teeth or tusks, not very sharp, but rather the shape of a cone: these are as white as the finest polished ivory, and are not covered by any skin or lips, and always in sight, which gives the creature a frightful appearance: in the lower jaw are holes opposite to these teeth, to receive them: when they clap their jaws together it causes a surprising noise, like that which is made by forcing a heavy plank with violence upon the ground, and may be heard at a great distance.

But what is yet more surprising to a stranger, is the incredible loud and terrifying roar, which they are capable of making, especially in the spring season, their breeding time. It most resembles very heavy distant thunder, not only shaking the air and waters, but causing the earth to tremble; and when hundreds and thousands are roaring at the same time, you can scarcely be persuaded, but that the whole globe is violently and dangerously agitated.

An old champion, who is perhaps absolute sovereign of a little lake or lagoon (when fifty less than himself are obliged to content themselves with swelling and roaring in little coves round about) darts forth from the reedy coverts all at once, on the surface of the waters, in a right line; at first seemingly as rapid as lightning, but gradually more slowly until he arrives at the center of the lake, when he stops. He now swells himself by drawing in wind and water through his mouth, which causes a loud sonorous rattling in the throat for near a minute, but it is immediately forced out again through his mouth and nostrils, with a loud noise, brandishing his tail in the air, and the vapor ascending from his nostrils like smoke. At other times, when swollen to an extent ready to burst, his head and tail lifted up, he spins or twirls round on the surface of the water. He acts his part like an Indian chief when rehearsing his feats of war; and then retiring, the exhibition is continued by others who dare to step forth, and strive to excel each other, to gain the attention of the favorite female.

Having gratified my curiosity at this general breeding-place and nursery of crocodiles, I continued my voyage up the river without being greatly disturbed by them. In my way I observed islets or floating fields of the bright green Pistia, decorated with other amphibious plants as Senecio Jacobea, Persicaria amphibia, Coreopsis bidens, Hydrocotyle fluitans, and many others of less note.

The swamps on the banks and islands of the river are generally three or four feet above the surface of the water, and very level; the timber large and growing thinly, more so than what is observed to be in the swamps below Lake George; the black rich earth is covered with moderately tall, and very succulent tender grass, which when chewed is sweet and agreeable to the taste, somewhat like young sugar-cane: it is a jointed decumbent grass, sending out radiculæ at the joints into the earth, and so spreads itself, by creeping over its surface.

The large timber trees which possess the low lands, are Acer rubrum, Ac. negundo, Ac. glaucum, Ulmus sylvatica, Fraxinus excelsior, Frax. aquatica, Ulmus suberifer, Gleditsia monosperma, Gledit. triacanthus, Diospyros Virginica, Nyssa aquatica, Nyssa sylvatica, Juglans cinerea, Quercus dentata, Quercus phillos, Hopea tinctoria, Corypha palma, Morus rubra, and many more. The palm grows on the edges of the banks, where they are raised higher than the adjacent level ground, by the accumulation of sand, river-shells, &c. I passed along several miles by those rich swamps: the channels of the river which encircle the several fertile islands I had passed, now uniting, formed one deep channel near three hundred yards over. The banks of the river on each side began to rise, and present shelly bluffs, adorned by beautiful orange groves, laurels and live oaks. And now appeared in sight a tree that claimed my whole attention: it was the Carica papaya, both male and female, which were in flower; and the latter both in flower and fruit, some of which were ripe, as large, and of the form of a pear, and of a most charming appearance.

This admirable tree is certainly the most beautiful of any vegetable production I know of; the towering laurel magnolia, and exalted palm, indeed exceed it in grandeur and magnificence, but not in elegance, delicacy, and gracefulness. It rises erect to the height of fifteen or twenty feet, with a perfectly straight tapering stem, which is smooth and polished, of a bright ash color, resembling leaf silver, curiously inscribed with the footsteps of the fallen leaves; and these vestiges are placed in a very regular uniform imbricated order, which has a fine effect, as if the little column were elegantly carved all over. Its perfectly spherical top is formed of very large lobe-sinuate leaves, supported on very long footstalks; the lower leaves are the largest as well as their petioles the longest, and make a graceful sweep or flourish, like the long s [ſ], or the branches of a sconce candlestick. The ripe and green fruit are placed round about the stem or trunk, from the lower-most leaves, where the ripe fruit are, and upwards almost to the top; the heart or inmost pithy part of the trunk is in a manner hollow, or at best consists of very thin porous medullæ or membranes. The tree very seldom branches or divides into limbs, I believe never unless the top is by accident broke off when very young: I saw one which had two tops or heads, the stem of which divided near the earth. It is always green, ornamented at the same time with flowers and fruit, which like figs come out singly from the trunk or

After resting and refreshing myself in these delightful shades, I left them with reluctance. Embarking again after the fervid heat of the meridian sun was abated, for some time I passed by broken ridges of shelly high land, covered with groves of live oaks, palm, Olea Americana, and orange trees; frequently observing floating islets and green fields of the Pistia near the shores of the river and lagoons.

Here is in this river, and in the waters all over Florida, a very curious and handsome species of birds, the people call them Snake Birds; I think I have seen paintings of them on the Chinese screens and other India pictures: they seem to be a species of cormorant or loon (Colymbus cauda elongata), but far more beautiful and delicately formed than any other species that I have ever seen. The head and neck of this bird are extremely small and slender, the latter very long indeed, almost out of all proportion; the bill long, straight, and slender, tapering from its ball to a sharp point; all the upper side, the abdomen and thighs, are as black and glossy as a raven's, covered with feathers so firm and elastic, that they in some degree resemble fish-scales; the breast and upper part of the belly are covered with feathers of a cream color; the tail is very long, of a deep black, and tipped with a silvery white, and when spread, represents an unfurled fan. They delight to sit in little peaceable communities, on the dry limbs of trees, hanging over the still waters, with their wings and tails expanded, I suppose to cool and air themselves, when at the same time they behold their images in the watery mirror. At such times, when we approach them, they drop off the limbs into the water as if dead, and for a minute or two are not to be seen; when on a sudden, at a vast distance, their long slender head and neck only appear, and have very much the appearance of a snake, and no other part of them is to be seen when swimming in the water, except sometimes the tip end of the tail. In the heat of the day they are seen in great numbers, sailing very high in the air, over lakes and rivers.

I doubt not but if this bird had been an inhabitant of the Tiber in Ovid's days, it would have furnished him with a subject for some beautiful and entertaining metamorphoses. I believe it feeds entirely on fish, for its flesh smells and tastes intolerably strong of it; it is scarcely to be eaten, unless constrained by insufferable hunger.

•　　•　　•

MICHEL GUILLAUME ST. JEAN DE CRÈVECOEUR

(1735–1813)

The third letter in Crèvecoeur's *Letters from an American Farmer* (1782) has probably been more widely quoted in modern discussions of American Civilization than the work of any other comparable writer except Alexis de Tocqueville, and even though emphasis on that one selection gives a misleading impression of Crèvecoeur's work it is worth reprinting here. The question of American identity, and especially of self-creation and self-definition in relation to European culture, has been a powerful theme in our literature for nearly two centuries.

Crèvecoeur himself was a prosperous farmer in Orange County, New York who had emigrated from his native France to Canada as a young man and, after some years in the army there, had moved to New York a few years after the fall of New France. Caught between the Loyalists and the Patriots during the Revolution, he had to leave New York in 1780, and he never reestablished his home in America, although he did come to New York as the French consul-general from 1783 to 1790. The third letter makes a memorable statement of American hopes for newness, the regeneration of tired ideas and refugees from all over Western Europe, the elevation of Europe's poor in America, the conviction of American abundance, the therapeutic qualities in the land. Later on, we must note, Crèvecoeur gives a less flattering characterization of American habits and possibilities and expresses a deep hostility to ideas and acts of "progress" on which he seems to look approvingly here. James C. Mohr has persuasively argued that Crèvecoeur intended both attitudes all along.

The text is from the first edition, 1782. A modern edition of other work by Crèvecoeur is *Sketches of Eighteenth-Century America: More Letters. . .*, ed. Henri L. Bourdin and others, 1925. See also Crèvecoeur's *18th-Century Travels in Pennsylvania and New York,* 1962.

Early biographies are Julia Mitchell, *St. Jean De Crèvecoeur,* 1916 and H. L. Rice,

Le Cultivateur Américain, 1933. A modern biography is Thomas Philbrick, *St. John De Crèvecoeur,* 1970. Two valuable critical appraisals are Leo Marx, *The Machine in the Garden,* 1964; and James C. Mohr, "Calculated Disillusionment: Crèvecoeur's Letters Reconsidered," *South Atlantic Quarterly,* 69 (1970):354–363.

Letters From an American Farmer[1]

from LETTER III.
WHAT IS AN AMERICAN.

I wish I could be acquainted with the feelings and thoughts which must agitate the heart and present themselves to the mind of an enlightened Englishman, when he first lands on this continent. He must greatly rejoice that he lived at a time to see this fair country discovered and settled; he must necessarily feel a share of national pride, when he views the chain of settlements which embellishes these extended shores. When he says to himself, this is the work of my countrymen, who, when convulsed by factions, afflicted by a variety of miseries and wants, restless and impatient, took refuge here. They brought along with them their national genius, to which they principally owe what liberty they enjoy, and what substance they possess. Here he sees the industry of his native country displayed in a new manner, and traces in their works the embryos of all the arts, sciences, and ingenuity which flourish in Europe. Here he beholds fair cities, substantial villages, extensive fields, an immense country filled with decent houses, good roads, orchards, meadows, and bridges, where an hundred years ago all was wild, woody and uncultivated! What a train of pleasing ideas this fair spectacle must suggest, it is a prospect which must inspire a good citizen with the most heartfelt pleasure. The difficulty consists in the manner of viewing so extensive a scene. He is arrived on a new continent; a modern society offers itself to his contemplation, different from what he had hitherto seen. It is not composed, as in Europe, of great lords who possess every thing, and of a herd of people who have nothing. Here are no aristocratical families, no courts, no kings, no bishops, no ecclesiastical dominion, no invisible power giving to a few a very visible one; no great manufacturers employing thousands, no great refinements of luxury. The rich and the poor are not so far removed from each other as they are in Europe. Some few towns excepted, we are all tillers of the earth, from Nova Scotia to West Florida. We are a people of cultivators, scattered over an immense territory, communicating with each other by means of good roads and navigable rivers, united by the silken bands of mild government, all respecting the laws, without dreading their power, because they are equitable. We are all animated with the spirit of an industry which is unfettered and unrestrained, because each person works for himself. If he travels through our rural districts he views not the hostile castle, and the haughty mansion contrasted with the clay-built hut and miserable cabin, where cattle and men help to keep each other warm,

[1] London, 1782.

and dwell in meanness, smoke, and indigence. A pleasing uniformity of decent competence appears throughout our habitations. The meanest of our log-houses is a dry and comfortable habitation. Lawyer or merchant are the fairest titles our towns afford; that of a farmer is the only appellation of the rural inhabitants of our country. It must take some time ere he can reconcile himself to our dictionary, which is but short in words of dignity, and names of honor. There, on a Sunday, he sees a congregation of respectable farmers and their wives, all clad in neat homespun, well mounted, or riding in their own humble wagons. There is not among them an esquire, saving the unlettered magistrate. There he sees a parson as simple as his flock, a farmer who does not riot on the labor of others. We have no princes, for whom we toil, starve, and bleed: we are the most perfect society now existing in the world. Here man is free as he ought to be; nor is this pleasing equality so transitory as many others are. Many ages will not see the shores of our great lakes replenished with inland nations, nor the unknown bounds of North America entirely peopled. Who can tell how far it extends? Who can tell the millions of men whom it will feed and contain? for no European foot has as yet travelled half the extent of this mighty continent!

The next wish of this traveller will be to know whence came all these people? They are a mixture of English, Scotch, Irish, French, Dutch, Germans, and Swedes. From this promiscuous breed, that race now called Americans have arisen. The eastern provinces must indeed be excepted; as being the unmixed descendants of Englishmen. I have heard many wish that they had been more intermixed also: for my part; I am no wisher, and think it much better as it has happened. They exhibit a most conspicuous figure in this great and variegated picture; they too enter for a great share in the pleasing perspective displayed in these thirteen provinces. I know it is fashionable to reflect on them, but I respect them for what they have done; for the accuracy and wisdom with which they have settled their territory; for the decency of their manners; for their early love of letters; their ancient college, the first in this hemisphere; for their industry; which to me who am but a farmer is the criterion of every thing. There never was a people, situated as they are, who with so ungrateful a soil have done more in so short a time. Do you think that the monarchical ingredients which are more prevalent in other governments, have purged them from all foul stains? Their histories assert the contrary.

In this great American asylum, the poor of Europe have by some means met together, and in consequence of various causes; to what purpose should they ask one another what countrymen they are? Alas, two-thirds of them had no country. Can a wretch who wanders about, who works and starves, whose life is a continual scene of sore affliction or pinching penury; can that man call England or any other kingdom his country? A country that had no bread for him, whose fields procured him no harvest, who met with nothing but the frowns of the rich, the severity of the laws, with jails and punishments; who owned not a single foot of the extensive surface of this planet? No! urged by a variety of motives, here they came. Every thing has tended to regenerate them; new laws, a new mode of living, a new social system; here they are become men: in Europe they were as so many useless plants, wanting vegitative mold, and refreshing showers; they withered, and were mowed down by want, hunger, and war; but now by the power of transplantation, like all other plants they have taken root and flourished! Formerly they were not numbered in any civil lists of their country, except in those of the poor; here they rank as citizens. By what invisible power has this surprising metamorphosis been performed? By that of the laws and that of their industry. The laws, the indulgent laws, protect them as they arrive, stamping on them the symbol of adoption; they receive ample rewards for their labors; these accumulated rewards procure them lands; those lands confer on them the title of freemen, and to that title every benefit is affixed which men can possibly require. This is the great operation daily performed by our laws. From whence proceed these laws? From our government. Whence that government? It is derived from the original genius and strong desire of the people ratified and confirmed by the crown. This is the great chain which links us all, this is the picture which every province exhibits, Nova Scotia excepted. There the crown has done all; either there were no people who had genius, or it was not much attended to: the consequence is, that the province is very thinly inhabited indeed; the power of the crown in conjunction with the musketos has prevented men from settling there. Yet some parts of it flourished once, and it contained a mild harmless set of people. But for the fault of a few leaders, the whole were banished. The greatest political error the crown ever committed in America, was to cut off men from a country which wanted nothing but men!

What attachment can a poor European emigrant have for a country where he had nothing? The knowledge of the language, the love of a few kindred as poor as himself, were the only cords that tied him: his country is now that which gives him land, bread, protection, and consequence: *Ubi panis ibi patria*,[2] is the motto of all emigrants. What then is the American, this new man? He is either an European, or the descendant of an European, hence that strange mixture of blood, which you will find in no other country, I could point out to you a family whose grandfather was an Englishman, whose wife was Dutch, whose son married a French woman, and whose present four sons have now four wives of different nations. *He* is an American, who leaving behind him all his ancient prejudices and manners, receives new ones from the new mode of life he has embraced, the new government he obeys, and the new rank he holds. He becomes an American by being

[2] "Where there is bread, there is my country."

received in the broad lap of our great *Alma Mater*.[3] Here individuals of all nations are melted into a new race of men, whose labors and posterity will one day cause great changes in the world. Americans are the western pilgrims, who are carrying along with them that great mass of arts, sciences, vigor, and industry which began long since in the East; they will finish the great circle. The Americans were once scattered all over Europe; here they are incorporated into one of the finest systems of population which has ever appeared, and which will hereafter become distinct by the power of the different climates they inhabit. The American ought therefore to love this country much better than that wherein either he or his forefathers were born. Here the rewards of his industry follow with equal steps the progress of his labor; his labor is founded on the basis of nature, *self-interest;* can it want a stronger allurement? Wives and children, who before in vain demanded of him a morsel of bread, now, fat and frolicksome, gladly help their father to clear those fields whence exuberant crops are to arise to feed and to clothe them all; without any part being claimed, either by a despotic prince, a rich abbot, or a mighty lord. Here religion demands but little of him; a small voluntary salary to the minister, and gratitude to God; can he refuse these? The American is a new man, who acts upon new principles; he must therefore entertain new ideas, and form new opinions. From involuntary idleness, servile dependence, penury, and useless labor, he has passed to toils of a very difficult nature, rewarded by ample subsistence.—This is an American.

British America is divided into many provinces, forming a large association, scattered along a coast 1500 miles extent and about 200 wide. This society I would fain examine, at least such as it appears in the middle provinces, if it does not afford that variety of tinges and gradations which may be observed in Europe, we have colors peculiar to ourselves. For instance, it is natural to conceive that those who live near the sea, must be very different from those who live in the woods; the intermediate space will afford a separate and distinct class.

Men are like plants; the goodness and flavor of the fruit proceeds from the peculiar soil and exposition in which they grow. We are nothing but what we derive from the air we breathe, the climate we inhabit, the government we obey, the system of religion we profess, and the nature of our employment. Here you will find but few crimes; these have acquired as yet no root among us. I wish I were able to trace all my ideas; if my ignorance prevents me from describing them properly, I hope I shall be able to delineate a few of the outlines, which are all I propose.

Those who live near the sea, feed more on fish than on flesh, and often encounter that boisterous element. This renders them more bold and enter-

---

[3] "Loving Mother."

prising; this leads them to neglect the confined occupations of the land. They see and converse with a variety of people; their intercourse with mankind becomes extensive. The sea inspires them with a love of traffic, a desire of transporting produce from one place to another; and leads them to a variety of resources which supply the place of labor. Those who inhabit the middle settlements, by far the most numerous, must be very different; the simple cultivation of the earth purifies them, but the indulgences of the government, the soft remonstrances of religion, the rank of independent freeholders, must necessarily inspire them with sentiments, very little known in Europe among people of the same class. What do I say? Europe has no such class of men; the early knowledge they acquire, the early bargains they make, give them a great degree of sagacity. As freemen they will be litigious; pride and obstinacy are often the cause of law suits; the nature of our laws and governments may be another. As citizens it is easy to imagine, that they will carefully read the newspapers, enter into every political disquisition, freely blame or censure governors and others. As farmers they will be careful and anxious to get as much as they can, because what they get is their own. As northern men they will love the cheerful cup. As Christians, religion curbs them not in their opinions; the general indulgence leaves every one to think for themselves in spiritual matters; the laws inspect our actions, our thoughts are left to God. Industry, good living, selfishness, litigiousness, country politics, the pride of freemen, religious indifference, are their characteristics. If you recede still farther from the sea, you will come into more modern settlements; they exhibit the same strong lineaments, in a ruder appearance. Religion seems to have still less influence, and their manners are less improved.

Now we arrive near the great woods, near the last inhabited districts; there men seem to be placed still farther beyond the reach of government, which in some measure leaves them to themselves. How can it pervade every corner; as they were driven there by misfortunes, necessity of beginnings, desire of acquiring large tracts of land, idleness, frequent want of economy, ancient debts; the re-union of such people does not afford a very pleasing spectacle. When discord, want of unity and friendship; when either drunkenness or idleness prevail in such remote districts, contention, inactivity, and wretchedness must ensue. There are not the same remedies to these evils as in a long established community. The few magistrates they have, are in general little better than the rest, they are often in a perfect state of war; that of man against man, sometimes decided by blows, sometimes by means of the law; that of man against every wild inhabitant of these venerable woods, of which they are come to dispossess them. There men appear to be no better than carnivorous animals of a superior rank, living on the flesh of wild animals when they can catch them, and when they are not able, they subsist on grain. He who would wish to see America in its proper light, and have a true idea of its feeble beginnings and barbarous rudiments, must visit our extended line of frontiers where the last settlers dwell, and where he may see the first labors of settlement, the mode of clearing the earth, in all their different appearances; where men are wholly left dependent on their native tempers, and on the spur of uncertain industry, which often fails when not sanctified by the efficacy of a few moral rules. There, remote from the power of example, and check of shame, many families exhibit the most hideous parts of our society. They are a kind of forlorn hope, preceding by ten or twelve years the most respectable army of veterans which come after them. In that space, prosperity will polish some, vice and the law will drive off the rest, who uniting again with others like themselves will recede still farther; making room for more industrious people, who will finish their improvements, convert the loghouse into a convenient habitation, and rejoicing that the first heavy labors are finished, will change in a few years that hitherto barbarous country into a fine fertile, well regulated district. Such is our progress, such is the march of the Europeans toward the interior parts of this continent. In all societies there are off-casts; this impure part serves as our precursors or pioneers; my father himself was one of that class, but he came upon honest principles, and was therefore one of the few who held fast; by good conduct and temperance, he transmitted to me his fair inheritance, when not above one in fourteen of his cotemporaries had the same good fortune.

Forty years ago this smiling country was thus inhabited; it is now purged, a general decency of manners prevails throughout, and such has been the fate of our best countries.

Exclusive of those general characteristics, each province has its own, founded on the government, climate, mode of husbandry, customs, and peculiarity of circumstances. Europeans submit insensibly to these great powers, and become, in the course of a few generations, not only Americans in general, but either Pennsylvanians, Virginians, or provincials under some other name. Whoever traverses the continent must easily observe those strong differences, which will grow more evident in time. The inhabitants of Canada, Massachusetts, the middle provinces, the southern ones will be as different as their climates; their only points of unity will be those of religion and language.

As I have endeavored to show you how Europeans become Americans; it may not be disagreeable to show you likewise how the various Christian sects introduced, wear out, and how religious indifference becomes prevalent. When any considerable number of a particular sect happen to dwell contiguous to each other, they immediately erect a temple, and there worship the Divinity agreeably to their own peculiar ideas. Nobody disturbs them. If any new sect springs up in Europe, it may happen that many of its professors will come and settle in America. As they bring their zeal with them, they are at liberty to make proselytes if they can, and to build a meeting and to follow the dictates of their consciences; for neither the government nor any other power interferes. If they are peaceable subjects, and are industrious, what is it to their neighbors how and in what manner they think fit to address their prayers to the Supreme Being? But if the sectaries are not settled close together, if they are mixed with other denominations, their zeal will cool for want of fuel, and will be extinguished in a little time. Then the Americans become as to religion, what they are as to country, allied to all. In them the name of Englishman, Frenchman, and European is lost, and in like manner, the strict modes of Christianity as practiced in Europe are lost also. This effect will extend itself still farther hereafter, and though this may appear to you as a strange idea, yet it is a very true one. I shall be able perhaps hereafter to explain myself better, in the mean while, let the following example serve as my first justification.

Let us suppose you and I to be travelling; we observe that in this house, to the right, lives a Catholic, who prays to God as he has been taught, and believes in transubstantiation; he works and raises wheat, he has a large family of children, all hale and robust; his belief, his prayers offend nobody. About one mile farther on the same road, his next neighbor may be a good honest plodding German Lutheran, who addresses himself to the same God, the God of all, agreeably to the modes he has been educated in, and believes in consubstantiation; by so doing he scandalizes nobody; he also works in his fields, embellishes the earth; clears swamps; etc. What has the world to do with his Lutheran principles? He persecutes nobody, and nobody persecutes him, he visits his neighbors, and his neighbors visit him. Next to him lives a seceder, the most enthusiastic of all sectaries; his zeal is hot and fiery, but separated as he is from others of the same complexion, he has no congregation of his own to resort to, where he might cabal and mingle religious pride with worldly obstinacy. He likewise raises good crops, his house is handsomely painted, his orchard is one of the fairest in the neighborhood. How does it concern the welfare of the country, or of the province at large, what this man's religious sentiments are, or really whether he has any at all? He is a good farmer, he is a sober, peaceable, good citizen: William Penn himself would not wish for more. This is the visible character, the invisible one is only guessed at, and is nobody's business. Next again lives a Low Dutchman, who implicitly believes the rules laid down by the synod of Dort. He conceives no other idea of a clergyman than that of an hired man; if he does his work well he will pay him the stipulated sum; if not he will dismiss him, and do without his sermons, and let his church be shut up for years! But notwithstanding this coarse idea, you will find his house and farm to be the neatest in all the country; and you will judge by his wagon and fat horses, that he thinks more of the affairs of this world than of those of the next. He is sober and laborious, therefore he is all he ought to be as to the affairs of this life; as for those of the next, he must trust to the great Creator. Each of these people instruct their children as well as they can, but these instructions are feeble compared to those which are given to the youth of the poorest class in Europe. Their children will therefore grow up less zealous and more indifferent in matters of religion than their parents. The foolish vanity; or rather the fury of making proselytes, is unknown here; they have no time, the seasons call for all their attention, and thus in a few years, this mixed neighborhood will exhibit a strange religious medley, that will be neither pure Catholicism nor pure Calvinism. A very perceptible indifference even in the first generation, will become apparent; and it may happen that the daughter of the Catholic will marry the son of the seceder, and settle by themselves at a distance from their parents. What religious education will they give their children? A very imperfect one. If there happens to be in the neighborhood any place of worship, we will suppose a Quaker's meeting; rather than not show their fine clothes, they will go to it, and some of them may perhaps attach themselves to that society. Others will remain in a perfect state of indifference; the children of these zealous parents will not be able to tell what their religious principles are, and their grandchildren still less. The neighborhood of a place of worship generally leads them to it, and the action of going thither, is the strongest evidence they can give of their attachment to any sect. The Quakers are the only people who retain a fondness for their own mode of worship; for be they ever so far separated from each other, they hold a sort of communion with the society, and seldom depart from its rules, at least in this country. Thus all sects are mixed as well as all nations; thus religious indifference is imperceptibly disseminated from one end of the continent to the other; which is at present one of the strongest characteristics of the Americans. Where this will reach no one can tell, perhaps it may leave a vacuum fit to receive other systems. Persecution, religious pride, the love of contradiction, are the food of what the world commonly calls religion. These motives have ceased here; zeal in Europe is confined; here it evaporates in the great distance it has to travel; there it is a grain of powder inclosed, here it burns away in the open air, and consumes without effect.

But to return to our back settlers. I must tell you, that there is something in the proximity of the woods, which is very singular. It is with men as it is with the plants and animals that grow and live in the forests; they are entirely different from those that live in the plains. I will candidly tell you all my thoughts but you are not to expect that I shall advance any reasons. By living in or near the woods, their actions are regulated by the wildness of the neighborhood. The deer often come to eat their grain, the wolves to destroy their sheep, the bears to kill their hogs, the foxes to catch their poultry. This surrounding hostility, immediately puts the gun into their hands; they watch these animals, they kill some; and thus by defending their property, they soon become professed hunters; this is the progress; once hunters, farewell to the plough. The chase renders them ferocious, gloomy, and unsociable; a hunter wants no neighbor, he rather hates them, because he dreads the competition. In a little time their success in the woods makes them neglect their tillage. They trust to the natural fecundity of the earth, and therefore do little; carelessness in fencing, often exposes what little they sow to destruction; they are not at home to watch; in order therefore to make up the deficiency, they go oftener to the woods. That new mode of life brings along with it a new set of manners, which I cannot easily describe. These new manners being grafted on the old stock, produce a strange sort of lawless profligacy; the impressions of which are indelible. The manners of the Indian natives are respectable, compared with this European medley. Their wives and children live in sloth and inactivity; and having no proper pursuits, you may judge what education the latter receive. Their tender minds have nothing else to contemplate but the example of their parents; like them they grow up a mongrel breed, half civilized, half-savage, except nature stamps on them some constitutional propensities. That rich, that voulptuous sentiment is gone which struck them so forcibly; the possession of their freeholds no longer conveys to their minds the same pleasure and pride. To all these reasons you must add, their lonely situation, and you cannot imagine what an effect on manners the great distances they live from each other has! Consider one of the last settlements in its first view; of what is it composed? Europeans who have not that sufficient share of knowledge they ought to have, in order to prosper; people who have suddenly passed from oppression, dread of government, and fear of laws, into the unlimited freedom of the woods. This sudden change must have a very great effect on most men, and on that class particularly. Eating of wild meat, whatever you may think, tends to alter their temper; though all the proof I can adduce, is, that I have seen it: and having no place of worship to resort to, what little society this might afford, is denied them. The Sunday meetings, exclusive of religious benefits, were the only social bonds that might have inspired them with some degree of emulation in neatness. Is it then surprising to see men thus situated, immersed in great and heavy labors, degenerate a little? It is rather a wonder the effect is not more diffusive. The Moravians and the Quakers are the only instances in exception to what I have advanced. The first never settle singly, it is a colony of the society which emigrates; they carry with them their forms, worship, rules, and decency: the others never begin so hard, they are always able to buy improvements, in which there is a great advantage, for by that time the country is recovered from its first barbarity. Thus our bad people are those who are half cultivators and half hunters; and the worst of them are those who have degenerated altogether into the hunting state. As old ploughmen and new men of the woods, as Europeans and new made Indians, they contract the vices of both; they adopt the moroseness and ferocity of a native, without his mildness, or even his industry at home. If manners are not refined, at least they are rendered simple and inoffensive by tilling the earth; all our wants are suplied by it, our time is divided between labor and rest, and leaves none for the commission of great misdeeds. As hunters it is divided between the toil of the chase, the idleness of repose, or the indulgence of inebriation. Hunting is but a licentious idle life, and if it does not always pervert good dispositions; yet, when it is united with bad luck, it leads to want: want stimulates that propensity to rapacity and injustice, too natural to needy men, which is the fatal gradation. After this explanation of the effects which follow by living in the woods, shall we yet vainly flatter ourselves with the hope of converting the Indians? We should rather begin with converting our back-settlers; and now if I dare mention the name of religion, its sweet accents would be lost in the immensity of these woods. Men thus placed, are not fit either to receive or remember its mild instructions; they want temples and ministers, but as soon as men cease to remain at home, and begin to lead an erratic life, let them be either tawny or white, they cease to be its disciples.

Thus have I faintly and imperfectly endeavored to trace our society from the sea to our woods; yet you must not imagine that every person who moves back, acts upon the same principles, or falls into the same degeneracy. Many families carry with them all their decency of conduct, purity of morals, and respect of religion; but these are scarce, the power of example is sometimes irresistible. Even among these back-settlers, their depravity is greater or less, according to what nation or province they belong. Were I to adduce proofs of this, I might be accused of partiality. If there happens to be some rich intervals, some fertile bottoms, in those remote districts, the people will there prefer tilling the land to hunting, and will attach themselves to it; but even on these fertile spots you may plainly perceive the inhabitants to acquire a great degree of rusticity and selfishness.

It is in consequence of this straggling situation, and the astonishing power it has on manners, that the back-settlers of both the Carolinas, Virginia, and many other parts, have been long a set of lawless people; it has been even dangerous to travel among them. Government can do nothing in so extensive a country, better it should wink at these irregularities, than that it should use means inconsistent with its usual mildness. Time will efface those stains: in proportion as the great body of population approaches them they will reform; and become polished and subordinate. Whatever has been said of the four New England provinces, no such degeneracy of manners has ever tarnished their annals; their back-settlers have been kept within the bounds of decency, and government, by means of wise laws, and by the influence of religion. What a detestable idea such people must have given to the natives of the Europeans! They trade with them, the worst of people are permitted to do that which none but persons of the best characters should be employed in. They get drunk with them, and often defraud the Indians. Their avarice, removed from the eyes of their superiors, knows no bounds, and aided by a little superiority of knowledge, these traders deceive them, and even sometimes shed blood. Hence those shocking violations, those sudden devastations which have so often stained our frontiers, when hundreds of innocent people have been sacrificed for the crimes of a few. It was in consequence of such behavior, that the Indians took the hatchet against the Virginians in 1774. Thus are our first steps trod, thus are our first trees felled, in general, by the most vicious of our people; and thus the path is opened for the arrival of a second and better class, the true American freeholders; the most respectable set of people in this part of the world: respectable for their industry, their happy independence, the great share of freedom they possess, the good regulation of their families, and for extending the trade and the dominion of our mother country.

Europe contains hardly any other distinctions but lords and tenants; this fair country alone is settled by freeholders, the possessors of the soil they cultivate, members of the government they obey, and the framers of their own laws, by means of their representatives. This is a thought which you have taught me to cherish; our distance from Europe, far from diminishing, rather adds to our usefulness and consequence as men and subjects. Had our forefathers remained there, they would only have crowded it, and perhaps prolonged those convulsions which had shook it so long. Every industrious European who transports himself here, may be compared to a sprout growing at the foot of a great tree; it enjoys and draws but a little portion of sap; wrench it from the parent roots, transplant it, and it will become a tree bearing fruit also. Colonists are therefore entitled to the consideration due to the most useful subjects; a hundred families barely existing in some parts of Scotland, will here in six years, cause an annual exportation of 10,000 bushels of wheat: 100 bushels being but a common quantity for an industrious family to sell, if they cultivate good land. It is here then that the idle may be employed, the useless become useful, and the poor become rich; but by riches I do not mean gold and silver, we have but little of those metals; I mean a better sort of wealth, cleared lands, cattle, good houses, good clothes, and an increase of people to enjoy them.

There is no wonder that this country has so many charms, and presents to Europeans so many temptations to remain in it. A traveler in Europe becomes a stranger as soon as he quits his own kingdom; but it is otherwise here. We know, properly speaking, no strangers; this is every person's country; the variety of our soils, situations, climates, governments, and produce, hath something which must please every body. No sooner does an European arrive, no matter of what condition, than his eyes are opened upon the fair prospect; he hears his language spoke, he retraces many of his own country manners, he perpetually hears the names of families and towns with which he is acquainted; he sees happiness and prosperity in all places disseminated; he meets with hospitality, kindness, and plenty everywhere: he beholds hardly any poor, he seldom hears of punishments and executions, and he wonders at the elegance of our towns, those miracles of industry and freedom. He cannot admire enough our rural districts, our convenient roads, good taverns, and our many accommodations; he involuntarily loves a country where everything is so lovely. When in England, he was a mere Englishman; here he stands on a larger portion of the globe, not less than its fourth part, and may see the productions of the north, in iron and naval stores; the provisions of Ireland, the grain of Egypt, the indigo, the rice of China. He does not find, as in Europe, a crowded society, where every place is overstocked; he does not feel that perpetual collision of parties, that difficulty of beginning, that contention which oversets so many. There is room for every body in America; has he any particular talent, or industry? he exerts it in order to procure a livelihood, and it succeeds. Is he a merchant? the avenues of trade are infinite; is he eminent in any respect? he will be employed and respected. Does he love a country life? pleasant farms present themselves; he may purchase what he wants, and thereby become an American farmer. Is he a laborer, sober and industrious? he need not go many miles, nor receive many informations before he will be hired, well fed at the table of his employer, and paid four or five times more than he can get in Europe. Does he want uncultivated lands? thousands of acres present themselves, which he may purchase cheap. Whatever be his talents or inclinations, if they are moderate, he may satisfy them. I do not mean that every one who comes will grow rich in a little time; no, but he may procure an easy, decent maintenance, by his industry. Instead of starving he will be fed, instead of being idle he will have employment; and these are riches enough for such men as come over here. The rich stay in Europe, it is only the middling and poor that emigrate. Would you wish to travel in independent idleness, from north to south, you will find easy access, and the most cheerful reception at every house; society without ostentation, good cheer without pride, and every decent diversion which the country affords, with little expense. It is no wonder that the European who has lived here a few years, is desirous to remain; Europe with all its pomp, is not to be compared to this continent, for men of middle stations, or laborers.

An European, when he first arrives, seems limited in his intentions, as well as in his views; but he very suddenly alters his scale; two hundred miles formerly appeared a very great distance, it is now but a trifle; he no sooner breathes our air than he forms schemes, and embarks in designs he never would have thought of in his own country. There the plenitude of society confines many useful ideas, and often extinguishes the most laudable schemes which here ripen into maturity. Thus Europeans become Americans.

But how is this accomplished in that crowd of low, indigent people, who flock here every year from all parts of Europe? I will tell you; they no sooner arrive than they immediately feel the good effects of that plenty of provisions we possess: they fare on our best food, and are kindly entertained; their talents, character, and peculiar industry are immediately inquired into, they find countrymen everywhere disseminated, let them come from whatever part of Europe. Let me select one as an epitome of the rest; he is hired, he goes to work, and works moderately; instead of being employed by a haughty person, he finds himself with his equal, placed at the substantial table of the farmer, or else at an inferior one as good; his wages are high, his bed is not like that bed of sorrow on which he used to lie; if he behaves with propriety, and is faithful, he is caressed, and becomes as it were a member of the family. He begins to feel the effects of a sort of resurrection; hitherto he had not lived, but simply vegetated; he now feels himself a man, because he is treated as such; the laws of his own country had overlooked him in his insignificancy; the laws of this cover him with their mantle. Judge what an alteration there must arise in the mind and the thoughts of this man; he begins to forget his former servitude and dependence, his heart involuntarily swells and glows; this first swell inspires him with those new thoughts which constitute an American. What love can he entertain for a country where his existence was a burden to him; if he is a generous good man, the love of this new adoptive parent will sink deep into his heart. He looks around, and sees many a prosperous person, who but a few years before was as poor as himself. This encourages him much, he begins to form some little scheme, the first, alas, he ever formed in his life. If he is wise he thus spends two or three years, in which time he acquires knowledge, the use of tools, the modes of working the lands, felling trees, etc. This prepares the foundation of a good name, the most useful acquisition he can make. He is encouraged, he has gained friends; he is advised and directed, he feels bold, he purchases some land; he gives all the money he has brought over, as well as what he has earned, and trusts to the God of harvest for the discharge of the rest. His good name procures him credit, he is now possessed of the deed, conveying to him and his posterity the fee simple and absolute property of two hundred acres of land, situated on such a river. What an epocha in this man's life! He is become a freeholder, from perhaps a German boor—he is now an American, a Pennsylvanian, an English subject. He is naturalized, his name is enrolled with those of the other citizens of the province. Instead of being a vagrant, he has a place of residence; he is called the inhabitant of such a county, or of such a district, and for the first time in his life counts for something; for hitherto he had been a cipher. I only repeat what I have heard many say, and no wonder their hearts should glow, and be agitated with a multitude of feelings, not easy to describe. From nothing to start into being; from a servant to the rank of a master; from being the slave of some despotic prince, to become a free man, invested with lands, to which every municipal blessing is annexed! What a change indeed! It is in consequence of that change that he becomes an American. This great metamorphosis has a double effect, it extinguishes all his European prejudices, he forgets that mechanism of subordination, that servility of disposition which poverty had taught him; and sometimes he is apt to forget it too much, often passing from one extreme to the other. If he is a good man, he forms schemes of future prosperity, he proposes to educate his children better than he has been educated himself; he thinks of future modes of conduct, feels an ardor to labor he never felt before. Pride steps in and leads him to every thing that the laws do not forbid: he respects them; with a heart-felt gratitude he looks toward the east, toward that insular government from whose wisdom all his new felicity is derived, and under whose wings and protection he now lives. These reflections constitute him the good man and the good subject. Ye poor Europeans, ye, who sweat, and work for the great—ye, who are obliged to give so many sheaves to the church, so many to your lords, so many to your government, and have hardly any left for yourselves—ye, who are held in less estimation than favorite hunters—or useless lap-dogs—ye, who only breathe the air of nature, because it cannot be withheld from you; it is here that ye can conceive the possibility of those feelings I have been describing; it is here the laws of naturalization invite everyone to partake of our great labors and felicity, to till unrented, untaxed lands! Many, corrupted beyond the power of amendment, have brought with them all their vices, and disregarding the advantages held to them, have gone on in their former career of iniquity, until they have been overtaken and punished by our laws. It is not every emigrant who succeeds; no, it is only the sober, the honest, and industrious: happy those to whom this transition has served as a powerful spur to labor, to prosperity, and to the good establishment of children, born in the days of their poverty; and who had no other portion to expect but the rags of their parents, had it not been for their happy emigration. Others again, have been led astray by this enchanting scene; their new pride, instead of leading them to the fields, has kept them in idleness; the idea of possessing lands is all that satisfies them—though surrounded with fertility, they have moldered away their time in inactivity, misinformed husbandry, and ineffectual endeavors. How much wiser, in general, the honest Germans than almost all other Europeans; they hire themselves to some of their wealthy landsmen, and in that apprenticeship learn every thing that is necessary. They attentively consider the prosperous industry of others, which imprints in their minds a strong desire of possessing the same advantages. This forcible idea never quits them, they launch forth, and by dint of sobriety, rigid parsimony, and the most persevering industry, they commonly succeed. Their astonishment at their first arrival from Germany is very great—it is to them a dream; the contrast must be very powerful indeed; they observe their countrymen flourishing in every place; they travel through whole counties where not a word of English is spoken; and in the names and the language of the people, they retrace Germany. They have been an useful acquisition to this continent, and to Pennsylvania in particular; to them it owes some share of its prosperity: to their mechanical knowledge and patience, it owes the finest mills in all America, the best teams of horses, and many other advantages. The recollection of their former poverty and slavery never quits them as long as they live.

The Scotch and the Irish might have lived in their own country perhaps as poor, but enjoying more civil advantages, the effects of their new situation do not strike them so forcibly, nor has it so lasting an effect. From whence the difference arises I know not, but out of twelve families of emigrants of each country, generally seven Scotch will succeed, nine German, and four Irish. The Scotch are frugal and laborious, but their wives cannot work so hard as German women, who on the contrary vie with their husbands, and often share with them the most severe toils of the field, which they understand better. They have therefore nothing to struggle against, but the common casualties of nature. The Irish do not prosper so well; they love to drink and to quarrel; they are litigious, and soon take to the gun, which is the ruin of every thing; they seem beside to labor under a greater degree of ignorance in husbandry than the others; perhaps it is that their industry had less scope, and was less exercised at home. I have heard many relate, how the land was parcelled out in that kingdom; their ancient conquest has been a great detriment to them, by over-setting their landed property. The lands possessed by a few, are leased down *ad infinitum,* and the occupiers often pay five guineas an acre. The poor are worse lodged there than anywhere else in Europe; their potatoes, which are easily raised, are perhaps an inducement to laziness: their wages are too low and their whiskey too cheap.

There is no tracing observation of this kind, without making at the same time very great allowances, as there are everywhere to be found, a great many exceptions. The Irish themselves, from different parts of that kingdom, are very different. It is difficult to account for this surprising locality, one would think on so small an island an Irishman must be an Irishman: yet it is not so, they are different in their aptitude to, and in their love of labor.

The Scotch on the contrary are all industrious and saving; they want nothing more than a field to exert themselves in, and they are commonly sure of succeeding. The only difficulty they labor under is, that technical American knowledge which requires some time to obtain; it is not easy for those who seldom saw a tree, to conceive how it is to be felled, cut up, and split into rails and posts.

. . .

IV
The Revolution and the Republic
1763-1815

The Treaty of Paris in 1763 virtually removed France as a serious threat to English colonization and left the colonists and the royal authorities free to recognize their inevitable conflicts of interest. American literature of the next 50 years is dominated by implicit and usually explicit assumptions concerning the nature of the republic. From John Adams's letter to the *Boston Evening Post* (1763) to the indignant letters and speeches by black writers and Indian orators, the question of civil justice and republican manners is central. Along with Benjamin Franklin, John Adams and Thomas Jefferson participated in these debates both during the Revolution and in the decades during which the new republic was being created and modified. Most of the other writers in this chapter concern themselves more with questions for the republic than with the separation from Great Britain. Notice how powerfully post-Revolutionary writers, Isaac Backus or Benjamin Banneker, appeal to the principles of the Declaration of Independence and to the revolutionary experience.

THOMAS PAINE

(1737-1809)

After a series of discouraging failures in various trades, Thomas Paine emigrated from England to America, armed with a letter of introduction from Benjamin Franklin, who recommended him as "an ingenious worthy young man" (he was 37) fit for some sort of clerical post. Here Paine quickly found his vocation. Within less than two years after his arrival he had written and published *Common Sense* (January 1776), the pamphlet that is generally agreed to have had more influence than any other single force on the popular decision in favor of national independence. He joined the Continental Army and continued to write with a genius for what has since become known as psychological warfare. Some of his phrases from *The American Crisis,* a series of letters that he began to publish during the Continental Army's worst moments, are memorized even today by schoolchildren throughout the country, and during the Revolution those phrases endeared Paine to the people and to George Washington himself. "These are the times that try men's souls," Paine wrote in the first number of *The Crisis,* wherein his scorn for "the summer soldier and the sunshine patriot" rallied patriots to stand by their suffering army in the next gloomy winter. That first letter was read to General Washington's troops on their way to surprise the Hessians in the symbolic victory at Trenton on Christmas Eve, 1776.

After the Treaty of Paris in 1783 Paine was rewarded with an estate that had been confiscated from Loyalists in New York, and with some money from the state and national governments, but within the next decade he became one of the most thoroughly detested of Revolutionary heroes. Like Joel Barlow, he spent most of these years in England and France as a defender of the French Revolution and an unsuccessful proponent of moderation in the French National Assembly. He was

Moncure Conway edited *The Writings of Thomas Paine,* 4 vols., 1894-1896; he also wrote *The Life of Thomas Paine,* 2 vols., 1892. A twentieth-century edition is *The Life and Works of Thomas Paine,* ed. Wm. Vander Weyde, 1925.

The best biography is David F. Hawke, *Paine,* 1974. See also Alfred O. Aldridge, *Man of Reason: The Life of Thomas Paine,* 1959; Haskell Pearson, *Thomas*

Paine, 1937; Leo Gurko, *Tom Paine, Freedom's Apostle,* 1957; I.M. Thompson, *The Religious Beliefs of Thomas Paine,* 1957.

Robert R. Palmer has written two important interpretive studies: "Tom Paine: Victim of the Rights of Men," *Pennsylvania Magazine of History and Biography,* 66 (1942): 161-175; and *The Age of the Democratic Revolution,* 1959.

banished from England (though he had already departed) after he had published *The Rights of Man,* a scornful attack on monarchy and an answer to Edmund Burke's *Reflections* on the French Revolution. Although Paine opposed the execution of King Louis XVI, argued for civil rights for dissenters, and was even imprisoned in Paris for a time, he came under increasing attack in England and the United States as a radical and, after he had published *The Age of Reason* (1795), an atheist. It did not matter that he was emphatically a Deist, convinced that a benevolent Creator had instituted principles of moral law in the order of nature. For many Christians, especially during the 1790's, when France seemed to represent anarchy and inevitable tyranny as well as infidelity, the distinction between Deism and atheism would have seemed unimportant. When Paine returned to the United States in 1802, he was reviled and even physically attacked, and the vicious animosity followed him beyond death; his body was denied burial in a Quaker cemetery, and years afterward his very bones were dug up and sent to England for some kind of admonitory display.

Although manifestly unjust, the vehemence of Anglo-American hostility toward Paine does show some understanding of a major quality in his mind and work. Like many self-taught American writers—from Benjamin Franklin before him to Herman Melville, Mark Twain, and Ambrose Bierce in the next century—Paine was much more skillful, and his vaunted "reason" much more effective, in ridiculing the fallacies or pretentiousness of established authority than in supporting the affirmative convictions that Paine wanted to establish in its place. It is the blasphemous ridicule of Biblical "superstition" that was unforgivably memorable on the one hand, and at the same time even a dispassionate reader might see that if used against his own political and religious faith, Paine's methods of theological criticism could not protect one from infidelity and anarchy. This problem becomes a central one in the American Renaissance, from the writings of William Ellery Channing and the Transcendentalists to those of Melville and, later on, Mark Twain and Henry Adams.

In a positive and memorable way, nonetheless, Paine recorded some of the strongest convictions on which Jeffersonian philosophers and writers of fiction from Irving and Cooper to Mark Twain and Henry James were agreed during much of the next century. The very title of *Common Sense* appeals to the ultimate principle of individual self-reliance in politics, just as Paine's declaration that his mind was his church carried the antisacerdotal prejudices of Protestant sentiment to the limit of their original tendency. The conviction that government exists for negative reasons, to restrain the excesses of the wicked, and the notion that it is "unnatural" for a vast continent (for so Paine represents the English colonies in America) to be controlled by a tiny island thousands of miles away—these beliefs have major consequences in American literature long after the political independence for which Paine articulated them had been won.

Common Sense[1]

Addressed to the Inhabitants of America, on the following Interesting Subjects, viz.:
  I. *Of the Origin and Design of Government in General; with Concise Remarks on the English Constitution.*
  II. *Of Monarchy and Hereditary Succession.*
  III. *Thoughts on the Present State of American Affairs.*
  IV. *Of the Present Ability of America; with some Miscellaneous Reflections.*

THOUGHTS ON THE PRESENT STATE OF AMERICAN AFFAIRS

In the following pages I offer nothing more than simple facts, plain arguments, and common sense: and have no other preliminaries to settle with the reader, than that he will divest himself of prejudice and prepossession, and suffer his reason and his feeling to determine for themselves: that he will put on, or rather that he will not put off, the true character of a man, and generously enlarge his views beyond the present day.

Volumes have been written on the subject of the struggle between England and America. Men of all ranks have embarked in the controversy, from different motives, and with various designs; but all have been ineffectual, and the period of debate is closed. Arms as the last resource decide the contest; the appeal was the choice of the King, and the continent[2] has accepted the challenge.

It hath been reported of the late Mr. Pelham[3] (who tho' an able minister was not without his faults) that on his being attacked in the House of Com-

[1] The text is the first edition, Philadelphia, 1776.

First published in January 1776, *Common Sense* had an extraordinary sale during that year. Nobody can measure the effect of a pamphlet on a complex national decision, but if *Common Sense* did not strongly influence opinion its immense sale coincided with a powerful development between January and July of sentiment for independence. Here Paine expressed the indignation and the faith that many colonists shared, and by making "the cause of America. . . the cause of all mankind" he anticipated the tone of the preamble to the Declaration.

[2] Paine's reference to the American colonies as "the continent" has important significance below, when he argues that it is absurd for a small island to govern a distant continent.

[3] Henry Pelham, Prime Minister from 1744 to 1754.

mons on the score that his measures were only of a temporary kind, replied, *"they will last my time."* Should a thought so fatal and unmanly possess the Colonies in the present contest, the name of Ancestors will be remembered by future generations with detestation.

The sun never shined on a cause of greater worth. 'Tis not the affair of a city, a county, a province, or a kingdom; but of a continent—of at least one eighth part of the habitable globe. 'Tis not the concern of a day, a year, or an age; posterity are virtually involved in the contest, and will be more or less affected even to the end of time by the proceedings now. Now is the seed-time of continental union, faith and honor. The least fracture now, will be like a name engraved with the point of a pin on the tender rind of a young oak; the wound would enlarge with the tree, and posterity read it in full grown characters.

By referring the matter from argument to arms, a new æra for politics is struck—a new method of thinking has arisen. All plans, proposals, etc. prior to the nineteenth of April, i. e. to the commencement of hostilities,[4] are like the almanacs of last year; which though proper then, are superseded and useless now. Whatever was advanced by the advocates on either side of the question then, terminated in one and the same point, viz. a union with Great Britain; the only difference between the parties was the method of effecting it; the one proposing force, the other friendship; but it has so far happened that the first has failed, and the second has withdrawn her influence.

As much has been said of the advantages of reconciliation, which, like an agreeable dream, has passed away and left us as we were, it is but right that we should examine the contrary side of the argument, and inquire into some of the many material injuries which these colonies sustain, and always will sustain, by being connected with and dependent on Great Britain. To examine that connection and dependence, on the principles of nature and common sense, to see what we have to trust to, if separated, and what we are to expect, if dependent.

I have heard it asserted by some, that as America has flourished under her former connection with Great Britain, the same connection is necessary toward her future happiness, and will always have the same effect.—Nothing can be more fallacious than this kind of argument.—We may as well assert that because a child has thrived upon milk, that it is never to have meat, or that the first twenty years of our lives is to become a precedent for the next twenty. But even this is admitting more than is true; for I answer roundly, that America would have flourished as much, and probably much more, had no European power taken any notice of her. The commerce by which she hath enriched herself are the necessaries of life, and will always have a market while eating is the custom of Europe.

[4] At Lexington and Concord, Massachusetts.

THOMAS PAINE

But she has protected us, say some. That she hath engrossed us is true, and defended the continent at our expense as well as her own, is admitted, and she would have defended Turkey from the same motive, *viz.* for the sake of trade and dominion.

Alas! we have been long led away by ancient prejudices and made large sacrifices to superstition. We have boasted the protection of Great Britain, without considering, that her motive was *interest* not *attachment;* and that she did not protect us from *our enemies* on *our account,* but from her enemies on her own account, from those who had no quarrel with us on any *other account,* and who will always be our enemies on the *same account.* Let Britain waive her pretensions to the continent, or the continent throw off the dependence, and we should be at peace with France and Spain were they at war with Britain. The miseries of Hanover's last war[5] ought to warn us against connections.

It hath lately been asserted in Parliament, that the colonies have no relation to each other but through the parent country, i.e. that Pennsylvania and the Jerseys, and so on for the rest, are sister colonies by the way of England; this is certainly a very roundabout way of proving relationship, but it is the nearest and only true way of proving enmity (or enemyship, if I may so call it). France and Spain never were, nor perhaps ever will be, our enemies as *Americans,* but as our being the *subjects of Great Britain.*

But Britain is the parent country, say some. Then the more shame upon her conduct. Even brutes do not devour their young, nor savages make war upon their families; wherefore, the assertion, if true, turns to her reproach; but it happens not to be true, or only partly so, and the phrase *parent* or *mother country* hath been jesuitically adopted by the King and his parasites, with a low papistical design of gaining an unfair bias on the credulous weakness of our minds. Europe, and not England, is the parent country of America. This new world hath been the asylum for the persecuted lovers of civil and religious liberty from *every part* of Europe. Hither have they fled, not from the tender embraces of the mother, but from the cruelty of the monster; and it is so far true of England, that the same tyranny which drove the first emigrants from home, pursues their descendants still.

In this extensive quarter of the globe, we forget the narrow limits of three hundred and sixty miles (the extent of England) and carry our friendship on a larger scale; we claim brotherhood with every European Christian, and triumph in the generosity of the sentiment.

It is pleasant to observe by what regular gradations we surmount the force of local prejudices, as we enlarge our acquaintance with the world. A man born in any town in England divided into parishes, will naturally asso-

[5] Paine blames the Seven Years' War (1756-1763), which was more costly to the American colonies than any previous war, on the ruling house of Hanover, the line of George III.

ciate most with his fellow parishioners (because their interests in many cases will be common) and distinguish him by the name of *neighbor;* if he meet him but a few miles from home, he drops the narrow idea of a street, and salutes him by the name of *townsman;* if he travel out of the county and meet him in any other, he forgets the minor divisions of street and town, and calls him *country-man, i.e. county-man;* but if in their foreign excursions they should associate in France, or any other part of *Europe,* their local remembrance would be enlarged into that of *Englishman.* And by a just parity of reasoning, all Europeans meeting in America, or any other quarter of the globe, are *countrymen;* for England, Holland, Germany, or Sweden, when compared with the whole, stand in the same places on the larger scale, which the divisions of street, town, and county do on the smaller ones; distinctions too limited for continental minds. Not one-third of the inhabitants, even of this province are of English descent. Wherefore, I reprobate the phrase of parent or mother country applied to England only, as being false, selfish, narrow and ungenerous.

But, admitting that we were all of English descent, what does it amount to? Nothing. Britain, being now an open enemy, extinguishes every other name and title: and to say that reconciliation is our duty, is truly farcical. The first king of England, of the present line (William the Conqueror) was a Frenchman, and half the peers of England are descendants from the same country; wherefore, by the same method of reasoning, England ought to be governed by France.

Much hath been said of the united strength of Britain and the colonies, that in conjunction they might bid defiance to the world: but this is mere presumption, the fate of war is uncertain, neither do the expressions mean anything, for this continent would never suffer itself to be drained of inhabitants, to support the British arms in either Asia, Africa or Europe.

Besides, what have we to do with setting the world at defiance? Our plan is commerce, and that, well attended to, will secure us the peace and friendship of all Europe; because it is the interest of all Europe to have America a *free port.* Her trade will always be a protection, and her barrenness of gold and silver secure her from invaders.

I challenge the warmest advocate of reconciliation to show a single advantage that this continent can reap, by being connected with Great Britain. I repeat the challenge, not a single advantage is derived. Our corn will fetch its price in any market in Europe, and our imported goods must be paid for buy them where we will.

But the injuries and disadvantages which we sustain by that connection, are without number; and our duty to mankind at large, as well as to ourselves, instructs us to renounce the alliance: because, any submission to, or dependence on, Great Britain, tends directly to involve this continent in European wars and quarrels, and set us at variance with nations who would otherwise seek our friendship, and against whom we have neither anger nor complaint. As Europe is our market for trade, we ought to form no partial connection with any part of it. 'Tis the true interest of America to steer clear of European contentions, which she can never do, while by her dependence on Britain, she is made the make-weight in the scale of British politics.

Europe is too thickly planted with kingdoms to be long at peace, and whenever a war breaks out between England and any foreign power, the trade of America goes to ruin, *because of her connection with Britain.* The next war may not turn out like the last, and should it not, the advocates for reconciliation now will be wishing for separation then, because neutrality in that case would be a safer convoy than a man of war. Everything that is right or reasonable pleads for separation. The blood of the slain, the weeping voice of nature cries, 'TIS TIME TO PART. Even the distance at which the Almighty hath placed England and America is a strong and natural proof that the authority of the one over the other, was never the design of heaven. The time likewise at which the continent was discovered, adds weight to the argument, and the manner in which it was peopled, increases the force of it.—The Reformation was preceded by the discovery of America: as if the Almighty graciously meant to open a sanctuary to the persecuted in future years, when home should afford neither friendship nor safety.

The authority of Great Britain over this continent, is a form of government, which sooner or later must have an end. And a serious mind can draw no true pleasure by looking forward, under the painful and positive conviction that what he calls "the present constitution" is merely temporary. As parents, we can have no joy, knowing that *this government* is not sufficiently lasting to insure anything which we may bequeath to posterity: and by a plain method of argument, as we are running the next generation into debt, we ought to do the work of it, otherwise we use them meanly and pitifully. In order to discover the line of our duty rightly, we should take our children in our hand, and fix our station a few years farther into life; that eminence will present a prospect which a few present fears and prejudices conceal from our sight.

Though I would carefully avoid giving unnecessary offense, yet I am inclined to believe, that all those who espouse the doctrine of reconciliation, may be included within the following descriptions.

Interested men, who are not to be trusted, weak men who *cannot* see, prejudiced men who *will not* see, and a certain set of moderate men who think better of the European world than it deserves; and this last class, by an ill-judged deliberation, will be the cause of more calamities to this continent than all the other three.

It is the good fortune of many to live distant from the scene of present sorrow; the evil is not sufficiently brought to *their* doors to make *them* feel the precariousness with which all American property is possessed. But let our imaginations transport us a few moments to Boston;[6] that seat of wretchedness will teach us wisdom, and instruct us for ever to renounce a power in whom we can have no trust. The inhabitants of that unfortunate city who but a few months ago were in ease and affluence, have now no other alternative than to stay and starve, or turn out to beg. Endangered by the fire of their friends if they continue within the city, and plundered by the soldiery if they leave it, in their present situation they are prisoners without the hope of redemption, and in a general attack for their relief they would be exposed to the fury of both armies.

Men of passive tempers look somewhat lightly over the offenses of Great Britain, and, still hoping for the best, are apt to call out, *come, come, we shall be friends again for all this*. But examine the passions and feelings of mankind: bring the doctrine of reconciliation to the touchstone of nature, and then tell me whether you can hereafter love, honor, and faithfully serve the power that hath carried fire and sword into your land? If you cannot do all these, then are you only deceiving yourselves, and by your delay bringing ruin upon posterity. Your future connection with Britain, whom you can neither love nor honor, will be forced and unnatural, and being formed only on the plan of present convenience, will in a little time fall into a relapse more wretched than the first. But if you say, you can still pass the violations over, then I ask, Hath your house been burnt? Hath your property been destroyed before your face? Are your wife and children destitute of a bed to lie on, or bread to live on? Have you lost a parent or child by their hands, and yourself the ruined and wretched survivor? If you have not, then are you not a judge of those who have. But if you have, and can still shake hands with the murderers, then are you unworthy the name of husband, father, friend, or lover, and whatever may be your rank or title in life, you have the heart of a coward, and the spirit of a sycophant.

This is not inflaming or exaggerating matters, but trying them by those feelings and affections which nature justifies, and without which we should be incapable of discharging the social duties of life, or enjoying the felicities of it. I mean not to exhibit horror for the purpose of provoking revenge, but to awaken us from fatal and unmanly slumbers, that we may pursue determinately some fixed object. 'Tis not in the power of Britain or of Europe to conquer America, if she doth not conquer herself by *delay* and *timidity*. The present winter is worth an age if rightly employed, but if lost or neglected the whole continent will partake of the misfortune; and there is no punishment which that man doth not deserve, be he who, or what, or where he will, that may be the means of sacrificing a season so precious and useful.

'Tis repugnant to reason, to the universal order of things; to all examples from former ages, to suppose, that this continent can long remain subject to

---

[6] Then under siege for six months.

any external power. The most sanguine in Britain doth not think so. The utmost stretch of human wisdom cannot, at this time, compass a plan, short of separation, which can promise the continent even a year's security. Reconciliation is *now* a fallacious dream. Nature has deserted the connection, and art cannot supply her place. For, as Milton wisely expresses, "never can true reconcilement grow where wounds of deadly hate have pierced so deep."[7]

Every quiet method for peace hath been ineffectual. Our prayers have been rejected with disdain; and hath tended to convince us that nothing flatters vanity or confirms obstinacy in kings more than repeated petitioning—and nothing hath contributed more than that very measure to make the kings of Europe absolute. Witness Denmark and Sweden. Wherefore, since nothing but blows will do, for God's sake let us come to a final separation, and not leave the next generation to be cutting throats under the violated unmeaning names of parent and child.

To say they will never attempt it again is idle and visionary; we thought so at the repeal of the Stamp Act, yet a year or two undeceived us; as well may we suppose that nations which have been once defeated will never renew the quarrel.

As to government matters, 'tis not in the power of Britain to do this continent justice: the business of it will soon be too weighty and intricate to be managed with any tolerable degree of convenience, by a power so distant from us, and so very ignorant of us; for if they cannot conquer us they cannot govern us. To be always running three or four thousand miles with a tale or a petition, waiting four or five months for an answer, which, when obtained, requires five or six more to explain it in, will in a few years be looked upon as folly and childishness.—There was a time when it was proper, and there is a proper time for it to cease.

Small islands not capable of protecting themselves, are the proper objects for government to take under their care; but there is something absurd in supposing a continent to be perpetually governed by an island. In no instance hath nature made the satellite larger than its primary planet; and as England and America, with respect to each other, reverse the common order of nature, it is evident that they belong to different systems. England to Europe: America to itself.

I am not induced by motives of pride, party or resentment to espouse the doctrine of separation and independence; I am clearly, positively, and conscientiously persuaded that 'tis the true interest of this continent to be so; that everything short of *that* is mere patchwork, that it can afford no lasting felicity—that it is leaving the sword to our children, and shrinking back at a

[7] *Paradise Lost*, Book IV, lines 98-99.

time when a little more, a little further, would have rendered this continent the glory of the earth.

As Britain hath not manifested the least inclination towards a compromise, we may be assured that no terms can be obtained worthy the acceptance of the continent, or any ways equal to the expense of blood and treasure we have been already put to.

The object contended for, ought always to bear some just proportion to the expense. The removal of North, or the whole detestable junto,[8] is a matter unworthy the millions we have expended. A temporary stoppage of trade was an inconvenience, which would have sufficiently balanced the repeal of all the acts complained of, had such repeals been obtained; but if the whole continent must take up arms, if every man must be a soldier, 'tis scarcely worth our while to fight against a contemptible ministry only. Dearly, dearly do we pay for the repeal of the acts,[9] if that is all we fight for; for, in a just estimation 'tis as great a folly to pay a bunker-hill price[10] for law as for land. As I have always considered the independency of this continent, as an event which sooner or later must arrive, so from the late rapid progress of the continent to maturity, the event cannot be far off. Wherefore, on the breaking out of hostilities, it was not worth the while to have disputed a matter which time would have finally redressed, unless we meant to be in earnest: otherwise it is like wasting an estate on a suit at law, to regulate the trespasses of a tenant whose lease is just expiring. No man was a warmer wisher for a reconciliation than myself, before the fatal nineteenth of April, 1775, but the moment the event of that day was made known, I rejected the hardened, sullen-tempered Pharaoh of England forever; and disdain the wretch, that with the pretended title of FATHER OF HIS PEOPLE can unfeelingly hear of their slaughter, and composedly sleep with their blood upon his soul.

But admitting that matters were now made up, what would be the event? I answer, the ruin of the continent. And that for several reasons.

First. The powers of governing still remaining in the hands of the King, he will have a negative over the whole legislation of this continent. And as he hath shown himself such an inveterate enemy to liberty, and discovered such a thirst for arbitrary power, is he, or is he not, a proper person to say to these colonies, *You shall make no laws but what I please!?* And is there any inhabitant of America so ignorant as not to know, that according to what is called the *present Constitution,* this continent can make no laws but what the King gives leave to; and is there any man so unwise as not to see, that

---

[8] Lord North, the Prime Minister, and his government.

[9] The so-called Intolerable Acts of the 1770's, in various measures asserting British control over the colonies and in some actually punishing them.

[10] The battle of Bunker Hill killed an extraordinary number, June 1775.

(considering what has happened) he will suffer no law to be made here but such as suits his purpose? We may be as effectually enslaved by the want of laws in America, as by submitting to laws made for us in England. After matters are made up (as it is called), can there be any doubt, but the whole power of the Crown will be exerted to keep this continent as low and humble as possible? Instead of going forward we shall go backward, or be perpetually quarrelling, or ridiculously petitioning.—We are already greater than the King wishes us to be, and will he not hereafter endeavor to make us less? To bring the matter to one point, Is the power who is jealous of our prosperity, a proper power to govern us? Whoever says No, to this question, is an Independent for independency means no more than this, whether we shall make our own laws, or, whether the King, the greatest enemy this continent hath, or can have, shall tell us *"there shall be no laws but such as I like."*

But the King, you'll say, has a negative in England; the people there can make no laws without his consent. In point of right and good order, it is something very ridiculous that a youth of twenty-one (which hath often happened) shall say to several millions of people older and wiser than himself, "I forbid this or that act of yours to be law." But in this place I decline this sort of reply, tho' I will never cease to expose the absurdity of it, and only answer that England being the King's residence, and America not so, makes quite another case. The King's negative here is ten times more dangerous and fatal than it can be in England; for *there* he will scarcely refuse his consent to a bill for putting England into as strong a state of defense as possible, and in America he would never suffer such a bill to be passed.

America is only a secondary object in the system of British politics, England consults the good of *this* country no further than it answers her *own* purpose. Wherefore, her own interest leads her to suppress the growth of *ours*, in every case which doth not promote *her* advantage, or in the least interfere with it. A pretty state we should soon be in under such a second-hand government, considering what has happened! Men do not change from enemies to friends by the alteration of a name: and in order to show that reconciliation *now* is a dangerous doctrine, I affirm, *that it would be policy in the King at this time to repeal the acts, for the sake of reinstating himself in the government of the provinces;* in order that HE MAY ACCOMPLISH BY CRAFT AND SUBTLETY, IN THE LONG RUN, WHAT HE CANNOT DO BY FORCE AND VIOLENCE IN THE SHORT ONE. Reconciliation and ruin are nearly related.

Secondly.—That as even the best terms which we can expect to obtain can amount to no more than a temporary expedient, or a kind of government by guardianship, which can last no longer than till the colonies come of age, so the general face and state of things in the interim will be unsettled and unpromising: emigrants of property will not choose to come to a country whose form of government hangs but by a thread, and who is every day tottering on the brink of commotion and disturbance: and numbers of the present inhabitants would lay hold of the interval to dispose of their effects, and quit the continent.

But the most powerful of all arguments is, that nothing but independence, i.e. a continental form of government, can keep the peace of the continent and preserve it inviolate from civil wars. I dread the event of a reconciliation with Britain *now*, as it is more than probable that it will be followed by a revolt somewhere or other, the consequences of which may be far more fatal than all malice of Britain.

Thousands are already ruined by British barbarity (thousands more will probably suffer the same fate). Those men have other feelings than us who have nothing suffered. All they *now* possess is liberty; what they have before enjoyed is sacrificed to its service, and having nothing more to lose they disdain submission. Besides, the general temper of the colonies, towards a British government will be like that of a youth who is nearly out of his time; they will care very little about her: and a government which cannot preserve the peace is no government at all, and in that case we pay our money for nothing; and pray what is it that Britain can do, whose power will be wholly on paper, should a civil tumult break out the very day after reconciliation? I have heard some men say, many of whom I believe spoke without thinking, that they dreaded an independence, fearing that it would produce civil wars: it is but seldom that our first thoughts are truly correct, and that is the case here; for there is ten times more to dread from a patched up connection than from independence. I make the sufferer's case my own, and I protest, that were I driven from house and home, my property destroyed, and my circumstances ruined, that as a man, sensible of injuries, I could never relish the doctrine of reconciliation, or consider myself bound thereby.

The colonies have manifested such a spirit of good order and obedience to continental government, as is sufficient to make every reasonable person easy and happy on that head. No man can assign the least pretense for his fears, on any other grounds, than such as are truly childish and ridiculous, viz., that one colony will be striving for superiority over another.

Where there are no distinctions there can be no superiority; perfect equality affords no temptation. The republics of Europe are all (and we may say always) in peace. Holland and Switzerland are without wars, foreign or domestic: monarchical governments, it is true, are never long at rest: the Crown itself is a temptation to enterprising ruffians at *home;* and that degree of pride and insolence ever attendant on regal authority, swells into a rupture with foreign powers in instances where a republican government, by being formed on more natural principles, would negotiate the mistake.

If there is any true cause of fear regarding independence, it is because no plan is yet laid down. Men do not see their way out.—Wherefore, as an opening into that business I offer the following hints; at the same time modestly affirming, that I have no other opinion of them myself, than that they may be the means of giving rise to something better. Could the straggling thoughts of individuals be collected, they would frequently form materials for wise and able men to improve into useful matter.

LET the assemblies be annual, with a president only. The representation more equal, their business wholly domestic, and subject to the authority of a Continental Congress.

Let each colony be divided into six, eight, or ten, convenient districts, each district to send a proper number of delegates to Congress, so that each colony send at least thirty. The whole number in Congress will be at least 390. Each Congress to sit and to choose a president by the following method. When the delegates are met, let a colony be taken from the whole thirteen colonies by lot, after which let the Congress choose (by ballot) a president from out of the delegates of that province. In the next Congress, let a colony be taken by lot from twelve only, omitting that colony from which the president was taken in the former Congress, and so proceeding on till the whole thirteen shall have had their proper rotation. And in order that nothing may pass into a law but what is satisfactorily just, not less than three-fifths of the Congress to be called a majority.—He that will promote discord, under a government so equally formed as this, would have joined Lucifer in his revolt.

But as there is a peculiar delicacy from whom, or in what manner, this business must first arise, and as it seems most agreeable and consistent that it should come from some intermediate body between the governed and the governors, that is, between the Congress and the People, Let a CONTINENTAL CONFERENCE be held in the following manner, and for the following purpose.

A committee of twenty-six members of Congress, *viz.* two for each colony. Two members from each house or assembly, or provincial convention; and five representatives of the People at large, to be chosen in the capital city or town of each province, for, and in behalf of the whole province, by as many qualified voters as shall think proper to attend from all parts of the province for that purpose; or, if more convenient, the representatives may be chosen in two or three of the most populous parts thereof. In this CONFERENCE, thus assembled, will be united the two grand principles of business, *knowledge* and *power*. The members of Congress, assemblies, or conventions, by having had experience in national concerns, will be able and useful counsellors, and the whole, being impowered by the people, will have a truly legal authority.

The conferring members being met, let their business be to frame a CONTINENTAL CHARTER, or Charter of the United Colonies (answering to what is called the Magna Charta of England), fixing the number and manner of choosing members of Congress, members of Assembly, with their date of sitting; and drawing the line of business and jurisdiction between them:

always remembering, that our strength is continental, not provincial. Securing freedom and property to all men, and above all things, the free exercise of religion, according to the dictates of conscience, with such other matter as it is necessary for a charter to contain. Immediately after which the said conference to dissolve, and the bodies which shall be chosen conformable to the said charter, to be the legislators and governors of this continent for the time being: whose peace and happiness, may God preserve. AMEN.

Should any body of men be hereafter delegated for this or some similar purpose, I offer them the following extracts from that wise observer on governments, DRAGONETTI.[11] "The science," says he, "of the politician consists in fixing the true point of happiness and freedom. Those men would deserve the gratitude of ages, who should discover a mode of government that contained the greatest sum of individual happiness, with the least national expense."

But where, say some, is the king of America? I'll tell you, Friend, he reigns above, and doth not make havoc of mankind like the Royal Brute of Great Britain. Yet that we may not appear to be defective even in earthly honors, let a day be solemnly set apart for proclaiming the Charter; let it be brought forth placed on the divine law, the Word of God; let a crown be placed thereon, by which the world may know, that so far as we approve of monarchy, that in America THE LAW IS KING. For as in absolute governments the king is law, so in free countries the law *ought* to BE king, and there ought to be no other. But lest any ill use should afterwards arise, let the Crown at the conclusion of the ceremony be demolished, and scattered among the People whose right it is.

A government of our own is our natural right: and when a man seriously reflects on the precariousness of human affairs, he will become convinced, that it is infinitely wiser and safer, to form a Constitution of our own in a cool deliberate manner, while we have it in our power, than to trust such an interesting event to time and chance. If we omit it now, some Massanello[12] may hereafter arise, who, laying hold of popular disquietudes, may collect together the desperate and the discontented, and by assuming to themselves the powers of government, finally sweep away the liberties of the continent like a deluge. Should the government of America return again into the hands of Britain, the tottering situation of things will be a temptation for some desperate adventurer to try his fortune; and in such a case, what relief can Britain give? Ere she could hear the news, the fatal business might be done; and ourselves suffering like the wretched Britons under the oppression of the conqueror. Ye that oppose independence now, ye know not what ye do; ye are opening a door to eternal tyranny, by keeping vacant the seat of govern-

[11] Giacinto Dragonetti (1738–1818), a judge in Naples. Paine cites Dragonetti on "Virtues and Rewards."

[12] Paine later added a note identifying Thomas Anello as a Neapolitan revolutionary leader who became king.

ment. There are thousands and tens of thousands, who would think it glorious to expel from the continent, that barbarous and hellish power, which hath stirred up the Indians and the Negroes to destroy us; the cruelty hath a double guilt, it is dealing brutally by us, and treacherously by them.

To talk of friendship with those in whom our reason forbids us to have faith, and our affections wounded thro' a thousand pores instruct us to detest, is madness and folly. Every day wears out the little remains of kindred between us and them; and can there be any reason to hope, that as the relationship expires, the affection will increase, or that we shall agree better when we have ten times more and greater concerns to quarrel over than ever?

Ye that tell us of harmony and reconciliation, can ye restore to us the time that is past? Can ye give to prostitution its former innocence? Neither can ye reconcile Britain and America. The last cord now is broken, the people of England are presenting addresses against us. There are injuries which nature cannot forgive; she would cease to be nature if she did. As well can the lover forgive the ravisher of his mistress, as the Continent forgive the murders of Britain. The Almighty hath implanted in us these inextinguishable feelings for good and wise purposes. They are the guardians of His image in our hearts. They distinguish us from the herd of common animals. The social compact would dissolve, and justice be extirpated from the earth, or have only a casual existence were we callous to the touches of affection. The robber and the murderer would often escape unpunished, did not the injuries which our tempers sustain, provoke us into justice.

O! ye that love mankind! Ye that dare oppose not only the tyranny but the tyrant, stand forth! Every spot of the old world is over-run with oppression. Freedom hath been hunted round the globe. Asia and Africa have long expelled her.—Europe regards her like a stranger, and England hath given her warning to depart. O receive the fugitive, and prepare in time an asylum for mankind.

OF THE PRESENT ABILITY OF AMERICA WITH SOME MISCELLANEOUS REFLECTIONS

I have never met a man either in England or America, who hath not confessed his opinion, that a separation between the countries would take place, one time or other: and there is no instance, in which we have shown less judgment; than in endeavoring to describe, what we call, the ripeness or fitness of the continent for independence.

As all men allow the measure, and vary only in their opinion of the time, let us, in order to remove mistakes, take a general survey of things, and endeavor if possible to find out the very time. But I need not go far, the inquiry ceases at once, for the *time hath found us.* The general concurrence, the glorious union of all things, proves the fact.

'Tis not in numbers but in unity that our great strength lies; yet our present numbers are sufficient to repel the force of all the world. The continent has at this time the largest body of armed and disciplined men of any power under heaven: and is just arrived at that pitch of strength, in which no single colony is able to support itself, and the whole, when united, is able to do anything. Our land force is more than sufficient, and as to naval affairs, we cannot be insensible that Britain would never suffer an American man of war to be built, while the continent remained in her hands. Wherefore, we should be no forwarder a hundred years hence in that branch than we are now; but the truth is, we should be less so, because the timber of the country is every day diminishing.

Were the continent crowded with inhabitants, her sufferings under the present circumstances would be intolerable. The more seaport-towns we had, the more should we have both to defend and to lose. Our present numbers are so happily proportioned to our wants, that no man need be idle. The diminution of trade affords an army, and the necessities of any army create a new trade.

Debts we have none; and whatever we may contract on this account will serve as a glorious memento of our virtue. Can we but leave posterity with a settled form of government, an independent constitution of its own, the purchase at any price will be cheap. But to expend millions for the sake of getting a few vile acts repealed, and routing the present ministry only, is unworthy the charge, and is using posterity with the utmost cruelty; because it is leaving them the great work to do, and a debt upon their backs from which they derive no advantage. Such a thought's unworthy a man of honor, and is the true characteristic of a narrow heart and a piddling politician.

The debt we may contract doth not deserve our regard if the work be but accomplished. No nation ought to be without a debt. A national debt is a national bond; and when it bears no interest, it is in no case a grievance. Britain is oppressed with a debt of upwards of one hundred and forty millions sterling, for which she pays upwards of four millions interest. And as a compensation for her debt, she has a large navy. America is without a debt, and without a navy; yet for a twentieth part of the English national debt, could have a navy as large again. The navy of England is not worth at this time more than three millions and a half sterling.

No country on the globe is so happily situated, or so internally capable of raising a fleet as America. Tar, timber, iron and cordage are her natural produce. We need go abroad for nothing. Whereas the Dutch, who make large profits by hiring out their ships of war to the Spaniards and Portuguese, are obliged to import most of the materials they use. We ought to view the building a fleet as an article of commerce, it being the natural manufactory of this country. 'Tis the best money we can lay out. A navy when finished is worth more than it cost: and is that nice point in national policy, in which commerce and protection are united. Let us build; if we want them not, we can sell; and by that means replace our paper currency with ready gold and silver.

In point of manning a fleet, people in general run into great errors; it is not necessary that one fourth part should be sailors. The *Terrible* privateer, Captain Death,[13] stood the hottest engagement of any ship last war, yet had not twenty sailors on board, though her complement of men was upwards of two hundred. A few able and social sailors will soon instruct a sufficient number of active landsmen in the common work of a ship. Wherefore we never can be more capable of beginning on maritime matters than now, while our timber is standing, our fisheries blocked up, and our sailors and shipwrights out of employ. Men of war, of seventy and eighty guns, were built forty years ago in New England, and why not the same now? Shipbuilding is America's greatest pride, and in which she will, in time, excel the whole world. The great empires of the east are mostly inland, and consequently excluded from the possibility of rivalling her. Africa is in a state of barbarism; and no power in Europe, hath either such an extent of coast, or such an internal supply of materials. Where nature hath given the one, she hath withheld the other; to America only hath she been liberal to both. The vast empire of Russia is almost shut out from the sea; wherefore her boundless forests, her tar, iron, and cordage are only articles of commerce.

In point of safety, ought we to be without a fleet? We are not the little people now, which we were sixty years ago; at that time we might have trusted our property in the streets, or fields rather, and slept securely without locks or bolts to our doors and windows. The case is now altered, and our methods of defense ought to improve with our increase of property. A common pirate, twelve months ago, might have come up the Delaware, and laid the city of Philadelphia under contribution for what sum he pleased; and the same might have happened to other places. Nay, any daring fellow, in a brig of 14 or 16 guns, might have robbed the whole continent, and carried off half a million of money. These are circumstances which demand our attention, and point out the necessity of naval protection.

Some perhaps will say, that after we have made it up with Britain, she will protect us. Can they be so unwise as to mean, that she will keep a navy in our harbors for that purpose? Common sense will tell us, that the power which hath endeavored to subdue us, is of all others, the most improper to defend us. Conquest may be effected under the pretense of friendship; and ourselves, after a long and brave resistance, be at last cheated into slavery. And if her ships are not to be admitted into our harbors, I would ask, how is

[13] A British privateer called the *Terrible* was commanded during the early part of the Seven Years' War by a man who called himself Captain Death.

she to protect us? A navy three or four thousand miles off can be of little use, and on sudden emergencies, none at all. Wherefore if we must hereafter protect ourselves, why not do it for ourselves? Why do it for another?

The English list of ships of war, is long and formidable, but not a tenth part of them are at any one time fit for service, numbers of them are not in being; yet their names are pompously continued in the list, if only a plank be left of the ship; and not a fifth part of such as are fit for service, can be spared on any one station at one time. The East and West Indies, Mediterranean, Africa, and other parts, over which Britain extends her claim, make large demands upon her navy. From a mixture of prejudice and inattention, we have contracted a false notion respecting the navy of England, and have talked as if we should have the whole of it to encounter at once, and, for that reason, supposed that we must have one as large; which not being instantly practicable, has been made use of by a set of disguised Tories to discourage our beginning thereon. Nothing can be further from truth than this; for if America had only a twentieth part of the naval force of Britain, she would be by far an over-match for her; because, as we neither have, nor claim any foreign dominion, our whole force would be employed on our own coast, where we should, in the long run, have two to one the advantage of those who had three or four thousand miles to sail over, before they could attack us, and the same distance to return in order to refit and recruit. And although Britain, by her fleet, hath a check over our trade to Europe, we have as large a one over her trade to the West Indies, which, by laying in the neighborhood of the continent lies entirely at its mercy.

Some method might be fallen on to keep up a naval force in time of peace, if we should not judge it necessary to support a constant navy. If premiums were to be given to merchants to build and employ in their service, ships mounted with 20, 30, 40, or 50 guns (the premiums to be in proportion to the loss of bulk to the merchant), fifty or sixty of those ships, with a few guardships on constant duty, would keep up a sufficient navy, and that without burdening ourselves with the evil so loudly complained of in England, of suffering their fleet in time of peace to lie rotting in the docks. To unite the sinews of commerce and defense is sound policy; for when our strength and our riches play into each other's hand, we need fear no external enemy.

In almost every article of defense we abound. Hemp flourishes even to rankness, so that we need not want cordage. Our iron is superior to that of other countries. Our small arms equal to any in the world. Cannon we can cast at pleasure. Saltpeter and gunpowder we are every day producing. Our knowledge is hourly improving. Resolution is our inherent character, and courage has never yet forsaken us. Wherefore, what is it that we want? Why is it that we hesitate? From Britain we can expect nothing but ruin. If she is once admitted to the government of America again, this continent will not be worth living in. Jealousies will be always arising; insurrections will be constantly happening; and who will go forth to quell them? Who will venture his life to reduce his own countrymen to a foreign obedience? The difference between Pennsylvania and Connecticut, respecting some unlocated lands, shows the insignificance of a British government, and fully proves that nothing but continental authority can regulate continental matters.

Another reason why the present time is preferable to all others, is, that the fewer our numbers are, the more land there is yet unoccupied, which, instead of being lavished by the King on his worthless dependents, may be hereafter supplied, not only to the discharge of the present debt, but to the constant support of government. No nation under heaven hath such an advantage as this.

The infant state of the colonies, as it is called, so far from being against is an argument in favor of independence. We are sufficiently numerous, and were we more so we might be less united. 'Tis a matter worthy of observation, that the more a country is peopled, the smaller their armies are. In military numbers, the ancients far exceeded the moderns: and the reason is evident, for trade being the consequence of population, men became too much absorbed thereby to attend to anything else. Commerce diminishes the spirit both of patriotism and military defense. And history sufficiently informs us, that the bravest achievements were always accomplished in the nonage of a nation. With the increase of commerce England hath lost its spirit. The city of London, notwithstanding its numbers, submits to continued insults with the patience of a coward. The more men have to lose, the less willing are they to venture. The rich are in general slaves to fear, and submit to courtly power with the trembling duplicity of a spaniel.

Youth is the seed-time of good habits as well in nations as in individuals. It might be difficult, if not impossible, to form the continent into one government half a century hence. The vast variety of interests, occasioned by an increase of trade and population, would create confusion. Colony would be against colony. Each being able would scorn each other's assistance: and while the proud and foolish gloried in their little distinctions, the wise would lament that the union had not been formed before. Wherefore the present time is the true time for establishing it. The intimacy which is contracted in infancy, and the friendship which is formed in misfortune, are of all others the most lasting and unalterable. Our present union is marked with both these characters: we are young, and we have been distressed; but our concord hath withstood our troubles, and fixes a memorable era for posterity to glory in.

The present time likewise, is that peculiar time which never happens to a nation but once, viz. the time of forming itself into a government. Most nations have let slip the opportunity, and by that means have been compelled to receive laws from their conquerors, instead of making laws for themselves. First, they had a king, and then a form of government; whereas the articles or charter of government should be formed first, and men dele-gated to execute them afterwards: but from the errors of other nations let us learn wisdom, and lay hold of the present opportunity—*to begin government at the right end.*

When William the Conqueror subdued England, he gave them law at the point of the sword; and, until we consent that the seat of government in America be legally and authoritatively occupied, we shall be in danger of having it filled by some fortunate ruffian, who may treat us in the same manner, and then, where will be our freedom? where our property?

As to religion, I hold it to be the indispensable duty of government to protect all conscientious professors thereof, and I know of no other business which government has to do therewith. Let a man throw aside that narrow-ness of soul, that selfishness of principle, which the niggards of all professions are so unwilling to part with, and he will be at once delivered of his fears on that head. Suspicion is the companion of mean souls, and the bane of all good society. For myself, I fully and conscientiously believe, that it is the will of the Almighty that there should be a diversity of religious opinions among us. It affords a larger field for our Christian kindness: were we all of one way of thinking, our religious dispositions would want matter for probation; and on this liberal principle I look on the various denominations among us, to be like children of the same family, differing only in what is called their Chris-tian names.

In pages 566 and 567 I threw out a few thoughts on the propriety of a continental charter (for I only presume to offer hints, not plans) and in this place, I take the liberty of re-mentioning the subject, by observing, that a charter is to be understood as a bond of solemn obligation, which the whole enters into, to support the right of every separate part, whether of religion, professional freedom, or property. A right reckoning makes long friends.

I have heretofore likewise mentioned the necessity of a large and equal representation; and there is no political matter which more deserves our attention. A small number of electors, or a small number of representatives, are equally dangerous. But if the number of representatives be not only small, but unequal, the danger is increased. As an instance of this, I mention the following; when the petition of the associates was before the House of Assembly of Pennsylvania, twenty-eight members only were present; all the Bucks County members, being eight, voted against it, and had seven of the Chester members done the same, this whole province had been governed by two counties only; and this danger it is always exposed to. The unwarrant-able stretch likewise, which the House made in their last sitting, to gain an undue authority over the delegates of that province, ought to warn the people at large, how they trust power out of their hands. A set of instructions for their delegates were put together, which in point of sense and business would have dishonored a school-boy, and after being approved by a few, a very few, without doors, were carried into the House, and there passed in behalf of the whole colony; whereas, did the whole colony know with what ill-will that house had entered on some necessary public measures, they would not hesitate a moment to think them unworthy of such a trust.

Immediate necessity makes many things convenient, which if continued would grow into oppressions. Expedience and right are different things. When the calamities of America required a consultation, there was no method so ready, or at that time so proper, as to appoint persons from the several houses of assembly for that purpose; and the wisdom with which they have proceeded hath preserved this continent from ruin. But as it is more than probable that we shall never be without a CONGRESS, every well wisher to good order must own that the mode for choosing members of that body, deserves consideration. And I put it as a question to those who make a study of mankind, whether representation and election is not too great a power for one and the same body of men to possess? When we are planning for posterity, we ought to remember that virtue is not hereditary.

It is from our enemies that we often gain excellent maxims, and are frequently surprised into reason by their mistakes. Mr. Cornwall (one of the Lords of the Treasury) treated the petition of the New-York Assembly with contempt, because *that* house, he said, consisted but of twenty-six members, which trifling number, he argued, could not with decency be put for the whole. We thank him for his involuntary honesty.°

TO CONCLUDE, however strange it may appear to some, or however unwilling they may be to think so, matters not, but many strong and striking reasons may be given to show, that nothing can settle our affairs so expeditiously as an open and determined DECLARATION FOR INDEPENDENCE. Some of which are,

First.—It is the custom of nations, when any two are at war, for some other powers, not engaged in the quarrel, to step in as mediators, and bring about the preliminaries of a peace: but while America calls herself the subject of Great Britain, no power, however well disposed she may be, can offer her mediation. Wherefore, in our present state we may quarrel on forever.

Secondly.—It is unreasonable to suppose, that France or Spain will give us any kind of assistance, if we mean only to make use of that assistance for the purpose of repairing the breach, and strengthening the connection between Britain and America; because, those powers would be sufferers by the consequences.

Thirdly.—While we profess ourselves the subjects of Britain, we must, in the eyes of foreign nations, be considered as rebels. The precedent is somewhat dangerous to *their peace*, for men to be in arms under the name of subjects: we, on the spot, can solve the paradox; but to unite resistance and subjection, requires an idea much too refined for common understanding.

Fourthly.—Were a manifesto to be published, and despatched to foreign

---

° Those who would fully understand of what great consequence a large and equal representation is to a State, should read [James] Burgh's Political Disquisitions.

courts, setting forth the miseries we have endured, and the peaceful methods which we have ineffectually used for redress; declaring at the same time, that not being able any longer to live happily or safely under the cruel disposition of the British court, we have been driven to the necessity of breaking off all connections with her; at the same time, assuring all such courts of our peaceable disposition towards them, and of our desire of entering into trade with them; such a memorial would produce more good effects to this continent, than if a ship were freighted with petitions to Britain.[14]

Under our present denomination of British subjects, we can neither be received nor heard abroad: the custom of all courts is against us, and will be so, until by an independence we take rank with other nations.

These proceedings may at first seem strange and difficult, but like all other steps which we have already passed over, will in a little time become familiar and agreeable: and until an Independence is declared, the continent will feel itself like a man who continues putting off some unpleasant business from day to day, yet knows it must be done, hates to set about it, wishes it over, and is continually haunted with the thoughts of its necessity.

[14] Compare the Declaration of Independence, below, p. 615.

The Age of Reason[1]

TO MY FELLOW CITIZENS OF THE UNITED STATES OF AMERICA

I put the following work under your protection. It contains my opinion upon Religion. You will do me the justice to remember, that I have always strenuously supported the right of every man to his own opinion, however different that opinion might be to mine. He who denies to another this right, makes a slave of himself to his present opinion, because he precludes himself the right of changing it.

The most formidable weapon against errors of every kind is Reason. I have never used any other, and I trust I never shall.

Your affectionate friend and fellow citizen,

THOMAS PAINE.

Luxembourg, 8th Pluviose,

Second Year of the French Republic, one and indivisible.

January 27, O.S. 1794

[1] Paris, 1795.

THE AGE OF REASON, BEING AN
INVESTIGATION OF TRUE AND OF FABULOUS
THEOLOGY
[From PART ONE]

It has been my intention, for several years past, to publish my thoughts upon Religion. I am well aware of the difficulties that attend the subject; and, from that consideration, had reserved it to a more advanced period of life. I intended it to be the last offering I should make to my fellow citizens of all nations; and that at a time, when the purity of the motive that induced me to it, could not admit of a question, even by those who might disapprove the work.

The circumstance that has now taken place in France, of the total abolition of the whole national order of priesthood, and of everything appertaining to compulsive systems of religion, and compulsive articles of faith, has not only precipitated my intention, but rendered a work of this kind exceedingly necessary; lest, in the general wreck of superstition, of false systems of government, and false theology, we lose sight of morality, of humanity, and of the theology that is true.

As several of my colleagues, and others of my fellow citizens of France, have given me the example of making their voluntary and individual profession of faith, I also will make mine; and I do this with all that sincerity and frankness with which the mind of man communicates with itself.

I believe in one God, and no more; and I hope for happiness beyond this life.

I believe the equality of man, and I believe that religious duties consist in doing justice, loving mercy, and endeavoring to make our fellow creatures happy.

But lest it should be supposed that I believe many other things in addition to these, I shall, in the progress of this work, declare the things I do not believe, and my reasons for not believing them.

I do not believe in the creed professed by the Jewish church, by the Roman church, by the Greek church, by the Turkish church, by the Protestant church, nor by any church that I know of. My own mind is my own church.

All national institutions of churches, whether Jewish, Christian, or Turkish, appear to me no other than human inventions set up to terrify and enslave mankind, and monopolize power and profit.

I do not mean by this declaration to condemn those who believe otherwise. They have the same right to their belief as I have to mine. But it is necessary to the happiness of man, that he be mentally faithful to himself.

Infidelity does not consist in believing, or in disbelieving: it consists in professing to believe what he does not believe.[2]

It is impossible to calculate the moral mischief, if I may so express it, that mental lying has produced in society. When a man has so far corrupted and prostituted the chastity of his mind, as to subscribe his professional belief to things he does not believe, he has prepared himself for the commission of every other crime. He takes up the trade of a priest for the sake of gain, and in order to *qualify* himself for that trade, he begins with a perjury. Can we conceive anything more destructive to morality than this?

Soon after I had published the pamphlet, COMMON SENSE, in America, I saw the exceeding probability that a revolution in the system of government, would be followed by a revolution in the system of religion. The adulterous connection of church and state, wherever it had taken place, whether Jewish, Christian, or Turkish, had so effectually prohibited, by pains and penalties, every discussion upon established creeds, and upon first principles of religion, that until the system of government should be changed, those subjects could not be brought fairly and openly before the world: but that whenever this should be done, a revolution in the system of religion would follow. Human inventions and priest-craft would be detected; and man would return to the pure, unmixed, and unadulterated belief of one God, and no more.

Every national church or religion has established itself by pretending some special mission from God communicated to certain individuals. The Jews have their Moses; the Christians their Jesus Christ, their apostles and saints; and the Turks their Mahomet; as if the way to God was not open to every man alike.

Each of those churches show certain books which they call *revelation*, or the word of God. The Jews say that their word of God was given by God to Moses face to face; the Christians say, that their word of God came by divine inspiration; and the Turks say, that their word of God (the Koran) was brought by an angel from heaven. Each of those churches accuses the other of unbelief; and, for my own part, I disbelieve them all.

As it is necessary to affix right ideas to words, I will, before I proceed further into the subject, offer some observations on the word *revelation*. Revelation, when applied to religion, means something communicated *immediately* from God to man.

No one will deny or dispute the power of the Almighty to make such a communication if He pleases. But admitting, for the sake of a case, that something has been revealed to a certain person, and not revealed to any other person, it is revelation to that person only. When he tells it to a second

[2] In this paragraph and the next, Paine makes an extreme statement of a central Protestant belief in the thought of Thomas Hooker, Cot- ton Mather, R. W. Emerson, Thoreau, Hawthorne, Melville, Mark Twain.

person, a second to a third, a third to a fourth, and so on, it ceases to be a revelation to all those persons. It is revelation to the first person only, and *hearsay* to every other; and consequently, they are not obliged to believe it.

It is a contradiction in terms and ideas to call anything a revelation that comes to us at second hand, either verbally or in writing. Revelation is necessarily limited to the first communication. After this, it is only an account of something which that person says was a revelation made to him; and though he may find himself obliged to believe it, it cannot be incumbent upon me to believe it in the same manner, for it was not a revelation made to *me*, and I have only his word for it that it was made to *him*.

When Moses told the children of Israel that he received the two tables of the commandments from the hand of God, they were not obliged to believe him, because they had no other authority for it than his telling them so; and I have no other authority for it than some historian telling me so. The commandments carry no internal evidence of divinity with them. They contain some good moral precepts, such as any man qualified to be a law-giver or a legislator could produce himself, without having recourse to supernatural intervention.°

When I am told that the Koran was written in heaven, and brought to Mahomet by an angel, the account comes to near the same kind of hearsay evidence, and second hand authority, as the former. I did not see the angel myself, and therefore I have a right not to believe it.

When also I am told that a woman, called the Virgin Mary, said, or gave out, that she was with child without any cohabitation with a man, and that her betrothed husband, Joseph, said, that an angel told him so, I have a right to believe them or not: such a circumstance required a much stronger evidence than their bare word for it: but we have not even this; for neither Joseph nor Mary wrote any such matter themselves. It is only reported by others that *they said so*. It is hearsay upon hearsay, and I do not choose to rest my belief upon such evidence.

It is, however, not difficult to account for the credit that was given to the story of Jesus Christ being the Son of God. He was born at a time when the heathen mythology had still some fashion and repute in the world, and that mythology had prepared the people for the belief of such a story. Almost all the extraordinary men that lived under the heathen mythology were reputed to be the sons of some of their gods. It was not a new thing at that time to believe a man to have been celestially begotten: the intercourse of gods with women was then a matter of familiar opinion. Their Jupiter, according to their accounts, had cohabited with hundreds: the story, therefore, had nothing in it either new, wonderful, or obscene: it was comfortable to the opinions that then prevailed among the people called Gentiles, or mytholo-

---

° This is, however, necessary to except the declaration which says, that God *visits the* *sins of the fathers upon the children*. It is contrary to every principle of moral justice.

gists, and it was those people only that believed it. The Jews who had kept strictly to the belief of one God, and no more, and who had always rejected the heathen mythology, never credited the story.

It is curious to observe how the theory of what is called the Christian church, sprung out of the tail of the heathen mythology. A direct incorporation took place in the first instance, by making the reputed founder to be celestially begotten. The trinity of gods that then followed was no other than a reduction of the former plurality, which was about twenty or thirty thousand. The statue of Mary succeeded the statue of Diana of Ephesus. The deification of heroes, changed into the canonization of saints. The mythologists had gods for everything; the Christian mythologists had saints for everything. The church became as crowded with the one, as the pantheon had been with the other; and Rome was the place of both. The Christian theory is little else than the idolatry of the ancient mythologists, accommodated to the purposes of power and revenue; and it yet remains to reason and philosophy to abolish the amphibious fraud.

Nothing that is here said can apply, even with the most distant disrespect, to the *real* character of Jesus Christ. He was a virtuous and an amiable man. The morality that he preached and practiced was of the most benevolent kind; and though similar systems of morality had been preached by Confucius, and by some of the Greek philosophers, many years before; by the Quakers since; and by many good men in all ages; it has not been exceeded by any.

Jesus Christ wrote no account of himself, of his birth, parentage, or anything else. Not a line of what is called the New Testament is of his writing. The history of him is altogether the work of other people; and as to the account given of his resurrection and ascension, it was the necessary counterpart to the story of his birth. His historians, having brought him into the world in a supernatural manner, were obliged to take him out again in the same manner, or the first part of the story must have fallen to the ground.

The wretched contrivance with which this latter part is told, exceeds everything that went before it. The first part, that of the miraculous conception, was not a thing that admitted of publicity; and therefore the tellers of this part of the story, had this advantage, that though they might not be credited, they could not be detected. They could not be expected to prove it, because it was not one of those things that admitted of proof, and it was impossible that the person of whom it was told could prove it himself.

But the resurrection of a dead person from the grave, and his ascension through the air, is a thing very different as to the evidence it admits of, to the invisible conception of a child in the womb. The resurrection and ascension, supposing them to have taken place, admitted of public and ocular demonstration, like that of the ascension of a balloon, or the sun at noon day, to all Jerusalem at least. A thing which everybody is required to believe, requires that the proof and evidence of it should be equal to all, and universal; and as the public visibility of this last related act was the only evidence that could give sanction to the former part, the whole of it falls to the ground, because that evidence never was given. Instead of this, a small number of persons, not more than eight or nine, are introduced as proxies for the whole world, to say, they *saw it*, and all the rest of the world are called upon to believe it. But it appears that Thomas did not believe the resurrection; and, as they say, would not believe, without having ocular and manual demonstration himself. *So neither will I;* and the reason is equally as good for me and for every other person, as for Thomas.[3]

It is in vain to attempt to palliate or disguise this matter. The story, so far as relates to the supernatural part, has every mark of fraud and imposition stamped upon the face of it. Who were the authors of it is as impossible for us now to know, as it is for us to be assured, that the books in which the account is related, were written by the persons whose names they bear. The best surviving evidence we now have respecting this affair is the Jews. They are regularly descended from the people who lived in the times this resurrection and ascension is said to have happened, and they say, *it is not true.* It has long appeared to me a strange inconsistency to cite the Jews as a proof of the truth of the story. It is just the same as if a man were to say, I will prove the truth of what I have told you, by producing the people who say it is false.

That such a person as Jesus Christ existed, and that he was crucified, which was the mode of execution at that day, are historical relations strictly within the limits of probability. He preached most excellent morality, and the equality of man; but he preached also against the corruptions and avarice of the Jewish priests; and this brought upon him the hatred and vengeance of the whole order of priest-hood. The accusation which those priests brought against him, was that of sedition and conspiracy against the Roman government, to which the Jews were then subject and tributary; and it is not improbable that the Roman government might have some secret apprehension of the effects of his doctrine as well as the Jewish priests; neither is it improbable that Jesus Christ had in contemplation the delivery of the Jewish nation from the bondage of the Romans. Between the two, however, this virtuous reformer and revolutionist lost his life.

It is upon this plain narrative of facts, together with another case I am going to mention, that the Christian mythologists, calling themselves the Christian church, have erected their fable, which for absurdity and extravagance is not exceeded by anything that is to be found in the mythology of the ancients.

The ancient mythologists tell that the race of Giants made war against Jupiter, and that one of them threw an hundred rocks against him at one throw; that Jupiter defeated him with thunder, and confined him afterwards

[3] See John 20:24-29.

under Mount Etna; and that every time the Giant turns himself, Mount Etna belches fire. It is here easy to see that the cirumstance of the mountain, that of its being a volcano, suggested the idea of the fable; and that the fable is made to fit and wind itself up with that circumstance.

The Christian mythologists tell that their Satan made war against the Almighty, who defeated him, and confined him afterwards, not under a mountain, but in a pit. It is here easy to see that the first fable suggested the idea of the second; for the fable of Jupiter and the Giants was told many hundred years before that of Satan.

Thus far the ancient and the Christian mythologists differ very little from each other. But the latter have contrived to carry the matter much farther. They have contrived to connect the fabulous part of the story of Jesus Christ, with the fable orginating from Mount Etna: and in order to make all the parts of the story tie together, they have taken to their aid the traditions of the Jews; for the Christian mythology is made up partly from the ancient mythology, and partly from the Jewish traditions.

The Christian mythologists, after having confined Satan in a pit, were obliged to let him out again, to bring on the sequel of the fable. He is then introduced into the garden of Eden in the shape of a snake, or a serpent, and in that shape he enters into familiar conversation with Eve, who is no ways surprised to hear a snake talk; and the issue of this tête-à-tête is, that he persuades her to eat an apple, and the eating of that apple, damns all mankind.

After giving Satan this triumph over the whole creation, one would have supposed that the church mythologists would have been kind enough to send him back again to the pit; or, if they had not done this, that they would have put a mountain upon him[4] (for they say that their faith can remove a mountain) or have put him *under* a mountain, as the former mythologists had done, to prevent his getting again among the women, and doing more mischief. But instead of this, they leave him at large without even obliging him to give his parole. The secret of which is, that they could not do without him; and after being at the trouble of making him, they bribed him to stay. They promised him ALL the Jews, ALL the Turks by anticipation, nine-tenths of the world beside, and Mahomet into the bargain. After this, who can doubt the bountifulness of the Christian mythology?

Having thus made an insurrection and a battle in heaven, in which none of the combatants could be either killed or wounded—put Satan into the pit—let him out again—given him a triumph over the whole creation—damned all mankind by the eating of an apple, these Christian mythologists bring the two ends of their fable together. They represent this virtuous and amiable man, Jesus Christ, to be at once both God and man, and also the Son

[4] In this paragraph the comical tone and the argument are striking, like those of Mark Twain a century later. See "Little Bessie would Assist Providence."

of God, celestially begotten on purpose to be sacrificed, because, they say, that Eve in her longing had eaten an apple.

Putting aside everything that might excite laughter by its absurdity, or detestation by its profaneness, and confining ourselves merely to an examination of the parts, it is impossible to conceive a story more derogatory to the Almighty, more inconsistent with His wisdom, more contradictory to His power, than this story is.

In order to make for it a foundation to rise upon, the inventors were under the necessity of giving to the being, whom they call Satan, a power equally as great, if not greater, than they attribute to the Almighty. They have not only given him the power of liberating himself from the pit, after what they call his fall, but they have made that power increase afterwards to infinity. Before this fall, they represent him only as an angel of limited existence, as they represent the rest. After his fall, he becomes, by their account, omnipresent. He exists everywhere, and at the same time. He occupies the whole immensity of space.

Not content with this deification of Satan, they represent him as defeating by stratagem, in the shape of an animal of the creation, all the power and wisdom of the Almighty. They represent him as having compelled the Almighty to the *direct necessity* either of surrendering the whole of the creation to the government and sovereignty of this Satan, or of capitulating for its redemption by coming down upon earth, and exhibiting Himself upon a cross in the shape of a man.

Had the inventors of this story told it the contrary way, that is, had they represented the Almighty as compelling Satan to exhibit *himself* on a cross in the shape of a snake, as a punishment for his new transgression, the story would have been less absurd, less contradictory. But instead of this, they make the transgressor triumph, and the Almighty fall.

That many good men have believed this strange fable and lived very good lives under that belief (for credulity is not a crime) is what I have no doubt of. In the first place, they were educated to believe it, and they would have believed anything else in the same manner. There are also many who have been so enthusiastically enraptured by what they conceived to be the infinite love of God to man, in making a sacrifice of Himself, that the vehemence of the idea has forbidden and deterred them from examining into the absurdity and profaneness of the story. The more unnatural anything is, the more is it capable of becoming the object of dismal admiration.

But if objects for gratitude and admiration are our desire, do they not present themselves every hour to our eyes? Do we not see a fair creation prepared to receive us the instant we were born—a world furnished to our hands that cost us nothing? Is it we that light up the sun; that pour down the rain; and fill the earth with abundance? Whether we sleep or wake, the vast machinery of the universe still goes on.[5] Are these things, and the blessings they indicate in future, nothing to us? Can our gross feelings be excited by no other subjects than tragedy and suicide? Or is the gloomy pride of man become so intolerable, that nothing can flatter it but a sacrifice of the Creator?

I know that this bold investigation will alarm many, but it would be paying too great a compliment to their credulity to forbear it upon that account. The times and the subject demand it to be done. The suspicion that the theory of what is called the Christian church is fabulous, is becoming very extensive in all countries: and it will be consolation to men staggering under that suspicion, and doubting what to believe and what to disbelieve, to see the subject freely investigated. I therefore pass on to an examination of the books called the Old and the New Testament.

These books, beginning with Genesis and ending with Revelations (which by the bye is a book of riddles that requires a Revelation to explain it) are, we are told, the word of God. It is therefore proper for us to know who told us so, that we may know what credit to give to the report. The answer to this question is, that nobody can tell, except that we tell one another so. The case, however, historically appears to be as follows:

When the church mythologists established their system, they collected all the writings they could find, and managed them as they pleased. It is a matter altogether of uncertainty to us whether such of the writings as now appear, under the name of the Old and the New Testament, are in the same state in which those collectors say they found them; or whether they added, altered, abridged, or dressed them up.

Be this as it may, they decided by *vote* which of the books, out of the collection they had made, should be the WORD OF GOD and which should not. They rejected several: they voted others to be doubtful, such as the books called the Apocraphy; and those books which had a majority of votes, were voted to be the word of God. Had they voted otherwise, all the people, since calling themselves Christians, had believed otherwise; for the belief of the one comes from the vote of the other. Who the people were that did all this, we know nothing of; they called themselves by the general name of the church; and this is all we know of the matter.

As we have no other external evidence or authority for believing those books to be the word of God than what I have mentioned, which is no evidence or authority at all, I come, in the next place, to examine the internal evidence contained in the books themselves.

[5] The emphasis on divine creation is characteristic of Deists and especially of Jeffersonian writers in this country. So, too, is the emphasis on the *"machinery"* of the Universe." Of course the question "Is it we that light up the sun" echoes the Book of Job—and the preface to Edward Taylor's *God's Determinations*, above, p. 291.

In the former part of this essay, I have spoken of revelation. I now proceed further with that subject, for the purpose of applying it to the books in question.

Revelation is a communication of something, which the person, to whom that thing is revealed, did not know before. For if I have done a thing, or seen it done, it needs no revelation to tell me I have done it, or seen it, nor to enable me to tell it, or to write it.

Revelation, therefore, cannot be applied to anything done upon earth of which man is himself the actor or the witness; and consequently all the historical and anecdotal part of the Bible, which is almost the whole of it, is not within the meaning and compass of the word revelation, and therefore is not the word of God.

When Samson ran off with the gate-posts of Gaza, if he ever did so (and whether he did or not is nothing to us) or when he visited his Delilah, or caught his foxes,[6] or did anything else, what has revelation to do with these things? If they were facts, he could tell them himself; or his secretary, if he kept one, could write them, if they were worth either telling or writing; and if they were fictions, revelation could not make them true; and whether true or not, we are neither the better nor the wiser for knowing them.—When we contemplate the immensity of that Being, who directs and governs the incomprehensible WHOLE, of which the utmost ken of human sight can discover but a part, we ought to feel shame at calling such paltry stories the word of God.

As to the account of the creation, with which the book of Genesis opens, it has all the appearance of being a tradition which the Israelites had among them before they came into Egypt; and after their departure from that country they put it at the head of their history, without telling, as it is most probable they did not know, how they came by it. The manner in which the account opens, shows it to be traditionary. It begins abruptly. It is nobody that speaks. It is nobody that hears. It is addressed to nobody. It has neither first, second, nor third person. It has every criterion of being a tradition. It has no voucher. Moses does not take it upon himself by introducing it with the formality that he uses on other occasions, such as that of saying, *"The Lord spake unto Moses, saying."*

Why it has been called the Mosaic account of the creation, I am at a loss to conceive. Moses, I believe, was too good a judge of such subjects to put his name to that account. He had been educated among the Egyptians, who were a people as well skilled in science, and particularly in astronomy, as any people of their day; and the silence and caution that Moses observes, in not authenticating the account, is a good negative evidence that he neither told it, nor believed it.—The case is, that every nation of people has been world-makers, and the Israelites had as much right to set up the trade of world-

[6] See the Book of Judges.

making as any of the rest; and as Moses was not an Israelite, he might not choose to contradict the tradition. The account, however, is harmless; and this is more than can be said for many other parts of the Bible.

When we read the obscene stories, the voluptuous debaucheries, the cruel and torturous executions, the unrelenting vindictiveness, with which more than half the Bible is filled, it would be more consistent that we called it the word of a demon, than the word of God. It is a history of wickedness, that has served to corrupt and brutalize mankind; and, for my own part, I sincerely detest it,[7] as I detest everything that is cruel.

We scarcely meet with anything, a few phrases excepted, but what deserves either our abhorrence, or our contempt, till we come to the miscellaneous parts of the Bible. In the anonymous publication, the Psalms and the book of Job, more particularly in the latter, we find a great deal of elevated sentiment reverentially expressed of the power and benignity of the Almighty; but they stand on no higher rank than many other compositions on similar subjects, as well before that time as since.

The proverbs, which are said to be Solomon's, though most probably a collection (because they discover a knowledge of life, which his situation excluded him from knowing), are an instructive table of ethics. They are inferior in keenness to the proverbs of the Spaniards, and not more wise and economical than those of the American Franklin.

All the remaining parts of the Bible, generally known by the name of the prophets, are the works of the Jewish poets and itinerant preachers, who mixed poetry, anecdote, and devotion together; and those works still retain the air and style of poetry, though in translation.

. . .

---

[7] This statement in particular is not calculated to please the great majority of potential readers in the United States. Doubting the Bible might be comprehensible. Detesting it was probably not.

THOMAS JEFFERSON

(1743–1826)

The presidential section of this anthology of literature may seem strange to American students in the last quarter of the twentieth century, for even though several recent presidents have published books that presumably they themselves wrote, we know that they depend heavily on speech writers and that no modern president has won national attention largely through his skill as a writer. John Adams, Thomas Jefferson, and James Madison were all among the intellectual as well as the literary leaders of their day, and the political essay was one of the major means they used in addressing the national public. Even if none of them had been elected to the presidency, their political writings would be among the most important American literary documents of their time.

Jefferson, of course, was unrivaled except by Franklin in the extraordinary versatility of his accomplishments. His curiosity and ingenuity extended all the way from architecture and mechanical invention to educational, agricultural, and political experiment and to musical composition and performance. Trained for the law in Williamsburg, he quickly became a young leader in the legislature, where he eventually achieved one of the three acts for which, at the end of a long, distinguished life, he expressly wished to be remembered—the bill to disestablish the Anglican Church in Virginia and to allow complete relig-

The standard edition is *The Papers of Thomas Jefferson,* ed. Julian P. Boyd and others, 1950. For later works not yet completed in this edition, see *The Works of Thomas Jefferson,* 12 vols., ed. Paul L. Ford, 1904. Ford also edited *Thomas Jefferson's Correspondence,* 1916. Later editions of the correspondence include *Correspondence Between John Adams and Thomas Jefferson,* ed. Paul Wilstach, 1925; *The Adams-Jefferson Letters,* ed., L. J. Cappon, 1959.

The most extensive and detailed biography is Dumas Malone, *Jefferson and His Time,* 5 vols., 1948–1974. Valuable studies include Adrienne Koch, *The Philosophy of Thomas Jefferson,* 1943; C. A. Bowers, *Jefferson and Hamilton,* 1925, and *Jeffer-son in Power,* 1936; Merrill D. Peterson, *The Jefferson Image on the American Mind,* 1960, and *Thomas Jefferson and the New Nation,* 1970. See also Henry Adams, *History of the United States During the Administration of Thomas Jefferson,* 4 vols., 1889–1891. Single-volume editions are *The Complete Jefferson,* ed. Saul K. Padover, 1943; *Life and Selected Writings of Alexander Hamilton and Thomas Jefferson,* ed. A. Koch and W. Peden, 1946, and *Notes on the State of Virginia,* ed. W. Peden, 1955. Edwin Gittleman has published a valuable literary study of the Declaration of Independence, "Jefferson's 'Slave Narrative': The Declaration of Independence as a Literary Text," *Early American Literature,* 8 (1974): 239–256.

Portrait of Thomas Jefferson, by Charles Willson Peale (1741–1827). *(Library of Congress.)*

ious liberty in the Commonwealth. The second of those three accomplishments was his authorship of the Declaration of Independence, and the third was his founding of the University of Virginia in Charlottesville near his home. Among the achievements he did *not* specify were not only his service as Governor of Virginia and President of the United States but also his complete design of two great buildings that remain among the most beautiful architectural works in the United States: his home at Monticello and the University of Virginia. He was Secretary of State in Washington's first administration. He was founder and leader of the Republican Party. He presided, in an unprecedented and for him an inconsistent extension of presidential authority, over the purchase of the Louisiana Territory. He designed a newly efficient moldboard for wooden plows, and a portable music stand for string quartets, a pair of swinging doors that open simultaneously by pressure on either one, a weather vane that could be read from a safe position under cover, and a writing device that automatically made two copies at once.

Besides the Declaration of Independence Jefferson's most important literary works were *Summary of the Rights of British America, Notes on Virginia,* his two presidential inaugural addresses, his autobiography, and a variety of his letters. Here we reprint the section of his autobiography that describes the composition of the Declaration of Independence, and several chapters from his *Notes on Virginia.*

Jefferson is as important to our literature for what he represented, what he believed, as for any of his individual literary works. For it was through his version of Deistic, agrarian, practical republicanism that many of the central, unquestioned assumptions underlying American literary culture became acceptable outside the range of direct Puritan influence. The idea of workmanship, for example, and of the Creator as a supreme model to be emulated in the building of a new republic on a continental scale; the preference for agrarian over urban nurture as the best source of strength for the Republic; the conviction that "a ploughman," because he had "not been led astray by artificial rules," would decide a moral issue with at least as much wisdom as "a professor"; the conviction that no error was as dangerous as the suppression of free speech, so long as "truth is left free to combat" error; the convicton that "that government is best which governs least"; the declaration that all men are created equal—all these, though sometimes contradicted in Jefferson's writing and practice, came into general acceptance at least partly through the writings of Jefferson and his associates. (The best book on that subject is Daniel Boorstin, *The Lost World of Thomas Jefferson.*)

Jefferson, though unquestionably a great figure, has been a puzzling, sometimes almost enigmatic and often controversial one ever since his active days. As Merrill Peterson has shown, "the Jefferson image on the American mind" has changed drastically during such crises as the battle over slavery and "states' rights," and the modern battle over growing federal power. Jefferson has been adopted as a hero by people whose influence he would almost surely have opposed, and those who share some of his populist sympathies have in some ways openly favored giving the federal government extraordinary powers (as Jefferson himself now and then did while President) to achieve their goals.

Perhaps the most puzzling riddle of all is Jefferson's relation to slavery. Not only as the author of the declaration that "all men are created equal" but also as the man who in the same document blamed the British government for foisting slavery and the slave trade on the American colonies, Jefferson seems even more incongruous than other Revolutionary leaders as the owner of a large number of slaves—as Benjamin Banneker emphatically reminded him (see below, p. 689). He did detest the system, but his capacity to live with the incongruity remains a challenge to the historical imagination and to the historical judgment.

Notes on the State of Virginia.[1]

[These notes were composed during the American Revolution, in answer to queries by a French correspondent.]

QUERY IV.
A NOTICE OF ITS MOUNTAINS?

For the particular geography of our mountains I must refer to Fry and Jefferson's map of Virginia; and to Evan's analysis of this map of America, for a more philosophical view of them than is to be found in any other work. It is worthy of notice, that our mountains are not solitary and scattered confusedly over the face of the country; but that they commence at about one hundred and fifty miles from the sea-coast, are disposed in ridges, one behind another, running nearly parallel with the sea-coast, though rather approaching it as they advance north-eastwardly. To the south-west, as the

---

[1] London, 1787. A small edition had been printed privately in 1785.

tract of country between the sea-coast and the Mississippi becomes narrower, the mountains converge into a single ridge, which, as it approaches the Gulf of Mexico, subsides into plain country, and gives rise to some of the waters of that gulf, and particularly to a river called the Apalachicola, probably from the Apalachies, an Indian nation formerly residing on it. Hence the mountains giving rise to that river, and seen from its various parts, were called the Apalachian mountains, being in fact the end or termination only of the great ridges passing through the continent. European geographers, however, extended the name northwardly as far as the mountains extended; some giving it, after their separation into different ridges, to the Blue Ridge, others to the North Mountain, others to the Alleghany, others to the Laurel Ridge, as may be seen by their different maps. But the fact I believe is, that none of these ridges were ever known by that name to the inhabitants, either native or emigrant, but as they saw them so called in European maps. In the same direction, generally, are the veins of limestone, coal, and other minerals hitherto discovered; and so range the falls of our great rivers. But the courses of the great rivers are at right angles with these. James and Potomac penetrate through all the ridges of mountains eastward of the Alleghany; that is, broken by no water course. It is in fact the spine of the country between the Atlantic on one side, and the Mississippi and St. Lawrence on the other. The passage of the Potomac through the Blue Ridge is, perhaps, one of the most stupendous scenes in nature. You stand on a very high point of land. On your right comes up the Shenandoah, having ranged along the foot of the mountain an hundred miles to seek a vent. On your left approaches the Potomac, in quest of a passage also. In the moment of their junction, they rush together against the mountain, rend it asunder, and pass off to the sea. The first glance of this scene hurries our senses into the opinion, that this earth has been created in time, that the mountains were formed first, that the rivers began to flow afterwards, that in this place, particularly, they have been dammed up by the Blue Ridge of mountains, and have formed an ocean which filled the whole valley; that continuing to rise they have at length broken over at this spot, and have torn the mountain down from its summit to its base. The piles of rock on each hand, but particularly on the Shenandoah, the evident marks of their disrupture and avulsion from their beds by the most powerful agents of nature, corroborate the impression. But the distant finishing which nature has given to the picture, is of a very different character. It is a true contrast to the foreground. It is as placid and delightful as that is wild and tremendous. For the mountain being cloven asunder, she presents to your eye, through the cleft, a small catch of smooth blue horizon, at an infinite distance in the plain country, inviting you, as it were, from the riot and tumult roaring around, to pass through the breach and participate of the calm below. Here the eye ultimately composes itself; and that way, too, the road happens actually to lead. You cross the Potomac above the junction, pass along its side through the base of the mountain for three miles, its terrible precipices hanging in fragments over you, and within about twenty miles reach Fredericktown, and the fine country round that. This scene is worth a voyage across the Atlantic. Yet here, as in the neighborhood of the Natural Bridge, are people who have passed their lives within half a dozen miles, and have never been to survey these monuments of a war between rivers and mountains, which must have shaken the earth itself to its center. (B.)

The height of our mountains has not yet been estimated with any degree of exactness. The Alleghany being the great ridge which divides the waters of the Atlantic from those of the Mississippi, its summit is doubtless more elevated above the ocean than that of any other mountain. But its relative height, compared with the base on which it stands, is not so great as that of some others, the country rising behind the successive ridges like the steps of stairs. The mountains of the Blue Ridge, and of these the Peaks of Otter, are thought to be of a greater height, measured from their base, than any others in our country, and perhaps in North America. From data, which may found a tolerable conjecture, we suppose the highest peak to be about four thousand feet perpendicular, which is not a fifth part of the height of the mountains of South America, nor one-third of the height which would be necessary in our latitude to preserve ice in the open air unmelted through the year. The ridge of mountains next beyond the Blue Ridge, called by us the North Mountain, is of the greatest extent; for which reason they were named by the Indians the endless mountains.

A substance supposed to be pumice, found floating on the Mississippi, has induced a conjecture that there is a volcano on some of its waters; and as these are mostly known to their sources, except the Missouri, our expectations of verifying the conjecture would of course be led to the mountains which divide the waters of the Mexican Gulf from those of the South Sea; but no volcano having ever yet been known at such a distance from the sea, we must rather suppose that this floating substance has been erroneously deemed pumice.

QUERY V.
ITS CASCADES AND CAVERNS?

The only remarkable cascade in this country is that of the Falling Spring in Augusta. It is a water of James' river where it is called Jackson's river, rising in the warm spring mountains, about twenty miles south-west of the warm spring, and flowing into that valley. About three-quarters of a mile from its source it falls over a rock two hundred feet into the valley below. The sheet of water is broken in its breadth by the rock, in two or three places, but not at all in its height. Between the sheet and the rock, at the bottom, you may walk across dry. This cataract will bear no comparison with that of Niagara

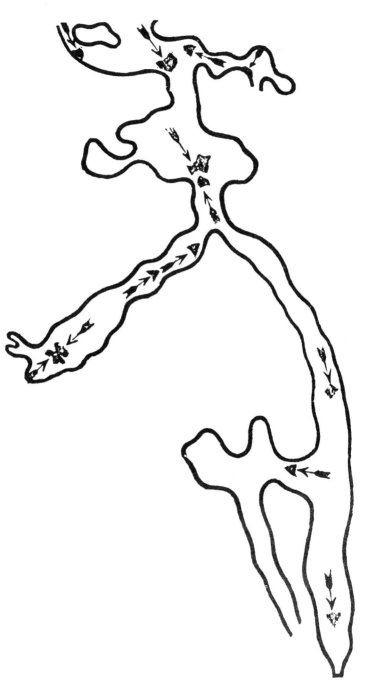

An eye-draft of Madison's cave, on a scale of 50 feet to the inch. The arrows show where it descends or ascends. *[Jefferson's note]*

as to the quantity of water composing it; the sheet being only twelve or fifteen feet wide above and somewhat more spread below; but it is half as high again, the latter being only one hundred and fifty-six feet, according to the mensuration made by order of M. Vaudreuil, Governor of Canada, and one hundred and thirty according to a more recent account.

In the lime-stone country there are many caverns of very considerable extent. The most noted is called Madison's Cave, and is on the north side of the Blue Ridge, near the intersection of the Rockingham and Augusta line with the south fork of the southern river of Shenandoah. It is in a hill of about two hundred feet perpendicular height, the ascent of which, on one side, is so steep that you may pitch a biscuit from its summit into the river which washes its base. The entrance of the cave is, in this side, about two-thirds of the way up. It extends into the earth about three hundred feet, branching into subordinate caverns, sometimes ascending a little, but more generally descending, and at length terminates, in two different places, at basins of water of unknown extent, and which I should judge to be nearly on a level with the water of the river; however, I do not think they are formed by refluent water from that, because they are never turbid; because they do not rise and fall in correspondence with that in times of flood or of drought; and because the water is always cool. It is probably one of the many reservoirs with which the interior parts of the earth are supposed to abound, and yield supplies to the fountains of water, distinguished from others only by being accessible. The vault of this cave is of solid lime-stone, from twenty to forty or fifty feet high; through which water is continually percolating. This, trickling down the sides of the cave, has incrusted them over in the form of elegant drapery; and dripping from the top of the vault generates on that and on the base below, stalactites of a conical form, some of which have met and formed massive columns.

Another of these caves is near the North Mountain, in the county of Frederick, on the lands of Mr. Zane. The entrance into this is on the top of an extensive ridge. You descend thirty or forty feet, as into a well, from whence the cave extends, nearly horizontally, four hundred feet into the earth, preserving a breadth of from twenty to fifty feet, and a height of from five to twelve feet. After entering this cave a few feet, the mercury, which in the open air was 50°, rose to 57° of Fahrenheit's thermometer, answering to 11° of Reaumur's, and it continued at that to the remotest parts of the cave. The uniform temperature of the cellars of the observatory of Paris, which are ninety feet deep, and of all subterraneous cavities of any depth, where no chemical agencies may be supposed to produce a factitious heat, has been found to be 10° of Reaumur, equal to 54½° of Fahrenheit. The temperature of the cave above mentioned so nearly corresponds with this, that the difference may be ascribed to a difference of instruments.

At the Panther gap, in the ridge which divides the waters of the Crow and the Calf pasture, is what is called the *Blowing Cave*. It is in the side of a hill, is of about one hundred feet diameter, and emits constantly a current of air of such force as to keep the weeds prostrate to the distance of twenty yards before it. This current is strongest in dry, frosty weather, and in long spells of rain weakest. Regular inspirations and expirations of air, by caverns and fissures, have been probably enough accounted for by supposing them combined with intermitting fountains; as they must of course inhale air while their reservoirs are emptying themselves, and again emit it while they are filling. But a constant issue of air, only varying in its force as the weather is drier or damper, will require a new hypothesis. There is another blowing cave in the Cumberland mountain, about a mile from where it crosses the Carolina line. All we know of this is, that it is not constant, and that a fountain of water issues from it.

The *Natural Bridge*, the most sublime of nature's works, though not comprehended under the present head, must not be pretermitted. It is on the ascent of a hill, which seems to have been cloven through its length by some great convulsion. The fissure, just at the bridge, is, by some admeasurements, two hundred and seventy feet deep, by others only two hundred and five. It is about forty-five feet wide at the bottom and ninety feet at the top; this of course determines the length of the bridge, and its height from the water. Its breadth in the middle is about sixty feet, but more at the ends, and the thickness of the mass, at the summit of the arch, about forty feet. A part of this thickness is constituted by a coat of earth, which gives growth to many large trees. The residue, with the hill on both sides, is one solid rock of limestone. The arch approaches the semi-elliptical form; but the larger axis of the ellipsis, which would be the cord of the arch, is many times longer than the transverse. Though the sides of this bridge are provided in some parts with a parapet of fixed rocks, yet few men have resolution to walk to them, and look over into the abyss. You involuntarily fall on your hands and feet, creep to the parapet, and peep over it. Looking down from this height about a minute, gave me a violent head-ache. If the view from the top be painful and intolerable, that from below is delightful in an equal extreme. It is impossible for the emotions arising from the sublime to be felt beyond what they are here; so beautiful an arch, so elevated, so light, and springing as it were up to heaven! The rapture of the spectator is really indescribable! The fissure continuing narrow, deep, and straight, for a considerable distance above and below the bridge, opens a short but very pleasing view of the North Mountain on one side and the Blue Ridge on the other, at the distance each of them of about five miles. This bridge is in the county of Rockbridge, to which it has given name, and affords a public and commodious passage over a valley which cannot be crossed elsewhere for a considerable distance. The stream passing under it is called Cedar-creek. It is a water of James' river, and sufficient in the driest seasons to turn a grist-mill, though its fountain is not more than two miles above.[1]

QUERY XVII.
RELIGION

THE DIFFERENT RELIGIONS RECEIVED INTO THAT STATE?

The first settlers in this country were emigrants from England, of the English church, just at a point of time when it was flushed with complete victory over the religious of all other persuasions. Possessed, as they became, of the powers of making, administering, and executing the laws, they showed equal intolerance in this country with their Presbyterian brethren, who had emigrated to the northern government. The poor Quakers were flying from persecution in England. They cast their eyes on these new countries as asylums of civil and religious freedom; but they found them free only for the reigning sect. Several acts of the Virginia assembly of 1659, 1662, and 1693, had made it penal in parents to refuse to have their children baptized; had prohibited the unlawful assembling of Quakers; had made it penal for any master of a vessel to bring a Quaker into the state; had ordered those already here, and such as should come thereafter, to be imprisoned till they should

---

[1] Don Ulloa mentions a break, similar to this, in the province of Angaraez, in South America. It is from sixteen to twenty-two feet wide, one hundred and eleven feet deep, and of 1.3 miles continuance, English measure. Its breadth at top is not sensibly greater than at bottom. But the following fact is remarkable, and will furnish some light for conjecturing the probable origin of our natural bridge. "Esta caxa, o cauce está cortada en péna viva con tanta precision, que las desigualdades del un lado entrantes, corresponden á las del otro lado salientes, como si aquella altura se hubiese abierto expresamente, con sus bueltas y tortuosidades, para darle transito á los aguas por entre los dos morallones que la forman; siendo tal su igualdad, que si llegasen á juntarse se endentarian uno con otro sin dextar hueco." Not. Amer. ii. §10. Don Ulloa inclines to the opinion that this channel has been effected by the wearing of the water which runs through it, rather than that the mountain should have been broken open by any convulsion of nature. But if it had been worn by the running of the water, would not the rocks which form the sides, have been worn plain! or if, meeting in some parts with veins of harder stone, the water had left prominences on the one side, would not the same cause have sometimes, or perhaps generally, occasioned prominences on the other side also? Yet Don Ulloa tells us, that on the other side there are always corresponding cavities, and that these tally with the prominences so perfectly, that, were the two sides to come together they would fit in all their indentures, without leaving any void. I think that this does not resemble the effect of running water, but looks rather as if the two sides had parted asunder. The sides of the break, over which is the natural bridge of Virginia, consisting of a veiny rock which yields to time, the correspondence between the salient and re-entering inequalities, if it existed at all, has now disappeared. This break has the advantage of the one described by Don Ulloa in its finest circumstance; no portion in that instance having held together, during the separation of the other parts, so as to form a bridge over the abyss. [Jefferson's note.]

abjure the country; provided a milder punishment for their first and second return, but death for their third; had inhibited all persons from suffering their meetings in or near their houses, entertaining them individually, or disposing of books which supported their tenets. If no capital execution took place here, as did in New-England, it was not owing to the moderation of the church, or spirit of the legislature, as may be inferred from the law itself; but to historical circumstances which have not been handed down to us. The Anglicans retained full possession of the country about a century. Other opinions began then to creep in, and the great care of the government to support their own church, having begotten an equal degree of indolence in its clergy, two-thirds of the people had become dissenters at the commencement of the present revolution. The laws indeed were still oppressive on them, but the spirit of the one party had subsided into moderation, and of the other had risen to a degree of determination which commanded respect.

The present state of our laws on the subject of religion is this. The convention of May 1776, in their declaration of rights, declared it to be a truth, and a natural right, that the exercise of religion should be free; but when they proceeded to form on that declaration the ordinance of government, instead of taking up every principle declared in the bill of rights, and guarding it by legislative sanction, they passed over that which asserted our religious rights, leaving them as they found them. The same convention, however, when they met as a member of the general assembly in October 1776, repealed all *acts of Parliament* which had rendered criminal the maintaining any opinions in matters of religion, the forbearing to repair to church, and the exercising any mode of worship; and suspended the laws giving salaries to the clergy, which suspension was made perpetual in October 1779. Statutory oppressions in religion being thus wiped away, we remain at present under those only imposed by the common law, or by our own acts of assembly. At the common law, *heresy* was a capital offense, punishable by burning. Its definition was left to the ecclesiastical judges, before whom the conviction was, till the statute of the i El. c. i. circumscribed it, by declaring, that nothing should be deemed heresy, but what had been so determined by authority of the canonical scriptures, or by one of the four first general councils, or by some other council having for the grounds of their declaration the express and plain words of the Scriptures. Heresy, thus circumscribed, being an offense at the common law, our act of assembly of October 1777, c. 17. gives cognizance of it to the general court, by declaring, that the jurisdiction of that court shall be general in all matters at the common law. The execution is by the writ *de hæretico comburendo*. By our own act of assembly of 1705, c. 30, if a person brought up in the Christian religion denies the being of a God, or the Trinity, or asserts there are more gods than one, or denies the Christian religion to be true, or the Scriptures to be of divine authority, he is punishable on the first offense by incapacity to hold any office or employment ecclesiastical, civil, or military; on the second by disability to sue, to take any gift or legacy, to be guardian, executor, or administrator, and by three years imprisonment, without bail. A father's right to the custody of his own children being founded in law on his right of guardianship, this being taken away, they may of course be severed from him, and put, by the authority of a court, into more orthodox hands. This is a summary view of that religious slavery, under which a people have been willing to remain, who have lavished their lives and fortunes for the establishment of their civil freedom.

The error seems not sufficiently eradicated, that the operations of the mind, as well as the acts of the body, are subject to the coercion of the laws.[1] But our rulers can have authority over such natural rights only as we have submitted to them. The rights of conscience we never submitted, we could not submit. We are answerable for them to our God. The legitimate powers of government extend to such acts only as are injurious to others. But it does me no injury for my neighbor to say there are twenty gods, or no god. It neither picks my pocket nor breaks my leg. If it be said, his testimony in a court of justice cannot be relied on, reject it then, and be the stigma on him. Constraint may make him worse by making him a hypocrite, but it will never make him a truer man. It may fix him obstinately in his errors, but will not cure them. Reason and free inquiry are the only effectual agents against error. Give a loose to them, they will support the true religion, by bringing every false one to their tribunal, to the test of their investigation. They are the natural enemies of error, and of error only. Had not the Roman government permitted free inquiry, Christianity could never have been introduced. Had not free inquiry been indulged, at the era of the Reformation, the corruptions of Christianity could not have been purged away. If it be restrained now, the present corruptions will be protected, and new ones encouraged. Was the government to prescribe to us our medicine and diet, our bodies would be in such keeping as our souls are now. Thus in France the emetic was once forbidden as a medicine, and the potato as an article of food. Government is just as infallible too when it fixes systems in physics. Galileo[2] was sent to the Inquisition for affirming that the earth was a sphere: the government had declared it to be as flat as a trencher, and Galileo was obliged to abjure his error. This error however at length prevailed, the earth became a globe, and Descartes[3] declared it was whirled round its axis by a vortex. The government in which he lived was wise enough to see that this was no question of civil jurisdiction, or we should all have been involved by authority in vortices. In fact, the vortices have been exploded, and the New-

---

[1] Furneaux passim. [Jefferson's note.] The reference is to Philip Furneaux, *Letters to the Honorable Mr. Justice Blackstone, Concerning His Exposition of the Act of Toleration* . . . . London, 1770.

[2] Galileo Galilei (1564-1642), Italian scientist and philosopher, whose astronomical obser-

vations supported the Copernican theory of the solar system but who was forced by the Inquisition to deny that the earth revolves around the sun.

[3] René Descartes (1596-1650), French philosopher and mathematician.

tonian principle of gravitation is now more firmly established, on the basis of reason, than it would be were the government to step in, and to make it an article of necessary faith. Reason and experiment have been indulged, and error has fled before them. It is error alone which needs the support of government. Truth can stand by itself. Subject opinion to coercion: whom will you make your inquisitors? Fallible men; men governed by bad passions, by private as well as public reasons. And why subject it to coercion? To produce uniformity. But is uniformity of opinion desirable? No more than of face and stature. Introduce the bed of Procrustes[4] then, and as there is danger that the large men may beat the small, make us all of a size, by lopping the former and stretching the latter. Difference of opinion is advantageous in religion. The several sects perform the office of a Censor morum[5] over each other. Is uniformity attainable? Millions of innocent men, women, and children, since the introduction of Christianity, have been burnt, tortured, fined, imprisoned; yet we have not advanced one inch towards uniformity. What has been the effect of coercion? To make one-half the world fools, and the other half hypocrites. To support roguery and error all over the earth. Let us reflect that it is inhabited by a thousand millions of people. That these profess probably a thousand different systems of religion. That ours is but one of that thousand. That if there be but one right, and ours that one, we should wish to see the 999 wandering sects gathered into the fold of truth. But against such a majority we cannot effect this by force. Reason and persuasion are the only practicable instruments. To make way for these, free inquiry must be indulged; and how can we wish others to indulge it while we refuse it ourselves. But every state, says an inquisitor, has established some religion. No two, say I, have established the same. Is this a proof of the infallibility of establishments? Our sister states of Pennsylvania and New York, however, have long subsisted without any establishment at all. The experiment was new and doubtful when they made it. It has answered beyond conception. They flourish infinitely. Religion is well supported; of various kinds, indeed, but all good enough; all sufficient to preserve peace and order: or if a sect arises, whose tenets would subvert morals, good sense has fair play, and reasons and laughs it out of doors, without suffering the state to be troubled with it. They do not hang more malefactors than we do. They are not more disturbed with religious dissensions. On the contrary, their harmony is unparalleled, and can be ascribed to nothing but their unbounded tolerance, because there is no other circumstance in which they differ from every nation on earth. They have made the happy discovery, that the way to silence religious disputes, is to take no notice of them. Let us too give this experiment fair play, and get rid, while we may, of those tyrannical laws. It is true, we are as yet secured against them by the spirit of the times.

---

[4] A giant in Greek fable, Procrustes lengthened or shortened his captives to make them fit his unchangeable iron beds.

[5] A moral critic, or critic of morals, customs.

I doubt whether the people of this country would suffer an execution for heresy, or a three years imprisonment for not comprehending the mysteries of the Trinity. But is the spirit of the people an infallible, a permanent reliance? Is it government? Is this the kind of protection we receive in return for the rights we give up? Besides, the spirit of the times may alter, will alter. Our rulers will become corrupt, our people careless. A single zealot may commence persecutor, and better men be his victims. It can never be too often repeated, that the time for fixing every essential right on a legal basis is while our rulers are honest, and ourselves united. From the conclusion of this war we shall be going down hill. It will not then be necessary to resort every moment to the people for support. They will be forgotten, therefore, and their rights disregarded. They will forget themselves, but in the sole faculty of making money, and will never think of uniting to effect a due respect for their rights. The shackles, therefore, which shall not be knocked off at the conclusion of this war, will remain on us long, will be made heavier and heavier, till our rights shall revive or expire in a convulsion.

QUERY XVIII.
MANNERS

THE PARTICULAR CUSTOMS AND MANNERS THAT MAY HAPPEN TO BE RECEIVED IN THAT STATE? [SLAVERY]

It is difficult to determine on the standard by which the manners of a nation may be tried, whether *catholic,* or *particular.* It is more difficult for a native to bring to that standard the manners of his own nation, familiarized to him by habit. There must doubtless be an unhappy influence on the manners of our people produced by the existence of slavery among us. The whole commerce between master and slave is a perpetual exercise of the most boisterous passions, the most unremitting despotism on the one part, and degrading submissions on the other. Our children see this, and learn to imitate it; for man is an imitative animal. This quality is the germ of all education in him. From his cradle to his grave he is learning to do what he sees others do. If a parent could find no motive either in his philanthropy or his self-love, for restraining the intemperance of passion towards his slave, it should always be a sufficient one that his child is present. But generally it is not sufficient. The parent storms, the child looks on, catches the lineaments of wrath, puts on the same airs in the circle of smaller slaves, gives a loose to his worst of passions, and thus nursed, educated, and daily exercised in tyranny, cannot but be stamped by it with odious peculiarities. The man must be a prodigy who can retain his manners and morals undepraved by such circumstances. And with what execration should the statesman be loaded, who permitting one-half the citizens thus to trample on the rights of the other, transforms those into despots, and these into enemies, destroys the morals of the one

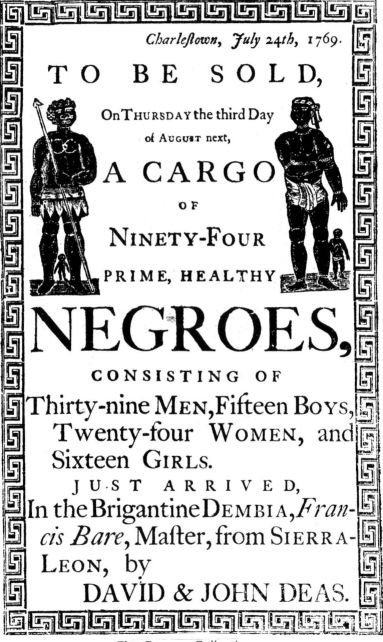

Charlestown, July 24th, 1769.

TO BE SOLD,

On THURSDAY the third Day of AUGUST next,

A CARGO

OF

NINETY-FOUR

PRIME, HEALTHY

NEGROES,

CONSISTING OF

Thirty-nine MEN, Fifteen BOYS, Twenty-four WOMEN, and Sixteen GIRLS.

JUST ARRIVED,

In the Brigantine DEMBIA, *Francis Bare*, Master, from SIERRA-LEON, by

DAVID & JOHN DEAS.

part, and the amor patriae[1] of the other. For if a slave can have a country in this world, it must be any other in preference to that in which he is born to live and labor for another: in which he must lock up the faculties of his nature, contribute as far as depends on his individual endeavors to the evanishment of the human race, or entail his own miserable condition on the endless generations proceeding from him. With the morals of the people, their industry also is destroyed. For in a warm climate, no man will labor for himself who can make another labor for him. This is so true, that of the proprietors of slaves a very small proportion indeed are ever seen to labor. And can the liberties of a nation be thought secure when we have removed their only firm basis, a conviction in the minds of the people that these liberties are of the gift of God? That they are not to be violated but with his wrath? Indeed I tremble for my country when I reflect that God is just: that His justice cannot sleep for ever: that considering numbers, nature and natural means only, a revolution of the wheel of fortune, an exchange of situation, is among possible events: that it may become probable by supernatural interference! The Almighty has no attribute which can take side with us in such a contest.—But it is impossible to be temperate and to pursue this subject through the various considerations of policy, of morals, of history natural and civil. We must be contented to hope they will force their way into every one's mind. I think a change already perceptible, since the origin of the present revolution. The spirit of the master is abating, that of the slave rising from the dust, his condition mollifying, the way I hope preparing, under the auspices of heaven, for a total emancipation, and that this is disposed, in the order of events, to be with the consent of the masters, rather than by their extirpation.

[1] Love of country.

From The Autobiography of Thomas Jefferson[1]

[HIS EARLY LIFE AND CAREER]

January 6, 1821. At the age of 77, I begin to make some memoranda, and state some recollections of dates and facts concerning myself, for my own more ready reference, and for the information of my family.

[1] Published posthumously, in 1829, by his grandson, Jefferson's autobiography was written when Jefferson was 78, in 1821. The text here is from Paul Ford's edition of Jefferson's *Works*, 12 vols., New York (1892-1894).

The tradition in my father's family was, that their ancestor came to this country from Wales, and from near the mountain of Snowdon, the highest in Great Britain. I noted once a case from Wales, in the law reports, where a person of our name was either plaintiff or defendant; and one of the same name was secretary to the Virginia Company. These are the only instances in which I have met with the name in that country. I have found it in our early records; but the first particular information I have of any ancestor was of my grandfather, who lived at the place in Chesterfield called Ozborne's, and owned the lands afterwards the glebe of the parish. He had three sons; Thomas who died young, Field who settled on the waters of Roanoke and left numerous descendants, and Peter, my father, who settled on the lands I still own, called Shadwell, adjoining my present residence. He was born February 29, 1707-8, and intermarried 1739, with Jane Randolph, of the age of 19, daughter of Isham Randolph, one of the seven sons of that name and family settled at Dungeoness in Goochland. They trace their pedigree far back in England and Scotland, to which let every one ascribe the faith and merit he chooses.

My father's education had been quite neglected; but being of a strong mind, sound judgment, and eager after information, he read much and improved himself, insomuch that he was chosen, with Joshua Fry, professor of Mathematics in William and Mary College, to continue the boundary line between Virginia and North Carolina, which had been begun by Colonel Byrd; and was afterwards employed with the same Mr. Fry, to make the first map of Virginia which had ever been made, that of Captain Smith being merely a conjectural sketch. They possessed excellent materials for so much of the country as is below the Blue Ridge; little being then known beyond that ridge. He was the third or fourth settler, about the year 1737, of the part of the country in which I live. He died August 17th, 1757, leaving my mother a widow, who lived till 1776, with six daughters and two sons, myself the elder. To my younger brother he left his estate on James river, called Snowden, after the supposed birth place of the family: to myself, the lands on which I was born and live. He placed me at the English school at five years of age; and at the Latin at nine, where I continued until his death. My teacher, Mr. Douglas, a clergyman from Scotland, with the rudiments of the Latin and Greek languages, taught me the French; and on the death of my father, I went to the Reverend Mr. Maury, a correct classical scholar, with whom I continued two years; and then, to wit, in the spring of 1760, went to William and Mary College where I continued two years. It was my great good fortune, and what probably fixed the destinies of my life, that Dr. William Small of Scotland, was then professor of Mathematics, a man profound in most of the useful branches of science, with a happy talent of communication, correct and gentlemanly manners, and an enlarged and liberal mind. He, most happily for me, became soon attached to me, and made me his daily companion when not engaged in the school; and from his conversation I got my first views of the expansion of science, and of the system of things in which we are placed. Fortunately, the philosophical chair became vacant soon after my arrival at college, and he was appointed to fill it *per interim:* and he was the first who ever gave, in that college, regular lectures in Ethics, Rhetoric and Belles lettres. He returned to Europe in 1762, having previously filled up the measure of his goodness to me, by procuring for me, from his most intimate friend George Wythe, a reception as a student of law, under his direction, and introduced me to the acquaintance and familiar table of Governor Fauquier, the ablest man who had ever filled that office. With him, and at his table, Dr. Small and Mr. Wythe, his *amici omnium horarum,*[2] and myself, formed a *partie quarree,*[3] and to the habitual conversations on these occasions I owed much instruction. Mr. Wythe continued to be my faithful and beloved mentor in youth, and my most affectionate friend through life. In 1767, he led me into the practice of the law at the bar of the general court, at which I continued until the Revolution shut up the courts of justice.[°]

In 1769, I became a member of the legislature by the choice of the county in which I live, and so continued until it was closed by the Revolution. I made one effort in that body for the permission of the emancipation of slaves, which was rejected: and indeed, during the regal government, nothing liberal could expect success. Our minds were circumscribed within narrow limits, by an habitual belief that it was our duty to be subordinate to the mother country in all matters of government, to direct all our labors in subservience to her interests, and even to observe a bigoted intolerance for all religions but hers. The difficulties with our representatives were of habit and despair, not of reflection and conviction. Experience soon proved that they could bring their minds to rights, on the first summons of their attention. But the King's Council, which acted as another house of legislature, held their places at will, and were in most humble obedience to that will: the Governor too, who had a negative on our laws, held by the same tenure, and with still greater devotedness to it: and, last of all, the Royal negative closed the last door to every hope of amelioration.

On the 1st of January, 1772, I was married to Martha Skelton, widow of Bathurst Skelton, and daughter of John Wayles, then twenty-three years old. Mr. Wayles was a lawyer of much practice, to which he was introduced more by his great industry, punctuality and practical readiness, than by eminence in the science of his profession. He was a most agreeable companion, full of pleasantry and good humor, and welcomed in every society. He acquired a handsome fortune, and died in May, 1773, leaving three daughters:

---

[2] Friends of all hours.
[3] That is, a party of four. The phrase, spelled with a "c" rather than "q," is still used to indicate the right number for a game of bridge or other cards.

[°] For a sketch of the life and character of Mr. Wythe, see my letter of August 31, 1820, to Mr. John Saunderson. [In an Appendix.]

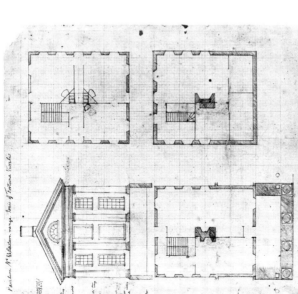

Thomas Jefferson's drawings for a pavilion at the University of Virginia.
Thomas Jefferson's drawings for the Rotunda, University of Virginia.
Photograph of Thomas Jefferson's home at Monticello. *(George Laycock/Photo Researchers.)*

the portion which came on that event to Mrs. Jefferson, after the debts should be paid, which were very considerable, was about equal to my own patrimony, and consequently doubled the ease of our circumstances.

When the famous Resolutions of 1765, against the Stamp-act, were proposed, I was yet a student of law in Williamsburg. I attended the debate, however, at the door of the lobby of the House of Burgesses, and heard the splendid display of Mr. Henry's talents as a popular orator.[4] They were great indeed; such as I have never heard from any other man. He appeared to me to speak as Homer wrote. Mr. Johnson, a lawyer, and member from the Northern neck, seconded the resolutions, and by him the learning and logic of the case were chiefly maintained. My recollections of these transactions may be seen page 60 of the life of Patrick Henry, by Wirt, to whom I furnished them.

In May, 1769, a meeting of the General Assembly was called by the Governor, Lord Botetourt. I had then become a member; and to that meeting became known the joint resolutions and address of the Lords and Commons of 1768-9, on the proceedings in Massachusetts. Counter-resolutions, and an address to the King by the House of Burgesses, were agreed to with little opposition, and a spirit manifestly displayed itself of considering the cause of Massachusetts as a common one. The Governor dissolved us: but we met the next day in the Apollo [room] of the Raleigh tavern, formed ourselves into a voluntary convention, drew up articles of association against the use of any merchandise imported from Great Britain, signed and recommended them to the people, repaired to our several counties, and were re-elected without any other exception than of the very few who had declined assent to our proceedings.

Nothing of particular excitement occurring for a considerable time, our countrymen seemed to fall into a state of insensibility to our situation; the duty on tea, not yet repealed, and the declaratory act of a right in the British Parliament, to bind us by their laws in all cases whatsoever, still suspended over us. But a court of enquiry held in Rhode Island in 1762, with a power to send persons to England to be tried for offenses committed here, was considered, at our session of the spring of 1773, as demanding attention. Not thinking our old and leading members up to the point of forwardness and zeal which the times required, Mr. Henry, Richard Henry Lee, Francis L. Lee, Mr. Carr and myself agreed to meet in the evening, in a private room of the Raleigh, to consult on the state of things. There may have been a member or two more whom I do not recollect. We were all sensible that the most urgent of all measures was that of coming to an understanding with all the

[4] Patrick Henry (1736-1799) declared in this debate: "Caesar had his Brutus, Charles the First had his Cromwell, and George the Third—may he profit from their example!" Ten years later Henry made the memorable speech insisting on a choice between liberty and death.

other colonies, to consider the British claims as a common cause to all, and to produce a unity of action: and for this purpose that a committee of correspondence in each colony would be the best instrument for intercommunication: and that their first measure would probably be, to propose a meeting of deputies from every colony, at some central place, who should be charged with the direction of the measures which should be taken by all. We therefore drew up the resolutions which may be seen in Wirt, page 87. The consulting members proposed to me to move them, but I urged that it should be done by Mr. Carr, my friend and brother-in-law, then a new member, to whom I wished an opportunity should be given of making known to the house his great worth and talents. It was so agreed; he moved them, they were agreed to *nem. con.*[5] and a committee of correspondence[6] appointed, of whom Peyton Randolph, the speaker, was chairman. The Governor (then Lord Dunmore) dissolved us, but the committee met the next day, prepared a circular letter to the speakers of the other colonies, inclosing to each a copy of the resolutions, and left it in charge with their chairman to forward them by expresses.

The origination of these committees of correspondence between the colonies, has been since claimed for Massachusetts, and [John] Marshall[7] has given in to this error, although the very note of his appendix to which he refers, shows that their establishment was confined to their own towns. This matter will be seen clearly stated in a letter of Samuel Adams Wells to me of April 2nd, 1819, and my answer of May 12th. I was corrected by the letter of Mr. Wells in the information I had given Mr. Wirt, as stated in his note, page 87, that the messengers of Massachusetts and Virginia crossed each other on the way, bearing similar propositions; for Mr. Wells shows that Massachusetts did not adopt the measure, but on the receipt of our proposition, delivered at their next session. Their message, therefore, which passed ours, must have related to something else, for I well remember Peyton Randolph's informing me of the crossing of our messengers.

The next event which excited our sympathies for Massachusetts, was the Boston port bill, by which that port was to be shut up on the 1st of June, 1774. This arrived while we were in session in the spring of that year. The lead in the House, on these subjects, being no longer left to the old members, Mr. Henry, R. H. Lee, Fr. L. Lee, three or four other members, whom I do not recollect, and myself, agreeing that we must boldly take an unequivocal stand in the line with Massachusetts, determined to meet and consult on the proper measures, in the council chamber, for the benefit of

---

[5] Latin abbreviation for "nobody opposed."

[6] Committees of correspondence, formed in the scattered colonies, were a major means of keeping sympathetic people in other colonies informed of local events, so that some

common action might be possible against the British authorities.

[7] Life of Washington, vol. ii. p. 151. [Jefferson's note.]

the library in that room. We were under conviction of the necessity of arousing our people from the lethargy into which they had fallen, as to passing events; and thought that the appointment of a day of general fasting and prayer, would be most likely to call up and alarm their attention. No example of such a solemnity had existed since the days of our distresses in the war of '55, since which a new generation had grown up. With the help, therefore, of Rushworth, whom we rummaged over for the revolutionary precedents and forms of the Puritans of that day, preserved by him, we cooked up a resolution, somewhat modernizing their phrases, for appointing the 1st day of June, on which the port bill was to commence, for a day of fasting, humiliation and prayer, to implore Heaven to avert from us the evils of civil war, to inspire us with firmness in support of our rights, and to turn the hearts of the King and Parliament to moderation and justice. To give greater emphasis to our proposition, we agreed to wait the next morning on Mr. Nicholas, whose grave and religious character was more in unison with the tone of our resolution, and to solicit him to move it. We accordingly went to him in the morning. He moved it the same day; the 1st of June was proposed; and it passed without opposition. The Governor dissolved us, as usual. We retired to the Apollo, as before, agreed to an association, and instructed the committee of correspondence to propose to the corresponding committees of the other colonies, to appoint deputies to meet in Congress at such place, *annually,* as should be convenient, to direct, from time to time, the measures required by the general interest: and we declared that an attack on any one colony, should be considered as an attack on the whole. This was in May. We further recommended to the several counties to elect deputies to meet at Williamsburg, the 1st of August ensuing, to consider the state of the colony, and particularly to appoint delegates to a general Congress, should that measure be acceded to by the committees of correspondence generally. It was acceded to; Philadelphia was appointed for the place, and the 5th of September for the time of meeting. We returned home, and in our several counties invited the clergy to meet assemblies of the people on the 1st of June, to perform the ceremonies of the day, and to address to them discourses suited to the occasion. The people met generally, with anxiety and alarm in their countenances, and the effect of the day, through the whole colony, was like a shock of electricity, arousing every man and placing him erect and solidly on his center. They chose, universally, delegates for the convention. Being elected one for my own county, I prepared a draught of instructions to be given to the delegates whom we should send to the Congress, which I meant to propose at our meeting. In this I took the ground that, from the beginning, I had thought the only one orthodox or tenable, which was, that the relation between Great Britain and these colonies was exactly the same as that of England and Scotland, after the accession of James and until the union, and the same as her present relations with Hanover, having the same executive chief, but no other necessary political connection; and that our emigration from England to this country gave her no more rights over us, than the emigrations of the Danes and Saxons gave to the present authorities of the mother country, over England. In this doctrine, however, I had never been able to get any one to agree with me but Mr. Wythe. He concurred in it from the first dawn of the question, What was the political relation between us and England? Our other patriots, Randolph, the Lees, Nicholas, Pendleton, stopped at the half-way house of John Dickinson, who admitted that England had a right to regulate our commerce, and to lay duties on it for the purposes of regulation, but not of raising revenue. But for this ground there was no foundation in compact, in any acknowledged principles of colonization, nor in reason: expatriation being a natural right, and acted on as such, by all nations, in all ages. I set out for Williamsburg some days before that appointed for our meeting, but was taken ill of a dysentery on the road, and was unable to proceed. I sent on, therefore, to Williamsburg two copies of my draught, the one under cover to Peyton Randolph, who I knew would be in the chair of the convention, the other to Patrick Henry. Whether Mr. Henry disapproved the ground taken, or was too lazy to read it (for he was the laziest man in reading I ever knew) I never learned: but he communicated it to nobody. Peyton Randolph informed the convention he had received such a paper from a member, prevented by sickness from offering it in his place, and he laid it on the table for perusal. It was read generally by the members, approved by many, though thought too bold for the present state of things; but they printed it in pamphlet form, under the title of 'A summary view of the rights of British America.' It found its way to England, was taken up by the opposition, interpolated a little by Mr. Burke so as to make it answer opposition purposes, and in that form ran rapidly through several editions.

·   ·   ·

[THE DECLARATION OF INDEPENDENCE]

In Congress, Friday, June 7, 1776.[8] The delegates from Virginia moved, in obedience to instructions from their constituents, that the Congress should declare that these United colonies are, and of right ought to be, free and independent states, that they are absolved from all allegiance to the British crown, and that all political connection between them and the state of Great Britain is, and ought to be, totally dissolved; that measures should be imme-

[8] Here, in the original manuscript, commence the "two preceding sheets" referred to by Mr. Jefferson, page 20, as containing "notes" taken by him "whilst these things were going on." They are easily distinguished from the body of the MS. in which they were inserted by him, being of a paper very different in size, quality and color, from that on which the latter is written [Paul Ford's note.]

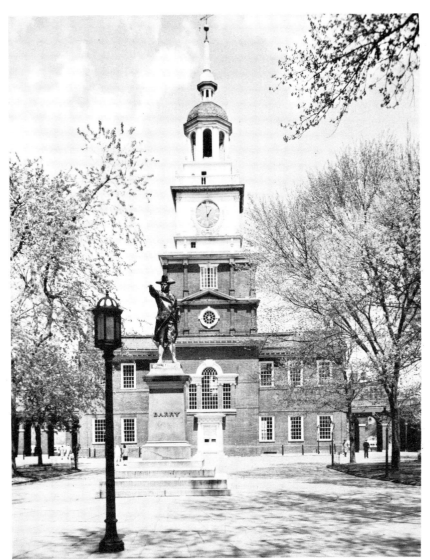

Independence Hall, Philadelphia, Pennsylvania. Completed in 1741, designed by Governor Andrew Hamilton. The white steeple was added in 1781. The Declaration of Independence, the Articles of Confederation, and the U.S. Constitution were signed here. *(Pennsylvania Department of Commerce, Bureau of Travel Development.)*

diately taken for procuring the assistance of foreign powers, and a Confederation be formed to bind the colonies more closely together.

The House being obliged to attend at that time to some other business, the proposition was referred to the next day, when the members were ordered to attend punctually at ten o'clock.

Saturday, June 8. They proceeded to take it into consideration, and referred it to a committee of the whole, into which they immediately resolved themselves, and passed that day and Monday the 10th in debating on the subject.

It was argued by Wilson, Robert R. Livingston, E. Rutledge, Dickinson and others—

That, though they were friends to the measures themselves, and saw the impossibility that we should ever again be united with Great Britain, yet they were against adopting them at this time:

That the conduct we had formerly observed was wise and proper now, of deferring to take any capital step till the voice of the people drove us into it:

That they were our power, and without them our declarations could not be carried into effect:

That the people of the middle colonies (Maryland, Delaware, Pennsylvania, the Jerseys and New York) were not yet ripe for bidding adieu to British connection, but that they were fast ripening, and, in a short time, would join in the general voice of America:

That the resolution, entered into by this House on the 15th of May, for suppressing the exercise of all powers derived from the crown, had shown, by the ferment into which it had thrown these middle colonies, that they had not yet accommodated their minds to a separation from the mother country:

That some of them had expressly forbidden their delegates to consent to such a declaration, and others had given no instructions, and consequently no powers to give such consent:

That if the delegates of any particular colony had no power to declare such colony independent, certain they were, the others could not declare it for them; the colonies being as yet perfectly independent of each other:

That the assembly of Pennsylvania was now sitting above stairs, their convention would sit within a few days, the convention of New York was now sitting, and those of the Jerseys and Delaware counties would meet on the Monday following, and it was probable these bodies would take up the question of Independence, and would declare to their delegates the voice of their state:

That if such a declaration should now be agreed to, these delegates must retire, and possibly their colonies might secede from the Union:

That such a secession would weaken us more than could be compensated by any foreign alliance:

That in the event of such a division, foreign powers would either refuse to join themselves to our fortunes, or, having us so much in their power as that desperate declaration would place us, they would insist on terms proportionably more hard and prejudicial:

That we had little reason to expect an alliance with those to whom alone, as yet, we had cast our eyes:

That France and Spain had reason to be jealous of that rising power, which would one day certainly strip them of all their American possesions:

That it was more likely they should form a connection with the British court, who, if they should find themselves unable otherwise to extricate themselves from their difficulties, would agree to a partition of our territories, restoring Canada to France, and the Floridas to Spain, to accomplish for themselves a recovery of these colonies:

That it would not be long before we should receive certain information of the disposition of the French court, from the agent whom we had sent to Paris for that purpose:

That if this disposition should be favorable, by waiting the event of the present campaign, which we all hoped would be successful, we should have reason to expect an alliance on better terms:

That this would in fact work no delay of any effectual aid from such ally, as, from the advance of the season and distance of our situation, it was impossible we could receive any assistance during this campaign:

That it was prudent to fix among ourselves the terms on which we would form alliance, before we declared we would form one at all events:

And that if these were agreed on, and our Declaration of Independence ready by the time our Ambassador should be prepared to sail, it would be as well, as to go into that Declaration at this day.

On the other side, it was urged by J. Adams, Lee, Wythe and others, that no gentleman had argued against the policy or the right of separation from Britain, nor had supposed it possible we should ever renew our connection; that they had only opposed its being now declared:

That the question was not whether, by a Declaration of Independence, we should make ourselves what we are not; but whether we should declare a fact which already exists:

That, as to the people or Parliament of England, we had always been independent of them, their restraints on our trade deriving efficacy from our acquiescence only, and not from any rights they possessed of imposing them, and that so far, our connection had been federal only, and was now dissolved by the commencement of hostilities:

That, as to the King, we had been bound to him by allegiance, but that this bond was now dissolved by his assent to the late act of Parliament, by which he declares us out of his protection, and by his levying war on us, a fact which had long ago proved us out of his protection; it being a certain position in law, that allegiance and protection are reciprocal, the one ceasing when the other is withdrawn:

That James the II. never declared the people of England out of his protection, yet his actions proved it and the Parliament declared it:

No delegates then can be denied, or ever want, a power of declaring an existent truth:

That the delegates from the Delaware counties having declared their constituents ready to join, there are only two colonies, Pennsylvania and Maryland, whose delegates are absolutely tied up, and that these had, by their instructions, only reserved a right of confirming or rejecting the measure:

That the instructions from Pennsylvania might be accounted for from the times in which they were drawn, near a twelvemonth ago, since which the face of affairs has totally changed:

That within that time, it had become apparent that Britain was determined to accept nothing less than a *carte-blanche,* and that the King's answer to the Lord Mayor, Aldermen and Common Council of London, which had come to hand four days ago, must have satisfied every one of this point:

That the people wait for us to lead the way:

That *they* are in favor of the measure, though the instructions given by some of their *representatives* are not:

That the voice of the representatives is not always consonant with the voice of the people, and that this is remarkably the case in these middle colonies:

That the effect of the resolution of the 15th of May has proved this, which, raising the murmurs of some in the colonies of Pennsylvania and Maryland, called forth the opposing voice of the freer part of the people, and proved them to be the majority even in these colonies:

That the backwardness of these two colonies might be ascribed, partly to the influence of proprietary power and connections, and partly, to their having not yet been attacked by the enemy:

That these causes were not likely to be soon removed, as there seemed no probability that the enemy would make either of these the seat of this summer's war:

That it would be vain to wait either weeks or months for perfect unanimity, since it was impossible that all men should ever become of one sentiment on any question:

That the conduct of some colonies, from the beginning of this contest, had given reason to suspect it was their settled policy to keep in the rear of the confederacy, that their particular prospect might be better, even in the worst event:

That, therefore, it was necessary for those colonies who had thrown themselves forward and hazarded all from the beginning, to come forward now also, and put all again to their own hazard.

That the history of the Dutch revolution, of whom three states only con-federated at first, proved that a secession of some colonies would not be so dangerous as some apprehended:

That a declaration of Independence alone could render it consistent with European delicacy, for European powers to treat with us, or even to receive an Ambassador from us:

That till this, they would not receive our vessels into their ports, nor acknowledge the adjudications of our courts of admiralty to be legitimate, in cases of capture of British vessels:

That though France and Spain may be jealous of our rising power, they must think it will be much more formidable with the addition of Great Britain; and will therefore see it their interest to prevent a coalition; but should they refuse, we shall be but where we are; whereas without trying, we shall never know whether they will aid us or not:

That the present campaign may be unsuccessful, and therefore we had better propose an alliance while our affairs wear a hopeful aspect:

That to wait the event of this campaign will certainly work delay, be-cause, during this summer, France may assist us effectually, by cutting off those supplies of provisions from England and Ireland, on which the enemy's armies here are to depend; or by setting in motion the great power they have collected in the West Indies, and calling our enemy to the defense of the possessions they have there:

That it would be idle to lose time in settling the terms of alliance, till we had first determined we would enter into alliance:

That it is necessary to lose no time in opening a trade for our people, who will want clothes, and will want money too, for the payment of taxes:

And that the only misfortune is, that we did not enter into alliance with France six months sooner, as, besides opening her ports for the vent of our last year's produce, she might have marched an army into Germany, and prevented the petty princes there, from selling their unhappy subjects to subdue us.

It appearing in the course of these debates, that the colonies of New York, New Jersey, Pennsylvania, Delaware, Maryland, and South Carolina were not yet matured for falling from the parent stem, but that they were fast advancing to that state, it was thought most prudent to wait a while for them, and to postpone the final decision to July 1st: but, that this might occasion as little delay as possible, a committee was appointed to prepare a Declaration of Independence. The committee were John Adams, Dr. Frank-lin, Roger Sherman, Robert R. Livingston, and myself. Committees were also appointed, at the same time, to prepare a plan of confederation for the colonies, and to state the terms proper to be proposed for foreign alliance. The committee for drawing the Declaration of Independence, desired me to do it. It was accordingly done, and being approved by them, I reported it to the House on Friday, the 28th of June, when it was read and ordered to lie on the table. On Monday, the 1st of July, the House resolved itself into a committee of the whole, and resumed the consideration of the original motion made by the delegates of Virginia, which, being again debated through the day, was carried in the affirmative by the votes of New Hampshire, Connecticut, Massachusetts, Rhode Island, New Jersey, Maryland, Virginia, North Carolina and Georgia. South Carolina and Pennsylvania voted against it. Delaware had but two members present, and they were divided. The delegates from New York declared they were for it themselves, and were assured their constituents were for it; but that their instructions having been drawn near a twelvemonth before, when reconciliation was still the general object, they were enjoined by them to do nothing which should impede that object. They therefore thought themselves not justifiable in voting on either side, and asked leave to withdraw from the question; which was given them. The committee rose and reported their resolution to the House. Mr. Edward Rutledge, of South Carolina, then requested the determination might be put off to the next day, as he believed his colleagues, though they disapproved of the resolution, would then join in it for the sake of unanimity. The ultimate question, whether the House would agree to the resolution of the committee, was accordingly postponed to the next day, when it was again moved, and South Carolina concurred in voting for it. In the mean time, a third member had come post from the Delaware counties, and turned the vote of that colony in favor of the resolution. Members of a different sentiment attending that morning from Pennsylvania also, her vote was changed, so that the whole twelve colonies who were authorized to vote at all, gave their voices for it; and, within a few days,[9] the convention of New York approved of it, and thus supplied the void occasioned by the withdrawing of her delegates from the vote.

Congress proceeded the same day to consider the Declaration of Independence, which had been reported and laid on the table the Friday preceding, and on Monday referred to a committee of the whole. The pusillanimous idea that we had friends in England worth keeping terms with, still haunted the minds of many. For this reason, those passages which conveyed censures on the people of England were struck out, lest they should give them offense. The clause too, reprobating the enslaving the inhabitants of Africa, was struck out in complaisance to South Carolina and Georgia, who had never attempted to restrain the importation of slaves, and who, on the contrary, still wished to continue it. Our northern brethren also, I believe, felt a little tender under those censures; for though their people had very few slaves themselves, yet they had been pretty considerable carriers of them to others. The debates having taken up the greater parts of the 2nd,

[9] July 9.

3rd, and 4th days of July, were, on the evening of the last, closed; the Declaration was reported by the committee, agreed to by the House, and signed by every member present, except Mr. Dickinson. As the sentiments of men are known not only by what they receive, but what they reject also, I will state the form of the Declaration as originally reported. The parts struck out by Congress shall be distinguished by a black line drawn under them;° and those inserted by them shall be placed in the margin, or in a concurrent column.

A Declaration by the Representatives of the United States of America, in *General* Congress assembled.

When, in the course of human events, it becomes necessary for one people to dissolve the political bands which have connected them with another, and to assume among the powers of the earth the separate and equal station to which the laws of nature and of nature's God entitle them, a decent respect to the opinions of mankind requires that they should declare the causes which impel them to the separation.

We hold these truths to be self evident: that all men are created equal; that they are endowed by their creator with [*inherent and*] inalienable rights; that among these are life,   *certain* liberty and the pursuit of happiness;[10] that to secure these rights, governments are instituted among men, deriving their just powers from the consent of the governed; that whenever any form of government becomes destructive of these ends, it is the right of the people to alter or to abolish it, and to institute new government, laying its foundation on such principles, and organizing its powers in such form, as to them shall seem most likely to effect their safety and happiness. Prudence, indeed, will dictate that governments long established should not be changed for light and transient causes; and accordingly all experience hath shewn that mankind are more disposed to suffer while evils are sufferable, than to right themselves by abolishing the forms to which they are accustomed. But when a long train of abuses and usurpations [*begun at a distinguished period and*] pursuing invariably the same object, evinces a design to reduce them under absolute despotism, it is their right, it is their duty to throw off such government, and to provide new guards for their future security. Such has been the patient

---

° In this publication, the parts struck out are printed in *italics* and inclosed in brackets.

[10] The original phrase in John Locke's *Second Treatise of Government* is "life, liberty, and estate" or property. Jefferson apparently substituted "the pursuit of happiness." These two paragraphs of the preamble declare principles that encouraged the popular forces in revolutionary movements around the world, from France to India.

"Congress Voting Independence" by Robert Edge Pine, completed by Edward Savage. (*The Historical Society of Pennsylvania.*)

sufferance of these colonies; and such is now the necessity which constrains them to [*expunge*] their former sys-   *alter*
tems of government. The history of the present king of
Great Britain is a history of [*unremitting*] injuries and   *repeated*
usurpations, [*among which appears no solitary fact to
contradict the uniform tenor of the rest, but all have*] in   *all having*
direct object the establishment of an absolute tyranny
over these states. To prove this, let facts be submitted to a candid
world [*for the truth of which we pledge a faith yet unsullied by falsehood.*]

He has refused his assent to laws the most wholesome and necessary
for the public good.

He has forbidden his governors to pass laws of immediate and pressing importance, unless suspended in their operation till his assent
should be obtained; and, when so suspended, he has utterly neglected
to attend to them.

He has refused to pass other laws for the accommodation of large
districts of people, unless those people would relinquish the right of
representation in the legislature, a right inestimable to them, and formidable to tyrants only.

He has called together legislative bodies at places unusual, uncomfortable, and distant from the depository of their public records, for
the sole purpose of fatiguing them into compliance with his measures.

He has dissolved representative houses repeatedly [*and continually*]
for opposing with manly firmness his invasions on the rights of the
people.

He has refused for a long time after such dissolutions to cause others
to be elected, whereby the legislative powers, incapable of annihilation, have returned to the people at large for their exercise, the state
remaining, in the mean time, exposed to all the dangers of invasion
from without and convulsions within.

He has endeavored to prevent the population of these states; for
that purpose obstructing the laws for naturalization of foreigners, refusing to pass others to encourage their migrations hither, and raising
the conditions of new appropriations of lands.

He has [*suffered*] the administration of justice [*totally*   *obstructed*
to cease in some of these states] refusing his assent to   *by*
laws for establishing judiciary powers.

He has made [*our*] judges dependant on his will alone for the tenure
of their offices, and the amount and payment of their salaries.

He has erected a multitude of new offices, [*by a self-assumed
power*] and sent hither swarms of new officers to harrass our people
and eat out their substance.

He has kept among us in times of peace standing armies [*and ships of war*] without the consent of our legislatures.

He has affected to render the military independent of, and superior to, the civil power.

He has combined with others to subject us to a jurisdiction foreign to our constitutions and unacknowledged by our laws, giving his assent to their acts of pretended legislation for quartering large bodies of armed troops among us; for protecting them by a mock trial from punishment for any murders which they should commit on the inhabitants of these states; for cutting off our trade with all parts of the world; for imposing taxes on us without our consent;
for depriving us [ ] of the benefits of trial by jury; for   *in many cases*
transporting us beyond seas to be tried for pretended
offences; for abolishing the free system of English laws in a neighboring province, establishing therein an arbitrary government, and enlarging its boundaries, so as to render it at once an example and fit
instrument for introducing the same absolute rule into
these [*states*]; for taking away our charters, abolishing our   *colonies*
most valuable laws, and altering fundamentally the forms of our governments; for suspending our own legislatures, and declaring themselves invested with power to legislate for us in all cases whatsoever.

He has abdicated government here [*withdrawing   by declaring
his governors, and declaring us out of his allegiance   us out of his
and protection.*]   protection and
    waging war
He has plundered our seas, ravaged our coasts,   against us.
burnt our towns and destroyed the lives of our people.

He is at this time transporting large armies of foreign mercenaries to complete the works of death,
desolation and tyranny already begun with circum-   *scarcely par-*
stances of cruelty and perfidy [ ] unworthy the head   *alleled in the*
of a civilized nation.   *most barba-*
He has constrained our fellow citizens taken cap-   *rous ages and*
tive on the high seas to bear arms against their coun-   *totally*
try, to become the executioners of their friends and
brethren, or to fall themselves by their hands.   *excited do-*
He has [ ] endeavored to bring on the inhabitants   *mestic insur-*
of our frontiers the merciless Indian savages, whose   *rections*
known rule of warfare is an undistinguished destruc-   *among us, and*
tion of all ages, sexes and conditions [*of existence.*]   *has*

[*He has incited treasonable insurrections of our fellow citizens, with the allurements of forfeiture and confiscation of our property.*

He has waged cruel war against human nature itself, violating its

*most sacred rights of life and liberty in the persons of a distant people
who never offended him, captivating and carrying them into slavery in
another hemisphere, or to incur miserable death in their transportation
thither. This piratical warfare, the opprobrium of* INFIDEL *powers, is the
warfare of the* CHRISTIAN *king of Great Britain. Determined to keep
open a market where* MEN *should be bought and sold, he has prostituted his negative for suppressing every legislative attempt to prohibit
or to restrain this execrable commerce. And that this assemblage of
horrors might want no fact of distinguished die, he is now exciting
those very people to rise in arms among us, and to purchase that liberty
of which he has deprived them, by murdering the people on whom he
also obtruded them: thus paying off former crimes committed against
the* LIBERTIES *of one people, with crimes which he urges them to commit against the* LIVES *of another.*]

In every stage of these oppressions we have petitioned for redress in
the most humble terms: our repeated petitions have been answered
only by repeated injuries.

A prince whose character is thus marked by every act which
may define a tyrant is unfit to be the ruler of a [ ] people [*who   free
mean to be free. Future ages will scarcely believe that the har-
diness of one man adventured, within the short compass of twelve
years only, to lay a foundation so broad and so undisguised for tyranny
over a people fostered and fixed in principles of freedom.*]

Nor have we been wanting in attentions to our British brethren. We
have warned them from time to time of attempts   *an unwarrantable*
by their legislature to extend [*a*] jurisdiction over
[*these our states*]. We have reminded them of the   *us*
circumstances of our emigration and settlement
here, [*no one of which could warrant so strange a pretension: that these
were effected at the expence of our own blood and treasure, unassisted
by the wealth or the strength of Great Britain: that in constituting
indeed our several forms of government, we had adopted one common
king, thereby laying a foundation for perpetual league and amity with
them: but that submission to their parliament was no part of our constitution, nor ever in idea, if history may be credited:
and,*] we [ ] appealed to their native justice and mag-   *have*
nanimity [*as well as to*] the ties of our common kin-   *and we have*
dred to disavow these usurpations which [*were likely conjured them
to*] interrupt our connection and correspondence.   *by*
They too have been deaf to the voice of justice and of
consanguinity, [*and when occasions have been given   would inevi-
them, by the regular course of their laws, of removing   tably*
from their councils the disturbers of our harmony, they have, by their
free election, re-established them in power. At this very time too, they
are permitting their chief magistrate to send over not only soldiers of*

our common blood, but Scotch and foreign mercenaries to invade and destroy us. These facts have given the last stab to agonizing affection, and manly spirit bids us to renounce for ever these unfeeling brethren. We must endeavor to forget our former love for them, and hold them as we hold the rest of mankind, enemies in war, in peace friends. We might have been a free and a great people together; but a communication of grandeur and of freedom, it seems, is below their dignity. Be it so, since they will have it. The road to happi- We must therefore *ness and to glory is open to us too. We will* and hold them *tread it apart from them, and]* acquiesce in the as we hold the necessity which denounces our [*eternal*] separa- rest of mankind, tion [ ]! enemies in war,
in peace friends.
We therefore the representatives of the United States of America in General Congress *assembled, do in the name, and by the authority of the good people of these [states reject and renounce all allegiance and subjection to the kings of Great Britain and all others who may hereafter claim by, through or under them; we utterly dissolve all political connection which may heretofore have subsisted between us and the people or parliament of Great Britain: and finally we do assert and declare these colonies to be free and independent states,] and that as free and independent states, they have full power to levy war, conclude peace, contract alliances, establish commerce, and to do all other acts and things which independent states may of right do.*

And for the support of this declaration, we mutually pledge to each other our lives, our fortunes, and our sacred honor.[11]

We therefore the representatives of the United States of America in General Congress assembled, appealing to the supreme judge of the world for the rectitude of our intentions, do in the name, and by the authority of the good people of these colonies, solemnly publish and declare, that these united colonies are, and of right ought to be free and independent states; that they are absolved from all allegiance to the British crown, and that all political connection between them and the state of Great Britain is, and ought to be, totally dissolved; and that as free and independent states, they have full power to levy war, conclude peace, contract alliances, establish commerce, and to do all other acts and things which independent states may of right do.

And for the support of this declaration, with a firm reliance on the protection of divine providence, we mutually pledge to each other our lives, our fortunes, and our sacred honour.

The Declaration thus signed on the 4th, on paper, was engrossed on parchment, and signed again on the 2nd of August.

---

[11] The revised version of the final two paragraphs follows below.

JOHN ADAMS

(1735–1826)

Generally acknowledged as one of the chief inventors of "checks and balances" in the United States Constitution, John Adams had won distinction as a moderate but firm Revolutionary leader in the 1760's and 1770's, and although the record of his Presidency will always be marred by the notorious Alien and Sedition Acts he was a brave defender of civil liberties before and after that trying period of undeclared war against France. One can see the quality of his mind and principles in his defense of the Massachusetts constitution and in his famous correspondence with Thomas Jefferson. Less well known are his letters under the name of Humphry Ploughjogger and his autobiography, which especially in the narrative of his childhood and youth creates an attractive picture of family life and Massachusetts politics in the decades before the Revolution. Adams, like Jefferson and Franklin, thought of the self to be represented in all these works—letters, political debate, autobiography—as essentially a public presence, whose emotional and private life were of no great value or proper interest to the reader. We know that Adams, for example, had a passionate temper, as some of his rhetoric indicates clearly enough, but the requirements of public discourse, even in autobiography, obliged him to express as his proper self the thoughts, however unique, of a rational, public-spirited mind. Neither for Adams nor for Jefferson or Franklin was the autobiography in any modern sense confessional.

The complete title of Adams's three-volume work on the American constitutions is *A Defense of the Constitutions of Government of the United States of America against the attack of M. Turgot, in his letter to Dr. Price, dated the twenty-second of March, 1778.* Adams wrote the

The standard nineteenth-century edition is *The Works of John Adams*, 10 vols., ed. Charles Francis Adams, 1850–1856, but the Adams papers are now being reedited. See *The Diary and Autobiography of John Adams*, 4 vols., ed. Lyman Butterfield and others, 1961; *Familiar Letters of John Adams and His Wife Abigail Adams During the Revolution*, ed. Charles Francis Adams, 1876; *Correspondence of John Adams and Thomas Jefferson, 1812–1826*, ed. Paul Wistach, 1925; *The Book of Abigail and John*, 1975.

The most extensive recent biography is Page Smith, *John Adams*, 2 vols. 1962. Recent evaluations include Clinton Rossiter, "The Legacy of John Adams," *Yale Review*, 46 (1957): 528–550; John R. Howe, *The Changing Political Thought of John Adams*, 1966; Earl N. Harbert, "John Adams' Private Voice: The Diary and Autobiography," *Tulane Studies in English*, 15 (1967): 89–105; Peter Shaw, *The Character of John Adams*, 1975.

book in considerable haste in 1786 and 1787, while he was serving as Minister to Great Britain and therefore unable to participate in the Constitutional Convention in Philadelphia. The constitutions that he defends here are those of several American states, but he concentrates especially on the Massachusetts constitution of 1780, much of which he himself drafted. Besides answering Turgot's criticism of the separation of powers, Adams was also concerned about a popular debtors' rebellion under Daniel Shays in Massachusetts (1786-1787) and about proposals by Benjamin Franklin, Thomas Paine, and others for a government dominated by the legislature.

In the long preface that is reprinted here Adams states clearly his fundamental principle, which is almost the same as that of John Cotton, the Puritan minister who had written on limited government in the 1630's: all government must be limited, because any man given power will use every ounce of it that he is permitted to use. The legislature must therefore be limited by and separate from the executive and judiciary, and the legislature itself must consist of a popular branch and a senate that represents established wealth and culture.

Letters to *The Boston Evening Post* and *The Boston Gazette*[1]

[Under the name of Humphry Ploughjogger, Adams wrote a number of letters to Boston newspapers about political issues in the 1760's. Here we print a letter (1763) on the prospect of a standing army, and another (1767) ridiculing an antirepublican argument by a learned antagonist. Adams's extension of analogy in the idiom of the farmer is unusually effective. Although later a Federalist, Adams knew how to appeal to common sense and plebeian sympathies. His use of this character and style establishes him in a long tradition that includes Brother Jonathan, Simon Suggs, and Huckleberry Finn.]

LETTER TO *THE BOSTON EVENING POST,* MARCH 14, 1763

Boston, the third of March 1763.

Lofing Sun,

Thes fue lins cums to let you no, that I am very wel at prisent, thank God fer it, hoping that you and the family are so too. I haf bin here this fortnite and it is fiftene yeres you no sins I was here laste, and ther is grate altera-

---

[1] The texts of this letter and the next were prepared and edited by Helen Saltman, from *The Boston Evening Post*, March 14, 1763, and *The Boston Gazette*, January 5, 1767.

shons both in the plase and peple. the grate men dus nothin but quaril with one anuther and put peces in the nues paper aginst one anuther, and sum sayes one is rite, and others sayes tuther is rite and they dont know why or wherefor, there is not base such bad work amungst us when we are a goin to ordane a minstur as ther is amungst these grete Fokes, and they say there is going to be a standin armey to be kept in pay all pece time and I am glad of it Ime sure for then muney will be plenty and we can sell off our sauce and meat, but some other peple says we shull be force to pay um and that will be bad on tuther hand becaus we haf pade taksis enuf alredy amungst us, and they say we are despretly in det now but howsomever we dont pay near upon it so much as bostun folks and thats som cumfurt but I hop our depetys will be so wise as to take care we shant pay no more for that, the Boston peple are grave dedly proud for I see seven or eight chirch minsturs[2] tuther day and they had ruffles on and grate ty wigs with matter a bushel of hair on um that cums haf way down there baks, but I dont wonder they go so fin for there is a parcel of peple in Lundun that chuses um as they say and pays um, but our M - - - - -[3] thinks themselfs well off if they can get a toe shirt to go to Leckshan[4] in, but that is not their sorts for if they ant well pade they cant help it and they ort to be for the bible says the laburrer is wurthy of his hier and they that prech the Gospel should live by the Gospel, but Ime dredful afrade that now there is somany of these minsturs here that they will try to bring in popiree among us and then the pritandur will come and we shall all be made slaves an I have bote your juse harp and intend to come home next week and tell your mother so. so no more at prisent but that I am

Your lofeing father

Humphry Ploughjogger.

LETTER TO *THE BOSTON GAZETTE,*
JANUARY 5, 1767

Messieurs Edes & Gill,
Please to insert the following
To The Learned Philanthrop

In your first Treatise, I find these Words, "Whatever tends to create in the Minds of the People, a Contempt of the Persons of those who hold the highest Offices in the State, tends to induce in the Minds of the People a

---

[2] Anglicans, or Church of England ministers, chosen not by their respective congregations but by authorities in London.

[3] That is, ministers?

[4] A tow shirt to go to the Annual Election in.

Belief that Subordination is not necessary, and is no essential Part of Government."—Now if I understand the Meaning of your high-flown Words, for the Gizzard of me, I can't see the Truth of them—Should any one say, and in Print too, that the Steeple of Dr. Sewall's Meeting-House, was old, and decayed, and rotten, as it was the last Time I see it, and in Danger of Falling on the Heads of the People in the Street, would this tend to induce in the Minds of the People, a Belief that a Steeple was not necessary to a Meeting-House, and that any Meeting-House, might as well be turned topsy-turvey, and the Steeple stuck down into the Earth, instead of being erected into the Air? Again, suppose the Sweep of my Cyder-Mill, was cracked and shivered, so that it had not Strength to grind an Apple, or to turn the Rolls, if one of my Neighbours should tell me of this, would this tend to create in me a Belief, that a Sweep was no necessary Part of a Cyder-Mill, and that the Sweep might as well be placed where the Rolls are, or where the Hopper is, or the Trough, as here we commonly put it? Once more, I have a Mare that is old, and lean, and hipped, and stifled, and spavined, and heavy, and botty, and has lost her Mane and Tail, and both her Ears, by the naughty Boys. Now if I should put this Jade into a Horse Cart, and lead her through the Town in the Sight of all the People, I believe they would one and all, despise my old Beast, and laugh at her too, and if any of them came near her, and she should kick 'em and bite 'em, they would hate her too; but would all this their Contempt and Laughter and Hatred, tend to induce in their Minds a Belief that a Horse was not necessary to draw a Horse Cart, and that a Cart might as well be put before a Horse, as a Horse before a Cart?

This now seems to be strong Rashosination, so do you answer my Questions directly, not find Fault with my Pointing and Spelling as you served Mr. X, who our School-Master tells me is a Man of better Sense than you are, and Spells and Points better too, notwithstanding your Braggadocio airs.

So I remain your's to Sarve.

H. P[l]oughjogger

P. S. I'm so well known in the larned World, that I tho't it not worth while to write my Name out at length, but you may print it so if you pleas.

° I do think he might just have mention'd me, and quoted some lines at me, or something———— for instance he might have said,

> Joggs slowly on, unkowing what he fought [sought?]
> And whistled as he went for want of thought.

A Defense of the Constitutions of Government[1]

From **the Preface**

The arts and sciences, in general, during the three or four last centuries have had a regular course of progressive improvement. The inventions in mechanic arts, the discoveries in natural philosophy, navigation, and commerce, and the advancement of civilization and humanity have occasioned changes in the condition of the world and the human character which would have astonished the most refined nations of antiquity. A continuation of similar exertions is every day rendering Europe more and more like one community, or single family. Even in the theory and practice of government, in all the simple monarchies considerable improvements have been made. The checks and balances of republican governments have been in some degree adopted at the courts of princes. By the erection of various tribunals to register the laws and exercise the judicial power—by indulging the petitions and remonstrances of subjects until by habit they are regarded as rights—a control has been established over ministers of state and the royal councils, which, in some degree, approaches the spirit of republics. Property is generally secure and personal liberty seldom invaded. The press has great influence, even where it is not expressly tolerated; and the public opinion must be respected by a minister, or his place becomes insecure. Commerce begins to thrive; and if religious toleration were established, personal liberty a little more protected by giving an absolute right to demand a public trial in a certain reasonable time, and the states were invested with a few more privileges, or rather restored to some that have been taken away, these governments would be brought to as great a degree of perfection, they would approach as near to the character of governments of laws and not of men, as their nature will probably admit of. In so general a refinement, or more properly a reformation of manners and improvement in science, is it not unaccountable that the knowledge of the principles and construction of free governments, in which the happiness of life, and even the further progress of improvement in education and society, in knowledge and virtue, are so deeply interested, should have remained at a full stand for two or three thousand years?

According to a story in Herodotus,[2] the nature of monarchy, aristocracy, and democracy, and the advantages and inconveniences of each were as well understood at the time of the neighing of the horse of Darius as they are at this hour. A variety of mixtures of these simple species were conceived and attempted with various success by the Greeks and Romans. Representations

---

[1] The text is based on The C. F. Adams edition.

[2] Greek historian of the fifth century B.C.

instead of collections of the people; a total separation of the executive from the legislative power, and of the judicial from both; and a balance in the legislature by three independent, equal branches are perhaps the only three discoveries in the constitution of a free government since the institution of Lycurgus. Even these have been so unfortunate that they have never spread: the first has been given up by all the nations, excepting one, which had once adopted it; and the other two, reduced to practice, if not invented, by the English nation, have never been imitated by any other except their own descendants in America.

While it would be rash to say that nothing further can be done to bring a free government in all its parts still nearer to perfection, the representations of the people are most obviously susceptible of improvement. The end to be aimed at in the formation of a representative assembly seems to be the sense of the people, the public voice. The perfection of the portrait consists in its likeness. Numbers, or property, or both should be the rule; and the proportions of electors and members an affair of calculation. The duration should not be so long that the deputy should have time to forget the opinions of his constituents. Corruption in elections is the great enemy of freedom. Among the provisions to prevent it, more frequent elections and a more general privilege of voting are not all that might be devised. Dividing the districts, diminishing the distance of travel, and confining the choice to residents would be great advances towards the annihilation of corruption. The modern aristocracies of Holland, Venice, Bern, etc., have tempered themselves with innumerable checks by which they have given a great degree of stability to that form of government; and though liberty and life can never be there enjoyed so well as in a free republic, none is perhaps more capable of profound sagacity. We shall learn to prize the checks and balances of a free government and even those of the modern aristocracies if we recollect the miseries of Greece, which arose from its ignorance of them. The only balance attempted against the ancient kings was a body of nobles; and the consequences were perpetual alternations of rebellion and tyranny and the butchery of thousands upon every revolution from one to the other. When kings were abolished, aristocracies tyrannized; and then no balance was attempted but between aristocracy and democracy. This, in the nature of things, could be no balance at all, and therefore the pendulum was forever on the swing.

It is impossible to read in Thucydides[3] his account of the factions and confusions throughout all Greece, which were introduced by this want of an equilibrium, without horror. "During the few days that Eurymedon, with his troops, continued at Corcyra, the people of that city extended the massacre to all whom they judged their enemies. The crime alleged was their attempt

[3] Greek historian of the Pelopponesian War, in the fifth century B.C.

to overturn the democracy. Some perished merely through private enmity; some by the hands of the borrower on account of the money they had lent. Every kind of death, every dreadful act was perpetrated. Fathers slew their children; some were dragged from altars; some were butchered at them; numbers, immured in temples, were starved. The contagion spread through the whole extent of Greece; factions raged in every city, the licentious many contending for the Athenians and the aspiring few for the Lacedæmonians. The consequence was seditions in cities with all their numerous and tragical incidents."

"Such things ever will be," says Thucydides, "so long as human nature continues the same." But if this nervous historian had known a balance of three powers, he would not have pronounced the distemper so incurable but would have added—*so long as parties in cities remain unbalanced*. He adds—"Words lost their signification; brutal rashness was fortitude; prudence, cowardice; modesty, effeminacy; and being wise in everything, to be good for nothing: the hot temper was manly valor; calm deliberation, plausible knavery; he who boiled with indignation was trustworthy; and he who presumed to contradict was ever suspected. Connection of blood was less regarded than transient acquaintance; associations were not formed for mutual advantage consistent with law, but for rapine against all law; trust was only communication of guilt; revenge was more valued than never to have suffered an injury; perjuries were masterpieces of cunning; the dupes only blushed, the villains most impudently triumphed.

"The source of all these evils was a thirst of power, from rapacious and ambitious passions. The men of large influence, some contending for the just equality of the democratical and others for the fair decorum of aristocratical government, by artful sounds embarrassed those communities for their own private lucre by the keenest spirit, the most daring projects, and most dreadful machinations. Revenge, not limited by justice or the public welfare, was measured only by such retaliation as was judged the sweetest—by capital condemnations, by iniquitous sentences, and by glutting the present rancor of their hearts with their own hands. The pious and upright conduct was on both sides disregarded; the moderate citizens fell victims to both. Seditions introduced every species of outrageous wickedness into the Grecian manners. Sincerity was laughed out of countenance; the whole order of human life was confounded; the human temper, too apt to transgress in spite of laws, now having gained the ascendant over law, seemed to glory that it was too strong for justice and an enemy to all superiority."

Mr. Hume[4] has collected from Diodorus Siculus alone a few massacres which happened in only sixty of the most polished years of Greece:—"From

---

[4] David Hume (1711-1766), Scottish philosopher and historian. The quotation is from "On the Populousness of Ancient Nations."

Sybaris, 500 nobles banished; of Chians, 600 citizens; at Ephesus, 340 killed, 1000 banished; of Cyrenians, 500 nobles killed, all the rest banished; the Corinthians killed 120, banished 500; Phæbidas banished 300 Bœotians. Upon the fall of the Lacedæmonians, democracies were restored in many cities and severe vengeance taken of the nobles; the banished nobles, returning, butchered their adversaries at Phialæ, in Corinth, in Megara, in Phliasia, where they killed 300 of the people; but these, again revolting, killed above 600 of the nobles, and banished the rest. In Arcadia, 1400 banished, besides many killed; the banished retired to Sparta and Pallantium; the latter were delivered up to their countrymen and all killed. Of the banished from Argos and Thebes, there were 500 in the Spartan army. The people before the usurpation of Agathocles had banished 600 nobles; afterwards that tyrant, in concurrence with the people, killed 4000 nobles and banished 6000, and killed 4000 people at Gela; his brother banished 8000 from Syracuse. The inhabitants of Ægesta, to the number of 40,000, were killed, man, woman, and child, for sake of their money; all the relations of the Libyan army, father, brothers, children, killed; 7000 exiles killed after capitulation. These numbers, compared with the population of those cities, are prodigious; yet Agathocles was a man of character and not to be suspected of wanton cruelty contrary to the maxims of his age."

Such were the fashionable outrages of unbalanced parties. In the name of human and divine benevolence, is such a system as this to be recommended to Americans in this age of the world? Human nature is as incapable now of going through revolutions with temper and sobriety, with patience and prudence, or without fury and madness, as it was among the Greeks so long ago. The latest revolution that we read of was conducted, at least on one side, in the Grecian style, with laconic energy; and with a little Attic salt, at least, without too much patience, foresight, and prudence on the other. Without three orders and an effectual balance between them in every American constitution, it must be destined to frequent unavoidable revolutions; though they are delayed a few years, they must come in time. The United States are large and populous nations in comparison with the Grecian commonwealths or even the Swiss cantons; and they are growing every day more disproportionate and therefore less capable of being held together by simple governments. Countries that increase in population so rapidly as the States of America did, even during such an impoverishing and destructive war as the last was, are not to be long bound with silken threads; lions, young or old, will not be bound by cobwebs. It would be better for America, it is nevertheless agreed, to ring all the changes with the whole set of bells and go through all the revolutions of the Grecian States, rather than establish an absolute monarchy among them, notwithstanding all the great and real improvements which have been made in that kind of government.

The objection to it is not because it is supported by nobles and a subordination of ranks; for all governments, even the most democratical, are supported by a subordination of offices and of ranks too. None ever existed without it but in a state of anarchy and outrage, in a contempt of law and justice, no better than no government. But the nobles in the European monarchies support them more by opposing than promoting their ordinary views. The kings are supported by their armies; the nobles support the crown, as it is in full possession of the gift of all employments; but they support it still more by checking its ministers and preventing them from running into abuses of power and wanton despotism; otherwise the people would be pushed to extremities and insurrections. It is thus that the nobles reconcile the monarchical authority to the obedience of the subjects; but take away the standing armies and leave the nobles to themselves, and in a few years they would overturn every monarchy in Europe and erect aristocracies.

It is become a kind of fashion among writers to admit, as a maxim, that if you could be always sure of a wise, active, and virtuous prince, monarchy would be the best of governments. But this is so far from being admissible that it will forever remain true that a free government has a great advantage over a simple monarchy. The best and wisest prince, by means of a freer communication with his people and the greater opportunities to collect the best advice from the best of his subjects, would have an immense advantage in a free state over a monarchy. A senate consisting of all that is most noble, wealthy, and able in the nation, with a right to counsel the crown at all times, is a check to ministers and a security against abuses such as a body of nobles who never meet and have no such right can never supply. Another assembly composed of representatives chosen by the people in all parts gives free access to the whole nation and communicates all its wants, knowledge, projects, and wishes to government; it excites emulation among all classes, removes complaints, redresses grievances, affords opportunities of exertion to genius, though in obscurity, and gives full scope to all the faculties of man; it opens a passage for every speculation to the legislature, to administration, and to the public; it gives a universal energy to the human character, in every part of the state, such as never can be obtained in a monarchy.

There is a third particular which deserves attention both from governments and people. In a simple monarchy the ministers of state can never know their friends from their enemies; secret cabals undermine their influence and blast their reputation. This occasions a jealousy, ever anxious and irritated, which never thinks the government safe without an encouragement of informers and spies throughout every part of the state, who interrupt the tranquility of private life, destroy the confidence of families in their own domestics and in one another, and poison freedom in its sweetest retirements. In a free government, on the contrary, the ministers can have no enemies of consequence but among the members of the great or little council, where every man is obliged to take his side and declare his opinions upon every question. This circumstance alone to every manly mind would be sufficient to decide the preference in favor of a free government. Even secrecy, where the executive is entire in one hand, is as easily and surely preserved in a free government as in a simple monarchy; and as to dispatch, all the simple monarchies of the whole universe may be defied to produce greater or more numerous examples of it than are to be found in English history. An Alexander or a Frederic, possessed of the prerogatives only of a king of England. and leading his own armies, would never find himself embarrassed or delayed in any honest enterprise. He might be restrained, indeed, from running mad and from making conquests to the ruin of his nation merely for his own glory; but this is no argument against a free government.

There can be no free government without a democratical branch in the constitution. Monarchies and aristocracies are in possession of the voice and influence of every university and academy in Europe. Democracy, simple democracy, never had a patron among men of letters. Democratical mixtures in government have lost almost all the advocates they ever had out of England and America. Men of letters must have a great deal of praise and some of the necessaries, conveniences, and ornaments of life. Monarchies and aristocracies pay well and applaud liberally. The people have almost always expected to be served gratis and to be paid for the honor of serving them; and their applauses and adorations are bestowed too often on artifices and tricks, on hypocrisy and superstition, on flattery, bribes, and largesses. It is no wonder then that democracies and democratical mixtures are annihilated all over Europe except on a barren rock, a paltry fen, an inaccessible mountain, or an impenetrable forest. The people of England, to their immortal honor, are hitherto an exception; but, to the humiliation of human nature, they show very often that they are like other men. The people in America have now the best opportunity and the greatest trust in their hands that Providence ever committed to so small a number since the transgression of the first pair; if they betray their trust, their guilt will merit even greater punishment than other nations have suffered and the indignation of Heaven. If there is one certain truth to be collected from the history of all ages, it is this: that the people's rights and liberties and the democratical mixture in a constitution can never be preserved without a strong executive, or, in other words, without separating the executive from the legislative power. If the executive power or any considerable part of it is left in the hands either of an aristocratical or a democratical assembly, it will corrupt the legislature as necessarily as rust corrupts iron or as arsenic poisons the human body; and when the legislature is corrupted, the people are undone.

The rich, the well-born, and the able acquire an influence among the people that will soon be too much for simple honesty and plain sense in a house of representatives. The most illustrious of them must, therefore, be separated from the mass and placed by themselves in a senate; this is, to all honest and useful intents, an ostracism. A member of a senate of immense wealth, the most respected birth, and transcendent abilities has no influence in the nation in comparison of what he would have in a single representative assembly. When a senate exists, the most powerful man in the state may be safely admitted into the house of representatives because the people have it in their power to remove him into the senate as soon as his influence becomes dangerous. The senate becomes the great object of ambition and the richest and the most sagacious wish to merit an advancement to it by services to the public in the house. When he has obtained the object of his wishes, you may still hope for the benefits of his exertions without dreading his passions; for the executive power being in other hands, he has lost much of his influence with the people and can govern very few votes more than his own among the senators.

It was the general opinion of ancient nations that the Divinity alone was adequate to the important office of giving laws to men. The Greeks entertained this prejudice throughout all their dispersions; the Romans cultivated the same popular delusion; and modern nations, in the consecration of kings and in several superstitious chimeras of divine right in princes and nobles, are nearly unanimous in preserving remnants of it. Even the venerable magistrates of Amersfort devoutly believe themselves God's viceregents. Is it that obedience to the laws can be obtained from mankind in no other manner? Are the jealousy of power and the envy of superiority so strong in all men that no consideration of public or private utility are sufficient to engage their submission to rules for their own happiness? Or is the disposition to imposture so prevalent in men of experience that their private views of ambition and avarice can be accomplished only by artifice? It was a tradition in antiquity that the laws of Crete were dictated to Minos by the inspiration of Jupiter. This legislator and his brother Rhadamanthus were both his sons; once in nine years they went to converse with their father, to propose questions concerning the wants of the people; and his answers were recorded as laws for their government. The laws of Lacedæmon were communicated by Apollo to Lycurgus; and, lest the meaning of the deity should not have been perfectly comprehended or correctly expressed, they were afterwards confirmed by his oracle at Delphos. Among the Romans Numa was indebted for those laws which procured the prosperity of his country to his conversations with Egeria. The Greeks imported these mysteries from Egypt and the East, whose despotisms from the remotest antiquity to this day have been founded in the same solemn empiricism, their emperors and nobles being all descended from their gods. Woden and Thor were divinities too; and their posterity ruled a thousand years in the north by the strength of a like credulity. Manco Capac was the child of the sun, the visible deity of the Peruvians, and transmitted his divinity, as well as his earthly dignity and authority, through a line of Incas. And the rudest tribes of savages in North America have certain families from which their leaders are always chosen under the immediate protection of the god War. There is nothing in which mankind have been more unanimous; yet nothing can be inferred from it more than this, that the multitude have always been credulous and the few are always artful.

The United States of America have exhibited, perhaps, the first example of governments erected on the simple principles of nature; and if men are now sufficiently enlightened to disabuse themselves of artifice, imposture, hypocrisy, and superstition, they will consider this event as an era in their history. Although the detail of the formation of the American governments is at present little known or regarded either in Europe or in America, it may hereafter become an object of curiosity. It will never be pretended that any persons employed in that service had interviews with the gods or were in any degree under the inspiration of Heaven, more than those at work upon ships or houses, or laboring in merchandise or agriculture; it will forever be acknowledged that these governments were contrived merely by the use of reason and the senses, as Copley painted Chatham; West, Wolf; and Trumbull, Warren and Montgomery; as Dwight, Barlow, Trumbull, and Humphries composed their verse, and Belknap and Ramsay history; as Godfrey invented his quadrant, and Rittenhouse his planetarium; as Boylston practiced inoculation, and Franklin electricity; as Paine exposed the mistakes of Raynal, and Jefferson those of Buffon, so unphilosophically borrowed from the despicable dreams of De Pau.[5] Neither the people nor their conventions, committees, or subcommittees considered legislation in any other light than as ordinary arts and sciences, only more important. Called without expectation and compelled without previous inclination, though undoubtedly at the best period of time, both for England and America, suddenly to erect new systems of laws for their future government, they adopted the method of a wise architect in erecting a new palace for the residence of his sovereign. They determined to consult Vitruvius, Palladio, and all other writers of reputation in the art; to examine the most celebrated buildings, whether they remain entire or in ruins; to compare these with the principles of writers; and to inquire how far both the theories and models were founded in nature or created by fancy; and when this was done, so far as their circumstances would allow, to adopt the advantages and reject the inconveniences of all. Unembarrassed by attachments to noble families, hereditary lines and successions, or any considerations of royal blood, even the pious mystery of holy oil had no more influence than that other one of holy water. The people were universally too enlightened to be imposed on by artifice; and their

[5] Here Adams appeals to the achievements of American painters: John Singleton Copley, who painted a portrait of William Pitt, the Earl of Chatham; Benjamin West, who painted a portrait of General Wolfe, hero of Quebec; and John Trumbull, who painted grand scenes of the death of two American Revolutionary heroes. The American writers mentioned next are Timothy Dwight, Joel Barlow, John Trumbull, and David Humphreys, the so-called Connecticut Wits; and the historians Jeremy Belknap and David Ramsay.

leaders, or more properly followers, were men of too much honor to attempt it. Thirteen governments thus founded on the natural authority of the people alone, without a pretense of miracle or mystery, and which are destined to spread over the northern part of that whole quarter of the globe, are a great point gained in favor of the rights of mankind. The experiment is made and has completely succeeded; it can no longer be called in question whether authority in magistrates and obedience of citizens can be grounded on reason, morality, and the Christian religion, without the monkery of priests or the knavery of politicians. As the writer was personally acquainted with most of the gentlemen in each of the states who had the principal share in the first draughts, the following work was really written to lay before the public a specimen of that kind of reading and reasoning which produced the American constitutions.

It is not a little surprising that all this kind of learning should have been unknown to any illustrious philosopher and statesman, and especially one who really was what he has been often called, "a well of science." But if he could be unacquainted with it or it could have escaped his memory, we may suppose millions in America have occasion to be reminded of it. The writer has long seen with anxiety the facility with which philosophers of greatest name have undertaken to write of American affairs without knowing anything of them and have echoed and reëchoed each other's visionary language. Having neither talents, leisure, nor inclination to meet such champions in the field of literary controversy, he little thought of venturing to propose to them any questions. Circumstances, however, have lately occurred which seem to require that some notice should be taken of one of them. If the publication of these papers should contribute anything to turn the attention of the younger gentlemen of letters in America to this kind of inquiry, it will produce an effect of some importance to their country. The subject is the most interesting that can engage the understanding or the heart; for whether the end of man, in this stage of his existence, be enjoyment, or improvement, or both, it can never be attained so well in a bad government as a good one.

·   ·   ·

The institutions now made in America will not wholly wear out for thousands of years. It is of the last importance, then, that they should begin right. If they set out wrong, they will never be able to return, unless it be by accident, to the right path. After having known the history of Europe and of England in particular, it would be the height of folly to go back to the institutions of Woden and of Thor, as the Americans are advised to do. If they had been counselled to adopt a single monarchy at once, it would have been less mysterious.

Robertson, Hume, and Gibbon[6] have given such admirable accounts of the feudal institutions and their consequences that it would have been, perhaps, more discreet to have referred to them without saying anything more upon the subject. To collect together the legislation of the Indians would take up much room but would be well worth the pains. The sovereignty is in the nation, it is true, but the three powers are strong in every tribe; and their royal and aristocratical dignities are much more generally hereditary, from the popular partiality to particular families and the superstitious opinion that such are favorites of the God of War, than late writers upon this subject have allowed.

GROSVENOR SQUARE, January 1, 1787.

[6] Eighteenth-century British historians.

JAMES MADISON

(1751–1836)

James Madison's chief contribution to American letters is the series of essays he wrote in association with Alexander Hamilton and John Jay to persuade the people of New York to ratify the United States Constitution in 1788. The numbers of "The Federalist" that Madison wrote display the qualities for which he was admired in politics throughout his long career—clarity, shrewdness, practical good sense, and an unspectacular ability to reason for the public good. In the Federalist #10, for example, Madison turns against the antifederalists one of the chief arguments against giving the central government new powers—the size of the country. Agreeing with most national leaders of the day that partisanship or "factions" would be dangerous to the public good, Madison argues here that the conflict of economic or sectional interests over so broad an area will make it more difficult than in individual

The standard edition is *The Writings of James Madison*, 9 vols., ed. Gaillard Hunt, 1900-1910. A new edition will be definitive: *The Papers of James Madison*, ed. W. T. Hutchinson and others, 1962-.

The most thorough modern biography is Irving Brant, *James Madison*, 6 vols., 1941-1961. See also Ralph L. Ketcham, *James Madison; A Biography*, 1971. A one-volume edition of the Federalist papers is *The Federalist*, ed. Benjamin Wright, 1961. For commentary, see Douglass Adair, "'That Politics May Be Reduced to a Science': David Hume, James Madison, and the Tenth Federalist," *Huntington Library Quarterly*, 20 (1957): 343-360.

towns or states for special groups to pervert governmental decisions to their own purposes. And in the sixty-eighth paper he discusses the impeachment process by which the executive, the authority most feared by opponents of the new Constitution in those days when royal governors and the claims of King George II were still well remembered, could be restrained. Both these lucid analyses are of course especially relevant to issues in our much larger and more powerful country today.

Madison served in the Virginia constitutional convention in 1776, soon after he had broken off advanced religious and Hebrew studies at Princeton, from which he had graduated in 1771 and where he had befriended Hugh Henry Brackenridge and Philip Freneau. He helped to write the Virginia Bill of Rights and was elected to the Continental Congress in 1780. He was one of the chief advocates of the federal Constitutional Convention of 1787, and his notes of that long historic meeting, published several years after his death, are an invaluable source for study of the Founders' methods and intentions. He is generally recognized as having achieved strong influence on the assignment of great power to the federal government. Within two years after the establishment of the new government, however, Madison had become a leader of the Republican party that opposed many of Alexander Hamilton's commercial and banking policies, and Madison settled also into opposition to the pro-English, anti-French policies of the Washington and Adams administrations. He became Secretary of State under Jefferson and succeeded him for two terms as the fourth President of the United States. When Jefferson died in 1826 Madison became Rector of the new University of Virginia, until two years before his own death 10 years later.

The Federalist No. 10
[On Factions][1]

November 22, 1787

To the People of the State of New York.

Among the numerous advantages promised by a well constructed Union, none deserves to be more accurately developed than its tendency to break

---

[1] First published in *The Daily Advertiser*, November 22, 1787, then in *The New York* *Packet* and *The Independent Journal* on the 23rd and 24th, respectively.

and control the violence of faction. The friend of popular governments, never finds himself so much alarmed for their character and fate, as when he contemplates their propensity to this dangerous vice. He will not fail therefore to set a due value on any plan which, without violating the principles to which he is attached, provides a proper cure for it. The instability, injustice and confusion introduced into the public councils, have in truth been the mortal diseases under which popular governments have everywhere perished; as they continue to be the favorite and fruitful topics from which the adversaries to liberty derive their most specious declamations. The valuable improvements made by the American Constitutions on the popular models, both ancient and modern, cannot certainly be too much admired; but it would be an unwarrantable partiality, to contend that they have as effectually obviated the danger on this side as was wished and expected. Complaints are everywhere heard from our most considerate and virtuous citizens, equally the friends of public and private faith, and of public and personal liberty; that our governments are too unstable; that the public good is disregarded in the conflicts of rival parties; and that measures are too often decided, not according to the rules of justice, and the rights of the minor party; but by the superior force of an interested and over-bearing majority. However anxiously we may wish that these complaints had no foundation, the evidence of known facts will not permit us to deny that they are in some degree true. It will be found indeed, on a candid review of our situation, that some of the distresses under which we labor, have been erroneously charged on the operation of our governments; but it will be found, at the same time, that other causes will not alone account for many of our heaviest misfortunes; and particularly, for that prevailing and increasing distrust of public engagements, and alarm for private rights, which are echoed from one end of the continent to the other. These must be chiefly, if not wholly, effects of the unsteadiness and injustice, with which a factious spirit has tainted our public administrations.

By a faction I understand a number of citizens, whether amounting to a majority or minority of the whole, who are united and actuated by some common impulse of passion, or of interest, adverse to the rights of other citizens, or to the permanent and aggregate interests of the community.

There are two methods of curing the mischiefs of faction: the one, by removing its causes; the other, by controlling its effects.

There are again two methods of removing the causes of faction: the one by destroying the liberty which is essential to its existence; the other, by giving to every citizen the same opinions, the same passions, and the same interests.

It could never be more truly said than of the first remedy, that it is worse than the disease. Liberty is to faction, what air is to fire, an aliment without which it instantly expires. But it could not be a less folly to abolish liberty, which is essential to political life, because it nourishes faction, than it would be to wish the annihilation of air, which is essential to animal life, because it imparts to fire its destructive agency.

The second expedient is as impracticable, as the first would be unwise. As long as the reason of man continues fallible, and he is at liberty to exercise it, different opinions will be formed. As long as the connection subsists between his reason and his self-love, his opinions and his passions will have a reciprocal influence on each other; and the former will be objects to which the latter will attach themselves. The diversity in the faculties of men from which the rights of property originate, is not less an insuperable obstacle to a uniformity of interests. The protection of these faculties is the first object of government. From the protection of different and unequal faculties of acquiring property, the possession of different degrees and kinds of property immediately results: and from the influence of these on the sentiments and views of the respective proprietors, ensues a division of the society into different interests and parties.

The latent causes of faction are thus sown in the nature of man; and we see them everywhere brought into different degrees of activity, according to the different circumstances of civil society. A zeal for different opinions concerning religion, concerning government and many other points, as well of speculation as of practice; an attachment to different leaders ambitiously contending for pre-eminence and power; or to persons of other descriptions whose fortunes have been interesting to the human passions, have in turn divided mankind into parties, inflamed them with mutual animosity, and rendered them much more disposed to vex and oppress each other, than to co-operate for their common good. So strong is this propensity of mankind to fall into mutual animosities, that where no substantial occasion presents itself, the most frivolous and fanciful distinctions have been sufficient to kindle their unfriendly passions, and excite their most violent conflicts. But the most common and durable source of factions, has been the various and unequal distribution of property. Those who hold, and those who are without property, have ever formed distinct interests in society. Those who are creditors, and those who are debtors, fall under a like discrimination. A landed interest, a manufacturing interest, a mercantile interest, a monied interest, with many lesser interests, grow up of necessity in civilized nations, and divide them into different classes, actuated by different sentiments and views. The regulation of these various and interfering interests forms the principal task of modern legislation, and involves the spirit of party and faction in the necessary and ordinary operations of government.

No man is allowed to be a judge in his own cause; because his interest would certainly bias his judgment, and, not improbably, corrupt his integrity. With equal, nay with greater reason, a body of men, are unfit to be both judges and parties, at the same time; yet, what are many of the most important acts of legislation, but so many judicial determinations, not indeed concerning the rights of single persons, but concerning the rights of large bodies of citizens; and what are the different classes of legislators, but advocates and parties to the causes which they determine? Is a law proposed concerning private debts? It is a question to which the creditors are parties on one side, and the debtors on the other. Justice ought to hold the balance between them. Yet the parties are and must be themselves the judges; and the most numerous party, or, in other words, the most powerful faction must be expected to prevail. Shall domestic manufactures be encouraged, and in what degree, by restrictions on foreign manufactures? are questions which would be differently decided by the landed and the manufacturing classes; and probably by neither, with a sole regard to justice and the public good. The apportionment of taxes on the various descriptions of property, is an act which seems to require the most exact impartiality; yet, there is perhaps no legislative act in which greater opportunity and temptation are given to a predominant party, to trample on the rules of justice. Every shilling with which they over-burden the inferior number, is a shilling saved to their own pockets.

It is in vain to say, that enlightened statesmen will be able to adjust these clashing interests, and render them all subservient to the public good. Enlightened statesmen will not always be at the helm: nor, in many cases, can such an adjustment be made at all, without taking into view indirect and remote considerations, which will rarely prevail over the immediate interest which one party may find in disregarding the rights of another, or the good of the whole.

The inference to which we are brought, is, that the *causes* of faction cannot be removed; and that relief is only to be sought in the means of controlling its *effects*.

If a faction consists of less than a majority, relief is supplied by the republican principle, which enables the majority to defeat its sinister views by regular vote: it may clog the administration, it may convulse the society; but it will be unable to execute and mask its violence under the forms of the Constitution. When a majority is included in a faction, the form of popular government on the other hand enables it to sacrifice to its ruling passion or interest, both the public good and the rights of other citizens. To secure the public good, and private rights, against the danger of such a faction, and at the same time to preserve the spirit and the form of popular government, is then the great object to which our enquiries are directed: let me add that it is the great desideratum, by which alone this form of government can be rescued from the opprobrium under which it has so long labored, and be recommended to the esteem and adoption of mankind.

By what means is this object attainable? Evidently by one of two only. Either the existence of the same passion or interest in a majority at the same time, must be prevented; or the majority, having such co-existent passion or interest, must be rendered, by their number and local situation, unable to concert and carry into effect schemes of oppression. If the impulse and the opportunity be suffered to coincide, we well know that neither moral nor religious motives can be relied on as an adequate control. They are not found to be such on the injustice and violence of individuals, and lose their efficacy in proportion to the number combined together; that is, in proportion as their efficacy becomes needful.

From this view of the subject, it may be concluded, that a pure democracy, by which I mean, a society, consisting of a small number of citizens, who assemble and administer the government in person, can admit of no cure for the mischiefs of faction. A common passion or interest will, in almost every case, be felt by a majority of the whole; a communication and concert results from the form of government itself; and there is nothing to check the inducements to sacrifice the weaker party, or an obnoxious individual. Hence it is, that such democracies have ever been spectacles of turbulence and contention; have ever been found incompatible with personal security, or the rights of property; and have in general been as short in their lives, as they have been violent in their deaths. Theoretic politicians, who have patronized this species of government, have erroneously supposed, that by reducing mankind to a perfect equality in their political rights, they would, at the same time, be perfectly equalized and assimilated in their possessions, their opinions, and their passions.

A republic, by which I mean a government in which the scheme of representation takes place, opens a different prospect, and promises the cure for which we are seeking. Let us examine the points in which it varies from pure democracy, and we shall comprehend both the nature of the cure, and the efficacy which it must derive from the union.

The two great points of difference between a democracy and a republic are, first, the delegation of the government, in the latter, to a small number of citizens elected by the rest: secondly, the greater number of citizens, and greater sphere of country, over which the latter may be extended.

The effect of the first difference is, on the one hand to refine and enlarge the public views, by passing them through the medium of a chosen body of citizens, whose wisdom may best discern the true interest of their country, and whose patriotism and love of justice, will be least likely to sacrifice it to temporary or partial considerations. Under such a regulation, it may well happen that the public voice pronounced by the representatives of the people, will be more consonant to the public good, than if pronounced by the people themselves convened for the purpose. On the other hand, the effect may be inverted. Men of factious tempers, of local prejudices, or of sinister designs, may by intrigue, by corruption or by other means, first obtain the suffrages, and then betray the interests of the people. The question resulting is, whether small or extensive republics are most favorable to the election of proper guardians of the public weal: and it is clearly decided in favor of the latter by two obvious considerations.

In the first place it is to be remarked that however small the republic may be, the representatives must be raised to a certain number, in order to guard against the cabals of a few; and that however large it may be, they must be limited to a certain number, in order to guard against the confusion of a multitude. Hence the number of representatives in the two cases, not being in proportion to that of the constituents, and being proportionally greatest in the small republic, it follows, that if the proportion of fit characters, be not less, in the large than in the small republic, the former will present a greater option, and consequently a greater probability of a fit choice.

In the next place, as each representative will be chosen by a greater number of citizens in the large than in the small republic, it will be more difficult for unworthy candidates to practice with success the vicious arts, by which elections are too often carried; and the suffrages of the people being more free, will be more likely to center on men who possess the most attractive merit, and the most diffusive and established characters.

It must be confessed, that in this, as in most other cases, there is a mean, on both sides of which inconveniencies will be found to lie. By enlarging too much the number of electors, you render the representative too little acquainted with all their local circumstances and lesser interests; as by reducing it too much, you render him unduly attached to these, and too little fit to comprehend and pursue great and national objects. The Federal Constitution forms a happy combination in this respect; the great and aggregate interests being referred to the national, the local and particular, to the state legislatures.

The other point of difference is, the greater number of citizens and extent of territory which may be brought within the compass of republican, than of democratic government; and it is this circumstance principally which renders factious combinations less to be dreaded in the former, than in the latter. The smaller the society, the fewer probably will be the distinct parties and interests composing it; the fewer the distinct parties and interests, the more frequently will a majority be found of the same party; and the smaller the number of individuals composing a majority, and the smaller the compass within which they are placed, the more easily will they concert and execute their plans of oppression. Extend the sphere, and you take in a greater variety of parties and interests; you make it less probable that a majority of the whole will have a common motive to invade the rights of other citizens; or if such a common motive exists, it will be more difficult for all who feel it to discover their own strength, and to act in unison with each other. Besides other impediments, it may be remarked, that where there is a consciousness of unjust or dishonorable purposes, communication is always checked by distrust, in proportion to the number whose concurrence is neoossary.

Hence it clearly appears, that the same advantage, which a republic has over a democracy, in controlling the effects of faction, is enjoyed by a large over a small republic—is enjoyed by the Union over the states composing it. Does this advantage consist in the substitution of representatives, whose enlightened views and virtuous sentiments render them superior to local prejudices, and to schemes of injustice? It will not be denied, that the representation of the Union will be most likely to possess these requisite endowments. Does it consist in the greater security afforded by a greater variety of parties, against the event of any one party being able to outnumber and oppress the rest? In an equal degree does the encreased variety of parties, comprised within the Union, encrease this security? Does it, in fine, consist in the greater obstacles opposed to the concert and accomplishment of the secret wishes of an unjust and interested majority? Here, again, the extent of the Union gives it the most palpable advantage.

The influence of factious leaders may kindle a flame within their particular States, but will be unable to spread a general conflagration through the other States: a religious sect, may degenerate into a political faction in a part of the confederacy; but the variety of sects dispersed over the entire face of it, must secure the national councils against any danger from that source: a rage for paper money, for an abolition of debts, for an equal division of property, or for any other improper or wicked project, will be less apt to pervade the whole body of the Union, than a particular member of it; in the same proportion as such a malady is more likely to taint a particular county or district, than an entire State.

In the extent and proper structure of the Union, therefore, we behold a republican remedy for the diseases most incident to republican government. And according to the degree of pleasure and pride, we feel in being Republicans, ought to be our zeal in cherishing the spirit, and supporting the character of Federalists.

PUBLIUS.

ISAAC BACKUS

(1724–1806)

Isaac Backus was baptized in the First Congregational Church of Norwich, Connecticut, to which his parents belonged, but he belongs in American literary and cultural history as a Baptist who probably did more than any other northerner to establish religious liberty as a fundamental principle of the Republic. Backus was converted during the Great Awakening, when he was 17 years old, and he and his mother soon joined a Separatist church. Within a few years he found himself in violation of a new Massachusetts law (1742) that forbade anyone to preach without express permission of the ordained ministers, for he preached as a "lay exhorter" in Massachusetts and Rhode Island as well as Connecticut, and in 1748 both his mother and his brother were jailed in Norwich for refusing to pay taxes for support of the established minister there.

From that time forward, Backus was increasingly committed to the fight for separation of church and state. His commitment was intensified when, after his marriage to a Baptist in 1749, he himself came to oppose infant baptism and (in 1756) to accept ordination as pastor of the First Baptist Church of Middleboro, for Baptists opposed taxes for ministers' salaries, and their ministers received no state support. Backus took the case for religious equality to King George III and then to the Continental Congress, but despite the cogency of his arguments, he was not successful until (after his death) the Massachusetts constitution was revised in the nineteenth century.

The standard text and the source of this selection is *Isaac Backus on Church, State, and Calvinism: Pamphlets, 1754–1789,* ed. William G. McLoughlin, 1968. Recent studies include William G. McLoughlin, *Issac Backus and the American Pietistic Tradition,* 1967; William G. McLoughlin, *New England Dissent, 1630–1833: The Baptists and the Separation of Church and State,* 1971.

From An Appeal
to the Public for Religious Liberty,
Against the Oppressions
of the Present Day.[1]

CONCLUSION

And now dear countrymen, we beseech you seriously to consider of these things. The great importance of a general union through this country in order to the preservation of our liberties has often been pleaded for with propriety, but how can such a union be expected so long as that dearest of all rights, equal liberty of conscience, is not allowed? Yea, how can any reasonably expect that HE who has the hearts of kings in His hand will turn the heart of our earthly sovereign to hear the pleas for liberty of those who will not hear the cries of their fellow subjects under their oppressions? Has it not been plainly proved that so far as any man gratifies his own inclinations without regard to the universal law of equity so far he is in bondage? So that it is impossible for anyone to tyrannize over others without thereby becoming a miserable slave himself, a slave to raging lust and a slave to guilty fears of what will be the consequence. We are told that the father of Cyrus, though a heathen, "Had often taught him to consider that the prudence of men is very short and their views very limited, that they cannot penetrate into futurity, and that many times what they think must needs turn to their advantage proves their ruin, whereas the gods, being eternal, know all things, future as well as past, and inspire those that love them to undertake what is most expedient for them, which is a favor and protection they owe to no man and grant only to those that invoke and consult them." And we are told by the same author,[2] of another wise heathen who said, "'Tis observable that those that fear the Deity most are least afraid of man." And shall not Christians awake to a most hearty reverence of HIM who has said (and will ever make good His word) *With what measure ye mete, it shall be measured to you again.*[3]

Suffer us a little to expostulate with our fathers and brethren who inhabit the land to which our ancestors fled for religious liberty. You have lately been accused with being disorderly and rebellious by men in power who profess a great regard for order and the public good. And why don't you believe them and rest easy under their administrations? You tell us you cannot because you are taxed where you are not represented. And is it not

---

[1] Boston, 1778.

[2] Rollin in his ancient history. [Backus's note.]

[3] See Luke 6:38 and Mark 4:24.

really so with us? You do not deny the right of the British Parliament to impose taxes within her own realm; only complain that she extends her taxing power beyond her proper limits. And have we not as good right to say you do the *same thing?* And so that wherein you judge others you condemn yourselves? Can three thousand miles possibly fix such limits to taxing power as the difference between civil and sacred matters has already done? One is only a difference of *space*, the other is so great a difference in the *nature* of things as there is between *sacrifices to God* and the *ordinances of man*. This we trust has been fully proved.

If we ask why have you not been easy and thankful since the Parliament has taken off so many of the taxes that they had laid upon us, you answer that they still claim a power to tax us when and as much as they please. And is not that the very difficulty before us? In the year 1747 our legislature passed an act to free the Baptists in general from ministerial taxes for ten years. Yet because they [the Baptists] increased considerably, when that time was about half expired they [the legislature] broke in upon the liberty they had granted and made a new act wherein no Baptist church nor minister was allowed to have any such exemption till they had *first* obtained certificates from three other churches. By which the late Mr. John Proctor observed (in a remonstrance that he drew and which was presented to our court) that they had, as far as in them lay, "disfranchised, unchurched, and usurped an illegal power over all the religious societies of the people in said act called anabaptists throughout this province; for where is it possible for the poor anabaptists to find the *first* three authenticated ministers and churches to authenticate the first three!" So we have now related a case in which a number of our brethren were put to new cost for copies to notify others with hope of relief to themselves and yet in the same session of court they had a worse burden laid upon them than before. And their repeated cries and then the petition of our united churches were all rejected.

A very great grievance which our country has justly complained of is that by some late proceedings a man's house or locks cannot secure either his person or his property from oppressive officers. Pray then consider what our brethren have suffered at Ashfield.

Many think it hard to be frowned upon only for pleading for their rights and laying open particular acts of encroachment thereon. But what frowns have we met with for no other crime? And as the present contest between Great Britain and America is not so much about the greatness of the taxes already laid, as about a submission to their taxing power, so (though what we have already suffered is far from being a trifle, yet) our greatest difficulty at present concerns the submitting to a taxing power in ecclesiastical affairs. It is supposed by many that we are exempted from such taxes, but they are greatly mistaken. For all know that paper is a money article and writing upon it is labor, and this tax we must pay every year as a token of submission to their power, or else they will lay a heavier tax upon us. And we have one difficulty in submitting to this power which our countrymen have not in the other case, that is, our case affects the conscience as theirs does not. And equal liberty of conscience is one essential article in our CHARTER which constitutes this government and describes the extent of our rulers' authority and what are the rights and liberties of the people. And in the confession of faith which our rulers and their ministers have published to the world they say, "God alone is Lord of the conscience and hath left it free from the doctrines and commandments of men which are in *anything* contrary to His word *or not contained in it.* So that to believe such doctrines or to obey such commands out of conscience is to *betray* true liberty of conscience, and the requiring of an implicit faith and an absolute blind obedience is to destroy liberty of conscience and reason also."

And a most famous historian of theirs,[4] after mentioning some former violations of that liberty says, "The great noise that hath been made in the world about the *persecution* made in New England I will now stop with only transcribing the words uttered in the sermon to the first great and general assembly of the Massachusetts Bay, after the two colonies of Massachusetts and Plymouth were by Royal Charter united, 2 *Chron.* xii, 12:

> Things will *go well* when magistrates are great promoters of the thing that good is and what the Lord requireth of them. I do not mean that it would be well for the *civil* magistrate with *civil* penalty to compel men to this or that *way of worship* which they are *conscientiously* indisposed unto. He is most properly the officer of *human society,* and a Christian by non-conformity to this or that *imposed way of worship* does not break the terms on which he is to enjoy the benefits of human society. A man has a *right* unto his life, his estate, his liberty, and his family although he should not come up unto these and those blessed *institutions* of our Lord. *Violences* may bring the erroneous to be hypocrites, but they will never bring them to be believers. No, they naturally prejudice men's minds against the *cause* which is therein pretended for as being a weak, a wrong, an evil cause.[5]

These things were then delivered and were received with the *thanks* of the house of representatives and ten years after were spread by the historian through the nation with the express design of stopping any further complaints about New England's persecutions. But if the constitution of this government gives the magistrate no other authority than what belongs to *civil society,* we desire to know how he ever came to *impose* any particular *way of worship* upon any town or precinct whatsoever? And if a man has a right to his *estate,* his *liberty* and his *family* notwithstanding his non-con-

[4] Cotton Mather. See Backus's note after the quotation. Notice that Mather's "life, . . .estate, . . .liberty" is very close to John Locke's phrase, borrowed and revised by Thomas Jefferson for The Declaration of Independence.

[5] *Magnalia,* b[ook] 7, pp. 28, 29.

formity to the magistrate's way of worship, by what authority has any man had his goods spoiled, his land sold, or his person imprisoned, and thereby deprived of the enjoyment both of his liberty and his family for no crime at all against the peace or welfare of the state but only because he refused to conform to, or to support an *imposed* way of worship, or an *imposed* minister.[6]

In a celebrated oration for liberty, published last spring in Boston, a maxim was recited which carries its own evidence with it which is this, NO MAN CAN GIVE THAT WHICH IS ANOTHER'S. Yet have not our legislature from time to time made acts to empower the major part of the inhabitants in towns and precincts to *give away* their neighbors' estates to what ministers they please! And can we submit to such doctrines and commandments of men and not *betray* true liberty of conscience!

[6] Many pretend that without a tax to support ministers that the public would suffer for want of due encouragement of useful learning. But *human* learning is surely as needful for physicians and lawyers as for *spiritual* teachers. And dare any deny that the affairs of law and physic fall more directly under the notice of the state than divinity does? Why then do our legislature leave every man, and woman too, at liberty to choose their own lawyer and physician and not oblige them either to employ or pay any other though the majority may prefer them? Can any better reason be rendered for this difference in conduct than this, viz., It has been found an easier matter to *impose* upon people about their souls than about their bodies or their temporal estates! [Backus's note.]

* * *

ROYALL TYLER

(1757–1826)

On his way to a distinguished legal career that culminated in his service as Chief Justice of the Supreme Court of Vermont and as Professor of Law at the University of Vermont, Royall Tyler distinguished himself also as a man of letters. He is now remembered especially as the author

The present text of *The Contrast* is based on the first edition, Philadelphia, 1790. For Tyler's verse, see *The Verse of Royall Tyler*, ed. Marius B. Péladeau, 1967; for his prose, see *The Prose of Royall Tyler*, ed. Marius B. Péladeau, 1972, although the authorship of some of the selections has been challenged.

The best critical biography is George Thomas Tanselle, *Royall Tyler*, 1967. For Tyler in the history of American drama, see Arthur Hobson Quinn, *A History of the American Drama from the Beginning to the Civil War*, 1943. See also Constance Rourke, *The Roots of American Culture and Other Essays*, 1942.

of the first American comedy that was professionally produced (*The Contrast*, 1787), but he continued to write plays, essays, and satirical verse in association with the Federalist critic Joseph Dennie, and he published one novel, *The Algerine Captive* (1797). Along with eighteenth-century attorneys from Thomas Hutchinson and Thomas Jefferson to Hugh Henry Brackenridge and Joel Barlow, Tyler represents the flourishing young literary culture of relatively isolated men of letters, a generation before lawyers as well as clergymen and physicians contributed richly to the literature of the American Renaissance.

In *The Contrast* itself, which he apparently wrote in less than a month, probably after he had seen a performance of Richard Brinsley Sheridan's *The School for Scandal,* Tyler establishes themes that recur in American literature from the preface to Thomas Hooker's *Survey of the Sum of Church Discipline,* to Henry James and Mark Twain, Sinclair Lewis and Ernest Hemingway. He sees danger in the provincial imitation of European manners, and like Joel Barlow and Washington Irving he represents that danger not only through his humorless Colonel Manly but also through the conventionally comic figure of Jonathan, the rustic Yankee.

Sonnet to an Old Mouser[1]

Child of lubricious art! of sanguine sport!
Of *pangful mirth!* sweet ermin'd sprite!
Who lov'st, with silent, *velvet step,* to court
The bashful bosom of the night.

Whose elfin eyes can pierce night's sable gloom,   5
And witch her *fairy prey* with guile,
Who sports fell frolic o'er the grisly tomb,
And gracest death with dimpling smile!

Daughter of ireful mirth, sportive in rage
Whose joy should shine in sculptur'd base relief,   10
Like Patience, in rapt Shakespeare's deathless page,
Smiling in marble at wan grief.

Oh, come and teach me all thy barb'rous joy,
To sport with sorrow first, and then destroy.

[1] Published in the *Farmer's Weekly Museum,* April 1, 1799. The text is from Joseph Dennie's reprint in *The Port Folio,* 1801.

Spondee's Mistresses[1]

I

Let Cowley, soft in am'rous verse
The rovings of his love rehearse,
  With passion most unruly,
Boast how he woo'd sweet Amoret,
The sobbing Jane, and sprightly Bet,   5
The lily fair and smart brunette,
  In sweet succession truly.

II

But list, ye lovers, and you'll swear,
I rov'd with him beyond compare,
  And was far more unlucky.   10
For never yet in Yankee coast
Were found such girls, who so could boast,
An honest lover's heart to roast,
  From Casco to Kentucky.

III

When first the girls nicknam'd me beau,   15
And I was all for dress and show,
  I set me out a courting.
A romping Miss, with heedless art,
First caught, then almost broke, my heart,
MISS CONDUCT nam'd, we soon did part,   20
  I did not like sporting.

IV

The next coquet, who rais'd a flame,
Was far more grave, and somewhat lame,
  She in my heart did rankle.
She conquer'd, with a sudden glance,   25
The spiteful slut was called MISS CHANCE;
I took the gypsy out to dance;
  She almost broke my ankle.

---

[1] The allusion here is to Abraham Cowley's *The Mistress: or, Several Copies of Love Verses* (1647), in different metrical forms expressing the poet's suffering to his love. Tyler's poem was first published in the *Farmer's Museum*, April 15, 1700. Text from Joseph Dennie's *Port Folio*.

V

A thoughtless girl, just in her teens,
Was the next fair, whom Love it seems   30
   Had made me prize most highly,
I thought to court a lovely mate,
But, how it made my heart to ache,
It was that jade, the vile MISS TAKE;
   In troth, Love did it slyly.   35

VI

And last, MISS FORTUNE, whimpering, came,
Cur'd me of Love's tormenting flame,
   And all my beau pretenses;
In Widow's Weeds, the prude appears;
See now—she drowns me with her tears,   40
With bony fist, now slaps my ears,
   And brings me to my senses.

Choice of a Wife[1]

Fluttering lovers, giddy boys,
Sighing soft for Hymen's joys,
Would you shun the tricking arts,
Beauty's traps for youthful hearts,
Would you treasure in a wife,   5
Riches, which shall last through life;
Would you in your choice be nice,
Hear Minerva's sage advice.

   Be not caught with shape, nor air,
Coral lips, nor flowing hair;   10
Shape and jaunty air may cheat,
Coral lips may speak deceit.
Girls unmask'd would you descry,
Fix your fancy on the eye;
NATURE there has truth design'd,   15
'Tis the eye, that speaks the mind.
Shun the proud, disdainful eye,
Frowning fancied dignity,
Shun the eye with vacant glare;
COLD INDIFFERENCE WINTERS THERE.   20

---

[1] Published in *The New Hampshire and Vermont Journal,* December 6, 1796.

Shun the eager orb of fire
Gloating with impure desire;
Shun the wily eye of prude,
Looking coy to be pursued.
From the jilting eye refrain,   25
Glancing love, and now disdain.
Fly the fierce, satiric eye,
Shooting keen severity;
For Nature thus, her truth design'd
And made the eye proclaim the mind.   30

PROLOGUE [to The Contrast]

*Written by a young gentleman of New-York, and spoken
by Mr. Wignell.*

Exult, each patriot heart!—this night is shewn
A piece, which we may fairly call our own;
Where the proud titles of "My Lord! Your Grace!"
To humble *Mr.* and plain *Sir* give place.
Our Author pictures not from foreign climes
The fashions or the follies of the times;
But has confin'd the subject of his work
To the gay scenes—the circles of New-York.
On native themes his Muse displays her pow'rs;
If ours the faults, the virtues too are ours.
Why should our thoughts to distant countries roam,
When each refinement may be found at home?
Who travels now to ape the rich or great,
To deck an equipage and roll in state;
To court the graces, or to dance with ease,
Or by hypocrisy to strive to please?
Our free-born ancestors such arts despis'd;
Genuine sincerity alone they priz'd;
Their minds, with honest emulation fir'd,
To solid good—not ornament—aspir'd;
Or, if ambition rous'd a bolder flame,
Stern virtue throve, where indolence was shame.

But modern youths, with imitative sense,
Deem taste in dress the proof of excellence;
And spurn the meanness of your homespun arts,
Since homespun habits would obscure their parts;

Whilst all, which aims at splendour and parade,
Must come from Europe, *and be ready made.*
Strange! we should thus our native worth disclaim,
And check the progress of our rising fame.
Yet *one*, whilst imitation bears the sway,
Aspires to nobler heights, and points the way.
Be rous'd, my friends! his bold example view;
Let your own Bards be proud to copy *you!*
Should rigid critics reprobate our play,
At least the patriotic heart will say,
"Glorious our fall, since in a noble cause.
"The bold *attempt alone* demands applause."
Still may the wisdom of the Comic Muse
Exalt your merits, or your faults accuse.
But think not, 'tis her aim to be severe;—
We all are mortals, and as mortals err.
If candour pleases, we are truly blest;
Vice trembles, when compell'd to stand confess'd.
Let not light Censure on your faults offend,
Which aims not to expose them, but amend.
Thus does our Author to your candour trust;
Conscious, the *free* are generous, as just.

JOEL BARLOW

(1754-1812)

The career of Joel Barlow, like those of Freneau, Brackenridge, Paine, and Brown, shows that the man of letters in the early years of the Republic was likely to be found scrambling among a variety of incom-

The standard edition is *The Works of Joel Barlow,* introduction by William K. Bottorff and Arthur L. Ford, 1970.

The best modern biography is James L. Woodress, *A Yankee's Odyssey: The Life of Joel Barlow,* 1958. See also Charles B. Todd, *Life and Letters of Joel Barlow,* 1886; Theodore A. Zunder, *The Early Days of Joel Barlow, A Connecticut Wit,* 1934; Leon Howard, *The Connecticut Wits,* 1943.

Recent commentaries include Theodore Grieder, "Joel Barlow's The Hasty Pudding: A Study in American Neo-Classicism," *British Association for American Studies Bulletin* (1965): 35-42; Robert O. Arner, "The Smooth and Emblematic Song: Joel Barlow's The Hasty Pudding," *Early American Literature,* 7 (1972): 76-91.

patible roles: schoolteacher, army chaplain, journalist, diplomat, attorney, poet-publisher, entrepreneur, storekeeper, land speculator, political adviser, revolutionary consultant, and pamphleteer. Barlow won local distinction as a poet during his undergraduate years at Yale, and at the same time he also fought in the Continental Army. After his graduation from Yale in 1778 he taught school for a while, then returned to study for an advanced degree. He became chaplain in the Third Massachusetts Brigade in 1780. By that time he was well along in the composition of an epic called *The Vision of Columbus,* and after the war ended he spent some time trying to sell enough subscriptions to have that long work profitably published. He became for a time an editor of a weekly newspaper, *The American Mercury,* most of which he is said to have written, and he went briefly into partnership with Noah Webster in another publishing enterprise. In 1786 he was admitted to the bar, and during the next year he collaborated with other "Connecticut Wits" in writing a satirical poem called *The Anarchiad. The Vision of Columbus* was published at last in 1787 and was highly praised in this country, where it sold enough copies to earn Barlow some money.

The next year, however, Barlow's employment as attorney and sales agent for a vast land-speculation scheme in the Ohio River Valley took him to Europe, where he stayed for 17 more years. In Paris he befriended Thomas Jefferson, and as the French Revolution developed he became associated in London with Thomas Paine, Joseph Priestley, and other friends of the Revolution. He published in 1792 *Advice to the Privileged Orders,* in answer to Edmund Burke's strictures on the Revolution, and he became, through Thomas Paine's influence and the danger that Barlow might be charged with sedition in England, first a citizen of France and then, hurriedly, a resident of Paris, where he tried but failed to win election to the National Assembly. It was in 1793, during the Reign of Terror, which he had tried to prevent, that he wrote his best poem, *The Hasty Pudding.* In the next decade Barlow engaged successfully in commerce in Germany, accepted diplomatic assignments, wrote and published letters in criticism of anti-French policies of American Federalists, and at last returned to the United States in 1804. Here he began a new epic in collaboration with the inventor Robert Fulton; he began work at President Jefferson's insistence on a pro-Republican history of the United States; he published a revised edition *(The Columbiad)* of his epic on Columbus; and he worked as an adviser to Presidents Jefferson and Madison. In 1811 Madison sent him to France to negotiate a treaty with Napoleon, and it was while working on that negotiation during Napoleon's retreat from Moscow in 1812 that Barlow contracted pneumonia in Poland and died.

The Hasty Pudding is one of the finest American poems before Emily Dickinson, and the reasons for its extraordinarily high quality are formal and cultural as well as circumstantial. The historical accident of coming upon corn-meal mush (or strong memories of it) at an inn in the Alps during the Reign of Terror, and after a five-year absence from his native Connecticut, would be reason enough for the strong rush of homesickness and the affectionate idealization of a pastoral, republican Conneticut in the poem. But the form, too, helps to account for Barlow's success and for the continuing delight that *The Hasty Pudding* brings to readers nearly two centuries later. The mock-heroic form was much more appropriate to the self-assertion of provincial Americans than the heavy Vergilian or Miltonic rhetoric could ever be. Here as in Irving's *History of New York* and Brackenridge's *Modern Chivalry* the provincial writer could show his mastery of a European form while masking his self-doubt in humor, and he could show American virtue by deflating the presumptuousness (even though he sometimes concedes the reality) of European grandeur.

The Hasty Pudding[1]

Omne tulit punctum qui miscuit utile dulci.[2]
He makes a good breakfast who mixes pudding
with molasses.

PREFACE

A simplicity in diet, whether it be considered with reference to the happiness of individuals or the prosperity of a nation, is of more consequence than we are apt to imagine. In recommending so important an object to the rational part of mankind, I wish it were in my power to do it in such a manner as would be likely to gain their attention. I am sensible that it is one of those subjects in which example has infinitely more power than the most convincing arguments or the highest charms of poetry. Goldsmith's *Deserted Village*, though possessing these two advantages in a greater degree than any other work of the kind, has not prevented villages in England from being deserted. The apparent interest[3] of the rich individuals, who form the taste

---

[1] The text is the first separate American printing, New Haven, 1796.

[2] Barlow's translation is part of the joke. A more conventional translation of this famous line from Horace's *Ars Poetica* is, "He has won all approval who has mixed the useful with the sweet, pleasant, or agreeable."

[3] That is, economic self-interest.

as well as the laws in that country, has been against him; and with that interest it has been vain to contend.

The vicious habits which in this little piece I endeavor to combat, seem to me not so difficult to cure. No class of people has any *interest* in supporting them; unless it be the interest which certain families feel in vying with each other in sumptuous entertainments. There may indeed be some instances of depraved appetites, which no arguments will conquer; but these must be rare. There are very few persons but what would always prefer a plain dish for themselves, and would prefer it likewise for their guests, if there were no risk of reputation in the case. This difficulty can only be removed by example; and the example should proceed from those whose situation enables them to take the lead in forming the manners of a nation. Persons of this description in America, I should hope, are neither above nor below the influence of truth and reason, when conveyed in language suited to the subject.

Whether the manner I have chosen to address my arguments to them be such as to promise any success is what I cannot decide. But I certainly had hopes of doing some good, or I should not have taken the pains of putting so many rhymes together.—The example of domestic virtues has doubtless a great effect. I only wish to rank *simplicity of diet* among the virtues. In that case I should hope it will be cherished and more esteemed by others than it is at present.

THE AUTHOR

CANTO I

Ye Alps audacious, thro' the heav'ns that rise,
To cramp the day and hide me from the skies;
Ye Gallic flags,[4] that o'er their heights unfurl'd,
Bear death to kings, and freedom to the world,
I sing not you. A softer theme I chuse,   5
A virgin theme, unconscious of the Muse,
But fruitful, rich, well suited to inspire
The purest frenzy of poetic fire.
   Despise it not, ye Bards to terror steel'd,
Who hurl your thunders round the epic field;   10
Nor ye who strain your midnight throats to sing
Joys that the vineyard and the still-house bring;
Or on some distant fair your notes employ,
And speak of raptures that you ne'er enjoy.

[4] The French had recently (1792) taken Savoy from Sardinia.

I sing the sweets I know, the charms I feel,   15
My morning incense, and my evening meal,
The sweets of Hasty-Pudding. Come, dear bowl,
Glide o'er my palate, and inspire my soul.
The milk beside thee, smoking from the kine,
Its substance mingled, married in with thine,   20
Shall cool and temper thy superior heat,
And save the pains of blowing while I eat.
    Oh! could the smooth, the emblematic song
Flow like thy genial juices o'er my tongue,
Could those mild morsels in my numbers chime,   25
And, as they roll in substance, roll in rhyme,
No more thy aukward unpoetic name
Should shun the Muse, or prejudice thy fame;
But rising grateful to th' accustom'd ear,
All Bards should catch it, and all realms revere!   30
    Assist me first with pious toil to trace
Thro' wrecks of time thy lineage and thy race;
Declare what lovely squaw, in dayes of yore,
(Ere great Columbus sought thy native shore)
First gave thee to the world; her works of fame   35
Have liv'd indeed, but liv'd without a name.
Some tawny Ceres,[5] goddess of her days,
First learn'd with stones to crack the well-dry'd maise,
Thro' the rough seive to shake the golden show'r,
In boiling water stir the yellow flour: 40
The yellow flour, bestrew'd and stir'd with haste,
Swells in the flood and thickens to a paste,
Then puffs and wallops, rises to the brim,
Drinks the dry knobs that on the surface swim;
The knobs at last the busy ladle breaks,   45
And the whole mass its true consistence takes.
    Could but her sacred name, unknown so long,
Rise, like her labors, to the son of song,
To her, to them, I'd consecrate my lays,
And blow her pudding with the breath of praise.   50
If 'twas Oella, whom I sang before,[6]
I here ascribe her one great virtue more.
Not thro' the rich Peruvian realms alone
The fame of Sol's sweet daughter should be known,

---

[5] Goddess of grain.

[6] In *The Vision of Columbus*, Barlow had written of Oella and Manco Capac, progenitors of the Incas of Peru. Oella, daughter of the Sun, was the first woman to spin cloth and to perform other domestic arts.

But o'er the world's wide clime should live secure,   55
Far as his rays extend, as long as they endure.
   Dear Hasty-Pudding, what unpromis'd joy
Expands my heart, to meet thee in Savoy!
Doom'd o'er the world thro' devious paths to roam,
Each clime my country, and each house my home,   60
My soul is sooth'd, my cares have found an end,
I greet my long-lost, unforgotten friend.
   For Thee thro' Paris, that corrupted town,
How long in vain I wandered up and down,
Where shameless Bacchus,[7] with his drenching hoard,   65
Cold from his cave usurps the morning board.
London is lost in smoke and steep'd in tea;
No Yankey there can lisp the name of thee;
The uncouth word, a libel on the town,
Would call a proclamation from the crown.[8]   70
For climes oblique, that fear the sun's full rays,
Chill'd in their fogs, exclude the generous maize;
A grain whose rich luxuriant growth requires
Short gentle showers, and bright etherial fires.
   But here, tho' distant from our native shore,   75
With mutual glee we meet and laugh once more.
The same! I know thee by that yellow face,
That strong complexion of true Indian race.
Which time can never change, nor soil impair,
Nor Alpine snows, nor Turkey's morbid air;   80
For endless years, thro' every mild domain,
Where grows the maize, there thou art sure to reign.
   But man, more fickle, the bold licence claims,
In different realms to give thee different names.
Thee the soft nations round the warm Levant   85
Polanta call, the French of course *Polante*.
Ev'n in thy native regions, how I blush
To hear the Pennsylvanians call thee *Mush!*
On Hudson's banks, while men of Belgic spawn[9]
Insult and eat thee by the name *Suppawn*.   90
All spurious appellations, void of truth,
I've better known thee from my earliest youth,
Thy name is *Hasty-Pudding*; thus our sires
Were wont to greet thee fuming from their fires;

[7] God of wine.
[8] Probably Barlow refers here to the English proclamation (May 1792) forbidding the publication of seditious matter. In a later note Barlow said that "a certain King" had been trying "to prevent American principles from being propagated in his country."

[9] Here Barlow strains for a rhyme to refer to the Dutch settlers of New York. The word *Suppawn* was an Indian term.

And while they argu'd in thy just defence   95
With logic clear, they thus explain'd the sense:—
"In *haste* the boiling cauldron, o'er the blaze,
Receives and cooks the ready-powder'd maize;
In *haste* 'tis served, and then in equal *haste*,
With cooling milk, we make the sweet repast.   100
No carving to be done, no knife to grate
The tender ear, and wound the stony plate;
But the smooth spoon, just fitted to the lip,
And taught with art the yielding mass to dip,
By frequent journeys to the bowl well stor'd,   105
Performs the hasty honors of the board."
Such is thy name, significant and clear,
A name, a sound to every Yankey dear,
But most to me, whose heart and palate chaste
Preserve my pure hereditary taste.   110
 There are who strive to stamp with disrepute
The luscious food, because it feeds the brute;
In tropes of high-strain'd wit, while gaudy prigs
Compare thy nursling man to pamper'd pigs;
With sovereign scorn I treat the vulgar jest,   115
Nor fear to share thy bounties with the beast.
What though the generous cow gives me to quaff
The milk nutritious; am I then a calf?
Or can the genius of the noisy swine,
Though nurs'd on pudding, thence lay claim to mine?   120
Sure the sweet song, I fashion to thy praise,
Runs more melodious than the notes they raise.
 My song resounding in its grateful glee,
No merit claims; I praise myself in thee.
My father lov'd thee thro' his length of days;   125
For thee his fields were shaded o'er with maize;
From thee what health, what vigor he possesst,
Ten sturdy freemen from his loins attest;
Thy constellation rul'd my natal morn,
And all my bones were made of Indian corn.   130
Delicious grain! whatever form it take,
To roast or boil, to smother or to bake,
In every dish 'tis welcome still to me,
But most, my Hasty-Pudding, most in thee.

Let the green Succatash with thee contend,   135
Let beans and corn their sweetest juices blend,
Let butter drench them in its yellow tide,
And a long slice of bacon grace their side;
Not all the plate, how fam'd soe'er it be,
Can please my palate like a bowl of thee.   140
    Some talk of Hoe-Cake, fair Virginia's pride,
Rich Johnny-cake this mouth has often tri'd;
Both please me well, their virtues much the same,
Alike their fabric, as allied their fame,
Except in dear New-England, where the last   145
Receives a dash of pumpkin in the paste,
To give it sweetness and improve the taste.
But place them all before me, smoaking hot,
The big, round dumplin rolling from the pot;
The pudding of the bag, whose quivering breast,   150
With suet lin'd, leads on the Yankey feast;
The Charlotte brown,[10] within whose crusty sides
A belly soft the pulpy apple hides;
The yellow bread, whose face like amber glows,
And all of Indian that the bake-pan knows—   155
You tempt me not—my fav'rite greets my eyes,
To that lov'd bowl my spoon by instinct flies.

CANTO II

To mix the food by vicious rules of art,
To kill the stomach and to sink the heart,
To make mankind to social virtue sour,   160
Cram o'er each dish, and be what they devour;
For this the kitchen Muse first fram'd her book,
Commanding sweat to stream from every cook;
Children no more their antic gambols tri'd,
And friends to physic wonder'd why they died.   165
    Not so the Yankey—his abundant feast,
With simples furnish'd, and with plainness drest,
A numerous offspring gathers round the board,
And cheers alike the servant and the lord;
Whose well-bought hunger prompts the joyous taste,   170
And health attends them from the short repast.
    While the full pail rewards the milk-maid's toil,
The mother sees the morning cauldron boil;
To stir the pudding next demands their care,
To spread the table and the bowls prepare;   175

---

[10] A kind of pie or cake.

To feed the children, as their portions cool,
And comb their heads, and send them off to school.
    Yet may the simplest dish some rules impart,
For nature scorns not all the aids of art.
Ev'n Hasty-Pudding, purest of all food,   180
May still be bad, indifferent, or good,
As sage experience the short process guides,
Or want of skill, or want of care presides.
Whoe'er would form it on the surest plan,
To rear the child and long sustain the man;   185
To shield the morals while it mends the size,
And all the powers of every food supplies,
Attend the lessons that the Muse shall bring,
Suspend your spoons, and listen while I sing.
    But since, O man! thy life and health demand   190
Not food alone, but labour from thy hand,
First in the field, beneath the sun's strong rays,
Ask of thy mother earth the needful maize;
She loves the race that courts her yielding soil,
And gives her bounties to the sons of toil.   195
    When now the ox, obedient to thy call,
Repays the loan that fill'd the winter stall,
Pursue his traces o'er the furrow'd plain,
And plant in measur'd hills the golden grain.
But when the tender germe begins to shoot,   200
And the green spire declares the sprouting root,
Then guard your nursling from each greedy foe,
Th' insidious worm, the all-devouring crow.
A little ashes, sprinkled round the spire,
Soon steep'd in rain, will bid the worm retire;   205
The feather'd robber with his hungry maw
Swift flies the field before your man of straw,
A frightful image, such as school-boys bring
When met to burn the Pope, or hang the King.[11]
    Thrice in each season, through each variant row   210
Wield the strong plow-share and the faithful hoe;
The faithful hoe, a double task that takes,
To till the summer corn, and roast the winter cakes.
    Slow springs the blade, while check'd by chilling rains,
Ere yet the sun the seat of Cancer gains;[12]   215

---

[11] On November 5, Guy Fawkes Day, English and Anglo-American Protestants celebrated the discovery of the Gunpowder plot of 1605.

[12] Reaching the Tropic of Cancer on June 21.

But when his fiercest fires emblaze the land,
Then start the juices, then the roots expand;
Then, like a column of Corinthian[13] mould,
The stalk struts upward, and the leaves unfold;
The busy branches all the ridges fill,   220
Entwine their arms, and kiss from hill to hill.
Here cease to vex them, all your cares are done;
Leave the last labors to the parent sun;
Beneath his genial smiles the well-drest field,
When autumn calls, a plenteous crop shall yield.   225
   Now the strong foliage bears the standards high,
And shoots the tall top-gallants to the sky;
The suckling ears their silky fringes bend,
And pregnant grown, their swelling coats distend;
The loaded stalk, while still the burthen grows,   230
O'erhangs the space that runs between the rows;
High as a hop-field waves the silent grove,
A safe retreat for little thefts of love,
When the pledg'd roasting-ears invite the maid,
To meet her swain beneath the new-form'd shade;   235
His generous hand unloads the cumbrous hill,
And the green spoils her ready basket fill;
Small compensation for the two-fold bliss,
The promis'd wedding and the present kiss.
   Slight depredations these; but now the moon   240
Calls from his hollow tree the sly raccoon;
And while by night he bears his prize away,
The bolder squirrel labors thro' the day.
Both thieves alike, but provident of time,
A virtue rare, that almost hides their crime.   245
Then let them steal the little stores they can,
And fill their gran'ries from the toils of man;
We've one advantage where they take no part,
With all their wiles they ne'er have found the art
To boil the Hasty-Pudding; here we shine   250
Superior far to tenants of the pine;
This envy'd boon to man shall still belong,
Unshar'd by them in substance or in song.
   At last the closing season browns the plain,
And ripe October gathers in the grain;   255

[13] In the Corinthian order of Greek architecture, the capital is decorated in a way that might resemble the tassels and green leaves of corn stalks.

Deep loaded carts the spacious corn-house fill,
The sack distended marches to the mill;
The lab'ring mill beneath the burthen groans,
And show'rs the future pudding from the stones;
Till the glad house-wife greets the powder'd gold,   260
And the new crop exterminates the old.
Ah, who can sing what every wight must feel,
The joy that enters with the bag of meal,
A general jubilee pervades the house,
Wakes every child and gladdens every mouse.   265

CANTO III

The days grow short; but tho' the falling sun
To the glad swain proclaims his day's work done,
Night's pleasing shades his various tasks prolong,
And yield new subjects to my various song.
For now, the corn-house fill'd, the harvest home,   270
Th' invited neighbors to the *Husking* come;
A frolic scene, where work, and mirth, and play,
Unite their charms, to chace the hours away.
Where the huge heap lies center'd in the hall,
The lamp suspended from the cheerful wall,   275
Brown corn-fed nymphs, and strong hard-handed beaux,
Alternate rang'd, extend in circling rows,
Assume their seats, the solid mass attack;
The dry husks rustle, and the corn-cobs crack;
The song, the laugh, alternate notes resound,   280
And the sweet cider trips in silence round.
The laws of Husking every wight can tell;
And sure no laws he ever keeps so well:
For each red ear a general kiss he gains,
With each smut ear he smuts the luckless swains;   285
But when to some sweet maid a prize is cast,
Red as her lips, and taper as her waist,
She walks the round, and culls one favor'd beau,
Who leaps, the luscious tribute to bestow.
Various the sport, as are the wits and brains   290
Of well-pleas'd lasses and contending swains;
Till the vast mound of corn is swept away,
And he that gets the last ear, wins the day.
Meanwhile the house-wife urges all her care,
The well-earn'd feast to hasten and prepare.   295

The sifted meal already waits her hand,
The milk is strain'd, the bowls in order stand,
The fire flames high; and, as a pool (that takes
The headlong stream that o'er the mill-dam breaks)
Foams, roars and rages, with incessant toils,   300
So the vext cauldron rages, roars and boils.
    First with clean salt she seasons well the food,
Then strews the flour, and thickens all the flood.
Long o'er the simmering fire she lets it stand;
To stir it well demands a stronger hand;   305
The husband takes his turn; and round and round
The ladle flies; at last the toil is crown'd;
When to the board the thronging huskers pour,
And take their seats as at the corn before.
    I leave them to their feast. There still belong   310
More copious matters to my faithful song.
For rules there are, tho' ne'er unfolded yet,
Nice rules and wise, how pudding should be ate.[14]
    Some with molasses line the luscious treat,
And mix, like Bards, the useful with the sweet.   315
A wholesome dish, and well deserving praise,
A great resource in those bleak wintry days,
When the chill'd earth lies buried deep in snow,
And raging Boreas dries the shivering cow.
    Blest cow! thy praise shall still my notes employ,   320
Great source of health, the only source of joy;
Mother of Egypt's God[15]—but sure, for me,
Were I to leave my God, I'd worship thee.
How oft thy teats these pious hands have prest!
How oft thy bounties proved my only feast!   325
How oft I've fed thee with my fav'rite grain!
And roar'd, like thee, to find thy children slain!
    Ye swains who know her various worth to prize,
Ah! house her well from Winter's angry skies.
Potatoes, pumpkins, should her sadness cheer,   330
Corn from your crib, and mashes from your beer;
When spring returns she'll well acquit the loan,
And nurse at once your infants and her own.
    Milk then with pudding I should always chuse;
To this in future I confine my Muse,   335

---

[14] Probably pronounced to rhyme exactly
with *yet*.

[15] The mother of Osiris was depicted as a
cow.

Till she in haste some farther hints unfold,
Well for the young, nor useless to the old.
First in your bowl the milk abundant take,
Then drop with care along the silver lake
Your flakes of pudding; these at first will hide   340
Their little bulk beneath the swelling tide;
But when their growing mass no more can sink,
When the soft island looms above the brink,
Then check your hand; you've got the portion's due,
So taught our sires, and what they taught is true. [16]   345
    There is a choice in spoons. Tho' small appear
The nice distinction, yet to me 'tis clear.
The deep-bowl'd Gallic spoon, contriv'd to scoop
In ample draughts the thin diluted soup,
Performs not well in these substantial things,   350
Whose mass adhesive to the metal clings;
Where the strong labial muscles must embrace
The gentle curve, and sweep the hollow space.
With ease to enter and discharge the freight,
A bowl less concave but still more dilate,   355
Becomes the pudding best. The shape, the size,
A secret rests unknown to vulgar eyes.
Experienc'd feeders can alone impart
A rule so much above the lore of art.
These tuneful lips, that thousand spoons have tried,   360
With just precision could the point decide,
Tho' not in song; the muse but poorly shines
In cones, and cubes, and geometric lines,
Yet the true form, as near as she can tell,
Is that small section of a goose-egg shell,   365
Which in two equal portions shall divide
The distance from the centre to the side.

[16] "There are various ways of preparing and eating it; with molasses, butter, sugar, cream, and fried. Why so excellent a thing cannot be eaten alone? Nothing is perfect alone, even man who boasts of so much perfection is nothing without his fellow substance. In eating, beware of the lurking heat that lies deep in the mass; dip your spoon gentle, take shallow dips and cool it by degrees. It is sometimes necessary to blow. This is indicated by certain signs which every experienced feeder knows. They should be taught to young beginners. I have known a child's tongue blistered for want of this attention, and then the schooldame would insist that the poor thing had told a lie. A mistake: the falsehood was in the faithless pudding. A prudent mother will cool it for her child with her own sweet breath. The husband, seeing this, pretends his own wants blowing too from the same lips. A sly deceit of love. She knows the cheat, but feigning ignorance, lends her pouting lips and gives a gentle blast, which warms the husband's heart more than it cools his pudding." [Barlow's note.]

Fear not to slaver; 'tis no deadly sin.
Like the free Frenchman, from your joyous chin
Suspend the ready napkin; or, like me,   370
Poise with one hand your bowl upon your knee;
Just in the zenith your wise head project,
Your full spoon, rising in a line direct,
Bold as a bucket, heeds no drops that fall,
The wide-mouth'd bowl will surely catch them all.   375

HUGH HENRY BRACKENRIDGE

(1748-1816)

Although he had written some satirical verse while an undergraduate at Princeton, Hugh Henry Brackenridge did not hit upon his most effectively comic, mock-heroic literary form until he had misspent some years trying to write in a grand style appropriate to the heroic drama or the epic. Here and in other ways, of course, his development resembles that of Joel Barlow. For the Princeton graduation in 1771, Brackenridge collaborated with Philip Freneau on a dramatic poem called *The Rising Glory of America,* and for the same ceremony when he received his Master's degree in divinity three years later he composed and read an equally grand *Poem on Divine Revelation.* He published a drama called *The Battle of Bunker's Hill* (1776); served as a chaplain in the Continental Army; published other grave works, including *The Death of General Montgomery, at the Siege of Quebec* (1777); and in 1779 founded and edited *The United States Magazine: A Repository of History, Politics, and Literature,* which survived for only a year. In 1780 he became an attorney, and the following year, at the age of 31, he moved to the frontier town of Pittsburgh, where both his legal career and the memorable part of his literary career flourished.

From the time of the Revolution Brackenridge's literary imagination had been closely tied to his notion of the Republic and its political needs. In *Modern Chivalry,* the first volume of which he published in 1792, he found a way to offer serious instruction to his countrymen while entertaining them. His delightful introduction, like the notice

The best edition is *Modern Chivalry*, ed. Claude M. Newlin, 1937. Newlin has also written a biography, *The Life and Writings of Hugh Henry Brackenridge,* 1932. See also Daniel Marder, *Hugh Henry Brackenridge,* 1967.

that Mark Twain was to prefix to *Huckleberry Finn* in the 1880's, warns the reader to expect no content in the book, but only a perfect model of literary form. In a generally picaresque form, with Captain Farrago venturing forth like Don Quixote on a plow horse and attended by a stereotype of the illiterate Irish immigrant, Brackenridge is able to display the social and political issues in comic action and then to comment (as Henry Fielding, for example, had done in *Tom Jones*) ironically, but sometimes with explicit seriousness in his own person. He displays his mastery of Swiftian satirical techniques—most delightfully in the Captain's response to a challenge to a duel (Book III, Chapter IV)—and it is clear that he had long delighted in classical satirists, but he also demonstrates a shrewd understanding of political and social realities in the American West during the first years of the Republic. From the bogus or exploitative Indian treaty to the dangers of circumstantial evidence and the realities of class conflict in American political elections, *Modern Chivalry* raises complex issues about the nature and cost of democracy. Brackenridge has already broken with the Federalists by this time, but he does not avoid the question of competence implicit in the eligibility of every man for election to public office. His answer comes in a plea for mutual respect among different classes and kinds of talent—at one point he even says that the motto for his entire volume is, let the carpenter stick to his last—but he does mean genuine respect. The weaver's skill is not less good than that of the gentleman who has been educated for the conduct of public affairs, but it is different. At the same time Brackenridge anticipates in a different form, even as he tries to combat, the delightfully notorious motto of the fictitious rascal Simon Suggs: "It is good to be shifty in a new country."

Modern Chivalry is tied closely to real politics in a more literal way. Brackenridge published the first three volumes in 1792 and 1793, but the Whiskey Insurrection had occurred before he published Volume IV (1797), and Part II was not published until 1804 and 1805, by which time Brackenridge had been appointed to the Pennsylvania Supreme Court and the controversy between Jeffersonian Republicans and the Judiciary had become a major issue. Brackenridge had striven to mediate successfully between the genuinely aggrieved Whiskey insurrectionists and the military force sent by President Washington in 1794. Maligned by both sides in the disputes, Brackenridge found himself defending in real life the principles he had enunciated in his fiction, and that experience along with similar ones in the ensuing decade was reflected in the later volumes of *Modern Chivalry.*

In our sensitive age, which has been called to notice explicitly the racial condescension that was quietly accepted or simply unrecognized in American life, the stock figure of Teague Oregan, the illiterate

Irish "bog-trotter," will surely offend some readers. Without defending the conception or the execution of such a type, one ought to notice two relevant facts: that Brackenridge frankly introduces Teague as an abstraction ("I shall say nothing of the character of this man, because the very name imports what he was"), and that the stock figures of such ethnic groups were often in nineteenth- and early twentieth-century representations acceptable within the groups themselves. (See Oscar Handlin, *The Uprooted,* Chapter 7.)

Modern Chivalry[1]

BOOK I

INTRODUCTION

It has been a question for some time past, what would be the best means to fix the English language. Some have thought of Dictionaries, others of Institutes, for that purpose. Swift, I think it was, who proposed, in his letters to the Earl of Oxford, the forming an academy of learned men, in order by their observations and rules, to settle the true spelling, accentuation, and pronunciation, as well as the proper words, and the purest, most simple, and perfect phraseology of language. It has always appeared to me, that if some great master of style should arise, and without regarding sentiment, or subject, give an example of good language in his composition, which might serve as a model to future speakers and writers, it would do more to fix the orthography, choice of words, idiom of phrase, and structure of sentence, than all the Dictionaries and Institutes that have been ever made. For certainly, it is much more conducive to this end. to place before the eyes what is good writing, than to suggest it to the ear, which may forget in a short time all that has been said.

It is for this reason, that I have undertaken this work; and that it may attain the end the more perfectly, I shall consider language only, not in the least regarding the matter of the work; but as musicians, when they are about to give the most excellent melody, pay no attention to the words that are set to music; but take the most unmeaning phrases, such as sol, fa, la; so here, culling out the choicest flowers of diction, I shall pay no regard to the idea; for it is not in the power of human ingenuity to attain two things perfectly at once. Thus we see that they mistake greatly, who think to have a clock that can at once tell the hour of the day, the age of the moon, and the

[1] The text is the 1793 edition.

day of the week, month, or year; because the complexness of the machine hinders that perfection which the simplicity of the works and movements can alone give. For it is not in nature to have all things in one. If you are about to choose a wife, and expect beauty, you must give up family and fortune; or if you attain these, you must at least want good temper, health, or some other advantage: so to expect good language and good sense, at the same time, is absurd, and not in the compass of common nature to produce. Attempting only one thing, therefore, we may entertain the idea of hitting the point of perfection. It has been owing to an inattention to this principle, that so many fail in their attempts at good writing. A Jack of all Trades, is proverbial of a bungler; and we scarcely ever find any one who excels in two parts of the same art; much less in two arts at the same time. The smooth poet wants strength; and the orator of a good voice, is destitute of logical reason and argument. How many have I heard speak, who, were they to attempt voice only, might be respectable; but undertaking, at the same time, to carry sense along with them, they utterly fail, and become contemptible. One thing at once, is the best maxim that ever came into the mind of man. This might be illustrated by a thousand examples; but I shall not trouble myself with any; as it is not so much my object to convince others as to show the motives by which I myself am governed. Indeed, I could give authority which is superior to all examples; *viz.* that of the poet Horace; who, speaking on this very subject of excellence in writing, says, *Quidvis,* that is, whatever you compose, let it be, *simplex duntaxit & unum:* that is, simple, and one thing only.

It will be needless for me to say any thing about the critics; for as this work is intended as a model or rule of good writing, it cannot be the subject of criticism. It is true, Homer has been criticized by a Zoilus and an Aristotle; but the one contented himself with pointing out defects; the other, beauties. But Zoilus has been censured, Aristotle praised; because in a model there can be no defect; error consisting in a deviation from the truth, and faults, in an aberration from the original of beauty; so that where there are no faults there can be no food for criticism, taken in the unfavorable sense of finding fault with the productions of an author. I have no objections, therefore, to any praise that may be given to this work; but to censure or blame must appear absurd; because it cannot be doubted but that it will perfectly answer the end proposed.

Being a book without thought, or the smallest degree of sense, it will be useful to young minds, not fatiguing their understandings, and easily introducing a love of reading and study. Acquiring language at first by this means, they will afterwards gain knowledge. It will be useful especially to young men of light minds intended for the bar or pulpit. By heaping too much upon them, style and matter at once, you surfeit the stomach, and turn away the appetite from literary entertainment, to horse-racing and cock-fighting. I shall consider myself, therefore, as having performed an acceptable service, to all weak and visionary people, if I can give them something to read without the trouble of thinking. But these are collateral advantages of my work, the great object of which is, as I have said before, to give a model of perfect stile in writing. If hereafter any author of supereminent abilities, should choose to give this style a body, and make it the covering to some work of sense, as you would wrap fine silk round a beautiful form, so that there may be, not only vestment, but life in the object, I have no objections; but shall be rather satisfied with having it put to so good a use.

CHAPTER I
[RACING]

John Farrago, was a man of about fifty-three years of age, of good natural sense, and considerable reading; but in some things whimsical, owing perhaps to his greater knowledge of books than of the world; but, in some degree, also, to his having never married, being what they call an old bachelor, a characteristic of which is, usually, singularity and whim. He had the advantage of having had in early life, an academic education; but having never applied himself to any of the learned professions, he had lived the greater part of his life on a small farm, which he cultivated with servants or hired hands, as he could conveniently supply himself with either. The servant that he had at this time, was an Irishman, whose name was Teague Oregan. I shall say nothing of the character of this man, because the very name imports what he was.

A strange idea came into the head of Captain Farrago about this time; for, by the bye, I had forgot to mention that having been chosen captain of a company of militia in the neighborhood, he had gone by the name of Captain ever since; for the rule is, once a captain, and always a captain; but, as I was observing, the idea had come in to his head, to saddle an old horse that he had, and ride about the world a little, with his man Teague at his heels, to see how things were going on here and there, and to observe human nature. For it is a mistake to suppose, that a man cannot learn man by reading him in a corner, as well as on the widest space of transaction. At any rate, it may yield amusement.

It was about a score of miles from his own house, that he fell in with what we call Races. The jockeys seeing him advance, with Teague by his side, whom they took for his groom, conceived him to be some person who had brought his horse to enter for the purse. Coming up and accosting him, said they, You seem to be for the races, Sir; and have a horse to enter. Not at all, said the Captain; this is but a common palfrey, and by no means remarkable for speed or bottom; he is a common plough horse which I have used on my farm for several years, and can scarce go beyond a trot; much less match himself with your blooded horses that are going to take the field on this occasion.

The jockeys were of opinion, from the speech, that the horse was what they call a bite, and that under the appearance of leanness and stiffness, there was concealed some hidden quality of swiftness uncommon. For they had heard of instances, where the most knowing had been taken in by mean looking horses; so that having laid two, or more, to one, they were nevertheless bit by the bet; and the mean looking nags, proved to be horses of a more than common speed and bottom. So that there is no trusting appearances. Such was the reasoning of the jockeys. For they could have no idea, that a man could come there in so singular a manner, with a groom at his foot, unless he had some great object of making money by the adventure. Under this idea, they began to interrogate him with respect to the blood and pedigree of his horse; whether he was of the Dove, or the bay mare that took the purse; and was imported by such a one at such a time? whether his sire was Tamerlane or Bajazet?

The Captain was irritated at the questions, and could not avoid answering.—Gentlemen, said he, it is a strange thing that you should suppose that it is of any consequence what may be the pedigree of a horse. For even in men it is of no avail. Do we not find that sages have had blockheads for their sons; and that blockheads have had sages? It is remarkable, that as estates have seldom lasted three generations, so understanding and ability have seldom been transmitted to the second. There never was a greater man, take him as an orator and philosopher than Cicero: and never was there a person who had greater opportunities than his son Marcus; and yet he proved of no account or reputation. This is an old instance, but there are a thousand others. Chesterfield and his son are mentioned. It is true, Philip and Alexander may be said to be exceptions: Philip of the strongest possible mind; capable of almost everything we can conceive; the deepest policy and the most determined valor; his son Alexander not deficient in the first, and before him in the last; if it is possible to be before a man than whom you can suppose nothing greater. It is possible, in modern times, that Tippo Saib may be equal to his father Hyder Ali. Some talk of the two Pitts. I have no idea that the son is, in any respect, equal to old Sir William. The one is a labored artificial minister; the other spoke with the thunder, and acted with the lightning of the gods. I will venture to say, that when the present John Adamses, and Lees, and Jeffersons, and Jays, and Henrys, and other great men, who figure upon the stage at this time, have gone to sleep with their fathers, it is an hundred to one if there is any of their descendants who can fill their places. Was I to lay a bet for a great man, I would sooner pick up the brat of a tinker, than go into the great houses to choose a piece of stuff for a man of genius. Even with respect to personal appearance, which is more in the power of natural production, we do not see that beauty always produces beauty; but on the contrary, the homeliest persons have oftentimes the best favored offspring; so that there is no rule or reason in these things. With respect to this horse, therefore, it can be of no moment whether he is blooded or studed, or what he is. He is a good old horse, used to the plough, and carries my weight very well; and I have never yet made enquiry with respect to his ancestors, or affronted him so much as to cast up to him the defect of parentage. I bought him some years ago from Neil Thomas, who had him from a colt. As far as I can understand, he was of a brown mare that John M'Neis had; but of what horse I know no more than the horse himself. His gaits are good enough, as to riding a short journey of seven or eight miles, or the like; but he is rather a pacer than a trotter; and though his bottom may be good enough in carrying a bag to the mill, or going in the plough, or the sled, or the harrow, &c. yet his·wind is not so good, nor his speed, as to be fit for the heats.

The jockeys thought the man a fool, and gave themselves no more trouble about him.

The horses were now entered, and about to start for the purse. There was Black and all Black, and Snip, John Duncan's Barbary Slim, and several others. The riders had been weighed, and when mounted, the word was given. It is needless to describe a race; everybody knows the circumstances of it. It is sufficient to say, that from the bets that were laid, there was much anxiety, and some passion in the minds of those concerned: so, that as two of the horses, Black and all-Black, and Slim, came out near together; there was dispute and confusion. It came to kicking and cuffing in some places. The Captain was a good deal hurt with such indecency amongst gentlemen, and advancing, addressed them in the following manner: Gentlemen, this is an unequal amd unfair proceeding. It is unbecoming modern manners, or even the ancient. For at the Olympic games of Greece, where were celebrated horse and chariot races, there was no such hurry scurry as this; and in times of chivalry itself, where men ate, drank, and slept on horseback, though there was a great deal of pell-melling, yet no such disorderly work as this. If men had a difference, they couched their lances, and ran full tilt at one another; but no such indecent expressions, as villain, scoundrel, liar, ever came out of their mouths. There was the most perfect courtesy in those days of heroism and honor; and this your horse-racing, which is a germ of the amusement of those times, ought to be conducted on the same principles of decorum, and good breeding.

As he was speaking, he was jostled by someone in the crowd, and thrown from his horse; and had it not been for Teague, who was at hand, and helped him on again, he would have suffered damage. As it was, he received a contusion in his head, of which he complained much; and having left the race-ground, and coming to a small cottage, he stopped a little, to alight and dress the wound. An old woman who was there, thought they ought to take a little of his water, and see how it was with him; but the Captain having no faith in telling disorders by the urine, thought proper to send for a surgeon who was hard by, to examine the bruise, and apply bandages. The surgeon attended, and examining the part, pronounced it a contusion of the cerebrum. But as there appeared but little laceration, and no fracture, simple or compound, the pia mater could not be injured; nor even could there be more than a slight impression on the dura mater. So that trepaning did not at all appear necessary. A most fortunate circumstance; for a wound in the head, is of all places the most dangerous; because there can be no amputation to save life. There being but one head to a man, and that being the residence of the five senses, it is impossible to live without it. Nevertheless, as the present case was highly dangerous, as it might lead to a subsultus tendinum, or lock-jaw, it was necessary to apply cataplasms in order to reduce inflammation, and bring about a sanative disposition of the parts. Perhaps it might not be amiss, to take an anodyne as a refrigerant. Many patients had been lost by the ignorance of empirics prescribing bracers; whereas, in the first stage of a contusion, relaxing and antifebrile medicines are proper. A little phlebotomy was no doubt necessary, to prevent the bursting of the blood vessels.

The Captain hearing so many hard words, and bad accounts of this case, was much alarmed. Nevertheless he did not think it could be absolutely so dangerous. For it seemed to him that he was not sick at heart, or under any mortal pain. The surgeon observed, that in this case he could not himself be a judge. For the very part was affected by which he was to judge, *viz.* the head; that it was no uncommon thing for men in the extremest cases to imagine themselves out of danger; whereas in reality, they were in the greatest possible: that notwithstanding the symptoms were mild, yet from the contusion, a mortification might ensue. Hypocrates, who might be styled an elementary physician, and has a treatise on this very subject, is of opinion, that the most dangerous symptom is a topical insensibility; but among the moderns, Sydenham considers it in another point of view, and thinks that where there is no pain, there is as great reason to suppose that there is no hurt, as that there is a mortal one. Be this as it may, antiseptic medicines might be very proper.

The Captain hearing so much jargon, and conscious to himself that he was by no means in so bad a state as this son of Esculapius would represent, broke out into some passion. It is, said he, the craft of your profession to make the case worse than it is, in order to increase the perquisites. But if there is any faith in you, make the same demand, and let me know your real judgment. The surgeon was irritated with his distrust, and took it into his head to fix some apprehension in the mind of his patient, if possible, that his case was not without danger. Looking steadfastly at him for some time, and feeling his pulse, there is, said he, an evident delirium approaching. This argues an affection of the brain, but it will be necessary, after some soporiferous draughts, to put the patient to sleep. Said the Captain, If you will give me about a pint of whiskey and water, I will try to go to sleep myself. A deleterious mixture, in this case, said the surgeon, cannot be proper; especially a distillation of that quality. The Captain would hear no more; but requesting the man of the cabin, to let him have the spirits proposed, drank a pint or two of grog, and having bound up his head with a handkerchief, went to bed.

CHAPTER II
CONTAINING SOME GENERAL REFLECTIONS

The first reflection that arises, is, the good sense of the Captain; who was unwilling to impose his horse for a racer; not being qualified for the course. Because, as an old lean beast, attempting a trot, he was respectable enough; but going out of his nature and affecting speed, he would have been contemptible. The great secret of preserving respect, is the cultivating and showing to the best advantage the powers that we possess, and the not going beyond them. Everything in its element is good, and in their proper sphere all natures and capacities are excellent. This thought might be turned into a thousand different shapes, and clothed with various expressions; but after all, it comes to the old proverb at last, *Ne sutor ultra crepidam,* Let the cobler stick to his last; a sentiment we are about more to illustrate in the sequel of this work.

The second reflection that arises, is, the simplicity of the Captain; who was so unacquainted with the world, as to imagine that jockeys and men of the turf could be composed by reason and good sense; whereas there are no people who are by education of a less philosophic turn of mind. The company of horses is by no means favorable to good taste and genius. The rubbing and currying them, but little enlarges the faculties, or improves the mind; and even riding, by which a man is carried swiftly through the air, though it contributes to health, yet stores the mind with few or no ideas; and as men naturally consimilate with their company, so it is observable that your jockeys are a class of people not far removed from the sagacity of a good horse. Hence most probably the fable of the centaur, among the ancients; by which they held out the moral of the jockey and the horse being one beast.

A third reflection is, that which he exprest; *viz.* the professional art of the surgeon to make the most of the case, and the technical terms used by him. I have to declare, that it is with no attempt at wit, that the terms are set down, or the art of the surgeon hinted at; because it is so commonplace a thing to ridicule the peculiarities of a profession, that it savors of mean parts to indulge it. For a man of real genius will never walk in the beaten track, because his object is what is new and uncommon. This surgeon does not appear to have been a man of very great ability; but the Captain was certainly wrong in declining his prescriptions; for the maxim is, *Unicuique in arte, sua perito, credenaum est;* every one is to be trusted in his profession.

CHAPTER III
[AN ELECTION]

The Captain rising early next morning, and setting out on his way, had now arrived at a place where a number of people were convened, for the purpose of electing persons to represent them in the legislature of the state. There was a weaver who was a candidate for this appointment, and seemed to have a good deal of interest among the people. But another, who was a man of education, was his competitor. Relying on some talent of speaking which he thought he possessed, he addressed the multitude.

Said he, Fellow citizens, I pretend not to any great abilities; but am conscious to myself that I have the best good will to serve you. But it is very astonishing to me that this weaver should conceive himself qualified for the trust. For though my acquirements are not great, yet his are still less. The mechanical business which he pursues, must necessarily take up so much of his time, that he cannot apply himself to political studies. I should therefore think it would be more answerable to your dignity, and conducive to your interest, to be represented by a man at least of some letters, than by an illiterate handicraftsman like this. It will be more honorable for himself, to remain at his loom and knot threads, than to come forward in a legislative capacity: because, in the one case, he is in the sphere where God and nature has placed him; in the other, he is like a fish out of water, and must struggle for breath in a new element.

Is it possible he can understand the affairs of government, whose mind has been concentered to the small object of weaving webs; to the price by the yard, the grist of the thread, and such like matters as concern a manufacturer of cloths? The feet of him who weaves, are more occupied than the head, or at least as much; and therefore the whole man must be, at least, but in half accustomed to exercise his mental powers. For these reasons, all other things set aside, the chance is in my favor, with respect to information. However, you will decide, and give your suffrages to him or to me, as you shall judge expedient.

The Captain hearing these observations, and looking at the weaver, could not help advancing, and undertaking to subjoin something in support of what had been just said. Said he, I have no prejudice against a weaver more than another man. Nor do I know any harm in the trade; save that from the sedentary life in a damp place, there is usually a paleness of the countenance: but this is a physical, not a moral evil. Such usually occupy subterranean apartments; not for the purpose, like Demosthenes, of shaving their heads, and writing over eight times the history of Thucydides, and perfecting a style of oratory; but rather to keep the thread moist; or because this is considered but as an inglorious sort of trade, and is frequently thrust away into cellars, and damp outhouses, which are not occupied for a better use.

But to rise from the cellar to the senate house, would be an unnatural hoist. To come from counting threads, and adjusting them to the splits of a reed, to regulate the finances of a government, would be preposterous; there being no congruity in the case. There is no analogy between knotting threads and framing laws. It would be a reversion of the order of things. Not that a manufacturer of linen or woolen, or other stuff, is an inferior character, but a different one, from that which ought to be employed in affairs of state. It is unnecessary to enlarge on this subject; for you must all be convinced of the truth and propriety of what I say. But if you will give me leave to take the manufacturer aside a little, I think I can explain to him my ideas on the subject; and very probably prevail with him to withdraw his pretensions. The people seeming to acquiesce, and beckoning to the weaver, they drew aside, and the Captain addressed him in the following words:

Mr. Traddle, said he, for that was the name of the manufacturer, I have not the smallest idea of wounding your sensibility; but it would seem to me, it would be more your interest to pursue your occupation, than to launch out into that of which you have no knowledge. When you go to the senate house, the application to you will not be to warp a web; but to make laws for the commonwealth. Now, suppose that the making these laws, requires a knowledge of commerce, or of the interests of agriculture, or those principles upon which the different manufacturers depend, what service could you render. It is possible you might think justly enough; but could you speak? You are not in the habit of public speaking. You are not furnished with those common-place ideas, with which even very ignorant men can pass for knowing something. There is nothing makes a man so ridiculous as to attempt what is above his sphere. You are no tumbler for instance; yet should you give out that you could vault upon a man's back; or turn head over heels, like the wheels of a cart; the stiffness of your joints would encumber you; and you would fall upon your backside to the ground. Such a squash as that would do you damage. The getting up to ride on the state is an unsafe thing to those who are not accustomed to such horsemanship. It is a disagreeable thing for a man to be laughed at, and there is no way of keeping oneself from it but by avoiding all affectation.

While they were thus discoursing, a bustle had taken place among the crowd. Teague hearing so much about elections, and serving the government, took it into his head, that he could be a legislator himself. The thing was not displeasing to the people, who seemed to favor his pretensions; owing, in some degree, to there being several of his countrymen among the crowd; but more especially to the fluctuation of the popular mind, and a disposition to what is new and ignoble. For though the weaver was not the most elevated object of choice, yet he was still preferable to this tatter-demalion, who was but a menial servant, and had so much of what is called the brogue on his tongue, as to fall far short of an elegant speaker.

The Captain coming up, and finding what was on the carpet, was greatly chagrined at not having been able to give the multitude a better idea of the importance of a legislative trust; alarmed also, from an apprehension of the loss of his servant. Under these impressions he resumed his address to the multitude. Said he, This is making the matter still worse, gentlemen: this servant of mine is but a bog-trotter; who can scarcely speak the dialect in which your laws ought to be written; but certainly has never read a single treatise on any political subject; for the truth is, he cannot read at all. The young people of the lower class, in Ireland, have seldom the advantage of a good education; especially the descendants of the ancient Irish, who have most of them a great assurance of countenance, but little information, or literature. This young man, whose family name is Oregan, has been my servant for several years. And, except a too great fondness for women, which now and then brings him into scrapes, he has demeaned himself in a manner tolerable enough. But he is totally ignorant of the great principles of legislation; and more especially, the particular interests of the government. A free government is a noble possession to a people: and this freedom consists in an equal right to make laws, and to have the benefit of the laws when made. Though doubtless, in such a government, the lowest citizen may become chief magistrate; yet it is sufficient to possess the right; not absolutely necessary to exercise it. Or even if you should think proper, now and then, to show your privilege, and exert, in a signal manner, the democratic prerogative, yet is it not descending too low to filch away from me a hireling, which I cannot well spare, to serve your purpose. You are surely carrying the matter too far, in thinking to make a senator of this hostler; to take him away from an employment to which he had been bred, and put him to another, to which he has served no apprenticeship: to set those hands which have been lately employed in currying my horse, to the draughting bills, and preparing business for the house.

The people were tenacious of their choice, and insisted on giving Teague their suffrages; and by the frown upon their brows, seemed to indicate resentment at what had been said; as indirectly charging them with want of judgment; or calling in question their privilege to do what they thought proper. It is a very strange thing, said one of them, who was a speaker for the rest, that after having conquered Burgoyne and Cornwallis, and got a government of our own, we cannot put in it whom we please. This young man may be your servant, or another man's servant; but if we choose to make him a delegate, what is that to you. He may not be yet skilled in the matter, but there is a good day a-coming. We will impower him; and it is better to trust a plain man like him, than one of your high flyers, that will make laws to suit their own purposes.

Said the Captain, I had much rather you would send the weaver, though I thought that improper, than to invade my household, and thus detract from me the very person that I have about me to brush my boots and clean my spurs. The prolocutor of the people gave him to understand that his surmises were useless, for the people had determined on the choice, and Teague they would have, for a representative.

Finding it answered no end to expostulate with the multitude, he requested to speak a word with Teague by himself. Stepping aside, he said to him, composing his voice, and addressing him in a soft manner; Teague, you are quite wrong in this matter they have put into your head. Do you know what it is to be a member of a deliberate body? What qualifications are necessary? Do you understand anything of geography? If a question should be, to make a law to dig a canal in some part of the state, can you describe the bearing of the mountains, and the course of the rivers? Or if commerce is to be pushed to some new quarter, by the force of regulations, are you competent to decide in such a case? There will be questions of law, and astronomy on the carpet. How you must gape and stare like a fool, when you come to be asked your opinion of these subjects? Are you acquainted with the abstract principles of finance; with the funding public securities; the ways and means of raising the revenue; providing for the discharge of the public debts, and all other things which respect the economy of the government? Even if you had knowledge, have you a facility of speaking. I would suppose you would have too much pride to go to the house just to say, Ay, or No. This is not the fault of your nature, but of your education; having been accustomed to dig turf in your early years, rather than instructing yourself in the classics, or common school books.

When a man becomes a member of a public body, he is like a raccoon, or other beast that climbs up the fork of a tree; the boys pushing at him with pitch-forks, or throwing stones, or shooting at him with an arrow, the dogs barking in the mean time. One will find fault with your not speaking; another with your speaking, if you speak at all. They will have you in the newspapers, and ridicule you as a perfect beast. There is what they call the caricatura; that is, representing you with a dog's head, or a cat's claw. As you have a red head, they will very probably make a fox of you, or a sorrel horse, or a brindled cow. It is the devil in hell to be exposed to the squibs and crackers of the gazette wits and publications. You know no more about these matters than a goose; and yet you would undertake rashly, without advice, to enter on the office; nay, contrary to advice. For I would not for a thousand guineas, though I have not the half of it to spare, that the breed of the Oregans should come to this; bringing on them a worse stain than stealing sheep; to which they are addicted. You have nothing but your character, Teague, in a new country to depend upon. Let it never be said, that you quitted an honest livelihood, the taking care of my horse, to follow the new fangled whims of the times, and to be a statesman.

Teague was moved chiefly with the last part of the address, and consented to give up the object.

The Captain, glad of this, took him back to the people, and announced his disposition to decline the honor which they had intended him.

Teague acknowledged that he had changed his mind, and was willing to remain in a private station.

The people did not seem well pleased with the Captain; but as nothing more could be said about the matter, they turned their attention to the weaver, and gave him their suffrages.

CHAPTER IV
[A CONJURER]

Captain Farrago leaving this place, proceeded on his way; and at the distance of a mile or two, met a man with a bridle in his hand; who had lost a horse, and had been at a conjurer's to make enquiry, and recover his property.

It struck the mind of the Captain to go to this conjuring person, and make a demand of him, what was the cause that the multitude were so disposed to elevate the low to the highest station. He had rode but about a mile, when the habitation of the conjurer, by the direction and description of the man who had lost the horse had given, began to be in view. Coming up to the door, and enquiring if that was not where conjurer Kolt lived, they were answered Yes. Accordingly alighting, and entering the domicile, all those things took place which usually happen, or are described in cases of this nature, *viz.* there was the conjurer's assistant, who gave the Captain to understand that master had withdrawn a little, but would be in shortly.

In the meantime, the assistant endeavored to draw from him some account of the occasion of his journey; which the other readily communicated; and the conjurer, who was listening through a crack in the partition, overheard. Finding it was not a horse or a cow, or a piece of linen that was lost, but an abstract question of political philosophy which was to be put, he came from his lurking place, and entered, as if not knowing that any person had been waiting for him.

After mutual salutations, the Captain gave him to understand the object which he had in view by calling on him.

Said the conjurer, This lies not at all in my way. If it had been a dozen of spoons, or a stolen watch, that you had to look for, I could very readily, by the assistance of my art, have assisted you in the recovery; but as to this matter of man's imaginations and attachments in political affairs, I have no more understanding than another man.

It is very strange, said the Captain, that you who can tell by what means a thing is stolen, and the place where it is deposited, though at a thousand miles distance, should know so little of what is going on in the breast of man, as not to be able to develop his secret thoughts, and the motives of his actions.

It is not of our business, said the other; but should we undertake it, I do not see that it would be very difficult to explain all that puzzles you at present. There is no need of a conjurer to tell why it is that the common people are more disposed to trust one of their own class, than those who may affect to be superior. Besides, there is a certain pride in man, which leads him to elevate the low, and pull down the high. There is a kind of creating power exerted in making a senator of an unqualified person; which when the author has done, he exults over the work, and like the Creator Himself when he made the world, sees that "it is very good." Moreover, there is in every government a patrician class, against whom the spirit of the multitude naturally militates: and hence a perpetual war; the aristocrats endeavoring to detrude the people, and the people contending to obtrude themselves. And it is right it should be so; for by this fermentation, the spirit of democracy is kept alive.

The Captain, thanking him for his information, asked him what was to pay; at the same time pulling out half a crown from a green silk purse which he had in his breeches pocket. The conjurer gave him to understand, that as the solution of these difficulties was not within his province he took nothing for it. The Captain expressing his sense of his disinterested service, bade him adieu.

CHAPTER V
CONTAINING REFLECTIONS

A democracy is beyond all question the freest government: because under this, every man is equally protected by the laws, and has equally a voice in making them. But I do not say an equal voice; because some men have stronger lungs than others, and can express more forcibly their opinions of public affairs. Others, though they may not speak very loud, yet have a faculty of saying more in a short time; and even in the case of others, who speak little or none at all, yet what they do say containing good sense, comes with greater weight; so that all things considered, every citizen, has not, in this sense of the word, an equal voice. But the right being equal, what great harm if it is unequally exercised? Is it necessary that every man should become a statesman? No more than that every man should become a poet or a painter. The sciences, are open to all; but let him only who has taste and genius pursue them. If any man covets the office of a bishop, says St. Paul, he covets a good work. But again, he adds this caution, Ordain not a novice, lest being lifted up with pride, he falls into the condemnation of the Devil. It is indeed making a devil of a man to lift him up to a state to which he is not suited. A ditcher is a respectable character, with his over-alls on, and a spade in his hand; but put the same man to those offices which require the head whereas he has been accustomed to impress with his foot, and there appears a contrast between the individual and the occupation.

There are individuals in society, who prefer honor to wealth; or cultivate political studies as a branch of literary pursuits; and offer themselves to serve public bodies, in order to have an opportunity of discovering their knowledge, and exercising their judgment. It must be chagrining to these, and hurtful to the public, to see those who have no talent this way, and ought to have no taste, preposterously obtrude themselves upon the government. It is the same as if a brick-layer should usurp the office of a tailor, and come with his square and perpendicular, to take the measure of a pair of breeches.

It is proper that those who cultivate oratory, should go to the house of orators. But for an Ay and No man to be ambitious of that place, is to sacrifice his credit to his vanity.

I would not mean to insinuate that legislators are to be selected from the more wealthy of the citizens, yet a man's circumstances ought to be such as afford him leisure for study and reflection. There is often wealth without taste or talent. I have no idea, that because a man lives in a great house and has a cluster of bricks or stones about his backside, that he is therefore fit for a legislator. There is so much pride and arrogance with those who consider themselves the first in a government, that it deserves to be checked by the populace, and the evil most usually commences on this side. Men associate with their own persons, the adventitious circumstances of birth and fortune: So that a fellow blowing with fat and repletion, conceives himself superior to the poor lean man, that lodges in an inferior mansion. But as in all cases, so in this, there is a medium. Genius and virtue are independent of rank and fortune; and it is neither the opulent, nor the indigent, but the man of ability and integrity that ought to be called forth to serve his country: and while, on the one hand, the aristocratic part of the government, arrogates a right to represent; on the other hand, the democratic contends the point; and from this conjunction and opposition of forces, there is produced a compound resolution, which carries the object in an intermediate direction. When we see therefore, a Teague Oregan lifted up, the philosopher will reflect, that it is to balance some purse-proud fellow, equally as ignorant, that comes down from the sphere of aristocratic interest.

But every man ought to consider for himself, whether it is his use to be this draw-back, on either side. For as when good liquor is to be distilled, you throw in some material useless in itself to correct the effervescence of the spirit; so it may be his part to act as a sedative. For though we commend the effect, yet still the material retains but its original value.

But as the nature of things is such, let no man who means well to the commonwealth, and offers to serve it, be hurt in his mind when someone of meaner talents is preferred. The people are a sovereign, and greatly despotic; but, in the main, just.

I have a great mind, in order to elevate the composition, to make quotations from the Greek and Roman history. And I am conscious to myself, that I have read the writers on the government of Italy and Greece, in ancient, as well as in modern times. But I have drawn a great deal more from reflection on the nature of things, than from all the writings I have ever read. Nay, the history of the election, which I have just given, will afford a better lesson to the American mind, than all that is to be found in other examples. We have seen here, a weaver a favored candidate, and in the next instance, a bog-trotter superseding him. Now it may be said, that this is fiction; but fiction, or no fiction, the nature of the thing will make it a reality. But I return to the adventures of the Captain, whom I have upon my hands; and who, as far as I can yet discover, is a good honest man; and means what is benevolent and useful; though his ideas may not comport with the ordinary manner of thinking, in every particular.

FROM BOOK IV
[DUELING]

CHAPTER II

Detaining some time in a village, there was a great deal said about a certain Miss Fog, who was the belle of the place. Her father had made a fortune by the purchase of public securities. A garrison having been at this place, and troops quartered here, he had been employed as an issuing commissary! When the commissioners sat to adjust unliquidated claims, he had a good deal in his power, by vouching for the accounts of the butcher, and baker, and wood-cutter, and water-drawer, and waggoner, and all others of all occupations whatsoever, whose claims were purchased by himself in the mean time, and when the certificates issued in their names, they were to his use. The butcher and baker, no doubt, long before had been paid out of the flesh killed, or bread baked; because it is a good maxim, and a scriptural expression, "Muzzle not the ox that treadeth out the corn." But the public has a broad back, and a little vouching, by a person interested, is not greatly felt. These certificates, though at first of little value, and issued by the commissioners with the liberality of those who give what is of little worth, yet by the funding acts of the government, having become, in value, equal to gold and silver, the commissary had a great estate thrown upon him; so that from low beginnings, he had become a man of fortune and consequence. His family, and especially the eldest daughter, shared the advantage; for she had become the object of almost all wooers. The Captain, though an old bachelor, as we have said, had not wholly lost the idea of matrimony. Happening to be in a circle, one evening, where Miss Fog was, he took a liking to her, in all respects save one, which was, that she seemed, on her part, to have taken a liking to a certain Mr. Jacko, who was there present; and to whose attention she discovered a facility of acquiescence. The Captain behaved, for the present, as if he did not observe the preference; but the following day, waiting on the young lady at her father's house, he drew her into conversation, and began to reason with her, in the following manner:

Miss Fog, said he, you are a young lady of great beauty, great sense, and fortune still greater than either.—This was a sad blunder in a man of gallantry, but the lady not being of the greatest sensibility of nerve, did not perceive it.—On my part, said he, I am a man of years, but a man of some reflection; and it would be much more advisable in you to trust my experience, and the mellowness of my disposition in a state of matrimony, than the vanity and petulance of this young fop Jacko, for whom you show a partiality. The color coming into the young lady's face at this expression, she withdrew, and left him by himself. The Captain struck with the rudeness, withdrew·also, and, calling Teague from the kitchen, mounted his horse and set off.

The next morning, shortly after he had got out of bed, and had just come downstairs at his lodging, and was buttoning the knees of his breeches, a light airy looking young man, with much bowing and civility, entered the hall of the public house, and enquiring if this was not Captain Farrago to whom he had the honor to address himself, delivered him a paper. On the perusal, it was found to be a challenge from Mr. Jacko.

The fact was, that Miss Fog, in order the more to recommend herself to her suitor, had informed him of the language of the Captain. The young man, though he had no great stomach for the matter, yet according to the custom of these times, could do no less than challenge. The bearer was what is called his second.

The Captain having read the paper, and pausing a while, said, Mr. Second, for that I take to be your style and character, is it consistent with reason or common sense, to be the aider or abettor of another man's folly; perhaps the prompter: for it is no uncommon thing with persons to inflame the passions of their friends, rather than allay them. This young woman, for I shall not call her lady, from vanity, or ill-nature, or both, has become a talebearer to her lover, who, I will venture to say, thanks her but little for it; as she has thereby rendered it necessary for him to take this step. You, in the meantime, are not blameless, as it became you to have declined the office, and thereby furnished an excuse to your friend for not complying with the custom. For it would have been a sufficient apology with the lady to have said, although he was disposed to fight, yet he could get no one to be his armorbearer or assistant. It could have been put upon the footing, that all had such regard for his life, that no one would countenance him in risking it. You would have saved him by this means, all that uneasiness which he feels at present, lest I should accept his challenge. I am not so unacquainted with human nature, as not to know how disagreeable it must be to think of having a pistol ball lodged in the groin or the left breast, or, to make the best of it, the pan of the knee broke, or the nose cut off or some wound less than mortal given; disagreeable, especially to a man in the bloom of life, and on the point of marriage with a woman to whose person or fortune he has no exception. I would venture to say, therefore, there will be no great difficulty in appeasing this Orlando Furioso, that has sent me the challenge. Did you know the state of his mind, you would find him at prayers at this moment, that I would ease his fears, and make some apology. A very slight one would suffice. I dare say, his resentment against Miss Fog is not slight, and that he would renounce her person and fortune both, to get quit of the duel. But the opinion of the world is against him, and he must fight. Do you think he has any great gratitude to you for your services on this occasion. He had much rather you had, in the freedom of friendship, given him a kick on the backside, when he made application to you; and told him, that it did not become him to quarrel about a woman, who had, probably, consulted but her own vanity, in giving him the information. In that case, he would have been more pleased with you a month hence, than he is at present. I do not know that he has an overstock of sense; nevertheless, he cannot be just such a fool, as not to consider, that you, yourself, may have pretensions to this belle, and be disposed to have him out of the way before you. He must be a fool, indeed, if he does not reflect, that you had much rather see us fight than not; from the very same principle that we take delight in seeing a cock-match, or a horse-race. The spectacle is new, and produces a brisk current of thought through the mind; which is a constituent of pleasure, the absence of all movement giving none at all.

What do you suppose I must think of you, Mr. Second; I, who have read books, and thought a little on the subject; have made up my mind in these matters, and account the squires that bring challenges from knights, as people of but very small desert. Thinking men have condemned the duel, and laws have prohibited it; but these miscreants still keep it up, by being the conductors of the fluid. My indignation, therefore, falls on such, and I have long ago fixed on the mode of treating them. It is this: a stout athletic man calls upon me, with a challenge in his hand, I knock him down, if I can, without saying a word. If the natural arm be not sufficient for this purpose, I avail myself of any stone, wooden, or iron instrument that I cast my eye upon, not just to take away his life, if I can help it; but to hit the line as exactly as possible, between actual homicide, and a very bad wound. For in this case, I should conceive, a battery could be justifiable, or at least excusable, and the fine not very great; the bearing a challenge being a breach of the peace, in the first instance. This would be my conduct with a stout athletic man, whom I might think it dangerous to encounter with fair warning, and on equal terms. But in the present case, where—(here the second began to show signs of fear, raising himself, and inclining backwards, opening his eyes wider, and casting a look towards the door)—where, continued the Captain, I have to do with a person of your slender make, I do not adopt that surprise, or use an artificial weapon; but with these fists, which have been used in early life to agricultural employments, I shall very deliberately impress a blow. The second rising to his feet began to recede a little. Be under no apprehensions, said the Captain; I shall use no unfair method of biting, gouging, or wounding the private parts. Nay, as you appear to be a young man of a delicate constitution, I shall only choke a little. You will give me leave to take you by the throat in as easy a manner as possible.

In the mean time, the second had been withdrawing towards the door, and the Captain with outstretched arms, in a sideway direction, proceeding to intercept him. In an instant, he was seized by the neck, and the exclamation of murder which he made at the first grasp, began to die away in hoarse guttural murmurs of one nearly strangled, and laboring for breath. The Captain meaning that he should be more alarmed than hurt, dismissed him with a salutation of his foot on the backside, as a *claude ostium,* as he went out. You may be, said he, a gentleman in the opinion of the world; but you are a low person in mine; and so it shall be done to everyone who shall come upon such an errand.

• • •

CHAPTER IV
[THE CAPTAIN'S REPLY TO A CHALLENGE]

On reflection, it seemed advisable to the Captain to write an answer to the card which Colonel, or Major Jacko, or whatever his title may have been, had sent him this morning. It was as follows:

SIR, I have two objections to this duel matter. The one is, lest I should hurt you; and the other is, lest you should hurt me. I do not see any good it would do me to put a bullet through any part of your body. I could make no use of you when dead, for any culinary purpose, as I would a rabbit or a turkey. I am no cannibal to feed on the flesh of men. Why then shoot down a human creature, of which I could make no use. A buffalo would be better meat. For though your flesh might be delicate and tender; yet it wants the firmness and consistency which takes and retains salt. At any rate it would not be fit for long sea voyages. You might make a good barbecue, it is true, being of the nature of a raccoon or an opossum; but people are not in the habit of barbecuing anything human now. As to your hide, it is not worth the taking off, being little better than that of a year old colt.

It would seem to me a strange thing to shoot at a man that would stand still to be shot at; in as much as I have been heretofore used to shoot at things flying, or running, or jumping. Were you on a tree now like a squirrel, endeavoring to hide yourself in the branches, or like a raccoon, that after much eyeing and spying I observe at length in the crotch of a tall oak, with boughs and leaves intervening, so that I could just get a sight of his hinder parts, I should think it pleasurable enough to take a shot at you. But as it is, there is no skill or judgment requisite either to discover or take you down.

As to myself, I do not much like to stand in the way of anything that is harmful. I am under apprehensions you might hit me. That being the case, I think it most advisable to stay at a distance. If you want to try your pistols, take some object, a tree or a barn door about my dimensions. If you hit that, send me word, and I shall acknowledge that if I had been in the same place, you might also have hit me.

J. FARRAGO.

CHAPTER V
CONTAINING REFLECTIONS

Captain Farrago was a good man, but unacquainted with the world. His ideas were drawn chiefly from what may be called the old school; the Greek and Roman notions of things. The combat of the duel was to them unknown. Though it seems strange, that a people who were famous for almost all arts and sciences, should have remained ignorant of its use. I do not conceive how, as a people, they could exist without it. But so it was, they actually were without the knowledge of it. For we do not find any trace of this custom in the poets or historians of all antiquity.

I do not know at what period, precisely, the custom was introduced; or to whom it was owing; but omitting this disquisition, we content ourselves with observing, that it has produced as great an improvement in manners, as the discovery of the loadstone, and mariners compass, has in navigation. Not that I mean to descant, at full length, on the valuable effects of it; but simply to observe, that it is a greater aid to government than the alliance of church and state itself. If Dr. Warburton had had leisure, I could wish he had written a treatise upon it. Some effect to ridicule it, as carrying to a greater length small differences, than the aggravation may justify. As for instance, a man is angry enough with you to give you a slap in the face; but the custom says, he must shoot you through the head. I think the smaller the aggravation, the nicer the sense of honor. The heaviest mind will resent a gross affront; but to kill a man where there is no affront at all, shows a great sensibility. It is immaterial whether there is or is not an injury, provided the world thinks there is; for it is the opinion of mankind we are to consult. It is a duty which we owe them to provide for their amusement. *Non nascimur nobis ipsis;* we are not born for ourselves, but for others. *Decorum pro patria mori;* it is a becoming thing to die for one's country; and shall it not also be accounted honorable to throw one's life away for the entertainment of a few particular neighbors and acquaintances. It is true, the tears that will be shed upon your grave, will not make the grass grow; but you will have the consolation, when you leave the world, to have fallen in the bed of honor.

It is certainly a very noble institution, that of the duel; and it has been carried to very great perfection, in some respects. Nevertheless, I would submit it to the public, whether still farther improvement might not be made in the laws and regulations of it. For instance, could it not be reduced nearer to an equality of chances, by proportioning the caliber, or bore of the pistol; the length of the barrel, also, to the size of the duellist who holds it; or by fixing the ratio of distance in proportion to the bulk of combatants. To explain myself: When I am to fight a man of small size, I ought to have a longer pistol than my adversary, because my mark is smaller; or I ought to be permitted to come nearer to him. For it is altogether unfair that men of unequal bulk should fire at equal distances, and with equal calibers. The smaller size multiplied by the larger space, or larger pistol, would equal the larger size multiplied by the smaller space or smaller pistol. If this amendment of the duel laws should be approved by men of honor, let it be added to the code.

BOOK V

CHAPTER I
[AN INDIAN TREATY-MAKER]

Not long after this, being at a certain place, the Captain was accosted by a stranger in the following manner: Captain Farrago, said he, I have heard of a young man in your service who talks Irish. Now, Sir, my business is that of an Indian treaty-maker; and am on my way with a party of kings, and half kings, to the commissioners, to hold a treaty. My king of the Kickapoos, who was a Welsh blacksmith, took sick by the way, and is dead. I have heard of this lad of yours, and could wish to have him a while to supply his place. The treaty will not last longer than a couple of weeks; and as the government will probably allow three or four thousand dollars for the treaty, it will be in our power to make it worth your while, to spare him for that time. Your king of the Kickapoos, said the Captain; what does that mean? Said the stranger, it is just this: You have heard of the Indian nations to the westward, that occasionally make war upon the frontier settlements. It has been a policy of government, to treat with these, and distribute goods. Commissioners are appointed for that purpose. Now you are not to suppose that it is an easy matter to catch a real chief, and bring him from the woods; or if at some expense one was brought, the goods would go to his use; whereas, it is much more profitable to hire substitutes and make chiefs of our own: and as some unknown gibberish is necessary, to pass for an Indian language, we generally make use of Welsh, or Low Dutch, or Irish; or pick up an ingenious fellow here and there, who can imitate a language by sounds of his own, in his mouth, and throat. But we prefer one who can speak a real tongue, and give more for him. We cannot afford you a great deal at this time for the use of your man; because it is not a general treaty where 20,000 or 30,000 dollars are appropriated for the purpose of holding it; but an occasional, or what we call a running treaty, by way of brightening the chain, and holding fast friendship. The commissioners will doubtless be glad to see us, and procure from government an allowance for the treaty. For the more treaties, the more use for commissioners. The business must be kept up, and treaties made if there are none of themselves. My Pianksha, and Choctaw chiefs, are very good fellows; the one of them a Scotch pedlar that talks the Erse; the other has been some time in Canada, and has a little broken Indian, God knows what language; but has been of great service in assisting to teach the rest some Indian custom and manners. I have had the whole of them for a fortnight past under my tuition, teaching them war songs and dances, and to make responses at the treaty. If your man is tractable, I can make him a Kickapoo in about nine days. A breech-clout and leggins, that I took off the blacksmith that died, I have ready to put on him. He must have part of his head shaved, and painted, with feathers on his crown; but the paint will rub off, and the hair grow in a short time, so that he can go about with you again.

It is a very strange affair, said the Captain. Is it possible that such deception can be practiced in a new country. It astonishes me, that the government does not detect such imposition. The government, said the Indian treaty-man, is at a great distance. It knows no more of Indians than a cow does of Greek. The legislature, hears of wars and rumors of wars, and supports the executive in forming treaties. How is it possible for men who live remote from the scene of action, to have adequate ideas of the nature of Indians, or the transactions that are carried on in their behalf? Do you think the one half of those savages that come to treat, are real representatives of the nation? Many of them are not savages at all; but weavers and pedlars, as I have told you, picked up to make kings and chiefs. I speak of those particularly that come trading down to inland towns, or the metropolis. I would not communicate these mysteries of our trade, were it not that I confide in your good sense, and have occasion for your servant.

It is a mystery of iniquity, said the Captain. Do you suppose that I would countenance such a fraud upon the public? I do not know, said the other; it is a very common thing for men to speculate, nowadays. If you will not, another will. An 100 dollars might as well be in your pocket as another man's. I will give you that for the use of your servant, for a week or two, and say no more about it. It is an idea new to me entirely, said the Captain, that Indian princes, whom I have seen escorted down as such, were no more than trumpery, disguised, as you mention; that such should be introduced to polite assemblies, and have the honor to salute the fair ladies with a kiss, the greatest beauties thinking themselves honored by having the salutation of a sovereign? It is so, said the other; I had a red headed bricklayer once, whom I passed for a Chippawa; and who has dined with clubs, and sat next the President. He was blind of an eye, and was called blind Sam by the traders. I have given it out that he was a great warrior, and had lost his eye by an arrow, in a contest with a rival nation. These things are now reduced to a system; and it is so well known to those who are engaged in the traffic, that we think nothing of it.

How the devil, said the Captain, do you get speeches made, and interpret them so as to pass for truth. That is an easy matter, said the other; Indian speeches are nearly all alike. You have only to talk of burying hatchets under large trees, kindling fires, brightening chains; with a demand, at the latter end, of blankets for the backside, and rum to get drunk with.

I much doubt, said the Captain, whether treaties that are carried on in earnest are of any great use. Of none at all, said the other; especially as the practice of giving goods prevails; because this is an inducement to a fresh war. This being the case, it can be no harm to make a farce of the whole matter; or rather a profit of it; by such means as I propose to you, and have pursued myself.

After all, said the Captain, I cannot but consider it as a kind of contra-band and illicit traffic; and I must be excused from having any hand in it, I shall not betray your secret, but I shall not favor it. It would ill become me, whose object in riding about in this manner, is to give just ideas on subjects, to take part in such ill-gotten gain.

The Indian treaty-man finding it in vain to say more, withdrew.

BENJAMIN BANNEKER

(1731–1806)

The essential biographical facts about this admirable man are con-tained in his own letter to Thomas Jefferson and in the brief note that was appended, along with Jefferson's reply, to Banneker's letter when it was published in 1791. Banneker thus takes his place in American literature as one of the first in a long line of Afro-American charac-ters—especially in autobiography but also in fiction—whose primary duty is to stand forth as, in Emerson's phrase, "a man speaking among men," to show the skeptical or evidently indifferent white audience that a black man is a complete man. Banneker's eloquence does not preclude extraordinary subtlety, for in the fourteenth chapter of *Notes on Virginia* Jefferson had doubted whether a black person could be found "capable of tracing and comprehending the investigations of Euclid"; and in the same passage Jefferson had said that he "never yet could . . . find that a black had uttered a thought above the level of plain narration."

An early account is Henry E. Baker, "Ben-jamin Banneker, The Negro Mathemati-cian and Astronomer," *Journal of Negro History*, 3 (1918): 99–118. For Banneker's place in American history, see John Hope Franklin, *From Slavery to Freedom, a His-tory of Negro Americans,* 1969.

Copy of a Letter
from Benjamin Banneker
to the Secretary of State

1792[1]

Maryland, Baltimore County, August 19, 1791.

SIR,

I am fully sensible of the greatness of that freedom which I take with you on the present occasion; a liberty which seemed to me scarcely allowable, when I reflected on that distinguished and dignified station in which you stand, and the almost general prejudice and prepossession, which is so prevalent in the world against those of my complexion.

I suppose it is a truth too well attested to you, to need a proof here, that we are a race of beings who have long labored under the abuse and censure of the world; that we have long been looked upon with an eye of contempt; and that we have long been considered rather as brutish than human, and scarcely capable of mental endowments.

Sir, I hope I may safely admit, in consequence of that report which hath reached me, that you are a man far less inflexible in sentiments of this nature, than many others; that you are measurably friendly and well disposed towards us; and that you are willing and ready to lend your aid and assistance to our relief from those many distresses and numerous calamities to which we are reduced.

Now Sir, if this is founded in truth, I apprehend you will embrace every opportunity to eradicate that train of absurd and false ideas and opinions which so generally prevails with respect to us; and that your sentiments are concurrent with mine, which are, that one universal Father hath given being to us all; and that He hath not only made us all of one flesh, but that He hath also, without partiality, afforded us all the same sensations and endowed us all with the same faculties; and that however variable we may be in society or religion, however diversified in situation or color, we are all of the same family, and stand in the same relation to Him.

Sir, if these are sentiments of which you are fully persuaded, I hope you cannot but acknowledge that it is the indispensable duty of those who maintain for themselves the rights of human nature, and who possess the obligations of Christianity, to extend their power and influence to the relief of every part of the human race from whatever burden or oppression they may

---

[1] This brief letter, with Thomas Jefferson's brief reply, was published separately in Philadelphia, 1792.

unjustly labor under; and this, I apprehend, a full conviction of the truth and obligation of these principles should lead all to.

Sir, I have long been convinced that if your love for yourselves, and for those inestimable laws which preserved to you the rights of human nature, was founded on sincerity, you could not but be solicitous that every individual, of whatever rank or distinction, might with you equally enjoy the blessings thereof; neither could you rest satisfied short of the most active effusion of your exertions, in order to their promotion from any state of degradation, to which the unjustifiable cruelty and barbarism of men may have reduced them.[2]

Sir, I freely and cheerfully acknowledge that I am of the African race, and in that color which is natural to them of the deepest dye; and it is under a sense of the mose profound gratitude to the Supreme Ruler of the Universe that I now confess to you that I am not under that state of tyrannical thraldom and inhuman captivity to which too many of my brethren are doomed, but that I have abundantly tasted of the fruition of those blessings, which proceed from that free and unequalled liberty with which you are favored; and which, I hope, you will willingly allow you have mercifully received from the immediate hand of that Being from whom proceedeth every good and perfect gift.

Sir, suffer me to recall to your mind that time in which the arms and tyranny of the British crown were exerted, with every powerful effort, in order to reduce you to a state of servitude: look back, I entreat you, on the variety of dangers to which you were exposed; reflect on that time in which every human aid appeared unavailable, and in which even hope and fortitude wore the aspect of inability to the conflict, and you cannot but be led to a serious and grateful sense of your miraculous and providential preservation; you cannot but acknowledge, that the present freedom and tranquillity which you enjoy you have mercifully received, and that it is the peculiar blessing of Heaven.

This, Sir, was a time when you clearly saw into the injustice of a state of slavery, and in which you had just apprehensions of the horrors of its condition. It was now that your abhorrence thereof was so excited, that you publicly held forth this true and invaluable doctrine, which is worthy to be recorded and remembered in all succeeding ages: "We hold these truths to be self-evident, that all men are created equal; that they are endowed by their Creator with certain unalienable rights, and that among these are, life, liberty, and the pursuit of happiness."

Here was a time in which your tender feelings for yourselves had engaged you thus to declare you were then impressed with proper ideas of the great violation of liberty, and the free possession of those blessings to which you

[2] Here Banneker expresses one of the earliest published allusions to the contradiction between slavery and the Declaration of Independence. Compare Frederick Douglass and David Walker, below.

were entitled by nature; but, Sir, how pitiable is it to reflect, that although you were so fully convinced of the benevolence of the Father of mankind, and of His equal and impartial distribution of these rights and privileges which He hath conferred upon them, that you should at the same time counteract His mercies, in detaining by fraud and violence so numerous a part of my brethren under groaning captivity and cruel oppression, that you should at the same time be found guilty of that most criminal act, which you professedly detested in others, with respect to yourselves.

I suppose that your knowledge of the situation of my brethren is too extensive to need a recital here; neither shall I presume to prescribe methods by which they may be relieved, otherwise than by recommending to you and all others, to wean yourselves from those narrow prejudices which you have imbibed with respect to them, and as Job proposed to his friends, "put your soul in their souls' stead";[3] thus shall your hearts be enlarged with kindness and benevolence towards them; and thus shall you need neither the direction of myself or others, in what manner to proceed herein.

And now, Sir, although my sympathy and affection for my brethren hath caused my enlargement thus far, I ardently hope that your candor and generosity will plead with you in my behalf, when I make known to you, that it was not originally my design; but having taken up my pen in order to direct to you, as a present, a copy of an Almanac which I have calculated for the succeeding year, I was unexpectedly and unavoidably led thereto.

This calculation is the production of my arduous study, in this my advanced stage of life; for having long had unbounded desires to become acquainted with the secrets of nature, I have had to gratify my curiosity herein, through my own assiduous application to Astronomical Study, in which I need not recount to you the many difficulties and disadvantages which I have had to encounter.

And although I had almost declined to make my calculation for the ensuing year, in consequence of that time which I had allotted therefor, being taken up at the Federal Territory, by the request of Mr. Andrew Ellicott; yet finding myself under several engagements to printers of this state, to whom I had communicated my design, on my return to my place of residence, I industriously applied myself thereto, which I hope I have accomplished with correctness and accuracy; a copy of which I have taken the liberty to direct to you, and which I humbly request you will favorably receive; and although you may have the opportunity of perusing it after the publication, yet I choose to send it to you in manuscript previous thereto, that thereby you might not only have an earlier inspection, but that you might also view it in my own hand writing.

And now, Sir, I shall conclude, and subscribe myself, with the most profound respect,

Your most obedient humble servant,

[3] Job 16:2–5.

BENJAMIN BANNEKER.

PHILIP FRENEAU

(1752–1832)

Starting out with hopes of becoming a clergyman, Philip Freneau acquired at Princeton the friendships and the interest that would eventually lead him into political journalism, maritime adventure (running British blockades during the Revolution), and rather imitative poetry. He was especially friendly with James Madison and Hugh Henry Brackenridge, with whom he wrote *The Rising Glory of America* and who published some of Freneau's early verse in *The United States Magazine*. Captured and imprisoned by the British in 1780, Freneau wrote increasingly vehement prose and verse attacking agents of the Crown. He spent a few years as captain of a merchantman after the war, and then he founded the *National Gazette* as an anti-Federalist newspaper at a time when the Jeffersonian party needed a regular voice. That paper failed in 1793, but Freneau continued to struggle for solvency through other journalistic ventures in New Jersey and New York.

Freneau is remembered today largely for the power of his journalism (as in the creation of Robert Slender, O.S.M.—One of the Swinish Multitude) and for a few poems on characteristically American subjects—the honeysuckle, the Indian student, a particular battle.

The standard text of the poetry is *The Poems of Philip Freneau,* 3 vols., ed. F. L. Pattee, 1902–1907.

The best biography is Lewis Leary, *That Rascal Freneau,* 1941. Studies include Nelson F. Adkins, *Philip Freneau and the Cosmic Enigma: The Religious and Philosophical Speculations of an American Poet,* 1949; Jacob Axelrod, *Philip Freneau: Champion of Democracy,* 1967; Philip Merrill Marsh, *The Works of Philip Freneau, a Critical Study,* 1968.

A one-volume edition, with an excellent introduction, is H. H. Clark, *Poems of Freneau,* 1929.

On The Memorable Victory Obtained by the Gallant Captain John Paul Jones, of the Bon Homme Richard, over the *Serapis*. . .[1]

1.

O'er the rough main with flowing sheet
The guardian of a numerous fleet,
    Seraphis from the Baltic came;
A ship of less tremendous force
Sail'd by her side the self-same course,   5
Countess of Scarb'ro' was her name.

2.

And now their native coasts appear,
Britannia's hills their summits rear
    Above the German main;
Fond to suppose their dangers o'er,   10
They southward coast along the shore,
Thy waters, gentle Thames, to gain.

3.

Full forty guns Seraphis bore,
And Scarb'ro's Countess twenty-four,
    Mann'd with Old England's boldest tars—   15
What flag that rides the Gallic seas
Shall dare attack such piles as these,
Design'd for tumults and for wars!

4.

Now from the top-mast's giddy height
A seaman cry'd—"Four sail in sight   20
    Approach with favouring gales,"
Pearson, resolv'd to save the fleet,
Stood off to sea these ships to meet,
    And closely brac'd his shivering sails.

[1] The text is the 1795 edition. The poem celebrates Jones's finest military victory, achieved during a raid along the English coast in a merchant-ship that had been converted to military use and named in honor of Benjamin Franklin's Poor Richard. The battle was fought September 23, 1779. Herman Melville gives quite a different tone to the battle, and to Jones's character, in *Israel Potter* (1855).

5.

With him advanc'd the Countess bold,   25
Like a black tar in wars grown old:
    And now these floating piles drew nigh;
But, muse, unfold what chief of fame
In th'other warlike squadron came,
    Whose standards at his mast head fly.   30

6.

'Twas JONES, brave JONES, to battle led
As bold a crew as ever bled
    Upon the sky surrounded main;
The standards of the Western World
Were to the willing winds unfurl'd   35
    Denying Britain's tyrant reign.

7.

The *Good Man Richard* led the line;
The *Alliance* next: with these combine
    The Gallic ship they *Pallas* call:
The *Vengeance*, arm'd with sword and flame,   40
These to attack the Britons came—
    But *two* accomplish'd all.[2]

8.

Now Phoebus sought his pearly bed:[3]
But who can tell the scenes of dread,
    The horrors of that fatal night!   45
Close up these floating castles came;
The Good Man Richard bursts in flame;
    Seraphis trembled at the sight.

9.

She felt the fury of *her* ball;
Down, prostrate down, the Britons fall;   50
    The decks were strew'd with slain:
JONES to his foe his vessel lash'd;
And, while the black artillery flash'd,
    Loud thunders shook the main.

---

[2] That is, two ships did virtually all the fighting for the American side. Jones's *Bonhomme Richard* captured the *Serapis*, and the *Pallas* captured the *Countess of Scarborough*.

[3] The sun (Phoebus) set.

10.

Alas! that mortals should employ   55
Such murdering engines, to destroy
    That frame by heav'n so nicely join'd;
Alas! that e'er the god decreed
That brother should by brother bleed,
    And pour'd such madness in the mind.   60

11.

But thou, brave JONES, no blame shalt bear;
The rights of men demand thy care:
    For *these* you dare the greedy waves—
No tyrant on destruction bent
Has plann'd thy conquests—thou art sent   65
    To humble tyrants and their slaves.

12.

See!—dread Serapis flames again—
And art thou, JONES, among the slain,
    And sunk to Neptune's caves below—
He lives—though crowds around him fall,   70
Still he, unhurt, survives them all;
    Almost alone he fights the foe.

13.

And can thy ship these strokes sustain?
Behold thy brave companions slain,
    All clasp'd in ocean's dark embrace.   75
STRIKE, OR BE SUNK—the Briton cries—
SINK, IF YOU CAN—the chief replies,[4]
    Fierce lightnings blazing in his face.

14

Then to the side three guns he drew,
(Almost deserted by his crew)   80
    And charg'd them deep with woe:
By *Pearson's* flash he aim'd the balls;
His main-mast totters—down it falls—
    Tremendous was the blow.

[4] Jones is said to have replied: "I have not begun to fight."

15

Pearson as yet disdain'd to yield,   85
But scarce his secret fears conceal'd,
    And thus was heard to cry—
"With hell, not mortals, I contend;
What art thou—human, or a fiend,
    That dost my force defy?   90

16.

"Return, my lads, the fight renew."
So call'd bold Pearson to his crew;
    But call'd, alas! in vain;
Some on the decks lay maim'd and dead;
Some to their deep recesses fled,   95
    And more were bury'd in the main.

17.

Distress'd, forsaken, and alone,
He haul'd his tatter'd standard down,
    And yielded to his gallant foe;
Bold *Pallas* soon the *Countess* took,   100
Thus both their haughty colours struck,
    Confessing what the brave can do.

18.

But, Jones, too dearly didst thou buy
These ships possest so gloriously,
    Too many deaths disgrac'd the fray: 105
Thy barque, that bore the conquering flame,
That the proud Briton overcame,
    Even she forsook thee on thy way;

19.

For when the morn began to shine,
Fatal to her, the ocean brine   110
    Pour'd through each spacious wound;
Quick in the deep she disappear'd:—
But JONES to friendly Belgia steer'd,
    With conquest and with glory crown'd.

20.

Go on, great man, to daunt the foe,   115
And bid the haughty Britons know
    They to our *Thirteen Stars* shall bend;
Those *Stars* that, veil'd in dark attire,
Long glimmer'd with a feeble fire,
    But radiant now ascend.   120

21.

Bend to the the Stars that flaming rise
In western, not in eastern, skies,
    Fair Freedom's reign restor'd—
So when the magi, come from far,
Beheld the God-attending Star,
    They trembled and ador'd.[5]   125

[5] Here Freneau associates American destiny with the same divine plan that announced the birth of Jesus to the Wise Men. He associates the birth of the new republic with the birth of the new religion.

To the Memory of the Brave Americans, under General Greene, in South Carolina, who fell in the action of September 8, 1781

At Eutaw springs the valiant died:
    Their limbs with dust are cover'd o'er—
Weep on, ye springs, your tearful tide;
    How many heroes are no more!

If in this wreck of ruin, they   5
    Can yet be thought to claim a tear,
O smite thy gentle breast, and say
    The friends of freedom slumber here!

Thou, who shalt trace this bloody plain,
    If goodness rules thy generous breast,   10
Sigh for the wasted rural reign;
    Sigh for the shepherds sunk to rest!

Stranger, their humble graves adorn;
    You too may fall, and ask a tear:
'Tis not the beauty of the morn   15
    That proves the evening shall be clear—

They saw their injur'd country's woe;
    The flaming town, the wasted field;
Then rush'd to meet the insulting foe;
    They took the spear—but left the shield.   20

Led by thy conquering standards, GREENE,
    The Britons they compell'd to fly:
None distant view'd the fatal plain,
    None griev'd in such a cause to die—

But, like the Parthian,[1] fam'd of old,   25
    Who, flying, still their arrows threw;
These routed Britons, full as bold,
    Retreated, and retreating slew.

Now rest in peace, our patient band;
    Though far from nature's limits thrown,   30
We trust they find a happier land,
    A brighter Phoebus of their own.

[1] Persian horsemen who used retreat as a deceptive tactic, then went on the offensive again.

The Wild Honey Suckle[1]

Fair flower, that dost so comely grow,
Hid in this silent dull retreat,
Untouch'd thy honey'd blossoms blow:
Unseen thy little branches greet:
    No roving foot shall crush thee here,   5
    No busy hand provoke a tear.

By Nature's self in white array'd,
She bade thee shun the vulgar eye,
And planted here the guardian shade,
And sent soft waters murmuring by;   10
    Thus quietly thy summer goes,
    Thy days declining to repose.

Smit with those charms, that must decay,
I grieve to see your future doom;
They died—nor were those flowers less gay,   15
The flowers that did in Eden bloom;
    Unpitying frosts, and Autumn's power
    Shall leave no vestige of this flower.

[1] First published in 1786. The text follows Lewis Leary's version of the first printing. See *That Rascal Freneau*, p. 144. The tone and theme of this poem are much less simply tied to a mechanistic Deism than is the poem "On the Uniformity and Perfection of Nature," below, p. 699.

From morning suns and evening dews
At first, thy little being came: 20
If nothing once, you nothing lose,
For when you die you are the same;
　　　The space between, is but an hour,
　　　The frail duration of a flower.

Lines Occasioned by A Visit to an Old Indian Burying Ground[1]

In spite of all the learn'd have said,
I still my old opinion keep;
The *posture* that *we* give the dead,
Points out the soul's eternal sleep.

Not so the ancients of these lands—   5
The Indian, when from life releas'd,
Again is *seated* with his friends,
And shares again the joyous feast.[2]

His imag'd birds, and painted bowl,
And venison, for a journey dress'd,   10
Bespeak the nature of the soul,
ACTIVITY, that knows no rest.

His bow, for action ready bent,
And arrows, with a head of stone,
Can only mean that life is spent,   15
And not the finer essence gone.

Thou, stranger, that shalt come this way,
No fraud upon the dead commit—
Observe the swelling turf and say
They do not *lie*, but here they *sit*.   20

Here still a lofty rock remains,
On which a curious eye may trace
(Now wasted, half, by wearing rains)
The fancies of a ruder race.

[1] First published in *The American Museum*, November 1787. The text is the 1795 edition.

[2] Freneau observes that "the North American Indians bury their dead in a sitting posture. . . ."

Here still an aged elm aspires,   25
Beneath whose far projecting shade
(And which the shepherd still admires)
The children of the forest play'd!

There oft a restless Indian queen,
(Pale Shebah with her braided hair)   30
And many a barbarous form is seen
To chide the man that lingers there.

By midnight moons, o'er moistening dews,
In vestments for the chace array'd,
The hunter still the deer pursues,   35
The hunter and the deer, a shade!

And long shall timorous Fancy see
The painted chief and pointed spear,
And Reason's self shall bow the knee
To shadows and delusions here.   40

On the Uniformity and Perfection of Nature[1]

On one fix'd point all nature moves,
Nor deviates from the track she loves;
Her system drawn from reason's source,
She scorns to change her wonted course.

Could she descend from that great plan   5
To work unusual things for man,
To suit the insect of an hour—
This would betray a want of power,

Unsettled in its first design
And erring, when it did combine   10
The parts that form the vast machine,
The figures sketch'd on nature's scene.

---

[1] The text is from the 1815 edition, the year this poem first appeared. The emphasis on order and regularity here, and the image of the vast machine typify the cool rationalism against which American Romantics—as in Emerson's objection to "the pale negations of Unitarianism"—rebelled. Freneau, of course, did not always limit his poetry, or his other literary expression, to so cool a view of the natural world.

Perfections of the great first cause
Submit to no contracted laws,
But all-sufficient, all-supreme,   15
Include no trivial views in them.

Who looks through nature with an eye
That would the scheme of heaven descry
Observes her constant, still the same
In all her laws, through all her frame.   20

No imperfection can be found
In all that is, above, around,—
All nature made, in reason's sight,
Is order all, and *all is right*.[2]

[2] Perhaps an echo of Alexander Pope's
"Whatever is, is right," in *Essay on Man*
(1732), the last line of the first Epistle.

JUPITER HAMMON

(1711-c.1800)

Toward the end of the eighteenth century a number of black voices began to command attention, and their message to be transcribed, on the subject of slavery and liberty. Whether in a sermon, an oration, a petition to the authorities, or an autobiography, the various speakers addressed themselves to the cruelty and the fundamental contradiction of American chattel slavery. Repeatedly in the writings of former slaves that appeared during the next 60 years, the question of their authenticity was raised, and so we often have certification printed along with the texts as an essential part of the literary record—as at the end of a speech by young Peter Williams in 1808 and in the *Narrative of the Life of Frederick Douglass, . . .Written by Himself,* in 1845.

The range of tone in these works is broad. A citizen of the United States in the 1970's can notice that some of the basic issues—militancy against some form of moderation or accommodation—have persisted

The text may be found in *Early Negro Writing, 1760-1837,* ed. Dorothy Porter, 1972.

for nearly 200 years. Jupiter Hammon addresses "the Negroes of New York" on the assumption that they are all slaves and that many of them do not wish to be free. He concentrates much of the time on obedience to masters, religious improvement, the life after death, the evils of thievery and drunkenness, and the value of learning to read the Bible. It is difficult to tell at this distance how much of his admonitory condescension in this address was an obligatory concession for one who wished to get his advice for survival and his respect for liberty into print—or how seriously he meant his statement that he himself did not wish to be free. Surely the same paragraph in which he makes that statement shows a strong ironic appreciation of the contrast between the price paid for American independence in the Revolution and the willingness of white Americans to hold slaves. But the tone of Benjamin Banneker, James Forten, and William Hamilton is starkly different from that of Hammon.

Jupiter Hammon was also the first black writer to publish a poem in the American colonies (1760). (His second published poem was written to Phillis Wheatley, after some of her work had been published, in 1778.)

An Address to the
Negroes In the State of New York[1]

"Of a truth I perceive that God is no respecter of persons:
"But in every Nation, he that feareth him and worketh righteousness, is accepted with him," *Acts.* 34, 35.

TO THE PUBLIC

As this address is wrote in a better style than could be expected from a slave, some may be ready to doubt of the genuineness of the production. The author, as he informs in the title page, is a servant of Mr. Lloyd, and has been remarkable for his fidelity and abstinence from those vices, which he warns his brethren against. The manuscript wrote in his own hand, is in our possession. We have made no material alterations in it, except in the spelling, which we found needed considerable correction.

The Printers.

New York, 20th. Feb. 1787.

[1] New York, 1787.

AN ADDRESS TO THE NEGROES
OF THE STATE OF NEW YORK

When I am writing to you with a design to say something to you for your good, and with a view to promote your happiness, I can with truth and sincerity join with the apostle Paul, when speaking of his own nation the Jews, and say that "I have great heaviness and continual sorrow in my heart for my brethren, my kinsmen according to the flesh." Yes my dear brethren, when I think of you, which is very often, and of the poor, despised and miserable state you are in, as to the things, of this world, and when I think of your ignorance and stupidity, and the great wickedness of the most of you, I am pained to the heart. It is at times almost too much for human nature to bear, and I am obliged to turn my thoughts from the subject or endeavor to still my mind, by considering that it is permitted thus to be by that God who governs all things, who setteth up one and pulleth down another. While I have been thinking on this subject, I have frequently had great struggles in my own mind, and have been at a loss to know what to do. I have wanted exceedingly to say something to you, to call upon you with the tenderness of a father and friend, and to give you the last, and I may say dying advice, of an old man, who wishes your best good in this world, and in the world to come. But while I have had such desires, a sense of my own ignorance and unfitness to teach others has frequently discouraged me from attempting to say anything to you; yet when I thought of your situation, I could not rest easy.

When I was at Hartford in Connecticut, where I lived during the war, I published several pieces which were well received, not only by those of my own color, but by a number of the white people, who thought they might do good among their servants. This is one consideration, among others, that emboldens me now to publish what I have written to you. Another is, I think you will be more likely to listen to what is said, when you know it comes from a Negro, one your own nation and color, and therefore can have no interest in deceiving you, or in saying anything to you, but what he really thinks is your interest and duty to comply with. My age, I think, gives me some right to speak to you, and reason to expect you will hearken to my advice. I am now upwards of seventy years old, and cannot expect, though I am well, and able to do almost any kind of business, to live much longer. I have passed the common bounds set for man, and must soon go the way of all the earth. I have had more experience in the world than the most of you, and I have seen a great deal of the vanity and wickedness of it. I have great reason to be thankful that my lot has been so much better than most slaves have had. I suppose I have had more advantages and privileges than most of you who are slaves have ever known, and I believe more than many white people have enjoyed, for which I desire to bless God, and pray that He may bless those who have given them to me. I do not, my dear friends, say these things about myself to make you think that I am wiser or better than others; but that you might hearken, without prejudice, to what I have to say to you on the following particulars.

1st. Respecting obedience to masters. Now whether it is right, and lawful, in the sight of God, for them to make slaves of us or not, I am certain that while we are slaves, it is our duty to obey our masters, in all their lawful commands, and mind them unless we are bid to do that which we know to be sin, or forbidden in God's word. The apostle Paul says, "Servants be obedient to them that are your masters according to the flesh, with fear and trembling in singleness in your heart as unto Christ: Not with eye service, as men pleasers, but as the servants of Christ doing the will of God from the heart: With good will doing service to the Lord, and not to men: Knowing that whatever thing a man doeth the same shall he receive of the Lord, whether he be bond or free."[2] Here is a plain command of God for us to obey our masters. It may seem hard for us, if we think our masters wrong in holding us slaves, to obey in all things, but who of us dare dispute with God! He has commanded us to obey, and we ought to do it cheerfully, and freely. This should be done by us, not only because God commands, but because our own peace and comfort depend upon it. As we depend upon our masters, for what we eat and drink and wear, and for all our comfortable things in this world, we cannot be happy unless we please them. This we cannot do without obeying them freely, without muttering or finding fault. If a servant strives to please his master and studies and takes pains to do it, I believe there are but few masters who would use such a servant cruelly. Good servants frequently make good masters. If your master is really hard, unreasonable and cruel, there is no way so likely for you to convince him of it, as always to obey his commands, and try to serve him, and take care of his interest, and try to promote it all in your power. If you are proud and stubborn and always finding fault, your master will think the fault lies wholly on your side, but if you are humble, and meek, and bear all things patiently, your master may think he is wrong, if he does not, his neighbors will be apt to see it, and will befriend you, and try to alter his conduct. If this does not do, you must cry to Him, who has the hearts of all men in His hands, and turneth them as the rivers of waters are turned.

2d. The particular I would mention, is honesty and faithfulness. You must suffer me now to deal plainly with you, my dear brethren, for I do not mean to flatter, or omit speaking the truth, whether it is for you, or against you. How many of you are there who allow yourselves in stealing from your

[2] Compare 1 Peter 2:18.

masters. It is very wicked for you not to take care of your masters' goods, but how much worse is it to pilfer and steal from them, whenever you think you shall not be found out. This you must know is very wicked and provoking to God. There are none of you so ignorant, but that you must know that this is wrong. Though you may try to excuse yourselves, by saying that your masters are unjust to you, and though you may try to quiet your consciences in this way, yet if you are honest in owning the truth you must think it is as wicked, and on some accounts more wicked to steal from your masters, than from others.

We cannot certainly, have any excuse either for taking anything that belongs to our masters without their leave, or for being unfaithful in their business. It is our duty to be faithful, *not with eye service as men pleasers.* We have no right to stay when we are sent on errands, any longer than to do the business we were sent upon. All the time spent idly, is spent wickedly, and is unfaithfulness to our masters. In these things I must say, that I think many of you are guilty. I know that many of you endeavor to excuse yourselves, and say that you have nothing that you can call your own, and that you are under great temptations to be unfaithful and take from your masters. But this will not do, God will certainly punish you for stealing and for being unfaithful. All that we have to mind is our own duty. If God has put us in bad circumstances, that is not our fault and He will not punish us for it. If any are wicked in keeping us so, we cannot help it, they must answer to God for it. Nothing will serve as an excuse to us for not doing our duty. The same God will judge both them and us. Pray then my dear friends, fear to offend in this way, but be faithful to God, to your masters, and to your own souls.

The next thing I would mention, and warn you against, is profaneness. This you know is forbidden by God. Christ tells us, "swear not at all," and again it is said "thou shalt not take the name of the Lord thy God in vain, for the Lord will not hold him guiltless, that taketh his name in vain." Now though the great God has forbidden it, yet how dreadfully profane are many, and I don't know but I may say the most of you? How common is it to hear you take the terrible and awful name of the great God in vain?—To swear by it, and by Jesus Christ, His Son—How common is it to hear you wish damnation to your companions, and to your own souls—and to sport with in the name of Heaven and Hell, as if there were no such places for you to hope for, or to fear. Oh my friends, be warned to forsake this dreadful sin of profaneness. Pray my dear friends, believe and realize, that there is a God— that He is great and terrible beyond what you can think—that He keeps you in life every moment—and that He can send you to that awful Hell, that you laugh at, in an instant, and confine you there forever, and that He will certainly do it, if you do not repent. You certainly do not believe, that there is a God, or that there is a Heaven or Hell, or you would never trifle with them. It would make you shudder, if you heard others do it, if you believe them as much, as you believe anything you see with your bodily eyes.

I have heard some learned and good men say, that the heathen, and all that worshiped false gods, never spoke lightly or irreverently of their gods, they never took their names in vain, or jested with those things which they held sacred. Now why should the true God, who made all things, be treated worse in this respect, than those false gods, that were made of wood and stone. I believe it is because Satan tempts men to do it. He tried to make them love their false gods, and to speak well of them, but he wishes to have men think lightly of the true God, to take His holy name in vain, and to scoff at, and make a jest of all things that are really good. You may think that Satan has not power to do so much, and have so great influence on the minds of men: but the Scripture says, "he goeth about like a roaring Lion, seeking whom he may devour—that he is the prince of the power of the air—and that he rules in the hearts of the children of disobedience,—and that wicked men are led captive by him, to do his will."[3] All those of you who are profane, are serving the Devil. You are doing what he tempts and desires you to do. If you could see him with your bodily eyes, would you like to make an agreement with him, to serve him, and do as he bid you? I believe most of you would be shocked at this, but you may be certain that all of you who allow yourselves in this sin, are as really serving him, and to just as good purpose, as if you met him, and promised to dishonor God, and serve him with all your might. Do you believe this? It is true whether you believe it or not. Some of you to excuse yourselves, may plead the example of others, and say that you hear a great many white people, who know more than such poor ignorant Negroes as you are, and some who are rich and great gentlemen, swear, and talk profanely, and some of you may say this of your masters, and say no more than is true. But all this is not a sufficient excuse for you. You know that murder is wicked. If you saw your master kill a man, do you suppose this would be any excuse for you, if you should commit the same crime? You must know it would not; nor will your hearing him curse and swear, and take the name of God in vain, or any other man, be he ever so great or rich, excuse you. God is greater than all other beings, and Him we are bound to obey. To Him we must give an account for every idle word that we speak. He will bring us all, rich and poor, white and black, to His judgment seat. If we are found among those who *feared His name*, and *trembled at His work*, we shall be called good and faithful servants. Our slavery will be at an end, and though ever so mean, low, and despised in this world, we shall sit with God in His kingdom as kings and priests, and rejoice forever, and ever. Do not then, my dear friends, take God's holy name in vain, or speak profanely in any way. Let not the example of others lead you into the sin, but reverence and fear that great and fearful name, the Lord our God.

[3] See 1 Peter 5:8.

I might now caution you against other sins to which you are exposed, but as I meant only to mention those you were exposed to, more than others, by your being slaves, I will conclude what I have to say to you, by advising you to become religious, and to make religion the great business of your lives.

Now I acknowledge that liberty is a great thing, and worth seeking for, if we can get it honestly, and by our good conduct, prevail on our masters to set us free. Though for my own part I do not wish to be free, yet I should be glad if others, especially the young Negroes, were to be free, for many of us, who are grown up slaves, and have always had masters to take care of us, should hardly know how to take care of ourselves, and it may be more for our own comfort to remain as we are.[4] That liberty is a great thing we may know from our own feelings, and we may likewise judge so from the conduct of the white people, in the late war. How much money has been spent, and how many lives has been lost, to defend their liberty? I must say that I have hoped that God would open their eyes, when they were so much engaged for liberty, to think of the state of the poor blacks, and to pity us. He has done it in some measure, and has raised us up many friends, for which we have reason to be thankful, and to hope in His mercy. What may be done further, He only knows, for *known unto God are all His ways from the beginning.*[5] But this, my dear brethren, is by no means the greatest thing we have to be concerned about. Getting our liberty in this world, is nothing to our having the liberty of the children of God. Now the Bible tells us that we are all by nature, sinners, that we are slaves to sin and Satan, and that unless we are converted, or born again, we must be miserable forever. Christ says, except a man be born again, he cannot see the kingdom of God, and all that do not see the kingdom of God, must be in the kingdom of darkness. There are but two places where all go after death, white and black, rich and poor; those places are Heaven and Hell. Heaven is a place made for those who are born again, and who love God, and it is a place where they will be happy forever. Hell is a place made for those who hate God, and are His enemies, and where they will be miserable to all eternity. Now you may think you are not enemies to God, and do not hate Him. But if your heart has not been changed, and you have not become true Christians, you certainly are enemies to God, and have been opposed to Him ever since you were born. Many of you, I suppose, never think of this, and are almost as ignorant as the beasts that perish. Those of you who can read I must beg you to read the Bible, and whenever you can get time, study the Bible, and if you can get no other time, spare some of your time from sleep, and learn what the mind and

---

[4] Notice the ambiguity in this sentence and the next, and the peculiar logic. Hammon seems to say that he wants young people to become free *because* many old slaves would not know how to take care of themselves if they were freed. In the next sentence, more-over, he acknowledges his own feeling "that liberty is a great thing." His appeal to the Revolution, though more subtle than that of Banneker, makes the same point.

[5] Acts 15:18.

will of God is. But what shall I say to them who cannot read? This lay with great weight on my mind, when I thought of writing to my poor brethren, but I hope that those who can read will take pity on them and read what I have to say to them. In hopes of this I will beg of you to spare no pains in trying to learn to read. If you are once engaged you may learn. Let all the time you can get be spent in trying to learn to read. Get those who can read to learn you, but remember, that what you learn for, is to read the Bible. If there was no Bible, it would be no matter whether you could read or not. Reading other books would do you no good. But the Bible is the Word of God, and tells you what you must do to please God; it tells you how you may escape misery, and be happy forever. If you see most people neglect the Bible, and many that can read never look into it, let it not harden you and make you think lightly of it, and that it is a book of no worth. All those who are really good, love the Bible, and meditate on it day and night. In the Bible God has told us everything it is necessary we should know in order to be happy here and hereafter. The Bible is a revelation of the mind and will of God to men. Therein we may learn what God is. That He made all things by the power of His Word; and that He made all things for His own glory, and not for our glory. That He is over all, and above all His creatures, and more above them than we can think or conceive—that they can do nothing without Him—that He upholds them all, and will over-rule all things for His own glory. In the Bible likewise we are told what man is. That he was at first made holy, in the image of God, that he fell from that state of holiness, and became an enemy to God, and that since the fall, all the imaginations of the thoughts of his heart, are evil and only evil, and that continually. That the carnal mind is not subject to the law of God, neither indeed can be. And that all mankind, were under the wrath and curse of God, and must have been forever miserable, if they had been left to suffer what their sins deserved. It tells us that God, to save some of mankind, sent His Son into this world to die, in the room and stead of sinners, and that now God can save from eternal misery all that believe in His Son, and take Him for their Saviour, and that all are called upon to repent, and believe in Jesus Christ. It tells us that those who do repent, and believe, and are friends to Christ, shall have many trials and sufferings in this world, but that they shall be happy forever, after death, and reign with Christ to all eternity. The Bible tells us that this world is a place of trial, and that there is no other time or place for us to alter, but in this life. If we are Christians when we die, we shall awake to the resurrection of life; if not, we shall awake to the resurrection of damnation. It tells us, we must all live in Heaven or Hell, be happy or miserable, and that without end. The Bible does not tell us of but two places, for all to go to. There is no place for innocent folks that are not Christians. There is no place for ignorant folks, that did not know how to be Christians. What I mean is, that there is no place besides Heaven and Hell. These two places will receive all mankind, for Christ says, there are but two sorts, *he [that] is not*

with me is against me, and he that gathereth not with me, scattereth abroad.
The Bible likewise tells us that this world, and all things in it shall be burnt
up—and that "God has appointed a day in which He will judge the world,
and that He will bring every secret thing whether it be good or bad into
judgment—that which is done in secret shall be declared on the house top."
I do not know, nor do I think any can tell, but that the day of judgment may
last a thousand years. God could tell the state of all His creatures in a
moment, but then everything that everyone has done, through his whole life
is to be told, before the whole world of angels and men. There, Oh how
solemn is the thought! You and I must stand, and hear everything we have
thought or done, however secret, however wicked and vile, told before all
the men and women that ever have been, or ever will be, and before all the
angels, good and bad.

Now my dear friends seeing the Bible is the Word of God, and everything
in it is true, and it reveals such awful and glorious things, what can be more
important than that you should learn to read it; and when you have learned
to read, that you should study it day and night. There are some things very
encouraging in God's word for such ignorant creatures as we are; for God
hath not chosen the rich of this world.[6] Not many rich, not many noble are
called, but God hath chosen the weak things of this world, and things which
are not, to confound things that are: and when the great and the rich refused
coming to the gospel feast, the servant was told, to go into the highways, and
hedges, and compel those poor creatures that he found there to come in.
Now my brethren it seems to me, that there are no people that ought to
attend to the hope of happiness in another world so much as we do. Most of
us are cut off from comfort and happiness here in this world, and can expect
nothing from it. Now seeing this is the case, why should we not take care to
be happy after death? Why should we spend our whole lives in sinning
against God, and be miserable in this world, and in the world to come? If we
do thus, we shall certainly be the greatest fools. We shall be slaves here, and
slaves forever. We cannot plead so great temptations to neglect religion as
others. Riches and honors which drown the greater part of mankind, who
have the Gospel, in perdition, can be little or no temptations to us.

We live so little time in this world that it is no matter how wretched and
miserable we are, if it prepares us for heaven. What is forty, fifty, or sixty
years, when compared to eternity? When thousands and millions of years
have rolled away, this eternity will be no nigher coming to an end. Oh how
glorious is an eternal life of happiness! And how dreadful, an eternity of
misery. Those of us who have had religious masters, and have been taught to
read the Bible, and have been brought by their example and teaching to a

---

[6] Here, too, the social message may be less
subservient to the masters than the tone of
the whole address would lead one to believe.

sense of divine things, how happy shall we be to meet them in heaven, where we shall join them in praising God forever. But if any of us have had such masters, and yet have lived and died wicked, how will it add to our misery to think of our folly. If any of us who have wicked and profane masters should become religious, how will our estates be changed in another world. Oh my friends, let me intreat of you to think on these things, and to live as if you believed them to be true. If you become Christians you will have reason to bless God forever, that you have been brought into a land where you have heard the Gospel, though you have been slaves. If we should ever get to Heaven, we shall find nobody to reproach us for being black, or for being slaves. Let me beg of you my dear African brethren, to think very little of your bondage in this life, for your thinking of it will do you no good. If God designs to set us free, He will do it, in His own time, and way; but think of your bondage to sin and Satan, and do not rest, until you are delivered from it.

We cannot be happy, if we are ever so free or ever so rich, while we are servants of sin, and slaves to Satan. We must be miserable here, and to all eternity.

I will conclude what I have to say with a few words to those Negroes who have their liberty. The most of what I have said to those who are slaves may be of use to you, but you have more advantages, on some accounts, if you will improve your freedom, as you may do, than they. You have more time to read God's holy Word, and to take care of the salvation of your souls. Let me beg of you to spend your time in this way, or it will be better for you, if you had always been slaves. If you think seriously of the matter, you must conclude, that if you do not use your freedom, to promote the salvation of your souls, it will not be of any lasting good to you. Besides all this, if you are idle, and take to bad courses, you will hurt those of your brethren who are slaves, and do all in your power to prevent their being free. One great reason that is given by some for not freeing us, I understand, is that we should not know how to take care of ourselves, and should take to bad courses. That we should be lazy and idle, and get drunk and steal. Now all those of you, who follow any bad courses, and who do not take care to get an honest living by your labor and industry, are doing more to prevent our being free than anybody else. Let me beg of you then for the sake of your own good and happiness, in time, and for eternity, and for the sake of your poor brethren, who are still in bondage to lead quiet and peaceable lives in all godliness and honesty, and may God bless you, and bring you to His kingdom, for Christ's sake, Amen.

PHILLIS WHEATLEY

(c. 1753–1784)

Brought from Africa to Boston in a slave ship when she was only eight years old, Phillis Wheatley became the household servant to the wife of John Wheatley. Her prodigious mastery of the new language, her mastery of the Bible within less than two years, and her wide reading in classical history and contemporaneous poetry made her famous in Boston. When some of her translations and original poems were published during her teens, she was sought out as a correspondent by some eminent Englishmen, who arranged that she visit London in 1773. She was emancipated after the death of Mrs. Wheatley in 1773, and five years later she married a free black man named John Peters. Of their three children none survived her, and she herself—apparently separated from her husband—died young and extremely poor.

Wheatley's poetry is understandably imitative and conventional, but her achievement at so early an age and under such conditions has an important significance in American literary history. She was not the last black writer whose literary training and potential audience were defined or at least strongly affected by the conventions, the language, and the needs of an alien white society. That problem remains a live issue in the 1970's, as it was nearly a century ago for Paul Laurence Dunbar and Charles Chesnutt. In this volume some of its nineteenth-century meaning can be observed in the selection from the writings of Frederick Douglass.

Recent biographies are Shirley Graham, *The Story of Phillis Wheatley,* 1969; William G. Allen, *Wheatley, Banneker and Horton,* 1970. *The Poems of Phillis Wheatley* have been edited, in the text used here, by Julian D. Mason, 1966. Kenneth Silverman has edited "Four New Letters by Phillis Wheatley," *Early American Literature,* 8 (1974), 257–271.

An Hymn to the Evening.

Soon as the sun forsook the eastern main
The pealing thunder shook the heav'nly plain;
Majestic grandeur! From the zephyr's wing,
Exhales the incense of the blooming spring.
Soft purl the streams, the birds renew their notes,   5
And through the air their mingled music floats.

Frontispiece for an English edition of Phillis Wheatley's poems. *(The Granger Collection.)*

Through all the heav'ns what beauteous dyes are spread!
But the west glories in the deepest red:
So may our breasts with ev'ry virtue glow,
The living temples of our God below!   10

Fill'd with the praise of him who gives the light,
And draws the sable curtains of the night,
Let placid slumbers soothe each weary mind,
At morn to wake more heav'nly, more refin'd;
So shall the labors of the day begin   15
More pure, more guarded from the snares of sin.

Night's leaden sceptre seals my drowsy eyes,
Then cease, my song, till fair *Aurora* rise.

Liberty and Peace, a Poem.[1]

LO! Freedom comes. Th' prescient Muse foretold,
    All Eyes th' accomplish'd Prophecy behold:
Her Port describ'd, "*She moves divinely fair,*
Olive and Laurel bind her golden Hair."
She, the bright Progeny of Heaven, descends,   5
And every Grace her sovereign Step attends;
For now kind Heaven, indulgent to our Prayer,
In smiling *Peace* resolves the Din of *War.*
Fix'd in *Columbia*[2] her illustrious Line,
And bids in thee her future Councils shine.   10
To every Realm her Portals open'd wide,
Receives from each the full commercial Tide.
Each Art and Science now with rising Charms
Th' expanding Heart with Emulation warms.
E'en great *Britannia* sees with dread Surprize,   15
And from the dazzl'ing Splendor turns her Eyes!
Britain, whose Navies swept th' *Atlantic* o'er,
And Thunder sent to every distant Shore:
E'en thou, in Manners cruel as thou art,
The Sword resign'd, resume the friendly Part!   20
For *Galia's*[3] Power espous'd *Columbia's* Cause,
And new-born *Rome* shall give *Britannia* Law,

---

[1] This poem, one of the two published under the poet's married name, was printed as a pamphlet in 1784. The Treaty of Paris ended the Revolutionary War in 1783, two years after the fighting had stopped.

[2] The United States.

[3] France's.

Nor unremember'd in the grateful Strain,
Shall princely *Louis'* friendly Deeds remain;
The generous Prince th' impending Vengeance eye's,   25
Sees the fierce Wrong, and to the rescue flies.
Perish that Thirst of boundless Power, that drew
On *Albion's*[4] Head the Curse to Tyrants due.
But thou appeas'd submit to Heaven's decree,
That bids this Realm of Freedom rival thee!   30
Now sheathe the Sword that bade the Brave atone
With guiltless Blood for Madness not their own.
Sent from th' Enjoyment of their native Shore.
Ill-fated—never to behold her more!
From every Kingdom on *Europa's* Coast   35
Throng'd various Troops, their Glory, Strength and Boast.
With heart-felt pity fair *Hibernia*[5] saw
Columbia menac'd by the Tyrant's Law:
On hostile Fields fraternal Arms engage,
And mutual Deaths, all dealt with mutual Rage;   40
The Muse's Ear hears mother Earth deplore
Her ample Surface smoak with kindred Gore:
The hostile Field destroys the social Ties,
And ever-lasting Slumber seals their Eyes.
Columbia mourns, the haughty Foes deride,   45
Her Treasures plunder'd, and her Towns destroy'd:
Witness how *Charlestown's* curling Smoaks arise,
In sable Columns to the clouded Skies!
The ample Dome, high-wrought with curious Toil,
In one sad Hour the savage Troops despoil.   50
Descending *Peace* and Power of War confounds;
From every Tongue celestial *Peace* resounds:
As for the East th' illustrious King of Day,
With rising Radiance drives the Shades away,
So Freedom comes array'd with Charms divine,   55
And in her Train Commerce and Plenty shine.
Britannia owns her Independent Reign,
Hibernia, Scotia, and the Realms of *Spain;*
And great *Germania's* ample Coast admires
The generous Spirit that *Columbia* fires.   60
Auspicious Heaven shall fill with fav'ring Gales,
Where e'er *Columbia* spreads her swelling Sails:
To every Realm shall *Peace* her Charms display,
And Heavenly *Freedom* spread her golden Ray.

[4] England's.   [5] Ireland.

ABSALOM JONES

(1746–1818)

Absalom Jones was founder and Rector of St. Thomas's, the African Episcopal Church in Philadelphia, and he was the first black rector in America. Besides this petition to the federal government in 1799, he published a sermon in 1808, *A Thanksgiving Sermon* to commemorate the official abolition of the African slave trade. The abolition was required by the Constitution, which allowed 20 more years for the trade when it was adopted in 1788. Jones had previously distinguished himself by organizing black people for service to the afflicted in Philadelphia during the yellow fever plague of 1793. And in 1814, after Washington, D.C. had been burned by British troops, Jones organized black men to build a defensive perimeter there.

Petition of Absalom Jones and Seventy-Three Others[1]

TO THE PRESIDENT, SENATE, AND HOUSE OF REPRESENTATIVES.

The Petition of the People of Color, free men, within the City and Suburbs of Philadelphia, humbly showeth,

That, thankful to God, our Creator, and to the Government under which we live, for the blessings and benefits granted to us in the enjoyment of our natural right to liberty, and the protection of our persons and property from the oppression and violence which so great a number of like color and national descent are subject to, we feel ourselves bound, from a sense of these blessings, to continue in our respective allotments, and to lead honest and peaceable lives, rendering due submission unto the laws, and exciting and encouraging each other thereto, agreeable to the uniform advice of our friends of every denomination; yet while we feel impressed with grateful sensations for the Providential favor we ourselves enjoy, we cannot be insen-

---

[1] The text is from John Parrish, *Remarks on the Slavery of Black People. . .*, Philadelphia, 1806.

sible of the condition of our afflicted brethren, suffering under various circumstances, in different parts of these states; but deeply sympathizing with them, are incited by a sense of social duty, and humbly conceive ourselves authorized to address and petition you on their behalf, believing them to be objects of your representation in your public councils, in common with ourselves and every other class of citizens within the jurisdiction of the United States, according to the design of the present Constitution, formed by the General Convention, and ratified in the different states, as set forth in the preamble thereto in the following words, viz. "We, the people of the United States, in order to form a more perfect union, establish justice, insure domestic tranquillity, provide for the common defense, and to secure the blessings of liberty to ourselves and posterity, do ordain, etc." We apprehend this solemn compact is violated, by a trade carried on in a clandestine manner, to the coast of Guinea, and another equally wicked, practiced openly by citizens of some of the southern states, upon the waters of Maryland and Delaware; men sufficiently callous to qualify them for the brutal purpose, are employed in kidnapping those of our brethren that are free, and purchasing others of such as claim a property in them; thus, those poor helpless victims, like droves of cattle, are seized, fettered, and hurried into places provided for this most horrid traffic, such as dark cellars and garrets, as is notorious at Northwestfork, Chestertown, Eastown, and divers other places. After a sufficient number is obtained, they are forced on board vessels, crowded under hatches, without the least commiseration, left to deplore the sad separation of the dearest ties in nature, husband from wife, and parents from children; thus packed together, they are transported to Georgia and other places and there inhumanly exposed to sale. Can any commerce, trade, or transaction so detestable shock the feeling of man, or degrade the dignity of his nature equal to this? And how increasingly is the evil aggravated, when practiced in a land high in profession of the benign doctrines of our Blessed Lord, who taught His followers to do unto others as they would they should do unto them. Your petitioners desire not to enlarge, though volumes might be filled with the sufferings of this grossly abused part of the human species, seven hundred thousand of whom, it is said, are now in unconditional bondage in these states: but conscious of the rectitude of our motives in a concern so nearly affecting us, and so effectually interesting to the welfare of this country, we cannot but address you as guardians of our rights, and patrons of equal and national liberties, hoping you will view the subject in an impartial, unprejudiced light. We do not ask for an immediate emancipation of all, knowing that the degraded state of many, and their want of education, would greatly disqualify for such a change; yet, humbly desire you may exert every means in your power to undo the heavy burdens, and prepare the way for the oppressed to go free, that every yoke may be broken. The law not long since enacted by Congress, called the Fugitive Bill, is in its execution found to be attended with circumstances peculiarly hard and distressing; for many of our afflicted brethren, in order to avoid the barbarities wantonly exercised upon them, or through fear of being carried off by those men-stealers, being forced to seek refuge by flight, they are then, by armed men, under color of this law, cruelly treated, or brought back in chains to those that have no claim upon them. In the Constitution and the Fugitive Bill, no mention is made of black people, or slaves: therefore, if the Bill of Rights, or the Declaration of Congress are of any validity, we beseech, that as we are men, we may be admitted to partake of the liberties and unalienable rights therein held forth; firmly believing that the extending of justice and equity to all classes would be a means of drawing down the blessing of Heaven upon this land, for the peace and prosperity of which, and the real happiness of every member of the community, we fervently pray. Philadelphia, 30th of December, 1799.

Absalom Jones and others. 73 subscribers.

WILLIAM HAMILTON

(Dates of birth and death unknown)

William Hamilton gave one of many addresses to commemorate the abolition of slavery in New York. What makes this oration memorable now is not only the appeal to the Declaration of Independence but the militant content and tone. Years earlier, Hamilton had stressed the value of knowing the geographical location and something of the history and cultural grandeur of Africa. Here he praises the universal principles of the Declaration even while he deplores Thomas Jefferson's inconsistency and the widespread racial prejudice of white Americans.

The text is from *Early Negro Writing, 1760–1837,* ed. Dorothy Porter, 1972.

An Oration
delivered in the African zion church,
on the Fourth of July, 1827,
In Commemoration of the Abolition of
Domestic Slavery
in this state.

Liberty! kind goddess! brightest of the heavenly deities that guide the affairs of men.

Oh Liberty! where thou art resisted and irritated, thou art terrible as the raging sea, and dreadful as a tornado. But where thou art listened to, and obeyed, thou art gentle as the purling stream that meanders through the mead; as soft and as cheerful as the zephyrs that dance upon the summer's breeze, and as bounteous as autumn's harvest.

To thee, the sons of Afric, in this once dark, gloomy, hopeless, but now fairest, brightest, and most cheerful of thy domain, do owe a double oblation of gratitude. Thou hast entwined and bound fast the cruel hand of oppression—thou hast by the powerful charm of reason, deprived the monster of his strength—he dies, he sinks to rise no more.

Thou hast loosened the hard bound fetters by which we were held; and by a voice sweet as the music of heaven, yet strong and powerful, reaching to the extreme boundaries of the state of New York, hath declared that we the people of color, the sons of Afric, are free!

My brethren and fellow citizens, I hail you all. This day we stand redeemed from a bitter thralldom. Of us it may be truly said, "the last agony is o'er," the Africans are restored! No more shall the accursed name of slave be attached to us—no more shall *Negro* and *slave* be synonymous.

Fellow citizens, I come to felicitate you on the victory obtained—not by a sanguinary conflict with the foe—there are left no fields teeming with blood; not a victory obtained by fierce-flaming, death-dealing ordnance, vomiting forth fire and horrible destruction—no thousands made to lick the dust—no groans of the wounded and the dying. But I come to felicitate you on the victory obtained by the principles of liberty, such as are broadly and indelibly laid down by the glorious sons of '76; and are contained in the ever memorable words prefixed to the Declaration of Independence of these United States: viz. "We hold these truths to be self-evident, that all men are created equal, and endowed by their Creator with certain unalienable rights; and that among these are life, liberty, and the pursuit of happiness." A victory obtained by these principles over prejudice, injustice, and foul oppression.

This day has the state of New York regenerated herself—this day has she been cleansed of a most foul, poisonous, and damnable stain. I stand amazed at the quiet, yet rapid progress the principles of liberty have made. A semi-century ago, the people of color, with scarcely an exception, were all slaves. It is true, that many in the city, who remained here in the time of the revolution (when their masters left at the approach of the British), and many too from the country, who became a kind of refugee, obtained their liberty by leaving the country at the close of the war, or a few years' respite from slavery: for such as were found remaining after the Revolution, were again claimed by their masters. Yes, we were in the most abject state of slavery that can be conceived, except that of our brethren at the South, whose miseries are a little more enhanced. Without going back to the times of Negro plot, when a kind of fanaticism seized the people of New York,[1] something similar in its bearing and effect to the sad circumstance that took place among the people of New England, in their more puritanic times, and about a half century before the fancied plot, when they put to death the good people for being witches.

Yes, my brethren, in this state we have been advertised, and bought, and sold like any commodity. In this state we have suffered cruelly; suffered by imprisonment, by whipping, and by scourging.

I have seen men chained with iron collars to their necks. I have seen—but hold! Let me proceed no farther. Why enter into the blood-chilling detail of our miseries? It would only dampen those joys that ought to glow and sparkle on every countenance: it would only give vent to feelings that would not be reconcilable with the object of our assembling.

The cause of emancipation has ever had its votaries, but they stood single and alone. After the Revolution, they drew nearer together.

That venerable body of religionists, called Friends, ought ever to be held in grateful remembrance by us. Their public speakers were the first to enter their protest against the deadly sin of slaveholding; and so zealous did its members become, that the church, or more technically, the meeting, passed laws; first forbidding its members from holding slaves for life, next forbidding the use of slaves altogether. But the most powerful lever, or propelling cause, was the Manumission Society. Although many of its members belonged to the just-named society, yet very many were members of other religious societies, and some did not belong to any, but who were philanthropists indeed. How sweet it is to speak of good men! Nature hath not made us calumniators—calumny yields us no pleasure: if it does, it is satanic pleasure: but to speak of good men yields a pleasure such as the young feel, when talking of their lovers, or the parent feels, when telling of the prattle of their infants.

---

[1] In 1741, in response to an alleged conspiracy of slaves to rebel, many black people were executed, some burned at the stake, during a period of several "fanatical" weeks of official vengeance in New York City. The comparison to New England, where convicted witches were not burned but hanged, is just.

In speaking of the Manumission Society, we are naturally drawn to its first founders. These must have been good men: the prejudice of the times forbade any other but men of good and virtuous minds from having any lot or part in the matter. Any other must have shrunk from the undertaking. I am, therefore, about to name men who ought to be deeply inscribed on your memories, and in your hearts: the names of Washington and Jefferson should not be pronounced in the hearing of your children, until they could clearly and distinctly pronounce the names I am about to give. First, that great and good statesman, the right honorable John Jay, the first President of the Manumission Society. Blessed God! how good it is he has lived to see, as a reward, the finishing of a work he helped to begin.

Next, the good John Murray, peace attends his memory, he was a man that calumny never did approach, but what she bit her tongue: he was the first Treasurer: next, the not only harmless, but good Samuel Franklin, the first-Vice-President; next the zealous, the virtuous, the industrious John Keese, the first Secretary; next, general Alexander Hamilton, that excellent soldier, and most able civilian and financier, and first of his profession at the bar. Next, that man of more than sterling worth, Robert Bowne.

The other names which I shall give, are of equal worth with those already mentioned, and are as follows:

Alexander M'Dougal, Colonel Robert Troup, John Lawrence, Peter Yates, Melancton Smith, William Goforth, Ebenezer S. Burling, Laurence Embree, Zebulon Bartow, Elijah Cock, William Shotwell, Joseph Laurence, James Cogswell, Matthew Vicker, William Backhouse, William Cartman, Thomas Burling, Thomas Bowne, Leonard M. Cutting.

These are the men that formed the Manumission Society, and stamped it with those best of principles, found in the preamble to the constitution, framed by them. It is too excellent to pass over, and is as follows: "The benevolent Creator, and Father of all men; having given to them all an equal right to life, liberty and property, no sovereign power on earth can justly deprive them of either but in conformity to impartial laws, to which they have expressly or tacitly consented; it is our duty both as free citizens and Christians, not only to regard with compassion the injustice done to those among us, who are held as slaves, but to endeavor by all lawful ways and means, to enable them to share equally with us, that civil and religious liberty, with which an indulgent Providence has blessed these states; and to which these our brethren are as much entitled as ourselves."

It was on the 25th January, 1785, these gentlemen held their first meeting, and on the fourth of the following month, they adopted a constitution, headed by the just mentioned most liberal and excellent preamble.

To enter into a detail of the services rendered us by this society would be out of my power. Even those that have come within my knowledge would occupy more time (though pleasing to relate) by far than we have on hand. Suffice it to say that through the efforts of this society, our situation has been much meliorated, and very many of our brethren have been liberated from slavery. The Society, between the time of its formation and 1813, obtained many salutary laws relative to our emancipation and well usage. But by a revision of the laws of the state about this time, some had been changed in their intent, while others had become nugatory.

Being alarmed, the Society made strong efforts to regain the lost ground. The years between 1813 and 1817 were spent by the Society in vigorous efforts, by which, however, they gained little more than an accession of strength. But prior to the session that brought forth the law that gave rise to this rejoicing, three gentlemen, whom I shall name with pride and much glorying, viz. Mr. Joseph Curtis, Mr. John Murray, and Mr. Thomas Addis Emmet, waited on the then governor Mr. Daniel D. Tompkins. He was a man, who, if he had faults, his virtues overwhelmed them, angels vied with each other the privilege of conveying him to a better state. From the governor, who always was our friend, these gentlemen obtained a ready promise that he would introduce the subject of emancipation in his message to the legislature, and recommend to them the fixing on a time for its accomplishment, which promise he faithfully performed.

I have named some of the men to whom our gratitude is due. Did I name them as they rise on the altar of my heart, I should name many equally worthy, and equally noted; and some, although not of so public a character, who have yet rendered equal services. The Manumission Society have labored hard and incessantly in order to bring us from our degraded situation, and restore us to the rights of men. It has stood, a phalanx, firm and undaunted, amid the flames of prejudice, and the shafts of calumny. How pleasing it is, they have a reward. Our Heavenly Father hath fixed the highest sensations of pleasure to good and virtuous actions.

My Brethren, our enemies have assumed various attitudes: sometimes they have worn a daring front, and blasphemously have said, the Negroes have no souls, they are not men, they are a species of the ourang outang. Sometimes, in more mild form, they say, they are a species inferior to white men. Then again they turn to blasphemy, and say, God hath made them to be slaves.

Let us look at them, and we shall see, with all their pomp, and pride, and hauteur, they are more the objects of pity and commiseration, than of anger and hate. Well may it be said, "the wicked are like the troubled sea." It is hard breathing in their atmosphere. Are not deeds of injustice the harrowers up of fears of revenge, in proportion to their turpitude? We have a fair portrait in the Southern states. In order to see it more clearly, contrast the Southern and Northern sections of the union. Would the people of the North exchange situations for the slaves of the South, ten times told? Reverse the question, and what must be the answer? Do the people of the North need nightly patrols to save them from insurrections? How sweet is the sleep of the virtuous! The hoverings around their nocturnal rest are soothing angels—

the wicked dream of being pursued by furies. In the South, a poor, single, solitary man of color, cannot enter their country, but through their dread of soul, they seize him and imprison him. They are like him that has murdered his neighbor, who starts at everyone that looks him in the face.

It would be foolishness in me, my brethren, to tell you that by all the rules laid down by naturalists for determining the species of a creature, that we have souls, and are men. We too irresistibly feel that we have, and are such. We can more easily doubt that we exist, than doubt that we are men. To the second proposition, and my soul for it, if there is any difference in the species, that difference is in favor of the people of color.

Man is a moral being, and ought to be governed by his reason. The lessons of reason are the lessons of morality. If we measure souls at all, we ought to measure them by the scale of morality. What does he gain that can enter into the most abstruse reasoning about matter and its properties; that is acquainted with the anatomy of every creature; or can tell you of all the heavenly bodies, of plants, and their satellites, of their diameters, and their distances, their diurnal rotations, their revolutions around their primaries, and degrees of their inclination to their orbits, and times of their revolution around the sun, if when he is done, he sits down to the intoxicating draught, until he is deprived of his reason, and becomes like a stupid beast? How much does such an abstruse reasoner gain, by the proper rule over him, who only reasons himself into sober and virtuous habits?

I know that I ought to speak with caution; but an ambidexter philosopher,[2] who can reason contrarywise, first tells you "that all men are created equal, and that they are endowed with the unalienable rights of life, liberty, and the pursuit of happiness," next proves that one class of men are not equal to another, which by the bye, does not agree with axioms in geometry, that deny that things can be equal, and at the same time unequal to one another—suppose that such philosopher should keep around him a number of slaves, and at the same time should tell you, that God hath no attribute to favor the cause of the master in case of an insurrection of the slaves. Would not such a reasoner only show a heterogeneous mind? Although he should be called an abstruse reasoner, what kind of superiority does he discover? Does he not reason, and act, like one that battles with the elements? Does he reason like a man of true moral principles? Does he set a good example? Does he act in conformity to true philosophy? True philosophy teaches, that man should act in conformity to his reason, and reason, and the law of God and nature, declare that all men are equal, and that life, liberty, and the pursuit of happiness are their unalienable rights.

It is a maxim among civilians that the principles of government and acts of the legislator should be in unison. What ought to be considered the most

[2] The allusion is to Thomas Jefferson. See above, pp. 687–689, 601.

vital principles of our general government, are contained in the words already mentioned, as standing in front of the Declaration of Independence; and in that article of the Constitution, that declares that no person shall be deprived of life, liberty, or property, without due course of law. What a jargon does that law of the United States form with the principles here laid down, that gives to one class of men the right to arrest, wherever they may find them within its jurisdiction, another class of men, and retain them as their lawful property? This, no doubt, is superior legislation, and bespeaks superior minds.

In these United States, among white men, there is an almost universal prejudice against the amalgamation of the blood of the white and black population, which goes so far as to create in them the supercilious fear, or rather the horrible sensation, that the pretty white will be changed thereby to the dingy mulatto. Yes, true it is, and true though it is white men masters do amalgamate the blood, and the children of such amalgamation they hold as slaves: and worse, they sell as slaves. It is said by a Frenchman of high note, that the American will sell his dog for money; I do not know that the Frenchman will not do the same. But this I do know, that white men sell the children of their own begetting, for sordid gold.

Authority and gold are their gods, their household gods, their sanctuary gods, and the highest gods of their sanctum sanctorum. What titillation of soul they receive from these gods! How bold! how venturous! how stubborn! how pliant! how wise! how simple! how everything but virtuous they are!

I am sorry to break from this unravelling so soon, for I did mean to unravel this mystery of superiority. But it is necessary that we devote a few moments to a subject of vital interest to us. And here let me particularly address the youth. With you rests the high responsibility of redeeming the character of our people. White men say you are not capable of the study of what may be called abstruse literature, and that you are deficient in moral character. I feel, I know, that these assertions are as false as hell. Yet I do know, you are sunk into the deepest frivolity and lethargy that any people can be sunk. Oh Heavens! that I could rouse you. Has this frivolity taken from you all shame? Has this lethargy taken from you all ambition? Youth of my people, I look to you. Shall this degrading charge stand unrepelled by contrary facts? Oh! That I could enflame you with proper ambition. Your honor, your character, your happiness, your well-being, all, all are at stake, and involved in the question at issue. And it is for you to retrieve or acknowledge that your fathers have been slaves deservedly.

First, my young friends, let me invite you to the path of virtue. It is a straight, open path, strewed with the sweetest aromatics: it is the path of pleasure, the path of honor, the path of respectability. Vice, from which I would call you, is its opposite; it is a crooked, thorny way, full of stinking weeds, the path of trouble, debasement, misery, and destruction.

Next, I would invite you to the study of the sciences. Here lies an open field of pleasure, that is increased at every step you take therein. If you have labor, be assured that your compensation is infinite. It has been the policy of white men to give you a high opinion of your advancement, when you have made but smattering attainments. They know that a little education is necessary for the better accomplishing the menial services you are in the habit of performing for them. They do not wish you to be equal with them—much less superior. Therefore, in all advancements they assist in (I speak of them generally) they will take care that you do not rise above mediocrity.

My young friends, it is a laudable ambition that prompts us to the highest standing in literature. Is there anything noble or praiseworthy obtained by sneaking conduct? Why look up to others, when we may obtain the highest standing ourselves? There is a height of knowledge which you may easily attain to, that when arrived at, you will look down with amazement, at the depth of ignorance you have risen from. I am sorry to say it; but I speak with the intention to quicken you, that, properly speaking, there is none learned among us. If there is, now is the time to show themselves; it is worse than felony to keep back. It is too true, that men of prime genius among us, that have possessed high talents for improvement, have suffered improper considerations to keep them down. Therefore, my young friends, I look to you, and pray you, by all that proper pride you feel in being men, that you show yourselves such, by performing acts of worth equal with other men. Why not form yourselves into literary companies for the study of the sciences? The expense would not be as great as you incur for useless gratifications, beside the advantage of receiving pleasure, infinitely beyond what those gratifications afford.

I would now turn to the female part of this assembly, particularly the young. It is for you to form the manners of the men. My female friends, it is for you, not by proud, but modest conduct, to lead them in the true line of decorum and gentle manners. First, I would have you discountenance that loud vocability of gabble, that too much characterizes us in the street: I would look upon him, or her, that hailed me with too loud, or vulgar accents, as one who had forgot what is due to female modesty. Next, and most of consequence, I would have you prefer his affections and company most, who endeavors most to improve his mind. If you give preference to men of understanding, depend on it, they will endeavor to make themselves suitable to your wishes. But above all, endeavor to improve your own minds. I know that in the ability to improve, you are more than a match for white females, in all proper female education. Here, let me close, with our best thanks and wishes to the State of New York.

POEMS AND SPEECHES BY AMERICAN INDIANS

The following poems and speeches represent the translated, written record of an oral literature that expresses two paradoxical qualities in Indian experience: an almost timeless relationship of anonymous poets to cyclical nature, and the indignant reaction of specific leaders to specific threats on particular occasions by the invading Anglo-American society.

This Newly Created World[1]

WINNEBAGO

Pleasant it looked,
this newly created world.
Along the entire length and breadth
of the earth, our grandmother,
extended the green reflection 5
of her covering
and the escaping odors
were pleasant to inhale.

[1] The text is an original translation in Paul Radin, *The Road of Life and Death,* New York, 1945, p. 254. These lines were not a separate poem in the Winnebago "Ritual of Awards," part four of "The Medicine Rite." They were published separately for the first time in a selection from Radin's translation.

War Song[1]

SIOUX

clear the way
in a sacred manner
I come
the earth
is mine 5

[1] Translated from the Sioux by Frances Densmore, in "Teton Sioux Music," *Bureau of American Ethnology, Bulletin no. 61,* 1918, p. 351.

Song[1]

OJIBWA

Whence does he dawn, the buck?
Whence does he dawn,
the buck, the buck, the buck?

[1] Translated from the Chippewa by Frances Densmore, in "Chippewa Music II," *Bureau* *of American Ethnology, Bulletin No. 53,* 1913, p. 201.

Magic Formula to Make an Enemy Peaceful[1]

NAVAHO

Put your feet down with pollen.
Put your hands down with pollen.
Put your head down with pollen.
Then your feet are pollen;
Your hands are pollen;   5
Your body is pollen;
Your mind is pollen;
Your voice is pollen.
The trail is beautiful.
Be still.   10

[1] Translated from the Navaho by Washington Matthews, in *Navajo Legends,* Boston, 1897, p. 109.

Spring Song[1]

OJIBWA

as my eyes
search the prairie
I feel the summer in the spring

[1] The text is Frances Densmore, "Chippewa Music III," p. 254.

Offering[1]

ZUNI

That our earth mother may wrap herself
In a fourfold robe of white meal;
That she may be covered with frost flowers;
That yonder on all the mossy mountains
The forests may huddle together with the cold;　　　5
That their arms may be broken by the snow,
In order that the land may be thus,
I have made my prayer sticks into living beings.

[1] Translated from the Zuñi by Ruth Bvnzel, in "Introduction to Zuñi Ceremonialism," *Bureau of American Ethnology, 47th Annual Report, 1929-30,* pp. 483-484.

Is This Real?[1]

PAWNEE

Let us see, is this real,
Let us see, is this real,
This life I am living?
You, Gods, who dwell everywhere,
Let us see, is this real,　　　5
This life I am living?

[1] Translated from the Pawnee by D. G. Brinton, in *Essays of an Americanist,* Philadelphia, 1890, p. 292.

A Speech by Powhatan[1]

[Powhatan was the head of the Algonquin Confederacy when Captain John Smith reported this speech, made in 1609.]

[1] The text is from C. Bradbury, *Lives of Celebrated American Indians,* Boston, 1843, pp. 179-180.

Why will you take by force what you may obtain by love? Why will you destroy us who supply you with food? What can you get by war? . . . We are unarmed, and willing to give you what you ask, if you come in a friendly manner. . . .

I am not so simple as not to know it is better to eat good meat, sleep comfortably, live quietly with my women and children, laugh and be merry with the English, and being their friend, trade for their copper and hatchets, than to run away from them. . . .

Take away your guns and swords, the cause of all our jealousy, or you may die in the same manner.

A Speech by Canassatego[1]

[Canassatego, an Iroquois, rebuked the Anglo-American negotiators in 1742.]

Canassatego: We received from the Proprietors yesterday, some goods in consideration of our release of the lands on the west side of Susquehanna. It is true, we have the full quantity according to agreement; but if the Proprietor had been here himself, we think, in regard of our numbers and poverty, he would have made an addition to them. If the goods were only to be divided amongst the Indians present, a single person would have but a small portion; but if you consider what numbers are left behind, equally entitled with us to a share, there will be extremely little. We therefore desire, if you have the keys of the Proprietor's chest, you will open it, and take out a little more for us.

We know our lands are now become more valuable: the white people think we do not know their value; but we are sensible that the land is everlasting, and the few goods we receive for it are soon worn out and gone. For the future we will sell no lands but when Brother Onas[2] is in the country; and we will know beforehand the quantity of the goods we are to receive. Besides, we are not well used with respect to the lands still unsold by us. Your people daily settle on these lands, and spoil our hunting.—We must insist on your removing them, as you know they have no right to settle to the northward of *Kittochtinny-Hills.*—In particular, we renew our com-

---

[1] The text is Benjamin Franklin's printing of this speech in *The Treaty held with the Indians of the Six Nations, at Philadelphia, in 1742* (Philadelphia, 1742).

[2] The proprietor of Pennsylvania.

plaints against some people who are settled at *Juniata,* a branch of *Susque-hanna,* and all along the banks of that river, as far as *Mahaniay;* and desire they may be forthwith made to go off the land; for they do great damage to our cousins the *Delawares.*

We have further to observe, with respect to the lands lying on the west side of *Susquehanna,* that though Brother *Onas* (meaning the Proprietor) has paid us for what his people possess, yet some parts of that country have been taken up by persons whose place of residence is to the south of this province, from whom we have never received any consideration. This affair was rec-ommended to you by our chiefs at our last treaty; and you then, at our earnest desire, promised to write a letter to that person who has the author-ity over those people, and to procure us his answer: as we have never heard from you on this head, we want to know what you have done in it. If you have not done anything, we now renew our request, and desire you will inform the person whose people are seated on our lands, that that country belongs to us, in right of conquest; we having bought it with our blood, and taken it from our enemies in fair war; and we expect, as owners of that land, to receive such a consideration for it as the land is worth. We desire you will press him to send us a positive answer: let him say *Yes* or *No:* if he says Yes, we will treat with him; if No, we are able to do ourselves justice; and we will do it, by going to take payment ourselves.

It is customary with us to make a present of skins whenever we renew our treaties. We are ashamed to offer our brethren so few; but your horses and cows have eat the grass our deer used to feed on. This has made them scarce, and will, we hope, plead in excuse for our not bringing a larger quantity: if we could have spared more we would have given more; but we are really poor; and desire you'll not consider the quantity, but, few as they are, accept them in testimony of our regard.

A Speech by Pachgantschilias[1]

[*A Moravian missionary named John G. Heckewelder heard Pachgantschilias deliver this speech in 1787. Compare H. H. Brackenridge, Modern Chivalry, above pp. 685–687.*]

I admit that there are good white men, but they bear no proportion to the bad; the bad must be the strongest, for they rule. They do what they please. They enslave those who are not of their color, although created by the same

---

[1] The text is from Helen Hunt Jackson, *A Century of Dishonor,* Boston, 1889, pp. 32, 33.

Great Spirit who created them. They would make slaves of us if they could; but as they cannot do it, they kill us. There is no faith to be placed in their words. They are not like the Indians, who are only enemies while at war, and are friends in peace. They will say to an Indian, "My friend; my brother!" They will take him by the hand, and, at the same moment, destroy him. And so you [Christian Indians] will also be treated by them before long. Remember that this day I have warned you to beware of such friends as these. I know the Long-knives. They are not to be trusted.

A Speech by Tecumseh[1]

[Tecumseh was the elected leader of a large number of Western nations. In 1810 he protested the sale of Indiana lands five years before. Here he addresses Governor William Henry Harrison, whom he confronted reluctantly a year later, when Harrison more or less deliberately provoked the conflict that became known as the battle of Tippecanoe. Henry Adams's version in History of the United States during the Administration of James Madison *is an excellent account.]*

Houses are built for you to hold councils in; Indians hold theirs in the open air. I am a Shawnee. My forefathers were warriors. Their son is a warrior. From them I take my only existence. From my tribe I take nothing. I have made myself what I am. And I would that I could make the red people as great as the conceptions of my own mind, when I think of the Great Spirit that rules over us all. . . . I would not then come to Governor Harrison to ask him to tear up the treaty. But I would say to him, "Brother, you have the liberty to return to your own country."

You wish to prevent the Indians from doing as we wish them, to unite and let them consider their lands as the common property of the whole. You take the tribes aside and advise them not to come into this measure. . . . You want by your distinctions of Indian tribes, in allotting to each a particular, to make them war with each other. You never see an Indian endeavor to make the white people do this. You are continually driving the red people, when at last you will drive them onto the great lake, where they can neither stand nor work.

Since my residence at Tippecanoe, we have endeavored to level all distinctions, to destroy village chiefs, by whom all mischiefs are done. It is they who sell the land to the Americans. Brother, this land that was sold, and the goods that was given for it, was only done by a few. . . . In the future we are

[1] The text is from Samuel G. Drake, *Book of the Indians of North America*, Boston, 1833, Book V, 121–122.

prepared to punish those who propose to sell land to the Americans. If you continue to purchase them, it will make war among the different tribes, and, at last I do not know what will be the consequences among the white people. Brother, I wish you would take pity on the red people and do as I have requested. If you will not give up the land and do cross the boundary of our present settlement, it will be very hard, and produce great trouble between us.

The way, the only way to stop this evil is for the red men to unite in claiming a common and equal right in the land, as it was at first, and should be now—for it was never divided, but belongs to all. No tribe has the right to sell, even to each other, much less to strangers. . . . *Sell a country! Why not sell the air, the great sea, as well as the earth?* Did not the Great Spirit make them all for the use of his children?

How can we have confidence in the white people?

When Jesus Christ came upon the earth you killed Him and nailed Him to the cross. You thought He was dead, and you were mistaken. You have Shakers among you and you laugh and make light of their worship.

Everything I have told you is the truth. The Great Spirit has inspired me.

[The following speech was made to other Indian groups in 1811].

Where today are the Pequot? Where are the Narragansett, the Mohican, the Pocanet, and other powerful tribes of our people? They have vanished before the avarice and oppression of the white man, as snow before the summer sun. . . . Will we let ourselves be destroyed in our turn, without making an effort worthy of our race? Shall we, without a struggle, give up our homes, our lands, bequeathed to us by the Great Spirit? The graves of our dead and everything that is dear and sacred to us? . . . I know you will say with me, Never! Never! . . .

Sleep not longer, O Choctaws and Chickasaws, in false security and delusive hopes. . . . Will not the bones of our dead be plowed up, and their graves turned into plowed fields?

V
Beginnings of
American Romanticism

Scholars from Perry Miller and Yvor Winters to Sacvan Bercovitch have
perceived the North American origins of romanticism in New England
Puritan thought—especially in the Puritans' emphasis on intensive
self-examination, the individual will, the amoral if not hostile wildness
of American nature, and the heart or affections as the center of religious experience. Among the forerunners of American romanticism,
one can also cite Jefferson, Bartram, and Freneau, all of whom stress
the beauty of Nature and the importance of personal response to that
beauty. In Charles Brockden Brown and Washington Irving, then, we
do not isolate an exclusive source of American romanticism; we underline the complexity of literary and intellectual history. Irving's *History of New York by Diedrich Knickerbocker* contains, in its nostalgia
for the past and its emotional preference of placid New Amsterdam to
the energetic yankee-ism that conquered it, attitudes that are clearly
appropriate to the definition of romanticism in our next chapter. But
Knickerbocker's History also fits into the sort of mock-heroic tradition
that we have represented in Barlow's *The Hasty Pudding* and Brackenridge's *Modern Chivalry*. It is "The Author's Account of Himself" and
"Reflections of the Moslem Domination of Spain" that mark Irving
decisively as romantic. In Charles Brockden Brown, moreover, the conventions of Gothic mystery and horror become romantic as the author
explores what Henry James later admired in Nathaniel Hawthorne:
"the deeper psychology," the mysterious depths of the psyche.

CHARLES BROCKDEN BROWN

(1771–1810)

In his very brief life Charles Brockden Brown made a permanent mark in American letters. His work cannot be adequately represented in an anthology, but these prefaces to three of his five novels give some indication of his intentions, of his methods, and of the kind of audience he presumed to be listening to him.

Brown had been favorably impressed by the work of William Godwin toward social reform in England, and he wrote both *Alcuin: A Dialogue* (1798) and his first two Gothic novels under that influence. *Alcuin* concerned women's rights, but the novels were powerful, if often technically clumsy explorations of the human psyche under stress. The disputed "miraculous" phenomena that Brown defends as actual in his preface to *Wieland* include spontaneous combustion, ventriloquism (or biloquism, as Brown called it), and a religious man's murder of his entire family under what he takes to be a divine command (related to some of the ventriloquist's ambiguous projections of his voice). Under these extreme circumstances Brown represents the psychological conduct of three personality types: a young woman, who narrates most of the story in letters, and who though painfully susceptible to emotional and intuitive influences strives to govern her conduct by reasoning according to experimental evidence (that is, the evidence of her own experience, her own senses); her fiancé, who obliges her to strive for such control but whose rationalizations from circumstantial evidence allow his own unacknowledged feelings to do grave injustice to her; and the young woman's brother, the religious fanatic who is deluded into murder and suicide. All three, as Warner Berthoff has brilliantly shown, misread the evidence, and the epistemological conundrums that will preoccupy Hawthorne and Melville in some of their best works are thus posed for the first time in American

The standard edition is *Charles Brockden Brown's Novels,* 6 vols., 1887 (reprinted 1963, 1968).

An early biography is William Dunlap, *The Life of Charles Brockden Brown,* 2 vols., 1815. Recent biographies include Harry R. Warfel, *Charles Brockden Brown: American Gothic Novelist,* 1949; David Lee Clark, *Charles Brockden Brown: Pioneer Voice of America,* 1952; Donald A. Ringe, *Charles Brockden Brown,* 1966. See also Warner B. Berthoff, "Adventures of the Young Man: An Approach to Charles Brockden Brown," *American Quarterly,* 9 (1957): 421–434; and the entire fall 1974 issue of *Early American Literature,* which is devoted to Brown. See especially therein the articles by William L. Hedges and Michael Davitt Bell.

fiction. (Compare the genuine perplexity of Thomas Shepard, Samuel Sewall, Nathan Cole.)

Arthur Mervyn explores some of the same issues in a setting that emphasizes the real horror and intense pressure of life among the survivors (of whom C. B. Brown was one) during the year of the yellow fever plague in Philadelphia (1793). *Edgar Huntly* was the first American novel to try to capitalize on native scenery and the action of American Indians.

Brown could not survive as a novelist. After publishing six novels in three years, he edited two different magazines, each in turn dedicated to practical information and the encouragement of American literature. The *Literary Magazine and American Register*, the first of these, survived for five years, and the second, *The American Register*, continued until Brown's death in 1810. In these years he wrote extensively about American history and contemporary politics, and he spoke with some regret about his hastily written Gothic romances. But despite their flaws the best of those works did survive to be useful to Hawthorne and Poe long after Brown had died of consumption. And despite their faults they still carry remarkable power today.

[Preface to *Wieland,* or *The Transformation*]

ADVERTISEMENT.[1]

The following work is delivered to the world as the first of a series of performances, which the favorable reception of this will induce the writer to publish. His purpose is neither selfish nor temporary, but aims at the illustration of some important branches of the moral constitution of man. Whether this tale will be classed with the ordinary or frivolous sources of amusement, or be ranked with the few productions whose usefulness secures to them a lasting reputation, the reader must be permitted to decide.

The incidents related are extraordinary and rare. Some of them, perhaps, approach as nearly to the nature of miracles as can be done by that which is not truly miraculous. It is hoped that intelligent readers will not disapprove of the manner in which appearances are solved, but that the solution will be found to correspond with the known principles of human nature. The power which the principal person is said to possess can scarcely be denied to be

[1] From the first edition.

real. It must be acknowledged to be extremely rare; but no fact, equally uncommon, is supported by the same strength of historical evidence.

Some readers may think the conduct of the younger Wieland impossible. In support of its possibility the writer must appeal to physicians and to men conversant with the latent springs and occasional perversions of the human mind. It will not be objected that the instances of similar delusion are rare, because it is the business of moral painters to exhibit their subject in its most instructive and memorable forms. If history furnishes one parallel fact, it is a sufficient vindication of the writer; but most readers will probably recollect an authentic case, remarkably similar to that of Wieland.

It will be necessary to add, that this narrative is addressed, in an epistolary form, by the lady whose story it contains, to a small number of friends, whose curiosity, with regard to it, had been greatly awakened. It may likewise be mentioned, that these events took place between the conclusion of the French and the beginning of the revolutionary war.[2] The memoirs of Carwin, alluded to at the conclusion of the work, will be published or suppressed according to the reception which is given to the present attempt.

C. B. R.

September 3, 1798.

[2] That is, between 1763 and 1775.

[Preface to *Arthur Mervyn*][1]

The evils of pestilence by which this city[2] has lately been afflicted will probably form an era in its history. The schemes of reformation and improvement to which they will give birth, or, if no efforts of human wisdom can avail to avert the periodical visitations of this calamity, the change in manners and population which they will produce, will be, in the highest degree, memorable. They have already supplied new and copious materials for reflection to the physician and the political economist. They have not been less fertile of instruction to the moral observer, to whom they have furnished new displays of the influence of human passions and motives.

Amidst the medical and political discussions which are now afloat in the community relative to this topic, the author of these remarks has ventured to methodize his own reflections, and to weave into an humble narrative, such incidents as appeared to him most instructive and remarkable among those which came within the sphere of his own observation. It is everyone's duty to profit by all opportunities of inculcating on mankind the lessons of justice

[1] From the first edition.   [2] Philadelphia.

and humanity. The influences of hope and fear, the trials of fortitude and constancy, which took place in this city, in the autumn of 1793, have, perhaps, never been exceeded in any age. It is but just to snatch some of these from oblivion, and to deliver to posterity a brief but faithful sketch of the condition of this metropolis during that calamitous period. Men only require to be made acquainted with distress for their compassion and their charity to be awakened. He that depicts, in lively colors, the evils of disease and poverty, performs an eminent service to the sufferers, by calling forth benevolence in those who are able to afford relief, and he who portrays examples of disinterestedness and intrepidity, confers on virtue the notoriety and homage that are due to it, and rouses in the spectators, the spirit of salutary emulation.

In the following tale a particular series of adventures is brought to a close; but these are necessarily connected with the events which happened subsequent to the period here described. These events are not less memorable than those which form the subject of the present volume, and may hereafter be published either separately or in addition to this.

C. B. B.

[Preface to *Edgar Huntly*][1]

TO THE PUBLIC.

The flattering reception that has been given, by the public, to Arthur Mervyn, has prompted the writer to solicit a continuance of the same favor, and to offer to the world a new performance.

America has opened new views to the naturalist and politician; but has seldom furnished themes to the moral painter. That new springs of action, and new motives to curiosity should operate; that the field of investigation, opened to us by our own country, should differ essentially from those which exist in Europe, may be readily conceived. The sources of amusement to the fancy and instruction to the heart, that are peculiar to ourselves, are equally numerous and inexhaustible. It is the purpose of this work to profit by some of these sources; to exhibit a series of adventures, growing out of the condition of our country, and connected with one of the most common and most wonderful diseases or affections of the human frame.

One merit the writer may at least claim; that of calling forth the passions and engaging the sympathy of the reader, by means hitherto unemployed by preceding authors. Puerile superstition and exploded manners; Gothic cas-

---

[1] From the first edition.

tles and chimeras; are the materials usually employed for this end. The incidents of Indian hostility, and the perils of the western wilderness, are far more suitable; and, for a native of America to overlook these, would admit of no apology. These, therefore, are, in part, the ingredients of this tale, and these he has been ambitious of depicting in vivid and faithful colors. The success of his efforts must be estimated by the liberal and candid reader.

C. B. B.

WASHINGTON IRVING

(1783–1859)

Although prevailing critical judgment during the last 50 years has treated him chiefly as a transitional figure, Washington Irving deserves close study as one of the few major American writers, and one of the most versatile, in the two centuries before the Civil War. In the years before 1840 he was not only the first American writer to be generally praised in England but the author most widely respected among young writers in his own country. Deceptively urbane, and in his later years vulnerable to the charge of social complacency, he has too often been dismissed as sentimental and superficial. It is true that Walt Disney's animated cartoon version of "The Legend of Sleepy Hollow" succeeds in representing the essential atmosphere of that minor masterpiece, but Irving's best work has nonetheless an admirable social range and depth.

The youngest of 11 children, Irving grew up in the family of a strict Presbyterian father but was apparently allowed to attend the theater

The standard edition in progress is *The Works of Washington Irving*, ed. Henry Pochmann and others, 1969—. Until this edition is completed, the best complete edition is *Irving's Works*, author's revised edition, 40 vols., 1848; but the 1809 and 1812 editions of Knickerbocker's *History of New York* are livelier than the revised version.

The standard biography is Stanley T. Williams, *The Life of Washington Irving*, 2 vols., 1935. Other studies are Edward Wagenknecht, *Washington Irving: Modera-*

tion Displayed, 1962; William L. Hedges, *Washington Irving, An American Study*, 1965. See also Philip Young, "Fallen from Time: The Mythic Rip Van Winkle," *Kenyon Review*, 22 (1960): 547-573, and Martin Roth, *Comedy and America: The Lost World Of Washington Irving*, 1976.

One volume editions are *Washington Irving: Representative Selections*, ed. Henry H. Pochmann, American Writers Series, and *Selected Writings of Washington Irving*, ed. Saxe Commins, 1945.

and to read freely in eighteenth-century English literature. He read law and eventually, under some pressure, made gestures toward entering the family mercantile business, but his vocation was plainly literary, and his subject concerned from the beginning relations between European culture and the provincial American republic.

Irving, like Brackenridge and Barlow before him, found the mock-heroic stance and an aggressively irreverent humor appropriate to his embarrassing situation as a provincial writer mediating between a rude young culture and the awesome traditions of England and Europe. As William L. Hedges has demonstrated, Irving made shrewd use of pseudonymous narrators for this purpose in his early works. In a period of intense new concentration on national orgins and national history in England and Western Europe, Irving achieved through Diedrich Knickerbocker a strong position for the American writers who were only too painfully aware of their country's lack of history. The ironic, sophisticated intelligence behind the mask of Knickerbocker displays its mastery not only of polite English literary forms but also of eighteenth-century historiography. And it displays rather brashly a subtle understanding of the most advanced implications of historical skepticism. The very title, *A History of New York from the Creation of the World to the End of the Dutch Dynasty*, ridicules the pretentiousness of all human history, European as well as Dutch-American; the presumptuousness of European historians and the vulnerability of mythical European heroes are inevitably suggested by the caricature of squat Hendrick Hudson and the devastating chapter on the right of conquest. These important qualities cannot be perceived in the usual anthology selection, a chapter or two from the later books on Governor Peter Stuyvesant or the satire on President Thomas Jefferson. By reprinting a rather large part of Book I, we hope to make the nature of this neglected masterpiece accessible to students, to encourage them to read the entire volume, and to establish a context for evaluating Irving's achievement.

Both in the *History of New York* and in *The Sketch Book* (1820), which immediately won him a splendid reputation in England, Irving's subject is the relationship between modern progress and tradition in America as well as the subtle relationships of European and American culture. As the "sauntering" narrator Geoffrey Crayon looks for the "picturesque" corners rather than the grand monuments of English history, he reminds us in a way of Diedrich Knickerbocker; and as Rip Van Winkle and the townspeople in "The Legend of Sleepy Hollow" resist the bustling progress of commercial industry, they remind us of the fat, phlegmatic Dutchmen who in Knickerbocker's *History* were displaced by the swarming, energetic Yankees. The conflict between busy "doing" and contented or meditative "being" will recur in the works of Thoreau, Henry James, and others.

Irving lived abroad from 1815 to 1832, and throughout that period he continued to write effectively of relations between Europe and Anglo-American culture. Just as he had exploited the vogue of national folklore in "Rip Van Winkle," he now profited from the new interest in Spain and Spanish history. He invented a Spanish friar as the narrator of *The Chronicle of the Conquest of Granada*, celebrating the heroic leadership of Queen Isabella, yet lamenting the inevitable fall of the Moorish dynasty. But when the journals of Christopher Columbus were made available for the first time by a Spanish historian, Irving wrote in his own person a biography that won him praise as the leading American historian of his time, and that book remained for more than a century the best study in English of Columbus. In 1832 Irving published his "Spanish sketchbook," *Tales of the Alhambra,* based on his extended residence in that ruined palace and on his arduous and occasionally dangerous journey across Spain on horseback.

Irving was nearly 50 when he returned to the United States, and in his last 25 years he enjoyed the role of an eminent, influential man of letters. But if he was done with literary innovation he had not renounced energetic, adventurous travel. He was past 50 when he made the long journey that enabled him to write *A Tour on the Prairie* (1835), and even older when he visited the trading post at Astoria and when he returned to Madrid as United States minister to the Spanish court. In these years, too, he extended his series on Columbus and lesser explorers; he prepared new, sometimes less crude and therefore less vigorous editions of his own earlier work; and he wrote the five-volume *Life of Washington* that he regarded as the crowning work of his literary career.

In the literary history of his time Irving was a central figure both because of his innovative achievement and because of the example he set younger writers. He adapted conventions of late-eighteenth-century English literature to American needs, and in *The Sketch-Book* he made major contributions to the development of the short story and to the theme of American relationships to European literary culture and historical tradition. In most of his work before 1832, moreover, he found important ways to make the fashionably sentimental interest of European literature in the past relevant to the needs of his own self-conscious new nation, which regarded itself as the country of the future. Nor should it be forgotten that Irving was extraordinarily generous to younger writers. He was the central figure in the establishment of a Knickerbocker circle, and he was also kind to particular writers—especially to the historians William H. Prescott and John L. Motley, both of whom he might well have ignored or impeded as potential rivals.

A History of New York, from the Beginning of the World to the End of the Dutch Dynasty.[1]

TO THE PUBLIC

"To rescue from oblivion the memory of former incidents, and to render a just tribute of renown to the many great and wonderful transactions of our Dutch progenitors, Diedrich Knickerbocker, native of the city of New-York, produces this historical essay.*" Like the great Father of History[2] whose words I have just quoted, I treat of times long past, over which the twilight of uncertainty had already thrown its shadows, and the night of forgetfulness was about to descend forever. With great solicitude had I long beheld the early history of this venerable and ancient city, gradually slipping from our grasp, trembling on the lips of narrative old age, and day by day dropping piece meal into the tomb. In a little while, thought I, and those reverend Dutch burghers, who serve as the tottering monuments of good old times, will be gathered to their fathers; their children engrossed by the empty pleasures of insignificant transactions of the present age, will neglect to treasure up the recollections of the past, and posterity shall search in vain, for memorials of the days of the Patriarchs. The origin of our city will be buried in eternal oblivion, and even the names and achievements of Wouter Van Twiller, Willam Kieft, and Peter Stuyvesant, be enveloped in doubt and fiction, like those of Romulus and Remus, of Charlemagne, King Arthur, Rinaldo, and Godfrey of Bologne.

Determined therefore, to avert if possible this threatened misfortune, I industriously sat myself to work, to gather together all the fragments of our infant history which still existed, and like my revered prototype, Herodotus, where no written records could be found, have endeavored to continue the chain of history by well authenticated traditions.

In this arduous undertaking, which has been the whole business of a long and solitary life, it is incredible the number of learned authors I have consulted; and all to but little purpose. Strange as it may seem, though such multitudes of excellent works have been written about this country, there are none extant which give any full and satisfactory account of the early

---

[1] The text is the second edition, New York, 1812. We omit the opening account of the finding of Knickerbocker's manuscript.

*Beloe's Herodotus.

[2] Herodotus has long been called the father of history. By beginning with him, Irving underlines both the awkward parallel between the great historians and Knickerbocker, and Washington Irving's familiarity with European scholarship and literature. In the Preface and in the history, Knickerbocker will soon parade before us a long list of ancient and modern authorities, from Xenophon to Bolingbroke.

history of New York, or of its three first Dutch governors. I have, however, gained much valuable and curious matter from an elaborate manuscript written in exceeding pure and classic low dutch, excepting a few errors in orthography, which was found in the archives of the Stuyvesant family. Many legends, letters and other documents have I likewise gleaned, in my researches among the family chests and lumber garrets of our respectable Dutch citizens; and I have gathered a host of well authenticated traditions from divers excellent old ladies of my acquaintance, who requested that their names might not be mentioned. Nor must I neglect to acknowledge how greatly I have been assisted by that admirable and praiseworthy institution, the NEW YORK HISTORICAL SOCIETY, to which I here publicly return my sincere acknowledgments.

In the conduct of this inestimable work I have adopted no individual model, but on the contrary have simply contented myself with combining and concentrating the excellencies of the most approved ancient historians. Like Xenophon, I have maintained the utmost impartiality, and the strictest adherence to truth throughout my history. I have enriched it, after the manner of Sallust, with various characters of ancient worthies, drawn at full length and faithfully colored. I have seasoned it with profound political speculations like Thucydides, sweetened it with the graces of sentiment like Tacitus, and infused into the whole the dignity, the grandeur and magnificence of Livy.

I am aware that I shall incur the censure of numerous very learned and judicious critics, for indulging too frequently in the bold excursive manner of my favorite Herodotus. And to be candid, I have found it impossible always to resist the allurements of those pleasing episodes, which like flowery banks and fragrant bowers, beset the dusty road of the historian, and entice him to turn aside, and refresh himself from his wayfaring. But I trust it will be found, that I have always resumed my staff, and addressed myself to my weary journey with renovated spirits, so that both my readers and myself, have been benefited by the relaxation.

Indeed, though it has been my constant wish and uniform endeavor, to rival Polybius himself, in observing the requisite unity of History, yet the loose and unconnected manner in which many of the facts herein recorded have come to hand, rendered such an attempt extremely difficult. This difficulty was likewise increased, by one of the grand objects contemplated in my work, which was to trace the rise of sundry customs and institutions in this best of cities, and to compare them when in the germ of infancy, with what they are in the present old age of knowledge and improvement.

But the chief merit on which I value myself, and found my hopes for future regard, is that faithful veracity with which I have compiled this invaluable little work; carefully winnowing away the chaff of hypothesis, and discarding the tares of fable, which are too apt to spring up and choke the seeds of truth and wholesome knowledge.—Had I been anxious to captivate the superficial throng, who skim like swallows over the surface of literature; or had I been anxious to commend my writings to the pampered palates of literary epicures, I might have availed myself of the obscurity that overshadows the infant years of our city, to introduce a thousand pleasing fictions. But I have scrupulously discarded many a pithy tale and marvellous adventure, whereby the drowsy ear of summer indolence might be enthralled; jealously maintaining that fidelity, gravity, and dignity, which should ever distinguish the historian. "For a writer of this class," observes an elegant critic, "must sustain the character of a wise man, writing for the instruction of posterity; one who has studied to inform himself well, who has pondered his subject with care, and addresses himself to our judgment, rather than to our imagination."

Thrice happy, therefore, is this our renowned city, in having incidents worthy of swelling the theme of history; and doubly thrice happy is it in having such a historian as myself, to relate them. For after all, gentle reader, cities *of themselves*, and in fact, empires *of themselves*, are nothing without an historian. It is the patient narrator who records their prosperity as they rise—who blazons forth the splendor of their noontide meridian—who props their feeble memorials as they totter to decay—who gathers together their scattered fragments as they rot—and who piously at length collects their ashes into the mausoleum of his work,[3] and rears a triumphal monument, to transmit their renown to all succeeding ages.

What has been the fate of many fair cities of antiquity, whose nameless ruins encumber the plains of Europe and Asia, and awaken the fruitless inquiry of the traveller?—they have sunk into dust and silence, they have perished from remembrance for want of a historian! The philanthropist may weep over their desolation—the poet may wander among their mouldering arches and broken columns, and indulge the visionary flights of his fancy—but alas! alas! the modern historian, whose pen, like my own, is doomed to confine itself to dull matter of fact, seeks in vain among their oblivious remains, for some memorial that may tell the instructive tale, of their glory and their ruin.

"Wars, conflagrations, deluges," says Aristotle, "destroy nations, and with them all their monuments, their discoveries, and their vanities—The torch of science had more than once been extinguished and rekindled—a few individuals, who have escaped by accident, reunite the thread of generations."

The same sad misfortune which has happened to so many ancient cities, will happen again, and from the same sad cause, to nine-tenths of those

---

[3] It would be tedious and costly to point out every double meaning in this work, but the mausoleum near the end of this passage in seeming praise of the historian's power deserves especial notice as a warning to read with attention to the author's lively and deadly wit. In the next paragraph Irving mocks the conventional sighs that he and other contemporaries breathed all too easily as they contemplated the mortality of nations.

which now flourish on the face of the globe. With most of them the time for recording their history is gone by; their origin, their foundation, together with the early stages of their settlement, are forever buried in the rubbish of years; and the same would have been the case with this fair portion of the earth, if I had not snatched it from obscurity in the very nick of time, at the moment that those matters herein recorded, were about entering into the wide-spread insatiable maw of oblivion—if I had not dragged them out, as it were, by the very locks, just as the monster's adamantine fangs were closing upon them forever! And here have I, as before observed, carefully collected, collated, and arranged them, scrip and scrap, "*punt en punt, gat en gat,*" and commenced in this little work, a history to serve as a foundation, on which other historians may hereafter raise a noble superstructure, swelling in process of time, until *Knickerbocker's New York* may be equally voluminous, with *Gibbon's Rome*, or *Hume and Smollett's England!*

And now indulge me for a moment, while I lay down my pen, skip to some little eminence at the distance of two or three hundred years ahead; and casting back a bird's eye glance, over the waste of years that is to roll between; discover myself—little I!—at this moment the progenitor, prototype, and precursor of them all, posted at the head of this host of literary worthies, with my book under my arm, and New York on my back, pressing forward like a gallant commander, to honor and immortality!

Such are the vainglorious imaginings that will now and then enter into the brain of the author—that irradiate, as with celestial light, his solitary chamber, cheering his weary spirits, and animating him to persevere in his labors. And I have freely given utterance to these rhapsodies whenever they have occurred; not, I trust, from an unusual spirit of egotism, but merely that the reader may for once have an idea, how an author thinks and feels while he is writing—a kind of knowledge very rare and curious, and much to be desired.

BOOK I

CHAPTER IV.
SHOWING THE GREAT DIFFICULTY PHILOSOPHERS HAVE HAD IN PEOPLING AMERICA—AND HOW THE ABORIGINES CAME TO BE BEGOTTEN BY ACCIDENT—TO THE GREAT RELIEF AND SATISFACTION OF THE AUTHOR.

The next inquiry[1] at which we arrive in the regular course of our history, is to ascertain, if possible, how this country was originally peopled; a point

---

[1] In the first three chapters Knickerbocker has considered the creation and population of the world, and the discovery of America, ironically ridiculing both the idea of discovery (the natives being unaware that they are lost) and the uncertainty of conflicting evidence about the date of discovery. Now he will expose the preposterous ignorance and credulity of learned authorities.

fruitful of incredible embarrassments; for unless we prove that the Aborigines did absolutely come from somewhere, it will be immediately asserted in this age of scepticism, that they did not come at all; and if they did not come at all, then was this country never populated—a conclusion perfectly agreeable to the rules of logic, but wholly irreconcilable to every feeling of humanity, inasmuch as it must syllogistically prove fatal to the innumerable Aborigines of this populous region.

To avert so dire a sophism, and to rescue from logical annihilation so many millions of fellow creatures, how many wings of geese have been plundered! what oceans of ink have been benevolently drained! and how many capacious heads of learned historians have been addled and forever confounded! I pause with reverential awe, when I contemplate the ponderous tomes in different languages, with which they have endeavored to solve this question, so important to the happiness of society, but so involved in clouds of impenetrable obscurity. Historian after historian has engaged in the endless circle of hypothetical argument, and after leading us a weary chase through octavos, quartos, and folios, has let us out at the end of his work, just as wise as we were at the beginning. It was doubtless some philosophical wild goose chase of the kind, that made the old poet Macrobius rail in such a passion at curiosity, which he anathematizes most heartily, as "an irksome agonizing care, a superstitious industry about unprofitable things, an itching humor to see what is not to be seen, and to be doing what signifies nothing when it is done." But to proceed:

Of the claims of the children of Noah to the original population of this country I shall say nothing, as they have already been touched upon in my last chapter. The claimants next in celebrity, are the descendants of Abraham. Thus Christoval Colon (vulgarly called Columbus) when he first discovered the gold mines of Hispaniola immediately concluded, with a shrewdness that would have done honor to a philosopher, that he had found the ancient Ophir, from whence Solomon procured the gold for embellishing the temple at Jerusalem; nay, Colon even imagined that he saw the remains of furnaces of veritable Hebraic construction, employed in refining the precious ore.

So golden a conjecture, tinctured with such fascinating extravagance, was too tempting not to be immediately snapped at by the gudgeons of learning, and accordingly, there were divers profound writers, ready to swear to its correctness, and to bring in their usual load of authorities, and wise surmises, wherewithal to prop it up. Vetablus and Robertus Stephens declared nothing could be more clear—Arius Montanus without the least hesitation, asserts that Mexico was the true Ophir, and the Jews the early settlers of the country. While Possevin, Becan, and several other sagacious writers, lug in a *supposed* prophecy of the fourth book of Esdras, which being inserted in the mighty hypothesis, like the keystone of an arch, gives it, in their opinion, perpetual durability.

Scarce, however, have they completed their goodly superstructure, than in trudges a phalanx of opposite authors, with Hans de Laet the great Dutchman at their head, and at one blow, tumbles the whole fabric about their ears. Hans, in fact, contradicts outright all the Israelitish claims to the first settlement of this country, attributing all those equivocal symptoms, and traces of Christianity and Judaism, which have been said to be found in divers provinces of the new world, to the *Devil*, who has always affected to counterfeit the worship of the true Deity. "A remark," says the knowing old Padre d'Acosta, "made by all good authors who have spoken of the religion of nations newly discovered, and founded besides on the authority of the *fathers of the church.*"

Some writers again, among whom it is with great regret I am compelled to mention Lopez de Gomara, and Juan de Leri, insinuate that the Canaanites, being driven from the land of promise by the Jews, were seized with such a panic that they fled without looking behind them, until stopping to take breath, they found themselves safe in America. As they brought neither their national language, manners, nor features, with them, it is supposed they left them behind in the hurry of their flight—I cannot give my faith to this opinion.

I pass over the supposition of the learned Grotius, who being both an ambassador and a Dutchman to boot, is entitled to great respect; that North America was peopled by a strolling company of Norwegians, and that Peru was founded by a colony from China—Manco or Mungo Capac, the first Incas, being himself a Chinese. Nor shall I more than barely mention, that father Kircher ascribes the settlement of America to the Egyptians, Budbeck to the Scandinavians, Charron to the Gauls, Juffredus Petri to a skating party from Friesland, Milius to the Celtæ, Marinocus the Sicilian to the Romans, Le Compte to the Phœnicians, Postel to the Moors, Martyn d'Angleria to the Abyssinians, together with the sage surmise of De Laet, that England, Ireland and the Orcades may contend for that honor.

Nor will I bestow any more attention or credit to the idea that America is the fairy region of Zipangri, described by that dreaming traveller Marco Polo the Venetian; or that it comprises the visionary island of Atlantis, described by Plato. Neither will I stop to investigate the heathenish assertion of Paracelsus, that each hemisphere of the globe was originally furnished with an Adam and Eve. Or the more flattering opinion of Dr. Romayne, supported by many nameless authorities, that Adam was of the Indian race—or the startling conjecture of Buffon, Helvetius, and Darwin, so highly honorable to mankind, that the whole human species is accidentally descended from a remarkable family of monkeys!

This last conjecture, I must own, came upon me very suddenly and very ungraciously. I have often beheld the clown in a pantomine, while gazing in stupid wonder at the extravagant gambols of a harlequin, all at once electrified by a sudden stroke of the wooden sword across his shoulders. Little did

I think at such times, that it would ever fall to my lot to be treated with equal discourtesy, and that while I was quietly beholding these grave philosophers, emulating the eccentric transformations of the hero of pantomime, they would on a sudden turn upon me and my readers, and with one hypothetical flourish metamorphose us into beasts! I determined from that moment not to burn my fingers with any more of their theories, but content myself with detailing the different methods by which they transported the descendants of these ancient and respectable monkeys, to this great field of theoretical warfare.

This was done either by migrations by land or transmigrations by water. Thus Padre Joseph D'Acosta enumerates three passages by land, first by the north of Europe, secondly by the north of Asia, and thirdly by regions southward of the straits of Magellan. The learned Grotius marches his Norwegians by a pleasant route across frozen rivers and arms of the sea, through Iceland, Greenland, Estotiland and Naremberga. And various writers, among whom are Angleria, De Hornn and Buffon, anxious for the accommodation of these travellers, have fastened the two continents together by a strong chain of deductions—by which means they could pass over dryshod. But should even this fail, Pinkerton, that industrious old gentleman, who compiles books, and manufactures Geographies, has constructed a natural bridge of ice, from continent to continent, at the distance of four or five miles from Behring's straits—for which he is entitled to the grateful thanks of all the wandering aborigines who ever did, or ever will pass over it.

It is an evil much to be lamented, that none of the worthy writers above quoted, could ever commence his work, without immediately declaring hostilities against every writer who had treated of the same subject. In this particular, authors may be compared to a certain sagacious bird, which in building its nest, is sure to pull to pieces the nests of all the birds in its neighborhood. This unhappy propensity tends grievously to impede the progress of sound knowledge. Theories are at best but brittle productions, and when once committed to the stream, they should take care that like the notable pots which were fellow voyagers, they do not crack each other.

For my part, when I beheld the sages I have quoted, gravely accounting for unaccountable things, and discoursing thus wisely about matters forever hidden from their eyes, like a blind man describing the glories of light, and the beauty and harmony of colors, I fell back in astonishment at the amazing extent of human ingenuity.[2]

If—cried I to myself, these learned men can weave whole systems out of nothing, what would be their productions were they furnished with substan-

---

[2] In this paragraph and the next sentence Irving expresses the chief value of the comical mode to upstart, modern, American writers. Compare Herman Melville, "Hawthorne and His Mosses," and Mark Twain, *The Innocents Abroad*—and Thoreau's *Walden* and Emerson's "American Scholar."

tial materials—if they can argue and dispute thus ingeniously about subjects beyond their knowledge, what would be the profundity of their observations, did they but know what they were talking about! Should old Rhadamanthus, when he comes to decide upon their conduct while on earth, have the least idea of the usefulness of their labors, he will undoubtedly class them with those notorious wise men of Gotham, who milked a bull, twisted a rope of sand, and wove a velvet purse from a sow's ear.

My chief surprise is, that among the many writers I have noticed, no one has attempted to prove that this country was peopled from the moon—or that the first inhabitants floated hither on islands of ice, as white bears cruise about the northern oceans—or that they were conveyed hither by balloons, as modern aeronauts pass from Dover to Calais—or by witchcraft, as Simon Magus posted among the stars—or after the manner of the renowned Scythian Abaris, who like the New England witches on full-blooded broomsticks, made most unheard of journeys on the back of a golden arrow, given him by the Hyperborean Apollo.

But there is still one mode left by which this country could have been peopled, which I have reserved for the last, because I consider it worth all the rest, it is—*by accident!* Speaking of the islands of Solomon, New Guinea, and New Holland, the profound father Charlevoix observes, "in fine, all these countries are peopled, and *it is possible,* some have been so *by accident.* Now if it could have happened in that manner, why might it not have been at the *same time,* and by the *same means,* with *the other* parts of the globe?" This ingenious mode of deducing certain conclusions from possible premises, is an improvement in syllogistic skill, and proves the good father superior even to Archimedes, for he can turn the world without anything to rest his lever upon. It is only surpassed by the dexterity with which the sturdy old Jesuit, in another place, cuts the gordian knot—"Nothing" says he, "is more easy. The inhabitants of both hemispheres are certainly the descendants of the same father. The common father of mankind, received an express order from Heaven, to people the world, and *accordingly it has been peopled.* To bring this about, it was necessary to overcome all difficulties in the way, *and they have also been overcome!*" Pious Logician! How does he put all the herd of laborious theorists to the blush, by explaining in five words, what it has cost them volumes to prove they knew nothing about!

They have long been picking at the lock, and fretting at the latch, but the honest father at once unlocks the door by bursting it open, and when he has it once ajar, he is at full liberty to pour in as many nations as he pleases. This proves to a demonstration that a little piety is better than a cart load of philosophy, and is a practical illustration of that Scriptural promise—"By faith ye shall move mountains."

From all the authorities here quoted, and a variety of others which I have consulted, but which are omitted through fear of fatiguing the unlearned reader—I can only draw the following conclusions, which luckily however, are sufficient for my purpose—First, That this part of the world has actually *been peopled* (Q. E. D.)[3] to support which, we have living proofs in the numerous tribes of Indians that inhabit it. Secondly, That it has been peopled in five hundred different ways, as proved by a cloud of authors, who from the positiveness of their assertions seem to have been eye-witnesses to the fact—Thirdly, that the people of this country had a *variety of fathers*, which as it may not be thought much to their credit by the common run of readers, the less we say on the subject the better. The question therefore, I trust, is forever at rest.

CHAPTER V.
IN WHICH THE AUTHOR PUTS A MIGHTY QUESTION TO THE ROUT, BY THE ASSISTANCE OF THE MAN IN THE MOON—WHICH NOT ONLY DELIVERS THOUSANDS OF PEOPLE FROM GREAT EMBARRASSMENT, BUT LIKEWISE CONCLUDES THIS INTRODUCTORY BOOK.

The writer of a history may, in some respects, be likened unto an adventurous knight, who having undertaken a perilous enterprise, by way of establishing his fame, feels bound in honor and chivalry, to turn back for no difficulty nor hardship, and never to shrink or quail whatever enemy he may encounter. Under this impression, I resolutely draw my pen and fall to with might and main, at those doughty questions and subtle paradoxes, which, like fiery dragons and bloody giants, beset the entrance to my history, and would fain repulse me from the very threshold. And at this moment a gigantic question has started up, which I must needs take by the beard and utterly subdue, before I can advance another step in my historic undertaking—but I trust this will be the last adversary I shall have to contend with, and that in the next book I shall be enabled to conduct my readers in triumph into the body of my work.

The question which has thus suddenly arisen, is, what right had the first discoverers of America to land and take possession of a country, without first gaining the consent of its inhabitants, or yielding them an adequate compensation for their territory?—a question which has withstood many fierce assaults, and has given much distress of mind to multitudes of kind hearted folk. And indeed, until it be totally vanquished, and put to rest, the worthy people of America can by no means enjoy the soil they inhabit, with clear right and title, and quiet, unsullied consciences.

The first source of right, by which property is acquired in a country, is DISCOVERY. For as all mankind have an equal right to anything, which has never before been appropriated, so any nation, that discovers an uninhabited

---

[3] Quod erat demonstrandum. Which was to be proved.

country, and takes possession thereof, is considered as enjoying full property, and absolute, unquestionable empire therein.°

This proposition being admitted, it follows clearly, that the Europeans who first visited America, were the real discoverers of the same; nothing being necessary to the establishment of this fact, but simply to prove that it was totally uninhabited by man. This would at first appear to be a point of some difficulty, for it is well known, that this quarter of the world abounded with certain animals, that walked erect on two feet, had something of the human countenance, uttered certain unintelligible sounds, very much like language, in short, had a marvellous resemblance to human beings. But the zealous and enlightened fathers, who accompanied the discoverers, for the purpose of promoting the kingdom of heaven, by establishing fat monasteries and bishoprics on earth, soon cleared up this point, greatly to the satisfaction of his holiness the pope, and of all Christian voyagers and discoverers.

They plainly proved, and as there were no Indian writers arose on the other side, the fact was considered as fully admitted and established, that the two-legged race of animals before mentioned, were mere cannibals, detestable monsters, and many of them giants—which last description of vagrants have, since the times of Gog, Magog, and Goliath,[2] been considered as outlaws, and have received no quarter in either history, chivalry or song. Indeed, even the philosophic Bacon, declared the Americans to be people proscribed by the laws of nature, inasmuch as they had a barbarous custom of sacrificing men, and feeding upon man's flesh.

Nor are these all the proofs of their utter barbarism: among many other writers of discernment, Ulloa tells us "their imbecility is so visible, that one can hardly form an idea of them different from what one has of the brutes. Nothing disturbs the tranquillity of their souls, equally insensible to disasters, and to prosperity. Though half naked, they are as contented as a monarch in his most splendid array. Fear makes no impression on them, and respect as little."—All this is furthermore supported by the authority of M. Bouguer. "It is not easy," says he,"to describe the degree of their indifference for wealth and all its advantages. One does not well know what motives to propose to them when one would persuade them to any service. It is vain to offer them money, they answer that they are not hungry." And Vanegas confirms the whole, assuring us that "ambition they have none, and are more desirous of being thought strong than valiant. The objects of ambition with us, honor, fame, reputation, riches, posts, and distinctions are unknown among them. So that this powerful spring of action, the cause of so much *seeming* good and *real* evil in the world has no power over them. In a word,

---

°Grotius. Puffendorf, b. 5. c. 4. Vattel, b. 1. c. 18, & c.[1]

[1] Here and below, Irving cites actual commentators on international law and equity, while mocking them.

[2] Gog and Magog are the names of nations to be led by Satan in a war against the Kingdom of God. See Revelation 20: 7-8. Goliath was the Philistine giant slain by David. See 1 Samuel 17: 4-51.

these unhappy mortals may be compared to children, in whom the development of reason is not completed."

Now all these peculiarities, although in the unenlightened states of Greece, they would have entitled their possessors to immortal honor, as having reduced to practice those rigid and abstemious maxims, the mere talking about which, acquired certain old Greeks the reputation of sages and philosophers;—yet were they clearly proved in the present instance, to betoken a most abject and brutified nature, totally beneath the human character. But the benevolent fathers, who had undertaken to turn these unhappy savages into dumb beasts, by dint of argument, advanced still stronger proofs; for as certain divines of the sixteenth century, and among the rest Lullus affirm—the Americans go naked, and have no beards!—"They have nothing," says Lullus, "of the reasonable animal, except the mask."—And even that mask was allowed to avail them but little, for it was soon found that they were of a hideous copper complexion—and being of a copper complexion, it was all the same as if they were Negroes—and Negroes are black, "and black," said the pious fathers, devoutly crossing themselves "is the color of the Devil!" Therefore, so far from being able to own property, they had no right even to personal freedom, for liberty is too radiant a deity, to inhabit such gloomy temples. All which circumstances plainly convinced the righteous followers of Cortés and Pizarro,[3] that these miscreants had no title to the soil that they infested—that they were a perverse, illiterate, dumb, beardless, *black-seed*—mere wild beasts of the forests, and like them should either be subdued or exterminated.

From the foregoing arguments, therefore, and a variety of others equally conclusive, which I forbear to enumerate, it was clearly evident that this fair quarter of the globe when first visited by Europeans, was a howling wilderness, inhabited by nothing but wild beasts; and that the transatlantic visitors acquired an incontrovertible property therein, by the *right of discovery*.

This right being fully established, we now come to the next, which is the right acquired by *cultivation*. "The cultivation of the soil," we are told, "is an obligation imposed by nature on mankind. The whole world is appointed for the nourishment of its inhabitants: but it would be incapable of doing it, was it uncultivated. Every nation is then obliged by the law of nature to cultivate the ground that has fallen to its share. Those people, like the ancient Germans and modern Tartars, who, having fertile countries, disdain to cultivate the earth, and choose to live by rapine, are wanting to themselves, and *deserve to be exterminated as savage and pernicious beasts.*"°

Now it is notorious, that the savages knew nothing of agriculture, when first discovered by the Europeans, but lived a most vagabond, disorderly, unrighteous life,—rambling from place to place, and prodigally rioting upon

---

[3] Spanish conquerors, respectively, of Mexico and Peru in the sixteenth century.

° Vattel-B. i. ch. 17. See likewise Grotius, Puffendorf, etc.

the spontaneous luxuries of nature, without tasking her generosity to yield them anything more; whereas it has been most unquestionably shown, that heaven intended the earth should be ploughed and sown, and manured, and laid out into cities, and towns, and farms, and country seats, and pleasure grounds, and public gardens, all which the Indians knew nothing about—therefore they did not improve the talents providence had bestowed on them—therefore they were careless stewards—therefore they had no right to the soil—therefore they deserved to be exterminated.

It is true the savages might plead that they drew all the benefits from the land which their simple wants required—they found plenty of game to hunt, which, together with the roots and uncultivated fruits of the earth, furnished a sufficient variety for their frugal repasts;—and that as heaven merely designed the earth to form the abode, and satisfy the wants of man; so long as those purposes were answered, the will of heaven was accomplished.—But this only proves how undeserving they were of the blessings around them—they were so much the more savages, for not having more wants; for knowledge is in some degree an increase of desires, and it is this superiority both in the number and magnitude of his desires, that distinguishes the man from the beast. Therefore the Indians, in not having more wants, were very unreasonable animals; and it was but just that they should make way for the Europeans, who had a thousand wants to their one, and therefore would turn the earth to more account, and by cultivating it, more truly fulfill the will of heaven. Besides—Grotius and Lauterbach, and Puffendorff, and Titius, and many wise men beside, who have considered the matter properly, have determined, that the property of a country cannot be acquired by hunting, cutting wood, or drawing water in it—nothing but precise demarcation of limits, and the intention of cultivation, can establish the possession. Now as the savages (probably from never having read the authors above quoted) had never complied with any of these necessary forms, it plainly followed that they had no right to the soil, but that it was completely at the disposal of the first comers, who had more knowledge, more wants, and more elegant, that is to say, artificial desires than themselves.

In entering upon a newly discovered, uncultivated country, therefore, the newcomers were but taking possession of what, according to the aforesaid doctrine, was their own property—therefore in opposing them, the savages were invading their just rights, infringing the immutable laws of nature, and counteracting the will of heaven—therefore they were guilty of impiety, burglary and trespass on the case,—therefore they were hardened offenders against God and man—therefore they ought to be exterminated.

But a more irresistible right than either that I have mentioned, and one which will be the most readily admitted by my reader, provided he be blessed with bowels of charity and philanthropy, is the right acquired by civilization. All the world knows the lamentable state in which these poor savages were found. Not only deficient in the comforts of life, but what is still worse, most piteously and unfortunately blind to the miseries of their situation. But no sooner did the benevolent inhabitants of Europe behold their sad condition than they immediately went to work to ameliorate and improve it. They introduced among them rum, gin, brandy, and the other comforts of life—and it is astonishing to read how soon the poor savages learned to estimate these blessings: they likewise made known to them a thousand remedies, by which the most inveterate diseases are alleviated and healed, and that they might comprehend the benefits and enjoy the comforts of these medicines, they previously introduced among them the diseases, which they were calculated to cure. By these and a variety of other methods was the condition of these poor savages wonderfully improved; they acquired a thousand wants, of which they had before been ignorant, and as he has most sources of happiness, who has most wants to be gratified, they were doubtlessly rendered a much happier race of beings.

But the most important branch of civilization, and which has most strenuously been extolled, by the zealous and pious fathers of the Romish Church, is the introduction of the Christian faith. It was truly a sight that might well inspire horror, to behold these savages, stumbling among the dark mountains of paganism, and guilty of the most horrible ignorance of religion. It is true, they neither stole nor defrauded; they were sober, frugal, continent, and faithful to their word; but though they acted right habitually, it was all in vain, unless they acted so from precept. The newcomers therefore used every method, to induce them to embrace and practice the true religion— except indeed that of setting them the example.

But notwithstanding all these complicated labors for their good, such was the unparalleled obstinacy of these stubborn wretches, that they ungratefully refused to acknowledge the strangers as their benefactors, and persisted in disbelieving the doctrines they endeavored to inculcate; most insolently alleging, that from their conduct, the advocates of Christianity did not seem to believe in it themselves. Was not this too much for human patience?—would not one suppose, that the benign visitants from Europe, provoked at their incredulity, and discouraged by their stiff-necked obstinacy, would forever have abandoned their shores, and consigned them to their original ignorance and misery?—But no—so zealous were they to effect the temporal comfort and eternal salvation of these pagan infidels, that they even proceeded from the milder means of persuasion, to the more painful and troublesome one of persecution—Let loose among them whole troops of fiery monks and furious bloodhounds—purified them by fire and sword, by stake and faggot; in consequence of which indefatigable measures, the cause of Christian love and charity was so rapidly advanced, that in a very few years, not one-fifth of the number of unbelievers existed in South America, that were found there at the time of its discovery.

What stronger right need the European settlers advance to the country than this? Have not whole nations of uninformed savages been made acquainted with a thousand imperious wants and indispensable comforts, of which they were before wholly ignorant—Have they not been literally hunted and smoked out of the dens and lurking places of ignorance and infidelity, and absolutely scourged into the right path? Have not the temporal things, the vain baubles and filthy lucre of this world, which were too apt to engage their worldly and selfish thoughts, been benevolently taken from them; and have they not instead thereof, been taught to set their affections on things above?—And finally, to use the words of a reverend Spanish father, in a letter to his superior in Spain—"Can anyone have the presumption to say, that these savage Pagans, have yielded anything more than an inconsiderable recompense to their benefactors; in surrendering to them a little pitiful tract of this dirty sublunary planet, in exchange for a glorious inheritance in the kingdom of Heaven!"

Here then are three complete and undeniable sources of right established, any one of which was more than ample to establish a property in the newly discovered regions of America. Now, so it has happened in certain parts of this delightful quarter of the globe, that the right of discovery has been so strenuously asserted—the influence of cultivation so industriously extended, and the progress of salvation and civilization so zealously prosecuted, that, what with their attendant wars, persecutions, oppressions, diseases, and other partial evils that often hang on the skirts of great benefits—the savage aborigines have, somehow or another, been utterly annihilated—and this all at once brings me to a fourth right, which is worth all the others put together—For the original claimants to the soil being all dead and buried, and no one remaining to inherit or dispute the soil, the Spaniards, as the next immediate occupants, entered upon the possession as clearly as the hangman succeeds to the clothes of the malefactor—and as they have Blackstone,° and all the learned expounders of the law on their side, they may set all actions of ejectment at defiance—and this last right may be entitled, the RIGHT BY EXTERMINATION, or in other words, the RIGHT BY GUN-POWDER.

But lest any scruples of conscience should remain on this head, and to settle the question of right forever, his holiness Pope Alexander VI, issued a mighty bull, by which he generously granted the newly discovered quarter of the globe to the Spaniards and Portuguese; who, thus having law and gospel on their side, and being inflamed with great spiritual zeal, showed the Pagan savages neither favor nor affection, but prosecuted the work of discovery, colonization, civilization, and extermination, with ten times more fury than ever.

Thus were the European worthies who first discovered America clearly entitled to the soil; and not only entitled to the soil, but likewise to the eternal thanks of these infidel savages, for having come so far, endured so

° Bl. Com. B. II. c.i.

many perils by sea and land, and taken such unwearied pains, for no other purpose but to improve their forlorn, uncivilized and heathenish condition—for having made them acquainted with the comforts of life; for having introduced among them the light of religion, and finally—for having hurried them out of the world, to enjoy its reward!

But as argument is never so well understood by us selfish mortals, as when it comes home to ourselves, and as I am particularly anxious that this question should be put to rest forever, I will suppose a parallel case, by way of arousing the candid attention of my readers.

Let us suppose then, that the inhabitants of the moon, by astonishing advancement in science, and by a profound insight into that ineffable lunar philosophy, the mere flickerings of which have of late years dazzled the feeble optics, and addled the shallow brains of the good people of our globe—let us suppose, I say, that the inhabitants of the moon, by these means, had arrived at such a command of their *energies*, such an enviable state of *perfectibility*, as to control the elements, and navigate the boundless regions of space. Let us suppose a roving crew of these soaring philosophers, in the course of an aerial voyage of discovery among the stars, should chance to alight upon this outlandish planet.

And here I beg my readers will not have the uncharitableness to smile, as is too frequently the fault of volatile readers, when perusing the grave speculations of philosophers. I am far from indulging in any sportive vein at present; nor is the supposition I have been making so wild as many may deem it. It has long been a very serious and anxious question with me and many a time and oft, in the course of my overwhelming cares and contrivances for the welfare and protection of this my native planet, have I lain awake whole nights, debating in my mind, whether it were most probable we should first discover and civilize the moon, or the moon discover and civilize our globe. Neither would the prodigy of sailing in the air and cruising among the stars be a whit more astonishing and incomprehensible to us, than was the European mystery of navigating floating castles, through the world of waters, to the simple savages. We have already discovered the art of coasting along the aerial shores of our planet, by means of balloons, as the savages had, of venturing along their sea coasts in canoes; and the disparity between the former, and the aerial vehicles of the philosophers from the moon, might not be greater, than that, between the bark canoes of the savages, and the mighty ships of their discoverers. I might here pursue an endless chain of similar speculations; but as they would be unimportant to my subject, I abandon them to my reader, particularly if he be a philosopher, as matters well worthy his attentive consideration.

To return then to my supposition—let us suppose that the aerial visitants I have mentioned, possessed of vastly superior knowledge to ourselves; that is to say, possessed of superior knowledge in the art of extermination—riding on Hypogriffs—defended with impenetrable armor—armed with concentrated sunbeams, and provided with vast engines, to hurl enormous moon-stones: in short, let us suppose them, if our vanity will permit the supposi-tion, as superior to us in knowledge, and consequently in power, as the Europeans were to the Indians, when they first discovered them. All this is very possible, it is only our self-sufficiency that makes us think otherwise; and I warrant the poor savages, before they had any knowledge of the white men, armed in all the terrors of glittering steel and tremendous gun-powder, were as perfectly convinced that they themselves were the wisest, the most virtuous, powerful, and perfect of created beings as are, at this present moment, the lordly inhabitants of old England, the volatile populace of France, or even the self-satisfied citizens of this most enlightened republic.

Let us, suppose, moreover, that the aerial voyagers, finding this planet to be nothing but a howling wilderness, inhabited by us, poor savages and wild beasts, shall take formal possession of it, in the name of his most gracious and philosophic excellency, the man in the moon. Finding, however, that their numbers are incompetent to hold it in complete subjection, on account of the ferocious barbarity of its inhabitants; they shall take our worthy Pres-ident, the King of England, the Emperor of Hayti, the mighty Bonaparte, and the great King of Bantam, and returning to their native planet, shall carry them to court, as were the Indian chiefs led about as spectacles in the courts of Europe.

Then making such obeisance as the etiquette of the court requires, they shall address the puissant man in the moon, in, as near as I can conjecture, the following terms:

"Most serene and mighty Potentate, whose dominions extend as far as eye can reach, who rideth on the Great Bear, useth the sun as a looking glass, and maintaineth unrivalled control over tides, madmen, and sea-crabs. We, thy liege subjects, have just returned from a voyage of discovery, in the course of which we have landed and taken possession of that obscure little dirty planet, which thou beholdest rolling at a distance. The five uncouth monsters, which we have brought into this august presence, were once very important chiefs among their fellow savages, who are a race of beings totally destitute of the common attributes of humanity; and differing in everything from the inhabitants of the moon, inasmuch as they carry their heads upon their shoulders, instead of under their arms—have two eyes instead of one—are utterly destitute of tails and of a variety of unseemly complexions, par-ticulary of a horrible whiteness—instead of pea green.

"We have moreover found these miserable savages sunk into a state of the utmost ignorance and depravity, every man shamelessly living with his own wife, and rearing his own children, instead of indulging in that community of wives enjoined by the law of nature, as expounded by the philosophers of the moon. In a word, they have scarcely a gleam of true philosophy among them, but are, in fact, utter heretics, ignoramuses, and barbarians. Taking compassion, therefore, on the sad condition of these sublunary wretches, we have endeavored, while we remained on their planet, to introduce among them the light of reason—and the comforts of the moon.—We have treated them to mouthfuls of moonshine, and draughts of nitrous oxide, which they swallowed with incredible voracity, particularly the females; and we have likewise endeavored to instill into them the precepts of lunar philosophy. We have insisted upon their renouncing the contemptible shackles of religion and common sense, and adoring the profound, omnipotent and all perfect energy, and the ecstatic, immutable, immovable perfection. But such was the unparalleled obstinacy of these wretched savages, that they persisted in cleaving to their wives, and adhering to their religion, and absolutely set at nought the sublime doctrines of the moon—nay, among other abominable heresies, they even went so far as blasphemously to declare, that this ineffable planet was made of nothing more nor less than green cheese!"

At these words, the great man in the moon (being a very profound philosopher) shall fall into a terrible passion, and possessing equal authority over things that do not belong to him, as did whilom his holiness the Pope, shall forthwith issue a formidable bull, —specifying, "That—whereas a certain crew of Lunatics have lately discovered and taken possession of a newly discovered planet, called *the earth*—and that whereas it is inhabited by none but a race of two-legged animals that carry their heads on their shoulders instead of under their arms; cannot talk the lunatic language; have two eyes instead of one; are destitute of tails, and of a horrible whiteness, instead of pea green—therefore, and for a variety of other excellent reasons—they are considered incapable of possessing any property in the planet they infest, and the right and title to it are confirmed to its original discoverers.—And furthermore, the colonists who are now about to depart to the aforesaid planet, are authorized and commanded to use every means to convert these infidel savages from the darkness of Christianity, and make them thorough and absolute lunatics."

In consequence of this benevolent bull, our philosophic benefactors go to work with hearty zeal. They seize upon our fertile territories, scourge us from our rightful possessions, relieve us from our wives, and when we are unreasonable enough to complain, they will turn upon us and say—miserable barbarians! ungrateful wretches!—have we not come thousands of miles to improve your worthless planet!—have we not fed you with moonshine—have we not intoxicated you with nitrous oxide—does not our moon give you light every night, and have you the baseness to murmur, when we claim a pitiful return for all these benefits? But finding that we not only persist in absolute contempt of their reasoning and disbelief in their philosophy, but even go so far as daringly to defend our property, their patience shall be exhausted, and they shall resort to their superior powers of argument—hunt us with hypogriffs, transfix us with concentrated sunbeams, demolish our cities with moonstones; until having by main force, converted us to the true faith, they shall graciously permit us to exist in the torrid deserts of Arabia, or the frozen regions of Lapland, there to enjoy the blessings of civilization and the charms of lunar philosophy—in much the same manner as the re-formed and enlightened savages of this country, are kindly suffered to inhabit the inhospitable forests of the north, or the impenetrable wildernesses of South America.

Thus, I hope, I have clearly proved, and strikingly illustrated, the right of the early colonists to the possession of this country—and thus is this gigantic question, completely vanquished—so having manfully surmounted all obstacles, and subdued all opposition, what remains but that I should forthwith conduct my readers, into the city which we have been so long in a manner besieging.—But hold, before I proceed another step, I must pause to take breath and recover from the excessive fatigue I have undergone, in preparing to begin this most accurate of histories. And in this I do but imitate the example of a renowned Dutch tumbler of antiquity, who took a start of three miles for the purpose of jumping over a hill, but having run himself out of breath by the time he reached the foot, sat himself quietly down for a few moments to blow, and then walked over it at his leisure.

From The Sketch-Book of Geoffrey Crayon, Gent.[1]

[The Sketch-Book was first published in seven installments in New York, in 1819 and 1820. In that version there were 25 chapters besides the introduction and conclusion, but then Irving added more. Most of the book consisted of essays and sketches about life in England—"Westminster Abbey," "Rural Life in England," "Bracebridge Hall" (which is still performed annually at a lodge in Yosemite National Park at Christmas time). Mixed in among these were some sentimental tales, some humorous sketches, a critical essay on English misunderstandings of America, and a few essays and tales about American life—not only the two famous stories reprinted below, but a historical essay on "Philip of Pokanoket," the leader named and killed in King Philip's War.]

THE AUTHOR'S ACCOUNT OF HIMSELF.

"I am of this mind with Homer, that as the snaile that crept out of her shel was turned eftsoons into a toad, and thereby was forced to make a stoole to sit on; so the traveller that stragleth from his owne country is in a short time transformed into so monstrous a shape, that he is faine to alter his mansion with his manners, and to live where he can, not where he would."

Lyly's EUPHUES.

---

[1] The text is the 1848 edition. In this preface Irving creates another persona to narrate his sketches and stories, although Geoffrey Crayon, the "author" described here, also uses Diedrich Knickerbocker to narrate both "Rip Van Winkle" and "The Legend of Sleepy Hollow." Notice here the defensive distinction between the glories of America and those of Europe.

I was always fond of visiting new scenes, and observing strange characters and manners. Even when a mere child I began my travels, and made many tours of discovery into foreign parts and unknown regions of my native city, to the frequent alarm of my parents, and the emolument of the town-crier. As I grew into boyhood, I extended the range of my observations. My holiday afternoons were spent in rambles about the surrounding country. I made myself familiar with all its places famous in history or fable. I knew every spot where a murder or robbery had been committed, or a ghost seen. I visited the neighboring villages, and added greatly to my stock of knowledge, by noting their habits and customs, and conversing with their sages and great men. I even journeyed one long summer's day to the summit of the most distant hill, whence I stretched my eye over many a mile of terra incognita, and was astonished to find how vast a globe I inhabited.

This rambling propensity strengthened with my years. Books of voyages and travels became my passion, and in devouring their contents, I neglected the regular exercises of the school. How wistfully would I wander about the pier-heads in fine weather, and watch the parting ships, bound to distant climes—with what longing eyes would I gaze after their lessening sails, and waft myself in imagination to the ends of the earth!

Further reading and thinking, though they brought this vague inclination into more reasonable bounds, only served to make it more decided. I visited various parts of my own country; and had I been merely a lover of fine scenery, I should have felt little desire to seek elsewhere its gratification, for on no country have the charms of nature been more prodigally lavished. Her mighty lakes, like oceans of liquid silver; her mountains, with their bright aerial tints; her valleys, teeming with wild fertility; her tremendous cataracts, thundering in their solitudes; her boundless plains, waving with spontaneous verdure; her broad deep rivers, rolling in solemn silence to the ocean; her trackless forests, where vegetation puts forth all its magnificence; her skies, kindling with the magic of summer clouds and glorious sunshine; no, never need an American look beyond his own country for the sublime and beautiful of natural scenery.

But Europe held forth the charms of storied and poetical association.[2] There were to be seen the masterpieces of art, the refinements of highly-cultivated society, the quaint peculiarities of ancient and local custom. My native country was full of youthful promise: Europe was rich in the accumu-

---

[2] That is, American natural splendor would inspire awe in any sensitive observer; Europe's special charm came through to an observer whose psyche had already been prepared to associate remembered lore of human action with the scenes taken in by the eye. Here Europe is the country of the past, and that emphasis is often repeated in American literature at least until World War I.

lated treasures of age. Her very ruins told the history of times gone by, and every mouldering stone was a chronicle. I longed to wander over the scenes of renowned achievement—to tread, as it were, in the footsteps of antiquity—to loiter about the ruined castle—to meditate on the falling tower—to escape, in short, from the commonplace realities of the present, and lose myself among the shadowy grandeurs of the past.

I had, beside all this, an earnest desire to see the great men of the earth. We have, it is true, our great men in America: not a city but has an ample share of them. I have mingled among them in my time, and been almost withered by the shade into which they cast me; for there is nothing so baleful to a small man as the shade of a great one, particularly the great man of a city. But I was anxious to see the great men of Europe; for I had read in the works of various philosophers, that all animals degenerated in America, and man among the number. A great man of Europe, thought I, must therefore be as superior to a great man of America, as a peak of the Alps to a highland of the Hudson; and in this idea I was confirmed, by observing the comparative importance and swelling magnitude of many English travellers among us, who, I was assured, were very little people in their own country. I will visit this land of wonders, thought I, and see the gigantic race from which I am degenerated.

It has been either my good or evil lot to have my roving passion gratified. I have wandered through different countries, and witnessed many of the shifting scenes of life. I cannot say that I have studied them with the eye of a philosopher; but rather with the sauntering gaze with which humble lovers of the picturesque stroll from the window of one print-shop to another; caught sometimes by the delineations of beauty, sometimes by the distortions of caricature, and sometimes by the loveliness of landscape. As it is the fashion for modern tourists to travel pencil in hand, and bring home their port-folios filled with sketches, I am disposed to get up a few for the entertainment of my friends. When, however, I look over the hints and memorandums I have taken down for the purpose, my heart almost fails me at finding how my idle humor has led me aside from the great objects studied by every regular traveller who would make a book. I fear I shall give equal disappointment with an unlucky landscape painter, who had travelled on the continent, but, following the bent of his vagrant inclination, had sketched in nooks, and corners, and by-places. His sketch-book was accordingly crowded with cottages, and landscapes, and obscure ruins; but he had neglected to paint St. Peter's, or the Coliseum; the cascade of Terni, or the bay of Naples; and had not a single glacier or volcano in his whole collection.

Rip Van Winkle.[1]

A POSTHUMOUS WRITING OF DIEDRICH KNICKERBOCKER.

> *By Woden, God of Saxons,*
> *From whence comes Wednesday, that is Wodensday,*
> *Truth is a thing that ever I will keep*
> *Unto thylke day in which I creep into*
> *My sepulchre——*
>
> Cartwright.

The following Tale was found among the papers of the late Diedrich Knickerbocker, an old gentleman of New York, who was very curious in the Dutch history of the province, and the manners of the descendants from its primitive settlers. His historical researches, however, did not lie so much among books as among men; for the former are lamentably scanty on his favorite topics; whereas he found the old burghers, and still more their wives, rich in that legendary lore, so invaluable to true history. Whenever, therefore, he happened upon a genuine Dutch family, snugly shut up in its low-roofed farmhouse, under a spreading sycamore, he looked upon it as a little clasped volume of black-letter, and studied it with the zeal of a book-worm.

The result of all these researches was a history of the province during the reign of the Dutch governors, which he published some years since. There have been various opinions as to the literary character of his work, and, to tell the truth, it is not a whit better than it should be. Its chief merit is its scrupulous accuracy, which indeed was a little questioned on its first appearance, but has since been completely established; and it is now admitted into all historical collections, as a book of unquestionable authority.

The old gentleman died shortly after the publication of his work, and now that he is dead and gone, it cannot do much harm to his memory to say that his time might have been much better employed in weightier labors. He, however, was apt to ride his hobby his own way; and though it did now and then kick up the dust a little in the eyes of his neighbors, and grieve the spirit of some friends, for whom he felt the truest deference and affection; yet his errors and follies are remembered "more in sorrow than in anger," and it begins to be suspected, that he never intended to injure or offend. But however his memory may be appreciated by critics, it is still held dear by many folks, whose good opinion is well worth having; particularly by certain biscuit-bakers, who have gone so far as to imprint his likeness on their new-

---

[1] Both "Rip Van Winkle" and "The Legend of Sleepy Hollow" explore American issues, lore, and character while the author borrows the central action from German folklore. See especially the works listed above by H.A. Pochmann and Philip Young. Crayon cites a German source in his note at the end of the tale.

"The Return of Rip Van Winkle," a painting by John Quidor (1801–1881). The painting was shown at the National Academy in 1829. (National Gallery of Art, Washington, D.C. Andrew Mellon Collection, 1942.)

year cakes; and have thus given him a chance for immortality, almost equal to the being stamped on a Waterloo Medal, or a Queen Ann's Farthing.

———————

Whoever has made a voyage up the Hudson must remember the Kaatskill mountains. They are a dismembered branch of the great Appalachian family, and are seen away to the west of the river, swelling up to a noble height, and lording it over the surrounding country. Every change of season, every change of weather, indeed, every hour of the day, produces some change in the magical hues and shapes of these mountains, and they are regarded by all the good wives, far and near, as perfect barometers. When the weather is fair and settled, they are clothed in blue and purple, and print their bold outlines on the clear evening sky; but, sometimes, when the rest of the landscape is cloudless, they will gather a hood of gray vapors about their summits, which, in the last rays of the setting sun, will glow and light up like a crown of glory.

At the foot of these fairy mountains, the voyager may have descried the light smoke curling up from a village, whose shingle-roofs gleam among the trees, just where the blue tints of the upland melt away into the fresh green of the nearer landscape. It is a little village of great antiquity, having been founded by some of the Dutch colonists, in the early times of the province, just about the beginning of the government of the good Peter Stuyvesant (may he rest in peace!) and there were some of the houses of the original settlers standing within a few years, built of small yellow bricks brought from Holland, having latticed windows and gable fronts, surmounted with weather-cocks.

In that same village, and in one of these very houses (which, to tell the precise truth, was sadly time-worn and weather-beaten), there lived many years since, while the country was yet a province of Great Britain, a simple good-natured fellow of the name of Rip Van Winkle. He was a descendant of the Van Winkles who figured so gallantly in the chivalrous days of Peter Stuyvesant, and accompanied him to the siege of Fort Christina. He inherited, however, but little of the martial character of his ancestors. I have observed that he was a simple good-natured man; he was, moreover, a kind neighbor, and an obedient hen-pecked husband. Indeed, to the latter circumstance might be owing that meekness of spirit which gained him such universal popularity; for those men are most apt to be obsequious and conciliating abroad, who are under the discipline of shrews at home. Their tempers, doubtless, are rendered pliant and malleable in the fiery furnace of domestic tribulation; and a curtain lecture is worth all the sermons in the world for teaching the virtues of patience and long-suffering. A termagant wife may, therefore, in some respects, be considered a tolerable blessing; and if so, Rip Van Winkle was thrice blessed.

Certain it is, that he was a great favorite among all the good wives of the village, who, as usual, with the amiable sex, took his part in all family squabbles; and never failed, whenever they talked those matters over in their evening gossipings, to lay all the blame on Dame Van Winkle. The children of the village, too, would shout with joy whenever he approached. He assisted at their sports, made their playthings, taught them to fly kites and shoot marbles, and told them long stories of ghosts, witches, and Indians. Whenever he went dodging about the village, he was surrounded by a troop of them, hanging on his skirts, clambering on his back, and playing a thousand tricks on him with impunity; and not a dog would bark at him throughout the neighborhood.

The great error in Rip's composition was an insuperable aversion to all kinds of profitable labor. It could not be from the want of assiduity or perseverance; for he would sit on a wet rock, with a rod as long and heavy as a Tartar's lance, and fish all day without a murmur, even though he should not be encouraged by a single nibble. He would carry a fowling-piece on his shoulder for hours together, trudging through woods and swamps, and up hill and down dale, to shoot a few squirrels or wild pigeons. He would never refuse to assist a neighbor even in the roughest toil, and was a foremost man at all country frolics for husking Indian corn, or building stone-fences; the women of the village, too, used to employ him to run their errands, and to do such little odd jobs as their less obliging husbands would not do for them. In a word Rip was ready to attend to anybody's business but his own; but as to doing family duty, and keeping his farm in order, he found it impossible.

In fact, he declared it was of no use to work on his farm; it was the most pestilent little piece of ground in the whole country; everything about it went wrong, and would go wrong, in spite of him. His fences were continually falling to pieces; his cow would either go astray, or get among the cabbages; weeds were sure to grow quicker in his fields than anywhere else; the rain always made a point of setting in just as he had some out-door work to do; so that though his patrimonial estate had dwindled away under his management, acre by acre, until there was little more left than a mere patch of Indian corn and potatoes, yet it was the worst conditioned farm in the neighborhood.

His children, too, were as ragged and wild as if they belonged to nobody. His son Rip, an urchin begotten in his own likeness, promised to inherit the habits, with the old clothes of his father. He was generally seen trooping like a colt at his mother's heels, equipped in a pair of his father's cast-off galligaskins, which he had much ado to hold up with one hand, as a fine lady does her train in bad weather.

Rip Van Winkle, however, was one of those happy mortals, of foolish, well-oiled dispositions, who take the world easy, eat white bread or brown, whichever can be got with least thought or trouble, and would rather starve on a penny than work for a pound. If left to himself, he would have whistled life away in perfect contentment; but his wife kept continually dinning in his ears about his idleness, his carelessness, and the ruin he was bringing on his family. Morning, noon, and night, her tongue was incessantly going, and everything he said or did was sure to produce a torrent of household eloquence. Rip had but one way of replying to all lectures of the kind, and that, by frequent use, had grown into a habit. He shrugged his shoulders, shook his head, cast up his eyes, but said nothing. This, however, always provoked a fresh volley from his wife; so that he was fain to draw off his forces, and take to the outside of the house—the only side which, in truth, belongs to a henpecked husband.

Rip's sole domestic adherent was his dog Wolf, who was as much henpecked as his master; for Dame Van Winkle regarded them as companions in idleness, and even looked upon Wolf with an evil eye, as the cause of his master's going so often astray. True it is, in all points of spirit befitting an honorable dog, he was as courageous an animal as ever scoured the woods—but what courage can withstand the ever-during and all-besetting terrors of a woman's tongue? The moment Wolf entered the house his crest fell, his tail drooped to the ground, or curled between his legs, he sneaked about with a gallows air, casting many a sidelong glance at Dame Van Winkle, and at the least flourish of a broomstick or ladle, he would fly to the door with yelping precipitation.

Times grew worse and worse with Rip Van Winkle as years of matrimony rolled on; a tart temper never mellows with age, and a sharp tongue is the only edged tool that grows keener with constant use. For a long while he used to console himself, when driven from home, by frequenting a kind of perpetual club of the sages, philosophers, and other idle personages of the village; which held its sessions on a bench before a small inn, designated by a rubicund portrait of His Majesty George the Third. Here they used to sit in the shade through a long lazy summer's day, talking listlessly over village gossip, or telling endless sleepy stories about nothing. But it would have been worth any statesman's money to have heard the profound discussions that sometimes took place, when by chance an old newspaper fell into their hands from some passing traveller. How solemnly they would listen to the contents, as drawled out by Derrick Van Bummel, the schoolmaster, a dapper learned little man, who was not to be daunted by the most gigantic word in the dictionary; and how sagely they would deliberate upon public events some months after they had taken place.

The opinions of this junto were completely controlled by Nicholas Vedder, a patriarch of the village, and landlord of the inn, at the door of which he took his seat from morning till night, just moving sufficiently to avoid the sun and keep in the shade of a large tree; so that the neighbors could tell the hour by his movements as accurately as by a sun-dial. It is true he was rarely heard to speak, but smoked his pipe incessantly. His adherents, however (for every great man has his adherents), perfectly understood him, and knew how to gather his opinions. When anything that was read or related displeased him, he was observed to smoke his pipe vehemently, and to send forth short, frequent and angry puffs; but when pleased, he would inhale the smoke slowly and tranquilly, and emit it in light and placid clouds; and sometimes, taking the pipe from his mouth, and letting the fragrant vapor curl about his nose, would gravely nod his head in token of perfect approbation.

From even this stronghold the unlucky Rip was at length routed by his termagant wife, who would suddenly break in upon the tranquillity of the assemblage and call the members all to naught; nor was that august personage, Nicholas Vedder himself, sacred from the daring tongue of this terrible virago, who charged him outright with encouraging her husband in habits of idleness.

Poor Rip was at last reduced almost to despair; and his only alternative, to escape from the labor of the farm and clamor of his wife, was to take gun in hand and stroll away into the woods. Here he would sometimes seat himself at the foot of a tree, and share the contents of his wallet with Wolf, with whom he sympathized as a fellow-sufferer in persecution. "Poor Wolf," he would say, "thy mistress leads thee a dog's life of it; but never mind, my lad, whilst I live thou shalt never want a friend to stand by thee!" Wolf would wag his tail, look wistfully in his master's face, and if dogs can feel pity I verily believe he reciprocated the sentiment with all his heart.

In a long ramble of the kind on a fine autumnal day, Rip had unconsciously scrambled to one of the highest parts of the Kaatskill mountains. He was after his favorite sport of squirrel shooting, and the still solitudes had echoed and re-echoed with the reports of his gun. Panting and fatigued, he threw himself, late in the afternoon, on a green knoll, covered with mountain herbage, that crowned the brow of a precipice. From an opening between the trees he could overlook all the lower country for many a mile of rich woodland. He saw at a distance the lordly Hudson, far, far below him, moving on its silent but majestic course, with the reflection of a purple cloud, or the sail of a lagging bark, here and there sleeping on its glassy bosom, and at last losing itself in the blue highlands.

On the other side he looked down into a deep mountain glen, wild, lonely, and shagged, the bottom filled with fragments from the impending cliffs, and scarcely lighted by the reflected rays of the setting sun. For some time Rip lay musing on this scene; evening was gradually advancing; the mountains began to throw their long blue shadows over the valleys; he saw that it would be dark long before he could reach the village, and he heaved a heavy sigh when he thought of encountering the terrors of Dame Van Winkle.

As he was about to descend, he heard a voice from a distance, hallooing, "Rip Van Winkle! Rip Van Winkle!" He looked round, but could see nothing but a crow winging its solitary flight across the mountain. He thought his fancy must have deceived him, and turned again to descend, when he heard the same cry ring through the still evening air; "Rip Van Winkle! Rip Van Winkle!"—at the same time Wolf bristled up his back, and giving a low growl, skulked to his master's side, looking fearfully down into the glen. Rip now felt a vague apprehension stealing over him; he looked anxiously in the same direction, and perceived a strange figure slowly toiling up the rocks, and bending under the weight of something he carried on his back. He was surprised to see any human being in this lonely and unfrequented place, but supposing it to be someone of the neighborhood in need of his assistance, he hastened down to yield it.

On nearer approach he was still more surprised at the singularity of the stranger's appearance. He was a short square-built old fellow, with thick bushy hair, and a grizzled beard. His dress was of the antique Dutch fashion—a cloth jerkin strapped round the waist—several pair of breeches, the outer one of ample volume, decorated with rows of buttons down the sides, and bunches at the knees. He bore on his shoulder a stout keg, that seemed full of liquor, and made signs for Rip to approach and assist him with the load. Though rather shy and distrustful of this new acquaintance, Rip complied with his usual alacrity; and mutually relieving one another, they clambered up a narrow gully, apparently the dry bed of a mountain torrent. As they ascended, Rip every now and then heard long rolling peals, like distant thunder, that seemed to issue out of a deep ravine, or rather cleft, between lofty rocks, toward which their rugged path conducted. He paused for an instant, but supposing it to be the muttering of one of those transient thunder-showers which often take place in mountain heights, he proceeded. Passing through the ravine, they came to a hollow, like a small amphitheater, surrounded by perpendicular precipices, over the brinks of which impending trees shot their branches, so that you only caught glimpses of the azure sky and the bright evening cloud. During the whole time Rip and his companion had labored on in silence; for though the former marvelled greatly what could be the object of carrying a keg of liquor up this wild mountain, yet there was something strange and incomprehensible about the unknown, that inspired awe and checked familiarity.

On entering the amphitheater, new objects of wonder presented themselves. On a level spot in the center was a company of odd-looking personages playing at nine-pins. They were dressed in a quaint outlandish fashion; some wore short doublets, others jerkins, with long knives in their belts, and most of them had enormous breeches, of similar style with that of the guide's. Their visages, too, were peculiar: one had a large beard, broad face, and small piggish eyes: the face of another seemed to consist entirely of nose, and was surmounted by a white sugar-loaf hat set off with a little red cock's tail. They all had beards, of various shapes and colors. There was one who seemed to be the commander. He was a stout old gentleman, with a weather-beaten countenance; he wore a laced doublet, broad belt and hanger, high-crowned hat and feather, red stockings, and high-heeled shoes, with roses in them. The whole group reminded Rip of the figures in an old Flemish painting, in the parlor of Dominie Van Shaick, the village parson, and which had been brought over from Holland at the time of the settlement.

What seemed particularly odd to Rip was, that though these folks were evidently amusing themselves, yet they maintained the gravest faces, the most mysterious silence, and were, withal, the most melancholy party of pleasure he had ever witnessed. Nothing interrupted the stillness of the scene but the noise of the balls, which, whenever they were rolled, echoed along the mountains like rumbling peals of thunder.

As Rip and his companion approached them, they suddenly desisted from their play, and stared at him with such fixed statue-like gaze, and such strange, uncouth, lack-luster countenances, that his heart turned within him, and his knees smote together. His companion now emptied the contents of the keg into large flagons, and made signs to him to wait upon the company. He obeyed with fear and trembling; they quaffed the liquor in profound silence, and then returned to their game.

By degrees Rip's awe and apprehension subsided. He even ventured, when no eye was fixed upon him, to taste the beverage, which he found had much of the flavor of excellent Hollands. He was naturally a thirsty soul, and was soon tempted to repeat the draught. One taste provoked another; and he reiterated his visits to the flagon so often that at length his senses were overpowered, his eyes swam in his head, his head gradually declined, and he fell into a deep sleep.

On waking, he found himself on the green knoll whence he had first seen the old man of the glen. He rubbed his eyes—it was a bright sunny morning. The birds were hopping and twittering among the bushes, and the eagle was wheeling aloft, and breasting the pure mountain breeze. "Surely," thought Rip, "I have not slept here all night." He recalled the occurrences before he fell asleep. The strange man with a keg of liquor—the mountain ravine—the wild retreat among the rocks—the woe-begone party at nine-pins—the flagon—"Oh! that flagon! that wicked flagon!" thought Rip—"what excuse shall I make to Dame Van Winkle!"

He looked round for his gun, but in place of the clean well-oiled fowling-piece, he found an old firelock lying by him, the barrel incrusted with rust, the lock falling off, and the stock worm-eaten. He now suspected that the grave roisters of the mountain had put a trick upon him, and, having dosed him with liquor, had robbed him of his gun. Wolf, too, had disappeared, but he might have strayed away after a squirrel or partridge. He whistled after him and shouted his name, but all in vain; the echoes repeated his whistle and shout, but no dog was to be seen.

He determined to revisit the scene of the last evening's gambol, and if he met with any of the party, to demand his dog and gun. As he rose to walk, he found himself stiff in the joints, and wanting in his usual activity. "These mountain beds do not agree with me," thought Rip, "and if this frolic should lay me up with a fit of the rheumatism, I shall have a blessed time with Dame Van Winkle." With some difficulty he got down into the glen: he found the gully up which he and his companion had ascended the preceding evening; but to his astonishment a mountain stream was now foaming down it, leaping from rock to rock, and filling the glen with babbling murmurs. He, however, made shift to scramble up its sides, working his toilsome way through thickets of birch, sassafras, and witch-hazel, and sometimes tripped up or entangled by the wild grapevines that twisted their coils or tendrils from tree to tree, and spread a kind of network in his path.

At length he reached to where the ravine had opened through the cliffs to the amphitheater; but no traces of such opening remained. The rocks presented a high impenetrable wall over which the torrent came tumbling in a sheet of feathery foam, and fell into a broad deep basin, black from the shadows of the surrounding forest. Here, then, poor Rip was brought to a stand. He again called and whistled after his dog; he was only answered by the cawing of a flock of idle crows, sporting high in air about a dry tree that overhung a sunny precipice; and who, secure in their elevation, seemed to look down and scoff at the poor man's perplexities. What was to be done? The morning was passing away, and Rip felt famished for want of his breakfast. He grieved to give up his dog and gun; he dreaded to meet his wife; but it would not do to starve among the mountains. He shook his head, shouldered the rusty firelock, and, with a heart full of trouble and anxiety, turned his steps homeward.

As he approached the village he met a number of people, but none whom he knew, which somewhat surprised him, for he had thought himself acquainted with everyone in the country round. Their dress, too, was of a different fashion from that to which he was accustomed. They all stared at him with equal marks of surprise, and whenever they cast their eyes upon him, invariably stroked their chins. The constant recurrence of this gesture induced Rip, involuntarily, to do the same, when, to his astonishment, he found his beard had grown a foot long!

He had now entered the skirts of the village. A troop of strange children ran at his heels, hooting after him, and pointing at his gray beard. The dogs, too, not one of which he recognized for an old acquaintance, barked at him as he passed. The very village was altered; it was larger and more populous. There were rows of houses which he had never seen before, and those which had been his familiar haunts had disappeared. Strange names were over the doors—strange faces at the windows—everything was strange. His mind now misgave him; he began to doubt whether both he and the world around him were not bewitched. Surely this was his native village, which he had left but the day before. There stood the Kaatskill mountains—there ran the silver Hudson at a distance—there was every hill and dale precisely as it had always been—Rip was sorely perplexed—"That flagon last night," thought he, "has addled my poor head sadly!"

It was with some difficulty that he found the way to his own house, which he approached with silent awe, expecting every moment to hear the shrill voice of Dame Van Winkle. He found the house gone to decay—the roof fallen in, the windows shattered, and the doors off the hinges. A half-starved dog that looked like Wolf was skulking about it. Rip called him by name, but the cur snarled, showed his teeth, and passed on. This was an unkind cut indeed—"My very dog," sighed poor Rip, "has forgotten me!"

He entered the house, which, to tell the truth, Dame Van Winkle had always kept in neat order. It was empty, forlorn, and apparently abandoned. This desolateness overcame all his connubial fears—he called loudly for his wife and children—the lonely chambers rang for a moment with his voice, and then all again was silence.

He now hurried forth, and hastened to his old resort, the village inn—but it too was gone. A large rickety wooden building stood in its place, with great gaping windows, some of them broken and mended with old hats and petticoats, and over the door was painted, "the Union Hotel, by Jonathan Doolittle." Instead of the great tree that used to shelter the quiet little Dutch inn of yore, there now was reared a tall naked pole, with something on the top that looked like a red night-cap, and from it was fluttering a flag, on which was a singular assemblage of stars and stripes—all this was strange and incomprehensible. He recognized on the sign, however, the ruby face of King George, under which he had smoked so many a peaceful pipe; but even this was singularly metamorphosed. The red coat was changed for one of blue and buff, a sword was held in the hand instead of a scepter, the head was decorated with a cocked hat, and underneath was painted in large characters, GENERAL WASHINGTON.

There was, as usual, a crowd of folk about the door, but none that Rip recollected. The very character of the people seemed changed. There was a busy, bustling, disputatious tone about it, instead of the accustomed phlegm and drowsy tranquillity. He looked in vain for the sage Nicholas Vedder, with his broad face, double chin, and fair long pipe, uttering clouds of tobacco-smoke instead of idle speeches; or Van Bummel, the schoolmaster, doling forth the contents of an ancient newspaper. In place of these, a lean, bilious-looking fellow, with his pockets full of handbills, was haranguing vehemently about rights of citizens—elections—members of congress—liberty—Bunker's Hill—heroes of seventy-six—and other words, which were a perfect Babylonish jargon to the bewildered Van Winkle.

The appearance of Rip, with his long grizzled beard, his rusty fowling-piece, his uncouth dress, and an army of women and children at his heels, soon attracted the attention of the tavern politicians. They crowded round him, eyeing him from head to foot with great curiosity. The orator bustled up to him, and, drawing him partly aside, inquired "on which side he voted?" Rip stared in vacant stupidity. Another short but busy little fellow pulled him by the arm, and, rising on tiptoe, inquired in his ear, "Whether he was Federal or Democrat?" Rip was equally at a loss to comprehend the question; when a knowing, self-important old gentleman, in a sharp cocked hat, made his way through the crowd, putting them to the right and left with his elbows as he passed, and planting himself before Van Winkle, with one arm akimbo, the other resting on his cane, his keen eyes and sharp hat penetrating, as it were, into his very soul, demanded in an austere tone, "what brought him to the election with a gun on his shoulder, and a mob at his heels, and whether he meant to breed a riot in the village?"—"Alas! gentlemen," cried Rip, somewhat dismayed, "I am a poor quiet man, a native of the place, and a loyal subject of the king, God bless him!"

Here a general shout burst from the by-standers—"A tory! a tory! a spy! a refugee! hustle him! away with him!" It was with great difficulty that the self-important man in the cocked hat restored order; and, having assumed a tenfold austerity of brow, demanded again of the unknown culprit, what he came there for, and whom he was seeking? The poor man humbly assured him that he meant no harm, but merely came there in search of some of his neighbors, who used to keep about the tavern.

"Well—who are they?—name them."

Rip bethought himself a moment, and inquired, "Where's Nicholas Vedder?"

There was a silence for a little while, when an old man replied, in a thin piping voice, "Nicholas Vedder! why, he is dead and gone these eighteen years! There was a wooden tombstone in the church-yard that used to tell all about him, but that's rotten and gone too."

"Where's Brom Dutcher?"

"Oh, he went off to the army in the beginning of the war; some say he was killed at the storming of Stony Point—others say he was drowned in a squall at the foot of Antony's Nose. I dont' know—he never came back again."

"Where's Van Bummel, the schoolmaster?"

"He went off to the wars too, was a great militia general, and is now in Congress."

Rip's heart died away at hearing of these sad changes in his home and friends, and finding himself thus alone in the world. Every answer puzzled him too, by treating of such enormous lapses of time, and of matters which he could not understand: war—congress—Stony Point;—he had no courage to ask after any more friends, but cried out in despair, "Does nobody here know Rip Van Winkle?"

"Oh, Rip Van Winkle!" exclaimed two or three, "Oh, to be sure! that's Rip Van Winkle yonder, leaning against the tree."

Rip looked, and beheld a precise counterpart of himself, as he went up the mountain: apparently as lazy, and certainly as ragged. The poor fellow was now completely confounded. He doubted his own identity, and whether he was himself or another man. In the midst of his bewilderment, the man in the cocked hat demanded who he was, and what was his name?

"God knows," exclaimed he, at his wit's end; "I'm not myself—I'm somebody else—that's me yonder—no—that's somebody else got into my shoes—I was myself last night, but I fell asleep on the mountain, and they've changed my gun, and everything's changed, and I'm changed, and I can't tell what's my name, or who I am!"

The by-standers began now to look at each other, nod, wink significantly, and tap their fingers against their foreheads. There was a whisper, also, about securing the gun, and keeping the old fellow from doing mischief, at the very suggestion of which the self-important man in the cocked hat retired with some precipitation. At this critical moment a fresh comely woman pressed through the throng to get a peep at the gray-bearded man. She had a chubby child in her arms, which, frightened at his looks, began to cry. "Hush, Rip," cried she, "hush, you little fool; the old man won't hurt you." The name of the child, the air of the mother, the tone of her voice, all awakened a train of recollections in his mind. "What is your name, my good woman?" asked he.

"Judith Gardenier."

"And your father's name?"

"Ah, poor man, Rip Van Winkle was his name, but it's twenty years since he went away from home with his gun, and never has been heard of since—his dog came home without him; but whether he shot himself, or was carried away by the Indians, nobody can tell. I was then but a little girl."

Rip had but one question more to ask; but he put it with a faltering voice: "Where's your mother?"

"Oh, she too had died but a short time since; she broke a blood-vessel in a fit of passion at a New England peddler."

There was a drop of comfort, at least, in this intelligence. The honest man could contain himself no longer. He caught his daughter and her child in his arms. "I am your father!" cried he—"Young Rip Van Winkle once—old Rip Van Winkle now!—Does nobody know poor Rip Van Winkle?"

All stood amazed, until an old woman, tottering out from among the crowd, put her hand to her brow, and peering under it in his face for a moment, exclaimed, "Sure enough! it is Rip Van Winkle—it is himself! Welcome home again, old neighbor—Why, where have you been these twenty long years?"

Rip's story was soon told, for the whole twenty years had been to him but as one night. The neighbors stared when they heard it; some were seen to wink at each other, and put their tongues in their cheeks: and the self-important man in the cocked hat, who, when the alarm was over, had returned to the field, screwed down the corners of his mouth, and shook his head—upon which there was a general shaking of the head throughout the assemblage.

It was determined, however, to take the opinion of old Peter Vanderdonk, who was seen slowly advancing up the road. He was a descendant of the historian of that name, who wrote one of the earliest accounts of the province. Peter was the most ancient inhabitant of the village, and well versed in all the wonderful events and traditions of the neighborhood. He recollected Rip at once, and corroborated his story in the most satisfactory manner. He assured the company that it was a fact, handed down from his ancestor the historian, that the Kaatskill mountains had always been haunted by strange beings. That it was affirmed that the great Hendrick Hudson, the first discoverer of the river and country, kept a kind of vigil there every twenty years, with his crew of the Half-moon; being permitted in this way to revisit the scenes of his enterprise, and keep a guardian eye upon the river, and the great city called by his name. That his father had once seen them in their old Dutch dresses playing at nine-pins in a hollow of the mountain; and that he himself had heard, one summer afternoon, the sound of their balls, like distant peals of thunder.

To make a long story short, the company broke up, and returned to the more important concerns of the election. Rip's daughter took him home to live with her; she had a snug, well-furnished house, and a stout cheery farmer for a husband, whom Rip recollected for one of the urchins that used to climb upon his back. As to Rip's son and heir, who was the ditto of himself, seen leaning against the tree, he was employed to work on the farm; but evinced an hereditary disposition to attend to anything else but his business.

Rip now resumed his old walks and habits; he soon found many of his former cronies, though all rather the worse for the wear and tear of time; and preferred making friends among the rising generation, with whom he soon grew into great favor.

Having nothing to do at home, and being arrived at that happy age when a man can be idle with impunity, he took his place once more on the bench at the inn door, and was reverenced as one of the patriarchs of the village, and a chronicle of the old times "before the war." It was some time before he could get into the regular track of gossip, or could be made to comprehend the strange events that had taken place during his torpor. How that there had been a revolutionary war—that the country had thrown off the yoke of old England—and that, instead of being subject of his Majesty George the Third, he was now a free citizen of the United States. Rip, in fact, was no politician; the changes of states and empires made but little impression on him; but there was one species of despotism under which he had long groaned, and that was—petticoat government. Happily that was at an end; he had got his neck out of the yoke of matrimony, and could go in and out whenever he pleased, without dreading the tyranny of Dame Van Winkle. Whenever her name was mentioned, however, he shook his head, shrugged his shoulders, and cast up his eyes; which might pass either for an expression of resignation to his fate, or joy at his deliverance.

He used to tell his story to every stranger that arrived at Mr. Doolittle's hotel. He was observed, at first, to vary on some points every time he told it, which was, doubtless, owing to his having so recently awaked. It at last settled down precisely to the tale I have related, and not a man, woman, or child in the neighborhood, but knew it by heart. Some always pretended to doubt the reality of it, and insisted that Rip had been out of his head, and that this was one point on which he always remained flighty. The old Dutch inhabitants, however, almost universally gave it full credit. Even to this day they never hear a thunderstorm of a summer afternoon about the Kaatskill, but they say Hendrick Hudson and his crew are at their game of nine-pins; and it is a common wish of all hen-pecked husbands in the neighborhood, when life hangs heavy on their hands, that they might have a quieting draught out of Rip Van Winkle's flagon.

NOTE.

The foregoing Tale, one would suspect, had been suggested to Mr. Knicker-bocker by a little German superstition about the Emperor Frederick *der Rothbart,* and the Kypphaüser mountain: the subjoined note, however, which he had appended to the tale, shows that it is an absolute fact, narrated with his usual fidelity:

"The story of Rip Van Winkle may seem incredible to many, but neverthe-less I give it my full belief, for I know the vicinity of our old Dutch settle-ments to have been very subject to marvellous events and appearances. Indeed, I have heard many stranger stories than this, in the villages along the Hudson; all of which were too well authenticated to admit of a doubt. I have even talked with Rip Van Winkle myself, who, when last I saw him, was a very venerable old man, and so perfectly rational and consistent on every other point, that I think no conscientious person could refuse to take this into the bargain; nay, I have seen a certificate on the subject taken before a country justice and signed with a cross, in the justice's own handwriting. The story, therefore, is beyond the possibility of doubt.

D.K."

POSTSCRIPT.

The following are travelling notes from a memorandum-book of Mr. Knickerbocker:

The Kaatsberg, or Catskill mountains, have always been a region full of fable. The Indians considered them the abode of spirits, who influenced the weather, spreading sunshine or clouds over the landscape, and sending good or bad hunting seasons. They were ruled by an old squaw spirit, said to be their mother. She dwelt on the highest peak of the Catskills, and had charge of the doors of day and night to open and shut them at the proper hour. She hung up the new moons in the skies, and cut up the old ones into stars. In times of drought, if properly propitiated, she would spin light summer clouds out of cobwebs and morning dew, and send them off from the crest of the mountain, flake after flake, like flakes of carded cotton, to float in the air; until, dissolved by the heat of the sun, they would fall in gentle showers, causing the grass to spring, the fruits to ripen, and the corn to grow an inch an hour. If displeased, however, she would brew up clouds black as ink, sitting in the midst of them like a bottle-bellied spider in the midst of its web; and when these clouds broke, woe betide the valleys!

In old times, say the Indian traditions, there was a kind of Manitou or Spirit, who kept about the wildest recesses of the Catskill Mountains, and took a mischievous pleasure in wreaking all kinds of evils and vexations upon the red men. Sometimes he would assume the form of a bear, a panther, or a deer, lead the bewildered hunter a weary chase through tangled forests and among ragged rocks; and then spring off with a loud ho! ho! leaving him aghast on the brink of a beetling precipice or raging torrent.

The favorite abode of this Manitou is still shown. It is a great rock or cliff on the loneliest part of the mountains, and, from the flowering vines which clamber about it, and the wild flowers which abound in its neighborhood, is known by the name of the Garden Rock. Near the foot of it is a small lake, the haunt of the solitary bittern, with water-snakes basking in the sun on the leaves of the pond-lilies which lie on the surface. This place was held in great awe by the Indians, insomuch that the boldest hunter would not pursue his game within its precincts. Once upon a time, however, a hunter who had lost his way, penetrated to the garden rock, where he beheld a number of gourds placed in the crotches of trees. One of these he seized and made off with it, but in the hurry of his retreat he let it fall among the rocks, when a great stream gushed forth, which washed him away and swept him down precipices, where he was dashed to pieces, and the stream made its way to the Hudson, and continues to flow to the present day; being the identical stream known by the name of the Kaaters-kill.

The Legend of Sleepy Hollow.

FOUND AMONG THE PAPERS OF THE LATE DIEDRICH KNICKERBOCKER.

> *A pleasing land of drowsy head it was,*
> *Of dreams that wave before the half-shut eye;*
> *And of gay castles in the clouds that pass,*
> *For ever flushing round a summer sky.*
> Castle of Indolence.[1]

In the bosom of one of those spacious coves which indent the eastern shore of the Hudson, at that broad expansion of the river denominated by the ancient Dutch navigators the Tappan Zee, and where they always prudently shortened sail, and implored the protection of St. Nicholas when they crossed, there lies a small market-town or rural port, which by some is called Greensburgh, but which is more generally and properly known by the name of Tarry Town.[2] This name was given, we are told, in former days, by the good housewives of the adjacent country, from the inveterate propensity of their husbands to linger about the village tavern on market days. Be that as it may, I do not vouch for the fact, but merely advert to it, for the sake of being precise and authentic. Not far from this village, perhaps about two miles, there is a little valley, or rather lap of land, among high hills, which is one of the quietest places in the whole world. A small brook glides through it, with just murmur enough to lull one to repose; and the occasional whistle of a quail, or tapping of a woodpecker, is almost the only sound that ever breaks in upon the uniform tranquillity.

I recollect that, when a stripling, my first exploit in squirrel-shooting was in a grove of tall walnut trees that shades one side of the valley. I had wandered into it at noon time, when all nature is peculiarly quiet, and was startled by the roar of my own gun, as it broke the Sabbath stillness around, and was prolonged and reverberated by the angry echoes. If ever I should wish for a retreat, whither I might steal from the world and its distractions, and dream quietly away the remnant of a troubled life, I know of none more promising than this little valley.

From the listless repose of the place, and the peculiar character of its inhabitants, who are descendants from the original Dutch settlers, this sequestered glen has long been known by the name of SLEEPY HOLLOW, and its rustic lads are called the Sleepy Hollow Boys throughout all the neighboring

[1] A poem by James Thomson (1700–1748).
[2] Irving lived in this old Dutch village in his last 25 years, and his grave is at Sleepy Hollow.

country. A drowsy, dreamy influence seems to hang over the land, and to pervade the very atmosphere. Some say that the place was bewitched by a high German[3] doctor, during the early days of the settlement; others, that an old Indian chief, the prophet or wizard of his tribe, held his pow-wows there before the country was discovered by Master Hendrick Hudson. Certain it is, the place still continues under the sway of some witching power, that holds a spell over the minds of the good people, causing them to walk in a continual reverie. They are given to all kinds of marvellous beliefs; are subject to trances and visions; and frequently see strange sights, and hear music and voices in the air. The whole neighborhood abounds with local tales, haunted spots, and twilight superstitions; stars shoot and meteors glare oftener across the valley than in any other part of the country, and the nightmare,[4] with her whole nine fold, seems to make it the favorite scene of her gambols.

The dominant spirit, however, that haunts this enchanted region, and seems to be commander-in-chief of all the powers of the air, is the apparition of a figure on horseback without a head. It is said by some to be the ghost of a Hessian trooper,[5] whose head had been carried away by a cannon-ball, in some nameless battle during the revolutionary war; and who is ever and anon seen by the country folk, hurrying along in the gloom of night, as if on the wings of the wind. His haunts are not confined to the valley, but extend at times to the adjacent roads, and especially to the vicinity of a church at no great distance. Indeed, certain of the most authentic historians of those parts, who have been careful in collecting and collating the floating facts concerning this specter, allege that the body of the trooper, having been buried in the church-yard, the ghost rides forth to the scene of battle in nightly quest of his head; and that the rushing speed with which he sometimes passes along the Hollow, like a midnight blast, is owing to his being belated, and in a hurry to get back to the church-yard before daybreak.

Such is the general purport of this legendary superstition, which has furnished materials for many a wild story in that region of shadows; and the specter is known, at all the country firesides, by the name of the Headless Horseman of Sleepy Hollow.

It is remarkable that the visionary propensity I have mentioned is not confined to the native inhabitants of the valley, but is unconsciously imbibed by everyone who resides there for a time. However wide awake they may have been before they entered that sleepy region, they are sure, in a little time, to inhale the witching influence of the air, and begin to grow imaginative—to dream dreams, and see apparitions.

---

[3] That is, from the German highlands.
[4] Personified as a female succubus or demon. The reference is to her nine familiars.

[5] Hessian soldiers were hired by the British government to help put down the rebellion of 1775.

I mention this peaceful spot with all possible laud; for it is in such little retired Dutch valleys, found here and there embosomed in the great State of New York, that population, manners, and customs, remain fixed; while the great torrent of migration and improvement, which is making such incessant changes in other parts of this restless country, sweeps by them unobserved. They are like those little nooks of still water which border a rapid stream; where we may see the straw and bubble riding quietly at anchor, or slowly revolving in their mimic harbor, undisturbed by the rush of the passing current. Though many years have elapsed since I trod the drowsy shades of Sleepy Hollow, yet I question whether I should not still find the same trees and the same families vegetating in its sheltered bosom.

In this by-place of nature, there abode, in a remote period of American history, that is to say, some thirty years since, a worthy wight of the name of Ichabod Crane; who sojourned, or, as he expressed it, "tarried," in Sleepy Hollow, for the purpose of instructing the children of the vicinity. He was a native of Connecticut; a state which supplies the Union with pioneers for the mind as well as for the forest, and sends forth yearly its legions of frontier woodsmen and country schoolmasters. The cognomen of Crane was not inapplicable to his person. He was tall, but exceedingly lank, with narrow shoulders, long arms and legs, hands that dangled a mile out of his sleeves, feet that might have served for shovels, and his whole frame most loosely hung together. His head was small, and flat at top, with huge ears, large green glassy eyes, and a long snipe nose, so that it looked like a weather-cock, perched upon his spindle neck, to tell which way the wind blew. To see him striding along the profile of a hill on a windy day, with his clothes bagging and fluttering about him, one might have mistaken him for the ge-nius of famine descending upon the earth, or some scarecrow eloped from a cornfield.

His school-house was a low building of one large room, rudely con-structed of logs; the windows partly glazed, and partly patched with leaves of old copy-books. It was most ingeniously secured at vacant hours, by a withe twisted in the handle of the door, and stakes set against the window shutters; so that, though a thief might get in with perfect ease, he would find some embarrassment in getting out; an idea most probably borrowed by the architect, Yost Van Houten, from the mystery of an eel-pot. The school-house stood in a rather lonely but pleasant situation, just at the foot of a woody hill, with a brook running close by, and a formidable birch tree growing at one end of it. From hence the low murmur of his pupils' voices, conning over their lessons, might be heard in a drowsy summer's day, like the hum of a beehive; interrupted now and then by the authoritative voice of the master, in the tone of menace or command; or, peradventure, by the appalling sound of the birch, as he urged some tardy loiterer along the flowery path of knowledge. Truth to say, he was a conscientious man, and

ever bore in mind the golden maxim, "Spare the rod and spoil the child."—
Ichabod Crane's scholars certainly were not spoiled.

I would not have it imagined, however, that he was one of those cruel
potentates of the school, who joy in the smart of their subjects; on the
contrary, he administered justice with discrimination rather than severity;
taking the burden off the backs of the weak, and laying it on those of the
strong. Your mere puny stripling, that winced at the least flourish of the rod,
was passed by with indulgence; but the claims of justice were satisfied by
inflicting a double portion on some little, tough, wrong-headed, broad-
skirted Dutch urchin, who sulked and swelled and grew dogged and sullen
beneath the birch. All this he called "doing his duty by their parents"; and
he never inflicted a chastisement without following it by the assurance, so
consolatory to the smarting urchin, that "he would remember it, and thank
him for it the longest day he had to live."

When school hours were over, he was even the companion and playmate
of the larger boys; and on holiday afternoons would convoy some of the
smaller ones home, who happened to have pretty sisters, or good housewives
for mothers, noted for the comforts of the cupboard. Indeed it behooved
him to keep on good terms with his pupils. The revenue arising from his
school was small, and would have been scarcely sufficient to furnish him
with daily bread, for he was a huge feeder, and though lank, had the dilating
powers of an anaconda; but to help out his maintenance, he was, according
to country custom in those parts, boarded and lodged at the houses of the
farmers, whose children he instructed. With these he lived successively a
week at a time; thus going the rounds of the neighborhood, with all his
worldly effects tied up in a cotton handkerchief.

That all this might not be too onerous on the purses of his rustic patrons,
who are apt to consider the costs of schooling a grievous burden, and schoolmasters as mere drones, he had various ways of rendering himself both useful
and agreeable. He assisted the farmers occasionally in the lighter labors of
their farms; helped to make hay; mended the fences; took the horses to
water; drove the cows from pasture; and cut wood for the winter fire. He
laid aside, too, all the dominant dignity and absolute sway with which he
lorded it in his little empire, the school, and became wonderfully gentle and
ingratiating. He found favor in the eyes of the mothers, by petting the children, particularly the youngest; and like the lion bold, which whilom so
magnanimously the lamb did hold, he would sit with a child on one knee,
and rock a cradle with his foot for whole hours together.

In addition to his other vocations, he was the singing-master of the neighborhood, and picked up many bright shillings by instructing the young folks
in psalmody. It was a matter of no little vanity to him, on Sundays, to take his
station in front of the church gallery, with a band of chosen singers; where,
in his own mind, he completely carried away the palm from the parson.
Certain it is, his voice resounded far above all the rest of the congregation;

and there are peculiar quavers still to be heard in that church, and which may even be heard half a mile off, quite to the opposite side of the mill-pond, on a still Sunday morning, which are said to be legitimately descended from the nose of Ichabod Crane. Thus, by divers little make-shifts in that ingenious way which is commonly denominated "by hook and by crook," the worthy pedagogue got on tolerably enough, and was thought, by all who understood nothing of the labor of headwork, to have a wonderfully easy life of it.

The schoolmaster is generally a man of some importance in the female circle of a rural neighborhood; being considered a kind of idle gentlemanlike personage, of vastly superior taste and accomplishments to the rough country swains, and, indeed, inferior in learning only to the parson. His appearance, therefore, is apt to occasion some little stir at the tea-table of a farmhouse, and the addition of a supernumerary dish of cakes or sweetmeats, or, peradventure, the parade of a silver tea-pot. Our man of letters, therefore, was peculiarly happy in the smiles of all the country damsels. How he would figure among them in the church-yard, between services on Sundays! gathering grapes for them from the wild vines that overrun the surrounding trees; reciting for their amusement all the epitaphs on the tombstones; or sauntering, with a whole bevy of them, along the banks of the adjacent mill-pond; while the more bashful country bumpkins hung sheepishly back, envying his superior elegance and address.

From his half itinerant life, also, he was a kind of travelling gazette, carrying the whole budget of local gossip from house to house; so that his appearance was always greeted with satisfaction. He was, moreover, esteemed by the women as a man of great erudition, for he had read several books quite through, and was a perfect master of Cotton Mather's history of New England Witchcraft,[6] in which, by the way, he most firmly and potently believed.

He was, in fact, an odd mixture of small shrewdness and simple credulity. His appetite for the marvellous, and his powers of digesting it, were equally extraordinary; and both had been increased by his residence in this spell-bound region. No tale was too gross or monstrous for his capacious swallow. It was often his delight, after his school was dismissed in the afternoon, to stretch himself on the rich bed of clover, bordering the little brook that whimpered by his school-house, and there con over old Mather's direful tales, until the gathering dusk of the evening made the printed page a mere mist before his eyes. Then, as he wended his way, by swamp and stream and awful woodland, to the farmhouse where he happened to be quartered, every sound of nature, at that witching hour, fluttered his excited imagina-

---

[6] Probably the reference is *The Wonders of the Invisible World* (London, 1693), but of course Mather wrote of New England witchcraft trials in at least two other works, the biography of Phips (see above, pp. 271-281) and *Late Memorable Providences* (Boston, 1689).

tion: the moan of the whip-poor-will° from the hill-side; the boding cry of the tree-toad, that harbinger of storm; the dreary hooting of the screech-owl, or the sudden rustling in the thicket of birds frightened from their roost. The fire-flies, too, which sparkled most vividly in the darkest places, now and then startled him, as one of uncommon brightness would stream across his path; and if, by chance, a huge blockhead of a beetle came winging his blundering flight against him, the poor varlet was ready to give up the ghost, with the idea that he was struck with a witch's token. His only resource on such occasions, either to drown thought, or drive away evil spirits, was to sing psalm tunes;—and the good people of Sleepy Hollow, as they sat by their doors of an evening, were often filled with awe, at hearing his nasal melody, "in linked sweetness long drawn out,"[7] floating from the distant hill, or along the dusky road.

Another of his sources of fearful pleasure was, to pass long winter evenings with the old Dutch wives, as they sat spinning by the fire, with a row of apples roasting and spluttering along the hearth, and listen to their marvellous tales of ghosts and goblins, and haunted fields, and haunted brooks, and haunted bridges, and haunted houses, and particularly of the headless horseman, or galloping Hessian of the Hollow, as they sometimes called him. He would delight them equally by his anecdotes of witchcraft, and of the direful omens and portentous sights and sounds in the air, which prevailed in the earlier times of Connecticut; and would frighten them woefully with speculations upon comets and shooting stars; and with the alarming fact that the world did absolutely turn round, and that they were half the time topsy-turvy!

But if there was a pleasure in all this, while snugly cuddling in the chimney corner of a chamber that was all of a ruddy glow from the crackling wood fire, and where, of course, no specter dared to show his face, it was dearly purchased by the terrors of his subsequent walk homewards. What fearful shapes and shadows beset his path amidst the dim and ghastly glare of a snowy night!—With what wistful look did he eye every trembling ray of light streaming across the waste fields from some distant window!—How often was he appalled by some shrub covered with snow, which, like a sheeted specter, beset his very path!—How often did he shrink with curdling awe at the sound of his own steps on the frosty crust beneath his feet; and dread to look over his shoulder, lest he should behold some uncouth being tramping close behind him!—and how often was he thrown into complete dismay by some rushing blast, howling among the trees, in the idea that it was the Galloping Hessian on one of his nightly scourings!

All these, however, were mere terrors of the night, phantoms of the mind

---

° The whip-poor-will is a bird which is only heard at night. It receives its name from its note, which is thought to resemble those words.

[7] Quoted from John Milton, "L'Allegro."

that walk in darkness; and though he had seen many specters in his time, and been more than once beset by Satan in divers shapes, in his lonely perambulations, yet daylight put an end to all these evils; and he would have passed a pleasant life of it, in despite of the Devil and all his works, if his path had not been crossed by a being that causes more perplexity to mortal man than ghosts, goblins, and the whole race of witches put together, and that was— a woman.

Among the musical disciples who assembled, one evening in each week, to receive his instructions in psalmody, was Katrina Van Tassel, the daughter and only child of a substantial Dutch farmer. She was a blooming lass of fresh eighteen; plump as a partridge; ripe and melting and rosy cheeked as one of her father's peaches, and universally famed, not merely for her beauty, but her vast expectations. She was withal a little of a coquette, as might be perceived even in her dress, which was a mixture of ancient and modern fashions, as most suited to set off her charms. She wore the ornaments of pure yellow gold, which her great-great-grandmother had brought over from Saardam; the tempting stomacher of the olden time; and withal a provokingly short petticoat, to display the prettiest foot and ankle in the country round.

Ichabod Crane had a soft and foolish heart towards the sex; and it is not to be wondered at, that so tempting a morsel soon found favor in his eyes; more especially after he had visited her in her paternal mansion. Old Baltus Van Tassel was a perfect picture of a thriving, contented, liberal-hearted farmer. He seldom, it is true, sent either his eyes or his thoughts beyond the boundaries of his own farm; but within those everything was snug, happy, and well-conditioned. He was satisfied with his wealth, but not proud of it; and piqued himself upon the hearty abundance, rather than the style in which he lived. His stronghold was situated on the banks of the Hudson, in one of those green sheltered, fertile nooks, in which the Dutch farmers are so fond of nestling. A great elm tree spread its broad branches over it; at the foot of which bubbled up a spring of the softest and sweetest water, in a little well, formed of a barrel; and then stole sparkling away through the grass, to a neighboring brook, that bubbled along among alders and dwarf willows. Hard by the farmhouse was a vast barn, that might have served for a church; every window and crevice of which seemed bursting forth with the treasures of the farm; the flail was busily resounding within it from morning to night; swallows and martins skimmed twittering about the eaves; and rows of pigeons, some with one eye turned up, as if watching the weather, some with their heads under their wings, or buried in their bosoms, and others swelling, and cooing, and bowing about their dames, were enjoying the sunshine on the roof. Sleek unwieldy porkers were grunting in the repose and abundance of their pens; whence sallied forth, now and then, troops of sucking pigs, as if to snuff the air. A stately squadron of snowy geese were riding in an adjoining pond, convoying whole fleets of ducks; regiments of turkeys were gobbling through the farmyard, and guinea fowls fretting about it, like ill-tempered housewives, with their peevish discontented cry. Before the barn door strutted the gallant cock, that pattern of a husband, a warrior, and a fine gentleman, clapping his burnished wings, and crowing in the pride and gladness of his heart—sometimes tearing up the earth with his feet, and then generously calling his ever-hungry family of wives and children to enjoy the rich morsel which he had discovered.

The pedagogue's mouth watered, as he looked upon this sumptuous promise of luxurious winter fare. In his devouring mind's eye, he pictured to himself every roasting-pig running about with a pudding in his belly, and an apple in his mouth; the pigeons were snugly put to bed in a comfortable pie, and tucked in with a coverlet of crust; the geese were swimming in their own gravy; and the ducks pairing cosily in dishes, like snug married couples, with a decent competency of onion sauce. In the porkers he saw carved out the future sleek side of bacon, and juicy relishing ham; not a turkey but he beheld daintily trussed up, with its gizzard under its wing, and, peradventure, a necklace of savory sausages; and even bright chanticleer himself lay sprawling on his back, in a side-dish, with uplifted claws, as if craving that quarter which his chivalrous spirit disdained to ask while living.

As the enraptured Ichabod fancied all this, and as he rolled his great green eyes over the fat meadow-lands, the rich fields of wheat, of rye, of buckwheat, and Indian corn, and the orchards burdened with ruddy fruit, which surrounded the warm tenement of Van Tassel, his heart yearned after the damsel who was to inherit these domains, and his imagination expanded with the idea, how they might be readily turned into cash, and the money invested in immense tracts of wild land, and shingle palaces in the wilderness. Nay, his busy fancy already realized his hopes, and presented to him the blooming Katrina, with a whole family of children, mounted on the top of a wagon loaded with household trumpery, with pots and kettles dangling beneath; and he beheld himself bestriding a pacing mare, with a colt at her heels, setting out for Kentucky, Tennessee, or the Lord knows where.

When he entered the house the conquest of his heart was complete. It was one of those spacious farmhouses, with high-ridged, but lowly-sloping roofs, built in the style handed down from the first Dutch settlers; the low projecting eaves forming a piazza along the front, capable of being closed up in bad weather. Under this were hung flails, harness, various utensils of husbandry, and nets for fishing in the neighboring river. Benches were built along the sides for summer use; and a great spinning-wheel at one end, and a churn at the other, showed the various uses to which this important porch might be devoted. From this piazza the wondering Ichabod entered the hall, which formed the center of the mansion and the place of usual residence. Here, rows of resplendent pewter, ranged on a long dresser, dazzled his eyes. In one corner stood a huge bag of wool ready to be spun; in another a quantity of linsey-woolsey just from the loom; ears of Indian corn, and strings of dried apples and peaches, hung in gay festoons along the walls, mingled with the gaud of red peppers; and a door left ajar gave him a peep into the best parlor, where the claw-footed chairs, and dark mahogany tables, shone like mirrors; andirons, with their accompanying shovel and tongs, glistened from their covert of asparagus tops; mock-oranges and conch-shells decorated the mantelpiece; strings of various colored birds' eggs were suspended above it: a great ostrich egg was hung from the center of the room, and a corner cupboard, knowingly left open, displayed immense treasures of old silver and well-mended china.

From the moment Ichabod laid his eyes upon these regions of delight, the peace of his mind was at an end, and his only study was how to gain the affections of the peerless daughter of Van Tassel. In this enterprise, however, he had more real difficulties than generally fell to the lot of a knight-errant of yore, who seldom had anything but giants, enchanters, fiery dragons, and such like easily-conquered adversaries, to contend with; and had to make his way merely through gates of iron and brass, and walls of adamant, to the castle keep, where the lady of his heart was confined; all which he achieved as easily as a man would carve his way to the center of a Christmas pie; and then the lady gave him her hand as a matter of course. Ichabod, on the contrary, had to win his way to the heart of a country coquette, beset with a labyrinth of whims and caprices, which were forever presenting new difficulties and impediments; and he had to encounter a host of fearful adversaries of real flesh and blood, the numerous rustic admirers, who beset every portal to her heart; keeping a watchful and angry eye upon each other, but ready to fly out in the common cause against any new competitor.

Among these the most formidable was a burly, roaring, roistering blade, of the name of Abraham, or, according to the Dutch abbreviation, Brom Van Brunt, the hero of the country round, which rang with his feats of strength and hardihood. He was broad-shouldered and double-jointed, with short curly black hair, and a bluff, but not unpleasant countenance, having a mingled air of fun and arrogance. From his Herculean frame and great powers of limb, he had received the nickname of BROM BONES, by which he was universally known. He was famed for great knowledge and skill in horsemanship, being as dexterous on horseback as a Tartar. He was foremost at all races and cock-fights; and, with the ascendancy which bodily strength acquires in rustic life, was the umpire in all disputes, setting his hat on one side, and giving his decisions with an air and tone admitting of no gainsay or appeal. He was always ready for either a fight or a frolic; but had more mischief than ill-will in his composition; and, with all his overbearing roughness, there was a strong dash of waggish good humor at bottom. He had three or four boon companions, who regarded him as their model, and at the head of whom he scoured the country, attending every scene of feud or merriment for miles round. In cold weather he was distinguished by a fur cap, surmounted with a flaunting fox's tail; and when the folks at a country gathering descried this well-known crest at a distance, whisking about among a squad of hard riders, they always stood by for a squall. Sometimes his crew would be heard dashing along past the farmhouses at midnight, with whoop and halloo, like a troop of Don Cossacks;[8] and the old dames, startled out of their sleep, would listen for a moment till the hurry-scurry had clattered by, and then exclaim, "Ay, there goes Brom Bones and his gang!" The neighbors looked upon him with a mixture of awe, admiration, and good will; and when any madcap prank, or rustic brawl, occurred in the vicinity, always shook their heads, and warranted Brom Bones was at the bottom of it.

This rantipole hero had for some time singled out the blooming Katrina for the object of his uncouth gallantries, and though his amorous toyings were something like the gentle caresses and endearments of a bear, yet it was whispered that she did not altogether discourage his hopes. Certain it is, his advances were signals for rival candidates to retire, who felt no inclination to cross a lion in his amours; insomuch, that when his horse was seen tied to Van Tassel's paling, on a Sunday night, a sure sign that his master was courting, or, as it is termed, "sparking," within, all other suitors passed by in despair, and carried the war into other quarters.

Such was the formidable rival with whom Ichabod Crane had to contend, and, considering all things, a stouter man than he would have shrunk from the competition, and a wiser man would have despaired. He had, however, a happy mixture of pliability and perseverance in his nature; he was in form and spirit like a supple-jack—yielding, but tough; though he bent, he never broke; and though he bowed beneath the slightest pressure, yet, the moment it was away—jerk! he was as erect, and carried his head as high as ever.

To have taken the field openly against his rival would have been madness; for he was not a man to be thwarted in his amours, any more than that stormy lover, Achilles.[9] Ichabod, therefore, made his advances in a quiet and gently-insinuating manner. Under cover of his character of singing-master, he made frequent visits at the farmhouse; not that he had anything to apprehend from the meddlesome interference of parents, which is so often a stumbling-block in the path of lovers. Balt Van Tassel was an easy indulgent soul; he loved his daughter better even than his pipe, and, like a reasonable man and an excellent father, let her have her way in everything. His notable little wife, too, had enough to do to attend to her housekeeping and manage her poultry; for, as she sagely observed, ducks and geese are foolish things, and must be looked after, but girls can take care of themselves. Thus while the busy dame bustled about the house, or plied her spinning-wheel at one

---

[8] That is, horsemen along the Don River in Russia.

[9] Achilles, the Greek hero, was killed before he could marry the daughter of Priam, King of Troy, but he persisted in his suit after his death, and in response the victorious Greeks killed her so that she could join him.

end of the piazza, honest Balt would sit smoking his evening pipe at the other, watching the achievements of a little wooden warrior, who, armed with a sword in each hand, was most valiantly fighting the wind on the pinnacle of the barn. In the meantime, Ichabod would carry on his suit with the daughter by the side of the spring under the great elm, or sauntering along in the twilight, that hour so favorable to the lover's eloquence.

I profess not to know how women's hearts are wooed and won. To me they have always been matters of riddle and admiration. Some seem to have but one vulnerable point, or door of access; while others have a thousand avenues, and may be captured in a thousand different ways. It is a great triumph of skill to gain the former, but a still greater proof of generalship to maintain possession of the latter, for the man must battle for his fortress at every door and window. He who wins a thousand common hearts is therefore entitled to some renown; but he who keeps undisputed sway over the heart of a coquette, is indeed a hero. Certain it is, this was not the case with the redoubtable Brom Bones; and from the moment Ichabod Crane made his advances, the interests of the former evidently declined; his horse was no longer seen tied at the palings on Sunday nights, and a deadly feud gradually arose between him and the preceptor of Sleepy Hollow.

Brom, who had a degree of rough chivalry in his nature, would fain have carried matters to open warfare, and have settled their pretensions to the lady, according to the mode of those most concise and simple reasoners, the knights-errant of yore—by single combat; but Ichabod was too conscious of the superior might of his adversary to enter the lists against him: he had overheard a boast of Bones, that he would "double the schoolmaster up, and lay him on a shelf of his own school-house"; and he was too wary to give him an opportunity. There was something extremely provoking in this obstinately pacific system; it left Brom no alternative but to draw upon the funds of rustic waggery in his disposition, and to play off boorish practical jokes upon his rival. Ichabod became the object of whimsical persecution to Bones, and his gang of rough riders. They harried his hitherto peaceful domains; smoked out his singing school, by stopping up the chimney; broke into the school-house at night, in spite of its formidable fastenings of withe and window stakes, and turned everything topsy-turvy: so that the poor schoolmaster began to think all the witches in the country held their meetings there. But what was still more annoying, Brom took all opportunities of turning him into ridicule in presence of his mistress, and had a scoundrel dog whom he taught to whine in the most ludicrous manner, and introduced as a rival of Ichabod's to instruct her in psalmody.

In this way matters went on for some time, without producing any material effect on the relative situation of the contending powers. On a fine autumnal afternoon, Ichabod, in pensive mood, sat enthroned on the lofty stool whence he usually watched all the concerns of his little literary realm. In his hand he swayed a ferule, that scepter of despotic power; the birch of justice reposed on three nails, behind the throne, a constant terror to evil doers; while on the desk before him might be seen sundry contraband articles and prohibited weapons, detected upon the persons of idle urchins; such as half-munched apples, popguns, whirligigs, fly-cages, and whole legions of rampant little paper game-cocks. Apparently there had been some appalling act of justice recently inflicted, for his scholars were all busily intent upon their books, or slyly whispering behind them with one eye kept upon the master; and a kind of buzzing stillness reigned throughout the school-room. It was suddenly interrupted by the appearance of a Negro,[10] in tow-cloth jacket and trousers, a round-crowned fragment of a hat, like the cap of Mercury, and mounted on the back of a ragged, wild, half-broken colt, which he managed with a rope by way of halter. He came clattering up to the school door with an invitation to Ichabod to attend a merry-making or "quilting frolic," to be held that evening at Mynheer Van Tassel's; and having delivered his message with that air of importance, and effort at fine language, which a Negro is apt to display on petty embassies of the kind, he dashed over the brook, and was seen scampering away up the hollow, full of the importance and hurry of his mission.

All was now bustle and hubbub in the late quiet school-room. The scholars were hurried through their lessons, without stopping at trifles; those who were nimble skipped over half with impunity, and those who were tardy, had a smart application now and then in the rear, to quicken their speed, or help them over a tall word. Books were flung aside without being put away on the shelves, inkstands were overturned, benches thrown down, and the whole school was turned loose an hour before the usual time, bursting forth like a legion of young imps, yelping and racketing about the green, in joy at their early emancipation.

The gallant Ichabod now spent at least an extra half hour at his toilet, brushing and furbishing up his best, and indeed only suit of rusty black, and arranging his looks by a bit of broken looking-glass, that hung up in the school-house. That he might make his appearance before his mistress in the true style of a cavalier, he borrowed a horse from the farmer with whom he was domiciliated, a choleric old Dutchman, of the name of Hans Van Ripper, and, thus gallantly mounted, issued forth, like a knight-errant in quest of adventures. But it is meet I should, in the true spirit of romantic story, give some account of the looks and equipments of my hero and his steed. The animal he bestrode was a broken-down plough-horse, that had outlived almost everything but his viciousness. He was gaunt and shagged, with a ewe neck and a head like a hammer; his rusty mane and tail were tangled and knotted with burrs; one eye had lost its pupil, and was glaring and spectral; but the other had the gleam of a genuine devil in it. Still he must have had fire and mettle in his day, if we may judge from the name he bore of Gun-

[10] Here, and again below, Irving's technique of caricature is no more sensitive than Brack-enridge's was to the implications of racial stereotypes.

powder. He had, in fact, been a favorite steed of his master's, the choleric Van Ripper, who was a furious rider, and had infused, very probably, some of his own spirit into the animal; for, old and brokendown as he looked, there was more of the lurking devil in him than in any young filly in the country.

Ichabod was a suitable figure for such a steed. He rode with short stirrups, which brought his knees nearly up to the pommel of the saddle; his sharp elbows stuck out like grasshoppers'; he carried his whip perpendicularly in his hand, like a scepter, and, as his horse jogged on, the motion of his arms was not unlike the flapping of a pair of wings. A small wool hat rested on the top of his nose, for so his scanty strip of forehead might be called; and the skirts of his black coat fluttered out almost to the horse's tail. Such was the appearance of Ichabod and his steed, as they shambled out of the gate of Hans Van Ripper, and it was altogether such an apparition as is seldom to be met with in broad daylight.

It was, as I have said, a fine autumnal day, the sky was clear and serene, and nature wore that rich and golden livery which we always associate with the idea of abundance. The forests had put on their sober brown and yellow, while some trees of the tenderer kind had been nipped by the frosts into brilliant dyes of orange, purple, and scarlet. Streaming files of wild ducks began to make their appearance high in the air; the bark of the squirrel might be heard from the groves of beech and hickory nuts, and the pensive whistle of the quail at intervals from the neighboring stubble-field.

The small birds were taking their farewell banquets. In the fullness of their revelry, they fluttered, chirping and frolicking, from bush to bush, and tree to tree, capricious from the very profusion and variety around them. There was the honest cock-robin, the favorite game of stripling sportsmen, with its loud querulous note; and the twittering blackbirds flying in sable clouds; and the golden-winged woodpecker, with his crimson crest, his broad black gorget, and splendid plumage; and the cedar bird, with its redtipt wings and yellow-tipt tail, and its little monteiro cap of feathers; and the blue-jay, that noisy coxcomb, in his gay light-blue coat and white underclothes; screaming and chattering, nodding and bobbing and bowing, and pretending to be on good terms with every songster of the grove.

As Ichabod jogged slowly on his way, his eye, ever open to every symptom of culinary abundance, ranged with delight over the treasures of jolly autumn. On all sides he beheld vast store of apples; some hanging in oppressive opulence on the trees; some gathered into baskets and barrels for the market; others heaped up in rich piles for the cider-press. Farther on he beheld great fields of Indian corn, with its golden ears peeping from their leafy coverts, and holding out the promise of cakes and hasty pudding; and the yellow pumpkins lying beneath them, turning up their fair round bellies to the sun, and giving ample prospects of the most luxurious of pies; and anon he passed the fragrant buckwheat fields, breathing the odor of the bee-hive, and as he beheld them, soft anticipations stole over his mind of dainty slapjacks, well buttered, and garnished with honey or treacle, by the delicate little dimpled hand of Katrina Van Tassel.

Thus feeding his mind with many sweet thoughts and "sugared supposi-tions," he journeyed along the sides of a range of hills which look out upon some of the goodliest scenes of the mighty Hudson. The sun gradually wheeled his broad disk down into the west. The wide bosom of the Tappan Zee lay motionless and glassy, excepting that here and there a gentle undu-lation waved and prolonged the blue shadow of the distant mountain. A few amber clouds floated in the sky, without a breath of air to move them. The horizon was of a fine golden tint, changing gradually into a pure apple green, and from that into the deep blue of the mid-heaven. A slanting ray lingered on the woody crests of the precipices that overhung some parts of the river, giving greater depth to the dark-gray and purple of their rocky sides. A sloop was loitering in the distance, dropping slowly down with the tide, her sail hanging uselessly against the mast; and as the reflection of the sky gleamed along the still water, it seemed as if the vessel was suspended in the air.

It was toward evening that Ichabod arrived at the castle of the Heer Van Tassel, which he found thronged with the pride and flower of the adjacent country. Old farmers, a spare leathern-faced race, in homespun coats and breeches, blue stockings, huge shoes, and magnificent pewter buckles. Their brisk withered little dames, in close crimped caps, long-waisted short-gowns, homespun petticoats, with scissors and pincushions, and gay calico pockets hanging on the outside. Buxom lasses, almost as antiquated as their mothers, excepting where a straw hat, a fine ribbon, or perhaps a white frock, gave symptoms of city innovation. The sons, in short square-skirted coats with rows of stupendous brass buttons, and their hair generally queued in the fashion of the times, especially if they could procure an eel-skin for the purpose, it being esteemed, throughout the country, as a potent nourisher and strengthener of the hair.

Brom Bones, however, was the hero of the scene, having come to the gathering on his favorite steed Daredevil, a creature, like himself, full of mettle and mischief, and which no one but himself could manage. He was, in fact, noted for preferring vicious animals, given to all kinds of tricks, which kept the rider in constant risk of his neck, for he held a tractable well-broken horse as unworthy of a lad of spirit.

Fain would I pause to dwell upon the world of charms that burst upon the enraptured gaze of my hero, as he entered the state parlor of Van Tas-sel's mansion. Not those of the bevy of buxom lasses, with their luxurious display of red and white; but the ample charms of a genuine Dutch country tea-table, in the sumptuous time of autumn. Such heaped-up platters of cakes of various and almost indescribable kinds, known only to experienced Dutch housewives! There was the doughty doughnut, the tenderer oly koek,[11] and the crisp and crumbling cruller; sweet cakes and short cakes, ginger cakes and honey cakes, and the whole family of cakes. And then there were apple pies and peach pies and pumpkin pies; besides slices of ham and smoked beef; and moreover delectable dishes of preserved plums, and peaches, and pears, and quinces; not to mention broiled shad and roasted chickens; together with bowls of milk and cream, all mingled higgledy-pig-gledy, pretty much as I have enumerated them, with the motherly tea-pot sending up its clouds of vapor from the midst—Heaven bless the mark! I want breath and time to discuss this banquet as it deserves, and am too eager to get on with my story. Happily, Ichabod Crane was not in so great a hurry as his historian, but did ample justice to every dainty.

He was a kind and thankful creature, whose heart dilated in proportion as his skin was filled with good cheer; and whose spirits rose with eating as some men's do with drink. He could not help, too, rolling his large eyes round him as he ate, and chuckling with the possibility that he might one day be lord of all this scene of almost unimaginable luxury and splendor. Then, he thought, how soon he'd turn his back upon the old school-house; snap his fingers in the face of Hans Van Ripper, and every other niggardly patron, and kick any itinerant pedagogue out of doors that should dare to call him comrade!

Old Baltus Van Tassel moved about among his guests with a face dilated with content and good humor, round and jolly as the harvest moon. His hospitable attentions were brief, but expressive, being confined to a shake of the hand, a slap on the shoulder, a loud laugh, and a pressing invitation to "fall to, and help themselves."

And now the sound of the music from the common room, or hall, summoned to the dance. The musician was an old grayheaded Negro, who had been the itinerant orchestra of the neighborhood for more than half a century. His instrument was as old and battered as himself. The greater part of the time he scraped on two or three strings, accompanying every movement of the bow with a motion of the head; bowing almost to the ground, and stamping with his foot whenever a fresh couple were to start.

Ichabod prided himself upon his dancing as much as upon his vocal powers. Not a limb, not a fiber about him was idle; and to have seen his loosely hung frame in full motion, and clattering about the room, you would have thought Saint Vitus himself, that blessed patron of the dance, was figuring before you in person. He was the admiration of all the Negroes; who, having gathered, of all ages and sizes, from the farm and the neighborhood, stood forming a pyramid of shining black faces at every door and window, gazing with delight at the scene, rolling their white eyeballs, and showing grinning rows of ivory from ear to ear. How could the flogger of urchins be otherwise than animated and joyous? The lady of his heart was his partner in the dance,

[11] An oily cake, much like a doughnut.

and smiling graciously in reply to all his amorous oglings; while Brom Bones, sorely smitten with love and jealousy, sat brooding by himself in one corner.

When the dance was at an end, Ichabod was attracted to a knot of the sager folks, who, with old Van Tassel, sat smoking at one end of the piazza, gossiping over former times, and drawing out long stories about the war.

This neighborhood, at the time of which I am speaking, was one of those highly-favored places which abound with chronicle and great men. The British and American line had run near it during the war; it had, therefore, been the scene of marauding, and infested with refugees, cow-boys,[12] and all kinds of border chivalry. Just sufficient time had elapsed to enable each storyteller to dress up his tale with a little becoming fiction, and, in the indistinctness of his recollection, to make himself the hero of every exploit.

There was the story of Doffue Martling, a large blue-bearded Dutchman, who had nearly taken a British frigate with an old iron nine-pounder from a mud breastwork, only that his gun burst at the sixth discharge. And there was an old gentleman who shall be nameless, being too rich a mynheer to be lightly mentioned, who, in the battle of White-plains, being an excellent master of defense, parried a musket ball with a small sword, insomuch that he absolutely felt it whiz round the blade, and glance off at the hilt: in proof of which, he was ready at any time to show the sword, with the hilt a little bent. There were several more that had been equally great in the field, not one of whom but was persuaded that he had a considerable hand in bringing the war to a happy termination.

But all these were nothing to the tales of ghosts and apparitions that succeeded. The neighborhood is rich in legendary treasures of the kind. Local tales and superstitions thrive best in these sheltered long-settled retreats; but are trampled under foot by the shifting throng that forms the population of most of our country places. Besides, there is no encouragement for ghosts in most of our villages, for they have scarcely had time to finish their first nap, and turn themselves in their graves, before their surviving friends have travelled away from the neighborhood; so that when they turn out at night to walk their rounds, they have no acquaintance left to call upon. This is perhaps the reason why we so seldom hear of ghosts except in our long-established Dutch communities.

The immediate cause, however, of the prevalence of supernatural stories in these parts, was doubtless owing to the vicinity of Sleepy Hollow. There was a contagion in the very air that blew from that haunted region; it breathed forth an atmosphere of dreams and fancies infecting all the land. Several of the Sleepy Hollow people were present at Van Tassel's, and, as usual, were doling out their wild and wonderful legends. Many dismal tales

---

[12] James Fenimore Cooper wrote a memorable account of these Loyalist or Tory marauders in one episode of *The Spy* (1821).

were told about funeral trains, and mourning cries and wailings heard and seen about the great tree where the unfortunate Major André[13] was taken, and which stood in the neighborhood. Some mention was made also of the woman in white, that haunted the dark glen at Raven Rock, and was often heard to shriek on winter nights before a storm, having perished there in the snow. The chief part of the stories, however, turned upon the favorite specter of Sleepy Hollow, the headless horseman, who had been heard several times of late, patrolling the country; and, it was said, tethered his horse nightly among the graves in the church-yard.

The sequestered situation of this church seems always to have made it a favorite haunt of troubled spirits. It stands on a knoll, surrounded by locust trees and lofty elms, from among which its decent whitewashed walls shine modestly forth, like Christian purity beaming through the shades of retirement. A gentle slope descends from it to a silver sheet of water, bordered by high trees, between which, peeps may be caught at the blue hills of the Hudson. To look upon its grass-grown yard, where the sunbeams seem to sleep so quietly, one would think that there at least the dead might rest in peace. On one side of the church extends a wide woody dell, along which raves a large brook among broken rocks and trunks of fallen trees. Over a deep black part of the stream, not far from the church, was formerly thrown a wooden bridge; the road that led to it, and the bridge itself, were thickly shaded by overhanging trees, which cast a gloom about it, even in the daytime; but occasioned a fearful darkness at night. This was one of the favorite haunts of the headless horseman; and the place where he was most frequently encountered. The tale was told of old Brouwer, a most heretical disbeliever in ghosts, how he met the horseman returning from his foray into Sleepy Hollow, and was obliged to get up behind him; how they galloped over bush and brake, over hill and swamp, until they reached the bridge; when the horseman suddenly turned into a skeleton, threw old Brouwer into the brook, and sprang away over the tree-tops with a clap of thunder.

This story was immediately matched by a thrice marvellous adventure of Brom Bones, who made light of the galloping Hessian as an arrant jockey. He affirmed that, on returning one night from the neighboring village of Sing Sing, he had been overtaken by this midnight trooper; that he had offered to race with him for a bowl of punch, and should have won it too, for Daredevil beat the goblin horse all hollow, but, just as they came to the church bridge, the Hessian bolted, and vanished in a flash of fire.

All these tales, told in that drowsy undertone with which men talk in the dark, the countenances of the listeners only now and then receiving a casual gleam from the glare of a pipe, sank deep in the mind of Ichabod. He repaid

---

[13] The British officer who was executed for espionage after he was captured near Tarrytown, New York.

them in kind with large extracts from his invaluable author, Cotton Mather, and added many marvellous events that had taken place in his native state of Connecticut, and fearful sights which he had seen in his nightly walks about Sleepy Hollow.

The revel now gradually broke up. The old farmers gathered together their families in their wagons, and were heard for some time rattling along the hollow roads, and over the distant hills. Some of the damsels mounted on pillions behind their favorite swains, and their light-hearted laughter, mingling with the clatter of hoofs, echoed along the silent woodlands, sounding fainter and fainter until they gradually died away—and the late scene of noise and frolic was all silent and deserted. Ichabod only lingered behind, according to the custom of country lovers, to have a tête-à-tête with the heiress, fully convinced that he was now on the high road to success. What passed at this interview I will not pretend to say, for in fact I do not know. Something, however, I fear me, must have gone wrong, for he certainly sallied forth, after no very great interval, with an air quite desolate and chopfallen.—Oh these women! these women! Could that girl have been playing off any of her coquettish tricks?—Was her encouragement of the poor pedagogue all a mere sham to secure her conquest of his rival?—Heaven only knows, not I!—Let it suffice to say, Ichabod stole forth with the air of one who had been sacking a hen-roost, rather than a fair lady's heart. Without looking to the right or left to notice the scene of rural wealth, on which he had so often gloated, he went straight to the stable, and with several hearty cuffs and kicks, roused his steed most uncourteously from the comfortable quarters in which he was soundly sleeping, dreaming of mountains of corn and oats, and whole valleys of timothy and clover.

It was the very witching time of night that Ichabod, heavy-hearted and crestfallen, pursued his travel homewards, along the sides of the lofty hills which rise above Tarry-town, and which he had traversed so cheerily in the afternoon. The hour was as dismal as himself. Far below him, the Tappan Zee spread its dusky and indistinct waste of waters, with here and there the tall mast of a sloop, riding quietly at anchor under the land. In the dead hush of midnight, he could even hear the barking of the watch dog from the opposite shore of the Hudson; but it was so vague and faint as only to give an idea of his distance from this faithful companion of man. Now and then, too, the long-drawn crowing of a cock, accidentally awakened, would sound far, far off, from some farmhouse away among the hills—but it was like a dreaming sound in his ear. No signs of life occurred near him, but occasionally the melancholy chirp of a cricket, or perhaps the guttural twang of a bull-frog, from a neighboring marsh, as if sleeping uncomfortably, and turning suddenly in his bed.

All the stories of ghosts and goblins that he had heard in the afternoon, now came crowding upon his recollection. The night grew darker and darker; the stars seemed to sink deeper in the sky, and driving clouds occasionally hid them from his sight. He had never felt so lonely and dismal. He was, moreover, approaching the very place where many of the scenes of the ghost stories had been laid. In the center of the road stood an enormous tulip tree, which towered like a giant above all the other trees of the neighborhood, and formed a kind of landmark. Its limbs were gnarled, and fantastic, large enough to form trunks for ordinary trees, twisting down almost to the earth, and rising again into the air. It was connected with the tragical story of the unfortunate André, who had been taken prisoner hard by; and was universally known by the name of Major André's tree. The common people regarded it with a mixture of respect and superstition, partly out of sympathy for the fate of its ill-starred namesake, and partly from the tales of strange sights and doleful lamentations told concerning it.

As Ichabod approached this fearful tree, he began to whistle: he thought his whistle was answered—it was but a blast sweeping sharply through the dry branches. As he approached a little nearer, he thought he saw something white, hanging in the midst of the tree—he paused and ceased whistling; but on looking more narrowly, perceived that it was a place where the tree had been scathed by lightning, and the white wood laid bare. Suddenly he heard a groan—his teeth chattered and his knees smote against the saddle: it was but the rubbing of one huge bough upon another, as they were swayed about by the breeze. He passed the tree in safety, but new perils lay before him.

About two hundred yards from the tree a small brook crossed the road, and ran into a marshy and thickly-wooded glen, known by the name of Wiley's swamp. A few rough logs, laid side by side, served for a bridge over this stream. On that side of the road where the brook entered the wood, a group of oaks and chestnuts, matted thick with wild grapevines, threw a cavernous gloom over it. To pass this bridge was the severest trial. It was at this identical spot that the unfortunate André was captured, and under the covert of those chestnuts and vines were the sturdy yeomen concealed who surprised him. This has ever since been considered a haunted stream, and fearful are the feelings of the schoolboy who has to pass it alone after dark.

As he approached the stream his heart began to thump; he summoned up, however, all his resolution, gave his horse half a score of kicks in the ribs, and attempted to dash briskly across the bridge; but instead of starting forward, the perverse old animal made a lateral movement, and ran broadside against the fence. Ichabod, whose fears increased with the delay, jerked the reins on the other side, and kicked lustily with the contrary foot: it was all in vain; his steed started, it is true, but it was only to plunge to the opposite side of the road into a thicket of brambles and alder bushes. The schoolmaster now bestowed both whip and heel upon the starveling ribs of old Gunpowder, who dashed forward, snuffling and snorting, but came to a stand just by the bridge, with a suddenness that had nearly sent his rider sprawling over his head. Just at this moment a plashy tramp by the side of the bridge caught the sensitive ear of Ichabod. In the dark shadow of the grove, on the margin of the brook, he beheld something huge, misshapen, black and towering. It stirred not, but seemed gathered up in the gloom, like some gigantic monster ready to spring upon the traveller.

The hair of the affrighted pedagogue rose upon his head with terror. What was to be done? To turn and fly was now too late; and besides, what chance was there of escaping ghost or goblin, if such it was, which could ride upon the wings of the wind? Summoning up, therefore, a show of courage, he demanded in stammering accents—"Who are you?" He received no reply. He repeated his demand in a still more agitated voice. Still there was no answer. Once more he cudgelled the sides of the inflexible Gunpowder, and, shutting his eyes, broke forth with involuntary fervor into a psalm tune. Just then the shadowy object of alarm put itself in motion, and, with a scramble and a bound, stood at once in the middle of the road. Though the night was dark and dismal, yet the form of the unknown might now in some degree be ascertained. He appeared to be a horseman of large dimensions, and mounted on a black horse of powerful frame. He made no offer of molestation or sociability, but kept aloof on one side of the road, jogging along on the blind side of old Gunpowder, who had now got over his fright and waywardness.

Ichabod, who had no relish for this strange midnight companion, and bethought himself of the adventure of Brom Bones with the Galloping Hessian, now quickened his steed, in hopes of leaving him behind. The stranger, however, quickened his horse to an equal pace. Ichabod pulled up, and fell into a walk, thinking to lag behind—the other did the same. His heart began to sink within him; he endeavored to resume his psalm tune, but his parched tongue clove to the roof of his mouth, and he could not utter a stave. There was something in the moody and dogged silence of this pertinacious companion, that was mysterious and appalling. It was soon fearfully accounted for. On mounting a rising ground, which brought the figure of his fellow-traveller in relief against the sky, gigantic in height, and muffled in a cloak, Ichabod was horror-struck, on perceiving that he was headless!—but his horror was still more increased, on observing that the head, which should have rested on his shoulders, was carried before him on the pommel of the saddle: his terror rose to desperation; he rained a shower of kicks and blows upon Gunpowder, hoping, by a sudden movement, to give his companion the slip—but the specter started full jump with him. Away then they dashed, through thick and thin; stones flying, and sparks flashing at every bound. Ichabod's flimsy garments fluttered in the air, as he stretched his long lank body away over his horse's head, in the eagerness of his flight.

They had now reached the road which turns off to Sleepy Hollow; but Gunpowder, who seemed possessed with a demon, instead of keeping up it, made an opposite turn, and plunged headlong down hill to the left. This road leads through a sandy hollow, shaded by trees for about a quarter of a mile, where it crosses the bridge famous in goblin story, and just beyond swells the green knoll on which stands the whitewashed church.

As yet the panic of the steed had given his unskillful rider an apparent advantage in the chase; but just as he had got half way through the hollow, the girths of the saddle gave way, and he felt it slipping from under him. He seized it by the pommel, and endeavored to hold it firm, but in vain; and had just time to save himself by clasping old Gunpowder round the neck, when the saddle fell to the earth, and he heard it trampled under foot by his pursuer. For a moment the terror of Hans Van Ripper's wrath passed across his mind—for it was his Sunday saddle; but this was no time for petty fears; the goblin was hard on his haunches; and (unskillful rider that he was!) he had much ado to maintain his seat; sometimes slipping on one side, sometimes on another, and sometimes jolted on the high ridge of his horse's backbone, with a violence that he verily feared would cleave him asunder.

An opening in the trees now cheered him with the hopes that the church bridge was at hand. The wavering reflection of a silver star in the bosom of the brook told him that he was not mistaken. He saw the walls of the church dimly glaring under the trees beyond. He recollected the place where Brom Bones's ghostly competitor had disappeared. "If I can but reach that bridge," thought Ichabod, "I am safe." Just then he heard the black steed panting and blowing close behind him; he even fancied that he felt his hot breath. Another convulsive kick in the ribs, and old Gunpowder sprang upon the bridge; he thundered over the resounding planks; he gained the opposite side; and now Ichabod cast a look behind to see if his pursuer should vanish, according to rule, in a flash of fire and brimstone. Just then he saw the goblin rising in his stirrups, and in the very act of hurling his head at him. Ichabod endeavored to dodge the horrible missile, but too late. It encountered his cranium with a tremendous crash—he was tumbled headlong into the dust, and Gunpowder, the black steed, and the goblin rider, passed by like a whirlwind.

The next morning the old horse was found without his saddle, and with the bridle under his feet, soberly cropping the grass at his master's gate. Ichabod did not make his appearance at breakfast—dinner-hour came, but no Ichabod. The boys assembled at the schoolhouse, and strolled idly about the banks of the brook; but no school-master. Hans Van Ripper now began to feel some uneasiness about the fate of poor Ichabod, and his saddle. An inquiry was set on foot, and after diligent investigation they came upon his traces. In one part of the road leading to the church was found the saddle trampled in the dirt; the tracks of horses' hoofs deeply dented in the road, and evidently at furious speed, were traced to the bridge, beyond which, on the bank of a broad part of the brook, where the water ran deep and black, was found the hat of the unfortunate Ichabod, and close beside it a shattered pumpkin.

The brook was searched, but the body of the school-master was not to be discovered. Hans Van Ripper, as executor of his estate, examined the bundle which contained all his worldly effects. They consisted of two shirts and a half; two stocks for the neck; a pair or two of worsted stockings; an old pair of corduroy smallclothes; a rusty razor; a book of psalm tunes, full of dogs' ears; and a broken pitchpipe. As to the books and furniture of the school-house, they belonged to the community, excepting Cotton Mather's History of Witchcraft, a New England Almanac, and a book of dreams and fortune-telling; in which last was a sheet of foolscap much scribbled and blotted in several fruitless attempts to make a copy of verses in honor of the heiress of Van Tassel. These magic books and the poetic scrawl were forthwith consigned to the flames by Hans Van Ripper; who from that time forward determined to send his children no more to school; observing, that he never knew any good come of this same reading and writing. Whatever money the schoolmaster possessed, and he had received his quarter's pay but a day or two before, he must have had about his person at the time of his disappearance.

The mysterious event caused much speculation at the church on the following Sunday. Knots of gazers and gossips were collected in the churchyard, at the bridge, and at the spot where the hat and pumpkin had been found. The stories of Brouwer, of Bones, and a whole budget of others, were called to mind; and when they had diligently considered them all, and compared them with the symptoms of the present case, they shook their heads, and came to the conclusion that Ichabod had been carried off by the galloping Hessian. As he was a bachelor, and in nobody's debt, nobody troubled his head any more about him. The school was removed to a different quarter of the hollow, and another pedagogue reigned in his stead.

It is true, an old farmer, who had been down to New York on a visit several years after, and from whom this account of the ghostly adventure was received, brought home the intelligence that Ichabod Crane was still alive; that he had left the neighborhood, partly through fear of the goblin and Hans Van Ripper, and partly in mortification at having been suddenly dismissed by the heiress; that he had changed his quarters to a distant part of the country; had kept school and studied law at the same time, had been admitted to the bar, turned politician, electioneered, written for the newspapers, and finally had been made a justice of the Ten Pound Court. Brom Bones too, who shortly after his rival's disappearance conducted the blooming Katrina in triumph to the altar, was observed to look exceedingly knowing whenever the story of Ichabod was related, and always burst into a hearty laugh at the mention of the pumpkin; which led some to suspect that he knew more about the matter than he chose to tell.

The old country wives, however, who are the best judges of these matters, maintain to this day that Ichabod was spirited away by supernatural means; and it is a favorite story often told about the neighborhood round the winter evening fire. The bridge became more than ever an object of super-stitious awe, and that may be the reason why the road has been altered of late years, so as to approach the church by the border of the mill-pond. The school-house being deserted, soon fell to decay, and was reported to be haunted by the ghost of the unfortunate pedagogue; and the ploughboy, loitering homeward of a still summer evening, has often fancied his voice at a distance, chanting a melancholy psalm tune among the tranquil solitudes of Sleepy Hollow.

POSTSCRIPT, FOUND IN THE HANDWRITING OF MR. KNICKERBOCKER.

The preceding tale is given, almost in the precise words in which I heard it related at a Corporation meeting of the ancient city of Manhattoes, at which were present many of its sagest and most illustrious burghers. The narrator was a pleasant, shabby, gentlemanly old fellow, in pepper-and-salt clothes, with a sadly humorous face, and one whom I strongly suspected of being poor,—he made such efforts to be entertaining. When his story was con-cluded, there was much laughter and approbation, particularly from two or three deputy aldermen, who had been asleep a greater part of the time. There was, however, one tall, dry-looking old gentleman, with beetling eye-brows, who maintained a grave and rather severe face throughout: now and then folding his arms, inclining his head, and looking down upon the floor, as if turning a doubt over in his mind. He was one of your wary men, who never laugh, but upon good grounds—when they have reason and the law on their side. When the mirth of the rest of the company had subsided, and silence was restored, he leaned one arm on the elbow of his chair, and, sticking the other akimbo, demanded, with a slight but exceedingly sage motion of the head, and contraction of the brow, what was the moral of the story, and what it went to prove?

The story-teller, who was just putting a glass of wine to his lips, as a refreshment after his toils, paused for a moment, looked at his inquirer with an air of infinite deference, and, lowering the glass slowly to the table, observed, that the story was intended most logically to prove:—

"That there is no situation in life but has its advantages and pleasures—provided we will but take a joke as we find it:

"That, therefore, he that runs races with goblin troopers is likely to have rough riding of it.

"Ergo, for a country schoolmaster to be refused the hand of a Dutch heiress, is a certain step to high preferment in the state."

The cautious old gentleman knit his brows tenfold closer after this expla-nation, being sorely puzzled by the ratiocination of the syllogism; while, methought, the one in pepper-and-salt eyed him with something of a trium-phant leer. At length, he observed, that all this was very well, but still he thought the story a little on the extravagant—there were one or two points on which he had his doubts.

"Faith, sir," replied the story-teller, "as to that matter, I don't believe one-half of it myself."

D.K.

From Tales of the Alhambra, 1832[1]

[Long before the ruined palace became a center of tourism to be preserved by the Spanish government, Irving lived for some months in the Alhambra, and he used that experience as the basis for his "Spanish sketchbook" of tales and essays about Spain and his travels there. Here he meditates on the vanishing peoples—in a way that would remind citizens of the young United States of the American Indian nations— and perhaps the destiny of all nations.]

REFLECTIONS ON THE MOSLEM DOMINATION IN SPAIN

One of my favorite resorts is the balcony of the central window of the Hall of Ambassadors, in the lofty tower of Comares. I have just been seated there, enjoying the close of a long brilliant day. The sun, as he sank behind the purple mountains of Alhama, sent a stream of effulgence up the valley of the Darro, that spread a melancholy pomp over the ruddy towers of the Alhambra, while the Vega, covered with a slight sultry vapor that caught the setting ray, seemed spread out in the distance like a golden sea. Not a breath of air disturbed the stillness of the hour, and though the faint sound of music and merriment now and then arose from the gardens of the Darro, it but rendered more impressive the monumental silence of the pile which overshadowed me. It was one of those hours and scenes in which memory asserts an almost magical power, and, like the evening sun beaming on these mouldering towers, sends back her retrospective rays to light up the glories of the past.

As I sat watching the effect of the declining daylight upon this Moorish pile, I was led into a consideration of the light, elegant and voluptuous character prevalent throughout its internal architecture, and to contrast it with the grand but gloomy solemnity of the Gothic edifices, reared by the Spanish conquerors. The very architecture thus bespeaks the opposite and

[1] The text is the first American edition. The Alhambra is the ruined but still magnificent palace of the Moorish rulers of Granada, who were defeated by the Spanish armies of Ferdinand and Isabella in 1492.

irreconcilable natures of the two warlike people, who so long[2] battled here for the mastery of the Peninsula. By degrees I fell into a course of musing upon the singular features of the Arabian or Morisco Spaniards, whose whole existence is as a tale that is told, and certainly forms one of the most anomalous yet splendid episodes in history. Potent and durable as was their dominion, we have no one distinct title by which to designate them. They were a nation, as it were, without a legitimate country or a name. A remote wave of the great Arabian inundation, cast upon the shores of Europe, they seemed to have all the impetus of the first rush of the torrent. Their course of conquest from the rock of Gibraltar to the cliffs of the Pyrenees, was as rapid and brilliant as the Moslem victories of Syria and Egypt. Nay, had they not been checked on the plains of Tours, all France, all Europe, might have been overrun with the same facility as the empires of the East, and the crescent might at this day have glittered on the fanes of Paris and of London.

Repelled within the limits of the Pyrenees, the mixed hordes of Asia and Africa that formed this great irruption, gave up the Moslem principles of conquest, and sought to establish in Spain a peaceful and permanent dominion. As conquerors their heroism was only equalled by their moderation; and in both, for a time, they excelled the nations with whom they contended. Severed from their native homes, they loved the land given them, as they supposed, by Allah, and strove to embellish it with everything that could administer to the happiness of man. Laying the foundations of their power in a system of wise and equitable laws, diligently cultivating the arts and sciences, and promoting agriculture, manufactures and commerce, they gradually formed an empire unrivalled for its prosperity, by any of the empires of Christendom; and diligently drawing round them the graces and refinements that marked the Arabian empire in the East at the time of its greatest civilization, they diffused the light of oriental knowledge through the western regions of benighted Europe.

The cities of Arabian Spain became the resort of Christian artisans, to instruct themselves in the useful arts. The universities of Toledo, Cordova, Seville, and Granada were sought by the pale student from other lands, to acquaint himself with the sciences of the Arabs, and the treasured lore of antiquity; the lovers of the gay sciences resorted to Cordova and Granada, to imbibe the poetry and music of the East; and the steel-clad warriors of the North hastened thither, to accomplish themselves in the graceful exercises and courteous usages of chivalry.

If the Moslem monuments in Spain; if the Mosque of Cordova, the Alcazar of Seville and the Alhambra of Granada, still bear inscriptions fondly boasting of the power and permanency of their dominion, can the boast be derided as arrogant and vain? Generation after generation, century after century had passed away, and still they maintained possession of the land. A

---

[2] Over a period of eight centuries.

period had elapsed longer than that which has passed since England was subjugated by the Norman conqueror; and the descendants of Musa and Tarik might as little anticipate being driven into exile, across the same straits traversed by their triumphant ancestors, as the descendants of Rollo and William and their victorious peers may dream of being driven back to the shores of Normandy.

With all this, however, the Moslem empire in Spain was but a brilliant exotic that took no permanent root in the soil it embellished. Secured from all their neighbors of the West by impassable barriers of faith and manners, and separated by seas and deserts from their kindred of the East, they were an isolated people. Their whole existence was a prolonged though gallant and chivalric struggle for a foot-hold in a usurped land. They were the outposts and frontiers of Islamism. The Peninsula was the great battle ground where the Gothic conquerors of the North and the Moslem conquerors of the East, met and strove for mastery; and the fiery courage of the Arab was at length subdued by the obstinate and persevering valor of the Goth.

Never was the annihilation of a people more complete than that of the Morisco Spaniards. Where are they? Ask the shores of Barbary and its desert places. The exiled remnant of their once powerful empire disappeared among the barbarians of Africa, and ceased to be a nation. They have not even left a distinct name behind them, though for nearly eight centuries they were a distinct people. The home of their adoption and of their occupation for ages refuses to acknowledge them but as invaders and usurpers. A few broken monuments are all that remain to bear witness to their power and dominion, as solitary rocks left far in the interior bear testimony to the extent of some vast inundation. Such is the Alhambra. A Moslem pile in the midst of a Christian land; an Oriental palace amidst the Gothic edifices of the West; an elegant memento of a brave, intelligent and graceful people, who conquered, ruled, and passed away.

PART II

THE ROMANTIC ERA

1819-1869

INTRODUCTION

The Romantic movement in America developed from the literary, social, and political currents of Western Europe and the religious thought of seventeenth- and eighteenth-century America. These sources contributed to an Americanized Romanticism in which the concept of the common person became so paramount that it assumed many different aspects: transcendentalist and Yankee, idealist and humorist, prosperous Jacksonian and romantic nationalist, Westerner, Indian, reformer, immigrant, Southern yeoman, and slave. Romantic artists, like their European counterparts, were deeply concerned with the poetic expression of their sentiments toward nature as well as the uses to which organic form and the language of common people could be put; but the literary attitudes that influenced them were given a special intensity by the political meaning and promise of America. These authors created literature that turned upon the concept of the common American as a self-reliant, pragmatic individual who was unique and free at the same time that he was bound to the democracy. Throughout the writing of Emerson and the transcendentalists, abolitionists and slaves, political figures and poets and immigrants runs the theme of the religious and social freedom of the individual: having foregone the religion of one's ancestors or the nationality of one's birth, how does one preserve his identity as an American in a democracy that demands equality?

By midcentury, in the darkening shadows of a Civil War, Walt Whitman defined the problems of pluralism that characterized the Romantic period and that still lie at the paradoxical center of American culture:

> One's self I sing, a single separate person
> Yet utter the word Democratic, the word En-Masse.

1. THE ROMANTIC AESTHETIC

The roots of European romanticism are tangled, but they can be most usefully located in two significant figures of the eighteenth century: the French social commentator and educational theorist, Jean Jacques Rousseau, and the English religious leader, John Wesley.

In *The Social Contract* and *Emile,* Rousseau championed the natural goodness of the individual person and scorned the conventions of society; he rejected the concepts of original sin, the fall from grace and innate depravity, and stressed the moral validity of a person's inner experience and spontaneous feeling. "Man is born free," Rousseau announced in *The Social Contract,* "and is everywhere in chains." During the same period in England, the evangelist John Wesley was expressing views similar to Rousseau's. Wesley appealed to the unlettered common man and preached that he should repudiate the hierarchy of the church, its creeds and dogmas, and trust his own emotions, the value of his individual soul, the dignity of his person, and the salvation that comes through faith.

Rousseau and Wesley helped to create an intellectual climate in which Romantic writers flourished and came to dominate Western culture at the turn of the nineteenth century: philosophers like Fichte, Schelling, Schleiermacher, and Kant in Germany, and poets like Burns, Blake, Wordsworth, Coleridge, Byron, Shelley, and Keats in Great Britain. These authors, each from his singular perspective, created the writing that American Romantics revered; for them, as for Keats, the imagination was to "be compared to Adam's dream—he awoke and found it truth."

The influence of European philosophers, poets, and novelists was direct and profound. In the second edition of *The Lyrical Ballads* (1798), Wordsworth and Coleridge called for a revolution in aesthetics; in 1837 Emerson translated many of their thoughts concerning language and nature and the organic form into an American context. At the turn of the century, Gothic novelists peopled their works with ghosts and haunted chambers; Charles Brockden Brown, Irving, Poe, and Hawthorne borrowed their techniques and situated domestic demons in New York, Virginia, and Massachusetts. Sir Walter Scott described a vast world of romance that influenced northern novelists like Cooper and had so great an impact on southern writers and their conception of character that Mark Twain later held him responsible for the Civil War.

Americans fashioned Romanticism to their own needs, but their aesthetic attitudes were those of Europeans. They believed in the primacy of the imagination rather than the intellect, in poetry as a faith that holds greater importance than the material world—"poets are," as Emerson said, "liberating gods." Like the Europeans, Americans championed the single separate person and his particular response to the smallest grain of experience. Throughout this literature—and in much of American writing afterwards—man is alone, a creature not so engulfed and shaped by an established and class-oriented society, as one finds in the novels of Jane Austen, Dickens, and Thackeray, although with certain writers like Cooper, Simms, and Harriet Beecher Stowe these social forces do make themselves felt. In classical American literature, Emerson and Thoreau cherish their solitude in nature; Hawthorne views solitude as an isolation that is destructive; Melville sends Ahab into a loneliness of spirit that is finally monomaniacal; Poe creates solitary figures who live with their haunted imagination and the memory of their lost love; Whitman describes himself as a "solitary singer."

The solitary figure is found most often in nature, whether the setting provides the condition, as it does in *Walden,* for a person to live deliberately and rediscover himself or whether it becomes the metaphor, as in "Young Goodman Brown," of man's bewilderment, doubt, and suspicion. Nature is the great force of Romantic writers, and it is significant that the movement in America runs roughly from the static yet stately and eloquent poetry of Bryant, who was so influenced by Wordsworth, to the open, sensual, more "democratic" embrace of nature that one finds in Whitman—"I lean and loafe at my ease observing a spear of summer grass"—a poet who views the grass as the organic symbol of the American democracy. Nature signifies the miraculous in life for the Romantic artist, and he celebrates a rebirth of wonder, his own capacity to respond to his unlimited potentialities; thus Emerson asks at the outset of his first important essay, *Nature* (1836), "Why should not we also enjoy an original relation to the universe" and Thoreau closes *Walden* with a morning image, "Only that day dawns to which we are awake." These writers marvel at the miraculous in life, at the smallest natural object, finding constant correspondences between the large and the small:

And I know that the spirit of God is the brother of my own,
And that all the men ever born are also my brothers, and the women
   my sisters and lovers,
And that a kelson of the creation is love,
And limitless are leaves stiff or drooping in the fields,
And brown ants in the little wells beneath them,
And mossy scabs of the worm fence, heap'd stones, elder, mullein
   and poke-weed.

This reverence for nature can be measured in the attitudes that the authors had toward language and the concept of organic form. For Emerson, Thoreau, and Whitman, words were "the signs of natural facts"; in order to express the spirit of democracy, they felt that the poet would have to use the language of the common man and abjure a poetic diction that seemed distant from everyday experience. Thus the theory of organic form developed by Coleridge—such as the life is, Coleridge had written, such is the form—was adopted by American romantic artists as a primary principle in their work. For Emerson, all of nature is interrelated because it emanates from the oversoul, and poetry is simply the attempt to express metaphorically and organically the human spirit: "For it is not metres, but a metre-making argument that makes a poem—a thought so passionate and alive that like the spirit of a plant or an animal it has an architecture of its own and adorns nature

with a new thing." For Thoreau, the organic principle is the great discovery he makes in *Walden,* as he insists that "Nature is a greater and
more perfect art." For Whitman, the grass is the symbolic food on
which democracy feeds, organically connecting earth, animals, man,
and God. Poets such as Bryant, Whittier, Lowell, and Longfellow wrote
some of their finest verse in response to the natural beauty of New
England—a pastoral poetry, simply stated, about a waterfowl or a
snowbound family in Massachusetts. A sculptor like Horatio Greenough was centrally concerned with bridging form and function, and
his writings affected not only contemporaries like Emerson but his
disciple Louis Sullivan who, in turn, had a deep impact on Frank Lloyd
Wright. Painters were eager to represent the American landscape faithfully: Thomas Cole, Asher B. Durand, and Martin Heade turned to the
Hudson River Valley; George Catlin recorded the image of the Indian;
Karl Bodner, Alfred Miller, George Caleb Bingham, and Charles Deas
depicted the West; Albert Bierstadt painted the rough terrain of the
Rocky Mountains; and W. S. Mount painted the sandswept stretches of
Long Island. Later in the century, Thomas Eakins brought to his art a
regard for natural simplicity and a resistance to "mere decoration" that
was shared by writers like Emerson, Thoreau, and Whitman. Finally, in
the music of the period—particularly the spirituals of Negroes—the
natural emotions of common people are expressed unpretentiously so
that feeling and form are fused in an organic relationship to each
other.

The wonder of life that forms a natural expression in Bryant, Whittier, Emerson, Thoreau, and Whitman can also assume that other manifestation of Romanticism—the supernatural. For Poe and Hawthorne
especially, romance can provide a range of response far greater than
that of the realistic novel or story; and, as narrative artists rather than
essayists, they deal in the shadows and complexities of the mind, often
taking the reader beyond the mundane world so that the world will be
more real when he returns to it. In the preface to *The House of the
Seven Gables,* Hawthorne states his own view most clearly.

When a writer calls his work a Romance, it need hardly be observed that he wishes to claim a certain latitude, both as to its
fashion and material, which he would not have felt himself entitled to assume had he professed to be writing a novel. The latter
form of composition is presumed to aim at a very minute fidelity,
not merely to the possible, but to the probable and ordinary
course of man's experience. The former—while, as a work of art,
it must rigidly subject itself to laws, and while it sins unpardonably so far as it may swerve aside from the truth of the human
heart—has fairly a right to present that truth under circum-

stances, to a great extent, of the writer's own choosing or creation. If he think fit, also, he may so manage his atmospherical medium as to bring out or mellow the lights and deepen and enrich the shadows of the picture. He will be wise, no doubt, to make a very moderate use of the privileges here stated, and, especially, to mingle the Marvellous rather as a slight, delicate, and evanescent flavor, than as any portion of the actual substance of the dish offered to the public. He can hardly be said, however, to commit a literary crime even if he disregard this caution.

Hawthorne, Poe, and Melville take the reader into a romantic, sometimes Gothic world that is ultimately a commentary on the real world in which he lives. The unknown can be terrifying, a place of gloom and melancholy in "The Fall of the House of Usher" and "The Masque of the Red Death"; a nightmare of confusion in "My Kinsman, Major Molineux"; and a mystery in *Moby Dick,* which is never completely comprehended. The power of blackness can be grotesque or macabre in the work of Poe and his imitators; it can also be a vision of evil or of mystery and doubt in the fiction of Hawthorne and Melville. For Poe, Hawthorne, and Melville, the dark night of the soul is a reality that borders the natural world—a reality that penetrates into the unconscious and the exotic, which we, in an age enamored of psychoanalysis and the occult, are familiar with.

All of these ideas—man's natural goodness, the primacy of the imagination, solitude, the significance of nature and its smallest object, the force of common language and the desire for a literary expression that is truly organic, and the projection of a tragic and Gothic vision—naturally assume different forms and stylistic expression in these writers. We think of Emerson's style as largely aphoristic, abstract, oracular—the language of someone delivering a speech or a sermon. Thoreau's writing is more concrete and tense, firmly rooted to the objects he is describing. Hawthorne and Poe have a classical prose that is carefully wrought, whereas Melville's style is less constrained, more limpid and rich with allusion and, in the magnificent passages of *Moby Dick,* highly rhetorical and dramatic. In this period there is a declamatory literature reflected not only by Emerson's essays and Melville's *Moby Dick,* but by other forms of expression as well: the sermons of ministers like Theodore Parker and Lyman Beecher; the histories of Prescott, Bancroft, and Motley; the political "high" style of Daniel Webster and John C. Calhoun; the "low" speech of Seba Smith and Johnson J. Hooper; the passionate rhetoric of Frederick Douglass and other abolitionists; and the oracular poetry of Whitman. A democratic voice is represented by a solitary speaker who expresses himself in the first person as a man speaking among men.

However different the expression of all these writers, their thought returns to the individual and the circular correspondences that emanate from him: the soul in relationship to the body; the person in correspondence with nature, society, and the cosmos. The great question for Emerson, Thoreau, Hawthorne, and Melville is reliance on the self—on God within the self—and the correspondence of that self to a harmonious natural world in which it finds itself.

The Romantic aesthetic took root in America and assumed, for many artists and politicians, the singular shape of nationalism. In 1782 Crèvecoeur had asked, "What then is the American, this new man?" and he answered, "The American is a new man, who acts upon new principles; he must therefore entertain new ideas and new opinions." This theme was increasingly repeated, with many variations, until the Civil War, as novelists and poets drew verbal portraits of an American Eden in which a new Adam could begin again—along Cooper's forests, in Hawthorne's Salem, in Thoreau's Walden, and on Melville's ships. Emerson spoke for his generation when he said, in "The American Scholar," that "our day of dependence, our long apprenticeship to the learning of other lands, draws to a close. The millions that around us are rushing into life, cannot always be fed on the sere remains of foreign harvests. . . . We have listened too long to the courtly muses of Europe."

Oliver Wendell Holmes called "The American Scholar" our "intellectual Declaration of Independence." And, indeed, Emerson's essay reflects a cultural revolution of profound proportions—one that rebels not only against the political and literary domination of Europe but also against an American past that seems antidemocratic; a revolution that releases the life of the imagination in authors like Poe, Hawthorne, and Melville so that a complex American literature finally assumes distinctive characteristics; a revolution that touches transcendentalists, politicians, presidents, white and black orators of the South and the North, as the making of America is measured against its meaning.

2. THE CULTURAL REVOLUTION

Romanticism was indeed a liberating force in America, and the writers of the period considered themselves figures in a cultural revolution that had penetrated the religious, imaginative, and political life of the nation. Calvinism had stressed man's limitations, his foreordination, and his inability to save himself before an angry God who seeks to restrain Satan; unitarianism had then placed emphasis on historical Christianity and on man's limited place in a God-oriented universe. Romantic thinkers expressed their belief in the free individual—that single, separate person whose political freedom from England had its religious counterpart in the repudiation of Calvinism and (in the work of Emerson, Thoreau, and the transcendentalists) unitarianism. Religion was democratized and an emphasis was placed on Jesus and the personal expression of goodness. The sanctity of the free individual is the common strand that runs through Emerson's "American Scholar," Thoreau's "Civil Disobedience," Hawthorne and Melville's fiction, Cooper's Leatherstocking novels, Holmes's "Deacon's Masterpiece," and Whittier's "Ichabod," as well as through the slave narratives and abolitionist literature of the time.

Not only did the successful political and religious revolutions, based on the doctrines "that declared all men to be equal," make Calvinism and unitarianism seem incompatible with the emerging nation; certain cultural forces in America encouraged an individualism that rejected a religion more appropriate to another time in American culture. Rapid industrial expansion, the movement westward, the solidification of plantation life in the South, the election of Andrew Jackson, the significant development that all men now had the right to vote, the infectious concept of America as a new nation in a new world with a "manifest destiny," the creation of religions such as the Latter Day Saints, the widespread belief in a philosophy of progress and reform, and a growing sense of nationalism and later sectionalism—each of these cultural elements contributed to the American's faith in himself, his increasing sense of his own Americanness.

Writers conceived of their work in terms of space as well as time: *The Deerslayer, Moby Dick, Song of Myself,* and *Huckleberry Finn* are expressions of freedom—or of an attempt at freedom—and they anticipate an immigrant and black literature of movement across oceans, rivers, and the vast spaces of America. The sense of a broad continent and the possibility of moving westward was a fundamental myth that had its deepest roots in Romanticism: as people freed themselves spiritually and historically, so they sought physical liberation. Emigrants traveled to California and Oregon on wagons and caravans in search of gold and fur; Brigham Young led the Mormons to Utah; merchants developed their trade by using steamboats that sped down the Mississippi; in midcentury they used the hastily built railroads. Travel in America served to equalize people and underscored a national characteristic that would intensify with the expanding technocracy—the desire for speed. Indeed, as people moved westward, America became the nation it has since remained, a "democracy of haste."

The most sophisticated authors were infected by the romantic myth of the West. Although Emerson, Thoreau, and Melville did not actually migrate, they allude to the possibilities of the West in their writings; Whitman centers on this theme in much of his poetry—as in the westward movement of Lincoln's coffin in "When Lilacs Last in the Dooryard Bloom'd"—but especially in *Passage to India;* and other Easterners, from Washington Irving in *Astoria* (1836) to Bret Harte in "The Luck of Roaring Camp" (1868), conceived of the West as wild, primitive, romantic. An historian like Francis Parkman criticized the society of old and New England in a typically Romantic fashion; novelists and poets created myths about folk heroes such as Daniel Boone, David Crockett, Mike Fink, and Kit Carson; and James Fenimore Cooper developed the natural hero in Natty Bumppo of the Leatherstocking novels, a figure who moved inexorably westward in search of freedom from materialistic white men. A great theme of American literature—the clash between industrialized society and nature, between the machine and the garden—was born in this period. One finds it expressed in Horatio Greenough's sculpture of a struggle between Daniel Boone and an Indian warrior, the allegorical representation of society and primitivism; one sees it recreated in Mark Twain's *Life on the Mississippi;* one discovers its twentieth-century model in Faulkner's lamentation on the destruction of nature by rapacious men, *The Bear.* For each of these writers and artists the threat to nature invariably involves a threat to the freedom of the individual American.

3. THE LIFE OF THE IMAGINATION

"There is the grand truth about Nathaniel Hawthorne. He says no! in thunder; but the Devil himself cannot make him say *yes.* For all men who say *yes,* lie; and all men who say *no,*—why, they are in the happy condition of judicious unincumbered travellers in Europe; they cross frontiers in Eternity with nothing but a carpet-bag,—that is to say, the Ego."

Melville's famous description of Hawthorne, extreme though it may be, offers an approach to the imaginative life of Romantic authors, a way of distinguishing between a group of writers like Emerson, Thoreau, Whitman, Hawthorne, and Melville himself, whom we have come to regard as the major authors of the period, and another group like Bryant, Longfellow, Lowell, and Holmes, "minor" writers. The former reject an abiding dependence on European literary models, whereas Longfellow, Lowell, and Holmes see themselves as poets whose work is in the tradition of English literature; their writing is largely conventional, carefully wrought, and often poignant, but not disturbing or provocative. In certain instances, like Lowell's "Biglow Papers" or Holmes's "Deacon's Masterpiece," these poets do challenge convention but, for the most part, they accept their literary heritage and adapt it easily to the American setting. The same may be said, on a decidedly lower level of intensity and quality, of those innumerable novelists whom Hawthorne called "damned scribbling women," although there were at least as many men who churned out the sentimental fiction that anticipated the television soap operas of our own time. Names like John Neal, Lydia Huntley Sigourney, E. D. E. N. Southworth, John P. Kennedy, James Kirk Paulding, R. M. Bird, N. P. Willis, George Lippard, Augusta Jane Evans Wilson, and Margaret Junkin Preston are remembered now by literary historians only; but their sentimental fiction represents an aspect of the times that one does not always find in the essays of Emerson or the fiction of Hawthorne.

These conventional and sentimental characteristics of Romantic fiction and poetry can also be seen, from still another perspective, in the literature of the South. In the late eighteenth and early nineteenth centuries many of the most impressive American statesmen were Southerners. Washington, Jefferson, Madison, and Monroe provided "a cluster of leadership of talents," the historian Richard Morris has pointed out, that "has never appeared again in America. . . . Theirs was a society where the spirit of deference still prevailed, where an intellectually elite, a 'meritocracy,' could rule." It is significant that a culture in which learning was so highly regarded among the affluent should produce political thinkers and statesmen of the first rank but not novelists or poets or essayists. It is true that Southern intellectuals were naturally drawn to political affairs and viewed literature as an avocation; most Southerners who had literary interests were trained as lawyers. But, in the generation after the founding of the Republic, many of them—writers like John P. Kennedy, William Gilmore Simms, William A. Caruthers, Nathaniel Beverly Tucker, John Esten Cooke, and Paul Hamilton Hayne—had artistic ambitions and wrote voluminously.

The absence of profoundly original creative work in the South stems in part from the paucity of sophisticated readers, the agrarian conditions blocking a cultural life, the rigid views of sexuality, and other social conditions that discouraged artistic life. But a deeper reason lies in the unwillingness of Southern authors to explore the implications of democratization. A typical writer like Simms, for example, began in 1833 to write romances in the manner of Sir Walter Scott—*The Yemassee* (1835) is his best-known work in this genre. At the outset of his career, Simms was not especially concerned with political or social questions; but as he became more aware of the threat to slavocracy in the South, he began to champion the Southern past in romances like *Woodcraft* (1851), *The Forayers* (1855), and *Eutaw* (1856). During the 1850's Simms had a paternal affection for his slaves; but that feeling turned sour during the war and, in the Reconstruction era, he considered Southern Negroes ungrateful parasites. Finally, when a journalist visited Simms in 1867, he claimed that "Charleston, sir, . . . was the finest city in the world; not a large city, but the finest. South Carolina, sir, was the flower of modern civilization. Our people were the most hospitable, the most accomplished, having the highest degree of culture, and the highest sense of honor of any people, I will not say of America, sir, but of any country on the globe. And they are so still, even in their temporary desolation." This sort of defensiveness was shared by many Southerners and, after the war, those authors like Thomas Nelson Page who still regarded nostalgically the days when master, mistress, and slave were in their "proper" relationship to one another began to create a fiction of local manners, morality, and mores that was narrowly sectional and chauvinistic. Soon this attitude yielded to the more complex view of George Washington Cable, Joel Chandler Harris, and Kate Chopin. The only major author to emerge from the group of local colorists and regionalists was Mark Twain, and his greatest novel, *Huckleberry Finn,* is the first significant work to view the Negro as a human being rather than a problem. In recognizing the spiritual equality of Jim, Huckleberry Finn opens the questions of social equality and moral culpability; and not until these questions were deeply considered artistically, after the World War I, did Southern writers like William Faulkner, Allen Tate, and Robert Penn Warren produce, from varying perspectives, a complex literature of the first rank.

For most novelists and poets of the Romantic period, the tension involved in the rejection of a past belief or a present attitude is absent; they use stock devices and aesthetic attitudes in their work and never really question social mores and religious conflicts. But the major writers of this "Golden Age" in American literature do create defiant works—they do say no in thunder. "The Divinity School Address" deplores the emphasis on historical Christianity; *The Scarlet Letter* condemns the moral rigidity of the Puritans; the Leatherstocking novels criticize the destruction of nature in the name of civilization and progress; *Walden* is an indictment of man's superficial existence.

Part of Melville's demand for a significant native literature arose from his sense that the author must challenge traditions and beliefs that have become obsolescent. Although he could characterize Emerson as a "Plato who talks thro' his nose"—especially when Emerson did not seem to take sufficient account of tragedy and evil in the actual world—he had real admiration for him, for Melville thought of Emerson as a "diver," one of those writers willing to take chances and break with tradition. His deepest admiration, however, was for Hawthorne, who could record not only the affirmative side of man's condition but knew of his darker aspects as well: "For spite of all the Indian-summer sunlight on the hither side of Hawthorne's soul," wrote Melville, "the other side—like the dark half of the physical sphere—is shrouded in a blackness, ten times black. . . this great power in him derives its force from its appeals to that Calvinistic sense of Innate Depravity and Original Sin, from whose visitations, in some shape or other, no deeply thinking mind is always and wholly free. For, in certain moods, no man can weigh this world without throwing in something, somehow like Original Sin, to strike the uneven balance."

The fiction of Hawthorne, Melville, and Poe explores the dark side of man's nature and expresses an extraordinary "power of blackness" that is central to the Romantic imagination. Whereas many of the transcendentalists tend to view evil as illusory—"evil is the measles and mumps of the soul," Emerson writes, "cold without heat"—Hawthorne, Poe, and Melville make it a primary force in their work. Their fiction differs from that of mid-nineteenth-century English and French novelists in its tendency toward the symbolic. Hawthorne and Melville are reacting to a Calvinist tradition that stressed the elect and the damned, and their best work is theologically rooted. "Never to be sure where one stands with God," as Edmund Wilson suggests, "makes life extremely uncomfortable, and the constant obsession with infinite power makes it difficult to be interested in one's neighbor."

One reason for the symbolic quality in the romantic fiction of Hawthorne and Melville is the residual effect of the Calvinist tradition on their sensibility—Hawthorne himself wondered whether an entire life devoted to writing fiction was morally proper. Another important reason—particularly for Poe, whose fiction carries no real theological concerns—is the influence of European Gothicism. Still another reason is the unwillingness to view the human being in terms of his fallibility as a person—largely because of the lingering effects of Calvinism but also because of an audience that was morally inhibited and did not want the sort of exploration into private behavior that one finds in twentieth-century literature. Although Hawthorne, Melville, and Poe shared these attitudes and were controlled by them, they were, of course, deeply aware of the unconscious desires in their characters. Much of the power in their work stems from the tension between what they knew or sensed about human nature and how much they dared to state. In *The Scarlet Letter,* the central action—the seduction of Hester Prynne—occurs in the prehistory of the novel, and Hawthorne explores only the consequences of the sexual act; yet one feels the passion of Hester Prynne in the exposition of her thoughts, in the figure of her daughter, and in the occasional meetings with her vengeful husband and her lover Dimmesdale. For Poe eroticism assumed the guise of death, and it is pervasive in his best fiction as lovers are buried alive or return from the dead or haunt the living. In an important examination of major nineteenth-century American authors, *Studies in Classic American Literature,* D. H. Lawrence defines this problem succintly by stressing a "split in the American art and art-consciousness. On the top it is as nice as pie, goody-goody and lovey-dovey. . . .

Serpents [the classical American writers] were. . . . You *must* look through the surface of American art, and see the inner diabolism of the symbolic meaning. Otherwise it is all mere childishness."

4. SOCIAL AND POLITICAL THOUGHT

Hawthorne, Melville, and Poe are remembered for the intense expression of their private vision; but it would be a mistake to consider these authors as somehow distant from the social issues of their time. They lived in an era of reform, and they responded to it in some of their most interesting work: "Earth's Holocaust," "The Celestial Railroad," and *The Blithedale Romance; The Confidence Man* and "Bartleby, the Scrivener"; and *The Gold Bug.* Indeed, the reform movements that developed are the period's manifestation of a religious impulse that so many writers had inherited; and no account of American Civilization in the early nineteenth century would be complete without underscoring them.

The broadest moral and social movement throughout the Romantic era was Transcendentalism. Anticipated by William Ellery Channing's liberalized attitude toward Christianity, the transcendental faith was most forcefully formulated by Emerson in *Nature* (1836), "The American Scholar" (1837), and "The Divinity School Address" (1838). These seminal essays repudiate the cultural dependence on Europe and the slavish devotion to an historical Christianity; they explore the moral implications of democracy and demand a language and literature of the common man, a need for the American's belief in himself as a single, separate person. In the 1830's and 1840's, Thoreau, Bronson Alcott, Orestes Brownson, and dozens of other thinkers adapted transcendentalism to their own intellectual purposes; but for all of them certain tenets held constant—the belief in intuition or the inner light, the need for a harmony between man and nature, the faith in man's centrality and of God's presence within him. Sometimes transcendentalists spoke too abstractly about "spirit" and the "oversoul" and consequently encouraged the satirical thrusts of Hawthorne in "The Celestial Railroad" and "Earth's Holocaust" or of Melville in *The Confidence Man.* At times they tried to implement their ideas in concrete projects like Bronson Alcott's utopian experiment, Fruitlands, or the most famous social experiment of the time, Brook Farm, where George Ripley, Albert Brisbane, Parke Godwin, Orestes Brownson, and others were associated in the 1840's; but these experiments ultimately appeared unreal and absurd to a writer like Hawthorne, even though he himself lived at Brook Farm for a short time and wrote the best-known satire on the dangers of misguided reform, *The Blithedale Romance* (1853).

In addition to transcendentalism, which had the most profound and pervasive effect on all Romantic writers, many other utopian experiments arose. Dorothea Dix sought to correct the cruelties inflicted on the insane; Josiah Quincy, mayor of Boston and president of Harvard, instituted municipal reforms in Boston; the Reverend Thomas H. Gallaudet began a school for the deaf in Hartford; Dr. Samuel Howe worked toward improving the education of the blind; and George Rapp and Robert Dale Owen established utopian communities. Other movements expressed still more varied humanitarian impulses: Fourierism, vegetarianism, the water cure, phrenology, mesmerism, temperance, and feminism. No significant work of art resulted from all of these reforms. Whitman wrote a fragile temperance tract, *Franklin Evans* (1843); Albert Brisbane defended Fourierism in his *Social Destiny of Man;* Margaret Fuller championed women's rights in *Woman in the Nineteenth Century* (1845); and scores of abolitionists like Wendell Phillips, William Lloyd Garrison, Whittier, and Douglass filled the periodicals and newspapers with morally instructive essays that attacked the institution of slavery.

The major authors of this period maintained their independence and, like Thoreau, insisted that the only genuine reform is self-reform. Emerson, Thoreau, Hawthorne, and Melville were temperamentally resistant to movements and groups. Emerson celebrates Man in his essays but speaks little of individual men; Thoreau sets himself apart from society when he goes to Walden; Hawthorne struggles against a predilection toward solitude and satirizes crowds in his fiction; and Melville draws within himself, creating studies of isolation in "Bartleby" and "The Encantadas." Although these writers were committed to the concept of democracy, they did not like men in the mass, and it was not until Whitman wrote *Song of Myself* and *Democratic Vistas* that the implications of democratization were fully explored.

However resistant the classical American authors may have been to social action, they were inevitably drawn into humanitarian causes and particularly to the one reform movement that was not ephemeral, abolitionism. Under the leadership of William Lloyd Garrison, abolitionism began in 1835 as a reform that concentrated on individual improvement, then attacked the church and the government for their lack of moral purpose and, finally, became extremely active in social reform. Throughout the 1830's and 1840's, Emerson, Thoreau, Whittier, Lowell, and others expressed varying degrees of sympathy with the antislavery movement. Emerson remained customarily distant from the daily battle; Thoreau never joined an Abolitionist organization—like Emerson, he distrusted even those groups that represented his own views—but he grew more and more militant, delivering an address on

"Slavery in Massachusetts" in 1854 and rising to the defense of John Brown in "A Plea for Captain John Brown" (1859); Whittier was an impassioned abolitionist from the outset and significant poems like "From Massachusetts to Virginia" express his indignation at the abuses of slavery in the South.

The antislavery movement reached one of its most intense moments in 1850, when Daniel Webster, who had been considered by Northerners a liberal leader in the Senate, defended the Fugitive Slave Law. Emerson replied bitterly in his journals, "By God, I will not obey it," and published his indictment of the act in "The Fugitive Slave Law" (1854); Thoreau was outraged at Negroes being arrested in Boston and at an antislavery convention delivered "Slavery in Massachusetts"; Whittier characterized Webster as an Ichabod.

> So fallen! so lost! the light withdrawn
> Which once he wore!
> The glory from his gray hairs gone
> Forevermore!

In addition to the writings of white authors, Negroes who had been fortunate enough to receive an education were expressing their own views of slavery. David Walker delivered *An Appeal . . . to the Colored Citizens of the World* in 1829, pleading for a general uprising, and was characterized as "totally subversive" in the South; Nat Turner wrote his confessions, printed in 1832; David Ruggles defended antislavery workers of New York in his *Mirror of Liberty* (1839). W. W. Brown published the first novel by a black man in America, *Clotel, or the President's Daughter: A Narrative of Slave Life in the United States* (1853); and Samuel Ringgold brought out *Autobiography of a Fugitive Slave* (1855). The most effective spokesman for black people in the nineteenth century was Frederick Douglass, an orator and public figure of great consequence in the antislavery movement, whose three autobiographies—*Narrative of the Life of Frederick Douglass* (1845), *My Bondage and My Freedom* (1855), and *Life and Times of Frederick Douglass* (1881)—remain the most penetrating account of slavery that has been written from the point of view of a black man. Most of these slave narratives were scarcely known in the nineteenth century and therefore are not reflected in the histories of the period, although Douglass edited a newspaper and was widely read in England and the United States. In our own time, many of the narratives have been reprinted and have succeeded in rendering the full conditions of slavery and in humanizing the black man.

In the South, the issue of slavery was paramount for writers and politicians. During the 1820's and '30's authors like John Pendleton Kennedy in *Swallow Barn* and William A. Caruthers In *The Cavaliers of*

Virginia (1835) depicted Southern plantations in which master and slave live harmoniously in a natural setting of beauty. But John Calhoun was already championing states rights and white supremacy; and, as abolitionist sentiment developed in the North, a series of books and essays by Southerners defended the institution of slavery: George Fitzhugh's *Cannibals All!* (1857) and *Sociology of the South* (1859), William Grayson's *The Hireling and the Slave* (1854), and William Gilmore Simms' *Southward Ho!* (1859) and "The Morals of Slavery" (1845).

The literature of abolitionism, slavery, and the Civil War is of extraordinary social significance and often of considerable aesthetic power. It includes Frederick Douglass' *Narrative* (1845), Harriet Beecher Stowe's *Uncle Tom's Cabin* (1851), Melville's *Benito Cereno* (1853) and *Battle Pieces* (1866); Thoreau's "Slavery in Massachusetts" (1854) and "A Plea for Captain John Brown" (1859); Whittier's poetry; Whitman's *Drum Taps* (1865), and many documents by the leading political figures of the time—Daniel Webster, Henry Clay, John C. Calhoun, and Abraham Lincoln. The issues raised by the condition of slavery have never left the American consciousness; they challenge the essential principles of democracy: equality, freedom, and the dignity of each separate person in a pluralistic society. When Benito Cereno, in Melville's novel, is asked what casts a shadow over him, he replies, "The Negro," and speaks for a generation of antebellum Americans troubled by the relationship between the races, anticipating Richard Wright's remark a century later that "The Negro is America's metaphor" and James Baldwin's indictment of white America: "In the eyes of one's victim, one sees oneself. Walk through the streets of Harlem and see what we this country have become." Like so many other social and political issues in American history, slavery was given its first real definition during the Romantic period.

The Romantic movement is a pivotal moment in Western history. Arising from the age of industrialism and reason, it carries the germinating seeds of America's complex fate. It is a turning point for the release of man's creativity: not only in literature and painting, but in sciences such as physics, chemistry, and biology, and in social sciences such as psychology, sociology, and anthropology. Self-reliance frees the imagination to create the modern world—so thought Emerson, Thoreau, Whitman, the transcendentalists and others; so many modern thinkers believe today. Yet across the view of Romanticism as a creative and affirmative force falls the warning of Melville and Hawthorne that the celebration of the heart at the expense of the mind can lead to a destructive irrationality and self-reliant monomania—a fictional Ahab or Chillingworth, an actual Hitler.

In America, pragmatism has always served as a counterweight to idealism: there has been a philosophical current of common sense as well as of transcendental idealism throughout the history of this country. During the Great Awakening of the 1740's, Jonathan Edwards gave eloquent expression to a strain of idealism that had run through the sermons of Puritan ministers; at the same time Benjamin Franklin was voicing a pragmatic philosophy that would influence the Founding Fathers. In the nineteenth century, the more ethereal poetry and essays of transcendentalists were satirized by Hawthorne, Melville, and Poe—and there was enough of the Yankee in Emerson and the curmudgeon in Thoreau to control whatever tendencies they themselves had toward the purely transcendental. In the South and West, common sense and wit assumed the form of a frontier humor as writers like T. B. Thorpe, Seba Smith, and Johnson J. Hooper drew their materials from the most common experiences and poked fun at any tendency to idealize human experience—a strain that finds its most accomplished expression in Mark Twain.

It has indeed been a complex fate to be an American, for the paradoxes of the national character have been many: idealism juxtaposed to materialism; immigration as a source of freedom for those who then enslaved others; natural beauty marred by industrial rapacity; innovation and creativity followed by destruction and planned obsolescence; and individualism struggling against the egalitarianism of the masses. And the questions, first formulated in the Romantic period, are still aspects of an unresolved American fate. How can the individual remain a single, separate person whose uniqueness is not sacrificed to technology? How can he remain "good" in a highly computerized and centralized society conducive to the moral corruption of a Vietnam War or of Watergate? How does a democracy encourage the creativity of industry without relinquishing the beauty of nature? How does the individual remain imaginative when machines think for him? Or retain his singularity when his clothing, shelter, food, and entertainment are all mass produced? Or avoid the jargon of professions, the functional language of merchandizing? How does he preserve the sense of person in congested cities? How does an educational structure serve all of its people and yet nourish the possibility of personal excellence and achievement? How can Americans resolve the paradox expressed by Walt Whitman:

> One's self I sing, a single separate person
> Yet utter the word Democratic, the word En-Masse.

Perhaps this is the special tension of Americans, their peculiar complex fate. We still live with the fundamental questions of Romanticism, in the shadow of wars, after the closing of national boundaries, at the end of immigration movements—in the threat of an ever-increasing bureaucracy. If there is any way of retaining the uniqueness of the individual—the most compelling characteristic of Romanticism—it must arise from the sense of openness and healthy contradiction that has always been distinctively American, expressed once in the release from old religions and foreign muses; defined later in the movement westward and the creation of cities and then megalopolises; strengthened by immigration and now by an education for every person; defined finally by a pluralistic society that Whitman embraced more than 100 years ago when he expressed his own self-confidence as an American living in a contradictory culture:

> Do I contradict myself?
> Very well then I contradict myself,
> (I am large, I contain multitudes.)

I

The American Scene

THE LAND

WILLIAM CULLEN BRYANT

(1794-1878)

Although William Cullen Bryant was a poet throughout his life, he wrote his finest lyrics before he became editor of the *New York Evening Post* in 1829. From the publication of his first draft of "Thanatopsis" in 1811 until he left his law practice in Great Barrington, Massachusetts, for the more active trade of journalism, Bryant was the

The Poetical Works of William Cullen Bryant, Household Edition, 1876, was the last text published during Bryant's life, but the most popular edition is *The Life and Works of William Cullen Bryant,* 6 vol., ed. Parke Godwin, 1883-1884. A reliable volume is *William Cullen Bryant, Representative Selections,* with Introduction, Bibliography, and Notes (American Writers Series), ed. Tremaine McDowell, 1935.

The standard biography for years was Parke Godwin's *Biography,* 1883. The best recent study is Harry Houston Peckham, *Gotham Yankee: A Biography of William Cullen Bryant,* 1950.

Critical studies include William A. Brad-

ley, *William Cullen Bryant,* English Men of Letters Series, 1905; Allen Nevins, *The Evening Post: A Century of Journalism,* 1922; C. S. Johnson, *Politics and a Bellyful* 1962; Albert F. McLean, *William Cullen Bryant,* 1964; Charles Henry Brown, *William Cullen Bryant,* 1972.

Two essays that shed light on Bryant's relations with Cole are Donald A Ringe, "Kindred Spirits: Bryant and Cole," *American Quarterly,* VI (1954), and Charles Sanford, "The Concept of the Sublime in Bryant and Cole," *American Literature,* XXVII (1957).

The following selections are taken from *The Poetical Works.*

quintessential Romanticist. His works, influenced by the eighteenth-century graveyard poets Blair and Gray but especially by the Romantic poet Wordsworth, are various tributes to the power of nature and its effect on the human sensibility.

Bryant's childhood was good preparation for his role as America's first important Romantic poet. Born on a farm in Cummington, Massachusetts, he grew up in the Berkshire Hills. His father was a doctor and encouraged the boy's precocious interest in poetry. By the time Bryant was 14, he had written an anti-Jefferson satire, "The Embargo, or Sketches of the Times," which his Federalist father received with pleasure and helped to publish. In 1811, the first version of "Thanatopsis" appeared and, by 1821, after he had read *The Lyrical Ballads,* Bryant added the introductory lines and issued the poem as we now know it. Bryant is less pantheistic than Wordsworth and, though he had shed the outward trappings of his Calvinist and Federalist upbringing, the ominous Puritan God is still a force throughout his best poetry, transformed into a majesty and formidable presence.

"Thanatopsis" was included in Bryant's first volume, *Poems* (1821), together with "To A Waterfowl" and "Inscription for the Entrance to a Wood." In 1829 he became editor of the *New York Evening Post* and began a long career as a liberal journalist, supporting labor unions and radical democracy and attacking the Bank of the United States, infringements on free speech, and the corporate monopolies. Throughout the 1830's, Bryant was a Jacksonian Democrat. As the issue of slavery became increasingly associated with the Democrats, however, he supported the new Republican party of Lincoln and achieved preeminence because of his courage in defending democracy and liberalism.

Bryant was also a literary critic of note. In 1825 he delivered his *Lectures on Poetry* and, from that time until the appearance of his last volume, *Poets and Poetry of the English Language* in 1871, he stressed the moral significance of poetry and the need of the poet to express fundamental emotions in simple terms. These characteristics infuse his own poems, especially those in which he pays tribute to the American scene. As a verbal landscape artist he shared a deep respect for nature with his friends Thomas Cole and Asher B. Durand, the painters. It is altogether appropriate that the two human figures represented in Durand's painting, *Kindred Spirits,* should be Bryant and Cole.

WILLIAM CULLEN BRYANT

Thanatopsis[1]

To him who in the love of Nature holds
Communion with her visible forms, she speaks
A various language; for his gayer hours
She has a voice of gladness, and a smile
And eloquence of beauty, and she glides   5
Into his darker musings, with a mild
And healing sympathy, that steals away
Their sharpness, ere he is aware. When thoughts
Of the last bitter hour come like a blight
Over thy spirit, and sad images   10
Of the stern agony, and shroud, and pall,
And breathless darkness, and the narrow house,
Make thee to shudder, and grow sick at heart,—
Go forth, under the open sky, and list
To Nature's teachings, while from all around—   15
Earth and her waters, and the depths of air,—
Comes a still voice—
                    Yet a few days, and thee
The all-beholding sun shall see no more
In all his course; nor yet in the cold ground,   20
Where thy pale form was laid, with many tears,
Nor in the embrace of ocean, shall exist
Thy image. Earth, that nourished thee, shall claim
Thy growth, to be resolved to earth again,
And, lost each human trace, surrendering up   25
Thine individual being, shalt thou go
To mix forever with the elements,
To be a brother to the insensible rock

[1] "Thanatopsis" means a view of death. It was first published in the *North American Review*, September 1817. In a letter written in 1855, Bryant made the following comment about the poem: "I cannot give you any information of the occasion which suggested to my mind the idea of my poem Thanatopsis. It was written when I was seventeen or eighteen years old—I have not now at hand the memorandums which would enable me to be precise—and I believe it was composed in my solitary rambles in the woods. As it was first committed to paper, it began with the half-line —Yet a few days, and thee—and ended with the beginning of another line with the words—And make their bed with thee. The rest of the poem—the introduction and the close—was added some years afterward, in 1821, when I published a little collection of my poems at Cambridge."

The concentration on death indicates Bryant's debt to the "graveyard school" of poetry in England; like the poets Blair, Southey, Cowper, Collins, Young, and Gray, Bryant is concerned with the question of how a person shall confront death. Rejecting formal Calvinism, the poet expresses a stoic view of life that suggests that the individual will have to discover his own faith and be self-reliant.

And to the sluggish clod, which the rude swain
Turns with his share, and treads upon. The oak   30
Shall send his roots abroad, and pierce thy mould.

   Yet not to thine eternal resting-place
Shalt thou retire alone, nor couldst thou wish
Couch more magnificent. Thou shalt lie down
With patriarchs of the infant world, with kings,   35
The powerful of the earth, the wise, the good,
Fair forms, and hoary seers of ages past,
All in one mighty sepulchre. The hills
Rock-ribbed and ancient as the sun, the vales
Stretching in pensive quietness between;   40
The venerable woods—rivers that move
In majesty, and the complaining brooks
That make the meadows green; and, poured round all,
Old Ocean's gray and melancholy waste,—
Are but the solemn decorations all   45
Of the great tomb of man. The golden sun,
The planets, all the infinite host of heaven,
Are shining on the sad abodes of death,
Through the still lapse of ages. All that tread
The globe are but a handful to the tribes   50
That slumber in its bosom.—Take the wings
Of morning, pierce the Barcan wilderness,
Or lose thyself in the continuous woods
Where rolls the Oregon, and hears no sound,
Save his own dashings—yet the dead are there: 55
And millions in those solitudes, since first
The flight of years began, have laid them down
In their last sleep—the dead reign there alone.
So shalt thou rest, and what if thou withdraw
In silence from the living, and no friend   60
Take note of thy departure? All that breathe
Will share thy destiny. The gay will laugh
When thou are gone, the solemn brood of care
Plod on, and each one as before will chase
His favorite phantom; yet all these shall leave   65
Their mirth and their employments, and shall come
And make their bed with thee. As the long train
Of ages glide away, the sons of men,
The youth in life's green spring, and he who goes
In the full strength of years, matron and maid,   70
The speechless babe, and the gray-headed man—

Shall one by one be gathered to thy side,
By those, who in their turn shall follow them.

So live, that when thy summons comes to join
The innumerable caravan, which moves   75
To that mysterious realm, where each shall take
His chamber in the silent halls of death,
Thou go not, like the quarry-slave at night,
Scourged to his dungeon, but, sustained and soothed
By an unfaltering trust, approach thy grave,   80
Like one who wraps the drapery of his couch
About him, and lies down to pleasant dreams.

1817, 1821

To a Waterfowl[1]

Whither, midst falling dew,
While glow the heavens with the last steps of day,

Far, through their rosy depths, dost thou pursue
Thy solitary way?
Vainly the fowler's eye   5
Might mark thy distant flight, to do thee wrong,
As, darkly seen against the crimson sky,
Thy figure floats along.

Seek'st thou the plashy brink
Of weedy lake, or marge of river wide,   10

[1] In his biography of Bryant, Parke Godwin draws the image of young Bryant, in December 1815, walking toward Plainfield, Massachusetts, where he wished to practice law: "He walked up the hills, very forlorn and desolate indeed, not knowing what was to become of him in the big world which grew bigger as he ascended and yet darker with the coming on of night. The sun had already set, leaving behind it one of those brilliant seas of chrysolite and opal which often flood the New England skies. While he was looking on the rosy splendor with rapt admiration, a solitary bird made wing along the illuminated horizon. He watched the lone wanderer until it was lost in the distance, asking himself whither it had come and to what far home it was flying. When he went to the house where he was to stop for the night, his mind was still full of what he had seen and felt, and he wrote those lines. . .'To a Waterfowl.'

The last stanza suggests Bryant's new Unitarian faith and his belief in the omnipresence of God in nature.

Or where the rocking billows rise and sink
    On the chafed ocean side?

There is a Power, whose care
Teaches thy way along that pathless coast,—
The desert and illimitable air,   15
    Lone wandering, but not lost.

All day thy wings have fann'd,
At that far height, the cold thin atmosphere;
Yet stoop not, weary, to the welcome land,
    Though the dark night is near.   20

  And soon that toil shall end,
Soon shalt thou find a summer home, and rest,
And scream among thy fellows; reeds shall bend,
    Soon, o'er thy sheltered nest.

Thou'rt gone, the abyss of heaven   25
Hath swallowed up thy form, yet, on my heart
Deeply hath sunk the lesson thou hast given,
    And shall not soon depart.

He, who, from zone to zone,
Guides through the boundless sky thy certain flight,   30
In the long way that I must trace alone,
    Will lead my steps aright.

                          1818, 1821

Inscription for the Entrance to a Wood[1]

Stranger, if thou has learned a truth which needs
No school of long experience, that the world
Is full of guilt and misery, and hast seen
Enough of all its sorrows, crimes, and cares,
To tire thee of it, enter this wild wood   5
And view the haunts of Nature. The calm shade

---

[1] Many of Bryant's poems were the inspiration for Asher B. Durand's paintings: "Thanatopsis," for example, is visually represented in a landscape of the same title. This poem should be compared with Durand's "Mountain Forest." Both poet and artist were particularly concerned to make their landscapes uniquely American and to create the sense of a virgin land different from that of Europe.

Shall bring a kindred calm, and the sweet breeze
That makes the green leaves dance, shall waft a balm
To thy sick heart. Thou will find nothing here
Of all that pained thee in the haunts of men, 10
And made thee loathe thy life. The primal curse
Fell, it is true, upon the unsinning earth,
But not in vengeance. God hath yoked to guilt
Her pale tormentor, misery. Hence, these shades
Are still the abodes of gladness; the thick roof 15
Of green and stirring branches is alive
And musical with birds, that sing and sport
In wantonness of spirit; while below
The squirrel, with raised paws and form erect,
Chirps merrily. Throngs of insects in the shade 20
Try their thin wings and dance in the warm beam
That waked them into life. Even the green trees
Partake the deep contentment; as they bend
To the soft winds, the sun from the blue sky
Looks in and sheds a blessing on the scene. 25
Scarce less the cleft-born wild-flower seems to enjoy
Existence, than the winged plunderer
That sucks its sweets. The mossy rocks themselves
And the old and ponderous trunks of prostrate trees
That lead from knoll to knoll a causey rude 30
Or bridge the sunken brook, and their dark roots,
With all their earth upon them, twisting high,
Breathe fixed tranquillity. The rivulet
Sends forth glad sounds, and tripping o'er its bed
Of pebbly sands, or leaping down the rocks, 35
Seems, with continuous laughter, to rejoice
In its own being. Softly tread the marge,
Lest from her midway perch thou scare the wren
That dips her bill in water. The cool wind,
That stirs the stream in play, shall come to thee, 40
Like one that loves thee nor will let thee pass
Ungreeted, and shall give its light embrace.

To Cole, the Painter, Departing for Europe[1]

Thine eyes shall see the light of distant skies;
   Yet, COLE! thy heart shall bear to Europe's strand
   A living image of our own bright land,
Such as upon thy glorious canvas lies;
Lone lakes—savannas where the bison roves—   5
   Rocks rich with summer garlands—solemn streams—
   Skies, where the desert eagle wheels and screams—
Spring bloom and autumn blaze of boundless groves.
Fair scenes shall greet thee where thou goest—fair,
   But different—everywhere the trace of men,   10
Paths, homes, graves, ruins, from the lowest glen
To where life shrinks from the fierce Alpine air.
   Gaze on them, till the tears shall dim thy sight,
   But keep that earlier, wilder image bright.

1830, 1832

[1] Bryant had a close association with Thomas Cole, whose work is discussed on p. 831 and whose paintings are reproduced on pp. 832-833. This tribute to Cole was written when the artist went to Europe in 1829. Both Bryant and Cole are drawn in Asher B. Durand's famous painting, *Kindred Spirits* (p. 835), as two small cultured figures set against the magnificence of the Catskill Mountains. The juxtaposition of cultivated artists and the landscape suggests their harmony with the largeness and awesome power of nature.

THE HUDSON RIVER PAINTERS

In 1825, a Colonel John Trumbull, who belonged to a Bread and Cheese Club that included well-known artists, noticed three paintings in the window of a New York frameshop. Trumbull admired the paint-

Three of the authoritative studies of early American art are William Dunlap, *A History of the Rise and Progress of the Arts of Design in the United States,* 2 vols., 1834; 3 vols., 1918, 1965; James Jackson Jarves, *Art Hints, Architecture, Sculpture and Painting,* 1855, and Jarves, *The Art-Idea,* 1860.

Alan Burroughs, *Limners and Likenesses: Three Centuries of American Painting,* 1936, is comprehensive. More recent works include Virgil Barker, *American Painting, History and Interpretation,* 1950; James T. Flexner, *First Flowers of our Wilderness: American Painting,* 1947; *The Light of Distant Skies,* 1760-1835, 1954; *That Wilder Image,* 1962; Oliver Larkin, *Art and Life in America,* 1949, 1960; E. P. Richardson, *Painting in America,* 1952;

(Footnote continued next page.)

ings and "saw the American land depicted in all of its native peculiarity with powerful realism and yet a lover's eye." The landscapes had been painted by Thomas Cole and, at Trumbull's invitation, Cole joined the Bread and Cheese Club and came to know some of the leading painters of the period: Samuel B. Morse, Asher B. Durand, Washington Allston, John Kensett, Thomas Doughty, Frederic Church, Henry Inman, John Vanderlyn, and John Wesley Jarvis. Through this association and mutual encouragement, the Hudson River School of painting developed.

The Hudson River painters were primarily concerned with the Catskill Mountains, the Hudson River itself, and the rough terrain of upstate New York, although in time the school included painters like Albert Bierstadt and Thomas Moran, who drew landscapes of the Rocky Mountain region. These artists bring an enthusiasm and optimism to their work as well as a great sympathy for natural surroundings not yet contaminated by social forces. The romantic concept of nature is projected realistically: the paintings use light dramatically and emphasize detail, atmosphere, and climate. In the work of Cole, man is in harmony with nature; in the paintings of Doughty, man seems at odds with the landscape, a deeply lonely Byronic figure; in Durand's art, man is never dwarfed by his environment. Throughout these landscapes runs a moral commentary that suggests the power of God in nature.

John K. Howat, *The Hudson River and Its Painters,* 1972. A study that pays especial attention to literary connections is Barbara Novak, *American Painting of the Nineteenth Century: Realism, Idealism and the American Experience,* 1969. For studies of the individual painters represented in this volume, see the following: E. P. Richardson, *Washington Allston: A Study of the Romantic Artist in America,* 1948; Rev. Louis L. Noble, *The Course of Empire, Voyage of Life and Other Pictures of Thomas Cole,* 1853, 1964; Asher B. Durand, *The Life and Times of Asher B. Durand,* 1894; Bartlett Cowdrey and H. W. Williams, Jr., *William Sidney Mount, 1807-1868: An American Painter,* 1944; John Wilmerding, *Fitzhugh Lane, 1804-1865, American Marine Painter,* 1964; Robert McIntyre, *Martin Johnson Heade,* 1948.

WASHINGTON ALLSTON

(1779-1843)

Washington Allston went to London in 1801 to study painting under Benjamin West. He continued his work in Paris and Rome, beginning as a classical painter and becoming more and more romantic after his return to America in 1800. In his best work he tries to respond to

Washington Allston. "Moonlit Landscape," 1819. *(Courtesy, Museum of Fine Arts, Boston. Gift of William Sturgis Bigelow.)*

intuitive creation as well as to a long artistic tradition. His finest canvasses are those in which he captures man's loneliness and melancholy through a natural setting that binds the individual to permanent forces. *Moonlit Landscape* (1819) and *Landscape, American Scene: Time, Afternoon with a Southwest Haze* (1835) are fine examples of Allston's art.

Moonlit Landscape

It was Allston's view that "to give the whole truth in the midnight as well as in the daylight belongs to a master."

Upon his return from Europe, Allston recorded the following comments, which underlie his fanciful painting, *Moonlit Landscape:* "A homesickness which (in spite of some of the best and kindest friends, and every encouragement that I could wish as an artist) I could not overcome, brought me back to my own country in 1818. We made Boston Harbour on a clear evening in October. It was an evening to remember! The wind fell and left our ship almost stationary on a long low swell, as smooth as glass and undulating under one of our gorgeous autumnal skies like a prairie of amber. The moon looked down on us like a living thing, as if to bid us welcome, and the fanciful thought is still in my memory that she broke her image on the water to make partners for a dance of fireflies—and they *did* dance, if I ever saw dancing."

Landscape, American Scenery: Time, Afternoon with a Southwest Haze

" . . . The poet leaves his song half sung, or finishes it, beyond the scope of mortal ears, in a celestial choir. The painter—as Allston did—leaves half his conception on the canvas to sadden us with its imperfect beauty, and goes to picture forth the whole, if it be no irreverence to say so, in the hues of heaven. But rather such incomplete designs of this life will be perfected nowhere. This so frequent abortion of man's dearest projects must be taken as a proof that the deeds of earth, however etherealised by piety or genius, are without value, except as exercises and manifestations of the spirit."

—Nathaniel Hawthorne, "The Artist of the Beautiful"

THOMAS COLE

(1801-1848)

Born in England in 1801, Thomas Cole migrated to the United States with his family in 1818. After living in Philadelphia and Pittsburgh, the Coles moved to New York in 1825. Young Cole had already begun to paint and, from the sale of one painting, he took a trip upstate where, in his own words, "the spectacle of the Hudson River and the Catskill Mountains came upon him with the quality of a revelation." The wildness, power, and dignity of the landscape deeply affected him and appear as features in his most famous paintings: *The Voyage of Life: Manhood, Hudson Highlands, The Oxbow of the Connecticut, The Summer Sunset, Catskill Creek,* and *Scene from the Last of the Mohicans.*

Cole had a life-long friendship with William Cullen Bryant and shared the poet's view that nature has a deeply religious effect on the individual. For Cole, Nature and Art were indistinguishable.

That the true and the beautiful in Nature and Art are one and inseparable I have long been convinced. And that truth is the fixed and unchangeable standard of taste, that works of art, however they may tickle the fancy and amuse the eye of the multitude at the time—unless founded and built upon truth will pass away like the breeze that for the moment ruffles the surface of the lake. Those founded on truth are permanent and reflect the world in perfect beauty. What I mean by true in Nature is the fulfillment in themselves, the consummation . . . of created things, of the objects and purposes for which they were created. . . . By true in art I mean imitation of true nature and not the imitation of accidents nor merely the common imitation that takes nature indiscriminately. All nature is not true. The stunted pine, the withered fig-tree, the flowers whose petals are imperfect are not true.

The Voyage of Life (Manhood)

In the terrible and the grand . . . when the mind is astonished, the eye does not dwell on the minute but seizes the whole. In the forest, during an hour of tempest, it is not the bough playing in the wind, but

Thomas Cole. "The Oxbow" (The Connecticut River Near Northampton), 1836. *(The Metropolitan Museum of Art, Gift of Mrs. Russell Sage, 1908.)*

Thomas Cole. "The Course of Empire: The Consummation of Empire," 1836. (Courtesy of The New York Historical Society, New York City.)

833

the whole mass stooping to the blast that absorbs the attention: the detail, however fine, is comparatively unobserved. In a picture of such a subject detail should not attract the eye, but the whole. It should be, in this case, the aim of the artist to impress the spirit of the entire scene upon the mind of the beholder. . . . The finest scene in the world, one most fitted to awaken sensations of the sublime, is made up of minutest parts. These ought all to be given, but so given as to render them subordinate and ministrative to one effect.

—Thomas Cole

ASHER B. DURAND

(1796-1886)

Asher B. Durand was a close friend of Thomas Cole and William Cullen Bryant. Beginning as an engraver, Durand turned to the creation of portraits and then landscapes. Unlike Cole, Durand created paintings that were serene; but he shared Cole's belief that God and nature are one. Durand and Bryant brought out a volume, *The American Landscape,* which featured Durand's engravings and Bryant's text. The two men had a considerable influence on each other, and one can juxtapose the paintings with the poetry: Durand's *Monument Mountain* is described in Bryant's poem of the same name; his landscapes, *Mountain Forest, In the Woods,* and *The Edge of the Forest* are captured in Bryant's "Inscription for the Entrance to a Wood," "Autumn Woods," "A Forest Hymn," and "Among the Trees."

FREDERIC EDWIN CHURCH

(1826-1900)

Frederic Edwin Church studied under Thomas Cole and extended his master's view of nature into panoramic landscapes like *Niagara Falls* (1857) and *In the Heart of the Andes* (1859). So huge were these works that people needed cylinders to view their details.

Asher B. Durand. "Kindred Spirits," 1849. *(Collection of The New York Public Library, Astor, Lenox and Tilden Foundations.)*

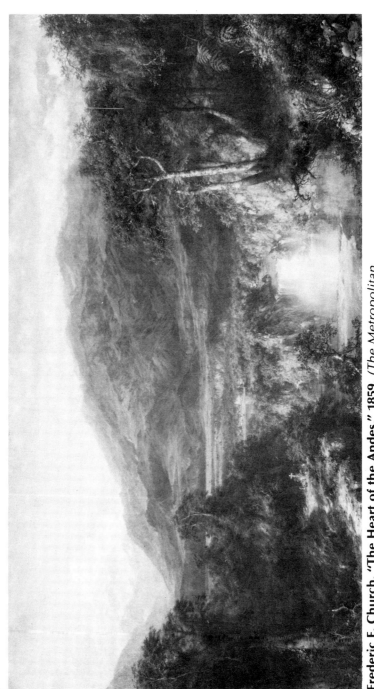

Frederic E. Church. "The Heart of the Andes," 1859. *(The Metropolitan Museum of Art, Bequest of Mrs. David Bows, 1909.)*

ALBERT BIERSTADT

(1830-1902)

Albert Bierstadt extended the vision of New England painters into the reaches of the Rocky Mountains. His *Merced River, Yosemite Valley* (1866) is a dramatic rendering of the rough and realistic aspects of the American landscape. The figures in the moving boat and on the ledge seem to be at one with the large mountains, not overwhelmed or dwarfed by them.

JOHN JAMES AUDUBON

(1785-1851)

Audubon approached the American landscape from still another point of view: he drew brilliant paintings of the birds in America. His collection, *The Birds of North America* (1827-1838), is still a classic in the field of ornithology.

Albert Bierstadt. "Merced River, Yosemite Valley." *(The Metropolitan Museum of Art, Gift of the sons of William Paton, 1909.)*

John J. Audubon. "Carolina Paroquet," 1825. *(Courtesy of The New York Historical Society, New York City.)*

NATURE, THE INDIVIDUAL, AND SOCIETY

RALPH WALDO EMERSON

(1803-1881)

The primary element in Ralph Waldo Emerson's life was theology. All of his ancestors had been preachers in the churches of Concord, and it was natural that his view of nature, society, and politics should be

The Collected Works of Ralph Waldo Emerson, 1971—, is and will be the standard edition. Until it is completed, the most useful texts may be found in The Complete Works of Ralph Emerson, The Centenary Edition, ed. E. W. Emerson and W. E. Forbes, 1909-1914; The Journals and Miscellaneous Notebooks of Ralph Waldo Emerson, Vol. I, ed. W. H. Gilman and others, 1961 (for a complete set, see The Journals of Ralph Waldo Emerson, 10 vols., ed. E. W. Emerson and W. E. Forbes, 1909-1914); The Letters of Ralph Waldo Emerson, 6 vols., ed. Ralph L. Rusk, 1939. Other collections of importance are Ralph Waldo Emerson: Early Lectures, ed. S. E. Whicher and R. E. Spiller, 1959; Vol. II, R. E. Spiller, 1964; Vol. III, R. E. Spiller and W. E. Williams, 1972.

The standard biography is Ralph L. Rusk, The Life of Ralph Waldo Emerson, 1949. Early studies are G. W. Cooke, Ralph Waldo Emerson, 1881; J. E. Cabot, A Memoir of Ralph Waldo Emerson, 2 vols., 1887; and G. E. Woodbury, Ralph Waldo Emerson, 1907.

Critical studies include Vivian C. Hopkins, Spires of Form: A Study of Emerson's Aesthetics, 1951; Sherman Paul, Emerson's Angle of Vision, 1952; Stephen Whicher,

Freedom and Fate: An Inner Life of Ralph Waldo Emerson, 1953; F. J. Carpenter, Emerson Handbook, 1953; Milton R. Konvitz and Stephen Whicher, eds. Emerson: A Collection of Critical Essays, Twentieth Century Views, 1962; Jonathan Bishop, Emerson on the Soul, 1964; Joel Porte, Emerson and Thoreau: Transcendentalists in Conflict, 1966; Jeffrey Duncan, The Power and Form of Emerson's Thought, 1973; H. H. Waggoner, Emerson as Poet, 1974; Edward Wagenknecht, Ralph Waldo Emerson: Portrait of a Balanced Soul, 1974, and David Levin, ed. Emerson-Prophecy, Metamorphosis, and Influence: Selected Papers from the English Institute, 1976. For an historical survey of Emersonian criticism, see Milton R. Konvitz, ed., The Recognition of Waldo Emerson, 1972.

A good and accessible collection is The Complete Essays and Other Writings, ed. Brooks Atkinson, 1940.

Nature, "The American Scholar," and "The Divinity School Address" are taken from The Collected Works of Ralph Waldo Emerson, ed. R. E. Spiller and A. R. Ferguson, 1972, a CEEA edition. The other texts are from Essays: Second Series, included in The Complete Works, ed. E. W. Emerson.

strongly religious. Through his theological training and his discovery of God within himself and nature, he witnessed the early growth of the nation and wrote its moral commentary. He was the American Scholar throughout the nineteenth century, that central figure whose numerous essays influenced the thought of Thoreau, Whitman, Emily Dickinson, Frost, and scores of lesser writers, the idealist whose writing was a moral touchstone for the fiction of Hawthorne, Melville, and others.

Emerson was born in Concord, Massachusetts on May 25, 1803. His father, William, was the minister of the First Church of Boston, a congregationalist who still adhered to the hereditary doctrine of human depravity but who questioned predestination, the Calvinist scheme of salvation, and the concept of the trinity, and who sympathized with the emerging Unitarianism that would soon dominate New England theology. In politics, William Emerson was far more conservative: he distrusted the reform measures of radicals and all modern innovations. Emerson's mother was a simple, pious woman who struggled to raise him and his four other brothers—William, Charles, Edward, and Robert—after the father's death in 1811 had reduced the family to poverty. Two other close relatives offered the growing boy a different religious perspective: his strong-minded and eccentric aunt, Mary Moody Emerson, who retained her faith in Calvinism and the Englightenment, and his step-grandfather, the Reverend Ezra Ripley of Concord, who was nominally a Unitarian but who still behaved like a latter-day Puritan.

Although these figures provided a connection with religious orthodoxy and the traditions of his ancestry, young Emerson responded more sympathetically to the progressive tendencies in Boston: the growing importance of Unitarianism, as articulated by William Ellery Channing, and the political independence of an America that had thrown off its "colonial complex." He attended the Boston Latin School from 1812 to 1817 and then Harvard College from 1817 to 1821; he was, unlike his brothers Charles and Edward, an ordinary student, who was uncertain of his future vocation, who tended to remain aloof from his fellow students, and who resisted the strict curriculum of the college. Unwillingly, he taught young ladies in his brother William's school; his real career was spent privately, as he read philosophy, history, and poetry, and began to write his own essays and poems. He had decided to become a minister, like his ancestors, and returned to Harvard, to the Divinity School, in 1825. Already he was under the strong influence of William Ellery Channing, resisting orthodoxy and embracing liberalism, expressing his new ideas of compensation and self-reliance as a young minister in various churches. In March 1829 he was ordained pastor of the Second Church in Boston.

Emerson's apprenticeship for his later career as lecturer and essayist was rapidly drawing to a close. In September 1829, he married Ellen Tucker, a girl he had been courting for more than a year; but she was never really healthy and, in 1831, she died of consumption. A year later he resigned his pastorate, unable to perform the rites of the church, unwilling to conspire with his congregation in the worship of the "dead forms of our grandfathers." Opposed to the institution, the history, the creeds, and the rites of the church, he wanted to teach ethics and not preach religious dogma; and when his church would not permit him to forego his own participation in the ceremony of the Last Supper—a rite perpetuated by St. Paul which, he claimed, had no valid authority—Emerson resigned his position. This was an act of considerable courage, a dramatic example of those elements that he would soon champion in his essays: self-reliance and the denial of historical and religious creeds. In the next four years he refined these ideas and produced the work on which he established his reputation: *Nature* (1836), "The American Scholar" (1837), and "The Divinity School Address" (1838). The significant and absorbing question to ask oneself, as a student of American Civilization, is why this young man, growing up in a traditional household, with the pedigree of a pilgrim and the comfortable future of a New England minister, should choose to take issue with inherited doctrines and declare an intellectual independence that would be a guide for his and later generations.

Privately, Emerson had more than the usual share of tragedy. His father died when he was eight; his brother Edward suffered a nervous breakdown in 1828 and died in 1834; his brother Charles died in 1836; his fourth brother Robert was mentally retarded; his first wife Ellen died after they had been married for only a year and a half; his son Waldo died when not yet six years old. In addition to an inordinate number of family misfortunes, he suffered himself. During his early twenties, his vision was impaired, his body plagued by rheumatic pains, and his lungs threatened by tuberculosis. By the time he formulated his concepts of self-reliance and the oversoul, he was well-acquainted with suffering and tragedy; indeed, it was not until he had returned from his European trip, taken after he resigned from the ministry, that he recovered his full health. His emphasis on action in "The American Scholar" and his denial of evil in "The Divinity School Address" stem in part from his feeling that man must be stoical despite personal suffering. Instead of resorting to any romantic pose or morbid self-pity because of his physical weakness, he took a pragmatic attitude and confronted experience, through his lectures and his writing, directly. The modern reader may feel that Emerson's essays are excessively affirmative and do not recognize sufficiently man's limitations, but Emerson was interested in appealing to the ideal and in creating a literature that goes beyond tragedy, a literature of thanksgiving.

Emerson's private need for self-assertion was given encouragement by the trip he made to Europe between 1832 and 1833. In England he met Coleridge, Wordsworth and, most important, Thomas Carlyle. These writers had broken with literary traditions and had celebrated in their poems and essays the common man, nature, the organic form in art, and the use of simple language. Emerson was intent on converting his career from minister to writer and scholar and, as a young man who had yet to prove himself, he was stimulated by the great writers of Europe. He returned to Concord with a renewed faith in himself.

The American society of his time was particularly consonant with Emerson's ideas. The Puritan heritage was in decline; political and cultural leaders stressed the new nation's independence of England; a cult of self-improvement was on everyone's lips; an adolescent America promised frontier expansion to the West and South and an industrial growth of extraordinary dimensions. Most important, democracy was committed to the common man and his future—it demanded a literature different from that of European nations, and Emerson became its most articulate and forceful spokesman. He became, as John Dewey said, the "philosopher of democracy." In his first important essay, *Nature* (1836), he announced his philosophical views: "Our age is retrospective. . . . Why should not we also enjoy an original relation to the universe? Why should not we have a poetry and philosophy of insight and not of tradition, and a religion by revelation to us, and not the history of theirs." In "The American Scholar," he wrote, as Oliver Wendell Holmes remarked, "our intellectual Declaration of Independence," and insisted that in America the scholar must be Man Thinking, an activist in whom self-reliance is the cardinal characteristic. In "The Divinity School Address," he refuted the exclusive divinity of Christ and the reverence for the history and institution of the church. These three essays define, with an extraordinary eloquence, the central ideas of Emerson and the thinkers of his age; and, with their publication, the literature of the American renaissance was given shape and substance.

In 1835 Emerson had married Lydia Jackson. The couple lived in Concord and raised their four children—Waldo, born in 1836, died in 1842; Ellen was born in 1839, Edith in 1841, and Edward in 1844. Emerson's *Essays, First Series* appeared in 1841 and included "History," "Self-Reliance," and "Compensation"; his *Essays: Second Series* was published in 1844 and included "The Poet" and "Experience." Throughout the next 30 years, his writing was prolific and highly influential: *Poems* (1847), *Representative Men* (1850), *English Traits* (1856), and *The Conduct of Life* (1860). His later work was more controlled by a sense of the individual's limitations and by an increasing respect for the powerful and successful person; the essays "Napoleon" from *Representative Men* and "Fate" from *The Conduct of Life* suggest his modified attitude. Emerson's writing also reflects a constant concern with the events of his time: he protested the government's treatment of the Cherokee Indians, attacked Daniel Webster for his support of the Fugitive Slave Law, and championed John Brown and other abolitionists in their opposition of slavery. But he mistrusted himself as a reformer, and when friends wanted him to join the Utopian experiment at Brook Farm in 1841, he declined—he was too much the individualist to become part of any community. He viewed himself as the American Scholar who articulated for a generation the correspondences between nature and the soul; the concepts of the oversoul and self-reliance and compensation; the belief in idealism, and the worth of the individual man.

James Russell Lowell called Emerson "a Plotinus-Montaigne"; John Dewey termed him "the philosopher of democracy"; George Santayana saw him as a Puritan Mystic with a poetic fancy and a gift for observation and epigram; Yvor Winter condemned him as a fraud; Newton Arvin characterized him as our bishop. Whatever the final judgment, no important critic of our native culture has avoided Emerson's work, for it is central to an understanding of American intellectual and literary history.

Nature¹

A subtle chain of countless rings
The next unto the farthest brings;
The eye reads omens where it goes,
And speaks all languages the rose;
And, striving to be man, the worm
Mounts through all the spires of form.²

INTRODUCTION

Our age is retrospective. It builds the sepulchres of the fathers. It writes biographies, histories, and criticism. The foregoing generations beheld God and nature face to face; we, through their eyes. Why should not we also enjoy an original relation to the universe? Why should not we have a poetry and philosophy of insight and not of tradition, and a religion by revelation to us, and not the history of theirs? Embosomed for a season in nature, whose floods of life stream around and through us, and invite us by the powers they supply, to action proportioned to nature, why should we grope among the dry bones of the past, or put the living generation into masquerade out of its faded wardrobe? The sun shines to-day also. There is more wool and flax in

¹ This essay is the first major statement of the transcendental faith. It contains most of Emerson's principle ideas: the significance of nature in the life of man; the need for self-reliance, solitude, and spiritual harmony; the belief in the oversoul; and the organic relationship of language to nature.

Emerson had thought about the subject for many years. In the journal that he kept on ship when he returned from England in 1833 he stated that "I like my book about Nature, and wish I knew where and how I ought to live" (*Journals*, III, 196). He had read Plato and the Neoplatonists, Swedenborg, Wordsworth, Coleridge, Goethe, and the German idealists. On his trip to Europe, after he had resigned from his ministry, he met the English writers and was especially influenced by Carlyle, with whom he established a lifelong relationship.

Emerson began to write the essay when he was living at the Manse in Concord, the home of his step-grandfather, Dr. Ripley, in 1834, and the same place in which Hawthorne was to write *Mosses from an Old Manse*. The first edition of *Nature* was published anonymously in the summer of 1836 and sold only 500 copies; it appeared again in 1849 as the first essay in *Nature, Addresses, and Lectures* (*Works*, I). Although the first edition had a small sale (approximately 500 copies in 13 years), it did reach influential thinkers and made a great impression on them. *Nature* is not profoundly original—one can find these ideas in the work of many writers of the time—but they are expressed with rare eloquence and power and with a comprehensiveness that make the essay perhaps the most significant expression of transcendentalism in American literature.

² The poem was the epigraph of *Nature* when it was republished in 1849 and was later incorporated in the 1867 volume, *May-Day and Other Pieces* (*Works*, IX, 165-166). In the first edition, Emerson used as an epigraph a quotation from Plotinus: "Nature is but an image or imitation of wisdom, the last thing of the soul; Nature being a thing which doth only do, but not know."

the fields. There are new lands, new men, new thoughts. Let us demand our own works and laws and worship.

Undoubtedly we have no questions to ask which are unanswerable. We must trust the perfection of the creation so far, as to believe that whatever curiosity the order of things has awakened in our minds, the order of things can satisfy. Every man's condition is a solution in hieroglyphic to those inquiries he would put. He acts it as life, before he apprehends it as truth. In like manner, nature is already, in its forms and tendencies, describing its own design. Let us interrogate the great apparition, that shines so peacefully around us. Let us inquire, to what end is nature?

All science has one aim, namely, to find a theory of nature. We have theories of races and of functions, but scarcely yet a remote approach to an idea of creation. We are now so far from the road to truth, that religious teachers dispute and hate each other, and speculative men are esteemed unsound and frivolous. But to a sound judgment, the most abstract truth is the most practical. Whenever a true theory appears, it will be its own evidence. Its test is, that it will explain all phenomena. Now many are thought not only unexplained but inexplicable; as language, sleep, madness, dreams, beasts, sex.

Philosophically considered, the universe is composed of Nature and the Soul. Strictly speaking, therefore, all that is separate from us, all which Philosophy distinguishes as the NOT ME,[3] that is, both nature and art, all other men and my own body, must be ranked under this name, NATURE. In enumerating the values of nature and casting up their sum, I shall use the word in both senses;—in its common and in its philosophical import. In inquiries so general as our present one, the inaccuracy is not material; no confusion of thought will occur. *Nature*, in the common sense, refers to essences unchanged by man; space, the air, the river, the leaf. *Art* is applied to the mixture of his will with the same things, as in a house, a canal, a statue, a picture. But his operations taken together are so insignificant, a little chipping, baking, patching, and washing, that in an impression so grand as that of the world on the human mind, they do not vary the result.

CHAPTER I. NATURE

To go into solitude, a man needs to retire as much from his chamber as from society. I am not solitary whilst I read and write, though nobody is with me. But if a man would be alone, let him look at the stars. The rays that come from those heavenly worlds, will separate between him and vulgar things.

---

[3] This definition of the NOT ME probably derives from the German philosopher Fichte. It appears in Carlyle's essay on Novalis (1829): "what Fichte means by his far-famed *Ich* and *Nicht-ich* [I and Not-I]." Carlyle uses this phrase, "the NOT ME," again in *Sartor Resartus* (1833-1834), Book II, Chapter 8.

One might think the atmosphere was made transparent with this design, to give man, in the heavenly bodies, the perpetual presence of the sublime. Seen in the streets of cities, how great they are! If the stars should appear one night in a thousand years, how would men believe and adore; and preserve for many generations the remembrance of the city of God which had been shown! But every night come out these envoys of beauty, and light the universe with their admonishing smile.

The stars awaken a certain reverence, because though always present, they are always inaccessible; but all natural objects make a kindred impression, when the mind is open to their influence. Nature never wears a mean appearance. Neither does the wisest man extort all her secret, and lose his curiosity by finding out all her perfection. Nature never became a toy to a wise spirit. The flowers, the animals, the mountains, reflected all the wisdom of his best hour, as much as they had delighted the simplicity of his childhood.

When we speak of nature in this manner, we have a distinct but most poetical sense in the mind. We mean the integrity of impression made by manifold natural objects. It is this which distinguishes the stick of timber of the wood-cutter, from the tree of the poet. The charming landscape which I saw this morning, is indubitably made up of some twenty or thirty farms. Miller owns this field, Locke that, and Manning the woodland beyond. But none of them owns the landscape. There is a property in the horizon which no man has but he whose eye can integrate all the parts, that is, the poet. This is the best part of these men's farms, yet to this their warranty-deeds give no title.

To speak truly, few adult persons can see nature. Most persons do not see the sun. At least they have a very superficial seeing. The sun illuminates only the eye of the man, but shines into the eye and the heart of the child. The lover of nature is he whose inward and outward senses are still truly adjusted to each other; who has retained the spirit of infancy even into the era of manhood. His intercourse with heaven and earth, becomes part of his daily food. In the presence of nature, a wild delight runs through the man, in spite of real sorrows. Nature says,—he is my creature, and maugre[4] all his impertinent griefs, he shall be glad with me. Not the sun or the summer alone, but every hour and season yields its tribute of delight; for every hour and change corresponds to and authorizes a different state of the mind, from breathless noon to grimmest midnight. Nature is a setting that fits equally well a comic or a mourning piece. In good health, the air is a cordial of incredible virtue. Crossing a bare common, in snow puddles, at twilight, under a clouded sky, without having in my thoughts any occurrence of special good fortune, I have enjoyed a perfect exhilaration. Almost I fear to think how glad I am. In the woods too, a man casts off his years, as the snake his slough, and at what

---

[4] In spite of.

period soever of life, is always a child. In the woods, is perpetual youth. Within these plantations of God, a decorum and sanctity reign, a perennial festival is dressed, and the guest sees not how he should tire of them in a thousand years. In the woods, we return to reason and faith. There I feel that nothing can befall me in life,—no disgrace, no calamity, (leaving me my eyes,) which nature cannot repair. Standing on the bare ground,—my head bathed by the blithe air, and uplifted into infinite space,—all mean egotism vanishes. I become a transparent eye-ball. I am nothing. I see all. The currents of the Universal Being circulate through me; I am part or particle of God. The name of the nearest friend sounds then foreign and accidental. To be brothers, to be acquaintances,—master or servant, is then a trifle and a disturbance. I am the lover of uncontained and immortal beauty. In the wilderness, I find something more dear and connate[5] than in streets or villages. In the tranquil landscape, and especially in the distant line of the horizon, man beholds somewhat as beautiful as his own nature.

The greatest delight which the fields and woods minister, is the suggestion of an occult relation between man and the vegetable. I am not alone and unacknowledged. They nod to me and I to them. The waving of the boughs in the storm, is new to me and old. It takes me by surprise, and yet is not unknown. Its effect is like that of a higher thought or a better emotion coming over me, when I deemed I was thinking justly or doing right.

Yet it is certain that the power to produce this delight, does not reside in nature, but in man, or in a harmony of both. It is necessary to use these pleasures with great temperance. For, nature is not always tricked in holiday attire, but the same scene which yesterday breathed perfume and glittered as for the frolic of the nymphs, is overspread with melancholy today. Nature always wears the colors of the spirit. To a man laboring under calamity, the heat of his own fire hath sadness in it. Then, there is a kind of contempt of the landscape felt by him who has just lost by death a dear friend. The sky is less grand as it shuts down over less worth in the population.

CHAPTER II. COMMODITY[6]

Whoever considers the final cause of the world, will discern a multitude of uses that enter as parts into that result. They all admit of being thrown into one of the following classes: Commodity; Beauty; Language; and Discipline.

Under the general name of Commodity, I rank all those advantages which our senses owe to nature. This, of course, is a benefit which is temporary and mediate, not ultimate, like its service to the soul. Yet although low, it is perfect in its kind, and is the only use of nature which all men apprehend.

[5] Of common origin.

[6] Emerson uses this term in its archaic sense: a physical material, or practical use or advantage.

The misery of man appears like childish petulance, when wc explore the steady and prodigal provision that has been made for his support and delight on this green ball which floats him through the heavens. What angels invented these splendid ornaments, these rich conveniences, this ocean of air above, this ocean of water beneath, this firmament of earth between? this zodiac of lights, this tent of dropping clouds, this striped coat of climates, this fourfold year? Beasts, fire, water, stones, and corn serve him. The field is at once his floor, his work-yard, his play-ground, his garden, and his bed.

> "More servants wait on man
> Than he'll take notice of."——[7]

Nature, in its ministry to man, is not only the material, but is also the process and the result. All the parts incessantly work into each other's hands for the profit of man. The wind sows the seed; the sun evaporates the sea; the wind blows the vapor to the field; the ice, on the other side of the planet, condenses rain on this; the rain feeds the plant; the plant feeds the animal; and thus the endless circulations of the divine charity nourish man.

The useful arts are but reproductions or new combinations by the wit of man, of the same natural benefactors. He no longer waits for favoring gales, but by means of steam, he realizes the fable of æolus's bag,[8] and carries the two and thirty winds in the boiler of his boat. To diminish friction, he paves the road with iron bars, and, mounting a coach with a ship-load of men, animals, and merchandise behind him, he darts through the country, from town to town, like an eagle or a swallow through the air. By the aggregate of these aids, how is the face of the world changed, from the era of Noah to that of Napoleon! The private poor man hath cities, ships, canals, bridges, built for him. He goes to the post-office, and the human race run on his errands; to the book-shop, and the human race read and write of all that happens, for him; to the court-house, and nations repair his wrongs. He sets his house upon the road, and the human race go forth every morning, and shovel out the snow, and cut a path for him.

But there is no need of specifying particulars in this class of uses. The catalogue is endless, and the examples so obvious, that I shall leave them to the reader's reflection, with the general remark, that this mercenary benefit is one which has respect to a farther good. A man is fed, not that he may be fed, but that he may work.

---

[7] The lines appear in "Man," by the English poet George Herbert (1593-1633).

[8] Aeolus is the king of the winds, according to Greek mythology. In the *Odyssey*, Book X, he gives Odysseus a bag that contains storm winds; the sailors open the bag and cause a storm to occur.

CHAPTER III. BEAUTY

A nobler want of man is served by nature, namely, the love of Beauty. The ancient Greeks called the world κόσμος,[9] beauty. Such is the constitution of all things, or such the plastic power of the human eye, that the primary forms, as the sky, the mountain, the tree, the animal, give us a delight *in and for themselves;* a pleasure arising from outline, color, motion, and grouping. This seems partly owing to the eye itself. The eye is the best of artists. By the mutual action of its structure and of the laws of light, perspective is produced, which integrates every mass of objects, of what character soever, into a well colored and shaded globe, so that where the particular objects are mean and unaffecting, the landscape which they compose, is round and symmetrical. And as the eye is the best composer, so light is the first of painters. There is no object so foul that intense light will not make beautiful. And the stimulus it affords to the sense, and a sort of infinitude which it hath, like space and time, make all matter gay. Even the corpse hath its own beauty. But beside this general grace diffused over nature, almost all the individual forms are agreeable to the eye, as is proved by our endless imitations of some of them, as the acorn, the grape, the pine-cone, the wheat-ear, the egg, the wings and forms of most birds, the lion's claw, the serpent, the butterfly, sea-shells, flames, clouds, buds, leaves, and the forms of many trees, as the palm.

For better consideration, we may distribute the aspects of Beauty in a threefold manner.

I. First, the simple perception of natural forms is a delight. The influence of the forms and actions in nature, is so needful to man, that, in its lowest functions, it seems to lie on the confines of commodity and beauty. To the body and mind which have been cramped by noxious work or company, nature is medicinal and restores their tone. The tradesman, the attorney comes out of the din and craft of the street, and sees the sky and the woods, and is a man again. In their eternal calm, he finds himself. The health of the eye seems to demand a horizon. We are never tired, so long as we can see far enough.

But in other hours, Nature satisfies the soul purely by its loveliness, and without any mixture of corporeal benefit. I have seen the spectacle of morning from the hill-top over against my house, from day-break to sun-rise, with emotions which an angel might share. The long slender bars of cloud float like fishes in the sea of crimson light. From the earth, as a shore, I look out into that silent sea. I seem to partake its rapid transformations: the active enchantment reaches my dust, and I dilate and conspire[10] with the morning wind. How does Nature deify us with a few and cheap elements! Give me

[9] The Greek word meaning order in the universe.

[10] Breathe in unison.

health and a day, and I will make the pomp of emperors ridiculous. The dawn is my Assyria;[11] the sun-set and moon-rise my Paphos,[12] and unimaginable realms of faerie; broad noon shall be my England of the senses and the understanding; the night shall be my Germany of mystic philosophy and dreams.

Not less excellent, except for our less susceptibility in the afternoon, was the charm, last evening, of a January sunset. The western clouds divided and subdivided themselves into pink flakes modulated with tints of unspeakable softness; and the air had so much life and sweetness, that it was a pain to come within doors. What was it that nature would say? Was there no meaning in the live repose of the valley behind the mill, and which Homer or Shakespeare could not re-form for me in words? The leafless trees become spires of flame in the sunset, with the blue east for their background, and the stars of the dead calices[13] of flowers, and every withered stem and stubble rimed with frost, contribute something to the mute music.

The inhabitants of cities suppose that the country landscape is pleasant only half the year. I please myself with observing the graces of the winter scenery, and believe that we are as much touched by it as by the genial influences of summer. To the attentive eye, each moment of the year has its own beauty, and in the same field, it beholds, every hour, a picture which was never seen before, and which shall never be seen again. The heavens change every moment, and reflect their glory or gloom on the plains beneath. The state of the crop in the surrounding farms alters the expression of the earth from week to week. The succession of native plants in the pastures and road-sides, which make the silent clock by which time tells the summer hours, will make even the divisions of the day sensible to a keen observer. The tribes of birds and insects, like the plants punctual to their time, follow each other, and the year has room for all. By water-courses, the variety is greater. In July, the blue pontederia or pickerel-weed blooms in large beds in the shallow parts of our pleasant river,[14] and swarms with yellow butterflies in continual motion. Art cannot rival this pomp of purple and gold. Indeed the river is a perpetual gala, and boasts each month a new ornament.

But this beauty of Nature which is seen and felt as beauty, is the least part. The shows of day, the dewy morning, the rainbow, mountains, orchards in blossom, stars, moonlight, shadows in still water, and the like, if too eagerly hunted, become shows merely, and mock us with their unreality. Go out of the house to see the moon, and 't is mere tinsel; it will not please as when its light shines upon your necessary journey. The beauty that shimmers in the yellow afternoons of October, who ever could clutch it? Go forth to

---

[11] Emerson refers to a golden age of the past.

[12] An ancient city on the island of Cyprus, where a cult of Aphrodite, the Greek goddess of love, flourished.

[13] "Calyxes," the outer envelope of a flower.

[14] The Concord River, a branch of the Merrimack.

find it, and it is gone: 't is only a mirage as you look from the windows of diligence.

2. The presence of a higher, namely, of the spiritual element is essential to its perfection. The high and divine beauty which can be loved without effeminacy, is that which is found in combination with the human will, and never separate. Beauty is the mark God sets upon virtue. Every natural action is graceful. Every heroic act is also decent, and causes the place and the bystanders to shine. We are taught by great actions that the universe is the property of every individual in it. Every rational creature has all nature for his dowry and estate. It is his, if he will. He may divest himself of it; he may creep into a corner, and abdicate his kingdom, as most men do, but he is entitled to the world by his constitution. In proportion to the energy of his thought and will, he takes up the world into himself. "All those things for which men plough, build, or sail, obey virtue;" said an ancient historian.[15] "The winds and waves," said Gibbon,[16] "are always on the side of the ablest navigators." So are the sun and moon and all the stars of heaven. When a noble act is done,—perchance in a scene of great natural beauty; when Leonidas[17] and his three hundred martyrs consume one day in dying, and the sun and moon come each and look at them once in the steep defile of Thermopylae; when Arnold Winkelried,[18] in the high Alps, under the shadow of the avalanche, gathers in his side a sheaf of Austrian spears to break the line for his comrades; are not these heroes entitled to add the beauty of the scene to the beauty of the deed? When the bark of Columbus nears the shore of America;—before it, the beach lined with savages, fleeing out of all their huts of cane; the sea behind; and the purple mountains of the Indian Archipelago around, can we separate the man from the living picture? Does not the New World clothe his form with her palm-groves and savannahs as fit drapery? Ever does natural beauty steal in like air, and envelope great actions. When Sir Harry Vane[19] was dragged up the Tower-hill, sitting on a sled, to suffer death, as the champion of the English laws, one of the multitude cried out to him, "You never sate on so glorious a seat." Charles II., to intimidate the citizens of London, caused the patriot Lord

---

[15] Gaius Sallustius Crispus (86-34 B.C.), a Roman author from whose book, *Cataline's Conspiracy*, the quotation is taken.

[16] Edward Gibbon (1737-1794), an English historian. The quotation is from his *The History of the Decline and Fall of the Roman Empire* (1776-1788), Volume II, Chapter 68.

[17] Leonidas was the King of Sparta who led the Spartan army against the Persians in 480 B. C. at the Battle of Thermopylae. See Herodotus, *History*, Book VII.

[18] A Swiss patriot who allegedly died heroically at the Battle of Sempach in 1386 where the Austrian troops were routed.

[19] Sir Henry Vane, the Younger (1613-1662), the fourth governor of the Massachusetts Bay Colony (1636-1637). He was later a leader of the Parliamentary party in England and was executed for high treason by Charles II after the restoration to power of the Stuart government.

Russel[20] to be drawn in an open coach, through the principal streets of the city, on his way to the scaffold. "But," to use the simple narrative of his biographer,[21] "the multitude imagined they saw liberty and virtue sitting by his side." In private places, among sordid objects, an act of truth or heroism seems at once to draw to itself the sky as its temple, the sun as its candle. Nature stretcheth out her arms to embrace man, only let his thoughts be of equal greatness. Willingly does she follow his steps with the rose and the violet, and bend her lines of grandeur and grace to the decoration of her darling child. Only let his thoughts be of equal scope, and the frame will suit the picture. A virtuous man is in unison with her works, and makes the central figure of the visible sphere. Homer, Pindar, Socrates, Phocion,[22] associate themselves fitly in our memory with the whole geography and climate of Greece. The visible heavens and earth sympathize with Jesus. And in common life, whosoever has seen a person of powerful character and happy genius, will have remarked how easily he took all things along with him,— the persons, the opinions, and the day, and nature became ancillary to a man.

3. There is still another aspect under which the beauty of the world may be viewed, namely, as it becomes an object of the intellect. Beside the relation of things to virtue, they have a relation to thought. The intellect searches out the absolute order of things as they stand in the mind of God, and without the colors of affection. The intellectual and the active powers seem to succeed each other in man, and the exclusive activity of the one, generates the exclusive activity of the other. There is something unfriendly in each to the other, but they are like the alternate periods of feeding and working in animals; each prepares and certainly will be followed by the other. Therefore does beauty, which, in relation to actions, as we have seen, comes unsought, and comes because it is unsought, remain for the apprehension and pursuit of the intellect; and then again, in its turn, of the active power. Nothing divine dies. All good is eternally reproductive. The beauty of nature reforms itself in the mind, and not for barren contemplation, but for new creation.

All men are in some degree impressed by the face of the world; some men even to delight. This love of beauty is Taste. Others have the same love in such excess, that, not content with admiring, they seek to embody it in new forms. The creation of beauty is Art.

[20] William Russell (1639-1683) was an English statesman who was executed for high treason under Charles II for involvement in the Rye House Plot. Lord Russell had spoken against the corrupt court and the Catholic party.

[21] *Life of William Lord Russell* (1819) by Lord John Russell.

[22] Homer was the Greek author of the heroic epics; Pindar was a Greek lyric poet of the fifth and sixth centuries whose themes were heroic; Socrates was a Greek philosopher, the teacher of Plato and others; Phocion was an Athenian general and statesman of the fourth century B.C., the subject of one of Plutarch's Lives.

The production of a work of art throws a light upon the mystery of humanity. A work of art is an abstract or epitome of the world. It is the result or expression of nature, in miniature. For although the works of nature are innumerable and all different, the result or the expression of them all is similar and single. Nature is a sea of forms radically alike and even unique. A leaf, a sun-beam, a landscape, the ocean, make an analogous impression on the mind. What is common to them all,—that perfectness and harmony, is beauty. Therefore the standard of beauty is the entire circuit of natural forms,—the totality of nature; which the Italians expressed by defining beauty "il piu nell' uno."[23] Nothing is quite beautiful alone: nothing but is beautiful in the whole. A single object is only so far beautiful as it suggests this universal grace. The poet, the painter, the sculptor, the musician, the architect, seek each to concentrate this radiance of the world on one point, and each in his several work to satisfy the love of beauty which stimulates him to produce. Thus is Art, a nature passed through the alembic of man. Thus in art, does nature work through the will of a man filled with the beauty of her first works.

The world thus exists to the soul to satisfy the desire of beauty. Extend this element to the uttermost, and I call it an ultimate end. No reason can be asked or given why the soul seeks beauty. Beauty, in its largest and pro-foundest sense, is one expression for the universe. God is the all-fair. Truth, and goodness, and beauty, are but different faces of the same All. But beauty in nature is not ultimate. It is the herald of inward and eternal beauty, and is not alone a solid and satisfactory good. It must therefore stand as a part and not as yet the last or highest expression of the final cause of Nature.

CHAPTER IV. LANGUAGE

A third use which Nature subserves to man is that of Language. Nature is the vehicle of thought, and in a simple, double, and threefold degree.

1. Words are signs of natural facts.
2. Particular natural facts are symbols of particular spiritual facts.
3. Nature is the symbol of spirit.

1. Words are signs of natural facts. The use of natural history is to give us aid in supernatural history. The use of the outer creation is to give us language for the beings and changes of the inward creation. Every word which is used to express a moral or intellectual fact, if traced to its root, is found to be borrowed from some material appearance. *Right* originally means *straight; wrong* means *twisted. Spirit* primarily means *wind; transgression,* the crossing of a *line; supercilious,* the *raising of the eye-brow.* We say the

---

[23] The many in one.

heart to express emotion, the *head* to denote thought; and *thought* and *emotion* are, in their turn, words borrowed from sensible things, and now appropriated to spiritual nature. Most of the process by which this transformation is made, is hidden from us in the remote time when language was framed; but the same tendency may be daily observed in children. Children and savages use only nouns or names of things, which they continually convert into verbs, and apply to analogous mental acts.

2. But this origin of all words that convey a spiritual import,—so conspicuous a fact in the history of language,—is our least debt to nature. It is not words only that are emblematic; it is things which are emblematic. Every natural fact is a symbol of some spiritual fact. Every appearance in nature corresponds to some state of the mind, and that state of the mind can only be described by presenting that natural appearance as its picture. An enraged man is a lion, a cunning man is a fox, a firm man is a rock, a learned man is a torch. A lamb is innocence; a snake is subtle spite; flowers express to us the delicate affections. Light and darkness are our familiar expression for knowledge and ignorance; and heat for love. Visible distance behind and before us, is respectively our image of memory and hope.

Who looks upon a river in a meditative hour, and is not reminded of the flux of all things? Throw a stone into the stream, and the circles that propagate themselves are the beautiful type of all influence. Man is conscious of a universal soul within or behind his individual life, wherein, as in a firmament, the natures of Justice, Truth, Love, Freedom, arise and shine. This universal soul, he calls Reason: it is not mine or thine or his, but we are its; we are its property and men. And the blue sky in which the private earth is buried, the sky with its eternal calm, and full of everlasting orbs, is the type of Reason. That which, intellectually considered, we call Reason, considered in relation to nature, we call Spirit. Spirit is the Creator. Spirit hath life in itself. And man in all ages and countries, embodies it in his language, as the FATHER.

It is easily seen that there is nothing lucky or capricious in these analogies, but that they are constant, and pervade nature. These are not the dreams of a few poets, here and there, but man is an analogist, and studies relations in all objects. He is placed in the centre of beings, and a ray of relation passes from every other being to him. And neither can man be understood without these objects, nor these objects without man. All the facts in natural history taken by themselves, have no value, but are barren like a single sex. But marry it to human history, and it is full of life. Whole Floras, all Linnæus' and Buffon's[24] volumes, are but dry catalogues of facts; but the most trivial of these facts, the habit of a plant, the organs, or work, or noise of an insect,

---

[24] Carolus Linnæus (1707-1778), a Swedish botanist, the author of the *Systema Naturae* and the originator of the nomenclature and classification of plants and animals. Comte de Buffon (1707-1788), a French naturalist, the author of the influential *Histoire Naturelle*, a 44-volume treatise of the biological sciences.

applied to the illustration of a fact in intellectual philosophy, or, in any way associated to human nature, affects us in the most lively and agreeable manner. The seed of a plant,—to what affecting analogies in the nature of man, is that little fruit made use of, in all discourse, up to the voice of Paul, who calls the human corpse a seed,[25]—"It is sown a natural body; it is raised a spiritual body." The motion of the earth round its axis, and round the sun, makes the day, and the year. There are certain amounts of brute light and heat. But is there no intent of an analogy between man's life and the seasons? And do the seasons gain no grandeur or pathos from that analogy? The instincts of the ant are very unimportant considered as the ant's; but the moment a ray of relation is seen to extend from it to man, and the little drudge is seen to be a monitor, a little body with a mighty heart, then all its habits, even that said to be recently observed, that it never sleeps, become sublime.

Because of this radical correspondence between visible things and human thoughts, savages, who have only what is necessary, converse in figures. As we go back in history, language becomes more picturesque, until its infancy, when it is all poetry; or, all spiritual facts are represented by natural symbols. The same symbols are found to make the original elements of all languages. It has moreover been observed, that the idioms of all languages approach each other in passages of the greatest eloquence and power. And as this is the first language, so is it the last. This immediate dependence of language upon nature, this conversion of an outward phenomenon into a type of somewhat in human life, never loses its power to affect us. It is this which gives that piquancy to the conversation of a strongnatured farmer or back-woodsman, which all men relish.[26]

Thus is nature an interpreter, by whose means man converses with his fellow men. A man's power to connect his thought with its proper symbol, and so to utter it, depends on the simplicity of his character, that is, upon his love of truth and his desire to communicate it without loss. The corruption of man is followed by the corruption of language. When simplicity of character and the sovereignty of ideas is broken up by the prevalence of secondary desires, the desire of riches, the desire of pleasure, the desire of power, the desire of praise,—and duplicity and falsehood take place of simplicity and truth, the power over nature as an interpreter of the will, is in a degree lost; new imagery ceases to be created, and old words are perverted to stand for things which are not; a paper currency is employed when there is no bullion

---

[25] See I Corinthians xv: 42-44.

[26] Although these thoughts concerning language are specifically Emersonian and are closely related to democratization in America, they owe their philosophical origin to Emanuel Swedenborg (1688-1772), whose *Heaven and Its Wonders and Hell* (1758), commonly called *Heaven and Hell*, influenced Emerson. "The whole natural world," Swedenborg wrote, "corresponds to the spiritual world; and not only the natural world collectively, but also its individual parts. . . ."

in the vaults. In due time, the fraud is manifest, and words lose all power to stimulate the understanding or the affections. Hundreds of writers may be found in every long-civilized nation, who for a short time believe, and make others believe, that they see and utter truths, who do not of themselves clothe one thought in its natural garment, but who feed unconsciously upon the language created by the primary writers of the country, those, namely, who hold primarily on nature.

But wise men pierce this rotten diction and fasten words again to visible things; so that picturesque language is at once a commanding certificate that he who employs it, is a man in alliance with truth and God. The moment our discourse rises above the ground line of familiar facts, and is inflamed with passion or exalted by thought, it clothes itself in images. A man conversing in earnest, if he watch his intellectual processes, will find that always a material image, more or less luminous, arises in his mind, cotemporaneous with every thought, which furnishes the vestment of the thought. Hence, good writing and brilliant discourse are perpetual allegories. This imagery is spontaneous. It is the blending of experience with the present action of the mind. It is proper creation. It is the working of the Original Cause through the instruments he has already made.

These facts may suggest the advantage which the country-life possesses for a powerful mind, over the artificial and curtailed life of cities. We know more from nature than we can at will communicate. Its light flows into the mind evermore, and we forget its presence. The poet, the orator, bred in the woods, whose senses have been nourished by their fair and appeasing changes, year after year, without design and without heed,—shall not lose their lesson altogether, in the roar of cities or the broil of politics. Long hereafter, amidst agitation and terror in national councils,—in the hour of revolution,—these solemn images shall reappear in their morning lustre, as fit symbols and words of the thoughts which the passing events shall awaken. At the call of a noble sentiment, again the woods wave, the pines murmur, the river rolls and shines, and the cattle low upon the mountains, as he saw and heard them in his infancy. And with these forms, the spells of persuasion, the keys of power are put into his hands.

3. We are thus assisted by natural objects in the expression of particular meanings. But how great a language to convey such peppercorn informations! Did it need such noble races of creatures, this profusion of forms, this host of orbs in heaven, to furnish man with the dictionary and grammar of his municipal speech? Whilst we use this grand cipher to expedite the affairs of our pot and kettle, we feel that we have not yet put it to its use, neither are able. We are like travellers using the cinders of a volcano to roast their eggs. Whilst we see that it always stands ready to clothe what we would say, we cannot avoid the question, whether the characters are not significant of themselves. Have mountains, and waves, and skies, no significance but what

we consciously give them, when we employ them as emblems of our thoughts? The world is emblematic. Parts of speech are metaphors because the whole of nature is a metaphor of the human mind. The laws of moral nature answer to those of matter as face to face in a glass. "The visible world and the relation of its parts, is the dial plate of the invisible." The axioms of physics translate the laws of ethics. Thus, "the whole is greater than its part"; "reaction is equal to action"; "the smallest weight may be made to lift the greatest, the difference of weight being compensated by time"; and many the like propositions, which have an ethical as well as physical sense. These propositions have a much more extensive and universal sense when applied to human life, than when confined to technical use.

In like manner, the memorable words of history, and the proverbs of nations, consist usually of a natural fact, selected as a picture or parable of a moral truth. Thus; A rolling stone gathers no moss; A bird in the hand is worth two in the bush; A cripple in the right way, will beat a racer in the wrong; Make hay whilst the sun shines; 'T is hard to carry a full cup even; Vinegar is the son of wine; The last ounce broke the camel's back; Long-lived trees make roots first;—and the like. In their primary sense these are trivial facts, but we repeat them for the value of their analogical import. What is true of proverbs, is true of all fables, parables, and allegories.

This relation between the mind and matter is not fancied by some poet, but stands in the will of God, and so is free to be known by all men. It appears to men, or it does not appear. When in fortunate hours we ponder this miracle, the wise man doubts, if, at all other times, he is not blind and deaf;

———"Can these things be,
And overcome us like a summer's cloud,
Without our special wonder?"[27]

for the universe becomes transparent, and the light of higher laws than its own, shines through it. It is the standing problem which has exercised the wonder and the study of every fine genius since the world began; from the era of the Egyptians and the Brahmins, to that of Pythagoras, of Plato, of Bacon, of Leibnitz, of Swedenborg.[28] There sits the Sphinx at the road-side, and from age to age, as each prophet comes by, he tries his fortune at reading her riddle. There seems to be a necessity in spirit to manifest itself in

[27] *Macbeth*, III, iv, 110-112.

[28] Pythagoras was a Greek philosopher of the sixth century who taught the transmigration of the souls; Plato (428 B.C.-347 B.C.), the great philosopher of Western idealism; Francis Bacon (1561-1626), an English philos-opher who founded inductive science; Gottfried Wilhelm von Leibnitz (1646-1716), a German mathematician and philosopher; Emanuel Swedenborg (1688-1772), a Swedish mystic of whom Emerson drew a full portrait in *Representative Men*.

material forms; and day and night, river and storm, beast and bird, acid and alkali, preëxist in necessary Ideas in the mind of God, and are what they are by virtue of preceding affections, in the world of spirit. A Fact is the end or last issue of spirit. The visible creation is the terminus or the circumference of the invisible world. "Material objects," said a French philosopher,[29] "are necessarily kinds of *scoriæ*[30] of the substantial thoughts of the Creator, which must always preserve an exact relation to their first origin; in other words, visible nature must have a spiritual and moral side."

This doctrine is abstruse, and though the images of "garment," "scoriæ," "mirror," &c., may stimulate the fancy, we must summon the aid of subtler and more vital expositors to make it plain. "Every scripture is to be interpreted by the same spirit which gave it forth,"—is the fundamental law of criticism. A life in harmony with nature, the love of truth and of virtue, will purge the eyes to understand her text. By degrees we may come to know the primitive sense of the permanent objects of nature, so that the world shall be to us an open book, and every form significant of its hidden life and final cause.

A new interest surprises us, whilst, under the view now suggested, we contemplate the fearful extent and multitude of objects; since "every object rightly seen, unlocks a new faculty of the soul." That which was unconscious truth, becomes, when interpreted and defined in an object, a part of the domain of knowledge,—a new weapon in the magazine of power.

CHAPTER V. DISCIPLINE

In view of this significance of nature, we arrive at once at a new fact, that nature is a discipline. This use of the world includes the preceding uses, as parts of itself.

Space, time, society, labor, climate, food, locomotion, the animals, the mechanical forces, give us sincerest lessons, day by day, whose meaning is unlimited. They educate both the Understanding and the Reason. Every property of matter is a school for the understanding,—its solidity or resistance, its inertia, its extension, its figure, its divisibility. The understanding adds, divides, combines, measures, and finds everlasting nutriment and room for its activity in this worthy scene. Meantime, Reason transfers all these lessons into its own world of thought, by perceiving the analogy that marries Matter and Mind.

1. Nature is a discipline of the understanding in intellectual truths. Our dealing with sensible objects is a constant exercise in the necessary lessons of

[29] J. G. E. Oegger, a French Swedenborgian writer. The book from which the quotation is taken is *Le Vrai Messie* (1829), translated by Elizabeth Peabody, a friend of Emerson's.

[30] Dross, slag.

difference, of likeness, of order, of being and seeming, of progressive arrangement; of ascent from particular to general; of combination to one end of manifold forces. Proportioned to the importance of the organ to be formed, is the extreme care with which its tuition[31] is provided,—a care pretermitted[32] in no single case. What tedious training, day after day, year after year, never ending, to form the common sense; what continual reproduction of annoyances, inconveniences, dilemmas; what rejoicing over us of little men; what disputing of prices, what reckonings of interest,—and all to form the Hand of the mind;—to instruct us that "good thoughts are no better than good dreams, unless they be executed!"[33]

The same good office is performed by Property and its filial systems of debt and credit. Debt, grinding debt, whose iron face the widow, the orphan, and the sons of genius fear and hate;—debt, which consumes so much time, which so cripples and disheartens a great spirit with cares that seem so base, is a preceptor whose lessons cannot be foregone, and is needed most by those who suffer from it most. Moreover, property, which has been well compared to snow,—"if it fall level to-day, it will be blown into drifts to-morrow,"—is merely the surface action of internal machinery, like the index on the face of a clock. Whilst now it is the gymnastics of the understanding, it is hiving in the foresight of the spirit, experience in profounder laws.

The whole character and fortune of the individual are affected by the least inequalities in the culture of the understanding; for example, in the perception of differences. Therefore is Space, and therefore Time, that man may know that things are not huddled and lumped, but sundered and individual. A bell and a plough have each their use, and neither can do the office of the other. Water is good to drink, coal to burn, wool to wear; but wool cannot be drunk, nor water spun, nor coal eaten. The wise man shows his wisdom in separation, in gradation, and his scale of creatures and of merits, is as wide as nature. The foolish have no range in their scale, but suppose every man is as every other man. What is not good they call the worst, and what is hateful, they call the best.

In like manner, what good heed, nature forms in us! She pardons no mistakes. Her yea is yea, and her nay, nay.[34]

The first steps in Agriculture, Astronomy, Zoölogy, (those first steps which the farmer, the hunter, and the sailor take,) teach that nature's dice are always loaded; that in their heaps and rubbish are concealed sure and useful results.

How calmly and genially the mind apprehends one after another the laws of physics! What noble emotions dilate the mortal as he enters into the

[31] Upbringing or guardianship.

[32] Overlooked.

[33] This is paraphrased from Francis Bacon's essay, "Of Great Place."

[34] Cf. Matthew, v: 37: "But let your communication be, Yea, yea; Nay, nay; for whatsoever is more than these cometh of evil."

counsels of the creation, and feels by knowledge the privilege to BE! His insight refines him. The beauty of nature shines in his own breast. Man is greater that he can see this, and the universe less, because Time and Space relations vanish as laws are known.

Here again we are impressed and even daunted by the immense Universe to be explored. "What we know, is a point to what we do not know." Open any recent journal of science, and weigh the problems suggested concerning Light, Heat, Electricity, Magnetism, Physiology, Geology, and judge whether the interest of natural science is likely to be soon exhausted.

Passing by many particulars of the discipline of nature we must not omit to specify two.

The exercise of the Will or the lesson of power is taught in every event. From the child's successive possession of his several senses up to the hour when he saith, "thy will be done!"[35] he is learning the secret, that he can reduce under his will, not only particular events, but great classes, nay the whole series of events, and so conform all facts to his character. Nature is thoroughly mediate. It is made to serve. It receives the dominion of man as meekly as the ass on which the Saviour rode.[36] It offers all its kingdoms[37] to man as the raw material which he may mould into what is useful. Man is never weary of working it up. He forges the subtile and delicate air into wise and melodious words, and gives them wing as angels of persuasion and command. More and more, with every thought, does his kingdom stretch over things, until the world becomes, at last, only a realized will,—the double of the man.

2. Sensible objects conform to the premonitions of Reason and reflect the conscience. All things are moral; and in their boundless changes have an unceasing reference to spiritual nature. Therefore is nature glorious with form, color, and motion, that every globe in the remotest heaven; every chemical change from the rudest crystal up to the laws of life; every change of vegetation from the first principle of growth in the eye of a leaf, to the tropical forest and antediluvian coal-mine; every animal function from the sponge up to Hercules, shall hint or thunder to man the laws of right and wrong, and echo the Ten Commandments. Therefore is nature ever the ally of Religion: lends all her pomp and riches to the religious sentiment. Prophet and priest, David, Isaiah, Jesus, have drawn deeply from this source.

This ethical character so penetrates the bone and marrow of nature, as to seem the end for which it was made. Whatever private purpose is answered by any member or part, this is its public and universal function, and is never

---

[35] Cf. Matthew, xxvi, 42 (Jesus at Gethsemane): "He went away again the second time, and prayed, saying, O my Father, if this cup may not pass away from me, except I drink it, thy will be done." See also Matthew, vi., 9, 10, The Lord's Prayer.

[36] Cf. John xii; 12-15.

[37] Cf. Matthew iv: 8.

omitted. Nothing in nature is exhausted in its first use. When a thing has served an end to the uttermost, it is wholly new for an ulterior service. In God, every end is converted into a new means. Thus the use of Commodity, regarded by itself, is mean and squalid. But it is to the mind an education in the great doctrine of Use, namely, that a thing is good only so far as it serves; that a conspiring of parts and efforts to the production of an end, is essential to any being. The first and gross manifestation of this truth, is our inevitable and hated training in values and wants, in corn and meat.

It has already been illustrated, in treating of the significance of material things, that every natural process is but a version of a moral sentence. The moral law lies at the centre of nature and radiates to the circumference. It is the pith and marrow of every substance, every relation, and every process. All things with which we deal, preach to us. What is a farm but a mute gospel? The chaff and the wheat, weeds and plants, blight, rain, insects, sun,—it is a sacred emblem from the first furrow of spring to the last stack which the snow of winter overtakes in the fields. But the sailor, the shepherd, the miner, the merchant, in their several resorts, have each an experience precisely parallel and leading to the same conclusion: because all organizations are radically alike. Nor can it be doubted that this moral sentiment which thus scents the air, and grows in the grain, and impregnates the waters of the world, is caught by man and sinks into his soul. The moral influence of nature upon every individual is that amount of truth which it illustrates to him. Who can estimate this? Who can guess how much firmness the sea-beaten rock has taught the fisherman? how much tranquillity has been reflected to man from the azure sky, over whose unspotted deeps the winds forevermore drive flocks of stormy clouds, and leave no wrinkle or stain? how much industry and providence and affection we have caught from the pantomime of brutes? What a searching preacher of self-command is the varying phenomenon of Health!

Herein is especially apprehended the Unity of Nature,—the Unity in Variety,—which meets us everywhere. All the endless variety of things make a unique, an identical impression. Xenophanes[38] complained in his old age, that, look where he would, all things hastened back to Unity. He was weary of seeing the same entity in the tedious variety of forms. The fable of Proteus[39] has a cordial truth. Every particular in nature, a leaf, a drop, a crystal, a moment of time is related to the whole, and partakes of the perfection of the whole. Each particle is a microcosm, and faithfully renders the likeness of the world.

Not only resemblances exist in things whose analogy is obvious, as when we detect the type of the human hand in the flipper of the fossil saurus,[40] but

---

[38] Greek philosopher, sixth century B.C.

[39] A sea god who could change his form when he wished. See the *Odyssey*, Book IV.

[40] A lizard.

also in objects wherein there is great superficial unlikeness. This architecture is called "frozen music," by De Staël and Goethe.[41] Vitruvius[42] thought an architect should be a musician. "A Gothic church," said Coleridge,[43] "is a petrified religion." Michael Angelo maintained, that, to an architect, a knowledge of anatomy is essential. In Haydn's oratorios,[44] the notes present to the imagination not only motions, as, of the snake, the stag, and the elephant, but colors also; as the green grass. The law of harmonic sounds reappears in the harmonic colors. The granite is differenced in its laws only by the more or less of heat, from the river that wears it away. The river, as it flows, resembles the air that flows over it; the air resembles the light which traverses it with more subtile currents; the light resembles the heat which rides with it through Space. Each creature is only a modification of the other; the likeness in them is more than the difference, and their radical law is one and the same. Hence it is, that a rule of one art, or a law of one organization, holds true throughout nature. So intimate is this Unity, that, it is easily seen, it lies under the undermost garment of nature, and betrays its source in universal Spirit. For, it pervades Thought also. Every universal truth which we express in words, implies or supposes every other truth. *Omne verum vero consonat.*[45] It is like a great circle on a sphere, comprising all possible circles; which, however, may be drawn, and comprise it, in like manner. Every such truth is the absolute Ens[46] seen from one side. But it has innumerable sides.

The same central Unity is still more conspicuous in actions. Words are finite organs of the infinite mind. They cannot cover the dimensions of what is in truth. They break, chop, and impoverish it. An action is the perfection and publication of thought. A right action seems to fill the eye, and to be related to all nature. "The wise man, in doing one thing, does all; or, in the one thing he does rightly, he sees the likeness of all which is done rightly."[47]

Words and actions are not the attributes of mute and brute nature. They introduce us to the human form, of which all other organizations appear to be degradations. When this organization appears among so many that surround it, the spirit prefers it to all others. It says, "From such as this, have I drawn joy and knowledge. In such as this, have I found and beheld myself. I will speak to it. It can speak again. It can yield me thought already formed

[41] Madame de Staël (1766-1817) in *Corinne ou L'Italie* (1807), Book IV, Chapter 3; Johann W. Von Goethe (1749-1832) in *Conversations with Eckermann* (the passage dated March 23, 1829).

[42] Marcus Vitruvius Pollio, a Roman architect of the first century B.C. See his *De Architectura*, Book I, Chapter 1, Section 8.

[43] See Coleridge's "Lecture on the General Character of the Gothic Mind in the Middle Ages," which appears in his *Literary Remains* (1836).

[44] Joseph Haydn (1732-1809).

[45] Every truth accords with every other truth.

[46] Abstract being or existence.

[47] Translated from Goethe. See Emerson's *Journals* for February 28, 1836.

and alive." In fact, the eye,—the mind,—is always accompanied by these forms, male and female; and these are incomparably the richest informations of the power and order that lie at the heart of things. Unfortunately, every one of them bears the marks as of some injury; is marred and superficially defective. Nevertheless, far different from the deaf and dumb nature around them, these all rest like fountain-pipes on the unfathomed sea of thought and virtue whereto they alone, of all organizations, are the entrances.

It were a pleasant inquiry to follow into detail their ministry to our education, but where would it stop? We are associated in adolescent and adult life with some friends, who, like skies and waters, are coextensive with our idea; who, answering each to a certain affection of the soul, satisfy our desire on that side; whom we lack power to put at such focal distance from us, that we can mend or even analyze them. We cannot chuse but love them. When much intercourse with a friend has supplied us with a standard of excellence, and has increased our respect for the resources of God who thus sends a real person to outgo our ideal; when he has, moreover, become an object of thought, and, whilst his character retains all its unconscious effect, is converted in the mind into solid and sweet wisdom,—it is a sign to us that his office is closing, and he is commonly withdrawn from our sight in a short time.

CHAPTER VI. IDEALISM

Thus is the unspeakable but intelligible and practicable meaning of the world conveyed to man, the immortal pupil, in every object of sense. To this one end of Discipline, all parts of nature conspire.

A noble doubt perpetually suggests itself, whether this end be not the Final Cause of the Universe; and whether nature outwardly exists. It is a sufficient account of that Appearance we call the World, that God will teach a human mind, and so makes it the receiver of a certain number of congruent sensations, which we call sun and moon, man and woman, house and trade. In my utter impotence to test the authenticity of the report of my senses, to know whether the impressions they make on me correspond with outlying objects, what difference does it make, whether Orion is up there in heaven, or some god paints the image in the firmament of the soul? The relations of parts and the end of the whole remaining the same, what is the difference, whether land and sea interact, and worlds revolve and intermingle without number or end,—deep yawning under deep, and galaxy balancing galaxy, throughout absolute space, or, whether, without relations of time and space, the same appearances are inscribed in the constant faith of man? Whether nature enjoy a substantial existence without, or is only in the apocalypse of the mind, it is alike useful and alike venerable to me. Be it what it may, it is ideal to me, so long as I cannot try the accuracy of my senses.

The frivolous make themselves merry with the Ideal theory, as if its consequences were burlesque; as if it affected the stability of nature. It surely does not. God never jests with us, and will not compromise the end of nature, by permitting any inconsequence in its procession. Any distrust of the permanence of laws, would paralyze the faculties of man. Their permanence is sacredly respected, and his faith therein is perfect. The wheels and springs of man are all set to the hypothesis of the permanence of nature. We are not built like a ship to be tossed, but like a house to stand. It is a natural consequence of this structure, that, so long as the active powers predominate over the reflective, we resist with indignation any hint that nature is more short-lived or mutable than spirit. The broker, the wheelwright, the carpenter, the toll-man, are much displeased at the intimation.

But whilst we acquiesce entirely in the permanence of natural laws, the question of the absolute existence of nature, still remains open. It is the uniform effect of culture on the human mind, not to shake our faith in the stability of particular phenomena, as of heat, water, azote;[48] but to lead us to regard nature as a phenomenon, not a substance; to attribute necessary existence to spirit; to esteem nature as an accident and an effect.

To the senses and the renewed understanding, belongs a sort of instinctive belief in the absolute existence of nature. In their view, man and nature are indissolubly joined. Things are ultimates, and they never look beyond their sphere. The presence of Reason mars this faith. The first effort of thought tends to relax this despotism of the senses, which binds us to nature as if we were a part of it, and shows us nature aloof, and, as it were, afloat. Until this higher agency intervened, the animal eye sees, with wonderful accuracy, sharp outlines and colored surfaces. When the eye of Reason opens, to outline and surface are at once added, grace and expression. These proceed from imagination and affection, and abate somewhat of the angular distinctness of objects. If the Reason be stimulated to more earnest vision, outlines and surfaces become transparent, and are no longer seen; causes and spirits are seen through them. The best, the happiest moments of life, are these delicious awakenings of the higher powers, and the reverential withdrawing of nature before its God.

Let us proceed to indicate the effects of culture. 1. Our first institution[49] in the Ideal philosophy is a hint from nature herself.

Nature is made to conspire with spirit to emancipate us. Certain mechanical changes, a small alteration in our local position apprizes us of a dualism. We are stangely affected by seeing the shore from a moving ship, from a balloon, or through the tints of an unusual sky. The least change in our point of view, gives the whole world a pictorial air. A man who seldom rides, needs only to get into a coach and traverse his own town, to turn the street into a puppetshow. The men, the women,—talking, running, bartering, fight-

---

[48] Nitrogen.   [49] Instruction.

ing,—the earnest mechanic, the lounger, the beggar, the boys, the dogs, are unrealized[50] at once, or, at least, wholly detached from all relation to the observer, and seen as apparent, not substantial beings. What new thoughts are suggested by seeing a face of country quite familiar, in the rapid movement of the rail-road car! Nay, the most wonted objects, (make a very slight change in the point of vision,) please us most. In a camera obscura,[51] the butcher's cart, and the figure of one of our own family amuse us. So a portrait of a well-known face gratifies us. Turn the eyes upside down, by looking at the landscape through your legs, and how agreeable is the picture, though you have seen it any time these twenty years!

In these cases, by mechanical means, is suggested the difference between the observer and the spectacle,—between man and nature. Hence arises a pleasure mixed with awe; I may say, a low degree of the sublime is felt from the fact, probably, that man is hereby apprized, that, whilst the world is a spectacle, something in himself is stable.

2. In a higher manner, the poet communicates the same pleasure. By a few strokes he delineates, as on air, the sun, the mountain, the camp, the city, the hero, the maiden, not different from what we know them, but only lifted from the ground and afloat before the eye. He unfixes the land and the sea, makes them revolve around the axis of his primary thought, and disposes them anew. Possessed himself by a heroic passion, he uses matter as symbols of it. The sensual man conforms thoughts to things; the poet conforms things to his thoughts. The one esteems nature as rooted and fast; the other, as fluid, and impresses his being thereon. To him, the refractory world is ductile and flexible; he invests dust and stones with humanity, and makes them the words of the Reason. The imagination may be defined to be, the use which the Reason makes of the material world. Shakspeare possesses the power of subordinating nature for the purposes of expression, beyond all poets. His imperial muse tosses the creation like a bauble from hand to hand, and uses it to embody any capricious shade of thought that is uppermost in his mind. The remotest spaces of nature are visited, and the farthest sundered things are brought together, by a subtile spiritual connexion. We are made aware that magnitude of material things is merely relative, and all objects shrink and expand to serve the passion of the poet. Thus, in his sonnets, the lays of birds, the scents and dyes of flowers, he finds to be the *shadow* of his beloved;[52] time, which keeps her from him, is his *chest;*[53] the suspicion she has awakened, is her *ornament;*

> The ornament of beauty is Suspect,
> A crow which flies in heaven's sweetest air.[54]

---

[50] Rendered unreal.

[51] An early device for projecting an image; the original camera.

[52] Cf. Shakespeare, Sonnet XCVIII.

[53] Cf. Shakespeare, Sonnet LXV, 10.

[54] Cf. Shakespeare, Sonnet LXX, 3-4.

His passion is not the fruit of chance; it swells, as he speaks, to a city, or a state.

> No, it was builded far from accident;
> It suffers not in smiling pomp, nor falls
> Under the brow of thralling discontent;
> It fears not policy, that heretic,
> That works on leases of short numbered hours,
> But all alone stands hugely politic.[55]

In the strength of his constancy, the Pyramids[56] seem to him recent and transitory. And the freshness of youth and love dazzles him with its resemblance to morning.

> Take those lips away
> Which so sweetly were forsworn;
> And those eyes,—the break of day,
> Lights that do mislead the morn.[57]

The wild beauty of this hyperbole, I may say, in passing, it would not be easy to match in literature.

This transfiguration which all material objects undergo through the passion of the poet,—this power which he exerts, at any moment, to magnify the small, to micrify the great,—might be illustrated by a thousand examples from his Plays. I have before me the Tempest, and will cite only these few lines.

> ARIEL. The strong based promontory
> Have I made shake, and by the spurs plucked up
> The pine and cedar.[58]

Prospero calls for music to soothe the frantic Alonzo, and his companions;

> A solemn air, and the best comforter
> To an unsettled fancy, cure thy brains
> Now useless, boiled within thy skull.[59]

---

[55] Cf. Shakespeare, Sonnet CXXIII, 5-7, 9-11.

[56] Cf. Shakespeare, Sonnet CXIII, 2.

[57] Cf. Shakespeare, *Measure for Measure*, IV, 1-4.

[58] *The Tempest*, V, i, 46-48. The lines are Prospero's.

[59] *Ibid.*, Act V., Sc. 1, 58-60.

Again;

> The charm dissolves apace
> And, as the morning steals upon the night,
> Melting the darkness, so their rising senses
> Begin to chase the ignorant fumes that mantle
> Their clearer reason.
>   Their understanding
> Begins to swell: and the approaching tide
> Will shortly fill the reasonable shores
> That now lie foul and muddy.[60]

The perception of real affinities between events, (that is to say, of *ideal* affinities, for those only are real,) enables the poet thus to make free with the most imposing forms and phenomena of the world, and to assert the predominance of the soul.

3. Whilst thus the poet delights us by animating nature like a creator, with his own thoughts, he differs from the philosopher only herein, that the one proposes Beauty as his main end; the other Truth. But, the philosopher, not less than the poet, postpones the apparent order and relations of things to the empire of thought. "The problem of philosophy," according to Plato,"is, for all that exists conditionally, to find a ground unconditioned and absolute."[61] It proceeds on the faith that a law determines all phenomena, which being known, the phenomena can be predicted. That law, when in the mind, is an idea. Its beauty is innate. The true philosopher and the true poet are one, and a beauty, which is truth, and a truth, which is beauty, is the aim of both. Is not the charm of one of Plato's and Aristotle's definitions, strictly like that of the Antigone of Sophocles?[62] It is, in both cases, that a spiritual life has been imparted to nature; that the solid seeming block of matter has been pervaded and dissolved by a thought; that this feeble human being has penetrated the vast masses of nature with an informing soul, and recognised itself in their harmony, that is, seized their law. In physics, when this is attained, the memory disburthens itself of its cumbrous catalogues of particulars, and carries centuries of observation in a single formula.

Thus even in physics, the material is ever degraded before the spiritual. The astronomer, the geometer, rely on their irrefragable analysis, and disdain the ·results of observation. The sublime remark of Euler[63] on his law of arches, "This will be found contrary to all experience, yet is true;" had already transferred nature into the mind, and left matter like an outcast corpse.

---

[60] *Ibid.*, Act V., Sc. 1, 64-68, 79-82.

[61] *The Republic,* Book V

[62] *Antigone* is a tragedy by Sophocles (496?-406 B.C.), a Greek dramatist.

[63] An eighteenth-century Swiss mathematician, quoted by Coleridge in *The Friend*, (1818), Sec. II. Essay VII.

4. Intellectual science has been observed to beget invariably a doubt of the existence of matter. Turgot[64] said, "He that has never doubted the existence of matter, may be assured he has no aptitude for metaphysical inquiries." It fastens the attention upon immortal necessary uncreated natures, that is, upon Ideas; and in their beautiful and majestic presence, we feel that our outward being is a dream and a shade. Whilst we wait in this Olympus of gods, we think of nature as an appendix to the soul. We ascend into their region, and know that these are the thoughts of the Supreme Being. "These are they who were set up from everlasting, from the beginning, or ever the earth was. When he prepared the heavens, they were there; when he established the clouds above, when he strengthened the fountains of the deep. Then they were by him, as one brought up with him. Of them took he counsel."[65]

Their influence is proportionate. As objects of science, they are accessible to few men. Yet all men are capable of being raised by piety or by passion, into their region. And no man touches these divine natures, without becoming, in some degree, himself divine. Like a new soul, they renew the body. We become physically nimble and lightsome; we tread on air; life is no longer irksome, and we think it will never be so. No man fears age or misfortune or death, in their serene company, for he is transported out of the district of change. Whilst we behold unveiled the nature of Justice and Truth, we learn the difference between the absolute and the conditional or relative. We apprehend the absolute. As it were, for the first time, *we exist.* We become immortal, for we learn that time and space are relations of matter; that, with a perception of truth, or a virtuous will, they have no affinity.

5. Finally, religion and ethics, which may be fitly called,—the practice of ideas, or the introduction of ideas into life,—have an analogous effect with all lower culture, in degrading nature and suggesting its dependence on spirit. Ethics and religion differ herein; that the one is the system of human duties commencing from man; the other, from God. Religion includes the personality of God; Ethics does not. They are one to our present design. They both put nature under foot. The first and last lesson of religion is, "The things that are seen, are temporal; the things that are unseen are eternal."[66] It puts an affront upon nature. It does that for the unschooled, which philosophy does for Berkeley and Viasa.[67] The uniform language that may be heard in the churches of the most ignorant sects, is,—'Contemn the unsub-

---

[64] Anne Robert Jacques Turgot (1727-1781), a French economist and statesman, comptroller-general of France under Louis XVI.

[65] Paraphrased from Proverbs viii: 23, 27, 28, 30. Emerson has changed the phrasing from first-person singular to third-person plural.

[66] Cf. II Corinthians: iv: 18.

[67] George Berkeley (1685-1753) was a British idealistic philosopher and churchman whose thought is connected with that of Viasa, legendary author of the Hindu and Sanskirt scriptures termed the Vedas, the source of Vedanta beliefs.

stantial shows of the world; they are vanities, dreams, shadows, unrealities; seek the realities of religion.' The devotee flouts nature. Some theosophists[68] have arrived at a certain hostility and indignation towards matter, as the Manichean[69] and Plotinus.[70] They distrusted in themselves any looking back to these flesh-pots of Egypt.[71] Plotinus was ashamed of his body. In short, they might all better say of matter, what Michael Angelo said of eternal beauty, "it is the frail and weary weed, in which God dresses the soul, which he has called into time."[72]

It appears that motion, poetry, physical and intellectual science, and religion, all tend to affect our convictions of the reality of the external world. But I own there is something ungrateful in expanding too curiously the particulars of the general proposition, that all culture tends to imbue us with idealism. I have no hostility to nature, but a child's love to it. I expand and live in the warm day like corn and melons. Let us speak her fair. I do not wish to fling stones at my beautiful mother, nor soil my gentle nest. I only wish to indicate the true position of nature in regard to man, wherein to establish man, all right education tends; as the ground which to attain is the object of human life, that is, of man's connexion with nature. Culture inverts the vulgar views of nature, and brings the mind to call that apparent, which it uses to call real, and that real, which it uses to call visionary. Children, it is true, believe in the external world. The belief that it appears only, is an afterthought, but with culture, this faith will as surely arise on the mind as did the first.

The advantage of the ideal theology over the popular faith, is this, that it presents the world in precisely that view which is most desirable to the mind. It is, in fact, the view which Reason, both speculative and practical, that is, philosophy and virtue, take. For, seen in the light of thought, the world always is phenomenal; and virtue subordinates it to the mind. Idealism sees the world in God. It beholds the whole circle of persons and things, of actions and events, of country and religion, nor as painfully accumulated, atom after atom, act after act, in an aged creeping Past, but as one vast

[68] Believers in direct revelation of divine knowledge through contemplation.

[69] Manichaeism was a widespread syncretic religious doctrine, pronounced heretical by the Church, originating in the third century. A Manichean was one who believed in the teachings of Manes, a third-century Persian prophet who stressed the conflict between good and evil, the forces of light and darkness, spirit and matter. He was mistakenly supposed to have taught that matter is essentially evil and that the soul comes from the principle of goodness.

[70] Plotinus (204?-270? A.D.) was a Neoplatonist philosopher who gave a mystical interpretation to Plato's philosophy. His work was widely known among the transcendentalists.

[71] Cf. Exodus, xvi: 3: "And the whole congregation of the children of Israel murmured against Moses and Aaron in the wilderness: And the children of Israel said unto them, Would to God we had died by the hand of the Lord in the land of Egypt, when we sat by the fleshpots, and when we did eat bread to the full. . . ."

[72] Cf. Michelangelo's Sonnet CXXIII, 9-11.

picture, which God paints on the instant eternity, for the contemplation of the soul. Therefore the soul holds itself off from a too trivial and microscopic study of the universal tablet. It respects the end too much, to immerse itself in the means. It sees something more important in Christianity, than the scandals of ecclesiastical history or the niceties of criticism; and, very incurious concerning persons or miracles, and not at all disturbed by chasms of historical evidence, it accepts from God the phenomenon, as it finds it, as the pure and awful form of religion in the world. It is not hot and passionate at the appearance of what it calls its own good or bad fortune, at the union or opposition of other persons. No man is its enemy. It accepts whatsoever befalls, as part of its lesson. It is a watcher more than a doer, and it is a doer, only that it may the better watch.

CHAPTER VII. SPIRIT

It is essential to a true theory of nature and of man, that it should contain somewhat progressive. Uses that are exhausted or that may be, and facts that end in the statement, cannot be all that is true of this brave lodging wherein man is harbored, and wherein all his faculties find appropriate and endless exercise. And all the uses of nature admit of being summed in one, which yields the activity of man an infinite scope. Through all its kingdoms, to the suburbs and outskirts of things, it is faithful to the cause whence it had its origin. It always speaks of Spirit. It suggests the absolute. It is a perpetual effect. It is a great shadow pointing always to the sun behind us.

The aspect of nature is devout. Like the figure of Jesus, she stands with bended head, and hands folded upon the breast. The happiest man is he who learns from nature the lesson of worship.

Of that ineffable essence which we call Spirit, he that thinks most, will say least. We can foresee God in the course and, as it were, distant phenomena of matter; but when we try to define and describe himself, both language and thought desert us, and we are as helpless as fools and savages. That essence refuses to be recorded in propositions, but when man has worshipped him intellectually, the noblest ministry of nature is to stand as the apparition of God. It is the great organ through which the universal spirit speaks to the individual, and strives to lead back the individual to it.

When we consider Spirit, we see that the views already presented do not include the whole circumference of man. We must add some related thoughts.

Three problems are put by nature to the mind; What is matter? Whence is it? and Whereto? The first of these questions only, the ideal theory answers. Idealism saith: matter is a phenomenon, not a substance. Idealism acquaints us with the total disparity between the evidence of our own being, and the evidence of the world's being. The one is perfect; the other, incapable of any assurance; the mind is a part of the nature of things; the world is a divine dream, from which we may presently awake to the glories and certainties of day. Idealism is a hypothesis to account for nature by other principles than those of carpentry and chemistry. Yet, if it only deny the existence of matter, it does not satisfy the demands of the spirit. It leaves God out of me. It leaves me in the splendid labyrinth of my perceptions, to wander without end. Then the heart resists it, because it baulks the affections in denying substantive being to men and women. Nature is so pervaded with human life, that there is something of humanity in all, and in every particular. But this theory makes nature foreign to me, and does not account for that consanguinity which we acknowledge to it.

Let it stand then, in the present state of our knowledge, merely as a useful introductory hypothesis, serving to apprize us of the eternal distinction between the soul and the world.

But when, following the invisible steps of thought, we come to inquire, Whence is matter? and Whereto? many truths arise to us out of the recesses of consciousness. We learn that the highest is present to the soul of man, that the dread universal essence, which is not wisdom, or love, or beauty, or power, but all in one, and each entirely, is that for which all things exist, and that by which they are; that spirit creates; that behind nature, throughout nature, spirit is present; that spirit is one and not compound; that spirit does not act upon us from without, that is, in space and time, but spiritually, or through ourselves. Therefore, that spirit, that is, the Supreme Being, does not build up nature around us, but puts it forth through us, as the life of the tree puts forth new branches and leaves through the pores of the old. As a plant upon the earth, so a man rests upon the bosom of God; he is nourished by unfailing fountains, and draws, at his need, inexhaustible power. Who can set bounds to the possibilities of man? Once inhale the upper air, being admitted to behold the absolute natures of justice and truth, and we learn that man has access to the entire mind of the Creator, is himself the creator in the finite. This view, which admonishes me where the sources of wisdom and power lie, and points to virtue as to

> "The golden key
> Which opes the palace of eternity."[74]

carries upon its face the highest certificate of truth, because it animates me to create my own world through the purification of my soul.

The world proceeds from the same spirit as the body of man. It is a remoter and inferior incarnation of God, a projection of God in the unconscious. But it differs from the body in one important respect. It is not, like that, now subjected to the human will. Its serene order is inviolable by us. It

[74] John Milton, *Comus,* 13-14.

is therefore, to us, the present expositor of the divine mind. It is a fixed point whereby we may measure our departure. As we degenerate, the contrast between us and our house is more evident. We are as much strangers in nature, as we are aliens from God. We do not understand the notes of birds. The fox and the deer run away from us; the bear and tiger rend us. We do not know the uses of more than a few plants, as corn and the apple, the potato and the vine. Is not the landscape, every glimpse of which hath a grandeur, a face of him? Yet this may show us what discord is between man and nature, for you cannot freely admire a noble landscape, if laborers are digging in the field hard by. The poet finds something ridiculous in his delight, until he is out of the sight of men.

CHAPTER VIII. PROSPECTS

In inquiries respecting the laws of the world and the frame of things, the highest reason is always the truest. That which seems faintly possible—it is so refined, is often faint and dim because it is deepest seated in the mind among the eternal verities. Empirical science is apt to cloud the sight, and, by the very knowledge of functions and processes, to bereave the student of the manly contemplation of the whole. The savant[75] becomes unpoetic. But the best read naturalist who lends an entire and devout attention to truth, will see that there remains much to learn of his relation to the world, and that it is not to be learned by any addition or subtraction or other comparison of known quantities, but is arrived at by untaught sallies of the spirit, by a continual self-recovery, and by entire humility. He will perceive that there are far more excellent qualities in the student than preciseness and infallibility; that a guess is often more fruitful than an indisputable affirmation, and that a dream may let us deeper into the secret of nature than a hundred concerted experiments.

For, the problems to be solved are precisely those which the physiologist and the naturalist omit to state. It is not so pertinent to man to know all the individuals of the animal kingdom, as it is to know whence and whereto is this tyrannizing unity in his constitution, which evermore separates and classifies things, endeavoring to reduce the most diverse to one form. When I behold a rich landscape, it is less to my purpose to recite correctly the order and superposition of the strata, than to know why all thought of multitude is lost in a tranquil sense of unity. I cannot greatly honor minuteness in details, so long as there is no hint to explain the relation between things and thoughts; no ray upon the *metaphysics* of conchology,[76] of botany, of the arts, to show the relation of the forms of flowers, shells, animals, architecture, to the mind, and build science upon ideas. In a cabinet of natural

---

[75] A scholar.   [76] A study of shells.

history,[77] we become sensible of a certain occult recognition and sympathy in regard to the most unwieldy and eccentric forms of beast, fish, and insect. The American who has been confined, in his own country, to the sight of buildings designed after foreign models, is surprised on entering York Minster[78] or St. Peter's at Rome, by the feeling that these structures are imitations also,—faint copies of an invisible archetype. Nor has science sufficient humanity, so long as the naturalist overlooks that wonderful congruity which subsists between man and the world; of which he is lord, not because he is the most subtile inhabitant, but because he is its head and heart, and finds something of himself in every great and small thing, in every mountain stratum, in every new law of color, fact of astronomy, or atmospheric influence which observation or analysis lay open. A perception of this mystery inspires the muse of George Herbert,[79] the beautiful psalmist of the seventeenth century. The following lines are part of his little poem on Man.

> "Man is all symmetry,
> Full of proportions, one limb to another,
> And to all the world besides.
> Each part may call the farthest, brother;
> For head with foot hath private amity,
> And both with moons and tides.

> "Nothing hath got so far
> But man hath caught and kept it as his prey;
> His eyes dismount the highest star;
> He is in little all the sphere.
> Herbs gladly cure our flesh, because that they
> Find their acquaintance there.

> "For us, the winds do blow,
> The earth doth rest, heaven move, and fountains flow;
> Nothing we see, but means our good,
> As our delight, or as our treasure;
> The whole is either our cupboard of food,
> Or cabinet of pleasure.

> "The stars have us to bed:
> Night draws the curtain; which the sun withdraws.
> Music and light attend our head.
> All things unto our flesh are kind,
> In their descent and being; to our mind,
> In their ascent and cause.

---

[77] A display case of classified specimens.
[78] The cathedral at York, England.

[79] The British metaphysical poet (1593-1633).

"More servants wait on man
Than he'll take notice of. In every path,
He treads down that which doth befriend him
When sickness makes him pale and wan.
Oh mighty love! Man is one world, and hath
Another to attend him."

The perception of this class of truths makes the eternal attraction which draws men to science, but the end is lost sight of in attention to the means. In view of this half-sight of science, we accept the sentence of Plato, that, "poetry comes nearer to vital truth than history." Every surmise and vaticination[80] of the mind is entitled to a certain respect, and we learn to prefer imperfect theories, and sentences, which contain glimpses of truth, to digested systems which have no one valuable suggestion. A wise writer will feel that the ends of study and composition are best answered by announcing undiscovered regions of thought, and so communicating, through hope, new activity to the torpid spirit.

I shall therefore conclude this essay with some traditions of man and nature, which a certain poet[81] sang to me; and which, as they have always been in the world, and perhaps reappear to every bard, may be both history and prophecy.

"The foundations of man are not in matter, but in spirit. But the element of spirit is eternity. To it, therefore, the longest series of events, the oldest chronologies are young and recent. In the cycle of the universal man, from whom the known individuals proceed, centuries are points, and all history is but the epoch of one degradation.

"We distrust and deny inwardly our sympathy with nature. We own and disown our relation to it, by turns. We are, like Nebuchadnezzar,[82] dethroned, bereft of reason, and eating grass like an ox. But who can set limits to the remedial force of spirit?

"A man is a god in ruins. When men are innocent, life shall be longer, and shall pass into the immortal, as gently as we awake from dreams. Now, the world would be insane and rabid, if these disorganizations should last for hundreds of years. It is kept in check by death and infancy. Infancy is the perpetual Messiah, which comes into the arms of fallen men, and pleads with them to return to paradise.

---

[80] Prophecy or revelation.

[81] [Amos] Bronson Alcott (1799-1888) was the transcendentalist who created the *Orphic Sayings* which appeared in *The Dial*, 1840. See p. 1621 for an account of Alcott's life and thought and for the *Orphic Sayings* themselves.

[82] Cf. Daniel iv; 31-33: ". . . there fell a voice from heaven, saying, 'O king Nebuchadnezzar, to thee it is spoken: The Kingdom is departed from thee. And they shall drive thee from men, and thy dwelling shall be with the beasts of the field: they shall make thee to eat grass as oxen. . .'"

"Man is the dwarf of himself. Once he was permeated and dissolved by spirit. He filled nature with his overflowing currents. Out from him sprang the sun and moon; from man, the sun; from woman, the moon. The laws of his mind, the periods of his actions externized themselves into day and night, into the year and the seasons. But, having made for himself this huge shell, his waters retired; he no longer fills the veins and veinlets; he is shrunk to a drop. He sees, that the structure still fits him, but fits him colossally. Say, rather, once it fitted him, now it corresponds to him from far and on high. He adores timidly his own work. Now is man the follower of the sun, and woman the follower of the moon. Yet sometimes he starts in his slumber, and wonders at himself and his house, and muses strangely at the resemblance betwixt him and it. He perceives that if his law is still paramount, if still he have elemental power, 'if his word is sterling yet in nature,' it is not conscious power, it is not inferior but superior to his will. It is Instinct." Thus my Orphic poet sang.[83]

At present, man applies to nature but half his force. He works on the world with his understanding alone. He lives in it, and masters it by a penny-wisdom; and he that works in it, is but a half-man, and whilst his arms are strong and his digestion good, his mind is imbruted and he is a selfish savage. His relation to nature, his power over it, is through the understanding; as by manure; the economic use of fire, wind, water, and the mariner's needle; steam, coal, chemical agriculture; the repairs of the human body by the dentist and the surgeon. This is such a resumption of power, as if a banished king should buy his territories inch by inch, instead of vaulting at once into his throne. Meantime, in the thick darkness, there are not wanting gleams of a better light,—occasional examples of the action of man upon nature with his entire force,—with reason as well as understanding. Such examples are; the traditions of miracles in the earliest antiquity of all nations; the history of Jesus Christ; the achievements of a principle, as in religious and political revolutions, and in the abolition of the Slave-trade; the miracles of enthusiasm,[84] as those reported of Swedenborg, Hohenlohe, and the Shakers; many obscure and yet contested facts, now arranged under the name of Animal Magnetism;[85] prayer; eloquence; self-healing; and the wisdom of children. These are examples of Reason's momentary grasp of the sceptre; the exer-

---

[83] Alcott. Orphic is used in the mystical sense, and is related to Orpheus, the musician of Greek mythology who, by virtue of his art, charmed beasts, trees, and rocks, as well as human beings.

[84] Literally this means "possession by a god; the ecstatic or frenzied religious states."

Alexander Leopold, Prince of Hohenlohe (1794-1849), was a German Catholic priest; the Shakers were a celibate religious sect that claimed instances of "possession."

[85] Hypnosis. It was given that term by Franc Anton Mesmer (1734-1815), an Austrian physician.

tions of a power which exists not in time or space, but an instantaneous in-streaming causing power. The difference between the actual and the ideal force of man is happily figured by the schoolmen, in saying, that the knowledge of man is an evening knowledge, *vespertina cognitio*, but that of God is a morning knowledge, *matutina cognitio*.

The problem of restoring to the world original and eternal beauty, is solved by the redemption of the soul. The ruin or the blank, that we see when we look at nature, is in our own eye. The axis of vision is not coincident with the axis of things, and so they appear not transparent but opake. The reason why the world lacks unity, and lies broken and in heaps, is, because man is disunited with himself. He cannot be a naturalist, until he satisfies all the demands of the spirit. Love is as much its demand, as perception. Indeed, neither can be perfect without the other. In the uttermost meaning of the words, thought is devout, and devotion is thought. Deep calls unto deep.[86] But in actual life, the marriage is not celebrated. There are innocent men who worship God after the tradition of their fathers, but their sense of duty had not yet extended to the use of all their faculties. And there are patient naturalists, but they freeze their subject under the wintry light of the understanding. Is not prayer also a study of truth,—a sally of the soul into the unfound infinite? No man ever prayed heartily, without learning something. But when a faithful thinker, resolute to detach every object from personal relations, and see it in the light of thought, shall, at the same time, kindle science with the fire of the holiest affections, then will God go forth anew into the creation.

It will not need, when the mind is prepared for study, to search for objects. The invariable mark of wisdom is to see the miraculous in the common. What is a day? What is a year? What is summer? What is woman? What is a child? What is sleep? To our blindness, these things seem unaffecting. We make fables to hide the baldness of the fact and conform it, as we say, to the higher law of the mind. But when the fact is seen under the light of an idea, the gaudy fable fades and shrivels. We behold the real higher law. To the wise, therefore, a fact is true poetry, and most beautiful of fables. These wonders are brought to our own door. You also are a man. Man and woman, and their social life, poverty, labor, sleep, fear, fortune, are known to you. Learn that none of these things is superficial, but that each phenomenon hath its roots in the faculties and affections of the mind. Whilst the abstract question occupies your intellect, nature brings it in the concrete to be solved by your hands. It were a wise inquiry for the closet, to compare,

[86] Cf. Psalms xlii: "Deep calleth unto deep at the noise of thy waterspouts: all thy waves and thy billows are gone over me."

point by point, especially at remarkable crises in life, our daily history, with the rise and progress of ideas in the mind.

So shall we come to look at the world with new eyes. It shall answer the endless inquiry of the intellect,—What is truth? and of the affections,—What is good? by yielding itself passive to the educated Will. Then shall come to pass what my poet said; "Nature is not fixed but fluid. Spirit alters, moulds, makes it. The immobility or bruteness of nature, is the absence of spirit; to pure spirit, it is fluid, it is volatile, it is obedient. Every spirit builds itself a house; and beyond its house, a world; and beyond its world, a heaven. Know then, that the world exists for you. For you is the phenomenon perfect. What we are, that only can we see. All that Adam had, all that Cæsar could, you have and can do. Adam called his house, heaven and earth; Cæsar called his house, Rome; you perhaps call yours, a cobbler's trade; a hundred acres of ploughed land; or a scholar's garret. Yet line for line and point for point, your dominion is as great as theirs, though without fine names. Build, therefore, your own world. As fast as you conform your life to the pure idea in your mind, that will unfold its great proportions. A correspondent revolution in things will attend the influx of the spirit. So fast will disagreeable appearances, swine, spiders, snakes, pests, mad-houses, prisons, enemies, vanish; they are temporary and shall be no more seen. The sordor and filths of nature, the sun shall dry up, and the wind exhale. As when the summer comes from the south, the snow-banks melt, and the face of the earth becomes green before it, so shall the advancing spirit create its ornaments along its path, and carry with it the beauty it visits, and the song which enchants it; it shall draw beautiful faces, and warm hearts, and wise discourse, and heroic arts, around its way, until evil is no more seen. The kingdom of man over nature, which cometh not with observation,—a dominion such as now is beyond his dream of God,—he shall enter without more wonder than the blind man feels who is gradually restored to perfect sight."

The American Scholar[1]

AN ORATION

*Delivered Before the Phi Beta Kappa Society,
at Cambridge, August 31, 1837*

MR. PRESIDENT, AND GENTLEMEN,

I greet you on the re-commencement of our literary year.[2] Our anniversary is one of hope, and, perhaps, not enough of labor. We do not meet for games of strength or skill, for the recitation of histories, tragedies 'and odes, like the ancient Greeks; for parliaments of love and poesy, like the Troubadours; nor for the advancement of science, like our contemporaries in the British and European capitals. Thus far, our holiday has been simply a friendly sign of the survival of the love of letters amongst a people too busy to give to letters any more. As such, it is precious as the sign of an indestructible instinct. Perhaps the time is already come, when it ought to be, and will be something else; when the sluggard intellect of this continent will look from under its iron lids and fill the postponed expectation of the world with something better than the exertions of mechanical skill. Our day of dependence, our long apprenticeship to the learning of other lands, draws to a close. The millions that around us are rushing into life, cannot always be fed on the sere remains of foreign harvests. Events, actions arise, that must be sung, that will sing themselves. Who can doubt that poetry will revive and lead in a new age, as the star in the constellation Harp[3] which now flames in our zenith, astronomers announce, shall one day be the pole-star for a thousand years?

In the light of this hope, I accept the topic which not only usage, but the nature of our association, seem to prescribe to this day,—the AMERICAN SCHOLAR. Year by year, we come up hither to read one more chapter of his

[1] This address was delivered at the Phi Beta Kappa exercises at Harvard on August 31, 1837. It made a deep impression on those students who gathered at noon in the meeting house across from Harvard Yard. Bronson Alcott remembered the occasion, "the mixed confusion, consternation, surprise, and wonder" of some of the audience; Oliver Wendell Holmes claimed that "this grand oration was our intellectual Declaration of Independence. . . the young men went out from it as if a prophet had been proclaiming to them 'Thus saith the Lord' "; and James Russell Lowell remembered the lecture "as an event without any former parallel in our literary annals, a scene to be always treasured in our memory for its picturesqueness and its inspiration. What crowded and breathless aisles, what windows clustering with eager heads, what enthusiasm of approval, what grim silence of foregone dissent! It was our Yankee version of a lecture by Abelard, our Harvard parallel to the last public appearance of Schelling."

[2] The academic year usually began around September 1.

[3] Emerson refers to Vega, the fourth brightest star and located in the constellation Lyra.

biography. Let us inquire what light new days and events have thrown on his character, his duties and his hopes.

It is one of those fables, which out of an unknown antiquity, convey an unlooked-for wisdom, that the gods, in the beginning, divided Man into men, that he might be more helpful to himself; just as the hand was divided into fingers, the better to answer its end.

The old fable covers a doctrine ever new and sublime; that there is One Man,—present to all particular men only partially, or through one faculty; and that you must take the whole society to find the whole man. Man is not a farmer, or a professor, or an engineer, but he is all. Man is priest, and scholar, and statesman, and producer, and soldier. In the *divided* or social state, these functions are parcelled out to individuals, each of whom aims to do his stint of the joint work, whilst each other performs his. The fable implies that the individual to possess himself, must sometimes return from his own labor to embrace all the other laborers. But unfortunately, this original unit, this fountain of power, has been so distributed to multitudes, has been so minutely subdivided and peddled out, that it is spilled into drops, and cannot be gathered. The state of society is one in which the members have suffered amputation from the trunk, and strut about so many walking monsters,—a good finger, a neck, a stomach, an elbow, but never a man.

Man is thus metamorphosed into a thing, into many things. The planter, who is Man sent out into the field to gather food, is seldom cheered by any idea of the true dignity of his ministry. He sees his bushel and his cart, and nothing beyond, and sinks into the farmer, instead of Man on the farm. The tradesman scarcely ever gives an ideal worth to his work, but is ridden by the routine of his craft, and the soul is subject to dollars. The priest becomes a form; the attorney, a statute-book; the mechanic, a machine; the sailor, a rope of a ship.

In this distribution of functions, the scholar is the delegated intellect. In the right state, he is, *Man Thinking*. In the degenerate state, when the victim of society, he tends to become a mere thinker, or, still worse, the parrot of other men's thinking.

In this view of him, as Man Thinking, the whole theory of his office is contained. Him nature solicits, with all her placid, all her monitory pictures. Him the past instructs. Him the future invites. Is not, indeed, every man a student, and do not all things exist for the student's behoof? And, finally, is not the true scholar the only true master? But, as the old oracle said, "All things have two handles. Beware of the wrong one." In life, too often, the scholar errs with mankind and forfeits his privilege. Let us see him in his school, and consider him in reference to the main influences he receives.

I. The first in time and the first in importance of the influences upon the mind is that of nature. Every day, the sun, and, after sunset, night and her stars. Ever the winds blow; ever the grass grows. Every day, men and

women, conversing, beholding and beholden. The scholar must needs stand
wistful and admiring before this great spectacle. He must settle its value in
his mind. What is nature to him? There is never a beginning, there is never
an end to the inexplicable continuity of this web of God, but always circular
power returning into itself. Therein it resembles his own spirit, whose beginning, whose ending he never can find—so entire, so boundless. Far, too, as
her splendors shine, system on system shooting like rays, upward, downward,
without centre, without circumference,—in the mass and in the particle
nature hastens to render account of herself to the mind. Classification begins.
To the young mind, every thing is individual, stands by itself. By and by, it
finds how to join two things, and see in them one nature; then three, then
three thousand; and so, tyrannized over by its own unifying instinct, it goes
on tying things together, diminishing anomalies, discovering roots running
under ground, whereby contrary and remote things cohere, and flower out
from one stem. It presently learns, that, since the dawn of history, there has
been a constant accumulation and classifying of facts. But what is classification but the perceiving that these objects are not chaotic, and are not foreign, but have a law which is also a law of the human mind? The astronomer
discovers that geometry, a pure abstraction of the human mind, is the measure of planetary motion. The chemist finds proportions and intelligible
method throughout matter: and science is nothing but the finding of analogy,
identity in the most remote parts. The ambitious soul sits down before each
refractory fact; one after another, reduces all strange constitutions, all new
powers, to their class and their law, and goes on forever to animate the last
fibre of organization, the outskirts of nature, by insight.

Thus to him, to this school-boy under the bending dome of day, is suggested, that he and it proceed from one root; one is leaf and one is flower;
relation, sympathy, stirring in every vein. And what is that Root? Is not that
the soul of his soul?—A thought too bold—a dream too wild. Yet when this
spiritual light shall have revealed the law of more earthly natures,—when he
has learned to worship the soul, and to see that the natural philosophy that
now is, is only the first gropings of its gigantic hand, he shall look forward to
an ever expanding knowledge as to a becoming creator. He shall see that
nature is the opposite of the soul, answering to it part for part. One is seal,
and one is print. Its beauty is the beauty of his own mind. Its laws are the
laws of his own mind. Nature then becomes to him the measure of his
attainments. So much of nature as he is ignorant of, so much of his own mind
does he not yet possess. And, in fine, the ancient precept, "Know thyself,"
and the modern precept, "Study nature," become at last one maxim.[4]

II. The next great influence into the spirit of the scholar, is, the mind of
the Past,—in whatever form, whether of literature, of art, of institutions, that

[4] This paragraph is one of Emerson's clearest statements of his theory of correspondences in which the microcosm and the macrocosm, the soul and the body, spirit and nature, are one.

mind is inscribed. Books are the best type of the influence of the past, and perhaps we shall get at the truth—learn the amount of this influence more conveniently—by considering their value alone.

The theory of books is noble. The scholar of the first age received into him the world around; brooded there on; gave it the new arrangement of his own mind, and uttered it again. It came into him—life; it went out from him—truth. It came to him—short-lived actions; it went out from him—immortal thoughts. It came to him—business; it went from him—poetry. It was—dead fact; now, it is quick thought. It can stand, and it can go. It now endures, it now flies, it now inspires. Precisely in proportion to the depth of mind from which it issued, so high does it soar, so long does it sing.

Or, I might say, it depends on how far the process had gone, of transmuting life into truth. In proportion to the completeness of the distillation, so will the purity and imperishableness of the product be. But none is quite perfect. As no air-pump can by any means make a perfect vacuum, so neither can any artist entirely exclude the conventional, the local, the perishable from his book, or write a book of pure thought that shall be as efficient, in all respects, to a remote posterity, as to contemporaries, or rather to the second age. Each age, it is found, must write its own books; or rather, each generation for the next succeeding. The books of an older period will not fit this.

Yet hence arises a grave mischief. The sacredness which attaches to the act of creation,—the act of thought,—is instantly transferred to the record. The poet chanting, was felt to be a divine man. Henceforth the chant is divine also. The writer was a just and wise spirit. Henceforward it is settled, the book is perfect; as love of the hero corrupts into worship of his statue. Instantly, the book becomes noxious. The guide is a tyrant. We sought a brother, and lo, a governor. The sluggish and perverted mind of the multitude, always slow to open to the incursions of Reason, having once so opened, having once received this book, stands upon it, and makes an outcry, if it is disparaged. Colleges are built on it. Books are written on it by thinkers, not by Man Thinking; by men of talent, that is, who start wrong, who set out from accepted dogmas, not from their own sight of principles. Meek young men grow up in libraries, believing it their duty to accept the views which Cicero, which Locke, which Bacon have given, forgetful that Cicero, Locke and Bacon[5] were only young men in libraries when they wrote these books.

[5] These authors were common to students of the time. Marcus Tullius Cicero (106-43 B.C.), a Roman philosopher and statesman, was studied for his oratory; John Locke (1632-1704), English philosopher, for his philosophy of empiricism, reflected in *Essay Concerning Human Understanding* (1690); and Francis Bacon (1561-1626), a Renaissance English philosopher who founded the inductive method of science as part of his general theories of knowledge, set down in *The Advancement of Learning* (1605) and *Novum Organum* (1620).

Hence, instead of Man Thinking, we have the bookworm. Hence, the book-learned class, who value books, as such; not as related to nature and the human constitution, but as making a sort of Third Estate[6] with the world and the soul. Hence, the restorers of readings, the emendators, the biblioma-niacs of all degrees.

This is bad; this is worse than it seems. Books are the best of things, well used; abused, among the worst. What is the right use? What is the one end which all means go to effect? They are for nothing but to inspire. I had better never see a book than to be warped by its attraction clean out of my own orbit, and made a satellite instead of a system. The one thing in the world of value, is, the active soul,—the soul, free, sovereign, active. This every man is entitled to; this every man contains within him, although in almost all men, obstructed, and as yet unborn. The soul active sees absolute truth; and utters truth, or creates. In this action, it is genius; not the privilege of here and there a favorite, but the sound estate of every man. In its essence, it is progressive. The book, the college, the school of art, the institu-tion of any kind, stop with some past utterance of genius. This is good, say they,—let us hold by this. They pin me down. They look backward and not forward. But genius always looks forward. The eyes of man are set in his forehead, not in his hindhead. Man hopes. Genius creates. To create,—to create,—is the proof of a divine presence. Whatever talents may be, if the man create not, the pure efflux of the Deity is not his:—cinders and smoke, there may be, but not yet flame. There are creative manners, there are creative actions, and creative words; manners, actions, words, that is, indica-tive of no custom or authority, but springing spontaneous from the mind's own sense of good and fair.

On the other part, instead of being its own seer, let it receive always from another mind its truth, though it were in torrents of light, without periods of solitude, inquest and self-recovery, and a fatal disservice is done. Genius is always sufficiently the enemy of genius by over-influence. The literature of every nation bear me witness. The English dramatic poets have Shakspear-ized now for two hundred years.

Undoubtedly there is a right way of reading,—so it be sternly subordi-nated. Man Thinking must not be subdued by his instruments. Books are for the scholar's idle times. When he can read God directly, the hour is too precious to be wasted in other men's transcripts of their readings. But when the intervals of darkness come, as come they must,—when the soul seeth not, when the sun is hid, and the stars withdraw their shining,—we repair to the lamps which were kindled by their ray to guide our steps to the East again, where the dawn is. We hear that we may speak. The Arabian proverb says, "A fig tree looking on a fig tree, becometh fruitful."

[6] Refers to the commons. The other two es-tates were the clergy and the nobility.

It is remarkable, the character of the pleasure we derive from the best books. They impress us ever with the conviction that one nature wrote and the same reads. We read the verses of one of the great English poets, of Chaucer, of Marvell, of Dryden, with the most modern joy,—with a pleasure, I mean, which is in great part caused by the abstraction of all *time* from their verses. There is some awe mixed with the joy of our surprise, when this poet, who lived in some past world, two or three hundred years ago, says that which lies close to my own soul, that which I also had wellnigh thought and said. But for the evidence thence afforded to the philosophical doctrine of the identity of all minds, we should suppose some preestablished harmony, some foresight of souls that were to be, and some preparation of stores for their future wants, like the fact observed in insects, who lay up food before death for the young grub they shall never see.

I would not be hurried by any love of system, by any exaggeration of instincts, to underrate the Book. We all know, that as the human body can be nourished on any food, though it were boiled grass and the broth of shoes, so the human mind can be fed by any knowledge. And great and heroic men have existed, who had almost no other information than by the printed page. I only would say, that it needs a strong head to bear that diet. One must be an inventor to read well. As the proverb says, "He that would bring home the wealth of the Indies, must carry out the wealth of the Indies." There is then creative reading, as well as creative writing. When the mind is braced by labor and invention, the page of whatever book we read becomes luminous with manifold allusion. Every sentence is doubly significant, and the sense of our author is as broad as the world. We then see, what is always true, that as the seer's hour of vision is short and rare among heavy days and months, so is its record, perchance, the least part of his volume. The discerning will read in his Plato or Shakspeare, only that least part,—only the authentic utterances of the oracle,—and all the rest he rejects, were it never so many times Plato's and Shakspeare's.

Of course, there is a portion of reading quite indispensable to a wise man. History and exact science he must learn by laborious reading. Colleges, in like manner, have their indispensable office,—to teach elements. But they can only highly serve us, when they aim not to drill, but to create; when they gather from far every ray of various genius to their hospitable halls, and, by the concentrated fires, set the hearts of their youth on flame. Thought and knowledge are natures in which apparatus and pretension avail nothing. Gowns, and pecuniary foundations, though of towns of gold, can never countervail the least sentence or syllable of wit.[7] Forget this, and our American colleges will recede in their public importance whilst they grow richer every year.

[7] In the archaic sense of knowledge.

III. There goes in the world a notion that the scholar should be a recluse, a valetudinarian,—as unfit for any handiwork or public labor, as a penknife for an axe. The so-called "practical men" sneer at speculative men, as if, because they speculate or *see*,[8] they could do nothing. I have heard it said that the clergy,—who are always more universally than any other class, the scholars of their day,—are addressed as women: that the rough, spontaneous conversation of men they do not hear, but only a mincing and diluted speech. They are often virtually disfranchised; and, indeed, there are advocates for their celibacy. As far as this is true of the studious classes, it is not just and wise. Action is with the scholar subordinate, but it is essential. Without it, he is not yet man. Without it, thought can never ripen into truth. Whilst the world hangs before the eye as a cloud of beauty, we cannot even see its beauty. Inaction is cowardice, but there can be no scholar without the heroic mind. The preamble of thought, the transition through which it passes from the unconscious to the conscious, is action. Only so much do I know, as I have lived. Instantly we know whose words are loaded with life, and whose not.

The world,—this shadow of the soul, or *other me*, lies wide around. Its attractions are the keys which unlock my thoughts and make me acquainted with myself. I run eagerly into this resounding tumult. I grasp the hands of those next me, and take my place in the ring to suffer and to work, taught by an instinct that so shall the dumb abyss be vocal with speech. I pierce its order; I dissipate its fear; I dispose of it within the circuit of my expanding life. So much only of life as I know by experience, so much of the wilderness have I vanquished and planted, or so far have I extended my being, my dominion. I do not see how any man can afford, for the sake of his nerves and his nap, to spare any action in which he can partake. It is pearls and rubies to his discourse. Drudgery, calamity, exasperation, want, are instructers in eloquence and wisdom. The true scholar grudges every opportunity of action past by, as a loss of power.

It is the raw material out of which the intellect moulds her splendid products. A strange process too, this, by which experience is converted into thought, as a mulberry leaf is converted into satin. The manufacture goes forward at all hours.

The actions and events of our childhood and youth are now matters of calmest observation. They lie like fair pictures in the air. Not so with our recent actions,—with the business which we now have in hand. On this we are quite unable to speculate. Our affections as yet circulate through it. We no more feel or know it, than we feel the feet, or the hand, or the brain of our body. The new deed is yet a part of life,—remains for a time immersed in our unconscious life. In some contemplative hour, it detaches itself from

---

[8] "Speculate" is derived from the Latin *spe-cere*, "to see."

the life like a ripe fruit, to become a thought of the mind. Instantly, it is raised, transfigured; the corruptible has put on incorruption.[9] Always now it is an object of beauty, however base its origin and neighborhood. Observe, too, the impossibility of antedating this act. In its grub state, it cannot fly, it cannot shine,—it is a dull grub. But suddenly, without observation, the self-same thing unfurls beautiful wings, and is an angel of wisdom. So is there no fact, no event, in our private history, which shall not, sooner or later, lose its adhesive inert form, and astonish us by soaring from our body into the empyrean.[10] Cradle and infancy, school and playground, the fear of boys, and dogs, and ferules,[11] the love of little maids and berries, and many another fact that once filled the whole sky, are gone already; friend and relative, profession and party, town and country, nation and world, must also soar and sing.

Of course, he who has put forth his total strength in fit actions, has the richest return of wisdom. I will not shut myself out of this globe of action and transplant an oak into a flower pot, there to hunger and pine; nor trust the revenue of some single faculty, and exhaust one vein of thought, much like those Savoyards,[12] who, getting their livelihood by carving shepherds, shepherdesses, and smoking Dutchmen, for all Europe, went out one day to the mountain to find stock, and discovered that they had whittled up the last of their pine trees. Authors we have in numbers, who have written out their vein, and who, moved by a commendable prudence, sail for Greece or Palestine, follow the trapper into the prairie, or ramble round Algiers to replenish their merchantable stock.

If it were only for a vocabulary the scholar would be covetous of action. Life is our dictionary. Years are well spent in country labors; in town—in the insight into trades and manufactures; in frank intercourse with many men and women; in science; in art; to the one end of mastering in all their facts a language, by which to illustrate and embody our perceptions. I learn immediately from any speaker how much he has already lived, through the poverty or the splendor of his speech. Life lies behind us as the quarry from whence we get tiles and copestones for the masonry of to-day. This is the way to learn grammar. Colleges and books only copy the language which the field and the work-yard made.

But the final value of action, like that of books, and better than books, is, that it is a resource. That great principle of Undulation in nature, that shows itself in the inspiring and expiring of the breath; in desire and satiety; in the ebb and flow of the sea, in day and night, in heat and cold, and as yet more deeply ingrained in every atom and every fluid, is known to us under the

---

[9] Cf. I Corinthians, xv: 54: "For this corruptible must put on incorruption, and this mortal must put on immortality."

[10] The highest heaven.

[11] Flat sticks used for beating.

[12] Inhabitants of Savoy in southeast France.

name of Polarity,—these "fits of easy transmission and reflection," as Newton[13] called them, are the law of nature because they are the law of spirit.

The mind now thinks; now acts; and each fit reproduces the other. When the artist has exhausted his materials, when the fancy no longer paints, when thoughts are no longer apprehended, and books are a weariness,—he has always the resource *to live.* Character is higher than intellect. Thinking is the function. Living is the functionary. The stream retreats to its source. A great soul will be strong to live, as well as strong to think. Does he lack organ or medium to impart his truths? He can still fall back on this elemental force of living them. This is a total act. Thinking is a partial act. Let the grandeur of justice shine in his affairs. Let the beauty of affection cheer his lowly roof. Those "far from fame" who dwell and act with him, will feel the force of his constitution in the doings and passages of the day better than it can be measured by any public and designed display. Time shall teach him that the scholar loses no hour which the man lives. Herein he unfolds the sacred germ of his instinct, screened from influence. What is lost in seemliness is gained in strength. Not out of those on whom systems of education have exhausted their culture, comes the helpful giant to destroy the old or to build the new, but out of unhandselled[14] savage nature, out of terrible Druids[15] and Berserkers, come at last Alfred[16] and Shakspeare.

I hear therefore with joy whatever is beginning to be said of the dignity and necessity of labor to every citizen. There is virtue yet in the hoe and the spade, for learned as well as for unlearned hands. And labor is every where welcome; always we are invited to work;[17] only be this limitation observed, that a man shall not for the sake of wider activity sacrifice any opinion to the popular judgments and modes of action.

I have now spoken of the education of the scholar by nature, by books, and by action. It remains to say somewhat of his duties.

They are such as become Man Thinking. They may all be comprised in self-trust. The office of the scholar is to cheer, to raise, and to guide men by showing them facts amidst appearances. He plies the slow, unhonored, and

[13] Sir Isaac Newton (1642-1727) was an English mathematician and physicist. This phrase is taken from *Optics* (1704).

[14] A rare word used by Emerson to mean "unequipped" or "unfurnished," with the sense of rawness and primitiveness. For the literal meaning see the Oxford English Dictionary. A "handsel" is a ceremonial gift for good luck.

[15] Druids were Ancient Pagan Celtic priests; Berserkers were savage warriors of Norse mythology.

[16] King Alfred (849-899) of England defeated the Danes and was considered the greatest of Saxon kings, largely responsible for promoting national identity, laws, and culture.

[17] This is a concept that Emerson undoubtedly owes to his association with Thomas Carlyle, the English essayist whom he had met in his trip abroad. Carlyle stressed the significance of work and discipline in man's moral life.

unpaid task of observation. Flamsteed and Herschel,[18] in their glazed observatories, may catalogue the stars with the praise of all men, and, the results being splendid and useful, honor is sure. But he, in his private observatory, cataloguing obscure and nebulous stars of the human mind, which as yet no man has thought of as such,—watching days and months, sometimes, for a few facts; correcting still his old records;—must relinquish display and immediate fame. In the long period of his preparation, he must betray often an ignorance and shiftlessness in popular arts, incurring the disdain of the able who shoulder him aside. Long he must stammer in his speech; often forego the living for the dead. Worse yet, he must accept—how often! poverty and solitude. For the ease and pleasure of treading the old road, accepting the fashions, the education, the religion of society, he takes the cross of making his own, and, of course, the self-accusation, the faint heart, the frequent uncertainty and loss of time which are the nettles and tangling vines in the way of the self-relying and self-directed; and the state of virtual hostility in which he seems to stand to society, and especially to educated society. For all this loss and scorn, what offset? He is to find consolation in exercising the highest functions of human nature. He is one who raises himself from private considerations, and breathes and lives on public and illustrious thoughts. He is the world's eye. He is the world's heart. He is to resist the vulgar prosperity that retrogrades ever to barbarism, by preserving and communicating heroic sentiments, noble biographies, melodious verse, and the conclusions of history. Whatsoever oracles the human heart in all emergencies, in all solemn hours has uttered as its commentary on the world of actions,—these he shall receive and impart. And whatsoever new verdict Reason from her inviolable seat pronounces on the passing men and events of to-day,—this he shall hear and promulgate.

These being his functions, it becomes him to feel all confidence in himself, and to defer never to the popular cry. He and he only knows the world. The world of any moment is the merest appearance. Some great decorum, some fetish of a government, some ephemeral trade, or war, or man, is cried up by half mankind and cried down by the other half, as if all depended on this particular up or down. The odds are that the whole question is not worth the poorest thought which the scholar has lost in listening to the controversy. Let him not quit his belief that a popgun is a popgun, though the ancient and honorable of the earth affirm it to be the crack of doom. In silence, in steadiness, in severe abstraction, let him hold himself; add observation to observation, patient of neglect, patient of reproach; and bide his own time,—happy enough if he can satisfy himself alone that this day he has seen something truly. Success treads on every right step. For the instinct is sure that prompts him to tell his brother what he thinks. He then learns that

[18] John Flamsteed (1646-1719), Sir [Frederick] William Herschel (1738-1882), and his son John Frederick William were English astronomers.

in going down into the secrets of his own mind, he has descended into the secrets of all minds. He learns that he who has mastered any law in his private thoughts, is master to that extent of all men whose language he speaks, and of all into whose language his own can be translated. The poet in utter solitude remembering his spontaneous thoughts and recording them, is found to have recorded that which men in crowded cities find true for them also. The orator distrusts at first the fitness of his frank confessions,—his want of knowledge of the persons he addresses,—until he finds that he is the complement of his hearers;—that they drink his words because he fulfils for them their own nature; the deeper he dives into his privatest secretest presentiment,—to his wonder he finds, this is the most acceptable, most public, and universally true. The people delight in it; the better part of every man feels, This is my music: this is myself.

In self-trust, all the virtues are comprehended. Free should the scholar be,—free and brave. Free even to the definition of freedom, "without any hindrance that does not arise out of his own constitution."[19] Brave; for fear is a thing which a scholar by his very function puts behind him. Fear always springs from ignorance. It is a shame to him if his tranquillity, amid dangerous times, arise from the presumption that like children and women, his is a protected class; or if he seek a temporary peace by the diversion of his thoughts from politics or vexed questions, hiding his head like an ostrich in the flowering bushes, peeping into microscopes, and turning rhymes, as a boy whistles to keep his courage up. So is the danger a danger still: so is the fear worse. Manlike let him turn and face it. Let him look into its eye and search its nature, inspect its origin,—see the whelping of this lion,—which lies no great way back; he will then find in himself a perfect comprehension of its nature and extent; he will have made his hands meet on the other side, and can henceforth defy it, and pass on superior. The world is his who can see through its pretension. What deafness, what stone-blind custom, what overgrown error you behold, is there only by sufferance,—by your sufferance. See it to be a lie, and you have already dealt it its mortal blow.

Yes, we are the cowed,—we the trustless. It is a mischievous notion that we are come late into nature; that the world was finished a long time ago. As the world was plastic and fluid in the hands of God, so it is ever to so much of his attributes as we bring to it. To ignorance and sin, it is flint. They adapt themselves to it as they may; but in proportion as a man has anything in him divine, the firmament flows before him, and takes his signet and form. Not he is great who can alter matter, but he who can alter my state of mind. They are the kings of the world who give the color of their present thought to all nature and all art, and persuade men by the cheerful serenity of their carrying the matter, that this thing which they do, is the apple which the ages have desired to pluck, now at last ripe, and inviting nations to the harvest.

---

[19] Freedom as defined by Immanuel Kant.

The great man makes the great thing. Wherever Macdonald sits, there is the head of the table. Linnæus makes botany the most alluring of studies and wins it from the farmer and the herb-woman. Davy, chemistry: and Cuvier, fossils.[20] The day is always his, who works in it with serenity and great aims. The unstable estimates of men crowd to him whose mind is filled with a truth, as the heaped waves of the Atlantic follow the moon.

For this self-trust, the reason is deeper than can be fathomed,—darker than can be enlightened. I might not carry with me the feeling of my audience in stating my own belief. But I have already shown the ground of my hope, in adverting to the doctrine that man is one. I believe man has been wronged: he has wronged himself. He has almost lost the light that can lead him back to his prerogatives. Men are become of no account. Men in history, men in the world of to-day are bugs, are spawn, and are called "the mass" and "the herd." In a century, in a millenium, one or two men; that is to say—one or two approximations to the right state of every man. All the rest behold in the hero or the poet their own green and crude being—ripened; yes, and are content to be less, so *that* may attain to its full stature. What a testimony—full of grandeur, full of pity, is borne to the demands of his own nature, by the poor clansman, the poor partisan, who rejoices in the glory of his chief. The poor and the low find some amends to their immense moral capacity, for their acquiescence in a political and social inferiority. They are content to be brushed like flies from the path of a great person, so that justice shall be done by him to that common nature which it is the dearest desire of all to see enlarged and glorified. They sun themselves in the great man's light, and feel it to be their own element. They cast the dignity of man from their downtrod selves upon the shoulders of a hero, and will perish to add one drop of blood to make that great heart beat, those giant sinews combat and conquer. He lives for us, and we live in him.

Men such as they are, very naturally seek money or power; and power because it is as good as money,—the "spoils," so called, "of office." And why not? for they aspire to the highest, and this, in their sleep-walking, they dream is highest. Wake them, and they shall quit the false good and leap to the true, and leave governments to clerks and desks. This revolution is to be wrought by the gradual domestication of the idea of Culture. The main enterprise of the world for splendor, for extent, is the upbuilding of a man. Here are the materials strown along the ground. The private life of one man shall be a more illustrious monarchy,—more formidable to its enemy, more

[20] Carolus Linnæus was an eighteenth-century Swedish philosopher who founded the binomial system of plant and animal classification; Sir Humphry Davy (1778-1829), an English chemist who discovered potassium and sodium, was a pioneer in electrolysis, and professor of chemistry at the Royal Institution; Baron Georges Leopold Chrétien Fréderic Dagobert Cuvier (1769-1832) was a French naturalist, paleontologist, comparative anatomist, and author of *Regne Animal*.

sweet and serene in its influence to its friend, than any kingdom in history. For a man, rightly viewed, comprehendeth the particular natures of all men. Each philosopher, each bard, each actor, has only done for me, as by a delegate, what one day I can do for myself. The books which once we valued more than the apple of the eye, we have quite exhausted. What is that but saying that we have come up with the point of view which the universal mind took through the eyes of that one scribe; we have been that man, and have passed on. First, one; then, another; we drain all cisterns, and waxing greater by all these supplies, we crave a better and more abundant food. The man has never lived that can feed us ever. The human mind cannot be enshrined in a person who shall set a barrier on any one side to this unbounded, unboundable empire. It is one central fire which flaming now out of the lips of Etna, lightens the capes of Sicily; and now out of the throat of Vesuvius, illuminates the towers and vineyards of Naples. It is one light which beams out of a thousand stars. It is one soul which animates all men.

But I have dwelt perhaps tediously upon this abstraction of the Scholar. I ought not to delay longer to add what I have to say, of nearer reference to the time and to this country.

Historically, there is thought to be a difference in the ideas which predominate over successive epochs, and there are data for marking the genius of the Classic, of the Romantic, and now of the Reflective or Philosophical age. With the views I have intimated of the oneness or the identity of the mind through all individuals, I do not much dwell on these differences. In fact, I believe each individual passes through all three. The boy is a Greek; the youth, romantic; the adult, reflective. I deny not, however, that a revolution in the leading idea may be distinctly enough traced.

Our age is bewailed as the age of Introversion. Must that needs be evil? We, it seems, are critical. We are embarrassed with second thoughts. We cannot enjoy any thing for hankering to know whereof the pleasure consists. We are lined with eyes. We see with our feet. The time is infected with Hamlet's unhappiness,—

"Sicklied o'er with the pale cast of thought." [21]

Is it so bad then? Sight is the last thing to be pitied. Would we be blind? Do we fear lest we should outsee nature and God, and drink truth dry? I look upon the discontent of the literary class as a mere announcement of the fact that they find themselves not in the state of mind of their fathers, and regret the coming state as untried; as a boy dreads the water before he has learned that he can swim. If there is any period one would desire to be born in,—is it not the age of Revolution; when the old and the new stand side by side,

[21] *Hamlet,* Act III, Sc. i, 1. 85.

and admit of being compared; when the energies of all men are searched by fear and by hope; when the historic glories of the old, can be compensated by the rich possibilities of the new era? This time, like all times, is a very good one, if we but know what to do with it.

I read with joy some of the auspicious signs of the coming days as they glimmer already through poetry and art, through philosophy and science, through church and state.

One of these signs is the fact that the same movement which effected the elevation of what was called the lowest class in the state, assumed in literature a very marked and as benign an aspect. Instead of the sublime and beautiful, the near, the low, the common, was explored and poetized. That which had been negligently trodden under foot by those who were harnessing and provisioning themselves for long journeys into far countries, is suddenly found to be richer than all foreign parts. The literature of the poor, the feelings of the child, the philosophy of the street, the meaning of household life, are the topics of the time. It is a great stride. It is a sign—is it not? of new vigor, when the extremities are made active, when currents of warm life run into the hands and the feet. I ask not for the great, the remote, the romantic; what is doing in Italy or Arabia; what is Greek art, or Provencal Minstrelsy; I embrace the common, I explore and sit at the feet of the familiar, the low. Give me insight into to-day, and you may have the antique and future worlds. What would we really know the meaning of? The meal in the firkin; the milk in the pan; the ballad in the street; the news of the boat; the glance of the eye; the form and the gait of the body;—show me the ultimate reason of these matters;—show me the sublime presence of the highest spiritual cause lurking, as always it does lurk, in these suburbs and extremities of nature; let me see every trifle bristling with the polarity that ranges it instantly on an eternal law; and the shop, the plough, and the ledger, referred to the like cause by which light undulates and poets sing;—and the world lies no longer a dull miscellany and lumber room, but has form and order; there is no trifle; there is no puzzle; but one design unites and animates the farthest pinnacle and the lowest trench.

This idea has inspired the genius of Goldsmith, Burns, Cowper, and, in a newer time, of Goethe, Wordsworth, and Carlyle. This idea they have differently followed and with various success. In contrast with their writing, the style of Pope, of Johnson, of Gibbon, looks cold and pedantic. This writing is blood-warm. Man is surprised to find that things near are not less beautiful and wondrous than things remote. The near explains the far. The drop is a small ocean. A man is related to all nature. This perception of the worth of the vulgar, is fruitful in discoveries. Goethe, in this very thing the most modern of the moderns, has shown us, as none ever did, the genius of the ancients.

There is one man of genius who has done much for this philosophy of life, whose literary value has never yet been rightly estimated;—I mean Emanuel

Swedenborg. The most imaginative of men, yet writing with the precision of a mathematician, he endeavored to engraft a purely philosophical Ethics on the popular Christianity of his time. Such an attempt, of course, must have difficulty which no genius could surmount. But he saw and showed the connexion between nature and the affections of the soul. He pierced the emblematic or spiritual character of the visible, audible, tangible world. Especially did his shade-loving muse hover over and interpret the lower parts of nature; he showed the mysterious bond that allies moral evil to the foul material forms, and has given in epical parables a theory of insanity, of beasts, of unclean and fearful things.

Another sign of our times, also marked by an analogous political move-ment is, the new importance given to the single person. Every thing that tends to insulate the individual,—to surround him with barriers of natural respect, so that each man shall feel the world is his, and man shall treat with man as a sovereign state with a sovereign state;—tends to true union as well as greatness. "I learned," said the melancholy Pestalozzi,[22] "that no man in God's wide earth is either willing or able to help any other man." Help must come from the bosom alone. The scholar is that man who must take up into himself all the ability of the time, all the contributions of the past, all the hopes of the future. He must be an university of knowledges. If there be one lesson more than another which should pierce his ear, it is, The world is nothing, the man is all; in yourself is the law of all nature, and you know not yet how a globule of sap ascends; in yourself slumbers the whole of Reason; it is for you to know all, it is for you to dare all. Mr. President and Gentle-men, this confidence in the unsearched might of man, belongs by all motives, by all prophecy, by all preparation, to the American Scholar. We have lis-tened too long to the courtly muses of Europe. The spirit of the American freeman is already suspected to be timid, imitative, tame. Public and private avarice make the air we breathe thick and fat. The scholar is decent, indo-lent, complaisant. See already the tragic consequence. The mind of his coun-try, taught to aim at low objects, eats upon itself. There is no work for any but the decorous and the complaisant. Young men of the fairest promise, who begin life upon our shores, inflated by the mountain winds, shined upon by all the stars of God, find the earth below not in unison with these,—but are hindered from action by the disgust which the principles on which busi-ness is managed inspire, and turn drudges, or die of disgust,—some of them suicides. What is the remedy? They did not yet see, and thousands of young men as hopeful now crowding to the barriers for the career, do not yet see, that if the single man plant himself indomitably on his instincts, and there

---

[22] Johann Henrich Pestalozzi (1746–1827) was a Swiss educational reformer, admired by the transcendentalists. He was melan-cholic because his theories did not seem to be successful during his lifetime. Pestalozzi's influence can be seen in Emerson's essay, "Education," in *Lectures and Biographical Sketches* (*Works*, X).

abide, the huge world will come round to him. Patience—patience;—with the shades of all the good and great for company; and for solace, the perspective of your own infinite life; and for work, the study and the communication of principles, the making those instincts prevalent, the conversion of the world. Is it not the chief disgrace in the world, not to be an unit;—not to be reckoned one character;—not to yield that peculiar fruit which each man was created to bear, but to be reckoned in the gross, in the hundred, or the thousand, of the party, the section, to which we belong; and our opinion predicted geographically, as the north, or the south. Not so, brothers and friends,—please God, ours shall not be so. We will walk on our own feet; we will work with our own hands; we will speak our own minds. The study of letters shall be no longer a name for pity, for doubt, and for sensual indulgence. The dread of man and the love of man shall be a wall of defence and a wreath of joy around all. A nation of men will for the first time exist, because each believes himself inspired by the Divine Soul which also inspires all men.

The Poet[1]

A moody child and wildly wise
Pursued the game with joyful eyes,
Which chose, like meteors, their way,
And rived the dark with private ray:
They overleapt the horizon's edge,
Searched with Apollo's privilege;
Through man, and woman, and sea, and star
Saw the dance of nature forward far;
Through worlds, and races, and terms, and times
Saw musical order, and pairing rhymes.[2]

[1] Emerson delivered a series of lectures in the winter of 1841 to 1842 and prominent among them was a discourse on the Poet. The essay, which was probably written in 1842, draws on his fundamental ideas concerning creativity and is his most important statement about the role of the poet. In the famous phrase, "For it is not metres, but a metre-making argument that makes a poem," Emerson expresses his view of the organic nature of the poetic act; for him, the idea is inextricably fused with its execution, and the relation of the poem to physical and human nature was all important. The organicism stressed in the essay can be seen in the written work of Horatio Greenough; in the later architecture of Louis Sullivan and Frank Lloyd Wright; and, of course, in the poetry of Whitman, Dickinson, Frost, and many others.

[2] These lines also appear, in another version, in Emerson's posthumous poem, "The Poet" (*Works*, IX, 311).

Olympian bards who sung
Divine ideas below,
Which always find us young,
And always keep us so.[3]

Those who are esteemed umpires of taste are often persons who have acquired some knowledge of admired pictures or sculptures, and have an inclination for whatever is elegant; but if you inquire whether they are beautiful souls; and whether their own acts are like fair pictures, you learn that they are selfish and sensual. Their cultivation is local, as if you should rub a log of dry wood in one spot to produce fire, all the rest remaining cold. Their knowledge of the fine arts is some study of rules and particulars, or some limited judgment of color or form, which is exercised for amusement or for show. It is a proof of the shallowness of the doctrine of beauty as it lies in the minds of our amateurs, that men seem to have lost the perception of the instant dependence of form upon soul. There is no doctrine of forms in our philosophy. We were put into our bodies, as fire is put into a pan to be carried about; but there is no accurate adjustment between the spirit and the organ, much less is the latter the germination of the former. So in regard to other forms, the intellectual men do not believe in any essential dependence of the material world on thought and volition. Theologians think it a pretty air-castle to talk of the spiritual meaning of a ship or a cloud, of a city or a contract, but they prefer to come again to the solid ground of historical evidence; and even the poets are contented with a civil and conformed manner of living, and to write poems from the fancy, at a safe distance from their own experience. But the highest minds of the world have never ceased to explore the double meaning, or shall I say the quadruple or the centuple of much more manifold meaning, of every sensuous fact; Orpheus, Empedocles, Heraclitus, Plato, Plutarch, Dante, Swedenborg,[4] and the masters of sculpture, picture and poetry. For we are not pans and barrows, nor even porters of the fire and torch-bearers, but children of the fire, made of it, and only the same divinity transmuted and at two or three removes, when we know least about it. And this hidden truth, that the fountains whence all this

---

[3] These lines occur also in "Ode to Beauty," ll. 60-64.

[4] Orpheus was the musician of Greek mythology whose music cast a spell on plants, animals, trees, and rocks; Empedocles was a pre-Socratic Greek philosopher who saw in all matter the alternations between harmony and discord; Heraclitus, a Greek philosopher, claimed that there was unity in all things, always subject to flux; Plato was an early fourth-century B.C. Greek philosopher who viewed material being as the shadow of spiritual reality; Plutarch expressed this same view in his biographies, *Parallel Lives of Noble Greeks and Romans;* Dante (1265-1321) wrote the *Divine Comedy,* which joined the experience of heaven, earth, and hell; Swedenborg was an eighteenth-century Swedish mystic, the author of *Heaven and Its Wonders and Hell* (1758) whose thought as a mystic was recorded in Emerson's *Representative Men.*

river of Time and its creatures floweth are intrinsically ideal and beautiful, draws us to the consideration of the nature and functions of the Poet, or the man of Beauty; to the means and materials he uses, and to the general aspect of the art in the present time.

The breadth of the problem is great, for the poet is representative. He stands among partial men for the complete man, and apprises us not of his wealth, but of the common wealth. The young man reveres men of genius, because, to speak truly, they are more himself than he is. They receive of the soul as he also receives, but they more. Nature enhances her beauty, to the eye of loving men, from their belief that the poet is beholding her shows at the same time. He is isolated among his contemporaries by truth and by his art, but with this consolation in his pursuits, that they will draw all men sooner or later. For all men live by truth and stand in need of expression. In love, in art, in avarice, in politics, in labor, in games, we study to utter our painful secret. The man is only half himself, the other half is his expression.

Notwithstanding this necessity to be published, adequate expression is rare. I know not how it is that we need an interpreter, but the great majority of men seem to be minors, who have not yet come into possession of their own, or mutes, who cannot report the conversation they have had with nature. There is no man who does not anticipate a supersensual utility in the sun and stars, earth and water. These stand and wait to render him a peculiar service. But there is some obstruction or some excess of phlegm in our constitution, which does not suffer them to yield the due effect. Too feeble fall the impressions of nature on us to make us artists. Every touch should thrill. Every man should be so much an artist that he could report in conversation what had befallen him. Yet, in our experience, the rays or appulses[5] have sufficient force to arrive at the senses, but not enough to reach the quick and compel the reproduction of themselves in speech. The poet is the person in whom these powers are in balance, the man without impediment, who sees and handles that which others dream of, traverses the whole scale of experience, and is representative of man, in virtue of being the largest power to receive and to impart.

For the universe has three children, born at one time, which reappear under different names in every system of thought, whether they be called cause, operation and effect; or, more poetically, Jove, Pluto, Neptune; or, theologically, the Father, the Spirit and the Son; but which we will call here the Knower, the Doer and the Sayer. These stand respectively for the love of truth, for the love of good, and for the love of beauty. These three are equal. Each is that which he is, essentially, so that he cannot be surmounted or analyzed, and each of these three has the power of the others latent in him and his own, patent.

[5] Powerful driving motions toward something.

The poet is the sayer, the namer, and represents beauty. He is a sovereign, and stands on the center. For the world is not painted or adorned, but is from the beginning beautiful; and God has not made some beautiful things, but Beauty is the creator of the universe. Therefore the poet is not any permissive potentate, but is emperor in his own right. Criticism is infested with a cant of materialism, which assumes that manual skill and activity is the first merit of all men, and disparages such as say and do not, overlooking the fact that some men, namely poets, are natural sayers, sent into the world to the end of expression, and confounds them with those whose province is action but who quit it to imitate the sayers. But Homer's words are as costly and admirable to Homer as Agamemnon's victories are to Agamemnon. The poet does not wait for the hero or the sage, but, as they act and think primarily, so he writes primarily what will and must be spoken, reckoning the others, though primaries also, yet, in respect to him, secondaries and servants; as sitters or models in the studio of a painter, or as assistants who bring building materials to an architect.

For poetry was all written before time was, and whenever we are so finely organized that we can penetrate into that region where the air is music, we hear those primal warblings and attempt to write them down, but we lose ever and anon a word or a verse and substitute something of our own, and thus miswrite the poem. The men of more delicate ear write down these cadences more faithfully, and these transcripts, though imperfect, become the songs of the nations. For nature is as truly beautiful as it is good, or as it is reasonable, and must as much appear as it must be done, or be known. Words and deeds are quite indifferent modes of the divine energy. Words are also actions, and actions are a kind of words.

The sign and credentials of the poet are that he announces that which no man foretold. He is the true and only doctor,[6] he knows and tells; he is the only teller of news, for he was present and privy to the appearance which he describes. He is a beholder of ideas and an utterer of the necessary and causal. For we do not speak now of men of poetical talents, or of industry and skill in meter, but of the true poet. I took part in a conversation the other day concerning a recent writer of lyrics,[7] a man of subtle mind, whose head appeared to be a music-box of delicate tunes and rhythms, and whose skill and command of language we could not sufficiently praise. But when the question arose whether he was not only a lyrist but a poet, we were obliged to confess that he is plainly a contemporary, not an eternal man. He does not stand out of our low limitations, like a Chimborazo[8] under the line, running up from a torrid base through all the climates of the globe, with belts of the herbage of every latitude on its high and mottled sides, but this

[6] Teacher.

[7] Probably Tennyson. Emerson later had a higher opinion of him.

[8] A mountain in Ecuador.

genius is the landscape-garden of a modern house, adorned with fountains and statues, with well-bred men and women standing and sitting in the walks and terraces. We hear, through all the varied music, the ground-tone of conventional life. Our poets are men of talents who sing, and not the children of music. The argument is secondary, the finish of the verses is primary.

For it is not meters, but a meter-making argument that makes a poem,— a thought so passionate and alive that like the spirit of a plant or an animal it has an architecture of its own, and adorns nature with a new thing. The thought and the form are equal in the order of time, but in the order of genesis the thought is prior to the form. The poet has a new thought; he has a whole new experience to unfold; he will tell us how it was with him, and all men will be the richer in his fortune. For the experience of each new age requires a new confession, and the world seems always waiting for its poet. I remember when I was young how much I was moved one morning by tidings that genius had appeared in a youth who sat near me at table. He had left his work and gone rambling none knew whither, and had written hundreds of lines, but could not tell whether that which was in him was therein told; he could tell nothing but that all was changed,—man, beast, heaven, earth and sea. How gladly we listened! how credulous! Society seemed to be compromised. We sat in the aurora of a sunrise which was to put out all the stars. Boston seemed to be at twice the distance it had the night before, or was much farther than that. Rome,—what was Rome? Plutarch and Shakespeare were in the yellow leaf,[9] and Homer no more should be heard of. It is much to know that poetry has been written this very day, under this very roof, by your side. What! that wonderful spirit has not expired! These stony moments are still sparkling and animated! I had fancied that the oracles were all silent, and nature had spent her fires; and behold! all night, from every pore, these fine auroras have been streaming. Every one has some interest in the advent of the poet, and no one knows how much it may concern him. We know that the secret of the world is profound, but who or what shall be our interpreter, we know not. A mountain ramble, a new style of face, a new person, may put the key into our hands. Of course the value of genius to us is in the veracity of its report. Talent may frolic and juggle; genius realizes and adds. Mankind in good earnest have availed so far in understanding themselves and their work, that the foremost watchman on the peak announces his news. It is the truest word ever spoken, and the phrase will be the fittest, most musical, and the unerring voice of the world for that time.

All that we call sacred history attests that the birth of a poet is the principal event in chronology. Man, never so often deceived, still watches for the arrival of a brother who can hold him steady to a truth until he has made it his own. With what joy I begin to read a poem which I confide in as

---

[9] See *Macbeth*, V, iii, 23. Byron wrote these words on his thirty-sixth birthday. [On This Day I Complete My Thirty-Sixth Year (1824)].

an inspiration! And now my chains are to be broken; I shall mount above these clouds and opaque airs in which I live,—opaque, though they seem transparent,—and from the heaven of truth I shall see and comprehend my relations. That will reconcile me to life and renovate nature, to see trifles animated by a tendency, and to know what I am doing. Life will no more be a noise; now I shall see men and women, and know the signs by which they may be discerned from fools and satans. This day shall be better than my birthday: then I became an animal; now I am invited into the science of the real. Such is the hope, but the fruition is postponed. Oftener it falls that this winged man, who will carry me into the heaven, whirls me into mists, then leaps and frisks about with me as it were from cloud to cloud, still affirming that he is bound heavenward; and I, being myself a novice, am slow in perceiving that he does not know the way into the heavens, and is merely bent that I should admire his skill to rise like a fowl or a flying fish, a little way from the ground or the water; but the all-piercing, all-feeding and ocular air of heaven that man shall never inhabit. I tumble down again soon into my old nooks, and lead the life of exaggerations as before, and have lost my faith in the possibility of any guide who can lead me thither where I would be.

But, leaving these victims of vanity, let us, with new hope, observe how nature, by worthier impulses, has insured the poet's fidelity to his office of announcement and affirming, namely by the beauty of things, which becomes a new and higher beauty when expressed. Nature offers all her creatures to him as a picture-language. Being used as a type, a second wonderful value appears in the object, far better than its old value; as the carpenter's stretched cord, if you hold your ear close enough, is musical in the breeze. "Things more excellent than every image," says Jamblichus,[10] "are expressed through images." Things admit of being used as symbols because nature is a symbol, in the whole, and in every part. Every line we can draw in the sand has expression; and there is no body without its spirit or genius. All form is an effect of character; all condition, of the quality of the life; all harmony, of health; and for this reason a perception of beauty should be sympathetic, or proper only to the good. The beautiful rests on the foundations of the necessary. The soul makes the body, as the wise Spenser teaches:—

> "So every spirit, as it is more pure,
> And hath in it the more of heavenly light,
> So it the fairer body doth procure
> To habit in, and it more fairly dight,
> With cheerful grace and amiable sight.
> For, of the soul, the body form doth take,
> For soul is form, and doth the body make."[11]

[10] A fourth-century Syrian Neoplatonic philosopher.

[11] Edmund Spenser, "An Hymn in Honour of Beautie" (1596), 127-33.

Here we find ourselves suddenly not in a critical speculation but in a holy place, and should go very warily and reverently. We stand before the secret of the world, there where Being passes into Appearance and Unity into Variety.

The Universe is the externization of the soul. Wherever the life is, that bursts into appearance around it. Our science is sensual, and therefore superficial. The earth and the heavenly bodies, physics and chemistry, we sensually treat, as if they were self-existent; but these are the retinue of that Being we have. "The mighty heaven," said Proclus, [12] "exhibits, in its transfigurations, clear images of the splendor of intellectual perceptions; being moved in conjunction with the unapparent periods of intellectual natures." Therefore science always goes abreast with the just elevation of the man, keeping step with religion and metaphysics; or the state of science is an index of our self-knowledge. Since every thing in nature answers to a moral power, if any phenomenon remains brute and dark it is because the corresponding faculty in the observer is not yet active.

No wonder then, if these waters be so deep, that we hover over them with a religious regard. The beauty of the fable proves the importance of the sense; to the poet, and to all others; or, if you please, every man is so far a poet as to be susceptible of these enchantments of nature; for all men have the thoughts whereof the universe is the celebration. I find that the fascination resides in the symbol. Who loves nature? Who does not? Is it only poets, and men of leisure and cultivation, who live with her? No; but also hunters, farmers, grooms and butchers, though they express their affection in their choice of life and not in their choice of words. The writer wonders what the coachman or the hunter values in riding, in horses and dogs. It is not superficial qualities. When you talk with him he holds these at as slight a rate as you. His worship is sympathetic; he has no definitions, but he is commanded in nature by the living power which he feels to be there present. No imitation or playing of these things would content him; he loves the earnest of the north wind, of rain, of stone and wood and iron. A beauty not explicable is dearer than a beauty which we can see to the end of. It is nature the symbol, nature certifying the supernatural, body overflowed by life which he worships with coarse but sincere rites.

The inwardness and mystery of this attachment drive men of every class to the use of emblems. The schools of poets and philosophers are not more intoxicated with their symbols than the populace with theirs. In our political parties, compute the power of badges and emblems. See the great ball which they roll from Baltimore to Bunker Hill! [13] In the political processions, Low-

---

[12] A Neoplatonic philosopher (410?-485) of Alexandria and Athens.

[13] The rolling balls were used in the Whig campaign for Harrison in 1840 to indicate his developing majority.

ell goes in a loom, and Lynn in a shoe, and Salem in a ship.[14] Witness the cider-barrel, the log-cabin, the hickory-stick, the palmetto, and all the cognizances of party. See the power of national emblems. Some stars, lilies, leopards, a crescent, a lion, an eagle, or other figure which came into credit God knows how, on an old rag of bunting, blowing in the wind on a fort at the ends of the earth, shall make the blood tingle under the rudest or the most conventional exterior. The people fancy they hate poetry, and they are all poets and mystics!

Beyond the universality of the symbolic language we are apprised of the divineness of this superior use of things, whereby the world is a temple whose walls are covered with emblems, pictures and commandments of the Deity,—in this, that there is no fact in nature which does not carry the whole sense of nature; and the distinctions which we make in events and in affairs, of low and high, honest and base, disappear when nature is used as a symbol. Thought makes everything fit for use. The vocabulary of an omniscient man would embrace words and images excluded from polite conversation. What would be base, or even obscene, to the obscene, becomes illustrious, spoken in a new connection of thought. The piety of the Hebrew prophets purges their grossness. The circumcision is an example of the power of poetry to raise the low and offensive. Small and mean things serve as well as great symbols. The meaner the type by which a law is expressed, the more pungent it is, and the more lasting in the memories of men; just as we choose the smallest box or case in which any needful utensil can be carried. Bare lists of words are found suggestive to an imaginative and excited mind, as it is related of Lord Chatham[15] that he was accustomed to read in Bailey's Dictionary when he was preparing to speak in Parliament. The poorest experience is rich enough for all the purposes of expressing thought. Why covet a knowledge of new facts? Day and night, house and garden, a few books, a few actions, serve us as well as would all trades and all spectacles. We are far from having exhausted the significance of the few symbols we use. We can come to use them yet with a terrible simplicity. It does not need that a poem should be long. Every word was once a poem. Every new relation is a new word. Also we use defects and deformities to a sacred purpose, so expressing our sense that the evils of the world are such only to the evil eye. In the old mythology, mythologists observe, defects are ascribed to divine natures, as lameness to Vulcan, blindness to Cupid, and the like,—to signify exuberances.

For as it is dislocation and detachment from the life of God that makes things ugly, the poet, who re-attaches things to nature and the Whole,—re-

---

[14] Three Massachusetts towns. Lowell was famous for its textile mills, Lynn for its shoe factories, and Salem for its shipping and commerce.

[15] William Pitt (1708-1778), Earl of Chatham, the famous English statesman and orator under George II.

attaching even artificial things and violation of nature, to nature, by a deeper insight,—disposes very easily of the most disagreeable facts. Readers of poetry see the factory-village and the railway, and fancy that the poetry of the landscape is broken up by these; for these works of art are not yet consecrated in their reading; but the poet sees them fall within the great Order not less than the beehive or the spider's geometrical web. Nature adopts them very fast into her vital circles, and the gliding train of cars she loves like her own. Besides, in a centered mind, it signifies nothing how many mechanical inventions you exhibit. Though you add millions, and never so surprising, the fact of mechanics has not gained a grain's weight. The spiritual fact remains unalterable, by many or by few particulars; as no mountain is of any appreciable height to break the curve of the sphere. A shrewd country-boy goes to the city for the first time, and the complacent citizen is not satisfied with his little wonder. It is not that he does not see all the fine houses and know that he never saw such before, but he disposes of them as easily as the poet finds place for the railway. The chief value of the new fact is to enhance the great and constant fact of Life, which can dwarf any and every circumstance, and to which the belt of wampum and the commerce of America are alike.

The world being thus put under the mind for verb and noun, the poet is he who can articulate it. For though life is great, and fascinates and absorbs; and though all men are intelligent of the symbols through which it is named; yet they cannot originally use them. We are symbols and inhabit symbols; workmen, work, and tools, words and things, birth and death, all are emblems but we sympathize with the symbols, and being infatuated with the economical uses of things, we do not know that they are thoughts. The poet, by an ulterior intellectual perception, gives them a power which makes their old use forgotten, and puts eyes and a tongue into every dumb and inanimate object. He perceives the independence of the thought on the symbol, the stability of the thought, the accidency[16] and fugacity[17] of the symbol. As the eyes of Lyncæus[18] were said to see through the earth, so the poet turns the world to glass, and shows us all things in their right series and procession. For through that better perception he stands one step nearer to things, and sees the flowing or metamorphosis; perceives that thought is multiform; that within the form of every creature is a force compelling it to ascend into a higher form; and following with his eyes the life, uses the forms which express that life, and so his speech flows with the flowing of nature. All the facts of the animal economy, sex, nutriment, gestation, birth, growth, are symbols of the passage of the world into the soul of man, to suffer there a change and reappear a new and higher fact. He uses forms according to the

---

[16] Accidental or chance character.
[17] Fleetingness, instability.
[18] In Greek mythology, the lookout on the ship *Argo;* Lyncæus was chosen for this position because he had the sharpest vision of all Jason's Argonauts.

life, and not according to the form. This is true science. The poet alone knows astronomy, chemistry, vegetation and animation, for he does not stop at these facts, but employs them as signs. He knows why the plain or meadow or space was strown with these flowers we call suns and moons and stars; why the great deep is adorned with animals, with men, and gods; for in every word he speaks he rides on them as the horses of thought.

By virtue of this science the poet is the Namer or Language-maker, naming things sometimes after their appearance, sometimes after their essence, and giving to every one its own name and not another's, thereby rejoicing the intellect, which delights in detachment or boundary. The poets made all the words, and therefore language is the archives of history, and, if we must say it, a sort of tomb of the muses. For though the origin of most of our words is forgotten, each word was at first a stroke of genius, and obtained currency because for the moment it symbolized the world to the first speaker and to the hearer. The etymologist finds the deadest word to have been once a brilliant picture. Language is fossil poetry. As the limestone of the continent consists of infinite masses of the shells of animalcules, so language is made up of images or tropes, which now, in their secondary use, have long ceased to remind us of their poetic origin. But the poet names the thing because he sees it, or comes one step nearer to it than any other. This expression or naming is not art, but a second nature, grown out of the first, as a leaf out of a tree. What we call nature is a certain self-regulated motion or change; and nature does all things by her own hands, and does not leave another to baptize her but baptizes herself; and this through the metamorphosis again. I remember that a certain poet[19] described it to me thus:—

Genius is the activity which repairs the decays of things, whether wholly or partly of a material and finite kind. Nature, through all her kingdoms, insures herself. Nobody cares for planting the poor fungus; so she shakes down from the gills of one agaric[20] countless spores, any one of which, being preserved, transmits new billions of spores tomorrow or next day. The new agaric of this hour has a chance which the old one had not. This atom of seed is thrown into a new place, not subject to the accidents which destroyed its parent two rods off. She makes a man; and having brought him to ripe age, she will no longer run the risk of losing this wonder at a blow, but she detaches from him a new self, that the kind may be safe from accidents to which the individual is exposed. So when the soul of the poet has come to ripeness of thought, she detaches and sends away from it its poems or songs,—a fearless, sleepless, deathless progeny, which is not exposed to the accidents of the weary kingdom of time; a fearless, vivacious offspring, clad with wings (such was the virtue of the soul out of which they came) which

---

[19] Emerson himself rearranging Plato's idea in his own style.   [20] A fungus of the mushroom type.

carry them fast and far, and infix them irrecoverably into the hearts of men. These wings are the beauty of a poet's soul. The songs, thus flying immortal from their mortal parent, are pursued by clamorous flights of censures, which swarm in far greater numbers and threaten to devour them; but these last are not winged. At the end of a very short leap they fall plump down and rot, having received from the souls out of which they came no beautiful wings. But the melodies of the poet ascend and leap and pierce into the deeps of infinite time.

So far the bard taught me, using his freer speech. But nature has a higher end, in the production of new individuals, than security, namely *ascension*, or the passage of the soul into higher forms. I knew in my younger days the sculptor who made the statue of the youth which stands in the public garden. He was, as I remember, unable to tell directly what made him happy or unhappy, but by wonderful indirections he could tell. He rose one day, according to his habit, before the dawn, and saw the morning break, grand as the eternity out of which it came, and for many days after, he strove to express this tranquillity, and lo! his chisel had fashioned out of marble the form of a beautiful youth, Phosphorus,[21] whose aspect is such that it is said all persons who look on it become silent. The poet also resigns himself to his mood, and that thought which agitated him is expressed, but *alter idem*,[22] in a manner totally new. The expression is organic, or the new type which things themselves take when liberated. As, in the sun, objects paint their images on the retina of the eye, so they, sharing the aspiration of the whole universe, tend to paint a far more delicate copy of their essence in his mind. Like the metamorphosis of things into higher organic forms is their change into melodies. Over everything stands its daemon or soul, and, as the form of the thing is reflected by the eye, so the soul of the thing is reflected by a melody. The sea, the mountain-ridge, Niagara, and every flower-bed, pre-exist, or super-exist, in precantations, which sail like odors in the air, and when any man goes by with an ear sufficiently fine, he overhears them and endeavors to write down the notes without diluting or depraving them. And herein is the legitimation of criticism, in the mind's faith that the poems are a corrupt version of some text in nature with which they ought to be made to tally. A rhyme in one of our sonnets should not be less pleasing than the iterated nodes of a seashell, or the resembling difference of a group of flowers. The pairing of the birds is an idyl, not tedious as our idyls are; a tempest is a rough ode, without falsehood or rant; a summer, with its harvest sown, reaped and stored, is an epic song, subordinating how many admirably executed parts. Why should not the symmetry and truth that modulate these glide into our spirits, and we participate the invention of nature?

[21] In Latin, the morning star, from the Greek for "light-bearer."

[22] Another of the same kind.

This insight, which expresses itself by what is called Imagination, is a very high sort of seeing, which does not come by study, but by the intellect being where and what it sees; by sharing the path or circuit of things through forms, and so making them translucid to others. The path of things is silent. Will they suffer a speaker to go with them? A spy they will not suffer; a lover, a poet, is the transcendency of their own nature,—him they will suffer. The condition of true naming, on the poet's part, is his resigning himself to the divine *aura*[23] which breathes through forms, and accompanying that.

It is a secret which every intellectual man quickly learns, that beyond the energy of his possessed and conscious intellect he is capable of a new energy (as of an intellect doubled on itself), by abandonment to the nature of things; that beside his privacy of power as an individual man, there is a great public power on which he can draw, by unlocking, at all risks, his human doors, and suffering the ethereal tides to roll and circulate through him; then he is caught up into the life of the Universe, his speech is thunder, his thought is law, and his words are universally intelligible as the plants and animals. The poet knows that he speaks adequately then only when he speaks somewhat wildly, or "with the flower of the mind"; not with the intellect used as an organ, but with the intellect released from all service and suffered to take its direction from its celestial life; or as the ancients were wont to express themselves, not with intellect alone but with the intellect inebriated by nectar. As the traveler who has lost his way throws his reins on his horse's neck and trusts to the instinct of the animal to find his road, so must we do with the divine animal who carries us through this world. For if in any manner we can stimulate this instinct, new passages are opened for us into nature; the mind flows into and through things hardest and highest, and the metamorphosis is possible.

This is the reason why bards love wine, mead, narcotics, coffee, tea, opium, the fumes of sandalwood and tobacco, or whatever other procurers of animal exhilaration. All men avail themselves of such means as they can, to add this extraordinary power to their normal powers; and to this end they prize conversation, music, pictures, sculpture, dancing, theaters, traveling, war, mobs, fires, gaming, politics, or love, or science, or animal intoxication,—which are several coarser or finer *quasi*-mechanical substitutes for the true nectar, which is the ravishment of the intellect by coming nearer to the fact. These are auxiliaries to the centrifugal tendency of a man, to his passage out into free space, and they help him to escape the custody of that body in which he is pent up, and of that jail-yard of individual relations in which he is enclosed. Hence a great number of such as were professionally expressers of Beauty, as painters, poets, musicians and actors, have been more than others wont to lead a life of pleasure and indulgence; all but the few who

[23] An "air" or appearance. Prophetic incantations.

received the true nectar; and, as it was a spurious mode of attaining free-dom, as it was an emancipation not into the heavens but into the freedom of baser places, they were punished for that advantage they won, by a dissipa-tion and deterioration. But never can any advantage be taken of nature by a trick. The spirit of the world, the great calm presence of the Creator, comes not forth to the sorceries of opium or of wine. The sublime vision comes to the pure and simple soul in a clean and chaste body. That is not an inspira-tion, which we owe to narcotics, but some counterfeit excitement and fury. Milton says that the lyric poet may drink wine and live generously, but the epic poet, he who shall sing of the gods and their descent unto men, must drink water out of a wooden bowl. For poetry is not "Devil's wine," but God's wine.[24] It is with this as it is with toys. We fill the hands and nurseries of our children with all manner of dolls, drums and horses; withdrawing their eyes from the plain face and sufficing objects of nature, the sun and moon, the animals, the water and stones, which should be their toys. So the poet's habit of living should be set on a key so low that the common influ-ences should delight him. His cheerfulness should be the gift of the sunlight; the air should suffice for his inspiration, and he should be tipsy with water. That spirit which suffices quiet hearts, which seems to come forth to such from every dry knoll of sere grass, from every pine stump and half-imbedded stone on which the dull March sun shines, comes forth to the poor and hungry, and such as are of simple taste. If thou fill thy brain with Boston and New York, with fashion and covetousness, and wilt stimulate thy jaded senses with wine and French coffee, thou shalt find no radiance of wisdom in the lonely waste of the pine woods.

If the imagination intoxicates the poet, it is not inactive in other men. The metamorphosis excites in the beholder an emotion of joy. The use of symbols has a certain power of emancipation and exhilaration for all men. We seem to be touched by a wand which makes us dance and run about happily, like children. We are like persons who come out of a cave or cellar into the open air. This is the effect on us of tropes, fables, oracles and all poetic forms. Poets are thus liberating gods. Men have really got a new sense, and found within their world another world, or nest of worlds; for, the metamorphosis once seen, we divine that it does not stop. I will not now consider how much this makes the charm of algebra and the mathematics, which also have their tropes, but it is felt in every definition; as when Aristotle defines *space* to be an immovable vessel in which things are contained,[25]—or when Plato defines a *line* to be a flowing point; or *figure* to be bound of solid; and many the like. What a joyful sense of freedom we have when Vitruvius announces the old

---

[24] See *Elegia Sexta* (*Elegy* VI), one of Mil-ton's Latin poems. Milton is speaking of the lyric poet as the writer of elegies. Emerson makes a free translation and paraphrase of Milton's words.

[25] See Aristotle, *Physics*, Book IV, 212a, 14.

opinion of artists that no architect can build any house well who does not know something of anatomy.[26] When Socrates, in Charmides, tells us that the soul is cured of its maladies by certain incantations, and that these incantations are beautiful reasons, from which temperance is generated in souls,[27] when Plato calls the world an animal, and Timaeus affirms that the plants also are animals,[28] or affirms a man to be a heavenly tree, growing with his root,[29] which is his head, upward; and, as George Chapman, following him, writes,

> "So in our tree of man, whose nervie root
> Springs in his top;"—[30]

when Orpheus speaks of hoariness as "that white flower which marks extreme old age"; when Proclus,[31] calls the universe the statue of the intellect; when Chaucer, in his praise of "Gentilesse," compares good blood in mean condition to fire, which, though carried to the darkest house betwixt this and the mount of Caucasus, will yet hold its natural office and burn as bright as if twenty thousand men did it behold;[32] when John saw, in the Apocalypse, the ruin of the world through evil, and the stars fall from heaven as the fig tree casteth her untimely fruit,[33] when Aesop reports the whole catalogue of common daily relations through the masquerade of birds and beasts;—we take the cheerful hint of the immortality of our essence and its versatile habit and escapes, as when the gypsies say of themselves "it is in vain to hang them, they cannot die."

The poets are thus liberating gods. The ancient British bards had for the title of their order, "Those who are free throughout the world."[34] They are free, and they make free. An imaginative book renders us much more service at first, by stimulating us through its tropes, than afterward when we arrive at the precise sense of the author. I think nothing is of any value in books excepting the transcendental and extraordinary. If a man is inflamed and

---

[26] Vitruvius Pollio, a Roman engineer and architect of the first century B.C., the age of Augustus, author of *On Architecture*.

[27] See Plato, *Charmides*, 157, one of the dialogues of Plato, in which Socrates is the chief speaker.

[28] See Plato, *Timaeus*, 30.

[29] *Ibid.*, 77. Timaeus is a principal speaker in the dialogue, which is named after him, in which the creation and nature of the world are discussed.

[30] From the Dedication of Chapman's 1609 translation of the *Iliad* to Prince Henry, 132-33.

[31] A Neoplatonic philosopher (410?-485) of Alexandria and Athens.

[32] See "The Wife of Bath's Tale," 11. 1139-1145. This was a favorite passage of Emerson's, according to his editor (*Works*, III, 300).

[33] See Revelations, vi: 13.

[34] In William Owen's *The Heroic Elegies and Other Pieces of Llywarc Hen*, 1792, the British poets, when attending a gathering outside their own province or outside Britain itself, retained the titles, "The Bards of the Isle, A Britain through the world," and "Those who are at liberty through the world."

carried away by his thought, to that degree that he forgets the authors and the public and heeds only this one dream which holds him like an insanity, let me read his paper, and you may have all the arguments and histories and criticism. All the value which attaches to Pythagoras, Paracelsus, Cornelius Agrippa, Cardan, Kepler, Swedenborg, Schelling, Oken,[35] or any other who introduces questionable facts into his cosmogony, as angels, devils, magic, astrology, palmistry, mesmerism, and so on, is the certificate we have of departure from routine, and that here is a new witness. That also is the best success in conversation, the magic of liberty, which puts the world like a ball in our hands. How cheap even the liberty then seems; how mean to study, when an emotion communicates to the intellect the power to sap and up-heave nature; how great the perspective! nations, times, systems, enter and disappear like threads in tapestry of large figure and many colors; dream delivers us to dream, and while the drunkenness lasts we will sell our bed, our philosophy, our religion, in our opulence.

There is good reason why we should prize this liberation. The fate of the poor shepherd, who, blinded and lost in the snowstorm, perishes in a drift within a few feet of his cottage door, is an emblem of the state of man. On the brink of the waters of life and truth, we are miserably dying. The inac-cessibleness of every thought but that we are in, is wonderful. What if you come near to it; you are as remote when you are nearest as when you are farthest. Every thought is also a prison; every heaven is also a prison. There-fore we love the poet, the inventor, who in any form, whether in an ode or in an action or in looks and behavior, has yielded us a new thought. He unlocks our chains and admits us to a new scene.

This emancipation is dear to all men, and the power to impart it, as it must come from greater depth and scope of thought, is a measure of intel-lect. Therefore all books of the imagination endure, all which ascend to that truth that the writer sees nature beneath him, and uses it as his exponent. Every verse or sentence possessing this virtue will take care of its own immortality. The religions of the world are the ejaculations of a few imagina-tive men.

But the quality of the imagination is to flow, and not to freeze. The poet did not stop at the color or the form, but read their meaning; neither may he

---

[35] Pythagoras was a pre-Socratic Greek mathematician and mystical philosopher; Paracelsus was the name for Theophrastus Bombastus von Hohenheim (1493-1541)—Paracelsus means "superior to Celsus," a Pla-tonic writer of the second century A.D., who was a German physician and writer on occult subjects; Cornelius Agrippa was Henry Cornelius Agrippa von Nettesheim (1486-1535), a German physician and author on oc-cult subjects, called a magician in his own time; Cardan was Girolamo Cardano (1501-76), an Italian physician and astrologer, au-thor of *De Subtilitate Rerum*, in which he anticipated certain modern principles; Kep-ler was a Renaissance German astronomer and mathematician; Swedenborg, an eigh-teenth-century Swedish mystic; Oken was Lorenz Oken (1779-1851), a German natural-ist who wrote *Die Zeugung* ("Procreation"), in which he states that all organisms are de-rived from cells or vesicles.

rest in this meaning, but he makes the same objects exponents of his new thought. Here is the difference betwixt the poet and the mystic, that the last nails a symbol to one sense, which was true sense for a moment, but soon becomes old and false. For all symbols are fluxional;[36] all language is vehicular[37] and transitive, and is good, as ferries and horses are, for conveyance, not as farms and houses are, for homestead. Mysticism consists in the mistake of an accidental and individual symbol for an universal one. The morning-redness happens to be the favorite meteor to the eyes of Jacob Behmen,[38] and comes to stand to him for truth and faith; and, he believes, should stand for the same realities to every reader. But the first reader prefers as naturally the symbol of a mother and child, or a gardener and his bulb, or a jeweler polishing a gem. Either of these, or of a myriad more, are equally good to the person to whom they are significant. Only they must be held lightly, and be very willingly translated into the equivalent terms which others use. And the mystic must be steadily told,—All that you say is just as true without the tedious use of that symbol as with it. Let us have a little algebra, instead of this trite rhetoric,—universal signs, instead of these village symbols,—and we shall both be gainers. The history of hierarchies seems to show that all religious error consisted in making the symbol too stark and solid, and was at last nothing but an excess of the organ of language.

Swedenborg, of all men in the recent ages, stands eminently for the translator of nature into thought. I do not know the man in history to whom things stood so uniformly for words. Before him the metamorphosis continually plays. Everything on which his eye rests, obeys the impulses of moral nature. The figs become grapes whilst he eats them. When some of his angels affirmed a truth, the laurel twig which they held blossomed in their hands. The noise which at a distance appeared like gnashing and thumping, on coming nearer was found to be the voice of disputants. The men in one of his visions, seen in heavenly light, appeared like dragons, and seemed in darkness; but to each other they appeared as men, and when the light from heaven shone into their cabin, they complained of the darkness, and were compelled to shut the window that they might see.

There was this perception in him which makes the poet or seer an object of awe and terror, namely that the same man or society of men may wear one aspect to themselves and their companions, and a different aspect to higher intelligences. Certain priests, whom he describes as conversing very learnedly together, appeared to the children who were at some distance, like dead horses; and many the like misappearances. And instantly the mind inquires whether these fishes under the bridge, yonder oxen in the pasture, those dogs in the yard, are immutably fishes, oxen and dogs, or only so

---

[36] Flowing.

[37] Capable of serving as a vehicle; from the literal to the intangible.

[38] Jakob Böhme (1575-1624), a German mystic. See "New England Reformers," p. 1688.

appear to me, and perchance to themselves appear upright men; and whether I appear as a man to all eyes. The Brahmins and Pythagoras propounded the same question, and if any poet has witnessed the transformation he doubtless found it in harmony with various experiences. We have all seen changes as considerable in wheat and caterpillars. He is the poet and shall draw us with love and terror, who sees through the flowing vest the firm nature, and can declare it.

I look in vain for the poet whom I describe. We do not with sufficient plainness or sufficient profoundness address ourselves to life, nor dare we chaunt our own times and social circumstance. If we filled the day with bravery, we should not shrink from celebrating it. Time and nature yield us many gifts, but not yet the timely man, the new religion, the reconciler, whom all things await. Dante's praise is that he dared to write his autobiography in colossal cipher, or into universality.[39] We have had no genius in America, with tyrannous eye, which knew the value of our incomparable materials, and saw, in the barbarism and materialism of the times, another carnival of the same gods whose picture he so much admires in Homer; then in the Middle Age; then in Calvinism. Banks and tariffs, the newspaper and caucus, Methodism and Unitarianism, are flat and dull to dull people, but rest on the same foundations of wonder as the town of Troy and the temple of Delphi, and are as swiftly passing away. Our log-rolling, our stumps and their politics, our fisheries, our Negroes and Indians, our boats and our repudiations,[40] the wrath of rogues and the pusillanimity of honest men, the northern trade, the southern planting, the western clearing. Oregon and Texas, are yet unsung. Yet America is a poem in our eyes; its ample geography dazzles the imagination, and it will not wait long for meters. If I have not found that excellent combination of gifts in my countrymen which I seek, neither could I aid myself to fix the idea of the poet by reading now and then in Chalmers's collection of five centuries of English poets.[41] These are wits more than poets, though there have been poets among them. But when we adhere to the ideal of the poet, we have our difficulties even with Milton and Homer. Milton is too literary, and Homer too literal and historical.

But I am not wise enough for a national criticism, and must use the old largeness a little longer, to discharge my errand from the muse to the poet concerning his art.

Art is the path of the creator to his work. The paths or methods are ideal and eternal, though few men ever see them; not the artist himself for years,

---

[39] Emerson is referring to the confessional quality of the *Divine Comedy*.

[40] Some of the states had refused to pay the debts they had incurred in the form of state bonds.

[41] Alexander Chalmers (1759-1834) was a Scottish editor and biographer, compiler of the well-known anthology, *The Works of the English Poets from Chaucer to Cowper*, in 21 volumes.

or for a lifetime, unless he come into the conditions. The painter, the sculptor, the composer, the epic rhapsodist, the orator, all partake one desire, namely to express themselves symmetrically and abundantly, not dwarfishly and fragmentarily. They found or put themselves in certain conditions, as, the painter and sculptor before some impressive human figures; the orator into the assembly of the people; and the others in such scenes as each has found exciting to his intellect; and each presently feels the new desire. He hears a voice, he sees a beckoning. Then he is apprised, with wonder, what herds of daemons hem him in. He can no more rest; he says, with the old painter, "By God it is in me and must go forth of me." He pursues a beauty, half seen, which flies before him. The poet pours out verses in every solitude. Most of the things he says are conventional, no doubt; but by and by he says something which is original and beautiful. That charms him. He would say nothing else but such things. In our way of talking we say "That is yours, this is mine"; but the poet knows well that it is not his; that it is as strange and beautiful to him as to you; he would fain hear the like eloquence at length. Once having tasted this immortal ichor,[42] he cannot have enough of it, and as an admirable creative power exists in these intellections, it is of the last importance that these things get spoken. What a little of all we know is said! What drops of all the sea of our science are baled up! and by what accident it is that these are exposed, when so many secrets sleep in nature! Hence the necessity of speech and song; hence these throbs and heart-beatings in the orator, at the door of the assembly, to the end namely that thought may be ejaculated as Logos, or Word.

Doubt not, O poet, but persist. Say "It is in me, and shall out." Stand there, balked and dumb, stuttering and stammering, hissed and hooted, stand and strive, until at last rage draw out of thee that *dream*-power which every night shows thee is thine own; a power transcending all limit and privacy, and by virtue of which a man is the conductor of the whole river of electricity. Nothing walks, or creeps, or grows, or exists, which must not in turn arise and walk before him as exponent of his meaning. Comes he to that power, his genius is no longer exhaustible. All the creatures by pairs and by tribes pour into his mind as into a Noah's ark, to come forth again to people a new world. This is like the stock of air for our respiration or for the combustion of our fireplace; not a measure of gallons, but the entire atmosphere if wanted. And therefore the rich poets, as Homer, Chaucer, Shakspeare, and Raphael, have obviously no limits to their works except the limits of their lifetime, and resemble a mirror carried through the street, ready to render an image of every created thing.

O poet! a new nobility is conferred in groves and pastures, and not in castles or by the sword-blade any longer. The conditions are hard, but equal.

---

[42] A mythological fluid supposed to have flowed in the blood of the Greek gods. Emerson is using the word here as a synonym for "nectar," the drink of the gods.

Thou shalt leave the world, and know the muse only. Thou shalt not know any longer the times, customs, graces, politics, or opinions of men, but shall take all from the muse. For the time of towns is tolled from the world by funereal chimes, but in nature the universal hours are counted by succeeding tribes of animals and plants, and by growth of joy on joy. God wills also that thou abdicate a manifold and duplex life, and that thou be content that others speak for thee. Others shall be thy gentlemen and shall represent all courtesy and worldly life for thee; others shall do the great and resounding actions also. Thou shalt lie close hid with nature, and canst not be afforded to the Capitol or the Exchange. The world is full of renunciations and appreticeships, and this is thine; thou must pass for a fool and a churl for a long season. This is the screen and sheath in which Pan has protected his well-beloved flower, and thou shalt be known only to thine own, and they shall console thee with tenderest love. And thou shalt not be able to rehearse the names of thy friends in thy verse, for an old shame before the holy ideal. And this is the reward; that the ideal shall be real to thee, and the impressions of the actual world shall fall like summer rain, copious, but not troublesome to thy invulnerable essence. Thou shalt have the whole land for thy park and manor, the sea for thy bath and navigation, without tax and without envy; the woods and the rivers thou shalt own, and thou shalt possess that wherein others are only tenants and boarders. Thou true land-lord! sea-lord! air-lord! Wherever snow falls or water flows or birds fly, wherever day and night meet in twilight, wherever the blue heaven is hung by clouds or sown with stars, wherever are forms with transparent boundaries, wherever are outlets into celestial space, wherever is danger, and awe, and love,—there is Beauty, plenteous as rain, shed for thee, and though thou shouldst walk the world over, thou shalt not be able to find a condition inopportune or ignoble.

From Representative Men

NAPOLEON;
OR, THE MAN OF THE WORLD[1]
FROM REPRESENTATIVE MEN

Among the eminent persons of the nineteenth century, Bonaparte is far the best known and the most powerful; and owes his predominance to the fidelity with which he expresses the tone of thought and belief, the aims of the

---

[1] This lecture was read in Exeter Hall, London, in 1848. For Emerson, Napoleon was the man of action incarnate—that contemporary hero who had largeness of intellect, firmness of will, and absolute self-confidence.

masses of active and cultivated men. It is Swedenborg's theory that every organ is made up of homogeneous particles; or as it is sometimes expressed, every whole is made of similars; that is, the lungs are composed of infinitely small lungs; the liver, of infinitely small livers; the kidney, of little kidneys, etc. Following this analogy, if any man is found to carry with him the power and affections of vast numbers, if Napoleon is France, if Napoleon is Europe, it is because the people whom he sways are little Napoleons.

In our society there is a standing antagonism between the conservative and the democratic classes; between those who have made their fortunes, and the young and the poor who have fortunes to make; between the interests of dead labor—that is, the labor of hands long ago still in the grave, which labor is now entombed in money stocks, or in land and buildings owned by idle capitalists—and the interests of living labor, which seeks to possess itself of land and buildings and money stocks. The first class is timid, selfish, illiberal, hating innovation, and continually losing numbers by death. The second class is selfish also, encroaching, bold, self-relying, always outnumbering the other and recruiting its numbers every hour by births. It desires to keep open every avenue to the competition of all, and to multiply avenues: the class of business men in America, in England, in France and throughout Europe; the class of industry and skill. Napoleon is its representative. The instinct of active, brave, able men, throughout the middle class every where, has pointed out Napoleon as the incarnate Democrat. He had their virtues and their vices; above all, he had their spirit or aim. That tendency is material, pointing at a sensual success and employing the richest and most various means to that end; conversant with mechanical powers, highly intellectual, widely and accurately learned and skilful, but subordinating all intellectual and spiritual forces into means to a material success. To be the rich man, is the end. "God has granted," says the Koran, "to every people a prophet in its own tongue." Paris and London and New York, the spirit of commerce, of money and material power, were also to have their prophet; and Bonaparte was qualified and sent.

Every one of the million readers of anecdotes or memoirs or lives of Napoleon, delights in the page, because he studies in it his own history. Napoleon is thoroughly modern, and, at the highest point of his fortunes, has the very spirit of the newspapers. He is no saint—to use his own word, "no capuchin,"[2] and he is no hero, in the high sense. The man in the street finds in him the qualities and powers of other men in the street. He finds him, like himself, by birth a citizen, who, by very intelligible merits, arrived at such a commanding position that he could indulge all those tastes which the common man possesses but is obliged to conceal and deny: good society, good books, fast travelling, dress, dinners, servants without number, personal weight, the execution of his ideas, the standing in the attitude of a benefactor

[2] A monk.

to all persons about him, the refined enjoyments of pictures, statues, music, palaces and conventional honors—precisely what is agreeable to the heart of every man in the nineteenth century, this powerful man possessed.

It is true that a man of Napoleon's truth of adaptation to the mind of the masses around him, becomes not merely representative but actually a monopolizer and usurper of other minds. Thus Mirabeau[3] plagiarized every good thought, every good word that was spoken in France. Dumont[4] relates that he sat in the gallery of the Convention and heard Mirabeau make a speech. It struck Dumont that he could fit it with a peroration, which he wrote in pencil immediately, and showed it to Lord Elgin,[5] who sat by him. Lord Elgin approved it, and Dumont, in the evening, showed it to Mirabeau. Mirabeau read it, pronounced it admirable, and declared he would incorporate it into his harangue to-morrow, to the Assembly. "It is impossible," said Dumont, "as, unfortunately, I have shown it to Lord Elgin." "If you have shown it to Lord Elgin and to fifty persons beside, I shall still speak it to-morrow": and he did speak it with much effect, at the next day's session. For Mirabeau, with his overpowering personality, felt that these things which his presence inspired were as much his own as if he had said them, and that his adoption of them gave them their weight. Much more absolute and centralizing was the successor to Mirabeau's popularity and to much more than his predominance in France. Indeed, a man of Napoleon's stamp almost ceases to have a private speech and opinion. He is so largely receptive, and is so placed, that he comes to be a bureau for all the intelligence, wit and power of the age and country. He gains the battle; he makes the code; he makes the system of weights and measures; he levels the Alps; he builds the road. All distinguished engineers, savants, statists, report to him: so likewise do all good heads in every kind: he adopts the best measures, sets his stamp on them, and not these alone, but on every happy and memorable expression. Every sentence spoken by Napoleon and every line of his writing, deserves reading, as it is the sense of France.

Bonaparte was the idol of common men because he had in transcendent degree the qualities and powers of common men. There is a certain satisfaction in coming down to the lowest ground of politics, for we get rid of cant and hypocrisy. Bonaparte wrought, in common with that great class he represented for power and wealth—but Bonaparte, specially, without any scruple as to the means. All the sentiments which embarrass men's pursuit of these objects, he set aside. The sentiments were for women and children. Fontanes,[6] in 1804, expressed Napoleon's own sense, when in behalf of the

---

[3] Comte de Mirabeau (1749–1791), the title of Honoré G. V. Riquetti, was a French revolutionist.

[4] Pierre Etienne Louis Dumont (1759–1829) was a friend of Mirabeau and recorded his activities in *Souvenirs sur Mirabeau* (1832).

[5] Lord Elgin, Seventh Earl of Elgin and Eleventh Earl of Kincardine (1766–1841), British diplomat and art connoisseur.

[6] Marquis de Louis Fontanes (1757–1821) was a poet and translator of Pope's *Essay on Man;* he was also a member of the Institute from 1795, and in 1804 president of the legislative body.

Senate he addressed him—"Sire, the desire of perfection is the worst disease that ever afflicted the human mind." The advocates of liberty and of progress are "ideologists"—a word of contempt often in his mouth—"Necker is an ideologist": "Lafayette is an ideologist."[7]

An Italian proverb, too well known, declares that "if you would succeed, you must not be too good." It is an advantage, within certain limits, to have renounced the dominion of the sentiments of piety, gratitude and generosity; since what was an impassable bar to us, and still is to others, becomes a convenient weapon for our purposes; just as the river which was a formidable barrier, winter transforms into the smoothest of roads.

Napoleon renounced, once for all, sentiments and affections, and would help himself with his hands and his head. With him is no miracle and no magic. He is a worker in brass, in iron, in wood, in earth, in roads, in buildings, in money and in troops, and a very consistent and wise master-workman. He is never weak and literary, but acts with the solidity and the precision of natural agents. He has not lost his native sense and sympathy with things. Men give way before such a man, as before natural events. To be sure there are men enough who are immersed in things, as farmers, smiths, sailors and mechanics generally; and we know how real and solid such men appear in the presence of scholars and grammarians: but these men ordinarily lack the power of arrangement, and are like hands without a head. But Bonaparte superadded to this mineral and animal force, insight and generalization, so that men saw in him combined the natural and the intellectual power, as if the sea and land had taken flesh and begun to cipher. Therefore the land and sea seem to presuppose him. He came unto his own and they received him. This ciphering operative knows what he is working with and what is the product. He knew the properties of gold and iron, of wheels and ships, of troops and diplomatists, and required that each should do after its kind.

The art of war was the game in which he exerted his arithmetic. It consisted, according to him, in having always more forces than the enemy, on the point where the enemy is attacked, or where he attacks: and his whole talent is strained by endless manœuvre and evolution, to march always on the enemy at an angle, and destroy his forces in detail. It is obvious that a very small force, skilfully and rapidly manœuvring so as always to bring two men against one at the point of engagement, will be an overmatch for a much larger body of men.

The times, his constitution and his early circumstances combined to develop this pattern democrat. He had the virtues of his class and the conditions for their activity. That common-sense which no sooner respects any end than it finds the means to effect it; the delight in the use of means; in the

---

[7] Jacques Necker (1732-1804), a French statesman and financier. Marquis de Marie Joseph-Lafayette (1757-1834) was a French reformer and general who aided United States troops against the British in the Revolutionary War.

choice, simplification and combining of means; the directness and thoroughness of his work; the prudence with which all was seen and the energy with
which all was done, make him the natural organ and head of what I may
almost call, from its extent, the *modern* party.

Nature must have far the greatest share in every success, and so in his.
Such a man was wanted, and such a man was born; a man of stone and iron,
capable of sitting on horseback sixteen or seventeen hours, of going many
days together without rest or food except by snatches, and with the speed
and spring of a tiger in action; a man not embarrassed by any scruples;
compact, instant, selfish, prudent, and of a perception which did not suffer
itself to be baulked or misled by any pretences of others, or any superstition
or any heat or haste of his own. "My hand of iron," he said, "was not at the
extremity of my arm, it was immediately connected with my head." He
respected the power of nature and fortune, and ascribed to it his superiority,
instead of valuing himself, like inferior men, on his opinionativeness, and
waging war with nature. His favorite rhetoric lay in allusion to his star; and
he pleased himself, as well as the people, when he styled himself the "Child
of Destiny." "They charge me," he said, "with the commission of great
crimes: men of my stamp do not commit crimes. Nothing has been more
simple than my elevation, 't is in vain to ascribe it to intrigue or crime; it was
owing to the peculiarity of the times and to my reputation of having fought
well against the enemies of my country. I have always marched with the
opinion of great masses and with events. Of what use then would crimes be
to me?" Again he said, speaking of his son, "My son can not replace me; I
could not replace myself. I am the creature of circumstances."

He had a directness of action never before combined with so much comprehension. He is a realist, terrific to all talkers and confused truth-obscuring
persons. He sees where the matter hinges, throws himself on the precise
point of resistance, and slights all other considerations. He is strong in the
right manner, namely by insight. He never blundered into victory, but won
his battles in his head before he won them on the field. His principal means
are in himself. He asks counsel of no other. In 1796 he writes to the Directory.[8] "I have conducted the campaign without consulting any one. I should
have done no good if I had been under the necessity of conforming to the
notions of another person. I have gained some advantages over superior
forces and when totally destitute of every thing, because, in the persuasion
that your confidence was reposed in me, my actions were as prompt as my
thoughts."

History is full, down to this day, of the imbecility of kings and governors.
They are a class of persons much to be pitied, for they know not what they
should do. The weavers strike for bread, and the king and his ministers,

---

[8] The executive body in charge of the French
government from 1795 to 1799.

knowing not what to do, meet them with bayonets. But Napoleon understood his business. Here was a man who in each moment and emergency knew what to do next. It is an immense comfort and refreshment to the spirits, not only of kings, but of citizens. Few men have any next; they live from hand to mouth, without plan, and are ever at the end of their line, and after each action wait for an impulse from abroad. Napoleon had been the first man of the world, if his ends had been purely public. As he is, he inspires confidence and vigor by the extraordinary unity of his action. He is firm, sure, self-denying, self-postponing, sacrificing every thing—money, troops, generals, and his own safety also, to his aim; not misled, like common adventurers, by the splendor of his own means. "Incidents ought not to govern policy," he said, "but policy, incidents." "To be hurried away by every event is to have no political system at all." His victories were only so many doors, and he never for a moment lost sight of his way onward, in the dazzle and uproar of the present circumstance. He knew what to do, and he flew to his mark. He would shorten a straight line to come at his object. Horrible anecdotes may no doubt be collected from his history, of the price at which he bought his successes; but he must not therefore be set down as cruel, but only as one who knew no impediment to his will; not bloodthirsty, not cruel—but woe to what thing or person stood in his way! Not bloodthirsty, but not sparing of blood—and pitiless. He saw only the object: the obstacle must give way. "Sire, General Clarke can not combine with General Junot,[9] for the dreadful fire of the Austrian battery."—"Let him carry the battery."—"Sire, every regiment that approaches the heavy artillery is sacrificed: Sire, what orders?"—"Forward, forward!" Seruzier, a colonel of artillery, gives, in his "Military Memoirs," the following sketch of a scene after the battle of Austerlitz.[10]—"At the moment in which the Russian army was making its retreat, painfully, but in good order, on the ice of the lake, the Emperor Napoleon came riding at full speed toward the artillery. 'You are losing time,' he cried; 'fire upon those masses; they must be engulfed: fire upon the ice!' The order remained unexecuted for ten minutes. In vain several officers and myself were placed on the slope of a hill to produce the effect: their balls and mine rolled upon the ice without breaking it up. Seeing that, I tried a simple method of elevating light howitzers. The almost perpendicular fall of the heavy projectiles produced the desired effect. My method was immediately followed by the adjoining batteries, and in less than no time we buried" some "thousands of Russians and Austrians under the waters of the lake."

In the plentitude of his resources, every obstacle seemed to vanish. "There shall be no Alps," he said; and he built his perfect roads, climbing by

[9] Andoche Junot (1771-1853) was an adjutant under Napoleon in Egypt.

[10] Austerlitz—a town in Moravia, Czechoslovakia, the site of Napoleon's victory over the Russian and Austrian armies (1805).

graded galleries their steepest precipices, until Italy was as open to Paris as any town in France. He laid his bones to, and wrought for his crown. Having decided what was to be done, he did that with might and main. He put out all his strength. He risked every thing and spared nothing, neither ammunition, nor money, nor troops, nor generals, nor himself.

We like to see every thing do its office after its kind, whether it be a milch-cow or a rattlesnake; and if fighting be the best mode of adjusting national differences (as large majorities of men seem to agree), certainly Bonaparte was right in making it thorough. The grand principle of war, he said, was that an army ought always to be ready, by day and by night and at all hours, to make all the resistance it is capable of making. He never economized his ammunition, but, on a hostile position, rained a torrent of iron—shells, balls, grape-shot—to annihilate all defence. On any point of resistance he concentrated squadron on squadron in overwhelming numbers until it was swept out of existence. To a regiment of horse-chasseurs at Lobenstein, two days before the battle of Jena,[11] Napoleon said, "My lads, you must not fear death; when soldiers brave death, they drive him into the enemy's ranks." In the fury of assault, he no more spared himself. He went to the edge of his possibility. It is plain that in Italy he did what he could, and all that he could. He came, several times, within an inch of ruin; and his own person was all but lost. He was flung into the marsh at Arcola. The Austrians were between him and his troops, in the *mêlée*, and he was brought off with desperate efforts. At Lonato, and at other places, he was on the point of being taken prisoner. He fought sixty battles. He had never enough. Each victory was a new weapon. "My power would fall, were I not to support it by new achievements. Conquest has made me what I am, and conquest must maintain me." He felt, with every wise man, that as much life is needed for conservation as for creation. We are always in peril, always in a bad plight, just on the edge of destruction and only to be saved by invention and courage.

This vigor was guarded and tempered by the coldest prudence and punctuality. A thunderbolt in the attack, he was found invulnerable in his intrenchments. His very attack was never the inspiration of courage, but the result of calculation. His idea of the best defence consists in being still the attacking party. "My ambition," he says, "was great, but was of a cold nature." In one of his conversations with Las Cases,[12] he remarked, "As to the moral courage, I have rarely met with the two-o'clock-in-the-morning kind: I mean unprepared courage; that which is necessary on an unexpected occasion, and which, in spite of the most unforeseen events, leaves full freedom

---

[11] A city of southern East Germany, the site of Napoleon's victory over Prussia (1806).

[12] Comte de Emannuel Dieudonne Las Cases (1766–1842), French historian, author of *At-* *las Historique* (1803–1804) and *Mémorial de Saint-Hélène* (1821–1823). He was fascinated by Napoleon's genius and insisted on sharing his exile.

of judgment and decision": and he did not hesitate to declare that he was himself eminently endowed with this two-o'clock-in-the-morning courage, and that he had met with few persons equal to himself in this respect.

Every thing depended on the nicety of his combinations, and the stars were not more punctual than his arithmetic. His personal attention descended to the smallest particulars. "At Montebello, I ordered Kellermann to attack with eight hundred horse, and with these he separated the six thousand Hungarian grenadiers, before the very eyes of the Austrian cavalry. This cavalry was half a league off and required a quarter of an hour to arrive on the field of action, and I have observed that it is always these quarters of an hour that decide the fate of a battle." "Before he fought a battle, Bonaparte thought little about what he should do in case of success, but a great deal about what he should do in case of a reverse of fortune." The same prudence and good sense mark all his behavior. His instructions to his secretary at the Tuileries[13] are worth remembering. "During the night, enter my chamber as seldom as possible. Do not awake me when you have any good news to communicate; with that there is no hurry. But when you bring bad news, rouse me instantly, for then there is not a moment to be lost." It was a whimsical economy of the same kind which dictated his practice, when general in Italy, in regard to his burdensome correspondence. He directed Bourrienne to leave all letters unopened for three weeks, and then observed with satisfaction how large a part of the correspondence had thus disposed of itself and no longer required an answer. His achievement of business was immense, and enlarges the known powers of man. There have been many working kings, from Ulysses to William of Orange,[14] but none who accomplished a tithe of this man's performance.

To these gifts of nature, Napoleon added the advantage of having been born to a private and humble fortune. In his later days he had the weakness of wishing to add to his crowns and badges the prescription of aristocracy; but he knew his debt to his austere education, and made no secret of his contempt for the born kings, and for "the hereditary asses," as he coarsely styled the Bourbons.[15] He said that "in their exile they had learned nothing, and forgot nothing." Bonaparte had passed through all the degrees of military service, but also was citizen before he was emperor, and so has the key to citizenship. His remarks and estimates discover the information and justness of measurement of the middle class. Those who had to deal with him found that he was not to be imposed upon, but could cipher as well as another man. This appears in all parts of his Memoirs, dictated at St. Helena. When the expenses of the empress, of his household, of his palaces, had

---

[13] A royal residence in Paris, France, begun in 1564 by Catherine de Médicis and burned in 1871; now the site of the Tuileries Gardens, a park near the Louvre.

[14] Latin name for Odysseus, King of Ithaca; William of Orange (1533-1584) was the founder of the Dutch Republic.

[15] French royal family.

accumulated great debts, Napoleon examined the bills of the creditors himself, detected overcharges and errors, and reduced the claims by considerable sums.

His grand weapon, namely the millions whom he directed, he owed to the representative character which clothed him. He interests us as he stands for France and for Europe; and he exists as captain and king only as far as the Revolution, or the interest of the industrious masses, found an organ and a leader in him. In the social interests, he knew the meaning and value of labor, and threw himself naturally on that side. I like an incident mentioned by one of his biographers at St. Helena. "When walking with Mrs. Balcombe, some servants, carrying heavy boxes, passed by on the road, and Mrs. Balcombe desired them, in rather an angry tone, to keep back. Napoleon interfered, saying 'Respect the burden, Madame.' " In the time of the empire he directed attention to the improvement and embellishment of the markets of the capital. "The market-place," he said, "is the Louvre of the common people." The principal works that have survived him are his magnificent roads. He filled the troops with his spirit, and a sort of freedom and companionship grew up between him and them, which the forms of his court never permitted between the officers and himself. They performed, under his eye, that which no others could do. The best document of his relation to his troops is the order of the day on the morning of the battle of Austerlitz, in which Napoleon promises the troops that he will keep his person out of reach of fire. This declaration, which is the reverse of that ordinarily made by generals and sovereigns on the eve of a battle, sufficiently explains the devotion of the army to their leader.

But though there is in particulars this identity between Napoleon and the mass of the people, his real strength lay in their conviction that he was their representative in his genius and aims, not only when he courted, but when he controlled, and even when he decimated them by his conscriptions. He knew, as well as any Jacobin[16] in France, how to philosophize on liberty and equality; and when allusion was made to the precious blood of centuries, which was spilled by the killing of the Duc d'Enghien,[17] he suggested, "Neither is my blood ditch-water." The people felt that no longer the throne was occupied and the land sucked of its nourishment, by a small class of legitimates, secluded from all community with the children of the soil, and holding the ideas and superstitions of a long-forgotten state of society. Instead of that vampyre, a man of themselves held, in the Tuileries, knowledge and ideas like their own, opening of course to them and their children all places of power and trust. The day of sleepy, selfish policy, ever narrowing the means and opportunities of young men, was ended, and a day of expansion

[16] A radical republican during the French Revolution.

[17] Duc d'Enghien (1772–1804) was shot on March 21, 1804, because Bonaparte believed in his complicity of conspiracy.

and demand was come. A market for all the powers and productions of man was opened; brilliant prizes glittered in the eyes of youth and talent. The old, iron-bound, feudal France was changed into a young Ohio or New York; and those who smarted under the immediate rigors of the new monarch, pardoned them as the necessary severities of the military system which had driven out the oppressor. And even when the majority of the people had begun to ask whether they had really gained any thing under the exhausting levies of men and money of the new master, the whole talent of the country, in every rank and kindred, took his part and defended him as its natural patron. In 1814, when advised to rely on the higher classes, Napoleon said to those around him, "Gentlemen, in the situation in which I stand, my only nobility is the rabble of the Faubourgs."

Napoleon met this natural expectation. The necessity of his position required a hospitality to every sort of talent, and its appointment to trusts; and his feeling went along with this policy. Like every superior person, he undoubtedly felt a desire for men and compeers, and a wish to measure his power with other masters, and an impatience of fools and underlings. In Italy, he sought for men and found none. "Good God!" he said, "how rare men are! There are eighteen millions in Italy, and I have with difficulty found two—Dandolo and Melzi."[18] In later years, with larger experience, his respect for mankind was not increased. In a moment of bitterness he said to one of his oldest friends, "Men deserve the contempt with which they inspire me. I have only to put some gold-lace on the coat of my virtuous republicans and they immediately become just what I wish them." This impatience at levity was, however, an oblique tribute of respect to those able persons who commanded his regard not only when he found them friends and coadjutors but also when they resisted his will. He could not confound Fox and Pitt, Carnot, Lafayette and Bernadotte,[19] with the danglers of his court; and in spite of the detraction which his systematic egotism dictated toward the great captains who conquered with and for him, ample acknowledgments are made by him to Lannes, Duroc, Kleber, Dessaix, Massena, Murat, Ney and Augereau.[20] If he felt himself their patron and the founder of their fortunes, as when he said "I made my generals out of mud"—he could not hide his satisfaction in receiving from them a seconding and support commensurate with the grandeur of his enterprise. In the Russian campaign he was so much impressed by the courage and resources of

[18] Enrico Dandolo (1108-1205) was a doge of Constantinople, eminent in learning and public affairs; Jose De Palafox y Melzi, the Duke of Saragossa (1775-1847) was a Spanish soldier, known for his defense of Saragossa in the Peninsular War (1808-1809).

[19] William Johnson Fox (1786-1864), English orator and political writer; William Pitt (1759-1806), English statesman; Nicholas M. Lazare Carnot (1753-1823), organizer of victory during the French Revolution; Jean Baptiste Jules Bernadotte (1763?-1844), general under Napoleon, King of Sweden (1818-1844).

[20] French military leaders.

Marshal Ney, that he said, "I have two hundred millions in my coffers, and I would give them all for Ney." The characters which he has drawn of several of his marshals are discriminating, and though they did not content the insatiable vanity of French officers, are no doubt substantially just. And in fact every species of merit was sought and advanced under his government. "I know," he said, "the depth and draught of water of every one of my generals." Natural power was sure to be well received at his court. Seventeen men in his time were raised from common soldiers to the rank of king, marshal, duke, or general; and the crosses of his Legion of Honor were given to personal valor, and not to family connexion. "When soldiers have been baptized in the fire of a battlefield, they have all one rank in my eyes."

When a natural king becomes a titular king, every body is pleased and satisfied. The Revolution entitled the strong populace of the Faubourg St. Antoine, and every horse-boy and powder-monkey in the army, to look on Napoleon as flesh of his flesh and the creature of *his* party; but there is something in the success of grand talent which enlists an universal sympathy. For in prevalence of sense and spirit over stupidity and malversation, all reasonable men have an interest; and as intellectual beings we feel the air purified by the electric shock, when material force is overthrown by intellectual energies. As soon as we are removed out of the reach of local and accidental partialities, Man feels that Napoleon fights for him; these are honest victories, this strong steam-engine does our work. Whatever appeals to the imagination, by transcending the ordinary limits of human ability, wonderfully encourages and liberates us. This capacious head, revolving and disposing sovereignly trains of affairs, and animating such multitudes of agents; this eye, which looked through Europe; this prompt invention; this inexhaustible resource—what events! what romantic pictures! what strange situations!—when spying the Alps, by a sunset in the Sicilian sea; drawing up his army for battle in sight of the Pyramids, and saying to his troops, "From the tops of those pyramids, forty centuries look down on you;" fording the Red Sea; wading in the gulf of the Isthmus of Suez. On the shore of Ptolemais, gigantic projects agitated him. "Had Acre fallen, I should have changed the face of the world." His army, on the night of the battle of Austerlitz, which was the anniversary of his inauguration as Emperor, presented him with a bouquet of forty standards taken in the fight. Perhaps it is a little puerile, the pleasure he took in making these contrasts glaring; as when he pleased himself with making kings wait in his antechambers, at Tilsit, at Paris and at Erfurt.

We can not, in the universal imbecility, indecision and indolence of men, sufficiently congratulate ourselves on this strong and ready actor, who took occasion by the beard, and showed us how much may be accomplished by the mere force of such virtues as all men possess in less degrees; namely, by punctuality, by personal attention, by courage and thoroughness. "The Austrians," he said, "do not know the value of time." I should cite him, in his earlier years, as a model of prudence. His power does not consist in any wild or extravagant force; in any enthusiasm like Mahomet's, or singular power of persuasion; but in the exercise of common-sense on each emergency, instead of abiding by rules and customs. The lesson he teaches is that which vigor always teaches—that there is always room for it. To what heaps of cowardly doubts is not that man's life an answer. When he appeared it was the belief of all military men that there could be nothing new in war; as it is the belief of men to-day that nothing new can be undertaken in politics, or in church, or in letters, or in trade, or in farming, or in our social manners and customs; and as it is at all times the belief of society that the world is used up. But Bonaparte knew better than society; and moreover knew that he knew better. I think all men know better than they do; know that the institutions we so volubly commend are go-carts and baubles; but they dare not trust their presentiments. Bonaparte relied on his own sense, and did not care a bean for other people's. The world treated his novelties just as it treats everybody's novelties—made infinite objection, mustered all the impediments; but he snapped his finger at their objections. "What creates great difficulty," he remarks, "in the profession of the land-commander, is the necessity of feeding so many men and animals. If he allows himself to be guided by the commissaries he will never stir, and all his expeditions will fail." An example of his common-sense is what he says of the passage of the Alps in winter, which all writers, one repeating after the other, had described as impracticable. "The winter," says Napoleon, "is not the most unfavorable season for the passage of lofty mountains. The snow is then firm, the weather settled, and there is nothing to fear from avalanches, the real and only danger to be apprehended in the Alps. On these high mountains there are often very fine days in December, of a dry cold, with extreme calmness in the air." Read his account, too, of the way in which battles are gained. "In all battles a moment occurs when the bravest troops, after having made the greatest efforts, feel inclined to run. That terror proceeds from a want of confidence in their own courage, and it only requires a slight opportunity, a pretence, to restore confidence to them. The art is, to give rise to the opportunity and to invent the pretence. At Arcola I won the battle with twenty-five horsemen. I seized that moment of lassitude, gave every man a trumpet, and gained the day with this handful. You see that two armies are two bodies which meet and endeavor to frighten each other; a moment of panic occurs, and that moment must be turned to advantage. When a man has been present in many actions, he distinguishes that moment without difficulty: it is as easy as casting up an addition."

This deputy of the nineteenth century added to his gifts a capacity for speculation on general topics. He delighted in running through the range of practical, of literary and of abstract questions. His opinion is always original and to the purpose. On the voyage to Egypt he liked, after dinner, to fix on three or four persons to support a proposition, and as many to oppose it. He gave a subject, and the discussions turned on questions of religion, the different kinds of government, and the art of war. One day he asked whether the planets were inhabited. On another, what was the age of the world. Then he proposed to consider the probability of the destruction of the globe, either by water or by fire: at another time, the truth or fallacy of presentiments, and the interpretation of dreams. He was very fond of talking of religion. In 1806 he conversed with Fournier, bishop of Montpellier, on matters of theology. There were two points on which they could not agree, viz. that of hell, and that of salvation out of the pale of the church. The Emperor told Josephine that he disputed like a devil on these two points, on which the bishop was inexorable. To the philosophers he readily yielded all that was proved against religion as the work of men and time, but he would not hear of materialism. One fine night, on deck, amid a clatter of materialism, Bonaparte pointed to the stars, and said, "You may talk as long as you please, gentlemen, but who made all that?" He delighted in the conversation of men of science, particularly of Monge and Berthollet[21] but the men of letters he slighted; they were "manufacturers of phrases." Of medicine too he was fond of talking, and with those of its practitioners whom he most esteemed— with Corvisart at Paris, and with Antonomarchi at St. Helena.[22] "Believe me," he said to the last, "we had better leave off all these remedies: life is a fortress which neither you nor I know any thing about. Why throw obstacles in the way of its defence? Its own means are superior to all the apparatus of your laboratories. Corvisart candidly agreed with me that all your filthy mixtures are good for nothing. Medicine is a collection of uncertain prescriptions, the results of which, taken collectively, are more fatal than useful to mankind. Water, air and cleanliness are the chief articles in my pharmacopœia."

His memoirs, dictated to Count Montholon and General Gourgaud[23] at St.

---

[21] Gaspard Monge (1746-1818), French mathematician, physicist and inventor of descriptive geometry; Comte Claude Louis Berthollet (1748-1822), French chemist.

[22] Baron De Jean Nicholas Corvisart-Desmarets (1755-1821), professor at the Collège de France; Francisco Antommarchi (1780-1838) was Napoleon's physician at St. Helena from 1818.

[23] Charles Montholon (1783-1853) was a French general and diplomat. With Gourgaud he published *Memories pour servir a l'histoire de France sous Napoléon, ecrits sous sa dictée.*

Helena, have great value, after all the deduction that it seems is to be made from them on account of his known disingenuousness. He has the good-nature of strength and conscious superiority. I admire his simple, clear narrative of his battles—good as Cæsar's; his good-natured and sufficiently respectful account of Marshal Wurmser and his other antagonists; and his own equality as a writer to his varying subject. The most agreeable portion is the Campaign in Egypt.

He had hours of thought and wisdom. In intervals of leisure, either in the camp or the palace, Napoleon appears as a man of genius directing on abstract questions the native appetite for truth and the impatience of words he was wont to show in war. He could enjoy every play of invention, a romance, a *bon mot*, as well as a stratagem in a campaign. He delighted to fascinate Josephine and her ladies, in a dim-lighted apartment, by the terrors of a fiction to which his voice and dramatic power lent every addition.

I call Napoleon the agent or attorney of the middle class of modern society; of the throng who fill the markets, shops, counting-houses, manufactories, ships, of the modern world, aiming to be rich. He was the agitator, the destroyer of prescription, the internal improver, the liberal, the radical, the inventor of means, the opener of doors and markets, the subverter of monopoly and abuse. Of course the rich and aristocratic did not like him. England, the centre of capital, and Rome and Austria, centres of tradition and genealogy, opposed him. The consternation of the dull and conservative classes, the terror of the foolish old men and old women of the Roman conclave, who in their despair took hold of any thing, and would cling to red hot iron—the vain attempts of statists to amuse and deceive him, of the emperor of Austria to bribe him; and the instinct of the young, ardent and active men every where, which pointed him out as the giant of the middle class, make his history bright and commanding. He had the virtues of the masses of his constituents: he had also their vices. I am sorry that the brilliant picture has its reverse. But that is the fatal quality which we discover in our pursuit of wealth, that it is treacherous, and is bought by the breaking or weakening of the sentiments; and it is inevitable that we should find the same fact in the history of this champion, who proposed to himself simply a brilliant career, without any stipulation or scruple concerning the means.

Bonaparte was singularly destitute of generous sentiments. The highest-placed individual in the most cultivated age and population of the world—he has not the merit of common truth and honesty. He is unjust to his generals; egotistic and monopolizing; meanly stealing the credit of their great actions from Kellermann, from Bernadotte; intriguing to involve his faithful Junot in hopeless bankruptcy, in order to drive him to a distance from Paris, because the familiarity of his manners offends the new pride of his throne. He is a boundless liar. The official paper, his "Moniteur," and all his bulletins, are proverbs for saying what he wished to be believed; and worse—he sat, in his premature old age, in his lonely island, coldly falsifying facts and dates and characters, and giving to history a theatrical *éclat*. Like all Frenchmen he has a passion for stage effect. Every action that breathes of generosity is poisoned by this calculation. His star, his love of glory, his doctrine of the immortality of the soul, are all French: "I must dazzle and astonish. If I were to give the liberty of the press, my power could not last three days." To make a great noise is his favorite design. "A great reputation is a great noise: the more there is made, the farther off it is heard. Laws, institutions, monuments, nations, all fall; but the noise continues, and resounds in after ages." His doctrine, of immortality is simply fame. His theory of influence is not flattering. "There are two levers for moving men—interest and fear. Love is a silly infatuation, depend upon it. Friendship is but a name. I love nobody. I do not even love my brothers: perhaps Joseph a little, from habit, and because he is my elder; and Duroc, I love him too; but why?—because his character pleases me: he is stern and resolute, and I believe the fellow never shed a tear. For my part I know very well that I have no true friends. As long as I continue to be what I am, I may have as many pretended friends as I please. Leave sensibility to women; but men should be firm in heart and purpose, or they should have nothing to do with war and government." He was thoroughly unscrupulous. He would steal, slander, assassinate, drown and poison, as his interest dictated. He had no generosity, but mere vulgar hatred; he was intensely selfish; he was perfidious; he cheated at cards; he was a prodigious gossip, and opened letters, and delighted in his infamous police, and rubbed his hands with joy when he had intercepted some morsel of intelligence concerning the men and women about him, boasting that "he knew every thing;" and interfered with the cutting the dresses of the women; and listened after the hurrahs and the compliments of the street, incognito. His manners were coarse. He treated women with low familiarity. He had the habit of pulling their ears and pinching their cheeks when he was in good humor, and of pulling the ears and whiskers of men, and of striking and horse-play with them, to his last days. It does not appear that he listened at keyholes, or at least that he was caught at it. In short, when you have penetrated through all the circles of power and splendor, you were not dealing with a gentleman, at last; but with an impostor and a rogue; and he fully deserves the epithet of *Jupiter Scapin*, or a sort of Scamp Jupiter.

In describing the two parties into which modern society divides itself—the democrat and the conservative—I said, Bonaparte represents the democrat, or the party of men of business, against the stationary or conservative party. I omitted then to say, what is material to the statement, namely that these two parties differ only as young and old. The democrat is a young conservative; the conservative is an old democrat. The aristocrat is the democrat ripe and gone to seed—because both parties stand on the one ground of the supreme value of property, which one endeavors to get, and the other to keep. Bonaparte may be said to represent the whole history of this party, its youth and its age; yes, and with poetic justice its fate, in his own. The counter-revolution, the counter-party, still waits for its organ and representative, in a lover and a man of truly public and universal aims.

Here was an experiment, under the most favorable conditions, of the powers of intellect without conscience. Never was such a leader so endowed and so weaponed; never leader found such aids and followers. And what was the result of this vast talent and power, of these immense armies, burned cities, squandered treasures, immolated millions of men, of this demoralized Europe? It came to no result. All passed away like the smoke of his artillery, and left no trace. He left France smaller, poorer, feebler, than he found it; and the whole contest for freedom was to be begun again. The attempt was in principle suicidal. France served him with life and limb and estate, as long as it could identify its interest with him; but when men saw that after victory was another war; after the destruction of armies, new conscriptions; and they who had toiled so desperately were never nearer to the reward—they could not spend what they had earned, nor repose on their down-beds, nor strut in their châteaux—they deserted him. Men found that his absorbing egotism was deadly to all other men. It resembled the torpedo, which inflicts a succession of shocks on any one who takes hold of it, producing spasms which contract the muscles of the hand, so that the man can not open his fingers: and the animal inflicts new and more violent shocks, until he paralyzes and kills his victim. So this exorbitant egotist narrowed, impoverished and absorbed the power and existence of those who served him; and the universal cry of France and of Europe in 1814 was, "Enough of him;" "*Assez de Bonaparte.*"

It was not Bonaparte's fault. He did all that in him lay to live and thrive without moral principle. It was the nature of things, the eternal law of man and of the world which baulked and ruined him; and the result, in a million experiments, will be the same. Every experiment, by multitudes or by individuals, that has a sensual and selfish aim, will fail. The pacific Fourier will be as inefficient as the pernicious Napoleon. As long as our civilization is essentially one of property, of fences, of exclusiveness, it will be mocked by delusions. Our riches will leave us sick; there will be bitterness in our laughter, and our wine will burn our mouth. Only that good profits which we can taste with all doors open, and which serves all men.

From Conduct of Life

FATE[1]

Delicate omens traced in air,
To the lone bard true witness bare;
Birds with auguries on their wings
Chanted undeceiving things,
Him to beckon, him to warn;
Well might then the poet scorn
To learn of scribe or courier
Hints writ in vaster character;
And on his mind, at dawn of day,
Soft shadows of the evening lay.
For the prevision is allied
Unto the thing so signified;
Or say, the foresight that awaits
Is the same Genius that creates.

It chanced during one winter a few years ago, that our cities were bent on discussing the theory of the Age. By an odd coincidence, four or five noted men were each reading a discourse to the citizens of Boston or New York, on the Spirit of the Times.[2] It so happened that the subject had the same prominence in some remarkable pamphlets and journals issued in London in the same season. To me, however, the question of the times resolved itself into a practical question of the conduct of life. How shall I live? We are incompetent to solve the times. Our geometry cannot span the huge orbits of the prevailing ideas, behold their return and reconcile their opposition. We can only obey our own polarity. 'T is fine for us to speculate and elect our course, if we must accept an irresistible dictation.

In our first steps to gain our wishes we come upon immovable limitations. We are fired with the hope to reform men. After many experiments we find

---

[1] "Fate" was the first lecture in a series that Emerson called "The Conduct of Life"; it was delivered at the Masonic Temple in Boston in December 1851. Emerson was dissatisfied with the essay, and he continued to revise it throughout the 1850's. In 1860 it appeared as the first essay in a volume entitled *The Conduct of Life (Works,* VI).

In "Fate," Emerson deals more directly and fully than anywhere else in his work with the role of determinism in human experience; he seems more realistic and pragmatic

than in his early essays. Although Emerson still stresses the significance of freedom, which he associates with "thought," he is also deeply conscious of fate, which he characterizes as "Nature." A full treatment of this tension between freedom and fate may be found in Stephen Whicher's critical study, *Freedom and Fate.*

[2] Emerson had lectured on "The Spirit of the Times" to a considerable audience in New York on January 29, 1850.

that we must begin earlier,—at school. But the boys and girls are not docile; we can make nothing of them. We decide that they are not of good stock. We must begin our reform earlier still,—at generation: that is to say, there is Fate, or laws of the world.

But if there be irresistible dictation, this dictation understands itself. If we must accept Fate, we are not less compelled to affirm liberty, the significance of the individual, the grandeur of duty, the power character. This is true, and that other is true. But our geometry cannot span these extreme points and reconcile them. What to do? By obeying each thought frankly, by harping, or, if you will, pounding on each string, we learn at last its power. By the same obedience to other thoughts we learn theirs, and then comes some reasonable hope of harmonizing them. We are sure that, though we know not how, necessity does comport with liberty, the individual with the world, my polarity with the spirit of the times. The riddle of the age has for each a private solution. If one would study his own time, it must be by this method of taking up in turn each of the leading topics which belong to our scheme of human life, and by firmly stating all that is agreeable to experience on one, and doing the same justice to the opposing facts in the others, the true limitations will appear. Any excess of emphasis on one part would be corrected, and a just balance would be made.

But let us honestly state the facts. Our America has a bad name for superficialness. Great men, great nations, have not been boasters and buffoons, but perceivers of the terror of life, and have manned themselves to face it. The Spartan, embodying his religion in his country, dies before its majesty without a question. The Turk, who believes his doom is written on the iron leaf in the moment when he entered the world, rushes on the enemy's sabre with undivided will. The Turk, the Arab, the Persian, accepts the foreordained fate:—

"On two days, it steads not to run from thy grave,
The appointed, and the unappointed day;
On the first, neither balm nor physician can save,
Nor thee, on the second, the Universe slay."[3]

The Hindoo under the wheel is as firm. Our Calvinists in the last generation had something of the same dignity. They felt that the weight of the Universe held them down to their place. What could *they* do? Wise men feel that there is something which cannot be talked or voted away,—a strap or belt which girds the world:—

[3] From the Persian poet Ali ben Abu, rendered in English by Emerson from the German translation by von Hammer-Purgstall.

"The Destinee, ministre general,
That executeth in the world over al,
The purveiance that God hath seen beforne,
So strong it is, that though the world had sworne
The contrary of a thing by yea or nay,
Yet sometime it shall fallen on a day
That falleth not oft in a thousand yeer;
For certainly, our appetités here,
Be it or warre, or pees, or hate, or love,
All this is ruled by the sight above."
—CHAUCER: *The Knight's Tale*[4]

The Greek Tragedy expressed the same sense. "Whatever is fated that will take place. The great immense mind of Jove is not to be transgressed."[5]

Savages cling to a local god of one tribe or town. The broad ethics of Jesus were quickly narrowed to village theologies, which preach an election or favoritism. And now and then an amiable parson, like Jung Stilling[6] or Robert Huntington,[7] believes in a pistareen[8] Providence, which, whenever the good man wants a dinner, makes that somebody shall knock at his door and leave a half-dollar. But Nature is no sentimentalist,—does not cosset or pamper us. We must see that the world is rough and surly, and will not mind drowning a man or a woman, but swallows your ship like a grain of dust. The cold, inconsiderate of persons, tingles your blood, benumbs your feet, freezes a man like an apple. The diseases, the elements, fortune, gravity, lightning, respect no persons. The way of Providence is a little rude. The habit of snake and spider, the snap of the tiger and other leapers and bloody jumpers, the crackle of the bones of his prey in the coil of the anaconda,— these are in the system, and our habits are like theirs. You have just dined, and however scrupulously the slaughter-house is concealed in the graceful distance of miles, there is complicity, expensive races—race living at the expense of race. The planet is liable to shocks from comets, perturbations from planets, rendings from earthquake and volcano, alterations of climate, precessions of equinoxes. Rivers dry up by opening of the forest. The sea changes its bed. Towns and counties fall into it. At Lisbon an earthquake

[4] "The Knight's Tale," 805-14.

[5] Aeschylus, *The Suppliants*, 11. 1047-1049.

[6] Johann Henrich Jung-Stilling (1740-1817), a German physician and mystical writer. Stilling is described sympathetically by his friend Goethe in his autobiography, *Poetry and Truth*.

[7] Robert Huntington was an English orientalist who lived from 1636 to 1701; but Emerson probably means William Huntington (1745-1813), who was a popular and eccentric preacher of his own time and who predicted the downfall of the papacy in the year 1870.

[8] A Spanish coin of small value.

killed men like flies.[9] At Naples three years ago ten thousand persons were crushed in a few minutes.[10] The scurvy at sea, the sword of the climate in the west of Africa, at Cayenne, at Panama, at New Orleans, cut off men like a massacre. Our western prairie shakes with fever and ague. The cholera, the small-pox, have proved as mortal to some tribes as a frost to the crickets, which, having filled the summer with noise, are silenced by a fall of the temperature of one night. Without uncovering what does not concern us, or counting how many species of parasites hang on a bombyx,[11] or groping after intestinal parasites or infusory[12] biters, or the obscurities of alternate generation,—the forms of the shark, the *labrus*,[13] the jaw of the sea-wolf paved with crushing teeth, the weapons of the grampus, and other warriors hidden in the sea, are hints of ferocity in the interiors of nature. Let us not deny it up and down. Providence has a wild, rough, incalculable road to its end, and it is of no use to try to whitewash its huge, mixed instrumentalities, or to dress up that terrific benefactor in a clean shirt and white neckcloth of a student in divinity.

Will you say, the disasters which threaten mankind are exceptional, and one need not lay his account for cataclysms every day? Ay, but what happens once may happen again, and so long as these strokes are not to be parried by us they must be feared.

But these shocks and ruins are less destructive to us than the stealthy power of other laws which act on us daily. An expense of ends to means is fate;—organization tyrannizing over character. The menagerie, or forms and powers of the spine, is a book of fate; the bill of the bird, the skull of the snake, determines tyrannically its limits. So is the scale of races, of temperaments; so is sex; so is climate; so is the reaction of talents imprisoning the vital power in certain directions. Every spirit makes its house; but afterwards the house confines the spirit.

The gross lines are legible to the dull; the cabman is phrenologist so far, he looks in your face to see if his shilling is sure. A dome of brow denotes one thing, a pot-belly another; a squint, a pug-nose, mats of hair, the pigment of the epidermis, betray character. People seem sheathed in their tough organization. Ask Spurzheim,[14] ask the doctors, ask Quetelet[15] if temperaments decide nothing?—or if there be anything they do not decide? Read the

---

[9] The earthquake that destroyed most of Lisbon and occasioned the writing of Voltaire's *Candide*.

[10] There was a highly destructive earthquake in Naples on December 17, 1857.

[11] The moth of the silkworm.

[12] Relating to the Infusoria, microscopic marine animals.

[13] A predatory fish.

[14] Johann Spurzheim (1776–1832) was a disciple of F. J. Gall, the founder of the pseudo-science of phrenology.

[15] Lambert Quételet (1796–1874) was a Belgian mathematician who helped to found the science of statistics.

description in medical books of the four temperaments[16] and you will think you are reading your own thoughts which you had not yet told. Find the part which black eyes and which blue eyes play severally in the company. How shall a man escape from his ancestors, or draw off from his veins the black drop which he drew from his father's or his mother's life? It often appears in a family as if all the qualities of the progenitors were potted in several jars,— some ruling quality in each son or daughter of the house; and sometimes the unmixed temperament, the rank unmitigated elixir, the family vice is drawn off in a separate individual and the others are proportionally relieved. We sometimes see a change of expression in our companion and say his father or his mother comes to the windows of his eyes, and sometimes a remote relative. In different hours a man represents each of several of his ancestors, as if there were seven or eight of us rolled up in each man's skin,—seven or eight ancestors at least; and they constitute the variety of notes for that new piece of music which his life is. At the corner of the street you read the possibility of each passenger in the facial angel, in the complexion, in the depth of his eye. His parentage determines it. Men are what their mothers made them. You may as well ask a loom which weaves huckabuck[17] why it does not make cashmere, as expect poetry from this engineer, or a chemical discovery from that jobber. Ask the digger in the ditch to explain Newton's laws; the fine organs of his brain have been pinched by overwork and squalid poverty from father to son for a hundred years. When each comes forth from his mother's womb, the gate of gifts closes behind him. Let him value his hands and feet, he has but one pair. So he has but one future, and that is already predetermined in his lobes and described in that little fatty face, pigeye, and squat form. All the privilege and all the legislation of the world cannot meddle or help to make a poet or a prince of him.

Jesus said, "When he looketh on her, he hath committed adultery."[18] But he is an adulterer before he has yet looked on the woman, by the superfluity of animal and the defect of thought in his constitution. Who meets him, or who meets her, in the street, sees that they are ripe to be each other's victim.

In certain men digestion and sex absorb the vital force, and the stronger these are, the individual is so much weaker. The more of these drones perish, the better for the hive. If, later, they give birth to some superior individual, with force enough to add to this animal a new aim and a complete apparatus to work it out, all the ancestors are gladly forgotten. Most men and most women are merely one couple more. Now and then one has a new cell or camarilla[19] opened in his brain,—an architectural, a musical, or a philological knack; some stray taste or talent for flowers, or chemistry, or pigments, or story-telling, a good hand for drawing, a good foot for dancing, an athletic

[16] The four psychological types of medical theory that divided human beings according to their constitutional make-up; this was a deterministic doctrine.

[17] A rough linen fabric used for toweling.

[18] A paraphrase of Matthew v.28.

[19] A small chamber.

frame for wide journeying, etc.— which skill nowise alters rank in the scale of nature, but serves to pass the time; the life of sensation going on as before. At last these hints and tendencies are fixed in one or in a succession. Each absorbs so much food and force as to become itself a new centre. The new talent draws off so rapidly the vital force that not enough remains for the animal functions, hardly enough for health; so that in the second generation, if the like genius appear, the health is visibly deteriorated and the generative force impaired.

People are born with the moral or with the material bias;—uterine brothers with this diverging destination; and I suppose, with high magnifiers, Mr. Frauenhofer[20] or Dr. Carpenter[21] might come to distinguish in the embryo, at the fourth day,—this is a Whig, and that a Free-soiler.

It was a poetic attempt to lift this mountain of Fate, to reconcile this despotism of race with liberty, which led the Hindoos to say, "Fate is nothing but the deeds committed in a prior state of existence."[22] I find the coincidence of the extremes of Eastern and Western speculation in the daring statement of Schelling,[23] "There is in every man a certain feeling that he has been what he is from all eternity, and by no means became such in time." To say it less sublimely,—in the history of the individual is always an account of his condition, and he knows himself to be a party to his present estate.

A good deal of our politics is physiological. Now and then a man of wealth in the heyday of youth adopts the tenet of broadest freedom. In England there is always some man of wealth and large connection, planting himself, during all his years of health, on the side of progress, who, as soon as he begins to die, checks his forward play, calls in his troops and becomes conservative. All conservatives are such from personal defects. They have been effeminated by position or nature, born halt and blind, through luxury of their parents, and can only, like invalids, act on the defensive. But strong natures, backwoodsmen, New Hampshire giants, Napoleons, Burkes,[24] Broughams,[25] Websters,[26] Kossuths,[27] are inevitable patriots, until their life ebbs and their defects and gout, palsy and money, warp them.

[20] Joseph von Frauenhofer (1787-1826) was a German optician and astronomer who improved the telescope.

[21] William B. Carpenter (1813-1885) was an English biologist, author of *The Microscope, Its Revelations and Uses* (1856).

[22] A concise summary of the central doctrine of Karma, in Hindu thought.

[23] Friedrich von Schelling (1775-1854) was a German philosopher, author of *A System of Transcendental Idealism* (1800). Schelling had a significant influence on Coleridge and, through him, on Emerson.

[24] Edmund Burke (1729-1797) was an English statesman.

[25] Henry Brougham (1778-1868) was also know as Baron Brougham and Vaux, an English Whig statesman, proponent of the Reform Bill of 1832, and Lord Chancellor.

[26] Daniel Webster (1782-1852), the American statesman and orator. See p. 1726.

[27] Louis Kossuth (1802-1894) was a Hungarian patriot and statesman who lead the Hungarian Revolution in 1848 and later made a visit to America, where he was welcomed by Emerson (see *Miscellanies; Works*, XI).

The strongest idea incarnates itself in majorities and nations, in the healthiest and strongest. Probably the election goes by avoirdupois weight, and if you could weigh bodily the tonnage of any hundred of the Whig and the Democratic party in a town on the Dearborn balance, as they passed the hay-scales, you could predict with certainty which party would carry it. On the whole it would be rather the speediest way of deciding the vote, to put the selectmen or the mayor and aldermen at the hay-scales.

In science we have to consider two things: power and circumstance. All we know of the egg, from each successive discovery, is, *another vesicle;* and if, after five hundred years you get a better observer or a better glass, he finds, within the last observed, another. In vegetable and animal tissue it is just alike, and all that the primary power or spasm operates is still vesicles, vesicles. Yes,—but the tyrannical Circumstance! A vesicle in new circumstances, a vesicle lodged in darkness, Oken[28] thought, became animal; in light, a plant. Lodged in the parent animal, it suffers changes which end in unsheathing miraculous capability in the unaltered vesicle, and it unlocks itself to fish, bird, or quadruped, head and foot, eye and claw. The Circumstance is Nature. Nature is what you may do. There is much you may not. We have two things,—the circumstance, and the life. Once we thought positive power was all. Now we learn that negative power, or circumstance, is half. Nature is the tyrannous circumstance, the thick skull, the sheathed snake, the ponderous, rock-like jaw; necessitated activity; violent direction; the conditions of a tool, like the locomotive, strong enough on its track, but which can do nothing but mischief off of it; of skates, which are wings on the ice but fetters on the ground.

The book of Nature is the book of Fate. She turns the gigantic pages,— leaf after leaf,—never re-turning one. One leaf she lays down, a floor of granite; then a thousand ages, and a bed of slate; a thousand ages, and a measure of coal; a thousand ages, and a layer of marl and mud: vegetable forms appear; her first misshapen animals, zoöphyte, trilobium, fish; then, saurians,—rude forms, in which she has only blocked her future statue, concealing under these unwieldy monsters the fine type of her coming king. The face of the planet cools and dries, the races meliorate, and man is born. But when a race has lived its term, it comes no more again.

The population of the world is a conditional population; not the best, but the best that could live now; and the scale of tribes, and the steadiness with which victory adheres to one tribe and defeat to another, is as uniform as the superposition of strata. We know in history what weight belongs to race. We see the English, French, and Germans planting themselves on every shore and market of America and Australia, and monopolizing the commerce of these countries. We like the nervous and victorious habit of our own branch

[28] Lorenz Oken (1779–1851) was a German naturalist.

of the family. We follow the step of the Jew, of the Indian, of the Negro. We see how much will has been expended to extinguish the Jew, in vain. Look at the unpalatable conclusions of Knox,[29] in his Fragment of Races;—a rash and unsatisfactory writer, but charged with pungent and unforgetable truths. "Nature respects race, and not hybrids." "Every race has its own *habitat*." "Detach a colony from the race, and it deteriorates to the crab."[30] See the shades of the picture. The German and Irish millions, like the Negro, have a great deal of guano in their destiny. They are ferried over the Atlantic and carted over America, to ditch and to drudge, to make corn cheap and then to lie down prematurely to make a spot of green grass on the prairie.

One more fagot of these adamantine bandages is the new science of Statistics. It is a rule that the most casual and extraordinary events, if the basis of population is broad enough, become matter of fixed calculation. It would not be safe to say when a captain like Bonaparte, a singer like Jenny Lind, or a navigator like Bowditch[31] would be born in Boston; but, on a population of twenty or two hundred millions, something like accuracy may be had.

'T is frivolous to fix pedantically the date of particular inventions. They have all been invented over and over fifty times. Man is the arch machine of which all these shifts drawn from himself are toy models. He helps himself on each emergency by copying or duplicating his own structure, just so far as the need is. 'T is hard to find the right Homer, Zoroaster, or Menu;[32] harder still to find the Tubal Cain,[33] or Vulcan, or Cadmus, or Copernicus, or Fust,[34] or Fulton, the indisputable inventor. There are scores and centuries of them. "The air is full of men." This kind of talent so abounds, this constructive tool-making efficiency, as if it adhered to the chemic atoms; as if the air he breathes were made of Vaucansons,[35] Franklins, and Watts.

Doubtless in every million there will be an astronomer, a mathematician, a comic poet, a mystic. No one can read the history of astronomy without perceiving that Copernicus, Newton, Laplace,[36] are not new men, or a new

---

[29] Robert Knox (1790-1862) was a Scottish anatomist and ethnologist. He wrote *The Races of Man, a Fragment* (1850), in which he held that human races are as different from one another biologically as animal species.

[30] The crab apple.

[31] Nathaniel Bowditch (1773-1838) was an American mathematician, author of the popular *New American Practical Navigator* (1802).

[32] Actually Manu, the legendary author of the Hindu code, *The Laws of Manu*. Both Emerson and Thoreau were interested in its translation.

[33] See Genesis iv:22.

[34] Johann Fust (ca. 1400-66) was an early German printer, associated with Gutenberg.

[35] Jacques de Vaucanson (1709-1782) was a French mathematician and inventor who improved on that hand-loom; he also invented a mechanical duck that could pick up grains and swallow them.

[36] Marquis de Laplace (1749-1827) was a French mathematician and astronomer, the author of *Mécanique Céleste*, a systematic work. He was also the first propounder of the hypothesis of the nebular origin of the solar system.

kind of men, but that Thales, Anaximenes, Hipparchus, Empedocles, Aristarchus, Pythagoras, Œnipodes,[37] had anticipated them; each had the same tense geometrical brain, apt for the same vigorous computation and logic; a mind parallel to the movement of the world. The Roman mile probably rested on a measure of a degree of the meridian. Mahometan and Chinese know what we know of leap-year, of the Gregorian calendar, and of the precession of the equinoxes. As in every barrel of cowries brought to New Bedford there shall be one *orangia*,[38] so there will, in a dozen millions of Malays and Mahometans, be one or two astronomical skulls. In a large city, the most casual things, and things whose beauty lies in their casualty, are produced as punctually and to order as the baker's muffin for breakfast. Punch makes exactly one capital joke a week; and the journals contrive to furnish one good piece of news every day.

And not less work the laws of repression, the penalties of violated functions. Famine, typhus, frost, war, suicide and effete races must be reckoned calculable parts of the system of the world.

These are pebbles from the mountain, hints of the terms by which our life is walled up, and which show a kind of mechanical exactness, as of a loom or mill in what we call casual or fortuitous events.

The force with which we resist these torrents of tendency looks so ridiculously inadequate that it amounts to little more than a criticism or protest made by a minority of one, under compulsion of millions. I seemed in the height of a tempest to see men overboard struggling in the waves, and driven about here and there. They glanced intelligently at each other, but 't was little they could do for one another; 't was much if each could keep afloat alone. Well, they had a right to their eye-beams, and all the rest was Fate.

We cannot trifle with this reality, this cropping-out in our planted gardens of the core of the world. No picture of life can have any veracity that does not admit the odious facts. A man's power is hooped in by a necessity which, by many experiments, he touches on every side until he learns its arc.

The element running through entire nature, which we popularly call Fate, is known to us as limitation. Whatever limits us we call Fate. If we are brute and barbarous, the fate takes a brute and dreadful shape. As we refine, our checks become finer. If we rise to spiritual culture, the antagonism takes a spiritual form. In the Hindoo fables, Vishnu follows Maya through all her ascending changes, from insect and crawfish up to elephant; whatever form she took, he took the male form of that kind, until she became at last woman

[37] Thales, Anaximenes, Empedocles, and Pythagoras were pre-Socratic Greek philosophers of the fifth and sixth centuries B.C.; Hipparchus was an astronomer of the second century B.C.; Aristarchus was a grammarian of the second century B.C.; Œnipides (i.e., Œnopides) was a Greek astronomer and mathematician of the fifth century B.C.
[38] South Pacific seashell.

and goddess, and he a man and a god.[39] The limitations refine as the soul purifies, but the ring of necessity is always perched at the top.

When the gods in the Norse heaven were unable to bind the Fenris Wolf with steel or with weight of mountains,—the one he snapped and the other he spurned with his heel,—they put round his foot a limp band softer than silk or cobweb, and this held him; the more he spurned it the stiffer it drew.[40] So soft and so stanch is the ring of Fate. Neither brandy, nor nectar, nor sulphuric ether, nor hell-fire, nor ichor, nor poetry, nor genius, can get rid of this limp band. For if we give it the high sense in which the poets use it, even thought itself is not above Fate; that too must act according to eternal laws, and all that is wilful and fantastic in it is in opposition to its fundamental essence.

And last of all, high over thought, in the world of morals, Fate appears as vindicator, levelling the high, lifting the low, requiring justice in man, and always striking soon or late when justice is not done. What is useful will last, what is hurtful will sink. "The doer must suffer," said the Greeks, "you would soothe a Deity not to be soothed." "God himself cannot procure good for the wicked," said the Welsh triad.[41] "God may consent, but only for a time," said the bard of Spain. The limitation is impassable by any insight of man. In its last and loftiest ascensions, insight itself and the freedom of the will is one of its obedient members. But we must not run into generalizations too large, but show the natural bounds or essential distinctions, and seek to do justice to the other elements as well.

Thus we trace Fate in matter, mind, and morals; in race, in retardations of strata, and in thought and character as well. It is everywhere bound or limitation. But Fate has its lord; limitation its limits,—is different seen from above and from below, from within and from without. For though Fate is immense, so is Power, which is the other fact in the dual world, immense. If Fate follows and limits Power, Power attends and antagonizes Fate. We must respect Fate as natural history, but there is more than natural history. For who and what is this criticism that pries into the matter? Man is not order of nature, sack and sack, belly and members, link in a chain, nor any ignominious baggage; but a stupendous antagonism, a dragging together of

---

[39] Vishnu was one of the three gods of the Hindu Trinity, together with Brahma and Siva, who saved mankind in a series of ten avatars or incarnations. Máyá was the goddess of illusion.

[40] The story of the Fenriswolf or Fenrir is recounted in the *Younger Edda* ("Gylfi's Mocking," 34). The Fenris Wolf is associated with Loki, god of discord in Norse mythology. The "limp band" with which the mon-

ster was bound was composed of six things, including the beard of a woman, the breath of a fish, and the spittle of a bird.

[41] See Edward Davies, *The Mythology and Rites of the British Druids* (1809), p. 79. A Welsh triad is "a form of composition characterized by an arrangement of subjects or statements in groups of three" (Oxford English Dictionary).

the poles of the Universe. He betrays his relation to what is below him,—thick-skulled, small-brained, fishy, quadrumanous, quadruped ill-disguised, hardly escaped into biped,—and has paid for the new powers by loss of some of the old ones. But the lightning which explodes and fashions planets, maker of planets and suns, is in him. On one side elemental order, sandstone and granite, rock-ledges, peat-bog, forest, sea and shore; and on the other part thought, the spirit which composes and decomposes nature,—here they are, side by side, god and devil, mind and matter, king and conspirator, belt and spasm, riding peacefully together in the eye and brain of every man.

Nor can he blink the freewill. To hazard the contradiction,—freedom is necessary. If you please to plant yourself on the side of Fate, and say, Fate is all; then we say, a part of Fate is the freedom of man. Forever wells up the impulse of choosing and acting in the soul. Intellect annuls Fate. So far as a man thinks, he is free. And though nothing is more disgusting than the crowing about liberty by slaves, as most men are, and the flippant mistaking for freedom of some paper preamble like a Declaration of Independence or the statute right to vote, by those who have never dared to think or to act,—yet it is wholesome to man to look not at Fate, but the other way: the practical view is the other. His sound relation to these facts is to use and command, not to cringe to them. "Look not on Nature, for her name is fatal," said the oracle. The too much contemplation of these limits induces meanness. They who talk much of destiny, their birth-star, etc., are in a lower dangerous plane, and invite the evils they fear.

I cited the instinctive and heroic races as proud believers in Destiny. They conspire with it; a loving resignation is with the event. But the dogma makes a different impression when it is held by the weak and lazy. 'T is weak and vicious people who cast the blame on Fate. The right use of Fate is to bring up our conduct to the loftiness of nature. Rude and invincible except by themselves are the elements. So let man be. Let him empty his breast of his windy conceits, and show his lordship by manners and deeds on the scale of nature. Let him hold his purpose as with the tug of gravitation. No power, no persuasion, no bribe shall make him give up his point. A man ought to compare advantageously with a river, an oak, or a mountain. He shall have not less the flow, the expansion, and the resistance of these.

'T is the best use of Fate to teach a fatal courage. Go face the fire at sea, or the cholera in your friend's house, or the burglar in your own, or what danger lies in the way of duty,—knowing you are guarded by the cherubim of Destiny. If you believe in Fate to your harm, believe it at least for your good.

For if Fate is so prevailing, man also is part of it, and can confront fate with fate. If the Universe have these savage accidents, our atoms are as savage in resistance. We should be crushed by the atmosphere, but for the reaction of the air within the body. A tube made of a film of glass can resist the shock of the ocean if filled with the same water. If there be omnipotence in the stroke, there is omnipotence of recoil.

1. But Fate against Fate is only parrying and defence: there are also the noble creative forces. The revelation of Thought takes man out of servitude into freedom. We rightly say of ourselves, we were born and afterward we were born again, and many times. We have successive experiences so important that the new forgets the old, and hence the mythology of the seven or the nine heavens. The day of days, the great day of the feast of life, is that in which the inward eye opens to the Unity in things, to the omnipresence of law:—sees that what is must be and ought to be, or is the best. This beatitude dips from on high down on us and we see. It is not in us so much as we are in it. If the air come to our lungs, we breathe and live; if not, we die. If the light come to our eyes, we see; else not. And if truth come to our mind we suddenly expand to its dimensions, as if we grew to worlds. We are as lawgivers; we speak for Nature; we prophesy and divine.

This insight throws us on the party and interest of the Universe, against all and sundry; against ourselves as much as others. A man speaking from insight affirms of himself what is true of the mind: seeing its immortality, he says, I am immortal; seeing its invincibility, he says, I am strong. It is not in us, but we are in it. It is of the maker, not of what is made. All things are touched and changed by it. This uses and is not used. It distances those who share it from those who share it not. Those who share it not are the flocks and herds. It dates from itself; not from former men or better men, gospel, or constitution, or college, or custom. Where it shines, Nature is no longer intrusive, but all things make a musical or pictorial impression. The world of men show like a comedy without laughter: populations, interests, government, history; 't is all toy figures in a toy house. It does not overvalue particular truths. We hear eagerly every thought and word quoted from an intellectual man. But in his presence our own mind is roused to activity, and we forget very fast what he says, much more interested in the new play of our own thought than in any thought of his. 'T is the majesty into which we have suddenly mounted, the impersonality, the scorn of egotisms, the sphere of laws, that engage us. Once we were stepping a little this way and a little that way; now we are as men in a balloon, and do not think so much of the point we have left, or the point we would make, as of the liberty and glory of the way.

Just as much intellect as you add, so much organic power. He who sees through the design, presides over it, and must will that which must be. We sit and rule, and, though we sleep, our dream will come to pass. Our thought, though it were only an hour old, affirms an oldest necessity, not to be separated from thought, and not to be separated from will. They must always have coexisted. It apprises us of its sovereignty and godhead, which refuse to be severed from it. It is not mine or thine, but the will of all mind. It is poured into the souls of all men, and the soul itself which constitutes them men. I know not whether there be, as is alleged, in the upper region of our atmosphere, a permanent westerly current which carries with it all atoms which rise to that height, but I see that when souls reach a certain clearness of perception they accept a knowledge and motive above selfishness. A breath of will blows eternally through the universe of souls in the direction of the Right and Necessary. It is the air which all intellects inhale and exhale, and it is the wind which blows the worlds into order and orbit.

Thought dissolves the material universe by carrying the mind up into a sphere where all is plastic. Of two men, each obeying his own thought, he whose thought is deepest will be the strongest character. Always one man more than another represents the will of Divine Providence to the period.

2. If thought makes free, so does the moral sentiment. The mixtures of spiritual chemistry refuse to be analyzed. Yet we can see that with the perception of truth is joined the desire that it shall prevail; that affection is essential to will. Moreover, when a strong will appears, it usually results from a certain unity of organization, as if the whole energy of body and mind flowed in one direction. All great force is real and elemental. There is no manufacturing a strong will. There must be a pound to balance a pound. Where power is shown in will, it must rest on the universal force. Alaric[42] and Bonaparte must believe they rest on a truth, or their will can be bought or bent. There is a bribe possible for any finite will. But the pure sympathy with universal ends is an infinite force, and cannot be bribed or bent. Whoever has had experience of the moral sentiment cannot choose but believe in unlimited power. Each pulse from that heart is an oath from the Most High. I know not what the word *sublime* means, if it be not the intimations, in this infant, of a terrific force. A text of heroism, a name and anecdote of courage, are not arguments but sallies of freedom. One of these is the verse of the Persian Hafiz,[43] "'T is written on the gate of Heaven, 'Woe unto him who suffers himself to be betrayed by Fate!' " Does the reading of history make us fatalists? What courage does not the opposite opinion show! A little whim of will to be free gallantly contending against the universe of chemistry.

But insight is not will, nor is affection will. Perception is cold, and goodness dies in wishes. As Voltaire said, 't is the misfortune of worthy people that they are cowards; "un des plus grands malheurs des honnêtes gens c'est qu'ils sont des lâches."[44] There must be a fusion of these two to generate the

---

[42] King of the Visigoths (c. 337–410), the conqueror of Rome in 410 A.D.
[43] Hafiz was a fourteenth-century Persian poet.

[44] "One of the greatest misfortunes of worthy people is that they are cowards."

energy of will. There can be no driving force except through the conversion of the man into his will, making him the will, and the will him. And one may say boldly that no man has a right perception of any truth who has not been reacted on by it so as to be ready to be its martyr.

The one serious and formidable thing in nature is a will. Society is servile from want of will, and therefore the world wants saviours and religions. One way is right to go; the hero sees it, and moves on that aim, and has the world under him for root and support. He is to others as the world. His approbation is honor; his dissent, infamy. The glance of his eye has the force of sunbeams. A personal influence towers up in memory only worthy, and we gladly forget numbers, money, climate, gravitation, and the rest of Fate.

We can afford to allow the limitation, if we know it is the meter of the growing man. We stand against Fate, as children stand up against the wall in their father's house and notch their height from year to year. But when the boy grows to man, and is master of the house, he pulls down that wall and builds a new and bigger. 'T is only a question of time. Every brave youth is in training to ride and rule this dragon. His science is to make weapons and wings of these passions and retarding forces. Now whether, seeing these two things, fate and power, we are permitted to believe in unity? The bulk of mankind believe in two gods. They are under one dominion here in the house, as friend and parent, in social circles, in letters, in art, in love, in religion; but in mechanics, in dealing with steam and climate, in trade, in politics, they think they come under another; and that it would be a practical blunder to transfer the method and way of working of one sphere into the other. What good, honest, generous men at home, will be wolves and foxes on 'Change! What pious men in the parlor will vote for what reprobates at the polls! To a certain point, they believe themselves the care of a Providence. But in a steamboat, in an epidemic, in war, they believe a malignant energy rules.

But relation and connection are not somewhere and sometimes, but everywhere and always. The divine order does not stop where their sight stops. The friendly power works on the same rules in the next farm and the next planet. But where they have not experience they run against it and hurt themselves. Fate then is a name for facts not yet passed under the fire of thought; for causes which are unpenetrated.

But every jet of chaos which threatens to exterminate us is convertible by intellect into wholesome force. Fate is unpenetrated causes. The water drowns ship and sailor like a grain of dust. But learn to swim, trim your bark, and the wave which drowned it will be cloven by it and carry it like its own foam, a plume and a power. The cold is inconsiderate of persons, tingles your blood, freezes a man like a dewdrop. But learn to skate, and the ice will give you a graceful, sweet, and poetic motion. The cold will brace your limbs and brain to genius, and make you foremost men of time. The cold and sea will train an imperial Saxon race, which nature cannot bear to lose, and after cooping it up for a thousand years in yonder England, gives a hundred Englands, a hundred Mexicos. All the bloods it shall absorb and domineer: and more than Mexicos, the secrets of water and steam, the spasms of electricity, the ductility of metals, the chariot of the air, the ruddered balloon are awaiting you.

The annual slaughter from typhus far exceeds that of war; but right drainage destroys typhus. The plague in the sea-service from scurvy is healed by lemon juice and other diets portable or procurable; the depopulation by cholera and small-pox is ended by drainage and vaccination; and every other pest is not less in the chain of cause and effect, and may be fought off. And whilst art draws out the venom, it commonly extorts some benefit from the vanquished enemy. The mischievous torrent is taught to drudge for man; the wild beasts he makes useful for food, or dress, or labor; the chemic explosions are controlled like his watch. These are now the steeds on which he rides. Man moves in all modes, by legs of horses, by wings of wind, by steam, by gas of balloon, by electricity, and stands on tiptoe threatening to hunt the eagle in his own element. There's nothing he will not make his carrier.

Steam was till the other day the devil which we dreaded. Every pot made by any human potter or brazier had a hole in its cover, to let off the enemy, lest he should lift pot and roof and carry the house away. But the Marquis of Worcester,[45] Watt, and Fulton bethought themselves that where was power was not devil, but was God; that it must be availed of, and not by any means let off and wasted. Could he lift pots and roofs and houses so handily? He was the workman they were in search of. He could be used to lift away, chain and compel other devils far more reluctant and dangerous, namely, cubic miles of earth, mountains, weight or resistance of water, machinery, and the labors of all men in the world; and time he shall lengthen, and shorten space.

It has not fared much otherwise with higher kinds of steam. The opinion of the million was the terror of the world, and it was attempted either to dissipate it, by amusing nations, or to pile it over with strata of society,—a layer of soldiers, over that a layer of lords, and a king on the top; with clamps and hoops of castles, garrisons, and police. But sometimes the religious principle would get in and burst the hoops and rive every mountain laid on top of it. The Fultons and Watts of politics, believing in unity, saw that it was a power, and by satisfying it (as justice satisfies everybody),

[45] Edward Somerset, Marquis of Worcester (1601-1667), author of *Century of. . .Inventions* (1663); he describes the possible invention of a primitive steam engine, along with other possible creations.

through a different disposition of society,—grouping it on a level instead of piling it into a mountain,—they have contrived to make of this terror the most harmless and energetic form of a State.

Very odious, I confess, are the lessons of Fate. Who likes to have a dapper phrenologist pronouncing on his fortunes? Who likes to believe that he has, hidden in his skull, spine, and pelvis, all the vices of a Saxon or Celtic race, which will be sure to pull him down,—with what grandeur of hope and resolve he is fired,—into a selfish, hunkstering, servil, dodging animal? A learned physician tells us the fact is invariable with the Neapolitan, that when mature he assumes the forms of the unmistakable scoundrel. That is a little overstated,—but may pass.

But these are magazines and arsenals. A man must thank his defects, and stand in some terror of his talents. A transcendent talent draws so largely on his forces as to lame him; a defect pays him revenues on the other side. The sufferance which is the badge of the Jew, has made him, in these days, the ruler of the rulers of the earth. If Fate is ore and quarry, if evil is good in the making, if limitation is power that shall be, if calamities, oppositions, and weights are wings and means,—we are reconciled.

Fate involves the melioration. No statement of the Universe can have any soundness which does not admit its ascending effort. The direction of the whole and of the parts is toward benefit, and in proportion to the health. Behind every individual closes organization; before him opens liberty,—the Better, the Best. The first and worse races are dead. The second and imperfect races are dying out, or remain for the maturing of higher. In the latest race, in man, every generosity, every new perception, the love and praise he extorts from his fellows, are certificates of advance out of fate into freedom. Liberation of the will from the sheaths and clogs of organization which he has outgrown, is the end and aim of this world. Every calamity is a spur and valuable hint; and where his endeavors do not yet fully avail, they tell as tendency. The whole circle of animal life—tooth against tooth, devouring war, war for food, a yelp of pain and a grunt of triumph, until at last the whole menagerie, the whole chemical mass is mellowed and refined for higher use—pleases at a sufficient perspective.

But to see how fate slides into freedom and freedom into fate, observe how far the roots of every creature run, or find if you can a point where there is no thread of connection. Our life is consentaneous and far-related. This knot of nature is so well tied that nobody was ever cunning enough to find the two ends. Nature is intricate, overlapped, interweaved and endless. Christopher Wren said of the beautiful King's College chapel, that "if anybody would tell him where to lay the first stone, he would build such another." But where shall we find the first atom in this house of man, which is all consent, inosculation and balance of parts?

The web of relation is shown in *habitat*, shown in hibernation. When hibernation was observed, it was found that whilst some animals became torpid in winter, others were torpid in summer; hibernation then was a false name. The *long sleep* is not an effect of cold, but is regulated by the supply of food proper to the animal. It becomes torpid when the fruit or prey it lives on is not in season, and regains its activity when its food is ready.

Eyes are found in light; ears in auricular air; feet on land; fins in water; wings in air; and each creature where it was meant to be, with a mutual fitness. Every zone has its own *Fauna*. There is adjustment between the animal and its food, its parasite, its enemy. Balances are kept. It is not allowed to diminish in numbers, nor to exceed. The like adjustments exist for man. His food is cooked when he arrives; his coal in the pit; the house ventilated; the mud of the deluge dried; his companions arrived at the same hour, and awaiting him with love, concert, laughter and tears. These are coarse adjustments, but the invisible are not less. There are more belongings to every creature than his air and his food. His instincts must be met, and he has predisposing power that bends and fits what is near him to his use. He is not possible until the invisible things are right for him, as well as the visible. Of what changes then in sky and earth, and in finer skies and earths, does the appearance of some Dante or Columbus apprise us!

How is this effected? Nature is no spendthrift, but takes the shortest way to her ends. As the general says to his soldiers, "If you want a fort, build a fort," so nature makes every creature do its own work and get its living,—is it planet, animal or tree. The planet makes itself. The animal cell makes itself;—then, what it wants. Every creature, wren or dragon, shall make its own lair. As soon as there is life, there is self-direction and absorbing and using of material. Life is freedom,—life in the direct ratio of its amount. You may be sure the new-born man is not inert. Life works both voluntarily and supernaturally in its neighborhood. Do you suppose he can be estimated by his weight in pounds, or that he is contained in his skin,—this reaching, radiating, jaculating fellow? The smallest candle fills a mile with its rays, and the papillæ of a man run out to every star.

When there is something to be done, the world knows how to get it done. The vegetable eye makes leaf, pericarp, root, bark, or thorn, as the need is; the first cell converts itself into stomach, mouth, nose, or nail, according to the want; the world throws its life into a hero or a shepherd, and puts him where he is wanted. Dante and Columbus were Italians, in their time; they would be Russians or Americans to-day. Things ripen, new men come. The adaptation is not capricious. The ulterior aim, the purpose beyond itself, the correlation by which planets subside and crystallize, then animate beasts and men,—will not stop but will work into finer particulars, and from finer to finest.

The secret of the world is the tie between person and event. Person makes event, and event person. The "times," "the age," what is that but a few profound persons and a few active persons who epitomize the times?— Goethe, Hegel, Metternich, Adams, Calhoun, Guizot, Peel, Cobden, Kossuth, Rothschild, Astor, Brunel, and the rest. The same fitness must be presumed between a man and the time and event, as between the sexes, or between a race of animals and the food it eats, or the inferior races it uses. He thinks his fate alien, because the copula is hidden. But the soul contains the event that shall befall it; for the event is only the actualization of its thoughts, and what we pray to ourselves for is always granted. The event is the print of your form. It fits you like your skin. What each does is proper to him. Events are the children of his body and mind. We learn that the soul of Fate is the soul of us, as Hafiz sings,—

> "Alas! till now I had not known,
> My guide and fortune's guide are one."

All the toys that infatuate men and which they play for,—houses, land, money, luxury, power, fame, are the selfsame thing, with a new gauze or two of illusion overlaid. And of all the drums and rattles by which men are made willing to have their heads broke, and are led out solemnly every morning to parade,—the most admirable is this by which we are brought to believe that events are arbitrary and independent of actions. At the conjuror's, we detect the hair by which he moves his puppet, but we have not eyes sharp enough to descry the thread that ties cause and effect.

Nature magically suits the man to his fortunes, by making these the fruit of his character. Ducks take to the water, eagles to the sky, waders to the sea margin, hunters to the forest, clerks to counting-rooms, soldiers to the frontier. Thus events grow on the same stem with persons; are sub-persons. The pleasure of life is according to the man that lives it, and not according to the work or the place. Life is an ecstasy. We know what madness belongs to love,—what power to paint a vile object in hues of heaven. As insane persons are indifferent to their dress, diet, and other accommodations, and as we do in dreams, with equanimity, the most absurd acts, so a drop more of wine in our cup of life will reconcile us to strange company and work. Each creature puts forth from itself its own condition and sphere, as the slug sweats out its slimy house on the pear-leaf, and the woolly aphides on the apple perspire their own bed, and the fish its shell. In youth we clothe ourselves with rainbows and go as brave as the zodiac. In age we put out another sort of perspiration,—gout, fever, rheumatism, caprice, doubt, fretting and avarice.

A man's fortunes are the fruit of his character. A man's friends are his magnetisms. We go to Herodotus and Plutarch for examples of Fate; but we are examples. *"Quisque suos patimur manes,"*[46] The tendency of every man to enact all that is in his constitution is expressed in the old belief that the efforts which we make to escape from our destiny only serve to lead us into it: and I have noticed a man likes better to be complimented on his position, as the proof of the last or total excellence, than on his merits.

A man will see his character emitted in the events that seem to meet, but which exude from and accompany him. Events expand with the character. As once he found himself among toys, so now he plays a part in colossal systems, and his growth is declared in his ambition, his companions and his performance. He looks like a piece of luck, but is a piece of causation; the mosiac, angulated[47] and ground to fit into the gap he fills. Hence in each town there is some man who is, in his brain and performance, an explanation of the tillage, production, factories, banks, churches, ways of living and society of that town. If you do not chance to meet him, all that you see will leave you a little puzzled; if you see him it will become plain. We know in Massachusetts who built New Bedford, who built Lynn, Lowell, Lawrence, Clinton, Fitchburg, Holyoke, Portland, and many another noisy mart. Each of these men, if they were transparent, would seem to you not so much men as walking cities, and wherever you put them they would build one.

History is the action and reaction of these two,—Nature and Thought; two boys pushing each other on the curbstone of the pavement. Everything is pusher or pushed; and matter and mind are in perpetual tilt and balance, so. Whilst the man is weak, the earth takes up him. He plants his brain and affections. By and by he will take up the earth, and have his gardens and vineyards in the beautiful order and productiveness of his thought. Every solid in the universe is ready to become fluid on the approach of the mind, and the power to flux[48] it is the measure of the mind. If the wall remain adamant, it accuses the want of thought. To a subtle force it will stream into new forms, expressive of the character of the mind. What is the city in which we sit here, but an aggregate of incongruous materials which have obeyed the will of some man? The granite was reluctant, but his hands were stronger, and it came. Iron was deep in the ground and well combined with stone, but could not hide from his fires. Wood, lime, stuffs, fruits, gums, were dispersed over the earth and sea, in vain. Here they are, within reach of every man's day-labor,—what he wants of them. The whole world is the flux of matter over the wires of thought to the poles or points where it would build. The races of men rise out of the ground preoccupied with a thought which rules them, and divided into parties ready armed and angry to fight for this metaphysical abstraction. The quality of the thought differences the Egyptian and the Roman, the Austrian and the American. The men who

[46] "Each of us undergoes his own particular penality." This line appears in the speech of Anchises to Aeneas in the Underworld and is concerned with the life history of the soul. Emerson is referring to the fatality of an individual's personal character.
[47] Constructed with corners.
[48] To make fluid.

come on the stage at one period are all found to be related to each other. Certain ideas are in the air. We are all impressionable, for we are made of them; all impressionable, but some more than others, and these first express them. This explains the curious contemporaneousness of inventions and discoveries. The truth is in the air, and the most impressionable brain will announce it first, but all will announce it a few minutes later. So women, as most susceptible, are the best index of the coming hour. So the great man, that is, the man most imbued with the spirit of the time, is the impressionable man,—of a fibre irritable and delicate, like iodine to light. He feels the infinitesimal attractions. His mind is righter than others because he yields to a current so feeble as can be felt only by a needle delicately poised.

The correlation is shown in defects. Möller,[49] in his Essay on Architecture, taught that the building which was fitted accurately to answer its end would turn out to be beautiful though beauty had not been intended. I find the like unity in human structures rather virulent and pervasive; that a crudity in the blood will appear in the argument; a hump in the shoulder will appear in the speech and handiwork. If his mind could be seen, the hump would be seen. If a man has a see-saw in his voice, it will run into his sentences, into his poem, into the structure of his fable, into his speculation, into his charity. And as every man is hunted by his own dæmon, vexed by his own disease, this checks all his activity.

So each man, like each plant, has his parasites. A strong, astringent, bilious nature has more truculent enemies than the slugs and moths that fret my leaves. Such an one has curculios, bores, knife-worms; a swindler ate him first, then a client, then a quack, then smooth, plausible gentlemen, bitter and selfish as Moloch.

This correlation really existing can be divined. If the threads are there, thought can follow and show them. Especially when a soul is quick and docile, as Chaucer sings:—

> "Or if the soule of proper kind
> Be so parfite as men find,
> That it wot what is to come,
> And that he warneth all and some
> Of everiche of hir aventures,
> By avisions or figures;
> But that our flesh hath no might
> To understand it aright
> For it is warned too derkely."[50]

[49] George Möller (1784-1852) was a German architect, author of *Denkmaler der deutschen Baukunst*, translated into English as *Essay on the Origin and Progress of Gothic Architecture* (1825).

[50] See Chaucer, *The House of Fame*, Proem, 11. 43-51.

Some people are made up of rhyme, coincidence, omen, periodicity, and presage: they meet the person they seek; what their companion prepares to say to them, they first say to him; and a hundred signs apprise them of what is about to befall.

Wonderful intricacy in the web, wonderful constancy in the design this vagabond life admits. We wonder how the fly finds its mate, and yet year after year, we find two men, two women, without legal or carnal tie, spend a great part of their best time within a few feet of each other. And the moral is that what we seek we shall find;[51] what we flee from flees from us; as Goethe said, "what we wish for in youth, comes in heaps on us in old age,"[52] too often cursed with the granting of our prayer: and hence the high caution, that since we are sure of having what we wish, we beware to ask only for high things.

One key, one solution to the mysteries of human condition, one solution to the old knots of fate, freedom, and foreknowledge, exists; the propounding, namely, of the double consciousness. A man must ride alternately on the horses of his private and his public nature, as the equestrians in the circus throw themselves nimbly from horse to horse, or plant one foot on the back of one and the other foot on the back of the other. So when a man is the victim of his fate, has sciatica in his loins and cramp in his mind; a club-foot and a club in his wit; a sour face and a selfish temper; a strut in his gait and a conceit in his affection; or is ground to powder by the vice of his race;—he is to rally on his relation to the Universe, which his ruin benefits. Leaving the dæmon who suffers, he is to take sides with the Deity who secures universal benefit by his pain.

To offset the drag of temperament and race, which pulls down, learn this lesson, namely, that by the cunning co-presence of two elements, which is throughout nature, whatever lames or paralyzes you draws in with it the divinity, in some form, to repay. A good intention clothes itself with sudden power. When a god wishes to ride, any chip or pebble will bud and shoot out winged feet and serve him for a horse.

Let us build altars to the Blessed Unity which holds nature and souls in perfect solution, and compels every atom to serve an universal end. I do not wonder at a snow-flake, a shell, a summer landscape, or the glory of the stars; but at the necessity of beauty under which the universe lies; that all is and must be pictorial; that the rainbow and the curve of the horizon and the arch of the blue vault are only results from the organism of the eye. There is no need for foolish amateurs to fetch me to admire a garden of flowers, or a sungilt cloud, or a waterfall, when I cannot look without seeing splendor and grace. How idle to choose a random sparkle here or there, when the indwell-

---

[51] See Matthew vii: 7.

[52] The motto to the second part of Goethe's autobiography, *Poetry and Truth*.

ing necessity plants the rose of beauty on the brow of chaos, and discloses the central intention of Nature to be harmony and joy.

Let us build altars to the Beautiful Necessity. If we thought men were free in the sense that in a single exception one fantastical will could prevail over the law of things, it were all one as if a child's hand could pull down the sun. If in the least particular one could derange the order of nature,—who would accept the gift of life?

Let us build altars to the Beautiful Necessity, which secures that all is made of one piece; the plaintiff and defendant, friend and enemy, animal and planet, food and eater are of one kind. In astronomy is vast space but no foreign system; in geology, vast time but the same laws as to-day. Why should we be afraid of Nature, which is no other than "philosophy and theology embodied"? Why should we fear to be crushed by savage elements, we who are made up of the same elements? Let us build to the Beautiful Necessity, which makes man brave in believing that he cannot shun a danger that is appointed, nor incur one that is not; to the Necessity which rudely or softly educates him to the perception that there are no contingencies; that Law rules throughout existence; a Law which is not intelligent but intelligence;—not personal nor impersonal—it disdains words and passes understanding; it dissolves persons; it vivifies nature; yet solicits the pure in heart to draw on all its omnipotence.

Concord Hymn

SUNG AT THE COMPLETION OF THE BATTLE MONUMENT,[1] JULY 4, 1837

By the rude bridge that arched the flood,
Their flag to April's breeze unfurled,
Here once the embattled farmers stood
And fired the shot heard round the world.

[1] The Battle Monument is for the Minute Men who had fought the British troops at Lexington and Concord, April 19, 1775. It had been established in the mid-1830's on land presented to the town by Emerson's step-grandfather, the Reverend Ezra Ripley. Emerson was not present at the dedication of the monument on July 4, 1837. Oliver Wendell Holmes called the poem "compact, expressive, sere, solemn, musical"; and Robert Frost characterized the first four lines as "surpassing any others ever written about soldiers" [*Daedalus*, LXXXVIII (Fall 1959), 718].

The foe long since in silence slept;   5
   Alike the conqueror silent sleeps;
And Time the ruined bridge has swept
   Down the dark stream which seaward creeps.

On this green bank, by this soft stream,
   We set to-day a votive stone;   10
That memory may their deed redeem,
   When, like our sires, our sons are gone.

Spirit, that made those heroes dare
   To die, and leave their children free,
Bid Time and Nature gently spare   15
   The shaft we raise to them and thee.

1837, 1876

Give All to Love[1]

Give all to love;
Obey thy heart;
Friends, kindred, days,
Estate, good-fame,
Plans, credit and the Muse,—   5
Nothing refuse.

'T is a brave master;
Let it have scope:
Follow it utterly,
Hope beyond hope: 10
High and more high

[1] This poem appears to be irresponsible, but it is in the history of Platonic thought and was echoed by Emerson elsewhere: in his essay "Love" (*Essays: First Series*) and in "Compensation" (*Ibid.*). Robert Frost notes that "Emerson supplies the emancipating formulae for giving an attachment up for an attraction, one nationality for another nationality, one love for another love. . . . Left to myself I have gradually come to see that what Emerson was meaning in 'Give All to Love' was, Give all to Meaning. The freedom is ours to insist on meaning" [see *Daedalus*, LXXXVIII (Fall 1959), 715–716].

It dives into noon,
With wing unspent,
Untold intent;
But it is a god,   15
Knows its own path
And the outlets of the sky.

It was never for the mean;
It requireth courage stout.
Souls above doubt,   20
Valor unbending,
It will reward,—
They shall return
More than they were,
And ever ascending.   25

Leave all for love;
Yet, hear me, yet,
One word more thy heart behoved,
One pulse more of firm endeavor,—
Keep thee to-day,   30
To-morrow, forever,
Free as an Arab
Of thy beloved.

Cling with life to the maid;
But when the surprise,   35
First vague shadow of surmise
Flits across her bosom young,
Of a joy apart from thee,
Free be she, fancy-free;
Nor thou detain her vesture's hem,   40
Nor the palest rose she flung
From her summer diadem.

Though thou loved her as thyself,
As a self of purer clay,
Though her parting dims the day,   45
Stealing grace from all alive;
Heartily know,
When half-gods go,
The gods arrive.

                                                         1847

Brahma[1]

If the red slayer think he slays,
  Or if the slain think he is slain,
They know not well the subtle ways
  I keep, and pass, and turn again.[2]

Far or forgot to me is near;   5
  Shadow and sunlight are the same;
The vanished gods to me appear;
  And one to me are shame and fame.

They reckon ill who leave me out;
  When me they fly, I am the wings;   10
I am the doubter and the doubt,
  And I the hymn the Brahmin sings.

The strong gods pine from my abode,[3]
  And pine in vain the sacred Seven,[4]
But thou, meek lover of the good!   15
  Find me, and turn thy back on heaven.[5]

1856   1857, 1867

[1] "Brahma" was published in the first issue of the *Atlantic Monthly* (November 1857). Emerson drew his thoughts from two volumes that he was particularly familiar with, the *Bhagavad-Gita* and the *Katha Upanishad*. Brahma is the Hindu supreme soul of the universe. As in his sources, Emerson is concerned with the illusory nature of death, the permanence of the real Self. The personal Self is only a part of the eternal Self, which is Brahma. The body may be born and die, but the Self has an indestructible life.

[2] Cf. *The Bhagavad-Gita*, translated by Charles Wilkins.
"The Man who believeth that it is the soul which killeth, and he who thinketh that the soul may be destroyed, are both alike deceived; for it neither killeth, nor is killed."

[3] Indra, the sky-god: Agni, the god of fire; and Yama, the god of death and immortality. All three are eventually absorbed in Brahma.

[4] The seven highest saints, in the Hindu pantheon.

[5] "Surrendering all the laws, come for refuge to me alone. I will deliver thee from all the laws, come for refuge to me alone. I will deliver thee from all sins; grieve not" [Krishna to Arjuna, *Bhagavad-Gita*, Lesson the Eighteenth, *Hindu Scriptures* (Everyman), p. 286].

Days[1]

Daughters of Time, the hypocritic Days,
Muffled and dumb like barefoot dervishes,
And marching single in an endless file,
Bring diadems and fagots in their hands.
To each they offer gifts after his will,   5
Bread, kingdoms, stars, and sky that holds them all.
I, in my pleached garden,[2] watched the pomp,
Forgot my morning wishes, hastily
Took a few herbs and apples, and the Day
Turned and departed silent. I, too late,   10
Under her solemn fillet saw the scorn.

1857, 1867

[1] "Days" first appeared in the *Atlantic Monthly* (November 1857).

[2] The branches of the shrubs are interwoven or pleached and rendered flat; in that sense they are artificial.

HORATIO GREENOUGH

(1805–1852)

Horatio Greenough grew up in Boston, was graduated from Harvard in 1825, and spent most of his career studying and practicing sculpture in Rome. Befriended by James Fenimore Cooper, Greenough did sculptures of Lafayette, Washington, Cooper, and John Quincy Adams. When he returned to the United States in 1843 to observe the installation of his *Washington,* he was deeply distressed at the negative reaction to the seminudity of the statue. He felt that American taste was provincial, and he turned his attention to describing the sort of sculp-

See *Form and Function, Remarks on Art by Horatio Greenough,* Harold A. Small, 1947. The first major literary critic to establish Greenough's relationship to Emer-son and the transcendentalists was F. O. Matthiessen, *American Renaissance,* 1941, pp. 140–52.

ture and art that he considered appropriate to the United States. Like Emerson, Thoreau, and Whitman, he wanted American art to be organic, and he advocated functional beauty. Although Greenough was not able to render his theories in his own work, he expressed the view of organic art that was to be repeated by Louis Sullivan and Frank Lloyd Wright and that became the formative principle of late nineteenth- and twentieth-century American sculpture and architecture.

American Architecture[1]

We have heard the learned in matters relating to art express the opinion that these United States are destined to form a new style of architecture. Remembering that a vast population, rich in material and guided by the experience, the precepts, and the models of the Old World, was about to erect durable structures for every function of civilized life, we also cherished the hope that such a combination would speedily be formed.

We forgot that, though the country was young, yet the people were old; that as Americans we have no childhood, no half-fabulous, legendary wealth, no misty, cloud-enveloped background. We forgot that we had not unity of religious belief, nor unity of origin; that our territory, extending from the white bear to the alligator, made our occupations dissimilar, our character and tastes various. We forgot that the Republic had leaped full-grown and armed to the teeth from the brain of her parent, and that a hammer had been the instrument of delivery. We forgot that reason had been the dry nurse of the giant offspring, and had fed her from the beginning with the strong bread and meat of fact; that every wry face the bantling ever made had been daguerreotyped, and all her words and deeds printed and labeled away in the pigeonholes of official bureaus.

Reason can dissect, but cannot originate; she can adopt, but cannot create; she can modify, but cannot find. Give her but a cockboat, and she will elaborate a line-of-battle ship; give her but a beam with its wooden tooth, and she turns out the patent plow. She is not young; and when her friends insist upon the phenomena of youth, then is she least attractive. She can imitate the flush of the young cheek, but where is the flash of the young eye? She buys the teeth—alas! she cannot buy the breath of childhood. The puny

[1] In *English Traits* (1856), Emerson said of this essay that it "announced in advance the leading thoughts of Mr. Ruskin on the *morality* in architecture, notwithstanding the antagonism of their views of the history of art." Greenough's "American Architecture" was first published in 1843, in the *United States Magazine and Democratic Review*. Ruskin's *Seven Lamps of Architecture*, in which he indicated his idea that the buildings and art of a people express their morality, first appeared in 1849.

cathedral of Broadway,[2] like an elephant dwindled to the size of a dog, measures her yearning for Gothic sublimity, while the roar of the Astor House, and the mammoth vase of the great reservoir, shows how she works when she feels at home and is in earnest.

The mind of this country has never been seriously applied to the subject of building. Intently engaged in matters of more pressing importance, we have been content to receive our notions of architecture as we have received the fashion of our garments and the form of our entertainments, from Europe. In our eagerness to appropriate, we have neglected to adapt, to distinguish,—nay, to understand. We have built small Gothic temples of wood and have omitted all ornaments for economy, unmindful that size, material, and ornament are the elements of effect in that style of building. Captivated by the classic symmetry of the Athenian models, we have sought to bring the Parthenon into our streets, to make the temple of Theseus work in our towns.[3] We have shorn them of their lateral colonnades, let them down from their dignified platform, pierced their walls for light, and, instead of the storied relief and the eloquent statue which enriched the frieze and graced the pediment, we have made our chimneytops to peer over the broken profile and tell, by their rising smoke, of the traffic and desecration of the interior. Still the model may be recognized, some of the architectural features are entire; like the captive king, stripped alike of arms and purple and drudging amid the Helots of a capital, the Greek temple, as seen among us, claims pity for its degraded majesty, and attests the barbarian force which has abused its nature and been blind to its qualities.

If we trace architecture from its perfection in the days of Pericles to its manifest decay in the reign of Constantine, we shall find that one of the surest symptoms of decline was the adoption of admired forms and models for purposes not contemplated in their invention. The forum became a temple; the tribunal became a temple; the theater was turned into a church; nay, the column, that organized member, that subordinate part, set up for itself, usurped unity, and was a monument! The great principles of architecture being once abandoned, correctness gave way to novelty, economy and vainglory associated produced meanness and pretension. Sculpture, too, had waned. The degenerate workmen could no longer match the fragments they sought to mingle, nor copy the originals they only hoped to repeat. The moldering remains of better days frowned contempt upon such impotent

---

[2] The reference is apparently to Trinity Church, which was completed in 1846. Trinity is a sizable church, but puny if compared with the great European cathedrals.

[3] "The public sentiments just now runs almost exclusively and popularly into the Grecian school. We build little besides temples for our churches, our banks, our taverns, our court-houses, and our dwellings. A friend of mine has just built a brewery on the model of the Temple of the Winds."—Aristabulus Bragg, in Cooper's novel, *Home As Found* (1838).

efforts, till, in the gradual coming of darkness, ignorance became contempt, and insensibility ceased to compare.

We say that the mind of this country has never been seriously applied to architecture. True it is that the commonwealth, with that desire of public magnificence which has ever been a leading feature of democracy, has called from the vasty deep of the past the spirits of the Greek, the Roman, and the Gothic styles; but they would not come when she did call to them! The vast cathedral, with its ever-open portals, towering high above the courts of kings, inviting all men to its cool and fragrant twilight, where the voice of the organ stirs the blood, and the dim-seen visions of saints and martyrs bleed and die upon the canvas amid the echoes of hymning voices and the clouds of frankincense—this architectural embodying of the divine and blessed words, "Come to me, ye who labor and are heavy laden, and I will give you rest!" demands a sacrifice of what we hold dearest. Its cornerstone must be laid upon the right to judge the claims of the church. The style of Greek architecture, as seen in the Greek temple, demands the aid of sculpture, insists upon every feature of its original organization, loses its harmony if a note be dropped in the execution, and when so modified as to serve for a customhouse or bank, departs from its orginal beauty and propriety as widely as the crippled gelding of a hackney coach differs from the bounding and neighing wild horse of the desert. Even where, in the fervor of our faith in shapes, we have sternly adhered to the dictum of another age, and have actually succeeded in securing the entire exterior which echoes the forms of Athens, the pile stands a stranger among us, and receives a respect akin to what we should feel for a fellow citizen in the garb of Greece. It is a makebelieve. It is not the real thing. We see the marble capitals; we trace the acanthus leaves of a celebrated model—incredulous;[4] it is not a temple.

The number and variety of our experiments in building show the dissatis-faction of the public taste with what has been hitherto achieved; the expense at which they have been made proves how strong is the yearning after excellence; the talents and acquirements of the artists whose services have been engaged in them are such as to convince us that the fault lies in the system, not in the men. Is it possible that out of this chaos order can arise?—that of these conflicting dialects and jargons a language can be born? When shall we have done with experiments? What refuge is there from the absur-dities that have successively usurped the name and functions of architecture? Is it not better to go on with consistency and uniformity, in imitation of an admired model, than incur the disgrace of other failures? In answering these questions let us remember with humility that all salutary changes are the work of many and of time; but let us encourage experiment at the risk of

---

[4] In Greenough's pseudonymous *Travels* this is "incredulous odi," for *incredulus odi* in Horace's line, "Quodcunque ostendis mihi sic incredulus odi" ("Scenes put before me in this way move only my incredulity and disgust").

license, rather than submit to an iron rule that begins by sacrificing reason, dignity, and comfort. Let us consult nature, and in the assurance that she will disclose a mine richer than was ever dreamed of by the Greeks, in arts as well as in philosophy. Let us regard as ingratitude to the author of nature the despondent idleness that sits down while one want is unprovided for, one worthy object unattained.

If, as the first step in our search after the great principles of construction, we but observe the skeletons and skins of animals, through all the varieties of beast and bird, of fish and insect, are we not as forcibly struck by their variety as by their beauty? There is no arbitrary law of proportion, no un-bending model of form. There is scarce a part of the animal organization which we do not find elongated or shortened, increased, diminished, or suppressed, as the wants of the genus of species dictate, as their exposure or their work require. The neck of the swan and that of the eagle, however different in character and proportion, equally charm the eye and satisfy the reason. We approve the length of the same member in grazing animals, its shortness in beasts of prey. The horse's shanks are thin, and we admire them; the greyhound's chest is deep, and we cry, beautiful! It is neither the pres-ence nor the absence of this or that part, or shape, or color, that wins our eye in natural objects; it is the consistency and harmony of the parts juxtaposed, the subordination of details to masses, and of masses to the whole.

The law of adaptation is the fundamental law of nature in all structure. So unflinchingly does she modify a type in accordance with a new position, that some philosophers have declared a variety of appearance to be the object aimed at; so entirely does she limit the modification to the demands of necessity, that adherence to one original plan seems, to limited intelligence, to be carried to the very verge of caprice. The domination of arbitrary rules of taste has produced the very counterpart of the wisdom thus displayed in every object around us; we tie up the camelopard to the rack; we shave the lion and call him a dog; we strive to bind the unicorn with his band in the furrow, and make him harrow the valleys after us!

When the savage of the South Sea islands shapes his war club, his first thought is of its use. His first efforts pare the long shaft, and mold the convenient handle; then the heavier end takes gradually the edge that cuts, while it retains the weight that stuns. His idler hour divides its surface by lines and curves, or embosses it with figures that have pleased his eye or are linked with his superstition. We admire its effective shape, its Etruscan-like quaintness, its graceful form and subtle outline, yet we neglect the lesson it might teach. If we compare the form of a newly invented machine with the perfected type of the same instrument, we observe, as we trace it through the phases of improvement, how weight is shaken off where strength is less needed, how functions are made to approach without impeding each other, how straight becomes curved, and the curve is straightened, till the straggling and cumbersome machine becomes the compact, effective, and beautiful engine.

So instinctive is the perception of organic beauty in the human eye, that we cannot withhold our admiration even from the organs of destruction. There is majesty in the royal paw of the lion, music in the motion of the brindled tiger; we accord our praise to the sword and the dagger, and shudder our approval of the frightful aptitude of the ghastly guillotine.

Conceiving destruction to be a normal element of the system of nature equally with production, we have used the word beauty in connection with it. We have no objection to exchange it for the word character, as indicating the mere adaptation of forms to functions, and would gladly substitute the actual pretensions of our architecture to the former, could we hope to secure the latter.

Let us now turn to a structure of our own, one which, from its nature and uses, commands us to reject authority, and we shall find the result of the manly use of plain good sense, so like that of taste, and genius too, as scarce to require a distinctive title. Observe a ship at sea! Mark the majestic form of her hull as she rushes through the water, observe the graceful bend of her body, the gentle transition from round to flat, the grasp of her keel, the leap of her bows, the symmetry and rich tracery of her spars and rigging, and those grand wind muscles, her sails. Behold an organization second only to that of an animal, obedient as the horse, swift as the stag, and bearing the burden of a thousand camels from pole to pole! What academy of design, what research of connoisseurship, what imitation of the Greek produced this marvel of construction? Here is the result of the study of man upon the great deep, where Nature spake of the laws of building, not in the feather and in the flower, but in winds and waves, and he bent all his mind to hear and to obey.[5] Could we carry into our civil architecture the responsibilities that weigh upon our shipbuilding, we should ere long have edifices as superior to the Parthenon, for the purposes that we require, as the *Constitution* or the *Pennsylvania* is to the galley of the Argonauts. Could our blunders on terra firma be put to the same dread test that those of shipbuilders are, little would be now left to say on this subject.

Instead of forcing the functions of every sort of building into one general form, adopting an outward shape for the sake of the eye or of association, without reference to the inner distribution, let us begin from the heart as the

---

[5] Greenough would not allow a figurehead, certainly not a carved wooden statue painted in imitation of marble, as an embellishment to a ship. Having remarked one that has lost both arms and a leg, he wrote: "I was delighted with another proof that I had found of the perfect organization of ships, viz., that the only part of the hull where function will allow a statue to stand without being in Jack's way is one where the plunge bath so soon demolishes it."—*Travels*, p. 179.

nucleus, and work outward. The most convenient size and arrangement of the rooms that are to constitute the building being fixed, the access of the light that may, of the air that must be wanted, being provided for, we have the skeleton of our building. Nay, we have all excepting the dress. The connection and order of parts, juxtaposed for convenience, cannot fail to speak of their relation and uses. As a group of idlers on the quay, if they grasp a rope to haul a vessel to the pier, are united in harmonious action by the cord they seize, as the slowly yielding mass forms a thorough-bass to their livelier movement, so the unflinching adaptation of a building to its position and use gives, as a sure product of that adaptation, character and expression.

What a field of study would be opened by the adoption in civil architecture of those laws of apportionment, distribution, and connection which we have thus hinted at? No longer could the mere tyro huddle together a crowd of ill-arranged, ill-lighted, and stifled rooms and, masking the chaos with the sneaking copy of a Greek façade, usurp the name of architect. If this anatomic connection and proportion has been attained in ships, in machines, and, in spite of false principles, in such buildings as made a departure from it fatal, as in bridges and in scaffolding, why should we fear its immediate use in all construction? As its first result, the bank would have the physiognomy of a bank, the church would be recognized as such, nor would the billiard room and the chapel wear same uniform of columns and pediment. The African king, standing in mock majesty with his legs and feet bare, and his body clothed in a cast coat of the Prince Regent, is an object whose ridiculous effect defies all power of face. Is not the Greek temple jammed in between the brick shops of Wall Street or Cornhill, covered with lettered signs, and occupied by groups of money-changers and applewomen, a parallel even for his African majesty?

We have before us a letter in which Mr. Jefferson recommends the model of the Maison Carrée for the State House at Richmond. Was he aware that the Maison Carrée is but a fragment, and that, too, of a Roman temple? He was; it is beautiful—is the answer. An English society erected in Hyde Park a cast in bronze of the colossal Achilles of the Quirinal, and, changing the head, transformed it into a monument to Wellington. But where is the distinction between the personal prowess, the invulnerable body, the heaven-shielded safety of the hero of the Iliad and the complex of qualities which makes the modern general? The statue is beautiful—is the answer. If such reasoning is to hold, why not translate one of Pindar's odes in memory of Washington, or set up in Carolina a colossal Osiris in honor of General Greene?

The monuments of Egypt and of Greece are sublime as expressions of their power and their feeling. The modern nation that appropriates them displays only wealth in so doing. The possession of means, not accompanied by the sense of propriety or feeling for the true, can do no more for a nation than it can do for an individual. The want of an illustrious ancestry may be compensated, fully compensated; but the purloining of the coat-of-arms of a defunct family is intolerable. That such a monument as we have described should have been erected in London while Chantrey flourished, when Flaxman's fame was cherished by the few, and Baily and Behnes were already known, is an instructive fact. That the illustrator of the Greek poets and of the Lord's Prayer should in the meanwhile have been preparing designs for George the Fourth's silversmiths, is not less so.

The edifices in whose construction the principles of architecture are developed may be classed as organic, formed to meet the wants of their occupants, or monumental, addressed to the sympathies, the faith, or the taste of a people. These two great classes of buildings, embracing almost every variety of structure, though occasionally joined and mixed in the same edifice, have their separate rules, as they have a distinct abstract nature. In the former class the laws of structure and apportionment, depending on definite wants, obey a demonstrable rule. They may be called machines each individual of which must be formed with reference to the abstract type of its species. The individuals of the latter class, bound by no other laws than those of the sentiment which inspires them, and the sympathies to which they are addressed, occupy the positions and assume the forms best calculated to render their parent feeling. No limits can be put to their variety; their size and richness have always been proportioned to the means of the people who have erected them.

If, from what has been thus far said, it shall have appeared that we regard the Greek masters as aught less than the true apostles of correct taste in building, we have been misunderstood. We believe firmly and fully that they can teach us; but let us learn principles, not copy shapes; let us imitate them like men, and not ape them like monkeys. Remembering what a school of art it was that perfected their system of ornament, let us rather adhere to that system in enriching what we invent than substitute novelty for propriety. After observing the innovations of the ancient Romans, and of the modern Italian masters in this department, we cannot but recur to the Horatian precept—

"exemplaria Graeca
Nocturna versate manu, versate diurna!"°

To conclude: The fundamental laws of building found at the basis of every style of architecture must be the basis of ours. The adaptation of the forms and magnitude of structures to the climate they are exposed to, and the offices for which they are intended, teaches us to study our own varied

° Apply Greek models, with a nocturnal
hand and with a daytime hand.

wants in these respects.[6] The harmony of their ornament with the nature that they embellished, and the institutions from which they sprang, calls on us to do the like justice to our country, our government, and our faith. As a Christian preacher may give weight to truth, and add persuasion to proof, by studying the models of pagan writers, so the American builder by a truly philosphic investigation of ancient art will learn of the Greeks to be American.

The system of building we have hinted at cannot be formed in a day. It requires all the science of any country to ascertain and fix the proportions and arrangements of the members of a great building, to plant it safely on the soil, to defend it from the elements, to add the grace and poetry of ornament to its frame. Each of these requisites to a good building requires a special study and a lifetime. Whether we are destined soon to see so noble a fruit may be doubtful; but we can, at least, break the ground and throw in the seed.

We are fully aware that many regard all matters of taste as matters of pure caprice and fashion. We are aware that many think our architecture already perfect; but we have chosen, during this sultry weather, to exercise a truly American right—the right of talking. This privilege, thank God, is unquestioned—from Miller,[7] who, robbing Béranger, translates into fanatical prose, "Finissons-en! le monde est assez vieux!" to Brisbane,[8] who declares that the same world has yet to begin, and waits a subscription of two hundred thousand dollars in order to start. Each man is free to present his notions on any subject. We have also talked, firm in the belief that the development of a nation's taste in art depends on a thousand deep-seated influences beyound the ken of the ignorant present; firm in the belief that freedom and knowledge will bear the fruit of refinement and beauty, we have yet dared to utter a few words of discontent, a few crude thoughts of what might be, and we feel the better for it. We promised ourselves nothing more than that satisfaction which Major Downing[9] attributes to every man "who has had his say, and then cleared out," and we already have a pleasant consciousness of what he meant by it.

---

[6] "The fault just now is perhaps to consult the books too rigidly, and to trust too little to invention; for no architecture, and especially no domestic architecture, can ever be above reproach, until climate, the uses of the edifice, and the situation, are respected as leading considerations. Nothing can be uglier, *per se*, than a Swiss cottage, or anything more beautiful under its precise circumstances. As regards these mushroom temples which are the offspring of Mammon. let them be dedicated to whom they may, I should exactly reverse the opinion and say, that while nothing can be much more beautiful, *per se*, nothing can be in worse taste than to put them where they are."—Cooper's *Home As Found* (1838).

[7] William Miller, founder of the sect of Millerites, who prophesied that the world would be destroyed in 1843.

[8] Albert Brisbane, the father of American Fourierism. Proposals for one of his communal "Associations" called for public subscription of $400,000 of capital stock, half of which must be paid in cash.

[9] Major Downing was the pseudonym of Seba Smith, in his letters in Yankee dialect.

HENRY DAVID THOREAU

(1817–1862)

Throeau's life was one of continuous self-examination. He wished to live organically, to simplify his external life so that he could concentrate on essentials. "There are two kinds of simplicity," he remarked, "—one that is akin to foolishness, the other to wisdom. The philosopher's style of living is only outwardly simple, but inwardly complex. The savage's style is both outwardly and inwardly simple." Civilization did not civilize man, Thoreau claimed, but lured him into a constant concern with details and a pursuit of outward trappings that left him with no real sense of himself. "Simplicity, simplicity, simplicity!" Thoreau demanded, and reduced his life to its barest realities so that he confronted nature and himself directly.

Thoreau was born on July 12, 1817, in Concord, Massachusetts. His grandfather had migrated from the Isle of Jersey and had been successful as a Boston merchant; but his father suffered several financial misfortunes and did not earn a comfortable living until he began to manufacture pencils in the mid-1820's. Thoreau had an older sister and brother, Helen and John, and a second sister, Sophia, who was born in

The standard edition is the *Writings of Henry David Thoreau,* the Walden Edition, 20 vols, 1906. It will be superseded by *The Writings of Henry D. Thoreau,* 25 vols., ed. W. Harding. Two volumes in this edition have been published: *Walden,* ed. J. Stanly, 1971, and *The Maine Woods,* ed. J. Moldenauer, 1972. Other important volumes are *Consciousness in Concord: Thoreau's Lost Journal,* (1840-1841), ed. Perry Miller, 1958; *The Heart of Thoreau's Journals,* ed. Odell Shepard, 1927, and *The Collected Poems,* ed. Carl Bode, 1964. *Correspondence of Henry David Thoreau,* ed. Carl Bode and Walter Harding, 1958. A good one-volume edition is *The Portable Thoreau,* ed. Carl Bode, 1947.

Older biographies are Henry Salt, *Life of Henry David Thoreau,* 1890; F. B. Sandborn, *The Life of Henry David Thoreau,* 1917, and Henry S. Canby,*Thoreau,* 1929. A more recent study is Walter Harding, *The Days of Henry Thoreau,* 1965.

Criticism includes Mark Van Doren, *Thoreau,* 1916; J. W. Krutch, *Henry David Thoreau,* 1948; R. L. Cook, *Passage to Walden,* 1949; Walter Harding, *Thoreau: A Century of Criticism,* 1954; Leo Stoller, *After Walden: Thoreau's Changing Views on Economic Man,* 1951; Sherman Paul, *The Shores of America: Thoreau's Inward Exploration,* 1958; Walter Harding, *The Thoreau Handbook,* 1959; Lauriat Lane, ed., *Approaches to Walden,* 1961; Milton Meltzer and Walter Harding, *Thoreau Profile,* 1962; Sherman Paul, ed., *Thoreau: A Collection of Critical Essays,* 1962; Joel Porte, *Emerson and Thoreau, Transcendentalists in Conflict,* 1966; Richard Ruland, ed., *Twentieth Century Interpretations of Walden,* 1968; Charles Anderson, *The Magic Cycle of Walden,* 1968; Wendell Glick, *The Recognition of Henry David Thoreau, Selected Criticism Since 1848,* 1969; Stanley Cavell, *The Senses of Walden,* 1972; William J. Wolf, *Thoreau: Mystic, Prophet, Ecologist,* 1974. The texts are taken from *The Writings.*

1819. His closest attachment was to John, with whom he conducted a progressive private school in his home after his graduation from Harvard College in 1837. The brothers were successful teachers, but they had to close their school when John fell ill; he died suddenly of lockjaw in 1842, and Henry was so deeply affected that he himself developed a sympathetic case of the same disease. In 1839 and 1840, Thoreau carried on a courtship of Ellen Sewall, but her father, who was a Unitarian minister, intervened because of Thoreau's radical tendencies, and the relationship ended.

The most significant association of Thoreau's life was with Emerson. The two met some time in 1837, when Emerson was establishing his reputation, and the older writer had a deeply liberating influence on Thoreau. Their ideas coincided and the friendship flourished so greatly that Thoreau lived as a handyman and disciple in Emerson's house from 1841 to 1843. During this time, Thoreau began to publish extensively in *The Dial,* and shared many of Emerson's editorial responsibilities. In turn, Emerson helped Thoreau in practical ways: he arranged to have him tutor his brother's sons on Staten Island; he offered him some land that he owned near Walden Pond; he asked Thoreau to take care of his house and family while he lectured in England. Differences between the men arose, however, as Thoreau developed his own distinct ideas. He gew to resent his role as Emerson's disciple, as simply the man who embodied Emerson's ideas. Emerson might note in his journal for 1852 that "Thoreau gives me, in flesh and blood and pertinacious Saxon belief, my own ethics"; he might consider Thoreau's ideas his own, "originally dressed." But, at the same time, Thoreau was commenting on Emerson in his own journal: "I yearn toward thee my friend, but I have not confidence in thee. We do not believe in the same God." From 1845, when he moved into his cabin beside Walden Pond, until his death in 1862, Thoreau maintained his independence.

Thoreau lived at Walden Pond for two years and two months. This was the central and critical experience of his life, during which he wrote *A Week on the Concord and Merrimack Rivers,* published in 1849, and the major portion of his most significant work, *Walden* (1854). In July 1846, he was imprisoned for the night because he refused to pay his poll tax to a government that supported slavery; this experience, recorded in his essay, "Civil Disobedience" (1849), reflected a concern with antislavery activities that became more militant as the country approached the Civil War; in 1854 he lectured on "Slavery in Massachusetts" and in 1859 on "A Plea for Captain John Brown." In *Walden* Thoreau issued a strong demand for simplicity, self-honesty, and harmony between nature and himself. His view of life at Walden drew heavily on all his senses: "See, hear, smell, taste, etc., while these senses are fresh and pure," he wrote in his journal. Unlike

Emerson, Alcott, and other writers, who were in essential agreement with his ideas, he immersed himself in the natural world and reported his feelings in a specific and concrete style. The consistent theme that runs through all of his writing is the need for the individual to reform himself, to come to terms with the reality within himself. He distrusted the modern cult of progress, and his work is largely a protest against the various ways that the new industrial and materialistic America infringed on the rights of the individual.

Thoreau's later work—*The Maine Woods* (1864), *Cape Cod* (1865), and *A Yankee in Canada* (1866)—was published posthumously and indicates his continued absorption in nature, his increasing attention to naturalistic detail, and a style of writing that is marked by wit, concision, and irony. But Thoreau's distinct characteristics are most effectively rendered in *Walden* and the social essays. *Walden* is the American classic of individualism and self-reliance. "Civil Disobedience," "Slavery in Massachusetts," and "A Plea for Captain John Brown" are seminal documents in the literature of protest, and they have exercised a considerable influence on modern social reformers like Mahatma Ghandi and Martin Luther King.

From Walden

WHERE I LIVED, AND WHAT I LIVED FOR[1]

At a certain season of our life we are accustomed to consider every spot as the possible site of a house. I have thus surveyed the country on every side within a dozen miles of where I live. In imagination I have bought all the farms in succession, for all were to be bought, and I knew their price. I walked over each farmer's premises, tasted his wild apples, discoursed on husbandry with him, took his farm at his price, at any price, mortgaging it to him in my mind; even put a higher price on it,—took every thing but a deed of it,—took his word for his deed, for I dearly love to talk,—cultivated it, and him too to some extent, I trust, and withdrew when I have enjoyed it long enough, leaving him to carry it on. This experience entitled me to be regarded as a sort of real-estate broker by my friends. Wherever I sat, there I might live, and the landscape radiated from me accordingly. What is a

---

[1] Thoreau's *Walden*, which was published in 1854, is the most sustained and brilliant expression of individualism in our literature. In the essay, "Where I Lived and What I Lived For," which is the second chapter of the book and contains its essential meaning, Thoreau contrasts city life—complex and frenetic—with the simple life of the country in which he was living. His basic themes are clearly underscored: simplicity, self-trust, and the organic life

house but a *sedes*, a seat?—better if a country seat. I discovered many a site for a house not likely to be soon improved, which some might have thought too far from the village, but to my eyes the village was too far from it. Well, there I might live, I said: and there I did live, for an hour, a summer and a winter life; saw how I could let the years run off, buffet the winter through, and see the spring come in. The future inhabitants of this region, wherever they may place their houses, may be sure that they have been anticipated. An afternoon sufficed to lay out the land into orchard, woodlot, and pasture, and to decide what fine oaks or pines should be left to stand before the door, and whence each blasted tree could be seen to the best advantage; and then I let it lie, fallow perchance, for a man is rich in proportion to the number of things which he can afford to let alone.

My imagination carried me so far that I even had the refusal of several farms,—the refusal was all I wanted,—but I never got my fingers burned by actual possession. The nearest that I came to actual possession was when I bought the Hollowell place, and had begun to sort my seeds, and collected materials with which to make a wheelbarrow to carry it on or off with; but before the owner gave me a deed of it, his wife—every man has such a wife—changed her mind and wished to keep it, and he offered me ten dollars to release him. Now, to speak the truth, I had but ten cents in the world, and it surpassed my arithmetic to tell, if I was that man who had ten cents, or who had a farm, or ten dollars, or all together. However, I let him keep the ten dollars and the farm too, for I had carried it far enough; or rather, to be generous, I sold him the farm for just what I gave for it, and, as he was not a rich man, made him a present of ten dollars, and still had my ten cents, and seeds, and materials for a wheelbarrow left. I found thus that I had been a rich man without any damage to my poverty. But I retained the landscape, and I have since annually carried off what it yielded without a wheelbarrow. With respect to landscapes,—

> "I am monarch of all I *survey*,
> My right there is none to dispute." [2]

I have frequently seen a poet withdraw, having enjoyed the most valuable part of a farm, while the crusty farmer supposed that he had got a few wild apples only. Why, the owner does not know it for many years when a poet has put his farm in rime, the most admirable kind of invisible fence, has fairly impounded it, milked it, skimmed it, and got all the cream, and left the farmer only the skimmed milk.

[2] William Cowper (1731-1800), the first stanza of his "Verses Supposed to Be Written by Alexander Selkirk." Selkirk was a Scottish sailor who lived for four years alone on an island and was the model for Defoe's Robinson Crusoe.

The real attractions of the Hollowell farm, to me, were: its complete retirement, being about two miles from the village, half a mile from the nearest neighbor, and separated from the highway by a broad field; its bounding on the river, which the owner said protected it by its fogs from frosts in the spring, though that was nothing to me; the gray color and ruinous state of the house and barn, and the dilapidated fences, which put such an interval between me and the last occupant; the hollow and lichen-covered apple trees, gnawed by rabbits, showing what kind of neighbors I should have; but above all, the recollection I had of it from my earliest voyages up the river, when the house was concealed behind a dense grove of red maples, through which I heard the house-dog bark. I was in haste to buy it, before the proprietor finished getting out some rocks, cutting down the hollow apple trees, and grubbing up some young birches which had sprung up in the pasture, or, in short, had made any more of his improvements. To enjoy these advantages I was ready to carry it on; like Atlas, to take the world on my shoulders,—I never heard what compensation he received for that,—and do all those things which had no other motive or excuse but that I might pay for it and be unmolested in my possession of it; for I knew all the while that it would yield the most abundant crop of the kind I wanted. If I could only afford to let it alone. But it turned out as I have said.

All that I could say, then, with respect to farming on a large scale—I have always cultivated a garden—was, that I had had my seeds ready. Many think that seeds improve with age. I have no doubt that time discriminates between the good and the bad; and when at last I shall plant, I shall be less likely to be disappointed. But I would say to my fellows, once for all, As long as possible live free and uncommitted. It makes but little difference whether you are committed to a farm or the county jail.

Old Cato,[3] whose "De Re Rustica" is my "Cultivator," says,—and the only translation I have seen makes sheer nonsense of the passage,—"When you think of getting a farm turn it thus in your mind, not to buy greedily; nor spare your pains to look at it, and do not think it enough to go round it once. The oftener you go there the more it will please you, if it is good." I think I shall not buy greedily, but go round and round it as long as I live, and be buried in it first, that it may please me the more at last.

The present was my next experiment of this kind, which I purpose to describe more at length, for convenience putting the experience of two years into one. As I have said, I do not propose to write an ode to dejection, but to brag as lustily as chanticleer in the morning, standing on his roost, if only to wake my neighbors up.

---

[3] Cato the Elder (234-149 B.C.) was a Roman statesman. The quotation is taken from *Do Agricultura* (or *De Re Rustica*), Chapter

1. *Cultivator* was the name of a magazine for farmers.

When first I took up my abode in the woods, that is, began to spend my nights as well as days there, which, by accident, was on Independence Day, or the Fourth of July, 1845, my house was not finished for winter, but was merely a defence against the rain, without plastering or chimney, the walls being of rough, weather-stained boards, with wide chinks, which made it cool at night. The upright white hewn studs and freshly planed door and window casings gave it a clean and airy look, especially in the morning, when its timbers were saturated with dew, so that I fancied that by noon some sweet gum would exude from them. To my imagination it retained throughout the day more or less of this auroral character, reminding me of a certain house on a mountain which I had visited a year before. This was an airy and unplastered cabin, fit to entertain a travelling god, and where a goddess might trail her garments. The winds which passed over my dwelling were such as sweep over the ridges of mountains, bearing the broken strains, or celestial parts only, of terrestrial music. The morning wind forever blows, the poem of creation is uninterrupted; but few are the ears that hear it. Olympus is but the outside of the earth everywhere.

The only house I had been the owner of before, if I except boat, was a tent, which I used occasionally when making excursions in the summer, and this is still rolled up in my garret; but the boat, after passing from hand to hand, has gone down the stream of time. With this more substantial shelter about me, I had made some progress toward settling in the world. This frame, so slightly clad, was a sort of crystallization around me, and reacted on the builder. It was suggestive somewhat as a picture in outlines. I did not need to go out doors to take the air, for the atmosphere within had lost none of its freshness. It was not so much within doors as being a door where I sat, even in the rainiest weather. The Harivansa[4] says, "An abode without birds is like a meat without seasoning." Such was not my abode, for I found myself suddenly neighbor to the birds; not by having imprisoned one, but having caged myself near them. I was not only nearer to some of those which commonly frequent the garden and the orchard, but to those wilder and more thrilling songsters of the forest which never, or rarely, serenade a villager,—the wood-thrush, the veery, the scarlet tanger, the field-sparrow, the whippoorwill, and many others.

I was seated by the shore of a small pond, about a mile and a half south of the village of Concord and somewhat higher than it, in the midst of an extensive wood between that town and Lincoln, and about two miles south of that our only field known to fame, Concord Battle Ground; but I was so low in the woods that the opposite shore, half a mile off, like the rest, covered with wood, was my most distant horizon. For the first week, whenever I looked out on the pond it impressed me like a tarn high up on the side of a mountain, its bottom far above the surface of other lakes, and, as the sun

---

[4] A fifth-century Hindu epic.

arose, I saw it throwing off its nightly clothing of mist, and here and there, by degrees, its soft ripples or its smooth reflecting surface was revealed, while the mists, like ghosts, were stealthily withdrawing in every direction into the woods, as at the breaking up of some nocturnal conventicle. The very dew seemed to hang upon the trees later into the day than usual, as on the sides of mountains.

This small lake was of most value as a neighbor in the intervals of a gentle rain-storm in August, when, both air and water being perfectly still, but the sky overcast, mid-afternoon had all the serenity of evening, and the wood thrush sang around, and was heard from shore to shore. A lake like this is never smoother than at such a time; and the clear portion of the air above it being shallow and darkened by clouds, the water, full of light and reflections, becomes a lower heaven itself so much the more important. From a hilltop near by, where the wood had been recently cut off, there was a pleasing vista southward across the pond, through a wide indentation in the hills which form the shore there, where their opposite sides sloping toward each other suggested a stream flowing out in that direction through a wooded valley, but stream there was none. That way I looked between and over the near green hills to some distant and higher ones in the horizon, tinged with blue. Indeed, by standing on tiptoe I could catch a glimpse of some of the peaks of the still bluer and more distant mountain ranges in the northwest, those true-blue coins from heaven's own mint, and also of some portion of the village. But in other directions, even from this point, I could not see over or beyond the woods which surrounded me. It is well to have some water in your neighborhood, to give buoyancy to and float the earth. One value even of the smallest well is, that when you look into it you see that earth is not continent but insular. This is as important as that it keeps butter cool. When I looked across the pond from this peak toward the Sudbury meadows, which in time of flood I distinguished elevated perhaps by a mirage in their seething valley, like a coin in a basin, all the earth beyond the pond appeared like a thin crust insulated and floated even by this small sheet of intervening water, and I was reminded that this on which I dwelt was but *dry land*.

Though the view from my door was still more contracted, I did not feel crowded or confined in the least. There was pasture enough for my imagination. The low shrub oak plateau to which the opposite shore arose stretched away toward the prairies of the West and the steppes of Tartary,[5] affording ample room for all the roving families of men. "There are none happy in the world but beings who enjoy freely a vast horizon,"—said Damodara,[6] when his herds required new and larger pastures.

[5] The large region in southeast central Russia.
[6] Krishna. In Hindu religion, he is the incarnation of the god Vishnu.

Both place and time were changed, and I dwelt nearer to those parts of the universe and to those eras in history which had most attracted me. Where I lived was as far off as many a region viewed nightly by astronomers. We are wont to imagine rare and delectable places in some remote and more celestial corner of the system, behind the constellation of Cassiopeia's Chair, far from noise and disturbance. I discovered that my house actually had its site in such a withdrawn, but forever new and unprofaned, part of the universe. If it were worth the while to settle in those parts near to the Pleiades or the Hyades, to Aldebaran or Altair,[7] then I was really there, or at an equal remoteness from the life which I had left behind, divided and twinkling with as fine a ray to my nearest neighbor, and to be seen only in moonless nights by him. Such was that part of creation where I had squatted;—

> "There was a shepherd that did live,
>   And held his thoughts as high
> As were the mounts whereon his flocks
>   Did hourly feed him by."[8]

What should we think of the shepherd's life if his flocks always wandered to higher pastures than his thoughts?

Every morning was a cheerful invitation to make my life of equal simplicity, and I may say innocence, with Nature herself. I have been as sincere a worshipper of Aurora[9] as the Greeks. I got up early and bathed in the pond; that was a religious exercise, and one of the best things which I did. They say that characters were engraven on the bathing tub of King Tching-thang[10] to this effect— "Renew thyself completely each day; do it again, and again, and forever again."[11] I can understand that. Morning brings back the heroic ages. I was as much affected by the faint hum of a mosquito making its invisible and unimaginable tour through my apartment at earliest dawn, when I was sitting with door and windows open, as I could be by any trumpet that ever sang of fame. It was Homer's requiem; itself an Iliad and Odyssey in the air, singing its own wrath and wanderings.[12] There was something cosmical about it; a standing advertisement, till forbidden, of the everlasting vigor and fertility of the world. The morning, which is the most memorable season of the day, is the awakening hour. Then there is least somnolence in us; and for an hour, at least, some part of us awakes which slumbers all the rest of the

---

[7] Constellations and stars.

[8] From an anonymous English poem that was first published in 1610.

[9] In classical mythology, the goddess of the dawn.

[10] Confucius.

[11] Confucius, *The Great Learning,* "Commentator of the Philosopher Tsang," II. i.

[12] The "wrath" of Achilles is the subject of the *Iliad,* the "wanderings" of Odysseus the subject of the *Odyssey.*

day and night. Little is to be expected of that day, if it can be called a day, to which we are not awakened by our Genius,[13] but by the mechanical nudgings of some servitor, are not awakened by our own newly acquired force and aspirations from within, accompanied by the undulations of celestial music, instead of factory bells, and a fragrance filling the air—to a higher life than we fell asleep from; and thus the darkness bear its fruit, and prove itself to be good, no less than the light. That man who does not believe that each day contains an earlier, more sacred, and auroral hour than he has yet profaned, has despaired of life, and is pursuing a descending and darkening way. After a partial cessation of his sensuous life, the soul of man, or its organs rather, are reinvigorated each day, and his Genius tries again what noble life it can make. All memorable events, I should say, transpire in morning time and in a morning atmosphere. The Vedas[14] say, "All intelligences awake with the morning." Poetry and art, and the fairest and most memorable of the actions of men, date from such an hour. All poets and heroes, like Memmon,[15] are the children of Aurora, and emit their music at sunrise. To him whose elastic and vigorous thought keeps pace with the sun, the day is a perpetual morning. It matters not what the clocks say or the attitudes and labors of men. Morning is when I am awake and there is a dawn in me. Moral reform is the effort to throw off sleep. Why is it that men give so poor an account of their day if they have not been slumbering? They are not such poor calculators. If they had not been overcome with drowsiness, they would have performed something. The millions are awake enough for physical labor; but only one in a million is awake enough for effective intellectual exertion, only one in a hundred millions to a poetic or divine life. To be awake is to be alive. I have never yet met a man who was quite awake. How could I have looked him in the face?

We must learn to reawaken and keep ourselves awake, not by mechanical aids, but by an infinite expectation of the dawn, which does not forsake us in our soundest sleep. I know of no more encouraging fact than the unquestionable ability of man to elevate his life by a conscious endeavor. It is something to be able to paint a particular picture, or to carve a statue, and so to make a few objects beautiful; but it is far more glorious to carve and paint the very atmosphere and medium through which we look, which morally we can do. To affect the quality of the day, that is the highest of arts. Every man is tasked to make his life, even in its details, worthy of the contemplation of his most elevated and critical hour. If we refused, or rather used up, such paltry infomation as we get, the oracles would distinctly inform us how this might be done.

[13] In Roman belief, the guardian spirit assigned to each person at birth.

[14] Ancient Hindu scriptures.

[15] The statue of Memmon at Thebes allegedly emitted music at dawn.

I went to the woods because I wished to live deliberately, to front only the essential facts of life, and see if I could not learn what it had to teach, and not, when I came to die, discover that I had not lived. I did not wish to live what was not life, living is so dear, nor did I wish to practice resignation, unless it was quite necessary. I wanted to live deep and suck out all the marrow of life, to live so sturdily and Spartan-like as to put to rout all that was not life, to cut a broad swath and shave close, to drive life into a corner, and reduce it to its lowest terms, and, if it proved to be mean, why then to get the whole and genuine meanness of it, and publish its meanness to the world; or if it were sublime, to know it by experience, and be able to give a true account of it in my next excursion. For most men, it appears to me, are in a strange uncertainty about it, whether it is of the devil or of God and have *somewhat hastily* concluded that, it is the chief end of man here to "glorify God and enjoy him forever."[16]

Still we live meanly, like ants; though the fable tells us that we were long ago changed into men;[17] like pygmies we fight with cranes;[18] it is error upon error, and clout upon clout, and our best virtue has for its occasion a superfluous and evitable wretchedness. Our life is frittered away by detail. An honest man has hardly need to count more than his ten fingers, or in extreme cases he may add his ten toes, and lump the rest. Simplicity, simplicity, simplicity! I say, let your affairs be as two or three, and not a hundred or a thousand; instead of a million count half a dozen, and keep your accounts on your thumb-nail. In the midst of this chopping sea of civilized life, such are the clouds and storms and quicksands and thousand-and-one items to be allowed for, that a man has to live, if he would not founder and go to the bottom and not make his port at all, by dead reckoning, and he must be a great calculator indeed who succeeds. Simplify, simplify. Instead of three meals a day, if it be necessary eat but one; instead of a hundred dishes, five; and reduce other things in proportion. Our life is like a German Confederacy, made up of petty states, with its boundary forever fluctuating, so that even a German cannot tell you how it is bounded at any moment. The nation itself, with all its so-called internal improvements, which, by the way, are all external and superficial, is just such an unwieldy and overgrown establishment, cluttered with furniture and tripped up by its own traps, ruined by luxury and heedless expense, by want of calculation and a worthy aim, as the million households in the land; and the only cure for it, as for them, is in a rigid economy, a stern and more than Spartan simplicity of life and elevation of purpose. It lives too fast. Men think that it is essential that the *Nation* have commerce, and export ice, and talk through a telegraph, and ride thirty

[16] The "Shorter Catechism" of *The New England Primer.*

[17] In Greek mythology, Zeus changed ants into men because of the prayers of Aeachus who had lost many of his people through a plague.

[18] See the *Iliad*, Book II, 5.

miles an hour, without a doubt, whether *they* do or not; but whether we should live like baboons or like men, is a little uncertain. If we do not get out sleepers,[19] and forge rails, and devote days and nights to the work, but go to tinkering upon our *lives* to improve *them*, who will build railroads? And if railroads are not built, how shall we get to Heaven in season? But if we stay at home and mind our business, who will want railroads? We do not ride on the railroad; it rides upon us. Did you ever think what those sleepers are that underlie the railroad? Each one is a man, an Irishman, or a Yankee man. The rails are laid on them, and they are covered with sand, and the cars run smoothly over them. They are sound sleepers, I assure you. And every few years a new lot is laid down and run over; so that, if some have the pleasure of riding on a rail, others have the misfortune to be ridden upon. And when they run over a man that is walking in his sleep, a supernumerary sleeper in the wrong position, and wake him up, they suddenly stop the cars, and make a hue and cry about it, as if this were an exception. I am glad to know that it takes a gang of men for every five miles to keep the sleepers down and level in their beds as it is, for this is a sign that they may sometime get up again.

Why should we live with such hurry and waste of life? We are determined to be starved before we are hungry. Men say that a stitch in time saves nine, and so they take a thousand stitches to-day to save nine to-morrow. As for *work*, we haven't any of any consequence. We have the Saint Vitus' dance, and cannot possibly keep our heads still. If I should only give a few pulls at the parish bell-rope, as for a fire, that is, without setting the bell, there is hardly a man on his farm in the outskirts of Concord, notwithstanding that press of engagements which was his excuse so many times this morning, nor a boy, nor a woman, I might almost say, but would forsake all and follow that sound, not mainly to save property from the flames, but, if we will confess the truth, much more to see it burn, since burn it must, and we, be it known, did not set it on fire,—or to see it put out, and have a hand in it, if that is done as handsomely; yes, even if it were the parish church itself. Hardly a man takes a half-hour's nap after dinner, but when he wakes he holds up his head and asks, "What's the news?" as if the rest of mankind had stood his sentinels. Some give directions to be waked every half-hour, doubtless for no other purpose; and then, to pay for it, they tell what they have dreamed. After a night's sleep the news is as indispensable as the breakfast. "Pray tell me anything new that has happened to a man anywhere on this globe,"—and he reads it over his coffee and rolls, that a man has had his eyes gouged out this morning on the Wachito River,[20] never dreaming the

---

[19] Railrod ties.

[20] The Ouachita begins in Arkansas and ends in Louisiana.

while that he lives in the dark unfathomed mammoth cave of this world, and has but the rudiment of an eye himself.

For my part, I could easily do without the post-office. I think that there are very few important communications made through it. To speak critically, I never received more than one or two letters in my life—I wrote this some years ago—that were worth the postage. The penny-post is, commonly, an institution through which you seriously offer a man that penny for his thoughts which is so often safely offered in jest. And I am sure that I never read any memorable news in a newspaper. If we read of one man robbed, or murdered, or killed by accident, or one house burned, or one vessel wrecked, or one steamboat blown up, or one cow run over on the Western Railroad,[21] or one mad dog killed, or one lot of grasshoppers in the winter,— we never need read of another. One is enough. If you are acquainted with the principle, what do you care for a myriad instances and applications? To a philosopher all *news*, as it is called, is gossip and they who edit and read it are old women over their tea. Yet not a few are greedy after this gossip. There was such a rush, as I hear, the other day at one of the offices to learn the foreign news by the last arrival, that several large squares of plate glass belonging to the establishment were broken by the pressure,—news which I seriously think a ready wit might write a twelvemonth, or twelve years, beforehand with sufficient accuracy. As for Spain, for instance, if you know how to throw in Don Carlos and the Infanta, and Don Pedro and Seville and Granada,[22] from time to time in the right proportions,—they may have changed the names a little since I saw the papers,—and serve up a bull-fight when other entertainments fail, it will be true to the letter, and give us as good an idea of the exact state or ruin of things in Spain as the most succinct and lucid reports under this head in the newspapers: and as for England, almost the last significant scrap of news from that quarter was the revolution of 1649;[23] and if you have learned the history of her crops for an average year, you never need attend to that thing again, unless your speculations are of a merely pecuniary character. If one may judge who rarely looks into the newspapers, nothing new does ever happen in foreign parts, a French revolution not excepted.

What news! how much more important to know what that is which was never old! "Kieou-he-yu (great dignitary of the state of Wei) sent a man to Khoung-tseu to know his news. Khoung-tseu caused the messenger to be seated near him, and questioned him in these terms: What is your master

[21] This railroad ran from Boston to Troy, New York, and later was absorbed into the Boston and Maine railroad.
[22] Don Carlos and Don Pedro contended for the throne after the death of King Ferdinand

in 1839. The Infanta, Princess Isabella, became Queen in 1843.
[23] The British monarchy was overthrown and Charles I was executed by the Puritans under Cromwell in 1649.

doing? The messenger answered with respect: My master desires to diminish
the number of his faults, but he cannot come to the end of them. The
messenger being gone, the philosopher remarked: What a worthy messenger! What a worthy messenger!"[24] The preacher, instead of vexing the ears
of drowsy farmers on their day of rest at the end of the week,—for Sunday
is the fit conclusion of an ill-spent week, and not the fresh and brave beginning of a new one,—with this one other draggle-tail of a sermon, should
shout with thundering voice, "Pause! Avast! Why so seeming fast, but deadly
slow?"

Shams and delusions are esteemed for soundest truths, while reality is
fabulous. If men would steadily observe realities only, and not allow themselves to be deluded, life, to compare it with such things as we know, would
be like a fairy tale and the Arabian Nights' Entertainments. If we respected
only what is inevitable and has a right to be, music and poetry would resound along the streets. When we are unhurried and wise, we perceive that
only great and worthy things have any permanent and absolute existence,
that petty fears and petty pleasures are but the shadow of the reality. This is
always exhilarating and sublime. By closing the eyes and slumbering, and
consenting to be deceived by shows, men establish and confirm their daily
life of routine and habit everywhere, which still is built on purely illusory
foundations. Children, who play life, discern its true law and relations more
clearly than men, who fail to live it worthily, but who think that they are
wiser by experience, that is, by failure. I have read in a Hindoo book, that
"there was a king's son, who, being expelled in infancy from his native city,
was brought up by a forester, and, growing up to maturity in that state,
imagined himself to belong to the barbarous race with which he lived. One
of his father's ministers having discovered him, revealed to him what he was,
and the misconception of his character was removed, and he knew himself to
be a prince. So soul," continues the Hindoo philosopher, "from the circumstances in which it is placed, mistakes its own character, until the truth is
revealed to it by some holy teacher, and then it knows itself to be
Brahma."[25] I perceive that we inhabitants of New England live this mean
life that we do because our vision does not penetrate the surface of things.
We think that that *is* which *appears* to be. If a man should walk through this
town and see only the reality, where, think you, would the "Mill-dam" go to?
If he should give us an account of the realities he beheld there, we should
not recognize the place in his description. Look at a meeting-house, or a
court-house, or a jail, or a shop, or a dwelling-house, and say what that thing
really is before a true gaze, and they would all go to pieces in your account
of them. Men esteem truth remote, in the outskirts of the system, behind the

[24] See Confucius, *Analects*, XIV, xxvi.

[25] In Hindu theology, Brahma is God the
Creator, the unchanging Self, the opposite of
Maya, which is illusion or the changing world
of physical appearances.

farthest star, before Adam and after the last man. In eternity there is indeed something true and sublime. But all these times and places and occasions are now and here. God himself culminates in the present moment, and will never be more divine in the lapse of all the ages. And we are enabled to apprehend at all what is sublime and noble only by the perpetual instilling and drenching of the reality that surrounds us. The universe constantly and obediently answers to our conceptions; whether we travel fast or slow, the track is laid for us. Let us spend our lives in conceiving then. The poet or the artist never yet had so fair and noble a design but some of his posterity at least could accomplish it.

Let us spend one day as deliberately as Nature, and not be thrown off the track by every nutshell and mosquito's wing that falls on the rails. Let us rise early and fast, or break fast, gently and without perturbation; let company come and let company go, let the bells ring and the children cry,—determined to make a day of it. Why should we knock under and go with the stream? Let us not be upset and overwhelmed in that terrible rapid and whirlpool called a dinner, situated in the meridian shallows. Weather this danger and you are safe, for the rest of the way is down hill. With unrelaxed nerves, with morning vigor, sail by it, looking another way, tied to the mast like Ulysses.[26] If the engine whistles, let it whistle till it is hoarse for its pains. If the bell rings, why should we run? We will consider what kind of music they are like. Let us settle ourselves, and work and wedge our feet downward through the mud and slush of opinion, and prejudice, and tradition, and delusion, and appearance, that alluvion which covers the globe, through Paris and London, through New York and Boston and Concord, through Church and State, through poetry and philosophy and religion, till we come to a hard bottom and rocks in place, which we can call *reality*, and say, This is, and no mistake; and then begin, having a *point d'appui*,[27] below freshet and frost and fire, a place where you might found a wall or a state, or set a lamp-post safely, or perhaps a gauge, not a Nilometer,[28] but a Realometer, that future ages might know how deep a freshet of shams and appearances had gathered from time to time. If you stand right fronting and face to face to a fact, you will see the sun glimmer on both its surfaces, as if it were a cimeter,[29] and feel its sweet edge dividing you through the heart and marrow, and so you will happily conclude your mortal career. Be it life or death, we crave only reality. If we are really dying, let us hear the rattle in our throats and feel cold in the extremities; if we are alive, let us go about our business.

---

[26] In Homer's *Odyssey*, Book XII, Ulysses (or Odysseus) has himself tied to the mast so that he will not be tempted to jump overboard like the sailors who hear the songs. Ulysses soon meets Charybdis, a whirlpool, in Book XII, but avoids it.

[27] A point of support or a foundation.

[28] An ancient device used to record the rise and fall of the Nile.

[29] Scimitar, a short curved sword.

Time is but the stream I go a-fishing in. I drink at it; but while I drink I see the sandy bottom and detect how shallow it is. Its thin current slides away, but eternity remains. I would drink deeper; fish in the sky, whose bottom is pebbly with stars. I cannot count one. I know not the first letter of the alphabet. I have always been regretting that I was not as wise as the day I was born. The intellect is a cleaver; it discerns and rifts its way into the secret of things. I do not wish to be any more busy with my hands than is necessary. My head is hands and feet. I feel all my best faculties concentrated in it. My instinct tells me that my head is an organ for burrowing, as some creatures use their snout and fore paws, and with it I would mine and burrow my way through these hills. I think that the richest vein is somewhere hereabouts; so by the divining-rod and thin rising vapors I judge; and here I will begin to mine.

CONCLUSION

To the sick the doctors wisely recommend a change of air and scenery. Thank Heaven, here is not all the world. The buckeye does not grow in New England, and the mockingbird is rarely heard here. The wild goose is more of a cosmopolite than we; he breaks his fast in Canada, takes a luncheon in the Ohio, and plumes himself for the night in a southern bayou. Even the bison, to some extent, keeps pace with the seasons, cropping the pastures of the Colorado only till a greener and sweeter grass awaits him by the Yellowstone. Yet we think that if rail fences are pulled down, and stone walls piled up on our farms, bounds are henceforth set to our lives and our fates decided. If you are chosen town clerk, forsooth, you cannot go to Tierra del Fuego[1] this summer: but you may go to the land of infernal fire nevertheless. The universe is wider than our views of it.

Yet we should oftener look over the tafferel of our craft, like curious passengers, and not make the voyage like stupid sailors picking oakum.[2] The other side of the globe is but the home of our correspondent. Our voyaging is only great-circle sailing,[3] and the doctors prescribe for diseases of the skin merely. One hastens to southern Africa to chase the giraffe; but surely that is not the game he would be after. How long, pray, would a man hunt giraffes if he could? Snipes and woodcocks also may afford rare sport; but I trust it would be nobler game to shoot one's self.—

[1] Islands off the tip of South America. The term means "Land of Fire."

[2] Fibers that are picked from old ropes and used for caulking. The word derives from "outcomb."

[3] Navigation between the shortest distance joining two points on the earth's surface.

"Direct your eye right inward, and you'll find
A thousand regions in your mind
Yet undiscovered. Travel them, and be
Expert in home-cosmography."[4]

What does Africa,—what does the West stand for? Is not our own interior white on the chart? black though it may prove, like the coast, when discovered. Is it the source of the Nile, or the Niger, or the Mississippi, or a Northwest Passage around this continent, that we would find? Are these the problems which most concern mankind? Is Franklin the only man who is lost, that his wife should be so earnest to find him? Does Mr. Grinnell[5] know where he himself is? Be rather the Mungo Park, the Lewis and Clark and Frobisher,[6] of your own streams and oceans; explore your own higher latitudes,—with shiploads of preserved meats to support you, if they be necessary; and pile the empty cans sky-high for a sign. Were preserved meats invented to preserve meat merely? Nay, be a Columbus to whole new continents and worlds within you, opening new channels, not of trade, but of thought. Every man is the lord of a realm beside which the earthly empire of the Czar is but a petty state, a hummock left by the ice. Yet some can be patriotic who have no *self*-respect, and sacrifice the greater to the less. They love the soil which makes their graves, but have no sympathy with the spirit which may still animate their clay. Patriotism is a maggot in their heads. What was the meaning of that South-Sea Exploring Expedition,[7] with all its parade and expense, but an indirect recognition of the fact that there are continents and seas in the moral world to which every man is an isthmus or an inlet, yet unexplored by him, but that it is easier to sail many thousand miles through cold and storm and cannibals, in a government ship, with five hundred men and boys to assist one, than it is to explore the private sea, the Atlantic and Pacific Ocean of one's being alone.—

"Erret, et extremos alter scrutetur Iberos.
Plus habet hic vitae, plus habet ille viae."

Let them wander and scrutinize the outlandish Australians.
I have more of God, they more of the road.[8]

---

[4] William Habbington (1605-1664), "To My Honoured Friend Sir Ed. P. Knight."

[5] Sir John Franklin (1786-1847) was an English explorer who was lost in his attempt to find the Northwest Passage in the Arctic in 1847. The American Henry Grinnell (1799-1847) led an expedition to search for him.

[6] Mungo Park was an eighteenth-century Scottish explorer of Africa; Sir Martin Frobisher was a sixteenth-century English explorer for the Northwest Passage.

[7] A U.S. Naval expedition that explored the South Pacific from 1838 to 1842.

[8] From "The Old Man of Verona," by Claudian (A.D. 400). Thoreau translates vitae (life) as "God" and alters Iberians to Australians.

It is not worth the while to go round the world to count the cats in Zanzibar. Yet do this even till you can do better, and you may perhaps find some "Symmes' Hole"[9] by which to get at the inside at last. England and France, Spain and Portugal, Gold Coast and Slave Coast, all front on this private sea; but no bark from them has ventured out of sight of land, though it is without doubt the direct way to India. If you would learn to speak all tongues and conform to the customs of all nations, if you would travel farther than all travellers, be naturalized in all climes, and cause the Sphinx[10] to dash her head against a stone, even obey the precept of the old philosopher,[11] and explore thyself. Herein are demanded the eye and the nerve. Only the defeated and deserters go to the wars, cowards that run away and enlist. Start now on that farthest western way, which does not pause at the Mississippi or the Pacific, nor conduct toward a worn-out China or Japan, but leads on direct, a tangent to this sphere, summer and winter, day and night, sun down, moon down, and at last earth down too.

It is said that Mirabeau[12] took to highway robbery "to ascertain what degree of resolution was necessary in order to place one's self in formal opposition to the most sacred laws of society." He declared that "a soldier who fights in the ranks does not require half so much courage as a footpad,"—"that honor and religion have never stood in the way of a well-considered and a firm resolve." This was manly, as the world goes; and yet it was idle, if not desperate. A saner man would have found himself often enough "in formal opposition" to what are deemed "the most sacred laws of society," through obedience to yet more sacred laws, and so have tested his resolution without going out of his way. It is not for a man to put himself in such an attitude to society, but to maintain himself in whatever attitude he find himself through obedience to the laws of his being, which will never be one of opposition to a just government, if he should chance to meet with such.

I left the woods for as good a reason as I went there. Perhaps it seemed to me that I had several more lives to live, and could not spare any more time for that one. It is remarkable how easily and insensibly we fall into a particular route, and make a beaten track for ourselves. I had not lived there a week before my feet wore a path from my door to the pondside; and though it is five or six years since I trod it, it is still quite distinct. It is true, I fear,

---

[9] John Symmes was a captain in the Army who tried to create an expedition to search for entrance holes in the earth at the North and South poles; he felt that the earth was hollow and inhabitable.

[10] In Greek mythology, the winged monster near Thebes strangled all those who could not solve the riddle she posed. When Oedipus solved the riddle, she destroyed herself

in the manner Thoreau describes. See Sophocles' *Oedipus Rex*.

[11] Thoreau is referring to the maxim, "Know Thyself," which was associated with Socrates (469?–399 B.C.), the Greek philosopher.

[12] Honore Riqueti Count de Mirabeau (1749-1791) was a leader of the French Revolution, a count, statesman, and orator.

that others may have fallen into it, and so helped to keep it open. The surface of the earth is soft and impressible by the feet of men; and so with the paths which the mind travels. How worn and dusty, then, must be the highways of the world, how deep the ruts of tradition and conformity! I did not wish to take a cabin passage, but rather to go before the mast and on the deck of the world, for there I could best see the moonlight amid the mountains. I do not wish to go below now.

I learned this, at least, by my experiment: that if one advances confidently in the direction of his dreams and endeavors to live the life which he has imagined, he will meet with a success unexpected in common hours. He will put some things behind, will pass an invisible boundary; new, universal, and more liberal laws will begin to establish themselves around and within him; or the old laws be expanded, and interpreted in his favor in a more liberal sense, and he will live with the license of a higher order of beings. In proportion as he simplifies his life, the laws of the universe will appear less complex, and solitude will not be solitude, nor poverty poverty, nor weakness weakness. If you have built castles in the air, your work need not be lost; that is where they should be. Now put the foundations under them.

It is a ridiculous demand which England and America make, that you shall speak so that they can understand you. Neither men nor toadstools grow so. As if that were important, and there were not enough to understand you without them. As if Nature could support but one order of understandings, could not sustain birds as well as quadrupeds, flying as well as creeping things, and *hush* and *whoa*, which Bright[13] can understand, were the best English. As if there were safety in stupidity alone. I fear chiefly lest my expression may not be *extra-vagant*[14] enough, may not wander far enough beyond the narrow limits of my daily experience, so as to be adequate to the truth of which I have been convinced. *Extra vagance!* it depends on how you are yarded. The migrating buffalo, which seeks new pastures in another latitude, is not extravagant like the cow which kicks over the pail, leaps the cowyard fence, and runs after her calf, in milking time. I desire to speak somewhere without bounds; like a man in a waking moment, to men in their waking moments; for I am convinced that I cannot exaggerate enough even to lay the foundation of a true expression. Who that has heard a strain of music feared then lest he should speak extravagantly any more forever? In view of the future or possible, we should live quite laxly and undefined in front, our outlines dim and misty on that side; as our shadows reveal an insensible perspiration toward the sun. The volatile truth of our words should continually betray the inadequacy of the residual statement. Their truth is instantly *translated;* its literal monument alone remains. The words

[13] The common term for an ox, for whom *hush* and *whoa* were driving calls.

[14] From the Latin *extra* ("beyond" or "outside") and *vagari* ("to wander").

which express our faith and piety are not definite; yet they are significant and fragrant like frankincense to superior natures.

Why level downward to our dullest perception always, and praise that as common sense? The commonest sense is the sense of men asleep, which they express by snoring. Sometimes we are inclined to class those who are once-and-a-half-witted with the half-witted, because we appreciate only a third part of their wit. Some would find fault with the morning red, if they ever got up early enough. "They pretend," as I hear, "that the verses of Kabir[15] have four different senses; illusion, spirit, intellect, and the exoteric doctrine of the Vedas"; but in this part of the world it is considered a ground for complaint if a man's writings admit of more than one interpretation. While England endeavors to cure the potato-rot, will not any endeavor to cure the brain-rot, which prevails so much more widely and fatally?

I do not suppose that I have attained to obscurity, but I should be proud if no more fatal fault were found with my pages on this score than was found with the Walden ice. Southern customers objected to its blue color, which is the evidence of its purity, as if it were muddy, and preferred the Cambridge ice, which is white, but tastes of weeds. The purity men love is like the mists which envelop the earth, and not like the azure ether beyond.

Some are dinning in our ears that we Americans, and moderns generally, are intellectual dwarfs compared with the ancients, or even the Elizabethan men. But what is that to the purpose? A living dog is better than a dead lion.[16] Shall a man go and hang himself because he belongs to the race of pygmies, and not be the biggest pygmy that he can? Let every one mind his own business, and endeavor to be what he was made.

Why should we be in such desperate haste to succeed and in such desperate enterprises? If a man does not keep pace with his companions, perhaps it is because he hears a different drummer. Let him step to the music which he hears, however measured or far away. It is not important that he should mature as soon as an apple tree or an oak. Shall he turn his spring into summer? If the condition of things which we were made for is not yet, what were any reality which we can substitute? We will not be shipwrecked on a vain reality. Shall we with pains erect a heaven of blue glass over ourselves, though when it is done we shall be sure to gaze still at the true ethereal heaven far above, as if the former were not?

There was an artist[17] in the city of Kouroo who was disposed to strive after perfection. One day it came into his mind to make a staff. Having considered that in an imperfect work time is an ingredient, but into a perfect

---

[15] Kabir (1450?–1518) was an Indian reformer. This quotation is translated from Garcin de Tassy, *Histoire de la Litterature Hindoui* (1839), the *History of Hindu Literature*.

[16] Cf. Ecclesiastes, ix: 4.

[17] This legend was created by Thoreau from the *Bhagavad-Gita*.

work time does not enter, he said to himself, It shall be perfect in all respects, though I should do nothing else in my life. He proceeded instantly to the forest for wood, being resolved that it should not be made of unsuitable material; and as he searched for and rejected stick after stick, his friends gradually deserted him, for they grew old in their works and died, but he grew not older by a moment. His singleness of purpose and resolution, and his elevated piety, endowed him, without his knowledge, with perennial youth. As he made no compromise with Time, Time kept out of his way, and only sighed at a distance because he could not overcome him. Before he had found a stick in all respects suitable the city of Kouroo was a hoary ruin, and he sat on one of its mounds to peel the stick. Before he had given it the proper shape the dynasty of the Candahars was at an end, and with the point of the stick he wrote the name of the last of that race in the sand, and then resumed his work. By the time he had smoothed and polished the staff Kalpa was no longer the pole-star; and ere he had put on the ferule and the head adorned with precious stones, Brahma had awoke and slumbered many times. [18] But why do I stay to mention these things? When the finishing stroke was put to his work, it suddenly expanded before the eyes of the astonished artist into the fairest of all the creations of Brahma. He had made a new system in making a staff, a world with full and fair proportions; in which, though the old cities and dynasties had passed away, fairer and more glorious ones had taken their places. And now he saw by the heap of shavings still fresh at his feet, that, for him and his work, the former lapse of time had been an illusion, and that no more time had elapsed than is required for a single scintillation from the brain of Brahma to fall on and inflame the tinder of a mortal brain. The material was pure, and his art was pure; how could the result be other than wonderful?

No face which we can give to a matter will stead us so well at last as the truth. This alone wears well. For the most part, we are not where we are, but in a false position. Through an infirmity of our natures, we suppose a case, and put ourselves into it, and hence are in two cases at the same time, and it is doubly difficult to get out. In sane moments we regard only the facts, the case that is. Say what you have to say, not what you ought. Any truth is better than make-believe. Tom Hyde, the tinker, standing on the gallows, was asked if he had anything to say. "Tell the tailors," said he, "to remember to make a knot in their thread before they take the first stitch." His companion's prayer is forgotton.

However mean your life is, meet it and live it; do not shun it and call it hard names. It is not so bad as you are. It looks poorest when you are richest. The faultfinder will find faults even in paradise. Love your life, poor as it is.

---

[18] In Hindu belief, a waking day and a night of sleep for Brahma lasted more than 4 billion years.

You may perhaps have some pleasant, thrilling glorious hours, even in a poorhouse. The setting sun is reflected from the windows of the almshouse as brightly as from the rich man's abode; the snow melts before its door as early in the spring. I do not see but a quiet mind may live as contentedly there, and have as cheering thoughts, as in a palace. The town's poor seem to me often to live the most independent lives of any. Maybe they are simply great enough to receive without misgiving. Most think that they are above being supported by the town; but it oftener happens that they are not above supporting themselves by dishonest means, which should be more disreputable. Cultivate poverty like a garden herb, like sage. Do not trouble yourself much to get new things, whether clothes or friends. Turn the old; return to them. Things do not change; we change. Sell your clothes and keep your thoughts. God will see that you do not want society. If I were confined to a corner of a garret all my days, like a spider, the world would be just as large to me while I had my thoughts about me. The philosopher[19] said: "From an army of three divisions one can take away its general, and put it in disorder; from the man the most abject and vulgar one cannot take away his thought." Do not seek so anxiously to be developed, to subject yourself to many influences to be played on; it is all dissipation. Humility like darkness reveals the heavenly lights. The shadows of poverty and meanness gather around us, "and lo! creation widens to our view."[20] We are often reminded that if there were bestowed on us the wealth of Crœsus,[21] our aims must still be the same, and our means essentially the same. Moreover, if you are restricted in your range by poverty, if you cannot buy books and newspapers, for instance, you are but confined to the most significant and vital experiences; you are compelled to deal with the material which yields the most sugar and the most starch. It is life near the bone where it is sweetest. You are defended from being a trifler. No man loses ever on a lower level by magnanimity on a higher. Superfluous wealth can buy superfluities only. Money is not required to buy one necessary of the soul.

I live in the angle of a leaden wall, into whose composition was poured a little alloy of bell-metal. Often, in the repose of my mid-day, there reaches my ears a confused *tintinnabulum*[22] from without. It is the noise of my contemporaries. My neighbors tell me of their adventures with famous gentlemen and ladies, what notabilities they met at the dinner-table; but I am no more interested in such things than in the contents of the Daily Times. The interest and the conversation are about costume and manners chiefly; but a goose is a goose still, dress it as you will. They tell me of California and

[19] Confucius. The quotation is from *Analects*, IX, xxv.

[20] From "Night and Death" by Joseph Blanco White (1775-1841), an English poet and ecclesiastic.

[21] Sixth-century B.C. ruler in Asia Minor known for his fabulous wealth.

[22] Latin for "a little tinkling bell."

Texas, of England and the Indies, of the Hon. Mr.——of Georgia or of Massachusetts, all transient and fleeting phenomena, till I am ready to leap from their court-yard like the Mameluke bey.[23] I delight to come to my bearings,—not walk in procession with pomp and parade, in a conspicuous place, but to walk even with the Builder of the universe, if I may,—not to live in this restless, nervous, bustling, trivial Nineteenth Century, but stand or sit thoughtfully while it goes by. What are men celebrating? They are all on a committee of arrangements, and hourly expect a speech from somebody. God is only the president of the day, and Webster is his orator. I love to weigh, to settle, to gravitate toward that which most strongly·and rightfully attracts me;—not hang by the beam of the scale and try to weigh less,—not suppose a case, but take the case that is; to travel the only path I can, and that on which no power can resist me. It affords me no satisfaction to commence to spring an arch before I have got a solid foundation. Let us not play at kittly-benders.[24] There is a solid bottom everywhere. We read that the traveller asked the boy if the swamp before him had a hard bottom. The boy replied that it had. But presently the traveller's horse sank in up to the girths, and he observed to the boy, "I thought you said that this bog had a hard bottom." "So it has," answered the latter, "but you have not got half way to it yet." So it is with the bogs and quicksands of society; but he is an old boy that knows it. Only what is thought, said, or done at a certain rare coincidence is good. I would not be one of those who will foolishly drive a nail into mere lath and plastering; such a deed would keep me awake nights. Give me a hammer, and let me feel for the furring.[25] Do not depend on the putty. Drive a nail home and clinch it so faithfully that you can wake up in the night and think of your work with satisfaction,—a work at which you would not be ashamed to invoke the Muse. So will help you God, and so only. Every nail driven should be as another rivet in the machine of the universe, you carrying on the work.

Rather than love, than money, than fame, give me truth. I sat at a table where were rich food and wine in abundance, and obsequious attendance, but sincerity and truth were not; and I went hungry from the inhospitable board. The hospitality was as cold as the ices. I thought that there was no need of ice to freeze them. They talked to me of the age of the wine and the fame of the vintage; but I thought of an older, a newer, and purer wine, of a more glorious vintage, which they had not got, and could not buy. The style, the house and grounds and "entertainment" pass for nothing with me. I called on the king, but he made me wait in his hall, and conducted like a man incapacitated for hospitality. There was a man in my neighborhood who

---

[23] *Bey* means prince in Turkish. One prince allegedly escaped the Massacre of the Mamelukes (an Egyptian military caste) in 1811 by leaping from the wall on to a horse.

[24] A children's dare game of skating or running on thin ice.

[25] The wooden supports beneath the lathwork.

lived in a hollow tree. His manners were truly regal. I should have done better had I called on him.

How long shall we sit in our porticoes practising idle and musty virtues, which any work would make impertinent? As if one were to begin the day with long-suffering, and hire a man to hoe his potatoes; and in the afternoon go forth to practise Christian meekness and charity with goodness aforethought! Consider the China pride and stagnant self-complacency of mankind. This generation inclines a little to congratulate itself on being the last of an illustrious line; and in Boston and London and Paris and Rome, thinking of its long descent, it speaks of its progress in art and science and literature with satisfaction. There are the Records of the Philosophical Societies, and the public Eulogies of *Great Men!* It is the good Adam contemplating his own virtue. "Yes, we have done great deeds, and sung divine songs, which shall never die,"—that is, as long as *we* can remember them. The learned societies and great men of Assyria,—where are they? What youthful philosophers and experimentalists we are! There is not one of my readers who has yet lived a whole human life. These may be but the spring months in the life of the race. If we have had the seven-years' itch, we have not seen the seventeen-year locust yet in Concord. We are acquainted with a mere pellicle of the globe on which we live. Most have not delved six feet beneath the surface, nor leaped as many above it. We know not where we are. Beside, we are sound asleep nearly half our time. Yet we esteem ourselves wise, and have an established order on the surface. Truly, we are deep thinkers, we are ambitious spirits! As I stand over the insect crawling amid the pine needles on the forest floor, and endeavoring to conceal itself from my sight, and ask myself why it will cherish those humble thoughts, and hide its head from me who might, perhaps, be its benefactor, and impart to its race some cheering information, I am reminded of the greater Benefactor and Intelligence that stands over me the human insect.

There is an incessant influx of novelty into the world and yet we tolerate incredible dulness. I need only suggest what kind of sermons are still listened to in the most enlightened countries. There are such words as joy and sorrow, but they are only the burden of a psalm, sung with a nasal twang, while we believe in the ordinary and mean. We think that we can change our clothes only. It is said that the British Empire is very large and respectable, and that the United States are a first-rate power. We do not believe that a tide rises and falls behind every man which can float the British Empire like a chip, if he should ever harbor it in his mind. Who knows what sort of seventeen-year locust will next come out of the ground? The government of the world I live in was not framed, like that of Britain, in after-dinner conversations over the wine.

The life in us is like the water in the river. It may rise this year higher than man has ever known it, and flood the parched uplands; even this may be the eventful year, which will drown out all our muskrats. It was not always dry land where we dwell. I see far inland the banks which the stream anciently washed, before science began to record its freshets. Every one has heard the story which has gone the rounds of New England, of a strong and beautiful bug which came out of the dry leaf of an old table of apple-tree wood, which had stood in a farmer's kitchen for sixty years, first in Connecticut, and afterward in Massachusetts,—from an egg deposited in the living tree many years earlier still, as appeared by counting the annual layers beyond it; which was heard gnawing out for several weeks, hatched perchance by the heat of an urn. Who does not feel his faith in a resurrection and immortality strengthened by hearing of this? Who knows what beautiful and winged life, whose egg has been buried for ages under many concentric layers of wood-enness in the dead dry life of society, deposited at first in the alburnum of the green and living tree, which has been gradually converted into the semblance of its well-seasoned tomb,—heard perchance gnawing out now for years by the astonished family of man, as they sat round the festive board,—may unexpectedly come forth from amidst society's most trivial and hand-selled furniture, to enjoy its perfect summer life at last!

I do not say that John or Jonathan[26] will realize all this; but such is the character of that morrow which mere lapse of time can never make to dawn. The light which puts out our eyes is darkness to us. Only that day dawns to which we are awake. There is more day to dawn. The sun is but a morning star.

[26] "John Bull" and "Brother Jonathan" personify the typical Englishman and American.

Sic Vita[1]

I am a parcel of vain strivings tied
By a chance bond together,
Dangling this way and that, their links
Were made so loose and wide,
Methinks,
For milder weather.   5

[1] "Sic Vita" was published in the *Dial*, II (July 1841), 81–82 and was reprinted in *A week on the Concord and Merrimack Rivers* (1849). The poem was written when Thoreau was still an undergraduate at Harvard, then wrapped round a bunch of violets, tied loosely with straw, and thrown into the window of Lucy Jackson Brown, a sister of Emerson's second wife, Lidian. Emerson thought highly of Thoreau's poetry and when he edited the *Dial* he stated that "My Henry Thoreau will be a great poet for such a company and one of these days for all companies."

A bunch of violets without their roots,
   And sorrel intermixed,
  Encircled by a wisp of straw
    Once coiled about their shoots,
        The law
     By which I'm fixed.   10

A nosegay which Time clutched from out
   Those fair Elysian fields,
  With weeds and broken stems, in haste,
   Doth make the rabble rout
        That waste
    The day he yields.   15

And here I bloom for a short hour unseen,
   Drinking my juices up,
  With no root in the land
   To keep my branches green
        But stand
    In a bare cup.   20

Some tender buds were left upon my stem
   In mimicry of life,
  But ah! the children will not know
   Till time has withered them,
        The wo
    With which they're rife.   25

But now I see I was not plucked for nought,
   And after in life's vase
  Of glass set while I might survive,
   But by a kind hand brought
        Alive
    To a strange place.   30

That stock thus thinned will soon redeem its hours,
   And by another year,
  Such as God knows, with freer air,
   More fruits and fairer flowers
        Will bear,
    While I droop here.   35

The Inward Morning[1]

Packed in my mind lie all the clothes
    Which outward nature wears,
And in its fashion's hourly change
    It all things else repairs.

In vain I look for change abroad,   5
    And can no difference find,
Till some new ray of peace uncalled
    Illumes my inmost mind.

What is it gilds the trees and clouds,
    And paints the heavens so gay,   10
But yonder fast abiding light
    With its unchanging ray?

Lo, when the sun streams through the wood
    Upon a winter's morn,
Where'er his silent beams intrude   15
    The murky night is gone.

How could the patient pine have known
    The morning breeze would come,
Or humble flowers anticipate
    The insect's noonday hum?   20

Till the new light with morning cheer
    From far streamed through the aisles,
And nimbly told the forest trees
    For many stretching miles.

I've heard within my inmost soul   25
    Such cheerful morning news,
In the horizon of my mind
    Have seen such orient hues,

As in the twilight of the dawn
    When the first birds awake,   30
Are heard within some silent wood,
    Where they the small twigs break,

---

[1] "The Inward Morning" was published in the *Dial*, III (October 1842) and reprinted in a *Week on the Concord and Merrimack Rivers* (1849).

Or in the eastern skies are seen
    Before the sun appears,
The harbingers of summer heats   35
    Which from afar he bears.

Stanzas[1]

Nature doth have her dawn each day,
    But mine are far between;
Content, I cry, for sooth to say,
    Mine brightest are, I ween.

For when my sun doth deign to rise,   5
    Though it be her noontide,
Her fairest field in shadow lies,
    Nor can my light abide.

Sometimes I bask me in her day,
    Conversing with my mate;   10
But if we interchange one ray,
    Forthwith her heats abate.

Through his discourse I climb and see,
    As from some eastern hill,
A brighter morrow rise to me   15
    Than lieth in her skill.

As 't were two summer days in one,
    Two Sundays come together,
Our rays united make one Sun,
    With fairest summer weather.   20

[1] "Stanzas" was published in the *Dial*, I
(January 1841), 314.

WALT WHITMAN

(1819–1892)

Of all the major Romantic writers in America Walt Whitman seems the easiest to know, the most familiar, and the most accessible to readers. He insisted that his poetry not be read as a "literary performance" and, indeed, his verse does seem free and open, inviting the casual reader to poke along at his ease. The notion is deceptive, however, one of a host of deceptions practiced by Whitman on the unwary; with all his apparent spontaneity and bluff good nature, he is often covert, devious, furtive, and sly. Late in life, particularly after his disabling stroke at the age of 54, Whitman cultivated a view of himself as the Good Grey Poet, a homespun bard and prophet. The image has unhappily remained, for with all its validity in terms of his fervent attachment to democracy, it has mislead readers into expecting a poetry of doctrine, of slogan, of trumpeted celebration. There is this quality in his poetry, to be sure, but few readers have been prepared for the special difficulties of his best works, which arise from the double nature of his successful verse, its startling immediacy, and its refusal to yield a definite meaning. The poetry is a beguiling assault of the reader's conventional sense of himself as a reader. To all readers who take the Good Grey

The standard edition, which presently includes nine published volumes, is *The Collected Writings of Walt Whitman,* General Editors: Gay Wilson Allen and Sculley Bradley, 1966—. Eighteen volumes are projected. This edition includes *Leaves of Grass,* Comprehensive Reader's Edition, ed. Harold Blodgett and Sculley Bradley, 1965. Until superseded by this edition, the most useful text is *Leaves of Grass,* ed. Emory Holloway, 1924, 1954. Another complete edition is *The Complete Writings of Walt Whitman,* 10 vols., ed. R. M. Bucke and others, 1902.

The standard biography is Gay Wilson Allen, *The Solitary Singer, A Critical Biography of Walt Whitman,* 1955. Allen has also published two other important studies: *Walt Whitman Handbook,* 1957, rev. 1975 and *A Reader's Guide to Walt Whitman,* 1970. The best early biographies are Emory Holloway, *Whitman, An Interpretation in Narrative,* 1926; Newton Arvin,

Whitman, 1938, and H. S. Canby, *Walt Whitman, An American,* 1943.

Recent biographies and criticism include the translation of Gay Wilson Allen, ed., *Walt Whitman Abroad,* 1955; Roger Asselineau, *The Evolution of Walt Whitman,* 2 vols., 1960, 1962; Richard Chase, *Walt Whitman Reconsidered,* 1955, and the pamphlet, "Walt Whitman," 1961; Milton Hindus, ed., *Leaves of Grass, One Hundred Years After,* 1955; J. E. Miller, *A Critical Guide to Leaves of Grass,* 1957; Roy Harvey Pearce, *Whitman, A Collection of Critical Essays,* 1962; H. J. Waskow, *Whitman, Explorations in Form,* 1966; E. H. Miller, *Walt Whitman's Poetry,* 1968; E. H. Miller, ed., *A Century of Whitman Criticism;* Ivan Marki, *The Trial of the Poet: An Interpretation of the First Edition of Leaves of Grass,* 1976; Richard M. Bucke, *Medical Mystic,* 1977.

The texts from *Leaves of Grass* are those of the edition of 1891-1892.

Poet at face value, he issues a warning, in "Whoever You Are Holding
Me Now in Hand":
  But these leaves conning you con at peril,
  For these leaves and me you will not understand,
  They will elude you at first and still more afterward, I will
  certainly elude you,
  Even while you should think you had unquestionably caught
  me, behold!
  Already you see I have escaped from you.

With calculation he plots against the security of readers who feel
"proud to get at the meaning of poems." His is a book, wrote Robert
Lewis Stevenson, only for those with "the gift of reading." He demands
participation; his "you" is the name of a presence for each reader to
experience as himself. "The process of reading," Whitman writes in
Democratic Vistas, "is not a half-sleep, but, in the highest sense, an
exercise, a gymnast's struggle." The reader "is to do something for
himself, must be on the alert, must himself or herself construct indeed
the poem. . .—the text furnishing the hints, the clue, the start of framework."

  Whitman's radical spirit is embodied most exactly in this conception of the active reader, the emergent "you" who will stand in
equality with the poet, for whom the poem is less a finished thing than
a beginning, a new channel into richer, deeper experience. Herein lies
his significant break with what George Santayana called the Genteel
Tradition, a tradition that cherishes "art," specifically of the European
past, over rough and brute contemporary life. "In Walt Whitman,"
Santayana wrote, "democracy is carried into psychology and morals.
The various sights, moods, and emotions are given each one vote; they
are declared to be all free and equal, and the innumerable commonplace moments of life are suffered to speak like the others. Those moments formerly reputed great are not excluded, but they are made to
march in the ranks with their companions—plain foot-soldiers and
servants of the hour." D. H. Lawrence makes a similar point in describing Whitman's poetry as "the unrestful, ungraspable poetry of the
sheer present, poetry whose very permanency lies in its wind-like transit. . . . The clue to all his utterances lies in the sheer appreciation of
the instant moment, life surging into utterance at its very well-head."

  Whitman's is a poetry of *sources,* in the root sense of engendering
acts: uttering, naming, and reconstituting a world of named things and
feelings. We sense a fresh world, freshly encountered and perceived. It
is a poetry of plenitude, of the "amplitude of time," of an abundance
that in its cumulative surge sometimes forces the self (the uttering,

generative voice) to step back, retreat, and reconstitute itself on different grounds. Identity is central to the ebb and flow movements of
Whitman's poetry, because at bottom the principle is the endless challenge posed by experience to any provisional version of reality. Thus
the elusiveness, the rhythms of contraction and expansion, the patterns of contradiction, all serve to maintain a fragile, ineffable sense of
life, of *livingness.* The poetry lives, in short, as long as the dialectic
between self and world, self and Other, remains tense, taut with potential, as in the crucial inscription, "One's-Self I sing, a simple separate person, /Yet utter the word Democratic, the word En-Masse."

For Whitman the poem is not a vehicle of abstract meaning but the
reader's opportunity for a personal liberation, a transformation—or, to
use a term Whitman appropriated from his master Emerson, a *translation* of experience into truth. Emerson wrote that the poet is essential
to the very being of a culture, since he "represents" the fullness of
being: "the man is only half himself, the other half is his expression."
The poet, the "sayer," is a liberating god, Emerson writes in his essay
"The Poet." "He is the only teller of news, for he was present and privy
to the appearance which he described;" "he unlocks our chains and
admits us to a new scene."

How well these epithets fit Whitman; no wonder Emerson saw immediately the value of the slim green volume titled *Leaves of Grass*
that he received from the author, previously unknown to him, in 1855.
"I find it the most extraordinary piece of wit and wisdom that America
had yet contributed," he wrote to Whitman, adding: "I greet you at the
beginning of a great career, which yet must have had a long foreground somewhere, for such a start." He must have recognized precisely the "tyrannous eye" he had called for in "The Poet": "We have
had yet no genius in America, with tyrannous eye, which knew the
value of our incomparable materials, and saw, in the barbarism and
materialism of the times, another carnival of the same gods whose
picture he so much admires in Homer." The emphasis falls here on the
act of seeing, which precedes and remains part and parcel of the act of
saying. Emerson's poet knows what the average man has forgotten,
that "every sensuous fact" had manifold meanings, is an emblem or
symbol, if properly seen. The poet endows facts with "a power" and
"puts eyes and a tongue into every dumb and inanimate object." And
by thus turning "the world to glass," the poet endows his adept reader
with equal powers of seeing, saying, and being. In such manner, by
"an ulterior intellectual perception," vivifying experience by detaching
fixed meanings from things, poets "make free." "To be is just as great
as to perceive or tell," echoes Whitman in his 1855 preface.

Whitman recorded late in life that he had been simmering and that Emerson had brought him to a boil. One can well imagine the effect of the Emersonian rhapsody of self-reliance on a young man like Whitman, whose early years read like a quest for selfhood as well as vocation. Emerson sanctioned individual experience above formal schooling, and this fit exactly the needs of a young man who, until his creation of "Walt Whitman a kosmos," had by turn tried his hand at school teaching, printing, typesetting, reporting, editing, and carpentry, whose life from his birth on rural Long Island had been one of movement in and out of jobs and places, and a variety of "roles": political campaigner, man about town, dandy, one of the roughs. In retrospect Whitman wrote that the purpose of *Leaves of Grass* (the title of the book that contained all his poems) was "to put *a Person,* a human being (myself, in the latter half of the Nineteenth Century, in America,) freely, fully and truly on record." The intention is perhaps comparable to Wordsworth's in *The Prelude,* except that Whitman's effort was not a reflection on experience but an attempt to give a voice to experience itself. Traces of his many vocations, his travels (including a trip to New Orleans with his brother in 1848, his family life (one brother died in an insane asylum, another was a congenital idiot, the wife of another became a prostitute, a sister suffered from melancholia, the father was ill-tempered, and the mother of Dutch and Quaker background, the chief source of strength in the family) take many forms in the poetry, as does the cosmopolitanism of New York in this period, where he had access to music, opera, museums, galleries, and books. Whitman tapped a novel resource for poetry—common experience. His route to poetry fell not through the colleges where most of the eminent literary figures of his day had received their training, but through printing shops and newspaper offices, political stumps and city streets. Whitman himself emerged from the "incomparable materials" Emerson spoke of; he was raised in and gave expression to their ambiance.

During the late 1830's and 1840's Whitman had contributed highly "literary" pieces to the New York press, conventional essays, poems, and sentimental fiction. After a series of editorial positions in the 1840's, ending with his being fired from the editorship of the prominent Brooklyn *Eagle* (the reason was his too-fervent commitment to the Free Soil movement), Whitman began keeping a notebook in which the first edition of *Leaves* germinated. After 1848 he worked mainly as a freelance writer, odd-jobber, and house-builder with his father. His book appeared in 1855, appropriately enough on July 4, privately printed and anonymous, the author identified not by name but by image (a visual emblem), in a photographic frontispiece of a bearded young man in workman's clothes. This unique large-sized volume in a green cover held 12 untitled poems. In 1856 an expanded second edition appeared, again at the author's own expense (neither edition sold many copies). By 1860 yet a third edition reached print, much expanded, this time printed commercially. All in all Whitman issued nine editions of his book, each enlarged and revised. The final or "death bed" edition (1891) is generally considered definitive, though scholars and critics argue that the earliest version of specific poems is usually the best.

It is clear that the years between the late 1840's when the first poems were in composition and 1860, when the book achieves its characteristic form, represent Whitman's most fertile period. Judging from the evidence of the superb sensual and covertly homosexual lyrics of "Children of Adam" and "Calamus" and the great longer poems, "Crossing Brooklyn Ferry," "Out of the Cradle Endlessly Rocking," and "As I Ebb'd with the Ocean of Life" (all composed between 1855 and 1860), Whitman must have experienced a profound crisis in these years. The 1855 edition also held poems of the underside of life, most notably the Baudelairean "The Sleepers," along with the heady poems of self-discovery and venturing forth; the poems of 1860 introduce a deeper note of loss, even of despair and self-loathing. Their preoccupation is with death and the discovery of the outlet of poetry in the awareness of mortality.

The Civil War was another sort of crisis. At first Whitman seems to have paid little serious attention to the outbreak of hostilities after the secession but in 1862, his brother George was wounded and Whitman traveled to the front in Virginia, beginning a momentous phase of his life as nurse and wound-dresser. The issue of these years was *Drum Taps* (1865), a book of often restrained death-ridden etchings of battle scenes, fed by a compassion that reaches moving heights in poems such as "The Wound-Dresser," and the stark, evocative prose sketches of *Specimen Days* (1822). In 1866 a sequel to *Drum Taps* appeared, including what many readers consider his greatest single poem, "When Lilacs Last in the Dooryard Bloom'd," an elegy on the death of Lincoln. After the war Whitman held a clerkship in the Bureau of Indian Affairs, but was dismissed after six months as the author of disreputable works; he found another government position in the Attorney General's office, and continued to revise his *Leaves* and make additions. In 1873 he suffered the stroke that left him paralyzed the rest of his life. He moved to Camden where he lived first with his brother, then in the famous Mickle Street house, living close to the edge of poverty, surrounded by a band of disciples and admirers, carrying a vast correspondence, still revising and polishing, and making occasional public appearances. In 1879 he traveled west as far as Nevada; he died in Camden on March 26, 1892.

Much of Whitman's prose writing in his last period was retrospective. In the preface to the 1855 edition he had written that the "proof of a poet is that his country absorbs him as affectionately as he has absorbed it." Except for a handful of Bohemians, off-beats, and transcendentalists, few of his countrymen were ready to take his work into their system, although he was sometimes enthusiastically received by prominent writers in England. Moreover, the Civil War and its aftermath, especially the erosion of public morality and the emergence of a fashionable cynicism, posed a challenge to his commitment to democracy. Typically, out of personal doubt and crisis, Whitman created a major literary work, this time, in 1870, the long essay *Democratic Vistas*. In this difficult, part-satiric, part-prophetic work, Whitman gives free rein to his disappointments, yet, in the end, transcends his doubts and concludes affirmatively. What emerges from the shifting perspectives, the dialectics of belief and doubt, is an illuminating sense of what democracy, equality, and America mean for Whitman, and of the relation of the poet to these concepts. The main argument of the essay is that if democracy denotes only a political system, if it does not, in Santayana's words, enter psychology and morals, if it remains a political system without becoming a culture (a way of life), then it fails in its historic mission. We learn in this remarkable essay that at the deepest level Whitman's poetry is inseparable from his vision of a culture of free men and women, living in mutuality and self-respect. We learn too that the American reality was in his eyes extremely difficult and problematic. It raises the existential question of what any man has to do with others, or the individual with the mass. Poetry plays the role of a mediation, the vehicle through which the democratic synthesis of the interests of the self and the interests of the mass can take place. It is a high order for poetry, but Whitman insists on it. Here, too, we find his clearest statements about the methods of poetry, its necessary indirection, its teaching through hints and clues instead of didactic message.

Much of Whitman has been and remains enigmatic for audiences who do not share his abiding conviction in the relationship between poetry, the soul, and the way people live with each other. Surely Whitman is a "presence" in modern poetry—his influence is felt in almost all twentieth-century American poets, from Pound and Eliot to Hart Crane, Wallace Stevens, and William Carlos Williams—but perhaps, as Hart Crane wrote, his "bequest" is "still to be realized in all its implications."

Preface to Leaves of Grass[1]
1855

America does not repel the past or what it has produced under its forms or amid other politics or the idea of castes or the old religions. . . accepts the lesson with calmness. . . is not so impatient as has been supposed that the slough still sticks to opinions and manners and literature while the life which served its requirements has passed into the new life of the new forms. . . perceives that the corpse is slowly borne from the eating and sleeping rooms of the house. . . perceives that it waits a little while in the door. . . that it was fittest for its days. . . that its action has descended to the stalwart and well-shaped heir who approaches. . . and that he shall be fittest for his days.

The Americans of all nations at any time upon the earth have probably the fullest poetical nature. The United States themselves are essentially the greatest poem. In the history of the earth hitherto to the largest and most stirring appear tame and orderly to their ampler largeness and stir. Here at last is something in the doings of man that corresponds with the broadcast doings of the day and night. Here is not merely a nation but a teeming nation of nations. Here is action untied from strings necessarily blind to particulars and details magnificently moving in vast masses. Here is the hospitality which forever indicates heroes. . . Here are the roughs and beards and space and ruggedness and nonchalance that the soul loves. Here the perfomance disdaining the trivial unapproached in the tremendous audacity of its crowds and groupings and the push of its perspective spreads with crampless and flowing breadth and showers of prolific and splendid extravagance. One sees it must indeed own the riches of the summer and winter, and need never be bankrupt while corn grows from the ground or the orchards drop apples or the bays contain fish or men beget children upon women.

Other states indicate themselves in their deputies. . . but the genius of the United States is not best or most in its executives or legislatures, nor in its ambassadors or authors or colleges or churches or parlors, nor even in its newspapers or inventors. . . but always most in the common people. Their manners speech dress friendships—the freshness and candor of their physiognomy—the picturesque looseness of their carriage. . . their deathless attachment to freedom—their aversion to anything indecorous or soft or mean—the practical acknowledgment of the citizens of one state by the citizens of all other states—the fierceness of their roused resentment—their curiosity and welcome of novelty—their self-esteem and wonderful sympathy—their susceptibility to a slight—the air they have of persons who never

---

[1] This preface, which appeared before the first edition of *Leaves of Grass* in 1855, is Whitman's clearest poetics for a democracy. It has the epigrammatic quality of Emerson's essays, which strongly influenced the writing, and the power of the poem, *"Song of Myself,"* which followed.

knew how it felt to stand in the presence of superiors—the fluency of their speech—their delight in music, the sure symptom of manly tenderness and native elegance of soul. . . their good temper and open-handedness—the terrible significance of their elections—the President's taking off his hat to them not they to him—these too are unrhymed poetry. It awaits the gigantic and generous treatment worthy of it.

The largeness of nature or the nation were monstrous without a corresponding largeness and generosity of the spirit of the citizen. Not nature nor swarming states nor streets and steamships nor prosperous business nor farms nor capital nor learning may suffice for the ideal of man. . . nor suffice the poet. No reminiscences may suffice either. A live nation can always cut a deep mark and can have the best authority the cheapest. . . namely from its own soul. This is the sum of the profitable uses of individuals or states and of present action and grandeur and of the subjects of poets.—As if it were necessary to trot back generation after generation to the eastern records! As if the beauty and sacredness of the demonstrable must fall behind that of the mythical! As if men do not make their mark out of any times! As if the opening of the western continent by discovery and what had transpired since in North and South America were less than the small theatre of the antique or the aimless sleepwalking of the middle ages! The pride of the United States leaves the wealth and finesse of the cities and all returns of commerce and agriculture and all the magnitude of geography or shows of exterior victory to enjoy the breed of full-sized men or one full-sized man unconquerable and simple.

The American poets are to enclose old and new for America is the race of races. Of them a bard is to be commensurate with a people. To him the other continents arrive as contributions. . . he gives them reception for their sake and his own sake. His spirit responds to his country's spirit. . . he incarnates its geography and natural life and rivers and lakes. Mississippi with annual freshets and changing chutes, Missouri and Columbia and Ohio and Saint Lawrence with the falls and beautiful masculine Hudson, do not embouchure where they spend themselves more than they embouchure into him. The blue breadth over the inland sea of Virginia and Maryland and the sea off Massachusetts and Maine and over Manhattan bay and over Champlain and Erie and over Ontario and Huron and Michigan and Superior, and over the Texan and Mexican and Floridian and Cuban seas and over the seas off California and Oregon, is not tallied by the blue breadth of the waters below more than the breadth of above and below is tallied by him. When the long Atlantic coast stretches longer and the Pacific coast stretches longer he easily stretches with them north and south. He spans between them also from east to west and reflects what is between them. On him rise solid growths that offset the growths of pine and cedar and hemlock and live oak and locust and chestnut and cypress and hickory and lime tree and cotton-

wood and tulip tree and cactus and wild vine and tamarind and persimmon. . . and tangles as tangled as any cane brake or swamp. . . and forests
coated with transparent ice and icicles hanging from the boughs and crackling in the wind. . . and sides and peaks of mountains. . . and pasturage sweet
and free as savannah or upland or prairie. . . with flights and songs and
screams that answer those of the wild pigeon and highhole and orchard
oriole and coot and surf duck and red-shouldered hawk and fish hawk and
white ibis and Indian hen and cat owl and water pheasant and quabird and
pied sheldrake and blackbird and mockingbird and buzzard and condor and
night heron and eagle. To him the hereditary countenance descends both
mother's and father's. To him enter the essences of the real things and past
and present events—of the enormous diversity of temperature and agriculture and mines—the tribes of red aborigines—the weatherbeaten vessels
entering new ports or making landings on rocky coasts—the first settlements
north or south—the rapid stature and muscle—the haughty defiance of '76,
and the war and peace and formation of the constitution. . . the union always
surrounded by blatherers and always calm and impregnable—the perpetual
coming of immigrants—the wharf-hem'd cities and superior marine—the
unsurveyed interior—the loghouses and clearings and wild animals and hunters and trappers. . . the free commerce—the fisheries and whaling and gold-
digging—the endless gestation of new states—the convening of Congress
every December, the members duly coming up from all climates and the
uttermost parts. . . the noble character of the young mechanics and of all
free American workmen and workwomen. . . the general ardor and friendliness and enterprise—the perfect equality of the female with the male. . . the
large amativeness—the fluid movement of the population—the factories and
mercantile life and laborsaving machinery—the Yankee swap—the New
York firemen and the target excursion—the southern plantation life—the
character of the northeast and of the northwest and southwest—slavery and
the tremulous spreading of hands to protect it, and the stern opposition to it
which shall never cease till it ceases or the speaking of tongues and the
moving of lips cease. For such the expression of the American poet is to be
transcendant and new. It is to be indirect and not direct or descriptive or
epic. Its quality goes through these to much more. Let the age and wars of
nations be chanted and let their eras and characters be illustrated and that
finish the verse. Not so the great psalm of the republic. Here the theme is
creative and has vista. Here comes one among the well-beloved stonecutters
and plans with decision and science and sees the solid and beautiful forms of
the future where there are now no solid forms.

Of all nations the United States with veins full of poetical stuff most need
poets and will doubtless have the greatest and use them the greatest. Their
Presidents shall not be their common referee so much as their poets shall. Of
all mankind the great poet is the equable man. Not in him but off from him
things are grotesque or eccentric or fail of their sanity. Nothing out of its

place is good and nothing in its place is bad. He bestows on every object or quality its fit proportions neither more nor less. He is the arbiter of the diverse and he is the key. He is the equalizer of his age and land. . . he supplies what wants supplying and checks what wants checking. If peace is the routine out of him speaks the spirit of peace, large, rich, thrifty, building vast and populous cities, encouraging agriculture and the arts and commerce—lighting the study of man, the soul, immortality—federal, state or municipal government, marriage, health, free trade, intertravel by land and sea. . . nothing too close, nothing too far off. . . the stars not too far off. In war he is the most deadly force of the war. Who recruits him recruits horse and foot. . . he fetches parks of artillery the best that engineer ever knew. If the time becomes slothful and heavy he knows how to arouse it. . . he can make every word he speaks draw blood. Whatever stagnates in the flat of custom or obedience or legislation he never stagnates. Obedience does not master him, he masters it. High up out of reach he stands turning a concentrated light. . . he turns the pivot with his finger. . . he baffles the swiftest runners as he stands and easily overtakes and envelops them. The time straying toward infidelity and confections and persiflage he withholds by his steady faith. . . he spreads out his dishes. . . he offers the sweet firm-fibred meat that grows men and women. His brain is the ultimate brain. He is no arguer. . . he is judgment. He judges not as the judge judges but as the sun falling around a helpless thing. As he sees the farthest he has the most faith. His thoughts are the hymns of the praise of things. In the talk on the soul and eternity and God off of his equal plane he is silent. He sees eternity less like a play with a prologue and denouement. . . he sees eternity in men and women. . . he does not see men and women as dreams or dots. Faith is the antiseptic of the soul. . . it pervades the common people and preserves them. . . they never give up believing and expecting and trusting. There is that indescribable freshness and unconsciousness about an illiterate person that humbles and mocks the power of the noblest expressive genius. The poet sees for a certainty how one not a great artist may be just as sacred and perfect as the greatest artist. . . The power to destroy or remold is freely used by him but never the power of attack. What is past is past. If he does not expose superior models and prove himself by every step he takes he is not what is wanted. The presence of the greatest poet conquers. . . not parleying or struggling or any prepared attempts. Now he has passed that way see after him! there is not left any vestige of despair or misanthropy or cunning or exclusiveness or the ignominy of a nativity or color or delusion of hell or the necessity of hell. . . and no man thenceforward shall be degraded for ignorance or weakness or sin.

The greatest poet hardly knows pettiness or triviality. If he breathes into anything that was before thought small it dilates with the grandeur and life of the universe. He is a seer. . . he is individual. . . he is complete in himself. . . the others are as good as he, only he sees it and they do not. He is not one of the chorus. . . he does not stop for any regulations. . . he is the president of regulation. What the eyesight does to the rest he does to the rest. Who knows the curious mystery of the eyesight? The other senses corroborate themselves, but this is removed from any proof but its own and foreruns the identities of the spiritual world. A single glance of it mocks all the investigations of man and all the instruments and books of the earth and all reasoning. What is marvelous? what is unlikely? what is impossible or baseless or vague? after you have once just opened the space of a peach pit and given audience to far and near and to the sunset and had all things enter with electric swiftness softly and duly without confusion or jostling or jam.

The land and sea, the animals fishes and birds, the sky of heaven and the orbs, the forests mountains and rivers, are not small themes. . . but folks expect of the poet to indicate more than the beauty and dignity which always attach to dumb real objects. . . they expect him to indicate the path between reality and their souls. Men and women perceive the beauty well enough. . . probably as well as he. The passionate tenacity of hunters, woodmen, early risers, cultivators of gardens and orchards and fields, the love of healthy women for the manly form, seafaring persons, drivers of horses, the passion for light and the open air, all is an old varied sign of the unfailing perception of beauty and of a residence of the poetic in outdoor people. They can never be assisted by poets to perceive. . . some may but they never can. The poetic quality is not marshalled in rhyme or uniformity or abstract addresses to things nor in melancholy complaints or good precepts, but is the life of these and much else and is in the soul. The profit of rhyme is that it drops seeds of a sweeter and more luxuriant rhyme, and of uniformity that it conveys itself into its own roots in the ground out of sight. The rhyme and uniformity of perfect poems show the free growth of metrical laws and bud from them as unerringly and loosely as lilacs or roses on a bush, and take shapes as compact as the shapes of chestnuts and oranges and melons and pears, and shed the perfume impalpable to form. The fluency and ornaments of the finest poems or music or orations or recitations are not independent but dependent. All beauty comes from beautiful blood and a beautiful brain. If the greatnesses are in conjunction in a man or woman it is enough. . . the fact will prevail through the universe. . . but the gaggery and gilt of a million years will not prevail. Who troubles himself about his ornaments or influency is lost. This is what you shall do: Love the earth and sun and the animals, despise riches, give alms to everyone that asks, stand up for the stupid and crazy, devote your income and labor to others, hate tyrants, argue not concerning God, have patience and indulgence toward the people, take off your hat to nothing known or unknown or to any man or number of men, go freely with powerful uneducated persons and with the young and with the mothers of families, read these leaves in the open air every season of every year of your life, re-examine all you have been told at school or church or in any book, dismiss whatever insults your own soul, and your own flesh shall be a great poem and have the richest fluency not only in its words but in the silent lines of its lips and face and between the lashes of your eyes and in every motion and joint of your body. . . .The poet shall not spend his time in unneeded work. He shall know that the ground is always ready plowed and manured. . . others may not know it but he shall. He shall go directly to the creation. His trust shall master the trust of everything he touches. . . and shall master all attachment.

The known universe has one complete lover and that is the greatest poet. He consumes an eternal passion and is indifferent which chance happens and which possible contingency of fortune or misfortune and persuades daily and hourly his delicious pay. What balks or breaks others is fuel for his burning progress to contact and amorous joy. Other proportions of the reception of pleasure dwindle to nothing to his proportions. All expected from heaven or from the highest he is rapport with in the sight of the daybreak or a scene of the winter woods or the presence of children playing or with his arm round the neck of a man or woman. His love above all love has leisure and expanse. . . he leaves room ahead of himself. He is no irresolute or suspicious lover. . . he is sure. . . he scorns intervals. His experience and the showers and thrills are not for nothing. Nothing can jar him. . . suffering and darkness cannot—death and fear cannot. To him complaint and jealousy and envy are corpses buried and rotten in the earth. . . he saw them buried. The sea is not surer of the shore or the shore of the sea than he is of the fruition of his love and of all perfection and beauty.

The fruition of beauty is no chance of hit or miss. . . it is inevitable as life. . . it is exact and plumb as gravitation. From the eyesight proceeds another eyesight and from the hearing proceeds another hearing and from the voice proceeds another voice eternally curious of the harmony of things with man. To these respond perfections not only in the committees that were supposed to stand for the rest but in the rest themselves just the same. These understand the law of perfection in masses and floods. . . that its finish is to each for itself and onward from itself. . . that it is profuse and impartial. . . that there is not a minute of the light or dark nor an acre of the earth or sea without it—nor any direction of the sky nor any trade or employment nor any turn of events. This is the reason that about the proper expression of beauty there is precision and balance. . . one part does not need to be thrust above another. The best singer is not the one who has the most lithe and powerful organ. . . the pleasure of poems is not in them that take the handsomest measure and similes and sound.

Without effort and without exposing in the least how it is done the greatest poet brings the spirit of any or all events and passions and scenes and persons some more and some less to bear on your individual character as you hear or read. To do this well is to compete with the laws that pursue and follow time. What is the purpose must surely be there and the clue of it must be there. . . and the faintest indication is the indication of the best and then becomes the clearest indication. Past and present and future are not disjoined but joined. The greatest poet forms the consistence of what is to be from what has been and is. He drags the dead out of their coffins and stands them again on their feet. . . he says to the past, Rise and walk before me that I may realize you. He learns the lesson. . . he places himself where the future becomes present. The greatest poet does not only dazzle his rays over character and scenes and passions. . . he finally ascends and finishes all. . . he exhibits the pinnacles that no man can tell what they are for or what is beyond. . . he glows a moment on the extremest verge. He is most wonderful in his last half-hidden smile or frown. . . by that flash of the moment of parting the one that sees it shall be encouraged or terrified afterwards for many years. The greatest poet does not moralize or make applications of morals. . . he knows the soul. The soul has that measureless pride which consists in never acknowledging any lessons but its own. But it has sympathy as measureless as its pride and the one balances the other and neither can stretch too far while it stretches in company with the other. The inmost secrets of art sleep with the twain. The greatest poet has lain close betwixt both and they are vital in his style and thoughts.

The art of art, the glory of expression and the sunshine of the light of letters is simplicity. Nothing is better than simplicity. . . nothing can make up for excess or for the lack of definiteness. To carry on the heave of impulse and pierce intellectual depths and give all subjects their articulations are powers neither common nor very uncommon. But to speak in literature with the perfect rectitude and insouciance of the movements of animals and the unimpeachableness of the sentiment of trees in the woods and grass by the roadside is the flawless triumph of art. If you have looked on him who has achieved it you have looked on one of the masters of the artists of all nations and times. You shall not contemplate the flight of the graygull over the bay or the mettlesome action of the blood horse or the tall leaning of sunflowers on their stalk or the appearance of the sun journeying through heaven or the appearance of the moon afterward with any more satisfaction than you shall contemplate him. The greatest poet has less a marked style and is more the channel of thoughts and things without increase or diminution, and is the free channel of himself. He swears to his art, I will not be meddlesome, I will not have in my writing my elegance or effect or originally to hang in the way between me and the rest like curtains. I will have nothing hang in the way, not the richest curtains. What I tell I tell for precisely what it is. Let who may exalt or startle or fascinate or sooth I will have purposes as health or heat or snow has and be as regardless of observation. What I experience or portray shall go from my composition without a shred of my composition. You shall stand by my side and look in the mirror with me.

The old red blood and stainless gentility of great poets will be proved by their unconstraint. A heroic person walks at his ease through and out of that custom or precedent or authority that suits him not. Of the traits of the brotherhood of writers savants musicians inventors and artists nothing is finer than silent defiance advancing from new free forms. In the need of poems philosophy politics mechanism science behavior, the craft, or any craft, he is greatest forever and forever who contributes the greatest original practical example. The cleanest expression is that which finds no sphere worthy of itself and makes one.

The messages of great poets to each man and woman are, Come to us on equal terms, Only then can you understand us, We are no better than you, What we enclose you enclose, What we enjoy you may enjoy. Did you suppose there could be only one Supreme? We affirm there can be unnumbered Supremes, and that one does not countervail another any more than one eyesight countervails another. . . and that men can be good or grand only of the consciousness of their supremacy within them. What do you think is the grandeur of storms and dismemberments and the deadliest battles and wrecks and the wildest fury of the elements and the power of the sea and the motion of nature and of the throes of human desires and dignity and hate and love? It is that something in the soul which says, Rage on, Whirl on. I tread master here and everywhere, Master of the spasms of the sky and of the shatter of the sea, Master of nature and passion and death, And of all terror and all pain.

The American bards shall be marked for generosity and affection and for encouraging competitors. . . They shall be kosmos. . . without monopoly or secrecy. . .glad to pass any thing to any one. . . hungry for equals night and day. They shall not be careful of riches and privilege. . . they shall perceive who the most affluent man is. The most affluent man is he that confronts all the shows he sees by equivalents out of the stronger wealth of himself. The American bard shall delineate no class of persons nor one or two out of the strata of interests nor love most nor truth most nor the soul most nor the body most. . .and not be for the eastern states more than the western or the northern states more than the southern.

Exact science and its practical movements are no checks on the greatest poet but always his encouragement and support. The outset and remembrance are there. . . there are the arms that lifted him first and brace him best. . . there he returns after all his goings and comings. The sailor and traveler. . . the anatomist chemist astronomer geologist phrenologist spiritualist mathematician historian and lexicographer are not poets, but they are the lawgivers of poets and their construction underlies the structure of every perfect poem. No matter what rises or is uttered they sent the seed of the conception of it. . . of them and by them stand the visible proofs of souls. . . always of their father-stuff must begotten the sinewy races of bards. If there shall be love and content between the father and the son and if the greatness of the son is the exuding of the greatness of the father there shall be love between the poet and the man of demonstrable science. In the beauty of poems are the tuft and final applause of science. Great is the faith of the flush of knowledge and of the investigation of the depths of qualities and things. Cleaving and circling here swells the soul of the poet yet is president of itself always. The depths are fathomless and therefore calm. The innocence and nakedness are resumed. . . they are neither modest nor immodest. The whole theory of the special and supernatural and all that was twined with it or educed out of it departs as a dream. What has ever happened. . . what happens and whatever may or shall happen, the vital laws enclose all. . . they are sufficient for any case and for all cases. . . none to be hurried or retarded. . . any miracle of affairs or persons inadmissible in the vast clear scheme where every motion and every spear of grass and the frames and spirits of men and women and all that concerns them are unspeakably perfect miracles all referring to all and each distinct and in its place. It is also not consistent with the reality of the soul to admit that there is anything in the known universe more divine than men and women.

Men and women and the earth and all upon it are simply to be taken as they are, and the investigation of their past and present and future shall be unintermitted and shall be done with perfect candor. Upon this basis philosophy speculated ever looking toward the poet, ever regarding the eternal tendencies of all toward happiness never inconsistent with what is clear to the senses and to the soul. For the eternal tendencies of all toward happiness make the only point of sane philosophy. Whatever comprehends less than that. . . whatever is less than the laws of light and of astronomical motion. . . or less than the laws that follow the thief the liar the glutton and the drunkard through this life and doubtless afterward. . . or less than vast stretches of time or the slow formation of density of the patient upheaving of strata—is of no account. Whatever would put God in a poem or system of philosophy as contending against some being or influence, is also of no account. Sanity and ensemble characterize the great master. . . spoilt in one principle all is spoilt. The great master has nothing to do with miracles. He sees health for himself in being one of the mass. . . he sees the hiatus in singular eminence. To the perfect shape comes common ground. To be under the general law is great for that is to correspond with it. The master knows that he is unspeakabley great and that all are unspeakably great. . . that nothing for instance is greater than to conceive children and bring them up well. . . that to be is just as great as to perceive or tell.

In the make of the great masters the idea of political liberty is indispensable. Liberty takes the adherence of heroes wherever men and women exist. . . but never takes any adherence or welcome from the rest more than from poets. They are the voice and exposition of liberty. They out of ages are worthy the grand idea. . . to them it is confided and they must sustain it. Nothing has precedence of it and nothing can wrap or degrade it. The attitude of great poets is to cheer up slaves and horrify despots. The turn of their necks, the sound of their feet, the motions of their wrists, are full of hazard to the one and hope to the other. Come nigh them awhile and though they neither speak or advise you shall learn the faithful American lesson. Liberty is poorly served by men whose good intent is quelled from one failure or two failures or any number of failures, or from the casual indifference or ingratitude of the people, or from the sharp show of the tushes of power, or the bringing to bear soldiers and cannon or any penal statutes. Liberty relies upon itself, invites no one, promises nothing, sits in calmness and light, is positive and composed, and knows no discouragement. The battle rages with many a loud alarm and frequent advance and retreat. . . the enemy triumphs. . . the prison, the handcuffs, the iron necklace and anklet, the scaffold, garrote and lead balls do their work. . the cause is asleep. . . the strong throats are choked with their own blood. . . the young men drop their eyelashes toward the ground when they pass each other. . . and is liberty gone out of that place? No never. When liberty goes it is not the first to go nor the second nor third to go. . . it waits for all the rest to go. . . it is the last. . . When the memories of the old martyrs are faded utterly away. . . when the large names of patriots are laughed at in the public halls from the lips of the orators. . . when the boys are no more christened after the same but christened after tyrants and traitors instead. . . when the laws of the free are grudgingly permitted and laws of informers and blood money are sweet to the taste of the people. . . when I and you walk abroad upon the earth stung with compassion at the sight of numberless brothers answering our equal friendship and calling no man master—and when we are elated with noble joy at the sight of slaves. . . when the soul retires in the cool communion of the night and surveys its experience and has much extasy over the word and deed that put back a helpless innocent person into the gripe of the gripers or into any cruel inferiority. . . when those in all parts of these states who could easier realize the true American character but do not yet—when the swarms of cringers, suckers, doughfaces, lice of politics, planners of sly involutions for their own preferment to city offices or state legislatures or the judiciary or congress or the presidency, obtain a response of love and natural deference from the people whether they get the offices or no. . . when it is better to be a bound booby and rogue in office at a high salary than the poorest free mechanic or farmer with his hat unmoved from his head and firm eyes and a candid and generous heart. . . and when servility by town or state or the federal government or any oppression on a large scale or small scale can be tried on without its own punishment following duly after in exact proportion against the smallest chance of escape. . . or rather when all life and all the souls of men and women are discharged from any part of the earth—then only shall the instinct of liberty be discharged from that part of the earth.

As the attributes of the poets of the kosmos concenter in the real body and soul and in the pleasure of things they possess the superiority of genuiness over all fiction and romance. As they emit themselves facts are showered over the light. . . the daylight is lit with more volatile light. . . also the deep between the setting and rising sun goes deeper many fold. Each precise object or condition or combination or process exhibits a beauty. . . the multiplication table its—old age its—the carpenter's trade its—the grand opera its. . . the huge hulled clean-shaped New York clipper at sea under steam or full sail gleams with unmatched beauty. . . the American circles and large harmonies of government gleam with theirs. . . and the commonest definite intentions and actions with theirs. The poets of the kosmos advance through all interpositions and coverings and turmoils and stratagems to first principles. They are of use. . . they dissolve poverty from its need and riches from its conceit. You large proprietor they say shall not realize or perceive more than anyone else. The owner of the library is not he who holds a legal title to it having bought and paid for it. Anyone and everyone is owner of the library who can read the same through all the varieties of tongues and sub-jects and styles, and in whom they enter with ease and take residence and force toward paternity and maternity, and make supple and powerful and rich and large. . . These American states strong and healthy and accom-plished shall receive no pleasure from violations of natural models and must not permit them. In paintings or moldings or carvings in mineral or wood, or in the illustrations of books or newspapers, or in any comic or tragic prints, or in the patterns of woven stuffs or anything to beautify rooms or furniture or costumes, or to put upon cornices or monuments or on the prows or sterns of ships, or to put anywhere before the human eye indoors or out, that which distorts honest shapes or which creates unearthly beings or places or contin-gencies is a nuisance and revolt. Of the human form especially it is so great it must never be made ridiculous. Of ornaments to a work nothing outre can be allowed. . . but those ornaments can be allowed that conform to the perfect facts of the open air and that flow out of the nature of the work and come irrepressibly from it and are necessary to the completion of the work. Most works are most beautiful without ornament. . . Exaggerations will be revenged in human physiology. Clean and vigorous children are jetted and conceived only in those communities where the models of natural forms are public every day. . . . Great genius and the people of these states must never be demeaned to romances. As soon as histories are properly told there is no more need of romances.

The great poets are also to be known by the absence in them of tricks and by the justification of perfect personal candor. Then folks echo a new cheap joy and a divine voice leaping from their brains: How beautiful is candor! All faults may be forgiven of him who has perfect candor. Henceforth let no man of us lie, for we have seen that openness wins the inner and outer world and that there is no single exception, and that never since our earth gathered itself in a mass have deceit or subterfuge or prevarication attracted its small-est particle or the faintest tinge of a shade—and that through the enveloping wealth and rank of a state or the whole republic of states a sneak or sly person shall be discovered and despised. . . and that the soul has never been once fooled and never can be fooled. . . and thrift without the loving nod of the soul is only a fetid puff. . . and there never grew up in any of the continents of the globe nor upon any planet or satellite or star, nor upon the asteroids, nor in any part of ethereal space, nor in the midst of density, nor under the fluid wet of the sea, nor in that condition which precedes the birth of babes, nor at any time during the changes of life, nor in that condition that follows what we term death, nor in any stretch of abeyance or action afterward of vitality, nor in any process of formation or reformation anywhere, a being whose instinct hated the truth.

Extreme caution or prudence, the soundest organic health, large hope and comparison and fondness for women and children, large alimentiveness and destructiveness and causality, with a perfect sense of the oneness of nature and the propriety of the same spirit applied to human affairs. . . these are called up of the float of the brain of the world to be parts of the greatest poet from his birth out of his mother's womb and from her birth out of her mother's. Caution seldom goes far enough. It has been thought that the prudent citizen was the citizen who applied himself to solid gains and did well for himself and his family and completed a lawful life without debt or crime. The greatest poet sees and admits these economies as he sees the economies of food and sleep, but has higher notions of prudence than to think he gives much when he gives a few slight attentions at the latch of the gate. The premises of the prudence of life are not the hospitality of it or the ripeness and harvest of it. Beyond the independence of a little sum laid aside for burial money, and of a few clapboards around and shingles overhead on a lot of American soil owned, and the easy dollars that supply the year's plain clothing and meals, the melancholy prudence of the abandonment of such a great being as a man is to the toss and pallor of years of moneymaking with all their scorching days and icy nights and all their stifling deceits and underhanded dodgings, or infinitesimals of parlors, or shameless stuffing while others starve. . . and all the loss of the bloom and odor of the earth and of the flowers and atmosphere and of the sea and of the true taste of the women and men you pass or have to do with in youth or middle age, and the issuing sickness and desperate revolt at the close of a life without elevation or naïveté, and the ghastly chatter of a death without serenity or majesty, is the great fraud upon modern civilization and forethought, blotching the surface and system which civilization undeniably drafts, and moistening with tears the immense features it spreads and spreads with such velocity before the reached kisses of the soul. . . . Still the right explanation remains to be made about prudence. The prudence of the mere wealth and respectability of the most esteemed life appears too faint for the eye to observe at all when little and large alike drop quietly aside at the thought of the prudence suitable for immortality. What is wisdom that fills the thinness of a year or seventy or eighty years to wisdom spaced out by ages and coming back at a certain time with strong reinforcements and rich presents and the clear faces of wedding

guests as far as you can look in every direction running gaily toward you?
Only the soul is of itself. . . all else has reference to what ensues. All that a
person does or thinks is of consequence. Not a move can a man or woman
make that affects him or her in a day or a month or any part of the direct
lifetime or the hour of death but the same affects him or her onward afterward through the indirect lifetime. The indirect is always as great and real as
the direct. The spirit receives from the body just as much as it gives to the
body. Not one name of word or deed. . . not of venereal sores or discolor-
ations. . . not the privacy of the onanist. . . not of the putrid veins of gluttons
or rum drinkers. . . not peculation or cunning or betrayal or 'murder. . . no
serpentine poison of those that seduce women. . . not the foolish yielding of
women. . . not prostitution. . . not of any depravity of young men. . . not of
the attainment of gain by discreditable means. . . not any nastiness of appetite. . . not any harshness of officers to men or judges to prisoners or fathers
to sons or sons to fathers or husbands to wives or bosses to their boys. . . not
of greedy looks or malignant wishes. . . nor any of the wiles practiced by
people upon themselves. . . ever is or ever can be stamped on the program
but it is duly realized and returned, and that returned in further performances. . . and they returned again. Nor can the push of charity or personal
force ever be anything else than the profoundest reason, whether it brings
arguments to hand or no. No specification is necessary. . . to add or subtract
or divide is in vain. Little or big, learned or unlearned, white or black, legal
or illegal, sick or well, from the first inspiration down the windpipe to the
last expiration out of it, all that a male or female does that is vigorous and
benevolent and clean is so much sure profit to him or her in the unshakable
order of the universe and through the whole scope of it forever. If the savage
or felon is wise it is well. . . if the greatest poet or savant is wise it is simply
the same. . . if the President or chief justice is wise it is the same. . . if the
young mechanic or farmer is wise it is no more or less. . . if the prostitute is
wise it is no more or less. The interest will come round. . . all will come
round. All the best actions of war and peace. . . all help given to relatives
and strangers and the poor and old and sorrowful and young children and
widows and the sick, and to all shunned persons. . . all furtherance of fugitives and of the escape of slaves. . . all the self-denial that stood steady and
aloof on wrecks and saw others take the seats of the boats. . . all offering of
substance or life for the good old cause, or for a friend's sake or opinion's
sake. . . all pains of enthusiasts scoffed at by their neighbors. . . all the vast
sweet love and precious suffering of mothers. . . all honest men baffled in
strifes recorded or unrecorded. . . all the grandeur and good of the few
ancient nations whose fragments of annals we inherit. . . and all the good of
the hundreds of far mightier and more ancient nations unknown to us by
name or date or location. . . all that was ever manfully begun, whether it
succeeded or not. . . all that has at any time been well suggested out of the
divine heart of man or by the divinity of his mouth or by the shaping of his

great hands. . . and all that is well thought or done this day on any part of the surface of the globe. . . or on any of the wandering stars or fixed stars by those there as we are here. . . or that is henceforth to be well thought or done by you whoever you are, or by anyone—these singly and wholly inured at their time and inure now and will inure always to the identities from which they sprung or shall spring. . . .Did you guess any of them lived only its moment? The world does not so exist. . . no parts palpable or impalpable so exist. . . no result exists now without being from its long antecedent result, and that from its antecedent, and so backward without the farthest mentionable spot coming a bit nearer to the beginning than any other spot. . . . Whatever satisfies the soul is truth. The prudence of the greatest poet answers at last the craving and glut of the soul, is not contemptuous of less ways of prudence if they conform to its ways, puts off nothing, permits no let-up for its own case or any case, has no particular sabbath or judgment day, divides not the living from the dead or the righteous from the unrighteous, is satisfied with the present, matches every thought or act by its correlative, knows no possible forgiveness or deputed atonement. . . knows that the young man who composedly periled his life and lost it has done exceeding well for himself, while the man who has not periled his life and retains it to old age in riches and ease has perhaps achieved nothing for himself worth mentioning. . . and that only that person has no great prudence to learn who has learnt to prefer real long-lived things, and favors body and soul the same, and perceives the indirect assuredly following the direct, and what evil or good he does leaping onward and waiting to meet him again—and who in his spirit in any emergency whatever neither hurries or avoids death.

The direct trial of him who would be the greatest poet is today. If he does not flood himself with the immediate age as with vast oceanic tides. . . and if he does not attract his own land body and soul to himself and hang on its neck with incomparable love and plunge his semitic muscle into its merits and demerits. . . and if he be not himself the age transfigured. . . and if to him is not opened the eternity which gives similitude to all periods and locations and processes and animate and inanimate forms, and which is the bond of time, and rises up from its inconceivable vagueness and infiniteness in the swimming shape of today, and is held by the ductile anchors of life, and makes the present spot the passage from what was to what shall be, and commits itself to the representation of this wave of an hour and this one of the sixty beautiful children of the wave—let him merge in the general run and wait his development. . . . Still the final test of poems or any character or work remains. The prescient poet projects himself centuries ahead and judges performer or performance after the changes of time. Does it live through them? Does it still hold on untired? Will the same style and the direction of genius to similar points be satisfactory now? Has no new discovery in science or arrival at superior planes of thought and judgment and behavior fixed him or his so that either can be looked down upon? Have the marches of tens and hundreds and thousands of years made willing detours to the right hand and the left hand for his sake? Is he beloved long and long after he is buried? Does the young man think often of hm? and the young woman think often of him? and do the middle-aged and the old think of him?

A great poem is for ages and ages in common and for all degrees and complexions and all departments and sects and for a woman as much as a man and a man as much as a woman. A great poem is no finish to a man or woman but rather a beginning. Has anyone fancied he could sit at last under some due authority and rest satisfied with explanations and realize and be content and full? To no such terminus does the greatest poet bring. . . . he brings neither cessation or sheltered fatness and ease. The touch of him tells in action. Whom he takes he takes with firm sure grasp into live regions previously unattained. . . thenceforward is no rest. . . they see the space and ineffable sheen that turn the old spots and lights into dead vacuums. The companion of him beholds the birth and progress of stars and learns one of the meanings. Now there shall be a man cohered out of tumult and chaos. . . the elder encourages the younger and shows him how. . . they two shall launch off fearlessly together till the new world fits an orbit for itself and looks unabashed on the lesser orbits of the stars and sweeps through the ceaseless rings and shall never be quiet again.

There will soon be no more priests. Their work is done. They may wait awhile. . . perhaps a generation or two. . . dropping off by degrees. A superior breed shall take their place. . . the gangs of kosmos and prophets en masse shall take their place. A new order shall arise and they shall be the priests of man, and every man shall be his own priest. The churches built under their umbrage shall be the churches of men and women. Through the divinity of themselves shall the kosmos and the new breed of poets be interpreters of men and women and of all events and things. They shall find their inspiration in real objects today, symptoms of the past and future. . . They shall not deign to defend immortality or God or the perfection of things or liberty or the exquisite beauty and reality of the soul. They shall arise in America and be responded to from the remainder of the earth.

The English language befriends the grand American expression. . . it is brawny enough and limber and full enough. On the tough stock of a race who through all change of circumstances was never without the idea of political liberty, which is the animus of all liberty, it has attracted the terms of daintier and gayer and subtler and more elegant tongues. It is the powerful language of resistance. . . it is the dialect of common sense. It is the speech of the proud and melancholy races and of all who aspire. It is the chosen tongue to express growth faith self-esteem freedom justice equality friendliness amplitude prudence decision and courage. It is the medium that shall well nigh express the inexpressible.

No great literature nor any style of behavior or oratory or social inter-course or household arrangements or public institutions or the treatment of bosses of employed people, nor executive detail or detail of the army or navy, nor spirit of legislation or courts or police or tuition or architecture or songs or amusements or the costumes of young men, can long elude the jealous and passionate instinct of American standards. Whether or no the sign appears from the mouths of the people, it throbs a live interrogation in every freeman's and freewoman's heart after that which passes by or this built to remain. Is it uniform with my country? Are its disposals without ignominious distinctions? Is it for the evergrowing communes of brothers and lovers, large, well united, proud beyond the old models, generous beyond all models? Is it something grown fresh out of the fields or drawn from the sea for use to me today here? I know that what answers for me an American must answer for any individual or nation that serves for a part of my materi-als. Does this answer? or is it without reference to universal needs? or sprung of the needs of the less developed society of special ranks? or old needs of pleasure overlaid by modern science and forms? Does this acknowledge liberty with audible and absolute acknowledgment, and set slavery at naught for life and death? Will it help breed one good shaped and well hung man, and a woman to be his perfect and independent mate? Does it improve manners? Is it for the nursing of the young of the republic? Does it solve readily with the sweet milk of the nipples of the breasts of the mother of many children? Has it too the old ever-fresh forbearance and impartiality? Does it look with the same love on the last born and those hardening toward stature, and on the errant, and on those who disdain all strength of assault outside of their own?

The poems distilled from other poems will probably pass away. The cow-ard will surely pass away. The expectation of the vital and great can only be satisfied by the demeanor of the vital and great. The swarms of the polished deprecating and reflectors and the polite float off and leave no remem-brance. America prepares with composure and good will for the visitors that have sent word. It is not intellect that is to be their warrant and welcome. The talented, the artist, the ingenious, the editor, the statesman, the eru-dite. . . they are not unappreciated. . . they fall in their place and do their work. The soul of the nation also does its work. No disguise can pass on it. . . no disguise can conceal from it. It rejects none, it permits all. Only toward as good as itself and toward the like of itself will it advance halfway. An indi-vidual is as superb as a nation when he has the qualities which make a superb nation. The soul of the largest and wealthiest and proudest nation may well go half-way to meet that of its poets. The signs are effectual. There is no fear of mistake. If the one is true the other is true. The proof of a poet is that his country absorbs him as affectionately as he has absorbed it.

Song of Myself[1]

1   I celebrate myself, and sing myself,
    And what I assume you shall assume,
    For every atom belonging to me as good belongs to you.

    I loafe and invite my soul,
    I lean and loafe at my ease observing a spear of summer grass.   5

    My tongue, every atom of my blood, form'd from this soil, this air,
    Born here of parents born here from parents the same,
      and their parents the same,
    I, now thirty-seven years old in perfect health begin,
    Hoping to cease not till death.

    Creeds and schools in abeyance,   10
    Retiring back a while sufficed at what they are, but never
      forgotten,
    I harbor for good or bad, I permit to speak at every hazard,
    Nature without check with original energy.

2   Houses and rooms are full of perfumes, the shelves are crowded
      with perfumes,
    I breathe the fragrance myself and know it and like it,   15
    The distillation would intoxicate me also, but I shall not let it.

    The atmosphere is not a perfume, it has no taste of the distillation,
      it is odorless,
    It is for my mouth forever, I am in love with it,
    I will go to the bank by the wood and become undisguised and
      naked,
    I am mad for it to be in contact with me.   20

    The smoke of my own breath,
    Echoes, ripples, buzz'd whispers, love-root, silk-thread, crotch and
      vine,
    My respiration and inspiration, the beating of my heart,
      the passing of blood and air through my lungs,
    The sniff of green leaves and dry leaves, and of the shore
      and dark-color'd sea-rocks, and of hay in the barn,
    The sound of the belch'd words of my voice loos'd to the eddies of
      the wind,   25

[1] The poem is Whitman's most brilliant early expression of his "barbaric yawp," the exaltation of the individual man and his physical nature.

    The first version, printed in 1855 with the preface, was untitled; in 1856 it was called "A Poem of Walt Whitman, an American"; in 1860 and 1867, "Walt Whitman"; and, in 1881, "Song of Myself."

A few light kisses, a few embraces, a reaching around of arms,
The play of shine and shade on the trees as the supple boughs wag,
The delight alone or in the rush of the streets, or along the fields,
    and hill-sides,
The feeling of health, the full-noon trill, the song of me rising from
    bed and meeting the sun.

Have you reckon'd a thousand acres much? have you reckon'd the
    earth much?   30
Have you practis'd so long to learn to read?
Have you felt so proud to get at the meaning of poems?

Stop this day and night with me and you shall possess the origin of
    all poems,
You shall possess the good of the earth and sun, (there are millions
    of suns left,)
You shall no longer take things at second or third hand, nor look
    through the eyes of the dead, nor feed on the spectres in books,   35
You shall not look through my eyes either, nor take things from me,
You shall listen to all sides and filter them from your self.

3 I have heard what the talkers were talking, the talk of the
    beginning and the end,
But I do not talk of the beginning or the end.

There was never any more inception than there is now,   40
Nor any more youth or age than there is now,
And will never be any more perfection than there is now,
Nor any more heaven or hell than there is now.
Urge and urge and urge,
Always the procreant urge of the world.   45

Out of the dimness opposite equals advance, always substance
    and increase, always sex,
Always a knit of identity, always distinction, always a breed of life.

To elaborate is no avail, learn'd and unlearn'd feel that it is so.

Sure as the most certain sure, plumb in the uprights, well
    entretied,[2] braced in the beams,

[2] Cross braced.

Stout as a horse, affectionate, haughty, electrical,   50
I and this mystery here we stand.

Clear and sweet is my soul, and clear and sweet is all that is not
    my soul.

Lack one lacks both, and the unseen is proved by the seen,
Till that becomes unseen and receives proof in its turn.

Showing the best and dividing it from the worst age vexes age,   55
Knowing the perfect fitness and equanimity of things,
    while they discuss I am silent, and go bathe and admire myself.

Welcome is every organ and attribute of me, and of any man
    hearty and clear
Not an inch nor a particle of an inch is vile, and none
    shall be less familiar than the rest.

I am satisfied—I see, dance, laugh, sing;
As the hugging and loving bed-fellow sleeps at my side through the
    night, and withdraws at the peep of the day with stealthy tread,   60
Leaving me baskets cover'd with white towels swelling the house
    with their plenty,
Shall I postpone my acceptation and realization and scream at my
    eyes,
That they turn from gazing after and down the road,
And forthwith cipher and show me to a cent,
Exactly the value of one and exactly the value of two, and which is
    ahead?   65

4   Trippers and askers surround me,
    People I meet, the effect upon me of my early life or the ward and
        city I live in, or the nation,
    The latest dates, discoveries, inventions, societies, authors old and
        new,
    My dinner, dress, associates, looks, compliments, dues,
    The real or fancied indifference of some man or woman I love,   70
    The sickness of one of my folks or of myself, or ill-doing or loss
        or lack of money, or depressions or exaltations,
    Battles, the horrors of fratricidal war, the fever of doubtful news,
        the fitful events;
    These come to me days and nights and go from me again,
    But they are not the Me myself.

Apart from the pulling and hauling stands what I am, 75
Stands amused, complacent, compassionating, idle, unitary,
Looks down, is erect, or bends an arm on an impalpable certain
    rest,
Looking with side-curved head curious what will come next,
Both in and out of the game and watching and wondering at it.

Backward I see in my own days where I sweated through fog
    with linguists and contenders, 80
I have no mockings or arguments, I witness and wait.

5 I believe in you my soul, the other I am must not abase itself to
    you,
And you must not be abased to the other.

Loafe with me on the grass, loose the stop from your throat,
Not words, not music or rhyme I want, not custom or lecture, not
    even the best, 85
Only the lull I like, the hum of your valved voice.

I mind how once we lay such a transparent summer morning,
How you settled your head athwart my hips and gently turn'd
    over upon me,
And parted the shirt from my bosom-bone, and plunged your
    tongue to my bare-stript heart,
And reach'd till you felt my beard, and reach'd till you held my
    feet. 90

Swiftly arose and spread around me the peace and knowledge
    that pass all the argument of the earth,
And I know that the hand of God is the promise of my own,
And I know that the spirit of God is the brother of my own,
And that all the men ever born are also my brothers,
    and the women my sisters and lovers, 95
And that a kelson[3] of the creation is love,
And limitless are leaves stiff or drooping in the fields,
And brown ants in the little wells beneath them,
And mossy scabs of the worm fence, heap'd stones, elder,
    mullein and poke-weed.

6 A child said *What is the grass?* fetching it to me with full hands; 100
How could I answer the child? I do not know what it is any more
    than he

[3] A timber or girder placed parallel with and
bolted to the keel for additional strength.

I guess it must be the flag of my disposition, out of hopeful green
    stuff woven

Or I guess it is the handkerchief of the Lord,
A scented gift and remembrancer designedly dropt,
Bearing the owner's name someway in the corners, that we may
    see and remark, and say *Whose?*   105

Or I guess the grass is itself a child, the produced babe of the
    vegetation.

Or I guess it is a uniform hieroglyphic,
And it means, Sprouting alike in broad zones and narrow zones,
Growing among black folks as among white,
Kanuck, Tuckahoe, Congressman, Cuff,[4] I give them the same,   110
    I receive them the same.

And now it seems to me the beautiful uncut hair of graves.

Tenderly will I use you curling grass,
It may be you transpire from the breasts of young men,
It may be if I had known them I would have loved them,
It may be you are from old people, or from offspring taken soon
    out of their mothers' laps,   115
And here you are the mothers' laps.

This grass is very dark to be from the white heads of old mothers,
Darker than the colorless beards of old men,
Dark to come from under the faint red roofs of mouths.

O I perceive after all so many uttering tongues,   120
And I perceive they do not come from the roofs of mouths for
    nothing.

I wish I could translate the hints about the dead young men and
    women,
And the hints about old men and mothers, and the offspring taken
    soon out of their laps.

What do you think has become of the young and old men?
And what do you think has become of the women and children?   125

[4] "Kanuck" is a French Canadian; "Tuckahoe" is a poor Virginian in the tidewater; and
"Cuff" is a black man.

They are alive and well somewhere,
The smallest sprout shows there is really no death,
And if ever there was it led forward life, and does not wait
    at the end to arrest it,
And ceas'd the moment life appear'd.

All goes onward and outward, nothing collapses,   130
And to die is different from what any one supposed, and luckier.

7 Has any one supposed it lucky to be born?
  I hasten to inform him or her it is just as lucky to die, and I know
      it.

  I pass death with the dying and birth with the new-wash'd babe,
      and am not contain'd between my hat and boots,
  And peruse manifold objects, no two alike and every one good,   135
  The earth good and the stars good, and their adjuncts all good.

  I am not an earth nor an adjunct of an earth,
  I am the mate and companion of people, all just as immortal
      and fathomless as myself,
  (They do not know how immortal, but I know.)

  Every kind for itself and its own, for me mine male and female,   140
  For me those that have been boys and that love women,
  For me the man that is proud and feels how it stings to be slighted,
  For me the sweet-heart and the old maid, for me mothers
      and the mothers of mothers,
  For me lips that have smiled, eyes that have shed tears,
  For me children and the begetters of children.   145

  Undrape! you are not guilty to me, nor stale nor discarded,
  I see through the broadcloth and gingham whether or no,
  And am around, tenacious, acquisitive, tireless, and cannot be
      shaken away.

8 The little one sleeps in its cradle,
  I lift the gauze and look a long time, and silently brush away flies
      with my hand   150

  The youngster and the red-faced girl turn aside up the bushy hill,
  I peeringly view them from the top.

  The suicide sprawls on the bloody floor of the bedroom,
  I witness the corpse with its dabbled hair, I note where the pistol
      has fallen.

The blab of the pave, tires of carts, sluff of boot-soles, talk of the
    promenaders. 155
The heavy omnibus, the driver with his interrogating thumb, the
    clank of the shod horses on the granite floor,
The snow-sleighs, clinking, shouted jokes, pelts of snow-balls,
The hurrahs for popular favorites, the fury of rous'd mobs,
The flap of the curtain'd litter, a sick man inside borne to the
    hospital,
The meeting of enemies, the sudden oath, the blows and fall, 160
The excited crowd, the policeman with his star quickly working
    his passage to the centre of the crowd,
The impassive stones that receive and return so many echoes,
What groans of over-fed or half-starv'd who fall sunstruck or in fits,
What exclamations of women taken suddenly who hurry home
    and give birth to babes,
What living and buried speech is always vibrating here,
    what howls restrain'd be decorum, 165
Arrests of criminals, slights, adulterous offers made, acceptances,
    rejections with convex lips,
I mind them or the show or resonance of them—I come and I
    depart.

9 The big doors of the country barn stand open and ready,
The dried grass of the harvest-time loads the slow-drawn wagon,
The clear light plays on the brown gray and green intertinged, 170
The armfuls are pack'd to the sagging mow.

I am there, I help, I came stretch'd atop of the load,
I felt its soft jolts, one leg reclined on the other,
I jump from the cross-beams and seize the clover and timothy,
And roll head over heels and tangle my hair full of wisps. 175

10 Alone far in the wilds and mountains I hunt,
Wandering amazed at my own lightness and glee,
In the late afternoon choosing a safe spot to pass the night,
Kindling a fire and broiling the fresh-kill'd game,
Falling asleep on the gather'd leaves with my dog and gun by my
    side. 180

The Yankee clipper is under her sky-sails, she cuts the sparkle and
    scud,
My eyes settle the land, I bend at her prow or shout joyously from
    the deck.

The boatmen and clam-diggers arose early and stopt for me,
I tuck'd my trouser-ends in my boots and went and had a good
    time;
You should have been with us that day round the chowder-kettle.   185

I saw the marriage of the trapper in the open air in the far west,
    the bride was a red girl,
Here father and his friends sat near cross-legged and dumbly
    smoking,
    they had moccasins to their feet and large thick blankets
    hanging from their shoulders,
On a bank lounged the trapper, he was drest mostly in skins,
    his luxuriant beard and curls protected his neck,
    he held his bride by the hand,
She had long eyelashes, her head was bare, her coarse straight
    locks
    descended upon her voluptuous limbs and reach'd to her feet.

The runaway slave came to my house and stopt outside,   190
I heard his motions crackling the twigs of the woodpile,
Through the swung half-door of the kitchen I saw him limpsy and
    weak,
And went where he sat on a log and led him in and assured him,
And brought water and fill'd a tub for his sweated body and
    bruis'd feet,
And gave him a room that enter'd from my own, and gave him
    some coarse clean clothes,   195
And remember perfectly well his revolving eyes and his
    awkwardness,
And remember putting plasters on the galls of his neck and ankles;
He staid with me a week before he was recuperated and pass'd
    north,
I had him sit next me at table, my fire-lock lean'd in the corner.

11 Twenty-eight young men bathe by the shore,   200
Twenty-eight young men and all so friendly;
Twenty-eight years of womanly life and all so lonesome.

She owns the fine house by the rise of the bank,
She hides handsome and richly drest aft the blinds of the window.

Which of the young men does she like the best?   205
Ah the homeliest of them is beautiful to her.

Where are you off to, lady? for I see you,
You splash in the water there, yet stay stock still in your room.

Dancing and laughing along the beach came the twenty-ninth
    bather,
The rest did not see her, but she saw them and loved them.   210

The beards of the young men glisten'd with wet,
    it ran from their long hair,
Little streams pass'd all over their bodies.

An unseen hand also pass'd over their bodies,
It descended tremblingly from their temples and ribs.

The young men float on their backs, their white bellies bulge to the
    sun, they do not ask who seizes fast to them,   215
They do not know who puffs and declines with pendant and
    bending arch,
They do not think whom they souse with spray.

12 The butcher-boy puts off his killing-clothes, or sharpens his knife
    at the stall in the market,
I loiter enjoying his repartee and his shuffle and break-down.[5]

Blacksmiths with grimed and hairy chests environ the anvil,   220
Each has his main-sledge, they are all out, there is a great heat in
    the fire.

From the cinder-strew'd threshold I follow their movements,
The lithe sheer of their waists plays even with their massive arms,
Overhand the hammers swing, overhand so slow, overhand so sure,
They do not hasten, each man hits in his place.   225

13 The negro holds firmly the reins of his four horses, the block swags
    underneath on its tied-over chain,
The negro drives the long dray of the stone-yard, steady and tall
    he stands pois'd on one leg on the string-piece,
His blue shirt exposes his ample neck and breast and loosens over
    his hip-band,
His glance is calm and commanding, he tosses the slouch of his hat
    away from his forehead,   230
The sun falls on his crispy hair and mustache, falls on the black
    of his polish'd and perfect limbs.

I behold the picturesque giant and love him, and I do not stop
    there,
I go with the team also.

---

[5] The "shuffle" is a sliding dance; the "break-
down" a festive and noisy dance.

In me the caresser of life wherever moving, backward as well as
    forward sluing
To niches aside and junior bending, not a person or object missing,   235
Absorbing all to myself and for this song.

Oxen that rattle the yoke and chain or halt in the leafy shade,
    what is that you express in your eyes?
It seems to me more than all the print I have read in my life.

My tread scares the wood-drake and wood-duck on my distant
    and day-long ramble,
They rise together, they slowly circle around.   240

I believe in those wing'd purposes,
And acknowledge red, yellow, white, playing within me,
And consider green and violet and the tufted crown intentional,
And do not call the tortoise unworthy because she is not something
    else,
And the jay in the woods never studied the gamut, yet trills pretty
    well to me,   245
And the look of the bay mare shames silliness out of me.

14 The wild gander leads his flock through the cool night,
Ya-honk he says, and sounds it down to me like an invitation,
The pert may suppose it meaningless, but I listening close,
Find its purpose and place up there toward the wintry sky.   250

The sharp-hoof'd moose of the north, the cat on the house-sill,
    the chickadee, the prairie-dog,
The litter of the grunting sow as they tug at her teats,
The brood of the turkey-hen and she with her half-spread wings,
I see in them and myself the same old law.

The press of my foot to the earth springs a hundred affections,   255
They scorn the best I can do to relate them.

I am enamour'd of growing out-doors,
Of men that live among cattle or taste of the ocean or woods,
Of the builders and steerers of ships and the wielders of axes and
    mauls, and the drivers of horses,
I can eat and sleep with them week in and week out.   260

What is commonest, cheapest, nearest, easiest, is Me,
Me going in for my chances, spending for vast returns,
Adorning myself to bestow myself on the first that will take me,
Not asking the sky to come down to my good will,
Scattering it freely forever.   265

¹⁵ The pure contralto sings in the organ loft,
The carpenter dresses his plank, the tongue of his foreplane
  whistles its wild ascending lisp,
The married and unmarried children ride home to their
  Thanksgiving dinner.
The pilot seizes the king-pin, he heaves down with a strong arm,
The mate stands braced in the whale-boat, lance and harpoon are
  ready, 270
The duck-shooter walks by silent and cautious stretches,
The deacons are ordain'd with cross'd hands at the altar,
The spinning-girl retreats and advances to the hum of the big
  wheel,
The farmer stops by the bars as he walks on a First-day[6] loafe
  and looks at the oats and rye,
The lunatic is carried at last to the asylum a confirm'd case, 275
(He will never sleep any more as he did in the cot
  in his mother's bed-room;)
The jour printer with gray head and gaunt jaws works at his case,[7]
He turns his quid of tobacco while his eyes blurr with the
  manuscript;
The malform'd limbs are tied to the surgeon's table,
What is removed drops horribly in a pail; 280
The quadroon girl is sold at the auction-stand, the drunkard nods
  by the bar-room stove,
The machinist rolls up his sleeves, the policeman travels his beat,
  the gate-keeper marks who pass,
The young fellow drives the express-wagon, (I love him,
  though I do not know him;)
The half-breed straps on his light boots to compete in the race,
The western turkey-shooting draws old and young,
  some lean on their rifles, some sit on logs, 285
Out from the crowds steps the marksman, takes his position, levels
  his piece;
The groups of newly-come immigrants cover the wharf or levee,
As the woolly-pates hoe in the sugar-field, the overseer views them
  from his saddle,
The bugle calls in the ball-room, the gentlemen run for their
  partners, the dancers bow to each other,
The youth lies awake in the cedar-roof'd garret and harks to the
  musical rain, 290

---

[6] The Quaker term for Sunday.   [7] The box that holds type.

The Wolverine[8] sets traps on the creek that helps fill the Huron,

The squaw wrapt in her yellow-hemm'd cloth is offering moccasins
and bead-bags for sale,

The connoisseur peers along the exhibition-gallery with half-shut
eyes bent sideways,

As the deck-hand makes fast the steamboat the plank is thrown
for the shore-going passengers,

The young sister holds out the skein while the elder sister winds it
off in a ball, and stops now and then for the knots,   295

The one-year wife is recovering and happy having a week ago
borne her first child,

The clean-hair'd Yankee girl works with her sewing-machine
or in the factory or mill,

The paving-man leans on his two-handed rammer, the reporter's
lead flies swiftly over the note-book, the sign-painter
is lettering with blue and gold,

The canal boy trots on the tow-path, the book-keeper counts at his
desk, the shoemaker waxes his thread,

The conductor beats time for the band and all the performers
follow him,   300

The child is baptized, the convert is making his first professions,

The regatta is spread on the bay, the race is begun, (how the white
sails sparkle!)

The drover watching his drove sings out to them that would stray,

The pedler sweats with his pack on his back,
(the purchaser higgling about the odd cent;)

The bride unrumples her white dress, the minute-hand of the clock
moves slowly,   305

The opium-eater reclines with rigid head and just-open'd lips,

The prostitute draggles her shawl, her bonnet bobs on her tipsy
and pimpled neck,

The crowd laugh at her blackguard oaths, the men jeer and wink
to each other

(Miserable! I do not laugh at your oaths nor jeer you;)   310

The President holding a cabinet council is surrounded by the great
Secretaries,

---

[8] A native of Michigan.

On the piazza walk three matrons stately and friendly with twined
    arms,
The crew of the fish-smack pack repeated layers of halibut in the
    hold,
The Missourian crosses the plains toting his wares and his cattle,
As the fare-collector goes through the train he gives notice
    by the jingling of loose change,   315
The floor-men are laying the floor, the tinners are tinning the roof,
    the masons are calling for mortar,
In single file each shouldering his hod pass onward the laborers;
Seasons pursuing each other the indescribable crowd is gather'd,
    it is the fourth of Seventh-month,[9] (what salutes of cannon and
    small arms!)
Seasons pursuing each other the plougher ploughs, the mower
    mows, and the winter grain falls in the ground;
Off on the lakes the pike-fisher watches and waits
    by the hole in the frozen surface,   320
The stumps stand thick round the clearing, the squatter strikes
    deep with his axe,
Flatboatmen make fast towards dusk near the cotton-wood or
    pecan-trees, drain'd by the Tennessee, or through those of the
    Arkansas,
Torches shine in the dark that hangs on the Chattahoochee or
    Altamahaw,
Patriarchs sit at supper with sons and grandsons and great-
    grandsons around them,   325
In walls of adobie,[10] in canvas tents, rest hunters and trappers
    after their days sport,
The city sleeps and the country sleeps,
The living sleep for their time, the dead sleep for their time,
The old husband sleeps by his wife and the young husband sleeps
    by his wife;
And these tend inward to me and I tend outward to them,   330
And such as it is to be of these more or less I am,
And of these one and all I weave the song of myself.

[9] The Quaker term for the Fourth of July.
[10] A sun-dried, unburned brick of clay and
straw—used for a Spanish house.

¹⁶ I am of old and young, of the foolish as much as the wise,
Regardless of others, ever regardful of others,
Maternal as well as paternal, a child as well as a man,   335
Stuff'd with the stuff that is coarse and stuff'd with the stuff that is
    fine,
One of the Nation of many nations, the smallest the same
    and the largest the same,
A Southerner soon as a Northern, a planter nonchalant and
    hospitable down by the Ocnee¹¹ I live,
A Yankee bound my own way ready for trade, my joints the
    limberest joints on earth and the sternest joints on earth,   340
A Kentuchian walking vale of the Elkhorn in my deer-skin leggings,
    a Louisianian or Georgian,
A boatman over lakes or bays or along coasts, a Hoosier, Badger,
    Buckeye;¹²
At home on Kanadian snow-shoes or up in the bush, or with
    fishermen off Newfoundland,
At home in the fleet of ice-boats, sailing with the rest and tacking,
At home on the hills of Vermont or in the woods of Maine, or the
    Texan ranch,   345
Comrade of Californians, comrade of free North-Westerners,
    (loving their big proportions,)
Comrade of raftsmen and coalmen, comrade of all who shake
    hands and welcome to drink and meat,
A learner with the simplest, a teacher of the thoughtfullest,
A novice beginning yet experient of myraids of seasons,
Of every hue and caste am I, of every rank and religion,   350
A farmer, mechanic, artist, gentleman, sailor, quaker,
Prisoner, fancy-man, rowdy, lawyer, physician, priest.

I resist any thing better than my own diversity,
Breathe the air but leave plenty after me,
And am not stuck up, and am in my place.   355

(The moth and the fish-eggs are in their place,
The bright suns I see the dark suns I cannot see are in their place,
The palpable is in its place and the impalpable is in its place.)

---

¹¹ Oconee is a river in Northeast Georgia.   ¹² Slang for Indiana, Wisconsin, Ohio.

17 These are really the thoughts of all men in all ages and lands,
    they are not original with me,
  If they are not yours as much as mine they are nothing, or next to
    nothing,   360
  If they are not the riddle and the untying of the riddle they are
    nothing,
  If they are not just as close as they are distant they are nothing.

  This is the grass that grows wherever the land is and the water is,
  This the common air that bathes the globe.

18 With music strong I come, with my cornets and my drums,   365
  I play not marches for accepted victors only, I play marches
    for conquer'd and slain persons.

  Have you heard that it was good to gain the day?
  I also say it is good to fall, battles are lost in the same spirit
    in which they are won.

  I beat and pound for the dead,
  I blow through my embouchures[13] my loudest and gayest for them.   370

  Vivas to those who have fail'd!
  And to those whose war-vessels sank in the sea!
  And to those themselves who sank in the sea!
  And to all generals that lost engagements, and all overcome heroes!
  And the numberless unknown heroes equal to the greatest heroes
    known!   375

19 This is the meal equally set, this the meat for natural hunger,
  It is for the wicked just the same as the righteous, I make
    appointments with.
  I will not have a single person slighted or left away,
  The kept-woman, sponger, thief, are hereby invited,
  The heavy-lipp'd slave is invited, the veneralee is invited;   380
  There shall be no difference between them and the rest.

  This the press of a bashful hand, this the float and odor of hair,
  This the touch of my lips to yours, this the murmur of yearning,
  This the far-off depth and height reflecting my own face,
  This the thoughtful merge of myself, and the outlet again.   385

  Do you guess I have some intricate purpose?
  Well I have, for the Fourth-month[14] showers have,
    and the mica on the side of a rock has.

---

[13] Mouthpieces of instruments.   [14] April.

Do you take it I would astonish?

Does the daylight astonish? does the early redstart twittering
through the woods?
Do I astonish more than they?   390

This hour I tell things in confidence,
I might not tell everybody, but I will tell you.

20 Who goes there? hankering, gross, mystical, nude;
How is it I extract strength from the beef I eat?

What is a man anyhow? what am I? what are you?   395

All I mark as my own you shall offset it with your own,
Else it were time lost listening to me.

I do not snivel that snivel the world over,
That months are vacuums and the ground but wallow and filth.

Whimpering and truckling fold with powders for invalids,
conformity goes to the fourth-remov'd,   400
I wear my hat as I please indoors or out.

Why should I pray? why should I venerate and be ceremonious?

Having pried through the strata, analyzed to a hair,
counsel'd with doctors and calculated close,
I find no sweeter fat than sticks to my own bones.

In all people I see myself, none more and not one a barley-corn
less,   405
And the good or bad I say of myself I say of them.

I know I am solid and sound,
To me the converging objects of the universe perpetually flow,
All are written to me, and I must get what the writing means.

I know I am deathless,   410
I know this orbit of mine cannot be swept by a carpenter's
compass,
I know I shall not pass like a child's carlacue cut with a burnt stick
at night.

I know I am august,
I do not trouble my spirit to vindicate itself or be understood,
I see that the elementary laws never apologize,   415
(I reckon I behave no prouder than the level I plant my house by,
after all.)

I exist as I am, that is enough,
If no other in the world be aware I sit content,
And if each and all be aware I sit content.

One world is aware and by far the largest to me, and that is
    myself,   420
And whether I come to my own to-day or in ten thousand or ten
    million years,
I can cheerfully take it now, or with equal cheerfulness I can wait.

My foothold is tenon'd and mortis'd in granite,
I laugh at what you call dissolution,
And I know the amplitude of time.   425

21 I am the poet of the Body and I am the poet of the Soul,
The pleasures of heaven are with me and the pains of hell are with
    me,
The first I graft and increase upon myself, the latter I translate
    into a new tongue.

I am the poet of the woman the same as the man,
And I say it is as great to be a woman as to be a man,   430
And I say there is nothing greater than the mother of men.

I chant the chant of dilation or pride,
We have had ducking and deprecating about enough,
I show that size is only deprecating about enough,
I show that size is only development.

Have you outstript the rest? are you the President?   435
It is a trifle, they will more than arrive there everyone, and still
    pass on.

I am he that walks with the tender and growing night,
I call to the earth and sea half-held by the night.

Press close bare-bosom'd night—press close magnetic nourishing
    night!
Night of south winds—night of the large few stars!   440
Still nodding night—mad naked summer night.

Smile O voluptuous cool-breath'd earth!
Earth of the slumbering and liquid trees!
Earth of departed sunset—earth of the mountains misty-topt!
Earth of the vitreous[15] pour of the full moon just tinged with blue!   445
Earth of shine and dark mottling the tide of the river!
Earth of the limpid gray of clouds brighter and clearer for my
    sake!
Far-swooping elbow'd earth—rich apple-blossom'd earth!
Smile, for your lover comes.

[15] Pertaining to glass.

Prodigal, you have given me love—therefore I to you give love!   450
O unspeakable passionate love.

22 You sea! I resign myself to you also—I guess what you mean,
I behold from the beach your crooked inviting fingers,
I believe you refuse to go back without feeling of me,
We must have a turn together, I undress, hurry me out of sight of
    the land,   455
Cushion me soft, rock me in billowy drowse,
Dash me with amorous wet, I can repay you.

Sea of stretch'd ground-swells,
Sea breathing broad and convulsive breaths,
Sea of the brine of life and of unshovell'd yet always-ready graves,   460
Howler and scooper of storms, capricious and dainty sea,
I am integral with you, I too am of one phase and of all phases.

Partaker of influx and efflux I, extoller of hate and conciliation,
Extoller of armies and those that sleep in each others' arms.

I am he attesting sympathy,   465
(Shall I make my list of things in the house and skip the house
    that supports them?)

I am not the poet of goodness only, I do not decline to be
the poet of wickedness also.

What blurt is this about virtue and about vice?
Evil propels me and reform of evil propels me, I stand indifferent,
My gait is no fault-finder's or rejecter's gait,   470
I moisten the roots of all that has grown.

Did you fear some scrofula[16] out of the unflagging pregnancy?
Did you guess the celestial laws are yet to be work'd over and
    rectified?

I find one side a balance and the antipodal side a balance,
Soft doctrine as steady help as stable doctrine,   475
Thought and deeds of the present our rouse and early start.

This minute that comes to me over the past decillions,[17]
There is no better than it and now.

What behaved well in the past or behaves well to-day is not such a
    wonder,
The wonder is always and always how there can be a mean man or
    an infidel.   480

_____

[16] Predisposition to tuberculosis and respira-   [17] One followed by 33 zeroes, 10^{33}.
tory catarrhs.

23 Endless unfolding of words of ages!
    And mine a word of the modern, the word En-Masse.

    A word of the faith that never balks,
    Here or henceforward it is all the same to me, I accept Time
        absolutely.

    It alone is without flaw, it alone rounds and completes all,   485
    That mystic baffling wonder alone completes all.

    I accept Reality and dare not question it,
    Materialism first and last imbuing.

    Hurrah for positive science! long live exact demonstration!
    Fetch stonecrop mixt with cedar and branches of lilac,   490
    This is the lexicographer, this the chemist, this made a grammar
        of the old cartouches, [18]
    These mariners put the ship through dangerous unknown seas,
    This is the geologist, this works with the scalpel, and this is a
        mathematician.

    Gentlemen, to you be first honors always!   495
    Your facts are useful, and yet they are not my dwelling,
    I but enter by them to an area of my dwelling.
    Less the reminders of properties told my words,
    And more the reminders they of life untold, and of freedom
        and extrication,

    And make short account of neuters and geldings, [19] and favor men
        and women fully equipt,
    And beat the gong of revolt, and stop with fugitives
        and them that plot and conspire.   500

24 Walt Whitman, a kosmos, of Manhattan the son,
    Turbulent, fleshy, sensual, eating, drinking and breeding,
    No sentimentalist, no stander above men and women or apart from
        them,
    No more modest than immodest.

    Unscrew the locks from the doors!   505
    Unscrew the doors themselves from their jambs!

    Whoever degrades another degrades me,
    And whatever is done or said returns at last to me.

---

[18] Scroll-like tablets used to provide space   [19] Castrated animals.
for inscriptions.

Through me the afflatus[20] surging and surging, through me
    the current and index.

I speak the pass-word primeval, I give the sign of democracy,   510
By God! I will accept nothing which all cannot have their
    counterpart of on the same terms.

Through me many long dumb voices,
Voices of the interminable generations of prisoners and slaves,
Voices of the diseas'd and despairing and of thieves and dwarfs,
Voices of cycles of preparation and accretion,   515
And of the threads that connect the stars, and of wombs
    and of the father-stuff,
And of the rights of them the others are down upon,
Of the deform'd, trivial, flat, foolish, despised,
Fog in the air, beetles rolling balls of dung.

Through me forbidden voices,   520
Voices of sexes and lusts, voices veil'd and I remove the veil,
Voices indecent by me clarified and transfigur'd.

I do not press my fingers across my mouth,
I keep as delicate around the bowels as around the head and heart,

Copulation is no more rank to me than death is.   525

I believe in the flesh and the appetites,
Seeing, hearing, feeling, are miracles, and each part and tag of me
    is a miracle.

Divine am I inside and out, and I make holy whatever I touch
    or am touch'd from,
The scent of these arm-pits aroma finer than prayer,
This head more than churches, bibles, and all the creeds.   530

If I worship one thing more than another it shall be the spread
    of my own body, or any part of it,
Translucent mould of me it shall be you!
Shaded ledges and rests it shall be you!
Firm masculine colter it shall be you!
Whatever goes to the tilth[21] of me it shall be you!   535
You my rich blood! your milky stream pale strippings of my life!
Breast that presses against other breasts it shall be you!
My brain it shall be your occult convolutions!
Root of wash'd sweet-flag! timorous pond-snipe! nest of guarded
    duplicate eggs! it shall be you!   540

---

[20] A creative impulse.   [21] The tilled earth.

Mix'd tussled hay of head, beard, brawn, it shall be you!
Trickling sap of maple, fibre of manly wheat, it shall be you!
Sun so generous it shall be you!
Vapors lighting and shading my face it shall be you!
You sweaty brooks and dews it shall be you!   545
Winds whose soft-tickling genitals rub against me it shall be you!
Broad muscular fields, branches of live oak, loving lounger
    in my winding paths, it shall be you!
Hands I have taken, face I have kiss'd, mortal I have ever touch'd,
    it shall be you.

I dote on myself, there is that lot of me and all so luscious,
Each moment and whatever happens thrills me with joy,   550
I cannot tell how my ankles bend, nor whence the cause of my
    faintest wish,
Nor the cause of the friendship I emit, nor the cause of the
    friendship I take again.

That I walk up my stoop, I pause to consider if it really be,
A morning-glory at my window satisfies me more than the
    metaphysics of books.

To behold the day-break!   555
The little light fades the immense and diaphanous shadows,
The air tastes good to my palate.

Hefts of the moving world at innocent gambols silently rising,
    freshly exuding,
Scooting obliquely high and low.

Something I cannot see puts upward libidinous prong,   560
Seas of bright juice suffuse heaven.

The earth by the sky staid with, the daily close of their junctions
The heav'd challenge from the east that, moment over my head,
The mocking taunt, See then whether you shall be master!

25 Dazzling and tremendous how quick the sun-rise would kill me,   565
If I could not now and always send sun-rise out of me.

We also ascend dazzling and tremendous as the sun,
We found our own O my soul in the calm and cool of the day-
    break.

My voice goes after what my eyes cannot reach,
With the twirl of my tongue I encompass worlds and volumes of
    worlds.   570

Speech is the twin of my vision, it is unequal to measure itself,
It provokes me forever, it says sarcastically,
Walt you contain enough, why don't you let it out then?

Come now I will not be tantalized, you conceive too much of
   articulation,
Do you not know O speech how the buds beneath you are folded?   575
Waiting in gloom, protected by frost,
The dirt receding before my prophetical screams,
I underlying causes to balance them at last,
My knowledge my live parts, it keeping tally with the meaning of
   all things,
Happiness, (which whoever hears me let him or her
   set out in search of this day.)   580

My final merit I refuse you, I refuse putting from me what I really
   am,

Encompass worlds, but never try to encompass me,
I crowd your sleekest and best by simply looking toward you.

Writing and talk do not prove me,
I carry the plenum of proof and every thing else in my face,   585
With the hush of my lips I wholly confound the skeptic.

26 Now I will do nothing but listen,
   To accrue what I hear into this song, to let sounds contribute
      toward it.

I hear bravuras of birds, bustle of growing wheat, gossip flames,
   clack of sticks cooking my meals,
I hear the sound I love, the sound of the human voice,   590
I hear all sounds running together, combined, fused or following,
Sounds of the city and sounds out of the city, sounds of the day
   and night,
Talkative young ones to those that like them,
   the loud laugh of work-people at their meals,
The angry base of disjointed friendship, the faint tones of the sick,
The judge with hands tight to the desk, his pallid lips
   pronouncing a death-sentence,   595
The heave' e' yo of stevedors unlading ships by the wharves,
   the refrain of the anchor-lifters,
The ring of alarm-bells, the cry of fire, the whirr of swift-streaking
   engines and hose-carts with premonitory tinkles and color'd
   lights,

The steam-whistle, the solid roll of the train of approaching cars,
The slow march play'd at the head of the association marching two
    and two,
(They go to guard some corpse, the flag-tops are draped with black
    muslin.)   600

I hear the violoncello, ('tis the young man's heart's complaint,)
I hear the key'd cornet, it glides quickly in through my ears,
It shakes mad-sweet pangs through my belly and breast.

I hear the chorus, it is a grand opera,
Ah this indeed is music—this suits me.

A tenor large and fresh as the creation fills me,   605
The orbic flex of his mouth is pouring and filling me full.

I hear the train'd soprano (what work with hers is this?)
The orchestra whirls me wider than Uranus[22] flies,
It wrenches such ardors from me I did not know I possess'd them,
It sails me, I dab with bare feet, they are lick'd by the indolent
    waves,   610
I am cut by bitter and angry hail, I lose my breath,
Steep'd amid honey'd morphine, my windpipe throttled in fakes of
    death,
At length let up again to feel the puzzle of puzzles,
And that we call Being.

27 To be in any form, what is that?   615
(Round and round we go, all of us, and ever come back thither,)
If nothing lay more develop'd the quahaug[23] in its callous shell
    were enough.

Mine is no callous shell,
I have instant conductors all over me whether I pass or stop,
They seize every object and lead it harmlessly through me.   620

I merely stir, press, feel with my fingers, and am happy,
To touch my person to some one else's is about as much as I can
    stand.

[22] The seventh planet from the sun, an early   [23] An edible, hard-shelled clam.
supreme god in Greek mythology, the per-
sonification of the sky.

28 Is this then a touch? quivering me to a new identity,
Flames and ether making a rush for my veins,
Treacherous tip of me reaching and crowding to help them,   625
My flesh and blood playing out lightning to strike
    what is hardly different from myself,
On all sides prurient provokers stiffening my limbs,
Straining the udder of my heart for its withheld drip,
Behaving licentious toward me, taking no denial,
Depriving me of my best as for a purpose,   630
Unbuttoning my clothes, holding me by the bare waist,
Deluding my confusion with the calm of the sunlight and pasture-
    fields,
Immodestly sliding the fellow-senses away,
They bribed to swap off with touch and go and graze at the edges
    of me,
No consideration, no regard for my draining strength or my anger,   635
Fetching the rest of the herd around to enjoy them a while,
Then all uniting to stand on a headland and worry me.

The sentries desert every other part of me,
They have left me helpless to a red marauder,
They all come to the headland to witness and assist against me.   640

I am given up by traitors,
I talk wildly, I have lost my wits, I and nobody else am the
    greatest traitor,
I went myself first to the headland, my own hands carried me
    there.

You villain touch! what are you doing? my breath is tight in its
    throat,
Unclench your floodgates, you are too much for me.   645

29 Blind loving wrestling touch, sheath'd hooded sharp-tooth'd touch!
Did it make you ache so, leaving me?

Parting track'd by arriving, perpetual payment of perpetual loan,
Rich showering rain, and recompense richer afterward.

Sprouts take and accumulate, stand by the curb prolific and vital,   650
Landscapes projected masculine, full-sized and golden.

30 All truths wait in all things,
They neither hasten their own delivery nor resist it,
They do not need the obstetric forceps of the surgeon,
The insignificant is as big to me as any,   655
(What is less or more than a touch.)

Logic and sermons never convince,
The damp of the night drives deeper into my soul.

(Only what proves itself to every man and woman is so,
Only what nobody denies is so.)   660

A minute and a drop of me settle my brain,
I believe the soggy clods shall become lovers and lamps,
And a compend of compends is the meat of a man or woman,
And a summit and flower there is the feeling they have for each
    other,
And they are to branch boundlessly out of that lesson until it
    becomes omnific,   665
And until one and all shall delight us, and we them.

31 I believe a leaf of grass is no less than the journey-work of the
    stars,
And the pismire[24] is equally perfect, and a grain of sand, and the
    egg of the wren,
And the tree-toad is a chef-d'œuvre for the highest,
And the running blackberry would adorn the parlors of heaven,

And the narrowest hinge in my hand puts to scorn all machinery, 670
And the cow crunching with depress'd head surpasses any statue,
And a mouse is miracle enough to stagger sextillions[25] of infidels.

I find I incorporate gneiss,[26] cola, long-threaded moss, fruits, grains,
    esculent[27] roots,
And am stucco'd with quadrupeds and birds all over,
And have distanced what is behind me for good reasons,   675
But call any thing back again when I desire it.

In vain the speeding or shyness,
In vain the plutonic rocks send their old heat against my approach,
In vain the mastodon retreats beneath its own powder'd bones,
In vain objects stand leagues off and assume manifold shapes,   680
In vain the ocean settling in hollows and the great monsters lying
    low,
In vain the buzzard houses herself with the sky,
In vain the snake slides through the creepers and logs,
In vain the elk takes to the inner passes of the woods,
In vain the razor-bill'd auk sails far north to Labrador,   685
I follow quickly, I ascend to the nest in the fissure of the cliff.

[24] An ant.   [27] Edible.
[25] One followed by 21 zeroes, 10^{21}.
[26] A kind of granite, in which the minerals
are arranged in layers.

³² I think I could turn and live with animals, they are so placid and
   self-contain'd,
I stand and look at them long and long.

They do not sweat and whine about their condition,
They do not lie awake in the dark and weep for their sins,   690
They do not make me sick discussing their duty to God,
Not one is dissatisfied, no one is demented with the mania of
   owning things.
Not one kneels to another, nor to his kind that lived thousands of
   years ago,
Not one is respectable or unhappy over the whole earth.

So they show their relations to me and I accept them,
They bring me tokens of myself, they evince them plainly in their
   possession.   695

I wonder where they get those tokens,
Did I pass that way huge times ago and negligently drop them?
Myself moving forward then and now and forever,
Gathering and showing more always and with velocity,
Infinite and omnigenous, and the like of these among them,   700
Not too exclusive toward the reaches of my remembrancers,
Picking out here one that I love, and now go with him on brotherly
   terms.

A gigantic beauty of a stallion, fresh and responsive to my caresses,
Head high in the forehead, wide between the ears,
Limbs glossy and supple, tail dusting the ground   705
Eyes full of sparkling wickedness, ears finely cut, flexibly moving.

His nostrils dilate as my heels embrace him,
His well-built limbs tremble with pleasure as we race around and
   return.

I but use you a minute, then I resign you, stallion,
Why do I need your paces when I myself out-gallop them?   710
Even as I stand or sit passing faster than you.

³³ Space and Time! now I see it is true, what I guess'd at,
What I guess'd when I loaf'd on the grass,
What I guess'd while I lay alone in my bed,
And again as I walk'd the beach under the paling stars of the
   morning.   715

My ties and ballasts leave me, my elbows rest in sea-gaps,
I skirt sierras, my palms cover continents,
I am afoot with my vision.

By the city's quadrangular houses—in log huts, camping with
    lumbermen,
Along the ruts of the turnpike, along the dry gulch and rivulet bed,   720
Weeding my onion-patch or hoeing rows of carrots and parsnips,
    crossing savannas,[28] trailing in forests,
Prospecting, gold-digging, girdling the trees of a new purchase,
Scorch'd ankle-deep by the hot sand, hauling my boat
    down the shallow river,
Where the panther walks to and fro on a limb overhead,
Where the buck turns furiously at the hunter,   725
Where the rattlesnake suns his flabby length on a rock,
    where the otter is feeding on fish,
Where the alligator in his tough pimples sleeps by the bayou,
Where the black bear is searching for roots or honey, where the
    beaver pats the mud with his paddle-shaped tail;
Over the growing sugar, over the yellow-flower'd cotton plant,
    over the rice in its low moist field,
Over the sharp-peak'd farm house, with its scallop'd scum
    and slender shoots from the gutters,   730
Over the western persimmon, over the long-leav'd corn,
    over the delicate blue-flower flax,
Over the white and brown buckwheat, a hummer and buzzer
    there with the rest,
Over the dusky green of the rye as it ripples and shades in the
    breeze;
Scaling mountains, pulling myself cautiously up, holding on by low
    scragged limbs,
Walking the path worn in the grass and beat through the leaves of
    the brush,   735
Where the quail is whistling betwixt the woods and the wheat-lot,
Where the bat flies in the Seventh-month eve, where the great
    gold-bug drops through the dark,
Where the brook puts out of the roots of the old tree and flows to
    the meadow,
Where cattle stand and shake away flies with the tremulous
    shuddering of their hides,
Where the cheese-cloth hangs in the kitchen, where andirons
    straddle
    the hearth-slab, where cobwebs fall in festoons from the rafters;   740

[28] Flat, treeless grassland in the tropics.

Where trip-hammers crash, where the press is whirling its
   cylinders,
Wherever the human heart beats with terrible throes under its ribs,
Where the pear-shaped balloon is floating aloft,
   (floating in it myself and looking composedly down,)
Where the lift-car is drawn on the slip-noose, where the heat
   hatches pale-green eggs in the dented sand,
Where the she-whale swims with her calf and never forsakes it,   745
Where the steam-ship trails hind-ways its long pennant of smoke,
Where the fin of the shark cuts like a black chip out of the water,
Where the half-burn'd brig is riding on unknown currents,
Where shells grow to her slimy deck, where the dead are
   corrupting below;
Where the dense-starr'd flag is borne at the head of the regiments,   750
Approaching Manhattan up by the long-stretching island,
Under Niagara, the cataract falling like a veil over my
   countenance,
Upon a door-step, upon the horse-block of hard wood outside,
Upon the race-course, or enjoying picnics or jigs or a good game of
   base-ball,
At he-festivals, with blackguard gibes, ironical license, bull-dances,
   drinking, laughter,   755
At the cider-mill tasting the sweets of the brown mash,
   sucking the juice through a straw,
At apple-peelings wanting kisses for all the red fruit I find,
At musters, beach-parties, friendly bees, huskings, house-raisings;
Where the mocking-bird sounds his delicious gurgles, cackles,
   screams, weeps,
Where the hay-rick stands in the barn-yard, where the dry-stalks
   are scatter'd, where the brood-cow waits in the hovel,   760
Where the bull advances to do his masculine work, where the stud
   to the mare, where the cock is treading the hen,
Where the heifers browse, where geese nip their food with short
   jerks,
Where sun-down shadows lengthen over the limitless and lonesome
   prairie,
Where herds of buffalo make a crawling spread of the square miles
   far and near,
Where the humming-bird shimmers, where the neck of the long-
   lived swan is curving and winding,   765
Where the laughing-gull scoots by the shore, where she laughs
   her near-human laugh,

Where bee-hives range on a gray bench in the garden
    half hid by the high weeds,
Where band-neck'd partridges roost in a ring on the ground
    with their heads out,
Where burial coaches enter the arch'd gates of a cemetery,
Where winter wolves bark amid wastes of snow and icicled trees,   770
Where the yellow-crown'd heron comes to the edge of the marsh
    at night and feeds upon small crabs,
Where the splash of swimmers and divers cools the warm noon,
Where the katy-did works her chromatic reed on the walnut-tree
    over the well,
Through patches of citrons and cucumbers with silver-wired leaves,
Through the salt-lick or orange glade, or under conical firs,   775
Through the gymnasium, through the curtain'd saloon,
    through the office or public hall;
Pleas'd with the native and pleas'd with the foreign,
Pleas'd with the new and old,
Pleas'd with the homely woman as well as the handsome,
Pleas'd with the quakeress as she puts off her bonnet and talks
    melodiously,
Pleas'd with the tune of the choir of the whitewash'd church,   780
Pleas'd with the earnest words of the sweating Methodist preacher,
    impress'd seriously at the camp-meeting;
Looking in at the shop-windows of Broadway the whole forenoon,
    flatting the flesh of my nose on the thick plate glass,
Wandering the same afternoon with my face turn'd up to the
    clouds, or down a lane or along the beach,
My right and left arms round the sides of two friends, and I in the
    middle;
Coming home with the silent and dark-cheek'd bush-boy,
    (behind me he rides at the drape of the day,)   785
Far from the settlements studying the print of animals' feet,
    or the moccasin print,
By the cot in the hospital reaching lemonade to a feverish patient,
Nigh the coffin'd corpse when all is still, examining with a candle;
Voyaging to every port to dicker and adventure,
Hurrying with the modern crowd as eager and fickle as any,   790
Hot toward one I hate, ready in my madness to knife him,
Solitary at midnight in my back yard, my thoughts gone from me a
    long while,

Walking the old hills of Judæa with the beautiful gentle God by
    my side,
Speeding through space, speeding through heaven and the stars,
Speeding amid the seven satellites and the broad ring,
    and the diameter of eighty thousand miles,   795
Speeding with tail'd meteors, throwing fire-balls like the rest,
Carrying the crescent child that carries its own full mother in its
    belly,
Storming, enjoying, planning, loving, cautioning,
Backing and filling, appearing and disappearing,
I tread day and night such roads.   800

I visit the orchards of spheres and look at the product,
And look at quintillions[29] ripen'd and look at quintillions green.

I fly those flights of a fluid and swallowing soul,
My course runs below the soundings of plummets.

I help myself to material and immaterial,   805
No guard can shut me off, no law prevent me.

I anchor my ship for a little while only,
My messengers continually cruise away or bring their returns to
    me.

I go hunting polar furs and the seal, leaping chasms with a pike-
    pointed staff, clinging to topples of brittle and blue.

I ascend to the foretruck,   810
I take my place late at night in the crow's-nest,
We sail the arctic sea, it is plenty light enough,
Through the clear atmosphere I stretch around on the wonderful
    beauty,
The enormous masses of ice pass me and I pass them,
    the scenery is plain in all directions,
The white-top't mountains show in the distance,
    I fling out my fancies toward them,   815
We are approaching some great battle-field in which we are soon
    to be engaged
We pass the colossal outposts of the encampment
    we pass with still feet and caution,
Or we are entering by the suburbs some vast and ruin'd city,
The blocks and fallen architecture more than all the living cities of
    the globe.

---

[29] One followed by eighteen zeroes, 1^{10}

I am a free companion, I bivouac by invading watchfires,   820
I turn the bridegroom out of bed and stay with the bride myself,
I tighten her all night to my thighs and lips.

My voice is the wife's voice, the screech by the rail of the stairs,
They fetch my man's body up dripping and drown'd.

I understand the large hearts of heroes,   825
The courage of present times and all times,
How the skipper saw the crowded and rudderless wreck of the
    steam-ship and Death chasing it up and down the storm,
How he knuckled tight and gave not back an inch, and was faithful
    of days and faithful of nights,
And chalk'd in large letters on a board, *Be of good cheer,*
    we will not desert you;
How he follow'd with them and tack'd with them three days
    and would not give it up,   830
How he saved the drifting company at last,
How the lank loose-gown'd women look'd when boated
    from the side of their prepared graves,
How the silent old-faced infants and the lifted sick,
    and the sharp-lipp'd unshaved men;
All this I swallow, it tastes good, I like it well, it becomes mine,
I am the man, I suffer'd, I was there.   835

The disdain and calmness of martyrs,
The mother of old, condemn'd for a witch, burnt with dry wood,
    her children gazing on,
The hounded slave that flags in the race, leans by the fence,
    blowing, cover'd with sweat,
The twinges that sting like needles his legs and neck,
    the murderous buckshot and the bullets,
All these I feel or am.   840

I am the hounded slave, I wince, at the bite of the dogs,
Hell and despair are upon me, crack and again crack the
    marksmen,
I clutch the rails of the fence, my gore drips, thinn'd with the ooze
    of my skin,
I fall on the weeds and stones,
The riders spur their unwilling horses, haul close,   845
Taunt my dizzy ears and beat me violently over the head with
    whip-stocks.

Agonies are one of my changes of garment,
I do not ask the wounded person how he feels,
  I myself become the wounded person,
My hurts turn livid upon me as I lean on a can and observe.

I am the mash'd fireman with breast-bone broken,   850
Tumbling walls buried me in their debris,
Heat and smoke I inspired, I heard the yelling shouts of my
    comrades,
I heard the distant click of their picks and shovels,
They have clear'd the beams away, they tenderly lift me forth.

I lie in the night air in my red shirt, the pervading hush is for my
    sake,   855
Painless after all I lie exhausted but not so unhappy,
White and beautiful are the faces around me,
    the heads are bared of their fire-caps,
The kneeling crowd fades with the light of the torches.

Distant and dead resuscitate,
They show as the dial or move as the hands of me, I am the clock
    myself.   860

I am an old artillerist, I tell of my fort's bombardment,
I am there again.

Again the long roll of the drummers,
Again the attacking cannon, mortars,
Again to my listening ears the cannon responsive.   865

I take part, I see and hear the whole,
The cries, curses, roar, the plaudits, for well-aim'd shots,
The ambulanza slowly passing trailing its red drip,
Workmen searching after damages, making indispensable repairs,
The fall of grenades through the rent roof, the fan-shaped
    explosion,   870
The whizz of limbs, heads, stone, wood, iron, high in the air.

Again gurgles the mouth of my dying general, he furiously waves
    with his hand,
He gasps through the clot, *Mind not me—mind—the
    entrenchments.*

³⁴ Now I tell what I knew in Texas in early youth,
(I tell not the fall of Alamo,³⁰   875
Not one escaped to tell the fall of Alamo,
The hundred and fifty are dumb yet at Alamo,)
'Tis the tale of the murder in cold blood
 of four hundred and twelve young men.

Retreating they had form'd in a hollow square with their baggage
 for breastworks,
Nine hundred lives out of the surrounding enemies, nine times their
 number was the price they took in advance,   880
Their colonel was wounded and their ammunition gone,
They treated for an honorable capitulation, receiv'd writing and
 seal, gave up their arms and march'd back prisoners of war.

They were the glory of the race of rangers,
Matchless with horse, rifle, song, supper, courtship,
Large, turbulent, generous, handsome, proud, and affectionate,   885
Bearded, sunburnt, drest in the free costume of hunters,
Not a single one over thirty years of age.

The second First-day morning they were brought out in squads
 and massacred, it was beautiful early summer,
The work commenced about five o'clock and was over by eight.

None obey'd the command to kneel,   890
Some made a mad and helpless rush, some stood stark and straight,
A few fell at once, shot in the temple or heart, the living and dead
 lay together,
The maim'd and mangled dug in the dirt, the new-comers saw
 them there,
Some half-kill'd attempted to crawl away,
These were despatch'd with bayonets or batter'd with the blunts of
 muskets,   895
A youth not seventeen years old seiz'd his assassin till two more
 came to release him,
The three were all torn and cover'd with the boy's blood.

---

³⁰ A Franciscan mission in San Antonio,
Texas; the site of the massacre of Texans by
Mexican forces in 1836.

At eleven o'clock began the burning of the bodies;
That is the tale of the murder of the four hundred and twelve
    young men.

35 Would you hear of an old-time sea-fight?   900
Would you learn who won by the light of the moon and stars?
List to the yarn, as my grandmother's father the sailor told it to
    me. [31]

Our foe was no skulk in his ship I tell you, (said he,)
His was the surly English pluck, and there is no tougher or truer,
    and never was, and never will be;
Along the lower'd eve he came horribly raking us.   905

We closed with him, the yards entangled, the cannon touch'd,
My captain lash'd fast with his own hands.

We had receiv'd some eighteen pound shots under the water,
On our lower-gun-deck two large pieces had burst at the first fire,
    killing all around and blowing up overhead.

Fighting at sun-down, fighting at dark,   910
Ten o'clock at night, the full moon well up, our leaks on the gain,
    and five feet of water reported,
The master-at-arms loosing the prisoners confined in the after-hold
    to give them a chance for themselves.

The transit to and from the magazine is now stopt by the sentinels,
They see so many strange faces they do not know whom to trust.

Our frigate takes fire,   915
The other asks if we demand quarter?
If our colors are struck and the fighting done?

Now I laugh content, for I hear the voice of my little captain,
We have not struck, he composedly cries, *we have just begun
    our part of the fighting.*

Only three guns are in use,   920
One is directed by the captain himself against the enemy's main-
    mast,
Two well serv'd with grape and canister silence his musketry
    and clear his decks.
The tops alone second the fire of this little battery, especially the
    main-top,
They hold out bravely during the whole of the action.

[31] The yarn is of John Paul Jones (1747–1792), a Scottish-born American naval officer in the Revolutionary War whose ship, *Bonhomme Richard,* was triumphant over the British *Serapis* in the sea fight of September 23, 1779.

Not a moment's cease,   925
The leaks gain fast on the pumps, the fire eats toward the powder-
    magazine.

One of the pumps has been shot away, it is generally thought we
    are sinking.

Serene stands the little captain,
He is not hurried, his voice is neither high nor low,
His eyes give more light to us than our battle-lanterns.   930

Toward twelve there in the beams of the moon they surrender to
    us.

36 Stretch'd and still lies the midnight,
    Two great hulls motionless on the breast of the darkness,
    Our vessel riddled and slowly sinking, preparations to pass to the
        one we have conquer'd,
    The captain on the quarter-deck coldly giving his orders
        through a countenance white as a sheet,   935
    Near by the corpse of the child that serv'd in the cabin,
    The dead face of an old salt with long white hair and carefully
        curl'd whisker
    The flames spite of all that can be done flickering aloft and below,
    The husky voices of the two or three officers yet fit for duty,
    Formless stacks of bodies and bodies by themselves,
        dabs of flesh upon the masts and spars,   940
    Cut of cordage, dangle of rigging, slight shock of the soothe of
        waves,
    Black and impassive guns, litter of powder-parcels, strong scent,
    A few large stars overhead, silent and mournful shining,

    Delicate sniffs of sea-breeze, smells of sedgy grass and fields by the
        shore, death-messages given in charge to survivors,
    The hiss of the surgeon's knife, the gnawing teeth of his saw,   945
    Wheeze, cluck, swash of falling blood, short wild scream,
        and long, dull, tapering groan,
    These so, these irretrievable.

37 You laggards there on guard! look to your arms!
    In at the conquer'd doors they crowd! I am possess'd!
    Embody all presences outlaw'd or suffering,   950
    See myself in prison shaped like another man,
    And feel the dull unintermitted pain.

For me the keepers of convicts shoulder their carbines and keep
  watch,
It is I let out in the morning and barr'd at night.

Not a mutineer walks handcuff'd to jail but I am handcuff'd to him
  and walk by his side,   955
(I am less the jolly one there, and more the silent one
  with sweat on my twitching lips.)

Not a youngster is taken for larceny but I go up too, and am tried
  and sentenced.

Not a cholera patient lies at the last gasp but I also lie at the last
  gasp,
My face is ash-color'd, my sinews gnarl, away from me people
  retreat.

Askers embody themselves in me and I am embodied in them,   960
I project my hat, sit shame-faced, and beg.

38 Enough! enough! enough!
Somehow I have been stunn'd. Stand back!
Give me a little time beyond my cuff'd head, slumbers, dreams,
  gaping,
I discover myself on the verge of a usual mistake.   965

That I could forget the mockers and insults!
That I could forget the trickling tears and the blows
  of the bludgeons and hammers!
That I could look with a separate look on my own crucifixion
  and bloody crowning.

I remember now,
I resume the overstaid fraction,   970
The grave of rock multiplies what has been confided to it, or to
  any graves,
Corpses rise, gashes heal, fastenings roll from me.

I troop forth replenish'd with supreme power, one of an average
  unending procession,
Inland and sea-coast we go, and pass all boundary lines,
Our swift ordinances on their way over the whole earth,   975
The blossoms we wear in our hats the growth of thousands of
  years.

Eleves,[32] I salute you! come forward!
Continue your annotations, continue your questionings.

---

[32] French for students.

³⁹ The friendly and flowing savage, who is he?
Is he waiting for civilization, or past it and mastering it?   980

Is he some Southwesterner rais'd out-doors? is he Kanadian?
Is he from the Mississippi country? Iowa, Oregon, California?
The mountains? prairie-life, bush-life? or sailor from the sea?

Wherever he goes men and women accept and desire him
They desire he should like them, touch them, speak to them, stay
     with them.   985

Behavior lawless as snow-flakes, words simple as grass,
     uncomb'd head, laughter, and naïvetè,
Slow-stepping feet, common features, common modes and
     emanations,
They descend in new forms from the tips of his fingers,
They are wafted with the odor of his body or breath,
     they fly out of the glance of his eyes.

⁴⁰ Flaunt of the sunshine I need not your bask—lie over!   990
You light surfaces only, I force surfaces and depths also.

Earth! you seem to look for something at my hands,
Say, old top-knot, what do you want?

Man or woman, I might tell how I like you, but cannot,
And might tell what it is in me and what it is in you, but cannot,   995
And might tell that pining I have, that pulse of my nights and days.

Behold, I do not give lectures or a little charity,
When I give I give myself.

You there, impotent, loose in the knees,
Open your scarf'd chops till I blow grit within you,   1000
Spread your palms and lift the flaps of your pockets,
I am not to be denied, I compel, I have stores plenty and to spare,
And any thing I have I bestow.

I do not ask who you are, that is not important to me,
You can do nothing and be nothing but what I will infold you.   1005

To cotton-field drudge or cleaner of privies I lean,
On his right cheek I put the family kiss,
And in my soul I swear I never will deny him.

On women fit for conception I start bigger and nimbler babes,
(This day I am jetting the stuff of far more arrogant republics.)   1010

To any one dying, thither I speed and twist the knob of the door,
Turn the bed-clothes toward the foot of the bed,
Let the physician and the priest go home.

I seize the descending man and raise him with resistless will,
O despairer, here is my neck,   1015
By God, you shall not go down! hang your whole weight upon me.

I dilate you with tremendous breath, I buoy you up,
Every room of the house do I fill with an arm'd force,
Lovers of me, bafflers of graves.

Sleep—I and they keep guard all night,   1020
Not doubt, not decease shall dare to lay finger upon you,
I have embraced you, and henceforth possess you to myself,
And when you rise in the morning you will find what I tell you is
    so.

41 I am he bringing help for the sick as they pant on their backs,
And for strong upright men I bring yet more needed help.   1025

I heard what was said of the universe,
Heard it and heard it of several thousand years;
It is middling well as far as it goes—but is that all?

Magnifying and applying come I,
Outbidding at the start the old cautious hucksters,   1030
Taking myself the exact dimensions of Jehovah,
Lithographing Kronos, Zeus his son, and Hercules his grandson,
Buying drafts of Osiris, Isis, Belus, Brahma, Buddha,
In my portfolio placing Manito loose, Allah on a leaf, the crucifix
    engraved.
With Odin and the hideous-faced Mexitli[33] and every idol and
    image,   1035
Taking them all for what they are worth and not a cent more,
Admitting they were alive and did the work of their days,
(They bore mites as for unfledg'd birds who have now to rise
    and fly and sing for themselves,)
Accepting the rough deific sketches to fill out better in myself,
    bestowing them freely on each man and woman I see,
Discovering as much or more in a framer framing a house,   1040
Putting higher claims for him there with his roll'd-up sleeves
    driving the mallet and chisel,
Not objecting to special revelations, considering a curl of smoke or
    a hair
    on the back of my hand just as curious as any revelation,
Lads ahold of fire-engines and hook-and-ladder ropes no less to me
    than the gods of the antique wars,
Minding their voices peal through the crash of destruction,

---

[33] The gods of many different faiths.

Their brawny limbs passing safe over charr'd laths, their white
    foreheads whole and unhurt out of the flames;   1045
By the mechanic's wife with her babe at her nipple interceding
    for every person born,
Three scythes at harvest whizzing in a row from three lusty angels
    with shirts bagg'd out of their waist,
The snag-tooth'd hostler with red hair redeeming sins past and to
    come,
Selling all he possesses, traveling on foot to fee lawyers for his
    brother and sit by him while he is tried for forgery;   1050
What was strewn in the amplest strewing the square rod about me,
    and not filling the square rod then,
The bull and the bug never worshipp'd half enough,
Dung and dirt more admirable than was dream'd,
The supernatural of no account, myself waiting my time
    to be one of the supremes,
The day getting ready for me when I shall do as much good as the
    best, and be as prodigious;   1055
By my life-lumps! becoming already a creator,
Putting myself here and now to the ambush'd womb of the
    shadows.

42 A call in the midst of the crowd,
My own voice, orotund sweeping and final.

Come my children,   1060
Come my boys and girls, my women, household and intimates,
Now the performer launches his nerve,
    he has pass'd his prelude on the reeds within.

Easily written loose-finger'd chords—I feel the thrum of your
    climax and close.

My head slues³⁴ round on my neck,
Music rolls, but not from the organ,   1065
Folks are around me, but they are no household of mine.

Ever the hard unsunk ground,
Ever the eaters and drinkers, ever the upward and downward sun,
    ever the air and the ceaseless tides,
Ever myself and my neighbors, refreshing, wicked, real,

---

³⁴ Twists sideways.

Ever the old inexplicable query, ever that thorn'd thumb,
    that breath of itches and thirsts,
Ever the vexer's hoot! hoot! till we find where the sly one hides
    and bring him forth,
Ever love, ever the sobbing liquid of life,
Ever the bandage under the chin, ever the trestles of death.

Here and there with dimes on the eyes walking,
To feed the greed of the belly the brains liberally spooning,
Tickets buying, taking, selling, but in to the feast never once going,
Many sweating, ploughing, thrashing, and then the chaff for
    payment receiving,
A few idly owning, and they the wheat continually claiming.

This is the city and I am one of the citizens,
Whatever interests the rest interests me, politics, wars, markets,
    newspapers, schools,
The mayor and councils, banks, tariffs, steamships, factories, stocks,
    stores, real estate and personal estate.

The little plentiful manikins skipping around in collars and tail'd
    coats,
I am aware who they are, (they are positively not worms or fleas,)
I acknowledge the duplicates of myself, the weakest and shallowest
    is deathless with me,
What I do and say the same waits for them,
Every thought that flounders in me the same flounders in them.

I know perfectly well my own egotism,
Know my omnivorous lines and must not write any less,
And would fetch you whoever you are flush with myself.

Not words of routine this song of mine,
But abruptly to question, to leap beyond yet nearer bring;
This printed and bound book—but the printer and the printing-
    office boy?
The well-taken photographs—but your wife or friend
    close and solid in your arms?
The black ship mail'd with iron, her mighty guns in ther turrets—
    but the pluck of the captain and engineers?
In the houses the dishes and fare and furniture—but the host and
    hostess,
    and the look out of their eyes?
The sky up there—yet here or next door, or across the way?
The saint and sages in history—but you yourself?
Sermons, creeds, theology—but the fathomless human brain,
And what is reason? and what is love? and what is life?

⁴³ I do not despise you priests, all time, the world over,   1100
My faith is the greatest of faiths and the least of faiths,
Enclosing worship ancient and modern and all between ancient
    and modern.
Believing I shall come again upon the earth after five thousand
    years,
Waiting responses from oracles, honoring the gods, saluting the sun,
Making a fetich³⁵ of the first rock or stump, powowing with sticks
    in the circle of obis,³⁶   1105
Helping the llama or brahmin as he trims the lamps of the idols,
Dancing yet through the streets in a phallic procession,
    rapt and austere in the woods a gymnosophist,³⁷
Drinking mead from the skull-cup, to Shastas and Vedas admirant,
    minding the Koran,³⁸
Walking the teokallis,³⁹ spotted with gore from the stone and knife,
    beating the serpent-skin drum,
Accepting the Gospels, accepting him that was crucified,
    knowing assuredly that he is divine,   1110
To the mass kneeling or the puritan's prayer rising, or sitting
    patiently in a pew,
Ranting and frothing in my insane crisis, or waiting dead-like
    till my spirit arouses me,
Looking forth on pavement and land, or outside of pavement and
    land,
Belonging to the winders of the circuit of circuits.

One of that centripetal and centrifugal gang I turn and talk
    like a man leaving charges before a journey.   1115

Down-hearted doubters dull and excluded,
Frivolous, sullen, moping, angry, affected, dishearten'd, atheistical,
I know every one of you, I know the sea of torment, doubt, despair
    and unbelief.

How the flukes splash!
How they contort rapid as lightning, with spasms and spouts of
    blood!   1120

---

³⁵ A material object believed among primitive cultures to have magical powers.

³⁶ A form of religious belief, of African origin, involving witchcraft.

³⁷ One of an ancient sect of Hindu ancestors, as reported in classical antiquity.

³⁸ In the Hindu religion, Shastas are the lessons, and Vedas the holy writings. The Koran is the sacred text of Islam, which contains the revelations made by Allah to Mohammed.

³⁹ Teocallis is a temple of ancient Mexico and Central America, built on a mound of truncated pyramidal shape. Whitman refers to the mound itself.

Be at peace bloody flukes of doubters and sullen mopers,
I take my place among you as much as among any,
The past is the push of you, me, all, precisely the same,
And what is yet untried and afterward is for you, me, all, precisely
    the same.

I do not know what is untried and afterward,   1125
But I know it will in its turn prove sufficient, and cannot fail.

Each who passes is consider'd, each who stops is consider'd,
    not a single one can it fail.

It cannot fail the young man who died and was buried,
Nor the young woman who died and was put by his side,
Nor the little child that peep'd in at the door, and then drew back
    and was never seen again,   1130

Nor the old man who has lived without purpose,
    and feels it with bitterness worse than gall,
Nor him in the poor house tubercled by rum and the bad disorder,
Nor the numberless slaughter'd and wreck'd, nor the brutish
    koboo [40] call'd the ordure of humanity,
Nor the sacs merely floating with open mouths for food to slip in,
Nor any thing in the earth, or down in the oldest graves of the
    earth,   1135
Nor any thing in the myriads of spheres, nor the myriads of
    myriads that inhabit them,
Nor the present, nor the least wisp that is known.

44   It is time to explain myself—let us stand up.

What is known I strip away,
I launch all men and women forward with me into the Unknown.   1140

The clock indicates the moment—but what does eternity indicate?

We have thus far exhausted trillions of winters and summers,
There are trillions ahead, and trillions ahead of them.

Births have brought us richness and variety,
And other births will bring us richness and variety,   1145

I do not call one greater and one smaller,
That which fills its period and place is equal to any.

[40] A native of Palembang on the east coast of
Sumatra.

Were mankind murderous or jealous upon you, my brother, my
    sister?
I am sorry for you, they are not murderous or jealous upon me,
All has been gentle with me, I keep no account with lamentation,   1150
(What have I to do with lamentation?)

I am an acme of things accomplish'd, and I an encloser of things to
    be.

My feet strike an apex of the apices of the stairs,
On every step bunches of ages, and larger bunches between the
    steps,
All below duly travel'd, and still I mount and mount.   1155

Rise after rise bow the phantoms behind me,
Afar down I see the huge first Nothing, I know I was even there,
I waited unseen and always, and slept through the lethargic mist,
And took my time, and took no hurt from the fetid carbon.

Long I was hugg'd close—long and long.   1160

Immense have been the preparations for me.
Faithful and friendly the arms that have help'd me.

Cycles ferried my cradle, rowing and rowing like cheerful
    boatmen,
For room to me stars kept aside in their own rings,
They sent influences to look after what was to hold me.   1165

Before I was born out of my mother generations guided me,
My embryo has never been torpid, nothing could overlay it.

For it the nebula cohered to an orb,
The long slow strata piled to rest it on,
Vast vegetables gave it sustenance,   1170
Monstrous sauroids[41] transported it in their mouths
    and deposited it with care.

All forces have been steadily employ'd to complete and delight me,
Now on this spot I stand with my robust soul.

45 O span of youth! ever-push'd elasticity!
O manhood, balanced, florid and full.   1175

My lovers suffocate me,
Crowding my lips, thick in the pores of my skin,
Jostling me through streets and public halls, coming naked to me at
    night,

[41] Lizards.

Crying by day, *Ahoy!* from the rocks of the river,
    swinging and chirping over my head,
Calling my name from flower-beds, vines, tangled underbrush,   1180
Lighting on every moment of my life,
Bussing my body with soft balsamic busses,
Noiselessly passing handfuls out of their hearts and giving them to
    be mine.

Old age superbly rising! O welcome, ineffable grace of dying days!

Every condition promulges not only itself,
    it promulges what grows after and out of itself,   1185
And the dark hush promulges as much as any.

I open my scuttle at night and see the far-sprinkled systems,
And all I see, multiplied as high as I can cypher, edge but the rim
    of the farther systems.

Wider and wider they spread, expanding, always expanding,
Outward and outward and forever outward.   1190

My sun has his sun and round him obediently wheels,
He joins with his partners a group of superior circuit,
And greater sets follow, making specks of the greatest inside them.

There is no stoppage and never can be stoppage,
If I, you, and the worlds, and all beneath or upon their surfaces,
    were this moment reduced back to a pallid float,
    it would not avail in the long run,   1195
We should surely bring up again where we now stand,
And surely go as much farther, and then farther and farther.

A few quadrillions of eras, a few octillions of cubic leagues,
    do not hazard the span or make it impatient,
They are but parts, anything is but a part.

See ever so far, there is limitless space outside of that,   1200
Count ever so much, there is limitless time around that.

My rendezvous is appointed, it is certain,
The Lord will be there and wait till I come on perfect terms,
The great Camerado, the lover true for whom I pine will be there.

46   I know I have the best of time and space, and was never measured
    and never will be measured.   1205

I tramp a perpetual journey, (come listen all!)
My signs are a rain-proof coat, good shoes, and a staff cut from the
    woods,
No friend of mine takes his ease in my chair,

I have not chair, no church, no philosophy,
I lead no man to a dinner-table, library, exchange,   1210
But each man and each woman of you I lead upon a knoll,
My left hand hooking you round the waist,
My right hand pointing to landscapes of continents and the public
    road.

Not I, not any one else can travel that road for you,
You must travel it for yourself.   1215

It is not far, it is within reach,
Perhaps you have been on it since you were born and did not
    know,
Perhaps it is everywhere on water and on land.

Shoulder your duds dear son, and I will mine, and let us hasten
    forth,
Wonderful cities and free nations we shall fetch as we go.   1220

If you tire, give me both burdens, and rest the chuff of your hand
    on my hip,
And in due time you shall repay the same service to me,
For after we start we never lie by again.

This day before dawn I ascended a hill and look'd at the crowded
    heaven,
And I said to my spirit, *When we become the enfolders of those
    orbs,*
*   and the pleasure and knowlege of every thing in them,*
*   shall we be fill'd and satisfied then?*   1225
And my spirit said, *No, we but level that lift to pass and continue
    beyond.*

You are also asking me questions and I hear you,
I answer that I cannot answer, you must find out for yourself.

Sit a while dear son,
Here are biscuits to eat and here is milk to drink,   1230
But as soon as you sleep and renew yourself in sweet clothes,
    I kiss you with a good-by kiss and open the gate for your egress
    hence.

Long enough have you dream'd contemptible dreams,
Now I wash the gum from your eyes,
You must habit yourself to the dazzle of the light and of every
    moment of your life.

Long have you timidly waded holding a plank by the shore,   1235
Now I will you to be a bold swimmer,
To jump off in the midst of the sea, rise again, nod to me, shout,
    and laughingly dash with your hair.

47 I am the teacher of athletes,
He that by me spreads a wider breast than my own proves the
    width of my own,
He most honors my style who learns under it to destroy the
    teacher.   1240

The boy I love, the same becomes a man not through derived
    power, but in his own right,
Wicked rather than virtuous out of conformity or fear,
Fond of his sweetheart, relishing well his steak,
Unrequited love or a slight cutting him worse than sharp steel cuts,
First-rate to ride, to fight, to hit the bull's eye, to sail a skiff,
    to sing a song or play on the banjo,   1245
Preferring scars and the beard and faces pitted with small-pox
    over all latherers,
And those well-tann'd to those that keep out of the sun.

I teach straying from me, yet who can stray from me?
I follow you whoever you are from the present hour,
My words itch at your ears till you understand them.   1250

I do not say these things for a dollar or to fill up the time
    while I wait for a boat,
(It is you talking just as much as myself, I act as the tongue of you,
Tied in your mouth, in mine it begins to be loosen'd.)

I swear I will never again mention love or death inside a house,
And I swear I will never translate myself at all, only to him or her
    who privately stays with me in the open air.   1255

If you would understand me go to the heights or water-shore,
The nearest gnat is an explanation, a drop or motion of waves a
    key,
The maul, the oar, the hand-saw, second my words.

No shutter'd room or school can commune with me,
But roughs and little children better than they.   1260

The young mechanic is closest to me, he knows me well,
The woodman that takes his axe and jug with him shall take me
    with him all day,

The farm-boy ploughing in the field feels good at the sound of my
  voice,
In vessels that sail my words sail, I go with fishermen and seamen
  and love them.

The soldier camp'd or upon the march is mine,   1265
On the night ere the pending battle many seek me, and I do not
  fail them,
On that solemn night (it may be their last) those that know me seek
  me.

My face rubs to the hunter's face when he lies down alone in his
  blanket,
The driver thinking of me does not mind the jolt of his wagon,
The young mother and old mother comprehend me,
                                                                  1270
The girl and the wife rest the needle a moment and forget where
  they are,
They and all would resume what I have told them.

48 I have said that the soul is not more than the body,
And I have said that the body is not more than the soul,
And nothing, not God, is greater to one than one's self is,   1275
And whoever walks a furlong[42] without sympathy walks to his own
  funeral
  Drest in his shroud,
And I or you pocketless of a dime may purchase the pick of the
  earth,
And to glance with an eye or show a bean in its pod
  confounds the learning of all times,
And there is no trade or employment but the yound man following
  it
  may become a hero,
And there is no object so soft but it makes a hub for the wheel'd
  universe,   1280
And I say to any man or woman, Let your soul stand cool and
  composed
  before a million universes.

And I say to mankind, Be not curious about God,
For I who am curious about each am not curious about God,
(No array of terms can say how much I am at peace about God
  and about death.)

---

[42] 1/8th of a mile or 220 yards.

I hear and behold God in every object, yet understand God not in
    the least,   1285
Nor do I understand who there can be more wonderful than
    myself.

Why should I wish to see God better than this day?

I see something of God each hour of the twenty-four,
    and each moment then,
In the faces of men and women I see God, and in my own face
    in the glass,
I find letters from God dropt in the street, and every one
    is sign'd by God's name,   1290
And I leave them where they are, for I know that wheresoe'er I
    go,
Others will punctually come for ever and ever.

49 And as to you Death, and you bitter hug of mortality,
    it is idle to try to alarm me.

To his work without flinching the accoucheur[43] comes,
I see the elder-hand pressing, receiving, supporting,   1295
I recline by the sills of the exquisite flexible doors,
And mark the outlet, and mark the relief and escape.

And as to you Corpse I think you are good manure,
    but that does not offend me,
I smell the white roses sweet-scented and growing,
I reach to the leafy lips, I reach to the polish'd breasts of melons.   1300

And as to you Life I reckon you are the leavings of many deaths,
(No doubt I have died myself ten thousand times before.)

I hear you whispering there O stars of heaven,
O suns—O grass of graves—O perpetual transfers and promotions,
If you do not say any thing how can I say any thing?   1305

Of the turbid pool that lies in the autumn forest,
Of the moon that descends the steeps of the soughing twilight,
Toss, sparkles of day and dusk—toss on the black stems that decay
    in the muck,
Toss to the moaning gibberish of the dry limbs.

I ascend from the moon, I ascend from the night,   1310
I perceive that the ghastly glimmer is noonday sunbeams reflected,
And debouch[44] to the steady and central from the offspring great
    or small.

---

43 The midwife.   44 To come out.

50 There is that in me—I do not know what it is—but I know it is in
    me.
Wrench'd and sweaty—calm and cool then my body becomes,
I sleep—I sleep long.   1315

I do not know it—it is without name—it is a word unsaid,
It is not in any dictionary, utterance, symbol.

Something it swings on more than the earth I swing on,
To it the creation is the friend whose embracing awakes me.

Perhaps I might tell more. Outlines! I plead for my brothers and
    sisters.   1320

Do you see O my brothers and sisters?
It is not chaos or death—it is form, union, plan—it is eternal life—
    it is Happiness.

51 The past and present wilt—I have fill'd them, emptied them,
And proceed to fill my next fold of the future.

Listener up there! what have you to confide to me?   1325
Look in my face while I snuff the sidle of evening,
(Talk honestly, no one else hears you, and I stay only a minute
    longer.)

Do I contradict myself?
Very well then I contradict myself,
(I am large, I contain multitudes.)   1330

I concentrate toward them that are nigh, I wait on the door-slab.

Who has done his day's work? who will soonest be through
    with his supper?
Who wishes to walk with me?

Will you speak before I am gone? will you prove already too late?

52 The spotted hawk swoops by and accuses me, he complains of my
    gab and my loitering.   1335

I too am not a bit tamed, I too am untranslatable,
I sound my barbaric yawp over the roofs of the world.

The last scud of day holds back for me,
It flings my likeness after the rest and true as any on the shadow'd
    wilds,
It coaxes me to the vapor and the dusk.   1340

I depart as air, I shake my white locks at the runaway sun,
I effuse[45] my flesh in eddies, and drift it in lacy jags.

I bequeath myself to the dirt to grow from the grass I love,
If you want me again look for me under your boot-soles.

You will hardly know who I am or what I mean,   1345
But I shall be good health to you nevertheless,
And filter and fibre your blood.

Failing to fetch me at first keep encouraged,
Missing me one place search another,
I stop somewhere waiting for you.   1350

1855

[45] To spread out or exude.

The Sleepers[1]

[1] I wander all night in my vision,
   Stepping with light feet, swiftly and noiselessly stepping and
     stopping,
   Bending with open eyes over the shut eyes of sleepers,
   Wandering and confused, lost to myself, ill-assorted, contradictory,
   Pausing, gazing, bending, and stopping.   5

How solemn they look there, stretch'd and still,
How quiet they breathe, the little children in their cradles.

The wretched features of ennuyés,[2] the white features of corpses,
   the livid faces of drunkards, the sick-gray faces of onanists,[3]
The gash'd bodies on battle-fields, the insane in their strong-door'd
   rooms,
   the sacred idiots, the new-born emerging from gates,
   and the dying emerging from gates,
The night pervades them and infolds them.   10

The married couple sleep calmly in their bed, he with his palm on
   the hip
   of the wife, and she with her palm on the hip of the husband,

[1] This poem is Whitman's attempt to project himself as a spirit among the sleepers of all lands and is one of the few surrealist verses of the nineteenth century. The poem was called "Night Poem" in 1856, "Sleep Mus-ings" in 1860 and 1867, and "The Sleepers" since 1871.

[2] Bored ones.

[3] Male masturbators.

The sisters sleep lovingly side by side in their bed,
The men sleep lovingly side by side in theirs,
And the mother sleeps with her little child carefully wrapt.

The blind sleep, and the deaf and dumb sleep, 15
The prisoner sleeps well in the prison, the runaway son sleeps,
The murderer that is to be hung next day, how does he sleep?
And the murder'd person, how does he sleep?

The female that loves unrequited sleeps,
And the male that loves unrequited sleeps, 20
The head of the money-maker that plotted all day sleeps,
And the enraged and treacherous dispositions, all, all sleep.

I stand in the dark with drooping eyes by the worst-suffering
    and the most restless,
I pass my hands soothingly to and fro a few inches from them,
The restless sink in their beds, they fitfully sleep. 25

Now I pierce the darkness, new beings appear,
The earth recedes from me into the night,
I saw that it was beautiful, and I see that what is not the earth is
    beautiful.

I go from bedside to bedside, I sleep close with the other sleepers
    each in turn,
I dream in my dream all the dreams of the other dreamers, 30
And I become the other dreamers.

I am a dance—play up there! the fit is whirling me fast!

I am the ever-laughing—it is new moon and twilight,
I see the hiding of douceurs,[4] I see nimble ghosts whichever way I
    look,
Cache and cache[5] again deep in the ground and sea,
    and where it is neither ground nor sea. 35

Well do they do their jobs those journeymen divine,
Only from me can they hide nothing, and would not if they could,
I reckon I am their boss and they make me a pet besides,
And surround me and lead me and run ahead when I walk,

To lift their cunning covers to signify me with stretch'd arms,
    and resume the way; 40
Onward we move a gay gang of blackguards! with mirth-shouting
    music
    and wild-flapping pennants of joy!

---

[4] French for sweetnesses.   [5] French for hide.

I am the actor, the actress, the voter, the politician,
The emigrant and the exile, the criminal that stood in the box,
He who has been famous and he who shall be famous after to-day,
The stammerer, the well-form'd person, the wasted or feeble
    person.   45

I am she who adorn'd herself and folded her hair expectantly,
My truant lover has come, and it is dark.

Double yourself and receive me darkness,
Receive me and my lover too, he will not let me go without him.

I roll myself upon you as upon a bed, I resign myself to the dusk.   50

He whom I call answers me and takes the place of my lover,
He rises with me silently from the bed.

Darkness, you are gentler than my lover, his flesh was sweaty and
    panting,
I feel the hot moisture yet that he left me.

My hands are spread forth, I pass them in all directions,   55
I would sound up the shadowy shore to which you are journeying.

Be careful darkness! already what was it touch'd me?
I thought my lover had gone, else darkness and he are one,
I hear the heart-beat, I follow, I fade away.

2 I descend my western course, my sinews are flaccid,   60
Perfume and youth course through me and I am their wake.

It is my face yellow and wrinkled instead of the old woman's,
I sit low in a straw-bottom chair and carefully darn my grandson's
    stockings.

It is I too, the sleepless widow looking out on the winter midnight,
I see the sparkles of starshine on the icy and pallid earth.   65

A shroud I see and I am the shroud, I wrap a body and lie in the
    coffin,
It is dark here under ground, it is not evil or pain here,
    it is blank here, for reasons.

(It seems to me that everything in the light and air ought to be
    happy,
Whoever is not in his coffin and the dark grave
    let him know he has enough.)

3 I see a beautiful gigantic swimmer swimming naked
    through the eddies of the sea,   70
His brown hair lies close and even to his head,
    he strikes out with courageous arms, he urges himself with his
    legs,
I see his white body, I see his undaunted eyes,
I hate the swift-running eddies that would dash him
    head-foremost on the rocks.

What are you doing you ruffianly red-trickled waves?
Will you kill the courageous giant?
    will you kill him in the prime of his middle age?

                                                  75

Steady and long he struggles,
He is baffled, bang'd, bruis'd, he holds out while his strength holds
    out,
The slapping eddies are spotted with his blood, they bear him away,
    they roll him, swing him, turn him,
His beautiful body is borne in the circling eddies,
    it is continually bruis'd on rocks,
Swiftly and out of sight is borne the brave corpse.   80

4 I turn but do not extricate myself,
    Confused, a past-reading, another, but with darkness yet.

The beach is cut by the razory ice-wind, the wreck-guns sound,
The tempest lulls, the moon comes floundering through the drifts.

I look where the ship helplessly heads end on, I hear the burst as
    she strikes,
    I hear the howls of dismay, they grow fainter and fainter.   85

I cannot aid with my wringing fingers,
I can but rush to the surf and let it drench me and freeze upon me.

I search with the crowd, not one of the company is wash'd to us
    alive,
In the morning I help pick up the dead and lay them in rows in a
    barn.

5 Now of the older war-days, the defeat at Brooklyn,[6]   90
    Washington stands inside the lines, he stands on the intrench'd hills
    amid a crowd of officers,

---

[6] The battle of Brooklyn Heights, August 27,
1776.

His face is cold and damp, he cannot repress the weeping drops,
He lifts the glass perpetually to his eyes, the color is blanch'd from
   his cheeks,
He sees the slaughter of the southern braves confided to him by
   their parents.

The same at last and at last when peace is declared,   95
He stands in the room of the old tavern,
   the well-belov'd soldiers all pass through
The officers speechless and slow draw near in their turns,
The chief encircles their necks with his arm
   and kisses them on the cheek,
He kisses lightly the wet cheeks one after another,
   he shakes hands and bids good-by to the army.

6 Now what my mother told me one day as we sat at dinner together,   100
   Of when she was a nearly grown girl living home with her parents
   on the old homestead.

A red squaw came one breakfast-time to the old homestead,
On her back she carried a bundle of rushes for rush-bottoming
   chairs,
Her hair, straight, shiny, coarse, black, profuse, half-envelop'd her
   face,
Her step was free and elastic, and her voice sounded exquisitely as
   she spoke.   105

My mother look'd in delight and amazement at the stranger,
She look'd at the freshness of her tall-borne face
   and full and pliant limbs,
The more she look'd upon her she loved her,
Never before had she seen such wonderful beauty and purity,
She made her sit on a bench by the jamb of the fireplace,
   she cook'd food for her,   110
She had no work to give her, but she gave her remembrance and
   fondness.

The red squaw staid all the forenoon,
   and toward the middle of the afternoon she went away,

O my mother was loth to have her go away,
All the week she thought of her, she watch'd for her many a month,
She remember'd her many a winter and many a summer,   115
But the red squaw never came nor was heard of there again.

7 A show of the summer softness—a contact of something unseen—
  an amour of the light and air,
I am jealous and overwhelm'd with friendliness,
And will go gallivant with the light and air myself.

O love and summer, you are in the dreams and in me,   120
Autumn and winter are in the dreams, the farmer goes with his
  thrift,
The droves and crops increase, the barns are well-fill'd.

Elements merge in the night, ships make tacks in the dreams,
The sailor sails, the exile returns home,
The fugitive returns unharm'd, the immigrant is back beyond
  months and years,   125
The poor Irishman lives in the simple house of his childhood
  with the well-known neighbors and faces,
They warmly welcome him, he is barefoot again, he forgets he is
  well off,
The Dutchman voyages home, and the Scotchman and Welshman
  voyage home, and the native of the Mediterranean voyages
  home,
To every port of England, France, Spain, enter well-fill'd ships,
The Swiss foots it toward his hills, the Prussian goes his way,
  the Hungarian his way, and the Pole his way,   130
The Swede returns, and the Dane and Norwegian return.

The homeward bound and the outward bound,
The beautiful lost swimmer, the ennuyé, the onanist,
  the female that loves unrequited, the money-maker,
The actor and actress, those through with their parts
  and those waiting to commence,
The affectionate boy, the husband and wife, the voter,
  the nominee that is chosen and the nominee that has fail'd,   135
The great already known and the great any time after to-day,
The stammerer, the sick, the perfect-form'd, the homely,
The criminal that stood in the box, the judge that sat and sentenced
  him,
  the fluent lawyers, the jury, the audience,
The laugher and weeper, the dancer, the midnight widow, the red
  squaw,

The consumptive, the erysipalite,[7] the idiot, he that is wrong'd,   140
The antipodes, and every one between this and them in the dark,
I swear they are averaged now—one is no better than the other,
The night and sleep have liken'd them and restored them.

I swear they are all beautiful,
Every one that sleeps is beautiful, every thing in the dim light is
    beautiful,   145
The wildest and bloodiest is over, and all is peace.

Peace is always beautiful,
The myth of heaven indicates peace and night.

The myth of heaven indicated the soul,
The soul is always beautiful, it appears more or it appears less,
    it comes or it lags behind,   150
It comes from its embower'd garden and looks pleasantly on itself
    and encloses the world,
Perfect and clean the genitals previously jetting,
    and perfect and clean the womb cohering,
The head well-grown proportion'd and plumb,
    and the bowels and joints proportion'd and plumb.

The soul is always beautiful,
The universe is duly in order, every thing is in its place,   155
What has arrived is in its place and what waits shall be in its place,
The twisted skull waits, the watery or rotten blood waits,
The child of the glutton or venerealee waits long, and the child
    of the drunkard waits long, and the drunkard himself waits long,
The sleepers that lived and died wait, the far advanced are to go on
    in their turns, and the far behind are to come on in their turns,
The diverse shall be no less diverse, but they shall flow and unite—
    they unite now.   160

[8] The sleepers are very beautiful as they lie unclothed,
They flow hand in hand over the whole earth from east to west
    as they lie unclothed,
The Asiatic and African are hand in hand,
    the European and American are hand in hand,
Learn'd and unlearn'd are hand in hand, and male and female are
    hand in hand,

---

[7] One who has an acute disease of the skin,
commonly called "St. Anthony's fire."

The bare arm of the girl crosses the bare breast of her lover,
    they press close without lust, his lips press her neck,   165
The father holds his grown or ungrown son in his arms with
    measureless love,
    and the son holds the father in his arms with measureless love,
The whiter hair of the mother shines on the white wrist of the
    daughter,
The breath of the boy goes with the breath of the man,
    friend is inarm'd by friend,
The scholar kisses the teacher and the teacher kisses the scholar,
    the wrong'd is made right,
The call of the slave is one with the master's call,
    and the master salutes the slave,   170
The felon steps forth from the prison, the insane becomes sane,
    the suffering of sick persons is reliev'd,
The sweatings and fevers stop, the throat that was unsound is
    sound,
    the lungs of the consumptive are resumed, the poor distress'd
    head is free,
The joints of the rheumatic move as smoothly as ever, and smoother
    than ever,
Stiflings and passages open, the paralyzed become supple,
The swell'd and convuls'd and congested awake to themselves in
    condition,   175
They pass the invigoration of the night
    and the chemistry of the night, and awake.

I too pass from the night,
I stay a while away O night, but I return to you again and love you.

Why should I be afraid to trust myself to you?
I am not afraid, I have been well brought forward by you,   180
I love the rich running day, but I do not desert her in whom I lay
    so long,
I know not how I came of you and I know not where I go with
    you,
    but I know I came well and shall go well.

I will stop only a time with the night, and rise betimes,
I will duly pass the day O my mother, and duly return to you.

1855

Scented Herbage of My Breast[1]

Scented herbage of my breast,
Leaves from you I glean, I write, to be perused best afterwards,
Tomb-leaves, body-leaves growing up above me above death,
Perennial, roots, tall leaves, O the winter shall not freeze you delicate
    leaves,
Every year shall you bloom again, out from where you retired
    you shall emerge again;   5
O I do not know whether many passing by will discover you
    or inhale your faint odor, but I believe a few will;
O slender leaves! O blossoms of my blood! I permit you to tell
    in your own way of the heart that is under you,
O I do not know what you mean there underneath yourselves,
    you are not happiness,
You are often more bitter than I can bear, you burn and sting me,
Yet you are beautiful to me you faint tinged roots, you make me think
    of death,   10
Death is beautiful from you, (what indeed is finally beautiful
    except death and love?)
O I think it is not for life I am chanting here my chant of lovers,
    I think it must be for death,
For how calm, how solemn it grows to ascend to the atmosphere of
    lovers,
Death or life I am then indifferent, my soul declines to prefer,
(I am not sure but the high soul of lovers welcomes death most,)   15
Indeed O death, I think now these leaves mean precisely the same as
    you mean,
Grow up taller sweet leaves that I may see! grow up out of my
    breast!
Spring away from the conceal'd heart there!
Do not fold yourself so in your pink-tinged roots timid leaves!
Do not remain down there so ashamed, herbage of my breast!   20
Come I am determin'd to unbare this broad breast of mine,
    I have long enough stifled and choked;
Emblematic and capricious blades I leave you, now you serve me not,
I will say what I have to say by itself,
I will sound myself and comrades only,
    I will never again utter a call only their call,   25
I will raise with it immortal reverberations through the States,

---

[1] The poem is the second in the volume
called *Calamus*, poems of manly attachment.

I will give an example to lovers to take permanent shape
    and will through the States,
Through me shall the words be said to make death exhilarating,
Give me your tone therefore O death, that I may accord with it,
Give me yourself, for I see that you belong to me now above all,   30
    and are folded inseparably together, you love and death are,
Nor will I allow you to balk me any more with what I was calling
    life,
For now it is convey'd to me that you are the purports[2] essential,
That you hide in these shifting forms of life, for reasons,
    and that they are mainly for you,
That you beyond them come forth to remain, the real reality,   35
That behind the mask of materials you patiently wait, no matter how
    long,
That you will one day perhaps take control of all,
That you will perhaps dissipate this entire show of appearance,
That may-be you are what it is all for, but it does not last so very
    long,
But you will last very long.   40

                                        1860

[2] The apparent meanings.

Whoever You Are Holding Me Now in Hand

Whoever you are holding me now in hand,
Without one thing all will be useless,
I give you fair warning before you attempt me further,
I am not what you supposed, but far different.

Who is he that would become my follower?   5
Who would sign himself a candidate for my affections?

The way is suspicious, the result uncertain, perhaps destructive,
You would have to give up all else, I alone would expect to be
    your sole and exclusive standard,
Your novitiate[1] would even then be long and exhausting,

[1] A beginner.

The whole past theory of your life and all conformity to the lives
    around you
        would have to be abandon'd,   10
Therefore release me now before troubling yourself any further,
    let go your hand from my shoulders,
Put me down and depart on your way.

Or else by stealth in some wood for trial,
Or back of a rock in the open air,
(For in any roof'd room of a house I emerge not, nor in company,   15
And in libraries I lie as one dumb, a gawk, or unborn, or dead,)
But just possibly with you on a high hill, first watching lest any person
    for miles around approach unawares,

Or possibly with you sailing at sea, or on the beach of the sea
    or some quiet island,
Here to put your lips upon mine I permit you,
With the comrade's long-dwelling kiss or the new husband's kiss,   20
For I am the new husband and I am the comrade.

Or if you will, thrusting me beneath your clothing,
Where I may feel the throbs of your heart or rest upon your hip,
Carry me when you go forth over land or sea;
For thus merely touching you is enough, is best,   25
And thus touching you would I silently sleep and be carried eternally.

But these leaves conning you con at peril,
For these leaves and me you will not understand
They will elude you at first and still more afterward, I will certainly
    elude you,
Even while you should think you had unquestionably caught me,
    behold!   30
Already you see I have escaped from you.

For it is not for what I have put into it that I have written this book,
Nor it is by reading it you will acquire it,
Nor do those know me best who admire me and vauntingly praise
    me,
Nor will the candidates for my love (unless at most a very few) prove
    victorious,   35
Nor will my poems do good only, they will do just as much evil,
    perhaps more,
For all is useless without that which you may guess at many times and
    not hit,
        that which I hinted at;
Therefore release me and depart on your way.

1860

I Saw in Louisiana a Live-Oak Growing

I saw in Louisiana a live-oak growing,
All alone stood it and the moss hung down from the branches,
Without any companion it grew there uttering joyous leaves of dark
    green
And its look, rude, unbending, lusty, made me think of myself,
But I wonder'd how it could utter joyous leaves standing alone there
    without its friend near, for I knew I could not,   5
And I broke off a twig with a certain number of leaves upon 'it,
    and twined around it a little moss,
And brought it away, and I have placed it in sight in my room,
It is not needed to remind me as of my own dear friends,
(For I believe lately I think of little else than of them,)
Yet it remains to me a curious token, it makes me think of manly
    love;   10
For all that, and though the live-oak glistens there in Louisiana
    solitary in a wide flat space,
Uttering joyous leaves all its life without a friend a lover near,
I know very well I could not.

                    1860

Out of the Cradle Endlessly Rocking[1]

Out of the cradle endlessly rocking,
Out of the mocking-bird's throat, the musical shuttle,
Out of the Ninth-month[2] midnight,
Over the sterile sands and the fields beyond, where the child
    leaving his bed wander'd alone, bareheaded, barefoot,
Down from the shower'd halo,   5
Up from the mystic play of shadows twining and twisting
    as if they were alive,
Out from the patches of briers and blackberries,
From the memories of the bird that chanted to me,
From your memories sad brother, from the fitful risings
    and fallings I heard,

---

[1] The poem is a revisitation of Whitman's childhood in Long Island. The setting moves Whitman to write about the search for the origins of the poet's song and of the origins of poetry itself. It first appeared as "A Child's Reminiscence" on December 24, 1859, in the New York *Saturday Press.*

[2] The Quaker term for September.

From under that yellow half-moon late-risen and swollen as if with
    tears,   10
From those beginning notes of yearning[3] and love there in the mist,
From the thousand responses of my heart never to cease,
From the myriad thence-arous'd words,
From the word stronger and more delicious than any,

From such as now they start the scene revisiting,   15
As a flock, twittering, rising, or overhead passing,
Borne hither, ere all eludes me, hurriedly,
A man, yet by these tears a little boy again,
Throwing myself on the sand, confronting the waves,
I, chanter of pains and joys, uniter of here and hereafter,   20
Taking all hints to use them, but swiftly leaping beyond them,
A reminiscence sing.

Once Paumanok,[4]
When the lilac-scent was in the air and Fifth-month[5] grass was
    growing,
Up this seashore in some briers,   25
Two feather'd guests from Alabama, two together,
And their nest, and four light-green eggs spotted with brown,
And every day the he-bird to and fro near at hand,
And every day the she-bird crouch'd on her nest, silent, with bright
    eyes,
And every day I, a curious boy, never too close, never disturbing
    them,   30
Cautiously peering, absorbing, translating.

Shine! shine! shine!
Pour down your warmth, great sun!
While we bask, we two together,

Two together!   35
Winds blow south, or winds blow north,
Day come white, or night come black,
Home, or rivers and mountains from home,
Singing all time, minding no time,
While we two keep together.   40

[3] Sickness.   [5] The Quaker term for May.
[4] The Indian term for Long Island.

Till of a sudden,
May-be kill'd, unknown to her mate,
One forenoon the she-bird crouch'd not on the nest,
Nor return'd that afternoon, nor the next,
Nor ever appear'd again.   45

And thenceforward all summer in the sound of the sea,
And at night under the full of the moon in calmer weather,
Over the hoarse surging of the sea,
Or flitting from brier to brier by day,
I saw, I heard at intervals the remaining one, the he-bird,   50
The solitary guest from Alabama.

Blow! blow! blow!
Blow up sea-winds along Paumanok's shore;
I wait and I wait till you blow my mate to me.

Yes, when the stars glisten'd,   55
All night long on the prong of a moss-scallop'd stake,
Down almost amid the slapping waves,
Sat the lone singer wonderful causing tears.

He call'd on his mate,
He pour'd forth the meanings which I of all men know.   60

Yes my brother I know,
The rest might not, but I have treasur'd every note,
For more than once dimly down to the beach gliding,
Silent, avoiding the moonbeams, blending myself with the shadows,
Recalling now the obscure shapes, the echoes,
   the sounds and sights after their sorts,   65
The white arms out in the breakers tirelessly tossing,
I, with bare feet, a child, the wind wafting my hair,
Listen'd long and long.

Listen'd to keep, to sing, now translating the notes,
Following you my brother.   70

Soothe! soothe! soothe!
Close on its wave soothes the wave behind,
And again another behind embracing and lapping, every one close,
But my love soothes not me, not me.

Low hangs the moon, it rose late,   75
It is lagging—O I think it is heavy with love, with love.

O madly the sea pushes upon the land,
With love, with love.

O night! do I not see my love fluttering out among the breakers?
What is that little black thing I see there in the white?   80

Loud! loud! loud!
Loud I call to you, my love!
High and clear I shoot my voice over the waves,
Surely you must know who is here, is here,
You must know who I am, my love.   85

Low-hanging moon!
What is that dusky spot in your brown yellow?
O it is the shape, the shape of my mate!
O moon do not keep her from me any longer.

Land! land! O land!   90
Whichever way I turn, O I think you could give me my mate
*   back again if you only would,*
For I am almost sure I see her dimly whichever way I look.

O rising stars!
Perhaps the one I want so much will rise, will rise with some of you.   95

O throat! O trembling throat!
Sound clearer through the atmosphere!
Pierce the woods, the earth,
Somewhere listening to catch you must be the one I want.

Shake out carols!   100
Solitary here, the night's carols!
Carols of lonesome love! death's carols!
Carols under that lagging, yellow, waning moon!
O under that moon where she droops almost down into the sea!
O reckless despairing carols.   105

But soft! sink low!
Soft! let me just murmur,
And do you wait a moment you husky-nois'd sea,
For somewhere I believe I heard my mate responding to me,
So faint, I must be still, be still to listen,   110
But not altogether still, for then she might not come immediately to
*   me.*

Hither my love!
Here I am! here!
With this just-sustain'd note I announce myself to you,
This gentle call is for you my love, for you.

Do not be decoy'd elsewhere,   115
That is the whistle of the wind, it is not my voice,
That is the fluttering, the fluttering of the spray,
Those are the shadows of leaves.

O darkness! O in vain!
O I am very sick and sorrowful   120

O brown halo in the sky near the moon, drooping upon the sea!
O troubled reflection in the sea!
O throat! O throbbing heart!
And I singing uselessly, uselessly all the night.

O past! O happy life! O songs of joy!   125
In the air, in the woods, over fields,
Loved! loved! loved! loved! loved!
But my mate no more, no more with me!
We two together no more.

The aria sinking,   130
All else continuing, the stars shining,
The winds blowing, the notes of the bird continuous echoing,
With angry moans the fierce old mother incessantly moaning,
On the sands of Paumanok's shore gray and rustling,
The yellow half-moon enlarged, sagging down, drooping,
    the face of the sea almost touching,   135
The boy ecstatic, with his bare feet the waves,
    with his hair the atmosphere dallying,
The love in the heart long pent, now loose, now at last tumultuously
    bursting
The aria's meaning, the ears, the soul, swiftly depositing,
The strange tears down the cheeks coursing,
The colloquy there, the trio, each uttering,   140
The undertone, the savage old mother incessantly crying,
To the boy's soul's questions sullenly timing, some drown'd secret
    hissing,
To the outsetting bard.

Demon or bird! (said the boy's soul,)
Is it indeed toward your mate you sing? or is it really to me? 145
For I, that was a child, my tongue's use sleeping, now I have heard you,
Now in a moment I know what I am for, I awake,
And already a thousand singers, a thousand songs,
   clearer, louder and more sorrowful than yours,
A thousand warbling echoes have started to life within me, never to die.

O you singer solitary, singing by yourself, projecting me, 150
O solitary me listening, never more shall I cease perpetuating you,
Never more shall I escape, never more the reverberations,
Never more the cries of unsatisfied love be absent from me,
Never again leave me to be the peaceful child I was before
   what there in the night,
By the sea under the yellow and sagging moon, 155
The messenger there arous'd, the fire, the sweet hell within,
The unknown want, the destiny of me.

O give me the clue! (it lurks in the night here somewhere,)
O if I am to have so much, let me have more!

A word then, (for I will conquer it,) 160
The word final, superior to all,
Subtle, sent up—what is it?—I listen:
Are you whispering it, and have been all the time, you sea-waves?
Is that it from your liquid rims and wet sands?

Whereto answering, the sea, 165
Delaying not, hurrying not,
Whisper'd me through the night, and very plainly before daybreak,
Lisp'd to me the low and delicious word death,
And again death, death, death, death,
Hissing melodious, neither like the bird nor like my arous'd child's heart, 170
But edging near as privately for me rustling at my feet,
Creeping thence steadily up to my ears and laving me softly all over,
Death, death, death, death, death.

Which I do not forget,
But fuse the song of my dusky demon and brother, 175
That he sang to me in the moonlight on Paumanok's gray beach,
With the thousand responsive songs at random,
My own songs awaked from that hour,
And with them the key, the word up from the waves,
The word of the sweetest song and all songs, 180
That strong and delicious word which, creeping to my feet,
(Or like some old crone rocking the cradle,
   swathed in sweet garments, bending aside,)
The sea whisper'd me.

1859

As I Ebb'd with the Ocean of Life

1 As I ebb'd with the ocean of life,
  As I wended the shores I know,
  As I walk'd where the ripples continually wash you Paumanok,
  Where they rustle up hoarse and sibilant,
  Where the fierce old mother endlessly cries for her castaways, 5
  I musing late in the autumn day, gazing off southward,
  Held by this electric self out of the pride of which I utter poems,
  Was seiz'd by the spirit that trails in the lines underfoot,
  The rim, the sediment that stands for all the water
    and all the land of the globe.

  Fascinated, my eyes reverting from the south, dropt,
    to follow those slender windrows, 10
  Chaff, straw, splinters of wood, weeds, and the sea-gluten,[1]
  Scum, scales from shining rocks, leaves of salt-lettuce, left by the
    tide,
  Miles walking, the sound of breaking waves the other side of me,
  Paumanok there and then as I thought the old thought of likenesses,
  These you presented to me you fish-shaped island, 15
  As I wended the shores I know,
  As I walk'd with that electric self seeking types.

2 As I wend to the shores I know not,
  As I list to the dirge, the voices of men and women wreck'd,
  As I inhale the impalpable breezes that set in upon me, 20

---

[1] Adhesive.

As the ocean so mysterious rolls toward me closer and closer,
I too but signify at the utmost a little wash'd-up drift,
A few sands and dead leaves to gather,
Gather, and merge myself as part of the sands and drift.

O baffled, balk'd, bent to the very earth,   25
Oppress'd with myself that I have dared to open my mouth,
Aware now that amid all that blab whose echoes recoil upon me
    I have not once had the least idea who or what I am,
But that before all my arrogant poems the real Me stands yet
    untouch'd,
    untold, altogether unreach'd,
Withdrawn far, mocking me with mock-congratulatory signs and
    bows,
With peals of distant ironical laughter at every word I have written,   30
Pointing in silence to these songs, and then to the sand beneath.

I perceive I have not really understood any thing, not a single
    object,
    and that no man ever can,
Nature here in sight of the sea taking advantage of me,
    to dart upon me and sting me,
Because I have dared to open my mouth to sing at all.

3 You oceans both, I close with you,   35
We murmur alike reproachfully rolling sands and drift,
    knowing not why,
These little shreds indeed standing for you and me and all.

You friable[2] shore with trails of debris,
You fish-shaped island, I take what is underfoot,
What is yours is mine my father.   40

I too Paumanok,
I too have bubbled up, floated the measureless float,
    and been wash'd on your shores,
I too am but a trail of drift and debris,
I too leave little wrecks upon you, you fish-shaped island.

I throw myself upon your breast my father,   45
I cling to you so that you cannot unloose me,
I hold you so firm till you answer me something.

Kiss me my father,
Touch me with your lips as I touch those I love,
Breathe to me while I hold you close the secret of the murmuring I
    envy.   50

[2] Readily crumbled, brittle.

⁴ Ebb, ocean of life, (the flow will return,)
Cease not your moaning you fierce old mother,
Endlessly cry for your castaways, but fear not, deny not me,
Rustle not up so hoarse and angry against my feet as I touch you
    or gather from you.

I mean tenderly by you and all,   55
I gather for myself and for this phantom looking down where we
    lead, and following me and mine.

Me and mine, loose windrows, little corpses,
Froth, snowy white, and bubbles,
(See, from my dead lips the ooze exuding at last,
See, the prismatic colors glistening and rolling,)   60
Tufts of straw, sands, fragments,
Buoy'd hither from many moods, one contradicting another,
From the storm, the long calm, the darkness, the swell,
Musing, pondering, a breath, a briny tear, a dab of liquid or soil,
Up just as much out of fathomless workings fermented and thrown,   65
A limp blossom or two, torn, just as much over waves floating,
    drifted at random,
Just as much for us that sobbing dirge of Nature,
Just as much whence we come that blare of the cloud-trumpets,
We, capricious, brought hither we know not whence, spread out
    before you,
You up there walking or sitting,   70
Whoever you are, we too lie in drifts at your feet.³

                               1860

³ Gay Wilson Allen, in *The Whitman Hand-book* (1956), calls attention to the pessimistic quality of these lines. Whitman was suffering at the time from mental depression and tragic brooding.

A Hand-Mirror

Hold it up sternly—see this it sends back, (who is it? is it you?)
Outside fair costume, within ashes and filth,
No more a flashing eye, no more a sonorous voice or springy step,
Now some slave's eye, voice, hands, step,
A drunkard's breath, unwholesome eater's face, venerealee's flesh,   5

Lungs rotting away piecemeal, stomach sour and cankerous,
Joints rheumatic, bowels clogged with abomination,
Blood circulating dark and poisonous streams,
Words babble, hearing and touch callous,   10
No brain, no heart left, no magnetism of sex;
Such from one look in this looking-glass ere you go hence,
Such a result so soon—and from such a beginning!

                                                                        1860

I Sit and Look Out

I sit and look out upon all the sorrows of the world,
    and upon all oppression and shame,
I hear secret convulsive sobs from young men at anguish with
    themselves, remorseful after deeds done,
I see in low life the mother misused by her children, dying,
    neglected, gaunt, desperate,
I see the wife misused by her husband, I see the treacherous seducer
    of young women,
I mark the ranklings of jealousy and unrequited love attempted to be
    hid, I see these sights on the earth,   5
I see the workings of battle, pestilence, tyranny, I see martyrs and
    prisoners,
I observe a famine at sea, I observe the sailors casting lots
    who shall be kill'd to preserve the lives of the rest,
I observe the slights and degradations cast by arrogant persons
    upon laborers, the poor, and upon negroes, and the like;
All these—all the meanness and agony without end I sitting look out
    upon,
See, hear, and am silent.   10

                                                                        1860

The Dalliance of the Eagles[1]

Skirting the river road, (my forenoon walk, my rest,)
Skyward in air a sudden muffled sound, the dalliance of the eagles,
The rushing amorous contact high in space together,
The clinching interlocking claws, a living, fierce, gyrating wheel,
Four beating wings, two beaks, a swirling mass tight grappling,   5
In tumbling turning clustering loops, straight downward falling,
Till o'er the river pois'd, the twain yet one, a moment's lull,
    A motionless still balance in the air, then parting, talons loosing,
Upward again on slow-firm pinions slanting, their separate diverse
    flight,
She hers, he his, pursuing.   10

1880

[1] The poem first appeared in the November
1880 issue of *Cope's Tobacco Plant.*

Cavalry Crossing a Ford[1]

A line in long array where they wind betwixt green islands,
They take a serpentine course, their arms flash in the sun—
    Hark to the musical clank,
Behold the silvery river, in it the splashing horses loitering stop to
    drink,
Behold the brown-faced men, each group, each person a picture,
    the negligent rest on the saddles,
Some emerge on the opposite bank, others are just entering the
    ford—while,
Scarlet and blue and snowy white,
The guidon flags[2] flutter gayly in the wind.

1865

[1] This and the next two poems were included
in *Drum Taps* (1865), Whitman's poetic record of the Civil War.

[2] The standard for a military unit.

Vigil Strange I Kept on the Field One Night

Vigil strange I kept on the field one night;
When you my son and my comrade dropt at my side that day,
One look I but gave which your dear eyes return'd with a look
    I shall never forget,
One touch of your hand to mine O boy, reach'd up as you lay on the
    ground,
Then onward I sped in the battle, the even-contested battle,   5
Till late in the night reliev'd to the place at last again I made my
    way,
Found you in death so cold dear comrade, found your body
    son of responding kisses, (never again on earth responding,)
Bared your face in the starlight, curious the scene,
    cool blew the moderate night-wind,
Long there and then in vigil I stood, dimly around me the battle-field
    spreading,
Vigil wondrous and vigil sweet there in the fragrant silent night,   10
But not a tear fell, not even a long-drawn sigh, long, long I gazed,
Then on the earth partially reclining sat by your side
    leaning my chin in my hands,
Passing sweet hours, immortal and mystic hours with you dearest
    comrade—not a tear, not a word,
Vigil of silence, love and death, vigil for you my son and my soldier,
As onward silently stars aloft, eastward new ones upward stole,   15
Vigil final for you brave boy, (I could not save you, swift was your
    death,
I faithfully loved you and cared for you living,
    I think we shall surely meet again,)
Till at latest lingering of the night, indeed just as the dawn appear'd,
My comrade I wrapt in his blanket, envelop'd well his form,
Folded the blanket well, tucking it carefully over head and carefully
    under feet.   20
And there and then and bathed by the rising sun, my son in his grave,
    in his rude-dug grave I deposited,
Ending my vigil strange with that, vigil of night and battle-field dim,
Vigil for boy of responding kisses, (never again on earth responding,)
Vigil for comrade swiftly slain, vigil I never forget, how as day
    brighten'd,
I rose from the chill ground and folded my soldier well in his blanket,   25
And buried him where he fell.

1865

A Sight in Camp in the Daybreak Gray and Dim[1]

A sight in camp in the daybreak gray and dim,
As from my tent I emerge so early sleepless,
As slow I walk in the cool fresh air the path near by the hospital tent,
Three forms I see on stretchers lying, brought out there untended
　　lying,
Over each the blanket spread, ample brownish woolen blanket,　　　　　　5
Gray and heavy blanket, folding, covering all.

Curious I halt and silent stand,
Then with the light fingers I from the face of the nearest the first
　　just lift the blanket;
Who are you elderly man so gaunt and grim, with well-gray'd hair,
　　and flesh all sunken about the eyes?
Who are you my dear comrade?　　　　　　　　　　　　　　　　　　10

Then to the second I step—and who are you my child and darling?
Who are you sweet boy with cheeks yet blooming?

Then to the third—a face nor child nor old, very calm,
　　as of beautiful yellow-white ivory;
Young man I think I know you—I think this face is the face
　　of the Christ himself,
Dead and divine and brother of all, and here again he lies.　　　　　15

1865

[1] The source of this poem is in Whitman's notebook of 1862–1863: "Sight at daybreak in camp in front of the hospital tent. Three dead men lying, each with a blanket spread over him—I lift up one and look at the young man's face, calm and yellow. 'tis strange' (Young man: I think this face of yours is the face of my 'dead Christ')."

When Lilacs Last in the Dooryard Bloom'd

1　When lilacs[1] last in the dooryard bloom'd,
　　And the great star[2] early droop'd in the western sky in the night,
　　I mourn'd, and yet shall mourn with ever-returning spring.

[1] The lilacs are associated with memories of Abraham Lincoln and come to symbolize love.

[2] President Lincoln, whose death was the occasion of the poem.

Ever-returning spring, trinity sure to me you bring,
Lilac blooming perennial and drooping star in the west,   5
And thought of him I love.

2 O powerful western fallen star!
  O shades of night—O moody, tearful night!
  O great star disappear'd—O the black murk that hides the star!
  O cruel hands that hold me powerless—O helpless soul of me!   10
  O harsh surrounding cloud that will not free my soul.

3 In the dooryard fronting an old farm-house near the white-wash'd
    palings,
  Stands the lilac-bush tall-growing with heart-shaped leaves of rich
    green,
  With many a pointed blossom rising delicate, with the perfume
    strong I love,
  With every leaf a miracle—and from this bush in the dooryard,   15
  With delicate-color'd blossoms and heart-shaped leaves of rich
    green,
  A sprig with its flower I break.

4 In the swamp in secluded recesses,
  A shy and hidden bird[3] is warbling a song.

  Solitary the thrush,   20
  The hermit withdrawn to himself, avoiding the settlements,
  Sings by himself a song.

  Song of the bleeding throat,
  Death's outlet song of life, (for well dear brother I know,
  If thou wast not granted to sing thou would'st surely die.)   25

5 Over the breast of the spring, the land, amid cities,
  Amid lanes and through old woods, where lately the violets peep'd
    from the ground, spotting the gray debris,
  Amid the grass in the fields each side of the lanes, passing the
    endless grass,
  Passing the yellow-spear'd wheat, every grain from its shroud
    in the dark-brown fields uprisen,
  Passing the apple-tree blows of white and pink in the orchards,   30
  Carrying a corpse to where it shall rest in the grave,
  Night and day journeys a coffin.[4]

[3] The poet.
[4] The coffin holds the immortal character of Lincoln, whose body was taken to Springfield, Illinois, where it was buried.

⁶ Coffin that passes through lanes and streets,
  Through day and night with the great cloud darkening the land,
  With the pomp of the inloop'd flags with the cities draped in black,   35
  With the show of the States themselves as of crape-veil'd women
    standing,
  With processions long and winding and the flambeaus of the night,
  With the countless torches lit, with the silent sea of faces
    and the unbared heads,
  With the waiting depot, the arriving coffin, and the sombre faces,
  With dirges through the night, with the thousand voices
    rising strong and solemn,   40
  With all the mournful voices of the dirges pour'd around the coffin,
  The dim-lit churches and the shuddering organs—
    where amid these you journey,
  With the tolling tolling bells' perpetual clang.
  Here, coffin that slowly passes,
  I give you my sprig of lilac.   45

⁷ (Nor for you, for one alone,
  Blossoms and branches green to coffins all I bring,
  For fresh as the morning, thus would I chant a song for you
    O sane and sacred death.

  All over bouquets of roses,   50
  O death, I cover you over with roses and early lilies,
  But mostly and now the lilac that blooms the first,
  Copious I break, I break the sprigs from the bushes,
  With loaded arms I come, pouring for you,
  For you and the coffins all of you O death.)   55

⁸ O western orb sailing the heaven,
  Now I know what you must have meant as a month since I walk'd,
  As I walk'd in silence the transparent shadowy night,
  As I saw you had something to tell as you bent to me night after
    night,
  As you droop'd from the sky low down as if to my side,
    (while the other stars all look'd on,)   60
  As we wander'd together the solemn night, (for something
    I know not what kept me from sleep,)
  As the night advanced, and I saw on the rim of the west
    how full you were of woe,
  As I stood on the rising ground in the breeze in the cool
    transparent night,

As I watch'd where you pass'd and was lost in the netherward
   black of the night,
As my soul in its trouble dissatisfied sank, as where you sad orb,   65
Concluded, dropt in the night, and was gone.

⁹ Sing on there in the swamp,
   O singer bashful and tender, I hear your notes, I hear your call,
   I hear, I come presently, I understand you,
   But a moment I linger, for the lustrous star has detain'd me,   70
   The star my departing comrade holds and detains me.

¹⁰ O how shall I warble myself for the dead one there I loved?
   And how shall I deck my song for the large sweet soul that has
      gone?
   And what shall my perfume be for the grave of him I love?

   Sea-winds blown from east and west,   75
   Blown from the Eastern sea and blown from the Western sea,
      till there on the prairies meeting,
   These and with these and the breath of my chant,
   I'll perfume the grave of him I love?

¹¹ O what shall I hang on the chamber walls?
   And what shall the pictures be that I hang on the walls,   80
   To adorn the burial-house of him I love?

   Pictures of growing spring and farms and homes,
   With the Fourth-month⁵ eve at sundown, and the gray smoke lucid
      and bright,
   With floods of the yellow gold of the gorgeous, indolent, sinking
      sun, burning, expanding the air,
   With the fresh sweet herbage under foot, and the pale green
      leaves, of the trees prolific,   85
   In the distance the flowing glaze, the breast of the river,
      with a wind-dapple here and there,
   With ranging hills on the banks, with many a line against the sky,
      and shadows,
   And the city at hand with dwellings so dense, and stacks of
      chimneys,
   And all the scenes of life and the workshops,
      and the workmen homeward returning.

⁵ The Quaker term for April.

¹² Lo, body and soul—this land,   90
My own Manhattan with spires, and the sparkling and hurrying
    tides, and the ships,
The varied and ample land, the South and the North in the light,
    Ohio's shores and flashing Missouri
And ever the far-spreading prairies cover'd with grass and corn.

Lo, the most excellent sun so calm and haughty,
The violet and purple morn with just-felt breezes,   95
The gentle soft-born measureless light,
The miracle spreading bathing all, the fulfill'd noon,
The coming eve delicious, the welcome night and the stars,
Over my cities shining all, enveloping man and land.

¹³ Sing on, sing on you gray-brown bird,   100
Sing from the swamps, the recesses, pour your chant from the
    bushes,
Limitless out of the dusk, out of the cedars and pines.

Sing on dearest brother, warble your reedy song,
Loud human song, with voice of uttermost woe.

O liquid and free and tender!   105
O wild and loose to my soul—O wondrous singer!
You only I hear—yet the star holds me, (but will soon depart,)
Yet the lilac with mastering odor holds me.

¹⁴ Now while I sat in the day and look'd forth,
In the close of the day with its light and the fields of spring,
    and the farmers preparing their crops,   110
In the large unconscious scenery of my land with its lakes and
    forest,
In the heavenly aerial beauty, (after the perturb'd winds and the
    storms,)
Under the arching heavens of the afternoon swift passing,
    and the voices of children and women,
The many-moving sea-tides, and I saw the ships how they sail'd,
And the summer approaching with richness, and the fields all busy
    with labor.   115
And the infinite separate houses, how they all went on,
    each with its meals and minutia of daily usages,
And the streets how their throbbings throbb'd, and the cities
    pent—lo, then and there,

Falling upon them all and among them all, enveloping me with the
    rest,
Appear'd the cloud, appear'd the long black trail,
And I knew death, its thought, and the sacred knowledge of death.   120

Then with the knowledge of death as walking one side of me,
And the thought of death close-walking the other side of me,
And I in the middle as with companions,
and as holding the hands of companions,
I fled forth to the hiding receiving night that talks not,
Down to the shores of the water, the path by the swamp in the
    dimness,   125
To the solemn shadowy cedars and ghostly pines so still.

And the singer so shy to the rest receiv'd me,
The gray-brown bird I know receiv'd us comrades three, And he
    sang the carol of death, and a verse for him I love.

From deep secluded recesses,   130
From the fragrant cedars and the ghostly pines so still,
Came the carol of the bird.

And the charm of the carol rapt me,
As I held as if by their hands my comrades in the night,
And the voice of my spirit tallied the song of the bird.   135

Come lovely and soothing death,
Undulate round the world, serenely arriving, arriving,
In the day, in the night, to all, to each,
Sooner or later delicate death.

Prais'd be the fathomless universe,   140
For life and joy, and for objects and knowledge curious,
And for love, sweet love—but praise! praise! praise!
For the sure-enwinding arms of cool-enfolding death.

Dark mother always gliding near with soft feet,
Have none chanted for thee a chant of fullest welcome?   145
Then I chant it for thee, I glorify thee above all,
I bring thee a song that when thou must indeed come, come
    unfalteringly.

Approach strong deliveress,
When it is so, when thou hast taken them I joyously sing the dead,
Lost in the loving floating ocean of thee,   150
Laved in the flood of thy bliss O death.

From me to thee glad serenades,
Dances for thee I propose saluting thee, adornments and feastings
    for thee,
And the sights of the open landscape and the high-spread sky are
    fitting,
And life and the fields, and the huge and thoughtful night.   155

The night in silence under many a star,
The ocean shore and the husky whispering wave whose voice I
    know,
And the soul turning to thee O vast and well-veil'd death,
And the body gratefully nestling close to thee.

Over the tree-tops I float thee a song,   160
Over the rising and sinking waves, over the myriad fields and the
    prairies wide,
Over the dense-pack'd cities all and the teeming wharves and ways,
I float this carol with joy, with joy to thee O death.

15 To the tally of my soul,
   Loud and strong kept up the gray-brown bird,   165
   With pure deliberate notes spreading filling the night.

   Loud in the pines and cedars dim,
   Clear in the freshness moist and the swamp-perfume,
   And I with my comrades there in the night.

   While my sight that was bound in my eyes unclosed,   170
   As to long panoramas of visions.

   And I saw askant the armies,
   I saw as in noiseless dreams hundreds of battle-flags,
   Borne through the smoke of the battles and pierc'd with missiles I
       saw them.
   And carried hither and yon through the smoke, and torn and
       bloody,   175
   And at last but a few shreds left on the staffs, (and all in silence,)
   And the staffs all splinter'd and broken.

   I saw battle-corpses, myriads of them,
   And the white skeletons of young men, I saw them,
   I saw the debris and debris of all the slain soldiers of the war,   180
   But I saw they were not as was thought,
   They themselves were fully at rest, they suffer'd not,
   The living remain'd and suffer'd, the mother suffer'd,
   And the wife and the child and musing comrade suffer'd,
   And the armies that remain'd suffer'd.   185

16 Passing the visions, passing the night,
Passing, unloosing the hold of my comrades' hands,
Passing the song of the hermit bird and the tallying song of my
  soul,
Victorious song, death's outlet song, yet varying ever-altering song,
As low and wailing, yet clear the notes, rising and falling, flooding
  the night,   190
Sadly sinking and fainting, as warning and warning,
  and yet again bursting with joy,

Covering the earth and filling the spread of the heaven,
As that powerful psalm in the night I heard from recesses,
Passing, I leave thee lilac with heart-shaped leaves,
I leave thee there in the door-yard, blooming, returning with
  spring.   195

I cease from my song for thee,
From my gaze on thee in the west, fronting the west, communing
  with thee,
O comrade lustrous with silver face in the night.

Yet each to keep and all, retrievements out of the night,
The song, the wondrous chant of the gray-brown bird,   200
And the tallying chant, the echo arous'd in my soul,
With the lustrous and drooping star with the countenance full of
  woe,
With the holders holding my hand nearing the call of the bird,
Comrades mine and I in the midst, and their memory ever to keep,
  for the dead I loved so well,
For the sweetest, wisest soul of all my days and lands—
  and this for his dear sake,   205
Lilac and star and bird twined with the chant of my soul,
There in the fragrant pines and the cedars dusk and dim.

1865–1866

The City Dead-House

By the city dead-house by the gate,
As idly sauntering wending my way from the clangor,
I curious pause, for lo, an outcast form, a poor dead prostitute
  brought,
Her corpse they deposit unclaim'd, it lies on the damp brick
  pavement,

The divine woman, her body, I see the body, I look on it alone,   5
That house once full of passion and beauty, all else I notice not,
Nor stillness so cold, nor running water from faucet,
    nor odors morbific[1] impress me,
But the house alone—that wondrous house—that delicate fair
    house—that ruin!
That immortal house more than all the rows of dwellings ever built!
Or white-domed capitol with majestic figure surmounted,
    or all the old high-spired cathedrals,   10
That little house alone more than them all—poor, desperate house!
Fair, fearful wreck—tenement of a soul—itself a soul,
Unclaim'd, avoided house—take one breath from my tremulous lips,
Take one tear dropt aside as I go for thought of you,
Dead house of love—house of madness and sin, crumbled, crush'd,   15
House of life, erewhile talking and laughing—but ah, poor house,
    dead even then,
Months, years, an echoing, garnish'd house—but dead, dead, dead.

                                 1867

[1] Causing or producing death.

This Compost[1]

Something startles me where I thought I was safest,
I withdraw from the still woods I loved,
I will not go now on the pastures to walk,
I will not strip the clothes from my body to meet my lover the sea,
I will not touch my flesh to the earth as to other flesh to renew me.   5

O how can it be that the ground itself does not sicken?
How can you be alive you growths of spring?
How can you furnish health you blood of herbs, roots, orchards,
    grain?
Are they not continually putting distemper'd corpses within you?
Is not every continent work'd over and over with sour dead?   10

[1] This poem was first published as "Poem of
Wonder at the Resurrection of the Wheat."

Where have you disposed of their carcasses?
Those drunkards and gluttons of so many generations?
Where have you drawn off all the foul liquid and meat?
I do not see any of it upon you to-day, or perhaps I am deceiv'd,
I will run a furrow with my plough, I will press my spade through the
    sod and turn it up underneath,   15
I am sure I shall expose some of the foul meat.

Behold this compost! behold it well!
Perhaps every mite has once form'd part of a sick person—yet
    behold!
The grass of spring covers the prairies,
The bean bursts noiselessly through the mould in the garden,   20
The delicate spear of the onion pierces upward,
The apple-buds cluster together on the apple-branches,
The resurrection of the wheat appears with pale visage out of its
    graves,
The tinge awakes over the willow-tree and the mulberry-tree,
The he-birds carol mornings and evenings while the she-birds sit on
    their nests,   25
The young of poultry break through the hatch'd eggs,
The new-born of animals appear, the calf is dropt from the cow,
    the colt from the mare,
Out of its little hill faithfully rise the potato's dark green leaves,
Out of its hill rises the yellow maize-stalk, the lilacs bloom in the
    dooryards,
The summer growth is innocent and disdainful above all those strata
    of sour dead.   30

What chemistry!
That the winds are really not infectious,
That this is no cheat, this transparent green-wash of the sea
    which is so amorous after me,
That it is safe to allow it to lick my naked body all over with its
    tongues,
That it will not endanger me with the fevers
    that have deposited themselves in it,   35
That all is clean forever and forever,
That the cool drink from the well tastes so good,
That blackberries are so flavorous and juicy,
That the fruits of the apple-orchard and the orange-orchard,
    that melons, grapes, peaches, plums, will none of them poison me,

That when I recline on the grass I do not catch any disease,   40
Though probably every spear of grass rises
   out of what was once a catching disease.

Now I am terrified at the Earth, it is that calm and patient,
It grows such sweet things out of such corruptions,
It turns harmless and stainless on its axis,
   with such endless successions of diseas'd corpses,
It distills such exquisite winds out of such infused fetor,   45
It renews with such unwitting looks its prodigal, annual, sumptuous
   crops,
It gives such divine materials to men, and accepts such leavings
   from them at last.

1856

Sparkles from the Wheel

Where the city's ceaseless crowd moves on the livelong day,
Withdrawn I join a group of children watching, I pause aside with
   them.

By the curb toward the edge of the flagging,
A knife-grinder works at his wheel sharpening a great knife,
Bending over he carefully holds it to the stone, by foot and knee,   5
With measur'd tread he turns rapidly, as he presses with light but
   firm box,
Forth issue then in copious golden jets,
Sparkles from the wheel.

The scene and all its belongings, how they seize and affect me,
The sad sharp-chinn'd old man with worn clothes
   and broad shoulder-band of leather,   10
Myself effusing and fluid, a phantom curiously floating,
   now here absorb'd and arrested,
The group, (an unminded point set in a vast surrounding,)
The attentive, quiet children, the loud, proud, restive base of the
   streets,
The low hoarse purr of the whirling stone, the light-press'd blade,
Diffusing, dropping, sideways-darting, in tiny showers of gold,
Sparkles from the wheel.   15

1871

Passage to India [1]

1 Singing my days,
Singing the great achievements of the present,
Singing the strong light works of engineers,
Our modern wonders, (the antique ponderous Seven outvied,)
In the Old World the east the Suez canal,   5
In the New by its mighty railroad spann'd,
The seas inlaid with eloquent gently wires;
Yet first to sound, and ever sound, the cry with thee O soul,
The Past! the Past! the Past!

The Past—the dark unfathom'd retrospect!   10
The teeming gulf—the sleepers and the shadows!
The past—the infinite greatness of the past!
For what is the present after all but a growth out of the past?
(As a projectile form'd, impell'd, passing a certain line, still keeps
    on,
So the present, utterly form'd, impell'd by the past.)   15

2 Passage O soul to India!
Eclaircise [2] the myths Asiatic, the primitive fables.

Not you alone proud truths of the world,
Nor you alone ye facts of modern science,
But myths and fables of eld, Asia's, Africa's fables,   20
The far-darting beams of the spirit, the unloos'd dreams,
The deep diving bibles and legend,
The daring plots of the poets, the elder religions;
O you temples fairer than lilies pour'd over by the rising sun!
O you fables spurning the known, eluding the hold of the known,
    mounting to heaven!   25
You lofty and dazzling towers, pinnacled, red as roses,
    burnish'd with gold!
Towers of fables immortal fashion'd from mortal dreams!
You too I welcome and fully the same as the rest!
You too with joy I sing.

Passage to India!   30
Lo, soul, seest thou not God's purpose from the first?
The earth to be spann'd, connected by network,

---

[1] The poem is an expression of Whitman's universalism, inspired by the opening of the Suez Canal (1869), linking Asia and Europe; the completion of a transcontinental railroad in the United States (1869), and the Atlantic Cable, linking Europe and America.
[2] French for clarify.

The races, neighbors, to marry and be given in marriage,
The oceans to be cross'd, the distant brought near,
The lands to be welded together.   35

A worship new I sing,
You captains, voyagers, explorers, yours,
You engineers, you architects, machinists, yours,
You, not for trade or transportation only,
But in God's name, and for thy sake O soul.   40

³ Passage to India!
Lo soul for thee of tableaus twain,
I see in one the Suez canal initiated, open'd,
I see the procession of steamships, the Empress Eugenie's leading
    the band,
I mark from on deck the strange landscape, the pure sky,
    the level sand in the distance,   45
I pass swiftly the picturesque groups, the workmen gather'd,
The gigantic dredging machines.

In one again, different, (yet thine, all thine, O soul, the same,)
I see over my own continent the Pacific railroad surmounting every
    barrier,
I see continual trains of cars winding along the Platte
    carrying freight and passengers,   50
I hear the locomotives rushing and roaring, and the shrill steam-
    whistle,
I hear the echoes reverberate through the grandest scenery in the
    world,
I cross the Laramie plains, I note the rocks in grotesque shapes, the
    buttes,
I see the plentiful larkspur and wild onions, the barren,
    colorless, sage-deserts,   55
I see in glimpses afar or towering immediately above me the great
    mountains, I see the Wind river and the Wahsatch mountains,
I see the Monument mountain and the Eagle's Nest, I pass the
    Promontory, I ascend the Nevadas,
I scan the noble Elk mountain and wind around its base,
I see the Humboldt range, I thread the valley and cross the river,
I see the clear waters of lake Tahoe, I see forests of majestic pines, 60
Or crossing the great desert, the alkaline plains, I behold enchanting
    mirages of waters and meadows,

Marking through these and after all, in duplicate slender lines,
Bridging the three or four thousand miles of land travel,
Tying the Eastern to the Western sea,   65
The road between Europe and Asia.

(Ah Genoese[3] thy dream! thy dream!
Centuries after thou art laid in thy grave,
The shore thou foundest verifies thy dream.)

[4] Passage to India!   70
Struggles of many a captain, tales of many a sailor dead,
Over my mood stealing and spreading they come,
Like clouds and cloudlets in the unreach'd sky.

Along all history, down the slopes,
As a rivulet running, sinking now, and now again to the surface
    rising,
A ceaseless thought, a varied train—lo, soul, to thee, thy sight, they
    rise,   75
The plans, the voyages again the expeditions;
Again Vasco de Gama[4] sails forth,
Again the knowledge gain'd, the mariner's compass,
Lands found and nations born, thou born America,
For purpose vast, man's long probation fill'd,   80
Thou rondure of the world at last accomplish'd.

[5] O vast Rondure, swimming in space,
Cover'd all over with visible power and beauty,
Alternate light and day and the teeming spiritual darkness,
Unspeakable high processions of sun and moon and countless stars
    above,   85
Below, the manifold grass and waters, animals, mountains, trees,
With inscrutable purpose, some hidden prophetic intention,
Now first it seems my thought begins to span thee.

Down from the gardens of Asia descending radiating,
Adam and Eve appear, then their myriad progeny after them,   90
Wandering, yearning, curious, with restless explorations,
With questionings, baffled, formless, feverish, with never-happy
    hearts,
With that sad incessant refrain, Wherefore unsatisfied soul?
    and Whither O mocking life?

---

[3] Christopher Columbus.
[4] Vasco da Gama (1469?-1524) was a Portu-   guese explorer and colonial administrator,
                                             the first to reach India by the sea.

Ah who shall soothe these feverish children?
Who justify these restless explorations?   95
Who speak the secret of impassive earth?
Who bind it to us? what is this separate Nature so unnatural?
What is this earth to our affections? (unloving earth,
    without a throb to answer ours,
Cold earth, the place of graves.)

Yet soul be sure the first intent remains, and shall be carried out,   100
Perhaps even now the time has arrived.

After the seas are all cross'd, (as they seem already cross'd,)
After the great captains and engineers have accomplish'd their
    work,
After the noble inventors, after the scientists, the chemist,
    the geologist, ethnologist,
Finally shall come the poet worthy that name,   105
The true son of God shall come singing his songs.

Then not your deeds only O voyagers, O scientists and inventors,
    shall be justified,
All these hearts as of fretted children shall be sooth'd,
All affection shall be fully responded to, the secret shall be told,
All these separations and gaps shall be taken up and hook'd
    and link'd together,   110
The whole earth, this cold, impassive, voiceless earth,
    shall be completely justified,
Trinitas divine shall be gloriously accomplish'd and compacted
    by the true son of God, the poet,
(He shall indeed pass the straits and conquer the mountains,
He shall double the cape of Good Hope to some purpose,)
Nature and Man shall be disjoin'd and diffused no more,   115
The true son of God shall absolutely fuse them.

6 Year at whose wide-flung door I sing!
Year of the purpose accomplish'd!
Year of the marriage of continents, climates and oceans!
(No mere doge of Venice now wedding the Adriatic,)   120
I see O year in you the vast terraqueous globe given and giving all,
Europe to Asia, Africa join'd, and they to the New World,
The lands, geographies, dancing before you, holding a festival
    garland,
As brides and bridegrooms hand in hand.

Passage to India! 125
Cooling airs from Caucasus far, soothing cradle of man,
The river Euphrates[5] flowing, the past lit up again.

Lo soul, the retrospect brought forward,
The old, most populous, wealthiest of earth's lands,
The streams of the Indus and the Ganges[6] and their many affluents, 130
(I my shores of America walking to-day behold, resuming all,)
The tale of Alexander[7] on his warlike marches suddenly dying,
On one side China and on the other side Persia and Arabia,
To the south the great seas and the bay of Bengal,
The flowing literatures, tremendous epics, religions, castes, 135
Old occult Brahma interminably far back, the tender and junior
    Buddha,
Central and southern empires and all their belongings, possessors,
The wars of Tamerlane,[8] the reign of Aurungzebe,[9]
The traders, rulers, explorers, Moslems, Venetians, Byzantium,
    the Arabs, Portuguese,
The first travelers famous yet, Marco Polo,[10] Batouta the Moor,[11] 140
Doubts to be solv'd the map incognita, blanks to be fill'd,
The foot of man unstay'd, the hands never at rest,
Thyself O soul that will not brook a challenge.The mediæval
    navigators rise before me,
The world of 1492, with its awaken'd enterprise, 145
Something swelling in humanity now like the sap of the earth in
    spring,
The sunset splendor of chivalry declining.

And who art thou sad shade?
Gigantic, visionary, thyself a visionary,
With majestic limbs and pious beaming eyes 150
Spreading around with every look of thine a golden world,
Enhuing it with gorgeous hues.

[5] A river of southwestern Asia, flowing some 2235 miles from east central Turkey, through northeastern Syria and central Iraq, to the Tigris River. It was thought to be the "cradle" of the West.

[6] Indus is a river rising in southwestern Tibet and flowing through Tibet and Pakistan to the Arabian Sea. The Ganges is a river in Northern India and East Pakistan, flowing from the Himalayas to the Bay of Bengal. It is sacred to the Hindus.

[7] Alexander the Great (356-323 B.C.) was king of Macedonia and conqueror of Greece,

the Persian Empire, and Egypt. He died on his return from India.

[8] Tamerlane (1336?-1405) was an Islamic conqueror of central Asia and eastern Europe.

[9] A seventeenth-century emperor of Hindustan.

[10] A Venetian traveler (1254?-1324?) at the court of Kublai Khan who traveled to Cathay.

[11] Baboutsh (1303-1377) went to Asia and Africa.

As the chief histrion,[12]
Down to the footlights walks in some great scene,
Dominating the rest I see the Admiral[13] himself,   155
(History's type of courage, action, faith,)
Behold him sail from Palos[14] leading his little fleet,
His voyage behold, his return, his great fame,
His misfortunes, calumniators, behold him a prisoner, chain'd,
Behold his dejection, poverty, death.   160

(Curious in time I stand, noting the efforts of heroes,
Is the deferment long? bitter the slander, poverty, death?
Lies the seed unreck'd for centuries in the ground? lo, to God's due
    occasion,
Uprising in the night, it sprouts, blooms,
And fills the earth with use and beauty.)   165

7 Passage indeed O soul to primal thought,
Not lands and seas alone, thy own clear freshness,
The young maturity of brood and bloom,
To realms of budding bibles.

O soul, repressless, I with thee and thou with me,   170
Thy circumnavigation of the world begin,
Of man, the voyage of his mind's return,
To reason's early paradise,
Back, back to wisdom's birth, to innocent intuitions,
Again with fair creation.   175

8 O we can wait no longer,
We too take ship O soul,
Joyous we too launch out on trackless seas,
Fearless for unknown shores on waves of ecstasy to sail,
Amid the wafting winds, (thou pressing me to thee, I thee to me, O
    soul,)   180
Caroling free, singing our song of God, Chanting our chant of
    pleasant exploration.

With laugh and many a kiss,
(Let others deprecate, let others weep for sin, remorse, humiliation,)
O soul thou pleasest me, I thee.   185

Ah more than any priest O soul we too believe in God,
But with the mystery of God we dare not dally.

---

[12] Performer.   [14] Columbus sailed from this Spanish seaport.
[13] Christopher Columbus.

O soul thou pleasest me, I thee,
Sailing these seas or on the hills, or walking in the night,
Thoughts, silent thoughts, of Time and Space and Death, like waters
 flowing, 190
Bear me indeed as through the regions infinite,
Whose air I breathe, whose ripples hear, lave me all over,
Bathe me O God in thee, mounting to thee,
I and my soul to range of thee.

O Thou transcendent, 195
Nameless, the fibre and the breath,
Light of the light, shedding forth universes, thou centre of them,
Thou mightier centre of the true, the good, the loving,
Thou moral, spiritual fountain—affection's source—thou reservoir,
(O pensive soul of me—O thirst unsatisfied—waitest not there? 200
Waitest not haply for us somewhere there the Comrade perfect?)
Thou pulse—thou motive of the stars, suns, systems,
That, circling, move in order, safe, harmonious,
Athwart the shapeless vastnesses of space,
How should I think, how breathe a single breath, how speak, if, out
 of myself, 205
I could not launch, to those, superior universes?

Swiftly I shrivel at the thought of God,
At Nature and its wonders, Time and Space and Death,
But that I, turning, call to thee O soul, thou actual Me,
And lo, thou gently masterest the orbs, 210
Thou matest Time, smilest content at Death,
And fillest, swellest full the vastnesses of Space.

Greater than stars or suns,
Bounding O soul thou journeyest forth;
What love than thine and ours could wider amplify? 215
What aspirations, wishes, outvie thine and ours O soul?
What dreams of the ideal? what plans of purity, perfection,
 strength?
What cheerful willingness for others' sake to give up all?
For others' sake to suffer all?

Reckoning ahead O soul, when thou, the time achiev'd, 220
The seas all cross'd, weather'd the capes, the voyage done,
Surrounded, copest, frontest God, yieldest, the aim attain'd,
As fill'd with friendship, love complete, the Elder Brother found,
The Younger melts in fondness in his arms.

9   Passage to more than India!   225
    Are thy wings plumed indeed for such far flights?
    O soul, voyagest thou indeed on voyages like those?
    Disportest thou on waters such as those?
    Soundest below the Sanscrit and Vedas?[15]
    Then have thy bent unleash'd.   230

    Passage to you, your shores, ye aged fierce enigmas!
    Passage to you, to mastership of you, ye strangling problems!
    You, strew'd with the wrecks of skeletons, that, living,
        never reach'd you.

    Passage to more than Inida!
    O secret of the earth and sky!   235
    Of you O waters of the sea! O winding creeks and rivers!
    Of you O woods and fields! of you strong mountains of my land!
    Of you O prairies! of you gray rocks!
    O morning red! O clouds! O rain and snows!
    O day and night, passage to you!   240

    O sun and moon and all you stars! Sirius and Jupiter![16]
    Passage to you!

    Passage, immediate passage! the blood burns in my veins!
    Away O soul! hoist instantly the anchor!
    Cut the hawsers—haul out—shake out every sail!   245
    Have we not stood here like trees in the ground long enough?
    Have we not grovel'd here long enough, eating and drinking like
        mere brutes?
    Have we not darken'd and dazed ourselves with books long
        enough?

    Sail forth—steer for the deep waters only,
    Reckless O soul, exploring, I with thee, and thou with me,   250
    For we are bound where mariner has not yet dared to go,
    And we will risk the ship, ourselves and all.

    O my brave soul!
    O farther farther sail!
    O daring joy, but safe! are they not all the seas of God?   255
    O farther, farther, farther sail!

                                                                  1871

[15] The oldest sacred writings of Hinduism, written in Sanskrit.

[16] Sirius is the brightest star in the sky; Jupiter is the fifth planet from the sun, the largest in the solar system.

Prayer of Columbus[1]

A batter'd, wreck'd old man,[2]
Thrown on this savage shore, far, far from home,
Pent by the sea and dark rebellious brows, twelve dreary months,
Sore, stiff with many toils, sicken'd and nigh to death,
I take my way along the island's edge,   5
Venting a heavy heart.

I am too full of woe!
Haply I may not live another day;
I cannot rest O God, I cannot eat or drink or sleep,
Till I put forth myself, my prayer, once more to Thee,   10
Breathe, bathe myself once more in Thee, commune with Thee,
Report myself once more to Thee.

Thou knowest my years entire, my life,
My long and crowded life of active work, not adoration merely;
Thou knowest the prayers and vigils of my youth,   15
Thou knowest my manhood's solemn and visionary meditations,
Thou knowest how before I commenced I devoted all to come to
    Thee,
Thou knowest I have in age ratified all those vows and strictly kept
    them,
Thou knowest I have not once lost nor faith nor ecstasy in Thee,
In shackles, prison'd, in disgrace, repining not,   20
Accepting all from Thee, as duly come from Thee.

All my emprises have been fill'd with Thee,
My speculations, plans, begun and carried on in thoughts of Thee,
Sailing the deep or journeying the land for Thee;
Intentions, purports, aspirations mine, leaving results to Thee.   25

O I am sure they really came from Thee,
The urge, the ardor, the unconquerable will,
The potent, felt, interior command, stronger than words,
A message from the Heavens whispering to me even in sleep,
These sped me on.   30

[1] The poem first appeared in *Harpers Maga-zine*, March 1874.

[2] Whitman had suffered a stroke and thought he would not recover.

By me and these the work so far accomplish'd,
By me earth's elder cloy'd and stifled lands uncloy'd, unloos'd,
By me the hemispheres rounded and tied, the unknown to the known.

The end I know not, it is all in Thee,
Or small or great I know not—haply what broad fields, what lands,   35
Haply the brutish measureless human undergrowth I know,
Transplanted there may rise to stature, knowledge, worthy Thee,
Haply the swords I know may there indeed be turn'd to, reaping-tools,
Haply the lifeless cross I know, Europe's dead cross, may bud and
    blossom there.

One effort more, my altar this bleak sand;   40
That Thou O God my life has lighted,
With ray of light, steady, ineffable, vouchsafed of Thee,
Light rare untellable, lighting the very light,
Beyond all signs, descriptions, languages;
For that O God, be it my latest word, here on my knees,   45
Old, poor, and paralyzed, I thank Thee.

My terminus near,
The clouds already closing in upon me,
The voyage balk'd, the course disputed, lost,
I yield my ships to Thee.   50

My hands, my limbs grow nerveless,
My brain feels rack'd, bewilder'd,
Let the old timbers part, I will not part,
I will cling fast to Thee, O God, though the waves buffet me,
Thee, Thee at least I know.   55

Is it the prophet's thought I speak, or am I raving?
What do I know of life? what of myself?
I know not even my own work past or present,
Dim ever-shifting guesses of it spread before me,
Of newer better worlds, their mighty parturition,   60
Mocking, perplexing me.

And these things I see suddenly, what mean they?
As if some miracle, some hand divine unseal'd my eyes,
Shadowy vast shapes smile through the air and sky,
And on the distant waves sail countless ships,   65
And anthems in new tongues I hear saluting me.

1874

Whispers of Heavenly Death

Whispers of heavenly death murmur'd I hear,
Labial gossip of night, sibilant chorals,
Footsteps gently ascending, mystical breezes wafted soft and low,
Ripples of unseen rivers, tides of a current flowing, forever flowing,
(Or is it the plashing of tears? the measureless waters of human tears?)   5

I see, just see skyward, great cloud-masses,
Mournfully slowly they roll, silently swelling and mixing,
With at times a half-dimm'd sadden'd far-off star,
Appearing and disappearing.

(Some parturition[1] rather, some solemn immortal birth;   10
On the frontiers to eyes impenetrable,
Some soul is passing over.)

                                                                    1868

[1] Childbirth.

A Noiseless Patient Spider

A noiseless patient spider,
I mark'd where on a little promontory it stood isolated,
Mark'd how to explore the vacant vast surrounding,
It launch'd forth filament, filament, filament, out of itself,
Ever unreeling them, ever tirelessly speeding them.   5

And you O my soul where you stand,
Surrounded, detached, in measureless oceans of space,
Ceaselessly musing, venturing, throwing, seeking the spheres to
    connect them,
Till the bridge you will need be form'd, till the ductile anchor hold,
Till the gossamer thread you fling catch somewhere, O my soul.   10

                                                                    1868

From Democratic Vistas
1871

As the greatest lessons of Nature through the universe are perhaps the lessons of variety and freedom, the same present the greatest lessons also in
New World politics and progress. If a man were asked, for instance, the

distinctive points contrasting modern European and American political and other life with the old Asiatic cultus, as lingering-bequeathed yet in China and Turkey, he might find the amount of them in John Stuart Mill's profound essay on Liberty[1] in the future, where he demands two main constituents, or sub-strata, for a truly grand nationality—1st, a large variety of character— and 2nd, full play for human nature to expand itself in numberless and even conflicting directions—(seems to be for general humanity much like the in- fluences that make up, in their limitless field, that perennial health-action of the air we call the weather—an infinite number of currents and forces, and contributions, and temperatures, and cross purposes, whose ceaseless play of counterpart upon counterpart brings constant restoration and vitality). With this thought—and not for itself alone, but all it necessitates, and draws after it—let me begin my speculations.

America, filling the present with greatest deeds and problems, cheerfully accepting the past, including feudalism (as, indeed, the present is but the legitimate birth of the past, including feudalism), counts, as I reckon, for her

---

[1] *"From a territorial area of less than nine hundred thousand square miles, the Union has expanded into over four millions and a half—fifteen times larger than that of Great Britain and France combined—with a shore-line, including Alaska, equal to the entire cir- cumference of the earth, and with a domain within these lines far wider than that of the Romans in their proudest days of conquest and renown. With a river, lake, and coastwise commerce estimated to over two thousand millions of dollars per year; with a railway traffic of four to six thousand millions per year, and the annual domestic exchanges of the country running up to nearly ten thou- sand millions per year; with over two thou- sand millions of dollars invested in manufac- turing, mechanical, and mining industry; with over five hundred millions of acres of land in actual occupancy, valued, with their appurtenances, at over seven thousand mil- lions of dollars, and producing annually crops valued at over three thousand millions of dol- lars; with a realm which, if the density of Belgium's population were possible, would be vast enough to include all the present inhabi- tants of the world; and with equal rights guaranteed to even the poorest and humblest of our forty millions of people—we can, with a manly pride akin to that which distin- guished the palmiest days of Rome, claim,"* etc., etc., etc.—Vice-President Colfax's Speech, July 4, 1870.

Later—London Times (Weekly), June 23, '82.

"The wonderful wealth-producing power of the United States defies and sets at naught the grave drawbacks of a mischievous protec- tive tariff, and has already obliterated, al- most wholly, the traces of the greatest of modern civil wars. What is especially remark- able in the present development of American energy and success is its wide and equable distribution. North and south, east and west, on the shores of the Atlantic and the Pacific, along the chain of the great lakes, in the val- ley of the Mississippi, and on the coasts of the Gulf of Mexico, the creation of wealth and the increase of population are signally exhibited. It is quite true, as has been shown by the recent apportionment of population in the House of Representatives, that some sec- tions of the Union have advanced, relatively to the rest, in an extraordinary and unex- pected degree. But this does not imply that the States which have gained no additional representatives or have actually lost some have been stationary or have receded. The fact is that the present tide of prosperity has risen so high that it has overflowed all barri- ers, and has filled up the backwaters, and established something like an approach to uniform success." [Whitman's note.]

justification and success (for who, as yet, dare claim success?) almost entirely on the future. Nor is that hope unwarranted. Today, ahead, though dimly yet, we see, in vistas, a copious, sane, gigantic offspring. For our New World I consider far less important for what it has done, or what it is, than for results to come. Sole among nationalities, these States have assumed the task to put in forms of lasting power and practicality, on areas of amplitude rivaling the operations of the physical kosmos, the moral political speculations of ages, long, long deferred, the democratic republican principle, and the theory of development and perfection by voluntary standards, and self-reliance. Who else, indeed, except the United States, in history, so far, have accepted in unwitting faith, and, as we now see, stand, act upon, and go security for, these things?

But preluding no longer, let me strike the keynote of the following strain. First premising that, though the passages of it have been written at widely different times (it is, in fact, a collection of memoranda, perhaps for future designers, comprehenders), and though it may be open to the charge of one part contradicting another—for there are opposite sides to the great question of democracy, as to every great question—I feel the parts harmoniously blended in my own realization and convictions, and present them to be read only in such oneness, each page and each claim and assertion modified and tempered by the others. Bear in mind, too, that they are not the result of studying up in political economy, but of the ordinary sense, observing, wandering among men, these States, these stirring years of war and peace. I will not gloss over the appalling dangers of universal suffrage in the United States. In fact, it is to admit and face these dangers I am writing. To him or her within whose thought rages the battle, advancing, retreating, between democracy's convictions, aspirations, and the people's crudeness, vice, caprices, I mainly write this essay. I shall use the words America and democracy as convertible terms. Not an ordinary one is the issue. The United States are destined either to surmount the gorgeous history of feudalism, or else prove the most tremendous failure of time. Not the least doubtful am I on any prospects of their material success. The triumphant future of their business, geographic and productive departments, or larger scales and in more varieties than ever, is certain. In those respects the republic must soon (if she does not already) outstrip all examples hitherto afforded, and dominate the world.

Admitting all this, with the priceless value of our political institutions, general suffrage (and fully acknowledging the latest, widest opening of the doors), I say that, far deeper than these, what finally and only is to make of our Western world a nationality superior to any hither known, and outtopping the past, must be vigorous, yet unsuspected Literatures, perfect personalities and sociologies, original, transcendental, and expressing (what, in highest sense, are not yet expressed at all) democracy and the modern. With these, and out of these, I promulgate new races of Teachers, and of perfect Women, indispensable to endow the birth-stock of a New World. For feudalism, caste, the ecclesiastic traditions, though palpably retreating from political institutions, still hold essentially, by their spirit, even in this country, entire possession of the more important fields, indeed the very subsoil, of education, and of social standards and literature.

I say that democracy can never prove itself byond cavil, until it founds and luxuriantly grows its own forms of art, poems, schools, theology, displacing all that exists, or that has been produced anywhere in the past, under opposite influences. It is curious to me that while so many voices, pens, minds, in the press, lecture rooms, in our Congress, etc., are discussing intellectual topics, pecuniary dangers, legislative problems, the suffrage, tariff and labor questions, and the various business and benevolent needs of America, with propositions, remedies, often worth deep attention, there is one need, a hiatus the profoundest, that no eye seems to perceive, no voice to state. Our fundamental want today in the United States, with closest, amplest reference to present conditions, and to the future, is of a class, and the clear idea of a class, of native authors, literatures, far different, far higher in grade, than any yet known, sacerdotal, modern, fit to cope with our occasions, lands, permeating the whole mass of American mentality, taste, belief, breathing into it a new breath of life, giving it decision, affecting politics far more than the popular superficial suffrage, with results inside and underneath the elections of Presidents or Congresses—radiating, begetting appropriate teachers, schools, manners, and, as its grandest result, accomplishing (what neither the schools nor the churches and their clergy have hitherto accomplished, and without which this nation will no more stand, permanently, soundly, than a house will stand without a sub-stratum), a religious and moral character beneath the political and productive and intellectual bases of the States. For know you not, dear, earnest reader, that the people of our land may all read and write, and may all possess the right to vote— and yet the main things may be entirely lacking?—(and this to suggest them).

Viewed, today, from a point of view sufficiently over-arching, the problem of humanity all over the civilized world is social and religious, and is to be finally met and treated by literature. The priest departs, the divine literatus comes. Never was anything more wanted than, today, and here in the States, the poet of the modern is wanted, or the great literatus of the modern. At all times, perhaps, the central point in any nation, and that whence it is itself really swayed the most and whence it sways others, is its national literature, especially its archetypal poems. Above all previous lands, a great original literature is surely to become the justification and reliance (in some respects the sole reliance of American democracy.)

Few are aware how the great literature penetrates all, gives hue to all, shapes aggregates and individuals, and, after subtle ways, with irresistible power, constructs, sustains, demolishes at will. Why tower, in reminiscence, above all the nations of the earth, two special lands, petty in themselves, yet inexpressibly gigantic, beautiful, columnar? Immortal Judah lives, and Greece immortal lives, in a couple of poems.

Nearer than this. It is not generally realized, but it is true, as the genius of Greece, and all the sociology, personality, politics, and religion of those wonderful states, resided in their literature or aesthetics, that what was afterwards the main support of European chivalry, the feudal, ecclesiastical, dynastic world over there—forming its osseous structure, holding it together for hundreds, thousands of years, preserving its flesh and bloom, giving it form, decision, rounding it out, and so saturating it in the conscious and unconscious blood, breed, belief, and intuitions of men, that it still prevails powerful to this day, in defiance of the mighty changes of time—was its literature, permeating to the very marrow, especially that major part, its enchanting songs, ballads, and poems:[2]

.   .   .

I say we had best look our times and lands searchingly in the face, like a physician diagnosing some deep disease. Never was there, perhaps, more hollowness at heart than at present, and here in the United States. Genuine belief seems to have left us. The underlying principles of the States are not honestly believed in (for all this hectic glow, and these melodramatic screamings), nor is humanity itself believed in. What penetrating eye does not everywhere see through the mask? The spectacle is appalling. We live in an atmosphere of hypocrisy throughout. The men believe not in the women, nor the women in the men. A scornful superciliousness rules in literature. The aim of all the *littérateurs* is to find something to make fun of. A lot of churches, sects, etc., the most dismal phantasms I know, usurp the name of religion. Conversation is a mass of badinage. From deceit in the spirit, the mother of all false deeds, the offspring is already incalculable. An acute and candid person, in the revenue department in Washington, who is led by the course of his employment to regularly visit the cities, north, south, and west, to investigate frauds, has talked much with me about his discoveries. The depravity of the business classes of our country is not less than has been supposed, but infinitely greater. The official services of America, national,

[2] *See, for hereditaments, specimens, Walter Scott's Border Minstrelsy, Percy's collection, Ellis's early English Metrical Romances, the European continental poems of Walter of Aquitania, and the Nibelungen, of pagan stock, but monkish-feudal redaction; the history of the Troubadours, by Fauriel; even the far-back cumbrous old Hindu epics, as indicating the Asian eggs out of which European chivalry was hatched; Ticknor's chapters on the Cid, and on the Spanish poems and poets of Calderon's time. Then always, and, of course, as the superbest poetic culmination-expression of feudalism, the Shakespearean dramas, in the attitudes, dialogue, characters, etc., of the princes, lords, and gentlemen, the pervading atmosphere, the implied and expressed standard of manners, the high port and proud stomach, the regal embroidery of style, etc.* [Whitman's note.]

state, and municipal, in all their branches and departments, except the judiciary, are saturated in corruption, bribery, falsehood, maladministration; and the judiciary is tainted. The great cities reek with respectable as much as non-respectable robbery and scoundrelism. In fashionable life, flippancy, tepid amours, weak infidelism, small aims, or no aims at all, only to kill time. In business (this all-devouring modern word, business), the one sole object is, by any means, pecuniary gain. The magician's serpent in the fable ate up all the other serpents; and moneymaking is our magician's serpent, remaining today sole master of the field. The best class we show, is but a mob of fashionably dressed speculators and vulgarians. True, indeed, behind this fantastic farce, enacted on the visible stage of society, solid things and stupendous labors are to be discovered, existing crudely and going on in the background, to advance and tell themselves in time. Yet the truths are none the less terrible. I say that our New World democracy, however great a success in uplifting the masses out of their sloughs, in materialistic development, products, and in a certain highly deceptive superficial popular intellectuality, is, so far, an almost complete failure in its social aspects, and in really grand religious, moral, literary, and aesthetic results. In vain do we march with unprecedented strides to empire so colossal, outvying the antique, beyond Alexander's, beyond the proudest sway of Rome. In vain have we annexed Texas, California, Alaska, and reach north for Canada and south for Cuba. It is as if we were somehow being endowed with a vast and more and more thoroughly appointed body, and then left with little or no soul.

· · ·

The purpose of democracy—supplanting old belief in the necessary absoluteness of established dynastic rulership, temporal, ecclesiastical, and scholastic, as furnishing the only security against chaos, crime, and ignorance—is, through many transmigrations and amid endless ridicules, arguments, and ostensible failures, to illustrate, at all hazards, this doctrine or theory that man, properly trained in sanest, highest freedom, may and must become a law, and series of laws, unto himself, surrounding and providing for, not only his own personal control, but all his relations to other individuals, and to the State; and that, while other theories, as in the past histories of nations, have proved wise enough, and indispensable perhaps for their conditions, *this*, as matters now stand in our civilized world, is the only scheme worth working from, as warranting results like those of Nature's laws, reliable, when once established, to carry on themselves.

The argument of the matter is extensive, and, we admit, by no means all on one side. What we shall offer will be far, far from sufficient. But while leaving unsaid much that should properly even prepare the way for the treatment of this many-sided question of political liberty, equality, or republicanism—leaving the whole history and consideration of the feudal plan and its products, embodying humanity, its politics and civilization, through the retrospect of past time (which plan and products, indeed, make up all of the past, and a large part of the present)—leaving unanswered, at least by any specific and local answer, many a well-wrought argument and instance, and many a conscientious declamatory cry and warning—as, very lately, from an eminent and venerable person abroad[3]—things, problems, full of doubt, dread, suspense (not new to me, but old occupiers of many an anxious hour in city's din, or night's silence), we still may give a page or so, whose drift is opportune. Time alone can finally answer these things. But as a substitute in passing, let us, even if fragmentarily, throw forth a short direct or indirect suggestion of the premises of that other plan, in the new spirit, under the new forms, started here in our America.

As to the political section of Democracy, which introduces and breaks ground for further and vaster sections, few probably are the minds, even in these republican States, that fully comprehend the aptness of that phrase, "the government of the people, by the people, for the people," which we inherit from the lips of Abraham Lincoln; a formula whose verbal shape is homely wit, but whose scope includes both the totality and all minutiae of the lesson.

The People! Like our huge earth itself, which, to ordinary scansion, is full of vulgar contradictions and offense, man, viewed in the lump, displeases, and is a constant puzzle and affront to the merely educated classes. The rare, cosmical, artist-mind, lit with the Infinite, alone confronts his manifold and oceanic qualities—but taste, intelligence and culture (so-called), have been against the masses, and remain so. There is plenty of glamour about the most damnable crimes and hoggish meannesses, special and general, of the feudal and dynastic world over there, with its *personnel* of lords and queens and courts, so well dressed and so handsome. But the People are ungrammatical, untidy, and their sins gaunt and ill bred.

Literature, strictly considered, has never recognized the People, and, whatever may be said, does not today. Speaking generally, the tendencies of literature, as hitherto pursued, have been to make mostly critical and querulous men. It seems as if, so far, there were some natural repugnance between a literary and professional life, and the rude rank spirit of the democracies. There is, in later literature, a treatment of benevolence, a charity business, rife enough it is true; but I know nothing more rare, even in this country,

---

[3] *Shooting Niagara.—I was at first roused to much anger and abuse by this essay from Mr. Carlyle, so insulting to the theory of America—but happening to think afterwards how I had more than once been in the like mood, during which his essay was evidently cast, and seen persons and things in the same light (indeed, some might say there are signs of the same feeling in these Vistas)—I have since read it again, not only as a study, expressing as it does certain judgments from the highest feudal point of view, but have read it with respect as coming from an earnest soul, and as contributing certain sharp-cutting metallic grains, which, if not gold or silver, may be good, hard, honest iron.* [Whitman's note.]

than a fit scientific estimate and reverent appreciation of the People—of their measureless wealth of latent power and capacity, their vast, artistic contrasts of lights and shades—with, in America, their entire reliability in emergencies, and a certain breadth of historic grandeur, of peace or war, far surpassing all the vaunted samples of book-heroes, or any *haut ton* coteries, in all the records of the world.

.   .   .   .

I say the mission of government, henceforth, in civilized lands, is not repression alone, and not authority alone, not even of law, nor by that favorite standard of the eminent writer, the rule of the best men, the born heroes and captains of the race (as if such ever, or one time out of a hundred, get into the big places, elective or dynastic)—but higher than the highest arbitrary rule, to train communities through all their grades, beginning with individuals and ending there again, to rule themselves. What Christ appeared for in the moral-spiritual field for human-kind, namely, that in respect to the absolute soul, there is in the possession of such by each single individual, something so transcendent, so incapable of gradations (like life), that, to that extent, it places all beings on a common level, utterly regardless of the distinctions of intellect, virtue, station, or any height or lowliness whatever—is tallied in like manner, in this other field, by democracy's rule that men, the nation, as a common aggregate of living identities, affording in each a separate and complete subject for freedom, worldly thrift and happiness, and for a fair chance for growth, and for protection in citizenship, etc., must, to the political extent of the suffrage or vote, if no further, be placed, in each and in the whole, on one broad, primary, universal, common platform.

The purpose is not altogether direct; perhaps it is more indirect. For it is not that democracy is of exhaustive account in itself. Perhaps, indeed, it is (like Nature), of no account in itself. It is that, as we see, it is the best, perhaps only, fit and full means, formulater, general caller-forth, trainer, for the million, not for grand material personalities only, but for immortal souls. To be a voter with the rest is not so much; and this, like every institute, will have its imperfections. But to become an enfranchised man, and now, impediments removed, to stand and start without humiliation, and equal with the rest; to commence, or have the road cleared to commence, the grand experiment of development, whose end (perhaps requiring several generations), may be the forming of a full-grown man or woman—that *is* something. To ballast the State is also secured, and in our times is to be secured, in no other way.

We do not (at any rate I do not), put it either on the ground that the People, the masses, even the best of them, are, in their latent or exhibited qualities, essentially sensible and good—nor on the ground of their rights;

but that good or bad, rights or no rights, the democratic formula is the only safe and preservative one for coming times. We endow the masses with the suffrage for their own sake, no doubt; then, perhaps still more, from another point of view, for community's sake. Leaving the rest to the sentimentalists, we present freedom as sufficient in its scientific aspect, cold as ice, reasoning, deductive, clear and passionless as crystal.

Democracy too is law, and of the strictest, amplest kind. Many suppose (and often in its own ranks the error), that it means a throwing aside of law, and running riot. But, briefly, it is the superior law, not alone that of physical force, the body, which, adding to, it supersedes with that of the spirit. Law is the unshakable order of the universe forever; and the law over all, and law of laws, is the law of successions; that of the superior law, in time, gradually supplanting and overwhelming the inferior one. (While, for myself, I would cheerfully agree—first covenanting that the formative tendencies shall be administered in favor, or at least not against it, and that this reservation be closely construed—that until the individual or community show due signs, or be so minor and fractional as not to endanger the State, the condition of authoritative tutelage may continue, and self-government must abide its time.) Nor is the aesthetic point, always an important one, without fascination for highest aiming souls. The common ambition strains for elevations, to become some privileged exclusive. The master sees greatness and health in being part of the mass; nothing will do as well as common ground. Would you have in yourself the divine, vast, general law? Then merge yourself in it.

And, topping democracy, this most alluring record, that it alone can bind, and ever seeks to bind, all nations, all men, of however various and distant lands, into a brotherhood, a family. It is the old, yet ever-modern dream of earth, out of her eldest and her youngest, her fond philosophers and poets. Not that half only, individualism, which isolates. There is another half, which is adhesiveness or love, that fuses, ties, and aggregates, making the races comrades, and fraternizing all. Both are to be vitalized by religion (sole worthiest elevator of man or State), breathing into the proud, material tissues, the breath of life. For I say at the core of democracy, finally, is the religious element. All the religions, old and new, are there. Nor may the scheme step forth, clothed in resplendent beauty and command, till these, bearing the best, the latest fruit, the spiritual, shall fully appear.

A portion of our pages we might indite with reference toward Europe, especially the British part of it, more than our own land, perhaps not absolutely needed for the home reader. But the whole question hangs together, and fastens and links all peoples. The liberalist of today has this advantage over antique or medieval times, that his doctrine seeks not only to individualize but to universalize. The great Solidarity has arisen. Of all dangers to a nation, as things exist in our day, there can be no greater one than having certain portions of the people set off from the rest by a line drawn—they not privileged as others, but degraded, humiliated, made of no account. Much quackery teems, of course, even on democracy's side, yet does not really affect the orbic quality of the matter. To work in, if we may so term it, and justify God, His divine aggregate, the People (or, the veritable horned and sharp-tailed Devil, *His* aggregate, if there be who convulsively insist upon it)—this, I say, is what democracy is for; and this is what our America means, and is doing—may I not say, has done? If not, she means nothing more, and does nothing more, than any other land. And, as by virtue of its cosmical, antiseptic power, Nature's stomach is fully strong enough not only to digest the morbific matter always presented, not to be turned aside, and perhaps, indeed, intuitively gravitating thither—but even to change such contributions into nutriment for highest use and life—so American democracy's. This is the lesson we, these days, send over to European lands by every western breeze.

And truly, whatever may be said, in the way of abstract argument, for or against the theory of a wider democratizing of institutions in any civilized country, much trouble might well be saved to all European lands by recognizing this palpable fact (for a palpable fact it is), that some form of such democratizing is about the only resource now left. *That*, or chronic dissatisfaction continued, mutterings which grow annually louder and louder, till, in due course, and pretty swiftly in most cases, the inevitable crisis, crash, dynastic ruin. Anything worthy to be called statesmanship in the Old World, I should say, among the advanced students, adepts, or men of any brains, does not debate today whether to hold on, attempting to lean back and monarchize, or to look forward and democratize—but *how*, and in what degree and part, most prudently to democratize.

. . .

I submit, therefore, that the fruition of democracy, on aught like a grand scale, resides altogether in the future. As, under any profound and comprehensive view of the gorgeous-composite feudal world, we see in it, through the long ages and cycles of ages, the results of a deep, integral, human and divine principle, or fountain, from which issued laws, ecclesia, manners, institutes, costumes, personalities, poems (hitherto unequaled), faithfully partaking of their source, and indeed only arising either to betoken it, or to furnish parts of that varied-flowing display, whose center was one and absolute—so, long ages hence, shall the due historian or critic make at least an equal retrospect, an equal history for the democratic principle. It too must be adorned, credited with its results—then, when it, with imperial power, through amplest time, has dominated mankind—has been the source and test of all the moral, aesthetic, social, political, and religious expressions and institutes of the civilized world—has begotten them in spirit and in form, and has carried them to its own unprecedented heights—has had (it is possible) monastics and ascetics, more numerous, more devout than the monks and priests of all previous creeds—has swayed the ages with a breadth and rectitude tallying Nature's own—has fashioned, systemized, and triumphantly finished and carried out, in its own interest, and with unparalleled success, a new earth and a new man.

Thus we presume to write, as it were, upon things that exist not, and travel by maps yet unmade, and a blank. But the throes of birth are upon us; and we have something of this advantage in seasons of strong formations, doubts, suspense—for then the afflatus of such themes haply may fall upon us, more or less; and then, hot from surrounding war and revolution, our speech, though without polished coherence, and a failure by the standard called criticism, comes forth, real at least as the lightnings.

And maybe we, these days, have, too, our own reward—(for there are yet some, in all lands, worthy to be so encouraged). Though not for us the joy of entering at the last the conquered city—not ours the chance ever to see with our own eyes the peerless power and splendid *éclat* of the democratic principle, arrived at meridian, filling the world with effulgence and majesty far beyond those of past history's kings, or all dynastic sway—there is yet, to whoever is eligible among us, the prophetic vision, the joy of being tossed in the brave turmoil of these times—the promulgation and the path, obedient, lowly reverent to the voice, the gesture of the god, or holy ghost, which others see not, hear not—with the proud consciousness that amid whatever clouds, seductions, or heart-wearying postponements, we have never deserted, never despaired, never abandoned the faith.

So much contributed, to be conned well, to help prepare and brace our edifice, our planned Idea—we still proceed to give it in another of its aspects—perhaps the main, the high façade of all. For to democracy, the leveler, the unyielding principle of the average, surely joined another principle, equally unyielding, closely tracking the first, indispensable to it, opposite (as the sexes are opposite), and whose existence, confronting and ever modifying the other, often clashing, paradoxical, yet neither the highest avail without the other, plainly supplies to these grand cosmic politics of ours, and to the launched forth mortal dangers of republicanism, today, or any day, the counterpart and offset whereby Nature restrains the deadly original relentlessness of all her first-class laws. This second principle is individuality, the pride and centripetal isolation of a human being in himself—identity—personalism. Whatever the name, its acceptance and thorough infusions through the organizations of political commonalty now shooting Aurora-like about the world, are of utmost importance, as the principle itself is needed for very life's sake. It forms, in a sort, or is to form, the compensating balance-wheel of the success working machinery of aggregate America.

And, if we think of it, what does civilization itself rest upon—and what object has it, what its religions, arts, schools, etc., but rich, luxuriant, varied personalism? To that, all bends; and it is because toward such result democracy alone, on anything like Nature's scale, breaks up the limitless fallows of human-kind, and plants the seed, and gives fair play, that its claims now precede the rest. The literature songs, aesthetics, etc., of a country are of importance principally because they furnish the materials and suggestions of personality for the women and men of that country, and enforce them in a thousand effective ways.[4] As the topmost claim of a strong consolidating of the nationality of these States is, that only by such powerful compaction can the separate States secure that full and free swing within their spheres, which is becoming to them, each after its kind, so will individuality, and unimpeded branchings, flourish best under imperial republic forms.

Assuming Democracy to be at present in its embryo condition, and that the only large and satisfactory justification of it resides in the future, mainly through the copious production of perfect characters among the people, and through the advent of a sane and pervading religiousness, it is with regard to the atmosphere and spaciousness fit for such characters, and of certain nutriment and cartoon-draftings proper for them, and indicating them for New World purposes, that I continue the present statement—an exploration, as of new ground, wherein, like other primitive surveyors, I must do the best I can, leaving it to those who come after me to do much better. (The service, in fact, if any, must be to break a sort of first path or track, no matter how rude and ungeometrical.)

We have frequently printed the word Democracy. Yet I cannot too often repeat that it is a word the gist of which still sleeps, quite unawakened, notwithstanding the resonance and the many angry tempests out of which its syllables have come, from pen or tongue. It is a great word whose history, I suppose, remains unwritten, because that history had yet to be enacted. It is,

---

[4] *After the rest is satiated, all interest culminates in the field of persons, and never flags there. Accordingly in this field have the great poets and literatures signally toiled. They too, in all ages, all lands, have been creators, fashioning, making types of men and women, as Adam and Eve are made in the divine fable. Behold, shaped, bred by orientalism, feudalism, through their long growth and culmination, and breeding back in return— (when shall we have an equal series, typical of democracy?)—behold, commencing in primal Asia (apparently formulated, in what beginning we know in the gods of the mythologies, and coming down thence), a few samples out of the countless product, bequeathed to the moderns, bequeathed to America as studies. For the men, Yudishtura, Rama, Arjuna, Solomon, most of the Old and New Testament characters; Achilles, Ulysses, Theseus, Prometheus, Hercules, Aeneas, Plu-*

tarch's heroes; the Merlin of Celtic bards; the Cid, Arthur and his knights, Siegfried and Hagen in the Nibelungen; Roland and Oliver; Roustam in the Shah-Nemah; and so on to Milton's Satan, Cervantes' Don Quixote, Shakespeare's Hamlet, Richard II, Lear, Marc Anthony, etc., and the modern Faust. These, I say, are models, combined, adjusted to other standards than America's, but of priceless value to her and hers.

Among women, the goddesses of the Egyptian, Indian, and Greek mythologies, certain Bible characters, especially the Holy Mother; Cleopatra, Penelope; the portraits of Brunhelde and Chriemhilde in the Nibelungen; Oriana, Una, etc.; the modern Consuelo, Walter Scott's Jeanie and Effie Deans, etc., etc. (Yet women portrayed or outlined at her best, or as perfect human mother, does not hitherto, it seems to me, fully appear in literature.) [Whitman's note.]

in some sort, younger brother of another great and often used word, Nature, whose history also waits unwritten. As I perceive, the tendencies of our day, in the States (and I entirely respect them), are toward those vast and sweeping movements, influences, moral and physical, of humanity, now and always current over the planet, in the scale of the impulses of the elements. Then it is also good to reduce the whole matter to the consideration of a single self, a man, a woman, on permanent grounds. Even for the treatment of the universal, in politics, metaphysics, or anything, sooner or later we come down to one single, solitary soul.

There is, in sanest hours, a consciousness, a thought that rises, independent, lifted out from all else, calm, like the stars, shining eternal. This is the thought of identity—yours for you, whoever you are, as mine for me. Miracle of miracles, beyond statement, most spiritual and vaguest of earth's dreams, yet hardest basic fact, and only entrance to all facts. In such devout hours, in the midst of the significant wonders of heaven and earth (significant only because of the Me in the center), creeds, conventions, fall away and become of no account before this simple idea. Under the luminousness of real vision, it alone takes possession, takes value. Like the shadowy dwarf in the fable, once liberated and looked upon, it expands over the whole earth, and spreads to the roof of heaven.

The quality of Being, in the object's self, according to its own central idea and purpose, and of growing therefrom and thereto—not criticism by other standards, and adjustments thereto—is the lesson of Nature. True, the full man wisely gathers, culls, absorbs; but if, engaged disproportionately in that, he slights or overlays the precious idiocrasy and special nativity and intention that he is, the man's self, the main thing, is a failure, however wide his general cultivation. Thus, in our times, refinement and delicatesse are not only attended to sufficiently, but threaten to eat us up, like a cancer. Already, the democratic genius watches, ill-pleased, these tendencies. Provision for a little healthy rudeness, savage virtue, justification of what one has in one's self, whatever it is, is demanded. Negative qualities, even deficiencies, would be a relief. Singleness and normal simplicity and separation, amid this more complex, more and more artificialized state of society—how pensively we yearn for them! how we would welcome their return!

In some such direction, then—at any rate enough to preserve the balance—we feel called to throw what weight we can, not for absolute reasons, but current ones. To prune, gather, trim, conform, and ever cram and stuff, and be genteel and proper, is the pressure of our days. While aware that much can be said even in behalf of all this, we perceive that we have not now to consider the question of what is demanded to serve a half-starved and barbarous nation, or set of nations, but what is most applicable, most pertinent, for numerous congeries of conventional, overcorpulent societies, already becoming stifled and rotten with flatulent, infidelistic, literature, and polite conformity and art. In addition to established sciences, we suggest a science as it were of healthy average personalism, on original-universal grounds, the object of which should be to raise up and supply through the States a copious race of superb American men and women, cheerful, religious, ahead of any yet known.

America has yet morally and artistically originated nothing. She seems singularly unaware that the models of persons, books, manners, etc., appropriate for former conditions and for European lands, are but exiles and exotics here. No current of her life, as shown on the surfaces of what is authoritatively called her society, accepts or runs into social or aesthetic democracy; but all the currents set squarely against it. Never, in the Old World, was thoroughly upholstered exterior appearance and show, mental and other, built entirely on the idea of caste, and on the sufficiency of mere outside acquisition—never were glibness, verbal intellect more the test, the emulation—more loftily elevated as head and sample—than they are on the surface of our republican States this day. The writers of a time hint the mottoes of its gods. The word of the modern, say these voices, is the word Culture.

We find ourselves abruptly in close quarters with the enemy. This word Culture, or what it has come to represent, involves, by contrast, our whole theme, and has been, indeed, the spur, urging us to engagement. Certain questions arise. As now taught, accepted and carried out, are not the processes of culture rapidly creating a class of supercilious infidels, who believe in nothing? Shall a man lose himself in countless masses of adjustments, and be so shaped with reference to this, that, and the other, that the simply good and healthy and brave parts of him are reduced and clipped away, like the bordering of box in a garden? You can cultivate corn and roses and orchards—but who shall cultivate the mountain peaks, the ocean, and the tumbling gorgeousness of the clouds? Lastly—is the readily given reply that culture only seeks to help, systematize, and put in attitude, the elements of fertility and power, a conclusive reply?

I do not so much object to the name, or word, but I should certainly insist, for the purposes of these States, on a radical change of category, in the distribution of precedence. I should demand a program of culture, drawn out, not for a single class alone, or for the parlors or lecture rooms, but with an eye to practical life, the west, the workingmen, the facts of farms and jackplanes and engineers, and of the broad range of the women also of the middle and working strata, and with reference to the perfect equality of women, and of a grand and powerful motherhood. I should demand of this program or theory a scope generous enough to include the widest human area. It must have for its spinal meaning the formation of a typical personality of character eligible to the uses of the high average of men—and *not* restricted by conditions ineligible to the masses. The best culture will always be that of the manly and courageous instincts, and loving perceptions, and of self-respect—aiming to form, over this continent, an idiocrasy of universal-ism which, true child of America, will bring joy to its mother, returning to her in her own spirit, recruiting myriads of offspring, able, natural, percep-tive, tolerant, devout believers in her, America, and with some definite in-stinct why and for what she has arisen, most vast, most formidable of historic births, and is, now and here, with wonderful step, journeying through Time.

The problem, as it seems to me, presented to the New World, is, under permanent law and order, and after preserving cohesion (ensemble-Individ-uality), at all hazards, to vitalize man's free play of special Personalism, recognizing in it something that calls ever more to be considered, fed, and adopted as the sub-stratum for the best that belongs to us (government indeed is for it), including the new aesthetic of our future.

To formulate beyond this present vagueness—to help line and put before us the species, or a specimen of the species, of the democratic ethnology of the future, is a work toward which the genius of our land, with peculiar encouragement, invites her well-wishers. Already certain limnings, more or less grotesque, more or less fading and watery, have appeared. We too (re-pressing doubts and qualms) will try our hand.

Attempting, then, however crudely, a basic model or portrait of personal-ity for general use for the manliness of the States (and doubtless that is most useful which is most simple and comprehensive for all, and toned low enough), we should prepare the canvas well beforehand. Parentage must consider itself in advance. (Will the time hasten when fatherhood and moth-erhood shall become a science—and the noblest science?) To our model, a clear-blooded, strong-fibered physique is indispensable; the questions of food, drink, air, exercise, assimilation, digestion, can never be intermitted. Out of these we descry a well-begotten selfhood—in youth, fresh, ardent, emotional, aspiring, full of adventure; at maturity, brave, perceptive, under control, neither too talkative nor too reticent, neither flippant nor somber; of the bodily figure, the movements easy, the complexion showing the best blood, somewhat flushed, breast expanded, and erect attitude, a voice whose sound outvies music, eyes of calm and steady gaze, yet capable also of flash-ing—and a general presence that holds its own in the company of the high-est. (For it is native personality, and that alone, that endows a man to stand before presidents or generals, or in any distinguished collection, with *aplomb*—and *not* culture, or any knowledge or intellect whatever.)

With regard to the mental-educational part of our model, enlargement of intellect, stores of cephalic knowledge, etc., the concentration thitherward of all the customs of our age, especially in America, is so overweening, and provides so fully for that part, that, important and necessary as it is, it really needs nothing from us here—except, indeed, a phrase of warning and re-straint. Manners, costumes, too, though important, we need not dwell upon here. Like beauty, grace of motion, etc., they are results. Causes, original things, being attended to, the right manners unerringly follow. Much is said, among artists, of "the grand style," as if it were a thing by itself. When a man, artist or whoever, has health, pride, acuteness, noble aspirations, he has the motive-elements of the grandest style. The rest is but manipulation (yet that is no small matter).

Leaving still unspecified sterling parts of any model fit for the future personality of America, I must not fail, again and ever, to pronounce myself on one, probably the least attended to in modern times—a hiatus, indeed, threatening its gloomiest consequences after us. I mean the simple, unsophisticated Conscience, the primary moral element. If I were asked to'specify in what quarter lie the grounds of darkest dread respecting the America of our hopes, I should have to point to this particular. I should demand the invariable application to individuality, this day and any day, of that old, evertrue plumb-rule of persons, eras, nations. Our triumphant modern civilizee, with its all-schooling and his wondrous appliances, will show himself but an amputation while this deficiency remains. Beyond (assuming a more hopeful tone), the vertebration of the manly and womanly personalism of our Western world, can only be, and is, indeed, to be (I hope), its all penetrating Religiousness.

The ripeness of Religion is doubtless to be looked for in this field of individuality, and is a result that no organization or church can ever achieve. As history is poorly retained by what the technists call history, and is not given out from their pages, except the learner has in himself the sense of the well-wrapt, never yet written, perhaps impossible to be written, history—so Religion, although casually arrested, and, after a fashion, preserved in the churches and creeds, does not depend at all upon them, but is a part of the identified soul, which, when greatest, knows not bibles in the old way, but in new ways—the identified soul, which can really confront Religion when it extricates itself entirely from the churches, and not before.

Personalism fuses this, and favors it. I should say, indeed, that only in the perfect uncontamination and solitariness of individuality may the spirituality of religion positively come forth at all. Only here, and on such terms, the meditation, the devout ecstasy, the soaring flight. Only here, communion with the mysteries, the eternal problems, whence? whither? Alone, and identity, and the mood—and the soul emerges, and all statements, churches, sermons, melt away like vapors. Alone, and silent thought and awe, and aspiration—and then the interior consciousness, like a hitherto unseen inscription, in magic ink, beams out its wondrous lines to the sense. Bibles may convey, and priests expound, but it is exclusively for the noiseless operation of one's isolated Self, to enter the pure ether of veneration, reach the divine levels, and commune with the unutterable.

. . .

Then there are mutterings (we will not now stop to heed them here, but they must be heeded), of something more revolutionary. The day is coming when the deep questions of woman's entrance amid the arenas of practical life, politics, the suffrage, etc., will not only be argued all around us, but may be put to decision, and real experiment.

Of course, in these States, for both man and woman, we must entirely recast the types of highest personality from what the oriental, feudal, ecclesiastical worlds bequeath us, and which yet possess the imaginative and aesthetic fields of the United States, pictorial and melodramatic, not without use as studies, but making sad work, and forming a strange anachronism upon the scenes and exigencies around us. Of course, the old undying elements remain. The task is, to successfully adjust them to new combinations, our own days. Nor is this so incredible. I can conceive a community, today and here, in which, on a sufficient scale, the perfect personalities, without noise meet; say in some pleasant western settlement or town, where a couple of hundred best men and women, of ordinary worldly status, have by luck been drawn together, with nothing extra of genius or wealth, but virtuous, chaste, industrious, cheeful, resolute, friendly and devout. I can conceive such a community organized in running order, powers judiciously delegated—farming, building, trade, courts, mails, schools, elections, all attended to; and then the rest of life, the main thing, freely branching and blossoming in each individual, and bearing golden fruit. I can see there, in every young and old man, after his kind, and in every woman after hers, a true personality, developed, exercised proportionately in body, mind, and spirit. I can imagine this case as one not necessarily rare or difficult, but in buoyant accordance with the municipal and general requirements of our times. And I can realize in it the culmination of something better than any stereotyped *éclat* of history or poems. Perhaps unsung, undramatized, unput in essays or biographies—perhaps even some such community already exists, in Ohio, Illinois, Missouri, or somewhere, practically fulfilling itself, and thus outvying, in cheapest vulgar life, all that has been hitherto shown in best ideal pictures.

In short, and to sum up, America, betaking herself to formative action (as it is about time for more solid achievement, and less windy promise), must, for her purposes, cease to recognize a theory of character grown of feudal aristocracies, or formed by merely literary standards, or from any ultramarine full-dress formulas of culture, polish, caste, etc., and must sternly promulgate her own new standard, yet old enough, and accepting the old, the perennial elements, and combining them into groups, unities, appropriate to the modern, the democratic, the west, and to the practical occasions and needs of our own cities, and of the agricultural regions. Ever the most precious in the common. Ever the fresh breeze of field, or hill or lake, is more than any palpitation of fans, though of ivory, and redolent with perfume; and the air is more than the costliest perfumes.

. . .

In the prophetic literature of these States (the reader of my speculations will miss their principal stress unless he allows well for the point that a new Literature, perhaps a new Metaphysics, certainly a new Poetry, are to be, in my opinion. the only sure and worthy supports and expressions of the American Democracy), Nature, true Nature, and the true idea of Nature, long absent, must, above all, become fully restored, enlarged, and must furnish the pervading atmosphere to poems, and the test of all high literary and aesthetic compositions. I do not mean the smooth walks, trimmed hedges, posys and nightingales of the English poets, but the whole orb, with its geologic history, the cosmos, carrying fire and snow, that rolls through the illimitable areas, light as a feather, though weighing billions of tons. Furthermore, as by what we now partially call Nature is intended, at most, only what is entertainable by the physical conscience, the sense of matter, and of good animal health—on these it must be distinctly accumulated, incorporated, that man, comprehending these, has, in towering superaddition, the moral and spiritual consciences, indicating his destination beyond the ostensible, the mortal.

To the heights of such estimate of Nature indeed ascending, we proceed to make observations for our Vistas, breathing rarest air. What is I believe called Idealism seems to me to suggest (guarding against extravagance, and ever modified even by its opposite) the course of inquiry and desert of favor for our New World metaphysics, their foundation of and in literature, giving hue to all.[5]

[5] *The culmination and fruit of literary artistic expression, and its final fields of pleasure for the human soul, are in metaphysics, including the mysteries of the spiritual world, the soul itself, and the question of the immortal continuation of our identity. In all ages, the mind of man has brought up here—and always will. Here, at least, of whatever race or era, we stand on common ground. Applause, too, is unanimous, antique or modern. Those authors who work well in this field—though their reward, instead of a handsome percentage, or royalty, may be but simply the laurel crown of the victors in the great Olympic games—will be dearest to humanity, and their works, however aesthetically defective, will be treasured forever. The altitude of literature and poetry has always been religion—and always will be. The Indian Vedas, the Nackas of Zoroaster, the Talmud of the Jews, the Old Testment, the Gospel of Christ and His disciples, Plato's works, the Koran of Mohammed, the Edda of Snorro, and so on toward our own day, to Swedenborg, and to the invaluable contributions of Leibnitz, Kant, and Hegel—these, with such poems only in which (while singing well of persons and events, of the passions of man, and the shows of the material universe), the religious tone, the consciousness of mystery, the recognition of the future, of the unknown, of Deity over and under all, and of the divine purpose, are never absent, but indirectly give tone to all—exhibit literature's real heights and elevations, towering up like the great mountains of the earth.*

Standing on this ground—the last, the
(Footnote continued next page.)

The elevating and etherealizing ideas of the unknown and of unreality must be brought forward with authority, as they are the legitimate heirs of the known, and of reality, and at least as great as their parents. Fearless of scoffing, and of the ostent,[6] let us take our stand, our ground, and never desert it, to confront the growing excess and arrogance of realism. To the cry, now victorious—the cry of sense, science, flesh, incomes, farms, merchandise, logic, intellect, demonstrations, solid perpetuities, buildings of brick and iron, or even the facts of the shows of trees, earth, rocks, etc., fear not, my brethren, my sisters, to sound out with equally determined voice, that conviction brooding within the recesses of every envisioned soul—illusions! apparitions! figments all! True, we must not condemn the show, neither absolutely deny it, for the indispensability of its meanings; but how clearly we see that, migrate in soul to what we can already conceive of superior and spiritual points of view, and palpable as it seems under present relations, it all and several might, nay certainly would, fall apart and vanish.

· · ·

In the future of these States must arise poets immenser far, and make great poems of death. The poems of life are great, but there must be the poems of the purports of life, not only in itself, but beyond itself. I have eulogized Homer, the sacred bards of Jewry, Aeschylus, Juvenal, Shakespeare, etc., and acknowledged their inestimable value. But (with perhaps the exception in some, not all respects, of the second-mentioned) I say there must, for future and democratic purposes, appear poets (dare I to say so?) of higher class even than any of those—poets not only possessed of the religious

highest, only permanent ground—and sternly criticizing from it, all works, either of the literary, or any art, we have peremptorily to dismiss every pretensive production, however fine its aesthetic or intellectual points, which violates or ignores, or even does not celebrate, the central divine idea of All, suffusing universe, of eternal trains of purpose, in the development, by however slow degrees, of the physical, moral, and spiritual cosmos. I say he has studied, meditated to no profit, whatever may be his mere erudition, who has not absorbed this simple consciousness and faith. It is not entirely new—but it is for Democracy to elaborate it, and look to build upon and expand from it, with uncompromising reliance. Above the doors of teaching the inscription is to appear, Though little or nothing can be absolutely known, perceived, except from a point of view which is evanescent, yet we know at least one permanency, that Time and Space, in the will of God, furnish successive chains, completions of material births and beginnings, solve all discrepancies, fears and doubts, and eventually fulfill happiness—and that the prophecy of those births, namely spiritual results, throws the true arch over all teaching, all science. The local considerations of sin, disease, deformity, ignorance, death, etc., and their measurement by the superficial mind, and ordinary legislation and theology, are to be met by science, boldly accepting, promulging this faith, and planting the seeds of superber laws—of the explication of the physical universe through the spiritual—and clearing the way for a religion, sweet and unimpugnable alike to little child or great savant. [Whitman's note.]

[6] In the archaic sense, an act of showing or exhibition.

fire and abandon of Isaiah, luxuriant in the epic talent of Homer, or for proud characters as in Shakespeare, but consistent with the Hegelian formulas, and consistent with modern science.[7] America needs, and the world needs, a class of bards who will, now and ever, so link and tally the rational physical being of man, with the ensembles of time and space, and with this vast and multiform show, Nature, surrounding him, ever tantalizing him, equally a part, and yet not a part of him as to essentially harmonize, satisfy, and put at rest. Faith, very old, now scared away by science, must be restored, brought back by the same power that caused her departure—restored with new sway, deeper, wider, higher than ever. Surely, this universal ennui, this coward fear, this shuddering at death, these low, degrading views, are not always to rule the spirit pervading future society, as it has the past, and does the present. What the Roman Lucretius[8] sought most nobly, yet all too blindly, negatively to do for his age and its successors, must be done positively by some great coming literatus, especially poet, who, remaining fully poet, will absorb whatever science indicates, with spiritualism, and out of them, and out of his own genius, will compose the great poem of death. Then will man indeed confront Nature, and confront time and space, both with science, and *con amore*, and take his right place, prepared for life, master of fortune and misfortune. And then that which was long wanted will be supplied, and the ship that had it not before in all her voyages, will have an anchor.

There are still other standards, suggestions, for products of high literatures. That which really balances and conserves the social and political world is not so much legislation, police, treaties, and dread of punishment, as the latent eternal intuitional sense, in humanity, of fairness, manliness, decorum, etc. Indeed, this perennial regulation, control, and oversight, by self-suppliance, is *sine qua non* to democracy; and a highest, widest aim of democratic literature may well be to bring forth, cultivate, brace, and strengthen this sense, in individuals and society. A strong mastership of the general inferior self by the superior self, is to be aided, secured, indirectly, but surely, by the literatus, in his works, shaping, for individual or aggregate democracy, a great passionate body, in and along with which goes a great masterful spirit.

•　　•　　•

[7] Homer (850-800 B.C.), the Greek epic poet of *The Iliad* and *The Odyssey;* Juvenal (A.D. 60?-140?), Roman lawyer and satirist. Hegelianism is the philosophy of George Wilhelm Friedrich Hegel (1770-1831), German philosopher whose doctrine of phenomenology attempts by dialectical method to make scientific the final truths of religion.

[8] Lucretius Caius (96?-55 B.C.) was a Roman philosophical poet and a disciple of Epicurus. His great work was *De Rerum Natura* (in six books).

Investigating here, we see, not that it is a little thing we have, in having the bequeathed libraries, countless shelves of volumes, records, etc.; yet how serious the danger, depending entirely on them, of the bloodless vein, the nerveless arm, the false application, at second or third hand. We see that the real interest of this people of ours in the theology, history, poetry, politics, and personal models of the past (the British islands, for instance, and indeed all the past), is not necessarily to mold ourselves or our literature upon them, but to attain fuller, more definite comparisons, warnings, and the insight to ourselves, our own present, and our own far grander, different, future history, religion, social customs, etc. We see that almost everything that has been written, sung, or stated, of old, with reference to humanity under the feudal and oriental institutes, religions, and for other lands, needs to be rewritten, resung, restated, in terms consistent with the institution of these States, and to come in range and obedient uniformity with them.

We see, as in the universes of the material cosmos, after meteorological, vegetable, and animal cycles, man at last arises, born through them, to prove them, concentrate them, to turn upon them with wonder and love—to command them, adorn them, and carry them upward into superior realms—so, out of the series of the preceding social and political universes, now arise these States. We see that while many were supposing things established and completed, really the grandest things always remain; and discover that the work of the New World is not ended, but only fairly begun.

We see our land, America, her literature, aesthetics, etc., as, substantially, the getting in form, or effusement and statement, of deepest basic elements and loftiest final meanings, of history and man—and the portrayal (under the eternal laws and conditions of beauty) of our own physiognomy, the subjective tie and expression of the objective, as from our own combination, continuation, and points of view—and the deposit and record of the national mentality, character, appeals, heroism, wars, and even liberties—where these, and all, culminate in native literary and artistic formulation, to be perpetuated; and not having which native, first-class formulation, she will flounder about, and her other, however imposing, eminent greatness, prove merely a passing gleam; but truly having which, she will understand herself, live nobly, nobly contribute, emanate, and, swinging, poised safely on herself, illumined and illuming, become a full-formed world, and divine Mother not only of material but spiritual worlds, in ceaseless succession through time—the main thing being the average, the bodily, the concrete, the democratic, the popular, on which all the superstructures of the future are to permanently rest.

WILLIAM SIDNEY MOUNT

(1807-1865)

William S. Mount was a genre painter who attempted to depict nature precisely as it is. "My best pictures," he wrote, "are those which I painted out of doors—I must follow my gift to paint figures out of doors as well as in doors, without regard to paint room. The longer an artist leaves nature the more feeble he gets. He therefore should constantly imitate God—one true picture from nature is worth a dozen from the imagination. Remember the air tints. The skys as seen from [Stony Brook] Long Island away from the City are remarkable for clearness—also the water in the harbor and sound are clear and transparent."

As a proponent of "plein-airiste" or open-air painting, Mount was influenced by his friends of the Hudson River School, Thomas Cole and Asher B. Durand. Like them, he adapted his views of nature to a form of painting called luminism in which the viewer is taken beyond realism into a subjectivity so intense that the emotions of the artist are projected into the object. The painter's personality is absent and the object is presented with so great a degree of clarity that it appears more real in the painting than it would be in actual life. The artist becomes, in Emerson's words, "a transparent eyeball."

Mount's art has much in common with the writings of Emerson, Thoreau, Whitman, Whittier, and Lowell. He was particularly interested in fusing the visual object and the thought as the poets wished to fuse the written word and the idea. Like them he had a tendency toward the transcendental state of mind; his work is a constant attempt to create a union between the real and the ideal.

Mount drew portraits and biblical scenes that express his religious inclinations. But his significant art is the representation of the American scene: realistic renderings like *Dancing on the Barn Floor* (1831), *Farmer's Nooning* (1830), *The Power of Music* (1847), *California News* (1850) and brilliant landscapes like *Eel Spearing at Setauket* and *Long Island Farmhouses.*

William Sidney Mount. **"Eel Spearing at Setauket," 1845.** *(Reproduced through the courtesy of the New York Historical Association, Cooperstown, New York.)*

William Sidney Mount, "Long Island Houses." *(The Metropolitan Museum of Art, Gift of Louise F. Wickham in memory of her father, William H. Wickham, 1928.)*

FITZHUGH LANE

(1804-1865)

Fitzhugh Lane was a native of Gloucester, Massachusetts. His work is a visual representation of Emerson's ideas as expressed in *Nature* (1836) and other essays: the painting is the object of the inner eye; matter is an extension of the mind; the Understanding simply translates the informing concept of the Reason. Lane is especially interested in the fixed moment in time, projected through an extended space; the foreground is often bare, the horizon firm and, if a person appears, he is in the midst of large spaces. Vision develops from the inner eye of the artist and moves outward. Lane is the first of many painters to project this interior mood. It is one of the central characteristics of American art and can be seen in the work of Martin Heade, Thomas Eakins, Winslow Homer, Oliver La Farge, Edward Hopper, Ben Shahn, and Andrew Wyeth.

Some of Fitzhugh Lane's better-known paintings are *Brace's Rock, Eastern Point, Gloucester* (1863); *Owl's Head, Penobscot Bay, Maine* (1862); *Sea Shore Sketch* (1854); *Off Mount Desert Island* (1856), and *Somes Sound, Mount Desert Island* (1850).

Fitzhugh Lane. "Off Mount Desert Island," 1856. *(Collection of the Brooklyn Museum.)*

MARTIN JOHNSON HEADE

(1819-1904)

Emerson's belief in the unity of nature is well illustrated by Martin Heade's *The Stranded Boat*. The distant figure in the painting is simply one object among many in a harmonious rendering of man and nature.

Heade's work has some Gothic and surrealist effects, as in *Approaching Storm, Beach Near New Port* (1860) and *Off Shore: After the Storm* (late 1860's). He also fuses a tendency toward impressionism with the realistic interest in light and atmosphere. Several of his paintings reveal his interest in specifying the time of day: *Dawn* (1862), *Sunset over the Marshes* (1863), and *Twilight, Sale Marshes* (n.d.); others reveal his sensitivity to light and space: *Lake George* (1817), *Salt Marshes, Newport, Rhode Island* (1863).

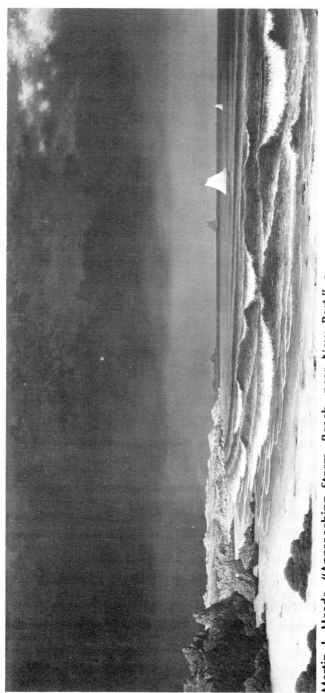

Martin J. Heade, "Approaching Storm, Beach, near New Port," c. 1860–1870. (Courtesy, Museum of Fine Arts, Boston, M & M Karolik Collection.)

THE WESTWARD MOVEMENT

DANIEL BOONE

(1734-1820)

The Wild West had a symbolic force of great magnitude on the imagination of Easterners. Francis Parkman deplored the civilization that had bred him and romanticized primitivism in *The Oregon Trail.* Timothy Dwight, Philip Freneau, Washington Irving, Walt Whitman, and many others imagined a freedom in the West—a "Passage to India"—that was linked to "the manifest destiny" of Americans. In James Fenimore Cooper's novels the migration westward assumed the form of an elaborate myth as Leatherstocking tried to withstand the destruction of the frontier. For many of these authors as well as for the average American, the one figure who symbolized the West most vividly was Daniel Boone.

Daniel Boone was a trailblazer in the forests of Kentucky who defended the new settlements against the Indians during the Revolutionary period. In a short time he assumed mythical proportions as the courageous figure who on the one hand opened up the frontier for settlers and at the same time was a fugitive from civilization. Byron celebrated Boone in *Don Juan* as the virtuous natural man, and Cooper assimilated characteristics of Boone into the figure of the aged Leatherstocking. There have been many versions of Daniel Boone's exploits: John Filson's *The Discovery, Settlement, and Present State of Kentucke* (1784); Daniel Byran's epic, *The Adventures of Daniel Boone* (1813), and Timothy Flint's biography, *The Life and Adventures of Daniel Boone* (1823). The most popular record of Boone's adventures was Flint's, which was reprinted 14 times and proved to be the most popular biography of the early nineteenth century.

The major renditions of Boone's adventures may be found in John Filson, *The Discovery, Settlement and Present State of Kentucke,* 1784; Daniel Bryan, *The Mountain Muse: Comprising the Adventures of Daniel Boone: And the Power of Virtuous and Refined Beauty,* 1813; Timothy Flint, *Biographical Memoir of Daniel Boone, The First Settler of Kentucky.* Interspersed with Incidents in the Early Annals of His Country, 1842.

For critical accounts of Flint, see James K. Folsom, *Timothy Flint,* 1965; Lawrence Elliott, *The Long Hunter: A New Life of Daniel Boone,* 1976.

The present selection is taken from Timothy Flint's *Biographical Memoir,* 1842.

The Life and Adventures of Daniel Boone

Rejoicing on account of the peace—Boone indulges his propensity for hunting—Kentucky increases in population—Some account of their conflicting land titles—Progress of civil improvement destroying the range of the hunter—Litigation of land titles—Boone loses his lands—Removes from Kentucky to the Kanawha—Leaves the Kanawha and goes to Missouri, where he is appointed Commandant.

The peace which followed the defeat of the northern tribes of Indians by General Wayne, was most grateful to the harassed settlers of the west. The news of it was received everywhere with the most lively joy. Everyone had cause of gratulation. The hardy warriors, whose exploits we have recounted, felt that they were relieved from the immense responsibilities which rested upon them as the guardians and protectors of the infant settlements. The new settlers could now clear their wild lands, and cultivate their rich fields in peace—without fearing the ambush and the rifles of a secret foe; and the tenants of the scattered cabins could now sleep in safety, and without the dread of being awakened by the midnight war whoop of the savage. Those who had been pent up in forts and stations joyfully sallied forth, and settled wherever the soil and local advantages appeared the most inviting.

Colonel Boone, in particular, felt that a firm and resolute perseverance had finally triumphed over every obstacle. That the rich and boundless valleys of the great west—the garden of the earth—and the paradise of hunters, had been won from the dominion of the savage tribes, and opened as an asylum for the oppressed, the enterprising, and the free of every land. He had travelled in every direction through this great valley. He had descended from the Alleghanies into the fertile regions of Tennessee, and traced the courses of the Cumberland and Tennessee Rivers. He had wandered with delight through the blooming forests of Kentucky. He had been carried prisoner by the Indians through the wilderness which is now the state of Ohio, to the great lakes of the north; he had traced the headwaters of the Kentucky, the Wabash, the Miamies, the Scioto, and other great rivers of the west, and had followed their meanderings to their entrance into the Ohio; he had stood upon the shores of this beautiful river, and gazed with admiration, as he pursued its winding and placid course through endless forests to mingle with the Mississippi; he had caught some glimmerings of the future, and saw with the prophetic eye of a patriot, that this great valley must soon become the abode of millions of freemen; and his heart swelled with joy, and warmed with a transport which was natural to a mind so unsophisticated and disinterested as his.

Boone rejoiced in a peace which put an end to his perils and anxieties, and which now gave him full leisure and scope to follow his darling pursuit of hunting. He had first been led to the country by that spirit of the hunter, which in him amounted almost to a passion. This propensity may be said to be natural to man. Even in cities and populous places we find men so fond of this pastime, that they ransack the cultivated fields and enclosures of the farmer, for the purpose of killing the little birds and squirrels, which, from their insignificance, have ventured to take their abode with civilized man. What then must have been the feelings of Boone, to find himself in the grand theater of the hunter—filled with buffaloes, deer, bears, wild turkeys, and other noble game!

The free exercise of this darling passion had been checked and restrained, ever since the first settlement of the country, by the continued wars and hostile incursions of the Indians. The path of the hunter had been ambushed by the wily savage, and he seldom ventured beyond the purlieus[1] of his cabin, or the station where he resided. He was now free to roam in safety through the pathless wilderness—to camp out in security whenever he was overtaken by night; and to pursue the game wherever it was to be found in the greatest abundance.

Civilization had not yet driven the primitive tenants of the forest from their favorite retreats. Most of the country was still in a state of nature— unsettled and unappropriated. Few fences or inclosures impeded the free range of the hunter, and very few buts and bounds warned him of his being about to trespass upon the private property of some neighbors. Herds of buffaloes and deer still fed upon the rich canebrake and rank vegetation of the boundless woods, and resorted to the numerous Licks for salt and drink.

Boone now improved this golden opportunity of indulging in his favorite pursuit. He loved to wander alone, with his unerring rifle upon his shoulder, through the labyrinths of the tangled forests, and to rouse the wild beast from his secret lair. There was to him a charm in these primeval solitudes which suited his peculiar temperament, and he frequently absented himself on these lonely expeditions for days together. He never was known to return without being loaded with the spoils of the chase. The choicest viands and titbits of all the forest-fed animals were constantly to be found upon his table. Not that Boone was an epicure; far from it. He would have been satisfied with a soldier's fare. In common with other pioneers of his time, he knew what it was to live upon roots and herbs for days together. He had suffered hunger and want in all its forms without a murmur or complaint. But when peace allowed him to follow his profession of a hunter, and to exercise that tact and superiority which so much distinguished him, he selected from the abundance and profusion of the game which fell victims to

---

[1] Outskirts or neighboring areas.

his skill, such parts as were most esteemed. His friends and neighbors were also, at all times, made welcome to a share of whatever he killed. And he continued to live in this primitive simplicity—enjoying the luxury of hunting, and of roving in the woods, and indulging his generous and disinterested disposition towards his neighbors, for several years after the peace.

In the meantime, while Boone had been thus courting solitude, and absorbed by the engrossing excitement of hunting, the restless spirit of immigration, and of civil and physical improvement, had not been idle. After the peace the tide of population poured into the country in a continual stream, and the busy spirit of civilization was everywhere making inroads into the ancient forests, and encroaching upon the dominions of the hunter.

JAMES FENIMORE COOPER

(1789-1851)

James Fenimore Cooper was the first American novelist to demonstrate on a broad scale the fictional possibilities of native history and customs. In a time when British critics wondered who in the four corners

The Works of James Fenimore Cooper, 48 vols., is now being published by the State University of New York. Until this edition appears in its entirety, the standard reference is The Works of James Fenimore Cooper, Mohawk Edition, 33 vols., 1895-1900. Other editions are Cooper's Novels, illustrated by F. O. C. Darley. 32 vols., 1859-1861; J. Fenimore Cooper's Works, Household Edition. 32 vols., 1876-1884. (Fifteen of the novels have prefaces written by Cooper's daughter, Susan.) Robert E. Spiller and P. C. Blackburn have prepared a valuable Descriptive Bibliography of the Writings of James Fenimore Cooper, 1934.

An early memoir is William Cullen Bryant, Memorial of James Fenimore Cooper, 1852. Thomas R. Lounsbury, James Fenimore Cooper, 1882, and Henry Walcott Boynton, James Fenimore Cooper, 1931, are still useful. Recent biographies include James Grossman, James Fenimore Cooper, 1949, 1967, and Donald A. Ringe, James Fenimore Cooper, 1962.

Critical studies include Robert E. Spiller, Fenimore Cooper, Critic of His Times, 1931; Yvor Winters, "Fenimore Cooper, or the Ruin of Times," in Maule's Curse, 1938; Edwin Cady, The Gentleman in America, 1949, Chapters 5 and 6; Roy Harvey Pearce, The Savages of America, 1953, 1965; Mary Cunningham, ed., James Fenimore Cooper: A Re-appraisal, 1954; Arvid Shulenberger, Cooper's Theory of Fiction: His Prefaces and Their Relation to His Novels, 1955; Thomas Philbrick, James Fenimore Cooper and the Development of American Sea Fiction, 1961; Marius Bewley, The Eccentric Design, 1959, especially Chapters 3, 4, 5; Warren S. Walker, ed., Leatherstocking and the Critics, 1965; G. Dekker, James Fenimore Cooper: The American Scott, 1967.

The text of the Preface is from the 1850 complete edition of The Leatherstocking Tales. The selection from The Prairie is from the author's revised edition, 1851.

of the world would want to read an American book, Cooper recreated an American past that appealed to world audiences. His best fiction— 30 novels in all—concentrates on the disappearance of the frontier and the force of the sea in American civilization. Cooper is a myth maker who not only weaves a fascinating fable but records the relationship of man and nature in a period when that relationship was surrendering to industrialism and to the destruction of the forest and plain.

Cooper was brought up in an aristocratic household. His father owned thousands of acres of land in upstate New York near the Otsego Lake and ruled more than 40,000 people who rented land from him. After his graduation from Yale, Cooper enlisted in the Navy, with the intention of pursuing a naval career; but he returned from the sea to marry into a family as aristocratic as his own and to settle down as a country squire in Cooperstown. His first book was allegedly written as the result of his wife's challenge when, upon reading an English novel, Cooper told her, "I believe I could write a better story myself." Within a year he had published *Precaution* (1820), a novel about English society. The next year he completed a story of the Revolutionary period, *The Spy,* and soon afterward began the famous Leatherstocking series with *The Pioneers* (1823). This group of novels is Cooper's finest achievement and, in addition to *The Pioneers,* includes *The Last of the Mohicans* (1826), *The Prairie* (1827), *The Pathfinder* (1940), and *The Deerslayer* (1841).

Cooper wrote voluminously throughout his life. One group of novels deals with the sea—*The Pilot* (1824), *The Red Rover* (1828), and *The Sea Lions* (1849); another depicts the evils of feudal society—*The Bravo* (1831), *The Heidenmauer* (1832), and *The Headsman* (1833); still another treats of the Anti-Rent War in New York State that raged on from 1839 to 1846—*Satanstoe* (1845), *The Chainbearer* (1845), and *The Redskins* (1846).

From 1826 until 1833, Cooper traveled in Europe with his family so that his children could have a finer education than he felt they would receive at home. Through his acquaintance with Lafayette, he became more and more interested in political affairs and wrote *Gleanings in Europe* (1837), a book that analyzes the limitations of governmental systems in the continental countries. When he returned home, Cooper analyzed the American system, opposing the Jacksonian democrats and emphasizing the need for a landed aristocratic class that would uphold standards in government, the arts, and education. *The American Democrat* (1838) is his best statement of this position.

As Mark Twain pointed out, in "Fenimore Cooper's Literary Offenses," Cooper has many limitations as a novelist: faulty and flat characterization; humorlessness; contrived plots, and verbosity. But he also had a mythoepic sensibility in his finest work, the ability to combine the qualities of realism and romanticism in tales that are uniquely American. The Leatherstocking series remains the most vivid rendering of the vanishing frontier in our literature, projected dramatically through characters like Natty Bumppo (variously called The Deerslayer and the Leatherstocking), the Indians Chingachcook and Uncas, and a host of white characters who either despoil the American landscape or try to preserve it as a "virgin land."

The mythic quality of Leatherstocking is captured in the selection that closes *The Prairie* and that describes his death. The first selection, the Preface, sets Cooper's novel in the context of the Leatherstocking Tales and indicates the scope of the series.

Preface to *The Leatherstocking Tales*

This series of stories, which has obtained the name of "The Leather-Stocking Tales," has been written in a very desultory and inartificial manner. The order in which the several books appeared was essentially different from that in which they would have been presented to the world, had the regular course of their incidents been consulted. In "The Pioneers," the first of the series written, the Leather-Stocking is represented as already old, and driven from his early haunts in the forest, by the sound of the axe, and the smoke of the settler. "The Last of the Mohicans," the next book in order of publication, carried the readers back to a much earlier period in the history of our hero, representing him as middle-aged, and in the fullest vigor of manhood. In "The Prairie," his career terminated, and he is laid in his grave. There, it was originally the intention to leave him, in the expectation that, as in the case of the human mass, he would soon be forgotten. But a latent regard for this character induced the author to resuscitate him in "The Pathfinder," a book that was not long after succeeded by "The Deerslayer," thus completing the series as it now exists.

While the five books that have been written were originally published in the order just mentioned, that of the incidents, insomuch as they are connected with the career of their principal character, is, as has been stated, very different. Taking the life of the Leather-Stocking as a guide, "The Deerslayer" should have been the opening book, for in that work he is seen just emerging into manhood; to be succeeded by "The Last of the Mohicans," "The Pathfinder," "The Pioneers," and "The Prairie." This arrangement embraces the order of events, though far from being that in which the books at first appeared. "The Pioneers" was published in 1822; "The Deerslayer" in 1841; making the interval between them nineteen years. Whether these progressive years have had a tendency to lessen the value of the last-named book by lessening the native fire of its author, or of adding somewhat in the way of improved taste and a more matured judgment, is for others to decide.

If anything from the pen of the writer of these romances is at all to outlive himself, it is, unquestionably, the series of "The Leather-Stocking Tales." To say this, is not to predict a very lasting reputation for the series itself, but simply to express the belief it will outlast any, or all, of the works from the same hand.

It is undeniable that the desultory manner in which "The Leather-Stocking Tales" were written, has, in a measure, impaired their harmony, and otherwise lessened their interest. This is proved by the fate of the two books last published, though probably the two most worthy an enlightened and cultivated reader's notice. If the facts could be ascertained, it is probable the result would show that of all those (in America, in particular) who have read the three first books of the series, not one in ten has a knowledge of the existence even of the last two. Several causes have tended to produce this result. The long interval of time between the appearance of "The Prairie" and that of "The Pathfinder," was itself a reason why the later books of the series should be overlooked. There was no longer novelty to attract attention, and the interest was materially impaired by the manner in which events were necessarily anticipated, in laying the last of the series first before the world. With the generation that is now coming on the stage this fault will be partially removed by the edition contained in the present work, in which the several tales will be arranged solely in reference to their connexion with each other.

The author has often been asked if he had any original in his mind, for the character of Leather-Stocking. In a physical sense, different individuals known to the writer in early life, certainly presented themselves as models, through his recollections; but in a moral sense this man of the forest is purely a creation. The idea of delineating a character that possessed little of civilization but its highest principles as they are exhibited in the uneducated, and all of savage life that is not incompatible with these great rules of conduct, is perhaps natural to the situation in which Natty was placed. He is too proud of his origin to sink into the condition of the wild Indian, and too much a man of the woods not to imbibe as much as was at all desirable, from his friends and companions. In a moral point of view it was the intention to illustrate the effect of seed scattered by the way side. To use his own language, his "gifts" were "white gifts," and he was not disposed to bring on them discredit. On the other hand, removed from nearly all the temptations of civilized life, placed in the best associations of that which is deemed savage, and favorably disposed by nature to improve such advantages, it appeared to the writer that his hero was a fit subject to represent the better qualities of both conditions, without pushing either to extremes.

There was no violent stretch of the imagination, perhaps, in supposing one of civilized associations in childhood, retaining many of his earliest lessons amid the scenes of the forest. Had these early impressions, however, not been sustained by continued, though casual connexion with men of his own color, if not of his own caste, all our information goes to show he would soon have lost every trace of his origin. It is believed that sufficient attention was paid to the particular circumstances in which this individual was placed to justify the picture of his qualities that has been drawn. The Delawares early attracted the attention of missionaries, and were a tribe unusually influenced by their precepts and example. In many instances they became Christians, and cases occurred in which their subsequent lives gave proof of the efficacy of the great moral changes that had taken place within them.

A leading character in a work of fiction has a fair right to the aid which can be obtained from a poetical view of the subject. It is in this view, rather than in one more strictly circumstantial, that Leather-Stocking has been drawn. The imagination has no great task in portraying to itself a being removed from the everyday inducements to err, which abound in civilized life, while he retains the best and simplest of his early impressions; who sees God in the forest; hears him in the winds; bows to him in the firmament that o'ercanopies all; submits to his sway in a humble belief of his justice and mercy; in a word, a being who finds the impress of the Deity in all the works of nature, without any of the blots produced by the expedients, and passion, and mistakes of man. This is the most that has been attempted in the character of Leather-Stocking. Had this been done without any of the drawbacks of humanity, the picture would have been, in all probabilty, more pleasing than just. In order to preserve the *vrai-semblable*,[1] therefore, traits derived from the prejudices, tastes, and even the weaknesses of his youth, have been mixed up with these higher qualities and longings, in a way, it is hoped, to represent a reasonable picture of human nature, without offering to the spectator a "monster of goodness."

It has been objected to these books that they give a more favorable picture of the red man than he deserves. The writer apprehends that much of this objection arises from the habits of those who have made it. One of his critics, on the appearance of the first work in which Indian character was portrayed, objected that its "characters were Indians of the school of Heckewelder,[2] rather than of the school of nature." These words quite probably contain the substance of the true answer to the objection. Heckewelder was an ardent, benevolent missionary, bent on the good of the red man, and seeing in him one who had the soul, reason, and characteristics of a fellow-being. The critic is understood to have been a very distinguished agent of the government, one very familiar with Indians, as they are seen at the councils

[1] Credible.

[2] John Gottlieb Ernestus Heckewelder (1743-1823) was a pioneer Moravian Church missionary to Indians in the Ohio region.

to treat for the sale of their lands, where little or none of their domestic qualities come in play, and where, indeed, their evil passions are known to have the fullest scope. As just would it be to draw conclusions of the general state of American society from the scenes of the capital, as to suppose that the negotiating of one of these treaties is a fair picture of Indian life.

It is the privilege of all writers of fiction, more particularly when their works aspire to the elevation of romances, to present the *beau-idéal* of their characters to the reader. This it is which constitutes poetry, and to suppose that the red man is to be represented only in the squalid misery or in the degraded moral state that certainly more or less belongs to his condition, is, we apprehend, taking a very narrow view of an author's privileges. Such criticism would have deprived the world of even Homer.

1850

FROM THE PRAIRIE

DEATH OF A HERO

The trapper was placed on a rude seat, which had been made with studied care, to support his frame in an upright and easy attitude. The first glance of the eye told his former friends, that the old man was at length called upon to pay the last tribute of nature. His eye was glazed and apparently as devoid of sight as of expression. His features were a little more sunken and strongly marked than formerly; but there, all change, so far as exterior was concerned, might be said to have ceased. His approaching end was not to be ascribed to any positive disease, but had been a gradual and mild decay of the physical powers. Life, it is true, still lingered in his system, but it was as though at times entirely ready to depart, and then it would appear to reanimate the sinking form, as if reluctant to give up the possession of a tenement, that had never been undermined by vice or corrupted by disease. It would have been no violent fancy to have imagined, that the spirit fluttered about the placid lips of the old woodsman, reluctant to depart from a shell, that had so long given it an honest and an honourable shelter.

His body was so placed as to let the light of the setting sun fall full upon the solemn features. His head was bare, the long, thin locks of gray fluttering lightly in the evening breeze. His rifle lay upon his knee, and the other accoutrements of the chase were placed at his side within reach of his hand. Between his feet lay the figure of a hound, with its head crouching to the earth as if it slumbered, and so perfectly easy and natural was its position, that a second glance was necessary to tell Middleton, he saw only the skin of Hector, stuffed, by Indian tenderness and ingenuity, in a manner to represent the living animal. ° ° °

When he had placed his guests in front of the dying man, Hard-Heart, after a pause, that proceeded as much from sorrow as decorum, leaned a little forward and demanded—

"Does my father hear the words of his son?"

"Speak," returned the trapper, in tones that issued from his inmost chest, but which were rendered awfully distinct by the death-like stillness, that reigned in the place. "I am about to depart from the village of the Loups, and shortly shall be beyond the reach of your voice."

"Let the wise chief have no cares for his journey," continued Hard-Heart with an earnest solicitude, that led him to forget, for the moment, that others were waiting to address his adopted parent; "a hundred Loups shall clear his path from briars."

"Pawnee, I die, as I have lived, a Christian man," resumed the trapper with a force of voice, that had the same startling effect on his hearers, as is produced by the trumpet, when its blast rises suddenly and freely on the air after its obstructed sounds have been heard struggling in the distance; "as I come into life, so will I leave it. Horses and arms are not needed to stand in the presence of the Great Spirit of my people. He knows my colour and according to my gifts will he judge my deeds."

"My father will tell my young men how many Mingoes he has struck and what acts of valour and justice he has done, that they may know how to imitate him."

"A boastful tongue is not heard in the heaven of a white man!" solemnly returned the old man. "What I have done He has seen. His eyes are always open. That which has been well done, he will remember; wherein I have been wrong will he not forget to chastise, though he will do the same in mercy. No, my son; a Pale-face may not sing his own praises, and hope to have them acceptable before his God!"

A little disappointed, the young partisan stepped modestly back, making way for the recent comers to approach. Middleton took one of the meagre hands of the trapper and struggling to command his voice, he succeeded in announcing his presence. The old man listened like one whose thoughts were dwelling on a very different subject, but when the other had succeeded in making him understand, that he was present, an expression of joyful recognition passed over his faded features—

"I hope you have not so soon forgotten those, whom you so materially served!" Middleton concluded. "It would pain me to think my hold on your memory was so light."

"Little that I have ever seen is forgotten," returned the trapper; "I am at the close of many weary days, but there is not one among them all, that I could wish to overlook. I remember you with the whole of your company; ay, and your gran'ther, that went before you. I am glad, that you have come back upon these plains, for I had need of one, who speaks the English, since little faith can be put in the traders of these regions. Will you do a favour, lad, to an old and dying man?"

"Name it," said Middleton; "it shall be done."

"It is a far journey to send such trifles," resumed the old man, who spoke at short intervals as strength and breath permitted; "A far and weary journey is the same; but kindnesses and friendships are things not to be forgotten. There is a settlement among the Otsego hills—"

"I know the place," interrupted Middleton, observing that he spoke with increasing difficulty; "proceed to tell me what you would have done."

"Take then this rifle, and pouch, and horn, and send them to the person, whose name is graven on the plates of the stock. A trader cut the letters with his knife, for it is long, that I have intended to send him such a token of my love!"

"It shall be so. Is there more that you could wish?"

"Little else have I to bestow. My traps I give to my Indian son; for honestly and kindly had he kept his faith. Let him stand before me."

Middleton explained to the chief, what the trapper had said, and relinquished his own place to the other.

"Pawnee," continued the old man, always changing his language to suit the person he addressed, and not unfrequently according to the ideas he expressed, "it is a custom of my people for the father to leave his blessing with the son, before he shuts his eyes forever. This blessing I give to you; take it, for the prayers of a Christian man will never make the path of a just warrior, to the blessed prairies, either longer or more tangled. May the God of a white man look on your deeds with friendly eyes, and may you never commit an act that shall cause him to darken his face. I know not whether we shall ever meet again. There are many traditions concerning the place of Good Spirits. It is not for one like me, old and experienced though I am, to set up my opinions against a nation's. You believe in the blessed prairies, and I have faith in the sayings of my fathers. If both are true, our parting will be final; but if it should prove, that the same meaning is hid under different words, we shall yet stand together, Pawnee, before the face of your Wahcondah, who will then be no other than my God. There is much to be said in favour of both religions, for each seems suited to its own people, and no doubt it was so intended. I fear I have not altogether followed the gifts of my colour, inasmuch as I find it a little painful to give up for ever the use of the rifle and the comforts of the chase. But then the fault has been my own, seeing that it could not have been His. Ay, Hector," he continued, leaning forward a little, and feeling for the ears of the hound, "our parting has come at last, dog, and it will be a long hunt. You have been an honest, and a bold, and a faithful hound. Pawnee, you cannot slay the pup on my grave, for where a Christian dog falls, there he lies forever; but you can be kind to him, after I am gone for the love you bear his master."

"The words of my father, are in my ears," returned the young partisan, making a grave and respectful gesture of assent. ° ° °

The old man made a long, and apparently a musing pause. At times he raised his eyes wistfully as if he would again address Middleton, but some innate feeling appeared always to suppress his words. The other, who observed his hesitation, enquired in a way most likely to encourage him to proceed, whether there was aught else, that he could wish to have done.

"I am without kith or kin in the wide world!" the trapper answered; "when I am gone, there will be an end of my race. We have never been chiefs, but honest, and useful in our way, I hope it cannot be denied, we have always proved ourselves. My father lies buried near the sea, and the bones of his son will whiten on the prairies—"

"Name the spot, and your remains shall be placed by the side of your father," interrupted Middleton.

"Not so, not so, Captain. Let me sleep, where I have lived, beyond the din of the settlements. Still I see no need, why the grave of an honest man should be hid, like a Red-skin in his ambushment. I paid a man in the settlements to make and put a graven stone at the head of my father's resting place. It was the value of twelve beaver-skins, and cunningly and curiously was it carved! Then it told to all comers that the body of such a Christian lay beneath; and it spoke of his manner of life, of his years, and of his honesty. When we had done with the Frenchers in the old war, I made a journey to the spot, in order to see that all was rightly performed, and glad I am to say the workman had not forgotten his faith."

"And such a stone you would have at your grave?"

"I! no, no, I have no son but Hard-Heart, and it is little, that an Indian knows of White fashions and usages. Besides I am his debtor, already, seeing it is so little I have done, since I have lived in his tribe. The rifle might bring the value of such a thing—but then I know, it will give the boy pleasure to hang the piece in his hall, for many is the deer and the bird that he has seen to destroy. No, no, the gun must be sent to him, whose name is graven on the lock!"

"But there is one, who would gladly prove his affection in the way you wish; he, who owes you not only his deliverance from so many dangers, but who inherits a heavy debt of gratitude from his ancestors. The stone shall be put at the head of your grave."

The old man extended his emaciated hand, and gave the other a squeeze of thanks.

"I thought you might be willing to do it, but I was backward in asking the favour," he said, "seeing that you are not of my kin. Put no boastful words on the same, but just the name, the age and the time of death, with something from the holy book; no more, no more. My name will then not be altogether lost on 'arth; I need no more." ° ° °

The trapper had remained nearly motionless for an hour. His eyes, alone, had occasionally opened and shut. When opened, his gaze seemed fastened on the clouds, which hung around the western horizon, reflecting the bright colours, and giving form and loveliness to the glorious tints of an American sunset. The hour—the calm beauty of the season—the occasion, all conspired to fill the spectators with solemn awe. Suddenly, while musing on the remarkable position, in which he was placed, Middleton felt the hand, which he held, grasp his own with incredible power, and the old man, supported on either side by his friends, rose upright to his feet. For a moment he looked about him, as if to invite all in presence to listen, (the lingering remnant of human frailty,) and then with a fine military elevation of the head, and with a voice that might be heard in every part of that numerous assembly, he pronounced the word—"Here!"

A movement so entirely unexpected, and the air of grandeur and humility, which were so remarkably united in the mien of the trapper, together with the clear and uncommon force of his utterance, produced a short period of confusion in the faculties of all present. When Middleton and Hard-Heart, who had each involuntarily extended a hand to support the form of the old man, turned to him again, they found, that the subject of their interest was removed forever beyond the necessity of their care. They mournfully placed the body in its seat, and Le Balafré arose to announce the termination of the scene to the tribe. The voice of the old Indian seemed a sort of echo from that invisible world, to which the meek spirit of the trapper had just departed.

"A valiant, a just and a wise warrior has gone on the path, which will lead him to the blessed grounds of his people!" he said, "When the voice of the Wahcondah called him, he was ready to answer. Go, my children; remember the just chief of the Pale-faces, and clear your own tracks from briars!"

The grave was made beneath the shade of some noble oaks. It has been carefully watched to the present hour by the Pawnees of the Loup, and is often shown to the traveller and the trader as a spot where a just White-man sleeps. In due time the stone was placed at its head, with the simple inscription, which the trapper had himself requested. The only liberty taken by Middleton was to add,—"May no wanton hand disturb his remains!"

1827

GEORGE CALEB BINGHAM

(1811-1879)

George Caleb Bingham was born in Virginia and moved with his family to Missouri. After studying at the Pennsylvania Academy of the Fine Arts, he went to Germany for three years and studied in Dusseldorf. He remained, however, an American artist who painted country and town life in the Midwest. His genre painting, *Fur Traders Descending the Missouri* (1845), is a good example of the poetic quality he brings to an ordinary scene. Bingham has often been compared with Mark Twain, since both artists drew their inspiration from the same Midwestern memories and experiences.

George Caleb Bingham, "Fur Traders Descending the Missouri," 1845.
(The Metropolitan Museum of Art, Morris K. Jessep Fund, 1933.)

George Caleb Bingham, "The County Election," 1851–1852. *(The St. Louis Art Museum.)*

George Caleb Bingham, "The Emigration of Daniel Boone," 1851–1852.
(Collection, Washington University, St. Louis.)

HUMOR

American humor has always been a deep reflection of the national character. In newspapers and almanacs, dramas, and travel books, Americans depicted politicians, Yankee peddlers, frontiersmen, and Southern gentlemen with a satirical thrust that often was more realistic than the stock types created by novelists. In an age when fictionists and poets often felt constrained by tradition and fixed attitudes toward morality, the humorists wrote in the vernacular and examined mores and customs from a fresh perspective. During the period from 1830 to 1860, three types of humor seem especially important: the Downeast, "cracker-box" wit, the Southwest tall tale, and the political satire of the "literary comedians."

Downeast humor appeared in the newspapers of the time and used primarily politics as a subject. Writers like Seba Smith and James Russell Lowell drew heavily on dialect, local types like the Yankee, and political figures. The humor of the Southwest was more raucous and exhuberant, since the customs of Tennessee, Georgia, Alabama, Louisi-

The best early work on American humor is Constance Rourke, *American Humor: A Study of the National Character,* 1931; but see also Henry Watterson, "The South in Light and Shade," *The Compromises of Life and Other Lectures and Addresses,* 1903, pp. 59-101; Jennette Tandy, *Cracker-box Philosophers in American Humor and Satire,* 1925; Franklin Meine, ed., *Tall Tales of the Southwest,* 1930; Richard Dorson, *Jonathan Draws the Long Bow,* 1946; Frank L. Owsley, *Plain Folk of the South,* 1949. Blair has written extensively on humor in this country. See his "The Popularity of Nineteenth-Century American Humorists," *American Literature,* III (May 1931), 174-194; *Horse Sense in American Humor from Benjamin Franklin to Ogden Nash,* 1942; and *Native American Humor,* 1960.

The texts of Jack Downing are from *The Life and Writings of Major Downing,* 1824; "The Debate in the Sennit" is No. V in *The Bigelow Papers,* 1848; "Mike Fink Beats Davy Crockett at a Shooting Match" is from *The Crockett Almanac,* 1840;

"Georgia Theatrics" is in *Georgia Scenes,* 1835, 1940; "The Big Bear of Arkansas" appeared in *The Spirit of the Times,* 1841; "Interview with President Lincoln" is in *Artemus Ward: His Book,* 1862; "Shows Why He Should Not Be Drafted" is in *The Nasby Papers,* 1864.

The several editions of Davy Crockett's life are *A Narrative of the Life of David Crockett. . . Written by Himself,* 1834; *An Account of Colonel Crockett's Tour to the North and Down East,* 1835; *The Autobiography of David Crockett,* With an Introduction by Hamlin Garland, 1923; *A Narrative of the Life of David Crockett,* Ed., Joseph J. Arpad, 1974.

Studies of these various figures include Constance Rourke, *Davy Crockett,* 1937; James A. Shackford, *David Crockett: The Man and the Legend,* 1956; John Donald Wade, *Augustus Baldwin Longstreet,* 1924; Mary Alice Wyman, *Two American Pioneers: Seba Smith and Elizabeth Oakes Smith,* 1927; Milton Rickels, *Thomas Bangs Thorpe,* 1962.

ana, Mississippi, Arkansas, and Missouri were dramatically and realistically rendered; this humor depends heavily on oral story-telling and the qualities of exaggeration and incongruity. Finally, literary comedians like Charles Farrar Browne, who created the character of Artemus Ward, and David Locke who invented Petroleum V. Nasby, spoofed Abraham Lincoln and other political figures in midcentury and developed a political satire that is still a prominent feature of popular culture. These journalists anticipate a long line of writers who; however sophisticated they may have been in politics and art, drew heavily on the democratizing quality of American humor: Abraham Lincoln, Mark Twain, Ernest Hemingway Ring Lardner, James Thurber, Will Rogers, William Faulkner, Ralph Ellison, Saul Bellow, Norman Mailer, and Philip Roth. The types change with time and place, but the qualities of exaggeration, incongruity, and cruelty recur.

Downeast

SEBA SMITH

(1792–1868)

Seba Smith created the *Jack Downing Papers,* which first appeared in the *Portland Courier* in 1830 and continued until 1859 under different titles: *The Life and Writings of Major Jack Downing* (1833); *The Select Letters of Major Jack Downing* (1834); *Way Down East* (1854); and *My Thirty Years Out of the Senate* (1859). Smith used the technique of the crackerbox philosopher and is best remembered for his political satire, projected through a series of letters written by Jack Downing.

From Jack Downing Papers

LETTER I. [JACK GOES TO PORTLAND]

Portland, Monday, Jan. 18, 1830.

To Cousin Ephraim Downing, up in Downingville:
Dear Cousin Ephraim:—I now take my pen in hand to let you know that I am well, hoping these few lines will find you enjoying the same blessing. When I come down to Portland I didn't think o' staying more than three or four days, if I could sell my load of ax handles, and mother's cheese, and cousin Nabby's bundle of footings; but when I got here I found Uncle Nat was gone a freighting down to Quoddy, and Aunt Sally said as how I shouldn't stir a step home till he come back agin, which won't be this month. So here I am, loitering about this great town, as lazy as an ox. Ax handles don't fetch nothing; I couldn't hardly give 'em away. Tell Cousin Nabby I sold her footings for nine-pence a pair, and took it all in cotton cloth. Mother's cheese come to seven-and-sixpence; I got her half a pound of shushon, and two ounces of snuff, and the rest in sugar. When Uncle Nat comes home I shall put my ax handles aboard of him, and let him take 'em to Boston next time he goes; I saw a feller tother day, that told me they'd fetch a good price there. I've been here now a whole fortnight, and if I could tell ye one half I've seen, I guess you'd stare worse than if you'd seen a catamount.[1] I've been to meeting, and to the museum, and to both Legislaters, the one they call the House, and the one they call the Sinnet. I spose Uncle Joshua is in a great hurry to hear something about these Legislaters; for you know he's always reading newspapers, and talking politics, when he can get anybody to talk with him. I've seen him when he had five tons of hay in the field well made, and a heavy shower coming up, stand two hours disputing with Squire W. about Adams and Jackson—one calling Adams a tory and a fed, and the other saying Jackson was a murderer and a fool; so they kept it up, till the rain began to pour down, and about spoilt all his hay.

Uncle Joshua may set his heart at rest about the bushel of corn that he bet 'long with the postmaster, that Mr. Ruggles would be Speaker of that Legislater they call the House; for he's lost it, slick as a whistle. As I hadn't much to do, I've been there every day since they've been a setting. A Mr. White, of Monmouth, was the Speaker the first two days; and I can't see why they didn't keep him in all the time; for he seemed to be a very clever, good-natured sort of man, and he had such a smooth, pleasant way with him, that I couldn't help feeling sorry when they turned him out and put in another.

---

[1] Short for catamountain. Any of various wild felines, like a mountain lion or lynx.

But some said he wasn't put in hardly fair; and I don't know as he was, for the first day, when they were all coming in and crowding round, there was a large, fat man, with a round, full, jolly sort of face, I suppose he was the captain, for he got up and commanded them to come to order, and then he told this Mr. White to whip into the chair quicker than you could say Jack Robinson. Some of 'em scolded about it, and I heard some, in a little room they called the lobby, say 'twas a mean trick; but I couldn't see why, for I thought Mr. White made a capital Speaker, and when *our* company turns out, the cap'n always has a right to do as he'a a mind to.

They kept disputing most all the time the first two days about a poor Mr. Roberts, from Waterborough. Some said he shouldn't have a seat because he adjourned the town meeting and wasn't fairly elected. Others said it was no such thing, and that he was elected as fairly as any of 'em. And Mr. Roberts himself said he was, and said he could bring men that would swear to it, and good men too. But, notwithstanding all this, when they came to vote, they got three or four majority that he shouldn't have a seat. And I thought it a needless piece of cruelty, for they wan't crowded, and there was a number of seats empty. But they would have it so, and the poor man had to go and stand up in the lobby.

Then they disputed awhile about a Mr. Fowler's having a seat. Some said he shouldn't have a seat, because when he was elected some of his votes were given for his father. But they were more kind to him than they were to Mr. Roberts, for they voted that he *should* have a seat; and I suppose it was because they thought he had a lawful right to inherit whatever was his father's. They all declared there was no party politics about it, and I don't think there was; for I noticed that all who voted that Mr. Roberts *should* have a seat, voted that Mr. Fowler should *not;* and all who voted that Mr. Roberts should *not* have a seat, voted that Mr. Fowler *should.* So, as they all voted *both* ways, they must have been conscientious, and I don't see how there could be any party about it.

It's a pity they couldn't be allowed to have two Speakers, for they seemed to be very anxious to choose Mr. Ruggles and Mr. Goodenow. They two had every vote except one, and if they had had *that,* I believe they would both have been chosen; as it was, however, they both came within a humbird's eye of it. Whether it was Mr. Ruggles voted for Mr. Goodenow, or Mr. Goodenow for Mr. Ruggles, I can't exactly tell; but I rather guess it was Mr. Ruggles voted for Mr. Goodenow, for he appeared to be very glad to see Mr. Goodenow in the chair, and shook hands with him as good-natured as could be. I would have given half my load of ax handles, if they could both have been elected and set up there together, they would have been so happy. But as they can't have but one Speaker at a time, and as Mr. Goodenow appears to understand the business very well, it is not likely Mr. Ruggles will be Speaker any this winter. So Uncle Joshua will have to shell out his bushel of corn, and I hope it will learn him better than to bet about politics again. Before I came from home, some of the papers said how there was a majority of ten or fifteen *National Republicans* in the Legislater, and the other party said there was a pretty clever little majority of *Democratic Republicans.* Well, now everybody says it has turned out jest as that queer little paper, called the Daily Courier, said 'twould. That paper said it was such a close rub it couldn't hardly tell which side would beat. And it's jest so, for they've been here now most a fortnight acting jest like two boys playin see-saw on a rail. First one goes up, and then 'tother; but I reckon one of the boys is rather heaviest, for once in a while he come down chuck, and throws the other up into the air as though he would pitch him head over heels. Your loving cousin till death.

JACK DOWNING

JAMES RUSSELL LOWELL

(1819–1891)*

Lowell's *Bigelow Papers* (1846–1848) is the best known example of downeast humor. Like Jack Downing, Hosea Bigelow is an uneducated Yankee who nevertheless has perceptive comments to make about politics. Lowell uses all the devices of this type of humor: illiterate spelling, crackerbox wit, comic portraits of famous people, and a diction that, in Lowell's language, sucks up the "feeding juices from the mother-earth of a rich common folk-talk."

From The Bigelow Papers, Second Series

SUNTHIN' IN THE PASTORAL LINE

TO THE EDITORS OF THE ATLANTIC MONTHLY

Jaalam, 17th May, 1862.

GENTLEMEN,—

At the special request of Mr. Biglow, I intended to inclose, together with his own contribution, (into which, at my suggestion, he has thrown a little more of pastoral sentiment than usual,) some passages from my sermon on

* For a full discussion of Lowell's life and work, see pp. 1498–1499.

the day of the National Fast, from the text, "Remember them that are in bonds, as bound with them," Heb. xiii. 3. But I have not leisure sufficient at present for the copying of them, even were I altogether satisfied with the production as it stands. I should prefer, I confess, to contribute the entire discourse to the pages of your respectable miscellany, if it should be found acceptable upon perusal, especially as I find the difficulty in selection of greater magnitude than I had anticipated. What passes without challenge in the fervour of oral delivery, cannot always stand the colder criticism of the closet. I am not so great an enemy of Eloquence as my friend Mr. Biglow would appear to be from some passages in his contibution for the current month. I would not, indeed, hastily suspect him of covertly glancing at myself in his somewhat caustick animadversions, albeit some of the phrases he girds at are not entire strangers to my lips. I am a more hearty admirer of the Puritans than seems now to be the fashion and believe, that, if they Hebraized a little too much in their speech, they showed remarkable practical sagacity as statesmen and founders. But such phenomena as Puritanism are the results rather of great religious than of merely social convulsions, and do not long survive them. So soon as an earnest conviction has cooled into a phrase, its work is over, and the best that can be done with it is to bury it. *Ite, missa est.*[1] I am inclined to agree with Mr. Biglow that we cannot settle the great political questions which are now presenting themselves to the nation by the opinions of Jeremiah or Ezekiel as to the wants and duties of the Jews in their time, nor do I believe that an entire community with their feelings and views would be practicable or even agreeable at the present day. At the same time I could wish that their habit of subordinating the actual to the moral, the flesh to the spirit, and this world to the other, were more common. They had found out, at least, the great military secret that soul weighs more than body.—But I am suddenly called to a sick-bed in the household of a valued parishioner.

With esteem and respect,
Your obedient servant,
HOMER WILBUR.

Once git a smell o' musk into a draw,
An' it clings hold like precerdents in law:
Your gra'ma'am put it there,—when, goodness knows,—
To jes' this-worldify her Sunday-clo'es;
But the old christ wun't sarve her gran'son's wife,
(For, 'thout new funnitoor, wut good in life?)
An'so ole clawfoot, from the precinks dread   5

---

[1] "Co, tho mass is finished."

O' the spare chamber, slinks into the shed
Where, dim with dust, it fust or last subsides
To holdin' seeds an fifty things besides;
But better days stick fast in heart an' husk,
An' all you keep in 't gits a scent o' musk.   10

Jes' so with poets: wut they've airly read
Gits kind o' worked into their heart an' head,
So 's 't they can't seem to write but jest on sheers
With furrin countries or played-out ideers,
Nor hev a feelin', ef it doos n't smack   15
O' wut some critter chose to feel 'way back:
This makes 'em talk o'daisies, larks, an' things,
Ez though we 'd nothin' here that blows an' sings,—
(Why, I'd give more for one live bobolink
Than a square mile o' larks in printer's ink,)—   20
This makes 'em think our fust o' May is May,
Which 't ain't, for all the almanicks can say.

O little city-gals, don't never go it
Blind on the word o' noospaper or poet!
They're apt to puff, an' May-day seldom looks,
Up in the country ez it doos in books;
They're no more like than hornets'-nests an' hives,   25
Or printed sarmons be to holy lives.
I with my trouses perched on cowhide boots,
Tuggin' my foundered feet out by the roots,
Hev seen ye come to fling on April's hearse
Your muslin nosegays from the milliner's,   30
Puzzlin' to find dry ground your queen to choose,
An' dance your throats sore in morocker shoes:
I've seen ye an' felt proud, thet, come wut would,
Our Pilgrim stock wuz pethed with hardihood.
Pleasure doos make us Yankees kind o'winch,   35
Ez though 't wuz sunthin' paid for by the inch;
But yit we du contrive to worry thru,
Ef Dooty tells us thet the thing's to du,
An' kerry a hollerday, ef we set out,
Ez stiddily ez though 't wuz a redoubt.   40

I, country-born an' bred, know where to find
Some blooms thet make the season suit the mind,
An' seem to metch the doubtin' bluebird's notes,—
Half-vent'rin' liverworts in furry coats,
Bloodroots, whose rolled-up leaves ef you oncuri,   45

Each on 'em 's cradle to a baby-pearl,—
But these are jes' Spring's pickets; sure ez sin,
The rebble frosts 'll try to drive 'em in;
For half our May's so awfully like May n't,
't would rile a Shaker or an evrige saint;   50
Though I own up I like our back'ard springs
That kind o' haggle with their greens an' things,
An' when you 'most give up, 'uthout more words
Toss the fields full o' blossoms, leaves, an' birds;
Thet's Northun natur', slow an' apt to doubt,
But when it *doos* git stirred, ther' 's no ginout!   55

Fust come the blackbirds clatt'rin' in tall trees,
An' settlin' things in windy Congresses,—
Queer politicians, though, for I'll be skinned
Ef all on 'em don't head aginst the wind.
'fore long the trees begin to show belief,—   60
The maple crimsons to a coral reef,
Then saffern swarms swing off from all the willers
So plump they look like yaller caterpillars,
Then gray hossches'nuts leetle hands unfold
Softer 'n a baby's be at three days old: 65
Thet 's robin-redbreast's almanick; he knows
Thet arter this ther' 's only blossom-snows;
So, choosin' out a handy crotch an' spouse,
He goes to plast'rin' his adobe house.

Then seems to come a hitch,—things lag behind,   70
Till some fine mornin' Spring makes up her mind,
An' ez, when snow-swelled rivers cresh their dams
Heaped-up with ice thet dovetails in an' jams,
A leak comes spiritin' thru some pin-hole cleft,
Grows stronger, fercer, tears out right an' left,   75
Then all the waters bow themselves an' come,
Suddin, in one gret slope o' shedderin' foam,
Jes' so our Spring gits everythin' in tune
An' gives one leap from Aperl into June:
Then all comes crowdin' in; afore you think,   80
Young oak-leaves mist the side-hill woods with pink;
The catbird in the laylock-bush is loud:
The orchards turn to heaps o' rosy cloud;
Red-cedars blossom tu, though few folks know it,
An' look all dipt in sunshine like a poet;   85

The lime-trees pile their solid stacks o' shade
An' drows'ly simmer with the bees' sweet trade;
In ellum-shrouds the flashin' hangbird clings
An' for the summer vy'ge his hammock slings;
All down the loose-walled lanes in archin' bowers   90
The barb'ry droops its strings o'golden flowers,
Whose shrinkin' hearts the school-gals love to try
With pins,—they'll worry yourn so, boys, bimeby!
But I don't love your cat'logue style,—do you?—
Ez ef to sell off Natur' by vendoo;   95
One word with blood in 't 's twice ez good ez two:
'nuff sed, June's bridesman, poet o' the year,
Gladness on wings, the bobolink, is here;
Half-hid in tip-top apple-blossoms he swings
Or climbs against the breeze with quiverin' wings,   100
Or, givin' way to 't in a mock despair,
Runs down, a brook o' laughter, thru the air.

I ollus feel the sap start in my veins
In Spring, with curus heats an' prickly pains,
Thet drive me, when I git a chance, to walk   105
Off by myself to hev a privit talk
With a queer critter thet can't seem to 'gree
Along o' me like most folks,—Mister Me.
Ther' 's times when I'm unsoshle ez a stone,
An' sort o' suffercate to be alone,—   110
I'm crowded jes' to think thet folks are nigh,
An' can't bear nothin' closer than the sky;
Now the wind 's full ez shifty in the mind
Ez wut it is ou'-doors, ef I ain't blind,
An' sometimes, in the fairest sou'west weather   115
My innard vane pints east for weeks together,
My natur' gits all goose-flesh, an' my sins
Come drizzlin' on my conscience sharp ez pins:
Wal, et sech times I jes' slip out o' sight
An' take it out in a fair stan'-up fight   120
With the one cuss I can't lay on the shelf,
The crook'dest stick in all the heap,—Myself.

'T wuz so las' Sabbath arter meetin'-time:
Findin' my feelin's would n't noways rhyme
With nobody's, but off the hendle flew   125
An' took things from an east-wind pint o' view,

I started off to lose me in the hills
Where the pines be, up back o' 'Sian's Mills:
Pines, ef you 're blue, are the best friends I know,
They mope an' sigh an' sheer your feelin's so,— 130
They hesh the ground beneath so, tu, I swan,
You half-forgit you've gut a body on.
Ther' 's a small school'us' there where four roads meet,
The door-steps hollered out by little feet, 135
An' side-posts carved with names whose owners grew
To gret men, some on 'em, an' deacons, tu;
't ain't used no longer, coz the town hez gut
A high-school, where they teach the Lord knows wut:
Three-story larnin' 's pop'lar now; I guess 140
We thriv' ez wal on jes' two stories less,
For it strikes me ther' 's sech a thing ez sinnin'
By overloadin' children's underpinnin':
Wal, here it wuz I larned my A B C,
An' it's a kind o' favorite spot with me. 145

We 're curus critters: Now ain't jes' the minute
Thet ever fits us easy while we're in it;
Long ez 't wuz futur', 't would be perfect bliss,—
Soon ez it's past, *thet* time's wuth ten o' this;
An' yit there ain't a man thet need be told 150
Thet Now's the only bird lays eggs o' gold.
A knee-high lad, I used to plot an' plan
An' think 't wuz life's cap-sheaf to be a man;
Now, gittin' gray, there's nothin' I enjoy
Like dreamin' back along into a boy:
So the ole school'us' is a place I choose 155
Afore all others, ef I want to muse;
I set down where I used to set, an' git
My boyhood back, an' better things with it,—
Faith, Hope, an' sunthin', et if is n't Cherrity, 160
It's want o' guile, an' thet 's ez gret a rerrity,—
While Fancy's cushin', free to Prince and Clown,
Makes the hard bench ez soft ez milkweed-down.

Now, 'fore I knowed, thet Sabbath arternoon
When I sot out to tramp myself in tune, 165
I found me in the school'us' on my seat,
Drummin' the march to No-wheres with my feet.

Thinkin' o' nothin', I've heerd ole folks say
Is a hard kind o' dooty in its way:
It's thinkin everythin' you ever knew,   170
Or ever hearn, to make your feelin's blue.
I sot there tryin' thet on for a spell:
I thought o' the Rebellion, then o'Hell,
Which some folks tell ye now is jest a metterfor
(A the'ry p'raps, it wun't *feel* none the better for):   175
I thought o' Reconstruction, wut we'd win
Patchin' our patent self-blow-up agin:
I thought ef this' ere milkin' o' the wits,
So much a month, warn't givin' Natur' fits,—
Ef folks warn't druv, findin' their own milk fail,   180
To work the cow thet hez an iron tail,
An' ef idees 'thout ripenin' in the pan
Would send up cream to humor ary man:
From this to thet I let my worryin' creep,
Till finally I must ha' fell asleep.   185

Our lives in sleep are some like streams thet glide
'twixt flesh an' sperrit boundin' on each side,
Where both shores' shadders kind o' mix an' mingle
In sunthin' thet ain't jes' like either single;
An' when you cast off moorin's from To-day,   190
An' down towards To-morrer drift away,
The imiges thet tengle on the stream
Make a new upside-down'ard world o' dream:
Sometimes they seem like sunrise-streaks and warnin's
O' wut 'll be in Heaven on Sabbath-mornin's   195
An', mixed right in ez ef jest out o' spite,
Sunthin' thet says your supper ain't gone right.
I'm gret on dreams, an' often when I wake,
I've lived so much it makes my mem'ry ache,   200
An' can't skurce take a cat-nap in my cheer
'thout hevin' 'em, some good, some bad, all queer,
Now I wuz settin' where I'd ben, it seemed,
An' ain't sure yit whether I r'ally dreamed,
Nor, ef I did, how long I might ha' slep',   205
When I hearn some un stompin' up the step,
An' lookin' round, ef two an' two make four,
I see a Pilgrim Father in the door.

He wore a steeple-hat, tall boots, an' spurs
With rowels to 'em big ez ches' nut-burrs,   210
An' his gret sword behind him sloped away
Long 'z a man's speech thet dunno wut to say.—
"Ef your name's Biglow, an' your given-name
Hosee," sez he, "it's arter you I came;
I'm your gret-gran 'ther multiplied by three."—   215
"My *wut?*" sez I.—"Your gret-gret-gret," sez he:
"You would n't ha' never ben here but for me.
Two hundred an' three year ago this May
The ship I come in sailed up Boston Bay;
I'd been a cunnle in our Civil War,—   220
But wut on airth hev *you* gut up one for?
Coz we du things in England, 't ain't for you
To git a notion you can du 'em tu:
I'm told you write in public prints: ef true,
It's nateral you should know a thing or two."—   225
"Thet air 's an argymunt I can't endorse,—
't would prove, coz you wear spurs, you kep' a horse:
For brains," sez I, "wutever you may think,
Ain't boun' to cash the drafs o' pen-an'-ink,—
Though mos' folks write ez ef they hoped jes' quickenin'   230
The churn would argoo skim-milk into thickenin';
But skim-milk ain't a thing to change its view
O' wut it 's meant for more 'n a smoky flue.
But du pray tell me, 'fore we furder go,
How in all Natur' did you come to know   235
'bout our affairs," sez I, "in Kingdom-Come?"—
"Wal, I worked round at sperrit-rappin' some,
An' danced the tables till their legs wuz gone,
In hopes o' larnin' wut wuz goin' on,"
Sez he, "but mejums lie so like all-split   240
Thet I concluded it wuz best to quit.
But, come now, ef you wun't confess to knowin',
You've some conjectures how the thing's a-goin."—
"Gran'ther," sez I, "a vane warn't never known
Nor asked to hev a jedgment of its own;   245
An' yit, ef 't ain't gut rusty in the jints,
It's safe to trust its say on certin pints:
It knows the wind's opinions to a T,
An' the wind settles wut the weather'll be."

"I never thought a scion of our stock   250
Could grow the wood to make a weathercock;
When I wuz younger 'n you, skurce more 'n a shaver,
No airthly wind," sez he, "could make me waver!"
(Ez he said this, he clinched his jaw an' forehead,
Hitchin' his belt to bring his sword-hilt forrard.)—   255
"Jes so it wuz with me," sez I, "I swow,
When *I* wuz younger 'n wut you see me now,—
Nothin' from Adam's fall to Huldy's bonnet,
Thet I warn't full-cocked with my jedgment on it;
But now I'm gittin' on in life, I find   260
It 's a sight harder to make up my mind,—
Nor I don't often try tu, when events
Will du it for me free of all expense.
The moral question's ollus plain enough,—
It's jes' the human-natur' side thet's tough;   265
Wut 's best to think may n't puzzle me nor you,—
The pinch comes in decidin' wut to *du;*
Ef you *read* History, all runs smooth ez grease,
Coz there the men ain't nothin' more 'n idees,—
But come to *make* it, ez we must to-day,   270
Th' idees hev arms an' legs an' stop the way:
It's easy fixin' things in facts an' figgers,—
They can't resist, nor warn't brought up with niggers;
But come to try your the'ry on,—why then
Your facts an' figgers change to ign'ant men   275
Actin' ez ugly—" —"Smite 'em hip an' thigh!"
Sez gran'ther, "and let every man-child die!
Oh for three weeks o' Cromwle an' the Lord!
Up, Isr'el, to your tents an' grind the sword!"—
"Thet kind o' thing worked wal in ole Judee,   280
But you forgit how long it's ben A. D.;
You think thet 's ellerkence,—I call it shoddy,
A think," sez I, "wun't cover soul nor body;
I like the plain all-wool o' common-sense,
Thet warms ye now, an' will a twelve-month hence.   285
You took to follerin' where the Prophets beckoned,
An', fust you knowed on, back come Charles the Second;
Now wut I want's to hev all *we* gain stick,
An' not to start Millennium too quick;
We hain't to punish only, but to keep,   290
An, the cure's gut to go a cent'ry deep."

"Wall, milk-an'-water ain't the best o' glue,"
Sez he, "an' so you'll find afore you're thru;
Ef reshness venters sunthin', shilly-shally
Loses ez often wut 's ten times the vally. 295
Thet exe of ourn, when Charles's neck gut split,
Opened a gap thet ain't bridged over yit:
Slav'ry 's your Charles, the Lord hez gin the exe"—
"Our Charles," sez I, "hez gut eight million necks.
The hardest question ain't the black man's right. 300
The trouble is to 'mancipate the white;
One 's chained in body an' can be sot free,
But t' other's chained in soul to an idee:
It's a long job, but we shall worry thru it;
Ef bagnets fail, the spellin'-book must du it." 305
"Hosee," sez he, "I think you're goin' to fail:
The rettlesnake ain't dangerous in the tail;
This 'ere rebellion 's nothing but the rettle,—
You'll stomp on thet an' think you've won the bettle;
It's Slavery thet's the fangs an' thinkin' head, 310
An' ef you want selvation, cresh it dead,—
An' cresh it suddin, or you'll larn by waitin'
Thet Chance wun't stop to listen to debatin'!"—
"God's truth!" sez I,—"an' ef I held the club,
An' knowed jes' where to strike,—but there 's the rub!"— 315
"Strike soon," sez he, "or you'll be deadly ailin',—
Folks thet's afeared to fail are sure o' failin';
God hates your sneakin creturs thet believe
He'll settle things they run away an' leave!"
He brought his foot down fercely, ez he spoke, 320
An' give me sech a startle thet I woke.

1862

Southwest

DAVY CROCKETT AND MIKE FINK

(1786-1836)   (1770?-1823?)

Colonel David Crockett of Tennessee was the personification of the "gamecock of the wilderness," that frontiersman who was "half man and half alligator" and about whose backwoods adventures many tall tales were created. He called himself the "Coonskin Congressman" from Tennessee, and his exploits figured in the conquest of the West and the Alamo, long after his death in 1836.

Mike Fink was known as the first flatboatman and the hero of such extraordinary exploits as suppressing seawolfs. It was rumored throughout the West that he could shoot more accurately than anyone else of his time.

The following yarn brings Davy Crockett and Mike Fink together in a typical tall tale. The speaker is Davy Crockett.

Mike Fink Beats Davy Crockett at a Shooting Match

ANONYMOUS

I expect, stranger, you think old Davy Crockett war never beat at the long rifle; but he war tho. I expect there's no man so strong, but what he will find some one stronger. If you havent heerd tell of one Mike Fink, I'll tell you something about him, for he war a helliferocious fellow, and made an almighty fine shot. Mike was a boatman on the Mississip, but he had a little cabbin on the head of the Cumberland, and a horrid handsome wife, that loved him the wickedest that ever you see. Mike only worked enough to find his wife in rags, and himself in powder, and lead, and whiskey, and the rest of the time he spent in nocking over bar and turkeys, and bouncing deer, and sometimes drawing a lead on an injun. So one night I fell in with him in the woods, where him and his wife shook down a blanket for me in his wigwam. In the morning sez Mike to me, 'I've got the handsomest wife, and the fastest horse, and the sharpest shooting iron in all Kentuck, and if any man dare doubt it, I'll be in his hair quicker than hell could scorch a feather.' This put my dander up, and sez I, 'I've nothing to say agin your wife, Mike, for it cant be denied she's a shocking handsome woman, and Mrs. Crockett's in Tennessee, and I've got no horses. Mike, I dont exactly like to tell you you lie about what you say about your rifle, but I'm d—d if you speak the truth, and I'll prove it. Do you see that are cat sitting on the top rail of your potato patch, about a hundred and fifty yards off? If she ever hears agin, I'll be shot if it shant be without ears.' So I plazed away, and I'll bet you a horse, the ball cut off both the old tom cat's ears close to his head, and shaved the hair off clean across the skull, as slick as if I'd done it with a razor, and the critter never stirred, nor knew he'd lost his ears till he tried to scratch 'em. 'Talk about your rifle after that, Mike!' sez I. 'Do you see that are sow away off furder than the eend of the world,' sez Mike, 'with a litter of pigs round her,' and he lets fly. The old sow give a grunt, but never stirred in her tracks, and Mike falls to loading and firing for dear life, till he hadn't left one of them are pigs enough tail to make a tooth-pick on. 'Now,' sez he, 'Col. Crockett, I'll be pretticularly ableedged to you if you'll put them are pig's tails on again,' sez he. 'That's onpossible, Mike,' sez I, 'but you've left one of 'em about an inch to steer by, and if it had a-been my work, I wouldn't have done it so wasteful. I'll mend your host,' and so I lets fly, and cuts off the apology he'd left the poor cretur for decency. I wish I may drink the whole of Old Mississip, without a drop of the rale stuff in it, if you wouldn't have thort the tail had been drove in with a hammer. That made Mike a kinder sorter wrothy, and he sends a ball after his wife as she was going to the spring after a gourd full of water, and nocked half her koom out of her head, without stirring a hair, and calls out to her to stop for me take a plizzard at what was left on it. The angeliferous critter stood still as a scarecrow in a cornfield, for she'd got used to Mike's tricks by long practiss. 'No, no, Mike,' sez I, 'Davy Crockett's hand would be sure to shake, if his iron war pointed within a hundred mile of a shemale, and I give up beat, Mike, and as we've had our eye-openers a-ready, we'll now take a flem-cutter, by way of an anti-formatic, and then we'll disperse.'

AUGUSTUS BALDWIN LONGSTREET

(1790–1870)

Augustus Baldwin Longstreet was a lawyer, judge, and editor who spoke, as he said, of "Georgia language" and "Georgia humor" and recorded faithfully his local region through oral humor. "Georgia Theatrics" is included in Longstreet's book, *Georgia Scenes* (1835).

From Georgia Scenes

GEORGIA THEATRICS

If my memory fail me not, the 10th of June, 1809, found me, at about eleven o'clock in the forenoon, ascending a long and gentle slope in what was called "The Dark Corner" of Lincoln. I believe it took its name from the moral darkness which reigned over that portion of the county at the time of which I am speaking. If in this point of view it was but a shade darker than the rest of the county, it was inconceivably dark. If any man can name a trick or sin which had not been committed at the time of which I am speaking, in the very focus of all the county's illumination (Lincolnton), he must himself be the most inventive of the tricky and the very Judas of sinners. Since that time, however (all humor aside), Lincoln has become a living proof "that light shineth in darkness." Could I venture to mingle the solemn with the ludicrous, even for the purposes of honorable contrast, I could adduce from this county instances of the most numerous and wonderful transitions from vice and folly to virtue and holiness which have ever, perhaps, been witnessed since the days of the apostolic ministry. So much, lest it should be thought by some that what I am about to relate is characteristic of the county in which it occurred.

Whatever may be said of the *moral* condition of the Dark Corner at the time just mentioned, its *natural* condition was anything but dark. It smiled in all the charms of spring; and spring borrowed a new charm from its undulating grounds, its luxuriant woodlands, its sportive streams, its vocal birds, and its blushing flowers.

Rapt with the enchantment of the season and the scenery around me, I was slowly rising the slope, when I was startled by loud, profane, and boisterous voices, which seemed to proceed from a thick covert of undergrowth about two hundred yards in the advance of me and about one hundred to the right of my road.

"You kin, kin you?"

"Yes, I kin, and am able to do it! Boo-oo-oo! Oh, wake snakes, and walk your chalks! Brimstone and—fire! Don't hold me, Nick Stoval! The fight's made up, and let's go at it—My soul if I don't jump down his throat, and gallop every chitterling out of him before you can say 'quit'!"

"Now, Nick, don't hold him! Jist let the wildcat come, and I'll tame him. Ned'll see me a fair fight! Won't you, Ned?"

"Oh, yes; I'll see you a fair fight, blast my old shoes if I don't!"

"That's sufficient, as Tom Haynes said when he saw the elephant. Now let him come!"

Thus they went on, with countless oaths interspersed, which I dare not even hint at, and with much that I could not distinctly hear.

In mercy's name! thought I, what band of ruffians has selected this holy season and this heavenly retreat for such pandemoniac riots! I quickened my gait, and had come nearly opposite to the thick grove whence the noise proceeded, when my eye caught, indistinctly and at intervals, through the foliage of the dwarf-oaks and hickories which intervened, glimpses of a man, or men, who seemed to be in a violent struggle; and I could occasionally catch those deep-drawn, emphatic oaths which men in conflict utter when they deal blows. I dismounted, and hurried to the spot with all speed. I had overcome about half the space which separated it from me, when I saw the combatants come to the ground, and, after a short struggle, I saw the upper-most one (for I could not see the other) make a heavy plunge with both his thumbs, and at the same instant I heard a cry in the accent of keenest torture, "Enough! My eye's out!"

I was so completely horror-struck that I stood transfixed for a moment to the spot where the cry met me. The accomplices in the hellish deed which had been perpetrated had all fled at my approach—at least, I supposed so, for they were not to be seen.

"Now, blast your corn-shucking soul!" said the victor (a youth about eighteen years old) as he rose from the ground—"come cutt'n' your shines 'bout me agin, next time I come to the courthouse, will you? Get your owl eye in agin if you can!"

At this moment he saw me for the first time. He looked excessively embarrassed, and was moving off, when I called to him, in a tone emboldened by the sacredness of my office and the iniquity of his crime, "Come back, you brute, and assist me in relieving your fellow-mortal, whom you have ruined forever!"

My rudeness subdued his embarrassment in an instant; and with a taunting curl of the nose, he replied, "You needn't kick before you're spurr'd. There a'n't nobody there, nor ha'n't been nother. I was jist seein' how I could 'a' fout." So saying, he bounded to his plough, which stood in the corner of the fence about fifty yards beyond the battle-ground.

And, would you believe it, gentle reader? his report was true. All that I had heard and seen was nothing more nor less than a Lincoln rehearsal, in which the youth who had just left me had played all the parts of all the characters in a court-house fight.

I went to the ground from which he had risen, and there were the prints of his two thumbs, plunged up to the balls in the mellow earth, about the distance of a man's eyes apart; and the ground around was broken up as if two stags had been engaged upon it.

THOMAS B. THORPE

(1815–1878)

T. B. Thorpe was a newspaper editor and painter who is best remembered for his tall tale, "The Big Bear of Arkansas." This tale is perhaps the most famous of the genre and makes great use of incongruity in achieving its humor. It appeared in *The Spirit of the Times* in 1841.

The Big Bear of Arkansas

A steamboat of the Mississippi frequently, in making her regular trips, carries between places varying from one to two thousand miles apart; and as these boats advertise to land passengers and freight at "all intermediate landings," the heterogeneous character of the passengers of one of these up-country boats can scarcely be imagined by one who has never seen it with his own eyes. Starting from New Orleans in one of these boats, you will find yourself associated with men from every state in the Union, and from every portion of the globe; and a man of observation need not lack for amusement or instruction in such a crowd, if he will take the trouble to read the great book of character so favourably opened before him. Here may be seen jostling together the wealthy Southern planter, and the pedlar of tin-ware from New England—the Northern merchant, and the Southern jockey—a venerable bishop, and a desperate gambler—the land speculator, and the honest farmer—professional men of all creeds and characters—Wolvereens, Suckers, Hoosiers, Buckeyes, and Corn-crackers, beside a "plentiful sprinkling" of the half-horse and half-alligator species of men, who are peculiar to "old Mississippi," and who appear to gain a livelihood simply by going up and down the river. In the pursuit of pleasure or business, I have frequently found myself in such a crowd.

On one occasion, when in New Orleans, I had occasion to take a trip of a few miles up the Mississippi, and I hurried on board the well-known "high-pressure-and-beat-every-thing" steamboat *Invincible*, just as the last note of the last bell was sounding; and when the confusion and bustle that is natural to a boat's getting under way had subsided, I discovered that I was associated in as heterogeneous a crowd as was ever got together. As my trip was to be of a few hours' duration only, I made no endeavours to become acquainted with my fellow passengers most of whom would be together many days. Instead of this, I took out of my pocket the "latest paper," and more critically than usual examined its contents; my fellow passengers at the same time disposed themselves in little groups. While I was thus busily employed in reading, and my companions were more busily employed in discussing such subjects as suited their humours best, we were startled most unexpectedly by a loud Indian whoop, uttered in the "Social hall," that part of the cabin fitted off for a bar; then was to be heard a loud crowing, which would not have continued to have interested us—such sounds being quite common in that place of spirits—had not the hero of these windy accomplishments stuck his head into the cabin and hallooed out, "Hurra for the Big Bar of Arkansaw!" and then might be heard a confused hum of voices, unintelligible, save in such broken sentences as "horse," "screamer," "lightning is slow," etc. As might have been expected, this continued interruption attracted the attention of every one in the cabin; all conversation dropped, and in the midst of this surprise the "Big Bar" walked into the cabin, took a chair, put his feet on the stove, and looking back over his shoulder, passed the general and familiar salute of "Strangers, how are you?" He then expressed himself as much at home as if he had been at "the Forks of Cypress," and "perhaps a little more so." Some of the company at this familiarity looked a little angry, and some astonished; but in a moment every face was wreathed in a smile. There was something about the intruder that won the heart on sight. He appeared to be a man enjoying perfect health and contentment: his eyes were as sparkling as diamonds, and good-natured to simplicity. Then his perfect confidence in himself was irresistibly droll. "Perhaps," said he, "gentlemen," running on without a person speaking, "perhaps you have been to New Orleans often; I never made *the first visit before*, and I don't intend to make another in a crow's life. I am thrown away in that ar place, and useless, that ar a fact. Some of the gentlemen that called me *green*—well, perhaps I am, said I, *but I arn't so at home;* and if I ain't off my trail much, the heads of them perlite chaps themselves wern't much the hardest; for according to my notion, they were real *know-nothings*, green as a pumpkin-vine—couldn't, in farming, I'll bet, raise a crop of turnips; and as for shooting, they'd miss a barn if the door was swinging, and that, too, with the best rifle in the country. And then they talked to me 'bout hunting, and laughed at my calling the principal game in Arkansaw poker, and high-low-jack. 'Perhaps,' said I, 'you prefer chickens and rolette'; at this they laughed harder than ever, and asked me if I lived in the woods, and didn't know what *game* was? At this I rather think I laughed. 'Yes,' I roared, and says, 'Strangers, if you'd asked me *how we got our meat* in Arkansaw, I'd a told you at once, and given you a list of varmints that would make a caravan, beginning with the bar, and ending off with the cat; that's *meat* though, not game.' Game, indeed, that's what city folks call it; and with them it means chippen-birds and shite-pokes; maybe such trash live in my diggens, but I arn't noticed them yet; a bird any way is too trifling. I never did shoot at but one, and I'd never forgiven myself for that, had it weighed less than forty pounds. I wouldn't draw a rifle on any thing less than that; and when I meet with another wild turkey of the same weight I will drap him."

"A wild turkey weighing forty pounds!" exclaimed twenty voices in the cabin at once.

"Yes, strangers, and wasn't it a whopper? You see, the thing was so fat that it couldn't fly far; and when he fell out of the tree, after I shot him, on striking the ground he bust open behind, and the way the pound gobs of tallow rolled out of the opening was perfectly beautiful."

"Where did all that happen?" asked a cynical-looking Hoosier.

"Happen! happened in Arkansaw: where else could it have happened, but in the creation state, the finishing-up country—a state where the *sile* runs downs to the centre of the 'arth, and government gives you a title to every inch of it? Then its airs—just breathe them, and they will make you snort like a horse. It's a state without a fault, it is."

"Excepting mosquitoes," cried the Hoosier.

"Well, stranger, except them; for it ar a fact that they are rather *enormous*, and do push themselves in somewhat troublesome. But, stranger, they never stick twice in the same place; and give them a fair chance for a few months, and you will get as much above noticing them as an alligator. They can't hurt my feelings, for they lay under the skin; and I never knew but one case of injury resulting from them, and that was to a Yankee; and they take worse to foreigners, any how, than they do to natives. But the way they used that fellow up! first they punched him until he swelled up and bustled; then he su-per-a-ted, as the doctor called it, until he was as raw as beef; then he took the ager, owing to the warm weather, and finally he took a steamboat and left the country. He was the only man that ever took mosquitoes to heart that I know of. But mosquitoes is natur, and I never find fault with her. If they ar large, Arkansaw is large, her varmints ar large, her trees ar large, her rivers ar large, and a small mosquito would be of no more use in Arkansaw than preaching in a cane-brake."

This knock-down argument in favour of big mosquitoes used the Hoosier up, and the logician started on a new track, to explain how numerous bear were in his "diggins," where he represented them to be "about as plenty as blackberries, and a little plentifuler."

Upon the utterance of this assertion, a timid little man near me inquired if the bear in Arkansaw ever attacked the settlers in numbers.

"No," said our hero, warming with the subject, "no, stranger, for you see it ain't the natur of bar to go in droves; but the way they squander about in pairs and single ones is edifying. And then the way I hunt them the old black rascals know the crack of my gun as well as they know a pig's squealing. They grow thin in our parts, it frightens them so, and they do take the noise dreadfully, poor things. That gun of mine is perfect *epidemic among bar;* if not watched closely, it will go off as quick on a warm scent as my dog Bowie-knife will: and then that dog—whew! why the fellow thinks that the world is full of bar, he finds them so easy. It's lucky he don't talk as well as think; for with his natural modesty, if he should suddenly learn how much he is ac-knowledged to be ahead of all other dogs in the universe, he would be astonished to death in two minutes. Strangers, the dog knows a bar's way as well as a horse-jockey knows a woman's; he always barks at the right times, bites at the exact place, and whips without getting a scratch. I never could tell whether he was made expressly to hunt bar, or whether bar was made expressly for him to hunt; any way, I believe they were ordained to go together as naturally as Squire Jones says a man and woman is, when he moralizes in marrying a couple. In fact, Jones once said, said he, 'Marriage according to law is a civil contract of divine origin; it's common to all coun-tries as well as Arkansaw, and people take to it as naturally as Jim Doggett's Bowie-knife takes to bar.'"

"What season of the year do your hunts take place?" inquired a gentle-manly foreigner, who, from some peculiarities of his baggage, I suspect to be an Englishman, on some hunting expedition, probably at the foot of the Rocky Mountains.

"The season for bar hunting, stranger," said the man of Arkansaw, "is generally all the year round, and the hunts take place about as regular. I read in history that varmints have their fat season, and their lean season. That is not the case in Arkansaw, feeding as they do upon the *spontenacious* produc-tions of the sile, they have one continued fat season the year round; though in winter things in this way is rather more greasy than in summer, I must admit. For that reason bar with us run in warm weather, but in winter, they only waddle. Fat, fat! it's an enemy to speed; it tames everything that has plenty of it. I have seen wild turkeys, from its influence, as gentle as chick-ens. Run a bar in this fat condition, and the way it improves the critter for eating is amazing; it sort of mixes the ile up with the meat, until you can't tell t'other from which. I've done this often. I recollect one perty morning in particular, of putting an old fellow on the stretch, and considering the weight he carried, he run well. But the dogs soon tired him down, and when I came up with him wasn't he in a beautiful sweat—I might say fever; and then to see his tongue sticking out of his mouth a feet, and his sides sinking and opening like a bellows, and his cheeks so fat he couldn't look cross. In this fix I blazed at him, and pitch me naked into a briar patch if the steam didn't come out of the bullet-hole ten foot in a straight line. The fellow, I reckon, was made on the high-pressure system, and the lead sort of bust his biler."

"That column of steam was rather curious, or else the bear must have been *warm*," observed the foreigner, with a laugh.

"Stranger, as you observe, that bar was WARM, and the blowing off of the steam show'd it, and also how hard the varmint had been run. I have no doubt if he had kept on two miles farther his insides would have been stewed; and I expect to meet with a varmint yet of extra bottom, who will run himself into a skinfull of bar's grease: it is possible, much onlikelier things have happened."

"Whereabouts are these bears so abundant?" inquired the foreigner, with increasing interest.

"Why, stranger, they inhabit the neighbourhood of my settlement, one of the prettiest places on old Mississippi—a perfect location, and no mistake; a place that had some defects until the river made the 'cut-off' at 'Shirt-tail bend,' and that remedied the evil, as it brought my cabin on the edge of the river—a great advantage in wet weather, I assure you, as you can now roll a barrel of whiskey into my yard in high water from a boat, as easy as falling off a log. It's a great improvement, as toting it by land in a jug, as I used to do, *evaporated* it too fast, and it became expensive. Just stop with me, stranger, a month or two, or a year if you like, and you will appreciate my place. I can give you plenty to eat; for besides hog and hominy you can have bar-ham, and bar-sausages, and a mattrass of bar-skins to sleep on, and a wildcat-skin, pulled off hull, stuffed with corn shucks, for a pillow. That bed would put you to sleep if you had the rheumatics in every joint of your body. I call that ar bed a *quietus*.[1] Then look at my land—the government ain' got another such a piece to dispose of. Such timber, and such bottom land, why you can't preserve any thing natural you plant in it unless you pick it young, things thar will grow out of shape so quick. I once planted in those diggins a few potatoes and beets; they took a fine start, and after that an ox team couldn't have kept them from growing. About that time I went off to old Kentucky on bisiness, and did not hear from them things in three months, when I accidentally stumbled on a fellow who had stopped at my place, with an idea of buying me out. 'How did you like things?' said I. 'Pretty well,' said he; 'the cabin is convenient, and the timber land is good; but that bottom land ain't worth the first red cent.' 'Why?' said I. 'Cause,' said he. 'Cause

---

[1] Release from life: death.

what?' said I. "Cause it's full of cedar stumps and Indian mounds,' said he, *'and it can't be cleared.'* 'Lord,' said I, 'them ar "cedar stumps" is beets, and them ar "Indian mounds" is tater hills.' As I expected, the crop was overgrown and useless; the sile is too rich, *and planting in Arkansaw is dangerous.* I had a good-sized sow killed in that same bottom land. The old thief stole an ear of corn, and took it down where she slept at night to eat. Well, she left a grain or two on the ground, and lay down on them; before morning the corn shot up, and the percussion killed her dead. I don't plant any more; natur intended Arkansaw for a hunting ground, and I go according to natur."

The questioner who thus elicited the description of our hero's settlement, seemed to be perfectly satisfied and said no more; but the "Big Bar of Arkansaw" rambled on from one thing to another with a volubility perfectly astonishing, occasionally disputing with those around him, particularly with a "live Sucker" from Illinois, who had the daring to say that our Arkansaw friend's stories "smelt rather tall."

In this manner the evening was spent; but conscious that my own association with so singular a personage would probably end before morning, I asked him if he would not give me a description of some particular bear hunt; adding that I took great interest in such things, though I was no sportsman. The desire seemed to please him, and he squared himself round towards me, saying, that he could give me an idea of a bar hunt that was never beat in this world, or in any other. His manner was so singular, that half of his story consisted in his excellent way of telling it, the great peculiarity of which was the happy manner he had of emphasizing the prominent parts of his conversation. As near as I can recollect, I have italicized them, and given the story in his own words.

"Stranger," said he, "in bar hunts *I am numerous,* and which particular one, as you say, I shall tell, puzzles me. There was the old she devil I shot at the Hurricane last fall—then there was the old hog thief I popped over at the Bloody Crossing, and then—Yes, I have it! I will give you an idea of a hunt, in which the greatest bar was killed that ever lived, *none excepted;* about an old fellow that I hunted, more or less, for two or three years; and if that ain't a particular bar hunt, I ain't got one to tell. But in the first place, stranger, let me say, I am pleased with you, because you ain't ashamed to gain information by asking, and listening, and that's what I say to Countess's pups every day when I'm home; and I have got great hopes of them ar pups, because they are continually *nosing* about; and though they stick it sometimes in the wrong place, they gain experience any how, and may learn something useful to boot. Well, as I was saying about this big bar, you see when I and some more first settled in our region, we were drivin to hunting naturally; we soon liked it, and after that we found it an easy matter to make the thing our business. One old chap who had pioneered 'afore us, gave us to understand that we had settled in the right place. He dwelt upon its merits until it was affecting, and showed us, to prove his assertion, more marks on the sassafras trees than I ever saw on a tavern door 'lection time. 'Who keeps that ar reckoning?' said I. 'The bar,' said he. 'What for?' said I. 'Can't tell,' said he; 'but so it is; the bar bite the bark and wood too, at the highest point from the ground they can reach, and you can tell, by the marks,' said he, 'the length of the bar to an inch.' 'Enough,' said I; 'I've learned something here a'ready, and I'll put it in practice.'

"Well, stranger, just one month from that time I killed a bar, and told its exact length before I measured it, by those very marks; and when I did that, I swelled up considerable—I've been a prouder man ever since. So I went on, larning something every day, until I was reckoned a buster, and allowed to be decidedly the best bar hunter in my district; and that is a reputation as much harder to earn than to be reckoned first man in Congress, as an iron ramrod is harder than a toadstool. Did the varmints grow over-cunning by being fooled with by green-horn hunters, and by this means get troublesome, they send for me as a matter of course; and thus I do my own hunting, and most of my neighbours'. I walk into the varmints though, and it has become about as much the same to me as drinking. It is told in two sentences—a bar is started, and he is killed. The thing is somewhat monotonous now—I know just how much they will run, where they will tire, how much they will growl, and what a thundering time I will have in getting them home. I could give you this history of the chase with all particulars at the commencement, I know the signs so well—*Stranger, I'm certain.* Once I met with a match though, and I will tell you about it; for a common hunt would not be worth relating.

"On a fine fall day, long time ago, I was trailing about for bar, and what should I see but fresh marks on the sassafras trees, about eight inches above any in the forests that I knew of. Says I, 'them marks is a hoax, or it indicates the d———t bar that was ever grown.' In fact, stranger, I couldn't believe it was real, and I went on. Again I saw the same marks, at the same height, and *I knew the thing lived.* That conviction came home to my soul like an earthquake. Says I, 'here is something a-purpose for me: that bar is mine, or I give up the hunting business.' The very next morning what should I see but a number of buzzards hovering over my cornfield. 'The rascal has been there,' said I, 'for that sign is certain': and, sure enough, on examining, I found the bones of what had been as beautiful a hog the day before, as was ever raised by a Buckeye. Then I tracked the critter out of the field to the woods, and all the marks he left behind, showed me that he was *the bar.*

"Well, stranger, the first fair chase I ever had with that big critter, I saw him no less than three distinct times at a distance: the dogs run him over eighteen miles and broke down, my horse gave out, and I was as nearly used up as a man can be, made on *my* principle, *which is patent.* Before this adventure, such things were unknown to me as possible; but, strange as it was, that bar got me used to it before I was done with him; for he got so at last, that he would leave me on a long chase *quite easy*. How he did it, I never could understand. That a bar runs at all, is puzzling; but how this one could tire down and bust a pack of hounds and a horse, that were used to overhauling everything they started after in no time, was past my understanding. Well, stranger, that bar finally got so sassy, that he used to help himself to a hog off my premises whenever he wanted one; the buzzards followed after what he left, and so between *bar and buzzard*, I rather think I was *out of pork*.

"Well, missing that bar so often took hold of my vitals, and I wasted away. The thing had been carried too far, and it reduced me in flesh faster than an ager. I would see that bar in every thing I did; *he hunted me*, and that, too, like a devil, which I began to think he was. While in this fix, I made preparations to give him a last brush, and be done with it. Having completed every thing to my satisfaction, I started at sunrise, and to my great joy, I discovered from the way the dogs run, that they were near him; finding his trail was nothing, for that had become as plain to the pack as a turnpike road. On we went, and coming to an open country, what should I see but the bar very leisurely ascending a hill, and the dogs close at his heels, either a match for him in speed, or else he did not care to get out of their way—I don't know which. But wasn't he a beauty, though? I loved him like a brother.

"On he went, until he came to a tree, the limbs of which formed a crotch about six feet from the ground. Into this crotch he got and seated himself, the dogs yelling all around it; and there he sat eyeing them as quiet as a pond in low water. A green-horn friend of mine, in company, reached shooting distance before me, and blazed away, hitting the critter in the centre of his forehead. The bar shook his head as the ball struck it, and then walked down from that tree as gently as a lady would from a carriage. 'Twas a beautiful sight to see him do that—he was in such a rage that he seemed to be as little afraid of the dogs as if they had been sucking pigs; and the dogs warn't slow in making a ring around him at a respectful distance, I tell you; even Bowie-knife, himself, stood off. Then the way his eyes flashed—why the fire of them would have singed a cat's hair; in fact that bar was in a *wrath all over*. Only one pup came near him, and he was brushed out so totally with the bar's left paw, that he entirely disappeared; and that made the old dogs more cautious still. In the meantime, I came up, and taking deliberate aim as a man should do, at his side, just back of his foreleg, *if my gun did not snap*, call me a coward, and I won't take it personal. Yes, stranger, *it snapped*, and I could not find a cap about my person. While in this predicament, I turned round to my fool friend—says I, 'Bill,' says I, 'you're an ass—you're a fool—you might as well have tried to kill that bar by barking the tree under his belly, as to have done it by hitting him in the head. Your shot has made a tiger of him, and blast me, if a dog gets killed or wounded when they come to blows, I will stick my knife into your liver, I will—' my wrath was up. I had lost my caps, my gun had snapped, the fellow with me had fired at the bar's head, and I expected every moment to see him close in with the dogs, and kill a dozen of them at least. In this thing I was mistaken, for the bar leaped over the ring formed by the dogs, and giving a fierce growl, was off—the pack, of course, in full cry after him. The run this time was short, for coming to the edge of a lake the varmint jumped in, and swam to a little island in the lake, which it reached just a moment before the dogs. 'I'll have him now,' said I, for I had found my caps in the *lining of my coat*—so, rolling a log into the lake, I paddled myself across to the island, just as the dogs had cornered the bar in a thicket. I rushed up and fired—at the same time the critter leaped over the dogs and came within three feet of me, running like mad; he jumped into the lake, and tried to mount the log I had just deserted, but every time he got half his body on it, it would roll over and send him under; the dogs, too, got around him, and pulled him about, and finally Bowie-knife clenched with him, and they sunk into the lake together. Stranger, about this time, I was excited, and I stripped off my coat, drew my knife, and intended to have taken a part with Bowie-knife myself, when the bar rose to the surface. But the varmint staid under—Bowie-knife came up alone, more dead than alive, and with the pack came ashore. 'Thank God,' said I, 'the old villain has got his deserts at last.' Determined to have the body, I cut a grape-vine for a rope, and dove down where I could see the bar in the water, fastened my queer rope to his leg, and fished him, with great difficulty, ashore. Stranger, may I be chawed to death by young alligators, if the thing I looked at wasn't a *she bar, and not the old critter after all*. The way matters got mixed on that island was onaccountably curious, and thinking of it made me more than ever convinced that I was hunting the devil himself. I went home that night and took to my bed—the thing was killing me. The entire team of Arkansaw in bar-hunting, acknowledged himself used up, and the fact sunk into my feelings like a snagged boat will in the Mississippi. I grew as cross as a bar with two cubs and a sore tail. The thing got out 'mong my neighbours, and I was asked how come on that individu-al that never lost a bar when once started? and if that same individ-u-al didn't wear telescopes when he turned a she bar, of ordinary size, into an old one, a little larger than a horse? 'Perhaps,' said I, 'friends'—getting wrathy—'perhaps you want to call somebody a liar.' 'Oh, no,' said they, 'we only heard such things as being *rather common* of late, but we don't believe one word of it; oh, no,'— and then they would ride off and laugh like so many hyenas over a dead nigger. It was too much, and I determined to catch that bar, go to Texas, or die,—and I made my preparations accordin'. I had the pack shut up and rested. I took my rifle to pieces and iled it. I put caps in every pocket about my person, *for fear of the lining*. I then told my neighbours, that on Monday morning—naming the day—I would start THAT BAR, and bring him home with me, or they might divide my settlement among them, the owner having disappeared. Well, stranger, on the morning previous to the great day of my hunting expedition, I went into the woods near my house, taking my gun and Bowie-knife along, just *from habit*, and there sitting down also from habit, what should I see, getting over my fence, but *the bar!* Yes, the old varmint was within a hundred yards of me, and the way he walked *over that fence*— stranger, he loomed up like a *black mist*, he seemed so large, and he walked right towards me. I raised myself, took deliberate aim, and fired. Instantly the varmint wheeled, gave a yell, and *walked through the fence* like a falling tree would through a cobweb. I started after, but was tripped up by my inexpressibles, which either from habit, or the excitement of the moment, were about my heels, and before I had really gathered myself up, I heard the old varmint groaning in a thicket near by, like a thousand sinners, and by the time I reached him he was a corpse. Stranger, it took five niggers and myself to put that carcase on a mule's back, and old long-ears waddled under the load, as if he was foundered in every leg of his body, and with a common whopper of a bar, he would have trotted off, and enjoyed himself. 'Twould astonish you to know how big he was: I made a *bedspread of his skin*, and the way it used to cover my bar mattress, and leave several feet on each side to tuck up, would have delighted you. It was in fact a creation bar, and if it had lived in Samson's time, and met him, in a fair fight, it would have licked him in the twinkling of a dice-box. But, strangers, I never like the way I hunted, and *missed him*. There is something curious about it, I could never understand,—and I never was satisfied at his giving in so easy at last. Perhaps, he had heard of my preparations to hunt him the next day, so he jist come in, like Capt. Scott's coon, to save his wind to grunt with in dying; but that ain't likely. My private opinion is, that that bar was an *unhuntable bar, and died when his time come.*"

When the story was ended, our hero sat some minutes with his auditors in a grave silence; I saw there was a mystery to him connected with the bear whose death he had just related, that had evidently made a strong impression on his mind. It was also evident that there was some superstitious awe connected with the affair,—a feeling common with all "children of the wood," when they meet with any thing out of their everyday experience. He was the first one, however, to break the silence, and jumping up, he asked all present to "liquor" before going to bed,—a thing which he did, with a number of companions, evidently to his heart's content.

Long before day, I was put ashore at my place of destination, and I can only follow with the reader, in imagination, our Arkansas friend, in his adventures at the "Forks of Cypress" on the Mississippi.

Literary Comedians

CHARLES FARRAR BROWNE

(1834–1867)

Charles Farrar Browne was the creator of Artemus Ward, who began as a traveling showman and ended as the persona of Browne himself, a lecturer who satirized politicians. Browne used comic spelling and bad grammar to achieve his comic effects. Artemus Ward poked fun at all political and social groups: the "Mormins," the Shakers, the advocates of woman's rights, Southerners, and Northerners. It is alleged that Lincoln, fond of the writings of Artemus Ward, read excerpts from Browne's work to the members of his cabinet as a form of comic relief before presenting to them the final draft of the Emancipation Proclamation.

From The Writings of Artemus Ward

INTERVIEW WITH PRESIDENT LINCOLN

I hav no politics. Nary a one. I'm not in the bisiness. If I was I spose I should holler versiffrusly in the streets at nite and go home to Betsy Jane smellen of coal ile and gin, in the mornin. I should go to the Poles arly. I should stay there all day. I should see to it that my nabers was thar. I should git carriges to take the kripples, the infirm and the indignant thar. I should be on guard agin frauds and sich. I should be on the look out for the infamus lise of the enemy, got up just be4 elecshun for perlitical effeck. When all was over and my candydart was elected, I should move heving & arth—so to speak—until I got orfice, which if I didn't git a orfice I should turn round and abooze the Administration with all my mite and maine. But I'm not in the bisniss. I'm in a far more respectful bisniss nor what pollertics is. I wouldn't giv two cents to be a Congresser. The wuss insult I ever received was when sertin citizens of Baldinsville axed me to run fur the Legislater. Sez I, "My friends, dostest think I'd stoop to that there?" They turned as white as a sheet. I spoke in my most orfullest tones, & they knowd I wasn't to be trifled with. They slunked out of site to onct.

There4, havin no politics, I made bold to visiot Old Abe at his humstid in Springfield. I found the old feller in his parler, surrounded by a perfeck swarm of orfice seekers. Knowin he had been capting of a flat boat on the roarin Mississippy I thought I'd address him in sailor lingo, so sez I "Old Abe, ahoy! Let out yer main-suls, reef hum the fore-castle & throw yer jib-poop overboard! Shiver my timbers, my harty!" (N. B. This is ginuine mariner langwidge. I know, becawz I've seen sailor plays acted out by them New York theater fellers.) Old Abe lookt up quite cross & sez, "Send in yer petition by & by. I can't possibly look at it now. Indeed, I can't. It's onpossible sir!"

"Mr. Linkin, who do you spect I air?" sed I.

"A orfice-seeker, to be sure?" sed he.

"Wall, sir," sed I, "you s never more mistaken in your life. You hain't gut a orfiss I'd take under no circumstances. I'm A. Ward. Wax figgers is my perfeshun. I'm the father of Twins, and they look like me—*both of them.* I cum to pay a friendly visit to the President eleck of the United States. If so be you wants to see me say so—if not, say so, & I'm orf like a jug handle."

"Mr. Ward, sit down. I am glad to see you, Sir."

"Repose in Abraham's Buzzum!" sed one of the orfice seekers, his idee bein to git orf a goak at my expense.

"Wall," sez I, "ef all you fellers repose in that there Buzzum thare'll be mity poor nussin for sum of you!" whereupon Old Abe buttoned his weskit clear up and blusht like a maidin of sweet 16. Jest at this pint of the conversation another swarm of orfice-seekers arrove & cum pilin into the parler. Sum wanted post orfices, sum wanted collectorships, sum wantid furrin missions, and all wanted sumthin. I thought Old Abe would go crazy. He hadn't more than had time to shake hands with 'em, before another tremenjis crowd cum porein onto his premises. His house and dooryard was now perfeckly overflowed with orfice seekers, all clameruss for a immejit interview with Old Abe. One man from Ohio, who had about seven inches of corn whiskey into him, mistook me for Old Abe and addrest me as "The Prahayrie Flower of the West!" Thinks I *you* want a offiss putty bad. Another man with a gold heded cane and a red nose told Old Abe he was "a seckind Washington & the Pride of the Boundliss West."

Sez I, "Squire, you wouldn't take a small post-offis if you could git it, would you?"

Sez he, "a patrit is abuv them things, sir!"

"There's a putty big crop of patrits this season, aint there Squire?" sez I, when *another* crowd of offiss seekers pored in. The house, door-yard, barn & woodshed was now all full, and when *another* crowd cum I told 'em not to go away for want of room as the hog pen was still empty. One patrit from a small town in Michygan went up on top the house, got into the chimney and slid down into the parler where Old Abe was endeverin to keep the hungry pack of orfice-seekers from chawin him up alive without benefit of clergy. The minit he reached the fire-place he jumpt up, brusht the soot out of his eyes, and yelled: "Don't make any pintment at the Spunkville postoffiss till you've read my papers. All the respectful men in our town is signers to that there dockyment!"

"Good God!" cride Old Abe, "they cum upon me from the skize—down the chimneys, and from the bowels of the yearth!" He hadn't more'n got them words out of his delikit mouth before two fat offiss-seekers from Wisconsin, in endeverin to crawl atween his legs for the purpuss of applyin for the tollgateship at Milwawky, upsot the President eleck & he would hev gone sprawlin into the fire-place if I hadn't caught him in these arms. But I hadn't morn'n stood him up strate before another man cum crashin down the chimney, his head strikin me vilently agin the inards and prostratin my voluptoous form onto the floor. "Mr. Linkin," shoutid the infatooated being, "my papers is signed by every clergyman in our town, and likewise the skoolmaster!"

Sez I, "you egrejis ass," gittin up & brushin the dust from my eyes, "I'll sign your papers with this bunch of bones, if you don't be a little more keerful how you make my bread basket a depot in the futer. How do you like that air perfumery?" sez I, shuving my fist under his nose. "Them's the kind of papers I'll giv you! Them's the papers *you* want!"

"But I workt hard for the ticket; I toiled night and day! The patrit should be rewarded!"

"Virtoo," sed I, holdin' the infatooated man by the coat-collar, "virtoo, sir, is its own reward. Look at me!" He did look at me, and qualed be4 my gaze. "The fact is," I continued, lookin' round on the hungry crowd, "there is scarcely a offiss for every ile lamp carrid round durin' this campane. I wish thare was. I wish thare was furrin missions to be filled on varis lonely Islands where eppydemics rage incessantly, and if I was in Old Abe's place I'd send every mother's son of you to them. What air you here for?" I continnered, warmin up considerable, "can't you giv Abe a minit's peace? Don't you see he's worrid most to death! Go home, you miserable men, go home & till the sile! Go to peddlin tinware—go to choppin wood—go to bilin' sope—stuff sassengers—black boots—git a clerkship on sum respectable manure cart—go round as original Swiss Bell Ringers—becum 'origenal and only' Campbell Minstrels—go to lecturin at 50 dollars a nite—inbark in the peanut bizniss—*write for the Ledger*—saw off your legs and go round givin concerts, with techin appeals to a charitable public, printed on your handbills—anything for a honest living, but don't come round here drivin Old Abe crazy by your outrajis cuttings up! Go home. Stand not upon the order of your goin', but go to onct! If in five minits from this time," sez I pullin' out my new sixteen dollar huntin cased watch, and brandishin' it before their eyes, "Ef in five minits from this time a single sole of you remains on these here premises, I'll go out to my cage near by, and let my Boy Constructor loose! & ef he gits amung you, you'll think old Solferino has cum again and no mistake!" You ought to hev seen them scamper, Mr. Fair. They run orf as tho Satun his self was arter them with a red hot pronged pitchfork. In five minits the premisis was clear.

"How kin I ever repay you, Mr. Ward, for your kindness?" sed Old Abe, advancin and shakin me warmly by the hand. "How kin I ever repay you, sir?"

"By givin the whole country a good, sound administration. By poerin' ile upon the troubled waturs, North and South. By pursooin' a patriotic, firm, and just course, and then if any State wants to secede, let 'em Sesesh!"

"How 'bout my Cabinit, Mister Ward?" sed Abe.

"Fill it up with Showmen sir! Showmen is devoid of politics. They hain't got any principles! They know how to cater for the public. They know what the public wants, North & South. Showmen, sir, is honest men. Ef you doubt their literary ability, look at their posters, and see small bills! Ef you want a Cabinit as is a Cabinit fill it up with showmen, but don't call on me. The moral wax figger perfeshun musn't be permitted to go down while there's a drop of blood in these vains! A. Linkin, I wish you well! Ef Powers or Walcutt wus to pick out a model for a beautiful man, I scarcely think they'd sculp you; but ef you do the fair thing by your country you'll make as putty a angel as any of us! A. Linkin, use the talents which Nature has put into you judishusly and firmly, and all will be well! A. Linkin, adoo!"

He shook me cordyully by the hand—we exchanged picters, so we could gaze upon each others' liniments when far away from one another—he at the hellum of the ship of State, and I at the hellum of the show bizniss—admittance only 15 cents.

DAVID ROSS LOCKE

(1833–1888)

David Ross Locke was a New Yorker who achieved his fame as a political humorist through the character of Petroleum V. Nasby, a rogue who mimicked all institutions. Charles Sumner valued the papers of Petroleum V. Nasby, and Abraham Lincoln so admired this work that he was reported to have said, "For the genius to write these things, I would gladly give up my office."

From Letters of Petroleum V. Nasby

SHOWS WHY HE SHOULD NOT BE DRAFTED[1]

August the 6th, 1862.

I see in the papers last nite that the Government hez institooted a draft, and that in a few weeks sum hundreds uv thousands uv peeceable citizens will be dragged to the tented field. I know not wat uthers may do, but ez for me, I cant go. Upon a rigid eggsaminashun uv my fizzleckle man, I find it wood be wus nor madnis for me to undertake a campane, to-wit:—

1. I'm bald-headid, and hev bin obliged to wear a wig these 22 years.
2. I hev dandruff in wat scanty hair still hangs around my venerable temples.
3. I hev a kronic katarr.
4. I hev lost, sence Stanton's order to draft, the use uv wun eye entirely, and hev kronic inflammashen in the other.
5. My teeth is all unsound, my palit aint eggsactly rite, and I hev hed bronkeetis 31 yeres last Joon. At present I hev a koff, the paroxizms uv wich is friteful to behold.
6. I'm holler-chestid, am short-winded, and hev alluz hed pains in my back and side.
7. I am afflictid with kronic diarrear and kostivniss. The money I hev paid (or promist to pay), for Jayneses karminnytiv balsam and pills wood astonish almost enny body.
8. I am rupchered in nine places, and am entirely enveloped with trusses.
9. I hev verrykose vanes, hev a white-swellin on wun leg and a fever sore on the uther; also wun leg is shorter than tother, though I handle it so expert that nobody never noticed it.
10. I hev korns and bunyons on both feet, wich wood prevent me from marchin.

I dont suppose that my political opinions, wich are aginst the prossekoo-shun uv this unconstooshnel war, wood hev any wate, with a draftin orfiser; but the above reesons why I cant go, will, I make no doubt, be suffishent.

PETROLEUM V. NASBY

[1] One of the most surprising results of the conscription was the amount of disease disclosed among men between "eighteen and forty-five," in districts where quotas could not be raised by volunteering. [Locke's note.]

II
The Life of the Imagination

NATHANIEL HAWTHORNE

(1804–1864)

In the eyes of his contemporaries, Hawthorne represented the most accomplished American storyteller and novelist. Edgar Allan Poe questioned Hawthorne's fondness of allegory but recognized the power and clarity of his moral perceptions and, when formulating his famous

The standard edition, though not yet complete, is *The Centenary Edition of the Works of Nathaniel Hawthorne,* ed. William Charvat, Roy Harvey Pearce, and Claude Simpson, textual Editors: Fredson Bowers and Matthew Bruccoli, 1962—.

A valuable though impressionistic account of Hawthorne's life and work is Henry James, *Hawthorne,* 1879. A good early study is George E. Woodberry, *Nathanial Hawthorne,* 1902. The most reliable factual biography is Randall Stewart, *Nathaniel Hawthorne, A Biography,* 1948. Other critical biographies are E. H. Davidson, *Hawthorne's Last Phase,* 1949; Mark Van Doren, *Nathaniel Hawthorne,* 1949, Edward Wagenknecht, *Nathaniel Hawthorne: Man and Writer,* 1961; and Terence Martin, *Nathaniel Hawthorne,* 1965.

Modern criticism of Hawthorne begins with Newton Arvin, *Hawthorne* (1929); Yvor Winters, *Maule's Curse,* 1938; and F. O. Matthiessen, *American Renaissance,* 1941, pp. 179-368. See also Lawrence S. Hall, *Hawthorne, Critic of Society,* 1944; Richard H. Fogle, *Hawthorne's Fiction: The Light and the Dark,* 1952; Hyatt Waggoner, *Hawthorne, A Critical Study,* 1955; Arlin Turner, *Nathaniel Hawthorne,* 1955; Roy R. Male, *Hawthorne's Tragic Vision,* 1957; Harry Levin, *Power of Blackness,* 1960; Hubert H. Hoeltje, *Inward Sky: The Mind and Heart of Nathaniel Hawthorne,* 1962; Millicent Bell, *Hawthorne's View of the Artist,* 1962; Frederic Crews, *The Sins of the Fathers: Hawthorne's Psychological Themes,* 1966; A. N. Kaul, ed., *Hawthorne, A Collection of Critical Essays,* 1966; David Levin, *In Defense of Historical Literature* (1967); Richard H. Brodhead, *Hawthorne, Melville, and the Novel,* 1976; Kenneth Dauber, *Rediscovering Hawthorne,* 1977; Edgar A. Dryden, *Nathaniel Hawthorne: The Poetics of Enchantment,* 1977.

The present texts are taken from the Centenary Edition.

definition of the short story, Poe used *Twice-Told Tales* as his example. Herman Melville was deeply indebted to Hawthorne as the first American writer to develop a mature vision of tragedy and evil, and he admired the older author for his ability to say "No, in thunder," for his "great power of blackness" that "derives its force from its appeal to that Calvinistic sense of Innate Depravity and Original Sin." After the Civil War, Henry James spoke for his generation when he characterized Hawthorne as "the greatest imaginative writer we have" and stressed Hawthorne's remarkable success in transcending the cultural limitations of provincial New England and discovering, in his own Puritan heritage, the social texture necessary for enduring literature. Throughout the subsequent history of American literary criticism, Hawthorne has maintained his solid reputation as the first distinctively American writer to draw on the American past, to explore the individual conscience in its struggle with sin and guilt and evil, and to create a small but impressive group of stories and novels, which are still compelling to readers as dark allegories of man's inhumanity to man.

Born on July 4, 1804, in Salem, Massachusetts, Hawthorne spent his early years with his mother and two sisters. His father, who was a sea captain, died in 1808, in Surinam, Dutch Guinea, while on a long voyage, and young Hawthorne grew up in a small house on Herbert Street, exposed to his mother's grief and solitude. He attended the local schools until he was admitted to Bowdoin College in 1821. At Bowdoin, where he was only an average student, he became a classmate of Franklin Pierce, the future president, and Henry Wadsworth Longfellow. After his graduation in 1825, Hawthorne returned to Salem, and lived in the seclusion of his mother's home for the next 12 years in what he called his haunted chamber. "This deserves to be called a haunted chamber," he wrote his future wife, Sophia Peabody, "for thousands upon thousands of visions have appeared to me in it; and some few of them have become visible to the world. If ever I should have a biographer, he ought to make great mention of this chamber in my memoirs, because so much of my lonely youth was wasted here, and here my mind and character were formed."

Hawthorne grew up in a country without a significant literature from which to develop his own artistic vision. It was natural that his first novel, *Fanshawe* (1828), should be a sentimental Gothic romance of pursuit and flight, since the tradition was well-established in England and Hawthorne accepted it as the simplest way of establishing himself as an author. He was never proud of *Fanshawe,* however, and attempted to suppress all available copies.

At the same time that he published *Fanshawe,* Hawthorne was creating the short stories on which his originality was based: "My Kinsman, Major Molineux," "The Gentle Boy," "The Gray Champion," "The Maypole of Merrymount," "Wakefield," and many others. From 1825 to 1832, in his haunted chamber, Hawthorne read extensively in Puritan history and came to know the experiences of his own family. His earliest American ancestor, William Hawthorne, had settled in Salem in 1637 and became well-known as a legislator, magistrate, Indian fighter, explorer, and as a bitter persecutor of innocent Quakers. "I know not whether these ancestors of mine bethought themselves to repent," Hawthorne wrote later in his life, "and ask pardon of Heaven for their cruelties; or whether they are now groaning under the heavy consequences of them, in another state of being. At all events, I, the present writer, as their representative, hereby take shame upon myself for their sakes, and pray that any curse incurred by them. . . may be now and henceforth removed."

Hawthorne published *Twice-Told Tales* in 1837 and, though the volume did not achieve great popularity, it did receive high critical acclaim from sophisticated readers; he had opened, in his own phrase, "an intercourse with the world." At the same time, Hawthorne had become engaged to Sophia Peabody of Salem and Boston, and sought to establish himself economically so that he could marry her. From 1839 to 1841 he worked as a measurer of salt and coal at the Boston custom house and then in April 1841, went to live at Brook Farm in West Roxbury, Massachusetts. He bought $1000 worth of stock in the cooperative and joined the socialist experiment, living among transcendentalists and other reformers who wished to prove that work need not be meaningless. But Hawthorne found farming dull and the cerebral socialists a trifle absurd as they struggled clumsily with their hands; he left Brook Farm in November. A decade later, he satirized the utopian experiment and transcendentalism generally in *The Blithedale Romance* (1852).

In the summer of 1842, Hawthorne married Sophia Peabody, and they settled in the Old Manse in Concord, where Emerson had lived for a brief time and written *Nature*. Although his fiction was published frequently during these years, Hawthorne could not earn enough money from his writing, and he accepted a political appointment from Massachusetts Democrats as a surveyor in the Salem custom house. In 1846 he published *Mosses from an Old Manse,* which included subtle psychological stories such as "Young Goodman Brown" and "Roger Malvin's Burial"; and after he lost his position as surveyor because of the Whig political victory, he devoted himself to full-time writing. Within a short period of time he produced a cluster of books that established him as the leading American fictionist: *The Scarlet Letter* (1850); *The House of the Seven Gables* (1851); *The Snow Image* and *The Twice-Told Tales* (1851); *The Blithedale Romance* (1852); *A Won-*

der Book for Girls and Boys (1852); and *Tanglewood Tales for Girls and Boys* (1853). This burst of creativity was the climax of Hawthorne's career; he did write one final novel, *The Marble Faun* (1860) but, for the most part, his later years were spent as a consul at Liverpool from 1853 to 1857—an appointment made possible by the election of his friend Franklin Pierce to the presidency—and in an attempt to complete several different romances: *Dr. Grimshawe's Secret, The Ancestral Footstep, Septimius Felton,* and *The Dolliver Romance.* Hawthorne died in 1864, a literary figure celebrated for a group of short stories— "Young Goodman Brown," "Roger Malvin's Burial," "My Kinsman, Major Molineux," "The Minister's Black Veil," "Ethan Brand," "Rappaccini's Daughter," "The Birthmark," and a few others—and *The Scarlet Letter* and *The House of the Seven Gables.*

This small body of work represents the first attempt of an American novelist and storyteller to formulate a vision of tragedy and evil in terms of his native history. The dominant intellectual currents of the time stressed those affirmative aspects of man's nature that made Calvinism seem an outworn religion; Hawthorne also regarded Puritan society with a jaundiced and critical eye, but he never repudiated the concept of original sin and man's propensity to evil. He criticized the transcendentalists and well-intentioned reformers in works like "The Celestial Railroad," "Earth's Holocaust," and *The Blithedale Romance,* regarding the transcendentalists as naively oblivious to sin and guilt, the reformers as people who failed to acknowledge the frailty of each individual person and who, in extreme moments, attempted to manipulate others to their will. In *The Scarlet Letter* and "Young Goodman Brown," he censured the Puritans for their unyielding and self-righteous judgment and for the imposition of their imperious will on the individual person. Indeed, the desire of a society or of an individual to manipulate the will of another, which takes the form of overweening pride, is the cardinal sin in Hawthorne's moral universe and a dominant theme in his art.

In the sermons of the Puritan ministers, Hawthorne found a deep concern with man's tragic condition—sin and evil, guilt and pride mark the writings of Cotton Mather and Jonathan Edwards—but little concern with the individual and the psychological consequences of his sinful nature. Hawthorne created a framework of tragedy, in which he explored the conscience of an isolated person as it responded to evil. Drawing on native materials, he did not create tragedy in the Aristotelian sense: his "heroes" are not princes or kings but ministers like the Reverend Dimmesdale in *The Scarlet Letter* or, more often, ordinary people like Young Goodman Brown, Robin Molineux, and Reuben Bourne. The tragedy in a Hawthorne tale is never completely comprehended by the central character, partially because he is not a large heroic figure with a deeper insight into human nature, partially because Hawthorne refused to enter too deeply into the personality of the individual. One never knows the inner life of a Hawthorne character or his daily existence, as one might in a realistic work of fiction; the character is often a type rather than a person, projected in a symbolic tale that always has a moral point to make. He shared with Emerson and the transcendentalists, Poe, and Melville a symbolic frame of mind, and he grappled with the same themes that obsessed them: self-reliance and self-reform; the correspondences between physical and human nature; and the significance of solitude and the individual's relationship to others. From one point of view, Hawthorne's fiction is a sharp critique of transcendentalism in that he questioned excessive reliance on the self and stressed the need for reformation of the individual person before grandiose social schemes were contemplated.

Yet Hawthorne should not be considered as only a symbolist or fabulist, an author who created moral tales that are somber commentaries on man's imperfect condition. He was also a shrewd observer of his contemporary scene, and he often betrayed a playful turn of mind in sketches like "A Rill from the Town Pump," "Sunday at Home," "The Toll Gatherer's Day," and "Birds and Bird Voices." Were we to become readers of Hawthorne's own time, an audience accustomed to the light essays of Irving or the casual observations of Nathaniel P. Willis and James Kirke Paulding, we would be struck by the pervasive presence of whimsy, of comic attitudes, of absurdity in Hawthorne's work. As Henry James reminds us, Hawthorne had, in early nineteenth-century America, "no Oxford, nor Eton, nor Harrow; no literature, no novels, museums, no pictures, no political society, no sporting class—no Epsom nor Ascot!"; and the thin texture of his social world—expressed in sketches like "Main Street," "Sights from a Steeple," "Little Annie's Ramble," "David Swan," and "Snow Flakes"—suggests why he needed the symbolic or allegoric tale when he wished to view the tragic frailties of man and why for him allegory was not a "lighter exercise of the imagination."

However tragic the situations in his fiction may be, Hawthorne always introduces a note of absurdity that prevents his "heroes" from ever being fully tragic: Robin Molineux is mocked and self-mocking; Goodman Brown is a "stern, a sad, a darkly meditative, distrustful" person who does not understand his tragedy; Wakefield carries a crafty smile toward everyone. Even in his most elaborate attempt at creating tragedy, *The Scarlet Letter,* Hawthorne checks himself. "Be true! Be true!" his moral reads. "Show finally to the world, if not your worst, yet some trait whereby the worst may be inferred!"

Hawthorne did not confront the tragic situations in his fiction directly but drew inferences from them. In addition to being a latter-day Puritan, a man absorbed with the history of his ancestors, an author

who brooded over such human conditions as evil, sin, guilt, and isolation, Hawthorne held an an ironic view of man's behavior that prevented him from creating an awesome tragic hero like Ahab in *Moby
Dick*. His prose is classically clear, his view of life ambiguously dark;
his characters are symbolically projected, yet human in their realistic
and often absurd limitations; his subject is the conscience of man as it
reflects on sin, yet he refrains from probing the guilt in too personal a
fashion; he is our first important writer to give imaginative force to our
historical past and creates the illusion of objectivity, yet his view of
Puritanism is partial, colored by the legacy of family guilt; he writes
dark tragedies, but he streaks his stories with an irony and satire that
humble man and remind him of his absurd condition. Caught in these
many paradoxes, Hawthorne created an impressive body of fiction—
inescapably American in its setting and characteristics, but broader
than any national boundaries in its concern with the nature of evil and
sin and guilt.

From the many paradoxes of his art emerges the recurrent theme
that connects Hawthorne with his contemporaries and with ourselves:
the evil inherent in any person's attempt to manipulate another. He
believed that each person must discover his own uniqueness, but reliance on the self must never be at the expense of others—therein lies
the sin of pride. He shared the democratic notion that man must always be a social self and retain his balance by respecting others.
Throughout his fiction, one finds a commentary on the excesses of
self-reliance and pride. He took his readers into the symbolic reaches
of romance, but he never forgot—nor allowed his readers to forget—
the separate person fixed in a moment of history, in a realistic place, in
situations that reminded him of his human limitations.

My Kinsman, Major Molineux[1]

After the kings of Great Britain had assumed the right of appointing the
colonial governors, the measures of the latter seldom met with the ready and
generous approbation which had been paid to those of their predecessors,

[1] This story was first published in *The Token* for 1832 and was included in a volume of tales, *The Snow Image* (1852). Many of Hawthorne's favorite themes are reflected in "My Kinsman, Major Molineux": the initiation into evil; the limitations of self-reliance; the corrosive results of one man's attempted manipulation of another; the effects of sin on human nature; the insidious manifestations of guilt; the isolation of human beings from one another. Hawthorne uses an allegorical technique in which Good and Evil, man and the devil, light and darkness are juxtaposed. But he does not resort solely to allegory; he places his tale in the historical context of eighteenth-century New England and underscores the conflicts between the colonists and the Crown governor.

under the original charters. The people looked with most jealous scrutiny to the exercise of power which did not emanate from themselves, and they usually rewarded their rulers with slender gratitude for the compliances by which, in softening their instructions from beyond the sea, they had incurred the reprehension of those who gave them. The annals of Massachusetts Bay will inform us, that of six governors in the space of about forty years from the surrender of the old charter, under James II., two were imprisoned by a popular insurrection; a third, as Hutchinson[2] inclines to believe, was driven from the province by the whizzing of a musket-ball; a fourth, in the opinion of the same historian, was hastened to his grave by continual bickerings with the House of Representatives; and the remaining two, as well as their successors, till the revolution, were favored with few and brief intervals of peaceful sway.[3] The inferior members of the court party, in times of high political excitement, led scarcely a more desirable life. These remarks may serve as a preface to the following adventures, which chanced upon a summer night, not far from a hundred years ago. The reader, in order to avoid a long and dry detail of colonial affairs, is requested to dispense with an account of the train of circumstances that had caused much temporary inflammation of the popular mind.

It was near nine o'clock of a moonlight evening, when a boat crossed the ferry with a single passenger, who had obtained his conveyance at that unusual hour by the promise of an extra fare. While he stood on the landing-place, searching in either pocket for the means of fulfilling his agreement, the ferryman lifted a lantern, by the aid of which, and the newly risen moon, he took a very accurate survey of the stranger's figure. He was a youth of barely eighteen years, evidently country-bred, and now, as it should seem, upon his first visit to town. He was clad in a coarse gray coat, well worn, but in excellent repair; his under garments were durably constructed of leather, and fitted tight to a pair of serviceable and well-shaped limbs; his stockings of blue yarn were the incontrovertible work of a mother or a sister; and on his head was a three-cornered hat, which in its better days had perhaps sheltered the graver brow of the lad's father. Under his left arm was a heavy cudgel formed of an oak sapling, and retaining a part of the hardened root; and his equipment was completed by a wallet, not so abundantly stocked as to incommode the vigorous shoulders on which it hung. Brown, curly hair,

---

[2] Thomas Hutchinson (1711–1780) was the last royal governor (1771–1774) and the author of *The History of the Colony of Massachusetts Bay.*

[3] The people of Massachusetts appealed to the charter and wished to control the colonial governors who were appointed by the Crown; but the Crown annulled the Massachusetts charter in 1684. "The six governors who followed each other "in the space of about forty years" were Simon Bradstreet (1679–1686, 1689–1692), Sir Edmund Andros (1686–1689), Sir William Phips (1692–1694), Richard Coote, Earl of Bellomont (1697–1700), Joseph Dudley (1702–1715), and Samuel Shute (1716–1722). Hawthorne uses Hutchinson's volume as his authority.

well-shaped features, and bright, cheerful eyes were nature's gifts, and worth all that art could have done for his adornment.

The youth, one of whose names was Robin, finally drew from his pocket the half of a little province bill of five shillings, which, in the depreciation in that sort of currency, did but satisfy the ferryman's demand, with the surplus of a sexangular piece of parchment, valued at three pence. He then walked forward into the town, with as light a step as if his day's journey had not already exceeded thirty miles, and with as eager an eye as if he were entering London city, instead of the little metropolis of a New England colony. Before Robin had proceeded far, however, it occured to him that he knew not whither to direct his steps; so he paused, and looked up and down the narrow street, scrutinizing the small and mean wooden buildings that were scattered on either side.

"This low hovel cannot be my kinsman's dwelling," thought he, "nor yonder old house, where the moonlight enters at the broken casement; and truly I see none hereabouts that might be worthy of him. It would have been wise to inquire my way of the ferryman, and doubtless he would have gone with me, and earned a shilling from the Major for his pains. But the next man I meet will do as well."

He resumed his walk, and was glad to perceive that the street now became wider, and the houses more respectable in their appearance. He soon discerned a figure moving on moderately in advance, and hastened his steps to overtake it. As Robin drew nigh, he saw that the passenger was a man in years, with a full periwig of gray hair, a wide-skirted coat of dark cloth, and silk stockings rolled above the knees. He carried a long and polished cane, which he struck down perpendicularly before him at every step; and at regular intervals he uttered two successive hems, of a peculiarly solemn and sepulchral intonation. Having made these observations, Robin laid hold of the skirt of the old man's coat, just when the light from the open door and windows of a barber's shop fell upon both their figures.

"Good evening to you, honored sir," said he, making a low bow, and still retaining his hold of the skirt. "I pray you tell me whereabouts is the dwelling of my kinsman, Major Molineux."

The youth's question was uttered very loudly; and one of the barbers, whose razor was descending on a well soaped chin, and another who was dressing a Ramillies wig,[4] left their occupations, and came to the door. The citizen, in the mean time, turned a long-favored countenance upon Robin, and answered him in a tone of excessive anger and annoyance. His two sepulchral hems, however, broke into the very centre of his rebuke, with

---

[4] A wig named after Ramillies, Belgium; it is a plaited wig, with a bow of ribbon tied at the top and bottom.

most singular effect, like a thought of the cold grave obtruding among wrathful passions.

"Let go my garment, fellow! I tell you, I know not the man you speak of. What! I have authority, I have—hem, hem—authority; and if this be the respect you show for your betters, your feet shall be brought acquainted with the stocks by daylight, tomorrow morning!"

Robin released the old man's skirt, and hastened away, pursued by an ill-mannered roar of laughter from the barber's shop. He was at first considerably surprised by the result of his question, but, being a shrewd youth, soon thought himself able to account for the mystery.

"This is some country representative," was his conclusion, "who has never seen the inside of my kinsman's door, and lacks the breeding to answer a stranger civilly. The man is old, or verily—I might be tempted to turn back and smite him on the nose. Ah, Robin, Robin! even the barber's boys laugh at you for choosing such a guide! You will be wiser in time, friend Robin."

He now became entangled in a succession of crooked and narrow streets, which crossed each other, and meandered at no great distance from the water-side. The smell of tar was obvious to his nostrils, the masts of vessels pierced the moonlight above the tops of the buildings, and the numerous signs, which Robin paused to read, informed him that he was near the centre of business. But the streets were empty, the shops were closed, and lights were visible only in the second stories of a few dwelling houses. At length, on the corner of a narrow lane, through which he was passing, he beheld the broad countenance of a British hero swinging before the door of an inn, whence proceeded the voices of many guests. The casement of one of the lower windows was thrown back, and a very thin curtain permitted Robin to distinguish a party at supper, round a well-furnished table. The fragrance of the good cheer steamed forth into the outer air, and the youth could not fail to recollect that the last remnant of his travelling stock of provision had yielded to his morning appetite, and that noon had found and left him dinnerless.

"Oh, that a parchment three-penny might give me a right to sit down at yonder table!" said Robin, with a sigh. "But the Major will make me welcome to the best of his victuals; so I will even step boldly in, and inquire my way to his dwelling."

He entered the tavern, and was guided by the murmur of voices and the fumes of tobacco to the public-room. It was a long and low apartment, with oaken walls, grown dark in the continual smoke, and a floor which was thickly sanded, but of no immaculate purity. A number of persons—the larger part of whom appeared to be mariners, or in some way connected with the sea—occupied the wooden benches, or leather bottomed chairs, conversing on various matters, and occasionally by lending their attention to some topic of general interest. Three or four little groups were draining as many bowls of punch, which the West India trade had long since made a familiar drink in the colony. Others, who had the appearance of men who lived by regular and laborious handicraft, preferred the insulated bliss of an unshared potation, and became more taciturn under its influence. Nearly all, in short, evinced a predilection for the Good Creature in some of its various shapes, for this is a vice to which, as Fast Day sermons of a hundred years ago will testify,[5] we have a long hereditary claim. The only guests to whom Robin's sympathies inclined him were two or three sheepish countrymen, who were using the inn somewhat after the fashion of a Turkish caravansary; they had gotten themselves into the darkest corner of the room, and heedless of the Nicotian[6] atmosphere, were supping on the bread of their own ovens, and the bacon cured in their own chimney-smoke. But though Robin felt a sort of brotherhood with these strangers, his eyes were attracted from them to a person who stood near the door, holding whispered conversation with a group of ill-dressed associates. His features were separately striking almost to grotesqueness, and the whole face left a deep impression on the memory. The forehead bulged out into a double prominence, with a vale between; the nose came boldly forth in an irregular curve, and its bridge was of more than a finger's breadth; the eyebrows were deep and shaggy, and the eyes glowed beneath them like fire in a cave.

While Robin deliberated of whom to inquire respecting his kinsman's dwelling, he was accosted by the innkeeper, a little man in a stained white apron, who had come to pay his professional welcome to the stranger. Being in a second generation from a French Protestant, he seemed to have inherited the courtesy of his parent nation; but no variety of circumstances was ever known to change his voice from the one shrill note in which he now addressed Robin.

"From the country, I presume, sir?" said he, with a profound bow. "Beg leave to congratulate you on your arrival, and trust you intend a long stay with us. Fine town here, sir, beautiful buildings, and much that may interest a stranger. May I hope for the honor of your commands in respect to supper?"

"The man sees a family likeness! the rogue has guessed that I am related to the Major!" thought Robin, who had hitherto experienced little superfluous civility.

All eyes were now turned on the country lad, standing at the door, in his worn three-cornered hat, gray coat, leather breeches, and blue yarn stockings, leaning on an oaken cudgel, and bearing a wallet on his back.

Robin replied to the couteous innkeeper, with such an assumption of confidence as befitted the Major's relative. "My honest friend," he said, "I shall make it a point to patronize your house on some occasion, when"—here

---

[5] The addresses delivered by the New England clergy on special days of public penance.

[6] The air of "nicotiana," that is, nicotine or tobacco.

he could not help lowering his voice—"when, I may have more than a parchment three-pence in my pocket. My present business," continued he, speaking with lofty confidence, "is merely to inquire my way to the dwelling of my kinsman, Major Molineux."

There was a sudden and general movement in the room, which Robin interpreted as expressing the eagerness of each individual to become his guide. But the innkeeper turned his eyes to a written paper on the wall, which he read, or seemed to read, with occasional recurrences to the young man's figure.

"What have we here?" said he, breaking his speech into little dry fragments. " 'Left the house of the subscriber, bounden servant,[7] Hezekiah Mudge,—had on, when he went away, gray coat, leather breeches, master's third-best hat. One pound currency reward to whosoever shall lodge him in any jail of the providence.' Better trudge, boy; better trudge!"

Robin had begun to draw his hand towards the lighter end of the oak cudgel, but a strange hostility in every countenance induced him to relinguish his purpose of breaking the courteous innkeeper's head. As he turned to leave the room, he encountered a sneering glance from the bold-featured personage whom he had before noticed; and no sooner was he beyond the door, than he heard a general laugh, in which the innkeeper's voice might be distinguished, like the dropping of small stones into a kettle.

"Now, is it not strange," thought Robin, with his usual shrewdness,—"is it not strange that the confession of an empty pocket should outweigh the name of my kinsman, Major Molineux? Oh, if I had one of those grinning rascals in the woods, where I and my oak sapling grew up together, I would teach him that my arm is heavy though my purse be light!"

On turning the corner of the narrow lane, Robin found himself in a spacious street, with an unbroken line of lofty houses on each side, and a steepled building at the upper end, whence the ringing of a bell announced the hour of nine. The light of the moon, and the lamps from the numerous shop-windows, discovered people promenading on the pavement, and amongst them Robin had hoped to recognize his hitherto inscrutable relative. The result of his former inquiries made him unwilling to hazard another, in a scene of such publicity, and he determined to walk slowly and silently up the street, thrusting his face close to that of every elderly gentleman, in search of the Major's lineaments. In his progress, Robin encountered many gay and gallant figures. Embroidered garments of showy colors, enormous periwigs, gold-laced hats, and silver-hilted swords glided past him and dazzled his optics. Travelled youths, imitators of the European fine gentlemen of the period, trod jauntily along, half dancing to the fashionable tunes

---

[7] An indentured servant who served his master for seven years before being granted his freedom.

which they hummed, and making poor Robin ashamed of his quiet and natural gait. At length, after many pauses to examine the gorgeous display of goods in the shop-windows, and after suffering some rebukes for the impertinence of his scrutiny into people's faces, the Major's kinsman found himself near the steepled building, still unsuccessful in his search. As yet, however, he had seen only one side of the thronged street; so Robin crossed, and continued the same sort of inquisition down the opposite pavement, with stronger hopes than the philosopher seeking an honest man, but with no better fortune. He had arrived about midway towards the lower end, from which his course began, when he overheard the approach of some one who struck down a cane on the flagstones at every step, uttering at regular intervals, two sepulchral hems.

"Mercy on us!" quoth Robin, recognizing the sound.

Turning a corner, which chanced to be close at his right hand, he hastened to pursue his researches in some other part of the town. His patience now was wearing low, and he seemed to feel more fatigue from his rambles since he crossed the ferry, than from his journey of several days on the other side. Hunger also pleaded loudly within him, and Robin began to balance the propriety of demanding, violently, and with lifted cudgel, the necessary guidance from the first solitary passenger whom he should meet. While a resolution to this effect was gaining strength, he entered a street of mean appearance, on either side of which a row of ill-built houses was straggling towards the harbor. The moonlight fell upon no passenger along the whole extent, but in the third domicile which Robin passed there was a half-opened door, and his keen glance detected a woman's garment within.

"My luck may be better here," said he to himself.

Accordingly, he approached the door, and beheld it shut closer as he did so; yet an open space remained, sufficing for the fair occupant to observe the stranger, without a corresponding display on her part. All that Robin could discern was a strip of scarlet petticoat, and the occasional sparkle of an eye, as if the moonbeams were trembling on some bright thing.

"Pretty mistress," for I may call her so with a good conscience, thought the shrewd youth, since I know nothing to the contrary,—"my sweet pretty mistress, will you be kind enough to tell me whereabouts I must seek the dwelling of my kinsman, Major Molineux?"

Robin's voice was plaintive and winning, and the female, seeing nothing to be shunned in the handsome country youth, thrust open the door, and came forth into the moonlight. She was a dainty little figure, with a white neck, round arms, and a slender waist, at the extremity of which her scarlet petticoat jutted out over a hoop, as if she were standing in a balloon. Moreover, her face was oval and pretty, her hair dark beneath the little cap, and her bright eyes possessed a sly freedom, which triumphed over those of Robin.

"Major Molineux dwells here," said this fair woman.

Now, her voice was the sweetest Robin had heard that night, yet he could not help doubting whether that sweet voice spoke Gospel truth. He looked up and down the mean street, and then surveyed the house before which they stood. It was a small, dark edifice of two stories, the second of which projected over the lower floor, and the front apartment had the aspect of a shop for petty commodities.

"Now, truly, I am in luck," replied Robin, cunningly, "and so indeed is my kinsman, the Major, in having so pretty a housekeeper. But I prithee trouble him to step to the door; I will deliver him a message from his friends in the country, and then go back to my lodgings at the inn."

"Nay, the Major has been abed this hour or more," said the lady of the scarlet petticoat; "and it would be to little purpose to disturb him to-night, seeing his evening draught was of the strongest. But he is a kind-hearted man, and it would be as much as my life's worth to let a kinsman of his turn away from the door. You are the good old gentleman's very picture, and I could swear that was his rainy-weather hat. Also he has garments very much resembling those leather small-clothes. But come in, I pray, for I bid you hearty welcome in his name."

So saying, the fair and hospitable dame took our hero by the hand; and the touch was light, and the force was gentleness, and though Robin read in her eyes what he did not hear in her words, yet the slender-waisted woman in the scarlet petticoat proved stronger than the athletic country youth. She had drawn his halfwilling footsteps nearly to the threshold, when the opening of a door in the neighborhood startled the Major's housekeeper, and, leaving the Major's kinsman, she vanished speedily into her own domicile. A heavy yawn preceded the appearance of a man, who, like the Moonshine of Pyramus and Thisbe,[8] carried a lantern, needlessly aiding his sister luminary in the heavens. As he walked sleepily up the street, he turned his broad, dull face on Robin, and displayed a long staff, spiked at the end.

"Home, vagabond, home!" said the watchman, in accents that seemed to fall asleep as soon as they were uttered. "Home, or we'll set you in the stocks by peep of day!"

"This is the second hint of this kind," thought Robin. "I wish they would end my difficulties, by setting me there to-night."

Nevertheless, the youth felt an instinctive antipathy towards the guardian of midnight order, which at first prevented him from asking his usual question. But just when the man was about to vanish behind the corner, Robin resolved not to lose the opportunity, and shouted lustily after him,—

"I say, friend! will you guide me to the house of my kinsman, Major Molineux?"

The watchman made no reply, but turned the corner and was gone; yet

[8] See Shakespeare, *Midsummer Night's Dream*, V, i, 130 ff. The comic characters in this play present the tragedy of "Pyramus and Thisbe."

Robin seemed to hear the sound of drowsy laughter stealing along the solitary street. At that moment, also, a pleasant titter saluted him from the open window above his head; he looked up, and caught the sparkle of a saucy eye; a round arm beckoned to him, and next he heard light footsteps descending the staircase within. But Robin, being of the household of a New England clergyman, was a good youth, as well as a shrewd one; so he resisted temptation, and fled away.

He now roamed desperately, and at random, through the town, almost ready to believe that a spell was on him, like that by which a wizard of his country had once kept three pursuers wandering, a whole winter night, within twenty paces of the cottage which they sought. The streets lay before him, strange and desolate, and the lights were extinguished in almost every house. Twice, however, little parties of men, among whom Robin distinguished individuals in outlandish attire, came hurrying along; but, though on both occasions, they paused to address him, such intercourse did not at all enlighten his perplexity. They did but utter a few words in some language of which Robin knew nothing, and perceiving his inability to answer, bestowed a curse upon him in plain English and hastened away. Finally, the lad determined to knock at the door of every mansion that might appear worthy to be occupied by his kinsman, trusting that perseverance would overcome the fatality that had hitherto thwarted him. Firm in this resolve, he was passing beneath the walls of a church, which formed the corner of two streets, when, as he turned into a shade of its steeple, he encountered a bulky stranger, muffled in a cloak. The man was proceeding with the speed of earnest business, but Robin planted himself full before him, holding the oak cudgel with both hands across his body as a bar to further passage.

"Halt, honest man, and answer me a question," said he, very resolutely. "Tell me, this instant, whereabouts is the dwelling of my kinsman, Major Molineux!"

"Keep your tongue between your teeth, fool, and let me pass!" said a deep, gruff voice, which Robin partly remembered. "Let me pass, or I'll strike you to the earth!"

"No, no, neighbor!" cried Robin, flourishing his cudgel, and then thrusting its larger end close to the man's muffled face. "No, no, I'm not the fool you take me for, nor do you pass till I have an answer to my question. Whereabouts is the dwelling of my kinsman, Major Molineux?"

The stranger, instead of attempting to force his passage, stepped back into the moonlight, unmuffled his face, and stared full into that of Robin.

"Watch here an hour, and Major Molineux will pass by," said he.

Robin gazed with dismay and astonishment on the unprecedented physiognomy of the speaker. The forehead with its double prominence, the broad hooked nose, the shaggy eyebrows, and fiery eyes were those which he had noticed at the inn, but the man's complexion had undergone a singular, or, more properly, a twofold change. One side of the face blazed an intense red, while the other was black as midnight, the division line being in the broad bridge of the nose; and a mouth which seemed to extend from ear to ear was black or red, in contrast to the color of the cheek. The effect was as if two individual devils, a fiend of fire and a fiend of darkness, had united themselves to form this infernal visage. The stranger grinned in Robin's face, muffled his party colored features, and was out of sight in a moment.

"Strange things we travellers see!" ejaculated Robin.

He seated himself, however, upon the steps of the church-door, resolving to wait the appointed time for his kinsman. A few moments were consumed in philosophical speculations upon the species of man who had just left him; but having settled this point shrewdly, rationally, and satisfactorily, he was compelled to look elsewhere for his amusement. And first he threw his eyes along the street. It was of more respectable appearance than most of those into which he had wandered; and the moon, creating, like the imaginative power, a beautiful strangeness in familiar objects, gave something of romance to a scene that might not have possessed it in the light of day. The irregular and often quaint architecture of the houses, some of whose roofs were broken into numerous little peaks, while others ascended, steep and narrow, into a single point, and others again were square; the pure snow-white of some of their complexions, the aged darkness of others, and the thousand sparklings, reflected from bright substances in the walls of many; these matters engaged Robin's attention for a while, and then began to grow wearisome. Next he endeavored to define the forms of distant objects, starting away, with almost ghostly indistinctness, just as his eye appeared to grasp them; and finally he took a minute survey of an edifice which stood on the opposite side of the street, directly in front of the church-door, where he was stationed. It was a large, square mansion, distinguished from its neighbors by a balcony, which rested on tall pillars, and by an elaborate Gothic window, communicating therewith.

"Perhaps this is the very house I have been seeking," thought Robin.

Then he strove to speed away the time, by listening to a murmur which swept continually along the street, yet was scarcely audible, except to an unaccustomed ear like his; it was a low, dull, dreamy sound, compounded of many noises, each of which was at too great a distance to be separately heard. Robin marvelled at this snore of a sleeping town, and marvelled more whenever its continuity was broken by now and then a distant shout, apparently loud where it originated. But altogether it was a sleep-inspiring sound, and, to shake off its drowsy influence, Robin arose, and climbed a window-frame, that he might view the interior of the church. There the moonbeams came trembling in, and fell down upon the deserted pews, and extended along the quiet aisles. A fainter yet more awful radiance was hovering around the pulpit, and one solitary ray had dared to rest upon the open page of the great Bible. Had nature, in that deep hour, become a worshipper in the house which man had builded? Or was that heavenly light the visible sanctity of the place,—visible because no earthly and impure feet were within the walls? The scene made Robin's heart shiver with a sensation of loneliness stronger than he had ever felt in the remotest depths of his native woods; so he turned away and sat down again before the door. There were graves around the church, and now an uneasy thought obtruded into Robin's breast. What if the object of his search, which had been so often and so strangely thwarted, were all the time mouldering in his shroud? What if his kinsman should glide through yonder gate, and nod and smile to him in dimly passing by?

"Oh that any breathing thing were here with me!" said Robin.

Recalling his thoughts from the uncomfortable track, he sent them over forest, hill, and stream, and attempted to imagine how that evening of ambiguity and weariness had been spent by his father's household. He pictured them assembled at the door, beneath the tree, the great old tree, which had been spared for its huge twisted trunk and venerable shade, when a thousand leafy brethren fell. There, at the going down of the summer sun, it was his father's custom to perform domestic worship, that the neighbors might come and join with him like brothers of the family, and that the wayfaring man might pause to drink at the fountain, and keep his heart pure by freshening the memory of home. Robin distinguished the seat of every individual of the little audience; he saw the good man in the midst, holding the Scriptures in the golden light that fell from the western clouds; he beheld him close the book and all rise up to pray. He heard the old thanksgivings for daily mercies, the old supplications for their continuance, to which he had so often listened in weariness, but which were now among his dear remembrances. He perceived the slight inequality of his father's voice when he came to speak of the absent one; he noted how his mother turned her face to the broad and knotted trunk; how his elder brother scorned, because the beard was rough upon his upper lip, to permit his features to be moved; how the younger sister drew down a low hanging branch before her eyes; and how the little one of all, whose sports had hitherto broken the decorum of the scene, understood the prayer for her playmate, and burst into clamorous grief. Then he saw them go in at the door; and when Robin would have entered also, the latch tinkled into its place, and he was excluded from his home.

"Am I here, or there?" cried Robin, starting; for all at once, when his thoughts had become visible and audible in a dream, the long, wide, solitary street shone out before him.

He aroused himself, and endeavored to fix his attention steadily upon the large edifice which he had surveyed before. But still his mind kept vibrating between fancy and reality; by turns, the pillars of the balcony lengthened into the tall, bare stems of pines, dwindled down to human figures, settled again into their true shape and size, and then commenced a new succession of changes. For a single moment, when he deemed himself awake, he could have sworn that a visage—one which he seemed to remember, yet could not absolutely name as his kinsman's—was looking towards him from the Gothic window. A deeper sleep wrestled with and nearly overcame him, but fled at the sound of footsteps along the opposite pavement. Robin rubbed his eyes, discerned a man passing at the foot of the balcony, and addressed him in a loud, peevish, and lamentable cry.

"Hallo, friend! must I wait here all night for my kinsman, Major Molineux?"

The sleeping echoes awoke, and answered the voice; and the passenger, barely able to discern a figure sitting in the oblique shade of the steeple, traversed the street to obtain a nearer view. He was himself a gentleman in the prime, of open, intelligent, cheerful, and altogether prepossessing countenance. Perceiving a country youth, apparently homeless and without friends, he accosted him in a tone of real kindness, which had become strange to Robin's ears.

"Well, my good lad, why are you sitting here?" inquired he. "Can I be of service to you in any way?"

"I am afraid not, sir," replied Robin, despondingly; "yet I shall take it kindly, if you'll answer me a single question. I've been searching, half the night, for one Major Molineux; now, sir, is there really such a person in these parts, or am I dreaming?"

"Major Molineux! The name is not altogether strange to me," said the gentleman, smiling. "Have you any objection to telling me the nature of your business with him?"

Then Robin briefly related that his father was a clergyman, settled on a small salary, at a long distance back in the country, and that he and Major Molineux were brothers' children. The Major, having inherited riches, and acquired civil and military rank, had visited his cousin, in great pomp, a year or two before; had manifested much interest in Robin and an elder brother, and, being childless himself, had thrown out hints respecting the future establishment of one of them in life. The elder brother was destined to succeed to the farm which his father cultivated in the interval of sacred duties; it was therefore determined that Robin should profit by his kinsman's generous intentions, especially as he seemed to be rather the favorite, and was thought to possess other necessary endowments.

"For I have the name of being a shrewd youth," observed Robin, in this part of his story.

"I doubt not you deserve it," replied his new friend, good-naturedly; "but pray proceed."

"Well, sir, being nearly eighteen years old, and well grown, as you see," continued Robin, drawing himself up to his full height, "I thought it high time to begin in the world. So my mother and sister put me in handsome trim, and my father gave me half the remnant of his last year's salary, and five days ago I started for this place, to pay the Major a visit. But, would you believe it, sir! I crossed the ferry a little after dark, and have yet found nobody that would show me the way to his dwelling; only, an hour or two since, I was told to wait here, and Major Molineux would pass by."

"Can you describe the man who told you this?" inquired the gentleman.

"Oh, he was a very ill-favored fellow, sir," replied Robin, "with two great bumps on his forehead, a hook nose, fiery eyes, and, what struck me as the strangest, his face was of two different colors. Do you happen to know such a man, sir?"

"Not intimately," answered the stranger, "but I chanced to meet him a little time previous to your stopping me. I believe you may trust his word, and that the Major will very shortly pass through this street. In the mean time, as I have a singular curiosity to witness your meeting, I will sit down here upon the steps and bear you company."

He seated himself accordingly, and soon engaged his companion in animated discourse. It was but of brief continuance, however, for a noise of shouting, which had long been remotely audible, drew so much nearer that Robin inquired its cause.

"What may be the meaning of this uproar?" asked he. "Truly, if your town be always as noisy, I shall find little sleep while I am an inhabitant."

"Why, indeed, friend Robin, there do appear to be three or four riotous fellows abroad to-night," replied the gentleman. "You must not expect all the stillness of your native woods here in our streets. But the watch will shortly be at the heels of these lads and"—

"Ay, and set them in the stocks by peep of day," interrupted Robin, recollecting his own encounter with the drowsy lanternbearer. "But, dear sir, if I may trust my ears, an army of watchmen would never make head against such a multitude of rioters. There were at least a thousand voices went up to make that one shout."

"May not a man have several voices, Robin, as well as two complexions?" said his friend.

"Perhaps a man may; but Heaven forbid that a woman should!" responded the shrewd youth, thinking of the seductive tones of the Major's housekeeper.

The sounds of a trumpet in some neighboring street now became so evident and continual, that Robin's curiosity was strongly excited. In addition to the shouts, he heard frequent bursts from many instruments of discord, and a wild and confused laughter filled up the intervals. Robin rose from the steps, and looked wistfully towards a point whither people seemed to be hastening.

"Surely some prodigious merry-making is going on," exclaimed he. "I have laughed very little since I left home, sir, and should be sorry to lose an opportunity. Shall we step round the corner by that darkish house, and take our share of the fun?"

"Sit down again, sit down, good Robin," replied the gentleman, laying his hand on the skirt of the gray coat. "You forget that we must wait here for your kinsman; and there is reason to believe that he will pass by, in the course of a very few moments."

The near approach of the uproar had now disturbed the neighborhood; windows flew open on all sides; and many heads, in the attire of the pillow, and confused by sleep suddenly broken, were protruded to the gaze of whoever had leisure to observe them. Eager voices hailed each other from house to house, all demanding the explanation, which not a soul could give. Half-dressed men hurried towards the unknown commotion, stumbling as they went over the stone steps that thrust themselves into the narrow footwalk. The shouts, the laughter, and the tuneless bray, the antipodes of music, came onwards with increasing din, till scattered individuals, and then denser bodies, began to appear round a corner at the distance of a hundred yards.

"Will you recognize your kinsman, if he passes in this crowd?" inquired the gentleman.

"Indeed, I can't warrant it, sir; but I'll take my stand here, and keep a bright lookout," answered Robin, descending to the outer edge of the pavement.

A mighty stream of people now emptied into the street, and came rolling slowly towards the church. A single horseman wheeled the corner in the midst of them, and close behind him came a band of fearful wind-instruments, sending forth a fresher discord now that no intervening building kept it from the ear. Then a redder light disturbed the moonbeams, and a dense multitude of torches shone along the street, concealing, by their glare, whatever object they illuminated. The single horseman, clad in a military dress, and bearing a drawn sword, rode onward as the leader, and, by his fierce and variegated countenance, appeared like war personified; the red of one cheek was an emblem of fire and sword; the blackness of the other betokened the mourning that attends them. In his train were wild figures in the Indian dress, and many fantastic shapes without a model, giving the whole march a visionary air, as if a dream had broken forth from some feverish brain, and were sweeping visibly through the midnight streets. A mass of people, inactive, except as applauding spectators, hemmed the procession in; and several women ran along the sidewalk, piercing the confusion of heavier sounds with their shrill voices of mirth or terror.

"The double-faced fellow has his eye upon me," muttered Robin, with an indefinite but an uncomfortable idea that he was himself to bear a part in the pageantry.

The leader turned himself in the saddle, and fixed his glance full upon the country youth, as the steed went slowly by. When Robin had freed his eyes from those fiery ones, the musicians were passing before him, and the torches were close at hand; but the unsteady brightness of the latter formed a veil which he could not penetrate. The rattling of wheels over the stones sometimes found its way to his ear, and confused traces of a human form appeared at intervals, and then melted into the vivid light. A moment more, and the leader thundered a command to halt: the trumpets vomited a horrid breath, and then held their peace; the shouts and laughter of the people died away, and there remained only a universal hum, allied to silence. Right before Robin's eyes was an uncovered cart. There the torches blazed the brightest, there the moon shone out like day, and there, in tar-and-feathery dignity, sat his kinsman, Major Molineux!

He was an elderly man, of large and majestic person, and strong square features, betokening a steady soul; but steady as it was his enemies had found means to shake it. His face was pale as death, and far more ghastly; the broad forehead was contracted in his agony, so that his eyebrows formed one grizzled line; his eyes were red and wild, and the foam hung white upon his quivering lip. His whole frame was agitated by a quick and continual tremor, which his pride strove to quell, even in those circumstances of overwhelming humiliation. But perhaps the bitterest pang of all was when his eyes met those of Robin; for he evidently knew him on the instant, as the youth stood witnessing the foul disgrace of a head grown gray in honor. They stared at each other in silence, and Robin's knees shook, and his hair bristled, with a mixture of pity and terror. Soon, however, a bewildering excitement began to seize upon his mind; the preceding adventures of the night, the unexpected appearance of the crowd, the torches, the confused din and the hush that followed, the spectre of his kinsman reviled by that great multitude,— all this, and, more than all, a perception of tremendous ridicule in the whole scene, affected him with a sort of mental inebriety. At that moment a voice of sluggish merriment saluted Robin's ears, he turned instinctively, and just behind the corner of the church stood the lantern-bearer, rubbing his eyes, and drowsily enjoying the lad's amazement. Then he heard a peal of laughter like the ringing of silvery bells; a woman twitched his arm, a saucy eye met his, and he saw the lady of the scarlet petticoat. A sharp, dry cachinnation appealed to his memory, and standing on tiptoe in the crowd, with his white apron over his head, he beheld the courteous little innkeeper. And lastly, there sailed over the heads of the multitude a great, broad laugh, broken in the midst by two sepulchral hems; thus, "Haw, haw, haw,—hem, hem,— haw, haw, haw, haw!"

The sound proceeded from the balcony of the opposite edifice, and thither Robin turned his eyes. In front of the Gothic window stood the old citizen, wrapped in a wide gown, his gray periwig exhanged for a nightcap, which was thrust back from his forehead, and his silk stockings hanging about his legs. He supported himself on his polished cane in a fit of convulsive merriment, which manifested itself on his solemn old features like a funny inscription on a tombstone. Then Robin seemed to hear the voices of the barbers, of the guests of the inn, and of all who had made sport of him that night. The contagion was spreading among the multitude, when all at once, it seized upon Robin, and he sent forth a shout of laughter that echoed through the street,—every man shook his sides, every man emptied his lungs, but Robin's shout was the loudest there. The cloud-spirits peeped from their silvery islands, as the congregated mirth went roaring up the sky! The Man in the Moon heard the far bellow. "Oho," quoth he, "the old earth is frolicsome to-night!"

When there was a momentary calm in that tempestuous sea of sound, the leader gave the sign, the procession resumed its march. On they went, like fiends that throng in mockery around some dead potentate, mighty no more, but majestic still in his agony. On they went, in counterfeited pomp, in senseless uproar, in frenzied merriment, trampling all on an old man's heart. On swept the tumult, and left a silent street behind.

·   ·   ·

"Well, Robin, are you dreaming?" inquired the gentleman, laying his hand on the youth's shoulder.

Robin started, and withdrew his arm from the stone post to which he had instinctively clung, as the living stream rolled by him. His cheek was somewhat pale, and his eye not quite as lively as in the earlier part of the evening.

"Will you be kind enough to show me the way to the ferry?" said he, after a moment's pause.

"You have, then, adopted a new subject of inquiry?" observed his companion, with a smile.

"Why, yes, sir," replied Robin, rather dryly. "Thanks to you, and to my other friends, I have at last met my kinsman, and he will scarce desire to see my face again. I begin to grow weary of a town life, sir. Will you show me the way to the ferry?"

"No, my good friend Robin,—not to-night, at least," said the gentleman. "Some few days hence, if you wish it, I will speed you on your journey. Or, if you prefer to remain with us, perhaps, as you are a shrewd youth, you may rise in the world without the help of your kinsman, Major Molineux."

1832, 1851

Young Goodman Brown[1]

Young Goodman Brown[2] came forth at sunset into the street at Salem village; but put his head back, after crossing the threshold, to exchange a parting kiss with his young wife. And Faith, as the wife was aptly named,

---

[1] This story first appeared in the *New England Magazine* (April 1835), and was reprinted in *Mosses from an Old Manse* (1846). The story uses the journey motif most effec-   tively: Young Goodman Brown goes from daylight, reality, piety, and faith into evil and forbidden knowledge—and his guide is Sa-   (Footnote continued next page.)

thrust her own pretty head into the street, letting the wind play with the pink ribbons of her cap while she called to Goodman Brown.

"Dearest heart," whispered she, softly and rather sadly, when her lips were close to his ear, "prithee put off your journey until sunrise and sleep in your own bed to-night. A lone woman is troubled with such dreams and such thoughts that she's afeared of herself sometimes. Pray tarry with me this night, dear husband, of all nights in the year."

"My love and my Faith," replied young Goodman Brown, "of all nights in the year, this one night must I tarry away from thee. My journey, as thou callest it, forth and back again, must needs be done 'twixt now and sunrise. What, my sweet, pretty wife, dost thou doubt me already, and we but three months married?"

"Then God bless you!" said Faith, with the pink ribbons; "and may you find all well when you come back."

"Amen!" cried Goodman Brown. "Say thy prayers, dear Faith, and go to bed at dusk, and no harm will come to thee."

So they parted; and the young man pursued his way until, being about to turn the corner by the meeting house, he looked back and saw the head of Faith still peeping after him with a melancholy air, in spite of her pink ribbons.

"Poor little Faith!" thought he, for his heart smote him, "What a wretch am I to leave her on such an errand! She talks of dreams, too. Methought as she spoke there was trouble in her face, as if a dream had warned her what work is to be done to-night. But no, no; 'twould kill her to think it. Well, she's a blessed angel on earth; and after this one night I'll cling to her skirts and follow her to heaven."

With this excellent resolve for the future, Goodman Brown felt himself justified in making more haste on his present evil purpose. He had taken a dreary road, darkened by all the gloomiest trees of the forest, which barely stood aside to let the narrow path creep through, and closed immediately behind. It was all as lonely as could be; and there is this peculiarity in such a solitude, that the traveller knows not who may be concealed by the innumerable trunks and the thick boughs overhead; so that with lonely footsteps he may yet be passing through an unseen multitude.

"There may be a devilish Indian behind every tree," said Goodman

---

tan, who appears at first in the shape of Brown's grandfather. Hawthorne was particularly interested in witchcraft as a result of his ancestor's involvement in the Salem trials of 1692, and he knew that spectral evidence had been a major issue in those trials, and that convictions had ceased after the court stopped accepting it. The question then was whether the Devil could assume the shape of

an innocent person. Notice how often the characters Brown sees in the forest are described as *figures, shapes, forms*—in seventeenth-century terms, specters.

[2] Hawthorne uses this name to give his central figure a position below that of the gentleman, for whom the term "Mr." would have been designated.

Brown to himself; and he glanced fearfully behind him as he added, "What if the devil himself should be at my very elbow!"

His head being turned back, he passed a crook of the road, and, looking forward again, beheld the figure of a man, in grave and decent attire, seated at the foot of an old tree. He arose at Goodman Brown's approach and walked onward side by side with him.

"You are late, Goodman Brown," said he. "The clock of the Old South was striking as I came through Boston;[3] and that is full fifteen minutes agone."

"Faith kept me back a while," replied the young man, with a tremor in his voice, caused by the sudden appearance of his companion, though not wholly unexpected.

It was now deep dusk in the forest, and deepest in that part of it where these two were journeying. As nearly as could be discerned, the second traveller was about fifty years old, apparently in the same rank of life as Goodman Brown, and bearing a considerable resemblance to him, though perhaps more in expression than features. Still they might have been taken for father and son. And yet, though the elder person was as simply clad as the younger and as simple in manner too, he had an indescribable air of one who knew the world, and who would not have felt abashed at the governor's dinner table or in King William's court,[4] were it possible that his affairs should call him thither. But the only thing about him that could be fixed upon as remarkable was his staff, which bore the likeness of a great black snake, so curiously wrought that it might almost be seen to twist and wriggle itself like a living serpent. This, of course, must have been an ocular deception, assisted by the uncertain light.

"Come, Goodman Brown," cried his fellow-traveller, "this is a dull pace for the beginning of a journey. Take my staff, if you are so soon weary."

"Friend," said the other, exchanging his slow pace for a full stop, "having kept covenant by meeting thee here, it is my purpose now to return whence I came. I have scruples touching the matter thou wot'st of."

"Sayest thou so?" replied he of the serpent, smiling apart. "Let us walk on, nevertheless, reasoning as we go; and if I convince thee not thou shalt turn back. We are but a little way in the forest yet."

"Too far! too far!" exclaimed the goodman, unconsciously resuming his walk. "My father never went into the woods on such an errand, nor his father before him. We have been a race of honest men and good Christians since the days of the martyrs; and shall I be the first of the name of Brown that ever took this path and kept—"

---

[3] The Boston Church which was established in 1669. The "figure" Brown sees has travelled between 20 and 30 miles in 15 minutes.

Notice below that Brown is "but a little way in the forest yet."

[4] William III, King of England, 1689-1702.

"Such company, thou wouldst say," observed the elder person, interpreting his pause. "Well said, Goodman Brown! I have been as well acquainted with your family as with ever a one among the Puritans; and that's no trifle to say. I helped your grandfather, the constable, when he lashed the Quaker woman so smartly through the streets of Salem;[5] and it was I that brought your father a pitch-pine knot, kindled at my own hearth, to set fire to an Indian village, in King Philip's war.[6] They were my good friends, both; and many a pleasant walk have we had along this path, and returned merrily after midnight. I would fain be friends with you for their sake."

"If it be as thou sayest," replied Goodman Brown, "I marvel they never spoke of these matters; or, verily, I marvel not, seeing that the least rumor of the sort would have driven them from New England. We are a people of prayer, and good works to boot, and abide no such wickedness."

"Wickedness or not," said the traveller with the twisted staff, "I have a very general acquaintance here in New England. The deacons of many a church have drunk the communion wine with me; the selectmen of divers towns make me their chairman; and a majority of the Great and General Court[7] are firm supporters of my interest. The governor and I, too—But these are state secrets."

"Can this be so?" cried Goodman Brown, with a stare of amazement at his undisturbed companion. "Howbeit, I have nothing to do with the governor and council; they have their own ways, and are no rule for a simple husbandman[8] like me. But, were I to go on with thee, how should I meet the eye of that good old man, our minister, at Salem village? Oh, his voice would make me tremble both Sabbath day and lecture day."[9]

Thus far the elder traveller had listened with due gravity; but now burst into a fit of irrepressible mirth, shaking himself so violently that his snakelike staff actually seemed to wriggle in sympathy.

"Ha,! ha! ha!" shouted he again and again; then composing himself. "Well, go on, Goodman Brown, go on; but, prithee, don't kill me with laughing."

"Well, then, to end the matter at once," said Goodman Brown, considerably nettled, "there is my wife, Faith. It would break her dear little heart; and I'd rather break my own."

"Nay, if that be the case," answered the other, "e'en go thy ways, Good-

---

[4] William III, King of England, 1689-1702.
[5] William Hawthorne (1607?-1681) allegedly drove Quaker women out of Salem. See the introduction to Hawthorne's work.
[6] King Philip's war was the most significant of the Indian wars in New England. King Philip was the name given by the English colonists to Metacomet, who was chief of the Wam-

panoag Indians and who died in the battle (1675-1676).

[7] The legislative body of colonial Massachusetts.

[8] A farmer or any humble man.

[9] The day of the midweek sermon, usually Thursday.

man Brown. I would not for twenty old women like the one hobbling before us that Faith should come to any harm."

As he spoke, he pointed his staff at a female figure on the path, in whom Goodman Brown recognized a very pious and exemplary dame, who had taught him his catechism in youth, and was still his moral and spiritual adviser, jointly with the minister and Deacon Gookin.

"A marvel, truly, that Goody Cloyse[10] should be so far in the wilderness at nightfall," said he. "But, with your leave, friend, I shall take a cut through the woods until we have left this Christian woman behind. Being a stranger to you, she might ask whom I was consorting with and whither I was going."

"Be it so," said his fellow-traveller. "Betake you to the woods, and let me keep the path."

Accordingly the young man turned aside, but took care to watch his companion, who advanced softly along the road until he had come within a staff's length of the old dame. She, meanwhile, was making the best of her way, with singular speed for so aged a woman, and mumbling some indistinct words—a prayer, doubtless—as she went. The traveller put forth his staff and touched her withered neck with what seemed the serpent's tail.

"The devil!" screamed the pious old lady.

"Then Goody Cloyse knows her old friend?" observed the traveller, confronting her and leaning on his writhing stick.

"Ah, forsooth, and is it your worship indeed?" cried the good dame. "Yea, truly is it, and in the very image of my old gossip, Goodman Brown, the grandfather of the silly fellow that now is. But—would your worship believe it?—my broomstick hath strangely disappeared, stolen, as I suspect, by the unhanged witch, Goody Cory, and that, too, when I was all anointed with the juice of smallage, and cinquefoil, and wolf's bane—"[11]

"Mingled with fine wheat and the fat of a new-born babe," said the shape of old Goodman Brown.

"Ah, your worship knows the recipe," cried the old lady, cackling aloud. "So, as I was saying, being all ready for the meeting, and no horse to ride on, I made up my mind to foot it; for they tell me there is a nice young man to be taken into communion to-night. But now your good worship will lend me your arm, and we shall be there in a twinkling."

"That can hardly be," answered her friend. "I may not spare you my arm, Goody Cloyse; but here is my staff, if you will."

So saying, he threw it down at her feet, where, perhaps, it assumed life, being one of the rods which its owner had formerly lent to the Egyptian

[10] Short for "Goodwife." Daniel Gookin (1612-1687), Goody Cloyse, Goody Cory, and Martha Carrier are historical people, and the women were sentenced to death for witchcraft by the court of which Hawthorne's ancestor was a member. Gookin was the author of *Historical Collections of the Indians of Massachusetts* (1674).

[11] "Smallage" is parsley; "cinquefoil" is a yellow rose; "wolf's bane" is aconite or monkshood, a poisonous plant.

magi. Of this fact, however, Goodman Brown could not take cognizance. He had cast up his eyes in astonishment, and, looking down again, beheld neither Goody Cloyse nor the serpentine staff, but his fellow-traveller alone, who waited for him as calmly as if nothing had happened.

"That old woman taught me my catechism," said the young man; and there was a world of meaning in this simple comment.

They continued to walk onward, while the elder traveller exhorted his companion to make good speed and persevere in the path, discoursing so aptly that his arguments seemed rather to spring up in the bosom of his auditor than to be suggested by himself. As they went, he plucked a branch of maple to serve for a walking stick, and began to strip it of the twigs and little boughs, which were wet with evening dew. The moment his fingers touched them they became strangely withered and dried up as with a week's sunshine. Thus the pair proceeded, at a good free pace, until suddenly, in a gloomy hollow of the road, Goodman Brown sat himself down on the stump of a tree and refused to go any farther.

"Friend," said he, stubbornly, "my mind is made up. Not another step will I budge on this errand. What if a wretched old woman do choose to go to the devil when I thought she was going to heaven: is that any reason why I should quit my dear Faith and go after her?"

"You will think better of this by and by," said his acquaintance, composedly. "Sit here and rest yourself a while; and when you feel like moving again, there is my staff to help you along."

Without more words, he threw his companion the maple stick, and was as speedily out of sight as if he had vanished into the deepening gloom. The young man sat a few moments by the roadside, applauding himself greatly, and thinking with how clear a conscience he should meet the minister in his morning walk, nor shrink from the eye of good old Deacon Gookin. And what calm sleep would be his that very night, which was to have been spent so wickedly, but so purely and sweetly now, in the arms of Faith! Amidst these pleasant and praiseworthy meditations, Goodman Brown heard the tramp of horses along the road, and deemed it advisable to conceal himself within the verge of the forest, conscious of the guilty purpose that had brought him thither, though now so happily turned from it.

On came the hoof tramps and the voices of the riders, two grave old voices, conversing soberly as they drew near. These mingled sounds appeared to pass along the road, within a few yards of the young man's hiding-place; but, owing doubtless to the depth of the gloom at that particular spot, neither the travellers nor their steeds were visible. Though their figures brushed the small boughs by the wayside, it could not be seen that they intercepted, even for a moment, the faint gleam from the strip of bright sky athwart which they must have passed. Goodman Brown alternately crouched and stood on tiptoe, pulling aside the branches and thrusting forth his head as far as he durst without discerning so much as a shadow. It vexed him the more, because he could have sworn, were such a thing possible, that he recognized the voices of the minister and Deacon Gookin, jogging along quietly, as they were wont to do, when bound to some ordination or ecclesiastical council. While yet within hearing, one of the riders stopped to pluck a switch.

"Of the two, reverend sir," said the voice like the deacon's, "I had rather miss an ordination dinner than to-night's meeting. They tell me that some of our community are to be here from Falmouth and beyond, and others from Connecticut and Rhode Island, besides several of the Indian powwows, who, after their fashion, know almost as much deviltry as the best of us. Moreover, there is a goodly young woman to be taken into communion."

"Mighty well, Deacon Gookin!" replied the solemn old tones of the minister. "Spur up, or we shall be late. Nothing can be done, you know, until I get on the ground."

The hoofs clattered again; and the voices, talking so strangely in the empty air, passed on through the forest, where no church had ever been gathered or solitary Christian prayed. Whither, then, could these holy men be journeying so deep into the heathen wilderness? Young Goodman Brown caught hold of a tree for support, being ready to sink down on the ground, faint and overburdened with the heavy sickness of his heart. He looked up to the sky, doubting whether there really was a heaven above him. Yet there was the blue arch, and the stars brightening in it.

"With heaven above and Faith below, I will yet stand firm against the devil!" cried Goodman Brown.

While he still gazed upward into the deep arch of the firmament and had lifted his hands to pray, a cloud, though no wind was stirring, hurried across the zenith and hid the brightening stars. The blue sky was still visible, except directly overhead, where this black mass of cloud was sweeping swiftly northward. Aloft in the air, as if from the depths of the cloud, came a confused and doubtful sound of voices. Once the listener fancied that he could distinguish the accents of townspeople of his own, men and women, both pious and ungodly, many of whom he had met at the communion table, and had seen others rioting at the tavern. The next moment, so indistinct were the sounds, he doubted whether he had heard aught but the murmur of the old forest, whispering without a wind. Then came a stronger swell of those familiar tones, heard daily in the sunshine at Salem village, but never until now from a cloud of night. There was one voice, of a young woman, uttering lamentations, yet with an uncertain sorrow, and entreating for some favor, which, perhaps, it would grieve her to obtain; and all the unseen multitude, both saints and sinners, seemed to encourage her onward.

"Faith!" shouted Goodman Brown, in a voice of agony and desperation; and the echoes of the forest mocked him, crying, "Faith! Faith!" as if bewildered wretches were seeking her all through the wilderness.

The cry of grief, rage, and terror was yet piercing the night, when the unhappy husband held his breath for a response. There was a scream, drowned immediately in a louder murmur of voices, fading into far-off laughter, as the dark cloud swept away, leaving the clear and silent sky above Goodman Brown. But something fluttered lightly down through the air and caught on the branch of a tree. The young man seized it, and beheld a pink ribbon.

"My Faith is gone!" cried he, after one stupefied moment. "There is no good on earth; and sin is but a name. Come, devil; for to thee is this world given."

And, maddened with despair, so that he laughed loud and long, did Goodman Brown grasp his staff and set forth again, at such a rate that he seemed to fly along the forest path rather than to walk or run. The road grew wilder and drearier and more faintly traced, and vanished at length, leaving him in the heart of the dark wilderness, still rushing onward with the instinct that guides mortal man to evil. The whole forest was peopled with frightful sounds—the creaking of the trees, the howling of wild beasts, and the yell of Indians; while sometimes the wind tolled like a distant church bell, and sometimes gave a broad roar around the traveller, as if all Nature were laughing him to scorn. But he was himself the chief horror of the scene, and shrank not from its other horrors.

"Ha! ha! ha!" roared Goodman Brown when the wind laughed at him. "Let us hear which will laugh loudest. Think not to frighten me with your deviltry. Come witch, come wizard, come Indian powwow, come devil himself, and here comes Goodman Brown. You may as well fear him as he fear you."

In truth, all through the haunted forest there could be nothing more frightful than the figure of Goodman Brown. On he flew among the black pines, brandishing his staff with frenzied gestures, now giving vent to an inspiration of horrid blasphemy, and now shouting forth such laughter as set all the echoes of the forest laughing like demons around him. The fiend in his own shape is less hideous than when he rages in the breast of man. Thus sped the demoniac on his course, until, quivering among the trees, he saw a red light before him, as when the felled trunks and branches of a clearing have been set on fire, and throw up their lurid blaze against the sky, at the hour of midnight. He paused, in a lull of the tempest that had driven him onward, and heard the swell of what seemed a hymn, rolling solemnly from a distance with the weight of many voices. He knew the tune; it was a familiar one in the choir of the village meeting house. The verse died heavily away, and was lengthened by a chorus, not of human voices, but of all the sounds of the benighted wilderness pealing in awful harmony together. Goodman Brown cried out; and his cry was lost to his own ear by its unison with the cry of the desert.

In the interval of silence he stole forward until the light glared full upon his eyes. At one extremity of an open space, hemmed in by the dark wall of the forest, arose a rock, bearing some rude, natural resemblance either to an altar or a pulpit, and surrounded by four blazing pines, their tops aflame, their stems untouched, like candles at an evening meeting. The mass of foliage that had overgrown the summit of the rock was all on fire, blazing high into the night and fitfully illuminating the whole field. Each pendent twig and leafy festoon was in a blaze. As the red light arose and fell, a numerous congregation alternately shone forth, then disappeared in shadow, and again grew, as it were, out of the darkness, peopling the heart of the solitary woods at once.

"A grave and dark-clad company," quoth Goodman Brown.

In truth they were such. Among them, quivering to and fro between gloom and splendor, appeared faces that would be seen next day at the council board of the province, and others which, Sabbath after Sabbath, looked devoutly heavenward, and benignantly over the crowded pews, from the holiest pulpits in the land. Some affirm that the lady of the governor was there. At least there were high dames well known to her, and wives of honored husbands, and widows, a great multitude, and ancient maidens, all of excellent repute, and fair young girls, who trembled lest their mothers should espy them. Either the sudden gleams of light flashing over the obscure field bedazzled Goodman Brown, or he recognized a score of the church members of Salem village famous for their especial sanctity. Good old Deacon Gookin had arrived, and waited at the skirts of that venerable saint, his revered pastor. But, irreverently consorting with these grave, reputable, and pious people, these elders of the church, these chaste dames and dewy virgins, there were men of dissolute lives and women of spotted fame, wretches given over to all mean and filthy vice, and suspected even of horrid crimes. It was strange to see that the good shrank not from the wicked, nor were the sinners abashed by the saints. Scattered also among their palefaced enemies were the Indian priests, or powwows, who had often scared their native forest with more hidious incantations than any known to English witchcraft.

"But where is Faith?" thought Goodman Brown; and, as hope came into his heart, he trembled.

Another verse of the hymn arose, a slow and mournful strain, such as the pious love, but joined to words which expressed all that our nature can conceive of sin, and darkly hinted at far more. Unfathomable to mere mortals is the lore of fiends. Verse after verse was sung; and still the chorus of the desert swelled between like the deepest tone of a mighty organ; and with the final peal of that dreadful anthem there came a sound, as if the roaring wind, the rushing streams, the howling beasts, and every other voice of the unconverted wilderness were mingling and according with the voice of guilty man in homage to the prince of all. The four blazing pines threw up a loftier flame, and obscurely discovered shapes and visages of horror on the smoke wreaths above the impious assembly. At the same moment the fire on the rock shot redly forth and formed a glowing arch above its base, where now appeared a figure. With reverence be it spoken, the figure bore no slight similitude, both in garb and manner, to some grave divine of the New England churches.

"Bring forth the converts!" cried a voice that echoed through the field and rolled into the forest.

At the word, Goodman Brown stepped forth from the shadow of the trees and approached the congregation, with whom he felt a loathful brotherhood by the sympathy of all that was wicked in his heart. He could have well nigh sworn that the shape of his own dead father beckoned him to advance, looking downward from a smoke wreath, while a woman, with dim features of despair, threw out her hand to warn him back. Was it his mother? But he had no power to retreat one step, nor to resist, even in thought, when the minister and good old Deacon Gookin seized his arms and led him to the blazing rock. Thither came also the slender form of a veiled female, led between Goody Cloyse, that pious teacher of the catechism, and Martha Carrier, who had received the devil's promise to be queen of hell. A rampant hag was she. And there stood the proselytes beneath the canopy of fire.

"Welcome, my children," said the dark figure, "to the communion of your race. Ye have found thus young your nature and your destiny. My children, look behind you!"

They turned; and flashing forth, as it were, in a sheet of flame, the fiend worshippers were seen; the smile of welcome gleamed darkly on every visage.

"There," resumed the sable form, "are all whom ye have reverenced from youth. Ye deemed them holier than yourselves, and shrank from your own sin, contrasting it with their lives of righteousness and prayerful aspirations heavenward. Yet here are they all in my worshipping assembly. This night it shall be granted you to know their secret deeds; how hoary-bearded elders of the church have whispered wanton words to the young maids of their households; how many a woman, eager for widow's weeds, has given her husband a drink at bedtime and let him sleep his last sleep in her bosom; how beardless youths have made haste to inherit their father's wealth; and how fair damsels—blush not, sweet ones—have dug little graves in the garden, and bidden me, the sole guest, to an infant's funeral. By the sympathy of your human hearts for sin ye all shall scent out all the places—whether in church, bed chamber, street, field, or forest—where crime has been committed, and shall exult to behold the whole earth one stain of guilt, one mighty blood spot. Far more than this. It shall be yours to penetrate, in every bosom, the deep mystery of sin, the fountain of all wicked arts, and which inexhaustibly supplies more evil impulses than human power—than my power at its utmost—can make manifest in deeds. And now, my children, look upon each other."

They did so; and, by the blaze of the hell-kindled torches, the wretched man beheld his Faith, and the wife her husband, trembling before that unhallowed altar.

"Lo, there ye stand, my children," said the figure, in a deep and solemn tone, almost sad with its despairing awfulness, as if his once angelic nature could yet mourn for our miserable race. "Depending upon one another's hearts, ye had still hoped that virtue were not all a dream. Now are ye undeceived. Evil is the nature of mankind. Evil must be your only happiness. Welcome again, my children, to the communion of your race."

"Welcome," repeated the fiend worshippers, in one cry of despair and triumph.

And there they stood, the only pair, as it seemed, who were yet hesitating on the verge of wickedness in this dark world. A basin was hollowed, naturally, in the rock. Did it contain water, reddened by the lurid light? or was it blood? or, perchance, a liquid flame? Herein did the shape of evil dip his hand and prepare to lay the mark of baptism upon their foreheads, that they might be partakers of the mystery of sin, more conscious of the secret guilt of others, both in deed and thought, than they could now be of their own. The husband cast one look at his pale wife, and Faith at him. What polluted wretches would the next glance show them to each other, shuddering alike at what they disclosed and what they saw!

"Faith! Faith!" cried the husband, "look up to heaven, and resist the wicked one."

Whether Faith obeyed, he knew not. Hardly had he spoken when he found himself amid calm night and solitude, listening to a roar of the wind which died heavily away through the forest. He staggered against the rock, and felt it chill and damp; while a hanging twig, that had been all on fire, besprinkled his cheek with the coldest dew.

The next morning young Goodman Brown came slowly into the street of Salem village, staring around him like a bewildered man. The good old minister was taking a walk along the graveyard to get an appetite for breakfast and meditate his sermon, and bestowed a blessing, as he passed, on Goodman Brown. He shrank from the venerable saint as if to avoid an anathema. Old Deacon Gookin was at domestic worship, and the holy words of his prayer were heard through the open window. "What God doth the wizard pray to?" quoth Goodman Brown. Goody Cloyse, that excellent old Christian, stood in the early sunshine at her own lattice, catechizing a little girl who had brought her a pint of morning's milk. Goodman Brown snatched away the child as from the grasp of the fiend himself. Turning the corner by the meeting house, he spied the head of Faith, with the pink ribbons, gazing anxiously forth, and bursting into such joy at sight of him that she skipped along the street and almost kissed her husband before the whole village. But Goodman Brown looked sternly and sadly into her face, and passed on without a greeting.

Had Goodman Brown fallen asleep in the forest and only dreamed a wild dream of a witch meeting?

Be it so, if you will; but alas! it was a dream of evil omen for young Goodman Brown. A stern, a sad, a darkly meditative, a distrustful, if not a desperate, man did he become from the night of that fearful dream. On the Sabbath day, when the congregation were singing a holy psalm, he could not listen, because an anthem of sin rushed loudly upon his ear and drowned all the blessed strain. When the minister spoke from the pulpit, with power and fervid eloquence and with his hand on the open Bible, of the sacred truths of our religion, and of saintlike lives and triumphant deaths, and of future bliss or misery unutterable, then did Goodman Brown turn pale, dreading lest the roof should thunder down upon the gray blasphemer and his hearers. Often, awaking suddenly at midnight, he shrank from the bosom of Faith; and at morning or eventide, when the family knelt down at prayer he scowled, and muttered to himself, and gazed sternly at his wife, and turned away. And when he had lived long, and was borne to his grave a hoary corpse, followed by Faith, an aged woman, and children and grandchildren a goodly procession, besides neighbors not a few, they carved no hopeful verse upon his tombstone; for his dying hour was gloom.

The Minister's Black Veil[1]

A PARABLE

The sexton stood in the porch of Milford meeting-house, pulling busily at the bell-rope. The old people of the village came stooping along the street. Children, with bright faces, tripped merrily beside their parents, or mimicked a graver gait, in the conscious dignity of their Sunday clothes. Spruce bachelors looked sidelong at the pretty maidens, and fancied that the Sabbath sunshine made them prettier than on week days. When the throng had mostly streamed into the porch, the sexton began to toll the bell, keeping his eye on the Reverend Mr. Hooper's door. The first glimpse of the clergyman's figure was the signal for the bell to cease its summons.

[1] The story was first published in *The Token* (1836) and was included in the *Twice-Told Tales* (1837). Hawthorne himself commented on the story: "Another clergyman in New England, Mr. Joseph Moody, of York, Maine, who died about eighty years since, made himself remarkable by the same eccentricity that is here related of the Reverend Mr. Hooper. In his case, however, the symbol had a different import. In early life he had accidentally killed a beloved friend; and from that day till the hour of his death, he hid his face from men." Hawthorne broadens and deepens the idea so that the veil becomes a universal symbol of man's guilt and sin—and of the ambiguity in all the signs men and women must try to read.

"But what has good Parson Hooper got upon his face?" cried the sexton in astonishment.

All within hearing immediately turned about, and beheld the semblance of Mr. Hooper, pacing slowing his meditative way towards the meeting-house. With one accord they started, expressing more wonder than if some strange minister were coming to dust the cushions of Mr. Hooper's pulpit.

"Are you sure it is our parson?" inquired Goodman Gray of the sexton.

"Of a certainty it is good Mr. Hooper," replied the sexton. "He was to have exchanged pulpits with Parson Shute, of Westbury; but Parson Shute sent to excuse himself yesterday, being to preach a funeral sermon."

The cause of so much amazement may appear sufficiently slight. Mr. Hooper, a gentlemanly person, of about thirty, though still a bachelor, was dressed with due clerical neatness, as if a careful wife had starched his band, and brushed the weekly dust from his Sunday's garb. There was but one thing remarkable in his appearance. Swathed about his forehead, and hanging down over his face, so low as to be shaken by his breath, Mr. Hooper had on a black veil.[2] On a nearer view it seemed to consist of two folds of crape, which entirely concealed his features, except the mouth and chin, but probably did not intercept his sight, further than to give a darkened aspect to all living and inanimate things. With this gloomy shade before him, good Mr. Hooper walked onward, at a slow and quiet pace, stooping somewhat, and looking on the ground, as is customary with abstracted men, yet nodding kindly to those of his parishioners who still waited on the meeting-house steps. But so wonder-struck were they that his greeting hardly met with a return.

"I can't really feel as if good Mr. Hooper's face was behind that piece of crape," said the sexton.

"I don't like it," muttered an old woman, as she hobbled into the meeting-house. "He has changed himself into something awful, only by hiding his face."

"Our parson has gone mad!" cried Goodman Gray, following him across the threshold.

A rumor of some accountable phenomenon had preceded Mr. Hooper into the meeting-house, and set all the congregation astir. Few could refrain from twisting their heads towards the door; many stood upright, and turned directly about; while several little boys clambered upon the seats, and came down again with a terrible racket. There was a general bustle, a rustling of the women's gowns and shuffling of the men's feet, greatly at variance with

[2] Cf. Poe's explanation of why Hooper put on the black veil, in his review of the *Twice-Told Tales:* "The moral put into the mouth of the dying minister will be supposed to convey the true import of the narrative; and that a crime of dark dye (having reference to the 'young lady') has been committed, is a point which only minds congenial with that of the author will perceive."

that hushed repose which should attend the entrance of the minister. But Mr. Hooper appeared not to notice the perturbation of his people. He entered with an almost noiseless step, bent his head mildly to the pews on each side, and bowed as he passed his oldest parishioner, a white-haired great-grandsire, who occupied an arm-chair in the centre of the aisle. It was strange to observe how slowly this venerable man became conscious of something singular in the appearance of his pastor. He seemed not fully to partake of the prevailing wonder, till Mr. Hooper had ascended the stairs, and showed himself in the pulpit face to face with his congregation, except for the black veil. That mysterious emblem was never once withdrawn. It shook with his measured breath, as he gave out the psalm; it threw its obscurity between him and the holy page, as he read the Scriptures; and while he prayed, the veil lay heavily on his uplifted countenance. Did he seek to hide it from the dread Being whom he was addressing?

Such was the effect of this simple piece of crape, that more than one woman of delicate nerves was forced to leave the meeting-house. Yet perhaps, the pale-faced congregation was almost as fearful a sight to the minister, as his black veil to them.

Mr. Hooper had the reputation of a good preacher, but not an energetic one: he strove to win his people heavenward by mild, persuasive influences, rather than to drive them thither by the thunders of the Word. The sermon which he now delivered was marked by the same characteristics of style and manner as the general series of his pulpit oratory. But there was something, either in the sentiment of the discourse itself, or in the imagination of the auditors, which made it greatly the most powerful effort that they had ever heard from their pastor's lips. It was tinged, rather more darkly than usual, with the gentle gloom of Mr. Hooper's temperament. The subject had reference to secret sin, and those sad mysteries which we hide from our nearest and dearest, and would fain conceal from our own consciousness, even forgetting that the Omniscient can detect them. A subtle power was breathed into his words. Each member of the congregation, the most innocent girl, and the man of hardened breast, felt as if the preacher had crept upon them, behind his awful veil, and discovered their hoarded iniquity of deed or thought. Many spread their clasped hands on their bosoms. There was nothing terrible in what Mr. Hooper said, at least, no violence; and yet, with every tremor of his melancholy voice, the hearers quaked. An unsought pathos came hand in hand with awe. So sensible were the audience of some unwonted attribute in their minister, that they longed for a breath of wind to blow aside the veil, almost believing that a stranger's visage would be discovered, though the form, gesture, and voice were those of Mr. Hooper.

At the close of the services, the people hurried out with indecorous confusion, eager to communicate their pent-up amazement, and conscious of lighter spirits the moment they lost sight of the black veil. Some gathered in little circles, huddled closely together, with their mouths all whispering in the centre; some went homeward alone, wrapt in silent meditation; some talked loudly, and profaned the Sabbath day with ostentatious laughter. A few shook their sagacious heads, intimating that they could penetrate the mystery; while one or two affirmed that there was no mystery at all, but only that Mr. Hooper's eyes were so weakened by the midnight lamp, as to require a shade. After a brief interval, forth came good Mr. Hooper also, in the rear of his flock. Turning his veiled face from one group to another, he paid due reverence to the hoary heads, saluted the middle aged with kind dignity as their friend and spiritual guide, greeted the young with mingled authority and love, and laid his hands on the little children's heads to bless them. Such was always his custom on the Sabbath day. Strange and bewildered looks repaid him for his courtesy. None, as on former occasions, aspired to the honor of walking by their pastor's side. Old Squire Saunders, doubtless by an accidental lapse of memory, neglected to invite Mr. Hooper to his table, where the good clergyman had been wont to bless the food, almost every Sunday since his settlement. He returned, therefore, to the parsonage, and, at the moment of closing the door, was observed to look back upon the people, all of whom had their eyes fixed upon the minister. A sad smile gleamed faintly from beneath the black veil, and flickered about his mouth, glimmering as he disappeared.

"How strange," said a lady, "that a simple black veil, such as any woman might wear on her bonnet, should become such a terrible thing on Mr. Hooper's face!"

"Something must surely be amiss with Mr. Hooper's intellects," observed her husband, the physician of the village. "But the strangest part of the affair is the effect of this vagary, even on a sober-minded man like myself. The black veil, though it covers only our pastor's face, throws its influence over his whole person, and makes him ghostlike from head to foot. Do you not feel it so?"

"Truly do I," replied the lady; "and I would not be alone with him for the world. I wonder he is not afraid to be alone with himself!"

"Men sometimes are so," said her husband.

The afternoon service was attended with similar circumstances. At its conclusion, the bell tolled for the funeral of a young lady. The relatives and friends were assembled in the house, and the more distant acquaintances stood about the door, speaking of the good qualities of the deceased, when their talk was interrupted by the appearance of Mr. Hooper, still covered with his black veil. It was now an appropriate emblem. The clergyman stepped into the room where the corpse was laid, and bent over the coffin, to take a last farewell of his deceased parishioner. As he stooped, the veil hung straight from his forehead, so that, if her eyelids had not been closed forever, the dead maiden might have seen his face. Could Mr. Hooper be fearful of her glance, that he so hastily caught back the black veil? A person who watched the interview between the dead and living, scrupled not to affirm, that, at the instant when the clergyman's features were disclosed, the corpse had slightly shuddered, rustling the shroud and muslin cap, though the countenance retained the composure of death. A superstitious old woman was the only witness of this prodigy. From the coffin Mr. Hooper passed into the chamber of the mourners, and thence to the head of the staircase, to make the funeral prayer. It was a tender and heart-dissolving prayer, full of sorrow, yet so imbued with celestial hopes, that the music of a heavenly harp, swept by the fingers of the dead, seemed faintly to be heard among the saddest accents of the minister. The people trembled, though they but darkly understood him when he prayed that they, and himself, and all of mortal race, might be ready, as he trusted this young maiden had been, for the dreadful hour that should snatch the veil from their faces. The bearers went heavily forth, and the mourners followed, saddening all the street, with the dead before them, and Mr. Hooper in his black veil behind.

"Why do you look back?" said one in the procession to his partner.

"I had a fancy," replied she, "that the minister and the maiden's spirit were walking hand in hand."

"And so had I, at the same moment," said the other.

That night, the handsomest couple in Milford village were to be joined in wedlock. Though reckoned a melancholy man, Mr. Hooper had a placid cheerfulness for such occasions, which often excited a sympathetic smile where livelier merriment would have been thrown away. There was no quality of his disposition which made him more beloved than this. The company at the wedding awaited his arrival with impatience, trusting that the strange awe, which had gathered over him throughout the day, would now be dispelled. But such was not the result. When Mr. Hooper came, the first thing that their eyes rested on was the same horrible black veil, which had added deeper gloom to the funeral, and could portend nothing but evil to the wedding. Such was its immediate effect on the guests that a cloud seemed to have rolled duskily from beneath the black crape, and dimmed the light of the candles. The bridal pair stood before the minister. But the bride's cold fingers quivered in the tremulous hand of the bridegroom, and her deathlike paleness caused a whisper that the maiden who had been buried a few hours before was come from her grave to be married. If ever another wedding was so dismal, it was that famous one where they tolled the wedding knell. After performing the ceremony, Mr. Hooper raised a glass of wine to his lips, wishing happiness to the new-married couple in a strain of mild pleasantry that ought to have brightened the features of the guests, like a cheerful gleam from the hearth. At that instant, catching a glimpse of his figure in the looking-glass, the black veil involved his own spirit in the horror with which it overwhelmed all others. His frame shuddered, his lips grew white, he spilt the untasted wine upon the carpet, and rushed forth into the darkness. For the Earth, too had on her Black Veil.

The next day, the whole village of Milford talked of little else than Parson Hooper's black veil. That, and the mystery concealed behind it, supplied a topic for discussion between acquaintances meeting in the street, and good women gossiping at their open windows. It was the first item of news that the tavern-keeper told to his guests. The children babbled of it on their way to school. One imitative little imp covered his face with an old black hand-kerchief, thereby so affrighting his playmates that the panic seized himself, and he well-nigh lost his wits by his own waggery.

It was remarkable that of all the busybodies and impertinent people in the parish, not one ventured to put the plain question to Mr. Hooper, where-fore he did this thing. Hitherto, whenever there appeared the slightest call for such interference, he had never lacked advisers, nor shown himself averse to be guided by their judgment. If he erred at all, it was by so painful a degree of self-distrust, that even the mildest censure would lead him to consider an indifferent action as a crime. Yet, though so well acquainted with this amiable weakness, no individual among his parishioners chose to make the black veil a subject of friendly remonstrance. There was a feeling of dread, neither plainly confessed nor carefully concealed, which caused each to shift the responsibility upon another, till at length it was found expedient to send a deputation of the church, in order to deal with Mr. Hooper about the mystery, before it should grow into a scandal. Never did an embassy so ill discharge its duties. The minister received them with friendly courtesy, but became silent, after they were seated, leaving to his visitors the whole burden of introducing their important business. The topic, it might be supposed, was obvious enough. There was the black veil swathed round Mr. Hooper's forehead, and concealing every feature above his placid mouth, on which, at times, they could perceive the glimmering of a melancholy smile. But that piece of crape, to their imagination, seemed to hang down before his heart, the symbol of a fearful secret between him and them. Were the veil but cast aside, they might speak freely of it, but not till then. Thus they sat a considerable time, speechless, confused, and shrinking uneasily from Mr. Hooper's eye, which they felt to be fixed upon them with an invisible glance. Finally, the deputies returned abashed to their constituents, pro-nouncing the matter too weighty to be handled, except by a council of the churches, if, indeed, it might not require a general synod.

But there was one person in the village unappalled by the awe with which the black veil had impressed all beside herself. When the deputies returned without an explanation, or even venturing to demand one, she, with the calm energy of her character, determined to chase away the strange cloud that appeared to be settling round Mr. Hooper, every moment more darkly than before. As his plighted wife, it should be her privilege to know what the black veil concealed. At the minister's first visit, therefore, she entered upon the subject with a direct simplicity, which made the task easier both for him and her. After he had seated himself, she fixed her eyes steadfastly upon the veil, but could discern nothing of the dreadful gloom that had so overawed the multitude: it was but a double fold of crape, hanging down from his forehead to his mouth, and slightly stirring with his breath.

"No," said she aloud, and smiling, "there is nothing terrible in this piece of crape, except that it hides a face which I am always glad to look upon. Come, good sir, let the sun shine from behind the cloud. First lay aside your black veil: then tell me why you put it on."

Mr. Hooper's smile glimmered faintly.

"There is an hour to come," said he, "when all of us shall cast aside our veils. Take it not amiss, beloved friend, if I wear this piece of crape till then."

"Your words are a mystery, too," returned the young lady. "Take away the veil from them, at least."

"Elizabeth, I will," said he, "so far as my vow may suffer me. Know, then, this veil is a type and a symbol, and I am bound to wear it ever, both in light and darkness, in solitude and before the gaze of multitudes, and as with strangers, so with my familiar friends. No mortal eye will see it withdrawn. This dismal shade must separate me from the world: even you, Elizabeth, can never come behind it!"

"What grievous affliction hath befallen you," she earnestly inquired, "that you should thus darken your eyes forever?"

"If it be a sign of mourning," replied Mr. Hooper, "I, perhaps, like most other mortals, have sorrows dark enough to be typified by a black veil."

"But what if the world will not believe that it is the type of an innocent sorrow?" urged Elizabeth. "Beloved and respected as you are, there may be whispers that you hide your face under the consciousness of secret sin. For the sake of your holy office, do away this scandal!"

The color rose into her cheeks as she intimated the nature of the rumors that were already abroad in the village. But Mr. Hooper's mildness did not forsake him. He even smiled again—that same sad smile, which always appeared like a faint glimmering of light, proceeding from the obscurity beneath the veil.

"If I hide my face for sorrow, there is cause enough," he merely replied; "and if I cover it for secret sin, what mortal might not do the same?"

And with this gentle, but unconquerable obstinacy did he resist all her entreaties. At length Elizabeth sat silent. For a few moments she appeared lost in thought, considering probably, what new methods might be tried to withdraw her lover from so dark a fantasy, which, if it had no other meaning, was perhaps a symptom of mental disease. Though of a firmer character than his own, the tears rolled down her cheeks. But, in an instant, as it were, a new feeling took the place of sorrow: her eyes were fixed insensibly on the black veil, when, like a sudden twilight in the air, its terrors fell around her. She arose, and stood trembling before him.

"And do you feel it then, at last?" said he mournfully.

She made no reply, but covered her eyes with her hand, and turned to leave the room. He rushed forward and caught her arm.

"Have patience with me, Elizabeth!" cried he, passionately. "Do not desert me, though this veil must be between us here on earth. Be mine, and hereafter there shall be no veil over my face, no darkness between our souls! It is but a mortal veil—it is not for eternity! O! you know not how lonely I am, and how frightened, to be alone behind my black veil. Do not leave me in this miserable obscurity forever!"

"Lift the veil but once, and look me in the face," said she.

"Never! It cannot be!" replied Mr. Hooper.

"Then farewell!" said Elizabeth.

She withdrew her arm from his grasp, and slowly departed, pausing at the door, to give one long shuddering gaze, that seemed almost to penetrate the mystery of the black veil. But, even amid his grief, Mr. Hooper smiled to think that only a material emblem had separated him from happiness, though the horrors, which it shadowed forth, must be drawn darkly between the fondest of lovers.

From that time no attempts were made to remove Mr. Hooper's black veil, or, by a direct appeal, to discover the secret which it was supposed to hide. By persons who claimed a superiority to popular prejudice, it was reckoned merely an eccentric whim, such as often mingles with the sober actions of men otherwise rational, and tinges them all with its own semblance of insanity. But with the multitude, good Mr. Hooper was irreparably a bugbear. He could not walk the street with any peace of mind, so conscious was he that the gentle and timid would turn aside to avoid him, and that others would make it a point of hardihood to throw themselves in his way. The impertinence of the latter class compelled him to give up his customary walk at sunset to the burial ground; for when he leaned pensively over the gate, there would always be faces behind the gravestones, peeping at his black veil. A fable went the rounds that the stare of the dead people drove him thence. It grieved him, to the very depth of his kind heart, to observe how the children fled from his approach, breaking up their merriest sports, while his melancholy figure was yet afar off. Their instinctive dread caused him to feel more strongly than aught else, that a preternatural horror was interwoven with the threads of the black crape. In truth, his own antipathy to the veil was known to be so great, that he never willingly passed before a mirror, nor stooped to drink at a still fountain, lest, in its peaceful bosom, he should be affrighted by himself. This was what gave plausibility to the whispers, that Mr. Hooper's conscience tortured him for some great crime too horrible to be entirely concealed, or otherwise than so obscurely intimated. Thus, from beneath the black veil, there rolled a cloud into the sunshine, an ambiguity of sin or sorrow, which enveloped the poor minister, so that love or sympathy could never reach him. It was said that ghost and fiend consorted with him there. With self-shudderings and outward terrors, he walked continually in its shadows, groping darkly within his own soul, or gazing through a medium that saddened the whole world. Even the lawless wind, it was believed, respected his dreadful secret, and never blew aside the veil. But still good Mr. Hooper sadly smiled at the pale visages of the wordly throng as he passed by.

Among all its bad influences, the black veil had the one desirable effect, of making its wearer a very efficient clergyman. By the aid of his mysterious emblem—for there was no other apparent cause—he became a man of awful power over souls that were in agony for sin. His converts always regarded him with a dread peculiar to themselves, affirming, though but figuratively, that, before he brought them to celestial light, they had been with him behind the black veil. Its gloom, indeed, enabled him to sympathize with all dark affections. Dying sinners cried aloud for Mr. Hooper, and would not yield their breath till he appeared; though ever, as he stooped to whisper consolation, they shuddered at the veiled face so near their own. Such were the terrors of the black veil, even when Death had bared his visage! Strangers came long distances to attend service at his church, with the mere idle purpose of gazing at his figure, because it was forbidden them to behold his face. But many were made to quake ere they departed! Once, during Governor Belcher's[3] administration, Mr. Hooper was appointed to preach the election sermon. Covered with his black veil, he stood before the chief magistrate, the council, and the representatives, and wrought so deep an impression, that the legislative measures of that year were characterized by all the gloom and piety of our earliest ancestral sway.

In this manner Mr. Hooper spent a long life, irreproachable in outward act, yet shrouded in dismal suspicions; kind and loving, though unloved, and dimly feared; a man apart from men, shunned in their health and joy, but ever summoned to their aid in mortal anguish. As years wore on, shedding their snows above his sable veil, he acquired a name throughout the New England churches, and they called him Father Hooper. Nearly all his parishioners, who were of mature age when he settled, had been borne away by many a funeral: he had one congregation in the church, and a more crowded one in the churchyard; and having wrought so late into the evening, and done his work so well, it was now good Father Hooper's turn to rest.

Several persons were visible by the shaded candle-light, in the death chamber of the old clergyman. Natural connections he had none. But there was the decorously grave, though unmoved physician, seeking only to mitigate the last pangs of the patient whom he could not save. There were the deacons, and other eminently pious members of his church. There, also, was the Reverend Mr. Clark, of Westbury, a young and zealous divine, who had ridden in haste to pray by the bedside of the expiring minister. There was the nurse, no hired hand-maiden of death, but one whose calm affection had

[3] Jonathan Belcher (1682-1757) was royal governor of the Massachusetts Bay Colony, 1730-1741.

endured thus long in secrecy, in solitude, amid the chill of age, and would not perish, even at the dying hour. Who, but Elizabeth! And there lay the hoary head of good Father Hooper upon the death pillow, with the black veil still swathed about his brow, and reaching down over his face, so that each more difficult gasp of his faint breath caused it to stir. All through life that piece of crape had hung between him and the world: it had separated him from cheerful brotherhood and woman's love, and kept him in that saddest of all prisons, his own heart; and still it lay upon his face, as if to deepen the gloom of his darksome chamber, and shade him from the sunshine of eternity.

For some time previous, his mind had been confused, wavering doubtfully between the past and the present, and hovering forward, as it were, at intervals, into the indistinctness of the world to come. There had been feverish turns, which tossed him from side to side, and wore away what little strength he had. But in his most convulsive struggles, and in the wildest vagaries of his intellect, when no other thought retained its sober influence, he still showed an awful solicitude lest the black veil should slip aside. Even if his bewildered soul could have forgotten, there was a faithful woman at his pillow, who, with averted eyes, would have covered that aged face, which she had last beheld in the comeliness of manhood. At length the death-stricken old man lay quietly in the torpor of mental and bodily exhaustion, with an imperceptible pulse, and breath that grew fainter and fainter, except when a long, deep, and irregular inspiration seemed to prelude the flight of his spirit.

The minister of Westbury approached the bedside.

"Venerable Father Hooper," said he, "the moment of your release is at hand. Are you ready for the lifting of the veil that shuts in time from eternity?"

Father Hooper at first replied merely by a feeble motion of his head; then, apprehensive, perhaps, that his meaning might be doubtful, he exerted himself to speak.

"Yea," said he, in faint accents, "my soul hath a patient weariness until that veil be lifted."

"And is it fitting," resumed the Reverend Mr. Clark, "that a man so given to prayer, of such a blameless example, holy in deed and thought, so far as mortal judgment may pronounce; is it fitting that a father in the church should leave a shadow on his memory, that may seem to blacken a life so pure? I pray you, my venerable brother, let not this thing be! Suffer us to be gladdened by your triumphant aspect as you go to your reward. Before the veil of eternity be lifted, let me cast aside this black veil from your face!"

And thus speaking, the Reverend Mr. Clark bent forward to reveal the mystery of so many years. But, exerting a sudden energy, that made all the beholders stand aghast, Father Hooper snatched both his hands from beneath the bedclothes, and pressed them strongly on the black veil, resolute to struggle, if the minister of Westbury would contend with a dying man.

"Never!" cried the veiled clergyman. "On earth, never!"

"Dark old man!" exclaimed the affrighted minister, "with what horrible crime upon your soul are you now passing to the judgment?"

Father Hooper's breath heaved; it rattled in his throat; but, with a mighty effort, grasping forward with his hands, he caught hold of life, and held it back till he should speak. He even raised himself in bed; and there he sat, shivering with the arms of death around him, while the black veil hung down, awful, at that last moment, in the gathered terrors of a lifetime. And yet the faint, sad smile, so often there, now seemed to glimmer from its obscurity, and linger on Father Hooper's lips.

"Why do you tremble at me alone?" cried he, turning his veiled face round the circle of pale spectators. "Tremble also at each other! Have men avoided me, and women shown no pity, and children screamed and fled, only for my black veil? What, but the mystery which it obscurely typifies, has made this piece of crape so awful? When the friend shows his inmost heart to his friend; the lover to his best beloved; when man does not vainly shrink from the eye of his Creator, loathsomely treasuring up the secret of his sin; then deem me a monster, for the symbol beneath which I have lived, and die! I look around me, and lo! on every visage a Black Veil!"

While his auditors shrank from one another, in mutual affright, Father Hooper fell back upon his pillow, a veiled corpse, with a faint smile lingering on the lips. Still veiled, they laid him in his coffin, and a veiled corpse they bore him to the grave. The grass of many years has sprung up and withered on that grave, the burial stone is moss-grown, and good Mr. Hooper's face is dust; but awful is still the thought that it mouldered beneath the Black Veil!

1836, 1837

Preface¹ to The House of the Seven Gables

When a writer calles his work a Romance, it need hardly be observed that he wishes to claim a certain latitude, both as to its fashion and material, which he would not have felt himself entitled to assume had he professed to

¹ Hawthorne's prefaces to *The House of the Seven Gables*, *The Blithedale Romance*, and *The Marble Faun* are important acts of criticism in which he attempts to make the fundamental distinction between the romance and the novel. Henry James was to discuss this idea in his study of Hawthorne (1879) when he praised his predecessor highly but held that "Hawthorne, in his allegorical moods, is nothing if not allegorical, and allegory, to my sense, is quite one of the light exercises of the imagination." Hawthorne's own prefaces not only justify allegory but the whole range of romance that he practiced in his art.

be writing a Novel. The latter form of composition is presumed to aim at a very minute fidelity, not merely to the possible, but to the probable and ordinary course of man's experience. The former—while, as a work of art, it must rigidly subject itself to laws, and while it sins unpardonably so far as it may swerve aside from the truth of the human heart—has fairly a right to present that under circumstances, to a great extent of the writer's own choosing or creation. If he think fit, also, he may so manage his atmospherical medium as to bring out or mellow the lights and deepen and enrich the shadows of the picture. He will be wise, no doubt, to make a very moderate use of the privileges here stated, and, especially, to mingle the Marvellous rather as a slight, delicate, and evanescent flavor, than as any portion of the actual substance of the dish offered to the public. He can hardly he said, however, to commit a literary crime even if he disregard this caution.

In the present work, the author has proposed to himself—but with what success, fortunately, it is not for him to judge—to keep undeviatingly within his immunities. The point of view in which this tale comes under the Romantic definition lies in the attempt to connect a bygone time with the very present that is flitting away from us. It is a legend prolonging itself, from an epoch now gray in the distance, down into our own broad daylight, and bringing along with it some of its legendary mist, which the reader, according to his pleasure, may either disregard, or allow it to float almost imperceptibly about the characters and events for the sake of a picturesque effect. The narrative, it may be, is woven of so humble a texture as to require this advantage, and, at the same time, to render it the more difficult of attainment.

Many writers lay very great stress upon some definite moral purpose, at which they profess to aim their works. Not to be deficient in this particular, the author has provided himself with a moral,—the truth, namely, that the wrong-doing of one generation lives into the successive ones, and, divesting itself of every temporary advantage, becomes a pure and uncontrollable mischief; and he would feel it a singular gratification if this romance might effectually convince mankind—or, indeed, any one man—of the folly of tumbling down an avalanche of ill-gotten gold, or real estate, on the heads of an unfortunate posterity, thereby to maim and crush them, until the accumulated mass shall be scattered abroad in its original atoms. In good faith, however, he is not sufficiently imaginative to flatter himself with the slightest hope of this kind. When romances do really teach anything, or produce any effective operation, it is usually through a far more subtle process than the ostensible one. The author has considered it hardly worth his while, therefore, relentlessly to impale the story with its moral as with an iron rod,—or, rather, as by sticking a pin through a butterfly,—thus at once depriving it of life, and causing it to stiffen in an ungainly and unnatural attitude. A high truth, indeed, fairly finely, and skilfully wrought out, brightening at every step, and crowning the final development of a work of fiction, may add an artistic glory, but is never any truer, and seldom any more evident, at the last page than at the first.

The reader may perhaps choose to assign an actual locality to the imaginary events of this narrative. If permitted by the historical connection,—which, though slight, was essential to his plan,—the author would very willingly have avoided anything of this nature. Not to speak of other objections, it exposes the romance to an inflexible and exceedingly dangerous species of criticism, by bringing his fancy-pictures almost into positive contact with the realities of the moment. It has been no part of his object, however, to describe local manners, nor in any way to meddle with the characteristics of a community for whom he cherishes a proper respect and a natural regard. He trusts not to be considered as unpardonably offending by laying out a street that infringes upon nobody's private rights, and appropriating a lot of land which had no visible owner, and building a house of materials long in use for constructing castles in the air. The personages of the tale—though they give themselves out to be of ancient stability and considerable prominence—are really of the author's own making, or, at all events, of his own mixing; their virtues can shed no lustre, nor their defects redound, in the remotest degree, to the discredit of the venerable town of which they profess to be inhabitants. He would be glad, therefore, if—especially in the quarter to which he alludes—the book may be read strictly as a Romance, having a great deal more to do with the clouds overhead than with any portion of the actual soil of the County of Essex.

Lenox, January 27, 1851.

Preface to The Blithedale Romance

In the "Blithedale" of this volume many readers will, probably, suspect a faint and not very faithful shadowing of Brook Farm, in Roxbury which (now a little more than ten years ago) was occupied and cultivated by a company of socialists. The author does not wish to deny that he had this community in his mind, and that (having had the good fortune, for a time, to be personally connected with it) he has occasionally availed himself of his actual reminiscences, in the hope of giving a more life-like tint to the fancy-sketch in the following pages. He begs it to be understood, however, that he has considered the institution itself as not less fairly the subject of fictitious handling than the imaginary personages whom he has introduced there. His whole treatment of the affair is altogether incidental to the main purpose of the romance; nor does he put forward the slightest pretensions to illustrate a theory, or elicit a conclusion, favorable or otherwise, in respect to socialism.

In short, his present concern with the socialist community is merely to establish a theatre, a little removed from the highway of ordinary travel, where the creatures of his brain may play their phantasmagorical antics, without exposing them to too close a comparison with the actual events of real lives. In the old countries, with which fiction has long been conversant, a certain conventional privilege seems to be awarded to the romancer; his work is not put exactly side by side with nature; and he is allowed a license with regard to every-day probability, in view of the improved effects which he is bound to produce thereby. Among ourselves, on the contrary there is as yet no such Faery Land, so like the real world, that, in a suitable remoteness, one cannot well tell the difference, but with an atmosphere of strange enchantment, beheld through which the inhabitants have a propriety of their own. This atmosphere is what the American romancer needs. In its absence, the beings of imagination are compelled to show themselves in the same category as actually living mortals; a necessity that generally renders the paint and pasteboard of their composition but too painfully discernible. With the idea of partially obviating this difficulty (the sense of which has always pressed very heavily upon him), the author has ventured to make free with his old and affectionately remembered home at Brook Farm, as being certainly the most romantic episode of his own life,—essentially a day-dream, and yet, a fact,— and thus offering an available foothold between fiction and reality. Furthermore, the scene was in good keeping with the personages whom he desired to introduce.

These characters, he feels it right to say, are entirely fictitious. It would, indeed (considering how few amiable qualities he distributes among his imaginary progeny), be a most grievous wrong to his former excellent associates, were the author to allow it to be supposed that he has been sketching any of their likenesses. Had he attempted it, they would at least have recognized the touches of a friendly pencil. But he has done nothing of the kind. The self-concentrated Philanthropist; the high-spirited Woman, bruising herself against the narrow limitations of her sex; the weakly Maiden, whose tremulous nerves endow her with Sibylline attributes; the Minor Poet, beginning life with strenuous aspirations which die out with his youthful fervor,— all these might have been looked for at Brook Farm, but, by some accident, never made their appearance there.

The author cannot close his reference to this subject without expressing a most earnest wish that some one of the many cultivated and philosophic minds, which took an interest in that enterprise, might now give the world its history. Ripley, with whom rests the honorable paternity of the institution, Dana, Dwight, Channing, Burton, Parker, for instance,—with others, whom he dares not name, because they veil themselves from the public eye,— among these is the ability to convey both the outward narrative and the inner truth and spirit of the whole affair, together with the lessons which those years of thought and toil must have elaborated, for the behoof of future experimentalists. Even the brilliant Howadji might find as rich a theme in his youthful reminiscences of Brook Farm, and a more novel one,— close at hand as it lies,—than those which he has since made so distant a pilgrimage to seek, in Syria and along the surrent of the Nile.

Concord, Mass., *May,* 1852.

Preface to The Marble Faun

It is now seven or eight years (so many, at all events, that I cannot precisely remember the epoch) since the author of this romance last appeared before the Public. It had grown to be a custom with him to introduce each of his humble publications with a familiar kind of preface, addressed nominally to the Public at large, but really to a character with whom he felt entitled to use far greater freedom. He meant it for that one congenial friend,—more comprehensive of his purposes, more appreciative of his success, more indulgent of his shortcomings, and in all respects, closer and kinder than a brother,—that all-sympathizing critic, in short, whom an author never actually meets, but to whom he implicitly makes his appeal whenever he is conscious of having done his best.

The antique fashion of Prefaces recognized this genial personage as the "Kind Reader," the "Gentle Reader," the "Beloved," the "Indulgent," or, at coldest, the "Honored Reader," to whom the prim old author was wont to make his preliminary explanation and apologies, with the certainty that they would be favorably received. I never personnally encountered, nor corresponded through the post with this representative essence of all delightful and desirable qualities which a reader can possess. But, fortunately for myself, I never therefore concluded him to be merely a mythic character. I had always a sturdy faith in his actual existence, and wrote for him year after year, during which the great eye of the Public (as well it might) almost utterly overlooked my small productions.

Unquestionably, this gentle, kind, benevolent, indulgent, and most beloved and honored Reader did once exist for me, and (in spite of the infinite chances against a letter's reaching its destination without a definite address) dully received the scrolls which I flung upon whatever wind was blowing, in the faith that they would find him out. But, is he extant now? In these many years, since he last heard from me, may he not have deemed his earthly task accomplished, and have withdrawn to the paradise of gentle readers, wherever it may be, to the enjoyments of which his kindly charity on my behalf must surely have entitled him? I have a sad foreboding that this may be the truth. The "Gentle Reader," in the case of any individual author, is apt to be extremely short-lived; he seldom outlasts a literary fashion, and, except in very rare instances, closes his weary eyes before the writer has half done with him. If I find him at all, it will probably be under some mossy-grave-stone, inscribed with a half-obliterated name which I shall never recognize.

Therefore, I have little heart or confidence (especially, writing as I do, in a foreign land, and after a long, long absence from my own) to presume upon the existence of that friend of friends, that unseen brother of the soul, whose apprehensive sympathy has so often encouraged me to be egotistical in my prefaces, careless though unkindly eyes should skim over what was never meant for them. I stand upon ceremony now; and, after stating a few particulars about the work which is here offered to the Public, must make my most reverential bow, and retire behind the curtain.

This Romance was sketched out during a residence of considerable length in Italy,[1] and has been rewritten and prepared for the press in England. The author proposed to himself merely to write a fanciful story, evolving a thoughtful moral, and did not propose attempting a portraiture of Italian manners and character. He has lived too long abroad not to be aware that a foreigner seldom acquires that knowledge of a country at once flexible and profound, which may justify him in endeavoring to idealize its traits.

Italy, as the site of his Romance, was chiefly valuable to him as affording a sort of poetic or fairy precinct, where actualities would not be so terribly insisted upon as they are, and must needs be, in America. No author, without a trial, can conceive of the difficulty of writing a romance about a country where there is no shadow, no antiquity, no mystery, no picturesque and gloomy wrong, nor anything but a commonplace prosperity, in broad and simple daylight, as is happily the case with my dear native land. It will be very long, I trust, before romance-writers may find congenial and easily handled themes, either in the annals of our stalwart republic, or in any characteristic and probable events of our individual lives. Romance and poetry, ivy, lichens, and wall-flowers, need ruin to make them grow.

In rewriting these volumes, the author was somewhat surprised to see the extent to which he had introduced descriptions of various Italian objects, antique, pictorial, and statuesque. Yet these things fill the mind everywhere in Italy, and especially in Rome, and cannot easily be kept from flowing out upon the page when one writes freely, and with self-enjoyment. And, again, while reproducing the book, on the broad and dreary sands of Redcar,[2] with

---

[1] The Hawthornes lived in Italy from 1858 to 1859.

[2] A town in Yorkshire, England, on the North Sea.

the gray German Ocean tumbling in upon me, and the northern blast always howling in my ears, the complete change of scene made these Italian reminiscences shine out so vividly that I could not find it in my heart to cancel them.

An act of justice remains to be performed towards two men of genius with whose productions the author has allowed himself to use a quite unwarrantable freedom. Having imagined a sculptor in this Romance, it was necessary to provide him with such works in marble as should be in keeping with the artistic ability which he was supposed to possess. With this view, the author laid felonious hands upon a certain bust of Milton, and a statue of a pearl-diver, which he found in the studio of MR. PAUL AKERS, and secretly conveyed them to the premises of his imaginary friend, in the Via Frezza. Not content even with these spoils, he committed a further robbery upon a magnificent statue of Cleopatra, the production of MR. WILLIAM W. STORY, an artist whom this country and the world will not long fail to appreciate. He had thoughts of appropriating, likewise, a certain door of bronze by MR. RANDOLPH ROGERS, representing the history of Columbus in a series of admirable bas-reliefs, but was deterred by an unwillingness to meddle with public property. Were he capable of stealing from a lady, he would certainly have made free with MISS HOSMER's admirable statue of Zenobia.

He now wishes to restore the above-mentioned beautiful pieces of sculpture to their proper owners, with many thanks, and the avowal of his sincere admiration. What he has said of them in the Romance does not partake of the fiction in which they are imbedded, but expresses his genuine opinion, which, he has little doubt, will be found in accordance with that of the Public. It is, perhaps, unnecessary to say, that, while stealing their designs, the Author has not taken a similar liberty with the personal characters of either of these gifted sculptors; his own man of marble being entirely imaginary.

Leamington, *December* 15, 1859.

Extracts From Journals

Hawthorne's journals provide an interesting record of his fictional sources as well as reflections on his contemporaries. From 1835 until 1862 he recorded his thoughts and observations. They have now been collected in modern editions and reveal Hawthorne as not only a sensitive artist but also a man fully alert to the social and political issues of his time.

THE SCARLET LETTER

June 15, 1838

The situation of a man in the midst of a crowd, yet as completely in the power of another, life and all, as if they two were in the deepest solitude.

1838

Character of a man who, in himself and his external circumstances, shall be equally and totally false; his fortune resting on baseless credit—his patriotism assumed—his domestic affections, his honor and honesty, all a sham. His own misery in the midst of it—it making the whole universe, heaven and earth alike an unsubstantial mockery to him.

January 4, 1839

The strange sensation of a person who feels himself an object of deep interest, and close observation, and various construction of all his actions, by another person.

1842 (?)

To trace out the influence of a frightful and disgraceful crime in debasing and destroying a character naturally high and noble, the guilty person being alone conscious of the crime.

November 17, 1847

A story of the effects of revenge, in diabolizing him who indulges in it.

EARTH'S HOLOCAUST[1]

1840

A bonfire to be made of the gallows and of all symbols of evil.

1844

When the reformation of the world is complete, a fire shall be made of the gallows; and the Hangman shall come and sit down by it, in solitude and despair. To him shall come the Last Thief, the Last Prostitute, the Last

[1] See pp. 1691–1706.

Drunkard, and other representatives of past crime and vice; and they shall hold a dismal merrymaking, quaffing the contents of the Drunkard's last Brandy Bottle.

BROOK FARM

April 13, 1841 [Brook Farm, Oak Hill]

Belovedest,[2] I have not yet taken my first lesson in agriculture, as thou mayst well suppose—except that I went to see our cows foddered, yesterday afternoon. We have eight of our own; and the number is now increased by a transcendental heifer belonging to Miss Margaret Fuller. She is very fractious, I believe, and apt to kick over the milk-pail. Thou knowest best, whether in these traits of character, she resembles her mistress. Thy husband intends to convert himself into a milkmaid this evening, but I pray Heaven that Mr. Ripley may be moved to assign him the kindliest cow in the herd, otherwise he will perform [his] duty with fear and trembling.

THOREAU

September 1, 1842

Mr. Thoreau dined with us yesterday.[3] He is a singular character—a young man with much of wild original nature still remaining in him; and so far as he is sophisticated, it is in a way and method of his own. He is as ugly as sin, long-nosed, queer-mouthed, and with uncouth and rustic, although courteous manners, corresponding very well with such an exterior. But his ugliness is of an honest and agreeable fashion, and becomes him much better than beauty. He was educated, I believe, at Cambridge, and formerly kept school in this town; but for two or three years back, he has repudiated all regular modes of getting a living, and seems inclined to lead a sort of Indian life among civilized men—an Indian life, I mean, as respects the absence of any systematic effort for a livelihood. He has been for some time an inmate of Mr. Emerson's family; and, in requital, he labors in the garden, and performs such other offices as may suit him—being entertained by Mr. Emerson for the sake of what true manhood there is in him. Mr. Thoreau is a keen and

[2] His fiancée, Sophia Peabody, whom he married on July 9, 1842. Hawthorne was at Brook Farm from April to November 1841.

[3] After Hawthorne's marriage to Sophia Peabody on July 9, 1842, the couple moved to the "Old Manse," in Concord, where they lived until 1845. The journals for these years also contain reflections on Emerson, Margaret Fuller, Ellery Channing, and other contemporaries.

delicate observer of nature—a genuine observer—which, I suspect, is almost as rare a character as even an original poet; and Nature, in return for his love, seems to adopt him as her especial child, and shows him secrets which few others are allowed to witness. He is familiar with beast, fish, fowl, and reptile, and has strange stories to tell of adventures and friendly passages with these lower brethren of mortality. Herb and flower, likewise, wherever they grow, whether in garden or wildwood, are his familiar friends. He is also on intimate terms with the clouds, and can tell the portents of storms. It is a characteristic trait, that he has a great regard for the memory of the Indian tribes, whose wild life would have suited him so well; and, strange to say, he seldom walks over a ploughed field without picking up an arrow-point, spearhead, or other relic of the red man, as if their spirits willed him to be the inheritor of their simple wealth.

With all this he has more than a tincture of literature—a deep and true taste for poetry, especially the elder poets, although more exclusive than is desirable, like all other Transcendentalists, so far as I am acquainted with them. He is a good writer—at least he has written one good article, a rambling disquisition on Natural History, in the last Dial, which, he says, was chiefly made up from journals of his own observations. Methinks this article gives a very fair image of his mind and character—so true, innate, and literal in observation, yet giving the spirit as well as the letter of what he sees, even as a lake reflects its wooded banks, showing every leaf, yet giving the wild beauty of the whole scene. Then there are passages in the article of cloudy and dreamy metaphysics, partly affected, and partly the natural exhalations of his intellect; and also passages where his thoughts seem to measure and attune themselves into spontaneous verse, as they rightfully may, since there is real poetry in him. There is a basis of good sense and of moral truth, too, throughout the article, which also is a reflection of his character; for he is not unwise to think and feel, however imperfect is his own mode of action. On the whole, I find him a healthy and wholesome man to know.

After dinner (at which we cut the first watermelon and muskmelon that our garden has grown), Mr. Thoreau and I walked up the bank of the river, and at a certain point he shouted for his boat. Forthwith a young man paddled it across, and Mr. Thoreau and I voyaged farther up the stream, which soon became more beautiful than any picture, with its dark and quiet sheet of water, half shaded, half sunny, between high and wooded banks. The late rains have swollen the stream so much that many trees are standing up to their knees, as it were, in the water, and boughs, which lately swung high in air, now dip and drink deep of the passing wave. As to the poor cardinals which glowed upon the bank a few days since, I could see only a few of their scarlet caps, peeping above the tide. Mr. Thoreau managed the boat so perfectly, either with two paddles or with one, that it seemed instinct with his own will, and to require no physical effort to guide it. He said that, when some Indians visited Concord a few years ago, he found that he had acquired, without a teacher, their precise method of propelling and steering a canoe. Nevertheless being in want of money, the poor fellow was desirous of selling the boat of which he was so fit a pilot, and which was built by his own hands; so I agreed to give him his price (only seven dollars), and accordingly became the possessor of the Musketaquid. I wish I could acquire the aquatic skill of the original owner at as reasonable a rate.

MELVILLE

November 20, 1856 [Southport]

A week ago last Monday, Herman Melville came to see me at the Consulate,[4] looking much as he used to do (a little paler, and perhaps a little sadder), in a rough outside coat, and with his characteristic gravity and reserve of manner. He had crossed from New York to Glasgow in a screw steamer, about a fortnight before, and had since been seeing Edinburgh, and other interesting places. I felt rather awkward at first, because this is the first time I have met him since my ineffectual attempt to get him a consular appointment from General Pierce. However, I failed only from real lack of power to serve him; so there was no reason to be ashamed, and we soon found ourselves on pretty much our former terms of sociability and confidence. Melville has not been well of late; he has been affected with neuralgic complaints in his head and his limbs, and no doubt has suffered from too constant literary occupation, pursued without much success latterly; and his writings, for a long while past, have indicated a morbid state of mind. So he left his place at Pittsfield, and has established his wife and family, I believe, with his father-in-law in Boston, and is thus far on his way to Constantinople. I do not wonder that he found it necessary to take an airing through the world, after so many years of toilsome pen-labor following after so wild and adventurous a youth as his was. I invited him to come and stay with us at Southport as long as he might remain in this vicinity; and, accordingly, he did come, on the next day, taking with him, by way of luggage, the least little bit of a bundle, which, he told me, contained a nightshirt and a toothbrush. He is a person of very gentlemanly instincts in every respect, save that he is a little heterodox in the matter of clean linen.

[4] From August 1853 to July 1857, Hawthorne was the American consul in Liverpool. Melville had just completed *The Confidence Man*, was negotiating for an English publisher, and was traveling in England, the continent, and Israel.

He stayed with us from Tuesday till Thursday; and, on the intervening day, we took a pretty long walk together, and sat down in a hollow among the sandhills (sheltering ourselves from the high, cool wind) and smoked a cigar. Melville, as he always does, began to reason of Providence and futurity, and of everything that lies beyond human ken, and informed me that he had 'pretty much made up his mind to be annihilated'; but still he does not seem to rest in that anticipation, and, I think, will never rest until he gets hold of a definite belief. It is strange how he persists—and has persisted ever since I knew him, and probably long before—in wandering to and fro over these deserts, as dismal and monotonous as the sandhills amid which we were sitting. He can neither believe, nor be comfortable in his unbelief; and he is too honest and courageous not to try to do one or the other. If he were a religious man, he would be one of the most truly religious and reverential; he has a very high and noble nature and is better worth immortality than most of us.

He went back with me to Liverpool on Thursday; and, the next day, Henry Bright met him at my office, and showed him whatever was worth seeing in town. On Saturday, Melville and I went to Chester together. I love to take every opportunity of going to Chester; it being the one only place, within easy reach of Liverpool, which possesses any old English interest. . . . We left Chester at about four o'clock; and I took the rail for Southport at half-past six, parting from Melville at a street-corner in Liverpool, in the rainy evening. I saw him again on Monday, however. He said that he already felt better than in America; but observed that he did not anticipate much pleasure in his rambles, for that the spirit of adventure is gone out of him. He certainly is much overshadowed since I saw him last; but I hope he will brighten as he goes onward. He sailed from Liverpool in a steamer on Tuesday, leaving his trunk behind him at my consulate, and taking only a carpet-bag to hold all his travelling-gear. This is the next best thing to going naked; and as he wears his beard and moustache, and so needs no dressing-case— nothing but a toothbrush—I do not know a more independent personage. He learned his travelling-habits by drifting about, all over the South Sea, with no other clothes or equipage than a red flannel shirt and a pair of duck trousers. Yet we seldom see men of less criticizable manners than he.

EDGAR ALLAN POE

(1809-1849)

From 1827 until 1849 Edgar Allan Poe functioned as a comprehensive man of letters: a Romantic poet, a hard-nosed critic, a prolific writer of detective and horror stories, fantasies, fables, hoaxes, riddles, grotesques, and science fiction. Poe succeeded in the genres of poetry, criticism, and fiction, establishing guidelines and definitions against which future artists and students of literature have measured themselves for more than a century; but he never quite became the gentleman of letters—the connoisseur of the fine arts—he so desperately wanted to be.

Certainly Poe was no connoisseur like James Russell Lowell, who wrote appreciative essays, collected in *My Study Windows and Among My Books,* and who characterized Poe as "3/5ths of him genius and 2/5ths sheer fudge"; nor did he have the commanding presence of Emerson, who called Poe the "jingle man." He lacked Hawthorne's controlled intensity and Melville's ability to pursue relentlessly and fully his tragic vision, although he shared their sensitivity to evil, trag-

The standard edition is still *The Complete Works of Edgar Allan Poe,* 17 vols., ed. James A. Harrison, 1902. It is being superseded by *Collected Works of Edgar Allan Poe,* ed. Thomas O. Mabbott, 1969—. Volume I *Poems* has been published. Other editions still in print are *Works of Edgar Allan Poe,* 10 vols., ed. E. C. Stedman and G. E. Woodberry, 1894-1895, reprinted in 1914. J. W. Ostrom has edited *The Letters of Edgar Allan Poe,* 2 vols., 1948, 1966. Killis Campbell has edited *The Poems of Edgar Allan Poe,* 1917, and *Poe's Short Stories,* 1927. A one-volume edition, *The Complete Poems and Stories of Edgar Allan Poe,* has been edited by A. H. Quinn and E. H. O'Neill, 1946.

The authoritative biography is Arthur Hobson Quinn, *Edgar Allan Poe: A Critical Biography,* 1941. Two earlier biographies are G. E. Woodberry, *The Life of Edgar Allan Poe, Personal and Literary,* 2 vols., 1885, rev., 1910, and Hervey Allen, *Israfel—The Life and Times of Edgar Allan Poe,* 2 vols., 1933. A Freudian analysis is M. Bonaparte, *The Life and Works of Edgar Poe, A Psychoanalytic Interpretation,* 1949.

Critical studies include Joseph Wood Krutch, *Edgar Allan Poe: A Study in Genius,* 1926; Killis Campbell, *The Mind of Poe and Other Studies,* 1933; N. B. Fagin, *The Histrionic Mr. Poe,* 1949; Yvor Winters, in *A Defense of Reason,* 1947; Allen Tate, in *The Forlorn Demon,* 1953; Patrick F. Quinn, *The French Face of Edgar Poe,* 1957; Harry Levin, *The Power of Blackness,* 1958; V. Buranelli, *Edgar Allan Poe,* 1961; Richard Wilbur, "The House of Poe," Anniversary Lectures; David H. Rein, *Edgar Allan Poe: The Inner Pattern,* 1960; Edward Wagenknecht, *Edgar Allan Poe, The Man Behind the Legend,* 1963; S. P. Moss, *Poe's Literary Battles,* 1963; E. W. Parks, *Edgar Allan Poe,* 1964; Robert Regan, ed., *Poe: A Collection of Critical Essays,* 1967; F. Stovall, *Edgar Poe the Poet,* 1969; Daniel Hoffman, *Poe, Poe, Poe, Poe, Poe, Poe, Poe,* 1972.

edy, and the power of blackness that so distinguished them from the transcendentalists. Unlike all of these authors—as well as others like Longfellow, Whittier, Holmes, and Bryant—Poe had no venerable family against which he could even rebel; he had no traditional career or financial support; he had no deep feeling for or against religion; and he was a Southerner in a literary world dominated by Northerners. Poe was in every sense an outsider, relishing and resenting in turn his role as the brooding romantic, the American Byron, the *enfant terrible* of American letters. He did not live to a hoary old age like most of his contemporaries, tempering youthful excesses with senescent wisdom: he abused himself so that he died by the time he was 40. But in the 20 years of his authorship, despite all of his ephemeral sketches and scattered writings on so many different subjects, he created a core of brilliant poems, short stories, and critical essays, and he managed, in his own erratic way, to function as a professional writer—the first of our professional writers. "In the darkness of his solitary confinement," Edmund Wilson has reminded us, "Poe is still a prince."

Many of Poe's problems stemmed naturally from the nervous sensibility he inherited from his parents, both of whom were wandering actors: the mother died in 1811, two years after Poe's birth, and the father disappeared. Poe was adopted by an affluent merchant, John Allan, and grew up in Richmond, Virginia. In 1815, the family went to England and returned to Richmond in 1820. Poe entered the University of Virginia at the age of 17, but did not remain for very long; he gambled sporadically, incurring many debts, and fell into a pattern of drinking whenever pressures became too acute. His stepfather grew impatient with him, cut off the little money that he had given Poe and removed the young man from the university. The two men, so temperamentally different from one another, were never really reconciled, and their relationship was marked by continual acrimony. Within three months of his return from the University, Poe had left his foster parent and gone to Boston to make his way as a poet.

Poe's first book of poems, *Tamerlane and Other Poems* (1827), was characterized by a pride and a fanciful quality that appeared in all of his work. It was not successful and Poe turned, in the first of many attempts to seek security, to the army, claimed to be 21 when he was only 19, changed his name to Edgar A. Perry, and stayed in the armed services until 1829, leaving to accept an appointment at West Point, as an enlisted man. Poe managed to reach the rank of Sergeant Major but, clearly, this Byronic poet was not destined for a military career—by 1829 he had published *Al Aaraaf, Tamerlane, and Minor Poems*. After leaving West Point, Poe approached his stepfather, who had remarried after his first wife's death, for financial assistance; but he was rebuffed. He then traveled to Baltimore in 1833 and lived in the home of his father's widowed sister, Maria Clemm, and her daughter, Virginia, whom he married in 1835 when she was 14 years and 3 months old.

Poe's literary career really began when he won a short story contest in 1833 for "The Manuscript in the Bottle." He came to the notice of various literary figures, served as the editor of a number of magazines—*The Southern Literary Messenger, The Messenger, Graham's Magazine, the Evening Mirror,* and the *Broadway Journal*—and tried, at different times, to establish his own journal. During these years Poe was a practicing and hard-working editor and, in that role, he became the first major literary critic in American culture.

As a critic, Poe commented on most of his contemporaries, both major and minor, and formulated general principles in fiction, poetry, satire, travel, and criticism that have endured until today. He also wrote extensively in each of these genres, so that one may measure his practice against his principles.

Poe's definition of the short story occurs in an essay he wrote on Hawthorne's *Mosses from an Old Manse.*

> A skillful literary artist has constructed a tale. If wise, he has not fashioned his thoughts to accommodate his incidents; but having conceived, with deliberate care, a certain unique or single *effect* to be wrought out, he then invents such incidents—he then combines such events as may best aid him in establishing this preconceived effect. If his very initial sentence tend not to the outbringing of this effect, then he has failed in his first step. In the whole composition there should be no word written, of preestablished design. And by such means, with such care and skill, a picture is at length painted which leaves in the mind of him who contemplates it with a kindred art, sense of the fullest satisfaction. The idea of the tale has been presented unblemished, because undisturbed; and this is an end unattainable by the novel. Undue brevity is just as exceptionable here as in the poem; but undue length is yet more to be avoided.

Poe's own most successful stories adhere to these principles: those that center on the death of a beautiful woman—"The Fall of the House of Usher," "Ligeia," "Berenice," "Morella," "Eleanora," and "The Oval Portait"; those that are more specifically "horror" stories—"The Tell-Tale Heart," "The Cask of Amontillado," "The Black Cat," and "The Pit and the Pendulum"; and tales of ratiocination or, as we have come to term them, the detective stories—"The Purloined Letter," "The Murders in the Rue Morgue," and "The Mystery of Marie Roget."

Poe had equally explicit views of poetry. For him, the long poem did not exist; and the poet who attempted an epic like "Paradise Lost" or "The Iliad" was really creating a series of short poems that were artificially stitched together. Above all, the poet should avoid didacticism and concentrate on one fundamental subject—the death of a beautiful lady. Through this subject the poet can express man's immortality and the elevation of his soul, and concern himself with beauty instead of truth: "Annabel Lee," "Ulalume," and "The Raven"—three of Poe's finest poems—are clear examples of these poetic principles.

Poe applied his critical views most vigorously to the work of his contemporaries. He could be caustic in his attack on Longfellow's ballads, claiming that Longfellow was affected, imitative, obtrusively didactic, and, on occasion, guilty of plagiarism; he understood the limitations of Irving, Bryant, and Cooper at a time when literary criticism was little more than literary appreciation. He may have exaggerated his own learning as part of the general pose he assumed—one critic has called him "the histrionic Mr. Poe"—and certainly he could be obsessively cruel whenever he personalized his criticism. But, despite all of his excesses and his large amount of ephemeral work, he did establish principles in the practice of poetry and fiction and he did create exemplary works in every genre.

The Raven and Other Poems appeared in 1845 and was the expression of Poe's fullest achievement as a poet. By that time he had published his greatest short stories—"The Fall of the House of Usher," "The Purloined Letter," and "The Murders in the Rue Morgue"—and the literary criticism that marked him as one of the few original aestheticians of his time. He could never make a living from his writings, however, and he rapidly disintegrated: Virginia, his wife, died in 1847; in a state of despair and financial destitution, Poe turned more and more to drink. In a rather pathetic way, he made romantic overtures to a series of older women toward the end of his life, each of whom in turn rebuffed him. In October 1849 he died of delerium tremens in a Baltimore hospital.

The duality between the pragmatic and the romantic was never reconciled in Poe's life and work: he remained a harsh critic but a tender poet, an analytic critic but a creator of the supernatural. As a poet he assumed the role of the Romantic in pursuit of supernal beauty. In much of his fiction he also escaped actuality and discovered horror and a power of blackness in a world of grotesques, the occult, and the deranged: his themes and characters anticipate the many different attempts by contemporary film makers and writers to explore the unknown. Whereas Hawthorne and Melville were concerned with the ethical dimensions of evil, Poe was fascinated by the way it developed from man's neuroses. His characters move between the worlds of the living and the dead, the sane and the insane, actuality and fantasy: characters return from the dead, a raven appears to drive a young poet mad; a person is obsessed by a black cat. Poe was a verbal landscapist of death who searched for unity in chaos, a logic and coherence in existence. He tried to survive in a society that democratized man, but he could not adapt—as a practical editor and critic, as a Romantic author—to the gritty qualities of America; he was highly narcissistic, perilously close in his greatest work to losing the sense of self in relation to others. His characters are European gentlemen even when they are destroying themselves, not so much in revolt against society, but contemptuous of it. Because society would not nourish the artist, the artist ridiculed society.

This duality between the actual and the romantic, between prose and poetry, between matter and mind, between thought and emotion finally reached such an exquisite tension that Poe could not contain it. Actuality dominated, and the imagination became repetitive, incapable of growth, and finally of expression. But for 22 years, from 1827 to 1849, Edgar Allan Poe not only created our most brilliant criticism but some of our most memorable short fiction and poetry. The dark world he explored is an inescapable part of the American mind, as recurrent in our serious and popular culture as the latest obsession with satanism, the occult, and science fiction.

Sonnet—To Science

Science! true daughter of Old Time thou art!
    Who alterest all things with thy peering eyes.
Why preyest thou thus upon the poet's heart,
    Vulture, whose wings are dull realities?
How should he love thee? or how deem thee wise?   5
    Who wouldst not leave him in his wandering
To seek for treasure in the jewelled skies,
    Albeit he soared with an undaunted wing?
Has thou not dragged Diana from her car?
    And driven the Hamadryad from the wood   10
To seek a shelter in some happier star?
    Hast thou not torn the Naiad from her flood,
The Elfin from the green grass, and from me
The summer dream beneath the tamarind[1] tree?

1829   1829, 1845

[1] An oriental tree.

Israfel

In heaven a spirit doth dwell
"Whose heart-strings are a lute";
None sing so wildly well
As the angel Israfel,
And the giddy stars (so legends tell)   5
Ceasing their hymns, attend the spell
    Of his voice, all mute.

Tottering above
    In her highest noon,
    The enamored moon   10
Blushes with love,
    While, to listen, the red levin[1]
    (With the rapid Pleiads, even,
    Which were seven)
    Pauses in Heaven.   15

And they say (the starry choir
    And the other listening things)
That Israfeli's fire
Is owing to that lyre
    By which he sits and sings—   20
The trembling living wire
    Of those unusual strings.

But the skies that angel trod,
    Where deep thoughts are a duty—
Where Love's a grown-up God—   25
    Where the Houri[2] glances are
Imbued with all the beauty
    Which we worship in a star.

Therefore, thou art not wrong,
    Israfeli, who despisest   30
An unimpassioned song;
To thee the laurels belong,
Best bard, because the wisest!
Merrily live, and long!

The ecstasies above   35
    With thy burning measures suit—
Thy grief, thy joy, thy hate, thy love,
    With the fervor of thy lute—
    Well may the stars be mute!

[1] Lightning.   [2] A nymph.

Yes, Heaven is thine; but this   40
   Is a world of sweets and sours;
   Our flowers are merely—flowers,
And the shadow of thy perfect bliss
   Is the sunshine of ours.

If I could dwell   45
Where Israfel
   Hath dwelt, and he where I,
He might not sing so wildly well
   A mortal melody,
While a bolder note than this might swell   50
   From my lyre within the sky.

1831, 1845

To Helen[1]

Helen, thy beauty is to me
   Like those Nicean[2] barks of yore,
That gently, o'er a perfumed sea,
   The weary, way-worn wanderer bore   5
To his own native shore.

On desperate seas long wont to roam,
   Thy hyacinth[3] hair thy classic face,
Thy Naiad[4] airs have brought me home
   To the glory that was Greece
   And the grandeur that was Rome.   10

[1] According to Poe, the inspiration for this poem was Mrs. Jane Stith Stanard, a Richmond friend who died in 1824. The woman is ideally created. He is particularly successful in evoking the image of Helen of Troy as a symbol of beauty and mystery that has vanished from the world but is still carried in the mind of the sympathetic poet.

[2] Poe's meaning is vague. He may have had in mind the sleeping Odysseus' return to Ithaca on a Phoenecian bark, described in Book XIII of the *Odyssey*. Milton also mentions the "Nyseian isle" in *Paradise Lost*, IV, 275. Twenty-six lines later, Milton describes Ad-

am's "hyacinthine locks." Poe uses the word primarily for its melodic effect.

[3] Poe was fond of this word. In "Ligeia," he describes the heroine's hair as "raven-black. . . glossy. . . luxuriant and naturally curling tresses, setting forth the full force of the Homeric epithet, 'hyacinthine!' " "Hyacinth" is taken from the flower with clustered blooms that bears the name of Hycianthus. Apollo caused the flower to spring from his blood and thus kept alive the image of Hyacinthus.

[4] A water-nymph.

Lo! in yon brilliant window-niche
How statue-like I see thee stand!
The agate lamp within thy hand,
Ah! Psyche,[5] from the regions which
Are Holy Land!   15

1823   1831, 1845

[5] The soul.

The Raven[1]

Once upon a midnight dreary, while I pondered, weak, and weary,
Over many a quaint and curious volume of forgotten lore—
While I nodded, nearly napping, suddenly there came a tapping,
As of some one gently rapping, rapping at my chamber door.
"'Tis some visitor," I muttered, "tapping at my chamber door—   5
             Only this and nothing more."

Ah, distinctly I remember it was in the bleak December,
And each separate dying ember wrought its ghost upon the floor.
Eagerly I wished the morrow;—vainly I had sought to borrow
From my books surcease of sorrow—sorrow for the lost Lenore—   10
For the rare and radiant maiden whom the angels name Lenore—
             Nameless here for evermore.

[1] "The Raven" is Poe's most captivating poetic drama. It describes a student's loss of reality as a consequence of losing his love and his immersion into madness. The varying stages of emotion—sadness, fear, hysteria, and despair—indicate why the poem has been so popular for those who view poetry as performance. In "The Raven," Poe fuses many of his most compelling themes and dramatic effects: the death of a beautiful lady: the sense of horror and mystery; the neurotic and psychotic states of mind; the brooding, Gothic setting: the Byronic sense of a lonely poet-student who confronts the despair of his own mind.

A year after the poem was published, Poe printed "The Philosophy of Composition," which was a cool and rational attempt at indicating how he had created the poem. The inspiration for the narrator's "Lost Lenore" has been traced to a childhood sweetheart, Miss Royster, and to Poe's wife, Virginia, who was seriously ill at the time and who died two years later, in 1847; but apart from any specific model, Lenore is also the abstraction of a lyric emotion that had obsessed Poe from the time he began to write poetry.

And the silken sad uncertain rustling of each purple curtain
Thrilled me—filled me with fantastic terrors never felt before;
So that now, to still the beating of my heart, I stood repeating: 15
"'Tis some visitor entreating entrance at my chamber door—
Some late visitor entreating entrance at my chamber door;
> This it is and nothing more."

Presently my soul grew stronger; hesitating then no longer,
"Sir," said I, "or Madam, truly your forgiveness I implore;   20
But the fact is I was napping, and so gently you came rapping,
And so faintly you came tapping, tapping at my chamber door,
That I scarce was sure I heard you"—here I open wide the door;—
> Darkness there and nothing more.

Deep into that darkness peering, long I stood there wondering,
    fearing,   25
Doubting, dreaming dreams no mortals ever dared to dream before;
But the silence was unbroken, and the stillness gave no token,
And the only word there spoken was the whispered word, "Lenore!"
This I whispered, and an echo murmured back the word,
    "Lenore!"—
> Merely this and nothing more.   30

Back into the chamber turning, all my soul within me burning,
Soon again I heard a tapping something louder than before.
"Surely," said I, "surely that is something at my windor lattice;
Let me see, then, what thereat it, and this mystery explore—
Let my heart be still a moment, and this mystery explore;—   35
> 'Tis the wind and nothing more."

Open here I flung the shutter, when, with many a flirt and flutter,
In there stepped a stately Raven of the saintly days of yore.
Not the least obeisance made he; not a minute stopped or stayed he,
But, with mien of lord or lady, perched above my chamber door—   40
Perched upon a bust of Pallas[2] just above my chamber door—
> Perched, and sat, and nothing more.

Then this ebony bird beguiling my sad fancy into smiling,
By the grave and stern decorum of the countenance it wore,
"Though thy crest be shorn and shaven, thou," I said, "art sure no
    craven,   45
Ghastly grim and ancient Raven wandering from Nightly shore—
Tell me what thy lordly name is on the Night's Plutonian shore!"[3]
> Quoth the Raven, "Nevermore."

[2] Pallas Athena, the goddess of wisdom.   [3] Pluto governed the infernal underworld.

Much I marvelled this ungainly fowl to hear discourse so plainly,
Though its answer little meaning—little relevancy bore;   50
For we cannot help agreeing that no living human being
Ever yet was blessed with seeing bird above his chamber door—
Bird or beast upon the sculptured bust above his chamber door,
                    With such name as "Nevermore."

But the Raven, sitting lonely on that placid bust, spoke only   55
That one word, as if his soul in that one word he did outpour.
Nothing farther then he uttered; not a feather then he fluttered—
Till I scarcely more than muttered; "Other friends have flown
    before—"
On the morrow *he* will leave me as my Hopes have flown before."
                    Then the bird said, "Nevermore."   60

Startled at the stillness broken by reply so aptly spoken,
"Doubtless," said I, "what it utters is its only stock and store,
Caught from some unhappy master whom unmerciful Disaster
Followed fast and followed faster till his songs one burden bore—
Till the dirges of his Hope that melancholy burden bore   65
                    Of 'Never—nevermore.' "

But the Raven still beguiling all my sad soul into smiling,
Straight I wheeled a cushioned seat in front of bird and bust and
    door;
Then, upon the velvet sinking, I betook myself to linking
Fancy unto fancy, thinking what this ominous bird of yore—   70
What this grim, ungainly, ghastly, gaunt, and ominous bird of yore
                    Meant in croaking "Nevermore."

This I sat engaged in guessing, but no syllable expressing
To the fowl whose fiery eyes now burned into my bosom's core;
This and more I sat divining, with my head at ease reclining   75
On the cushion's velvet lining that the lamp-light gloated o'er,
But whose velvet violet lining with the lamp-light gloating[4] o'er
                    She shall press, ah, nevermore!

[4] The word is used in the obscure sense of
"to refract light."

Then, methought, the air grew denser, perfumed from an unseen
    censer
Swung by Seraphim[5] whose foot-falls tinkled on the tufted floor.   80
"Wretch," I cried, "thy God hath lent thee—by these angels he hath
    sent thee
Respite—respite and nepenthe from thy memories of Lenore!
Quaff, oh quaff this kind nepenthe[6] and forget this lost Lenore!"
                  Quoth the Raven, "Nevermore."

"Prophet!" said I, "thing of evil!—prophet still, if bird or devil!—   85
Whether Tempter sent, or whether tempest tossed thee here ashore,
Desolate, yet all undaunted, on this desert land enchanted—
On this home by Horror haunted,—tell me truly, I implore—
Is there—*is* there balm in Gilead?[7]—tell me—tell me, I implore!"
                  Quoth the Raven, "Nevermore."   90

"Prophet!" said I, "thing of evil!—prophet still, if bird or devil!
By that heaven that bends above us—by that God we both adore—
Tell this soul with sorrow laden if, within the distant Aidenn,
It shall clasp a sainted maiden whom the angels name Lenore—
Clasp a rare and radiant maiden whom the angels name Lenore."   95
                  Quoth the Raven, "Nevermore."

"Be that word our sign of parting, bird or fiend!" I shrieked,
    upstarting—
"Get thee back into the tempest and the Night's Plutonian shore!
Leave no black plume as a token of that lie thy soul hath spoken!
Leave my loneliness unbroken!—quit the bust above my door!   100
Take thy beak from out my heart, and take thy form from off my
    door!"
                  Quoth the Raven, "Nevermore."

And the raven, never flitting, still is sitting, *still* is sitting
On the pallid bust of Pallas just above my chamber door;
And his eyes have all the seeming of a demon's that is dreaming,   105
And the lamp-light o'er him streaming throws his shadow on the floor;
And my soul from out that shadow that lies floating on the floor
           Shall be lifted—nevermore!

1842–1844   1845

[5] The highest order of angels.

[6] A drug that removes pain and sadness.

[7] Cf. Jeremiah viii: 22: "Is there no balm in Gilead?"

Annabel Lee[1]

It was many and many a year ago,
  In a kingdom by the sea,
That a maiden there lived whom you may know
  By the name of Annabel Lee;
And this maiden she lived with no other thought   5
  Than to love and be loved by me.

I was a child and *she* was a child,
  In this kingdom by the sea:
But we loved with a love that was more than love—
  I and my Annabel Lee;   10
With a love that the winged seraphs of heaven
  Coveted her and me.

And this was the reason that, long ago,
  In this kingdom by the sea,
A wind blew out of a cloud, chilling   15
  My beautiful Annabel Lee;
So that her high-born kinsman came
  And bore her away from me,
To shut her up in a sepulchre
  In this kingdom by the sea.   20

The angels, not half so happy in heaven,
  Went envying her and me—
Yes!—that was the reason (as all men know,
  In this kingdom by the sea)
That the wind came out of the cloud by night,   25
  Chilling and killing my Annabel Lee.

But our love it was stronger by far than the love
  Of those who were older than we—
  Of many far wiser than we—
And neither the angels in heaven above,   30
  Nor the demons down under the sea,
Can ever dissever my soul from the soul
  Of the beautiful Annabel Lee.

---

[1] "Annabel Lee" is one of the best-known examples of the incantatory quality of Poe's poetry. Although a meaning can be deduced from the words, much of the effect depends on the repetition of words, the mellifluous sound and beat of the lyrics. Poe became more and more prone to this type of poetry in his later years. "Annabel Lee" was published in the New York *Tribune* on October 9, 1849, two days after Poe's death.

For the moon never beams, without bringing me dreams
    Of the beautiful Annabel Lee;   35
And the stars never rise, but I feel the bright eyes
    Of the beautiful Annabel Lee;
And so, all the night-tide, I lie down by the side
Of my darling—my darling—my life and my bride,
      In the sepulchre there by the sea,   40
      In her tomb by the sounding sea.

1849, 1850

Ligeia[1]

And the will therein lieth, which dieth not. Who knoweth the mysteries of the will, with its vigor? For God is but a great will pervading all things by nature of its intentness. Man doth not yield himself to the angels, nor unto death utterly, save only through the weakness of his feeble will.—Joseph Glanvill[2]

I cannot, for my soul, remember how, when, or even precisely where, I first became acquainted with the lady Ligeia. Long years have since elapsed, and my memory is feeble through much suffering. Or, perhaps, I cannot *now* bring these points to mind, because, in truth, the character of my beloved, her rare learning, her singular yet placid cast of beauty, and the thrilling and enthralling eloquence of her low musical language, made their way into my heart by paces so steadily and stealthily progressive, that they have been unnoticed and unknown. Yet I believe that I met her first and most frequently in some large, old, decaying city near the Rhine. Of her family—I have surely heard her speak. That it is of a remotely ancient date cannot be doubted. Ligeia! Ligeia! Buried in studies of a nature more than all else adapted to deaden impressions of the outward world, it is by that sweet word alone—by Ligeia—that I bring before mine eyes in fancy the image of

[1] "Ligeia" was originally published in the *American Museum*, September 18, 1838. It is one of many stories that Poe wrote concerning life after death and the return from death of a beautiful lady: "Morella," "Berenice," "The Fall of the House of Usher," and "Eleonara" are other examples. In Poe's mind, death was closely associated with love, and many of these stories deal with interconnections between the two concepts. Poe considered "Ligeia" his finest story.

It is important to remember that the concern with death was an aspect of all forms of Romanticism. One finds it in landscapes of the Hudson River School as well as in the work of European artists like Gericault and Delacroix.

[2] Joseph Glanvill (1636-1680) was an English clergyman who believed in witchcraft and the preexistence of the soul. His most important book is *The Vanity of Dogmatizing*. The epigraph has not been discovered in Glavill's works.

her who is no more. And now, while I write, a recollection flashes upon me that I have *never known* the paternal name of her who was my friend and my betrothed, and who became the partner of my studies, and finally the wife of my bosom. Was it a playful charge on the part of my Ligeia? or was it a test of my strength of affection, that I should institute no inquiries upon this point? or was it rather a caprice of my own—a wildly romantic offering on the shrine of the most passionate devotion? I but indistinctly recall the fact itself—what wonder that I have utterly forgotten the circumstances which originated or attended it? And, indeed, if ever that spirit which is entitled *Romance*—if ever she, the wan and the misty-winged *Ashtophet*[3] of idolatrous Egypt, presided, as they tell, over marriages ill-omened, then most surely she presided over mine.

There is one dear topic, however, on which my memory fails me not. It is the *person* of Ligeia. In stature she was tall, somewhat slender, and, in her latter days, even emaciated. I would in vain attempt to portray the majesty, the quiet ease of her demeanor, or the incomprehensible lightness and elasticity of her footfall. She came and departed as a shadow. I was never made aware of her entrance into my closed study, save by the dear music of her low sweet voice, as she placed her marble hand upon my shoulder. In beauty of face no maiden ever equalled her. It was the radiance of an opium-dream—an airy and spirit-lifting vision more wildly divine than the phantasies which hovered about the slumbering souls of the daughters of Delos.[4] Yet her features were not of that regular mould which we have been falsely taught to worship in the classical labors of the heathen. "There is no exquisite beauty," says Bacon, Lord Verulam,[5] speaking truly of all the forms and *genera* of beauty, "without some *strangeness* in the proportion." Yet, although I saw that the features of Ligeia were not of a classic regularity—although I perceived that her loveliness was indeed "exquisite," and felt that there was much of "strangeness" pervading it, yet I have tried in vain to detect the irregularity and to trace home my own perception of "the strange." I examined the contour of the lofty and pale forehead—it was faultless—how cold indeed that word when applied to a majesty so divine!—the skin rivalling the purest ivory, the commanding extent and repose, the gentle prominence of the regions above the temples; and then the raven-black, the glossy, the luxuriant, and naturally-curling tresses, setting forth the full force of the Homeric epithet, "hyacinthine!"[6] I looked at the delicate outlines of the nose—and nowhere but in the graceful medallions of the

---

[3] An Egyptian adaptation of the Syrian love goddess Ashtoreth, who is associated with Astarte.

[4] The Aegean island that is the birthplace of Apollo, god of music and poetry, and Artemis, who was a virgin goddess and was

waited on by chaste maidens. Delos, where Apollo was born, was considered a shrine.

[5] This quotation is taken from Francis Bacon's essay, "Of Beauty." Bacon wrote "excellent," not "exquisite."

[6] See "To Helen," l. 7.

Hebrews had I beheld a similar perfection. There were the same luxurious smoothness of surface, the same scarcely perceptible tendency to the aquiline, the same harmoniously curved nostrils speaking the free spirit. I regarded the sweet mouth. Here was indeed the triumph of all things heavenly—the magnificent turn of the short upper lip—the soft, voluptuous slumber of the under—the dimples which sported, and the color which spoke—the teeth glancing back, with a brilliancy almost startling, every ray of the holy light which fell upon them in her serene and placid yet most exultingly radiant of all smiles. I scrutinized the formation of the chin—and, here too, I found the gentleness of breadth, the softness and the majesty, the fulness and the spirituality, of the Greek—the contour which the god Apollo revealed but in a dream, to Cleomenes,[7] the son of the Athenian. And then I peered into the large eyes of Ligeia.

For eyes we have no models in the remotely antique. It might have been, too, that in these eyes of beloved lay the secret to which Lord Verulam alludes. They were, I must believe, far larger than the ordinary eyes of our own race. They were even fuller than the fullest of the gazelle eyes of the tribe of the valley of Nourjahad.[8] Yet it was only at intervals—in moments of intense excitement—that this peculiarity became more than slightly noticeable in Ligeia. And at such moments was her beauty—in my heated fancy thus it appeared perhaps—the beauty of beings either above or apart from the earth—the beauty of the fabulous Houri[9] of the Turk. The hue of the orbs was the most brilliant of black, and, far over them, hung jettylashes of great length. The brows, slightly irregular in outline, had the same tint. The "strangeness," however, which I found in the eyes was of a nature distinct from the formation, or the color, or the brilliancy of the features, and must, after all, be referred to the *expression*. Ah, word of no meaning! behind whose vast latitude of mere sound we intrench our ignorance of so much of the spiritual. The expression of the eyes of Ligeia! How for long hours have I pondered upon it! How have I, through the whole of a midsummer night, struggled to fathom it! What was it—that something more profound than the well of Democritus[10]—which lay far within the pupils of my beloved? What *was* it? I was possessed with a passion to discover. Those eyes! those large, those shining, those divine orbs! they became to me twin stars of Leda,[11] and I to them devoutest of astrologers.

There is no point, among the many incomprehensible anomalies of the science of mind, more thrillingly exciting than the fact—never, I believe,

[7] An Athenian sculptor of the Venus de Medici.

[8] The setting of an oriental tale by Mrs. Frances Sheridan, *The History of Nourjahad* (1776).

[9] A nymph of the Mohammedan paradise.

[10] Democritus, a fifth-century B.C. Greek, called the "laughing philosopher." His famous aphorism, "Truth lies at the bottom of a well," is the source of Poe's line.

[11] The Gemini has two bright stars, Castor and Pollux, twin sons of the mortal Leda and the god Zeus. In the Greek legend, Zeus came to Leda in the form of a swan.

noticed in the schools—that in our endeavors to recall to memory something long forgotten, we often find ourselves *upon the very verge* of remembrance, without being able, in the end, to remember. And thus how frequently, in my intense scrutiny of Ligeia's eyes, have I felt approaching the full knowledge of their expression—felt it approaching—yet not quite be mine—and so at length entirely depart! And (strange, oh, strangest mystery of all!) I found, in the commonest objects of the universe, a circle of analogies to that expression. I mean to say that, subsequently to the period when Ligeia's beauty passed into my spirit, there dwelling as in a shrine, I derived, from many existences in the material world, a sentiment such as I felt always around, within me, by her large and luminous orbs. Yet not the more could I define that sentiment, or analyze, or even steadily view it. I recognized it, let me repeat, sometimes in the survey of a rapidly growing vine—in the contemplation of a moth, a butterfly, a chrysalis, a stream of running water. I have felt it in the ocean—in the falling of a meteor. I have felt it in the glances of unusually aged people. And there are one or two stars in heaven (one especially, a star of the sixth magnitude, double and changeable, to be found near the large star in Lyra[12]) in a telescopic scrutiny of which I have been made aware of the feeling. I have been filled with it by certain sounds from stringed instruments, and not unfrequently by passages from books. Among innumerable other instances, I well remember something in a volume of Joseph Glanvill, which (perhaps merely from its quaintness—who shall, say?) never failed to inspire me with the sentiment: "And the will therein lieth, which dieth not. Who knoweth the mysteries of the will, with its vigor? For God is but a great will pervading all things by nature of its intentness. Man doth not yield him to the angels, nor unto death utterly, save only through the weakness of his feeble will."

Length of years and subsequent reflection have enabled me to trace, indeed, some remote connection between this passage in the English moralist and a portion of the character of Ligeia. And *intensity* in thought, action, or speech was possible, in her, a result, or at least an index, of that gigantic volition which, during our long intercourse, failed to give other and more immediate evidence of its existence. Of all the women whom I have ever known, she, the outwardly calm, the ever-placid Ligeia, was the most violently a prey to the tumultuous vultures of stern passion. And of such passion I could form no estimate, save by the miraculous expansion of those eyes which at once so delighted and appalled me,—by the almost magical melody, modulation, distinctness, and placidity of her very low voice,—and by the fierce energy (rendered doubly effective by contrast with her manner of utterance) of the wild words which she habitually uttered.

---

[12] The large star to which Poe refers is Vega (Alpha Lyrae); the other star, Epsilon Lyrae, is invisible to the naked eye.

I have spoken of the learning of Ligeia: it was immense—such as I have never known in woman. In the classical tongues was she deeply proficient, and as far as my own acquaintance extended in regard to the modern dialects of Europe, I have never known her at fault. Indeed upon any theme of the most admired because simply the most abstruse of the boasted erudition of the Academy, have I *ever* found Ligeia at fault? How singularly—how thrillingly, this one point in the nature of my wife has forced itself, at this late period only, upon my attention! I said her knowledge was such as I have never known in woman—but where breathes the man who has traversed, and successfully, *all* the wide areas of moral, physical, and mathematical science? I saw not then what I now clearly perceive, that the acquisitions of Ligeia were gigantic, were astounding; yet I was sufficiently aware of her infinite supremacy to resign myself, with a child-like confidence, to her guidance through the chaotic world of metaphysical investigation at which I was most busily occupied during the earlier years of our marriage. With how vast a triumph—with how vivid a delight—with how much of all that is ethereal in hope did I *feel*, as she bent over me in studies but little sought—but less known,—that delicious vista by slow degrees expanding before me, down whose long, gorgeous, and all untrodden path, I might at length pass onward to the goal of a wisdom too divinely precious not to be forbidden!

How poignant, then, must have been the grief with which, after some years, I beheld my well-gounded expectations take wings to themselves and fly away! Without Ligeia I was but as a child groping benighted. Her presence, her readings alone, rendered vividly luminous the many mysteries of the transcendentalism in which we were immersed. Wanting the radiant lustre of her eyes, letters, lambent and golden, grew duller than Saturnian[13] lead. And now those eyes shone less and less frequently upon the pages over which I pored. Ligeia grew ill. The wild eyes blazed with a too—too glorious effulgence; the pale fingers became of the transparent waxen hue of the grave; and the blue veins upon the lofty forehead swelled and sank impetuously with the tides of the most gentle emotion. I saw that she must die—and I struggled desperately in spirit with the grim Azrael.[14] And the struggles of the passionate wife were, to my astonishment, even more energetic than my own. There had been much in her stern nature to impress me with the belief that, to her, death would have come without its terrors, but not so. Words are impotent to convey any just idea of the fierceness of resistance with which she wrestled with the Shadow. I groaned in anguish at the pitiable spectacle. I would have soothed—I would have reasoned; but in the intensity of her wild desire for life—for life—*but* for life—solace and reason were alike the uttermost of folly. Yet not until the last instance, amid the most

[13] *Saturnus* was Latin for lead in medieval alchemy, a process of turning lead into gold.
[14] The Angel of Death, in Mohammedan and Jewish religion, who divides the soul from the body.

convulsive writhings of her fierce spirit, was shaken the external placidity of her demeanor. Her voice grew more gentle—grew more low—yet I would not wish to dwell upon the wild meaning of the quietly uttered words. My brain reeled as I hearkened, entranced to a melody more than mortal—to assumptions and aspirations which mortality had never before known.

That she loved me I should not have doubted; and I might have been easily aware that, in a bosom such as hers, love would have reigned no ordinary passion. But in death only was I fully impressed with the strength of her affection. For long hours, detaining my hand, would she pour out before me the overflowing of a heart whose more than passionate devotion amounted to idolatry. How had I deserved to be so blessed by such confessions?—how had I deserved to be so cursed with the removal of my beloved in the hour of my making them? But upon this subject I cannot bear to dilate. Let me say only, that in Ligeia's more than womanly abandonment to a love, alas! all unmerited, all unworthily bestowed, I at length recognized the principle of her longing, with so wildly earnest a desire, for the life which was now fleeing so rapidly away. It is this wild longing—it is this eager vehemence of desire for life—*but* for life—that I have no power to portray—no utterance capable of expressing.

At high noon of the night in which she departed, beckoning me, peremptorily, to her side, she bade me repeat certain verses composed by herself not many days before. I obeyed her. They were these:—[15]

> *Lo! 'tis a gala night*
>   *Within the lonesome latter years!*
> *An angel throng, bewinged, bedight*
>   *In veils, and drowned in tears,*
> *Sit in a theatre, to see*
>   *A play of hope and fears,*
> *While the orchestra breathes fitfully*
>   *The music of the spheres.*
>
> *Mimes, in the form of God on high,*
>   *Mutter and mumble low,*
> *And hither and thither fly;*
>   *Mere puppets they, who come and go*
> *At bidding of vast formless things*
>   *That shift the scenery to and fro,*
> *Flapping from out their condor wings*
>   *Invisible Woe!*

[15] The poem was first included in the story when it appeared in the *Broadway Journal*, September 27, 1845.

That motley drama!—oh, be sure
  It shall not be forgot!
With its Phantom chased for evermore,
  By a crowd that seize it not,
Through a circle that ever returneth in
  To the self-same spot;
And much of Madness, and more of Sin
  And Horror, the soul of the plot!

But see, amid the mimic rout
  A crawling shape intrude!
A blood-red thing that writhes from out
  The scenic solitude!
It writhes!—it writhes!—with mortal pangs
  The mimes become its food,
And the seraphs sob at vermin fangs
  In human gore imbued.

Out—out are the lights—out all!
  And over each quivering form,
The curtain, a funeral pall,
  Comes down with the rush of a storm—
And the angels, all pallid and wan,
  Uprising, unveiling, affirm
That the play is the tragedy, "Man,"
  And its hero, the conqueror Worm.

"O God!" half shrieked Ligeia, leaping to her feet and extending her arms
aloft with a spasmodic movement, as I made an end of these lines—"O God!
O Divine Father!—shall these things be undeviatingly so?—shall this conqueror be not once conquered? Are we not part and parcel in Thee? Who—
who knoweth the mysteries of the will with its vigor? Man doth not yield him
to the angels, *nor unto death utterly,* save only through the weakness of his
feeble will."

And now, as if exhausted with emotion, she suffered her white arms to
fall, and returned solemnly to her bed of death. And as she breathed her last
sighs, there came mingled with them a low murmur from her lips. I bent to
them my ear, and distinguished, again, the concluding words of the passage
in Glanvill: *"Man doth not yield him to the angels, nor unto death utterly,
save only through the weakness of his feeble will."*

She died: and I, crushed into the very dust with sorrow, could no longer
endure the lonely desolation of my dwelling in the dim and decaying city by
the Rhine. I had no lack of what the world calls wealth. Ligeia had brought
me far more, very far more, than ordinarily falls to the lot of mortals. After

a few months, therefore, of weary and aimless wandering, I purchased and put in some repair, an abbey, which I shall not name, in one of the wildest and least frequented portions of fair England. The gloomy and dreary grandeur of the building, the almost savage aspect of the domain, the many melancholy and time-honored memories connected with both, had much in unison with the feelings of utter abandonment which had driven me into that remote and unsocial region of the country. Yet although the external abbey, with its verdant decay hanging about it, suffered but little alteration. I gave way, with a child-like perversity, and perchance with a faint hope of alleviating my sorrows, to a display of more than regal magnificence within. For such follies, even in childhood, I had imbibed a taste, and now they came back to me as if in the dotage of grief. Alas, I felt how much ever of incipient madness might have been discovered in the gorgeous and fantastic draperies, in the solemn carvings of Egypt, in the wild cornices and furniture, in the Bedlam[16] patterns of the carpets of tufted gold! I had become a bounden slave in the trammels of opium, and my labors and my orders had taken a coloring from my dreams. But these absurdities I must not pause to detail. Let me speak only of that one chamber, ever accursed, whither, in a moment of mental alienation, I led from the altar as my bride—as the successor of the unforgotten Ligeia—the fair-haired and blue-eyed Lady Rowena Trevanion, of Tremaine.

There is no individual portion of the architecture and decoration of that bridal chamber which is not now visibly before me. Where were the souls of the haughtly family of the bride, when, through thirst of gold, they permitted to pass the threshold of an apartment *so* bedecked, a maiden and a daughter so beloved? I have said, that I minutely remember the details of the chamber—yet I am sadly forgetful on topics of deep moment; and here there was no system, no keeping, in the fantastic display, to take hold upon the memory. The room lay in a high turret of the castellated abbey, was pentagonal in shape, and of capacious size. Occupying the whole southern face of the pentagon was the sole window—an immense sheet of unbroken glass from Venice—a single pane, and tinted of a leaden hue, so that the rays of either the sun or moon passing through it, fell with a ghastly lustre on the objects within. Over the upper portion of this huge window, extended the trellis-work of an aged vine, which clambered up the massy walls of the turret. The ceiling, of gloomy-looking oak, was excessively lofty, vaulted, and elaborately fretted with the wildest and most grotesque specimens of a semi-Gothic, semi-Druidical device. From out the most central recess of this melancholy vaulting, depended, by a single chain of gold with long links, a huge censer of the same metal, Saracenic[17] in pattern, and with many perforations so contrived that there writhed in and out of them, as if endured with a serpent vitality, a continual succession of parti-colored fires.

Some few ottomans and golden candelabra, of Eastern figure, were in various stations about; and there was the couch, too—the bridal couch—of an Indian model, and low, and sculptured of solid ebony, with a pall-like canopy above. In each of the angles of the chamber stood on end a gigantic sarcophagus of black granite, from the tombs of the kings over against Luxor,[18] with their aged lids full of immemorial sculpture. But in the draping of the apartment lay, alas! the chief phantasy of all. The lofty walls, gigantic in height—even unproportionably so—were hung from summit to foot, in vast folds, with a heavy and massive-looking tapestry—tapestry of a material which was found alike as a carpet on the floor, as a covering for the ottomans and the ebony bed, as a canopy for the bed and as the gorgeous volutes of the curtains which partially shaded the window. The material was the richest cloth of gold. It was spotted all over, at irregular intervals, with arabesque[19] figures, about a foot in diameter, and wrought upon the cloth in patterns of the most jetty black. But these figures partook of the true character of the arabesque only when regarded from a single point of view. By a contrivance now common, and indeed traceable to a very remote period of antiquity, they were made changeable in aspect. To one entering the room, they bore the appearance of simple monstrosities; but upon a farther advance, this appearance gradually departed; and, step by step, as the visitor moved his station in the chamber, he saw himself surrounded by an endless succession of the ghastly forms which belong to the superstition of the Norman,[20] or arise in the guilty slumbers of the monk. The phantasmagoric effect was vastly heightened by the artificial introduction of a strong continual current of wind behind the draperies—giving a hideous and uneasy animation to the whole.

In halls such as these—in a bridal chamber such as this—I passed, with the Lady of Tremaine, the unhallowed hours of the first month of our marriage—passed them with but little disquietude. That my wife dreaded the fierce moodiness of my temper—that she shunned me, and loved me but little—I could not help perceiving; but it gave me rather pleasure than otherwise. I loathed her with a hatred belonging more to demon than to man. My memory flew back (oh, with what intensity of regret!) to Ligeia, the beloved, the august, the beautiful, the entombed. I revelled in recollections of her purity, of her wisdom, of her lofty—her ethereal nature, of her passionate, her idolatrous love. Now, then, did my spirit fully and freely burn with more than all the fires of her own. In the excitement of my opium

---

[18] The old setting of Thebes, on the Nile river.

[19] A fanciful pattern of interlacing organic forms, like fruit and flowers.

[20] An abbreviation for Northman, one of the Scandinavians who occupied Normandy, in northern France.

dreams (for I was habitually fettered in the shackles of the drug), I would call aloud upon her name, during the silence of the night, or among the sheltered recesses of the glens by day, as if, through the wild eagerness, the solemn passion, the consuming ardor of my longing for the departed, I could restore her to the pathways she had abondoned—ah, *would* it be for ever?—upon the earth.

About the commencement of the second month of the marriage, the Lady Rowena was attacked with sudden illness, from which her recovery was slow. The fever which consumed her rendered her nights uneasy; and in her perturbed state of half-slumber, she spoke of sounds, and of motions, in and about the chamber of the turret, which I concluded had no origin save in the distemper of her fancy, or perhaps in the phantasmagoric influences of the chamber itself. She became at length convalescent—finally, well. Yet but a brief period elapsed, ere a second more violent disorder again threw her upon a bed of suffering; and from this attack her frame, at all times feeble, never altogether recovered. Her illnesses were, after this epoch, of alarming character, and of more alarming recurrence, defying alike the knowledge and the great exertions of her physicians. With the increase of the chronic disease, which had thus, apparently, taken too sure hold upon her constitution to be eradicated by human means, I could not fail to observe a similar increase in the nervous irritation of her temperament, and in her excitability by trivial causes of fear. She spoke again, and now more frequently and pertinaciously, of the sounds—of the slight sounds—and of the unusual motions among the tapestries, to which she had formerly alluded.

One night, near the closing in of September, she pressed this distressing subject with more than usual emphasis upon my attention. She had just awakened from an unquiet slumber, and I had been watching, with feelings half of anxiety, half of vague terror, the workings of her emaciated countenance. I sat by the side of her ebony bed, upon one of the ottomans of India. She partly arose, and spoke, in an earnest low whisper, of sounds which she *then* heard, but which I could not hear—of motions which she *then* saw, but which I could not perceive. The wind was rushing hurriedly behind the tapestries, and I wished to show her (what, let me confess it, I could not *all* believe) that those almost inarticulate breathings, and those very gentle variations of the figures upon the wall, were but the natural effects of that customary rushing of the wind. But a deadly pallor, overspreading her face, had proved to me that my exertions to reassure her would be fruitless. She appeared to be fainting, and no attendants were within call. I remembered where was deposited a decanter of light wine which had been ordered by her physicians, and hastened across the chamber to procure it. But, as I stepped beneath the light of the censer, two circumstances of a startling nature attracted my attention. I had felt that some palpable although invisible object had passed lightly by my person; and I saw that there lay upon the golden carpet, in the very middle of the rich lustre thrown from the censer, a shadow—a faint, indefinite shadow of angelic aspect—such as might be fancied for the shadow of a shade. But I was wild with the excitement of an immoderate dose of opium, and heeded these things but little, nor spoke of them to Rowena. Having found the wine, I recrossed the chamber, and poured out a gobletful, which I held to the lips of the fainting lady. She had now partially recovered, however, and took the vessel herself, while I sank upon an ottoman near me, with my eyes fastened upon her person. It was then that I became distinctly aware of a gentle foot-fall upon the carpet, and near the couch; and in a second thereafter, as Rowena was in the act of raising the wine to her lips, I saw, or may have dreamed that I saw, fall within the goblet, as if from some invisible spring in the atmosphere of the room three of four large drops of a brilliant and ruby colored fluid. If this I saw—not so Rowena. She swallowed the wine unhesitatingly, and I forbore to speak to her of a circumstance which must, after all, I considered, have been but the suggestion of a vivid imagination, rendered morbidly active by the terror of the lady, by the opium, and by the hour.

Yet I cannot conceal it from my own perception that, immediately subsequent to the fall of the ruby-drops, a rapid change for the worse took place in the disorder of my wife; so that, on the third subsequent night, the hands of her menials prepared her for the tomb, and on the fourth, I sat alone, with her shrouded body, in that fantastic chamber which had received her as my bride. Wild visions, opium-engendered, flitted, shadow-like, before me. I gazed with unquiet eye upon the sarcophagi in the angles of the room, upon the varying figures of the drapery, and upon the writhing of the parti-colored fires in the censer overhead. My eyes then fell, as I called to mind the circumstances of a former night, to the spot beneath the glare of the censer where I had seen the faint traces of the shadow. It was there, however, no longer; and breathing with greater freedom, I turned my glances to the pallid and rigid figure upon the bed. Then rushed upon me a thousand memories of Ligeia—and then came back upon my heart, with the turbulent violence of a flood, the whole of that unutterable woe with which I had regarded *her* thus enshrouded. The night waned; and still, with a bosom full of bitter thoughts of the one only and supremely beloved, I remained gazing upon the body of Rowena.

It might have been midnight, or perhaps earlier, or later, for I had taken no note of time, when a sob, low, gentle, but very distinct, startled me from my revery. I *felt* that it came from the bed of ebony—the bed of death. I listened in an agony of superstitious terror—but there was no repetition of the sound. I strained my vison to detect any motion in the corpse—but there was not the slightest perceptible. Yet I could not have been deceived. I *had* heard the noise, however faint, and my soul was awakened within me. I resolutely and perseveringly kept my attention riveted upon the body. Many minutes elapsed before any circumstance occurred tending to throw light upon the mystery. At length it became evident that a slight, a very feeble, and barely noticeable tinge of color had flushed up within the cheeks, and along the sunken small veins of the eyelids. Through a species of unutterable horror and awe, for which the language of mortality has no sufficiently energetic expression, I felt my heart cease to beat, my limbs grow rigid where I sat. Yet a sense of duty finally operated to restore my self-possession. I could no longer doubt that we had been precipitate in our preparations—that Rowena still lived. It was necessary that some immediate exertion be made; yet the turret was altogether apart from the portion of the abbey tenanted by the servants—there were none within call—I had no means of summoning them to my aid without leaving the room for many minutes—and this I could not venture to do. I therefore struggled alone in my endeavors to call back the spirit still hovering. In a short period it was certain, however, that a relapse had taken place; the color disappeared from both eyelid and cheek, leaving a wanness even more than that of marble; the lips became doubly shrivelled and pinched up in the ghastly expression of death; a repulsive clamminess and coldness overspread rapidly the surface of the body; and all the usual rigorous stiffness immediately supervened. I fell back with a shudder upon the couch from which I had been so startlingly aroused, and again gave myself up to passionate waking visions of Ligeia.

An hour thus elapsed, when (could it be possible?) I was a second time aware of some vague sound issuing from the region of the bed. I listened — in extremity of horror. The sound came again—it was a sigh. Rushing to the corpse, I saw—distinctly saw—a tremor upon the lips. In a minute afterward they relaxed, disclosing a bright line of the pearly teeth. Amazement now struggled in my bosom with the profound awe which had hitherto reigned there alone. I felt that my vision grew dim, that my reason wandered; and it was only by a violent effort that I at length succeeded in nerving myself to the task which duty thus once more had pointed out. There was now a partial glow upon the forehead and upon the cheek and throat; a perceptible warmth pervaded the whole frame; there was even a slight pulsation at the heart. The lady *lived;* and with redoubled ardor I betook myself to the task of restoration. I chafed and bathed the temples and the hands, and used every exertion which experience, and no little medical reading, could suggest. But in vain. Suddenly, the color fled, the pulsation ceased, the lips resumed the expression of the dead, and, in an instant afterward, the whole body took upon itself the icy chilliness, the livid hue, the intense rigidity, the sunken outline, and all the loathsome peculiarities of that which has been, for many days, a tenant of the tomb.

And again I sunk into visions of Ligeia—and again (what marvel that I shudder while I write?), *again* there reached my ears a low sob from the region of the ebony bed. But why shall I minutely detail the unspeakable horrors of that night? Why shall I pause to relate how, time after time, until near the period of the gray dawn, this hideous drama of revivification was repeated; how each terrific relapse was only into a sterner and apparently more irredeemable death; how each agony wore the aspect of a struggle with some invisible foe; and how each struggle was succeeded by I know not what change in the personal appearance of the corpse? Let me hurry to a conclusion.

The greater part of the fearful night had worn away, and she who had been dead once again stirred—and now more vigorously than hitherto, although arousing from a dissolution more appalling in its utter hopelessness than any. I had long ceased to struggle or to move, and remained sitting rigidly upon the ottoman, a helpless prey to a whirl of violent emotions, of which extreme awe was perhaps the least terrible, the least consuming. The corpse, I repeat, stirred, and now more vigorously than before. The hues of life flushed up with unwonted energy into the countenance—the limbs relaxed—and, save that the eyelids were yet pressed heavily together, and that the bandages and draperies of the grave still imparted their charnel character to the figure, I might have dreamed that Rowena had indeed shaken off, utterly, the fetters of Death. But if this idea was not, even then, altogether adopted, I could at least doubt no longer, when, arising from the bed, tottering, with feeble steps, with closed eyes, and with the manner of one bewildered in a dream, the thing that was enshrouded advanced boldly and palpably into the middle of the apartment.

I trembled not—I stirred not—for a crowd of unutterable fancies connected with the air, the stature, the demeanor, of the figure, rushing hurriedly through my brain, had paralyzed—had chilled me into stone. I stirred not—but gazed upon the apparition. There was a mad disorder in my thoughts—a tumult unappeasable. Could it, indeed, be the *living* Rowena who confronted me? Could it, indeed, be Rowena *at all* —the fair-haired, the blue-eyed Lady Rowena Trevanion of Tremaine? Why, *why* should I doubt it? The bandage lay heavily about the mouth—but then might it not be the mouth of the breathing Lady of Tremaine? And the cheeks—there were the roses as in her noon of life—yes, these might indeed be the fair cheeks of the living Lady of Tremaine. And the chin, with its dimples, as in health, might it not be hers?—but *had she then grown taller since her malady?* What inexpressible madness seized me with that thought? One bound, and I had reached her feet! Shrinking from my touch, she let fall from her head, unloosened, the ghastly cerements which had confined it, and there streamed forth into the rushing atmosphere of the chamber huge masses of long and dishevelled hair; *it was blacker than the raven wings of midnight!* And now slowly opened *the eyes* of the figure which stood before me. "Here then, at least," I shrieked aloud, "can I never—can I never be mistaken—these are the full, and the black, and the wild eyes—of my lost love—of the Lady—of the Lady Ligeia."

The Fall of the House of Usher[1]

Son cœur est un luth suspendu;

Sitôt qu'on le touche il résonne.[2]

—*De Béranger*

During the whole of a dull, dark, and soundless day in the autumn of the year, when the clouds hung oppressively low in the heavens, I had been passing alone, on horseback, through a singularly dreary tract of country, and at length found myself, as the shades of the evening drew on, within view of the melancholy House of Usher.[3] I know not how it was —but, with the first glimpse of the building, a sense of insufferable gloom pervaded my spirit. I say insufferable; for the feeling was unrelieved by any of that half-pleasurable, because poetic, sentiment with which the mind usually receives even the sternest natural images of the desolate or terrible. I looked upon the scene before me—upon the mere house, and the simple landscape features of the domain—upon the bleak walls—upon the vacant eye-like windows— upon a few rank sedges—and upon a few white trunks of decayed trees— with an utter depression of soul which I can compare to no earthly sensation more properly than to the after-dream of the reveller upon opium—the bitter lapse into every-day life—the hideous dropping off of the veil. There was an iciness, a sinking, a sickening of the heart—an unredeemed dreariness of thought which no goading of the imagination could torture into aught of the sublime. What was it—I paused to think—what was it that so unnerved me in the contemplation of the House of Usher? It was a mystery all insoluble; nor could I grapple with the shadowy fancies that crowded upon me as I pondered. I was forced to fall back upon the unsatisfactory conclusion, that while, beyond doubt, there *are* combinations of very simple natural objects which have the power of thus affecting us, still the analysis of this power lies among considerations beyond our depth. It was possible, I reflected, that a mere different arrangement of the particulars of the scene, of the details of the picture, would be sufficient to modify, or perhaps to annihilate its capacity for sorrowful impression; and, acting upon this idea, I reined my horse to the precipitous black and lurid tarn that lay in unruffled lustre by the dwell-

---

[1] "The Fall of the House of Usher" was initially published in *Burton's Gentleman's Magazine* (September 18, 1839). In this story, Poe's method is largely pictorial. There is little narrative, and the reader becomes absorbed in various states of mind: Usher's intellect and morbid fear of sensuality; his sister Madeline's emotional nature, and the all-inclusive house that embodies the two of them.

[2] Pierre Jean de Béranger (1780-1857) was a French poet. The lines are taken from "Le Refus" (11. 41-42): "His heart is a hanging lute:/If it be but touched, it resounds." See "Israfel," 1. 2.

[3] A theatrical couple, Mr. and Mrs. Luke Usher, were guardians of Poe's mother, Elizabeth Arnold, when she was an orphaned child-actress.

ing, and gazed down—but with a shudder even more thrilling than before—
upon the remodelled and inverted images of the gray sedge, and the ghastly
tree-stems, and the vacant and eye-like windows.

Nevertheless, in this mansion of gloom I now proposed to myself a sojourn
of some weeks. Its proprietor, Roderick Usher, had been one of my boon
companions in boyhood; but many years had elapsed since our last meeting.
A letter, however, had lately reached me in a distant part of the country—a
letter from him—which, in its wildly importunate nature, had admitted of no
other than a personal reply. The MS. gave evidence of nervous agitation.
The writer spoke of acute bodily illness—of a mental disorder which oppressed him—and of an earnest desire to see me, as his best and indeed his
only personal friend, with a view of attempting, by the cheerfulness of my
society, some alleviation of his malady. It was the manner in which all this,
and much more, was said—it was the apparent *heart* that went with his
request—which allowed me no room for hesitation; and I accordingly
obeyed forthwith what I still considered a very singular summons.

Although, as boys, we had been intimate associates, yet I really knew little
of my friend. His reserve had been always excessive and habitual. I was
aware, however, that his very ancient family had been noted, time out of
mind, for a peculiar sensibility of temperament, displaying itself, through
long ages, in many works of exalted art, and manifested, of late, in repeated
deeds of munificent yet unobtrusive charity, as well as in a passionate devotion to the intricacies, perhaps even more than to the orthodox and easily
recognizable beauties, of musical science. I had learned, too, the very remarkable fact, that the stem of the Usher race, all time-honored as it was,
had put forth, at no period, any enduring branch; in other words, that the
entire family lay in the direct line of descent, and had always, with very
trifling and very temporary variation, so lain. It was this deficiency, I considered, while running over in thought the perfect keeping of the character of
the premises with the accredited character of the people, and while specu-
lating upon the possible influence which the one, in the long lapse of centuries, might have exercised upon the other—it was this deficiency, perhaps, of
collateral issue, and the consequent undeviating transmission, from sire to
son, of the patrimony with the name, which had, at length, so identified the
two as to merge the original title of the estate in the quaint and equivocal
appellation of the "House of Usher"—an appellation which seemed to include, in the minds of the peasantry who used it, both the family and the
family mansion.

I have said that the sole effect of my somewhat childish experiment—that
of looking down within the tarn—had been to deepen the first singular
impression. There can be no doubt that the consciousness of the rapid increase of my superstition—for why should I not so term it?—served mainly
to accelerate the increase itself. Such, I have long known, is the paradoxical
law of all sentiments having terror as a basis. And it might have been for this

reason only, that, when I again uplifted my eyes to the house itself, from its image in the pool, there grew in my mind a strange fancy—a fancy so ridiculous, indeed, that I but mention it to show the vivid force of the sensations which oppressed me. I had so worked upon my imagination as really to believe that about the whole mansion and domain there hung an atmosphere peculiar to themselves and their immediate vicinity—an atmosphere which had no affinity with the air of heaven, but which had reeked up from the decayed trees, and the gray wall, and the silent tarn—a pestilent and mystic vapor, dull, sluggish, faintly discernible, and leaden-hued.

Shaking off from my spirit what *must* have been a dream, I scanned more narrowly the real aspect of the building. Its principal feature seemed to be that of an excessive antiquity. The discoloration of ages had been great. Minute fungi overspread the whole exterior, hanging in a fine tangled web-work from the eaves. Yet all this was apart from any extraordinary dilapidation. No portion of the masonry had fallen; and there appeared to be a wild inconsistency between its still perfect adaptation of parts, and the crumbling condition of the individual stones. In this there was much that reminded me of the specious totality of old wood-work which has rotted for long years in some neglected vault, with no disturbance from the breath of the external air. Beyond this indication of extensive decay, however, the fabric gave little token of instability. Perhaps the eye of a scrutinizing observer might have discovered a barely perceptible fissure, which, extending from the roof of the building in front made its way down the wall in a zigzag direction, until it became lost in the sullen waters of the tarn.

Noticing these things, I rode over a short causeway to the house. A servant in waiting took my horse, and I entered the Gothic archway of the hall. A valet, of stealthy step, thence conducted me, in silence, through many dark and intricate passages in my progress to the *studio* of his master. Much that I encountered on the way contributed, I know not how, to heighten the vague sentiments of which I have already spoken. While the objects around me—while the carvings of the ceilings, the sombre tapestries of the walls, the ebon blackness of the floors, and the phatasmagoric armorial trophies which rattled as I strode, were but matters to which, or to such as which, I had been accustomed from my infancy—while I hesitated not to acknowledge how familiar was all this—I still wondered to find how unfamiliar were the fancies which ordinary images were stirring up. On one of the staircases, I met the physician of the family. His countenance, I thought, wore a mingled expression of low cunning and perplexity. He accosted me with trepidation and passed on. The valet now threw open a door and ushered me into the presence of his master.

The room in which I found myself was very large and lofty. The windows were long, narrow, and pointed, and at so vast a distance from the black oaken floor as to be altogether inaccessible from within. Feeble gleams of encrimsoned light made their way through the trellissed panes, and served to render sufficiently distinct the more prominent objects around; the eye, however, struggled in vain to reach the remoter angles of the chamber, or the recesses of the vaulted and fretted ceiling. Dark draperies hung upon the walls. The general furniture was profuse, comfortless, antique, and tattered. Many books and musical instruments lay scattered about, but failed to give any vitality to the scene. I felt that I breathed an atmosphere of sorrow. An air of stern, deep, and irredeemable gloom hung over and pervaded all.

Upon my entrance, Usher arose from a sofa on which he had been lying at full length, and greeted me with a vivacious warmth which had much in it, I at first thought, of an overdone cordiality—of the constrained effort of the *ennuyé*[4] man of the world. A glance, however, at his countenance convinced me of his perfect sincerity. We sat down; and for some moments, while he spoke not, I gazed upon him with a feeling half of pity, half of awe. Surely, man had never before so terribly altered, in so brief a period, as had Roderick Usher! It was with difficulty that I could bring myself to admit the identity of the wan being before me with the companion of my early boyhood. Yet the character of his face had been at all times remarkable. A cadaverousness of complexion; an eye large, liquid, and luminous beyond comparison; lips somewhat thin and very pallid, but of a surpassingly beautiful curve; a nose of a delicate Hebrew model, but with a breadth of nostril unusual in similar formations; a finely moulded chin, speaking, in its want of prominence, of a want of moral energy; hair of a more than web-like softness and tenuity;—these features, with an inordinate expansion above the regions of the temple, made up altogether a countenance not easily to be forgotten. And now in the mere exaggeration of the prevailing character of these features, and of the expression they were wont to convey, lay so much of change that I doubted to whom I spoke. The now ghastly pallor of the skin, and the now miraculous lustre of the eye, above all things startled and even awed me. The silken hair, too, had been suffered to grow all unheeded, and as, in its wild gossamer texture, it floated rather than fell about the face, I could not, even with effort, connect its Arabesque[5] expression with any idea of simple humanity.

In the manner of my friend I was at once struck with an incoherence — an inconsistency; and I soon found this to arise from a series of feeble and futile struggles to overcome an habitual trepidancy—an excessive nervous agitation. For something of this nature I had indeed been prepared, no less by his letter, than by reminiscences of certain boyish traits, and by conclusions deduced from his peculiar physical confirmation and temperament.[6] His action was alternately vivacious and sullen. His voice varied rapidly from a tremulous indecision (when the animal spirits seemed utterly in abeyance)

[4] Bored.
[5] Fantastic interlacing.
[6] Poe believed in the phrenological assumption that character could be deduced from external characteristics.

to that species of energetic concision—that abrupt, weighty, unhurried, and hollow-sounding enunciation—that leaden, self-balanced, and perfectly modulated guttural utterance, which may be observed in the lost drunkard, or the irreclaimable eater of opium, during the periods of his most intense excitement.

It was thus that he spoke of the object of my visit, of his earnest desire to see me, and of the solace he expected me to afford him. He entered, at some length, into what he conceived to be the nature of his malady. It was, he said, a constitutional and a family evil, and one for which he despaired to find a remedy—a mere nervous affection, he immediately added, which would undoubtedly soon pass off. It displayed itself in a host of unnatural sensations. Some of these, as he detailed them, interested and bewildered me; although, perhaps, the terms and the general manner of their narration had their weight. He suffered much from a morbid acuteness of the senses; the most insipid food was alone endurable; he could wear only garments of certain texture; the odors of all flowers were oppressive; his eyes were tortured by even a faint light; and there were but peculiar sounds, and these from stringed instruments, which did not inspire him with horror.

To an anomalous species of terror I found him a bounden slave. "I shall perish," said he, "I *must* perish in this deplorable folly. Thus, thus and not otherwise, shall I be lost. I dread the events of the future, not in themselves, but in their results. I shudder at the thought of any, even the most trivial, incident, which may operate upon this intolerable agitation of soul. I have, indeed, no abhorrence of danger, except in its absolute effect—in terror. In this unnerved, in this pitiable, condition I feel that the period will sooner or later arrive when I must abandon life and reason together, in some struggle with the grim phantasm, FEAR."

I learned, moreover, at intervals, and through broken and equivocal hints, another singular feature of his mental condition. He was enchained by certain superstitious impressions in regard to the dwelling which he tenanted, and whence, for many years, he had never ventured forth—in regard to an influence whose superstitious force was conveyed in terms too shadowy here to be re-stated—an influence which some peculiarities in the mere form and substance of his family mansion had, by dint of long sufferance, he said, obtained over his spirit—an effect which the *physique* of the gray walls and turrets, and of the dim tarn into which they all looked down, had, at length, brought about upon the *morale* of his existence.

He admitted, however, although with hesitation, that much of the peculiar gloom which thus afflicted him could be traced to a more natural and far more palpable origin—to the severe and long-continued illness—indeed to the evidently approaching dissolution—of a tenderly beloved sister, his sole companion for long years, his last and only relative on earth, "Her decease," he said, with a bitterness which I can never forget, "would leave him (him, the hopeless and the frail) the last of the ancient race of the Ushers." While he spoke, the lady Madeline (for so was she called) passed through a remote portion of the apartment, and, without having noticed my presence, disappeared. I regarded her with an utter astonishment not unmingled with dread; and yet I found it impossible to account for such feelings. A sensation of stupor oppressed me as my eyes followed her retreating steps. When a door, at length, closed upon her, my glance sought instinctively and eagerly the countenance of the brother; but he had buried his face in his hands, and I could only perceive that a far more than ordinary wanness had overspread the emaciated fingers through which trickled many passionate tears.

The disease of the lady Madeline had long baffled the skill of her physicians. A settled apathy, a gradual wasting away of the person, and frequent although transient affections of a partially cataleptical character were the unusual diagnosis. Hitherto she had steadily borne up against the pressure of her malady, and had not betaken herself finally to bed; but on the closing in of the evening of my arrival at the house, she succumbed (as her brother told me at night with inexpressible agitation) to the prostrating power of the destroyer; and I learned that the glimpse I had obtained of her person would thus probably be the last I should obtain—that the lady, at least while living, would be seen by me no more.

For several days ensuing, her name was unmentioned by either Usher or myself; and during this period I was busied in earnest endeavors to alleviate the melancholy of my friend. We painted and read together, or I listened, as if in a dream, to the wild improvisations of his speaking guitar. And thus, as a closer and still closer intimacy admitted me more unreservedly into the recesses of his spirit, the more bitterly did I perceive the futility of all attempt at cheering a mind from which darkness, as if an inherent positive quality, poured forth upon all objects of the moral and physical universe in one unceasing radiation of gloom.

I shall ever bear about me a memory of the many solemn hours I thus spent alone with the master of the House of Usher. Yet I should fail in any attempt to convey an idea of the exact character of the studies, or of the occupations in which he involved me, or led me the way. An excited and highly distempered ideality threw a sulphureous lustre over all. His long improvised dirges will ring forever in my ears. Among other things, I hold painfully in mind a certain singular perversion and amplification of the wild air of the last waltz of Von Weber.[7] From the paintings over which his elaborate fancy brooded, and which grew, touch by touch, into vaguenesses at which I shuddered the more thrillingly, because I shuddered knowing not

---

[7] Karl Maria Von Weber (1786-1826) was a German Romantic composer who inspired Karl Gottlieb Reissiger, a contemporary of Poe's. "The Last Waltz of Von Weber" is No. 5 of Reissiger's *Danses Brilliantes*.

why—from these paintings (vivid as their images now are before me) I would in vain endeavor to educe more than a small portion which should lie within the compass of merely written words. By the utter simplicity, by the nakedness of his designs, he arrested and overawed attention. If ever mortal painted an idea, that mortal was Roderick Usher. For me at least, in the circumstances then surrounding me, there arose out of the pure abstractions which the hypochondriac contrived to throw upon his canvas, an intensity of intolerable awe, no shadow of which felt I ever yet in the contemplation of the certainly glowing yet too concrete reveries of Fuseli.[8]

One of the phantasmagoric conceptions of my friend, partaking not so rigidly of the spirit of abstraction, may be shadowed forth, although feebly, in words. A small picture presented the interior of an immensely long and rectangular vault or tunnel, with low walls, smooth, white, and without interruption or device. Certain accessory points of the design served well to convey the idea that this excavation lay at an exceeding depth below the surface of the earth. No outlet was observed in any portion of its vast extent, and no torch or other artificial source of light was discernible; yet a flood of intense rays rolled throughout, and bathed the whole in a ghastly and inappropriate splendor.[9]

I have just spoken of that morbid condition of the auditory nerve which rendered all music intolerable to the sufferer, with the exception of certain effects of stringed instruments. It was, perhaps, the narrow limits to which he thus confined himself upon the guitar which gave birth, in great measure, to the fantastic character of his performances. But the fervid *facility* of his *impromptus* could not be so accounted for. They must have been, and were, in the notes, as well as in the words of his wild fantasias (for he not unfrequently accompanied himself with rhymed verbal improvisations), the result of that intense mental collectedness and concentration to which I have previously alluded as observable only in particular moments of the highest artificial excitement. The words of one of these rhapsodies I have easily remembered. I was, perhaps, the more forcibly impressed with it as he gave it, because, in the under or mystic current of its meaning, I fancied that I perceived, and for the first time, a full consciousness on the part of Usher of the tottering of his lofty reason upon her throne. The verses, which were entitled "The Haunted Palace,"[10] ran very nearly, if not accurately, thus:—

[8] Henry Fuseli (1741-1825) is the anglicized name of the Swiss-born professor at the Royal Academy in London who was a painter of the fantastic. He was particularly well known for his illustrations of Milton and Shakespeare.

[9] Compare this paragraph with the lines from *Romeo and Juliet*, v, iii, 84-86: "A grave? Oh, no, a lantern, slaughtered youth;/ For here lies Juliet, and her beauty makes/ This vault a feasting presence full of light."

[10] "The Haunted Palace" was first published in the *Baltimore Museum*, April 1839.

I.

In the greenest of our valleys,
  By good angels tenanted,
Once a fair and stately palace—
  Radiant palace—reared its head.
In the monarch Thought's dominion—
  It stood there!
Never seraph spread a pinion
  Over fabric half so fair.

II.

Banners yellow, glorious, golden,
  On its roof did float and flow
(This—all this—was in the olden
  Time long ago);
And every gentle air that dallied,
  In that sweet day,
Along the ramparts plumed and pallid,
  A winged odor went away.

III

Wanderers in that happy valley
  Through two luminous windows saw
Spirits moving musically
  To a lute's well-tunèd law;
Round about a throne, where sitting
  (Porphyrogene!)[11]
In state his glory well befitting,
  The ruler of the realm was seen.

IV.

And all with pearl and ruby glowing
  Was the fair palace door,
Through which came flowing, flowing, flowing
  And sparkling evermore,
A troop of Echoes whose sweet duty
  Was but to sing,
In voices of surpassing beauty,
  The wit and wisdom of their king.

---

[11] Derives from the Greek *porphyra* ("purple") and —*genes* ("born")—"to the purple born." Purple is the color of royalty.

V

But evil things, in robes of sorrow,
Assailed the monarch's high estate;
(Ah, let us mourn, for never morrow
Shall dawn upon him, desolate!)
And, round about his home, the glory
That blushed and bloomed
Is but a dim-remembered story
Of the old time entombed.

VI.

And travellers now within that valley,
Through the red-litten windows see
Vast forms that move fantastically
To a discordant melody;
While, like, a rapid ghastly river,
Through the pale door;
A hideous throng rush out forever,
And laugh—but smile no more.

I well remember that suggestions arising from this ballad led us into a train of thought wherein there became manifest an opinion of Usher's which I mention not so much on account of its novelty (for other men have thought thus), as on account of the pertinacity with which he maintained it. This opinion, in its general form, was that of the sentience of all vegetable things.[12] But, in his disordered fancy, the idea had assumed a more daring character, and trespassed, under certain conditions, upon the kingdom of inorganization.[13] I lack words to express the full extent, or the earnest *abandon* of his persuasion. The belief, however, was connected (as I have previously hinted) with the gray stones of the home of his forefathers. The conditions of the sentence had been here, he imagined, fulfilled in the method of collocation of these stones—in the order of their arrangement, as well as in that of the many *fungi* which overspread them, and of the decayed trees which stood around—above all, in the long undisturbed endurance of this arrangement, and in its reduplication in the still waters of the tarn. Its evidence—the evidence of the sentience—was to be seen, he said (and I here started as he spoke), in the gradual yet certain condensation of an atmosphere of their own about the waters and the walls. The result was discoverable, he added, in that silent yet importunate and terrible influence which for centuries had moulded the destinies of his family, and which made *him* what I now saw him—what he was. Such opinions need no comment, and I will make none.

[12] "Watson, Dr. Percival, Spallanzani, and especially the Bishop of Llandaff."—See *Chemical Essays,* Vol. v." [Poe's note].

[13] The reality of inorganic matter.

Our books—the books which, for years, had formed no small portion of the mental existence of the invalid—were, as might be supposed, in strict keeping with this character of phantasm. We pored together over such works as the "Ververt et Chartreuse" of Gresset; the "Belphegor" of Machiavelli; the "Heaven and Hell' of Swedenborg; the "Subterranean Voyage of Nicholas Klimm" of Holberg; the "Chiromancy" of Robert Flud, of Jean D'Indaginé, and of Dela Chambre; the "Journey into the Blue Distance of Tieck; and the "City of the Sun" of Campanella. One favorite volume was a small octavo edition of the "Directorium Inquisitorium," by the Dominican Eymeric de Gironne; and there were passages in Pomponius Mela, about the old African Satyrs and Ægipans, over which Usher would sit dreaming for hours. His chief delight, however, was found in the perusal of an exceedingly rare and curious book in quarto Gothic—the manual of a forgotten church— the *Vigiliæ Mortuorum secundum Chorum Ecclesiæ Maguntinæ.*[14]

I could not help thinking of the wild ritual of this work, and of its probable influence upon the hypochondriac, when, one evening, having informed me abruptly that the lady Madeline was no more, he stated his intention of preserving her corpse for a fortnight (previously to its final interment), in one of the numerous vaults within the main walls of the building. The worldly reason, however, assigned for this singular proceeding, was one which I did not feel at liberty to dispute. The brother had been led to his resolution (so he told me) by consideration of the unusual character of the malady of the deceased, of certain obtrusive and eager inquiries on the part of her medical men, and of the remote and exposed situation of the burial-ground of the family. I will not deny that when I called to mind the sinister countenance of the person whom I met upon the staircase, on the day of my arrival at the house, I had no desire to oppose what I regarded as at best but a harmless, and by no means an unnatural, precaution.

[14] These books are intended to reveal Usher's state of mind—his vast knowledge and his concern with the occult—before his burial and the resurrection of his sister, Madeline. *Vert-Vert and Chartreuse*, by Jean Baptise Gresset (1709-1777), are anticlerical poetic satires; *Belphegor*, by Niccolo Machiavelli (1469-1527) is a demonic tale that sets out to prove that women are the curse of men; *Heaven and Hell* (1758), by Emanuel Swedenborg, the Swedish philosopher, scientist, and mystic, is concerned with spiritual identity after death; *Subterranean Voyage* (1741) is an imaginary voyage tale about death; Robert Flud (1574-1637) was an English physician, cabalist, and Rosicrucian; Jean D'Indaginé's *Chiromantia* (1522) and De La Chambre's *Discours Sur Les Principes de la Chironmancie* (1653) were studies of palmistry and divination; *Das Alte Bush* is the title of the work by Ludwig Tieck (1773-1853), a German romantic novelist and critic; *City of the Sun* (1643) by Tommaso Campanella (1568-1639), an Italian philosopher of the late Renaissance, creates a Utopia. Eymeric de Gironne was a fourteenth-century Spanish Inquisitor-General who left a record of his Inquisitorial proceedings that served as a guide for Torquemada. Pomponius Mela wrote *De Situ Orbis*, a geographical treatise of the first century, and describes strange beasts of foreign lands: "Aegipans" were supposed goatmen of Africa. The final title may be translated as "Vigils for the Dead according to the Choir of the Church of Mayence."

At the request of Usher, I personally aided him in the arrangements for the temporary entombment. The body having been encoffined, we two alone bore it to its rest. The vault in which we placed it (and which had been so long unopened that our torches, half smothered in its oppressive atmosphere, gave us little opportunity for investigation) was small, damp, and entirely without means of admission for light; lying, at great depth, immediately beneath that portion of the building in which was my own sleeping apartment. It had been used, apparently, in remote feudal times, for the worst purposes of a donjon-keep, and, in later days, as a place of deposit for powder, or some other highly combustible substance, as a portion of its floor, and the whole interior of a long archway through which we reached it, were carefully sheathed with copper. The door, of massive iron, had been also, similarly protected. Its immense weight caused an unusually sharp, grating sound, as it moved upon its hinges.

Having deposited our mournful burden upon tressels within this region of horror, we partially turned aside the yet unscrewed lid of the coffin, and looked upon the face of the tenant. A striking similitude between the brother and sister now first arrested my attention; and Usher, divining, perhaps, my thought, murmured out some few words from which I learned that the deceased and himself had been twins, and that sympathies of a scarcely intelligible nature had always existed between them. Our glances, however, rested not long upon the dead—for we could not regard her unawed. The disease which had thus entombed the lady in the maturity of youth, had left, as usual in all maladies of a strictly cataleptical character, the mockery of a faint blush upon the bosom and the face, and that suspiciously lingering smile upon the lip which is so terrible in death. We replaced and screwed down the lid, and, having secured the door of iron, made our way, with toil, into the scarcely less gloomy apartments of the upper portion of the house.

And now, some days of bitter grief having elapsed, an observable change came over the features of the mental disorder of my friend. His ordinary manner had vanished. His ordinary occupations were neglected or forgotten. He roamed from chamber to chamber with hurried, unequal, and objectless step. The pallor of his countenance had assumed, if possible, a more ghastly hue—but the luminousness of his eye had utterly gone out. The once occasional huskiness of his tone was heard no more; and a tremulous quaver, as if of extreme terror, habitually characterized his utterance. There were times, indeed, when I thought his unceasingly agitated mind was laboring with some oppressive secret, to divulge which he struggled for the necessary courage. At times, again, I was obliged to resolve all into the mere inexplicable vagaries of madness, for I beheld him gazing upon vacancy for long hours, in an attitude of the profoundest attention, as if listening to some imaginary sound. It was no wonder that his condition terrified—that it infected me. I felt creeping upon me, by slow yet certain degrees, the wild influences of his own fantastic yet impressive superstitions.

It was, especially, upon retiring to bed late in the night of the seventh or eighth day after the placing of the lady Madeline within the donjon, that I experienced the full power of such feelings. Sleep came not near my couch—while the hours waned and waned away. I struggled to reason off the nervousness which had dominion over me. I endeavored to believe that much, if not all of what I felt, was due to the bewildering influence of the gloomy furniture of the room—of the dark and tattered draperies, which, tortured into motion by the breath of a rising tempest, swayed fitfully to and fro upon the walls, and rustled uneasily about the decorations of the bed. But my efforts were fruitless. An irrepressible tremor gradually pervaded my frame; and, at length, there sat upon my very heart an incubus of utterly causeless alarm. Shaking this off with a gasp and a struggle, I uplifted myself upon the pillows, and, peering earnestly within the intense darkness of the chamber, hearkened—I know not why, except that an instinctive spirit prompted me—to certain low and indefinite sounds which came, through the pauses of the storm, at long intervals, I knew not whence. Overpowered by an intense sentiment of horror, unaccountable yet unendurable, I threw on my clothes with haste (for I felt that I should sleep no more during the night), and endeavored to arouse myself from the pitiable condition into which I had fallen, by pacing rapidly to and fro through the apartment.

I had taken but few turns in this manner, when a light step on an adjoining staircase arrested my attention. I presently recognized it as that of Usher. In an instant afterward he rapped, with a gentle touch, at my door, and entered, bearing a lamp. His countenance was, as usual, cadaverously wan—but, moreover, there was a species of mad hilarity in his eyes—an evidently restrained *hysteria* in his whole demeanor. His air appalled me—but any thing was preferable to the solitude which I had so long endured, and I even welcomed his presence as a relief.

"And you have not seen it?" he said abruptly, after having stared about him for some moments in silence—"you have not then seen it?—but, stay! you shall." Thus speaking, and having carefully shaded his lamp, he hurried to one of the casements, and threw it freely open to the storm.

The impetuous fury of the entering gust nearly lifted us from our feet. It was, indeed, a tempestuous yet sternly beautiful night, and one wildly singular in its terror and its beauty. A whirlwind had apparently collected its force in our vicinity; for there were frequent and violent alterations in the direction of the wind; and the exceeding density of the clouds (which hung so low as to press upon the turrets of the house) did not prevent our perceiving the life-like velocity with which they flew careering from all points against each other, without passing away into the distance. I say that even their exceeding density did not prevent our perceiving this—yet we had no glimpse of the moon or stars, nor was there any flashing forth of the lightning. But the under surfaces of the huge masses of agitated vapor, as well as all terrestrial objects immediately around us, were glowing in the unnatural light of a faintly luminous and distinctly visible gaseous exhalation which hung about and enshrouded the mansion.

"You must not—you shall not behold this!" said I, shuddering, to Usher, as I led him, with a gentle violence, from the window to a seat. "These appearances, which bewilder you, are merely electrical phenomena not un-common—or it may be that they have their ghastly origin in the rank miasma of the tarn. Let us close this casement;—the air is chilling and dangerous to your frame. Here is one of your favorite romances. I will read, and you shall listen:—and so we will pass away this terrible night together."

The antique volume which I had taken up was the "Mad Trist" of Sir Launcelot Canning;[15] but I had called it a favorite of Usher's more in sad jest than in earnest; for, in truth, there is little in its uncouth and unimaginative prolixity which could have had interest for the lofty and spiritual ideality of my friend. It was, however, the only book immediately at hand; and I in-dulged a vague hope that the excitement which now agitated the hypochon-driac, might find relief (for the history of mental disorder is full of similar anomalies) even in the extremeness of the folly which I should read. Could I have judged, indeed, by the wild over-strained air of vivacity with which he hearkened, or apparently hearkened, to the words of the tale, I might well have congratulated myself upon the success of my design.

I had arrived at that well-known portion of the story where Ethelred, the hero of the Trist, having sought in vain for peaceable admission into the dwelling of the hermit, proceeds to make good an entrance by force. Here, it will be remembered, the words of the narrative run thus:

"And Ethelred, who was by nature of a doughty heart, and who was now mighty withal, on account of the powerfulness of the wine which he had drunken, waited no longer to hold parley with the hermit, who, in sooth, was of an obstinate and maliceful turn, but, feeling the rain upon his shoulders, and fearing the rising of the tempest, uplifted his mace outright, and, with blows, made quickly room in the plankings of the door for his gauntleted hand; and now pulling therewith sturdily, he so cracked and ripped, and tore all asunder, that the noise of the dry and hollow-sounding wood alarumed and reverberated throughout the forest."

At the termination of this sentence I started and, for a moment, paused; for it appeared to me (although I at once concluded that my excited fancy had deceived me)—it appeared to me that, from some very remote portion of the mansion, there came, indistinctly to my ears, what might have been, in its exact similarity of character, the echo (but a stifled and dull one certainly) of the very cracking and ripping sound which Sir Launcelot had so particu-larly described. It was, beyond doubt, the coincidence alone which had arrested my attention; for, amid the rattling of the sashes of the casements,

[15] This book was probably invented by Poe. It has not been found.

and the ordinary commingled noises of the still increasing storm, the sound, in itself, had nothing, surely, which should have interested or disturbed me. I continued the story:

"But the good champion Ethelred, now entering within the door, was sore enraged and amazed to perceive no signal of the maliceful hermit, but, in the stead thereof, a dragon of a scaly and prodigious demeanor and of a fiery tongue, which sate in guard before a palace of gold, with a floor of silver; and upon the wall there hung a shield of shining brass with this legend enwritten—

> Who entereth herein, a conqueror hath bin;
> Who slayeth the dragon, the shield he shall win.

And Ethelred uplifted his mace, and struck upon the head of the dragon, which fell before him, and gave up his pesty breath, with a shriek so horrid and harsh, and withal so piercing, that Ethelred had fain to close his ears with his hands against the dreadful noise of it, the like whereof was never before heard."

Here again I paused abruptly, and now with a feeling of wild amazement—for there could be no doubt whatever that, in this instance, I did actually hear (although from what direction it proceeded I found it impossible to say) a low and apparently distant, but harsh, protracted, and most unusual screaming or grating sound—the exact counterpart of what my fancy had already conjured up for the dragons's unnatural shriek as described by the romancer.

Oppressed, as I certainly was, upon the occurrence of this second and most extraordinary coincidence, by a thousand conflicting sensations, in which wonder and extreme terror were predominant, I still retained sufficient presence of mind to avoid exciting, by any observation, the sensitive nervousness of my companion. I was by no means certain that he had noticed the sounds in question; although, assuredly, a strange alteration had, during the last few minutes, taken place in his demeanor. From a position fronting my own, he had gradually brought round his chair, so as to sit with his face to the door of the chamber; and thus I could but partially perceive his features, although I saw that his lips trembled as if he were murmuring inaudibly. His head had dropped upon his breast—yet I knew that he was not asleep, from the wide and rigid opening of the eye as I caught a glance of it in profile. The motion of his body, too, was at variance with this idea—for he rocked from side to side with a gentle yet constant and uniform sway. Having rapidly taken notice of all this, I resumed the narrative of Sir Launcelot, which thus proceeded:

"And now, the champion, having escaped from the terrible fury of the dragon, bethinking himself of the brazen shield, and of the breaking up of the enchantment which was upon it, removed the carcass from out of the way before him, and approached valorously over the silver pavement of the castle to where the shield was upon the wall; which in Sooth tarried not for his full coming, but fell down at his feet upon the silver floor, with a mighty great and terrible ringing sound."

No sooner had these syllables passed my lips, than—as if a shield of brass had indeed, at the moment, fallen heavily upon a floor of silver—I became aware of a distinct, hollow, metallic, and clangorous, yet apparently muffled, reverberation. Completely unnerved, I leaped to my feet; but the measured rocking movement of Usher was undisturbed. I rushed to the chair in which he sat. His eyes were bent fixedly before him, and throughout his whole countenance there reigned a stony rigidity. But, as I placed my hand upon his shoulder, there came a strong shudder over his whole person; a sickly smile quivered about his lips; and I saw that he spoke in a low, hurried, and gibbering murmur, as if unconscious of my presence. Bending closely over him, I at length drank in the hideous import of his words.

"Now hear it?—yes, I hear it, and *have* heard it. Long—long—long—many minutes, many hours, many days, have I heard it—yet I dared not—oh, pity me, miserable wretch that I am!—I dared not—I *dared* not speak! *We have put her living in the tomb!* Said I not that my senses were acute? I *now* tell you that I heard her first feeble movements in the hollow coffin. I heard them—many, many days ago—yet I dared not—*I dared not speak!* And now—to-night—Ethelred—ha! ha!—the breaking of the hermit's door, and the death-cry of the dragon, and the clangor of the shield—say, rather, the rending of her coffin, and the grating of the iron hinges of her prison, and her struggles within the coppered archway of the vault! Oh! whither shall I fly?[16] Will she not be here anon? Is she not hurrying to upbraid me for my haste? Have I not heard her footstep on the stair? Do I not distinguish that heavy and horrible beating of her heart? Madman!"—here he sprang furiously to his feet, and shrieked out his syllables, as if in the effort he were giving up his soul—*"Madman! I tell you that she now stands without the door!"*

As if in the superhuman energy of his utterance there had been found the potency of a spell, the huge antique panels to which the speaker pointed threw slowly back, upon the instant, their ponderous and ebony jaws. It was the work of the rushing gust—but then without those doors there *did* stand the lofty and enshrouded figure of the lady Madeline of Usher. There was blood upon her white robes, and the evidence of some bitter struggle upon every portion of her emaciated frame. For a moment she remained trembling and reeling to and fro upon the threshold—then, with a low moaning cry, fell heavily inward upon the person of her brother, and in her violent and now final death-agonies, bore him to the floor a corpse, and a victim to the terrors he had anticipated.

[16] "Whither shall I go from thy spirit? Or whither shall I flee from thy presence?" (Psalms 139:7.)

From that chamber, and from that mansion, I fled aghast. The storm was still abroad in all its wrath as I found myself crossing the old causeway. Suddenly there shot along the path a wild light, and I turned to see whence a gleam so unusual could have issued; for the vast house and its shadows were alone behind me. The radiance was that of the full, setting, and blood-red moon, which now shone vividly through that once barely discernible fissure, of which I have before spoken as extending from the roof of the building, in a zigzag direction, to the base. While I gazed, this fissure rapidly widened—there came a fierce breath of the whirlwind—the entire orb of the satellite burst at once upon my sight—my brain reeled as I saw the mighty walls rushing asunder—there was a long tumultuous shouting sound like the voice of a thousand waters—and the deep and dank tarn at my feet closed sullenly and silently over the fragments of the *"House of Usher."*

The Purloined Letter[1]

Nil sapientiae odiosius acumine nimio.[2]
Seneca

At Paris, just after dark one gusty evening in the autumn of 18--, I was enjoying the twofold luxury of meditation and a meerschaum, in company with my friend C. Auguste Dupin, in his little back library, or bookcloset, *au troisième, No. 33, Rue Dunôt, Faubourg St. Germain.*[3] For one hour at least we had maintained a profound silence; while each, to any casual observer, might have seemed intently and exclusively occupied with the curling eddies of smoke that oppressed the atmosphere of the chamber. For myself, how-ever, I was mentally discussing certain topics which had formed matter for conversation between us at an earlier period of the evening; I mean the affair of the Rue Morgue, and the mystery attending the murder of Marie Rogêt.[4]

[1] "The Purloined Letter" was first published in *The Gift* (January 1845). It is Poe's third story about his detective-hero Dupin and fol-lowed "The Murders in the Rue Morgue" and "The Mystery of Marie Roget." Poe called these narratives "tales of ratiocina-tion" and, in them, demonstrated how a bril-liant man, C. Auguste Dupin, could take a situation full of chaos and reduce it to clarity, unity, and simplicity. Dupin is a hero who is always in command of himself, outside soci-ety yet sensitive to all of society's problems. He has served as a model for fictional private investigators throughout the nineteenth and twentieth centuries.

[2] "Nothing is more repugnant to learning than too much insight." This epigraph is not in Seneca's writings.

[3] Poe describes Dupin's quarters in "The Murders in the Rue Morgue" (1841) as a "time-eaten and grotesque mansion. . . totter-ing to its fall in a retired and desolate portion of the Faubourg St. Germain." Dupin and the narrator live on the fourth floor (called *au troisème* in French) and go out only at night. In the daytime, they darken the room and "busy their souls in dreams" by candle-light.

[4] Poe refers to the first two murders solved by Dupin.

I looked upon it, therefore, as something of a coincidence, when the door of our apartment was thrown open and admitted our old acquaintance, Monsieur G——, the Prefect of the Parisian police.

We gave him a hearty welcome; for there was nearly half as much of the entertaining as of the contemptible about the man, and we had not seen him for several years. We had been sitting in the dark, and Dupin now arose for the purpose of lighting a lamp, but sat down again, without doing so, upon G——'s saying that he had called to consult us, or rather to ask the opinion of my friend, about some official business which had occasioned a great deal of trouble.

"If it is any point requiring reflection," observed Dupin, as he forebore to enkindle the wick, "we shall examine it to better purpose in the dark."

"That is another of your odd notions," said the Prefect, who had a fashion of calling every thing "odd" that was beyond his comprehension and thus lived amid an absolute legion of "oddities."

"Very true," said Dupin, as he supplied his visitor with a pipe, and rolled towards him a comfortable chair.

"And what is the difficulty now?" I asked. "Nothing more in the assassination way, I hope?"

"Oh no; nothing of that nature. The fact is, the business is *very* simple indeed, and I make no doubt that we can manage it sufficiently well ourselves; but then I thought Dupin would like to hear the details of it, because it is so excessively *odd*."

"Simple and odd." said Dupin.

"Why, yes; and not exactly that, either. The fact is, we have all been a good deal puzzled because the affair *is* so simple, and yet baffles us altogether."

"Perhaps it is the very simplicity of the thing which puts you at fault," said my friend.

"What nonsense you *do* talk!" replied the Prefect, laughing heartily.

"Perhaps the mystery is a little *too* plain," said Dupin.

"Oh, good heavens! who ever heard of such an idea?"

"A little *too* self-evident."

"Ha! ha! ha!—ha! ha! ha!—ho! ho! ho!"—roared our visitor, profoundly amused, "oh, Dupin, you will be the death of me yet!"

"And what, after all, *is* the matter on hand?" I asked.

"Why, I will tell you," replied the Prefect, as he gave a long, steady, and contemplative puff, and settled himself in his chair, "I will tell you in a few words; but, before I begin, let me caution you that this is an affair demanding the greatest secrecy, and that I should most probably lose the position I now hold, were it known that I confided it to any one."

"Proceed," said I.

"Or not," said Dupin.

"Well, then; I have received personal information, from a very high quarter, that a certain document of the last importance has been purloined from the royal apartments. The individual who purloined it is known; this beyond a doubt; he was seen to take it. It is known, also, that it still remains in his possession."

"How is this known?" asked Dupin.

"It is clearly inferred," replied the Prefect, "from the nature of the document, and from the non-appearance of certain results which would at once arise from its passing *out* of the robber's possession;—that is to say, from his employing it as he must design in the end to employ it."

"Be a little more explicit," I said.

"Well, I may venture so far as to say that the paper gives its holder a certain power in a certain quarter where such power is immensely valuable." The Prefect was fond of the cant of diplomacy.

"Still I do not quite understand," said Dupin.

"No? Well; the disclosure of the document to a third person who shall be nameless would bring in question the honor of a personage of most exalted station; and this fact gives the holder of the document an ascendancy over the illustrious personage whose honor and peace are so jeopardized."

"But this ascendancy," I interposed, "would depend upon the robber's knowledge of the loser's knowledge of the robber. Who would dare—"

"The thief," said G——, "is the Minister D——, who dares all things, those unbecoming as well as those becoming a man. The method of the theft was not less ingenious than bold. The document in question—a letter, to be frank—had been received by the personage robbed while alone in the royal *boudoir*. During its perusal she was suddenly interrupted by the entrance of the other exalted personage from whom especially it was her wish to conceal it. After a hurried and vain endeavor to thrust it in a drawer, she was forced to place it, open as it was, upon a table. The address, however, was uppermost, and, the contents thus unexposed, the letter escaped notice. At this juncture enters the Minister D——. His lynx eye immediately perceives the paper, recognizes the handwriting of the address, observes the confusion of the personage addressed, and fathoms her secret. After some business transactions, hurried through in his ordinary manner, he produces a letter somewhat similar to the one in question, opens it, pretends to read it, and then places it in close juxtaposition to the other. Again he converses, for some fifteen minutes, upon the public affairs. At length, in taking leave, he takes also from the table the letter to which he had no claim. Its rightful owner saw, but, of course, dared not call attention to the act, in the presence of the third personage who stood at her elbow. The Minister decamped; leaving his own letter—one of no importance—upon the table."

"Here, then," said Dupin to me, "you have precisely what you demand to make the ascendancy complete—the robber's knowledge of the loser's knowledge of the robber."

"Yes," replied the Prefect; "and the power thus attained has, for some months past, been wielded, for political purposes, to a very dangerous extent. The personage robbed is more thoroughly convinced, every day, of the necessity of reclaiming her letter. But this, of course, cannot be done openly. In fine, driven to despair, she has committed the matter to me."

"Than whom," said Dupin, amid a perfect whirlwind of smoke. "no more sagacious agent could, I suppose, be desired, or even imagined."

"You flatter me," replied the Prefect; "but it is possible that some such opinion may have been entertained."

"It is clear," said I, "as you observe, that the letter is still in possession of the Minister; since it is this possession, and not any employment of the letter, which bestows the power. With the employment the power departs."

"True," said G——; "and upon this conviction I proceeded. My first care was to make thorough search of the Minister's hotel; and here my chief embarrassment lay in the necessity of searching without his knowledge. Beyond all things, I have been warned of the danger which would result from giving him reason to suspect our design."

"But," said I, "you are quite *au fait*[5] in these investigations. The Parisian police have done this thing often before."

"Oh yes; and for this reason I did not despair. The habits of the Minister gave me, too, a great advantage. He is frequently absent from home all night. His servants are by no means numerous. They sleep at a distance from their master's apartment, and, being chiefly Neapolitans, are readily made drunk. I have keys, as you know, with which I can open any chamber or cabinet in Paris. For three months a night has not passed, during the greater part of which I have not been engaged, personally, in ransacking the D—— Hôtel. My honor is interested, and, to mention a great secret, the reward is enormous. So I did not abandon the search until I had become fully satisfied that the thief is a more astute man than myself. I fancy that I have investigated every nook and corner of the premises in which it is possible that the paper can be concealed."

"But is it not possible," I suggested, "that although the letter may be in the possession of the Minister, as it unquestionably is, he may have concealed it elsewhere than upon his own premises?"

"This is barely possible," said Dupin. "The present peculiar condition of affairs at court, and especially of those intrigues in which D——is known to be involved, would render the instant availability of the document—its susceptibility of being produced at a moment's notice—a point of nearly equal importance with its possession."

"It's susceptibility of being produced?" said I.

"That is to say, of being *destroyed*," said Dupin.

[5] Skilled.

"True," I observed; "the paper is clearly then upon the premises. As for its being upon the person of the Minister, we may consider that as out of the question."

"Entirely," said the Prefect. "He has been twice waylaid, as if by footpads, and his person rigorously searched under my own inspection."

"You might have spared yourself this trouble," said Dupin. "D——, I presume, is not altogether a fool, and, if not, must have anticipated these waylayings, as a matter of course."

"Not *altogether* a fool," said G——, "but then he's a poet, which I take to be only one remove from a fool."

"True," said Dupin, after a long and thoughtful whiff from his meerschaum, "although I have been guilty of certain doggerel myself."

"Suppose you detail," said I, "the particulars of your search."

"Why the fact is, we took our time, and we searched *every where*. I have had long experience in these affairs. I took the entire building, room by room; devoting the nights of a whole week to each. We examined, first, the furniture of each apartment. We opened every possible drawer; and I presume you know that, to a properly trained police agent, such a thing as a *secret* drawer is impossible. Any man is a dolt who permits a 'secret' drawer to escape him in a search of this kind. The thing is *so* plain. There is a certain amount of bulk—a space—to be accounted for in every cabinet. Then we have accurate rules. The fiftieth part of a line could not escape us. After the cabinets we took the chairs. The cushions we probed with the fine long needles you have seen me employ. From the tables we removed the tops."

"Why so?"

"Sometimes the top of a table, or other similarly arranged piece of furniture, is removed by the person wishing to conceal an article; then the leg is excavated, the article deposited within the cavity, and the top replaced. The bottoms and tops of bed-posts are employed in the same way."

"But could not the cavity be detected by sounding?" I asked.

"By no means, if, when the article is deposited, a sufficient wadding of cotton be placed around it. Besides, in our case, we were obliged to proceed without noise."

"But you could not have removed—you could not have taken to pieces *all* articles of furniture in which it would have been possible to make a deposit in the manner you mention. A letter may be compressed into a thin spiral roll, not differing much in shape or bulk from a large knitting-needle, and in this form it might be inserted into the rung of a chair, for example. You did not take to pieces all the chairs?"

"Certainly not; but we did better—we examined the rungs of every chair in the hotel, and, indeed, the jointings of every description of furniture, by the aid of a most powerful microscope. Had there been any traces of recent disturbance we should not have failed to detect it instantly. A single grain of gimlet-dust, for example, would have been as obvious as an apple. Any disorder in the glueing—any unusual gaping in the joints—would have sufficed to insure detection."

"I presume you looked to the mirrors, between the boards and the plates, and you probed the beds and the bed-clothes, as well as the curtains and carpets."

"That of course; and when we had absolutely completed every particle of the furniture in this way, then we examined the house itself. We divided its entire surface into compartments, which we numbered so that none might be missed; then we scrutinized each individual square inch throughout the premises, including the two houses immediately adjoining, with the microscope, as before."

"The two houses adjoining!" I exclaimed; "you must have had a great deal of trouble."

"We had; but the reward offered is prodigious."

"You include the *grounds* about the houses?"

"All the grounds are paved with brick. They gave us comparatively little trouble. We examined the moss between the bricks, and found it undisturbed."

"You looked among D——'s papers, of course, and into the books of the library?"

"Certainly; we opened every package and parcel; we not only opened every book, but we turned over every leaf in each volume, not contenting ourselves with a mere shake, according to the fashion of some of our police officers. We also measured the thickness of every book-*cover*, with the most accurate admeasurement, and applied to each the most jealous scrutiny of the microscope. Had any of the bindings been recently meddled with, it would have been utterly impossible that the fact should have escaped observation. Some five or six volumes, just from the hands of the binder, we carefully probed, longitudinally, with the needles."

"You explored the floors beneath the carpets?"

"Beyond doubt. We removed every carpet, and examined the boards with the microscope."

"And the paper on the walls?"

"Yes."

"You looked into the cellars?"

"We did."

"Then," I said, "you have been making a miscalculation, and the letter is *not* upon the premises, as you supposed."

"I fear you are right there," said the Prefect. "And now, Dupin, what would you advise me to do?"

"To make a thorough re-search of the premises."

"That is absolutely needless," replied G——. "I am not more sure that I breathe than I am that the letter is not at the Hotel."

"I have no better advice to give you," said Dupin. "You have, of course, an accurate description of the letter?"

"Oh yes!"—And here the Prefect, producing a memorandum-book, proceeded to read aloud a minute account of the internal, and especially of the external appearance of the missing document. Soon after finishing the perusal of this description, he took his departure, more entirely depressed in spirits than I had ever known the good gentleman before.

In about a month afterwards he paid us another visit, and found us occupied very nearly as before. He took a pipe and a chair and entered into some ordinary conversation. At length I said,—

"Well, but G——, what of the purloined letter? I presume you have at last made up your mind that there is no such thing as overreaching the Minister?"

"Confound him, say I—yes; I made the re-examination, however, as Dupin suggested—but it was all labor lost, as I knew it would be."

"How much was the reward offered, did you say?" asked Dupin.

"Why, a very great deal—a *very* liberal reward—I don't like to say how much, precisely; but one thing I *will* say, that I wouldn't mind giving my individual check for fifty thousand francs to any one who could obtain me that letter. The fact is, it is becoming of more and more importance every day; and the reward has been lately doubled. If it were trebled, however, I could do no more than I have done."

"Why, yes," said Dupin, drawlingly, between the whiffs of his meerschaum, "I really—think, G——, you have not exerted yourself—to the utmost in this matter. You might—do a little more, I think, eh?"

"How?"—in what way?"

"Why—puff, puff—you might—puff, puff—employ counsel in the matter, eh?—puff, puff, puff. Do you remember the story they tell of Abernethy!"[6]

"No; hang Abernethy!"

"To be sure! hang him and welcome. But, once upon a time, a certain rich miser conceived the design of sponging upon this Abernethy for a medical opinion. Getting up, for this purpose, an ordinary conversation in a private company, he insinuated his case to his physician, as that of an imaginary individual.

" 'We will suppose,' said the miser, 'that his symptoms are such and such; now, doctor, what would *you* have directed him to take?"

" 'Take!' said Abernethy, 'why, take *advice*, to be sure.' "

"But," said the Prefect, a little discomposed, "I am *perfectly* willing to take advice, and to pay for it. I would *really* give fifty thousand francs to any one who would aid me in the matter."

[6] John Abernethy, a well-known English surgeon (1764-1831).

"In that case," replied Dupin, opening a drawer, and producing a check-book, "you may as well fill me up a check for the amount mentioned. When you have signed it, I will hand you the letter."

I was astounded. The Prefect appeared absolutely thunder-stricken. For some minutes he remained speechless and motionless, looking incredulously at my friend with open mouth, and eyes that seemed starting from their sockets; then, apparently recovering himself in some measure, he seized a pen, and after several pauses and vacant stares, finally filled up and signed a check for fifty thousand francs, and handed it across the table to Dupin. The latter examined it carefully and deposited it in his pocket-book; then, un-locking an *escritoire*,[7] took thence a letter and gave it to the Prefect. This functionary grasped it in a perfect agony of joy, opened it with a trembling hand, cast a rapid glance at its contents, and then, scrambling and struggling to the door, rushed at length unceremoniously from the room and from the house, without having uttered a syllable since Dupin had requested him to fill up the check.

When he had gone, my friend entered into some explanations.

"The Parisian police," he said, "are exceedingly able in their way. They are persevering, ingenious, cunning, and thoroughly versed in the knowledge which their duties seem chiefly to demand. Thus, when G—— detailed to us his mode of searching the premises at the Hôtel D——, I felt entire confidence in his having made a satisfactory investigation—so far as his labors extended."

"So far as his labors extended?" said I.

"Yes," said Dupin. "The measures adopted were not only the best of their kind, but carried out to absolute perfection. Had the letter been deposited within the range of their search, these fellows would, beyond a question, have found it."

I merely laughed—but he seemed quite serious in all that he said.

"The measures, then," he continued, "were good in their kind, and well executed; their defect lay in their being inapplicable to the case, and to the man. A certain set of highly ingenious resources are, with the Prefect, a sort of Procrustean[8] bed, to which he forcibly adapts his designs. But he perpetu-ally errs by being too deep or too shallow, for the matter in hand; and many a schoolboy is a better reasoner than he. I knew one about eight years of age, whose success at guessing in the game of 'even and odd' attracted universal admiration. This game is simple, and is played with marbles. One player holds in his hand a number of these toys, and demands of another whether that number is even or odd. If the guess is right, the guesser wins one; if wrong, he loses one. The boy to whom I allude won all the marbles of the

---

[7] A writing desk.

[8] Procrustes was a mythical Greek thief who tied his victims to a bed, if they were too short, he stretched them to fit the bed and if they were too long, he cut off their legs.

school. Of course he had some principle of guessing; and this lay in mere observation and admeasurement of the astuteness of his opponents. For example, an arrant simpleton is his opponent, and, holding up his closed hand, asks, 'are they even or odd?' Our schoolboy replies, 'odd,' and loses; but upon the second trial he wins, for he then says to himself, the simpleton had them even upon the first trial, and his amount of cunning is just sufficient to make him have them odd upon the second; I will therefore guess odd';—he guesses odd, and wins. Now, with a simpleton a degree above the first, he would have reasoned thus: 'This fellow finds that in the first instance I guessed odd, and, in the second, he will propose to himself upon the first impulse, a simple variation from even to odd, as did the first simpleton; but then a second thought will suggest that this is too simple a variation, and finally he will decide upon putting it even as before. I will therefore guess even';—he guesses even, and wins. Now this mode of reasoning in the schoolboy, whom his fellows termed 'lucky'—what, in its analysis, is it?"

"It is merely," I said, "an identification of the reasoner's intellect with that of his opponent."

"It is," said Dupin; "and, upon inquiring of the boy by what means he effected the *thorough* identification in which his success consisted, I received answer as follows: 'When I wish to find out how wise, or how stupid, or how good, or how wicked is any one, or what are his thoughts at the moment, I fashion the expression of my face, as accurately as possible, in accordance with the expression of his, and then wait to see what thoughts or sentiments arise in my mind or heart, as if to match or correspond with the expression.' This response of the schoolboy lies at the bottom of all the spurious profundity which has been attributed to Rochefoucauld, to La Bougive, to Machiavelli, and to Campanella."[9]

"And the identification," I said, "of the reasoner's intellect with that of his opponent, depends, if I understand you aright, upon the accuracy with which the opponent's intellect is admeasured."

"For its practical value it depends upon this," replied Dupin; "and the Prefect and his cohort fail so frequently, first, by default of this identification, and, secondly, by ill-admeasurement, or rather through non-admeasurement of the intellect with which they are engaged. They consider only their *own* ideas of ingenuity; and, in searching for anything hidden, advert only to the modes in which *they* would have hidden it. They are right in this much—that their own ingenuity is a faithful representative of that of *the mass;* but when the cunning of the individual felon is diverse in character from their own, the felon foils them, of course. This always happens when it

[9] The Duc de la Rochefoucauld (1613-1680) wrote *Moral Maxims and Reflections.* La Bougive probably refers to "La Bruyère": Jean de la Bruyère (1645-1696) also depicted manners, morals, and character. Niccolo Machiavelli's famous study of the state is *The Prince* (1513). Tommaso Campanella's most important book is *The City of the Sun* (1643). These various authors appeal to Poe for their psychological penetration of character.

is above their own, and very usually when it is below. They have no variation of principle in their investigations; at best, when urged by some unusual emergency—by some extraordinary reward—they extend or exaggerate their old modes of *practice*, without touching their principles. What, for example, in this case of D——, has been done to vary the principle of action? What is all this boring, and probing, and sounding, and scrutinizing with the microscope, and dividing the surface of the building into registered square inches—what is it all but an exaggeration of *the application* of the one principle or set of principles of search, which are based upon the one set of notions regarding human ingenuity, to which the Prefect, in the long routine of his duty, has been accustomed? Do you not see he has taken it for granted that *all* men proceed to conceal a letter—not exactly in a gimlet-hole bored in a chair-leg—but, at least, in *some* out-of-the-way hole or corner suggested by the same tenor of thought which would urge a man to secrete a letter in a gimlet-hole bored in a chair-leg? And do you not see also, that such *recherchés*[10] nooks for concealment are adopted only for ordinary occasions, and would be adopted only by ordinary intellects; for, in all cases of concealment, a disposal of the article concealed—a disposal of it in this *recherché* manner—is, in the very instance, presumable and presumed; and thus its discovery depends, not at all upon the acumen, but altogether upon the mere care, patience, and determination of the seekers; and where the case is of importance—or, what amounts to the same thing in the *policial* eyes, when the reward is of magnitude,—the qualities in question have *never* been known to fail? You will now understand what I meant in suggesting that, had the purloined letter been hidden any where within the limits of the Prefect's examination—in other words, had the principle of its concealment been comprehended within the principles of the Prefect—its discovery would have been a matter altogether beyond question. This functionary, however, has been thoroughly mystified; and the remote source of his defeat lies in the supposition that the Minister is a fool, because he has acquired renown as a poet. All fools are poets; this the Prefect *feels;* and he is merely guilty of a *non distributio medii*[11] in thence inferring that all poets are fools."

"But is this really the poet?" I asked. "There are two brothers, I know; and both have attained reputation in letters. The Minister I believe has written learnedly on the Differential Calculus. He is a mathematician, and no poet."

"You are mistaken; I know him well; he is both. As poet *and* mathematician, he would reason well; as mere mathematician, he could not have reasoned at all, and thus would have been at the mercy of the Prefect."

"You surprise me," I said, "by these opinions, which have been contra-

[10] Esoteric, studied.
[11] An undistributed middle, faulty deduction in logic.

dicted by the voice of the world. You do not mean to set at naught the well-digested idea of centuries. The mathematical reason has long been regarded as *the* reason *par excellence.*"

" '*Il y a à parier,*' " replied Dupin, quoting from Chamfort, " '*que toute idée publique, toute convention reçue, est une sottise, car elle a convenu au plus grand nombre.*'[12] The mathematicians, I grant you, have done their best to promulgate the popular error to which you allude, and which is none the less an error for its promulgation as truth. With an art worthy a better cause, for example, they have insinuated the term 'analysis' into application to algebra. The French are the originators of this particular deception; but if a term is of any importance—if words derive any value from applicability— then 'analysis' conveys 'algebra' about as much as, in Latin, '*ambitus*' implies 'ambition,' '*religio*' 'religion,' or '*homines honesti*' a set of '*honorable* men.' "

"You have a quarrel on hand, I see," said I, "with some of the algebraists of Paris; but proceed."

"I dispute the availability, and thus the value, of that reason which is cultivated in any especial form other than the abstractly logical. I dispute, in particular, the reason educed by mathematical study. The mathematics are the science of form and quantity; mathematical reasoning is merely logic applied to observation upon form and quantity. The great error lies in supposing that even the truths of what is called *pure* algebra, are abstract or general truths. And this error is so egregious that I am confounded at the universality with which it has been received. Mathematical axioms are *not* axioms of general truth. What is true of *relation*—of form and quantity—is often grossly false in regard to morals, for example. In this latter science it is very usually *un*true that the aggregated parts are equal to the whole. In chemistry also the axiom fails. In the consideration of motive it fails; for two motives, each of given value, have not, necessarily, a value when united, equal to the sum of their values apart. There are numerous other mathematical truths which are only truths within the limits of *relation*. But the mathematician argues, from his *finite truths*, through habit, as if they were of absolutely general applicability—as the world indeed imagines them to be. Bryant, in his very learned 'Mythology,' mentions an analogous source of error, when he says that 'although the Pagan fables are not believed, yet we forget ourselves continually, and make inferences from them as existing realities.' With the algebraists, however, who are Pagans themselves, the 'Pagan fables' *are* believed, and the inferences are made, not so much through lapse of memory, as through an unaccountable addling of the brains. In short, I never yet encountered the mere mathematician who could be trusted out of equal roots, or one who did not clandestinely hold it as a point of his faith that $x^2 + px$ was absolutely and unconditionally equal to q. Say to one of these gentlemen, by way of experiment, if you please, that you believe occa-

---

[12] Nicolas Chamfort (1741-1794): "The chances are that any popular idea, any ac- cepted notion, is foolishness, since it has proved agreeable to the mass of mankind."

sions may occur where $x^2 + px$ is *not* altogether equal to q, and, having made him understand what you mean, get out of his reach as speedily as convenient, for, beyond doubt, he will endeavor to knock you down.

"I mean to say," continued Dupin, while I merely laughed at his last observations, "that if the Minister had been no more than a mathematician, the Prefect would have been under no necessity of giving me this check. I knew him, however, as both mathematician and poet, and my measures were adapted to his capacity, with reference to the circumstances by which he was surrounded. I knew him as a courtier, too, and as a bold *intriguant*.[13] Such a man, I considered, could not fail to be aware of the ordinary policial modes of action. He could not have failed to anticipate—and events have proved that he did not fail to anticipate—the waylayings to which he was subjected. He must have foreseen, I reflected, the secret investigations of his premises. His frequent absences from home at night, which were hailed by the Prefect as certain aids to his success, I regarded only as *ruses*, to afford opportunity for thorough search to the police, and thus the sooner to impress them with the conviction to which G——, in fact, did finally arrive—the conviction that the letter was not upon the premises. I felt, also, that the whole train of thought, which I was at some pains in detailing to you just now, concerning the invariable principle of policial action in searches for articles concealed—I felt that this whole train of thought would necessarily pass through the mind of the Minister. It would imperatively lead him to despise all the ordinary *nooks* of concealment. *He* could not, I reflected, be so weak as not to see that the most intricate and remote recess of his hotel would be as open as his commonest closets to the eyes, to the probes, to the gimlets, and to the microscopes of the Prefect. I saw, in fine, that he would be driven, as a matter of course, to *simplicity*, if not deliberately induced to it as a matter of choice. You will remember, perhaps, how desperately the Prefect laughed when I suggested, upon our first interview, that it was just possible this mystery troubled him so much on account of its being so *very* self-evident."

"Yes," said I, "I remember his merriment well. I really thought he would have fallen into convulsions."

"The material world," continued Dupin, "abounds with the very strict analogies to the immaterial; and thus some color of truth has been given to the rhetorical dogma, that metaphor, or simile, may be made to strengthen an argument, as well as to embellish a description. The principle of the *vis inertiæ*,[14] for example, seems to be identical in physics and metaphysics. It is not more true in the former, that a large body is with more difficulty set in motion than a smaller one, and that its subsequent *momentum* is commensurate with this difficulty, than it is, in the latter, that intellects of the vaster capacity, while more forcible, more constant, and more eventful in their movements than those of inferior grade, are yet the less readily moved, and

---

[13] A schemer.   [14] Inertia.

more embarrassed and full of hesitation in the first few steps of their progress. Again: have you ever noticed which of the street signs, over the shop
doors, are the most attractive of attention?"

"I have never given the matter a thought," I said.

"There is a game of puzzles," he resumed, "which is played upon a map.
One party playing requires another to find a given word—the name of town,
river, state or empire—any word, in short, upon the motely and perplexed
surface of the chart. A novice in the game generally seeks to embarrass his
opponents by giving them the most minutely lettered names; but the adept
selects such words as stretch, in large characters, from one end of the chart
to the other. These, like the over-largely lettered signs and placards of the
street, escape observation by dint of being excessively obvious; and here the
physical oversight is precisely analogous with the moral inapprehension by
which the intellect suffers to pass unnoticed those considerations which are
too obtrusively and too palpably self-evident. But this is a point, it appears,
somewhat above or beneath the understanding of the Prefect. He never
once thought it probable, or possible, that the Minister had deposited the
letter immediately beneath the nose of the whole world, by way of best
preventing any portion of that world from perceiving it.

"But the more I reflected upon the daring, dashing, and discriminating
ingenuity of D——; upon the fact that the document must always have been
at hand, if he intended to use it to good purpose; and upon the decisive
evidence, obtained by the Prefect, that it was not hidden within the limits of
that dignitary's ordinary search—the more satisfied I became that, to conceal
this letter, the Minister had resorted to the comprehensive and sagacious
expedient of not attempting to conceal it at all.

"Full of these ideas, I prepared myself with a pair of green spectacles,
and called one fine morning, quite by accident, at the Ministerial hotel. I
found G— — at home, yawning, lounging, and dawdling, as usual, and pretending to be in the last extremity of *ennui*. He is, perhaps, the most really
energetic human being now alive—but that is only when nobody sees him.

"To be even with him, I complained of my weak eyes, and lamented the
necessity of the spectacles, under cover of which I cautiously and thoroughly
surveyed the apartment, while seemingly intent only upon the conversation
of my host.

"I paid especial attention to a large writing-table near which he sat, and
upon which lay confusedly some miscellaneous letters and other papers,
with one or two musical instruments and a few books. Here, however, after
a long and very deliberate scrutiny, I saw nothing to excite particular suspicion.

"At length my eyes, in going the circuit of the room, fell upon a trumpery
filigree card-rack of pasteboard, that hung dangling by a dirty blue ribbon,
from a little brass knob just beneath the middle of the mantel-piece. In this
rack, which had three or four compartments, were five or six visiting cards
and a solitary letter. This last was much soiled and crumpled. It was torn

nearly in two, across the middle—as if a design, in the first instance, to tear it entirely up as worthless, had been altered, or stayed, in the second. It had a large black seal, being the D—— cipher *very* conspicuously, and was addressed, in a diminutive female hand, to D——, the Minister, himself. It was thrust carelessly, and even, as it seemed, contemptuously, into one of the upper divisions of the rack.

"No sooner had I glanced at this letter, than I concluded it to be that of which I was in search. To be sure, it was, to all appearance radically different from the one of which the Prefect had read us so minute a description. Here the seal was large and black, with the D—— cipher; there it was small and red, with the ducal arms of the S—— family. Here, the address, to the Minister, was diminutive and feminine; there the superscription, to a certain royal personage, was markedly bold and decided; the size alone formed a point of correspondence. But, then, the *radicalness* of these differences, which was excessive; the dirt; the soiled and torn condition of the paper, so inconsistent with the *true* methodical habits of D——, and so suggestive of a design to delude the beholder into an idea of the worthlessness of the document;—these things, together with the hyperobtrusive situation of this document, full in the view of every visitor, and thus exactly in accordance with the conclusions to which I had previously arrived at these things, I say, were strongly corroborative of suspicion, in one who came with the intention to suspect.

"I protracted my visit as long as possible, and, while I maintained a most animated discussion with the Minister, on the topic which I knew well had never failed to interest and excite him, I kept my attention really riveted upon the letter. In this examination, I committed to memory its external appearance and arrangement in the rack; and also fell, at length, upon a discovery which set at rest whatever trivial doubt I might have entertained. In scrutinizing the edges of the paper, I observed them to be more *chafed* than seemed necessary. They presented the *broken* appearance which is manifested when a stiff paper, having been once folded and pressed with a folder, is refolded in a reversed direction, in the same creases or edges which had formed the original fold. This discovery was sufficient. It was clear to me that the letter had been turned, as a glove, inside out, re-directed, and resealed. I bade the Minister good morning, and took my departure at once, leaving a gold snuff-box upon the table.

"The next morning I called for the snuff-box, when we resumed quite eagerly, the conversation of the preceding day. While thus engaged, however, a loud report, as if of a pistol, was heard immediately beneath the windows of the hotel, and was succeeded by a series of fearful screams, and the shouting of a mob. D—— — rushed to a casement, threw it open, and looked out. In the meantime, I stepped to the card-rack, took the letter, and put it in my pocket, and replaced it by a *fac-simile* (so far as regards externals), which I had carefully prepared at my lodgings; imitating the D—— cipher, very readily, by means of a seal formed of bread.

"The disturbance in the street had been occasioned by the frantic behavior of a man with a musket. He had fired it among a crowd of women and children. It proved, however, to have been without ball, and the fellow was suffered to go his way as a lunatic or a drunkard. When he had gone, D—— came from the window, whither I had followed him immediately upon securing the object in view. Soon afterwards I bade him farewell. The pretended lunatic was a man in my own pay."

"But what purpose had you," I asked, "in replacing the letter by a *fac-simile?* Would it not have been better, at the first visit, to have seized it openly, and departed?"

"D——," replied Dupin, "is a desperate man, and a man of nerve. His hotel, too, is not without attendants devoted to his interests. Had I made the wild attempt you suggest, I might never have left the Ministerial presence alive. The good people of Paris might have heard of me no more. But I had an object apart from these considerations. You know my political prepossessions. In this matter, I act as a partisan of the lady concerned. For eighteen months the Minister has had her in his power. She has now him in hers—since, being aware that the letter is not in his possession, he will proceed with his exactions as if it was. Thus will he inevitably commit himself, at once, to his political destruction. His downfall, too, will not be more precipitate than awkward. It is all very well to talk about the *facilis descensus Averni,*[15] but in all kinds of climbing, as Catalani said of singing, it is far more easy to get up than to come down. In the present instance I have no sympathy—at least no pity—for him who descends. He is that *monstrum horrendum,*[16] an unprincipled man of genius. I confess, however, that I should like very well to know the precise character of his thoughts, when, being defied by her whom the Prefect terms 'a certain personage,' he is reduced to opening the letter which I left for him in the card-rack."

"How? did you put any thing particular in it?"

"Why—it did not seem altogether right to leave the interior blank—that would have been insulting. D— —, at Vienna once, did me an evil turn, which I told him, quite good-humoredly, that I should remember. So, as I knew he would feel some curiosity in regard to the identity of the person who had outwitted him, I thought it a pity not to give him a clue. He is well acquainted with my MS., and I just copied into the middle of the blank sheet the words—

> —Un dessein si funeste,
> S'il n'est digne d'Atrée, est digne de Thyeste.[17]

They are to be found in Crébillon's *Atrée.*' "

---

[15] From Virgil's *Aeneid,* VI, 126: "the descent to the infernal regions is easy."
[16] A fearful monster. This phrase is also taken from Virgil.

[17] "A plan so deadly is worthy of Thyestes, if not of Atreus."

Twice-Told Tales,
by Nathaniel Hawthorne[1]

A REVIEW

We said a few hurried words about Mr. Hawthorne in our last number, with the design of speaking more fully in the present. We are still, however, pressed for room, and must necessarily discuss his volumes more briefly and more at random than their high merits deserve.

The book professes to be a collection of *tales*, yet is, in two respects, misnamed. These pieces are now in their third republication, and, of course, are thrice-told. Moreover, they are by no means *all* tales, either in the ordinary or in the legitimate understanding of the term. Many of them are pure essays; for example, "Sights from a Steeple," "Sunday at Home," "Little Annie's Ramble," "A Rill from the Town Pump," "The Toll-Gatherer's Day," "The Haunted Mind," "The Sister Years," "Snow-Flakes," "Night Sketches," and "Foot-Prints on the Sea-Shore." We mention these matters chiefly on account of their discrepancy with that marked precision and finish by which the body of the work is distinguished.

Of the essays just named, we must be content to speak in brief. They are each and all beautiful, without being characterized by the polish and adaptation so visible in the tales proper. A painter would at once note their leading or predominant feature, and style it *repose*. There is no attempt at effect. All is quiet, thoughtful, subdued. Yet this repose may exist simultaneously with high originality of thought; and Mr. Hawthorne has demonstrated the fact. At every turn we meet with novel combinations; yet these combinations never surpass the limits of the quiet. We are soothed as we read; and withal is a calm astonishment that ideas so apparently obvious have never occurred or been presented to us before. Herein our author differs materially from Lamb or Hunt or Hazlitt—who, with vivid originality of manner and expression, have less of the true novelty of thought than is generally supposed, and whose originality, at best, has an uneasy and meretricious quaintness, replete with startling effects unfounded in nature, and inducing trains of reflection which lead to no satisfactory result. The Essays of Hawthorne have much of the character of Irving, with more of originality, and less of finish; while, compared with the Spectator,[2] they have a vast superiority at all points. The

---

[1] This review appeared in *Graham's Magazine*, May 1842. Poe had the highest regard for Hawthorne's abilities, and he uses *Twice-Told Tales* (1837) to illustrate his famous definition of the short story. The sixth paragraph has become a classic formulation and should be applied to Poe's fiction as well as to Hawthorne's.

[2] The *Spectator* was written, edited, and published from 1711-1714 by Joseph Addison and Richard Steele.

Spectator, Mr. Irving, and Mr. Hawthorne have in common that tranquil and subdued manner which we have chosen to denominate *repose;* but, in the case of the two former, this repose is attained rather by the absence of novel combination, or of originality, than otherwise, and consists chiefly in the calm, quiet, unostentatious expression of commonplace thoughts, in an unambitious, unadulterated Saxon. In them, by strong effort, we are made to conceive the absence of all. In the essays before us the absence of effort is too obvious to be mistaken, and a strong undercurrent of *suggestion* runs continuously beneath the upper stream of the tranquil thesis. In short, these effusions of Mr. Hawthorne are the product of a truly imaginative intellect, restrained, and in some measure repressed, by fastidiousness of taste, by constitutional melancholy, and by indolence.

But it is of his tales that we desire principally to speak. The tale proper, in our opinion, affords unquestionably the fairest field for the exercise of the loftiest talent, which can be afforded by the wide domains of mere prose. Were we bidden to say how the highest genius could be more advantageously employed for the best display of its own powers, we should answer, without hesitation—in the composition of a rhymed poem, not to exceed in length what might be perused in an hour. Within this limit alone can the highest order of true poetry exist. We need only here say, upon this topic, that, in almost all classes of composition, the unity of effect or impression is a point of the greatest importance. It is clear, moreover, that this unity cannot be thoroughly preserved in productions whose perusal cannot be completed at one sitting. We may continue the reading of a prose composition, from the very nature of prose itself, much longer than we can persevere, to any good purpose, in the perusal of a poem. This latter, if truly fulfilling the demands of the poetic sentiment, induces an exaltation of the soul which cannot be long sustained. All high excitements are necessarily transient. Thus a long poem is a paradox. And, without unity of impression, the deepest effects cannot be brought about. Epics were the offspring of an imperfect sense of Art, and their reign is no more. A poem *too* brief may produce a vivid, but never an intense or enduring impression. Without a certain continuity of effort—without a certain duration or repetition of purpose—the soul is never deeply moved. There must be the dropping of the water upon the rock. De Béranger has wrought brilliant things—pungent and spirit-stirring—but, like all immasive bodies, they lack *momentum,* and thus fail to satisfy the Poetic Sentiment. They sparkle and excite, but, from want of continuity, fail deeply to impress. Extreme brevity will degenerate into epigrammatism; but the sin of extreme length is even more unpardonable. *In medio tutissimus ibis.*[3]

Were we called upon, however, to designate that class of composition which, next to such a poem as we have suggested, should best fulfil the

---

[3] "It is safest to keep to the middle way."

demands of high genius—should offer it the most advantageous field of exertion—we should unhesitatingly speak of the prose tale, as Mr. Hawthorne has here exemplified it. We allude to the short prose narrative, requiring from a half-hour to one or two hours in its perusal. The ordinary novel is objectionable, from its length, for reasons already stated in substance. As it cannot be read at one sitting, it deprives itself, of course, of the immense force derivable from *totality*. Worldly interest intervening during the pauses of perusal, modify, annul, or counteract, in a greater or less degree, the impressions of the book. But simple cessation in reading would, of itself, be sufficient to destroy the true unity. In the brief tale, however, the author is enabled to carry out the fulness of his intention, be it what it may. During the hour of perusal the soul of the reader is at the writer's control. There are no external or extrinsic influences—resulting from weariness or interruption.

A skilful literary artist has constructed a tale. If wise, he has not fashioned his thoughts to accommodate his incidents; but having conceived, with deliberate care, a certain unique or single *effect* to be wrought out, he then invents such incidents—he then combines such events as may best aid him in establishing this preconceived effect. If his very initial sentence tend not to the outbringing of this effect, then he has failed in his first step. In the whole composition there should be no word written, of which the tendency, direct or indirect, is not to the one pre-established design. And by such means, with such care and skill, a picture is at length painted which leaves in the mind of him who contemplates it with a kindred art, a sense of the fullest satisfaction. The idea of the tale has been presented unblemished, because undisturbed; and this is an end unattainable by the novel. Undue brevity is just as exceptionable here as in the poem: but undue length is yet more to be avoided.

We have said that the tale has a point of superiority even over the poem. In fact, while the *rhythm* of this latter is an essential aid in the development of the poem's highest idea—the idea of the Beautiful—the artificialities of this rhythm are an inseparable bar to the development of all points of thought or expression which have their basis in *Truth*. But Truth is often, and in very great degree, the aim of the tale. Some of the finest tales are tales of ratiocination. Thus the field of this species of composition, if not in so elevated a region on the mountain of Mind, is a table-land of far vaster extent than the domain of the mere poem. Its products are never so rich, but infinitely more numerous, and more appreciable by the mass of mankind. The writer of the prose tale, in short, may bring to his theme a vast variety of modes or inflections of thought and expression—(the ratiocinative, for example, the sarcastic, or the humorous) which are not only antagonistical to the nature of the poem, but absolutely forbidden by one of its most peculiar and indispensable adjuncts; we allude, of course, to rhythm. It may be added here, *par parenthèse*,[4] that the author who aims at the purely beautiful in a

---

[4] Parenthetically.

prose tale is laboring at a great disadvantage. For Beauty can be better treated in the poem. Not so with terror, or passion, or horror, or a multitude of such other points. And here it will be seen how full of prejudice are the usual animadversions against those *tales of effect*, many fine examples of which were found in the earlier numbers of *Blackwood*.[5] The impressions produced were wrought in a legitimate sphere of action, and constituted a legitimate although sometimes an exaggerated interest. They were relished by every man of genius: although there were found many men of genius who condemned them without just ground. The true critic will but demand that the design intended be accomplished, to the fullest extent, by the means most advantageously applicable.

We have very few American tales of real merit—we may say, indeed, none, with the exception of *The Tales of a Traveller* of Washington Irving, and these *Twice-Told Tales* of Mr. Hawthorne. Some of the pieces of Mr. John Neal[6] abound in vigor and originality; but, in general, his compositions of this class are excessively diffuse, extravagant, and indicative of an imperfect sentiment of Art. Articles at random are, now and then, met with in our periodicals which might be advantageously compared with the best effusions of the British Magazines; but, upon the whole, we are far behind our progenitors in this department of literature.

Of Mr. Hawthorne's tales we should say, emphatically, that they belong to the highest region of Art—an Art subservient to genius of a very lofty order. We had supposed, with good reason for so supposing, that he had been thrust into his present position by one of the impudent *cliques* which beset our literature, and whose pretensions it is our full purpose to expose at the earliest opportunity; but we have been most aggreeably mistaken. We know of few compositions which the critic can more honestly commend than these *Twice-Told Tales*. As Americans, we feel proud of the book.

Mr. Hawthorne's distinctive trait is invention, creation, imagination, originality—a trait which, in the literature of fiction, is positively worth all the rest. But the nature of the originality, so far as regards its manifestation in letters, is but imperfectly understood. The inventive or original mind as frequently displays itself in novelty of *tone* as in novelty of matter. Mr. Hawthorne is original at *all* points.

It would be a matter of some difficulty to designate the best of these tales; we repeat that, without exception, they are beautiful. "Wakefield" is remarkable for the skill with which an old idea—a well-known incident—is worked up or discussed. A man of whims conceives the purpose of quitting his wife and residing *incognito*, for twenty years, in her immediate neighborhood. Something of this kind actually happened in London. The force of Mr.

---

[5] The *Edinburgh Monthly Magazine* (1817) soon became *Blackwood's Magazine*.

[6] John Neal was a novelist, poet, and critic (1793–1876) who had written a favorable review of Poe's "Al Aaraaf" in the *Yankee*, his literary periodical.

Hawthorne's tale lies in the analysis of the motives which must or might have impelled the husband to such folly, in the first instance, with the possible causes of his perseverance. Upon this thesis a sketch of singular power has been constructed.

"The Wedding Knell" is full of the boldest imagination—an imagination fully controlled by taste. The most captious critic could find no flaw in this production.

"The Minister's Black Veil" is a masterly composition, of which the sole defect is that to the rabble its exquisite skill will be *caviare*. The *obvious* meaning of this article will be found to smother its insinuated one. The *moral* put into the mouth of the dying minister will be supposed to convey the *true* import of the narrative; and that a crime of dark dye (having reference to the "young lady") has been committed, is a point which only minds congenial with that of the author will perceive.

"Mr. Higginbotham's Catastrophe" is vividly original, and managed most dexterously.

"Dr. Heidegger's Experiment" is exceedingly well imagined, and executed with surpassing ability. The artist breathes in every line of it.

"The White Old Maid" is objectionable even more than the "Minister's Black Veil," on the score of its mysticism. Even with the thoughtful and analytic, there will be much trouble in penetrating its entire import.

"The Hollow of the Three Hills" we would quote in full had we space;— not as evincing higher talent than any of the other pieces, but as affording an excellent example of the author's peculiar ability. The subject is commonplace. A witch subjects the Distant and the Past to the view of a mourner. It has been the fashion to describe, in such cases, a mirror in which the images of the absent appear; or a cloud of smoke is made to arise, and thence the figures are gradually unfolded. Mr. Hawthorne has wonderfully heightened his effect by making the ear, in place of the eye, the medium by which the fantasy is conveyed. The head of the mourner is enveloped in the cloak of the witch, and within its magic folds there arise sounds which have an all-sufficient intelligence. Throughout this article also, the artist is conspicuous—not more in positive than in negative merits. Not only is all done that should be done, but (what perhaps is an end with more difficulty attained) there is nothing done which should not be. Every word *tells*, and there is not a word which does *not* tell.

In "Howe's Masquerade" we observe something which resembles plagiarism[7]—but which *may be* a very flattering coincidence of thought. We quote the passage in question.

---

[7] It was impossible for Hawthorne to have plagiarized from Poe, since his story appeared in the *Democratic Review* of May 1838—a year before Poe's "William Wilson" was first published. Poe often accused his contemporaries of plagiarism. His most notorious conflict was with Longfellow.

[Quotation.]

The idea here is, that the figure in the cloak is the phantom or reduplication of Sir William Howe; but in an article called "William Wilson," one of the *Tales of the Grotesque and Arabesque*, we have not only the same idea, but the same idea similarly presented in several respects. We quote two paragraphs, which our readers may compare with what has been already given. We have italicized, above, the immediate particulars of resemblance.

[Quotation.]

Here it will be observed that, not only are the two general conceptions identical, but there are various *points* of similarity. In each case the figure seen is the wraith or duplication of the beholder. In each case the scene is a masquerade. In each case the figure is cloaked. In each, there is a quarrel—that is to say, angry words pass between the parties. In each the beholder is enraged. In each the cloak and sword fall upon the floor. The "villain, un-muffle yourself," of Mr. H. is precisely paralleled by a passage at page 56 of "William Wilson."

In the way of objection we have scarcely a word to say of these tales. There is, perhaps, a somewhat too general or prevalent *tone*—a tone of melancholy and mysticism. The subjects are insufficiently varied. There is not so much of *versatility* evinced as we might well be warranted in expecting from the high powers of Mr. Hawthorne. But beyond these trivial exceptions we have really none to make. The style is purity itself. Force abounds. High imagination gleams from every page. Mr. Hawthorne is a man of truest genius. We only regret that the limits of our Magazine will not permit us to pay him that full tribute of commendation, which, under other circumstances, we should be so eager to pay.

From The Poetic Principle[1]

In speaking of the Poetic Principle, I have no design to be either thorough or profound. While discussing, very much at random, the essentiality of what we call Poetry, my principal purpose will be to cite for consideration, some few of those minor English or American poems which best suit my own taste, or which, upon my own fancy, have left the most definite impression. By "minor poems" I mean, of course, poems of little length. And here, in the

[1] This lecture, modified several times during the latter part of Poe's life, was published after his death in the New York *Home Journal*, August 31, 1850. Much of the material is a reworking of Poe's review of Longfellow's *Ballads*, which had appeared in April 1842. Poe takes issue with didacticism in poetry and makes the claim that the chief aim of poetry is the revelation of "supernal beauty" and of creating a musical effect. A poem has the singular function of elevating the soul.

beginning permit me to say a few words in regard to a somewhat particular principle, which, whether rightfully or wrongfully, has always had its influence in my own critical estimate of the poem. I hold that a long poem does not exist. I maintain that the phrase, "a long poem," is simply a flat contradiction in terms.

I need scarcely observe that a poem deserves its title only inasmuch as it excites, by elevating the soul. The value of the poem is in the ratio of this elevating excitement. But all excitements are, through a physical necessity, transient. That degree of excitement which would entitle a poem to be so called at all, cannot be sustained throughout a composition of any great length. After a lapse of half an hour, at the very utmost, it flags—fails—a revulsion ensues—and then the poem is, in effect, and in fact, no longer such.

There are, no doubt, many who have found difficulty in reconciling the critical dictum that the "Paradise Lost" is to be devoutly admired throughout, with the absolute impossibility of maintaining for it, during perusal, the amount of enthusiasm which that critical dictum would demand. This great work, in fact, is to be regarded as poetical, only when, losing sight of that vital requisite in all works of Art, Unity, we view it merely as a series of minor poems. If, to preserve its Unity—its totality of effect or impression— we read it (as would be necessary) at a single sitting, the result is but a constant alternation of excitement and depression. After a passage of what we feel to be true poetry, there follow, inevitably, a passage of platitude which no critical prejudgment can force us to admire; but if upon completing the work, we read it again; omitting the first book—that is to say, commencing with the second—we shall be surprised at now finding that admirable which we before condemned—that damnable which we had previously so much admired. It follows from all this that the ultimate, aggregate. or absolute effect of even the best epic under the sun, is a nullity:—and this is precisely the fact.

In regard to the Iliad, we have, if not positive proof, at least very good reason, for believing it intended as a series of lyrics; but, granting the epic intention, I can say only that the work is based in an imperfect sense of Art. The modern epic is, of the supposititious ancient model, but an inconsiderate and blindfold imitation. But the day of these artistic anomalies is over. If, at any time, any very long poem *were* popular in reality—which I doubt—it is at least clear that no long poem will ever be popular again.

That the extent of a poetical work is, *ceteris paribus*,[2] the measure of its merit, seems undoubtedly, when we thus state it, a proposition sufficiently absurd—yet we are indebted for it to the quarterly Reviews. Surely there can be nothing in mere *size*, abstractly considered there can be nothing in mere *bulk*, so far as a volume is concerned, which has so continuously elic-

[2] All other things being equal.

ited admiration from these saturnine pamphlets! A mountain, to be sure, by the mere sentiment of physical magnitude which it conveys, *does* impress us with a sense of sublime—but no man is impressed after *this* fashion by the material grandeur of even "The Columbiad."[3] Even the Quarterlies have not instructed us to be so impressed by it. *As yet*, they have not *insisted* on our estimating Lamartine[4] by the cubic foot, or Pollock by the pound—but what else are we to *infer* from their continual prating about "sustained effort"? If, by "sustained effort," any little gentleman has accomplished an epic, let us frankly commend him for the effort—if this indeed be a thing commendable,—but let us forbear praising the epic on the effort's account. It is to be hoped that common-sense, in the time to come, will prefer deciding upon a work of Art, rather by the impression it makes—by the effect it produces—than by the time it took to impress the effect, or by the amount of "sustained effort" which had been found necessary in effecting the impression. The fact is, that perseverance is one thing and genius quite another—nor can all the Quarterlies in Christendom confound them. By-and-by, this proposition, with many which I have been just urging, will be received as self-evident. In the meantime, by being generally condemned as falsities, they will not be essentially damaged as truths.

On the other hand, it is clear that a poem may be improperly brief. Undue brevity degenerates into mere epigrammatism. A *very* short poem, while now and then producing a brilliant or vivid, never produces a profound or enduring, effect. There must be the steady pressing down of the stamp upon the wax. De Béranger[5] has wrought innumerable things, pungent and spirit-stirring; but, in general, they have been too imponderous to stamp themselves deeply into the public opinion; and thus, as so many feathers of fancy, have been blown aloft only to be whistled down the wind.

·   ·   ·

While the epic mania—while the idea that, to merit in poetry, prolixity is indispensable—has, for some years past, been gradually dying out of the public mind, by mere dint of its own absurdity, we find it succeeded by a heresy too palpably false to be long tolerated, but one which, in the brief period it has already endured, may be said to have accomplished more in the

[3] *The Columbiad* is the long poem by Joel Barlow, published in 1807, which revives historical events from the time of Columbus to the French Revolution. For an account of Barlow, see p. 651.

[4] Alphonse Marie Louis de Lamartine (1790-1869) was a French poet, statesman, and historian, author of the *Meditations* (1820); the Pollacks were an illustrious English family.

Poe could be referring to David (1780-1847), a chief justice of Bombay; his brother, Jonathan (1783-1870), attorney general and chief baron to the exchequer; or George, field-marshal in India.

[5] Pierre de Beranger (1780-1857), French poet whose lyrics were colored by his politics, a curious compound of republicanism and Bonapartism.

corruption of our Poetical Literature than all its other enemies combined. I allude to the heresy of *The Didactic.* It has been assumed, tacitly and avowedly, directly and indirectly, that the ultimate object of all Poetry is Truth. Every poem, it is said, should inculcate a moral; and by this moral is the poetical merit of the work to be ajudged. We Americans especially have patronized this happy idea; and we Bostonians, very especially, have developed it in full. We have taken it into our heads that to write a poem simply for the poem's sake, and to acknowledge such to have been our design, would be to confess ourselves radically wanting in the true Poetic dignity and force:—but the simple fact is, that, would we but permit ourselves to look into our own souls, we should immediately there discover that under the sun there neither exists nor *can* exist any work more thoroughly dignified—more supremely noble than this very poem—this poem *per se*—this poem which is a poem and nothing more—this poem written solely for the poem's sake.

With as deep a reverence for the True as ever inspired the bosom of man, I would, nevertheless, limit, in some measure, its modes of inculcation. I would limit to enforce them. I would not enfeeble them by dissipation. The demands of Truth are severe; she has no sympathy with the myrtles.[6] All *that* which is so indispensable in Song, is precisely all *that* with which *she* has nothing whatever to do. It is but making her a flaunting paradox, to wreathe her in gems and flowers. In enforcing a truth, we need severity rather than efflorescence of language. We must be simple, precise, terse. We must be cool, calm, unimpassioned. In a word, we must be in that mood which, as nearly as possible, is the exact converse of the poetical. *He* must be blind indeed who does not perceive the radical and chasmal differences between the truthful and the poetical modes of inculcation. He must be theory-mad beyond redemption who, in spite of these differences, shall still persist in attempting to reconcile the obstinate oils and waters of Poetry and Truth.

Dividing the world of mind into its three most immediately obvious distinctions, we have the Pure Intellect, Taste, and the Moral Sense. I place Taste in the middle, because it is just this position which, in the mind, it occupies. It holds intimate relations with either extreme; but from the Moral Sense is separated by so faint a difference that Aristotle has not hesitated to place some of its operations among the virtues themselves. Nevertheless, we find the *offices* of the trio marked with a sufficient distinction. Just as the intellect concerns itself with Truth, so Taste informs us of the Beautiful, while the Moral Sense is regardful of Duty. Of this latter, while Conscience teaches the obligation, and Reason the expediency, Taste contents herself with displaying the charms:—waging war upon Vice soley on the ground of

[6] Plants that were sacred to Aphrodite (Venus).

her deformity—her disproportion—her animosity to the fitting, to the appropriate, to the harmonious—in a word, to Beauty.

An immortal instinct, deep within the spirit of man, is thus, plainly, a sense of the Beautiful. This it is which administers to his delight in the manifold forms, and sounds, and odors, and sentiments amid which he exists. And just as the lily is repeated in the lake, or the eyes of Amaryllis in the mirror, so is the mere oral or written repetition of these forms, and sounds, and colors, and odors, and sentiments, a duplicate source of delight. But this mere repetition is not poetry. He who shall simply sing, with however glowing enthusiasm, or with however vivid a truth of description, of the sights, and sounds, and odors, and colors, and sentiments which greet *him* in common with all mankind—he, I say, has yet failed to prove his divine title. There is still a something in the distance which he has been unable to attain. We have still a thirst unquenchable, to allay which he has not shown us the crystal springs. This thirst belongs to the immortality of Man. It is at once a consequence and an indication of his perennial existence. It is the desire of the moth for the star. It is no mere appreciation of the Beauty before us—but a wild effort to reach the Beauty above. Inspired by an ecstatic prescience of the glories beyond the grave, we struggle, by multiform combinations among the things and thoughts of Time, to attain a portion of that Loveliness whose very elements, perhaps, appertain to eternity alone. And thus when by Poetry—or when by Music, the most entrancing of the Poetic moods—we find ourselves melted into tears—not as the Abbate Gravina[7] supposes—through excess of pleasure, but through a certain petulant, impatient sorrow at our inability to grasp *now*, wholly, here on earth, at once and forever, those divine and rapturous joys, of which *through* the poem, or *through* the music, we attain to but brief and indeterminate glimpses.

The struggle to apprehend the supernal Loveliness—this struggle, on the part of souls fittingly constituted—has given to the world all *that* which it (the world) has ever been enabled at once to understand and *to feel* as poetic.

The Poetic Sentiment, of course, may develop itself in various modes—in Painting, in Sculpture, in Architecture, in the Dance—very especially in Music,—and very peculiarly, and with a wide field, in the composition of the Landscape Garden. Our present theme, however, has regard only to its manifestation in words. And here let me speak briefly on the topic of rhythm. Contenting myself with the certainty that Music, in its various modes of metre, rhythm, and rhyme, is of so vast a moment in Poetry as never to be wisely rejected—is so vitally important an adjunct, that he is simply silly who declines its assistance, I will not now pause to maintain its

[7] Gran Vincenzo Gravina was an Italian critic, the author of *Della Ragion Poetica* (1708).

absolute essentiality. It is in Music, perhaps, that the soul most nearly attains the great end for which, when inspired by the Poetic Sentiment, it struggles—the creation of supernal Beauty. It *may* be, indeed, that here this sublime end is, now and then, attained *in fact*. We are often made to feel, with a shivering delight, that from an earthly harp are stricken notes which *cannot* have been unfamiliar to the angels. And thus there can be little doubt that in the union of Poetry with Music in its popular sense, we shall find the widest field for the Poetic development. The old Bards and Minnesingers had advantages which we do not possess—and Thomas Moore, singing his own songs, was, in the most legitimate manner, perfecting them as poems.

To recapitulate, then:—I would define, in brief, the Poetry of words as *The Rhythmical Creation of Beauty*. Its sole arbiter is Taste. With the Intellect or with the Conscience, it has only collateral relations. Unless incidentally it has no concern whatever either with Duty or with Truth.

A few words, however, in explanation. *That* pleasure which is at once the most pure, the most elevating, and the most intense, is derived, I maintain, from the contemplation of the Beautiful. In the contemplation of Beauty we alone find it possible to attain that pleasurable elevation, or excitement, *of the soul*, which we recognize as the Poetic Sentiment, and which is so easily distinguished from Truth, which is the satisfaction of the Reason, or from Passion, which is the excitement of the Heart. I make Beauty, therefore,— using the word as inclusive of the sublime,—I make Beauty the province of the poem, simply because it is an obvious rule of Art that effects should be made to spring as directly as possible from their causes—no one as yet having been weak enough to deny that the peculiar elevation in question is at least *most readily* attainable in the poem. It by no means follows, however, that the incitements of Passion, or the precepts of Duty, or even the lessons of Truth, may not be introduced into a poem, and with advantage; for they may subserve, incidentally, in various ways, the general purposes of the work; but the true artist will always contrive to tone them down in proper subjection to that *Beauty* which is the atmosphere and the real essence of the poem.

HERMAN MELVILLE

(1819–1891)

During his lifetime, Herman Melville was primarily known as the author of *Typee* (1846) and *Omoo* (1847), a popularizer of life in the South Seas, the man who had lived among the cannibals and returned to describe his exotic adventures to the ladies and gentlemen of New England. From 1846 until 1857, Melville struggled to establish himself as a serious writer in an expanding American democracy, but his subsequent novels—*Redburn* (1849), *Mardi* (1849), *Whitejacket* (1850), *Moby Dick* (1851), *Pierre* (1852), and *The Confidence Man* (1857)—as

The standard edition is still *The Works of Herman Melville,* Standard Edition, 16 vols. 1922–1924; 1963. It is being superseded by *The Writings of Herman Melville,* The Northwestern-Newberry Edition, ed. Harrison Hayford, Hershel Parker, and G. Thomas Tanselle, 1968. The following volumes have been published: *Typee, Omoo,* and *Redburn.* See also the individual texts, with good introductions, of *The Complete Works of Herman Melville,* Howard P. Vincent, General Editor. The following volumes have been published: *Collected Poems,* ed. H. P. Vincent, 1945; *Piazza Tales,* ed. E. S. Oliver, 1948; *Pierre, or the Ambiguities,* ed. H. S. Murray, 1949; *Moby-Dick, or, the Whale,* ed. L. S. Mansfield and H. P. Vincent, 1952; *The Confidence-Man,* ed. E. S. Foster, 1954; *Clarel,* ed. W. E. Bezanson, 1960. *The Letters of Herman Melville,* ed. Merrell R. Davis and William H. Gilman, 1960. The best text of *Moby-Dick* is *Moby-Dick; A Norton Critical Edition,* ed. Harrison Hayford and Hershel Parker, 1967.

The finest modern biography is Leon Howard, *Herman Melville: A Biography,* 1951, which should be supplemented by Jay Leyda, *The Melville Log: A Documentary Life of Herman Melville, 1819–1891,* 2 vols., 1951. The first biography was Raymond Weaver, *Herman Melville, Mariner and Mystic,* 1921, 1961, followed by John Freeman, *Herman Melville,* 1926 and Lewis Mumford, *Herman Melville,* 1929.

Critical studies include Charles R. Anderson, *Melville in the South Seas,* 1939; F. O. Matthiessen, *The American Renaissance,* 1941; William Braswell, *Melville's Religious Thought,* 1943; W. E. Sedgwick, *Herman Melville; The Tragedy of Mind,* 1944; H. P. Vincent, *The Trying out of Moby Dick,* 1949; Richard Chase, *Herman Melville; A Critical Study,* 1949; Newton Arvin, *Herman Melville,* 1950; Lawrance Thompson, *Melville's Quarrel with God,* Eleanor Melville Metcalf, *Herman Melville; Cycle and Epicyle* 1953; Edward H. Rosenberry, *Melville and the Comic Spirit,* 1955; Perry Miller, *The Raven and the Whale,* 1956; James Baird, *Ishmael,* 1956; R. Fogle, *Melville's Shorter Tales,* 1960; Warner Berthoff, *The Example of Melville,* 1962; James Miller, *A Reader's Guide to Herman Melville,* 1962; Richard Chase, ed., *Melville: A Collection of Critical Essays,* 1962; Herman Melville. *The Battle Pieces of Herman Melville,* edited with introduction and notes by Hennig Cohen, 1963; K. Widmer, *The Ways of Nihilism. . . Melville's Short Novels,* 1970; H. Bruce Franklin, *The Wake of the Gods,* 1963; Herschel Parker, ed., *The Recognition of Herman Melville: Selected Criticism since 1846,* 1967; Robert B. Buckley, *The Method of Melville's Short Fiction,* 1975; T. Walter Herbert, Jr., *Moby-Dick and Calvinism: A World Dismantled,* 1977.

The texts are taken from *The Works of Herman Melville.*

well as many of his stories were not well received. Melville grew resentful that his most imaginative work was unappreciated—from 1851 to 1861 his income from books averaged $228 a year—and he retired from professional authorship, taking a position as a custom's inspector on the New York City docks, writing poetry throughout the 1870's and 1880's and, finally, composing *Billy Budd* (1891), a novel that was not discovered and published until 33 years after his death. This eclipse of Melville's reputation and the consequent decline of his career as well as of his personal affairs constitutes, as one critic has said, "the heaviest count in our literary annals against the American mind."

Herman Melville was born on August 1, 1819, in New York City, the third child of Allan and Maria Gansevoort Melville. His maternal ancestors had settled in Albany, New York, in the seventeenth century and established themselves as landed gentry. Melville's grandfather was a general in the American Revolution and his father, Allan Melville, was an important merchant and importer. By the time of Melville's birth, however, his father's importing business was suffering because of America's first postwar depression and, in 1830, the family of eight children was taken to Albany, New York. By 1832, the father was dead, and young Herman had to leave the Albany Academy where he had studied for two years at various jobs: in a bank, on his uncle's farm, in his brother's fur factory, and in an elementary school.

Throughout these years Melville was unable to settle on any occupation. He studied surveying in 1838 and began to write for local newspapers soon afterward; but he was restless in his relative poverty, looking for release from a confining life. By 1839 his uncle had arranged for his employment on a cargo ship sailing for Liverpool. After his return, Melville tried his hand at teaching, then traveled to Illinois to make his fortune in an uncle's lead mines; but another depression cut short his attempt and he came east again, shaving his whiskers now (as his older brother had advised him) so that he could be a presentable lawyer's clerk. But Melville had the wanderlust and he was feeling "a damp, drizzly November of the soul," as he later wrote of the narrator in *Moby Dick*; by 1841 he was once again on the sea—this time leaving New Bedford for a three-year voyage to the South Seas.

The trip that Melville took from 1841 until 1844 was the most important of his life, because it served as the background of his finest fiction. He traveled around Cape Horn and up the coast of South America to the Galapagos Island, the Marquesas, and other islands. On July 9, 1842, he jumped ship with a friend and was imprisoned for a month by a tribe of cannibals in the Typee valley before he was rescued on August 9 by an Australian whaling ship. Later he was kept in brief confinement in Tahiti until he was able to escape on another whaler, arriving in Honolulu in 1843. On August 17, he sailed aboard the frigate *United States,* but it was not until October 1844 that the ship reached Boston and Melville was mustered out of the Navy.

Upon his return to the United States, Melville set out to become an author. He quickly wrote *Typee* and *Omoo,* novels that record his experiences in the South Seas and that proved to be quite popular in both America and England. Melville was so encouraged by the sales of these novels and his future prospects as a professional writer that he married Elizabeth Shaw, daughter of the Chief Justice of Massachusetts, on August 4, 1847, and settled in New York to raise a family.

Although *Typee* and *Omoo* were primarily travelogues, calculated to please an audience that was eager for genuinely romantic adventures, one of Melville's major themes—the consequences of self-reliance—had already suggested itself. Melville had returned to an America in which transcendentalists like Emerson were making great claims for self-expression, for reliance on one's intuition, and he had seen the abuses to which this concept could be put. In *Typee,* he described the Romantic flight from a materialistic society into a primordial world, but already he viewed the protagonist as a victim of the chieftain's will; in *Omoo* he depicted missionaries who imposed their Christianity on the natives and converted self-reliance into the manipulation of others.

Melville became more and more critical of the transcendentalists and their celebration of the single solitary self, the beneficence of nature, and the primacy of spirit over flesh. He had been across the oceans and had seen the kinds of storms and natural disasters that inhibit one from Emersonian generalizations about the "loveliness of nature"; nature, Melville knew, also had the power to destroy. Emerson could write that "The terrors of the storm are chiefly confined to the parlor and the cabin. The drover, the sailor, buffets it all day, and his health renews itself at as vigorous a pulse under the sleet, as under the sun of June"; but Melville, upon reading this passage, commented, "To one who has weathered Cape Horn as a common sailor what stuff all this is." Emerson could extol the virtues of spirit, but Melville grew impatient with Emerson's need to affirm and finally characterized him as "a Plato who talks thro' his nose."

As a practical man and a novelist, Melville found it necessary to measure all of his ideas against the realities he had experienced. Between 1849 and 1852 he came fully to grips with the central doctrine of transcendentalism and burst forth with an expression of concentrated creativity rarely equalled in the history of American culture. In *Redburn* (1849) he translated his first trip abroad into the journey of young Redburn from innocence to evil, from adolescence to manhood; in *Mardi* (1849) he explored philosophically the assumptions of transcendentalism; in *Whitejacket* (1850) he deplored the flogging so prevalent on ships; and, in *Moby Dick* (1851), he dramatized the abuses of self-reliance as his central figure, Ahab, asserts his will against the will of God because of a monomaniacal pursuit of the whale that has taken his leg and that will ultimately destroy the men on his ship. In *Moby Dick,* Melville creates a heterogeneous democratic society of men, each pursuing whales for a different purpose—pleasure, livelihood, adventure, greed—and each finally the victim of a man who manipulates him by an imposition of will that takes no cognizance of other people, that refuses to recognize what John Dewey once called the "conjoint communicated experience" of a democracy and that can lead only to self-destruction.

For anyone to have created so many intense works of art in so short a time, certain intellectual and creative forces had to gather within him suddenly. When Melville returned from the South Seas in 1844, he began to read voraciously. He was deeply interested in philosophy and theology, and he turned to authors such as Thomas Browne, Goethe, Carlyle, and Emerson. All of Melville's life there was a tension between his own Calvinist past, which he repudiated, and the contemporary transcendentalism, which he could never fully accept. Many of his protagonists are idealistic, from Reburn to Billy Budd, but their optimism and self-reliance founders in the real world and encounters fate in the form of willful authoritarians who abuse their power: "Fixed Fate, Free Will, Foreknowledge absolute" were the issues that absorbed him.

The questions of fate, evil, tragedy, and human frailty, which he felt were evaded by Emerson and the transcendentalists, were dramatically present in the work of two writers who profoundly influenced him: Shakespeare and Hawthorne. In Shakespeare, Melville not only discovered the form of tragedy that was so compatible with his own views of art, but he felt the powerful use of language and the brilliant exploration of character; without the influence of Shakespeare many of the dramatic soliloquies, the extraordinary rhetoric, and the tragic dimensions of Ahab—as one of many characters—would be inconceivable. In the deepest creative sense, Shakespeare was a "liberating god" for Melville.

Hawthorne had an equally profound impact on Melville's sensibility. In 1850, Melville moved to the Berkshires and became friendly with Hawthorne, who lived in nearby Lenox. He had come upon Hawthorne's volume of short stories, *Mosses from an Old Manse,* and praised them lavishly in a review that he wrote in August 1850, at the time he was working on *Moby Dick.* Melville felt what he called a "shock of recognition" and responded most sensitively to the dark side of Hawthorne's imagination, to his examination of evil: "For spite of all the Indian-summer sunlight on the hither side of Hawthorne's soul, the other side—like the dark half of the physical sphere—is shrouded in a blackness, ten times blacker. . . . Certain it is, however, that this great power of blackness in him derives its force from its appeals to that Calvinistic sense of Innate Depravity and Original Sin, from whose visitations, in some shape or other, no deeply thinking mind is always and wholly free. For, in certain moods, no man can weigh this world without throwing in something, somehow like Original Sin, to strike the uneven balance." For Melville, Hawthorne's presence was a motivating force—"the American who up to the present day has evinced, in literature, the largest brain with the largest heart." Hawthorne had just published *The Scarlet Letter* (1850) and was working on *The House of the Seven Gables* (1851); he was at the peak of his creative powers. The many hours that Melville spent talking with his neighbor encouraged him to create his own American Tragedy, his own vision of evil and the dangers of uncontrolled self-reliance, and he dedicated *Moby Dick* to Hawthorne.

Melville continued to write throughout the 1850's. The stories in *The Piazza Tales*—"Benito Cereno," "Bartleby, the Scrivener," and others—drew on the themes that were so elaborately and dramatically presented in *Moby Dick:* the threat to individual freedom and the excesses of self-reliance, the need for man to recognize his commonalty with others, and the abuses of authority. But despite all of his attempts to speak to the American public, Melville lost his audience, and with the publication of *Pierre* (1852), a highly personal novel of a young man's self-destruction, even his family wondered about his sanity. By the time that *The Confidence Man* was published in 1857, Melville suffered from physical and nervous exhaustion; he had periodic attacks of rheumatism, sciatica, and neuralgia; he could not earn a living from his work, and his "quarrel with God" remained unabated. When he traveled to Europe in 1857, he visited Hawthorne, who had become American consul in Liverpool and who wrote at the time one of the most revealing descriptions of his friend. Melville, Hawthorne noted, was

> looking much as he used to do (a little paler, and perhaps a little sadder), in a rough outside coat, and with his characteristic gravity and reserve of manner. . . . Melville has not been well, of late; he has been affected with neuralgic complaints in his head and limbs, and no doubt has suffered from too constant literary occupations, pursued without much success, latterly; and his writings, for a long while past, have indicated a morbid state of mind. . . . (On Wednesday) we took a pretty long walk together, and sat down in a hollow among the sand hills (sheltering ourselves from the high, cool wind) and smoked a cigar. Melville, as he always

does, began to reason of Providence and futurity, and of everything that lies beyond human ken, and informed me that he had
"pretty much made up his mind to be annihilated"; but still he
does not seem to rest in that anticipation; and, I think, will never
rest until he gets hold of a definite belief. It is strange how he
persists—and has persisted ever since I knew him, and probably
long before—in wandering to-and-fro over these deserts, as dismal and monotonous as the sand hills amid which we were sitting. He can neither believe, nor be comfortable in his unbelief;
and he is too honest and courageous not to try to do one or the
other. If he were a religious man, he would be one of the truly
religious and reverential; he has a very high and noble nature,
and better worth immortality than most of us.

When Melville returned from the Holy Land in 1857, *The Confidence Man* was published. The book was a satire on transcendental
self-affirmation and caricatured figures such as Emerson and Thoreau.
It was unsuccessful and marked the end of Melville's active attempt to
be a self-sustaining author. He sold his property in Pittsfield, moved to
New York City and, throughout the 1860's, wrote poems concerning
the Civil War, which were later collected as *Battle Pieces and Aspects
of the War* (1866). For 20 years, from 1866 to 1886, Melville was a
customs inspector and wrote only poetry: "Clarel, A Poem and Pilgrimage in the Holy Land" (1876); "John Marr and Other Sailors" (1888),
and "Timoleon" (1891). He died in 1891, scarcely known to the literary
world, and his final novel, *Billy Budd,* which he had written in the last
three years of his life, was not published until 1924.

Although Melville's reputation was eclipsed during his own lifetime, it has enjoyed extraordinary growth in the past 40 years as critics
and scholars have found his work particularly congenial to the modern
sensibility. His use of myth and symbolism, satire and irony, and fantasy and dream appeals to our imagination; his relentless uncertainty
about eschatological problems commands our ambiguous and doubting minds; his response to natural and primitive forces, his sympathy
for human limitation, his scorn of cant and hypocrisy, his recognition
of and attempt to understand the sources of evil in an age when philosophical thinkers shun the problem—all these attitudes, as expressed
by a genuinely honest and open intelligence, persuade us that Melville's vision of the world is essentially ours.

At the center of Melville's fiction is his criticism of Emersonian self-
reliance, his deep skepticism about the nature of confidence and optimism—and authority. Much of the tension in Melville's work grows
out of his fear of power: power controls the significant figures of his
novels and stories; power lurks behind the most innocent of his tales

when it is not directly manifest; and the number of victims that groan beneath the heavy weight of authority is, of course, legion. Melville began as a nineteenth-century Romantic whose early ideas are at one with those of his literary predecessors and his contemporaries, but he became a skeptic whose views anticipate those of twentieth-century writers. Melville's withdrawal into cynicism and disenchantment permits us to measure the surrender of an early acceptance—one is tempted to say an ultimate need—of skepticism in our own time, though most contemporary authors seek to transcend the comic negation so evident in a book like *The Confidence Man*. Writing in the middle of the nineteenth century, Melville expressed a growing distrust in power, and the quality of that distrust points toward what surely must be one of the dominant themes of modern American literature—the nature of authority.

Hawthorne and His Mosses[1]

A papered chamber in a fine old farm-house—a mile from any other dwelling, and dipped to the eaves in foliage—surrounded by mountains, old woods, and Indian ponds—this, surely, is the place to write of Hawthorne. Some charm is in this northern air, for love and duty seem both impelling to the task. A man of a deep and noble nature has seized me in this seclusion. His wild, witch voice rings through me; or, in softer cadences, I seem to hear it in the songs of the hillside birds that sing in the larch trees at my window.

Would that all excellent books were foundlings, without father or mother, that so it might be, we could glorify them, without including their ostensible authors! Nor would any true man take exception to this—least of all, he who writes: "When the Artist rises high enough to achieve the Beautiful, the

---

[1] This essay was published in two installments on August 17 and 24, 1850, in the *Literary World*, a magazine edited by Melville's friend Evert A. Duyckinck. Melville did not know Hawthorne well at the time that he wrote the piece, and he signed it anonymously, as "a Virginian Spending July in Vermont." Melville's response to the *Mosses* occurs four years after the book's appearance in 1846 and initiates a kinship between the two writers that was to last for at least the next seven years. As Melville indicates, it is the "blackness in Hawthorne. . . that so fixes and fascinates" him and, as an author who was writing *Moby Dick* at the time, his deep emotions are understandable. Although the essay is burdened by its excessive statements about a nationalist literature and by comparisons between Hawthorne and Shakespeare, it does strike at the most profound source of creativity in Hawthorne's work: the power of blackness, ten times black, which has attracted all readers sensitive to his art. Perhaps the most fascinating aspect of this essay is not so much its commentary on Hawthorne's work as its revelation of Melville's state of mind as he created his masterpiece. It is, of course, no accident that Melville dedicated *Moby Dick* to Hawthorne.

symbol by which he makes it perceptible to mortal senses becomes of little value in his eyes, while his spirit possesses itself in the enjoyment of the reality."[2]

But more than this. I know not what would be the right name to put on the title page of an excellent book; but this I feel, that the names of all fine authors are fictitious ones, far more so than that of Junius[3]—simply standing, as they do, for the mystical, ever-eluding Spirit of all Beauty, which ubiquitously possesses men of genius. Purely imaginative as this fancy may appear, it nevertheless seems to receive some warranty from the fact that on a personal interview no great author has ever come up to the idea of his reader. But that dust of which our bodies are composed, how can it fitly express the nobler intelligence among us? With reverence be it spoken, that not even in the case of one deemed more than man, not even in our Savior, did his visible frame betoken anything of the augustness of the nature within. Else, how could those Jewish eye-witnesses fail to see heaven in his glance?

It is curious, how a man may travel along a country road, and yet miss the grandest or sweetest of prospects, by reason of an intervening hedge so like all other hedges as in no way to hint of the wide landscape beyond. So has it been with me concerning the enchanting landscape in the soul of this Hawthorne, this most excellent Man of Mosses. His *Old Manse* has been written now four years, but I never read it till a day or two since. I had seen it in the bookstores—heard of it often—even had it recommended to me by a tasteful friend, as a rare, quiet book, perhaps too deserving of popularity to be popular. But there are so many books called "excellent," and so much unpopular merit, that amid the thick stir of other things, the hint of my tasteful friend was disregarded; and for four years the Mosses on the Old Manse never refreshed me with their perennial green. It may be, however, that all this while, the book, like wine, was only improving in flavor and body. At any rate, it so chanced that this long procrastination eventuated in a happy result. At breakfast the other day, a mountain girl, a cousin of mine, who for the last two weeks has every morning helped me to strawberries and raspberries—which, like the roses and pearls in the fairy-tale, seemed to fall into the saucer from those strawberry-beds, her cheeks—this delightful creature, this charming Cherry, says to me—"I see you spend your mornings in the haymow; and yesterday I found there Dwight's *Travels in New England.* Now I have something far better than that—something more congenial to our summer on these hills. Take these raspberries, and then I will give you some moss."—"Moss!" said I.—"Yes, and you must take it to the barn with you, and good-by to 'Dwight.'"

[2] The last sentence of Hawthorne's "The Artist of the Beautiful."
[3] The pseudonym used by the author of a series of political "Letters" that appeared in England between 1769 and 1771. They were published in 1821 and 1822.

With that she left me, and soon returned with a volume, verdantly bound, and garnished with a curious frontispiece in green—nothing less than a fragment of real moss cunningly pressed to a fly-leaf.—"Why this," said I, spilling my raspberries, "this is the *Mosses from an Old Manse.*" "Yes," said cousin Cherry, "yes, it is that flowering Hawthorne."—"Hawthorne and Mosses," said I, "no more it is morning: it is July in the country: and I am off for the barn."

Stretched on that new-mown clover, the hillside breeze blowing over me through the wide barn door, and soothed by the hum of the bees in the meadows around, how magically stole over me this Mossy Man! And how amply, how bountifully, did he redeem that delicious promise to his guests in the Old Manse, of whom it is written: "Others could give them pleasure and amusement, or instruction—these could be picked up anywhere—but it was for me to give them rest. Rest, in a life of trouble! What better could be done for those weary and world-worn spirits?. . . what better could be done for anybody, who came within our magic circle, than to throw the spell of a magic spirit over him?"—So all that day, half-buried in the new clover, I watched this Hawthorne's "Assyrian dawn and Paphian sunset and moonrise, from the summit of our eastern hill."

The soft ravishments of the man spun me round about in a web of dreams, and when the book was closed, when the spell was over, this wizard "dismissed me, with but misty reminiscences, as if I had been dreaming of him."

What a wild moonlight of contemplative humor bathes that Old Manse!— the rich and rare distillment of a spicy and slowly oozing heart. No rollicking rudeness, no gross fun fed on fat dinners, and bred in the lees of wine—but a humor so spiritually gentle, so high, so deep, and yet so richly relishable, that it were hardly inappropriate in an angel. It is the very religion of mirth; for nothing so human but it may be advanced to that. The orchard of the Old Manse seems the visible type of the fine mind that has described it. Those twisted and contorted old trees that "stretch out their crooked branches, and take such hold of the imagination, that we remember them as humorists and odd fellows." And then, as surrounded by these grotesque forms, and hushed in the noonday repose of this Hawthorne's spell, how aptly might the still fall of his ruddy thoughts into your soul be symbolized by "the thump of a great apple, in the stillest afternoon, falling without a breath of wind, from the mere necessity of perfect ripeness!" For no less ripe than ruddy are the apples of the thoughts and fancies in this sweet Man of Mosses.

"Buds and Bird-Voices"—What a delicious thing is that!—"Will the world ever be so decayed, that spring may not renew its greenness?"—And the "Fire-Worship." Was ever the hearth so glorified into an altar before?

The mere title of that piece is better than any common work in fifty folio volumes.[4] How exquisite is this:

> Nor did it lessen the charm of his soft, familiar courtesy and helpful-ness, that the mighty spirit, were opportunity offered him, would run riot through the peaceful house, wrap its inmates in his terrible em-brace, and leave nothing of them save their whitened bones. This pos-sibility of mad destruction only made his domestic kindness the more beautiful and touching. It was so sweet of him, being endowed with such power, to dwell, day after day, and one long, lonesome night after another, on the dusky hearth, only now and then betraying his wild nature, by thrusting his red tongue out of the chimney-top! True, he had done much mischief in the world, and was pretty certain to do more; but his warm heart atoned for all. He was kindly to the race of man. . . .

But he has still other apples, not quite so ruddy, though full as ripe—apples that have been left to wither on the tree, after the pleasant autumn gathering is past. The sketch of "The Old Apple-Dealer" is conceived in the subtlest spirit of sadness; he whose "subdued and nerveless boyhood prefigured his abortive prime, which, likewise, contained within itself the prophecy and image of his lean and torpid age." Such touches as are in this piece cannot proceed from any common heart. They argue such a depth of tenderness, such a boundless sympathy with all forms of being, such an omnipresent love, that we must needs say that this Hawthorne is here almost alone—in his generation at least—in the artistic manifestation of these things. Still more. Such touches as these—and many, very many similar ones, all through his chapters—furnish clues, whereby we enter a little way into the intricate, profound heart where they originated. And we see that suffering, some time or other and in some shape or other—this only can enable any man to depict it in others. All over him, Hawthorne's melancholy rests like an Indian sum-mer, which, though bathing a whole country in one softness, still reveals the distinctive hue of every towering hill, and each far-winding vale.

But it is the least part of genius that attracts admiration. Where Haw-thorne is known, he seems to be deemed a pleasant writer, with a pleasant style—a sequestered, harmless man, from whom any deep and weighty thing would hardly be anticipated: a man who means no meanings. But there is no man, in whom humor and love, like mountain peaks, soar to such a rapt height, as to receive the irradiations of the upper skies; there is no man in whom humor and love are developed in that high form called genius—no such man can exist without also possessing, as the indispensable complement

<hr>

[4] Large books in which the sheets have been folded only once.

of these, a great, deep intellect, which drops down into the universe like a plummet. Or, love and humor are only the eyes, through which such an intellect views this world. The great beauty in such a mind is but the product of its strength. What, to all readers, can be more charming than the piece entitled "Monsieur du Miroir"; and to a reader at all capable of fully fathoming it, what, at the same time, can possess more mystical depth of meaning?—Yes, there he sits, and looks at me—this "shape of mystery," this "identical Monsieur du Miroir."—"Methinks I should tremble now, were his wizard power, of gliding through all impediments in search of me, to place him suddenly before my eyes."

How profound, nay, appalling, is the moral evolved by the "Earth's Holocaust," where—beginning with the hollow follies and affectations of the world—all vanities and empty theories and forms are, one after another, and by an admirably graduated, growing comprehensiveness, thrown into the allegorical fire, till, at length, nothing is left but the all-engendering heart of man; which remaining still unconsumed, the great conflagration is naught. Of a piece with this is "The Intelligence Office," a wondrous symbolizing of the secret workings in men's souls. There are other sketches, still more charged with ponderous import.

"The Christmas Banquet" and "The Bosom Serpent" would be fine subjects for a curious and elaborate analysis, touching the conjectural parts of the mind that produced them. For spite of all the Indian-summer sunlight on the hither side of Hawthorne's soul, the other side—like the dark half of the physical sphere—is shrouded in a blackness, ten times black. But this darkness but gives more effect to the ever-moving dawn, that forever advances through it, and circumnavigates his world. Whether Hawthorne has simply availed himself of this mystical blackness as a means to the wondrous effects he makes it to produce in his lights and shades; or whether there really lurks in him, perhaps unknown to himself, a touch of Puritanic gloom—this, I cannot altogether tell. Certain it is, however, that this great power of blackness in him derives its force from its appeals to that Calvinistic sense of Innate Depravity and Original Sin, from whose visitations, in some shape or other, no deeply thinking mind is always and wholly free. For, in certain moods, no man can weigh this world, without throwing in something, somehow like Original Sin to strike the uneven balance. At all events, perhaps no writer has ever wielded this terrific thought with greater terror than this same harmless Hawthorne. Still more: this black conceit pervades him, through and through. You may be witched by his sunlight, transported by the bright gildings in the skies he builds over you, but there is the blackness of darkness beyond; and even his bright gildings but fringe and play upon the edges of thunder-clouds.—In one word, the world is mistaken in this Nathaniel Hawthorne. He himself must often have smiled at its absurd misconception of him. He is immeasurably deeper than the plummet of the mere critic. For it is not the brain that can test such a man; it is only the heart. You cannot come to know greatness by inspecting it; there is no glimpse to be caught of it, except by intuition; you need not ring it, you but touch it, and you find it is gold.

Now it is that blackness in Hawthorne, of which I have spoken, that so fixes and fascinates me. It may be, nevertheless, that it is too largely developed in him. Perhaps he does not give us a ray of his light for every shade of his dark. But however this may be, this blackness it is that furnishes the infinite obscure of his background—that background, against which Shakespeare plays his grandest conceits, the things that have made for Shakespeare his loftiest but most circumscribed renown, as the profoundest of thinkers. For by philosophers Shakespeare is not adored as the great man of tragedy and comedy.—"Off with his head! so much for Buckingham!"[5] This sort of rant, interlined by another hand, brings down the house—those mistaken souls, who dream of Shakespeare as a mere man of Richard-the-Third humps, and Macbeth daggers. But it is those deep far-away things in him; those occasional flashings-forth of the intuitive Truth in him; those short, quick probings at the very axis of reality;—these are the things that make Shakespeare Shakespeare. Through the mouths of the dark characters of Hamlet, Timon, Lear, and Iago, he craftily says, or sometimes insinuates, the things which we feel to be so terrifically true that it were all but madness for any good man, in his own proper character, to utter, or even hint of them. Tormented into desperation, Lear the frantic king tears off the mask, and speaks the sane madness of vital truth. But, as I before said, it is the least part of genius that attracts admiration. And so, much of the blind, unbridled admiration that has been heaped upon Shakespeare has been lavished upon the least part of him. And few of his endless commentators and critics seem to have remembered, or even perceived, that the immediate products of a great mind are not so great as that undeveloped, and sometimes undevelopable yet dimly discernible greatness, to which these immediate products are but the infallible indices. In Shakespeare's tomb lies infinitely more than Shakespeare ever wrote. And if I magnify Shakespeare, it is not so much for what he did do, as for what he did not do or refrained from doing. For in this world of lies, Truth is forced to fly like a scared white doe in the woodlands; and only by cunning glimpses will she reveal herself, as in Shakespeare and other masters of the great Art of Telling the Truth—even though it be covertly, and by snatches.

But if this view of the all-popular Shakespeare be seldom taken by his readers, and if very few who extol him have ever read him deeply, or, perhaps, only have seen him on the tricky stage (which alone made, and is still making, him his mere mob renown)—if few men have time, or patience, or palate, for the spiritual truth as it is in that great genius—it is, then, no

[5] Colley Cibber had interpolated this line in his version of *Richard III* (1700).

matter of surprise that in a contemporaneous age, Nathaniel Hawthorne is a man as yet almost utterly mistaken among men. Here and there, in some quiet armchair in the noisy town, or some deep nook among the noiseless mountains, he may be appreciated for something of what he is. But unlike Shakespeare, who was forced to the contrary course by circumstances, Hawthorne (either from simple disinclination, or else from inaptitude) refrains from all the popularizing noise and show of broad farce, and blood-besmeared tragedy; content with the still, rich utterances of a great intellect in repose, and which sends few thoughts into circulation, except they be arterialized at his large warm lungs, and expanded in his honest heart.

Nor need you fix upon that blackness in him, if it suit you not. Nor, indeed, will all readers discern it, for it is, mostly, insinuated to those who may best understand it, and account for it; it is not obtruded upon every one alike.

Some may start to read of Shakespeare and Hawthorne on the same page. They may say, that if an illustration were needed, a lesser light might have sufficed to elucidate this Hawthorne, this small man of yesterday. But I am not, willingly, one of those who, as touching Shakespeare at least, exemplify the maxim of Rochefoucauld,[6] that "we exalt the reputation of some, in order to depress that of others"; who, to teach all noble-souled aspirants that there is no hope for them, pronounce Shakespeare absolutely unapproachable. But Shakespeare has been approached. There are minds that have gone as far as Shakespeare into the universe. And hardly a mortal man, who, at some time or other, has not felt as great thoughts in him as any you will find in *Hamlet*. We must not inferentially malign mankind for the sake of any one man, whoever he may be. This is too cheap a purchase of contentment for conscious mediocrity to make. Besides, this absolute and unconditional adoration of Shakespeare has grown to be a part of our Anglo-Saxon superstitions. The Thirty-Nine Articles[7] are now Forty. Intolerance has come to exist in this matter. You must believe in Shakespeare's unapproachability, or quit the country. But what sort of a belief is this for an American, a man who is bound to carry republican progressiveness into Literature, as well as into Life? Believe me, my friends, that men not very much inferior to Shakespeare are this day being born on the banks of the Ohio. And the day will come when you shall say; who reads a book by an Englishman that is a modern?[8] The great mistake seems to be that even with those Americans who look forward to the coming of a great literary genius among us, they

[6] The Duc de la Rochefoucauld wrote *Reflexions ou Sentences et Maximes Morales* (1665).

[7] These articles state the creed of the Anglican Church, established in 1571.

[8] This barb is for the question that Sydney Smith, the English critic for the *Edinburgh Review*, had asked: "In the four quarters of the globe who reads an American book? or goes to an American play? or looks at an American picture or statue?" (1820).

somehow fancy he will come in the costume of Queen Elizabeth's day, be a writer of dramas founded upon old English history, or the tales of Boccaccio.[9] Whereas great geniuses are parts of the times; they themselves are the times, and possess a correspondent coloring. It is of a piece with the Jews, who, while their Shiloh[10] was meekly walking in their streets, were still praying for his magnificent coming; looking for him in a chariot, who was already among them on an ass. Nor must we forget that, in his own lifetime, Shakespeare was not Shakespeare, but only Master William Shakespeare of the shrewd, thriving business firm of Condell,[11] Shakespeare & Co., proprietors of the Globe Theatre in London, and by a courtly author, of the name of Chettle,[12] was looked at as an "up-start crow" beautified "with other birds' feathers." For, mark it well, imitation is often the first charge brought against real originality. Why this is so, there is not space to set forth here. You must have plenty of sea-room to tell the Truth in; especially when it seems to have an aspect of newness, as America did in 1492, though it was then just as old, and perhaps older than Asia, only those sagacious philosophers, the common sailors, had never seen it before, swearing it was all water and moonshine there.

Now, I do not say that Nathaniel of Salem is greater than William of Avon, or as great. But the difference between the two men is by no means immeasurable. Not a very great deal more, and Nathaniel were verily William.

This, too, I mean—that if Shakespeare has not been equaled, give the world time, and he is sure to be surpassed, in one hemisphere or the other. Nor will it at all do to say that the world is getting gray and grizzled now, and has lost that fresh charm which she wore of old, and by virtue of which the great poets of past times made themselves what we esteem them to be. Not so. The world is as young today as when it was created and this Vermont morning dew is as wet to my feet as Eden's dew to Adam's. Nor has Nature been all over ransacked by our progenitors, so that no new charms and mysteries remain for this latter generation to find. Far from it. The trillionth part has not yet been said, and all that has been said but multiplies the avenues to what remains to be said. It is not so much paucity as superabundance of material that seems to incapacitate modern authors.

Let America then prize and cherish her writers; yea, let her glorify them. They are not so many in number as to exhaust her good will. And while she has good kith and kin of her own, to take to her bosom, let her not lavish her embraces upon the household of an alien. For believe it or not, England,

[9] Giovanni Boccaccio, fourteenth-century Italian author of the *Decameron*.

[10] A site of Jewish ritual and faith in Old Testament times. Melville's meaning here is "Messiah."

[11] Henry Condell was an editor of the First Folio Edition of Shakespeare's plays (1623).

[12] Henry Chettle (d. 1607?); the words are by Robert Greene, however, another Elizabethan playwright, in *A Groatsworth of Wit*.

after all, is, in many things, an alien to us. China has more bowels of real love for us than she. But even were there no strong literary individualities among us, as there are some dozen at least, nevertheless, let America first praise mediocrity even, in her own children, before she praises (for everywhere, merit demands acknowledgment from every one) the best excellence in the children of any other land. Let her own authors, I say, have the priority of appreciation. I was much pleased with a hot-headed Carolina cousin of mine, who once said "If there were no other American to stand by, in Literature—why, then, I would stand by Pop Emmons and his *Fredoniad*, [13] and till a better epic came along, swear it was not very far behind the *Iliad*." Take away the words, and in spirit he was sound.

Not that American genius needs patronage in order to expand. For that explosive sort of stuff will expand though screwed up in a vise, and burst it, though it were triple steel. It is for the nation's sake, and not for her authors' sake, that I would have America be heedful of the increasing greatness among her writers. For how great the shame, if other nations should be before her, in crowning her heroes of the pen! But this is almost the case now. American authors have received more just and discriminating praise (however loftily and ridiculously given, in certain cases) even from some Englishmen, than from their own countrymen. There are hardly five critics in America; and several of them are asleep. As for patronage, it is the American author who now patronizes his country, and not his country him. And if at times some among them appeal to the people for more recognition, it is not always with selfish motives, but patriotic ones.

It is true that but few of them as yet have evinced that decided originality which merits great praise. But that graceful writer, [14] who perhaps of all Americans has received the most plaudits from his own country for his productions—that very popular and amiable writer, however good, and self-reliant in many things, perhaps owes his chief reputation to the self-acknowledged imitation of a foreign model, and to the studied avoidance of all topics but smooth ones. But it is better to fail in originality than to succeed in imitation. He who has never failed somewhere, that man can not be great. Failure is the true test of greatness. And if it be said that continual success is a proof that a man wisely knows his powers, it is only to be added that, in that case, he knows them to be small. Let us believe it, then, once for all, that there is no hope for us in these smooth, pleasing writers that know their powers. Without malice, but to speak the plain fact, they but furnish an appendix to Goldsmith, and other English authors. And we want no American Goldsmiths; nay, we want no American Miltons. It were the vilest thing you could say of a true American author, that he were an American Tomp-

[13] Richard Emmons (1788-1840), *Fredoniad, or Independence Preserves—An Epic Poem of the War of 1812*. The "epic" was a failure.

[14] An allusion to Washington Irving.

kins.[15] Call him an American, and have done; for you cannot say a nobler thing of him.—But it is not meant that all American writers should studiously cleave to nationality in their writings; only this, no American writer should write like an Englishman, or a Frenchman; let him write like a man, for then he will be sure to write like an American. Let us away with this leaven of literary flunkyism towards England. If either must play the flunky in this thing, let England do it, not us. While we are rapidly preparing for that political supremacy among the nations, which prophetically awaits us at the close of the present century, in a literary point of view we are deplorably unprepared for it, and we seem studious to remain so. Hitherto, reasons might have existed why this should be; but no good reason exists now. And all that is requisite to amendment in this matter is simply this: that, while freely acknowledging all excellence, everywhere, we should refrain from unduly lauding foreign writers, and, at the same time, duly recognize the meritorious writers that are our own; those writers who breathe that un-shackled, democratic spirit of Christianity in all things, which now takes the practical lead in this world, though at the same time led by ourselves—us Americans. Let us boldly contemn all imitation, though it comes to us grace-ful and fragrant as the morning, and foster all originality, though, at first, it be crabbed and ugly as our own pine knots. And if any of our authors fail, or seem to fail, then, in the words of my enthusiastic Carolina cousin, let us clap him on the shoulder, and back him against all Europe for his second round. The truth is that, in our point of view, this matter of a national literature has come to such a pass with us that in some sense we must turn bullies, else the day is lost, or superiority so far beyond us, that we can hardly say it will ever be ours.

And now, my countrymen, as an excellent author, of your own flesh and blood—an unimitating, and, perhaps, in his way, an inimitable man—whom better can I commend to you, in the first place, that Nathaniel Hawthorne. He is one of the new and far better generation of your writers. The smell of your breeches and hemlocks is upon him; your own broad prairies are in his soul; and if you travel away inland into his deep and noble nature, you will hear the far roar of his Niagara. Give not over to future generations the glad duty of acknowledging him for what he is. Take that joy to yourself, in your own generation; and so shall he feel those grateful impulses in him that may possibly prompt him to the full flower of some still greater achievement in your eyes. And by confessing him, you thereby confess others; you brace the whole brotherhood. For genius, all over the world, stands hand in hand, and one shock of recognition runs the whole circle round.

[15] "Tompkins" was a popular British term for a butler.

In treating of Hawthorne, or rather of Hawthorne in his writings (for I never saw the man,[16] and in the chances of a quiet plantation life, remote from his haunts, perhaps never shall); in treating of his works, I say, I have thur far omitted all mention of his *Twice-Told Tales*, and *The Scarlet Letter*. Both are excellent, but full of such manifold, strange, and diffusive beauties, that time would all but fail me to point the half of them out. But there are things in those two books which, had they been written in England a century ago, Nathaniel Hawthorne had utterly displaced many of the bright names we now revere on authority. But I am content to leave Hawthorne to himself, and to the infallible finding of posterity; and however great may be the praise I have bestowed upon him, I feel, that in so doing, I have more served and honored myself than him. For, at bottom, great excellence is praise enough to itself; but the feeling of a sincere and appreciative love and admiration towards it—this is relieved by utterance; and warm, honest praise ever leaves a pleasant flavor in the mouth; and it is an honorable thing to confess to what is honorable in others.

But I cannot leave my subject yet. No man can read a fine author, and relish him to his very bones, while he reads, without subsequently fancying to himself some ideal image of the man and his mind. And if you rightly look for it, you will almost always find that the author himself has somewhere furnished you with his own picture. For poets (whether in prose or verse), being painters of Nature, are like their brethren of the pencil, the true portrait painters, who, in the multitude of likenesses to be sketched, do not invariably omit their own; and in all high instances, they paint them without any vanity, though, at times, with a lurking something, that would take several pages to properly define.

I submit it, then, to those best acquainted with the man personally, whether the following is not Nathaniel Hawthorne; and to himself, whether something involved in it does not express the temper of his mind—that lasting temper of all true, candid men—a seeker, not a finder yet:

A man now entered, in neglected attire, with the aspect of a thinker, but somewhat too rough-hewn and brawny for a scholar. His face was full of sturdy vigor, with some finer and keener attribute beneath; though harsh at first, it was tempered with the glow of a large, warm heart, which had force enough to heat his powerful intellect through and through. He advanced to the Intelligencer, and looked at him with a glance of such stern sincerity, that perhaps few secrets were beyond its scope.

"I seek for Truth," said he.

[16] This is not precisely true, since Melville had been on a picnic with Hawthorne and other authors before he wrote "Hawthorne and His Mosses."

Twenty-four hours have elapsed since writing the foregoing. I have just returned from the haymow, charged more and more with love and admiration of Hawthorne. For I have just been gleaning through the *Mosses*, picking up many things here and there that had previously escaped me. And I found that but to glean after this man is better than to be in at the harvest of others. To be frank (though, perhaps, rather foolish), notwithstanding what I wrote yesterday of these Mosses, I had not then culled them all; but had, nevertheless, been sufficiently sensible of the subtle essences in them as to write as I did. To what infinite height of loving wonder and admiration I may yet be borne, when by repeatedly banqueting on these Mosses, I shall have thoroughly incorporated their whole stuff into my being—that, I can not tell. But already I feel that this Hawthorne has dropped germinous seeds into my soul. He expands and deepens down, the more I contemplate him; and further, and further, shoots his strong New England roots into the hot soil of my Southern soul.

By careful reference to the "Table of Contents," I now find that I have gone through all the sketches, but that when I yesterday wrote I had not at all read two particular pieces to which I now desire to call special attention—"A Select Party," and "Young Goodman Brown." Here be it said to all those whom this poor fugitive scrawl of mine may tempt to the perusal of the *Mosses* that they must on no account suffer themselves to be trifled with, disappointed, or deceived by the triviality of many of the titles to these sketches. For in more than one instance the title utterly belies the piece. It is as if rustic demijohns containing the very best and costliest of Falernian and Tokay[17] were labeled "Cider," "Perry",[18] and "Elderberry Wine." The truth seems to be that, like many other geniuses, this Man of Mosses takes great delight in hoodwinking the world—at least with respect to himself. Personally, I doubt not that he rather prefers to be generally esteemed but a so-so sort of author; being willing to reserve the thorough and acute appreciation of what he is to that party most qualified to judge—that is, to himself. Besides, at the bottom of their natures, men like Hawthorne, in many things, deem the plaudits of that public such strong presumptive evidence of mediocrity in the object of them, that it would in some degree render them doubtful of their own powers, did they hear much and vociferous braying concerning them in the public pastures. True, I have been braying myself (if you please to be witty enough to have it so), but then I claim to be the first that has so brayed in this particular matter; and therefore, while pleading guilty to the charge, still claim all the merit due to originality.

But with whatever motive, playful or profound, Nathaniel Hawthorne has chosen to entitle his pieces in the manner he has, it is certain that some of

---

[17] Falnerian wine is from Falnerus in Italy and was drunk by the Romans; Tokay is a rich, sweet wine from Hungary.

[18] A fermented pear juice.

them are directly calculated to deceive—egregiously deceive—the superficial skimmer of pages. To be downright and candid once more, let me cheerfully say that two of these titles did dolefully dupe no less an eagle-eyed reader than myself; and that, too, after I had been impressed with a sense of the great depth and breadth of this American man. "Who in the name of thunder" (as the country people say in this neighborhood), "who in the name of thunder," would anticipate any marvel in a piece entitled "Young Goodman Brown"? You would of course suppose that it was a simple little tale, intended as a supplement to "Goody Two-Shoes."[19] Whereas it is deep as Dante; nor can you finish it, without addressing the author in his own words: "It is yours to penetrate, in every bosom, the deep mystery of sin." And with Young Goodman, too, in allegorical pursuit of his Puritan wife, you cry out in your anguish—

"Faith!" shouted Goodman Brown, in a voice of agony and desperation; and the echoes of the forest mocked him, crying—"Faith! Faith!" as if bewildered wretches were seeking her, all through the wilderness.

Now this same piece, "Young Goodman Brown," is one of the two that I had not at all read yesterday; and I allude to it now, because it is, in itself, such a strong positive illustration of that blackness in Hawthorne which I had assumed from the mere occasional shadows of it, as revealed in several of the other sketches. But had I previously perused "Young Goodman Brown," I should have been at no pains to draw the conclusion which I came to at a time when I was ignorant that the book contained one such direct and unqualified manifestation of it.

The other piece of the two referred to is entitled "A Select Party," which, in my first simplicity upon originally taking hold of the book, I fancied must treat of some pumpkin-pie party in Old Salem, or some chowder party on Cape Cod. Whereas, by all the gods of Peedee! it is the sweetest and sublimest thing that has been written since Spenser wrote. Nay, there is nothing in Spenser that surpasses it, perhaps, nothing that equals it. And the test is this: read any canto in *The Faery Queen*, and then read "A Select Party," and decide which pleases you the most—that is, if you are qualified to judge. Do not be frightened at this; for when Spenser was alive, he was thought of very much as Hawthorne is now, was generally accounted just such a "gentle" harmless man. It may be that, to common eyes, the sublimity of Hawthorne seems lost in his sweetness—as perhaps in this same "Select Party" of his, for whom he has builded so august a dome of sunset clouds, and served them on richer plate than Belshazzar's when he banqueted his lords in Babylon.[20]

---

[19] A nursery tale, probably written by Oliver Goldsmith.

[20] See Daniel, v: 1-4.

But my chief business now is to point out a particular page in this piece, having reference to an honored guest, who, under the name of "The Master Genius" but in the guise "of a young man of poor attire, with no insignia of rank or acknowledged eminence," is introduced to the Man of Fancy, who is the giver of the feast. Now the page having reference to this "Master Genius" so happily expresses much of what I yesterday wrote, touching the coming of the literary Shiloh of America, that I cannot but be charmed by the coincidence; especially, when it shows such a parity of ideas, at least in this one point, between a man like Hawthorne and a man like me.

And here, let me throw out another conceit of mine touching this American Shiloh, or "Master Genius," as Hawthorne calls him. May it not be, that this commanding mind has not been, is not, and never will be, individually developed in any one man? And would it, indeed, appear so unreasonable to suppose that this great fullness and overflowing may be, or may be destined to be, shared by a plurality of men of genius? Surely, to take the very greatest example on record, Shakespeare cannot be regarded as in himself the concretion of all the genius of his time, nor as so immeasurably beyond Marlowe, Webster, Ford, Beaumont, Jonson, that those great men can be said to share none of his power? For one, I conceive that there were dramatists in Elizabeth's day, between whom and Shakespeare the distance was by no means great. Let anyone, hitherto, little acquainted with those neglected old authors, for the first time read them thoroughly, and even read Charles Lamb's *Specimens*[21] of them, and he will be amazed at the wondrous ability of those Anaks[22] of men, and shocked at this renewed example of the fact that Fortune has more to do with fame than merit—though, without merit, lasting fame there can be none.

Nevertheless, it would argue too ill of my country were this maxim to hold good concerning Nathaniel Hawthorne, a man, who already, in some few minds, has shed "such a light as never illuminates the earth, save when a great heart burns as the household fire of a grand intellect."

The words are his—in "A Select Party"; and they are a magnificent setting to a coincident sentiment of my own, but ramblingly expressed yesterday, in reference to himself. Gainsay it who will, and I now write, I am Posterity speaking by proxy—and after times will make it more than good, when I declare that the American, who up to the present day, has evinced, in Literature, the largest brain with the largest heart—that man is Nathaniel Hawthorne. Moreover, that whatever Nathaniel Hawthorne may hereafter write, the *Mosses from an Old Manse* will be ultimately accounted his masterpiece. For there is a sure though a secret sign in some works which proves the culmination of the powers (only the developable ones, however) that produced them. But I am by no means desirous of the glory of a prophet. I

[21] *Specimens of English Dramatic Poets Contemporary with Shakespeare* (1808).

[22] A legendary race of giants. See Numbers xiii:33.

pray Heaven that Hawthorne may *yet* prove me an impostor in this prediction. Especially, as I somehow cling to the strange fancy that, in all men, hiddenly reside certain wondrous, occult properties—as in some plants and minerals—which by some happy but very rare accident (as bronze was discovered by the melting of the iron and brass in the burning of Corinth) may chance to be called forth here on earth, not entirely waiting for their better discovery in the more congenial, blessed atmosphere of heaven.

Once more—for it is hard to be finite upon an infinite subject, and all subjects are infinite. By some people, this entire scrawl of mine may be esteemed altogether unnecessary, inasmuch, "as years ago" (they may say) "we found out the rich and rare stuff in this Hawthorne, whom you now parade forth as if only *yourself* were the discoverer of this Portuguese diamond in our Literature."—But even granting all this—and adding to it, the assumption that the books of Hawthorne have sold by the five thousand— what does that signify? They should be sold by the hundred thousand, and read by the million, and admired by every one who is capable of admiration.

Letters to Hawthorne[1]

I

Pittsfield, Wednesday morning [April, 1851]

MY DEAR HAWTHORNE,

Concerning the young gentleman's shoes, I desire to say that a pair to fit him, of the desired pattern cannot be had in all Pittsfield,—a fact which sadly impairs that metropolitan pride I formerly took in the capital of Berkshire. Henceforth Pittsfield must hide its head. However, if a pair of *bootees* will at all answer, Pittsfield will be very happy to provide them. Pray mention all this to Mrs. Hawthorne, and command me.

"The House of the Seven Gables: A Romance. By Nathaniel Hawthorne. One vol. 16mo, pp. 344." The contents of this book do not belie its rich, clustering, romantic title. With great enjoyment we spent almost an hour in each separate gable. This book is like a fine old chamber, abundantly, but still judiciously, furnished with precisely that sort of furniture best fitted to furnish it. There are rich hangings, whereon are broidered scenes from tragedies. There is old china with rare devices, set about on the carved buffet; there are long and indolent lounges to throw yourself upon; there is an admirable sideboard, plentifully stored with good viands; there is a smell as

---

[1] The first three letters represent Melville's state of mind while he was writing *Moby Dick*. The fourth letter is Melville's response to Hawthorne's reaction to *Moby Dick*, a letter that has not been preserved.

of old wine in the pantry; and finally, in one corner, there is a dark little black-letter volume in golden clasps, entitled "Hawthorne: A Problem." It has delighted us; it has piqued a reperusal; it has robbed us of a day, and made us a present of a whole year of thoughtfulness; it has bred great exhilaration and exultation with the remembrance that the architect of the Gables resides only six miles off, and not three thousand miles away in England, say. We think the book, for pleasantness of running interest, surpasses the other works of the author. The curtains are now drawn; the sun comes in more; genialities peep out more. Were we to particularize what most struck us in the deeper passages, we would point out the scene where Clifford, for a moment, would fain throw himself forth from the window to join the procession; or the scene where the judge is left seated in his ancestral chair. Clifford is full of an awful truth throughout. He is conceived in the finest, truest spirit. He is no caricature. He is Clifford. And here we would say that, did circumstances permit, we should like nothing better than to devote an elaborate and careful paper to the full consideration and analysis of the purport and significance of what so strongly characterizes all of this author's writings. There is a certain tragic phase of humanity which, in our opinion, was never more powerfully embodied than by Hawthorne: we mean the tragicalness of human thought in its own unbiased, native, and profounder workings. We think that into no recorded mind has the intense feeling of the visible truth ever entered more deeply than into this man's. By visible truth, we mean the apprehension of the absolute condition of present things as they strike the eye of the man who fears them not, though they do their worst to him,—the man who, like Russia or the British Empire, declares himself a sovereign nature (in himself) amid the powers of heaven, hell, and earth. He may perish; but so long as he exists he insists upon treating with all Powers upon an equal basis. If any of those other Powers choose to withhold certain secrets, let them; that does not impair my sovereignty in myself; that does not make me tributary. And perhaps, after all, there is *no* secret. We incline to think that the Problem of the Universe is like the Freemason's[2] mighty secret, so terrible to all children. It turns out, at last, to consist in a triangle, a mallet, and an apron,—nothing more! We incline to think that God cannot explain His own secrets, and that He would like a little information upon certain points Himself. We mortals astonish Him as much as He us. But it is this *Being* of the matter; there lies the knot with which we choke ourselves. As soon as you say *Me*, a *God*, a *Nature*, so soon you jump off from your stool and hang from the beam. Yes, that word is the hangman. Take God out of the dictionary, and you would have Him in the street.

---

[2] A secret organization, founded in the eighteenth century and based on agnosticism and the brotherhood of man.

There is the grand truth about Nathaniel Hawthorne. He says NO! in thunder; but the Devil himself cannot make him say *yes*. *For all men who say yes*, lie; and all men who say *no*,—why, they are in the happy condition of judicious, unincumbered travellers in Europe; they cross the frontiers into Eternity with nothing but a carpet-bag,—that is to say, the Ego. Whereas those *yes*-gentry, they travel with heaps of baggage, and, damn them! they will never get through the Custom House. What's the reason, Mr Hawthorne, that in the last stages of metaphysics a fellow always falls to *swearing* so? I could rip an hour. You see, I began with a little criticism extracted for your benefit from the "Pittsfield Secret Review," and here I have landed in Africa.

Walk down one of these mornings and see me. No nonsense; come. Remember me to Mrs. Hawthorne and the children.

H. MELVILLE

P.S. The marriage of Phoebe with the daguerreo-typist is a fine stroke, because of his turning out to be a *Maule*. If you pass Hepzibah's cent-shop buy me a Jim Crow (fresh) and send it to me by Ned Higgins.

2

[June, 1851]

MY DEAR HAWTHORNE—

I should have been rumbling down to you in my pine-board chariot a long time ago, were it not that for some weeks past I have been more busy than you can well imagine,—out of doors,—building and patching and tinkering away in all directions. Besides, I had my crops to get in,—corn and potatoes (I hope to show you some famous ones by and by),—and many other things to attend to, all accumulating upon this one particular season. I work myself; and at night my bodily sensations are akin to those I have so often felt before, when a hired man, doing my day's work from sun to sun. But I mean to continue visiting you until you tell me that my visits are both supererogatory and superfluous. With no son of man do I stand upon any etiquette or ceremony, except the Christian ones of charity and honesty. I am told, my fellowman, that there is an aristocracy of the brain. Some men have boldly advocated and asserted it. Schiller[3] seems to have done so, though I don't know much about him. At any rate, it is true that there have been those who, whole earnest in behalf of political equality, still accept the intellectual estates. And I can well perceive, I think, how a man of superior mind can, by its intense cultivation, bring himself, as it were, into a certain spontaneous aristocracy of feeling,—exceedingly nice and fastidious,—similar to that

[3] J. C. F. von Schiller (1759-1805), German poet and critic.

which, in an English Howard,[4] conveys a torpedo-fish thrill at the slightest contact with a social plebeian. So, when you see or hear of my ruthless democracy on all sides, you may possibly feel a touch of a shrink, or something of that sort. It is but nature to be shy of a mortal who boldly declares that a thief in jail is as honorable a personage as Gen. George Washington. This is ludicrous. But Truth is the silliest thing under the sun. Try to get a living by the Truth—and go to the Soup Societies. Heavens! Let any clergyman try to preach the Truth from its very stronghold, the pulpit, and they would ride him out of his church on his own pulpit bannister. It can hardly be doubted that all Reformers are bottomed upon the truth, more or less; and to the world at large are not reformers almost universally laughingstocks? Why so? Truth is ridiculous to men. Thus easily in my room here do I, conceited and garrulous, reverse the test of my Lord Shaftesbury.[5]

It seems an inconsistency to assert unconditional democracy in all things, and yet confess a dislike to all mankind—in the mass. But not so.—But it's an endless sermon,—no more of it. I began by saying that the reason I have not been to Lenox is this,—in the evening I feel completely done up, as the phrase is, and incapable of the long jolting to get to your house and back. In a week or so, I go to New York, to bury myself in a third-story room, and work and slave on my "Whale"[6] while it is driving through the press. *That* is the only way I can finish it now,—I am so pulled thither and thither by circumstances. The calm, the coolness, the silent grass-growing mood in which a man *ought* always to compose,—that, I fear, can seldom be mine. Dollars damn me; and the malicious Devil is forever grinning in upon me, holding the door ajar. Mr dear Sir, a presentiment is on me,—I shall at last be worn out and perish, like an old nutmeg-grater, grated to pieces by the constant attrition of the wood, that is, the nutmeg. What I feel most moved to write, that is banned,—it will not pay. Yet, altogether, write the *other* way I cannot. So the product is a final hash, and all my books are botches. I'm rather sore, perhaps, in this letter; but see my hand! four blisters on this palm, made by hoes and hammers within the last few days. It is a rainy morning; so I am indoors, and all work suspended. I feel cheerfully disposed, and therefore I write a little bluely. Would the Gin[7] were here! If ever, my dear Hawthorne, in the eternal times that are to come, you and I shall sit down in Paradise, in some little shady corner by ourselves; and if we shall by any means be able to smuggle a basket of champagne there (I won't believe in a Temperance Heaven), and if we shall then cross our celestial legs in the celestial grass that is forever tropical, and strike our glasses and our heads together, till both musically ring in concert,—then, O my dear fellow-mortal,

---

[4] A symbol of aristocracy.
[5] Lord Shaftesbury (1671–1713) wrote *Characteristics* (1711). His "test" was to subject the truth to ridicule.
[6] *Moby Dick.*
[7] In Mohammedan mythology, a jinni is a spirit who can help people or harm them.

how shall we pleasantly discourse of all the things manifold which now so distress us,—when all the earth shall be but a reminiscence, yea, its final dissolution an antiquity. Then shall songs be composed as when wars are over: humorous, comic songs,—"Oh, when I lived in that queer little hole called the world," or, "Oh, when I toiled and sweated below," or, "Oh, when I knocked and was knocked in the fight"—yes, let us look forward to such things. Let us swear that, though now we sweat, yet it is because of the dry heat which is indispensable to the nourishment of the vine which is to bear the grapes that are to give us the champagne hereafter.

But I was talking about the "Whale." As the fishermen say, "he's in his flurry" when I left him some three weeks ago. I'm going to take him by his jaw, however, before long, and finish him up in some fashion or other. What's the use of elaborating what, in its very essence, is so short-lived as a modern book? Though I wrote the Gospels in this century, I should die in the gutter.—I talk all about myself, and this is selfishness and egotism. Granted. But how help it? I am writing to you; I know little about you, but something about myself. So I write about myself,—at least to you. Don't trouble yourself, though, about writing; and don't trouble yourself about visiting; and when you *do* visit, don't trouble yourself about talking. I will do all the writing and visiting and talking myself.—By the way, in the last "Dollar Magazine" I read "The Unpardonable Sin." He was a sad fellow, that Ethan Brand. I have no doubt you are by this time responsible for many a shake and tremor of the tribe of "general readers." It is a frightful poetical creed that the cultivation of the brain eats out the heart. But it's my *prose* opinion that in most cases, in those men who have fine brains and work them well, the heart extends down to hams. And though you smoke them with the fire of tribulation, yet, like veritable hams, the head only gives the richer and the better flavor. I stand for the heart. To the dogs with the head! I had rather be a fool with a heart, than Jupiter Olympus with his head. The reason the mass of men fear God, and *at bottom dislike* Him, is because they rather distrust His Heart, and fancy Him all brain like a watch. (You perceive I employ a capital initial in the pronoun referring to the Deity; don't you think there is a slight dash of flunkeyism in that usage?) Another thing. I was in New York for four-and twenty hours the other day, and saw a portrait of N.H. And I have seen and heard many flattering (in a publisher's point of view) allusions to the "Seven Gables." And I have seen "Tales" and "A New Volume" announced, by N.H. So upon the whole, I say to myself, this N.H. is in the ascendant. My dear Sir, they begin to patronize. All Fame is patronage. Let me be infamous; there is no patronage in *that*. What "reputation" H.M. has is horrible. Think of it! To go down to posterity is bad enough, any way; but to go down as a "man who lived among the cannibals"! When I speak of posterity, in reference to myself, I only mean the babies who will probably be born in the moment immediately ensuing upon my giving up the ghost. I shall go down to some of them, in all likelihood. "Typee" will be given to them, perhaps, with their gingerbread. I have come to regard this matter of Fame as the most transparent of all vanities. I read Solomon more and more, and every time see deeper and deeper and unspeakable meanings in him. I did not think of Fame, a year ago, as I do now. My development has been all within a few years past. I am like one of those seeds taken out of the Egyptian Pyramids, which, after being three thousand years a seed and nothing but a seed, being planted in English soil, it developed itself, grew to greenness, and then fell to mould. So I. Until I was twenty-five, I had no development at all. From my twenty-fifth year I date my life. Three weeks have scarcely passed, at any time between then and now, that I have not unfolded within myself. But I feel that I am now come to the inmost leaf of the bulb, and that shortly the flower must fall to the mould. It seems to me now that Solomon was the truest man who ever spoke, and yet that he a little *managed* the truth with a view to popular conservatism; or else there have been many corruptions and interpolations of the text.—In reading some of Goethe's sayings, so worshipped by his votaries, I came across this, *"Live in the all."* That is to say, your separate identity is but a wretched one,—good; but get out of yourself, spread and expand yourself, and bring to yourself the tinglings of life that are felt in the flowers and the woods, that are felt in the planets Saturn and Venus, and the Fixed Stars. What nonsense! Here is a fellow with a raging toothache. "My dear boy," Goethe says to him, "you are sorely afflicted with that tooth; but you must *live in the all,* and then you will be happy!" As with all great genius, there is an immense deal of flummery in Goethe, and in proportion to my own contact with him, a monstrous deal of it in me.

H. MELVILLE

P.S. "Amen!" saith Hawthorne.
N.B. This "all" feeling, though, there is some truth in. You must often have felt it, lying on the grass on a warm summer's day. Your legs seem to send out shoots into the earth. Your hair feels like leaves upon you head. This is the *all* feeling. But what plays the mischief with the truth is that men will insist upon the universal application of a temporary feeling or opinion.
P.S. You must not fail to admire my discretion in paying the postage on this letter.

3

Pittsfield, June 29, 1851.

MY DEAR HAWTHORNE—
    The clear air and open window invite me to write to you. For some time past I have been so busy with a thousand things that I have almost forgotten

when I wrote you last, and whether I received an answer. This most persuasive season has now for weeks recalled me from certain crotchety and overdoleful chimeras, the like of which men like you and me, and some others, forming a chain of God's posts round the world, must be content to encounter now and then, and fight them the best way we can. But come they will,— for, in the boundless, trackless, but still glorious wild wilderness through which these outposts run, the Indians do sorely abound, as well as the insignificant but still stinging mosquitoes. Since you have been here, I have been building some shanties of houses (connected with the old one) and likewise some shanties of chapters and essays. I have been ploughing and sowing and raising and painting and printing and praying,—and now begin to come out upon a less bristling time, and to enjoy the calm prospect of things from a fair piazza at the north of the old farmhouse here.

Nor entirely yet, tho', am I without something to be urgent with. The "Whale" is only half thro' the press; for, wearied with the long delays of the printers, and disgusted with the heat and dust of the Babylonish brick-kiln of New York, I came back to the country to feel the grass—and end the book reclining on it, if I may.—I am sure you will pardon this speaking all about myself; for if I *say* so much on that head, be sure all the rest of the world are thinking about themselves ten times as much. Let us speak, tho' we show all our faults and weaknesses,—for it is a sign of strength to be weak, to know it, and out with it,—not in set way and ostentatiously, tho', but incidentally and without premeditation.—But I am falling into my old foible,—preaching. I am busy, but shall not be very long. Come and spend a day here, if you can and want to; if not, stay in Lenox, and God give you long life. When I am quite free of my present engagements, I am going to treat myself to a ride and a visit to you. Have ready a bottle of brandy, because I always feel like drinking that heroic drink when we talk ontological heroics together. This is rather a crazy letter in some respects, I apprehend. If so, ascribe it to the intoxicating effects of the latter end of June operating upon a very susceptible and preadventure feeble temperament.

Shall I send you a fin of the "Whale" by way of a specimen mouthful? The tail is not yet cooked—tho' the hell-fire in which the whole book is broiled might not unreasonably have cooked it all ere this. This is the book's motto (the secret one), Ego non baptiso te in nomine—but make out the rest yourself.[8]

H. M.

[8] See Chapter 113 in Moby Dick: *"Ego non baptizo te in nomine patris, sed in nomine diaboli"* (I do not baptize you in the name of the father, but in the name of the Devil).

4

Pittsfield, Monday afternoon [November, 1851]

MY DEAR HAWTHORNE—

People think that if a man has undergone any hardship, he should have a reward; but for my part, if I have done the hardest possible day's work, and then come to sit down in a corner and eat my supper comfortably—why, then I don't think I deserve any reward for my hard day's work—for am I not now at peace? Is not my supper good? My peace and my supper are my reward, my dear Hawthorne. So your joy-giving and exultation-breeding letter is not my reward for my ditcher's work with that book, but is the good goddess's bonus over and above what was stipulated for—for not one man in five cycles, who is wise, will expect appreciative recognition from his fellows, or any one of them. Appreciation! Recognition! Is love appreciated? Why, ever since Adam, who has got to the meaning of his great allegory—the world? Then we pygmies must be content to have our paper allegories but ill comprehended. I say your appreciation is my glorious gratuity. In my proud, humble way,—a shepherd-king,—I was lord of a little vale in the solitary Crimea; but you have now given me the crown of India. But on trying it on my head, I found it fell down on my ears, notwithstanding their asinine length—for it's only such ears that sustain such crowns.

Your letter was handed me last night on the road going to Mr. Morewood's, and I read it there. Had I been home, I would have sat down at once and answered it. In me divine magnanimities are spontaneous and instantaneous—catch them while you can. The world goes round, and the other side comes up. So now I can't write what I felt. But I felt pantheistic then—your heart beat in my ribs and mine in yours, and both in God's. A sense of unspeakable security is in me this moment, on account of your having understood the book. I have written a wicked book, and feel spotless as the lamb. Ineffable socialities are in me. I would sit down and dine with you and all the gods in old Rome's Pantheon. It is a strange feeling—no hopefulness is in it, no despair. Content—that is it; and irresponsibility; but without licentious inclination. I speak now of my profoundest sense of being, not of an incidental feeling.

Whence come you, Hawthorne? By what right do you drink from my flagon of life? And when I put it to my lips—lo, they are yours and not mine. I feel that the Godhead is broken up like the bread at the Supper, and that we are the pieces. Hence this infinite fraternity of feeling. Now, sympathizing with the paper, my angel turns over another page. You did not care a penny for the book. But, now and then as you read, you understood the pervading thought that impelled the book—and that you praised. Was it not so? You were arch-angel enough to despise the imperfect body, and embrace the soul. Once you hugged the ugly Socrates because you saw the flame in the mouth, and heard the rushing of the demon,—the familiar,—and recognized the sound; for you have heard it in your own solitudes.

My dear Hawthorne, the atmospheric skepticisms steal into me now, and make me doubtful of my sanity in writing you thus. But, believe me, I am not mad, most noble Festus![9] But truth is ever incoherent, and when the big hearts strike together, the concussion is a little stunning. Farewell. Don't write a word about the book. That would be robbing me of my miserly delight. I am heartily sorry I ever wrote anything about you—it was paltry. Lord, when shall we be done growing? As long as we have anything more to do, we have done nothing. So, now, let us add Moby Dick to our blessing, and step from that. Leviathan is not the biggest fish;—I have heard of Krakens.[10]

This is a long letter, but you are not at all bound to answer it. Possibly, if you do answer it, and direct it to Herman Melville, you will missend it—for the very fingers that now guide this pen are not precisely the same that just took it up and put it on this paper. Lord, when shall we be done changing? Ah! it's a long stage, and no inn in sight, and night coming, and the body cold. But with you for a passenger, I am content and can be happy. I shall leave the world, I feel, with more satisfaction for having come to know you. Knowing you persuades me more than the Bible of our immortality.

What a pity, that, for your plain, bluff letter, you should get such gibberish! Mention me to Mrs. Hawthorne and to the children, and so, good-by to you, with my blessing.

HERMAN

P.S. I can't stop yet. If the world was entirely made up of Magians,[11] I'll tell you what I should do. I should have a paper-mill established at one end of the house, and so have an endless riband of foolscap rolling in upon my desk; and upon that endless riband I should write a thousand—a million—billion thoughts, all under the form of a letter to you. The divine magnet is on you, and my magnet responds. Which is the biggest? A foolish question—they are One.

P.P.S. Don't think that by writing me a letter, you shall always be bored with an immediate reply to it—and so keep both of us delving over a writing-desk eternally. No such thing! I sha'n't always answer your letters, and you may do just as you please.

[9] See Acts 26:25. St. Paul's words before the magistrate.

[10] In Norwegian mythology, sea monsters.

[11] Literally Persian priests, but Melville means magicians.

Bartleby the Scrivener[1]

A STORY OF WALL STREET

I am a rather elderly man. The nature of my avocations, for the last thirty years, has brought me into more than ordinary contact with what would seem an interesting and somewhat singular set of men, of whom, as yet, nothing, that I know of, has ever been written—I mean, the law-copyists, or scriveners. I have known very many of them, professionally and privately, and, if I pleased, could relate divers histories, at which good-natured gentlemen might smile, and sentimental souls might weep. But I waive the biographies of all other scriveners, for a few passages in the life of Bartleby, who was a scrivener, the strangest I ever saw, or heard of. While, of other law-copyists, I might write the complete life, of Bartleby nothing of that sort can be done. I believe that no materials exist, for a full and satisfactory biography of this man. It is an irreparable loss to literature. Bartleby was one of those beings of whom nothing is ascertainable, except from the original sources, and, in his case, those are very small. What my own astonished eyes saw of Bartleby, *that* is all I know of him, except, indeed, one vague report, which will appear in the sequel.

Ere introducing the scrivener, as he first appeared to me, it is fit I make some mention of myself, my *employés*, my business, my chambers, and general surroundings; because some such description is indispensable to an adequate understanding of the chief character about to be presented. Imprimis:[2] I am a man who, from his youth upwards, has been filled with a profound conviction that the easiest way of life is the best. Hence, though I belong to a profession proverbially energetic and nervous, even to turbu-

---

[1] The story appeared in two installments in November and December of 1853 in *Putnam's Monthly Magazine*. It was republished in *Piazza Tales* (1856). It is tempting to view Bartleby as a parable of Melville's fate as a writer in 1852. Melville had not achieved the success he wished in *Moby Dick*, and his next novel, *Pierre* (1852), suggested his despair. In "Bartleby," he portrays Wall Street as a kind of madhouse to which Bartleby refuses to adapt; many critics have suggested that Melville's refusal to continue writing popular tales like *Typee* and *Omoo* for commercial purposes is projected into Bartleby's refusal to be merely a copier of other men's thoughts. The parallels are clear: Bartleby is a scrivener, Melville a writer; Bartleby withdraws from the popular demands of society, Melville retreated himself; the figures in the story are Wall Street lawyers, Melville's brother Allan and his father-in-law Judge Shaw were lawyers who also came to his financial aid.

However justified these parallels, the story takes on an independent authority of its own and remains as one of Melville's most memorable achievements. Most interpretations of the story tend to concentrate on the figure of Bartleby, his growing madness, isolation, and forlornness; but it might be well to consider the significance of the employer himself and his developing sense of responsibility for Bartleby. The story is told from the employer's point of view and, to a great extent, Bartleby is a reflection of the narrator's humanity.

[2] In the first place.

lence, at times, yet nothing of that sort have I ever suffered to invade my peace. I am one of those unambitious lawyers who never address a jury, or in any way draw down public applause; but, in the cool tranquillity of a snug retreat, do a snug business among rich men's bonds, and mortgages, and title-deeds. All who know me, consider me an eminently *safe* man. The late John Jacob Astor,[3] a personage little given to poetic enthusiasm, had no hesitation in pronouncing my first grand point to be prudence; my next, method. I do not speak it in vanity, but simply record the fact, that I was not unemployed in my profession by the late John Jacob Astor; a name which, I admit, I love to repeat; for it hath a rounded and orbicular sound to it, and rings like unto bullion. I will freely add, that I was not insensible to the late John Jacob Astor's good opinion.

Some time prior to the period at which this little history begins, my avocations had been largely increased. The good old office, now extinct in the State of New York, of a Master in Chancery, had been conferred upon me. It was not a very arduous office, but very pleasantly remunerative. I seldom lose my temper; much more seldom indulge in dangerous indignation at wrongs and outrages; but I must be permitted to be rash here and declare, that I consider the sudden and violent abrogation of the office of Master in Chancery, by the new Constitution, as a—premature act; inasmuch as I had counted upon a life-lease of the profits, whereas I only received those of a few short years.[4] But this is by the way.

My chambers were up stairs, at No.—Wall Street. At one end, they looked upon the white wall of the interior of a spacious skylight shaft, pene-trating the building from top to bottom.

This view might have been considered rather tame than otherwise, defi-cient in what landscape painters call "life." But, if so, the view from the other end of my chambers offered, at least, a contrast, if nothing more. In that direction, my windows commanded an unobstructed view of a lofty brick wall, black by age and everlasting shade; which wall required no spy-glass to bring out its lurking beauties, but, for the benefit of all near-sighted spectators, was pushed up to within ten feet of my window-panes. Owing to the great height of the surrounding buildings, and my chambers being on the second floor, the interval between this wall and mine not a little resembled a huge square cistern.

At the period just preceding the advent of Bartleby, I had two persons as copyists in my employment, and a promising lad as an office-boy. First, Turkey; second, Nippers; third, Ginger Nut. These may seem names, the like of which are not usually found in the Directory. In truth, they were nick-names, mutually conferred upon each other by my three clerks, and were

---

[3] John Jacob Astor (1763-1848), a German-born American capitalist who rose from pen-ury to make his fortune on the western fur trade. At his death in 1848 he was the wealthiest person in America.

[4] Courts of Chancery handled equity law.

deemed expressive of their respective persons or characters. Turkey was a short, pursy Englishman, of about my own age—that is, somewhere not far from sixty. In the morning, one might say, his face was of a fine florid hue, but after twelve o'clock, meridian—his dinner hour—it blazed like a grate full of Christmas coals; and continued blazing—but, as it were, with a gradual wane—till six o'clock, P. M., or thereabouts; after which, I saw no more of the proprietor of the face, which, gaining its meridian with the sun, seemed to set with it, to rise, culminate, and decline the following day, with the like regularity and undiminished glory. There are many singular coincidences I have known in the course of my life, not the least among which was the fact, that, exactly when Turkey displayed his fullest beams from his red and radiant countenance, just then, too, at that critical moment, began the daily period when I considered his business capacities as seriously disturbed for the remainder of the twenty-four hours. Not that he was absolutely idle, or averse to business then; far from it. The difficulty was, he was apt to be altogether too energetic. There was a strange, inflamed, flurried, flighty reck-lessness of activity about him. He would be incautious in dipping his pen into his inkstand. All his blots upon my documents were dropped there after twelve o'clock, meridian. Indeed, not only would he be reckless, and sadly given to making blots in the afternoon, but, some days, he went further, and was rather noisy. At such times, too, his face flamed with augmented bla-zonry, as if cannel coal had been heaped on anthracite. He made an unpleas-ant racket with his chair; spilled his sand-box; in mending his pens, impa-tiently split them all to pieces, and threw them on the floor in a sudden passion; stood up, and leaned over his table, boxing his papers about in a most indecorous manner, very sad to behold in an elderly man like him. Nevertheless, as he was in many ways a most valuable person to me, and all the time before twelve o'clock, meridian, was the quickest, steadiest crea-ture, too, accomplishing a great deal of work in a style not easily to be matched—for these reasons, I was willing to overlook his eccentricities, though, indeed, occasionally, I remonstrated with him. I did this very gently, however, because, though the civilest, nay, the blandest and most reverential of men in the morning yet, in the afternoon, he was disposed, upon provoca-tion, to be slightly rash with his tongue—in fact, insolent. Now, valuing his morning services as I did, and resolved not to lose them—yet, at the same time, made uncomfortable by his inflamed ways after twelve o'clock—and being a man of peace, unwilling by my admonitions to call forth unseemly retorts from him, I took upon me, one Saturday noon (he was always worse on Saturdays) to hint to him, very kindly, that, perhaps, now that he was growing old, it might be well to abridge his labors; in short, he need not come to my chambers after twelve o'clock, but, dinner over, had best go home to his lodgings, and rest himself till tea-time. But no; he insisted upon his afternoon devotions. His countenance became intolerably fervid, as he oratorically assured me—gesticulating with a long ruler at the other end of the room—that if his services in the morning were useful, how indispensable, then, in the afternoon?

"With submission, sir," said Turkey, on this occasion, "I consider myself your right-hand man. In the morning I but marshal and deploy my columns; but in the afternoon I put myself at their head, and gallantly charge the foe, thus"—and he made a violent thrust with the ruler.

"But the blots, Turkey," intimated I.

"True; but, with submission, sir, behold these hairs! I am getting old. Surely, sir, a blot or two on a warm afternoon is not to be severely urged against gray hairs. Old age—even if it blot the page—is honorable. With submission, sir, we *both* are getting old."

This appeal to my fellow-feeling was hardly to be resisted. At all events, I saw that go he would not. So, I made up my mind to let him stay, resolving, nevertheless, to see to it that, during the afternoon, he had to do with my less important papers.

Nippers, the second on my list, was a whiskered, sallow, and, upon the whole, rather piratical-looking young man, of about five-and-twenty. I always deemed him the victim of two evil powers—ambition and indigestion. The ambition was evinced by a certain impatience of the duties of a mere copyist, an unwarrantable usurpation of strictly professional affairs such as the original drawing up of legal documents. The indigestion, seemed betokened in an occasional nervous testiness and grinning irritability, causing the teeth to audibly grind together over mistakes committed in copying; unnecessary maledictions, hissed, rather than spoken, in the heat of business; and especially by a continual discontent with the height of the table where he worked. Though of a very ingenious mechanical turn, Nippers could never get this table to suit him. He put chips under it, blocks of various sorts, bits of pasteboard, and at last went so far as to attempt an exquisite adjustment, by final pieces of folded blotting-paper. But no invention would answer. If, for the sake of easing his back, he brought the table-lid at a sharp angle well up towards his chin, and wrote there like a man using the steep roof of a Dutch house for his desk, then he declared that it stopped the circulation in his arms. If now he lowered the table to his waistbands, and stooped over it in writing, then there was a sore aching in his back. In short, the truth of the matter was, Nippers knew not what he wanted. Or, if he wanted anything, it was to be rid of a scrivener's table altogether. Among the manifestations of his diseased ambition was a fondness he had for receiving visits from certain ambiguous-looking fellows in seedy coats, whom he called his clients. Indeed, I was aware that not only was he, at times, considerable of a ward-politician, but he occasionally did a little business at the justices' courts, and was not unknown on the steps of the Tombs.[5] I have good reason to believe,

---

[5] The worst prison in New York City as well as the one of maximum security.

however, that one individual who called upon him at my chambers, and who, with a grand air, he insisted was his client, was no other than a dun, and the alleged title-deed, a bill. But, with all his failings, and the annoyances he caused me, Nippers, like his compatriot Turkey, was a very useful man to me; wrote a neat, swift hand; and, when he chose, was not deficient in a gentlemanly sort of deportment. Added to this, he always dressed in a gentlemanly sort of way; and so, incidentally, reflected credit upon my chambers. Whereas, with respect to Turkey, I had much ado to keep him from being a reproach to me. His clothes were apt to look oily, and smell of eating-houses. He wore his pantaloons very loose and baggy in summer. His coats were execrable; his hat not to be handled. But while the hat was a thing of indifference to me, inasmuch as his natural civility and deference, as a dependent Englishman, always led him to doff it the moment he entered the room, yet his coat was another matter. Concerning his coats, I reasoned with him; but with no effect. The truth was, I suppose, that a man with so small an income could not afford to sport such a lustrous face and a lustrous coat at one and the same time. As Nippers once observed, Turkey's money went chiefly for red ink. One winter day, I presented Turkey with a highly respectable-looking coat of my own—a padded gray coat, of a most comfortable warmth, and which buttoned straight up from the knee to the neck. I thought Turkey would appreciate the favor, and abate his rashness and obstreperousness of afternoons. But no; I verily believe that buttoning himself up in so downy and blanket-like a coat had a pernicious effect upon him—upon the same principle that too much oats are bad for horses. In fact, precisely as a rash, restive horse is said to feel his oats, so Turkey felt his coat. It made him insolent. He was a man whom prosperity harmed.

Though, concerning the self-indulgent habits of Turkey, I had my own private surmises, yet, touching Nippers, I was well persuaded that, whatever might be his faults in other respects, he was, at least, a temperate young man. But, indeed, nature herself seemed to have been his vintner, and, at his birth, charged him so thoroughly with an irritable, brandy-like disposition, that all subsequent potations were needless. When I consider how, amid the stillness of my chambers, Nippers would sometimes impatiently rise from his seat, and stooping over his table, spread his arms wide apart, seize the whole desk, and move it, and jerk it, with a grim, grinding motion on the floor, as if the table were a perverse voluntary agent, intent on thwarting and vexing him, I plainly perceive that, for Nippers, brandy-and-water were altogether superfluous.

It was fortunate for me that, owing to its peculiar cause—indigestion—the irritability and consequent nervousness of Nippers were mainly observable in the morning, while in the afternoon he was comparatively mild. So that, Turkey's paroxysms only coming on about twelve o'clock, I never had to do with their eccentricities at one time. Their fits relieved each other, like guards. When Nippers' was on, Turkey's was off; and *vice versa*. This was a good natural arrangement, under the circumstances.

Ginger Nut, the third on my list, was a lad, some twelve years old. His father was a carman, ambitious of seeing his son on the bench instead of a cart, before he died. So he sent him to my office, as student at law, errand-boy, cleaner and sweeper, at the rate of one dollar a week. He had a little desk to himself, but he did not use it much. Upon inspection, the drawer exhibited a great array of the shells of various sorts of nuts. Indeed, to this quick-witted youth, the whole noble science of the law was contained in a nutshell. Not the least among the employments of Ginger Nut, as well as one which he discharged with the most alacrity, was his duty as cake and apple purveyor for Turkey and Nippers. Copying lawpapers being proverbially a dry, husky sort of business, my two scriveners were fain to moisten their mouths very often with Spitzenbergs,[6] to be had at the numerous stalls nigh the Custom House and Post Office. Also, they sent Ginger Nut very frequently for that peculiar cake—small, flat, round, and very spicy—after which he had been named by them. Of a cold morning, when business was but dull, Turkey would gobble up scores of these cakes, as if they were mere wafers—indeed, they sell them at the rate of six or eight for a penny—the scrape of his pen blending with the crunching of the crisp particles in his mouth. Of all the fiery afternoon blunders and flurried rashness of Turkey, was his once moistening a ginger-cake between his lips, and clapping in on to a mortgage, for a seal. I came within an ace of dismissing him then. But he mollified me by making an oriental bow, and saying—

"With submission, sir, it was generous of me to find you in stationery on my own account."

Now my original business—that of a conveyancer and title hunter, and drawer-up of recondite documents of all sorts—was considerably increased by receiving the Master's office. There was now great work for scriveners. Not only must I push the clerks already with me, but I must have additional help.

In answer to my advertisement, a motionless young man one morning stood upon my office threshold, the door being open, for it was summer. I can see that figure now—pallidly neat, pitiably respectable, incurably forlorn! It was Bartleby.

After a few words touching his qualifications, I engaged him, glad to have among my corps of copyists a man of so singularly sedate an aspect, which I thought might operate beneficially upon the flighty temper of Turkey, and the fiery one of Nippers.

I should have stated before that ground-glass folding-doors divided my premises into two parts, one of which was occupied by my scriveners, the other by myself. According to my humor, I threw open these doors, or

---

[6] A kind of apple.

closed them. I resolved to assign Bartleby a corner by the folding-doors, but on my side of them, so as to have this quiet man within easy call, in case any trifling thing was to be done. I placed his desk close up to a small sidewindow in that part of the room, a window which originally had afforded a lateral view of certain grimy brickyards and bricks, but which, owing to subsequent erections, commanded at present no view at all, though it gave some light. Within three feet of the panes was a wall, and the light came down from far above, between two lofty buildings, as from a very small opening in a dome. Still further to a satisfactory arrangement, I procured a high green folding screen, which might entirely isolate Bartleby from my sight, though not remove him from my voice. And thus, in a manner, privacy and society were conjoined.

At first, Bartleby did an extraordinary quantity of writing. As if long famishing for something to copy, he seemed to gorge himself on my documents. There was no pause for digestion. He ran a day and night line, copying by sunlight and by candle-light. I should have been quite delighted with his application, had he been cheerfully industrious. But he wrote on silently, palely, mechanically.

It is, of course, an indispensable part of a scrivener's business to verify the accuracy of his copy, word by word. Where there are two or more scriveners in an office, they assist each other in this examination, one reading from the copy, the other holding the original. It is a very dull, wearisome, and lethargic affair. I can readily imagine that, to some sanguine temperaments, it would be altogether intolerable. For example, I cannot credit that the mettlesome poet, Byron, would have contentedly sat down with Bartleby to examine a law document of, say five hundred pages, closely written in a crimpy hand.

Now and then, in the haste of business, it had been my habit to assist in comparing some brief document myself, calling Turkey or Nippers for this purpose. One object I had, in placing Bartleby so handy to me behind the screen, was, to avail myself of his services on such trivial occasions. It was on the third day, I think, of his being with me, and before any necessity had arisen for having his own writing examined, that, being much hurried to complete a small affair I had in hand, I abruptly called to Bartleby. In my haste and natural expectancy of instant compliance, I sat with my head bent over the original on my desk, and my right hand sideways, and somewhat nervously extended with the copy, so that, immediately upon emerging from his retreat, Bartleby might snatch it and proceed to business without the least delay.

In this very attitude did I sit when I called to him, rapidly stating what it was I wanted him to do—namely, to examine a small paper with me. Imagine my surprise, nay, my consternation, when, without moving from his privacy, Bartleby, in a singularly mild, firm voice, replied, "I would prefer not to."

I sat awhile in perfect silence, rallying my stunned faculties. Immediately it occurred to me that my ears had deceived me, or Bartleby had entirely misunderstood my meaning. I repeated my request in the clearest tone I could assume; but in quite as clear a one came the previous reply, "I would prefer not to."

"Prefer not to," echoed I, rising in high excitement, and crossing the room with a stride. "What do you mean? Are you moonstruck? I want you to help me compare this sheet here—take it," and I thrust it towards him.

"I would prefer not to," said he.

I looked at him steadfastly. His face was leanly composed; his gray eye dimly calm. Not a wrinkle of agitation rippled him. Had there been the least uneasiness, anger, impatience or impertinence in his manner; in other words, had there been anything ordinarily human about him, doubtless I should have violently dismissed him from the premises. But as it was, I should have as soon thought of turning my pale plaster-of-paris bust of Cicero out of doors. I stood gazing at him awhile, as he went on with his own writing, and then reseated myself at my desk. This is very strange, thought I. What had one best do? But my business hurried me. I concluded to forget the matter for the present, reserving it for my future leisure. So, calling Nippers from the other room, the paper was speedily examined.

A few days after this, Bartleby concluded four lengthy documents, being quadruplicates of a week's testimony taken before me in my High Court of Chancery. It became necessary to examine them. It was an important suit, and great accuracy was imperative. Having all things arranged, I called Turkey, Nippers, and Ginger Nut, from the next room, meaning to place the four copies in the hands of my four clerks, while I should read from the original. Accordingly, Turkey, Nippers, and Ginger Nut had taken their seats in a row, each with his document in his hand, when I called to Bartleby to join this interesting group.

"Bartleby! quick, I am waiting."

I heard a slow scrape of his chair legs on the uncarpeted floor, and soon he appeared standing at the entrance of his hermitage.

"What is wanted?" said he, mildly.

"The copies, the copies," said I, hurriedly. "We are going to examine them. There"—and I held towards him the fourth quadruplicate.

"I would prefer not to," he said, and gently disappeared behind the screen.

For a few moments I was turned into a pillar of salt,[7] standing at the head of my seated column of clerks. Recovering myself, I advanced towards the screen and demanded the reason for such extraordinary conduct.

"*Why* do you refuse?"

---

[7] The punishment accorded Lot's wife (Genesis xix:26).

"I would prefer not to."

With any other man I should have flown outright into a dreadful passion, scorned all further words, and thrust him ignominiously from my presence. But there was something about Bartleby that not only strangely disarmed me, but, in a wonderful manner, touched and disconcerted me. I began to reason with him.

"These are your own copies we are about to examine. It is labor saving to you, because one examination will answer for your four papers. It is common usage. Every copyist is bound to help examine his copy. Is it not so? Will you not speak? Answer!"

"I prefer not to," he replied in a flute-like tone. It seemed to me that, while I had been addressing him, he carefully revolved every statement that I made; fully comprehended the meaning; could not gainsay the irresistible conclusion; but, at the same time, some paramount consideration prevailed with him to reply as he did.

"You are decided, then, not to comply with my request—a request made according to common usage and common sense?"

He briefly gave me to understand, that on that point my judgment was sound. Yes: his decision was irreversible.

It is not seldom the case that, when a man is browbeaten in some unprecedented and violently unreasonable way, he begins to stagger in his own plainest faith. He begins, as it were, vaguely to surmise that, wonderful as it may be, all the justice and all the reason is on the other side. Accordingly, if any disinterested persons are present, he turns to them for some reinforcement for his own faltering mind.

"Turkey," said I, "what do you think of this? Am I not right?" "With submission, sir," said Turkey, in his blandest tone, "I think that you are."

"Nippers," said I, "what do *you* think of it?"

"I think I should kick him out of the office."

(The reader of nice[8] perceptions will have perceived that, it being morning, Turkey's answer is couched in polite and tranquil terms, but Nippers replies in ill-tempered ones. Or, to repeat a previous sentence, Nippers' ugly mood was on duty, and Turkey's off.)

"Ginger Nut," said I, willing to enlist the smallest suffrage in my behalf, "what do *you* think of it?"

"I think, sir, he's a little *luny,*" replied Ginger Nut, with a grin.

"You hear what they say," said I, turning towards the screen, "come forth and do your duty."

But he vouchsafed no reply. I pondered a moment in sore perplexity. But once more business hurried me. I determined again to postpone the consideration of this dilemma to my future leisure. With a little trouble we made out to examine the papers without Bartleby, though at every page or two

[8] Precise.

Turkey deferentially dropped his opinion, that this proceeding was quite out of the common; while Nippers, twitching in his chair with a dyspeptic nervousness, ground out, between his set teeth, occasional hissing maledictions against the stubborn oaf behind the screen. And for his (Nippers') part, this was the first and the last time he would do another man's business without pay.

Meanwhile Bartleby sat in his hermitage, oblivious to everything but his own peculiar business there.

Some days passed, the scrivener being employed upon another lengthy work. His late remarkable conduct led me to regard his ways narrowly. I observed that he never went to dinner; indeed, that he never went anywhere. As yet I had never, of my personal knowledge, known him to be outside of my office. He was a perpetual sentry in the corner. At about eleven o'clock though, in the morning, I noticed that Ginger Nut would advance toward the opening in Bartleby's screen, as if silently beckoned thither by a gesture invisible to me where I sat. The boy would then leave the office, jingling a few pence, and reappear with a handful of ginger-nuts, which he delivered in the hermitage, receiving two of the cakes for his trouble.

He lives, then, on ginger-nuts, thought I; never eats a dinner, properly speaking; he must be a vegetarian, then, but no; he never eats even vegetables, he eats nothing but ginger-nuts. My mind then ran on in reveries concerning the probable effects upon the human constitution of living entirely on ginger-nuts. Ginger-nuts are so called, because they contain ginger as one of their peculiar constituents, and the final flavoring one. Now, what was ginger? A hot, spicy thing. Was Bartleby hot and spicy? Not at all. Ginger, then, had no effect upon Bartleby. Probably he preferred it should have none.

Nothing so aggravates an earnest person as a passive resistance. If the individual so resisted be of a not inhumane temper, and the resisting one perfectly harmless in his passivity, then, in the better moods of the former, he will endeavor charitably to construe to his imagination what proves impossible to be solved by his judgment. Even so, for the most part, I regarded Bartleby and his ways. Poor fellow! thought I, he means no mischief; it is plain he intends no insolence; his aspect sufficiently evinces that his eccentricities are involuntary. He is useful to me. I can get along with him. If I turn him away, the chances are he will fall in with some less indulgent employer, and then he will be rudely treated, and perhaps driven forth miserably to starve. Yes. Here I can cheaply purchase a delicious self-approval. To befriend Bartleby; to humor him in his strange wilfulness, will cost me little or nothing, while I lay up in my soul what will eventually prove a sweet morsel for my conscience. But this mood was not invariable with me. The passiveness of Bartleby sometimes irritated me. I felt strangely goaded on to encounter him in new opposition—to elicit some angry spark from him answerable to my own. But, indeed, I might as well have essayed to strike fire with my knuckles against a bit of Windsor soap. But one afternoon the evil impulse in me mastered me, and the following little scene ensued:

"Bartleby," said I, "when those papers are all copied, I will compare them with you."

"I would prefer not to."

"How? Surely you do not mean to persist in that mulish vagary?"

No answer.

I threw open the folding-doors nearby, and turning upon Turkey and Nippers, exclaimed:

"Bartleby a second time says, he won't examine his papers. What do you think of it, Turkey?"

It was afternoon, be it remembered. Turkey sat glowing like a brass boiler; his bald head steaming; his hands reeling among his blotted papers.

"Think of it?" roared Turkey. "I think I'll just step behind his screen, and black his eyes for him!"

So saying, Turkey rose to his feet and threw his arms into a pugilistic position. He was hurrying away to make good his promise, when I detained him, alarmed at the effect of incautiously rousing Turkey's combativeness after dinner.

"Sit down, Turkey," said I, "and hear what Nippers has to say. What do you think of it, Nippers? Would I not be justified in immediately dismissing Bartleby?"

"Excuse me, that is for you to decide, sir. I think his conduct quite unusual, and, indeed, unjust, as regards Turkey and myself. But it may only be a passing whim."

"Ah," exclaimed I, "you have strangely changed your mind, then—you speak very gently of him now."

"All beer," cried Turkey; "gentleness is effects of beer—Nippers and I dined together to-day. You see how gentle *I* am, sir. Shall I go and black his eyes?"

"You refer to Bartleby, I suppose. No, not to-day, Turkey," I replied; "pray, put up your fists."

I closed the doors, and again advanced towards Bartleby. I felt additional incentives tempting me to my fate. I burned to be rebelled against again. I remembered that Bartleby never left the office.

"Bartleby," said I, "Ginger Nut is away; just step around to the Post Office, won't you?" (it was but a three minutes' walk) "and see if there is anything for me."

"I would prefer not to."

"You *will* not?"

"I *prefer* not."

I staggered to my desk, and sat there in a deep study. My blind inveteracy returned. Was there any other thing in which I could procure myself to be ignominiously repulsed by this lean, penniless wight?—my hired clerk? What added thing is there, perfectly reasonable, that he will be sure to refuse to do?

"Bartleby!"

No answer.

"Bartleby," in a louder tone.

No answer.

"Bartleby," I roared.

Like a very ghost, agreeable to the laws of magical invocation, at the third summons, he appeared at the entrance of his hermitage.

"Go to the next room, and tell Nippers to come to me."

"I prefer not to," he respectfully and slowly said, and mildly disappeared.

"Very good, Bartleby," said I, in a quiet sort of serenely-severe self-possessed tone, intimating the unalterable purpose of some terrible retribution very close at hand. At the moment I half intended something of the kind. But upon the whole, as it was drawing towards my dinner-hour, I thought it best to put on my hat and walk home for the day, suffering much from perplexity and distress of mind.

Shall I acknowledge it? The conclusion of this whole business was, that it soon became a fixed fact of my chambers, that a pale young scrivener, by the name of Bartleby, had a desk there; that he copied for me at the usual rate of four cents a folio (one hundred words); but he was permanently exempt from examining the work done by him, that duty being transferred to Turkey and Nippers, out of compliment, doubtless, to their superior acuteness; moreover, said Bartleby was never, on any account, to be dispatched on the most trivial errand of any sort; and that even if entreated to take upon him such a matter, it was generally understood that he would "prefer not to"— in other words, that he would refuse pointblank.

As days passed on, I became considerably reconciled to Bartleby. His steadiness, his freedom from all dissipation, his incessant industry (except when he chose to throw himself into a standing revery behind his screen), his great stillness, his unalterableness of demeanor under all circumstances, made him a valuable acquisition. One prime thing was this—*he was always there*—first in the morning, continually through the day, and the last at night. I had a singular confidence in his honesty. I felt my most precious papers perfectly safe in his hands. Sometimes, to be sure, I could not, for the very soul of me, avoid falling into sudden spasmodic passions with him. For it was exceeding difficult to bear in mind all the time those strange peculiarities, privileges, and unheard-of exemptions, forming the tacit stipulations on Bartleby's part under which he remained in my office. Now and then, in the eagerness of dispatching pressing business, I would inadvertently summon Bartleby, in a short, rapid tone, to put his finger, say, on the incipient tie of a bit of red tape with which I was about compressing some papers. Of course, from behind the screen the usual answer, "I prefer not to," was sure to come; and then, how could a human creature, with the common infirmities of our nature, refrain from bitterly exclaiming upon such perverseness—such unreasonableness? However, every added repulse of this sort which I received only tended to lessen the probability of my repeating the inadvertence.

Here it must be said, that, according to the custom of most legal gentlemen occupying chambers in densely-populated law buildings, there were several keys to my door. One was kept by a woman residing in the attic, which person weekly scrubbed and daily swept and dusted my apartments. Another was kept by Turkey for convenience sake. The third I sometimes carried in my own pocket. The fourth I knew not who had.

Now, one Sunday morning I happened to go to Trinity Church, to hear a celebrated preacher, and finding myself rather early on the ground I thought I would walk round to my chambers for a while. Luckily I had my key with me; but upon applying it to the lock, I found it resisted by something inserted from the inside. Quite surprised, I called out; when to my consternation a key was turned from within; and thrusting his lean visage at me, and holding the door ajar, the apparition of Bartleby appeared, in his shirt-sleeves, and otherwise in a strangely tattered deshabille, saying quietly that he was sorry, but he was deeply engaged just then, and—preferred not admitting me at present. In a brief word or two, he moreover added, that perhaps I had better walk round the block two or three times, and by that time he would probably have concluded his affairs.

Now, the utterly unsurmised appearance of Bartleby, tenanting my law-chambers of a Sunday morning, with his cadaverously gentlemanly *nonchalance*, yet withal firm and self-possessed, had such a strange effect upon me, that incontinently I slunk away from my own door, and did as desired. But not without sundry twinges of impotent rebellion against the mild effrontery of this unaccountable scrivener. Indeed, it was his wonderful mildness chiefly, which not only disarmed me, but unmanned me, as it were. For I consider that one, for the time, is sort of unmanned when he tranquilly permits his hired clerk to dictate to him, and order him away from his own premises. Furthermore, I was full of uneasiness as to what Bartleby could possibly be doing in my office in his shirt-sleeves, and in an otherwise dismantled condition of a Sunday morning. Was anything amiss going on? Nay, that was out of the question. It was not to be thought of for a moment that Bartleby was an immoral person. But what could he be doing there?—copying? Nay again, whatever might be his eccentricities, Bartleby was an eminently decorous person. He would be the last man to sit down to his desk in any state approaching to nudity. Besides, it was Sunday; and there was something about Bartleby that forbade the supposition that he would by any secular occupation violate the proprieties of the day.

Nevertheless, my mind was not pacified; and full of a restless curiosity, at last I returned to the door. Without hindrance I inserted my key, opened it, and entered. Bartleby was not to be seen. I looked round anxiously, peeped behind his screen; but it was very plain that he was gone. Upon more closely examining the place, I surmised that for an indefinite period Bartleby must have ate, dressed, and slept in my office, and that too without plate, mirror, or bed. The cushioned seat of a rickety old sofa in one corner bore the faint impress of a lean, reclining form. Rolled away under his desk, I found a blanket; under the empty grate, a blacking box and brush; on a chair, a tin basin, with soap and a ragged towel; in a newspaper a few crumbs of ginger-nuts and a morsel of cheese. Yes, thought I, it is evident enough that Bartleby has been making his home here, keeping bachelor's hall all by himself. Immediately then the thought came sweeping across me, what miserable friendlessness and loneliness are here revealed! His poverty is great; but his solitude, how horrible! Think of it. Of a Sunday, Wall Street is deserted as Petra;[9] and every night of every day it is an emptiness. This building, too, which of week-days hums with industry and life, at nightfall echoes with sheer vacancy, and all through Sunday is forlorn. And here Bartleby makes his home; sole spectator of a solitude which he has seen all populous—a sort of innocent and transformed Marius brooding among the ruins of Carthage![10]

For the first time in my life a feeling of overpowering stinging melancholy seized me. Before, I had never experienced aught but a not unpleasing sadness. The bond of a common humanity now drew me irresistibly to gloom. A fraternal melancholy! For both I and Bartleby were sons of Adam. I remembered the bright silks and sparkling faces I had seen that day, in gala trim, swan-like sailing down the Mississippi of Broadway; and I contrasted them with the pallid copyist, and thought to myself, Ah, happiness courts the light, so we deem the world is gay; but misery hides aloof, so we deem that misery there is none. These sad fancyings—chimeras, doubtless, of a sick and silly brain—led on to other and more special thoughts, concerning the eccentricities of Bartleby. Presentiments of strange discoveries hovered round me. The scrivener's pale form appeared to me laid out, among uncaring strangers, in its shivering winding-sheet.

Suddenly I was attracted by Bartleby's closed desk, the key in open sight left in the lock.

I mean no mischief, seek the gratification of no heartless curiosity, thought I; besides, the desk is mine, and its contents, too, so I will make bold to look within. Everything was methodically arranged, the papers smoothly placed. The pigeon-holes were deep, and removing the files of documents, I groped into their recesses. Presently I felt something there, and dragged it out. It

[9] The ruins of an ancient city in Palestine that had been rediscovered in 1812.

[10] Caius Marius (155?-86 B. C.) was a Roman general and plebeian who had won great victories in Africa. He is brooding because despite his success he was banished from Rome as a result of political maneuvering by patricians. He lived in exile but, when he returned, he had his political enemies murdered.

was an old bandanna handkerchief, heavy and knotted. I opened it, and saw it was a saving's bank.

I now recalled all the quiet mysteries which I had noted in the man. I remembered that he never spoke but to answer; that, though at intervals he had considerable time to himself, yet I had never seen him reading—no, not even a newspaper; that for long periods he would stand looking out, at his pale window behind the screen, upon the dead brick wall; I was quite sure he never visited any refectory or eating-house; while his pale face clearly indicated that he never drank beer like Turkey, or tea and coffee even, like other men; that he never went anywhere in particular that I could learn; never went out for a walk, unless, indeed, that was the case at present; that he had declined telling who he was, or whence he came, or whether he had any relatives in the world; that though so thin and pale, he never complained of ill-health. And more than all, I remembered a certain unconscious air of pallid—how shall I call it?—of pallid haughtiness, say, or rather an austere reserve about him, which had positively awed me into my tame compliance with his eccentricities, when I feared to ask him to do the slightest incidental thing for me, even though I might know, from his long-continued motionlessness, that behind his screen he must be standing in one of those dead-wall reveries of his.

Revolving all these things, and coupling them with the recently discovered fact, that he made my office his constant abiding place and home, and not forgetful of his morbid moodiness; revolving all these things, a prudential feeling began to steal over me. My first emotions had been those of pure melancholy and sincerest pity; but just in proportion as the forlornness of Bartleby grew and grew to my imagination, did that same melancholy merge into fear, that pity into repulsion. So true it is, and so terrible, too, that up to a certain point the thought or sight of misery enlists our best affections; but, in certain special cases, beyond that point it does not. They err who would assert that invariably this is owing to the inherent selfishness of the human heart. It rather proceeds from a certain hopelessness of remedying excessive and organic ill. To a sensitive being, pity is not seldom pain. And when at last it is perceived that such pity cannot lead to effectual succor, common sense bids the soul be rid of it. What I saw that morning persuaded me that the scrivener was the victim of innate and incurable disorder. I might give alms to his body; but his body did not pain him; it was his soul that suffered, and his soul I could not reach.

I did not accomplish the purpose of going to Trinity Church that morning. Somehow, the things I had seen disqualified me for the time from church-going. I walked homeward, thinking what I would do with Bartleby. Finally, I resolved upon this—I would put certain calm questions to him the next morning, touching his history, etc., and if he declined to answer them openly and unreservedly (and I supposed he would prefer not), then to give him a twenty dollar bill over and above whatever I might owe him, and tell him his services were no longer required; but that if in any other way I could assist him, I would be happy to do so, especially if he desired to return to his native place, wherever that might be, I would willingly help to defray the expenses. Moreover, if, after reaching home, he found himself at any time in want of aid, a letter from him would be sure of a reply.

The next morning came.

"Bartleby," said I, gently calling to him behind his screen.

No reply.

"Bartleby," said I, in a still gentler tone, "come here; I am not going to ask you to do anything you would prefer not to do—I simply wish to speak to you."

Upon this he noiselessly slid into view.

"Will you tell me, Bartleby, where you were born?"

"I would prefer not to."

"Will you tell me *anything* about yourself?"

"I would prefer not to."

"But what reasonable objection can you have to speak to me? I feel friendly towards you."

He did not look at me while I spoke, but kept his glance fixed upon my bust of Cicero, which, as I then sat, was directly behind me, some six inches above my head.

"What is your answer, Bartleby?" said I, after waiting a considerable time for a reply, during which his countenance remained immovable, only there was the faintest conceivable tremor of the white attenuated mouth.

"At present I prefer to give no answer," he said, and retired into his hermitage.

It was rather weak in me I confess, but his manner, on this occasion, nettled me. Not only did there seem to lurk in it a certain calm disdain, but his perverseness seemed ungrateful, considering the undeniable good usage and indulgence he had received from me.

Again I sat ruminating what I should do. Mortified as I was at his behavior, and resolved as I had been to dismiss him when I entered my office, nevertheless I strangely felt something superstitious knocking at my heart, and forbidding me to carry out my purpose, and denouncing me for a villian if I dared to breathe one bitter word against this forlornest of mankind. At last, familiarly drawing my chair behind his screen, I sat down and said: "Bartleby, never mind, then, about revealing your history; but let me entreat you, as a friend, to comply as far as may be with the usages of this office. Say now, you will help to examine papers tomorrow or next day: in short, say now, that in a day or two you will begin to be a little reasonable:—say so, Bartleby."

"At present I would prefer not to be a little reasonable," was his mildly cadaverous reply.

Just then the folding-doors opened, and Nippers approached. He seemed suffering from an unusually bad night's rest, induced by severer indigestion than common. He overheard those final words of Bartleby.

"*Prefer not,* eh?" gritted Nippers—"I'd *prefer* him, if I were you, sir," addressing me—"I'd *prefer* him; I'd give him preferences, the stubborn mule! What is it, sir, pray, that he *prefers* not to do now?"

Bartleby moved not a limb.

"Mr. Nippers," said I, "I'd prefer that you would withdraw for the present."

Somehow, of late, I had got into the way of involuntarily using this word "prefer" upon all sorts of not exactly suitable occasions. And I trembled to think that my contact with the scrivener had already and seriously affected me in a mental way. And what further and deeper aberration might it not yet produce? This apprehension had not been without efficacy in determining me to summary measures.

As Nippers, looking very sour and sulky, was departing, Turkey blandly and deferentially approached.

"With submission, sir," said he, "yesterday I was thinking about Bartleby here, and I think that if he would but prefer to take a quart of good ale every day, it would do much towards mending him, and enabling him to assist in examining his papers."

"So you have got the word, too," said I, slightly excited.

"With submission, what word, sir?" asked Turkey, respectfully crowding himself into the contracted space behind the screen, and by so doing, making me jostle the scrivener. "What word, sir?"

"I would prefer to be left alone here," said Bartleby, as if offended at being mobbed in his privacy.

"*That's* the word, Turkey," said I—"*that's* it."

"Oh, *prefer?* oh yes—queer word. I never use it myself. But, sir, as I was saying, if he would but prefer—"

"Turkey," interrupted I, "you will please withdraw."

"Oh certainly, sir if you prefer that I should."

As he opened the folding-door to retire, Nippers at his desk caught a glimpse of me, and asked whether I would prefer to have a certain paper copied on blue paper or white. He did not in the least roguishly accent the word "prefer." It was plain that it involuntarily rolled from his tongue. I thought to myself, surely I must get rid of a demented man, who already has in some degree turned the tongues, if not the heads of myself and clerks. But I thought it prudent not to break the dismission at once.

The next day I noticed that Bartleby did nothing but stand at his window in his dead-wall revery. Upon asking him why he did not write, he said that he had decided upon doing no more writing.

"Why, how now? what next?" exclaimed I, "do no more writing?"

"No more."

"And what is the reason?"

"Do you not see the reason for yourself?" he indifferently replied.

I looked steadfastly at him, and perceived that his eyes looked dull and glazed. Instantly it occured to me, that his unexampled diligence in copying by his dim window for the first few weeks of his stay with me might have temporarily impaired his vision.

I was touched. I said something in condolence with him. I hinted that of course he did wisely in abstaining from writing for a while; and urged him to embrace that opportunity of taking wholesome exercise in the open air. This, however, he did not do. A few days after this, my other clerks being absent, and being in a great hurry to dispatch certain letters by the mail, I thought that, having nothing else earthly to do, Bartleby would surely be less inflexible than usual, and carry these letters to the post-office. But he blankly declined. So, much to my inconvenience, I went myself.

Still added days went by. Whether Bartleby's eyes improved or not, I could not say. To all appearance, I thought they did. But when I asked him if they did, he vouchsafed no answer. At all events, he would do no copying. At last, in reply to my urgings, he informed me that he had permanently given up copying.

"What!" exclaimed I; "suppose your eyes should get entirely well—better than ever before—would you not copy then?"

"I have given up copying," he answered, and slid aside.

He remained as ever, a fixture in my chamber. Nay—if that were possible—he became still more of a fixture than before. What was to be done? He would do nothing in the office; why should he stay there? In plain fact, he had now become a millstone to me, not only useless as a necklace, but afflictive to bear. Yet I was sorry for him. I speak less than truth when I say that, on his own account, he occasioned me uneasiness. If he would but have named a single relative or friend, I would instantly have written, and urged their taking the poor fellow away to some convenient retreat. But he seemed alone, absolutely alone in the universe. A bit of wreck in the mid-Atlantic. At length, necessities connected with my business tyrannized over all other considerations. Decently as I could, I told Bartleby that in six days' time he must unconditionally leave the office. I warned him to take measures, in the interval, for procuring some other abode. I offered to assist him in this endeavor, if he himself would but take the first step towards a removal. "And when you finally quit me, Bartleby," added I, "I shall see that you go not away entirely unprovided. Six days from this hour, remember."

At the expiration of that period, I peeped behind the screen, and lo! Bartleby was there.

I buttoned up my coat, balanced myself; advanced slowly towards him, touched his shoulder, and said, "The time has come; you must quit this place; I am sorry for you; here is money; but you must go."

"I would prefer not," he replied, with his back still towards me.

"You *must*."

He remained silent.

Now I had an unbounded confidence in this man's common honesty. He had frequently restored to me sixpences and shillings carelessly dropped upon the floor, for I am apt to be very reckless in such shirt-button affairs. The proceeding, then, which followed will not be deemed extraordinary.

"Bartleby," said I, "I owe you twelve dollars on account; here are thirty-two; the odd twenty are yours—Will you take it?" and I handed the bills towards him.

But he made no motion.

"I will leave them here, then," putting them under a weight on the table. Then taking my hat and cane and going to the door, I tranquilly turned and added—"After you have removed your things from these offices, Bartleby, you will of course lock the door—since every one is now gone for the day but you—and if you please, slip your key underneath the mat, so that I may have it in the morning. I shall not see you again; so good-bye to you. If, hereafter, in your new place of abode, I can be of any service to you, do not fail to advise me by letter. Good-bye, Bartleby, and fare you well."

But he answered not a word; like the last column of some ruined temple, he remained standing mute and solitary in the middle of the otherwise deserted room.

As I walked home in a pensive mood, my vanity got the better of my pity. I could not but highly plume myself on my masterly management in getting rid of Bartleby. Masterly I call it, and such it must appear to any dispassionate thinker. The beauty of my procedure seemed to consist in its perfect quietness. There was no vulgar bullying, no bravado of any sort, no choleric hectoring, and striding to and fro across the apartment, jerking out vehement commands for Bartleby to bundle himself off with his beggarly traps. Nothing of the kind. Without loudly bidding Bartleby depart—as an inferior genius might have done—I *assumed* the ground that depart he must; and upon that assumption built all I had to say. The more I thought over my procedure, the more I was charmed with it. Nevertheless, next morning, upon awakening, I had my doubts—I had somehow slept off the fumes of vanity. One of the coolest and wisest hours a man has, is just after he awakes in the morning. My procedure seemed as sagacious as ever—but only in theory. How it would prove in practice—there was the rub. It was truly a beautiful thought to have assumed Bartleby's departure; but, after all, that assumption was simply my own, and none of Bartleby's. The great point was, not whether I had assumed that he would quit me, but whether he would prefer to do so. He was more a man of preferences than assumptions.

After breakfast, I walked down town, arguing the probabilities *pro* and *con*. One moment I thought it would prove a miserable failure, and Bartleby would be found all alive at my office as usual; the next moment it seemed certain that I should find his chair empty. And so I kept veering about. At the corner of Broadway and Canal Street, I saw quite an excited group of people standing in earnest conversation.

"I'll take odds he doesn't," said a voice as I passed.

"Doesn't go?—done!" said I, "put up your money."

I was instinctively putting my hand in my pocket to produce my own, when I remembered that this was an election day. The words I had overheard bore no reference to Bartleby, but to the success or non-success of some candidate for the mayoralty. In my intent frame of mind, I had, as it were, imagined that all Broadway shared in my excitement, and were debating the same question with me, I passed on, very thankful that the uproar of the street screened my momentary absent-mindedness.

As I had intended, I was earlier than usual at my office door. I stood listening for a moment. All was still. He must be gone. I tried the knob. The door was locked. Yes, my procedure had worked to a charm; he indeed must be vanished. Yet a certain melancholy mixed with this: I was almost sorry for my brilliant success. I was fumbling under the door mat for the key, which Bartleby was to have left there for me, when accidentally my knee knocked against a panel, producing a summoning sound, and in response a voice came to me from within—"Not yet; I am occupied."

It was Bartleby.

I was thunderstruck. For an instant I stood like the man who, pipe in mouth, was killed one cloudless afternoon long ago in Virginia, by summer lightning, at his own warm open window he was killed, and remained leaning out there upon the dreamy afternoon, till some one touched him, when he fell.

"Not gone!" I murmured at last. But again obeying that wondrous ascendancy which the inscrutable scrivener had over me, and from which ascendancy, for all my chafing, I could not completely escape, I slowly went down stairs and out into the street, and while walking round the block, considered what I should next do in this unheard-of perplexity. Turn the man out by an actual thrusting I could not; to drive him away by calling him hard names would not do; calling in the police was an unpleasant idea; and yet, permit him to enjoy his cadaverous triumph over me—this, too, I could not think of. What was to be done? or, if nothing could be done, was there anything further that I could *assume* in the matter? Yes, as before I had prospectively assumed that Bartleby would depart, so now I might retrospectively assume that departed he was. In the legitimate carrying out of this assumption, I might enter my office in a great hurry, and pretending not to see Bartleby at all, walk straight against him as if he were air. Such a proceeding would in a singular degree have the appearance of a homethrust. It was hardly possible that Bartleby could withstand such an application of the doctrine of assumption. But upon second thoughts the success of the plan seemed rather dubious. I resolved to argue the matter over with him again.

"Bartleby," said I, entering the office, with a quietly severe expression, "I am seriously displeased. I am pained, Bartleby. I had thought better of you. I had imagined you of such a gentlemanly organization, that in any delicate dilemma a slight hint would suffice—in short, an assumption. But it appears I am deceived. Why," I added, unaffectedly starting, "you have not even touched that money yet," pointing to it, just where I had left it the evening previous.

He answered nothing.

"Will you, or will you not, quit me?" I now demanded in a sudden passion, advancing close to him.

"I would prefer *not* to quit you," he replied, gently emphasizing the *not*.

"What earthly right have you to stay here? Do you pay any rent? Do you pay my taxes? Or is this property yours?"

He answered nothing.

"Are you ready to go on and write now? Are your eyes recovered? Could you copy a small paper for me this morning? or help me examine a few lines? or step round to the post-office? In a word, will you do anything at all, to give a coloring to your refusal to depart the premises?"

He silently retired into his hermitage.

I was now in such a state of nervous resentment that I thought it but prudent to check myself at present from further demonstrations. Bartleby and I were alone. I remembered the tragedy of the unfortunate Adams and the still more unfortunate Colt in the solitary office of the latter; and how poor Colt, being dreadfully incensed by Adams, and imprudently permitting himself to get wildly excited, was at unawares hurried into his fatal act—an act which certainly no man could possibly deplore more than the actor himself.[11] Often it has occurred to me in my ponderings upon the subject that had that altercation taken place in the public street, or at a private residence, it would not have terminated as it did. It was the circumstance of being alone in a solitary office, up stairs, of a building entirely unhallowed by humanizing domestic associations—an uncarpeted office, doubtless, of a dusty, haggard sort of appearance—this it must have been, which greatly helped to enhance the irritable desperation of the hapless Colt.

But when this old Adam of resentment rose in me and tempted me concerning Bartleby, I grappled him and threw him. How? Why, simply by recalling the divine injunction: "A new commandment give I unto you, that ye love one another."[12] Yes, this it was that saved me. Aside from higher considerations, charity often operates as a vastly wise and prudent principle—a great safeguard to its possessor. Men have committed murder for jealousy's sake, and anger's sake, and hatred's sake, and selfishness' sake, and

[11] Samuel Adams was murdered by John C. Colt in January 1842. He committed suicide just before he was to be hanged.

[12] John, xiii:34. These are the words of Jesus to his disciples.

spiritual pride's sake; but no man, that ever I heard of, ever committed a diabolical murder for sweet charity's sake. Mere self-interest, then, if no better motive can be enlisted, should, especially with high-tempered men, prompt all beings to charity and philanthropy. At any rate, upon the occasion in question, I strove to drown my exasperated feelings toward the scrivener by benevolently construing his conduct. Poor fellow, poor fellow! thought I, he don't mean anything; and besides, he has seen hard times, and ought to be indulged.

I endeavored, also, immediately to occupy myself, and at the same time to comfort my despondency. I tried to fancy, that in the course of the morning, at such time as might prove agreeable to him, Bartleby, of his own free accord, would emerge from his hermitage and take up some decided line of march in the direction of the door. But no. Half-past twelve o'clock came, Turkey began to glow in the face, overturn his inkstand, and become generally obstreperous; Nippers abated down into quietude and courtesy; Ginger Nut munched his noon apple; and Bartleby remained standing at his window in one of his profoundest dead-wall reveries. Will it be credited? Ought I to acknowledge it? That afternoon I left the office without saying one further word to him.

Some days now passed, during which, at leisure intervals I looked a little into "Edwards on the Will," and "Priestley on Necessity."[13] Under the circumstances, those books induced a salutary feeling. Gradually I slid into the persuasion that these troubles of mine, touching the scrivener, had been all predestinated from eternity, and Bartleby was billeted upon me for some mysterious purpose of an all-wise Providence, which it was not for a mere mortal like me to fathom. Yes, Bartleby, stay there behind your screen, thought I; I shall persecute you no more; you are harmless and noiseless as any of these old chairs; in short, I never feel so private as when I know you are here. At last I see it, I feel it; I penetrate to the predestinated purpose of my life. I am content. Others may have loftier parts to enact; but my mission in this world, Bartleby, is to furnish you with office-room for such period as you may see fit to remain.

I believe that this wise and blessed frame of mind would have continued with me, had it not been for the unsolicited and uncharitable remarks obtruded upon me by my professional friends who visited the rooms. But thus it often is, that the constant friction of illiberal minds wears out at last the best resolves of the more generous. Though to be sure, when I reflected upon it, it was not strange that people entering my office should be struck by the peculiar aspect of the unaccountable Bartleby, and so be tempted to

[13] Jonathan Edwards, *The Freedom of the Will* (1754). See p. 310, for a full discussion of Edwards' life and thought. Joseph Priestley (1733-1805) was an English scientist and theologian; he was trained as a Calvinist but later expressed a belief in necessity and natural determinism.

throw out some sinister observations concerning him. Sometimes an attorney, having business with me, and calling at my office, and finding no one but the scrivener there, would undertake to obtain some sort of precise information from him touching my whereabouts; but without heeding his idle talk, Bartleby would remain standing immovable in the middle of the room. So after contemplating him in that position for a time, the attorney would depart, no wiser than he came.

Also, when a reference was going on, and the room full of lawyers and witnesses, and business driving fast, some deeply-occupied legal gentleman present, seeing Bartleby wholly unemployed, would request him to run round to his (the legal gentleman's) office and fetch some papers for him. Thereupon, Bartleby would tranquilly decline, and yet remain idle as before. Then the lawyer would give a great stare, and turn to me. And what could I say? At last I was made aware that all through the circle of my professional acquaintance, a whisper of wonder was running round, having reference to the strange creature I kept at my office. This worried me very much. And as the idea came upon me of his possibly turning out a long-lived man, and keeping occupying my chambers, and denying my authority; and perplexing my visitors; and scandalizing my professional reputation; and casting a general gloom over the premises; keeping soul and body together to the last upon his savings (for doubtless he spent but half a dime a day), and in the end perhaps outlived me, and claim possession of my office by right of his perpetual occupancy: as all these dark anticipations crowded upon me more and more, and my friends continually intruded their relentless remarks upon the apparition in my room; a great change was wrought in me. I resolved to gather all my faculties together, and forever rid me of this intolerable incubus.

Ere revolving any complicated project, however, adapted to this end, I first simply suggested to Bartleby the propriety of his permanent departure. In a calm and serious tone, I commended the idea to his careful and mature consideration. But, having taken three days to meditate upon it, he apprised me, that his original determination remained the same; in short, that he still preferred to abide with me.

What shall I do? I now said to myself, buttoning up my coat to the last button. What shall I do? what ought I to do? what does conscience say I *should* do with this man, or, rather, ghost. Rid myself of him, I must; go, he shall. But how? You will not thrust him, the poor, pale, passive mortal—you will not thrust such a helpless creature out of your door? you will not dishonor yourself by such cruelty? No, I will not, I cannot do that. Rather would I let him live and die here, and then mason up his remains in the wall. What, then, will you do? For all your coaxing, he will not budge. Bribes he leaves under your own paper-weight on your table; in short, it is quite plain that he prefers to cling to you.

Then something severe, something unusual must be done. What! surely you will not have him collared by a constable, and commit his innocent pallor to the common jail? And upon what ground could you procure such a thing to be done?—a vagrant, is he? What! he a vagrant, a wanderer, who refuses to budge? It is because he will *not* be a vagrant, then, that you seek to count him *as* a vagrant. That is too absurd. No visible means of support: there I have him. Wrong again: for indubitably he *does* support himself, and that is the only unanswerable proof that any man can show of his possessing the means so to do. Not more, then. Since he will not quit me, I must quit him. I will change my offices; I will move elsewhere, and give him fair notice, that if I find him on my new premises I will then proceed against him as a common trespasser.

Acting accordingly, next day I thus addressed him: "I find these chambers too far from the City Hall; the air is unwholesome. In a word, I propose to remove my offices next week, and shall no longer require your services. I tell you this now, in order that you may seek another place."

He made no reply, and nothing more was said.

On the appointed day I engaged carts and men, proceeded to my chambers, and, having but little furniture, everything was removed in a few hours. Throughout, the scrivener remained standing behind the screen, which I directed to be removed the last thing. It was withdrawn; and, being folded up like a huge folio, left him the motionless occupant of a naked room. I stood in the entry watching him a moment, while something from within me upbraided me.

I re-entered, with my hand in my pocket—and—and my heart in my mouth.

"Good-bye, Bartleby; I am going—good-bye, and God some way bless you; and take that," slipping something in his hand. But it dropped upon the floor, and then—strange to say—I tore myself from him whom I had so longed to be rid of.

Established in my new quarters, for a day or two I kept the door locked, and started at every footfall in the passages. When I returned to my rooms, after any little absence, I would pause at the threshold for an instant, and attentively listen, ere applying my key. But these fears were needless. Bartleby never came nigh me.

I thought all was going well, when a perturbed-looking stranger visited me, inquiring whether I was the person who had recently occupied rooms at No.—Wall Street.

Full of forebodings, I replied that I was.

"Then sir," said the stranger, who proved a lawyer, "you are responsible for the man you left there. He refuses to do any copying; he refuses to do anything; he says he prefers not to; and he refuses to quit the premises."

"I am very sorry, sir," said I, with assumed tranquillity, but an inward tremor, "but, really, the man you allude to is nothing to me—he is no relation or apprentice of mine, that you should hold me responsible for him."

"In mercy's name, who is he?"

"I certainly cannot inform you. I know nothing about him. Formerly I employed him as a copyist; but he has done nothing for me now for some time past."

"I shall settle him, then—good morning, sir."

Several days passed, and I heard nothing more; and, though I often felt a charitable prompting to call at the place and see poor Bartleby, yet a certain squeamishness, of I know not what, withheld me.

All is over with him, by this time, thought I, as last, when, through another week, no further intelligence reached me. But, coming to my room the day after, I found several persons waiting at my door in a high state of nervous excitement.

"That's the man—here he comes," cried the foremost one, whom I recognized as the lawyer who had previously called upon me alone.

"You must take him away, sir, at once," cried a portly person among them, advancing upon me, and whom I knew to be the landlord of No.— Wall Street. "These gentlemen, my tenants, cannot stand it any longer; Mr. B——," pointing to the lawyer, "has turned him out of his room, and he now persists in haunting the building generally, sitting upon the banisters of the stairs by day, and sleeping in the entry by night. Everybody is concerned; clients are leaving the offices; some fears are entertained of a mob; something you must do, and that without delay."

Aghast at this torrent, I fell back before it, and would fain have locked myself in my new quarters. In vain I persisted that Bartleby was nothing to me—no more than to any one else. In vain—I was the last person known to have anything to do with him, and they held me to the terrible account. Fearful, then, of being exposed in the papers (as one person present obscurely threatened), I considered the matter, and, at length, said, that if the lawyer would give me a confidential interview with the scrivener, in his (the lawyer's) own room, I would, that afternoon, strive my best to rid them of the nuisance they complained of.

Going up stairs to my old haunt, there was Bartleby silently sitting upon the banister of the landing.

"What are you doing here, Bartleby?" said I.

"Sitting upon the banister," he mildly replied.

I motioned him into the lawyer's room, who then left us.

"Bartleby," said I, "are you aware that you are the cause of great tribulation to me, by persisting in occupying the entry after being dismissed from the office?"

No answer.

"Now one of two things must take place. Either you must do something, or something must be done with you. Now what sort of business would you like to engage in? Would you like to re-engage in copying for some one?"

"No; I would prefer not to make any change."

"Would you like a clerkship in a dry-goods store?"

"There is too much confinement about that. No, I would not like a clerkship; but I am not particular."

"Too much confinement," I cried, "why, you keep yourself confined all the time!"

"I would prefer not to take a clerkship," he rejoined, as if to settle that little item at once.

"How would a bar-tender's business suit you? There is no trying of the eye-sight in that."

"I would not like it at all; though, as I said before, I am not particular."

His unwonted wordiness inspirited me. I returned to the charge.

"Well, then, would you like to travel through the country collecting bills for the merchants? That would improve your health."

"No, I would prefer to do something else."

"How, then, would going as a companion to Europe, to entertain some young gentleman with your conversation—how would that suit you?"

"Not at all. It does not strike me that there is anything definite about that. I like to be stationary. But I am not particular."

"Stationary you shall be, then," I cried, now losing all patience, and, for the first time in all my exasperating connection with him, fairly flying into a passion. "If you do not go away from these premises before night, I shall feel bound—indeed, I *am* bound—to—to—to quit the premises myself!" I rather absurdly concluded, knowing not with what possible threat to try to frighten his immobility into compliance. Despairing of all further efforts, I was precipitately leaving him, when a final thought occured to me—one which had not been wholly unindulged before.

"Bartleby," said I, in the kindest tone I could assume under such exciting circumstances, "will you go home with me now—not to my office, but my dwelling—and remain there till we can conclude upon some convenient arrangement for you at our leisure? Come, let us start now, right away."

"No: at present I would prefer not to make any change at all."

I answered nothing; but, effectually dodging every one by the suddenness and rapidity of my flight, rushed from the building, ran up Wall Street towards Broadway, and, jumping into the first omnibus, was soon removed from the pursuit. As soon as tranquillity returned, I distinctly perceived that I had now done all that I possibly could, both in respect to the demands of the landlord and his tenants, and with regard to my own desire and sense of duty, to benefit Bartleby, and shield him from rude persecution. I now strove to be entirely care-free and quiescent; and my conscience justified me in the attempt; though, indeed, it was not so successful as I could have wished. So fearful was I of being again hunted out by the incensed landlord and his exasperated tenants, that, surrendering my business to Nippers, for a few days, I drove about the upper part of the town and through the suburbs, in my rockaway; crossed over to Jersey City and Hoboken, and paid fugitive to Manhattanville and Astoria. In fact, I almost lived in my rockaway for the time.

When again I entered my office, lo, a note from the landlord lay upon the desk. I opened it with trembling hands. It informed me that the writer had sent to the police, and had Bartleby removed to the Tombs as a vagrant. Moreover, since I knew more about him than any one else, he wished me to appear at the place, and make a suitable statement of the facts. These tidings had a conflicting effect upon me. At first I was indignant; but, at last, almost approved. The landlord's energetic, summary disposition, had led him to adopt a procedure which I do not think I would have decided upon myself; and yet, as a last resort, under such peculiar circumstances, it seemed the only plan.

As I afterwards learned, the poor scrivener, when told that he must be conducted to the Tombs, offered not the slighest obstacle, but, in his pale, unmoving way, silently acquiesced.

Some of the compassionate and curious by-standers joined the party; and headed by one of the constables arm-in-arm with Bartleby, the silent procession filed its way through all the noise, and heat, and joy of the roaring thoroughfares at noon.

The same day I received the note, I went to the Tombs, or, to speak more properly, the Halls of Justice. Seeking the right officer, I stated the purpose of my call, and was informed that the individual I described was, indeed, within. I then assured the functionary that Bartleby was a perfectly honest man, and greatly to be compassionated, however unaccountably eccentric. I narrated all I knew, and closed by suggesting the idea of letting him remain in as indulgent confinement as possible, till something less harsh might be done—though, indeed, I hardly knew what. At all events, if nothing else could be decided upon, the alms-house must receive him. I then begged to have an interview.

Being under no disgraceful charge, and quite serene and harmless in all his ways, they had permitted him freely to wander about the prison, and, especially, in the inclosed glass-plated yards thereof. And so I found him there, standing all alone in the quietest of the yards, his face towards a high wall, while all around, from the narrow slits of the jail windows, I thought I saw peering out upon him the eyes of murderers and thieves.

"Bartleby!"

"I know you," he said, without looking round—"and I want nothing to say to you."

"It was not I that brought you here, Bartleby," said I, keenly pained at his implied suspicion. "And to you, this should not be so vile a place. Nothing reproachful attaches to you by being here. And see, it is not so sad a place as one might think. Look, there is the sky, and here is the grass."

"I know where I am," he replied, but would say nothing more, and so I left him.

As I entered the corridor again, a broad meat-like man, in an apron, accosted me, and jerking his thumb over his shoulder said—"Is that your friend?"

"Yes."

"Does he want to starve? If he does, let him live on the prison fare, that's all."

"Who are you?" asked I, not knowing what to make of such an unofficially speaking person in such a place.

"I am the grub-man. Such gentlemen as have friends here, hire me to provide them with something good to eat."

"Is this so?" said I, turning to the turnkey.

He said it was.

"Well, then," said I, slipping some silver into the grub-man's hands (for so they called him), "I want you to give particular attention to my friend there; let him have the best dinner you can get. And you must be as polite to him as possible."

"Introduce me, will you?" said the grub-man, looking at me with expression which seemed to say he was all impatience for an opportunity to give a specimen of his breeding.

Thinking it would prove of benefit to the scrivener, I acquiesced: and, asking the grub-man his name, went up with him to Bartleby.

"Bartleby, this is a friend; you will find him very useful to you."

"Your sarvant, sir, your sarvant," said the grub-man, making a low salutation behind his apron. "Hope you find it pleasant here, sir: nice grounds—cool apartments—hope you'll stay with us some time—try to make it agreeable. What will you have for dinner to-day?"

"I prefer not to dine to-day," said Bartleby, turning away. "It would disagree with me; I am unused to dinners." So saying, he slowly moved to the other side of the inclosure, and took up a position fronting the dead-wall.

"How's this?" said the grub-man, addressing me with a stare of astonishment. "He's odd, ain't he?"

"I think he is a little deranged," said I, sadly.

"Deranged? deranged is it? Well, now, upon my word, I thought that friend of yourn was a gentleman forger; they are always pale and genteel-like, them forgers. I can't help pity 'em—can't help it, sir. Did you know Monroe Edwards?" he added, touchingly, and paused. Then, laying his hand pietously on my shoulder, sighed, "he died of consumption at Sing-Sing.[14] So you weren't acquainted with Monroe?"

[14] The state prison at Ossining, New York.

"No, I was never socially acquainted with any forgers. But I cannot stop longer. Look to my friend yonder. You will not lose by it. I will see you again."

Some few days after this, I again obtained admission to the Tombs, and went through the corridors in quest of Bartleby; but without finding him.

"I saw him coming from his cell not long ago," said a turnkey, "may be he's gone to loiter in the yards."

So I went in that direction.

"Are you looking for the silent man?" said another turnkey, passing me. "Yonder he lies—sleeping in the yard there. 'Tis not twenty minutes since I saw him lie down."

The yard was entirely quiet. It was not accessible to the common prisoners. The surrounding walls, of amazing thickness, kept off all sounds behind them. The Egyptian character of the masonry weighed upon me with its gloom. But a soft imprisoned turf grew under foot. The heart of the eternal pyramids, it seemed, wherein, by some strange magic, through the clefts, grass-seed, dropped by birds, had sprung.

Strangley huddled at the base of the wall, his knees drawn up, and lying on his side, his head touching the cold stones, I saw the wasted Bartleby. But nothing stirred. I paused; then went close up to him; stooped over, and saw that his dim eyes were open; otherwise he seemed profoundly sleeping. Something prompted me to touch him. I felt his hand, when a tingling shiver ran up my arm and down my spine to my feet.

The round face of the grub-man peered upon me now. "His dinner is ready. Won't he dine to-day, either? Or does he live without dining?"

"Lives without dining," said I, and closed the eyes.

"Eh!—He's asleep, ain't he?"

"With kings and counselors,"[15] murmured I.

There would seem little need for proceeding further in this history. Imagination will readily supply the meagre recital of poor Bartleby's interment. But, ere parting with the reader, let me say, that if this little narrative has sufficiently interested him, to awaken curiosity as to who Bartleby was, and what manner of life he led prior to the present narrator's making his acquaintance, I can only reply, that in such curiosity I fully share, but am wholly unable to gratify it. Yet here I hardly know whether I should divulge one little item of rumor, which came to my ear a few months after the scrivener's decease. Upon what basis it rested, I could never ascertain; and hence, how true it is I cannot now tell. But, inasmuch as this vague report has not been without a certain suggestive interest to me, however sad, it may prove the same with some others; and so I will briefly mention it. The report

---

[15] See Job iii:13-14: "For now should I have lain still and been quiet, I should have slept; then had I been at rest, With kings and counselors of the earth, which built desolate places for themselves."

was this: that Bartleby had been a subordinate clerk in the Dead Letter Office of Washington, from which he had been suddenly removed by a change in the administration. When I think over this rumor, hardly can I express the emotions which seize me. Dead letters! does it not sound like dead men? Conceive a man by nature and misfortune prone to a pallid hopelessness, can any business seem more fitted to heighten it than that of continually handling these dead letters, and assorting them for the flames? For by the cart-load they are annually burned. Sometimes from out the folded paper the pale clerk takes a ring—the finger it was meant for, perhaps, moulders in the grave; a bank-note sent in swiftest charity—he whom it would relieve, nor eats nor hungers any more; pardon for those who died despairing; hope for those who died unhoping; good tidings for those who died stifled by unrelieved calamities. On errands of life, these letters speed to death.

Ah, Bartleby! Ah! humanity!

From The Encatadas

SKETCH EIGHTH: NORFOLK ISLE AND THE CHOLA WIDOW[1]

"At last they in an island did espy
A seemly woman sitting by the shore,
That with great sorrow and sad agony
Seemed some great misfortune to deplore,
And loud to them for succor called evermore."

"Black his eyes as the midnight sky,
White his neck as the driven snow,
Red his cheek as the morning light;—
Cold he lies in the ground below.
    My love is dead,
    Gone to his death-bed,
All under the cactus tree."

---

[1] *The Encantadas* was published in *Putnam's Monthly Magazine* in March, April, and May, 1854. It appeared again in *Piazza Tales* together with "Benito Cereno" and "Bartleby the Scrivener." The eighth sketch is probably the most powerful, recounting as it does the destructive force of nature, the healing power of love, the endurance of Hunilla, and the loneliness of human nature. *The Encantadas* represent the Galapagos Islands, which Melville had seen a few years earlier; clearly they are by no means "enchanted."

"Each lonely scene shall thee restore,
For thee the tear be duly shed;
Belov'd till life can charm no more,
And mourned till Pity's self be dead."[2]

Far to the northeast of Charles's Isle, sequestered from the rest, lies Norfolk Isle; and, however insignificant to most voyages, to me, through sympathy, that lone island has become a spot made sacred by the strongest trials of humanity.

It was my first visit to the Encantadas. Two days had been spent ashore in hunting tortoises. There was not time to capture many; so on the third afternoon we loosed our sails. We were just in the act of getting under way, the uprooted anchor yet suspended and invisibly swaying beneath the wave, as the good ship gradually turned her heel to leave the isle behind, when the seaman who heaved with me at the windlass paused suddenly, and directed my attention to something moving on the land, not along the beach, but somewhat back, fluttering from the height.

In view of the sequel of this little story, be it here narrated how it came to pass, that an object which partly from its being so small was quite lost to every other man on board, still caught the eye of my handspike companion. The rest of the crew, myself included, merely stood up to our spikes in heaving; whereas, unwontedly exhilarated at every turn of the ponderous windlass, my belted comrade leaped atop of it, with might and main giving a downward, thewey perpendicular heave, raised eye bent in cheery animation upon the slowly receding shore. Being high lifted above all others was the reason he perceived the object, otherwise unperceivable: and this elevation of his eye was owing to the elevation of his spirits; and this again—for truth must out—to a dram of Peruvian pisco, in guerdon for some kindness done, secretly administered to him that morning by our mulatto steward. Now, certainly, pisco does a deal of mischief in the world; yet seeing that, in the present case it was the means, though indirect, of rescuing a human being from the most dreadful fate, must we not also needs admit that sometimes pisco does a deal of good?

Glancing across the water in the direction pointed out, I saw some white thing hanging from an inland rock, perhaps half a mile from the sea.

"It is a bird; a white-winged bird; perhaps a—no; it is—it is a handkerchief!"

"Aye, a handkerchief!" echoed my comrade, and with a louder shout apprised the captain.

---

[2] Adapted from Spenser's *The Faerie Queene*, Bk. II, xii, 27, and Chatterton's "The Mynstrelles Song," stanza 2.

Quickly now—like the running out and training of a great gun—the log cabin spy-glass was thrust through the mizzen rigging from the high platform of the poop; whereupon a human figure was plainly seen upon the inland rock, eagerly waving towards us what seemed to be the handkerchief.

Our captain was a prompt, good fellow. Dropping the glass, he lustily ran forward, ordering the anchor to be dropped again; hands to stand by a boat, and lower away.

In a half-hour's time the swift boat returned. It went with six and came with seven; and the seventh a woman.

It is not artistic heartlessness, but I wish I could but draw in crayons; for this woman was a most touching sight; and crayons, tracing softly melancholy lines, would best depict the mournful image of the dark-damasked Chola widow.

Her story was soon told, and though given in her own strange language was as quickly understood, for our captain from long trading on the Chilian coast was well versed in the Spanish. A *cholo*, or half-breed Indian woman of Payta in Peru, three years gone by, with her young new-wedded husband Felipe, of pure Castilian blood, and her one only Indian brother, Truxill, Hunilla had taken passage on the main in a French whaler, commanded by a joyous man; which vessel, bound to the cruising grounds beyond the Enchanted Isles, proposed passing close by their vicinity. The object of the little party was to procure tortoise oil, a fluid which for its great purity and delicacy is held in high estimation wherever known; and it is well known all along this part of the Pacific coast. With a chest of clothes, tools, cooking utensils, a rude apparatus for trying out the oil, some casks of biscuits, and other things, not omitting two favourite dogs, of which faithful animal all the Cholos are very fond, Hunilla and her companions were safely landed at their chosen place; the Frenchman, according to the contract made ere sailing, engaged to take them off upon returning from a four months' cruise in the westward seas; which interval the three adventurers deemed quite sufficient for their purposes.

On the isle's lone beach they paid him in silver for their passage out, the stranger having declined to carry them at all except upon that condition; though willing to take evey means to insure the due fulfilment of his promise. Felipe had striven hard to have this payment put off to the period of the ship's return. But in vain. Still, they thought they had, in another way, ample pledge of the good faith of the Frenchman. It was arranged that the expenses of the passage home should not be payable in silver, but in tortoises; one hundred tortoises ready captured to the returning captain's hand. These the Cholos meant to secure after their own work was done, against the probable time of the Frenchman's coming back; and no doubt in prospect already felt, that in those hundred tortoises—now somewhere ranging in the isle's interior—they possessed one hundred hostages. Enough: the vessel sailed: the gazing three on shore answered the loud glee of the singing crew; and ere evening, the French craft was hull down in the distant sea, its masts three faintest lines which quickly faded from Hunilla's eye.

The stranger had given a blithesome promise, and had anchored it with oaths; but oaths and anchors equally will drag; nought else abides on fickle earth but unkept promises of joy. Contrary winds from out unstabled skies, on contrary moods of his more varying mind, or shipwreck and sudden death in solitary waves; whatever was the cause, the blithe stranger never was seen again.

Yet, however dire a calamity was here in store, misgivings of it ere due time never disturbed the Cholo's busy mind, now all intent upon the toil-some matter which had brought them hither. Nay, by swift doom coming like the thief at night, ere seven weeks went by, two of the little party were removed from all anxieties of land or sea. No more they sought to gaze with feverish fear, or still more feverish hope, beyond the present's horizon line; but into the furthest future their own silent spirits sailed. By persevering labour beneath that burning sun, Felipe and Truxill had brought down to their hut many scores of tortoises, and tried out the oil, when, elated with their good success, and to reward themselves for such hard work, they, too hastily, made a catamaran, or Indian raft, much used on the Spanish main, and merrily started a fishing trip just without a long reef with many jagged gaps, running parallel with the shore, about half a mile from it. By some bad tide or hap—or natural negligence of joyfulness (for though they could not be heard, yet by their gestures they seemed singing at the time), forced in deep water against that iron bar—the ill-made catamaran was overset, and came all to pieces; when, dashed by broad-chested swells between their broken logs and the sharp teeth of the reef, both adventurers perished before Hunilla's eyes.

Before Hunilla's eyes they sank. The real woe of this event passed before her sight as some sham tragedy on the stage. She was seated on a rude bower among the withered thickets, crowning a lofty cliff, a little back from the beach. The thickets were so disposed, that in looking upon the sea at large she peered out from among the branches as from the lattice of a high bal-cony. But, upon the day we speak of here, the better to watch the adventure of those two hearts she loved, Hunilla had withdrawn the branches to one side and held them so. They formed an oval frame through which the bluey boundless sea rolled like a painted one. And there, the invisible painter painted to her view the wave-tossed and disjointed raft, its once level logs slantingly unheaved, as raking masts, and the four struggling arms undistin-guishable among them; and then all subsided into smooth-flowing creamy waters, slowly drifting the splintered wreck; while first and last, no sound of any sort was heard. Death in a silent picture; a dream of the eye; such vanishing shapes as the mirage shows.

So instant was the scene, so trance-like its mild pictorial effect, so distant from her blasted tower and her common sense of things, that Hunilla gazed and gazed, nor raised a finger or a wail. But as good to sit thus dumb, in stupor staring on that dumb show, for all that otherwise might be done. With half a mile of sea between, could her two enchanted arms aid those four fated ones? The distance long, the time one sand. After the lightning is beheld, what fool shall ever stay the thunderbolt? Felipe's body was washed ashore, but Truxill's never came; only his gay, braided hat of golden straw— that same sunflower thing he waved to her, pushing from the strand—and now, to the last gallant, it still saluted her. But Felipe's body floated to the marge, with one arm encirclingly outstretched. Lock-jawed in grim death, the lover-husband softly clasped his bride—true to her even in death's dream. Ah, Heaven, when man thus keeps his faith, wilt thou be faithless who created the faithful one? But they cannot break faith who never plighted it.

It needs not be said what nameless misery now wrapped the lonely widow. In telling her own story she passed this almost entirely over, simply recounting the event. Construe the comment of her features as you might; from her mere words little would you have weened that Hunilla was herself the heroine of her tale. But not thus did she defraud us of our tears. All hearts bled that grief could be so brave.

She but showed us her soul's lid, and the strange ciphers thereon engraved; all within, with pride's timidity, was withheld. Yet was there one exception. Holding out her small olive hand before our captain, she said in mild and slowest Spanish, "Señor, I buried him:" then paused, struggled as against the writhed coilings of a snake, and cringing suddenly, leaped up, repeating in impassioned pain. "I buried him, my life, my soul!"

Doubtless it was by half-unconscious, automatic motions of her hands, that this heavy-hearted one performed the final offices for Felipe, and planted a rude cross of withered sticks—no green ones might be had—as the head of that lonely grave, where rested now in lasting uncomplaint and quiet haven he whom untranquil seas had overthrown.

But some dull sense of another body that should be interred, of another cross that should hallow another grave—unmade as yet; some dull anxiety and pain touching her undiscovered brother now haunted the oppressed Hunilla. Her hands fresh from the burial earth, she slowly went back to the beach, with unshaped purposes wandered there, her spellbound eye bent upon the incessant waves. But they bore nothing to her but a dirge, which maddened her to think that murderers should mourn. As time went by, and these things came less dreamingly to her mind, the strong persuasions of her Romish faith, which sets peculiar store by consecrated urns, prompted her to resume in waking earnest that pious search which had but been begun as in somnambulism. Day after day, week after week, she trod the cindery beach, till at length a double motive edged every eager glance. With equal longing she now looked for the living and the dead; the brother and the captain; alike vanished, never to return. Little accurate note of time had Hunilla taken under such emotions as were hers, and little, outside herself, served for calendar or dial. As to poor Crusoe in the self-same sea, no saint's bell pealed forth the lapse of week or month; each day went by unchallenged; no chanticleer announced those sultry dawns, no lowing herds those poisonous nights. All wonted and steadily recurring sounds, human or humanized by sweet fellowship with man, but one stirred that torrid trance,—the cry of dogs; save which nought but the rolling sea invaded it, an all pervading monotone; and to the widow that was the least loved voice she could have heard.

No wonder that as her thoughts now wandered to the unreturning ship, and were beaten back again, the hope against hope so struggled in her soul, that at length she desperately said, "Not yet, not yet; my foolish heart runs on too fast." She forced patience for some further weeks. But to those whom earth's sure indraft draws, patience or impatience is still the same.

Hunilla now sought to settle precisely in her mind, to an hour, how long it was since the ship had sailed; and then, with the same precision, how long a space remained to pass. But this proved impossible. What present day or month it was she could not say. Time was her labyrinth, in which Hunilla was entirely lost.

And now follows—

Against my own purposes a pause descends upon me here. One knows not whether nature doth not impose some secrecy upon him who has been privy to certain things. At least, it is to be doubted whether it be good to blazon such. If some books are deemed most baneful and their sale forbid, how then with deadlier facts, not dreams of doting men? Those whom books will hurt will not be proof against events. Events, not books, should be forbid. But in all things man sows upon the wind, which bloweth just there whither it listeth; for ill or good man cannot know. Often ill comes from the good, as good from ill.

When Hunilla—

Dire sight it is to see some silken beast long dally with a golden lizard ere she devour. More terrible, to see how feline Fate will sometimes dally with a human soul, and by a nameless magic make it repulse one sane despair with another which is but mad. Unwittingly I imp this cat-like thing, sporting with the heart of him who reads; for if he feel not, he does read in vain.

—"The ship sails this day, to-day," at last said Hunilla to herself; "this gives me certain time to stand on; without certainty I go mad. In loose ignorance I have hoped and hoped, now in firm knowledge I will but wait. Now I live and no longer perish in bewilderings. Holy Virgin, aid me! Thou wilt waft back the ship. Oh, past length of weary weeks—all to be dragged over—to buy the certainty of to-day, I freely give ye, though I tear ye from me!"

As mariners tossed in tempest on some desolate ledge patch them a boat out of the remnants of their vessel's wreck, and launch it in the self-same waves—see here Hunilla, this lone ship-wrecked soul, out of treachery invoking trust. Humanity, thou strong thing. I worship thee, not in the laurelled victor, but in this vanquished one.

Truly, Hunilla leaned upon a reed, a real one; no metaphor; a real Eastern reed. A piece of hollow cane, drifted from unknown isles, and found upon the beach, its once jagged ends rubbed smoothly even as by sandpaper; its golden glazing gone. Long ground between the sea and land, upper and nether stone, the unvarnished substance was filed bare, and wore another polish now, one with itself, the polish of its agony. Circular lines at intervals cut all round this surface, divided it into six panels of unequal length. In the first were scored the days, each tenth one marked by a longer and deeper notch; the second was scored for the number of sea-fowl eggs for sustenance, picked out from the rocky nests; the third, how many fish had been caught from the shore, the fourth, how many small tortoises found inland; the fifth, how many days of sun; the sixth, of clouds, which last, of the two, was the greater one. Long night of busy numbering, misery's mathematics, to weary her too-wakeful soul to sleep; yet sleep for that was none.

The panel of the days was deeply worn, the long tenth notches half effaced, as alphabets of the blind. Ten thousand times the longing widow had traced her finger over the bamboo—dull flute, which played on, gave no sound—as if counting birds flown by in air, would hasten tortoises creeping through the woods.

After the one hundred and eightieth day no further mark was seen; that last one was the faintest, as the first the deepest.

"There were more days," said our Captain; "many, many more; why did you not go on and notch them too, Hunilla?"

"Señor, ask me not."

"And meantime, did no other vessel pass the isle?"

"Nay, Señor;—but—"

"You do not speak; but *what* Hunilla?"

"Ask me not, Señor."

"You saw ships pass, far away; you waved to them; they passed on;—was that it, Hunilla?"

"Señor, be it as you say."

Braced against her woe, Hunilla would not—durst not—trust the weakness of her tongue. Then when our Captain asked whether any whale-boats had—

But no, I will not file this thing complete for scoffing souls to quote, and call it firm proof upon their side. The half shall here remain untold. Those two unnamed events which befell Hunilla on this isle, let them abide between her and her God. In nature, as in law, it may be libellous to speak some truths.

Still, how it was that, although our vessel had lain three days anchored nigh the isle, its one human tenant should not have discovered us till just upon the point of sailing, never to revisit so lone and far a spot; this needs explaining ere the sequel come.

The place where the French captain had landed the little party was on the farther and opposite end of the isle. There too it was that they had afterwards built their hut. Nor did the widow in her solitude desert the spot where her loved ones had dwelt with her, and where the dearest of the twain now slept his last long sleep, and all her plaints awaked him not, and he of husbands the most faithful during life.

Now, high broken land rises between the opposite extremities of the isle. A ship anchored at one side is invisible from the other. Neither is the isle so small but a considerable company might wander for days through the wilderness of one side, and never be seen, or their halloos heard, by any stranger holding aloof on the other. Hence Hunilla, who naturally associated the possible coming of ships with her own part of the isle, might to the end have remained quite ignorant of the presence of our vessel, were it not for a mysterious presentiment, borne to her, so our mariners averred, by this isle's enchanted air. Nor did the widow's answer undo the thought.

"How did you come to cross the isle this morning then, Hunilla?" said our Captain.

"Señor, something came flittering by me. It touched my cheek, my heart, Señor."

"What do you say, Hunilla?"

"I have said, Señor; something came through the air."

It was a narrow chance. For when in crossing the isle Hunilla gained the high land in the centre, she must then for the first have perceived our masts, and also marked that their sails were being loosed, perhaps even heard the echoing chorus of the windlass song. The strange ship was about to sail, and she behind. With all haste she now descends the height on the hither side, but soon loses sight of the ship among the sunken jungles at the mountains base. She struggles on through the withered branches, which seek at every step to bar her path, till she comes to the isolated rock, still some way from the water. This she climbs, to reassure herself. The ship is still in plainest sight. But now, worn out with over tension, Hunilla all but faints; she fears to step down from her giddy perch; she is feign to pause, there where she is, and as a last resort catches the turban from her head, unfurls and waves it over the jungles towards us.

During the telling of her story the mariners formed a voiceless circle round Hunilla and the Captain; and when at length the word was given to man the fastest boat, and pull round to the isle's thither side to bring away Hunilla's chest and the tortoise-oil—such alacrity of both cheery and sad obedience seldom before was seen. Little ado was made. Already the anchor had been recommitted to the bottom and the ship swung calmly to it.

But Hunilla insisted upon accompanying the boat as indispensable pilot to her hidden hut. So, being refreshed with the best the steward could supply, she started with us. Nor did ever any wife of the most famous admiral in her husband's barge receive more silent reverence of respect, than poor Hunilla from this boat's crew.

Rounding many a vitreous cape and bluff, in two hours' time we shot inside the fatal reef; wound into a secret cove, looked up along a green many-gabled lava wall, and saw the island's solitary dwelling.

It hung upon an impending cliff, sheltered on two sides by tangled thickets, and half-screened from view in front by juttings of the rude stairway, which climbed the precipice from the sea. Built of canes, it was thatched with long, mildewed grass. It seemed an abandoned hayrick, whose haymakers were now no more. The roof inclined but one way; the eaves coming to within two feet of the ground. And here was a simple apparatus to collect the dews, or rather doubly-distilled and finest winnowed rains, which, in mercy or in mockery, the night skies sometimes drop upon these blighted Encantadas. All along beneath the eave, a spotted sheet, quite weather-stained, was spread, pinned to short, upright stakes, set in the shallow sand. A small clinker, thrown into the cloth, weighed its middle down, thereby straining all moisture unto a calabash placed below. This vessel supplied each drop of water ever drunk upon the isle by the Cholos. Hunilla told us the calabash would sometimes, but not often, be half filled over night. It held six quarts, perhaps. "But," said she, "we were used to thirst. At Sandy Payta, where I live, no shower from heaven ever fell; all the water there is brought on mules from the inland vales."

Tied among the thickets were some twenty moaning tortoises, supplying Hunilla's lonely larder; while hundreds of vast tableted black bucklers, like displaced, shattered tombstones of dark slate, were also scattered round. These were the skeleton backs of those great tortoises from which Felipe and Truxill had made their precious oil. Several large calabashes and two goodly kegs were filled with it. In a pot near by were the caked crusts of a quantity which had been permitted to evaporate. "They meant to have strained it off next day," said Hunilla, as she turned aside.

I forgot to mention the most singular sight of all, though the first that greeted us after landing; memory keeps not in all things to the order of occurrence.

Some ten small, soft-haired, ringleted dogs, of a beautiful breed, peculiar to Peru, set up a concert of glad welcomings when we gained the beach, which was responded to by Hunilla. Some of these dogs had, since her windowhood, been born upon the isle, the progeny of the two brought from Payta. Owing to the jagged steeps and pitfalls, tortuous thickets, sunken clefts and perilous intricacies of all sorts in the interior, Hunilla, admonished by the loss of one favourite among them, never allowed these delicate creatures to follow her in her occasional bird's-nests climbs and other wanderings; so that, through long habituation, they offered not to follow, when that morning she crossed the land; and her own soul was then too full of other things to heed their lingering behind. Yet, all along she had so clung to them, that, besides what moisture they lapped up at early daybreak from the small scoop-holes among the adjacent rocks, she had shared the dew of her calabash among them; never laying by any considerable store against those prolonged and utter droughts, which in some disastrous seasons warp these isles.

Having pointed out, at our desire, what few things she would like transported to the ship—her chest, the oil, not omitting the live tortoises which she intended for a grateful present to our Captain—we immediately set to work, carrying them to the boat down the long, sloping stair of deeply-shadowed rock. While my comrades were thus employed, I looked, and Hunilla had disappeared.

It was not curiosity alone, but, it seems to me, something different mingled with it, which prompted me to drop my tortoises and once more gaze slowly around. I remembered the husband buried by Hunilla's hands. A narrow pathway led into a dense part of the thickets. Following it through many mazes, I came out upon a small, round, open space, deeply chambered there.

The mound rose in the middle; a bare heap of finest sand, like that unverdured heap found at the bottom of an hour-glass run out. At its head stood the cross of withered sticks; the dry, peeled bark still fraying from it; its transverse limb tied up with rope, and forlornly adroop in the silent air.

Hunilla was partly prostrate upon the grave; her dark head bowed and lost in her long, loosened Indian hair; her hands extended to the cross-foot, with a little brass crucifix clasped between; a crucifix worn featureless, like an ancient graven knocker long plied in vain. She did not see me, and I made no noise but slid aside and left the spot.

A few moments, ere all was ready for our going, she reappeared among us. I looked into her eyes, but saw no tear. There was something which seemed strangely haughty in her air, and yet it was the air of woe. A Spanish and an Indian grief, which would not visibly lament. Pride's height in vain abased to proneness on the rock; nature's pride subduing nature's torture.

Like pages the small and silken dogs surrounded her, as she slowly descended towards the beach. She caught the two most eager creatures in her arms:—"Mia Teeta! Mia Tometeeta!" and fondling them, inquired how many could we take on board.

The mate commanded the boat's crew; not a hard-hearted man but his way of life had been such that in most things, even in the smallest, simple utility was his leading motive.

"We cannot take them all, Hunilla; our supplies are short; the winds are unreliable; we may be a good many days going to Tombez. So take those you have, Hunilla; but no more."

She was in the boat; the oarsmen too were seated; all save one, who stood ready to push off and then spring himself. With the sagacity of their race, the dogs now seemed aware that they were in the very instant of being deserted upon a barren strand. The gunwales of the boat were high; its prow—presented inland—was lifted; so, owing to the water, which they seemed instinctively to shun, the dogs could not well leap into the little craft. But their busy paws had scraped the prow, as it had been some farmer's door shutting them out from shelter in a winter storm. A clamorous agony of alarm. They did not howl, or whine; they all but spoke.

"Push off! Give way!" cried the mate. The boat gave one heavy drag and lurch, and next moment shot swiftly from the beach, turned on her heel, and sped. The dogs ran howling along the water's marge; now pausing to gaze at the flying boat, then motioning as if to leap in chase, but mysteriously withheld themselves; and again ran howling along the beach. Had they been human beings hardly would they have more vividly inspired the sense of desolation. The oars were plied as confederate feathers of two wings. No one spoke. I looked back upon the beach, and then upon Hunilla, but her face was set in a stern dusky calm. The dogs crouching in her lap vainly licked her rigid hands. She never looked behind her; but sat motionless, till we turned a promontory of the coast and lost all sights and sounds astern. She seemed as one who, having experienced the sharpest of mortal pangs, was henceforth content to have all lesser heartstrings riven, one by one. To Hunilla, pain seemed so necessary, that pain in other beings—though by love and sympathy made her own—was unrepiningly to be borne. A heart of yearning in a frame of steel. A heart of earthly yearning, frozen by the frost which falleth from the sky.

The sequel is soon told. After a long passage, vexed by calms and baffling winds, we made the little port of Tombez in Peru, there to recruit the ship. Payta was not very distant. Our captain sold the tortoise oil to a Tombez merchant; and adding to the silver a contribution from all hands, gave it to our silent passenger, who knew not what the mariners had done.

The last seen of lone Hunilla she was passing into Payta town, riding upon a small gray ass; and before her on the ass's shoulders, she eyed the jointed workings of the beast's armorial cross.

From Battle-Pieces[1]

THE PORTENT[2]

Hanging from the beam,
　Slowly swaying (such the law),
Gaunt the shadow on your green,
　Shenandoah!
The cut is on the crown　　　　　　　　　　　　　5
　(Lo, John Brown),
And the stabs shall heal no more.

Hidden in the cap
　Is the anguish none can draw;
So your future veils its face,　　　　　　　　　　　10
　Shenandoah!
But the streaming beard is shown
　(Weird John Brown),
The meteor of the war.

1859　　　　　　　　　　　　　　　　　　　　　1866

---

[1] *Battle-Pieces and Aspects of the War* (1866) represents Melville's deep sensitivity to the Civil War. Although he never fought, he followed the war closely and was deeply troubled by the threat it posed to the nation. The following poems, as Melville indicated in his preface to the volume, "originated in an impulse imparted by the fall of Richmond."

[2] John Brown (1800–1859) captured the arse-nal at Harper's Ferry, Virginia, on October 16, 1859. Together with 21 followers, he was attempting to foment a slave insurrection, but he failed. On December 2, 1859, he was hanged on charges of "treason to the commonwealth" and of "conspiring with slaves to commit treason and murder." See pp. 1803–1804 for Brown's last statement to the court.

THE MARCH INTO VIRGINIA[1]

ENDING IN THE FIRST MANASSAS
(JULY 1861)

Did all the lets and bars appear
    To every just or larger end,
Whence should come the trust and cheer?
    Youth must its ignorant impulse lend—
Age finds place in the rear.   5
    All wars are boyish, and are fought by boys,
The champions and enthusiasts of the state:
    Turbid ardors and vain joys
        Not barrenly abate—
Stimulants to the power mature,   10
    Preparatives of fate.

Who here forecasteth the event?
What heart but spurns at precedent
And warnings of the wise,
Contemned foreclosures of surprise?   15
The banners play, the bugles call,
The air is blue and prodigal.
    No berrying party, pleasure-wooed,
No picnic party in the May,
Ever went less loth than they   20
    Into that leafy neighborhood.
In Bacchic[2] glee they file toward Fate,
Moloch's[3] uninitiate;
Expectancy, and glad surmise
Of battle's unknown mysteries.   25
All they feel is this: 'tis glory,
A rapture sharp, though transitory,
Yet lasting in belaureled story.
So they gayly go to fight,
Chatting left and laughing right.   30

---

[1] This was the first major engagement of the Civil War, on July 21, 1861, along Bull Run near Manassas Junction, a railroad depot between Richmond and the Shenandoah Valley. This battle resulted in a northern disaster as General Beauregard routed 30,000 Union soldiers. As Hennig Cohen has pointed out, this poem captures many of the dualities present in Melville's poetry: will and necessity, action and ideas, youth and age, and good and evil.

[2] Bacchus was the name given to Dionysus, the Greek god of wine.

[3] See Lev. xviii:21 and Amos v:26. The worship of Moloch required the sacrifice of children by burning.

But some who this blithe mood present,
   As on in lightsome files they fare,
Shall die experienced ere three days be spent—
   Perish, enlightened by the vollied glare;
Or shame survive, and like to adamant,   35
   The throe of Second Manassas share.

                       1861

MALVERN HILL[1]

Ye elms that wave on Malvern Hill
   In prime of morn and May,
Recall ye how McClellan's men
      Here stood at bay?[2]
While deep within yon forest dim   5
   Our rigid comrades lay—
Some with the cartridge in their mouth,
Others with fixed arms lifted South—
      Invoking so
The cypress glades? Ah wilds of woe!   10

The spires of Richmond, late beheld
   Through rifts in musket-haze,
Were closed from view in clouds of dust
      On leaf-walled ways,
Where streamed our wagons in caravan;   15
   And the Seven Nights and Days
Of march and fast, retreat and fight,
Pinched our grimed faces to ghastly plight—
      Does the elm wood
Recall the haggard beards of blood?   20

The battle-smoked flag, with stars eclipsed,
   We followed (it never fell!)—
In silence husbanded our strength—
      Received their yell;
Till on this slope we patient turned   25
   With cannon ordered well;
Reverse we proved was not defeat;
But ah, the sod what thousands meet!—
      Does Malvern Wood
Bethink itself, and muse and brood?   30

---

[1] The site of a battle on July 1, 1862, in which the northern General, G. B. McClellan, defeated Robert E. Lee.

[2] Refers to the battle preceding Malvern Hill.

> We elms of Malvern Hill
> Remember everything;
> But sap the twig will fill:
> Wag the world how it will.
> Leaves must be green in Spring.[3]

35

1862   1866

[3] *As You Like It*, II, vii, 23.

SHILOH[1]

A REQUIEM
(APRIL 1862)

Skimming lightly, wheeling still,
   The swallows fly low[2]
Over the field in clouded days,
   The forest-field of Shiloh—
Over the field where April rain   5
Solaced the parched one stretched in pain
Through the pause of night
That followed the Sunday fight
   Around the church of Shiloh—
The church so lone, the log-built one,   10
That echoed to many a parting groan
     And natural prayer
   Of dying foemen mingled there—
Foemen at morn, but friends at eve—
   Fame or country least their care: 15
(What like a bullet can undeceive!)
   But now they lie low,
While over them the swallows skim,
   And all is hushed at Shiloh.

1866

[1] Shiloh, Tennessee, is located near the Mississippi and Tennessee border and the scene of a furious battle on April 6, 1862, between the Federal armies, led by Grant and Buell, and the Confederates, under Johnston and Beauregard. There were great losses on both sides.
   The biblical Shiloh was a sanctuary town and a resting place of the Ark of the Covenant.

[2] Hennig Cohen points out that in Renaissance painting the swallow appears as the symbol of the Incarnation in Annunciation and Nativity scenes. It is also connected with the Resurrection because of the belief that the swallow hibernated in the mind from which it was born each spring.

From Timoleon

AFTER THE PLEASURE PARTY

LINES TRACED UNDER AN IMAGE OF AMOR[1] THREATENING

Fear me, virgin whosoever
Taking pride from love exempt,
Fear me, slighted. Never, never
Brave me, nor my fury tempt:
Downy wings, but wroth they beat   5
Tempest even in reason's seat.

Behind the house the upland falls
With many an ordorous tree—
White marbles gleaming through green halls,
Terrace by terrace, down and down,   10
And meets the starlit Mediterranean Sea.

'Tis Paradise. In such an hour
Some pangs that rend might take release.
Nor less perturbed who keeps this bower
Of balm, nor finds balsamic peace?   15
From whom the passionate words in vent
After long revery's discontent?

Tired of the homeless deep,
Look how their flight yon hurrying billows urge,
Hitherward but to reap   20
Passive repulse from the iron-bound verge!
Insensate, can they never know
'Tis mad to wreck the impulsion so?

An art of memory is, they tell:
But to forget! forget the glade   25
Wherein Fate sprung Love's ambuscade,
To flout pale years of cloistral life
And flush me in this sensuous strife.
'Tis Vesta[2] struck with Sappho's[3] smart,
No fable her delirious leap: 30
With more of cause in desperate heart,
Myself could take it—but to sleep!

---

[1] Latin word for sexual love; Cupid, or in Greek, Eros.

[2] The Roman goddess of the hearth-fire. Her fire was kept burning by the vestal virgins.

[3] Sappho was a poet who lived in Lesbos and who allegedly drowned herself because of an unrequited love.

Now first I feel, what all may ween,
That soon or late, if faded e'en,
One's sex asserts itself. Desire,   35
The dear desire through love to sway,
Is like the Geysers that aspire—
Through cold obstruction win their fervid way.
But baffled here—to take disdain,
To feel rule's instinct, yet not reign;   40
To dote, to come to this drear shame—
Hence the winged blaze that sweeps my soul
Like prairie fires that spurn control,
Where withering weeds incense the flame.

And kept I long heaven's watch for this,   45
Contemning love, for this, even this?
O terrace chill in Northern air,
O reaching ranging tube I placed
Against yon skies, and fable chased
Till, fool, I hailed for sister there   50
Starred Cassiopea[4] in Golden Chair.
In dream I throned me, nor I saw
In cell the idiot crowned with straw.

And yet, ah yet scarce ill I reigned,
Through self-illusion self-sustained,   55
When now—enlightened, undeceived—
What gain I barrenly bereaved!
Than this can be yet lower decline—
Envy and spleen, can these be mine?

The peasant girl demure that trod   60
Beside our wheels that climbed the way,
And bore along a blossoming rod
That looked the sceptre of May-day—
On her—to fire this petty hell,
His softened glance how moistly fell!   65
The cheat! on briars her buds were strung;
And wiles peeped forth from mien how meek.
The innocent bare-foot! young, so young!
To girls, strong man's a novice weak.
To tell such beads! And more remain,   70
Sad rosary of belittling pain.

[4] In classical mythology, the wife of an Ethiopian king and the mother of Andromeda. After her death she was put in the skies in the constellation of stars that bears her name. The constellation supposedly resembles a chair.

When after lunch and sallies gay,
Like the Decameron folk[5] we lay
In sylvan groups; and I—let be!
O, dreams he, can he dream that one   75
Because not roseate feels no sun?
The plain lone bramble thrills with Spring
As much as vines that grapes shall bring.

Me now fair studies charm no more.
Shall great thoughts writ, or high themes sung   80
Damask wan cheeks—unlock his arm
About some radiant ninny flung?
How glad with all my starry lore,
I'd buy the veriest wanton's rose
Would but my bee therein repose.   85

Could I remake me! or set free
This sexless bound in sex, then plunge
Deeper than Sappho, in a lunge
Piercing Pan's[6] paramount mystery!
For, Nature, in no shallow surge   90
Against thee either sex may urge,
Why hast thou made us but in halves—
Co-relatives? This makes us slaves.
If these co-relatives never meet
Self-hood itself seems incomplete.   95
And such the dicing of blind fate
Few matching halves[7] here meet and mate.
What Cosmic jest or Anarch blunder
The human integral clove asunder
And shied the fractions through life's gate?   100

Ye stars that long your votary knew
Rapt in her vigil, see me here!
Whither is gone the spell ye threw
When rose before me Cassiopea?

---

[5] The characters in Boccaccio's *Decameron* (1353).

[6] In Greek mythology, the god of pastures and flocks. Melville has him represent the mystery of nature.

[7] Refers to the myth in Plato's *Symposium* that in primeval times human beings were of both sexes and Zeus, because of their pride, divided them in two. Since then they have been unhappy, separated as man and woman, and each has been in search of the other.

Usurped on by love's stronger reign—   105
But lo, your very selves do wane:
Light breaks—truth breaks! Silvered no more,
But chilled by dawn that brings the gale
Shivers yon bramble above the vale,
And disillusion opens all the shore.   110

    One knows not if Urania[8] yet
The pleasure-party may forget;
Or whether she lived down the strain
Of turbulent heart and rebel brain;
For Amor so resents a slight,   115
And her's had been such haught disdain,
He long may wreak his boyish spite,
And boy-like, little reck the pain.

    One knows not, no. But late in Rome
(For queens discrowned a congruous home)   120
Entering Albani's porch[9] she stood
Fixed by an antique pagan stone
Colossal carved. No anchorite seer,
Not Thomas à Kempis,[10] monk austere,
Religious more are in their tone;   125
Yet far, how far from Christian heart
That form august of heathen Art.
Swayed by its influence, long she stood,
Till surged emotion seething down,
She rallied and this mood she won: 130

    Languid in frame for me,
To-day by Mary's convent shrine,
Touched by her picture's moving plea
In that poor nerveless hour of mine,
I mused—A wandered still must grieve.   135
Half I resolved to kneel and believe,
Believe and submit the veil take on.
But thee, armed Virgin![11] less benign,
Thee now I invoke, thou mightier one.

[8] The Greek muse of astronomy.

[9] Porch of a villa in Rome that Melville had
visited in 1857.

[10] A monastic scholar (1385-1471) who
wrote *The Imitation of Christ*.

[11] Athena, goddess of wisdom, whose statue
is also at the Villa Albani.

Helmeted woman—if such term   140
Befit thee, far from strife
Of that which makes the sexual feud
And clogs the aspirant life—
O self-reliant, strong and free,
Thou in whom power and peace unite,   145
Transcender! raise me up to thee,
Raise me and arm me!

              Fond appeal.
For never passion peace shall bring,
Nor Art inanimate for long
Inspire. Nothing may help or heal   150
While Amor incensed remembers wrong.
Vindictive, not himself he'll spare;
For scope to give his vengeance play
Himself he'll blaspheme and betray.

   Then for Urania, virgins everywhere,   155
O pray! Example take too, and have care.

                                  1891

ART

In placid hours well-pleased we dream
Of many a brave unbodied scheme.
But form to lend, pulsed life create,
What unlike things must meet and mate:
A flame to melt—a wind to freeze;   5
Sad patience—joyous energies;
Humility—yet pride and scorn;
Instinct and study; love and hate;
Audacity—reverence. These must mate,
And fuse with Jacob's mystic heart,   10
To wrestle with the angel—Art.[1]

1891   1891

[1] Jacob wrestled with an angel all night until
he was convinced that it was God (Gen.
xxxii:24–30).

Billy Budd[1]
Sailor

AN INSIDE NARRATIVE[2]

DEDICATED

TO

JACK CHASE[3]

ENGLISHMAN

Wherever that great heart may now be
Here on Earth or harbored in Paradise

Captain of the Maintop
in the year 1843
in the U. S. Frigate
United States

1

In the time before steamships, or then more frequently than now, a stroller along the docks of any considerable seaport would occasionally have his attention arrested by a group of bronzed mariners, man-of-war's men or merchant sailors in holiday attire, ashore on liberty. In certain instances they

[1] *Billy Budd* was not discovered among Melville's manuscripts until 1924. It was edited and published as an additional volume to *The Works* (1922-1924) and then edited definitively in 1962 by Harrison Hayford and Merton M. Sealts, Jr. The Hayford and Sealts edition, reprinted below, is particularly valuable, since it presents a reading text and a genetic text, indicating Melville's craftsmanship as he revised the novel from 1886 until 1891.

Billy Budd has been interpreted as "a catastrophe of innocence"; a "tragedy of justice"; a "testament of acceptance" or of "reconciliation" or of "resistance"; and a "ceremony of innocence." It is concerned with all of these subjects as well as with political justice, expedience, and absolute morality. The tale is in sharp contrast to the early ones, which record various acts of rebellion against authority. The facts of *Billy Budd*—the death of innocence, the historical distortion of Billy's actions, the sudden, ostensibly meaningless slaying of Captain Vere

by the *Atheist*—prepare the reader for a melancholic, bitter conclusion; but the final tone is not depressing, and largely because of the tragic terms in which the story is conveyed. In the deaths of Billy Budd and Captain Vere, Melville expresses his faith in the human spirit, however skeptical he may be about humanity, however muted in his faith.

[2] No definitive interpretation has been made of this phrase. It probably refers to the facts behind the story. *Billy Budd* was partially based upon the case of the *Somers*, an American naval brig, in 1842. A young sailor, Philip Spencer, was accused and convicted of mutiny and then hanged on board, along with two others. The executive officer who presided over the court that meted out the punishment was Guert Gansevoort, Melville's cousin. The case created a stir in the newspapers, particularly in terms of the justice or injustice of the harsh sentence.

[3] Jack Chase is described more fully in *White-Jacket.*

would flank, or like a bodyguard quite surround, some superior figure of their own class, moving along with them like Aldebaran[4] among the lesser lights of his constellation. That signal object was the "Handsome Sailor" of the less prosaic time alike of the military and merchant navies. With no perceptible trace of the vainglorious about him, rather with the offhand unaffectedness of natural regality, he seemed to accept the spontaneous homage of his shipmates.

A somewhat remarkable instance recurs to me. In Liverpool, now half a century ago, I saw under the shadow of the great dingy streetwall of Prince's Dock (an obstruction long since removed) a common sailor so intensely black that he must needs have been a native African of the unadulterate blood of Ham—a symmetric figure much above the average height. The two ends of a gay silk handkerchief thrown loose about the neck danced upon the displayed ebony of his chest, in his ears were big hoops of gold, and a Highland bonnet with a tartan band set off his shapely head. It was a hot noon in July; and his face, lustrous with perspiration, beamed with barbaric good humor. In jovial sallies right and left, his white teeth flashing into view, he rollicked along, the center of a company of his shipmates. These were made up of such an assortment of tribes and complexions as would have well fitted them to be marched up by Anacharsis Cloots[5] before the bar of the first French Assembly as Representatives of the Human Race. At each spontaneous tribute rendered by the wayfarers to this black pagon of a fellow— the tribute of a pause and stare, and less frequently an exclamation—the motley retinue showed that they took that sort of pride in the evoker of it which the Assyrian priests doubtless showed for their grand sculptured Bull when the faithful prostrated themselves.

To return. If in some cases a bit of a nautical Murat[6] in setting forth his person ashore, the Handsome Sailor of the period in question evinced nothing of the dandified Billy-be-Dam, an amusing character all but extinct now, but occasionally to be encountered, and in a form yet more amusing than the original, at the tiller of the boats on the tempestuous Erie Canal or, more likely, vaporing in the groggeries along the towpath. Invariably a proficient in his perilous calling, he was also more or less of a mighty boxer or wrestler. It was strength and beauty. Tales of his prowess were recited. Ashore he was the champion; afloat the spokesman; on every suitable occasion always foremost. Close-reefing topsails in a gale, there he was, astride the weather yardarm-end, foot in the Flemish horse as stirrup, both hands tugging at the earing as at a bridle, in very much the attidue of young Alexander curbing the fiery Bucephalus.[7] A superb figure, tossed up as by the horns of Taurus

[4] Regarded by the ancients as the "eye" of the Bull, the constellation Taurus.

[5] The Baron de Cloots (1755-1794) made a declaration of the rights of man before the French Assembly.

[6] Joachim Murat (1767?-1815) was one of Napoleon's generals. As the King of Naples he was known as "the Daddy King."

[7] War horse of Alexander the Great (356-323 B.C.)

against the thunderous sky, cheerily hallooing to the strenuous file along the spar.

The moral nature was seldom out of keeping with the physical make. Indeed, except as toned by the former, the comeliness and power, always attractive in masculine conjunction, hardly could have drawn the sort of honest homage the Handsome Sailor in some examples received from his less gifted associates.

Such a cynosure, at least in aspect, and something such too in nature, though with important variations made apparent as the story proceeds, was welkin-eyed Billy Budd—or Baby Budd, as more familiarly, under circumstances hereafter to be given, he at last came to be called—aged twenty-one, a foretopman of the British fleet toward the close of the last decade of the eighteenth century. It was not very long prior to the time of the narration that follows that he had entered the King's service, having been impressed on the Narrow Seas from a homeward-bound English merchantman into a seventy-four outward bound, H. M. S. *Bellipotent;* which ship, as was not unusual in those hurried days, having been obliged to put to sea short of her proper complement of men. Plump upon Billy at first sight in the gangway the boarding officer, Lieutenant Ratcliffe, pounced, even before the merchantman's crew was formally mustered on the quarter-deck for his deliberate inspection. And him only he elected. For whether it was because the other men when ranged before him showed to ill advantage after Billy, or whether he had some scruples in view of the merchantman's being rather shorthanded, however it might be, the officer contented himself with his first spontaneous choice. To the surprise of the ship's company, though much to the lieutenant's satisfaction, Billy made no demur. But, indeed, any demur would have been as idle as the protest of a goldfinch popped into a cage.

Noting this uncomplaining acquiescence, all but cheerful, one might say, the shipmaster turned a surprised glance of silent reproach at the sailor. The shipmaster was one of those worthy mortals found in every vocation, even the humbler ones—the sort of person whom everybody agrees in calling "a respectable man." And—nor so strange to report as it may appear to be—though a ploughman of the troubled waters, lifelong contending with the intractable elements, there was nothing this honest soul at heart loved better than simple peace and quiet. For the rest, he was fifty or thereabouts, a little inclined to corpulence, a prepossessing face, unwhiskered, and of an agreeable color—a rather full face, humanely intelligent in expression. On a fair day with a fair wind and all going well, a certain musical chime in his voice seemed to be the veritable unobstructed outcome of the innermost man. He had much prudence, much conscientiousness, and there were occasions when these virtues were the cause of overmuch disquietude in him. On a passage, so long as his craft was in any proximity to land, no sleep for Captain Graveling. He took to heart those serious responsibilities not so heavily borne by some shipmasters.

Now while Billy Budd was down in the forecastle getting his kit together, the *Bellipotent's* lieutenant, burly and bluff, nowise disconcerted by Captain Graveling's omitting to proffer the customary hospitalities on an occasion so unwelcome to him, an omission simply caused by preoccupation of thought, unceremoniously invited himself into the cabin, and also to a flask from the spirit locker, a receptacle which his experienced eye instantly discovered. In fact he was one of those sea dogs in whom all the hardship and peril of naval life in the great prolonged wars of his time never impaired the natural instinct for sensuous enjoyment. His duty he always faithfully did; but duty is sometimes a dry obligation, and he was for irrigating its aridity, whensoever possible, with a fertilizing decoction of strong waters. For the cabin's proprietor there was nothing left but to play the part of the enforced host with whatever grace and alacrity were practicable. As necessary adjuncts to the flask, he silently placed tumbler and water jug before the irrepressible guest. But excusing himself from partaking just then, he dismally watched the unembarrassed officer deliberately diluting his grog a little, then tossing it off in three swallows, pushing the empty tumbler away, yet not so far as to be beyond easy reach, at the same time settling himself in his seat and smacking his lips with high satisfaction, looking straight at the host.

These proceedings over, the master broke the silence; and there lurked a rueful reproach in the tone of his voice: "Lieutenant, you are going to take my best man from me, the jewel of 'em."

"Yes, I know," rejoined the other, immediately drawing back the tumbler preliminary to a replenishing. "Yes, I know. Sorry."

"Beg pardon, but you don't understand, Lieutenant. See here, now. Before I shipped that young fellow, my forecastle was a rat-pit of quarrels. It was black times, I tell you, aboard the *Rights* here. I was worried to that degree my pipe had no comfort for me. But Billy came; and it was like a Catholic priest striking peace in an Irish shindy. Not that he preached to them or said or did anything in particular; but a virtue went out of him, sugaring the sour ones. They took to him like hornets to treacle; all but the buffer of the gang, the big shaggy chap with the fire-red whiskers. He indeed, out of envy, perhaps, of the newcomer, and thinking such a "sweet and pleasant fellow," as he mockingly designated him to the others, could hardly have the spirit of a gamecock, must needs bestir himself in trying to get up an ugly row with him. Billy forebore with him and reasoned with him in a pleasant way—he is something like myself, Lieutenant, to whom aught like a quarrel is hateful—but nothing served. So, in the second dogwatch one day, the Red Whiskers in presence of the others, under pretense of showing Billy just whence a sirloin steak was cut—for the fellow had once been a butcher—insultingly gave him a dig under the ribs. Quick as lightning Billy let fly his arm. I dare say he never meant to do quite as much as he did, but anyhow he gave the burly fool a terrible drubbing. It took about half a minute, I should think. And, lord bless you, the lubber was astonished at the celerity. And will you believe it, Lieutenant, the Red Whiskers now really loves Billy—loves him, or is the biggest hypocrite that ever I heard of. But they all love him. Some of 'em do his washing, darn his old trousers for him; the carpenter is at odd times making a pretty little chest of drawers for him. Anybody will do anything for Billy Budd; and it's the happy family here. But now, Lieutenant, if that young fellow goes—I know how it will be aboard the *Rights*. Not again very soon shall I, coming up from dinner, lean over the capstan smoking a quiet pipe—no, not very soon again, I think. Ay, Lieutenant, you are going to take away the jewel of 'em; you are going to take away my peacemaker!" And with that the good soul had really some ado in checking a rising sob.

"Well," said the lieutenant, who had listened with amused interest to all this and now was waxing merry with his tipple; "well, blessed are the peacemakers, especially the fighting peacemakers. And such are the seventy-four beauties some of which you see poking their noses out of the portholes of yonder warship lying to for me," pointing through the cabin window at the *Bellipotent*. "But courage! Don't look so downhearted, man. Why, I pledge you in advance the royal approbation. Rest assured that His Majesty will be delighted to know that in a time when his hardtack is not sought for by sailors with such avidity as should be, a time also when some shipmasters privily resent the borrowing from them a tar or two for the service; His Majesty, I say, will be delighted to learn that *one* shipmaster at least cheerfully surrenders to the King the flower of his flock, a sailor who with equal loyalty makes no dissent.—But where's my beauty? Ah," looking through the cabin's open door, "here he comes; and, by Jove, lugging along his chest— Apollo with his portmanteau!—My man," stepping out to him, "you can't take that big box aboard a warship. The boxes there are mostly shot boxes. Put your duds in a bag, lad. Boot and saddle for the cavalryman, bag and hammock for the man-of-war's man."

The transfer from chest to bag was made. And, after seeing his man into the cutter and then following him down, the lieutenant pushed off from the *Rights-of-Man*.[8] That was the merchant ship's name, though by her master and crew abbreviated in sailor fashion into the *Rights*. The hardheaded Dundee owner was a staunch admirer of Thomas Paine, whose book in rejoinder to Burke's arraignment of the French Revolution had then been published for some time and had gone everywhere. In christening his vessel after the title of Paine's volume the man of Dundee was something like his contemporary shipowner, Stephen Girard[9] of Philadelphia, whose sympathies, alike with his native land and its liberal philosophers, he evinced by naming his ships after Voltaire, Diderot, and so forth.

But now, when the boat swept under the merchantman's stern, and officer and oarsmen were noting—some bitterly and others with a grin—the name emblazoned there; just then it was that the new recruit jumped up from the bow where the coxswain had directed him to sit, and waving hat to

---

[8] The title of the book by Thomas Paine. See p. 554.

[9] Girard (1750-1831) was a merchant and banker in Philadelphia.

his silent shipmates sorrowfully looking over at him from the taffrail, bade the lads a genial good-bye. Then, making a salutation as to the ship herself, "And good-bye to you too, old *Rights-of-Man.*"

"Down, sir!" roared the lieutenant, instantly assuming all the rigor of his rank, though with difficulty repressing a smile.

To be sure, Billy's action was a terrible breach of naval decorum. But in that decorum he had never been instructed; in consideration of which the lieutenant would hardly have been so energetic in reproof but for the concluding farewell to the ship. This he rather took as meant to convey a covert sally on the new recruit's part, a sly slur at impressment in general, and that of himself in especial. And yet, more likely, if satire it was in effect, it was hardly so by intention, for Billy, though happily endowed with the gaiety of high health, youth, and a free heart, was yet by no means of a satirical turn. The will to it and the sinister dexterity were alike wanting. To deal in double meanings and insinuations of any sort was quite foreign to his nature.

As to his enforced enlistment, that he seemed to take pretty much as he was wont to take any vicissitude of weather. Like the animals, though no philosopher, he was, without knowing it, practically a fatalist. And it may be that he rather liked this adventurous turn in his affairs, which promised an opening into novel scenes and martial excitements.

Aboard the *Bellipotent* our merchant sailor was forthwith rated as an able seaman and assigned to the starboard watch of the foretop. He was soon at home in the service, not at all disliked for his unpretentious good looks and a sort of genial happy-go-lucky air. No merrier man in his mess: in marked contrast to certain other individuals included like himself among the impressed portion of the ship's company; for these when not actively employed were sometimes, and more particularly in the last dogwatch when the drawing near of twilight induced revery, apt to fall into a saddish mood which in some partook of sullenness. But they were not so young as our foretopman, and no few of them must have known a hearth of some sort, others may have had wives and children left, too probably, in uncertain circumstances, and hardly any but must have had acknowledged kith and kin, while for Billy, as will shortly be seen, his entire family was practically invested in himself.

2

Though our new-made foretopman was well received in the top and on the gun decks, hardly here was he that cynosure he had previously been among those minor ship's companies of the merchant marine, with which companies only had he hitherto consorted.

He was young; and despite his all but fully developed frame, in aspect looked even younger than he really was, owing to a lingering adolescent expression in the as yet smooth face all but feminine in purity of natural complexion but where, thanks to his seagoing, the lily was quite suppressed and the rose had some ado visibly to flush through the tan.

To one essentially such a novice in the complexities of factitious life, the abrupt transition from his former and simpler sphere to the ampler and more knowing world of a great warship; this might well have abashed him had there been any conceit or vanity in his composition. Among her miscellaneous multitude, the *Bellipotent* mustered several individuals who however inferior in grade were of no common natural stamp, sailors more signally susceptive of that air which continuous martial discipline and repeated presence in battle can in some degree impart even to the average man. As the Handsome Sailor, Billy Budd's position aboard the seventy-four was something analogous to that of a rustic beauty transplanted from the provinces and brought into competition with the highborn dames of the court. But this change of circumstances he scarce noted. As little did he observe that something about him provoked an ambiguous smile in one or two harder faces among the bluejackets. Nor less unaware was he of the peculiar favorable effect his person and demeanor had upon the more intelligent gentlemen of the quarterdeck. Nor could this well have been otherwise. Cast in a mold peculiar to the finest physical examples of those Englishmen in whom the Saxon strain would seem not at all to partake of any Norman or other admixture, he showed in face that humane look of reposeful good nature which the Greek sculptor in some instances gave to his heroic strong man, Hercules. But this again was subtly modified by another and pervasive quality. The ear, small and shapely, the arch of the foot, the curve in mouth and nostril, even the indurated hand dyed to the orange-tawny of the toucan's[10] bill, a hand telling alike of the halyards and tar bucket; but, above all, something in the mobile expression, and every chance attitude and movement, something suggestive of a mother eminently favored by Love and the Graces; all this strangely indicated a lineage in direct contradiction to his lot. The mysteriousness here became less mysterious through a matter of fact elicited when Billy at the capstan was being formally mustered into the service. Asked by the officer, a small, brisk little gentleman as it chanced, among other questions, his place of birth, he replied, "Please, sir, I don't know."

"Don't know where you were born? Who was your father?"

"God knows, sir."

Struck by the straightforward simplicity of these replies, the officer next asked, "Do you know anything about your beginning?"

"No, sir. But I have heard that I was found in a pretty silk-lined basket hanging one morning from the knocker of a good man's door in Bristol."

"*Found*, say you? Well," throwing back his head and looking up and down the new recruit; "well, it turns out to have been a pretty good find. Hope they'll find some more like you, my man; the fleet sadly needs them."

Yes, Billy Budd was a foundling, a presumable by-blow,[11] and, evidently, no ignoble one. Noble descent was as evident in him as in a blood horse.

---

[10] A tropical bird whose beak is extremely large.   [11] Illegitimate child.

For the rest, with little or no sharpness of faculty or any trace of the wisdom of the serpent, nor yet quite a dove, he possessed that kind and degree of intelligence going along with the unconventional rectitude of a sound human creature, one to whom not yet has been proffered the questionable apple of knowledge. He was illiterate; he could not read, but he could sing, and like the illiterate nightingale was sometimes the composer of his own song.

Of self-consciousness he seemed to have little or none, or about as much as we may reasonably impute to a dog of Saint Bernard's breed.

Habitually living with the elements and knowing little more of the land than as a beach, or, rather, that portion of the terraqueous globe providentially set apart for dance-houses, doxies, and tapsters, in short what sailors call a "fiddler's green," his simple nature remained unsophisticated by those moral obliquities which are not in every case incompatible with that manufacturable thing known as respectability. But are sailors, frequenters of fiddlers' greens, without vices? No; but less often than with landsmen of their vices, so called, partake of crookedness of heart, seeming less to proceed from viciousness than exuberance of vitality after long constraint: frank manifestations in accordance with natural law. By his original constitution aided by the co-operating influences of his lot, Billy in many respects was little more than a sort of upright barbarian, much such perhaps as Adam presumably might have been ere the urbane Serpent wriggled himself into his company.

And here be it submitted that apparently going to corroborate the doctrine of man's Fall, a doctrine now popularly ignored, it is observable that where certain virtues pristine and unadulterate peculiarly characterize anybody in the external uniform of civilization, they will upon scrutiny seem not to be derived from custom or convention, but rather to be out of keeping with these, as if needed exceptionally transmitted from a period prior to Cain's city and citified man. The character marked by such qualities has to an unvitiated taste an untampered-with flavor like that of berries, while the man thoroughly civilized, even in a fair specimen of the breed, has to the same mortal palate a questionable smack as of a compounded wine. To any stray inheritor of these primitive qualities found, like Caspar Hauser,[12] wandering dazed in any Christian capital of our time, the good-natured poet's famous invocation, near two thousand years ago, of the good rustic out of his latitude in the Rome of the Caesars, still appropriately holds:

Honest and poor, faithful in word and thought,
What hath thee, Fabian, to the city brought?[13]

[12] Caspar Hauser (1812?-1833) was discovered in 1828 in Nuremberg, Germany. He was alleged to have noble birth but was brought up without any exposure to society. His case raised the question of what is human nature like without social conditioning.
[13] Martial, *Epigrams*, IV, 5.

Though our Handsome Sailor had as much of masculine beauty as one can expect anywhere to see; nevertheless, like the beautiful woman in one of Hawthorne's minor tales,[14] there was just one thing amiss in him. No visible blemish indeed, as with the lady; no, but an occasional liability to a vocal defect. Though in the hour of elemental uproar or peril he was everything that a sailor could be, yet under sudden provocation of strong heart-feeling his voice, otherwise singularly musical, as if expressive of the harmony within, was apt to develop an organic hesitancy, on fact more or less of a stutter or even worse. In this particular Billy was a striking instance that the arch interferer, the envious marplot of Eden, still has more or less to do with every human consignment of this planet of Earth. In every case, one way or another he is sure to slip in his little card, as much as to remind us—I too have a hand here.

The avowal of such an imperfection in the Handsome Sailor should be evidence not alone that he is not presented as a conventional hero, but also that the story in which he is the main figure is no romance.

3

At the time of Billy Budd's arbitrary enlistment into the *Bellipotent* that ship was on her way to join the Mediterranean fleet. No long time elapsed before the junction was effected. As one of that fleet the seventy-four participated in its movements, though at times on account of her superior sailing qualities, in the absence of frigates, dispatched on separate duty as a scout and at times on less temporary service. But with all this the story has little concernment, restricted as it is to the inner life of one particular ship and the career of an individual sailor.

It was the summer of 1797. In the April of that year had occurred the commotion at Spithead followed in May by a second and yet more serious outbreak in the fleet at the Nore.[15] The latter is known, and without exaggeration in the epithet, as "the Great Mutiny." It was indeed a demonstration more menacing to England than the contemporary manifestoes and conquering and proselyting armies of the French Directory. To the British Empire the Nore Mutiny was what a strike in the fire brigade would be to London threatened by general arson. In a crisis when the kingdom might well have anticipated the famous signal that some years later published along the naval line of battle what it was that upon occasion England expected of Englishmen; *that* was the time when at the mastheads of the three-deckers and seventy-fours moored in her own roadstead—a fleet the right arm of a Power then all but the sole free conservative one of the Old World—the bluejackets, to be numbered by thousands, ran up with huzzas the British colors with the union and cross wiped out; by that cancellation transmuting the flag of founded law and freedom defined, into the enemy's red meteor of unbridled

---

[14] "The Birthmark."
[15] Anchorage at the mouth of the Thames where the mutiny of 1797 in the British Navy occurred.

and unbounded revolt. Reasonable discontent growing out of practical grievances in the fleet had been ignited into irrational combustion as by live cinders blown across the Channel from France in flames.

The event converted into irony for a time those spirited strains of Dibdin[16]—as a song-writer no mean auxiliary to the English government at that European conjuncture—strains celebrating, among other things, the patriotic devotion of the British tar: "And as for my life, 'tis the King's!"

Such an episode in the Island's grand naval story her naval historians naturally abridge, one of them (William James)[17] candidly acknowledging that fain would he pass it over did not "impartiality forbid fastidiousness." And yet his mention is less a narration than a reference, having to do hardly at all with details. Nor are these readily to be found in the libraries. Like some other events in every age befalling states everywhere, including America, the Great Mutiny was of such character that national pride along the views of policy would fain shade it off into the historical background. Such events cannot be ignored, but there is a considerate way of historically treating them. If a well-constituted individual refrains from blazoning aught amiss or calamitous in his family, a nation in the like circumstance may without reproach be equally discreet.

Though after parleyings between government and the ring-leaders, and concessions by the former as to some glaring abuses, the first uprising—that at Spithead—with difficulty was put down, or matters for the time pacified; yet at the Nore the unforeseen renewal of insurrection on a yet larger scale, and emphasized in the conferences that ensued by demands deemed by the authorities not only inadmissible but aggressively insolent, indicated—if the Red Flag did not sufficiently do so—what was the spirit animating the men. Final suppression, however, there was; but only made possible perhaps by the unswerving loyalty of the marine corps and a voluntary resumption of loyalty among influential sections of the crews.

To some extent the Nore Mutiny may be regarded as analogous to the distempering irruption of contagious fever in a frame constitutionally sound, and which anon throws it off.

At all events, of these thousands of mutineers were some of the tars who not so very long afterwards—whether wholly prompted thereto by patriotism, or pugnacious instinct, or by both—helped to win a coronet for Nelson at the Nile, and the naval crown of crowns for him at Trafalgar. To the mutineers, those battles and especially Trafalgar were a plenary absolution and a grand one. For all that goes to make up scenic naval display and heroic magnificence in arms, those battles, especially Trafalgar, stand unmatched in human annals.

---

[16] Charles Dibdin (1745-1814) was an English dramatist and song writer.

[17] William James was the author of *The Na-* *val History of Great Britain* (6 vols., London, 1860).

4

In this matter of writing, resolve as one may to keep to the main road, some bypaths have an enticement not readily to be withstood. I am going to err into such a bypath. If the reader will keep me company I shall be glad. At the least, we can promise ourselves that pleasure which is wickedly said to be in sinning, for a literary sin the divergence will be.

Very likely it is no new remark that the inventions of our time have at last brought about a change in sea warfare in degree corresponding to the revolution in all warfare effected by the original introduction from China into Europe of gunpowder. The first European firearm, a clumsy contrivance, was, as is well known, scouted by no few of the knights as a base implement, good enough peradventure for weavers too craven to stand up crossing steel with steel in frank fight. But as ashore knightly valor, though shorn of its blazonry, did not cease with the knights, neither on the seas—though nowadays in encounters there a certain kind of displayed gallantry be fallen out of date as hardly applicable under changed circumstances—did the nobler qualities of such naval magnates as Don John of Austria, Doria, Van Tromp, Jean Bart, the long line of British admirals, and the American Decatur of 1812 become obsolete with their wooden walls.[18]

Nevertheless, to anybody who can hold the Present at its worth without being inappreciative of the Past, it may be forgiven, if to such an one the solitary old hulk at Portsmouth, Nelson's *Victory*, seems to float there, not alone as the decaying monument of a fame incorruptible, but also as a poetic reproach, softened by its picturesqueness, to the *Monitors* and yet mightier hulls of the European ironclads. And this not altogether because such craft are unsightly, unavoidably lacking the symmetry and grand lines of the old battleships, but equally for other reasons.

There are some, perhaps, who while not altogether inaccessible to that poetic reproach just alluded to, may yet on behalf of the new order be disposed to parry it; and this to the extent of iconoclasm, if need be. For example, prompted by the sight of the star inserted in the *Victory's* quarter-deck designating the spot where the Great Sailor fell, these martial utilitarians may suggest considerations implying that Nelson's ornate publication of his person in battle was not only unnecessary, but not military, nay, savored of foolhardiness and vanity. They may add, too, that at Trafalgar it was in effect nothing less than a challenge to death; and death came; and that but for his bravado the victorious admiral might possibly have survived the battle, and so, instead of having his sagacious dying injunctions overruled by his

---

[18] All famous admirals. Don John of Austria led the fleet of the Holy League in victory over the Turks at Lepanto (1671); Andrea Doria (1468-1560) liberated Genoa from the Turks and was known as "the Liberator of Genoa"; Maarten Tromp (1597-1653) was a commander of Dutch fleets in combat with Spain, Portugal, and Britain; Jean Bart led privateers against the Dutch (1686-1697); and the American Stephen Decatur was a naval hero during the War of 1812.

immediate successor in command, he himself when the contest was decided might have brought his shattered fleet to anchor, a proceeding which might have averted the deplorable loss of life by shipwreck in the elemental tempest that followed the martial one.

Well, should we set aside the more than disputable point whether for various reasons it was possible to anchor the fleet, then plausibly enough the Benthamites[19] of war may urge the above. But the *might-have-been* is but boggy ground to build on. And, certainly, in foresight as to the larger issue of an encounter, and anxious preparations for it—buoying the deadly way and mapping it out, as at Copenhagen—few commanders have been so painstakenly circumspect as this same reckless declarer of his person in fight.

Personal prudence, even when dictated by quite other than selfish considerations, surely is no special virtue in a military man; while an excessive love of glory, impassioning a less burning impulse, the honest sense of duty, is the first. If the name *Wellington* is not so much of a trumpet to the blood as the simpler name *Nelson*, the reason for this may perhaps be inferred from the above. Alfred[20] in his funeral ode on the victor of Waterloo ventures not to call him the greatest soldier of all time, though in the same ode he invokes Nelson as "the greatest sailor since our world began."

At Trafalgar Nelson on the brink of opening the fight sat down and wrote his last brief will and testament. If under the presentiment of the most magnificent of all victories to be crowned by his own glorious death, a sort of priestly motive led him to dress his person in the jewelled vouchers of his own shining deeds; if thus to have adorned himself for the altar and the sacrifice were indeed vainglory, then affectation and fustian is each more heroic line in the great epics and dramas, since in such lines the poet but embodies in verse those exaltations of sentiment that a nature like Nelson, the opportunity being given, vitalizes into acts.

5

Yes, the outbreak at the Nore was put down. But not every grievance was redressed. If the contractors, for example, were no longer permitted to ply some practices peculiar to their tribe everywhere, such as providing shoddy cloth, rations not sound, or false in the measure; not the less impressment, for one thing, went on. By custom sanctioned for centuries, and judicially maintained by a Lord Chancellor as late as Mansfield,[21] that mode of manning the fleet, a mode now fallen into a sort of abeyance but never formally renounced, it was not practicable to give up in those years. Its abrogation would have crippled the indispensable fleet, one wholly under canvas, no

---

[19] Jeremy Bentham (1748-1832) was the philosopher of utilitarianism.

[20] Cf. Tennyson's "Ode on the Death of the Duke of Wellington" (1852) Tennyson's line reads, "The greatest sailor since our world began."

[21] Baron Mansfield was William Murray, the British parliamentarian who became lord chief justice in 1756 and later a cabinet minister (1773-1788)

steam power, its innumerable sails and thousands of cannon, everything in short, worked by muscle alone; a fleet the more insatiate in demand for men, because then multiplying its ships of all grades against contingencies present and to come of the convulsed Continent.

Discontent foreran the Two Mutinies, and more or less it lurkingly survived them. Hence it was not unreasonable to apprehend some return of trouble sporadic or general. One instance of such apprehensions: In the same year with this story, Nelson, then Rear Admiral Sir Horatio, being with the fleet off the Spanish coast, was directed by the admiral in command to shift his pennant from the *Captain* to the *Theseus;* and for this reason: that the latter ship having newly arrived on the station from home, where it had taken part in the Great Mutiny, danger was apprehended from the temper of the men; and it was thought that an officer like Nelson was the one, not indeed to terrorize the crew into base subjection, but to win them, by force of his mere presence and heroic personality, back to an allegiance if not as enthusiastic as his own yet as true.

So it was that for a time, on more than one quarter-deck, anxiety did exist. At sea, precautionary vigilance was strained against relapse. At short notice an engagement might come on. When it did, the lieutenants assigned to batteries felt it incumbent on them, in some instances, to stand with drawn swords behind the men working the guns.

6

But on board the seventy-four in which Billy now swung his hammock, very little in the manner of the men and nothing obvious in the demeanor of the officers would have suggested to an ordinary observer that the Great Mutiny was a recent event. In their general bearing and conduct the commissioned officers of a warship naturally take their tone from the commander, that is if he have that ascendancy of character that ought to be his.

Captain the Honorable Edward Fairfax Vere, to give his full title, was a bachelor of forty or thereabouts, a sailor of distinction even in a time prolific of renowned seamen. Though allied to the higher nobility, his advancement had not been altogether owing to influences connected with that circumstance. He had seen much service, been in various engagements, always acquitting himself as an officer mindful of the welfare of his men, but never tolerating an infraction of discipline; thoroughly versed in the science of his profession, and intrepid to the verge of temerity, though never injudiciously so. For his gallantry in the West Indian waters as flag lieutenant under Rodney in that admiral's crowning victory over De Grasse,[22] he was made a post captain.

Ashore, in the garb of a civilian, scarce anyone would have taken him for a sailor, more especially that he never garnished unprofessional talk with

---

[22] Admiral George Brydges Rodney (1719-1792) defeated the French admiral DeGrasse off Martinique in 1782.

nautical terms, and grave in his bearing, evinced little appreciation of mere humor. It was not out of keeping with these traits that on a passage when nothing demanded his paramount action, he was the most undemonstrative of men. Any landsman observing this gentleman not conspicuous by his stature and wearing no pronounced insignia, emerging from his cabin to the open deck, and noting the silent deference of the officers retiring to leeward, might have taken him for the King's guest, a civilian aboard the King's ship, some highly honorable discreet envoy on his way to an important post. But in fact this unobtrusiveness of demeanor may have proceeded from a certain unaffected modesty of manhood sometimes accompanying a resolute nature, a modesty evinced at all times not calling for pronounced action, which shown in any rank of life suggests virtue aristocratic in kind. As with some others engaged in various departments of the world's more heroic activities, Captain Vere though practical enough upon occasion would at times betray a certain dreaminess of mood. Standing alone on the weather side of the quarter-deck, one hand holding by the rigging, he would absently gaze off at the blank sea. At the presentation of him then of some minor matter interrupting the current of his thoughts, he would show more or less irascibility; but instantly he would control it.

In the navy he was popularly known by the appellation "Starry Vere." How much a designation happened to fall upon one who whatever his sterling qualities was without any brilliant ones, was in this wise: A favorite kinsman, Lord Denton, a freehearted fellow, had been the first to meet and congratulate him upon his return to England from his West Indian cruise; and but the day previous turning over a copy of Andrew Marvell's[23] poems had lighted, not for the first time, however, upon the lines entitled "Appleton House," the name of one of the seats of their common ancestor, a hero in the German wars of the seventeenth century, in which poem occur the lines:

> This 'tis to have been from the first
> In a domestic heaven nursed,
> Under the discipline severe
> Of Fairfax and the starry Vere.

And so, upon embracing his cousin fresh from Rodney's great victory wherein he had played so gallant a part, brimming over with just family pride in the sailor of their house, he exuberantly exclaimed, "Give ye joy, Ed; give ye joy, my starry Vere!" This got currency, and the novel prefix serving in familiar parlance readily to distinguish the *Bellipotent's* captain from another Vere his senior, a distant relative, an officer of like rank in the navy, it remained permanently attached to the surname.

[23] Andrew Marvell (1621-1678), a British poet.

7

In view of the part that the commander of the *Bellipotent* plays in scenes shortly to follow, it may be well to fill out the sketch of him outlined in the previous chapter.

Aside from his qualities as a sea officer Captain Vere was an exceptional character. Unlike no few of England's renowned sailors, long and arduous service with signal devotion to it had not resulted in absorbing and *salting* the entire man. He had a marked leaning toward everything intellectual. He loved books, never going to sea without a newly replenished library, compact but of the best. The isolated leisure, in some cases so wearisome, falling at intervals to commanders even during a war cruise, never was tedious to Captian Vere. With nothing of that literary taste which less heeds the thing conveyed than the vehicle, his bias was toward those books to which every serious mind of superior order occupying any active post of authority in the world naturally inclines: books treating of actual men and events no matter of what era—history, biography, and unconventional writers like Montaigne, who, free from cant and convention, honestly and in the spirit of common sense philosophize upon realities. In this line of reading he found confirmation of his own more reserved thoughts—confirmation which he had vainly sought in social converse, so that as touching most fundamental topics, there had got to be established in him some positive convictions which he forefelt would abide in him essentially unmodified so long as his intelligent part remained unimpaired. In view of the troubled period in which his lot was cast, this was well for him. His settled convictions were as a dike against those invading waters of novel opinion social, political, and otherwise, which carried away as in a torrent no few minds in those days, minds by nature not inferior to his own. While other members of that aristocracy to which by birth he belonged were incensed at the innovators mainly because their theories were inimical to the privileged classes, Captain Vere disinterestedly opposed them not alone because they seemed to him insusceptible of embodiment in lasting institutions, but at war with the peace of the world and the true welfare of mankind.

With minds less stored than his and less earnest, some officers of his rank, with whom at times he would necessarily consort, found him lacking in the companionable quality, a dry and bookish gentleman, as they deemed. Upon any chance withdrawal from their company one would be apt to say to another something like this: "Vere is a noble fellow, Starry Vere. 'Spite the gazettes, Sir Horatio" (meaning him who became Lord Nelson) "is at bottom scarce a better seaman or fighter. But between you and me now, don't you think there is a queer streak of the pedantic running through him? Yes, like the King's yarn in a coil of navy rope?"

Some apparent ground there was for this sort of confidential criticism; since not only did the captain's discourse never fall into the jocosely familiar, but in illustrating of any point touching the stirring personages and events of the time he would be so apt to cite some historic character or incident of antiquity as he would be to cite from the moderns. He seemed unmindful of the circumstances that to his bluff company such remote allusions, however pertinent they might really be, were altogether alien to men whose reading was mainly confined to the journals. But considerateness in such matters is not easy to natures constituted like Captain Vere's. Their honesty prescribes to them directness, sometimes far-reaching like that of a migratory fowl that in its flight never heeds when it crosses a frontier.

8

The lieutenants and other commissioned gentlemen forming Captain Vere's staff it is not necessary here to particularize, nor needs it to make any mention of any of the warrant officers. But among the petty officers was one who, having much to do with the story, may as well be forthwith introduced. His portrait I essay, but shall never hit it. This was John Claggart, the master-at-arms. But that sea title may to landsmen seem somewhat equivocal. Originally, doubtless, that petty officer's function was the instruction of the men in the use of arms, sword or cutlass. But very long ago, owing to the advance in gunnery making hand-to-hand encounters less frequent and giving to niter and sulphur the pre-eminence over steel, that function ceased; the master-at-arms of a great warship becoming a sort of police charged among other matters with the duty of preserving order on the populous lower gun decks.

Claggart was a man about five-and-thirty, somewhat spare and tall, yet of no ill figure upon the whole. His hand was too small and shapely to have been accustomed to hard toil. The face was a notable one, the features all except the chin clearly cut as those on a Greek medallion; yet the chin, beardless as Tecumseh's,[24] had something of strange protuberant broadness in its make that recalled the prints of the Reverend Dr. Titus Oates, the historic deponent with the clerical drawl in the time of Charles II and the fraud of the alleged Popish Plot.[25] It served Claggart in his office that his eye could cast a tutoring glance. His brow was of the sort phrenologically associated with more than average intellect; silken jet curls partly clustering over it, making a foil to the pallor below, a pallor tinged with a faint shade of amber akin to the hue of time-tinted marbles of old. This complexion, singularly contrasting with the red or deeply bronzed visages of the sailors, and in part the result of his official seclusion from the sunlight, though it was not exactly displeasing, nevertheless seemed to hint of something defective or abnormal in the constitution and blood. But his general aspect and manner were so suggestive of an education and career incongruous with his naval

[24] An American Indian chief (1768?-1813).
[25] The Reverend Titus Oates (1649-1705), a reverend, created a scandal in London in 1678 by claiming that the Catholics were attempting to subvert England; this became known as the "Popish Plot."

function that when not actively engaged in it he looked like a man of high quality, social and moral, who for reasons of his own was keeping incog.[26] Nothing was known of his former life. It might be that he was an Englishman: and yet there lurked a bit of accent in his speech suggesting that possibly he was not such by birth, but through naturalization in early childhood. Among certain grizzled sea gossips of the gun decks and forecastle went a rumor perdue that the master-at-arms was a *chevalier* who had volunteered into the King's navy by way of compounding for some mysterious swindle whereof he had been arraigned at the King's Bench. The fact that nobody could substantiate this report was, of course, nothing against its secret currency. Such a rumor once started on the gun decks in reference to almost anyone below the rank of a commissioned officer would, during the period assigned to this narrative, have seemed not altogether wanting in credibility to the tarry old wiseacres of a man-of-war crew. And indeed a man of Claggart's accomplishments, without prior nautical experience entering the navy at mature life, as he did, and necessarily allotted at the start to the lowest grade in it; a man too who never made allusion to his previous life ashore; these were circumstances which in the dearth of exact knowledge as to his true antecedents opened to the invidious a vague field for unfavorable surmise.

But the sailors' dogwatch gossip concerning him derived a vague plausibility from the fact that now for some period the British navy could so little afford to be squeamish in the matter of keeping up the muster rolls, that not only were press gangs notoriously abroad both afloat and ashore, but there was little or no secret about another matter, namely, that the London police were at liberty to capture any able-bodied suspect, any questionable fellow at large, and summarily ship him to the dockyard or fleet. Furthermore, even among voluntary enlistments there were instances where the motive thereto partook neither of patriotic impulse not yet of a random desire to experience a bit of sea life and martial adventure. Insolvent debtors of minor grade, together with the promiscuous lame ducks of morality, found in the navy a convenient and secure refuge, secure because, once enlisted aboard a King's ship, they were as much in sanctuary as the transgressor of the Middle Ages harboring himself under the shadow of the altar. Such sanctioned irregularities, which for obvious reasons the government would hardly think to parade at the time and which consequently, and as affecting the least influential class of mankind, have all but dropped into oblivion, lend color to something for the truth whereof I do not vouch, and hence have some scruple in stating; something I remember having seen in print though the book I cannot recall; but the same thing was personally communicated to me now more than forty years ago by an old pensioner in a cocked hat with whom I had a

[26] An abbreviation for *incognito*, concealed identity.

most interesting talk on the terrace at Greenwich, a Baltimore Negro, a Trafalgar man. It was to this effect: In the case of a warship short of hands whose speedy sailing was imperative, the deficient quota, in lack of any other way of making it good, would be eked out by drafts culled direct from the jails. For reasons previously suggested it would not perhaps be easy at the present day directly to prove or disprove the allegation. But allowed as a verity, how significant would it be of England's straits at the time confronted by those wars which like a flight of harpies rose shrieking from the din and dust of the fallen Bastille. That era appears measurably clear to us who look back at it, and but read of it. But to the grandfathers of us graybeards, the more thoughtful of them, the genius of it presented an aspect like that of Camoëns' Spirit of the Cape,[27] an eclipsing menace mysterious and prodigious. Not America was exempt from apprehension. At the height of Napoleon's unexampled conquests, there were Americans who had fought at Bunker Hill who looked forward to the possibility that the Atlantic might prove no barrier against the ultimate schemes of this French portentous upstart from the revolutionary chaos who seemed in act of fulfilling judgment prefigured in the Apolcalypse.[28]

But the less credence was to be given to the gun-deck talk touching Claggart, seeing that no man holding his office in a man-of-war can ever hope to be popular with the crew. Besides, in derogatory comments upon anyone against whom they have a grudge, or for any reason or no reason mislike, sailors are much like landsmen: they are apt to exaggerate or romance it.

About as much was really known to the *Bellipotent's* tars of the master-at-arms' career before entering the service as an astronomer knows about a comet's travels prior to its first observable appearance in the sky. The verdict of the sea quidnuncs[29] has been cited only by way of showing what sort of moral impression the man made upon rude uncultivated natures whose conceptions of human wickedness were necessarily of the narrowest, limited to ideas of vulgar rascality—a thief among the swinging hammocks during a night watch, or the man-brokers and land-sharks of the seaports.

It was no gossip, however, but fact that though, as before hinted, Claggart upon his entrance into the navy was, as a novice, assigned to the least honorable section of a man-of-war's crew, embracing the drudgery, he did not long remain there. The superior capacity he immediately evinced, his constitutional sobriety, an ingratiating deference to superiors, together with a peculiar ferreting genius manifested on a singular occasion; all this, capped by a certain austere patriotism, abruptly advanced him to the position of master-at-arms.

[27] Luis Voz de Camoëns (1524-1580) was the Portuguese author of the epic, the *Lusiads*, which Melville admired. In the epic, Vasco de Gama escaped the "Spirit of the Cape" when he made his first successful voyage around Africa to India.
[28] Revelation, the last book of the Bible.
[29] A gossip.

Of this maritime chief of police the ship's corporals, so called, were the immediate subordinates, and compliant ones; and this, as is to be noted in some business departments ashore, almost to a degree inconsistent with entire moral volition. His place put various converging wires of underground influence under the chief's control, capable when astutely worked through his understrappers of operating to the mysterious discomfort, if nothing worse, of any of the sea commonalty.

9

Life in the foretop well agreed with Billy Budd. There, when not actually engaged on the yards yet higher aloft, the topmen, who as such had been picked out for youth and activity, constituted an aerial club lounging at ease against the smaller stun'sails rolled up into cushions, spinning yarns like the lazy gods, and frequently amused with what was going on in the busy world of the decks below. No wonder then that a young fellow of Billy's disposition was well content in such society. Giving no cause of offense to anybody, he was always alert at a call. So in the merchant service it had been with him. But now such a punctiliousness in duty was shown that his topmates would sometimes good-naturedly laugh at him for it. This heightened alacrity had its cause, namely, the impression made upon him by the first formal gangway-punishment he had ever witnessed, which befell the day following his impressment. It had been incurred by a little fellow, young, a novice afterguardsman absent from his assigned post when the ship was being put about; a dereliction resulting in a rather serious hitch to that maneuver, one demanding instantaneous promptitude in letting go and making fast. When Billy saw the culprit's naked back under the scourge, grid-ironed with red welts and worse, when he marked the dire expression in the liberated man's face as with his woolen shirt flung over him by the executioner he rushed forward from the spot to bury himself in the crowd, Billy was horrified. He resolved that never through remissness would he make himself liable to such a visitation or do or omit aught that might merit even verbal reproof. What then was his surprise and concern when ultimately he found himself getting into petty trouble occasionally about such matters as the stowage of his bag or something amiss in his hammock, matters under the police oversight of the ship's corporals of the lower decks, and which brought down on him a vague threat from one of them.

So heedful in all things as he was, how could this be? He could not understand it, and it more than vexed him. When he spoke to his young topmates about it they were either lightly incredulous or found something comical in his unconcealed anxiety. "Is it your bag, Billy?" said one. "Well, sew yourself up in it, bully boy, and then you'll be sure to know if anybody meddles with it."

Now there was a veteran aboard who because his years began to disqualify him for more active work had been recently assigned duty as mainmastman in his watch, looking to the gear belayed at the rail roundabout that great spar near the deck. At off-times the foretopman had picked up some acquaintance with him, and now in his trouble it occurred to him that he might be the sort of person to go to for wise counsel. He was an old Dansker long anglicized in the service, of few words, many wrinkles, and some honorable scars. His wizened face, time-tinted and weather-stained to the complexion of an antique parchment, was here and there peppered blue by the chance explosion of a gun cartridge in action.

He was an *Agamemnon* man, some two years prior to the time of this story having served under Nelson when still captain in that ship immortal in naval memory, which dismantled and in part broken up to her bare ribs is a grand skeleton in Haden's[30] etching. As one of a boarding party from the *Agamemnon* he had received a cut slantwise along one temple and cheek leaving a long pale scar like a streak of dawn's light falling athwart the dark visage. It was on account of that scar and the affair in which it was known that he had received it, as well as from his blue-peppered complexion, that the Dansker went among the *Bellipotent's* crew by the name of "Board-Her-in-the-Smoke."

Now the first time that his small weasel eyes happened to light on Billy Budd, a certain grim internal merriment set all his ancient wrinkles into antic play. Was it that his eccentric unsentimental old sapience, primitive in its kind, saw or thought it saw something which in contrast with the warship's environment looked oddly incongruous in the Handsome Sailor? But after slyly studying him at intervals, the old Merlin's equivocal merriment was modified; for now when the twain would meet, it would start in his face a quizzing sort of look, but it would be but momentary and sometimes replaced by an expression of speculative query as to what might eventually befall like that, dropped into a world not without some mantraps and against whose subtleties simple courage lacking experience and address, and without any touch of defensive ugliness, is of little avail; and where such innocence as man is capable of does yet in a moral emergency not always sharpen the faculties or enlighten the will.

However it was, the Dansker in his ascetic way rather took to Billy. Nor was this only because of a certain philosophic interest in such a character. There was another cause. While the old man's eccentricities, sometimes bordering on the ursine, repelled the juniors, Billy, undeterred thereby, revering him as a salt hero, would make advances, never passing the old *Agamemnon* man without a salutation marked by that respect which is seldom lost on the aged, however crabbed at times or whatever their station in life.

[30] Francis Seymour Haden (1818-1910) was an English surgeon who revived interest in etching.

There was a vein of dry humor, or what not, in the mastman; and, whether in freak of patriarchal irony touching Billy's youth and athletic frame, or for some other and more recondite reason, from the first in addressing him he always substituted *Baby* for Billy, the Dansker in fact being the originator of the name by which the foretopman eventually became known aboard ship.

Well then, in his mysterious little difficulty going in quest of the wrinkled one, Billy found him off duty in a dogwatch ruminating by himself, seated on a shot box of the upper gun deck, now and then surveying with a somewhat cynical regard certain of the more swaggering promenaders there. Billy recounted his trouble, again wondering how it all happened. The salt seer attentively listened, accompanying the foretopman's recital with queer twitchings of his wrinkles and problematical little sparkles of his small ferret eyes. Making an end of his story, the foretopman asked, "And now, Dansker, do tell me what you think of it."

The old man, shoving up the front of his tarpaulin and deliberately rubbing the long slant scar at the point where it entered the thin hair, laconically said, "Baby Budd, Jemmy Legs" (meaning the master-at-arms) "is down on you."

"*Jemmy Legs!*" ejaculated Billy, his welkin eyes expanding. "What for? Why, he calls me 'the sweet and pleasant young fellow,' they tell me."

"Does he so?" grinned the grizzled one; then said, "Ay, Baby lad, a sweet voice has Jemmy Legs."

"No, not always. But to me he has. I seldom pass him but there comes a pleasant word."

"And that's because he's down upon you, Baby Budd."

Such reiteration, along with the manner of it, incomprehensible to a novice, disturbed Billy almost as much as the mystery for which he had sought explanation. Something less unpleasingly oracular he tried to extract; but the old sea Chiron,[31] thinking perhaps that for the nonce he had sufficiently instructed his young Achilles, pursed his lips, gathered all his wrinkles together, and would commit himself to nothing further.

Years, and those experiences which befall certain shrewder men subordinated lifelong to the will of superiors, all this had developed in the Dansker[32] the pithy guarded cynicism that was his leading characteristic.

10

The next day an incident served to confirm Billy Budd in his incredulity as to the Dansker's strange summing up of the case submitted. The ship at noon, going large before the wind, was rolling on her course, and he below at dinner and engaged in some sportful talk with the members of his mess, chanced in a sudden lurch to spill the entire contents of his soup pan upon

---

[31] In Greek mythology, the wisest of the centaurs who helped the ailing Achilles.

[32] A Dane.

the new-scrubbed deck. Claggart, the master-at-arms, official rattan in hand, happened to be passing along the battery in a bay of which the mess was lodged, and the greasy liquid streamed just across his path. Stepping over it, he was proceeding on his way without comment, since the matter was nothing to take notice of under the circumstances, when he happened to observe who it was that had done the spilling. His countenance changed. Pausing, he was about to ejaculate something hasty at the sailor, but checked himself, and pointing down to the streaming soup, playfully tapped him from behind with his rattan, saying in a low musical voice peculiar to him at times, "Handsomely done, my lad! And handsome is as handsome did it, too!" And with that passed on. Not noted by Billy as not coming within his view was the involuntary smile, or rather grimace, that accompanied Claggart's equivocal words. Aridly it drew down the thin corners of his shapely mouth. But everybody taking his remark as meant for humorous, and at which therefore as coming from a superior they were bound to laugh "with counterfeited glee,"[33] acted accordingly: and Billy, tickled, it may be, by the allusion to his being the Handsome Sailor, merrily joined in; then addressing his messmates exclaimed, "There now, who says that Jemmy Legs is down on me!"

"And who said he was, Beauty?" demanded one Donald with some surprise. Whereat the foretopman looked a little foolish, recalling that it was only one person, Board-Her-in-the-Smoke, who had suggested what to him was the smoky idea that this master-at-arms was in any peculiar way hostile to him. Meantime that functionary, resuming his path, must have momentarily worn some expression less guarded than that of the bitter smile, usurping the face from the heart—some distorting expression perhaps, for a drummer-boy heedlessly frolicking from the opposite direction and chancing to come into light collision with his person was strangely disconcerted by his aspect. Nor was the impression lessened when the official, impetuously giving him a sharp cut with the rattan, vehemently exclaimed, "Look where you go!"

11

What was the matter with the master-at-arms? And, be the matter what it might, how could it have direct relation to Billy Budd, with whom prior to the affair of the spilled soup he had never come into any special contact official or otherwise? What indeed could the trouble have to do with one so little inclined to give offense as the merchant-ship's "peacemaker," even him who in Claggart's own phrase was "the sweet and pleasant young fellow"? Yes, why should Jemmy Legs, to borrow the Dansker's expression, be "down" on the Handsome Sailor? But, at heart and not for nothing, as the late chance encounter may indicate to the discerning, down on him, secretly down on him, he assuredly was.

[33] Cf. Oliver Goldsmith, "The Deserted Village," 201.

Now to invent something touching the more private career of Claggart, something involving Billy Budd, of which something the latter should be wholly ignorant, some romantic incident implying that Claggart's knowledge of the young bluejacket began at some period anterior to catching sight of him on board the seventy-four—all this, not so difficult to do, might avail in a way more or less interesting to account for whatever of enigma may appear to lurk in the case. But in fact there was nothing of the sort. And yet the cause necessarily to be assumed as the sole one assignable is in its very realism as much charged with that prime element of Radcliffian romance, the mysterious, as any that the ingenuity of the author of *The Mysteries of Udolpho*[34] could devise. For what can more partake of the mysterious than an antipathy spontaneous and profound such as is envoked in certain exceptional mortals by the mere aspect of some other mortal, however harmless he may be, if not called forth by this very harmlessness itself?

Now there can exist no irritating juxtaposition of dissimilar personalities comparable to that which is possible aboard a great warship fully manned and at sea. There, every day among all ranks, almost every man comes into more or less of contact with almost every other man. Wholly there to avoid even the sight of an aggravating object one must give it Jonah's toss[35] or jump overboard himself. Imagine how all this might eventually operate on some peculiar human creature the direct reverse of a saint!

But for the adequate comprehending of Claggart by a normal nature these hints are insufficient. To pass from a normal nature to him one must cross "the deadly space between." And this is best done by indirection.

Long ago an honest scholar, my senior, said to me in reference to one who like himself is now no more, a man so unimpeachably respectable that against him nothing was ever openly said though among the few something was whispered, "Yes, X——is a nut not to be cracked by the tap of a lady's fan. You are aware that I am the adherent of no organized religion, much less of any philosophy built into a system. Well, for all that, I think that to try and get into X——, enter his labyrinth and get out again, without a clue derived from some source other than what is known as 'knowledge of the world'— that were hardly possible, at least for me."

"Why," said I, "X——, however singular a study to some, is yet human, and knowledge of the world assuredly implies the knowledge of human nature, and in most of its varieties."

"Yes, but a superficial knowledge of it, serving ordinary purposes. But for anything deeper, I am not certain whether to know the world and to know human nature be not two distinct branches of knowledge, which while they may coexist in the same heart, yet either may exist with little or nothing of

---

[34] *The Mysteries of Udolpho* (1794), a popular Gothic romance, was written by Ann Radcliffe (1764-1823).

[35] The throwing overboard of an unlucky person or object.

the other. Nay, in an average man of the world, his constant rubbing with it blunts that finer spiritual insight indispensable to the understanding of the essential in certain exceptional characters, whether evil ones or good. In a matter of some importance I have seen a girl wind an old lawyer about her little finger. Nor was it the dotage of senile love. Nothing of the sort. But he knew law better than he knew the girl's heart. Coke and Blackstone[36] hardly shed so much light into obscure spiritual places as the Hebrew prophets. And who were they? Mostly recluses."

At the time, my inexperience was such that I did not quite see the drift of all this. It may be that I see it now. And, indeed, if that lexicon which is based on Holy Writ were any longer popular, one might with less difficulty define and denominate certain phenomenal men. As it is, one must turn to some authority not liable to the charge of being tinctured with the biblical element.

In a list of definitions included in the authentic translation of Plato, a list attributed to him, occurs this: "Natural Depravity: a depravity according to nature," a definition which, though savoring of Calvinism, by no means involves Calvin's dogma as to total mankind. Evidently its intent makes it applicable but to individuals. Not many are the examples of this depravity which the gallows and jail supply. At any rate, for notable instances, since these have no vulgar alloy of the brute in them, but invariably are dominated by intellectuality, one must go elsewhere. Civilization, especially if of the austerer sort, is auspicious to it. It folds itself in the mantle of respectability. It has its certain negative virtues serving as silent auxiliaries. It never allows wine to get within its guard. It is not going too far to say that it is without vices or small sins. There is a phenomenal pride in it that excludes them. It is never mercenary or avaricious. In short, the depravity here meant partakes nothing of the sordid or sensual. It is serious, but free from acerbity. Though no flatterer of mankind it never speaks ill of it.

But the thing which in eminent instances signalizes so exceptional a nature is this: Though the man's even temper and discreet bearing would seem to intimate a mind peculiarly subject to the law of reason, not the less in heart he would seem to riot in complete exemption from that law, having apparently little to do with reason further than to employ it as an ambidexter implement for effecting the irrational. That is to say: Toward the accomplishment of an aim which in wantonness of atrocity would seem to partake of the insane, he will direct a cool judgment sagacious and sound. These men are madmen, and of the most dangerous sort, for their lunacy is not continuous, but occasional, evoked by some special object; it is protectively secretive, which is as much to say it is self-contained, so that when, moreover, most active it is to the average mind not distinguishable from sanity, and for the reason above suggested: that whatever its aims may be—and the aim is never declared—the method and the outward proceeding are always perfectly rational.

Now something such an one was Claggart, in whom was the mania of an evil nature, not engendered by vicious training or corrupting books or licentious living, but born with him and innate, in short "a depravity according to nature."

Dark sayings are these, some will say. But why? Is it because they somewhat savor of Holy Writ in its phrase "mystery of iniquity"?[37] If they do, such savor was far enough from being intended, for little will it commend these pages to many a reader of today.

The point of the present story turning on the hidden nature of the master-at-arms has necessitated this chapter. With an added hint or two in connection with the incident at the mess, the resumed narrative must be left to vindicate, as it may, its own credibility.

12

That Claggart's figure was not amiss, and his face, save the chin, well molded, has already been said. Of these favorable points he seemed not insensible, for he was not only neat but careful in his dress. But the form of Billy Budd was heroic; and if his face was without the intellectual look of the pallid Claggart's, not the less was it lit, like his, from within, though from a different source. The bonfire in his heart made luminous the rose-tan in his cheek.

In view of the marked contrast between the persons of the twain, it is more than probable that when the master-at-arms in the scene last given applied to the sailor the proverb "Handsome is as handsome does," he there let escape an ironic inkling, not caught by the young sailors who heard it, as to what it was that had first moved him against Billy, namely, his significant personal beauty.

Now envy and antipathy, passions irreconcilable in reason, nevertheless in fact may spring conjoined like Chang and Eng in one birth.[38] Is Envy then such a monster? Well, though many an arraigned mortal has in hopes of mitigated penalty pleaded guilty to horrible actions, did ever anybody seriously confess to envy? Something there is in it universally felt to be more shameful than even felonious crime. And not only does everybody disown it, but the better sort are inclined to incredulity when it is in earnest imputed to an intelligent man. But since its lodgment is in the heart not the brain, no degree of intellect supplies a guarantee against it. But Claggart's was no vulgar form of the passion. Nor, as directed toward Billy Budd, did it partake of that streak of apprehensive jealousy that marred Saul's visage per-

---

[37] Cf. II Thessalonians ii: 7: "For the mystery of iniquity doth already work."

[38] These were the original Siamese twins (1811-1874), famous in Melville's time.

turbedly brooding on the comely young David.[39] Claggart's envy struck deeper. If askance he eyed the good looks, cheery health, and frank enjoyment of young life in Billy Budd, it was because these went along with a nature that, as Claggart magnetically felt, had in its simplicity never willed malice or experienced the reactionary bite of that serpent. To him, the spirit lodged within Billy, and looking out from his welkin eyes as from windows, that ineffability it was which made the dimple in his dyed cheek, suppled his joints, and dancing in his yellow curls made him pre-eminently the Handsome Sailor. One person excepted, the master-at-arms was perhaps the only man in the ship intellectually capable of adequately appreciating the moral phenomenon presented in Billy Budd. And the insight but intensified his passion, which assuming various secret forms within him, at times assumed that of cynic disdain, disdain of innocence—to be nothing more than innocent! Yet in an aesthetic way he saw the charm of it, the courageous free-and-easy temper of it, and fain would have shared it, but he despaired of it.

With no power to annul the elemental evil in him, though readily enough he could hide it; apprehending the good, but powerless to be it; a nature like Claggart's, surcharged with energy as such natures almost invariably are, what recourse is left to it but to recoil upon itself and, like the scorpion for which the Creator alone is responsible, act out to the end the part allotted it.

13

Passion, and passion in its profoundest, is not a thing demanding a palatial stage whereon to play its part. Down among the groundlings, among the beggars and rakers of the garbage, profound passion is enacted. And the circumstances that provoke it, however trivial or mean, are no measure of its power. In the present instance the stage is a scrubbed gun-deck, and one of the external provocations a man-of-war's man's spilled soup.

Now when the master-at-arms noticed whence came that greasy fluid streaming before his feet, he must have taken it—to some extent wilfully, perhaps—not for the mere accident it assuredly was, but for the sly escape of a spontaneous feeling on Billy's part more or less answering to the antipathy on his own. In effect a foolish demonstration, he must have thought, and very harmless, like the futile kick of a heifer, which yet were the heifer a shod stallion would not be so harmless. Even so was it that into the gall of Claggart's envy he infused the vitriol of his contempt. But the incident confirmed to him certain telltale reports purveyed to his ear by "Squeak," one of his more cunning corporals, a grizzled little man, so nicknamed by the sailors on account of his squeaky voice and sharp visage ferreting about the dark corners of the lower decks after interlopers, satirically suggesting to them the idea of a rat in a cellar.

From his chief's employing him as an implicit tool in laying little traps for

[39] Cf. I Samuel xviii: 9 ff.

the worriment of the foretopman—for it was from the master-at-arms that
the petty persecutions heretofore adverted to had proceeded—the corporal,
having naturally enough concluded that his master could have no love for
the sailor, made it his business, faithful understrapper that he was, to foment
the ill blood by perverting to his chief certain innocent frolics of the good-
natured foretopman, besides inventing for his mouth sundry contumelious
epithets he claimed to have overheard him let fall. The master-at-arms never
suspected the veracity of these reports, more especially as to the epithets, for
he well knew how secretly unpopular may become a master-at-arms, at least
a master-at-arms of those days, zealous in his function, and how the bluejackets shoot at him in private their raillery and wit; the nickname by which he
goes among them (Jemmy Legs) implying under the form of merriment their
cherished disrespect and dislike. But in view of the greediness of hate for
pabulum it hardly needed a purveyor to feed Claggart's passion.

An uncommon prudence is habitual with the subtler depravity, for it has
everything to hide. And in case of an injury but suspected, its secretiveness
voluntarily cuts it off from enlightenment or disillusion; and, not unreluctant-
ly, action is taken upon surmise as upon certainty. And the retaliation is apt
to be in monstrous disproportion to the supposed offense; for when in anybody was revenge in its exactions aught else but an inordinate usurer? But
how with Claggart's conscience? For though consciences are unlike as foreheads, every intelligence, not excluding the scriptural devils who "believe
and tremble," has one. But Claggart's conscience being but the lawyer to his
will, made ogres of trifles, probably arguing that the motive imputed to Billy
in spilling the soup just when he did, together with the epithets alleged,
these, if nothing more, made a strong case against him; nay, justified animosity into a sort of retributive righteousness. The Pharisee is the Guy Fawkes[40]
prowling in the hid chambers underlying some natures like Claggart's. And
they can really form no conception of an unreciprocated malice. Probably
the master-at-arms' clandestine persecution of Billy was started to try the
temper of the man; but it had not developed any quality in him that enmity
could make official use of or even pervert into plausible self-justification; so
that the occurrence at the mess, petty if it were, was a welcome one to that
peculiar conscience assigned to be the private mentor of Claggart; and, for
the rest, not improbably it put him upon new experiments.

14

Not many days after the last incident narrated, something befell Billy Budd
that more graveled him than aught that had previously occurred.

It was a warm night for the latitude; and the foretopman, whose watch at
the time was properly below, was dozing on the uppermost deck whither he
had ascended from his hot hammock, one of hundreds suspended so closely

[40] Guy Fawkes plotted to blow up the House
of Parliament in what has become known as
the Gunpowder Plot (1604-1605).

wedged together over a lower gun deck that there was little or no swing to them. He lay as in the shadow of a hillside, stretched under the lee of the booms, a piled ridge of spare spars amidships between foremast and mainmast among which the ship's largest boat, the launch, was stowed. Alongside of three other slumberers from below, he lay near that end of the booms which approaches the foremast; his station aloft on duty as a foretopman being just over the deck-station of the forecastlemen, entitling him according to usage to make himself more or less at home in that neighborhood.

Presently he was stirred into semiconsciousness by somebody, who must have previously sounded the sleep of the others, touching his shoulder, and then, as the foretopman raised his head, breathing into his ear in a quick whisper, "Slip into the lee forechains, Billy; there is something in the wind, Don't speak. Quick, I will meet you there," and disappearing.

Now Billy, like sundry other essentially good-natured ones, had some of the weaknesses inseparable from essential good nature; and among these was a reluctance, almost an incapacity of plumply saying *no* to an abrupt proposition not obviously absurd on the face of it, nor obviously unfriendly, nor iniquitous. And being of warm blood, he had not the phlegm tacitly to negative any proposition by unresponsive inaction. Like his sense of fear, his apprehension as to aught outside of the honest and natural was seldom very quick. Besides, upon the present occasion, the drowse from his sleep still hung upon him.

However it was, he mechanically rose and, sleepily wondering what could be in the wind, betook himself to the designated place, a narrow platform, one of six, outside of the high bulwarks and screened by the great deadeyes and multiple columned lanyards of the shrouds and backstays; and, in a great warship of that time, of dimensions commensurate to the hull's magnitude; a tarry balcony in short, overhanging the sea, and so secluded that one mariner of the *Bellipotent*, a Nonconformist old tar of a serious turn, made it even in daytime his private oratory.

In this retired nook the stranger soon joined Billy Budd. There was no moon as yet; a haze obscured the starlight. He could not distinctly see the stranger's face. Yet from something in the outline and carriage, Billy took him, and correctly, for one of the afterguard.

"Hist! Billy," said the man, in the same quick cautionary whisper as before. "You were impressed, weren't you? Well, so was I"; and he paused, as to mark the effect. But Billy, not knowing exactly what to make of this, said nothing. Then the other: "We are not only impressed ones, Billy. There's a gang of us.—Couldn't you—help—at a pinch?"

"What do you mean?" demanded Billy, here thoroughly shaking off his drowse.

"Hist, hist!" the hurried whisper now growing husky. "See here," and the man held up two small objects faintly twinkling in the night-light; "see, they are yours, Billy, if you'll only——"

But Billy broke in, and in his resentful eagerness to deliver himself his vocal infirmity somewhat intruded. "D—d—damme, I don't know what you are d—d—driving at, or what you mean, but you had better g—g—go where you belong!" For the moment the fellow, as confounded, did not stir; and Billy, springing to his feet, said, "If you d—don't start, I'll t—t—toss you back over the r—rail!" There was no mistaking this, and the mysterious emissary decamped, disappearing in the direction of the mainmast in the shadow of the booms.

"Hallo, what's the matter?" here came growling from a forecastleman awakened from the deck-doze by Billy's raised voice. And as the foretopman reappeared and was recognized by him: "Ah, Beauty, is it you? Well, something must have been the matter, for you st—st—stuttered."

"Oh," rejoined Billy, now mastering the impediment, "I found an afterguardsman in our part of the ship here, and I bid him be off where he belongs."

"And is that all you did about it, Foretopman?" gruffly demanded another, an irascible old fellow of brick-colored visage and hair who was known to his associate forecastlemen as "Red Pepper." "Such sneaks I should like to marry to the gunner's daughter!"—by that expression meaning that he would like to subject them to disciplinary castigation over a gun.

However, Billy's rendering of the matter satisfactorily accounted to these inquirers for the brief commotion, since of all the sections of a ship's company the forecastlemen, veterans for the most part and bigoted in their sea prejudices, are the most jealous in resenting territorial encroachments, especially on the part of any of the after guard, of whom they have but a sorry opinion—chiefly landsmen never going aloft except to reef or furl the mainsail, and in no wise competent to handle a marlinspike or turn in a deadeye, say.

15

This incident sorely puzzled Billy Budd. It was an entirely new experience, the first time in his life that he had ever been personally approached in underhand intriguing fashion. Prior to this encounter he had known nothing of the afterguardsman, the two men being stationed wide apart, one forward and aloft during his watch, the other on deck and aft.

What could it mean? And could they really be guineas, those two glittering objects the interloper had held up to his (Billy's) eyes? Where could the fellow get guineas? Why, even spare buttons are not so plentiful at sea. The more he turned the matter over, the more he was nonplussed, and made uneasy and discomfited. In his disgustful recoil from an overture which, though he but ill comprehended, he instinctively knew must involve evil of some sort, Billy Budd was like a young horse fresh from the pasture suddenly inhaling a vile whiff from some chemical factory, and by repeated snortings trying to get it out of his nostrils and lungs. This frame of mind barred all desire of holding further parley with the fellow, even were it but for the purpose of gaining some enlightenment as to his design in approaching him. And yet he was not without natural curiosity to see how such a visitor in the dark would look in broad day.

He espied him the following afternoon in his first dogwatch below, one of the smokers on that forward part of the upper gun deck allotted to the pipe. He recognized him by his general cut and build more than by his round freckled face and glassy eyes of pale blue, veiled with lashes all but white. And yet Billy was a bit uncertain whether indeed it were he—yonder chap about his own age chatting and laughing in freehearted way, leaning against a gun; a genial young fellow enough to look at, and something of a rattle-brain, to all appearance. Rather chubby too for a sailor, even an after-guardsman. In short, the last man in the world, one would think, to be overburdened with thoughts, especially those perilous thoughts that must needs belong to a conspirator in any serious project, or even to the underling of such a conspirator.

Although Billy was not aware of it, the fellow, with a side long watchful glance, had perceived Billy first, and then noting that Billy was looking at him, thereupon nodded a familiar sort of friendly recognition as to an old acquaintance, without interrupting the talk he was engaged in with the group of smokers. A day or two afterwards, chancing in the evening prome-nade on a gun deck to pass Billy, he offered a flying word of good-fellowship, as it were, which by its unexpectedness, and equivocalness under the cir-cumstances, so embarrassed Billy that he knew not how to respond to it, and let it go unnoticed.

Billy was now left more at a loss than before. The ineffectual speculations into which he was led were so disturbingly alien to him that he did his best to smother them. It never entered his mind that here was a matter which, from its extreme questionableness, it was his duty as a loyal bluejacket to report in the proper quarter. And, probably, had such a step been suggested to him, he would have been deterred from taking it by the thought, one of novice magnanimity, that it would savor overmuch of the dirty work of a telltale. He kept the think to himself. Yet upon one occasion he could not forbear a little disburdening himself to the old Dansker, tempted thereto perhaps by the influence of a balmy night when the ship lay becalmed; the twain, silent for the most part, sitting together on deck, their heads propped against the bulwarks. But it was only a partial and anonymous account that Billy gave, the unfounded scruples above referred to preventing full disclo-sure to anybody. Upon hearing Billy's version, the sage Dansker seemed to divine more than he was told; and after a little meditation, during which his wrinkles were pursed as into a point, quite effacing for the time that quizzing expression his face sometimes wore: "Didn't I say so, Baby Budd?"

"Say what?" demanded Billy.

"Why, *Jemmy Legs* is *down* on you."

"And what," rejoined Billy in amazement, "has *Jemmy Legs* to do with that cracked afterguardsman?"

"Ho, it was an afterguardsman, then. A cat's-paw, a cat's-paw!" And with that exclamation, whether it had reference to a light puff of air just then coming over the calm sea, or a subtler relation to the afterguardsman, there is no telling, the old Merlin gave a twisting wrench with his black teeth at his plug of tobacco, vouchsafing no reply to Billy's impetuous question, though now repeated, for it was his wont to relapse into grim silence when interrogated in skeptical sort as to any of his sententious oracles, not always very clear ones, rather partaking of that obscurity which invests most Delphic deliverances from any quarter.

Long experience had very likely brought this old man to that bitter prudence which never interferes in aught and never gives advice.

16

Yes, despite the Dansker's pithy insistence as to the master-at-arms being at the bottom of these strange experiences of Billy on board the *Bellipotent,* the young sailor was ready to ascribe them to almost anybody but the man who, to use Billy's own expression, "always had a pleasant word for him." This is to be wondered at. Yet not so much to be wondered at. In certain matters, some sailors even in mature life remain unsophisticated enough. But a young seafarer of the disposition of our athletic foretopman is much of a child-man. And yet a child's utter innocence is but its blank ignorance, and the innocence more or less wanes as intelligence waxes. But in Billy Budd intelligence, such as it was, had advanced while yet his simple-mindedness remained for the most part unaffected. Experience is a teacher indeed; yet did Billy's years make his experience small. Besides, he had none of that intuitive knowledge of the bad which in natures not good or incompletely so foreruns experience, and therefore may pertain, as in some instances it too clearly does pertain, even to youth.

And what could Billy know of man except of man as a mere sailor? And the old-fashioned sailor, the veritable man before the mast, the sailor from boyhood up, he, though indeed of the same species as a landsman, is in some respects singularly distinct from him. The sailor is frankness, the landsman is finesse. Life is not a game with the sailor, demanding the long head—no intricate game of chess where few moves are made in straightforwardness and ends are attained by indirection, an oblique, tedious, barren game hardly worth that poor candle burnt out in playing it.[41]

Yes, as a class, sailors are in character a juvenile race. Even their deviations are marked by juvenility, this more especially holding true with the

---

[41] Cf. *Macbeth,* Act V, Sc. 5, ll. 15-17.

sailors of Billy's time. Then too, certain things which apply to all sailors do more pointedly operate here and there upon the junior one. Every sailor, too, is accustomed to obey orders without debating them; his life afloat is externally ruled for him; he is not brought into that promiscuous commerce with mankind where unobstructed free agency on equal terms—equal superficially, at least—soon teaches one that unless upon occasion he exercise a distrust keen in proportion to the fairness of the appearance, some foul turn may be served him. A ruled undemonstrative distrustfulness is so habitual, not with businessmen so much as with men who know their kind in less shallow relations than business, namely, certain men of the world, that they come at last to employ it all but unconsciously; and some of them would very likely feel real surprise at being charged with it as one of their general characteristics.

17

But after the little matter at the mess Billy Budd no more found himself in strange trouble at times about his hammock or his clothes bag or what not. As to that smile that occasionally sunned him, and the pleasant passing word, these were, if not more frequent, yet if anything more pronounced than before.

But for all that, there were certain other demonstrations now. When Claggart's unobserved glance happened to light on belted Billy rolling along the upper gun deck in the leisure of the second dogwatch, exchanging passing broadsides of fun with other young promenaders in the crowd, that glance would follow the cheerful sea Hyperion[42] with a settled meditative and melancholy expression, his eyes strangely suffused with incipient feverish tears. Then would Claggart look like a man of sorrows. Yes, and sometimes the melancholy expression would have in it a touch of soft yearning, as if Claggart could even have loved Billy but for fate and ban. But this was an evanescence, and quickly repented of, as it were, by an immitigable look, pinching and shriveling the visage into the momentary semblance of a wrinkled walnut. But sometimes catching sight in advance of the foretopman coming in his direction, he would, upon their nearing, step aside a little to let him pass, dwelling upon Billy for the moment with the glittering dental satire of a Guise.[43] But upon any abrupt unforeseen encounter a red light would flash forth from his eye like a spark from an anvil in a dusk smithy. That quick, fierce light was a strange one, darted from orbs which in repose were of a color nearest approaching a deeper violet, the softest of shades.

Though some of these caprices of the pit could not but be observed by their object, yet were they beyond the construing of such a nature. And the

---

[42] God of the sun.
[43] The Guises were a rich and powerful family in sixteenth- and seventeenth-century France; their intrigues appealed to Alexander Dumas, and other novelists.

thews of Billy were hardly compatible with that sort of sensitive spiritual organization which in some cases instinctively conveys to ignorant innocence an admonition of the proximity of the malign. He thought the master-at-arms acted in a manner rather queer at times. That was all. But the occasional frank air and pleasant word went for what they purported to be, the young sailor never having heard as yet of the "too fair-spoken man."

Had the foretopman been conscious of having done or said anything to provoke the ill will of the official, it would have been different with him, and his sight might have been purged if not sharpened. As it was, innocence was his blinder.

So was it with him in yet another matter. Two minor officers, the armorer and captain of the hold, with whom he had never exchanged a word, his position in the ship not bringing him into contact with them, these men now for the first began to cast upon Billy, when they chanced to encounter him, that peculiar glance which evidences that the man from whom it comes has been some way tampered with, and to the prejudice of him upon whom the glance lights. Never did it occur to Billy as a thing to be noted or a thing suspicious, though he well knew the fact, that the armorer and captain of the hold, with the ship's yeoman, apothecary, and others of that grade, were by naval usage messmates of the master-at-arms, men with ears convenient to his confidential tongue.

But the general popularity that came from our Handsome Sailor's manly forwardness upon occasion and irresistible good nature, indicating no mental superiority tending to excite an invidious feeling, this good will on the part of most of his shipmates made him the less to concern himself about such mute aspects toward him as those whereto allusion has just been made, aspects he could not so fathom as to infer their whole import.

As to the afterguardsman, though Billy for reasons already given necessarily saw little of him, yet when the two did happen to meet, invariably came the fellow's offhand cheerful recognition, sometimes accompanied by a passing pleasant word or two. Whatever that equivocal young person's original design may really have been, or the design of which he might have been the deputy, certain it was from his manner upon these occasions that he had wholly dropped it.

It was as if his precocity of crookedness (and every vulgar villain is precocious) had for once deceived him, and the man he had sought to entrap as a simpleton had through his very simplicity ignominiously baffled him.

But shrewd ones may opine that it was hardly possible for Billy to refrain from going up to the afterguardsman and bluntly demanding to know his purpose in the initial interview so abruptly closed in the forechains. Shrewd ones may also think it but natural in Billy to set about sounding some of the other impressed men of the ship in order to discover what basis, if any, there was for the emissary's obscure suggestions as to plotting disaffection aboard. Yes, shrewd ones may so think. But something more, or rather something else than mere shrewdness is perhaps needful for the due understanding of such a character as Billy Budd's.

As to Claggart, the monomania in the man—if that indeed it were—as involuntarily disclosed by starts in the manifestations detailed, yet in general covered over by his self-contained and rational demeanor; this, like a subterranean fire, was eating its way deeper and deeper in him. Something decisive must come of it.

18

After the mysterious interview in the forechains, the one so abruptly ended there by Billy, nothing especially germane to the story occurred until the events now about to be narrated.

Elsewhere it has been said that in the lack of frigates (of course better sailers than line-of-battle ships) in the English squadron up the Straits at that period, the *Bellipotent* 74 was occasionally employed not only as an available substitute for a scout, but at times on detached service of more important kind. This was not alone because of her sailing qualities, not common in a ship of her rate, but quite as much, probably, that the character of her commander, it was thought, specially adapted him for any duty where under unforeseen difficulties a prompt initiative might have to be taken in some matter demanding knowledge and ability in addition to those qualities implied in good seamanship. It was on an expedition of the latter sort, a somewhat distant one, and when the *Bellipotent* was almost at her furthest remove from the fleet, that in the latter part of an afternoon watch she unexpectedly came in sight of a ship of the enemy. It proved to be a frigate. The latter, perceiving through the glass that the weight of men and metal would be heavily against her, invoking her light heels crowded sail to get away. After a chase urged almost against hope and lasting until about the middle of the first dogwatch, she signally succeeded in effecting her escape.

Not long after the pursuit had been given up, and ere the excitement incident thereto had altogether waned away, the master-at-arms, ascending from his cavernous sphere, made his appearance cap in hand by the mainmast respectfully waiting the notice of Captain Vere, then solitary walking the weather side of the quarterdeck, doubtless somewhat chafed at the failure of the pursuit. The spot where Claggart stood was the place allotted to men of lesser grades seeking some more particular interview either with the officer of the deck or the captain himself. But from the latter it was not often that a sailor or petty officer of those days would seek a hearing; only some exceptional cause would, according to established custom, have warranted that.

Presently, just as the commander, absorbed in his reflections, was on the point of turning aft in his promenade, he became sensible of Claggart's presence, and saw the doffed cap held in deferential expectancy. Here be it said that Captain Vere's personal knowledge of this petty officer had only begun at the time of the ship's last sailing from home, Claggart then for the first, in transfer from a ship detained for repairs, supplying on board the *Bellipotent* the place of a previous master-at-arms disabled and ashore.

No sooner did the commander observe who it was that now deferentially stood awaiting his notice than a peculiar expression came over him. It was not unlike that which uncontrollably will flit across the countenance of one at unawares encountering a person who, though known to him indeed, has hardly been long enough known for thorough knowledge, but something in whose aspect nevertheless now for the first provokes a vaguely repellent distaste. But coming to a stand and resuming much of his wonted official manner, save that a sort of impatience lurked in the intonation of the opening word, he said "Well? What is it, Master-at-arms?"

With the air of a subordinate grieved at the necessity of being a messenger of ill tidings, and while conscientiously determined to be frank yet equally resolved upon shunning overstatement, Claggart at this invitation, or rather summons to disburden, spoke up. What he said, conveyed in the language of no uneducated man, was to the effect following, if not altogether in these words, namely, that during the chase and preparations for the possible encounter he had seen enough to convince him that at least one sailor aboard was a dangerous character in a ship mustering some who not only had taken a guilty part in the late serious troubles, but others also who, like the man in question, had entered His Majesty's service under another form than enlistment.

At his point Captain Vere with some impatience interrupted him: "Be direct, man; say *impressed men.*"

Claggart made a gesture of subservience, and proceeded. Quite lately he (Claggart) had begun to suspect that on the gun decks some sort of movement prompted by the sailor in question was covertly going on, but he had not thought himself warranted in reporting the suspicion so long as it remained indistinct. But from what he had that afternoon observed in the man referred to, the suspicion of something clandestine going on had advanced to a point less removed from certainty. He deeply felt, he added, the serious responsibility assumed in making a report involving such possible consequences to the individual mainly concerned, besides tending to augment those natural anxieties which every naval commander must feel in view of extraordinary outbreaks so recent as those which, he sorrowfully said it, it needed not to name.

Now at the first broaching of the matter Captain Vere, taken by surprise, could not wholly dissemble his disquietude. But as Claggart went on, the former's aspect changed into restiveness under something in the testifier's manner in giving his testimony. However, he refrained from interrupting him. And Claggart, continuing, concluded with this: "God forbid, your honor, that the *Bellipotent's* should be the experience of the—"

"Never mind that!" here peremptorily broke in the superior, his face altering with anger, instinctively divining the ship that the other was about to name, one in which the Nore Mutiny had assumed a singularly tragical character that for a time jeopardized the life of its commander. Under the circumstances he was indignant at the purposed allusion. When the commissioned officers themselves were on all occasions very heedful how they referred to the recent events in the fleet, for a petty officer unnecessarily to allude to them in the presence of his captain, this struck him as a most immodest presumption. Besides, to his quick sense of self-respect it even looked under the circumstances something like an attempt to alarm him. Nor at first was he without some surprise that one who so far as he had hitherto come under his notice had shown considerable tact in his function should in this particular evince such lack of it.

But these thoughts and kindred dubious ones flitting across his mind were suddenly replaced by an intuitional surmise which, though as yet obscure in form, served practically to affect his reception of the ill tidings. Certain it is that, long versed in everything pertaining to the complicated gun-deck life, which like every other form of life has its secret mines and dubious side, the side popularly disclaimed, Captain Vere did not permit himself to be unduly disturbed by the general tenor of his subordinate's report.

Furthermore, if in view of recent events prompt action should be taken at the first palpable sign of recurring insubordination, for all that, not judicious would it be, he thought, to keep the idea of lingering disaffection alive by undue forwardness in crediting an informer, even if his own subordinate and charged among other things with police surveillance of the crew. This feeling would not perhaps have so prevailed with him were it not that upon a prior occasion the patriotic zeal officially evinced by Claggart had somewhat irritated him as appearing rather supersensible and strained. Furthermore, something even in the official's self-possessed and somewhat ostentatious manner in making his specifications strangely reminded him of a bandsman, a perjurous witness in a capital case before a courtmartial ashore of which when a lieutenant he (Captain Vere) had been a member.

Now the peremptory check given to Claggart in the matter of the arrested allusion was quickly followed up by this: "You say that there is at least one dangerous man aboard. Name him."

"William Budd, a foretopman, your honor."

"William Budd!" repeated Captain Vere with unfeigned astonishment. "And mean you the man that Lieutenant Ratcliffe took from the merchantman not very long ago, the young fellow who seems to be so popular with the men—Billy, the Handsome Sailor, as they call him?"

"The same, your honor; but for all his youth and good looks, a deep one. Not for nothing does he insinuate himself into the good will of his shipmates, since at the least they will at a pinch say—all hands will—a good word for him, and at all hazards. Did Lieutenant Ratcliffe happen to tell your honor of that adroit fling of Budd's, jumping up in the cutter's bow under the merchantman's stern when he was being taken off? It is even masked by that sort of goodhumored air that at heart he resents his impressment. You have but noted his fair cheek. A mantrap may be under the ruddy-tipped daisies."

Now the Handsome Sailor as a signal figure among the crew had naturally enough attracted the captain's attention from the first. Though in general not very demonstrative to his officers, he had congratulated Lieutenant Ratcliffe upon his good fortune in lighting on such a fine specimen of the *genus homo*, who in the nude might have posed for a statue of young Adam before the Fall. As to Billy's adieu to the ship *Rights-of-Man*, which the boarding lieutenant had indeed reported to him, but, in a deferential way, more as a good story than aught else, Captain Vere, though mistakenly understanding it as a satiric sally, had but thought so much the better of the impressed man for it; as a military sailor, admiring the spirit that could take an arbitrary enlistment so merrily and sensibly. The foretopman's conduct, too, so far as it had fallen under the captain's notice, had confirmed the first happy augury, while the new recruit's qualities as a "sailor-man" seemed to be such that he had thought of recommending him to the executive officer for promotion to a place that would more frequently bring him under his own observation, namely, the captaincy of the mizzentop, replacing there in the starboard watch a man not so young whom partly for that reason he deemed less fitted for the post. Be it parenthesized here that since the mizzentopmen have not to handle such breadths of heavy canvas as the lower sails on the mainmast and foremast, a young man if of the right stuff not only seems best adapted to duty there, but in fact is generally selected for the captaincy of that top, and the company under him are light hands and often but striplings. In sum, Captain Vere had from the beginning deemed Billy Budd to be what in the naval parlance of the time was called a "King's bargain": that is to say, for His Britannic Majesty's navy a capital investment at small outlay or none at all.

After a brief pause, during which the reminiscences above mentioned passed vividly through his mind and he weighed the import of Claggart's last suggestion conveyed in the phrase "mantrap under the daisies," and the more he weighed it the less reliance he felt in the informer's good faith, suddenly he turned upon him and in a low voice demanded: "Do you come to me, Master-at-arms, with so foggy a tale? As to Budd, cite me an act or spoken word of his confirmatory of what you in general charge against him. Stay," drawing nearer to him; "heed what you speak. Just now, and in a case like this, there is a yardarm-end for the false witness."

"Ah, your honor!" sighed Claggart, mildly shaking his shapely head as in sad deprecation of such unmerited severity of tone. Then, bridling—erecting himself as in virtuous self-assertion—he circumstantially alleged certain words and acts which collectively, if credited, led to presumptions mortally inculpating Budd. And for some of these averments, he added, substantiating proof was not far.

With gray eyes impatient and distrustful essaying to fathom to the bottom Claggart's calm violet ones, Captain Vere again heard him out; then for the moment stood ruminating. The mood he evinced, Claggart—himself for the time liberated from the other's scrutiny—steadily regarded with a look difficult to render: a look curious of the operation of his tactics, a look such as might have been that of the spokesman of the envious children of Jacob deceptively imposing upon the troubled patriarch the blood-dyed coat of young Joseph.[44]

Though something exceptional in the moral quality of Captain Vere made him, in earnest encounter with a fellow man, a veritable touchstone of that man's essential nature, yet now as to Claggart and what was really going on in him his feeling partook less of intuitional conviction than of strong suspicion clogged by strange dubieties. The perplexity he evinced proceeded less from aught touching the man informed against—as Claggart doubtless opined—than from considerations how best to act in regard to the informer. At first, indeed, he was naturally for summoning that substantiation of his allegations which Claggart said was at hand. But such a proceeding would result in the matter at once getting abroad, which in the present stage of it, he thought, might undesirably affect the ship's company. If Claggart was a false witness—that closed the affair. And therefore, before trying the accusation, he would first practically test the accuser; and he thought this could be done in a quiet, undemonstrative way.

The measure he determined upon involved a shifting of the scene, a transfer to a place less exposed to observation than the broad quarter-deck. For although the few gun-room officers there at the time had, in due observance of naval etiquette, withdrawn to leeward the moment Captain Vere had begun his promenade on the deck's weather side; and though during the colloquy with Claggart they of course ventured not to diminish the distance; and though throughout the interview Captain Vere's voice was far from high, and Claggart's silvery and low; and the wind in the cordage and the wash of the sea helped the more to put them beyond earshot; nevertheless, the interview's continuance already had attracted observation from some topmen aloft and other sailors in the waist or further forward.

Having determined upon his measures, Captain Vere forthwith took action. Abruptly turning to Claggart, he asked, "Master-at-arms, is it now Budd's watch aloft?"

"No, your honor."

Whereupon, "Mr. Wilkes!" summoning the nearest midshipman.

"Tell Albert to come to me." Albert was the captain's hammock-boy, a sort of sea valet in whose discretion and fidelity his master had much confidence. The lad appeared.

[44] Genesis xxxvii: 31-34.

"You know Budd, the foretopman?"

"I do, sir."

"Go find him. It is his watch off. Manage to tell him out of earshot that he is wanted aft. Contrive it that he speaks to nobody. Keep him in talk yourself. And not till you get well aft here, not till then let him know that the place where he is wanted is my cabin. You understand. Go.—Master-at-arms, show yourself on the decks below, and when you think it time for Albert to be coming with his man, stand by quietly to follow the sailor in."

19

Now when the foretopman found himself in the cabin, closeted there, as it were, with the captain and Claggart, he was surprised enough. But it was a surprise unaccompanied by apprehension or distrust. To an immature nature essentially honest and humane, forewarning intimations of subtler danger from one's kind come tardily if at all. The only thing that took shape in the young sailor's mind was this: Yes, the captain, I have always thought, looks kindly upon me. Wonder if he's going to make me his coxswain. I should like that. And may be now he is going to ask the master-at-arms about me.

"Shut the door there, sentry," said the commander; "stand without, and let nobody come in.—Now, Master-at-arms, tell this man to his face what you told of him to me," and stood prepared to scrutinize the mutually confronting visages.

With the measured step and calm collected air of an asylum physician approaching in the public hall some patient beginning to show indications of a coming paroxysm, Claggart deliberately advanced within short range of Billy and, mesmerically looking him in the eye, briefly recapitulated the accusation.

Not at first did Billy take it in. When he did, the rose-tan of his cheek looked struck as by white leprosy. He stood like one impaled and gagged. Meanwhile the accuser's eyes, removing not as yet from the blue dilated ones, underwent a phenomenal change, their wonted rich violet color blurring into a muddy purple. Those lights of human intelligence, losing human expression, were gelidly protruding like the alien eyes of certain uncatalogued creatures of the deep. The first mesmeristic glance was one of serpent fascination; the last was as the paralyzing lurch of the torpedo fish.

"Speak, man!" said Captain Vere to the transfixed one, struck by his aspect even more than by Claggart's. Speak! Defend yourself!" Which appeal caused but a strange dumb gesturing and gurgling in Billy; amazement at such an accusation so suddenly sprung on inexperienced nonage; this, and, it may be, horror of the accuser's eyes, serving to bring out his lurking defect and in this instance for the time intensifying it into a convulsed tongue-tie; while the intent head and entire form straining forward in an agony of ineffectual eagerness to obey the injunction to speak and defend himself, gave an expression to the face like that of a condemned vestal priestess in the moment of being buried alive, and in the first struggle against suffocation.

Though at the time Captain Vere was quite ignorant of Billy's liability to vocal impediment, he now immediately divined it, since vividly Billy's aspect recalled to him that of a bright young schoolmate of his whom he had once seen struck by much the same startling impotence in the act of eagerly rising in the class to be foremost in response to a testing question put to it by the master. Going close up to the young sailor, and laying a soothing hand on his shoulder, he said, "There is no hurry, my boy. Take your time, take your time." Contrary to the effect intended, these words so fatherly in tone, doubtless touching Billy's heart to the quick, prompted yet more violent efforts at utterance—efforts soon ending for the time in confirming the paralysis, and bringing to his face an expression which was as a crucifixion to behold. The next instant, quick as the flame from a discharged cannon at night, his right arm shot out, and Claggart dropped to the deck. Whether intentionally or but owing to the young athlete's superior height, the blow had taken effect full upon the forehead, so shapely and intellectual-looking a feature in the master-at-arms; so that the body fell over lengthwise, like a heavy plank tilted from erectness. A gasp or two, and he lay motionless.

"Fated boy," breathed Captain Vere in tone so low as to be almost a whisper, "what have you done! But here, help me."

The twain raised the felled one from the loins up into a sitting position. The spare form flexibly acquiesced, but inertly. It was like handling a dead snake. They lowered it back. Regaining erectness, Captain Vere with one hand covering his face stood to all appearance as impassive as the object at his feet. Was he absorbed in taking in all the bearings of the event and what was best not only now at once to be done, but also in the sequel? Slowly he uncovered his face; and the effect was as if the moon emerging from eclipse should reappear with quite another aspect than that which had gone into hiding. The father in him, manifested towards Billy thus far in the scene, was replaced by the military disciplinarian. In his official tone he bade the foretopman retire to a stateroom aft (pointing it out), and there remain till thence summoned. This order Billy in silence mechanically obeyed. Then going to the cabin door where it opened on the quarter-deck, Captain Vere said to the sentry without, "Tell somebody to send Albert here." When the lad appeared, his master so contrived it that he should not catch sight of the prone one. "Albert," he said to him, "tell the surgeon I wish to see him. You need not come back till called."

When surgeon entered—a self-poised character of that grave sense and experience that hardly anything could take him aback—Captain Vere advanced to meet him, thus unconsciously intercepting his view of Claggart, and, interrupting the other's wonted ceremonious salutation, said, "Nay. Tell me how it is with yonder man," directing his attention to the prostrate one.

The surgeon looked, and for all his self-command somewhat started at the abrupt revelation. On Claggart's always pallid complexion, thick black blood was now oozing from nostril and ear. To the gazer's professional eye it was unmistakably no living man that he saw.

"Is it so, then?" said Captain Vere, intently watching him. "I thought it. But verify it." Whereupon the customary tests confirmed the surgeon's first glance, who now, looking up in unfeigned concern, cast a look of intense inquisitiveness upon his superior. But Captain Vere, with one hand to his brow, was standing motionless. Suddenly, catching the surgeon's arm convulsively, he exclaimed, pointing down to the body, "It is the divine judgment on Ananias![45] Look!"

Disturbed by the excited manner he had never before observed in the *Bellipotent's* captain, and as yet wholly ignorant of the affair, the prudent surgeon nevertheless held his peace, only again looking an earnest interrogatory as to what it was that had resulted in such a tragedy.

But Captain Vere was now again motionless, standing absorbed in thought. Again starting, he vehemently exclaimed, "Struck dead by an angel of God! Yet the angel must hang!"

At these passionate interjections, mere incoherences to the listener as yet unapprised of the antecedents, the surgeon was profoundly discomposed. But now, as recollecting himself, Captain Vere in less passionate tone briefly related the circumstances leading up to the event. "But come; we must dispatch," he added. "Help me to remove him" (meaning the body) "to yonder compartment," designating one opposite that where the foretopman remained immured. Anew disturbed by a request that, as implying a desire for secrecy, seemed unaccountably strange to him, there was nothing for the subordinate to do but comply.

"Go now," said Captain Vere with something of his wonted manner. "Go now. I presently shall call a drumhead court. Tell the lieutenants what has happened, and tell Mr. Mordant" (meaning the captain of marines), "and charge them to keep the matter to themselves."

20

Full of disquietude and misgiving, the surgeon left the cabin. Was Captain Vere suddenly affected in his mind, or was it but a transient excitement, brought about by so strange and extraordinary a tragedy? As to the drumhead court, it struck the surgeon as impolitic, if nothing more. The thing to do, he thought, was to place Billy Budd in confinement, and in a way dictated by usage, and postpone further action in so extraordinary a case to such time as they should rejoin the squadron, and then refer it to the admiral. He recalled the unwonted agitation of Captain Vere and his excited exclamations, so at variance with his normal manner. Was he unhinged?

[45] Ananias was stricken dead for having lied to God. See Acts v: 1-5.

But assuming that he is, it is not so susceptible of proof. What then can the surgeon do? No more trying situation is conceivable than that of an officer subordinate under a captain whom he suspects to be not mad, indeed, but yet not quite unaffected in his intellects. To argue his order to him would be insolence. To resist him would be mutiny.

In obedience to Captain Vere, he communicated what had happened to the lieutenants and captain of marines, saying nothing as to the captain's state. They fully shared his own surprise and concern. Like him too, they seemed to think that such a matter should be referred to the admiral.

21

Who in the rainbow can draw the line where the violet tint ends and the orange tint begins? Distinctly we see the difference of the colors, but where exactly does the one first blendingly enter into the other? So with sanity and insanity. In pronounced cases there is no question about them. But in some supposed cases, in various degrees supposedly less pronounced, to draw the exact line of demarcation few will undertake, though for a fee becoming considerate some professional experts will. There is nothing namable but that some men will, or undertake to, do it for pay.

Whether Captain Vere, as the surgeon professionally and privately surmised, was really the sudden victim of any degree of aberration, every one must determine for himself by such light as this narrative may afford.

That the unhappy event which has been narrated could not have happened at a worse juncture was but too true. For it was close on the heel of the suppressed insurrections, an aftertime very critical to naval authority, demanding from every English sea commander two qualities not readily interfusable—prudence and rigor. Moreover, there was something crucial in the case.

In the jugglery of circumstances preceding and attending the event on board the *Bellipotent,* and in the light of that martial code whereby it was formally to be judged, innocence and guilt personified in Claggart and Budd in effect changed places. In a legal view the apparent victim of the tragedy was he who had sought to victimize a man blameless; and the indisputable deed of the latter, navally regarded, constituted the most heinous of military crimes. Yet more. The essential right and wrong involved in the matter, the clearer that might be, so much the worse for the responsibility of a loyal sea commander, inasmuch as he was not authorized to determine the matter on that primitive basis.

Small wonder then that the *Bellipotent's* captain, though in general a man of rapid decision, felt that circumspectness not less than promptitude was necessary. Until he could decide upon his course, and in each detail; and not only so, but until the concluding measure was upon the point of being enacted, he deemed it advisable, in view of all the circumstances, to guard as much as possible against publicity. Here he may or may not have erred. Certain it is, however, that subsequently in the confidential talk of more than one or two gun rooms and cabins he was not a little criticized by some officers, a fact imputed by his friends and vehemently by his cousin Jack Denton to professional jealousy of Starry Vere. Some imaginative ground for invidious comment there was. The maintenance of secrecy in the matter, the confining all knowledge of it for a time to the place where the homicide occurred, the quarter-deck cabin; in these particulars lurked some resemblance to the policy adopted in those tragedies of the palace which have occurred more than once in the capital founded by Peter the Barbarian.[46]

The case indeed was such that fain would the *Bellipotent's* captain have deferred taking any action whatever respecting it further than to keep the foretopman a close prisoner till the ship rejoined the squadron and then submitting the matter to the judgment of his admiral.

But a true military officer is in one particular like a true monk. Not with more of self-abnegation will the latter keep his vows of monastic obedience than the former his vows of allegiance to martial duty.

Feeling that unless quick action was taken on it, the deed of the foretopman, so soon as it should be known on the gun decks, would tend to awaken any slumbering embers of the Nore among the crew, a sense of the urgency of the case overruled in Captain Vere every other consideration. But though a conscientious disciplinarian, he was no lover of authority for mere authority's sake. Very far was he from embracing opportunities for monopolizing to himself the perils of moral responsibility, none at least that could properly be referred to an official superior or shared with him by his official equals or even subordinates. So thinking, he was glad it would not be at variance with usage to turn the matter over to a summary court of his own officers, reserving to himself, as the one on whom the ultimate accountability would rest, the right of maintaining a supervision of it, or formally or informally interposing at need. Accordingly a drumhead court was summarily convened, he electing the individuals composing it: the first lieutenant, the captain of marines, and the sailing master.

In associating an officer of marines with the sea lieutenant and the sailing master in a case having to do with a sailor, the commander perhaps deviated from general custom. He was prompted thereto by the circumstance that he took that soldier to be a judicious person, thoughtful, and not altogether incapable of grappling with a difficult case unprecedented in his prior experience. Yet even as to him he was not without some latent misgiving, for withal he was an extremely good-natured man, an enjoyer of his dinner, a sound sleeper, and inclined to obesity—a man who though he would always maintain his manhood in battle might not prove altogether reliable in a moral dilemma involving aught of the tragic. As to the first lieutenant and the

[46] Peter I, Czar of Russia (1682-1725).

sailing master, Captain Vere could not but be aware that though honest natures, of approved gallantry upon occasion, their intelligence was mostly confined to the matter of active seamanship and the fighting demands of their profession.

The court was held in the same cabin where the unfortunate affair had taken place. This cabin, the commander's, embraced the entire area under the poop deck. Aft, and on either side, was a small stateroom, the one now temporarily a jail and the other a deadhouse, and a yet smaller compartment, leaving a space between expanding forward into a goodly oblong of length coinciding with the ship's beam. A skylight of moderate dimension was overhead, and at each end of the oblong space were two sashed porthole windows easily convertible back into embrasures for short carronades.

All being quickly in readiness, Billy Budd was arraigned, Captain Vere necessarily appearing as the sole witness in the case, and as such temporarily sinking his rank, though singularly maintaining it in a matter apparently trivial, namely, that he testified from the ship's weather side, with that object having caused the court to sit on the lee side. Concisely he narrated all that had led up to the catastrophe, omitting nothing in Claggart's accusation and deposing as to the manner in which the prisoner had received it. At this testimony the three officers glanced with no little surprise at Billy Budd, the last man they would have suspected either of the mutinous design alleged by Claggart or the undeniable deed he himself had done. The first lieutenant, taking judicial primacy and turning toward the prisoner, said, "Captain Vere has spoken. Is it or is it not as Captain Vere says?"

In response came syllables not so much impeded in the utterance as might have been anticipated. They were these: "Captain Vere tells the truth. It is just as Captain Vere says, but it is not as the master-at-arms said. I have eaten the Kings bread and I am true to the King."

"I believe you, my man," said the witness, his voice indicating a suppressed emotion not otherwise betrayed.

"God will bless you for that, your honor!" not without stammering said Billy, and all but broke down. But immediately he was recalled to self-control by another question, to which with the same emotional difficulty of utterance he said, "No, there was no malice between us. I never bore malice against the master-at-arms. I am sorry that he is dead. I did not mean to kill him. Could I have used my tongue I would not have struck him. But he foully lied to my face and in presence of my Captain, and I had to say something, and I could only say it with a blow, God help me!"

In the impulsive aboveboard manner of the frank one the court saw confirmed all that was implied in words that just previously had perplexed them, coming as they did from the testifier to the tragedy and promptly following Billy's impassioned disclaimer of mutinous intent—Captain Vere's words, "I believe you, my man."

Next it was asked of him whether he knew of or suspected aught savoring of incipient trouble (meaning mutiny, though the explicit term was avoided) going on in any section of the ship's company.

The reply lingered. This was naturally imputed by the court to the same vocal embarrassment which had retarded or obstructed previous answers. But in main it was otherwise here, the question immediately recalling to Billy's mind the interview with the afterguardsman in the forechains. But an innate repugnance to playing a part at all approaching that of an informer against one's own shipmates—the same erring sense of uninstructed honor which had stood in the way of his reporting the matter at the time, though as a loyal man-of-war's man it was incumbent on him, and failure so to do, if charged against him and proven, would have subjected him to the heaviest of penalties; this, with the blind feeling now his that nothing really was being hatched, prevailed with him. When the answer came it was a negative.

"One question more," said the officer of marines, now first speaking and with a troubled earnestness. "You tell us that what the master-at-arms said against you was a lie. Now why should he have so lied, so maliciously lied, since you declare there was no malice between you?"

At that question, unintentionally touching on a spiritual sphere wholly obscure to Billy's thoughts, he was nonplussed, evincing a confusion indeed that some observers, such as can readily be imagined, would have construed into involuntary evidence of hidden guilt. Nevertheless, he strove some way to answer, but all at once relinquished the vain endeavor, at the same time turning an appealing glance towards Captain Vere as deeming him his best helper and friend. Captain Vere, who had been seated for a time, rose to his feet, addressing the interrogator. "The question you put to him comes naturally enough. But how can he rightly answer it?—or anybody else, unless indeed it be he who lies within there," designating the compartment where lay the corpse. "But the prone one there will not rise to our summons. In effect, though, as it seems to me, the point you make is hardly material. Quite aside from any conceivable motive actuating the master-at-arms, and irrespective of the provocation to the blow, a martial court must needs in the present case confine its attention to the blow's consequence, which consequence justly is to be deemed not otherwise than as the striker's deed."

This utterance, the full significance of which it was not at all likely that Billy took in, nevertheless caused him to turn a wistful interrogative look toward the speaker, a look in its dumb expressiveness not unlike that which a dog of generous breed might turn upon his master, seeking in his face some elucidation of a previous gesture ambiguous to the canine intelligence. Nor was the same utterance without marked effect upon the three officers, more especially the soldier. Couched in it seemed to them a meaning unanticipated, involving a prejudgment on the speaker's part. It served to augment a mental disturbance previously evident enough.

The soldier once more spoke, in a tone of suggestive dubiety addressing at once his associates and Captain Vere: "Nobody is present—none of the ship's company, I mean—who might shed lateral light, if any is to be had, upon what remains mysterious in this matter."

"That is thoughtfully put," said Captain Vere; "I see your drift. Ay, there is a mystery; but, to use a scriptural phrase, it is a 'mystery of iniquity,'[47] a matter for psychologic theologians to discuss. But what has a military court to do with it? Not to add that for us any possible investigation of it is cut off by the lasting tongue-tie of—him—in yonder," again designating the mortuary stateroom. "The prisoner's deed—with that alone we have to do."

To this, and particularly the closing reiteration, the marine soldier, knowing not how aptly to reply, sadly abstained from saying aught. The first lieutenant, who at the outset had not unnaturally assumed primacy in the court, now overrulingly instructed by a glance from Captain Vere, a glance more effective than words, resumed that primacy. Turning to the prisoner, "Budd," he said, and scarce in equable tones, "Budd, if you have aught further to say for yourself, say it now."

Upon this the young sailor turned another quick glance toward Captain Vere; then, as taking a hint from that aspect, a hint confirming his own instinct that silence was now best, replied to the lieutenant, "I have said all, sir."

The marine—the same who had been the sentinel without the cabin door at the time that the foretopman, followed by the master-at-arms, entered it—he, standing by the sailor throughout these judicial proceedings, was now directed to take him back to the after compartment originally assigned to the prisoner and his custodian. As the twain disappeared from view, the three officers, as partially liberated from some inward constraint associated with Billy's mere presence, simultaneously stirred in their seats. They exchanged looks of troubled indecision, yet feeling that decide they must and without long delay. For Captain Vere, he for the time stood—unconsciously with his back toward them, apparently in one of his absent fits—gazing out from a sashed porthole to windward upon the monotonous blank of the twilight sea. But the court's silence continuing, broken only at moments by brief consultations, in low earnest tones, this served to arouse him and energize him. Turning, he to-and-fro paced the cabin athwart; in the returning ascent to windward climbing the slant deck in the ship's lee roll, without knowing its symbolizing thus in his action a mind resolute to surmount difficulties even if against primitive instincts strong as the wind and the sea. Presently he came to a stand before the three. After scanning their faces he stood less as mustering his thoughts for expression than as one inly deliberating how best to put them to well-meaning men not intellectually mature, men with whom it was necessary to demonstrate certain principles that were axioms to himself.

[47] II Thess. ii. 7.

Similar impatience as to talking is perhaps one reason that deters some minds from addressing any popular assemblies.

When speak he did, something, both in the substance of what he said and his manner of saying it, showed the influence of unshared studies modifying and tempering the practical training of an active career. This, along with his phraseology, now and then was suggestive of the grounds whereon rested that imputation of a certain pedantry socially alleged against him by certain naval men of wholly practical cast, captains who nevertheless would frankly concede that His Majesty's navy mustered no more efficient officer of their grade than Starry Vere.

What he said was to this effect: "Hitherto I have been but the witness, little more; and I should hardly think not to take another to me, that of your coadjutor for the time, did I not perceive in you—at the crisis too—a troubled hesitancy, proceeding, I doubt not, from the clash of military duty with moral scruple—scruple vitalized by compassion. For the compassion, how can I otherwise than share it? But, mindful of paramount obligations, I strive against scruples that may tend to enervate decision. Not, gentlemen, that I hide from myself that the case is an exceptional one. Speculatively regarded, it well might be referred to a jury of casuists. But for us here, acting not as casuists or moralists, it is a case practical, and under martial law practically to be dealt with.

"But your scruples: do they move as in a dusk? Challenge them. Make them advance and declare themselves. Come now; do they import something like this: If, mindless of palliating circumstances, we are bound to regard the death of the master-at-arms as the prisoner's deed, then does that deed constitute a capital crime whereof the penalty is a mortal one. But in natural justice is nothing but the prisoner's overt act to be considered? How can we adjudge to summary and shameful death a fellow creature innocent before God, and whom we feel to be so?—Does that state it aright? You sign sad assent. Well, I too feel that, the full force of that. It is Nature. But do these buttons that we wear attest that our allegiance is to Nature? No, to the King. Though the ocean, which is inviolate Nature primeval, though this be the element where we move and have our being as sailors, yet as the King's officers lies our duty in a sphere correspondingly natural? So little is that true, that in receiving our commissions we in the most important regards ceased to be natural free agents. When war is declared are we the commissioned fighters previously consulted? We fight at command. If our judgments approve the war, that is but coincidence. So in other particulars. So now. For suppose condemnation to follow these present proceedings. Would it be so much we ourselves that would condemn as it would be martial law operating through us? For that law and the rigor of it, we are not responsible. Our vowed responsibility is in this: That however pitilessly that law may operate in any instances, we nevertheless adhere to it and administer it.

"But the exceptional in the matter moves the hearts within you. Even so too is mine moved. But let not warm hearts betray heads that should be cool. Ashore in a criminal case, will an upright judge allow himself off the bench to be waylaid by some tender kinswoman of the accused seeking to touch him with her tearful plea? Well, the heart here, sometimes the feminine in man, is as that piteous woman, and hard though it be, she must here be ruled out."

He paused, earnestly studying them for a moment; then resumed.

"But something in your aspect seems to urge that it is not solely the heart that moves in you, but also the conscience, the private conscience. But tell me whether or not, occupying the position we do, private conscience should not yield to that imperial one formulated in the code under which alone we officially proceed?"

Here the three men moved in their seats, less convinced than agitated by the course of an argument troubling but the more the spontaneous conflict within.

Perceiving which, the speaker paused for a moment; then abruptly changing his tone, went on.

"To steady us a bit, let us recur to the facts.—In wartime at sea a man-of-war's man strikes his superior in grade, and the blow kills. Apart from its effect the blow itself is, according to the Articles of War, a capital crime. Furthermore——"

"Ay, sir," emotionally broke in the officer of marines, "in one sense it was. But surely Budd purposed neither mutiny nor homicide."

"Surely not, my good man. And before a court less arbitrary and more merciful than a martial one, that plea would largely extenuate. At the Last Assizes[48] it shall acquit. But how here? We proceed under the law of the Mutiny Act. In feature no child can resemble his father more than that Act resembles in spirit the thing from which it derives—War. In His Majesty's service—in this ship, indeed—there are Englishman forced to fight for the King against their will. Against their conscience, for aught we know. Though as their fellow creatures some of us may appreciate their position, yet as navy officers what reck we of it? Still less recks the enemy. Our impressed men he would fain cut down in the same swath with our volunteers. As regards the enemy's naval conscripts, some of whom may even share our own abhorrence of the regicidal French Directory,[49] it is the same on our side. War looks but to the frontage, the appearance. And the Mutiny Act, War's child, takes after the father. Budd's intent or non-intent is nothing to the purpose.

[48] The Biblical Judgment Day.
[49] The executive council of the French First Republic (1795-1799).

"But while, put to it by those anxieties in you which I cannot but respect, I only repeat myself—while thus strangely we prolong proceedings that should be summary—the enemy may be sighted and an engagement result. We must do; and one of two things must we do—condemn or let go."

"Can we not convict and yet mitigate the penalty?" asked the sailing master, here speaking, and falteringly, for the first.

"Gentlemen, were that clearly lawful for us under the circumstances, consider the consequences of such clemency. The people" (meaning the ship's company) "have native sense; most of them are familiar with our naval usage and tradition; and how would they take it? Even could you explain to them—which our official position forbids—they, long molded by arbitrary discipline, have not that kind of intelligent responsiveness that might qualify them to comprehend and discriminate. No, to the people the foretopman's deed, however it be worded in the announcement, will be plain homicide committed in a flagrant act of mutiny. What penalty for that should follow, they know. But it does not follow. *Why?* they will ruminate. You know what sailors are. Will they not revert to the recent outbreak at the Nore? Ay. They know the well-founded alarm—the panic it struck throughout England. Your clement sentence they would account pusillanimous. They would think that we flinch, that we are afraid of them—afraid of practicing a lawful rigor singularly demanded at this juncture, lest it should provoke new troubles. What shame to us such a conjecture on their part, and how deadly to discipline. You see then, whither, prompted by duty and the law, I steadfastly drive. But I beseech you, my friends, do not take me amiss. I feel as you do for this unfortunate boy. But did he know our hearts, I take him to be that generous nature that he would feel even for us on whom in this military necessity so heavy a compulsion is laid."

With that, crossing the deck he resumed his place by the sashed porthole, tacitly leaving the three to come to a decision. On the cabin's opposite side the troubled court sat silent. Loyal lieges, plain and practical, though at bottom they dissented from some points Captain Vere had put to them, they were without the faculty, hardly had the inclination, to gainsay one whom they felt to be an earnest man, one too not less their superior in mind than in naval rank. But it is not improbable that even such of his words as were not without influence over them, less came home to them than his closing appeal to their instinct as sea officers: in the forethought he threw out as to the practical consequences to discipline, considering the unconfirmed tone of the fleet at the time, should a man-of-war's man's violent killing at sea of a superior in grade allowed to pass for aught else than a capital crime demanding prompt infliction of the penalty.

Not unlikely they were brought to something more or less akin to that harassed frame of mind which in the year 1842 actuated the commander of the U.S. brig-of-war *Somers* to resolve, under the so-called Articles of War, Articles modeled upon the English Mutiny Act, to resolve upon the execution at sea of a midshipman and two sailors as mutineers designing the seizure of the brig. Which resolution was carried out though in a time of peace and within not many days' sail of home. An act vindicated by a naval court of inquiry subsequently convened ashore. History, and here cited without comment. True, the circumstances on board the *Somers* were different from those on board the *Bellipotent*. But the urgency felt, well-warranted or otherwise, was much the same.

Says a writer whom few know, "Forty years after a battle it is easy for a noncombatant to reason about how it ought to have been fought. It is another thing personally and under fire to have to direct the fighting while involved in the obscuring smoke of it. Much so with respect to other emergencies involving considerations both practical and moral, and when it is imperative promptly to act. The greater the fog the more it imperils the steamer, and speed is put on though at the hazard of running somebody down. Little ween the snug card players in the cabin of the responsibilities of the sleepless man on the bridge."

In brief, Billy Budd was formally convicted and sentenced to be hung at the yardarm in the early morning watch, it being now night. Otherwise, as is customary in such cases, the sentence would forthwith have been carried out. In wartime on the field or in the fleet, a mortal punishment decreed by a drumhead court—on the field sometimes decreed by but a nod from the general—follows without delay on the heel of conviction, without appeal.

22

It was Captain Vere himself who of his own motion communicated the finding of the court to the prisoner, for that purpose going to the compartment where he was in custody and bidding the marine there to withdraw for the time.

Beyond the communication of the sentence, what took place at this interview was never known. But in view of the character of the twain briefly closeted in that stateroom, each radically sharing in the rarer qualities of our nature—so rare indeed as to be all but incredible to average minds however much cultivated—some conjectures may be ventured.

It would have been in consonance with the spirit of Captain Vere should he on this occasion have concealed nothing from the condemned one—should he indeed have frankly disclosed to him the part he himself had played in bringing about the decision, at the same time revealing his actuating motives. On Billy's side it is not improbable that such a confession would have been received in much the same spirit that prompted it. Not without a sort of joy, indeed, he might have appreciated the brave opinion of him implied in his captain's making such a confidant of him. Nor, as to the sentence itself, could he have been insensible that it was imparted to him as to one not afraid to die. Even more may have been. Captain Vere in end may have developed the passion sometimes latent under an exterior stoical or indifferent. He was old enough to have been Billy's father. The austere devotee of military duty, letting himself melt back into what remains primeval in our formalized humanity, may in end have caught Billy to his heart, even as Abraham may have caught young Isaacs on the brink of resolutely offering him up in obedience to the exacting behest.[50] But there is no telling the sacrament, seldom if in any case revealed to the gadding world, wherever under circumstances at all akin to those here attempted to be set forth two of great Nature's nobler order embrace. There is privacy at the time, inviolable to the survivor; and holy oblivion, the sequel to each diviner magnanimity, providentially covers all at last.

The first to encounter Captain Vere in act of leaving the compartment was the senior lieutenant. The face he beheld, for the moment one expressive of the agony of the strong, was to that officer, though a man of fifty, a startling revelation. That the condemned one suffered less than he who mainly had effected the condemnation was apparently indicated by the former's exclamation in the scene soon perforce to be touched upon.

23

Of a series of incidents within a brief term rapidly following each other, the adequate narration may take up a term less brief, especially if explanation or comment here and there seem requisite to the better understanding of such incidents. Between the entrance into the cabin of him who never left it alive; and him who when he did leave it left it as one of condemned to die; between this and the closeted interview just given, less than an hour and a half had elapsed. It was an interval long enough, however, to awaken speculations among no few of the ship's company as to what it was that could be detaining in the cabin the master-at-arms and the sailor; for a rumor that both of them had been seen to enter it and neither of them had been seen to emerge, this rumor had got abroad upon the gun decks and in the tops, the people of a great warship being in one respect like villagers, taking microscopic note of every outward movement or non-movement going on. When therefore, in weather not at all tempestuous, all hands were called in the second dogwatch, a summons under such circumstances nor usual in those hours, the crew were not wholly unprepared for some announcement extraordinary, one having connection too with the continued absence of the two men from their wonted haunts.

There was a moderate sea at the time; and the moon, newly risen and near to being at its full, silvered the white spar deck wherever not blotted by the clear-cut shadows horizontally thrown of fixtures and moving men. On either side the quarterdeck the marine guard under arms was drawn up; and

[50] Cf. Genesis xxii: 1-14.

Captain Vere, standing in his place surrounded by all the wardroom officers, addressed his men. In so doing, his manner showed neither more nor less than that properly pertaining to his supreme position aboard his own ship. In clear terms and concise he told them what had taken place in the cabin: that the master-at-arms was dead, that he who had killed him had been already tried by a summary court and condemned to death, and that the execution would take place in the early morning watch. The word *mutiny* was not named in what he said. He refrained too from making the occasion an opportunity for any preachment as to the maintenance of discipline, thinking perhaps that under existing circumstances in the navy the consequence of violating discipline should be made to speak for itself.

Their captain's announcement was listened to by the throng of standing sailors in a dumbness like that of a seated congregation of believers in hell listening to the clergyman's announcement of his Calvinistic text.

At the close, however, a confused murmur went up. It began to wax. All but instantly, then, at a sign, it was pierced and suppressed by shrill whistles of the boatswain and his mates. The word was given to about ship.

To be prepared for burial Claggart's body was delivered to certain petty officers of his mess. And here, not to clog the sequel with lateral matters, it may be added that at a suitable hour, the master-at-arms was committed to the sea with every funeral honor properly belonging to his naval grade.

In this proceeding as in every public one growing out of the tragedy strict adherence to usage was observed. Nor in any point could it have been at all deviated from, either with respect to Claggart or Billy Budd, without begetting undesirable speculations in the ship's company, sailors, and more particularly men-of-war's men, being of all men the greatest sticklers for usage. For similar cause, all communication between Captain Vere and the condemned one ended with the closeted interview already given, the latter being now surrendered to the ordinary routine preliminary to the end. His transfer under guard from the captian's quarters was effected without unusual precautions—at least no visible ones. If possible, not to let the men so much as surmise that their officers anticipate aught amiss from them is the tacit rule in a military ship. And the more that some sort of trouble should really be apprehended, the more do the officers keep that apprehension to themselves, though not the less unostentatious vigilance may be augmented. In the present instance, the sentry placed over the prisoner had strict orders to let no one have communication with him but the chaplain. And certain obtrusive measures were taken absolutely to insure this point.

24

In a seventy-four of the old order the deck known as the upper gun deck was the one covered over by the spar deck, which last, though not without its armament, was for the most part exposed to the weather. In general it was at all hours free from hammocks; those of the crew swinging on the lower gun deck and berth deck, the latter being not only a dormitory but also the place for the stowing of the sailor's bags, and on both sides lined with the large chests or movable pantries of the many messes of the men.

On the starboard side of the *Bellipotent's* upper gun deck, behold Billy Budd under sentry lying prone in irons in one of the bays formed by the regular spacing of the guns comprising the batteries on either side. All these pieces were of the heavier caliber of that period. Mounted on lumbering wooden carriages, they were hampered with cumbersome harness of breeching and strong side-tackles for running them out. Guns and carriages, together with the long rammers and shorter linstocks lodged in loops overhead—all these, as customary, were painted black; and the heavy hempen breechings, tarred to the same tint, wore the like livery of the undertakers. In contrast with the funereal hue of these surroundings, the prone sailor's exterior apparel, white jumper and white duck trousers, each more or less soiled, dimly glimmered in the obscure light of the bay like a patch of discolored snow in early April lingering at some upland cave's black mouth. In effect he is already in his shroud, or the garments that shall serve him in lieu of one. Over him but scarce illuminating him, two battle lanterns swing from two massive beams of the deck above. Fed with the oil supplied by the war contractors (whose gains, honest or otherwise, are in every land an anticipated portion of the harvest of death), with flickering splashes of dirty yellow light they pollute the pale moonshine all but ineffectually struggling in obstructed flecks through the open ports from which the tampioned[51] cannon protrude. Other lanterns at intervals serve but to bring out somewhat the obscurer bays which, like small confessionals or side-chapels in a cathedral, branch from the long dimvistaed broad aisle between the two batteries of the covered tier.

Such was the deck where now lay the Handsome Sailor. Through the rose-tan of his complexion no pallor could have shown. It would have taken days of sequestration from the winds and the sun to have brought about the effacement of that. But the skeleton in the cheekbone at the point of its angle was just beginning delicately to be defined under the warm-tinted skin. In fervid hearts self-contained, some brief experiences devour our human tissue as secret fire in a ship's hold consumes cotton in the bale.

But now lying between the two guns, as nipped in the vice of fate, Billy's agony, mainly proceeding from a generous young heart's virgin experience of the diabolical incarnate and effective in some men—tension of that agony was over now. It survived not the something healing in the closeted interview with Captain Vere. Without movement, he lay as in a trance, that adolescent expression previously noted as his taking on something akin to the look of a slumbering child in the cradle when the warm heart-glow of the

---

[51] Stuffed with a tampion.

still chamber at night plays on the dimples that at whiles mysteriously form in the cheek, silently coming and going there. For now and then in the gyved one's trance a serene happy light born of some wandering reminiscence or dream would diffuse itself over his face, and then away only anew to return.

The chaplain, coming to see him and finding him thus, and perceiving no sign that he was conscious of his presence, attentively regarded him for a space, then slipping aside, withdrew for the time, peradventure feeling that even he, the minister of Christ though receiving his stipend from Mars, had no consolation to proffer which could result in a peace transcending that which he beheld. But in the small hours he came again. And the prisoner, now awake to his surroundings, noticed his approach, and civilly, all but cheerfully, welcomed him. But it was to little purpose that in the interview following the good man sought to bring Billy Budd to some godly understanding that he must die, and at dawn. True, Billy himself freely referred to his death as a thing close at hand; but it was something in the way that children will refer to death in general, who yet among their other sports will play a funeral with hearse and mourners.

Not that like children Billy was incapable of conceiving what death really is. No, but he was wholly without irrational fear of it, a fear more prevalent in highly civilized communities than those so-called barbarous ones which in all respects stand nearer to unadulterate Nature. And, as elsewhere said, a barbarian Billy radically was—as much so, for all the costume, as his countrymen the Bristish captives, living trophies, made to march in the Roman triumph of Germanicus.[52] Quite as much as those later barbarians, young men probably, and picked specimens among the earlier British converts to Christianity, at least nominally such, taken to Rome (as today converts from lesser isles of the sea may be taken to London), of whom the Pope of that time, admiring the strangeness of their personal beauty so unlike the Italian stamp, their clear ruddy complexion and curled flaxen locks, exclaimed, "Angles" (meaning *English*, the modern derivative), "Angles, do you call them? And is it because they look so like angels?" Had it been later in time, one would think that the Pope had in mind Fra Angelico's[53] seraphs, some of whom, plucking apples in gardens of the Hesperides, have the faint rosebud complexion of the more beautiful English girls.

If in vain the good chaplain sought to impress the young barbarian with ideas of death akin to those conveyed in the skull, dial, and crossbones on old tombstones, equally futile to all appearance were his efforts to bring home to him the thought of salvation and a Savior. Billy listened, but less out of awe or reverence, perhaps, than from a certain natural politeness, doubtless at

[52] Germanicus Caesar (15 B.C.-19 A.D.), a Roman conqueror, was the nephew of Tiberius and famous for his victories over the German tribes.

[53] An Italian painter (1387-1455) of religious frescoes.

bottom regarding all that in much the same way that most mariners of his class take any discourse abstract or out of the common tone of the workaday world. And this sailor way of taking clerical discourse is not wholly unlike the way in which the primer of Christianity, full of transcendent miracles, was received long ago on tropic isles by any superior *savage,* so called—a Tahitian, say of Captain Cook's time or shortly after that time.[54] Out of natural courtesy he received, but did not appropriate. It was like a gift placed in the palm of an outreached hand upon which the fingers do not close.

But the *Bellipotent's* chaplain was a discreet man possessing the good sense of a good heart. So he insisted not in his vocation here. At the instance of Captain Vere, a lieutenant had apprised him of pretty much everything as to Billy; and since he felt that innocence was even a better thing than religion wherewith to go to Judgment, he reluctantly withdrew; but in his emotion not without first performing an act strange enough in an Englishman, and under the circumstances yet more so in any regular priest. Stooping over, he kissed on the fair cheek his fellow man, a felon in martial law, one whom though on the confines of death he felt he could never convert to a dogma; nor for all that did he fear for his future.

Marvel not that having been made acquainted with the young sailor's essential innocence the worthy man lifted not a finger to avert the doom of such a martyr to martial discipline. So to do would not only have been as idle as invoking the desert, but would also have been an audacious transgression of the bounds of his function, one as exactly prescribed to him by military law as that of the boatswain or any other naval officer. Bluntly put, a chaplain is the minister of the Prince of Peace serving in the host of the God of War—Mars. As such, he is as incongruous as a musket would be on the altar at Christmas. Why, then, is he there? Because he indirectly subserves the purpose attested by the cannon; because too he lends the sanction of the religion of the meek to that which practically is the abrogation of everything but brute Force.

25

The night so luminous on the spar deck, but otherwise on the cavernous ones below, levels so like the tiered galleries in a coal mine—the luminous night passed away. But like the prophet in the chariot disappearing in heaven and dropping his mantle to Elisha, the withdrawing night transferred its pale robe to the breaking day. A meek, shy light appeared in the East, where stretched a diaphanous fleece of white furrowed vapor. That light slowly waxed. Suddenly *eight bells* was struck aft, responded to by one louder

---

[54] Captain James Cook (1728-1779) was a British explorer who traveled to the Marquesas Islands, which Melville described in *Typee.*

metallic stroke from forward. It was four o'clock in the morning. Instantly the silver whistles were heard summoning all hands to witness punishment. Up through the great hatchways rimmed with racks of heavy shot the watch below came pouring, overspreading with the watch already on deck the space between the mainmast and foremast including that occupied by the capacious launch and the black booms tiered on either side of it, boat and booms making a summit of observation for the powder-boys and younger tars. A different group comprising one watch of topmen leaned over the rail of that sea balcony, no small one in a seventy-four, looking down on the crowd below. Man or boy, none spake but in whisper, and few spake at all. Captain Vere—as before, the central figure among the assembled commissioned officers—stood nigh the break of the poop deck facing forward. Just below him on the quarter-deck the mariners in full equipment were drawn up much as at the scene of the promulgated sentence.

At sea in the old time, the execution by halter of a military sailor was generally from the foreyard. In the present instance, for special reasons the mainyard was assigned. Under an arm of that yard the prisoner was presently brought up, the chaplain attending him. It was noted at the time, and remarked upon afterwards, that in this final scene the good man evinced little or nothing of the perfunctory. Brief speech indeed he had with the condemned one, but the genuine Gospel was less on his tongue than in his aspect and manner towards him. The final preparations personal to the latter being speedily brought to an end by two boatswain's mates, the consummation impended. Billy stood facing aft. At the penultimate moment, his words, his only ones, words wholly unobstructed in the utterance, were these: "God bless Captain Vere!" Syllables so unanticipated coming from one with the ignominious hemp about his neck—a conventional felon's benediction directed aft towards the quarters of honor; syllables too delivered in the clear melody of a singing bird on the point of launching from the twig—had a phenomenal effect, not unenhanced by the rare personal beauty of the young sailor, spiritualized now through late experiences so poignantly profound.

Without volition, as it were, as if indeed the ship's populace were but the vehicles of some vocal current electric, with one voice from alow and aloft came a resonant sympathetic echo: "God bless Captain Vere!" And yet at that instant Billy alone must have been in their hearts, even as in their eyes.

At the pronounced words and the spontaneous echo that voluminously rebounded them, Captain Vere, either through stoic self-control or a sort of momentary paralysis induced by emotional shock, stood erectly rigid as a musket in the ship-armorer's rack.

The hull, deliberately recovering from the periodic roll to leeward, was just regaining an even keel when the last signal, a preconcerted dumb one, was given. At the same moment it chanced that the vapory fleece hanging low in the East was shot through with a soft glory as of the fleece of the Lamb of God seen in mystical vision, and simultaneously therewith, watched by the wedged mass of upturned faces, Billy ascended; and, ascending, took the full rose of the dawn.

In the pinioned figure arrived at the yard-end, to the wonder of all no motion was apparent, none save that created by the slow roll of the hull in moderate weather, so majestic in a great ship ponderously cannoned.

26

When some days afterwards, in reference to the singularity just mentioned, the purser, a rather ruddy, rotund person more accurate as an accountant than profound as a philosopher, said at mess to the surgeon, "What testimony to the force lodged in will power," the latter, saturnine, spare, and tall, one in whom a discreet causticity went along with a manner less genial than polite, replied, "Your pardon, Mr. Purser. In a hanging scientifically conducted—and under special orders I myself directed how Budd's was to be effected—any movement following the completed suspension and originating in the body suspended, such movement indicates mechanical spasm in the muscular system. Hence the absence of that is no more attributable to will power, as you call it, than to horsepower—begging your pardon."

"But this muscular spasm you speak of, is not that in a degree more or less invariable in these cases?"

"Assuredly so, Mr. Purser."

"How then, my good sir, do you account for its absence in this instance?"

"Mr. Purser, it is clear that your sense of the singularity in this matter equals not mine. You account for it by what you call will power—a term not yet included in the lexicon of science. For me, I do not, with my present knowledge, pretend to account for it at all. Even should we assume the hypothesis that at the first touch of the halyards the action of Budd's heart, intensified by extraordinary emotion at its climax, abruptly stopped—much like a watch when in carelessly winding it up you strain at the finish, thus snapping the chain—even under that hypothesis how account for the phenomenon that followed?"

"You admit, then, that the absence of spasmodic movement was phenomenal."

"It was phenomenal, Mr. Purser, in the sense that it was an appearance the cause of which is not immediately to be assigned."

"But tell me, my dear sir, " pertinaciously continued the other, "was the man's death effected by the halter, or was it a species of euthanasia?"

"*Euthanasia*, Mr. Purser, is something like your *will power*: I doubt its authenticity as a scientific term—begging your pardon again. It is at once imaginative and metaphysical—in short, Greek.—But," abruptly changing his tone, "there is a case in the sick bay that I do not care to leave to my assistants. Beg your pardon, but excuse me." And rising from the mess he formally withdrew.

27

The silence at the moment of execution and for a moment or two continuing thereafter, a silence but emphasized by the regular wash of the sea against the hull or the flutter of a sail caused by the helmsman's eyes being tempted astray, this emphasized silence was gradually disturbed by a sound not easily to be verbally rendered. Whoever has heard the freshet-wave of a torrent suddenly swelled by pouring showers in tropical mountains, showers not shared by the plain; whoever has heard the first muffled murmur of its sloping advance through precipitous woods may form some conception of the sound now heard. The seeming remoteness of its source was because of its murmurous indistinctness, since it came from close by, even from the men massed on the ship's open deck. Being inarticulate, it was dubious in significance further than it seemed to indicate some capricious revulsion of thought or feeling such as mobs ashore are liable to, in the present instance possibly implying a sullen revocation on the men's part of their involuntary echoing of Billy's benediction. But ere the murmur had time to wax into clamor it was met by a strategic command, the more telling that it came with abrupt unexpectedness: "Pipe down the starboard watch, Boatswain, and see that they go."

Shrill as the shriek of the sea hawk, the silver whistles of the boatswain and his mates pierced that ominous low sound, dissipating it; and yielding to the mechanism of discipline the throng was thinned by one-half. For the remainder, most of them were set to temporary employments connected with trimming the yards and so forth, business readily to be got up to serve occasion by any officer of the deck.

Now each proceeding that follows a mortal sentence pronounced at sea by a drumhead court is characterized by promptitude not perceptibly merging into hurry, though bordering that. The hammock, the one which had been Billy's bed when alive, having already been ballasted with shot and otherwise prepared to serve for his canvas coffin, the last offices of the sea undertakers, the sailmaker's mates, were now speedily completed. When everything was in readiness a second call for all hands, made necessary by the strategic movement before mentioned, was sounded, now to witness burial.

The details of this closing formality it needs not to give. But when the tilted plank let slide its freight into the sea, a second strange human murmur was heard, blended now with another inarticulate sound proceeding from certain larger seafowl who, their attention having been attracted by the peculiar commotion in the water resulting from the heavy sloped dive of the shotted hammock into the sea, flew screaming to the spot. So near the hull did they come, that the stridor or bony creak of their gaunt double-jointed pinions was audible. As the ship under light airs passed on, leaving the burial spot astern, they still kept circling it low down with the moving shadow of their outstretched wings and the croaked requiem of their cries.

Upon sailors as superstitious as those of the age preceding ours, men-of-war's men too who had just beheld the prodigy of repose in the form suspended in air, and now foundering in the deeps; to such mariners the action of the seafowl, though dictated by mere animal greed for prey, was big with no prosaic significance. An uncertain movement began among them, in which some encroachment was made. It was tolerated but for a moment. For suddenly the drum beat to quarters, which familiar sound happening at least twice every day, had upon the present occasion a signal peremptoriness in it. True martial discipline long continued superinduces in average man a sort of impulse whose operation at the official word of command much resembles in its promptitude the effect of an instinct.

The drumbeat dissolved the multitude, distributing most of them along the batteries of the two covered gun decks. There, as wonted, the guns' crew stood by their respective cannon erect and silent. In due course the first officer, sword under arm and standing in his place on the quarter-deck, formally received the successive reports of the sworded lieutenants commanding the sections of batteries below; the last of which reports being made, the summed report he delivered with the customary salute to the commander. All this occupied time, which in the present case was the object in beating to quarters at an hour prior to the customary one. That such variance from usage was authorized by an officer like Captain Vere, a martinet as some deemed him, was evidence of the necessity for unusual action implied in what he deemed to be temporarily the mood of his men. "With mankind," he would say, "forms, measured forms, are everything; and that is the import couched in the story of Orpheus with his lyre spellbinding the wild denizens of the wood." And this he once applied to the disruption of forms going on across the Channel and the consequences thereof.

At this unwonted muster at quarters, all proceeded as at the regular hour. The band on the quarter-deck played a sacred air, after which the chaplain went through the customary morning service. That done, the drum beat the retreat; and toned by music and religious rites subserving the discipline and purposes of war, the men in their wonted orderly manner dispersed to the places allotted them when not at the guns.

And now it was full day. The fleece of low-hanging vapor had vanished, licked up by the sun that late had so glorified it. And the circumambient air in the clearness of its serenity was like smooth white marble in the polished block not yet removed from the marble-dealer's yard.

28

The symmetry of form attainable in pure fiction cannot so readily be achieved in a narration essentially having less to do with fable than with fact. Truth uncompromisingly told will always have its ragged edges; hence the conclusion of such a narration is apt to be less finished than an architectural finial.

How it fared with the Handsome Sailor during the year of the Great Mutiny has been faithfully given. But though properly the story ends with his life, something in way of sequel will not be amiss. Three brief chapters will suffice.

In the general rechristening under the Directory of the craft originally forming the navy of the French monarchy, the *St. Louis* line-of-battle ship was named the *Athée* (the *Atheist*). Such a name, like some other substituted ones in the Revolutionary fleet, while proclaiming the infidel audacity of the ruling power, was yet, though not so intended to be, the aptest name, if one consider it, ever given to a warship; far more so indeed than the *Devastation,* the *Erebus* (the *Hell*), and similar names bestowed upon the fighting ships.

On the return passage to the English fleet from the detached cruise during which occurred the events already recorded, the *Bellipotent* fell in with the *Athée*. An engagement ensued, during which Captain Vere, in the act of putting his ship alongside the enemy with a view of throwing his boarders across her bulwarks, was hit by a musket ball from a porthole of the enemy's main cabin. More than disabled, he dropped to the deck and was carried below to the same cockpit where some of his men already lay. The senior lieutenant took commad. Under him the enemy was finally captured, and though much crippled was by rare good fortune successfully taken into Gibraltar, an English port not very distant from the scene of the fight. There Captain Vere with the rest of the wounded was put ashore. He lingered for some days, but the end came. Unhappily he was cut off too early for the Nile and Trafalgar.[55] The spirit that spite its philosophic austerity may yet have indulged in the most secret of all passions, ambition, never attained to the fulness of fame.

Not long before death, while lying under the influence of that magical drug which, soothing the physical frame, mysteriously operates on the subtler element in man, he was heard to murmur words inexplicable to his attendant: "Billy Budd, Billy Budd." That these were not the accents of remorse would seem clear from what the attendant said to the *Bellipotent's* senior officer of marines, who, as the most reluctant to condemn the members of the drumhead court, too well knew, though here he kept the knowledge to himself, who Billy Budd was.

29

Some few weeks after the execution, among other matters under the head of "News for the Mediterranean," there appeared in a naval chronicle of the time, an authorized weekly publication, an account of the affair. It was doubtless for the most part written in good faith, though the medium, partly rumor, through which the facts must have reached the writer served to deflect and in part falsify them. The account was as follows:

[55] Admiral Nelson was victorious over Napoleon's navy at the Battle of the Nile (1798): he died at Trafalgar (1805), although again he was victorious.

"On the tenth of the last month a deplorable occurrence took place on board H.M.S. *Bellipotent*. John Claggart, the ship's master-at-arms, discovering that some sort of plot was incipient among an inferior section of the ship's company, and that the ringleader was one William Budd; he, Claggart, in the act of arraigning the man before the captain, was vindictively stabbed to the heart by the suddenly drawn sheath knife of Budd.

"The deed and the implement employed sufficiently suggest that though mustered into the service under an English name the assassin was no Englishman, but one of those aliens adopting English cognomens whom the present extraordinary necessities of the service have caused to be admitted into it in considerable numbers.

"The enormity of the crime and the extreme depravity of the criminal appear the greater in view of the character of the victim, a middle-aged man respectable and discreet, belonging to that minor official grade, the petty officers, upon whom, as none know better than the commissioned gentlemen, the efficiency of His Majesty's navy so largely depends. His function was a responsible one, at once onerous and thankless; and his fidelity in it the greater because of his strong patriotic impulse. In this instance as in so many other instances in these days, the character of this unfortunate man signally refutes, if refutation were needed, that peevish saying attributed to the late Dr. Johnson, that patriotism is the last refuge of a scoundrel.

"The criminal paid the penalty of his crime. The promptitude of the punishment has proved salutary. Nothing amiss is now apprehended aboard H.M.S. *Bellipotent*."

The above, appearing in a publication now long ago superannuated and forgotten, is all that hitherto has stood in human record to attest what manner of men respectively were John Claggart and Billy Budd.

30

Everything is for a term venerated in navies. And tangible object associated with some striking incident of the service is converted into a monument. The spar from which the foretopman was suspended was for some few years kept trace of by the bluejackets. Their knowledge followed it from ship to dockyard and again from dockyard to ship, still pursuing it even when at last reduced to a mere dockyard boom. To them a chip of it was a piece of the Cross. Ignorant though they were of the secret facts of the tragedy, and not thinking but that the penalty was somehow unavoidably inflicted from the naval point of view, for all that, they instinctively felt that Billy was a sort of man as incapable of mutiny as of wilful murder. They recalled the fresh young image of the Handsome Sailor, that face never deformed by a sneer or subtler vile freak of the heart within. This impression of him was doubtless deepened by the fact that he was gone, and in a measure mysteriously gone. On the gun decks of the *Bellipotent* the general estimate of his nature and its unconscious simplicity eventually found rude utterance from another foretopman, one of his own watch, gifted, as some sailors are, with an artless *poetic* temperament. The tarry hand made some lines which, after circulating among the shipboard crews for a while, finally got rudely printed at Portsmouth as a ballad. The title given to it was the sailor's.

BILLY IN THE DARBIES[56]

Good of the chaplain to enter Lone Bay
And down on his marrowbones here and pray
For the likes just o' me, Billy Budd.—But, look:
Through the port comes the moonshine astray!
It tips the guard's cutlass and silvers this nook;
But 'twill die in the dawning of Billy's last day.
A jewel-block they'll make of me tomorrow,
Pendant pearl from the yardarm-end
Like the eardrop I gave to Bristol Molly—
O, 'tis me, not the sentence they'll suspend.
Ay, ay, all is up; and I must up too,
Early in the morning, aloft from alow.
On an empty stomach now never it would do.
They'll give me a nibble—bit o' biscuit ere I go.
Sure, a messmate will reach me the last parting cup;
But, turning heads away from the hoist and the belay,
Heaven knows who will have the running of me up!
No pipe to those halyards.—But aren't it all sham?
A blur's in my eyes; it is dreaming that I am.
A hatchet to my hawser? All adrift to go?
The drum roll to grog, and Billy never know?
But Donald he had promised to stand by the plank;
So I'll shake a friendly hand ere I sink.
But—no! It is dead then I'll be, come to think.
I remember Taff the Welshman when he sank.
And his cheek it was like the budding pink.
But me they'll lash in hammock, drop me deep.
Fathoms down, fathoms down, how I'll dream fast asleep.
I feel it stealing now. Sentry, are you there?
Just ease these darbies at the wrist,
And roll me over fair!
I am sleepy, and the oozy weeds about me twist.

1886–1891   1924, 1948, 1962

---

[56] Handcuffs.

HENRY WADSWORTH LONGFELLOW

(1807–1882)

More than any of the well-known American poets in the nineteenth century, Henry Wadsworth Longfellow represented the popular taste of his time. He wrote didactic poems of affirmation and piety like "A Psalm of Life"; confessional poems of death like "The Cross of Snow"; and traditional works like "The Wreck of the Hesperus," "The Skeleton in Armor," "Evangeline," and "Hiawatha." Unlike Poe, he never questioned that poetry should be morally instructive, and the poems that expressed his view enjoyed greater currency than those of any other writer.

Longfellow was born in Portland, Maine, on February 27, 1807, a descendant of seventeenth-century New England families. He was always an active scholar and, after graduating from Bowdoin in 1825, traveled to Europe in preparation for the newly created chair of modern languages at the college, which he assumed in 1829. In 1936 he went to Harvard and became Professor of Modern Languages and Belles-Lettres. His mastery of French, German, Spanish, and Italian was substantial, and he enjoyed his role as professor; but in the 1830's and 1840's he began to write extensively and soon established a considerable reputation. His many volumes appeared regularly: *Hyperion,* a novel, and *Voices of the Night,* a collection of poems, in 1839; *Ballads and Other Poems* (1839); *Poems on Slavery* (1842); *The Spanish Student* (1843); *Evangeline* (1849); *Kavanaugh* (1850), a novel; *The Song of Hiawatha* (1855); *The Courtship of Miles Standish and Other Poems* (1858); *Tales of a Wayside Inn* (1863); *Kéramos: And Other Poems* (1878), and *Ultime Thule* (1880). With each new publication, Longfellow enhanced his reputation and popularity until he became, in the

The standard edition is the Complete Poetical and Prose Works, 11 vols., ed. H. E. Scudder, 1886. Scudder also edited a one-volume edition, *Complete Poetical Works,* 1893.

Samuel Longfellow, the poet's brother, wrote the standard biography, *The Life of Henry Wadsworth Longfellow,* 3 vol., 1886. T. W. Higginson's *Henry Wadsworth Longfellow,* 1902, is also useful. A recent authoritative biography and critical study is Newton Arvin, *Longfellow: His Life and Work,* 1963.

Critical studies include H. Gorman, *A Victorian American, Henry Wadsworth Longfellow,* 1926; James T. Hatfield, *New Light on Longfellow,* 1933; Lawrance Thompson, *Young Longfellow,* 1938, and Edward Wagenknecht, *Longfellow, A Full Length Portrait,* 1955, revised as *Henry Wadsworth Longfellow: Portrait of an American Humanist,* 1966; Cecil B. Williams, *Henry Wadsworth Longfellow,* 1964; Edward Hirsh, *Henry Wadsworth Longfellow,* 1964.

last years of his life, the most famous poet in America—one of "Our Poets," as Van Wyck Brooks said—"kindly, gray-bearded, or otherwise grizzled old man."

Modern poets and critics like Pound, Eliot, I. E. Richards, Allen Tate, and John Crowe Ransom rejected the sort of romantic poetry that Longfellow wrote; and, in the twentieth century, his reputation has suffered severely. He avoids the paradoxes, ambiguities, and ironies so attractive to the contemporary reader and writes simply and directly, often sentimentally—as so many people in his time admired—but on occasion eloquently and powerfully.

The Skeleton in Armor[1]

"Speak! speak! thou fearful guest
Who, with thy hollow breast
Still in rude armor drest,
   Comest to daunt me!
Wrapt not in Eastern balms,   5
But with thy fleshless palms
Stretched, as if asking alms,
   Why dost thou haunt me?"

Then, from those cavernous eyes
Pale flashes seemed to rise,   10
As when the Northern skies
   Gleam in December;
And, like the water's flow
Under December's snow,
Came a dull voice of woe   15
   From the heart's chamber.

"I was a Viking old!
My deeds, though manifold,
No Skald in song has told,
   No Saga taught thee!   20

[1] Longfellow imagined that a skeleton in armor, which had been uncovered at Fall River, was part of the remains of old Northern sailors who arrived at the coast of North America in the tenth century. The poem was originally published in *Knickerbocker Magazine* for January 1841, and was then collected in *Ballads and Other Poems* (1841). Like Coleridge's "The Ancient Mariner," the original version of the poem contained marginal notes.

Take heed, that in thy verse
Thou dost the tale rehearse,
Else dread a dead man's curse;
    For this I sought thee.

"Far in the Northern Land,   25
By the wild Baltic's strand,
I, with my childish hand,
    Tamed the gerfalcon;[2]
And, with my skates fast-bound,
Skimmed the half-frozen Sound,   30
That the poor whimpering hound
    Trembled to walk on.

"Oft to his frozen lair
Tracked I the grisly bear,
While from my path the hare   35
    Fled like a shadow;
Oft through the forest dark
Followed the were-wolf's bark,
Until the soaring lark
    Sang from the meadow.   40

"But when I older grew,
Joining a corsair's crew,
O'er the dark sea I flew
    With the marauders.
Wild was the life we led;   45
Many the souls that sped,
Many the hearts that bled,
    By our stern orders.

"Many a wassail-bout
Wore the long Winter out;   50
Often our midnight shout
    Set the cocks crowing,
As we the Berserk's[3] tale
Measured in cups of ale,
Draining the oaken pail,   55
    Filled to o'erflowing.

[2] A large Arctic falcon.

[3] Berserkers were mythological Norse warriors of great passion.

"Once as I told in glee
Tales of the stormy sea,
Soft eyes did gaze on me,
   Burning yet tender;   60
And as the white stars shine
On the dark Norway pine,
On that dark heart of mine
   Fell their soft splendor.

"I wooed the blue-eyed maid,   65
Yielding, yet half afraid,
And in the forest's shade
   Our vows were plighted.
Under its loosened vest
Fluttered her little breast,   70
Like birds within their nest
   By the hawk frighted.

"Bright in her father's hall
Shields gleamed upon the wall,
Loud sang the minstrels all,   75
   Chanting his glory;
When of old Hildebrand
I asked his daughter's hand,
Mute did the minstrels stand.
   To hear my story.   80

"While the brown ale he quaffed,
Loud then the champion laughed,
And as the wind-gusts waft
   The sea-foam brightly,
So the loud laugh of scorn,   85
Out of those lips unshorn,
From the deep drinking-horn
   Blew the foam lightly.

"She was a Prince's child,
I but a Viking wild,   90
And though she blushed and smiled,
   I was discarded!
Should not the dove so white
Follow the sea-mew's[4] flight,
Why did they leave that night   95
   Her nest unguarded?

---

[4] European sea gull.

"Scarce had I put to sea,
Bearing the maid with me,
Fairest of all was she
   Among the Norsemen!   100
When on the white sea-strand,
Waving his armed hand,
Saw we old Hildebrand,
   With twenty horsemen.

"Then launched they to the blast,   105
Bent like a reed each mast,
Yet we were gaining fast,
   When the wind failed us;
And with a sudden flaw
Came round the gusty Skaw,[5]   110
So that our foe we saw
   Laugh as he hailed us.

"And as to catch the gale
Round veered the flapping sail,
'Death!' was the helmsman's hail,   115
   'Death without quarter!'
Mid-ships with iron keel
Struck we her ribs of steel;
Down her black hulk did reel
   Through the black water!   120

"As with his wings aslant,
Sails the fierce cormorant,
Seeking some rocky haunt,
   With his prey laden,—
So toward the open main,   125
Beating to sea again,
Through the wild hurricane,
   Bore I the maiden.

"Three weeks we westward bore,
And when the storm was o'er   130
Cloud-like we saw the shore
   Stretching to leeward;
There for my lady's bower
Built I the lofty tower,[6]
Which, to this very hour,   135
   Stands looking seaward.

[5] Cape Skagen, the northern point of Jutland in Denmark.

[6] The Newport tower. The origins of this tower are controversial.

"There lived we many years;
Time dried the maiden's tears;
She had forgot her fears,
   She was a mother;   140
Death closed her mild blue eyes,
Under that tower she lies;
Ne'er shall the sun arise
   On such another!

"Still grew my bosom then,   145
Still as a stagnant fen!
Hateful to me were men,
   The sunlight hateful!
In the vast forest here,
Clad in my warlike gear,   150
Fell I upon my spear,
   Oh, death was grateful!

"Thus, seamed with many scars,
Bursting these prison bars,
Up to its native stars   155
   My soul ascended!
There from the flowing bowl
Deep drinks the warrior's soul,
Skoal! to the Northland! *skoal!*"
   Thus the tale ended.   160

1840   1841

Mezzo Cammin[1]

WRITTEN AT BOPPARD ON THE RHINE
AUGUST 25, 1842, JUST BEFORE LEAVING FOR
HOME

Half of my life is gone, and I have let
   The years slip from me and have not fulfilled
   The aspiration of my youth, to build
   Some tower of song with lofty parapet.

[1] The title is taken from the first lines of Dante's *Divina Commedia: Nel mezzo del cam min di nostra vita* ("Midway upon the journey of our life.") Like Dante, Longfellow was 35 years of age. The sonnet was included in *The Belfry of Bruges* (1846).

No indolence, nor pleasure, nor the fret   5
    Of restless passions that would not be stilled,
    But sorrow, and a care that almost killed,[2]
    Kept me from what I may accomplish yet;
Though, half-way up the hill, I see the Past
    Lying beneath me with its sounds and sights,—   10
    A city in the twilight dim and vast,
With smoking roofs, soft bells, and gleaming lights,—
    And hear above me on the autumnal blast
The cataract of Death far thundering from the heights.

1842   [1845] 1846

[2] Longfellow's first wife had died of tuberculosis in 1835.

The Jewish Cemetery at Newport[1]

How strange it seems! These Hebrews in their graves,
    Close by the street of this fair seaport town,
Silent beside the never-silent waves,
    At rest in all this moving up and down!

The trees are white with dust, that o'er their sleep   5
    Wave their broad curtains in the southwind's breath,
While underneath these leafy tents they keep
    The long, mysterious Exodus of Death.

And these sepulchral stones, so old and brown,
    That pave with level flags their burial-place,   10
Seem like the tablets of the Law, thrown down
    And broken by Moses at the mountain's base.

The very names recorded here are strange,
    Of foreign accent, and of different climes;
Alvares and Rivera interchange   15
    With Abraham and Jacob of old times.

[1] This poem first appeared in *Putnam's Monthly Magazine* for July 1854, although it was originally written in 1852. It was included in the "Birds of Passage" section of *The Courtship of Miles Standish* (1858). The cemetery is near a synagogue that was no longer used in Longfellow's time, and it becomes for the poet a symbol of Jewish tragedy, exile, and persecution, as well as a memory of past greatness.

"Blessed by God! for he created Death!"
  The mourners said, "and Death is rest and peace;"
Then added, in the certainty of faith,
  "And giveth Life that nevermore shall cease."   20

Closed are the portals of their Synagogue,
  No Psalms of David now the silence break,
No Rabbi reads the ancient Decalogue
  In the grand dialect the Prophets spake.

Gone are the living, but the dead remain,   25
  And not neglected; for a hand unseen,
Scattering its bounty, like a summer rain,
  Still keeps their graves and their remembrance green.

How came they here? What burst of Christian hate,
  What persecution, merciless and blind,   30
Drove o'er the sea—that desert desolate—
  These Ishmaels and Hagars of mankind?

They lived in narrow streets and lanes obscure,
  Ghetto and Judenstrass, in mirk and mire;
Taught in the school of patience to endure   35
  The life of anguish and the death of fire.

All their lives long, with the unleavened bread
  And bitter herbs of exile and its fears,
The wasting famine of the heart they fed,
  And slaked its thirst and marah of their tears.   40

Anathema maranatha![2] was the cry
  That rang from town to town, from street to street;
At every gate the accursed Mordecai
  Was mocked and jeered, and spurned by Christian feet.

Pride and humiliation hand in hand   45
  Walked with them through the world where 'er they went;
Trampled and beaten were they as the sand,
  And yet unshaken as the continent.

---

[2] I Corinthians xvi:22 "Anathema" in Greek means "devoted to destruction" and "Mara-natha" in Aramaic means "at the coming of The Lord."

For in the background figures vague and vast
   Of patriarchs and of prophets rose sublime,   50
And all the great traditions of the Past
   They saw reflected in the coming time.

And thus forever with reverted look
   The mystic volume of the world they read,
Spelling it backward like a Hebrew book,   55
   Till life became a Legend of the Dead.

But ah! what once has been shall be no more!
   The groaning earth in travail and in pain
Brings forth its races, but does not restore,
   And the dead nations never rise again.   60

1854, 1858

The Cross of Snow[1]

In the long, sleepless watches of the night,
   A gentle face—the face of one long dead—
   Looks at me from the wall, where round its head
   The night-lamp casts a halo of pale light.
Here in this room she died; and soul more white   5
   Never through martyrdom of fire was led
   To its repose; nor can in books be read
   The legend of a life more benedight.
There is a mountain in the distant West
   That, sun-defying, in its deep ravines   10
   Displays a cross of snow upon its side.
Such is the cross I wear upon my breast
   These eighteen years, through all the changing scenes
   And seasons, changeless since the day she died.

1879   1886

[1] This poem was not published during Longfellow's lifetime. It was discovered after Longfellow's death by his brother Samuel, who printed it in the second volume of his *Life* (1886). The poem is concerned with the deep feeling Longfellow had for his second wife, Frances Appelton, who burned to death in 1861 before Longfellow could save her.

Ultima Thule[1]

DEDICATION: TO G. W. G.[2]

With favoring winds, o'er sunlit seas,
We sailed for the Hesperides,[3]
The land where golden apples grow;
But that, ah! that was long ago.

How far since then the ocean streams   5
Have swept us from the land of dreams,
That land of fiction and of truth,
The lost Atlantis[4] of our youth!

Whither, ah, whither? are not these
The tempest-haunted Orcades,[5]   10
Where sea-gulls scream, and breakers roar,
And wreck and sea-weed line the shore?

Ultima Thule! Utmost Isle!
Here in thy harbors for awhile
We lower our sails, awhile we rest   15
From the unending endless quest.

1879   1880

---

[1] Ultime Thule refers to the region of the earth that is the furthest north and still habitable—in that sense, the ultimate journey of man. The poem first appeared in *Ultime Thule* (1880).

[2] The poem is dedicated to George Washington Greene, a friend of Longfellow's since his youth.

[3] The "blessed Isles" of Greek mythology. The golden apples grew in Hesperides.

[4] A place of ultimate happiness that had allegedly sunk into the earth.

[5] Islands off the Scottish coast.

JOHN GREENLEAF WHITTIER

(1807–1892)

John Greenleaf Whittier viewed the individual and society from the point of view of the humanitarian. Born on December 17, 1807, in Haverhill, Massachusetts, he was raised in simple natural surroundings by a pious Quaker family that stressed the significance of the Bible. After a brief experience as a student at the Haverhill Academy, he became interested in political reform and wrote for a variety of newspapers—The Haverhill *Gazette, The New England Weekly,* The Essex *Transcript.* By 1833 he had established his reputation as a radical journalist and a polemical poet.

Much of Whittier's best-known poetry during his lifetime was written in protest to slavery. It tends too often to be obviously polemical and sentimental, and only a few poems like "Massachusetts to Virginia" and "Ichabod" are worth reprinting; they appear in the sections concerned with political expression and abolitionism. The poems represented here are direct expressions of Whittier's faith in the common man; in them, he frees himself of simply making meters and creates, as Emerson urges in "The Poet," a metermaking argument of considerable force. A second group of poems, which draw on Whittier's interest in American folklore, are ballads like "Barbara Frietchie" and "Skipper Ireson's Ride," and they are among the finest of their kind in American literature. The final group, which has proved to be Whittier's most popular, can be called genre poems; they were written toward the

The standard text is *The Writings of John Greenleaf Whittier,* Riverside Edition, 7 vols., ed. Horace E. Scudder, 1888–1889. Scudder also edited a one-volume edition, *The Complete Poetical Works of John Greenleaf Whittier, Representative Selections,* with introduction, bibliography, and notes, ed. by G. R. Carpenter, 1935. C. Franklin Currier has edited a *Bibliography of John Greenleaf Whittier,* 1937.

The standard biography is Samuel T. Pickard, *Life and Letters of John Greenleaf Whittier,* 2 vols., 1894, rev. 1907. See also G. R. Carpenter, *Whittier,* 1903, and Bliss Perry, *John Greenleaf Whittier: A Sketch of His Life,* 1907.

Criticism may be found in A. Mordell, *Quaker Militant, John Greenleaf Whittier,* 1933; Whitman Bennett, *Whittier, Bard of Freedom,* 1941; John A. Pollard, *John Greenleaf Whittier: Friend of Man,* 1949; George Arms, *The Fields were Green: A New View of Bryant, Whittier, Holmes, Lowell, and Longfellow, With a Selection of Their Poems,* 1953; John B. Pickard, *John Greenleaf Whittier: An Introduction and Interpretation,* 1961; Lewis Leary, *John Greenleaf Whittier,* 1961; Edward Wagenknecht, *John Greenleaf Whittier, A Portrait in Paradox,* 1967.

The poems are reprinted from *The Complete Poems of John Greenleaf Whittier, Representative Selections.*

middle of Whittier's career and express a profound attachment to the simple life conducted in nature and amidst his family. As a poet of the commonplace, Whittier wrote "Telling the Bees," "Maud Muller," and "Snow-Bound." These poems as well as the others reprinted here suggest why Whittier was known as "the people's poet." Throughout his work the sentiments of the Americans of his time are reflected: their fondness for romance, their idealism and religious faith, and their attachment to a particular place and to a closely knit family. Whittier captured these popular feelings and expressed them in concrete poetry that still creates a faithful picture of nineteenth-century New England life.

Skipper Ireson's Ride[1]

Of all the rides since the birth of time,
Told in story or sung in rhyme,—
On Apuleius's[2] Golden Ass,
Or one-eyed Calender's[3] horse of brass,
Witch astride of a human back,   5
Islam's prophet[4] on Al-Borák,—
The strangest ride that ever was sped
Was Ireson's, out from Marblehead!
    Old Floyd Ireson, for his hard heart,
    Tarred and feathered and carried in a cart   10
    By the women of Marblehead!

Body of turkey, head of owl,
Wings a-droop like a rained-on fowl,
Feathered and ruffled in every part.
Skipper Ireson stood in the cart.   15
Scores of women, old and young,
Strong of muscle, and glib of tongue,

[1] This poem was published in the *Atlantic Monthly* for December 1857, and included in *Home Ballads and Poems* (1860). Whittier stated that the ballad "was founded solely on a fragment of rhyme [the refrain sung by the women] which I heard from one of my early schoolmates, a native of Marblehead." The local legend, according to Whittier, "dated back at least a century." In 1879 Samuel Roads published his *History of Marblehead;* he calls Ireson "Benjamin" instead of Floyd and maintains that Ireson did not forsake his ship but, instead, the crew, which then accused Ireson of desertion. Whittier agreed with Roads' account of the incident.

[2] The *Golden Ass of Apuleius*, a Roman satirist and rhetorician of the second century, recounts the story of a man who was metamorphosed into a golden ass.

[3] The Calender is a wandering dervish. In the *Arabian Nights* (the "Story of the Third Calendar"), the calender killed the rider of the "Horse of brass" and subsequently lost his eye.

[4] Mohammed. Al-Borák was a mythical winged creature who took Mohammed to the highest reaches of heaven.

Pushed and pulled up the rocky lane,
Shouting and singing the shrill refrain:
    "Here's Flud Oirson, fur his horrd horrt,   20
    Torr'd an' furtherr'd an' corr'd in a corrt
      By the women o' Morble'ead!"

Wrinkled scolds with hands on hips,
Girls in bloom of cheek and lips,
Wild-eyed free-limbed, such as chase   25
Bacchus round some antique vase,
Brief of skirt, with ankles bare,
Loose of kerchief and loose of hair,
With conch-shells blowing and fish-horns' twang,
Over and over the Maenads sang: 30
    "Here's Flud Oirson, fur his horrd horrt,
    Torr'd an' furtherr'd an' corr'd in a corrt
      By the women o' Morble'ead!"

Small pity for him!—He sailed away
From a leaking ship in Chaleur Bay,—   35
Sailed away from a sinking wreck,
With his own town's-people on her deck!
"Lay by! lay by!" they called to him.
Back he answered, "Sink or swim!
Brag of your catch of fish again!"   40
And off he sailed through the fog and rain!
    Old Floyd Ireson, for his hard heart,
    Tarred and feathered and carried in a cart
      By the women of Marblehead!

Fathoms deep in dark Chaleur   45
That wreck shall lie forevermore.
Mother and sister, wife and maid,
Looked from the rocks of Marblehead
Over the moaning and rainy sea,—
Looked for the coming that might not be!   50
What did the winds and the sea-birds say
Of the cruel captain who sailed away—?
    Old Floyd Ireson, for his hard heart,
    Tarred and feathered and carried in a cart
      By the women of Marblehead!   55

Through the street, on either side,
Up flew windows, doors swung wide;
Sharp-tongued spinsters, old wives gray,
Treble lent the fish-horn's bray.

Sea-worn grandsires, cripple-bound, 60
Hulks of old sailors run aground,
Shook head, and fist, and hat, and cane,
And cracked with curses the hoarse refrain:
   "Here's Flud Oirson, fur his horrd horrt,
   Torr'd an' furtherr'd an' corr'd in a corrt 65
      By the women o' Morble'ead!"

Sweetly along the Salem road
Bloom of orchard and lilac showed.
Little the wicked skipper knew
Of the fields so green and the sky so blue. 70
Riding there in his sorry trim,
Like an Indian idol glum and grim,
Scarcely he seemed the sound to hear
Of voices shouting, far and near:
   "Here's Flud Oirson, fur his horrd horrt, 75
   Torr'd an' futherr'd an' corr'd in a corrt
      By the women o' Morble'ead!"

"Hear me, neighbors!" at last he cried,—
"What to me is this noisy ride?
What is the shame that clothes the skin 80
To the nameless horror that lives within?
Waking or sleeping, I see a wreck,
And hear a cry from a reeling deck!
Hate and curse me,—I only dread
The hand of God and the face of the dead!" 85
   Said old Floyd Ireson, for his hard heart,
   Tarred and feathered and carried in a cart
      By the women of Marblehead!

Then the wife of the skipper lost at sea
Said, "God has touched him! why should we!" 90
Said an old wife mourning her only son,
"Cut the rogue's tether and let him run!"
So with soft relentings and rude excuse,
Half scorn, half pity, they cut him loose,
And gave him a cloak to hide him in, 95
And left him alone with his shame and sin.

Poor Floyd Ireson, for his hard heart,
Tarred and feathered and carried in a cart
      By the women of Marblehead!

1857, 1860

Telling the Bees[1]

Here is the place; right over the hill
  Runs the path I took;
You can see the gap in the old wall still,
  And the stepping-stones in the shallow brook.

There is the house, with the gate red-barred, 5
  And the poplars tall;
And the barn's brown length, and the cattle-yard,
  And the white horns tossing above the wall.

There are the beehives ranged in the sun;
  And down by the brink 10
Of the brook are her poor flowers, weed-o'errun,
  Pansy and daffodil, rose and pink.

A year has gone, as the tortoise goes,
  Heavy and slow;
And the same rose blows, and the same sun glows, 15
  And the same brook sings of a year ago.

There's the same sweet clover-smell in the breeze;
  And the June sun warm
Tangles his wings of fire in the trees,
  Setting, as then, over Fernside farm. 20

I mind me how with a lover's care
  From my Sunday coat
I brushed off the burrs, and smoothed my hair,
  And cooled at the brookside my brow and throat.

Since we parted, a month had passed,— 25
  To love, a year;
Down through the beeches I looked at last
  On the little red gate and the well-sweep near.

I can see it all now,—the slantwise rain
  Of light through the leaves, 30
The sundown's blaze on her window-pane,
  The bloom of her roses under the eaves.

[1] This poem was first published in the *Atlantic Monthly* for April 1858, and then included in *Home Ballads and Other Poems* (1860), where Whittier has the following note to the poem: "A remarkable custom, brought from the Old Country, formerly prevailed in the rural districts of New England. On the death of a member of the family, the bees were at once informed of the event, and their hives dressed in mourning. This ceremonial was supposed to be necessary to prevent the swarms from leaving their hives and seeking a new home."

It was actually Whittier's mother, not his sister, who had died at his home, "Fernside farm," the year before.

Just the same as a month before,—
    The house and the trees,
The barn's brown gable, the vine by the door,—   35
    Nothing changed but the hives of bees.

Before them, under the garden wall,
    Forward and back,
Went drearily singing the chore-girl small,
    Draping each hive with a shred of black.   40

Trembling, I listened: the summer sun
    Had the chill of snow;
For I knew she was telling the bees of one
    Gone on the journey we all must go!

Then I said to myself, "My Mary weeps   45
    For the dead to-day:
Haply her blind old grandsire sleeps
    The fret and the pain of his age away."

But her dog whined low; on the doorway sill,
    With his cane to his chin,   50
The old man sat; and the chore-girl still
    Sung to the bees stealing out and in.

And the song she was singing ever since
    In my ear sounds on:—
"Stay at home, pretty bees, fly not hence!   55
    Mistress Mary is dead and gone!"

                      1858, 1860

Snow-Bound

[Snow-Bound first appeared as a booklet in 1866 and proved to be one of Whittier's most popular poems. He introduced the poem with a long explanatory note.]

To the Memory of
The Household It Describes,
This Poem Is Dedicated by the Author

The inmates of the family at the Whittier homestead who are referred to in the poem were my father, mother, my brother and two sisters, and my uncle and aunt both unmarried. In addition, there was the district school-master who boarded with us. The "not unfeared, half-welcome guest" was Harriet Livermore, daughter of Judge Livermore, of New Hampshire, a young woman of fine natural ability, enthusiastic, eccentric, with slight control over her violent temper, which sometimes made her religious profession doubtful. She was equally ready to exhort in schoolhouse prayer-meetings and dance in a Washington ball-room while her father was a member of Congress. She early embraced the doctrine of the Second Advent, and felt it her duty to proclaim the Lord's speedy coming. With this message she crossed the Atlantic and spent the greater part of a long life in travelling over Europe and Asia. She lived some time with Lady Hester Stanhope, a woman as fantastic and mentally strained as herself, on the slope of Mt. Lebanon, but finally quarrelled with her in regard to two white horses with red marks on their backs which suggested the idea of saddles, on which her titled hostess expected to ride into Jerusalem with the Lord. A friend of mine found her, when quite an old woman, wandering in Syria with a tribe of Arabs, who with the Oriental notion that madness is inspiration, accepted her as their prophetess and leader. At the time referred to in *Snow-Bound* she was boarding at the Rocks Village about two miles from us.

In my boyhood, in our lonely farm-house, we had scanty sources of information; few books and only a small weekly newspaper. Our only annual was the Almanac. Under such circumstances story-telling was a necessary resource in long winter evenings. My father when a young man had traversed the wilderness to Canada, and could tell us of his adventures with Indians and wild beasts, and of his sojourn in the French villages. My uncle was ready with his record of hunting and fishing and, it must be confessed, with stories which he at least half believed, of witchcraft and apparitions. My mother, who was born in the Indian-haunted region of Somersworth, New Hampshire, between Dover and Portsmouth, told us of the inroads of the savages, and the narrow escape of her ancestors, She described strange people who lived on the Piscataqua and Cocheco, among whom was Bantam the sorcerer. I have in my possession the wizard's "conjuring book," which he solemnly opened when consulted. It is a copy of Cornelius Agrippa's *Magic* printed in 1651, dedicated to Dr. Robert Child, who, like Michael Scott, had learned

> "the art of glammorie
> In Padua beyond the sea,"

and who is famous in the annals of Massachusetts, where he was at one time a resident, as the first man who dared petition the General Court for liberty of conscience. The full title of the book is *Three Books of Occult Philosophy, by Henry Cornelius Agrippa, Knight, Doctor of both Laws, Counsellor to Cæsar's Sacred Majesty and Judge of the Prerogative Court.*

> *"As the Spirits of Darkness be stronger in the dark, so Good Spirits, which be Angels of Light, are augmented not only by the Divine light of the Sun, but also by our common Wood Fire: and as the Celestial Fire drives away dark spirits, so also this our Fire of Wood doth the same."*

Snow-Bound

A WINTER IDYL
TO THE MEMORY OF THE HOUSEHOLD
IT DESCRIBES THIS POEM IS DEDICATED
BY THE AUTHOR

"As the Spirits of Darkness be stronger in the dark, so good Spirits which be Angels of Light, are augmented not only by the Divine Light of the Sun, but also, by our common Wood Fire: and as the Celestial Fire drives away dark spirits so also this our Fire of Wood doth the same."—COR. AGRIPPA, OCCULT PHILOSOPHY, Book I. ch. v.[1]

> "Announced by all the trumpets of the sky,
> Arrives the snow; and, driving o'er the fields,
> Seems nowhere to alight; the whited air
> Hides hills and woods, the river and the heaven,
> And veils the farm-house at the garden's end.
> The sled and traveller stopped, the courier's feet
> Delayed, all friends shut out, the housemates sit
> Around the radiant fireplace, enclosed
> In a tumultuous privacy of storm."
>
> —EMERSON, THE SNOW-STORM.

The sun that brief December day
Rose cheerless over hills of gray,
And, darkly circled, gave at noon
A sadder light than waning moon.
Slow tracing down the thickening sky   5
Its mute and ominous prophecy,
A portent seeming less than threat,
It sank from sight before it set.
A chill no coat, however stout,
Of homespun stuff could quite shut out,   10
A hard, dull bitterness of cold,
That checked, mid-vein, the circling race
Of life-blood in the sharpened face,
The coming of the snow-storm told.
The wind blew east; we heard the roar   15
Of Ocean on his wintry shore,
And felt the strong pulse throbbing there
Beat with low rhythm our inland air.

[1] Cornelius Heinrich Agrippa (1486–1535) was a German writer on the occult and a physician.

Meanwhile we did our nightly chores,
Brought in the wood from out of doors,   20
Littered the stalls, and from the mows,
Raked down the herd's-grass[2] for the cows:
Heard the horse whinnying for his corn;
And, sharply clashing horn on horn,
Impatient down the stanchion rows   25
The cattle shake their walnut bows,[3]
While, peering from his early perch
Upon the scaffold's pole of birch
The cock his crested helmet bent
And down his querulous challenge sent.   30

Unwarmed by any sunset light
The gray day darkened into night,
A night made hoary with the swarm
And whirl-dance of the blinding storm,
As zigzag, wavering to and fro   35
Crossed and recrossed the winged snow:
And ere the early bedtime came
The white drift piled the window-frame,
And through the glass the clothes-line posts
Looked in like tall and sheeted ghosts.   40

So all night long the storm roared on:
The morning broke without a sun;
In tiny spherule[4] traced with lines
Of Nature's geometric signs,
In starry flake, and pellicle,   45
All day the hoary meteor fell;
And, when the second morning shone,
We looked upon a world unknown,
On nothing we could call our own.
Around the glistening wonder bent   50
The blue walls of the firmament,
No cloud above, no earth below,—
A universe of sky and snow!
The old familiar sights of ours
Took marvellous shapes; strange domes and towers   55
Rose up where sty or corn-crib stood,
Or garden-wall, or belt of wood;

[2] Timothy or redtop, which were used as fodder.

[3] Upright posts used for controlling cattle; walnut bows are the collars attached to the stanchions.

[4] A long pole on a pivot with a bucket at the end to be dipped into the well.

A smooth white mound the brush-pile showed,
A fenceless drift that once was road;
The bridle-post an old man sat   60
With loose-flung coat and high cocked hat;
The well-curb had a Chinese roof;
And even the long sweep, high aloof,
In its slant splendor, seemed to tell
Of Pisa's leaning miracle.   65
A prompt, decisive man, no breath
Our father wasted: "Boys, a path!"
Well pleased, (for when did farmer boy
Count such a summons less than joy?)
Our buskins[5] on our feet we drew;   70
With mittened hands, and caps drawn low,
To guard our necks and ears from snow,
We cut the solid whiteness through.
And, where the drift was deepest, made
A tunnel walled and overlaid   75
With dazzling crystal: we had read
Of rare Aladdin's wondrous cave,
And to our own his name we gave,
With many a wish the luck were ours
To test his lamp's supernal powers.   80
We reached the barn with merry din,
And roused the prisoned brutes within.
The old horse thrust his long head out,
And grave with wonder gazed about;
The cock his lusty greeting said,   85
And forth his speckled harem led;
The oxen lashed their tails, and hooked,
And mild reproach of hunger looked;
The horned patriarch of the sheep,
Like Egypt's Amun[6] roused from sleep,   90
Shook his sage head with gesture mute,
And emphasized with stamp of foot.
All day the gusty north-wind bore
The loosening drift its breath before;
Low circling round its southern zone,   95
The sun through dazzling snow-mist shone.
No church-bell lent its Christian tone
To the savage air, no social smoke
Curled over woods of snow-hung oak.

---

[5] Leather boots.   [6] An Egyptian god with the head of a ram.

A solitude made more intense   100
By dreary-voicèd elements,
The shrieking of the mindless wind,
The moaning tree-boughs swaying blind,
And on the glass the unmeaning beat
Of ghostly finger-tips of sleet.   105
Beyond the circle of our hearth
No welcome sound of toil or mirth
Unbound the spell, and testified
Of human life and thought outside.
We minded[7] that the sharpest ear   110
The buried brooklet could not hear,
The music of whose liquid lip
Had been to us companionship,
And, in our lonely life, had grown
To have an almost human tone.   115

As night drew on, and, from the crest
Of wooded knolls that ridged the west,
The sun, a snow-blown traveller, sank
From sight beneath the smothering bank,
We piled, with care, our nightly stack   120
Of wood against the chimney-back,—
The oaken log, green, huge, and thick,
And on its top the stout back-stick;
The knotty forestick laid apart,
And filled between with curious art   125
The ragged brush; then, hovering near,
We watched the first red blaze appear,
Heard the sharp crackle, caught the gleam
On whitewashed wall and sagging beam,
Until the old, rude-furnished room   130
Burst, flower-like, into rosy bloom;
While radiant with a mimic flame
Outside the sparkling drift became,
And through the bare-boughed lilac-tree
Our own warm hearth seemed blazing free.   135
The crane and pendent trammels[8] showed,
The Turks' heads[9] on the andirons glowed;

---

[7] Knew.   [9] Turbanlike ornaments.

[8] Pothooks that hung from the metal arm or
crane in the fireplace.

While childish fancy, prompt to tell
The meaning of the miracle,
Whispered the old rhyme: *"Under the tree,*   140
When fire outdoors burns merrily,
There the witches are making tea."

The moon above the eastern wood
Shone at its full; the hill-range stood
Transfigured in the silver flood,   145
Its blown snows flashing cold and keen,
Dead white, save where some sharp ravine
Took shadow, or the sombre green
Of hemlocks turned to pitchy black
Against the whiteness at their back.   150
For such a world and such a night
Most fitting that unwarming light,
Which only seemed where'er it fell
To make the coldness visible.

Shut in from all world without,   155
We sat the clean-winged hearth about,
Content to let the north-wind roar
In baffled rage at pane and door,
While the red logs before us beat
The frost-line back with tropic heat;   160
And ever, when a louder blast
Shook beam and rafter as it passed,
The merrier up its roaring draught
The great throat of the chimney laughed;
The house-dog on his paws outspread   165
Laid to the fire his drowsy head,
The cat's dark silhouette on the wall
A couchant tiger's seemed to fall;
And, for the winter fireside meet,
Between the andirons' straddling feet,   170
The mug of cider simmered slow,
The apples sputtered in a row,
And, close at hand, the basket stood
With nuts from brown October's wood.

What matter how the night behaved?   175
What matter how the north-wind raved?
Blow high, blow low, not all its snow
Could quench our hearth-fire's ruddy glow.

O Time and Change!—with hair as gray
As was my sire's that winter day,   180
How strange it seems, with so much gone
Of life and love, to still live on!
Ah, brother![10] only I and thou
Are left of all that circle now,—
The dear home faces whereupon   185
That fitful firelight paled and shone.
Henceforth, listen as we will,
The voices of that hearth are still;
Look where we may, the wide earth o'er
Those lighted faces smile no more.   190
We tread the paths their feet have worn,
    We sit beneath their orchard trees,
    We hear, like them, the hum of bees
And rustle of the bladed corn;
We turn the pages that they read,   195
    Their written words we linger o'er,
But in the sun they cast no shade,
No voice is heard, no sign is made,
    No step is on the conscious floor!
Yet Love will dream, and Faith will trust,   200
(Since He who knows our need is just,)
That somehow, somewhere, meet we must.
Alas for him who never sees
The stars shine through his cypress-trees!
Who, hopeless, lays his dead away,   205
Nor looks to see the breaking day
Across the mournful marbles play!
Who hath not learned, in hours of faith,
    The truth to flesh and sense unknown,
That life is ever lord of Death   210
    And Love can never lose its own!

We sped the time with stories old,
Wrought puzzles out, and riddles told,
Or stammered from our school-book lore[11]
"The Chief of Gambia's golden shore."[12]   215
How often since, when all the land
Was clay in Slavery's shaping hand,
As if a far-blown trumpet stirred
The languorous sin-sick air, I heard:

---

[10] Matthew Franklin Whittier (1812-1883).

[11] Caleb Bingham's *The American Primer*.

[12] "The African Chief" by Mrs. S. W. Morton (1759-1846), a Boston poet.

"Does not the voice of reason cry, 220
Claim the first right which Nature gave,
From the red scourge of bondage fly,
Nor deign to live a burdened slave!"
Our father[13] rode again his ride
On Memphremagog's[14] wooded side; 225
Sat down again to moose and samp[15]
In trapper's hut and Indian camp;
Lived o'er the old idyllic ease
Beneath St. François'[16] hemlock-trees;
Again for him the moonlight shone 230
On Norman cap and bodiced zone;
Again he heard the violin play
Which led the village dance away.
And mingled in its merry whirl
The grandam and the laughing girl. 235
Or, nearer home, our steps he led
Where Salisbury's[17] level marshes spread
    Mile-wide as flies the laden bee;
Where merry mowers, hale and strong,
Swept, scythe on scythe, their swaths along 240
    The low green prairies of the sea.
We shared the fishing off Boar's Head
    And round the rocky Isles of Shoals[18]
    The hake-broil on the drift-wood coals;
The chowder on the sand-beach made, 245
Dipped by the hungry, steaming hot
With spoons of clam-shell from the pot.
We heard the tales of witchcraft old,
And dream and sign and marvel told
To sleepy listeners as they lay 250
Stretched idly on the salted hay,
Adrift along the winding shores,
When favoring breezes deigned to blow
The square sail of the gundelow
And idle lay the useless oars. 255

---

[13] John Whittier (1760–1830).
[14] A lake between Vermont and Quebec.
[15] Corn-meal mush.
[16] A French-Canadian village, north of Lake Memphremagog.

[17] A town in northern Massachusetts, east of the Haverhill farmstead.
[18] Off the New Hampshire coast. Boar's Head is a promontory on the coast.

Our mother,[19] while she turned her wheel
Or run the new-knit stocking-heel,
Told how the Indian hordes came down
At midnight on Cocheco[20] town,
And how her own great-uncle bore   260
His cruel scalp-mark to fourscore.
Recalling, in her fitting phrase,
    So rich and picturesque and free,
    (The common unrhymed poetry
Of simple life and country ways,)   265
The story of her early days,—
She made us welcome to her home;
Old hearths grew wide to give us room;
We stole with her a frightened look
At the gray wizard's conjuring-book,   270
The fame whereof went far and wide
Through all the simple country-side;
We heard the hawks at twilight play,
The boat-horn on Piscataqua,[21]
The loon's weird laughter far away;   275
We fished her little trout-brook, knew
What flowers in wood and meadow grew,
What sunny hillsides autumn-brown
She climbed to shake the ripe nuts down,
Saw where in sheltered cove and bay   280
The ducks' black squadron anchored lay,
And heard the wild-geese calling loud
Beneath the gray November cloud.

Then, haply, with a look more grave,
And soberer tone, some tale she gave   285
From painful Sewel's ancient tome,[22]
Beloved in every Quaker home,
Of faith fire-winged by martyrdom,
Or Chalkley's Journal,[23] old and quaint,—
Gentlest of skippers, rare sea-saint!—   290

[19] Abigail Hussey Whittier (1781-1857).

[20] On the Cocheco River, above Portsmouth, New Hampshire. An Indian raid had taken place there.

[21] A river on the border of Maine and New Hampshire.

[22] William Sewel, a Dutch Quaker, was the author of *History of the Rise, Increase, and Progress of the People Called the Quakers* (Dutch, 1717; English, 1725).

[23] Thomas Chalkley (1675-1741), a Quaker sea captain and missionary, was the author of *The Journal of Thomas Chalkley* (1747).

Who, when the dreary calms prevailed,
And water-butt and bread-cask failed,
And cruel, hungry eyes pursued
His portly presence mad for food,
With dark hints muttered under breath   295
Of casting lots for life or death,
Offered, if Heaven withheld supplies,
To be himself the sacrifice.
Then, suddenly, as if to save
The good man from his living grave,   300
A ripple on the water grew,
A school of porpoise flashed in view.
"Take, eat,"[24] he said, "and be content;
These fishes in my stead are sent
By Him who gave the tangled ram   305
To spare the child of Abraham."[25]

Our uncle,[26] innocent of books,
Was rich in lore of fields and brooks,
The ancient teachers never dumb
Of Nature's unhoused lyceum.   310
In moons and tides and weather wise,
He read the clouds as prophecies,
And foul or fair could well divine,
By many an occult hint and sign,
Holding the cunning-warded keys   315
To all the woodcraft mysteries;
Himself to Nature's heart so near
That all her voices in his ear
Of beast or bird had meanings clear,
Like Apollonius[27] of old,   320
Who knew the tales the sparrows told,
Or Hermes,[28] who interpreted
What the sage cranes of Nilus said;
A simple, guileless, childlike man,
Content to live where life began;   325

[24] Cf. Matthew xxvi: 26-27: "Jesus took bread, and blessed it, and brake it, and gave it to the disciples, and said, Take, eat; this is my body."

[25] Cf. Genesis, xxii: 7-14

[26] Moses Whittier (died 1824).

[27] Apollonius of Tyre was a Greek miracle writer of the first century.

[28] Hermes Trismegesitus was the mythical author of the occult *Hermetic Books* of Egypt. The "Nilus" is the Nile River.

Strong only on his native grounds,
The little world of sights and sounds
Whose girdle was the parish bounds,
Whereof his fondly partial pride
The common features magnified,   330
As Surrey hills to mountains grew
In White of Selborne's[29] loving view,—
He told how teal and loon he shot,
And how the eagle's eggs he got,
The feats on pond and river done,   335
The prodigies of rod and gun;
Till, warming with the tales he told,
Forgotten was the outside cold,
The bitter wind unheeded blew,
From ripening corn the pigeons flew,   340
The partridge drummed i' the wood, the mink
Went fishing down the river-bank;
In fields with bean or clover gay,
The woodchuck, like a hermit gray,
   Peered from the doorway of his cell;   345
The muskrat plied the mason's trade,
And tier by tier his mud-walls laid;
And from the shagbark overhead
   The grizzled squirrel dropped his shell.
Next, the dear aunt,[30] whose smile of cheer   350
And voice in dreams I see and hear,—
The sweetest woman ever Fate
Perverse denied a household mate,
Who, lonely, homeless, not the less
Found peace in love's unselfishness,   355
And welcome wheresoe'er she went,
A calm and gracious element,
Whose presence seemed the sweet income
And womanly atmosphere of home,—
Called up her girlhood memories,   360
The huskings and the apple-bees,
The sleigh-rides and the summer sails,
Weaving through all the poor details

[29] Gilbert White (1721-1793), a naturalist of Surrey County, England, wrote *The Natural History and Antiquities of Selborne* (1789).

[30] Mercy Hussey, his mother's sister, died in 1846.

And homespun warp of circumstance
A golden woof-thread of romance.   365
For well she kept her genial mood
And simple faith of maidenhood;
Before her still a cloud-land lay,
The mirage loomed across her way;
The morning dew, that dries so soon   370
With others, glistened at her noon;
Through years of toil and soil and care,
From glossy tress to then gray hair,
All unprofaned she held apart
The virgin fancies of the heart.   375
Be shame to him of woman born
Who hath for such but thought of scorn.

There, too, our elder sister[31] plied
Her evening task the stand beside;
A full, rich nature, free to trust,   380
Truthful and almost sternly just,
Impulsive, earnest, prompt to act,
And make her generous thought a fact,
Keeping with many a light disguise
The secret of self-sacrifice.   385
O heart sore-tried! thou hast the best,
That Heaven itself could give thee,—rest,
Rest from all bitter thoughts and things!
    How many a poor one's blessing went
    With thee beneath the low green tent   390
Whose curtain never outward swings!
As one who held herself a part
Of all she saw, and let her heart
    Against the household bosom lean,
Upon the motley-braided mat   395
Our youngest and our dearest[32] sat,
Lifting her large, sweet, asking eyes,
    Now bathed in the unfading green
And holy peace of Paradise.
Oh, looking from some heavenly hill,   400
    Or from the shade of saintly palms,
    Or silver reach of river calms,
Do those large eyes behold me still?

[31] Mary Caldwell Whittier (1806-1861).
[32] Elizabeth Hussey Whittier had died at the
age of 48, "one little year ago" (1864).

With me one little year ago:—
The chill weight of the winter snow   405
   For months upon her grave has lain;
And now, when summer south-winds blow
   And brier and harebell bloom again,
I tread the pleasant paths we trod,
I see the violet-sprinkled sod   410
Whereon she leaned, too frail and weak
The hillside flowers she loved to seek,
Yet following me where'er I went
With dark eyes full of love's content.
The birds are glad; the brier-rose fills   415
The air with sweetness; all the hills
Stretch green to June's unclouded sky;
But still I wait with ear and eye
For something gone which should be nigh,
A loss in all familiar things,   420
In flower that blooms, and bird that sings.
And yet, dear heart! remembering thee,
   Am I not richer than of old?
Safe in thy immortality,
   What change can reach the wealth I hold?   425
   What chance can mar the pearl and gold
Thy love hath left in trust with me?
And while in life's late afternoon,
   Where cool and long the shadows grow,
I walk to meet the night that soon   430
   Shall shape and shadow overflow,
I cannot feel that thou art far,
Since near at need the angels are;
And when the sunset gates unbar,
   Shall I not see thee waiting stand,   435
And, white against the evening star,
   The welcome of thy beckoning hand?

Brisk wielder of the birch and rule,
The master of the district school[33]
Held at the fire his favored place,   440
Its warm glow lit a laughing face
Fresh-hued and fair, where scarce appeared
The uncertain prophecy of beard.

[33] George Haskell (1799-1876).

He teased the mitten-blinded cat,
Played cross-pins on my uncle's hat, 445
Sang songs, and told us what befalls
In classic Dartmouth's college halls.
Born the wild Northern hills among,
From whence his yeoman father wrung
By patient toil subsistence scant, 450
Not competence and yet not want,
He early gained the power to pay
His cheerful, self-reliant way;
Could doff at ease his scholar's gown
To peddle wares from town to town; 455
Or through the long vacation's reach
In lonely lowland districts teach,
Where all the droll experience found
At stranger hearths in boarding round,
The moonlit skater's keen delight, 460
The sleigh-drive through the frosty night,
The rustic-party, with its rough
Accompaniment of blind-man's-buff,
And whirling-plate, and forfeits paid,
His winter task a pastime made. 465
Happy the snow-locked homes wherein
He tuned his merry violin,
Or played the athlete in the barn,
Or held the good dam's winding-yarn,
Or mirth-provoking versions told 470
Of classic legends rare and old,
Wherein the scenes of Greece and Rome
Had all the commonplace of home,
And little seemed at best the odds
'Twixt Yankee pedlers and old gods; 475
Where Pindus-born Arachthus[34] took
The guise of any grist-mill brook,
And dread Olympus at his will
Became a huckleberry hill.

A careless boy that night he seemed; 480
    But at his desk he had the look
And air of one who wisely schemed,
    And hostage from the future took
    In trained thought and lore of book.

[34] A legendary river that rose in the Pindus
Mountains of Greece.

Large-brained, clear-eyed, of such as he 485
Shall Freedom's young apostles be,
Who, following in War's bloody trail,
Shall every lingering wrong assail;
All chains from limb and spirit strike,
Uplift the black and white alike; 490
Scatter before their swift advance
The darkness and the ignorance,
The pride, the lust, the squalid sloth,
Which nurtured Treason's monstrous growth,
Made murder pastime, and the hell 495
Of prison-torture possible;
The cruel lie of caste refute,
Old forms remould, and substitute
For Slavery's lash the freeman's will,
For blind routine, wise-handed skill; 500
A school-house plant on every hill,
Stretching in radiate nerve-lines thence
The quick wires of intelligence;
Till North and South together brought
Shall own the same electric thought, 505
In peace a common flag salute,
And, side by side in labor's free
And unresentful rivalry,
Harvest the fields wherein they fought.

Another guest that winter night 510
Flashed back from lustrous eyes the light.
Unmarked by time, and yet not young,
The honeyed music of her tongue
And words of meekness scarcely told
A nature passionate and bold, 515
Strong, self-concentred, spurning guide,
Its milder features dwarfed beside
Her unbent will's majestic pride.
She sat among us, at the best,
A not unfeared, half-welcome guest, 520
Rebuking with her cultured phrase
Our homeliness of words and ways.
A certain pard-like, treacherous grace
Swayed the lithe limbs and dropped the lash,
Lent the white teeth their dazzling flash; 525
And under low brows, black with night,
Rayed out at times a dangerous light;

The sharp heat-lightnings of her face
Presaging ill to him whom Fate
Condemned to share her love or hate.   530
A woman tropical, intense
In thought and act, in soul and sense,
She blended in a like degree
The vixen and the devotee,
Revealing with each freak or feint   535
   The temper of Petruchio's Kate,[35]
The raptures of Siena's saint.[36]
Her tapering hand and rounded wrist
Had facile power to form a fist;
The warm, dark languish of her eyes   540
Was never safe from wrath's surprise.
Brows saintly calm and lips devout
Knew every change of scowl and pout;
And the sweet voice had notes more high
And shrill for social battle-cry.   545

Since then what old cathedral town
Has missed her pilgrim staff and gown,
What convent-gate has held its lock
Against the challenge of her knock!
Through Smyrna's plague-hushed thoroughfares,   550
Up sea-set Malta's rock stairs,
Gray olive slopes of hills that hem
   Thy tombs and shrines, Jerusalem,
Or startling on her desert throne
The crazy Queen of Lebanon[37]   555
With claims fantastic as her own,
Her tireless feet have held their way;
And still, unrestful, bowed, and gray,
She watches under Eastern skies,
   With hope each day renewed and fresh,   560
   The Lord's quick coming in the flesh,
Whereof she dreams and prophesies!

Where'er her troubled path may be,
   The Lord's sweet pity with her go!
The outward wayward life we see,   565
The hidden springs we may not know.

---

[35] Cf. Shakespeare's *Taming of the Shrew.*
[36] St. Catherine of Siene (1347–1380).

[37] Lady Hester Lucy Stanhope (1776–1839).
See Whittier's Introduction to the poem.

Nor is it given us to discern
  What threads the fatal sisters spun,
  Through what ancestral years has run
The sorrow with the woman born,   570
What forged her cruel chain of moods,
What set her feet in solitudes,
  And held the love within her mute,
What mingled madness in the blood,
  A life-long discord and annoy,   575
  Water of tears with oil of joy,
And hid within the folded bud
  Perversities of flower and fruit.
It is not ours to separate
  The tangled skein of will and fate,   580
To show what metes and bounds should stand
Upon the soul's debatable land,
And between choice and Providence
Divide the circle of events;
But He who knows our frame is just,   585
Merciful and compassionate,
And full of sweet assurances
And hope for all the language is,
That He remembereth we are dust![38]

At last the great logs, crumbling low,   590
Sent out a dull and duller glow,
The bull's-eye watch that hung in view,
Ticking its weary circuit through,
Pointed with mutely warning sign
Its black hand to the hour of nine.   595
That sign the pleasant circle broke:
My uncle ceased his pipe to smoke,
Knocked from its bowl the refuse gray,
And laid it tenderly away;
Then roused himself to safely cover   600
The dull red brands with ashes over.
And while, with care, our mother laid
The work aside, her steps she stayed
One moment, seeking to express
Her grateful sense of happiness   605
For food and shelter, warmth and health,
And love's contentment more than wealth,

[38] Cf. Psalms ciii: 9–14.

With simple wishes (not the weak
Vain prayers which no fulfilment seek,
But such as warm the generous heart,   610
O'er-prompt to do with Heaven its part)
That none might lack, that bitter night,
For bread and clothing, warmth and light.

Within our beds awhile we heard
The wind that round the gables roared,   615
With now and then a ruder shock,
Which made our very bedsteads rock.
We heard the loosened clapboards tost,
The board-nails snapping in the frost;
.And on us, through the unplastered wall,   620
Felt the light sifted snow-flakes fall.
But sleep stole on, as sleep will do
When hearts are light and life is new;
Faint and more faint the murmurs grew,
Till in the summer-land of dreams   625
They softened to the sound of streams,
Low stir of leaves, and dip of oars,
And lapsing waves on quiet shores.

Next morn we wakened with the shout
Of merry voices high and clear;   630
And saw the teamsters drawing near
To break the drifted highways out.
Down the long hillside treading slow
We saw the half-buried oxen go,
Shaking the snow from heads uptost,   635
Their straining nostrils white with frost.
Before our door the straggling train
Drew up, and added team to gain.
The elders threshed their hands a-cold,
    Passed, with the cider-mug, their jokes   640
    From lip to lip; the younger folks
Down the loose snow-banks, wrestling, rolled,
Then toiled again the cavalcade
    O'er windy hill, through clogged ravine,
    And woodland paths that wound between   645
Low drooping pine-boughs winter-weighed.
From every barn a team afoot,
At every house a new recruit,
Where, drawn by Nature's subtlest law,
Haply the watchful young men saw   650

Sweet doorway pictures of the curls
And curious eyes of merry girls,
Lifting their hands in mock defence
Against the snow-ball's compliments,
And reading in each missive tost   655
The charm with Eden never lost.

We heard once more the sleigh-bells' sound;
   And, following where the teamsters led,
The wise old Doctor[39] went his round,
Just pausing at our door to say,   660
In the brief autocratic way
Of one who, prompt at Duty's call,
Was free to urge her claim on all,
   That some poor neighbor sick abed
At night our mother's aid would need.   665
For, one in generous thought and deed,
   What mattered in the sufferer's sight
   The Quaker matron's inward light,
The Doctor's mail of Calvin's creed?
All hearts confess the saints elect   670
   Who, twain in faith, in love agree,
And melt not in an acid sect
   The Christian pearl of charity!

So days went on: a week had passed
Since the great world was heard from last.   675
The Almanac we studied o'er,
Read and reread our little store
Of books and pamphlets, scarce a score;
One harmless novel, mostly hid
From younger eyes, a book forbid,   680
And poetry, (or good or bad,
A single book was all we had,)
Where Ellwood's[40] meek, drab-skirted Muse,
   A stranger to the heathen Nine,
   Sang, with a somewhat nasal whine,   685
The wars of David and the Jews.
At last the floundering carrier bore
The village paper to our door.
Lo! broadening outward as we read,
To warmer zones the horizon spread;   690

[39] Dr. Elias Weld was the family physician who lent Whittier many of his books.

[40] Thomas Ellwood (1639-1714), an English Quaker, wrote the epic *Davideis* (1712).

In panoramic length unrolled
We saw the marvels that it told.
Before us passed the painted Creeks,[41]
   And daft McGregor[42] on his raids
   In Costa Rica's everglades.   695
And up Taygetos winding slow
Rode Ypsilanti's Mainote Greeks,[43]
A Turk's head at each saddle-bow!
Welcome to us its week-old news,
Its corner for the rustic Muse,   700
   Its monthly gauge of snow and rain,
Its record, mingling in a breath
The wedding bell and dirge of death:
Jest, anecdote, and love-lorn tale,
The latest culprit sent to jail;   705
Its hue and cry of stolen and lost,
Its vendue[44] sales and goods at cost,
   And traffic calling loud for gain.
We felt the stir of hall and street,
The pulse of life that round us beat;   710
The chill embargo of the snow
Was melted in the genial glow;
Wide swung again our ice-locked door,
And all the world was ours once more!

Clasp, Angel of the backward look   715
   And folded wings of ashen gray
   And voice of echoes far away,
The brazen covers of thy book;
The weird palimpsest old and vast,
Wherein thou hid'st the spectral past;   720
Where, closely mingling, pale and glow
The characters of joy and woe;
The monographs of outlived years,
Or smile-illumed or dim with tears,
   Green hills of life that slope to death,   725
And haunts of home, whose vistaed trees
Shade off to mournful cypresses
   With the white amaranths[45] underneath.

---

[41] The Creek Indians of Alabama were subdued by Andrew Jackson in 1814 and put on a reservation in 1821.

[42] Gregor McGregor tried to establish a colony in Costa Rica in 1819.

[43] In 1820, when the Greeks sought independence from Turkey, General Ypsilanti (1792-1828) triumphed in a battle at Mt. Taygetos on the Peloponnesus.

[44] Auction

[45] Legendary flowers that never die.

Even while I look, I can but heed
 The restless sands' incessant fall,   730
Importunate hours that hours succeed,
Each clamourous with its own sharp need,
 And duty keeping pace with all.
Shut down and clasp the heavy lids;
I hear again the voice that bids   735
The dreamer leave his dream midway
For larger hopes and graver fears:
Life greatens in these later years,
The century's aloe[46] flowers today!

Yet, haply, in some lull of life,   740
Some Truce of God which breaks its strife,
The worlding's eyes shall gather dew,
 Dreaming in throngful city ways
Of winter joys his boyhood knew;
And dear and early friends—the few   745
Who yet remain—shall pause to view
 These Flemish pictures of old days;
Sit with me by the homestead hearth,
And stretch the hands of memory forth
 To warm them at the wood-fire's blaze!   750
And thanks untraced to lips unknown
Shall greet me like the odors blown
From unseen meadows newly mown,
Or lilies floating in some pond,
Wood-fringed, the wayside gaze beyond;   755

Traveller owns the grateful sense
Of sweetness near, he knows not whence,
And, pausing, takes with forehead bare
The benediction of the air.

          1866

[46] A plant, known for its bitterness, that was said to bloom only once in a hundred years and that was used in embalming the body of Jesus (cf. John xix: 39–40).

OLIVER WENDELL HOLMES

(1809-1894)

Oliver Wendell Holmes was born on August 29, 1809 in Cambridge, Massachusetts. His father was a minister of Calvinist stock, caught between authoritarian ministers and a liberal parish that finally dismissed him because of his conservative tendencies. As a boy, Holmes took issue with his father's orthodoxy and remained throughout his life a critic of Calvinism. After his graduation from Harvard in 1829, he went to the Dane Law School, but turned to medicine in 1833 and received his M. D. from the Harvard Medical School in 1836. He had already begun to write poetry—the famous "Old Ironsides" appeared in 1830 and "The Last Leaf" in 1831; but his most serious concern at this point in his life was medicine, and he grew absorbed in research on subjects such as puerperal fever. Holmes published *Homoepathy and Its Kindred Delusions* in 1842, *The Contagiousness of Puerperal Fever* in 1843, and three novels—*Elsie Venner* (1860), *The Guardian Angel* (1867), and *A Moral Antipathy* (1885)—that are concerned with medical subjects and that suggest his liberal views and his belief in the primacy of reason. Holmes revered science in the way that his ancestors were devoted to religion.

Holmes is primarily remembered for a poetry of wit and urbanity. His most famous work, *The Autocrat of the Breakfast-Table,* appeared in 1858, followed by *The Professor at the Breakfast-Table* in 1859, and by *The Poet at the Breakfast-Table* in 1872. In these books he was able to capture the spontaneous qualities of conversation for which he was so famous and to satirize the religious, medical, and social pretensions of his day. His best-known poem, "The Deacon's Masterpiece," remains the classic spoof of Calvinist logic and rigid thinking.

The standard edition is *The Writings of Oliver Wendell Holmes,* Riverside Edition, 13 vols., 1891. A one-volume edition, *The Complete Poetical Works of Oliver Wendell Holmes,* was edited by H. E. Scudder, 1895. See also *Oliver Wendell Holmes: Representative Selections,* ed. S. I. Hayakawa and H. M. Jones, American Writers Series, 1939. Franklin T. Currier and Eleanor M. Tilton edited *A Bibliography of Oliver Wendell Holmes,* 1953. Franklin T. Baker edited *The Autocrat of the Breakfast-Table* (1928).

The standard biography is John Torrey Morse, *Life and Letters of Oliver Wendell Holmes,* 2 vols., 1896. Recent studies, which include criticism, are M. A. De-Wolfe Howe, *Holmes of the Breakfast-Table,* 1939; P. Obendorf, *The Psychiatric Novels of Oliver Wendell Holmes, 1943;* Eleanor M. Tilton, *Amiable Autocrat,* 1947; Miriam R. Small, *Oliver Wendell Holmes,* 1962.

The selection from *The Autocrat* is taken from *The Writings of Oliver Wendell Holmes;* the poems are reprinted from *The Complete Poetical Works of Oliver Wendell Holmes.*

The Chambered Nautilus[1]

This is the ship of pearl, which, poets feign,
    Sails the unshadowed main,—
    The venturous bark that flings
On the sweet summer wind its purpled wings
In gulfs enchanted, where the Siren[2] sings,   5
    And coral reefs lie bare,
Where the cold sea-maids rise to sun their streaming hair.

Its webs of living gauze no more unfurl;
    Wrecked is the ship of pearl!
    And every chambered cell,   10
Where its dim dreaming life was wont to dwell,
As the frail tenant shaped his growing shell,
    Before thee lies revealed,—
Its irised ceiling rent, its sunless crypt unsealed!

Year after year beheld the silent toil   15
    That spread his lustrous coil;
    Still, as the spiral grew,
He left the past year's dwelling for the new,
Stole with soft step its shining archway through,
    Built up its idle door,   20
Stretched in his last-found home, and knew the old no more.

Thanks for the heavenly message brought by thee,
    Child of the wandering sea,
    Cast from her lap, forlorn!
From thy dead lips a clearer note is born   25
Than ever Triton blew from wreathèd horn![3]
    While on mine ear it rings,
Through the deep caves of thought I hear a voice that sings:—

[1] This poem first appeared in the February 1858 issue of the *Atlantic Monthly* and was included in *The Autocrat of the Breakfast-Table* (1858).

    The nautilus is a cephalopod of the South Pacific and Indian Oceans, described by Holmes in *The Autocrat of the Breakfast-Table,* Sec. IV, as having a "series of enlarging compartments successively dwelt in by the animal that inhabits the shell, which is built in a widening spiral."

[2] In classical mythology, an alluring sea-nymph.

[3] Cf. Wordsworth, "The World Is Too Much With Us," 14: "Or hear old Triton blow his wreathed horn."

Build thee more stately mansions, O my soul,
   As the swift seasons roll!   30
   Leave thy low-vaulted past!
Let each new temple, nobler than the last,
Shut thee from heaven with a dome more vast,
   Till thou at length art free,
Leaving thine outgrown shell by life's unresting sea!   35

1858

From The Autocrat of the Breakfast-Table[1]

CHAPTER XI

[The company looked flustered one morning when I came in,—so much so, that I inquired of my neighbor, the divinity-student, what had been going on. It appears that the young fellow whom they call John had taken advantage of my being a little late (I having been rather longer than usual dressing that morning) to circulate several questions involving a quibble or play upon words,—in short, containing that indignity to the human understanding, condemned in the passages from the distinguished moralist of the last century and the illustrious historian of the present, which I cited on a former occasion, and known as a *pun*. After breakfast, one of the boarders handed me a small roll of paper containing some of the questions and their answers. I subjoin two or three of them, to show what a tendency there is to frivolity and meaningless talk in young persons of a certain sort, when not restrained by the presence of more reflective natures.—It was asked, "Why tertian and quartan fevers were like certain short-lived insects." Some interesting physiological relation would be naturally suggested. The inquirer blushes to find that the answer is in the paltry equivocation, that they *skip* a day or two.—"Why an Englishman must go to the Continent to weaken his grog or punch." The answer proves to have no relation whatever to the temperance-movement, as no better reason is given than that island—(or, as it is absurdly

---

[1] *The Autocrat of the Breakfast-Table* first appeared as two essays in *The New England Magazine* in 1831. When James Russell Lowell became editor of the *Alantic Monthly* in 1857, he asked Holmes to continue the series for the magazine. Reminiscent of eighteenth-century British wit, the essays in the *Atlantic Monthly* are told from the point of view of the Autocrat, a garrulous conversationalist who is surrounded by a divergent cast of characters of all social classes: a minister, poet, landlady, servant, and a sweet young girl.

written, *ile* and) water won't mix.—But when I came to the next question and its answer, I felt that patience ceased to be a virtue. "Why an onion is like a piano" is a query that a person of sensibility would be slow to propose; but that in an educated community an individual could be found to answer it in these words,—"Because it smell odious," *quasi*, it's melodious,—is not credible, but true. I can show you the paper.

Dear reader, I beg your pardon for repeating such things. I know most conversations reported in books are altogether above such trivial details, but folly will come up at every table as surely as purslane and chick-weed and sorrel will come up in gardens.[2] This young fellow ought to have talked philosophy, I know perfectly well; but he didn't,—he made jokes.]

I am willing,—I said,—to exercise your ingenuity in a rational and contemplative manner.—No, I do not proscribe certain forms of philosophical speculation which involve an approach to the absurd or the ludicrous, such as you may find, for example, in the folio of the Reverend Father Thomas Sanchez, in his famous Disputations, "De Sancto Matrimonio."[3] I will therefore turn this levity of yours to profit by reading you a rhymed problem, wrought out by my friend the Professor.

THE DEACON'S MASTERPIECE:[4]

OR THE WONDERFUL "ONE-HOSS-SHAY."

A LOGICAL STORY.

Have you heard of the wonderful one-hoss-shay,
That was built in such a logical way
It ran a hundred years to a day,
And then, of a sudden, it—ah, but stay,
I'll tell you what happened without delay,
Scaring the parson into fits,
Frightening people out of their wits,—
Have you ever heard of that, I say?

[2] Purslane is a trailing weed; sorrel is a plant with acid-flavored leaves.

[3] Thomas Sanchez (1550-1610) was a Jesuit casuist who became director of the school at Granada. His *De Sacramento Matrimonii* (1592) deals with the legal, moral, and religious questions that arise out of marriage.

[4] This poem first appeared in the September 1858 number of the *Atlantic Monthly*. It has long been considered Holmes' most famous attack on the Calvinist faith, particularly the tenets of original sin and predestination; but in the context of the *Autocrat*, it seems to be more an example of Holmes' rationalistic thought, his view that however perfect a logical system may be, it will not survive if its premises are faulty.

Seventeen hundred and fifty-five,
Georgius Secundus[5] was then alive,—
Snuffy old drone from the German hive;
That was the year when Lisbon-town
Saw the earth open and gulp her down,[6]
And Braddock's[7] army was done so brown,
Left without a scalp to its crown.
It was on the terrible earthquake-day
That the Deacon finished the one-hoss-shay.[8]

Now in building of chaises, I tell you what,
There is always *somewhere* a weakest spot,—
In hub, tire, felloe,[9] in spring or thill,[10]
In panel, or crossbar, or floor, or sill,
In screw, bolt, thoroughbrace,[11]—lurking still,
Find it somewhere you must and will,—
Above or below, or within or without,—
And that's the reason, beyond a doubt,
A chaise *breaks down*, but doesn't *wear out*.

But the Deacon swore (as Deacons do,
With an "I dew vum," or an "I tell *yeou*, ")
He would build one shay to beat the taown
'n' the keounty 'n' all the kentry raoun';
It should be so built that it *couldn'* break daown,
—"Fur," said the Deacon, "'t's mighty plain
Thut the weakes' place mus' stan' the strain;
'n' the way t' fix it, uz I maintain,
                    Is only jest
T' make that place uz strong uz the rest."

So the Deacon inquired of the village folk
Where he could find the strongest oak,
That couldn't be split nor bent nor broke,—
That was for spokes and floor and sills;
He sent for lancewood to make the thills;

---

[5] George II, King of England (1727-1760), belonged to the German house of Hanover.

[6] A catastrophic earthquake in Lisbon in 1755.

[7] General Edward Braddock (1695-1755) was the British commander-in-chief who was defeated and killed in the French and Indian Wars on July 9, 1755.

[8] Acutally Jonathan Edwards published his *The Freedom of the Will* in 1754. The logic of Edwards' Calvinist theology is one example of Holmes' satire.

[9] The outer wooden rim of a wheel.

[10] The shaft to which the horse is harnessed.

[11] A leather support that connected the carriage's body and the springs.

The crossbars were ash, from the straightest trees,
The panels of white-wood, that cuts like cheese,
But lasts like iron for things like these;
The hubs of logs from the "Settler's ellum,"—
Last of its timber,—they couldn't sell 'em,
Never an axe had seen their chips,
And the wedges flew from between their lips,
Their blunt ends frizzled like celery-tips;
Step and prop-iron, bolt and screw,
Spring, tire, axle, and linchpin[12] too,
Steel of the finest, bright and blue;
Thoroughbrace bison-skin, thick and wide;
Boot, top, dasher, from tough old hide
Found in the pit when the tanner died.
That was the way he "put her through."—
"There!" said the Deacon, "naow she'll dew."

Do! I tell you, I rather guess
She was a wonder, and nothing less!
Colts grew horses, beards turned gray,
Deacon and deaconess dropped away,
Children and grand-children—where were they?
But there stood the stout old one-hoss-shay
As fresh as on Lisbon-earthquake-day!

EIGHTEEN HUNDRED;—it came and found
The Deacon's Masterpiece strong and sound.
Eighteen hundred increased by ten;—
"Hahnsum kerridge" they called it then.
Eighteen hundred and twenty came;—
Running as usual; much the same.
Thirty and forty at last arrive,
And then come fifty, and FIFTY-FIVE.

Little of all we value here
Wakes on the morn of its hundredth year
Without both feeling and looking queer.
In fact, there's nothing that keeps its youth,
So far as I know, but a tree and truth.
(This is a moral that runs at large;
Take it.—You're welcome.—No extra charge.)

[12] Like a cotter pin.

FIRST OF NOVEMBER,—the Earthquake-day.—
There are traces of age in the one-hoss-shay,
A general flavor of mild decay,
But nothing local, as one may say.
There couldn't be,—for the Deacon's art
Had made it so like in every part
That there wasn't a chance for one to start.
For the wheels were just as strong as the thills,
And the floor was just as strong as the sills,
And the panels just as strong as the floor,
And the whippletree[13] neither less nor more,
And the back-crossbar as strong as the fore,
And spring and axle and hub *encore.*
And yet, *as a whole,* it is past a doubt
In another hour it will be *worn out!*

First of November, 'Fifty-five!
This morning the parson takes a drive.
Now, small boys, get out of the way!
Here comes the wonderful one-hoss-shay,
Drawn by a rat-tailed, ewe-necked bay.
"Huddup!" said the parson.—Off went they.

The parson was working his Sunday's text,—
Had got to *fifthly,* and stopped perplexed
At what the—Moses—was coming next.
All at once the horse stood still,
Close by the meet'n'-house on the hill.
—First a shiver, and then a thrill,
Then something decidedly like a spill,—
And the parson was sitting upon a rock,
At half-past nine by the meet'n'-house clock,—
Just the hour of the Earthquake shock!
—What do you think the parson found,
When he got up and stared around?
The poor old chaise in a heap or mound,
As if it had been to the mill and ground.
You see, of course, if you're not a dunce,
How it went to pieces all at once,—
All at once, and nothing first,—
Just as bubbles do when they burst.

End of the wonderful one-hoss-shay.
Logic is logic. That's all I say.

[13] A bar on the frame behind the horse, to
which the side harness is attached.

—I think there is one habit,—I said to our company a day or two afterwards,—worse than that of punning. It is the gradual substitution of cant or
slang terms for words which truly characterize their objects. I have known
several very genteel idiots whose whole vocabulary had deliquesced into
some half dozen expressions. All things fell into one of two great categories,—*fast* or *slow*. Man's chief end was to be a *brick*. When the great
calamities of life overtook their friends, these last were spoken of as being *a
good deal cut up*. Nine tenths of human existence were summed up in the
single word, *bore*. These expressions come to be the algebraic symbols of
minds which have grown too weak or indolent to discriminate. They are the
blank checks of intellectual bankruptcy;—you may fill them up with what
idea you like; it makes no difference, for there are no funds in the treasury
upon which they are drawn. Colleges and good-for-nothing smoking-clubs
are the places where these conversational fungi spring up most luxuriantly.
Don't think I undervalue the proper use and application of a cant word or
phrase. It adds piquancy to conversation, as a mushroom does to a sauce. But
it is no better than a toadstool, odious to the sense and poisonous to the
intellect, when it spawns itself all over the talk of men and youths capable of
talking, as it sometimes does. As we hear slang phraseology, it is commonly
the dish-water from the washings of English dandyism, schoolboy or
fullgrown, wrung out of a three-volume novel which had sopped it up, or
decanted from the pictured urn of Mr. Verdant Green, and diluted to suit
the provincial climate.

—The young fellow called John spoke up sharply and said, it was "rum"
to hear me "pitchin' into feller" for "goin' it in the slang line," when I used
all the flash words myself just when I pleased.

—I replied with my usual forbearance.—Certainly, to give up the algebraic symbol because *a* or *b* is often a cover for ideal nihility, would be
unwise. I have heard a child laboring to express a certain condition, involving a hitherto undescribed sensation (as it supposed), all of which could have
been sufficiently explained by the participle—*bored*. I have seen a country-
clergyman, with a one-story intellect and a one-horse vocabulary, who has
consumed his valuable time (and mine) freely, in developing an opinion of a
brother-minister's discourse which would have been abundantly characterized by a peach-down-lipped sophomore in the one word—*slow*. Let us
discriminate, and be shy of absolute proscription. I am omniverbivorous by
nature and training. Passing by such words as are poisonous, I can swallow
most others, and chew such as I cannot swallow.

Dandies are not good for much, but they are good for something. They
invent or keep in circulation those conversational blank checks or counters
just spoken of, which intellectual capitalists may sometimes find it worth
their while to borrow of them. They are useful, too, in keeping up the
standard of dress, which, but for them, would deteriorate, and become, what
some old fools would have it, a matter of convenience, and not of taste and
art. Yes, I like dandies well enough,—on one condition.

—What is that, Sir?—said the divintiy-student.

—That they have pluck. I find that lies at the bottom of all true dandyism. A little boy dressed up very fine, who puts his finger in his mouth and takes to crying, if other boys make fun of him, looks very silly. But if he turns red in the face and knotty in the fists, and makes an example of the biggest of his assailants, throwing off his fine Leghorn[14] and his thickly-buttoned jacket, if necessary, to consummate the act of justice, his small toggery takes on the splendors of the crested helmet that frightened Astyanax.[15] You remember that the Duke said his dandy officers were his best officers. The "Sunday blood," the super-superb sartorial equestrian of our annual Fast-day, is not imposing or dangerous. But such fellows as Brummel and D'Orsay and Bryon[16] are not to be snubbed quite so easily. Look out for "la main de fer sous le gant de velours"[17] (which I printed in English the other day without quotation-marks, thinking whether any *scarabæus criticus* would add this to his globe and roll in glory with it into the newspapers,—which he didn't do it, in the charming pleonasm of the London language, and therefore I claim the sole merit of exposing the same). A good many powerful and dangerous people have had a decided dash of dandyism about them. There was Alcibiades,[18] the "curled son of Clinias" an accomplished young man, but what would be called "swell" in these days. There was Aristoteles, a very distinguished writer, of whom you have heard,—a philosopher, in short, whom it took centuries to learn, centuries to unlearn, and is now going to take a generation or more to learn over again. Regular dandy he was. So was Marcus Antonius; and though he lost his game, he played for big stakes, and it wasn't his dandyism that spoiled his chance. Petrarch was not to be despised as scholar or a poet, but he was one of the same sort. So was Sir Humphrey Davy; so was Lord Palmerston, formerly, if I am not forgetful.[19] Yes,—a dandy is good for someting as such; and dandies such as I was just speaking of have rocked this planet like a cradle,—aye, and left it swinging to this day.—Still, if I were you, I wouldn't go to the tailor's, on the strength of these remarks, and run up a long bill which will render pockets a superfluity in your next suit. *"Elegans nascitur, non fit."* A man is born a dandy, as he is born a poet. There are heads that can't wear hats; there are necks that can't fit cravats; there are jaws that can't fill out collars—(Willis touched this last

[14] A hat.

[15] Astyanax was the young son of Hector and Andromache, killed by the conquering Greeks.

[16] Beau Brummel (1778-1840), Count D'Orsay (1801-1852), and Lord Byron (1788-1824) were known as dandies in their time.

[17] The iron hand under the velvet glove.

[18] Alcibiades (450?-404 B. C.), an Athenian general, was a protégé of Socrates.

[19] Marcus Aurelius Antoninus (121-180 A. D.), a Roman emperor and Stoic philosopher; Francesco Petrarch (1304-1374), an Italian humanist poet; Sir Humphry Davy (1778-1829), a British chemist who discovered the 12 chemical elements; Lord Palmerston (1784-1865), prime minister of Great Britain from 1855 to 1858 and 1859 to 1865.

point in one of his earlier ambrotypes, if I remember rightly); there are *tournures* nothing can humanize, and movements nothing can subdue to the gracious suavity or elegant languor or stately serenity which belong to different styles of dandysim.

We are forming an aristocracy, as you may observe, in this country,—not a *gratiâ-Dei*, nor a *jure-divino* one,—but a *de-facto* upper stratum of being, which floats over the turbid waves of common life like the iridescent film you may have seen spreading over the water about our wharves,—very splendid, though its origin may have been tax, tallow, train-oil, or other such unctuous commodities. I say, then, we are forming an aristocracy; and, transitory as its individual life often is, it maintains itself tolerably, as whole. Of course money is its corner-stone. But now observe this. Money kept for two or three generations transforms a race,—I don't mean merely in manners and hereditary culture, but in blood and bone. Money buys air and sunshine, in which children grow up more kindly, of course, than in close, back streets; it buys country places to give them happy and healthy summers, good nursing, good doctoring, and the best cuts of beef and mutton. When the spring-chickens come to market—I beg your pardon,—that is not what was I going to speak of. As the young females of each successive season come on, the finest specimens among them, other things being equal, are apt to attract those who can afford the expensive luxury of beauty. The physical character of the next generation rises in consequence. It is plain that certain families have in this way acquired an elevated type of face and figure, and at its small circle of city-connections we may sometimes find models of both sexes which one of the rural counties would find it hard to match from all its townships put together. Because there is a good deal of running down, of degeneration and waste of life, among the richer classes, you must not overlook the equally obvious fact I have just spoken of,—which in one or two generations more will be, I think, much more patent than just now.

The weak point in our chryso-aristocracy is the same I have alluded to in connnection with cheap dandyism. Its thorough manhood, its high-caste gallantry, are not so manifest as the plate-glass of its windows and the more or less legitimate heraldry of its coach-panels. It is very curious to observe of how small account military folks are held among our Northern people. Our young men must gild their spurs, but they need not win them. The equal division of property keeps the younger sons of rich people above the necessity of military service. Thus the army loses an element of refinement, and the moneyed upper class forgets what it is to count heroism among its virtues. Still I don't believe in any aristocracy without pluck as its backbone. Ours may show it when the time comes if it ever does come.*

---

* The marble tablets and memorial windows in our churches and monumental buildings bear evidence as to whether the young men of favored social position proved worthy of their privileges or not during the four years of trial which left us a nation.

—These United States furnish the greatest market for intellectual *green fruit* of all the places in the world. I think so, at any rate. The demand for intellectual labor is so enormous and the market so far from nice, that young talent is apt to fare like unripe gooseberries,—get plucked to make a fool of. Think of a country which buys eighty thousand copies of the "Proverbial Philosophy" while the author's admiring countrymen have been buying twelve thousand! How can one let his fruit hang in the sun until it gets fully ripe, while there are eighty thousand such hungry mouths ready to swallow it and proclaim its praise? Consequently, there never was such a collection of crude pippins and half-grown windfalls as our native literature displays among its fruits. There are literary green-groceries at every corner, which will buy anything, from a button-pear to a pine-apple. It takes a long apprenticeship to train a whole people to reading and writing. The temptation of money and fame is too great for young people. Do I not remember that glorious moment when the Late Mr.——we won't say who,—editor of the——we won't say what, offered me the sum of fifty cents *per* double-columned quarto page for shaking my young boughs over his foolscap apron? Was it not an intoxicating vision of gold and glory? I should doubtless have revelled in its wealth and splendor, but for learning that the *fifty cents* was to be considered a rhetorical embellishment, and by no means a literal expression of past fact or present intention.

—Beware of making your moral staple consist of the negative virtues. It is good to abstain, and teach others to abstain, from all that is sinful or hurtful. But making a business of it leads to emaciation of character, unless one feeds largely also on the more nutritious diet of active sympathetic benevolence.

—I don't believe one word of what you are saying,—spoke up the angular female in black bombazine.

I am sorry you disbelieve it, Madam,—I said, and added softly to my next neighbor,—but you prove it.

The young fellow sitting near me winked; and the divinity-student said, in an undertone,—*Optime dictum.*

Your talking Latin,—said I,—reminds me of an odd trick of one of my old tutors. He read so much of that language, that his English half turned into it.

He got caught in town, one hot summer, in pretty close quarters, and wrote, or began to write, a series of city pastorals. Eclogues he called them, and meant to have published them by subscription. I remember some of his verses, if you want to hear them.—You, Sir (addressing myself to the divinity-student), and all such as have been through college, or what is the same thing, received an honorary degree, will understand them without a dictionary. The old man had a great deal to say about "æstivation,"[20] as he called it, in opposition, as one might say, to *hibernation.* Intramural æstivation, or

[20] The act of spending or passing the summer.

town-like in summer, he would say, is a peculiar form of suspended existence, or semiasphyxia. One wakes up from it about the beginning of the last
week in September. This is what I remember of his poem:—

ÆSTIVATION.

An Unpublished Poem, by my late Latin Tutor.

In candent ire the solar splendor flames;
The foles, languescent, pend from arid rames;
His humid front the cive, anheling, wipes,
And dreams of erring on ventiferous ripes.

How dulce to vive occult to mortal eyes,
Dorm on the herb with none to supervise,
Carp the suave berries from the crescent vine,
And bibe the flow from longicaudate kine!

To me, alas! no verdurous visions come,
Save you exiguous pool's conferva-scum,—
No concave vast repeats the tender hue
That laves my milk-jug with celestial blue!

Me wretched! Let me curr to quercine shades!
Effund your albid hausts, lactiferous maids!
Oh, might I vole to some umbrageous clump,—
Depart,—be off,—excede,—evade,—erump!

—I have lived by the sea-shore and by the mountains.—No, I am not
going to say which is best. The one where your place is is the best for you.
But this difference there is: you can domesticate mountains, but the sea is
feræ naturæ. You may have a hut, or know the owner of one, on the moun-
tain-side; you see a light half-way up its ascent in the evening, and you know
there is a home, and you might share it. You have noted certain trees, perhaps; you know the particular zone where the hemlocks look so black in
October, when the maples and beeches have faded. All its reliefs and inta-
glios have electrotyped themselves in the medallions that hang round the
walls of your memory's chamber.—The sea remembers nothing. It is feline.
It licks your feet,—its huge flanks purr very pleasantly for you; but it will
crack your bones and eat you, for all that, and wipe the crimsoned foam
from its jaws as if nothing had happened. The mountains give their lost
children berries and water; the sea mocks their thirst and lets them die. The
mountains have a grand, stupid, lovable tranquillity; the sea has a fascinating,
treacherous intelligence. The mountains lie about like huge ruminants, their
broad backs awful to look upon, but safe to handle. The sea smooths its
silver scales until you cannot see their joints,—but her shining is that of a

snake's belly, after all.—In deeper suggestiveness I find as great a difference. The mountains dwarf mankind and foreshorten the procession of its long generations. The sea drowns out humanity and time; it has no sympathy with either; for it belongs to eternity, and of that it sings its monotonous song forever and ever.

Yet I should love to have a little box by the sea-shore. I should love to gaze out on the wild feline element from a front window of my own, just as I should love to look on a caged panther, and see it stretch its shining length, and then curl over and lap its smooth sides, and by-and-by begin to lash itself into rage and show its white teeth and spring at its bars, and howl the cry of its mad, but, to me, harmless fury.—And then,—to look at it with that inward eye,—who does not love to shuffle off time and its concerns, at intervals,—to forget who is President and who is Governor, what race he belongs to, what language he speaks, which golden-headed nail of the firmament his particular planetary system is hung upon, and listen to the great liquid metronome as it beats its solemn measure, steadily swinging when the solo or duet of human life began, and to swing just as steadily after the human chorus has died out and man is a fossil on its shores?

—What should decide one, in choosing a summer residence?—Constitutions, first of all. How much snow could you melt in an hour, if you were planted in a hogshead of it? Comfort is essential to enjoyment. All sensitive people should remember that persons in easy circumstances suffer much more from cold in summer—that is, the warm half of the year—than in winter, or the other half. You must cut your climate to your constitution, as much as your clothing to your shape. After this, consult your taste and convenience. But if you would be happy in Berkshire, you must carry mountains in your brain; and if you would enjoy Nahant, you must have an ocean in your soul. Nature plays at dominos with you; you must match her piece, or she will never give it up to you.

—The schoolmistress said, in a rather mischievous way, that she was afraid some minds or souls would be a little crowded, if they took in the Rocky Mountains or the Atlantic.

Have you ever read the little book called "The Stars and the Earth?"—said I.—Have you seen the Declaration of Independence photographed in a surface that a fly's foot would cover? The forms or conditions of Time and Space, as Kant[21] will tell you, are nothing in themselves,—only our way of looking at things. You are right, I think, however, in recognizing the idea of Space as being quite as applicable to minds as to the outer world. Every man of reflection is vaguely conscious of an imperfectly-defined circle which is

---

[21] Immanuel Kant (1724–1804), German philosopher.

drawn about his intellect. He has a perfectly clear sense that the fragments of his intellectual circle include the curves of many other minds of which he is cognizant. He often recognizes these as manifestly concentric with his own, but of less radius. On the other hand, when we find a portion of an arc on the outside of our own, we say it *intersects* ours, but are very slow to confess or to see that it *circumscribes* it. Every now and then a man's mind is stretched by a new idea or sensation, and never shrinks back to its former dimensions. After looking at the Alps, I felt that my mind had been stretched beyond the limits of elasticity, and fitted so loosely on my old ideas of space that I had to spread these to fit it.

—If I thought I should ever see the Alps!—said the schoolmistress.

Perhaps you will, some time or other,—I said.

It is not very likely,—she answered.—I have had one or two opportunities, but I had rather be anything than governess in a rich family.

[Proud, too, you little soft-voiced woman! Well, I can't say I like you any the worse for it. How long will school-keeping take to kill you? Is it possible the poor thing works with her needle, too? I don't like those marks on the side of her forefinger.

Tableau. Chamouni.[22] Mont Blanc in full view. Figures in the foreground; two of them standing apart; one of them a gentleman of—oh,—ah,—yes! the other a lady in white cashmere, leaning on his shoulder.—The ingenuous reader will understand that this was an internal, private, personal, subjective diorama, seen for one insant on the background of my own consciousness, and abolished into black nonentity by the first question which recalled me to actual life, as suddenly as if one of those iron shop-binds (which I always pass at dusk with a shiver, expecting to stumble over some poor but honest shop-boy's head, just taken off by its sudden and unexpected descent, and left outside upon the sidewalk) had come down in front of it "by the run."]

—Should you like to hear what moderate wishes life brings one to at last? I used to be very ambitious,—wasteful, extravagant, and luxurious in all my fancies. Read too much in the "Arabian Nights." Must have the lamp,—couldn't do without the ring. Exercise every morning on the brazen horse. Plump down into castles as full of little milk-white princesses as a nest is of young sparrows. All love me dearly at once.—Charming idea of life, but too high-colored for the reality. I have out-grown all this; my tastes have become exceedingly primitive,—almost, perhaps, ascetic. We carry happiness into our condition, but must not hope to find it there. I think you will be willing to hear some lines which embody the subdued and limited desires of my maturity.

[22] Chamonix is a valley of eastern France, north of Mont Blanc; the site of the resort town of Chamonix-Mont-Blanc.

CONTENTMENT.

"Man wants but little here below."

Little I ask; my wants are few;
   I only wish a hut of stone,
(A *very plain* brown stone will do,)
      That I may call my own;—
And close at hand is such a one,
In yonder street that fronts the sun.

Plain is quite enough for me;
   Three courses are as good as ten;—
If Nature can subsist on three,
      Thank Heaven for three. Amen!
I always thought cold victual nice;—
My *choice* would be vanilla-ice.

I care not much for gold or land;—
   Give me a mortgage here and there,—
Some good bank-stock,—some note of hand
      Or trifling railroad share;—
I only ask that Fortune send
A *little* more than I shall spend.

Honors are silly toys, I know,
   And titles are but empty names;—
I would, *perhaps,* be Plenipo,—
      But only near St. James;—
I'm very sure I should not care
To fill our Gubernator's chair.

Jewels are baubles; 't is a sin
   To care for such unfruitful things;—
One good-sized diamond in a pin,—
      Some, *not so large,* in rings,—
A ruby and a pearl, or so,
Will do for me;—I laugh at show.
My dame should dress in cheap attire;
   (Good, heavy silks are never dear;)—
I own perhaps I *might* desire
      Some shawls of true cashmere,—
Some marrowy crapes of China silk,
Like wrinkled skins on scalded milk.

I would not have the horse I drive
   So fast that folks must stop and stare:
An easy gait—two, forty-five—
     Suits me; I do not care;—
Perhaps, for just a *single spurt*,
Some seconds less would do no hurt.

Of pictures, I should like to own
   Titians and Raphaels three or four.—
I love so much their style and tone,—
     One Turner, and no more,—
(A landscape,—foreground golden dirt,—
The sunshine painted with a squirt.)—

Of books but few,—some fifty score
   For daily use, and bound for wear;
The rest upon an upper floor;—
     Some *little* luxury *there*
Of red morocco's gilded gleam,
And vellum rich as country cream.

Busts, cameos, gems,—such things as these
   Which others often show for pride,
I value for their power to please,
     And selfish churls deride;—
One Stradivarius, I confess,
Two Meerschaums, I would fain possess.

Wealth's wasteful tricks I will not learn,
   Nor ape the glittering upstart fool;—
Shall not carved tables serve my turn,
     But *all* must be of buhl?[23]
Give grasping pomp its double share,—
I ask but *one* recumbent chair.

Thus humble let me live and die,
   Nor long for Midas' golden touch,
If Heaven more generous gifts deny,
     I shall not miss them *much*,—
Too grateful for the blessing lent
Of simple tastes and mind content!

[23] A style of furniture decoration in which elaborate designs are inlaid with tortoise-shells and ivory.

MY LAST WALK WITH THE SCHOOLMISTRESS.

(A Parenthesis.)

I can't say just how many walks she and I had taken together before this one. I found the effect of going out every morning was decidedly favorable on her health. Two pleasing dimples, the places for which were just marked when she came, played, shadowy, in her freshening cheeks when she smiled and nodded good-morning to me from the schoolhouse-steps.

I am afraid I did the greater part of the talking. At any rate, if I should try to report all that I said during the first half-dozen walks we took together, I fear that I might receive a gentle hint from my friends the publishers, that a separate volume, at my own risk and expense, would be the proper method of bringing them before the public.

—I would have a woman as true as Death. At the first real lie which works from the heart outward, she should be tenderly chloroformed into a better world, where she can have an angel for a governess, and feed on strange fruits which will make her all over again, even to her bones and marrow.—Whether gifted with the accident of beauty or not, she should have been moulded in the rose-red clay of Love, before the breath of life made a moving mortal of her. Love-capacity is a congenital endowment; and I think, after a while, one gets to know the warm-hued natures it belongs to from the pretty pipe-clay counterfeits of them.—Proud she may be, in the sense of respecting herself; but pride, in the sense of contemning others less gifted than herself, deserves the two lowest circles of a vulgar woman's Inferno, where the punishments are Smallpox and Bankruptcy.—She who nips off the end of a brittle courtesy, as one breaks the tip of an icicle, to bestow upon those whom she ought cordially and kindly to recognize, proclaims the fact that she comes not merely of low blood, but of bad blood. Consciousness of unquestioned position makes people gracious in proper measure to all; but if a woman put on airs with her real equals, she has something about herself or her family she is ashamed of, or ought to be. Middle, and more than middle-aged people, who know family histories, generally see through it. An official of standing was rude to me once. Oh, that is the maternal grandfather,—said a wise old friend to me,—he was a boor.— Better too few words, from the woman we love, than too many: while she is silent, Nature is working for her; while she talks, she is working for herself.— Love is sparingly soluble in the words of men; therefore they speak much of it; but one syllable of woman's speech can dissolve more of it than a man's heart can hold.

—Whether I said any or all of these things to the schoolmistress, or not,— whether I stole them out of Lord Bacon,—whether I cribbed them from Balzac,—whether I dipped them from the ocean of Tupperian wisdom,—or whether I have just found them in my head, laid there by that solemn fowl,

Experience (who, according to my observation, cackles oftener than she drops real live eggs), I cannot say. Wise men have said more foolish things,—and foolish men, I don't doubt, have said as wise things. Anyhow, the schoolmistress and I had pleasant walks and long talks, all of which I do not feel bound to report.

—You are a stranger to me, Ma'am.—I don't doubt you would like to know all I said to the schoolmistress.—I sha'n't do it;—I had rather get the publishers to return the money you have invested in these pages. Besides, I have forgotten a good deal of it. I shall tell only what I like of what I remember.

—My idea was, in the first place, to search out the picturesque spots which the city affords a sights of, to those who have eyes. I know a good many, and it was a pleasure to look at them in company with my young friend. There were the shrubs and flowers in the Franklin-Place front-yards or borders: Commerce is just putting his granite foot upon them. Then there are certain small seraglio-gardens, into which one can get a peep through the crevices of high fences,—one in Myrtle Street, or at the back of it,—here and there one at the North and South ends. Then the great elms in Essex Street. Then the stately horse-chestnuts in that vacant lot in Chambers Street, which hold their outspread hands over your head (as I said in my poem the other day), and look as if they were whispering, "May grace, mercy, and peace be with you!"—and the rest of that benediction. May, there are certain patches of ground, which, having lain neglected for a time, Nature, who always has her pockets full of seeds, and holes in all her pockets, has covered with hungry plebeian growths, which fight for life with each other, until some of them get broad-leaved and succulent, and you have a coarse vegetable tapestry which Raphael would not have disdained to spread over the foreground of his masterpiece. The Professor pretends that he found such a one in Charles Street, which, in its dare-devil impudence of rough-and-tumble vegetation, beat the pretty-behaved flower-beds of the Public Garden as ignominiously as a group of young tatterdemalions playing pitch-and-toss beats a row of Sunday-school-boys with their teacher at their head.

But then the Professor has one of his burrows in that region, and puts everything in high colors relating to it. That is his way about everything.—I hold any man cheap,—he said,—of whom nothing stronger can be uttered than that all his geese are swans.—How is that, Professor?—said I;—I should have set you down for one of that sort.—Sir,—said he,—I am proud to say, that Nature has so far enriched me, that I cannot own so much as a *duck* without seeing in it as pretty a swan as ever swam the basin in the garden of the Luxembourg. And the Professor showed the whites of his eyes devoutly, like one returning thanks after a dinner of many courses.

I don't know anything sweeter than this leaking in Nature through all the cracks in the walls and floors of cities. You heap up a million tons of hewn rocks on a square mile or two of earth which was green once. The trees look down from the hill-sides and ask each other, as they stand on tiptoe,—"What are these people about?" And the small herbs at their feet look up and whisper back,—"We will go and see." So the small herbs pack themselves up in the least possible bundles, and wait until the wind steals to them at night and whispers,—"Come with me." Then they go softly with it into the great city,—one to a cleft in the pavement, one to a spout on the roof, one to a seam in the marbles over a rich gentleman's bones and one to the grave without a stone where nothing but a man is buried,—and there they grow, looking down on the generations of men from mouldy roofs, looking up from between the less-trodden pavements, looking out through iron cemetery-railings. Listen to them, when there is only a light breath stirring, and you will hear them saying to each other,—"Wait awhile!" The words run along the telegraph of those narrow green lines that border the roads leading from the city, until they reach the slope of the hills, and the trees repeat in low murmurs to each other,—"Wait awhile!" By-and-by the flow of life in the streets ebbs, and the old leafy inhabitants—the smaller tribes always in front—saunter in, one by one, very careless seemingly, but very tenacious, until they swarm so that the great stones gape from each other with the crowding of their roots, and the feldspar begins to be picked out of the granite to find them food. At last the trees take up their solemn line of march, and never rest until they have encamped in the market-place. Wait long enough and you will find an old doting oak hugging a huge worn block in its yellow underground arms; that was the corner-stone of the State-House. Oh, so patient she is, this imperturbable Nature!

—Let us cry!—

But all this has nothing to do with my walks and talks with the schoolmistress. I did not say that I would not tell you someting about them. Let me alone, and I shall talk to you more than I ought to, probably. We never tell our secrets to people that pump for them.

Books we talked about, and education. It was her duty to know something of these, and of course she did. Perhaps I was somewhat more learned than she, but I found that the difference between her reading and mine was like that of a man's and a woman's dusting a library. The man flaps about with a bunch of feathers; the woman goes to work softly with a cloth. She does not raise half the dust, nor fill her own eyes and mouth it,—but she goes into all the corners and attends to the leaves as much as to the covers.—Books are the *negative* pictures of thought, and the more sensitive the mind that receives their images, the more nicely the finest lines are reproduced. A woman (of the right kind), reading after a man, follows him as Ruth followed the reapers of Boaz, and her gleanings are often the finest of the wheat.

But it was in talking of Life that we came most nearly together. I thought I knew something about that,—that I could speak or write about it somewhat to the purpose.

To take up this fluid earthly being of ours as a sponge sucks up water,—to be steeped and soaked in its realities as a hide fills its pores lying seven years in a tan-pit,—to have winnowed every wave of it as a mill-wheel works up the stream that runs through the flume upon its float-boards,—to have curled up the keenest spasms and flattened out in the laxest languors of this breathing-sickness, which keeps certain parcels of matter uneasy for three or four score years,—to have fought all the devils and clasped all the angels of its delirium,—and then, just at the point when the white-hot passions have cooled down to cherry-red, plunge our experience into the ice-cold stream of some human language or other, one might think would end in a rhapsody with something of spring and temper in it. All this I thought my power and province.

The schoolmistress had tried life, too. Once in a while one meets with a single soul greater than all the living pageant which passes before it. As the pale astronomer sits in his study with sunken eyes and thin fingers, and weighs Uranus or Neptune as in a balance, so there are meek, slight women who have weighed all which this planetary life can offer, and hold it like a bauble in the palm of their slender hands. This was one of them. Fortune had left her, sorrow had baptized her; the routine of labor and the loneliness of almost friendless city-life were before her. Yet, as I looked upon her tranquil face, gradually regaining a cheerfulness which was often sprightly, as she became interested in the various matters we talked about and places we visited, I saw that eye and lip and every shifting lineament were made for love,—unconscious of their sweet office as yet, and meeting the cold aspect of Duty with the natural graces which were meant for the reward of nothing less than the Great Passion.

—I never addressed one word of love to the schoolmistress in the course of these pleasant walks. It seemed to me that we talked of everything but love on that particular morning. There was, perhaps, a little more timidity and hesitancy on my part than I have commonly shown among our people at the boarding-house. In fact, I considered myself the master at the breakfast-table; but, somehow, I could not command myself just then so well as usual. The truth is, I had secured a passage to Liverpool in the steamer which was to leave at noon,—with the condition, however, of being released in case circumstances occurred to detain me. The schoolmistress knew nothing about all this, of course, as yet.

It was on the Common that we were walking. The *mall*, or boulevard of our Common, you know, has various branches leading from it in different directions. One of these runs down from opposite Joy Street southward across the whole length of the Common to Boylston Street. We called it the long path, and were fond of it.

I felt very weak indeed (though of a tolerably robust habit) as we came opposite the head of this path on that morning. I think I tried to speak twice without making myself distinctly audible. At last I got out the question,—

Will you take the long path with me?—Certainly,—said the schoolmistress,—with much pleasure.—Think,—I said,—before you answer: if you take the long path with me now, I shall interpret it that we are to part no more!—The schoolmistress stepped back with a sudden movement, as if an arrow had struck her.

One of the long granite blocks used as seats was hard by,—the one you may still see close by the Gingko-tree.—Pray, sit down,—I said,—No, no, she answered, softly,—I will walk the *long path* with you!

—The old gentleman who sits opposite met us walking, arm in arm, about the middle of the long path, and said, very charmingly,—"Good-morning, my dears!"

JAMES RUSSELL LOWELL

(1819-1891)

James Russell Lowell was born on February 22, 1819, in Cambridge, Massachusetts, a child of parents whose families were of Puritan stock. He prepared to be a lawyer, after his graduation from Harvard in 1838, but by 1841 he had published his first volume of poems, *A Year's Life,* and was launched on a literary career.

Lowell was an active political poet and abolitionist; a professor of modern languages at Harvard; and the first editor of the successful *Atlantic Monthly* in 1857 and *The North American Review* in 1864. He burst into fame early in his career, during the "annus mirabilis" of

The standard edition is *The Writings of James Russell Lowell In Prose and Poetry,* 10 vols., ed. James Russell Lowell, Riverside Edition, 1890. See also *The Complete Writings of James Russell Lowell,* 16 vols. ed. C. E. Norton, Elmwood Edition, 1904. A one-volume edition, *The Complete Poetical Works of James Russell Lowell,* was edited by H. E. Scudder, 1897, and *A Bibliography of James Russell Lowell,* was edited by George W. Cooke, 1906. *The Letters of James Russell Lowell,* 2 vols., were edited by C. E. Norton, 1893.

The authoritative biography is Horace E. Scudder, *James Russell Lowell; A Biography,* 2 vols., 1901.

Studies include E. E. Hale, *James Russell Lowell and His Friends,* 1899; Ferris Greenslet, *James Russell Lowell; His Life and Works,* 1905; J. J. Reilly, *James Russell Lowell as a Critic,* 1915; Richard Criom Beatty, *James Russell Lowell,* 1942; Leon Howard, *A Victorian Knight-Errant, A study of the Early Career of James Russell Lowell,* 1952; Martin Duberman, *James Russell Lowell,* 1966; Claire McGlinchee, *James Russell Lowell,* 1967; Edward Wagenknecht, *James Russell Lowell,* 1971.

The poems are reprinted from *The Writings of James Russell Lowell in Prose and Poetry.*

1848, when he published *The Bigelow Papers,* First Series, a satire on this country's involvement in the Mexican and the Civil wars; *The Fable for Critics,* a perceptive commentary on Lowell's contemporaries, and *The Vision of Sir Launfal.* But he was an active writer all of his life, and his work shows a great breadth of interest—even though it lacks a certain focus. At the end of his career, he also wrote literary criticism, published in *My Study Windows* (1871) and *Among My Books* (1870, 1876).

The Present Crisis[1]

When a deed is done for Freedom, through the broad earth's
 aching breast
Runs a thrill of joy prophetic, trembling on from east to west,
And the slave, where'er he cowers, feels the soul within him climb
To the awful verge of manhood, as the energy sublime
Of a century bursts full-blossomed on the thorny stem of Time.   5

Through the walls of hut and palace shoots the instantaneous
 throe,
When the travail of the Ages wrings earth's systems to and fro;
At the birth of each new Era, with a recognizing start,
Nation wildly looks at nation, standing with mute lips apart,
And glad Truth's yet mightier man-child leaps beneath the Future's
 heart.   10

So the Evil's triumph sendeth, with a terror and a chill,
Under continent to continent, the sense of coming ill,
And the slave, where'er he cowers, feels his sympathies with God
In hot tear-drops ebbing earthward, to be drunk up by the sod,
Till a corpse crawls round unburied, delving in the nobler clod.   15

For mankind are one in spirit, and an instinct bears along,
Round the earth's electric circle, the swift flash of right or wrong;
Whether conscious or unconscious, yet Humanity's vast frame
Through its ocean-sundered fibres feels the gush of joy or shame;—
In the gain or loss of one race all the rest have equal claim.   20

[1] This poem was first published in the Boston *Courier* for December 11, 1844 and later collected in *Poems: Second Series* (1848). It was occasioned by the proposed annexation of Texas, which Lowell felt would lead to an extension of slavery.

Once to every man and nation comes the moment to decide,
In the strife of Truth with Falsehood, for the good or evil side;
Some great cause, God's new Messiah, offering each the bloom or
    blight,
Parts the goats upon the left hand, and the sheep upon the right,[2]
And the choice goes by forever 'twixt that darkness and that light.   25

Hast thou chosen, O my people, on whose party thou shalt stand,
Ere the Doom from its worn sandals shakes the dust against our
    land?[3]
Though the cause of Evil prosper, yet 'tis Truth alone is strong,
And, albeit she wander outcast now, I see around her throng
Troops of beautiful, tall angels, to enshield her from all wrong.   30

Backward look across the ages and the beacon-moments see,
That, like peaks of some sunk continent, jut through Oblivion's sea;
Not an ear in court or market for the low foreboding cry
Of those Crises, God's stern winnowers, from whose feet earth's
    chaff must fly;
Never shows the choice momentous till the judgment hath passed by.   35

Careless seems the great Avenger;[4] history's pages but record
One death-grapple in the darkness 'twixt old systems and the Word;
Truth forever on the scaffold, Wrong forever on the throne,—
Yet that scaffold sways the future, and, behind the dim unknown,
Standeth God within the shadow, keeping watch above his own.   40

We see dimly in the Present what is small and what is great,
Slow of faith how weak an arm may turn the iron helm of fate,
But the soul is still oracular; amid the market's din,
List the ominous stern whisper from the Delphic cave[5] within,—
"They enslave their children's children who make compromise with
    sin."   45

Slavery, the earth-born Cyclops, fellest of the giant brood,
Sons of brutish Force and Darkness, who have drenched the earth
    with blood,
Famished in his self-made desert, blinded by our purer day,
Gropes in yet unblasted regions for his miserable prey;—
Shall we guide his gory fingers where our helpless children play?   50

[2] Cf. Matthew xxv: 31–33.   [4] God. Cf. I Thessalonians v:6.
[3] Cf. Luke ix. 5.   [5] A grotto on Mount Parnassus.

Then to side with Truth is noble when we share her wretched crust,
Ere her cause bring fame and profit, and 'tis prosperous to be just;
Then it is the brave man chooses, while the coward stands aside,
Doubting in his abject spirit, till his Lord is crucified,
And the multitude make virtue of the faith they had denied.   55

Count me o'er earth's chosen heroes,—they were souls that stood
    alone,
While the men they agonized for hurled the contumelious stone,
Stood serene, and down the future saw the golden beam incline
To the side of perfect justice, mastered by their faith divine,
By one man's plain truth to manhood and to God's supreme design.   60

By the light of burning heretics Christ's bleeding feet I track,
Toiling up new Calvaries ever with the cross that turns not back,
And these mounts of anguish number how each generation learned
One new word of that grand *Credo* which in prophet-hearts hath
    burned
Since the first man stood God-conquered with his face to heaven
    upturned.   65

For Humanity sweeps onward: where to-day the martyr stands,
On the morrow crouched Judas[6] with the silver in his hands;
Far in front the cross stands ready and the crackling fagots burn,
While the hooting mob of yesterday in silent awe return
To glean up the scattered ashes into History's golden urn.   70

'Tis as easy to be heroes as to sit the idle slaves
Of a legendary virtue carved upon our father's graves,
Worshippers of light ancestral make the present light a crime;—
Was the Mayflower launched by cowards, steered by men behind
    their time?
Turn those tracks toward Past or Future, that make Plymouth Rock
    sublime?   75
They were men of present valor, stalwart old iconoclasts,
Unconvinced by axe or gibbet that all virtue was the Past's;
But we make thier truth our falsehood, thinking that hath made us
    free,
Hoarding it in mouldy parchments, while our tender spirits flee
The rude grasp of that great Impulse which drove them across the
    sea.   80

[6] The one disciple who betrayed Christ for
30 pieces of silver. Cf. xxv:3.

They have rights who dare maintain them; we are traitors to our sires,
Smothering in their holy ashes Freedoms' new-lit altar fires;
Shall we make their creed our jailer? Shall we, in our haste to slay,
From the tombs of the old prophets steal the funeral lamps away
To light up the martyr-fagots round the prophets of to-day? 85
New occasions teach new duties; Time makes ancient good uncouth;
They must upward still, and onward, who would keep abreast of
    Truth;
Lo, before us gleam her camp-fires! we ourselves must Pilgrims be,
Launch our Mayflower, and steer boldly through the desperate winter
    sea,
Nor attempt the Future's portal with the Past's blood-rusted key. 90

1844, 1848

Ode Recited at the Harvard Commemoration[1]

JULY 21, 1865

I

    Weak-winged is song,
Nor aims at that clear-ethered height
Whither the brave deed climbs for light:
    We seem to do them wrong,
Bringing our robin's-leaf to deck their hearse 5
Who in warm life-blood wrote their nobler verse,
Our trivial song to honor those who come
With ears attuned to strenuous trump and drum,
And shaped in squadron-strophes their desire,
Live battle-odes whose lines were steel and fire: 10
    Yet sometimes feathered words are strong,
A gracious memory to buoy up and save
From Lethe's dreamless ooze, the common grave
    Of the unventurous throng.

---

[1] This poem was read to alumni of Harvard College on July 21, 1865, to honor the Harvard students who had fought in the Civil War. It was published in the *Atlantic Monthly* for September 1865.

II

Today our Reverend Mother[2] welcomes back   15
  Her wisest Scholars, those who understood
The deeper teaching of her mystic tome,
  And offered their fresh lives to make it good:
      No lore of Greece or Rome,
No science peddling with the names of things,   20
Or reading stars to find inglorious fates,
      Can lift our life with wings
Far from Death's idle gulf that for the many waits,
      And lengthen out our dates
With that clear fame whose memory sings   25
In many hearts to come, and nerves them and dilates:
Nor such thy teaching, Mother of us all!
      Not such the Trumpet-call
      Of thy diviner mood,
      That could thy sons entice   30
From happy homes and toils, the fruitful nest
Of those half-virtues which the world calls best,
      Into War's tumult rude;
      But rather far that stern device
The sponsors chose that round thy cradle stood   35
    In the dim, unventured wood,
    The VERITAS[3] that lurks beneath
    The letter's unprolific sheath,
  Life of whate'er makes life worth living,
Seed-grain of high emprise, immortal food,   40
  One heavenly thing whereof earth hath the giving.

III

Many loved Truth, and lavished life's best oil
  Amid the dust of books to find her,
Content at last, for guerdon of their toil,
  With the cast mantle she hath left behind her.   45
    Many in sad faith sought for her,
Many with crossed hands sighed for her;
    But these, our brothers, fought for her,
    At life's dear peril wrought for her,
    So loved her that they died for her,   50
    Tasting the raptured fleetness
    Of her divine completeness:
    Their higher instinct knew

Their alma mater, Harvard College.   [3] Truth, on the Harvard College seal.

Those love her best who to themselves are true,
And what they dare to dream of, dare to do;   55
    They followed her and found her
    Where all may hope to find,
Not in the ashes of the burnt-out mind,
But beautiful, with danger's sweetness round her.
    Where faith made whole with deed   60
    Breathes its awakening breath
    Into the lifeless creed,
    They saw her plumed and mailed,
    With sweet, stern face unveiled,
And all-repaying eyes, look proud on them in death.   65

IV

Our slender life runs rippling by, and glides
    Into the silent hollow of the past;
      What is there that abides
    To make the next age better for the last?
      Is earth too poor to give us   70
    Something to live for here that shall outlive us?
      Some more substantial boon
Than such as flows and ebbs with Fortune's fickle moon?
      The little that we see
      From doubt is never free;   75
      The little that we do
      Is but half-nobly true;
      With our laborious hiving
What men call treasure, and the gods call dross,
    Life seems a jest of Fate's contriving,   80
    Only secure in every one's conniving,
A long account of nothings paid with loss,
Where we poor puppets, jerked by unseen wires,
    After our little hour of strut and rave,
With all our pasteboard passions and desires,   85
Loves, hates, ambitions, and immortal fires,
    Are tossed pell-mell together in the grave.
    But stay! no age was e'er degenerate,
    Unless men held it at too cheap a rate,
    For in our likeness still we shape our fate.   90
      Ah, there is something here
    Unfathomed by the cynic's sneer,
    Something that gives our feeble light
    A high immunity from the Night,
    Something that leaps life's narrow bars   95

To claim its birthright with the hosts of heaven;
  A seed of sunshine that can leaven
  Our earthly dullness with the beams of stars,
     And glorify our clay
  With light from fountains elder than the Day;   100
    A conscience more divine than we,
    A gladness fed with secret tears,
    A vexing, forward-reaching sense
    Of some more noble permanence;
      A light across the sea,   105
  Which haunts the soul and will not let it be,
Still beaconing from the heights of undegenerate years.

V

    Whither leads the path
    To ampler fates that leads?
    Not down through flowery meads,   110
    To reap an aftermath
  Of youth's vainglorious weeds,
  But up the steep, amid the wrath
And shock of deadly-hostile creeds,
  Where the world's best hope and stay   115
By battle's flashes gropes a desperate way,
And every turf the fierce foot clings to bleeds.
  Peace hath her not ignoble wreath,
  Ere yet the sharp, decisive word
Light the black lips of cannon, and the sword   120
    Dreams in its easeful sheath;
But some day the live coal behind the thought,
    Whether from Baäl's stone obscene,
    Or from the shrine serene
    Of God's pure altar brought,   125
Bursts up in flame; the war of tongue and pen
Learns with what deadly purpose it was fraught,
And, helpless in the fiery passion caught,
Shakes all the pillared state with shock of men:
Some day the soft Ideal that we wooed   130
Confronts us fiercely, foe-beset, pursued,
And cries reproachful: "Was it, then, my praise,
And not myself was loved? Prove now thy truth;
I claim of thee the promise of thy youth;
Give me thy life, or cower in empty phrase,   135
The victim of thy genius, not its mate!"

Life may be given in many ways,
And loyalty to Truth be sealed
As bravely in the closet as the field,
    So bountiful is Fate;   140
    But then to stand beside her,
    When craven churls deride her,
To front a lie in arms and not to yield,
    This shows, methinks, God's plan
    And measure of a stalwart man,   145
    Limbed liked the old heroic breeds,
    Who stand self-poised on manhood's solid earth,
  Not forced to frame excuses for his birth,
Fed from within with all the strength he needs.

VI

Such was he, our Martyr-Chief,   150
    Whom late the Nation he had led,
    With ashes on her head,
Wept with the passion of an angry grief:
Forgive me, if from present things I turn
To speak what in my heart will beat and burn,   155
    Nature, they say, doth dote,
    And cannot make a man
    Save on some worn-out plan,
    Repeating us by rote: 160
For him her Old-World moulds aside she threw,
    And choosing sweet clay from the breast
    Of the unexhausted West,
With stuff untainted shaped a hero new,
Wise, steadfast, in the strength of God, and true,   165
    How beautiful to see
Once more a shepherd of mankind indeed,
Who loved his charge, but never loved to lead;
One whose meek flock the people joyed to be,
    Not lured by any cheat of birth,   170
    But by his clear-grained human worth,
And brave old wisdom of sincerity!
    They knew that outward grace is dust;
    They could not choose but trust
In that sure-footed mind's unfaltering skill,   175
    And supple-tempered will
That bent like perfect steel to spring again and thrust.
    His was no lonely mountain-peak of mind,
    Thrusting to thin air o'er our cloudy bars,
    A sea-mark now, now lost in vapors blind;   180

Broad prairie rather, genial, level-lined,
Fruitful and friendly for all human kind,
Yet also nigh to heaven and loved to loftiest stars.
 Nothing of Europe here,
Or, then, of Europe fronting mornward still, 185
 Ere any names of Serf and Peer
 Could Nature's equal scheme deface
 And thwart her genial will;
 Here was a type of the true elder race,
And one of Plutarch's men[4] talked with us face to face. 190
 I praise him not; it were too late;
And some innative weakness there must be
In him who condescends to victory
Such as the Present gives, and cannot wait,
 Safe in himself as in a fate. 195
 So always firmly he:
 He knew to bide his time,
 And can his fame abide,
Still patient in his simple faith sublime,
 Till the wise years decided. 200
 Great captain, with their guns and drums,
 Disturb our judgment for the hour,
 But at last silence comes;
 These all are gone, and, standing like a tower,
Our children shall behold his fame. 205
 The kindly-earnest, brave, foreseeing man,
Sagacious, patient, dreading praise, not blame,
 New birth of our new soil, the first American.

VII
Long as man's hope insatiate can discern
 Or only guess some more inspiring goal 210
 Outside of Self, enduring as the pole,
Along whose course the flying axles burn
Of spirits bravely-pitched, earth's manlier brood;
 Long as below we cannot find
The meed that stills the inexorable mind; 215
So long this faith to some ideal Good,
Under whatever mortal names it masks,
Freedom, Law, Country, this ethereal mood
That thanks the Fates for their severer tasks,
 Feeling its challenged pulses leap, 220
 While others skulk in subterfuges cheap,

[4] Lincoln is compared to a hero in Plutarch's
Parallel Lives.

And, set in Danger's van, has all the boon it asks,
Shall win man's praise and women's love,
 Shall be a wisdom that we set above
All other skills and gifts to culture dear,   225
 A virtue round whose forehead we inwreathe
 Laurels that with a living passion breathe
When other crowns grow, while we twine them, sear.
 What brings us thronging these high rites to pay,
And seal these hours the noblest of our year,   230
 Save that our brothers found this better way?

VIII

We sit here in the Promised Land
That flows with Freedom's honey and milk;[5]
 But 'twas they won it. sword in hand,
Making the nettle danger soft for us as silk.   235
 We welcome back our bravest and our best;—
 Ah me! not all! some come not with the rest,
Who went forth brave and bright as any here!
I strive to mix some gladness with my strain,
   But the sad strings complain,   240
   And will not please the ear:
I sweep them for a pæan, but they wane
   Again and yet again
Into a dirge, and die way, in pain.
In these brave ranks I only see the gaps,   245
Thinking of dear ones whom the dumb turf wraps,
Dark to the triumph which they died to gain:
  Fitlier may others greet the living,
  For me the past is unforgiving;
   I with uncovered head   250
   Salute the sacred dead,
Who went, and who return not.—Say not so!
'Tis not the grapes of Canaan[6] that repay,
But the high faith that failed not by the way;
Virtue treads paths that end not in the grave;   255
No ban of endless night exiles the brave;
   And to the saner mind
We rather seem the dead that stayed behind.
Blow, trumpets, all your exultations blow!
For never shall their aureoled presence lack: 260
I see them muster in a gleaming row,
With every youthful brows that nobler show;

---

[5] Cf. Exodus iii: 8.   [6] Cf. Numbers xiii: 23–27.

We find in our dull road their shining track;
      In every nobler mood
We feel the orient of their spirit glow,   265
Part of our life's unalterable good,
Of all our saintlier aspiration;
      They come transfigured back,
Secure from change in their high-hearted ways,
Beautiful evermore, and with the rays   270
Of morn on their white Shields of Expectation!

IX

      But is there hope to save
  Even this ethereal essence from the grave?
What ever 'scaped Oblivion's subtle wrong
Save a few clarion names, or golden threads of song?   275
      Before my musing eye
    The mighty ones of old sweep by,
Disvoicèd now and insubstantial things,
As noisy once as we; poor ghosts of kings,
Shadows of empire wholly gone to dust,   280
And many races, nameless long ago,
To darkness driven by that imperious gust
Of ever-rushing Time that here doth blow:
O visionary world, condition strange,
  Where naught abiding is but only Change,   285
Where the deep-bolted stars themselves still shift and range!
  Shall we to more continuance make pretence?
Renown builds tombs: a life-estate is Wit;
      And, bit by bit,
The cunning years steal all from us but woe;   290
  Leaves are we, whose decays no harvest sow.
      But, when we vanish hence,
Shall they lie forceless in the dark below,
Save to make green their little length of sods,
Or deepen pansies for a year or two,   295
Who now to us are shining-sweet as gods?
Was dying all they had the skill to do?
That were not fruitless: but the Soul resents
Such short-lived service, as if blind events
Ruled without her, or earth could so endure;   300
She claims a more divine investiture
Of longer tenure than Fame's airy rents;
What'er she touches doth her nature share;
Her inspiration haunts the ennobled air,
      Gives eyes to mountains, blind,   305

Ears to the deaf earth, voices to the wind,
And her clear trump sings succor everywhere
By lonely bivouacs to the wakeful mind:
For soul inherits all that soul could dare:
   Yea, Manhood hath a wider span   310
And larger privilege of life than man.
The single deed, the private sacrifice,
So radiant now through proudly-hidden tears,
Is covered up erelong from mortal eyes
With thoughtless drift of the deciduous years;   315
But that high privilege that makes all men peers,
That leap of heart whereby a people rise
   Up to a noble anger's height,
And, flamed on by the Fates, not shrink, but grow more
  bright,
  That swift validity in noble veins,
   Of choosing danger and disdaining shame,
    Of being set on flame
  By the pure fire that flies all contact base
But wraps its chosen with angelic might,
   These are imperishable gains,   325
  Sure as the sun, medicinal as light,
  These hold great futures in their lusty reins
And certify to earth a new imperial race.

X

   Who now shall sneer?
  Who dare again to say we trace   330
  Our lines to a plebeian race?
   Roundhead and Cavalier![7]
Dumb are those names erewhile in battle loud;
Dream-footed as the shadow of a cloud,
   They flit across the ear: 335
That is best blood that hath most iron in't,
To edge resolve with, pouring without stint
   For what makes manhood dear.
   Tell us not of Plantagenets,
Hapsburgs, and Guelfs,[8] whose thin bloods crawl   340
Down from some victor in a border-brawl!
   How poor their outworn coronets,

[7] Roundheads were the Puritan supporters of Cromwell in the English Civil War and settled in Massachusetts; Cavaliers followed Charles I and settled in Virginia.

[8] The Plantagenets ruled England from 1154 to 1399; the Hapsburgs ruled the Holy Roman Empire from the fifteenth to the eighteenth centuries; the Guelphs dominated Italy in the thirteenth and fourteenth centuries.

Matched with one leaf of that plain civic wreath
Our brave for honor's blazon shall bequeath,
   Through whose desert a rescued Nation sets   345
Her heel on treason, and the trumpet hears
Shout victory, tingling Europe's sullen ears
   With vain resentments and more vain regrets!

XI

   Not in anger, not in pride,
   Pure from passion's mixture rude   350
   Ever to base earth allied,
   But with far-heard gratitude.
   Still with heart and voice renewed,
To heroes living and dear martyrs dead,
The strain should close that consecrates our brave.   355
   Lift the heart and lift the head!
      Lofty be its mood and grave,
      Not without a martial ring,
      Not without a prouder tread
      And a peal of exultation: 360
      Little right has he to sing
      Through whose heart in such an hour
      Beats no march of conscious power,
      Sweeps no tumult of elation!
      'Tis no Man we celebrate,   365
      By his country's victories great,
A hero half, and half the whim of Fate,
      But the pith and marrow of a Nation
      Drawing force from all her men,
      Highest, humblest, weakest, all,   370
      For her time of need, and then
      Pulsing it again through them,
   Till the basest can no longer cower,
   Feeling his soul spring up divinely tall,
   Touched but in passing by her mantle-hem.   375
   Come back, then, noble pride, for 'tis her dower!
      How could poet ever tower,
      If his passions, hopes, and fears,
      If his triumphs and his tears;
      Kept not measure with his people?   380
Boom, cannon, boom to all the winds and waves!
Clash out, glad bells, from every rocking steeple!
Banners, advance with triumph, bend your staves!
      And from every mountain-peak
      Let beacon-fire to answering beacon speak,   385

Katahdin tell Monadnock, Whiteface[9] he,
And so leap on in light from sea to sea,
    Till the glad news be sent
    Across a kindling continent,
Making earth feel more firm and air breathe braver: 390
"Be proud! for she is saved, and all have helped to save her!
  She that lifts up the manhood of the poor,
  She of the open soul and open door,
  With room about her hearth for all mankind!
  The fire is dreadful in her eyes no more;   395
  From her bold front the helm she doth unbind,
  Sends all her handmaid armies back to spin,
  And bids her navies, that so lately hurled
  Their crashing battle, hold their thunders in,
  Swimming like birds of calm along the unharmful shore.   400
  No challenge sends she to the elder world,
  That looked askance and hated; a light scorn
  Plays o'er her mouth, as round her mighty knees
  She calls her children back, and waits the morn
Of nobler day, enthroned between her subject seas."   405

XII

Bow down, dear Land, for thou hast found release!
  Thy God, in these distempered days,
  Hath taught thee the sure wisdom of His ways,
And through thine enemies hath wrought thy peace!
  Bow down in prayer and praise!   410
No poorest in thy borders but may now
Lift to the juster skies a man's enfranchised brow.
O Beautiful! my Country! ours once more!
Smoothing thy gold of war-dishevelled hair
O'er such sweet brows as never other wore,   415
    And letting thy set lips,
      Freed from wrath's pale eclipse,
The rosy edges of their smile lay bare,
What words divine of lover or of poet
Could tell our love and make thee know it,   420
Among the Nations bright beyond compare?
  What were our lives without thee?
  What all our lives to save thee?
  We reck not what we gave thee;
  We will not dare to doubt thee,   425
But ask whatever else, and we will dare!

1865   1865

[9] Mountain ranges in Maine, New Hampshire, and New York.

From A Fable for Critics[1]

READER! *walk up at once (it will soon be too late) and buy at a perfectly ruinous rate*

A

FABLE FOR CRITICS;

OR, BETTER,

(I like, as a thing that the reader's first fancy may strike, an old-fashioned title-page, such as presents a tabular view of the volume's contents,)

A GLANCE

AT A FEW OF OUR LITERARY PROGENIES

(Mrs. Malaprop's word)[2]

FROM

THE TUB OF DIOGENES;[3]

A VOCAL AND MUSICAL MEDLEY,

THAT IS,

A SERIES OF JOKES

BY A WONDERFUL QUIZ

who accompanies himself with a rub-a-dub-dub, full of spirit and grace, on the top of the tub.

Set forth in October, the 21st day, In the year '48, G. P. Putnam, Broadway.

It being the commonest mode of procedure, I premise a few candid remarks.

TO THE READER:—

This trifle, begun to please only myself and my own private fancy, was laid on the shelf. But some friends, who had seen it, induced me, by dint of

[1] This poem is perhaps the most discriminating account of the major American writers of mid-nineteenth century written by a contemporary. Lowell was a well-read man who knew the literary worlds of New York and Philadelphia, and he had a satirical, critical eye that could make the New England writers more human than they appear in other works of the time. *A Fable for Critics* probably owes something to Alexander Pope's *Dunciad,* Leigh Hunt's *Feast of the Poets,* and Byron's *English and Scotch Reviewers.* The speaker appears to be a critic who is giving an account of American authors to Phoebus Apollo, Greek god of poetry. Lowell draws his list of writers from two early anthologies, edited by Rufus W. Griswold, *The Poets and Poetry of America* (1842) and *The Prose Writers of America* (1847). Gris-wold is called "Tityrus," which means shepherd.

In the second edition of the poem, Lowell wrote the following prefatory note: "the *jeu d'esprit* was extemporized, I may fairly say, so rapidly was it written, purely for my own amusement and with no thought of publication. I sent daily installments of it to a friend in New York, the late Charles F. Briggs. He urged me to let it be printed, and I at last consented to its anonymous publication. The secret was kept till after several persons had laid claim to its authorship."

[2] Mrs. Malaprop is a character in Sheridan's *The Rivals* (1775) who constantly misused words.

[3] Diogenes (412?-323 B.C.), A Greek philosopher who allegedly lived in a tub and searched for an honest man in the world.

saying they liked it, to put it in print. That is, having come to that very conclusion, I asked their advice when 't would make no confusion. For (though in the gentlest of ways) they had hinted it was scarce worth the while, I should doubtless have printed it.

I began it, intending a Fable, a frail, slender thing, rhyme-winged, with a sting in its tail. But, by addings and alterings not previously planned, digressions chance-hatched, like birds' eggs in the sand, and dawdlings to suit every whimsey's demand (always freeing the bird which I held in my hand, for the two perched, perhaps out of reach, in the tree),—it grew by degrees to the size which you see. I was like the old woman that carried the calf, and my neighbors, like hers, no doubt, wonder and laugh; and when, my strained arms with their grown burthen full, I call it my Fable, they call it a bull.

Having scrawled at full gallop (as far as that goes) in a style that is neither good verse nor bad prose, and being a person whom nobody knows, some people will say I am rather more free with my readers than it is becoming to be, that I seem to expect them to wait on my leisure in following wherever I wander at pleasure, that, in short, I take more than a young author's lawful ease, and laugh in a queer way so like Mephistopheles,[4] that the public will doubt, as they grope through my rhythm, if in truth I am making fun *of* them or *with* them.

So the excellent Public is hereby assured that the sale of my book is already secured. For there is not a poet throughout the whole land but will purchase a copy or two out of hand, in the fond expectation of being amused in it, by seeing his betters cut up and abused in it. Now, I find, by a pretty exact calculation, there are something like ten thousand bards in the nation, of that special variety whom the Review and Magazine critics call *lofty* and *true*, and about thirty thousand (*this* tribe is increasing) of the kinds who are termed *full of promise* and *pleasing*. The Public will see by a glance at this schedule, that they cannot expect me to be over-sedulous about courting *them*, since it seems I have got enough fuel made sure of for boiling my pot.

As for such of our poets as find not their names mentioned once in my pages, with praises or blames, let them SEND IN THEIR CARDS, without further DELAY, to my friend G. P. PUTNAM, Esquire, in Broadway, where a LIST will be kept with the strictest regard to the day and the hour of receiving the card. Then, taking them up as I chance to have time (that is, if the names can be twisted in rhyme), I will honestly give each his PROPER POSITION, at the rate of ONE AUTHOR to each NEW EDITION. Thus a PREMIUM is offered sufficiently HIGH as the magazines say when they tell their best lie) to induce bards to CLUB their resources and buy the balance of every edition, until they have all of them fairly been run through the mill.

One word to such readers (judicious and wise) as read books with something behind the mere eyes, of whom in the country, perhaps, there are two,

---

[4] The villain of Goethe's *Faust*, the Devil's Messenger.

including myself, gentle reader, and you. All the characters sketched in this slight *jeu d'esprit*, though, it may be, they seem here and there, rather free, and drawn from a somewhat too cynical stand-point, are *meant* to be faithful, and that is the grand point, and none but an owl would feel sore at a rub from a jester who tells you, without any subterfuge, that he sits in Diogenes' tub.

o o o

"There comes Emerson first, whose rich words, every one,
Are like gold nails[5] in temples to hang trophies on,
Whose prose is grand verse, while his verse, the Lord knows,
Is some of it pr—No, 'tis not even prose;
I'm speaking of metres; some poems have welled   5
From those rare depths of soul that have ne'er been excelled;
They're not epics, but that doesn't matter a pin,
In creating, the only hard thing's to begin;
A grass-blade's no easier to make than an oak;
If you've once found the way, you've achieved the grand stroke;   10
In the worst of his poems are mines of rich matter,
But thrown in a heap with a crash and a clatter;
Now it is not one thing nor another alone
Makes a poem, but rather the general tone,
The something pervading, uniting the whole,   15
The before unconceived, unconceivable soul,
So that just in removing this trifle or that, you
Take away, as it were, a chief limb of the statue;
Roots, wood, bark, and leaves singly perfect may be,
But, clapt hodge-podge together, they don't make a tree.   20

"But, to come back to Emerson (whom, by the way,
I believe we left waiting),—his is, we may say,
A Greek head on right Yankee shoulders, whose range
Has Olympus for one pole, for t'other the Exchange;
He seems, to my thinking (although I'm afraid)   25
The comparison must, long ere this, have been made),
A Plotinus-Montaigne,[6] where the Egyptian's gold mist
And the Gascon's shrewd wit cheek-by-jowl coexist;
All admire, and yet scarcely six converts he's got
To I don't (nor they either) exactly know what;   30

[5] Cf. Ecclesiastes xii:11.

[6] Plotinus (205-270) was a Roman philosopher whose thought is a revision of Platonic idealism; Michel Eyquem de Montaigne (1533-1592) was a French skeptic whose character is recorded in Emerson's *Representative Men*. The Plotinus-Montaigne image refers to the mixture of idealism and Yankee skepticism in Emerson.

For though he builds glorious temples, 'tis odd
He leaves never a doorway to get in a god.
'Tis refreshing to old-fashioned people like me
To meet such a primitive Pagan as he,
In whose mind all creation is duly respected   35
As parts of himself—just a little projected;
And who's willing to worship the stars and the sun,
A convert to—nothing but Emerson.
So perfect a balance there is in his head,
That he talks of things sometimes as if they were dead;   40
Life, nature, love, God, and affairs of that sort,
He looks at as merely ideas; in short,
As if they were fossils stuck round in a cabinet,
Of such vast extent that our earth's a mere dab in it;
Composed just as he is inclined to conjecture her,   45
Namely, one part pure earth, ninety-nine parts pure lecturer;
You are filled with delight at his clear demonstration,
Each figure, word, gesture, just fits the occasion,
With the quiet precision of science he'll sort 'em,
But you can't help suspecting the whole a *post mortem*.   50

        "There are persons, mole-blind to the soul's make and style,
Who insist on a likeness 'twixt him and Carlyle;[7]
To compare him with Plato[8] would be vastly fairer,
Carlyle's the more burly, but E. is the rarer;
He sees fewer objects, but clearlier, truelier,   55
If C.'s as original, E.'s more peculiar;
That he's more of a man you might say of the one,
Of the other he's more of an Emerson;
C.'s the Titan, as shaggy of mind as of limb,—
E. the clear-eyed Olympian, rapid and slim;   60
The one's two thirds Norseman, the other half Greek,
Where the one's most abounding, the other's to seek;
C.'s generals require to be seen in the mass,—
E.'s specialties gain if enlarged by the glass;
C. gives nature and God his own fits of the blues,   65
And rims common-sense things with mystical hues,—
E. sits in a mystery calm and intense,
And looks coolly around him with sharp common-sense;

---

[7] Thomas Carlyle (1795-1881) was an English essayist who had a great influence on Emerson.

[8] Plato (427-347 B.C.) was a Greek philosopher.

C. shows you how every-day matters unite
With the dim transdiurnal recesses of night,— 70
While E., in a plain, preternatural way,
Makes mysteries matters of mere every day;
C. draws all his characters quite *à la* Fuseli,[9]—
Not sketching their bundles of muscles and thews illy,
He paints with a brush so untamed and profuse 75
They seem nothing but bundles of muscles and thews;
E. is rather like Flaxman, lines strait and severe,
And a colorless outline, but full, round, and clear;—
To the men he thinks worthy he frankly accords
The design of a white marble statue in words. 80
C. labors to get at the centre, and then
Takes a reckoning from there of his actions and men;
E. calmly assumes, the said centre as granted,
And, given himself, has whatever is wanted.

"He has imitators in scores, who omit 85
No part of the man but his wisdom and wit,—
Who go carefully o'er the sky-blue of his brain,
And when he has skimmed it once, skim it again;
If at all they resemble him, you may be sure it is
Because their shoals mirror his mists and obscurities, 90
As a mud-puddle seems deep as heaven for a minute,
While a cloud that floats o'er is reflected within it.

                      °   °   °

"There is Bryant, as quiet, as cool, and as dignified,
As a smooth, silent iceberg, that never is ignified,
Save when by reflection 'tis kindled o' nights 95
With a semblance of flame by the chill Northern Lights.
He may rank (Griswold[10] says so) first bard of your nation
(There's no doubt that he stands in supreme iceolation),
Your topmost Parnassus[11] he may set his heel on,
But no warm applauses come, peal following peal on,— 100
He's too smooth and too polished to hang any zeal on:
Unqualified merits, I'll grant, if you choose, he has 'em,
But he lacks the one merit of kindling enthusiasm;
If he stir you at all, it is just, on my soul,
Like being stirred up with the very North Pole. 105

[9] Johann Henrich Fuseli (1742-1825) was a Swiss engraver who illustrated Milton's *Paradise Lost* in great physical detail.

[10] Rufus Wilmot Griswold (1815-1857), editor and critic. See headnote.

[11] Parnassus was a mountain in Greece that was sacred to Apollo and the Muses.

"He is very nice reading in summer, but *inter*
Nos[12] we don't want *extra* freezing in winter;
Take him up in the depth of July, my advice is,
When you feel an Egyptian devotion to ices[13]
But, deduct all you can, there's enough that's right good in him.   110
He has a true soul for field, river, and wood in him;
And his heart, in the midst of brick walls, or where'er it is,
Glows, softens, and thrills with the tenderest charities—
To you mortals that delve in this trade-ridden planet?
No, to old Berkshire's hills, with their limestone and granite.   115
If you're one who *in loco* (add *foco* here) *desipis*,[14]
You will get of his outermost heart (as I guess) a piece;
But you'd get deeper down if you came as a precipice,
And would break the last seal of its inwardest fountain,
If you only could palm yourself off for a mountain.   120
Mr. Quivis,[15] or somebody quite as discerning.
Some scholar who's hourly expecting his learning.
Calls B. the American Wordsworth; but Wordsworth
May be rated at more than your whole tuneful herd's worth.
No, don't be absurd, he's an excellent Bryant;   125
But, my friends, you'll endanger the life of your client,
By attempting to stretch him up into a giant:
If you choose to compare him, I think there are two per-
sons fit for a parallel—Thomson and Cowper,[16]
I don't mean exactly,—there's something of each,   130
There's T.'s love of nature, C.'s penchant to preach;
Just mix up their minds so that C.'s spice of craziness
Shall balance and neutralize T.'s turn for laziness,
And it gives you a brain cook, quite frictionless, quiet,
Whose internal police nips the buds of all riot,—   135
A brain like a permanent strait-jacket put on
The heart that strives vainly to burst off a button,—
A brain which, without being slow or mechanic,
Does more than a larger less drilled, more volcanic;
He's a Cowper condensed, with no craziness bitten,   140
And the advantage that Wordsworth before him had written.

[12] Lowell puns by adding "extra" to *intro nos;* among ourselves.

[13] A pun on the name of Isis, Egyptian goddess.

[14] Refers to the saying, "You can be foolish in a particular place." *Loco foco* was the name of the liberal political faction of the time.

[15] "Whoever-he-is."

[16] James Thomson (1700-1748), a Scottish poet of *The Season's* (1730); Willaim Cowper (1731-1800), English poet, was the author of *Olney Hymns,* and suffered periodically from insanity. Lowell added a note: "To demonstrate quickly and easily how per-/-versely absurd 'tis to sound this name *Cowper,/ As people in general call him super,/* I remark that he rhymes it himself with horse-trooper."

"But, my dear little bardlings, don't prick up your ears
Nor suppose I would rank you and Bryant as peers;
If I call him an iceberg, I don't mean to say
There is nothing in that which is grand in its way;   145
He is almost the one of your poets that knows
How much grace, strength, and dignity lie in Repose;
If he sometimes falls short, he is too wise to mar
His thought's modest fulness by going too far;
'Twould be well if your authors should all make a trial   150
Of what virtue there is in severe self-denial,
And measure their writings by Hesiod's[17] staff,
Which teaches that all has less value than half.

"There is Whittier, whose swelling and vehement heart
Strains the strait-breasted drab of the Quaker apart,   155
And reveals the live Man, still supreme and erect,
Underneath the bemummying wrappers of sect;
There was ne'er a man born who had more of the swing
Of the true lyric bard and all that kind of thing;
And his failures arise (though he seem not to know it)   160
From the very same cause that has made him a poet,—
A fervor of mind which knows no separation
'Twixt simple excitement and pure inspiration,
As my Pythoness[18] erst sometimes erred from not knowing
If 'twere I or mere wind through her tripod was blowing;   165
Let his mind once get head in its favorite direction
And the torrent of verse bursts the dams of reflection,
While, borne with the rush of the metre along,
The poet may chance to go right or go wrong,
Content with the whirl and delirium of song;   170
Then his grammar's not always correct, nor his rhymes,
And he's prone to repeat his own lyrics sometimes,
Not his best, though, for those are struck off at white-heats
When the heart in his breast like a trip-hammer beats,
And can ne'er be repeated again any more   175
Than they could have been carefully plotted before:
Like old what's-his-name[19] there at the battle of Hastings
(Who, however, gave more than mere rhythmical bastings),

[17] A Greek poet of the eighth century B.C., author of *Works of Days*, who wrote, "Fools! they know not how much half exceeds the whole."

[18] Chief priestess at Apollo's oracle at Delphi. She was seated on a tripod over a vaporous chasm and went into a trance, during which she uttered Apollo's prophecies.

[19] Taillefer, the armed minstrel who sang *The Song of Roland* as he led the Norman horsemen of William the Conqueror into the battle of Hastings (on October 14, 1066).

Our Quaker leads off metaphorical fights
For reform and whatever they call human rights,   180
Both singing and striking in front of the war,
And hitting his foes with the mallet of Thor;[20]
Anne haec, one exclaims, on beholding his knocks,
Vestis filii tui,[21] O leather-clad Fox?[22]
Can that be thy son, in the battle's mid din,   185
Preaching brotherly love and then driving it in
To the brain of the tough old Goliath[23] of sin,
With the smoothest of pebbles from Castaly's spring[24]
Impressed on his hand hard moral sense with a sling?

   "All honor and praise to the right-hearted bard   190
Who was true to The Voice when such service was hard,
Who himself was so free he dared sing for the slave
When to look but a protest in silence was brave;
All honor and praise to the women and men
Who spoke out for the dumb and the downtrodden then!   195
It needs not to name them, already for each
I see History preparing the statue and niche;
They were harsh, but shall *you* be so shocked at hard words
Who have beaten your pruning-hooks up into swords,
Whose rewards and hurrahs men are surer to gain   200
By the reaping of men and of women than grain?
Why should *you* stand aghast at their fierce wordy war, if
You scalp one another for Bank or for Tariff?
Your calling them cut-throats and knaves all day long
Doesn't prove that the use of hard language is wrong;   205
While the World's heart beats quicker to think of such men
As signed Tyranny's doom with a bloody steel-pen,
While on Fourth-of-Julys beardless orators fright one
With hints at Harmodius and Aristogeiton,[25]
You need not look shy at your sisters and brothers   210
Who stab with sharp words for the freedom of others;—

---

[20] Norse god of war and thunder.

[21] Cf. Genesis xxxvii:32: "Is this indeed the coat of your son?" The words of Joseph's brother to his father Jacob.

[22] George Fox (1624-1691), founder of the Society of Friends (Quakers). He wore leather breeches.

[23] Cf. I Samuel xvii: 49. The Philistine giant who was slain by the stone from David's slingshot.

[24] A spring on Mount Parnassus that was sacred to Apollo and the Muses. Its waters allegedly inspired poetry.

[25] Harmodius and Aristogeiton were assassins of Hipparchus, the Athenian tyrant.

No, a wreath, twine a wreath for the loyal and true
Who, for sake of the many, dared stand with the few,
Not of blood-spattered laurel for enemies braved,
But of broad, peaceful oak-leaves for citizens saved!   215

o   o   o

"There is Hawthorne, with genius so shrinking and rare
That you hardly at first see the strength that is there;
A frame so robust, with a nature so sweet,
So earnest, so graceful, so lithe and so fleet,
Is worth a descent from Olympus to meet;   220
'Tis as if a rough oak that for ages had stood,
With his gnarled bony branches like ribs of the wood,
Should bloom, after cycles of struggle and scathe,
With a single anemone trembly and rathe;
His strength is so tender, his wildness so meek,   225
That a suitable parallel sets one to seek,—
He's a John Bunyan Fouqué, a Puritan Tieck; [26]
When Nature was shaping him, clay was not granted
For making so full-sized a man as she wanted,
So, to fill out her model, a little she spared   230
From some finer-grained stuff for a woman prepared,
And she could not have hit a more excellent plan
For making him fully and perfectly man.

o   o   o

"Here's Cooper, who's written six volumes to show
He's as good as a lord: well, let's grant that he's so;   235
If a person prefer that description of praise,
Why, a coronet's certainly cheaper than bays;
But he need take no pains to convince us he's not
(As his enemies say) the American Scott. [27]
Choose any twelve men, and let C. read aloud   240
That one of his novels of which he's most proud,
And I'd lay any bet that, without ever quitting
Their box, they'd be all, to a man, for acquitting.
He has drawn you one character, though, that is new,
One wildflower he's plucked that is wet with the dew   245

[26] Lowell juxtaposes Hawthorne's several characteristics: John Bunyan (1628-1688), the English author, wrote *The Pilgrim's Progress* (1678-84), a Christian allegory; Baron Friedrich de la Motte-Fouqué (1777-1843), the German author, wrote the allegorical fairy tale *Undine* (1811); Ludwig Tieck (1773-1853) was a German author who wrote romantic novels and plays.

[27] Contemporary critics had compared Cooper's fiction with that of Sir Walter Scott (1771-1832), which Lowell feels was excessive.

Of this fresh Western world, and, the thing not to mince,
He has done naught but copy it ill ever since,
His Indians, with proper respect be it said,
Are just Natty Bumppo[28] daubed over with red,
And his very Long Toms[29] are the same useful Nat,   250
Rigged up in duck pants and a sou'-wester hat,
(Though once in a Coffin, a good change was found
To have slipt the old fellow away underground).
All his other men-figures are clothes upon sticks,
The *dernière chemise*[30] of a man in a fix,   255
(As a captain besieged, when his garrison's small,
Sets up caps upon poles to be seen o'er the wall);
And the women he draws from one model don't vary,
All sappy as maples and flat as a prairie.
When a character's wanted, he goes to the task   260
As a cooper would do in composing a cask;
He picks out the staves, of their qualities heedful,
Just hoops them together as tight as is needful,
And, if the best fortune should crown the attempt, he
Has made at the most something wooden and empty.   265

"Don't suppose I would underrate Cooper's abilities;
If I thought you'd do that, I should feel very ill at ease;
The men who have given to *one* character life
And objective existence are not very rife;
You may number them all, both prose-writers and singers,   270
Without overrunning the bounds of your fingers,
And Natty won't go to oblivion quicker
Than Adams the parson or Primrose the vicar.[31]

"There is one thing in Cooper I like, too, and that is
That on manners he lectures his countrymen gratis,   275
Not precisely so either, because, for a rarity,
He is paid for his tickets in unpopularity.
Now he may overcharge his American pictures,
But you'll grant there's a good deal of truth in his strictures;
And I honor the man who is willing to sink   280
Half his present repute for the freedom to think,

---

[28] Leatherstocking, the hero of Cooper's *Leatherstocking Tales.*

[29] Long Tom Coffin was a character in *The Pilot* (1824).

[30] Literally, "last shirt"; French slang for "last resort."

[31] Parson Adams is the friend of the hero in Henry Fielding's *Joseph Adams* (1742); Dr. Primrose is a character in Oliver Goldsmith's *The Vicar of Wakefield* (1766).

And, when he has thought, be his cause strong or weak,
Will risk t'other half for the freedom to speak,
Caring naught for what vengeance the mob has in store,
Let that mob be the upper ten thousand or lower. 285

"There are truths you Americans need to be told,
And it never'll refute them to swagger and scold;
John Bull, looking o'er the Atlantic, in choler
At your aptness for trade, says you worship the dollar;
But to scorn such eye-dollar-try's what very few do, 290
And John goes to that church as often as you do.
No matter what John says, don't try to outcrow him,
'Tis enough to go quietly on and outgrow him;
Like most fathers, Bull hates to see Number One
Displacing himself in the mind of his son, 295
And detests the same faults in himself he'd neglected
When he sees them again in his child's glass reflected;
To love one another you're too like by half.
If he is a bull, you're a pretty stout calf,
And tear your own pasture for naught but to show 300
What a nice pair of horns you're beginning to grow.

"There are one or two things I should just like to hint,
For you don't often get the truth told you in print;
The most of you (this is what strikes all beholders)
Have a mental and physical stoop in the shoulders; 305
Though you ought to be free as the winds and the waves,
You've the gait and the manners of run-away slaves;
Though you brag of your New World, you don't half believe in it,
And as much of the Old as is possible weave in it;
Your goddess of freedom, a tight, buxom girl, 310
With lips like a cherry and teeth like a pearl,
With eyes bold as Herë's,[32] and hair floating free,
And full of the sun as the spray of the sea,
Who can sing at a husking or romp at a shearing,
Who can trip through the forests alone without fearing, 315
Who can drive home the cows with a song through the grass,
Keeps glancing aside into Europe's cracked glass,
Hides her red hands in gloves, pinches up her lithe waist,
And makes herself wretched with transmarine taste;
She loses her fresh country charm when she takes 320
Any mirror except her own rivers and lakes.

[32] Herë, or Hera, the goddess of women, the
sister and wife of Zeus.

"You steal Englishmen's books and think Englishmen's thought,
With their salt on her tail your wild eagle is caught;
Your literature suits its each whisper and motion
To what will be thought of it over the ocean;   325
The cast clothes of Europe your statesmanship tries
And mumbles again the old blarneys and lies;—
Forget Europe wholly, your viens throb with blood,
To which the dull current in hers is but mud;
Let her sneer, let her say your experiment fails,   330
In her voice there's a tremble e'en now while she rails,
And your shore will soon be in the nature of things
Covered thick with gilt driftwood of castaway kings,
Were alone, as it were in a Longfellow's Waif[33]
Her fugitive pieces will find themselves safe.   325
O my friends, thank your God, if you have one, that he
'Twixt the Old World and you set the gulf of a sea;
Be strong-backed, brown-handed, upright as your pines,
By the scale of a hemisphere shape your designs,
Be true to yourselves and this new nineteenth age,   340
As a statue by Powers, or a picture by Page,[34]
Plow, sail, forge, build, carve, paint, all things make new,
To your own New-World instincts contrive to be true,
Keep your ears open wide to the Future's first call,
Be whatever you will, but yourselves first of all,   345
Stand fronting the dawn on Toils heaven-scaling peaks,
And become my new race of more practical Greeks.—
Hem! your likeness at present, I shudder to tell o't,
Is that you have your slaves, and the Greek had his helot."[35]

                              ⚬   ⚬   ⚬

"There comes Poe, with his raven, like Barnaby Rudge,[36]   350
Three-fifths of him genius and two fifths sheer fudge,
Who talks like a book of iambs and pentameters,
In a way to make people of common sense damn metres,
Who has written some things quite the best of their kind,
But the heart somehow seems all squeezed out by the mind,   355
Who—But hey-day! What's this? Messieurs Mathews[37] and Poe,

[33] An anthology of poetry edited by Longfellow (1845).

[34] Hiram Powers (1805-1873) was an American sculptor; William Page (1811-1885) drew scenes of American history.

[35] A Spartan serf who could be freed only by the state.

[36] A raven is central to the action of Dickens' novel *Barnaby Rudge* (1841).

[37] Cornelius Mathews (1817-1889) was a New York editor and novelist who, like Poe, attacked Longfellow.

You mustn't fling mud-balls at Longfellow so,
Does it make a man worse that his character's such
As to make his friends love him (as you think) too much?
Why, there is not a bard at this moment alive   360
More willing than he that his fellows should thrive;
While you are abusing him thus, even now
He would help either one of you out of a slough;
You may say that he's smooth and all that till you're hoarse,
But remember that elegance also is force;   365
After polishing granite as much as you will,
The heart keeps its tough old persistency still;
Deduct all you can, *that* still keeps you at bay;
Why, he'll live till men weary of Collins and Gray.[38]
I'm not over-fond of Greek meters in English,[39]   370
To me rhyme's gain, so it be not too jinglish,
And your modern hexameter verses are no more
Like Greek ones than sleek Mr. Pope[40] is like Homer;
As the roar of the sea to the coo of a pigeon is,
So, compared to your moderns, sounds old Melesigenes;[41]   375
I may be too partial, the reason, perhaps, o't is
That I've heard the old blind man[42] recite his own rhapsodies,
And my ear with that music impregnate may be,
Like the poor exiled shell with the soul of the sea,
Or as one can't bear Strauss[43] when his nature is cloven   380
To its deeps within deeps by the stroke of Beethoven;[44]
But, set that aside, and 'tis truth that I speak,
Had Theocritus[45] written in English, not Greek,
I believe that his exquisite sense would scarce change a line
In that rare, tender, virgin-like pastoral Evangeline.   385
That's not ancient nor modern, its place is apart
Where time has no sway, in the realm of pure Art,
'Tis a shrine of retreat from Earth's hubbub and strife
As quiet and chaste as the author's own life.

¤   ¤   ¤

[38] William Collins (1721-1759) and Thomas Gray (1716-1771) were pre-Romantic poets.

[39] Longfellow's *Evangeline* was written in hexameters.

[40] Alexander Pope (1688-1744) translated Homer's *Iliad* into heroic couplets (1715-1726).

[41] "Born in Melos": Homer.

[42] Homer.

[43] Johann Strauss (1804-1849) was a Viennese composer of waltzes.

[44] Ludwig van Beethoven (1770-1827) was a German composer of symphonies, concertos, and sonatas.

[45] A third-century B.C. Greek pastoral poet.

"What! Irving? thrice welcome, warm heart and fine brain, 390
You bring back the happiest spirit from Spain,[46]
And the gravest sweet humor, that ever were there
Since Cervantes[47] met death in his gentle despair;
Nay, don't be embarrassed, nor look so beseeching,
I sha'n't run directly against my own preaching, 395
And having just laughed at their Raphaels and Dantes,
Go to setting you up beside matchless Cervantes;
But allow me to speak what I honestly feel,—
To a true poet-heart add the fun of Dick Steele,
Throw in all of Addison,[48] *minus* the chill, 400
With the whole of that partnership's stock and good-will,
Mix well, and while stirring, hum o'er, as a spell,
The fine *old* English Gentleman,[49] simmer it well,
Sweeten just to your own private liking, then strain, 405
That only the finest and clearest remain,
Let it stand out of doors till a soul it receives
From the warm lazy sun loitering down through green leaves,
And you'll find a choice nature, not wholly deserving
A name either English or Yankee—just Irving." 410

⁂   ⁂   ⁂

"There's Holmes, who is matchless among you for wit;
A Leyden-jar[50] always full-charged, from which flit
The electrical tingles of hit after hit;
In long poems 'tis painful sometimes, and invites
A thought of the way the new Telegraph[51] writes, 415
Which pricks down its little sharp sentences spitefully
As if you got more than you'd title to rightfully,
And you find yourself hoping its wild father Lightning
Would flame in for a second and give you a fright'ning.
He has perfect sway of what I call a sham metre, 420
But many admire it, the English pentameter,
And Campbell,[52] I think, wrote most commonly worse,
With less nerve, swing, and fire in the same kind of verse,

---

[46] Washington Irving's *Alhambra* (1832) was set in Spain. Irving had returned from an ambassadorship to Spain in 1845.

[47] Miguel de Cervantes Saavedra (1547-1616) was the author of *Don Quixote* (1605, 1615), a satire of Spanish life and chivalry.

[48] Sir Richard Steele (1672-1729) and Joseph Addison (1672-1719) collaborated on the eighteenth-century periodical, *The Spectator*.

[49] Refers to an essay by Irving from *Bracebridge Hall*, "The English Country Gentleman."

[50] A condenser of static electricity.

[51] The Morse code, introduced in 1844 by Samuel F. B. Morse (1791-1872).

[52] Thomas Campbell (1777-1844) was a Scottish poet.

Nor e'er achieved aught in't so worthy of praise
As the tribute of Holmes to the grand *Marseillaise*.[53]   425
You went crazy last year over Bulwer's New Timon;[54]
Why, if B., to the day of his dying, should rhyme on,
Heaping verses on verses and tomes upon tomes,
He could ne'er reach the best point and vigor of Holmes.
His are just the fine hands, too, to weave you a lyric   430
Full of fancy, fun, feeling, or spiced with satiric
In a measure so kindly you doubt if the toes
That are trodden upon are your own or your foes'.

"There is Lowell, who's striving Parnassus to climb
With a whole bale of *isms* tied together with rhyme,   435
He might get on alone, spite of brambles and boulders,
But he can't with that bundle he has on his shoulders,
The top of the hill he will ne'er come nigh reaching
Till he learns the distinction 'twix singing and preaching;
His lyre has some chords that would ring pretty well,   440
But he'd rather by half make a drum of the shell,
And rattle away till he's old as Methusalem,[55]
At the head of a march to the last new Jerusalem."

      ✿   ✿   ✿

1848

[53] In Holmes's *Poetry: A Metrical Essay*, Sec. II (1836).

[54] E. G. E. Lytton-Bulwer-Lytton (1803-

1883), *The New Timon: A Romance of London* (1846).

[55] Cf. Genesis v: 27.

WILLIAM GILMORE SIMMS

(1806–1870)

William Gilmore Simms was a significant and representative writer of the antebellum South. Novelist, critic, poet, correspondent, and editor, Simms was a substantial man of letters who commented on almost every aspect of Southern life. Beginning his career as a romantic novelist—his best-known work is *The Yemassee* (1835)—he became more and more sectional in his thinking, and the progress of his career is an illuminating reflection of one dominant aspect of Southern thought before the Civil War.

Simms was born on April 17, 1806, in Charleston, South Carolina. After his mother's death in 1808, his father went to Mississippi, and the boy was brought up by his maternal grandmother. He studied law briefly and was admitted to the bar, but his real interest was in writing and, by 1830, he was editor of the Charleston *City Gazette* and the author of several volumes of poetry. The great influence on Simms as well as on most Southern writers was Sir Walter Scott; Simms adopted Scott's techniques of fictionalizing historical events and of presenting realistically a wide variety of characters. His most important group of novels are those that celebrate the heroic battles of the South during the American Revolution:*The Partisan* (1835), *Mellichampe* (1836), *The Kinsman* (later called *The Scout,* 1841), *Katherine Walton* (1851), *Woodcraft* (1852), *The Forayer* (1855), and *Eutaw* (1856). In these novels he saw the South as a developing region of cultural and historical

The standard text is *The Writings of William Gilmore Simms,* published by J. J. S. Redfield, 1853–1859, and supervised by Simms himself. A new edition of 15 volumes is being prepared: J. C. Guilds and J. B. Meriwether, eds., *The Centennial Edition of the Writings of William Gilmore Simms,* 1969—. *The Letters of William Gilmore Simms,* 5 vols., Mary C. Simms Oliphant, Alfred Taylor Odell, T. C. Duncan Eaves, 1952–1956. For a complete descriptive bibliography of books by Simms, see A. S. Salley, *Catalogue of the Salley Collection of the Works of William Gilmore Simms,* 1943. James B. Merriwether has compiled *A Check List of the Separate Writings of William Gilmore Simms,* 1961.

The first important critical biography is William P. Trent, *William Gilmore Simms,* 1892. Simms' work is appraised in most studies of the American novel, but see especially Vernon L. Parrington, *Main Currents in American Thought,* II, 1927; Alexander Cowie, *The Rise of the American Novel,* 1948; Ernest Leisy *The American Historical Novel,* 1950; Jay B. Hubbell, *The South in American Literature,* 1954. Edd M. Parks has written *William Gilmore Simms As a Literary Critic,* 1961. A recent assessment is J. V. Ridgely, *William Gilmore Simms,* 1962.

The text from *The Yemassee* is taken from *The Writings of William Gilmore Simms.*

superiority, with a distinct social order in which blacks, Indians, poor whites, and planters had their predestined roles. In the 1830's and 1840's his paternalistic views were expressed romantically in literature and were not strident; but, as the South took issue with the North, Simms became a vigorous apologist for slavery and a champion of the Southern way of life.

Simm's literary attitudes were most clearly expressed in the introductions to his various novels. The preface of *The Yemassee* is a succinct statement of his concept of the romance and the novel.

Preface to The Yemassee

TO PROFESSOR

SAMUEL HENRY DICKSON, M.D.,

OF SOUTH CAROLINA.

My Dear Dickson,—

It is now nearly twenty years since I first inscribed the Romance of "The Yemassee" with your name. The great good fortune which attended the publication in the favor of the public, the repeated editions which have been called for, and the favourable opinions of most of the critics, who, from time to time, have sat in judgment upon it, seem to justify me in endeavouring to retouch and perpetuate the old inscription in the new and improved edition of my various writings which it is meant to herald. You will see, if you do me the honour again to glance over the pages of this story, that I have done something towards making it more acceptable to the reader. I could not change the plan of the story in any wise. That is beyond my control. I could make no material alterations of any kind; since such a labor is always undertaken with pain, and implies a minuteness of examination which would be excessively tedious to a writer who has long dismissed the book from his thoughts, in the more graceful occupation of fresh imaginings and new inventions. It is my great regret that I can now do so little towards rendering the story more worthy of the favor it has found. I am now fully conscious of its defects and crudities. No one can be more so than myself. In reading it over, for the small revision which I have made, I am absolutely angry with myself, as Scott is reported to have been Hogg while reading one of the stories of the Shepherd, at having spoiled and botched so much excellent material. I see now a thousand passages, through which had I the leisure, and could I muster courage for the effort, I should draw the pen, with the hope to substitute better thoughts, and improved situations, in a more appropriate and graceful style. But I need say to you how coldly and reluctantly would such a task be undertaken, by one who has survived his youth, and who must economize all his enthusiasm for the new creations of his fancy. I can only bestow a touch of the pruning knife here and there, cutting off the more obtrusive excrescences, and leaving minor ones to the indifference or the indulgence of the reader.

Something, perhaps should be said of the story as a whole. When I wrote, there was little understood, by readers generally, in respect to the character of the red men; and, of the opinions entertained on the subject, many, according to my own experience, I knew to be incorrect. I had seen the red men of the south in their own homes, on frequent occasions, and had arrived at conclusions in respect to them, and their habits and moral nature, which seemed to me to remove much of that air of mystery which was supposed to disguise most of their ordinary actions. These corrections of the vulgar opinions will be found unobtrusively given in the body of the work, and need not be repeated here. It needs only that I should say that the rude portraits of the red man, as given by those who see him in degrading attitudes only, and in humiliating relation with the whites, must not be taken as just delineation of the same being in his native woods, unsubdued, a fearless hunter, and without any degrading consciousness of inferiority, and still more degrading habits, to make him wretched and ashamed. My portraits, I contend, are true to the Indian as our ancestors knew him at early periods, and as our people, in certain situations, may know him still. What liberties I have taken with the subject, are wholly with his mythology. That portion of the story, which the reverend critics, with one exception, recognised as sober history, must be admitted to be a pure invention—one, however, based upon such facts and analogies as, I venture to think, will not discredit the proprieties of the invention.

What I shall add to these statements, must be taken from the old preface, which I shall somewhat modify.

You will note that I call "The Yemassee" a romance, and not a novel. You will permit me to insist upon the distinction. I am unwilling that the story shall be examined by any other than those standards which have governed me in its composition; and unless the critic is prepared to adopt with me those leading principles, in accordance with which the book has been written, the sooner we part company the better.

Supported by the authority of common sense and practice, to say nothing of Pope—

> "In every work regard the writer's end,
> Since none can compass more than they intend—"

I have surely a right to insist upon this particular. It is only when an author departs from his own standard (speaking of his labours as a work of art), that he offends against propriety and merits censure. Reviewing "Atlantis," a fairy tale, full of fanciful machinery, and without a purpose, save the embodiment to the mind's eye of some of those

> "Gay creatures of the element,
> That, in the colour of the rainbow live,
> And play i' the flighted clouds—"

one of my critics—then a very distinguished writer—gravely remarked, in a very popular periodical, "Magic is now beyond the credulity of eight years;" and yet the author *set out* to make a tale of magic, *knowing* it to be thus beyond the range of the probable—knowing that all readers were equally sagacious—and never, for a moment, contemplated the deception of any sober citizen.

The question briefly is—What are the standards of the modern Romance? What is the modern Romance itself? The reply is immediate. The modern Romance is the substitute which the people of the present day offer for the ancient epic. The form is changed; the matter is very much the same; at all events, it differs much more seriously from the English novel than it does from the epic and the drama, because the difference is one of material, even more than of fabrication. The reader who, reading Ivanhoe, keeps Richardson and Fielding beside him, will be at fault in every step of his progress. The domestic novel of those writers, confined to the felicitous narration of common and daily occuring events, and the grouping and delineation of characters in ordinary conditions of society, has altogether a different sort of composition; and if, in a strange doggedness, or simplicity of spirit, such a reader happens to pin his faith to such writers alone, circumscribing the boundless horizon of art to the domestic circle, the Romances of Maturin, Scott, Bulwer,[1] and others of the present day, will be little better than rhapsodical and intolerable nonsense.

When I say that our Romance is the substitute of modern times for the epic or the drama, I do not mean to say that they are exactly the same things, and yet, examined thoroughly, and *[sic]* the differences between them are very slight. These differences depend on the material employed, rather than upon the particular mode in which it is used. The Romance is of loftier origin than the Novel. It approximates the poem. It may be described as an amalgam of the two. It is only with those who are apt to insist upon poetry as

---

[1] Samuel Richardson (1689-1761) and Henry Fielding (1707-1754) were eighteenth-century English novelists; Charles Maturin (1782-1824) was an Irish dramatist and romancer; Sir Walter Scott (1771-1832) was a Scottish poet and historical novelist; Bulwer-Lytton (1803-1873) was an English novelist, playwright, essayist, poet, and politician.

verse, and to confound rhyme with poetry, that the resemblance is unappar-ent. The standards of the Romance—take such a story, for example, as the Ivanhoe of Scott, or the Salathiel of Croly,[2]—are very much those of the epic. It invests individuals with an absorbing interest—it hurries them rap-idly through crowding and exacting events, in a narrow space of time—it requires the same unities of plan, of purpose, and harmony of parts, and it seeks for its adventures among the wild and wonderful. It does not confine itself to what is known, or even what is probable. It grasps at the possible; and, placing a human agent in hitherto untried situations, it exercises its ingenuity in extricating him from them, while describing his feelings and his fortunes in his progress. The task has been well or ill done, in proportion to the degree of ingenuity and knowledge which the romancer exhibits in car-rying out the details, according to such proprieties as are called for by the circumstances of the story. These proprieties are the standards set up at his starting, and to which he is required religiously to confine himself.

"The Yemassee" is proposed as an *American* romance. It is so styled as much of the material could have been furnished by no other country. Some-thing too much of extravagance—so some may think,—even beyond the usual license of fiction—may enter into certain parts of the narrative. On this subject, it is enough for me to say, that the popular faith yields abundant authority for the wildest of its incidents. The natural romance of our country has been my object, and I have not dared beyond it. For the rest—for the general peculiarities of the Indians, in their undergraded condition—my au-thorities are numerous in all the writers who have written from their own experience. My chief difficulty, I may add, has risen rather from the discrimi-nation necessary in picking and choosing, than from any deficiency of the material itself. It is needless to add that the historical events are strictly true, and that the outline is to be found in the several chronicles devoted to the region of country in which the scene is laid. A slight anachronism occurs in one of the early chapters, but it has little bearing upon the story, and is altogether unimportant.

But I must not trespass upon your patience, if I do upon your attention. If you read "The Yemassee" *now*, with such changes of mood and judgment as I must acknowledge in my own case, I can hardly hope that it will please you as it did twenty years ago. And yet, my friend, could we both read it as we did then! Ah! how much more grateful our faith than our knowledge! How much do we lose by our gains—how much do our acquisitions cost us!

Yours faithfully,

W. GILMORE SIMMS.

Charleston, *June,* 1853.

[2] George Croly (1780-1860), Irish poet, ro-mancer-writer, biographer and preacher, wrote the romance, *Salathiel.*

WILLIAM HICKLING PRESCOTT

(1796-1859)

Historical writing in nineteenth-century America was in the romantic vein: replete with vivid characterization, varied adventures and picturesque landscapes; concerned with the lives of heroes and great events instead of with common people and ordinary existence; and rendered in a flourishing rhetoric befitting grand themes. The most significant histories of the period were George Bancroft's *The History of the United States* (1834), William Hickling Prescott's *The Conquest of Mexico* (1843), John Lathrop Motley's *The Rise of the Dutch Republic* (1856), and Francis Parkman's *Montcalm and Wolfe* (1884). *The Conquest of Mexico* is a fine historical study, the product of skillful and indefatigable research. Generally accurate in its account of Cortes' conquest of the Aztec Civilization in Mexico, Prescott's three-volume history is still highly readable. With bold and dramatic strokes, Prescott draws his themes: the victory of civilization over barbarism, Christianity over Paganism, and moral leadership over immorality and cannibalism. One of the most impressive and representative scenes is Prescott's description of the seizure of Montezuma.

The standard edition is *The Works of William H. Prescott*, 14 vols., 1863. For criticism, see David Levin, *History and Romantic Art: Bancroft, Prescott, Motley, and Parkman*, 1967. Clinton Harvey Gardiner, *William Hickling Prescott*, 1969.

The text from *The Conquest of Mexico* is taken from *The Works of William H. Prescott*.

From The Conquest of Mexico

CHAPTER III.

ANXIETY OF CORTÉS.—SEIZURE OF MONTEZUMA.—HIS TREATMENT BY THE SPANIARDS.—EXECUTION OF HIS OFFICERS.— MONTEZUMA IN IRONS.—REFLECTIONS.

1519

The Spaniards had been now a week in Mexico. During this time they had experienced the most friendly treatment from the emperor. But the mind of

Cortes[1] was far from easy. He felt that it was quite uncertain how long this amiable temper would last. A hundred circumstances might occur to change it. Montezuma[2] might very naturally feel that maintenance of so large a body too burdensome on his treasury. The people of the capital might become dissatisfied at the presence of so numerous an armed force within their walls. Many causes of disgust might arise betwixt the soldiers and the citizens. Indeed, it was scarcely possible that a rude, licentious soldiery, like the Spaniards, could be long kept in subjection without active employment.[3] The danger was even greater with the Tlascalans, a fierce race now brought into daily contact with the nation who held them in loathing and detestation. Rumors were already rife among the allies, whether well founded or not, of murmurs among the Mexicans accompanied by menaces of raising the bridges.

Even should the Spaniards be allowed to occupy their present quarters unmolested, it was not advancing the great object of the expedition. Cortés was not a whit nearer gaining the capital, so essential to his meditated subjugation of the country; and any day he might receive tidings that the crown, or, what he most feared, the governor of Cuba, had sent a force of superior strength to wrest from him a conquest but half achieved. Disturbed by these anxious reflections, he resolved to extricate himself from his embarrassment by one bold stroke. But he first submitted the affair to a council of the officers in whom he most confided, desirous to divide with them the responsibility of the act, and, no doubt, to interest them more heartily in its execution by making it in some measure the result of their combined judgments.

When the general had briefly stated the embarrassments of their position, the council was divided in opinion. All admitted the necessity of some instant action. One party were for retiring secretly from the city, and getting beyond the causeways before their march could be intercepted. Another advised that it should be done openly, with the knowledge of the emperor, of whose good will they had had so many proofs. But both these measures seemed alike impolitic. A retreat under these circumstances, and so abruptly made, would have the air of a flight. It would be construed into distrust of themselves; and anything like timidity on their part would be sure not only to bring on them the Mexicans, but the contempt of their allies, who would, doubtless, join in the general cry.

As to Montezuma, what reliance could they place on the protection of a prince so recently their enemy, and who, in his altered bearing, must have taken counsel of his fears rather than his inclinations?

[1] Hernando Cortés (1485-1547), the Spanish explorer, conqueror of the Aztecs, and colonial administrator of New Spain.
[2] Montezuma II (1480?-1520), the last Aztec emperor in Mexico, who was overthrown by Cortés.
[3] "We Spaniards," says Cortés, frankly, "are apt to be somewhat unmanageable and troublesome." Rel. Seg., ap. Lorenzana, p. 84. [Author's note.]

Even should they succeed in reaching the coast, their situation would be little better. It would be proclaiming to the world that, after all their lofty vaunts, they were unequal to the enterprise. Their only hopes of their sovereign's favor, and of pardon for their irregular proceedings, were founded on success. Hitherto, they had only made the discovery of Mexico; to retreat would be to leave conquest and the fruits of it to another. In short, to stay and to retreat seemed equally disastrous.

In this perplexity, Cortés proposed an expedient which none but the most daring spirit, in the most desperate extremity, would have conceived. This was to march to the royal palace and bring Montezuma to the Spanish quarters, by fair means if they could persuade him, by force if necessary,— at all events, to get possession of his person. With such a pledge, the Spaniards would be secure from the assault of the Mexicans, afraid by acts of violence to compromise the safety of their prince. If he came by his own consent, they would be deprived of all apology for doing so. As long as the emperor remained among the Spaniards, it would be easy, by allowing him a show of sovereignty, to rule on his name, until they had taken measures for securing their safety and the success of their enterprise. The idea of employing a sovereign as a tool for the government of his own kingdom, if a new one in the age of Cortés, is certainly not so in ours.

A plausible pretext for the seizure of the hospitable monarch—for the most barefaced action seeks to veil itself under some show of decency—was afforded by a circumstance of which Cortés had received intelligence at Cholula. He had left, as we have seen, a faithful officer, Juan de Escalante, with a hundred and fifty men, in garrison at Vera Cruz, on his departure for the capital. He had not been long absent when his lieutenant received a message from an Aztec chief named Quauhpopoca, governor of a district to the north of the Spanish settlement, declaring his desire to come in person and tender his allegiance to the Spanish authorities at Vera Cruz. He requested that four of the white men might be sent to protect him against certain unfriendly tribes through which his road lay. This was not an uncommon request, and excited no suspicion in Escalante. The four soldiers were sent; and on their arrival two of them were murdered by the false Aztec. The other two made their way back to the garrison.

The commander marched at once, with fifty of his men, and several thousand Indian allies, to take vengeance on the cacique.[4] A pitched battle followed. The allies fled from the redoubted Mexicans. The few Spaniards stood firm, and with the aid of their fire-arms and the blessed Virgin, who was distinctly seen hovering over their ranks in the van, they made good the field against the enemy. It cost them dear, however; since seven or eight Christians were slain, and among them the gallant Escalante himself, who died of his injuries soon after his return to the fort. The Indian prisoners

---

[4] An Indian chief.

captured in the battle spoke of the whole proceeding as having taken place at the instigation of Montezuma.

One of the Spaniards fell into the hands of the natives, but soon after perished of his wounds. His head was cut off and sent to the Aztec emperor. It was uncommonly large and covered with hair; and, as Montezuma gazed on the ferocious features, rendered more horrible by death, he seemed to read in them the dark lineaments of the destined destroyers of his house. He turned from it with a shudder, and commanded that it should be taken from the city, and not offered at the shrine of any of his gods.

Although Cortés had received intelligence of this disaster at Cholula, he had concealed it within his own breast, or communicated it to very few only of his most trusty officers, from apprehension of the ill effect it might have on the spirits of the common soldiers.

The cavaliers whom Cortés now summoned to the council were men of the same mettle with their leader. Their bold, chivalrous spirits seemed to court danger for its own sake. If one or two, less adventurous, were startled by the proposal he made, they were soon overruled by the others, who, no doubt, considered that a desperate disease required as desperate a remedy.

That night Cortés was heard pacing his apartment to and fro, like a man oppressed by thought or agitated by strong emotion. He may have been ripening in his mind the daring scheme for the morrow. In the morning the soldiers heard mass as usual, and Father Olmedo invoked the blessing Heaven on their hazardous enterprise. Whatever might be the cause in which he was embarked, the heart of the Spaniard was cheered with the conviction that the saints were on his side.

Having asked an audience from Montezuma, which was readily granted, the general made the necessary arrangements for his enterprise. The principal part of his force was drawn up in the court-yard, and he stationed a considerable detachment in the avenues leading to the palace, to check any attempt at rescue by the populace. He ordered twenty-five or thirty of the soldiers to drop in at the palace, as if by accident, in groups of three or four at a time, while the conference was going on with Montezuma. He selected five cavaliers, in whose courage and coolness he placed most trust, to bear him company: Pedro de Alvarado, Gonzalo de Sandoval, Francisco de Lujo, Velasquez de Leon, and Alonso de Avila,—brilliant names in the annals of the Conquest. All were clad, as well as the common soldiers, in complete armor, a circumstance of too familiar occurrence to excite suspicion.

The little party were graciously received by the emperor, who soon, with the aid of the interpreters, became interested in a sportive conversation with the Spaniards, while he indulged his natural munificence by giving them presents of gold and jewels. He paid the Spanish general the particular compliment of offering him one of his daughters as his wife; an honor which the latter respectfully declined, on the ground that he was already accommodated with one in Cuba, and that his religion forbade a plurality.

When Cortés perceived that a sufficient number of his soldiers were assembled, he changed his playful manner, and in a serious tone briefly acquainted Montezuma with the treacherous proceedings in the *tierra caliente,* and the accusation of him as their author. The emperor listened to the charge with surprise, and disavowed the act, which he said could only have been imputed to him by his enemies. Cortés expressed his belief in his declaration, but added that, to prove it true, it would be necessary to send for Quauhpopoca and his accomplices, that they might be examined and dealt with according to their deserts. To this Montezuma made no objection. Taking from his wrist, to which it was attached, a precious stone, the royal signet, on which was cut the figure of the War-god, he gave it to one of his nobles, with orders to show it to the Aztec governor, and require his instant presence in the capital, together with all those who had been accessory to the murder of the Spaniards. If he resisted, the officer was empowered to call in the aid of the neighboring towns to enforce the mandate.

When the messenger had gone, Cortés assured the monarch that this prompt compliance with his request convinced him of his innocence. But it was important that his own sovereign should be equally convinced of it. Nothing would promote this so much as for Montezuma to transfer his residence to the palace occupied by the Spaniards, till on the arrival of Quauhpopoca the affair could be fully investigated. Such an act of condescension would, of itself, show a personal regard for the Spaniards, incompatible with the base conduct alleged against him, and would fully absolve him from all suspicion!

Montezuma listened to this proposal, and the flimsy reasoning with which it was covered, with looks of profound amazement. He became pale as death; but in a moment his face flushed with resentment, as, with the pride of offended dignity, he exclaimed, "When was it ever heard that a great prince, like myself, voluntarily left his own palace to become a prisoner in the hands of strangers!"

Cortés assured him he would not go as a prisoner. He would experience nothing but respectful treatment from the Spaniards, would be surrounded by his own household, and hold intercourse with his people as usual. In short, it would be but a change of residence, from one of his palaces to another, a circumstance of frequent occurrence with him. It was in vain. "If I should consent to such a degradation," he answered, "my subjects never would." When further pressed, he offered to give up one of his sons and two of his daughters to remain as hostages with the Spaniards, so that he might be spared this disgrace.

Two hours passed in this fruitless discussion, till a high-mettled cavalier, Velasquez de Leon, impatient of the long delay, and seeing that the attempt, if not the deed, must ruin them, cried out, "Why do we waste words on this barbarian? We have gone too far to recede now. Let us seize him, and, if he resists, plunge our swords into his body!" The fierce tone and menacing gestures with which this was uttered alarmed the monarch, who inquired of Marina what the angry Spaniard said. The interpreter explained it in as gentle a manner as she could, beseeching him, "to accompany the white men to their quarters, where he would be treated with all respect and kindness, while to refuse them would but expose himself to violence, perhaps to death." Marina, doubtless, spoke to her sovereign as she thought, and no one had better opportunity of knowing the truth than herself.

This last appeal shook the resolution of Montezuma. It was in vain that the unhappy prince looked around for sympathy or support. As his eye wandered over the stern visages and iron forms of the Spaniards, he felt that his hour was indeed come; and, with a voice scarcely audible from emotion, he consented to accompany the strangers,—to quit the palace whither he was never more to return. Had he possessed the spirit of the first Montezuma, he would have called his guards around him, and left his life-blood on the threshold, sooner than have been dragged a dishonored captive across it. But his courage sank under circumstances. He felt he was the instrument of an irresistible Fate!

No sooner had the Spaniards got his consent, than orders were given for the royal litter. The nobles who bore and attended it could scarcely believe their senses when they learned their master's purpose. But pride now came to Montezuma's aid, and, since he must go, he preferred that it should appear to be with his own free will. As the royal retinue, escorted by the Spaniards, marched through the street with downcast eyes and dejected mien, the people assembled in crowds, and a rumor rang among them that the emperor was carried off by force to the quarters of the white men. A tumult would have soon arisen but for the intervention of Montezuma himself, who called out of the people to disperse, as he was visiting his friends of his own accord; thus sealing his ignominy by a declaration which deprived his subjects of the only excuse for resistance. On reaching the quarters, he sent out his nobles with similar assurances to the mob, and renewed orders to return to their homes.

He was received with ostentatious respect by the Spaniards, and selected the suite of apartments which best pleased him. They were soon furnished with fine cotton tapestries, feather-work, and all the elegancies of Indian upholstery. He was attended by such of his household as he chose, his wives and his pages, and was served with his usual pomp and luxury at his meals. He gave audience, as in his own palace, to his subjects, who were admitted to his presence, few indeed, at a time, under the pretext of greater order and decorum. From the Spaniards themselves he met with a formal deference. No one, not even the general himself, approached him without doffing his casque and rendering the obeisance due to his rank. Nor did they ever sit in his presence, without being invited by him to do so.

With all this studied ceremony and show of homage, there was one circumstance which too clearly proclaimed to his people that their sovereign was a prisoner. In the front of the palace a patrol of sixty men was established, and the same number in the rear. Twenty of each corps mounted guard at once, maintaining a careful watch, day and night. Another body, under command of Velasquez de Leon, was stationed in the royal antechamber. Cortés punished any departure from duty, or relaxation of vigilance, in these sentinels, with the utmost severity. He felt, as indeed every Spaniard must have felt, that the escape of the emperor now would be their ruin. Yet the task of this unintermitting watch sorely added to their fatigues. "Better this dog of a kind should die," cried a soldier one day, "than that we should wear out our lives in this manner." The words were uttered in the hearing of Montezuma, who gathered something of their import, and the offender was severely chastised by order of the general. Such instances of disrespect however, were very rare. Indeed, the amiable deportment of the monarch, who seemed to take a pleasure in the society of his jailers, and who never allowed a favor or attention from the meanest soldier to go unrequited, inspired the Spaniards with as much attachment as they were capable of feeling—for a barbarian.

Things were in this posture, when the arrival of Quauhpopoca from the coast was announced. He was accompanied by his son and fifteen Aztec chiefs. He had travelled all the way, borne, as became his high rank, in a litter. On entering Montezuma's presence he threw over his dress the coarse robe of *nequen,* and made the usual humiliating acts of obeisance. The poor parade of courtly ceremony was the more striking when placed in contrast with the actual condition of the parties.

The Aztec governor was coldly received by his master, who referred the affair (had he the power to do otherwise?) to the examination of Cortés. It was, doubtless, conducted in a sufficiently summary manner. To the general's query, whether the cacique was the subject of Montezuma, he replied, "And what other sovereign could I serve?" implying that his sway was universal. He did not deny his share in the transaction, nor did he seek to shelter himself under the royal authority till sentence of death was passed on him and his followers, when they all laid the blame of their proceedings on Montezuma. They were condemned to be burnt alive in the area before the palace. The funeral piles were made of heaps of arrows, javelins, and other weapons, drawn by the emperor's permission from the arsenals round the great *teocalli,* where they had been stored to supply means of defence in times of civic tumult or insurrection. By this politic precaution Cortés proposed to remove a ready means of annoyance in case of hostilities with the citizens.

To crown the whole of these extraordinary proceedings, Cortés, while preparations for the execution were going on, entered the emperor's apartment, attended by a soldier bearing fetters in his hands. With a severe aspect, he charged the monarch with being the original contriver of the violence offered to the Spaniards, as was now proved by the declaration of his own instruments. Such a crime, which merited death in a subject, could not be atoned for, even by a sovereign, without some punishment. So saying, he ordered the soldier to fasten the fetters on Montezuma's ankles. He coolly waited till it was done, then, turning his back on the monarch, quitted the room.

Montezuma was speechless under the infliction of this last insult. He was like one struck down by a heavy blow, that deprives him of all his faculties. He offered no resistance. But, though he spoke not a word, low, ill-suppressed moans, from time to time, intimated the anguish of his spirit. His attendants, bathed in tears, offered him their consolations. They tenderly held his feet in their arms, and endeavored by inserting their shawls and mantles, to relieve them from the pressure of the iron. But they could not reach the iron which had penetrated into his soul. He felt that he was no more a king.

Meanwhile, the execution of the dreadful doom was going forward in the court-yard. The whole Spanish force was under arms, to check any interruption that might be offered by the Mexicans. But none was attempted. The populace gazed in silent wonder regarding it as the sentence of the emperor. The manner of the execution, too, excited less surprise, from their familiarity with similar spectacles, aggravated, indeed, by additional horrors, in their own diabolic sacrifices. The Aztec lord and his companions, bound hand and foot to the blazing piles, submitted without a cry or a complaint to their terrible fate. Passive fortitude is the virtue of the Indian warrior; and it was the glory of the Aztec, as of the other races on the North American continent, to show how the spirit of the brave man may triumph over torture and the agonies of death.

When the dismal tragedy was ended, Cortés reentered Montezuma's apartment. Kneeling down, he unclasped his shackles with his own hand, expressing at the same time his regret that so disagreeable a duty as that of subjecting him to such a punishment had been imposed on him. This last indignity had entirely crushed the spirit of Montezuma; and the monarch whose frown, but a week since, would have made the nations of Anahuac tremble to their remotest borders, was now craven enough to thank his deliverer for his freedom, as for a great and unmerited boon.

Not long after, the Spanish general, conceiving that his royal captive was sufficiently humbled, expressed his willingness that he should return, if he inclined, to his own palace. Montezuma declined it; alleging, it is said, that his nobles had more than once importuned him to resent his injuries by taking arms against the Spaniards, and that, were he in the midst of them, it would be difficult to avoid it, or to save his capital from bloodshed and anarchy. The reason did honor to his heart, if it was the one which influenced him. It is probable that he did not care to trust his safety to those haughty and ferocious chieftains, who had witnessed the degradation of their master, and must despise his pusillanimity, as a thing unprecedented in an Aztec monarch. It is also said that, when Marina conveyed to him the permission of Cortés, the other interpreter, Aguilar, gave him to understand the Spanish officers never would consent that he should avail himself of it.

Whatever were his reasons, it is certain that he declined the offer; and the general, in a well-feigned or real ecstasy, embraced him, declaring "that he loved him as a brother, and that every Spaniard would be zealously devoted to his interests, since he had shown himself so mindful of theirs!" Honeyed words, "which," says the shrewd old chronicler who was present, "Montezuma was wise enough to know the worth of."

The events recorded in this chapter are certainly some of the most extraordinary on the page of history. That a small body of men, like the Spaniards, should have entered the palace of a mighty prince, have seized his person in the midst of his vassals, have borne him off a captive to their quarters,—that they should have put to an ignominious death before his face his high officers, for executing, probably, his own commands, and have crowned the whole by putting the monarch in irons like a common malefactor,—that this should have been done, not to a drivelling dotard in the decay of his fortunes, but to a proud monarch in the plentitude of his power, in the very heart of his capital, surrounded by thousands and tens of thousands, who trembled at his nod and would have poured out their blood like water in his defence,—that all this should have been done by a mere handful of adventurers, is a thing too extravagant, altogether too improbable, for the pages of romance! It is, nevertheless, literally true. Yet we shall not be prepared to acquiesce in the judgments of contemporaries who regarded these acts with admiration. We may well distrust any grounds on which it is attempted to justify the kidnapping of a friendly sovereign,—by those very persons, too, who were reaping the full benefit of his favors.

To view the matter differently, we must take the position of the Conquerors and assume with them the original right of conquest. Regarded from this point of view, many difficulties vanish. If conquest were a duty, whatever was necessary to effect it was right also. Right and expedient become convertible terms. And it can hardly be denied that the capture of the monarch was expedient, if the Spaniards would maintain their hold on the empire.

The execution of the Aztec governor suggests other considerations. If he were really guilty of the perfidious act imputed to him by Cortés, and if Montezuma disavowed it, the governor deserved death, and the general was justified by the law of nations in inflicting it. It is by no means so clear, however, why he should have involved so many in this sentence; most, perhaps all, of whom must have acted under his authority. The cruel manner of the death will less startle those who are familiar with the established penal codes in most civilized nations in the sixteenth century.

But, if governor deserved death, what pretence was there for the outrage on the person of Montezuma? If the former was guilty, the latter surely was not. But, if the cacique only acted in obedience to orders, the responsibility was transferred to the sovereign who gave the orders. They could not both stand in the same category.

It is vain, however, to reason on the matter on any abstract principles of right and wrong, or to suppose that the Conquerors troubled themselves with the refinements of casuistry. Their standard of right and wrong, in reference to the natives, was a very simple one. Despising them as an outlawed race, without God in the world, they, in common with their age, held it to be their "mission" (to borrow the cant phrase of our own day) to conquer and to convert. The measures they adopted certainly facilitated the first great work of conquest. By the execution of the caciques they struck terror not only into the capital, but throughout the country. It proclaimed that not a hair of a Spaniard was to be touched with impunity! By rendering Montezuma contemptible in his own eyes and those of his subjects, Cortés deprived him of the support of his people and forced him to lean on the arm of the stranger. It was a politic proceeding,—to which few men could have been equal who had a touch of humanity in their natures.

A good criterion of the moral sense of the actors in these events is afforded by the reflections of Bernal Diez, made some fifty years, it will be remembered, after the events themselves, when the fire of youth had become extinct, and the eye, glancing back through the vista half a century, might be supposed to be unclouded by the passions and prejudices which throw their mist over the present. "Now that I am an old man," says the veteran, "I often entertain myself with calling to mind the heroical deeds of early days, till they are as fresh as the events of yesterday. I think of the seizure of the Indian monarch, his confinement in irons, and the execution of his officers, till all these things seem actually passing before me. And, as I ponder on our exploits, I feel that it was not of ourselves that we performed them, but that it was the providence of God which guided us. Much food is there here for meditation!" There is so, indeed, and for a meditation not unpleasing, as we reflect on the advance, in speculative morality at least, which the nineteenth century has made over the sixteenth. But should not the consciousness of this teach us charity? Should it not make us the more distrustful of applying the standard of the present to measure the actions of the past?

III
Varieties of Thought: Religious, Social, and Political Reform

One of the most significant expressions of democratization in the period before the Civil War was the broad movement toward social and political reform. Almost every American institution and practice was examined in terms of its effect on the common man. Reformers attacked the evils of intemperance, the injustices inflicted on women and black people, and the limitations of churches, schools, prisons, and asylums.

The period was particularly receptive to the reformation of social ills. Romanticism was deeply influenced by Christianity in America, with its emphasis on charity, compassion, and moral conscience, and by the Enlightenment of eighteenth-century England, which maintained a belief in the perfectibility of man. By the middle of the century the deleterious effects of the Industrial Revolution had underscored the need to reform social injustice and to assert the dignity of the common man. However muted this religious impulse might become in later generations, social reform has remained as one of the irrepressible characteristics of American culture, manifesting itself in movements like abolitionism in mid-nineteenth century, the labor movement at the turn of the twentieth century, the socialism of the 1930's, and the many peace and civil rights demonstrations of our own time.

Social reformers had their adversaries and critics. One group of formidable opponents were Southerners who depended economically on slavery and defended the institution with increasing vigor in the period before the Civil War. Another group constituted Northern industrial leaders who challenged reform because of their own financial interests. Finally, particular writers like Hawthorne felt that the only genuine reform is the reform of the human heart; together with Poe, Melville, and other skeptics, Hawthorne satirized the eccentricities of many reformers for what he took to be a naivety about the nature of man and the function of democratic institutions.

Social reform in America assumed special dimensions because of the conflict that had arisen between aristocracy and democracy. Jeffersonian democrats had been patricians who clearly represented a ruling class; at the same time, they had committed themselves ideologically to liberty, equality, fraternity, and the natural rights of the common man. As these principles translated themselves into social action within a democracy, the leaders of commerce became more and more concerned and the lines were drawn, in this generation, between Jacksonian democrats and businessmen.

Every important thinker and political figure commented on the central issue of democracy and aristocracy. Alexis de Tocqueville offers perceptive observations of a Frenchman sympathetic to the new forces of American democracy. James Fenimore Cooper, in *The American Democrat,* represents the position of the Federalist or aristocrat, and Andrew Jackson, as the first frontier President, speaks for the common man insofar as he is threatened by the banking interests of aristocrats. These prefatory statements set the cultural context for documents from the major movements of religious, social, and political reform—transcendentalism, feminism, education, prison life, and temperance—as well as for the moral judgment of Emerson in "New England Reformers" and the satirical account of Hawthorne in "Earth's Holocaust."

ALEXIS DE TOCQUEVILLE

(1805–1859)

Alexis de Tocqueville was a French aristocrat who visited America in 1831 to observe the penitentiary system and to acquaint himself with democratic customs. In the course of his visit, he became more and

The most reliable edition of *Democracy in America* is the one originally edited by Henry Reeve and finally published in two volumes by Phillips Bradley from 1945 to 1958. A handy one-volume edition has been edited by J. P. Mayer and Max Lerner (1966).

Good general studies include J. P. Mayer, *Alexis de Tocqueville: A Biographical Study and Political Science,* 1960 and Marvin Zetterbaum, *Toqueville and the Problem of Democracy,* 1967.

more concerned with the problems of democracy. His study, *Democracy in America* (1840), remains probably the most important commentary on American institutions written by a foreigner.

De Tocqueville is particularly concerned with the ability of people to govern themselves and the preservation of their individual liberties as they may be usurped by the tyranny of the majority. Although he admired the liberalizing influences of democracy in America, he feared that egalitarianism would lead to mediocrity in the arts. The special value of *Democracy in America* is its perception into the tensions of American democracy—especially the issues of self-government and freedom—and its remarkable portrait of the American character.

From Democracy in America

THE PRINCIPLE OF EQUALITY
SUGGESTS TO THE AMERICANS THE IDEA
OF THE INDEFINITE PERFECTIBILITY
OF MAN

Equality suggests to the human mind several ideas which would not have originated from any other source, and it modifies almost all those previously entertained. I take as an example the idea of human perfectibility, because it is one of the principal notions that the intellect can conceive, and because it constitutes of itself a great philosophical theory, which is every instant to be traced by its consequences in the practice of human affairs. Although man has many points of resemblance with the brute creation, one characteristic is peculiar to himself—he improves: they are incapable of improvement. Mankind could not fail to discover this difference from its earliest period. The idea of perfectibility is therefore as old as the world; equality did not give birth to it, although it has imparted to it, a novel character.

When the citizens of a community are classed according to their rank, their profession, or their birth, and when all men are constrained to follow the career which happens to open before them, everyone thinks that the utmost limits of human power to be discerned in proximity to himself, and none seeks any longer to resist the inevitable law of his destiny. Not indeed that an aristocratic people absolutely contests man's faculty of self-improvement, but they do not hold it to be indefinite; amelioration they conceive, but not change: they imagine that the future condition of society may be better, but not essentially different; and whilst they admit that mankind has made vast strides in improvement, and may still have some to make, they assign to it beforehand certain impassable limits. Thus they do not presume that they have arrived at the supreme good or at absolute truth (what people or what man was ever wild enough to imagine it?) but they cherish a persuasion that they have pretty nearly reached that degree of greatness and knowledge which our imperfect nature admits of; and as nothing moves about them they are willing to fancy that everything is in its fit place. Then it is that the legislator affects to lay down eternal laws; that kings and nations will raise none but imperishable monuments; and that the present generation undertakes to spare generations to come the care of regulating their destinies.

In proportion as castes disappear and the classes of society approximate—as manners, customs, and laws vary, from the tumultuous intercourse of men—as new facts arise—as new truths are brought to light—as ancient opinions are dissipated, and others take their place—the image of an ideal perfection, forever on the wing, presents itself to the human mind. Continual changes are then every instant occurring under the observation of every man: the position of some is rendered worse; and he learns but too well, that no people and no individual, how enlightened soever they may be, can lay claim to infallibility;—the condition of others is improved; whence he infers that man is endowed with an indefinite faculty of improvement. His reverses teach him that none may hope to have discovered absolute good—his success stimulates him to the never-ending pursuit of it. Thus, forever seeking—forever falling, to rise again—often disappointed, but not discouraged—he tends unceasingly towards that unmeasured greatness so indistinctly visible at the end of the long track which humanity has yet to tread. It can hardly be believed how many facts naturally flow from the philosophical theory of the indefinite perfectibility of man, or how strong an influence it exercises even on men who, living entirely for the purposes of action and not of thought, seem to conform their actions to it, without knowing anything about it. I accost an American sailor, and I inquire why the ships of his country are built so as to last but for short time; he answers without hesitation that the art of navigation is every day making such rapid progress that the finest vessel would become almost useless if it lasted beyond a certain number of years. In these words, which fell accidentally and on a particular subject from a man of rude attainments, I recognize the general and systematic idea upon which a great people directs all its concerns.

Aristocratic nations are naturally too apt to narrow the scope of human perfectibility; democratic nations to expand it beyond compass.

OF INDIVIDUALISM
IN DEMOCRATIC COUNTRIES

I have shown how it is that in ages of equality every man seeks for his opinions within himself: I am now about to show how it is that, in the same ages, all his feelings are turned towards himself alone. Individualism[1] is a novel expression, to which a novel idea has given birth. Our father's were only acquainted with egotism. Egotism is a passionate and exaggerated love of self, which leads a man to connect everything with his own person, and to prefer himself to everything in the world. Individualism is a mature and calm feeling, which disposes each member of the community to sever himself from the mass of his fellow-creatures; and to draw apart with his family and his friends; so that, after he has thus formed a little circle of his own, he willingly leaves society at large to itself. Egotism originates in blind instinct: individualism proceeds from erroneous judgment more than from depraved feelings; it originates as much in the deficiencies of the mind as in the perversity of the heart. Egotism blights the germ of all virtue; individualism, at first, only saps the virtues of public life; but, in the long run, it attacks and destroys all others, and is at length absorbed in downright egotism. Egotism is a vice as old as the world, which does not belong to one form of society more than to another: individualism is of democratic origin, and it threatens to spread in the same ratio as the equality of conditions.

Amongst aristocratic nations, as families remain for centuries in the same condition, often on the same spot, all generations become as it were contemporaneous. A man almost always knows his forefathers, and respects them: he thinks he already sees his remote descendants, and he loves them. He willingly imposes duties on himself towards the former and the latter; and he will frequently sacrifice his personal gratifications to those who went before and to those who will come after him. Aristocratic institutions have, moreover, the effect of closely binding every man to several of his fellow-citizens. As the classes of an aristocratic people are strongly marked and permanent, each of them is regarded by its own members as a sort of lesser country, more tangible and more cherished than the country at large. As in aristocratic communities all the citizens occupy fixed positions, one above the other, the result is that each of them always sees a man above himself whose patronage is necessary to him, and below himself another man whose cooperation he may claim. Men living in aristocratic ages are therefore almost always closely attached to something placed out of their own sphere, and they are often disposed to forget themselves. It is true that in those ages the notion of human fellowship is faint, and that men seldom think of sacrificing themselves for mankind; but they often sacrifice themselves for other men. In democratic ages, on the contrary, when the duties of each individual to the race are much more clear, devoted service to any one man becomes more rare; the bond of human affection is extended, but it is relaxed.

---

[1] I adopt the expression of the original, however strange it may seem to the English ear, partly because it illustrates the remark on the introduction of general terms into democratic language which was made in a preceding chapter, and partly because I know of no English word exactly equivalent to the expression. The chapter itself defines the meaning attached to it by the author. [Translator's note.]

Amongst democratic nations new families are constantly springing up, others are constantly falling away, and all that remain change their condition; the woof of time is every instant broken, and the track of generations effaced. Those who went before are soon forgotten; of those who will come after no one has any idea: the interest of man is confined to those in close propinquity to himself. As each class approximates to other classes, and intermingles with them, its members become indifferent and as strangers to one another. Aristocracy had made a chain of all the members of the community, from the peasant to the king: democracy breaks that chain, and severs every link of it. As social conditions become more equal, the number of persons increases who, although they are neither rich enough nor powerful enough to exercise any great influence over their fellow-creatures, have nevertheless acquired or retained sufficient education and fortune to satisfy their own wants. They owe nothing to any man, they expect nothing from any man; they acquire the habit of always considering themselves as standing alone, and they are apt to imagine that their whole destiny is in their hands. Thus not only does democracy make every man forget his ancestors, but it hides his descendants, and separates his contemporaries from him; it throws him back forever upon himself alone, and threatens in the end to confine him entirely within the solitude of his own heart.

INDIVIDUALISM STRONGER AT THE CLOSE OF A DEMOCRATIC REVOLUTION THAN AT OTHER PERIODS

The period when the construction of democratic society upon the ruins of an aristocracy has just been completed, is especially that at which this separation of men from one another, and the egotism resulting from it, most forcibly strike the observation. Democratic communities not only contain a large number of independent citizens, but they are constantly filled with men who, having entered but yesterday upon their independent condition, are intoxicated with their new power. They entertain a presumptuous confidence in their strength, and as they do not suppose that they can henceforward ever have occasion to claim the assistance of their fellow-creatures, they do not scruple to show that they care for nobody but themselves.

An aristocracy seldom yields without a protracted struggle, in the course of which implacable animosities are kindled between the different classes of society. These passions survive the victory, and traces of them may be observed in the midst of the democratic confusion which ensues. Those members of the community who were at the top of the late gradations of rank cannot immediately forget their former greatness; they will long regard themselves as aliens in the midst of the newly composed society. They look upon all those whom this state of society has made their equals as oppressors, whose destiny can excite no sympathy; they have lost sight of their former equals, and feel no longer bound by a common interest to their fate: each of them, standing aloof, thinks that he is reduced to care for himself alone. Those, on the contrary, who were formerly at the foot of the social scale, and who have been brought up to the common level by a sudden revolution, cannot enjoy their newly acquired independence without secret uneasiness; and if they meet with some of their former superiors on the same footing as themselves, they stand aloof from them with an expression of triumph and of fear. It is, then, commonly at the outset of democratic society that citizens are most disposed to live apart. Democracy leads men not to draw near to their fellow-creatures; but democratic revolutions lead them to shun each other, and perpetuate in a state of equality the animosities which the state of inequality engendered. The great advantage of the Americans is that they have arrived at a state of democracy without having to endure a democratic revolution; and that they are born equal, instead of becoming so.

1840

JAMES FENIMORE COOPER

(1789–1851)*

The American Democrat is an eloquent defense of aristocracy. Cooper was dissatisfied with what he characterized as "the tyranny of opinion" in Jacksonian America and the tendency on the part of reformers and political leaders to champion the masses. As a member of the patrician class, he felt the need to defend his own status. *The American Democrat* has become a classic of conservative thought in America.

For a description of works by and about Cooper, see p. 1135. Valuable studies of Cooper as a social critic include R. E. Spiller, *Fenimore Cooper, Critic of his Times,* 1931; J. F. Ross, *The Social Criti-cism of Fenimore Cooper,* 1933; Dorothy Waples, *The Whig Myth of James Fenimore Cooper,* 1938.
* For a full introduction to Cooper, see pp. 1135–1137.

From The American Democrat

AN ARISTOCRAT AND A DEMOCRAT

We live in an age when the words aristocrat and democrat are much used, without regard to the real significations. An aristocrat is one of a few who possess the political power of a country; a democrat, one of the many. The words are also properly applied to those who entertain notions favorable to aristocratical or democratical forms of government. Such persons are not necessarily either aristocrats or democrats in fact, but merely so in opinion. Thus a member of democratical government may have an aristocratical bias, and vice versa.

To call a man who has the habits and opinions of a gentleman, an aristocrat from that fact alone, is an abuse of terms and betrays ignorance of the true principles of government, as well as of the world. It must be an equivocal freedom under which every one is not the master of his own innocent acts and associations; and he is a sneaking democrat indeed who will submit to be dictated to, in those habits over which neither law nor morality assumes a right of control.

Some men fancy that a democrat can only be one who seeks the level, social, mental and moral, of the majority, as rule that would at once exclude all men of refinement, education, and taste from the class. These persons are enemies of democracy, as they at once render it impracticable. They are usually great sticklers for their own associations and habits, too, though unable to comprehend any of a nature that are superior. They are, in truth, aristocrats in principle, though assuming a contrary pretension, the groundwork of all their feelings and arguments being self. Such is not the intention of liberty, whose aim is to leave every man to be the master of his own acts; denying hereditary honors, it is true, as unjust and unnecessary, but not denying the inevitable consequences of civilization.

The law of God is the only rule of conduct in this, as in other matters. Each man should do as he would be done by. Were the question put to the greatest advocate of indiscriminate association, whether he would submit to have his company and habits dictated to him, he would be one of the first to resist the tyranny; for they who are the most rigid in maintaining their own claims in such matters, are usually the loudest in decrying those whom they fancy to be better off than themselves. Indeed, it may be taken as a rule in social intercourse, that he who is the most apt to question the pretensions of others is the most conscious of the doubtful position he himself occupies; thus establishing the very claims he affects to deny, by letting his jealousy of it be seen. Manners, education, and refinement, are positive things, and they bring with them innocent tastes which are productive of high enjoyments; and it is as unjust to deny their possessors their indulgence as it would be to insist on the less fortunate's passing the time they would rather devote to athletic amusements, in listening to operas for which they have no relish, sung in a language they do not understand.

All that democracy means, is as equal a participation in rights as is practicable; and to pretend that social equality is a condition of popular institutions is to assume that the latter are destructive of civilization, for, as nothing is more self-evident than the impossibility of raising all men to the highest standard of tastes and refinement, the alternative would be to reduce the entire community to the lowest. The whole embarrassment on this point exists in the difficulty of making men comprehend qualities they do not themselves possess. We can all perceive the difference between ourselves and our inferiors, but when it comes to a question of the difference between us and our superiors, we fail to appreciate merits of which we have no proper conceptions. In face of this obvious difficulty, there is the safe and just governing rule, already mentioned, or that of permitting every one to be the undisturbed judge of his own habits and associations, so long as they are innocent and do not impair the rights of others to be equally judges for themselves. If follows that social intercourse must regulate itself, independently of institutions, with the exception that the latter, while they withhold no natural, bestow no factitious advantages beyond those which are inseparable from the rights of property, and general civilization.

In a democracy, men are just as free to aim at the highest attainable places in society, as to attain the largest fortunes; and it would be clearly unworthy of all noble sentiment to say that the grovelling competition for money shall alone be free, while that which enlists all the liberal acquirements and elevated sentiments to the race, is denied the democrat. Such an avowal would be at once a declaration of the inferiority of the system, since nothing but ignorance and vulgarity could be its fruits.

The democratic gentleman must differ in many essential particulars from the aristocratical gentleman, though in their ordinary habits and tastes they are virtually identical. Their principles vary, and, to a slight degree, their deportment accordingly. The democrat, recognizing the right of all to participate in power, will be more liberal in his general sentiments, a quality of superiority in itself, but in conceding this much to his fellow man, he will proudly maintain his own independence of vulgar domination as indispensable to his personal habits. The same principles and manliness that would induce him to depose a royal despot would induce him to resist a vulgar tyrant.

There is no more capital, though more common error, than to suppose him an aristocrat who maintains his independence of habits; for democracy asserts the control of the majority, only in matters of law, and not in matters of custom. The very object of the institution is the utmost practicable personal liberty, and to affirm the contrary would be sacrificing the end to the means.

An aristocrat, therefore, is merely one who fortifies his exclusive privileges by positive institutions, and a democrat, one who is willing to admit of a free competition in all things. To say, however, that the last supposes this competition will lead to nothing is an assumption that means are employed without any reference to an end. He is the purest democrat who best maintains his rights, and no rights can be dearer to a man of cultivation than exemptions from unseasonable invasions on his time by the coarse minded and ignorant.

1838

ANDREW JACKSON

(1767-1845)

As the first president of the common man, Andrew Jackson was eager to destroy the National Bank, the institution that represented aristocracy and wealth and that, in Jackson's view, discouraged a government of the people. Jackson's reelection in 1832 was an endorsement by the people that the National Bank should not be perpetuated.

A biography of Andrew Jackson is H. S. Bassett, *The Life of Andrew Jackson,* 2 vols., 1911. Scholarly studies include James Marquis; *Andrew Jackson, The Border Captain,* 1933; and Arthur Schlesinger, Jr., *The Age of Jackson,* 1945.

From Jackson's Bank Veto Message

Washington, July 10, 1832

To the Senate:

The bill "to modify and continue" the act entitled "An act to incorporate the subscribers to the Bank of the United States" was presented to me on the 4th July instant. Having considered it with that solemn regard to the principles of the Constitution which the day was calculated to inspire, and come to the conclusion that it ought not to become a law, I herewith return it to the Senate, in which it originated, with my objections.

A bank of the United States is in many respects convenient for the Government and useful to the people. Entertaining this opinion, and deeply impressed with the belief that some of the powers and privileges possessed by the existing bank are unauthorized by the Constitution, subversive of the rights of the States, and dangerous to the liberties of the people, I felt it my duty at an early period of my Administration to call the attention of Congress to the practicability of organizing an institution combining all its advantages and obviating these objections. I sincerely regret that in the act before me I can perceive none of those modifications of the bank charter which are necessary, in my opinion, to make it compatible with justice, with sound policy, or with the Constitution of our country.

The present corporate body, denominated the president, directors and company of the Bank of the United States, will have existed at the time this act is intended to take effect twenty years. It enjoys an exclusive privilege of banking under the authority of the General Government, a monopoly of its favor and support, and, as a necessary consequence, almost a monopoly of the foreign and domestic exchange. The powers, privileges, and favors bestowed upon it in the original charter, by increasing the value of the stock far above its par value, operated as a gratuity of many millions to the stockholders.

An apology may be found for the failure to guard against this result in the consideration that the effect of the original act of incorporation could not be certainly foreseen at the time of its passage. The act before me proposes another gratuity to the holders of the same stock, and in many cases to the same men, of at least seven millions more. This donation finds no apology in any uncertainty as to the effect of the act. On all hands it is conceded that its passage will increase at least 20 or 30 per cent more the market price of the stock, subject to the payment of the annuity of $200,000 per year secured by the act, thus adding in a moment one-fourth to its par value. It is not our own citizens only who are to receive the bounty of our Government. More than eight millions of the stock of this bank are held by foreigners. By this act the American Republic proposes virtually to make them a present of some millions of dollars. For these gratuities to foreigners, and to some of our own opulent citizens the act secures no equivalent whatever. They are the certain gains of the present stockholders under the operation of this act, after making full allowance for the payment of the bonus.

Every monopoly and all exclusive privileges are granted at the expense of the public, which ought to receive a fair equivalent. The many millions which this act proposes to bestow on the stockholders of the existing bank must come directly or indirectly out of the earnings of the American people. It is due to them, therefore, if their Government sell monopolies and exclusive privileges, that they should at least exact for them as much as they are worth in open market. The value of the monopoly in this case may be correctly ascertained. The twenty-eight millions of stock would probably be at an advance of 50 per cent, and command in market at least $42,000,000, subject to the payment of the present bonus. The present value of the monopoly, therefore, is $17,000,000, and this the act proposes to sell for three millions, payable in fifteen annual installments of $200,000 each.

It is not conceivable how the present stockholders can have any claim to the special favor of the Government. The present corporation has enjoyed its monopoly during the period stipulated in the original contract. If we must have such a corporation, why should not the Government sell out the whole stock and thus secure to the people the full market value of the privileges granted? Why should not Congress create and sell twenty-eight millions of stock, incorporating the purchases with all the powers and privileges secured in this act and putting the premium upon the sales into the Treasury?

But this act does not permit competition in the purchase of this monopoly. It seems to be predicated on the erroneous idea that the present stockholders have a prescriptive right not only to the favor but to the bounty of Government. It appears that more than a fourth part of the stock is held by foreigners and the residue is held by a few hundred of our own citizens, chiefly of the richest class. For their benefit does this act exclude the whole American people from competition in the purchase of this monopoly and dispose of it for many millions less than it is worth. This seems the less excusable because some of our citizens not now stockholders petitioned that the door of competition might be opened, and offered to take a charter on terms much more favorable to the Government and country.

But this proposition, although made by men whose aggregate wealth is believed to be equal to all the private stock in the existing bank, has been set aside, and the bounty of our Government is proposed to be again bestowed on the few who have been fortunate enough to secure the stock and at this moment wield the power of the existing institution. I can not perceive the justice or policy of this course. If our Government must sell monopolies, it would seem to be its duty to take nothing less than their full value, and if gratuities must be made once in fifteen or twenty years let them not be bestowed on the subjects of a foreign government nor upon a designated and favored class of men in our own country. It is but justice and good policy as far as the nature of the case will admit, to confine our favors to our own fellow-citizens, and let each in his turn enjoy an opportunity to profit by our bounty. In the bearings of the act before me upon these points I find ample reasons why it should not become a law.

It has been urged as an argument in favor of rechartering the present bank that the calling in its loans will produce great embarrassment and distress. The time allowed to close its concerns is ample, and if it has been well managed its pressure will be light, and heavy only in case its managment has been bad. If, therefore, it shall produce distress, the fault will be its own, and it would furnish a reason against renewing a power which has been so obviously abused. But will there ever be a time when this reason will be less powerful? To acknowledge its force is to admit that the bank ought to be perpetual, and as a consequence the present stockholders and those inheriting their rights as successors be established a privileged order, clothed both with great political power and enjoying immense pecuniary advantages from their connection with the Government.

The modifications of the existing charter proposed by this act are not such, in my view, as make it consistent with the rights of the States or the liberties of the people. The qualification of the right of the bank to hold real estate, the limitation of its power to establish branches, and the power reserved to Congress to forbid the circulation of small notes are restrictions comparatively of little value or importance. All the objectionable principles of the existing corporation, and most of its odious features, are retained without alleviation. . . .

In another of its bearings this provision is fraught with danger. Of the twenty-five directors of this bank five are chosen by the Government and twenty by the citizen stockholders. From all voice in these elections the foreign stockholders are excluded by the charter. In proportion, therefore, as the stock is transferred to foreign holders the extent of suffrage in the choice of directors is curtailed. Already is almost a third of the stock in foreign hands and not represented in elections. It is constantly passing out of the country, and this act will accelerate its departure. The entire control of the institution would necessarily fall into the hands of a few citizen stockholders, and the ease with which the object would be accomplished would be a temptation to designing men to secure that control in their own hands by monopolizing the remaining stock. There is danger that a president and directors would then be able to elect themselves from year to year, and without responsibility or control manage the whole concerns of the bank during the existence of its charter. It is easy to conceive that great evils to our country and its institutions might flow from such a concentration of power in the hands of a few men irresponsible to the people.

Is there no danger to our liberty and independence in a bank that in its nature has so little to bind it to our country? The president of the bank has told us that most of the State banks exist by its forbearance. Should its influence become concentered, as it may under the operation of such an act as this, in the hands of a self-elected directory whose interests are identified with those of the foreign stockholders, will there not be cause to tremble for the purity of our elections in peace and for the independence of our country in war? Their power would be great whenever they might choose to exert it; but if this monopoly were regularly renewed every fifteen or twenty years on terms proposed by themselves, they might seldom in peace put forth their strength to influence elections or control the affairs of the nation. But if any private citizen or public functionary should interpose to curtail its powers or prevent a renewal of its privileges, it can not be doubted that he would be made to feel its influence.

Should the stock of the bank principally pass into the hands of the subjects of a foreign country, and we should unfortunately become involved in a war with that country, what would be our condition? Of the course which would be pursued by a bank almost wholly owned by the subjects of a foreign power, and managed by those whose interests, if not affections, would run in the same direction there can be no doubt. All its operations within would be in aid of the hostile fleets and armies without. Controlling our currency, receiving our public moneys, and holding thousands of our citizens in dependence, it would be more formidable and dangerous than the naval and military power of the enemy.

If we must have a bank with private stockholders, every consideration of sound policy and every impulse of American feeling admonishes that it should be *purely American*. Its stockholders should be composed exclusively of our own citizens, who at least ought to be friendly to our Government and willing to support it in times of difficulty and danger. So abundant is domestic capital that competition in subscribing for the stock of local banks has recently led almost to riots. To a bank exclusively of American stockholders, possessing the powers and privileges granted by this act, subscriptions for $200,000,000 could readily be obtained. Instead of sending abroad the stock of the bank in which the Government must deposit its funds and on which it must rely to sustain its credit in times of emergency, it would rather seem to be expedient to prohibit its sale to aliens under penalty of absolute forfeiture.

It is maintained by the advocates of the bank that its constitutionality in all its features ought to be considered as settled by precedent and by the decision of the Supreme Court. To this conclusion I can not assent. Mere precedent is a dangerous source of authority, and should not be regarded as deciding questions of constitutional power except where the acquiescence of the people and the States can be considered as well settled. So far from this being the case on this subject, an argument against the bank might be based on precedent. One Congress, in 1791, decided in favor of a bank; another, in 1811, decided against it. One Congress in 1815, decided against a bank; another in 1816, decided in its favor. Prior to the present Congress, therefore, the precedents drawn from that source were equal. If we resort to the States, the expressions of legislative, judicial, and executive opinions against the bank have been probably to those in its favor as 4 to 1. There is nothing in precedent, therefore, which, if its authority were admitted, ought to weigh in favor of the act before me.

If the opinion of the Supreme Court covered the whole ground of this act, it ought not to control the coordinate authorities of this Government. The Congress, the Executive, and the Court must each for itself be guided by its own opinion of the Constitution. Each public officer who takes an oath to support the Constitution swears that he will support it as he understands it, and not as it is understood by others. It is as much the duty of the House of

Representatives, of the Senate, and of the President to decide upon the constitutionality of any bill or resolution which may be presented to them for passage or approval as it is of the supreme judges when it may be brought before them for judicial decision. The opinion of the judges has no more authority over Congress than the opinion of Congress has over the judges, and on that point the President is independent of both. The authority of the Supreme Court must not, therefore, be permitted to control the Congress or the Executive when acting in their legislative capacities, but to have only such influence as the force of their reasoning may deserve. . . .

On two subjects only does the Constitution recognize in Congress the power to grant exclusive privileges or monopolies. It declares that "Congress shall have power to promote the progress of science and useful arts by securing for limited times to authors and inventors the exclusive right to their respective writings and discoveries." Out of this express delegation of power have grown our laws of patents and copyrights. As the Constitution expressly delegates to Congress the power to grant exclusive privileges in these cases as the means of executing the substantive power "to promote the progress of science and useful arts," it is consistent with the fair rules of construction to conclude that such a power was not intended to be granted as a means of accomplishing any other end. On every other subject which comes within the scope of Congressional power there is an ever-living discretion in the use of proper means, which can not be restricted or abolished without an amendment of the Constitution. Every act of Congress, therefore, which attempts by grants of monopolies or sale of exclusive privileges for a limited time, or a time without limit, to restrict or extinguish its own discretion in the choice of means to execute its delegated powers is equivalent to a legislative amendment of the Constitution, and palpably unconstitutional. . . .

Suspicions are entertained and charges are made of gross abuse and violation of its charter. And investigation unwillingly conceded and so restricted in time as necessarily to make it incomplete and unsatisfactory discloses enough to excite suspicion and alarm. In the practices of the principal bank partially unveiled, in the absence of important witnesses, and in numerous charges confidently made and as yet wholly uninvestigated there was enough to induce a majority of the committee of investigation—a committee which was selected from the most able and honorable members of the House of Representatives—to recommend a suspension of further action upon the bill and a prosecution of the inquiry. As the charter had yet four years to run, and as a renewal now was not necessary to the successful prosecution of its business, it was to have been expected that the bank itself, conscious of its purity and proud of its character, would have withdrawn its application for the present, and demanded the severest scrutiny into all its transactions. In their declining to do so there seems to be an additional reason why the functionaries of the Government should proceed with less haste and more caution in the renewal of their monopoly.

The bank is professedly established as an agent of the executive branch of the Government, and its constitutionality is maintained on that ground. Neither upon the propriety of present action nor upon the provisions of this act was the Executive consulted. It has had no opportunity to say that it neither needs nor wants an agent clothed with such powers and favored by such exemptions. There is nothing in its legitimate functions which makes it necessary or proper. Whatever interest or influence, whether public or private, has given birth to this act, it can not be found either in the wishes or necessities of the executive department, by which present action is deemed premature, and the powers conferred upon its agent not only unnecessary, but dangerous to the Government and country.

It is to be regretted that the rich and powerful too often bend the acts of government to their selfish purposes. Distinctions in society will always exist under every just government. Equality of talents, of education, or of wealth can not be produced by human institutions. In the full enjoyment of the gifts of Heaven and the fruits of superior industry, economy, and virtue, every man is equally entitled to protection by law; but when the laws undertake to add to these natural and just advantages artificial distinctions, to grant titles, gratuities, and exclusive privileges, to make the rich richer and the potent more powerful, the humble members of society—the farmers, mechanics, and laborers—who have neither the time nor the means of securing like favors to themselves, have a right to complain of the injustice of their Government. There are no necessary evils in government. Its evils exist only in its abuses. If it would confine itself to equal protection, and, as Heaven does its rains, shower its favors alike on the high and the low, the rich and the poor, it would be an unqualified blessing. In the act before me there seems to be a wide and unnecessary departure from these just principles.

Nor is our Government to be maintained or our Union preserved by invasions of the rights and powers of the several States. In thus attempting to make our General Government strong we make it weak. Its true strength consists in leaving individuals and States as much as possible to themselves—in making itself felt, not in its power, but in its beneficence; not in its control, but in its protection; not in binding the States more closely to the center, but leaving each to move unobstructed in its proper orbit.

Experience should teach us wisdom. Most of the difficulties our Government now encounters and most of the dangers which impend over our Union have sprung from an abandonment of the legitimate objects of Government by our national legislation, and the adoption of such principles as are embodied in this act. Many of our rich men have not been content with equal protection and equal benefits, but have besought us to make them richer by act of Congress. By attempting to gratify their desires we have in the results of our legislation arrayed section against section, interest against interest, and man against man, in a fearful commotion which threatens to shake the foundations of our Union. It is time to pause in our career to review our principles, and if possible revive that devoted patriotism and spirit of compromise which distinguished the sages of the Revolution and the fathers of our Union. If we can not at once, in justice to interests vested under improvident legislation, make our Government what it ought to be, we can at least take a stand against all new grants of monopolies and exclusive privileges, against any prostitution of our Government to the advancement of the few at the expense of the many, and in favor of compromise and gradual reform in our code of laws and system of political economy.

I have now done my duty to my country. If sustained by my fellow-citizens, I shall be grateful and happy; if not, I shall find in the motives which impel me ample grounds for contentment and peace. In the difficulties which surround us and the dangers which threaten our institutions there is cause for neither dismay nor alarm. For relief and deliverance let us firmly rely on that kind Providence which I am sure watches with peculiar care over the destinies of our Republic, and on the intelligence and wisdom of our countrymen. Through *His* abundant goodness and *their* patriotic devotion our liberty and Union will be preserved.   ANDREW JACKSON

1832

REFORM

Religion

The transcendental movement, which emerged between 1815 and 1836 and which flourished from 1836 until the Civil War, set the stage for religious and social reform in American life. In a period of great industrial expansion and Jacksonian individualism, transcendentalism was the religious expression of the new democracy. It shared the spirit of self-confidence in its revolt against rational conservatism and in its reformation of the church. The movement encouraged subsequent reforms that sought to correct social ills and resulted in the most meaningful literature in American culture: the essays of Emerson and Thoreau, the poetry of Whitman, the fiction of Hawthorne, Melville, Poe, and scores of lesser authors.

The historical roots of transcendentalism reach into the colonial period. These nineteenth-century descendents of the Puritans also believed in "the inner light" and the primary significance of ethical values in the conduct of life. Their moral doctrines, which connect them with the Puritans, were altered by the democratizing influence of the Revolutionary period. Writers like Franklin and Jefferson had translated the religious fervor of Puritan thinkers into its social applications; at the same time, they "Americanized" the rational enlightenment of European philosophers so that a resistance to authority and a nationalistic spirit became notable characteristics of transcendentalism. In place of the distinctions between the "elect" and the "damned," a cult of perfectibility developed that insisted on the equality of all souls; instead of the inner light or "revelation" of God, there was the moral "intuition" of man himself; in contrast to an historical approach to Christianity, championed by conservative Unitarians like Andrews Norton, there was the call for a "saturnalia of faith" in the present moment.

The following selections attempt to render the complexity of the transcendental movement and to illuminate its central conflicts. After reading Ellery Channing's preliminary statement, one can appreciate more fully Emerson's radical essay, "The Divinity School Address," which is the central document opposing the historical approach to Christianity and which drew a sharp rebuttal from Andrews Norton in "The Latest Form of Infidelity." Norton, in turn, elicited the anger of George Ripley, Theodore Parker, and others. Thus the controversy between the old and the new, the conservative and the radical raged on as other writers—Bronson Alcott, Jones Very, Margaret Fuller, and Henry David Thoreau—championed the new faith that seemed so compatible with the new democracy.

WILLIAM ELLERY CHANNING

(1780–1842)

The guiding intelligence of Boston Unitarianism at the critical moment of declaring independence from the traditional Congregational Puritanism, William Ellery Channing was also a powerful voice in the literary culture of New England for more than 20 years after he had delivered his most celebrated sermon. He was a sweet-tempered moderate with a rare ability to maintain friendly relations with mutually hostile colleagues to his left and right. He was also a skillful writer and an effective proponent of a "national literature" (the title of one of his essays), and he befriended and encouraged Emerson and other young transcendentalist writers.

Channing's famous sermon at the ordination of Jared Sparks in Baltimore is a major document in the history of American letters, both for its own qualities and for what it resists and what it portends. Even without historical knowledge, any careful reader will notice the cautious, defensive tone of the first paragraphs. What made the situation so tense was that Unitarians had been preaching in Boston churches for decades, without any need to withdraw from the Congregational polity. So long as the members of a congregation did not object, a minister could quietly ignore Trinitarian doctrines and, by preaching "the fatherhood of God and the brotherhood of man," avoid open controversy—yet retain control of a powerful church. But both local complaints and the publication of a sensational book by one Thomas Belsham (*Unitarianism*, London, 1815) forced Unitarian leaders to consider declaring themselves. Channing was assigned the task, and he chose the moment of Sparks's ordination as his opportunity. His defensive tone is intended to reassure conservatives that he speaks for pious, thoughtful, substantial citizens instead of for revolutionary infidels, and it is also intended to set an example of reasoned debate.

The standard text is *The Works of William Ellery Channing*, 6 vols., 1841–1843.

Early biographies are W. H. Channing, *The Life of William Ellery Channing*, and J. W. Chadwick, *William Ellery Channing, Minister of Religion*, 1903. More recent studies include David P. Edgell, *William Ellery Channing, An Intellectual Portrait*, 1954; Conrad Wright, *The Beginnings of Unitarianism in America*, 1955; Arthur W. Brown, *Always Young For Liberty*, 1956, and *William Ellery Channing*, 1961; Madeleine H. Rice, *Federal Street Pastor: The Life of William Ellery Channing*, 1961; Jack Mendelsohn, *Channing, the Reluctant Radical*, 1971; Robert N. Hudspeth, *Ellery Channing*, 1973.

The sermon is reprinted from *The Works of William Ellery Channing*.

The form, then, and the method of inquiry and argument, represent for Unitarians like Channing an essential part of the creed. A careful reader of the sermon will not fail to notice that Channing spends much energy and time on the question of method: how we should read the Bible, how the Deity chooses to treat us, how we decide on religious doctrine, and how we debate with others. The effort of Unitarian thinkers as Channing represents them is to achieve within a Christian framework what Benjamin Franklin tried to do with his projected Society of the Free and Easy—to reduce to a minimum fundamental doctrines and then to stake all on a method of rational inquiry.

It is this emphasis on free inquiry and open discussion that seemed to welcome or at least provoke much more wildly speculative inquiry than Channing would approve. And of course, by seeming to care very little about doctrine, Channing and others left themselves open to ridicule by local writers like James Russell Lowell, who said:

> They believed—faith, I'm puzzled—I think I may call
> Their belief a belief in nothing at all
> Or something of that sort. I think they all went
> For a general union of total dissent.

Part of that dissent came from Ralph Waldo Emerson and other spiritually questioning and spiritually hungry, excitable young minds. It was the "pale negations" of Unitarianism that Emerson found inadequate, along with the stolidly dogmatic insistence of some Unitarians that belief in the reality (the "historicity") of Christ's miracles was essential to the Unitarian faith. For an understanding of the strong religious impulse behind transcendentalism, students should read Channing's sermon here, and then Emerson's address to the Harvard Divinity School in 1838.

Channing's collected works have been published. His essays on Milton and on National Literature, along with his sermons "Likeness to God" and "The Moral Argument against Calvinism," are worthy of attention. Channing was a beloved spiritual and cultural leader in the Boston area throughout his career as a minister in Boston.

[Unitarian Christianity]
A
Sermon
Delivered at the Ordination of the Rev.
Jared Sparks[1]

I THESS. V. 21.
Prove all things; hold fast that which is good.

The peculiar circumstances of this occasion not only justify, but seem to demand a departure from the course generally followed by preachers at the introduction of a brother into the sacred office. It is usual to speak of the nature, design, duties and advantages of the Christian ministry; and on these topicks I should now be happy to insist, did I not remember that a minister is to be given this day to a religious society, whose peculiarities of opinion have drawn upon them much remark, and may I not add, much reproach. Many good minds, many sincere Christians, I am aware, are apprehensive that the solemnities of this day are to give a degree of influence to principles which they deem false and injurious. The fears and anxieties of such men I respect; and, believing that they are grounded in part on mistake, I have thought it my duty to lay before you as clearly as I can, some of the distinguishing opinions of that class of Christians in our country, who are known to sympathize with this religious society. I must ask your patience, for such a subject is not to be despatched in a narrow compass. I must also ask you to remember, that it is impossible to exhibit, in a single discourse, our view of every doctrine of revelation, much less the differences of opinion which are known to subsist among ourselves. I shall confine myself to topicks on which our sentiments have been misrepresented, or which distinguish us most widely from others. May I not hope to be heard with candor. God deliver us all from prejudice, and unkindness, and fill us with the love of truth and virtue.

There are two natural divisions under which my thoughts will be arranged. I shall endeavor to unfold, 1st, the principles which we adopt in interpreting the Scriptures. And 2dly, some of the doctrines which the Scriptures, so interpreted, seem to us clearly to express.

I. We regard the Scriptures as the record of God's successive revelation to mankind, and particularly of the last and most perfect revelation of His will by Jesus Christ. Whatever doctrines seem to us to be clearly taught in the Scriptures, we receive without reserve or exception. We do not, however, attach equal importance to all the books in this collection. Our religion,

---

[1] The text is the first edition, Boston, 1819.

we believe, lies chiefly in the New Testament. The dispensation of Moses, compared with that of Jesus, we consider as imperfect, earthly, obscure, adapted to the childhood of the human race, a preparation for a nobler system, and chiefly useful now as serving to confirm and illustrate the Christian Scriptures. Jesus Christ is the only master of Christians, and whatever He taught, either during His personal ministry, or by His inspired apostles, we regard as of divine authority, and profess to make the rule of our lives.

This authority, which we give to the Scriptures, is a reason, we conceive, for studying them with peculiar care, and for inquiring anxiously into the principles of interpretation, by which their true meaning may be ascertained. The principles adopted by the class of Christians, in whose name I speak, need to be explained, because they are often misunderstood. We are particularly accused of making an unwarrantable use of reason in the interpretation of Scripture. We are said to exalt reason above revelation, to prefer our own wisdom to God's. Loose and undefined charges of this kind, are circulated so freely, and with such injurious intentions, that we think it due to ourselves, and to the cause of truth, to express our views with some particularity.

Our leading principle in interpreting Scripture is this, that the Bible is a book written for men, the language of men, and that its meaning is to be sought in the same manner, as that of other books. We believe that God, when He condescends to speak and write, submits, if we may so say, to the established rules of speaking and writing. How else would the Scriptures avail us more than if communicated in an unknown tongue.

Now all books, and all conversation, require in the reader or hearer the constant exercise of reason; or their true import is only to be obtained by continual comparison and inference. Human language, you well know, admits various interpretations, and every word and every sentence must be modified and explained according to the subject which is discussed, according to the purposes, feelings, circumstances and principles of the writer, and according to the genius and idioms of the language which he uses. These are acknowledged principles in the interpretation of human writings; and a man, whose words we should explain without reference to these principles, would reproach us justly with a criminal want of candor, and an intention of obscuring or distorting his meaning.

Were the Bible written in a language and style of its own, did it consist of words, which admit but a single sense, and of sentences wholly detached from each other, there would be no place for the principles now laid down. We could not reason about it, as about other writings. But such a book would be of little worth; and perhaps, of all books, the Scriptures correspond least to this description. The word of God bears the stamp of the same hand, which we see in his works. It has infinite connections and dependencies. Every proposition is linked with others, and is to be compared with others, that its full and precise import may be understood. Nothing stands alone. The New Testament is built on the Old. The Christian dispensation is a continuation of the Jewish, the completion of a vast scheme of providence, requiring great extent of view in the reader. Still more, the Bible treats of subjects on which we receive ideas from other sources besides itself; such subjects as the nature, passions, relations, and duties of man; and it expects us to restrain and modify its language by the known truths which observation and experience furnish on these topicks.

We profess not to know a book, which demands a more frequent exercise of reason than the Bible. In addition to the remarks now made on its infinite connections, we may observe, that its style nowhere affects the precision of science, or the accuracy of definition. Its language is singularly glowing, bold and figurative, demanding more frequent departures from the literal sense, than that of our own age and country, and consequently demands more continual exercise of judgment.—We find too, that the different portions of this book, instead of being confined to general truths, refer perpetually to the times when they were written, to states of society, to modes of thinking, to controversies in the church, to feelings and usages which have passed away, and without the knowledge of which we are constantly in danger of extending to all times, and places, what was of temporary and local application.—We find, too, that some of these books are strongly marked by the genius and character of their respective writers, that the Holy Spirit did not so guide the apostles as to suspend the peculiarities of their minds, and that a knowledge of their feelings, and of the influence under which they were placed, is one of the preparations for understanding their writings. With these views of the Bible, we feel it our bounden duty to exercise our reason upon it perpetually, to compare, to infer, to look beyond the letter to the spirit, to seek in the nature of the subject, and the aim of the writer, his true meaning; and, in general, to make use of what is known, for explaining what is difficult, and for discovering new truths.

Need I descend to particulars to prove that the Scriptures demand the exercise of reason. Take, for example, the style in which they generally speak of God, and observe how habitually they apply to Him human passions and organs. Recollect the declarations of Christ, that He came not to send peace, but a sword; that unless we eat His flesh, and drink His blood, we have no life in us; that we must hate father and mother, pluck out the right eye; and a vast number of passages equally bold and unlimited. Recollect the unqualified manner in which it is said of Christians, that they possess all things, know all things, and can do all things. Recollect the verbal contradiction between Paul and James, and the apparent clashing of some parts of Paul's writing, with the general doctrines and end of Christianity. I might extend the enumeration indefinitely, and who does not see, that we must limit all these passages by the known attributes of God, of Jesus Christ, and of human nature, and by the circumstances under which they were written, so as to give the language a quite different import from what it would require, had it been applied to different beings, or used in different connections.

Enough has been said to show in what sense we make use of reason in interpreting Scripture. From a variety of possible interpretations, we select that which accords with the nature of the subject, and the state of the writer, with the connection of the passage, with the general strain of Scripture, with the known character and will of God, and with the obvious and acknowledged laws of nature. In other words, we believe that God never contradicts, in one part of Scripture, what He teaches in another; and never contradicts, in revelation, what He teaches in his works and providence. And we, therefore, distrust every interpretation, which, after deliberate attention, seems repugnant to any established truth. We reason about the Bible precisely as civilians do about the constitution under which we live; who, you know, are accustomed to limit one provision of that venerable instrument by others, and to fix the precise import of its parts by inquiring into its general spirit, into the intentions of its authors, and into the prevalent feelings, impressions, and circumstances of the time when it was framed. Without these principles of interpretation, we frankly acknowledge, that we cannot defend the divine authority of the Scriptures. Deny us this latitude, and we must abandon this book to its enemies.[2]

We do not announce these principles as original, or peculiar to ourselves; all Christians occasionally adopt them, not excepting those, who most vehemently decry them, when they happen to menace some favourite article of their creed. All Christians are compelled to use them in their controversies with infidels. All sects employ them in their warfare with one another. All willingly avail themselves of reason, when it can be pressed into the service of their own party, and only complain of it, when its weapons wound themselves. None reason more frequently than our adversaries. It is astonishing what a fabric they rear from a few slight hints about the fall of our first parents; and how ingeniously they extract from detached passages, mysterious doctrines about the divine nature. We do not blame them for reasoning so abundantly, but for violating the fundamental rules of reasoning, for sacrificing the plain to the obscure, and the general strain of Scripture, to a scanty number of insulated texts.

We object strongly to the contemptuous manner in which human reason is often spoken of by our adversaries, because it leads, we believe, to universal skepticism. If reason be so dreadfully darkened by the fall, that its most decisive judgments on religion are unworthy of trust, then Christianity, and even natural theology, must be abandoned; for the existence and veracity of

[2] It is important to notice that both the Unitarians, as in this line, and the Trinitarians or Calvinists insisted on their respective positions as the last stronghold against infidelity. See also the first sentence of the paragraph after the next one. Unitarians were embarrassed when Emerson and others did, in effect, abandon the Bible.

God, and the divine original of Christianity, are conclusions of reason, and must stand or fall with it. If revelation be at war with this faculty, it subverts itself, for the great question of its truth is left by God to be decided at the bar of reason. It is worthy of remark, how nearly the bigot and the skeptic approach. Both would annihilate our confidence in our faculties, and both throw doubt and confusion over every truth. We honor revelation too highly to make it the antagonist of reason, or to believe, that it calls us to renounce our highest powers.

We indeed grant, that the use of reason in religion, is accompanied with danger. But we ask any honest man to look back on the history of the church, and say, whether the renunciation of it be not still more dangerous. Besides, it is a plain fact, that men reason as erroneously on all subjects, as on religion. Who does not know the wild and groundless theories, which have been framed in physical and political science? But who ever supposed, that we must cease to exercise reason on nature and society, because men have erred for ages in explaining them? We grant, that the passions continually, and sometimes fatally, disturb the rational faculty in its inquiries into revelation. The ambitious contrive to find doctrines in the Bible, which favor their love of dominion. The timid and dejected discover there a gloomy system, and the mystical and fanatical, a visionary theology. The vicious can find examples or assertions on which to build the hope of a late repentance, or of acceptance on easy terms; the falsely refined contrive to light on doctrines which have not been soiled by vulgar handling. But the passions do not distract the reason in religious, any more than in other inquiries, which excite strong and general interest; and this faculty, of consequence, is not to be renounced in religion, unless we are prepared to discard it universally. The true inference from the almost endless errors, which have darkened theology, is, not that we are to neglect and disparage our powers, but to exert them more patiently, circumspectly, uprightly. The worst errors, after all, have sprung up in that church, which proscribes reason, and demands from its members implicit faith. The most pernicious doctrines have been the growth of the darkest times, when the general credulity encouraged bad men and enthusiasts to broach their dreams and inventions, and to stifle the faint remonstrances of reason, by the menaces of everlasting perdition. Say what we may, God has given us a rational nature, and will call us to account for it. We may let it sleep, but we do so at our peril. Revelation is addressed to us as rational beings. We may wish, in our sloth, that God had given us a system, demanding no labor of comparing, limiting and inferring. But such a system would be at variance with the whole character of a present existence; and it is the part of wisdom to take revelation, as it is given to us, and to interpret it by the help of the faculties, which it everywhere supposes, and on which it is founded.

To the views now given, an objection is commonly urged from the character of God. We are told, that God, being infinitely wiser than men, His discoveries will surpass human reason. In a revelation from such a teacher, we ought to expect propositions, which we cannot reconcile with one another, and which may seem to contradict established truths; and it becomes us not to question or explain them away, but to believe, and adore, and to submit our weak and carnal reason, to the divine word. To this objection, we have two short answers. We say, first, that it is impossible that a teacher of infinite wisdom, should expose those, whom He would teach, to infinite error. But if once we admit, that propositions, which in their literal sense appear plainly repugnant to one another, or to any known truth, are still to be literally understood and received, what possible limit can we set to the belief of contradictions? What shelter have we from the wildest fanaticism, which can always quote passages, that in their literal and obvious sense, give support to its extravagancies? How can the Protestant escape from transubstantiation,[3] a doctrine most clearly taught us, if the submission of reason, now contended for, be a duty? How can we ever hold fast the truth of revelation, for if one apparent contradiction may be true, so may another, and the proposition, that Christianity is false, through involving inconsistency, may still be a verity.

We answer again, that, if God be infinitely wise, He cannot sport with the understandings of his creatures. A wise teacher discovers his wisdom in adapting himself to the capacities of his pupils, not in perplexing them with what is unintelligible, not in distressing them with the apparent contradiction, not in filling them with a sceptical distrust of their powers. An infinitely wise teacher, who knows the precise extent of our minds, and the best method of enlightening them, will surpass all other instructors in bringing down truth to our apprehension, and in showing its loveliness and harmony. We ought, indeed, to expect occasional obscurity in such a book as the Bible, which was written for past and future ages, as well as for the present. But God's wisdom is a pledge, that whatever is necessary for *us*, and necessary for salvation, is revealed too plainly to be mistaken, and too consistently, to be questioned by a sound and upright mind. It is not the mark of wisdom, to use an unintelligible phraseology, to communicate what is above our capacities, to confuse and unsettle the intellect, by appearances of contradiction. We honor our heavenly Teacher too much to ascribe to Him such a revelation. A revelation is a gift of light. It cannot thicken and multiply our perplexities.

II. Having thus stated the principles according to which we interpret Scriptures, I now proceed to the second great head of this discourse, which

---

[3] It was this doctrine that many Protestants had for centuries insisted as the chief obstacle to a union of Protestant and Roman Catholic churches. Transubstantiation is the doctrine that "the bread and wine of the Eucharist are transformed into the true presence of Christ." Channing taunts orthodox Protestants here by reminding them of Jesus' literal words at the Last Supper: "This is my body. . . .This is my blood." Matthew 26:26-28.

is, to state some of the views, which we derive from that sacred book, particularly those which distinguish us from other Christians.

First. We believe in the doctrine of GOD's UNITY, or that there is one God, and one only. To this truth we give infinite importance, and we feel ourselves bound to take heed, lest any man spoil us of it by vain philosophy. The proposition, *that there is one God,* seems to us exceedingly plain. We understand by it, that there is one being, one mind, one person, one intelligent agent, and one only, to whom underived and infinite perfection and dominion belong. We conceive, that these words could have conveyed no other meaning to the simple and uncultivated people, who were set apart to be the depositaries of this great truth, and who were utterly incapable of understanding those hairbreadth distinctions between *being* and *person,* which the sagacity of latter ages has discovered. We find no intimation, that this language was to be taken in an unusual sense, or that God's unity was a quite different thing from the oneness of other intelligent beings.

We object to the doctrine of the Trinity, that it subverts the unity of God. According to this doctrine, there are three infinite and equal persons, possessing supreme divinity, called the Father, Son, and Holy Ghost. Each of these persons, as described by theologians, has His own particular consciousness, will, and perceptions. They love each other, converse with each other, and delight in each other's society. They perform different parts in man's redemption, each having his appropriate office, and neither doing the work of the other. The Son is mediator, and not the Father. The Father sends the Son, and is not Himself sent; nor is He conscious, like the Son, of taking flesh. Here then, we have three intelligent agents, possessed of different consciousnesses, different wills, and different perceptions, performing different acts, and sustaining different relations; and if these things do not imply and constitute three minds or beings, we are utterly at a loss to know how three minds or beings are to be formed. It is difference of properties, and acts, and consciousness, which leads us to the belief of different intelligent beings, and if this mark fail us, our whole knowledge falls; we have no proof, that all the agents and persons in the universe are not one and the same mind. When we attempt to conceive of three Gods, we can do nothing more, than represent to ourselves three agents, distinguished from each other by similar marks and peculiarities to those, which separate the persons of the Trinity; and when common Christians hear these persons spoken of as conversing with each other, loving each other, and performing different acts, how can they help regarding them as different beings, different minds?

We do then, with all earnestness, though without reproaching our brethren, protest against the unnatural and unscriptural doctrine of the Trinity. "To us," as to the apostle and the primitive Christians, "there is one God, even the Father." With Jesus, we worship the Father, as the only living and true God.[4] We are astonished, that any man can read the New Testament,

---

[4] John, 17.

and avoid the conviction, that the Father alone is God. We hear our Saviour continually appropriating this character to the Father. We find the Father continually distinguished from Jesus by this title. "God sent his Son." "God anointed Jesus." Now, how singular and inexplicable is this phraseology, which fills the New Testament, if this title belong equally to Jesus, and if a principal object of this book is to reveal Him as God, as partaking equally with the Father in supreme divinity. We challenge our opponents to adduce one passage in the New Testament, where the word God means three persons, where it is not limited to one person, and where, unless turned from its usual sense by the connexion, it does not mean the Father. Can stronger proof be given, that the doctrine of three persons in the Godhead, is not a fundamental doctrine of Christianity?

This doctrine, were it true, must, from its difficulty, singularity, and importance, have been laid down with great clearness, guarded with great care, and stated with all possible precision. But where does this statement appear? From the many passages, which treat of God, we ask for one, one only, in which we are told, that He is a threefold being, or, that He is three persons, or, that He is Father, Son, and Holy Ghost. On the contrary, in the New Testament, where, at least, we might expect many express assertions of this nature, God is declared to be one, without the least attempt to prevent the acceptation of the words in their common sense; and He is always spoken of and addressed in the singular number, that is, in language which was universally understood to intend a single person, and to which no other idea could have been attached, without an express admonition. So entirely do the Scriptures abstain from stating the Trinity, that when our opponents would insert it into their creeds and doxologies, they are compelled to leave the Bible, and to invent forms of words altogether unsanctioned by scriptural phraseology. That a doctrine so strange, so liable to misapprehension, so fundamental as this is said to be, and requiring such careful exposition, should be left so undefined and unprotected, to be made out by inference, and to be hunted through distant and detached parts of Scripture, this is a difficulty, which, we think, no ingenuity can explain.

We have another difficulty. Christianity, it must be remembered, was planted and grew up amidst sharp-sighted enemies, who overlooked no objectionable part of the system, and who must have fastened with great earnestness on a doctrine involving such apparent contradictions as the Trinity. We cannot conceive an opinion against which, the Jews, who prided themselves on their adherence to God's unity, would have raised an equal clamour. Now, how happens it, that in the apostolic writings, which relate so much to objections against Christianity, and to the controversies, which grew out of this religion, not *one word* is said, implying that objections were brought against the gospel from the doctrine of the Trinity, not one word is uttered in its defense and explanation, not a word to rescue it from reproach and mistake? This argument has almost the force of demonstration. We are persuaded, that had three divine persons been announced by the first preachers of Christianity, all equal, and all infinite, one of whom was the very Jesus, who had lately died on a cross, this peculiarity of Christianity would have almost absorbed every other, and the great labor of the apostles would have been to repel the continual assaults, which it would have awakened. But the fact is, that not a whisper of objection to Christianity, on that account, reaches our ears from the apostolic age. In the epistles we see not a trace of controversy called forth by the Trinity.

We have further objections to this doctrine, drawn from its practical influence. We regard it as unfavorable to devotion, by dividing and distracting the mind in its communion with God. It is a great excellence of the doctrine of God's unity, that it offers to US ONE OBJECT of supreme homage, adoration and love, one infinite Father, one Being of Beings. one original and fountain, to whom we may refer all good, on whom all our powers and affections may be concentrated, and whose lovely and venerable nature may pervade all our thoughts. True piety, when directed to an undivided Deity, has a chasteness, a singleness, most favorable to religious awe, and love. Now the Trinity sets before us three distinct objects of supreme adoration; three infinite persons, having equal claims on our hearts; three divine agents, performing different offices, and to be acknowledged and worshipped in different relations. And is it possible, we ask, that the weak and limited mind of man can attach itself to these with the same power and joy, as to *one infinite Father*, the only First Cause, in whom all the blessings of nature and redemption meet, as their center and source? Must not devotion be distracted by the equal and rival claims of three equal persons, and must not the worship of the conscientious, consistent Christian be disturbed by apprehension, lest he withhold from one or another of these, his due proportion of homage?

We also think, that the doctrine of the Trinity injures devotion, not only by joining to the Father other objects of worship, but by taking from the Father the supreme affection, which is his due, and transferring it to the Son. This is a most important view. That Jesus Christ, if exalted into the infinite Divinity, should be more interesting than the Father, is precisely what might be expected from history, and from the principles of human nature. Men want an object of worship like themselves, and the great secret of idolatry lies in this propensity. A God, clothed in our form, and feeling our wants and sorrows, speaks to our weak nature more strongly, than a Father in heaven, a pure spirit, invisible, and unapproachable, save by the reflecting and purified mind.—We think too, that the peculiar offices ascribed to Jesus by the popular theology, make Him the most attractive person in the Godhead. The Father is the depositary of the justice, the vindicator of the rights, the avenger of the laws of the Divinity. On the other hand, the Son, the brightness of the divine mercy, stands between the incensed Deity and guilty humanity, exposes His meek head to the storms, and His compassionate breast to the sword of the divine justice, bears our whole load of punishment, and purchases, with His blood, every blessing which descends from heaven. Need we state the effect of these representations, especially on common minds, for whom Christianity was chiefly designed, and whom it seeks to bring to the Father, as the loveliest being? We do believe, that the worship of a bleeding, suffering God, tends strongly to absorb the mind, and to draw it from other objects, just as the human tenderness of the Virgin Mary has given her so conspicuous a place in the devotions of the church of Rome. We believe too, that this worship, though attractive, is not most fitted to spiritualize the mind, that it awakens human transport, rather than that deep veneration of the moral perfections of God, which is the essence of piety.

Secondly. Having thus given our views of the unity of God, I proceed to observe, that we believe in the *unity of Jesus Christ.* We believe that Jesus is one mind, one soul, one being, as truly one as we are, and equally distinct from the one God. We complain of the doctrine of the Trinity, that not satisfied with making God three beings, it makes Jesus Christ two beings, and thus introduces infinite confusion into our conceptions of His character. This corruption of Christianity, alike repugnant to common sense, and to the general strain of Scripture, is a remarkable proof of the power of a false philosophy in disfiguring the simple truth of Jesus.

According to this doctrine, Jesus Christ, instead of being one mind, one conscious intelligent principle, whom we can understand, consists of two souls, two minds, the one divine, the other human; the one weak, the other almighty; the one ignorant, the other omniscient. Now we maintain, that this is to make Christ two beings. To denominate Him one person, one being, and yet to suppose him made up of two minds, infinitely different from each other, is to abuse and confound language, and to throw darkness over all our conceptions of intelligent natures. According to the common doctrines, each of these two minds in Christ has its own consciousness, its own will, its own perceptions. They have in fact no common properties. The divine mind feels none of the wants and sorrows of the human, and the human is infinitely removed from the perfection and happiness of the divine. Can you conceive of two beings in the universe more distinct? We have always thought that one person was constituted and distinguished by one consciousness. The doctrine, that one and the same person should have two consciousnesses, two wills, two souls infinitely different from each other, this we think an enormous tax on human credulity.

We say, that if a doctrine, so strange, so difficult, so remote from all the previous conceptions of men, be indeed a part, and an essential part of revelation, it must be taught with great distinctness, and we ask our brethren to point to some plain, direct passage, where Christ is said to be composed of two minds infinitely different, yet constituting one person. We find none. Our opponents, indeed, tell us, that this doctrine is necessary to the harmony of the Scriptures, that some texts ascribe to Jesus Christ human, and others divine properties, and that to reconcile these, we must suppose two minds, to which these properties may be referred. In other words, for the purpose of reconciling certain difficult passages, which a just criticism can in a great degree, if not wholly, explain, we must invent an hypothesis vastly more difficult, and involving gross absurdity. We are to find our way out of a labyrinth by a clue, which conducts us into mazes infinitely more inextricable.

Surely if Jesus Christ felt that He consisted of two minds, and that this was a leading feature of His religion, His phraseology respecting himself would have been colored by this peculiarity. The universal language of men is framed upon the idea, that one person is mind, and one soul; and when the multitude heard this language from the lips of Jesus, they must have taken it in its usual sense, and must have referred to a single soul, all which he spoke, unless expressly instructed to interpret it differently. But where do we find this instruction? Where do you meet, in the New Testament, the phraseology which abounds in Trinitarian books, and which necessarily grew from the doctrine of two natures in Jesus. Where does this divine teacher say, This I speak as God, and this as man; this is true only of my human mind, this only of my divine? Where do we find in the epistles a trace of this strange phraseology? Nowhere. It was not needed in that day. It was demanded by the errors of a later age.

We believe then, that Christ's is one mind, one being, and I add, a being distinct from the one God. That Christ is not the one God, not the same being with the Father, is a necessary inference from our former head, in which we saw that the doctrine of three persons in God is a fiction. But on so important a subject, I would add a few remarks. We wish, that our opponents would weigh one striking fact. Jesus, in His preaching, continually spoke of God. The word was always in His mouth. We ask, does He, by this word, ever mean himself? We say, *never*. On the contrary, He most plainly distinguishes between God and himself, and so do his disciples, How this is to be reconciled with the idea, that the manifestation of Christ, as God, was a primary object of Christianity, our adversaries must determine.

If we examine the passages in which Jesus is distinguished from God, we shall see, that they not only speak of him as another being, but seem to labor to express His inferiority. He is continually spoken of as the Son of God, sent of God, receiving all His powers from God, working miracles because God was with Him, judging justly because God taught Him, having claims on our belief, because He was anointed and sealed by God, and as able of Himself to do nothing. The New Testament is *filled* with this language. Now we ask, what impression this language was fitted and intended to make? Could any, who heard it, have imagined, that Jesus was the *very God*, to whom He was so industriously declared to be inferior, the *very being*, by whom He was sent, and from whom He professed to have received his message and power?

Let it here be remembered, that the human birth, and bodily form, and humble circumstances, and mortal sufferings of Jesus, must all have prepared men to interpret, in the most unqualified manner, the language in which His inferiority to God was declared. Why then was this language used so continually, and without limitation, if Jesus were the Supreme Deity, and if this truth were an essential part of His religion? I repeat it, the human condition and sufferings of Christ, tended strongly to exclude from men's minds the idea of His proper Godhead; and of course, we should expect to find in the New Testament perpetual care and effort to counteract this tendency, to hold Him forth as the same being with His Father, if this doctrine were, as is pretended, the soul and center of his religion. We should expect to find the phraseology of Scripture cast into the mold of this doctrine, to hear familiarly of God the Son, of our Lord God Jesus, and to be told, that to us there is one God, even Jesus. But instead of this, the inferiority of Christ pervades the New Testatment. It is not only implied in the general phraseology, but repeatedly and decidedly expressed, and unaccompanied with any admonition to prevent its application of His whole nature. Could it then have been the great design of the sacred writers, to exhibit Jesus as the Supreme God?

I am aware, that these remarks will be met by two or three texts, in which Christ is called God, and by a class of passages, not very numerous, in which divine properties are said to be ascribed to Him. To these we offer one plain answer. We say, that it is one of the most established and obvious principles of criticism, that language is to be explained according to the known properties of the subject to which it is applied. Every man knows, that the same words convey very different ideas, when used in relation to different beings. Thus, Solomon *built* the temple in a different manner from the architect, whom he employed; and God *repents* differently from man. Now, we maintain, that the known properties and circumstances of Christ, His birth, sufferings, and death, His constant habit of speaking of God as a distinct being from Himself, His praying to God, His ascribing to God all His power and offices, these acknowledged properties of Christ, we say, oblige us to interpret the comparatively few passages, which are thought to make him the supreme God, in a manner consistent with His distinct and inferior nature. It is our duty to explain such texts by the rule, which we apply to other texts, in which human beings are called Gods, and are said to be partakers of the divine nature, to know and possess all things, and to be filled with all God's fulness. These latter passages we do not hesitate to modify, and restrain, and turn from the most obvious sense, because this sense is opposed to the known properties of the beings to whom they relate; and we maintain, that we adhere to the same principle, and use no greater latitude in explaining, as we do, the passages which are thought to support the Godhead of Christ.

Trinitarians profess to derive some important advantages from their mode of viewing Christ. It furnishes them, they tell us, with an infinite atonement, for it shows them an infinite being, suffering for their sins. The confidence with which this fallacy is repeated astonishes us. When pressed with the question, whether they really believe, that the infinite and unchangeable God suffered and died on the cross, they acknowledge that this is not true, but that Christ's human mind alone sustained the pains of death. How have we then an infinite sufferer? This language seems to us an imposition on common minds, and very derogatory to God's justice, as if this attribute could be satisfied by a sophism and a fiction.

We are also told, that Christ is a more interesting object, that His love and mercy are more felt, when He is received as the Supreme God, who left His glory to take humanity and to suffer for men. That Trinitarians are strongly moved by this representation, we do not mean to deny, but we think their emotions altogether founded on a misapprehension of their own doctrines. They talk of the second person of the Trinity leaving His glory, and His Father's bosom, to visit and save the world. But this second person, being the unchangeable and infinite God, was evidently incapable of parting with the least degree of His perfection and felicity. At the moment of His taking flesh, He was as intimately present with His Father as before, and equally with His Father filled heaven, and earth, and immensity. This, Trinitarians acknowledge, and still they profess to be touched and overwhelmed by the amazing humiliation of this immutable being!——But not only does their doctrine, when fully explained, reduce Christ's humiliation to a fiction, it almost wholly destroys the impressions with which His cross ought to be received. According to their doctrine, Christ was, comparatively, no sufferer at all. It is true, His human mind suffered; but this, they tell us, was an infinitely small part of Jesus, bearing no more proportion to His whole nature, than a single hair of our heads to the whole body; or, than a drop to the ocean. The divine mind of Christ, that which was most properly Himself, was infinitely happy, at the very moment of the suffering of His humanity. Whilst hanging on the cross, he was the happiest being in the universe, as happy as the infinite Father; so that, his pains, compared with his felicity, were nothing. This, Trinitarians do, and must acknowledge. It follows necessarily, from the immutableness of the divine nature, which they ascribe to Christ; so that their system, justly viewed, robs His death of interest, weakens our sympathy with His sufferings, and is, of all others, most unfavorable to a love of Christ, founded on a sense of his sacrifices for mankind. We esteem our own views to be vastly more affecting, especially those of us, who believe in Christ's pre-existence.[5] It is our belief, that Christ's humiliation, was real and entire, that the whole Saviour, and not a part of Him, suffered, that His crucifixion was a scene of deep and unmixed agony. As we stand round His cross, our minds are not distracted, or our sensibility weakened,

[5] As he explains below, Channing does not claim that all Unitarians agree on all doctrines concerning Jesus.

by contemplating Him as composed of incongruous and infinitely differing minds, and as having a balance of infinite felicity. We recognize, in the dying Jesus, but one mind. This, we think, renders His sufferings, and His patience and love in bearing them, incomparably more impressive and affecting, than the system we oppose.

Thirdly. Having thus given our belief on two great points, namely, that there is one God, and that Jesus Christ is a being distinct from, and inferior to God, I now proceed to another point on which we lay still greater stress. We believe in the *moral perfection of God.* We consider no part of theology so important as that which treats of God's moral character; and we value our views of Christianity chiefly, as they assert His amiable, and venerable attributes.

It may be said, that in regard to this subject, all Christians agree, that all ascribe to the Supreme Being, infinite justice, goodness, and holiness. We reply, that it is very possible to speak of God magnificently, and to think of Him meanly; to apply to His person high-sounding epithets, and to His government, principles which make Him odious. The heathens called Jupiter the greatest and the best; but his history was black with cruelty and lust. We cannot judge of men's real ideas of God, by their general language, for in all ages, they have hoped to soothe the Deity by adulation. We must inquire into their particular views of His purposes, of the principles of His administration, and of His disposition towards his creatures.

We conceive that Christians have generally leaned towards a very injurious view of the Supreme Being. They have too often felt, as if he were raised, by His greatness and sovereignty, above the principles of morality, above those eternal laws of equity and rectitude, to which all other beings are subjected. *We* believe, that in no being, is the sense of right so strong, so omnipotent, as in God. We believe that His almighty power is entirely submitted to His perception of rectitude; and this is the ground of our piety. It is not because He is our Creator merely, but because He created us for good and holy purposes; it is not because His will is irresistible, but because His will is the perfection of virtue, that we pay Him allegiance. We cannot bow before a being, however great and powerful, who governs tyrannically. We respect nothing but excellence, whether on earth, or in heaven. We venerate not the loftiness of God's throne, but the equity and goodness in which it is established.

We believe that God is infinitely good, kind, benevolent, in the proper sense of these words; good in disposition, as well as in act; good not to a few, but to all; good to every individual, as well as to the general system.

We believe too, that God is just; but we never forget, that His justice is the justice of a good being, dwelling in the same mind, and acting in harmony with perfect benevolence. By this attribute we understand God's infinite regard to virtue, or moral worth, expressed in a moral government; that is, in giving excellent and equitable laws, and in conferring such rewards, and inflicting such punishments, as are most fitted to secure their observance. God's justice has for its end the highest virtue of the creation, and it punishes for this end alone, and thus it coincides with benevolence; for virtue and happiness, though not the same, are inseparably conjoined.

God's justice thus viewed, appears to us to be in perfect harmony with His mercy. According to the prevalent systems of theology, these attributes are so discordant and jarring, that to reconcile them is the hardest task, and the most wonderful achievement of infinite wisdom. To *us* they seem to be intimate friends, always at peace, breathing the same spirit, and seeking the same end. By God's mercy, we understand not a blind instinctive compassion, which forgives without reflection, and without regard to the interests of virtue. *This*, we acknowledge, would be incompatible with justice, and also with enlightened benevolence. God's mercy, as we understand it, desires strongly the happiness of the guilty, but only through their penitence. It has a regard to character as truly as His justice. It defers punishment, and suffers long, that the sinner may return to his duty, but leaves the impenitent and unyielding, to the fearful retribution threatened in God's word.

To give our views of God, in one word, we believe in His *parental character*. We ascribe to Him, not only the name, but the dispositions and principles of a father. We believe that He has a father's concern for His creatures, a father's desire for their improvement, a father's equity in proportioning His commands to their powers, a father's joy in their progress, a father's readiness to receive the penitent, and a father's justice for the incorrigible. We look upon this world as a place of education, in which He is training men by mercies and sufferings, by aids and temptations, by means and opportunities of various virtues, by trials of principle, by the conflicts of reason and passion, by a discipline suited to free and moral beings, for union with himself, and for a sublime and ever growing virtue in heaven.

Now we object to the systems of religion, which prevail among us, that they are adverse, in a greater or less degree, to these purifying, comforting, and honorable views of God, that they take from us our Father in heaven, and substitute for Him a being, whom we cannot love if we would, and whom we ought not to love if we could.[6] We object, particularly on this ground, to that system, which arrogates to itself the name of orthodoxy, and which is now most industriously propagated through our country. This system teaches, that God brings us into existence wholly depraved, so that under the innocent features of our childhood, is hidden a nature averse to all good, and propense to all evil; and it teaches that God regards us with displeasure before we have acquired power to understand our duties, or reflect upon our actions. Now if there be one plain principle of morality, it is this, that we are accountable beings, only because we have consciences, a

[6] This is the main principle of Channing's later sermon, "The Moral Argument against Calvinism." Compare the sermons of Shep- ard and Edwards, above, pp. 94-128; 310-357.

power of knowing and performing our duty, and that in as far as we want this power, we are incapable of sin, guilt, or blame. We should call a parent a monster, who should judge and treat his children in opposition to this principle, and yet this enormous immorality is charged on our Father in Heaven.
310-357.

This system, also, teaches, that God selects from the corrupt mass of men a number to be saved, and that they are plucked, by an irresistible agency, from the common ruin, whilst the rest are commanded, under penalty of aggravated woe, to make a change in their characters, which their natural corruption places beyond their power, and are also promised pardon on conditions, which necessarily avail them nothing, unless they are favored with a special operation of God's grace, which He is predetermined to withhold. This mockery of mercy, this insult offered to the misery of the non-elect, by hollow proffers of forgiveness, completes the dreadful system which is continually obtruded upon us as the gospel, and which strives to monopolize the reputation of sanctity.

That this religious system does not produce all the effects on character, which might be anticipated, we most joyfully admit. It is often, very often, counteracted by nature, conscience, common sense, by the general strain of Scripture, by the mild example and precepts of Christ, and by the many positive declarations of God's universal kindness, and perfect equity. But still we think that we see occasionally its unhappy influence. It discourages the timid, gives excuses to the bad, feeds the vanity of the fanatical, and offers shelter to the bad feelings of the malignant. By shocking, as it does the fundamental principles of morality, and by exhibiting a severe and partial Deity, it tends strongly to pervert the moral faculty, to form a gloomy, fobidding, and servile religion, and to lead men to substitute censoriousness, bitterness, and persecution, for a tender and impartial charity. We think too, that this system, which begins with degrading human nature, may be expected to end in pride; for pride grows out of a consciousness of high distinctions, however obtained, and no distinction is so great as that, which is made between the elected and abandoned of God.

The false and dishonorable views of God, which have now been stated, we feel ourselves bound to resist unceasingly. Other errors we can pass over with comparative indifference. But we ask our opponents to leave to us a GOD, worthy of our love and trust, in whom our moral sentiments may delight, in whom our weaknesses and sorrows may find refuge. We cling to the divine perfections. We meet them everywhere in creation, we read them in the Scriptures, we see a lovely image of them in Jesus Christ; and gratitude, love and veneration call on us to assert them. Reproached, as we often are, by men, it is our consolation and happiness, that one of our chief offenses is the zeal with which we vindicate the dishonored goodness and rectitude of God.

Fourthly. Having thus spoken of the unity of God; of the unity of Jesus, and his inferiority to God; and of the perfections of the divine character; I now proceed to give our views of the *mediation of Christ* and *of the purposes of His mission.* With regard to the great object, which Jesus came to accomplish, there seems to be no possibility of mistake. We believe, that He was sent by the Father to effect a moral, or spiritual deliverance of mankind; that is, to rescue men from sin and its consequences, and to bring them to a state of everlasting purity and happiness. We believe, too, that He accomplishes this sublime purpose by a variety of methods; by His instructions respecting God's unity, parental character, and moral government, which are admirably fitted to reclaim the world from idolatry, and impiety, to the knowledge, love, and obedience of the Creator; by His promises of pardon to the penitent, and of divine assistance to those, who labor for progress in moral excellence; by the light which He has thrown on the path of duty; by His own spotless example, in which the loveliness and sublimity of virtue shine forth to warm and quicken, as well as guide us to perfection; by His threatenings against incorrigible guilt; by His glorious discoveries of immortality; by His sufferings and death; by that signal event, the resurrection, which powerfully bore witness to His divine mission, and brought down to men's senses a future life; by His continual intercession, which obtains for us spiritual aid and blessings; and by the power with which He is invested of raising the dead, judging the world, and conferring the everlasting rewards, promised to the faithful.

We have no desire to conceal the fact, that a difference of opinion exists among us, in regard to an interesting part of Christ's mediation; I mean, in regard to the precise influence of His death, on our forgiveness. Some suppose, that this event contributes to our pardon, as it was a principal means of confirming His religion, and of giving it a power over the mind; in other words, that it procures forgiveness by leading to that repentance and virtue, which is the great and only condition on which forgiveness is bestowed. Many of us are dissatisfied with this explanation, and think that the Scriptures ascribe the remission of sins to Christ's death, with an emphasis so peculiar, that we ought to consider this event as having a special influence in removing punishment, as a condition or method of pardon, without which, repentance would not avail us, at least to that extent, which is now promised by the gospel.

Whilst, however, we differ in explaining the connection between Christ's death and human forgiveness, a connection, which we all gratefully acknowledge, we agree in rejecting many sentiments, which prevail in regard to His mediation. The idea, which is conveyed to common minds by the popular system, that Christ's death has an influence in making God placable or merciful, in quenching His wrath, in awakening His kindness towards men, we reject with horror. We believe, that Jesus, instead of making the Father merciful, is sent by the Father's mercy to be our Saviour; that He is nothing to the human race, but what He is by God's appointment; that He communicates nothing but what God empowers Him to bestow; that our Father in heaven is originally, essentially and eternally placable, and disposed to forgive; and that His unborrowed, underived, and unchangeable love, is the only fountain of what flows to us through His Son. We conceive, that Jesus is dishonored, not glorified, by ascribing to Him an influence, which clouds the splendor of divine benevolence.

We farther agree in rejecting as unscriptural and absurd, the explanation given by the popular system, of the manner in which Christ's death procures forgiveness for men. This system teaches, that man having sinned against an infinite being, is infinitely guilty, and some even say, that a single transgression, though committed in our early and inconsiderate years, merits the eternal pains of hell.[7] Thus, an infinite penalty is due from every human being; and God's justice insists, that it shall be borne either by the offender, or a substitute. Now, from the nature of the case, no substitute is adequate to the work of sustaining the full punishment of a guilty world, save the infinite God himself; and accordingly, God took on Him human nature, that He might pay to his own justice the debt of punishment incurred by men, and might enable Himself to exercise mercy. Such is the prevalent system. Now, to us, this doctrine seems to carry on its front, strong marks of absurdity, and we maintain that Christianity ought not to be encumbered with it, unless it be laid down in the New Testament fully and expressly. We ask our adversaries, then, to point to some plain passages where it is taught. We ask for one text, in which we are told that God took human nature, that He might appease His own anger towards men, or make an infinite satisfaction to his own justice;—for one text, which tells us, that human guilt is infinite, and requires a correspondent substitute; that Christ's sufferings owe their efficacy to their being borne by an infinite being; or that His divine nature gives infinite value to the sufferings of the human. Not one word of this description can we find in the Scriptures; not a text, which even hints at these strange doctrines. They are altogether, we believe, the fictions of theologians. Christianity is in no degree responsible for them. We are astonished at their prevalence. What can be plainer, than that God cannot, in any sense, be a sufferer, or bear a penalty in the room of His creatures? How dishonorable to Him is the supposition, that His justice is now so severe as to exact infinite punishment for the sins of frail and feeble men, and now so easy and yielding as to accept the limited pains of Christ's human soul, as a full equivalent for the infinite and endless woes due from the world? How plain is it also, according to this doctrine, that God, instead of being plenteous in forgiveness, never forgives; for it is absurd to speak of men as forgiven, when their whole punishment is borne by a substitute. A scheme more fitted to bring

[7] See Edwards's "The Justice of God in the Damnation of Sinners." above, p. 334.

Christianity into contempt, and less suited to give comfort to a guilty and troubled mind, could not, we think, be easily invented.

We believe too, that this system is unfavorable to the character. It naturally leads men to think, that Christ came to change God's mind, rather than their own, that the highest object of His mission, was to avert punishment, rather than to communicate holiness, and that a large part of religion consists in disparaging good works and human virtue, for the purpose of magnifying the value of Christ's vicarious sufferings. In this way, a sense of the infinite importance, and indispensable necessity of personal improvement is weakened, and high sounding praises of Christ's cross, seem often to be substituted for obedience to his precepts. For ourselves, we have not so learned Jesus. Whilst we gratefully acknowledge, that He came to rescue us from punishment, we believe, that He was sent on a still nobler errand, namely, to deliver us from sin itself, and to form us to a sublime and heavenly virtue. We regard Him as a Saviour, chiefly as He is the light, physician, and guide of the dark, diseased, and wandering mind. No influence in the universe seems to us so glorious, as that over the character; and no redemption so worthy of thankfulness, as the restoration of the soul to purity. Without this, pardon, were it possible, would be of little value. Why pluck the sinner from hell, if a hell be left to burn in his own breast? Why raise him to heaven, if he remain a stranger to its sanctity and love? With these impressions, we are accustomed to value the gospel, chiefly, as it abounds in effectual aids, motives, excitements to a generous and divine virtue. In this virtue, as in a common centre, we see all its doctrines, precepts, promises meet, and we believe, that faith in this religion, is of no worth, and contributes nothing to salvation, any farther than as it uses these doctrines, precepts, promises, and the whole life, character, sufferings, and triumphs of Jesus, as the means of purifying the mind, of changing it into the likeness of his celestial excellence.

Fifthly. Having thus stated our views of the highest object of Christ's mission, that it is the recovery of men to virtue, or holiness, I shall now, in the last place, give our views of the *nature of Christian virtue,* or *true holiness.* We believe that all virtue has its foundation in the moral nature of man, that is, in conscience, or his sense of duty, and in the power of forming his temper and life according to conscience. We believe that these moral faculties are the grounds of responsibility, and the highest distinctions of human nature, and that no act is praiseworthy, any farther than it springs from their exertion. We believe, that no dispensations infused into us without our own moral activity, are of the nature of virtue, and therefore, we reject the doctrine of irresistible divine influence on the human mind, molding it into goodness, as marble is hewn into a statue. Such goodness, if this word may be used, would not be the object of moral approbation, any more than the instinctive affections of inferior animals, or the constitutional amiableness of human beings.

By these remarks, we do not mean to deny the importance of God's aid or Spirit; but by His Spirit, we mean a moral, illuminating and persuasive influence, not physical, not compulsory, not involving a necessity of virtue. We object, strongly, to the idea of many Christians respecting man's impotence and God's irresistible agency on the heart,[8] believing that they subvert our responsibility and the laws of our moral nature, that they make men machines, that they cast on God the blame of all evil deeds, that they discourage good minds, and inflate the fanatical with wild conceits of immediate and sensible inspiration.

Among the virtues, we give the first place to the *love of God*. We believe, that this principle is the true end and happiness of our being, that we were made for union with our Creator, that His infinite perfection is the only sufficient object and true resting place for the insatiable desires and unlimited capacities of the human mind, and that without Him, our noblest sentiments, admiration, veneration, hope, and love, would wither and decay. We believe too, that the love of God is not only essential to happiness, but to the strength and perfection of all the virtues; that conscience, without the sanction of God's authority and retributive justice, would be a weak director; that benevolence, unless nourished by communion with His goodness, and encouraged by His smile, could not thrive amidst the selfishness and thanklessness of the world; and that self-government, without a sense of the divine inspection, would hardly extend beyond an outward and partial purity. God, as He is essentially goodness, holiness, justice, and virtue, so He is the life, motive, and sustainer of virtue in the human soul.

But whilst we earnestly inculcate the love of God, we believe that great care is necessary to distinguish it from counterfeits. We think that much, which is called piety, is worthless.[9] Many have fallen into the error, that there can be no excess in feelings, which have God for their object; and, distrusting as coldness, that self-possession, without which virtue and devotion lose all their dignity, they have abandoned themselves to extravagancies, which have brought contempt on piety. Most certainly, if the love of God be that, which often bears its name, the less we have of it, the better. If religion be the shipwreck of understanding, we cannot keep too far from it. On this subject, we always speak plainly. We cannot sacrifice our reason to the reputation of zeal. We owe it to truth and religion, to maintain, that fanaticism, partial insanity, sudden impressions, and ungovernable transports, are anything, rather than piety.

---

[8] Compare Edward's "A Divine and Supernatural Light," above, p. 314, and Emerson's Divinity School Address, below, pp. 1588-1602. "Faith makes us, and not we it."

[9] The following lines resemble these objections of Charles Chauncy to enthusiasm, above, pp. 378-389.

We conceive, that the true love of God, is a moral sentiment, founded on a clear perception, and consisting in a high esteem and veneration of his moral perfections. Thus, it perfectly coincides, and is in fact the same thing with the love of virtue, rectitude, and goodness. You will easily judge then, what we esteem the surest and only decisive signs of piety. We lay no stress on strong excitements. We esteem *him*, and *him only* a pious man, who practically conforms to God's moral perfection and government, who shows his delight in God's benevolence, by loving and serving his neighbor; his delight in God's justice, by being resolutely upright; his sense of God's purity, by regulating his thoughts, imagination, and desires; and whose conversation, business, and domestic life are swayed by a regard to God's presence and authority. In all things else men may deceive themselves. Disordered nerves may give them strange sights, and sounds, and impressions. Texts of Scripture may come to them as from Heaven. Their whole souls may be moved, and their confidence in God's favor be undoubting. But in all this there is no religion. The question is, do they love God's commands, in which His character is fully displayed, and give up to these their habits and passions. Without this, ecstasy is a mockery. One surrender of desire to God's will, is worth a thousand transports. We do not judge of the bent of men's minds by their raptures, any more than we judge of the direction of a tree during a storm. We rather suspect loud profession, for we have observed, that deep feeling is generally noiseless, and least seeks display.

We would not, by these remarks, be understood as wishing to exclude from religion warmth, and even transport. We honor, and highly value true religious sensibility. We believe, that Christianity is intended to act powerfully on our whole nature, on the heart, as well as the understanding and the conscience. We conceive of heaven as a state, where the love of God will be exalted into an unbounded fervor and joy; and we desire, in our pilgrimage here, to drink into the spirit of that better world. But we think, that religious warmth is only to be valued, when it springs naturally from an improved character, when it comes unforced, when it is the recompense of obedience, when it is the warmth of a mind, which understands God by being like Him, and when, instead of disordering, it exalts the understanding, invigorates conscience, gives a pleasure to common duties, and is seen to exist in connection with cheerfulness, judiciousness, and a reasonable frame of mind. When we observe a fervor, called religious, in men whose general character expresses little refinement and elevation, and whose piety seems at war with reason, we pay it little respect. We honor religion too much to give its sacred name to a feverish, forced, fluctuating zeal, which has litte power over the life.

Another important branch of virtue, we believe to be love to Christ. The greatness of the work of Jesus, the spirit with which He executed it, and the sufferings which He bore for our salvation, we feel to be strong claims on our gratitude and veneration. We see in nature no beauty to be compared with the loveliness of His character, nor do we find on earth a benefactor, to whom we owe an equal debt. We read His history with delight, and learn from it the perfection of our nature. We are particularly touched by his death, which was endured for our redemption, and by that strength of charity, which triumphed over His pains. His resurrection is the foundation of our hope of immortality. His intercession gives us boldness to draw nigh to the throne of grace, and we look up to heaven with new desire, when we think, that if we follow Him here, we shall there see His benignant countenance, and enjoy His friendship forever.

I need not express to you our views on the subject of the *benevolent virtues*. We attach such importance to these, that we are sometimes reproached with exalting them above piety. We regard the spirit of love, charity, meekness, forgiveness, liberality, and beneficence, as the badge and distinction of Christians, as the brightest image we can bear of God, as the best proof of piety. On this subject, I need not, and cannot enlarge, but there is one branch of benevolence, which I ought not to pass over in silence, because we think that we conceive of it more highly and justly, that many of our brethren. I refer to the duty of candor, charitable judgment, expecially towards those who differ in religious opinion. We think, that in nothing have Christians so widely departed from their religion, as in this particular. We read with astonishment and horror, the history of the church, and sometimes when we look back on the fires of persecution, and the zeal of Christians building up walls of separation, and in giving up one another to perdition, we feel as if we were reading the records of an infernal, rather than a heavenly kingdom. An enemy to every religion, if asked to describe a Christian, would, with some show of reason, depict him as an idolater of his own distinguishing opinions, covered with badges of party, shutting his eyes on the virtues, and his ears on the arguments of his opponents, arrogating all excellence to his own sect, and all saving power to his own creed, sheltering under the name of pious zeal, the love of domination, the conceit of infallibility, and the spirit of intolerance, and trampling on men's rights under the pretense of saving their souls.

We can hardly conceive of a plainer obligation on beings of our frail and fallible nature, who are instructed in the duty of candid judgment, than to abstain from condemning men of apparent conscientiousness and sincerity, who are chargeable with no crime but that of differing from us in the interpretation of the Scriptures, and differing too, on topics of great and acknowledged obscurity. We are astonished at the hardihood of those, who, with Christ's warnings sounding in their ears, take on them the responsibility of making creeds for his church, and cast out professors of virtuous lives for imagined errors, for the guilt of thinking for themselves. We know that zeal for truth, is the cover for this usurpation of Christ's prerogative; but we think that zeal for truth, as it is called, is very suspicious, except in men, whose capacities and advantages, whose patient deliberations and whose improvements in humility, mildness, and candor, give them a right to hope that their views are more just, than those of their neighbors. Much of what passes for truth, we look upon with little respect, for it often appears to thrive most luxuriantly where other virtues shoot up thinly and feebly; and we have no gratitude for those reformers, who would force upon us a doctrine, which has not sweetened their own tempers, or made them better men than their neighbors.

We are accustomed to think much of the difficulties attending religious inquiries; difficulties springing from the slow development of our minds, from the power of early impressions, from the state of society, from human authority, from the general neglect of the reasoning powers, from the want of just principles of criticism, and of important helps in interpreting Scripture, and from various other causes. We find, that on no subject have men, and even good men, engrafted so many strange conceits, wild theories, and fictions of fancy, as on religion, and remembering, as we do, that we ourselves are sharers of the common frailty, we dare not assume infallibility in the treatment of our fellow Christians, or encourage in common Christians, who have little time for investigation, the habit of denouncing and condemning other denominations, perhaps more enlightened and virtuous than their own. Charity, forbearance, a delight in the virtues of different sects, a backwardness to censure and condemn, these are virtues, which, however poorly practised by us, we admire and recommend, and we would rather join ourselves to the church in which they abound than to any other communion, however elated with the belief of its own orthodoxy, however strict in guarding its creed, however burning with zeal against imagined error.

I have thus given the distinguishing views of those Christians in whose names I have spoken. We have embraced this sytem, not hastily or lightly, but after much deliberation, and we hold it fast, not merely because we believe it to be true, but because we regard it as purifying truth, as a doctrine according to godliness, as able to "work mightily" and to "bring forth fruit" in them who believe. That we wish to spread it, we have no desire to conceal; but we think, that we wish its diffusion, because we regard it as more friendly to practical piety and pure morals, than the opposite doctrines, because it gives clearer and nobler views of duty, and stronger motives to its perfomance, because it recommends religion at once to the understanding and heart, because it asserts the lovely and venerable attributes of God, because it tends to restore the benevolent spirit of Jesus to His divided and afflicted church, and because it cuts off every hope of God's favor, except that which springs from practical uniformity to the life and precepts of Christ. We see nothing in our views to give offense, save their purity, and it is their purity, which makes us seek and hope their extension through the world.

I now turn to the usual addresses of the day.

My friend and brother;—You are this day to take upon you important duties, to be clothed with an office, which the Son of God did not disdain; to devote yourself to that religion, which the most hallowed lips have preached, and the most precious blood sealed. We trust that you will bring to this work a willing mind, a firm purpose, a martyr's spirit, a readiness to toil and suffer for the truth, a devotion of your best powers to the interests of piety and virtue. I have spoken of the doctrines, which you will probably preach; but I do not mean, that you are to give yourself to controversy. You will remember, that good practice is the end of preaching, and will labor to make your people holy livers, rather than skilful disputants. Be careful, lest the desire of defending what you deem truth, and of repelling reproach and misrepresentation, turn you aside from your great business, which is to fix in men's minds a living conviction of the obligation, sublimity and happiness of Christian virtue. The best way to vindicate your sentiments, is to show, in your preaching and life, their intimate connection with Christian morals, with a high and delicate sense of duty, with candor towards your opposers, with inflexible integrity, and with an habitual reverence for God. If any light can pierce and scatter the clouds of prejudice, it is that of a pure example. You are to preach a system which has nothing to recommend it, but its fitness to make men better; which has no unintelligible doctrine for the mystical, no extravagancies for the fanatical, no dreams for the visionary, no contradictions for the credulous, which asks no sacrifice of men's understanding, but only of the passions and vices; and the best and only way to recommend such a system is, to show forth its power in purifying and exalting the character. My brother, may your life preach more loudly than your lips. Be to the people a pattern of all good works, and may your instructions derive authority from a well grounded belief in your hearers, that you speak from the heart, that you preach from experience, that the truth which you dispense has wrought powerfully in your own heart, that God, and Jesus, and heaven are not merely words on your lips, but most affecting realities to your mind, and springs of hope and consolation, and strength, in all your trials. Thus laboring, may you reap abundantly, and have a testimony of your faithfulness, not only on your own conscience, but in the esteem, love, virtues, and improvements of your people.

Brethren of this church and society.—We rejoice with you in the prospects of this day. We rejoice in the zeal, unanimity and liberality, with which you have secured to yourselves the administration of God's word and ordinances, according to your own understanding of the Scriptures. We thank God, that he has disposed you to form an association, on the true principles of Christianity and of Protestantism, that you have solemnly resolved to call no man master in religion, to take your faith from no human creed, to submit your consciences to no human authority, but to repair to the gospel, to read it with your own eyes, to exercise upon it your own understanding, to search it, as if not a sect existed around you, and to follow it wherever it may lead you. Brethren, hold fast your Christian and Protestant liberty. We wish you continued peace, and growing prosperity. We pray God, that your good works may glorify your Christian profession, that your candor, and serious attention may encourage our young brother, in the arduous work to which you have called him, and that your union with him, beginning in hope, may continue in joy, and may issue in the friendship and union of heaven.

To all who hear me, I would say, with the apostle; *Prove all things, hold fast that which is good.*[10] Do not, brethren, shrink from the duty of searching God's word for yourselves through fear of human censure and denunciation. Do not think that you may innocently follow the opinions, which prevail around you, without investigation, on the ground, that Christianity is now so purified from errors, as to need no laborious research. There is much reason to believe, that Christianity is at this moment dishonored by gross and cherished corruptions. If you remember the darkness, which hung over the gospel for ages; if you consider the impure union, which still subsists in almost every Christian country between the church, and the state, and which enlists mens' selfishness, and ambition, on the side of established error; if you recollect in what degree the spirit of intolerance has checked free inquiry, not only before, but after the reformation; you will see that Christianity cannot have freed itself from all the human inventions which disfigured it under the papal tyranny. No. Much stubble is yet to be burnt; much rubbish to be removed; many gaudy decorations, which a false taste has hung around Christianity, must be swept away; and the earth-born fogs, which have long shrouded it, must be scattered, before this divine fabric will rise before us in its native, and awful majesty, in its harmonious proportions, in its mild and celestial splendors.[11] This glorious reformation in the church, we hope, under God's blessing, from the demolition of human authority in matters of religion, from the fall of those hierarchies, huge establishments, general convocations or assemblies, and other human institutions, by which the minds of individuals are oppressed under the weight of numbers, and a papal dominion is perpetuated in the Protestant church. Our earnest prayer to God is, that He will overturn, and overturn, and overturn the strongholds of spiritual usurpation, until HE shall come, whose right it is to rule the minds of men; that the conspiracy of ages against the liberty of Christians may be brought to an end; that the servile assent, so long yielded to human creeds, may give place to honest and fearless inquiry into the Scriptures; and that Christianity, thus purified from error, may put forth its almighty energy, and prove itself, by its ennobling influence on the mind, to be indeed "the power of God unto salvation."

[10] See 1 Thessalonians 5:21.
[11] Here Channing shows that, despite great changes in doctrine, he stands squarely in the tradition of William Bradford and other reformers determined to restore Christianity to its primitive purity. See above, p. 23.

NOTE

The author intended to add some notes to this discourse, but they would necessarily be more extended than the occasion would justify. He wished to offer some remarks on the word *mystery,* but can only refer his readers to the dissertation of that subject, in the inestimable work of Dr. Campbell on the Gospels. He was prevented, by the limits of the discourse, from enlarging on that very interesting topick, the great end of our Saviour's mission; and he would refer those, who wish to obtain definite views on this point, to an admirable treatise on the design of Christianity, by Bishop Fowler, which may be found in Bishop Watson's tracts. Had I time, I should be happy to notice the principal texts adduced in the Trinitarian controversy, particularly those which are either interpolations, or false or doubtful readings, or false or doubtful translations, such as 1 John v. 7. Acts xx. 28. 1 Tim. iii. 16. Philipp. ii. 6, &c. These last texts should be dismissed from the controversy, and they cannot be needed, if the doctrine, which they are adduced to support, be a fundamental truth of Christianity. A fundamental truth cannot, certainly, want the aid of four or five doubtful passages; and Trinitarians betray the weakness of their cause, in the eagerness with which they struggle for those I have named. But I cannot enlarge. The candor of the reader will excuse many omissions in a sermon, which is necessarily too limited to do more, than give the most prominent views of a subject.

RALPH WALDO EMERSON

(1803–1881)*

Emerson's address is the most eloquent denunciation of the historical approach to Christianity in American literature. Delivered before the senior class of the Harvard Divinity School on July 15, 1838, the speech deeply angered the officers of the School. In his refutation of tradition and the divinity of Christ, Emerson was denying the ideological premises of leaders like Andrews Norton. His celebration of an indwelling God or the Intuition and his distinction between the Reason and the Understanding are central statements in the literature of transcendentalism.

*For a full Introduction to Emerson, see
pp. 840–844.

An Address
Delivered Before the Senior Class in Divinity College, Cambridge, Sunday Evening, 15 July, 1838[1]

In this refulgent summer it has been a luxury to draw the breath of life. The grass grows, the buds burst, the meadow is spotted with fire and gold in the tint of flowers. The air is full of birds, and sweet with the breath of the pine, the balm-of-Gilead, and the new hay. Night brings no gloom to the heart with its welcome shade. Through the transparent darkness the stars pour their almost spiritual rays. Man under them seems a young child, and his huge globe a toy. The cool night bathes the world as with a river, and prepares his eyes again for the crimson dawn. The mystery of nature was never displayed more happily. The corn and the wine have been freely dealt to all creatures, and the never-broken silence with which the old bounty goes forward, has not yielded yet one word of explanation. One is constrained to respect the perfection of this world, in which our senses converse. How wide; how rich; what invitation from every property it gives to every faculty of man! In its fruitful soils; in its navigable sea; in its mountains of metal and stone; in its forests of all woods; in its animals; in its chemical ingredients; in the powers and path of light, heat, attraction, and life, it is well worth the pith and heart of great men to subdue and enjoy it. The planters, the mechanics, the inventors, the astronomers, the builders of cities, and the captains, history delights to honor.

But the moment the mind opens, and reveals the laws which traverse the universe, and make things what they are, then shrinks the great world at once into a mere illustration and fable of this mind. What am I? and What is? asks the human spirit with a curiosity new-kindled, but never to be quenched. Behold these outrunning laws, which our imperfect apprehension can see tend this way and that, but not come full circle. Behold these infinite relations, so like, so unlike; many, yet one. I would study, I would know, I would admire forever. These works of thought have been the entertainments of the human spirit in all ages.

A more secret, sweet, and overpowering beauty appears to man when his heart and mind open to the sentiment of virtue. Then instantly he is instructed in what is above him. He learns that his being is without bound;

---

[1] Emerson had been invited to deliver this address by the senior class instead of by the officers of the Harvard Divinity School. He spoke on Sunday evening, July 15, 1838, and so offended the conservative clergymen that school officials disclaimed any responsibility for it. The essay is a direct criticism of the historical approach to church matters, as demonstrated by Andrews Norton; a refutation of the divinity of Christ; and a call for a new faith, residing in personal self-reliance.

that, to the good, to the perfect, he is born, low as he now lies in evil and weakness.[2] That which he venerates is still his own, though he has not realized it yet. He *ought*. He knows the sense of that grand word, though his analysis fails entirely to render account of it. When in innocency, or when by intellectual perception, he attains to say,—"I love the Right; Truth is beautiful within and without, forevermore. Virtue, I am thine: save me: use me: thee will I serve, day and night, in great, in small, that I may be not virtuous, but virtue:"—then is the end of the creation answered, and God is well pleased.

The sentiment of virtue is a reverence and delight in the presence of certain divine laws. It perceives that this homely game of life we play, covers, under what seem foolish details, principles that astonish. The child amidst his baubles, is learning the action of light, motion, gravity, muscular force; and in the game of human life, love, fear, justice, appetite, man, and God, interact. These laws refuse to be adequately stated. They will not by us or for us be written out on paper, or spoken by the tongue. They elude, evade our persevering thought, and yet we read them hourly in each other's faces, in each other's actions, in our own remorse. The moral traits which are all globed into every virtuous act and thought,—in speech, we must sever, and describe or suggest by painful enumeration of many particulars. Yet, as this sentiment is the essence of all religion, let me guide your eye to the precise objects of the sentiment, by an enumeration of some of those classes of facts in which this element is conspicuous.

The intuition of the moral sentiment is an insight of the perfection of the laws of the soul. These laws execute themselves. They are out of time, out of space, and not subject to circumstance. Thus; in the soul of man there is a justice whose retributions are instant and entire. He who does a good deed, is instantly ennobled himself. He who does a mean deed, is by the action itself contracted. He who puts off impurity, thereby puts on purity. If a man is at heart just, then in so far is he God; the safety of God, the immortality of God, the majesty of God do enter into that man with justice. If a man dissemble, deceive, he deceives himself, and goes out of acquaintance with his own being. A man in the view of absolute goodness, adores, with total humility. Every step so downward, is a step upward. The man who renounces himself, comes to himself by doing.

See how this rapid intrinsic energy worketh everywhere, righting wrongs, correcting appearances, and bringing up facts to a harmony with thoughts. Its operation in life, though slow to the senses, is, at last, as sure as in the soul. By it, a man is made the Providence to himself, dispensing good to his goodness, and evil to his sin. Character is always known. Thefts never enrich; alms never impoverish; murder will speak out of stone walls. The least

[a] Compare with similar statements made in "The Poet."

admixture of a lie,—for example, the smallest mixture of vanity, the least attempt to make a good impression, a favorable appearance,—will instantly vitiate the effect. But speak the truth, and all nature and all spirits help you with unexpected furtherance. Speak the truth, and all things alive or brute are vouchers, and the very roots of the grass underground there, do seem to stir and move to bear you witness. See again the perfection of the Law as it applies itself to the affections, and becomes the law of society. As we are, so we associate. The good, by affinity, seek the good; the vile, by affinity, the vile. Thus of their own volition, souls proceed into heaven, into hell.

These facts have always suggested to man the sublime creed, that the world is not the product of manifold power, but of one will, of one mind; and that one mind is everywhere active, in each ray of the star, in each wavelet of the pool; and whatever opposes that will, is everywhere baulked and baffled, because things are made so, and not otherwise. Good is positive. Evil is merely privative, not absolute. It is like cold, which is the privation of heat. All evil is so much death or nonentity. Benevolence is absolute and real. So much benevolence as a man hath, so much life hath he. For all things proceed out of this same spirit, which is differently named love, justice, temperance, in its different applications, just as the ocean receives different names on the several shores which it washes. All things proceed out of the same spirit, and all things conspire with it. Whilst a man seeks good ends, he is strong by the whole strength of nature. In so far as he roves from these ends, he bereaves himself of power, of auxiliaries; his being shrinks out of all remote channels, he becomes less and less, a mote, a point, until absolute badness is absolute death.

The perception of this law of laws always awakens in the mind a sentiment which we call the religious sentiment, and which makes our highest happiness. Wonderful is its power to charm and to command. It is a mountain air. It is the embalmer of the world. It is myrrh and storax, and chlorine and rosemary. It makes the sky and the hills sublime, and the silent song of the stars is it. By it, is the universe made safe and habitable, not by science or power. Thought may work cold and intransitive in things, and find no end or unity. But the dawn of the sentiment of virtue on the heart, gives and is the assurance that Law is sovereign over all natures; and the worlds, time, space, eternity, do seem to break out into joy.

This sentiment is divine and deifying. It is the beatitude of man. It makes him illimitable. Through it, the soul first knows itself. It corrects the capital mistake of the infant man, who seeks to be great by following the great, and hopes to derive advantages *from another*,—by showing the fountain of all good to be in himself, and that he, equally with every man, is an inlet into the deeps of Reason. When he says, "I ought;" when love warms him; when he chooses, warned from on high, the good and great deed; then, deep melodies wander through his soul from Supreme Wisdom. Then he can worship, and be enlarged by his worship; for he can never go behind this sentiment. In the sublimest flights of the soul, rectitude is never surmounted, love is never outgrown.

This sentiment lies at the foundation of society, and successively creates all forms of worship. The principle of veneration never dies out. Man fallen into superstition, into sensuality, is never wholly without the visions of the moral sentiment. In like manner, all the expressions of this sentiment are sacred and permanent in proportion to their purity. The expressions of this sentiment affect us deeper, greatlier, than all other compositions. The sentences of the oldest time, which ejaculate this piety, are still fresh and fragrant. This thought dwelled always deepest in the minds of men in the devout and contemplative East; not alone in Palestine, where it reached its purest expression, but in Egypt, in Persia, in India, in China. Europe has always owed to oriental genius, its divine impulses. What these holy bards said, all sane men found agreeable and true. And the unique impression of Jesus upon mankind, whose name is not so much written as ploughed into the history of this world, is proof of the subtle virtue of this infusion.

Meantime, whilst the doors of the temple stand open, night and day, before every man, and the oracles of this truth cease never, it is guarded by one stern condition; this, namely; It is an intuition. It cannot be received at second hand. Truly speaking, it is not instruction, but provocation, that I can receive from another soul. What he announces, I must find true in me, or wholly reject; and on his word, or as his second, be he who he may, I can accept nothing. On the contrary, the absence of this primary faith is the presence of degradation. As is the flood so is the ebb. Let this faith depart, and the very words it spake, and the things it made, become false and hurtful. Then falls the church, the state, art, letters, life. The doctrine of the divine nature being forgotten, a sickness infects and dwarfs the constitution. Once man was all; now he is an appendage, a nuisance. And because the indwelling Supreme Spirit cannot wholly be got rid of, the doctrine of it suffers this perversion, that the divine nature is attributed to one or two persons, and denied to all the rest, and denied with fury. The doctrine of inspiration is lost; the base doctrine of the majority of voices, usurps the place of the doctrine of the soul. Miracles, prophecy, poetry, the ideal life, the holy life, exist as ancient history merely; they are not in the belief, nor in the aspiration of society; but, when suggested, seem ridiculous. Life is comic or pitiful, as soon as the high ends of being fade out of sight, and man becomes near-sighted, and can only attend to what addresses the senses.

These general views, which, whilst they are general, none will contest, find abundant illustration in the history of religion, and especially in the history of the Christian church. In that, all of us have had our birth and nurture. The truth contained in that, you, my young friends, are now setting forth to teach. As the Cultus, or established worship of the civilized world, it has great historical interest for us. Of its blessed words, which have been the consolation of humanity, you need not that I should speak. I shall endeavor to discharge my duty to you, on this occasion, by pointing out two errors in its administration, which daily appear more gross from the point of view we have just now taken.

Jesus Christ belonged to the true race of prophets. He saw with open eye the mystery of the soul. Drawn by its severe harmony, ravished with its beauty, he lived in it, and had his being there. Alone in all history, he estimated the greatness of man. One man was true to what is in you and me. He saw that God incarnates himself in man, and evermore goes forth anew to take possession of his world. He said, in this jubilee of sublime emotion, "I am divine. Through me, God acts; through me, speaks. Would you see God, see me; or, see thee, when thou also thinkest as I now think." But what a distortion did his doctrine and memory suffer in the same, in the next, and the following ages! There is no doctrine of the Reason which will bear to be taught by the Understanding. The understanding caught this high chant from the poet's lips, and said, in the next age, "This was Jehovah come down out of heaven. I will kill you, if you say he was a man." The idioms of his language, and the figures of his rhetoric, have usurped the place of his truth; and churches are not built on his principles, but on his tropes. Christianity became a Mythus, as the poetic teaching of Greece and of Egypt, before. He spoke of miracles; for he felt that man's life was a miracle, and all that man doth, and he knew that this daily miracle shines, as the man is diviner. But the very word Miracle, as pronounced by Christian churches, gives a false impression; it is Monster. It is not one with the blowing clover and the falling rain.

He felt respect for Moses and the prophets; but no unfit tenderness at postponing their initial revelations, to the hour and the man that now is; to the eternal revelation in the heart. Thus was he a true man. Having seen that the law in us is commanding, he would not suffer it to be commanded. Boldly, with hand, and heart, and life, he declared it was God. Thus was he a true man. Thus is he, as I think, the only soul in history who has appreciated the worth of a man.

I. In thus contemplating Jesus, we become very sensible of the first defect of historical Christianity. Historical Christianity has fallen into the error that corrupts all attempts to communicate religion. As it appears to us, and as it has appeared for ages, it is not the doctrine of the soul, but an exaggeration of the personal, the positive, the ritual. It has dwelt, it dwells, with noxious exaggeration about the *person* of Jesus. The soul knows no persons. It invites every man to expand to the full circle of the universe, and will have no preferences but those of spontaneous love. But by this eastern monarchy of a Christianity, which indolence and fear have built, the friend of man is made the injurer of man. The manner in which his name is surrounded with expressions, which were once sallies of admiration and love, but are now petrified into official titles, kills all generous sympathy and liking. All who hear me, feel, that the language that describes Christ to Europe and America, is not the style of friendship and enthusiasm to a good and noble heart, but is appropriated and formal,—paints a demigod, as the Orientals or the Greeks would describe Osiris or Apollo. Accept the injurious impositions of our early catechetical instruction, and even honesty and self-denial were but splendid sins, if they did not wear the Christian name. One would rather be

"A pagan suckled in a creed outworn,"

than to be defrauded of his manly right in coming into nature, and finding not names and places, not land and professions, but even virtue and truth foreclosed and monopolized. You shall not be a man even. You shall not own the world; you shall not dare, and live after the infinite Law that is in you, and in company with the infinite Beauty which heaven and earth reflect to you in all lovely forms; but you must subordinate your nature to Christ's nature; you must accept our interpretations; and take his portrait as the vulgar draw it.

That is always best which gives me to myself. The sublime is excited in me by the great stoical doctrine, Obey thyself. That which shows God in me, fortifies me. That which shows God out of me, makes me a wart and a wen. There is no longer a necessary reason for my being. Already the long shadows of untimely oblivion creep over me, and I shall decease forever.

The divine bards are the friends of my virtue, of my intellect, of my strength. They admonish me, that the gleams which flash across my mind, are not mine, but God's; that they had the like, and were not disobedient to the heavenly vision. So I love them. Noble provocations go out from them, inviting me also to emancipate myself; to resist evil; to subdue the world; and to Be. And thus by his holy thoughts, Jesus serves us, and thus only. To aim to convert a man by miracles, is a profanation of the soul. A true conversion, a true Christ, is now, as always, to be made, by the reception of beautiful sentiments. It is true that a great and rich soul, like his, falling among the simple, does so preponderate, that, as his did, it names the world. The world seems to them to exist for him, and they have not yet drunk so deeply of his sense, as to see that only by coming again to themselves, or to God in themselves, can they grow forevermore. It is a low benefit to give me something; it is a high benefit to enable me to do somewhat of myself. The time is coming when all men will see, that the gift of God to the soul is not a vaunting, overpowering, excluding sanctity, but a sweet, natural goodness, a goodness like thine and mine, and that so invites thine and mine to be and to grow.

The injustice of the vulgar tone of preaching is not less flagrant to Jesus, than it is to the souls which it profanes. The preachers do not see that they make his gospel not glad, and shear him of the locks of beauty and the attributes of heaven. When I see a majestic Epaminondas,[3] or Washington; when I see among my contemporaries, a true orator, an upright judge, a dear friend; when I vibrate to the melody and fancy of a poem; I see beauty that is to be desired. And so lovely, and with yet more entire consent of my human being, sounds in my ear the severe music of the bards that have sung of the true God in all ages. Now do not degrade the life and dialogues of Christ out of the circle of this charm, by insulation and peculiarity. Let them lie as they befel, alive and warm, part of human life, and of the landscape, and of the cheerful day.

2. The second defect of the traditionary and limited way of using the mind of Christ is a consequence of the first; this, namely; that the Moral Nature, that Law of laws, whose revelations introduce greatness,—yea, God himself, into the open soul, is not explored as the fountain of the established teaching in society. Men have come to speak of the revelation as somewhat long ago given and done, as if God were dead. The injury to faith throttles the preacher; and the goodliest of institutions becomes an uncertain and inarticulate voice.

It is very certain that it is the effect of conversation with the beauty of the soul, to beget a desire and need to impart to others the same knowledge and love. If utterance is denied, the thought lies like a burden on the man. Always the seer is a sayer. Somehow his dream is told. Somehow he publishes it with solemn joy. Sometimes with pencil on canvas; sometimes with chisel on stone; sometimes in towers and aisles of granite, his soul's worship is builded; sometimes in anthems of indefinite music; but clearest and most permanent, in words.

The man enamored of this excellency, becomes its priest or poet. The office is coeval with the world. But observe the condition, the spiritual limitation of the office. The spirit only can teach. Not any profane man, not any sensual, not any liar, not any slave can teach, but only he can give, who has; he only can create, who is. The man on whom the soul descends, through whom the soul speaks, alone can teach. Courage, piety, love, wisdom, can teach; and every man can open his door to these angels, and they shall bring him the gift of tongues. But the man who aims to speak as books enable, as synods use, as the fashion guides, and as interest commands, babbles. Let him hush.

To this holy office, you propose to devote yourselves. I wish you may feel your call in throbs of desire and hope. The office is the first in the world. It is of that reality, that it cannot suffer the deduction of any falsehood. And it is my duty to say to you, that the need was never greater of new revelation

[3] A Theban statesman and general (c. 418-362 B. C.). He was noted for his honesty and self-command.

than now. From the views I have already expressed, you will infer the sad conviction, which I share, I believe, with numbers, of the universal decay and now almost death of faith in society. The soul is not preached. The Church seems to totter to its fall, almost all life extinct. On this occasion, any complaisance, would be criminal, which told you, whose hope and commission it is to preach the faith of Christ, that the faith of Christ is preached.

It is time that this ill-suppressed murmur of all thoughtful men against the famine of our churches; this moaning of the heart because it is bereaved of the consolation, the hope, the grandeur, that come alone out of the culture of the moral nature; should be heard through the sleep of indolence, and over the din of routine. This great and perpetual office of the preacher is not discharged. Preaching is the expression of the moral sentiment in application to the duties of life. In how many churches, by how many prophets, tell me, is man made sensible that he is an infinite Soul; that the earth and heavens are passing into his mind; that he is drinking forever the soul of God? Where now sounds the persuasion, that by its very melody imparadises my heart, and so affirms its own origin in heaven? Where shall I hear words such as in elder ages drew men to leave all and follow,—father and mother, house and land, wife and child? Where shall I hear these august laws of moral being so pronounced, as to fill my ear, and I feel ennobled by the offer of my uttermost action and passion? The test of the true faith, certainly, should be its power to charm and command the soul, as the laws of nature control the activity of the hands,—so commanding that we find pleasure and honor in obeying. The faith should blend with the light of rising and setting suns, with the flying cloud, the singing bird, and the breath of flowers. But now the priest's Sabbath has lost the splendor of nature; it is unlovely; we are glad when it is done; we can make, we do make, even sitting in our pews, a far better, holier, sweeter, for ourselves.

Whenever the pulpit is usurped by a formalist, then is the worshipper defrauded and disconsolate. We shrink as soon as the prayers begin, which do not uplift, but smite and offend us. We are fain to wrap our cloaks about us, and secure, as best we can, a solitude that hears not. I once heard a preacher who sorely tempted me to say, I would go to church no more. Men go, thought I, where they are wont to go, else had no soul entered the temple in the afternoon. A snowstorm was falling around us. The snowstorm was real; the preacher merely spectral; and the eye felt the sad contrast in looking at him, and then out of the window behind him, into the beautiful meteor of the snow. He had lived in vain. He had no one word intimating that he had laughed or wept, was married or in love, had been commended, or cheated, or chagrined. If he had ever lived and acted, we were none the wiser for it. The capital secret of his profession, namely, to convert life into truth, he had not learned. Not one fact in all his experience, had he yet imported into his doctrine. This man had ploughed, and planted, and talked, and bought, and sold; he had read books; he had eaten and drunken; his head aches; his heart throbs; he smiles and suffers; yet was there not a surmise, a hint, in all the discourse, that he had ever lived at all. Not a line did he draw out of real history. The true preacher can always be known by this, that he deals out to the people his life,—life passed through the fire of thought. But of the bad preacher, it could not be told from his sermon, what age of the world he fell in; whether he had a father or a child; whether he was a freeholder or a pauper; whether he was a citizen or a countryman; or any other fact of his biography.

It seemed strange that the people should come to church. It seemed as if their houses were very unentertaining, that they should prefer this thought-less clamor. It shows that there is a commanding attraction in the moral sentiment, that can lend a faint tint of light to dulness and ignorance, coming in its name and place. The good hearer is sure he has been touched some-times; is sure there is somewhat to be reached, and some word that can reach it. When he listens to these vain words, he comforts himself by their relation to his remembrance of better hours, and so they clatter and echo unchallenged.

I am not ignorant that when we preach unworthily, it is not always quite in vain. There is a good ear, in some men, that draws supplies to virtue out of very indifferent nutriment. There is poetic truth concealed in all the common-places of prayer and of sermons, and though foolishly spoken, they may be wisely heard; for, each is some select expression that broke out in a moment of piety from some stricken or jubilant soul, and its excellency made it remembered. The prayers and even the dogmas of our church, are like the zodiac of Denderah,[4] and the astronomical monuments of the Hindoos, wholly insulated from anything now extant in the life and business of the people.They mark the height to which the waters once rose. But this docility is a check upon the mischief from the good and devout. In a large portion of the community, the religious service gives rise to quite other thoughts and emotions. We need not chide the negligent servant. We are struck with pity, rather, at the swift retribution of his sloth. Alas for the unhappy man that is called to stand in the pulpit, and *not* give bread of life. Everything that befals, accuses him. Would he ask contributions for the missions, foreign or domestic? Instantly his face is suffused with shame, to propose to his parish, that they should send money a hundred or a thousand miles, to furnish such poor fare as they have at home, and would do well to go the hundred or the thousand miles, to escape. Would he urge people to a godly way of living; and can he ask a fellow creature to come to Sabbath meetings, when he and they all know what is the poor uttermost they can hope for therein? Will he invite them privately to the Lord's Supper? He dares not. If no heart warm this rite, the hollow, dry, creaking formality is too plain, than that he can

---

[4] An ancient city in Egypt in which the people worshipped the goddess Hathor.

face a man of wit and energy, and put the invitation without terror. In the street, what has he to say to the bold village blasphemer? The village blasphemer sees fear in the face, form, and gait of the minister.

Let me not taint the sincerity of this plea by any oversight of the claims of good men. I know and honor the purity and strict conscience of numbers of the clergy. What life the public worship retains, it owes to the scattered company of pious men, who minister here and there in the churches, and who, sometimes accepting with too great tenderness the tenet of the elders, have not accepted from others, but from their own heart, the genuine impulses of virtue, and so still command our love and awe, to the sanctity of character. Moreover, the exceptions are not so much to be found in a few eminent preachers, as in the better hours, the truer inspirations of all,—nay, in the sincere moments of every man. But with whatever exception, it is still true, that tradition characterizes the preaching of this country; that it comes out of the memory, and not out of the soul; that it aims at what is usual, and not at what is necessary and eternal; that thus, historical Christianity destroys the power of preaching, by withdrawing it from the exploration of the moral nature of man, where the sublime is, where are the resources of astonishment and power. What a cruel injustice it is to that Law, the joy of the whole earth, which alone can make thought dear and rich; that Law whose fatal sureness the astronomical orbits poorly emulate, that it is travestied and depreciated, that it is behooted and behowled, and not a trait, not a word of it articulated. The pulpit in losing sight of this Law, loses all its inspiration, and gropes after it knows not what. And for want of this culture, the soul of the community is sick and faithless. It wants nothing so much as a stern, high, stoical, Christian discipline, to make it know itself and the divinity that speaks through it. Now man is ashamed of himself; he skulks and sneaks through the world, to be tolerated, to be pitied, and scarcely in a thousand years does any man dare to be wise and good, and so draw after him the tears and blessings of his kind.

Certainly there have been periods when, from the inactivity of the intellect on certain truths, a greater faith was possible in names and persons. The Puritans in England and America, found in the Christ of the Catholic Church, and in the dogmas inherited from Rome, scope for their austere piety, and their longings for civil freedom. But their creed is passing away, and none arises in its room. I think no man can go with his thoughts about him, into one of our churches, without feeling that what hold the public worship had on me, is gone or going. It has lost its grasp on the affection of the good, and the fear of the bad. In the country, neighborhoods, half parishes are *signing off*,—to use the local term. It is already beginning to indicate character and religion to withdraw from the religious meetings. I have heard a devout person, who prized the Sabbath, say in bitterness of heart, "On Sundays, it seems wicked to go to church." And the motive, that holds the best there, is now only a hope and a waiting. What was once a mere circumstance, that the best and the worst men in the parish, the poor and the rich, the learned and the ignorant, young and old, should meet one day as fellows in one house, in sign of an equal right in the soul,—has come to be a paramount motive for going thither.

My friends, in these two errors, I think, I find the causes of that calamity of a decaying church and a wasting unbelief, which are casting malignant influences around us, and making the hearts of good men sad. And what greater calamity can fall upon a nation, than the loss of worship? Then all things go to decay. Genius leaves the temple, to haunt the senate, or the market. Literature becomes frivolous. Science is cold. The eye of youth is not lighted by the hope of other worlds, and age is without honor. Society lives to trifles, and when men die, we do not mention them.

And now, my brothers, you will ask, What in these desponding days can be done by us? The remedy is already declared in the ground of our complaint of the Church. We have contrasted the Church with the Soul. In the soul, then, let the redemption be sought. In one soul, in your soul, there are resources for the world. Wherever a man comes, there comes revolution. The old is for slaves. When a man comes, all books are legible, all things transparent, all religions are forms. He is religious. Man is the wonderworker. He is seen amid miracles. All men bless and curse. He saith yea and nay, only. The stationariness of religion; the assumption that the age of inspiration is past, that the Bible is closed; the fear of degrading the character of Jesus by representing him as a man; indicate with sufficient clearness the falsehood of our theology. It is the office of a true teacher to show us that God is, not was; that He speaketh, not spake. The true Christianity,—a faith like Christ's in the infinitude of man,—is lost. None believeth in the soul of man, but only in some man or person old and departed. Ah me! no man goeth alone. All men go in flocks to this saint or that poet, avoiding the God who seeth in secret. They cannot see in secret; they love to be blind in public. They think society wiser than their soul, and know not that one soul, and their soul, is wiser than the whole world. See how nations and races flit by on the sea of time, and leave no ripple to tell where they floated or sunk, and one good soul shall make the name of Moses, or of Zeno,[5] or of Zoroaster, reverend forever. None assayeth the stern ambition to be the Self of the nation, and of nature, but each would be an easy secondary to some Christian scheme, or sectarian connexion, or some eminent man. Once leave your own knowledge of God, your own sentiment, and take secondary knowledge, as St. Paul's, or George Fox's, or Swedenborg's,[6] and you get wide from God with every year

[5] Zeno was a Greek philosopher of the late fourth and early third centuries B. C. He established the Stoic school of philosophy; Zoroaster was a man whose name was used for an ancient Persian religion.

[6] George Fox (1624-1691) founded the Soci-

ety of Friends or Quakers in opposition to the Presbyterian faith: Emmanuel Swedenborg (1688-1722) was a mystical thinker whom Emerson described at length in *Representative Men*.

this secondary form lasts, and if, as now, for centuries,—the chasm yawns to that breadth, that men can scarcely be convinced there is in them anything divine.

Let me admonish you, first of all, to go alone; to refuse the good models, even those most sacred in the imagination of men, and dare to love God without mediator or veil. Friends enough you shall find who will hold up to your emulation Wesleys and Oberlins,[7] Saints and Prophets. Thank God for these good men, but say, "I also am a man." Imitation cannot go above its model. The imitator dooms himself to hopeless mediocrity. The inventor did it, because it was natural to him, and so in him it has a charm. In the imitator, something else is natural, and he bereaves himself of his own beauty, to come short of another man's.

Yourself a newborn bard of the Holy Ghost,—cast behind you all conformity, and acquaint men at first hand with Deity. Be to them a man. Look to it first and only, that you are such; that fashion, custom, authority, pleasure, and money are nothing to you,—are not bandages over your eyes, that you cannot see,—but live with the privilege of the immeasurable mind. Not too anxious to visit periodically all families and each family in your parrish connexion,—when you meet one of these men or women, be to them a divine man; be to them thought and virtue; let their timid aspirations find in you a friend; let their trampled instincts be genially tempted out in your atmosphere; let their doubts know that you have doubted, and their wonder feel that you have wondered. By trusting your own soul, you shall gain a greater confidence in other men. For all our penny-wisdom, for all our soul-destroying slavery to habit, it is not to be doubted, that all men have sublime thoughts; that all men do value the few real hours of life; they love to be heard; they love to be caught up into the vision of principles. We mark with light in the memory the few interviews, we have had in the dreary years of routine and of sin, with souls that made our souls wiser; that spoke what we thought; that told us what we knew; that gave us leave to be what we inly were. Discharge to men the priestly office, and, present or absent, you shall be followed with their love as by an angel.

And, to this end, let us not aim at common degrees of merit. Can we not leave, to such as love it, the virtue that glitters for the commendation of society, and ourselves pierce the deep solitudes of absolute ability and worth? We easily come up to the standard of goodness in society. Society's praise can be cheaply secured, and almost all men are content with those easy merits; but the instant effect of conversing with God, will be, to put them away. There are sublime merits; persons who are not actors, not speakers, but influences; persons too great for fame, for display; who disdain

[7] John Wesley (1703-1791) was a British evangelist who established Methodism ʊʊʊ the general introduction to Romanticism, pp. 803-804; Jean Frédéric Oberlin (1740-1826) was a Protestant clergyman of Alsace, who was much concerned with educational reform.

eloquence; to whom all we call art and artist, seems too nearly allied to show and by-ends, to the exaggeration of the finite and selfish, and loss of the universal. The orators, the poets, the commanders encroach on us only as fair women do, by our allowance and homage. Slight them by preoccupation of mind, slight them, as you can well afford to do, by height and universal aims, and they instantly feel that you have right, and that it is in lower places that they must shine. They also feel your right; for they with you are open to the influx of the all-knowing Spirit, which annihilates before its broad noon the little shades and gradations of intelligence in the compositions we call wiser and wisest.

In such high communion, let us study the grand strokes of rectitude: a bold benevolence, an independence of friends, so that not the unjust wishes of those who love us, shall impair our freedom, but we shall resist for truth's sake the freest flow of kindness, and appeal to sympathies far in advance; and,—what is the highest form in which we know this beautiful element,— a certain solidity of merit, that has nothing to do with opinion, and which is so essentially and manifestly virtue, that it is taken for granted, that the right, the brave, the generous step will be taken by it, and nobody thinks of commending it. You would compliment a coxcomb doing a good act, but you would not praise an angel. The silence that accepts merit as the most natural thing in the world, is the highest applause. Such souls, when they appear, are the Imperial Guard of Virtue, the perpetual reserve, the dictators of fortune. One needs not praise their courage,—they are the heart and soul of nature. O my friends, there are resources in us on which we have not drawn. There are men who rise refreshed on hearing a threat; men to whom a crisis which intimidates and paralyzes the majority—demanding not the faculties of prudence and thrift, but comprehension, immovableness, the readiness of sacrifice,—comes graceful and beloved as a bride. Napoleon said of Massena, that he was not himself until the battle began to go against him; then, when the dead began to fall in ranks around him, awoke his powers of combination, and he put on terror and victory as a robe. So it is in rugged crises, in unweariable endurance, and in aims which put sympathy out of question, that the angel is shown. But these are heights that we can scarce remember and look up to, without contrition and shame. Let us thank God that such things exist.

And now let us do what we can to rekindle the smouldering, nigh quenched fire of the altar. The evils of the church that now is, are manifest. The question returns, What shall we do? I confess, all attempts to project and establish a Cultus with new rites and forms, seem to me vain. Faith makes us, and not we it, and faith makes its own forms. All attempts to contrive system, are as cold as the new worship introduced by the French to the goddess of Reason,—today, pasteboard and fillagree, and ending to-morrow in madness and murder. Rather let the breath of new life be breathed by you through the forms already existing. For, if once you are alive, you shall find they shall become plastic and new. The remedy to their deformity is, first, soul, and second, soul, and evermore, soul. A whole popedom of forms, one pulsation of virtue can uplift and vivify. Two inestimable advantages Christianity has given us; first; the Sabbath, the jubilee of the whole world; whose light dawns welcome alike into the closet of the philosopher, into the garret of toil, and into prison cells, and everywhere suggests, even to the vile, a thought of the dignity of spiritual being. Let it stand forevermore, a temple, which new love, new faith, new sight shall restore to more than its first splendor to mankind. And secondly, the institution of preaching,—the speech of man to men,—essentially the most flexible of all organs, of all forms. What hinders that now, everywhere, in pulpits, in lecture-rooms, in houses, in fields, wherever the invitation of men or your own occasions lead you, you speak the very truth, as your life and conscience teach it, and cheer the waiting, fainting hearts of men with new hope and new revelation?

I look for the hour when that supreme Beauty, which ravished the souls of those Eastern men, and chiefly of those Hebrews, and through their lips spoke oracles to all time, shall speak in the West also. The Hebrew and Greek Scriptures contain immortal sentences, that have been bread of life to millions. But they have no epical integrity; are fragmentary; are not shown in their order to the intellect. I look for the new Teacher, that shall follow so far those shining laws, that he shall see them come full circle; shall see their rounding complete grace; shall see the world to be the mirror of the soul; shall see the identity of the law of gravitation with purity of heart; and shall show that the Ought, that Duty, is one thing with Science, with Beauty, and with Joy.

ORESTES BROWNSON

(1803–1876)

During his life, Orestes Brownson underwent a series of religious conversions: as a Presbyterian in 1822, as a Universalist in 1824, as a Unitarian in the late 1820's, as a transcendentalist during the 1830's, and then

The standard text is *The Works of Orestes A. Brownson,* 20 vols., ed. H. F. Brownson, 1882–1887. Brownson also wrote the standard biography, *Orestes A. 'Brownson's Early Life, Middle Life, Latter Life,* 3 vols., 1898–1900. Some later studies include S. A. Raemers, *America's Foremost Philosopher,* 1931; A. M. Schlesinger, *Orestes A.*

Brownson: A Pilgrim's Progress, 1939, 1963; Theodore Maynard, *Orestes Brownson: Yankee, Radical, Catholic,* 1943; Lapati, Amenio, D., *Oresks A. Brownson,* 1965.

The text is from *The Works of Orestes A. Brownson.*

as a Catholic in 1844. His most influential period was between 1834 and 1844 when he enunciated the transcendental faith most vigorously and denounced Unitarianism. This essay, which first appeared in the *Boston Quarterly Review* (October 1838), a journal Brownson edited, is typical of the author's spontaneous courage.

Emersons's Address

This is in some respects a remarkable address,—remarkable for its own character and for the place where and the occasion on which it was delivered. It is not often, we fancy, that such an address is delivered by a clergyman in a Divinity College to a class of young men just ready to go forth into the churches as preachers of the Gospel of Jesus Christ. Indeed it is not often that a discourse teaching doctrines like the leading doctrines of this, is delivered by a professedly religious man, anywhere or on any occasion.

We are not surprised that this address should have produced some excitement and called forth some severe censures upon its author; for we have long known that there are comparatively few who can hear with calmness the utterance of opinions to which they do not subscribe. Yet we regret to see the abuse which has been heaped upon Mr. Emerson. We ought to learn to tolerate all opinions, to respect every man's right to form and to utter his own opinions whatever they may be. If we regard the opinions as unsound, false, or dangerous, we should meet them calmly, refute them if we can; but be careful to respect, and to treat with all Christian meekness and love, him who entertains them . . .

In dismissing this address, we can only say that we have spoken of it freely, but with no improper feeling to its author. We love bold speculation; we are pleased to find a man who dares tell us what and precisely what he thinks, however unpopular his views may be. We have no disposition to check his utterance, by giving his views a bad name, although we deem them unsound. We love progress, and progress cannot be effected without freedom. Still we wish to see a certain sobriety, a certain reserve in all speculations, something like timidity about rushing off into an unknown universe, and some little regret in departing from the faith of our fathers.

Nevertheless, let not the tenor of our remarks be mistaken. Mr. Emerson is the last man in the world we should suspect of conscious hostility to religion and morality. No one can know him or read his productions without feeling a profound respect for the singular purity and uprightness of his character and motives. The great object he is laboring to accomplish is one in which he should receive the hearty cooperation of every American scholar, of every friend of truth, freedom, piety, and virtue. Whatever may be the character of his speculations, whatever may be the moral, philosophical, or theological system which forms the basis of his speculations, his real object is not the inculcation of any new theory on man, nature, or God; but to induce men to think for themselves on all subjects, and to speak from their own full hearts and earnest convictions. His object is to make men scorn to be slaves to routine, to custom, to established creeds, to public opinion, to the great names of this age, of this country, or of any other. He cannot bear the idea that a man comes into the world to-day with the field of truth monopolized and foreclosed. To every man lies open the whole field of truth, in morals, in politics, in science, in theology, in philosophy. The labors of past ages, the revelations of prophets and bards, the discoveries of the scientific and the philosophic, are not to be regarded as superseding our own exertions and inquiries, as impediments to the free action of our own minds, but merely as helps, as provocations to the freest and fullest spiritual action of which God has made us capable.

This is the real end he has in view, and it is a good end. To call forth the free spirit, to produce the conviction here implied, to provoke men to be men, self-moving, self-subsisting men, not mere puppets, moving but as moved by the reigning mode, the reigning dogma, the reigning school, is a grand and praiseworthy work, and we should reverence and aid, not abuse and hinder him who gives himself up soul and body to its accomplishment. So far as the author of the address before us is true to this object, earnest in executing this work, he has our hearty sympathy, and all the aid we, in our humble sphere, can give him. In laboring for this object, he proves himself worthy of his age and his country, true to religion and to morals, In calling, as he does, upon the literary men of our community, in the silver tones of his rich and eloquent voice, and above all by the quickening influence of his example, to assert and maintain their independence throughout the whole domain of thought, against every species of tyranny that would encroach upon it, he is doing his duty; he is doing a work the effects of which will be felt for good far and wide, long after men shall have forgotten the puerility of his conceits, the affectations of his style, and the unphilosophical character of his speculations. The doctrines he puts forth, the positive instructions, for which he is now censured, will soon be classed where they belong: but the influence of his free spirit, and free utterance, the literature of this country will long feel and hold in grateful remembrance.

ANDREWS NORTON

(1786–1853)

Andrews Norton was a Professor of Sacred Literature in the Harvard Divinity School from 1819 to 1830. As a consequence, he taught Emerson, George Ripley, James Freeman Clarke, Francis Hedge, and other exponents of transcendentalism. Norton was a conservative Unitarian who believed in the historical Christianity that Emerson repudiated in "The Divinity School Address"; he was indeed, as his enemies said, "the hard-headed Pope," and published in 1838 his most elaborate treatise, *The Evidence of the Genuineness of the Gospels* (1837–1844).

It is no accident then that Norton denounced Emerson in the essay for which he has become best known, "The Latest Form of Infidelity." Norton, who accuses Emerson of thinking that man is "a new-born bard of the Holy Ghost," seeks to establish the "miraculous" nature of Christianity, not of the individual. The history of Christianity, in Norton's view, is essential as the supporting evidence of divine faith in the "unseen and the eternal," in "the great objects of religion," and man must view himself as "a creature of a day," with limited control over his destiny. Norton stressed man's reason, Emerson man's intuition; Norton made great claims for historical Christianity, Emerson repudiated it; Norton stressed the "belief in authority," Emerson felt that authority must reside within the heart of man.

Norton's essay provoked sharp responses from other transcendentalists: George Ripley issued an immediate attack called "The Latest Form of Infidelity Examined"; and Theodore Parker published "The Previous Questions between Mr. Andrews Norton and His Alumni." With these and other rebuttals, transcendentalism became a dominant culture and religious force throughout New England.

Andrews Norton's essay reminds us that the transcendental movement was not one that only celebrated nature, self-reliance, and the oversoul. The conflict between Norton and the new generation was a cultural conflict between "the party of the past" and "the party of the future"; a religious conflict between liberal Unitarianism and transcendentalism, and a social conflict between the old order and the new, burgeoning democracy.

No biography or critical study has thus far been written. For a picture of Norton in the context of his struggle with the transcendentalists, see Perry Miller, ed., *The Transcendentalists*. "The Latest Form of Infidelity" is reprinted from this text.

A Discourse on the Latest Form of Infidelity

The present state of things imposes responsibilities upon all, who know the value of our faith and have ability to maintain it. Let us then employ this occasion in considering some of those opinions now prevalent, which are at war with a belief in Christianity. . .

The latest form of infidelity is distinguished by assuming the Christian name, while it strikes directly at the root of faith in Christianity, and indirectly of all religion, by denying the miracles attesting the divine mission of Christ . . .

If it were not the abuse of language that has prevailed, it would be idle to say, that, in denying the miracles of Christianity, the truth of Christianity is denied. It has been vaguely alleged, that the internal evidences of our religion are sufficient, and that miraculous proof is not wanted; but this can be said by no one who understands what Christianity is, and what its internal evidences are. On this ground, however, the miracles of Christ were not indeed expressly denied, but were represented by some of the founders of the modern school of German infidelity, as only prodigies, adapted to rouse the attention of a rude people, like the Jews; but not required for the conviction of men of more enlightened minds. By others, the accounts of them in the Gospels have been admitted as in the main true, but explained as only exaggerated and discolored relations of natural events. But now, without taking the trouble to go through this tedious and hopeless process of misinterpretation, there are many who avow their disbelief of all that is miraculous in Christianity, and still affect to call themselves Christians. But Christianity was a revelation from God; and, in being so, it was itself a miracle. No proof of his divine commission could be afforded, but through miraculous displays of God's power. Nothing is left that can be called Christianity, if its miraculous character be denied. Its essence is gone; its evidence is annihilated. Its truths, involving the highest interests of man, the facts which it makes known, and which are implied in its very existence as a divine revelation, rest no longer on the authority of God. All the evidence, if evidence it can be called, which it affords of its doctrines, consists in the real or pretended assertions of an individual, of whom we know very little, except that his history must have been most grossly misrepresented . . .

The rejection of Christianity, in any proper sense of the word, the denial that God revealed himself by Christ, the denial of the truth of the Gospel history, or, as it is called in the language of the sect, the rejection of *historical* Christianity, is, of course, accompanied by the rejection of all that mass of evidence, which, in the view of a Christian, establishes the truth of his religion. This evidence, it is said, consists only of probabilities. We want certainty. The dwellers in the regions of shadows complain, that the solid earth is not stable enough for them to rest on. They have firm footing on the clouds.

To the demand for certainty, let it come from whom it may, I answer, that I know of no absolute certainty, beyond the limit of momentary consciousness, a certainty that vanishes the instant it exists, and is lost in the region of metaphysical doubt. Beyond this limit, absolute certainty, so far as human reason may judge, cannot be the privilege of any finite being. When we talk of certainty, a wise man will remember what he is, and the narrow bounds of his wisdom and of his powers. . . A creature of a day, just endued with the capacity of thought, at first receiving all his opinions from those who have preceded him, entangled among numberless prejudices, confused by his passions, perceiving, if the eyes of his understanding are opened, that the sphere of his knowledge is hemmed in by an infinity of which he is ignorant, from which unknown region, clouds are often passing over, and darkening what seemed clearest to his view,—such a being cannot pretend to attain, by his unassisted powers, any assurance concerning the unseen and the eternal, the great objects of religion. If men had been capable of comprehending their weakness and ignorance, and of reflecting deeply on their condition here, a universal cry would have risen from their hearts, imploring their God, if there were one, to reveal himself, and to make known to them their destiny. Their wants have been answered by God before they were uttered. Such is the belief of a Christian; and there is no question more worthy of consideration than whether this belief be well founded. It can be determined only by the exercise of that reason which God has given us for our guidance in all that concerns us. There can be no intuition, no direct perception, of the truth of Christianity, no metaphysical certainty. But it would be folly, indeed, to reject the testimony of God concerning all our higher relations and interests, because we can have no assurance, that he has spoken through Christ, except such as the condition of our nature admits of . . .

In one sense, and an obvious sense of the word, religion is a universal want of man. It is required for the development of his moral and spiritual powers. He is suffering, tempted, and imperfect; and he needs it for consolation, for strength to resist, and for encouragement to make progress. . . But religious principle and feeling, however important, are necessarily founded on the belief of certain facts; of the existence and providence of God, and of man's immortality. Now the evidence of these facts is not intuitive; and whatever ground for the belief of them may be afforded by the phenomena of nature, or the ordinary course of events, it is certain, that the generality of men have never been able by their unassisted reason to obtain assurance concerning them. Out of the sphere of those enlightened by divine revelation, neither the belief nor the imagination of them has operated with any considerable effect to produce the religious character. . .

But the rejection of Christianity on the ground just stated, and the pretence that the only true universal source of religion is to be found in the common nature of man, have been connected by many with the rejection of all the reasoning by which those facts that are the basis of religion may be otherwise rendered probable; and often with the rejection of all belief in the facts themselves. The religion of which they speak, therefore, exists merely, if it exists at all, in undefined and unintelligible feelings, having reference perhaps to certain imaginations, the result of impressions communicated in childhood, or produced by the visible signs of religious belief existing around us, or awakened by the beautiful and magnificent spectacles which nature presents. Sometimes, as we have elsewhere seen, they are represented as being excited by a system of pantheism; a doctrine that rejects all proper religious belief, and does not admit of being stated in words expressing a rational meaning. In this case, whatever feelings may exist, they can have no claim to be called religious.

There is, then, no mode of establishing religious belief, but by the exercise of reason, by investigation, by forming a probable judgment upon facts. Christianity, in requiring this process, requires nothing more than any other form of religion must do. He who on this account rejects it, cannot have recourse to Natural Religion. This can offer him no relief from the necessity of reasoning; and still less can it pretend to give him any higher assurance than Christianity affords. If its voice be listened to, it will only direct him back to Christianity. If he will not refrain from using the name of religion, his only resource to escape the difficulty and uncertainty of reasoning, is to take refuge in some cloud of mysticism, that belies the form of religion . . .

But we have not, it may be said, yet removed the difficulty, that the evidence and character of Christianity, in order to be properly understood, require investigations which are beyond the capacity or the opportunities of a great majority of men . . . The reply is, that it is to be received on the same ground as we receive all other truths, of which we have not ourselves mastered the evidences; for the same reason that we do not reject all that vast amount of knowledge which is not the result of our own deductions. Our belief in those truths, the evidence of which we cannot fully examine for ourselves, is founded in a greater or less degree on the testimony of others, who have examined their evidence, and whom we regard as intelligent and trustworthy . . . This reliance on the knowledge of others may be called *belief on trust*, or *belief on authority;* but perhaps a more proper name for it would be *belief on testimony*, the testimony of those who have examined a subject to their conviction of the truth of certain facts . . . The admission of this principle does not weaken the force of its evidences in the mind of any man of correct judgment. In maintaining, therefore, that the thorough investigation of the evidences and character of our religion requires much knowledge and much thought, and the combined and continued labor of different minds, we maintain nothing that gives to Christianity a different character from what belongs to all the higher and more important branches of knowledge, and nothing inconsistent with its being in its nature a universal religion.

GEORGE RIPLEY

(1802-1880)

When George Ripley graduated from the Harvard Divinity School he was already a leader of Unitarianism. He published widely throughout the 1830's and helped Margaret Fuller edit *The Dial* from 1840 to 1841. In 1841 Ripley became President of The Brook Farm Association, and he and his wife struggled with the utopian experiment until its collapse in 1847. Most of his later years were spent paying the debts incurred by Brook Farm and in publishing scattered articles that spread the transcendental gospel.

When Andrews Norton published his attack on Emerson, Ripley was prepared for a counterthrust. In his essay, he underscores one of the main elements of transcendentalism: its democratic sympathies. Ripley accuses Norton of retaining a conservative position that is antipathetic to a developing nation committed to the equality of all men and women.

For studies of Ripley see Octavius B. Frothingham, *George Ripley*, 1882; Charles Robert Crowe, *George Ripley, Transcendentalist and Utopian Socialist*, 1967.

The text is taken from Perry Miller, *The Transcendentalists,* 1900.

The Latest Form of Infidelity Examined

In the hope, that the Cambridge Theological School would be true to these momentous obligations, would answer to the piercing cry of our country and age for a free and generous theology, would be a tower of safety and strength against every foe of mental liberty, we have loved it with an exceeding love. Her name has been written on the very palms of our hands: they would sooner forget their cunning, than we could forget her welfare: she had taught us to search boldly, though meekly and reverently, into the mysteries of God and the mind of Christ; we took pleasure in her stones and even honored her dust; we valued her reputation, her influence, her usefulness, as if it had been our own; we looked to her, perhaps with exaggerated, yet with pardonable confidence, as the great hope of a progressive theology in our native land, as the fountain from which a bright and benignant light would radiate beyond the mountains of New England, and shine upon the broad and pleasant meadows of the West. This feeling has been shared in common with almost all our clergymen. We have endeavored to diffuse it in our societies; it has kindled the enthusiasm of our most nobleminded young men; our opulent citizens have not escaped its influence; and nearly the whole of our religious community have regarded the School at Cambridge as their favorite child . . .

In our happy state of society, as there is no very broad line of distinction between the clergy and the rest of the community, they had shared in the influences, which, within the last few years, have acted so strongly on the public mind; with intelligent and reflecting men of every pursuit and persuasion, many of them had been led to feel the necessity of a more thorough reform in theology; they were not satisfied that the denial of the Trinity and its kindred doctrines gave them possession of all spiritual truth; they wished to press forward in the course which they had begun, to ascend to higher views, to gain a deeper insight into Christianity, to imbibe more fully its divine spirit, and to apply the truths of revelation to the wants of society and the progress of man.

Their experience as pastors had brought them into contact with a great variety of minds; some of which were dissatisfied with the traditions they had been taught; the religion of the day seemed too cold, too lifeless, too mechanical for many of their flock; they were called to settle difficulties in theology of which they had not been advised in the school; objections were presented by men of discernment and acuteness, which could not be set aside by the learning of books; it was discovered that many had become unable to rest their religious faith on the foundation of a material philosophy; and that a new direction must be given to their ideas, or they would be lost to Christianity, and possibly to virtue. The wants of such minds could not be concealed; they were known to the ministers, if not to the world; to neglect them would have been a sin; the wandering sheep in the wilderness excited more interest than the ninety and nine which were safe in the fold, and to restore them to the good shepherd was counted a paramount duty.

In the course of the inquiries which they had entered into, for their own satisfaction and the good of their people, they had become convinced of the superiority of the testimony of the soul to the evidence of the external senses; the essential character of Christianity, as a principle of spiritual faith, of reliance on the Universal Father, and of the intrinsic equality and brotherhood of man, was made more prominent than the historical circumstances with which it was surrounded, at its introduction into the world; and the signatures of truth and divinity which it bore on its front were deemed stronger proofs of its origin with God, than even the works of might which were wrought by its Author for the benefit of man. They cherished a firm and sincere conviction of the importance of these views, and their adaptation to the peculiar wants and highest interests of the community. They never disguised the results to which they had come; they gave them a due proportion of attention in their public services; they rejoiced in their discussion, even when it was called forth by rude attacks; though sometimes misunderstood, they were not discouraged; they knew the community they lived in, which will not suffer a good man to be put down; and with a calm confidence in truth, they were content to wait for the prevalence of their views. They regarded them as the natural result of liberal inquiry in theology, chastened and purified by the influence of religious sentiment, and guided by the lights of an elevated spiritual philosophy. In the exercise of their ministry, they had been confirmed in the soundness of their ideas; their benign effects were visible among the people of their charge; and these effects were thought to be in harmony with the spirit of Christ, nay, the necessary product of the religion which he announced. They saw their opinions rapidly spreading among the younger members of the profession, while they were regarded with charity, if not with approbation, by those whom they most honored among their seniors. No difference of speculation had estranged them from the hearts of their brethren; no breach had been made in the sympathy which was the pervading principle of their association; the understanding had been sacredly observed, if not formally expressed, that a profession of faith in Christ, and a sincere and virtuous character were the conditions of fellowship, rather than any agreement in theological opinion . . .

By the exclusive principle, I mean the assumption of the right for an individual, or for any body of individuals, to make their own private opinions the measure of what is fundamental in the Christian faith. As liberal Christians, we have long contended against this principle, as contrary to the very essence of Protestantism; we have claimed the inherent right of private judgment, as essential to Christian freedom; we have resisted, to the uttermost, every attempt to impose controverted points of opinion on the universal belief of the church. We have welcomed every man as a brother, who acknowledged Christ as his Master; we have not presumed to sit in judgment on any Christian's claim to discipleship; we have refused to entertain the question, whether he were entitled to the Christian name; we have felt that it was not ours to give or to withhold; and that the decision in all cases, must rest with himself. In was not because our exclusive brethren made a belief in the Trinity, a test of allegiance to Christ, that we accused them of inconsistency with the liberty of the Gospel; but because they presumed to erect any standard whatever, according to which the faith of individuals should be made to conform to the judgment of others. It was not any special application of the principle, that we objected to; it was the principle itself; and assuredly, the exercise of this principle does not change its character, by reason of the source from which it proceeds. Nay, is it not aggravated by the fact, that it is sustained, not by those with whom it forms a part of their religion, but by those whose religion is identified with hostility to it?

But the doctrine which lies at the foundation of your whole Discourse is a signal manifestation of the exclusive principle. You propose your own convictions,—and convictions, which it will appear in the sequel of this letter, are directly at war with the prevailing faith of the Church,—as the criterion of genuine Christian belief. You maintain that the truth of Christianity can be supported by no other evidence than that which appears satisfactory to yourself; that unless we are persuaded of the divine origin of our religion by the arguments which you deem valid, we cannot be persuaded at all; and that to speak of faith in the revelations of the Gospel, unless that faith be built on the only basis which you pronounce to be good, is, in itself, a proof of delusion or insincerity. You make no allowance for the immeasurable variety of mind which is found everywhere, for the different direction which early education, natural temperament, and peculiar associations impart to men's habits of thinking, for the shifting lights which the same evidence presents, according to the circumstances in which it arrests the attention, or for the changes acquired by language and the ideas which it conveys, in the progress of ages; but you advance your principle, with the same want of reserve or qualification that a teacher of the Infallible Church would have exhibited before the Reformation; you declare that a certain kind of evidence, in your view, establishes the truth of Christianity, and that he who rests his faith on any other is an infidel, notwithstanding his earnest and open professions to the contrary. You thus, in fact, deny the name of Christian to not a few individuals in your audience, although you avoid discussing the grounds by which their opinions are supported. For it is perfectly well known that many of our most eminent clergymen,—I will not refrain from speaking of them as they deserve, on account of my personal sympathy with their views,—repose their belief in the divine origin of Christianity on a different foundation from that which you approve as the only tenable one. Men whose names are almost a passport to the opinions they adopt, whose lives are a guaranty against all suspicion of guile, whose fervent devotion to every cause that promises the extension of religion or the good of man has become proverbial, whose candor and transparency of character is a constant memorial of the simplicity of Christ, are inclined to rest their convictions of the divinity of the Gospel on evidence which commends itself to their minds, although you may pronounce it to be valueless and deceptive. Among those who adopt this view of Christianity are clergymen who have never enjoyed the benefit of your instructions, but whose minds have been kept open to every fresh access of light, as well as their younger brethren who are deeply indebted to your counsels and example in the pursuit of truth, and who have obtained from your influence in former years, something of that spirit of freedom, for which they are now condemned . . .

The doctrine, that miracles are the only evidence of a divine revelation, if generally admitted, would impair the religious influence of the Christian ministry. It would separate the pastor of a church from the sympathies of his people, confine him in a sphere of thought remote from their usual interests, and give an abstract and scholastic character to his services in the pulpit. The great object of his endeavors would be to demonstrate the truth of the Christian history; the weapons of his warfare would be carnal, and not spiritual; drawn from grammars, and lexicons, and mouldy traditions, not from the treasures of the human heart. The miracles being established to the satisfaction of an inquisitive generation, nothing would remain but to announce the truth on their authority; for as all other evidence is without value, and this alone sufficient, it would be a waste of time to direct the attention to the divine glory of Christ and his revelation; this is beyond the reach of human "perception"; none but enthusiasts can make use of it. The minister would rely for success on his skill in argument, rather than on his sympathy with man; on the knowledge he gains within the walls of the University, rather than on the experience which may be learned in the homes of his people. He would trust more to his logical demonstration of the evidences of Christianity, than to the faithful exhibition of Christian truth to the naked human heart. But, I believe, not a wise and experienced pastor can be found, who will not say that, as a general rule, the discussion of the historical evidence is ill adapted to the pulpit, and that the effects of such preaching on society at large, or on the individual conscience, are too minute to be estimated . . .

On the contrary, I have known great and beneficial effects to arise from the simple exhibition of the truth of the Gospel to the heart and conscience, by earnest men, who trusted to the intuitive power of the soul, for the perception of its divinity. The revelation of Christ is addressed to the better nature of man; "my sheep," said he, "hear my voice, and follow me, and I give unto them eternal life"; "the light shines in darkness, and the darkness comprehendeth it not," but the "children of light" look upward and are blest; it meets with a cordial reception from those who are burdened with the consciousness of sin, who are seeking for higher things, who are "feeling after God, if haply they may find him"; and this fact is the foundation of the minister's success. If you confine him to the demonstration of the miracles; if you deny him intimate access to the soul, by the truth which he bears; if you virtually tell him the internal evidence of Christianity is a delusion, that our personal experience of its power is no proof of its divinity, and that the glorious Gospel of the blessed God is to be believed only because learned men vouchsafe to assure the humble Christian of its truth; you deprive the minister of all inward force; you make him little better than a logical machine; and much as I value a sound logic in its proper place, I am sure it is not the instrument which is mighty through God to the pulling down of the strong holds of sin. It may detect error; but it cannot give so much as a glimpse of the glory of Christ. It may refute fallacies; but it cannot bind the heart to the love of holiness. A higher power is necessary for this purpose; and such a power God has granted to man in the divine gift of Christianity, which corresponds to his inmost wants, and bears the pledge of its truth in its effects on the soul . . .

You maintain that "extensive learning" is usually requisite for those who would influence their fellow-men on religious subjects. But Jesus certainly did not take this into consideration in the selection of the twelve from the mass of the disciples; he committed the promulgation of his religion to "unlearned and ignorant" men; the sublimest truths were entrusted to the most common minds; and, in this way, "God made foolish the wisdom of the world" . . .

Christ honored man. He felt the worth of the soul. He knew its intimate connexion with God. He believed in the omnipresence of the Deity; but taught, that of all temples the "upright heart and pure" was the most acceptable. He saw that the parade of wisdom, which books impart, was as nothing before "the light that enlighteneth every human mind." The whole course of his nation's history was an illustration of the fact, "that poor mechanics are wont to be God's great ambassadors to mankind." Hence, he gave no preference to Nicodemus, that master in Israel, or to the wealthy Joseph of Arimathea, who, we may presume, had devoted his leisure to the cultivation of his mind, over Matthew the publican, or the sons of the fisherman Zebedee;[1] and while the former were hesitating between their convictions and their comforts at home, the latter were going barefoot from city to city to preach the kingdom of God. Christ established no college of Apostles; he did not revive the school of the prophets which had died out; he paid no distinguished respect to the pride of learning; indeed, he sometimes intimates that it is an obstacle to the perception of truth; and thanks God, that while he has hid the mysteries of the kingdom of Heaven from the wise and prudent, he has made them known to men as ignorant as babes of the lore of the schools . . .

Once more, I am obliged to differ from your conclusion with regard to the practical importance of scholars to the interests of religion. Perhaps I may venture to hope, that I am not likely to be accused of indifference to human learning. But I cannot fall in with the extravagant pretensions that you urge in its favor. I deny that it entitles its possessor to the claim of infallibility. True learning, in my opinion, is as modest as it is inquisitive; it searches for truth with a lowly and reverent aspect; it never counts itself to have yet attained; it never presumes to assert that it can gain no further light on any subject; conscious of frailty, it communes with all wise teachers; and in meek self-dependence, compares the lessons they announce with the oracles of God. Such learning blesses both its disciples and those to whom they are sent; the former obtain from the latter no less instruction than they give; their reverence for man is too deep to permit the exercise of scorn; and in free and trusting intercourse with all varieties of their fellow men, they feel

[1] Nicodemus was a Pharisee and a member of the Sanhedrin who defended Christ when he was denounced by other Pharisees; Joseph of Arimathea, the subject of many legends, is the Israelite who provided the tomb for Jesus; Matthew was one of the 12 apostles, according to legend the author of the first gospel; Zebedee was a fisherman whose sons James and John became disciples of Jesus. Cf. Matthew 4:21.

that they are living to learn; they are growing old in the pursuit of wisdom, with the freshness of children, λῃράσκονσι διδασκόμενοι; and the thought, that no clearer views of truth were yet to visit their minds, would almost bring them to the grave before their time.

A more sincere veneration for human beings I cannot feel, than for scholars of this character. I honor the learned, when they devote their attainments to the service of society; when they cherish a stronger interest in the welfare of their brethren, than in the luxury of their books; when they bring the researches of science to the illustration of truth, the correction of abuses, and the aid of the sufferer; but if they do not acknowledge a higher light than that which comes from the printed page; if they confound the possession of erudition with the gift of wisdom; and above all, if they presume to interfere in the communion of the soul with God, and limit the universal bounty of Heaven within their "smoky cells," I can only utter my amazement.

THEODORE PARKER

(1810–1860)

Theodore Parker, who came from a family of farmers, was a widely read transcendentalist. Unlike many of his contemporaries, he wrote in a straightforward, plain style; his rebuttal of Andrews Norton is couched in terms that would appeal to the common man of his time. Like Emerson, Brownson, and Ripley, Parker argues against historical Christianity and the limitations of man.

The standard text is *The Works of Theodore Parker*, 15 vols. 1907–1913.

A biography is John Weiss, *Life and Correspondence of Theodore Parker*, 2 vols. 1864.

Critical studies include Octavius Frothingham, *Theodore Parker*, 1874, John W. Chadwick, *Theodore Parker, Preacher and Reformer*, 1900, Henry Steel Commager, *Theodore Parker*, 1936, 1960; and Robert C. Albrecht, *Theodore Parker*, 1971.

The Previous Question
between Mr. Andrews Norton and
His Alumni Moved and Handled
in a Letter to all Those
Gentlemen

Now since all religion in general starts from the germs, and primary essential truths of religion, which are innate with man; since it is promoted by religious geniuses who, inspired by God, appeal to these innate germs and truths, in man; since all religions are fundamentally the same, and only specific variations of one and the same genus, and since, therefore, Christianity is one religion among many, though it is the highest, and even a perfect religion—it follows incontestably that Christianity also must start from these same points. Accordingly we find history verifying philosophy, for Christ always assumes these great facts, viz. the existence of God, and man's sense of dependence upon him, as facts given in man's nature. He attempted to excite in man a more living consciousness of these truths, and to give them a permanent influence on the whole character and life. His words were attended to, just as the words of Homer or Socrates, and the works of Phidias or Mozart[1] were attended to. But admiration for his character, and the influence of his doctrines, was immeasurably greater than in their case, because he stood in the very highest department of human interest, and spoke of matters more concerning than poetry or philosophy, sculpture or music. Now, if he assumed as already self-evident and undoubted, these two primary and essential truths of religion, which had likewise been assumed by all his predecessors—and if no miracle was needed to attest and give authority to his doctrines respecting those very foundations and essentials of religion, no man can consistently demand a miracle as a proof that Christ spoke the truth when he taught doctrines of infinitely less importance, which were themselves unavoidable conclusions from these two admitted truths. Gentlemen, I am told by my minister, who is an argumentative man, it is a maxim in logic, that what is true of the genus, is true also of the species. If, therefore, the two fundamentals of religion, which in themselves involve all necessary subordinate truths thereof, be assumed by Christ as self-evident, already acknowledged, and therefore at no time, and least of all at that time, requiring a miracle to substantiate them, I see not how it can be maintained, that a miracle was needed to establish inferior truths that necessarily followed from them. It would be absurd to suppose a miracle needed on the

[1] Homer was the Greek epic poet who is traditionally believed to be the author of the *Iliad* and the *Odyssey*: Socrates (470?-399 B. C.) was the Greek philosopher and teacher; Phidias was an Athenian sculptor of the fifth century B. C.; Wolfgang Amadeus Mozart (1756-1791) was the famous Austrian composer.

part of Socrates, to convince men that he uttered the truth, since no miracle could be a *direct* proof of that fact; and still more absurd would it be, while the most sublime doctrines, as soon as he affirmed them, were admitted as self-evident, to demand miraculous proofs for the truth of the legitimate and necessary deductions therefrom.

Still further, Gentlemen, Christianity is either the perfection of a religion whose germs and first truths are innate in the soul, or it is the perfection of a religion whose germs and first truths are not innate in the soul. If we take the latter alternative, I admit, that, following the common opinion, miracles would be necessary to establish the divine authority of the mediator of this religion; for devout men measuring the new doctrines by reason, conscience, and the religious sentiment—the only standard within their reach—and finding this doctrine contrary and repugnant thereto, must, of necessity, repel this religion, because it was unnatural, unsatisfactory, and useless to them. To open my meaning a little more fully by an illustration,—should a man present to my eyes a figure as the Ideal of Beauty, if that figure revolted my taste; were repugnant to my sense of harmony in outline, and symmetry of parts, I should say it could not be so; but if he had satisfactory credentials to convince me that he came direct from God, and to prove that this figure was indeed the Ideal of Beauty to the archangels, who had an aesthetic constitution more perfect than that of men, and therefore understood beauty better than I could do, I should admit the fact; but must, in that case, reject his Ideal Beauty, because it was the Ideal of Deformity, relatively, to my sense, inasmuch as it was repugnant to the first principles of human taste. Now if a religion whose germs and first truths are not innate in man, should be presented by a mediator furnished with credentials of his divine office, that are satisfactory to all men, the religion must yet be rejected. The religion must be made for man's religious nature, as much as the shoe must be made for the foot. God has laid the foundation of religion in man, and the religion built up in man must correspond to that foundation, otherwise it can be of no more use to him than St. Anthony's sermon was to the fishes.[2] There was nothing in the fishes to receive the doctrine. But if we take the other alternative, and admit that Christianity is the perfection of a religion whose germs and first truths are innate in man, and confessed to be so, by him who brings, and those who accept the religion, I see no need, or even any use of miracles, to prove the authority of this mediator. To illustrate as before; if some one brings me an image, as the Ideal of Beauty, and that image correspond to my idea of the Beautiful, though it rise never so much above it, I ask no external fact to convince me of the beauty of the image, or the authority of him who brings it. I have all the evidence of its excellent beauty that I need

[2] St. Anthony (250–356 A. D.?) was the father of monachism who, after 20 years of seclusion, was persuaded to leave his retreat; he founded a famous monastery.

or wish for; all that is possible. If Raphael[3] had wrought miracles, his works would have had no more value than now, for their value depends on no foreign authority; but on their corresponding to ideal excellence . . .

Gentlemen, I believe that Jesus, like other religious teachers, wrought miracles. I should come to this conclusion, even if the Evangelists[4] did not claim them for him; nay, I should admit that his miracles would be more numerous and extraordinary, more benevolent in character and motive, than the miracles of his predecessors. This would naturally follow, if his power and obedience were more perfect than theirs. But I see not how a miracle proves a doctrine, and I even conjecture we do not value him for the miracles; but the miracles for him. I take it no one would think much of his common miracles, if they were not wrought by the God-man. The divine character of Christ gives value to the miracles, which cannot give divinity to Christ, or even prove it is there, as I take it; for many Christians believed Apollonius of Tyana[5] wrought miracles, but they placed no value on them, because they had little respect for Apollonius of Tyana himself. The miracles of the Greek mythology, seem to have had no influence on the mind of the nation, because no great life lay at the bottom of these miracles. The same may be said of the miracles of the middle ages, and even of more modern times. We say these were not real miracles, and the saying is perhaps true, for the most part, but to such as believed them, they were just as good as true; yet their effect was trifling, because there was no great soul which worked these miracles. It may be said these differ in character from the Christian miracles, and the saying has its side of truth, if only the canonical miracles are included; but it is not true if the other miracles of Christian tradition are taken into account, for here malicious miracles are sometimes ascribed to him. But men found comfort in these stories only because they believed in the divinity of the character which lay at the bottom of the Christian movement . . .

Now, since these things are so, it seems to me much easier, more natural, and above all more true, to ground Christianity on the truth of its doctrines, and its sufficiency to satisfy all the moral and religious wants of man in the highest conceivable state, than to rest it on miracles, which, at best, could only be a sign, and not a proof of its excellence, and which, beside, do themselves require much more evidence to convince man of their truth, than Christianity requires without them. To me, the spiritual elevation of Jesus is a more convincing proof of his divinity, than the story of his miraculous transfiguration; and the words which he uttered, and the life which he lived,

[3] Raphael (1483–1520) was an Italian Renaissance painter and architect.
[4] The Evangelists were the authors of the four New Testament Gospels: Matthew, Mark, Luke, and John.
[5] Apollonius of Tyana (3 B. C.–c. A. D. 97)

was a Greek philosopher, leading exponent of Neo-Pythagoreanism, who traveled to India, met the Magi at Babylon on his way, and returned as a famous man, widely regarded as a wonder worker.

are more satisfactory evidence of his divine authority, than all his miracles, from the transformation of water into wine, to the resurrection of Lazarus.[6] I take him to be the most perfect religious incarnation of God, without putting his birth on the same level with that of Hercules.[7] I see the story of his supernatural conception, as a picture of the belief in the early Christian church, and find the divine character in the general instructions and heavenly life of Christ. I need no miracle to convince me that the sun shines, and just as little do I need a miracle to convince me of the divinity of Jesus and his doctrines, to which a miracle, as I look at it, can add just nothing. Even the miracle of the resurrection does not prove the immortality of the soul.

Gentleman, I would say a word to that portion of your number who rest Christianity solely, or chiefly on the miracles. I would earnestly deprecate your theology. Happily, with the unlearned, like myself, this miracle-question is one of *theology,* and not of *religion,* which latter may, and does exist, under the most imperfect and vicious theology. But do you wish that we should rest our theology and religion—for you make it a religious question—on ground so insecure? on a basis which every scoffer may shake, if he cannot shake down—a basis which you acknowledge to be insecure when other religions claim to rest on it, and one from which your own teachers are continually separating fragments? To the mass of Christians, who are taught to repose their faith on miracles, those of the Old are as good as those of the New Testament, both of which are insecure. One of your number, a man not to be named without respect for his talents, his learning, and, above all, for his conscientious piety, a man whom it delights me to praise, though from afar—at one blow, of his Academic Lectures, fells to the ground all the most stupendous miracles of the Old Testament; and another, a party in this contest, has long ago removed several miracles from the text of the New Testament, and thrown discredit—unconsciously—upon the rest. If the groundwork of Christianity is thus to be left at the mercy of scoffers, or scholars and critics, who decide by principles that are often arbitrary, and must be uncertain, what are we the unlearned, who have little time for investigating such matters—and to whom Latin schools and colleges have not opened their hospitable doors—what are we to do? You tell us that we must not fall back on the germs and first truths of religion in the soul. You tell us that Chrsit *"established a relation between man and God, that could not otherwise exist,"* and the ONLY proof that this relation is *real,* and that he had authority to establish it; is found in the particular miracles he wrought, which miracles cannot, at this day, be *proved* real. Thus you repel us from the belief that the relation between God and man is founded in the nature of

[6] Lazarus was the brother of Mary and Martha whom Jesus raised from the dead. Cf. John 11:1–44.

[7] Hercules was the son of Zeus and Alc-meme, a hero of extraordinary strength and courage who won immortality by performing the 12 labors demanded by Hera.

things, and was established at our creation, and that the authority of Christianity is not personal with Jesus, but rests on the eternal nature of Truth. Thus you make us rest our moral and religious faith, for time and eternity, on evidence too weak to be trusted in a trifling case that comes before a common court of justice. You make our religion depend entirely on something outside, on strange events which happened, it is said, two thousand years ago, of which we can never be certain, and on which yourselves often doubt, at least of the more and less. Gentlemen, we cannot be critics, but we would be Christians. If you strike away a part of the Bible, and deny—what philosophy must deny—the perfect literal truth of the first chapter of Genesis, or the book of Jonah, or any part which claims to be literally true, and is not literally true, for us you have destroyed all value in miracles as evidence—exclusive and irrefragable—for the truth of Christianity. Gentlemen, with us, Christianity is not a thing of speculation, but a matter of life, and I beseech you, in behalf of numbers of my fellows, pious and unlearned as myself, to do one of two things, either to prove that the miraculous stories in the Bible are perfectly true, that is, that there is nothing fictitious or legendary from Genesis to Revelations, which yet professes to be historical, and that the authors of the Bible were never mistaken as to facts or judgments thereon; or leave us to ground our belief in Christianity on its truth,—which is obvious to every spiritual eye that is open,—on its fitness to satisfy our wants; on its power to regenerate and restore degraded and fallen man; on our faith in Christ, which depends not on his birth, or ascension; on his miraculous powers of healing, creating, or transforming; but on his words of truth and holiness; on his divine life; on the undisputed fact that he was ONE WITH GOD. Until you do one of these things, we shall mourn in our hearts, and repeat the old petition "God save Christianity from its friends, its enemies we care not for." You may give us your miracles, and tell us they are sufficient witness, but hungering and thirsting, we shall look unto Christ, and say, "Lord, to whom shall we go, Thou only hast the words of everlasting life," and we believe on Thee, for thy words and life proclaim themselves divine, and these no man can take from us.

AMOS BRONSON ALCOTT

(1799–1888)

When Emerson chose to conclude his essay *Nature* "with some traditions of man and nature, which a certain poet sang to me," he was paying great tribute to his friend, Bronson Alcott, whom he referred to as "the Orphic Poet." Alcott was a Neoplatonic thinker whose philosophy, taken from his journals, is captured in the phrase that Emerson quotes: "The foundations of man are not in matter, but in spirit. But the spirit is eternity."

Alcott shared Emersons's ethereal tendencies, but he lacked his wit and directness. During his life he held various teaching positions. He tried to establish a communal society, Fruitlands, near Harvard, Massachusetts, and he published in the many journals of the time. But he was never able to earn a living, and he depended on financial help from his wife, his daughters (especially Louisa, the author of *Little Women*), and his friends.

Alcott's best-known and most representative writings are his *Orphic Sayings*. The first 50 of them appeared in *The Dial* in July 1840.

Odell Shepard edited *The Journals of Bronson Alcott*, 1938. Shepard has also written the best biography, *Pedlar's Progress: The Life of Bronson Alcott*, 1937. The early biography, Frank B. Sanborn and William T. Harris, *A. Bronson Alcott: His Life and Philosophy*, 2 vols., 1893 is still useful.

A personal account is Elizabeth P. Peabody, *Record of a School, Exemplifying the General Principles of Spiritual Character*, 1835. Recent studies include George E. Haefner, *A Critical Estimate of the Educational Theories and Practices of A. Bronson Alcott*, 1937 and Dorothy McCuskey, *Bronson Alcott, Teacher*, 1940.

Orphic Sayings

I

Thou art, my heart, a soul-flower, facing ever and following the motions of thy sun, opening thyself to her vivifying ray, and pleading thy affinity with the celestial orbs. Thou dost

the livelong day
Dial on time thine own eternity.

II. ENTHUSIASM

Believe, youth, that your heart is an oracle; trust her instinctive auguries, obey her divine leadings; nor listen too fondly to the uncertain echoes of your head. The heart is the prophet of your soul, and ever fulfills her prophecies; reason is her historian; but for the prophecy the history would not be. Great is the heart: cherish her; she is big with the future, she forebodes renovations. Let the flame of enthusiasm fire alway your bosom. Enthusiasm is the glory and hope of the world. It is the life of sanctity and genius; it has wrought all miracles since the beginning of time.

III. HOPE

Hope deifies man; it is the apotheosis of the soul; the prophecy and fulfilment of her destinies. The nobler her aspirations, the sublimer her conceptions of the Godhead. As the man, so his God: God is his idea of excellence; the complement of his own being.

IV. IMMORTALITY

The grander my conception of being, the nobler my future. There can be no sublimity of life without faith in the soul's eternity. Let me live superior to sense and custom, vigilant always, and I shall experience my divinity; my hope will be infinite, nor shall the universe contain, or content me. But if I creep daily from the haunts of an ignoble past, like a beast from his burrow, neither earth nor sky, man nor God, shall appear desirable or glorious; my life shall be loathsome to me, my future reflect my fears. He alone, who lives nobly, oversees his own being, believes all things, and partakes of the eternity of God.

V. VOCATION

Engage in nothing that cripples or degrades you. Your first duty is self-culture, self-exaltation: you may not violate this high trust. Your self is sacred, profane it not. Forge no chains wherewith to shackle your own members. Either subordinate your vocation to your life, or quit it forever: it is not for you; it is condemnation of your own soul. Your influence on others is commensurate with the strength that you have found in yourself. First cast the demons from your own bosom, and then shall your word exorcise them from the hearts of others.

VI. SENSUALISM

He who marvels at nothing, who feels nothing to be mysterious, but must needs bare all things to sense, lacks both wisdom and piety. Miracle is the mantle in which these venerable natures wrap themselves, and he, who seeks curiously to rend this asunder, profanes their sacred countenance to enter by stealth into the Divine presence. Sanctity, like God, is ever mysterious, and all devout souls reverence her. A wonderless age is godless: an age of reverence, an age of piety and wisdom.

VII. SPIRITUALISM

Piety is not scientific; yet embosoms the facts that reason develops in scientific order to the understanding. Religion, being a sentiment, is science yet in synthetic relations; truth yet undetached from love; thought not yet severed from action. For every fact that eludes the analysis of reason, conscience affirms its root in the supernatural. Every synthetic fact is supernatural and miraculous. Analysis by detecting its law resolves it into science, and renders it a fact of the understanding. Divinely seen, natural facts are symbols of spiritual laws. Miracles are of the heart; not of the head: indigenous to the soul; not freaks of nature, not growths of history. God, man, nature, are miracles.

VIII. MYSTICISM

Because the soul is herself mysterious, the saint is a mystic to the worldling. He lives to the soul; he partakes of her properties, he dwells in her atmosphere of light and hope. But the worldling, living to sense, is identified with the flesh; he dwells amidst the dust and vapors of his own lusts, which dim his vision, and obscure the heavens wherein the saint beholds the face of God.

IX. ASPIRATION

The insatiableness of her desires is an augury of the soul's eternity. Yearning for satisfaction, yet ever balked of it from temporal things, she still prosecutes her search for it, and her faith remains unshaken amidst constant disappointments. She would breathe life, organize light; her hope is eternal; a never-ending, still-beginning quest of the Godhead in her own bosom; a perpetual effort to actualize her divinity in time. Intact, aspirant, she feels the appulses of both spiritual and material things; she would appropriate the realm she inherits by virtue of her incarnation: infinite appetencies direct all her members on finite things; her vague strivings, and Cyclopean motions, confess an aim beyond the confines of transitory natures; she is quivered with heavenly desires: her quarry is above the stars: her arrows are snatched from the armory of heaven.

X. APOTHEOSIS

Every soul feels at times her own possibility of becoming a God; she cannot rest in the human, she aspires after the Godlike. This instinctive tendency is an authentic augury of its own fulfilment. Men shall become Gods. Every act of admiration, prayer, praise, worship, desire, hope, implies and predicts the future apotheosis of the soul.

XI. DISCONTENT

All life is eternal; there is none other; and all unrest is but the struggle of the soul to reassure herself on her inborn immortality; to recover her lost intuition of the same, by reason of her descent amidst the lusts and worship of the idols of flesh and sense. Her discomfort reveals her lapse from innocence; her loss of the divine presence and favor. Fidelity alone shall instaurate the Godhead in her bosom.

XII. TEMPTATION

Greater is he, who is above temptation, than he, who, being tempted, overcomes. The latter but regains the state from which the former has not fallen. He who is tempted has sinned; temptation is impossible to the holy.

XIII. CHOICE

Choice implies apostacy. The pure, unfallen soul is above choice. Her life is unbroken, synthetic; she is a law to herself, and finds no lusts in her members warring against the instincts of conscience. Sinners choose; saints act from instinct and intuition: there is no parley of alien forces in their being.

XIV. INSTINCT AND REASON

Innocent, the soul is quick with instincts of unerring aim; then she knows by intuition what lapsed reason defines by laborious inference; her appetites and affections are direct and trustworthy. Reason is the left hand of instinct;

it is tardy, awkward, but the right is ready and dextrous. By reasoning the soul strives to recover her lost intuitions; groping amidst the obscure darkness of sense, by means of the fingers of logic, for treasures present always and available to the eye of conscience. Sinners must needs reason; saints behold.

XV. IDENTITY AND DIVERSITY

It is the perpetual effort of conscience to divorce the soul from the dominion of sense; to nullify the dualities of the apparent, and restore the intuition of the real. The soul makes a double statement of all her facts; to conscience and sense; reason mediates between the two. Yet though double to sense, she remains single and one in herself; one in conscience, many in understanding; one in life, diverse in function and number. Sense, in its infirmity, breaks this unity to apprehend in part what it cannot grasp at once. Understanding notes diversity; conscience alone divines unity, and integrates all experience in identity of spirit. Number is predicable of body alone; not of spirit.

XVI. CONSCIENCE

Ever present, potent, vigilant, in the breast of man, there is that which never became a party in his guilt, never consented to a wrong deed, nor performed one, but holds itself above all sin, impeccable, immaculate, immutable, the deity of the heart, the conscience of the foul, the oracle and interpreter, the judge and executor of the divine law.

XVII. THEOCRACY

In the theocracy of the soul majorities do not rule. God and the saints; against them the rabble of sinners, with clamorous voices and uplifted hand, striving to silence the oracle of the private heart. Beelzebub[1] marshals majorities. Prophets and reformers are alway special enemies of his and his minions. Multitudes ever lie. Every age is a Judas,[2] and betrays its Messiahs into the hands of the multitude. The voice of the private, not popular heart, is alone authentic.

---

[1] Beelzebub according to Milton's *Paradise Lost*, was the chief of the fallen angels, next to Satan in power.

[2] Judas, known as "Judas Iscariot," was one of the 12 apostles; he betrayed Jesus.

XVIII. SPEECH

There is a magic in free speaking, especially on sacred themes, most potent and resistless. It is refreshing, amidst the inane common-places bandied in pulpits and parlors, to hear a hopeful word from an earnest, upright soul. Men rally around it as to the lattice in summer heats, to inhale the breeze that flows cool and refreshing from the mountains, and invigorates their languid frames. Once heard, they feel a buoyant sense of health and hopefulness, and wonder that they should have lain sick, supine so long, when a word has power to raise them from their couch, and restore them to soundness. And once spoken, it shall never be forgotten; it charms, exalts; it visits them in dreams, and haunts them during all their wakeful hours. Great, indeed, is the delight of speech; sweet the sound of one's bosom thought, as it returns laden with the fragrance of a brother's approval.

XIX. THOUGHT AND ACTION

Great thoughts exalt and deify the thinker; still more ennobling is the effect of great deeds on the actor. The dilation and joy of the soul at these visitations of God is like that of the invalid, again inhaling the mountain breeze after long confinement in chambers: she feels herself a noble bird, whose eyrie is in the empyrean that she is made to bathe her bosom and plume herself in the ether of thought; to soar and sing amidst the seraphim, beholding the faces of Apollo and Jove.[3]

XX. ACTION

Action translates death into life; fable into verity; speculation into experience; freeing man from the sorceries of tradition and the torpor of habit. The eternal Scripture is thus expurgated of the falsehoods interpolated into it by the supineness of the ages. Action mediates between conscience and sense: it is the gospel of the understanding.

XXI. ORIGINALITY

Most men are on the ebb; but now and then a man comes riding down sublimely in high hope from God on the flood tide of the soul, as she sets into the coasts of time, submerging old landmarks, and laying waste the labors of centuries. A new man wears channels broad and deep into the banks of the

[3] Apollo, in Greek mythology, was the god of the sun, prophecy, music, medicine, and poetry: Jove is the god Jupiter, patron of the Roman state and supreme among the gods.

ages; he washes away ancient boundaries, and sets afloat institutions, creeds, usages, which clog the ever flowing Present, stranding them on the shores of the Past. Such deluge is the harbinger of a new world, a renovated age. Hope builds an ark; the dove broods over the assuaged waters; the bow of promise gilds the east; the world is again repeopled and replanted. Yet the sons of genius alone venture into the ark: while most pass the rather down the sluggish stream of usage into the turbid pool of oblivion. Thitherward the retreating tide rolls, and wafted by the gales of inglorious ease, or urged by the winds of passion, they glide down the Lethean waters, and are not. Only the noble and heroic outlive in time their exit from it.

XXII. VALOR

The world, the state, the church, stand in awe of a man of probity and valor. He threatens their order and perpetuity: an unknown might slumbers in him; he is an augury of revolutions. Out of the invisible God, he comes to abide awhile amongst men; yet neither men nor time shall remain as at his advent. He is a creative element, and revises men, times, life itself. A new world preexists in his ideal. He overlives, outlives, eternizes the ages, and reports to all men the will of the divinity whom he serves.

XXIII. CHARACTER

Character is the only legitimate institution; the only regal influence. Its power is infinite. Safe in the citadel of his own integrity, principalities, powers, hierarchies, states, capitulate to the man of character at last. It is the temple which the soul builds to herself, within whose fanes genius and sanctity worship, while the kneeling ages bend around them in admiration and love.

XXIV. BREAD

The hunger of an age is alike a presentiment and pledge of its own supply. Instinct is not only prophetic but provident. When there is a general craving for bread, that shall assuredly be satisfied; bread is even then growing in the fields. Now, men are lean and famishing; but, behold, the divine Husbandman has driven his share through the age, and sown us bread that we may not perish; yea, the reapers even are going forth, a blithe and hopeful company, while yet the fields weep with the dews of the morning, and the harvests wave in yellow ripeness. Soon shall a table be spread, and the age rejoice in the fulness of plenty.

XXV. PROPHET

The prophet, by disciplines of meditation and valor, faithful to the spirit of the heart, his eye purified of the notes of tradition, his life of the vestiges of usage, ascends to the heights of immediate intuition: he rends the veil of sense; he bridges the distance between faith and sight, and beholds spiritual verities without scripture or mediator. In the presence of God, he communes with him face to face.

XXVI. METHOD

To benefit another, either by word or deed, you must have passed from the state in which he is, to a higher. Experience is both law and method of all tuition, all influence. This holds alike of physical as of spiritual truths; the demonstration must be epical; the method living, not empirical.

XXVII. BALANCES

I am not partial to your man who always holds his balance in hand, and must weigh forthwith whatsoever of physical or metaphysical haberdashery chances to be laid on his counter. I have observed that he thinks more of the accuracy and polish of his scales, than of the quality of the wares in which he deals. He never questions his own levity. But yet these balance-men are useful: it is convenient to have standards of market values. These are the public's approved sealers of weights and measures, who determine the worth of popular wares by their favorite weights, lucre and usage. It is well for the ages, that Genius rectifies both scales and men by a truer standard, quite wide of marts or markets.

XXVIII. PRUDENCE

Prudence is the footprint of Wisdom.

XXIX. REVELATION

The standing problem of Genius is to divine the essential verity intimated in the life and literature of the Past, divesting it of historical interpolations; separating the foreign from the indigenous, and translating the letter of the universal scripture into the spirit of contemporaneous life and letters.

XXX. CRITICISM

To just criticism unity of mind is essential. The critic must not esteem difference as real as sameness, and as permanent in the facts of nature. This tendency is fatal to all sound and final thinking: it never penetrates to the roots of things. All creative minds have been inspired and guided by the law of unity: their problem is ever to pierce the coarse and superficial rind of diversity, and discover the unity in whose core is the heart and seed of all things.

XXXI. CALCULUS

We need, what Genius is unconsciously seeking, and, by some daring generalization of the universe, shall assuredly discover, a spiritual calculus, a novum organon, whereby nature shall be divined in the soul, the soul in God, matter in spirit, polarity resolved into unity; and that power which pulsates in all life, animates and builds all organizations, shall manifest itself as one universal deific energy, present alike at the outskirts and centre of the universe, whose centre and circumference are one; omniscient, omnipotent, self-subsisting, uncontained, yet containing all things in the unbroken synthesis of its being.

XXXII. GENERATION AND CORRUPTION

The soul decomposes the substances of nature in the reverse order of their composition: read this backward for the natural history of their genesis and growth. Generation and corruption are polar or adverse facts. The tree first dies at the top: to raze the house we first remove the tiling. The decomposition and analysis are from without, according to the order of sense, not of soul. All investigations of nature must be analytic through the order of decay. Science begins and ends in death; poesy in life; philosophy in organization; art in creation.

XXXIII. EACH AND ALL

Life eludes all scientific analysis. Each organ and function is modified in substance and varied in effect, by the subtile energy which pulsates throughout the whole economy of things, spiritual and corporeal. The each is instinct with the all; the all unfolds and reappears in each. Spirit is all in all. God, man, nature, are a divine synthesis, whose parts it is impiety to sunder. Genius must preside devoutly over all investigations, or analysis, with her murderous knife, will seek impiously to probe the vitals of being.

XXXIV. GOD

God organizes never his attributes fully in single structures. He is instant, but never extant wholly, in his works. Nature does not contain, but is contained in him; she is the memoir of his life; man is a nobler scripture, yet fails to outwrite the godhead. The universe does not reveal, eternities do not publish the mysteries of his being. He subjects his noblest works to minute and constant revision; his idea ever transcends its form; he moulds anew his own idols; both nature and man are ever making, never made.

XXXV. NATURE

Nature seems remote and detached, because the soul surveys her by means of the extremest senses, imposing on herself the notion of difference and remoteness through their predominance, and thereby losing that of her own oneness with it. Yet nature is not separate from me; she is mine alike with my body; and in moments of true life, I feel my identity with her; I breathe, pulsate, feel, think, will, through her members, and know of no duality of being. It is in such moods of soul that prophetic visions are beheld, and evangels published for the joy and hope of mankind.

XXXVI. FLUX

Solidity is an illusion of the senses. To faith, nothing is solid: the nature of the soul renders such fact impossible. Modern chemistry demonstrates that nine tenths of the human body are fluid, and substances of inferior order in lesser proportion. Matter is ever pervaded and agitated by the omnipresent soul. All things are instinct with spirit.

XXXVII. SEPULTURE AND RESURRECTION

That which is visible is dead: the apparent is the corpse of the real; and undergoes successive sepultures and resurrections. The soul dies out of organs; the tombs cannot confine her; she eludes the grasp of decay; she builds and unseals the sepulchres. Her bodies are fleeting, historical. Whatsoever she sees when awake is death; when asleep dream.

XXXVIII. TIME

Organizations are mortal; the seal of death is fixed on them at birth. The young Future is nurtured by the Past, yet aspires to a nobler life, and revises, in his maturity, the traditions and usages of his day, to be supplanted by the sons and daughters whom he begets and ennobles. Time, like fabled Saturn, now generates, and, ere even their sutures be closed, devours his own offspring. Only the children of the soul are immortal; the births of time are premature and perishable.

XXXIX. EMBRYON

Man is a rudiment and embryon of God: eternity shall develop in him the divine image.

XL. ORGANIZATION

Possibly organization is no necessary function or mode of spiritual being. The time may come, in the endless career of the soul, when the facts of incarnation, birth, death, descent into matter and ascension from it, shall comprise no part of her history; when she herself shall survey this human life with emotions akin to those of the naturalist, on examining the relics of extinct races of beings; when mounds, sepulchres, monuments, epitaphs, shall serve but as memoirs of a past state of existence; a reminiscence of one metempsychosis of her life in time.

XLI. SPIRIT AND MATTER

Divined aright, there is nothing purely organic; all things are vital and inorganic. The microscope is developing this sublime fact. Sense looking at the historic surface beholds what it deems matter, yet is but spirit in fusion, fluent, pervaded by her own immanent vitality and trembling to organize itself. Neither matter nor death are possible: what seem matter and death are sensuous impressions, which, in our sanest moments, the authentic instincts contradict. The sensible world is spirit in magnitude, outspread before the senses for their analysis, but whose synthesis is the soul herself, whose prothesis is God. Matter is but the confine of spirit limning her to sense.

XLII. ORDER

The soul works from centre to periphery, veiling her labors from the ken of the senses. Her works are invisible till she has rounded herself in surface, where she completes her organizations. Appearance, though first to sense, is last in the order of generation: she recoils on herself at the acme of sense, revealing herself in reversed order. Historical is the sequel of genetic life.

XLIII. GENESIS

The popular genesis is historical. It is written to sense not to the soul. Two principles, diverse and alien, interchange the Godhead and sway the world by turns. God is dual. Spirit is derivative. Identity halts in diversity. Unity is actual merely. The poles of things are not integrated: creation globed and orbed. Yet in the true genesis, nature is globed in the material, souls orbed in the firmament. Love globes, wisdom orbs, all things. As magnet the steel, so spiritual attracts matter, which trembles to traverse the poles of diversity, and rest in the bosom of unity. All genesis is of love. Wisdom is her form: beauty her costume.

XLIV. GRAVITATION

Love and gravity are a twofold action of one life, whose conservative instincts in man and nature preserve inviolate the harmony of the immutable and eternal law of spirit. Man and nature alike tend toward the Godhead. All seeming divergence is overruled by this omnipotent force, whose retributions restore universal order.

XLV. LOVE

Love designs; thought sketches, action sculptures the works of spirit. Love is divine, conceiving, creating, completing, all things. Love is the Genius of Spirit.

XLVI. LIFE

Life, in its initial state, is synthetic; then feeling, thought, action are one and indivisible: love is its manifestation. Childhood and woman are samples and instances. But thought disintegrates and breaks this unity of soul: action alone restores it. Action is composition; thought decomposition. Deeds executed in love are graceful, harmonious, entire; enacted from thought merely, they are awkward, dissonant, incomplete: a manufacture, not creations, not works of genius.

XLVII. ACTUAL AND IDEAL

The actual and ideal are twins of one mother, Reality, who failing to incarnate her conceptions in time, meanwhile contents herself with admiring in each the complement of the other, herself integrant of both. Always are the divine Gemini intertwined; Pan and Psyche, man and woman, the soul and nature.

XLVIII. BEAUTY

All departures from perfect beauty are degradations of the divine image. God is the one type, which the soul strives to incarnate in all organizations. Varieties are historical: the one form embosoms all forms; all having a common likeness at the base of difference. Human heads are images, more or less perfect, of the soul's or God's head. But the divine features do not fix in flesh; in the coarse and brittle clay. Beauty is fluent; art of highest order represents her always in flux, giving fluency and motion to bodies solid and immovable to sense. The line of beauty symbolizes motion.

XLIX. TRANSFIGURATION

Never have we beheld a purely human face; as yet, the beast, demon, rather than the man or God, predominate in its expression. The face of the soul is not extant in flesh. Yet she has a face, and virtue and genius shall one day reveal her celestial lineaments: a beauty, a majesty, shall then radiate from her that shall transcend the rapt ideal of love and hope. So have I seen glimpses of this spiritual glory, when, inspired by some thought or sentiment, she was transfigured from the image of the earthly to that of the heavenly, the ignoble melting out of her features, lost in the supersensual life.

L. PROMETHEUS[4]

Know, O man, that your soul is the Prometheus, who, receiving the divine fires, builds up this majestic statue of clay, and moulds it in the deific image, the pride of gods, and model and analogon of all forms. He chiselled that godlike brow, arched those mystic temples from whose fanes she herself looks forth, formed that miraculous globe above, and planted that sylvan grove below; graved those massive blades yoked in armed powers; carved that heaven-containing bosom, wreathed those puissant thighs, and hewed those stable columns, diffusing over all the grandeur, the grace of his own divine lineaments, and delighting in this cunning work of his hand. Mar not its beauty, spoil not its symmetry, by the deforming lines of lust and sin: dethroning the divinity incarnated therein, and transforming yourself into the satyr and the beast.

---

[4] Prometheus, in Greek mythology, was a Titan who stole fire from Olympus and gave it to man. He is associated with creativity.

JONES VERY

(1810–1888)

Jones Very embodied the transcendental vision *in extremis.* After graduating from Harvard in 1836, he served on the faculty as a tutor in Greek until his claim that he beheld visions called into question his sanity and he was asked to resign. He became, in a sense, the mad poet of the transcendental movement. Despite Very's eccentricities, Alcott's remark still possesses a certain truth: Very's sonnets and essays "surpass any that have since appeared in subtlety and simplicity of execution."

A recent selection of Very's best poetry is *Jones Very; Selected Poems,* ed. Nathan Lyons, 1966. Very's work first received the attention of modern critics through Yvor Winters, in his *Maules Curse, Seven Studies in the History of American Obscuran-* *tism* 1938. Two subsequent studies are William Irving Bartlett, *Jones Very, Emerson's "Brave Saint,"* 1942 and Edwin Gittleman, *Jones Very: The Effective Years, 1833–1840,* 1967.

The New Birth

'Tis a new life;—thoughts move not as they did
With slow uncertain steps across my mind,
In thronging haste fast pressing on they bid
The portals open to the viewless wind
That comes not save when in the dust is laid   5
The crown of pride that gilds each mortal brow,
And from before man's vision melting fade
The heavens and earth;—their walls are falling now.—
Fast crowding on, each thought asks utterance strong;
Storm-lifted waves swift rushing to the shore,   10
On from the sea they send their shouts along,
Back through the cave-worn rocks their thunders roar;
And I a child of God by Christ made free
Start from death's slumbers to Eternity.

Thy Brother's Blood

I have no brother,—they who meet me now
Offer a hand with their own wills defiled,
And, while they wear a smooth unwrinkled brow,
Know not that Truth can never be beguiled;
Go wash the hand that still betrays thy guilt;—   5
Before the spirit's gaze what stain can hide?
Abel's red blood upon the earth is spilt,
And by thy tongue it cannot be denied;
I hear not with the ear,—the heart doth tell
Its secret deeds to me untold before;   10
Go, all its hidden plunder quickly sell,
Then shalt thou cleanse thee from thy brother's gore,
Then will I take thy gift;—that bloody stain
Shall not be seen upon thy hand again.

The Hand and Foot

The hand and foot that stir not, they shall find
Sooner than all the rightful place to go:
Now in their motion free as roving wind,
Though first no snail so limited and slow;
I mark them full of labor all the day,   5
Each active motion made in perfect rest;
They cannot from their path mistaken stray,
Though 'tis not theirs, yet in it they are blest;
The bird has not their hidden track found out,
The cunning fox though full of art he be;   10
It is the way unseen, the certain route,
Where ever bound, yet thou art ever free;
The path of Him, whose perfect law of love
Bids spheres and atoms in just order move.

The Fox and the Bird

The bird that has no nest,
The Fox that has no hole;
He's wiser than the rest,
Her eggs are never stole.

She builds where none can see, 5
He hides where none can find;
The bird can rest where'er she be,
He freely moves as wind.

Thou hast not found her little young,
E'en though thou'st sought them long; 10
Though from thine earliest day they've sung,
Thou hast not heard their song.

Thou hast not found that Fox's brood,
That nestle under ground;
Though through all time his burrow's stood, 15
His whelps thou'st never found.

Women's Rights

Woman's equality was a natural result of the transcendental metaphysic and the antislavery movement, although writers like Emerson and Holmes could not conceive of women voting. At the World Anti-Slavery Convention in London in 1840, some American women delegates were excluded, and they equated the discrimination against blacks with the similar discrimination against themselves as women. The Seneca Falls convention was held on July 19, 1848, and, as one can see in the phrasing of the document, the Declaration of Independence is brought up to date to include women.

The Seneca Falls Declaration of Sentiments and Resolutions July 19, 1848

1. DECLARATION OF SENTIMENTS

When, in the course of human events, it becomes necessary for one portion of the family of man to assume among the people of the earth a position different from that which they have hitherto occupied, but one to which the laws of nature and of nature's God entitle them, a decent respect to the opinions of mankind requires that they should declare the causes that impel them to such a course.

We hold these truths to be self-evident: that all men and women are created equal; that they are endowed by their Creator with certain inalienable rights; that among these are life, liberty, and the pursuit of happiness; that to secure these rights governments are instituted, deriving their just powers from the consent of the governed. Whenever any form of government becomes destructive of these ends, it is the right of those who suffer from it to refuse allegiance to it, and to insist upon the institution of a new government laying its foundation on such principles, and organizing its powers in such form, as to them shall seem most likely to effect their safety and happiness. Prudence, indeed, will dictate that governments long established should not be changed for light and transient causes; and accordingly all experience hath shown that mankind are more disposed to suffer while evils are sufferable, than to right themselves by abolishing the forms to which they are accustomed. But when a long train of abuses and usurpations, pursuing invariably the same object, evinces a design to reduce them under absolute despotism, it is their duty to throw off such government, and to provide new guards for their future security. Such has been the patient sufferance of the women under this government, and such is now the necessity which constrains them to demand the equal station to which they are entitled.

The history of mankind is a history of repeated injuries and usurpations on the part of man toward woman, having in direct object the establishment of an absolute tyranny over her. To prove this, let facts be submitted to a candid world.

He has never permitted her to exercise her inalienable right to the elective franchise.

He has compelled her to submit to laws, in the formation of which she had no voice.

He has withheld from her rights which are given to the most ignorant and degraded men—both natives and foreigners.

Having deprived her of this first right of a citizen, the elective franchise, thereby leaving her without representation in the halls of legislation, he has oppressed her on all sides.

He has made her, if married, in the eye of the law, civilly dead.

He has taken from her all right in property, even to the wages she earns.

He has made her, morally, an irresponsible being, as she can commit many crimes with impunity, provided they be done in the presence of her husband. In the covenant of marriage, she is compelled to promise obedience to her husband, he becoming, to all intents and purposes, her master—the law giving him power to deprive her of her liberty, and to administer chastisement.

He has so framed the laws of divorce, as to what shall be the proper causes, and in case of separation, to whom the guardianship of the children shall be given, as to be wholly regardless of the happiness of women—the law, in all cases, going upon a false supposition of the supremacy of man, and giving all power into his hands.

After depriving her of all rights as a married woman, if single, and the owner of property, he has taxed her to support a government which recognizes her only when her property can be made profitable to it.

He has monopolized nearly all the profitable employments, and from those she is permitted to follow, she receives but a scanty remuneration. He closes against her all the avenues to wealth and distinction which he considers most honorable to himself. As a teacher of theology, medicine, or law, she is not known.

He has denied her the facilities for obtaining a thorough education, all colleges being closed against her.

He allows her in Church, as well as State, but a subordinate position, claiming Apostolic authority for her exclusion from the ministry, and with some exceptions, from any public participation in the affairs of the Church.

He has created a false public sentiment by giving to the world a different code of morals for men and women, by which moral delinquencies which exclude women from society, are not only tolerated, but deemed of little account in man.

He has usurped the prerogative of Jehovah himself, claiming it as his right to assign for her a sphere of action, when that belongs to her conscience and to her God.

He has endeavored, in every way that he could, to destroy her confidence in her own powers, to lessen her self-respect and to make her willing to lead a dependent and abject life.

Now, in view of this entire disfranchisement of one-half the people of this country, their social and religious degradation—in view of the unjust laws above mentioned and because women do feel themselves aggrieved, oppressed, and fraudulently deprived of their most sacred rights, we insist that they have immediate admission to all the rights and privileges which belong to them as citizens of the United States.

In entering upon the great work before us, we anticipate no small amount of misconception, misrepresentation, and ridicule; but we shall use every instrumentality within our power to effect our object. We shall employ agents, circulate tracts, petition the State and National legislatures, and endeavor to enlist the pulpit and the press in our behalf. We hope this Convention will be followed by a series of Conventions embracing every part of the country.

2. RESOLUTIONS

Whereas, The great precept of nature is conceded to be, that "man shall pursue his own true and substantial happiness." Blackstone in his Commentaries remarks,[1] that this law of Nature being coeval with mankind, and dictated by God himself, is of course superior in obligation to any other. It is binding over all the globe, in all countries and at all times; no human laws are of any validity if contrary to this, and such of them as are valid, derive all their force, and all their validity, and all their authority, mediately and immediately, from this original; therefore,

Resolved, That all laws which prevent woman from occupying such a station in society as her conscience shall dictate, or which place her in a position inferior to that of man, are contrary to the great precept of nature, and therefore of no force or authority.

Resolved, That woman is man's equal—was intended to be so by the Creator, and the highest good of the race demands that she should be recognized as such.

Resolved, That the women of this country ought to be enlightened in regard to the laws under which they live, that they may no longer publish their degradation by declaring themselves satisfied with their present position, nor their ignorance, by asserting that they have all the rights they want.

Resolved, That inasmuch as man, while claiming for himself intellectual superiority, does accord to woman moral superiority, it is pre-eminently his duty to encourage her to speak and teach, as she has an opportunity, in all religious assemblies.

Resolved, That the same amount of virtue, delicacy, and refinement of behavior that is required of woman in the social state, should also be required of man, and the same transgressions should be visited with equal severity on both man and woman.

Resolved, That the objection of indelicacy and impropriety, which is so often brought against woman when she addresses a public audience, comes with a very ill-grace from those who encourage, by their attendance, her appearance on the stage, in the concert, or in feats of the circus.

Resolved, That woman has too long rested satisfied in the circumscribed limits which corrupt customs and a perverted application of the Scriptures have marked out for her, and that it is time she should move in the enlarged sphere which her great Creator has assigned her.

Resolved, That it is the duty of the women of this country to secure to themselves their sacred right to the elective franchise.

Resolved, That the equality of human rights results necessarily from the fact of the identity of the race in capabilities and responsibilities.

Resolved, That the speedy success of our cause depends upon the zealous and untiring efforts of both men and women, for the overthrow of the mo-

---

[1] William Blackstone (1723–1780) was a British jurist, the author of the *Commentaries.*

nopoly of the pulpit, and for the securing to women an equal participation with men in the various trades, professions, and commerce.

Resolved, therefore, That, being invested by the creator with the same capabilities, and the same consciousness of responsibility for their exercise, it is demonstrably the right and duty of woman, equally with man, to promote every righteous cause by every righteous means; and especially in regard to the great subjects of morals and religion, it is self-evidently her right to participate with her brother in teaching them, both in private and in public, by writing and by speaking, by any instrumentalities proper to be used, and in any assemblies proper to be held; and this being a self-evident truth growing out of the divinely implanted principles of human nature, and custom or authority adverse to it, whether modern or wearing the hoary sanction of antiquity, is to be regarded as a self-evident falsehood, and at war with mankind.

MARGARET FULLER

(1810–1850)

The one transcendentalist who considered women's rights comprehensively and deeply was Margaret Fuller, and her most important single work on the subject is *Woman in the Nineteenth Century* (1845). Margaret Fuller was well trained for her role. As the daughter of a congressman from Newburyport, she was trained in the classics of western culture. Like many of the transcendentalists, she grew particularly interested in German philosophy and literature, and conducted "conversations" in the Boston area. From 1840 to 1842 she edited the *Dial* and wrote literary criticism for Horace Greeley's *New York Tribune*. She traveled in Europe, where she married an Italian aristocrat, Marquis Angelo Ossoli. Upon her return to America, with their child, she was drowned in a shipwreck off Fire Island on July 19, 1850. In addition to her pamphlet, *Woman in the Nineteenth Century* (1845), her books include *Summer on the Lakes* (1843), *Papers on Literature and Art* (1846), and *Life Without and Life Within* (1859).

The standard text is *Collected Works*, ed. A. B. Fuller, 4 vols., 1855–1860. See also *Memoirs of Margaret Fuller Ossoli*, 2 vols., ed. R. W. Emerson, W. H. Channing, and J. F. Clarke, 1852. Two early biographies are J. W. Howe, *Margaret Fuller*, 1883, and T. W. Higginson, *Margaret Fuller Ossoli*, 1884. Modern biographies are Madeleine Stern, *The Life of Margaret Fuller*, 1942 and Mason Wade, *Margaret Fuller, Whetstone of Genius*, 1940, and Arthur W. Brown, *Margaret Fuller*, 1964. Wade has edited a useful collection, *The Writings of Margaret Fuller*, 1941.

In *Woman in the Nineteenth Century*, Margaret Fuller stresses the importance of sexual equality in a democracy. For her, the first step was the intellectual emancipation of her sex so that men and women would achieve a more harmonious relationship. When one considers the absence of any real treatment of the significance of women in the literature of her contemporaries, Margaret Fuller's document assumes particular significance. Edgar Allen Poe may have liked to classify the race into three categories, "men, women, and Margaret Fuller," but her point of view was essential in an age when women were scarcely represented as full and complex human beings.

From Woman in the Nineteenth Century

Frailty, thy name is WOMAN.[1]
    The Earth waits for her Queen.

The connection between these quotations may not be obvious but it is strict. Yet would any contradict us, if we made them applicable to the other side and began also,

Frailty, thy name is MAN.
    The Earth waits for its King?

Yet Man, if not yet fully installed in his powers, has given much earnest of his claims. Frail he is indeed—how frail, how impure! Yet often has the vein of gold displayed itself amid the baser ores, and Man has appeared before us in princely promise worthy of his future.

If oftentimes we see the prodigal son feeding on the husks in the fair field no more his own, anon we raise the eyelids, heavy from bitter tears, to behold in him the radiant apparition of genius and love, demanding not less than the all of goodness, power, and beauty. We see that in him the largest claim finds a due foundation. That claim is for no partial sway, no exclusive possession. He cannot be satisfied with any one gift of life, any one department of knowledge or telescopic peep at the heavens. He feels himself called to understand and aid Nature, that she may through his intelligence be raised and interpreted; to be a student of and servant to the universe-spirit; and king of his planet, that as an angelic minister he may bring it into conscious harmony with the law of that spirit.

[1] Cf. *Hamlet*, Act I, Sc 11, 146.

In clear, triumphant moments many times has rung through the spheres the prophecy of his jubilee; and those moments, though past in time, have been translated into eternity by thought; the bright signs they left hang in the heavens as single stars or constellations and already a thickly sown radiance consoles the wanderer in the darkest night. Other heroes since Hercules[2] have fulfilled the Zodiac of beneficent labors, and then given up their mortal part to the fire without a murmur; while no God dared deny that they should have their reward,

> Siquis tamen, Hercule, siquis
> Forte Deo doliturus erit, data præmia nollet,
> Sed meruise dari sciet, invitus que probabit,
> Assensere Dei.[3]

Sages and lawgivers have bent their whole nature to the search for truth, and thought themselves happy if they could buy, with the sacrifice of all temporal ease and pleasure, one seed for the future Eden. Poets and priests have strung the lyre with the heartstrings, poured out their best blood upon the altar, which, reared anew from age to age, shall at last sustain the flame pure enough to rise to highest heaven. Shall we not name with as deep a benediction those who, if not so immediately or so consciously in connection with the eternal truth, yet led and fashioned by a divine instinct serve no less to develop and interpret the open secret of love passing into life, energy creating for the purpose of happiness; the artist whose hand, drawn by a pre-existent harmony to a certain medium, molds it to forms of life more highly and completely organized than are seen elsewhere, and by carrying out the intention of Nature reveals her meaning to those who are not yet wise enough to divine it; the philosopher who listens steadily for laws and causes, and from those obvious infers those yet unknown; the historian who in faith that all events must have their reason and their aim records them, and thus fills archives from which the youth of prophets may be fed; the man of science dissecting the statements, testing the facts, and demonstrating order, even where he cannot its purpose?

Lives, too, which bear none of these names have yielded tones of no less significance. The candlestick set in a low place has given light as faithfully where it was needed as that upon the hill. In close alleys, in dismal nooks, the Word has been read as distinctly as when shown by angels to holy men in the dark prison. Those who till a spot of earth scarcely larger than is

---

[2] Hercules was the son of Zeus and Alcmene, a hero of extraordinary strength and courage who won immortality by performing the 12 labors demanded by Hera.

[3] If anyone, however, Hercules,

By chance will suffer for God, if anyone he will be unwilling
That rewards be given but he will know that they ought to be given
The gods assented.

wanted for a grave have deserved that the sun should shine upon its sod till violets answer.

So great has been from time to time the promise, that in all ages men have said the gods themselves came down to dwell with them; that the All-Creating wandered on the earth to taste in a limited nature the sweetness of virtue; that the All-Sustaining incarnated himself to guard in space and time the destinies of this world; that heavenly genius dwelt among the shepherds to sing to them and teach them how to sing. Indeed,

Der stets den Hirten gnädig sich bewies.

"He has constantly shown himself favorable to shepherds."

And the dwellers in green pastures and natural students of the stars were selected to hail first among men the holy child, whose life and death were to present the type of excellence which has sustained the heart of so large a portion of mankind in these later generations.

Such marks have been made by the footsteps of *man* (still, alas, to be spoken of as the *ideal* man) wherever he has passed through the wilderness of *men*, and whenever the pygmies stepped in one of those, they felt dilate within the breast somewhat that promised nobler stature and purer blood. They were impelled to forsake their evil ways of decrepit skepticism and covetousness of corruptible possessions. Convictions flowed in upon them. They, too, raised the cry: God is living now, today; and all beings are brothers, for they are his children. Simple words enough, yet which only angelic natures can use or hear in their full, free sense.

These were the triumphant moments; but soon the lower nature took its turn, and the era of a truly human life was postponed.

Thus is Man still a stranger in his inheritance, still a pleader, still a pilgrim. Yet his happiness is secure in the end. And now no more a glimmering consciousness but assurance begins to be felt and spoken, that the highest ideal Man can form of his own powers is that which he is destined to attain. Whatever the soul knows how to seek, it cannot fail to obtain. This is the Law and the Prophets. Knock and it shall be opened; seek and ye shall find. It is demonstrated; it is a maxim. Man no longer paints his proper nature in some form, and says, "Prometheus had it; it is God-like"; but "Man must have it; it is human." However disputed by many, however ignorantly used or falsified by those who do receive it, the fact of a universal, unceasing revelation has been too clearly stated in words to be lost sight of in thought; and sermons preached from the text, "Be ye perfect," are the only sermons of a pervasive and deep-searching influence.

But among those who meditate upon this text there is a great difference of view as to the way in which perfection shall be sought.

"Through the intellect," say some. "Gather from every growth of life its seed of thought; look behind every symbol for its law; if thou canst *see* clearly, the rest will follow."

"Through the life," say others. "Do the best thou knowest today. Shrink not from frequent error in this gradual, fragmentary state. Follow thy light for as much as it will show thee; be faithful as far as thou canst, in hope that faith presently will lead to sight. Help others without blaming their need of thy help. Love much, and be forgiven."

"It needs not intellect, needs not experience," says a third. "If you took the true way, your destiny would be accomplished in a purer and more natural order. You would not learn through facts of thought or action, but express through them the certainties of wisdom. In quietness yield thy soul to the causal soul. Do not disturb thy apprenticeship by premature effort; neither check the tide of instruction by methods of thy own. Be still; seek not, but wait in obedience. Thy commission will be given."

Could we indeed say what we want, could we give a description of the child that is lost, he would be found. As soon as the soul can affirm clearly that a certain demonstration is wanted, it is at hand. When the Jewish prophet described the Lamb as the expression of what was required by the coming era, the time drew nigh. But we say not, see not as yet clearly what we would. Those who call for a more triumphant expression of love, a love that cannot be crucified, show not a perfect sense of what has already been given. Love has already been expressed that made all things new, that gave the worm its place and ministry as well as the eagle; a love to which it was alike to descend into the depths of hell, or to sit at the right hand of the Father.

Yet no doubt a new manifestation is at hand, a new hour in the day of Man. We cannot expect to see any one sample of completed being, when the mass of men still lie engaged in the sod, or use the freedom of their limbs only with wolfish energy. The tree cannot come to flower till its root be free from the cankering worm, and its whole growth open to air and light. While any one is base, none can be entirely free and noble. Yet something new shall presently be shown of the life of man, for hearts crave, if minds do not know how to ask it.

Among the strains of prophecy, the following by an earnest mind of a foreign land, written some thirty years ago, is not yet outgrown; and it has the merit of being a positive appeal from the heart, instead of a critical declaration what Man should *not* do.

"The ministry of Man implies that he must be filled from the divine fountains which are being engendered through all eternity, so that at the mere name of his master he may be able to cast all his enemies into the abyss; that he may deliver all parts of nature from the barriers that imprison them; that he may purge the terrestrial atmosphere from the poisons that infect it; that he may preserve the bodies of men from the corrupt influences that surround and the maladies that afflict them; still more, that he may keep their souls pure from the malignant insinuations which pollute and the gloomy images that obscure them; that he may restore its serenity to the Word, which false words of men fill with mourning and sadness; that he may satisfy the desires of the angels, who await from him the development of the marvels of nature; that in fine his world may be filled with God, as eternity is."°

Another attempt we will give, by an obscure observer of our own day and country, to draw some lines of the desired image. It was suggested by seeing the design of Crawford's *Orpheus* , and connecting with the circumstance of the American in his garret at Rome making choice of this subject, that of Americans here at home showing such ambition to represent the character by calling their prose and verse "Orphic sayings," "Orphics."[4] We wish we could add that they have shown that musical apprehension of the progress of Nature through her ascending gradations which entitled them so to do, but their attempts are frigid though sometimes grand; in their strain we are not warmed by the fire which fertilized the soil of Greece.

Orpheus was a lawgiver by theocratic commission. He understood Nature, and made her forms move to his music. He told her secrets in the form of hymns, Nature as seen in the mind of God. His soul went forth toward all beings, yet could remain sternly faithful to a chosen type of excellence. Seeking what he loved, he feared not death nor hell; neither could any shape of dread daunt his faith in the power of the celestial harmony that filled his soul.

It seemed significant of the state of things in this country that the sculptor should have represented the seer at the moment when he was obliged with his hand to shade his eyes.

> Each Orpheus[5] must to the depths descend;
> For only thus the Poet can be wise;
> Must make the sad Persephone[6] his friend,
> And buried love to second life arise;
> Again his love must lose through too much love,
> Must lose his life by living life too true,
> For what he sought below is passed above,
> Already done is all that he would do;
> Must tune all being with his single lyre,
> Must melt all rocks free from their primal pain,
> Must search all nature with his one soul's fire,
> Must bind anew all forms in heavenly chain.
> If he already sees what he must do,
> Well may he shade his eyes from the far-shining view.

°St. Martin.

[4] The reference is to Alcott's *Orphic Sayings*. See p. 1621-1633.

[5] Orpheus was the legendary Thracian poet and musician to whom the establishment of the Orphic mysteries was ascribed.

[6] Persephone, in Greek mythology, was the wife of Pluto and queen of the underworld.

A better comment could not be made on what is required to perfect Man, and place him in that superior position for which he was designed, than by the interpretation of Bacon[7] upon the legends of the Siren coast. "When the wise Ulysses passed," says he, "he caused his mariners to stop their ears with wax, knowing there was in them no power to resist the lure of that voluptuous song. But he, the much experienced man, who wished to be experienced in all, and use all to the service of wisdom, desired to hear the song that he might understand its meaning. Yet, distrusting his own power to be firm in his better purpose, he caused himself to be bound to the mast, that he might be kept secure against his own weakness. But Orpheus passed unfettered, so absorbed in singing hymns to the gods that he could not even hear those sounds of degrading enchantment."

Meanwhile not a few believe, and men themselves have expressed the opinion, that the time is come when Eurydice[8] is to call for an Orpheus rather than Orpheus for Eurydice; that the idea of Man, however imperfectly brought out, has been far more so than that of Woman; that she, the other half of the same thought, the other chamber of the heart of life, needs now take her turn in the full pulsation, and that improvement in the daughters will best aid in the reformation of the sons of this age.

It should be remarked that as the principle of liberty is better understood, and more nobly interpreted, a broader protest is made in behalf of Woman. As men become aware that few men have had a fair chance, they are inclined to say that no women have had a fair chance. The French Revolution, that strangely disguised angel, bore witness in favor of Woman, but interpreted her claims no less ignorantly than those of Man. Its idea of happiness did not rise beyond outward enjoyment, unobstructed by the tyranny of others. The title it gave was *citoyen, citoyenne;*[9] and it is not unimportant to Woman that even this species of quality was awarded her. Before, she could be condemned to perish on the scaffold for treason, not as a citizen but as a subject. The right with which this title then invested a human being was that of bloodshed and license. The Goddess of Liberty was impure. As we read the poem addressed to her not long since by Béranger,[10] we can scarcely refrain from tears as painful as the tears of blood that flowed when "such crimes were committed in her name." Yes! Man, born to purify and animate the unintelligent and the cold, can in his madness degrade and pollute no less the fair and the chaste. Yet truth was prophesied in the ravings of that hideous fever caused by long ignorance and abuse. Europe is conning a valued lesson from the bloodstained page. The same tendencies further unfolded will bear good fruit in this country.

---

[7] Francis Bacon (1561-1626), English philosopher and essayist.

[8] Eurydice, in Greek mythology, was the wife of Orpheus, who was permitted by Pluto to follow her husband out of Hades, provided that he refrain from looking back at her; Orpheus did look back, and Eurydice was doomed to remain in the underworld.

[9] Citizen.

[10] Pierre Jean De Beranger (1780-1857) was a French poet.

Yet by men in this country, as by the Jews when Moses was leading them to the promised land, everything has been done that inherited depravity could do to hinder the promise of Heaven from its fulfillment. The cross, here as elsewhere, has been planted only to be blasphemed by cruelty and fraud. The name of the Prince of Peace has been profaned by all kinds of injustice toward the Gentile whom he said he came to save. But I need not speak of what has been done toward the Red Man, the Black Man. Those deeds are the scoff of the world; and they have been accompanied by such pious words that the gentlest would not dare to intercede with, "Father, forgive them, for they know not what they do."

Here as elsewhere the gain of creation consists always in the growth of individual minds, which live and aspire as flowers bloom and birds sing in the midst of morasses; and in the continual development of that thought, the thought of human destiny, which is given to eternity adequately to express, and which ages of failure only seemingly impede. Only seemingly; and whatever seems to the contrary, this country is as surely destined to elucidate a great moral law as Europe was to promote the mental culture of Man.

Though the national independence be blurred by the servility of individuals; though freedom and equality have been proclaimed only to leave room for a monstrous display of slavedealing and slavekeeping; though the free American so often feels himself free, like the Roman, only to pamper his appetites and his indolence through the misery of his fellow-beings; still it is not in vain that the verbal statement has been made, "All men are born free and equal." There it stands, a golden certainty wherewith to encourage the good, to shame the bad. The New World may be called clearly to perceive that it incurs the utmost penalty if it reject or oppress the sorrowful brother. And if men are deaf, the angels hear. But men cannot be deaf. It is inevitable that an external freedom, an independence of the encroachments of other men such as has been achieved for the nation, should be so also for every member of it. That which has once been clearly conceived in the intelligence cannot fail sooner or later to be acted out. It has become a law as irrevocable as that of the Medes[11] in their ancient dominion; men will privately sin against it, but the law, as expressed by a leading mind of the age,°

> Tutti fatti a sembianze d'un Solo,
> Figli tutti d'un solo riscatto,
> In qual'ora, in qual parte del suolo
> Trascorriamo quest' aura vital,
> Siam fratelli, siam stretti ad un patto:
> Maladetto colui che lo infrange,
> Che s'innalza sul fiacco che piange
> Che contrista uno spirito immortal.

[11] Inhabitants of ancient Media.   °Manzoni.

(All made in the likeness of the One,
    All children of one ransom,
In whatever hour, in whatever part of the soil,
    We draw this vital air,
We are brothers; we must be bound by one compact;
    Accursed he who infringes it,
Who raises himself upon the weak who weep,
    Who saddens an immortal spirit.)

This law cannot fail of universal recognition. Accursed be he who willingly saddens an immortal spirit—doomed to infamy in later, wiser ages, doomed in future stages of his own being to deadly penance only short of death. Accursed be he who sins in ignorance, if that ignorance be caused by sloth.

We sicken no less at the pomp than the strife of words. We feel that never were lungs so puffed with the wind of declamation on moral and religious subjects as now. We are tempted to implore these "word-heroes," these word-Catos,[12] word-Christs, to beware of cant above all things; to remember that hypocrisy is the most hopeless as well as the meanest of crimes, and that those must surely be polluted by it who do not reserve a part of their morality and religion for private use. Landor[13] says that he cannot have a great deal of mind who cannot afford to let the larger part of it lie fallow; and what is true of genius is not less so of virtue. The tongue is a valuable member, but should appropriate but a small part of the vital juices that are needful all over the body. We feel that the mind may "grow black and rancid in the smoke" even "of altars." We start up from the harangue to go into our closet and shut the door. There inquires the spirit, "Is this rhetoric the bloom of healthy blood, or a false pigment artfully laid on?" And yet again we know where is so much smoke, must be some fire; with so much talk about virtue and freedom, must be mingled some desire for them; that it cannot be in vain that such have become the common topics of conversation among men rather than schemes for tyranny and plunder, that the very newspapers see it best to proclaim themselves "Pilgrims," "Puritans," "Heralds of Holiness." The king that maintains so costly a retinue cannot be a mere boast or Barabbas fiction.[14] We have waited here long in the dust, we are tired and hungry, but the triumphal procession must appear at last.

°Dr. Johnson's one piece of advice should be written on every door: "Clear your mind of cant." But Byron, to whom it was so acceptable, in clearing away the noxious vine shook down the building. Sterling's emendation is worthy of honor: "Realize your cant, not cast it off."

[12] Marcus Porcius Cato the Elder, known as "the Censor." (234-149 B. C.).

[13] Walter Savage Landor (1775-1864) was an English poet.

[14] Barabbas was a condemned thief whose release was demanded of Pilate by the multitude instead of that of Jesus. Cf. Mark 15:6-11, John 18:40.

Of all its banners, none has been more steadily upheld, and under none have more valor and willingness for real sacrifices been shown, than that of the champions of the enslaved African. And this band it is which, partly from a natural following out of principles, partly because many women have been prominent in that cause, makes just now the warmest appeal in behalf of Woman.

Though there has been a growing liberality on this subject, yet society at large is not so prepared for the demands of this party, but that its members are and will be for some time coldly regarded as the Jacobins of their day.

"Is it not enough," cries the irritated trader, "that you have done all you could to break up the national union and thus destroy the prosperity of our country, but now you must be trying to break up family union, to take my wife away from the cradle and the kitchen-hearth to vote at polls and preach from a pulpit? Of course, if she does such things, she cannot attend to those of her own sphere. She is happy enough as she is. She has more leisure than I have—every means of improvement, every indulgence."

"Have you asked her whether she was satisfied with these *indulgences?*"

"No, but I know she is. She is too amiable to desire what would make me unhappy, and too judicious to wish to step beyond the sphere of her sex. I will never consent to have our peace disturbed by any such discussions."

" 'Consent—you?' It is not consent from you that is in question—it is assent from your wife."

"Am not I the head of my house?"

"You are not the head of your wife. God has given her a mind of her own."

"I am the head, and she the heart."

"God grant you play true to one another, then! I suppose I am to be grateful that you did not say she was only the hand. If the head represses no natural pulse of the heart, there can be no question as to your giving your consent. Both will be of one accord, and there needs but to present any question to get a full and true answer. There is no need of precaution, of indulgence, or consent. But our doubt is whether the heart *does* consent with the head, or only obeys its decrees with a passiveness that precludes the exercise of its natural powers, or a repugnance that turns sweet qualities to bitter, or a doubt that lays waste the fair occasions of life. It is to ascertain the truth that we propose some liberating measures."

Thus vaguely are these questions proposed and discussed at present. But their being proposed at all implies much thought and suggests more. Many women are considering within themselves what they need that they have not, and what they can have if they find they need it. Many men are considering whether women are capable of being and having more than they are and have, *and* whether, if so, it will be best to consent to improvement in their condition.

This morning, I open the Boston *Daily Mail,* and find in its "poet's corner" a translation of Schiller's "Dignity of Woman."[15] In the advertisement of a book on America, I see in the table of contents this sequence, "'Republican Institutions. American Slavery. American Ladies."

I open the *Deutsche Schnellpost,* published in New York, and find at the head of a column, *Juden-und Frauen-emanzipation in Ungarn* ("Emancipation of Jews and Women in Hungary").

The past year has seen action in the Rhode Island legislature to secure married women rights over their own property, where men showed that a very little examination of the subject could teach them much; an article in the *Democratic Review* on the same subject more largely considered, written by a woman impelled, it is said, by glaring wrong to a distinguished friend, having shown the defects in the existing laws and the state of opinion from which they spring; and an answer from the revered old man, J. Q. Adams, in some respects the Phocion of his time,[16] to an address made him by some ladies. To this last I shall again advert in another place.

These symptoms of the times have come under my view quite accidentally: one who seeks may each month or week collect more.

The numerous party, whose opinions are already labeled and adjusted too much to their mind to admit of any new light, strive by lectures on some model woman of bridelike beauty and gentleness, by writing and lending little treatises intended to mark out with precision the limits of Woman's sphere and Woman's mission, to prevent other than the rightful shepherd from climbing the wall, or the flock from using any chance to go astray.

Without enrolling ourselves at once on either side, let us look upon the subject from the best point of view which today offers; no better, it is to be feared, than a high house-top. A high hilltop or at least a cathedralspire would be desirable.

It may well be an Anti-Slavery party that pleads for Woman, if we consider merely that she does not hold property on equal terms with men; so that if a husband dies without making a will, the wife, instead of taking at once his place as head of the family, inherits only a part of his fortune, often brought him by herself, as if she were a child or ward only, not an equal partner.

We will not speak of the innumerable instances in which profligate and idle men live upon the earnings of industrious wives; or if the wives leave them and take with them the children to perform the double duty of mother and father, follow from place to place and threaten to rob them of the children, if deprived of the rights of a husband as they call them, planting themselves in their poor lodgings, frightening them into paying tribute by

---

[15] Johann Christoph Friedrich von Schiller (1759–1805), German poet, dramatist, and historian.

[16] Phocion (c. 402–317 B. C.) was an Athenian general and statesman.

taking from them the children, running into debt at the expense of these otherwise so overtasked helots. Such instances count up by scores within my own memory. I have seen the husband who had stained himself by a long course of low vice, till his wife was wearied from her heroic forgiveness by finding that his treachery made it useless, and that if she would provide bread for herself and her children, she must be separate from his ill fame— I have known this man come to install himself in the chamber of a woman who loathed him, and say she should never take food without his company. I have known these men steal their children, whom they knew they had no means to maintain, take them into dissolute company, expose them to bodily danger, to frighten the poor woman to whom, it seems, the fact that she alone had borne the pangs of their birth and nourished their infancy does not give an equal right to them. I do believe that this mode of kidnaping—and it is frequent enough in all classes of society—will be by the next age viewed as it is by Heaven now, and that the man who avails himself of the shelter of men's laws to steal from a mother her own children, or arrogate any superior right in them, save that of superior virtue, will bear the stigma he deserves in common with him who steals grown men from their motherland, their hopes, and their homes.

I said we will not speak of this now; yet I *have* spoken, for the subject makes me feel too much. I could give instances that would startle the most vulgar and callous; but I will not, for the public opinion of their own sex is already against such men, and where cases of extreme tyranny are made known, there is private action in the wife's favor. But she ought not to need this, nor, I think, can she long. Men must soon see that as on their own ground Woman is the weaker party, she ought to have legal protection which would make such oppression impossible. But I would not deal with "atrocious instances" except in the way of illustration, neither demand from men a partial redress in some one matter, but go to the root of the whole. If principles could be established, particulars would adjust themselves aright. Ascertain the true destiny of Woman; give her legitimate hopes, and a standard within herself; marriage and all other relations would by degrees be harmonized with these.

But to return to the historical progress of this matter. Knowing that there exists in the minds of men a tone of feeling toward women as toward slaves, such as is expressed in the common phrase, "Tell that to women and children"; that the infinite soul can only work through them in already ascertained limits; that the gift of reason, Man's highest prerogative, is allotted to them in much lower degree; that they must be kept from michief and melancholy by being constantly engaged in active labor, which is to be furnished and directed by those better able to think, &c., &c.—we need not multiply instances, for who can review the experience of last week without recalling words which imply, whether in jest or earnest, these views or views like these—knowing this, can we wonder that many reformers think that measures are not likely to be taken in behalf of women, unless their wishes could be publicly represented by women?

"That can never be necessary," cry the other side. "All men are privately influenced by women; each has his wife, sister, or female friends, and is too much biased by these relations to fail of representing their interests; and if this is not enough, let them propose and enforce their wishes with the pen. The beauty of home would be destroyed, the delicacy of the sex be violated, the dignity of halls of legislation degraded by an attempt to introduce them there. Such duties are inconsistent with those of a mother"; and then we have ludicrous pictures of ladies in hysterics at the polls, and senate chambers filled with cradles.

But if in reply we admit as truth that Woman seems destined by nature rather for the inner circle, we must add that the arrangements of civilized life have not been as yet such as to secure it to her. Her circle, if the duller, is not the quieter. If kept from "excitement," she is not from drudgery. Not only the Indian squaw carries the burdens of the camp, but the favorites of Louis XIV accompany him in his journeys, and the washerwoman stands at her tub and carries home her work at all seasons and in all states of health. Those who think the physical circumstances of Woman would make a part in the affairs of national government unsuitable are by no means those who think it impossible for Negresses to endure field work even during pregnancy, or for seamstresses to go through their killing labors.

As to the use of the pen, there was quite as much opposition to Woman's possessing herself of that help to free agency as there is now to her seizing on the rostrum or the desk; and she is likely to draw, from a permission to plead her cause that way, opposite inferences to what might be wished by those who now grant it.

As to the possiblity of her filling with grace and dignity any such position, we should think those who had seen the great actresses and heard the Quaker preachers of modern times would not doubt that Woman can express publicly the fullness of thought and creation without losing any of the peculiar beauty of her sex. What can pollute and tarnish is to act thus from any motive except that something needs to be said or done. Woman could take part in the processions, the songs, the dances of old religion; no one fancied her delicacy was impaired by appearing in public for such a cause.

As to her home, she is not likely to leave it more than she now does for balls, theaters, meetings for promoting missions, revival meetings, and others to which she flies in hope of an animation for her existence commensurate with what she sees enjoyed by men. Governors of ladies' fairs are no less engrossed by such a charge than the governor of a state by his; presidents of Washingtonian societies no less away from home than presidents of conventions. If men look straitly to it, they will find that unless their lives are domestic, those of the women will not be. A house is no home unless it contains food and fire for the mind as well as for the body. The female

Greek of our day is as much in the street as the male to cry, "What news?" We doubt not it was the same in Athens of old. The woman, shut out from the market-place, made up for it at the religious festivals. For human beings are not so constituted that they can live without expansion. If they do not get it in one way, they must in another perish.

As to men's representing women fairly at present, while we hear from men who owe to their wives not only all that is comfortable or graceful but all that is wise in the arrangement of their lives the frequent remark, "You cannot reason with a woman"—when from those of delicacy, nobleness, and poetic culture falls the contemptuous phrase "women and children," and that in no light sally of the hour, but in works intended to give a permanent statement of the best experiences—when not one man in the million, shall I say? no, not in the hundred million, can rise above the belief that Woman was made *for Man*—when such traits as these are daily forced upon the attention, can we feel that Man will always do justice to the interests of Woman? Can we think that he takes a sufficiently discerning and religious view of her office and destiny *ever* to do her justice, except when prompted by sentiment—accidentally or transiently, that is, for the sentiment will vary according to the relations in which he is placed? The lover, the poet, the artist are likely to view her nobly. The father and the philosopher have some chance of liberality; the man of the world, the legislator for expediency none.

Under these circumstances, without attaching importance in themselves to the changes demanded by the champions of Woman, we hail them as signs of the times. We would have every arbitrary barrier thrown down. We would have every path laid open to Woman as freely as to Man. Were this done and slight temporary fermentation allowed to subside, we should see crystallizations more pure and of more various beauty. We believe the divine energy would pervade nature to a degree unknown in the history of former ages, and that no discordant collision but a ravishing harmony of the spheres would ensue.

Yet then and only then will mankind be ripe for this, when inward and outward freedom for Woman as much as for Man shall be acknowledged as a *right*, not yielded as a concession. As the friend of the Negro assumes that one man cannot by right hold another in bondage, so should the friend of Woman assume that Man cannot by right lay even well-meant restrictions on Woman. If the Negro be a soul, if the woman be a soul, appareled in flesh, to one Master only are they accountable. There is but one law for souls, and if there is to be an interpreter of it, he must come not as man or son of man, but as son of God.

Were thought and feeling once so far elevated that Man should esteem himself the brother and friend, but nowise the lord and tutor, of Woman— were he really bound with her in equal worship—arrangements as to function and employment would be of no consequence. What Woman needs is not as a woman to act or rule, but as a nature to grow, as an intellect to discern, as a soul to live freely and unimpeded to unfold such powers as were given her when we left our common home. If fewer talents were given her, yet if allowed the free and full employment of these, so that she may render back to the giver his own with usury, she will not complain; nay, I dare to say she will bless and rejoice in her earthly birthplace, her earthly lot. Let us consider what obstructions impede this good era, and what signs give reason to hope that it draws near.

I was talking on this subject with Miranda, a woman, who, if any in the world could, might speak without heat and bitterness of the position of her sex. Her father was a man who cherished no sentimental reverence for Woman, but a firm belief in the equality of the sexes. She was his eldest child, and came to him at an age when he needed a companion. From the time she could speak and go alone, he addressed her not as a plaything but as a living mind. Among the few verses he ever wrote was a copy addressed to this child, when the first locks were cut from her head; and the reverence expressed on this occasion for that cherished head, he never belied. It was to him the temple of immortal intellect. He respected his child, however, too much to be an indulgent parent. He called on her for clear judgment, for courage, for honor and fidelity; in short, for such virtues as he knew. In so far as he possessed the keys to the wonders of this universe, he allowed free use of them to her, and by the incentive of a high expectation he forbade, so far as possible, that she should let the privilege lie idle.

Thus this child was early led to feel herself a child of the spirit. She took her place easily not only in the world of organized being, but in the world of mind. A dignified sense of self-dependence was given as all her portion, and she found it a sure anchor. Herself securely anchored, her relations with others were established with equal security. She was fortunate in a total absence of those charms which might have drawn to her bewildering flatteries, and in a strong electric nature which repelled those who did not belong to her and attracted those who did. With men and women her relations were noble—affectionate without passion, intellectual without coldness. The world was free to her, and she lived freely in it. Outward adversity came and inward conflict, but that faith and self-respect had early been awakened which must always lead at last to an outward serenity and an inward peace.

Of Miranda I had always thought as an example, that the restraints upon the sex were insuperable only to those who think them so, or who noisily strive to break them. She had taken a course of her own, and no man stood in her way. Many of her acts had been unusual, but excited no uproar. Few helped but none checked her; and the many men who knew her mind and her life showed to her confidence as to a brother, gentleness as to a sister. And not only refined, but very coarse men approved and aided one in whom they saw resolution and clearness of design. Her mind was often the leading one, always effective.

When I talked with her upon these matters and had said very much what I have written, she smilingly replied: "And yet we must admit that I have been fortunate, and this should not be. My good father's early trust gave the first bias, and the rest followed of course. It is true that I have had less outward aid in after years than most women; but that is of little consequence. Religion was early awakened in my soul—a sense that what the soul is capable to ask it must attain, and that though I might be aided and instructed by others, I must depend on myself as the only constant friend. This self-dependence, which was honored in me, is deprecated as a fault in most women. They are taught to learn their rule from without, not to unfold it from within.

"This is the fault of Man, who is still vain, and wishes to be more important to Woman than by right he should be."

"Men have not shown this disposition toward you," I said.

"No, because the position I early was enabled to take was one of self-reliance. And were all women as sure of their wants as I was, the result would be the same. But they are so overloaded with precepts by guardians who think that nothing is so much to be dreaded for a woman as originality of thought or character, that their minds are impeded by doubts till they lose their chance of fair, free proportions. The difficulty is to get them to the point from which they shall naturally develop self-respect and learn self-help.

"Once I thought that men would help to forward this state of things more than I do now. I saw so many of them wretched in the connections they had formed in weakness and vanity. They seemed so glad to esteem women whenever they could.

" 'The soft arms of affection,' said one of the most discerning spirits, 'will not suffice for me, unless on them I see the steel bracelets of strength.'

"But early I perceived that men never in any extreme of despair wished to be women. On the contrary, they were ever ready to taunt one another at any sign of weakness with,

Art thou not like the women, who—

"The passage ends various ways, according to the occasion and rhetoric of the speaker. When they admired any woman, they were inclined to speak of her as 'above her sex.' Silently I observed this, and feared it argued a rooted skepticism which for ages had been fastening on the heart and which only an age of miracles could eradicate. Ever I have been treated with great sincerity; and I look upon it as a signal instance of this, that an intimate friend of the other sex said in a fervent moment that I 'deserved in some star to be a man.' He was much surprised when I disclosed my view of my position and hopes, when I declared my faith that the feminine side, the side of love, of beauty, of holiness, was now to have its full chance, and that if either were better, it was better now to be a woman; for even the slightest achievement of good was furthering an especial work of our time. He smiled incredulously. 'She makes the best she can of it,' thought he. 'Let Jews believe the pride of Jewry, but I am of the better sort, and know better.'

"Another used as highest praise in speaking of a character in literature, the words 'a manly woman.'

"So in the noble passage of Ben Jonson:

> I meant the day-star should not brighter ride,
>   Nor shed like influence from its lucent seat;
> I meant she should be courteous, facile, sweet,
>   Free from that solemn vice of greatness, pride;
> I meant each softest virtue there should meet,
>   Fit in that softer bosom to abide,
> Only a learned and a *manly* soul
>   I purposed her, that should with even powers
> The rock, the spindle, and the shears control
>   Of destiny, and spin her own free hours."[17]

"Methinks," said I, "you are too fastidious in objecting to this. Jonson in using the word 'manly' only meant to heighten the picture of this, the true, the intelligent fate with one of the deeper colors."

"And yet," said she, "so invariable is the use of this word when a heroic quality is to be described, and I feel so sure that persistence and courage are the most womanly no less than the most manly qualities, that I would exchange these words for others of a larger sense, at the risk of marring the fine tissue of the verse. Read, 'A heavenward and instructed soul,' and I should be satisfied. Let it not be said, wherever there is energy or creative genius, 'She has a masculine mind.' "

[17] Epigrammes, LXXVI, "On Lucy Countesse of Bedford," 7-16.

Education

HORACE MANN

(1796–1859)

Horace Mann was a leading figure of nineteenth-century reform in education. Although he was a successful lawyer in Dedham, Massachusetts, and a representative to the Massachusetts State Legislature, Mann left his legal career to become secretary of the state board of education. Together with contemporaries such as Henry Barnard, he stressed the close relationship between public education and political democracy and popularized the idea that education is a major force in the cure of social ills. From 1853 until his death, Mann was president of Antioch College in Ohio.

Horace Mann's thought is reflected in his many reports and lectures. An important single work is the *Common School Journal,* from which the following selection is taken.

The standard life and text is *Life and Works of Horace Mann,* 3 vols., ed. M. T. P. Mann, 1865–1868. See also *Selective and Critical Bibliography of Horace Mann,* Federal Writers Project , 1937.

An older work is B. A. Hinsdale, *Horace Mann,* 1898. Modern studies include Merle Curti, *The Social Ideas of American Educators,* 1935, E. I. F. Williams, *Horace Mann, Educational Statesman,* 1937, and Jonathan Meserli, *Horace Mann,* 1971.

From Common School Journal

Animated by these feelings, we again enroll ourselves as a soldier in this cause,—not in the presumptious expectation that we can achieve aught that is worthy of its name; but, at the same time, not without hope that, while we uphold its banner, others may rally around it, and bear it on to victory.

Education derives arguments for its support from a more comprehensive range of considerations than ever united their advocacy for any other human interest. Health, freedom, wisdom, virtue, time, eternity, plead in its behalf. Some causes have reference to temporal interests; some to eternal;—education embraces both.

The view which invests education with the awful prerogative of projecting its consequences forward through the whole length of the illimitable future, will not be objected to by the champions of any religious creed. Those who believe that the destiny of the human soul is irrevocably fixed for weal or woe by its state or condition when its exit from life is made,—who believe that, as it is then sanctified, or unregenerated, it must go out from this world, through an opposite avenue, and into an opposite eternity,—will equally believe and maintain the tendency of intellectual and moral guidance, or neglect, especially during the impressible period of youth, to turn its course into the broad, or into the narrow way. Those, also, who believe that, although the soul should enter the spiritual world "unhouselled, unanointed, unanealed," yet that it will not be cut off from hope, but will be allowed to pass through other cycles of probation,

"Till the foul crimes done in its days of nature
    Are burnt and purged away,"

will of course believe and maintain that, the lighter the burden of sin which weighs it down, at its entrance into another life, the sooner will its recuperative energies enable it to rise from its guilty fall, and to ascend to the empyrean of perfect happiness. There is still another class, who interpret the Scriptures to promise universal beatitude to the whole human race, at the instant of death. They maintain that the soul leaves every earthly impurity in the foul tabernacle of flesh, where each had polluted the other during life, and at once springs aloft to be robed in garments of purity. But even they do not suppose that the spirit, though ransomed and cleansed by omnipotent grace, can overleap the immense moral spaces it has lost, and at once engage in the services of the upper temple, with that seraphic ardor which burns in bosoms, where its flame had been kindled while yet on earth. In other words, if the dogma of the theologians were true, that there are in heaven seven orders of celestial spirits, they will allow, that a wretch who died perpetrating sacrilege with his hands, and blaspheming God with his tongue, cannot, at once, and without a single rehearsal, strike the harp and sing hosannas in unison with the highest perfected spirits, but must forever be somewhat procrastinated in his ascent from order to order, in the celestial hierarchy.

In regard to Intellectual Education, no man can offer a single reason for arresting its progress, and confining it where it now is, which would not be equally available for reducing its present amount. He who would degrade the intellectual standing of Massachusetts to the level of Ireland, would degrade Ireland to the level of the interior of Africa, or of the Batta Islands. Nor could even the rank of savage life claim any immunity from still lower debasement. In the "lowest deep," there would be some whose selfishness would demand the opening of a still "lower deep." There would be no halting post until the race had reached the limits of degradation in troglodytes[1] and monkeys, and the godlike faculty of reason had been lost in the

[1] Prehistoric cave dwellers.

mechanism of animal instinct. The useful and elegant arts that minister to the comfort of man, and gladden his eye with beauty; poetry and eloquence that ravish the soul; philosophy that comprehends the workmanship of the heavens, and reads, in the present condition of the earth, as in the leaves of a book, the records of myriads of ages gone by; language by which we are taught by all the generations that are past, and by which we may teach all the generations that are to come;—all these would be sunk in oblivion, and all the knowledge possessed by the descendants of Bacon, and Newton, and Franklin,[2] would be to chatter and mow, to burrow in a hole, and crack nuts with the teeth. Such is the catastrophe to which we should come, could those prevail, who would make the present horizon of human knowledge stationary.

Physical Education is not only of great importance on its own account, but, in a certain sense, it seems to be invested with the additional importance of both intellectual and moral; because, although we have frequent proofs, that there may be a human body without a soul, yet, under our present earthly conditions of existence, there cannot be a human soul without a body. The statue must lie prostrate, without a pedestal; and, in this sense, the pedestal is as important as the statue.

The present generation is suffering incalculably under an ignorance of physical education. It is striving to increase the number of pleasurable sensations, without any knowledge of the great laws of health and life, and thus defeats its own object. The sexes respectively, are deteriorating from their fathers, and especially from their mothers, in constitutional stamina. The fifteen millions of the United States, at the present day, are by no means five times the three millions of the revolutionary era. Were this degeneracy attributable to mother Nature, we should compare her to a fraudulent manufacturer, who, having established his name in the market for the excellence of his fabrics, should avail himself of his reputation to palm off subsequent bales or packages, with the same stamp or earmark, but of meaner quality. Thus it is with the present race, as compared with their ancestors,—short in length, deficient in size and weight, and sleazy in texture. The activity and boldness of the sanguine temperament, and the enduring nature of the fibrous, which belonged to the olden time, are succeeded by the weak refinements of the nervous, and the lolling, lackadaisical, fashionable sentimentality of the lymphatic. The old hearts of oak are gone. Society is suffering under a curvature of the spine. If deterioration holds on, at its present rate, especially in our cities, we shall soon be a bed-rid people. There will be a land of ghosts and shadows this side of Acheron and the Elysian fields.[3]

[2] Francis Bacon (1561-1626), English philosopher and essayist; Isaac Newton (1642-1727), English mathematician, scientist, and philosopher; Benjamin Franklin (1706-1790), American statesman, author, and scientist.

[3] In Greek mythology, Acheron is the river of woe over which Charon ferried the souls of the dead to Hades. The Elysian Fields, in Greek mythology, are a place of ideal happiness.

Where are the young men, and, emphatically, where are the young women, who promise a green and vigorous age at seventy? The sweat and toil of the field and of the household are despised, and no substitute is provided for these invigorating exercises. Even professed connoisseurs, who lounge and dawdle in the galleries of art, and labor to express their weak rapture of the Jove-like stature and sublime strength of Hercules, or at the majestic figure of Venus,[4] beneath whose ample zone there resides the energy which prevents grace from degenerating into weakness,—even they will belie, in dress and contour, all the power and beauty they profess to admire. There is a general effeminacy in our modes of life, as compared with the indurating exposures of our ancestors. Our double-windows; our air-tight houses; our heated and unventilated apartments, from nursery to sleeping-room, and church; the multitude of our garments of fur, and down, and woollen, numerous as the integuments around an Egyptian mummy,—beneath which we shrink, and cower, and hide ourselves from our best friend, the north-west wind; our carriages, in which we ride when we should be on foot;—all these enervating usages, *without any equivalent of exercise or exposure,* are slackening the whole machinery of life. More weakly children are born, than under the vigorous customs and hardy life of our fathers; and, what is still more significant, a far greater proportion of these puny children, under our tender and delicate nursing, are reared than was formerly done. A weak cohesion still exists in many a thread of life, which, under the rough handling of former times, would have been snapped. Amid hardship and exposure, the young were toughened or destroyed. Nature passed round among them, as a gardener among the plants, and weeded out the blasted and mildewed. She shook the tree, till the sickly fruits fell off. She did not preserve these, as the stock from which to produce the still more degraded fruits of a second season. But, under the modern hothouse system, the puny and feeble are saved. They grow up without strength, passing from the weakness of childhood to that of age, without taking the vigor of manhood in their course. By the various appliances of art, indeed, the stooping frame can be kept upright and the shrunken be rounded out, into the semblance of humanity. But these cheats give no internal, organic force. Though the arts of bolstering up the human figure, and of giving to its unsightly angles the curvilinear forms of grace, should grow into science, and its practice should be the most lucrative of professions, yet not one element of genuine beauty or dignity will be thereby gained. Such arts can never bestow elasticity and vigor upon the frame, nor suffuse "the human face divine" with the roseate hues of health. The complexion will still be wan, the pulse feeble, the motions languid. The eye will have no fire. The imagination will lose its power to turn all light into rainbows. The intellect will never be sufficiently expanded to receive *a sys-*

---

[4] Hercules is the son of Zeus and Alcmene, a hero of extraordinary strength and courage who won immortality by performing the 12 labors demanded by Hera. Venus, in Roman mythology, is the goddess of love and beauty.

tem of truths, and single truths cut out from their connections, and adopted without reference to kindred truths, always mislead. The affections will fall, like Lucifer,[5] from the upper, to fasten upon objects, in the nether sphere. In a word, the forces of the soul will retreat from the fore-head to the hind-head, and the brow, that "dome of thought, and palace of the soul," will be narrow and "villainously low"; for it is here that Nature sets her signet, and stamps her child a philosopher or a cretin. Here she will not suffer her signatures to be counterfeited, for neither tailors nor mantua-makers can insert their cork or padding beneath the tables of the skull.

We have now pointed, as with the finger and rapidly, towards those grand relations in which mankind stand to the cause of education. These relations lie all around us. They connect us with the universe of matter, and with the universe of mind; and hence the necessity of our possessing knowledge, for it is only by knowledge that we can adjust ourselves to the objects to which we are related. These truths also point to the future; and hence the necessity that we should regulate our conduct according to them, for every act of life is a step carrying us further towards, or further from, the goal of our being.

To promote this object, at once so comprehensive and so enduring, is among the first duties of governments; it is also among the first duties of individuals. It is the duty of the great and powerful, in their broad sphere of action; and it is no less the duty of the humble and obscure, in their narrower circle. Let every one contribute "according to his ability."

The labor of another year, in endeavoring to advance the well-being of our fellow-men, through enlightenment, and the impulse of higher motives, is the mite which we propose to cast into the "treasury" of the Lord. We ask others to cast in of their abundance. We ask all to receive into their minds the great idea of social improvement, to contemplate, and strive to imbody in human form, the sublime law of progression,—the possibility and the practicability of an ever-upward ascension in the scale of being. The race can be made happier and better than it is. There are innumerable sufferings which spring from ignorance. The knowledge will dispel, and relieve multitudes who are now tormented with unnecessary and gratuitous pain. There are innumerable sufferings springing from fountains of perverted feeling, which have no necessary existence, which are no part of the inevitable lot of humanity. These, like the debasing customs of savage life, like the foul superstitions and idolatries of paganism, can be cast off, as a garment which we have outgrown. There are ten thousand existing causes of misery and crime, which need not be reproduced and perpetuated in the coming generation. Many, nay, most, of the burdens which mankind have borne, which we now bear, may be lightened, before they are cast upon our successors. Save, O, save the myriads of innocent beings who are just landing upon the shores of time;—save them from the contaminations of the world into which they are

---

[5] Lucifer is the archangel cast from Heaven
for leading a revolt of the angels; Satan.

sent; teach not their unpolluted lips to utter curses, nor their hands to up-hold injustice, nor their feet to wander in forbidden paths. Even those who take the darkest views of human nature, and who proclaim the most fearful auguries concerning its ultimate destiny,—even they will admit that the young are less vicious than the old; that childhood has a simplicity and an ingenuousness which intercourse with the world corrupts and debauches. They will admit that there is a guilelessness, an uncalculating affection, a sensibility to wrong, in the breasts of the young, which the arts and customs of the world deprave and harden. It is we, who by our ignorances, and our apathy, by our parsimony and our pride, create in them diseases which even the brute creations do not suffer, because they do not abuse the natures which God has given them. Why should we, who, in our considerate moments, would not punish even the wretch suspected of crime, until guilt is fastened upon him by indubitable proof, and who, even then, profess to pity him, as he meets the just retributions of a violated law,—why should we lead children astray by our evil customs and practices, and bring down upon them those penalties, which, in the self-executing law of God, will assuredly follow transgression? To punish the innocent has been regarded with abhorrence and execration in all ages of the world; but to tempt innocence to the commission of those offences which incur punishment, is far more cruel, because guilt is infinitely worse than the punishment which avenges it. Why should innocent childhood be tormented with pains not of its own procuring,—with pains which the follies and the vices of ancestors seem to have prepared, and made ready against its coming? Why should the new-born generations be ushered into a world worse than themselves; to breathe in physical and moral contaminations which they did not scatter; to die of maladies engendered by those who should have been their protectors and guardian spirits?

It is in our power to rescue children from these calamities. It is in our power to guard them from the contagion of guilt, from that subtilist of poisons, an evil example. They can be restrained from entering paths where others have fallen and perished. No rude child of ignorance, left to himself in the wild wilderness where he was born, ever reached to a thousandth part of that depravity, which has been achieved as a common thing, by those whose birthplace was in a land of boasted civilization. Civilization, then, has not accomplished its object. It has given more power than rectitude,—the ability to perform great things without that moral sovereignty, before which the greatest and grandest achievements stand condemned, if not consecrated by goodness.

And here we would inquire what sphere of patriotic exertion is left open for the lover of his country, but the sphere of improving the rising generation through the instrumentality of a more perfect and efficient system for their education? We call our fathers *patriots*, because they loved their country and made sacrifices for its welfare. But what was their country? A vast tract of wilderness territory did not constitute it. It was not unconscious, insentient plains, or rivers, or mountains, however beautifully and majestically they might spread, or flow, or shine, beneath the canopy of heaven. Their country was chiefly their descendants, the human beings who were to throng these vast domains, the sentient, conscious natures which were to live here,—and living, to enjoy or suffer. The question with them was, whether this should be a land of liberty or bondage, of light or darkness, of religion or superstition. It was to redeem and elevate the millions who, in the providence of God, should people these wide-spreading realms, that they engaged in a cause where those who suffered death seemed to suffer least, where the survivors most challenge our sympathy. But we have no battles to fight by land or sea, against a foreign foe. We have no fathers, or brothers, or sons, in the camp, suffering cold, and hunger, and nakedness. We have no edifice of government to rear, with exhausting study and anxiety. These labors are done and ended, and we have entered into the rich inheritance. What, then, shall we do that we may be patriotic? How shall our love of country, if any we have, be made manifest? How, but by laboring for our descendants,—not in the same way, but with the same fidelity, as our fathers labored for us? Otherwise, there is no moral consanguinity between ourselves and them. Otherwise, we are not of their blood, but gentiles and heathens, boasting a lineage which our acts and lives belie. It is mockery to say, "We have Abraham as our father," while we perform the deeds of pagans. The only sphere, then, left open for our patriotism, is the improvement of our children,—not the few, but the many; not a part of them, but all. This is but one field of exertion, but it opens an infinite career; for the capacities of mankind can go on developing, improving, perfecting, as long as the cycles of eternity revolve. For this improvement of the race, a high, a generous, an expansive education is the true and efficient means. There is not a good work which the hand of man has ever undertaken, which his heart has ever conceived, which does not require a good education for its helper. There is not an evil afflicting the earth, which can be extirpated, until the auxiliary of education shall lend its mighty aid. If an angel were to descend from heaven to earth, on an errand of mercy and love, he would hasten to accomplish his mission by illuminating the minds and purifying the hearts of children. The Saviour took little children in his arms and blessed them; he did not, by any miraculous exertion of power, bar up all passages to sin and error, and at once make mankind the passive recipients of perfection. He left it for us to be agents and co-workers with him in their redemption. He gave to us, not so much the boon of being blessed, as the more precious, the heavenly boon of blessing others. For this end, an instrument has been put into our hands, fully adequate to the accomplishment of so divine a purpose. We have the power to train up children in accordance with those wise and benign laws which the Creator has stamped upon their physical, their intellectual, and their moral nature; and of this stewardship we must assuredly give account. May it be rendered with joy, and not with sorrow!

Temperance

WALT WHITMAN

(1819-1892)

The temperance movement was one of the most widespread of all reforms in the early nineteenth century. Stories and poems were written by Lucius Sargent and Lydia Huntly Sigourney (the "Sweet Singer of Hartford"); plays like *Ten Nights in a Barroom* by Timothy Shay Arthur; novels such as *Franklin Evans* by Walt Whitman; and hundreds of tracts by hundreds of forgotten, but once-popular authors.

Heavy drinking was viewed as a social evil for a variety of reasons: it was destructive of family life; it decreased the efficiency of workers in industry; and it prevented the citizenry from implementing the laws with common sense and reason. By 1825 there were more than a million Americans who advocated total abstinence; by the 1850's 13 states had enacted prohibition legislation.

For a full description of works by and about Whitman, see pp. 989-994.

The following selection is taken from *Franklin Evans, The Early Poems and the Fiction,* ed. Thomas L. Brasher, pp. 236-239, 1963, Volume 6 in *The Collected Writings of Walt Whitman,* general editors, Gay Wilson Allen and Sculley Bradley, 1963—.

From Franklin Evans

CHAPTER XXV
CONCLUSION

As works of fiction have often been made the vehicle of morality, I have adopted the novel experiment of making one of the sort a messenger of the cause of Temperance. And though I know not what the decision of the reader may be, I am too strongly armed in the honesty of my intentions, to suppose that there can be any doubt as to the propriety of the *moral* intended to be conveyed—or to fear any attack upon the story, as regards its principles.

To expatiate upon the ruins and curses which follow the habitual use of strong drink, were at this time almost a stale homily. A great revolution has come to pass within the last eight to ten years. The dominion of the Liquor Fiend has been assaulted and battered. Good men and strong have come up to the work of attack. Warriors, with large hands, and with girded loins, are waiting with resolution, and their energies are devoted to the battle. They are taking the place of those who are wearied, and in their turn give way to others, who have new and greater strength. Will the old fortress yield? It *must*, sooner or later. It may be compared to some ivy-crowned castle, some strong tower of the olden time, with its flanked battlements, and its guards pacing on the top of its walls, and laughing to scorn all the devices of those who came against it. The red banner floated on its topmost height—inscribed with its fearful watchword, "Disgrace and Death!" And a million victims came every year, and yielded themselves to their ruin under its control. But the foes of the Castle of Orgies stepped forth in array, and swore to one another that they would devote their lives to the work of reform. Long did that haughty structure resist every blow—firmly did it defy every besieger. But the might of a good motive is more than the highest strength of wickedness; and at last the bars of the gates began to give way, and the thick walls cracked. An outpost was driven in, and a tower fell. How tremendous the shout then that arose from the men who were fighting the good fight, and the faces of their antagonists paled with fear! So they kept on. And other parts of the foundation were undermined, and the heavy stanchions were burst asunder, and the forces of the Red Fiend have been routed, band after band, until but a little are left; and they will soon have to retreat, and go the way of their brethren.

The good of the present age are smiling upon the cause of Temperance. It is indeed a holy cause. How many widows' tears it has assuaged—and how many poor wretched men it has taken by the hand, and led to reputation and comfort once more. It seems to me, that he who would speak of the efforts of the Termperance Societies with a sneer, is possessed of a very heedless and bigoted, or a very wicked disposition. It is true, that the dictates of a classic and most refined taste, are not always observed by these people; and the fashionable fop, the exquisite, or the pink of what is termed "quality," might feel not at home among them. But to persons with clear heads, and with breasts where philanthropy and a desire for the good of their fellows have a resting-place, I am fully content to leave the decision whether, after all, there be not a good deal of *intellectuality* engaged in the Temperance movement.

The Reformers have one great advantage, too, which makes up for any want of polish, or grace. They are sincere, and speak with the convictions of their own experience. In all ages, a revolution for the better, when started, has found its advocates among the poorer classes of men. From them, it gradually rises, until it pervades all ranks of society. It has happened so in this case. The few men who met together in Baltimore, and formed a compact with themselves to abstain from those practices which had been so injurious to them, little thought how their principles were to spread, and how they would be pointed back to with admiration, from the rich as well as the poor—the learned as well as the ignorant.

They called themselves WASHINGTONIANS. Long may the name be honored—and long may it continue to number among those who are proud to style themselves by the title—upright and noble spirits, determined never to turn back from the work, or to discredit the name they bear, and the Society to which they belong!

Any one who has attended the meetings of the temperance people, cannot but be amazed and delighted at the enthusiasm which pervades them. It is not confined to one sex, or to any particular age or class. It spreads over all. Men and women join in it. Young people, even boys and girls, are inoculated with the fervor, and are heard about the streets, singing the temperance songs, and conversing upon the principles of the doctrine, by which their fathers or brothers have been regenerated and made happy. The enthusiasm I mention, has not been limited, either, to one City or one State. It is felt over every part of this Republic, and accounts come to us of the wondrous doings of Temperance in Maine, while the same hour, in the Western mail, we receive the story of how many new converts there are in Illinois. Perhaps on no occasion has there been a spectacle so full of moral splendor. A whole nation forsaking an evil mania, which has hitherto made it the mark of scorn to those who, coming from abroad, have noticed this one foul blot in contradistinction to all the other national good qualities—and turning a goodly portion of its mighty powers to the business of preventing others from forming the same habits; and redeem [redeeming], as far as practicable, those who have already formed them: I consider it a sight which we may properly call on the whole world to admire!

In the story which has been narrated in the preceding pages, there is given by a faint idea of the dangers which surround our young men in this great city. On all sides, and at every step, some temptation assails them; but all the others joined together, are nothing compared with the seductive enchantments which have been thrown around the practice of intoxication, in some five or six of the more public and noted taverns called "musical saloons," or some other name which is used to hide their hideous nature. These places are multiplying. The persons engaged in the sale of ardent spirits are brought to see that their trade, unless they can join something to it, as a make-weight, will shortly vanish into thin air, and their gains along with it. Thus they have hit upon the expedient of MUSIC, as a lure to induce customers, and in too many cases with fatally extensive success.

I would warn that youth whose eye may scan over these lines, with a voice which speaks to him, not from idle fear, but the sad knowledge of experience, how bitter are the consequences attending, these musical drinking-shops. They are the fit portals of ruin and inevitably lead thither. I have known more than one young man, whose prospects for the future were good—in whom hope was strong, and energy not wanting—but all poisoned by these pestilent places, where the mind and the body are both rendered effeminate together.

To conclude, I would remark that, if my story meets with that favor which writers are perhaps too fond of relying upon, my readers may hear from me again, in the [a] method similar to that which has already made us acquainted.

THE AUTHOR.

Reform for the Insane

DOROTHEA DIX

(1802–1887)

Dorothea Dix was an outspoken opponent of the subhuman conditions suffered by the insane in Massachusetts prisons. Her *Memorial to the Legislature of Massachusetts* (1843) is well documented and underscores Ms. Dix's central point: the insane should not be treated as depraved animals but as sick people who need therapy in publicly supported institutions.

An early biography is Francis Tiffany, *Life of Dorothea Lynde Dix,* 1890. More recent studies are H. E. Marshall, *Dorothea Dix, Forgotten Samaritan,* 1937 and Dorothy Clarke Wilson, *Stranger and Traveler,* 1975.

The text is from *Memorial to the Legislature of Massachusetts,* 1843.

From Memorial to the Legislature of Massachusetts

. . . About two years since leisure afforded opportunity and duty prompted me to visit several prisons and almshouses in the vicinity of this metropolis, I found, near Boston, in the jails and asylums for the poor, a numerous class brought into unsuitable connection with criminals and the general mass of paupers. I refer to idiots and insane persons, dwelling in circumstances not only adverse to their own physical and moral improvement, but productive of extreme disadvantages to all other persons brought into association with them. I applied myself diligently to trace the causes of these evils, and sought to supply remedies. As one obstacle was surmounted, fresh difficulties appeared. Every new investigation has given depth to the conviction that it is only by decided, prompt, and vigorous legislation the evils to which I refer, and which I shall proceed more fully to illustrate, can be remedied. I shall be obliged to speak with great plainness, and to reveal many things revolting to the taste, and from which my woman's nature shrinks with peculiar sensitiveness. But truth is the highest consideration. *I tell what I have seen*—painful and shocking as the details often are—that from them you may feel more deeply the imperative obligation which lies upon you to prevent the possibility of a repetition or continuance of such outrages upon humanity. If I inflict pain upon you, and move you to horror, it is to acquaint you with sufferings which you have the power to alleviate, and make you hasten to the relief of the victims of legalized barbarity.

I come to present the strong claims of suffering humanity. I come to place before the Legislature of Massachusetts the condition of the miserable, the desolate, the outcast. I come as the advocate of helpless, forgotten, insane, and idiotic men and women; of beings sunk to a condition from which the most unconcerned would start with real horror; of beings wretched in our prisons, and more wretched in our almshouses. And I cannot suppose it needful to employ earnest persuasion, or stubborn argument, in order to arrest and fix attention upon a subject only the more strongly pressing in its claims because it is revolting and disgusting in its details.

I must confine myself to few examples, but am ready to furnish other and more complete details, if required. If my pictures are displeasing, coarse, and severe, my subjects, it must be recollected, offer no tranquil, refined, or composing features. The condition of human beings, reduced to the extremest states of degradation and misery, cannot be exhibited in softened language, or adorn a polished page.

I proceed, gentlemen, briefly to call your attention to the *present* state of insane persons confined within this Commonwealth, in *cages, closets, cellars, stalls, pens! Chained, naked, beaten with rods,* and *lashed* into obedience.

As I state cold, severe *facts*, I feel obliged to refer to persons, and detinitely to indicate localities. But it is upon my subject, not upon localities or individuals, I desire to fix attention; and I would speak as kindly as possible of all wardens, keepers, and other responsible officers, believing that *most* of these have erred not through hardness of heart and wilful cruelty so much as want of skill and knowledge, and want of consideration. Familiarity with suffering, it is said, blunts the sensibilities, and where neglect once finds a footing other injuries are multiplied. This is not all, for it may justly and strongly be added that, from the deficiency of adequate means to meet the wants of these cases, it has been an absolute impossibility to do justice in this matter. Prisons are not constructed in view of being converted into county hospitals, and almshouses are not founded as receptacles for the insane. And yet, in the face of justice and common sense, wardens are by law compelled to receive, and the masters of almshouses not to refuse, insane and idiotic subjects in all stages of mental disease and privation.

It is the Commonwealth, not its integral parts, that is accountable for most of the abuses which have lately and do still exist. I repeat it, it is defective legislation which perpetuates and multiplies these abuses. In illustration of my subject, I offer the following extracts from my Note-book and Journal:—

Springfield. In the jail, one lunatic woman, furiously mad, a State pauper, improperly situated, both in regard to the prisoners, the keepers, and herself. It is a case of extreme self-forgetfulness and oblivion to all the decencies of life, to describe which would be to repeat only the grossest scenes. She is much worse since leaving Worcester. In the almshouse of the same town is a woman apparently only needing judicious care, and some well-chosen employment, to make it unnecessary to confine her in solitude, in a dreary unfurnished room. Her appeals for employment and companionship are most touching, but the mistress replied "she had no time to attend to her."

· · ·

Lincoln. A woman in a cage. *Medford.* One idiotic subject chained, and one in a close stall for seventeen years. *Pepperell.* One often doubly chained, hand and foot; another violent; several peaceable now. *Brookfield.* One man caged, comfortable. *Granville.* One often closely confined; now losing the use of his limbs from want of exercise. *Charlemont.* One man caged. *Savoy.* One man caged. *Lenox.* Two in the jail, against whose unfit condition there the jailer protests.

Dedham. The insane disadvantageously placed in the jail. In the almshouse, two females in stalls, situated in the main building; lie in wooden bunks filled with straw; always shut up. One of these subjects is supposed curable. The overseers of the poor have declined giving her a trial at the hospital, as I was informed, on account of expense.

· · ·

Besides the above, I have seen many who, part of the year, are chained or caged. The use of cages all but universal. Hardly a town but can refer to some not distant period of using them; chains are less common; negligences frequent; wilful abuse less frequent than sufferings proceeding from ignorance, or want of consideration. I encountered during the last three months many poor creatures wandering reckless and unprotected through the country. Innumerable accounts have been sent me of persons who had roved away unwatched and unsearched after; and I have heard that responsible persons, controlling the almshouses, have not thought themselves culpable in sending away from their shelter, to cast upon the chances of remote relief, insane men and women. These, left on the highways, unfriended and incompetent to control or direct their own movements, sometimes have found refuge in the hospital, and others have not been traced. But I cannot particularize. In traversing the State, I have found hundreds of insane persons in every variety of circumstance and condition, many whose situation could not and need not be improved; a less number, but that very large, whose lives are the saddest pictures of human suffering and degradation. I give a few illustrations; but description fades before reality.

Danvers. November. Visited the almshouse. A large building, much out of repair. Understand a new one is in contemplation. Here are from fifty-six to sixty inmates, one idiotic, three insane; one of the latter in close confinement at all times.

Long before reaching the house, wild shouts, snatches of rude songs, imprecations and obscene language, fell upon the ear, proceeding from the occupant of a low building, rather remote from the principal building to which my course was directed. Found the mistress, and was conducted to the place which was called *"the home"* of the *forlorn* maniac, a young woman, exhibiting a condition of neglect and misery blotting out the faintest idea of comfort, and outraging every sentiment of decency. She had been, I learnt, "a respectable person, industrious and worthy. Disappointments and trials shook her mind, and, finally, laid prostrate reason and self-control. She became a maniac for life. She had been at Worcester Hospital for a considerable time, and had been returned as incurable." The mistress told me she understood that, "while there, she was comfortable and decent." Alas, what a change was here exhibited! She had passed from one degree of violence to another, in swift progress. There she stood, clinging to or beating upon the bars of her caged apartment, the contracted size of which afforded space only for increasing accumulations of filth, a *foul* spectacle. There she stood with naked arms and dishevelled hair, the unwashed frame invested with fragments of unclean garments, the air so extremely offensive, though ventilation was afforded on all sides save one, that it was not possible to remain beyond a few moments without retreating for recovery to the outward air. Irritation of body, produced by utter filth and exposure, incited her to the horrid process of tearing off her skin by inches. Her face, neck, and person were thus disfigured to hideousness. She held up a fragment just rent off. To my exclamation of horror, the mistress replied: "Oh, we can't help it. Half the skin is off sometimes. We can do nothing with her; and it makes no difference what she eats, for she consumes her own filth as readily as the food which is brought her."

. . .

Some may say these things cannot be remedied, these furious maniacs are not to be raised from these base conditions. I *know* they are. Could give *many* examples. Let *one* suffice. A young woman, a pauper, in a distant town, Sandisfield, was for years a raging maniac. A cage, chains, and *the whip* were the agents for controlling her, united with harsh tones and profane language. Annually, with others (the town's poor), she was put up at auction, and bid off at the lowest price which was declared for her. One year, not long past, an old man came forward in the number of applicants for the poor wretch. He was taunted and ridiculed. "What would he and his old wife do with such a mere beast?" "My wife says yes," replied he, "and I shall take her." She was given to his charge. He conveyed her home. She was washed, neatly dressed, and placed in a decent bedroom, furnished for comfort and opening into the kitchen. How altered her condition! As yet *the chains* were not off. The first week she was somewhat restless, at times violent, but the quiet, kind ways of the old people wrought a change. She received her food decently, forsook acts of violence, and no longer uttered blasphemies or indecent language. After a week the chain was lengthened, and she was received as a companion into the kitchen. Soon she engaged in trivial employments. "After a fortnight," said the old man, "I knocked off the chains and made her a free woman." She is at times excited, but not violently. They are careful of her diet. They keep her very clean. She calls them "father" and "mother." Go there now, and you will find her "clothed," and, though not perfectly in her "right mind," so far restored as to be a safe and comfortable inmate.

Newburyport. Visited the almshouse in June last. Eighty inmates. Seven insane, one idiotic. Commodious and neat house. Several of the partially insane apparently very comfortable. Two very improperly situated; namely, an insane man, not considered incurable, in an out-building, whose room opened upon what was called "the dead room," affording, in lieu of companionship with the living, a contemplation of corpses. The other subject was a woman in a *cellar.* I desired to see her. Much reluctance was shown. I pressed the request. The master of the house stated that she was *in the cellar;* that she was *dangerous to be approached;* that she had lately attacked his wife, and *was often naked.* I persisted, "If you will not go with me, give me the keys and I will go alone." Thus importuned, the outer doors were opened. I descended the stairs from within. A strange, unnatural noise seemed to proceed from beneath our feet. At the moment I did not much regard it. My conductor proceeded to remove a padlock, while my eye explored the wide space in quest of the poor woman. All for a moment was still. But judge my horror and amazement, when a door to a closet *beneath* the *staircase* was opened, revealing in the imperfect light a female apparently wasted to a skeleton, partially wrapped in blankets, furnished for the narrow bed on which she was sitting. Her countenance furrowed, not by age, but suffering, was the image of distress. In that contracted space, unlighted, unventilated, she poured forth the wailings of despair. Mournfully she extended her arms and appealed to me: "Why am I consigned to hell? dark—dark—I used to pray, I used to read the Bible—I have done no crime in my heart. I had friends. Why have all forsaken me!—my God, my God, why hast *thou* forsaken me!" Those groans, those wailings, come up daily, mingling with how many others, a perpetual and sad memorial. When the good Lord shall require an account of our stewardship, what shall all and each answer?

Perhaps it will be inquired how long, how many days or hours, was she imprisoned in these confined limits? *For years!* In another part of the cellar were other small closets, only better, because higher through the entire length, into one of which she by turns was transferred, so as to afford opportunity for fresh whitewashing, etc.

Saugus. December 24. Thermometer below zero; drove to the poorhouse; was conducted to the master's family-room by himself; walls garnished with handcuffs and chains, not less than five pairs of the former; did not inquire how or on whom applied; thirteen pauper inmates; one insane man; one woman insane; one idiotic man; asked to see them; the two men were shortly led in; appeared pretty decent and comfortable. Requested to see the other insane subject; was denied decidedly; urged the request, and finally secured a reluctant assent. Was led through an outer passage into a lower room, occupied by the paupers; crowded; not neat; ascended a rather low flight of stairs upon an open entry, through the floor of which was introduced a stove-pipe, carried along a *few feet,* about six inches above the floor, through which it was reconveyed below. From this entry opens a room of moderate size, having a sashed window; floor, I think painted; apartment *entirely* unfurnished; no chair, table, nor bed; neither, what is seldom missing, a bundle of straw or lock of hay; cold, very cold, the first movement of my conductor was to throw open a window, a measure imperatively necessary for those who entered. *On the floor* sat a woman, her limbs immovably contracted, so that the knees were brought upward to the chin; the face was concealed; the head rested on the folded arms. For clothing she appeared to have been furnished with *fragments* of many discharged garments. These were folded about her, yet they little benefited her, if one might judge by the constant shuddering which almost convulsed her poor crippled frame. Woeful was this scene. Language is feeble to record the misery she was suffering and had suffered. In reply to my inquiry if she could not change her position, I was answered by the master in the negative, and told that the contraction of limbs was occasioned by "neglect and exposure in former years," but *since she had been crazy,* and before she fell under the charge, as I inferred, of her present *guardians.* Poor wretch! she, like many others, was an example of what humanity becomes when the temple of reason falls in ruins, leaving the mortal part to injury and neglect, and showing how much can be endured of privation, exposure, and disease without extinguishing the lamp of life.

Passing out, the man pointed to a something, revealed to more than one sense, which he called "her bed; and we throw some blankets over her at night." Possibly this is done; others like myself, might be pardoned a doubt if they could have seen all I saw and heard abroad all I heard. The *bed,* so called, was about *three* feet long, and from a half to three-quarters of a yard wide; of old ticking or tow cloth was the case; the contents might have been a *full handful* of hay or straw. My attendant's exclamations on my leaving the house were emphatic, and can hardly be repeated.

.   .   .

It may not appear much more credible than the fact above stated, that a few months since a young woman in a state of complete insanity was confined entirely naked in a pen or stall in a barn. There, unfurnished with clothes, without bed and without fire, she was left—but not alone. Profligate men and idle boys had access to the den, whenever curiosity or vulgarity prompted. She is now removed into the house with other paupers; and for this humanizing benefit she was indebted to the remonstrances, in the first instance, *of an insane man.*

Another town now owns a poorhouse, which I visited, and am glad to testify to the present comfortable state of the inmates; but there the only provision the house affords for an insane person, should one, as is not improbable, be conveyed there, is a closet in the celler, formed by the arch upon which the chimney rests. This has a closed door, not only securing the prisoners, but excluding what of light and pure air might else find admission.

Abuses assuredly cannot always or altogether be guarded against; but, if in the civil and social relations all shall have "done what they could," no ampler justification will be demanded at the great tribunal.

Of the dangers and mischiefs sometimes following the location of insane persons in our almshouses, I will record but one more example. In Worcester has for several years resided a young woman, a lunatic pauper of decent life and respectable family. I have seen her as she usually appeared, listless and silent, almost or quite sunk into a state of dementia, sitting one amidst the family, "but not of them." A few weeks since, revisiting that almshouse, judge my horror and amazement to see her negligently bearing in her arms a young infant, of which I was told she was the unconscious parent. Who was the father, none could or would declare. Disqualified for the performance of maternal cares and duties, regarding the helpless little creature with a perplexed or indifferent gaze, she sat a silent, but, oh, how eloquent, a pleader for the protection of others of her neglected and outraged sex! Details of that black story would not strengthen the cause. Needs it a mightier plea than the sight of that forlorn creature and her wailing infant? Poor little child, more than orphan from birth, in this unfriendly world! A demented mother, a father on whom the sun might blush or refuse to shine!

·   ·   ·

The greatest evils in regard to the insane and idiots in the prisons of this Commonwealth are found at Ipswich and Cambridge, and distinguish these places only, as I believe, because the numbers are larger, being more than twenty in each. Ipswich has the advantage over Cambridge in having fewer furious subjects, and in the construction of the buildings, though these are so bad as to have afforded cause for presentment by the grand jury some time since. It is said that the new County House, in progress of building, will meet the exigencies of the case. If it is meant that the wing in the new prison, to be appropriated to the insane, will provide accommodation for all the insane and idiotic paupers in the county, I can only say that it could receive no more than can be gathered in the three towns of Salem, Newburyport, and Ipswich, supposing these are to be removed, there being in Ipswich twenty-two in the prison and eight in the almshouse; in Salem almshouse, seventeen uniformly crazy, and two part of the time deranged; and in that of Newburyport eleven, including idiots. Here at once are sixty. The returns of 1842 exhibit an aggregate of one hundred and thirty-five. Provision is made in the new prison for fifty-seven of this class, leaving seventy-eight unprovided for, except in the almshouses. From such a fate, so far as Danvers, Saugus, East Bradford, and some other towns in the county reveal conditions of insane subjects, we pray they may be exempt.

I have the verbal and written testimony of many officers of this Commonwealth, who are respectable alike for their integrity and the fidelity with which they discharge their official duties, and whose opinions, based on experience, are entitled to consideration, that the occupation of prisons for the detention of lunatics and of idiots is, under all circumstances, an evil, subversive alike of good order, strict discipline, and good morals. I transcribe a few passages which will place this mischief in its true light. The sheriff of Plymouth County writes as follows: "I am decidedly of the opinion that the county jail is a very improper place for lunatics and idiots. The last summer its bad effects were fully realized here, not only by the prisoners in jail, but the disturbance extended to the inhabitants dwelling in the neighborhood. A foreigner was sentenced by a justice of the peace to thirty days' confinement in the house of correction. He was to all appearance a lunatic or madman.

He destroyed every article in his room, even to his wearing apparel, his noise and disturbance was incessant for hours, day and night. I consider prisons places for the safe keeping of prisoners, and all these are equally entitled to humane treatment from their keepers, without regard to the cause of commitment. We have in jails no conveniences to make the situation of lunatics and idiots much more decent than would be necessary for the brute creation, and impossible to prevent the disturbance of the inmates under the same roof."

· · ·

It is not few, but many, it is not a part, but the whole, who bear unqualified testimony to this evil. A voice strong and deep comes up from every almshouse and prison in Massachusetts where the insane are or have been protesting against such evils as have been illustrated in the preceding pages.

Gentlemen, I commit to you this sacred cause. Your action upon this subject will effect the present and future condition of hundreds and of thousands.

In this legislation, as in all things, may you exercise that "wisdom which is the breath of the power of God."

Respectfully submitted,
D. L. Dix.

1843

RALPH WALDO EMERSON

(1803–1881)*

Although he was always reluctant to join any specific social experiment, Emerson was sympathetic to the moral implications of reform movements; and he was, of course, the great figure from whom so many others drew their inspiration.

In this essay, delivered first as a lecture on March 3, 1844, Emerson measures social reform in its American manifestations, recognizing the absurd as well as the more serious aspects of various efforts. His conclusions are consistent with his principles: no single reform—Fourier-

*For a full introduction to Emerson, see
pp. 840–844.

ism, education, temperance, or any of the socialist attempts—should consider itself more important than any other. The error with contemporary reformers, in Emerson's view, is that they look for specialized results, whereas genuine reform must be inward.

New England Reformers[1]

A LECTURE READ BEFORE THE SOCIETY IN AMORY HALL,[2] ON SUNDAY, MARCH 3, 1844

> In the suburb, in the town,
> On the railway, in the square,
> Came a beam of goodness down
> Doubling daylight everywhere:
> Peace now each for malice takes,
> Beauty for his sinful weeds,
> For the angel Hope aye makes
> Him an angel whom she leads.

Whoever has had opportunity of acquaintance with society in New England during the last twenty-five years, with those middle and with those leading sections that may constitute any just representation of the character and aim of the community, will have been struck with the great activity of thought and experimenting. His attention must be commanded by the signs that the Church, or religious party, is falling from the Church nominal, and is appearing in temperance and non-resistance societies,[3] on movements of abolitionists and of socialists; and in very significant assemblies called Sabbath and Bible Conventions; composed of ultraists, of seekers, of all the soul of the soldiery of dissent, and meeting to call in question the authority of the Sabbath, of the priesthood, and of the Church. In these movements nothing was more remarkable than the discontent they begot in the movers. The spirit of protest and of detachment drove the members of these Conventions to bear testimony against the Church, and immediately afterwards to declare their

[1] This lecture was delivered at the height of the Reform movement. Emerson sympathized with the many tendencies to examine the moral life of America, but he was also aware of the humorous excesses to which reformers often carried their ideas. In this essay he tries to see the entire movement in the broadest perspective and stresses the need for self-reform.

[2] The liberal Church of the Disciples in Boston. Emerson's friend, James Freeman Clarke, was the minister.

[3] Emerson is thinking of a convention like the Chardon Street Convention, which had been called by the Friends of Universal Reform in Boston in 1840. See his essay, "Chardon Street Convention," in *Lectures and Biographical Sketches* in *Works*, X, 371–77.

discontent with these Conventions, their independence of their colleagues, and their impatience of the methods whereby they were working. They defied each other, like a congress of kings, each of whom had a realm to rule, and a way of his own that made concert unprofitable. What a fertility of projects for the salvation of the world! One apostle thought all men should go to farming, and another that no man should buy or sell, that the use of money was the cardinal evil; another that the mischief was in our diet, that we eat and drink damnation. These made unleavened bread, and were foes to the death to fermentation. It was in vain urged by the housewife that God made yeast, as well as dough, and loves fermentation just as dearly as he loves vegetation; that fermentation develops the saccharine element in the grain, and makes it more palatable and more digestible. No; they wish the pure wheat, and will die but it shall not ferment. Stop, dear Nature, these incessant advances of thine; let us scotch these ever-rolling wheels! Others attacked the system of agriculture, the use of animal manures in farming, and the tyranny of man over brute nature; these abuses polluted his food. The ox must be taken from the plough and the horse from the cart, the hundred acres of the farm must be spaded, and the man must walk, wherever boats and locomotives will not carry him. Even the insect world was to be defended—that had been too long neglected, and a society for the protection of ground-worms, slugs and mosquitos was to be incorporated without delay. With these appeared the adepts of homœopathy, of hydropathy, of mesmerism, of phrenology, and their wonderful theories of the Christian miracles! Others assailed particular vocations, as that of the lawyer, that of the merchant, of the manufacturer, of the clergyman, of the scholar. Others attacked the institution of marriage as the fountain of social evils. Others devoted themselves to the worrying of churches and meetings for public worship; and the fertile forms of antinomianism[4] among the elder puritans seemed to have their match in the plenty of the new harvest of reform.

With this din of opinion and debate there was a keener scrutiny of institutions and domestic life than any we had known; there was sincere protesting against existing evils, and there were changes of employment dictated by conscience. No doubt there was plentiful vaporing, and cases of backsliding might occur. But in each of these movements emerged a good result, a tendency to the adoption of simpler methods, and an assertion of the sufficiency of the private man. Thus it was directly in the spirit and genius of the age, what happened in one instance when a church censured and threatened to excommunicate one of its members on account of the somewhat hostile part to the church which his conscience led him to take in the anti-slavery

[4] Emerson is referring to Ann Hutchinson, a seventeenth-century heretic of Massachusetts Bay whose teachings disturbed the magistrates of the colony. Ann Hutchinson (1591-1643) believed that salvation depended wholly on conviction of divine grace, a doctrine for which she was excommunicated by a synod of churches and banished from the Massachusetts Bay Colony.

business; the threatened individual immediately excommunicated the church, in a public and formal process. This has been several times repeated: it was excellent when it was done the first time, but of course loses all value when it is copied. Every project in the history of reform, no matter how violent and surprising, is good when it is the dictate of a man's genius and constitution, but very dull and suspicious when adopted from another. It is right and beautiful in any man to say, "I will take this coat, or this book, or this measure of corn of yours"—in whom we see the act to be original, and to flow from the whole spirit and faith of him; for then that taking will have a giving as free and divine; but we are very easily disposed to resist the same generosity of speech when we miss originality and truth to character in it.

There was in all the practical activities of New England for the last quarter of a century, a gradual withdrawal of tender consciences from the social organizations. There is observable throughout, the contest between mechanical and spiritual methods, but with a steady tendency of the thoughtful and virtuous to a deeper belief and reliance on spiritual facts.

In politics, for example, it is easy to see the progress of dissent. The country is full of rebellion; the country is full of kings. Hands off! let there be no control and no interference in the administration of the affairs of this kingdom of me. Hence the growth of the doctrine and of the party of Free Trade, and the willingness to try that experiment, in the face of what appear incontestable facts. I confess, the motto of the Globe newspaper[5] is so attractive to me that I can seldom find much appetite to read what is below it in its columns: "The world is governed too much." So the country is frequently affording solitary examples of resistance to the government, solitary nullifiers,[6] who throw themselves on their reserved rights; nay, who have reserved all their rights; who reply to the assessor and to the clerk of court that they do not know the State, and embarrass the courts of law by non-juring and the commander-in-chief of the militia by non-resistance.[7]

The same disposition to scrutiny and dissent appeared in civil, festive, neighborly, and domestic society. A restless, prying, conscientious criticism broke out in unexpected quarters. Who gave me the money with which I bought my coat? Why should professional labor and that of the counting-house be paid so disproportionately to the labor of the porter and woodsawyer? This whole business of Trade gives me to pause and think, as it constitutes false relations between men; inasmuch as I am prone to count myself relieved of any responsibility to behave well and nobly to that person whom I pay with money; whereas if I had not that commodity, I should be put on

[5] The Washington *Daily Globe*.

[6] Bronson Alcott had refused to pay his poll tax in Concord in 1843 as a protest against his government; he was arrested but not imprisoned. Thoreau protested in a similar fash- ion in 1846; see his essay, "Resistance to Civil Government."

[7] In 1839 William Lloyd Garrison and others founded the New England Non-Resistance Society to advocate pacifism.

my good behavior in all companies, and man would be a benefactor to man, as being himself his only certificate that he had a right to those aids and services which each asked of the other, Am I not too protected a person? is there not a wide disparity between the lot of me and the lot of thee, my poor brother, my poor sister? Am I not defrauded of my best culture in the loss of those gymnastics which manual labor and the emergencies of poverty constitute? I find nothing healthful or exalting in the smooth conventions of society; I do not like the close air of saloons.[8] I begin to suspect myself to be a prisoner, though treated with all this courtesy and luxury. I pay a destructive tax in my conformity.

The same insatiable criticism may be traced in the efforts for the reform of Education. The popular education has been taxed with a want of truth and nature. It was complained that an education to things was not given. We are students of words: we are shut up in schools, and colleges, and recitation-rooms, for ten or fifteen years, and come out at last with a bag of wind, a memory of words, and do not know a thing. We cannot use our hands, or our legs, or our eyes, or our arms. We do not know an edible root in the woods, we cannot tell our course by the stars, nor the hour of the day by the sun. It is well if we can swim and skate. We are afraid of a horse, of a cow, of a dog, of a snake, of a spider. The Roman rule was to teach a boy nothing that he could not learn standing. The old English rule was, "All summer in the field, and all winter in the study." And it seems as if a man should learn to plant, or to fish, or to hunt, that he might secure his subsistence at all events, and not be painful to his friends and fellow-men. The lessons of science should be experimental also. The sight of a planet through a telescope is worth all the course on astronomy; the shock of the electric spark in the elbow, outvalues all the theories; the taste of the nitrous oxide, the firing of an artificial volcano, are better than volumes of chemistry.

One of the traits of the new spirit is the inquisition it fixed on our scholastic devotion to the dead languages. The ancient languages, with great beauty of structure, contain wonderful remains of genius, which draw, and always will draw, certain like-minded men—Greek men, and Roman men—in all countries, to their study; but by a wonderful drowsiness of usage they had exacted the study of *all* men. Once (say two centuries ago), Latin and Greek had a strict relation to all the science and culture there was in Europe, and the Mathematics had a momentary importance at some era of activity in physical science. These things became stereotyped as *education,* as the manner of men is. But the Good Spirit never cared for the colleges, and though all men and boys were now drilled in Latin, Greek and Mathematics, it had quite left these shells high and dry on the beach, and was now creating and feeding other matters at other ends of the world. But in a hundred high schools and colleges this warfare against common-sense still goes on. Four, or

---

[8] Salons, drawing rooms.

six, or ten years, the pupil is parsing Greek and Latin, and as soon as he leaves the University, as it is ludicrously styled, he shuts those books for the last time. Some thousands of young men are graduated at our colleges in this country every year, and the persons who, at forty years, still read Greek, can all be counted on your hand. I never met with ten. Four or five persons I have seen who read Plato.

But is not this absurd, that the whole liberal talent of this country should be directed in its best years on studies which lead to nothing? What was the consequence? Some intelligent persons said or thought, "Is that Greek and Latin some spell to conjure with, and not words of reason? If the physician, the lawyer, the divine, never use it to come at their ends, I need never learn it to come at mine. Conjuring is gone out of fashion and I will omit this conjugating, and go straight to affairs." So they jumped the Greek and Latin, and read law, medicine, or sermons, without it. To the astonishment of all, the self-made men took even ground at once with the oldest of the regular graduates, and in a few months the most conservative circles of Boston and New York had quite forgotten who of their gownsmen was college-bred, and who was not.

One tendency appears alike in the philosophical speculation and in the rudest democratical movements, through all the petulance and all the puerility, the wish, namely to cast aside the superfluous and arrive at short methods; urged, as I suppose, by an intuition that the human spirit is equal to all emergencies, alone, and that man is more often injured than helped by the means he uses.

I conceive this gradual casting off of material aids and the indication of growing trust in the private self-supplied powers of the individual, to be the affirmative principle of the recent philosophy, and that it is feeling its own profound truth and is reaching forward at this very hour to the happiest conclusions. I readily concede that in this, as in every period of intellectual activity, there has been a noise of denial and protest; much was to be resisted, much was to be got rid of by those who were reared in the old, before they could begin to affirm and to construct. Many a reformer perishes in his removal of rubbish; and that makes the offensiveness of the class. They are partial; they are not equal to the work they pretend. They lose their way; in the assault on the kingdom of darkness they expend all their energy on some accidental evil, and lose their sanity and power of benefit. It is of little moment that one or two or twenty errors of our social system be corrected, but of much that the man be in his senses.

The criticism and attack on institutions, which we have witnessed, has made one thing plain, that society gains nothing whilst a man, not himself renovated, attempts to renovate things around him: he has become tediously good in some particular but negligent or narrow in the rest; and hypocrisy and vanity are often the disgusting result.

It is handsomer to remain in the establishment better than the establishment, and conduct that in the best manner, than to make a sally against evil by some single improvement, without supporting it by a total regeneration. Do not be so vain of your one objection. Do you think there is only one? Alas! my good friend, there is no part of society or of life better than any other part. All our things are right and wrong together. The wave of evil washes all our institutions alike. Do you complain of our Marriage? Our marriage is no worse than our education, our diet, our trade, our social customs. Do you complain of the laws of Property? It is a pedantry to give such importance to them. Can we not play the game of life with these counters, as well as with those? in the institution of property, as well as out of it? Let into it the new and renewing principle of love, and property will be universality. No one gives the impression of superiority to the institution, which he must give who will reform it. It makes no difference what you say, you must make me feel that you are aloof from it; by your natural and supernatural advantages do easily see to the end of it—do see how man can do without it. Now all men are on one side. No man deserves to be heard against property. Only Love, only an Idea, is against property as we hold it.

I cannot afford to be irritable and captious, nor to waste all my time in attacks. If I should go out of church whenever I hear a false sentiment I could never stay there five minutes. But why come out? the street is as false as the church, and when I get to my house, or to my manners, or to my speech, I have not got away from the lie. When we see an eager assailant of one of these wrongs, a special reformer, we feel like asking him, What right have you, sir, to your one virtue? Is virtue piecemeal? This is a jewel amidst the rags of a beggar.

In another way the right will be vindicated. In the midst of abuses, in the heart of cities, in the aisles of false churches, alike in one place and in another—wherever, namely, a just and heroic soul finds itself, there it will do what is next at hand, and by the new quality of character it shall put forth it shall abrogate that old condition, law, or school in which it stands, before the law of its own mind.

If partiality was one fault of the movement party, the other defect was their reliance on Association.[9] Doubts such as those I have intimated drove many good persons to agitate the questions of social reform. But the revolt against the spirit of commerce, the spirit of aristocracy, and the inveterate abuses of cities, did not appear possible to individuals; and to do battle against numbers they armed themselves with numbers, and against concert they relied on new concert.

[9] The Fourierist Socialists used this term to identify their cooperative society.

Following or advancing beyond the ideas of St. Simon, of Fourier, and of Owen,[10] three communities[11] have already been formed in Massachusetts on kindred plans, and many more in the country at large. They aim to give every member a share in the manual labor, to give an equal reward to labor and to talent, and to unite a liberal culture with an education to labor. The scheme offers, by the economies of associated labor and expense, to make every member rich, on the same amount of property that, in separate families, would leave every member poor. These new associations are composed of men and women of superior talents and sentiments; yet it may easily be questioned whether such a community will draw, except in its beginnings, the able and the good; whether those who have energy will not prefer their chance of superiority and power in the world, to the humble certainties of the association; whether such a retreat does not promise to become an asylum to those who have tried and failed, rather than a field to the strong; and whether the members will not necessarily be fractions of men, because each finds that he cannot enter it without some compromise. Friendship and association are very fine things, and a grand phalanx of the best of the human race, banded for some catholic object; yes, excellent; but remember that no society can ever be so large as one man. He, in his friendship, in his natural and momentary associations, doubles or multiplies himself; but in the hour in which he mortgages himself to two or ten or twenty, he dwarfs himself below the stature of one.

But the men of less faith could not thus believe, and to such, concert appears the sole specific of strength. I have failed, and you have failed, but perhaps together we shall not fail. Our housekeeping is not satisfactory to us, but perhaps a phalanx, a community, might be. Many of us have differed in opinion, and we could find no man who could make the truth plain, but possibly a college, or an ecclesiastical council, might. I have not been able either to persuade my brother or to prevail on myself to disuse the traffic or the potation of brandy, but perhaps a pledge of total abstinence might effectually restrain us. The candidate my party votes for is not to be trusted with a dollar, but he will be honest in the Senate, for we can bring public opinion to bear on him. Thus concert was the specific in all cases. But concert is neither better nor worse, neither more nor less potent, than individual force. All the men in the world cannot make a statue walk and speak, cannot make a drop of blood, or a blade of grass, any more than one man can. But let there be one man, let there be truth in two men, in ten men, then is concert for the first time possible; because the force which moves the world is a new quality, and can never be furnished by adding whatever quantities of a

[10] Comte de Saint-Simon (1760–1858), F. C. N. Fourier (1772–1837), and Robert Owen (1771–1858) were Utopian Socialists who influenced American reformers.

[11] West Roxbury (Brook Farm, 1841), Milford (Hopedale, 1842), and Harvard (Fruitlands, 1842). By the time this essay was written, Fruitlands no longer existed.

different kind. What is the use of the concert of the false and the disunited? There can be no concert in two, where there is no concert in one. When the individual is not *individual*, but is dual; when his thoughts look one way and his actions another; when his faith is traversed by his habits; when his will, enlightened by reason, is warped by his sense; when with one hand he rows and with the other backs water, what concert can be?

I do not wonder at the interest these projects inspire. The world is awaking to the idea of union, and these experiments show what it is thinking of. It is and will be magic. Men will live and communicate, and plough, and reap, and govern, as by added ethereal power, when once they are united; as in a celebrated experiment, by expiration and respiration exactly together, four persons lift a heavy man from the ground by the little finger only, and without sense of weight. But this union must be inward, and not one of covenants, and is to be reached by a reverse of the methods they use. The union is only perfect when all the uniters are isolated. It is the union of friends who live in different streets or towns. Each man, if he attempts to join himself to others, is on all sides cramped and diminished of his proportion; and the stricter the union the smaller and the more pitiful he is. But leave him alone, to recognize in every hour and place the secret soul; he will go up and down doing the works of a true member, and, to the astonishment of all, the work will be done with concert, though no man spoke. Government will be adamantine without any governor. The union must be ideal in actual individualism.

I pass to the indication in some particulars of that faith in man, which the heart is preaching to us in these days, and which engages the more regard, from the consideration that the speculations of one generation are the history of the next following.

In alluding just now to our system of education, I spoke of the deadness of its details. But it is open to graver criticism than the palsy of its members: it is a system of despair. The disease with which the human mind now labors is want of faith. Men do not believe in a power of education. We do not think we can speak to divine sentiments in man, and we do not try. We renounce all high aims. We believe that the defects of so many perverse and so many frivolous people who make up society, are organic, and society is a hospital of incurables. A man of good sense but of little faith, whose compassion seemed to lead him to church as often as he went there, said to me that "he liked to have concerts, and fairs, and churches, and other public amusements go on." I am afraid the remark is too honest, and comes from the same origin as the maxim of the tyrant, "If you would rule the world quietly, you must keep it amused." I notice too that the ground on which eminent public servants urge the claims of popular education is fear; "This country is filling up with thousands and millions of voters, and you must educate them to keep them from our throats." We do not believe that any education, any system of philosophy, any influence of genius, will ever give depth of insight to a superficial mind. Having settled ourselves into this infidelity, our skill is expended to procure alleviations, diversion, opiates. We adorn the victim with manual skill, his tongue with languages, his body with inoffensive and comely manners. So have we cunningly hid the tragedy of limitation and inner death we cannot avert. Is it strange that society should be devoured by a secret melancholy which breaks through all its smiles and all its gayety and games?

But even one step farther our infidelity has gone. It appears that some doubt is felt by good and wise men whether really the happiness and probity of men is increased by the culture of the mind in those disciplines to which we give the name of education. Unhappily too the doubt comes from scholars, from persons who have tried these methods. In their experience the scholar was not raised by the sacred thoughts amongst which he dwelt, but used them to selfish ends. He was a profane person, and became a showman, turning his gifts to a marketable use, and not to his own sustenance and growth. It was found that the intellect could be independently developed, that is, in separation from the man, as any single organ can be invigorated, and the result was monstrous. A canine appetite for knowledge was generated, which must still be fed but was never satisfied, and this knowledge, not being directed on action, never took the character of substantial, humane truth, blessing those whom it entered. It gave the scholar certain powers of expression, the power of speech, the power of poetry, of literary art, but it did not bring him to peace or to beneficence.

When the literary class betray a destitution of faith, it is not strange that society should be disheartened and sensualized by unbelief. What remedy? Life must be lived on a higher plane. We must go up to a higher platform, to which we are always invited to ascend; there, the whole aspect of things changes. I resist the scepticism of our education and of our educated men. I do not believe that the differences of opinion and character in men are organic. I do not recognize, beside the class of the good and the wise, a permanent class of sceptics, or a class of conservatives, or of malignants, or of materialists. I do not believe in two classes. You remember the story of the poor woman who importuned King Philip of Macedon to grant her justice, which Philip refused: the woman exclaimed, "I appeal": the king, astonished, asked to whom she appealed: the woman replied, "From Philip drunk to Philip sober."[12] The text will suit me very well. I believe not in two classes of men, but in man in two moods, in Philip drunk and Philip sober. I think, according to the good-hearted word of Plato, "Unwillingly the soul is deprived of truth." Iron conservative, miser, or thief, no man is but by a supposed necessity which he tolerates by shortness or torpidity of sight. The

---

[12] This anecdote is related by Valerius Maximus (who flourished in the first century A. D.) in *Facta et Dicta Memorabilia.*

soul lets no man go without some visitations and holidays of a diviner presence. It would be easy to show, by a narrow scanning of any man's biography, that we are not so wedded to our paltry performances of every kind but that every man has at intervals the grace to scorn his performances, in comparing them with his belief of what he should do; that he puts himself on the side of his enemies, listening gladly to what they say of him, and accusing himself of the same things.

What is it men love in Genius, but its infinite hope, which degrades all it has done? Genius counts all its miracles poor and short. Its own idea is never executed. The Iliad, the Hamlet, the Doric column, the Roman arch, the Gothic minster, the German anthem, when they are ended, the master casts behind him. How sinks the song in the waves of melody which the universe pours over his soul! Before that gracious Infinite out of which he drew these few strokes, how mean they look, though the praises of the world attend them. From the triumphs of his art he turns with desire to this greater defeat. Let those admire who will. With silent joy he sees himself to be capable of a beauty that eclipses all which his hands have done; all which human hands have ever done.

Well, we are all the children of genius, the children of virtue—and feel their inspirations in our happier hours. Is not every man sometimes a radical in politics? Men are conservatives when they are least vigorous, or when they are most luxurious. They are conservatives after dinner, or before taking their rest; when they are sick, or aged. In the morning, or when their intellect or their conscience has been aroused; when they hear music, or when they read poetry, they are radicals. In the circle of the rankest tories that could be collected in England, Old or New, let a powerful and stimulating intellect, a man of great heart and mind act on them, and very quickly these frozen conservators will yield to the friendly influence, these hopeless will begin to hope, these haters will begin to love, these immovable statues will begin to spin and revolve. I cannot help recalling the fine anecdote which Warton relates of Bishop Berkeley,[13] when he was preparing to leave England with his plan of planting the gospel among the American savages. "Lord Bathurst told me that the members of the Scriblerus Club being met at his house at dinner, they agreed to rally Berkeley, who was also his guest, on his scheme at Bermudas. Berkeley, having listened to the many lively things they had to say, begged to be heard in his turn, and displayed his plan with such an astonishing and animating force of eloquence and enthusiasm that they were struck dumb, and, after some pause, rose up all together with earnestness, exclaiming, 'Let us set out with him immediately.' " Men in all ways are better than they seem. They like flattery for the moment, but they

[13] Joseph Warton recounts this story about Berkeley in *Essay on the Writings and Genius of Pope*, II, 198.

know the truth for their own. It is a foolish cowardice which keeps us from trusting them and speaking to them rude truth. They resent your honesty for an instant, they will thank you for it always. What is it we heartily wish of each other? Is it to be pleased and flattered? No, but to be convicted and exposed, to be shamed out of our nonsense of all kinds, and made men of, instead of ghosts and phantoms. We are weary of gliding ghostlike through the world, which is itself so slight and unreal. We crave a sense of reality, though it comes in strokes of pain. I explain so—by this man-like love of truth—those excesses and errors into which souls of great vigor, but not equal insight, often fall. They feel the poverty at the bottom of all the seeming affluence of the world. They know the speed with which they come straight through the thin masquerade, and conceive a disgust at the indigence of nature: Rousseau, Mirabeau, Charles Fox, Napoleon, Byron—and I could easily add names nearer home, of raging riders, who drive their steeds so hard, in the violence of living to forget its illusion: they would know the worst, and tread the floors of hell.[14] The heroes of ancient and modern fame, Cimon, Themistocles, Alcibiades, Alexander, Cæsar, have treated life and fortune as a game to be well and skilfully played, but the stake not to be so valued but that any time it could be held as a trifle light as air, and thrown up. Cæsar, just before the battle of Pharsalia, discourses with the Egyptian priest concerning the fountains of the Nile, and offers to quit the army, the empire, and Cleopatra, if he will show him those mysterious sources.[15]

The same magnanimity shows itself in our social relations, in the preference, namely, which each man gives to the society of superiors over that of his equals. All that a man has will he give for right relations with his mates. All that he has will he give for an erect demeanor in every company and on each occasion. He aims at such things as his neighbors prize, and gives his days and nights, his talents and his heart, to strike a good stroke, to acquit himself in all men's sight as a man. The consideration of an eminent citizen, of a noted merchant, of a man of mark in his profession; a naval and military honor, a general's commission, a marshal's baton, a ducal coronet, the laurel of poets, and anyhow procured, the acknowledgment of eminent merit— have this lustre for each candidate that they enable him to walk erect and unashamed in the presence of some persons before whom he felt himself inferior. Having raised himself to this rank, having established his equality with class after class of those with whom he would live well, he still finds certain others before whom he cannot possess himself, because they have somewhat fairer, somewhat grander, somewhat purer, which extorts homage of him. Is his ambition pure? then will his laurels and his possessions seem

---

[14] Preserved by Plutarch in "Consolation to Apollonius," the sentence reads: "It is an expression of Pindar, that we are held to the dark bottom of hell by necessities as hard as iron" (*Essays and Miscellanies,* ed. by A. H. Clough and William W. Goodwin, I, 303).

[15] See Lucan, *De Bello Civili,* X, 172-92.

worthless: instead of avoiding these men who make his fine gold dim, he will cast all behind him and seek their society only, woo and embrace this his humiliation and mortification, until he shall know why his eye sinks, his voice is husky, and his brilliant talents are paralysed in this presence. He is sure that the soul which gives the lie to all things will tell none. His constitution will not mislead him. If it cannot carry itself as it ought, high and unmatchable in the presence of any man; if the secret oracles whose whisper makes the sweetness and dignity of his life do here withdraw and accompany him no longer—it is time to undervalue what he has valued, to dispossess himself of what he has acquired, and with Cæsar to take in his hand the army, the empire and Cleopatra, and say, "All these will I relinquish, if you will show me the fountains of the Nile." [16] Dear to us are those who love; the swift moments we spend with them are a compensation for a great deal of misery; they enlarge our life; but dearer are those who reject us as unworthy, for they add another life: they build a heaven before us whereof we had not dreamed, and thereby supply to us new powers out of the recesses of the spirit, and urge us to new and unattempted performances.

As every man at heart wishes the best and not inferior society, wishes to be convicted of his error and to come to himself so he wishes that the same healing should not stop in his thought, but should penetrate his will or active power. The selfish man suffers more from his selfishness than he from whom that selfishness withholds some important benefit. What he most wishes is to be lifted to some higher platform, that he may see beyond his present fear the transalpine good, so that his fear, his coldness, his custom may be broken up like fragments of ice, melted and carried away in the great stream of good will. Do you ask my aid? I also wish to be a benefactor. I wish more to be a benefactor and servant than you wish to be served by me; and surely the greatest good fortune that could befall me is precisely to be so moved by you that I should say, "Take me and all mine, and use me and mine freely to your ends!" for I could not say it otherwise than because a great enlargement had come to my heart and mind, which made me superior to my fortunes. Here we are paralyzed with fear; we hold on to our little properties, house and land, office and money, for the bread which they have in our experience yielded us, although we confess that our being does not flow through them. We desire to be made great; we desire to be touched with that fire which shall command this ice to stream, and make our existence a benefit. If therefore we start objections to your project, O friend of the slave, or friend of the poor or of the race, understand well that it is because we wish to drive you to drive us into your measures. We wish to hear ourselves confuted. We are haunted with a belief that you have a secret which it would highliest advantage us to learn, and we would force you to impart it to us, though it should bring us to prison or to worse extremity.

[16] See the allusion to Lucan above.

Nothing shall warp me from the belief that every man is a lover of truth. There is no pure lie, no pure malignity in nature. The entertainment of the proposition of depravity[17] is the last profligacy and profanation. There is no scepticism, no atheism but that. Could it be received into common belief, suicide would unpeople the planet. It has had a name to live in some dogmatic theology, but each man's innocence and his real liking of his neighbor have kept it a dead letter. I remember standing at the polls one day when the anger of the political contest gave a certain grimness to the faces of the independent electors, and a good man at my side,[18] looking on the people, remarked, "I am satisfied that the largest part of these men, on either side, mean to vote right." I suppose considerate observers, looking at the masses of men in their blameless and in their equivocal actions, will assent, that in spite of selfishness and frivolity, the general purpose in the great number of persons is fidelity. The reason why any one refuses his assent to your opinion, or his aid to your benevolent design, is in you: he refuses to accept you as a bringer of truth, because though you think you have it, he feels that you have it not. You have not given him the authentic sign.

If it were worth while to run into details this general doctrine of the latent but ever soliciting Spirit, it would be easy to adduce illustration in particulars of a man's equality to the Church, of his equality to the State, and of his equality to every other man. It is yet in all men's memory that, a few years ago, the liberal churches[19] complained that the Calvinistic church denied to them the name of Christian. I think the complaint was confession: a religious church would not complain. A religious man, like Behmen,[20] Fox,[21] or Swedenborg, is not irritated by wanting the sanction of the Church, but the Church feels the accusation of his presence and belief.

It only needs that a just man should walk in our streets to make it appear how pitiful and inartificial a contrivance is our legislation. The man whose part is taken and who does not wait for society in anything, has a power which society cannot choose but feel. The familiar experiment called the hydrostatic paradox, in which a capillary column of water balances the ocean, is a symbol of the relation of one man to the whole family of men. The wise Dandamis, on hearing the lives of Socrates, Pythagoras and Diogenes read, "judged them to be great men every way, excepting that they were too much subjected to the reverence of the laws, which to second and authorize, true virtue must abate very much of its original vigor."

And as a man is equal to the Church and equal to the State, so he is equal to every other man. The disparities of power in men are superficial; and all

[17] The Calvinist dogma of Total Depravity.
[18] Edmund Hosmer, a farmer and friend of Emerson.
[19] Unitarian churches.
[20] Jakob Boehme, a German mystic of the late sixteenth and early seventeenth centuries, the author of *Aurora*.
[21] George Fox (1624-1691), founder of the Society of Friends.

frank and searching conversation, in which a man lays himself open to his brother, apprises each of their radical unity. When two persons sit and converse in a thoroughly good understanding, the remark is sure to be made, See how we have disputed about words! Let a clear, apprehensive mind, such as every man knows among his friends, converse with the most commanding poetic genius, I think it would appear that there was no inequality such as men fancy, between them; that a perfect understanding, a like receiving, a like perceiving, abolished differences; and the poet would confess that his creative imagination gave him no deep advantage, but only the superficial one that he could express himself and the other could not; that his advantage was a knack, which might impose on indolent men but could not impose on lovers of truth; for they know the tax of talent, or what a price of greatness the power of expression too often pays. I believe it is the conviction of the purest men that the net amount of man and man does not much vary. Each is incomparably superior to his companion in some faculty. His want of skill in other directions has added to his fitness for his own work. Each seems to have some compensation yielded to him by his infirmity, and every hinderance operates as a concentration of his force.

These and the like experiences intimate that man stands in strict connection with a higher fact never yet manifested. There is power over and behind us, and we are the channels of its communications. We seek to say thus and so, and over our head some spirit sits which contradicts what we say. We would persuade our fellow to this or that; another self within our eyes dissuades him. That which we keep back, this reveals. In vain we compose our faces and our words; it holds uncontrollable communication with the enemy, and he answers civilly to us, but believes the spirit. We exclaim, "There's a traitor in the house!" but at last it appears that he is the true man, and I am the traitor. This open channel to the highest life is the first and last reality, so subtle, so quiet, yet so tenacious, that although I have never expressed the truth, and although I have never heard the expression of it from any other, I know that the whole truth is here for me. What if I cannot answer your questions? I am not pained that I cannot frame a reply to the question, What is the operation we call Providence? There lies the unspoken thing, present, omnipresent. Every time we converse we seek to translate it into speech, but whether we hit or whether we miss, we have the fact. Every discourse is an approximate answer: but it is of small consequence that we do not get it into verbs and nouns, whilst it abides for contemplation forever.

If the auguries of the prophesying heart shall make themselves good in time, the man who shall be born, whose advent men and events prepare and foreshow, is one who shall enjoy his connection with a higher life, with the man within man; shall destroy distrust by his trust, shall use his native but forgotten methods, shall not take counsel of flesh and blood, but shall rely on the Law alive and beautiful which works over our heads and under our feet.

Pitiless, it avails itself of our success when we obey it, and of our ruin when we contravene it. Men are all secret believers in it, else the word justice would have no meaning: they believe that the best is the true; that right is done at last; or chaos would come. It rewards actions after their nature, and not after the design of the agent. "Work," it saith to man, "in every hour, paid or unpaid, see only thou work, and thou canst not escape the reward: whether thy work be fine or coarse, planting corn or writing epics, so only it be honest work, done to thine own approbation, it shall earn a reward to the senses as well as to the thought: no matter how often defeated, you are born to victory. The reward of a thing well done, is to have done it."

As soon as a man is wonted to look beyond surfaces, and to see how this high will prevails without an exception or an interval, he settles himself into serenity. He can already rely on the laws of gravity, that every stone will fall where it is due; the good globe is faithful, and carries us securely through the celestial spaces, anxious or resigned, we need not interfere to help it on: and he will learn one day the mild lesson they teach, that our own orbit is all our task, and we need not assist the administration of the universe. Do not be so impatient to set the town right concerning the unfounded pretensions and the false reputation of certain men of standing. They are laboring harder to set the town right concerning themselves, and will certainly succeed. Suppress for a few days your criticism on the insufficiency of this or that teacher or experimenter, and he will have demonstrated his insufficiency to all men's eyes. In like manner, let a man fall into the divine circuits, and he is enlarged. Obedience to his genius is the only liberating influence. We wish to escape from subjection and a sense of inferiority, and we make self-denying ordinances, we drink water, we eat grass, we refuse the laws, we go to jail: it is all in vain; only by obedience to his genius, only by the freest activity in the way constitutional to him, does an angel seem to arise before a man and lead him by the hand out of all the wards of the prison.

That which befits us, embosomed in beauty and wonder as we are, is cheerfulness and courage, and the endeavor to realize our aspirations. The life of man is the true romance, which when it is valiantly conducted will yield the imagination a higher joy than any fiction. All around us what powers are wrapped up under the coarse mattings of custom, and all wonder prevented. It is so wonderful to our neurologists that a man can see without his eyes, that it does not occur to them that it is just as wonderful that he should see with them; and that is ever the difference between the wise and the unwise: the latter wonders at what is unusual, the wise man wonders at the usual. Shall not the heart which has received so much, trust the Power by which it lives? May it not quit other leadings, and listen to the Soul that has guided it so gently and taught it so much, secure that the future will be worthy of the past?

NATHANIEL HAWTHORNE

(1804-1864)*

As a writer who believed in original sin and the flawed character of man, Hawthorne viewed social reform with great skepticism. He felt that the ideas of progress and the perfectibility of human nature, which Americans had adapted from eighteenth-century thinkers, were naive and could indeed be pernicious. Throughout his fiction, especially in *The House of the Seven Gables, The Blithedale Romance,* and stories like "The Celestial Railroad" and "Earth's Holocaust," he satirized various reformers. For Hawthorne, reforming other people carried with it an arrogance that could easily lead to overt manipulation. Self-reform was the only genuine way in which social and moral evils could be abolished.

*For a full introduction to Hawthorne,
see pp. 1182-1187.

Earth's Holocaust [1]

Once upon a time—but whether in the time past or time to come is a matter of little or no moment—this wide world had become so overburdened with an accumulation of wornout trumpery that the inhabitants determined to rid themselves of it by a general bonfire. The site fixed upon at the representation of the insurance companies, and as being as central a spot as any other on the globe, was one of the broadest prairies of the West, where no human habitation would be endangered by the flames, and where a vast assemblage of spectators might commodiously admire the show. Having a taste for sights of this kind, and imagining, likewise, that the illumination of the bonfire might reveal some profundity of moral truth heretofore hidden in mist or darkness, I made it convenient to journey thither and be present. At my arrival, although the heap of condemned rubbish was as yet comparatively

[1] Hawthorne had a deep distrust of reform. The reformers' belief in eighteenth-century doctrines such as the idea of progress and the perfectibility of human nature seemed to him another example of the pride of intellect, which was a cardinal sin in Hawthorne's moral universe. In "Earth's Holocaust" as well as in *The Blithedale Romance,* he satirizes the reformers for their naive belief that they can change social institutions; the only reform possible, he felt, was within the human being himself. The story was first published in 1844 and was reprinted in *Mosses from an Old Manse* (1844).

small, the torch had already been applied. Amid that boundless plain, in the dusk of the evening, like a far off star alone in the firmament, there was merely visible one tremulous gleam, whence none could have anticipated so fierce a blaze as was destined to ensue. With every moment, however, there came foot travellers, women holding up their aprons, men on horseback, wheelbarrows, lumbering baggage wagons, and other vehicles, great and small, and from far and near laden with articles that were judged fit for nothing but to be burned.

"What materials have been used to kindle the flame?" inquired I of a bystander; for I was desirous of knowing the whole process of the affair from beginning to end.

The person whom I addressed was a grave man, fifty years old or thereabout, who had evidently come thither as a looker on. He struck me immediately as having weighed for himself the true value of life and its circumstances, and therefore as feeling little personal interest in whatever judgment the world might form of them. Before answering my question, he looked me in the face by the kindling light of the fire.

"Oh, some very dry combustibles," replied he, "and extremely suitable to the purpose—no other, in fact, than yesterday's newspapers, last month's magazines, and last year's withered leaves. Here now comes some antiquated trash that will take fire like a handful of shavings."

As he spoke some rough-looking men advanced to the verge of the bonfire, and threw in, as it appeared, all the rubbish of the herald's office—the blazonry of coat armor, the crests and devices of illustrious families, pedigrees that extended back, like lines of light, into the mist of the dark ages, together with stars, garters, and embroidered collars, each of which, as paltry a bawble as it might appear to the uninstructed eye, had once possessed vast significance, and was still, in truth, reckoned among the most precious of moral or material facts by the worshippers of the gorgeous past. Mingled with this confused heap, which was tossed into the flames by armfuls at once, were innumerable badges of knighthood, comprising those of all the European sovereignties, and Napoleon's decoration of the Legion of Honor, the ribbons of which were entangled with those of the ancient order of St. Louis.[2] There, too, were the medals of our own society of Cincinnati,[3] by means of which, as history tells us, an order of hereditary knights came near being constituted out of the king quellers of the revolution. And besides, there were the patents of nobility of German counts and barons, Spanish grandees, and English peers, from the worm-eaten instruments signed by William the Conqueror down to the bran new parchment of the latest lord who has received his honors from the fair hand of Victoria.

[2] Louis IX of France (1226-1270).
[3] The Society of the Cincinnati was established by Revolutionary Army officers in 1783. Washington was the president. The eldest sons were to continue as members.

At sight of the dense volumes of smoke, mingled with vivid jets of flame, that gushed and eddied forth from this immense pile of earthly distinctions, the multitude of plebeian spectators set up a joyous shout, and clapped their hands with an emphasis that made the welkin[4] echo. That was their moment of triumph, achieved, after long ages, over creatures of the same clay and the same spiritual infirmities, who had dared to assume the privileges due only to Heaven's better workmanship. But now there rushed towards the blazing heap a grayhaired man, of stately presence, wearing a coat, from the breast of which a star, or other badge of rank, seemed to have been forcibly wrenched away. He had not the tokens of intellectual power in his face; but still there was the demeanor, the habitual and almost native dignity, of one who had been born to the idea of his own social superiority, and had never felt it questioned till that moment.

"People," cried he, gazing at the ruin of what was dearest to his eyes with grief and wonder, but nevertheless with a degree of stateliness,—"people, what have you done? This fire is consuming all that marked your advance from barbarism, or that could have prevented your relapse thither. We, the men of the privileged orders, were those who kept alive from age to age the old chivalrous spirit; the gentle and generous thought; the higher, the purer, the more refined and delicate life. With the nobles, too, you cast off the poet, the painter, the sculptor—all the beautiful arts; for we were their patrons, and created the atmosphere in which they flourish. In abolishing the majestic distinctions of rank, society loses not only its grace, but its steadfastness"—

More he would doubtless have spoken; but here there arose an outcry, sportive, contemptuous, and indignant, that altogether drowned the appeal of the fallen nobleman, insomuch that, casting one look of despair at his own half-burned pedigree, he shrunk back into the crowd, glad to shelter himself under his new-found insignificance.

"Let him thank his stars that we have not flung him into the same fire!" shouted a rude figure, spurning the embers with his foot. "And henceforth let no man dare to show a piece of musty parchment as his warrant for lording it over his fellows. If he have strength of arm, well and good; it is one species of superiority. If he have wit, wisdom, courage, force of character, let these attributes do for him what they may; but from this day forward no mortal must hope for place and consideration by reckoning up the mouldy bones of his ancestors. That nonsense is done away."

"And in good time," remarked the grave observer by my side, in a low voice, however, "if no worse nonsense comes in its place: but, at all events, this species of nonsense has fairly lived out its life."

There was little space to muse or moralize over the embers of this time-honored rubbish; for, before it was half burned out, there came another multitude from beyond the sea, bearing the purple robes of royalty, and the

[4] The curved vault of the sky.

crowns, globes, and sceptres of emperors and kings. All these had been condemned as useless bawbles, playthings at best, fit only for the infancy of the world or rods to govern and chastise it in its nonage, but with which universal manhood at its full-grown stature could no longer brook to be insulted. Into such contempt had these regal insignia now fallen that the gilded crown and tinselled robes of the player king from Drury Lane Theatre had been thrown in among the rest, doubtless as a mockery of his brother monarchs on the great stage of the world. It was a strange sight to discern the crown jewels of England glowing and flashing in the midst of the fire. Some of them had been delivered down from the time of the Saxon princes; others were purchased with vast revenues, or perchance ravished from the dead brows of the native potentates of Hindostan;[5] and the whole now blazed with a dazzling lustre, as if a star had fallen in that spot and been shattered into fragments. The splendor of the ruined monarchy had no reflection save in those inestimable precious stones. But enough on this subject. It were but tedious to describe how the Emperor of Austria's mantle was converted to tinder, and how the posts and pillars of the French throne became a heap of coals, which it was impossible to distinguish from those of any other wood. Let me add, however, that I noticed one of the exiled Poles stirring up the bonfire with the Czar of Russia's sceptre, which he afterwards flung into the flames.[6]

"The smell of singed garments is quite intolerable here," observed my new acquaintance, as the breeze enveloped us in the smoke of a royal wardrobe. "Let us get to windward and see what they are doing on the other side of the bonfire."

We accordingly passed around, and were just in time to witness the arrival of a vast procession of Washingtonians,—as the votaries of temperance call themselves nowadays,—accompanied by thousands of the Irish disciples of Father Mathew, with that great apostle at their head.[7] They brought a rich contribution to the bonfire—being nothing less than all the hogsheads and barrels of liquor in the world, which they rolled before them across the prairie.

"Now, my children," cried Father Mathew, when they reached the verge of the fire, "one shove more, and the work is done. And now let us stand off and see Satan deal with his own liquor."

Accordingly, having placed their wooden vessels within reach of the flames, the procession stood off at a safe distance, and soon beheld them burst into a blaze that reached the clouds and threatened to set the sky itself on fire. And well it might; for here was the whole world's stock of spirituous

[5] A region in northern India.

[6] Czar Nicholas I put down rebellions in the Russian section of Poland in the 1830's.

[7] Theobald Mathew was an Irish priest and temperance advocate. He toured America from 1849 to 1851 and convinced more than half a million people to take the pledge.

liquors, which, instead of kindling a frenzied light in the eyes of individual topers as of yore, soared upwards with a bewildering gleam that startled all mankind. It was the aggregate of that fierce fire which would otherwise have scorched the hearts of millions. Meantime numberless bottles of precious wine were flung into the blaze, which lapped up the contents as if it loved them, and grew, like other drunkards, the merrier and fiercer for what it quaffed. Never again will the insatiable thirst of the fire fiend be so pampered. Here were the treasures of famous bon vivants—liquors that had been tossed on ocean, and mellowed in the sun, and hoarded long in the recesses of the earth—the pales, the gold, the ruddy juice of whatever vineyards were most delicate—the entire vintage of Tokay[8]—all mingling in one stream with the vile fluids of the common pothouse, and contributing to heighten the selfsame blaze. And while it rose in a gigantic spire that seemed to wave against the arch of the firmament and combine itself with the light of stars, the multitude gave a shout as if the broad earth were exulting in its deliverance from the curse of ages.

But the joy was not universal. Many deemed that human life would be gloomier than ever when that brief illumination should sink down. While the reformers were at work, I overheard muttered expostulations from several respectable gentlemen with red noses and wearing gouty shoes; and a ragged worthy, whose face looked like a hearth where the fire is burned out, now expressed his discontent more openly and boldly.

"What is this world good for," said the last toper, "now that we can never be jolly any more? What is to comfort the poor man in sorrow and perplexity? How is he to keep his heart warm against the cold winds of this cheerless earth? And what do you propose to give him in exchange for the solace that you take away? How are old friends to sit together by the fireside without a cheerful glass between them? A plague upon your reformation! It is a sad world, a cold world, a selfish world, a low world, not worth an honest fellow's living in, now that good fellowship is gone forever!"

This harangue excited great mirth among the bystanders; but, preposterous as was the sentiment, I could not help commiserating the forlorn condition of the last toper, whose boon companions had dwindled away from his side, leaving the poor fellow without a soul to countenance him in sipping his liquor, nor indeed any liquor to sip. Not that this was quite the true state of the case; for I had observed him at a critical moment filch a bottle of fourth-proof brandy that fell beside the bonfire and hide it in his pocket.

The spirituous and fermented liquors being thus disposed of, the zeal of the reformers next induced them to replenish the fire with all the boxes of tea and bags of coffee in the world. And now came the planters of Virginia, bringing their crops and tobacco. These, being cast upon the heap of inutility, aggregated it to the size of a mountain, and incensed the atmosphere

[8] A wine made in Tokay, Hungary.

with such potent fragrance that methought we should never draw pure breath again. The present sacrifice seemed to startle the lovers of the weed more than any that they had hitherto witnessed.

"Well, they've put my pipe out," said an old gentleman flinging it into the flames in a pet. "What is this world coming to? Everything rich and racy—all the spice of life—is to be condemned as useless. Now that they have kindled the bonfire, if these nonsensical reformers would fling themselves into it, all would be well enough!"

"Be patient," responded a stanch conservative; "it will come to that in the end. They will first fling us in, and finally themselves."

From the general and systematic measures of reform I now turned to consider the individual contributions to this memorable bonfire. In many instances these were of a very amusing character. One poor fellow threw in his empty purse, and another a bundle of counterfeit or insolvable bank notes. Fashionable ladies threw in their last season's bonnets, together with heaps of ribbons, yellow lace, and much other half-worn milliner's ware, all of which proved even more evanescent in the fire than it had been in the fashion. A multitude of lovers of both sexes—discarded maids or bachelors and couples mutually weary of one another—tossed in bundles of perfumed letters and enamored sonnets. A hack politician, being deprived of bread by the loss of office, threw in his teeth, which happened to be false ones. The Rev. Sydney Smith—having voyaged across the Atlantic for that sole purpose—came up to the bonfire with a bitter grin and threw in certain repudiated bonds, fortified though they were with the broad seal of a sovereign state.[9] A little boy of five years old, in the premature manliness of the present epoch, threw in his playthings; a college graduate his diploma; an apothecary, ruined by the spread of homœopathy,[10] his whole stock of drugs and medicines; a physician his library; a parson his old sermons; and a fine gentleman of the old school his code of manners, which he had formerly written down for the benefit of the next generation. A widow, resolving on a second marriage, slyly threw in her dead husband's miniature. A young man, jilted by his mistress, would willingly have flung his own desperate heart into the flames, but could find no means to wrench it out of his bosom. An American author, whose works were neglected by the public, threw his pen and paper into the bonfire, and betook himself to some less discouraging occupation. It somewhat startled me to overhear a number of ladies, highly respectable in appearance, proposing to fling their gowns and petticoats into the flames, and assume the garb, together with the manners, duties, offices, and responsibilities, of the opposite sex.

---

[9] The Reverend Sydney Smith (1771-1845) was an English writer for the *Edinburgh Review*. He exposed Pennsylvania's fraud in repudiating its debts.

[10] Medical treatment that relied on drugs that produced symptoms similar to those of the disease being treated.

What favor was accorded to this scheme I am unable to say, my attention being suddenly drawn to a poor, deceived, and half-delirious girl, who, exclaiming that she was the most worthless thing alive or dead, attempted to cast herself into the fire amid all that wrecked and broken trumpery of the world. A good man, however, ran to her rescue.

"Patience, my poor girl!" said he, as he drew her back from the fierce embrace of the destroying angel. "Be patient, and abide Heaven's will. So long as you possess a living soul, all may be restored to its first freshness. These things of matter and creations of human fantasy are fit for nothing but to be burned when once they have had their day; but your day is eternity!"

"Yes," said the wretched girl, whose frenzy seemed now to have sunk down into deep despondency,—"yes and the sunshine is blotted out of it!"

It was now rumored among the spectators that all the weapons and munitions of war were to be thrown into the bonfire, with the exception of the world's stock of gunpowder, which, as the safest mode of disposing of it, had already been drowned in the sea. This intelligence seemed to awaken great diversity of opinion. The hopeful philanthropist esteemed it a token that the millennium was already come; while persons of another stamp, in whose view mankind was a breed of bulldogs, prophesied that all the old stoutness, fervor, nobleness, generosity, and magnanimity of the race would disappear,—these qualities, as they affirmed, requiring blood for their nourishment. They comforted themselves, however, in the belief that the proposed abolition of war was impracticable for any length of time together.

Be that as it might, numberless great guns, whose thunder had long been the voice of battle,—the artillery of the Armada, the battering trains of Marlborough, and the adverse cannon of Napoleon and Wellington,[11]—were trundled into the midst of the fire. By the continual addition of dry combustibles, it had now waxed so intense that neither brass nor iron could withstand it. It was wonderful to behold how these terrible instruments of slaughter melted away like playthings of wax. Then the armies of the earth wheeled around the mighty furnace, with their military music playing triumphant marches, and flung in their muskets and swords. The standard-bearers, likewise, cast one look upward at their banners, all tattered with shot holes and inscribed with the names of victorious fields; and, giving them a last flourish on the breeze, they lowered them into the flame, which snatched them upward in its rush towards the clouds. This ceremony being over, the world was left without a single weapon in its hands, except possibly a few old king's arms and rusty swords and other trophies of the Revolution in some of our state armories. And now the drums were beaten and the trumpets brayed all together, as a prelude to the proclamation of universal and

[11] John Churchill was the Duke of Marlborough and defeated the French at Blenheim in 1704; Arthur Wellesley was the Duke of Wellington and defeated Napoleon at Waterloo in 1815.

eternal peace and the announcement that glory was no longer to be won by blood, but that it would henceforth be the contention of the human race to work out the greatest mutual good, and that beneficence, in the future annals of the earth, would claim the praise of valor. The blessed tidings were accordingly promulgated, and caused infinite rejoicings among those who had stood aghast at the horror and absurdity of war.

But I saw a grim smile pass over the seared visage of a stately old commander,—by his warworn figure and rich military dress, he might have been one of Napoleon's famous marshals,—who, with the rest of the world's soldiery, had just flung away the sword that had been familiar to his right hand for half a century.

"Ay! ay!" grumbled he. "Let them proclaim what they please; but, in the end, we shall find that all this foolery has only made more work for the armorers and cannon founders."

"Why, sir," exclaimed I, in astonishment, "do you imagine that the human race will ever so far return on the steps of its past madness as to weld another sword or cast another cannon?"

"There will be no need," observed, with a sneer, one who neither felt benevolence nor had faith in it. "When Cain wished to slay his brother, he was at no loss for a weapon."

"We shall see," replied the veteran commander. "If I am mistaken, so much the better; but in my opinion, without pretending to philosophize about the matter, the necessity of war lies far deeper than these honest gentlemen suppose. What! is there a field for all the petty disputes of individuals? and shall there be no great law court for the settlement of national difficulties? The battle field is the only court where such suits can be tried."

"You forget, general," rejoined I, "that, in this advanced stage of civilization, Reason and Philanthropy combined will constitute just such a tribunal as is requisite."

"Ah, I had forgotten that, indeed!" said the old warrior, as he limped away.

The fire was now to be replenished with materials that had hitherto been considered of even greater importance to the well being of society than the warlike munitions which we had already seen consumed. A body of reformers had travelled all over the earth in quest of the machinery by which the different nations were accustomed to inflict the punishment of death. A shudder passed through the multitude as these ghastly emblems were dragged forward. Even the flames seemed at first to shrink away, displaying the shape and murderous contrivance of each in a full blaze of light, which of itself was sufficient to convince mankind of the long and deadly error of human law. Those old implements of cruelty; those horrible monsters of mechanism; those inventions which seemed to demand something worse than man's natural heart to contrive, and which had lurked in the dusky nooks of ancient prisons, the subject of terror-stricken legend,—were now brought forth to view. Headsmen's axes, with the rust of noble and royal blood upon them, and a vast collection of halters that had choked the breath of plebeian victims, were thrown in together. A shout greeted the arrival of the guillotine, which was thrust forward on the same wheels that had borne it from one to another of the blood-stained streets of Paris. But the loudest roar of applause went up, telling the distant sky of the triumph of the earth's redemption, when the gallows made its appearance. An ill-looking fellow, however, rushed forward, and, putting himself in the path of the reformers, bellowed hoarsely, and fought with brute fury to stay their progress.

It was little matter of surprise, perhaps, that the executioner should thus do his best to vindicate and uphold the machinery by which he himself had his livelihood and worthier individuals their death; but it deserved special note that men of a far different sphere—even of that consecrated class in whose guardianship the world is apt to thrust its benevolence—were found to take the hangman's view of the question.

"Stay, my brethren!" cried one of them. "You are misled by a false philanthropy; you know not what you do. The gallows is a Heaven-ordained instrument. Bear it back, then, reverently, and set it up in its old place, else the world will fall to speedy ruin and desolation!"

"Onward! onward!" shouted a leader in the reform. "Into the flames with the accursed instrument of man's blood policy! How can human law inculcate benevolence and love while it persists in setting up the gallows as its chief symbol? One heave more, good friends, and the world will be redeemed from its greatest error."

A thousand hands, that nevertheless loathed the touch, now lent their assistance, and thrust the ominous burden far, far into the centre of the raging furnace. There its fatal and abhorred image was beheld, first black, then a red coal, then ashes.

"That was well done!" exclaimed I.

"Yes, it was well done," replied, but with less enthusiasm than I expected, the thoughtful observer who was still at my side; "well done, if the world be good enough for the measure. Death, however, is an idea that cannot easily be dispensed with in any condition between the primal innocence and that other purity and perfection which perchance we are destined to attain after travelling round the full circle; but, at all events, it is well that the experiment should now be tried."

"Too cold! too cold!" impatiently exclaimed the young and ardent leader in this triumph. "Let the heart have its voice here as well as the intellect. And as for ripeness, and as for progress, let mankind always do the highest, kindest, noblest thing that, at any given period, it has attained the perception of; and surely that thing cannot be wrong nor wrongly timed."

I know not whether it were the excitement of the scene, or whether the good people around the bonfire were really growing more enlightened every instant; but they now proceeded to measures in the full length of which I was hardly prepared to keep them company. For instance, some threw their marriage certificates into the flames, and declared themselves candidates for a higher, holier, and more comprehensive union than that which had subsisted from the birth of time under the form of the connubial tie. Others hastened to the vaults of banks and to the coffers of the rich,—all of which were open to the first comer on this fated occasion,—and brought entire bales of paper money to enliven the blaze, and tons of coin to be melted down by its intensity. Henceforth, they said, universal benevolence, uncoined and exhaustless, was to be the golden currency of the world. At this intelligence the bankers and speculators in the stocks grew pale, and a pickpocket, who had reaped a rich harvest among the crowd, fell down in a deadly fainting fit. A few men of business burned their day-books and ledgers, the notes and obligations of their creditors, and all other evidences of debts due to themselves; while perhaps a somewhat larger number satisfied their zeal for reform with the sacrifice of any uncomfortable recollection of their own indebtment. There was then a cry that the period was arrived when the title deeds of landed property should be given to the flames, and the whole soil of the earth revert to the public, from whom it had been wrongfully abstracted and most unequally distributed among individuals. Another party demanded that all written constitutions, set forms of government, legislative acts, statute books, and everything else on which human invention had endeavored to stamp its arbitrary laws, should at once be destroyed, leaving the consummated world as free as the man first created.

Whether any ultimate action was taken with regard to these propositions is beyond my knowledge; for, just then, some matters were in progress that concerned my sympathies more nearly.

"See! see! What heaps of books and pamphlets!" cried a fellow, who did not seem to be a lover of literature. "Now we shall have a glorious blaze!"

"That's just the thing!" said a modern philosopher. "Now we shall get rid of the weight of dead men's thought, which has hitherto pressed so heavily on the living intellect that it has been incompetent to any effectual self-exertion. Well done, my lads! Into the fire with them! Now you are enlightening the world indeed!"

"But what is to become of the trade?" cried a frantic bookseller.

"Oh, by all means let them accompany their merchandise," coolly observed an author. "It will be a noble funeral pile!"

The truth was, that the human race had now reached a stage of progress so far beyond what the wisest and wittiest men of former ages had ever dreamed of that it would have been a manifest absurdity to allow the earth to be any longer encumbered with their poor achievements in the literary line. Accordingly a thorough and searching investigation had swept the bookseller's shops, hawkers' stands, public, and private libraries, and even the little book-shelf by the country fireside, and had brought the world's entire mass of printed paper, bound or in sheets, to swell the already mountainous bulk of our illustrious bonfire. Thick, heavy folios, containing the labors of lexicographers, commentators and encyclopedists, were flung in, and falling among the embers with a leaden thump, smouldered away to ashes like rotten wood. The small, richly gilt French tomes of the last age, with the hundred volumes of Voltaire among them, went off in a brilliant shower of sparkles and little jets of flame; while the current literature of the same nation burned red and blue, and threw an infernal light over the visages of the spectators, converting them all to the aspect of party-colored fiends. A collection of German stories emitted a scent of brimstone. The English standard authors made excellent fuel, generally exhibiting the properties of sound oak logs. Milton's works, in particular, sent up a powerful blaze, gradually reddening into a coal, which promised to endure longer than almost any other material of the pile. From Shakespeare there gushed a flame of such marvellous splendor that men shaded their eyes as against the sun's meridian glory; nor even when the works of his own elucidators were flung upon him did he cease to flash forth a dazzling radiance from beneath the ponderous heap. It is my belief that he is blazing as fervidly as ever.

"Could a poet but light a lamp at that glorious flame," remarked I, "he might then consume the midnight oil to some good purpose."

"That is the very thing which modern poets have been too apt to do, or at least to attempt," answered a critic. "The chief benefit to be expected from this conflagration of past literature undoubtedly is, that writers will henceforth be compelled to light their lamps at the sun or stars."

"If they can reach so high," said I; "but that task requires a giant, who may afterwards distribute the light among inferior men. It is not every one that can steal the fire from heaven like Prometheus; but, when once he had done the deed, a thousand hearths were kindled by it."

It amazed me much to observe how indefinite was the proportion between the physical mass of any given author and the property of brilliant and long-continued combustion. For instance, there was not a quarto volume of the last century—nor, indeed, of the present—that could compete in that particular with a child's little gilt-covered book, containing Mother Goose's Melodies. The Life and Death of Tom Thumb[12] outlasted the biography of Marlborough. An epic, indeed a dozen of them, was converted to white ashes before the single sheet of an old ballad was half consumed. In more than one case, too, when volumes of applauded verse proved incapable of anything better than a stifling smoke, an unregarded ditty of some nameless bard—perchance in the corner of a newspaper—soared up among the stars with a flame as brilliant as their own. Speaking of the properties of flame, methought Shelley's poetry emitted a purer light than almost any other pro-

---

[12] *The Tragedy of Tragedies or, The Life and Death of Tom Thumb the Great* was a burlesque tragedy by Henry Fielding (1730).

ductions of his day, contrasting beautifully with the fitful and lurid gleams and gushes of black vapor that flashed and eddied from the volumes of Lord Byron. As for Tom Moore, [13] some of his songs diffused an odor like a burning pastil.

I felt particular interest in watching the combustion of American authors, and scrupulously noted by my watch the precise number of moments that changed most of them from shabbily-printed books to indistinguishable ashes. It would be invidious, however, if not perilous, to betray these awful secrets; so that I shall content myself with observing that it was not invariably the writer most frequent in the public mouth that made the most splendid appearance in the bonfire. I especially remember that a great deal of excellent inflammability was exhibited in a thin volume of poems by Ellery Channing; although, to speak the truth, there were certain portions that hissed and spluttered in a very disagreeable fashion. A curious phenomenon occurred in reference to several writers, native as well as foreign. Their books, though of highly respectable figure, instead of bursting into a blaze, or even smouldering out their substance in smoke, suddenly melted away in a manner that proved them to be ice.

If it be no lack of modesty to mention my own works, it must here be confessed that I looked for them with fatherly interest, but in vain. Too probably they were changed to vapor by the first action of the heat; at best, I can only hope that, in their quiet way, they contributed a glimmering spark or two to the splendor of the evening.

"Alas! and woe is me!" thus bemoaned himself a heavy-looking gentleman in green spectacles. "The world is utterly ruined, and there is nothing to live for any longer. The business of my life is snatched from me. Not a volume to be had for love or money!"

"This," remarked the sedate observer beside me, "is a bookworm—one of those men who are born to gnaw dead thoughts. His clothes, you see, are covered with the dust of libraries. He has no inward fountain of ideas; and, in good earnest, now that the old stock is abolished, I do not see what is to become of the poor fellow. Have you no word of comfort for him?"

"My dear sir," said I to the desperate bookworm, "is not Nature better than a book? Is not the human heart deeper than any system of philosophy? Is not life replete with more instruction than past observers have found it possible to write down in maxims? Be of good cheer. The great book of Time is still spread wide open before us; and, if we read it aright, it will be to us a volume of eternal truth."

"Oh, my books, my books, my precious printed books!" reiterated the forlorn bookworm. "My only reality was a bound volume; and now they will not leave me even a shadowy pamphlet!"

---

[13] Thomas Moore (1779-1852) was an Irish poet.

In fact, the last remnant of the literature of all the ages was now descending upon the blazing heap in the shape of a cloud of pamphlets from the press of the New World. These likewise were consumed in the twinkling of an eye, leaving the earth, for the first time since the days of Cadmus,[14] free from the plague of letters—an enviable field for the authors of the next generation.

"Well, and does anything remain to be done?" inquired I somewhat anxiously. "Unless we set fire to the earth itself, and then leap boldly off into infinite space, I know not that we can carry reform to any farther point."

"You are vastly mistaken, my good friend," said the observer. "Believe me, the fire will not be allowed to settle down without the addition of fuel that will startle many persons who have lent a willing hand thus far."

Nevertheless there appeared to be a relaxation of effort for a little time, during which, probably, the leaders of the movement were considering what should be done next. In the interval, a philosopher threw his theory into the flames,—a sacrifice which, by those who knew how to estimate it, was pronounced the most remarkable that had yet been made. The combustion, however, was by no means brilliant. Some indefatigable people, scorning to take a moment's ease, now employed themselves in collecting all the withered leaves and fallen boughs of the forest, and thereby recruited the bonfire to a greater height than ever. But this was mere by-play.

"Here comes the fresh fuel that I spoke of," said my companion.

To my astonishment, the persons who now advanced into the vacant space around the mountain fire bore surplices and other priestly garments, mitres, crosiers, and a confusion of Popish and Protestant emblems, with which it seemed their purpose to consummate the great act of faith. Crosses from the spires of old cathedrals were cast upon the heap with as little remorse as if the reverence of centuries, passing in long array beneath the lofty towers, had not looked up to them as the holiest of symbols. The font in which infants were consecrated to God, the sacramental vessels whence piety received the hallowed draught, were given to the same destruction. Perhaps it most nearly touched my heart to see among these devoted relics fragments of the humble communion tables and undecorated pulpits which I recognized as having been torn from the meeting-houses of New England. Those simple edifices might have been permitted to retain all of sacred embellishment that their Puritan founders had bestowed, even though the mighty structure of St. Peter's had sent its spoils to the fire of this terrible sacrifice. Yet I felt that these were but the externals of religion, and might most safely be relinquished by spirits that best knew their deep significance.

"All is well," said I, cheerfully. "The woodpaths shall be the aisles of our cathedral,—the firmament itself shall be its ceiling. What needs an earthly

[14] According to Greek legend, the inventor of the alphabet.

roof between the Deity and his worshippers? Our faith can well afford to lose all the drapery that even the holiest men have thrown around it, and be only the more sublime in its simplicity."

"True," said my companion; "but will they pause here?"

The doubt implied in his question was well founded. In the general destruction of books already described, a holy volume, that stood apart from the catalogue of human literature, and yet, in one sense, was at its head, had been spared. But the Titan of innovation,—angel or fiend, double in his nature, and capable of deeds befitting both characters,—at first shaking down only the old and rotten shapes of things, had now, as it appeared, laid his terrible hand upon the main pillars which supported the whole edifice of our moral and spiritual state. The inhabitants of the earth had grown too enlightened to define their faith within a form of words, or to limit the spiritual by any analogy to our material existence. Truths which the heavens trembled at were now but a fable of the world's infancy. Therefore, as the final sacrifice of human error, what else remained to be thrown upon the embers of that awful pile except the book which, though a celestial revelation to past ages, was but a voice from a lower sphere as regarded the present race of man? It was done! Upon the blazing heap of falsehood and wornout truth—things that the earth had never needed, or had ceased to need, or had grown childishly weary of—fell the ponderous church Bible, the great old volume that had lain so long on the cushion of the pulpit, and whence the pastor's solemn voice had given holy utterance on so many a Sabbath day. There, likewise, fell the family Bible, which the long-buried patriarch had read to his children,—in prosperity or sorrow, by the fireside and in the summer shade of trees,—and had bequeathed downward as the heirloom of generations. There fell the bosom Bible, the little volume that had been the soul's friend of some sorely-tried child of dust, who thence took courage, whether his trial were for life or death, steadfastly confronting both in the strong assurance of immortality.

All these were flung into the fierce and riotous blaze; and then a mighty wind came roaring across the plain with a desolate howl, as if it were the angry lamentation of the earth for the loss of heaven's sunshine; and it shook the gigantic pyramid of flame and scattered the cinders of half-consumed abominations around upon the spectators.

"This is terrible!" said I, feeling that my cheek grew pale, and seeing a like change in the visages about me.

"Be of good courage yet," answered the man with whom I had so often spoken. He continued to gaze steadily at the spectacle with a singular calmness, as if it concerned him merely as an observer. "Be of good courage, nor yet exult too much; for there is far less both of good and evil in the effect of this bonfire than the world might be willing to believe."

"How can that be?" exclaimed I, impatiently. "Has it not consumed everything? Has it not swallowed up or melted down every human or divine appendage of our mortal state that had substance enough to be acted on by fire? Will there be anything left us to-morrow morning better or worse than a heap of embers and ashes?"

"Assuredly there will," said my grave friend. "Come hither to-morrow morning, or whenever the combustible portion of the pile shall be quite burned out, and you will find among the ashes everything really valuable that you have seen cast into the flames. Trust me, the world of to-morrow will again enrich itself with the gold and diamonds which have been cast off by the world of to-day. Not a truth is destroyed nor buried so deep among the ashes but it will be raked up at last."

This was a strange assurance. Yet I felt inclined to credit it, the more especially as I beheld among the wallowing flames a copy of the Holy Scriptures, the pages of which, instead of being blackened into tinder, only assumed a more dazzling whiteness as the finger marks of human imperfection were purified away. Certain marginal notes and commentaries, it is true, yielded to the intensity of the fiery test, but without detriment to the smallest syllable that had flamed from the pen of inspiration.

"Yes; there is the proof of what you say," answered I, turning to the observer; "but if only what is evil can feel the action of the fire, then, surely, the conflagration has been of inestimable utility. Yet, if I understand aright, you intimate a doubt whether the world's expectation of benefit would be realized by it."

"Listen to the talk of these worthies," said he, pointing to a group in front of the blazing pile; "possibly they may teach you something useful without intending it."

The persons whom he indicated consisted of that brutal and most earthy figure who had stood forth so furiously in defence of the gallows,—the hangman, in short,—together with the last thief and the last murderer, all three of whom were clustered about the last toper. The latter was liberally passing the brandy bottle, which he had rescued from the general destruction of wines and spirits. This little convivial party seemed at the lowest pitch of despondency, as considering that the purified world must needs be utterly unlike the sphere that they had hitherto known, and therefore but a strange and desolate abode for gentlemen of their kidney.

"The best counsel for all of us is," remarked the hangman, "that, as soon as we have finished the last drop of liquor, I help you, my three friends, to a comfortable end upon the nearest tree, and then hang myself on the same bough. This is no world for us any longer."

"Poh, poh, my good fellows!" said a dark-complexioned personage, who now joined the group,—his complexion was indeed fearfully dark, and his eyes glowed with a redder light than that of the bonfire; "be not so cast down, my dear friends; you shall see good days yet. There's one thing that these wiseacres have forgotten to throw into the fire, and without which all the rest of the conflagration is just nothing at all; yes, though they had burned the earth itself to a cinder."

"And what may that be?" eagerly demanded the last murderer.

"What but the human heart itself?" said the dark-visaged stranger, with a portentous grin. "And, unless they hit upon some method of purifying that foul cavern, forth from it will reissue all the shapes of wrong and misery— the same old shapes or worse ones—which they have taken such a vast deal of trouble to consume to ashes. I have stood by this livelong night and laughed in my sleeve at the whole business. Oh, take my word for it, it will be the old world yet!"

This brief conversation supplied me with a theme for lengthened thought. How sad a truth, if true it were, that man's agelong endeavor for perfection had served only to render him the mockery of the evil principle, from the fatal circumstance of an error at the very root of the matter! The heart, the heart,—there was the little yet boundless sphere wherein existed the original wrong of which the crime and misery of this outward world were merely types. Purify that inward sphere, and the many shapes of evil that haunt the outward, and which now seem almost our only realities, will turn to shadowy phantoms and vanish of their own accord; but if we go no deeper than the intellect, and strive, with merely that feeble instrument, to discern and rectify what is wrong, our whole accomplishment will be a dream, so unsubstantial that it matters little whether the bonfire, which I have so faithfully described, were what we choose to call a real event and a flame that would scorch the finger, or only a phosphoric radiance and a parable of my own brain.

1844/1846

HENRY DAVID THOREAU

(1817–1862)*

This essay, commonly known as "Civil Disobedience," first appeared in Elizabeth Peabody's *Aesthetic Papers* (1848). Thoreau was opposed to the imperialism of the American government, which he felt was a result of the Mexican War. He connected it with the Southern slavocracy that was condoned, it seemed to him, by the government in Washington.

* For a full introduction to Thoreau, see
pp. 962–964.

"Civil Disobedience" has had a significant influence on the thinking of Tolstoy, Mahatma Ghandi, and Martin Luther King. Although it is a seminal document for all reformers, the essay is really concerned with self-reform and the affirmation of defiant individualism against a state that always is in danger of being tyrannical.

Civil Disobedience[1]

I heartily accept the motto,—"That government is best which governs least";[2] and I should like to see it acted up to more rapidly and systematically. Carried out, it finally amounts to this, which also I believe,—"That government is best which governs not at all"; and when men are prepared for it, that will be the kind of government which they will have. Government is at best but an expedient; but most governments are usually, and all governments are sometimes, inexpedient. The objections which have been brought against a standing army, and they are many and weighty, and deserve to prevail, may also at last be brought against a standing government. The standing army is only an arm of the standing government. The government itself, which is only the mode which the people have chosen to execute their will, is equally liable to be abused and perverted before the people can act through it. Witness the present Mexican wars,[3] the work of comparatively a few individuals using the standing government as their tool; for, in the outset, the people would not have consented to this measure.

This American government,—what is it but a tradition, though a recent one, endeavoring to transmit itself unimpaired to posterity, but each instant

[1] This address was delivered in the Concord Lyceum in February 1848 and published a year later in Elizabeth Peabody's *Aesthetic Papers*. It is a classic statement of individual passive resistance to the government's laws. Thoreau felt it shameful to be associated with a government that was also a slave's government, and he believed that the evil was so great that there was no time to change the laws except by breaking them. Note the many contrasts that he establishes in the mind of the reader: expediency versus conscience; prudence, spiritual laws; rule of might, rule of right; history (of slavery), the idea; the pragmatic, the ideal; the state, nature; society, the individual.

Thoreau's essay became internationally known when Tolstoy attested to its influence and Mahatma Ghandi acknowledged that it had inspired his own doctrine of passive resistance. In our own time, the most famous examples of civil disobedience and passive resistance have been those of Martin Luther King and the anti-Vietnam protesters during the 1960's.

[2] This phrase was the motto of the *United States Magazine and Democratic Review* (1837-1849). See the writings of Thomas Paine and Thomas Jefferson for earlier expressions of the same idea.

[3] The Mexican War (1846-1848) was chiefly precipitated by the United States' annexation of Texas. Abolitionists and reformers saw it as a way for northern textile manufacturers and southern cotton-planters as well as politicians to extend the slaveholding territory.

losing some of its integrity? It has not the vitality and force of a single living man; for a single man can bend it to his will. It is a sort of wooden gun to the people themselves. But it is not the less necessary for this; for the people must have some complicated machinery or other, and hear its dins, to satisfy that idea of government which they have. Governments show thus how successfully men can be imposed on, even impose on themselves, for their own advantage. It is excellent, we must all allow. Yet this government never of itself furthered any enterprise, but by the alacrity with which it got out of its way. It does not keep the country free. It does not settle the West. It does not educate. The character inherent in the American people has done all that has been accomplished; and it would have done somewhat more, if the government had not sometimes got in its way. For government is an expedient by which men would fain succeed in letting one another alone; and, as has been said, when it is most expedient, the governed are most let alone by it. Trade and commerce, if they were not made of India-rubber, would never manage to bounce over the obstacles which legislators are continually putting in their way; and, if one were to judge these men wholly by the effects of their actions and not partly by their intentions, they would deserve to be classed and punished with those mischievous persons who put obstructions on the railroads.

But, to speak practically and as a citizen, unlike those who call themselves no-government men, I ask for, not at once no government, but *at once* a better government. Let every man make known what kind of government would command his respect, and that will be one step toward obtaining it.

After all, the practical reason why, when the power is once in the hands of the people, a majority are permitted, and for a long period continue, to rule is not because they are most likely to be in the right, nor because this seems fairest to the minority, but because they are physically the strongest. But a government in which the majority rule in all cases cannot be based on justice, even as far as men understand it. Can there not be a government in which majorities do not virtually decide right and wrong, but conscience?— in which majorities decide only those questions to which the rule of expediency is applicable? Must the citizen ever for a moment, or in the least degree, resign his conscience to the legislator? Why has every man a conscience, then? I think that we should be men first, and subjects afterward. It is not desirable to cultivate a respect for the law, so much as for the right. The only obligation which I have a right to assume is to do at any time what I think right. It is truly enough said, that a corporation has no conscience; but a corporation of conscientious men is a corporation *with* a conscience. Law never made men a whit more just; and, by means of their respect for it, even the well-disposed are daily made the agents of injustice. A common and natural result of an undue respect for law is, that you may see a file of soldiers, colonel, captain, corporal, privates, powdermonkeys, and all, marching in admirable order over hill and dale to the wars, against their wills, ay, against their common sense and consciences, which makes it very steep marching indeed, and produces a palpitation of the heart. They have no doubt that it is a damnable business in which they are concerned; they are all peaceably inclined. Now, what are they? Men at all? or small movable forts and magazines, at the service of some unscrupulous man in power? Visit the Navy-Yard, and behold a marine, such a man as an American government can make, or such as it can make a man with its black arts,—a mere shadow and reminiscence of humanity, a man laid out alive and standing, and already, as one may say, buried under arms with funeral accompaniments, though it may be,—

> "Not a drum was heard, not a funeral note,
>   As his corse to the rampart we hurried;
> Not a soldier discharged his farewell shot
>   O'er the grave where our hero we buried."[4]

The mass of men serve the state thus, not as men mainly, but as machines, with their bodies. They are the standing army, and the militia, jailors, constables, posse comitatus,[5] etc. In most cases there is no free exercise whatever of the judgment or of the moral sense; but they put themselves on a level with wood and earth and stones; and wooden men can perhaps be manufactured that will serve the purpose as well. Such command no more respect than men of straw or a lump of dirt. They have the same sort of worth only as horses and dogs. Yet such as these even are commonly esteemed good citizens. Others—as most legislators, politicians, lawyers, ministers, and office-holders—serve the state chiefly with their heads; and, as they rarely make any moral distinctions, they are as likely to serve the Devil, without *intending* it, as God. A very few, as heroes, patriots, martyrs, reformers in the great sense, and *men*, serve the state with their consciences also, and so necessarily resist it for the most part; and they are commonly treated as enemies by it. A wise man will only be useful as a man, and will not submit to be "clay," and "stop a hole to keep the wind away,"[6] but leave that office to his dust at least:—

> "I am too high-born to be propertied,
> To be a secondary at control,
> Or useful serving-man and instrument
> To any sovereign state throughout the world."[7]

[4] The opening lines of "Burial of Sir John Moore at Corunna," by the Irish clergyman-poet Charles Wolfe (1791–1823).

[5] The body of men available to assist the county sheriff—a "posse."

[6] Cf. Shakespeare, *Hamlet*, Act V, Sc. 1, 236–37.

[7] Cf. Shakespeare, *King John*, Act V. Sc. 2, 79–82.

He who gives himself entirely to his fellow-men appears to them useless and selfish; but he who gives himself partially to them is pronounced a benefactor and philanthropist.

How does it become a man to behave toward this American government to-day? I answer, that he cannot without disgrace be associated with it. I cannot for an instant recognize that political organization as *my* government which is the *slave's* government also.

All men recognize the right of revolution; that is, the right to refuse allegiance to, and to resist, the government, when its tyranny or its inefficiency are great and unendurable. But almost all say that such is not the case now. But such was the case, they think, in the Revolution of '75.[8] If one were to tell me that this was a bad government because it taxed certain foreign commodities brought to its ports, it is most probable that I should not make an ado about it, for I can do without them. All machines have their friction; and possibly this does enough good to counterbalance the evil. At any rate, it is a great evil to make a stir about it. But when the friction comes to have its machine, and oppression and robbery are organized, I say, let us not have such a machine any longer. In other words, when a sixth of the population of a nation which has undertaken to be the refuge of liberty are slaves, and a whole country[9] is unjustly overrun and conquered by a foreign army, and subjected to military law, I think that it is not too soon for honest men to rebel and revolutionize. What makes this duty the more urgent is the fact that the country so overrun is not our own, but ours is the invading army.

Paley,[10] a common authority with many on moral questions, in his chapter on the "Duty of Submission to Civil Government, " resolves all civil obligation into expediency; and he proceeds to say, "that so long as the interest of the whole society requires it, that is, so long as the established government cannot be resisted or changed without public inconveniency, it is the will of God that the established government be obeyed, and no longer. . . . This principle being admitted, the justice of every particular case of resistance is reduced to a computation of the quantity of the danger and grievance on the one side, and of the probability and expense of redressing it on the other." Of this, he says, every man shall judge for himself. But Paley appears never to have contemplated those cases to which the rule of expediency does not apply, in which a people, as well as an individual, must do justice, cost what it may. If I have unjustly wrested a plank from a drowning man, I must restore it to him though I drown myself. This, according to Paley, would be

---

[8] The American Revolution began with the Battle of Lexington and Concord on April 29, 1775.

[9] Mexico.

[10] William Paley (1743–1805) was a British philosopher, the author of *Principles of a Moral and Political Philosophy* (1785), an expression of his utilitarianism. The quotation comes from this volume.

inconvenient. But he that would save his life, in such a case, shall lose it.[11] This people must cease to hold slaves, and to make war on Mexico, though it cost them their existence as a people.

In their practice, nations agree with Paley; but does any one think that Massachusetts does exactly what is right at the present crisis?

> "A drab of state, a cloth-o'-silver slut,
> To have her train borne up, and her soul trail in the dirt."[12]

Practically speaking, the opponents to a reform in Massachusetts are not a hundred thousand politicians at the South, but a hundred thousand merchants and farmers here, who are more interested in commerce and agriculture than they are in humanity, and are not prepared to do justice to the slave and to Mexico, *cost what it may*. I quarrel not with far-off foes, but with those who, near at home, coöperate with, and do the bidding of, those far away, and without whom the latter would be harmless. We are accustomed to say, that the mass of men are unprepared; but improvement is slow, because the few are not materially wiser or better than the many. It is not so important that many should be as good as you, as that there be some absolute goodness somewhere; for that will leaven the whole lump.[13] There are thousands who are *in opinion* opposed to slavery and to the war, who yet in effect do nothing to put an end to them; who, esteeming themselves children of Washington and Franklin, sit down with their hands in their pockets, and say that they know not what to do, and do nothing; who even postpone the question of freedom to the question of free-trade, and quietly read the prices-current along with the latest advices from Mexico, after dinner, and, it may be, fall asleep over them both. What is the price-current of an honest man and patriot to-day? They hesitate, and they regret, and sometimes they petition; but they do nothing in earnest and with effect. They will wait, well disposed, for others to remedy the evil, that they may no longer have it to regret. At most, they give only a cheap vote, and a feeble countenance and God-speed, to the right, as it goes by them. There are nine hundred and ninety-nine patrons of virtue to one virtuous man. But it is easier to deal with the real possessor of a thing than with the temporary guardian of it.

All voting is a sort of gaming, like checkers or backgammon, with a slight moral tinge to it, a playing with right and wrong, with moral questions; and betting naturally accompanies it. The character of the voters is not staked. I

---

[11] Cf. Luke, ix. 24: "For whosoever will save his life shall lose it; but whosoever will lose his life for my sake, the same shall save it."

[12] Cyril Tourneur, *The Revenger's Tragedie* (1607), IV, iv, 71-2.

[13] Cf. I Corinthians, v: 6: "Your glorying is not good. Know ye not that a little leaven leaveneth the whole lump."

cast my vote, perchance, as I think right; but I am not vitally concerned that that right should prevail. I am willing to leave it to the majority. Its obligation, therefore, never exceeds that of expediency. Even voting *for the right* is *doing* nothing for it. It is only expressing to men feebly your desire that it should prevail. A wise man will not leave the right to the mercy of chance, nor wish it to prevail through the power of the majority. There is but little virtue in the action of masses of men. When the majority shall at length vote for the abolition of slavery, it will be because they are indifferent to slavery, or because there is but little slavery left to be abolished by their vote. *They* will then be the only slaves. Only *his* vote can hasten the abolition of slavery who asserts his own freedom by his vote.

I hear of a convention to be held at Baltimore,[14] or elsewhere, for the selection of a candidate for the Presidency, made up chiefly of editors, and men who are politicians by profession; but I think, what is it to any independent, intelligent, and respectable man what decision they may come to? Shall we not have the advantage of his wisdom and honesty, nevertheless? Can we not count upon some independent votes? Are there not many individuals in the country who do not attend conventions? But no: I find that the respectable man, so called, has immediately drifted from his position, and despairs of his country, when his country has more reason to despair of him. He forthwith adopts one of the candidates thus selected as the only *available* one, thus proving that he is himself *available* for any purposes of the demagogue. His vote is of no more worth than that of any unprincipled foreigner or hireling native, who may have been bought. O for a man who is a *man*, and, as my neighbor says, has a bone in his back which you cannot pass your hand through! Our statistics are at fault: the population has been returned too large. How many *men* are there to a square thousand miles in this country? Hardly one. Does not America offer any inducement for men to settle here? The American has dwindled into an Odd Fellow,[15]—one who may be known by the development of his organ of gregariousness, and a manifest lack of intellect and cheerful self-reliance; whose first and chief concern, on coming into the world, is to see that the Almshouses are in good repair; and, before yet he has lawfully donned the virile garb,[16] to collect a fund for the support of the widows and orphans that may be; who, in short, ventures to live only by the aid of the Mutual Insurance company, which has promised to bury him decently.

It is not a man's duty, as a matter of course, to devote himself to the eradication of any, even the most enormous wrong; he may still properly have other concerns to engage him; but it is his duty, at least, to wash his

[14] The Democratic convention at Baltimore, May 1848.

[15] The Independent Order of Odd Fellows, a secret fraternal society.

[16] Cf. the *toga virilis*, worn by Roman boys during their fourteenth year.

hands of it, and, if he gives it no thought longer, not to give it practically his support. If I devote myself to other pursuits and contemplations, I must first see, at least, that I do not pursue them sitting upon another man's shoulders. I must get off him first, that he may pursue his contemplations too. See what gross inconsistency is tolerated. I have heard some of my townsmen say, "I should like to have them order me out to help put down an insurrection of the slaves, or to march to Mexico;—see if I would go"; and yet these very men have each, directly by their allegiance, and so indirectly, at least, by their money, furnished a substitute. The soldier is applauded who refuses to serve in an unjust war by those who do not refuse to sustain the unjust government which makes the war; is applauded by those whose own act and authority he disregards and sets at naught; as if the state were penitent to that degree that it hired one to scourge it while it sinned, but not to that degree that it left off sinning for a moment. Thus, under the name of Order and Civil Government, we are all made at last to pay homage to and support our own meanness. After the first blush of sin comes its indifference; and from immoral it becomes, as it were, unmoral, and not quite unnecessary to that life which we have made.

The broadest and most prevalent error requires the most disinterested virtue to sustain it. The slight reproach to which the virtue of patriotism is commonly liable, the noble are most likely to incur. Those who, while they disapprove of the character and measures of a government, yield to it their allegiance and support are undoubtedly its most conscientious supporters, and so frequently the most serious obstacles to reform. Some are petitioning the state to dissolve the Union, to disregard the requisitions of the President. Why do they not dissolve it themselves,—the union between themselves and the state,—and refuse to pay their quota into its treasury? Do not they stand in the same relation to the state that the state does to the Union? And have not the same reasons prevented the state from resisting the Union which have prevented them from resisting the state?

How can a man be satisfied to entertain an opinion merely, and enjoy it? Is there any enjoyment in it, if his opinion is that he is aggrieved? If you are cheated out of a single dollar by your neighbor, you do not rest satisfied with knowing that you are cheated, or with saying that you are cheated, or even with petitioning him to pay you your due; but you take effectual steps at once to obtain the full amount, and see that you are never cheated again. Action from principle, the perception and the performance of right, changes things and relations; it is essentially revolutionary, and does not consist wholly with anything which was. It not only divides states and churches, it divides families; ay, it divides the *individual* separating the diabolical in him from the divine.

Unjust laws exist: shall we be content to obey them, or shall we endeavor to amend them, and obey them until we have succeeded, or shall we transgress them at once? Men generally, under such a government as this, think that they ought to wait until they have persuaded the majority to alter them. They think that, if they should resist, the remedy would be worse than the evil. But it is the fault of the government itself that the remedy *is* worse than the evil. *It* makes it worse. Why is it not more apt to anticipate and provide for reform? Why does it not cherish its wise minority? Why does it cry and resist before it is hurt? Why does it not encourage its citizens to be on the alert to point out its faults, and *do* better than it would have them? Why does it always crucify Christ, and excommunicate Copernicus and Luther, and pronounce Washington and Franklin rebels?

One would think that a deliberate and practical denial of its authority was the only offense never contemplated by government; else, why has it not assigned its definite, its suitable and proportionate penalty? If a man who has no property refuses but once to earn nine shillings for the state, he is put in prison for a period unlimited by any law that I know, and determined only by the discretion of those who placed him there; but if he should steal ninety times nine shillings from the state, he is soon permitted to go at large again.

If the injustice is part of the necessary friction of the machine of government let it go, let it go: perchance it will wear smooth,—certainly the machine will wear out. If the injustice has a spring, or a pulley, or a rope, or a crank, exclusively for itself, then perhaps you may consider whether the remedy will not be worse than the evil; but if it is of such a nature that it requires you to be the agent of injustice to another, then, I say, break the law. Let your life be a counter friction to stop the machine. What I have to do is to see, at any rate, that I do not lend myself to the wrong which I condemn.

As for adopting the ways which the state has provided for remedying the evil, I know not of such ways. They take too much time, and a man's life will be gone. I have other affairs to attend to. I came into this world, not chiefly to make this a good place to live in, but to live in it, be it good or bad. A man has not everything to do, but something; and because he cannot do *everything*, it is not necessary that he should do *something* wrong. It is not my business to be petitioning the Governor or the Legislature any more than it is theirs to petition me; and if they should not hear my petition, what should I do then? But in this case the state has provided no way: its very Constitution is the evil. This may seem to be harsh and stubborn and unconciliatory; but it is to treat with the utmost kindness and consideration the only spirit that can appreciate or deserves it. So is all change for the better, like birth and death, which convulse the body.

I do not hesitate to say, that those who call themselves Abolitionists should at once effectually withdraw their support, both in person and property, from the government of Massachusetts and not wait till they constitute a majority of one, before they suffer the right to prevail through them. I think that it is enough if they have God on their side, without waiting for that other one. Moreover, any man more right than his neighbors constitutes a majority of one already.

I meet this American government, or its representative, the state government, directly, and face to face, once a year—no more—in the person of its tax-gatherer; this is the only mode in which a man situated as I am necessarily meets it; and it then says distinctly, Recognize me; and the simplest, most effectual, and, in the present posture of affairs, the indispensablist mode of treating with it on this head, of expressing your little satisfaction with and love for it, is to deny it then. My civil neighbor, the tax-gatherer, is the very man I have to deal with,—for it is, after all, with men and not with parchment that I quarrel,—and he has voluntarily chosen to be an agent of the government. How shall he ever know well what he is and does as an officer of the government, or as a man, until he is obliged to consider whether he shall treat me, his neighbor, for whom he has respect, as a neighbor and well-disposed man, or as a maniac and disturber of the peace, and see if he can get over this obstruction to his neighborliness without a ruder and more impetuous thought or speech corresponding with his action. I know this well, that if one thousand, if one hundred, if ten men whom I could name,—if ten *honest* men only,—ay, if *one* HONEST man, in this State of Massachusetts, *ceasing to hold slaves,* were actually to withdraw from this copartnership, and be locked up in the county jail therefore, it would be the abolition of slavery in America. For it matters not how small the beginning may seem to be: what is once well done is done forever. But we love better to talk about it: that we say is our mission. Reform keeps many scores of newspapers in its service, but not one man. If my esteemed neighbor, the State's ambassador,[17] who will devote his days to the settlement of the question of human rights in the Council Chamber, instead of being threatened with the prisons of Carolina, were to sit down the prisoner of Massachusetts, that State which is so anxious to foist the sin of slavery upon her sister,—though at present she can discover only an act of inhospitality to be the ground of a quarrel with her,— the Legislature would not wholly waive the subject the following winter.

Under a government which imprisons any unjustly, the true place for a just man is also a prison. The proper place to-day, the only place which Massachusetts has provided for her freer and less desponding spirits, is in her prisons, to be put out and locked out of the State by her own act, as they have already put themselves out by their principles. It is there that the fugitive slave, and the Mexican prisoner on parole, and the Indian come to plead the wrongs of his race should find them; on that separate, but more free and honorable ground, where the State places those who are not *with*

---

[17] Samuel Hoar (1778-1856) was a Concord lawyer and Congressman who was sent to Charleston, South Carolina to represent Negro seamen from Massachusetts who were threatened by arrest and enslavement. Hoar was forcibly evicted by the South Carolina legislature.

1716
HENRY DAVID THOREAU

her, but *against* her,—the only house in a slave State in which a free man can abide with honor. If any think that their influence would be lost there, and their voices no longer afflict the ear of the State, that they would not be as an enemy within its walls, they do not know by how much truth is stronger than error, nor how much more eloquently and effectively he can combat injustice who has experienced a little in his own person. Cast your whole vote, not a strip of paper merely, but your whole influence. A minority is powerless while it conforms to the majority; it is not even a minority then; but it is irresistible when it clogs by its whole weight. If the alternative is to keep all just men in prison, or give up war and slavery, the State will not hesitate which to choose. If a thousand men were not to pay their tax-bills this year, that would not be a violent and bloody measure, as it would be to pay them, and enable the State to commit violence and shed innocent blood. This is, in fact, the definition of a peaceable revolution, if any such is possible. If the tax-gatherer, or any other public officer, asks me, as one has done, "But what shall I do?" my answer is, "If you really wish to do anything, resign your office." When the subject has refused allegiance, and the officer has resigned his office, then the revolution is accomplished. But even suppose blood should flow. Is there not a sort of blood shed when the conscience is wounded? Through this wound a man's real manhood and immortality flow out, and he bleeds to an everlasting death. I see this blood flowing now.

I have contemplated the imprisonment of the offender, rather than the seizure of his goods,—though both will serve the same purpose,—because they who assert the purest right, and consequently are most dangerous to a corrupt State, commonly have not spent much time in accumulating property. To such the State renders comparatively small service, and a slight tax is wont to appear exorbitant, particularly if they are obliged to earn it by special labor with their hands. If there were one who lived wholly without the use of money, the State itself would hesitate to demand it of him. But the rich man—not to make any invidious comparison—is always sold to the institution which makes him rich. Absolutely speaking, the more money, the less virtue; for money comes between a man and his objects, and obtains them for him; and it was certainly no great virtue to obtain it. It puts to rest many questions which he would otherwise be taxed to answer; while the only new question which it puts is the hard but superfluous one, how to spend it. Thus his moral ground is taken from under his feet. The opportunities of living are diminished in proportion as what are called the "means" are increased. The best thing a man can do for his culture when he is rich is to endeavor to carry out those schemes which he entertained when he was poor. Christ answered the Herodians according to their condition. "Show me the tribute money," said he;—and one took a penny out of his pocket;—if you use money which has the image of Cæsar on it and which he has made current and valuable, that is, *if you are men of the State*, and gladly enjoy the advantages of Cæsar's government, then pay him back some of his own when he demands it. "Render therefore to Cæsar that which is Cæsar's, and to God those things which are God's,"[18] leaving them no wiser than before as to which was which; for they did not wish to know.

When I converse with the freest of my neighbors, I perceive that, whatever they may say about the magnitude and seriousness of the question, and their regard for the public tranquillity, the long and the short of the matter is, that they cannot spare the protection of the existing government, and they dread the consequences to their property and families of disobedience to it. For my own part, I should not like to think that I ever rely on the protection of the State. But, if I deny the authority of the State when it presents its tax-bill, it will soon take and waste all my property, and so harass me and my children without end. This is hard. This makes it impossible for a man to live honestly, and at the same time comfortably, in outward respects. It will not be worth the while to accumulate property; that would be sure to go again. You must hire or squat somewhere, and raise but a small crop, and eat that soon. You must live within yourself, and depend upon yourself always tucked up and ready for a start, and not have many affairs. A man may grow rich in Turkey even, if he will be in all respects a good subject of the Turkish government. Confucius[19] said: "If a state is governed by the principles of reason, poverty and misery are subjects of shame; if a state is not governed by the principles of reason, riches and honors are the subjects of shame." No: until I want the protection of Massachusetts to be extended to me in some distant Southern port, where my liberty is endangered, or until I am bent solely on building up an estate at home by peaceful enterprise, I can afford to refuse allegiance to Massachusetts, and her right to my property and life. It costs me less in every sense to incur the penalty of disobedience to the State than it would to obey. I should feel as if I were worth less in that case.

Some years ago, the State met me in behalf of the Church, and commanded me to pay a certain sum toward the support of a clergyman whose preaching my father attended, but never I myself. "Pay," it said, "or be locked up in the jail."[20] I declined to pay. But, unfortunately, another man saw fit to pay it. I did not see why the schoolmaster should be taxed to support the priest, and not the priest the schoolmaster; for I was not the State's schoolmaster, but I supported myself by voluntary subscription. I did not see why the lyceum should not present its tax-bill, and have the State to back its demand, as well as the Church. However, at the request of the selectmen, I condescended to make some such statement as this in writ-

---

[18] Cf. Matthew, xxii: 15-22.

[19] The *Analects* by Confucius (551?-479? B. C.) were popular among transcendentalists.

[20] Thoreau did not pay his church taxes in 1838, but he was not imprisoned; he did go to jail in July 1846 for refusing to pay his poll tax.

ing:—"Know all men by these presents, that I, Henry Thoreau, do not wish to be regarded as a member of any incorporated society which I have not joined." This I gave to the town clerk; and he has it. The State, having thus learned that I did not wish to be regarded as a member of that church, has never made a like demand on me since; though it said that it must adhere to its original presumption that time. If I had known how to name them, I should then have signed off in detail from all the societies which I never signed on to; but I did not know where to find a complete list.

I have paid no poll-tax for six years. I was put into a jail once on this account, for one night; and, as I stood considering the walls of solid stone, two or three feet thick, the door of wood and iron, a foot thick, and the iron grating which strained the light, I could not help being struck with the foolishness of that institution which treated me as if I were mere flesh and blood and bones, to be locked up. I wondered that it should have concluded at length that this was the best use it could put me to, and had never thought to avail itself of my services in some way. I saw that, if there was a wall of stone between me and my townsmen, there was a still more difficult one to climb or break through before they could get to be as free as I was. I did not for a moment feel confined, and the walls seemed a great waste of stone and mortar. I felt as if I alone of all my townsmen had paid my tax. They plainly did not know how to treat me, but behaved like persons who are underbred. In every threat and in every compliment there was a blunder; for they thought that my chief desire was to stand the other side of that stone wall. I could not but smile to see how industriously they locked the door on my meditations, which followed them out again without let or hindrance, and *they* were really all that was dangerous. As they could not reach me, they had resolved to punish my body; just as boys, if they cannot come at some person against whom they have a spite, will abuse his dog. I saw that the State was half-witted, that it was timid as a lone woman with her silver spoons, and that it did not know its friends from its foes, and I lost all my remaining respect for it, and pitied it.

Thus the State never intentionally confronts a man's sense, intellectual or moral, but only his body, his senses. It is not armed with superior wit or honesty, but with superior physical strength. I was not born to be forced. I will breathe after my own fashion. Let us see who is the strongest. What force has a multitude? They only can force me who obey a higher law than I. They force me to become like themselves. I do not hear of *men* being *forced* to live this way or that by masses of men. What sort of life were that to live? When I meet a government which says to me, "Your money or your life," why should I be in haste to give it my money? It may be in a great strait, and not know what to do: I cannot help that. It must help itself; do as I do. It is not worth the while to snivel about it. I am not responsible for the successful working of the machinery of society. I am not the son of the engineer. I perceive that, when an acorn and a chestnut fall side by side, the one does not remain inert to make way for the other, but both obey their own laws, and spring and grow and flourish as best they can, till one, perchance, overshadows and destroys the other. If a plant cannot live according to its nature, it dies; and so a man.

The night in prison was novel and interesting enough. The prisoners in their shirt-sleeves were enjoying a chat and the evening air in the doorway, when I entered. But the jailer said, "Come, boys, it is time to lock up"; and so they dispersed, and I heard the sound of their steps returning into the hollow apartments. My room-mate was introduced to me by the jailer as "a first-rate fellow and a clever[21] man." When the door was locked, he showed me where to hang my hat, and how he managed matters there. The rooms were white washed once a month; and this one, at least, was the whitest, most simply furnished, and probably the neatest apartment in the town. He naturally wanted to know where I came from, and what brought me there; and, when I had told him, I asked him in my turn how he came there, presuming him to be an honest man, of course; and, as the world goes, I believe he was. "Why," said he, "they accuse me of burning a barn; but I never did it." As near as I could discover, he had probably gone to bed in a barn when drunk, and smoked his pipe there; and so a barn was burnt. He had the reputation of being a clever man, had been there some three months waiting for his trial to come on, and would have to wait as much longer; but he was quite domesticated and contented, since he got his board for nothing, and thought that he was well treated.

He occupied one window, and I the other; and I saw that if one stayed there long, his principal business would be to look out the window. I had soon read all the tracts that were left there, and examined where former prisoners had broken out, and where a grate had been sawed off, and heard the history of the various occupants of that room; for I found that even here there was a history and a gossip which never circulated beyond the walls of the jail. Probably this is the only house in the town where verses are composed, which are afterward printed in a circular form, but not published. I was shown quite a long list of verses which were composed by some young men who had been detected in an attempt to escape, who avenged themselves by singing them.

I pumped my fellow-prisoner as dry as I could, for fear I should never see him again; but at length he showed me which was my bed, and left me to blow out the lamp.

It was like traveling into a far country, such as I had never expected to behold, to lie there for one night. It seemed to me that I never had heard the town-clock strike before, nor the evening sounds of the village; for we slept with the windows open, which were inside the grating. It was to see my native village in the light of the Middle Ages, and our Concord was turned

[21] Honest.

into a Rhine stream, and visions of knights and castles passed before me. There were the voices of old burghers that I heard in the streets. I was an involuntary spectator and auditor of whatever was done and said in the kitchen of the adjacent village-inn,—a wholly new and rare experience to me. It was a closer view of my native town. I was fairly inside of it. I never had seen its institutions before. This is one of its peculiar institutions; for it is a shire town. I began to comprehend what its inhabitants were about.

In the morning, our breakfasts were put through the hole in the door, in small oblong-square tin pans, made to fit, and holding a pint of chocolate, with brown bread, and an iron spoon. When they called for the vessels again, I was green enough to return what bread I had left; but my comrade seized it, and said that I should lay that up for lunch or dinner. Soon after he was let out to work at haying in a neighboring field, whither he went every day, and would not be back till noon; so he bade me good-day, saying that he doubted if he should see me again.

When I came out of prison,—for some one interfered, and paid that tax,[22]—I did not perceive that great changes had taken place on the common, such as he observed who went in a youth and emerged a tottering and gray-headed man; and yet a change had to my eyes come over the scene,—the town, and State, and country,—greater than any that mere time could effect. I saw yet more distinctly the State in which I lived. I saw to what extent the people among whom I lived could be trusted as good neighbors and friends; that their friendship was for summer weather only; that they did not greatly propose to do right; that they were a distinct race from me by their prejudices and superstitions, as the Chinamen and Malays are; that in their sacrifices to humanity they ran no risks, not even to their property; that after all they were not so noble but they treated the thief as he had treated them, and hoped, by a certain outward observance and a few prayers, and by walking in a particular straight though useless path from time to time, to save their souls. This may be to judge my neighbors harshly; for I believe that many of them are not aware that they have such an institution as the jail in their village.

It was formerly the custom in our village, when a poor debtor came out of jail, for his acquaintances to salute him, looking through their fingers, which were crossed to represent the grating of a jail window, "How do ye do?" My neighbors did not thus salute me, but first looked at me, and then at one another, as if I had returned from a long journey. I was put into jail as I was going to the shoemaker's to get a shoe which was mended. When I was let out the next morning, I proceeded to finish my errand, and, having put on my mended shoe, joined a huckleberry party, who were impatient to put themselves under my conduct; and in half an hour,—for the horse was soon

[22] The story has it that Emerson paid the tax; but this seems apochryphal. His Aunt Maria probably paid the tax.

tackled,—was in the midst of a huckleberry field, on one of our highest hills, two miles off, and then the State was nowhere to be seen.

This is the whole history of "My Prisons."[23]

I have never declined paying the highway tax, because I am as desirous of being a good neighbor as I am of being a bad subject; and as for supporting schools, I am doing my part to educate my fellow-countrymen now. It is for no particular item in the tax-bill that I refuse to pay it. I simply wish to refuse allegiance to the State, to withdraw and stand aloof from it effectually. I do not care to trace the course of my dollars, if I could, till it buys a man or a musket to shoot with,—the dollar is innocent,—but I am concerned to trace the effects of my allegiance. In fact, I quietly declare war with the State, after my fashion, though I will still make what use and get what advantage of her I can, as is usual in such cases.

If others pay the tax which is demanded of me, from a sympathy with the State, they do but what they have already done in their own case, or rather they abet injustice to a greater extent than the State requires. If they pay the tax from a mistaken interest in the individual taxed, to save his property, or prevent his going to jail, it is because they have not considered wisely how far they let their private feelings interfere with the public good.

This, then, is my position at present. But one cannot be too much on his guard in such a case, lest his action be biased by obstinacy or an undue regard for the opinions of men. Let him see that he does only what belongs to himself and to the hour.

I think sometimes, Why, this people mean well, they are only ignorant; they would do better if they knew how: why give your neighbors this pain to treat you as they are not inclined to? But I think again, This is no reason why I should do as they do, or permit others to suffer much greater pain of a different kind. Again, I sometimes say to myself, When many millions of men, without heat, without ill will, without personal feeling of any kind, demand of you a few shillings only, without the possibility, such is their constitution, of retracting or altering their present demand, and without the possibility, on your side, of appeal to any other millions, why expose yourself to this overwhelming brute force? You do not resist cold and hunger, the winds and the waves, thus obstinately; you quietly submit to a thousand similar necessities. You do not put your head into the fire. But just in proportion as I regard this as not wholly a brute force, but partly a human force, and consider that I have relations to those millions as to so many millions of men, and not of mere brute or inanimate things, I see that appeal is possible, first and instantaneously, from them to the Maker of them, and, secondly, from them to themselves. But if I put my head deliberately into the fire, there is no appeal to fire or to the Maker of fire, and I have only myself to

[23] English translation of the title *Le Mie Prigioni*, a record of his Austrian imprison- ment by the Italian patriot and poet Silvio Pellico (1789-1864).

blame. If I could convince myself that I have any right to be satisfied with men as they are, and to treat them accordingly, and not according, in some respects, to my requisitions and expectations of what they and I ought to be, then, like a good Mussulman and fatalist, I should endeavor to be satisfied with things as they are, and say it is the will of God. And, above all, there is this difference between resisting this and a purely brute or natural force, that I can resist this with some effect; but I cannot expect, like Orpheus,[24] to change the nature of the rocks and trees and beasts.

I do not wish to quarrel with any man or nation. I do not wish to split hairs, to make fine distinctions, or set myself up as better than my neighbors. I seek rather, I may say, even an excuse for conforming to the laws of the land. I am but too ready to conform to them. Indeed, I have reason to suspect myself on this head; and each year, as the tax-gatherer comes round, I find myself disposed to review the acts and position of the general and State governments, and the spirit of the people, to discover a pretext for conformity.

> "We must affect our country as our parents,
> And if at any time we alienate
> Our love or industry from doing it honor,
> We must respect effects and teach the soul
> Matter of conscience and religion,
> And not desire of rule or benefit."

I believe that the State will soon be able to take all my work of this sort out of my hands, and then I shall be not better a patriot than my fellow-countrymen. Seen from a lower point of view, the Constitution, with all its faults, is very good; the law and the courts are very respectable; even this State and this American government are, in many respects, very admirable, and rare things, to be thankful for, such as a great many have described them; but seen from a point of view a little higher, they are what I have described them; seen from a higher still, and the highest, who shall say what they are, or that they are worth looking at or thinking of at all?

However, the government does not concern me much, and I shall bestow the fewest possible thoughts on it. It is not many moments that I live under a government, even in this world. If a man is thought-free, fancy-free, imagination-free, that which *is not* never for a long time appearing *to be* to him, unwise rulers or reformers cannot fatally interrupt him.

I know that most men think differently from myself; but those whose lives are by profession devoted to the study of these or kindred subjects content me as little as any. Statesmen and legislators, standing so completely within the institution, never distinctly and nakedly behold it. They speak of moving

[24] Orpheus was a legendary Greek poet and musician.

society, but have no resting-place without it. They may be men of a certain experience and discrimination, and have no doubt invented ingenious and even useful systems, for which we sincerely thank them; but all their wit and usefulness lie within certain not very wide limits. They are wont to forget that the world is not governed by policy and expediency. Webster never goes behind government, and so cannot speak with authority about it.[25] His words are wisdom to those legislators who contemplate no essential reform in the existing government; but for thinkers, and those who legislate for all time, he never once glances at the subject. I know of those whose serene and wise speculations on this theme would soon reveal the limits of his mind's range and hospitality. Yet, compared with the cheap professions of most reformers, and the still cheaper wisdom and eloquence of politicians in general, his are almost the only sensible and valuable words, and we thank Heaven for him. Comparatively, he is always strong, original, and, above all, practical. Still, his quality is not wisdom, but prudence, The lawyer's truth is not Truth, but consistency or a consistent expediency. Truth is always in harmony with herself, and is not concerned chiefly to reveal the justice that may consist with wrong-doing. He well deserves to be called, as he has been called, the Defender of the Constitution. There are really no blows to be given by him but defensive ones. He is not a leader, but a follower. His leaders are the men of '87. "I have never made an effort," he says, "and never propose to make an effort; I have never countenanced an effort, and never mean to countenance an effort, to disturb the arrangement as originally made, by which the various States came into the Union." Still thinking of the sanction which the Constitution gives to slavery, he says, "Because it was a part of the original compact,—let it stand." Notwithstanding his special acuteness and ability, *he is* unable to take a fact out of its merely political relations, and behold it as it lies absolutely to be disposed of by the intellect,—what, for instance, it behooves a man to do here in America to-day with regard to slavery,—but ventures, or is driven, to make some such desperate answer as the following, while professing to speak absolutely, and as a private man,—from which what new and singular code of social duties might be inferred? "The manner," says he, "in which the governments of those States where slavery exists are to regulate it is for their own consideration, under their responsibility to their constituents, to the general laws of propriety, humanity, and justice, and to God. Associations formed elsewhere, springing from a feeling of humanity, or other cause, have nothing whatever to do with it. They have never received any encouragement from me, and they never will."[26]

[25] Webster was a defender of the Constitution and took a position of compromise and pragmatism in the issue of slavery; he was therefore scorned by many abolitionists and Northerners, notably Thoreau and Whittier.

See the section on Webster, pp. 1726-1729, and Whittier's "Ichabod," p. 1730.

[26] These extracts have been inserted since the lecture was read.

They who know of no purer sources of truth, who have traced up its stream no higher, stand, and wisely stand, by the Bible and the Constitution, and drink at it there with reverence and humility; but they who behold where it comes trickling into this lake or that pool, gird up their loins once more, and continue their pilgrimage toward its fountainhead.

No man with a genius for legislation has appeared in America. They are rare in the history of the world. There are orators, politicians, and eloquent men, by the thousand; but the speaker has not yet opened his mouth to speak who is capable of settling the much-vexed questions of the day. We love eloquence for its own sake, and not for any truth which it may utter, or any heroism it may inspire. Our legislators have not yet learned the comparative value of free-trade and of freedom, of union, and of rectitude, to a nation. They have no genius or talent for comparatively humble questions of taxation and finance, commerce and manufactures and agriculture. If we were left solely to the wordy wit of legislators in Congress for our guidance, uncorrected by the seasonable experience and the effectual complaints of the people, America would not long retain her rank among the nations. For eighteen hundred years, though perchance I have no right to say it, the New Testament has been written; yet where is the legislator who has wisdom and practical talent enough to avail himself of the light which it sheds on the science of legislation?

The authority of government, even such as I am willing to submit to,—for I will cheerfully obey those who know and can do better than I, and in many things even those who neither know nor can do so well,—is still an impure one: to be strictly just, it must have the sanction and consent of the governed. It can have no pure right over my person and property but what I concede to it. The progress from an absolute to a limited monarchy, from a limited monarchy to a democracy, is a progress toward a true respect for the individual. Even the Chinese philosopher was wise enough to regard the individual as the basis of the empire. Is a democracy, such as we know it, the last improvement possible in government? Is it not possible to take a step further towards recognizing and organizing the rights of man? There will never be a really free and enlightened State until the State comes to recognize the individual as a higher and independent power, from which all its own power and authority are derived, and treats him accordingly. I please my self with imagining a State as last which can afford to be just to all men, and to treat the individual with respect as a neighbor; which even would not think it inconsistent with its own repose if a few were to live aloof from it, not meddling with it, nor embraced by it, who fulfilled all the duties of neighbors and fellow-men. A State which bore this kind of fruit, and suffered it to drop off as fast as it ripened, would prepare the way for a still more perfect and glorious State, which also I have imagined, but not yet anywhere seen.

POLITICAL EXPRESSION

Oratory:
The Art of Rhetoric in the
Political Forum

Oratory has always been a primary form of literature in America. Early legislators were well trained in the art of rhetoric, and Puritan preachers like Increase Mather and Jonathan Edwards delivered sermons that depended heavily on the technique of persuasion and the public effect of the spoken word. During the Great Awakening of the 1730's and 1740's, when a preacher such as George Whitefield was denied a pulpit in an established church, he went to the people and spoke in common language charged with emotion.

The oratory of the Church naturally yielded to the rhetoric of the political forum and, during the Revolutionary period, legislative speech making became important in the drafting of the Constitution. The most significant period of forensic debate was between 1820 and 1860, when oratory largely shaped public affairs. The essays of Channing, Emerson, Parker, and the transcendentalists were deeply influenced by the forms of the sermon and the address, and they were usually first delivered before public audiences. In political life, the great thinkers were senators; Webster, Clay, and Calhoun—the most eloquent of American statesmen—often raised oratory to the level of art and spoke before large audiences at ceremonial occasions.

The subjects of these speeches varied. Webster's most famous addresses include funeral orations on Jefferson and Adams as well as statements before the United States Senate; the addresses of Calhoun and Clay tend to be exclusively political. Reformers like Wendell Phillips, Horace Mann, and Dorothea Dix spoke on temperance, education, and prison reform. The most impassioned and impressive rhetoricians turned their forensic skills to the central subject of the period—slavery—and the list of orators who commented on America's "national sin" is formidable: the senators Webster and Calhoun; the abolitionists Garrison, Curtis, and Whittier; the black orator Frederick Douglass; and, finally, Abraham Lincoln. In an age when the newspaper was not yet influential and when libraries were not readily available, oratory was the chief means of public communication.

DANIEL WEBSTER

(1782–1852)

Daniel Webster was the most impressive speaker on ceremonial occasions in the period before the Civil War. From 1818 to 1830, he delivered a series of public addresses that were models of their kind and had a deep impact on the sensibility of American schoolchildren: "The Plymouth Oration" (1820), "The First Bunker Hill Address" (1825), and "The Eulogy of Adams and Jefferson" (1820). A boy like Emerson followed Webster wherever he went, "from court-house to senate-chamber, from caucus to street," and admitted that he "owed to him a hundred fine hours and two or three moments of eloquence."

The standard edition of Webster's work is *The Writings and Speeches of Daniel Webster,* National Edition, 18 vols., 1903. A biography is C. M. Fuess, *Daniel Webster,* 2 vols., 1930. Recent studies include Gerald W. Johnson, *America's Silver Age,* 1939, Robert F. Dalzell, *Daniel Webster and the Trial of American Nationalism, 1843–1852,* 1974; Sydney Nathans, *Daniel Webster and Jacksonian Democracy,* 1973.

The Constitution and The Union (Seventh of March Speech, 1850)

[Until 1850 Webster was a Northern Hero, the statesman who transcended his section and represented the broadest interests of the Union. On March 7, 1850, however, he delivered a speech entitled "The Constitution and the Union," which attempted to strike a compromise between the antislavery movement and the proponents of secession, so that the Union could be preserved; as a consequence of this speech, his heroic image was shattered. Webster tries to mediate between the North and South, recognizing that secession can lead only to conflagration; but this note of conciliation was mocked by the antislavery forces, and he was vilified in the Northern press. He died two years later.]

MR. PRESIDENT,—I wish to speak to-day, not as a Massachusetts man, nor as a northern man, but as an American, and a member of the Senate of the United States. It is fortunate that there is a Senate of the United States; a body not yet moved from propriety, not lost to a just sense of its own dignity and its own high responsibilities, and a body to which the country looks, with confidence, for wise, moderate, patriotic, and healing counsels. It is not to be denied that we live in the midst of strong agitations, and are surrounded by

Daguerreotype of Daniel Webster. *(The Metropolitan Museum of Art, Gift of I.N. Pheeps Stokes, Edward S. Hawes, Alice Mary Hawes, Marion Augusta Hawes, 1937.)*

very considerable dangers to our institutions and government. The imprisoned winds are let loose. The East, the West, the North, and the stormy South, all combine to throw the whole sea into commotion, to toss its billows to the skies, and disclose its profoundest depths. I do not affect to regard myself, Mr. President, as holding, or as fit to hold, the helm in this combat with the political elements; but I have a duty to perform, and I mean to perform it with fidelity—not without a sense of existing dangers, but not without hope. I have a part to act, not for my own security or safety, for I am looking out for no fragment upon which to float away from the wreck, if wreck there must be, but for the good of the whole, and the preservation of the whole; and there is that which will keep me to my duty during this struggle, whether the sun and the stars shall appear, or shall not appear for many days. I speak to-day for the preservation of the Union. "Hear me for my cause." I speak to-day, out of a solicitous and anxious heart, for the restoration to the country of that quiet and that harmony which make the blessings of this union so rich and so dear to us all. These are the topics that I propose to myself to discuss; these are the motives, and the sole motives, that influence me in the wish to communicate my opinions to the Senate and the country; and if I can do anything, however little, for the promotion of these ends, I shall have accomplished all that I desire. . . .

Mr. President, I should much prefer to have heard, from every member on this floor, declarations of opinion that this Union could never be dissolved, than the declaration of opinion that in any case, under the pressure of circumstances, such a dissolution was possible. I hear with pain, and anguish, and distress, the word secession, especially when it falls from the lips of those who are eminently patriotic, and known to the country, and known all over the world, for their political services. Secession! Peaceable secession! Sir, your eyes and mine are never destined to see that miracle. The dismemberment of this vast country without convulsion! The breaking up of the fountains of the great deep without ruffling the surface! Who is so foolish— I beg every body's pardon—as to expect to see any such thing? Sir, he who sees these States, now revolving in harmony around a common centre, and expects to see them quit their places and fly off without convulsion, may look the next hour to see the heavenly bodies rush from their spheres, and jostle against each other in the realms of space, without producing the crush of the universe. There can be no such thing as a peaceable secession. Peaceable secession is an utter impossibility. Is the great Constitution under which we live—covering this whole country—is it to be thawed and melted away by secession, as the snows on the mountain melt under the influence of a vernal sun—disappear almost unobserved, and die off? No, sir! No, sir! I will not state what might produce the disruption of the states; but, sir, I see it as plainly as I see the sun in heaven—I see that disruption must produce such a war as I will not describe, in its twofold characters. . . .

Sir, I may express myself too strongly, perhaps—but some things, some moral things, are almost as impossible, as other natural or physical things;

and I hold the idea of a separation of these States—those that are free to form one government, and those that are slaveholding to form another—as a moral impossibility. We could not separate the States by any such line, if we were to draw it. We could not sit down here to-day and draw a line of separation, that would satisfy any five men in the country. There are natual causes that would keep and tie us together, and there are social and domestic relations which we could not break if we would, and which we should not, if we could. Sir, nobody can look over the face of this country at the present moment—nobody can see where its population is the most dense and growing—without being ready to admit, and compelled to admit, that ere long, America will be in the valley of the Mississippi. . . .

And now, Mr. President, instead of speaking of the possibility or utility of secession, instead of dwelling in these caverns of darkness, instead of groping with those ideas so full of all that is horrid and horrible, let us come out into the light of day; let us enjoy the fresh air of liberty and union; let us cherish those hopes which belong to us; let us devote ourselves to those great objects that are fit for our consideration and our action; let us raise our conceptions to the magnitude and the importance of the duties that devolve upon us; let our comprehension be as broad as the country for which we act, our aspirations as high as its certain destiny; let us not be pigmies in a case that calls for men. Never did there devolve, on any generation of men, higher trusts than now devolve upon us for the preservation of this Constitution and the harmony and peace of all who are destined to live under it. Let us make our generation one of the strongest and brightest links in that golden chain which is destined, I fully believe, to grapple the people of all the States to this Constitution, for ages to come. It is a great popular constitutional Government, guarded by legislation, law, and by judicature, and defended by the affections of the whole people. No monarchical throne presses the States together; no iron chain of military power encircles them; they live and stand upon a Government popular in its form, representative in its character, founded upon principles of equality, and calculated, we hope, as to last forever, In all its history, it has been beneficent; it has trodden down no man's liberty; it has crushed no State. Its daily respiration is liberty and patriotism; its yet youthful veins are full of enterprise, courage, and honorable love of glory and renown. Large before, the country has now, by recent events, become vastly larger. This republic now extends, with a vast breadth, across the whole continent. The two great seas of the world wash the one and other shore. We realize on a mighty scale, the beautiful description of the ornamental border of the buckler of Achilles—

> Now the broad shield complete the artist crowned,
> With his last band, and poured the ocean round;
> In living silver seemed the waves to roll.
> And beat the buckler's verge, and bound the whole.

JOHN GREENLEAF WHITTIER

(1807–1892)*

Whittier's poem "Ichabod" is a direct result of Webster's Seventh of March speech and suggests the response of abolitionists. Whittier supplied his own revealing note to the poem in his collected *Writings* (1888): "This poem was the outcome of the surprise and grief and forecast of evil consequence which I felt on reading the seventh of March speech of Daniel Webster in support of the 'compromise' and the Fugitive Slave Bill. No partisan or personal enmity dictated it. On the contrary my admiration of the splendid personality and intellectual power of the great Senator was never stronger than when I laid down his speech, and, in one of the saddest moments of life, penned my protest."

* For a full introduction to Whittier, see pp. 1451–1452.

Ichabod

So fallen! so lost! the light withdrawn
    Which once he wore!
The glory from his gray hairs gone
    Forevermore!

Revile him not, the Tempter hath   5
    A snare for all;
And pitying tears, not scorn and wrath,
    Befit his fall!

Oh, dumb be passion's stormy rage,
    When he who might   10
Have lighted up and led his age,
    Falls back in night.

Scorn! would the angels laugh, to mark
    A bright soul driven,
Fiend-goaded, down the endless dark,   15
    From hope and heaven!

Let not the land once proud of him
    Insult him now,
Nor brand with deeper shame his dim,
    Dishonored brow.   20

But let its humbled sons, instead,
    From sea to lake,
A long lament, as for the dead,
    In sadness make.

Of all we loved and honored, naught   25
    Save power remains;
A fallen angel's pride of thought,
    Still strong in chains.

All else is gone; from those great eyes
    The soul has fled: 30
When faith is lost, when honor dies,
    The man is dead!

Then pay the reverence of old days
    To his dead fame;
Walk backward, with averted gaze,   35
    And hide the shame!

1850

JOHN C. CALHOUN

(1782–1850)

Calhoun was the major spokesman for the South in the period before the war. From 1833 until his death in 1850 he vigorously defended the doctrine of states' rights. He denounced the tariff on imported goods and opposed any tendency to centralize power in the national government. As the representative of the slaveholding aristocracy, Calhoun was in direct disagreement with Webster, who supported New Eng-

The standard text is *The Works of John C. Calhoun*, 6 vols., ed. R. K. Cralle, 1853–1856.

For accounts of Calhoun's life, see W. M. Meigs, *The Life of John C. Calhoun*, 2 vols., 1917; Gerald Mortimer Cupers, *John C. Calhoun, Opportunist; a reappraisal*, 1960; Richard Nelson Current, *John C. Calhoun*, 1963.

Daguerreotype of John C. Calhoun. *(The Granger Collection.)*

land manufacturing interests and took a more moderate and broadly nationalistic position.

Calhoun believed that the country was governed by a federal constitution and that the states, not the people, were the actual constituents. Each state therefore had inalienable rights, including the right to possess its own property. Slaves were considered property by Calhoun, and any state that prohibited slavery was therefore violating the Constitution.

One of Calhoun's most famous and representative speeches was delivered on March 3, 1850, four days before Webster delivered his own compromise address on the issues of secession and slavery and less than a month before Calhoun himself died. Indeed, Calhoun was too ill to deliver the address, and a colleague read it to the Senate for him.

Speech on the Slavery Question

I have, Senators, believed from the first that the agitation of the subject of slavery would, if not prevented by some timely and effective measure, end in disunion. Entertaining this opinion, I have, on all proper occasions, endeavored to call the attention of both the two great measure to prevent so great a disaster, but without success. The agitation has been permitted to proceed, with almost no attempt to resist it, until it has reached a point when it can no longer be disguised or denied that the Union is in danger. You have thus had forced upon you the greatest and the gravest question that can ever come under your consideration—How can the Union be preserved?

To give a satisfactory answer to this mighty question, it is indispensable to have an accurate and thorough knowledge of the nature and the character of the cause by which the Union is endangered. Without such knowledge it is impossible to pronounce, with any certainty, by what measure it can be saved; just as it would be impossible for a physician to pronounce, in the case of some dangerous disease, with any certainty, by what remedy the patient could be saved, without similar knowledge of the nature and character of the cause which produced it. The first question, then, presented for consideration, in the investigation I propose to make, in order to obtain such knowledge, is—What is it that has endangered the Union?

To this question there can be but one answer,—that the immediate cause is the almost universal discontent which pervades all the States composing the Southern section of the Union. This widely-extended discontent is not of recent origin. It commenced with the agitation of the slavery question, and has been increasing ever since. The next question, going one step further back, is—What has caused this widely diffused and almost universal discontent?

It is a great mistake to suppose, as is by some, that it originated with demagogues, who excited the discontent with the intention of aiding their personal advancement, or with the disappointed ambition of certain politicians, who resorted to it as the means of retrieving their fortunes. On the contrary, all the great political influences of the section were arrayed against excitement, and exerted to the utmost to keep the people quiet. The great mass of the people of the South were divided, as in the other section, into Whigs and Democrats. The leaders and the presses of both parties in the South were very solicitous to prevent excitement and to preserve quiet; because it was seen that the effects of the former would necessarily tend to weaken, if not destroy, the political ties which united them with their respective parties in the other section. Those who know the strength of party ties will readily appreciate the immense force which this cause exerted against agitation, and in favor of preserving quiet. But, great as it was, it was not sufficient to prevent the widespread discontent which now pervades the section. No; some cause, far deeper and more powerful than the one supposed, must exist, to account for discontent so wide and deep. The question then recurs—What is the cause of this discontent? It will be found in the belief of the people of the Southern States, as prevalent as the discontent itself, that they cannot remain, as things now are, consistently with honor and safety, in the Union. The next question to be considered, is—What has caused this belief?

One of the causes is, undoubtedly, to be traced to the long-continued agitation of the slave question on the part of the North, and the many aggressions which they have made on the rights of the South during the time. I will not enumerate them at present, as it will be done hereafter in its proper place.

There is another lying back of it—with which this is intimately connected—that may be regarded as the great and primary cause. This is to be found in the fact that the equilibrium between the two sections, in the Government as it stood when the constitution was ratified and the Government put in action, has been destroyed. At that time there was nearly a perfect equilibrium between the two, which afforded ample means to each to protect itself against the aggression of the other; but, as it now stands, one section has the exclusive power of controlling the Government, which leaves the other without any adequate means of protecting itself against its encroachment and oppression. To place this subject distinctly before you, I have, Senators, prepared a brief statistical statement, showing the relative weight of the two sections in the Government under the first census of 1790 and last census of 1840.

According to the former, the population of the United States, including Vermont, Kentucky, and Tennessee, which then were in their incipient condition of becoming States, but were not actually admitted, amounted to 3,929,827. Of this number the Northern States had 1,997,899, and the Southern 1,952,072, making a difference of only 45,827 in favor of the former States. The number of States, including Vermont, Kentucky, and Tennessee, were sixteen; of which eight, including Vermont, belonged to the Northern section, and eight, including Kentucky and Tennessee, to the Southern,— making an equal division of the States between the two sections under the first census. There was a small preponderance in the House of Representatives, and in the Electoral College, in favor of the Northern, owing to the fact that, according to the provisions of the constitution, in estimating federal numbers five slaves count but three; but it was too small to affect sensibly the perfect equilibrium which, with that exception, existed at the time. Such was the equality of the two sections when the States composing them agreed to enter into a Federal Union. Since then the equilibrium between them has been greatly disturbed.

According to the last census the aggregate population of the United States amounted to 17,063,357, of which the Northern section contained 9,728,920, and the Southern 7,334,437, making a difference, in round numbers, of 2,400,000. The number of States had increased from sixteen to twenty-six, making an addition of ten States. In the mean time the position of Delaware had become doubtful as to which section she properly belonged. Considering her as neutral, the Northern States will have thirteen and the Southern States twelve, making a difference in the Senate of two Senators in favor of the former. According to the apportionment under the census of 1840, there were two hundred and twenty-three members of the House of Representatives, of which the Northern States had one hundred and thirty-five, and the Southern States (considering Delaware as neutral) eighty-seven, making a difference in favor of the former in the House of Representatives of forty-eight. The difference in the Senate of two members, added to this, gives to the North in the electoral college, a majority of fifty. Since the census of 1840, four States have been added to the Union—Iowa, Wisconsin, Florida, and Texas. They leave the difference in the Senate as it stood when the census was taken; but add two to the side of the North in the House, making the present majority in the House in its favor fifty, and in the electoral college fifty-two.

The result of the whole is to give the Northern section a predominance in every department of the Government, and thereby concentrate in it the two elements which constitute the Federal Government,—majority of States, and a majority of their population, estimated in federal numbers. Whatever section concentrates the two in itself possesses the control of the entire Government.

But we are just at the close of the sixth decade, and the commencement of the seventh. The census is to be taken this year, which must add greatly to the decided preponderance of the North in the House of Representatives and in the electoral college. The prospect is, also, that a great increase will be added to its present preponderance in the Senate, during the period of the decade, by the addition of new States. Two territories, Oregon and Minnesota, are already in progress, and strenuous efforts are making to bring in three additional States from the territory recently conquered from Mexico; which, if successful, will add three other States in a short time to the Northern section, making five States; and increasing the present number of its States from fifteen to twenty, and of its Senators from thirty to forty. On the contrary, there is not a single territory in progress in the Southern section, and no certainty that any additional State will be added to it during the decade. The prospect then is, that the two sections in the Senate, should the efforts now made to exclude the South from the newly acquired territories succeed, will stand, before the end of the decade, twenty Northern States to fourteen Southern (considering Delaware as neutral), and forty Northern Senators to twenty-eight Sourthern. This great increase of Senators, added to the great increase of members of the House of Representatives and the electoral college on the part of the North, which must take place under the next decade, will effectually and irretrievably destroy the equilibrium which existed when the Government commenced.

Had this destruction been the operation of time, without the interference of Government, the South would have had no reason to complain; but such was not the fact. It was caused by the legislation of this Government, which was appointed, as the common agent of all, and charged with the protection of the interests and security of all. The legislation by which it has been effected, may be classed under three heads. The first, is that series of acts by which the South has been excluded from the common territory belonging to all the States as members of the Federal Union—which have had the effect of extending vastly the portion allotted to the Northern section, and restricting within narrow limits the portion left the South. The next consists in adopting a system of revenue and disbursements, by which an undue proportion of the burden of taxation has been imposed upon the South, and an undue proportion of its proceeds appropriated to the North; and the last is a system of political measures, by which the original character of the Government has been radically changed. I propose to bestow upon each of these, in the order they stand, a few remarks, with the view of showing that it is owing to the action of this Government, that the equilibrium between the two sections has been destroyed, and the whole powers of the system centered in a sectional majority.

The first of the series of acts by which the South was deprived of its due share of the territories, originated with the confederacy which preceded the existence of this Government. It is to be found in the provision of the ordinance of 1787. Its effect was to exclude the South entirely from that vast and fertile region which lies between the Ohio and the Mississippi rivers, now embracing five States and one territory. The next of the series is the Missouri compromise, which excluded the South from that large portion of Louisiana which lies north of 36° 30', excepting what is included in the State of Missouri. The last of the series excluded the South from the whole of the Oregon Territory. All these, in the slang of the day, were what are called slave territories, and not free soil; that is, territories belonging to slaveholding powers and open to the emigration of masters with their slaves. By these several acts, the South was excluded from 1,238,025 square miles—an extent of country considerably exceeding the entire valley of the Mississippi. To the South was left the portion of the Territory of Louisiana lying south of 36° 30', and the portion north of it included in the State of Missouri, with the portion lying south of 36° 30', including the States of Louisiana and Arkansas, and the territory lying west of the latter, and south of 36° 30', called the Indian country. These, with the Territory of Florida, now the State, make, in the whole, 283,503 square miles. To this must be added the territory acquired with Texas. If the whole should be added to the Southern section, it would make an increase of 325,520, which would make the whole left to the South, 609,023. But a large part of Texas is still in contest between the two sections, which leaves it uncertain what will be the real extent of the portion of territory that may be left to the South.

I have not included the territory recently acquired by the treaty with Mexico. The North is making the most strenuous efforts to appropriate the whole to herself, by excluding the South from every foot of it. If she should succeed, it will add to that from which the South has already been excluded 526,078 square miles, and would increase the whole which the North has appropriated to herself, to 1,764,023, not including the portion that she may succeed in excluding us from in Texas. To sum up the whole, the United States, since they declared their independence, have acquired 2,373,046 square miles of territory, from which the North will have excluded the South, if she should succeed in monopolizing the newly acquired territories, about three-fourths of the whole, leaving to the South but one-fourth.

Such is the first and great cause that has destroyed the equilibrium between the two sections in the Government.

The next is the system of revenue and disbursements which has been adopted by the Government. It is well known that the Government has derived its revenue mainly from duties on imports. I shall not undertake to show that such duties must necessarily fall mainly on the exporting States, and that the South, as the great exporting portion of the Union, has in reality paid vastly more than her due proportion of the revenue; because I deem it unnecessary, as the subject has on so many occasions been fully discussed. Nor shall I, for the same reason, undertake to show that a far greater portion of the revenue has been disbursed at the North, than its due share; and that the joint effect of these causes has been, to transfer a vast amount from South to North, which, under an equal system of revenue and disbursements, would not have been lost to her. If to this be added, that many of the duties were imposed, not for revenue, but for protection,—that is, intended to put money, not in the treasury, but directly into the pocket of the manufacturers,—some conception may be formed of the immense amount which, in the long course of sixty years, has been transferred from South to North. There are no data by which it can be estimated with any certainty; but it is safe to say, that it amounts to hundreds of millions of dollars. Under the most moderate estimate, it would be sufficient to add greatly to the wealth of the North, and thus greatly increase her population by attracting emigration from all quarters to that section.

This, combined with the great primary cause, amply explains why the North has acquired a preponderance in every department of the Government by its disproportionate increase of population and States. The former, as has been shown, has increased, in fifty years, 2,400,000 over that of the South. This increase of population, during so long a period, is satisfactorily accounted for, by the number of emigrants, and the increase of their descendants, which have been attracted to the Northern section from Europe and the South, in consequence of the advantages derived from the causes assigned. If they had not existed—if the South had retained all the capital which has been extracted from her by the fiscal action of the Government; and, if it had not been excluded by the ordinance of 1787 and the Missouri compromise, from the region lying between the Ohio and the Mississippi rivers, and between the Mississippi and the Rocky Mountains north of 36° 30'—it scarcely admits of a doubt, that it would have divided the emigration with the North, and by retaining her own people, would have at least equalled the North in population under the census of 1840, and probably under that about to be taken. She would also, if she had retained her equal rights in those territories, have maintained an equality in the number of States with the North, and have preserved the equilibrium between the two sections that existed at the commencement of the Government. The loss, then, of the equilibrium is to be attributed to the action of this Government.

But while these measures were destroying the equilibrium between the two sections, the action of the Government was leading to a radical change in its character, by concentrating all the power of the system in itself. The occasion will not permit me to trace the measures by which this great change has been consumated. If it did, it would not be difficult to show that the process commenced at an early period of the Government; and that it proceeded, almost without interruption, step by step, until it absorbed virtually its entire powers; but without going through the whole process to establish the fact, it may be done satisfactorily by a very short statement.

That the Government claims, and practically maintains the right to decide in the last resort, as to the extent of its powers, will scarcely be denied by any one conversant with the political history of the country. That it also claims the right to resort to force to maintain whatever power it claims, against all opposition is equally certain. Indeed it is apparent, from what we daily hear, that this has become the prevailing and fixed opinion of a great majority of the community. Now, I ask, what limitation can possibly be placed upon the powers of a government claiming and exercising such rights? And, if none can be, how can the separate governments of the States maintain and protect the powers reserved to them by the constitution—or the people of the several States maintain those which are reserved to them, and among others, the sovereign powers by which they ordained and established, not only their separate State Constitutions and Governments, but also the Constitution and Government of the United States? But, if they have no constitutional means of maintaining them against the right claimed by this Government, it necessarily follows, that they hold them at its pleasure and discretion, and that all the powers of the system are in reality concentrated in it. It also follows, that the character of the Government has been changed in consequence, from a federal republic, as it originally came from the hands of its framers, into a great national consolidated democracy. It has indeed, at present, all the characteristics of the latter, and not one of the former, although it still retains its outward form.

The result of the whole of these causes combined is—that the North has acquired a decided ascendency over every department of this Government, and through it a control over all the powers of the system. A single section governed by the will of the numerical majority, has now, in fact, the control of the Government and the entire powers of the system. What was once a constitutional federal republic, is now converted, in reality, into one as absolute as that of the Autocrat of Russia, and as despotic in its tendency as any absolute government that ever existed.

As, then, the North has the absolute control over the Government, it is manifest, that on all questions between it and the South, where there is a diversity of interests, the interest of the latter will be sacrificed to the former, however oppressive the effects may be; as the South possesses no means by which it can resist, through the action of the Government. But if there was no question of vital importance to the South, in reference to which there was a diversity of views between the two sections, this state of things might be endured, without the hazard of destruction to the South. But such is not the fact. There is a question of vital importance to the Southern section, in reference to which the views and feelings of the two sections are as opposite and hostile as they can possibly be.

I refer to the relation between the two races in the Southern section, which constitutes a vital portion of her social organization. Every portion of the North entertains views and feelings more or less hostile to it. Those most opposed and hostile, regard it as a sin, and consider themselves under the most sacred obligation to use every effort to destroy it. Indeed, to the extent that they conceive that they have power, they regard themselves as implicated in the sin, and responsible for not suppressing it by the use of all and every means. Those less opposed and hostile, regard it as a crime—an offence against humanity, as they call it; and although not so fanatical, feel themselves bound to use all efforts to effect the same object; while those who are least opposed and hostile, regard it as a blot and a stain on the character of what they call the Nation, and feel themselves accordingly bound to give it no countenance or support. On the contrary, the Southern section regards the relation as one which cannot be destroyed without subjecting the two races to the greatest calamity, and the section to poverty, desolation, and wretchedness; and accordingly they feel bound, by every consideration of interest and safety, to defend it.

This hostile feeling on the part of the North towards the social organization of the South long lay dormant, but it only required some cause to act on those who felt most intensely that they were responsible for its continuance, to call it into action. The increasing power of this Government, and of the control of the Northern section over all its departments, furnished the cause. It was this which made an impression on the minds of many, that there was little or no restraint to prevent the Government from doing whatever it might choose to do. This was sufficient of itself to put the most fanatical portion of the North in action, for the purpose of destroying the existing relation between the two races in the South.

The first organized movement towards it commenced in 1835. Then, for the first time, societies were organized, presses established, lecturers sent forth to excite the people of the North, and incendiary publications scattered over the whole South, through the mail. The South was thoroughly aroused. Meetings were held everywhere, and resolutions adopted, calling upon the North to apply a remedy to arrest the threatened evil, and pledging themselves to adopt measures for their own protection, if it was not arrested. At the meeting of Congress, petitions poured in from the North, calling upon Congress to abolish slavery in the District of Columbia, and to prohibit, what they called, the internal slave trade between the States—announcing at the same time, that their ultimate object was to abolish slavery, not only in the District, but in the States and throughout the Union. At this period, the number engaged in the agitation was small, and possessed little or no personal influence.

Neither party in Congress had, at that time, any sympathy with them or their cause. The members of each party presented their petitions with great reluctance. Nevertheless, small and contemptible as the party then was, both of the great parties of the North dreaded them. They felt, that though small, they were organized in reference to a subject which had a great and a commanding influence over the Northern mind. Each party, on that account, feared to oppose their petitions, lest the opposite party should take advantage of the one who might do so, by favoring them. The effect was, that both united in insisting that the petitions should be received, and that Congress should take jurisdiction over the subject. To justify their course, they took the extraordinary ground, that Congress was bound to receive petitions on every subject, however objectionable they might be, and whether they had, or had not, jurisdiction over the subject. These views prevailed in the House of Representatives, and partially in the Senate; and thus the party succeeded in their first movements, in gaining what they proposed—a position in Congress from which agitation could be extended over the whole Union. This was the commencement of the agitation, which has ever since continued, and which, as is now acknowledged, has endangered the Union itself.

As for myself, I believe at that early period, if the party who got up the petitions should succeed in getting Congress to take jurisdiction, that agitation would follow, and that it would in the end, if not arrested, destroy the Union. I then so expressed myself in debate, and called upon both parties to take grounds against assuming jurisdiction; but in vain. Had my voice been heeded, and had Congress refused to take jurisdiction, by the united votes of all parties, the agitation which followed would have been prevented, and the fanatical zeal that gives impulse to the agitation, and which has brought us to our present perilous condition, would have become extinguished, from the want of fuel to feed the flame. *That* was the time for the North to have shown her devotion to the Union; but, unfortunately, both of the great parties of that section were so intent on obtaining or retaining party ascendancy, that all other considerations were overlooked or forgotten.

What has since followed are but natural consequences. With the success of their first movement, this small fanatical party began to acquire strength; and with that, to become an object of courtship to both the great parties. The necessary consequence was a further increase of power, and a gradual tainting of the opinions of both of the other parties with their doctrines, until the infection has extended over both; and the great mass of the population of the North, who, whatever may be their opinion of the original abolition party, which still preserves its distinctive organization, hardly ever fail, when it comes to acting, to co-operate in carrying out their measures. With the increase of their influence, they extended the sphere of their action. In a short time after the commencement of their first movement, they had acquired sufficient influence to induce the legislatures of most of the Northern States to pass acts, which in effect abrogated the clause of the constitution that provides for the delivery up of fugitive slaves. Not long after, petitions followed to abolish slavery in forts, magazines, and dockyards, and all other places where Congress had exclusive power of legislation. This was followed by petitions and resolutions of legislatures of the Northern States from all territories acquired, or to be acquired, and to prevent the admission of any State hereafter into the Union, which, by its constitution, does not prohibit slavery. And Congress is invoked to do all this, expressly with the view to the final abolition of slavery in the States. That has been avowed to be the ultimate object from the beginning of the agitation until the present time; and yet the great body of both parties of the North, with the full knowledge of the fact, although disavowing the abolitionists, have co-operated with them in almost all their measures.

Such is a brief history of the agitation, as far as it has yet advanced. Now I ask, Senators, what is there to prevent its further progress, until it fulfils the ultimate end proposed, unless some decisive measure should be adopted to prevent it? Has any one of the causes, which has added to its increase from its original small and contemptible beginning until it has attained its present magnitude, diminished in force? Is the original cause of the movement—that slavery is a sin, and ought to be suppressed—weaker now than at the commencement? Or is the abolition party less numerous or influential, or have they less influence with, or control over the two great parties of the North in elections? Or has the South greater means of influencing or controlling the movements of this Government now, than it had when the agitation commenced? To all these questions but one answer can be given: No—no—no. The very reverse is true. Instead of being weaker, all the elements in favor of agitation are stronger now than they were in 1835, when it first commenced, while all the elements of influence on the part of the South are weaker. Unless something decisive is done, I again ask, what is to stop this agitation, before the great and final object at which it aims—the abolition of slavery in the States—is consummated? Is it, then, not certain, that if something is not done to arrest it, the South will be forced to choose between abolition and secession? Indeed, as events are now moving, it will not require the South to secede, in order to dissolve the Union. Agitation will of itself effect it, of which its past history furnishes abundant proof—as I shall next proceed to show.

It is a great mistake to suppose that disunion can be effected with a single blow. The cords which bound these States together in one common Union, are far too numerous and powerful for that. Disunion must be the work of time. It is only through a long process, and successively, that the cords can be snapped, until the whole fabric falls asunder. Already the agitation of the slavery question has snapped some of the most important, and has greatly weakened all the others, as I shall proceed to show.

The cords that bind the States together are not only many, but various in character. Some are spiritual or ecclesiastical; some political; others social. Some appertain to the benefit conferred by the Union, and others to the feeling of duty and obligation.

The strongest of those of a spiritual and ecclesiastical nature, consisted in the unity of the great religious denominations, all of which originally embraced the whole Union. All these denominations, with the exception, perhaps, of the Catholics, were organized very much upon the principle of political institutions. Beginning with smaller meetings, corresponding with the political divisions of the country, their organization terminated in one great central assemblage, corresponding very much with the character of

Congress. At these meetings the principle clergymen and lay members of the respective denominations, from all parts of the Union, met to transact business relating to their common concerns. It was not confined to what appertained to the doctrines and discipline of the respective denominations, but extended to plans for disseminating the Bible—establishing missions, distributing tracts—and of establishing presses for the publication of tracts, newspapers, and periodicals, with a view of diffusing religious information—and for the support of their respective doctrines and creeds. All this combined contributed greatly to strengthen the bonds of the Union. The ties which held each denomination together formed a strong cord to hold the whole Union together; but, powerful as they were, they have not been able to resist the explosive effect of slavery agitation.

This first of these cords which snapped, under its explosive force, was that of the powerful Methodist Episcopal Church. The numerous and strong ties which held it together, are all broken, and its unity gone. They now form separate churches; and, instead of that feeling of attachment and devotion to the interests of the whole church which was formerly felt, they are now arrayed into two hostile bodies, engaged in litigation about what was formerly their common property.

The next cord that snapped was that of the Baptists—one of the largest and most respectable of the denominations. That of the Presbyterians is not entirely snapped, but some of its strands have given way. That of the Episcopal Church is the only one of the four great Protestant denominations which remains unbroken and entire.

The strongest cord, of a political character, consists of the many and powerful ties that had held together the two great parties which have, with some modifications, existed from the beginning of the Government. They both extended to every portion of the Union, and strongly contributed to hold all its parts together. But this powerful cord has fared no better than the spiritual. It resisted, for a long time, the explosive tendency of the agitation, but has finally snapped under its force—if not entirely, in a great measure. Nor is there one of the remaining cords which has not been greatly weakened. To this extent the Union has already been destroyed by agitation, in the only way it can be, by sundering and weakening the cords which bind it together.

If the agitation goes on, the same force, acting with increased intensity, as has been shown, will finally snap every cord, when nothing will be left to hold the States together except force. But, surely, that can, with no propriety of language, be called a Union, when the only means by which the weaker is held connected with the stronger portion is *force*. It may, indeed, keep them connected; but the connection will partake much more of the character of subjugation, on the part of the weaker to the stronger, than the union of free, independent, and sovereign States, in one confederation, as they stood in the early stages of the Government, and which only is worthy of the sacred name of Union.

Having now, Senators, explained what it is that endangers the Union, and traced it to its cause, and explained its nature and character, the question again recurs—How can the Union be saved? To this I answer, there is but one way by which it can be—and that is—by adopting such measures as will satisfy the States belonging to the Southern section, that they can remain in the Union consistently with their honor and their safety. There is, again, only one way by which this can be effected, and that is—by removing the causes by which this belief has been produced. Do this, and discontent will cease— harmony and kind feelings between the sections be restored—and every apprehension of danger to the Union removed. The question, then, is—How can this be done? But, before I undertake to answer this question, I propose to show by what the Union cannot be saved.

It cannot, then, be saved by eulogies on the Union, however splendid or numerous. The cry of "Union, Union—the glorious Union!" can no more prevent disunion than the cry of "Health, health—glorious health!" on the part of the physician, can save a patient lying dangerously ill. So long as the Union, instead of being regarded as a protector, is regarded in the opposite character, by not much less than a majority of the States, it will be in vain to attempt to conciliate them by pronouncing eulogies on it.

Besides this cry of Union comes commonly from those whom we cannot believe to be sincere. It usually comes from our assailants. But we cannot believe them to be sincere; for, if they loved the Union, they would necessarily be devoted to the constitution. It made the Union,—and to destroy the constitution would be to destroy the Union. But the only reliable and certain evidence of devotion to the constitution is, to abstain, on the one hand, from violating it, and to repel, on the other, all attempts to violate it. It is only by faithfully performing these high duties that the constitution can be preserved, and with it the Union.

But how stands the profession of devotion to the Union by our assailants, when brought to this test? Have they abstained from violating the constitution? Let the many acts passed by the Northern States to set aside and annul the clause of the constitution providing for the delivery up of fugitive slaves answer. I cite this, not that it is the only instance (for there are many others), but because the violation in this particular is too notorious and palpable to be denied. Again: have they stood forth faithfully to repel violations of the constitution? Let their course in reference to the agitation of the slavery question, which was commenced and has been carried on for fifteen years, avowedly for the purpose of abolishing slavery in the States—an object all acknowledged to be unconstitutional—answer. Let them show a single instance, during this long period, in which they have denounced the agitators or their attempts to effect what is admitted to be unconstitutional, or a single measure which they have brought forward for that purpose. How can we, with all these facts before us, believe that they are sincere in their profession of devotion to the Union, or avoid believing their profession is but intended to increase the vigor of their assaults and to weaken the force of our resistance?

Nor can we regard the profession of devotion to the Union, on the part of those who are not our assailants, as sincere, when they pronounce eulogies upon the Union, evidently with the intent of charging us with disunion, without uttering one word of denunciation against our assailants. If friends of the Union, their course should be to unite with us in repelling these assaults, and denouncing the authors as enemies of the Union. Why they avoid this, and pursue the course they do, it is for them to explain.

Nor can the Union be saved by invoking the name of the illustrious Southerner whose mortal remains repose on the western bank of the Potomac. He was one of us—a slaveholder and a planter. We have studied his history, and find nothing in it to justify submission to wrong. On the contrary, his great fame rests on the solid foundation, that, while he was careful to avoid doing wrong to others, he was prompt and decided in repelling wrong. I trust that, in this respect, we profited by his example.

Nor can we find any thing in history to deter us from seceding from the Union, should it fail to fulfil the objects for which it was instituted, by being permanently and hopelessly converted into the means of oppressing instead of protecting us. On the contrary, we find much in his example to encourage us, should we be forced to the extremity of deciding between submission and disunion.

There existed then, as well as now, a union—that between the parent country and her then colonies. It was a union that had much to endear it to the people of the colonies. Under its protecting and superintending care, the colonies were planted and grew up and prospered, through a long course of years, until they became populous and wealthy. Its benefits were not limited to them. Their extensive agricultural and other productions, gave birth to a flourishing commerce, which richly rewarded the parent country for the trouble and expense of establishing and protecting them. Washington was born and grew up to manhood under that union. He acquired his early distinction in its service, and there is every reason to believe that he was devotedly attached to it. But his devotion was a rational one. He was attached to it, not as an end, but as a means to an end. When it failed to fulfil its end, and, instead of affording protection, was converted into the means of oppressing the colonies, he did not hesitate to draw his sword, and head the great movement by which that union was for ever severed, and the independence of these States established. This was the great and crowning glory of his life, which has spread his fame over the whole globe, and will transmit it to the latest posterity.

Nor can the plan proposed by the distinguished Senator from Kentucky, nor that of the administration, save the Union. I shall pass by, without remark, the plan proposed by the Senator, and proceed directly to the consideration of that of the administration. I however assure the distinguished and able Senator, that, in taking this course, no disrespect whatever is intended to him or his plan. I have adopted it, because so many Senators of distinguished abilities, who were present when he delivered his speech, and explained his plan, and who were fully capable to do justice to the side they support, have replied to him.

The plan of the administration cannot save the Union, because it can have no effect whatever, towards satisfying the States composing the Southern section of the Union, that they can, consistently with safety and honor, remain in the Union. It is, in fact, but a modification of the Wilmot Proviso. It proposes to effect the same object,—to exclude the South from all territory acquired by the Mexican treaty. It is well known that the South is united against the Wilmot Proviso, and has committed itself by solemn resolutions, to resist, should it be adopted. Its opposition *is not to the name*, but that which it *proposes to effect*. That, the Southern States hold to be unconstitutional, unjust, inconsistent with their equality as members of the common Union, and calculated to destroy irretrievably the equilibrium between the two sections. These objections equally apply to what, for brevity, I will call the Executive Proviso. There is no difference between it and the Wilmot, except in the mode of effecting the object; and in that respect, I must say, that the latter is much the least objectionable. It goes to its object openly, boldly, and distinctly. It claims for Congress unlimited power over the territories and proposes to assert it over the territories, acquired from Mexico, by a positive prohibition of slavery. Not so the Executive Proviso. It takes an indirect course, and in order to elude the Wilmot Proviso, and thereby avoid encountering the united and determined resistance of the South, it denies, by implication, the authority of Congress to legislate for the territories, and claims the right as belonging exclusively to the inhabitants of the territories. But to effect the object of excluding the South, it takes care, in the mean time, to let in emigrants freely from the Northern States and all other quarters, except from the South, which it takes special care to exclude by holding up to them the danger of having their slaves liberated under the Mexican laws. The necessary consequence is to exclude the South from the territory, just as effectually as would the Wilmot Proviso. The only difference in this respect is, that what one proposes to effect directly and openly, the other proposes to effect indirectly and covertly.

But the Executive Proviso is more objectionable that the Wilmot, in another and more important particular. The latter, to effect its object, inflicts a dangerous wound upon the constitution, by depriving the Southern States, as joint partners and owners of the territories, of their rights in them; but it inflicts no greater wound than is absolutely necessary to effect its object. The former, on the contrary, while it inflicts the same wound, inflicts others equally great, and, if possible, greater, as I shall next proceed to explain.

In claiming the right for the inhabitants, instead of Congress, to legislate for the territories, the Executive Proviso assumes that the sovereignty over the territories is vested in the former: or to express it in the language used in a resolution offered by one of the Senators from Texas (General Houston, now absent), they have "the same inherent right of self-government as the people in the states." The assumption is utterly unfounded, unconstitutional, without example, and contrary to the entire practice of the Government, from its commencement to the present time. . . .

Having now shown what cannot save the Union, I return to the question with which I commenced, How can the Union be saved? There is but one way by which it can with any certainty; and that is, by a full and final settlement, on the principle of justice, of all the questions at issue between the two sections. The South asks for justice, simple justice, and less she ought not to take. She has no compromise to offer, but the constitution; and no concession or surrender to make. She has already surrendered so much that she has little left to surrender. Such a settlement would go to the root of the evil, and remove all cause of discontent, by satisfying the South, that she could remain honorably and safely in the Union, and thereby restore the harmony and fraternal feelings between the sections, which existed anterior to the Missouri agitation. Nothing else can, with any certainty, finally and for ever settle the questions at issue, terminate agitation, and save the Union.

But can this be done? Yes, easily; not by the weaker party, for it can of itself do nothing—not even protect itself—but by the stronger. The North has only to will it to accomplish it—to do justice by conceding to the South an equal right in the acquired territory, and to do her duty by causing the stipulations relative to fugitive slaves to be faithfully fulfilled—to cease the agitation of the slave question, and to provide for the insertion of a provision in the constitution, by an amendment, which will restore to the South, in substance, the power she possessed of protecting herself, before the equilibrium between the sections was destroyed by the action of this Government. There will be no difficulty in devising such a provision—one that will protect the South, and which, at the same time, will improve and strengthen the Government, instead of impairing and weakening it.

But will the North agree to this? It is for her to answer the question. But, I will say, she cannot refuse, if she has half the love of the Union which she professes to have, or without justly exposing herself to the charge that her love of power and aggrandizement is far greater than her love of the Union. At all events, the responsibility of saving the Union rests on the North, and not on the South. The South cannot save it by any act of hers, and the North may save it without any sacrifice, whatever, unless to do justice, and to perform her duties under the constitution, should be be regarded by her as a sacrifice.

It is time, Senators, that there should be an open and manly avowal on all sides, as to what is intended to be done. If the question is not now settled, it is uncertain whether it ever can hereafter be; and we, as the representatives of the States of this Union, regarded as governments, should come to a distinct understanding as to our respective views, in order to ascertain whether the great questions at issue can be settled or not. If you, who represent the stronger portion, cannot agree to settle them on the broad principle of justice and duty, say so; and let the States we both represent agree to separate and part in peace. If you are unwilling we should part in peace, tell us so; and we shall know what to do, when you reduce the question to submission or resistance. If you remain silent, you will compel us to infer by your acts what you intend. In that case, California will become the test question. If you admit her, under all the difficulties that oppose her admission, you compel us to infer that you intend to exclude us from the whole of the acquired territories, with the intention of destroying, irretrievably, the equilibrium between the two sections. We would be blind not to perceive in that case, that your real objects are power and aggrandizement, and infatuated not to act accordingly.

I have now, Senators, done my duty in expressing my opinions fully, freely, and candidly, on this solemn occasion. In doing so, I have been governed by the motives which have governed me in all the stages of the agitation of the slavery question since its commencement. I have exerted myself, during the whole period, to arrest it, with the intention of saving the Union, if it could be done; and if it could not, to save the section where it has pleased Providence to cast my lot, and which I sincerely believe has justice and the constitution on its side. Having faithfully done my duty to the best of my ability, both to the Union and my section, throughout this agitation, I shall have the consolation, let what will come, that I am free from all responsibility.

1850

HENRY CLAY

(1777–1852)

Henry Clay came to the United States Senate in 1806, having migrated from Virginia, the state of his birth, to Kentucky. He asserted a nationalistic attitude by urging the creation of a strong navy and militia so

The standard text is *The Works of Henry Clay*, 10 vols., ed. Calvin Colton, 1904. A biography is G. G. Van Deusen, *The Life of Henry Clay*, 1937. Recent studies are Bernard Mayo, *Henry Clay, Spokesman of the New West*, 1937, and Carl Schurz, Henry Clay, 1968.

the country could wage the War of 1812 and thus finally declare its independence from English domination.

Much of Clay's middle career was spent in an attempt to create a balanced economy for America in what he called "The American System." He tried to mediate between those who wanted the National Bank and those who defended Jackson, between the commercial interests represented by Webster and the agrarianism championed by Calhoun. After his pursuit of the presidency had failed, Clay returned to the Senate in his old age and assumed his characteristic role of pacificator, attempting to persuade Americans that the only sensible course of action was the preservation of the Union. But, by the time Clay was making his compromise proposals, sectional antagonism had grown too great and the country was traveling inexorably toward Civil War.

Clay's Resolutions
January 29, 1850

(U. S. SENATE JOURNAL,
31st CONGRESS, 1st SESSION, P. 118FF.)

It being desirable, for the peace, concord, and harmony of the Union of these States, to settle and adjust amicably all existing questions of controversy between them arising out of the institution of slavery upon a fair, equitable and just basis: therefore,

1. *Resolved*, That California, with suitable boundaries, ought, upon her application to be admitted as one of the States of this Union, without the imposition by Congress of any restriction in respect to the exclusion or introduction of slavery within those boundaries.

2. *Resolved*, That as slavery does not exist by law, and is not likely to be introduced into any of the territory acquired by the United States from the republic of Mexico, it is inexpedient for Congress to provide by law either for its introduction into, or exclusion from, any part of the said territory; and that appropriate territorial governments ought to be established by Congress in all of the said territory, not assigned as the boundaries of the proposed State of California, without the adoption of any restriction or condition on the subject of slavery.

3. *Resolved*, That the western boundary of the State of Texas ought to be fixed on the Rio del Norte, commencing one marine league from its mouth, and running up that river to the southern line of New Mexico; thence with that line eastwardly, and so continuing in the same direction to the line as established between the United States and Spain, excluding any portion of New Mexico, whether lying on the east or west of that river.

4. *Resolved,* That it be proposed to the State of Texas, that the United States will provide for the payment of all that portion of the legitimate and bona fide public debt of that State contracted prior to its annexation to the United States, and for which the duties on foreign imports were pledged by the said State to its creditors, not exceeding the sum of——dollars, in consideration of the said duties so pledged having been no longer applicable to that object after the said annexation, but having thenceforward become payable to the United States; and upon the condition, also, that the said State of Texas shall, by some solemn authentic act of her legislature or of a convention, relinquish to the United States any claim which it has to any part of New Mexico.

5. *Resolved,* That it is inexpedient to abolish slavery in the District of Columbia whilst that institution continues to exist in the State of Maryland, without the consent of that State, without the consent of the people of the District, and without just compensation to the owners of slaves within the District.

6. *But, resolved,* That it is expedient to prohibit, within the District, the slave trade in slaves brought into it from States or places beyond the limits of the District, either to be sold therein as merchandise, or to be transported to other markets without the District of Columbia.

7. *Resolved,* That more effectual provision ought to be made by law, according to the requirement of the constitution, for the restitution and delivery of persons bound to service or labor in any State, who may escape into any other State or Territory in the Union. And,

8. *Resolved,* That Congress has no power to promote or obstruct the trade in slaves between slaveholding States; but that the admission or exclusion of slaves brought from one into another of them, depends exclusively upon their own particular laws.

THE NORTHERN PERSPECTIVE; ABOLITIONISM

The most compelling and dramatic reform movement in the North between 1820 and 1860 was abolitionism. The movement largely took the form of oratory: in sermons by Theodore Parker and Henry Ward Beecher; in public addresses by Wendell Phillips and William Lloyd Garrison; in *cris de couer* by John Brown, and in speeches by writers like Thoreau, which have become part of our literary heritage. In addition to its use as a political weapon, oratory was effective because it appealed to the common man: it was and has remained a form particularly characteristic of a democracy. These speeches are often of transient interest: they tend to be hortatory, moralistic, and judgmental. But few documents reflect so well a major strand in New England thought as the speakers sought to function in the role of the nation's conscience.

WENDELL PHILLIPS

(1811–1884)

Wendell Phillips was an eloquent champion of the black man throughout the pre-Civil War period. His speech, "Murder of Lovejoy," helped to establish his fame and placed him among the great orators of the time as well as among the most influential abolitionists. It was delivered on November 7, 1837, at a meeting in Faneuil Hall, Boston, and was occasioned by the murder of the Reverend Elijah Lovejoy, an abolitionist editor, by a mob in Alton, Illinois. Lovejoy had been trying to protect his printing press from destruction. After the murder, the attorney-general of Massachusetts, James T. Austin, defended the mob and characterized Lovejoy as a fool. Phillips, who was 26 years old, made his first public appearance in delivering this speech.

Phillips' work appears in *Speeches, Lectures, and Letters,* 1969. Louis Filler has collected some of Phillips' most important work in *Wendell Phillips in Civil Rights and Freedom,* 1965. Modern studies include James J. Green, *Wendell Phillips,* 1943; Oscar Sherwin, *Prophet of Liberty, A Biography of Wendell Phillips,* 1945; Irving Bartlett, *Wendell Phillips, Brahmin Radical,* 1961; Lorenzo Sears, *Wendell Phillips,* 1967.

The Murder of Lovejoy

Mr. Chairman:—We have met for the freest discussion of these resolutions, and the events which gave rise to them. I hope I shall be permitted to express my surprise at the sentiments of the last speaker, James Austin [who had come to the defense of the mob that had murdered Lovejoy],—surprise not only at such sentiments from such a man, but at the applause they have received within these walls. A comparison has been drawn between the events of the Revolution and the tragedy at Alton. We have heard it asserted here, in Faneuil Hall, that Great Britain had a right to tax the Colonies, and we have heard the mob at Alton, the drunken murderers of Lovejoy, compared to those patriot fathers who threw the tea overboard! Fellow-citizens, is this Faneuil Hall Doctrine? The mob at Alton were met to wrest from a citizen his just rights,—met to resist the laws. We have been told that our fathers did the same; and the glorious mantle of Revolutionary precedent has been thrown over the mobs of our day. . . . To draw the conduct of our ancestors into a precedent for mobs, for a right to resist laws we ourselves have enacted, is an insult to their memory. The difference between the excitements of those days and our own, which the gentleman in kindness to the latter has overlooked, is simply this: the men of that day went for the right, as secured by the laws. They were the people rising to sustain the laws and constitution of the Province. The rioters of our day go for their own wills, right or wrong. Sir, when I heard the gentleman lay down principles which place the murderers of Alton side by side with Otis and Hancock, with Quincy and Adams, I thought those pictured lips would have broken into voice to rebuke the recreant American,—the slanderer of the dead. The gentleman said that he should sink into insignificance if he dared to gainsay the principles of these resolutions. Sir, for the sentiments he has uttered, on soil consecrated by the prayers of Puritans and the blood of patriots, the earth should have yawned and swallowed him up. . . .

Throughout that terrible night I find nothing to regret but this, that within the limits of our country, civil authority should have been so prostrated as to oblige a citizen to arm in his own defense, and to arm in vain. The gentleman says Lovejoy was presumptuous and imprudent,—he "died as the fool dieth." And a reverend clergyman of the city tells us that no citizen has a right to publish opinions disagreeable to the community! If any mob follows such publication, on *him* rests its guilt! He must wait, forsooth, till the people come up to it and agree with him! This libel on liberty goes on to say that the want of right to speak as we think is an evil inseparable from republican institutions! If this be so, what are they worth? Welcome the despotism of the Sultan, where one knows what he may publish and what he may not, rather than the tyranny of this many-headed monster, the mob, where we know not what we may do or say, till some fellow-citizen has tried it, and paid for the lesson with his life. This clerical absurdity chooses as a check for the abuses of the press, not the *law*, but the dread of a mob. By so doing, it deprives not only the individual and the minority of their rights, but the majority also, since the expression of *their* opinion may sometimes provoke disturbance from the minority. A few men may make a mob as well as many. The majority, then, have no right, as Christian men, to utter their sentiments, if by any possibility it may lead to a mob! Shades of Hugh Peters and John Cotton,[1] save us from such pulpits!

---

[1] Hugh Peters (1598-1660), an English Independent divine; John Cotton (1585-1652), English divine, preached in Boston from 1633, and opposed Roger Williams.

Imprudent to defend the liberty of the press! Why? Because the defence was unsuccessful? Does success gild crime into patriotism, and the want of it change heroic self-devotion to imprudence? Was Hampden imprudent when he drew the sword and threw away the scabbard? Yet he, judged by that single hour, was unsuccessful. After a short exile, the race he hated sat again upon the throne.

Imagine yourself present when the first news of Bunker Hill battle reached a New England town. The tale would have run thus: "The patriots are routed,—the redcoats victorious,—Warren lies dead upon the field." With what scorn would that *Tory* have been received who should have charged Warren with *imprudence!* who should have said that, bred a physician, he was "out of place" in that battle, and "died as the *fool dieth*"! How would the intimation have been received that Warren and his associates should have waited a better time? But if success be indeed the only criterion of prudence, *Respice finem,*—wait till the end.

Presumptuous to assert the freedom of the press on American ground! Is the assertion of such freedom before the age? So much before the age as to leave one no right to make it because it displeases the community? Who invents this libel on his country? It is this very thing which entitles Lovejoy to greater praise. The disputed right which provoked the Revolution—taxation without representation—is far beneath that for which he died. One word, gentlemen. As much as *thought* is better than money, so much is the cause in which Lovejoy died nobler than a mere question of taxes. James Otis[2] thundered in this Hall when the King did but touch his *pocket.* Imagine, if you can, his indignant eloquence, had England offered to put a gag upon his lips.

The question that stirred the Revolution touched our civil interests. *This* concerns us not only as citizens, but as immortal beings. Wrapped up in its fate, saved or lost with it, are not only the voice of the statesman, but the instructions of the pulpit, and the progress of our faith.

The clergy "marvellously out of place" where free speech is battled for,—liberty of speech on national sins? Does the gentleman remember that freedom to preach was first gained, dragging in its train freedom to print? I thank the clergy here present, as I reverence their predecessors, who did not so far forget their country in their immediate profession as to deem it duty to separate themselves from the struggle of '76,—the Mayhews and Coopers, who remembered they were citizens before they were clergymen.

Mr. Chairman, from the bottom of my heart I thank that brave little band at Alton for resisting. We must remember that Lovejoy had fled from city to city,—suffered the destruction of three presses patiently. At length he took counsel with friends, men of character, of tried integrity, of wide views, of

[2] James Otis (1725–1783), American revolutionary leader and pamphleteer.

Christian principle. They thought the crisis had come: it was full time to assert the laws. They saw around them, not a community like our own, of fixed habits, of character moulded and settled, but one "in the gristle, not yet hardened into the bone of manhood." The people there, children of our older States, seem to have forgotten the blood-tried principles of their fathers the moment they lost sight of our New England hills. Something was to be done to show them the priceless value of the freedom of the press, to bring back and set right their wandering and confused ideas. He and his advisers looked out on a community staggering like a drunken man, indifferent to their rights and confused in their feelings. Deaf to argument, haply they might be stunned into sobriety. They saw that of which we cannot judge, the *necessity* of resistance. Insulted law called for it. Public opinion, fast hastening on the downward course, must be arrested.

Does not the event show they judged rightly? Absorbed in a thousand trifles, how has the nation all at once come to a stand? Men begin, as in 1776 and 1640, to discuss principles, to weigh characters, to find out where they are. Haply we may awake before we are borne over the precipice.

I am glad, Sir, to see this crowded house. It is good for us to be here. When Liberty is in danger, Faneuil Hall has the right, it is her duty, to strike the key-note for these United States. I am glad, for one reason, that remarks such as those to which I have alluded have been uttered here. The passage of these resolutions, in spite of this opposition, led by the Attorney-General of the Commonwealth, will show more clearly, more decisively, the deep indignation with which Boston regards this outrage.

WILLIAM LLOYD GARRISON

(1805–1879)

In 1831 William Lloyd Garrison established the most famous of the antislavery journals, *The Liberator*. The theme of the newspaper was persistent throughtout the antislavery movement: those who are oppressed in America, and specifically black people, should be freed im-

The *Works* appeared in 1905. For a representative collection of Garrison's work see *Documents of Upheaval, Selections from William Lloyd Garrison's The Liberator, 1831–1865,* ed. Truman Nelson, 1966. Russell B. Nye, *William Lloyd Garrison and the Humanitarian Reformers,* 1955.

Studies include John L. Thomas, *The Liberator, William Lloyd Garrison, A Biography,* 1963; Martin Duberman, *The Anti-Slavery Vanguard: New Essays on the Abolitionists,* 1965; Austin Warren, "William Lloyd Garrison," in *The New England Conscience,* 1967.

mediately. There is a radical, apocalyptic tone to Garrison's writing that assumes a distinctly religious character, effectively captured in the following selection, from the first number of *The Liberator.*

From The Liberator
January 1, 1831

TO THE PUBLIC

In the month of August, I issued proposals for publishing *"The Liberator"* in Washington City; but the enterprise, though hailed in different sections of the country, was palsied by public indifference. Since that time, the removal of the *Genius of Universal Emancipation* to the Seat of Government has rendered less imperious the establishment of a similar periodical in that quarter.

During my recent tour for the purpose of exciting the minds of the people by a series of discourses on the subject of slavery, every place that I visited gave fresh evidence of the fact, that a greater revolution in public sentiment was to be effected in the free states—*and particularly in New England*—than at the south. I found contempt more bitter, opposition more active, detraction more relentless, prejudice more stubborn, and apathy more frozen, than among slave owners themselves. Of course, there were individual exceptions to the contrary. This state of things afflicted, but did not dishearten me. I determined, at every hazard, to lift up the standard of emancipation in the eyes of the nation, *within sight of Bunker Hill and in the birth place of liberty.* That standard is now unfurled; and long may it float, unhurt by the spoliations of time or the missiles of a desperate foe—yea, till every chain be broken, and ever bondman set free! Let Southern oppressors tremble—let their secret abettors tremble—let their Northern apologists tremble—let all the enemies of the persecuted blacks tremble.

I deem the publication of my original Prospectus unnecessary, as it has obtained a wide circulation. The principles therein inculcated will be steadily pursued in this paper, excepting that I shall not array myself as the political partisan of any man. In defending the great cause of human rights, I wish to derive the assistance of all religions and of all parties.

Assenting to the "self evident truth" maintained in the American Declaration of Independence, "that all men are created equal, and endowed by their Creator with certain inalienable rights—among which are life, liberty and the pursuit of happiness," I shall strenuously contend for the immediate enfranchisement of our slave population. In Park-Street Church, on the Fourth of July, 1829, in an address on slavery, I unreflectingly assented to the popular but pernicious doctrine of *gradual* abolition. I seize this opportunity to make a full and unequivocal recantation, and thus publicly to ask pardon of my God, of my country, and of my brethren the poor slaves, for having uttered a sentiment so full of timidity, injustice and absurdity. A similar recantation, from my pen, was published in the *Genius of Universal Emancipation* at Baltimore, in September, 1829. My conscience is now satisfied.

I am aware, that many object to the severity of my language; but is there not cause for severity? I *will be* as harsh as truth, and as uncompromising as justice. On this subject. I do not wish to think, or speak, or write, with moderation. No! No! Tell a man whose house is on fire, to give a moderate alarm; tell him to moderately rescue his wife from the hands of the ravisher; tell the mother to gradually extricate her babe from the fire into which it has fallen;—but urge me not to use moderation in a cause like the present. I am in earnest—I will not equivocate—I will not excuse—I will not retreat a single inch—*AND I WILL BE HEARD*. The apathy of the people is enough to make every statue leap from its pedestal, and to hasten the resurrection of the dead.

It is pretended, that I am retarding the cause of emancipation by the coarseness of my invective, and the precipitancy of my measures. *The charge is not true.* On this question my influence,—humble as it is,—is felt at this moment to a considerable extent, and shall be felt in coming years—not perniciously, but beneficially—not as a curse, but as a blessing; and posterity will bear testimony that I was right. I desire to thank God, that he enables me to disregard "the fear of man which bringeth a snare," and to speak his truth in its simplicity and power. . . .

William Lloyd Garrison.

JOHN GREENLEAF WHITTIER

(1807–1892)

As a muckraking journalist and polemical poet who was bitterly opposed to slavery, Whittier drew on his humanitarian impulses and expressed his faith in the common man. His work appeared in William Lloyd Garrison's *Liberator,* the *Pennsylvania Freeman,* and the *National Era,* where he denounced intemperance, the squalid conditions of prisons, and discrimination against women, American Indians, and Negroes. Although he was aware of all the political and social arguments against these injustices, he based his opposition on religious grounds: slavery was a moral evil, intemperance blurred the reason that God had given to man, woman was man's equal before God. He despised war and feared that the impending conflict between North and South would mean that "Democracy [was] divided against itself"; but his antipathy for slavery was so great that he yielded to the moral necessity of the Civil War as the will of God.

Of all the strictly "literary" figures of the Romantic period, Whittier was the most impassioned opponent of slavery. For 30 years he composed tracts, essays, and poems that called for the liberation of black people. A tract like *Justice and Expediency; or, Slavery Considered with a View to Its Rightful and Effectual Abolition* (1833) sold more than 5000 copies. Too many of Whittier's abolitionist essays and poems have a slanted, moralistic tone, further marred by trite expressions, tired abstractions, and platitudes not present in his nature poetry. One abolitionist poem, however, that reflects Whittier's highmindedness without being unfairly accusatory of Southerners, is "From Massachusetts to Virginia."

Massachusetts to Virginia

The blast from Freedom's Northern hills, upon its Southern way,
Bears greeting to Virginia from Massachusetts Bay:
No word of haughty challenging, nor battle bugle's peal,
Nor steady tread of marching files, nor clang of horsemen's steel,

No trains of deep-mouthed cannon along our highways go;   5
Around our silent arsenals untrodden lies the snow;
And to the land-breeze of our ports, upon their errands far,
A thousand sails of commerce swell, but none are spread for war.

We hear thy threats,Virginia! thy stormy words and high
Swell harshly on the Southern winds which melt along our sky;   10
Yet not one brown, hard hand foregoes its honest labor here,
No hewer of our mountain oaks suspends his axe in fear.

Wild are the waves which lash the reefs along St. George's bank;
Cold on the shores of Labrador the fog lies white and dank;
Through storm, and wave, and blinding mist, stout are the hearts
    which man   15
The fishing-smacks of Marblehead, the sea-boats of Cape Ann.

The cold north light and wintry sun glare on their icy forms,
Bent grimly o'er their straining lines or wrestling with the storms;
Free as the winds they drive before, rough as the waves they roam,
They laugh to scorn the slaver's threat against their rocky home.   20

JOHN GREENLEAF WHITTIER

What means the Old Dominion? Hath she forgot the day
When o'er her conquered valleys swept the Briton's steel array?
How, side by side with sons of hers, the Massachusetts men
Encountered Tarleton's charge of fire, and stout Cornwallis, then?

Forgets she how the Bay State, in answer to the call   25
Of her old House of Burgesses, spoke out from Faneuil Hall?
When, echoing back her Henry's cry,[1] came pulsing on each breath
Or Northern winds the thrilling sounds of "Liberty or Death!"

What asks the Old Dominion? If now her sons have proved
False to their fathers' memory, false to the faith they loved;   30
If she can scoff at Freedom, and its great charter spurn,
Must we of Massachusetts from truth and duty turn?

We hunt your bondmen, flying from Slavery's hateful hell;
Our voices, at your bidding, take up the bloodhound's yell;
We gather, at your summons, above our fathers' graves,   35
From Freedom's holy altar-horns to tear your wretched slaves!

Thank God! not yet so vilely can Massachusetts bow;
The spirit of her early time is with her even now;
Dream not because her Pilgrim blood moves slow and calm and cool,
She thus can stoop her chainless neck, a sister's slave and tool!   40

All that a sister State should do, all that a free State may,
Heart, hand, and purse we proffer, as in our early day;
But that one dark loathsome burden ye must stagger with alone,
And reap the bitter harvest which ye yourselves have sown!

Hold, while ye may, your struggling slaves, and burden God's free air   45
With woman's shriek beneath the lash, and manhood's wild despair;
Cling closer to the "cleaving curse" that writes upon your plains
The blasting of Almighty wrath against a land of chains.

Still shame your gallant ancestry, the cavaliers of old,
By watching round the shambles where human flesh is sold;   50
Gloat o'er the new-born child, and count his market value, when
The maddened mother's cry of woe shall pierce the slaver's den!

Lower than plummet soundeth,[2] sink the Virginia name;
Plant, if ye will, your fathers' graves with rankest weeds of shame;
Be, if ye will, the scandal of God's fair universe;   55
We wash our hands forever of your sin and shame and curse.

---

[1] Patrick Henry (1736-1799), American Revolutionary leader and orator.

[2] Cf. Shakespeare, *The Tempest*, III, 3, 101.

A voice from lips whereon the coal from Freedom's shrine hath been,
Thrilled, as but yesterday, the hearts of Berkshire's mountain men:
The echoes of that solemn voice are sadly lingering still
In all our sunny valleys, on every wind-swept hill.   60

And when the prowling man-thief came hunting for his prey
Beneath the very shadow of Bunker's shaft of gray,
How, through the free lips of the son, the father's warning spoke;
How, from its bonds of trade and sect, the Pilgrim city broke!

A hundred thousand right arms were lifted up on high,   65
A hundred thousand voices sent back their loud reply;
Through the thronged towns of Essex the startling summons rang,
And up from bench and loom and wheel her young mechanics
    sprang!

The voice of free, broad Middlesex, of thousands as of one,
The shaft of Bunker calling to that of Lexington;   70
From Norfolk's ancient villages, from Plymouth's rocky bound
To where Nantucket feels the arms of ocean close her round;

From rich and rural Worcester, where through the calm repose
Of cultured vales and fringing woods the gentle Nashua flows,
To where Wachuset's wintry blasts the mountain larches stir,   75
Swelled up to Heaven the thrilling cry of "God save Latimer!"

And sandy Barnstable rose up, wet with the salt sea spray;
And Bristol sent her answering shout down Narragansett Bay!
Along the broad Connecticut old Hampden felt the thrill,
And the cheer of Hampshire's woodmen swept down from Holyoke
    Hill.   80

The voice of Massachusetts! Of her free sons and daughters,
Deep calling unto deep aloud, the sound of many waters![3]
Against the burden of that voice what tyrant power shall stand?
No fetters in the Bay State! No slave upon her land!

Look to it well, Virginians! In calmness we have borne,   85
In answer to our faith and trust, your insult and your scorn;
You've spurned our kindest counsels; you've hunted for our lives:
And shaken round our hearths and homes your manacles and gyves!

We wage no war, we lift no arm, we fling no torch within
The fire-damps of the quaking mine beneath your soil of sin;   90
We leave ye with your bondmen, to wrestle, while ye can,
With the strong upward tendencies and god-like soul of man!

[3] Cf. Psalms xlii: 7: Ezekiel xliii:2.

But for us and for our children, the vow which we have given
For freedom and humanity is registered in heaven;
No slave-hunt in our borders,—no pirate on our strand!   95
No fetters in the Bay State,—no slave upon our land!

1843

FREDERICK DOUGLASS

(1817–1895)

Frederick Douglass was the most distinguished black orator and writer in nineteenth-century America. As an abolitionist, he delivered many antislavery addresses and, through his awesome stage manner, acquired a reputation as an "African Prince." In 1847 Douglass broke with William Lloyd Garrison and began his own career in journalism and literature.

The standard text of the autobiography is *My Life and Times of Frederick Douglass,* revised and enlarged from *My Bondage and My Freedom,* 1892, 1941, 1962. *Narrative of the Life of Frederick Douglass* has been edited by Benjamin Quarles from the 1845 *Narrative,* 1960.

An early biography is Charles W. Chesnutt, *Frederick Douglass,* 1899. Recent studies include Shirley Graham, *There Was Once a Slave: The Heroic Story of Frederick Douglass,* 1947; Benjamin Quarles, *Frederick Douglass,* 1948; Philip S. Foner, *Frederick Douglass, A Biography,* 1964; Arna W. Bontemps, *Free at Last,* 1971.

What to the Slave Is the Fourth of July?

EXTRACT FROM AN ORATION, AT ROCHESTER, JULY 5, 1852

Fellow-Citizens—Pardon me, and allow me to ask, why am I called upon to speak here to-day? What have I, or those I represent, to do with your national independence? Are the great principles of political freedom and of natural justice, embodied in that, Declaration of Independence extended to us? and am I, therefore, called upon to bring our humble offering to the national altar, and to confess the benefits, and express devout gratitude for the blessings, resulting from your independence to us?

Daguerreotype, about 1855, of Frederick Douglass. *(The Granger Collection.)*

Would to God, both for your sakes and ours, that an affirmative answer could be truthfully returned to these questions! Then would my task be light, and my burden easy and delightful. For who is there so cold that a nation's sympathy could not warm him? Who so obdurate and dead to the claims of gratitude, that would not thankfully acknowledge such priceless benefits? Who so stolid and selfish, that would not give his voice to swell the hallelujahs of a nation's jubilee, when the chains of servitude had been torn from his limbs? I am not that man. In a case like that, the dumb might eloquently speak, and the "lame man leap as an hart."

But, such is not the state of the case. I say it with a sad sense of the disparity between us. I am not included within the pale of this glorious anniversary! Your high independence only reveals the immeasurable distance between us. The blessings in which you this day rejoice, are not enjoyed in common. The rich inheritance of justice, liberty, prosperity, and independence, bequeathed by your fathers, is shared by you, not by me. The sunlight that brought life and healing to you, has brought stripes and death to me. This Fourth of July is *yours*, not *mine*. *You* may rejoice, *I* must mourn. To drag a man in fetters into the grand illuminated temple of liberty, and call upon him to join you in joyous anthems, were inhuman mockery and sacrilegious irony. Do you mean, citizens, to mock me, by asking me to speak to-day? If so, there is a parallel to your conduct. And let me warn you that it is dangerous to copy the example of a nation whose crimes, towering up to heaven, were thrown down by the breath of the Almighty, burying that nation in irrecoverable ruin! I can to-day take up the plaintive lament of a peeled and woe-smitten people.

"By the rivers of Babylon, there we sat down. Yea! we wept when we remembered Zion.[1] We hanged our harps upon the willows in the midst thereof. For there, they that carried us away captive, required of us a song; and they who wasted us required of us mirth, saying, Sing us one of the songs of Zion. How can we sing the Lord's song in a strange land? If I forget thee, O Jerusalem, let my right hand forget her cunning. If I do not remember thee, let my tongue cleave to the roof of my mouth."

Fellow-citizens, above your national, tumultuous joy, I hear the mournful wail of millions, whose chains, heavy and grievous yesterday, are to-day rendered more intolerable by the jubilant shouts that reach them. If I do forget, if I do not faithfully remember those bleeding children of sorrow this day, "may my right hand forget her cunning, and may my tongue cleave to the roof of my mouth!" To forget them, to pass lightly over their wrongs, and to chime in with the popular theme, would be treason most scandalous and shocking, and would make me a reproach before God and the world. My

---

[1] Babylon, the capital of ancient Babylonia, is the term used for any place of captivity or exile. Zion, the Jewish homeland, is a term often used to describe an idealized harmonious community. The quotation is from Psalms CXXXVII, 1-6.

subject, then, fellow-citizen, is AMERICAN SLAVERY. I shall see this day and its popular characteristics from the slave's point of view. Standing there, identified with the American bondman, making his wrongs mine, I do not hesitate to declare, with all my soul, that the character and conduct of this nation never looked blacker to me than on this Fourth of July. Whether we turn to the declarations of the past, or to the professions of the present, the conduct of the nation seems equally hideous and revolting. America is false to the past, false to the present, and solemnly binds herself to be false to the future. Standing with God and the crushed and bleeding slave on this occasion, I will, in the name of the constitution and the bible, which are disregarded and trampled upon, dare to call in question and to denounce, with all the emphasis I can command, everything that serves to perpetuate slavery—the great sin and shame of America! "I will not equivocate; I will not excuse;" I will use the severest language I can command; and yet not one word shall escape me that any man, whose judgment is not blinded by prejudice, or who is not at heart a slaveholder, shall not confess to be right and just.

But I fancy I hear some one of my audience say, it is just in this circumstance that you and your brother abolitionists fail to make a favorable impression on the public mind. Would you argue more, and denounce less, would you persuade more and rebuke less, your cause would be much more likely to succeed. But, I submit, where all is plain there is nothing to be argued. What point in the anti-slavery creed would you have me argue? On what branch of the subject of the people of this country need light? Must I undertake to prove that the slave is a man? That point is conceded already. Nobody doubts it. The slaveholders themselves acknowledge it in the enactment of laws for their government. They acknowledge it when they punish disobedience on the part of the slave. There are seventy-two crimes in the state of Virginia, which, if committed by a black man (no matter how ignorant he be), subject him to the punishment of death; while only two of these same crimes will subject a white man to the like punishment. What is this but the acknowledgement that the slave is a moral, intellectual, and responsible being. The manhood of the slave is conceded. It is admitted in the fact that southern statute books are covered with enactments forbidding, under severe fines and penalties, the teaching of the slave to read or write. When you can point to any such laws, in reference to the beasts of the field, then I may consent to argue the manhood of the slave. When the dogs in your streets, when the fowls of the air, when the cattle on your hills, when the fish of the sea, and the reptiles that crawl, shall be unable to distinguish the slave from a brute, then will I argue with you that the slave is a man!

For the present, it is enough to affirm the equal manhood of the Negro race. Is it not astonishing that, while we are plowing, planting, and reaping, using all kinds of mechanical tools, erecting houses, constructing bridges, building ships, working in metals of brass, iron, copper, silver, and gold; that, while we are reading, writing, and cyphering, acting as clerks, merchants, and secretaries, having among us lawyers, doctors, ministers, poets, authors, editors, orators, and teachers; that, while we are engaged in all manner of enterprises common to other men—digging gold in California, capturing the whale in the Pacific, feeding sheep and cattle on the hillside, living, moving, acting, thinking, planning, living in families as husbands, wives, and children, and, above all, confessing and worshiping the Christian's God, and looking hopefully for life and immortality beyond the grave—we are called upon that we are men!

Would you have me argue that man is entitled to liberty? that he is the rightful owner of his own body? You have already declared it. Must I argue the wrongfulness of slavery? Is that a question for republicans? Is it to be settled by the rules of logic and argumentation, as a matter beset with great difficulty, involving a doubtful application of the principle of justice, hard to be understood? How should I look to-day in the presence of Americans, dividing and subdividing a discourse, to show that men have a natural right to freedom, speaking of it relatively and positively, negatively and affirmatively? To do so, would be to make myself ridiculous, and to offer an insult to your understanding. There is not a man beneath the canopy of heaven that does not know that slavery is wrong *for him.*

What! am I to argue that it is wrong to make men brutes, to rob them of their liberty, to work them without wages, to keep them ignorant of their relations to their fellow-men, to beat them with sticks, to flay their flesh with the lash, to load their limbs with irons, to hunt them with dogs, to sell them at auction, to sunder their families, to knock out their teeth, to burn their flesh, to starve them into obedience and submission to their masters? Must I argue that a system, thus marked with blood and stained with pollution, is wrong? No; I will not. I have better employment for my time and strength than such arguments would imply.

What, then, remains to be argued? Is it that slavery is not divine; that God did not establish it; that our doctors of divinity are mistaken? There is blasphemy in the thought. That which is inhuman cannot be divine. Who can reason on such a proposition! They that can, may! I cannot. The time for such argument is past.

At a time like this, scorching irony, not convincing argument, is needed. Oh! had I the ability, and could I reach the nation's ear, I would to-day pour out a fiery stream of biting ridicule, blasting reproach, withering sarcasm, and stern rebuke. For it is not light that is needed, but fire; it is not the gentle shower, but thunder. We need the storm, the whirlwind, and the earthquake. The feeling of the nation must be quickened; the conscience of the nation must be roused; the propriety of the nation must be startled; the hypocrisy of the nation must be exposed; and its crimes against God and man must be proclaimed and denounced.

What to the American slave is your Fourth of July? I answer, a day that reveals to him, more than all other days in the year, the gross injustice and cruelty to which he is the constant victim. To him, your celebration is a sham; your boasted liberty, an unholy license; your national greatness, swelling vanity; your sounds of rejoicing are empty and heartless; your denunciations of tyrants, brass-fronted impudence; your shouts of liberty and equality, hollow mockery; your prayers and hymns, your sermons and thanksgivings, with all your religious parade and solemnity, are to him mere bombast, fraud, deception, impiety, and hypocrisy—a thin veil to cover up crimes which would disgrace a nation of savages. There is not a nation on the earth guilty of practices more shocking and bloody, than are the people of these United States, at this very hour.

Go where you may, search where you will, roam through all the monarchies and despotisms of the old world, travel through South America, search out every abuse, and when you have found the last, lay your facts by the side of every-day practices of this nation, and you will say with me, that, for revolting barbarity and shameless hypocrisy, America reigns without a rival.

HARRIET BEECHER STOWE

(1811–1896)

Uncle Tom's Cabin was the most influential indictment of slavery in the history of American fiction. Within a year of its publication the novel had sold 305,000 copies in America and more than 2 million copies in foreign countries. Stage versions were produced long after the Civil War so that the characters were converted into caricatures who represented various conditions of slavery: Uncle Tom as the long-suffering, deeply religious, and essentially passive black man; George, the young black militant; Eliza, the afflicted Negro mother; St. Clare, the benevolent but vapid plantation owner; George Shelby, the liberal Southerner; and Simon Legree, the inhuman plantation owner. *Uncle*

The standard text is *The Writings of Harriet Beecher Stowe*, 16 vols., 1869. Early biographies include Annie Fields, *Life and Letters of Harriet Beecher Stowe*, 1897; C. E. Stowe, *Life of Harriet Beecher Stowe*, 1889; K. N. and C. E. Stowe, *Harriet Beecher Stowe*, 1911, and Catherine Gilberison, *Harriet Beecher Stowe*, 1937. Recent studies are Forrest Wilson, *Crusader in Crinoline: The Life of Harriet Beecher Stowe*, 1941; Charles H. Forten,

The Rungless Ladder; Harriet Beecher Stowe and New England Puritanism, 1959; John R. Adams, *Harriet Beecher Stowe*, 1963; Edward C. Wagenknecht, *Harriet Beecher Stowe: The Known and the Unknown,* 1965; Alice C. Crozier, *The Novels of Harriet Beecher Stowe*, 1969. An important essay is James Baldwin, "Everybody's Protest Novel," *Partisan Review,* 16 (1949), reprinted in *Notes of a Native Son,* 1955.

Harriet Beecher Stowe, *(The Metropolitan Museum of Art.)*

Tom's Cabin is a deeply religious book—which, as Harriet Beecher Stowe said, came to her "in visions, one after the other"—and its moral passion carries the reader along, even when he knows that the plot and style of the book seem preposterously sentimental.

Harriet Beecher Stowe had grown up in a religious New England family. Her father, Lyman Beecher, was a famous Presbyterian preacher; one of her brothers was Henry Ward Beecher, a well-known minister from Brooklyn; and her husband, Calvin Stowe, was also a minister and scholar. The couple had an austere and penurious life together, but their religious faith gave them a strength in the midst of adversity—these forces found their way into *Uncle Tom's Cabin*. Fiction itself was of little interest to Harriet Beecher Stowe; her literary sensibility was formed by the sermon, and her famous novel is really a kind of fictionalized sermon. Its central subject, and the subject of all her work, as Edmund Wilson has pointed out, is the crisis in Calvinist theology. The Beecher family in which she was raised and the Stowe family into which she married were steeped in the Calvinist faith, but it was a faith that was crumbling. Mrs. Stowe herself was concerned that the spirit of Jesus was absent from the practice of Calvinism, and she created *Uncle Tom's Cabin* as a kind of morality drama, in which the characters assume mythical proportions.

It may be true, as James Baldwin pointed out 100 years later, that *Uncle Tom's Cabin* "is a very bad novel, having in its self-righteous, virtuous sentimentality, much in common with *Little Women*"; it is also true that *Uncle Tom's Cabin* "is a catalogue of violence . . . [a book] not intended to do anything more than prove that slavery was wrong"; and, finally, there is indeed a similarity between novels of social protest like *Uncle Tom's Cabin* and *Native Son,* a "categorization" of character instead of a real attempt to explore its "beauty, dread, power." Baldwin's essay, "Everybody's Protest Novel," should be read as a contemporary revulsion against the protest novel, whether in the hands of a white or black author. But, as he recognizes, this tradition has been strong in American letters and particularly in the work of black authors. The seminal novel in that tradition is *Uncle Tom's Cabin,* and it should be read in the context of the literature, the songs, and the pamphlets that precede the Civil War. When seen together with works as various as Thoreau's "Slavery in Massachusetts" or Julia Ward Howe's "Battle Hymn of the Republic," it is revealed as a central document of American civilization.

From Uncle Tom's Cabin

CHAPTER XL
THE MARTYR

"Deem not the just by Heaven forgot!
  Though life its common gifts deny,—
Thou, with a crushed and bleeding heart,
  And spurned of man, he goes to die!
For God hath marked each sorrowing day,
  And numbered every bitter tear;
And heaven's long years of bliss shall pay
  For all his children suffer here."

—Bryant.

The longest day must have its close,—the gloomiest night will wear on to a morning. An eternal, inexorable lapse of moments is ever hurrying the day of the evil to an eternal night, and the night of the just to an eternal day. We have walked with our humble friend thus far in the valley of slavery; first through flowery fields of ease and indulgence, then through heart-breaking separations from all that man holds dear. Again, we have waited with him in a sunny island, where generous hands concealed his chains with flowers; and, lastly, we have followed him when the last ray of earthly hope went out in night, and seen how, in the blackness of earthly darkness, the firmament of the unseen has blazed with stars of new and significant lustre.

The morning star now stands over the tops of the mountains, and gales and breezes, not of earth, show that the gates of day are unclosing.

The escape of Cassy and Emmeline irritated the before surly temper of Legree to the last degree; and his fury, as was to be expected, fell upon the defenceless head of Tom. When he hurriedly announced the tidings among his hands, there was a sudden light in Tom's eye, a sudden upraising of his hands, that did not escape him. He saw that he did not join the muster of the pursuers. He thought of forcing him to do it; but, having had, of old, experience of his inflexibility when commanded to take part in any deed of inhumanity, he would not, in his hurry, stop to enter into any conflict with him.

Tom, therefore, remained behind, with a few who had learned of him to pray, and offered up prayers for the escape of the fugitives.

When Legree returned, baffled and disappointed, all the long-working hatred of his soul towards his slave began to gather in a deadly and desperate form. Had not this man braved him,—steadily, powerfully, resistlessly,—ever since he bought him? Was there not a spirit in him which, silent as it was, burned on him like the fires of perdition?

"I *hate* him!" said Legree, that night, as he sat up in his bed; "I *hate* him! And isn't he MINE? Can't I do what I like with him? Who's to hinder, I wonder?" And Legree clenched his fist, and shook it, as if he had something in his hands that he could rend in pieces.

But, then, Tom was a faithful, valuable, servant; and, although Legree hated him the more for that, yet the consideration was still somewhat of a restraint to him.

The next morning, he determined to say nothing, as yet; to assemble a party, from some neighboring plantations, with dogs and guns; to surround the swamp, and go about the hunt systematically. If it succeeded, well and good; if not, he would summon Tom before him, and—his teeth clenched and his blood boiled—*then* he would break that fellow down, or——there was a dire inward whisper, to which his soul assented.

Ye say that the *interest* of the master is a sufficient safeguard for the slave. In the fury of man's mad will, he will wittingly, and with open eye, sell his own soul to the devil to gain his ends; and will he be more careful of his neighbor's body?

"Well," said Cassy, the next day, from the garret, as she reconnoitered through the knot-hole, "the hunt's going to begin again, to-day!"

Three or four mounted horsemen were curvetting about, on the space front of the house; and one or two leashes of strange dogs were struggling with the Negroes who held them, baying and barking at each other.

The men were, two of them, overseers of plantations in the vicinity; and others were some of Legree's associates at the tavern-bar of a neighboring city, who had come for the interest of the sport. A more hard-favored set, perhaps, could not be imagined. Legree was serving brandy, profusely, round among them, as also among the Negroes, who had been detailed from the various plantations for this service; for it was an object to make every service of this kind, among the Negroes, as much of a holiday as possible.

Cassy placed her ear at the knot-hole; and, as the morning air blew directly towards the house, she could overhear a good deal of the conversation. A grave sneer overcast the dark, severe gravity of her face, as she listened, and heard them divide out the ground, discuss the rival merits of the dogs, give orders about firing, and the treatment of each, in case of capture.

Cassy drew back; and, clasping her hands, looked upward, and said, "O, great Almighty God! we are *all* sinners; but what have *we* done, more than all the rest of the world, that we should be treated so?"

There was a terrible earnestness in her face and voice, as she spoke.

"If it wasn't for *you,* child," she said, looking at Emmeline, "I'd *go* out to them; and I'd thank any one of them that *would* shoot me down; for what use will freedom be to me? Can it give me back my children, or make me what I used to be?"

Emmeline, in her child-like simplicity, was half afraid of the dark moods of Cassy. She looked perplexed, but made no answer. She only took her hand, with a gentle, caressing movement.

"Don't!" said Cassy, trying to draw it away; "you'll get me to loving you; and I never mean to love anything, again!"

"Poor Cassy!" said Emmeline, "don't feel so! If the Lord gives us liberty, perhaps he'll give you back your daughter; at any rate, I'll be like a daughter to you. I know I'll never see my poor old mother again! I shall love you, Cassy, whether you love me or not!"

The gentle, child-like spirit conquered. Cassy sat down by her, put her arm round her neck, stroked her soft, brown hair; and Emmeline then wondered at the beauty of her magnificent eyes, now soft with tears.

"O, Em!" said Cassy, "I've hungered for my children, and thirsted for them, and my eyes fail with longing for them! Here! here!" she said, striking her breast, "it's all desolate, all empty! If God would give me back my children, then I could pray."

"You must trust him, Cassy," said Emmeline; "he is our Father!"

"His wrath is upon us." said Cassy; "he has turned away in anger."

"No, Cassy! He will be good to us! Let us hope in Him," said Emmeline,—"I always have had hope."

·   ·   ·

The hunt was long, animated, and thorough, but unsuccessful; and, with grave, ironic exultation, Cassy looked down on Legree, as, weary and dispirited, he alighted from his horse.

"Now, Quimbo," said Legree, as he stretched himself down in the sitting-room, "you jest go and walk that Tom up here, right away! The old cuss is at the bottom of this yer whole matter; and I'll have it out of his old black hide, or I'll know the reason why!"

Sambo and Quimbo, both, though hating each other, were joined in one mind by a no less cordial hatred of Tom. Legree had told them, at first, that he had bought him for a general overseer, in his absence; and this had begun an ill will, on their part, which had increased, in their debased and servile natures, as they saw him becoming obnoxious to their master's displeasure. Quimbo, therefore, departed, with a will, to execute his orders.

Tom heard the message with a forewarning heart; for he knew all the plan of the fugitives' escape, and the place of their present concealment;— he knew the deadly character of the man he had to deal with, and his despotic power. But he felt strong in God to meet death, rather than betray the helpless.

He sat his basket down by the row, and, looking up, said, "Into thy hands I commend my spirit! Thou hast redeemed me, oh Lord God of truth!" and then quietly yielded himself to the rough, brutal grasp with which Quimbo seized him.

"Ay, ay!" said the giant, as he dragged him along; "ye'll cotch it, now! I'll boun' Mas'r's back's up *high!* No sneaking out, now! Tell ye, ye'll get it, and no mistake! See how ye'll look, now, helpin' Mas'r's niggers to run away! See what ye'll get!"

The savage words none of them reached that ear!— a higher voice there was saying, "Fear not them that kill the body, and, after that, have no more that they can do." Nerve and bone of that poor man's body vibrated to those words, as if touched by the finger of God; and he felt the strength of a thousand souls in one. As he passed along, the trees and bushes, the huts of his servitude, the whole scene of his degradation, seemed to whirl by him as the landscape by the rushing car. His soul throbbed,—his home was in sight,—and the hour of release seemed at hand.

"Well, Tom!" said Legree, walking up, and seizing him grimly by the collar of his coat, and speaking through his teeth, in a paroxysm of determined rage, "do you know I've made up my mind to KILL you?"

"It's very likely, Mas'r," said Tom, calmly.

"I *have,*" said Legree, with grim, terrible calmness, "*done—just—that—thing,* Tom, unless you'll tell me what you know about these yer gals!"

Tom stood silent.

"D'ye hear!" said Legree, stamping, with a roar like that of an incensed lion. "Speak!"

"*I han't got nothing to tell, Mas'r,*" said Tom, with a slow, firm, deliberate utterance.

"Do you dare to tell me, ye old black Christian, ye don't *know?*" said Legree.

Tom was silent.

"Speak!" thundered Legree, striking him furiously. "Do you know anything?"

"I know, Mas'r; but I can't tell anything. *I can die!*"

Legree drew in a long breath; and, suppressing his rage, took Tom by the arm, and, approaching his face almost to his said, in a terrible voice, "Hark'e, Tom!—ye think, 'cause I've let you off before, I don't mean what I say; but, this time, I've *made up my mind,* and counted the cost. You've always stood it out agin' me: now, I'll *conquer ye, or kill ye!*—one or t'other. I'll count every drop of blood there is in you, and take 'em, one by one, till ye give up!"

Tom looked up to his master, and answered, "Mas'r, if you was sick, or in trouble, or dying, and I could save ye, I'd *give* ye my heart's blood; and if taking every drop of blood in this poor body would save your precious soul, I'd give 'em freely, as the Lord gave his for me. O, Mas'r! don't bring this great sin on your soul! It will hurt you more than 'twill me! Do the worst you can, my troubles'll be over soon; but, if ye don't repent, yours won't *never* end!"

Like a strange snatch of heavenly music, heard in the lull of a tempest, this burst of feeling made a moment's black pause. Legree stood aghast, and looked at Tom; and there was such a silence, that the tick of the old clock could be heard, measuring, with silent touch, the last moments of mercy and probation to that hardened heart.

It was but a moment. There was one hesitating pause,—one irresolute, relenting thrill,—and the spirit of evil came back, with seven-fold vehemence; and Legree, foaming with rage, smote his victim to the ground.

.   .   .

Scenes of blood and cruelty are shocking to our ear and heart. What man has nerve to do, man has not nerve to hear. What brother-man and brother-Christian must suffer, cannot be told us, even in our secret chamber, it so harrows up the soul! And yet, oh my country; these things are done under the shadow of thy laws! O, Christ! thy church sees them, almost in silence!

But, of old, there was One whose suffering changed an instrument of torture, degradation and shame, into a symbol of glory, honor, and immortal life; and, where His spirit is, neither degrading stripes, nor blood, nor insults, can make the Christian's last struggle less than glorious.

Was he alone, that long night, whose brave, loving spirit was bearing up, in that old shed, against buffeting and brutal stripes?

Nay! There stood by him ONE,—seen by him alone,—"like unto the Son of God."

The tempter stood by him, too,—blinded by furious, despotic will,—every moment pressing him to shun that agony by the betrayal of the innocent. But the brave, true heart was firm on the Eternal Rock. Like his Master, he knew that, if he saved others, himself he could not save; nor could utmost extremity wring from him words, save of prayer and holy trust.

"He's most gone, Mas'r," said Sambo, touched, in spite of himself, by the patience of his victim.

"Pay away, till he give up! Give it to him!—give to him!" shouted Legree. "I'll take every drop of blood he has, unless he confesses!"

Tom opened his eyes, and looked upon his master. "Ye poor miserable crittur!" he said, "there an't no more ye can do! I forgive ye, with all my soul!" and he fainted entirely away.

"I be'lieve, my soul, he's done for, finally," said Legree, stepping forward, to look at him. "Yes, he is! Well, his mouth's shut up, at last,—that's one comfort!"

Yes, Legree; but who shall shut up that voice in thy soul? that soul, past repentance, past prayer, past hope, in whom the fire that never shall be quenched is already burning!

Yet Tom was not quite gone. His wondrous words and pious prayers had struck upon the hearts of the imbruted blacks, who had been the instruments of cruelty upon him; and, the instant Legree withdrew, they took him down, and, in their ignorance, sought to call him back to life,—as if *that* were any favor to him.

"Sartin, we's been doin' a dreadful wicked thing!" said Sambo; "hopes Mas'r'll have to 'count for it, and not we."

They washed his wounds,—they provided a rude bed, of some refuse cotton, for him to lie down on; and one of them, stealing up to the house, begged a drink of brandy of Legree, pretending that he was tired, and wanted it for himself. He brought it back, and poured it down Tom's throat.

"O, Tom!" said Quimbo, "we's been awful wicked to ye!"

"I forgive ye, with all my heart!" said Tom, faintly.

"O, Tom! do tell us who is *Jesus*, anyhow?" said Sambo;—"Jesus, that's been a standin' by you so, all this night—Who is he?"

The word roused the failing, fainting spirit. He poured forth a few energetic sentences of that wondrous One,—his life, his death, his everlasting presence, and power to save.

They wept,—both the two savage men.

"Why didn't I never hear this before?" said Sambo; "but I do believe!—I can't help it! Lord Jesus, have mercy on us!"

"Poor critturs!" said Tom, "I'd be willing to b'ar all I have, if it'll only bring ye to Christ! O, Lord! give me these two more souls, I pray!"

That prayer was answered!

HENRY DAVID THOREAU

(1817–1862)*

Among Thoreau's militant speeches, "Slavery in Massachusetts" (1854) and "A Plea for Captain John Brown" (1859) are the most memorable. With these two addresses Thoreau joined the abolitionists and went beyond the pacifism expressed in "Civil Disobedience." His humor becomes more bitter and his manner more arch and demanding.

Thoreau's anger was inflamed by the passage of the Fugitive Slave Law (1850) and specifically by the decision of Massachusetts judges to return the Negro fugitives Thomas Simms and Anthony Burns to slavery in 1851. In "Slavery in Massachusetts," which was delivered on July 4, 1854, Thoreau put his own state on trial and attacked the expedience of judges and newspapers. In "A Plea for Captain John Brown," delivered on October 30, 1859, while John Brown was in prison, he justifies violence and, in effect, condemns nonviolent solutions to the evil of slavery.

*For a full introduction to Thoreau, see pp. 962–964.

Slavery in Massachusetts

I lately attended a meeting of the citizens of Concord, expecting, as one among many, to speak on the subject of slavery in Massachusetts; but I was surprised and disappointed to find that what had called my townsmen together was the destiny of Nebraska, and not of Massachusetts, and that what I had to say would be entirely out of order. I had thought that the house was on fire, and not the prairie; but though several of the citizens of Massachusetts are now in prison for attempting to rescue a slave from her own clutches, not one of the speakers at that meeting expressed regret for it, not one even referred to it. It was only the disposition of some wild lands a thousand miles off which appeared to concern them. The inhabitants of Concord are not prepared to stand by one of their own bridges, but talk only of taking up a position on the highlands beyond the Yellowstone River. Our Buttricks and Davises and Hosmers are retreating thither, and I fear that they will leave no Lexington Common between them and the enemy. There is not one slave in Nebraska; there are perhaps a million slaves in Massachusetts.

They who have been bred in the school of politics fail now and always to face the facts. Their measures are half measures and makeshifts merely. They put off the day of settlement indefinitely, and meanwhile the debt accumulates. Though the Fugitive Slave Law had not been the subject of discussion on that occasion, it was at length faintly resolved by my townsmen, at an adjourned meeting, as I learn, that the compromise compact of 1820 having been repudiated by one of the parties, "Therefore, . . . the Fugitive Slave Law of 1850 must be repealed."[1] But this is not the reason why an iniquitous law should be repealed. The fact which the politician faces is merely that there is less honor among thieves than was supposed, and not the fact that they are thieves.

As I had no opportunity to express my thoughts at that meeting, will you allow me to do so here?

Again it happens that the Boston Court-House is full of armed men, holding prisoner and trying a MAN, to find out if he is not really a SLAVE. Does any one think that justice or God awaits Mr. Loring's decision? For him to sit there deciding still, when this question is already decided from eternity to eternity, and the unlettered slave himself and the multitude around have long since heard and assented to the decision, is simply to make himself ridiculous. We may be tempted to ask from whom he received his commission, and who he is that received it; what novel statutes he obeys, and what precedents are to him of authority. Such an arbiter's very existence is an impertinence. We do not ask him to make up his mind, but to make up his pack.

[1] The law whereby fugitive slaves had to be returned to their owners in the South. See also Emerson's essay "The Fugitive Slave Law," Webster's speech, pp. 1726–1720, and Whittier's response in his poem "Ichabod," p. 1730.

I listen to hear the voice of a Governor, Commander-in-Chief of the forces of Massachusetts. I hear only the creaking of crickets and the hum of insects which now fill the summer air. The Governor's exploit is to review the troops on muster days. I have seen him on horseback, with his hat off, listening to a chaplain's prayer. It chances that that is all I have ever seen of a Governor. I think that I could manage to get along without one. If he is not of the least use to prevent my being kidnapped, pray of what important use is he likely to be to me? When freedom is most endangered, dwells in the deepest obscurity. A distinguished clergyman told me that he chose the profession of a clergyman because it afforded the most leisure for literary pursuits. I would recommend to him the profession of a Governor.

Three years ago, also, when the Sims tragedy was acted,[2] I said to myself, There is such an officer, if not such a man, as the Governor of Massachusetts,—what has he been about the fortnight? Has he had as much as he could do to keep on the fence during this moral earthquake? It seemed to me that no keener satire could have been aimed at, no more cutting insult have been offered to that man, than just what happened,—the absence of all inquiry after him in that crisis. The worst and the most I chance to know of him is that he did not improve that opportunity to make himself known, and worthily known. He could at least have *resigned* himself into fame. It appeared to be forgotten that there was such a man or such an office. Yet no doubt he was endeavoring to fill the gubernatorial chair all the while. He was no Governor of mine. He did not govern me.

But at last, in the present case, the Governor was heard from. After he and the United States government had perfectly succeeded in robbing a poor innocent black man of his liberty for life, and, as far as they could, of his Creator's likeness in his breast, he made a speech to his accomplices, at a congratulatory supper!

I have read a recent law of this State, making it penal for any officer of the "Commonwealth" to "detain or aid in the . . . detention," anywhere within its limits, "of any person, for the reason that he is claimed as a fugitive slave." Also, it was a matter of notoriety that a writ of replevin to take the fugitive out of the custody of the United States Marshal could not be served for want of sufficient force to aid the officer.

I had thought that the Governor was, in some sense, the executive officer of the State; that it was his business, as a Governor, to see that the laws of the State were executed; while, as a man, he took care that he did not, by so doing, break the laws of humanity; but when there is any special important use for him, he is useless, or worse than useless, and permits the laws of the State to go unexecuted. Perhaps I do not know what are the duties of a Governor; but if to be a Governor requires to subject one's self to so much

[2] In 1851 Massachusetts had surrendered the fugitive slave, Thomas Sims, to his master.

ignominy without remedy, if it is to put a restraint upon my manhood, I shall take care never to be Governor of Massachusetts. I have not read far in the statutes of this Commonwealth. It is not profitable reading. They do not always say what is true; and they do not always mean what they say. What I am concerned to know is, that that man's influence and authority were on the side of the slaveholder, and not of the slave,—of the guilty, and not of the innocent,—of injustice, and not of justice. I never saw him of whom I speak; indeed, I did not know that he was Governor until this event occurred. I heard of him and Anthony Burns[3] at the same time, and thus, undoubtedly, most will hear of him. So far am I from being governed by him. I do not mean that it was anything to discredit that I had not heard of him, only that I heard what I did. The worst I shall say of him is, that he proved no better than the majority of his constituents would be likely to prove. In my opinion, he was not equal to the occasion.

The whole military force of the State is at the service of Mr. Suttle, a slaveholder from Virginia, to enable him to catch a man whom he calls his property; but not a soldier is offered to save a citizen of Massachusetts from being kidnapped! Is this what all these soldiers, all this *training*, have been for these seventy-nine years past? Have they been trained merely to rob Mexico and carry back fugitive slaves to their masters?

These very nights I heard the sound of a drum in our streets. There were men *training* still; and for what? I could with an effort pardon the cockerels of Concord for crowing still, for they, perchance, had not been beaten that morning; but I would not excuse this rub-a-dub of the "trainers." The slave was carried back by exactly such as these; *i.e.*, by the soldier, of whom the best you can say in this connection is that he is a fool made conspicuous by a painted coat.

Three years ago, also, just a week after the authorities of Boston assembled to carry back a perfectly innocent man, and one whom they knew to be innocent, into slavery, the inhabitants of Concord caused the bells to be rung and the cannons to be fired, to celebrate their liberty,—and the courage and love of liberty of their ancestors who fought at the bridge. As if *those* three millions had fought for the right to be free themselves, but to hold in slavery three million others. Nowadays, men wear a fool's-cap, and call it a liberty-cap. I do not know but there are some who, if they were tied to a whipping-post, and could but get one hand free, would use it to ring the bells and fire the cannons to celebrate *their* liberty. So some of my townsmen took the liberty to ring and fire. That was the extent of their freedom; and when the sound of the bells died away, their liberty died away also; when the powder was all expended, their liberty went off with the smoke.

[3] Anthony Burns was another fugitive slave returned to his master.

The joke could be no broader if the inmates of the prisons were to subscribe for all the powder to be used in such salutes, and hire the jailers to do the firing and ringing for them, while they enjoyed it through the grating.

This is what I thought about my neighbors.

Every humane and intelligent inhabitant of Concord, when he or she heard those bells and those cannons, thought not with pride of the events of the 19th of April, 1775, but with shame of the events of the 12th of April, 1851. But now we have half buried that old shame under a new one.

Massachusetts sat waiting Mr. Loring's decision, as if it could in any way affect her own criminality. Her crime, the most conspicuous and fatal crime of all, was permitting him to be the umpire in such a case. It was really the trial of Massachusetts. Every moment that she now hesitated to set this man free, every moment that she now hesitates to atone for her crime, she is convicted. The Commissioner on her case is God; not Edward G. God, but simply God.

I wish my countrymen to consider, that whatever the human law may be, neither an individual nor a nation can ever commit the least act of injustice against the obscurest individual without having to pay the penalty for it. A government which deliberately enacts injustice, and persists in it, will at length even become the laughing-stock of the world.

Much has been said about American slavery, but I think that we do not even yet realize what slavery is. If I were seriously to propose to Congress to make mankind into sausages, I have no doubt that most of the members would smile at my proposition, and if any believed me to be in earnest, they would think that I proposed something much worse than Congress had ever done. But if any of them will tell me that to make a man into a sausage would be much worse,—would be any worse,—than to make him into a slave,—than it was to enact the Fugitive Slave Law,—I will accuse him of foolishness, of intellectual incapacity, of making a distinction without a difference. The one is just as sensible a proposition as the other.

I hear a good deal said about trampling this law under foot. Why, one need not go out of his way to do that. This law rises not to the level of the head or the reason; its natural habitat is in the dirt. It was born and bred, and has its life, only in the dust and mire, on a level with the feet; and he who walks with freedom, and does not with Hindoo mercy avoid treading on every venomous reptile, will inevitably tread on it, and so trample it under foot,—and Webster,[4] its maker, with it, like the dirt-bug and its ball.

Recent events will be valuable as a criticism on the administration of justice in our midst, or, rather, as showing what are the true resources of justice in any community. It has come to this, that the friends of liberty, the friends of the slave, have shuddered when they have understood that his fate

[4] Daniel Webster (1782–1852), Senator from Massachusetts and the greatest of American orators. He supported the Fugitive Slave Law in his March 7 speech. See pp. 1726–1729.

was left to the legal tribunals of the country to be decided. Free men have no faith that justice will be awarded in such a case. The judge may decide this way or that; it is a kind of accident, at best. It is evident that he is not a competent authority in so important a case. It is no time, then, to be judging according to his precedents, but to establish a precedent for the future. I would much rather trust to the sentiment of the people. In their vote you would get something of some value, at least, however small; but in the other case, only the trammeled judgment of an individual, of no significance, be it which way it might.

It is to some extent fatal to the courts, when the people are compelled to go behind them. I do wish to believe that the courts were made for fair weather, and for very civil cases merely, but think of leaving it to any court in the land to decide whether more than three millions of people, in this case a sixth part of a nation, have a right to be freemen or not! But it has been left to the courts of *justice*, so called,—to the Supreme Court of the land,—and, as you all know, recognizing no authority but the Constitution, it has decided that the three millions are and shall continue to be slaves. Such judges as these are merely the inspectors of a pick-lock and murderer's tools, to tell him whether they are in working order or not, and there they think that their responsibility ends. There was a prior case on the docket, which they, as judges appointed by God, had no right to skip; which having been justly settled, they would have been saved from this humiliation. It was the case of the murderer himself.

The law will never make men free; it is men who have got to make the law free. They are the lovers of law and order who observe the law when the government breaks it.

Among human beings, the judge whose words seal the fate of a man furthest into eternity is not he who merely pronounces the verdict of the law, but he, whoever he may be, who, from a love of truth, and unprejudiced by any custom or enactment of men, utters a true opinion or *sentence* concerning him. He it is that *sentences* him. Whoever can discern truth has received his commission from a higher source than the chiefest justice in the world who can discern only law. He finds himself constituted judge of the judge. Strange that it should be necessary to state such simple truths!

I am more and more convinced that, with reference to any public question, it is more important to know what the country thinks of it than what the city thinks. The city does not *think* much. On any moral question, I would rather have the opinion of Boxboro' than of Boston and New York put together. When the former speaks, I feel as if somebody *had* spoken, as if *humanity* was yet, and a reasonable being had asserted its rights,—as if some unprejudiced men among the country's hills had at length turned their attention to the subject, and by a few sensible words redeemed the reputation of the race. When, in some obscure country town, the farmers come together to a special town-meeting, to express their opinion on some subject which is vexing the land, that, I think, is the true Congress, and the most respectable one that is ever assembled in the United States.

It is evident that there are, in this Commonwealth at least, two parties, becoming more and more distinct,—the party of the city, and the party of the country. I know that the country is mean enough, but I am glad to believe that there is a slight difference in her favor. But as yet she has few, if any organs, through which to express herself. The editorials which she reads, like the news, come from the seaboard. Let us, the inhabitants of the country, cultivate self-respect. Let us not send to the city for aught more essential than our broadcloths and groceries; or, if we read the opinions of the city, let us entertain opinions of our own.

Among measures to be adopted, I would suggest to make as earnest and vigorous an assault on the press as has already been made, and with effect, on the church. The church has much improved within a few years; but the press is, almost without exception, corrupt. I believe that in this country the press exerts a greater and a more pernicious influence than the church did in its worst period. We are not a religious people, but we are a nation of politicians. We do not care for the Bible, but we do care for the newspaper. At any meeting of politicians,—like that at Concord the other evening, for instance,—how impertinent it would be to quote from the Bible! how impertinent it would be to quote from the Constitution! The newspaper is a Bible which we read every morning and every afternoon, standing and sitting, riding and walking. It is a Bible which every man carries in his pocket, which lies on every table and counter, and which the mail, and thousands of missionaries, are continually dispersing. It is, in short, the only book which America has printed, and which America reads: So wide is its influence. The editor is a preacher whom you voluntarily support. Your tax is commonly one cent daily, and it costs nothing for pew hire. But how many of these preachers preach the truth? I repeat the testimony of many an intelligent foreigner, as well as my own convictions, when I say, that probably no country was ever ruled by so mean a class of tyrants as, with a few noble exceptions, are the editors of the periodical press in *this* country. And as they live and rule only by their servility, and appealing to the worse, and not the better, nature of man, the people who read them are in the condition of the dog that returns to his vomit.

The *Liberator* and the *Commonwealth* were the only papers in Boston, as far as I know, which made themselves heard in condemnation of the cowardice and meanness of the authorities of that city, as exhibited in '51. The other journals, almost without exception, by their manner of referring to and speaking of the Fugitive Slave Law, and the carrying back of the slave Sims, insulted the common sense of the country, at least. And, for the most part, they did this, one would say, because they thought so to secure the approbation of their patrons, not being aware that a sounder sentiment prevailed to any extent in the heart of the Commonwealth. I am told that some of them have improved of late; but they are still eminently time-serving. Such is the character they have won.

But, thank fortune, this preacher can be even more easily reached by the weapons of the reformer than could the recreant priest. The free men of New England have only to refrain from purchasing and reading these sheets, have only to withhold their cents, to kill a score of them at once. One whom I respect told me that he purchased Mitchells' *Citizen* in the cars, and then threw it out the window. But would not his contempt have been more fatally expressed if he had not bought it?

Are they Americans? are they New Englanders? are they inhabitants of Lexington and Concord and Framingham, who read and support the Boston *Post, Mail, Journal, Advertiser, Courier,* and *Times?* Are these the Flags of our Union? I am not a newspaper reader, and may omit to name the worst.

Could slavery suggest a more complete servility than some of these journals exhibit? Is there any dust which their conduct does not lick, and make fouler still with its slime? I do not know whether the Boston *Herald* is still in existence, but I remember to have seen it about the streets when Sims was carried off. Did it not act its part well,—serve its master faithfully? How could it have gone lower on its belly? How can a man stoop lower than he as low? do more than put his extremities in the place of the head he has? than make his head his lower extremity? When I have taken up this paper with my cuffs turned up, I have heard the gurgling of the sewer through every column. I have felt that I was handling a paper picked out of the public gutters, a leaf from the gospel of the gambling-house, the groggery, and the brothel, harmonizing with the gospel of the Merchants' Exchange.

The majority of the men of the North, and of the South and East and West, are not men of principle. If they vote, they do not send men to Congress on errands of humanity; but while their brothers and sisters are being scourged and hung for loving liberty, while—I might here insert all that slavery implies and is—it is the mismanagement of wood and iron and stone and gold which concerns them. Do what you will, O Government, with my wife and children, my mother and brother, my father and sister, I will obey your commands to the letter. It will indeed grieve me if you hurt them, if you deliver them to overseers to be hunted by hounds or to be whipped to death; but, nevertheless, I will peaceably pursue my chosen calling on this fair earth, until perchance, one day, when I have put on mourning for them dead. I shall have persuaded you to relent. Such is the attitude, such are the words of Massachusetts.

Rather than do thus, I need not say what match I would touch, what system endeavor to blow up; but as I love my life, I would side with the light, and let the dark earth roll from under me, calling my mother and my brother to follow.

I would remind my countrymen that they are to be men first, and Americans only at a late and convenient hour. No matter how valuable law may be to protect your property, even to keep soul and body together, if it do not keep you and humanity together.

I am sorry to say that I doubt if there is a judge in Massachusetts who is prepared to resign his office, and get his living innocently, whenever it is required of him to pass sentence under a law which is merely contrary to the law of God. I am compelled to see that they put themselves, or rather are by character, in this respect, exactly on a level with the marine who discharges his musket in any direction he is ordered to. They are just as much tools, and as little men. Certainly, they are not the more to be respected, because their master enslaves their understandings and consciences, instead of their bodies.

The judges and lawyers,—simply as such, I mean,—and all men of expediency, try this case by a very low and incompetent standard. They consider, not whether the Fugitive Slave Law is right, but whether it is what they call *constitutional*. Is virtue constitutional, or vice? Is equity constitutional, or iniquity? In important moral and vital questions, like this, it is just as impertinent to ask whether a law is constitutional or not, as to ask whether it is profitable or not. They persist in being the servants of the worst of men, and not the servants of humanity. The question is, not whether you or your grandfather, seventy years ago, did not enter into an agreement to serve the Devil, and that service is not accordingly now due; but whether you will not now, for once and at last, serve God,—in spite of your own past recreancy, or that of your ancestor,—by obeying that eternal and only just CONSTITU-TION, which He, and not any Jefferson or Adams, has written in your being.

The amount of it is, if the majority vote the Devil to be God, the minority will live and behave accordingly,—and obey the successful candidate, trusting that, some time or other, by some Speaker's casting-vote, perhaps, they may reinstate God. This is the highest principle I can get out or invent for my neighbors. These men act as if they believed that they could safely slide down a hill a little way,—or a good way,—and would surely come to a place, by and by, where they could begin to slide up again. This is expediency, or choosing that course which offers the slightest obstacles to the feet, that is, a downhill one. But there is no such thing as accomplishing a righteous reform by the use of "expediency." There is no such thing as sliding up hill. In morals the only sliders are backsliders.

Thus we steadily worship Mammon, both school and state and church, and on the seventh day curse God with a tintamar from one end of the Union to the other.

Will mankind never learn that policy is not morality,—that it never secures any moral right, but considers merely what is expedient? chooses the available candidate,—who is invariably the Devil,—and what right have his constituents to be surprised, because the Devil does not behave like an angel of light? What is wanted is men, not of policy, but of probity,—who recognize a higher law than the Constitution, or the decision of the majority. The fate of the country does not depend on how you vote at the polls,—the worst man is as strong as the best at that game; it does not depend on what kind of paper you drop into the ballot-box once a year, but on what kind of man you drop from your chamber into the street every morning.

What should concern Massachusetts is not the Nebraska Bill, nor the Fugitive Slave Bill, but her own slaveholding and servility. Let the State dissolve her union with the slaveholder. She may wriggle and hesitate, and ask leave to read the Constitution once more; but she can find no respectable law or precedent which sanctions the continuance of such a union for an instant.

Let each inhabitant of the State dissolve his union with her, as long as she delays to do her duty.

The events of the past month teach me to distrust Fame. I see that she does not finely discriminate, but coarsely hurrahs. She considers not the simple heroism of an action, but only as it is connected with its apparent consequences. She praises till she is hoarse the easy exploit of the Boston tea party, but will be comparatively silent about the braver and more disinterestedly heroic attack on the Boston Court-House, simply because it was unsuccessful!

Covered with disgrace, the State has sat down coolly to try for their lives and liberties the men who attempted to do its duty for it. And this is called *justice!* They who have shown that they can behave particularly well may perchance be put under bonds for *their good behavior.* They whom truth requires at present to plead guilty are, of all the inhabitants of the State, preëminently innocent. While the Governor, and the Mayor, and countless officers of the Commonwealth are at large, the champions of liberty are imprisoned.

Only they are guiltless who commit the crime of contempt of such a court. It behooves every man to see that his influence is on the side of justice, and let the courts make their own characters. My sympathies in this case are wholly with the accused, and wholly against their accusers and judges. Justice is sweet and musical; but injustice is harsh and discordant. The judge still sits grinding at his organ, but it yields no music, and we hear only the sound of the handle. He believes that all the music resides in the handle, and the crowd toss him their coppers the same as before.

Do you suppose that that Massachusetts which is now doing these things,—which hesitates to crown these men, some of whose lawyers, and even judges, perchance, may be driven to take refuge in some poor quibble, that they may not wholly outrage their instinctive sense of justice,—do you suppose that she is anything but base and servile? that she is the champion of liberty?

Show me a free state, and a court truly of justice, and I will fight for them, if need be; but show me Massachusetts, and I refuse her my allegiance, and express contempt for her courts.

The effect of a good government is to make life more valuable,—of a bad one, to make it less valuable. We can afford that railroad and all merely material stock should lose some of its value, for that only compels us to live more simply and economically; but suppose that the value of life itself should be diminished! How can we make a less demand on man and nature, how live more economically in respect to virtue and all noble qualities, than we do? I have lived for the last month—and I think that every man in Massachusetts capable of the sentiment of patriotism must have had a similar experience—with the sense of having suffered a vast and indefinite loss. I did not know at first what ailed me. At last it occurred to me that what I had lost was a country. I had never respected the government near to which I lived, but I had foolishly thought that I might manage to live here, minding my private affairs, and forget it. For my part, my old and worthiest pursuits have lost I cannot say how much of their attraction, and I feel that my investment in life here is worth many per cent. less since Massachusetts last deliberately sent back an innocent man, Anthony Burns, to slavery. I dwelt before, per-haps, in the illusion that my life passed somewhere only *between* heaven and hell, but now I cannot persuade myself that I do not dwell *wholly within* hell. The site of that political organization called Massachusetts is to me morally covered with volcanic scoriæ and cinders, such as Milton describes in the infernal regions. If there is any hell more unprincipled than our rulers, and we, the ruled, I feel curious to see it. Life itself being worth less, all things with it, which minister to it, are worth less. Suppose you have a small library, with pictures to adorn the walls,—a garden laid out around,—and contemplate scientific and literary pursuits, and discover all at once that your villa, with all its contents, is located in hell, and that the justice of the peace has a cloven foot and a forked tail,—do not these things suddenly lose their value in your eyes?

I feel that, to some extent, the State has fatally interfered with my lawful business. It has not only interrupted me in my passage through Court Street on errands of trade, but it has interrupted me and every man on his onward and upward path, on which he had trusted soon to leave Court Street far behind. What right had it to remind me of Court Street? I have found that hollow which even I had relied on for solid.

I am surprised to see men going about their business as if nothing had happened. I say to myself, "Unfortunates! they have not heard the news." I am surprised that the man whom I just met on horseback sould be so earnest to overtake his newly bought cows running away,—since all property is insecure, and if they do not run away again, they may be taken away from him when he gets them. Fool! does he not know that his seed-corn is worth less this year,—that all beneficent harvests fail as you approach the empire of hell? No prudent man will build a stone house under these circumstances, or engage in any peaceful enterprise which it requires a long time to accom-plish. Art is as long as ever, but life is more interrupted and less available for a man's proper pursuits. It is not an era of repose. We have used up all our inherited freedom. If we would save our lives, we must fight for them.

I walk toward one of our ponds; but what signifies the beauty of nature when men are base? We walk to lakes to see our serenity reflected in them; when we are not serene, we go not to them. Who can be serene in a country where both the rulers and the ruled are without prinicple? The remembrance of my country spoils my walk. My thoughts are murder to the State, and involuntarily go plotting against her.

But it chanced the other day that I scented a white water-lily, and a season I had waited for had arrived. It is the emblem of purity. It burst up so pure and fair to the eye, and so sweet to the scent, as if to show us what purity and sweetness reside in, and can be extracted from, the slime and muck of earth. I think I have plucked the first one that has opened for a mile. What confirmation of our hopes is in the fragrance of this flower! I shall not so soon despair of the world for it, notwithstanding slavery, and the cowardice and want of principle of Northern men. It suggests what kind of laws have prevailed longest and widest, and still prevail, and that the time may come when man's deeds will smell as sweet. Such is the odor which the plant emits. If Nature can compound this fragrance still annually, I shall believe her still young and full of vigor, her integrity and genius unimpaired, and that there is virtue even in man, too, who is fitted to perceive and love it. It reminds me that Nature has been partner to no Missouri Compromise.[5] I scent no compromise in the fragrance of the water-lily. It is not a *Nymphœa DOUGLASII*. In it, the sweet, and pure, and innocent are wholly sundered from the obscene and baleful. I do not scent in this the time-serving irresolution of a Massachusetts Governor, nor of a Boston Mayor. So behave that the odor of your actions may enhance the general sweetness of the atmosphere, that when we behold or scent a flower, we may not be reminded how inconsistent your deeds are with it; for all odor is but one form of advertisement of a moral quality, and if fair actions had not been performed, the lily would not smell sweet. The foul slime stands for the sloth and vice of man, the decay of humanity; the fragrant flower that springs from it, for the purity and courage which are immortal.

Slavery and servility have produced no sweet-scented flower annually, to charm the senses of men, for they have no real life: they are merely a decaying and a death, offensive to all healthy nostrils. We do not complain that they *live*, but that they do not *get buried.* Let the living bury them: even they are good for manure.

---

[5] The Missouri Compromise, largely implemented by Henry Clay, was established when Missouri was admitted as a slave state but with the proviso that slavery would be forever excluded from the territory acquired by the Louisiana Purchase north of the parallel 36° 30′, the southern boundary of Missouri.

A Plea for Captain John Brown

I trust that you will pardon me for being here. I do not wish to force my thoughts upon you, but I feel forced myself. Little as I know of Captain Brown, I would fain do my part to correct the tone and statements of the newspapers, and of my countrymen generally, respecting his character and actions. It costs us nothing to be just. We can at least express our sympathy with, and admiration of, him and his companions, and that is what I now propose to do.

First, as to his history. I will endeavor to omit, as much as possible, what you have already read. I need not describe his person to you, for probably most of you have seen and will not soon forget him. I am told that his grandfather, John Brown, was an officer in the Revolution; that he himself was born in Connecticut about the beginning of this century, but early went with his father to Ohio. I heard him say that his father was a contractor who furnished beef to the army there, in the war of 1812; that he accompanied him to the camp, and assisted him in that employment, seeing a good deal of military life,—more, perhaps, than if he had been a soldier; for he was often present at the councils of the officers. Especially, he learned by experience how armies are supplied and maintained in the field,—a work which, he observed, requires at least as much experience and skill as to lead them in battle. He said that few persons had any conception of the cost, even the pecuniary cost, of firing a single bullet in war. He saw enough, at any rate, to disgust him with a military life; indeed, to excite in him a great abhorrence of it; so much so, that though he was tempted by the offer of some petty office in the army, when he was about eighteen, he not only declined that, but he also refused to train when warned, and was fined for it. He then resolved that he would never have anything to do with any war, unless it were a war for liberty.

When the troubles in Kansas began, he sent several of his sons thither to strengthen the party of the Free State men, fitting them out with such weapons as he had; telling them that if the troubles should increase, and there should be need of him, he would follow, to assist them with his hand and counsel. This, as you all know, he soon after did; and it was through his agency, far more than any other's, that Kansas was made free.

For a part of his life he was a surveyor, and at one time he was engaged in wool-growing, and he went to Europe as an agent about that business. There, as everywhere, he had his eyes about him, and made many original observations. He said, for instance, that he saw why the soil of England was so rich, and that of Germany (I think it was) so poor, and he thought of writing to some of the crowned heads about it. It was because in England the peasantry live on the soil which they cultivate, but in Germany they are gathered into villages at night. It is a pity that he did not make a book of his observations.

I should say that he was an old-fashioned man in his respect for the Constitution, and his faith in the permanence of this Union. Slavery he deemed to be wholly opposed to these, and he was its determined foe.

He was by descent and birth a New England farmer, a man of great common sense, deliberate and practical as that class is, and tenfold more so. He was like the best of those who stood at Concord Bridge once, on Lexington Common, and on Bunker Hill, only he was firmer and higher principled than any that I have chanced to hear of as there. It was no abolition lecturer that converted him. Ethan Allen and Stark,[1] with whom he may in some respects be compared, were rangers in a lower and less important field. They could bravely face their country's foes, but he had the courage to face his country herself when she was in the wrong. A Western writer says, to account for his escape from so many perils, that he was concealed under a "rural exterior;" as if, in that prairie land, a hero should, by good rights, wear a citizen's dress only.

He did not go to the college called Harvard, good old Alma Mater as she is. He was not fed on the pap that is there furnished. As he phrased it, "I know no more of grammar than one of your calves." But he went to the great university of the West, where he sedulously pursued the sudy of Liberty, for which he had early betrayed a fondness, and having taken many degrees, he finally commenced the public practice of Humanity in Kansas, as you all know. Such were *his humanities,* and not any study of grammar. He would have left a Greek accent slanting the wrong way, and righted up a falling man.

He was one of that class of whom we hear a great deal, but, for the most part, see nothing at all,—the Puritans. It would be in vain to kill him. He died lately in the time of Cromwell,[2] but he reappeared here. Why should he not? Some of the Puritan stock are said to have come over and settled in New England. They were a class that did something else than celebrate their forefathers' day, and eat parched corn in remembrance of that time. They were neither Democrats nor Republicans, but men of simple habits, straightforward, prayerful; not thinking much of rulers who did not fear God, not making compromises, nor seeking after available candidates.

"In his camp," as one has recently written, and as I have myself heard him state, "he permitted no profanity; no man of loose morals was suffered to remain there, unless, indeed, as a prisoner of war. 'I would rather,' said he, 'have the smallpox, yellow fever, and cholera, all together in my camp, than a man without principle. . . . It is a mistake, sir, that our people make,

[1] Heroes of the American Revolution.

[2] Oliver Cromwell (1599-1658) was an English military, political, and religious leader,

the Lord Protector of the Commonwealth from 1653 to 1658.

when they think that bullies are the best fighters, or that they are the fit men to oppose these Southerners. Give me men of good principles,—God-fearing men,—men who respect themselves, and with a dozen of them I will oppose any hundred such men as these Buford ruffians.' " He said that if one offered himself to be a soldier under him, who was forward to tell what he could or would do if he could only get sight of the enemy, he had but little confidence in him.

He was never able to find more than a score or so of recruits whom he would accept, and only about a dozen, among them his sons, in whom he had perfect faith. When he was here some years ago, he showed to a few a little manuscript book,—his "orderly book" I think he called it,—containing the names of his company in Kansas, and the rules by which they bound themselves; and he stated that several of them had already sealed the contract with their blood. When some one remarked that, with the addition of a chaplain, it would have been a perfect Cromwellian troop, he observed that he would have been glad to add a chaplain to the list, if he could have found one who could fill that office worthily. It is easy enough to find one for the United States army. I believe that he had prayers in his camp morning and evening, nevertheless.

He was a man of Spartan habits, and at sixty was scrupulous about his diet at your table, excusing himself by saying that he must eat sparingly and fare hard, as became a soldier, or one who was fitting himself for difficult enterprises, a life of exposure.

A man of rare common sense and directness of speech, as of action; a transcendentalist above all, a man of ideas and principles,—that was what distinguished him. Not yielding to a whim or transient impulse, but carrying out the purpose of a life. I noticed that he did not overstate anything, but spoke within bounds. I remember, particularly, how, in his speech here, he referred to what his family had suffered in Kansas, without ever giving the least vent to his pent-up fire. It was a volcano with an ordinary chimney-flue. Also referring to the deeds of certain Border Ruffians, he said, rapidly paring away his speech, like an experienced soldier, keeping a reserve of force and meaning, "They had a perfect right to be hung." He was not in the least a rhetorician, was not talking to Buncombe or his constituents anywhere, had no need to invent anything but to tell the simple truth, and communicate his own resolution; therefore he appeared incomparably strong, and eloquence in Congress and elsewhere seemed to me at a discount. It was like the speeches of Cromwell compared with those of an ordinary king.

As for his tact and prudence, I will merely say, that at a time when scarcely a man from the Free States was able to reach Kansas by any direct route, at least without having his arms taken from him, he, carrying what imperfect guns and other weapons he could collect, openly and slowly drove an ox-cart through Missouri, apparently in the capacity of a surveyor, with his surveying compass exposed in it, and so passed unsuspected, and had ample opportunity to learn the designs of the enemy. For some time after his arrival he still followed the same profession. When, for instance, he saw a knot of the ruffians on the prairie, discussing, of course, the single topic which then occupied their minds, he would, perhaps, take his compass and one of his sons, and proceed to run an imaginary line right through the very spot on which that conclave had assembled, and when he came up to them, he would naturally pause and have some talk with them, learning their news, and, at last, all their plans perfectly; and having thus completed his real survey he would resume his imaginary one, and run on his line till he was out of sight.

When I expressed surprise that he could live in Kansas at all, with a price set upon his head, and so large a number, including the authorities, exasperated against him, he accounted for it by saying, "It is perfectly well understood that I will not be taken." Much of the time for some years he has had to skulk in swamps, suffering from poverty and from sickness, which was the consequence of exposure, befriended only by Indians and a few whites. But though it might be known that he was lurking in a particular swamp, his foes commonly did not care to go in after him. He could even come out into a town where there were more Border Ruffians than Free State men, and transact some business, without delaying long, and yet not be molested; for, said he, "no little handful of men were willing to undertake it, and a large body could not be got together in season."

As for his recent failure, we do not know the facts about it. It was evidently far from being a wild and desperate attempt. His enemy, Mr. Vallandigham, is compelled to say that "It was among the best planned and executed conspiracies that ever failed."

Not to mention his other successes, was it a failure, or did it show a want of good management, to deliver from bondage a dozen human beings, and walk off with them by broad daylight, for weeks if not months, at a leisurely pace, through one State after another, for half the length of the North, conspicuous to all parties, with a price set upon his head, going into a courtroom on his way and telling what he had done, thus convincing Missouri that it was not profitable to try to hold slaves in his neighborhood?—and this, not because the government menials were lenient, but because they were afraid of him.

Yet he did not attribute his success, foolishly, to "his star," or to any magic. He said, truly, that the reason why such greatly superior numbers quailed before him was, as one of his prisoners confessed, because they lacked a cause,—a kind of armor which he and his party never lacked. When the time came, a few men were found willing to lay down their lives in defense of what they knew to be wrong; they did not like that this should be their last act in this world.

But to make haste to *his* last act, and its effects.

The newspapers seem to ignore, or perhaps are really ignorant of the fact that there are at least as many as two or three individuals to a town throughout the North who think much as the present speaker does about him and his enterprise. I do not hesitate to say that they are an important and growing party. We aspire to be something more than stupid and timid chattels, pretending to read history and our Bibles, but desecrating every house and every day we breathe in. Perhaps anxious politicians may prove that only seventeen white men and five negroes were concerned in the late enterprise; but their very anxiety to prove this might suggest to themselves that all is not told. Why do they still dodge the truth? They are so anxious because of a dim consciousness of the fact, which they do not distinctly face, that at least a million of the free inhabitants of the United States would have rejoiced if it had succeeded. They at most only criticize the tactics. Though we wear no crape, the thought of that man's position and probable fate is spoiling many a man's day here at the north for other thinking. If any one who has seen him here can pursue successfully any other train of thought, I do not know what he is made of. If there is any such who gets his usual allowance of sleep, I will warrant him to fatten easily under any circumstances which do not touch his body or purse. I put a piece of paper and pencil under my pillow, and when I could not sleep I wrote in the dark.

On the whole, my respect for my fellow-men, except as one may outweigh a million, is not being increased these days. I have noticed the cold-blooded way in which newspaper writers and men generally speak of this event, as if an ordinary malefactor, though one of unusual "pluck,"—as the Governor of Virginia is reported to have said, using the language of the cockpit, "the gamest man he ever saw,"—had been caught, and were about to be hung. He was not dreaming of his foes when the governor thought he looked so brave. It turns what sweetness I have to gall, to hear, or hear of, the remarks of some of my neighbors. When we heard at first that he was dead, one of my townsmen observed that "he died as the fool dieth;" which, pardon me, for an instant suggested a likeness in him dying to my neighbor living. Others, craven-hearted, said disparagingly, that "he threw his life away," because he resisted the government. Which way have they thrown *their* lives, pray?—such as would praise a man for attacking singly an ordinary band of thieves or murderers. I hear another ask, Yankee-like, "what will he gain by it?" as if he expected to fill his pockets by this enterprise. Such a one has no idea of gain by in this worldly sense. If it does not lead to a "surprise" party, if he does not get a new pair of boots, or a vote of thanks, it must be a failure. "But he won't gain anything by it." Well, no, I don't suppose he could get four-and-six-pence a day for being hung, take the year round; but then he stands a chance to save a considerable part of his soul,— and *such* a soul!—when *you* do not. No doubt you can get more in your market for a quart of milk than for a quart of blood, but that is not the market that heroes carry their blood to.

Such do not know that like the seed is the fruit, and that, in the moral world, when good seed is planted, good fruit is inevitable, and does not depend on our watering and cultivating; that when you plant, or bury, a hero in his field, a crop of heroes is sure to spring up. This is a seed of such force and vitality, that it does not ask our leave to germinate.

The momentary charge at Balaklava, in obedience to a blundering command, proving what a perfect machine the soldier is, has, properly enough, been celebrated by a poet laureate; but the steady, and for the most part successful, charge of this man, for some years, against the legions of Slavery, in obedience to an infinitely higher command, is as much more memorable than that as an intelligent and conscientious man is superior to a machine. Do you think that that will go unsung?

"Served him right,"—"A dangerous man,"—"He is undoubtedly insane." So they proceed to live their sane, and wise, and altogether admirable lives, reading their Plutarch a little, but chiefly pausing at that feat of Putnam, who was let down into a wolf's den; and in this wise they nourish themselves for brave and patriotic deeds some time or other. The Tract Society could afford to print that story of Putnam. You might open the district schools with the reading of it, for there is nothing about Slavery or the Chruch in it; unless it occurs to the reader that some pastors are *wolves* in sheep's clothing. "The American Board of Commissioners for Foreign Missions," even, might dare to protest against *that* wolf. I have heard of boards, and of American boards, but it chances that I never heard of this particular lumber till lately. And yet I hear of Northern men, and women, and children, by families, buying a "life-membership" in such societies as these. A life-membership in the grave! You can get buried cheaper than that.

Our foes are in our midst and all about us. There is hardly a house but is divided against itself, for our foe is the all but universal woodenness of both head and heart, the want of vitality in man, which is the effect of our vice; and hence are begotten fear, superstition, bigotry, persecution, and slavery of all kinds. We are mere figure-heads upon a hulk, with livers in the place of hearts. The curse is the worship of idols, which at length changes the worshipper into a stone image himself; and the New Englander is just as much an idolater as the Hindoo. This man was an exception, for he did not set up even a political graven image between him and his God.

A church that can never have done with excommunicating Christ while it exists! Away with your broad and flat churches, and your narrow and tall churches! Take a step forward, and invent a new style of out-houses. Invent a salt that will save you, and defend our nostrils.

The modern Christian is a man who has consented to say all the prayers in the liturgy, provided you will let him go straight to bed and sleep quietly afterward. All his prayers begin with "Now I lay me down to sleep," and he is forever looking forward to the time when he shall go to his "*long* rest." He has consented to perform certain old-established charities, too, after a fashion, but he does not wish to hear of any new-fangled ones; he doesn't wish to have any supplementary articles added to the contract, *to fit it to* the present time. He shows the whites of his eyes on the Sabbath, and the blacks all the rest of the week. The evil is not merely a stagnation of blood, but a stagnation of spirit. Many, no doubt, are well disposed, but sluggish by constitution and by habit, and they cannot conceive of a man who is actuated by higher motives than they are. Accordingly they pronounce this man insane, for they know that *they* could never act as he does, as long as they are themselves.

We dream of foreign countries, of other times and races of men, placing them at a distance in history or space; but let some significant event like the present occur in our midst, and we discover, often, this distance and this strangeness between us and our nearest neighbors. *They* are our Austrias, and Chinas, and South Sea Islands. Our crowded society becomes well spaced all at once, clean and handsome to the eye,—a city of magnificent distances. We discover why it was that we never got beyond compliments and surfaces with them before; we become aware of as many versts between us and them as there are between a wandering Tartar and a Chinese town. The thoughtful man becomes a hermit in the thoroughfares of the market-place. Impassable seas suddenly find their level between us, or dumb steppes stretch themselves out there. It is the difference of constitution, of intelligence, and faith, and not streams and mountains, that make the true and impassable boundaries between individuals and between states. None but the like-minded can come plenipotentiary to our court.

I read all the newspapers I could get within a week after this event, and I do not remember in them a single expression of sympathy for these men. I have since seen one noble statement, in a Boston paper, not editorial. Some voluminous sheets decided not to print the full report of Brown's words to the exclusion of other matter. It was as if a publisher should reject the manuscript of the New Testament, and print Wilsons' last speech. The same journal which contained this pregnant news was chiefly filled, in parallel columns, with the reports of the political conventions that were being held. But the descent to them was too steep. They should have been spared this contrast,—been printed in an extra, at least. To turn from the voices and deeds of earnest men to the *cackling* of political conventions! Office-seekers and speechmakers, who do not so much as lay an honest egg, but wear their breast bare upon an egg of chalk! Their great game is the game of straws, or rather that universal aboriginal game of the platter, at which the Indians cried *hub, bub!* Exclude the reports of religious and political conventions, and publish the words of a living man.

But I object not so much to what they have omitted as to what inserted. Even the *Liberator* called it "a misguided, wild, and apparently insane— effort." As for the herd of newspapers and magazines, I do not chance to know an editor in the country who will deliberately print anything which he knows will ultimately and permanently reduce the number of his subscribers. They do not believe that it would be expedient. How then can they print truth? If we do not say pleasant things, they argue, nobody will attend to us. And so they do like some traveling auctioneers, who sing an obscene song, in order to draw a crowd around them. Republican editors, obliged to get their sentences ready for the morning edition, and accustomed to look at everything by the twilight of politics, express no admiration, nor true sorrow even, but call these men "deluded fanatics,"—"mistaken men,"—"insane," or "crazed." It suggests what a *sane* set of editors we are blessed with, *not* "mistaken men;" who know very well on which side their bread is buttered, at least.

A man does a brave and humane deed, and at once, on all sides, we hear people and parties declaring, "I didn't do it, nor countenance *him* to to do it, in any conceivable way. It can't be fairly inferred from my past career." I, for one, am not interested to hear you define your position. I don't know that I ever was or ever shall be. I think it is mere egotism, or impertinent at this time. Ye needn't take so much pains to wash your skirts of him. No intelligent man will ever be convinced that he was any creature of yours. He went and came, as he himself informs us, "under the auspices of John Brown and nobody else." The Republican party does not perceive how many his *failure* will make to vote more correctly than they would have them. They have counted the votes of Pennsylvania & Co., but they have not correctly counted Captain Brown's vote. He has taken the wind out of their sails,—the little wind they had,—and they may as well lie to and repair.

What though he did not belong to your clique! Though you may not approve of his method or his principles, recognize his magnanimity. Would you not like to claim kindredship with him in that, though in no other thing he is like, or likely, to you? Do you think that you would lose your reputation so? What you lost at the spile, you would gain at the bung.

If they do not mean all this, then they do not speak the truth, and say what they mean. They are simply at their old tricks still.

"It was always conceded to him," *says one who calls him crazy*, "that he was a conscientious man, very modest in his demeanor, apparently inoffensive, until the subject of Slavery was introduced, when he would exhibit a feeling of indignation unparalleled."

The slave-ship is on her way, crowded with its dying victims; new cargoes are being added in mid-ocean; a small crew of slaveholders, countenanced by a large body of passengers, is smothering four millions under the hatches, and yet the politican asserts that the only proper way by which deliverance is to be obtained is by "the quiet diffusion of the sentiments of humanity," without any "outbreak." As if the sentiments of humanity were ever found unaccompanied by its deeds, and you could disperse them, all finished to order, the pure article, as easily as water with a watering-pot, and so lay the dust. What is that that I hear cast overboard? The bodies of the dead that have found deliverance. That is the way we are "diffusing" humanity, and its sentiments with it.

Prominent and influential editors, accustomed to deal with politicians, men of an infinitely lower grade, say, in their ignorance, that he acted "on the principle of revenge." They do not know the man. They must enlarge themselves to conceive of him. I have no doubt that the time will come when they will begin to see him as he was. They have got to conceive of a man of faith and of religious principle, and not a politician or an Indian; of a man who did not wait till he was personally interfered with or thwarted in some harmless business before he gave his life to the cause of the oppressed.

If Walker may be considered the representative of the South, I wish I could say that Brown was the representative of the North. He was a superior man. He did not value his bodily life in comparison with ideal things. He did not recognize unjust human laws, but resisted them as he was bid. For once we are lifted out of the trivialness and dust of politics into the region of truth and manhood. No man in America has ever stood up so persistently and effectively for the dignity of human nature, knowing himself for a man, and the equal of any and all governments. In that sense he was the most American of us all. He needed no babbling lawyer, making false issues, to defend him. He was more than a match for all the judges that American voters, or officeholders of whatever grade, can create. He could not have been tried by a jury of his peers, because his peers did not exist. When a man stands up serenely against the condemnation and vengeance of mankind, rising above them literally *by a whole body,*—even though he were of late the vilest murderer, who has settled that matter with himself,—the spectacle is a sublime one,—didn't ye know it, ye *Liberators,* ye *Tribunes,* ye *Republicans?*—and we become crminal in comparison. Do yourselves the honor to recognize him. He needs none of your respect.

As for the Democratic journals, they are not human enough to affect me at all. I do not feel indignation at anything they may say.

I am aware that I anticipate a little,—that he was still, at the last accounts, alive in the hands of his foes; but that being the case, I have all along found myself thinking and speaking of him as physically dead.

I do not believe in erecting statues to those who still live in our hearts, whose bones have not yet crumbled in the earth around us, but I would rather see the statue of Captain Brown in the Massachusetts State-House yard than that of any other man whom I know. I rejoice that I live in this age, that I am his contemporary.

What a contrast, when we turn to that political party which is so anxiously shuffling him and his plot out of its way, and looking around for some available slaveholder, perhaps, to be its candidate, at least for one who will execute the Fugitive Slave Law, and all those other unjust laws which he took up arms to annul!

Insane! A father and six sons, and one son-in-law, and several more men besides,—as many at least as twelve disciples,—all struck with insanity at once; while the sane tyrant holds with a firmer grip than ever his four millions of slaves, and a thousand sane editors, his abettors, are saving their country and their bacon! Just as insane were his efforts in Kansas. Ask the tyrant who is his most dangerous foe, the sane man or the insane? Do the thousands who know him best, who have rejoiced at his deeds in Kansas, and have afforded him material aid there, think him insane? Such a use of this word is a mere trope with most who persist in using it, and I have no doubt that many of the rest have already in silence retracted their words.

Read his admirable answers to Mason and others. How they are dwarfed and defeated by the contrast! On the one side, half-brutish, half-timid questioning; on the other, truth, clear as lightning, crashing into their obscene temples. They are made to stand with Pilate, and Gessler,[3] and the Inquisition. How ineffectual their speech and action! and what a void their silence! They are but helpless tools in this great work. It was no human power that gathered them about this preacher.

What have Massachusetts and the North sent a few *sane* representatives to Congress for, of late years?—to declare with effect what kind of sentiments? All their speeches put together and boiled down—and probably they themselves will confess it—do not match for manly directness and force, and for simple truth, the few casual remarks of crazy John Brown on the floor of the Harper's Ferry engine-house,—that man whom you are about to hang,to send to the other world, though not to represent *you* there. No, he was not our representative in any sense. He was too fair a specimen of man to represent the like of us. Who, then, *were* his constituents? If you read his words understandingly you will find out. In his case there is no idle eloquence, no made, nor maiden speech, no compliments to the oppressor. Truth is his inspirer, and earnestness the polisher of his sentences. He could afford to lose his Sharps rifles,while he retained his faculty of speech,—a Sharps rifle of infinitely surer and longer range.

And the New York *Herald* reports the conversation *verbatim!* It does not know of what undying words it is made the vehicle.

I have no respect for the penetration of any man who can read the report of that conversation and still call the principal in it insane. It has the ring of a saner sanity than an ordinary discipline and habits of life, than an ordinary organization, secure. Take any sentence of it,—"Any questions that I can honorably answer, I will; not otherwise. So far as I am myself concerned, I have told everything truthfully. I value my word, sir." The few who talk about his vindictive spirit, while they really admire his heroism, have no test by which to detect a noble man, no amalgam to combine with his pure gold. They mix their own dross with it.

It is a relief to turn from these slanders to the testimony of his more truthful, but frightened jailers and hangmen. Governor Wise speaks far more

[3] Pontius Pilate (A.D. 26?-36?), Roman official, procurator of Judea, who was assumed to have authorized the execution of Jesus; Hermann Gessler was a tyrannical steward of Austria in the early fourteenth century, defied by the Swiss patriot William Tell.

justly and appreciatingly of him than any Northern editor, or politician, or public personage, than I chance to have heard from. I know that you can afford to hear him again on this subject. He says: "They are themselves mistaken who take him to be a madman. . . . He is cool, collected, and indomitable, and it is but just to him to say that he was humane to his prisoners. . . . And he inspired me with great trust in his integrity as a man of truth. He is fanatic, vain and garrulous" (I leave that part to Mr. Wise), "but firm, truthful, and intelligent. His men, too, who survive, are like him. . . . Colonel Washington says that he was the coolest and firmest man he ever saw in defying danger and death. With one son dead by his side, and another shot through, he felt the pulse of his dying son with one hand, and held his rifle with the other, and commanded his men with the utmost composure, encouraging them to be firm, and to sell their lives as dear as they could. Of the three white prisoners, Brown, Stevens, and Coppoc, it was hard to say which was most firm." Almost the first Northern men whom the slaveholder has learned to respect!

The testimony of Mr. Vallandigham, though less vaulable, is of the same purport, that "it is vain to underrate either the man or his conspiracy. . . . He is the farthest possible removed from the ordinary ruffian, fanatic, or madman."

"All is quiet at Harper's Ferry," say the journals. What is the character of that calm which follows when the law and the slaveholder prevail? I regard this event as a touchstone designed to bring out, with glaring distinctness, the character of this government. We needed to be thus assisted to see it by the light of history. It needed to see itself. When a government puts forth its strength on the side of injustice, as ours to maintain slavery and kill the liberators of the slave, it reveals itself a merely brute force, or worse, a demoniacal force. It is the head of the Plug-Uglies. It is more manifest than ever that tyranny rules. I see this government to be effectually allied with France and Austria in oppressing mankind. There sits a tyrant holding fettered four millions of slaves; here comes their heroic liberator. This most hypocritical and diabolical government looks up from its seat on the gasping four millions, and inquires with an assumption of innocence: "What do you assault me for? Am I not an honest man? Cease agitation this subject, or I will make a slave of you, too, or else hang you."

We talk about *representative* government; but what a monster of a government is that where the noblest faculties of the mind, and the *whole* heart, are not *represented*. A semi-human tiger or ox, stalking over the earth, with its heart taken out and the top of its brain shot away. Heroes have fought well on their stumps when their legs were shot off, but I never heard of any good done by such a government as that.

The only government that I recognize—and it matters not how few are at the head of it, or how small its army—is that power that establishes justice in the land, never that which establishes injustice. What shall we think of a government to which all the truly brave and just men in the land are enemies, standing between it and those whom it oppresses? A government that pretends to be Christian and crucifies a million Christs every day!

Treason! Where does such treason take its rise? I cannot help thinking of you as you deserve, ye governments. Can you dry up the fountains of thought? High treason, when it is resistance to tyranny here below, has its origin in, and is first committed by, the power that makes and forever recreates man. When you have caught and hung all these human rebels, you have accomplished nothing but your own guilt, for you have not struck at the fountain-head. You presume to contend with a foe against whom West Point cadets and rifled cannon *point* not. Can all the art of the cannon founder tempt matter to turn against its maker? Is the form in which the founder thinks he casts it more essential than the constitution of it and of himself?

The United States have a coffle of four millions of slaves. They are determined to keep them in this condition; and Massachusetts is one of the confederated overseers to prevent their escape. Such are not all the inhabitants of Massachusetts, but such are they who rule and are obeyed here. It was Massachusetts, as well as Virginia, that put down this insurrection at Harper's Ferry. She sent the marines there, and she will have *to pay the penalty of her sin.*

Suppose that there is a society in this State that out of its own purse and magnanimity saves all the fugitive slaves that run to us, and protects our colored fellow-citizens, and leaves the other work to the government, so called. Is not that government fast losing its occupation, and becoming contemptible to mankind? If private men are obliged to perform the offices of government, to protect the weak and dispense justice, then the government becomes only a hired man, or clerk, to perform menial or indifferent services. Of course, that is but the shadow of a government whose existence necessitates a Vigilant Committee. What should we think of the Oriental Cadi even, behind whom worked in secret a Vigilant Committee. But such is the character of our Northern States generally; each has its Vigilant Committee. And, to a certain extent, these crazy governments recognize and accept this relation. They say, virtually, "We'll be glad to work for you on these terms, only don't make a noise about it." And thus the government, its salary being insured, withdraws into the back shop, taking the Constitution with it, and bestows most of its labor on repairing that. When I hear it at work sometimes, as I go by, it reminds me, at best, of those farmers who in winter contrive to turn a penny by following the coopering business. And what kind of spirit is their barrel made to hold? They speculate in stocks, and bore holes in mountains, but they are not competent to lay out even a decent highway. The only *free* road, the Underground Railroad, is owned and managed by the Vigilant Committee. *They* have tunneled under the whole breadth of the land. Such a government is losing its power and respectability as surely as water runs out of a leaky vessel, and is held by one that can contain it.

I hear many condemn these men because they were so few. When were the good and the brave ever in a majority? Would you have had him wait till that time came?—till you and I came over to him? The very fact that he had no rabble or troop of hirelings about him would alone distinguish him from ordinary heroes. His company was small indeed, because few could be found worthy to pass muster. Each one who there laid down his life for the poor and oppressed was a picked man, culled out of many thousand, if not millions; apparently a man of principle, of rare courage, and devoted humanity; ready to sacrifice his life at any moment for the benefit of his fellow-man. It may be doubted if there were as many more their equals in these respects in all the country,—I speak of his followers only,—for their leader, no doubt, scoured the land far and wide, seeking to swell his troop. These alone were ready to step between the oppressor and the oppressed. Surely they were the very best men you could select to be hung. That was the greatest compliment which this country could pay them. They were ripe for her gallows. She has tried a long time, she has hung a good many, but never found the right one before.

When I think of him, and his six sons, and his son-in-law, not to enumerate the others, enlisted for this fight, proceeding coolly, reverently, humanely to work, for months if not years, sleeping and waking upon it, summering and wintering the thought, without expecting any reward but a good conscience, while almost all America stood ranked on the other side,—I say again that it affects me as a sublime spectacle. If he had had any journal advocating *"his cause,"* any organ, as the phrase is, monotonously and wearisomely playing the same old tune, and then passing round the hat, it would have been fatal to his efficiency. If he had acted in any way so as to be let alone by the government, he might have been suspected. It was the fact that the tyrant must give place to him, or he to the tyrant, that distinguished him from all the reformers of the day that I know.

It was his peculiar doctrine that a man has a perfect right to interfere by force with the slaveholder, in order to rescue the slave. I agree with him. They who are continually shocked by slavery have some right to be shocked by the violent death of the slaveholder, but no others. Such will be more shocked by his life than by his death. I shall not be forward to think him mistaken in his method who quickest succeeds to liberate the slave. I speak for the slave when I say that I prefer the philanthropy of Captain Brown to that philanthropy which neither shoots me nor liberates me. At any rate, I do not think it is quite sane for one to spend his whole life in talking or writing about this matter, unless he is continuously inspired, and I have not done so. A man may have other affairs to attend to. I do not wish to kill nor to be killed, but I can foresee circumstances in which both these things would be by me unavoidable. We preserve the so-called peace of our community by deeds of petty violence every day. Look at the policeman's billy and hand-cuffs! Look at the jail! Look at the gallows! Look at the chaplain of the regiment! We are hoping only to live safely on the outskirts of *this* provisional army. So we defend ourselves and our hen-roosts, and maintain slavery. I know that the mass of my countrymen think that the only righteous use that can be made of Sharps rifles and revolvers is to fight duels with them, when we are insulted by other nations, or to hunt Indians, or shoot fugitive slaves with them, or the like. I think that for once the Sharps rifles and the revolvers were employed in a righteous cause. The tools were in the hands of one who could use them.

The same indignation that is said to have cleared the temple once will clear it again. The question is not about the weapon, but the spirit in which you use it. No man has appeared in America, as yet, who loved his fellow-man so well, and treated him so tenderly. He lived for him. He took up his life and he laid it down for him. What sort of violence is that which is encouraged, not by soldiers, but by peaceable citizens, not so much by laymen as by ministers of the Gospel, not so much by the fighting sects as by the Quakers, and not so much by Quaker men as by Quaker women?

This event advertises me that there is such a fact as death,—the possibility of a man's dying. It seems as if no man had ever died in America before; for in order to die you must first have lived. I don't believe in the hearses, and palls, and funerals that they have had. There was no death in the case, because there had been no life; they merely rotted or sloughed off, pretty much as they had rotted or sloughed along. No temple's veil was rent, only a hole dug somewhere. Let the dead bury their dead. The best of them fairly ran down like a clock. Franklin,—Washington,—they were let off without dying; they were merely missing one day. I hear a good many pretend that they are going to die; or that they have died, for aught that I know. Non-sense! I'll defy them to do it. They haven't got life enough in them. They'll deliquesce like fungi, and keep a hundred eulogists mopping the spot where they left off. Only half a dozen or so have died since the world began. Do you think that you are going to die, sir? No! there's no hope of you. You haven't got your lesson yet. You've got to stay after school. We make a needlesss ado about captial punishment,—taking lives, when there is no life to take. *Memento mori!* We don't understand that sublime sentence which some worthy got sculptured on his grave stone once. We've interpreted it in a groveling and sniveling sense; we've wholly forgotten how to die.

But be sure you do die nevertheless. Do your work, and finish it. If you know how to begin, you will know when to end.

These men, in teaching us how to die, have at the same time taught us how to live. If this man's acts and words do not create a revival, it will be the severest possible satire on the acts and words that do. It is the best news that America has ever heard. It has already quickened the feeble pulse of the North, and infused more and more generous blood into her veins and heart than any number of years of what is called commercial and political prosperity could. How many a man who was lately contemplating suicide has now something to live for!

One writer says that Brown's peculiar monomania made him to be "dreaded by the Missourians as a supernatural being." Sure enough, a hero in the midst of us cowards is always so dreaded. He is just that thing. He shows himself superior to nature. He has a spark of divinity in him.

> "Unless above himself he can
> Erect himself, how poor a thing is man!"[4]

Newspaper editors argue also that it is a proof of his *insanity* that he thought he was appointed to do this work which he did,—that he did not suspect himself for a moment! They talk as if it were impossible that a man could be "divinely appointed" in these days to do any work whatever; as if vows and religion were out of date as connected with any man's daily work; as if the agent to abolish slavery could only be somebody appointed by the President, or by some political party. They talk as if a man's death were a failure, and his continued life, be it of whatever character, were a success.

When I reflect to what a cause this man devoted himself, and how religiously, and then reflect to what cause his judges and all who condemn him so angrily and fluently devote themselves, I see that they are as far apart as the heavens and earth are asunder.

The amount of it is, our *"leading men"* are a harmless kind of folk, and they know *well enough* that *they* were not divinely appointed, but elected by the votes of their party.

Who is it whose safety requires that Captain Brown be hung? Is it indispensable to any Northern man? Is there no resource but to cast this man also to the Minotaur? If you do not wish it, say so distinctly. While these things are being done, beauty stands veiled and music is a screeching lie. Think of him,—of his rare qualities!—such a man as it takes ages to make, and ages to understand; no mock hero, nor the representative of any party. A man such as the sun may not rise upon again in this benighted land. To whose making went the costliest material, the finest adamant; sent to be the redeemer of those in captivity; and the only use to which you can put him is to hang him at the end of a rope! You who pretend to care for Christ crucified, consider what you are about to do to him who offered himself to be the saviour of four millions of men.

Any man knows when he is justified, and all the wits in the world cannot enlighten him on that point. The murderer always knows that he is justly punished; but when a government takes the life of a man without the consent of his conscience, it is an audacious government, and is taking a step

---

[4] From Samuel Daniel, *To the Lady Margaret Countess of Cumberland*, St. 12. Quoted by Wordsworth in *The Excursion*, Bk IV, 1. 330.

towards its own dissolution. Is it not possible that an individual may be right and a government wrong? Are laws to be enforced simply because they were made? or declared by any number of men to be good, if they are *not* good? Is there any necessity for a man's being a tool to perform a deed of which his better nature disapproves? Is it the intention of lawmakers that *good* men shall be hung ever? Are judges to interpret the law according to the letter, and not the spirit? What right have *you* to enter into a compact with yourself that you *will* do thus or so, against the light within you? Is it for *you* to *make up* your mind,—to form any resolution whatever,—and not accept the convictions that are forced upon you, and which ever pass your understanding? I do not believe in lawyers, in that mode of attacking or defending a man, because you descend to meet the judge on his own ground, and, in cases of the highest importance, it is of no consequence whether a man breaks a human law or not. Let lawyers decide trivial cases. Business men may arrange that among themselves. If they were the interpreters of the everlasting laws which rightfully bind man, that would be another thing. A counterfeiting law-factory, standing half in a slave land and half in a free! What kind of laws for free men can you expect from that?

I am here to plead his cause with you. I plead not for his life, but for his character,—his immortal life; and so it becomes your cause wholly, and is not his in the least. Some eighteen hundred years ago Christ was crucified; this morning, perchance, Captain Brown was hung. These are the two ends of a chain which is not without its links. He is not Old Brown any longer; he is an angel of light.

I see now that it was necessary that the bravest and humanest man in all the country should be hung. Perhaps he saw it himself. I *almost fear* that I may yet hear of his deliverance, doubting if a prolonged life, if *any* life, can do as much good as his death.

"Misguided!" "Garrulous!" "Insane!" "Vindictive!" So ye write in your easy-chairs, and thus he wounded responds from the floor of the Armory, clear as a cloudless sky, true as the voice of nature is: "No man sent me here; it was my own prompting and that of my Maker. I acknowledge no master in human form."

And in what a sweet and noble strain he proceeds, addressing his captors, who stand over him: "I think, my friends you are guilty of a great wrong against God and humanity, and it would be perfectly right for any one to interfere with you so far as to free those you willfully and wickedly hold in bondage."

And, referring to his movement: "It is, in my opinion, the greatest service a man can render to God."

"I pity the poor in bondage that have none to help them; that is why I am here; not to gratify any personal animosity, revenge, or vindictive spirit. It is my sympathy with the oppressed and the wronged, that are as good as you, and as precious in the sight of God."

You don't know your testament when you see it.

"I want you to understand that I respect the rights of the poorest and weakest of colored people, oppressed by the slave power, just as much as I do those of the most wealthy and powerful"

"I wish to say, furthermore, that you had better, all you people at the South, prepare yourselves for a settlement of that question, that must come up for settlement sooner than you are prepared for it. The sooner you are prepared the better. You may dispose of me very easily. I am nearly disposed of now; but this question is still to be settled,—this negro question, I mean; the end of that is not yet."

I foresee the time when the painter will paint that scene, no longer going to Rome for a subject; the poet will sing it; the historian record it; and, with the Landing of the Pilgrims and the Declaration of Independence, it will be the ornament of some future national gallery, when at least the present form of slavery shall be no more here. We shall then be at liberty to weep for Captain Brown. Then, and not till then, we will take our revenge.

JOHN BROWN

(1800–1859)

"Without the shedding of blood there is no remission of sins."

John Brown was a Kansas farmer who had used guerilla warfare in attacking slavery with a zeal that suggested emotional instability. Some of his activities, like the Pottawatomie massacre, were especially bloodthirsty, despite Brown's claim, that "they were decreed by Almighty God, ordained from Eternity." His career as a saint and a martyr was climaxed by his attempt to incite a slavery insurrection at Harper's Ferry, Virginia, in 1859. Brown was sentenced to death for "treason to the Commonwealth, conspiring with slaves to commit treason and murder." He carried himself with such great dignity and stoicism as he went to his hanging that Emerson compared him to Christ, and the more militant Northerners viewed him as a martyr and an inspiration.

Studies include F. B. Sanborn, *The Life and Letters of John Brown,* 1885; H. D. Thoreau, *Anti-Slavery and Reform Papers,* 1890; W. E. B. Dubois, *John Brown,* 1909; P. G. Villard, *John Brown: A Biography, Fifty Years After,* 1910; R. P. Warren, *John Brown, The Making of a Martyr,* 1929; James C. Malin, *John Brown and the Legend of Fifty-Six,* 1942, and Stephen B. Oates, *To Purge this Land with Blood: A Biography of John Brown,* 1970; Richard Owen Boyer, *The Legend of John Brown,* 1972; Truman John Nelson, *The Old Man: John Brown at Harper's Ferry,* 1973, and Benjamin Quarles, *Allies for Freedom: Blacks and John Brown,* 1974.

John Brown, *(The Metropolitan Museum of Art.)*

John Brown's Last Speech

I have, may it please the Court, a few words to say.

In the first place, I deny everything but what I have all along admitted,—the design on my part to free the slaves. I intended certainly to have made a clean thing of that matter, as I did last winter, when I went into Missouri and there took slaves without the snapping of a gun on either side, moved them through the country, and finally left them in Canada. I designed to have done the same thing again, on a larger scale. That was all I intended. I never did intend murder, or treason, or the destruction of property, or to excite or incite slaves to rebellion, or to make insurrection.

I have another objection; and that is, it is unjust that I should suffer such a penalty. Had I interfered in the manner which I admit, and which I admit has been fairly proved (for I admire the truthfulness and candor of the greater portion of the witnesses who have testified in this case),—had I so interfered in behalf of the rich, the powerful, the intelligent, the so-called great, or in behalf of any of their friends,—either father, mother, brother, sister, wife, or children, or any of that class,—and suffered and sacrificed what I have in this interference, it would have been all right; and every man in this court would have deemed it an act worthy of reward rather than punishment.

This court acknowledges, as I suppose, the validity of the law of God. I see a book kissed here which I suppose to be the Bible, or at least the New Testament. That teaches me that all things whatsoever I would that men should do to me, I should do even so to them. It teaches me, further, to "remember them that are in bonds, as bound with them." I endeavored to act up to that instruction. I say, I am yet too young to understand that God is any respecter of persons. I believe that to have interfered as I have done—as I have always freely admitted I have done—in behalf of His despised poor, was not wrong, but right. Now, if it is deemed necessary that I should forfeit my life for the furtherance of the ends of justice, and mingle my blood further with the blood of my children and with the blood of millions in this slave country whose rights are disregarded by wicked, cruel, and unjust enactments,—I submit; so let it be done!

Let me say one word further.

I feel entirely satisfied with the treatment I have received on my trial. Considering all the circumstances, it has been more generous than I expected. But I felt no consciousness of guilt. I have stated from the first what was my intention, and what was not. I never had any design against the life of any person, nor any disposition to commit treason, or excite slaves to rebel, or make any general insurrection. I never encouraged any man to do so, but always discouraged any idea of that kind.

Let me say, also, a word in regard to the statements made by some of those connected with me. I hear it has been stated by some of them that I have induced them to join me. But the contrary is true. I do not say this to injure them, but as regretting their weakness. There is not one of them but joined me of his own accord, and the greater part of them at their own expense. A number of them I never saw, and never had a word of conversation with, till the day they came to me; and that was for the purpose I have stated.

Now I have done.

1859

Songs

The songs of the North were charged with religious fervor and celebrated the men as soldiers "in the army of the Lord." The Federal's favorite song was "John Brown's Body," which was set to the tune of a popular Southern revival hymn, "Say, brothers, will you meet us." In 1861 some soldiers from a Massachusetts regiment fitted the words to the tune and, when they sang it in New York on July 24, 1861, the song became instantly popular.

John Brown's Body

Words: anonymous
Music: "Say, Brothers, Will You Meet Us?" (ascribed to William Steffe)

1. John Brown's body lies a-mouldering in the grave,
   John Brown's body lies a-mouldering in the grave,
   John Brown's body lies a-mouldering in the grave,
   But his soul goes marching on.

Chorus:
   Glory, glory, hallelujah,
   Glory, glory, hallelujah,
   Glory, glory, hallelujah,
   His soul goes marching on.

2. He's gone to be a soldier in the Army of the Lord,
   His soul goes marching on. (Chorus)

3. John Brown's knapsack is strapped upon his back,
   His soul goes marching on.   (Chorus)

3. John Brown died that the slaves might be free,
   But his soul goes marching on.   (Chorus)

5. The stars above in Heaven now are looking kindly down,
   On the grave of old John Brown.   (Chorus)

Battle-Hymn of the Republic

[Mrs. Julia Ward Howe, a humanitarian reformer and abolitionist, wrote the "Battle-Hymn of the Republic" after having visited an army camp near Washington, D.C. She was so moved by what she saw in the camp that she awoke the morning after her experience to write down the song in one extended mood. The words were fitted to the tune of "John Brown's Body." The poem itself was published in the Atlantic Monthly, February 1862.]

Mine eyes have seen the glory of the coming of the Lord:
He is trampling out the vintage where the grapes of wrath are stored;
He hath loosed the fateful lightning of his terrible swift sword;
   His truth is marching on.

I have seen Him in the watch-fires of a hundred circling camps;
They have builded Him an altar in the evening dews and damps;
I can read His righteous sentence by the dim and flaring lamps;
   His day is marching on.

I have read a fiery gospel, writ in burnished rows of steel:
"As ye deal with my contemners, so with you my grace shall deal;
Let the Hero, born of woman, crush the serpent with his heel,
   Since God is marching on."

He has sounded forth the trumpet that shall never call retreat;
He is sifting out the hearts of men before his judgment-seat:
Oh! be swift my soul, to answer Him! be jubilant, my feet!
   Our God is marching on.

In the beauty of the lilies Christ was born across the sea,
With a glory in his bosom that transfigures you and me:
As he died to make men holy, let us die to make men free,
   While God is marching on.

Tenting on the Old Camp Ground

[This song was composed by Walter Kitteredge, a Northern ballad singer. It was published in 1864 and became a favorite of both Northern and Southern troops.]

We're tenting tonight on the old camp ground,
Give us a song to cheer
Our weary hearts, a song of home
And friends we love so dear.

Many are the hearts that are weary tonight,
Wishing for the war to cease;
Many of the hearts that are looking for the right
To see the dawn of peace.

Tenting tonight, tenting tonight
Tenting on the old camp ground.

THE BLACK PERSPECTIVE

Before the first flowering of black culture in the work of Booker T. Washington, W. E. B. DuBois, Paul Dunbar, and Charles W. Chestnut, most significant black literature was polemical and autobiographical. The polemical tradition was initiated by Benjamin Baneker, Absalom Jones, and William Hamilton, although the most distinguished early utterance was the nonmilitant "address to the Negroes in the State of New York in 1787" by Jupiter Hammon. During the period before the Civil War, the speeches and autobiographies of David Walker, Nat Turner, and Frederick Douglass were forthright in their denunciation of slavery. It was natural that autobiography should become a major genre of black writing in America, first in the form of slave narratives written by William Wells Brown, Samuel Ringgold Ward, and Frederick Douglass; then in the accounts of self-improvement by Booker T. Washington, Kelly Miller, and a host of early twentieth-century black leaders; and, finally, in the more sophisticated treatment of Richard Wright's *Black Boy* (1945) and Ralph Ellison's *Invisible Man* (1952).

Another reflection of the black experience during this period took the form of spirituals. Unable to articulate their inward feelings about slavery and displacement, blacks gave form to their suffering and alienation through spirituals. These laments, together with folk songs that originated in slavery and that are now called "the blues," are among America's most creative and distinctive music.

DAVID WALKER

(1785–1830)

David Walker's Appeal of 1829 was labeled "totally subversive" in the South because it "called for slave insurrections." It is one of the first expressions of overt militancy.

A recent edition of David Walker's *Appeal* has been edited by Charles M. Wilste, 1965. It is also included in Herbert Aptheker's *One Continual Cry*, 1965, and Richard Barksdale and Kenneth Kinnamon, eds., *Black Writers of America*, 1972.

An interesting early essay is Clement Eaton, "A Dangerous Pamphlet in the Old South," *The Journal of Southern History*, II (1936), 323–334. For analyses of Walker, see Vernon Loggins, *The Negro Author*, 1931: Lerone Bennet, Jr., *Pioneers in Protest*, 1968: Melvin Dummer, ed., *Black History: A Reappraisal*, 1969, and Benjamin Quarles, *Black Abolitionists, 1969*.

From David Walker's Appeal

It will be recollected, that I, in the first edition of my "Appeal,"[1] promised to demonstrate in the course of which, viz. in the course of my Appeal, to the satisfaction of the most incredulous mind, that we Coloured People of these United States, are, the most wretched, degraded and abject set of beings that ever lived since the world began, down to the present day, and, that, the white Christians of America, who hold us in slavery, (or, more properly speaking, pretenders to Christianity,) treat us more cruel and barbarous than any Heathen nation did any people whom it had subjected, or reduced to the same condition, that the Americans (who are, notwithstanding, looking for the Millennial day) have us. All I ask is, for a candid and careful perusal of this the third and last edition of my Appeal, where the world may see that we, the Blacks or Coloured People, are treated more cruel by the white Christians of America, than devils themselves ever treated a set of men, women and children on this earth.

It is expected that all coloured men, women and children,[2] of every nation, language and tongue under heaven, will try to procure a copy of this Appeal and read it, or get some one to read it to them, for it is designed

[1] See my Preamble in first edition, first page also.

[2] Who are not deceitful, abject, and servile

to resist the cruelties and murders inflicted upon us by the white slave holders, our enemies by nature.

more particularly for them. Let them remember, that though our cruel oppressors and murderers, may (if possible) treat us more cruel, as Pharaoh did
the children of Israel, yet the God of the Ethiopians, has been pleased to
hear our moans in consequence of oppression; and the day of our redemption from abject wretchedness draweth near, when we shall be enabled, in
the most extended sense of the word, to stretch forth our hands to the
LORD Our GOD, but there must be a willingness on our part, for GOD to
do these things for us, for we may be assured that he will not take us by the
hairs of our head against our will and desire, and drag us from our very,
mean, low and abject condition.

PREAMBLE

My dearly beloved Brethren and Fellow Citizens:—Having travelled over a
considerable portion of these United States, and having, in the course of my
travels, taken the most accurate observations of things as they exist—the
result of my observations has warranted the full and unshaken conviction,
that we, (coloured people of these United States,) are the most degraded,
wretched, and abject set of beings that ever lived since the world began; and
I pray God that none like us ever may live again until time shall be no more.
They tell us of the Israelites in Egypt, the Helots in Sparta, and of the Roman
Slaves, which last were made up from almost every nation under heaven,
whose sufferings under those ancient and heathen nations, were, in comparison with ours, under this enlightened and Christian nation, no more than a
cypher—or, in other words, those nations of antiquity, had but little more
among them than the name and form of slavery; while wretchedness and
endless miseries were reserved, apparently in a phial, to be poured out upon
our fathers, ourselves and our children, by *Christian* Americans!

These positions I shall endeavour, by the help of the Lord, to demonstrate
in the course of this APPEAL, to the satisfaction of the most incredulous
mind—and may God Almighty, who is the Father of our Lord Jesus Christ,
open your hearts to understand and believe the truth.

The *causes*, my brethren, which produce our wretchedness and miseries,
are so very numerous and aggravating, that I believe the pen only of a
Josephus or a Plutarch, can well enumerate and explain them. Upon subjects, then, of such incomprehensible magnitude, so impenetrable, and so
notorious, I shall be obliged to omit a large class of, and content myself with
giving you an exposition of a few of those, which do indeed rage to such an
alarming pitch, that they cannot but be a perpetual source of terror and
dismay to every reflecting mind.

I am fully aware, in making this appeal to my much afflicted and suffering
brethren, that I shall not only be assailed by those whose greatest earthly
desires are, to keep us in abject ignorance and wretchedness, and who are of

the firm conviction that Heaven has designed us and our children to be slaves and *beasts of burden* to them and their children. I say, I do not only expect to be held up to the public as an ignorant, impudent and restless disturber of the public peace, by such avaricious creatures, as well as a mover of insubordination—and perhaps put in prison or to death, for giving a superficial exposition of our miseries, and exposing tyrants. But I am persuaded, that many of my brethren, particularly those who are ignorantly in league with slaveholders or tyrants, who acquire their daily bread by the blood and sweat of their more ignorant brethren—and not a few of those too, who are too ignorant to see an inch beyond their noses, will rise up and call me cursed—Yea, the jealous ones among us will perhaps use more abject subtlety, by affirming that this work is not worth perusing, that we are well situated, and there is no use in trying to better our condition, for we cannot. I will ask one question here.—Can our condition be any worse?—Can it be more mean and abject? If there are any changes, will they not be for the better, though they may appear for the worst at first? Can they get us any lower? Where can they get us? They are afraid to treat us worse, for they know well, the day they do it they are gone. But against all accusations which may or can be preferred against me, I appeal to Heaven for my motive in writing—who knows that my object is, if possible, to awaken in the breasts of my afflicted, degraded and slumbering brethren, a spirit of inquiry and investigation respecting our miseries and wretchedness in this REPUBLICAN LAND OF LIBERTY!!!!!!

The sources from which our miseries are derived, and on which I shall comment, I shall not combine in one, but shall put them under distinct heads and expose them in their turn; in doing which, keeping truth on my side, and not departing from the strictest rules of morality, I shall endeavour to penetrate, search out, and lay them open for your inspection. If you cannot or will not profit by them, I shall have done *my* duty to you, and my country and my God.

And as the inhuman system of *slavery*, is the *source* from which most of our miseries proceed, I shall begin with that *curse to nations*, which has spread terror and devastation through so many nations of antiquity, and which is raging to such a pitch at the present day in Spain and in Portugal. It had one tug in England, in France, and in the United States of America; yet the inhabitants thereof, do not learn wisdom, and erase it entirely from their dwellings and from all with whom they have to do. The fact is, the labour of slaves comes too cheap to the avaricious usurpers, and is (as they think) of such great utility to the country where it exists, that those who are actuated by sordid avarice only, overlook the evils, which will as sure as the Lord lives, follow after the good. In fact, they are so happy to keep in ignorance and degradation, and to receive the homage and the labour of the slaves, they forget that God rules in the armies of heaven his ears continually open to the cries, tears and groans of his oppressed people; and being a just and holy Being will at one day appear fully in behalf of the oppressed, and arrest the progress of the avaricious oppressors; for although the destruction of the oppressors God may not effect by the oppressed, yet the Lord our God will bring other destructions upon them—for not infrequently will he cause them to rise up one against another, to be split and divided, and to oppress each other, and sometimes to open hostilities with sword in hand.

So you may ask, what is the matter with this united and happy people?—Some say it is the cause of political usurpers, tyrants, oppressors, &c. But has not the Lord an oppressed and suffering people among them? Does the Lord condescend to hear their cries and see their tears in consequence of oppression? Will he let the oppressors rest comfortably and happy always? Will he not cause the very children of the oppressors to rise up against them, and ofttimes put them to death? "God works in many ways his wonders to perform."

I will not here speak of the destructions which the Lord brought upon Egypt, in consequence of the oppression and consequent groans of the oppressed—of the hundreds and thousands of Egyptians whom God hurled into the Red Sea for afflicting his people in their land—of the Lord's suffering people in Sparta or Lacedemon, the land of the truly famous Lycurgus—nor have I time to comment upon the cause which produced the fierceness with which Sylla usurped the title, and absolutely acted as dictator of the Roman people—the conspiracy of Cataline—the conspiracy against, and murder of Caesar in the Senate house—the spirit with which Marc Anthony made himself master of the commonwealth—his associating Octavius and Lipidus with himself in power—their dividing the provinces of Rome among themselves—their attack and defeat, on the plains of Phillippi, of the last defenders of their liberty, (Brutus and Cassius)—the tyranny of Tiberius, and from him to the final overthrow of Constantinople by the Turkish Sultan, Mahomed II. A.D. 1453.

I say, I shall not take up time to speak of the *causes* which produced so much wretchedness and massacre among those heathen nations, for I am aware that you know too well, that God is just, as well as merciful!—I shall call your attention a few moments to that *Christian* nation, the Spaniards—while I shall leave almost unnoticed, that avaricious and cruel people, the Portuguese, among whom all true hearted Christians and lovers of Jesus Christ, must evidently see the judgments of God displayed. To show the judgments of God upon the Spaniards, I shall occupy but a little time, leaving a plenty of room for the candid and unprejudiced to reflect.

All persons who are acquainted with history, and particularly the Bible, who are not blinded by the God of this world, and are not actuated solely by avarice—who are able to lay aside prejudice long enough to view candidly and impartially, things as they were, are, and probably will be—who are willing to admit that God made man to serve Him *alone*, and that man should have no other Lord or Lords but Himself—that God Almighty is the *sole proprietor* or *master* of the WHOLE human family, and will not on any consideration admit of a colleague, being unwilling to divide his glory with another—and who can dispense with prejudice long enough to admit that we are *men*, notwithstanding our *improminent noses* and *woolly heads*, and believe that we feel for our fathers, mothers, wives and children, as well as the whites do for theirs.—I say, all who are permitted to see and believe these things, can easily recognize the judgments of God among the Spaniards. Though others may lay the cause of the fierceness with which they cut each other's throats, to some other circumstances, yet they who believe that God is a God of justice, will believe that SLAVERY *is the principal cause.*

While the Spaniards are running about upon the field of battle cutting each other's throats, has not the Lord an afflicted and suffering people in the midst of them, whose cries and groans in consequence of oppression are continually pouring into the ears of the God of justice? Would they not cease to cut each other's throats, if they could? But how can they? The very support which they draw from government to aid them in perpetrating such enormities, does it not arise in a great degree from the wretched victims of oppression among them? And yet they are calling for PEACE!—PEACE!! Will any peace be given unto them? Their destruction may indeed be procrastinated awhile, but can it continue long, while they are oppressing the Lord's people? Has He not the hearts of all men in His hand? Will he suffer one part of his creatures to go on oppressing another like brutes always, with impunity? And yet, those avaricious wretches are calling for PEACE!!!! I declare, it does appear to me, as though some nations think God is asleep, or that he made the Africans for nothing else but to dig their mines and work their farms, or they cannot believe history, sacred or profane.

I ask every man who has a heart, and is blessed with the privilege of believing—Is not God a God of justice to *all* his creatures? Do you say he is? Then if he gives peace and tranquillity to tyrants, and permits them to keep our fathers, our mothers, ourselves and our children in eternal ignorance and wretchedness, to support them and their families, would he be to us a God of *justice?* I ask, O ye *Christians!!!* who hold us and our children in the most abject ignorance and degradation, that ever a people were afflicted with since the world began—I say, if God gives you peace and tranquillity, and suffers you thus to go on afflicting us, and our children, who have never given you the least provocation—would he be to us *a God of justice?* If you will allow that we are MEN, who feel for each other, does not the blood of our fathers and of us their children, cry aloud to the Lord of Sabaoth against you, for the cruelties and murders with which you have, and do continue to afflict us. But it is time for me to close my remarks on the suburbs, just to enter more fully into the interior of this system of cruelty and oppression.

ARTICLE I: OUR WRETCHEDNESS IN CONSEQUENCE OF SLAVERY

My beloved Brethren:—The Indians of North and of South America—the Greeks—the Irish, subjected under the King of Great Britain—the Jews, that ancient people of the Lord—the inhabitants of the islands of the sea—in fine, all the inhabitants of the earth, (except however, the sons of Africa) are called *men,* and of course are, and ought to be free. But we, (coloured people) and our children are *brutes!!* and of course are, and *ought to be* SLAVES to the American people and their children forever!! to dig their mines and work their farms; and thus go on enriching them, from one generation to another with our *blood* and our *tears!!!!*

I promised in a preceding page to demonstrate to the satisfaction of the most incredulous, that we, (coloured people of these United States of America) are the *most wretched, degraded* and *abject* set of beings that *ever lived* since the world began, and that the white Americans having reduced us to the wretched state of *slavery,* treat us in that condition *more cruel* (they being an enlightened and Christian people,) than any heathen nation did any people whom it had reduced to our condition. These affirmations are so well confirmed in the minds of all unprejudiced men, who have taken the trouble to read histories, that they need no elucidation from me. But to put them beyond all doubt, I refer you in the first place to the children of Jacob, or of Israel in Egypt, under Pharaoh and his people. Some of my brethren do not know who Pharaoh and the Egyptians were—I know it to be a fact, that some of them take the Egyptians to have been a gang of *devils,* not knowing any better, and that they (Egyptians) having got possession of the Lord's people, treated them *nearly* as cruel as *Christian Americans* do us, at the present day. For the information of such, I would only mention that the Eygptians, were Africans or coloured people, such as we are—some of them yellow and others dark—a mixture of Ethiopians and the natives of Egypt— about the same as you see the coloured people of the United States at the present day.—I say, I call your attention then, to the children of Jacob, while I point out particularly to you his son Joseph, among the rest, in Eygpt.

"And Pharaoh, said unto Joseph, thou shalt be over my house, and according unto thy word shall all my people be ruled: only in the throne will I be greater than thou."[3]

"And Pharaoh said unto Joseph, see, I have set thee over all the land of Egypt."[4]

"And Pharaoh said unto Joseph, I am Pharaoh, and without thee shall no man lift up his hand or foot in all the land of Egypt."[5]

---

[3] See Genesis, chap. xli.

[4] Genesis, chap. xli, 44

[5] Genesis, chap. xli, 44

Now I appeal to heaven and to earth, and particularly to the American people themselves, who cease not to declare that our condition is not *hard,* and that we are comparatively satisfied to rest in wretchedness and misery, under them and their children. Not, indeed, to show me a coloured President, a Governor, a Legislator, a Senator, a Mayor, or an Attorney at the Bar.—But to show me a man of colour, who holds the low office of a Constable, or one who sits in a Juror Box, even on a case of one of his wretched brethren, throughout this great Republic!!—But let us pass Joseph the son of Israel a little farther in review, as he existed with that heathen nation.

"And Pharaoh called Joseph's name Zaphnathpaaneah; and he gave him a wife Asenath the daughter of Potipherah priest of On. And Joseph went out over all the land of Egypt."[6]

Compare the above, with the American institutions. Do they not institute laws to prohibit us from marrying among the whites? I would wish, candidly, however, before the Lord, to be understood, that I would not give a *pinch of snuff* to be married to any white person I ever saw in all the days of my life. And I do say it, that the black man, or man of colour, who will leave his own colour (provided he can get one, who is good for any thing) and marry a white woman, to be a double slave to her, just because she is *white,* ought to be treated by her as he surely will be, viz: as a NIGGER!!!! It is not, indeed, what I care about inter-marriages with the whites, which induced me to pass this subject in review; for the Lord knows, that there is a day coming when they will be glad enough to get into the company of the blacks, notwithstanding, we are, in this generation, levelled by them, almost on a level with the brute creation: and some of us they treat even worse than they do the brutes that perish. I only made this extract to show how much lower we are held, and how much more cruel we are treated by the Americans, than were the children of Jacob, by the Egyptians.—We will notice the sufferings of Israel some further, under *heathen Pharaoh,* compared with ours under the *enlightened Christians of America.*

"And Pharaoh spake unto Joseph, saying, thy father and thy brethren are come unto thee:"

"The land of Egypt is before thee: in the best of the land makes thy father and brethren to dwell; in the land of Goshen let them dwell: and if thou knowest any men of activity among them, then make them rulers over my cattle."[7]

I ask those people who treat us so *well,* Oh! I ask them, where is the most barren spot of land which they have given unto us? Israel had the most fertile land in all Egypt. Need I mention the very notorious fact, that I have known a poor man of colour, who laboured night and day, to acquire a little money, and having acquired it, he vested it in a small piece of land, and got

[6] Genesis, chap. xli, 45.   [7] Genesis, chap. xlvii, 5,6.

him a house erected thereon, and having paid for the whole, he moved his family into it, where he was suffered to remain but nine months, when he was cheated out of his property by a white man, and driven out of door! And is not this the case generally? Can a man of colour buy a piece of land and keep it peaceably? Will not some white man try to get it from him, even if it is in a *mud hole?* I need not comment any farther on a subject, which all, both black and white, will readily admit. But I must, really, observe that in this very city, when a man of colour dies, if he owned any real estate it most generally falls into the hands of some white person. The wife and children of the deceased may weep and lament if they please, but the estate will be kept snug enough by its white possessor.

But to prove farther that the condition of the Israelites was better under the Egyptians than ours is under the whites. I call upon the professing Christians, I call upon the philanthropist, I call upon the very tyrant himself, to show me a page of history, either sacred or profane, on which a verse can be found, which maintains, that the Egyptians heaped the *insupportable insult* upon the children of Israel, by telling them that they were not of the *human family.* Can the whites deny this charge? Have they not, after having reduced us to the deplorable condition of slaves under their feet, held us up as descending originally from the tribes of *Monkeys* or *Orang-Outangs?* O! my God! I appeal to every man of feeling—is not this unsupportable? Is it not heaping the most gross insult upon our miseries, because they have got us under their feet and we cannot help ourselves? Oh! pity us we pray thee, Lord Jesus, Master.—Has Mr. Jefferson declared to the world, that we are inferior to the whites, both in the endowments of our bodies and of minds? It is indeed surprising, that a man of such great learning, combined with such excellent natural parts, should speak so of a set of men in chains. I do not know what to compare it to, unless, like putting one wild deer in an iron cage, where it will be secured, and hold another by the side of the same, then let it go, and expect the one in the cage to run as fast as the one at liberty. So far, my brethren, were the Eygptians from heaping these insults upon their slaves, that Pharaoh's daughter took Moses, a son of Israel for her own, as will appear by the following.

"And Pharaoh's daughter said unto her, [Moses' mother] take this child away, and nurse it for me, and I will pay thee thy wages. And the woman took the child [Moses] and nursed it.

"And the child grew, and she brought him unto Pharaoh's daughter and he became her son. And she called his name Moses: and she said because I drew him out of the water."[8]

In all probability, Moses would have become Prince Regent to the throne, and no doubt, in process of time but he would have been seated on the throne of Egypt. But he had rather suffer shame, with the people of God, than to enjoy pleasures with that wicked people for a season. O! that the

[8] See Exodus, chap. ii, 9, 10.

coloured people were long since of Moses' excellent disposition, instead of courting favour with, and telling news and lies to our *natural enemies*, against each other—aiding them to keep their hellish chains of slavery upon us. Would we not before this time, have been respectable men, instead of such wretched victims of oppression as we are? Would they be able to drag our mothers, our fathers, our wives, our children and ourselves, around the world in chains and hand-cuffs as they do, to dig up gold and silver for them and theirs? This question, my brethren, I leave for you to digest; and may God Almighty force it home to your hearts. Remember that unless you are united, keeping your tongues within your teeth, you will be afraid to trust your secrets to each other, and thus perpetuate our miseries under the *Christians!!!!!* Addition.—Remember, also to lay humble at the feet of our Lord and Master Jesus Christ, with prayers and fastings. Let our enemies go on with their butcheries, and at once fill up their cup. Never make an attempt to gain our freedom or *natural right,* from under our cruel oppressors and murderers, until you see your way clear[9]—when that hour arrives and you move, be not afraid or dismayed; for be you assured that Jesus Christ the King of heaven and of earth who is the God of justice and of armies, will surely go before you. And those enemies who have for hundreds of years stolen our *rights,* and kept us ignorant of Him and His divine worship, he will remove. Millions of whom, are this day, so ignorant and avaricious, that they cannot conceive how God can have an attribute of justice, and show mercy to us because it pleased Him to make us black—which colour, Mr. Jefferson calls unfortunate!!!!!! As though we are not as thankful to our God, for having made us as it pleased himself, as they (the whites), are for having made them white. They think because they hold us in their infernal chains of slavery, that we wish to be white, or of their colour—but they are dreadfully deceived—we wish to be just as it pleased our Creator to have made us, and no avaricious and unmerciful wretches, have any business to make slaves of, or hold us in slavery. How would they like for us to make slaves of, and hold them in cruel slavery, and murder them as they do us?—But is Mr. Jefferson's assertion true? viz. "that it is unfortunate for us that our Creator has been pleased to make us *black.*" We will not take his say so, for the fact. The world will have an opportunity to see whether it is unfortunate for us, that our Creator *has made us* darker than the *whites.*

---

[9] It is not to be understood here, that I mean for us to wait until God shall take us by the hair of our heads and drag us out of abject wretchedness and slavery, nor do I mean to convey the idea for us to wait until our enemies shall make preparations, and call us to seize those preparations, take it away from them, and put every thing before us to death, in order to gain our freedom which God has given us. For you must remember that we are men as well as they. God has been pleased to give us two eyes, two hands, two feet, and some sense in our heads as well as they. They have no more right to hold us in slavery than we have to hold them, we have just as much right, in the sight of God, to hold them and their children in slavery and wretchedness, as they have to hold us, and no more.

Fear not the number and education of our *enemies*, against whom we shall have to contend for our lawful right; guaranteed to us by our Maker; for why should we be afraid, when God is, and will continue, (if we continue humble) to be on our side?

The man who would not fight under our Lord and Master Jesus Christ, in the glorious and heavenly cause of freedom and of God—to be delivered from the most wretched, abject and servile slavery, that ever a people was afflicted with since the foundation of the world, to the present day—ought to be kept with all of his children or family, in slavery, or in chains, to be butchered by his *cruel enemies.*

I saw a paragraph, a few years since, in a South Carolina paper, which, speaking of the barbarity of the Turks, it said: "The Turks are the most barbarous people in the world—they treat the Greeks more like *brutes* than human beings." And in the same paper was an advertisement, which said: "Eight well built Virginia and Maryland *Negro fellows* and four *wenches* will positively be *sold* this day, *to the highest bidder!*" And what astonished me still more was, to see in this same *humane* paper!! the cuts of three men, with clubs and budgets on their backs, and an advertisement offering a considerable sum of money for their apprehension and delivery. I declare, it is really so amusing to hear the Southerners and Westerners of this country talk about *barbarity,* that it is positively, enough to make a man *smile.*

The sufferings of the Helots among the Spartans, were somewhat severe, it is true, but to say that theirs, were as severe as ours among the Americans, I do most strenuously deny—for instance, can any man show me an article on a page of ancient history which specifies, that, the Spartans chained, and hand-cuffed the Helots, and dragged them from their wives and children, children from their parents, mothers from their suckling babes, wives from their husband, driving them from one end of the country to the other? Notice the Spartans were heathens, who lived long before our Divine Master made his appearance in the flesh.

Can Christian Americans deny these barbarous cruelties? Have you not, Americans, having subjected us under you, added to these miseries, by insulting us in telling us to our face, because we are helpless, that we are not of the human family? I ask you, O! Americans, I ask you, in the name of the Lord, can you deny these charges? Some perhaps may deny, by saying, that they never thought or said that we were not men. But do not actions speak louder than *words?*—have they not made provisions for the Greeks, and Irish? Nations who have never done the least thing for them, while *we*, who have enriched their country with our blood and tears—have dug up gold and silver for them and their children, from generation to generation, and are in more miseries than any other people under heaven, are not seen, but by comparatively, a handful of the American people? There are indeed, more ways to kill a dog, besides choking it to death with butter. Further—The Spartans or Lacedemonians, had some frivolous pretext, for enslaving the

Helots, for they (Helots) while being free inhabitants of Sparta, stirred up an intestine commotion, and were, by the Spartans subdued, and made prisoners of war. Consequently they and their children were condemned to perpetual slavery.[10]

I have been for years troubling the pages of historians, to find out what our fathers have done to the *white Christians of America*, to merit such condign punishment as they have inflicted on them, and do continue to inflict on us their children. But I must aver, that my researches have hitherto been to no effect. I have therefore, come to the immoveable conclusion, that they (Americans) have, and do continue to punish us for nothing else, but for enriching them and their country. For I cannot conceive of any thing else. Nor will I ever believe otherwise, until the Lord shall convince me.

The world knows, that slavery as it existed among the Romans, (which was the primary cause of their destruction) was, comparatively speaking, no more than a *cypher*, when compared with ours under the Americans. Indeed I should not have noticed the Roman slaves, had not the very learned and penetrating Mr. Jefferson said, "when a master was murdered, all his slaves in the same house, or within hearing, were condemned to death."—Here let me ask Mr. Jefferson, (but he is gone to answer at the bar of God, for the deeds done in his body while living,) I therefore ask the whole American people, had I not rather die, or be put to death, than to be a slave to any tyrant, who takes not only my own, but my wife and children's lives by the inches? Yea, would I meet death with avidity far! far!! in preference to such *servile submission* to the murderous hands of tyrants. Mr. Jefferson's very severe remarks on us have been so extensively argued upon by men whose attainments in literature, I shall never be able to reach, that I would not have meddled with it, were it not to solicit each of my brethren, who has the spirit of a man, to buy a copy of Mr. Jefferson's "Notes on Virginia," and put it in the hand of his son. For let no one of us suppose that the refutations which have been written by our white friends are enough—they are *whites*—we are *blacks*.[11]

We, and the world wish to see the charges of Mr. Jefferson refuted by the blacks *themselves*, according to their chance; for we must remember that what the whites have written respecting this subject, is other men's labours, and did not emanate from the blacks. I know well, that there are some talents and learning among the coloured people of this country, which we have not a chance to develop, in consequence of oppression; but our oppression ought not to hinder us from acquiring all we can. For we will have a chance to develop them by and by. God will not suffer us, always to be oppressed. Our sufferings will come to an *end*, in spite of all the Americans

---

[10] See Dr. Goldsmith's *History of Greece.* See also, *Plutarch's Lives.* The Helots subdued by Agis, king of *Sparta.*

[11] See his *Notes on Virginia.*

this side of *eternity*. Then we will want all the learning and talents among ourselves, and perhaps more, to govern ourselves.—"Every dog must have its day," the American's is coming to an end.

But let us review Mr. Jefferson's remarks respecting us some further. Comparing our miserable fathers, with the learned philosophers of Greece, he says: "Yet notwithstanding these and other discouraging circumstances among the Romans, their slaves were often their rarest artists. They excelled too, in science, insomuch as to be usually employed as tutors to their master's children; Epictetus, Terence and Phaedrus, were slaves,—but they were of the race of whites. It is not their *condition* then, but *nature*, which has produced the distinction."[12] See this, my brethren!! Do you believe that this assertion is swallowed by millions of the whites? Do you know that Mr. Jefferson was one of as great characters as ever lived among the whites? See his writing for the world, and public labours for the United States of America. Do you believe that the assertions of such a man, will pass away into oblivion unobserved by this people and the world? If you do you are much mistaken—See how the American people treat us—have we souls in our bodies? Are we men who have any spirits at all? I know that there are many *swell-bellied* fellows among us, whose greatest object is to fill their stomachs. Such I do not mean—I am after those who know and feel, that we are MEN, as well as other people; to them, I say, that unless we try to refute Mr. Jefferson's arguments respecting us, we will only establish them.

But the slaves among the Romans. Every body who has read history, knows, that as soon as a slave among the Romans obtained his freedom, he could rise to the greatest eminence in the State, and there was no law instituted to hinder a slave from buying his freedom. Have not the Americans instituted laws to hinder us from obtaining our freedom? Do any deny this charge? Read the laws of Virginia, North Carolina, &c. Further: have not the Americans instituted laws to prohibit a man of colour from obtaining and holding any office whatever, under the government of the United States of America? Now, Mr. Jefferson tells us, that our condition is not so hard, as the slaves were under the Romans!!!!!!

It is time for me to bring this article to a close. But before I close it, I must observe to my brethren that at the close of the first Revolution in this country, with Great Britain, there were but thirteen States in the Union, now there are twenty-four, most of which are slave-holding States, and the whites are dragging us around in chains and in handcuffs, to their new States and Territories to work their mines and farms, to enrich them and their children—and millions of them believing firmly that we being a little darker than they, were made by our Creator to be an inheritance to them and their children for ever—the same as a parcel of *brutes*.

[12] See his *Notes on Virginia*.

Are we MEN!!—I ask you, O my brethren! are we *MEN?* Did our Creator make us to be slaves to dust and ashes like ourselves? Are they not dying worms as well as we? Have they not to make their appearance before the tribunal of Heaven, to answer for the deeds done in the body, as well as we? Have we any other Master as well as ours?—What right then, have we to obey and call any other Master, but Himself? How we could be so *submissive* to a gang of men, whom we cannot tell whether they are *as good* as ourselves or not, I never could conceive. However, this is shut up with the Lord, and we cannot precisely tell—but I declare, we judge men by their works.

The whites have always been an unjust, jealous, unmerciful, avaricious and blood-thirsty set of beings, always seeking after power and authority.— We view them all over the confederacy of Greece, where they were first known to be any thing, (in consequence of education) we see them there, cutting each other's throats—trying to subject each other to wretchedness and misery—to effect which, they used all kinds of deceitful, unfair, and unmerciful means. We view them next in Rome, where the spirit of tyranny and deceit raged still higher. We view them in Gaul, Spain, and in Britain.— In fine, we view them all over Europe, together with what were scattered about in Asia and Africa, as heathens, and we see them acting more like devils than accountable men. But some may ask, did not the blacks of Africa, and the mulattoes of Asia, go on in the same way as did the whites of Europe. I answer, no—they never were half so avaricious, deceitful and unmerciful as the whites, according to their knowledge.

But we will leave the whites or Europeans as heathens, and take a view of them as Christians, in which capacity we see them as cruel, if not more so than ever. In fact, take them as a body, they are ten times more cruel, avaricious and unmerciful than ever they were; for while they were heathens, they were bad enough it is true, but it is positively a fact that they were not quite so audacious as to go and take vessel loads of men, women and children, and in cold blood, and through devilishness, throw them into the sea, and murder them in all kind of ways. While they were heathens, they were too ignorant for such barbarity. But being Christians, enlightened and sensible, they are completely prepared for such hellish cruelties.

Now suppose God were to give them more sense, what would they do? If it were possible, would they not *dethrone* Jehovah and seat themselves upon his throne? I therefore, in the name and fear of the Lord God of Heaven and of earth, divested of prejudice either on the side of my colour or that of the whites, advance my suspicion of them, whether they are *as good by nature* as we are or not. Their actions, since they were known as a people have been the reverse, I do indeed suspect them, but this, as I before observed, is shut up with the Lord, we cannot exactly tell, it will be proved in succeeding generations.—The whites have had the essence of the gospel as it was preached by my master and his apostles—the Ethiopians have not, who are to have it in its meridian splendor—the Lord will give it to them to their satisfaction. I hope and pray my God, that they will make good use of it, that it may be well with them.[13]

[13] It is my solemn belief, that if ever the world becomes Christianized, (which must certainly take place before long) it will be through the means, under God of the *Blacks*, who are now held in wretchedness, and degradation, by the white *Christians* of the world, who before they learn to do justice to us before our Maker—and be reconciled to us, and reconcile us to them, and by that means have clear consciences before God and man.—Send out Missionaries to convert the Heathens, many of whom after they cease to worship gods, which neither see nor hear, become ten times more the children of Hell, than ever they were, why what is the reason? Why the reason is obvious, they must learn to do justice at home, before they go into distant lands, to display their charity, Christianity, and benevolence; when they learn to do justice, God will accept their offering, (no man may think that I am against Missionaries for I am not, my object is to see justice done at home, before we go to convert the heathens.)

NAT TURNER

(1800?–1831)

In 1831, Nat Turner led the first serious slave insurrection in American history. With 40 other blacks, Turner attacked several plantations in southeastern Virginia and slew 57 whites. In retaliation many Negroes were tortured, and 20 of them, including Turner, were hanged. Turner's rebellion led to more severe slave codes and greater surveillance of free Negroes in the South.

For an authoritative account of Turner's rebellion, see Herbert Aptheker's *Nat Turner's Slave Rebellion*, 1966.
The reaction of black scholars and artists to William Styron's fictional rendering of Turner's rebellion appears in John Henrik Clarke, ed., *William Styron's Nat Turner: Ten Black Writers Respond*, 1968. See also Stephen B. Oates, *The Fires of Jubilee; Nat Turner's Fierce Rebellion*, 1975.

From The Confessions of Nat Turner

The leader of the late Insurrection in Southampton, Va. As fully and voluntarily made to Thomas R. Gray, in the prison where he was confined, and acknowledged by him to be such when read before the Court of Southampton; with the certificate, under seal of the Court convened at Jerusalem, Nov. 5, 1831, for his trial.

DISTRICT OF COLUMBIA, TO WIT:

Be it remembered, That on this tenth day of November, Anno Domini, eighteen hundred and thirty-one, Thomas R. Gray of the said District, deposited in this office the title of a book, which is in the words as following:

"The Confessions of Nat Turner, the leader of the late insurrection in Southampton, Virginia, as fully and voluntarily made to Thomas R. Gray, in the prison where he was confined, and acknowledged by him to be such when read before the Court of Southampton; with the certificate, under seal, of the Court convened at Jerusalem, November 5, 1831, for his trial. Also, an authentic account of the whole insurrection, and with lists of the whites who were murdered, and of the Negroes brought before the Court of Southampton, and there sentenced, &. the right whereof he claims as proprietor, in conformity with an Act of Congress, entitled 'An act to amend the several acts respecting Copy Rights.' "

[Seal.]

EDMUND J. LEE, Clerk of the District. In testimony that the above is a true copy, from the record of the District Court for the District of Columbia, I, Edmund J. Lee, the Clerk thereof, have hereunto set my hand and affixed the seal of my office, this 10th day of November, 1831.

EDMUND J. LEE, C. D. C.

TO THE PUBLIC

The late insurrection in Southampton has greatly excited the public mind, and led to a thousand idle, exaggerated and mischievous reports. It is the first instance in our history of an open rebellion of the slaves, and attended with such atrocious circumstances of cruelty and destruction, as could not fail to leave a deep impression, not only upon the minds of the community where this fearful tragedy was wrought, but throughout every portion of our country, in which this population is to be found. Public curiosity has been on the stretch to understand the origin and progress of this dreadful conspiracy, and the motives which influence its diabolical actors. The insurgent slaves had all been destroyed, or apprehended, tried and executed, (with the exception of the leader,) without revealing any thing at all satisfactory, as to the motives which governed them, or the means by which they expected to accomplish their object. Every thing connected with the sad affair was wrapt in mystery, until Nat Turner, the leader of this ferocious band, whose name has resounded throughout our widely extended empire, was captured. This "great Bandit" was taken by a single individual, in a cave near the residence of his late owner, on Sunday, the thirtieth of October, without attempting to make the slightest resistance, and on the following day safely lodged in the jail of the County. His captor was Benjamin Phipps, armed with a shot gun well charged. Nat's only weapon was a small light sword which he immediately surrendered, and begged that his life might be spared. Since his confinement, by permission of the Jailor, I have had ready access to him, and finding that he was willing to make a full and free confession of the origin, progress and consummation of the insurrectory movements of the slaves of which he was the contriver and head; I determined for the gratification of public curiosity to commit his statements to writing, and publish them, with little or no variation, from his own words. That this is a faithful record of his confessions, the annexed certificate of the County Court of Southampton, will attest. They certainly bear one stamp of truth and sincerity. He makes no attempt (as all the other insurgents who were examined did,) to exculpate himself, but frankly acknowledges his full participation in all the guilt of the transaction. He was not only the contriver of the conspiracy, but gave the first blow towards its execution.

It will thus appear, that whilst every thing upon the surface of society wore a calm and peaceful aspect; whilst not one note of preparation was heard to warn the devoted inhabitants of woe and death, a gloomy fanatic was revolving in the recesses of his own dark, bewildered, and overwrought mind, schemes of indiscriminate massacre to the whites. Schemes too fearfully executed as far as his fiendish band proceeded in their desolating march. No cry for mercy penetrated their flinty bosoms. No acts of remembered kindness made the least impression upon these remorseless murderers. Men, women and children, from hoary age to helpless infancy were involved in the same cruel fate. Never did a band of savages do their work of death more unsparingly. Apprehension for their own personal safety seems to have been the only principle of restraint in the whole course of their bloody proceedings. And it is not the least remarkable feature in this horrid transaction, that a band actuated by such hellish purposes, should have resisted so feebly, when met by the whites in arms. Desperation alone, one would think, might have led to greater efforts. More than twenty of them attacked Dr. Blunt's house on Tuesday morning, a little before day-break, defended by two men and three boys. They fled precipitately at the first fire; and their future plans of mischief, were entirely disconcerted and broken up. Escaping thence, each individual sought his own safety either in concealment, or by returning home, with the hope that his participation might escape detection, and all were shot down in the course of a few days, or captured and brought to trial and punishment. Nat has survived all his followers, and the gallows will speedily close his career. His own account of the conspiracy is submitted to the public without comment. It reads an awful, and it is hoped, a useful lesson, as to the operations of a mind like his, endeavoring to grapple with things beyond its reach. How it first became bewildered and confounded, and finally corrupted and led to the conception and perpetration of the most atrocious and heart-rending deeds. It is calculated also to demonstrate the policy of our laws in restraint of this class of our population, and to induce all those entrusted with their execution, as well as our citizens generally, to see that they are strictly and rigidly enforced. Each particular community should look to its own safety, whilst the general guardians of the laws, keep a watchful eye over all. If Nat's statements can be relied on, the insurrection in this county was entirely local, and his designs confided but to a few, and these in his immediate vicinity. It was not instigated by motives of revenge or sudden anger, but the results of long deliberation, and a settled purpose of mind. The offspring of gloomy fanaticism, acting upon materials but too well prepared for such impressions. It will be long remembered in the annals of our country, and many a mother as she presses her infant darling to her bosom, will shudder at the recollection of Nat Turner, and his band of ferocious miscreants.

Believing the following narrative, by removing doubts and conjectures from the public mind which otherwise must have remained, would give general satisfaction, it is respectfully submitted to the public by their ob't serv't,

T. R. GRAY

Jerusalem, Southampton, Va. Nov. 5, 1831.

We the undersigned, members of the Court convened at Jerusalem, on Saturday, the 5th day of Nov. 1831, for the trial of Nat, *alias* Nat Turner, a negro slave, late the property of Putnam Moore, deceased, do hereby certify, that the confessions of Nat, to Thomas R. Gray, was read to him in our presence, and that Nat acknowledged the same to be full, free, and voluntary; and that furthermore, when called upon by the presiding Magistrate of the Court, to state if he had any thing to say, why sentence of death should not be passed upon him, replied he had nothing further than he had communicated to Mr. Gray. Given under our hands and seals at Jerusalem, this 5th day of November, 1831.

JEREMIAH COBB,	[Seal.]
THOMAS PRETLOW,	[Seal.]
JAMES W. PARKER,	[Seal.]
CARR BOWERS,	[Seal.]
SAMUEL B. HINES,	[Seal.]
ORRIS A. BROWNE,	[Seal.]

STATE OF VIRGINIA, SOUTHAMPTON COUNTY, TO WIT:

I, James Rochelle, Clerk of the County Court of Southampton in the State of Virginia, do hereby certify, that Jeremiah Cobb, Thomas Pretow, James W. Parker, Carr Bowers, Samuel B. Hines, and Orris A. Browne, esqr's are acting Justices of the Peace, in and for the County aforesaid, and were members of the Court which convened at Jerusalem, on Saturday the 5th day of November, 1831, for the trial of Nat *alias* Nat Turner, a negro slave, late the property of Putnam Moore, deceased, who was tried and convicted, as an insurgent in the late insurrection in the county of Southampton aforesaid, and that full faith and credit are due, and ought to be given to their acts as Justices of the peace aforesaid.

[Seal.]

> In testimony whereof, I have hereunto set my hand and caused the seal of the Court aforesaid, to be affixed this 5th day of November, 1831

JAMES ROCHELLE,
C. S. C. C.

CONFESSION

Agreeable to his own appointment, on the evening he was committed to prison, with permission of the jailer, I visited NAT on Tuesday the 1st November, when, without being questioned at all, he commenced his narrative in the following words:—

SIR,—You have asked me to give a history of the motives which induced me to undertake the late insurrection, as you call it—To do so I must go back to the days of my infancy, and even before I was born. I was thirty-one years of age the 2nd of October last, and born the property of Benj. Turner, of this county. In my childhood a circumstance occurred which made an indelible impression on my mind, and laid the ground work of that enthusiasm, which has terminated so fatally to many, both white and black, and for which I am about to atone at the gallows. It is here necessary to relate this circumstance—trifling as it may seem, it was the commencement of that belief which has grown with time, and even now, sir, in this dungeon, helpless and forsaken as I am, I cannot divest myself of. Being at play with other children, when three or four years old, I was telling them something, which my mother overhearing, said it had happened before I was born—I stuck to my story, however, and related somethings which went, in her opinion, to confirm it—others being called on were greatly astonished, knowing that these things had happened, and caused them to say in my hearing, I surely would be a prophet, as the Lord had shewn me things that had happened before my birth. And my father and mother strengthened me in this my first impression, saying in my presence, I was intended for some great purpose, which they had always thought from certain marks on my head and breast— [a parcel of excrescences which I believe are not at all uncommon, particularly among negroes, as I have seen several with the same. In this case he has either cut them off or they have nearly disappeared]—My grandmother, who was very religious, and to whom I was much attached—my master, who belonged to the church, and other religious persons who visited the house, and whom I often saw at prayers, noticing the singularity of my manners, I suppose, and my uncommon intelligence for a child, remarked I had too much sense to be raised, and if I was, I would never be of any service to any one as a slave—To a mind like mine, restless, inquisitive and observant of every thing that was passing, it is easy to suppose that religion was the subject to which it would be directed, and although this subject principally occupied my thoughts—there was nothing that I saw or heard of to which my attention was not directed—The manner in which I learned to read and write, not only had great influence on my own mind, as I acquired it with the most perfect ease, so much so, that I have no recollection whatever of learning the alphabet—but to the astonishment of the family, one day, when a book was shewn to me to keep me from crying, I began spelling the names of different objects—this was a source of wonder to all in the neighborhood, particularly the blacks—and this learning was constantly improved at all opportunities—when I got large enough to go to work, while employed, I was reflecting on many things that would present themselves to my imagination, and whenever an opportunity occurred of looking at a book, when the school children were getting their lessons, I would find many things that the fertility of my own imagination had depicted to me before; all my time, not devoted to my master's service, was spent either in prayer, or in making experiments in casting different things in moulds made of earth, in attempting to make paper, gun-powder, and many other experiments, that although I could not perfect, yet convinced me of its practicability if I had the means.[1] I was not addicted to stealing in my youth, nor have ever been—Yet such was the confidence of the negroes in the neighborhood, even at this early period of my life, in my superior judgment, that they would often carry me with them when they were going on any roguery, to plan for them. Growing up among them, with this confidence in my superior judgment, and when this, in their opinions, was perfected by Divine inspiration, from the circumstances already alluded to in my infancy, and which belief was ever

[1] When questioned as to the manner of manufacturing those different articles, he was found well informed on the subject.

afterwards zealously inculcated by the austerity of my life and manners, which became the subject of remark by white and black.—Having soon discovered to be great, I must appear so, and therefore studiously avoided mixing in society, and wrapped myself in mystery, devoting my time to fasting and prayer—By this time, having arrived to man's estate, and hearing the scriptures commented on at meetings, I was struck with that particular passage which says: "Seek ye the kingdom of Heaven and all things shall be added unto you." I reflected much on this passage, and prayed daily for light on this subject—As I was praying one day at my plough, the spirit spoke to me, saying "Seek ye the kingdom of Heaven and all things shall be added unto you." *Question*—what do you mean by the Spirit. *Ans.* The Spirit that spoke to the prophets in former days—and I was greatly astonished, and for two years prayed continually, whenever my duty would permit—and then again I had the same revelation, which fully confirmed me in the impression that I was ordained for some great purpose in the hands of the Almighty. Several years rolled round, in which many events occurred to strengthen me in this my belief. At this time I reverted in my mind to the remarks made of me in my childhood, and the things that had been shewn me—and as it had been said of me in my childhood by those by whom I had been taught to pray, both white and black, and in whom I had the greatest confidence, that I had too much sense to be raised, and if I was, I would never be of any use to any one as a slave. Now finding I had arrived to man's estate, and was a slave, and these revelations being made known to me, I began to direct my attention to this great object, to fulfil the purpose for which, by this time, I felt assured I was intended. Knowing the influence I had obtained over the minds of my fellow servants, (not by the means of conjuring and such like tricks—for to them I always spoke of such things with contempt) but by the communion of the Spirit whose revelations I often communicated to them, and they believed and said my wisdom came from God. I now began to prepare them for my purpose, by telling them something was about to happen that would terminate in fulfilling the great promise that had been made to me—About this time I was placed under an overseer, from whom I ran away—and after remaining in the woods thirty days, I returned, to the astonishment of the negroes on the plantation, who thought I had made my escape to some other part of the country, as my father had done before. But the reason of my return was, that the Spirit appeared to me and said I had my wishes directed to the things of this world, and not to the kingdom of Heaven, and that I should return to the service of my earthly master—"For he who knoweth his Master's will, and doeth it not, shall be beaten with many stripes, and thus have I chastened you." And the negroes found fault, and murmured against me, saying that if they had my sense they would not serve any master in the world. And about this time I had a vision—and I saw white spirits and black spirits engaged in battle, and the sun was darkened—tho thunder rolled in the Heavens, and blood flowed in streams—and I heard a voice saying, "Such is your luck, such you are called to see, and let it come rough or smooth, you must surely bear it." I now withdrew myself as much as my situation would permit, from the intercourse of my fellow servants, for the avowed purpose of serving the Spirit more fully—and it appeared to me, and reminded me of the things it had already shown me, and that it would then reveal to me the knowledge of the elements, the revolution of the planets, the operation of tides, and changes of the seasons. After this revelation in the year of 1825, and the knowledge of the elements being made known to me, I sought more than ever to obtain true holiness before the great day of judgment should appear, and then I began to receive the true knowledge of faith. And from the first steps of righteousness until the last, was I made perfect; and the Holy Ghost was with me, and said, "Behold me as I stand in the Heavens"—and I looked and saw the forms of men in different attitudes—and there were lights in the sky to which the children of darkness gave other names than what they really were—for they were the lights of the Savior's hands, stretched forth from east to west, even as they were extended on the cross on Calvary for the redemption of sinners. And I wondered greatly at these miracles, and prayed to be informed of a certainty of the meaning thereof—and shortly afterwards, while laboring in the field, I discovered drops of blood on the corn as though it were dew from heaven—and I communicated it to many, both white and black, in the neighborhood—and I then found on the leaves in the woods hieroglyphic characters, and numbers, with the forms of men in different attitudes, portrayed in blood, and representing the figures I had seen before in the heavens. And now the Holy Ghost had revealed itself to me, and made plain the miracles it had shown me—For as the blood of Christ had been shed on this earth, and had ascended to heaven for the salvation of sinners, and was now returning to earth again in the form of dew—and as the leaves on the trees bore the impression of the figures I had seen in the heavens, it was plain to me that the Savior was about to lay down the yoke he had borne for the sins of men, and the great day of judgment was at hand. About this time I told these things to a white man, (Etheldred T. Brantley) on whom it had a wonderful effect—and he ceased from his wickedness, and was attacked immediately with a cutaneous eruption, and blood oozed from the pores of his skin, and after praying and fasting nine days, he was healed, and the Spirit appeared to me again, and said, as the Savior had been baptised so should we be also—and when the white people would not let us be baptised by the church, we went down into the water together, in the sight of many who reviled us, and were baptised by the Spirit—After this I rejoiced greatly, and gave thanks to God. And on the 12th of May, 1828, I heard a loud noise in the heavens, and the Spirit instantly appeared to me and said the Serpent was loosened, and Christ had laid down the yoke he had borne for the sins of men, and that I should take it on and fight against the Serpent, for the time was fast approaching when the first should be last and the last should be first. *Ques.* Do you not find yourself mistaken now? *Ans.* Was not Christ crucified? And by signs in the heavens that it would make known to me when I should commence the great work—and until the first sign appeared, I should conceal it from the knowledge of men—And on the appearance of the sign, (the eclipse of the sun last February) I should arise and prepare myself, and slay my enemies with their own weapons. And immediately on the sign appearing in the heavens, the seal was removed from my lips, and I communicated the great work laid out for me to do, to four in whom I had the greatest confidence, (Henry, Hark, Nelson, and Sam)—It was intended by us to have begun the work of death on the 4th July last—Many were the plans formed and rejected by us, and it affected my mind to such a degree, that I fell sick, and the time passed without our coming to any determination how to commence—Still forming new schemes and rejecting them, when the sign appeared again, which determined me not to wait longer.

Since the commencement of 1830, I had been living with Mr. Joseph Travis, who was to me a kind master, and placed the greatest confidence in me; in fact, I had no cause to complain of his treatment to me. On Saturday evening, the 20th of August, it was agreed between Henry, Hark and myself, to prepare a dinner the next day for the men we expected, and then to concert a plan, as we had not yet determined on any. Hark, on the following morning, brought a pig, and Henry brandy, and being joined by Sam, Nelson, Will and Jack, they prepared in the woods a dinner, where, about three o'clock, I joined them.

Q. Why were you so backward in joining them.

A. The same reason that had caused me not to mix with them for years before.

I saluted them on coming up, and asked Will how came he there, he answered, his life was worth no more than others, and his liberty as dear to him. I asked him if he thought to obtain it? He said he would, or lose his life. This was enough to put him in full confidence. Jack, I knew, was only a tool in the hands of Hark, it was quickly agreed we should commence at home (Mr. J. Travis') on that night, and until we had armed and equipped ourselves, and gathered sufficient force, neither age nor sex was to be spared, (which was invariably adhered to). We remained at the feast, until about two hours in the night, when we went to the house and found Austin; they all went to the cider press and drank, except myself. On returning to the house, Hark went to the door with an axe, for the purpose of breaking it open, as we knew we were strong enough to murder the family, if they were awaked by the noise; but reflecting that it might create an alarm in the neighborhood, we determined to enter the house secretly, and murder them whilst sleeping. Hark got a ladder and set it against the chimney, on which I ascended, and hoisting a window, entered and came down stairs, unbarred the door, and removed the guns from their places. It was then observed that I must spill the first blood. On which, armed with a hatchet, and accompanied by Will, I entered my master's chamber, it being dark, I could not give a death blow, the hatchet glanced from his head, he sprang from the bed and called his wife, it was his last word, Will laid him dead, with a blow of his axe, and Mrs. Travis shared the same fate, as she lay in bed. The murder of this family, five in number, was the work of a moment, not one of them awoke; there was a little infant sleeping in a cradle, that was forgotten, until we had left the house and gone some distance, when Henry and Will returned and killed it; we got here, four guns that would shoot, and several old muskets, with a pound or two of powder. We remained some time at the barn, where we paraded; I formed them in a line as soldiers, and after carrying them through all the manoeuvres I was master of marched them off to Mr. Salathul Francis', about six hundred yards distant. Sam and Will went to the door and knocked. Mr. Francis asked who was there, Sam replied it was him, and he had a letter for him, on which he got up and came to the door; they immediately seized him, and dragging him out a little from the door, he was dispatched by repeated blows on the head; there was no other white person in the family. We started from there for Mrs. Reese's, maintaining the most perfect silence on our march, where finding the door unlocked, we entered, and murdered Mrs. Reese in her bed, while sleeping; her son awoke, but it was only to sleep the sleep of death, he had only time to say who is that, and he was no more. From Mrs. Reese's we went to Mrs. Turner's, a mile distant, which we reached about sunrise, on Monday morning. Henry, Austin, and Sam, went to the still, where, finding Mr. Peebles, Austin shot him, and the rest of us went to the house; as we approached, the family discovered us, and shut the door. Vain hope! Will, with one stroke of his axe, opened it, and we entered and found Mrs. Turner and Mrs. Newsome in the middle of a room, almost frightened to death. Will immediately killed Mrs. Turner, with one blow of his axe. I took Mrs. Newsome by the hand, and with the sword I had when I was apprehended, I struck her several blows over the head, but not being able to kill her, as the sword was dull. Will turning around and discovering it, despatched her also. A general destruction of property and search for money and ammunition, always succeded the murders. By this time my company amounted to fifteen, and nine men mounted, who started for Mrs. Whitehead's, (the other six were to go through a by way to Mr. Bryant's, and rejoin us at Mrs. Whitehead's,) as we approached the house we discovered Mr. Richard Whitehead standing in the cotton patch, near the lane fence; we called him over into the lane, and Will, the executioner, was near at hand, with his fatal axe, to send him to an untimely grave. As we pushed on to the house, I discovered some one run round the garden, and thinking it was some of the white family, I pursued them, but finding it was a servant girl belonging to the house, I returned to commence the work of death, but they whom I left, had not been idle; all the family were already murdered, but Mrs. Whitehead and her daughter

Margaret. As I came round to the door I saw Will pulling Mrs. Whitehead out of the house, and at the step he nearly severed her head from her body, with his broad axe. Miss Margaret, when I discovered her, had concealed herself in the corner, formed by the projection of clear cap from the house; on my approach she fled, but was soon overtaken, and after repeated blows with a sword, I killed her by a blow on the head, with a fence rail. By this time, the six who had gone by Mr. Bryant's, rejoined us, and informed me they had done the work of death assigned them. We again divided, part going to Mr. Richard Porter's, and from thence to Nathaniel Francis', the others to Mr. Howell Harris', and Mr. T. Doyles. On my reaching Mr. Porter's, he had escaped with his family. I understood there, that the alarm had already spread, and I immediately returned to bring up those sent to Mr. Doyles, and Mr. Howell Harris'; the party I left going on to Mr. Francis', having told them I would join them in that neighborhood. I met those sent to Mr. Doyles' and Mr. Harris' returning, having met Mr. Doyle on the road and killed him; and learning from some who joined them, that Mr. Harris was from home, I immediately pursued the course taken by the party gone on before; but knowing they would complete the work of death and pillage, at Mr. Francis' before I could get there, I went to Mr. Peter Edwards', expecting to find them there, but they had been here also. I then went to Mr. John T. Barrow's, they had been here and murdered him. I pursued on their track to Capt. Newit Harris', where I found the greater part mounted, and ready to start; the men now amounting to about forty, shouted and hurraed as I rode up, some were in the yard, loading their guns, others drinking. They said Captain Harris and his family had escaped, the property in the house they destroyed, robbing him of money and other valuables. I ordered them to mount and march instantly, this was about nine or ten o'clock, Monday morning. I proceeded to Mr. Levi Waller's, two or three miles distant. I took my station in the rear, and as it was my object to carry terror and devastation wherever we went, I placed fifteen or twenty of the best armed and most relied on, in front, who generally approached the houses as fast as their horses could run; this was for two purposes, to prevent escape and strike terror to the inhabitants—on this account I never got to the houses, after leaving Mrs. Whitehead's, until the murders were committed, except in one case. I sometimes got in sight in time to see the work of death completed, viewed the mangled bodies as they lay, in silent satisfaction, and immediately started in quest of other victims—Having murdered Mrs. Waller and ten children, we started for Mr. William Williams'—having killed him and two little boys that were there; while engaged in this, Mrs. Williams fled and got some distance from the house, but she was pursued, overtaken, and compelled to get up behind one of the company, who brought her back, and after showing her the mangled body of her lifeless husband, she was told to get down and lay by his side, where she was shot dead. I then started for Mr. Jacob Williams', where the family were murdered—Here we found a young man named Drury, who had come on business with Mr. Williams—he was pursued, overtaken and shot. Mrs. Vaughan was the next place we visited—and after murdering the family here, I determined on starting for Jerusalem—Our number amounted now to fifty or sixty, all mounted and armed with guns, axes, swords and clubs—On reaching Mr. James W. Parker's gate, immediately on the road leading to Jerusalem, and about three miles distant, it was proposed to me to call there, but I objected, as I knew he was gone to Jerusalem, and my object was to reach there as soon as possible; but some of the men having relations at Mr. Parker's it was agreed that they might call and get his people. I remained at the gate on the road, with seven or eight; the others going across the field to the house, about half a mile off. After waiting some time for them, I became impatient, and started to the house for them, and on our return we were met by a party of white men, who had pursued our blood-stained track, and who had fired on those at the gate, and dispersed them, which I knew nothing of, not having been at that time rejoined by any of them—Immediately on discovering the whites, I ordered my men to halt and form, as they appeared to be alarmed—The white men, eighteen in number, approached us in about one hundred yards, when one of them fired, (this was against the positive orders of Captain Alexander P. Peete, who commanded, and who had directed the men to reserve their fire until within thirty paces)—And I discovered about half of them retreating, I then ordered my men to fire and rush on them; the few remaining stood their ground until we approached within fifty yards, when they fired and retreated. We pursued and overtook some of them who we thought we left dead; (they were not killed) after pursuing them about two hundred yards, and rising a little hill, I discovered they were met by another party, and had halted, and were reloading their guns, (this was a small party from Jerusalem who knew the negroes were in the field, and had just tied their horses to await their return to the road, knowing that Mr. Parker and family were in Jerusalem, but knew nothing of the party that had gone in with Captain Peete; on hearing the firing they immediately rushed to the spot and arrived just in time to arrest the progress of these barbarous villians, and save the lives of their friends and fellow citizens). Thinking that those who retreated first, and the party who fired on us at fifty or sixty yards distant, had all fallen back to meet others with ammunition. As I saw them reloading their guns, and more coming up than I saw at first, and several of my bravest men being wounded, the others became panick struck and squandered over the field; the white men pursued and fired on us several times. Hark had his horse shot under him, and I caught another for him as it was running by me; five or six of my men were wounded, but none left on the field; finding myself defeated here I instantly determined to go through a private way, and cross the Nottoway river at the Cypress Bridge, three miles below Jerusalem, and attack that place in the rear, as I expected they would look for me on the other road, and I had a great desire to get there to procure arms and

ammunition. After going a short distance in this private way, accompanied
by about twenty men, I overtook two or three who told me the others were
dispersed in every direction. After trying in vain to collect a sufficient force
to proceed to Jerusalem, I determined to return, as I was sure they would
make back to their old neighborhood, where they would rejoin me, make
new recruits, and come down again. On my way back, I called at Mrs.
Thomas's, Mrs. Spencer's, and several other places, the white families having
fled, we found no more victims to gratify our thirst for blood, we stopped at
Maj. Ridley's quarter for the night, and being joined by four of his men, with
the recruits made since my defeat, we mustered now about forty strong.
After placing out sentinels, I laid down to sleep, but was quickly roused by
a great racket; starting up, I found some mounted, and others in great confusion; one of the sentinels having given the alarm that we were about to be
attacked, I ordered some to ride round and reconnoitre, and on their return
the others being more alarmed, not knowing who they were, fled in different
ways, so that I was reduced to about twenty again; with this I determined to
attempt to recruit, and proceed on to rally in the neighborhood, I had left.
Dr. Blunt's was the nearest house, which we reached just before day; on
riding up the yard, Hark fired a gun. We expected Dr. Blunt and his family
were at Maj. Ridley's, as I knew there was a company of men there; the gun
was fired to ascertain if any of the family were at home; we were immediately fired upon and retreated, leaving several of my men. I do not know
what became of them, as I never saw them afterwards. Pursuing our course
back and coming in sight of Captain Harris', where we had been the day
before, we discovered a party of white men at the house, on which all
deserted me but two, (Jacob and Nat), we concealed ourselves in the woods
until near night, when I sent them in search of Henry, Sam, Nelson, and
Hark, and directed them to rally all they could, at the place we had had our
dinner the Sunday before, where they would find me, and I accordingly
returned there as soon as it was dark and remained until Wednesday evening, when discovering white men riding around the place as though they
were looking for some one, and none of my men joining me, I concluded
Jacob and Nat had been taken, and compelled to betray me. On this I gave
up all hope for the present; and on Thursday night after having supplied
myself with provisions from Mr. Travis's, I scratched a hole under a pile of
fence rails in a field, where I concealed myself for six weeks, never leaving
my hiding place but for a few minutes in the dead of night to get water
which was very near; thinking by this time I could venture out, I began to go
about in the night and eaves drop the houses in the neighborhood; pursuing
this course for about a fortnight and gathering little or no intelligence, afraid
of speaking to any human being, and returning every morning to my cave
before the dawn of day. I know not how long I might have led this life, if
accident had not betrayed me, a dog in the neighborhood passing by my
hiding place one night while I was out, was attracted by some meat I had in
my cave, and crawled in and stole it, and was coming out just as I returned.

A few nights after, two negroes having started to go hunting with the same dog, and passed that way, the dog came again to the place, and having just gone out to walk about, discovered me and barked, on which thinking myself discovered, I spoke to them to beg concealment. On making myself known they fled from me. Knowing then they would betray me, I immediately left my hiding place, and was pursued almost incessantly until I was taken a fortnight afterwards by Mr. Benjamin Phipps, in a little hole I had dug out with my sword, for the purpose of concealment, under the top of a fallen tree. On Mr. Phipps' discovering the place of my concealment, he cocked his gun and aimed at me. I requested him not to shoot and I would give up, upon which he demanded my sword. I delivered it to him, and he brought me to prison. During the time I was pursued, I had many hair breadth escapes, which your time will not permit you to relate. I am here loaded with chains, and willing to suffer the fate that awaits me.

I here proceeded to make some inquiries of him, after assuring him of the certain death that awaited him, and that concealment would only bring destruction on the innocent as well as guilty, of his own color, if he knew of any extensive or concerted plan. His answer was, I do not. When I questioned him as to the insurrection in North Carolina happening about the same time, he denied any knowledge of it; and when I looked him in the face as though I would search his inmost thoughts, he replied, "I see sir, you doubt my word; but can you not think the same ideas, and strange appearances about this time in the heaven's might prompt others, as well as myself, to this undertaking." I now had much conversation with and asked him many questions, having forborne to do so previously, except in the cases noted in parenthesis; but during his statement, I had, unnoticed by him, taken notes as to some particular circumstances, and having the advantage of his statement before me in writing, on the evening of the third day that I had been with him, I began a cross examination, and found his statement corroborated by every circumstance coming within my own knowledge or the confessions of others who had been either killed or executed, and whom he had not seen nor had any knowledge since 22d of August last, he expressed himself fully satisfied as to the impracticability of his attempt. It has been said he was ignorant and cowardly, and that his object was to murder and rob for the purpose of obtaining money to make his escape. It is notorious, that he was never known to have a dollar in his life; to swear an oath, or drink a drop of spirits. As to his ignorance, he certainly never had the advantages of education, but he can read and write, (it was taught him by his parents,) and for natural intelligence and quickness of apprehension, is surpassed by few men I have ever seen. As to his being a coward, his reason as given for not resisting Mr. Phipps, shews the decision of his character. When he saw Mr. Phipps present his gun, he said he knew it was impossible for him to escape as the woods were full of men; he therefore thought it was better to surrender, and trust to fortune for his escape. He is a complete fanatic, or plays his part most admirably. On other subjects he possesses an uncommon share of intelligence, with a mind capable of attaining any thing; but warped and perverted by the influence of early impressions. He is below the ordinary stature, though strong and active, having the true negro face, every feature of which is strongly marked. I shall not attempt to describe the effect of his narrative, as told and commented on by himself, in the condemned hole of the prison. The calm, deliberate composure with which he spoke of his late deeds and intentions, the expression of his fiend-like face when excited by enthusiasm, still bearing the stains of the blood of helpless innocence about him; clothed with rags and covered with chains; yet daring to raise his manacled hands to heaven, with a spirit soaring above the attributes of man; I looked on him and my blood curdled in my veins.

I will not shock the feelings of humanity, nor wound afresh the bosoms of the disconsolate sufferers in this unparalleled and inhuman massacre, by detailing the deeds of their fiend-like barbarity. There were two or three who were in the power of these wretches, had they known it, and who escaped in the most providential manner. There were two whom they thought they left dead on the field at Mr. Parker's, but who were only stunned by the blows of their guns, as they did not take time to re-load when they charged on them. The escape of a little girl who went to school at Mr. Waller's, and where the children were collecting for that purpose, excited general sympathy. As their teacher had not arrived, they were at play in the yard, and seeing the negroes approach, she ran up on a dirt chimney, (such as are common to log houses,) and remained there unnoticed during the massacre of the eleven that were killed at this place. She remained on her hiding place till just before the arrival of a party, who were in pursuit of the murderers, when she came down and fled to a swamp, where, a mere child as she was, with the horrors of the late scene before her, she lay concealed until the next day, when seeing a party go up to the house, she came up, and on being asked how she escaped, replied with the utmost simplicity, "The Lord helped her." She was taken up behind a gentleman of the party, and returned to the arms of her weeping mother. Miss Whitehead concealed herself between the bed and the mat that supported it, while they murdered her sister in the same room, without discovering her. She was afterwards carried off, and concealed for protection by a slave of the family, who gave evidence against several of them on their trial. Mrs. Nathaniel Francis, while concealed in a closet heard their blows, and the shrieks of the victims of these ruthless savages; they then entered the closet, where she was concealed, and went out without discovering her. While in this hiding place, she heard two of her women in a quarrel about the division of her clothes. Mr. John T. Baron, discovering them approaching his house, told his wife to make her escape, and scorning to fly, fell fighting on his own threshold. After firing his rifle, he discharged his gun at them, and then broke it over the villain who first approached him, but he was overpowered, and slain. His bravery, however, saved from the hands of these monsters, his lovely and amiable wife, who will long lament a husband so deserving of her love. As directed by him, she attempted to escape through the garden, when she was caught and held by one of her servant girls, but another coming to her rescue, she fled to the woods, and concealed herself. Few indeed, were those who escaped their work of death. But fortunate for society, the hand of retributive justice has overtaken them; and not one that was known to be concerned has escaped.

The Commonwealth,	Charged with making insurrection, and plotting
vs.	to take away the lives of divers free white per-
Nat Turner	sons,

&c. on the 22d of August, 1831.

The court composed of———, having met for the trial of Nat Turner, the prisoner was brought in and arraigned, and upon his arraignment pleaded *Not guilty;* saying to his counsel, that he did not feel so.

On the part of the Commonwealth, Levi Waller was introduced, who being sworn, deposed as follows: *(agreeably to Nat's own Confession.)* Col. Trezvant[2] was then introduced, who being sworn, narrated Nat's Confession to him, as follows: *(his Confession as given to Mr. Gray.)* The prisoner introduced no evidence, and the case was submitted without argument to the court, who having found him guilty, Jeremiah Cobb, Esq. Chairman, pronounced the sentence of the court, in the following words: "Nat Turner! Stand up. Have you any thing to say why sentence of death should not be pronounced against you?"

Ans. I have not. I have made a full confession to Mr. Gray, and I have nothing more to say.

Attend then to the sentence of the Court. You have been arraigned and tried before this court, and convicted of one of the highest crimes in our criminal code. You have been convicted of plotting in cold blood, the indiscriminate destruction of men, of helpless women, and of infant children. The evidence before us leaves not a shadow of doubt, but that your hands were often imbrued in the blood of the innocent; and your own confession tells us that they were stained with the blood of a master; in your own language, "too indulgent." Could I stop here, your crime would be sufficiently aggravated. But the original contriver of a plan, deep and deadly, one that never can be effected, you managed so far to put it into execution, as to deprive us of many of our most valuable citizens; and this was done when they were asleep, and defenseless; under circumstances shocking to humanity. And while upon this part of the subject, I cannot but call your attention to the poor misguided wretches who have gone before you. They are not few in number—they were your bosom associates; and the blood of all cries aloud, and calls upon you, as the author of their misfortune. Yes! You forced them

---

[2] The committing Magistrate.

unprepared, from Time to Eternity. Borne down by this load of guilt, your only justification is, that you were led away by fanaticism. If this be true, from my soul I pity you; and while you have my sympathies, I am, nevertheless called upon to pass the sentence of the court. The time between this and your execution, will necessarily be very short; and your only hope must be in another world. The judgment of the court is, that you be taken hence to the jail from whence you came, thence to the place of execution, and on Friday next, between the hours of 10 A. M. and 2 P.M. be hung by the neck until you are dead! dead! dead! and may the Lord have mercy upon your soul.

A LIST OF PERSONS MURDERED IN THE INSURRECTION, ON THE 21st AND 22nd OF AUGUST, 1831.

Joseph Travers and wife and three children, Mrs. Elizabeth Turner, Hartwell Prebles, Sarah Newsome, Mrs. P. Reese and son William, Trajan Doyle, Henry Bryant and wife and child, and wife's mother, Mrs. Catharine Whitehead, son Richard and four daughters and grand-child, Salathiel Francis, Nathaniel Francis' overseer and two children, John T. Barrow, George Vaughan, Mrs. Levi Waller and ten children, William Williams, wife and two boys, Mrs. Caswell Worrell and child, Mrs. Rebecca Vaughan, Ann Eliza Vaughan, and son Arthur, Mrs. John K. Williams and child, Mrs. Jacob Williams and three children, and Edwin Drury—amounting to fifty-five.

A LIST OF NEGROES BROUGHT BEFORE THE COURT OF SOUTHAMPTON, WITH THEIR OWNERS' NAMES, AND SENTENCE.

Daniel,	Richard Porter,	Convicted.
Moses,	J. T. Barrow,	Do.
Tom,	Caty Whitehead,	Discharged.
Jack and Andrew,	Caty Whitehead,	Con. and transported
Jacob,	Geo. H. Charlton,	Disch'd without trial.
Isaac,	Ditto,	Convi. and transported.
Jack,	Everett Bryant,	Discharged.
Nathan,	Benj. Blunt's estate,	Convicted.
Nathan, Tom, and	Nathaniel Francis,	Convicted and transported
Davy, (boys,)	Elizabeth Turner,	Convicted.
Davy,	Thomas Ridley,	Do.
Curtis,	Do.	Do.
Stephen,	Benjamin Edwards,	Convicted and transp'd.
Hardy and Isham,	Nathaniel Francis,	Convicted.
Sam,	Joseph Travis' estate.	Do.
Hark,	Do.	Do. and transported.
Moses, (a boy,)	Levi Waller,	Convicted.
Davy,	Jacob Williams,	Do.
Nelson,	Edm'd Turner's estate	Do.
Nat,	Wm. Reese's estate	Do.
Dred,	Nathaniel Francis,	Do.

A LIST OF NEGROES BROUGHT BEFORE THE COURT OF SOUTHAMPTON, WITH THEIR OWNERS' NAMES, AND SENTENCE.

Arnold, Artist, (free)		Discharged.
Sam,	J. W. Parker,	Acquitted.
Ferry and Archer,	J. W. Parker,	Disch'd. without trial.
Jim,	William Vaughan,	Acquitted.
Bob,	Temperance Parker,	Do.
Davy,	Joseph Parker,	
Daniel,	Solomon D. Parker	Disch'd without trial.
Thomas Haithcock, (free,)		Sent on for further trial.
Joe,	John C. Turner,	Convicted.
Lucy,	John T. Barrow,	Do.
Matt,	Thomas Ridley,	Acquitted.
Jim,	Richard Porter,	Do.
Exum Artes, (free,)		Sent on for further trial.
Joe,	Richard P. Briggs,	Disch'd without trial.
Bury Newsome, (free,)		Sent on for further trial.
Stephen,	James Bell,	Acquitted.
Jim and Isaac,	Samuel Champion,	Convicted and trans'd.
Preston,	Hannah Williamson	Acquitted.
Frank,	Solomon D. Parker	Convi'd and transp'd.
Jack and Shadrach,	Nathaniel Simmons	Acquitted.
Nelso,	Benj. Blunt's estate,	Do.
Sam,	Peter Edwards,	Convicted.
Archer,	Arthur G. Reese,	Acquitted.
Isham Turner, (free,)		Sent on for further trial.
Nat Turner,	Putnam Moore, dec'd.	Convicted.

FREDERICK DOUGLASS

(1817–1895)

Frederick Douglass was born a slave at Tuckahoe, Maryland and brought up on the plantation of Colonel Edward Lloyd. He was sent to Baltimore when he was 10 and was taught to read by his master's wife, Mrs. Hugh Auld. In 1838 he escaped from Maryland, went to New York, married, and gained his freedom. Douglass soon became a well-known abolitionist, reformer journalist, and orator. Late in his life, he served as consul general to Haiti.

The following selection, which appeared in *The Liberator,* September 22, 1848, is a letter that Douglass wrote to his former master, Thomas Auld.

Letter to His Master

THOMAS AULD:

Sir—The long and intimate, though by no means friendly relation which unhappily subsisted between you and myself, leads me to hope that you will easily account for the great liberty which I now take in addressing you in this open and public manner. The same fact may possibly remove any disagreeable surprise which you may experience on again finding your name coupled with mine, in any other way than in an advertisement, accurately describing my person, and offering a large sum for my arrest. In thus dragging you again before the public, I am aware that I shall subject myself to no inconsiderable amount of censure. I shall probably be charged with an unwarrantable, if not a wanton and reckless disregard of the rights and proprieties of private life. There are those North as well as South who entertain a much higher respect for rights which are merely conventional, than they do for rights which are personal and essential. Not a few there are in our country, who, while they have no scruples against robbing the laborer of the hard earned results of his patient industry, will be shocked by the extremely indelicate manner of bringing your name before the public. . . .

I have selected this day on which to address you, because it is the anniversary of my emancipation; and knowing of no better way, I am led to this as the best mode of celebrating that truly important event. Just ten years ago this beautiful September morning, yon bright sun beheld me a slave—a poor, degraded chattel—trembling at the sound of your voice, lamenting that I was a man, and wishing myself a brute. The hopes which I had treasured up for weeks of a safe and successful escape from your grasp, were powerfully confronted at this last hour by dark clouds of doubt and fear, making my person shake and my bosom to heave with the heavy contest between hope and fear. I have no words to describe to you the deep agony of soul which I experienced on that never to be forgotten morning—(for I left by daylight). I was making a leap in the dark. The probabilities, so far as I could by reason determine them, were stoutly against the undertaking. The preliminaries and precautions I had adopted previously, all worked badly. I was like one going to war without weapons—ten chances of defeat to one of victory. One in whom I had confided, and one who had promised me assistance, appalled by fear at the trial hour, deserted me, thus leaving the responsibility of success or failure solely with myself. You, sir, can never know my feelings. As I look back to them, I can scarcely realize that I have passed through a scene so trying. Trying however as they were, and gloomy as was the prospect, thanks be to the Most High, who is ever the God of the oppressed, at the moment which was to determine my whole earthly career. His grace was sufficient, my mind was made up, I embraced the golden opportunity, took the morning tide at the flood, and a free man, young, active and strong, is the result. . . .

Since I left you, I have had a rich experience. I have occupied stations which I never dreamed of when a slave. Three out of the ten years since I left you, I spent as a common laborer on the wharves of New Bedford, Massachusetts. It was there I earned my first free dollar. It was mine, I could spend it as I pleased. I could buy hams or herring with it, without asking any odds of any body. That was a precious dollar to me. You remember when I used to make seven or eight, or even nine dollars a week in Baltimore, you would take every cent of it from me every Saturday night, saying that I belonged to you, and my earnings also. I never liked this conduct on your part—to say the best, I thought it a little mean. I would not have served you so. But let that pass. I was a little awkward about counting money in New England fashion when I first landed in New Bedford. I like to have betrayed myself several times. I caught myself saying phip, for fourpence; and at one time a man actually charged me with being a runaway, whereupon I was silly enough to become one by running away from him, for I was greatly afraid he might adopt measures to give me again into slavery, a condition I then dreaded more than death.

I soon, however, learned to count money, as well as to make it, and got on swimmingly. I married soon after leaving you; in fact, I was engaged to be married before I left you; and instead of finding my companion a burden, she was truly a helpmeet. She went to live at service, and I to work on the wharf, and though we toiled hard the first winter, we never lived more happily. After remaining in New Bedford for three years, I met with Wm. Lloyd Garrison, a person of whom you have *possibly* heard, as he is pretty generally known among slave-holders. He put it into my head that I might make myself serviceable to the cause of the slave by devoting a portion of my time to telling my own sorrows, and those of other slaves which had come under my observation. This was the commencement of a higher state of existence than any to which I had ever aspired. I was thrown into society the most pure, enlightened and benevolent that the country affords. Among these I have never forgotten you, but have invariably made you the topic of conversation—thus giving you all the notoriety I could do. I need not tell you that the opinion formed of you in these circles, is far from being favorable. They have little respect for your honesty, and less for your religion.

But I was going on to relate to you something of my interesting experience. I had not long enjoyed the excellent society to which I have referred, before the light of its excellence exerted a beneficial influence on my mind and heart. Much of my early dislike of white persons was removed, and their manners, habits and customs, so entirely unlike what I had been used to in the kitchen-quarters on the plantations of the South, fairly charmed me, and gave me a strong disrelish for the coarse and degrading customs of my former condition. I therefore made an effort so to improve my mind and deportment as to be somewhat fitted to the station to which I seemed almost providentially called. The transition from degradation to respectability was indeed great, and to get from one to the other without carrying some marks of one's former condition, is truly a difficult matter. I would not have you think that I am now entirely clear of all plantation peculiarities, but my friends here, while they entertain the strongest dislike to them, regard me with that charity to which my past life somewhat entitles me, so that my condition in this respect is exceedingly pleasant. So far as my domestic affairs are concerned, I can boast of as comfortable a dwelling as your own. I have an industrious and neat companion, and four dear children—the oldest a girl of nine years, and three fine boys, the oldest eight, the next six, and the youngest four years old. The three oldest are now going regularly to school—two can read and write, and the other can spell with tolerable correctness words of two syllables: Dear fellows! they are all in comfortable beds, and are sound asleep, perfectly secure under my own roof. There are no slaveholders here to rend my heart by snatching them from my arms, or blast a mother's dearest hopes by tearing them from her bosom. These dear children are ours—not to work up into rice, sugar and tobacco, but to watch over, regard, and protect, and to rear them up in the nurture and admonition of the gospel—to train them up in the paths of wisdom and virtue, and, as far as we can to make them useful to the world and to themselves. Oh! sir, a slaveholder never appears to me so completely an agent of hell, as when I think of and look upon my dear children. It is then that my feelings rise above my control. I meant to have said more with respect to my own prosperity and happiness, but thoughts and feelings which this recital has quickened unfit me to proceed further in that direction. The grim horrors of slavery rise in all their ghastly terror before me, the wails of millions pierce my heart, and chill my blood. I remember the chain, the gag, the bloody whip, the death-like gloom overshadowing the broken spirit of the fettered bondman, the appalling liability of his being torn away from wife and children, and sold like a beast in the market. Say not that this is a picture of fancy. You well know that I wear stripes on my back inflicted by your direction; and that you, while we were brothers in the same church, caused this right hand, with which I am now penning this letter, to be closely tied to my left, and my person dragged at the pistol's mouth, fifteen miles, from the Bay side to Easton to be sold like a beast in the market, for the alleged crime of intending to escape from your possession. All this and more you remember, and know to be perfectly true, not only of yourself, but of nearly all of the slaveholders around you.

At this moment, you are probably the guilty holder of at least three of my own dear sisters, and my only brother in bondage. These you regard as your property. They are recorded on your ledger, or perhaps have been sold to human flesh mongers, with a view to filling your own ever-hungry purse. Sir, I desire to know how and where these dear sisters are. Have you sold them?

or are they still in your possession? What has become of them? are they living or dead? And my dear old grand-mother, whom you turned out like an old horse, to die in the woods—is she still alive? Write and let me know all about them. If my grandmother be still alive, she is of no service to you, for by this time she must be nearly eighty years old—too old to be cared for by one to whom she has ceased to be of service, send her to me at Rochester, or bring her to Philadelphia, and it shall be the crowning happiness of my life to take care of her in her old age. Oh! she was to me a mother, and a father, so far as hard toil for my comfort could make her such. Send me my grand-mother! that I may watch over and take care of her in her old age. And my sisters, let me know all about them. I would write to them, and learn all I want to know of them, without disturbing you in any way, but that, through your unrighteous conduct, they have been entirely deprived of the power to read and write. You have kept them in utter ignorance, and have therefore robbed them of the sweet enjoyments of writing or receiving letters from absent friends and relatives. Your wickedness and cruelty committed in this respect on your fellow-creatures, are greater than all the stripes you have laid upon my back, or theirs. It is an outrage upon the soul—a war upon the immortal spirit, and one for which you must give account at the bar of our common Father and Creator. . . .

I will now bring this letter to a close, you shall hear from me again unless you let me hear from you. I intend to make use of you as a weapon with which to assail the system of slavery—as a means of concentrating public attention on the system, and deepening their horror of trafficking in the souls and bodies of men. I shall make use of you as a means of exposing the character of the American church and clergy—and as a means of bringing this guilty nation with yourself to repentance. In doing this I entertain no malice towards you personally. There is no roof under which you would be more safe than mine, and there is nothing in my house which you might need for your comfort, which I would not readily grant. Indeed, I should esteem it a privilege, to set you an example as to how mankind ought to treat each other.

I am your fellow man, but not your slave,

FREDERICK DOUGLASS.

CHARLOTTE FORTEN

(1838–1914)

Charlotte Forten was the granddaughter of James Forten, an affluent sailmaker. She grew up in Philadelphia and was sent by her father to Salem, Massachusetts, where she became a school teacher until her health declined. In her youth she kept a diary that reveals the moral paradoxes of her childhood: brilliant in school, she was scorned by those same girls who had befriended her in class. During the Civil War, she taught blacks in South Carolina and, afterwards, settled in Philadelphia, marrying Francis Grimke, an active champion of Negro rights.

A modern edition of Charlotte Forten's *Journal*, with an introduction and notes, is by Ray Allen, 1953.

From The Journal of Charlotte Forten

Wednesday, Sept. 12. To-day school commenced.—Most happy am I to return to the companionship of my studies,—ever my most valued friends. It is pleasant to meet the scholars again; most of them greeted me cordially, and were it not for the thought that *will* intrude, of the want of *entire sympathy* even of those I know and like best, I should greatly enjoy their society. There is one young girl and only one—Miss [Sarah] B[rown] who I believe thoroughly and heartily appreciates anti-slavery,—*radical* anti-slavery, and has no prejudice against color. I wonder that every colored person is not a misanthrope. Surely we have everything to make us hate mankind. I have met girls in the schoolroom[—]they have been thoroughly kind and cordial to me,—perhaps the next day met them in the street—they feared to recognize me; these I can but regard now with scorn and contempt,—once I liked them, believing them incapable of such meanness. Others give the most distant recognition possible.—I, of course, acknowledge no such recognitions, and they soon cease entirely. These are but trifles, certainly, to the great, public wrongs which we as a people are obliged to endure. But to those who experience them, these apparent trifles are most wearing and discouraging; even to the child's mind they reveal volumes of deceit and heartlessness, and early teach a lesson of suspicion and distrust. Oh! it is hard to go through life meeting contempt with contempt, hatred with hatred, fearing, with too good reason, to love and trust hardly any one whose skin is white,—however lovable, attractive and congenial in seeming. In the bitter, passionate feelings of my soul again and again there rises the questions "When, oh! when shall this cease?" "Is there no help?" "How long oh! how long must we continue to suffer—to endure?" Conscience answers it is wrong, it is ignoble to despair; let us labor earnestly and faithfully to acquire knowledge, to break down the barriers of prejudice and oppression. Let us take courage; never ceasing to work,—hoping and believing that if not for us, for another generation there is a better, brighter day in store,—when slavery and prejudice shall vanish before the glorious light of Liberty and Truth; when the rights of every colored man shall everywhere be acknowledged and respected, and he shall be treated as a *man* and a *brother!*

Spirituals

Spirituals represent the common experience of black people: their suffering, alienation, and melancholy as well as their stoicism and desire for freedom. Derived from an African instead of European tradition, these lyrics include spirituals, workaday songs, chaingang songs, "shouts," ballads and, ultimately, blues. They constitute a unique American art form.

Sometimes I Feel Like a Motherless Child

Sometimes I feel like a motherless child,
Sometimes I feel like a motherless child,
Sometimes I feel like a motherless child,
A long ways from home;
A long ways from home.
True believer, A long ways from home,
A long ways from home.

Sometimes I feel like I'm almos' gone,
Sometimes I feel like I'm almos' gone,
Sometimes I feel like I'm almos' gone,
Way up in de heab'nly lan',
Way up in de heab'nly lan'.
True believer, way up in de heab'mly lan',
Way up in de heab'nly lan'.

Sometimes I feel like a motherless child,
Sometimes I feel like a motherless child,
Sometimes I feel like a motherless child,
A long ways from home.

Go Down Moses

Go down, Moses
'Way down in Egypt land,
Tel ole Pharaoh,
To let my people go.
Go down, Moses
'Way down in Egypt land,
Tell ole Pharaoh,
To let my people go.

When Israel was in Egypts land:
Let my people go,
Oppressed so hard they could not stand,
Let my people go.
"When spoke the Lord,"
bold Moses said;
Let me people go
If not I'll smite your first born dead
Let my people go.

Go down, Moses,
'Way down in Egypt land,
Tell ole Pharaoh,
To let my people go.
O let me people go.

Steal Away to Jesus

Steal away, steal away, steal away to Jesus!
Steal away, steal away home,
I ain't got long to stay here.
Steal away, steal away, steal away to Jesus!
Steal away, steal away, steal away home,

I ain't got long to stay here.
My Lord, He calls me
He calls me by the thunder,
The trumpet sounds within a my soul,
I ain't got long to stay here.

Steal away, steal away, steal away to Jesus!
Steal away, steal away home,
I ain't got long to stay here,
Steal away, steal away. steal away to Jesus!
Steal away, steal away home,
I ain't got long to stay here.
Green trees a bending, po' sinner stand a trembling,
The trumpet sounds within a my soul,
I ain't got long to stay here,
Oh, Lord I ain't got long to stay here.

Joshua Fit De Battle Ob Jerico

Joshua fit de battle ob Jericho, Jerico, Jerico
Joshua fit de battle ob Jerico,
An' de walls come tumblin' down.

You may talk about yo' king ob Gideon,
You may talk about yo' man ob Saul,
Dere's none like good ole Joshua
At de battle ob Jerico.

Up to de walls ob Jerico,
He marched with spear in han',
"Go blow dem ran horns," Joshua cried
'Kase de battle am in my han."

Den de lam' ram sheep horns begin to blow,
Trumpets begin to soun',
Joshua a commanded de chollen to shout,
An' de walls comes tumblin' down,
Dat mornin'
Joshua fit de battle ob Jerico, Jerico, Jerico,
Joshua fit de battle ob Jerico,
An' de walls come tumblin' down.

Swing Low Sweet Chariot

Swing low sweet chariot,
Comin' for to carry me home,
Swing low sweet chariot,
Comin' for to carry me home,
O swing low sweet chariot,
Comin' for to carry me home,
Swing low sweet chariot,
Comin' for to carry me home.

I look'd over Jordan, an' what did I see,
Comin' for to carry me home
A band of angels comin' after me,
Comin' for to carry me home.

If you get a dere befo' I do,
Comin' for to carry me home
Tell all my friends I'm comin' too
Comin' for to carry me home.

O, Swing low sweet chariot,
Comin' for to carry me home,
Swing low sweet chariot,
Comin' for to carry me home
Comin' for to carry me home.

THE SOUTHERN PERSPECTIVE

From the perspective of many Southerners, slavery was contradictory to the philosophy of natural rights and, especially in Virginia, they gave their slaves freedom. During the Revolutionary period, the reluctance to free slaves resulted from a fear that racial tensions would occur and, after Southerners realized that it was impracticable to return slaves to Africa, they claimed that the evils of freed black people outweighed the evils of slavery. As the impact of the Enlightenment waned in the South, slavery became an institution.

The invention of the cotton gin confirmed the need for slavery in the minds of most Southerners, and the plantation system quickly spread into Georgia, Alabama, and Mississippi. The lower South then drew its slaves from the upper regions as the rapid production of cotton justified slavery economically. A proslavery argument developed that maintained that the institution was beneficial to the nation as a whole, and arguments that have been repeated for more than a century were soon marshalled: the Bible sanctioned slavery; the Negro was inferior; slavocracy was part of a less commercial and inhuman way of life than Northern industrialism. These arguments were augmented by other positions: the defense of states rights rather than the centralized government; the opposition to a centralized banking system; and the need for free trade.

GEORGE FITZHUGH

(1806-1881)

Fitzhugh's most famous apologies for slavery are *Sociology for the South; or, The Failure of a Free Society* (1854) and *Cannibals All or, Slavery Without Masters* (1857). Fitzhugh stressed the positive effects of slavery, concentrating on a comparison between the exploitation of industrial workers in the North with the paternalistic and benevolent support of blacks by the Southern slaveholders.

See Clement Eaton, "The South and Northern Radicalism," *New England Quarterly,* VIII (June 1935). A study that places Fitzhugh's thought in its social context is W. S. Jenkins, *Pro-Slavery Thought in The Old South,* (1935).

Negro Slavery

We have already stated that we should not attempt to introduce any new theories of government and of society, but merely try to justify old ones, so far as we could deduce such theories from ancient and almost universal practices. Now it has been the practice in all countries and in all ages, in some degree, to accommodate the amount and character of government control to the wants, intelligence, and moral capacities of the nations or individuals to be governed. A highly moral and intellectual people, like the free citizens of ancient Athens, are best governed by a democracy. For a less moral and intellectual one, a limited and constitutional monarchy will answer. For a people either very ignorant or very wicked, nothing short of military despotism will suffice. So among individuals, the most moral and well-informed members of society require no other government than law.

They are capable of reading and understanding the law, and have sufficient self-control and virtuous disposition to obey it. Children cannot be governed by mere law; first, because they do not understand it, and secondly, because they are so much under the influence of impulse, passion and appetite, that they want sufficient self-control to be deterred or governed by the distant and doubtful penalties of the law. They must be constantly controlled by parents or guardians, whose will and orders shall stand in the place of law for them. Very wicked men must be put into penitentiaries; lunatics into asylums, and the most wild of them into strait-jackets, just as the most wicked of the sane are manacled with irons; and idiots must have committees to govern and take care of them. Now, it is clear the Athenian democracy would not suit a negro nation, nor will the government of mere law suffice for the individual negro. He is but a grown up child, and must be governed as a child, not as a lunatic or criminal. The master occupies towards him the place of parent or guardian. We shall not dwell on this view, for no one will differ with us who thinks as we do of the negro's capacity, and we might argue till dooms-day, in vain, with those who have a high opinion of the negro's moral and intellectual capacity.

Secondly. The negro is improvident; will not lay up in summer for the wants of winter; will not accumulate in youth for the exigencies of age. He would become an insufferable burden to society. Society has the right to prevent this, and can only do so by subjecting him to domestic slavery. In the last place, the negro race is inferior to the white race, and living in their midst, they would be far outstripped or outwitted in the chase of free competition. Gradual but certain extermination would be their fate. We presume the maddest abolitionist does not think the negro's providence of habits and money-making capacity at all to compare to those of the whites. This defect of character would alone justify enslaving him, if he is to remain here. In Africa or the West Indies, he would become idolatrous, savage and cannibal, or be devoured by savages and cannibals. At the North he would freeze or starve.

We would remind those who deprecate and sympathize with negro slavery, that his slavery here relieves him from a far more cruel slavery in Africa, or from idolatry and cannibalism, and every brutal vice and crime that can disgrace humanity; and that it christianizes, protects, supports and civilizes him; that it governs him far better than free laborers at the North are governed. There, wife-murder has become a mere holiday pastime; and where so many wives are murdered, almost all must be brutally treated. Nay, more: men who kill their wives or treat them brutally, must be ready for all kinds of crime, and the calendar of crime at the North proves the inference to be correct. Negroes never kill their wives. If it be objected that legally they have no wives, then we reply, that in an experience of more than forty years, we never yet heard of a negro man killing a negro woman. Our negroes are not only better off as to physical comfort than free laborers, but their moral condition is better.

But abolish negro slavery, and how much of slavery still remains. Soldiers and sailors in Europe enlist for life; here, for five years. Are they not slaves who have not only sold their liberties, but their lives also? And they are worse treated than domestic slaves. No domestic affection and self-interest extend their ægis over them. No kind mistress, like a guardian angel, provides for them in health, tends them in sickness, and soothes their dying pillow. Wellington at Waterloo was a slave. He was bound to obey, or would, like Admiral Byng, have been shot for gross misconduct, and might not, like a common laborer, quit his work at any moment. He had sold his liberty, and might not resign without the consent of his master, the king. The common laborer may quit his work at any moment, whatever his contract; declare that liberty is an alienable right, and leave his employer to redress by a useless suit for damages. The highest and most honorable position on earth was that of the slave Wellington; the lowest, that of the free man who cleaned his boots and fed his hounds. The African cannibal, caught, christianized and enslaved, is as much elevated by slavery as was Wellington. The kind of slavery is adapted to the men enslaved. Wives and apprentices are slaves; not in theory only, but often in fact. Children are slaves to their parents, guardians and teachers. Imprisoned culprits are slaves. Lunatics and idiots are slaves also. Three-fourths of free society are slaves, no better treated, when their wants and capacities are estimated, than negro slaves. The masters in free society, or slave society, if they perform properly their duties, have more cares and less liberty than the slaves themselves. "In the sweat of thy face shalt thou earn thy bread!" made all men slaves, and such all *good men* continue to be.

Negro slavery would be changed immediately to some form of peonage, serfdom or villienage, if the negroes were sufficiently intelligent and provident to manage a farm. No one would have the labor and trouble of management, if his negroes would pay in hires and rents one-half what free tenants pay in rent in Europe. Every negro in the South would be soon liberated, if he would take liberty on the terms that white tenants hold it. The fact that he cannot enjoy liberty on such terms, seems conclusive that he is only fit to be a slave.

But for the assaults of the abolitionists, much would have been done ere this to regulate and improve Southern slavery. Our negro mechanics do not work so hard, have many more privileges and holidays, and are better fed and clothed than field hands, and are yet more valuable to their masters. The slaves of the South are cheated of their rights by the purchase of Northern manufactures which they could produce. Besides, if we would employ our slaves in the coarser processes of the mechanic arts and manufacturers, such as brick making, getting and hewing timber for ships and houses, iron mining and smelting, coal mining, grading railroads and plank roads, in the manufacture of cotton, tobacco, &c., we would find a vent in new employments for their increase, more humane and more profitable than the vent afforded by new states and territories. The nice and finishing processes of manufactures and mechanics should be reserved for the whites, who only are fitted for them, and thus, by diversifying pursuits and cutting off dependence on the North, we might benefit and advance the interests of our whole population. Exclusive agriculture has depressed and impoverished the South. We will not here dilate on this topic, because we intend to make it the subject of a separate essay. Free trade doctrines, not slavery, have made the South agricultural and dependent, given her a sparse and ignorant population, ruined her cities, and expelled her people.

Would the abolitionists approve of a system of society that set white children free, and remitted them at the age of fourteen, males and females, to all the rights, both as to person and property, which belong to adults? Would it be criminal or praiseworthy to do so? Criminal, of course. Now, are the average of negroes equal in formation, in native intelligence, in prudence or providence, to well-informed white children of fourteen? We who have lived with them for forty years, think not. The competition of the world would be too much for the children. They would be cheated out of their property and debased in their morals. Yet they would meet every where with sympathizing friends of their own color, ready to aid, advise and assist them. The negro would be exposed to the same competition and greater temptations, with no greater ability to contend with them, with these additional difficulties. He would be welcome nowhere; meet with thousands of enemies and no friends. If he went North, the white laborers would kick him and cuff him, and drive him out of employment. If he went to Africa, the savages would cook him and eat him. If he went to the West Indies, they would not let him in, or if they did, they would soon make of him a savage and idolater.

We have a further question to ask. If it be right and incumbent to subject children to the authority of parents and guardians, and idiots and lunatics to committees, would it not be equally right and incumbent to give the free negroes masters, until at least they arrive at years of discretion, which very few ever did or will attain? What is the difference between the authority of a parent and of a master? Neither pay wages, and each is entitled to the services of those subject to him. The father may not sell his child forever, but may hire him out till he is twenty-one. The free negro's master may also be restrained from selling. Let him stand *in loco parentis,* and call him papa instead of master. Look closely into slavery, and you will see nothing so hideous in it; or if you do, you will find plenty of it at home in its most hideous form.

The earliest civilization of which history gives account is that of Egypt. The negro was always in contact with that civilization. For four thousand years he has had opportunities of becoming civilized. Like the wild horse, he must be caught, tamed and domesticated. When his subjugation ceases he again runs wild, like the cattle on the Pampas of the South, or the horses on the prairies of the West. His condition in the West Indies proves this.

It is a common remark, that the grand and lasting architectural structures of antiquity were the results of slavery. The mighty and continued association of labor requisite to their construction, when mechanic art was so little advanced, and labor-saving process unknown, could only have been brought about by a despotic authority, like that of the master over his slaves. It is, however, very remarkable, that whilst in taste and artistic skill the world seems to have been retrograding ever since the decay and abolition of feudalism, in mechanical invention and in great utilitarian operations requiring the wielding of immense capital and much labor, its progress has been unexampled. Is it because capital is more despotic in its authority over free laborers than Roman masters and feudal lords were over their slaves and vassals?

Free society has continued long enough to justify the attempt to generalize its phenomena, and calculate its moral and intellectual influences. It is obvious that, in whatever is purely utilitarian and material, it incites invention and stimulates industry. Benjamin Franklin , as a man and a philosopher, is the best exponent of the working of the system. His sentiments and his philosophy are low, selfish, atheistic and material. They tend directly to make man a mere "featherless biped," well-fed, well-clothed and comfortable, but regardless of his soul as "the beasts that perish."

Since the Reformation the world has as regularly been retrograding in whatever belongs to the departments of genius, taste and art, as it has been progressing in physical science and its application to mechanical construction. Mediæval Italy rivalled if it did not surpass ancient Rome, in poetry, in sculpture, in painting, and many of the fine arts. Gothic architecture reared its monuments of skill and genius throughout Europe, till the 15th century; but Gothic architecture died with the Reformation. The age of Elizabeth was the Augustan age of England. The men who lived then acquired their sentiments in a world not yet deadened and vulgarized by puritanical cant and leveling demagoguism. Since then men have arisen who have been the fashion and the go for a season, but none have appeared whose names will descend to posterity. Liberty and equality made slower advances in France. The age of Louis XIV was the culminating point of French genius and art. It then shed but a flickering and lurid light. Frenchmen are servile copyists of Roman art, and Rome had no art of her own. She borrowed from Greece; distorted and deteriorated what she borrowed; and France imitates and falls below Roman distortions. The genius of Spain disappeared with Cervantes; and now the world seems to regard nothing as desirable except what will make money and what costs money. There is not a poet, an orator, a sculptor, or painter in the world. The tedious elaboration necessary to all the productions of high art would be ridiculed in this money-making, utilitarian, charlatan age. Nothing now but what is gaudy and costly excites admiration. The public taste is debased.

But far the worst feature of modern civilization, which is the civilization of free society, remains to be exposed. Whilst labor-saving processes have probably lessened by one half, in the last century, the amount of work needed for comfortable support, the free laborer is compelled by capital and competition to work more than he ever did before, and is less comfortable. The organization of society cheats him of his earnings, and those earnings go to swell the vulgar pomp and pageantry of the ignorant millionaires, who are the only great of the present day. These reflections might seem, at first view, to have little connexion with negro slavery; but it is well for us of the South not to be deceived by the tinsel glare and glitter of free society, and to employ ourselves in doing our duty at home, and studying the past, rather than in insidious rivalry of the expensive pleasures and pursuits of men whose sentiments and whose aims are low, sensual and grovelling.

Human progress consisting in moral and intellectual improvement, and there being no agreed and conventional standard weights or measures of moral and intellectual qualities and quantities, the question of progress can never be accurately decided. We maintain that man has not improved, because in all save the mechanic arts he reverts to the distant past for models to imitate, and he never imitates what he can excel.

We need never have white slaves in the South, because we have black ones. Our citizens, like those of Rome and Athens, are a privileged class. We should train and educate them to deserve the privileges and to perform the duties which society confers on them. Instead of, by a low demagoguism, depressing their self-respect by discourses on the equality of man, we had better excite their pride by reminding them that they do not fulfil the menial offices which white men do in other countries. Society does not feel the burden of providing for the few helpless paupers in the South. And we should recollect that here we have but half the people to educate, for half are negroes; whilst at the North they profess to educate all. It is in our power to spike this last gun of the abolitionists. We should educate all the poor. The abolitionists say that it is one of the necessary consequences of slavery that the poor are neglected. It was not so in Athens, and in Rome, and should not be so in the South. If we had less trade with and less dependence on the North, all our poor might be profitably and honorably employed in trades, professions and manufactures. Then we should have a rich and denser population. Yet we but marshal her in the way that she was going. The South is already aware of the necessity of a new policy, and has begun to act on it. Every day more and more is done for education, the mechanic arts, manufactures and internal improvements. We will soon be independent of the North.

We deem this peculiar question of negro slavery of very little importance. The issue is made throughout the world on the general subject of slavery in the abstract. The argument has commenced. One set of ideas will govern and control after awhile the civilized world. Slavery will every where be abolished, or every where be re-instituted. We think the opponents of practical, existing slavery, are stopped by their own admission; nay, that unconsciously, as socialists, they are the defenders and propagandists of slavery, and have furnished the only sound arguments on which its defence and justification can be rested. We have introduced the subject of negro slavery to afford us a better opportunity to disclaim the purpose of reducing the white man any where to the condition of negro slaves here. It would be very unwise and unscientific to govern white men as you would negroes. Every shade and variety of slavery has existed in the world. In some cases there has been much of legal regulation, much restraint of the master's authority; in others, none at all. The character of slavery necessary to protect the whites in Europe should be much milder than negro slavery, for slavery is only needed to protect the white man, whilst it is more necessary for the government of the negro even than for his protection. But even negro slavery should not be outlawed. We might and should have laws in Virginia, as in Louisiana, to make the master subject to presentment by the grand jury and to punishment, for any inhuman or improper treatment or neglect of his slave.

We abhor the doctrine of the "Types of Mankind;" first, because it is at war with scripture, which teaches us that the whole human race is descended from a common parentage; and, secondly, because it encourages and incites brutal masters to treat negroes, not as weak, ignorant and dependent brethren, but as wicked beasts, without the pale of humanity. This Southerner is the negro's friend, his only friend. Let no intermeddling abolitionist, no refined philosophy, dissolve this friendship.

WILLIAM J. GRAYSON

(1788–1863)

William J. Grayson was a congressional representative from South Carolina who took a more moderate position than Fitzhugh. He admitted some of the evils of slavery, but the burden of his most famous work, *The Hireling and the Slave (1856)*, is that the Northern factory

A collection of Grayson's work is *Selected Poems of William J. Grayson*, selected and compiled by Mrs. William H. Armstrong, 1907. For a brief account, see B. L.

Parrington, *The Romantic Revolution in America*, 1800–1860, in *Main Currents in American Thought*, pp. 103–108.

worker—the hireling—is a slave to commercialism whereas the Southern slave has security that comes from the ordered life of the plantation. *The Hireling and the Slave*, written in heroic couplets, is modeled on the poetry of the eighteenth century. It depicts slaves at play, hunting possums, fishing contentedly, and celebrating Christmas holidays. Grayson's poem remains as perhaps the most notable reply to Harriet Beecher Stowe's *Uncle Tom's Cabin.*

From The Hireling and the Slave

And yet the life, so unassailed by care,
So blest with moderate work, with ample fare,
With all the good an pauper Hireling needs,
The happier Slave on each plantation leads;
Safe from harassing doubts and annual fears,　　　　　5
He dreads no famine, in unfruitful years;
If harvest fail from inauspicious skies,
The Master's providence his food supplies;
No paupers perish here for want of bread,
Or lingering live, by foreign bounty fed;　　　　　10
No exiled trains of homeless peasants go,
In distant climes, to tell their tales of woe;
For other fortune, free from care and strife,
For work, or bread, attends the Negro's life,
And Christian Slaves may challenge as their own,　　　　　15
The blessings claimed in fabled states alone—
The cabin home, not comfortless, though rude,
Light daily labour, and abundant food,
The sturdy health, that temperate habits yield,
The cheerful song, that rings in every field,　　　　　20
The long, loud laugh, that freemen seldom share,
Heaven's boon to bosoms unapproached by care,
And boisterous jest and humour unrefined,
That leave, though rough, no painful sting behind;
While, nestling near, to bless their humble lot,　　　　　25
Warm social joys surround the Negro's cot,
The evening dance its merriment imparts,
Love, with his rapture, fills their youthful hearts,
And placid age, the task of labour done,
Enjoys the summer shade, the winter's sun,　　　　　30
And, as through life no pauper want he knows,
Laments no poorhouse penance at its close.

HINTON ROWAN HELPER

(1829-1909)

Helper's antislavery document, *The Impending Crisis of the South: How to Meet It (1857),* caused a sensation when it was first published, and it was widely circulated in the North at the same time as it was in the South. Slavery, in Helper's view, would lead to the economic ruin of the South because, in the long run, it was less profitable than granting the black man freedom. *The Impending Crisis* had an effect on Northerners that was second only to *Uncle Tom's Cabin,* since it attacked the oligarchy in the South and championed the cause of the poor Southern white.

The Impending Crisis of the South: Know How To Meet It has been edited by George M. Frederickson, 1968. A study is

Hugh C. Bailey, *Hinton Rowan Helper, Abolitionist and Racist,* 1965.

From The Free and the Slave States.

It is a fact well known to every intelligent Southerner that we are compelled to go to the North for almost every article of utility and adornment, from matches, shoepegs and paintings up to cotton-mills, steamships and statuary; that we have no foreign trade, no princely merchants, nor respectable artists; that, in comparison with the free states, we contribute nothing to the literature, polite arts and inventions of the age; that, for want of profitable employment at home, large numbers of our native population find themselves necessitated to emigrate to the West, whilst the free states retain not only the larger proportion of those born within their own limits, but induce, annually, hundreds of thousands of foreigners to settle and remain amongst them; that almost everything produced at the North meets with ready sale, while, at the same time, there is no demand, even among our own citizens, for the productions of Southern industry; that, owing to the absence of a proper system of business amongst us, the North becomes, in one way or another, the proprietor and dispenser of all our floating wealth, and that we are dependent on Northern capitalists for the means necessary to build our railroads, canals and other public improvements; that if we want to visit a foreign country, even though it may lie directly South of us, we find no convenient way of getting there except by taking passage through a Northern port; and that nearly all the profits arising from the exchange of commodities, from insurance and shipping offices, and from the thousand and one industrial pursuits of the country, accrue to the North, and are there invested in the erection of those magnificent cities and stupendous works of art which dazzle the eyes of the South, and attest the superiority of free institutions!

The North is the Mecca of our merchants, and to it they must and do make two pilgrimages per annum—one in the spring and one in the fall. All our commercial, mechanical, manufactural, and literary supplies come from there. We want Bibles, brooms, buckets and books, and we go to the North; we want pens, ink, paper, wafers and envelopes, and we go to the North; we want shoes, hats, handkerchiefs, umbrellas and pocket knives, and we go to the North; we want furniture, crockery, glassware and pianos, and we go to the North; we want toys, primers, school books, fashionable apparel, machinery, medicines, tombstones, and a thousand other things, and we go to the North for them all. Instead of keeping our money in circulation at home, by patronizing our own mechanics, manufacturers, and laborers, we send it all away to the North, and there it remains; it never falls into our hands again.

In one way or another we are more or less subservient to the North every day of our lives. In infancy we are swaddled in Northern muslin; in childhood we are humored with Northern gewgaws; in youth we are instructed out of Northern books; at the age of maturity we sow our "wild oats" on Northern soil; in middle-life we exhaust our wealth, energies and talents in the dishonorable vocation of entailing our dependence on our children and on our children's children, and, to the neglect of our own interests and the interests of those around us, in giving aid and succor to every department of Northern power; in the decline of life we remedy our eye-sight with Northern spectacles, and support our infirmities with Northern canes; in old age we are drugged with Northern physic; and, finally, when we die, our inanimate bodies, shrouded in Northern cambric, are stretched upon the bier, borne to the grave in a Northern carriage, entombed with a Northern spade, and memorized with a Northern slab!

But it can hardly be necessary to say more in illustration of this unmanly and unnational dependence, which is so glaring that it cannot fail to be apparent to even the most careless and superficial observer. All the world sees, or ought to see, that in a commercial, mechanical, manufactural, financial, and literary point of view, we are as helpless as babes; that, in comparison with the Free States, our agricultural resources have been greatly exaggerated, misunderstood and mismanaged; and that, instead of cultivating among ourselves a wise policy of mutual assistance and co-operation with respect to individuals, and of self-reliance with respect to the South at large, instead of giving countenance and encouragement to the industrial enterprises projected in our midst, and instead of building up, aggrandizing and beautifying our own States, cities and towns, we have been spending our substance at the North, and are daily augmenting and strengthening the very power which now has us so completely under its thumb.

It thus appears, in view of the preceding statistical facts and arguments, that the South, at one time the superior of the North in almost all the ennobling pursuits and conditions of life, has fallen far behind her competitor, and now ranks more as the dependency of a mother country than as the equal confederate of free and independent States. Following the order of our task, the next duty that devolves upon us is to trace out the causes which have conspired to bring about this important change, and to place on record the reasons, as we understand them. . . .

HENRY TIMROD

(1828–1867)

Although Henry Timrod prepared to be a lawyer and a teacher, he never really settled into either profession. He was fundamentally a lyric poet, deeply influenced by Wordsworth and the Romantics. When war broke out, the Northern market for his work vanished and he spent his last years in poverty. Unable to serve during the Civil War, he expressed his patriotism through poetry, and his most famous poems— "The Confederate Ode," "The Cotton Boll," "Carolina," and "Charleston"—are tributes to the South and specifically to South Carolina.

P. H. Hayne edited *Poems of Henry Timrod,* 1873. Timrod's work is in a modern scholarly edition, *Collected Poems, A Variorum,* ed. Edd Winfield Parks and Aileen Athens, 1965. Parks has also edited, with introduction, *The Essays of Henry Timrod,* 1942.

Early biographies are Henry Tazewell, *Henry Timrod, Laureate of the Confederacy,* 1928 and Clare Virginia Pettigrew, *Harp of the South,* 1936. See also Jay B. Hubbell, ed., *The Last Years of Henry Timrod, 1864–1867,* 1941, and E. W. Parks, *Henry Timrod,* 1964.

Charleston

Calm as that second summer which precedes
  The first fall of the snow,
In the broad sunlight of heroic deeds,
  The City bides the foe.

As yet, behind their ramparts stern and proud,   5
    Her bolted thunders sleep—
Dark Sumter, like a battlemented cloud,
    Looms o'er the solemn deep.

No Calpe frowns from lofty cliff or scar
    To guard the holy strand;   10
But Moultrie holds in leash her dogs of war
    Above the level sand.

And down the dunes a thousand guns lie couched,
    Unseen, beside the flood—
Like tigers in some Orient jungle crouched   15
    That wait and watch for blood.

Meanwhile, through streets still echoing with trade,
    Walk grave and thoughtful men,
Whose hands may one day wield the patriot's blade
    As lightly as the pen.   20

And maidens, with such eyes as would grow dim
    Over a bleeding hound,
Seem each one to have caught the strength of him
    Whose sword she sadly bound.

Thus girt without and garrisoned at home,   25
    Day patient following day,
Old Charleston looks from roof, and spire, and dome,
    Across her tranquil bay.

Ships, through a hundred foes, from Saxon lands
    And spicy Indian ports,   30
Bring Saxon steel and iron to her hands,
    And summer to her courts.

But still, along yon dim Atlantic line,
    The only hostile smoke   35
Creeps like a harmless mist above the brine,
    From some frail, floating oak.

Shall the spring dawn, and she still clad in smiles,
    And with an unscathed brow,
Rest in the strong arms of her palm-crowned isles,   40
    As fair and free as now?

We know not; in the temple of the Fates
    God has inscribed her doom;
And, all untroubled in her faith, she waits
    The triumph or the tomb.   45

Ode

SUNG ON THE OCCASION
OF DECORATING THE GRAVES
OF THE CONFEDERATE DEAD,
AT MAGNOLIA CEMETERY,
CHARLESTON, S.C., 1866

Sleep sweetly in your humble graves,   1
    Sleep, martyrs of a fallen cause!—
Though yet no marble column craves
    The pilgrim here to pause.

In seeds of laurels in the earth,   5
    The garlands of your fame are sown;
And, somewhere, waiting for its birth,
    The shaft is in the stone.

Meanwhile, your sisters for the years
    Which hold in trust your storied tombs,   10
Bring all they now can give you—tears,
    And these memorial blooms.

Small tributes, but your shades will smile
    As proudly on these wreaths to-day,
As when some cannon-moulded pile   15
    Shall overlook this Bay.

Stoop, angels, hither from the skies!
    There is no holier spot of ground,
Than where defeated valor lies
    By mourning beauty crowned.   20

JEFFERSON DAVIS

(1808–1889)

Jefferson Davis was a graduate of West Point who married into an aristocratic family of Mississippi. He served as a secretary of war in Buchanan's administration, opposing the industrial North and the antislavery movement. The following speech, his first inaugural address as President of the Confederate States, is an expression of his Southern nationalism. In time it became clear that Davis was neither tempermentally nor physically capable of leading the Confederacy.

The standard text is *Jefferson Davis, His Letters, Papers, and Speeches,* 10 vols., ed. Dunbar, 1923. See also the earlier Jefferson Davis, *The Rise and Fall of the Confederate Government,* 2 vols., 1881.

A biography is Robert McElroy, *Jefferson Davis, The Unreal and The Real,* 2 vols., 1939. A study is B. J. Hendrick, *Statesmen of the Lost Cause: Jefferson Davis and His Cabinet,* 1939.

Inaugural Address of Jefferson Davis

Gentlemen of the Congress of the Confederate States of America, Friends, and Fellow-Citizens: Called to the difficult and responsible station of Chief Magistrate of the Provisional Government which you have instituted, I approach the discharge of the duties assigned to me with humble distrust of my abilities, but with a sustaining confidence in the wisdom of those who are to guide and aid me in the administration of public affairs, and an abiding faith in the virtue and patriotism of the people. Looking forward to the speedy establishment of a permanent government to take the place of this, which by its greater moral and physical power will be better able to combat with many difficulties that arise from the conflicting interests of separate nations, I enter upon the duties of the office to which I have been chosen with the hope that the beginning of our career, as a Confederacy, may not be obstructed by hostile opposition to our enjoyment of the separate existence and independence we have asserted, and which, with the blessing of Providence, we intend to maintain.

Our present political position has been achieved in a manner unprecedented in the history of nations. It illustrates the American idea that governments rest on the consent of the governed, and that it is the right of the people to alter or abolish them at will whenever they become destructive of the ends for which they were established. The declared purpose of the

Photograph of Jefferson Davis, *(The Granger Collection.)*

compact of the Union from which we have withdrawn was to "establish justice, insure domestic tranquillity, provide for the common defense, promote the general welfare, and secure the blessings of liberty to ourselves and our posterity"; and when, in the judgment of the sovereign States composing this Confederacy, it has been perverted from the purposes for which it was ordained, and ceased to answer the ends for which it was established, a peaceful appeal to the ballot box declared that, so far as they are concerned, the Government created by that compact should cease to exist. In this they merely asserted the right which the Declaration of Independence of July 4, 1776, defined to be "inalienable." Of the time and occasion of its exercise they as sovereigns were the final judges, each for itself. The impartial and enlightened verdict of mankind will vindicate the rectitude of our conduct; and He who knows the hearts of men will judge of the sincerity with which we have labored to preserve the Government of our fathers in its spirit.

The right solemnly proclaimed at the birth of the United States, and which has been solemnly affirmed and reaffirmed in the Bills of Rights of the States subsequently admitted into the Union of 1789, undeniably recognizes in the people the power to resume the authority delegated for the purposes of government. Thus the sovereign States here represented have proceeded to form this Confederacy; and it is by abuse of language that their act has been denominated a revolution. They formed a new alliance, but within each State its government has remained; so that the rights of person and property have not been disturbed. The agent through which they communicated with foreign nations is changed, but this does not necessarily interrupt their international relations. Sustained by the consciousness that the transition from the former Union to the present Confederacy has not proceeded from a disregard on our part of just obligations, or any failure to perform every constitutional duty, moved by no interest or passion to invade the rights of others, anxious to cultivate peace and commerce with all nations, if we may not hope to avoid war, we may at least expect that posterity will acquit us of having needlessly engaged in it. Doubly justified by the absence of wrong on our part, and by wanton aggression on the part of others, there can be no cause to doubt that the courage and patriotism of the people of the Confederate States will be found equal to any measure of defense which their honor and security may require.

An agricultural people, whose chief interest is the export of commodities required in every manufacturing country, our true policy is peace, and the freest trade which our necessities will permit. It is alike our interest and that of all those to whom we would sell, and from whom we would buy, that there should be the fewest practicable restrictions upon the interchange of these commodities. There can, however, be but little rivalry between ours and any manufacturing or navigating community, such as the Northeastern States of the American Union. It must follow, therefore, that mutual interest will invite to good will and kind offices on both parts. If, however, passion or lust or dominion should cloud the judgment or inflame the ambition of those States, we must prepare to meet the emergency and maintain by the final arbitrament of the sword, the position which we have assumed among the nations of the earth.

We have entered upon the career of independence, and it must be inflexibly pursued. Through many years of controversy with our late associates of the Northern States, we have vainly endeavored to secure tranquillity and obtain respect for the rights to which we were entitled. As a necessity, not a choice, we have resorted to the remedy of separation, and henceforth our energies must be directed to the conduct of our own affairs, and the perpetuity of the Confederacy which we have formed. If a just perception of mutual interest shall permit us peaceably to pursue our separate political career, my most earnest desire will have been fulfilled. But if this be denied to us, and the integrity of our territory and jurisdiction be assailed, it will but remain for us with firm resolve to appeal to arms and invoke the blessing of Providence on a just cause.

As a consequence of our new condition and relations, and with a view to meet anticipated wants, it will be necessary to provide for the speedy and efficient organization of branches of the Executive department having special charge of foreign intercourse, finance, military affairs, and the postal service. For purposes of defense, the Confederate States may, under ordinary circumstances, rely mainly upon the militia; but it is deemed advisable, in the present condition of affairs, that there should be a well-instructed and disciplined army, more numerous than would usually be required on a peace establishment. I also suggest that, for the protection of our harbors and commerce of the high seas, a navy adapted to those objects will be required. But this, as well as other subjects appropriate to our necessities, have doubtless engaged the attention of Congress.

With a Constitution differing only from that of our fathers in so far as it is explanatory of their well-known intent, freed from sectional conflicts, which have interfered with the pursuit of the general welfare, it is not unreasonable to expect that States from which we have recently parted may seek to unite their fortunes to ours under the Government which we have instituted. For this your Constitution makes adequate provision; but beyond this, if I mistake not the judgment and will of the people, a reunion with the States from which we have separated is neither practicable nor desirable. To increase the power, develop the resources, and promote the happiness of the Confederacy, it is requisite that there should be so much of homogeneity that the welfare of every portion shall be the aim of the whole. When this does not exist, antagonisms are engendered which must and should result in separation.

Actuated solely by the desire to preserve our own rights, and promote our own welfare, the separation by the Confederate States has been marked by no aggression upon others, and followed by no domestic convulsion. Our industrial pursuits have received no check, the cultivation of our fields has progressed as heretofore, and, even should we be involved in war, there would be no considerable diminution in the production of the staples which have constituted our exports, and in which the commercial world has an interest scarcely less than our own. This common interest of the producer and consumer can only be interrupted by exterior force which would obstruct the transmission of our staples to foreign markets—a course of conduct which would be as unjust, as it would be detrimental, to manufacturing and commercial interests abroad.

Should reason guide the action of the Government from which we have separated, a policy so detrimental to the civilized world, the Northern States included, could not be dictated by even the strongest desire to inflict injury upon us; but, if the contrary should prove true, a terrible responsibility will rest upon it, and the suffering of millions will bear testimony to the folly and wickedness of our aggressors. In the meantime there will remain to us, besides the ordinary means before suggested, the well-known resources for retaliation upon the commerce of an enemy.

Experience in public stations, of subordinate grade to this which your kindness has conferred, has taught me that toil and care and disappointment are the price of official elevation. You will see many errors to forgive, many deficiencies to tolerate; but you shall not find in me either want of zeal or fidelity to the cause that is to me the highest in hope, and of most enduring affection. Your generosity has bestowed upon me an undeserved distinction, one which I neither sought nor desired. Upon the continuance of that sentiment, and upon your wisdom and patriotism, I rely to direct and support me in the performance of the duties required at my hands.

We have changed the constituent parts, but not the system of government. The Constitution framed by our fathers is that of these Confederate States. In their exposition of it, and in the judicial construction it has received, we have a light which reveals its true meaning.

Thus instructed as to the true meaning and just intepretation of that instrument, and ever remembering that all offices are but trusts held for the people, and that powers delegated are to be strictly construed, I will hope by due diligence in the performance of my duties, though I may disappoint your expectation, yet to retain, when retiring, something of the good will and confidence which welcome my entrance into office.

It is joyous in the midst of perilous times to look around upon a people united in heart, where one purpose of high resolve animates and actuates the whole; where the sacrifices to be made are not weighed in the balance against honor and right and liberty and equality. Obstacles may retard, but they cannot long prevent, the progress of a movement sanctified by its justice and sustained by a virtuous people. Reverently let us invoke the God of our fathers to guide and protect us in our efforts to perpetuate the principles which by his blessing they were able to vindicate, establish, and transmit to their posterity. With the continuance of his favor ever gratefully acknowledged, we may hopefully look forward to success, to peace, and to prosperity.

1861

Songs

When read for their sense as well as their rhythm, the songs of the South during the Civil War are militant, written to rouse the passion of soldiers. Like the Northern songs, there is a strong religious strain in all of them.

Maryland, My Maryland

This song was composed by James R. Randall in a burst of emotion when he heard that his classmate, marching with the sixth Massachusetts regiment in Baltimore, had been wounded. Anti-union riots in Baltimore supplied a further impetus for the poem. The words were later put to the tune of the German Christmas carol, "Tannenbaum, O Tannenbaum," by a Baltimore woman who sang it to Beauregard's Maryland troops.

Maryland, My Maryland

1 The despot's heel is on thy shore
Maryland, my Maryland!
His torch is at they temple door,
Maryland, my Maryland!
Avenge the patriotic gore
That flecked the streets of Baltimore,
And be the battle queen of yore,
Maryland, my Maryland!

2 Hark to an exiled son's appeal,
Maryland, my Maryland!
My Mother State, to thee I kneel,
Maryland, my Maryland!

For life or death, for woe or weal,
Thy peerless chivalry reveal,
And gird thy beauteous limbs with steel,
    Maryland, my Maryland!

3 Thou wilt not cower in the dust,
        Maryland, my Maryland!
    Thy beaming sword shall never rust,
        Maryland, my Maryland!
    Remember Carroll's sacred trust,
    Remember Howard's warlike thrust,
    And all thy slumberers with the just,
        Maryland, my Maryland!

4 Come! 'tis the red dawn of the day,
        Maryland, my Maryland!
    Come! with thy panoplied array
        Maryland, my Maryland!
    With Ringgold's spirit for the fray,
    With Watson's blood at Monterey,
    With fearless Lowe and dashing May,
        Maryland, my Maryland!

5 Dear mother, burst the tyrant's chain,
        Maryland, my Maryland!
    Virginia should not call in vain,
        Maryland, my Maryland!
    She meets her sisters on the plain,
    "*Sic temper!*" 'tis the proud refrain
    That baffles minions back amain,
        Maryland, my Maryland!
    Arise in majesty again,
        Maryland, my Maryland!

Marchin Through Georgia

1 Bring the gold old bugle, boys, we'll sing another song;
   Sing it with a spirit that will start the world along,
   Sing it as we used to sing it fifty thousand strong,
       While we were marching through Georgia.

   Hurrah! Hurrah!
   We bring the jubilee!
   Hurrah! Hurrah!

The flag that makes you free
So we sang the chorus from Atlanta to the sea,
While we were marching through Georgia.

2 How the darkeys shouted when they heard the joyful sound!
How the turkeys gobbled which our commissary found!
How the sweet potatoes even started from the ground,
    While we were marching through Georgia. (Chorus)

3 Yes, and there were Union men who wept with joyful tears,
When they saw the honored flag they had not seen for years;
Hardly could they be restrained from breaking forth in cheers,
    While we were marching through Georgia. (Chorus)

4 "Sherman's dashing Yankee boys will never reach the coast!"
So the saucy Rebels said, and 'twas a handsome boast;
Had they not forgot, alas! to reckon with the host,
    While we were marching through Georgia. (Chorus)

5 So we made a thoroughfare for Freedom and her train,
Sixty miles in latitude, three hundred to the main;
Treason fled before us, for resistance was in vain,
    While we were marching through Georgia. -(Chorus)

Dixie is Land

"Dixie" was first sung by Daniel Decater Emmett, a Southerner who lived in Ohio, on Broadway in 1859, as a "walk-around" song for Dan Bryant's Minstrels. It was the first song to gain popularity during the Civil War.

Dixie's Land

1 I wish I was in de land ob cotton,
  Old times dar am not forgotten,
    Look away! Look away!
    Look away! Dixie Land.
  In Dixie Land whar I was born in,
  Early on one frosty mornin',
    Look away! Look away!
    Look away! Dixie Land.

Den I wish I was in Dixie,
Hooray! Hooray!
In Dixie Land I'll take my stand,
To lib and die in Dixie,
Away, Away, Away down south in Dixie,
Away, Away, Away down south in Dixie.

2 Ole missus marry "Will de weaber,"
Willium was a gay deceaber;
   Look away! Look away!
   Look away! Dixie Land.
But when he put his arm around 'er,
He smiled as fierce as a forty pounder,
   Look away! Look away!
   Look away! Dixie Land. (Chorus)

3 His face was sharp as a butcher's cleaber,
But dat did not seem to greab 'er;
   Look away, etc.
Ole missus acted de foolish part,
And died for a man dat broke her heart,
   Look away, etc.- (Chorus)

4 Now here's a health to the next old Missus,
An' all de gals dat want to kiss us;
   Look away, etc.
But if you want to drive 'way sorrow,
Come and hear dis song tomorrow,
   Look away, etc. (Chorus)

5 Dar's buckwheat cakes and Injun batter,
Makes you fat or a little fatter;
   Look away, etc.
Den hoe it hown an' scratch your grabble,
To Dixie's Land I'm bound to trabble,
   Look away, etc. (Chorus)

The Old Folks at Home

Stephen Foster composed the most memorable ante-bellum minstrel songs. Ironically, he had not traveled South until he composed "The Old Folks at Home." This song, like "Old Black Joe," is a mythical rendering of plantation life before the Civil War when this life from Foster's point of view was idyllic for both slave and master.

THE OLD FOLKS AT HOME

Way down upon de Swanee ribber,
    Far, far away,
Dere's wha my heart is turning ebber,
    Dere's wha de old folks stay.
All up and down de whole creation,
    Sadly I roam,
Still longin' for de old plantation,
    And for de old folks at home.
        All de world am sad and dreary,
            Eb'rywhere I roam.
        Oh! darkies, how my heart grows weary,
        Far from de old folks at home.

All round de little farm I wander'd
    When I was young,
Den many happy days I squander'd,
    Many de songs I sung.
When I was playin' wid my brudder,
    Happy was I,
Oh, take me to my kind old mudder,
    Dere let me live and die.

One little hut among de bushes,
    One dat I love,
Still sadly to my mem'ry rushes,
    No matter where I rove.
When will I see de bees a-humming
    All round de comb?
When will I hear de banjo tumming
    Down in my good old home?

THE CIVIL WAR

ABRAHAM LINCOLN

(1809–1865)

As the country became more of a nation than a collection of states and shifted from a plantation aristocracy in the South to a commercial enterprise in the North, the West began to assume greater importance. From this region Lincoln emerged, bringing with him the belief in the common man and a dislike of slavery, his frontier humor, a deep knowledge of the Bible, and a moral purpose that was raised to the level of poetic and dignified eloquence in numerous addresses, letters, and essays. For Americans in the period between 1861 and 1865, Lincoln was the national hero, the symbol of national unity.

Born in Hardin County, Kentucky, Lincoln was taken early in his youth into southern Indiana. His mother died when he was nine, but she had a deep religious influence on him; his stepmother encouraged him in his ambitions, although the boy had only a year of formal schooling. After migrating with his family to Illinois, he finally settled in New Salem, near Springfield, taking up various occupations: rail splitter, storekeeper, postmaster, and lawyer. Soon Lincoln had won office to the Illinois legislature and after a brief period as a circuit-riding lawyer, he went to Congress in 1847 as a Whig representative. When he opposed slavery, he lost the nomination to office in 1849 and returned to private practice. He was defeated in 1855 in his attempt to

The standard text is *The Complete Works of Abraham Lincoln,* 2 vol. ed. J. G. Nicolay and John Hay, 1905–1906. See also *An Autobiography of Abraham Lincoln,* compiled by N. W. Stephenson, 1926; *Abraham Lincoln: His Speeches and Writing,* ed. R. P. Basler; and *The Collected Works of Abraham Lincoln,* 9 vols., ed. R. P. Basler, 1953.

An impressionistic biography is Carl Sandburg, *Abraham Lincoln,* 6 vols., 1926, 1939. See also Albert H. Beveridge, *Abraham Lincoln, 1809–1858,* 2 vols., 1928. The best biography is James G. Randall, *Lincoln,* 3 vol., 1945, 1947. See also Dixon Wecter, "The Democrat as Hero" in *The Hero in America,* 1941: Stefan Lorant, *Lincoln: A Picture Story of His Life,* 1952; Courtland Canby, ed., *Lincoln and the Civil War,* 1960; Herbert Joseph Edwards and John Erskin Hankins, *Lincoln the Writer,* 1962; Edmund Wilson, "Abraham Lincoln," in *Patriotic Gore,* 1962, pp. 99–130; and Stephen B. Oates, *With Malice Toward None: the Life of Abraham Lincoln,* 1977

Abraham Lincoln, *(Library of Congress.)*

win a seat in the senate and again in 1858, as a representative of the newly formed Republican party. His defeat by Stephen Douglass helped him to achieve a national reputation, because he had delivered powerful speeches that opposed both the extension of slavery and abolition. When Lincoln ran successfully for the presidency in 1860, his major position was the preservation of the Union. He held consistently to this argument during the Civil War as he led the North to

"Field Where General Reynolds Fell, Gettysburg." *(Photograph by Timothy O'Sullivan. Courtesy of The New York Historical Society, New York City.)*

Shadows-on-the-Teche, New Iberia, Louisiana. Greek revival planta-tion home built in 1831. *(Courtesy National Trust for Historic Preserva-tion.)*

victory. On April 14, 1865, he was assassinated in Ford's Theatre in Washington.

Two of Lincoln's most poignant and remarkable speeches are repre-sented here: The Gettysburg Address, and the Second Inaugural Ad-dress, delivered only six weeks before his assassination.

The Gettysburg Address[1]

Delivered at the Dedication of the National Cemetery, November 19, 1863

Fourscore and seven years ago our fathers brought forth on this continent a new nation, conceived in liberty, and dedicated to the proposition that all men are created equal.

Now we are engaged in a great civil war, testing whether that nation, or any nation so conceived and so dedicated, can long endure. We are met on a great battle-field of that war. We have come to dedicate a portion of that field as a final resting-place for those who here gave their lives that that nation might live. It is altogether fitting and proper that we should do this.

But, in a larger sense, we cannot dedicate—we cannot consecrate—we cannot hallow—this ground. The brave men, living and dead, who struggled here, have consecrated it far above our poor power to add or detract. The world will little note nor long remember what we say here, but it can never forget what they did here. It is for us, the living, rather, to be dedicated here to the unfinished work which they who fought here have thus far so nobly advanced. It is rather for us to be here dedicated to the great task remaining before us—that from these honored dead we take increased devotion to that cause for which they gave the last full measure of devotion; that we here highly resolve that these dead shall not have died in vain; that this nation, under God, shall have a new birth of freedom; and that government of the people, by the people, for the people, shall not perish from the earth.[2]

---

[1] This address was delivered at Gettysburg, Pennsylvania on November 19, 1863. The orator of the day was actually Edward Ever-ett, who spoke for two hours. Lincoln spoke for no more than two minutes, but his speech has remained the classic statement of faith in democracy.

[2] Theodore Parker had used this phrase in an antislavery speech in 1850.

Second Inaugural Address

FELLOW COUNTRYMEN:

At this second appearing to take the oath of the presidential office, there is less occasion for an extended address than there was at the first. Then a statement, somewhat in detail, of course to be pursued, seemed fitting and proper. Now, at the expiration of four years, during which public declarations have been constantly called forth on every point and phase of the great contest which still absorbs the attention and engrosses the energies of the nation, little that is new could be presented. The progress of our arms, upon which all else chiefly depends, is as well known to the public as to myself; and it is, I trust, reasonably satisfactory and encouraging to all. With high hope for the future, no prediction in regard to it is ventured.

On the occasion corresponding to this four years ago, all thoughts were anxiously directed to an impending civil war. All dreaded it—all sought to avert it. While the inaugural address was being delivered from this place, devoted altogether to saving the Union without war, insurgent agents were in the city seeking to destroy it without war—seeking to dissolve the Union, and divide effects, by negotiation. Both parties deprecated war; but one of them would make war rather than let the nation survive; and the other would accept war rather than let it perish. And the war came.

One-eighth of the whole population were colored slaves, not distributed generally over the Union, but localized in the Southern part of it. These slaves constituted a peculiar and powerful interest. All knew that this interest was, somehow, the cause of the war. To strengthen, perpetuate, and extend this interest was the object for which the insurgents would rend the Union, even by war; while the government claimed no right to do more than to restrict the territorial enlargement of it.

Neither party expected for the war the magnitude or the duration which it has already attained. Neither anticipated that the cause of the conflict might cease with, or even before, the conflict itself should cease. Each looked for an easier triumph, and a result less fundamental and astounding. Both read the same Bible, and pray to the same God; and each invokes his aid against the other. It may seem strange that any men should dare to ask a just God's assistance in wringing their bread from the sweat of other men's faces; but let us judge not, that we be not judged.[1] The prayers of both could not be answered—that of neither has been answered fully.

The Almighty has his own purposes. "Woe unto the world because of offences! for it must needs be that offences come; but woe to that man by

[1] Cf. Matthew vii: 1.

whom the offence cometh."[2] If we shall suppose that American slavery is one of those offences which, in the providence of God, must needs come, but which, having continued through his appointed time, he now wills to remove, and that he gives to both North and South this terrible war, as the woe due to those by whom the offence came, shall we discern therein any departure from those divine attributes which the believers in a living God always ascribe to him? Fondly do we hope—fervently do we pray—that this mighty scourge of war may speedily pass away. Yet, if God wills that it continue until all the wealth piled by the bondman's two hundred and fifty years of unrequited toil shall be sunk, and until every drop of blood drawn with the lash shall be paid by another drawn with the sword, as was said three thousand years ago, so still it must be said, "The judgments of the Lord are true and righteous altogether."[3]

With malice toward none; with charity for all: with firmness in the right, as God gives us to see the right, let us strive on to finish the work we are in; to bind up the nation's wounds; to care for him who shall have borne the battle, and for his widow, and his orphan—to do all which may achieve and cherish a just and lasting peace among ourselves, and with all nations.

[2] Cf. Matthew xviii: 7.   [3] Cf. Psalms xix: 9.

GENERAL BIBLIOGRAPHY

I. REFERENCE WORKS

Dictionary of American Biography. Allen Johnson, and Dumas Malone, Editors. Twenty volumes plus supplements, 1928-1958.

Handlin, O., A. M. Schlesinger, S. E. Morison, and others, Editors. *Harvard Guide to American History,* 1954.

Hart, J. D. *The Oxford Companion to American Literature,* 4th Edition, 1965.

Kunitz, S. J., and Howard Haycraft, Editors. *American Authors, 1600-1900,* 1944.

―――. *Twentieth Century Authors,* 1942. Supplement, 1955.

Leary, Lewis, Editor. *Articles on American Literature, 1900-1950,* 1954; *1950-1967,* 1970.

Millett, F. B. *Contemporary American Authors, A Critical Survey and 219 Bibliographies,* 1940.

Morris, R. B., ed., *Encyclopedia of American History,* 1953.

Mott, F. L. *American Journalism: A History of Newspapers in the United States Through 250 Years, 1690 to 1940,* 1941. Revised, 1951.

―――. *A History of American Magazines.* Four volumes, 1938-1957.

Quinn, Arthur Hobson, ed., *The Literature of the American People,* 1951.

Reader's Guide to Periodical Literature. Annual, 1900―.

Spiller, R. E., and others, eds. *Literary History of the United States.* Two-volume edition, 1953. Bibliography Supplement prepared by Richard M. Ludwig, 1959. Supplement II, 1970.

Stovall, Floyd. *Eight American Authors,* 1956.

Trent, W. P., John Erskine, S. P. Sherman, and Carl Van Doren, Editors, *Cambridge History of American Literature.* Four volumes, 1917-1921.

Who's Who in America. Biennial, 1899―.

Woodress, James. *American Literary Scholarship.* Annual, 19―.

―――. *Dissertations in American Literature, 1891-1955.* 1957.

II. GENERAL STUDIES

A. LITERARY HISTORY AND CRITICISM

American Writers Series. H. H. Clark, General Editor, 1934―. Twenty-eight volumes published.

Bercovitch, Sacvan, ed. *The Revaluation of Puritanism*, 1974.

———. *The Puritan Origins of the American Self*, 1975.

Blair, Walter. *Native American Humor (1800-1900)*, 1947.

Brown, Sterling. *Negro Poetry and Drama*, 1937.

Chase, Richard. *The American Novel and Its Tradition*, 1957.

Clark, H. H., Editor. *Transitions in American Literary History*, 1954.

Cowie, Alexander. *The Rise of the American Novel*, 1948.

Cunliffe, Marcus. *The Literature of the United States*, 1954.

Davis, Richard Beale. *Intellectual Life in the Colonial South, 1585-1763*, 1977.

Emerson, Everett, ed. *Major Writers of Early American Literature*, 1972.

Fiedler, Leslie. *Love and Death in the American Novel*, 1960.

Feidelson, Charles. *Symbolism in American Literature*, 1953.

Gelpi, Albert J. *The Tenth Muse*, 1975.

Hoffman, Daniel. *Form and Fable in American Literature*, 1965.

Hoffman, Frederick J. *The Art of Southern Fiction*, 1967.

Hubbell, Jay. *The South in American Literature, 1607-1900*, 1954.

Hughes, Glenn. *A History of the American Theatre, 1700-1950*, 1951.

Lawrence, D. H. *Studies in Classic American Literature*, 1923.

Leisy, E. E. *The American Historical Novel*, 1950.

Levin, David. *In Defense of Historical Literature*, 1967.

Lewis, R. W. B. *The American Adam: Innocence, Tragedy, and Tradition in the Nineteenth Century*, 1955.

Loggins, Vernon. *The Negro Author*, 1931.

Marx, Leo. *The Machine in the Garden: Technology and the Pastoral Ideal in America*, 1964.

Matthiessen, F. O. *American Renaissance: Art and Expression in the Age of Emerson and Whitman*, 1941.

May, Henry. *The Enlightenment in America*, 1976.

Mencken, H. L. *The American Language: An Inquiry into the Development of English in the United States*, 1919. Revised, 1936. Supplement I, 1945. Supplement II, 1948.

Meserve, Walter. *An Emerging Entertainment: The Drama of the American People from the Beginnings to 1828*, 1977

Parrington, V. L. *Main Currents in American Thought: An Interpretation of American Literature from the Beginnings to 1920*. Three volumes, 1927-1930.

Pearce, Roy Harvey. *The Continuity of American Poetry*, 1961.

Poirier, Richard. *A World Elsewhere: The Place of Style in American Literature*, 1966.

Pritchard, J. P. *Criticism in America*, 1956.

Quinn, Arthur Hobson. *American Fiction: An Historical and Critical Survey*, 1936.

———. *A History of the American Drama: From the Beginning to the Civil War*, 1923. Revised, 1943.

———. *A History of the American Drama: From the Civil War to the Present Day*. Two volumes, 1927. Reissued in one volume, 1936.

———, Murdock, K. B., Clarence Gohdes, and G. F. Whicher. *The Literature of the American People*, 1951.

Rourke, Constance. *American Humor: A Study of the National Character,* 1931.

Seely, John. *Prophetic Waters: The River in Early American Life and Literature,* 1977.

Silverman, Kenneth. *A Cultural History of the American Revolution,* 1976.

Smith, Henry Nash. *Virgin Land: The American West as Symbol and Myth,* 1950.

Spencer, B. T. *The Quest of Nationality: An American Literary Campaign,* 1957.

Spengermann, William C. *The Adventurous Muse: The Poetics of American Fiction, 1789-1900,* 1977.

Spiller, R. W. *The Cycle of American Literature: An Essay in Historical Criticism,* 1956.

Stewart, Randall. *American Literature and the Christian Tradition,* 1958.

Taylor, W. F. *The Economic Novel in America,* 1942.

Tyler, M. C. *A History of American Literature During the Colonial Period, 1607-1765.* Two volumes, 1878. Revised edition, 1897. One volume, 1949.

———. *The Literary History of the American Revolution, 1763-1783.* Two volumes, 1897; one volume, 1941.

Waggoner, Hyatt, *American Poets: From the Puritans to the Present,* 1968.

Williams, Stanley T. *The Spanish Background of American Literature,* 1955.

Wilson, Edmund, Editor. *The Shock of Recognition.*

———. *Patriotic Gore: Studies in the Literature of the American Civil War,* 1962.

B. HISTORY

Bailyn, Bernard. *The Ideological Origins of the American Revolution,* 1977.

Bailyn, Bernard, David B. Davis, David H. Donald, et al. *The Great Republic: A History of the American People,* 1977.

Baritz, Loren. *City on a Hill: A History of Ideas and Myths in America,* 1964.

Buck, Paul H. *The Road to Reunion, 1865-1900,* 1937.

Beard, C. A., and M. R. Beard. *The Rise of American Civilization.* Four volumes, 1927-1942.

Billington, R. A. *Westward Expansion: A History of the American Frontier,* 1949.

Burnham, John C., Editor. *Science in America, 19—.*

Butcher, Margaret. *The Negro in American Culture,* 1956.

Cargill, Oscar. *Intellectual America: Ideas on the March,* 1941.

Cash, W. J. *The Mind of the South,* 1941.

Chronicles of America Series. Allen Johnson, General Editor. Fifty volumes, 1918-1921. Six supplementary volumes, Allen Nevins, Editor, 1950-1951.

Commager, Henry S. *The American Mind: An Interpretation of American Thought and Character Since the 1880's,* 1950.

Curti, Merle. *The Growth of American Thought,* 1943.

Dorfman, Joseph. *The Economic Mind in American Civilization.* Three volumes, 1946-1949 (through World War I).

Fish, C. R. *The Rise of the Common Man, 1830-50,* 1927.

Franklin, John Hope. *From Slavery to Freedom: A History of American Negroes*, 3rd edition, revised and enlarged, 1967.

Gabriel, R. H. *The Course of American Thought*, 1943.

Gaustad, Edwin Scott. *A Religious History of America*, 1943.

Hesseltine, W. B. *A History of the South*. Revised, 1943.

Horton, Rod W., and Herbert Edwards. *Backgrounds of American Literary Thought*, 1952.

Howe, Irving. *A World More Attractive: A View of Modern Literature and Politics*, 1963.

Lasch, Christopher. *The New Radicalism in America, 1899-1963: The Intellectual as a Social Type*, 1965.

Lerner, Max. *America as a Civilization*, 19—.

Lomax, Alan. *The Folk Songs of North America*, 1960.

Lynn, Kenneth S., Editor. *The Comic Tradition in America*, 1958.

Miller, Perry. *Errand in the Wilderness*, 1963.

———. *The Life of the Mind in America from the Revolution to the Civil War*, 1965.

———. *The New England Mind: The Seventeenth Century*, 1939.

———. *The New England Mind: From Colony to Province*, 1953.

———. *The Raven and the Whale: The War of the Words and Wits in the Era of Poe and Melville*, 1956.

Morison, Samuel Eliot, and Henry S. Commager. *The Growth of the American Republic*. Two volumes, revised, 1950.

Myrdal, Gunnar. *An American Dilemma: The Negro Problem and Modern Democracy*. Two volumes, 1944.

Nevins, Allan. *The Emergence of Modern America, 1865-1878*, 1927.

Nichols, R. F. *The Disruption of American Democracy*, 1948.

Redding, J. Saunders. *The Lonesome Road: The Story of the Negro's Part in America*.

Reingold, Nathan, Editor. *Science in Nineteenth Century America*, 1946.

Rosenberg, Bernard, and David N. White. *Mass Culture: The Popular Arts in America*, 1957.

Schlesinger, A. M. *The Rise of the City, 1878-1898*, 1933.

———. *The Rise of Modern America, 1865-1951*, 1951.

Schlesinger, A. M., Jr. *The Age of Jackson*, 1945.

Schneider, H. W. *History of American Philosophy*, 1946.

Stampp, Kenneth. *The Peculiar Institution*, 1956.

Washburn, Wilcomb E. and John Aubrey. *The North American Indian Captivity*, 1977.

Stephenson, W. J., and E. M. Coulter, Editors. *A History of the South*. Six volumes, 1948-1953.

Washburn, Wilcomb E. and John Aubrey. *The North American Indian Captivity*, 1977.

Wish, Harvey. *Society and Thought in America*. Two volumes, 1950-1952.

C. ART

Andrews, Wayne. *Architecture in America: A Photographic History*, 1960.

Dunlap, William. *A History of the Rise and Progress of the Arts of Design in the United States*. Two volumes, 1834. Reissued, edited with additions by F. W. Bayley and C. E. Goodspeed. Three volumes. Revised, enlarged edition, edited by Alexander Wyckoff, preface by William P. Campbell. Three volumes, 1965.

Barker, Virgil. *American Painting: History and Interpretation*, 1950.

Burroughs, Alan. *Liners and Likenesses: Three Centuries of American Painting*, 1936.

Eliot, Alexander. *Three Hundred Years of American Painting*, 1957.

Flexner, James Thomas. *First Flowers of our Wilderness: American Painting*, 1947.

———. *The Light of Distant Skies, 1760-1835*, 1954.

———. *That Wilder Image*, 1962.

Jarves, James Jackson. *Art Hints, Architecture, Sculpture, and Painting*, 1855.

———. *The Art-Idea*, 1864; reissued, 1960.

———. *Art Thoughts*,

LaFollette, Suzanne. *Art in America From Colonial Times to the Present Day*, 1929.

Larkin, Oliver W. *Art and Life in America*. New York, 1960.

Richardson, E. P. *Painting in America*, 1956.

———. *A Short History of Painting in America*, 1963.

Whiffen, Marcus. *American Architecture Since 1780: A Guide to the Styles*, 1969.

D. MUSIC

Chase, Gilbert. *America's Music From the Pilgrims to the Present*, 1953.

Howard, J. J., and G. K. Bellows. *A Short History of Music in America*, 1957.

Jackson, G. P. *White and Negro Spirituals: Their Life Span and Kinship*, 1943.

Lomax, Alan. *The Folk Songs of North America*, 1960.

Index

Authors and selection included in these volumes are indicated by bold face type. Page numbers on which main discussion of an author or the page on which an individual selection begins are indicated by bold face type. Titles of works referred to but not included in these volumes are in bold face italic.

This book was designed by Suzanne Bennett.
Picture research was done by Abi Gail Solomon.
Debra Schwartz supervised production.

THE EDITORS

Volume 1

David Levin. Commonwealth Professor of English, University of Virginia. Harvard Ph.D. He has also taught at Stanford, University of Strasbourg, University of Toulouse, and the University of Madrid. Chief publications: articles and books on American literature, especially historical literature, including fiction and autobiography. *History as Romantic Art: Bancroft, Prescott, Motley, and Parkman; In Defense of Historical Literature;* and he is now writing a biography of Cotton Mather. Edited books: *What Happened In Salem? Documents Pertaining to the Salem Witchcraft Trials; Bonifacius, An essay Upon The Good by Cotton Mather;* and *The Puritan in the Enlightenment: Franklin and Edwards.*

Theodore L. Gross (General Editor). Vice-President for Institutional Advancement and Professor of English, The City College of The City University of New York. Columbia Ph.D. He has also taught at Barnard College, University of Nancy, and the University of Nice. Author of *The Heroic Ideal in American Literature; Hawthorne, Melville, Crane: A Critical Bibliography* (with S. Wertheim); *Thomas Nelson Page;* and *Albion W. Tourgée.* Edited books: *The Literature of American Jews; A Nation of Nations; Representative Men;* and *Dark Symphony: The Development of Negro Literature in America* (Coeditor, James Emanuel).

Volume 2

Alan Trachtenberg. Professor of American Studies and English, Yale University. Minnesota Ph.D. He has also taught at Pennsylvania State University and the University of New Mexico. Author of *Brooklyn Bridge: Fact and Symbol.* Edited books: *Democratic Vistas, 1865-1880; The City: American Experience* (Coeditors Peter Bunnell and Peter Neil); *Memoirs of Waldo Frank;* and *Critics of Culture.*

Benjamin DeMott. Professor of English, Amherst College. Harvard Ph.D. He has also taught at MIT, Yale, the City University of New York, and Birmingham University (England). He has written two novels, *The Body's Cage* and *A Married Man,* and is the author of numerous works on cultural commentary: *Hells & Benefits; You Don't Say; Supergrow; Surviving the Seventies;* and *Scholarship for Society.* He has been a book critic for *Harper's,* a contributing editor for *Saturday Review,* and is a columnist for *The Atlantic Monthly.*